Aerodine's

Pilot Travel Guide

Second Edition
National Coverage

Over 1,300 Fly-in Restaurants And Resorts
130 Articles About Attractions Near Airports
Special Aviation Museum Section

Nearby golf courses; Skiing; Outdoor activities;
Lodging; Available transportation;
Local tourism contacts and aviation services

Second Edition

Editor/Publisher
And Author
Kenneth J. Keifer

Aerodine's Pilot Travel Guide is published by Aerodine Magazine, P.O. Box 247, Palatine, Illinois 60078. ISBN: 0-9659068-0-9

How To Order:

Aerodine's Pilot Travel Guide may be purchased by mailing your check or money order or by telephone orders using VISA or MASTERCARD for $64.95 plus $6.00 for postage and handling, payable to Aerodine Magazine, P.O. Box 247, Palatine, Illinois 60078. Your copy will be shipped as soon as possible after we receive your payment. Discounts are available if placing larger orders. For information regarding individual orders, wholesale rates, advertising, or submitted information, call Aerodine Magazine at 847-358-4355. *(See page 1,008, 1,009 for Order Form).*

Acknowledgments

Special thanks are given to Mrs. Adeline Keifer for spending countless hours editing and reviewing the text and contents of our original book published in 1993. And Gail LeSeur as assistant editor in the production of the Second Edition along with Judy Stille of Stille Office Services for final proofreading. Also, if not for the support and financial contributions of Adeline Keifer, Clint J. Keifer and Lloyd Keifer, this publication would not have been possible.

We also want to award special appreciation to contributors and advertisers including persons operating and working at restaurants, resorts and points of interest, along with airport personnel, for taking the time to fill out questionnaires and participate in telephone interviews used in obtaining information.

Last, but certainly not least, we want to also thank our readers for informing us about new places that they have visited and informing us of any changes to existing establishments already in the book. In addition to our own research, this enables us to update information in a timely manner so we, in turn, can inform others with future and updated versions of this publication.

COVER PHOTOS:
The cover of the book was designed and created by Kenneth Keifer editor and publisher of Aerodine Magazine. The following list of pictures were submitted to Aerodine Magazine for promotional use by various public relations departments: Boating scene, by: Kentucky Department of Parks; Tennis and Skiing scene, by: Wintergreen Resort, Wintergreen, Virginia; Horse riding scene, Alisal Guest Ranch And Resort, Santa Ynez, California; Dining scene, by: Aerodine Magazine; Pool side photo by: Innisbrook Hilton Resort, Tarpon Springs, FL and the center aircraft picture is a twin engine Piper Cheyenne, by: Piper Aircraft Corporation, Vero Beach, Florida.

Aerodine Magazine
P.O. Box 247
Palatine, IL 60078
Phone: 847-358-4355

Disclaimer and Limitation of Liabilities:

The staff of Aerodine Magazine has acquired information by the most accurate source available at the time of printing and with the best intentions. Information has been acquired through questionnaires, correspondence and telephone interviews along with personal visits to various facilities.

As with any material of this nature, information may become inaccurate over the course of time. Aerodine Magazine, a subsidiary of Four K Flying Service, Inc., assumes no responsibility for inaccurate information submitted by contributors, nor does it assume liability for incidental or consequential damages in connection with or arising out of furnishing information within this publication.

It is the sole responsibility of the reader to verify all information by contacting the appropriate personnel regarding the establishment of intended use, in advance and prior to visiting that facility. In no way should this publication be used as a substitute for proper pre-flight planning or updated and current published documents critical to safe flight. It is the sole responsibility of the pilot to determine the condition of airport and runways of intended use by calling the appropriate authority in advance to determine if circumstances and conditions exist for safe flight.

Introduction

Due to the growing success in publishing aviation-related travel guides since 1983, Aerodine Magazine has finally prepared what may well be the most popular book available for aviation lovers all across the United States. Not only is this publication designed to serve recreational pilots in search of new places to fly on weekends for enjoyment, but is also devoted to satisfying the demanding needs of cross country pleasure and business air travelers.

There were several important considerations taken into account when preparing this book. Our objective was to satisfy the needs of a wide spectrum of general aviation enthusiasts. As an example: The weekend flyer enjoys planning local trips to visit nearby airport restaurants, resorts, golf courses, aviation museums, fishing spots, parks, points of interest and all sorts of near airport attractions within roughly a two hour flight from home base. Likewise, cross-country air travelers enjoy learning about new places to fly for enjoyment, and can use this book to select destination as well as food and fuel stops along their course of flight. Resorts, bed and breakfast establishments, sports and dude ranches located near airports, have been featured and serve as excellent vacation destinations. In order to provide the reader with additional information, and to help verify accommodations, we have included the phone number and address of local chambers of commerce or tourism council. Available meeting and conference locations have been included as well. In addition, flying clubs are always looking for new places to arrange activities and social events combined with convenient restaurant accommodations for their membership. A complete publication containing all the information mentioned above is what Aerodine has strived to create.

This book contains over 1,300 detailed fly-in restaurant and resort descriptions obtained by interviewing owners and managers of each facility. Articles about attractions, points of interest, aviation museums and resorts have also been featured, including a special section in the back portion of the book containing over 90 aviation museums.

Each of the facilities within this publication are arranged in a logical and systematic order offering the reader quick information at a glance. *Italicized print* within the one-half or full page segments, describe the establishment featured, restaurant information, containing items like hours of operation, types of food served, decor, distance and direction from the nearest airport, average prices per meal, banquet or group accommodations and much more. In a few instances, information about a particular restaurant of choice was unattainable. Each facility was given three chances to respond. After attempts by phone and questionnaires failed, we moved onto the next available restaurant at that same location.

Airport information has also been provided, along with excerpts from the latest government-published Airport Facility Directory (AFD) available before printing. In most cases, this section is positioned just left of the airport diagram and includes the following: airport location from nearest geographical town, coordinate, elevation, fuel, runway length and composition, attendance, common frequencies, airport notes, and fixed based operators and telephone numbers. A section located in the upper right hand portion of each page segment includes the area code, reference number for that location and a listing of additional nearby restaurants if any. Following this is a listing of nearby lodging establishments in the area, available courtesy cars, rental cars and ground transportation, meeting rooms and tourism councils. The notes under "Attraction" describe subject matter of particular interest for the traveler and destination choices. Golf courses, parks, nearby resorts, fishing, bed and breakfasts, recreational establishments, quaint towns, etc., are just some of the items presented.

The book is laid out in chapters by state. Index sheets along with a location map for each chapter provide the reader with information for determining what sites lie along their particular route of flight.

Each establishment featured within the full or half-page segments are issued a reference number displayed in the upper right hand corner. This number corresponds to the same establishment listed on the index sheet and location map at the front of each state chapter.

Although we have tried to represent all popular establishments located near airports across the country, it is likely we might have overlooked a few. In addition to our own research, some of the most interesting fly-in destinations were obtained directly from readers like yourself. If you should know about a particular point of interest or a favorite dining location situated near an airport, we would be most grateful if you would inform us so we, in turn, can share this information with others in future editions. Your input would be greatly appreciated.

Suggestions on how we may better serve your needs are also of great value to us. Please keep in mind that the information published in this book was obtained with the best intentions and efforts put forth. Even though we strive to provide our readers with the latest, most current information possible at the time of printing, we suggest, as a supplement to your normal pre-flight planning, that you call the restaurant and, most importantly the airport management to verify runway conditions before your intended flight. A little preparation on your part will ensure that every one of your planned fly-outs will be a joyful and memorable success. Happy Flying!

Table of Contents

Table of Contence Continued

Page Number

ALABAMA

LOCATION MAP

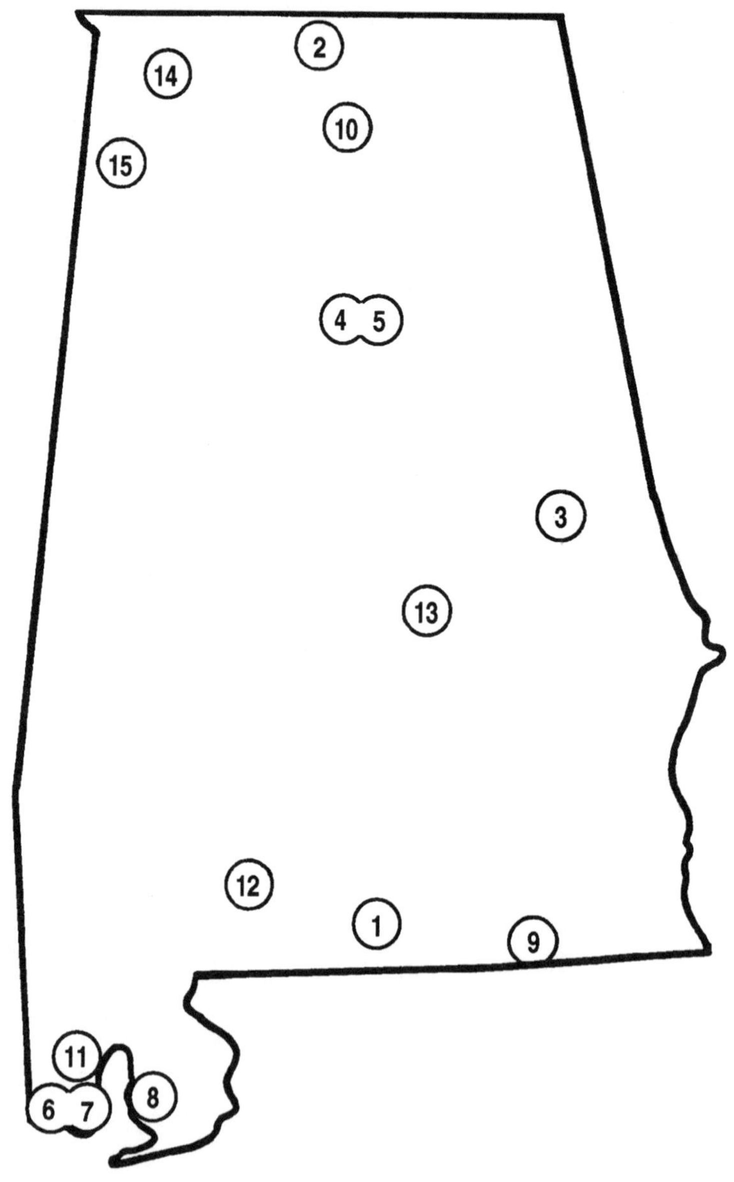

Not to be used for navigational purposes

ALABAMA

CROSS FILE INDEX

Location Number	City or Town	Airport Name And Identifier	Name of Attraction
1	Andalusia	Andalusia-opp (79J)	The Charter House Inn
2	Ardmore	Ardmore Arpt. (1M3)	Maw's Eatin' Place
3	Auburn	Opelika Robert G. Pitts (AUO)	Shoney's Restaurant
4	Birmingham	Birmingham Intl. (BHM)	Host Marriott
5	Birmingham	Birmingham Intl. (BHM)	V.J. On The Runway
6	Dauphin Island	Dauphin Island Arpt. (4R9)	Seafood Galley
7	Dauphin Island	Dauphin Island Arpt. (4R9)	Seafood House
8	Fairhope	Fairhope Muni. (4R4)	Marriott's Grand Motel
9	Geneva	Geneva Muni. Arpt. (33J)	Price's Diner
10	Huntsville	Intl.-Carl T. Jones Field (HSV)	Veranda Room
11	Mobile	Mobile Arpt./Bates Field (MOB)	Jerry's Catering
12	Monroeville	Monroe Co. Arpt. (MVC)	David's Catfish House
13	Montgomery	Dannelly Field (MGM)	Jerry's Catering
14	Muscle Shoals	Muscle Shoals Reg. (MSL)	Renaissance Grille
15	Red Bay	Red Bay Muni. Arpt. (M26)	Jack's Drive Inn

Articles

City or town	Nearest Airport and Identifier	Name of Attraction
Birmingham, AL	Birmingham Arpt. (BHM)	Southern Museum of Flight
Enterprise, AL	Enterprise Muni. (EDN)	U.S. Army Aviation Museum
Guntersville, AL	Guntersville Muni. Arpt. (8A1)	Ryder's Fighter Museum

AL-79J - ANDALUSIA
ANDALUSIA-OPP (AIRPORT)

(Area Code 205) 1

Restaurants Near Airport:
The Charter House Inn 3 mi W. Phone: 222-7511

Lodging: The Charter House Inn (3 miles west) 222-7511
Meeting Rooms: None reported
Transportation: The Charter House Inn will provide free courtesy transportation (except for Suday afternoons and evenings). Also Muscle Shoals Aviation
Information: Opp & Covington Co. Chamber of Commerce, P.O. Box 148, Opp, AL 36467, Phone: 493-3070

The Charter House Inn:

The Charter House Inn is a restaurant and lodging facility that is located approximately 3 miles west of Andalusia-Opp Airport. Restaurant hours vary from 6:00 a.m. to 9:30 p.m. Monday through Friday, 6:00 a.m. to 10:00 a.m. and 5:00 p.m. to 9:30 p.m. on Saturday, and 6:00 a.m. to 2:00 p.m. on Sunday. Enjoy its cozy, modern atmosphere while relaxing in the Brass Rail Lounge, or indulge in some of the fine food in the comfortable dining area. The restaurant features delicious appetizers such as fried mushrooms and shrimp cocktails, while specializing in entrees such as steak, chicken, and seafood. In addition, the inn boasts a popular Sunday through Friday lunch buffet and weekend breakfast buffet. There are also nightly dinner specials including the following: Monday-country fried steak, Tuesday-chicken breast, Wednesday-spaghetti w/meat sauce, Thursday-chicken fingers, Friday-All-You-Can-Eat catfish nuggets, and Saturday-prime rib. Average prices range from $4.50 for breakfast, $6.00 for lunch, and $11.00 for dinner. The Charter House Inn also provides sleeping accommodations, which include 62 comfortable rooms of contemporary decor that are filled with all of the necessary amenities. There is also an outdoor swimming pool, volleyball court, tennis court, jogging trail and a 1-1/2 mile nature trail. The restaurant will provide free courtesy transportation (except for Sunday afternoons and evenings). For more information, call The Charter House Inn at 222-7511.

Airport Information:

ANDALUSIA - ANDALUSIA-OPP (AIRPORT) (79J)
4 mi east of town N31-18.53 W86-23.63 Elev: 330 Fuel: 100LL, Jet-A
Rwy 11-29: H5000x100 (Asph) Attended: Monday through Saturday 1330-0100Z, Sun 1400-0100Z. Later hours available upon request. CTAF/Unicom: 122.8 App/Dep Con: 133.45 Tower: 119.55 (1330-0530Z) Monday-Friday, except holidays. Gnd Con: 121.9
FBO: Airport Authority Phone: 222-6598

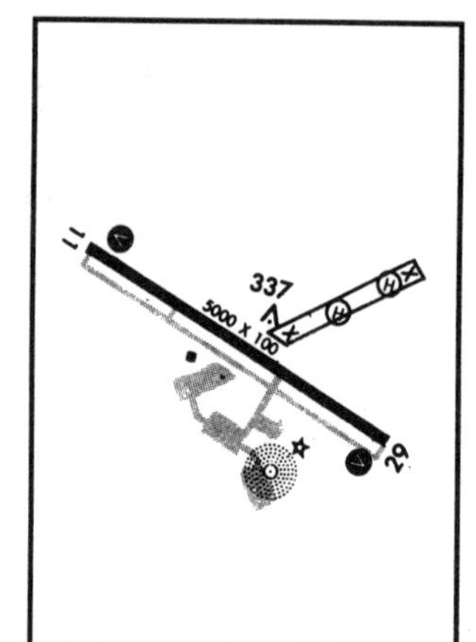

AL-1M3 - ARDMORE
ARDMORE AIRPORT

(Area Code AL-205 & TN-615) 2

Restaurants Near Airport:

Mildred's Rest.	3-4 mi.	Phone: 420-8393
Nancy's Place	3-4 mi.	Phone: 420-8393
Peoples Choice	3-4 mi.	Phone: 205-423-3490

Lodging: Budget Inn (3 blocks) 423-6699.
Meeting Rooms: None reported
Transportation: With advance notice appreciated, the airport manager can arrange an airport courtesy for short term use. Call Ardmore Aviation at 206-423-2736..
Information: Alabama Bureau of Tourism & Travel, 532 South Perry Street, Montgomery, AL 36104, Phone: 205-242-4169.

People's Choice Restaurant & Ardmore Cheese Co:

The restaurant, within walking distance from the Ardmore Airport, has been closed. However, thanks to the input from one of our readers, we learned about another restaurant in the area as well as a short side trip to the Ardmore Cheese Company. During our conversation with the airport manager we learned, that if given a little notice, he would provide a courtesy car for local visits into town. He indicated that there are a number of nice restaurants 3 to 5 miles from the airport. One of these restaurants caught our interest, known as the People's Choice Restaurant. This family-style establishment is about 3 or 4 miles from the airport and offers a casual atmosphere. It is open between 6:30 a.m. and 9 p.m., 7 days a week. They specialize in seafood buffets offered on Wednesday and Saturday evenings from 4 p.m. until 9 p.m. Prices are reasonable at $9.99 for all you can eat. This restaurant also features a breakfast and lunch buffet for only $4.00 to $5.00. The restaurant can seat about 100 people. The staff is friendly and the cooks are masters at their trade. Barbecued ribs are another specialty at People's Choice. For information call 205-423-3490. After you enjoy a fine meal, why not visit the Ardmore Cheese Company and pick up some cheese to take home with you. During our conversation with the owner of the cheese store, we learned that the Ardmore Cheese Company was a major cheese manufacturer and distribution center. For 50 years, cheese was prepared, packaged and shipped to all parts of the United States. In 1991 the manufacturing of cheese at this location was suspended; however, the company has grown and today has become a major distributor of mail order cheeses. A special catalog containing their unique cheeses is available by calling 615-427-2191. Why is the area code different from the restaurant? Because the state line of Tennessee and Alabama runs right down Main Street through town. To reach town from the airport, simply go 2 miles east on 53 until reaching Main Street, make a left on Main and take it into town. The Ardmore Cheese Company is only about one mile from People's Choice Restaurant. For more information call the airport manager at 205-423-2736.

Airport Information:

ARDMORE - ARDMORE AIRPORT (1M3)
2 mi southwest of town N34-58.67 W86-53.08 Elev: 920 Rwy 01-19: 2700x100 (Turf)
Attended: Mon-Fri daylight hours. Unicom: 122.9
FBO: Ardmore Aviation Phone: 423-2736

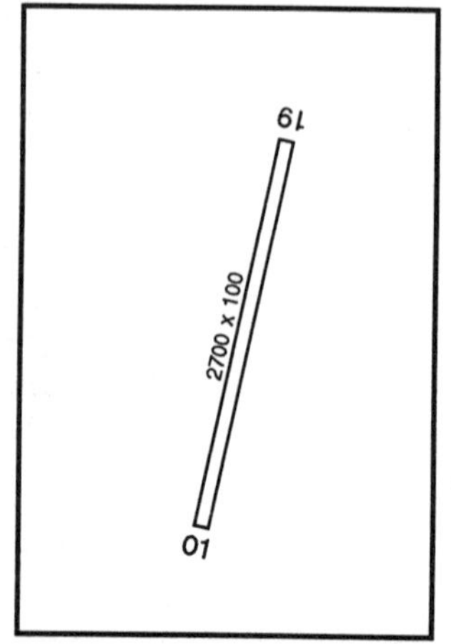

Not to be used for navigational purposes

AL-AUO - AUBURN
OPELIKA ROBERT G. PITTS AIRPORT

(Area Code 334)

3

Shoney's Restaurant:

Shoney's Restaurant is located about one mile from the airport by courtesy car or a little less if you decide to walk across the golf course. This family style restaurant is open from 6 a.m. to 12 a.m. Sunday through Thursday and 6 a.m. to 2 a.m. Friday and Saturday. Their menu contains items like shrimp, steak, New York strip 8 oz & 9 oz cuts. They also provide a breakfast bar from 6 a.m. to 11 a.m. Monday through Friday and from 6 a.m. to 2 p.m. on weekends. Average prices run $3.99 for breakfast, $5.00 to $9.00 for lunch and $7.00 to $12.00 for dinner. The restaurant has cloth awnings on the outside of the building which makes it easy to spot from the road. There is seating for 180 persons in their main dining room, as well as a back room used for groups up to 42 people. The staff at this facility takes pride in customer satisfaction. For more information call Shoney's Restaurant at 826-6224.

Restaurants Near Airport:

Harper Valley Cafe	(2 mi Free Trans)	Phone: 745-5476
Ivy's restaurant	2 mi	Phone: 800-346-7974
Red Lobster	2 mi	Phone: 821-4474
Shoney's Restaurant	1 mi	Phone: 826-6224

Lodging: Auburn Conference Center and Motor Lodge (Free trans) 821-7001; Auburn Univ. Hotel Conference Center 821-8200; Heart of Auburn Motel 887-3462; Holiday Inn 745-6331.
Meeting Rooms: Auburn Conference Center and Motor Lodge (free trans) 821-7001; Auburn Univ. Hotel Conference Center (convention facilities) 821-8200;
Transportation: Airport courtesy car available through fixed base operators. Call Auburn University Aviation at 844-4597.
Information: Chamber of Commerce, 714 East Glenn Avenue, P.O. Box 1370, Auburn, AL 36830. Phone: 887-7011.

Attractions:

Golf Course reported adjacent to airport. For information call Auburn University Aviation at 844-4597.

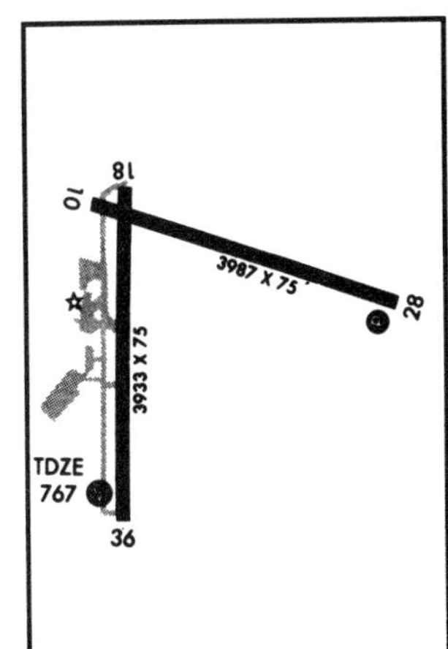

Airport Information:

AUBURN - OPELIKA ROBERT G. PITTS AIRPORT (AUO)
2 mi east of town N32-36.87 W85-25.86 Elev: 776 Fuel: 100LL, Jet-A
Rwy 10-28: H3987x75 (Asph) Rwy 18-36: H3933x75 (Asph-Grvd) Attended: 1300-0100Z
Unicom: 123.0
FBO: Auburn University Aviation Phone: 844-4597

AL-BHM - BIRMINGHAM
BIRMINGHAM INTERNATIONAL

(Area Code 205)

4, 5

Host Marriott.

This snack bar is located within the new terminal building at the Birmingham Airport. The cafe is open from 5 a.m. to 11 p.m. and serves pizza made on the premises and lite fare along with Colombo frozen yogurt and fresh fruit daily. Average prices run $4.50 for breakfast, $5.60 for lunch and $6.00 for dinner. For information call 592-4362.

V. J. On The Runway:

V. J. On The Runway is located on the north side of Birmingham International Airport. (Note: In June of 1995, the restaurant informed us that they may be moving a short distance down the road from the airport sometime in the near future.) V.J.'s is a modern style cafe, which is open between 6 a.m. and 8 p.m. Monday through Friday, and 7 a.m. and 7 p.m. on Saturday. It is closed on Sundays. The menu varies daily, featuring tasty dishes such as baked ham, smoked sausage, roast beef, cooked fresh collard greens, green beans, buttered beans, and an assortment of homemade pies. With advanced notice, the restaurant will cater to parties of 20 or more, as well as to pilots on-the-go. AMR Combs will provide courtesy transportation to and from the airport. For more information, please call V. J. On The Runway at 833-5351.

Restaurants Near Airport:

Dobbs Houses, Inc.	On Site	Phone: 592-4362
Holiday Inn Airport	1 mi S	Phone: 591-6900
Ramada Inn Airport	1 mi S	Phone: 591-7900
Rime Garden Suites	5 mi SE	Phone: 951-1200

Lodging: Free airport transportation by the following: Days Inn 592-6110; Holiday Inn-78 (East Airport Area) 596-8211; Holiday Inn-Airport 591-6900; Holiday Inn Homewood 942-2041; Ramada Inn-Airport 591-7900; Red Mountain Inn 942-2031; Rime Garden Suites 951-1200; UAB University Inn 933-7700; Embassy Suites 879-7400; Mountain Brook Inn 870-3100; Sheraton Perimeter Park South 967-2700; Tutwiler 322-2100; Wynfrey At Riverchase Galleria 987-1600;
Meeting Rooms: Dobbs Houses, Inc. (On Airport) 592-4362; All lodging facilities listed above have meeting room accommodations. Wynfrey At Riverchase Galleria 987-1600 has accommodations for conventions.
Transportation: Courtesy Car (FBO) Also Rental Cars: Avis 592-8901; Budget 595-2403; Dollar 595-5000; Hertz 591-6090; National 592-7259;
Information: Greater Birmingham Convention & Visitors Bureau, 2027 1st Ave North Commerce Center, 3rd Floor, 35203, Phone: 252-9825

Attractions:

Art Museum (3 mi); Civil Rights Museum (3 mi); Birmingham Zoo (5 mi); Botanical Gardens (5 mi); Five Pts South (5 mi); Riverchase Galleria Mall (15 mi).

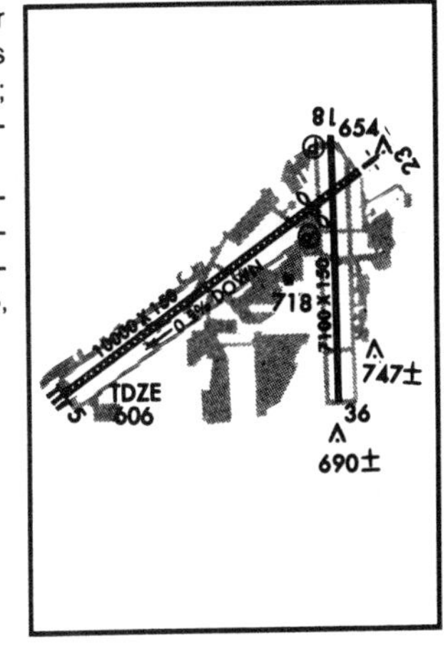

Airport Information:

BIRMINGHAM - BIRMINGHAM AIRPORT (BHM)
4 mi northeast N33-33.78 W86-45.21 Elev: 644
Fuel: 100LL, Jet-A Rwy: 05-23: H10000x150 (Asph-Grvd)
Rwy 18-36: H7100x150 (Asph-Grvd) Attended: continuously Atis: 119.4 Unicom: 122.95 App/Dep Con: 127.675, 123.8 Tower: 119.9, 118.25 Gnd Con: 121.7 Clnc Del: 125.675 Pre-Taxi Clnc: 125.675
FBO: AMR COMBS Birmingham Phone: 849-5520
FBO: Raytheon Aircraft Service Phone: 591-6830

Southern Museum of Flight

In a modern fully-equipped shop on the premises, airplanes are refurbished for display or rebuilt from bare bones of antique "basket case." Plans currently are underway to double the present display facility to accommodate the museum's flourishing collection of aircraft and tributes to explorers of the skies.

Located just two blocks east of the Birmingham Municipal Airport, the Southern Museum of Flight is a non-profit operation. The Birmingham Aero Club originally conceived and sponsored the museum and still contributes to its operation. The Southern Museum of Flight is now municipally owned and operated. All contributions, whether monetary or for display, are tax deductible.

The museum is open Tuesday through Saturday from 9:30 a.m. to 5:00 p.m. and Sunday from 1:00 p.m. to 4:30 p.m. For more information and details on group rates and scheduling, contact the Southern Museum of Flight at 205-833-8226.(Information submitted by museum).

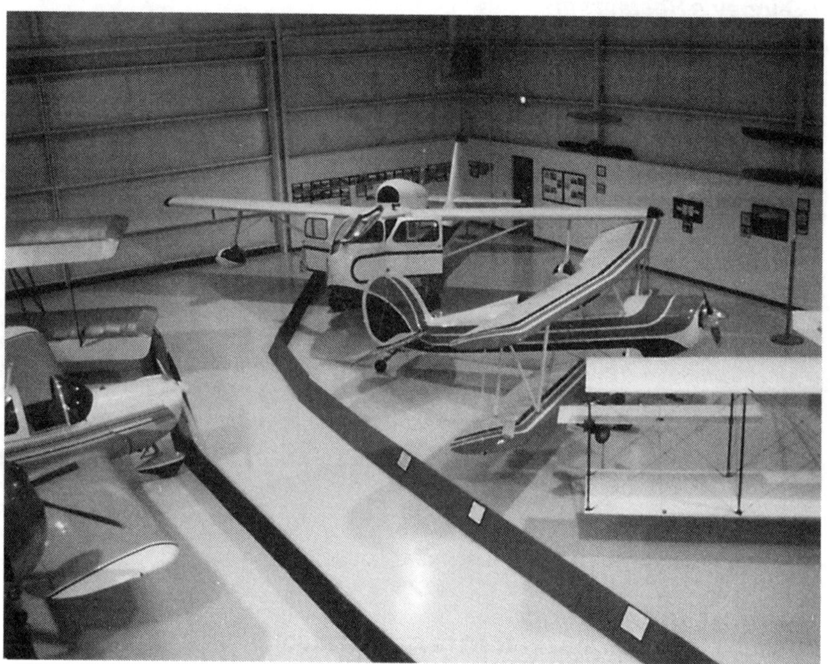

Southern Museum of Flight only 2 blks east of the Birmingham Arpt.

Photo by: Southern Museum of Flight

AL-4R9 - DAUPHIN ISLAND
DAUPHIN ISLAND AIRPORT

(Area Code 334) 6, 7

The Seafood Galley:

The Seafood Galley restaurant is located about 3/4th of a mile from the Dauphin Island Airport. Fly-in guests can either walk to the restaurant or simply call for free transportation. The restaurant is open 7 days a week from 6 a.m.. to 10 p.m. during summer months and until 9 p.m. during the winter. Specialties of the house include a full breakfast selection. Lunch and dinner entrees feature selections like "Poor Boy's" hamburgers, cheeseburgers, pizza's, BBQ ribs, chopped steak, T-bone, rib-eyes, casseroles, fried, grilled, blacken and steamed seafood, and seafood augratin. A nice complement of desserts and appetizers are also available. Average prices run $5.00 for breakfast, $6.00 for lunch. $6.00 to $14.00 for dinner. There is seating for about 200 people with additional group seating for up to 70 people. Mirrored columns decorate the center of the restaurant. with white wicker chairs and brown tables in the dining room. Accommodations for groups can easily be arranged along with buffet styled selections. A public beach is located across the street from the restaurant as well as couple of gift shops and women's clothing store adjacent to the restaurant. If you plan to walk from the airport take the first road to the right and go until you reach a dead end. then turn right on Danville Blvd. to the east. The restaurant should be on your right side, or better yet just call the restaurant at 861-8000 for transportation.

Seafood House Restaurant & Lounge:

The Seafood House is located about 1 mile from the Dauphin Island Airport, and will provide their fly-in guests with courtesy transportation to and from the restaurant and airport. This unique restaurant serves as a combination family style, "come-as-you-are" restaurant, while serving entrees more in tune to a fine dining facility. Their menu features oysters on the half shell, grilled fish, prime rib and rib eye steak. Average prices range from $5.00 for lunch to around $10.00 for dinner. On Friday nights they offer a seafood buffet from 6 p.m. to 9 p.m. On Saturday nights the chef prepares a prime rib special. In the lounge on Sunday, their appetizers include their famous crawfish bowl. The restaurant is located right at the marina where boats of all kinds are always coming and going. There is seating for 75 in the main dining room, with an additional 45 in their lounge. The Seafood House Restaurant is open during the summer between 11 a.m. and 10:30 p.m. 7 days a week. In the winter they open at 4 p.m. until 10 p.m. on weekdays and 11 a.m. to 10:30 p.m. on weekends. For more information, you can call this establishment at 861-7169.

Restaurants Near Airport:

Seafood Gallery	3/4 mi	Phone: 861-8000
Seafood House	1 mi	Phone: 861-7169

Lodging: Bayou Heron (1/2 mile) 861-5534; Gulf Breeze (1/2 mile) 861-7344.

Meeting Rooms: None Reported

Transportation: The Seafood House will pick pilots and their guests up at the airport.

Information: Mobile Convention & Visitor Bureau, One St Louis Center, Suite 2002, Mobile, AL 36602, Phone: 433-5100 or 800-666-6282.

Attractions:

18 hole golf course reported on the island. For information you can call "Aldofe Golf Club at 861-2433. Also: Fort Gaines is located on the east side of the island and was constructed between 1821 and 1861. This five sided fort serves as a museum of the Confederacy. This attraction is open daily except on December 25th. For information call 861-6992.

Airport Information:

DAUPHIN ISLAND - DAUPHIN ISLAND AIRPORT (4R9)
0 mi northwest of town 30-15-37N 88-07-39W Rwy 12-30: H3000x80 (Asph) Attended: unattended Unicom: 122.8 Notes: CAUTION: birds on and in vicinity of airport, Extensive banner tow operations around island coast line and north to Mobile.
Dauphin Island Airport Phone: 824-2831

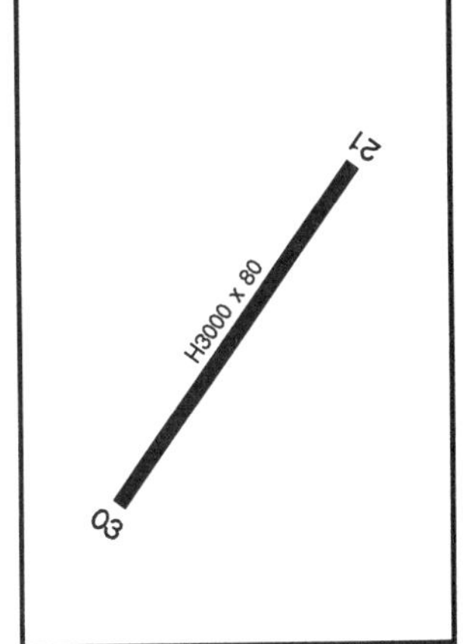

U.S. Army Aviation Museum

Enterprise, AL (AL-EDN)

The Army Aviation Museum Foundation, incorporated under the laws of the State of Alabama as a nonprofit organization, was formed on March 9, 1970. The purpose of the Foundation is to provide a proper permanent building to house and preserve the U.S. Army Aviation Museum, its memorabilia and artifacts. The museum serves to safeguard many one-of-a-kind aircraft and aviation related items, educate the aviation student and public, and generate an interest in and understanding of Army Aviation.

Situated between the south Alabama cities of Ozark, Enterprise, and Dothan, the U.S. Army Aviation Museum is easily accessible off U.S. Highway 84 and 231. The Museum, a new 87,000 square foot facility, is located in Building 6000 at the U.S. Army Aviation Center, Fort Rucker, Alabama. The Museum collection maintains many unique aircraft and research and development experiments in both fixed and rotor wing flight, to include one of the largest helicopter collection in the world. The aircraft display traces the history of Army aviation from its beginning. The significant aircraft on display start with the Army's first helicopter, the R-4, through the current attack helicopter, the AH-64 Apache; as well as a look at the development and employment of the light airplane. June 6, 1942 marked the beginning of light aviation as an organic part of the U.S. Army. Light aircraft on display include "Piper Cub" type airplanes and L-4 observation craft used for field artillery fire direction. In addition to the exhibits at the museum is the U.S. Army Aviation Gift Shop containing items like souvenirs, prints & posters, pilot supplies, jewelry, T-shirts, hats and much more. The museum hours are 9 a.m. to 4 p.m. seven days a week, closed Thanksgiving Day, Christmas Day, News Year's Eve and New Years Day. Admission is free. We believe the nearest general aviation airport is Enterprise Municipal (EDN) in the town of Enterprise, Alabama. For available transportation call the City of Enterprise (FBO) at 334-347-1211 or Enterprise Aviation, Inc. at 334-393-7727. For further information about the U.S. Army Aviation Museum, call 334-598-9465. (Information submitted by museum.)

AL-4R4 - FAIRHOPE
FAIRHOPE MUNICIPAL

(Area Code 205) **8**

Marriott's Grand Hotel:

Marriott's Grand Hotel is located on the Eastern shore of Mobile Bay, just 8 miles west of the Fairhope Municipal Airport in Point Clear. Known as the "Queen of Southern Resorts", this 147 year-old secluded bayside resort enchants guests with authentic Southern hospitality. It has three separate buildings and 16 cottages which house 307 guests. There is also 23,000 square feet of meeting space for various sized functions. The resort offers a variety of activities for the whole family. For the avid golfer, the 36-hole Lakewood Golf Club has a par 72 Azalea course and a par 71 Dogwood course, which is accented by steep bunkers, winding, magnolia-lined fairways, island greens and magnificent views of Mobile Bay. Tennis players will enjoy the Grand's Tennis Club which offers eight rubico-covered courts (two are lighted), a full service pro shop, and experienced tennis instructors. For nature -seekers, there are miles of walking, jogging, biking and horseback riding trails which meander through secluded gardens and 300-year-old moss-draped oaks. During the summer months, children age 5-12 are welcome to join the numerous educational and entertaining activities of the Grand Fun Camp. Kids will have a great time exploring the history of Point Clear and the great heritage of the South, as well as tackling team tennis, sidewalk chalking, bashing balloons and fishing. All guests can enjoy taking a dip in Mobile Bay or the 468,000 gallon pool, or even go windsurfing or aqua biking. They can charter a boat for sightseeing and fishing excursions. The Grand has a 34-slip marina with full facilities and docking privileges for guests, and is home to the resort's 111-foot yacht, "Southern Comfort". Pavilion Wharf offers plenty of fishing and crab trapping. For the ambitious guest, the chef at the Grand will prepare the catch-of-the-day for dinner that evening. The hotel personnel will provide courtesy transportation for fly-in guests. For information call 800-544-9933 or 928-9201.

Restaurants Near Airport:
Marriott's Grand Hotel 8 mi W. Phone: 928-9201

Lodging: Marriott's Grand Hotel (3 miles) 928-9201; Baron Motel (4 mi.) 928-2328; Homestead Grand Victorian (5 miles) 990-6132;

Meeting Rooms: Baron Motel 928-2328; Marriott's Grand Hotel 928-9201

Transportation: Marriott's Grand Hotel (courtesy car to and from airport) 928-9201; Homestead Grand Victorian 990-6132; Rental Cars: Enterprise/ will deliver 928-6810

Information: Eastern Shore Chamber of Commerce, 327 Fairhope Avenue, Fairhope, AL 36532. Phone: 205-928-6387

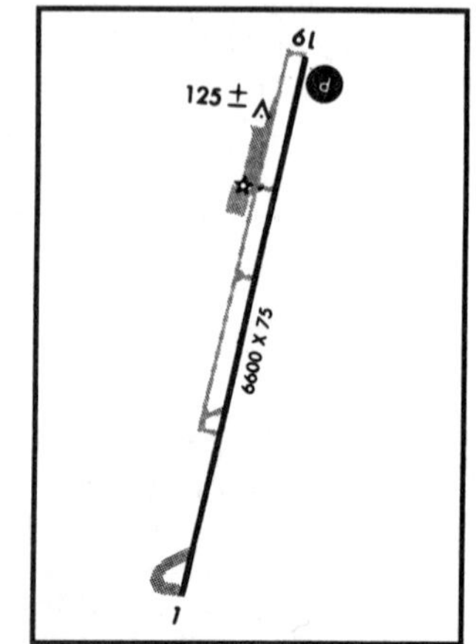

Airport Information:

FAIRHOPE - FAIRHOPE MUNICIPAL (4R4)
3 mi southeast of town N30-27.73 W87-52.68 Elev: 94 Fuel: 100LL, Jet-A Rwy 01-19: H6600x75 (Asph) Attended: 1200-0200Z CTAF/Unicom: 122.8 Notes: after hours call 800-681-0917.
FBO: Clark Aviation **Phone 37-8227**

AL-33J - GENEVA
GENEVA MUNICIPAL AIRPORT

(Area Code 334) 9

Price's Diner:

Price's Diner is located 3/4th of a mile southeast of the Geneva Municipal Airport. When speaking with the owner, we learned that he was also a pilot and would be happy to provide fly-in guests with courtesy transportation to and from his facility if possible, due to limited staff. The restaurant is open between 9:00 a.m. and 9:30 p.m. 7 days a week. The menu contains such items as hamburgers, barbecued entrees, chicken plates, rib-eye steak, shrimp, and specializes in catfish dinners. Average prices run $3.40 to $5.00 for lunch and about $4.50 to $6.00 for dinner. The restaurant can seat about 50 to 60 persons, and has a contemporary atmosphere. Fly-in groups and parties are welcome with advance notice. Meals can be prepared-to-go as well. For more information, call Price's Diner at 684-2576.

Restaurants Near Airport:
Price's Diner 3/4 mi Phone: 684-2576

Lodging: Eunola Motel (2 miles) 684-3646.

Meeting Rooms: None Reported

Transportation: The owner of Price's Diner informed us that they would do their best to provide fly-in guests with transportation to and from their restaurant.

Information: Alabama Bureau of Tourism & Travel, 532-South Perry Street, Montgomery, AL 36104, Phone: 205-242-4169

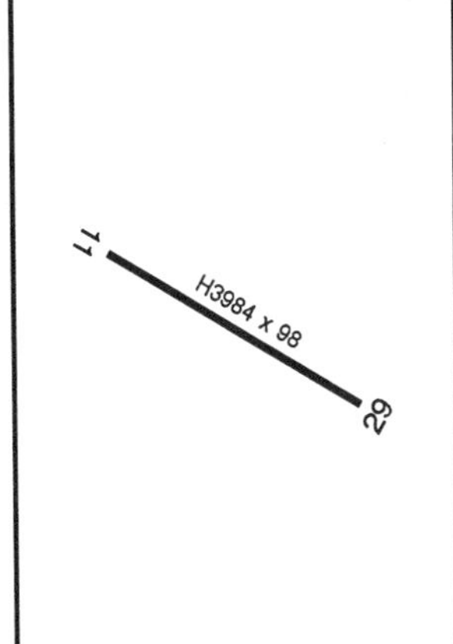

Airport Information:

GENEVA - GENEVA MUNICIPAL AIRPORT (33J)
2 mi north of town N31-03.34 W85-52.00 Elev: 101 Fuel: 100LL,
Rwy 11-29: H3984x98 (Asph) Attended: Mon-Fri 2100-0100Z, Sat-Sun 1400-2300Z
Unicom: 122.8 Notes: Extensive ultralight activity in vicinity of airport.
Geneva Aviation **Phone: 684-3591**

Ryder's Replica Fighter Museum

GUNTERSVILLE, AL (AL-8A1)

File photo by: Aerodine Magazine

In northeast Alabama's beautiful rolling hills, there is a beautiful resort area at the southernmost point of the Tennessee River. The Tennessee Valley Authority built Guntersville Dam, which formed that part of the river into a 69,000 acre lake with 949 miles of shoreline. The area draws tourists and vacationers from all over the world, and Frank Ryder chose this scenic spot to build Ryder's Replica Fighter Museum only a few short years ago.

Located at the Guntersville Airport, seven spotless hangars now display the nearly 40 WW-I replica aircraft, as well as the magnificent art collection, a recently added collection of vintage aircraft engines and propellers, an extensive aviation reference library and archives, and a vast array of artifacts and memorabilia. Beautiful large-scale unmanned aircraft, including a series of 15-footers, hang from the museum's beams, as well as a 32-foot zeppelin.

Additional airworthy replica fighters are presently under construction in virtually every corner of the United States by some of the finest and most experienced craftsmen in the WW-I field. These projects include a SPAD 7, SPAD 13, Morane-Saulnier BB, Sopwith 1-1/2 Strutter, SE5, Pfalz Dr-I Triplane and a Fokker D-VII. Several of them will be powered by such rare original engines as Mercedes, Hispano-Suiza, and even the much sought after original LeRhone and Gnome rotary engines.

Unlike many other museums, nearly all of the Ryder's aircraft on display are flown regularly. The planes are shuffled in and out of the museum's hangars for frequent exercise. With a few exceptions, such as the stunning black 80% scale Albatros DVa, most are full-size replicas accurately depicting many aircraft which, if originals did exist, would be far too rare, valuable and historically significant to risk flying. The main deviation from authenticity is the substitution of more modern and reliable engines such as Warner, Ranger, Lycoming and Continental, and the addition of brakes and tail wheels for safe handling. Four different aircraft from the collection have won Grand Champion Replica at Sun 'n Fun Fly-in for four years in a row.

On the rare occasions when the planes are exhibited at major fly-ins such as Oshkosh or Sun 'n Fun, they are flown there, not trailered. The exhibit halls feature aircraft from the movie "The Blue Max". Where round engines cowls are now housing flat four cylinder Lycomings, special false front engine kits have been designed to give the convincing appearance of the actual rotary engines. In others, such as the six-cylinder opposed Continental powered Halberstadts, a very convincing representation of the Mercedes is visible on top of the cowling. The graphics, such as propeller decals, fuselage script, squadron emblems, and elaborate colorful marking and insignia have been given careful attention to complete the detailing and visual impact of these replicas.

There are numerous display cases

throughout the museum featuring aeronautica of every type. These include such rarities as original instruments, machine guns, uniforms, exquisite models by such notables as the aviation artist Charles Hubbel, and personal memorabilia such as the Christmas 1917 presentation gold watch inscribed to Douglas Campbell, America's first ace.

Recently added and now distributed through the museum is The Gertler Collection, a display of rare pre-1919 aero engines. These range from such standards as the Curtiss OX-5, Liberty, Hispano Suizas, LeRhones, Gnomes and Anzanis to such rarities as the Roberts, Curtiss VX, Sturtevant, Hall-Scout, Gregoire-Gyp. Humber, Salmson and Lawrance A-3. Visitors fascinated by the amazing rotary engines are also drawn to a cut-away Gnome and a post war "Quick" conversion of a LeRhone rotary to the static radial configuration, as well as the early 50 h.p. Gnome, which contributed so much to the development of early aviation.

The art collection attractively exhibited throughout the museum covers illustration in all media, including pencil, pastels, pen and ink, acrylic water colors, oil on canvas, prints, lithos and originals. There are a great many works signed by not only the artists, but by the famous WW-I flyers that are the subjects. All of the art displayed throughout the museum was personally hung by Frank Ryder.

The newest feature of the museum is a series of walkways, giving visitors access to view the ongoing projects and repairs in the expanded workshop area. There is also a corridor to the storage hangar which houses thousands of extra WW-I aircraft parts, accessories and memorabilia, as well as additional WW-I replicas awaiting assembly or completion.

Still in the planning stage is a major exhibit of WW-I instruments and cockpit items which includes literally hundreds of original WW-I altimeters, tachometers, fuel gages, switches, pumps, compasses, seat belts, hand crank magnetos, cockpit placards, throttle quadrants and other interesting cockpit items.

Five restored antique autos, trucks and even an ambulance of WW-I are displayed as typical military support vehicles with a period military motorcycle to arrive soon.

There is a clean, well organized gift shop which offers collectibles and souvenirs in all price ranges, for all ages and tastes. Two of the most popular items are T-shirts of various designs and a fifty-minute video tape of all of the highlights of past AERODROME Conventions.

File Photo by: Aerodine Magazine

WW-I planes currently on display:

Albatros DVa, Albatros DV a (80% scale), Caudron 272, DeHavilland DH5, Fokker Dr-1 (4), Fokker D-VII (2), Fokker D-VIII, Fokker E-III, Halberstadt CL-IV, Martinsyde Buzzard, Neiuport 17 (3/4 scale) (2), Nieuport 24, Nieuport 28 (3), Pfalz D-III, SE5a (85% scale) (3), Siemens Schuckert D-IV, Sopwith Camel, Sopwith Pup, Sopwith Pup (3/4 scale), Sopwith Triplane, plus more soon to arrive.

The museum's new airplanes undergo extensive testing and frequent modification. Older veteran aircraft are kept airworthy and receive updating and more detailing as we try to make them as interesting as possible not only to the WW-I buff, but to the general public as well. The constant state of improvement and activity keeps the friendly, courteous museum staff eager and willing to provide insight and answer the questions of our visitors, many of whom have become regulars.

Ryder's Replica Fighter Museum is open daily, and hours are 9:00 a.m. to 4:00 p.m. The museum is closed some holidays, but will remain open during the "Aerodrome Convention". Admission is $5.00 for adults (age 16 and over), $2.50 for youths (age 6 through 15) and free for children (age 5 and under). Members of THE FIRST WARPLANES organization are admitted for half price with a membership card. For information call or write the:

RYDER'S REPLICA FIGHTER MUSEUM
Airport Rd. - 20446 U.S. Hwy. 431 N.
P.O. Box 366
Guntersville, AL 35976
Phone: 205-582-4309

This is one of several articles about the museum that was featured in "The First Warplanes Magazine", and was written by: Executive Director Joe Gertler

AERODROME A World War One fly-in convention

One event that should not be missed, is the annual Aerodrome Convention held at Gadsden, Alabama. This extravaganza of WW-I flying aircraft attracts over 50,000 visitors, and is growing by leaps and bounds each year it is held. Reservations at nearby hotels and motels are at a premium during the convention. In past years the show was held at Guntersville, Alabama but was moved to Gadsden Municipal Airport in order to accept the growing number of visitors and fly-in enthusiasts. For information about planned or scheduled events, accommodations and information kits, you can call the Ryder's Replica Fighter Museum at 205-582-4340. Information about rental cars, lodging and nearby restaurants can also be obtained by calling the Gadsden -Etowah Tourism Board at 205-549-0351.

AL-HSV - HUNTSVILLE INTL-CARL T. JONES FIELD

(Area Code 205) 10

Restaurants Near Airport:

Veranda Room Restaurant On Site Phone: 772-9661

Veranda Room Sheraton Inn Restaurant:

The Veranda Room is located adjacent to Huntsville Aviation and is part of the Sheraton Inn complex. This family style facility is open from 5:30 a.m. to 2:00 p.m. and then again from 3:00 p.m. to 10 p.m. 7 days a week. Their menu includes an assortment of breakfast items along with sandwiches, plate lunches, a variety of basic lunch and dinner selections as well as choice steaks. Average prices run $5.25 for breakfast, $5,95 for lunch and $12.95 for dinner. Meals can be prepared for carry-out or in-flight catering, which is one of their specialties. The dining room can seat 107 people and has a bright and cheery decor. Pictures of space art and photographs decorate the walls. Small or large groups can easily be handled in a number of conference rooms, available to accommodate from 10 to 250 people. For more information, call their switch board at 772-9661 and ask for the Veranda Room Restaurant.

Lodging: The following establishments provide transportation to and from the airport: Executive Inn 772-7170; Hilton 533-1400; Holiday Inn Research Park 830-0600; Holiday Inn-Space Center 837-7171; Marriott 830-2222; Radisson Suite Hotel 882-9400. Sheraton Inn-Huntsville Airport (on site) 772-9661.

Meeting Rooms: The following establishments provide transportation to and from the airport: Executive Inn 772-7170; Hilton (convention facilities) 533-1400; Holiday Inn Research Park 830-0600; Holiday Inn-Space Center 837-7171; Marriott (Convention facilities) 830-2222; Radisson Suite Hotel 882-9400. Sheraton Inn-Huntsville Airport (on site) 772-9661.

Transportation: FBO courtesy car available; Taxi: Executive Connection 772-0186; Alabama Yellow 533-3600; Rental Cars: Alamo 792-5000; American 461-9915; Avis 772-7811; Budget 534-6464; Hertz 772-9331; National 800-227-7368.

Information: Tourist Information Center, Convention & Visitors Bureau, Von Braun Civic Center, 700 Monroe Street, Huntsville, AL 35801, Phone: 551-2230 or 800-772-2348.

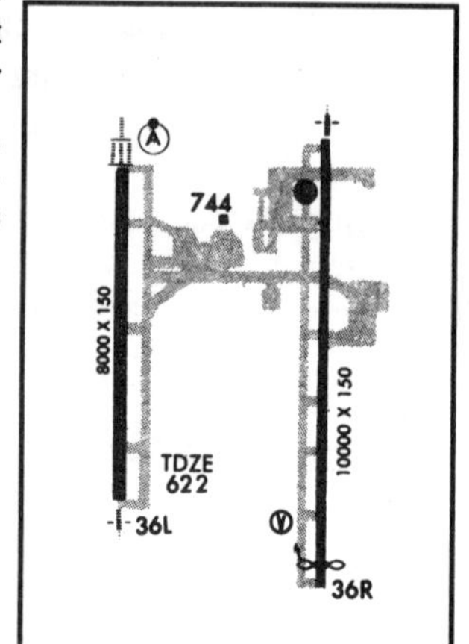

Airport Information:

HUNTSVILLE - HUNTSVILLE INTL-CARL T. JONES FIELD (HSV)
9 mi southwest of town N34-38.42 W86-46.39 Elev: 630 Fuel: 100LL, Jet-A
Rwy 18L-36R: H10000x150 (Asph-Grvd) Rwy 18R-36L: H8000x150 (Asph-Grvd) Attended: continuously Unicom: 122.95 Atis: 121.25 Tower: 127.6 Gnd Con: 121.9
Clnc Del: 120.35
FBO: Signature Flight Support Phone: 772-9341

AL-MOB - MOBILE MOBILE AIRPORT/BATES FLD (MOB)

(Area Code 205) 11

Restaurants Near Airport:

Cuco's	3 miles	Phone: N/A
Jerry's	On Site	Phone: 633-0877
Ruby Tuesday	3 miles	Phone: N/A

Jerry's Catering:

Jerry's Restaurant is located in the airport terminal building on Mobile Airport/Bates Field. This is a cafeteria styled restaurant is open from 5:30 a.m. to 10 p.m. 7 days a week. Their specialties include turkey clubs, fish sandwiches, corn dogs, hamburgers, hotdogs, and items from their steam line. They also offer a salad bar. Average prices run $3.50 for breakfast, and $4.75 for lunch and dinner. The restaurant can seat up to 75 persons. A big part of Jerry's services include catering to corporated pilots on the go. Sandwich trays, cheese and fruit trays as well as box lunches can be prepared. For more information call Jerry's Catering at 633-0877.

Lodging: Shuttle service to and from airport provided by the following: Howard Johnson Motor Lodge 471-2402; Holiday Inn I-65 342-3220; Mobil Hilton 476-6400; Ramada Inn I-65; Hampton Inn 344-4942; Warren Inn 342-0100; Holiday Inn Tillman's Corner 666-5600;

Meeting Rooms: Meeting rooms are available through the Mobil Airport Authority 633-4510; and also at Mobile Air Center 633-5000.

Transportation: Mobil Air Center has courtesy transportation. Avis Rent A Car 633-4745; Budget Rent-A-Car 633-8444; Hertz Rent-A-Car 633-4000; National Car Rental 633-4003; Yellow Cab 432-7711; Mobil Bay Limo: 633-5691.

Information: Mobile Convention & Visitors Corporation, One St. Louis Center, Ste. 2002, Mobile, AL 36602, Phone: 433-5100 or 800-666-6282.

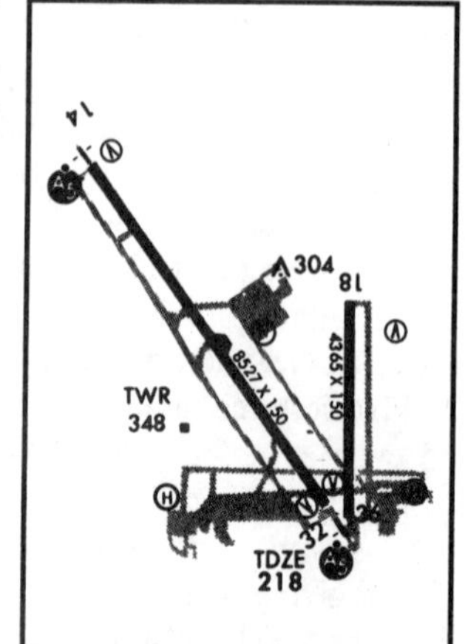

Airport Information:

MOBILE - MOBILE AIRPORT (MOB)
11 mi west of airport 30-41-28N 88-14-34W Elev: 218 Fuel: 100LL, Jet-A
Rwy 14-32: H8527x150 (Asph-Grvd) Rwy 18-36: H4365x150 (Asph-Grvd)
Attended: continuously Atis: 124.75 Unicom: 122.95 Mobil App/Dep Con: 118.5 (320-139 degrees) 121.0 (140-319 degrees) Tower: 118.3 Gnd Con: 121.9
Clnc Del: 119.85 Public Phone 24hrs
FBO: Mobile Air Center Phone: 633-5000
FBO: Aero-One Phone: 633-5396

AL-MVC - MONROEVILLE MONROE COUNTY AIRPORT

(Area Code 334)

12

David's Catfish House:

David's Catfish House is situated 1/4 mile from the Monroe County Airport. This facility is within walking distance from the airport, according to restaurant staff. This is a family style establishment that is open 11 a.m. to 9 p.m. Tuesday through Saturday. (Closed on Sundays) Of course, their specialty is catfish, however they also feature many other delicious selections such as steaks, hamburgers and chicken dishes. Many of their entrees are served with all-you-can-eat portions. Their main dining room can hold 125 persons. There is another room, which is used for special occasions, that will accommodate 50 guests. In-flight catering is also available. For more information, call the restaurant at 575-3460.

Restaurants Near Airport:

David's Catfish House	1/4 mi	Phone: 575-3460
Huddle House	1/4 mi	Phone: 743-4833
Mac's	1-1/2 mi	Phone: 575-7149

Lodging: Econo Lodge (3 miles) 575-3312; Monroe Motor Court (2 miles) 575-3177.

Meeting Rooms: None Reported

Transportation: Rental Cars: Avis 575-4235;

Information: Alabama Bureau of Tourism & Travel, 401 Adams Ave, P.O. Box 4927, Montgomery, AL 36103-4927, Phone: 334-242-4169.

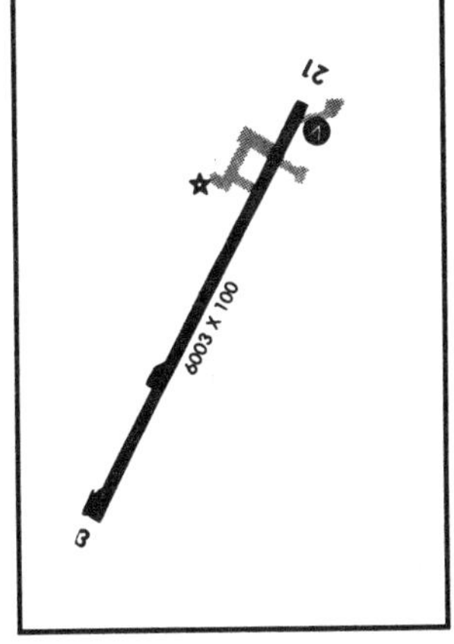

Airport Information:

MONROEVILLE - MONROE COUNTY AIRPORT (MVC)
3 mi south of town N31-2748 W87-21.06 Elev: 419 Fuel: 100LL, Jet-A
Rwy 03-21: H6003x100 (Asph) Attended: Mon-Fri 1330-2300Z, Sat 1400-2300Z, Sun 1600-2300Z Unicom: 123.0
FBO: Monroeville Aviation & Avionics Phone: 575-4235

AL-MGM - MONTGOMERY DANNELLY FIELD

(Area Code 334)

13

Jerry's Catering:

Jerry's Catering is located in the terminal building at the Montgomery/Dannelly Airport. This family style restaurant can be reached by shuttle service from the fixed base operators on the field. Their hours are from 5:30 a.m. to 8 p.m. 7 days a week. Their menu contains selections like Philly cheese steak sandwiches, burgers, turkey clubs, chicken, tuna and cold plate sandwiches. A full breakfast line is also offered. Average prices run about $3.50 to $5.95 for most items. Specials are also available on weekdays. The restaurant can accommodate up to 50 persons. Large plate glass windows allow customers to enjoy the view looking out over the airport as well as the passenger waiting areas. Fly-in groups and clubs are welcome if advance notice is given. All selection off their menu can be prepared for carry-out. For more information call Jerry's Catering at 284-8151.

Restaurants Near Airport:

Jerry's Catering	On Site	Phone: 284-8151

Lodging: The following provide free transportation: Best Western Peddler's Inn 288-0610; Governor's House 288-2800; Holiday Inn Airport 281-1660.

Meeting Rooms: Best Western Peddler's Inn 288-0610; Days Inn 281-8000; Holiday Inn Airport 281-1660.

Transportation: Taxi: Lane; Yellow. Rental Cars: Avis; Budget; Hertz; or National.

Information: Montgomery Area Chamber of Commerce, 41 Commerce Street, P.O. Box 79, Montgomery, AL 36101, or call Visitors Information Center at 262-0013.

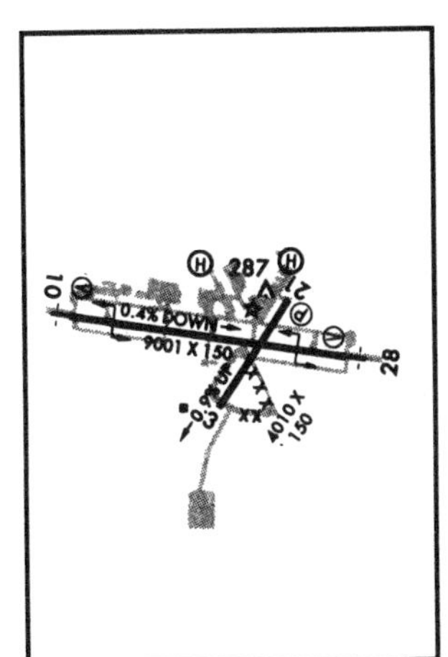

Airport Information:

MONTGOMERY - DANNELLY FIELD (MGM)
6 mi southwest of town N32-18.04 W86-23.64 Elev: 221 Fuel: 100LL, Jet-A
Rwy 10-28: H9001x150 (Asph-Grvd) Rwy 03-21: H4010x150 (Asph) Attended: continuously
Atis 124.425 Unicom: 122.95 Montgomery App/Dep Con: 124.0 South, 121.2 North
Tower: 119.7 Gnd Con: 121.7 Clnc Del: 118.3 Notes: CAUTION: (See Airport Facility Directory for comments)
FBO: Montgomery Aviation Corp. Phone: 288-7334

AL-MSL - MUSCLE SHOALS
MUSCLE SHOALS REGIONAL

(Area Code 205) 14

Renaissance Grille:

The Renaissance Grille is located about 4 miles north of the Muscle Shoals Regional Airport. Restaurant hours are from 11 a.m. to 10 p.m. Monday through Thursday, closing at 11 p.m. on Friday and Saturday and 9 p.m. on Sunday. The restaurant is situated at the top of a 300-foot-tall tower, and offers a 360-degree unrestricted view of the Wilson Lock and Dam on the Tennessee River. While enjoying the panoramic view of the river, be sure to catch a glimpse of the dining room's gracious Victorian decor. Although there is no breakfast menu, the restaurant offers a various assortment of delicious lunch and dinner entrees such as sandwiches, steaks, seafoods, and pastas. Some of the specialties include: chicken gumbo, quiche, chicken and beef kabobs, ribs, and the seafood "Catch of the Day". There are also homemade cheesecakes and brownies for dessert. Average prices vary for lunch and dinner, but they do not run above $18.00. The Grille will cater to parties of 20 or more, if reservations are made in advance. For more information, call the Renaissance Grille at 718-0092. Muscle Shoals Aviation will provide free courtesy transportation to and from the restaurant. Call 383-2270 for further information.

Restaurants Near Airport:

Cambelli	4 mi	Phone: 389-8952
Court Street Cafe	5 mi	Phone: 767-4300
George's Steak Pit	4 mi	Phone: 381-1534
Renaissance Grille	4 mi	Phone: 718-0092

Lodging: Executive Inn (3 miles) 766-2331; Holiday Inn (3 miles) 381-4710; Master Hosts Inn (5 miles) 764-5421; Ramada Inn (3 miles) 381-3743; Tourway Inn (8 miles) 766-2620
Meeting Rooms: None Reported
Transportation: Taxi services: Tuscumbia 383-1818; Yellow Cab Florence 766-1000
Information: Chamber of Commerce of the Shoals, 104 S. Pine Street, Florence, AL 35630, Phone: 764-4661

Attraction:

The Renaissance Tower, one of the tallest structures in the state, also includes the AlabamaShoals Aquar-ium and an 80-seat theater.

Airport Information:

Muscle Shoals - Muscle Shoals Regional Airport (MSL)
1 mi east of town N34-44.72 W87-36.61 Elev: 550 Fuel: 100LL, Jet-A Rwy 11-29: H6693x150 (Asph-Grvd) Rwy 18-36: H4000x100 (Asph) Attended: continuously CTAF: 123.6
Unicom: 122.95 Notes: During calm winds, runway 29 is preferred.
FBO: Muscle Shoals Aviation Phone: 383-2270
FBO: Aerial Services, Inc. Phone: 386-7597

Photo by: Tennessee Valley Exhibit Commission

The Renaissance Grille is situated at the top of the 300-foot-tall Renaissance Tower in Florence, Alabama. It offers a 360-degree unrestricted view of the Wilson Lock and Dam on the Tennessee River.

AL-M26 - RED BAY
RED BAY MUNICIPAL AIRPORT

(Area Code 205) 15

Jack's Drive Inn:

Jack's Drive Inn is located 1/4 mile from the Red Bay Municipal Airport. This family style restaurant is open from 8 a.m. to 9 p.m. Monday through Thursday and from 8 a.m. to 10 p.m. on Friday and Saturday. Their entrees include a full breakfast line, fish, barbecue, chicken plates, chicken fingers, fried shrimp, steak, as well as many different types of sandwiches. They also have a salad bar. Monday through Friday they provide a buffet from 10:30 a.m. to 2:00 p.m. There are two dining rooms available within the restaurant able to accommodate a total of 120 persons. Groups and parties are welcome. When flying into the Red Bay airport, be alert for any children or vehicles that may be crossing the runway. For more information about Jack's restaurant, call 356-9931.

Restaurants Near Airport:
Jack's Drive Inn 1/4 mi Phone: 356-9931

Lodging: None Reported

Meeting Rooms: None Reported

Transportation: None Reported

Information: Alabama Bureau of Tourism & Travel, 401 Adams Ave, P.O. Box 4927, Montgomery , AL 36103-4927, Phone: 334-242-4169.

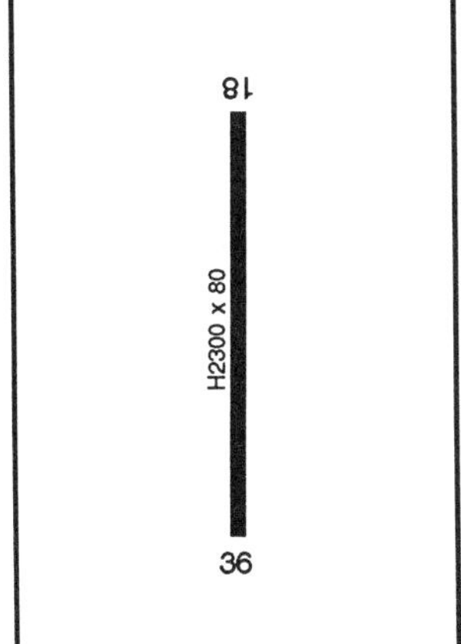

Airport Information:

RED BAY - RED BAY MUNICIPAL AIRPORT (M26)
1 mi northwest of town N34-27.01 W88-09.00 Elev: 620 Rwy 18-36: H2300x80 (Asph)
Attended: unattended CTAF: 122.9 Notes: CAUTION: children, dogs, cars may be on runway.
Red Bay Airport Phone: 356-4455

Promote General Aviation Just Take A Friend Flying

ARIZONA

LOCATION MAP

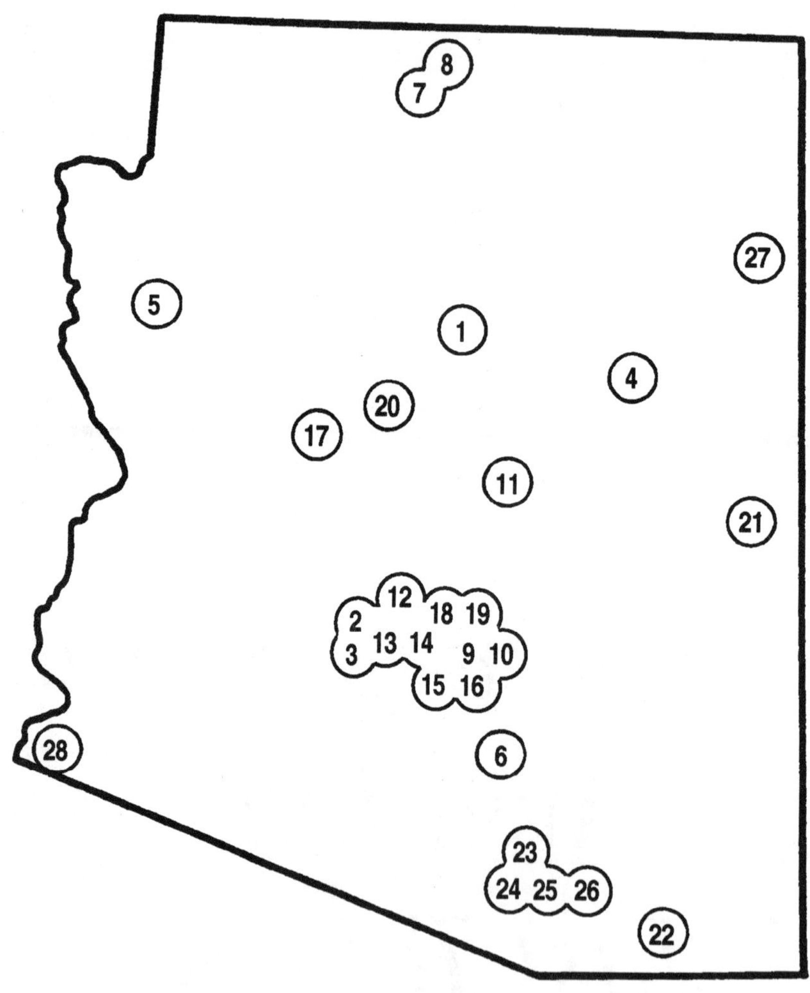

Not to be used for navigational purposes

ARIZONA

CROSS FILE INDEX

Location Number	City or Town	Airport Name And Identifier	Name of Attraction
1	Flagstaff	Flagstaff Pulliam Arpt. (FLG)	Little America Hotel
2	Glendale	Glendale Muni. (GEU)	Right Stuff Cafe
3	Goodyear	Phoenix-Goodyear Muni. (GYR)	Wigwam Resort
4	Holbrook	Holbrook Muni. (P14)	Denny's Restaurant
5	Kingman	Kingman Arpt. (IGM)	Maggie's Flightline Diner
6	Marana	Pinal Airpark (MZJ)	Elinor's Restaurant
7	Marble Canyon	Cliff Dwellers Lodge Arpt. (AZ03)	Cliff Dwellers Lodge
8	Marble Canyon	Marble Canyon Arpt. (L41)	Marble Canyon Lodge
9	Mesa	Falcon Field (FFZ)	Anzio Landing Rest.
10	Mesa	Falcon Field (FFZ)	Arizona Golf Resort
11	Payson	Payson Arpt. (E69)	Crosswind Restaurant
12	Phoenix	Deer Valley Muni. (DVT)	Deer Valley Arpt. Rest.
13	Phoenix	Phoenix Ski Harbor Intl.(PHX)	CA1 Service
14	Phoenix	Phoenix Ski Harbor Intl.(PHX)	Left Seat
15	Phoenix	Williams Gateway Arpt. (IWA)	Flight Deck Restaurant
16	Phoenix	Williams Gateway Arpt. (IWA)	Williams Golf Snack Bar
17	Prescott	Ernest A. Love Field (PRC)	Nancy's Skyway Rest.
18	Scottsdale	Scottsdale Muni. Arpt. (SDL)	Left Seat Restaurant
19	Scottsdale	Scottsdale Muni. Arpt. (SDL)	Thunderbird Restaurant
20	Sedona	Sedona Arpt. (SEZ)	Airport Restaurant
21	Springerville	Springerville Babbitt Field (Q35)	Mike's Steakhouse
22	Tombstone	Tombstone Muni. Arpt. (P29)	Top O' The Hill
23	Tucson	Ryan Airfield (RYN)	Wings Restaurant
24	Tucson	Tucson Intl. Arpt. (TUS)	El Charro (CA1 Services)
25	Tucson	Tucson Intl. Arpt. (TUS)	Sutters Tower Rest.
26	Tucson	Tucson Intl. Arpt. (TUS)	Tanque Verde Ranch
27	Window Rock	Window Rock Airport (P34)	Navajo Nation Inn
28	Yuma Mcas	Yuma Intl. Arpt. (YUM)	Sky Chief Restaurant

Articles

City or Town	Nearest Airport and Identifier	Name of Attraction
Goodyear, AZ	Goodyear Muni. (GYR)	The Wigwam Resort
Mesa, AZ	Falcon Fld. (FFZ)	Champlin Fighter Museum
Pima, AZ	Tucson Intl. Arpt. (TUS)	Pima Air Museum

AZ-FLG - FLAGSTAFF
FLAGSTAFF PULLIAM AIRPORT

(Area Code 602) 1

Restaurants Near Airport:
Little America Hotel 5 mi Phone: 779-2741

Little America Hotel:

Little America Hotel is located in scenic Northern Arizona, only 5 miles from Flagstaff Pulliam Airport. The hotel,open 365 days a year, is situated on over 400 acres of Ponderosa Pine forest. It provides 248 spacious guest rooms and suites that are richly furnished, offering the right blend of style and comfort to suit your needs. All rooms feature a 31-inch TV, cozy goose down pillows, imported marble, and spacious bath and dressing areas. Some also include private saunas, wet bars and fireplaces. For your dining pleasure, the Little America Restaurant is open 24 hours. It offers a full-service menu, along with cocktails. The Western Gold Dining Room, open 5:00 p.m. to 10:00 p.m., features affordable, first-class fare in an relaxed atmosphere. The American Ballroom offers a scrumptious Sunday Champagne Brunch from 9:00 a.m. to 2:00 p.m. Convention and banquet facilities are also available. For your shopping needs, the Gift Shop, open 24 hours, features fine fashions, authentic Indian jewelry, arts and crafts, and a gourmet food section. Little America Hotel also offers recreational activities, such as swimming in an olympic-size pool, jogging, badminton, croquet, tennnis, racquetball, and a health club. The hotel provides free 24-hour shuttle service to and from Flagstaff Pulliam Airport. For more information, contact the Little America Hotel at 779-2741.

Lodging: Little America Hotel (5 miles) 779-2741; Holiday Inn (4 miles) 774-1100; Motel Six (4 miles) 774-3757, 774-1801; Quality Inn (3 miles) 774-8771; Quality Suites (4 miles) 774-4333
Meeting Rooms: Little America Hotel 779-2741
Transportation: Little America Hotel provides free courtesy transportation to and from Flagstaff Pulliam Airport; Rental Cars: Avis 774-8421; Budget 779-0306; Hertz 774-4452
Information: Chamber and Visitor's Center, 101 W. Santa Fe, Flagstaff, AZ 86001-5598, Phone: 774-9541

Attractions: Walnut Canyon National Monument contains over 300 rock dwellings (dating back to 11 A.D.) in rugged canyons and cliffs 400 feet in depth. Visitor center and museum on premises, located 12 miles east of Flagstaff off U.S. 66 and I-40, for information call 526-3367; Fairfield Snowbowl (Skiing) 11,300 foot level on Mt. Agassiz and 9,954 foot level at Hart Prairie, vertical drop 2,300 foot drop, longest run 2.5 miles, Phone: 779-6126; Little America (Resort) 6 miles from airport with free transportation, 248 units, conference rooms, entertainment, tennis and golf privileges. For information call 779-2741.

Airport Information:

FLAGSTAFF - FLAGSTAFF PULLIAM AIRPORT (FLG)
4 miles south of town N35-08.31 W111-40.27 Elev: 7011 Fuel: 100LL, Jet-A Rwt 03-21: H6999x150 (Asph-Pfc) Attended: 1300-0600Z CTAF: 120.0 Atis: 125.8 Unicom: 122.95 App/Dep Con: 124.5 Tower: 120.0 NFCT (Apr1-Sep 30 1300-0400Z, Oct 1-Mar 31 1400-0200Z) Gnd Con: 121.9 Notes: Fuel avbl 1400-0300Z, fee other hours. Deer in airport vicinity. Rwy 03-21 windshear and turbulence at both ends of rwy when surface winds exceed 10 knots. Airport may be CLOSED for snow removal. CAUTION-removal equipment may be on rwy other times.
FBO: Alpine Air Service Phone: 779-5178

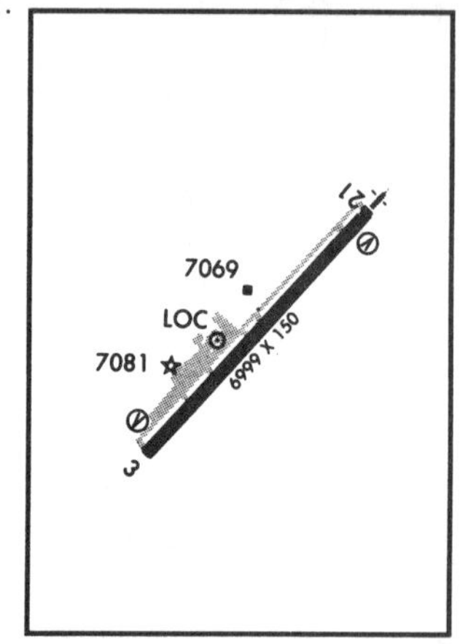

Photo by: Little America Hotel

Not to be used for navigational purposes

AZ-GEU - GLENDALE
GLENDALE - GLENDALE MUNICIPAL

(Area Code 602)

2

Restaurants Near Airport:

The Right Stuff Cafe	On Site	Phone: 872-1234
Wigwam Resort	7 mi	Phone: 935-3811

Lodging: Wigwam Resort (300 plus units, 7 miles, Trans.) 935-3811; Windmill Inn (6 miles) 800-547-4747.

Meeting Rooms: Conference and meeting rooms available at lodging facilities listed above.

Transportation: Rental Car: 872-1368

Information: Glendale Chamber of Commerce, 7105 North 59th Avenue, P.O. Box 249, Glendale, AZ 85311, Phone: 937-4754 or 800-ID-SUNNY.

The Right Stuff Cafe:

The Right Stuff Cafe is located within the terminal building. This combination cafe and family style restaurant is open between 7 a.m. and 3 p.m. 7 days a week. This is a full service restaurants that provides many items on their menu, some of which are named after certain types of aircraft and aviation terms. Their "Three Point Landing" club sandwich is one of their favorites along with Mexican dishes, like their popular Quesadilla. For dessert they offer cakes, pies, cinnamon rolls and muffins. Their "Mile High Pie" is a favorite with many customers. Average prices run between $2.99 and $6.00 for breakfast, and $3.75 to $5.25 for lunch. The restaurant is decorated with pictures of the space shuttle as well as other memorabilia. It offers a bright and sunny atmosphere. It also has been recently remodeled. Seating capacity is 78 in their main dining room. A nearby conference room can accommodate between 40 and 50 persons for groups and parties. For more information you can call the restaurant at 872-1234.

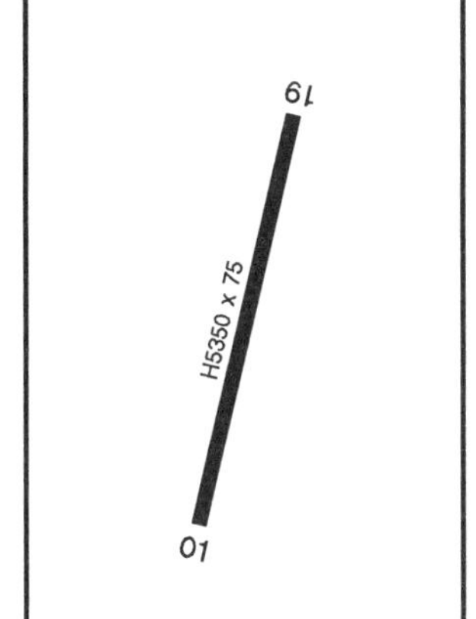

Airport Information:

GLENDALE - GLENDALE MUNICIPAL AIRPORT (GEU)
6 mi west of town N33-31.64 W112-17.71 Elev: 1066 Fuel: 80, 100, Jet-A
Rwy 01-19: H5350x75 (Asph) Attended: Mon-Fri 1300-0530Z, Sat-Sun 1400-0200
Tower: 121.0 Gnd Con: 118.0 Public Phone 24hrs Notes: Overnight parking, single $3.75, Twin $5.25
FBO: Airport Manager Phone: 931-5555

AZ-GYR - GOODYEAR
PHOENIX-GOODYEAR MUNICIPAL AIRPORT

(Area Code 602) 3

Wigwam Resort (Restaurants):

The Wigwam Resort is located in Litchfield Park, Arizona, just 5 miles from Phoenix-Goodyear Municipal Airport. Wigwam dining is an experience that guests will always enjoy. Members of the resort's highly-skilled culinary team have come from the best cooking schools in the world to create dishes using ingredients unique to the region and recipes from ancient southwestern cultures. At the Arizona Kitchen, the faint aroma of mesquite flows in the open kitchen adorned with red brick floors, decorative ceramic tile and shining copper. The Arizona is open Tuesday through Saturday 6:00 p.m. to 10:30 p.m., and it features award-winning southwestern cuisine. Specialties include: pizzas, meats, and fish and game grilled over aromatic woods. The Arizona Kitchen also features entertainment by guitarist Bryun Kayler, who performs neo-classical music. The Terrace Dining Room is open daily for breakfast from 6:30 a.m. to 10:30 a.m., for lunch from 11:00 a.m. to 2:00 p.m., and for dinner from 5:00 p.m. to 10:00 p.m. (jacket and tie required for dinner). A Sunday brunch is offered from 11:30 a.m. to 5:00 p.m. The Terrace serves delicious continental cuisine, and offers private rooms for groups. Entertainment is provided by The Bill Wise Trio, Monday through Saturday, 6:30 p.m. to 10:00 p.m. The Grille on the Greens serves breakfast from 7:00 a.m. to 11:00 a.m., lunch from 11:00 a.m. to 3:00 p.m., and dinner from 6:00 p.m. to 10:00 p.m. The Grille, is located just off the golf courses' starting tees, and serves a variety of traditional favorites, such as grilled prime steaks, live Maine lobster and other scrumptious fare. Different dinner buffets are featured on varying nights of the week. The Pool Cabana, open daily from 9:30 a.m. until dark, is a year-round, casual poolside dining spot, featuring salads, grilled burgers, milk shakes and specialty drinks. The Arizona Bar, which is open from 6:00 p.m. to 1:00 a.m., offers entertainment and dancing nightly in a lodge bar setting. It is also the perfect place to catch a sports event on television or play a game of billiards. The Kachina Lounge is located just outside the Arizona Kitchen and down the hall from the Terrace Dining Room. This cozy spot offers an adjoining oudoor fire pit for before-dinner or after-dinner cocktails, and relaxation by the piano. (Note:The resort has noted that restaurant hours and entertainment fluctuate seasonally.) For more information about restaurants, rates and accommodations at The Wigwam Resort, call 800-327-0396 or 935-3811.

Restaurants Near Airport:
The Wigwam Resort 5 mi Phone: 935-3811

Lodging: The Wigwam Resort (5 miles) 935-3811; Phoenix-Goodyear Inn (2 miles) 932-3210; Super 8 Motel (2-1/2 miles) 932-9622; Crossroads Inn (3 miles) 932-9191; Kings Inn (15 miles) 977-7621;

Meeting Rooms: The Wigwam Resort 935-3811

Transportation: Taxi Service: Westside 932-1692, 370-6612; Rental Cars: Budget 925-0543; Enterprise 974-0974

Information: Tri-City West Chamber of Commerce, 501 W. Van Buren, Suite K, Avondale, AZ 85323, Phone: 932-2260

See Article about the Wigwam Resort.

Attractions:

The Phoenix area has plenty to see and do. Also, for guests who are staying at The Wigwam Resort, the in-house tours department can help plan memorable trips and activities. Visit the Grand Canyon or Sedona; take hot-air balloon rides on or off property; Take desert Jeep tours; visiting the Heard Museum; Wildlife World Zoo; and Desert Botanical Gardens. There is plenty of shopping in Scottsdale, shopping and entertainment in Arizona Center, Wigwam Outlet Stores, and Camp Pow Wow for kids.There are also nearby attractions, such as Turf Paradise thoroughbred racing from October through May, Acrosanti-Paolo Solero's City of the Future in Mayor, and the Gila River Indian Crafts Center, located 30 miles south of Phoenix. For more information about attractions, call 932-2260.

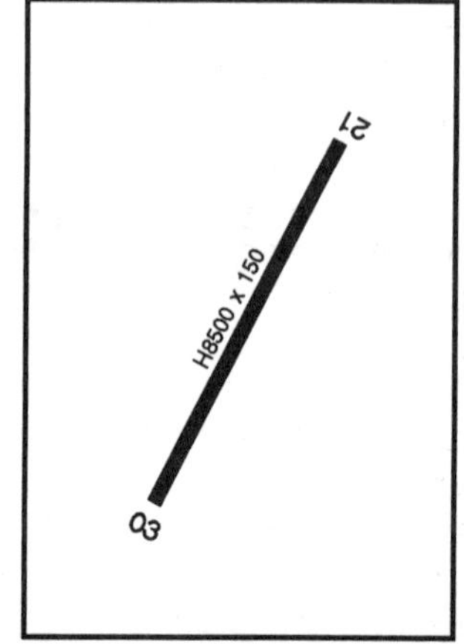

Airport Information:

GOODYEAR - PHOENIX-GOODYEAR MUNICIPAL AIRPORT (GYR)
1 mi southwest of twon N33-25.37 W112-22.56 Elev: 968 Fuel: 100LL, Jet-A Rwy 03-21: H8500x150 (Asph) Attended: 1300-0400Z CTAF: 120.1 Atis: 118.35 (1300-0400Z) Unicom: 122.95 Luke App/Dep Con: 134.1 (5001' and above) 120.5 (5000' and below) (1330-0530Z) Albuquerque Center App/Dep Con: 128.45 (0530-1330Z) Goodyear Tower: 120.1 (1300-0400Z) Gnd Con: 121.7 Notes: See "Airport Facility Directory" for comments about runway information.
FBO: City of Phoenix Phone: 932-1200, 932-4550

The Wigwam Resort

The Wigwam Resort is located in Litchfield Park, Arizona, just 17 miles west of downtown Phoenix. This popular vacation destination was once a private club built in 1918 to serve as lodging for visiting executives of the Goodyear Tire and Rubber Company. The resort, which is one of the most charming resorts in the Southwest, is situated on 463 acres of orange and palm trees, emerald green lawns and flower gardens. During their stay, guests will enjoy comfortable rooms, fabulous food, and plenty of recreational activities. They will also experience the rugged beauty and historical intrigue that Arizona has to offer. The resort's convenient location allows for easy trips through the desert to fascinating Indian ruins, historical attractions and national parks, such as the Grand Canyon.

Photo by: The Wigwam Resort The Wigwam Resort Fireplace Lounge

Guests will luxuriate in the comfort of the 331 quiet, private and spacious casitas are arranged in a quaint village setting. The casita rooms range in size from 480 to 612 square feet, and they provide a level of comfort reminiscent of accommodations built during an era when extended stays were common. Each guest casita includes a private patio on which to enjoy refreshments or simply soak in the sun. Unique decor, such as hand-blown glassware, wool Berber carpeting and comfortable, custom southwestern furnishings give each room its own special flair. The rooms also feature walk-in closets, spacious tiled bathrooms, plush terrycloth bathrobes, hair dryers and make-up mirrors, stocked mini-bars, two telephones, data ports, sewing kits, in-room safe deposit boxes, and twice-daily maid service. Some casitas also include fireplaces, wet bars and bathrooms with double vanities. Seventy luxury suites, including two Presidential suites, feature parlors for entertaining, and up to three bedrooms. Many include stone fireplaces.

Wigwam Resort's private conference registration area and adjoining business center makes it easy for those who are traveling on business to have a pleasant meeting experience from beginning to end. The resort offers state-of-the-art meeting facilities that are conveniently located just steps from guest casitas. Ballrooms, garden terrace areas, breakout and committee rooms, and private dining rooms cover 30,000 feet of meeting space. There are 25 meetings rooms equipped to accommodate meetings for groups ranging from 10 to 900. Executive groups may enjoy the Oraibi Suite for board meetings. For larger gatherings, the 10,800 square-foot Wigwam Ballroom features a built-in rear-screen projection booth, 18-foot ceilings and programmable lighting. For receptions or presentation breaks, large indoor foyers and spacious outdoor private terraces serve as ideal locations for refreshment service.

Wigwam is the only resort in Arizona that features three 18-hole championship golf courses: the Gold Course, the Blue Course, and the Red Course. The Gold Couse is a Silver Medal award winner designed by Robert Trent Jones, Sr., and it is 7,074 yards. The Blue Course, which was also designed by Jones, is 6,030 yards. The Red Course, which was designed by Robert "Red" Lawrence, is 6,865 yards. Guests have guaranteed tee times, as well as four putting greens, golf carts, pro-shop. Golf lessons by professional instructors are available. Junior clinics are offered free to young guests on weekends. The resort's staff are available to help coordinate group events, tournaments and scoring.

The resort also offers a plethora of other activities for all ages. There are two swimming pools, water volleyball, water slide, hot tubs and a poolside cabana. There are also nine lighted plexi-pave tennis courts, a stadium court and pro shop, badminton, basketball and sand volleyball courts, horseback rides, hayrides, trap and skeet shooting, bicycling, ping pong, croquet, shuffleboard, jogging, and a fitness center with exercise equipment, a sauna, whirlpool and steam room. An on-site beauty salon is also available for hair styling, pedicures, manicures and facials.

Away from the grounds, there are dozens of recreational adventures to explore. The in-house tours department can help plan memorable trips and activities. Enjoy a trip to the Grand Canyon or Sedona, hot-air balloon rides on or off property, desert Jeep tours, the Heard Museum, Wildlife World Zoo, Desert Botanical Gardens, shopping in Scottsdale, shopping and entertainment in Arizona Center, Wigwam Outlet Stores, or Camp Pow Wow for kids. There are also nearby attractions, such as Turf Paradise thoroughbred

Photo by: The Wigwam Resort

The Wigwam Resort Pool Cabana

racing from October through May, Acrosanti - Paolo Solero's City of the Future in Mayor, and the Gila River Indian Crafts Center, located 30 miles south of Phoenix.

Wigwam dining is an experience that guests will always enjoy. Members of the resort's highly-skilled culinary team have come from the best cooking schools in the world to create dishes using ingredients unique to the region and recipes from ancient southwestern cultures. At the Arizona Kitchen, the faint aroma of mesquite flows in the open kitchen adorned with red brick floors, decorative ceramic tile and shining copper. The Arizona is open Tuesday through Saturday 6:00 p.m. to 10:30 p.m., and it features award-winning southwestern cuisine. Specialties include: pizzas, meats, fish and game grilled over aromatic woods. The Arizona Kitchen also features entertainment by guitarist Bryun Kayler, who performs neo-classical music. The Terrace Dining Room is open daily for breakfast from 6:30 a.m. to 10:30 a.m., for lunch from 11:00 a.m. to 2:00 p.m., and for dinner from 5:00 p.m. to 10:00 p.m. (jacket and tie required for dinner). A Sunday brunch is offered from 11:30 a.m. to 5:00 p.m. The Terrace serves delicious continental cuisine, and offers private rooms for groups. Entertainment is provided by The Bill Wise Trio, Monday through Saturday, 6:30 p.m. to 10:00 p.m.

The Grille on the Greens serves breakfast from 7:00 a.m. to 11:00 a.m., lunch from 11:00 a.m. to 3:00 p.m., and dinner from 6:00 p.m. to 10:00 p.m. The Grille, is located just off the golf courses' starting tees. It serves a variety of traditional favorites, such as grilled prime steaks, live Maine lobster and other scrumptious fare. Different dinner buffets are featured on varying nights of the week. The Pool Cabana, open daily from 9:30 a.m. until dark, is a year-round, casual poolside dining spot, featuring salads, grilled burgers, milk shakes and specialty drinks.

The Arizona Bar, which is open from 6:00 p.m. to 1:00 a.m., offers entertainment and dancing nightly in a lodge bar setting. It is also the perfect place to catch a sports event on television or play a game of billiards. The Kachina Lounge is located just outside the Arizona Kitchen and down the hall from the Terrace Dining Room. This cozy spot offers an adjoining oudoor fire pit for before-dinner or after-dinner cocktails, and relaxation by the piano. (Note: The resort has noted that restaurant hours and entertainment fluctuate seasonally.)

The Wigwam also helps coordinate activities, events and presentations of every type and size. The staff can create custom arrangements to meet specific requests for props, decor, catering and service. An in-house design department can create elaborate custom props for themes, such as an Evening on the Orient Express, Night on the Santa Fe Trail, Phantom of the Opera, and Get Your Kicks on Route 66. An abundance of oudoor function areas are available at the resort, including the East Pool Patio, Sunset Point, and a nearby Old West film studio.

The Phoenix-Goodyear Municipal Airport is located only 5 miles from the resort. It has a 8,500'x150 asphalt runway. The Wigwam Resort will provide transportation to and from the airport for a $6.00 fee. The overnight parking fee is $5.00 for singles and $7.00 for twins, but is waived with a fuel purchase.

For more information about activities, rates and accommodations at The Wigwam Resort, call 800-327-0396 or 935-3811. (Information submitted by The Wigwam Resort)

AZ-P14 - HOLBROOK
HOLBROOK MUNICIPAL AIRPORT

(Area Code 520) 4

Denny's Restaurant:

Denny's Restaurant is located about 300 yards from the airport parking area. This is a family style facility that is open 24 hours, 7 days a week. Their specialty entrees include omelettes, pancakes, and egg dishes along with assorted sandwiches, 7 types of burgers, steaks, seafood and chicken plates. They also provide a nice dessert selection. Prices average about $5.50 for most selections. The restaurant has a seating capacity of 117 persons, with a southwestern decor. You can see the airport activity from the restaurant. Fly-in groups are also welcome. For more information about this restaurant call 524-2893.

Restaurants Near Airport:

Denny's Restaurant	300 yds	Phone: 524-2893
Jerry's	1/2 mi.	Phone: 524-2364

Lodging: Arizonian Inn (Adj Arpt) 524-2611; Comfort Inn 1/2 mi 524-6131; Motel 6 (Adj Arpt) 524-2666; Whiting Brothers Motel Adj Arpt. 524-6298; Motel 66 (1/2 mile) 524-6234.

Meeting Rooms: None Reported

Transportation: None Reported

Information: Holbrook-Petrified Forest Chamber of Commerce, 100 East Arizona Street, Holbrook, AZ 86025, Phone: 524-6558.

NO AIRPORT DIAGRAM AVAILABLE

Airport Information:

HOLBROOK - HOLBROOK MUNICIPAL AIRPORT (P14)
3 mi northeast of town N34-56.33 W110-08.37 Elev: 5257 Fuel: 100LL
Rwy 03-21: H6627x75 (Asph-Afsc) Rwy 11-29: 3200x120 (Dirt) Attended: continuously
Unicom: 122.8
FBO: Triple A Aviation Phone: 524-3267

AZ-IGM - KINGMAN
KINGMAN AIRPORT

(Area Code 520) 5

Maggie's Flightline Diner:

Maggie's Flightline Diner is a very popular restaurant with pilots from all over the area. The diner is situated mid-field at the Kingman Airport, under the WW-II control tower. This cafe is open between 6 a.m. and 3 p.m., 7 days a week. Their menu offers a variety of entrees. For breakfast they specialize in items like omelets, biscuits & gravy with eggs, as well as side orders. For lunch, they feature hamburgers, hot dogs, salads, and shrimp items. Desserts include homemade pies and peach cobblers. The average price per meal are very reasonable, averaging $3.50 for breakfast, and $3.75 for lunch. The restaurant is decorated in western style. Accommodations for fly-in groups and parties are also available if advance notice is given. For more information about Maggie's Flightline Diner, call 757-7474.

Restaurants Near Airport:

Dam Bar Steak House	7 mi	Phone: 753-3523
Golden Corral Steakhouse	8 mi SW	Phone: 753-1505
House of Chan	19 mi W.	Phone: 753-3232
Maggie's Flightline Diner	On Site	Phone: 757-7474

Lodging: Kings Inn 753-6101; Motel 6 757-7151; Quality Inn 753-4747; Wayfarer's Inn 753-6271.

Meeting Rooms: Quality Inn (7 miles) 753-5531.

Transportation: Kingman Cab 753-3624; Rental Cars: Hertz 753-5588; Budget 757-3361

Information: Chamber of Commerce, P.O. Box 1150, Kingman, AZ 86402, Phone: 753-6106.

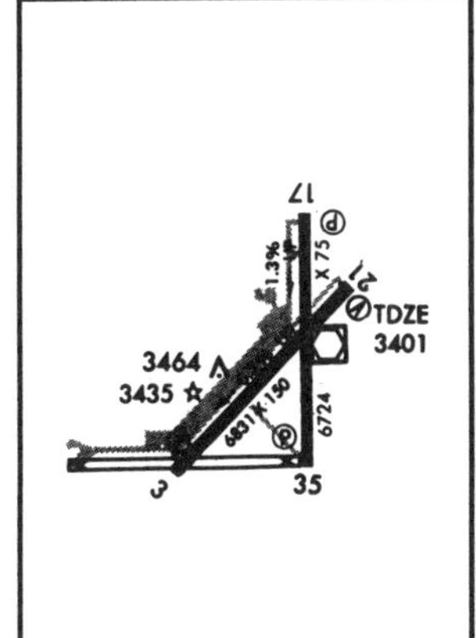

Airport Information:

KINGMAN - KINGMAN AIRPORT (IGM)
8 mi northeast of town N35-15.57 W113-56.28 Elev: 3446 Fuel: 80, 100LL, Jet-A
Rwy 03-21: H6831x150 (Asph) Rwy 17-35: H6724x75 (Asph-Conc) Attended 1400-0130Z
Unicom: 122.8 Public Phone 24hrs Notes: Overnight parking, Singles $3.00, Twins $5.00
FBO: Ari'Zona Aircraft Service Phone: 757-7744
FBO: Kingman Aero Service Phone: 757-1335

AZ-MZJ - MARANA PINAL AIRPARK

6

Restaurants Near Airport: (Area Code 602)
Elinor's Restaurant 1/4 mi (On Site) Phone: 682-4181

Elinor's Restaurant:

Elinor's Restaurant is located within walking distance about 1/4 mile from the aircraft parking area, within the terminal area. This cafeteria is open weekdays. Breakfast hours are 6:30 a.m. to 8:00 a.m., Lunch is served from 11:00 a.m. to 1:00 p.m. Elinor's Restaurant provides a full assortment of breakfast items along with other entrees. Average prices run $4.75 for breakfast and $5.75 for lunch. The seating capacity of this facility is 175 persons. Special group accommodations can be arranged. For more information about the Pinal Airpark Restaurant you can call 682-4181 ext. 534.

Lodging: Everybody's Inn (On Site) 682-4181 ext 534; Roadrunner Inn (On Site) 682-4181 ext 534; Quality Inn (Courtesy trans) 746-3932; Ramada Inn (Courtesy trans) 624-8341.

Meeting Rooms: None Reported

Transportation: Evergreen Air Center (FBO) can accommodate courtesy transportation within airport property and adjacent facilities. Many of the lodging and resort establishments listed above provide courtesy transportation. See "lodging" listed above.

Information: Arizona Office of Tourism, 1100 West Washington, Phoenix, AZ 85007 or call 602-542-TOUR, 800-842-8257.

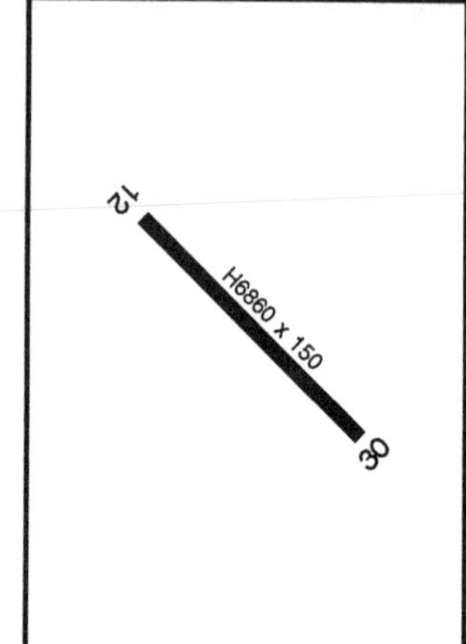

Airport Information:

MARANA - PINAL AIRPARK (MZJ)
7 mi northwest of town N32-30.64 W111-19.67 Elev: 1891 Fuel: 100LL, Jet-A
Rwy 12-30: H6860x150 (Asph) Attended: 1400-0630Z Unicom 123.05 Public Phone 24hrs
Notes: no landing fee CAUTION: Heavy military activity and parachute training.
Airport Manager Phone: 682-4181
FBO: Evergreen Air Center Phone: 682-4181

AZ-AZ03 - MARBLE CANYON CLIFF DWELLERS LODGE AIRPORT

7

Restaurants Near Airport: (Area Code 602)
Cliff Dwellers Lodge 3/10th mi Phone: 355-2228

Cliff Dwellers Lodge:

The Cliff Dwellers Lodge is located about 1/4 mile from the airstrip. Courtesy transportation can be arranged with prior notice, by calling the lodge in advance and simply buzzing the strip when you arrive. Future arrangements for obtaining a courtesy car at the airport may be available. Walking the short distance to the lodge can also be accomplished with no problem. The lodge itself contains a 21 room motel along with a family style restaurant. This restaurant is open between 6 a.m and 2 p.m. then again from 5 p.m. to 9 p.m., 7 days a week. Specialty items that are offered include a full breakfast line, chicken dishes, steaks, hamburgers, chili, seafood, sandwiches, as well as soups and salads. They also offer specials off their menu throughout the week. Average prices range from $3.00 to $5.00 for breakfast & lunch and between $3.00 to $15.00 for dinner. The lodge and restaurant provides a rustic appearance with knotty pine and wood paneling with an old southwestern styled decor. Seating capacity within their dining room is between 30 and 50 persons. For more information on the accommodations and the service of the Cliff Dwellers Lodge, you can call 355-2228.

Lodging: Cliff Dwellers Lodge (3/10th of a mile) 355-2228.

Meeting Rooms: None Reported

Transportation: Courtesy transportation to and from airport can be arranged by Cliff Dwellers Lodge if you call in advance. Upon arrival, buzz the strip and they will come out and pick you up. Accommodations for airport courtesy cars may be forthcoming. Call the lodge at 355-2228 for information.

Information: Arizona Office of Tourism, 1100 West Washington, Phoenix, AZ 85007 or call 602-542-TOUR.

Attractions:

River rafting trips are available down the Colorado River. Various trip durations can be arranged. For information you can contact the Grand Canyon National Park, P.O. Box 129, Grand Canyon, AZ 86023 or call 638-7888. Trout fishing is also available within this area. Call Cliff Dwellers Lodge at 355-2228 for information.

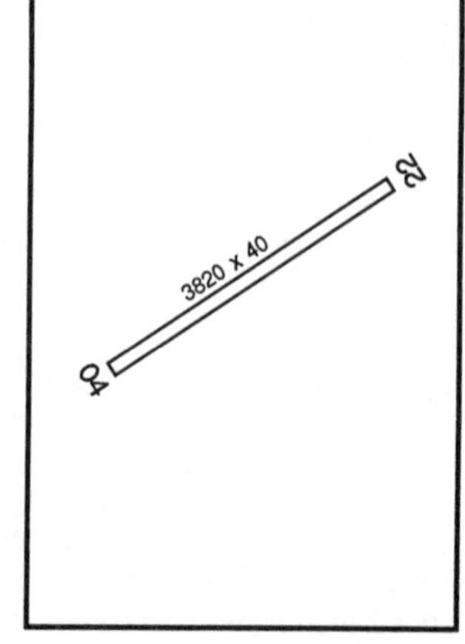

Airport Information:

MARBLE CANYON - CLIFF DWELLERS LODGE AIRPORT (AZ03)
7 mi southwest of town 36-44-04N 111-45-07W Elev: 4217 Rwy 04-22: 3820x40 (Dirt)
Attended: unattended CTAF: 122.9 Notes: CAUTION: See Airport Facility Directory for runway conditions and remarks.
Cliff Dwellers Lodge Phone: 355-2228

Not to be used for navigational purposes

AZ-L41 - MARBLE CANYON
MARBLE CANYON AIRPORT

Marble Canyon Lodge:

The restaurant at Marble Canyon Lodge is located across the highway and within walking distance from the aircraft tiedown area. A complete menu is designed for you and your family. Specialized entrees include a wide selection of American dishes including seafood, steaks, sandwiches, Navajo taco salad, soups, vegetarian meals, garden fresh salad bar and home baked pies, and desserts. A buffet is served on Saturday nights, along with daily specials. Prices range from $5.95 for breakfast, $5.95 for lunch and $8.95 for dinner. The restaurant decor is Western and offers guests a scenic view of cliffs and high desert terrain. Restaurant hours are from 7:00 a.m. to 8:30 p.m. during the week and 6:30 a.m. to 9:00 p.m. on weekends. Fly-in groups are welcome, with pre-arranged buffets or outdoor Bar-B-Ques and cookouts. Combined with the lodge, this facility has 52 units, and 8 condos. For information call 355-2225.

(Area Code 520) 8

Restaurants Near Airport:
Marble Canyon Lodge 300 yds Phone: 355-2225

Lodging: Marble Canyon Lodge, see description below.

Meeting Rooms: Marble Canyon Lodge

Transportation: Shuttle service provided by Marble Canyon Lodge, also this facility is located only 300 yards from airport and is well within walking distance.

Information: Marble Canyon Lodge, Marble Canyon, AZ 86036, or call 520-355-2225.

Airport Information:

MARBLE CANYON - MARBLE CANYON AIRPORT (L41)
1 mi southwest of town N36-48.75 W111-38.79
Elev: 3603 Rwy 03-21: H3790x25 (ASPH)
Attended: daylight hrs. CTAF: 122.9 VOR: 219 degrees and 11.7 NM to field. Notes: No line of sight btn rwy ends. $5.00 overnight parking.

21
H3790 x 25
03

Marble Canyon Lodge and Guide Service

Outfitters of Indian & River Expeditions:

Marble Canyon Lodge offers their guests a wide variety of activities in the beauty of the Southwest. Located on the Colorado River at the base of the 2,500 foot Vermilion Cliffs, the lodge is five miles from Lees Ferry, the tremendous tailwater trout fishery created by Glen Canyon dam and starting point for rafting trips through the Grand Canyon. The lodge is also a starting point for excursions into the Paria Canyon Primitive Area, Zion National Park, Lake Powell, Bryce Canyon, Glen Canyon and the North and South Rims of the Grand Canyon.

Established in 1929, the Marble Canyon Lodge retains its original rustic charm and offers a full range of services to the traveler all within walking distance of the air strip. Located at the lodge are a trading post, full service bar, coffee shop and dining room, 52 units and 8 condos. The trading post carries a selection of Southwestern jewelry, river running gear, fishing tackle and souvenirs. Of special note is the book section, offering nearly 400 titles (!). The dining room includes a wide range of American dishes, vegetarian meals, a garden fresh salad bar and nightly specials. Prices average $5.95 for breakfast, $5.95 for lunch and $8.95 for dinner. In addition Western style outdoor barbecues can be arranged for groups. Restaurant hours are 6:30 a.m. to 9:00 p.m. The Lodge offers guests clean, quiet rooms all, with air conditioning and individual temperature controls. Many offer a picture window view of surrounding cliffs and the vast desert landscape. In addition, house keeping units with full kitchens are available.

Fishing the Colorado: Located five miles from the lodge, the Colorado River at Lee's Ferry offers the visiting angler some of the finest trout fishing in the West. This 15 mile tailwater below Glen Canyon dam provides a year round angling opportunity for rainbow trout averaging 15-17 inches and a good chance of a fish of 20 inches of better. Utilizing one of their powerful jet or prop boats, you and your guide will access the runs and riffles below the 700-1500 foot red sandstone cliffs of Glen Canyon. The scenery alone is worth the trip! During the late fall and winter the fishing is primarily sight casting to large spawning rainbow in water 1-3 feet depth. As warmer weather arrives, abundant midge hatches provide nymph and dry fly fishing opportunities in shallow riffles and still backwaters. **Marble Canyon Guide Service** may be contacted at 1-800-533-7339.

AZ-FFZ - MESA
FALCON FIELD

(Area Code 602)

9, 10

Anzio Landing Italian Restaurant:

This popular restaurant is located on the northeast corner of Falcon Field adjacent to the approach end of runway 22L. (If you have been grounded, you can find them on Higley Road, just south of McDowell). After landing, you can taxi right up to their building and take advantage of one of their lighted tie-downs. The restaurant is open Monday through Thursday from 11 a.m. to 9 p.m., and Friday and Saturday from 11 a.m. to 10 p.m., closed on Sunday. Specialties of the house include fresh made garlic bread sticks, pasta fagioli, seafood stuffed mushrooms, and Fettuccine Alfredo, along with a children's menu for your little ones. Dinner selections include a variety of spaghetti dishes, pastas, steak, chicken, veal and seafood. Prices range from $4.95 to $7.95 at lunch, and $6.95 to $13.95 at dinner. Happy Hour is served in the lounge from 2:30 until 6:00 six days a week--don't miss the 24-foot Cessna over the bar! Rex & Mary Ellen Griswold are the owners of this establishment and have a special interest in aviation. Rex's father flew with the "Flying Tigers" in China, so the decor within the restaurant itself contains a variety of WW-II flying memorabilia. While you are enjoying a fine meal, you can view planes taking off and landing, the mountains in the distance and spectacular sunsets during the twilight hour. They have private rooms which can accommodate parties of 15 to 100, and are great for fly-in groups or any special occasion. Private and corporate caterings are also available for pilots on-the-go. Combining your dining experience with a trip to the Champlin Fighter Museum on the airport, makes for an exciting way to spend the day, especially for aviation enthusiasts. For reservations or more information you can call the restaurant at 832-1188.

Arizona Golf Resort:

One of the many distinct advantages of The Arizona Golf Resort is the complete range of activities for guests to enjoy without ever leaving the grounds. The resort's own meticulously manicured championship golf course is right at your doorstep. For relaxation or competition you'll find the course fits your game. Loosen up on the driving range and practice chipping, then perfect your stroke on the velvet putting green and you'll be ready for a great round of golf. A professional PGA staff offers expert instruction. There's tennis and swimming, spas to invigorate your body and panoramic views to restore your soul as you take a leisurely stroll or ride a bike through the resort's 150 lush acres. The Arizona Golf Resort has 4,000 square feet of meeting accommodations in their Fairway Conference Center. 160 spacious deluxe rooms and luxurious fairway suites are available with complimentary in-room coffee service. There are several locations on resort property that offer dining. Annabelle's Restaurant has an informal dining atmosphere in a most elegant setting. Breakfast, lunch and dinner are served. On Sunday they feature a brunch. Specialties include fresh fish, prime rib, steaks and vegetarian selections. Anna's Lounge and Grill is another establishment at the resort that offers deli selections, salads and light entrees. Live entertainment is featured from local entertainers. In addition to Annabelle's and Annas Lounge and Grill, the resort also has a pool-side patio and the 19th Green Cafe that overlooks the golf course. Car rentals can be arranged through the resort. The resort is located only 4 miles, or 10 minutes by car, from Mesa, Falcon Field (FFZ). For information call the resort at 832-3202 or 800-528-8282.

Restaurants Near Airport:

Anzio Landing Restaurant	On Site	Phone: 832-1188
Arizona Golf Resort	4 mi	Phone: 832-3202
Camelot Restaurant	2 mi E.	Phone: 832-0158
Red Mountain Ranch CC	3-1/2 mi E	Phone: 981-6501

Lodging: Arizona Golf Resort 4 mi 800-528-8282, 832-3202; Best Western Mezona 834-9233; Hilton-Pavilion 833-5555; Quality Inn-Royal Mesa 833-1231; Rodeway Inn 985-3600; Sheraton Mesa 898-8300; Starway Motel 832-5961.Lexington Hotel Suites 964-2897; Arizona Golf Resort & Conference Center 832-3202 or 800-528-8282.

Meeting Rooms: Anzio Landing Restaurant (On Field) 832-1188; Catus Aviation (On Field) 832-4100; Champlin Fighter Museum (On Field) 830-4540; Camelot Restaurant (2 miles E.) 832-0158; Arizona Golf Resort & Conference Center (5 miles from airport) 832-3202 or 800-582-8282 outside of AZ.

Transportation: Rental Cars: Mesa Leasing 985-4610; Master Leasing 832-2582: Taxi service: 834-4545.

Information: Convention & Visitors Bureau, 120 North Center Street, Mesa, AZ 85201, Phone: 969-1307.

Attractions:

Champlin Air Museum (on field) 830-4540; Arizona Golf Resort 4 mi 800-528-8282, 832-3202; Camelot Golf Course (2 miles) 6210 East McKellips; Saguaro Lake (20 miles) 986-5546; Canyon Lake (30 miles) 986-5546.

Champlin Fighter Museum
Mesa - Falcon Field
See article next page

Airport Information:

MESA - FALCON FIELD (FFZ)

5 mi northeast of town 33-27-39N 111-43-40W Elev: 1392 Fuel: 80, 100LL, Jet-A
Rwy 04R-22L: H5100x100 (Asph) Rwy 04L-22R: H3800x75 (Asph) Attended: 1300-0300Z Public phone 24hrs Atis: 118.25 Unicom: 122.95 Tower: 124.6
Gnd Con: 121.3 Notes: No landing fee. Overnight Parking: Single $3.50/night & Twin $4.50/night, For service after hours call 602-898-4055 CAUTION: traffic pattern for Rwy 04R-22L, 04L-22R are northwest of the airport and overlap. (See Airport Facility Directory).

FBO: Executive Aviation/SAS, **Phone: 832-0704**
FBO: Cactus Aviation, **Phone: 832-4100**

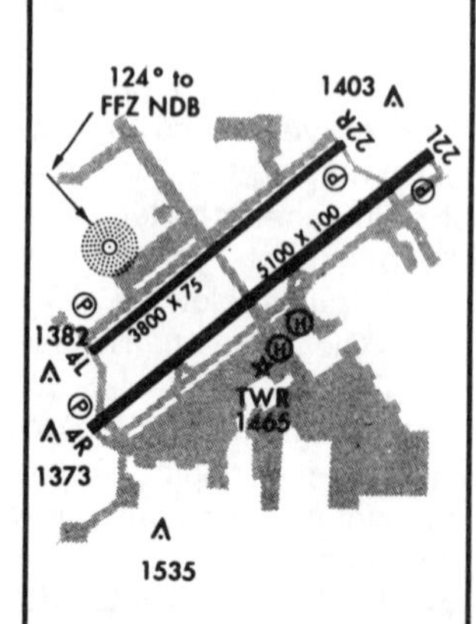

Photo by: Champlin Fighter Museum

World War Two Focke-Wulf 190D

Champlin Fighter Museum:

Mesa - Falcon Field (AZ-FFZ)

Unlike most other aviation museums which include all types of military aircraft, the Champlin Fighter Museum is devoted solely to fighter aircraft and the pilots who flew them. From the fragile wood and fabric aircraft of WW-1 to the thundering jets of Vietnam, the complete evolution of fighter aircraft is depicted in one museum. An educational plus entertainment experience is in store for those who remember and for those who want to learn more about the great air battles of history. Over 700 personally autographed photos of Aces from 15 countries are on display, spanning the history of aerial warfare from the First World War through Vietnam. Plus see personal articles and mementos of such heros of the air, as Von Richtofen and Joe Foss, and featuring 48 specially commissioned oil paintings of Second World War aircraft in action. These displays and more memorabilia from the personal collections of the American Fighter Aces Association are headquartered at the museum. Historical films of warbirds in action can be seen on videos documenting the evolution of the fighter, plus World War II bombers on actual combat footage, in their own movie theater. The most complete private collection of historic automatic weapons

Photo by: Champlin Fighter Museum

A complete collection of historic automatic weapons

are also on display. Over 200 arms from 14 countries representing a complete history of the machine gun from the earliest models in 1895 to the present. Included are aircraft mounted, anti-aircraft, tripod mounted and personal weapons - some still packed in original crates and never fired. Many extremely rare models are featured such as the German Kummelauf, designed to shoot around corners, as well as the most complete selection of Thompson "Tommy" submachine guns ever assembled. You and your friends are invited to browse their outstanding selection of rare aviation books and literature, original oil paintings, lithographs, model planes, jewelry, toys and souvenirs. One of the finest selection of aviation gifts and books are available. Admission: Adults $5.00, Children (14 and under) $2.50 and tour groups half price. The museum is open between 10 a.m. and 5 p.m. 7 days a week. Banquet and meeting facilities are available at the museum. For information, you can write to: Champlin Fighter Museum, 4636 Fighter Aces Drive, Mesa, Arizona 85205 or call 602-830-4540. Come take a flight into history to the Golden Age of Air Power at the Champlin Fighter Museum. It's a day the whole family will enjoy and remember for years to come. (Submitted by Champlin Fighter Museum).

Aircraft On Display

Rumpler Taube	Messerschmitt 109E
Fokker E-III	Focke-Wulf 190D
Fokker Dr.I	Spitfire MK IX
Fokker D-VII	Curtiss P-40N
Fokker D-VIII	North American P-51D
Albatros D-Va	Republic P-47D-2
Pfalz D-XII	Lockheed P-38L
Sopwith Camel	Grumman FM-2 Wildcat
Sopwith Pup	Goodyear F2G-1
Sopwith Snipe	Grumman F6F-3 Hellcat
Sopwith Triplane	MiG-15
Spad XIII	Mig-17
SE 5a	North American F86
Nieuport 27	Sabre
Avatik D-II	McDonnell Douglas F4

Photo by: Champlin Fighter Museum

A beautifully restored Albatros D-XII, one of 15 WW-I vintage aircraft on display.

AZ-E69 - PAYSON
PAYSON AIRPORT

(Area Code 520)

11

Crosswind Restaurant:

The Crosswind Restaurant is situated on the Payson Airport and is very close to the aircraft parking area. This family style restaurant specializes in preparing hearty selections including breakfasts specials for their guests. They are open throughout the week from 6 a.m. to 8 p.m. Their breakfast menu include fourteen different types of omelets available from the traditional to specialized creations by their chef. In addition to breakfast items, they serve a variety of luncheon, dinner and dessert choices. Homemade pies, sugar free pies, apple pies, French pies and cinnamon rolls are some of their customers favorites. The restaurant has been remodeled and decorated with all sorts of aviation items from paintings on the wall to framed posters. There are large windows all the way around that allow a view of the airport and its activity. Seating capacity is about 28 persons. Patio tables allow guests to enjoy a meal outdoors while watching the aircraft. After the restaurant closes down for the day, it reverts into a pilots lounge where you can still obtain cold sandwiches and coffee. Carry-out meals are also available from anything on their menu. For more information about the Crosswind Restaurant, call 474-1613.

Restaurants Near Airport:

The Crosswinds Restaurant	On Site	Phone: 474-1613

Lodging: Majestic Mountain Inn (4 mi., Trans) 474-0185 or 800-408-2442; Payson Lo Lodge 2 mi 474-2382; Payson Pueblo Inn (5 miles) Phone: 1-800-888-9828; Payson Super 8, 2 mi 474-4526; Swiss Village 1 mi. 474-3241.

Meeting Rooms: None Reported

Transportation: Chapman Auto 474-5261

Information: Chamber of Commerce, 1006 South Beeline Highway, P.O. Box 1380, Payson, AZ 85547, Phone: 474-4515 or 800-552-3068.

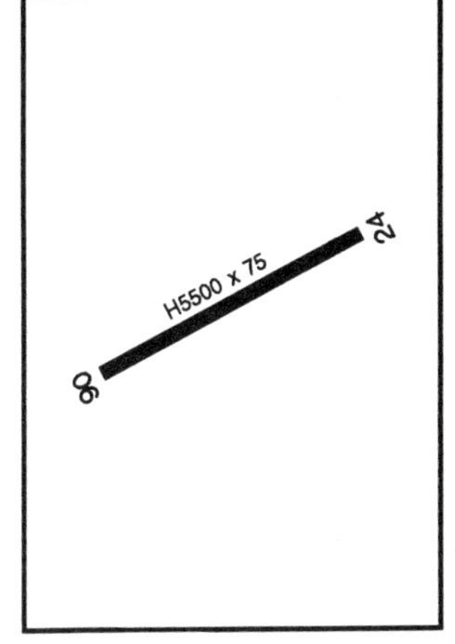

Airport Information:

PAYSON - PAYSON AIRPORT (E69)
1 mi west of town N34-15.41 W111-20.36 Elev: 5156 Fuel: 80, 100LL, Jet-A
Rwy 06-24: H5500x75 (Asph) Attended: 1500-0000Z Unicom: 122.8 Public Phone 24hrs
Notes: Overnight parking $2.00, Overnight camping available with prior permission.
FBO: Paige Aviation Fuels Phone: 474-2005

AZ-DVT - PHOENIX
DEER VALLEY MUNICIPAL

(Area Code 602)

12

Deer Valley Airport Restaurant:

The Airport Restaurant is located on the Deer Valley Municipal Airport. This family style restaurant has available aircraft parking in front of their facility. Their hours are from 6:30 a.m. to 9:00 p.m. 7 days a week. The menu contains a nice selection of breakfast items, as well as hot and cold sandwiches, burgers, fish and chips, baked cod fish, shrimp, homemade desserts, soups and salads. They also have a salad bar available. Meals average $4.00 for breakfast, $5.00 for lunch and $7.00 for dinner. The restaurant can seat up to a total of 200 people with available space for 60 people in the main dining room along with outside seating. This facility has booths, counter space, carpeting throughout the restaurant, hanging plants and a wood ceiling that all contributes to its comfortable and casual atmosphere. Fly-in custumers along with groups are always welcome. Catered parties as well as carry out meals can also be arranged. For more information call 582-5454.

Restaurants Near Airport:

Bill Johnson's	3 mi S.	Phone: 863-7921
Deer Valley Airport	On Site	Phone: 582-5454
T.J. Hannigan's	1/2 mi S.	Phone: 581-0098
Wings N Things	1 mi W.	Phone: 869-0774

Lodging: Sheraton Greenway 993-0800; Ramada Inn Metro-center 866-7000; Fountain Suites hotel 375-1777; Holiday Inn Corporate Center 943-2341.

Meeting Rooms: Accommodations for meeting and conference rooms can be arranged with advance notice through the airport managers office at 869-0975. Also Sheraton Greenway, Ramada Inn Metro-center and Fountain Suites Hotel all have meeting rooms. Holiday Inn Corporate Center has convention facilities available. See lodging listed above for phone numbers.

Transportation: Taxi: Checker Cab 257-1818; Yellow 252-5252; Car Rental: Dollar Rent-A-Car 861-0366.

Information: The Phoenix & Valley of the Sun Convention & Visitors Bureau, One Arizona Center, 400 E. Van Buren Street, Suite 600, Phoenix, AZ 85004, Phone: 254-6500 or 252-5588. For public transit information call 257-8426.

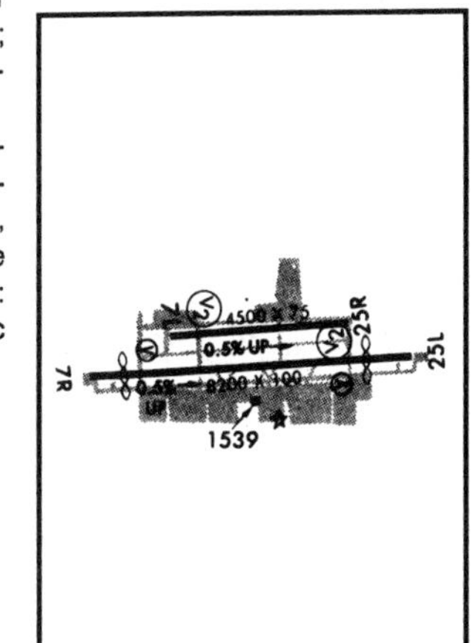

Airport Information:

PHOENIX - DEER VALLEY MUNICIPAL AIRPORT (DVT)
15 mi north of town N33-41.30 W112-04.93 Elev: 1476 Fuel: 80, 100LL, Jet-A
Rwy 07R-25L: H8200x100 (Asph) Rwy 07L-25R: H4500x75 (Asph) Attended 1300-0400Z
Atis: 126.5 Unicom: 122.95 Phoenix App/Dep Con: 120.7 Tower: 118.4 Gnd Con: 121.8
Clnc Del: 119.5 Notes: Overnight parking $3.75 singles, $6.25 twins.
FBO: Thunderbird Aviation Phone: 869-9174 FBO: Westwind Aviation Phone: 869-0866
Deer Valley Airport Phone: 869-0975

AZ-PHX - PHOENIX
PHOENIX SKI HARBOR INTL.

(Area Code 602) 13, 14

CA1 Services: - (Lefty South Rim):

CA1 Services offers several food service facilities within terminal #2, on the Phoenix Ski Harbor International Airport. The Lefty South Rim restaurant is a grill located in the lobby area. This establishment is open between 5 a.m. and 8 p.m. daily. Specialties of the house include a grilled tuna Caesar salad prepared in full customer view. Lefty's famous bacon cheeseburger is a favorite with many customers. Other selections are also available. Prices average $4.25 for breakfast items and around $5.95 for lunch and dinner choices. The decor of the restaurant is contemporary - situated under a famous mural of the Phoenix region - South Rim/Grand Canyon. All Items on their menu can be prepared for carry-out. A 20% discount is offered to all airline employees. In addition to this are the "Desert Sun" and Pizza Americo's, also operated by CA! Services. For information call 273-4837.

Left Seat:

The Left Seat restaurant is located on the Phoenix Ski Harbor Airport. This family style establishment has a historical background as one of the first proprietors on the field. It is also a favorite meeting place for aviation groups as well. In fact during our interview the management was catering a dinner for the distinguished group known as the "QB's" or the Quiet Birdman organization. The restaurant hours are from 6 a.m. to 2 p.m. They are also open weekends and evenings for private banquets. Specialties on their menu include chicken fried steak, Huevo's Ranchero's and Chorizo. Their main dining room can seat about 150 persons. The wall of the restaurant are decorated with all types of aviation pictures. For information about the Left Seat call 220-9407.

Restaurants Near Airport:

CA1 Services	On Site	Phone: 273-4837
Left Seat	On Site	Phone: 220-9407
Road House	1/2 mi	Phone: 273-0321

Lodging: Best Western Airport Inn 273-7251; Comfor Inn-Airport 275-5746; Courtyard By Marriott 966-4300; Doubletree Suites 225-0500; Embassy Suites Camelhead 244-8800; Hampton Inn-Airport-Tempe 438-8688; Hilton Inn-Airport East 273-7778; LaQuinta Inn 967-5900; Rodeway Inn-Airport West 273-1211; Travelodge-Airport 275-7651; Wydham Garden Hotel PHX 220-4400; (All within short distance from airport).

Meeting Rooms: Courtyard By Marriott 966-4300; Embassy Suites Camelhead 244-8800; Hampton Inn-Airport-Tempe 438-8688; Hilton Inn-Airport East 273-7778;

Transportation: Rental Cars: Alamo 244-0897; Avis 800-331-1212; Budget 800-527-0700; Courtesy 273-7503; Dollar 800-421-6868; Enterprize 225-0588; Hertz 800-654-3131; National 800-227-7368.

Information: Phoenix & Valley of the Sun Convention & Visitors Bureau, One Arizona Center, 400 east Van Buren Street, Suite 600, Phoenix, AZ 85004, Phone: 254-6500.

Attractions:

The Phoenix area contains many attractions for the visitor: Arizona Hall of Fame Museum presents exhibits about famous people who have contributed to Arizona's culture. Phone: 255-2110 or 542-4581; Arizona Mining & Mineral Museum displays collections of minerals and many ores samples maintained by the Arizona Department of Mines and Mineral Resources, 255-3791; Desert Botanical Garden contains 150 acres of cactus, plants and floral arrangements. Self-guided nature walk, cactus exhibits and group lectures explain the living dessert of the world. Phone: 941-1217; Mystery Castle is a popular attraction containing interesting and unique stone and sand castle's build over a period by one individual. (Oct-early July Tues-Sun). Phone: 268-1581; Phoenix Mountains Preserve covers over 23,000 acres of land containing mountains and deserts situated north and south of the city. Numerous recreational activities are available. Squaw Peak Park, Echo Canyon, South Mountain and North Mountain Recreational Area. Phone: 262-6861; Phoenix Zoo exhibits over 1,300 animals, reptiles and birds on display. Rare and exotic collections of wild life can be enjoyed. A children's zoo, refreshment centers and safari train tours are on the premises. Phone: 273-1341; The Heard Museum is another very popular Museum that explains the Southwestern Native American Culture. Primitive and even prehistoric art forms are displayed along with the rare Goldwater Kachina doll collection. Phone: 252-8848.

Airport Information:

PHOENIX - PHOENIX SKY HARBOR INTERNATIONAL (PHX)

3 mi east of town N33-26.17 W112-00.57 Elev: 1133 Fuel: 100LL, Jet-A Rwy 08L-26R: H11001x150 (Asph-Grvd) Rwy 08R-26L: H10300x150 (Asph-Grvd) Attended: continuously Atis: ARR 121.2 Dep 124.3 Unicom: 122.95 App/Dep Con: numerous depending on direction and altitude. Tower: 118.7, 120.9 Gnd Con: 121.9 (north) 125.0 (south) Clnc Del: 118.1 Notes: See current AFD for information.

FBO: Cutter Aviation	**Phone: 273-1237**	**FBO: Sawyer Aviation**	**Phone: 273-3770**
FBO: GTA Aviation	**Phone: 273-7704**	**FBO: Sky Harbor Executive**	**Phone: 273-3770**

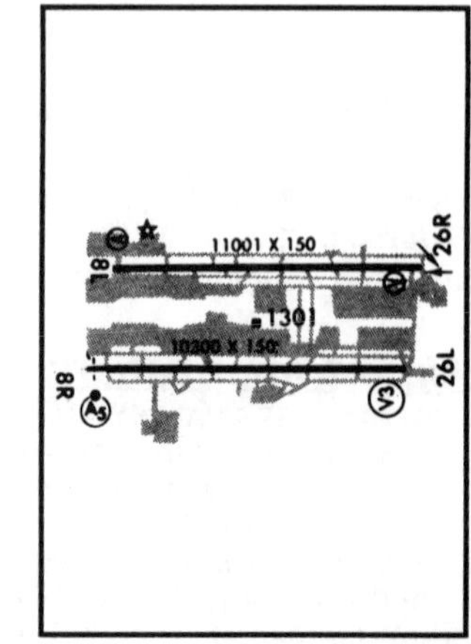

AZ-IWA - PHOENIX WILLIAMS GATEWAY

(Area Code 602) 15, 16

Flight Deck Restauant:

The Flight Deck Restaurant is situated within the terminal building on the Phoenix-Williams Gateway Airport. This restaurant has cafeteria-style service and is open 7:30 a.m. to 6 p.m. Monday through Friday. Future plans may extend hours through the weekend as well. Specialties of the house include their delicious breakfast bagel. For lunch they feature a variety of submarine sandwiches served with the freshest cuts of chicken and beef. This restaurant is unique and attracts many local cliental because the military pilots conducting practice maneuvers often fly-in and land at this airport. We were told by the management that guests can see war-birds like the McDonnell Douglas Harrier and North American T-28 Trojan frequently land nearby. Infact, the Flight Deck has a patio outside their door, where they have outdoor barbecues during the months between September and May on Wednesday and Friday between 10:30 a.m. and 1 p.m. The inside of the restaurant has about 7 tables. Outside on their patio they have about 10 picnic tables. Groups and fly-in clubs are welcome with advanced notice. In-flight catering is also available either through the FBO or by directly contacting the restaurant. For more information call 988-9517

Williams Golf Course Snack Bar:

The Williams Golf Course and Snack Bar is situated about 1/2 mile from the Phoenix-Williams Gateway Airport. During our conversation with the management we learned that fly-in guests normally obtain airport taxi service from the FBO to the golf course. Courtesy transportation may also be available. This 18 hole golf course is a matured establishment with large trees, lakes and bunkers providing challenging play for the average golfer. Future plans for the course include upgrades to make it even more challenging. A snack bar is located at the pro-shop. The grill is open from 7 a.m. to 4 p.m. Breakfast is served until 10:30 a.m. Lunch items include their popular 1/3rd deluxe hamburger or cheeseburgers, Phili-sandwiches, soups and much more. Daily specials are often available. From their dining room guests can enjoy a nice view overlooking the course. Prices including beverage average $5.00 for breakfast and between $4.00 and $7.00 for lunch. Groups can contact the tournament coordinator by calling 988-9419. For more information about the golf course or snack bar call 988-9405.

Restaurants Near Airport:

AZ Golf Resort	5 mi	Phone: 832-3202
Cosmos Italian Restaurant	1/2 mi	Phone: 988-1061
Flight Deck Restaurant	Trml Bldg	Phone: 988-9517
Williams Golf Course Snack Bar	1/2 mi	Phone: 988-9405

Lodging: AZ Golf Resort 5 miles 832-3202 or 800-528-8282; Best Western of Williams (trans, 3-1/2 mi) 800-635-4445; Courtyard by Marriott 461-3000 or 800-321-2211; Mesa Hilton 10 mi 833-5555; Sheraton Mesa 10 mi 898-8300.

Meeting Rooms: AZ Golf Resort 5 miles 832-3202 or 800-528-8282; Best Western of Williams (trans, 3-1/2 mi) 800-635-4445; Courtyard by Marriott 461-3000 or 800-321-2211; Mesa Hilton 10 mi 833-5555; Sheraton Mesa 10 mi 898-8300.

Transportation: Car rental: Thrifty 924-8666; Taxi service: Citywide 277-7100; Supershuttle 244-9000.

Information: Phoenix & Valley of the Sun Convention & Visitors Bureau, One Arizona Center, 400 east Van Buren Street, Suite 600, Phoenix, AZ 85004, Phone: 254-6500.

Attractions:

The Phoenix area contains many attractions for the visitor: Arizona Hall of Fame Museum presents exhibits about famous people who have contributed to Arizona's culture. Phone: 255-2110 or 542-4581; Arizona Mining & Mineral Museum displays collections of minerals and many ore samples maintained by the Arizona Department of Mines and Mineral Resources, 255-3791; Desert Botanical Garden contains 150 acres of cactus, plants and floral arrangements. Self-guided nature walk, cactus exhibits and group lectures explain the living dessert of the world. Phone: 941-1217; Mystery Castle is a popular attraction containing interesting and unique stone and sand castles built over a period by one individual. (Oct-early July, Tues-Sun). Phone: 268-1581; Phoenix Mountains Preserve covers over 23,000 acres of land containing mountains and deserts situated north and south of the city. Numerous recreational activities are available. Squaw Peak Park, Echo Canyon, South Mountain and North Mountain Recreational Area. Phone: 262-6861; Phoenix Zoo exhibits over 1,300 animals, reptiles and birds on display. Rare and exotic collections of wild life can be enjoyed. A children's zoo, refreshment centers and safari train tours are on the premises. Phone: 273-1341; The Heard Museum is another very popular Museum that explains the Southwestern Native American Culture. Primitive and even prehistoric art forms are displayed along with the rare Goldwater Kachina doll collection. Phone: 252-8848.

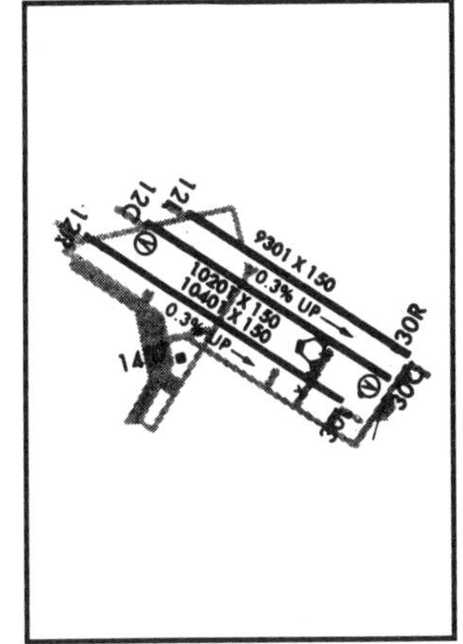

Airport Information:

PHOENIX - WILLIAMS GATEWAY (IWA)

9 mi east of town N33-18.47 W111-39.33 Elev: 1380 Fuel: 100LL, Jet-A Rwy 12R-30L: H1040x150 (Conc) Rwy 12C-30C: H1020x150 (Conc) Rwy 12L-30R: H9301x150 (Conc) Attended: Mon-Fri 1300-0800Z, Sat-Sun 1300-0400Z CTAF: 120.6 Atis:133.5 Phoenix App/Dep Con: 124.9 Willie Tower: 120.6 Gnd Con: 128.25 Clnc Del: 118.8

FBO: William Greater Airport Service Phone: 988-3443

AZ-PRC - PRESCOTT
ERNEST A. LOVE FIELD

(Area Code 520) 17

Nancy's Skyway Restaurant:

Nancy's Skyway Restaurant is situated in the terminal building on the Ernest A. Love Airport. Aircraft parking is available right outside their facility. This is a family style establishment open between 6:30 and 4 p.m. 7 days a week. Their menu provides daily specials, such as burgers, club sandwiches, soups and salads along with a nice selection of breakfast choices. Average prices for a meal run $4.00 to $5.00 for breakfast, and $5.00 to $6.00 for lunch. They can seat about 65 to 75 persons within the restaurant. Their decor is aviation oriented with lots of airplane pictures and model aircraft hanging from the ceiling. Fly-in groups are welcome. For larger groups please let them know in advance that you are coming. Carry-out meals can also be prepared. For more information call 445-6971.

Restaurants Near Airport:

Par For The Course	100 yds SE.	Phone: 778-5330
Skyway Restaurant	On Site	Phone: 445-6971

Lodging: Antelope Hills Inn 1/2 mi 778-6000; Sheraton Resort & Conference Center 776-1666; Prescottonian (10 miles) 445-3096.
Meeting Rooms: Prescott Resort & Conference Center 776-1666.
Transportation: Airport courtesy cars available; Both restaurants listed above are well within walking distance. Also rental cars available: Hertz 776-1399; Budget 778-3806.
Information: Chamber of Commerce, 117 W Goodwin Street, P.O. Box 1147, Prescott, AZ 86302, Phone: 445-2000.

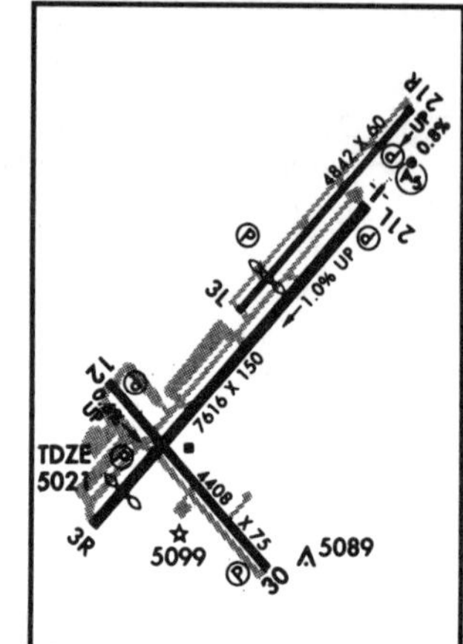

Attractions:

Antelope Hills Golf Course adjacent to Ernest A. Love Field, 445-0583; Sheraton Resort (10 miles); Prescott National Forest (15 miles); Granite Dells (4 miles); Granite Basin Lake and Watson Lake (4 miles); Whiskey Row (Downtown 10 miles); Sharlot Hall Museum (Downtown);

Airport Information:

PRESCOTT - ERNEST A. LOVE FIELD (PRC)
7 mi north of town N34-39 W112-25.29 Elev: 5042 Fuel: 100LL, Jet-A
Rwy 03R-21L: H7616x150 (Asph-Pfc) Rwy 03L-21R: H4842x60 (Asph) Rwy 11-29: H4408x75 (Asph) Attended: 1200-0700Z Atis: 127.2 Unicom: 122.95 Tower: 125.3 Grnd Con: 121.7 Notes: Overnight aircraft parking: $4.00 single, $5.00 multi, waived with fuel purchase; CAUTION: density altitude.

FBO: City of Prescott **Phone: 445-7860**
FBO: Prescott Pilot Shop **Phone: 776-8615**

AZ-SDL - SCOTTSDALE
SCOTTSDALE MUNICIPAL AIRPORT

(Area Code 602)

18, 19

Left Seat Restaurant and Lounge:

This family style restaurant is located within the terminal building of the Scottsdale Municipal Airport. Entrees include "All American Food", along with daily specials. Prices range from $4.50 for breakfast, and $6.00 for lunch. Restaurant hours are weekdays from 7 a.m. to 4 p.m. and weekends from 7 a.m. to 3 p.m. (Bar is open until 9 p.m.). The restaurant will cater to pilots on-the-go as well as provide accommodations for fly-in groups. For information call 991-2030.

Thunderbird Restaurant and Silver Wings Lounge:

The Thunderbird Restaurant is conveniently located just steps across the street from Scottsdale Airport's building, in the Best Western Thunderbird Suites Hotel. The Thunderbird Restaurant has a full service dining room that offers an American/Continental menu in addition to their salad bar, in an atmosphere of casual elegance. Hours are: 6:30 a.m. - 2 p.m. Breakfast/Lunch. 2 p.m. - 9 p.m. in the lounge. Dining Room is open for dinner from 5 p.m. to 9 p.m. Prices are within a moderate range. One can take a journey through aeronautical history while enjoying a beverage or light snack midst aviation memorabilia in the "Silver Wings Lounge". The decor is impressive with over 50 models and 100 aviation related photographs. Enjoy their large screen TV & Happy hour during the hours of 4 p.m. - 7 p.m. Lodging: Best Western Thunderbird Suites, 120 spacious 2-room suites, 4 story adjacent to Scottsdale Airport. Each suite has a wet bar, refrigerator, 2 televisions, 2 phones, and microwaves & video rentals are also available. Each room looks into their courtyard, and one can enjoy their heated pool and Jacuzzi. Special Pilot rates are available with identification. For additional information please call them at: 951-4000 or 1-800-334-1977.

Restaurants Near Airport:

Dallas House	Adj Arpt	Phone: 948-3651
Princess Resort	3 mi N.	Phone: 585-4848
The Left Seat	On Site	Phone: 991-2030
The Thunderbird	On Site	Phone: 951-4000

Lodging: Best Western Thunderbird Suites, 120 suites, 4 story adjacent to airport, Phone: 951-4000; Princess Resort, 3 mi. north of airport, off Scottsdale Rd just north of Bell Rd., 525 units, 82 suites, 48 acres with beautiful and luxurious resort like atmosphere, 36 hole golf course, three heated pools, convention facilities, Phone: 585-4848.

Transportation: Budget Rental Cars, Phone: 249-6124 Hertz Rental Cars, Phone: 948-2400. Also discount car rental is located in hotel lobby of the Best Western Thunderbird, 951-2191.

Convention Facilities: Best Western Thunderbird can accommodate up to 100 people with catering and audio/visual equipment if needed call 951-4000, or 800-334-1977.(See above), Princess Resort (See lodging above).

Information: Scottsdale Chamber of Commerce, Scottsdale Airport - 15000 N. Airport Drive, Scottsdale, AZ 85260, 800-877-1117.

Attractions:

Corporate Jets Grand Canyon Air Tours, flights over rim of Grand Canyon, 1/2 day flights departing Scottsdale Municipal Airport Phone: 948-2400. Rawhide 1880's Western Town, This is a re-created old west town featuring an old style restaurant steakhouse, and saloon, stagecoach rides, mock shootouts, shops and much more. Phone: 563-5111 or 563-5600. McCormick Railroad Park, encompassing 30 acres of land, with train rides, shops exhibiting artifacts and model railroad equipment. Phone: 994-2310

Airport Information:

SCOTTSDALE - SCOTTSDALE MUNICIPAL AIRPORT (SDL)
9 mi north of town N33-37.37 W111-54.63 Elev: 1508
Fuel: 100LL, Jet-A Rwy 03-21: H8251x75 (ASPH) Attended: 1200-0500Z Atis: 118.6 Unicom: 122.95
Tower: 119.9 Gnd Con: 121.6 Clnc Del: 124.8
Notes: Parking 1st 8 hrs (Free), 24 hrs ($3.50 single engine, $4.50 twin engine) and ($13.00 for jets). All restaurants within walking distance except Scottsdale Princess Resort.

Courtyard of the Thunderbird Inn

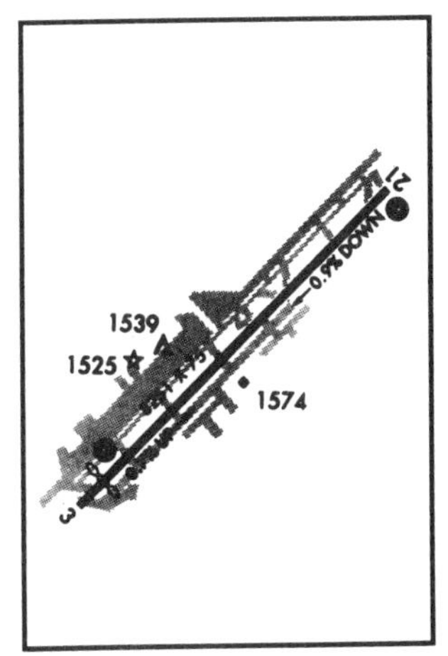

AZ-SEZ - SEDONA
SEDONA AIRPORT

(Area Code 520)

20

Restaurants Near Airport:
Airport Restaurant On Site Phone: 282-3576

Lodging: Sky Ranch Lodge (On Site) 282-6400 Poco Diablo (Free trans) 282-7333; Los Abrigados Resort (Free trans) 282-1777; Enchantment Resort (Airport trans) 282-2900;

Meeting Rooms: Meeting and conference room is available on the airport 282-4487; Also, Poco Diablo 282-7333; Los Abrigados Resort 282-1777; Enchantment Resort 282-2900.

Transportation: Bob's Taxi 282-1234; Bell Ruck 282-4222; Rental Cars: Budget 282-4602; Sedona Jeep 282-2227.

Information: Sedona-Oak Creek Canyon Chamber of Commerce, P.O. Box 478, Sedona, AZ 86339, Phone; 282-7722.

Airport Restaurant:

The Airport Restaurant is located right on the Sedona Airport and is situated well within walking distance, located only a couple hundred feet from the aircraft parking areas. The airport located on a mesa, overlooks the town of Sedona. The view and surrounding terrain is spectacular, while the restaurant offers a quaint and charming atmosphere of an old country inn. Antiques as well as items gathered over the years decorate the restaurant and provide a charming and pleasant decor. The view from the restaurant provides a full view of the airport and its activities, with each seat in the house offering a front row seat. This family style establishment is open from 7 a.m. to 3 p.m. every day except on Christmas. Their hours may soon be extended from 5 p.m. to 8 p.m. during the winter season and 5 p.m. to 9 p.m. during the summer. A full bar is also available on the premises. Specialized entrees include Mexican dishes, roast beef, chicken Teriyaki, roast loin of pork, along with a variety of delicious sandwiches as well as pita sandwiches. Daily specials include prime rib on Friday and Saturday, and leg of lamb on Sunday. Many flying clubs and associations visit this facility regularly for great atmosphere and good food. For more information you can call the Airport Restaurant at 282-3576.

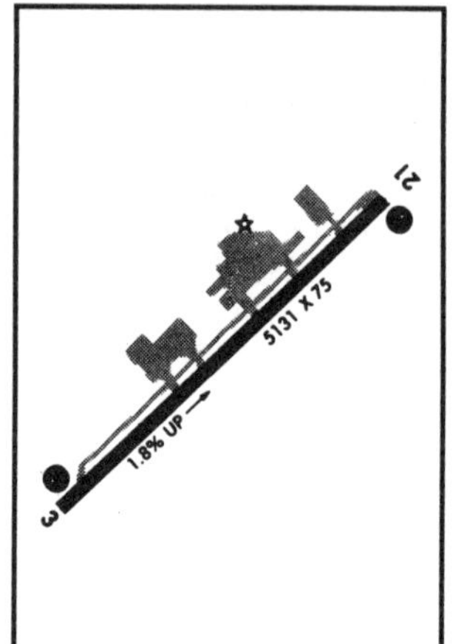

Airport Information:

SEDONA - SEDONA AIRPORT (SEZ)
2 mi southwest of town N34-50.92 W111-47.31 Elev: 4827 Fuel: 100LL, Jet-A
Rwy 03-21: H5131x75 (Asph) Attended: June-Aug 1400-0100Z, Sept-May 1500-0000Z
Unicom: 122.8 Public Phone 24hrs
FBO: Red Rock Aviation Phone: 282-1046

AZ-Q35 - SPRINGERVILLE
SPRINGERVILLE BABBITT FIELD

(Area Code 520)

21

Restaurants Near Airport:
Dick's Bakery N/A Phone: 333-5433
Mike's Steakhouse 2mi E. Phone: 333-4022

Lodging: El Jo Motor Inn (Free Transportation 2 miles) 333-4314; Reed's Motor Lodge 2 miles 333-4323; Sunrise Inn Best Western 2 mi 333-2540; Springville Inn 2 miles 333-4365; Whitings 1 mile 333-2655.

Meeting Rooms: None Reported

Transportation: Aerocrafter "FBO" can accommodate courtesy transportation to nearby facilities with advanced notice for its customers in addition to rental cars 333-5746.

Information: Arizona Office of Tourism, 1100 West Washington, Phoenix, Arizona 85007, Phone: 602-542-TOUR.

Mike's Steakhouse & Lounge:

Mike's Steakhouse & Lounge is considered a family style restaurant about 2-1/2 miles from the Springerville Airport on Hwy 60 & "D" street east towards Socorro, NM. Courtesy transportation can be arranged in advance by calling the restaurant or with Aerocrafter "FBO" at the airport. They provide courtesy transportation to nearby facilities for their customers. The restaurant is open daily from 4 p.m. to 9 p.m. all year long. Their lounge stays open until 1 a.m. They specialize in steaks, shrimp, monk fish "Poor man's lobster", chicken and cheeseburgers cooked on an open pit grill. Specials like prime rib are usually offered on Friday and Saturday night. Average prices run between $8.95 and $15.95 for dinner. The restaurant is decorated with antiques and has pictures of the West. Parties and groups are always welcome with accommodations for up to 90 people in their large dinning room. For information call the restaurant at 333-4022.

Attractions:

Fishing lake 2 miles; CASA Malapais - New Archeological Find; Sunrise Ski Resort 22 miles, Greer Cross Country Skiing 15 miles.

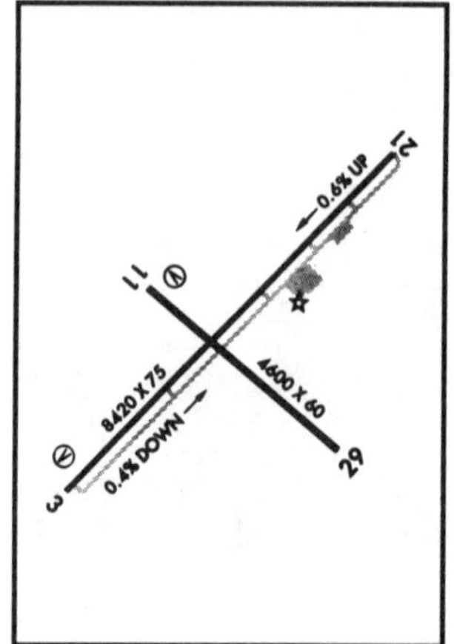

Airport Information:

SPRINGERVILLE - SPRINGERVILLE BABBITT FIELD (Q35)
1 mi west of town N34-07.72 W109-18.69 Elev: 7051 Fuel: 100LL, Jet-A
Rwy 03-21: H8420x75 (Asph) Rwy 11-29: H4600x60 (Asph) Attended: Apr-Oct 1400-0200Z, Nov-Mar dawn to dusk Unicom: 122.8 Public Phone 24hrs Notes: No landing fees, no overnight fee when gas is purchased.
FBO: Aerocrafter Phone: 333-5746

AZ-P29 - TOMBSTONE
TOMBSTONE MUNICIPAL AIRPORT

(Area Code 602) 22

Top O'The Hill:

The Top O' The Hill restaurant is located 3 miles northwest of the Tombstone Municipal Airport. Transportation to the restaurant can be arranged by calling the restaurant prior to your arrival and setting up a specific time and date that you will be landing at the airport. There is no telephone at the airport nor is the airport attended. You can also call City Hall at 457-3562 for transportation. Top O' The Hill is a family style restaurant that is open 7 days a week from 7 a.m. to 8 p.m. Specialties include Mexican dishes as well as roast beef, shrimp, chicken, chicken fried steak, steaks, pork chops, barbecued ribs, along with soups, and salads. Daily specials are also available. Prices average $3.95 for breakfast, and lunch and about $6.95 for dinner. This facility will be happy to arrange accommodations for group fly-ins and parties. the restaurant is located across the street from the famous "Boothill" graveyard and just 1/2 mile south of the Best Western lodge on Hwy 80. For information call 457-3461.

Restaurants Near Airport:

Longhorn Restaurant	3 mi NW	Phone: 457-3405
Lucky Cuss Restaurant	3 mi NW	Phone: 457-3561
Top O The Hill	3 mi NW	Phone: 457-3461
Wagon Wheel Restaurant	3 mi NW	Phone: 457-3656

Lodging: Adobe Lodge Motel 457-3641; Best Western Lookout Lodge (4 miles NW of Airport) 457-2223; Larian Motel 457-2272; Tombstone Motel 457-3478.

Transportation: There is no phone at the airport so it will be necessary to arrange advanced transportation through the restaurant of your choice or call City Hall at 457-3562. Exact time and date must be given so someone can meet you at the airport and take your party to the restaurant, or nearby facilities.

Attraction:

The town of Tombstone is most famous for the gun battle fought between the Earps and the Clantons in 1881 at the OK Corral. "Helldorado" is an annual, three day event held in Mid-October depicting some of the historical events which happened during the 1880's. For information call the Tombstone Courthouse State Historic Park at 457-3326 or Silver Nugget Museum at 457-3310.

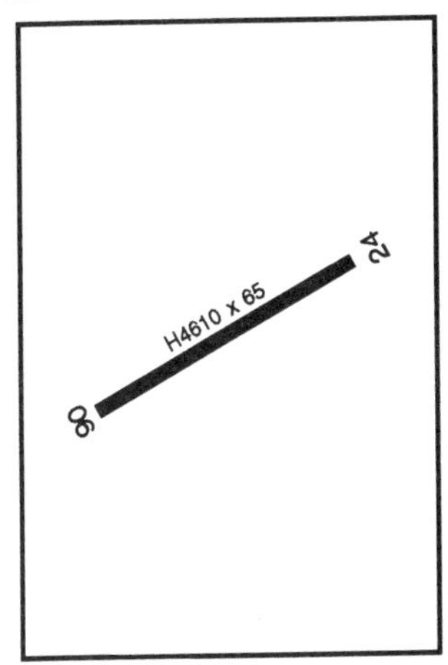

Airport Information:

TOMBSTONE - TOMBSTONE MUNICIPAL AIRPORT (P29)
3 mi southeast of town N31-40.26 W110-01.37 Elev: 4743 Rwy 06-24: H4610x65 (Asph-Asfc)
CTAF: 122.9 Attended: unattended No Public Phone on the field. Prior arrangements must be made for exact time and date you plan to arrive at the airport, so someone can meet you and take you to nearby facilities. Call City Hall 602-457-3461 or 3256 or restaurant to arrange transportation.

AZ-RYN - TUCSON
RYAN AIRFIELD

(Area Code 602) 23

Wings Restaurant:

The Wings Restaurant is located right on the Tucson Ryan Airfield. This cafe style restaurant is open from 6 a.m. to 8 p.m. and Friday and Saturday until 9 p.m. After landing at Ryan Airfield, you can taxi up and park your aircraft adjacent to the restaurant. Their menu includes items like pot roast, hamburgers, sandwiches, soups and salads. They make their own bread and bake it on the premises. Other specials offered are the Friday fish fry with cod for only $4.95, Saturday and Sunday they prepare specials in prime rib, stuffed chicken or pork and London broil dinners. Average prices run $2.00 to $3.00 for breakfast, $3.25 to $4.25 for lunch and $4.25 to $10.00 for dinner. They can seat up to 100 persons in their main dining area. This restaurant displays open beamed ceilings and widows along the back of the restaurant, that allow a fine view of the aircraft parking area. For more information about Wings Restaurant, call 883-9455.

Restaurants Near Airport:

Wings Restaurant	On Site	Phone: 883-9455

Lodging: None Reported

Meeting Rooms: None Reported

Transportation: None Reported

Information: Metropolitan Tucson Convention & Visitors Bureau, 130 South Scott Avenue, Tucson, AZ 85701, Phone: 624-1889.

Attractions:

Old Tucson (Temporarily closed due to fire. However may re-open in the future.) is an old west attraction as well as a current filming sight for western movies. Famous for its part in the movie "Arizona". There are mock gun fights with stunt shows daily, along with narrow gauge train and stage coach rides available to the visitor. This attraction is located at 201 South Kinney Road (10 miles) Phone: 883-6457; Also the Desert Museum located at 2021 North Kinney Road (12 miles) Phone: 883-2702.

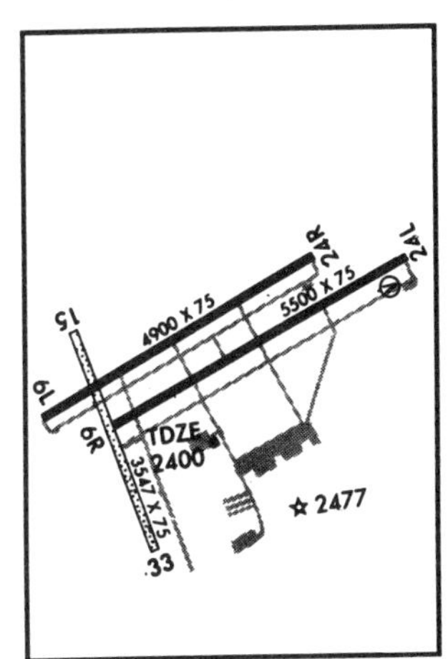

Airport Information:

TUCSON - RYAN AIRFIELD (RYN)
10 mi southwest of town 32-08-29N 111-10-24W Elev: 2415 Fuel: 80, 100LL
Rwy 06R-24L: H5500x75 (Asph) Rwy 06L-24R H4900x75 Rwy 16-34: 3547x75 (Dirt)
Attended 1300-0100Z Tower: 125.8 Gnd Con: 118.2 Public Phone 24hrs
Notes: CAUTION: runway 16-34 not visible from tower. Runway 06 preferential runway up to 10 knots tailwind. No landing fees, overnight parking $3.50.
Ryan Airfield Phone: 573-8100

AZ-TUS - TUCSON
TUCSON INTERNATIONAL AIRPORT

(Area Code 520)

24, 25, 26

El Charro Restaurant (CA1 Services):

This family-style restaurant is part of the CA1 Services organizations. It is a family-style establishment that is located on the Tucson International Airport (TUS) on the third level next to Delta Airlines. The restaurant hours are 10:30 a.m. to 9 p.m. A lounge named Toma Tia is situated adjacent to the restaurant. They specialize in preparing Mexican dishes. Carne Seca is very popular with many of their customers. Prices average around $7.00 for lunch and dinner. Groups are welcome with advanced notice appreciated. Anything on their menu can be prepared to go, if requested. In-flight catering is also available. In addition to this restaurant we were informed that there are also two food courts areas on the concourse level. For more information call 573-8225.

Sutters Tower Restaurant:

The Sutters Tower Restaurant is located on the Tucson International Airport. This family-style restaurant is situated near the executive tower and is open from 5:30 a.m. to 5 p.m. Monday through Saturday and on Sunday from 5:30 a.m. to 3 p.m. Their menu includes a full breakfast line with omelets, steak and eggs, as well as a wide selection of other entrees like hamburgers, sandwiches, soups, pies and desserts. The restaurant can seat 80 people in their dining room along with counter service. Many of their customers are air travelers, as well as nearby Air National Guard and Air Medical Helicopter personnel. For more information call 889-8641.

Tanque Verde Ranch:

Tanque Verde Ranch is one of America's old time cattle and guest ranches, and it is recognized as one of the last luxurious outposts of the Old West. The ranch is located on 640 acres in the desert foothills of the Tanque Verde, Rincon, and Catalina Mountains. The ranch's east border is part of the rugged Coronado National Forest, with the Saguaro National Park to the south. The ranch features 65 authentically decorated rooms and spacious, elegant casitas that are air-conditioned and offer beautiful desert and mountain views. Most rooms have adobe fireplaces and private outside patios. Tanque Verde Ranch features plenty of activities for its guests, such as horseback riding, tennis, sports, swimming, guided hikes, nature programs, spa facilities, and a variety of informative and entertaining evening programs. Championship golf is nearby and special group activities are easily arranged. There are also meeting rooms with spectacular views located throughout the ranch. The ranch also features Arizona's largest stable with over 130 well trained ranch horses. The ranch offers walking rides for beginners and loping rides for more experienced riders. Morning and afternoon rides, as well as all-day rides are also available. Guests can ride through the old mesquite corrals and fix their own "Cowboy" breakfast of chili, eggs and blueberry pancakes; They can mount up for an all-day trip and explore the terrain of the Old West with its giant Saguaros and prickly cacti; They can hike the Sonoran Desert and study animal habitats with the ranch's staff naturalists. Or watch a glorious sunset from the historic Ranch Ramada, and then relive the day in the cozy Gourmet Dining Room. For guests, the ranch offers the Full American Plan which includes breakfast, lunch and dinner. Tucson International Airport is located about 18 miles from Tanque Verde Ranch. With a minimum stay of 4 nights, the ranch will provide free transportation to and from the airport. Otherwise, the shuttle fee is $15.00. If traveling from the airport by car, turn right on Valencia, then take Valencia to Kolb Street and turn north (left). Next, take Kolb north to Speedway Boulevard, then travel east on the Boulevard through the foothills, until you come to 14301 E. Speedway. Travel time is estimated to be about 30 minutes. For more information about activities, rates and accommodations at Tanque Verde Ranch, call 800-234-DUDE (3833) or 296-6275.

Restaurants Near Airport:

CA1 Services	On Site	Phone: 573-8225
Inn at the Airport	1 mile	Phone: 746-0271
Sutters Tower Restaurant	On Site	Phone: 889-8641
Tanque Verde Ranch	18 mi	Phone: 296-6275

Lodging: Transportation is provided by the following: Tanque Verde Ranch (18 miles) 296-6275; Inn at the Airport (1 mile) 746-0271; Holiday Inn (4 miles) 746-1161; Howard Johnson's (5 miles) 623-7792; Courtyard By Marriott 573-0000; Embassy Suites Hotel & Conference Center 573-0700; Hampton Inn-Airport 889-5789; Holiday Inn-Airport 889-5789; Quality Inn-Airport 746-3932; Ramada Inn-Airport 294-5250; Viscount Suite Hotel 745-6500.

Meeting Rooms: Tanque Verde Ranch 296-6275; Also, most of the lodging facilities listed above have meeting rooms.

Transportation: Tanque Verde Ranch will provide free transportation with a minimum stay of 4 nights. Also, rental cars: Avis 746-3278, Budget 573-1207; Dollar 573-1100; Hertz 889-5731; National 573-8050

Information: Metropolitan Tucson Convention & Visitors Bureau, 130 S. Scott Avenue, Tucson, AZ 85701, Phone: 624-1889.

Attractions:

Pima Air Museum is located about 5 miles from the Tucson International Airport. The museum contains over 180 vintage and current aircraft on display, comprised both of civilian and military types, from the 1903 Wright Flyer to the "SR-71 Blackbird." Admission hours 9 a.m. to 5 p.m. everyday, except Christmas Day. Adults $5.00, children under 10 free. Indoor and outdoor displays, gift shop, and snack bar on premises; Also located at nearby Green Valley, AZ, is the Pima Titan Missile Museum, the only intercontinental ballistic missile complex in the world that is open to the public. Take Interstate 19 south to exit 69 west. Hours 9 a.m. to 5 p.m. For reservations, call 791-2929 for the Air Museum or 625-7736 for the Titan Missile Museum, or write to Tucson Air Museum Foundation 600 E. Valencia, Tucson, AZ 85706, Phone: 574-9658.

Airport Information:

TUCSON - TUCSON INTERNATIONAL AIRPORT (TUS)

6 mi south of town N32-06.98 W110-56.48 Elev: 2641 Fuel: 100, 100LL, Jet-A Rwy 11L-29R: H10994x150 (Asph-Grvd) Rwy 11R-29L: H9117x75 (Asph) Rwy 03-21: H7000x150 (Asph-Pfc) Attended: continuously Atis: 123.8 Unicom: 122.95 Tower: 118.3, 119.0 Gnd Con: 124.4 Clnc Del: 126.65 Public Phone 24hrs Notes: Overnight parking fee is $10.00 for both singles and twins, but is waived with a fuel purchase.

FBO: KBM Air Phone: 294-8214
FBO: Spirit Aviation Phone: 889-0593
FBO: Leading Edge Av. Phone: 295-9815
FBO: Tucson Executive Phone: 573-8128

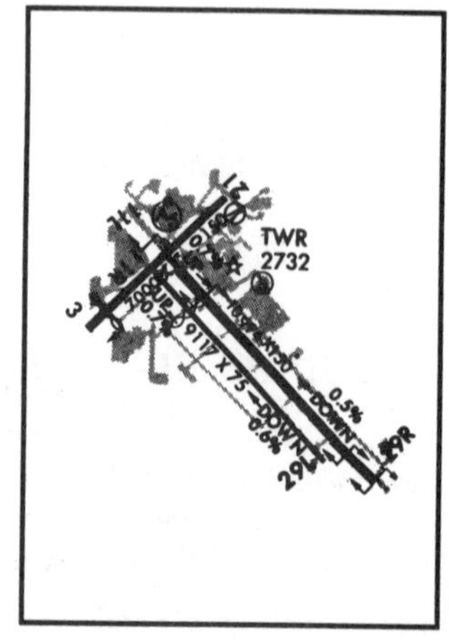

Not to be used for navigational purposes

Pima Air Museum

Photo by: Tucson Air Museum Foundation

The Tucson Air Museum Foundation contains the Pima Air Museum. Titan Missile Museum and the Home of the Arizona Aviation Hall of Fame & the 390 Memorial Museum. In 1966, a group of military and civilian enthusiasts presented to Pima County, their concept of an air museum for Tucson. On May 2, 1967 the Pima County Board of Supervisors appointed a committee to locate and obtain a site for such a museum. Authorization was given on July 18 of that year for incorporation of the Tucson Air Museum Foundation of the Pima County, a non profit educational corporation responsible for the operation of Pima Air Museum.

Under the Federal Parks Act, Pima County obtained a 320 acre parcel of government land from the Bureau of Land Management. The $800.00 purchase price was provided by the Foundation with the land being deeded to Pima County for a regional park. Approximately 30 acres of that portion was fenced in for the museum, and perimeter lighting and well for drinking water was installed. The original area has now been expanded to approximately 75 fenced-in acres.

In October 1969, 35 Air Force aircraft which the Military Aircraft Storage and Disposition Center had displayed along Gold Links Road, became the nucleus of the museum. They were moved to the new site in August of 1973, following inspection and certification by the Air Force Museum.

The dream became reality when on May 8, 1976, as an official Bi-centennial event, the Pima Air Museum was dedicated and opened to the public. The collection which by then had grown to 75 aircraft, continues to grow and as of now contains more than 200 examples. Many contain many airplanes at once, as they are worked through the various stages of restoration by highly skilled staff and volunteers.

In May 1986 the Pima Air Museum opened the Titan Missile Museum, located in Green Valley, Arizona. This museum is the only Intercontinental Ballistic Missile (ICBM) complex open to the public. Fifty-four Titan missile sites were located in the United States; 18 in Arizona, 18 in Arkansas, and 18 in Kansas. All have been destroyed except for the site which has been preserved as a museum. It stands today as it stood on alert for 19 years, accurate in every detail except for the empty booster and re-entry vehicle in the silo. One hour guided tours begin every half-hour. Walking shoes are required (no heels). The tour descends 55 steps to a level 35 feet underground. Special tours may be arranged for handicapped via an elevator. Reservations are suggested. However, walk-ins are also welcome.

The Pima Air Museum is located approximately 5 miles from the Tucson International Airport (TUS). Fly-in visitors can arrange transportation through the fixed base operators on the field: Taxi and rental car service are available to the Pima Air Museum. However, if desiring to visit the Titan Missile Museum located some 20 to 25 miles from the Air Museum, a rental car would be necessary. Avis, Budget, Hertz and National are all available at the Tucson International Airport. There are also two restaurants located on the airport. For information about the Pima Air Museum call 502-574-9658 for a recording describing admission and location. For a direct number to the museum call their administration office at 520-574-0646. Reservations for visiting the Titan Missile Museum can be arranged by calling 520-791-2929. (Information obtained from Tucson Air Museum Foundation.)

Photo by: Tucson Air Museum Foundation

AZ-P34 - WINDOW ROCK WINDOW ROCK AIRPORT

(Area Code 520)

27

Navajo Nation Inn:

The Navajo Nation Inn is located within walking distance and across the street from the Window Rock Airport. This combination family style and fine dining facility is open between 6:30 a.m. and 9:00 p.m. 7 days a week. Their menu specializes in American, Native American and Mexican foods, as well as Indian food. Daily specials are available. Average prices run $5.00 for breakfast, $6.00 for lunch and $8.00 for dinner. The decor of this establishment is modern with carpeting, booths, tables and local art and paintings hanging from the walls. The main dining room can seat about 72 people. In addition to the restaurant, they have a 56 room motel located next door with accommodations for larger groups and parties. Meeting and conference rooms can hold up to 50 people and 150 people in the "Day Room". A small zoo is also located nearby. For more information you can call the Navajo Nation Inn at 871-4108.

Restaurants Near Airport:

Los Verdes Cafe	2-1/4 mi W.	Phone: N/A
Navajo Nation Inn	1/4 mi	Phone: 871-4108
Tuller Cafe	2 mi W.	Phone: 871-4687

Lodging: Navajo Nation Inn (1/4 mi. Across the street) Phone: 871-4108.

Meeting Rooms: Navajo Nation Inn (1/4 mi . Across the street) Phone: 871-4108.

Transportation: None reported

Information: Navajoland Tourism Dept., P.O. Box 663, Window Rock, AZ 86515, Phone: 871-6659 or 871-7371.

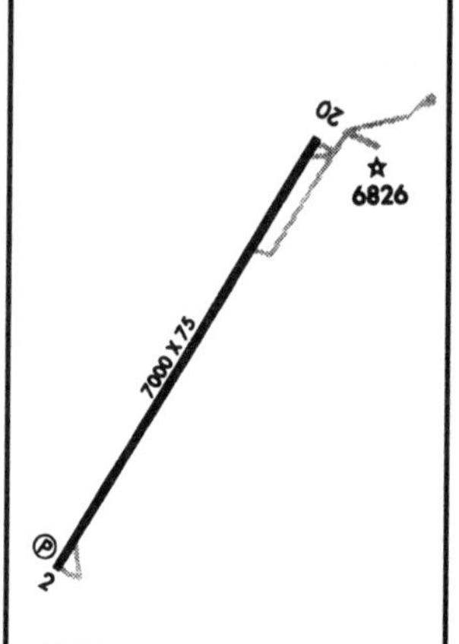

Airport Information:

WINDOW ROCK - WINDOW ROCK AIRPORT (P34)
1 mi south of town   N35-39.12 W109-04.04   Elev: 6739   Fuel: none reported
Rwy 02-20: H7000x75 (Asph)   Attended Mon-Fri 1500-0000Z   Unicom: 122.8
Notes: No landing fee reported
FBO: Navajo Air Transportation   Phone: 871-6466

AZ-YUM - YUMA MCAS YUMA INTERNATIONAL AIRPORT

(Area Code 520)

28

Sky Chief:

The Sky Chief is located about 6 blocks from the airport. Some people walk to the restaurant from the airport. However, courtesy shuttle service is available through Bet-Ko Air (FBO). The restaurant hours are 11 a.m. to 2 p.m. and 5 p.m. to 10 p.m. during the week and 5 p.m. to 10 p.m. on weekends. Their lounge is open from 11 a.m. to 12:30 a.m. but closed on Sunday. Entrees on their menu include steak and lobster, chicken, seafood, cod, prime rib along with lighter fare such as sandwiches, soups and salads including a salad bar. They also offer an assortment of appetizers as well. The main dining room can accommodate up to 80 persons. There are booths along both sides of the restaurant with tables in between. Groups up to 30 people can be served with advance notice. Meals-to-go are also available. The Sky Chief also provides live entertainment from 7 p.m. to 12 a.m. For more information you can call 726-0847.

Restaurants Near Airport:

Mandarine Palace	1 mi	Phone: 344-2805
Pilot House	On Site	Phone: 726-6530
Sky Chief	6 Blks	Phone: 726-0847

Lodging: Chilton Motor Hotel 1 mi.) 344-1050; Holiday Inn Express (Trans) 334-1420; Raddisson Suites Inn Yuma (Trans) 726-4830.

Meeting Rooms: Holiday Inn Express (Trans) 334-1420; Raddisson Suites Inn Yuma (Trans) 726-4830.

Transportation: Bet-Ko Air, Inc can accommodate courtesy transportation to nearby facilities; Taxi Service: Cactus Gold 343-7520; City Taxi 782-0111; Also Rental Cars: Avis 726-5737; Budget 344-1822; Hertz 726-5160.

Information: Yuma County Chamber of Commerce, 377 Main Street, P.O. Box 230, Yuma, AZ 85364, Phone: 782-2567.

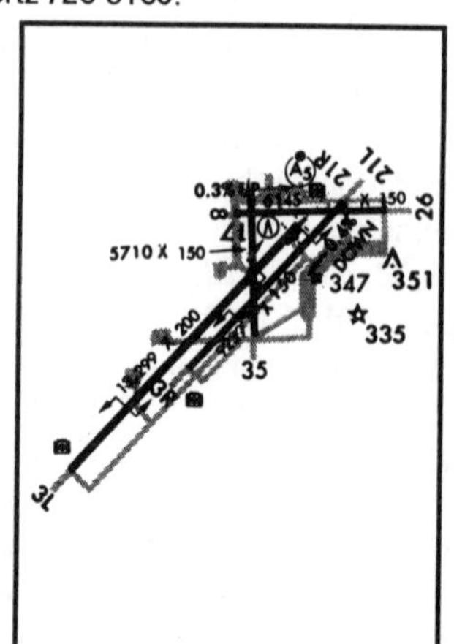

Airport Information:

YUMA MCAS - YUMA INTERNATIONAL AIRPORT (YUM)
3 mi south of town   N32-3939 W114-36.36   Elev: 213   Fuel: 100, Jet-A
Rwy 03L-21R: H13299x200 (Conc)   Rwy 03R-21L: H9239x150 (Asph-Conc)
Rwy 08-26: H6145x150 (Asph-Conc)   Rwy 17-35: H5710x150 (Asph-Conc)   Attended: continuously   Atis: 118.8   Unicom: 122.95   Tower: 119.3, 126.2   GND Con: 121.9
Clnc Del: 118.0   Caution: Joint use civil-military airport. Important advisory to all civil and air carrier operations. Refer to current Airport Facility Directory for updated information.
FBO: Bet-Ko Air, Inc.   Phone: 726-1116
FBO: Sun Western Flyers   Phone: 726-4715

ARKANSAS

LOCATION MAP

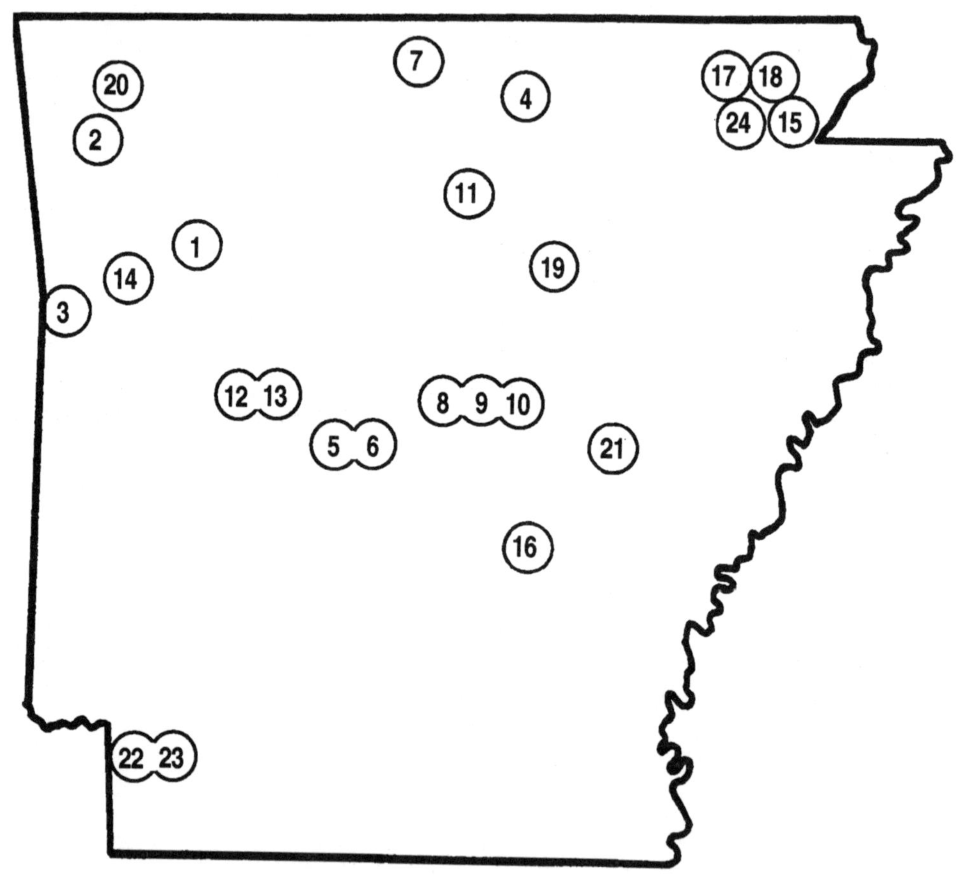

Not to be used for navigational purposes

ARKANSAS

CROSS FILE INDEX

Location Number	City or Town	Airport Name And Identifier	Name of Attraction
1	Clarksville	Clarksville Muni Arpt. (H35)	Western Sizzlin
2	Fayetteville	Drake Field (FYV)	Airport Restaurant
3	Fort Smith	Fort Smith Muni. Arpt. (FSM)	Cloud Nine Restaurant
4	Horseshoe Bend	Horseshoe Bend Arpt. (6M2)	Carriage Room
5	Hot Springs	Memorial Field (HOT)	Lake Hamilton Resort
6	Hot Springs	Memorial Field (HOT)	Wildwood 1884 B & B
7	Lakeview	Gaston's White River Resort (3M0)	Gaston's Restaurant
8	Little Rock	Adams Field Arpt. (LIT)	Ashley's Restaurant
9	Little Rock	Adams Field Arpt. (LIT)	Flight Deck Restaurant
10	Little Rock	Adams Field Arpt. (LIT)	River Crossing (Dobbs)
11	Mountain View	Harry E. Wilcox Mem. Field (7M2)	Ozark Folk Center Rest.
12	Mount Ida	Bearce Airport (7M3)	Crystal Inn Restaurant
13	Mount Ida	Bearce Airport (7M3)	Mountain Harbor Resort
14	Ozark	Franklin County Arpt. (7M5)	Wiederkehr Weikeller R.
15	Paragould	Kirk Field (PGR)	Oak's Restaurant
16	Pine Bluff	Grider Field (PBF)	Grider Field Restaurant
17	Pocahontas	Nick Wilson Field (M70)	Bonanza Restaurant
18	Pocahontas	Nick Wilson Field (M70)	Dairy Queen
19	Searcy	Searcy Muni. (M07)	AJ's Cookie Basket
20	Springdale	Springdale Muni. Arpt. (ASG)	Hickory Hangar
21	Stuttgart	Stuttgart Muni. Arpt. (SGT)	Mallard Restaurant
22	Texarkana	Texarkana Reg. (TXK)	Wings Restaurant
23	Texarkana	Texarkana Reg. (TXK)	Park Place
24	Walnut Ridge	Walnut Ridge Reg. Arpt. (ARG)	Walnut Ridge Arpt. Rest.

Articles

City or Town	Nearest Airport and Identifier	Name of Attraction
Mountain View, AR	Mt. View Wilcox Mem Fld. (7M2)	Ozark Folk Center State Park

AR-H35 - CLARKSVILLE
CLARKSVILLE MUNI AIRPORT

(Area Code 501) 1

Western Sizzlin:

This family style restaurant is located about 3 miles west of the Clarksville Municipal Airport. Courtesy transportation can be arranged with Evans Airport Service F.B.O. When leaving the airport turn west onto Highway 64 and go approximately 2-1/2 miles to exit 55 and I-40. This restaurant serves steak, potato and salad bar in addition to a complete vegetable bar plus dessert. Ice cream is included with the meal. Their complete hot vegetable bar and dessert bar is offered every day of the week. Average prices run $5.90 for lunch and $6.00 to $7.00 for dinner. The restaurant is open 11 a.m. to 9 p.m. Sunday through Thursday. Friday and Saturday they are open from 11 a.m. to 10 p.m. The decor is contemporary with seating for up to 265 persons. Accommodations for parties up to 100 persons can easily be arranged. All meals can be prepared-to-go. Delivery to the airport could be arranged. However, advance reservations must be made. For information call 754-6400.

Restaurants Near Airport:

Back Door Bar-B-Que	1/2 mi N	Phone: 754-8096
Simons Ole S Pancake Hse	2 mi SW	Phone: 754-2525
Western Sizzlin	3 mi W	Phone: 754-6400
Woodards Family Restaurant	2 mi SW	Phone: 754-3776

Lodging: Days Inn (5 mi, trans) 754-8555; Sherwood Motor Inn (Best Western, free shuttle, 2 miles) 754-7900; Super 8 Motel (Two miles) 754-8800;
Meeting Rooms: Woodards Family Inn (2 miles southwest of airport) 754-3776; Western Sizzlin Restaurant (3 mi west) 754-6400.
Transportation: Airport manager has private vehicle for customers and short term use, with advance notice; Also: Whitson Morgan Rental Cars 754-3020.
Information: Russellville Chamber of Commerce, 1019 West Main Street, P.O. Box 822, Russellville, AR 72801, Phone: 968-2530.

Attractions:

Clarksville Country Club is located 4 miles southwest, 754-3026; All kind of lakes and parks are located near the airport for those who enjoy outdoor sports.

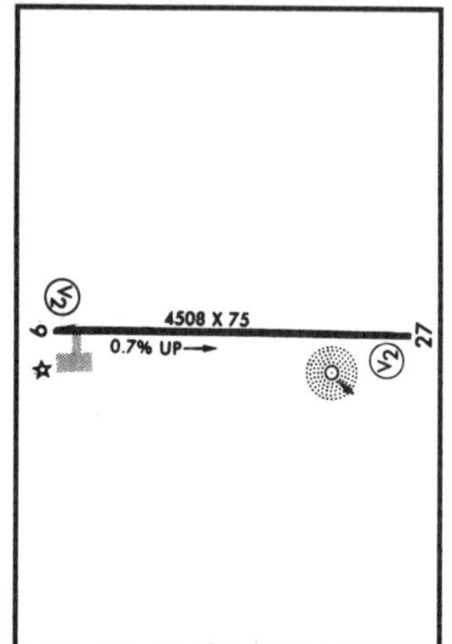

Airport Information:

CLARKSVILLE - CLARKSVILLE MUNICIPAL AIRPORT (H35)
3 mi east of town N35-28.24 W93-25.63 Elev: 481 Fuel: 100LL, Jet-A
Rwy 09-27: H4508x75 (Asph) Attended: unattended Unicom: 122.8
FBO: Airport Service Phone: 754-8899
FBO: JMB Aviation (Mechanic) Phone: 754-7713

AR-FYV - FAYETTEVILLE
DRAKE FIELD

(Area Code 501) 2

Airport Restaurant:

The Airport Restaurant is located within the terminal building at the Drake Field. This restaurant is within walking distance from the aircraft parking area. They are open from 6 a.m. to 10 p.m. Sunday through Friday, and from 6 a.m. to 7 p.m. on Saturday. The main dining room can seat 50 persons, with tables on one side of the restaurant, as well as counter service. Their menu includes cheeseburgers, hamburgers, French dip, fried chicken steak fingers, and sandwiches. Average prices run about $5.00 for most entrees. Most everything on their menu can also be prepared for carry-out. Group fly-ins and parties are welcome. For more information you can call the Airport Restaurant at 442-8599.

Restaurants Near Airport:

Airport Restaurant	On Site	Phone: 442-8599
Old Post Office	4 mi	Phone: 442-5588
Park Inn Restaurant	4 mi	Phone: 521-1166
Tim's Pizza	4 mi	Phone: 521-5551

Lodging: Clarion Inn (trans) 521-1166; Hilton Hotel (trans) 442-5555; Best Western 6 mi. 442-3041.
Meeting Rooms: Air Museum 521-4947; Airport Manager's Office 521-4750; Aero Tech Services (FBO) 442-4343.
Transportation: Aero Tech Services (FBO) can accommodate courtesy transportation to nearby facilities 443-4343; Also, Car Rental: Avis 442-8812; Budget 442-2055; Hertz 521-3400; National 442-7562; Airport Limousine 443-3529; Hatfield Limousine 521-3185; Taxi: C & H Taxi Service 421-1900.
Information: Chamber of Commerce, 123 West Mountain Street, P.O. Box 4216, Fayetteville, AR 72702-4216, Phone: 521-1710.

Attractions:

The Arkansas Air Museum is located right on the Fayetteville Drake Field. This museum exhibits historical and racing aircraft from World War I and II. All the aircraft are kept in flying condition. In addition to the aircraft, they also have engines and aviation related instruments. The museum charges no admission at this time. They are open from 11 a.m. to 4 p.m. Wednesday through Saturday and from 1 p.m. to 4 p.m. on Sunday. Allow at least 30 minutes to tour this museum. Open special hours for groups with prior notice. Also in the area is Beaver Lake, 30-40 miles, Champions Golf Course, Bella Vista Golf, Devil's Den State Park. (See "Information" listed above)

Airport Information:

FAYETTEVILLE - DRAKE FIELD (FYV)
3 mi south of town N36-00.31 W94-10.20 Elev: 1251 Fuel: 100LL, Jet-A
Rwy 16-34: H6006x100 (Asph-Grvd) Attended: 1100-0500Z Atis: 133.1 Unicom: 122.95
Tower: 128.0 Gnd Con: 121.8 Public Phone 24hrs
FBO: Aero Tech Services Phone: 443-4343.

AR-FSM - FORT SMITH
FORT SMITH MUNICIPAL AIRPORT

(Area Code 501)

3

Cloud Nine Restaurant:

Cloud Nine Restaurant is located in the terminal building at the Fort Smith Municipal Airport. This cafe is open between 6 a.m. and 6 p.m. 7 days a week. You can reach the restaurant by walking from the nearby aircraft parking ramp. Their menu includes specialty items like hamburgers, Cajun chicken, and club sandwiches. This restaurant is also known for its delicious homemade desserts including their large cinnamon rolls, to the mouth watering pie baked to perfection. In-flight catering is also available with advanced notice. In addition to the restaurant, they also have a small gift shop located adjacent to the dining area. For more information call the Cloud Nine Restaurant at 648-1189.

Restaurants Near Airport:

Cloud 9 Restaurant	On Site	Phone: 648-1189
Luby's	1 mi E.	Phone: N/A
Red Lobster	2 mi E.	Phone: 452-9010
Western Sizzlin	3 mi W.	Phone: 646-7715

Lodging: Best Western Trade Winds Inn (Free trans) 785-4121; Days Inn (Free trans) 783-0271; Holiday Inn (Free trans) 783-1000; Ramada Inn 646-2931; Kings Row Inn 452-4200; Sheraton Inn 452-4110; Fifth Season Inn 452-4880.

Meeting Rooms: Best Western Trade Winds 785-4121; Days Inn 783-0271; Holiday Inn 783-1000; Sheraton Inn 452-4110; Fifth Season Inn 452-4880.

Transportation: TAC Air (FBO) provides courtesy transportation to nearby facilities; Also, Razorback Taxi 646-5366; Avis 646-5588; Budget 646-9101; Hertz 646-7823; National 646-3471; Thrifty Car Rental 648-9568.

Information: Chamber of Commerce, 612 Garrison Avenue, P.O. Box 1668, Fort Smith, AR 72902, Phone: 783-6118.

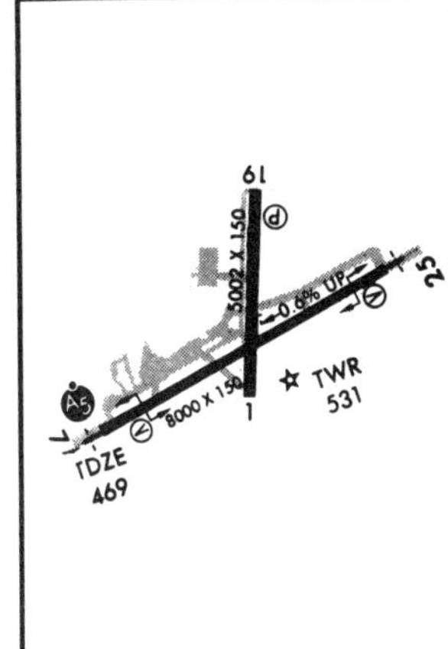

Airport Information:

FORT SMITH - FORT SMITH MUNICIPAL AIRPORT (FSM)
3 mi southeast of town N35-20.20 W94-22.05 Elev: 469 Fuel: 100LL, Jet-A,
Rwy 07-25: H8000x150 (Asph-Grvd) Rwy 01-19: H50002x150 (Asph-Grvd)
Attended: continuously Atis: 126.3 Unicom: 122.95 Tower: 118.3 Gnd Con: 121.9
Clnc Del 133.85 Public Phone 24hrs
FBO: TAC Air Phone: 646-1611

AR-6M2 - HORSESHOE BEND
HORSESHOE BEND AIRPORT

(Area Code 501)

4

Hillhigh Hotel & Spa
Carriage Room Supper Club:

This restaurant is located in the Hillhigh Hotel & Spa. Immediate pick-up service by free shuttle is available to restaurant guests at no charge by calling from the pilots lounge or if fly-in guests prefer, they may walk 4 blocks to the restaurant. This fine dining facility is open Tuesday through Saturday from 7 a.m. to 2 p.m. and 5 p.m. to 9 p.m. On Sunday they are open from 10 a.m. to 2 p.m. and closed on Monday. A complete menu from appetizers to desserts of homemade pies and cakes are available. Prime rib is their specialty. Prices range from $4.25 for breakfast, $4.95 for lunch and $12.95 for dinner. Daily specials at lunch and dinner are provided. Their beautifully appointed dining room with soft chandelier lighting, original art works, fine oak woodwork and detailing, overlooks the golf course and landscaped grounds. Flying groups frequently arrange their outings and conventions at this facility. They have hosted the Navion Flying Organization for 10 consecutively. Catering service for private and corporate pilots can also be arranged. The restaurant and lounge is connected to the Hillhigh Hotel and Spa with 76 rooms, health club, indoor pool, lighted golf course, beauty salon and much more. For information call 670-5141. (See "Attractions" listed above)

Restaurants Near Airport:

Carriage Room Rest.	1/2 mi W	Phone: 670-5141
Club House Restaurant	1/2 mi N	Phone: 670-4232
Bob & Ginney's Rest.	1/4 mi W	Phone: 670-4273

Lodging: Hillhigh Hotel & Spa, (Free Transportation, 1/2 mile west of airport), Phone: 670-5141. (Carriage Room Restaurant at same location).

Meeting Rooms: Hillhigh Hotel & Spa, contains accommodations for meeting and business conventions. (Free Transportation, 1/2 mile west of airport), Phone: 670-5141.

Transportation: There is a courtesy car for guests visiting the Hillhigh Hotel & Spa. Transportation is provided to and from the Horseshoe Bend Airport by calling 670-5141. Rental Cars can be arranged through: Hobbs Auto Sales 670-5500; or Turkey Mtn. Motors 322-7110.

Information: Horseshoe Bend Area Chamber of Commerce, P.O. Box 4083 - FS Horseshoe Bend, AR 72512, Phone: 670-5433

Attractions:

Hillhigh Hotel & Spa - "Horseshoe Bend is in an area of the Ozarks known for its famed natural wonders. An hour's drive will take you to Blanchard Springs Caverns within the Ozark National Forest to the southwest or to Mammoth Springs State Park to the north to see the world's largest spring. The White River, a half hour away, is renowned for its trout fishing. The world record German brown trout came from its waters. Although Hillhigh Hotel & Spa is a self-contained vacation hotel, all around it lies the resort community of Horseshoe Bend, where a larger world of recreational possibilities are only moments away. The town is situated upon the eastern Ozark's pristine Strawberry River. And while the community is certainly "Out of the way", it is easily accessible by highway or by air. It has its own 4,530-foot paved and lighted airstrip. Four lakes lie within the community: Diamond, Pioneer, North and the larger 645-acre Crown Lake, where Box Houn' Marina access is located. A challenging 18-hole championship golf course, about 4 blocks from the airport, is also available to guests.

Conventions: Considering a business meeting, a retreat, an association event or a seminar in the Ozarks? Hillhigh Hotel & Spa offers all the pluses of an Ozark vacation headquarters combined with all the meeting space and banquet arrangements required for groups. This establishment can provide special banquet seating plans, menus and makes sure all the details are handled efficiently to insure your meeting is a success.

Accommodations at Hillhigh Hotel & Spa: Besides the eighty spacious rooms and suites in this quality hotel, they provide the advantages of a full fledged health spa complete with a fully equipped exercise center, large indoor swimming pool, tennis court, a champagne whirlpool, sauna, jacuzzi, and even an expertly staffed beauty salon.

The gourmet restaurant "Carriage Room Supper Club and Lounge" has a menu providing entrees as varied as the tastes of their visitors. Club privileges are also available to their guests. For more information about this facility call 670-5141. (Submitted by: Hillhigh Hotel & Spa)

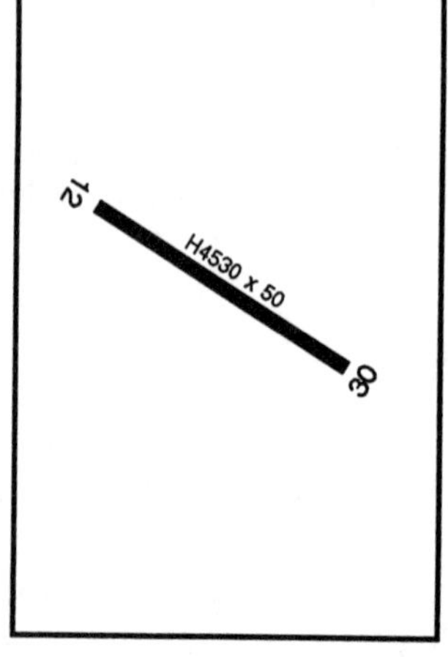

Airport Information:

HORSESHOE BEND - HORSESHOE BEND AIRPORT (6M2)
1 mi northeast of town N36-13.00 W91-45.01 Elev: 770 Fuel: 100LL, Mogas
Rwy 12-30: H4530x50 (Asph) Attended: unattended Unicom: 122.8 Public Phone: 24hrs
FBO: Air Quest Aviation **Phone: 670-5994**
FBO: Horseshoe Bend Municipal **Phone: 670-5113**

(Area Code 501)

5, 6

AR-HOT - HOT SPRINGS MEMORIAL FIELD

Lake Hamilton Resort:

This resort is located on Lake Hamilton estimated about 2 to 3 miles northwest of the airport. This resort offers luxury all-suite rooms with lake view balconies, and equipped with refrigerator, wet bar and coffee service. In addition they also have indoor and outdoor pools and jacuzzis, Lollipop lounge, licensed child-care facility, full service marina with water sports rentals. Their Hanford's Restaurant and Champagne Alley . The restaurant is open from 6 a.m. to 10 p.m. Some additional entertainment included at this resort are golf privileges, swimming beach, dancing, game room, motorboat rentals, fishing guides, a lakeside gazebo and much more. Convention facilities are also present.. Pilots landing at Hot Springs Memorial Airport can call the resort for courtesy transportation. For information call the Lake Hamilton Resort at 767-5511.

Wildwood 1884 Bed & Breakfast Inn:

With a glimpse of the elegant eighties Victorian charm the Wildwood 1884 Bed & Breakfast Inn is located about 6 miles east and just 10 minutes by car from the Hot Springs Memorial Airport. Transportation to and from the establishment is provided for their guests. This Queen Anne Victorian home is situated on one acre of land, and is listed in the National Register of Historic Places. Located only six blocks from the downtown district of Hot Springs allows guest sthe flexibility of shopping and site seeing. All rooms within the Inn have 15' ceilings and are named after the owners' children. Some include private porches, and are furnished with beautiful antique furnishings. For information you can call 624-4267.

Restaurants Near Airport:

Lake Hamilton Resort	3 mi W of city	Phone: 767-5511
Sawmill Depot	3 mi NE of Arpt.	Phone: 623-3082

Lodging: Arlington Resort Hotel 623-7771; Avanelle Motor Lodge 321-133; Best Western Sands Motel 624-1258; Hill Whehttey Inn 624-4441; Hilton Inn 800-445-8667; Lake Hamilton Resort 767-5511; Majestic Hotel & Spa 623-5511; Royale Vista Inn 624-5551; Wildwood 1884 Bed & Breakfast Inn Phone: 624-4267.

Meeting Rooms: Avanelle Motor Lodge 321-1332; Best Western Sands Motel 624-1258; Hilton Inn 623-6600; Majestic Hotel & Spa 623-5511; Royale Vista Inn 624-5551; Sheraton Inn-Lodge Resort 767-5511; Lake Hamilton Resort (Convention facilities) 767-5511.

Transportation: Taxi service reported on airport; Rental cars: Avis 623-3602; Discount Auto 321-1611; Hertz 623-7591; National 624-6252.

Information: Hot Springs Convention & Visitors Bureau 134 Convention Blvd., P.O Box K, Hot Springs, AR 71902. Phone: 501-321-2277 or 800-772-2489.

Attractions:

Hot Springs Mountain Tower (est 4 mi. NE of airport) overlooks 140 miles of beautiful Arkansas countryside including Hot Springs National Park and the Quachita Mountains. Call 623-6035 for information. Oaklawn Jockey Club (2 to 3 mi. east of airport) offers Thoroughbred racing in addition to special racing events held throughout the season. For information call 800-OAKLAWN. In addition contact the Hot Springs Convention & Visitors Bureau for further information by calling 321-2277 or 800-772-2489.

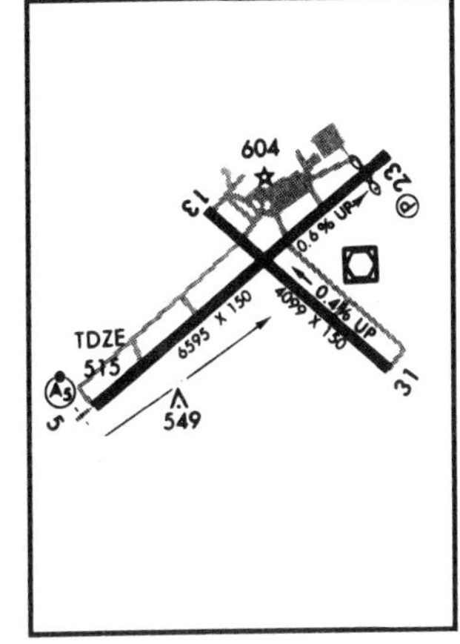

Airport Information:

HOTSPRINGS - MEMORIAL FIELD (HOT)
3 mi southwest of town N34-28.68 W93-05.77 Elev: 540 Fuel: 100LL, Jet-A
Rwy 05-23: H6595x150 (Asph-Grvd) Rwy 13-31: H4099x150 (Asph) Attended: 1130-0400Z
CTAF/Unicom: 123.0
FBO: City of Hot Springs Phone: 624-3306

AR-3M0 - LAKEVIEW
GASTON'S WHITE RIVER RESORT AIRPORT

(Area Code 501) 7

Gaston's Restaurant:

Gaston's Restaurant is located about 200' from their own private airstrip. The aircraft parking area is adjacent to the runway. This fine dining facility offers a nice selection of entrees as well as specializing in such items as rainbow trout, barbeques, steaks, homemade bread, appetizers, soups and much much more. Prices average $5.00 for breakfast, $7.00 for lunch and about $15.00 for dinner. On Sunday they offer a brunch beginning at 10 a.m. to 2 p.m. Gaston's will be more than happy to accommodate fly-in groups or parties, and can easily prepare and arrange catering for pilots on-the-go. The restaurant is open from 6:30 a.m. to 10 p.m. For more information call the restaurant at 431-5203 or the resort at 431-5202.

Restaurants Near Airport:
Gaston's Restaurant On Site Phone: 431-5203

Lodging: Gaston's White River Resort, (On airport) air conditioned cottages, bedroom cottages and private cottages with kitchens. Sizes vary from cottages for two up to lodges with 10 private bedrooms, meeting rooms and patios. Some with decks and fireplaces. Phone: 431-5202.

Meeting Rooms: Gaston's White River Resort contains accommodations for meetings and conferences. (See Lodging listed above)

Transportation: Courtesy car available. However, resort is adjacent to runway and within 200' of aircraft parking.

Information: Gaston's White River Resort, Lakeview, Arkansas 72642, Phone: 501-431-5202; Restaurant, 501-431-5203.

Dining room at Gaston's White River Resort

Attractions:

Gaston's Resort is a clean modern facility providing guests with everything they need for a complete vacation year around. Equipped with its own 3,200'x75' turf landing strip, makes this facility especially accessible to private and corporate aircraft users. The resort is positioned on the Kansas City chart and is located 298 degrees from the Flippen VOR, about 6 miles. Amenities include a play ground for the kids, swimming pool, tennis court, game room and nearby golf course, or hike along the river on their 1.7 mile nature trail. There is plenty to do for everyone in the family. But at Gaston's, the main pastime is fishing for rainbow and brown trout, and enjoying nature. The White River has a worldwide reputation as one of the finest trout streams around. The beautiful scenery along the river is a photographer's and nature lover's dream come true. Gaston's offers boats and motors with full dock service. Their experienced and state licensed guides are expert outdoorsmen, friendly and very handy with a boat and motor. Enjoying the outdoors does not mean "roughing It." Their cottages are comfortable and clean. They offer bedroom cottages with two double beds and private cottages with kitchens. Sizes vary from cottages for two up to lodges with 10 private bedrooms, meeting rooms and patios. Some even have large redwood decks plus wood burning fireplaces. From their restaurant you will enjoy a fine meal while experiencing a beautiful view overlooking the White River. The restaurant is decorated with old tools, antiques and photography from the past that enhances the casual atmosphere. Enjoy fine wines and beverages of your choice, seafood, steaks, and of course, rainbow trout, to their own homemade desserts. Their gift shop offers many unique items, finely-crafted collectibles and a large variety of souvenirs. Bait, fishing supplies and the newest available fishing tackle are all available in their sporting goods shop. As their special guest, you'll enjoy all the comforts and amenities that make Gaston's a truly unique experience. For information you can call the resort at 431-5202 or the restaurant at 431-5203.

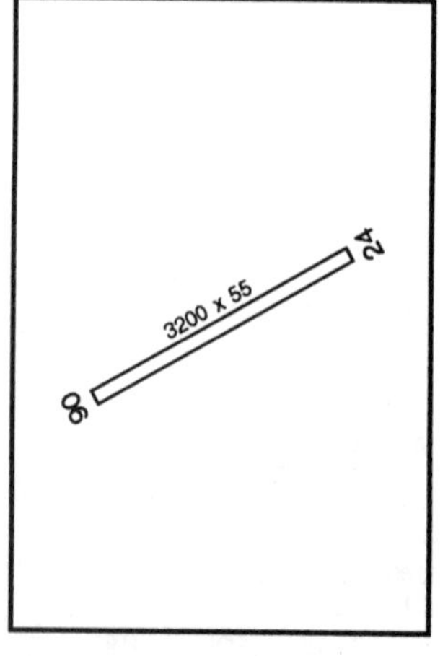

Airport Information:

LAKEVIEW - GASTONS AIRPORT (3M0)
1 mi south of town N36-20.92 W92-33.43 Elev: 479 Fuel: 100LL
Rwy 06-24: 3200x55 (Turf) Attended: continuously Unicom: 122.8
Notes: All aircraft land on runway 24, takeoff on runway 06., No landing fees charged.
FBO: Non reported; Resort phone: 431-5203

AR-LIT - LITTLE ROCK ADAMS FIELD AIRPORT

(Area Code 501) 8,9,10

Restaurants Near Airport

Ashley's Restaurant	6 mi SE	Phone: 374-7474
Flight Deck Rest.	On Site	Phone: 375-3245
River Crossing (Dobbs)	On Site	Phone: 374-3552

Lodging: Best Western Inn Towne 375-2100; Comfort Inn (1 mile, free trans.) 490-2010; Capital Hotel (6 mi southeast) 374-7474. Diamond Inn 376-3661; Holiday Inn Airport (1 mile, free trans.) 490-1000; Masters Economy Inn 372-4392; Radisson Legacy Hotel 374-0100;

Meeting Rooms: Flight Deck Restaurant has a conference room that will accommodate up to 12 persons. Their "Patio Room" can be reserved for up to 30 people (reservations required). Also; Best Western Inn Towne 375-2100; Camelot (Convention Facilities) 372-4371; Capital Hotel (Ashley's Restaurant) 374-7474; Radisson Legacy 374-0100.

Transportation: Ashley's Restaurant (Capital Hotel, 6 miles southeast of the airport) can be reached by free airport shuttle service; Airport Courtesy Car; Rental Cars: Avis; Budget; Dollar; Hertz; & National. (Call FBO's listed below)

Information: Little Rock Convention & Visitors Bureau, Statehouse Plaza, P.O. Box 3232, Little Rock, AR 72203, Phone: 376-4781.

Attractions:

Arkansas capitol building in Little Rock, AR (3 miles) Phone 682-5080.

Ashley's Restaurant:

Ashley's Restaurant is located in the Capital Hotel 6 miles southeast of the Little Rock Regional Airpark. This facility does not provide courtesy transportation for fly-in guests, however if you are in the mood for fine dining in an elegant setting, you might consider arranging free airport shuttle service, short term rental car use or taxi service (est. $10.00 one way) from the airport. Ashley's Restaurant serves breakfast between 6 a.m. and 10 a.m; Lunch from 11 a.m. to 2 p.m. and dinner from 6 p.m. to 11 p.m. They also serve a Sunday brunch between 11 a.m. and 2 p.m. that is reported to be popular with their customers. Their dining room has white linen covered tables, candles and fresh flowers arrangements. A marble entrance way along with crystal chandelier in the foyer add to the romantic surroundings. In addition to the main dining room, they offer 5 banquet rooms able to seat 110 persons for dining or 250 persons for receptions. Average prices run $8.00 for breakfast, $12.00 for lunch and $33.00 for dinner. Valet parking is also available. For more information about Ashley's Restaurant call 374-7474.

The Flight Deck Restaurant:

The Flight Deck Restaurant is conveniently situated in the general aviation terminal building on the east side of the airport. Pilots can park their aircraft at Central Flying Service and simply walk to the terminal building where The Flight Deck Restaurant is located. Breakfast is served from 7:15 a.m. to 10:30 a.m. One specialty on this portion of the menu includes their "Hill County Breakfast" which features 2 country fresh eggs, 3 slices of bacon or 2 sausage patties, toast or biscuits & gravy and fresh brewed coffee for around $5.00. Other selections on their menu include "On The Wing" salads, appetizers and side orders. "Deck Specialties" include club sandwiches with your choice of 7 different breads & 5 dressings. One specialty of the house is their burgers. "The Greatest Cheeseburger in Aviation History" grilled with jalapeno cheese, lettuce, tomato, pickle, onions, mayonnaise & mustard. Other burgers include their Bacon & Cheddar, Swiss & Mushroom Burger, Salad Burger and Chili Cheeseburger. Pilots on the go can order sandwich trays, box lunches, fingerfood assortment and gourmet trays. These trays contain selections like their seafood platter, cheese tray, special fruit tray and fruit & cheese combination tray. Please provide some lead time for preparing in-flight requests. If arranging a luncheon with clients or friends, the Flight Deck has a conference room that can accommodate 12 persons. Their patio room for meetings up to 30 people can be reserved with advance notice. For information you can call Central Flying Service at 501-375-3245.

River Crossing (Dobbs):

The River Crossing Restaurant is located within the main air carrier terminal building on the Little Rock Adams Field Airport. General aviation aircraft are restricted from this area due to heavy jet aircraft use. This cafeteria is joined by a snack bar known as the River Crossing Deli & Grill and is open from 5:30 a.m. to 9 p.m. Southern fried chicken is served each day in addition to other items on their menu. Guests are welcome to relax in the quiet dining room which overlooks the air field. Average prices run $3.00 for breakfast, and about $7.00 for lunch and dinner. Catering service is also available for almost any occasion. For information call 374-3552.

Airport Information:

LITTLE ROCK - ADAMS FIELD AIRPORT (LIT)

2 mi east of town N34-43.74 W92-13.48 Elev: 260 Fuel: 100LL, Jet A, B
Rwy 04R-22L: H7200x150 (Conc-Grvd) Rwy 04L-22R: H7173x150 (Asph-Grvd)
Rwy 18-36: H5124x150 (Asph) Attended: continuously Atis: 125.65 Unicom: 122.95
App/Dep Con: 124.2, 119.5 Tower: 118.7 Gnd Con: 121.9 Clnc Del 118.95
Pre Taxi Clnc: 118.95 Public Phone 24hrs

FBO: AR. Aerospace, Inc.	**Phone: 372-1501**
FBO: Central Flying Service, Inc.	**Phone: 375-3245**
FBO: Omni Air	**Phone: 374-5022**

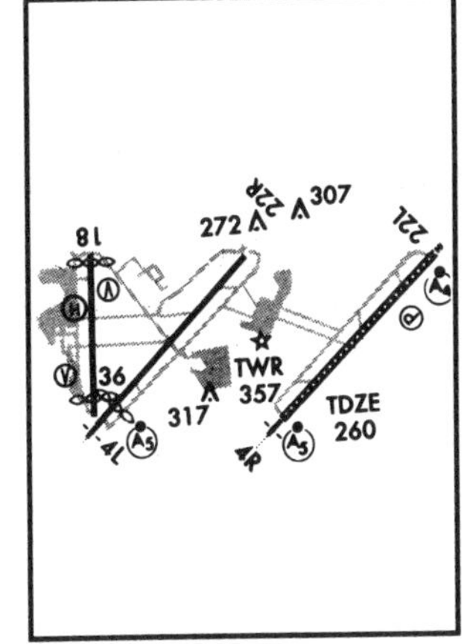

AR-7M2 - MOUNTAIN VIEW
HARRY E WILCOX MEMORIAL FLD.

11

Ozark Folk Center Restaurant:

This fine dining restaurant is located within the Ozark Folk Center lodge about 1-1/2 miles from the Harry E Wilcox Memorial Airport. Transportation can be arranged with the airport manager in advance. The lodge, will also provide transportation but only if they know in advance that you are flying in and landing at the Wilcox Memorial Airport (See transportation). Specialties of the house include catfish, soup and salad bar, smoked turkey, barbecued foods, country ham, southern fried chicken, ham and beans chicken and dumplings, and homemade pie's. Prices range from $3 to $5 for breakfast, $4 to $7 for lunch and $5 to $11 for dinner. No liquor is served as this is a dry county. Daily specials are offered along with Sunday buffets. The decor is traditional with a country like atmosphere. The restaurant is open 7 days a week from 7 a.m. to 8 p.m. April 3rd through December 6th. On special occasions they open during the winter on a limited basis. Their restaurant has two private dining rooms as well as the main dinning area. Catering is also available to pilots on-the-go if advance notice is given. For information you can call the restaurant or the lodge at either 269-3851 or 1-800-243-FOLK.

Airport Information:

MOUNTAIN VIEW - HARRY E WILCOX MEMORIAL FIELD (7M2)
2 mi east of town N35-51.87 W92-05.53 Elev: 802 Fuel: 100LL Rwy 09-27: H4502x50 (Asph) Attended: Mon-Fri 1400-2300Z Unicom: 122.7 Public Phone 24hrs
FBO: Airport Manager Phone: 269-3142

(Area Code 501)

Restaurants Near Airport:

Joshua's Ozark	1 mi NW	Phone: 269-4136
Journeyman	1 mi W	Phone: 269-2323
Ozark Folk Center	1-1/2 mi NW	Phone: 269-3851

Lodging: Ozark Folk Center Inn at Mountain View (Aprox. 1-1/2 miles from airport with free transportation, (advance notice required), 60 rooms, restaurant, pool, private patios, bellhops, Phone: 269-3851; or 1-800-243-FOLK; Dogwood Motel (Walking distance, 100 yards or free airport transportation), 30 rooms, Pool, near restaurant, Phone: 269-3871; Commercial Hotel, (Restored Country Inn), 8 rooms Phone: 269-4383; Redbud Motel, Phone: 269-4375; Fiddlers Inn, Phone: 269-2828; Mountain View Hotel, Phone: 269-3209

Meeting Rooms: Ozark Folk Center is a state operated facility which can accommodate those individuals interested in arranging conventions or business meetings. Phone: 269-3851 or 1-800-243-FOLK. Ask to speak with Public Information Officer, Debra Mullins.(See "Lodging" listed above)

Transportation: Courtesy car available at the airport if advance notice is given, Phone: 269-3142; Also Ozark Folk Center will provide transportation with advance reservations, Phone: 269-3851 or 1-800-243-FOLK. Rental Cars: Lackey Motors, Phone: 269-3211.

Information: Mountain View Area Chamber of Commerce, P.O. Box 133, Mountain View, AR 72560, Phone: 269-8068; Stone Country Council on Tourism Information Center, P.O. Box 253, Mountain View, AR 72560, Phone: 269-8098.

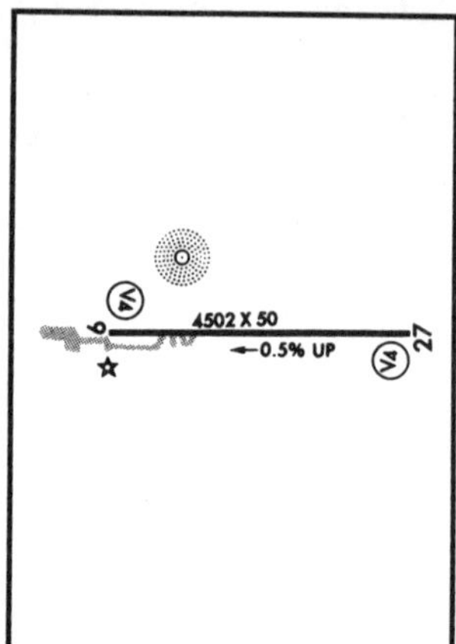

Ozark Folk Center State Park

About This Region:

The Ozark Center State Park in Mountain View, Arkansas, invites you to visit Mountain View on your next tour through Arkansas. Mountain View is located in the heart of the Ozark foothills of north central Arkansas. This area is rich in a natural heritage of mountain scenery, and offers many entertainment attractions. The Ozark Folk Center is an Arkansas State Park dedicated to the preservation of traditional Ozark mountain crafts, music, and culture. Their facilities include a 60 unit lodge (120 double occupancy), a beautiful stone and glass hilltop restaurant, conference and meeting facilities and gift shop. During their regular season, April through November, visitors are treated to over 24 traditional craft demonstrations daily in their craft area. These demonstrations recreate a way of life found in the Ozark mountains prior to 1920. Live musical performances feature the traditional sounds of the region. Each show features local musicians performing traditional Ozark mountain music, including square dances, gospel music, jig dancing, waltzing, and ballads, presented as they were over 60 years ago. Programs are scheduled six nights per week at 7:30 p.m. in their large auditorium. The area has much to offer in relaxing entertainment. Located nearby is Blanchard Springs Caverns, "The cave discovery of the century," where your group may enjoy the cavern tours, nature trails, and picnic area. Other activities include hiking, swimming in the clear mountain streams, horseback riding, touring historic downtown Mountain View and the many local antique and craft shops, and guided fishing and canoe trips down the scenic White River. You may also enjoy the many traditional music programs found in the Mountain View area. For more information , call 501-269-3871 or 1-800-243-FOLK. (For Information on convention facilities contact Public Information Officer, Debra Mullins at either phone number listed).

Photo by: Ark. Dept. of Parks & Tourism — Ozark Folk Center

Attractions:

The Ozark Folk Center State Park is located 1-1/2 miles northwest of the Harry E Wilcox Memorial Airport in Mountain View. This is the largest park in the state of Arkansas. Encompassing 915 acres, this park contains a living settlement dedicated to the heritage of preserving the life styles and folk music between the years of 1820's through the 1920's. This settlement contains 50 buildings with exhibits of crafts, basketry, quiltmaking, woodcarvings, reenacted gatherings and music shows. For information call 269-3851 or 1-800-243-FOLK; Blanchard Springs Caverns, are located about 8 miles northwest of the town of Mountain View along State Highway 14. These caverns display spectacular crystalline formations with underground rivers, and enormous chambers. Guided tours are given, with a movie presentation. One tour lasts approximately 1 hour, along the Dripstone Trail. The other tour lasts 1-3/4 hours along the more strenuous 1-1/4 mile Discovery Trail. Daily guided tours are given throughout the entire year except Monday and Tuesday between November through March. Senior Citizen rates available. Call 757-2211;

Annual Events:

These events include the Arkansas Folk Festival, held the third weekend in April; The Merle Travis Tribute, held in May; Arkansas State Fiddler's Contest at the Ozark Folk Center in September; And the Harvest Festival, with concerts, jamborees, contests, demonstrations, and fiddlers, in October, (Information) submitted by the Ozark Folk Center).

Photo by: Ark. Dept. of Parks & Tourism — Arkansas Folk Festival, held the third weekend in April

AR-7M3 - MOUNT IDA BEARCE AIRPORT

(Area Code 501) 12,13

The Crystal Inn Motel And Restaurant:

The "Crystal Inn Motel and Restaurant" is located at the northeast corner of the Mount Ida Airport. This family style restaurant is open from 7 a.m. to 7 p.m. on Monday, Tuesday, & Thursday and from 7 a.m. to 8 p.m. on Friday and Saturday and from 7 a.m. to 2:00 or 3:00 p.m on Sunday. They are closed on Wednesday. The Crystal Inn is within walking distance from the aircraft parking lot. The restaurant serves breakfast lunch and dinner. They have daily breakfast specials of $1.99 to $3.95 Monday through Friday and a breakfast buffets on Saturday and Sunday for only $3.95. On Friday and Saturday nights they have a seafood buffet with salad bar for $6.95. On Sunday there is a lunch buffet with salad bar for $5.95. The restaurant and motel having been recently remodeled, provides a comfortable home style atmosphere. For information call 867-2643.

Mountain Harbor Resort:

Mountain Harbor Resort is located on the shore of the largest and most beautiful lake in Arkansas, nestled into the mountains on 600 acres of cool green forest. Only 30 minutes from Hot Springs Mountain Harbor is a world apart. From your deck you can enjoy the incredible beauty of the lake at sunset or at sunrise over Hickorynut Mountain. You can fish until your heart is content. You can walk for miles on the logging roads in the surrounding National Forest or lose yourself in one of a thousand hideaway coves. Take plenty of time and drink in the ever-changing wonder of mountains, sun, sand and lake.

Settle into a luxurious condominium. Soak your tensions away in a private jacuzzi spa and then relax in richly appointed surroundings. Whether a family, a group or simply a couple seeking privacy and intimacy, you'll appreciate our condominiums. No two condominiums are exactly alike. Available by the day, week or month, these homes include fully equipped kitchens, color cable TV, a choice of two to four bedrooms with daily housekeeping service. Each is a comfortable retreat where your needs have been thoughtfully considered. Or you may choose more rustic accommodations that capture the feel and texture of the Quachita Mountains. All of their guest rooms and cabins are comfortably furnished and convenient guest rooms come with balconies or porches which overlook the lake or the natural wooded landscape. Come enjoy your stay at Mountain Harbor in an environment of casual good taste. They want every minute you spend with them to be something very special.

Restaurants Near Airport:
Crystal Inn & Restaurant On Site Phone: 867-2643
Mountain Harbor Resort 7 mi Phone: 867-2191

Lodging: Crystal Inn Motel & Restaurant (On site, 12 units) 867-2643; Mountain Harbor Resort, (Free Trans 7 miles) Off U.S. 270 East, Mount Ida 867-2191.

Meeting Rooms: Mountain Harbor Resort (Free Trans 7 miles) 867-2191.

Transportation: Fowler Aviation can provide courtesy transportation for short distances and if prior notice is given 867-4140

Information: Mount Ida Area Chamber of Commerce, P.O. Box 6, Mount Ida, AR 71957-0006, Phone: 501-867-2727

Anxious to see what is cooking? The dining accommodations offer a full range of entrees. The atmosphere is friendly and rustic and the view is spectacular of their lake. The Lodge Restaurant is known as the gathering place for old friends and new faces, too. Try one of their special buffets, or for a real treat, their picnic takeouts. Then afterwards, indulge yourself with their freshly-baked desserts. For breakfast, lunch or dinner, you will find a touch of country hospitality in everything they serve at the Lodge Restaurant. For business conferences or family reunions, their chef can custom design your menu - from island cookouts to superb banquets - your meal will be an unforgettable experience.

When you have the urge to get on the water, they have one of the largest marinas in the mid-south to serve you. Their marina has everything you need for any kind of lake activity. They rent ski boats, fishing boats, party barges and water toys. For certified divers, they have scuba air and a complete dive ship. Their marina store has everything from suntan lotion to fishing lures and bate. Whether you plan to come for a vacation or a conference, you needn't choose between business and pleasure. At Mountain Harbor, you can enjoy both. (Free airport transportation) For information call Mountain Harbor Resort at 867-2191.

Attractions: Mount Ida is known as the crystal capital and there are many gift shops and crystal mines to choose from. Crystal digging, fishing and boating on Lake Quachita, stock car racing and much more. Denby Point Lodge & Marina, Phone: 867-3651; Crystal House at the Robins Mining Co. (US 270 & Ark. 27 South) One of the oldest mines in Arkansas, phone: 867-2530; Ocus Stanley & Son Rock & Mineral Museum, 867-3556; Wegner Quartz Crystal Mines (Owley Road off Ark. 27 South) phone: 867-2309. Mountain Harbor Resort, (For lodging: Free trans 10 miles) contains 69 units, open year around, single rooms and kitchenettes, cottages, conference facilities, fishing guides, gift shop plus restaurant, featuring lakeview and island cookouts and unique catering, Phone: 867-2191.

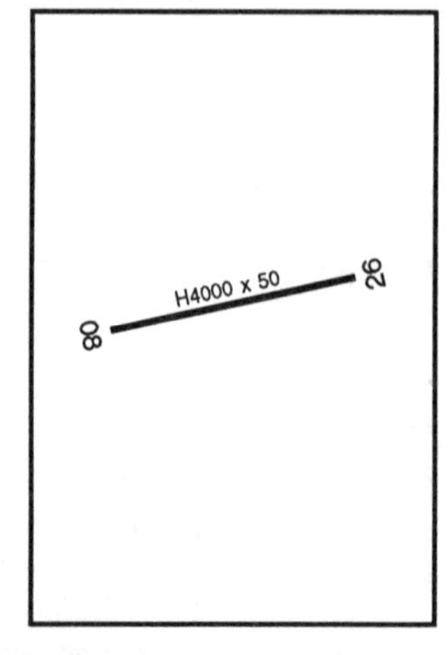

Airport Information:

MOUNT IDA - BEARCE AIRPORT (7M3)
5 mi east of town N34-31.76 W93-31.63 Elev: 643 Fuel: 100LL, Jet-A
Rwy 08-26: H4000x50 (ASPH) Attended: daylight hours Unicom: 122.9 Public Phone 24hrs
Notes: No landing fee, overnight tiedowns $3.00 per night; FBO, full maintenance, piston, prop jet.
FBO: Fowler Aviation, Phone: 867-4140

AR-7M5 - OZARK
FRANKLIN COUNTY AIRPORT

(Area Code 501)

14

Wiederkehr Weinkeller Restaurant:

This fine dining facility is located approximately 8-10 miles east of the Franklin County Airport. A detailed "Swiss" menu including German, French, Italian schnitzel, quiche, lasagna, and American steaks. Lunch is served from 11 a.m. to 3 p.m. and dinner 5 p.m. to 9 p.m. The restaurant is open Monday through Saturday and on Sunday from noon to 9 p.m. Average prices range from $10.00 for lunch and $20.00 for dinner. With prior reservations, private parties are welcome featuring buffet styled lunches and dinners. Daily specials are also available Monday through Saturday. The decor of this restaurant is patterned after a Swiss mountain chalet. Gray Aviation is reported to have courtesy cars available. For information or reservations call 501-468-3551.

Restaurants Near Airport:

Ozark Restaurat	2 mi. S.	Phone: 501-667-3327
Pizza Hut	2 mi. S.	Phone: 501-667-4741
River Valley	2 mi. S.	Phone: N/A
Weinkeller	8 mi. E.	Phone: 501-468-3551

Lodging: Oxford Inn - On SR23 1 blk N. of jct 64; Phone: 501-667-1131, restaurant adj., Ozark Motel - 3/4 mi W. on 64 & SR 23; 3 mi. S. of jct I-40 & SR 23, restaurant adj.

Transportation:
Gray Aviation (FBO) - 501-667-4796, Holley Ford Company - 501-667-4796

Information: Ozark Area Chamber of Commerce; P.O. Box 283, Ozark, AR 72949-0283.

Attractions:

Post Familie Vineyards & Winery; Phone: 501-468-2741, located at the intersection of Ark 186 & US 64. Tours run approximately 45 minutes at no charge and include gift shops, wine and juice tasting (Open-Seasonal; 8 a.m. to 7 p.m. Mon-Sat., Wiederkehr Wine Cellars, Inc., Rt.1, Box 14 Altus, AR 72821, Located at Ark 186 South, Phone: 501-468-3551. This is one of the oldest and largest wineries in mid-America and has been in business since 1880. Tours run approx. 45 minutes between 9 a.m. and 4:30 p.m. A wine fest is also held each year in September. (Arkansas Group Travel Planner); Also: Arkansas River State Park campgrounds, City Lake, golf.

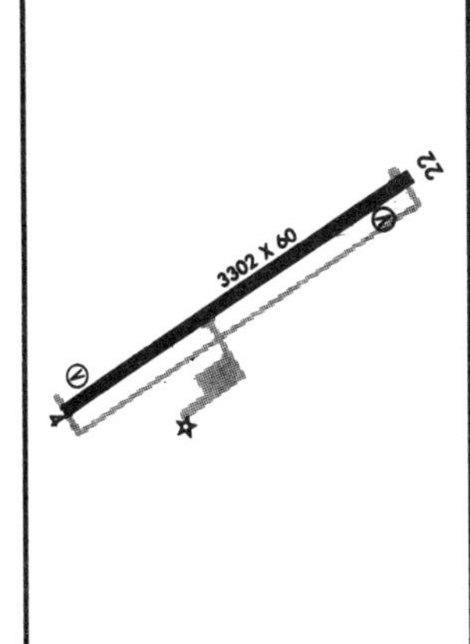

Airport Information:

OZARK - FRANKLIN CO. AIRPORT (7M5)
24 southeast of town, N35-30.64 W93-50.36 Elev: 648, Fuel: 100LL, Rwy 04-22: H3302x60 (ASPH), Attended Mon-Sat 1400-2300Z, Unicom 122.8
FBO: Gray Aviation, Phone: 501-667-4796.

Promote General Aviation Just Take A Friend Flying

AR-PGR - PARAGOULD
KIRK FIELD

(Area Code 501) 15

Oak's Restaurant:

Oak's Restaurant is situated within the Ramada Inn located about 1/4 mile from the airport. This full service family style restaurant is open 11 a.m. to 2 p.m. and from 5 p.m. to 9 p.m. The main dining room seats about 160 persons. Food is also served in the lounge. Their menu contains a wide selection of entrees including appetizers, steaks, seafood, catfish, sandwiches, a noon buffet from 11 a.m. to 2 p.m. with over 50 different items, and 4 main entrees as well as a soup and salad bar. This establishment offers dining, lodging with over 80 rooms, an indoor swimming pool and hot tub. There are 5 separate banquet rooms and a convention center at this location. Small or large groups are no problem, as this facility will cater to your needs. For more information about the restaurant or lodging accommodations call either 236-7164 for the restaurant or 239-2121 for motel or convention information.

Restaurants Near Airport:

Burger King Restaurant	Adj Arpt	Phone: 239-5503
Oaks (Ramada Inn)	Adj Arpt	Phone: 236-7164

Lodging: Ramada Inn (Adjacent Airport) 239-2121

Meeting Rooms: Ramada Inn (Adjacent Airport) 239-2121

Transportation: City Cab 236-7701;

Information: Arkansas Department of Parks and Tourism, 1 Capitol Mall, Little Rock, AR 72201, Phone: 501-682-7777 or 800/NATURAL.

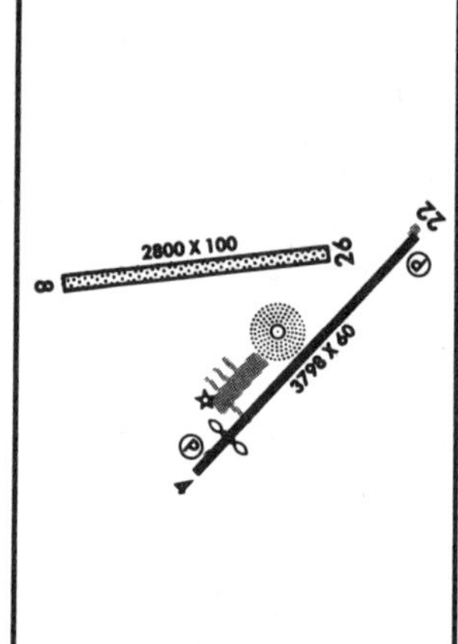

Airport Information:

PARAGOULD - KIRK FIELD (PGR)
1 mi northwest of town N36-03.82 W90-30.60 Elev: 291 Fuel: 100LL, Jet-A
Rwy 04-22: H3798x60 (Asph) Rwy 08-26: 2800x100 (Turf) Attended: 1400-2300Z
Unicom: 122.8
FBO: Airport Commision Phone: 236-7879

AR-PBF - PINE BLUFF
GRIDER FIELD

(Area Code 501) 16

Grider Field Restaurant:

This family style restaurant is situated right on the Pine Bluff Grider Field Airport within the main terminal building. The restaurant is centrally located on the field and can easily be reached without the need for courtesy transportation. This facility is open from 7 a.m. to 3 p.m. Monday through Saturday. Specialties of the house include sandwiches, specialty burgers, homemade pies and desserts made from scratch, and daily plate lunches. Prices are very reasonable. The restaurant is modern and decorated with an aviation theme, in addition to large windows facing the taxiway providing a view of airport operations. Griders Field Restaurant will be happy to cater to fly-in guests as well as business travelers or parties. Meals can also be prepared for carry-out. For more information call 536-4293.

Restaurants Near Airport:

Grider Field Restaurant	On Site	Phone: 536-4293
Holiday Inn Restaurant	3 mi NW.	Phone: 535-8640
Jones Cafe	2 mi N.	Phone: N/A

Lodging: Admiral Benbow Inn 535-8300; Holiday Inn 535-8640; Wilson World 535-3111.

Meeting Rooms: Admiral Benbow Inn (4 miles) 535-8300; Holiday Inn (3 miles) 535-8640.

Transportation: Taxi Service 534-2222; Rental Cars: Avis 535-3322.

Information: Pine Bluff Convention & Tourism Bureau, 1 Convention Center Plaza, Pine Bluff, AR 71601, Phone: 536-7600

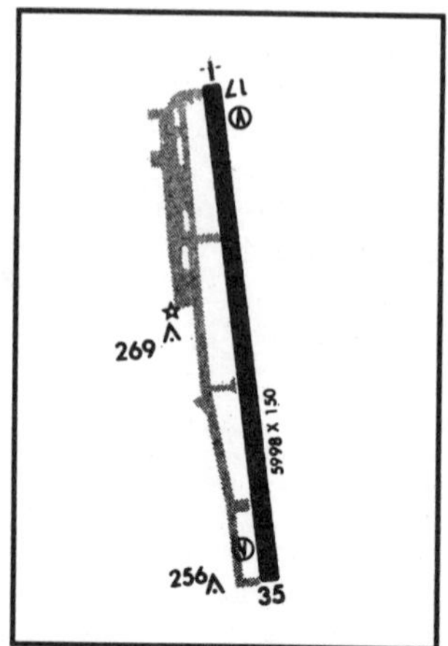

Airport Information:

PINE BLUFF - GRIDER FIELD (PBF)
4 mi southeast of town N34-10.50 W91-56.08 Elev: 206 Fuel: 100LL, Jet-A
Rwy 17-35: H5998-150 (Asph) Attended: 1300-0300Z CTAF/Unicom: 123.0
Public Phone 24 hrs Notes: For attendant after hours call 541-9346 or 536-3109.
Grider Field Airport Phone: 534-4131

AR-M70 - POCAHONTAS NICK WILSON FIELD

(Area Code 501) 17,18

Restaurants Near Airport:

Bonanza Rest.	Adj Arpt	Phone: 892-5489
Dairy Queen	2 blks	Phone: 892-3071
McDonald	3 blks	Phone: N/A
Sonic Drive-Inn	2 blks	Phone: N/A

Lodging: Cottonwood Inn (1 block) 892-2581; Hillcrest Motel (2 miles) 892-4527; Town House motel (2 blks) 892-4531.
Meeting Rooms: None Reported
Transportation: Airport Courtesy transportation may be available if advance notice is given and depending on available staff.
Information: Chamber of Commerce, 121 E. Everett Street, P.O. Box 466, Pocahontas, AR 72455, Phone: 892-3956.

Bonanza Restaurant:

The Bonanza Restaurant is situated across the street from the Nick Wilson Field, and about 1/2 mile from the aircraft parking ramp. This restaurant is open between 11 a.m. and 9 p.m. 7 days a week. They specialize in a variety of steaks, like rib-eye, t-bone, strip steak ,filets and chopped sirloin, as well as chicken, and seafood dishes. Average prices run around $6.99 for most main course entrees. There is a salad bar available in addition to the menu items. The decor is contemporary with tables and booths. They can seat up to 240 persons within the main dining room. Groups and parties are always welcome. Carry-out meals can be prepared on request. For more information call 892-5489.

Dairy Queen:

The Dairy Queen restaurant is located only 2 blocks from the Pocahontas Nick Wilson Field. This facility specializes in ice cream and other delights that we all enjoy so much, such as banana splits, sundaes, shakes, sodas etc. They also provide a full compliment of entrees, including hamburgers, catfish, shrimp, chicken strips, barbecue platters, pizza burgers and much more. Average prices run between $2.00 and $4.00 for most items. They also offer daily specials on many menu creations. The restaurant has counter service with seating for up to 65 persons. All items available on their menu are prepared to go. This particular restaurant has been successfully doing business for over 36 years. For more information call the Dairy Queen at 892-3071.

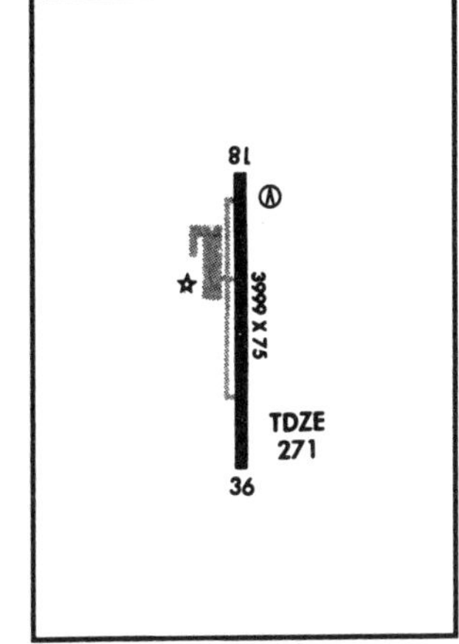

Airport Information:

POCAHONTAS - NICK WILSON FIELD (M70)
1 mi southeast of town N36-14.73 W90-57.31 Elev: 271 Fuel: 100LL
Rwy 18-36: H3999x75 (Asph) Attended: 1400-2300Z Unicom: 122.8 Notes: Fuel available nights, call 869-2260
Pocahontas Municipal Airport **Phone: 892-5606**

AR-M07 - SEARCY SEARCY MUNICIPAL AIRPORT

(Area Code 501) 19

AJ's Cookie Basket:

AJ's Cookie Basket is located about one mile from the Searcy Municipal Airport. From the airport you can travel left on Main street into town, about 1 mile to the court square and Market street. AJ's has red and white awnings on the outside of their building and should be easy to find. A courtesy car can be arranged at the airport in advance. Also a rental car can be obtained if you so choose. This cafe styled restaurant is open between 8 a.m. and 2:30 p.m. Monday through Friday. They offer daily specials including lasagna on Mondays, Poppy seed chicken on Tuesday, cache Wednesday, Mexican & chicken on Thursday, and on Fridays their menu varies. 10 different sandwiches are available including several soups and salads. A freshly baked cookie is served with each meal. Average prices run around $5.00 per selection. The restaurant has a light and airy atmosphere and can accommodate about 45 persons. The people at AJ's Cookie Basket will be happy to cater to your group functions. Also they can prepare gift baskets, if desired. For more information about this restaurant call 279-2888.

Restaurants Near Airport:

AJ's Cookie Basket	1 mi	Phone: 279-2888

Lodging: King's Inn (4 mi) 268-8252; Shoney's Inn (4 mi. trans) 268-0654

Meeting Rooms: None reported

Transportation: Holt rental cars 268-0353

Information: Searcy Chamber of Commerce 200 S. Spring Street, Searcy, AR 72143-6797, Phone: 501-268-2458.

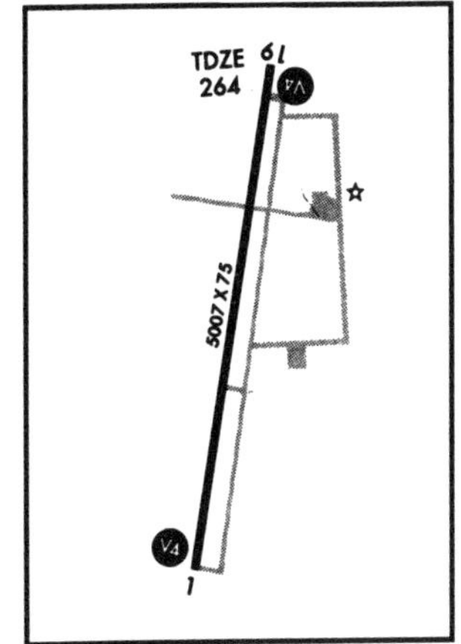

Airport Information:

Searcy - Searcy Municipal (M07)
3 mi south of town N35-12.72 W91-44.23 Elev: 264 Fuel: 100LL, Jet-A, Mogas Rwy 01-19: H5007x75 (Asph Attended: daylight Unicom: 122.7 Notes: For fuel after hours call 501-268-6009 (fee charged).
Airport Manager **Phone: 501-268-4186**

AR-ASG - SPRINGDALE
SPRINGDALE MUNICIPAL AIRPORT

20

Hickory Hangar:

The Hickory Hangar Restaurant is located on the second floor of the terminal building at the Springdale Municipal Airport. This cafe is open from 6 a.m. to 2 p.m. Monday through Friday and on Saturday and Sunday between 7 a.m. and 2 p.m. Entrees consist of breakfast items served all day like pancakes, waffles and oat-meal. Lunch items include meatloaf, Lasagna, smoked meats, barbecued dishes, and sliced sandwich meats. Additional selections include, their cleverly named "Captain Witt" or Half Witt chef salads. The restaurant runs parallel to the main runway and provides a view of arriving and departing aircraft, along with the surrounding mountains. Group accommodations can be arranged. Country BBQ's and "Hungary Baskets" can be prepared for carry-out. Catering for box meals like sandwiches & chips, or hot meals can also be arranged. The restaurant is decorated with pictures of aircraft and aviation memorabilia. Two months out of the year their out-door patio can be used for dining. This restaurant can handle up to 40 persons. For exclusive use of the restaurant, reserve time after 2:30 p.m. Allow at least a 4 day notice. For information call the restaurant at 756-3339.

Restaurants Near Airport: **(Area Code 501)**

A-Q Chicken House	2 mi N.	Phone: 751-4633
Hickory Hangar	On Site	Phone: 756-3339

Lodging: Executive Inn 1 mile 756-6101; Holiday Inn 2 miles 751-8300; Best Western Heritage 1 mile 751-3100.
Meeting Rooms: There is a free conference room in the terminal building at Springdale Municipal Airport. Also Executive Inn and Holiday Inn both have accommodations for meetings and conferences.
Transportation: Springdale Air Service can provide local courtesy transportation with advance notice, Phone: 751-4462.
Information: Chamber of Commerce, 700 West Emma, Box 166, Springdale, AR 72764, Phone: 751-4694.

Attractions: The Withrow Spring State park is located about 20 miles east of Springdale Airport, and exhibits moutainous terrain within its 700 acre region. War Eagle River contains towering bluffs and a large boiling spring at its base. The State Park also provides a number of activities such as hiking, camping, concessions, & canoe rentals. For information call 559-2593. Also Beaver Lake and Ridge Battlefield National Park are located near the Springdale area.

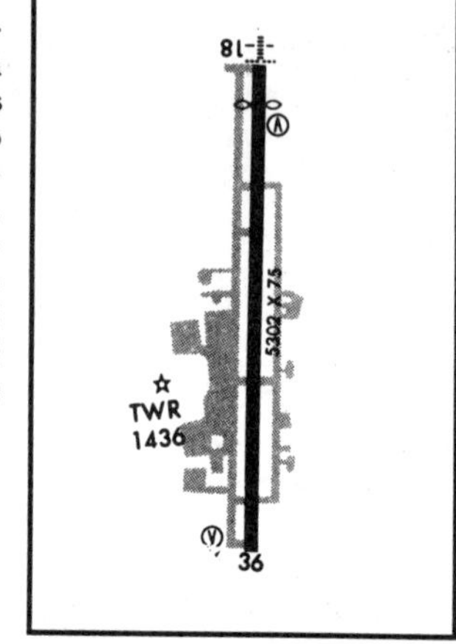

Airport Information:

SPRINGDALE - SPRINGDALE MUNICIPAL AIRPORT (ASG)
1 mi southeast of town N36-10.58 W94-07.16 Elev: 1353 Fuel: 100LL, Jet-A
Rwy 18-36: H5302x75 (Asph) Attended: Mon-Fri continuously, and Sat-Sun 1200-0000Z
Unicom: 122.95 Tower: 118.2 Gnd Con: 121.6 Public Phone 24hrs
FBO: Springdale Air Service, Inc. Phone: 751-4462

AR-SGT - STUTTGART
STUTTGART MUNICIPAL AIRPORT

(Area Code 501)

21

Mallard Restaurant:

The Mallard Restaurant, according to the management, is located 2 or 3 blocks from the Stuttgart Municipal Airport. This is a family style restaurant open between 5 a.m. and 8 p.m. Monday through Saturday and 5 a.m. to 2 p.m. on Sunday. Their menu includes items like t-bone steak, rib-eye steak, chicken fried steak, hamburger steak, catfish platters, hamburgers, cheeseburgers, and club sandwiches as well as a complete breakfast menu, which is available all day. Average prices run $4.00 for breakfast, $5.00 for lunch and $7.00 for dinner. They also offer plate lunch specials served mainly on weekdays. Their main dining room can seat 75 people comfortably, while their back dining room seats as many as 100 people for banquets, parties and receptions. This is a popular restaurant with many pilots. They usually serve between 20 and 30 fly-in groups each Sunday for breakfast. For more information, call the Mallard Restaurant at 673-1171.

Restaurants Near Airport:

Mallard Restaurant	2-3 blks	Phone: 673-1171

Lodging: Best Western (7 miles) 673-2575; Town House (7 miles) 673-2611.

Meeting Rooms: None Reported

Transportation: Avis Rental Car (With 48 hour prior notice) 673-2960.

Information: Chamber of Commerce, 507 S. Main, P.O. Box 932, Stuttgart, AR 72160, Phone: 673-1602.

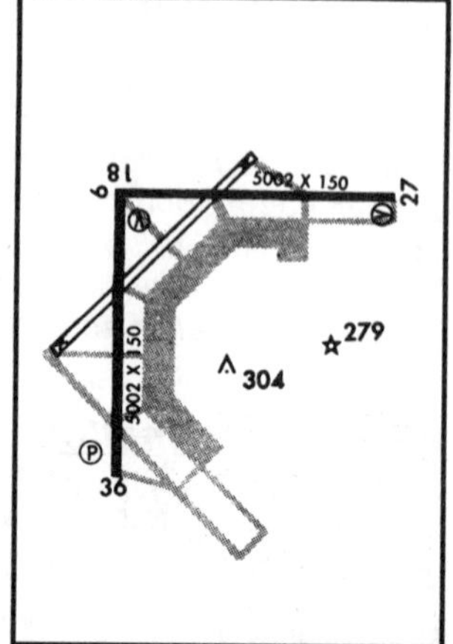

Airport Information:

STUTTGART - STUTTGART MUNICIPAL AIRPORT (SGT)
7 mi north of town N34-36.03 W91-34.47 Elev: 224 Fuel: 100LL, Jet-A
Rwy 09-27: H5002x150 (Conc) Rwy 18-36: H5002x150 (Conc) Attended: Nov-Jan 1400-0300Z, Feb-Oct 1400-2300Z Unicom: 122.8 Notes: For fuel nights call 673-2360
FBO: Farmer Aerial Seeders Phone: 673-1821
Arpt Manager Phone: 673-2960

AR-TXK - TEXARKANA
TEXARKANA REGIONAL-WEBB FLD.

(Area Code AR-501, TX-903)

22,23

Wings Restaurant:

Wings restaurant is situated in the main terminal building at the Texarkana Regional airport. This restaurant has a modern atmosphere and is decorated with aviation related memorabilia, including real props and a painted mural on the wall. Daily lunch specials are served along with other light fare. The average prices for meals are $4.50 for breakfast, and $5.00 for lunch and dinner. The people at Wings restaurant will prepare sandwiches trays and some box lunches for pilots on the go. For more information you can call the restaurant at 501-774-1309.

Park Place:

The Park Place restaurant would be classified as a fine dining facility, and is located about 1-1/2 miles from the Texarkana Regional-Webb Field. To reach this facility you take Arkansas Blvd. beyond the overpass and watch for the restaurant on your right side. The outside of the restaurant has a rustic and spread out-appearance. The restaurant decor inside offers an elegant atmosphere with soft lighting. There are skylights and lots of wood trim. The foyer has a brick covered walkway to the main dining area. Their kitchen is open from 6 p.m. to 11 p.m. Monday through Friday. Specialties on their menu include USDA choice meats, including Prime rib, Brechet of beef (Ponchartrain), Filet Mignon, and Rib-eye, just to mention a few. Seafood selections include Alaska crab legs, Lobster tail, fried frog legs, barbequed shrimp, Troute Enpapillote and swordfish. Average prices run between $12.95 and $13.95 for most items. Menu selections range from $9.95 to $23.95. Lobster selections are at market price. The Park Place restaurant has accommodations for groups or business conferences. There are two rooms that can serve 20 persons, one room that can handle 25 to 28 persons and another room that can seat 90 persons. When calling TAC Air (FBO) at 501-773-6969, we learned that customers can obtain transportation to the restaurant and back. For more information about the Park Place restaurant, call 501-772-2201.

Restaurants Near Airport:

Brangus	3 mi	Phone: 501-772-6988
Feed House	2 mi	Phone: 501-773-0595
Park Place	1-1/2 mi	Phone: 501-772-2201
Wings	On-Site	Phone: 501-774-1309

Lodging:
Best Western Kings Row Inn (free arpt trans 2 mi.) 501-774-3851; Holiday Inn Express (free arpt trans) 903-792-3366; Holiday Inn I-30 (airport trans 3 mi.) 501-774-3521; Ramada Inn (4-1/2 mi.) 794-3131; Sheraton Texarkana (3 mi.) 501-792-3222.

Meeting Rooms:
TAC Air (FBO) has a small conference room with accommodations for 2 to 25 persons. Phone 501-773-6969. Also: Best Western Kings Row Inn (2 mi.) 501-774-3851; Holiday Inn Express 903-792-3366; Holiday Inn I-30 501-774-3521.

Transportation:
Rental Cars available through Avis 773-1861; Budget 772-7386; Hertz 773-1192; National 772-8111. Also Taxi service by calling Yellow Cab at 774-4141.

Information:
Texarkana Chamber of Commerce, 819 State Line Avenue, P.O. Box 1464, Texarkana, TX 75504; Phone: 903-792-7191

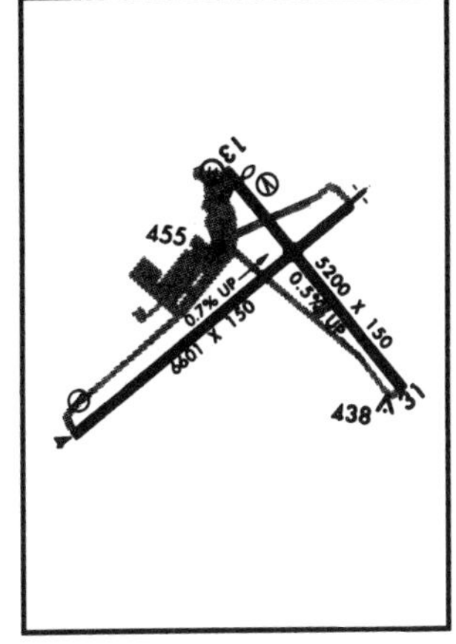

Airport Information:

Texarkana - Texarkana Regional-Webb Field (TXK)
3 mi northeast of town N33-27.22 W93-59.46 Elev: 389 Fuel: 100LL, Jet-A Rwy 04-22: H6601x150 (Asph) Rwy 13-31: H5200x150 (Asph) Attended: continuously Atis: 120.2 Unicom: 122.95 Tower: 125.7 Gnd Con: 121.7
FBO: TAC Air Phone: 501-773-6969

AR-ARG - WALNUT RIDGE
WALNUT RIDGE REGIONAL AIRPORT

(Area Code 501) 24

Walnut Ridge Airport Restaurant:

The Walnut Ridge Airport Restaurant is managed by Bertco Aviation and is situated adjacent to the terminal building at the Walnut Ridge Airport. This restaurant is open 10 a.m. to 2 p.m. Monday through Saturday. Their menu contains items like shrimp, chicken platters, sandwiches, hamburgers, and cheeseburgers. Average prices run $4.00 to $5.00 for most items on their menu. Daily specials are also provided. The decor of this facility has a country atmosphere with seating for up to 48 persons in their main dining room. Guests can enjoy a view of the whole airport from the dining room. A private dining area is also available for parties, banquets and meetings. Meals can be prepared to go as well. For more information about this restaurant, you can call them at 886-5432.

Restaurants Near Airport:
Walnut Ridge Airport Restaurant On Site Phone: 886-5432

Lodging: Alamo Court (8 miles) 886-2441.

Meeting Rooms: Alamo Court (8 miles) 886-2441; Walnut Ridge Airport Restaurant can accommodate groups 886-5432.

Transportation: Airport courtesy car available with advance notice.

Information: Walnut Ridge Chamber of Commerce, 117 NW 2nd Street, P.O. Box 842, Walnut Ridge, AR 72476, Phone: 886-3232.

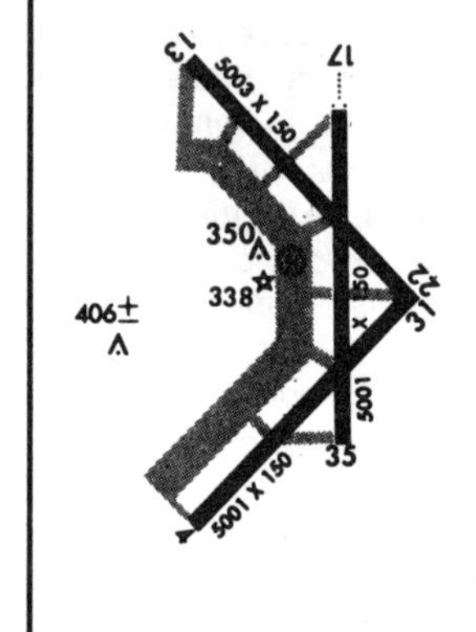

Airport Information:

WALNUT RIDGE - WALNUT RIDGE REGIONAL AIRPORT (ARG)
4 mi northeast N36-07.52 W90-55.48 Elev: 273 Fuel: 100LL, Jet-A
Rwy 13-31: H5003x150 (Conc) Rwy 04-22: H5001x150 (Conc) Rwy 17-35: H5001x150 (Conc) Attended 1400-0000Z Unicom: 122.8 Memphis Center App/Dep Con: 127.4
FBO: American Aviation **Phone: 886-2418**
FBO: Bertco Aviation **Phone: 886-5432**

CALIFORNIA

LOCATION MAP

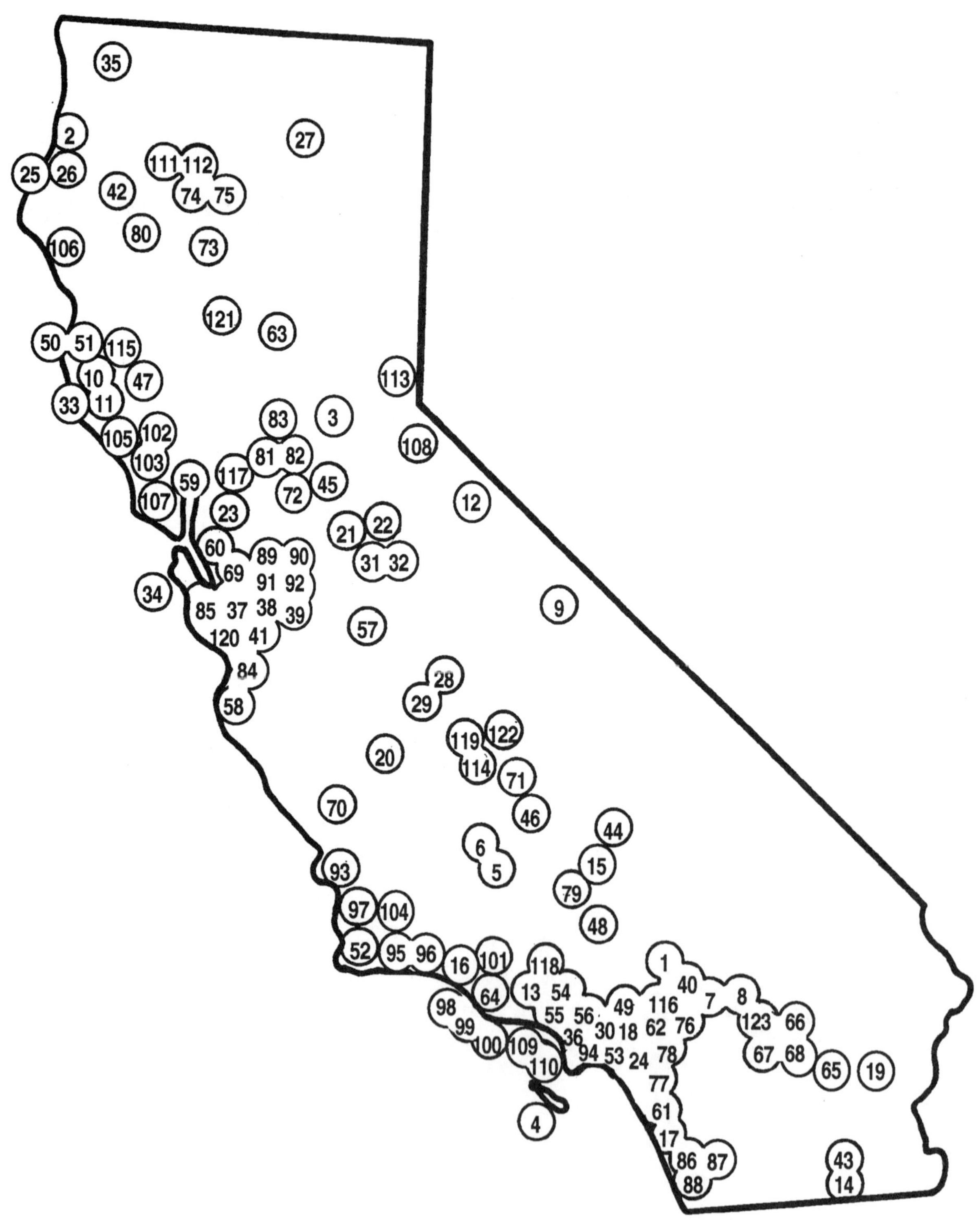

CALIFORNIA

CROSS FILE INDEX

Location Number	City or Town	Airport Name And Identifier	Name of Attraction
1	Apple Valley	Apple Valley Arpt. (APV)	Wings Cafe
2	Arcata/Eureka	Arcata Arpt. (ACV)	Silver Lining Restaurant
3	Auburn	Auburn Muni. Arpt. (AUN)	Wings Grill & Flight Line
4	Avalon	Catalina Arpt. (AVX)	Runway Cafe Restaurant
5	Bakersfield	Bakersfield Muni. Arpt. (L45)	Skyway Coffee Shop
6	Bakersfield	Meadows Field Arpt. (BFL)	Anton's Arpt. Bar & Grill
7	Big Bear City	Big Bear City Arpt. (L35)	Landings Cafe
8	Big Bear City	Big Bear City Arpt. (L35)	Mandarin Garden
9	Bishop	Bishop Arpt. (BIH)	Pete & Al's Cafe
10	Boonville	Boonville Arpt. (Q17)	Buckhorn Rest.
11	Boonville	Boonville Arpt. (Q17)	The Toll Hse Rest. & Inn
12	Bridgeport	Bryant Fld. (O57)	Bridgeport Inn
13	Burbank	Glendale-Pasadena Arpt. (BUR)	Air Hollywood Bar & Grill
14	Calexico	Calexico Intl. Arpt. (CXL)	Rosa's Plane Food
15	California City	California City Muni. (L71)	Ready Room Restaurant
16	Camarillo	Camarillo Arpt. (CMA)	Waypoint Cafe
17	Carlsbad	McClellan-Palomar Arpt. (CRQ)	Palomar Airport Cafe
18	Chino	Chino Arpt. (CNO)	Flo's Arpt. Cafe
19	Chiriaco Summit	Chiriaco Summit Arpt. (L77)	Summit Coffee Shop
20	Coalinga	Harris Ranch Arpt. (308)	Harris Ranch Restaurant
21	Columbia	Columbia Arpt. (O22)	Columbia City Hotel
22	Columbia	Columbia Arpt. (O22)	Columbia House
23	Concord	Buchanan Field (CCR)	Atrium Court Restaurant
24	Corona	Corona Muni. Arpt. (L66)	Bob's Cafe
25	Eureka	Eureka Muni. (O33)	Samoa Arpt. B&B
26	Eureka	Murray Field (EKA)	Pacific Clipper Cafe
27	Fall River Mills	Fall River Mills Arpt. (089)	Rvr. MillsGolf&CoffeeShp
28	Fresno	Fresno Air Trml. Arpt. (FAT)	CA1 Services
29	Fresno	Chandler Downtown (FCH)	Chabela's Restaurant
30	Fullerton	Fullerton Muni. Arpt. (FUL)	Tartuffles Restaurant
31	Groveland	Pine Mountain Lake (Q68)	Corsair Coffee Shop
32	Groveland	Pine Mountain Lake (Q68)	Inn at Sugar Pine (B&B)
33	Gualala	Ocean Ridge (Q69)	Gualala Country Inn
34	Half Moon Bay	Half Moon Bay (HAF)	The Shore Bird
35	Happy Camp	Happy Camp Arpt. (36S)	Indian Creek Cafe
36	Hawthorne	Hawthorne Muni. Arpt. (HHR)	Nat's Arpt. Cafe
37	Hayward	Hayward Air Trml. (HWD)	Carrow's Restaurant
38	Hayward	Hayward Air Trml. (HWD)	Manzella's Seafood Loft
39	Hayward	Hayward Air Trml. (HWD)	Skywest Bar & Grill
40	Hesperia	Hesperia Arpt. (L26)	Hesperia Arpt. Rest.
41	Hollister	Hollister Muni. Arpt. (307)	Silver Wings Restaurant

CROSS FILE INDEX
(California Continued)

Location Number	City or Town	Airport Name And Identifier	Name of Attraction
42	Hyampom	Hyampom Arpt. (Q75)	Hyampom Cafe & Bar
43	Imperial	Imperial County Arpt. (IPL)	La Hacienda Rest.
44	Inyokern	Inyokern Arpt. (IYK)	Two Sisters Restaurant
45	Jackson	Westover Field Amador Co. (O70)	Imperial Hotel
46	Kernville	Kern Valley Arpt. (L05)	Arpt. Coffee Shop
47	Lakeport	Lampson Field (102)	Sky Room Restaurant
48	Lancaster	General WM. J. Fox Airfield (WJF)	Sly Fox Cafe
49	La Vern	Brackett Field (POC)	Norm's Hangar Rest.
50	Ltl.Rvr/Mendocino	Little River Arpt. (048)	Cafe Beaujolais
51	Ltl.Rvr/Mendocino	Little River Arpt. (048)	Historic Medocino & Coast
52	Lompoc	Lompoc Arpt. (LPC)	Bravo Pizza
53	Long Beach	Long Beach/Daugherty Fld.(LGB)	The Prop Room
54	Los Angeles	Los Angeles Intl. Arpt. (LAX)	CA1 Services
55	Los Angeles	Los Angeles Intl. Arpt. (LAX)	Century Cafe
56	Los Angeles	Los Angeles Intl. Arpt. (LAX)	Wynsor's
57	Merced	Merced Muni./Macready Fld. (MCE)	Hangar Cafe
58	Monterey	Monterey Peninsula Arpt. (MRY)	Golden Tee Restaurant
59	Napa	Napa Co. Arpt. (APC)	Jonesy's Steak House
60	Oakland	Metropolitan Oakland Intl. (OAK)	CA1 Services
61	Oceanside	Oceanside Muni. Arpt. (L32)	The Grove Restaurant
62	Ontario	Ontario Intl. Arpt. (ONT)	Host (Marriott)
63	Oroville	Oroville Muni. Arpt. (OVE)	Table Mt. Golf Course
64	Oxnard	Oxnard Arpt. (OXR)	Hangar 5
65	Palm Springs	Bermuda Dunes (UDD)	Murph's Gaslight
66	Palm Springs	Palm Springs Regl. Arpt. (PSP)	CA1 Services
67	Palm Springs	Palm Springs Regl. Arpt. (PSP)	Doubletree Resort
68	Palm Springs	Palm Springs Regl. Arpt. (PSP)	Million Air Deli
69	Palo Alto	Palo Alto of Santa Clara Co. (PAO)	Harry's Hof Brau Rest.
70	Paso Robles	Paso Robles Muni. Arpt. (PRB)	Amelia's Restaurant
71	Porterville	Porterville Muni. Arpt. (PTV)	Annie's Restaurant
72	Rancho Murieta	Murieta Arpt. (RIU)	Riders Steakhouse
73	Red Bluff	Red Bluff Muni. Arpt. (RBL)	BJ's Arpt. Restaurant
74	Redding	Benton Field Arpt. (O85)	Airport Cafe
75	Redding	Redding Muni. Arpt. (RDD)	Chu's Restaurant
76	Rialto	Rialto Muni./Miro Field (L67)	Airport Diner
77	Riverside	Riverside Muni. Arpt. (RAL)	D & D Airport Cafe
78	Riverside (Rubidoux)	Flabob Arpt. (RIR)	Silver Wings Cafe
79	Rosamond	Rosamond Skypark Arpt. (LOO)	Golden Cantina Rest.
80	Ruth	Ruth Arpt. (Q95)	Flying AA Ranch Rest.
81	Sacramento	Sacramento Exec. Arpt. (SAC)	Marie Callendar Rest.
82	Sacramento	Sacramento Exec. Arpt. (SAC)	Tailspin Deli

CROSS FILE INDEX
(California Continued)

Location Number	City or Town	Airport Name And Identifier	Name of Attraction
83	Sacramento	Sacramento Metro Arpt. (SMF)	The Vista Dining Room
84	Salinas	Salinas Muni. Arpt. (SNS)	Salinas Arpt. Bar & Grill
85	San Carlos	San Carlos Arpt. (SQL)	Sky Kitchen Restaurant
86	San Diego	Montgomery Field (MYF)	94th Aero Squadron
87	San Diego	Montgomery Field (MYF)	Casa Machado
88	San Diego	San Diego Intl.-Lindbergh (SAN)	Marriott Host
89	San Jose	San Jose Intl. Arpt. (SJC)	94th Aero Squadron
90	San Jose	San Jose Intl. Arpt. (SJC)	CA1 Services
91	San Jose	San Jose Intl. Arpt. (SJC)	Flying Gift Shop & Deli
92	San Jose	San Jose Intl. Arpt. (SJC)	Jora's Restaurant
93	San Luis Obispo Co.	Mc Chesney Field (SBP)	Spirit of San Luis
94	Santa Ana	John Wayne/Orange Co. (SNA)	Orange Grill Rest. (Host)
95	Santa Barbara	Santa Barbara Muni. (SBA)	Beachside Bar Cafe
96	Santa Barbara	Santa Barbara Muni. (SBA)	Elephant Bar Restaurant
97	Santa Maria	Santa Maria Public Arpt. (SMX)	Pepper Garcia's
98	Santa Monica	Santamonica Muni. (SMO)	DC3 Restaurant
99	Santa Monica	Santamonica Muni. (SMO)	Spitfire Grill
100	Santa Monica	Santamonica Muni. (SMO)	Typhoon Restaurant
101	Santa Paula	Santa Paula Arpt. (SZP)	Logsdon Restaurant
102	Santa Rosa	Sonoma Co. Arpt. (STS)	Sellini Grill
103	Santa Rosa	Sonoma Co. Arpt. (STS)	Skylane Deli
104	Santa Ynez	Santa Ynez Arpt. (IZA)	Santa Ynez Attractions
105	Sea Ranch	Sea Ranch Assoc. (CA51)	The Sea Ranch
106	Shelter Cove	Shelter Cove Arpt. (0Q5)	Points of Interest
107	Sonoma	Sonoma Skypark (0Q9)	Sonoma Inn & Spa
108	South Lake Tahoe	Lake Tahoe Arpt. (TVL)	Harvey's Resort Hotel
109	Torrance	Torrance Municipal Arpt. (TOA)	CoCo's Bakery & Rest.
110	Torrance	Torrance Municipal Arpt. (TOA)	Del Conte's Restaurnat
111	Trinity Center	Trinity Center (O86)	The Sasquatch Cafe
112	Trinity Center	Trinity Center (O86)	Trinity Center Inn B & B
113	Truckee	Truckee-Tahoe Arpt. (TRK)	Northstar-at-Tahoe
114	Tulare	Mefford Fld. Arpt. (TLR)	Pitching Wedge Rest.
115	Ukiah	Ukiah Muni. Arpt. (UKI)	Beacon Restaurant
116	Upland	Cable Arpt. (CCB)	Cable Arpt. Cafe
117	Vacaville	Nut Tree Arpt. (O45)	Coffee Tree Restaurant
118	Van Nuys	Van Nuys Arpt. (VNY)	Landings Restaurant
119	Visalia	Visalia Muni. Arpt. (VIS)	Picific Grill
120	Watsonville	Watsonville Muni. Arpt. (WVI)	Zuniga's Mexican Rest.
121	Willows	Willows-Glenn Co. Arpt. (WLW)	Willow Brook Rest.
122	Woodlake	Woodlake Arpt. (O42)	Woodlake Outpost
123	Yucca Valley	Yucca Valley Arpt. (L22)	Cross Roads Restaurant

CROSS FILE INDEX
(California Continued)

Articles

City or town	Nearest Airport and Identifier	Name of Attraction
Avalon, CA	Catalina Arpt. (AVX)	Catalina Island
California City, CA	California City, (L71)	Air Force Flight Test Cntr.
Chino, CA	Chino Arpt. (CNO)	Planes of Fame Museum
Chiriaco-Summit, CA	Chiriaco-Summit Arpt. (L77)	General Patton's Memorial
Palm Springs, CA	Palm Springs Reg. (PSP)	Palm Springs Air Museum
Santa Monica, CA	Santa Monica Muni. (SMO)	Museum of Flying
Santa Ynez, CA	Santa Ynez (IZA)	Alisal Guest Ranch & Resort
Sonoma, CA	Sonoma Skypark (0Q9)	Sonoma Mission Inn & Spa
South Lake Tahoe, CA	Lake Tahoe (TVL)	Heavenly Resort (Lk. Tahoe)
South Lake Tahoe, CA	Lake Tahoe (TVL)	Lake Tahoe's South Shore
Truckee-Tahoe, CA	Truckee-Tahoe (TRK)	Northstare-at-Tahoe
Ukiah, CA	Ukiah Muni. (UKI)	Vichy Springs Resort

CA-APV - APPLE VALLEY
APPLE VALLEY AIRPORT

(Area Code 619) 1

Airport Wings Cafe:

The Wings Cafe is situated in the terminal building on the Apple Valley Airport. This cafe style restaurant is open Tuesday through Sunday from 7 a.m. to 3 p.m. Their menu includes breakfast specials on weekends, along with all types of sandwiches and hamburger selections. Be sure to try their famous "Sticky Buns", homemade deserts, soups and delicious pies. They also offer ultralight selections for those watching their gross weight. Average prices run between $5.00 and $6.00. This restaurant can seat 30 persons and offers a quaint atmosphere, with large windows allowing guests a view overlooking the runway and ramp at the airport. There are also beautiful pen and ink drawings hanging on the wall which are priced to sell. They have a banquet room able to accommodate up to 25 guests for private parties or business gatherings. In-flight catering is a service also provided by this establishment. Their "Black Box Specials" are meals-to-go for the traveler in a hurry. For more information call the Airport Wings Cafe at 247-6239.

Restaurants Near Airport:
Airport Wings Cafe On Site Phone: 247-6239

Lodging: OJA Motel (5 miles) 242-3614; Sunset Inn (Free trans) 243-2342.

Meeting Rooms: None Reported

Transportation: Enterprise 241-1187.

Information: Victorville Chamber of Commerce, 14174 Green Tree Blvd, Victorville, CA 92393, 245-6506; San Bernardino Area Chamber of Commerce, 546 West 6th Street, P.O. Box 658, San Bernardino, CA 92402, 714-885-7515.

Attractions:

Roy Rogers Museum, 15650 Seneca, Victorville, CA 92392, 619-243-4547.

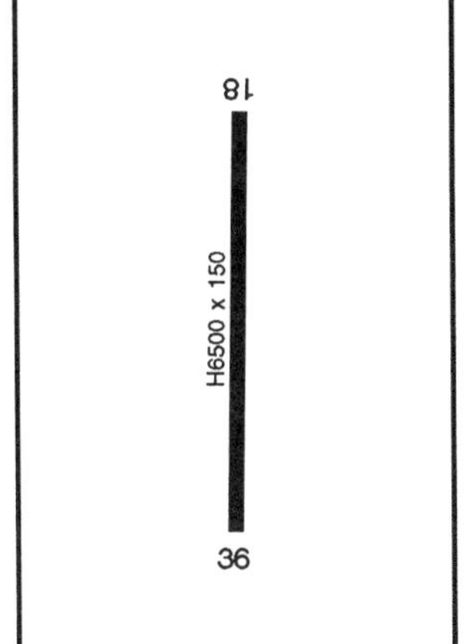

Airport Information:

APPLE VALLEY - APPLE VALLEY AIRPORT (APV)
3 mi north of town N34-3475 W117-11.17 Elev: 3059 Fuel: 80, 100LL, Jet-A
Rwy 18-36: H6500x150 (Asph) Attended: 1430-0100Z Unicom: 122.8 Public Phone 24hrs
Notes: No landing fee, $5.00 per night.
FBO: Lin's Flying Service Phone: 247-9007 Arpt. Manager Phone: 247-2371
FBO: Midfield Aviation Phone: 247-5766

CA-ACV - ARCATA/EUREKA
ARCATA AIRPORT

(Area Code 707) 2

Silver Lining Restaurant:

The Silver Lining Restaurant is located upstairs in the terminal building, at the Arcata Airport. This combination family and fine dining restaurant is open 7 days a week from 8:30 a.m. to 9:00 p.m. Their menu includes steak and seafood selections. Some of their specialty dishes include Chicken Marsale, New York pepper steak, Fettuccini Ricotta, Fresh salmon, Seafood Fettuccini and Southwestern Chicken. Their main dining room can seat 60 persons. Guests can see the entire landing strip from the restaurant, as well as the ocean and beach located nearby. They also have a conference room available with seating for up to 25 persons. With advance notice in-flight catering is also part of their services. For more information call the Silver Lining Restaurant at 839-0304.

Restaurants Near Airport:
Silver Lining Restaurant On Site Phone: 839-0304

Lodging: Eureka Inn (Shuttle) 442-6441; North Coast Inn (Shuttle) 822-4861; Red Lion Inn (20 miles, Shuttle reported) 445-0844.

Meeting Rooms: Eureka Inn 442-6441; North Coast Inn 822-4861; Red Lion Inn 445-8525.

Transportation: Taxi service available by calling 358-5031.

Information: Arcadia Chamber of Commerce, 388 W. Huntington Drive, Arcadia, CA 91007, 818-447-2159; Eureka Chamber of Commerce, 2112 Broadway, Eureka, CA 95501, 707-442-3738 or 800-356-6381; San Francisco Convention & Visitors Bureau, P.O. Box 429097, San Francisco, CA 94102-9097, Phone: 415-391-2000.

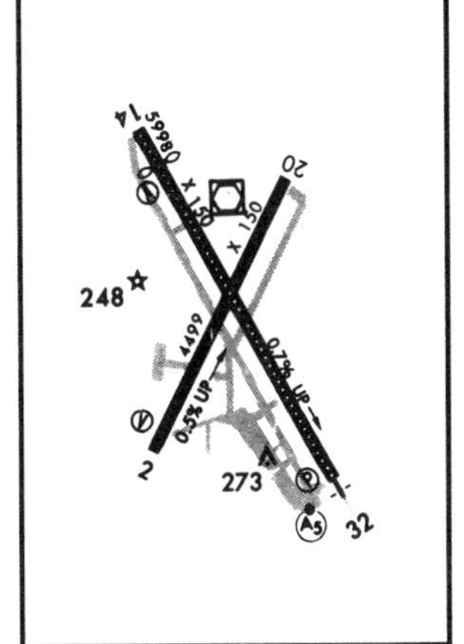

Airport Information:

ARCATA/EUREKA - ARCATA AIRPORT (ACV)
7 mi north of town N40-58.69 W124-06.52 Elev: 218 Fuel: 100LL, Jet-A
Rwy 14-32:H5998x150 (Asph-Pfc) Rwy 02-20: H4499x150 (Asph-Grvd) Attended: Sun-Fri 1400-0700Z, Sat 1500-0200Z CTAF: 123.65
FBO: County of Humboldt Phone: 839-5401

CA-AUN - AUBURN
AUBURN MUNICIPAL AIRPORT

(Area Code 916)

3

Restaurants Near Airport:
Wings Restaurant Adj Arpt Phone: 885-0428

Lodging: Auburn Inn (Trans) 885-1800

Meeting Rooms: Auburn Inn (Trans) 885-1800

Transportation: Cab 885-2227; Auburn Rent-A-Car 885-2400.

Information: Chamber of Commerce, 601 Lincoln Way, Auburn, CA 95603, Phone: 885-5616.

Attractions:

Old Town Auburn: Visitors can walk and visit the restored section of town retaining its historical value as a boomtown during the gold rush in the mid 1800's. (See "Information" listed above).

Wings Grill & Flight Line:

The Wings Grill & Flight Line, is a combination fixed base operation and full service restaurant, both on the Auburn Municipal Airport. Aircraft parking is available adjacent to the restaurant facility. Their dining establishment is open 7 days a week between 7 a.m. and 3 p.m. Items on their menu include fresh waffles, a large assortment of omelets and egg dishes as well as specialty items for lunch like hamburgers, cheeseburgers, sandwiches, grilled turkey, Ortega jack cheese and much more. Average prices run around $6.00 for most selections. Their dining room can seat up to 35 persons in addition to a nice outdoor dining patio furnished with tables that can seat an extra 38 people. The restaurant itself also contains an aviation theme decorated with a number of airplane related items as well as aircraft pictures. One unique feature included in this operation, is a pilot's supply store displaying pilot supplies, clothing, caps, books, maps and flight chart materials. They are also an authorized NOS chart dealer as well. 1/2 hour sight-seeing flights over the foot hills and surrounding area as well as flight training is another service offered by the owner. For more information call the Wings Grill & Flight Line at 885-0428.

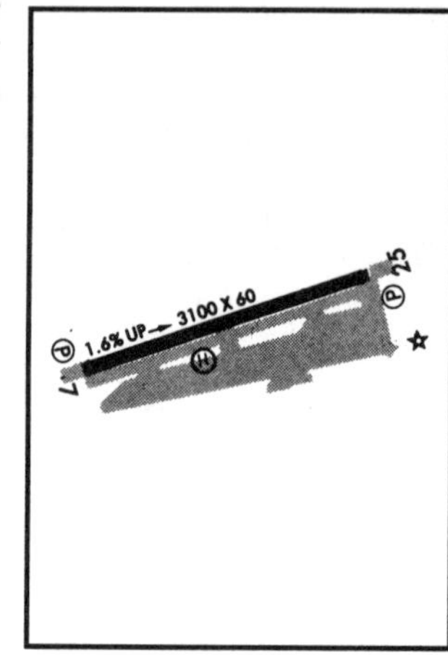

Airport Information:

AUBURN - AUBURN MUNICIPAL AIRPORT (AUN)
3 mi north of town N38-57.16 W121-04.90 Elev: 1520 Fuel: 80, 100, Mogas
Rwy 07-25: H3100x60 (Asph) Attended: May-Sep 1600-0200Z, Oct-Apr 1600-0100Z
Unicom: 122.7 Public Phone 24hrs Notes: $2.00 overnight parking fee
FBO: Wings Airport Service Phone: 823-0744

CA-AVX - AVALON
CATALINA AIRPORT

(Area Code 310)

4

Restaurants Near Airport:
Runway Cafe On Site Phone: 510-2196

Lodging: Cloud 7 Hotel (10 miles) 510-0454; El Terado (10 miles) 510-0831; Hotel Catalina (10 miles) 510-0027; Hotel St. Lauren 510-2299; Pavillion Lodge 510-2000; Inn On Mt Ada 510-2030.

Meeting Rooms: Hotel Catalina 510-0027

Transportation: Taxi: Avalon 510-0025; Catalina Airport Shuttle Bus 510-0143.

Information: Catalina Island Chamber of Commerce & Visitors Bureau, P.O. Box 217, Avalon, CA 90704, Phone: 510-1520.

Attractions:

Catalina Island tours and trips offer boat and bus tours to several attractions in the area 510-2000; Catalina Island Museum 510-2414. Avalon Casino, theatre, golfing, and fishing.

Runway Cafe Restaurant:

The Runway Cafe Restaurant is situated on the Catalina Airport, and is well within walking distance from aircraft parking. This cafe is open from 8:30 a.m. to 5 p.m. 7 days a week year around. Their menu includes specialty items like buffalo burgers, soft tacos, chicken breast plates, a variety of sandwiches, vegetarian dishes, and a full breakfast menu that is served until 12 noon. Average prices run about $6.00 for most selections. This restaurant has a Spanish decor with seating for about 60 people inside and seating for about 140 persons on their outdoor patio. There is also a small gift shop adjacent to the restaurant. During our conversation with the management, we learned that this area is somewhat isolated apart from the hustle and bustle of the city and offers guests a view of buffalo herds and wild countryside. In 1919 the Wrigley Jr chewing gum magnate, and owner of the Chicago Cubs base ball team, bought the island, and to this day it remains preserved through the conservation program as a wild life refuge. Within town there are many gift shops, restaurants and lodging establishment for the tourist. There is reported to be a landing fee of about $7.00-$15.00 for all aircraft operating in or out of the field. Also we might mention that prior permission is required by UNICOM 122.7 before landing or taking off at this airport. For more information about the Runway Cafe Restaurant you can call 510-2196.

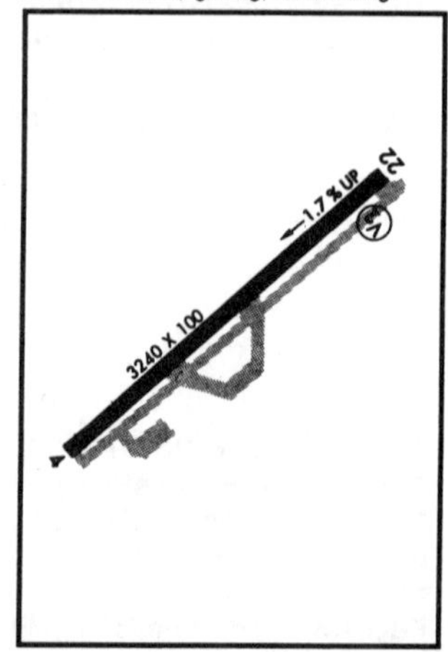

Airport Information:

AVALON - CATALINA AIRPORT (AVX)
6 mi northwest of town N33-2430 W118-24.95 Elev: 1602 Rwy 04-22: H3240x100 (Asph) Attended: Apr 15-Oct 15 1600-0300Z, Oct 16-Apr 14 1600-0100Z Unicom: 122.7
Notes: Landing Fee $7.00 to $15.00 Reported. Public use, approval required through UNICOM prior to takeoff or landing.
Catalina Airport Phone: 310-510-0143.

Catalina Island

Catalina Island is located just 22 miles off the Southern California coast. Although the island is close to the bustle of the city, its air is smog-free and its atmosphere is peaceful. Vacationers can enjoy water sports such as snorkeling, parasailing, deep sea fishing, and jet skiing. They can even go glass bottom boating, or they can just stick to land, relax on the beach and soak in the sun. Go camping, biking, hiking or horseback riding.

The island offers plenty of shopping and dining. There are a variety of clothing stores,including beachwear and other activewear shops, as well as souvenir shops, jewelry stores and galleries. The youngsters will enjoy the children's stores and the sweet shops.

Speaking of food, the choices of restaurants range from fast food restaurants to fine dining. Enjoy pizza, fresh seafood and hamburgers, as well as delicious Mexican and Italian food.

Lodging on Catalina Island is not hard to find. For the outdoorsman, the island has plenty of campsites to choose from. Campers can enjoy exotic scenery, while keeping an eye out for fox, quail, buffalo and bald eagles. There are also several hotels, Bed and Breakfasts, cottages and vacation rentals that provide comfortable accommodations.

Visitors can explore the island via scheduled bus service between Avalon and Two Harbors.The Catalina Safari Shuttle Bus stops at picnic sites, beaches, trails campgrounds and the airport. They can take guided sightseeing tours with Catalina Safari Tours and explore the natural history of the islands.The Catalina West End Dive Center provides scuba and snorkeling boat trips, beach dives, equipment rental, certifications and refresher courses. Complete resort dive packages are also available. Catalina Island Kayaks explore fascinating coves, reefs, caves and offshore islands. Dive kayaks and advanced level kayaks are also available.

Year-round vacationers can take the daily or nightly Starlight Undersea Tour, which is a semi-submersible vessel, or take the Inland Motor Tour, which includes a tour of El Rancho Escondido and Catalina Island Arabians. For extra enjoyment, they can take the Casino Tour, which includes ballroom, theatre, and a museum pass. Also, they can take daily or nightly tours on the Glass Bottom Boat, or take the Avalon Scenic Tour, or the Skyline Drive. May through September is the perfect time for taking a coastal cruise to Seal Rocks or a Flying Fish Boat Trip, or go twilight dining at Two Harbors.

Photo by: Catalina Island Chamber of Commerce

The City of Avalon and Avalon Bay serve as the gateway to Catalina Island.

Catalina Airport is located on the island, about 6 miles northwest of Avalon. It has a 3,240'x100 asphalt runway. Prior permission is required by Unicom: 122.7 before landing or taking off at this airport. There is a $5.00 landing fee. The Catalina Airport Shuttle Bus will provide transportation to and from the airport. Call 510-0143 for more information. Taxi service is also available at 510-0025. For further information about activities and accommodations on Catalina Island, contact the Catalina Island Chamber of Commerce and Visitors Bureau at 510-1520. (Information submitted by Catalina Island Chamber of Commerce and Visitors Bureau)

Photo by: Catalina Island Chamber of Commerce & Santa Catalina Island Company

The Green Pleasure Pier is great for fishing, renting boats, or "catching" a bite to eat.

CA-L45 - BAKERSFIELD
BAKERSFIELD MUNICIPAL AIRPORT

(Area Code 805)

5

Skyway Coffee Shop:

The Airpark Galley & Grill is located right on the flight line to the Bakersfield Municipal Airport. Pilots can easily walk to the restaurant from where they tie down their aircraft. This family style restaurant is open Monday through Thursday between 6:00 a.m. and 2 p.m., Friday between 6 a.m. and 9 p.m., Saturday from 6 a.m. to 9 p.m. and Sunday from 6 a.m. to 2 p.m. Please call this restaurant as hours may vary. Their menu includes a full breakfast line including omelets. Additional entrees include prime rib, fish and chips, a variety of sandwiches, barbecue beef and French dip. On Friday and Saturday they feature Halibut. Their dining room can seat 75 to 80 persons. The decor has an aviation theme. Banquet facilities are also available to accommodate about 40 additional persons. Groups and parties are welcome. Meals can also be prepared to-go as well. In fact, they even provide in-flight catering. For more information call the Skyway Coffee Shop at 831-7111.

Restaurants Near Airport:
Skyway Coffee Shop On Site Phone: 831-7111

Lodging: Bakers Field Lodge (Pilot discount) 327-7901.

Meeting Rooms: None Reported

Transportation: Yellow Cab 325-5041; Avis 397-2860; Standard Rent-A-Car 832-2431.

Information: Chamber of Commerce, 1033 Truxtun Avenue, P.O. Box 1947, Bakersfield, CA 93303, Phone: 327-4421.

Attraction:

Valley Grande Golf Course (1 mile) Sequioa National Park (11 miles) Kern Company Museum (7 miles). See "Information" listed above.

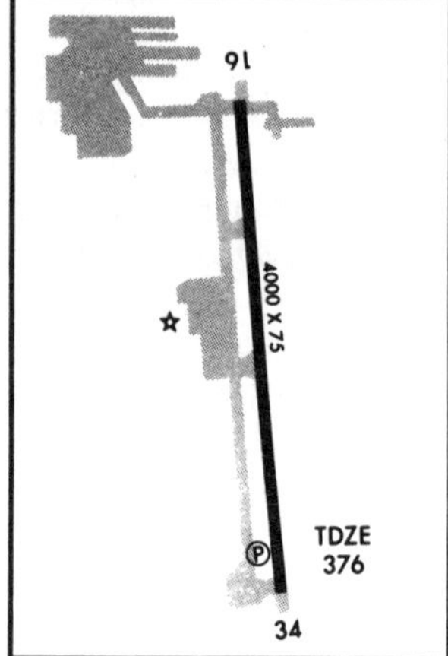

Airport Information:

BAKERSFIELD - BAKERSFIELD MUNICIPAL AIRPORT (L45)
3 mi south of town N35-19.49 W118-59.75 Elev: 376 Fuel: 80, 100LL
Rwy 16-34: H4000x75 (Asph) Attended: 1500-0100Z Unicom: 122.8 Public Phone 24hrs
Notes: runway lighting activated after 2200 hrs; Overnight parking $2.00;
Bakersfield Municipal Airport Phone: 326-3155
FBO: C & B Flying Service (Fuel) Phone: 832-2252
FBO: S & S Flight Center Phone: 831-6247

CA-BFL - BAKERSFIELD
MEADOWS FIELD AIRPORT

(Area Code 805)

6

Anton's At The Airport:

Anton's At The Airport , is located adjacent to the terminal and general aviation area. According to the management, this establishment combines a snack bar, cafe, family style and fine dining restaurant at one location. We were told that this is one of the most popular dining facilities throughout the Bakersfield area. Their hours are from 6:00 a.m. to 10 p.m. each day except Sunday until 8 p.m. Some of their specialties include fresh seafood (flown in daily), aged premium beef, Prime rib, Felet Mignon, lobster, roasted rack of lamb and southwestern specialties which are just a small part of the culinary delights that await you. The food, service and ambiance attract many fly-in customers from all over the California region. This facility boasts of its new cocktail lounge with piano bar as well as a very extensive menu with everything from Haute Cuisine to lite fare. The restaurant is restored in a 1950's Art Deco look with all new furniture, fixtures, bar and furnishings. The panoramic view of the airfield and mountains beyond are beautiful. Accommodations for meetings and banquets can be arranged in two rooms with a seating capacity of 150 persons. A complete in flight menu services everything from snack trays to hot meals for corporate jets. This restaurant along with the newly renovated Skyway Inn Motel (adjacent) make for a very convenient stopping point for cross country travelers as well as fly-in dining customers. For information call 399-9321.

Restaurants Near Airport:
Anton's At The Airport On Site Phone: 399-9321

Lodging: The following offer free shuttle service: Best Western (4 miles) 327-9651; Ramada Inn (5 miles) 327-0681; Rio Bravo (13 miles) 872-5000; Rio Mirada (4 miles) 324-5555; Sheraton Valley Inn (7 miles) 325-9700; Also Skyway House Motel (Adj Arpt) 399-9321.

Meeting Rooms: Skyway Inn Motel has two banquet meeting rooms available. For information call 399-9321.

Transportation: Avis 399-1718; Budget 399-2367; Hertz 393-2044; National 393-2068; Buses and taxi service is also reported.

Information: Chamber of Commerce, 1033 Truxtun Avenue, Suite C, P.O. Box 1947, Bakersfield, CA, 93303, Ph.327-4421.

Airport Information:

BAKERSFIELD - MEADOWS FIELD AIRPORT (BFL)
3 mi northwest of town N35-26.02 W119-03.41 Elev: 507 Fuel: 80, 100, 100LL, Jet-A
Rwy 12L-30R: H10857x150 (Asph-Grvd) Rwy 12R-30L: H3700x75 (Asph) Attended: 1330-0700Z
Atis: 118.6 Unicom: 122.95 Bakersfield App Con: 118.9 (N), 118.8 (S) Bakersfield Dep Con: 126.45 (N & S) Tower: 118.1 Gnd Con: 121.7 Notes: Overnight parking fees differ between FBO's.
FBO: Mercury Aviation Phone: 391-4900 **FBO: Lloyd's Aviation Serv. Phone: 393-1334**
FBO: Lloyd's Aircraft Main. Phone: 393-1588

CA-L35 - BIG BEAR CITY
BIG BEAR CITY AIRPORT

(Area Code 714)

7, 8

Restaurants Near Airport:

Landings Cafe	On Site	Phone: 585-3762
Mandarin Garden	On Site	Phone: 585-1818

Lodging: Big Bear Inn (Shuttle reported) 866-3471; Eagles Nest (Shuttle reported) 866-6465; Motel 6 (1/2 mile) 585-6666.
Meeting Rooms: Big Bear Inn 866-3471.
Transportation: Big Bear Cab 866-4444; Rental Cars: Big Bear 585-6447.
Information: Chamber of Commerce, 41647 Big Bear Blvd., Box 2860, Phone: 866-4607.

Attraction:
Golf course, parks, fishing lakes and skiing in winter within the immediate vicinity.

Landings Cafe:
The Landings Cafe is also reported to be located within the terminal building at the Big Bear City Airport. This cafe serves lighter fare, and is situated on the ground level under the Mandarin Garden restaurant. For information call the Landings Cafe restaurant at 585-3762.

Mandarin Garden:
The Mandarin Garden is located upstairs in the terminal building, at the Big Bear City Airport. This is a fine dining establishment that is open 7 days a week from 11 a.m. to 10 p.m. They specialize in Mandarin, Cantonese and American dishes, including famous selections like Peking duck, lobster, Live Maine Lobster & Crab, sweet punge shrimp, sweet & sour pork, Oriental seafood dishes, steaks, hamburgers and much more. Daily specials are also available. Their dining room can accommodate 150 persons within two dining areas. They also have a banquet area that can seat 60 persons as well as their bar with 120 available seats. Groups and parties are always welcome. However, large parties should make advance reservations. In-flight catering is also provided. For more information call the Mandarin Garden at 585-1818.

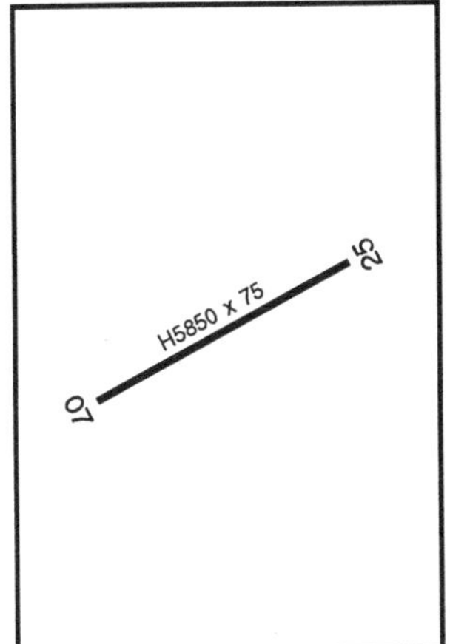

Airport Information:
BIG BEAR CITY - BIG BEAR CITY AIRPORT (L35)
1 mi northwest of town 34-15-49N 116-51-13W Elev: 6750 Fuel: 100LL, Jet-A
Rwy 07-25: H5850x75 (Asph) Attended: 1600-0100Z Unicom: 122.7 Notes: Mountains in all quadrants. No landing fees, only overnight parking fee $3.50 Single and $4.50 for twins.

FBO: Aero Haven **Phone: 585-9663**
FBO: Callaway Aviation **Phone: 585-4303**
FBO: Resort Aviation **Phone: 585-8388**
FBO: Aero Specialties **Phone: 585-3086**

CA-BIH - BISHOP
BISHOP AIRPORT

(Area Code 619)

9

Restaurants Near Airport:

Bishop's Grill	2 mi W.	Phone: 873-3911
Jack's Waffle Shop	2 mi W.	Phone: 872-7971
Lee's Chinese Food	2 mi W.	Phone: 872-2189

Lodging: Best Western Westerner (2-1/2 miles) 873-3544; Elm's Motel (2-1/2 miles) 873-8118.

Meeting Rooms: Best Western Westerner 873-3544.

Transportation: Shuttle Bus reported at airport; Car Rental: Eastern Sierra Auto 873-4291;

Information: Bishop Chamber of Commerce, 690 N. Main Street, Bishop, CA 93514, 873-8405.

Pete & Al's Cafe:

According to the airport management, this restaurant has been closed. We were informed however, that there may be another restaurant establishment re-opening in the future. It is uncertain as to when this may occur.

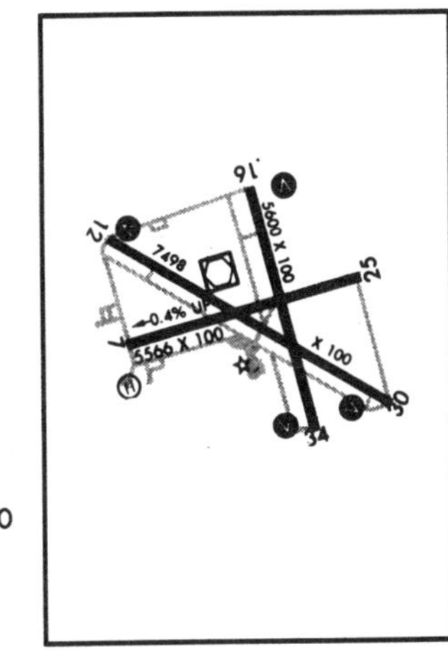

Attractions:
"Bishop is located in the "Deepest Valley" (Owens Valley), and is surrounded by mountains and unique scenery. Close attractions include, Yosemite and Kings Canyon, Sequoia National Park, Death Valley, great winter skiing and summer fishing, and back packing in the Sierra Nevada Wilderness." (By Pete & Als Restaurant).

Airport Information:
BISHOP - BISHOP AIRPORT (BIH)
2 mi east of town N37-22.39 W118-21.82 Elev: 4120 Fuel: 100LL, Jet-A
Rwy 12-30: H7498x100 (Asph-Pfc) Rwy 16-34: H5600x100 (Asph-Pfc) Rwy 07-25: H5566x100 (Asph) Attended: 1530-0200Z Unicom: 123.0 Public Phone 24hrs

FBO: Hangar One Aero Service **Phone: 873-7500**
FBO: Bishop County Airport **Phone: 872-2971**

CA-Q17 - BOONVILLE
BOONVILLE - BOONVILLE AIRPORT

(Area Code 707)

10, 11

Buckhorn Restaurant:

The Buckhorn Saloon, the brew pub for Anderson Valley Brewing Company, is located 1/2 to 3/4 of a mile from the Boonville Airport. After landing you can walk past the High School to Hwy 128 and turn right, then go approx 1/3 mile to the restaurant. Transportation is available, prior arrangements requested. This family style restaurant is situated on the upper level of the Anderson Valley Brewing Company and is open 7 days, June through November, and Thursday through Monday during winter months. Hours are 11 a.m. to 10 p.m. Specialties include fish & chips, burgers and soups. Prices run about $7.00 for lunch and $11.00 for dinner. The decor features collectibles from breweries around the world. Groups are welcom with advance arrangements. The Boonville Hotel is located across the street from The Buckhorn Saloon. For information call 895-2337.

The Toll House Restaurant & Inn:

The Toll House Restaurant and Inn is located 4 miles from the Boonville Airport, and welcomes guests year around. Courtesy transportation is provided given advance notice. In the heart of Mendocino's wine country, just 125 miles north of San Francisco, this charming property features some of northern California's most beautiful land. This secluded 360 acre ranch offers you quiet surroundings for relaxing and taking in the scenery, while providing for a variety of activities. The Toll House Restaurant prepares menu selections daily using the finest fresh ingredients available. Seasonally, wild game is featured. This fine dining establishment is open from 6 p.m. to 8 p.m. Thursday through Monday, as well as Sunday for brunch, and on all holidays. Prices average $7.00 to $10.00 for breakfast and $25.00 to $30.00 for dinner selections. The Inn and restaurant is beautifully restored in 1912 Victorian style. This facility offers a memorable setting for a group meeting, wedding, or romantic getaway. Activities in the area include area wineries, horseback riding, swimming, fishing (1/2 mile river frontage), hiking and a great deal more. For information and reservations call the Toll House at 895-3630.

Restaurants Near Airport:

Anderson Creek Inn	1.5 mi	Phone: 895-3091
Buckhorn Saloon	3/4 mi	Phone: 895-2337
Bear Wallow Lodge	4 mi.	Phone: 895-3335
Toll House Inn	4 mi.	Phone: 895-3630

Lodging: Anderson Creek Inn (1-1/2 mile) 895-3091; Bear Wallow Lodge (4 miles) 895-3335; Boonville Hotel (3/4 mile) 895-2210; Toll House Inn (4 miles) 895-3630;

Meeting Rooms: Toll House (4 miles) 895-3630; Boonville Hotel (3/4 mile) 895-2210; Buckhorn Saloon (3/4 mile) 895-2337.

Transportation: Transportation can be arranged through Mr Joe Fox (Airport Manager) at 895-3483.

Information: Greater Ukiah Chamber of Commerce, 495-E E Perkins Street, Ukiah, CA 95482, Phone: 462-4705.

Airport Information:

BOONVILLE - BOONVILLE AIRPORT (Q17)

1 mi northwest of town   N39-00.76 W123-22.97   Elev: 371   Rwy 12-30: H3240x40 (Asph)
Attended: unattended   CTAF: 122.7   Notes: Overnight parking fees: $1.00/night, $10/week, $100/year
Airport Manager   Phone: 895-3483

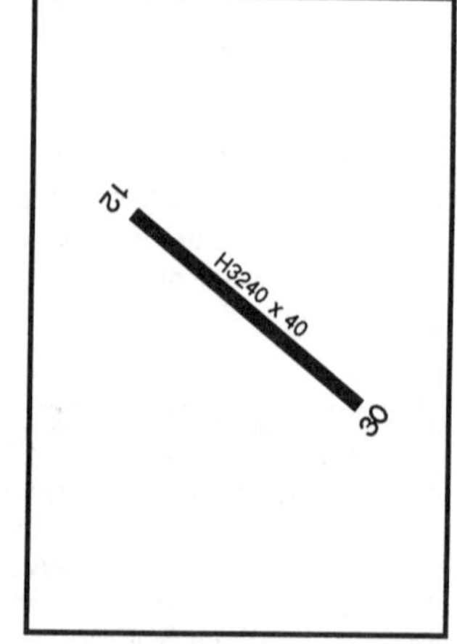

CA-O57 - BRIDGEPORT BRYANT FIELD

(Area Code 619) **12**

Bridgeport Inn:

The Bridgeport Inn is a restaurant and lodging facility that is located about 1/3 mile south of Bryant Field. This is a combination family restaurant for lunch and fine dining facility during evening meals. House specialties include rack of lamb, Australian lobster tail, prime rib, shrimp dishes, assorted steaks, pastas and a complete choice of breakfast entrees. Prices run $6.00 for lunch and $14.00 for dinner. Restaurant hours are 8 a.m. to 10 p.m. 7 days a week. Daily specials are offered for breakfast, lunch and dinner. This establishment offers a unique decor with a beautiful Victorian motif. The dining room has laced table cloths, laced drapes on the windows and candles on each table. Their large parlor includes room for special occasions with a player piano, bar and pot bellied stove. The Bridgeport Inn has the original Victorian two story building that was built in 1977, surrounding this building is a recently constructed addition which houses lodging units for their guests. Some of the units contain standard accommodations.

Restaurants Near Airport:
Bridgeport Inn 1/3 mi. Phone: 932-7380

Lodging: Bridgeport Inn 1/3rd mi. 932-7380; Silver Maple 1/3 mi. 932-8521; Walker River Lodge 2 blks 932-7380 Westerner Motel 2 blks 932-7241.
Meeting Rooms: Bridgeport Inn 1/3rd mi. 932-7380.
Transportation: Bridgeport Inn will furnish courtesy transportation fro the airport and their facility. 932-7380;
Information: Bridgeport Inn 932-7380. Bryant Field Airport 932-7043;

Others offer the European plan with common bathroom arrangements. In addition the Bridgeport Inn can easily be reached from the airport. Guests can call for courtesy transportation. While there you might enjoy visiting the attractions in the area. Reservations are suggested especially during summer months for dinner. If walking, leave the airport and walk up the road towards town about 300 yds to Saint Clair street then turn left and go 1 block. For information call the Bridgeport Inn at 932-7380.

Attractions:

Their are numerous attractions within this region. If you like fishing, you can literally drop a line in the water only 100 feet from the airport; Yosemite National Park is located only 20 miles south west of the town of Bridgeport. Also one popular attraction visited by many vacationers is Bodie State Historic Park. This 320 acre park and ghost town displays an accurate depiction of what it was like during the 1800's gold rush. Over 150 buildings have been preserved in a state of arrested decay making it the only site to maintain the look of a real ghost town. During our conversation with the Bridgeport Inn manager we learned this particular town is not commercialized like other historic towns, however it still is occupied by locals. A walking tour and self guided brochure takes you through the main part of town. For information call 647-6445. Also: just south of Bridgeport is the, lunar-like terrain of Mono Lake. Millions of years of volcanic activity has created lava-strewn islands.

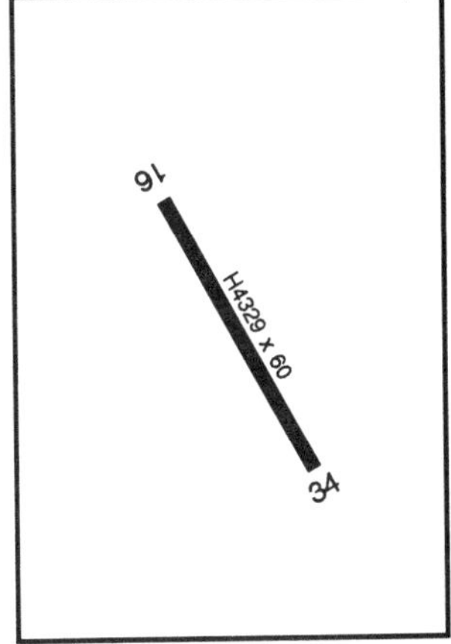

Airport Information:

BRIDGEPORT - BRYANT FIELD (O57)
0 mi northeast of town N38-15.75 W119-13.54 Elev: 6468 Fuel: 80, 100LL Rwy 16-34: H4329x60 (Asph) Attended: unattended CTAF: 122.9 Notes: For fuel call 619-932-7153 Rotating bcn located 1/2 mile east of the airport on top of hill.
Airport Manager Phone: 932-7043

CA-BUR - BURBANK GLENDALE-PASADENA AIRPORT

(Area Code 818) **13**

Air Hollywood Bar & Grill:

The Air Hollywood Bar & Grill is located in the terminal building at the Glendale-Pasadena Airport. This restaurant is open from 6 a.m. to 9 p.m. Sunday through Friday and Saturday from 6 a.m. to 7 p.m. They serve many Chinese and American dishes including their specialties like stir-fry, Chinese chicken salads, chili, soups, sandwiches, and a full breakfast line. Average prices run $6.50 for breakfast and $8.50 for most dinner items. Daily specials are also provided on their menu as well. During our conversation with the manager of the restaurant, we learned that the restaurant decor is visually appealing and exhibits a unique aviation theme, with videos, soundtracks and music recordings from aviation movies. The chef that prepares meals for their guests, is a member of the "USA American Gold Meddle Chef" just recently elected to compete in the "International Culinary Exposition", held in Frankfort every year since 1904. Their motto is to "Provide world class food for world class travelers." For more information about this restaurant call 972-1337.

Restaurants Near Airport:
Air Hollywood Bar & Grill On Site Phone: 972-1337

Lodging: Burbank Airport Hilton (Adj Arpt, trans) 843-6000; Holiday Inn (2 miles) 841-4770; Ramada Inn (1 mile) 843-5955.

Meeting Rooms: Burbank Airport Hilton (Convention facilities) 843-6000.

Transportation: Taxi service on field; Rental Cars: Avis, Dollar, Hertz, National.

Information: Greater Los Angeles Visitors & Convention Bureau, 633 W. Fifth Street, Suite 6000, Los Angeles, CA 90071, Phone: 213-624-7300.

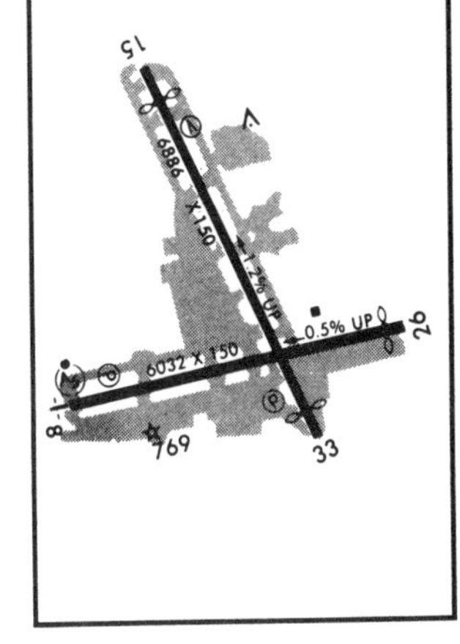

Airport Information:

BURBANK - GLENDALE-PASADENA AIRPORT (BUR)
3 mi northwest of town N34-12.04 W118-21.51 Elev: 775 Fuel: 100LL, Jet-A, Mogas Rwy 15-33: H6885x150 (Asph-Grvd) Rwy 08-26: H6032x150 (Asph-Grvd) Attended: continuously Atis: 134.5 Unicom: 122.95 App/Dep: 135.05, 134.2, 124.6, 120.4 Tower: 118.7 Gnd Con: 123.9 Clnc Del: 118.0
FBO: Professional Pilot Training Phone: 567-4458

CA-CXL - CALEXICO
CALEXICO INTL AIRPORT

(Area Code 619) 14

Rosa's Plane Food:

The Rosa's Plane Food Restaurant is situated on the Calexico International Airport. Guests can easily walk to the restaurant from the aircraft tie-down areas. According to the management at the airport, this establishment provides a casual atmosphere with additional amenities like a pool table and game room. Restaurant hours are between 9 a.m. and 7 p.m., 7 days a week. Their menu specializes in Mexican cuisine. This is a full service facility providing breakfast, lunch and dinner selections. For more information about the Rosa's Plane Food Restaurant call 357-6660.

Restaurants Near Airport:
Rosa's Plane Food Restaurant On Site Phone: 357-6660

Lodging: De Anza Hotel 357-1112; Don Juan (1 mile) 357-3231; El Rancho Motel (Est. 1-2 mile) 357-2468; Hollies Fiesta Hotel (1 mile) 357-3271.

Meeting Rooms: De Anza Hotel 357-1112; Hollies Motel 357-3271.

Transportation: Border Taxi 357-6161; Calexico Taxi 357-1119; California Taxi 357-2414.

Information: Chamber of Commerce, P.O. Box 948, Calexico, CA 92232, Phone: 357-1166.

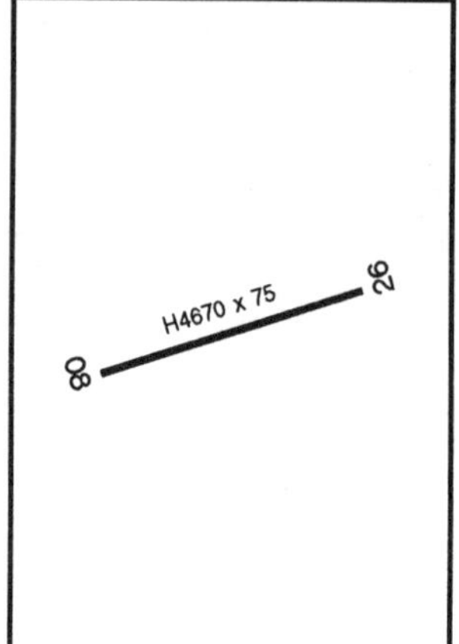

Airport Information:

CALEXICO - CALEXICO INTERNATIONAL AIRPORT (CXL)
1 mi west of town N32-40.17 W115-30.80 Elev: 00 Fuel: 100LL, Jet-A
Rwy 08-26: H4670x75 (Asph-Afsc) Attended: 1600-0100Z Unicom: 122.8
Calexico Airport Phone: 768-2175
FBO: Jaax Flying Service Phone: 357-4647, 800-544-3449

CA-L71 - CALIFORNIA CITY
CALIFORNIA CITY MUNICIPAL

(Area Code 619) 15

Ready Room Restaurant:

During our conversation with the airport manager we learned that California City Municipal airport has received many improvements over the past several years. A new 3,000 square foot terminal building was recently built, along with runway, taxiway and ramp improvements. Transportation to nearby attractions is no problem; infact, the local dial-a-ride service has their office right in the terminal. Nearby Edwards Air Force Base also provides shuttle service to their location. The Ready Room restaurant opened its doors on February 14, 1997. It has an aviation theme and provides guests with a cozy atmosphere complete with aviation-related memorabilia and items and photos of NASA projects. A number of previous articles from the golden age of aviation pioneering still remain on display. This restaurant offers a full selection of breakfast, lunch and dinner choices. A special sandwich on their menu is called the "Rat-Fink-Burger." Its a delicious hamburger smothered with mushrooms, cheese and chili. The management of the restaurant also specializes in featuring buffets through the week and weekends. The view from the restaurant overlooks the Sierra Madre Mountain range and Tehachapi peak to the west. For more information about the airport services, available ground transportation, attractions in the area or restaurant services call the California City Airport manager at 619-373-4867.

Restaurants Near Airport:
Ready Room Trml bldg. Phone: Arpt mgr. 373-4867

Lodging: Econo Lodge est. 15-20 miles 805-824-2463; Motel Six 12 mi 824-4571; Silver Saddle Ranch Club 12 mi 373-8617;
Meeting Rooms: Call the airport manager at 373-4867
Transportation: Dial-a-ride office located right in the airport terminal building. Also shuttle service available to and from Edwards Air Force Base. Courtesy transportation also reported available. Call the airport manager for information about these services. Phone: 373-4867.
Information: Chamber of Commerce, 44335 Lowtree Street, Lancaster, CA 93534; Phone: 948-4518.

Attractions:

Air Force Flight Test Center at Edwards Air Force Base contains a museum and public tours of the facility. The tour provided by the Flight Test Historical Foundation begins with a 1/2 hour movie followed by a bus tour of portions of the base and flight areas. A NASA tour is also available. For information about either of these tours contact Public Affairs at 805-277-3510. Also see the article about this attraction.

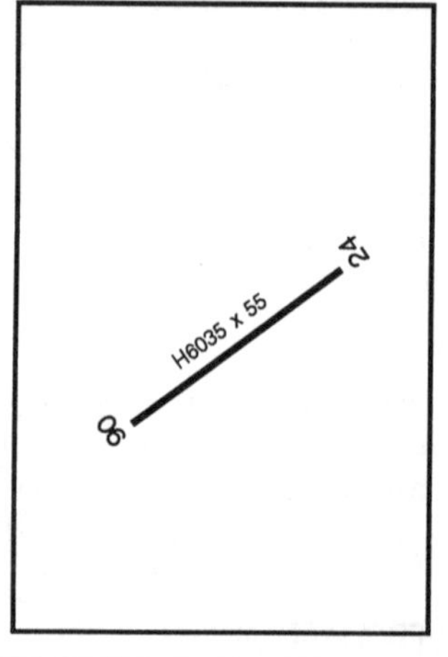

Airport Information:

CALIFORNIA CITY - CALIFORNIA CITY MUNICIPAL (L71)
10 mi northwest of town N35-09.11 W118-00.84 Rwy 06-24: H6035x55 (Asph) Attended: 1600-0100 Unicom: 122.7 Notes: Parachute Jumping and extensive glider traffic and sky diving activity daily. See current AFD for information.
FBO: California City Airport Phone: 373-4867

Air Force Flight Test Center Museum

Edwards AFB - California City, CA (L71) or Lancaster, CA (WJF)

Aviation, particularly aeronautical flight testing, has been one of the most exciting and dramatic parts of 20th Century life. The truly revolutionary events of this period were centered around the Air Force Flight Test Center at Edwards Air Force Base. In terms of the number and magnitude of events that have occurred there over the past five decades, no other place in the world can match the aviation/aerospace heritage of Edwards AFB. Little of the heritage of this era remains and the interested researcher or visitor must travel far from where the aviation history was made to see the craft responsible for these feats - if they exist at all.

It was precisely for this reason, because the heritage of flight research and flight testing accomplished at Edwards was being lost, that a group of concerned citizens banded together to form the Flight Test Historical Foundation. Their purpose? - to create a new aerospace museum at Edwards AFB that would preserve and interpret our nation's magnificent flight test heritage and the history of Edwards AFB.

The Foundation's dreams are finally taking shape - the Air Force Flight Test Center Museum is in the making. Over 300 acres have been set aside on Edwards AFB to develop a museum complex, and an extensive collection of aircraft, artifacts, and aviation memorabilia is being assembled to provide the historic basis for dramatic and educational exhibits. Samples of aircraft tested at Edwards are currently on display in various locations around the base, on the proposed museum's Jimmy Doolittle Airpark, and at the museum's Blackbird Airpark at Air Force Plant 42, approximately 36 miles away in Palmdale.

Visitors to the future museum will view a one-of-a-kind Fairchild Republic YA-10B, the first General Dynamics F-111A, the prototype Lockheed A-12 "Blackbird," the only surviving NF-104A rocket-assisted aerospace trainer, a Douglas TB-26B, and a number of other rare aircraft such as the PA-48 Enforcer, P-59B, SR-71A, X-1E, X-21, and XP-81, along with many other aircraft and aerospace-related artifacts. Additionally, suitable aircraft that reflect the breadth and scope of Edward's history will continue to be acquired by the museum as they become available.

Current plans call for the remodeling of a small visitor center and gift shop in an existing facility, followed, as funds become available, by construction of a major museum complex housing exhibit halls, a gift shop, research center, library, theater, and restoration facilities. The wide-range exhibits area will also include a Society of Experimental Test Pilots Heritage Hall.

The Air Force Flight Test Center (AFFTC)) Museum is currently in the embryonic stages of development. It will be one of 30 such museums throughout the Air Force and will interpret the history of the AFFTC, Edwards AFB and its antecedents, and the history of USAF flight test. There are currently 57 aircraft in the collection, with 13 on display (12 at Edwards and one at the AFFTC-managed Blackbird Airpark in Palmdale) and the others in storage and/or restoration. Other artifacts in the collection include aircraft propulsion systems, hardware, life support equipment, personal memorabilia, photographs, test reports, and technical drawings. A private non-profit organization, the Flight Test Historical Foundation, has been formed to raise funds for construction of the museum on 335 acres of land set aside on Edwards AFB for museum development. An existing facility in the base shopping area, is currently being remodeled to serve as an interim museum until the permanent museum is constructed. This small "starter museum" will provide space for exhibits, a video presentation area, a small work area, a gift shop, and administrative offices.

The projected opening date of the interim museum was in the spring of 1992. The museum will be open to the public Tuesday through Sunday, free of charge. Entry to Edwards AFB is controlled so visitors must have a valid driver's license or other photo I.D. (and current vehicle registration if arriving by auto) in their possession when requesting a visitor's pass at one of the three base entry gates. Occasionally, entry to the base is prohibited for other than official travel. They recommend visitors call the museum prior to making travel plans to visit Edwards AFB.

During our conversation with the public affairs office, we learned that there are tours available for the public. The Flight Test Historical Foundation on Fridays offers a tour that begins with a 1/2 hour film followed by a 1 hour bus trip to view portions of the base and flight areas. NASA also features tours Monday through Friday between 10:15 a.m. and 1:15 p.m. Visitors can arrange to take both tours as they are scheduled work together. For information about the museum and Flight Test Historical Foundation tour call the public affairs number 805-277-3510. For NASA tours call 805-258-3460. A recording message about the tours is available by calling 805-277-6082 or 6083.

One additional annual attraction is the airshow and anniversary celebrations of flight, held in October of each year. Several outstanding aerial performers are on hand.

If flying in to see the museum, the closest civilian airport is California City Muni. (L71) about 14 miles north and west from the northern main entrance to the base. Dial-a-ride transportation service is available at the terminal building. Shuttle service from the Air Force Base is also accessible. For airport information on transportation airport services etc. call the airport managers office at 619-373-4867. General WM. J. Fox Airfield (WJF) in Lancaster, CA. is another good choice. This airport has rental cars available. As well as nearby lodging facilities if planning to stay overnight. Fixed Base Operators that serve fuel on the field include: Comarco, Inc Flight Service Branch 805-940-1709. Rental cars situated at Fox Airfield include: Avis 945-5825, Enterprise 945-4611 and Hertz 942-5824. See location number 49 for information about lancaster and the Sly Fox Cafe on the field. For museum information call 805-277-8050. (Information obtained from the Flight Test Historical Foundation.)

Public Affairs: 805-277-3510
Tours: 805-277-3517
Pre-recorded message:
805-277-6082 or 6083.
NASA tours: 805-258-3460

CA-CMA - CAMARILLO
CAMARILLO AIRPORT

16

Waypoint Cafe:

The Waypoint Cafe is located within walking distance to aircraft parking at the Camarillo Airport. We were told that if you park your airplane at Channel Island Aviation you can walk to the cafe. This restaurant is open 7 days a week between 7 a.m. and 6 p.m. Monday through Saturday and 8 a.m. to 6 p.m. on Sundays. Specialties of the house include BBQ tri tip sandwiches, Cesa with chicken, patty melts, tuna melts, 4 different hamburgers, chili dogs, tacos, salads, and soup of the day. Various Mexican entrees are also offered. Breakfast dishes are served all day like their popular Eggs Benedict special and hot cakes. In addition to seating for 75 within the restaurant, outdoor seating is also available with seating for 30 additional place settings. The decor of the restaurant is enhanced with all types of aviation photos on loan from local pilots. Lots of windows provide a nice view of the surrounding area. In-flight catering is another service of the Waypoint Cafe Items from their menu, fruit, cheese, salads, and sandwich trays are all available for pilots on the go. Catering on the premises can also be arranged for your special fly-in club or business get together. For more information call the restaurant at 388-2535.

Restaurants Near Airport: **(Area Code 805)**
Waypoint Cafe On Site Phone: 388-2535

Lodging: Country Inn (1-1/2 mi) 447-3529; Radisson Hotel (988-0130)
Meeting Rooms: Country Inn (1-1/2 mi) 447-3529;
Transpertation: Rental Cars: Enterprise 389-8922; Rent-A-Wreck 987-1816
Information: Chamber of Commerce, 632 Las Posas Road, Camarillo, CA 93010, Phone: 484-4383.

Attractions:

Confederate Air Force is situated on the airport. Fisherman's Warf-Channel Island Harbor is a popular attraction near the towns of Ventura and Oxnard, CA. about 8 miles from the airport. Paradise Cove just south of the town of Oxnard offers a picturesque setting, with sailboats, and schooners anchored within the cove surrounded by rocky cliffs. Nearby Islands along the region attract many fishing and charter boats.

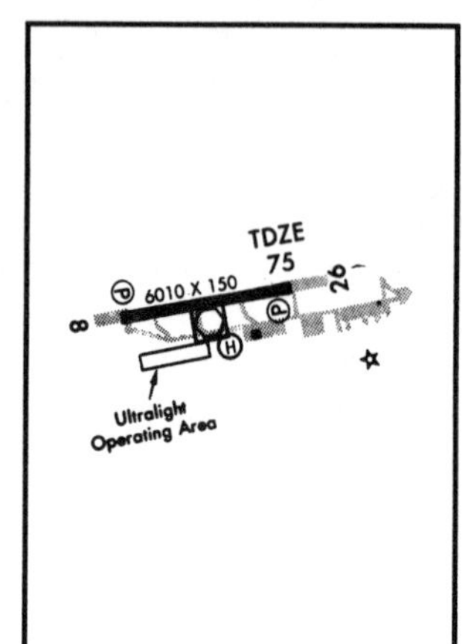

Airport Information:

CAMARILLO - CAMARILLO (CMA)
3 mi west of town N34-12.83 W119-05.66 Elev: 75 Fuel: 80, 100LL, Jet-A Rwy 08-26: H6010x150 (Asph-Conc) Attended: continuously Atis: 119.2 Tower: 128.2 Gnd Con: 121.8 CAUTION: High performance military aircraft ops in vicinity of airport. No takeoffs between 0800-1300Z.
FBO: Channel Islands Aviation **Phone: 987-1301**
FBO: Western Cardinal **Phone: 482-2586**

CA-CRQ - CARLSBAD
McCLELLAN-PALOMAR AIRPORT

17

Palomar Airport Cafe:

The Palomar Runway Cafe is located on the McClellan-Palomar Airport. This cafe style restaurant is open 7 days a week from 7 a.m. to 5 p.m. Their menu selections include a full breakfast line, hamburgers, club sandwiches, pastrami sandwiches, diet plates, chef salads and homemade soups. Average prices run between $2.45 and $5.95 for most choices. Daily specials are also available. The restaurant has seating for 49 persons and provides a very open and airy atmosphere with tables, booths and large windows providing guests with a great view overlooking the runway. Photographs and pictures of aircraft are also mounted on the walls, in addition to aviation styled wall paper. They even have an outdoor deck able to accommodate up to 25 persons. Groups limiting their size to 10 persons are welcome. Meals can be prepared for carry-out as well. Their services also include in-flight catering. For more information call the Palomar Runway Cafe at 438-9669.

Restaurants Near Airport: **(Area Code 619)**
Palomar Airport Cafe On Site Phone: 438-9669

Lodging: Best Western (3 miles) 483-7880; La Costa Resort & Spa (3 miles, trans) 438-9111; Lexington Hotel Suites (Trans) 438-2285; Olympic Golf Resort Hotel (1/2 mile) 438-8330; Surf Motel (3 miles) 729-7961.

Meeting Rooms: Best Western 483-7880; La Costa Hotel & Spa 438-9111; Lexington Hotel Suites 438-2285; Olympic Golf Resort Hotel 438-8330.

Transportation: Taxi Service: Yellow Cab 722-4214, Rental Cars: Avis 931-1393.

Information: Convention & Visitors Bureau, P.O. Box 1246, Carlsbad, CA 92018, Phone: 434-6093 or 800-227-5722.

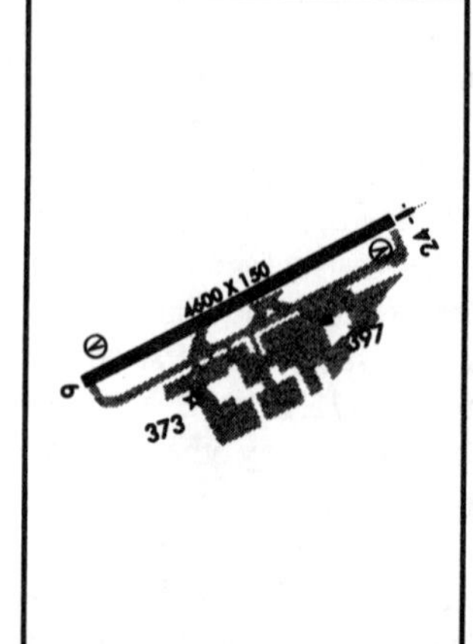

Airport Information:

CARLSBAD - McCLELLAN-PALOMAR AIRPORT (CRQ)
3 mi southeast of town N33-07.69 N117-16.82 Elev: 328 Fuel: 100LL, Jet-A
Rwy 06-24: H4600x150 (Asph-Pfc) Attended: continuously Atis: 120.15 Unicom: 122.95
Tower: 118.6 Gnd Con: 121.8
FBO: Gibbs Aviation Service **Phone: 438-7603**
FBO: Western Flight **Phone: 438-6800 or 800-523-4038**

CA-CNO - CHINO
CHINO AIRPORT

(Area Code 909) 18

Restaurants Near Airport:
Flo's Airport Cafe On Site Phone: 597-3416

Lodging: Best Western Pine Tree (1-2 miles) 628-6021; Comfort Inn - Airport South (1-2 miles) 986-3556; Travelodge - Ontario (1-2 miles) 984-1775.

Meeting Rooms: Comfort Inn - Airport South 986-3556.

Transportation: Rent-A-Wreck 983-3711.

Information: Los Angeles Convention and Visitors Bureau, 633 W. Fifth Street, Suite 6000, Los Angeles, CA 90071, Phone: 213-624-7300.

Flo's Airport Cafe:

Flo's Airport Cafe is located directly across from the airport transient parking area. This combination cafe and family style restaurant is open 7 days a week between 5:30 a.m. and 7 p.m. Specialties include biscuits and gravy, steak and eggs, sausage omelets, and many additional breakfast items including egg dishes, etc. For lunch and dinner they feature pork chops, shrimp, seafood platters, low calorie dishes, hamburgers, grilled ham and cheese sandwiches, fried breast of chicken, turkey plates, deluxe combination plates, roast pork, soups, salads, and for dessert, homemade pies, cobblers and cream pies. Average prices run $3.95 for breakfast, $4.25 for lunch and around $5.50 for dinner. Daily specials are also available throughout the week. The restaurant can accommodate up to 150 persons, and displays a very rustic and country decor. Pictures of aircraft as well as other artist's works are on display throughout the restaurant and within a special gallery for guests to enjoy. Many groups visit this establishment on a regular basis in numbers as high as 45 to 50 at one time. Advance notice would be appreciated if you plan to arrange a large fly-in or get together. For more information call Flo's Airport Cafe at 597-3416.

Planes of Fame Museum
See Article this page

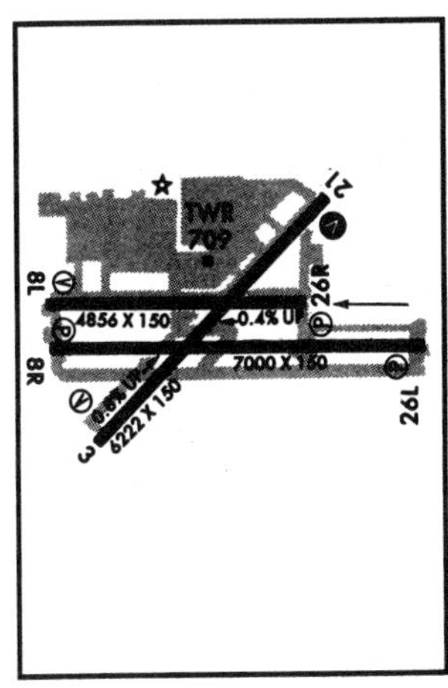

Airport Information:

CHINO - CHINO AIRPORT (CNO)
3 mi southeast of town N33-58.51 W117-38.21 Elev: 650 Fuel: 100LL, Jet-A
Rwy 08R-26L: H7000x150 Rwy 03-21: H6221x150 (Asph) Rwy 08L-26R: H4856x150 (Asph)
Attended: 1500-0300Z Atis: 121.15 Unicom: 122.95 Tower: 118.5 Gnd Con: 121.6
Public Phone 24hrs Notes: Overnight parking fees $5.00 singles, $8.50 twins.
FBO: Flight Craft Phone: 597-1731

Planes of Fame Museum

Chino, CA (CA-CNO)

Established on January 12, 1957, The Air Museum was the very first aviation museum of its type west of the Rocky Mountains, a pioneer in the "flying museum" concept. The Air Museum continually strives to restore as many of the aircraft in its collection as possible, to flying condition in order to show them off in their natural element - the sky. Of the more than 110 aircraft currently in the Planes of Fame collection, over two dozen are flyable, and new projects are always in progress.

Projects currently nearing completion at The Air Museum include the restoration to flying condition of: a British Supermarine Spitfire Mk. XIX; an original Japanese Aichi D3A "Val" dive bomber; the last surviving Northrop N9M-B Flying Wing; and the Bell YP-59A Airacomet, the first American jet aircraft.

As a true warbird sanctuary, a number of the aircraft in The Air Museum's collection are the very last surviving examples of their types left in the world. Included in this category are the museum's Ryan FR-1 Fireball, Japanese Mitsubishi J2M3 Raiden interceptor, the Horton Ho.IV flying wing glider and the Japanese Mitsubishi J8M-1 Shusui rocket-powered interceptor. Furthermore, The Air Museum's Japanese 12A Guardsman, Boeing P-12E/FHB-3 pursuit and Boeing P-26A "Peashooter" are the only authentic flyable examples of these particular types.

Located on the Chino Airport, the old Cal Aero Flight Academy of WW-II is historic in itself. The Air Museum operates both a traditional warbird museum and a separate fighter Jets Museum. The Air Museum is open to the public every day of the week from 9 a.m. until 5 p.m. except for Thanksgiving and Christmas. Admission to either the warbird collection or the Fighter Jets Museum is $7.95 for adults, $1.95 for juniors under 12 and free for kids under 5 when accompanied by adults. Combination tickets for admission to both museums are available at $8.00 for adults and $2.00 for juniors.

The Air Museum also hosts monthly special events, many of which involve flying activities and generally scheduled for the first Saturday of each month. Information about the special events can be obtained by calling The Air Museum at 909-597-3722.

GENERAL PATTON
MEMORIAL MUSEUM
★★★★

Photo by: General Patton Memorial Museum

Entrance to the Memorial Museum, Thirty miles East of Indio, CA

CA-L77 - CHIRIACO SUMMIT
CHIRIACO SUMMIT AIRPORT

(Area Code 619) 19

Restaurants Near Airport:
Summit Coffee Shop walk dist. Phone: 227-3227

Lodging: Hotel Datetree (30 miles west, Indio, CA) 800-292-5599; Indian Wells Hotel 800-248-3220.
Meeting Rooms: None reported
Transportation: None reported
Information: Patton Memorial Military Museum 227-3483.

Attractions:

General Patton Memorial and Museum within walking distance, Phone: 227-3483; The weekend before Veterans' Day attracts between 2,000 and 4,000 guest including high ranking officials. Live entertainment, music, Civil War and Indian encampments, food and beverage consessions, are all part of this galla event. For informaton call 227-3483.

Chiriaco Summit Coffee Shop:

The General Patton Memorial Museum and Chiriaco Summit Coffee Shop are located within walking distance, or 1/4 mile, from the Chiriaco Summit Airport. The restaurant serves hearty meals including breakfast, lunch and dinner. This combination truck stop, cafe and mini mart is open 24 hours a day (closed major holidays). Breakfast entrees include several egg dishes accompanied with sausage, pork chops, chicken fried steak, corned beef hash and, yes, Spam. French toast, buttermilk pancakes and biscuits and gravy are available. Their dinner selections include fried chicken, chicken strips, pork chops, liver & onions, New York strip steak and deep fried shrimp. Prices average $5.50 for breakfast and lunch, and around $7.00 to $12.00 for dinner. Guests can tour the memorial and learn about the veterans who served under General Patton, enjoy looking at variety of armored vehicles and tanks on display. Then top your day off with a meal at the Chiriaco Summit Coffee Shop before heading on to your next destination. The Annual Veterans' Day Celebration is held the weekend before Veterans' Day. It is an event that is enjoyed by everyone. (See Article). For restaurant information call 227-3227.

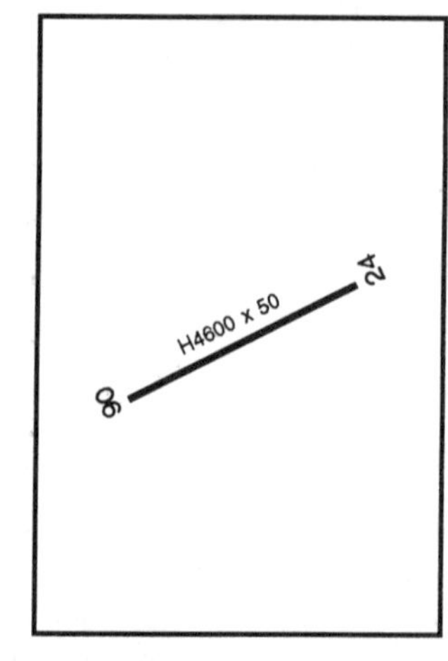

Airport Information:

CHIRIACO SUMMIT - CHIRIACO SUMMIT (L77)
1 mi northeast of town - (Indio, CA 30 miles west) N33-39.92 W115-42.63 Elev: 1713 Rwy 06-24: H4600x50 (Asph) Attended: unattended CTAF: 122.9 Notes: Pilot visibility is limited to 1400' from either end of Rwy 06-24; Also tie-down ropes etc. recommended due to windy conditions.
Airport Manager Phone: 227-3227

General Patton's Memorial Museum Desert Training Center:

It was in the middle of southeastern California's Mojave Desert... a bleak, inhospitable, remote, vast expanse of cactus, scrub and sand. Temperatures ranged from below freezing to 120 in the shade. There was little water and vegetation. Dust storms could blind men and cloudbursts were frequent. The area's elevations ranged from the desert floor to 7,000 feet above sea level.

But to Major General George Smith Patton Jr., U.S. Army, the land was nothing less than enchanting. It was in early March of 1942 when Patton, commander of the Army's First (I) Corps and his staff first surveyed the area. Patton had been ordered by the War Department to locate, establish and command a training center to train troops for desert warfare. The Army's rationale was that American forces soon would be required to fight the German enemy in North Africa. France had been defeated. The British had failed to hold the Balkans and Greece. And German General Rommel had arrived in Libya to join their Italian allies. The U.S. military felt that North Africa was the first place they could get the enemy.

So Patton, enamored with the area's endless terrain and super suitability for armored combat training, established the Desert Training Center in late March 1942, making his headquarters at Camp Young near Shavers Summit (now known as Chiriaco Summit) which today is the locale of the Patton Museum.

Construction of the Desert Training Center soon was underway and troop began arriving at once. The area was expanded in size and scope and ultimately was 350 miles wide and 250 miles deep, ranging from Pamona, CA eastward to Phoenix, AZ and from Yuma, AZ to Boulder City, NV. The area's name was changed to the California-Arizona Maneuver Area and Iron Mountain, Camp Granite, Camp Essex, Camp Ibis, Camp Hyder, Camp Horn, Camp Laquna, Camp Pilot Knob and Camp Bouse. The camps were massive tent cities containing tanks and repair shops, hospitals, aviation facilities and anti-aircraft and field artillery units.

The camps trained nearly 1 million American servicemen and women. CAMA was the world's largest military installation, both in size and population. In late July of 1943, for example, there were 10,996 officers, 514 flight personnel, 604 nurses and hospital attendants and 179,536 enlisted personnel assigned to the 11 camps, for a total of 191,620.

Training at the camps was rigid and exacting. Soldiers were required to run a mile in 10 minutes while carrying rifles and full packs. Troops trained throughout the hot days and sought shelter in tents at night. Water was strictly rationed and salt tablets were issued to ward off dehydration and heat prostration. Food was standard field rations, scorpions, tarantulas and rattlesnakes were held at bay by pouring diesel fuel on the ground near mess and living areas.

Photo by: General Patton Memorial Museum

One of several tanks on display at the Memorial.

Sand was everywhere... it found its way into food, water, weapons, engines, bedrolls, clothing, tents and trooper's eyes and mouths. Choking clouds of dust were omnipresent as tanks and other vehicles raced across the California, Arizona and Nevada deserts.

Patton commanded the camps for four months, departing in early August of 1942 to lead Operation Torch, the allied assault on German-held North Africa which began in November of that year. His contributions to the training, discipline and regimen at CAMA were numerous. Often piloting his own plane, he crisscrossed the maneuver area, giving orders by radio to the tank crews below. He called in experts on the desert who lectured him on living in that difficult environment. Noted among them were Roy Chapman Andrews, the famed explorer of Asia's Gobi Desert, and Sir Hubert Wilkins, the Australian-born authority on tropical clothing.

On April 30, 1944, two years after its inception, the California-Arizona Maneuver Area (CAMA) was closed by the Army, and abandoned to the mercies of the desert. But their legacy and the legacy of General George Patton remains, as manifested in the General George Patton Memorial Museum which has risen in the California desert near his headquarters at Camp Young.

The museum is a non profit institution run by a board of directors. This Memorial pays tribute to all veterans. The General Patton Memorial Museum is open 7 days a week between 9:30 a.m. and 4:30 p.m., closed Thanksgiving, Christmas and Easter. A 26-minute movie describes the museum, desert training center and Patton's war campaigns. Outdoors are 17 tanks and vehicles on display. Plan on at least 1 to 1-1/2 hours when touring the center. Admission is $3.50 for seniors 62 and above, $4.00 for adults and/or children over 12 years old, and under 12 years, free with adult. Group rates are also available.

A very interesting occasion is held each year at the memorial site attracting between 2,000 and 4,000 people. The weekend before Veterans' Day a celebration takes place. Special tribute and recognition is given to those veterans on active duty who serve and have served the

CA-3O8 - COALINGA HARRIS RANCH AIRPORT

(Area Code 209)

20

Harris Ranch Restaurant:

This combination family style and fine dining facility is located on the northeast side of the Coalinga Municipal Airport. The restaurant is within walking distance from aircraft parking. Their hours during the winter months are 7 a.m. to 10 p.m. and in the summer from 6 a.m. to 11 p.m. The specialties of the house include mostly beef entrees in addition to Mexican dishes, salads, hot and cold sandwiches, fish, chicken, duck, prawns and lobster. Their menu also includes a selection of appetizers. Buffets are served including items like beef, seafood and Mexican foods. The restaurant is decorated in early Californian decor and accented in Mexican. This facility contains various banquet accommodations which can handle a small group up to a large party of over 320 people. (Weddings, luncheons, meetings, etc.) For pilots on-the-go, meals can be prepared for carry-out. Average prices run $7.80 for breakfast, $10.00 for lunch and $18.00 for dinner. In addition to the restaurant, the Harris Ranch has 88 rooms and suites within walking distance from the airport and restaurant. For more information call 935-0717.

Restaurants Near Airport:

Fountain Court Dining Rm	Adj Arpt	Phone: 935-0717
Harris Ranch Restaurant	Adj Arpt	Phone: 935-0717
Jockey Club	Adj Arpt	Phone: 935-0717

Lodging: Harris Ranch Inn on premises.

Meeting Rooms: Harris Ranch Restaurant & Inn on airport.

Transportation: None reported

Information: Harris Ranch Restaurant & Inn 935-0717.

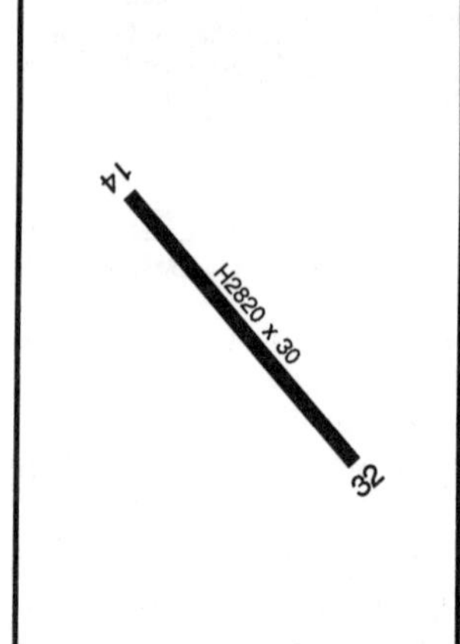

Airport Information:

COAlINGA - HARRIS RANCH (3O8)

9 mi northeast of town N36-14-.88 W120-14.26 Elev: 470 Fuel: 100LL Rwy 14-32: H2820x30 (Asph) Attended: 1400-0300Z Unicom: 122.9 Public Phone 24hrs Notes: Electrical P-line 30' AGL two tenths mile south of airport. Also: No landing fee

FBO: Harris Ranch Texaco Phone: 935-0717, 935-2939 or 935-0717 ext 592

CA-O22 - COLUMBIA
COLUMBIA AIRPORT

(Area Code 209)

21, 22

Columbia City Hotel:

This hotel contains a fine dining facility, located about 1 mile from the Columbia Airport. You can either walk along a marked path into town, information obtained from restaurant, or call the restaurant in advance and arrange transportation (very limited staff). The restaurant is part of a 10-room bed & breakfast inn. This dining facility is open for dinner Tuesday through Sunday from 5:00 to 8:30 p.m., and Sunday brunch between 11 a.m. and 2 p.m. Their dinner menu consists of a 4 course meal which includes a choice of appetizers, soup, salad, 5-6 entrees of your choice, and a dessert selection. Menus change monthly and feature the freshest ingredients of the season. Prices range from $26.00 to $31.00 for dinner and $7.00 to $9.00 for Sunday Brunch. Banquet facilities and private meeting rooms for up to 50 people can be arranged. Group lunches and dinner menus are also available. For more information call the restaurant at 532-1479.

Restaurants Near Airport:

Columbia City Hotel	1 mi	Phone: 532-1479
Columbia House	1 mi	Phone: 532-5134
Egg Cellar	1-1/4mi	Phone: 532-5988

lodging: Columbia City Hotel & Restaurant 532-1479; Columbia Inn 533-0446; Gem Motel 532-4508;
Meeting Rooms: The City Hotel can accommodate up to 50 people within their private meeting rooms or banquet facilities. Call 532-1479 for more information.
Transportation: Bald Eagle Aviation Rental Cars 533-4616; Enterprise 533-1759; EZ Rental Cars 532-2204; Hammond Ford 532-5593; Taxi service: Gold Country 533-1759; Vintage Cab 533-2181; Note: Columbia City Hotel may provide transportation depending on available staff. Call ahead to make arrangements in advance 532-1479.
Information: Columbia Chamber of Commerce at P.O. Box 1824 Columbia, CA 95310, 532-0150 or call Columbia State Historic Park at 532-4301 or 532-0150.

Columbia House:

The Columbia House is a family run operation open 8 a.m. to 5 p.m. on weekends and 8 a.m. to 3 p.m. weekdays. Specialties of the house include their 8 ounce char-broiled chicken breast and New York steak and their famous "Pastie" a turn over meat pie, prepared with either chicken, beef sirloin, pork or tenderloin. A full breakfast line is also available. Prices average $3.00 to $5.00 for most selections. The restaurant can accommodate up to 200 people. Groups are welcome. They will even open the restaurant during off hours to serve catered parties. The Columbia House provides casual dining. For information call 532-5134.

Attractions:

One of our readers informed us that Air-camping is very popular with many of the pilots in the region. Daily camping fees are $6.00. Contact the FBO's or airport manager at 533-5685, for more information. The Fallon Theater provides theater productions and performances to many vacationers year around. For information call the Columbia Chamber of Commerce at 532-0150; Also the Columbia State Historic Park became famous as the "Gem of the Southern Mines" during the great gold rush in the mid 1800s. More than 5,000 people crowded the streets. At today's prices over 1.5 billion dollars of the precious metal was brought in and weighed on the Fargo Express Company scales. As with many gold mining settlements, a great fire swept through this town on two separate occasions, but from the ashes sprang new and improved buildings made of fireproof brick and iron "Fire Doors" built to withstand future fires. Today this town has become a national monument preserved in a style that mirrors the very existence of life as it existed back in days of the great California Gold Rush. As a living community, Columbia State Historic Park provides a blend of historical museums, hotels, shops and restaurants in the traditional appearance as when they were first constructed over 135 years ago. Another attraction in the area is the Fallon Theater which provides productions and plays held year round. The Columbia Airport, located only a short distance from the town center, makes this attraction a convenient place to arrange a visit with your friends or a group fly-out. During your visit, you can walk the streets and visit shops, museums and restaurants while watching the local merchants ply their trades.

Photo by: Columbia City Hotel

Airport Information:

COLUMBIA - COLUMBIA AIRPORT (O22)
1 mi southwest of town N38-01.83 W120-24.87 Elev: 2118 Fuel: 80, 100LL, Jet-A
Rwy 17-35: H4670x75 (Asph) Rwy 11-29: 2600x100 (Turf) Attended: 1600-0100Z
Unicom: 123.05 Public Phone 24hrs Notes: Overnight Tiedowns (Single) $2.60, (Twins) $5.25; CAUTION: Deer on and in vicinity of airport; Rwy 11 departures prohibited due to conflict with main runway; Rwy 29 not recommended during winter operations from Nov.-Mar.; Ultralight activity; All flights over Columbia State Park prohibited; Consult Airport Facility Directory and AIM for updated information;

FBO: Bald Eagle Aviation,	**Phone: 533-4616**	**FBO: Courtney Aviation**	**Phone: 532-2345**
FBO: Airworld Enterprise,	**Phone: 533-2802**	**FBO: JS Aviation**	**Phone: 532-3855**
FBO: Columbia Aviation,	**Phone: 533-1900**		

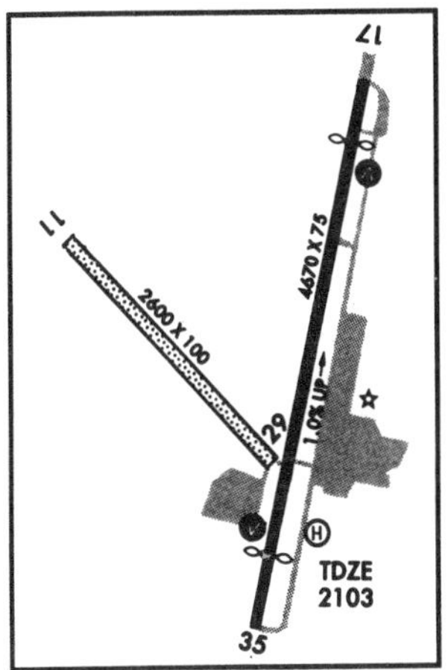

CA-CCR - CONCORD BUCHANAN FIELD

Restaurants Near Airport: (Area Code 510) **23**

Atrium Court (Sheraton) On Site Phone: 825-7700

Lodging: Concord Hilton (1 mile) 827-2000; Holiday Inn (1 mile, trans) 687-5500; Sheraton Concord Hotel (On Airport, trans) 825-7700.

Meeting Rooms: Hilton Concord (Convention facilities) 827-2000; Holiday Inn 687-5500; Sheraton Concord Hotel, (On Airport, Conference Center) 825-7700.

Transportation: Taxi Service: Bills 685-8280; Martinez 228-0420; Rental Cars: Avis 685-4400; Budget 689-7685; Dollar 674-0600; Hertz 685-2686.

Information: Concord Convention & Visitors Bureau, 2151 Salvio Street, Concord, CA 94520, Phone: 685-1184.

Atrium Court Restaurant (Sheraton Concord):

The Atrium Court Restaurant is located within the Sheraton Hotel on the Concord Buchanan Airport. According to the restaurant management you can park your aircraft in the transient area and simply walk through the gate to the hotel. This combination family style and fine dining facility is open 7 days a week from 6:30 a.m. to 2 p.m. for lunch, then re-opens for dinner between 5 p.m. and 10 p.m. Their menu offers selections like prime rib, steaks, pasta, all types of sandwiches, soup and salads and a full breakfast line offered until 11:30 a.m. Average prices run $6.00 for breakfast, $9.00 for lunch and $16.00 for dinner choices. The main dining area can accommodate 150 people. On Sunday they offer a champagne brunch from 10 a.m. to 2 p.m. The atmosphere is casual and provides a magnificent decor, within their atrium and balconies overlooking a beautiful courtyard, planting areas with streams and a swimming pool. In-flight catering is also provided by the Atrium Court Restaurant. The Sheraton Hotel also has accommodations for group meetings and conferences. There are 323 rooms for lodging as well as many other amenities such as a putting green, indoor swimming pool, spa, fitness center, pool tables, and live entertainment in the Hangar Lounge Call 510-825-7700.

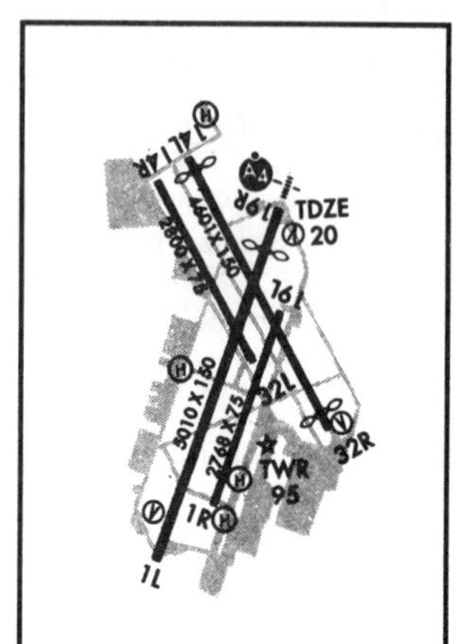

Airport Information:

CONCORD - BUCHANAN FIELD (CCR)
1 mi west of town N37-59.37 W122-03.42 Elev: 23 Fuel: 100, 100LL, Jet-A1+
Rwy 14L-32R: H4601x150 (Asph-Conc-Pfc) Rwy 01L-19R: H4400x150 (Asph-Conc Pfc)
Rwy 14R-32L: H2800x75 (Asph) Rwy 01R-19L: H2768x75 (Asph) Attended: continuously
Atis: 124.7 Unicom: 122.95 Concord Tower: 123.9 (Left runways), 119.7 (Right runways)
Gnd Con: 121.9 Clnc Del: 118.75
FBO: Navajo Aviation Phone: 685-1150
FBO: Pacific States Aviation Phone: 685-4400

CA-AJO - CORONA CORONA MUNICIPAL AIRPORT

(Area Code 909) **24**

Restaurants Near Airport:
Bob's Cafe On Site Phone: 734-2570

Lodging: Comfort Inn 371-7185; Crest Motel (4 miles) 737-4817; Flaming Arrow Motel 737-0491; Kings Inn (2 miles) 734-4241; Motel 6 (2 miles) 735-6408; Travel Lodge (2 miles) 272-4800.

Meeting Rooms: None Reported

Transportation: Yellow Cab 684-1234; Also Rental Cars: Budget 371-3540; Enterprise 272-8000; Hobo 736-1411; Thrifty 371-4094; Ugly Duckling 736-0458.

Information: Long Beach Area Convention and Visitors Council, One World Trade Center, #300, Long Beach, CA 90831, Phone: 436-3645 or 800-4-LB-STAY.

Bob's Cafe:

Bob's Cafe is located on the east end of the airport and is reported to be within walking distance from aircraft parking area. According to the airport office the restaurant is situated near the transient line. This cafe is open between 6 a.m. and 5 p.m. Menu items include omelets, chili, hamburgers, chicken fried steak, steak burgers, salads and soups as well as desserts and pies. Their dining room can seat about 100 persons and they also have an outdoor patio that can seat 45 to 50 persons. Meals can be prepared for carry-out if requested. For more information about Bob's Cafe call 734-2570.

Airport Information:

CORONA - CORONA MUNICIPAL AIRPORT (AJO)
3 mi northwest of town N33-53.86 W117-36.15 Elev: 533 Fuel: 80, 100LL
Rwy 07-25: H3200x60 (Asph) Remarks: Attended: 1600-0200Z Unicom: 122.8
Public Phone 24hrs Notes: Overnight parking $3.00 per night all aircraft.
FBO: Corona Air Service (Fuel) Phone: 737-1300
FBO: Chrisaire Aviation (Self serve) Phone: 736-6151

CA-O33 - EUREKA
EUREKA MUNICIPAL

(Area Code 707)

25

(Meals served only to overnight B & B Guests)

Samoa Airport Bed & Breakfast:

The Samoa Airport Bed & Breakfast is situated right on the airport. You can find this establishment by looking for a white building on the east side of the runway. The airport was used as a blimp base during WWII. The operators of this Bed and Breakfast remodeled the offers quarters to accommodate their guests. They decorated the interior with aviation memorabilia. According to the management the Bed & Breakfast contains a lounge and dining room. They serve breakfast, juice, egg dishes, muffins, coffee and fruit. Many of their guest are fighter pilots that use their facility for overnight lodging. Their room rate is $60.00 per night. They invite guests to enjoy an evening with clean comfortable and quiet accommodations. For more information you can call them at 445-0765.

Restaurants Near Airport:

Samoa Airport Bed & Breakfast	On Site	Phone: 445-0765
Samoa Cook House	3 mi N.	Phone: 442-1659

Lodging: Samoa Airport Bed & Breakfast (On Site) 445-0765

Meeting Rooms: Samoa Airport Hospitality Hall has accommodations for 60 plus persons.

Transportation: Yellow Cab 442-4551; Enterprise Car Rental 800-325-8007; Avis 800-831-2847.

Information: Eureka/Humboldt County Convention and Visitors Bureau, 1034 Second Street, Eureka, CA 95501 707-443-5097, 800-338-7352 (within CA). 800-346-3482 (outside CA).

Attractions:

Airport is situated adjacent to beach. Activities include sport fishing. Redwoods within 30 min drive of field. Also Old Town - Eureka.

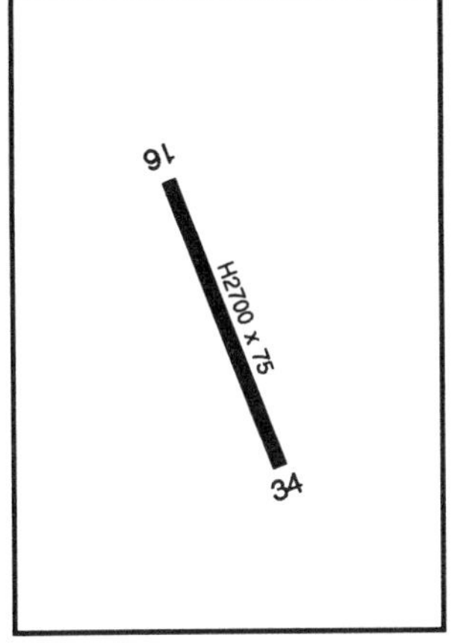

Airport Information:

EUREKA - EUREKA MUNICIPAL (O33)
2 mi west of city N40-46.86 W124-12.74 Elev: 20 Rwy 16-34: H2700x75 (Asph)
CTAF: 122.9 Public Ohone 24 hrs. Notes: No landing fee's or overnight fee's for guest of Samoa B & B; Day use only, airport reported CLOSED nights. AFD reportes "Unattended"
FBO: Airport Manager Phone: 441-4186
FBO: Samoa Airport B & B Phone: 445-0765

CA-EKA - EUREKA
MURRAY FIELD

(Area Code 707)

26

Pacific Clipper Cafe:

The Pacific Clipper Cafe can be found in the terminal, and Northern Air FBO building. This cafe serves a menu consisting of a variety of entrees. However, they are most famous for their prize winning cheese cake. On Sunday, they offer a champagne brunch. Prices off their menu range between $5.50 for breakfast and $6.00 for lunch. Their restaurant hours are from 7 a.m. to 3 p.m. on Tuesday through Saturday, and 9 a.m. to 2 p.m. on Sunday. Arranging group get-togethers or dinner parties are no problem. Likewise, they are also available for catering, should the need arise. They are closed on Monday. The decor of the restaurant portrays a unique aeronautical theme, particularly directed toward flying boats. For more information call the restaurant at 444-9338.

Restaurants Near Airport

Pacific Clipper Cafe	On Site	Phone: 444-9338

Lodging: Eureka Inn, (3 miles from airport) 7th and 1st street, Eureka, 442-6441; Red Lion Inn, (2 miles from airport) 1929 4th Street, Eureka, 445-0844

Transportation: Yellow Cab 442-4551; Contact FBO for availability of rental cars.

Conference: Meeting rooms are available at the Pacific Clipper/ Northern Air, seating about 12 persons, and located on the field. Generally available between 7 a.m. and 5 p.m.

Information: Eureka Chamber of Commerce, 2112 Broadway, Eureka, CA 95501, or call 707-442-3738 or 800-356-6381.

Attractions: Eureka Municipal Golf Course, 4750 Fairway Drive in Eureka, Phone:443-4808; Patricks Point State Park in the town of Trinidad about 23 miles north of airport.

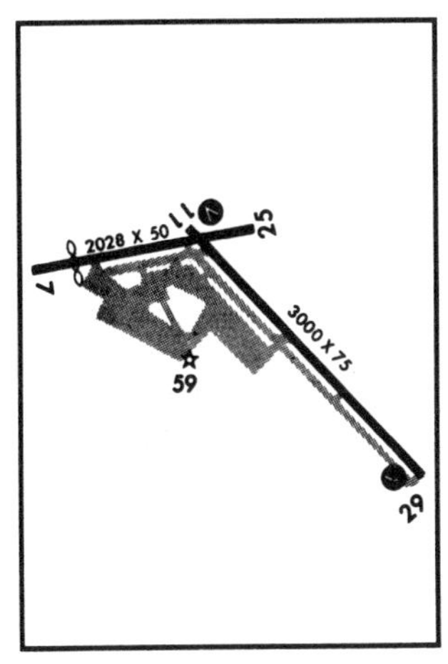

Airport Information:

EUREKA - MURRAY FIELD (EKA)
3 mi east of town N40-48.26 W124-06.90 Elev: 07 Fuel: 100
Rwy 11-29: H3000x75 (ASPH) Rwy 07-25: H2030x50 (ASPH) Attended: 1630-0130Z
Unicom: 122.7 Public Phone 24 hrs
FBO: Northern Air Phone: 445-9653 or 443-3179

CA-089 - FALL RIVER MILLS
FALL RIVER MILLS AIRPORT

(Area Code 916) 27

Fall River Mills Golf Course and Coffee Shop:

The Fall River Mills Golf course is located about 2 miles from the Fall River Mills Airport. Free courtesy transportation is available to fly in customers. Their is a small coffee shop connected with the pro shop. The snack bar is open from 7 a.m. to 3 p.m. and depending on the number of golfers, remains open throughout the dinner hour. Their menu includes a variety of sandwiches like French dip, hamburgers, cheeseburgers, hot-dogs, fries and potato chips. A special meal of the day is usually prepared by the staff. Average prices run $6.00 for lunch. Groups as large as 60 people have been served in the past. If flying in with a sizable group, please let them know in advance so they can accommodate your party. The pro shop is in the same building as the snack bar. The golf course is a championship 18 hole course. Reservations and tee times can be reserved as far as two week in advance if needed. For more information you can call the pro-shop at 336-5555 or the snack bar at 336-6575.

Restaurants Near Airport:

Country Club Restaurant	1 mi W.	Phone: 336-6576
Fall River Golf Course Cafe	2 mi (Trans)	Phone: 336-5555
Fall River Hotel & Rest.	1/2 mi W.	Phone: 336-5550
Friends Cafe	1/2 mi W.	Phone: 336-5120

Lodging: Fall River Hotel & Restaurant, (1/2 mile west of airport), Phone: 336-5550

Meeting Rooms: Contact airport manager at 336-5669 or Fall River Hotel & Restaurant at 336-5550.

Transportation: Contact the airport manager at 336-5669.

Attractions:

Fall River Valley Golf & Country Club is located 2 miles from the airport with free transportation. Phone: 336-5555; Also Fall River is a Blue Ribbon trout fishery as in nearby Hat Creek. Fly fishing is one of the activities that is enjoyed by many in this area.

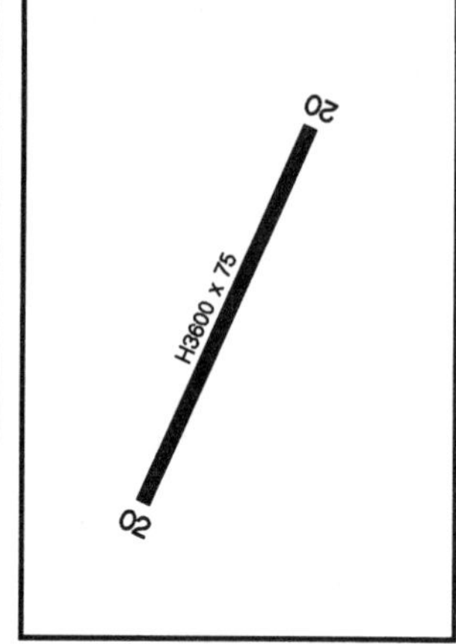

Airport Information:

FALL RIVER MILLS - FALL RIVER MILLS AIRPORT (089)
1 mile north of town N43-01.13 W121-26.00 Elev: 3323 Fuel: 100LL, Jet-A
Rwy 02-20: H3600x75 (ASPH) Attended: 1600-0100Z Unicom: 122.8
Public Phone 24hrs **Notes: For attendant other hours call 916-336-6115 (Service Charge);**
Ramp Use Fee large aircraft is $10.00/landing; Tie down: $5.00 twin & $3.00 single.

CA-FAT - FRESNO
FRESNO AIR TERMINAL AIRPORT

(Area Code 209) 28

CA1 Services:

Concession Aire, Inc. has constructed a new dining facility located in the main terminal building at the Fresno Air Terminal Airport. During our conversation with the corporate office we learned this new establishment combines a cafe with a deli and fine dining restaurant. Their hours are from 5 a.m. to 8 p.m. 7 days a week. A coffee shop adjacent to the restaurant will provide freshly baked goods as well as a deli case with sandwiches, espresso bar and yogurt bar. On the other side of the coffee shop is the Kitty Hawk Lounge which serves hot appetizers and gourmet items. This is a fine place to relax and enjoy yourself between flights or while waiting for your party. From the lounge area, guests are able to view the activity on the ramp as well as arriving and departing aircraft. In addition to the restaurant, Concessionaire, Inc. provides In-flight catering for business aircraft, local-charter and scheduled air carrier flights. Most of the fixed base operators should have access to menus for that purpose. For more information contact the restaurant at 251-8208.

Restaurants Near Airport:

CA1 Services	On Site	Phone: 251-8208
Hill Fire Restaurant	1/2 mi	Phone: 252-4401
Tower Coffee Shop	On Site	Phone: 255-8101

Lodging: Airport Piccadilly (Adj Airport, trans) 251-6000; Holiday Inn (1 block, free trans) 252-3611.

Meeting Rooms: Airport Piccadilly 251-6000; Holiday Inn 252-3611.

Transportation: Courtesy and taxi service available at airport; Rental Cars: Avis 251-5001; Budget 251-5515; Dollar 252-4000; Hertz 251-5055; National 251-5577.

Information: Fresno Visitors Bureau, 808 M Street, Fresno, CA 93721, Phone: 233-0836 or 800-788-0836

Attractions:

Pilot shop is located on the airport (9 a.m. to 5:30 p.m.). For information call the California Pilot Ship at at 251-1913.

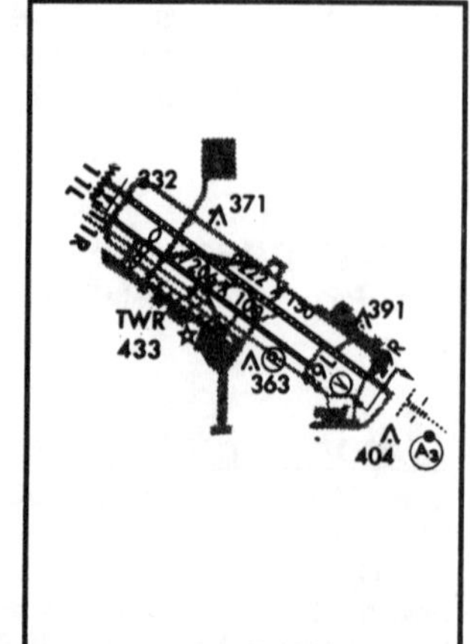

Airport Information:

FRESNO - FRESNO AIR TERMINAL AIRPORT (FAT)
5 mi northeast of town N36-46.57 W119-43.09 Elev: 333 Fuel: 100, Jet-A
Rwy 11L-29R: H9222x150 (Asph-Pfc) Rwy 11R-29L: H7206x100 (Asph) Attended: continuously Atis: 121.35 Unicom: 122.95 App/Dep Con: 132.35, 119.6, 118.5 Tower: 118.2
Gnd Con: 121.7 Clnc Del: 124.35
FBO: Corporate Aircraft Phone: 251-1555 FBO: Western Piper Sales Phone: 252-2926
FBO: Wofford Flying Serv Phone: 454-7501

CA-FCH - FRESNO
FRESNO CHANDLER DOWNTOWN

(Area Code 209)

29

Chabela's Mexican/American Restaurant:

The Flying Saucer Restaurant is located right in front of the transit aircraft parking ramp. This cafe styled restaurant is open 7 days a week between 7:00 a.m. and 3:00 p.m. They specialize in preparing Mexican cuisine. Some of the items presented are hamburgers, bacon cheeseburgers, beef, chicken and pork chowmaine, rice vegetable and stir fried selections as well as a full breakfast line. Average prices run $3.90 for breakfast and about $5.00 for most luncheon selections. Their main dining area can seat up to 25 persons comfortably, with counter and table service. A view of the airport can be enjoyed from the restaurant through large windows. Groups can, and often do arrange meeting and social events at this facility, making use of their conference and banquet rooms available to accommodate up to 30 persons. The decor of the dining area displays an aviation theme with model airplanes hanging from the ceiling. Meals can also be prepared to go. For more information about the Flying Saucer call 497-1416.

Restaurants Near Airport:

Chabela's	On Site	Phone: 497-1416
Chihuahua (Mex)	2 mi E.	Phone: 266-9964
El Torito Rest.	3 mi SE.	Phone: 485-2991

Lodging: Holiday Inn Cntr. Plaza (3-1/2 miles) 268-1000; Fresno Hilton 485-9000.

Meeting Rooms: A conference room is available on the airport, for information call airport superintendent at 488-4456. The Chabela's (On Site) has a banquet room reported available for up to 30 persons.

Transportation: American Cab 485-0404; Bull Dog Cab 224-1071; City Cab 228-8282; Checker Cab 456-1234.

Information: Fresno Visitors Bureau, 808 M Street, Fresno, CA 93721, Phone: 233-0836 or 800-543-8488.

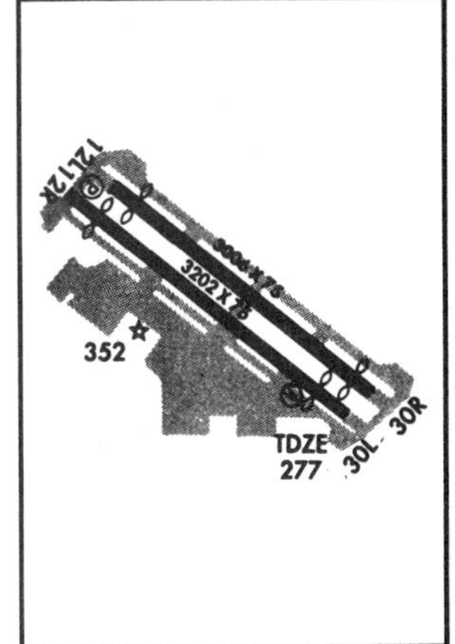

Airport Information:

FRESNO - FRESNO CHANDLER DOWNTOWN AIRPORT (FCH)
2 mi west of town N36-43.94 W119-49.19 Elev: 278 Fuel: 80, 100LL
Rwy 12R-30L: H3202x75 (Asph) Rwy 12L-30R: H3006x75 (Asph) Attended: 1600-0100Z Unicom: 123.0 Public Phone 24hrs Notes: Parking fees $2.00/day after first 4 hours; Jeromye Avery, C.A.E., Airport Superintendent 488-4456.
FBO: Buchner Aero Specialties **Phone: 233-9547**
FBO: Frank X. Ruiz Avionics, Inc. **Phone: 233-0700**

CA-FUL - FULLERTON
FULLERTON MUNICIPAL AIRPORT

(Area Code 714)

30

Tartuffles:

Tartuffles is a combination family style restaurant and coffee shop. This facility can easily be reached by walking from the aircraft tie-down area, according to the restaurant management. They are open 7 days a week between 7 a.m. and 4 p.m., except on holidays like Christmas, New Years Eve and Thanksgiving etc. Their menu includes items such as hamburgers, club sandwiches, grilled ham and cheese sandwiches, chicken salad plates, French dip, and a nice salad bar available from lunch until closing. Average prices run $4.00 for breakfast, and $5.50 for lunch. Daily specials are also available. One such special very popular with their customers is the 1/2 sandwich, soup and salad bar selection offered for only $4.75. The decor of this establishment is modern and clean with booths and tables in addition to an enclosed patio that can seat about 30 people. The main dining room can also accommodate up to 80 persons. Larger groups and parties are welcome, with advance notice appreciated. Meals can be ordered to go as well. For more information call 870-9235.

Restaurants Near Airport:

Tartuffles	On Site	Phone: 870-9235
The Hobbit	8.5 mi SE.	Phone: 997-1972

Lodging: Holiday Inn (1-1/2 mile, Free trans) 522-7000.

Meeting Rooms: Holiday Inn (Free trans) 522-7000; Griswolds (Convention facilities) 635-9000.

Transportation: Taxi Service: Yellow Cab 535-2211; West Coast Cab 547-8000; Rental Cars: Avis 871-8271; Budget 995-3454; Dollar 773-9527; Nationwide 680-0855.

Information: Anaheim /Orange County Visitor & Convention Bureau, 800 West Katella Avenue, P.O. Box 4270, Anaheim, CA 92803, Phone: 714-999-8999.

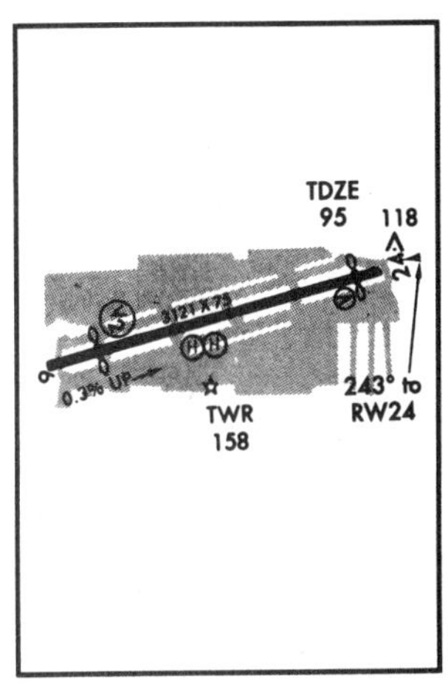

Airport Information:

FULLERTON - FULLERTON MUNICIPAL AIRPORT (FUL)
3 mi west of town N33-52.32 W117-58.79 Elev: 96 Fuel: 100LL, Jet-A Rwy 06-24: H3121x75 (Asph) Attended: 1400-0600Z Atis: 125.05 Unicom: 122.95 Tower: 119.1 Gnd Con: 121.8 Public Phone 24hrs Notes: No landing fees, Overnight parking $5.25 singles, $7.50 twins, $10.00 cabins class; Airport Notes: Rwy 6 is primary calm wind runway after tower closes. Climb to 1100 prior to turns (Follow R/R tracks) R/W heading till 800' or beach blvd.
FBO: Aviation Facilities, Inc. **Phone: 870-9931**
FBO: General Aviation **Phone: 526-6611**

CA-Q68 - GROVELAND PINE MOUNTAIN LAKE

(Area Code 209) 31, 32

Corsair Coffee Shop:

The Corsair Coffee Shop is located on the southwest corner of the Pine Mountain Lake Airport near Groveland, California. This family-style restaurant is easy to find and is situated about 100 yards from the aircraft transit parking lot. They are open Mondays from 8 a.m. to 2 p.m., Thursdays and Fridays from 8 a.m. to 7 p.m., and Saturdays and Sundays from 8 a.m. to 2 p.m. Their menu includes breakfast items that are served all day. For lunch a variety of sandwiches are offered including steak, hamburgers, cheeseburgers, sausage, patty melts, BLT's, tuna, turkey, and ham & cheese. Their dinner entrees include sirloin steak, deep fried chicken, chicken nuggets, served daily; chicken fried steak as a special on Thursdays, and sliced roast turkey that is carved from a special roast served as a special on Fridays. This is one of the favorites with many customers. This dish comes with dressing, gravy, vegetable, cranberry sauce and bread. They even offer a child's plate. Average prices run 85 cents to $7.00 for breakfast. For lunch prices range from $2.25 to $7.00. And for dinner choices range from $7.00 to $9.00. The restaurant has lots of pictures and models of airplanes in addition to aviation magazines and books. They often prepare meals for local club fly-ins when advance notice is given. The restaurant has seating for 25 persons and some outdoor seating available in the summer months. For information call 962-6793.

The Inn at Sugar Pine Ranch: (Bed & Breakfast)

This bed and breakfast is located about 3 or 4 miles from the Groveland Pine Mountain Lake Airport. One of our readers landed at this airport and chose to stay at The Inn at Sugar Pine Ranch for a few days. He was so impressed with this facility, that he asked the management to contact us so we could place them in our book. After speaking with the management I can understand why this particular facility should be included. This bed & breakfast is situated on 60 acres of countryside. The refurbished 1860 farm house containing the lodging facility was at one time part of a wood mill. The farm house was enlarged in 1905 to include more space, it contained three private rooms with private baths. The up-town cottage has four rooms with private baths and entrances. Also there are five separate cottages in the pines all with private baths. Today the land contain stands of sugar pines, oaks and incense cedars that add to the peaceful country setting. A national forest adjoins the property across the street. If planning to visit points of interest in the area, this bed & breakfast makes for a nice central base from which to make short excursions to local attractions. Yosemit e National Park and the Cathedral Mountain Range is situated about 22 miles east of their property. Additional attractions include historical gold mining towns in the area and river rafting. Transportation to and from the airport can be arranged by calling the inn. Rental cars can also be obtained at the airport. For more information about The Inn at Sugar Pine Ranch call 962-7823.

Restaurants Near Airport:

Corsair Coffee Shop	On Site	Phone: 962-6793
The Inn at Sugar Pine B&B	3-4 mi	Phone: 962-7823

Lodging: Groveland Hotel & Restaurant (trans, 4 miles) 962-4000; Hotel Charlotte (4 miles) 962-6455; Bed & Breakfast Inn at Sugar Pine Ranch (3-4 mi trans) 962-7823; Mother Lode 962-7057.

Transportation: Rental cars: Johnnie's Chevron 962-6234; Also: Mother Load Aviation (FBO) can help arrange transportation by calling 962-6472.

Information: Modesto Convention & Visitors Bureau, 1114 J Street, P.O. Box 844, Modesto CA 95353, Phone; 577-5757.

Airport Information:

GROVELAND - PINE MOUNTAIN LAKE (Q68)
3 mi northeast of town N37-51.70 W120-10.71 Elev: 2930 Fuel: 80, 100LL Rwy 09-27: H3625x50 (Asph) Attended: 1600-0100Z Unicom: 123.05 Public Phone 24hrs
Notes: Fuel available through unicom; Fee for overnight parking. Transient parking avbl. Ldg fee.
FBO: Airport Manager (off site) Phone: 533-5685
FBO: Mother Lode Aviation Phone: 962-6472

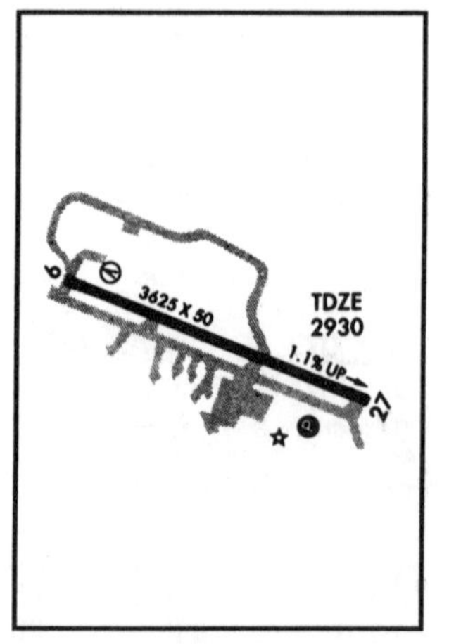

CA-Q69 - GUALALA OCEAN RIDGE

(Area Code 707)

Gualala Country Inn: (Dining nearby)

The Gualala Country Inn is a lodging facility situated within the town of Gualala, California. The town offers a casual and unhurried setting to enjoy the spectacular Pacific Ocean. Recreational activities include camping, cycling, hiking, beaching, whale watching. bird and wildlife watching, sailing, scuba diving, river swimming, tennis, golf, horseback riding and picnicking. There are also excellent boutiques, original craft shops, and art galleries to explore. Within the town dining possibilities range from casual snacks to gourmet cuisine. The people at the Gualala Country Inn will be happy to shuttle guests from the airport to their establishment. According to the management, once you arrive at their location, ground transportation is not necessary because most dining and downtown shops are within walking distance. The Inn overlooks the Pacific Ocean, Gualala Beach and river. It also offers an excellent vantage point to watch the fall and spring migration of the California Gray Whales. Rooms are tastefully decorated with nostalgic oak furniture, warm comforters, and queen size beds. Their Surf, Sunset, & Sea Spray rooms have woodburning fireplaces and a two person whirlpool spa. Room rates run between $71.00 and $145.00/night. All rooms have private baths, telephones, and cable color TV. For information call 800-564-4466 in California or 707-884-4343 outside California.

Restaurants Near Airport:

Dining within town	0 miles	N/A
St. Orres	5-7 mi	884-3335

Lodging: Gualala Country Inn (Free arpt. trans.) 884-4343; St Orres 884-3303; Whale Watch 884-3667.
Meeting Rooms: Sea Ranch Lodge (Pvt. Airstrip) 785-2371;
Transportaton: Gualala Country Inn will provide guests with free transportation to Inn 884-4343;
Information: Fort Bragg-Mendocino Coast Chamber of Commerce, 322 N. Main St, P.O. Box 1141, Fort Bragg, CA 95437. Phone: 961-6300.

Attractions: The Gualala River has ancient forests with towering redwoods. Enjoy sunbathing in the summer and steelhead fishing in the winter. Point Arena Lighthouse is another popular attraction with a 115 foot tall structure. Tours are given, call 882-2777; Sea Ranch Golf Links are open to the public (nine holes) 785-2371; Horseback riding through back country trails and giant redwood forests, call Gualala Country Inn 884-4343 or Sea Ranch Lodge 785-2371 for local information.

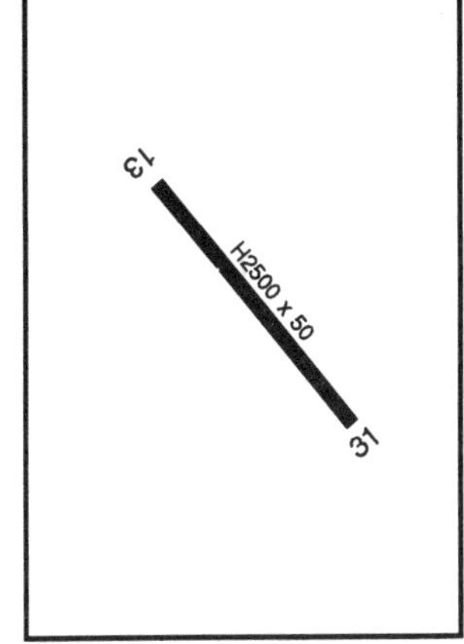

Airport Information:

GUALALA - OCEAN RIDGE (Q69)
3 north of town N38-48.08 W123-31.82 Elev: 940 Rwy 13-31: H2500x50 (Asph) Attended: unattended. Unicom: 122.8 Notes: Airport avalable for use from 1400-0600Z only. CLOSED all other hours. Deer frequently on runway. Rwy 13-31 undulated. Extreme turbulance in windy conditions. Consult Airport Facility Directory for further information. Also "Anchor Bay MOA" overlies region.
Airport Informaton: Phone: 707-884-3573 or 884-3579

CA-HAF - HALF MOON BAY HALF MOON BAY - HALF MOON BAY

(Area Code 415)

34

The Shore Bird:

Known as "Cape Cod on the California Coast", This popular restaurant boasts a unique Cape Cod building and seaside location, and is located only 1/2 mile southeast of the Half Moon Bay Airport. To reach the restaurant park your plane on the south end of the airport and follow the path across the foot bridge towards the harbor (About 100 yard walk). Fresh flowers, a garden patio, and fireplaces in the bar and dining rooms add to the restaurants cozy and romantic atmosphere. Umbrella covered tables offer guests "Outdoor Waterfront Dining". Fresh seafood is their specialty, but a varied menu also includes steaks and pastas. Homemade salad dressings and desserts are also a specialty. Sunday Brunch is a particular favorite because of a wide variety of unusual brunch entrees. Each lady at brunch or dinner receives a long-stemmed rose. The dining rooms and a more casual Seafood Cafe all have views of Pillar Point Harbor and the ocean. Located just north of Half Moon Bay, at the edge of the harbor. Prices average $8.00 to $15.00 for most selections. The restaurant is open 7 days a week from 11:30 a.m. to 9 p.m. on Monday through Friday, 11:30 a.m. to 9 p.m. on Saturday and from 11:00 a.m. to 9 p.m. on Sunday. Continuous service is provided in the Seafood Cafe from 11:30 a.m. daily. For information call 728-5541.

Restaurants Near Airport:

Half Moon Bay Coffee	On Site	Phone: 573-3701
Harbor Inn	1 mi SE	Phone: 726-2329
Pillar Point Inn	1/2 mi SE	Phone: 728-7377
Shore Bird	1/2 mi SE	Phone: 728-5541

Lodging: Mill Rose (Local Airport Transportation) 726-9794; Best Western Half Moon Lodge 726-9000; Pillar Point 728-7377.
Meeting Rooms: Best Western Half Moon Lodge 726-9000; Pillar Point 728-7377.
Transportation: Yellow Cab 368-9999; Coast (Rental) Car At terminal; Janies Ford (Rental) 726-4496
Information: San Francisco Conv. & Visitors Bureau, P.O. Box 6977, San Francisco, CA 94101, Phone: 415-974-6900.

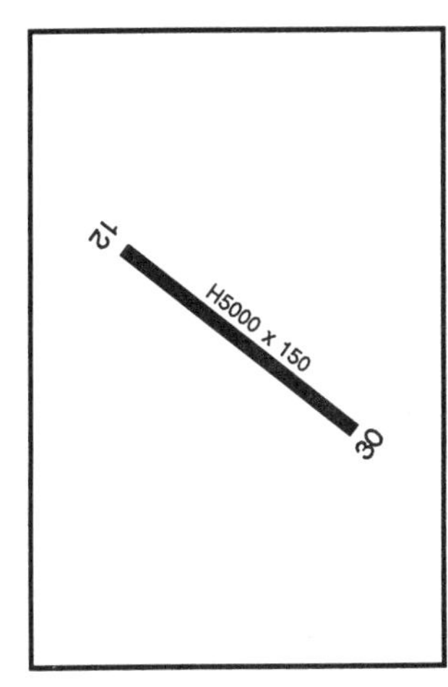

Airport Information:

HALF MOON BAY - HALF MOON BAY AIRPORT (HAF)
5 mi northwest of town N37-30.83 W122-30.07 Elev: 67 Fuel: 100LL Rwy 12-30: H5000x150 (Asph-Conc) Attended: 1600-0100Z Unicom: 122.8 Public Phone 24hrs
Notes: No landing fee. Transient parking $4.00 per night.
West Coast Aviation Phone: 728-3323

Photo Compliments of The Shore Bird Restaurant

The Shore Bird Restaurant has been in service since 1970

CA-36S - HAPPY CAMP
HAPPY CAMP AIRPORT

(Area Code 916) 35

Indian Creek Cafe:

The Indian Creek Cafe is located 1/2 mile from the Happy Camp Airport. You can call the restaurant after landing and they will come and pick you up, or you can simply walk to their facility. This restaurant is a fine dining facility, and is open from 6 a.m. to 8:30 p.m. on weekdays. On weekends they are open from 7 a.m. to 8:30 p.m. (Closed the last 2-3 weeks in December). They have a large menu featuring seafood, Mexican, steaks, chicken, vegetarian meals, home-made breads, soups, and desserts along with daily specials. Prices run $6.00 for breakfast, $7.00 for lunch and $14.00 for dinner. The decor is western and caters to groups if advance notice is given. All items from their 20 page menu can be prepared for carry-out. This restaurant has been awarded a "AAA" rating. For reservations you can call 493-5180.

Restaurants Near Airport:

Elk Creek Lodge	1-3mi E.	Phone: 493-2208
Indian Creek Cafe	1/2 mi E.	Phone: 493-5180
The Woodsman Cafe	3/4 mi E.	Phone: 493-2733

Lodging: Elk Creek Campground at Happy Camp, CA offers lodging and entertainment for fly-in guests (Free Pick-up) 493-2208. Forest Lodge (1 mile) 493-5424; Rustic Inn (1 mile) 493-2658;

Transportation: The Indian Creek Cafe will provide transportation for fly-in guests. Also Elk Creek Campground will pick-up.

Information: Happy Camp Chamber of Commerce, 63810 Hwy. 96, Happy Camp, CA 96039, Phone: 916-493-2900.

Attractions:

Eagle Nest Golf Course (20 miles north) 22112 Klamath River Road, Klamath River, CA 465-9276; Beaver Creek Lodge (20 miles north) 16606 Hwy 96, Klamath River, CA 465-2331; Wilderness Packers (2 miles south) 313 Indian Creek Road, Happy Camp, CA 493-2793; Elk Creek Lodge is located about 1 mile from the Happy Camp Airport and offers camping, fishing and various outdoor activities as well as motel suites. They will pick up guests at the airport. For informaton call 493-2208.

Airport Information:

HAPPY CAMP - HAPPY CAMP AIRPORT (36S)

0 mi southwest of town N41-47.44 W123-23.34 Elev: 1209 Rwy 04-22: H3000x50 (Asph)

Attended: unattended CTAF: 122.9 Public Phone 24hrs Notes: None reported.

Airport Informaton: Phone: 916-842-8250

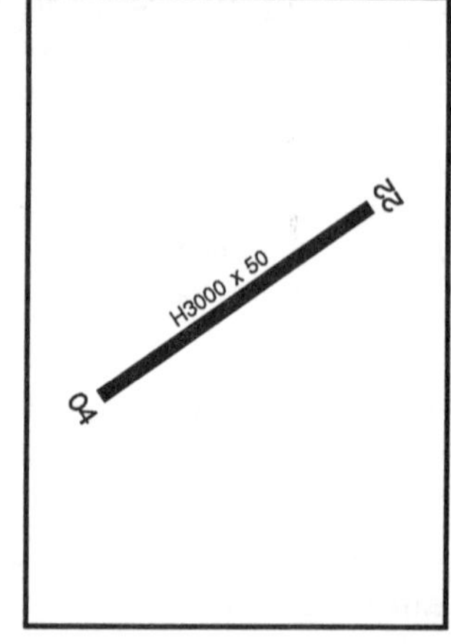

CA-HHR - HAWTHORNE
HAWTHORNE MUNICIPAL

(Area Code 310) 36

Nat's Airport Cafe:

Nat's Airport Cafe is located on the Hawthorne Municipal Airport. This family restaurant is open Monday through Friday between 6:30 a.m. and 8 p.m. and Saturday and Sunday from 7 a.m. to 4 p.m. Specialties on their menu include prime rib dinners, turkey, steaks, club sandwiches, Eggs Benedict, omelets, homemade biscuits, rolls, pies and pastries. Daily specials are also offered including soup or salad and dessert. Average prices run $4.00 for breakfast, $5.00 for lunch and $6.00 for dinner. The restaurant has a contemporary decor. Banquet rooms are available with seating up to 500 people. Nat's Airport Cafe is more than happy to accommodate catered meals for small or large groups and parties. In-flight catering is also available. For more information call Nat's Airport Cafe at 973-4152.

Restaurants Near Airport:
Nat's Airport Cafe On Site Phone: 973-4152

Lodging: Cockatoo Hotel 1 mi 679-2291; Ramada Inn 1-2/2 mi 536-9800.

Meeting Rooms: Banquet or group luncheons available through Nat's Airport Cafe (On Site) 973-4152.

Transportation: Taxi Service: Gardena 538-5111; Rental Cars: Call FBO to arrange.

Attractions:

Beach 3-1/2 miles west of airport; Hollywood Park Race Track 3 miles north with casino. Western Museum of Flight; Great Western Forum 2-1/2 miles northeast; Dodgers Stadium 7 miles north.

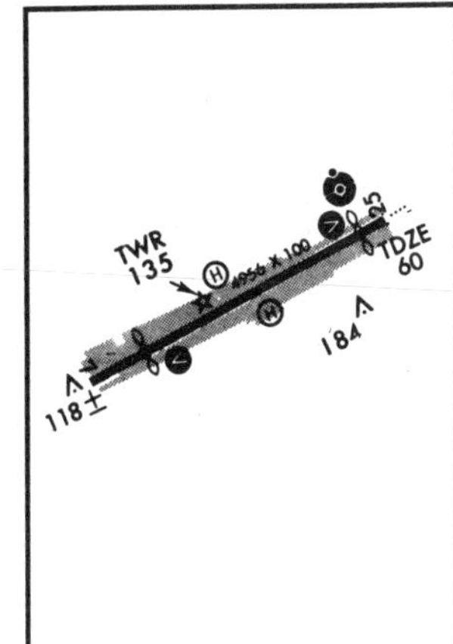

Airport Information:

HAWTHORNE - HAWTHORNE MUNICIPAL (HHR)
1 mi east of town N33-55.37 W118-20.11 Elev: 63 Fuel: 100LL, Jet-A Rwy 07-25: H4956x100 (Conc) Attended: 1500-0400 Z Atis: 118.4 Tower: 121.1 Gnd Con: 125.0 Notes: Fuel available during schedualed times. call 310-332-5241; CAUTION: Check AFD for information.

FBO: City of Hawthorne **Phone: 970-7215**
FBO: Northrop Grumman Aviation **Phone: 332-5241**
FBO: Security Aviation **Phone: 676-4673 or 676-2206**

CA-HWD HAYWARD
HAYWARD AIR TERMINAL

(Area Code 510)

37, 38, 39

Carrow's Restaurant:

According to the management, fly-in guests can simply taxi their aircraft in and tie down adjacent to the terminal building and walk a short distance down "A" Street to Hesperian Blvd. to reach the terminal building. This family style restaurant is open 24 hours a day, 7 days a week. Entree selections include a variety of choices, including daily specials at all meal periods. Average prices run $4.50 for breakfast, $5.00 for lunch and $6.00 for dinner selections. The interior of the restaurant has a contemporary family decor. For more information call the Carrow's Restaurant at 782-5686.

Manzella's Seafood Loft:

The Manzella's Seafood Loft is located near the end of runway 28 Left, and according to the restaurant manager you can taxi over to their aircraft parking area and walk right into the restaurant. They currently have 4 tie-downs available. This restaurant specializes in seafood, prime rib and steaks. They also have veal, chicken and pasta dishes. The restaurant is open Mon-Fri from 11:00 a.m. to 9:00 p.m. and Sat from 5:00 p.m. to 10:00 p.m. (Closed Sunday) There is live music on Thur, Fri, & Sat nights. Meals generally run between $7.00 to $14.00 for lunch and $9.50 to $19.00 for dinner. This facility has a rustic decor, and can accommodate 20-225 persons for meetings or fly-in club gatherings. They also provide catering if requested. Shuttle service is available between the Executive Inn and this restaurant. For information about this fine dining facility, call (510) 887-6040.

Skywest Bar & Grill:

The Skywest Bar & Grill is located off the north end of runway 10R, on the golf course at the northwest end of the Hayward Air Terminal Airport. Fly-in customers can tie-down in front of the terminal building and contact the airport administration staff for shuttle service by calling 293-8678, or park at one of the FBO's on the field that offers shuttle service over to the restaurant via Skywest Drive. Their hours are from 6 a.m. to 6 p.m. seven days a week except on Christmas. Specialties of the house include, omelets, pancakes, eggs for breakfast, as well as hot and cold sandwiches for lunch and dinner. Daily specials such as chicken dishes and special barbecues are available. The restaurant decor is sports oriented with a casual atmosphere. Groups of 20 or more are welcome with advance notice. Catering for larger groups of 25 and up can be arranged in advance. A wide variety of foods can be prepared to fit the customer's request. For information call 276-1533.

Restaurants Near Airport:

Carrow's Restaurant	On Site NW	Phone: 782-5686
Manzella's Seafood Loft	On Site SW	Phone: 887-6040
Skywest Bar & Grill	On Site Terml.	Phone: 276-1533

Lodging: Executive Inn (On Airport) Phone: 732-6300, Vagabond Inn (On Airport) 100 rooms, 2 story, heated pool, cafe on premises open 24 hrs, meeting rooms, Phone: 785-5480; Best Western Inn (360 W. A Street) Phone: 785-8700.
Transportation: FBO: Flightcraft (Courtesy cars available) Phone: 785-5510, Atlas Rent-A-Car Phone: 352-8400, Able Rent-A-Car Phone: 489-4444, Budget Rental Phone: 889-1464, Alameda Co Transit Phone: 582-3035, Bart Phone: 783-2278, Yellow Cab Phone: 581-4321.
Information: Hayward Chamber of Commerce, 22300 Foothill Blvd., Suite 303, Hayward, CA 94541, Phone: 510-537-2424.

Attractions:

Skywest Golf Course: (Adjacent Airport - North Side) Although located on the airport, Skywest Golf Course is operated by the Hayward Area Parks District. The golf course not only hosts a restaurant and lounge (through a concession), but a pro shop as well. It is a fully mature par 72, 18 hole championship golf course. Patrons have a choice of a daily 9-hole rate or the full 18-hole rate. Power and hand carts are available. The golf course staff is available to assist in tournament management including organization, registration and scoring. Tee prizes and awards, special promotions, clinics with professional staff, photography, printing and catering are all available to customers. For information call 278-6188; **Kennedy Park:** (Adjacent airport - northeast side of field) Tennis, petting zoo, train rides & picnic grounds, Phone: 887-9730; Shuttle service is available at both Executive Inn and Vagabond Inn (On Airport) offers "Golf Package" accommodations, 100 rooms, heated pool, cafe on premises open 24 hrs, meeting rooms, Phone: 785-5480; **Movie Theater:** A nine (9) screen movie theater is located on the airport immediately adjacent to Carrow's Restaurant. Although the theater is within walking distance from the golf course, restaurants and hotels, vehicle parking is plentiful for theater patrons.

Airport Information:

HAYWARD - HAYWARD AIR TERMINAL (HWD)
2 mi west of town N37-39.56 W122-07.34 Elev: 47 Fuel 100LL, Jet-A
Rwy 10R-28L: H5024-x150 (ASPH) Rwy 10L-28R: H3107x75 (ASPH) Attended: 1600-0100Z
Atis: 126.7 Unicom: 122.95 Bay App Con: 124.4, 134.5 Bay Dep Con: 124.4, 134.5
Tower: 120.2, 118.9 Gnd Con: 121.4 Clnc Del: 124.35 Public Phone 24 hrs
Notes: No landing fee, $5.00 per night 0-3500 lbs., $7.00 3501-12500 lbs. and $10.00 12501-25000 lbs., The Hayward Air Terminal is a noise sensitive airport, For noise information contact the airport office at Phone: 293-8692. (Violators will be cited).
FBO: California Airways Phone: 887-7686
FBO: Flightcraft (Exxon) Phone: 785-5511

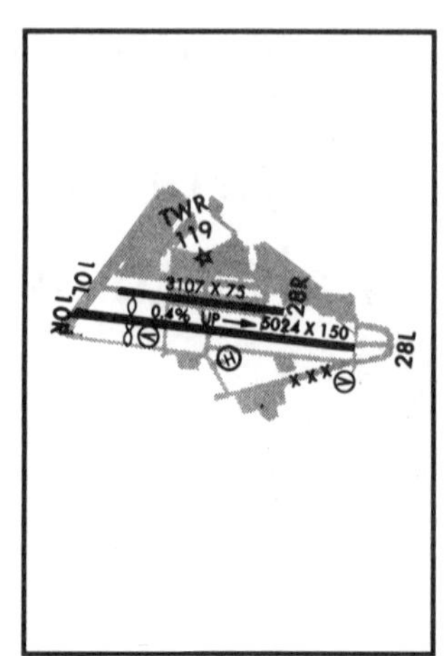

Not to be used for navigational purposes

CA-L26 - HESPERIA
HESPERIA AIRPORT

(Area Code 619)

Hesperia Airport Restaurant:

The Hesperia Airport Restaurant is located on the grounds of the Hesperia Airport. This facility is open Tuesday through Sunday from 7 a.m. to 3:00 p.m. Their menu includes hamburgers, steaks, sandwiches to order, breakfast selections and omelets as well as homemade soups and salads. Their dining area can seat 70 persons and is furnished with tables and booths, pictures of airplanes and large windows where guests can see airplanes takeoff and land from the airport. The view from the restaurant also provides a great view of the Santa-Fe rail road tracks which run parallel to the runway. A banquet room is also available for groups as large as 45 persons in the upstairs portion of the restaurant. Everything on their menu can be prepared for carry-out as well. For more information call the Hesperia Airport Restaurant at 948-1177.

Attractions:

Hesperia Country Club (Golf) 244-3701; Hesperia Lake Park 244-5951, (Both within 5 to 10 miles).

Airport Information:

HESPERIA - HESPERIA AIRPORT (L26)
3 mi south of town N34-22.63 W117-18.95 Elev: 3390 Fuel: 80, 100LL
Rwy 03-21: H3910x50 (Asph) Attended: 1600-0200Z Unicom: 123.0
Public Phone 24hrs Notes: Overnight tie-downs $5.00
FBO: Hesperia Aviation Phone: 948-1177

Restaurants Near Airport:
Hesperia Airport Rest. On Site Phone: 948-1177

Lodging: Motel on property for fly-in clients only (Reservations required) 948-1005.

Meeting Rooms: A very small meeting could be accommodated at the airport, by pre-arrangement. Other facilities located in Hesperia or Victorville (5 to 10 miles away) call 948-1005.

Transportation: Hi Desert Taxi 949-8294; Yellow Cab 244-0900; Hesperia Car Rental 949-0460; Enterprise Rentals 244-5542; For rental cars call on arrival.

Information: California Division of Tourism, P.O. Box 1499, Sacramento, CA 95812, Phone: 800-862-2543.

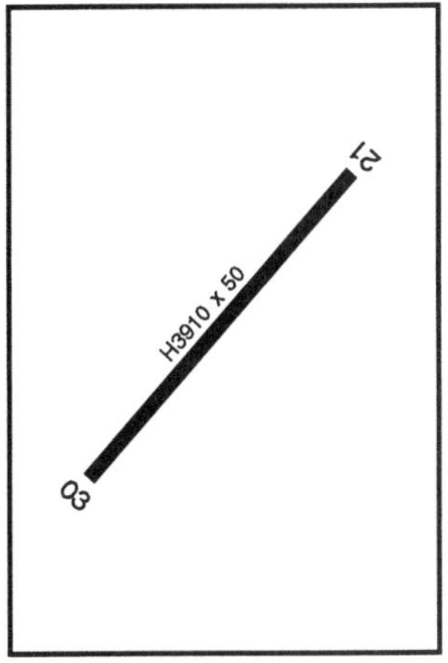

CA-307 - HOLLISTER
HOLLISTER MUNICIPAL AIRPORT

(Area Code 408)

41

Silver Wings Restaurant:

The Silver Wings Restaurant is situated on the Hollister Municipal Airport, and is within walking distance from the aircraft parking area. This is a family style restaurant that is open for breakfast and lunch 7 days a week between 6 a.m. and 3 p.m. For dinner they are open Tuesday through Saturday from 5 p.m. to 9 p.m. They specialize in serving breakfast and lunch. Their menu includes a full compliment of egg dishes, steak and eggs, omelets, pancakes as well as lunch entrees like hot and cold sandwiches, hamburgers, cheeseburgers, chicken fried steaks, soups and salads. Daily specials are also available every day except on Weekends. Their main dining room can seat 50 persons and exhibits an aviation theme with photographs of aircraft that are donated by local pilots right on the field. Average prices run $4.00 to $8.00 for breakfast & lunch and $8.00 to $12.00 for dinner. Groups as large as 30 people can be served if advance notice is made. Meals from their menu can also be prepared-to-go as well. Most major credit cards are accepted. For more information about the Silver Wing Restaurant call 637-1566.

Airport Information:

HOLLISTER - HOLLISTER MUNICIPAL AIRPORT (307)
3 mi north of town N36-53.60 W121-24.62 Elev: 230 Fuel: 100LL, Jet-A
Rwy 13-31: H6350x100 (Asph) Rwy 06-24: H3150x100 (Asph) Attended: 1600-0100Z
Unicom: 123.0 Public Phone 24hrs Notes: No landing fees, overnight parking $3.00 per aircraft
FBO: OK Aviation Phone: 636-9291

Restaurants Near Airport:
Silver Wings Restaurant On Site Phone: 637-1566

Lodging: Weibe Motel 637-5801; Hollister Inn 637-1641.

Meeting Rooms: None Reported

Transportation: Hollister Taxi 637-3778; Starlight Limousine 636-0579.

Information: California Division of Tourism, P.O. Box 1499, Sacramento, CA 95812, Phone: 800-862-2543.

Attractions:

Ridgemark Golf & Country Club, (Approx. 5 miles) 3800 Airline Hwy, Hollister, Phone: 637-1010.

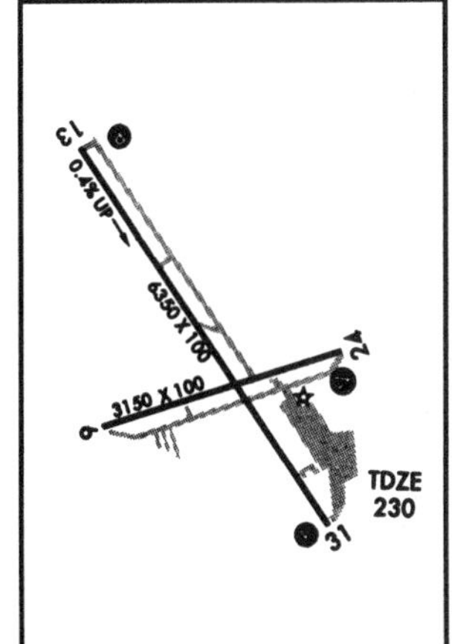

CA-Q75 - HYAMPOM
HYAMPOM AIRPORT

(Area Code 916) 42

Hyampom Cafe & Bar:

Hyampom Cafe & Bar is located about 1/4 mile from the Hyampom Airport. This combination restaurant, tavern and general store, is open between 10 a.m. and 8 p.m. 5 days a week between Friday and Tuesday, (Closed on Wednesday and Thursday). A variety of meals are available with specialties of the house being New York steak, hamburgers, chicken burgers, chicken strips, sandwiches, chili and hot dogs. Daily specials are offered throughout the week, such as roast beef, ham, chicken, and teriyaki beef to mention a few. The cafe can accommodate 25 persons. An outdoor deck will soon be constructed and also available for customer use, according to the management. Larger groups of 20 or more are welcome. However, please give 1 week notice. Guests visiting this location are welcome to stay at the Hyampom Ziegler's Trails' End is located only 50 yards from the Hyampom Cafe & Bar. In addition, fishing, hunting and recreational guide service is also available through Patton's Pack Station. (See "Attractions"). For information about the Hyampom Cafe & Bar call 628-4929, 800-566-5266.

Restaurants Near Airport:
Hyampom Cafe & Bar 1/4 mi E. Phone: 628-4116
Valley View Inn 4-5 mi E. Phone: N/A

Lodging: Gail & Bob's Motel (1/2 mile) 7 units are available with advance reservations, Phone: 628-4758.
Meeting Rooms: None Reported
Transportation: Ziegler's Trail' End within walking dist; Both Hyampom Cafe & Bar 628-4116 and Gail & Bob's Resort Motel 628-4758 will provide courtesy transportation if requested in advance.
Information: California Division of Tourism, P.O. Box 1499, Sacramento, CA 95812, Phone: 800-862-2543.

Attractions:

Ziegler's Trails' End: (Submitted) located 1/2 mile from the Hyampom Airport will be glad to pick you up by prearrangement. This facility is open year around, and has 7 all electric cabins with full kitchen facilities, electric heat, air conditioned and carpeted floors. Attractions and services include hunting, fishing, hiking, bicycling and swimming. Additional activities include Indian Valley, river tubing as well as Great Blue Heron feeding along the river. For information call 628-4929 or 800-566-5266.

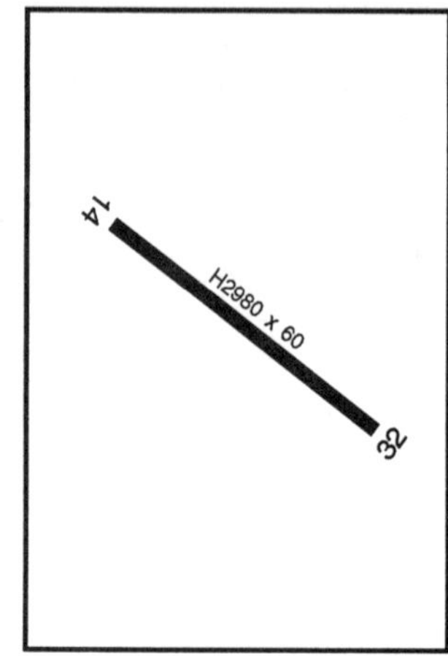

Airport Information:

HYAMPOM - HYAMPOM AIRPORT (Q75)
1 mi northwest of town N40-37.66 N123-28.24 Elev: 1250 Rwy 14-32: H2980x60 (Asph) Attended: unattended Unicom: 122.8 Public Phone 24hrs located near cafe and bar 1/4 mile from airport. Notes: Right traffic Rwy. 14.
Airport Operator Phone: 628-4466

CA-IPL - IMPERIAL
IMPERIAL COUNTY AIRPORT

(Area Code 619) 43

La Hacienda Restaurant:

The La Hacienda Restaurant specializes in preparing Mexican cuisine and is located only 1/8 mile from the Imperial County Airport. Fly-in guests can easily walk to the restaurant from the airfield. This family style facility is open Tuesday through Saturday during the summer months between 11 p.m. and 9 p.m. Times may change during winter months. Sunday and Monday they are reported closed. Their menu displays many fine Mexican entrees as well as combination plates and platters. Average prices run about $5.00 to $6.00 for most selections. Their main dining room can accommodate up to 135 persons and is decorated in a Spanish decor. Groups and parties are welcome. Advance notice is appreciated especially if your group is a large one. For more information regarding this establishment please call the La Hacienda Restaurant at 355-1640.

Restaurants Near Airport:
La Hacienda Restaurant 1/8 mi E. Phone: 355-1640

Lodging: Ramada Inn (5 miles, south of field) 352-5152.

Meeting Rooms: Conference Room located in the airport terminal building. Call Rebecca at 339-4323 for information.

Transportation: Taxi Service: City Cab 352-6141; Yellow Cab 352-3100; Dial-A-Ride 352-5110; Rental Cars: Avis 355-2408; Hertz 355-2401.

Information: California Division of Tourism, P.O. Box 1499, Sacramento, CA 95812, Phone: 800-862-2543.

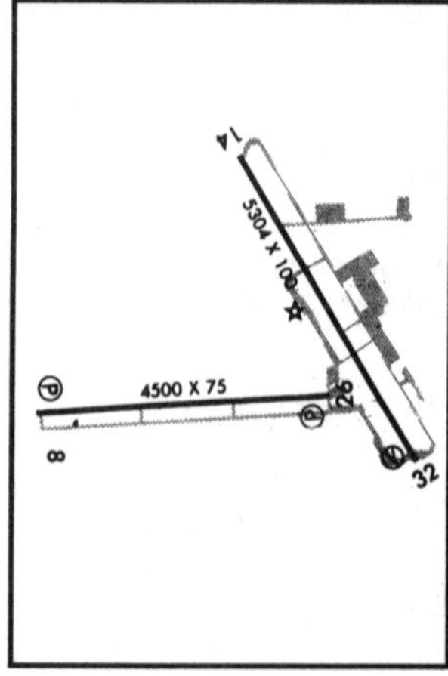

Airport Information:

IMPERIAL - IMPERIAL COUNTY AIRPORT (IPL)
1 mi south of town N32-50.05 W115-34.72 Elev: -56 Fuel: 100LL, Jet-A
Rwy 14-32: H5304x100 (Asph-Pfc) Rwy 08-26: H4500x75 (Asph) Attended: 1600-0100Z
Unicom: 122.7 Public Phone 24hrs Notes: Overnight tie-down, singles $3.00, twins $5.00
FBO: Imperial Flying Service Phone: 353-1375

CA-IYK - INYOKERN
INYOKERN AIRPORT

44

(Area Code 619)

Restaurants Near Airport:

Two Sisters	1 mi	Phone: 377-4012

Lodging: Carriage Inn (10 miles) 446-7910; Heritage Inn 446-6543; Mayfair (1 mile) 377-2416; Motel 5 (2 miles) 377-6711.
Meeting Rooms: Airport has conference room; Also City of Ridgecrest has a facility which can accommodate up to 500 persons; Carriage Inn 446-7910; Heritage Inn 446-6543.
Transportation: United Cab 371-4737; Arrow Cab 375-5777; Rental Cars: Avis 446-5566; Budget 446-7957; Hertz 446-7717.
Information: Inyokern Chamber of Commerce, 1249 Broadway, P.O. Box 232, Inyokern, CA 93527, Phone: 377-4712.

Two Sisters Restaurant:

The Two Sisters Restaurant provides free pick up service for fly-in guests arriving at the Inyokern Airport. This family style restaurant is situated 1 mile from the airfield and is open 365 days out of the year. They open at 6 a.m. for breakfast. They also offer a country breakfast buffet between 7:30 a.m. and 11:30 a.m. on Saturday and Sunday as well as a salad buffet lunch (or order from the menu) beginning at 11 a.m. A full dinner buffet is offered Monday through Saturday between 5 p.m. to 10 p.m., and 12 noon to 9 p.m. on Sunday. Their dinner menu includes luscious steaks, shrimp, fried chicken and many more gourmet entrees. A sumptuous buffet is served nightly with Tuesday night featuring authentic Mexican dishes, Friday night is Icelandic codfish, Saturday night is barbecued beef ribs and Sunday is roast beef. Their lunch menu includes hot and cold sandwiches, soup of various kinds, salads, hamburgers, milk shakes, soda drinks and salad buffet. The dining area can seat about 150 persons with a banquet room available for parties or groups. Organ & Piano music nightly, adds to the casual atmosphere for your dining pleasure. Whether you dine in the Tiki Room or in the main dining room you and your party will remember the great food, entertainment and a warm aloha welcome of the Two Sisters Restaurant. For information call 377-4012.

Attractions:

Points of interest reported : Museums; Death Valley National Forest; Lake Isabella; Red Rock Canyon State Park; Sequoia National Forest; Pacific Crest Trail.

NO AIRPORT DIAGRAM AVAILABLE

Airport Information:

INYOKERN - INYOKERN AIRPORT (IYK)
1 mi northwest of town   N35-39.53 W117-49.77   Elev: 2455   Fuel: 80, 100LL, Jet-A
Rwy 15-33: H7100x75 (Asph)   Rwy 02-20: H6000x75 (Asph)   Rwy 10-28: H4070x75 (Asph)
Attended: dawn-dusk   Unicom: 122.8   Public Phone 24hrs   Notes: No landing fees, overnight parking $3.50.
FBO: Inyokern Aero   Phone: 377-5709

CA-O70 - JACKSON
WESTOVER FIELD AMADOR CO.

45

(Area Code 209)

Restaurants Near Airport:

Imperial Hotel	2.5 mi N	Phone: 267-9172
Sutter Creek Palace	1 mi N.	Phone: 267-9852
Sutter Hill C. Shp	1/2 mi N	Phone: N/A
Teresa's Place	2 mi S.	Phone: 223-2376

Lodging: Amador Inn (Best Western in Jackson, 3 miles) 223-0211; Linda Vista (1 mile) 223-1096; Foxes Bed & Breakfast, (Sutter Creek, 1-1/2 miles) 267-5882; Imperial Hotel (2.5 miles) 267-9172.
Meeting Rooms: Aparicios Hotel 1 mi 267-9177; Best Western 2 mi 223-0211; Hanford House 1 mi 267-0747; Imperial Hotel 2.5 mi 267-9172; Vista Motel 1 mi 223-1096.
Transportation: Imperial Hotel will pick pilots up (2.5 miles) 267-9172; Busses during the week days are available, Amador Rapid Transit System (223 Bus); Taxi service: Pioneer Cab Company 223-3335; Rental Cars: Hollman Car Rental 267-5113;
Information: El Dorado County Chamber of Commerce, 542 Main Street, Placerville, CA 95667, Phone: 626-2344.

Imperial Hotel:

The Imperial Hotel is located 2-1/2 miles north of the Westover/ Amador County Airport on Highway 49. This combination fine dining and lodging facility will provide transportation for fly-in guests. The restaurant is open Monday through Saturday 5 p.m. to 9 p.m. for dinner. A full service lounge accompanies the restaurant. A few of the specialties featured on their menu include: Filet Mignon served with brandy sauce, roasted sword fish with lemon grass mustered sauce, vegetable Napoleon served with roasted red bell pepper and served with Currants and pine nuts, Grilled pork chops on a bead of sour cherry sauce, Desserts include homemade ice cream with additional favorites like Expresso Gelato, Chocolate Moose Bombb, Creme Brulee and Tiramisu. Prices range from $13.00 to $20.00 for most selections. The restaurant is located within an 1879 Gothic red brick two story building which serves also as a bed and breakfast facility. "It was restored in 1988 and equipped with a restaurant and full bar. A restful atmosphere and innovative menu combine to create ideal dining conditions". For Information call 267-9172.

Attractions:

Fishing at Lake Pardee & Lake Amador (12 miles); Skiing at Kirkwood 65 miles and Iron Mountain 45 miles away.

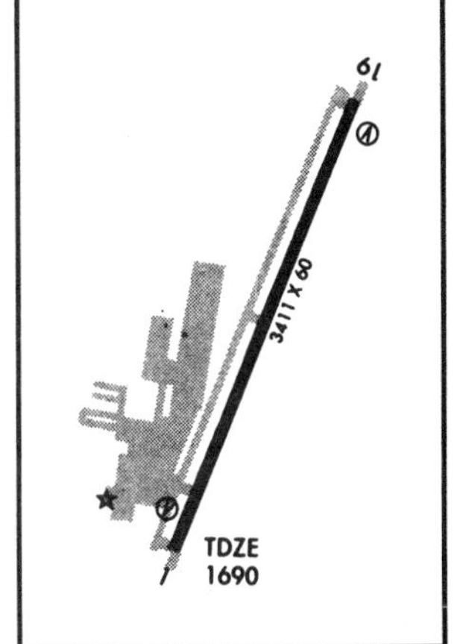

Airport Information:

JACKSON - WESTOVER FIELD AMADOR COUNTY (O70)
2 mi northwest of town   N38-22.61 W120-47.64   Elev: 1690   Fuel: 80, 100LL
Rwy 01-19: H3411x60 (Asph)   Attended: Mon-Fri 1600-0100Z, Sat-Sun 1700-0000Z
Public Phone 24hrs   Unicom: 122.8   Notes: Rwy 19 preferred runway; Overnight tie-down $2.00 all aircraft; Group fly-ins welcome, limited camping on the airport; Home of the Annual West Coast National Swift Fly-in.
FBO: Classic Acrft. Serv.   Phone: 223-2376

CA-L05 - KERNVILLE
KERN VALLEY AIRPORT

46

(Area Code 619)

Restaurants Near Airport:
Airport Coffee Shop On Site Phone: 376-2852

Airport Coffee Shop:

The Airport Coffee Shop is located adjacent to the Kern Valley Airport. The coffee shop is open from 7 a.m. to 5 p.m. 7 days a week. This establishment specializes in serving breakfast and lunch entrees. A full breakfast line including omelets as well as patty melts, hamburgers, bacon burgers, bratwurst, and much more is available off their menu. Average prices run $3.00 to $4.75 for breakfast, and $2.50 to $3.00 for lunch. The restaurant resembles a little old house with seating for about 17 inside and 20 to 25 on their outdoor deck. Groups are also welcome if advance notice is given. Airplane pictures on the walls give it that special touch providing an aviation theme. Meals can also be prepared-to-go if requested. For more information call the Airport Coffee Shop at 376-2852.

Lodging: Hi Ho Resort Lodge (1 miles) 376-2671; The Kernville Inn (3-1/2 miles) 376-2206; The Neill House (Bed & Breakfast (3-1/2 miles) 376-2771; Whispering Pines Bed & Breakfast (5 miles) 376-2334

Meeting Rooms: Facilities listed above are reported to have some accommodations for meeting rooms.

Transportation: None Reported,

Information: Chamber of Commerce, 11447, Kernville Road, P.O. Box 397, Kernville, CA 93238. Phone: 376-2629.

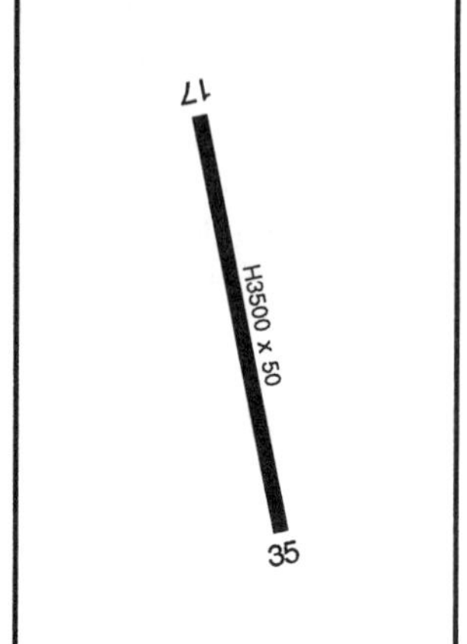

Attractions:

100Yards from the famous Kern River & Lake Isabella. Golf courses located only 2 miles from airport, also excellent fishing for trout (river) bass, bluegill, catfish, etc. White water river rafting is also a very popular sport of the area, in addition to many other attractions and points of interest within the Sequoia National Forest region.

Airport Information:

KERNVILLE - KERN VALLEY AIRPORT (L05)
3 mi south of town N35-43.70 W118-25.19 Elev: 2614 Fuel: 100LL
Rwy 17-35: H3500x50 (Asph) Attended: daylight Hours (No night operations) Unicom: 122.8
FBO: Nelson Aviation Phone: 376-2852

CA-1O2 - LAKEPORT
LAMPSON FIELD

47

(Area Code 707)

Restaurants Near Airport:
Sky Room Restaurant 100 ft SW. Phone: 263-6261

Sky Room Restaurant:

The Sky Room Restaurant is located adjacent to the Lampson Airport about 50 feet from the transient tie-down area. This fine dining establishment is open from 9 a.m. to 12 p.m. for breakfast, 11 a.m. to 3 p.m. for lunch and 4 p.m. to 9 p.m. for dinner. On Saturday and Sunday they offer a champagne breakfast from 9 a.m. to 12 p.m. Their menu specializes in ground beef selections like their broiled ground beef steak, New York steak sandwiches, fresh fish, and prime rib. Average prices run $5.75 for lunch and $10.95 for dinner choices. A two dinner special is offered complete with appetizer, salad, fresh baked bread for only $20.50. Daily specials are also available. Their dining room can seat up to 65 persons. The restaurant is decorated with cloth covered tables, each with flower settings, carpeted floors, and large windows allowing guests a view of the airport, runway system and landing and departing aircraft. Larger fly-in groups up to 20 persons can be accommodated if advance notice is given. Meals can also be prepared-to-go if requested. For more information call the Sky Room Restaurant at 263-6261.

Lodging: Anchorage Inn (5 miles) 263-5417; Clear Lake Inn (5 miles) 263-3551; Konocti Harbor Inn (9 miles, east of field) 279-4281; Skylark Motel (5 miles) 263-6151.

Meeting Rooms: Konocti Harbor Inn (9 miles East) 279-4281.

Transportation: Lake County Rent-A-Car 263-4036; Lake County Transit 263-7433.

Information: California Division of Tourism, P.O. Box 1499, Sacramento, CA 95812, Phone: 800-862-2543.

Attractions:

Clear Lake (2 miles-Fishing & boating); Clear Lake State Park (5 miles).

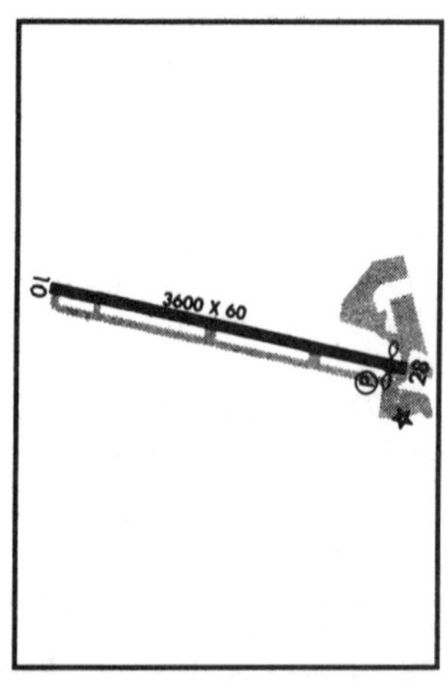

Airport Information:

LAKEPORT - LAMPSON FIELD (1O2)
3 mi south of town N38-59.41 W122-53.98 Elev: 1380 Fuel: 80, 100LL,
Rwy 10-28: H3600x60 (Asph) Attended: 1600-0100Z Unicom: 122.8 Public Phone 24hrs Notes: No landing fees, Overnight tie-down fees $3.00 for singles and $5.00 for twins.
FBO: Lake Aero Styling & Repair Phone: 263-0412
FBO: Tom's Aircraft Enterprises Phone: 263-9330

CA-WJF - LANCASTER GENERAL WM. J. FOX AIRFIELD

(Area Code 805)

48

Restaurants Near Airport:

Don Cuco's (Mex)	9 mi S.	Phone: 948-4651
JE's Old Fire Hse.	18 mi S.	Phone: 273-0833
Sly Fox Cafe	On Site	Phone: 949-2284
Tony Roma's	7 mi S.	Phone: 949-ROMA

Sly Fox Cafe:

The Sly Fox Cafe is located in the terminal building at the Lancaster General WM. J. Fox Airfield. Aircraft transient parking is situated only about 30 feet from the terminal building entrance. This restaurant is classified as a family style establishment, and is open for business between 8 a.m. and 5 p.m. Monday through Wednesday and 8 a.m. to 9 p.m. Thursday through Sunday. Their menu features a varied breakfast selection including omelets, and all types of egg dishes. For lunch they serve cold sandwiches, hamburgers, salads, and homemade potato salad as well as soups. Daily specials are also available. Average prices run $6.00 for breakfast and about $5.00 for lunch. Their main dining area can accommodate up to 50 persons. There is additional seating in their glassed in patio area. Larger groups and parties should give advance notice. In-flight catering is also provided however let them know you are coming in advance if a special order or tray is to be prepared. Otherwise, everything on their menu can be prepared for carry-out upon request. For more information call the Sly Fox Cafe at, 949-2284.

Lodging: Best West Antelope Valley 5-6 mi 948-4651; Desert Inn (8 miles, free trans) 942-8401; Ramada Inn 5-6 mi 273-1200; Rio Mirada (8 miles, shuttle) 949-3423.
Meeting Rooms: Best West Antelope Valley 948-4651; Desert Inn 942-8401; Rio Mirada 949-3423.
Transportation: A.V Taxi 942-8294; Rental Cars: Avis 945-5825; Budget 945-4448; Dollar Rent-A-Car 945-7100; Hertz 942-5824.
Information: Chamber of Commerce, 44335 Lowtree Street, Lancaster, CA 93534; Phone: 948-4518.

Attractions:

Airforce Flight Test Center at Edwards AFB. (See article) Public Affairs: 805-277-3510; Apollo Park, (Adj Airport) fishing lake, picnic area, and children's play area. Phone: 945-8290.

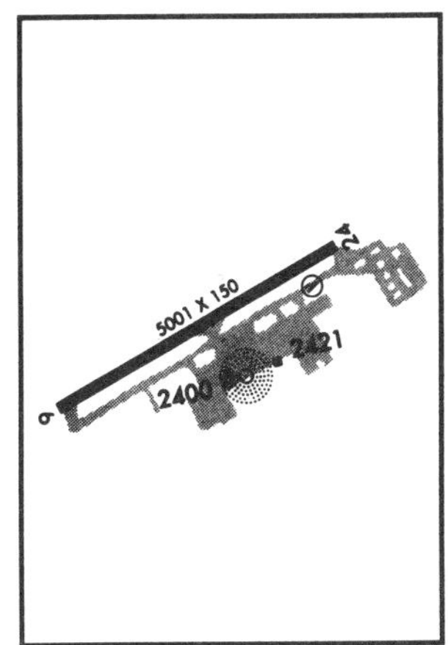

Airport Information:

LANCASTER - GENERAL WM. J. FOX AIRFIELD (WJF)
4 mi northwest of town N34-44.46 W118-13.14 Elev: 2347 Fuel: 100LL, Jet-A Rwy 06-24: H5001x150 (Asph-Afsc) Attended: contiuously Atis: 126.3 Unicom: 122.95 Fox Tower: 120.3 Gnd Con: 121.7 Public Phone 24hrs Notes: Overnight parking fees $5.00 and $10.00; Landing fees for commercial operations only. Managers request: Never leave aircraft untied (County Ordinance 9979); Also U.S.F.S. Tanker Operations June through November.
FBO: Comarco, Inc. Phone: 940-1709

CA-POC - LA VERNE BRACKETT FIELD

(Area Code 909)

49

Restaurants Near Airport:
Norm's Hangar Restaurant On Site Phone: 596-6675

Norm's Hangar Restaurant:

Norm's Hangar Restaurant is located next to the transient parking area. Fly-in guests can walk to the restaurant with no problem. This family style facility is open 7 days a week between 7 a.m. to 3 p.m. Their menu includes items specializing in breakfast and lunch. Some of the choices are omelets, pancake sandwiches, biscuits and gravy, hamburgers and cheeseburgers, club sandwiches, French dip sandwiches and soups & salads. Specials include a choice of sandwich, and cup of soup for a reasonable amount. Averagemenu prices run between $2.50 and $4.95 for breakfast and $4.00 to $4.25 for lunch. Their establishment contains seating for 56 per sons within the restaurant itself, and about 32 on their patio outside. The outdoor patio dining area is especially popular with many customers, and provides a great view of the airport activity and runway system. Groups and parties are also welcome. If your party is large in numbers, please let them know in advance when your group is planning to fly in. In-flight catering is another service available. However, special cheese trays or fruit trays might take extra time to prepare. Regular box lunches or items right off their menu its no problem. For more information about the Norm's Hangar Restaurant, call 596-6675.

Lodging: Embassy Suites (Est. 1-3 miles) 818-915-3441; Shilo Inn (Est. 1-3 miles) 714-598-0073.
Meeting Rooms: Embassy Suites 818-915-3441; Shilo Inn 714-598-0073.
Transportation: Taxi Service: Call 714-622-1313; Also Rental Cars: Budget 714-623-0558; Hertz 819-966-7458; Rent-A-Wreck 714-946-7841.
Information: California Division of Tourism, P.O. Box 1499, Sacramento, CA 95812, Phone: 800-862-2543.

Attractions:

Golf Course located next to airport; Puddingstone Lake and County Park (Adj Arpt. - 2 miles to parking area).

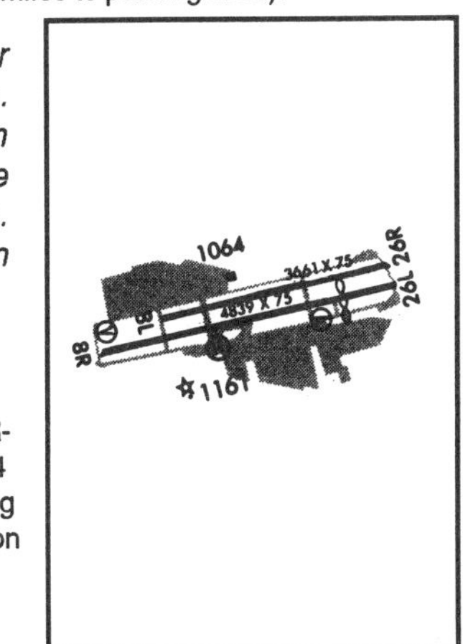

Airport Information:

LA VERNE - BRACKETT FIELD (POC)
1 mi southwest of town N34-05.50 W117-46.91 Elev: 1011 Fuel: 100LL, Jet-A Rwy 08R-26L: H4839x75 (Asph) Rwy 08L-26R: H3661x75 (Asph) Attended: continuously Atis: 124.4 Unicom: 122.95 Tower: 118.2 Gnd Con: 125.0 Public Phone 24hrs Notes: Overnight parking $5.00 single, $10.00 twin. There are 21 fixed base operators doing business on the field. For information contact airport manager's office.
Brackett Field Airport Phone: 714-593-1395 FBO: Comarco, Inc. Phone: 593-1395
Air Desert Pacific Phone: 596-6059 FBO: West-Air Inst. Phone: 593-5117

CA-048 - LITTLE RIVER/MENDOCINO LITTLE RIVER AIRPORT

(Area Code 707)

50, 51

Cafe Beaujolais:

Cafe Beaujolais is a very popular Victorian-styled restaurant that attracts many people throughout the year. Infact, several famous movie stars have visited this establishment on repeated occasions guaranteed a quiet and private meal away from fans and autograph intrusions. The Cafe Beaujolais prepares a variety of delicious meals made from local produce and area-grown ingredients, organically cultivated. Once arriving at the restaurant one's first impression might be a bit deceiving with a simple entrance-way into this Victorian home. But once inside the restaurant you will be overwhelmed by the beautiful back yard English-designed country garden with paths and walkways. Recently rare and exotic plants and flowers are on display with a Mediterranean flair. Many guest enjoy a quiet stroll through the garden while their reservation time approaches. On some Saturdays they even give guided tours of the garden. Cafe Beaujolais specializes in entrees such as bread made fresh from their brick oven, oven poached salmon, roast chicken, broiled sword fish, Mexican, Thai and French dishes are very popular. Their chef, famous for French excellence, prepares delicious desserts. Fruit in season is often used, like apple crisp or fig torts and chocolate mousse cake are to die for. The restaurant has two separate dining areas. The main room can seat up to 40 persons. A private dining room overlooking the garden can be reserved for groups or private occasions. When visiting this restaurant ,we suggest you land at Little River Airport which is about 6 miles southeast of the town of Mendocino. Rental cars are available through Coast Flyers, Inc. 937-1224. For more information call the Cafe Beaujolais at 937-5614.

Historic Mendocino Town & Coast: (Attractions)

Thanks to one of our contributors, we learned about the wonderful attractions near the town of Mendocino. The entire area along Route 1 Coastal Highway is known for its breathtaking scenery, natural beauty, coastal surf and vistas and famous restaurants. When flying in to this area you will want to land at Little River Airport (048). Once there you can obtain your rental car through Coast Flyers, Inc. at 707-937-1224. Advance reservations are suggested. The town of Mendocino is located 6 miles north from the airport. Over 80 miles of coastal scenery can be enjoyed. There are numerous bed and breakfast establishments throughout the region. Some of the most popular Inns include the Albion River Inn 6 miles south of Mendocino along California Route 1, 937-1919; ElK Cove, in the town of Elk, CA, about 15 miles south of Mendocino along CA1, Phone: 877-3321; Harbor House also situated in the town of Elk along CA1, Phone: 877-3203; Headlands (jct of Howard and Albion St., Mendocino, CA) 877-3203; Hill House 937-0554; Joshua Grindle (Free arpt. trans.) 937-4143; Mendocino Inn 937-0511; and Stanford Inn By The Sea (Free arpt trans.) 937-5615.

Restaurants Near Airport:

Albion River Inn	6 mi.	Phone: 937-1919
Cafe Beaujolais	6 mi	Phone: 937-5614

Lodging: Albion River Inn (along CA Route 1, Albion, CA) 937-1919; Elk Cove Inn (Free Trans. along CA Route 1, ELk, CA) 877-3321; Harbor House (along CA Route 1, Elk, CA) 877-3203; Headlands Inn (jct of Howard & Albion Streets, Mendocino, CA) 937-4431. Hill House 937-0554; Mendocino Inn 937-0511; Stanford Inn By The Sea (Free arpt. trans) 937-5615.

Meeting Rooms: Cafe Beaujolais (restaurant) has a small room available for private meetings. Phone: 937-5614; Hill House Inn 937-0554.

Transportation: Rental cars are available through Coast Flyers, Inc. 937-1224.

Information: Fort Bragg-Mendocino Coast Chamber of Commerce, 332 N. Main Street, P.O. Box 1141, Fort Bragg, CA 95437, Phone: 961-6300 or 800-726-2780

Attractions:

Mendocino Coastal Town offers many things to see and do. A number of fine bed & breakfast Inns are available as well as fine dining restaurants. The scenery is what attracts many people each year. (See *Information*).

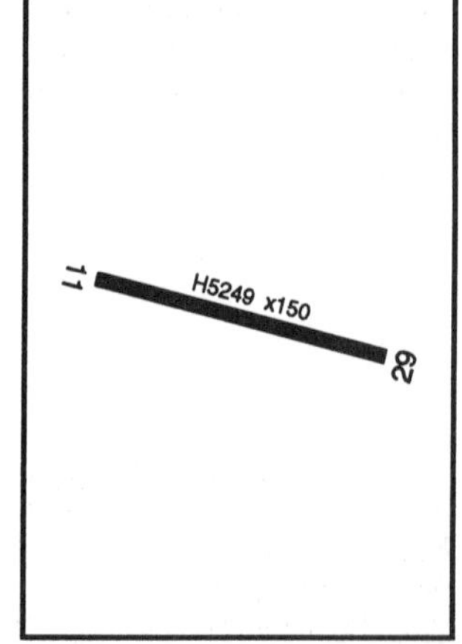

Airport Information:

LITTLE RIVER - LITTLE RIVER AIRPORT (048)
3 mi southeast of town N39-15.72 W123-45.22 Elev: 572 Fuel: 100LL Rwy 11-29: H5249x150 (Asph) Attended: Wed-Mon 1600-0100Z Unicom: 122.7
FBO: Coast Flyers, Inc. Phone: 937-1224

Not to be used for navigational purposes

CA-LPC - LOMPOC
LOMPOC AIRPORT

(Area Code 805)

52

Bravo Pizza:

Bravo Pizza is located in the Central Plaza shopping center directly south of the Lompoc Airport and is situated well within walking distance from Marshall Aviation. This restaurant is unique inasmuch as it has an Italian concept with a French flair. The owner of the restaurant not only specializes in preparing the finest ingredients into making mouth watering pizzas but he is also a pilot himself and enjoys the common interests of fellow airmen. Some of the specialties of the house include "White Pizza" which is made without tomato sauce, and includes olive oil, fresh garlic, along with four different types of cheeses blended together. Bar-B-Qued chicken pizza; Pasta Pizza, "Tri-tip Rancher Pizza", and Baga Bueno Pizza (Hot Latin Pizza) made with refried beans Italian sausage, along with the traditional pizza's like cheese and pepperoni, Italian, and salami. Another pizza specially prepared is their Salmon Pizza. Specials include their personal pizza for only $2.50; buy one pizza and get the second for 1/2 price; dinner salads for $1.25 and drinks for 50 cents. This family style restaurant can be seen from the airport. The building has a beige exterior with blue trim. The atmosphere is warm and friendly. In-flight catering can also be arranged as well. Bravo Pizza is open from 11 a.m. to 10 p.m. 7 days a week. In the future, the owner of Bravo Pizza may be opening a restaurant facility on the airport. For more information call Bravo Pizza at 737-6181.

Restaurants Near Airport:

Boston Market	WalkDist.	Phone:735-5944
Brovo Pizza	Walk Dist.	Phone: 737-6181
Carrows	Walk Dist.	Phone: 7360702
"KFC"	Walk Dist.	Phone: 736-0846

Lodging: Quality Inn (Adj. Arpt.) 735-8555

Meeting Rooms: Quality Inn (Adj. Arpt.) will accommodate meeting & conferences. Phone: 735-8555; Embassy Suites 735-8311; Inn of Lompoc 735-7744.

Transportation: Service Taxi 736-3636; Budget Rental Cars 735-5053; Enterprise Car Rental 735-4147; Lompoc Car Rental (On arpt.) 735-1631; Lompoc Transit 736-4722;

Information: Lompoc Valley Chamber of Commerce, 111 South "I" Street, Lompoc, CA 93436 Phone: 736-4567

Attractions:

One of our readers contributed this attraction for all to enjoy. Hidden in a peaceful valley and removed from the main highways, the town of Lompoc offers a quiet blend of scenic beauty, exciting history and gentle recreation. Flowers are celebrated with gusto in the town of Lompoc. The mild, sunny climate and rich soil provide ideal conditions for growing flowers. Over the years, this town has played a major role in the cultivation and distribution of flowers. Their seeds used for resale in stores all across the country. From June through September, the city is bordered by acres of vivid zinnias, marigolds, sweet peas, petunias and other blossoms. The popular Lompoc Flower Festival is held the last weekend each June. Flower field tours by bus show off hundreds of acres of flower fields. Narrators give you insight into the flower seed industry and the many types of flowers grown there. You can tour the flower fields on your own at other times of the year. Pick up a self-guided 19 mile flower field tour brochure from the Lompoc Valley Chamber of Commerce. While visiting the town of Lompoc you can also visit La Purisima Mission and step back into the early 1800's. A California State Historic Park, La Purisima is the state's most fully restored mission. Four times a year costumed docents enact everyday chores during Mission Life Days. Candle dipping, soap making, spinning and weaving are demonstrated. During Purisima's People Day, held four weekends each year, members of a volunteer group assume the roles of various 1820 Mission residents. For information about scheduled tours or local events, contact the Lompoc Community Chamber of Commerce at 736-4567. (Information supplied by Chamber of Commerce).

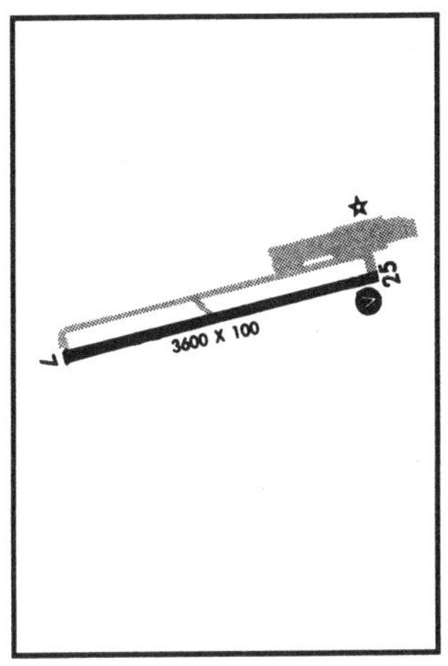

Airport Information:

LOMPOC - LOMPOC AIRPORT (LPC)

2 mi north of town N34-39.94 W120-28.00 Elev: 87 Fuel: 80, 100LL, Jet-A Rwy: 07-25: H3600x100 (Asph) Attended 1600-0200Z Unicom: 122.7 Phone: 24hrs

FBO: Marshall Aviation Phone: 736-0034 or 736-8854

CA-LGB - LONG BEACH
LONG BEACH (DAUGHERTY FLD)

(Area Code 310)

53

The Prop Room Cafe & Bar (CA1 Services):

The Prop Room Cafe & Bar is situated in the main terminal building on the upper level. This cafe styled restaurant is open between 6 a.m. and 6 p.m. 7 days a week except Saturday when they close at 2 p.m. Their menu contains a full breakfast selection, including omelets, French toast, muffins along with appetizers, nacho's, soups & salads, Mexican items, all types of deli sandwiches, club sandwiches, hamburgers, patty melts and meatloaf which happens to be a favorite with many of their customers. Average cost for breakfast runs between $3.75 and $5.50, lunches averages about $6.95. Their main dining area can seat 100 persons and is decorated in Art Deco design with different levels that allow a view of the airport and runways. Groups and parties between 20 and 60 persons can easily be accommodated with advance notice. Meals can also be prepared to go as well. For more information call 420-3733.

Airport Information:

LONG BEACH - LONG BEACH (DAUGHERTY FLD) (LGB)
3 mi northeast of town 33-49-04N 118-09-03W Elev 57 Fuel: 100LL, Jet-A
Rwy 12-30: H10000x200 (Asph-Grvd) Rwy 07L-25R: H6192x200 (Asph) Rwy 07R-25L: H5420x150 (Asph) Rwy 16R-34L: H4470x75 (Asph) Rwy 16L-34R: H4267x75 (Asph)
Attended: continuously Atis: 127.75 Unicom: 122.95 Long Beach Tower: 119.4, 120.5
Gnd Con: 133.0, 121.6 Clnc: 118.15 Public Phone 24hrs Notes: No landing fees reported for general aviation aircraft. Parking fees vary by FBO's (Not run by city airport).

FBO: Atlantic Aviation Phone: 426-5500
FBO: Martin Aviation Phone: 420-3500
FBO: Petrowings Limited Phone: 420-1846
FBO: Executive Terml. II Jet Ctr. Phone: 498-1482

Restaurants Near Airport:

Charley Brown's	2 mi W.	Phone: 427-5488
Marriot Hotel (Cafe Terrace)	1 mi S.	Phone: 425-5210
The Prop Room Cafe & Bar	On Site	Phone: 420-3733
Velvet Turtle	3 mi W.	Phone: 426-0391

Lodging: Marriott Hotel (1 mile) 425-5210; Holiday Inn (1-3 miles) 597-4401; Residence Inn (1-3 miles) 595-0909
Meeting Rooms: Atlantic Aviation (On Site) 426-5500, Marriott Hotel 425-5210; Holiday Inn 597-4401.
Transportation: United Checker Cab (On Site); Avis 988-3255; Budget 421-0143; Dollar 421-8841; Hertz 420-2444; National 421-8877.
Information: Long Beach Area Convention and Visitors Council, One World Trade Center, #300, Long Beach, CA 90831-0300, Phone: 436-3645.

Attractions:

Skylinks Golf Course 421-3388; Lakewood Country Club (Golf) 429-9711, Queen Mary 435-3511, Spruce Goose 435-3511, El Dorado Golf 431-4019. (All within 10 miles of airport).

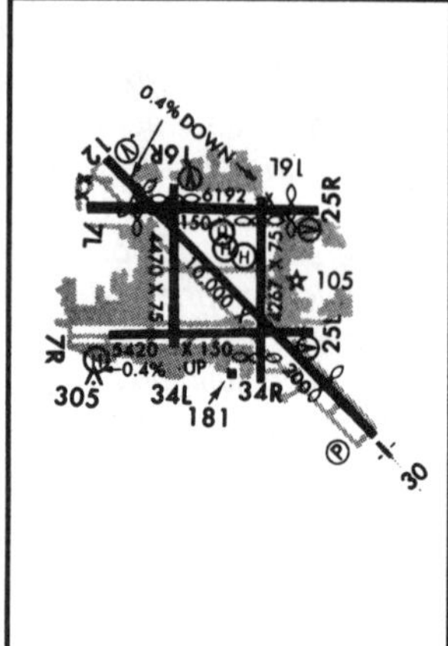

Not to be used for navigational purposes

CA-LAX - LOS ANGELES
LOS ANGELES INTL. AIRPORT

(Area Code 310)

54, 55, 56

CA1 Services - Encounter Restaurant:

This fine dining establishment is located on the Los Angeles International Airport. The restaurant opens at 10 a.m. and remains open throughout the dinner hours. They serve a wide variety of regional cuisine including fresh seafood flown in daily. The decor of this restaurant displays a modern appearance. The colors, lights and sound add to the exceptional dining experience. Top Los Angeles chefs prepare unique dishes in an atmosphere like none other. Prices average $14.00 to $16.00 for lunch and $32.00 to $34.00 for dinner. Catering is also available as well. For information call 215-5149.

Century Cafe:

This family style restaurant is located directly across the street from the Los Angeles International Airport. Complimentary shuttle service is available 24hrs a day to and from the airport and restaurant. The Century Cafe is open 365 days a year from 6 :00 a.m. to Midnight. They serve a full breakfast, lunch and dinner. The menu includes soups, salads, sandwiches, ice cream & desserts, appetizers and entrees including chef's specials. Average prices run $9.00 for breakfast, $10.00 for lunch and $12.00 for dinner. Buffets can be arranged for larger groups staying in house for conventions, if booked and planned in advance. The decor creates a cheerful atmosphere and the dress code is casual. Monday through Friday they offer a "Pasta Bar" from 11:30 a.m. to 2 p.m. For more information call 670-9000 ext. 6451.

Wynsor's:

The management and staff of Wynsor's restaurant would like to extend to you an evening of enjoyment and relaxation at their restaurant and lounge. Wynsor's is located off the main lobby in the Wyndham Hotel, situated at the entrance way to the Los Angeles International Airport. The interior of the restaurant is dominated by mahogany walls with brass trimming. The subdued lighting gives an elegant but not overly formal atmosphere, and the traditional colonial theme is tied together by the deep comfortable seating, and polished wood and brass. The focal point of the restaurant is a unique brass rotisserie located on an island surrounded by their bountiful salad and dessert buffet. Wynsor"s offer hearty fare ranging from truly American to continental cuisine. The portions are abundant and the unlimited salad and dessert buffets complete the plentiful image. No one leaves Wynsor's hungry! For those looking for a lighter meal, Wynsor's salad buffet is available for lunch and dinner. Their hours are 11:15 a.m. to 2:30 p.m. for lunch Monday through Friday, 5:30 p.m. to 10:30 p.m. for dinner. Monday through Saturday and 5:30 p.m. to 10 p.m. on Sunday for dinner. Friday and Saturday night the music picks up with a band and dancing from 9:00 p.m. to 1:00 a.m. Their lounge is open from 11:15 a.m. to 1:00 a.m. daily. For information call 670-9000 ext 6450.

Airport Information:

LOS ANGELES - LOS ANGELES INTERNATIONAL AIRPORT (LAX)
9 mi southwest of town N33-56.55 W118-24.48 Elev: 126 Fuel: 100LL, Jet-A
Rwy 07L-25R: H12091x150 (Conc-Grvd) Rwy 07R-25L: H11096x200 (Conc-Grvd)
Rwy 06R-24L: H10285x150 (Conc-Grvd) Rwy 06L-24R: H8925x150 (Conc-Grvd) Attended: continuously Atis Arrival: 133.8 Atis Dep: 135.65 Unicom: 122.95 Socal App Con: 128.5, 124.9, 124.5, 124.3 Socal Dep Con 125.2, 124.3 Tower: 133.9 (N. Complex), 120.95 (S. Complex), 119.8, 120.35 (Helicopters)
Gnd Con: 121.75 (S. Complex); 121.65 (N. Complex) Clnc Del: 121.4
FBO: Mercury Aviation Phone: 215-5745

Restaurants Near Airport:

CA1 Service Encounter Rest.	On Site	Phone: 215-5149
Century Cafe	Entrance to Arpt.	Phone: 670-9000 ext. 6451
Wynsor's	Entrance to Arpt.	Phone: 670-9000 ext. 6450

Lodging: Airport Marina 670-8111; Crown Sterling Suites 640-3600; Crowne Plaza-L.A. Intl. Arpt. 642-7500; Doubletree Club 322-0999; Doubletree-L.A. Arpt. 216-5858; Hilton & Towers-Los Angeles Arpt. 410-4000; Marriott-Arpt. 641-5700; Quality Hotel-Los Angeles Arpt. 645-2200; Renaissance 337-2800; Sheraton Gateway 642-1111; Wyndham Hotel (At entrance to Intl. Arpt.) 337-9000.

Meeting Rooms: All facilities listed under lodging contain accommodations for meetings. The following have convention facilities available: Hilton & Towers-Los Angeles Arpt. 410-4000; Marriott-Arpt. 641-5700; Quality Hotel-Los Angeles Arpt. 645-2200; Renaissance 337-2800; Sheraton Gateway 642-1111; Wyndham Hotel (At entrance to Intl. Arpt.) 337-9000.

Transportation: Shuttle bus, & courtesy car reported; Also Taxi Service: Bell Cab 221-2355; Beverly Hills 273-6611; Checker 464-2246; Independent Cab 385-8294; L.A. Taxi 627-7000; United Checker 834-1121; Valley Cab 787-1900; Rental Cars: Alamo 627-7000; Avis 646-5600; Budget 645-4500; Dollar 645-9333; Hertz 646-4861; National 670-4950; Rent-A-Wreck 800-423-2158.

Information: The Greater Los Angeles Visitors & Convention Bureau, 633 West Fifth Street, Suite 6000, Los Angeles, CA 90071 Phone: 213-624-7300.

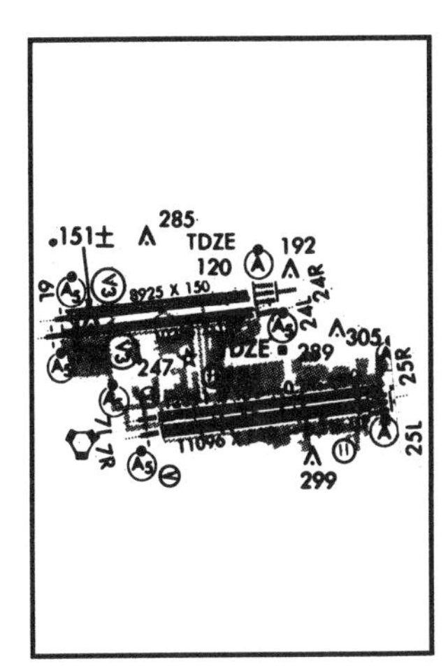

CA-MCE - MERCED
MERCED MUNI/MACREADY FLD.

(Area Code 209) 57

Restaurants Near Airport:

Buchanan's CA Cuisine	1-1/2 mi	Phone: 723-3041
Hangar Cafe	On Site	Phone: 723-6201

Lodging: Gatway Motel (2 miles) 722-5734; New Merced Motel (2 miles) 722-7481; Pine Cone Inn (1 mile, Best Western) 723-3711.
Meeting Rooms: Pine Cone Inn (Best Western) 723-3711.
Transportation: Merced Transit Bus 385-6849; Merced Taxi 722-9293; Rental Cars: Aide 722-8084; Hertz 384-1627.
Information: Chamber of Commerce, 690 W 16th St., Merced, CA 95340, Phone: 384-3333 or 800-446-5353.

Hangar Cafe:

The Hangar Cafe is situated right on the Merced Municipal/ Macready Field, and is located well within walking distance from the aircraft tie-down area. This facility is open from 7 a.m. to 3 p.m. 6 days a week, (Closed on Sundays). They specialize in preparing breakfast and lunch selections. Choices off their menu include hamburgers, bacon cheese-burgers, foot long hot dogs, chili dogs, tuna melts, ham and cheese sandwiches, grilled cheese sandwiches, BLT's, and patty melts along with a complete breakfast line. Average prices run $2.40 to $5.00 for breakfast and $2.40 to $4.50 for most luncheon selections. Daily specials are also available. Their main dining room can seat 48 persons and exhibits an aviation decorated decor including model airplanes, plants, and a nice view of the airport. In-flight catering (Cheese trays etc.) are available for customers who call ahead. Everything on their menu can be prepared-to-go if requested. For more information call 723-6201.

Attractions:

Castle Air Museum is located 7 miles from the Merced Municipal/Macready Airport, in the heart of the San Joaquin Valley, adjacent to Castle Air Force Base. The outdoor museum contains about 30 varieties of military aircraft as well as the indoor museum exhibiting a fascinating collection of war-time memorabilia, along with a gift shop and restaurant on the premises. Hours of operation are 10 a.m. to 4 p.m. daily except on New Years Day, Easter, Thanksgiving and Christmas. For information call 723-2178. Also in this region are several other points of interest: Yosemite National Park (80 miles) Lake Yosemite (10 miles) Lakes McClure & Mc Swain (45 miles), San Luis Reservoir (45 miles), San Luis-Kesterson & Merced National Wildlife Refuges (45 miles).

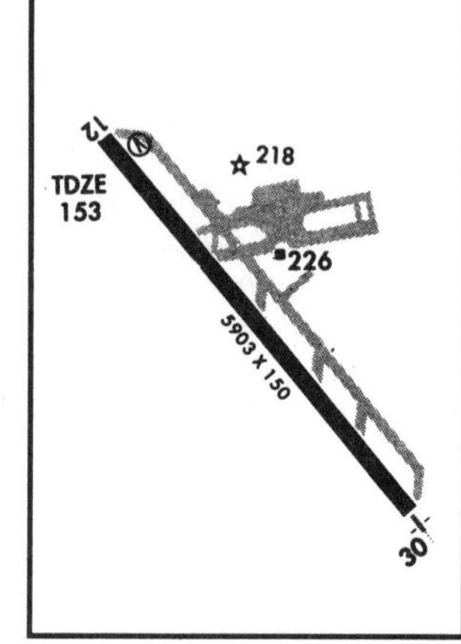

Airport Information:

MERCED - MERCED MUNICIPAL/MACREADY FIELD (MCE)
2 mi southwest of town N37-17.08 W120-30.83 Elev: 153 Fuel: 80, 100LL, Jet-A
Rwy 12-30: H5903x150 (Asph-Pfc) Attended: Nov-Jan 1600-0200Z, Feb-Oct 1600-0100Z Unicom: 122.7 Public Phone 24hrs Notes: Overnight tie-down fees: $3.00 singles, $4.00 twins; Avoid right turns which will position aircraft over city.
FBO: Sky Trek Aviation Phone: 722-6300

CA-MRY - MONTEREY
MONTEREY PENINSULA AIRPORT

(Area Code 408) 58

Restaurants Near Airport:

Golden Tee	On Site	Phone: 373-1232

Lodging: Courtesy transportation provided by the following: Monterey Sheraton 649-4232; Beach Hotel (Best Western) 394-3321; Way Station Inn 372-2945.

Meeting Rooms: Monterey Conference Center is available for larger meetings. For smaller group meetings the FBO's and the airport Board Room is available at $50.00/day or $25.00 for 1/2 the day. Monterey Peninsula Airport District 373-3731 or see FBO's listed below.

Information: Monterey Peninsula Chamber of Commerce and Visitors & Convention Bureau, 380 Alvarado Street, P.O. Box 1770, Monterey Peninsula, CA 93940, Phone: 649-1770

Golden Tee Restaurant:

The Golden Tee restaurant is located 100 yards away from the aircraft parking ramp at the Monterey Peninsula Airport. This combination family style and fine dining facility is open everyday from 9:30 a.m. to 9 p.m. The restaurant offers main courses with fresh seafood, Italian specialties and prime steaks. Average prices run $5.00 for breakfast, $8.00 for lunch and $13.00 for dinner. Lunch and dinner specials are offered every day. Accom-modations for groups and parties can easily be arranged for up to 30 persons. Catering service is also available. The owners have been in business for over 30 years at this location. A large portion of their business is from local clientele as well as fly-in groups. The remainder is from the public using the airline service. According to manage-ment, this restaurant has been rated as one of the top airport establishments in the country. For more informa-tion about the Golden Tee restaurant call 373-1232.

Attractions:

Pebble Beach and Spanish Bay Golf Course as well as others in the area. Cannery Row, Monterey Bay Aquarium, Big Sur (1/2 hour south along the coast), 17 Mile Drive, Carmel Basilica Mission Inn, and shopping in downtown Carmel. (See "Information" listed above)

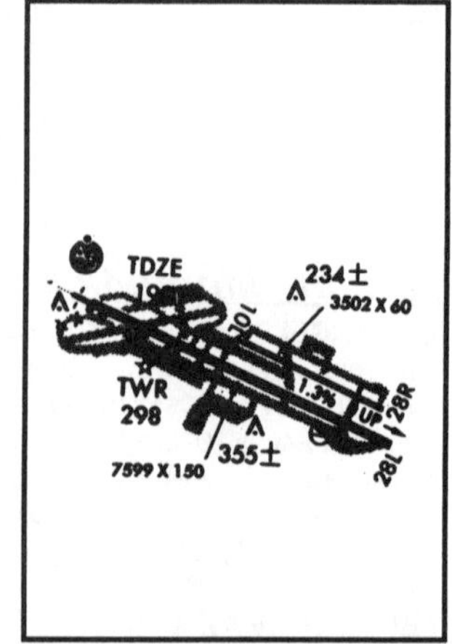

Airport Information:

MONTEREY - MONTEREY PENINSULA AIRPORT (MRY)
3 mi southeast of town N36-35.22 W121-05.58 Elev: 254 Fuel: 100, Jet-A
Rwy 10R-28L: H7598x150 (Asph-Grvd-Pfc) Rwy 10L-28R: H3501x60 (Asph) Attended: continuously Atis: 119.25 Unicom 122.95 App/Dep Con: 133.0, 127.15 Tower 118.4 Gnd Con: 121.9 Clnc Del: 135.45 Public Phone 24hrs
FBO: Del Monte East Phone: 373-3201
FBO: Del Monte West Phone: 373-3451

CA-APC - NAPA
NAPA COUNTY AIRPORT

(Area Code 707) 59

Restaurants Near Airport:

Embassy Suites	6 mi N.	Phone: 253-9546
Highway 29 Cafe	3 mi	Phone: 224-6303
Jonsey's Steak House	On Site	Phone: 255-2003
Silverado Country Club	10 mi	Phone: 255-2970

Jonesy's Famous Steak House:

This family styled facility is situated conveniently within the administration building at the Napa County Airport. The view from the restaurant overlooks the activities on the field. This restaurant also combines a small coffee shop and lounge in addition to the main dining room. The restaurant opens at 11:30 a.m. Tuesday through Sunday and closes at 8 p.m. on Sunday and 9 p.m. on Friday and Saturday. Entrees consist of several delicious steak selections uniquely prepared in full view, on a dry grill weighed down by Sacramento river rocks which sear the meat and lock in juices. This is their famous 50 year tradition of fine cooking. Top sirloin, filet mignon, sirloin club and New york steaks are available, in addition to poultry, sandwiches and fresh seafood choices. Appetizers, soups, salads and side orders are also provided as well as child portions. Daily lunch and dinner specials, along with holiday buffets (Easter) are offered. Prices range under $10.00 for lunch and average $ 15.00 for dinner. The decor of the restaurant is elegant with linen service but offers a casual atmosphere. Banquets facilities are available. For information call the restaurant at 255-2003.

Lodging: Silverado Country Club (10 miles) 255-2970; Embassy Suites (6 miles) 253-9546; Clarion Inn (4 miles) 253-7433.
Meeting Rooms: Airport Terminal Building can accommodate up to 30 people in their conference rooms, Phone: 253-9546. In addition the Jonsey's Steak House can handle 100 people if needed, Phone: 217-2003.
Transportation: No transportation is necessary to visit Jonsey's Steak House. It is located in the administration building overlooking the airport; Also, Yellow Cab 226-3731; Budget Car Rental 224-7845; Evans Transport 255-1559.
Information: Napa Chamber of Commerce, 1556 First Street, Napa, CA 94559, Phone: 226-7455. or the Convention & Visitors Bureau, 1310 Town Center Mall, Napa, CA 94559, Phone: 226-7459.

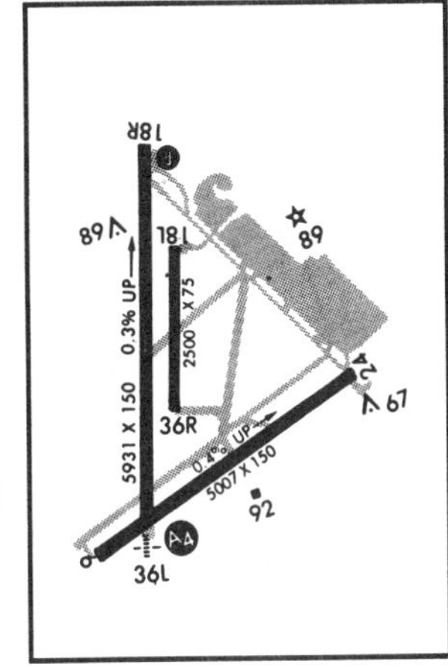

Airport Information:

NAPA - NAPA COUNTY AIRPORT (APC)
5 mi south of town N38-12.79 W122-16.84 Elev: 33 Fuel: 100LL, Jet-A
Rwy 18R-36L: H5931x150 (Conc) Rwy 06-24: H5007x150 (Conc) Rwy 18L-36R: H2500x75 (Asph)
Attended: 1600-0500Z Atis: 124.05 Unicom: 122.95 Tower: 118.7 Gnd Con: 121.7 Public
Phone 24hrs Notes: overnight parking fees vary $3.00 to $15.00.
FBO: Bridgeford Flying Serv. Phone: 644-1658
FBO: IASCO Phone: 224-3609

CA-OAK - OAKLAND
METROPOLITAN OAKLAND INTL.

(Area Code 510) 60

Restaurants Near Airport:

CA1 Services	On Site	Phone: 577-4931

CA1 Services:

Located on the Metropolitan Oakland International Airport are two main Buffeterias owned and operated by CA1 Services. One is located in the number 1 terminal and the other is at the number 2 terminal. Courtesy transportation may be available through the fixed base operators, or taxi service can be arranged. According to information received, both of these restaurants begin operation at 5:15 a.m. and close at 8:45 p.m. Some of the specialties available are fried chicken, Salisbury steak, fettucini, chicken Chasseur, halibut, baked chicken, beef burgundy, and all types of sandwiches, cheeseburgers and hamburgers. Average prices run between $3.95 and $4.50 for breakfast, and $6.75 for lunch & dinner. The decor is similar to a cafeteria, with cooks and servers to help you with your particular selection. The buffeteria section can seat 200 persons. Another section located nearby, has accommodations for about 10 persons and provides full table service. Meals can also be prepared-to-go if requested. For information about this and other food services on the airport, call CA1 Services at 577-4931.

Lodging: Claremont Resort Hotel & Tennis Club (Free trans) 843-3000; Days Inn (2 miles) 800-325-2525; Hilton Oakland Airport Hotel (1 mile) 635-5000; Holiday Inn-Oakland Airport (2 miles) 562-5311; Hyatt Oakland Airport Hotel (1 mile) 562-6100; Park Plaza Hotel (1 mile) 635-5300; Six Pence Inn of America (2-1/2 miles) 638-1180.
Meeting Rooms: Claremont Resort Hotel & Tennis Club (Free trans, convention facilities) 843-3000 or 7924; Hilton Oakland Airport 635-5000; Holiday Inn-Oakland Airport 562-5311; Hyatt Oakland Airport 562-6100.
Transportation: Taxi Service: Associated 893-4991; Goodwill 836-1234; Taxi 261-4100; Yellow 444-1234; Also Rental Cars: Avis 562-2216; Budget 568-4770; Dollar 577-4915; Hertz 568-1177; National 632-2225; Rent-A-Wreck 538-3818.
Information: Convention and Visitors Bureau, 1000 Broadway, Suite 200, Oakland, CA 94607, Phone: 839-9000 or 800-262-5526.

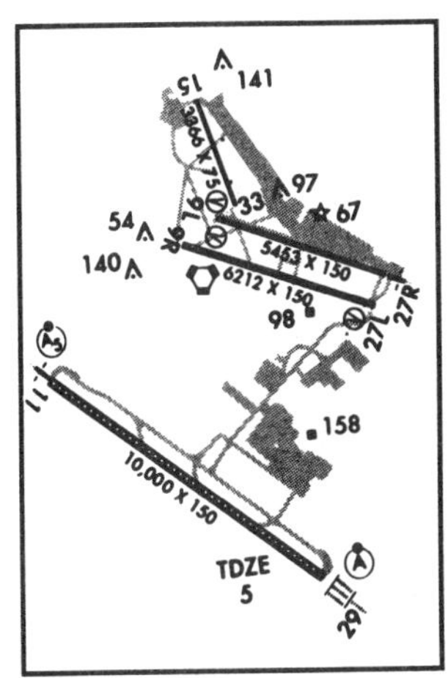

Airport Information:

OAKLAND - METROPOLITAN OAKLAND INTL. (OAK)
4 mi south of town N37-43.28 W122-13.24 Elev: 06 Fuel: 100LL, Jet-A
Rwy 11-29: H10000x150 (Asph-Pfc) Rwy 09R-27L: H6212x150 (Asph-Pfc) Rwy 09L-27R: H5453x150 (Asph) Rwy 15-33: H3366x75 (Asph) Attended: continuously Atis: 128.5
Unicom: 122.95 Oakland Tower: 118.3, 127.2, 124.9 Gnd Con: 121.75, 121.9 Clnc Del: 121.1
FBO: Kaiser Air Oakland Jet Center Phone: 569-9622
FBO: Precision Aircraft & Repair Phone: 632-5466

CA-L32 - OCEANSIDE
OCEANSIDE MUNICIPAL AIRPORT

(Area Code 619)

61

The Grove Restaurant:

The Grove Restaurant is about a 5 to 7 minute walk from the Oceanside Municipal Airport located straight up Airport Road then make a left to the restaurant. This is a combination family style and fine dining facility. Menu selections include prime rib, fish and chips, liver and onions, boneless breast of chicken, fresh fish, barbecued ribs, prawns, all types of sandwiches, and salads. Average prices run $4.00 to $7.00 for lunch and $7.00 to $15.00 for dinner. Usually three different daily specials are offered during lunch each day. Their dining areas can seat between 150 and 200 persons in all. Three different dining rooms make up the restaurant with colonial furnishings consisting of high backed chairs and booths. A banquet room is also available that can seat 100 extra persons. Carry-out meals are available on request as well. The grounds surrounding the restaurant display beautiful orange groves and walkways. A time and temperature sign provides a visible landmark for the Grove Restaurant. For more information call 757-7711.

Restaurants Near Airport:

Airport Deli	5 min walk	Phone: 439-3229
Grove Restaurant	5 min walk	Phone: 757-7711

Lodging: Marty's Valley Inn (7 min walk, Best Western) 757-7700.

Meeting Rooms: Marty's Valley Inn (Conference facilities) 757-7700.

Transportation: Taxi Service: Yellow Cab 722-4214; Rental Cars: Carpenters Avis 757-7800; Enterprise Car 931-1111.

Information: Chamber of Commerce, Tourism Promotion, 928 North Hill Street, Oceanside, CA 92054 Phone: 721-1101.

Attractions:

San Luis Rey Mission 757-3250; Beaches and Harbor facilities (2 miles west).

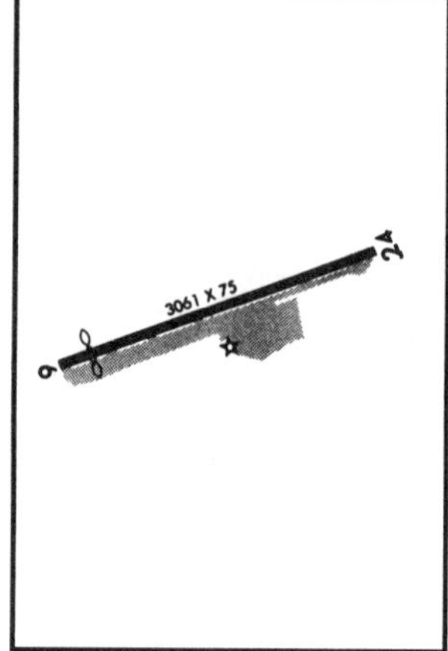

Airport Information:

OCEANSIDE - OCEANSIDE MUNICIPAL AIRPORT (L32)
2 mi northeast of town N33-13.07 W117-21.12 Elev: 28 Fuel: 80, 100LL
Rwy 06-24: H3061x75 (Asph) Attended: Apr-Oct 1600-0200Z, Nov-Mar 1600-0100Z
Unicom: 123.0 Public Phone 24hrs Notes: No landing fees, Overnight parking fees $2.50 singles and $3.50 for twins. Please check with the airport for noise abatement procedures. Departure procedures strictly enforced on noise abatement.
FBO: Airport Management Phone: 966-4511

CA-ONT - ONTARIO
ONTARIO INTL. AIRPORT

(Area Code 909)

62

Host (Marriott):

Host International, Inc. operates a number of food and beverage service facilities on the field. 2 lounges, 3 snack bars, 1 Taco Bell Restaurant and a cafeteria style restaurant all reported to be within the terminal building on the Ontario International Airport. The cafeteria is open at various times throughout the day in conjunction with scheduled air carrier arrival and departure peak hours. 5:45 a.m. for breakfast, 1 p.m. for lunch and between 8 p.m. and 11 p.m. for dinner. Their menu features hamburgers, hot meals, full course dinners, hotdogs, tacos, and desserts, Ice cream, and pastries. Average prices run about $4.50 for most entrees. Meal specials are prepared and available every day. Seating in their dining area consists of 200 settings within their table or booth areas. Groups and parties are welcome. In addition to the restaurant, there are two airport gift shops on the premises as well. For more information about any of these dining establishments call Host International at 983-9835.

Restaurants Near Airport:

Clarion Restaurant	1/2 mi	Phone: 986-8811
Host (Marriott)	On Site	Phone: 983-9835
Holiday Inn	1 mile	Phone: 983-3604
Ontario Arpt Hilton	1 mile	Phone: 980-0400

Lodging: Best Western Ontario Airport (Free trans) 983-9600; Marriott/Clarion Hotel-Ontario Airport (Free trans) 986-8811; Compri At Ontario Airport (Free trans) 391-6411; Hilton Ontario Airport (Free trans) 980-0400; Holiday Inn-Ontario Intl. Airport (Free trans) 983-3604; Lexington Suites (Free trans) 983-8484; Quality Inn (Free trans) 988-8466; Red Lion (Free trans) 983-0909;
Meeting Rooms: Best Western Ontario Arpt 983-9600; Marriott/Clarion Hotel-Ontario Arpt (Convention facilities) 986-8811; Compri At Ontario Arpt 391-6411; Hilton Ontario Arpt (Convention facilities) 980-0400; Holiday Inn-Ontario Intl. Arpt 983-3604; Lexington Suites 983-8484; Quality Inn 988-8466; Red Lion 983-0909.
Transportation: Taxi Service: Yellow Cab 986-1138; Rental Cars: Avis 983-3689; Budget 984-1785; Dollar 986-4541; Hertz 986-2024; National 988-7444; Thrifty 983-1949.
Information: Visitors and Convention Bureau, 421 North Euclid, Ontario, CA 91762, Phone: 984-2450.

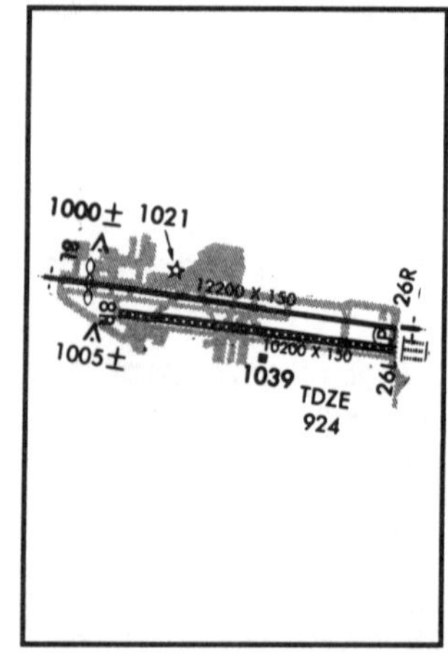

Airport Information:

ONTARIO - ONTARIO INTERNATIONAL AIRPORT (ONT)
2 mi east of town N34-03.36 W117-36.07 Elev: 943 Fuel: 100LL, Jet-A Rwy 08L-26R: H12200x150 (Asph-Conc-Grvd) Rwy 08R-26L: H10200x150 (Conc-Grvd) Attended: continuously Atis 124.25 App/Dep Con: 135.4, 134.0, 127.25, 125.5, 119.65 Tower: 120.6
Gnd Con: 121.9 Clnc Del: 118.1 Notes: CAUTION: Large numbers of starlings and crows may occur on approach to Rwy 26L/26R, Hawks, eagles and owls have been spotted in vicinity of airport.
FBO: Raytheon Aircraft Services Phone: 390-2370

CA-OVE - OROVILLE
OROVILLE MUNICIPAL AIRPORT

(Area Code 916)

63

Table Mountain Golf Course:

The Table Mountain Golf Course Restaurant is located adjacent to the Oroville Municipal Airport. This cafe style facility is open Monday through Thursday between 8 a.m. and 4 p.m., and Friday, Saturday and Sunday between 7 a.m. and 3 p.m. The restaurant and bar area can seat 100 persons. Their menu provides selections like a variety of sandwiches, hamburgers, patty melts, chili burgers, chili dogs, soup and salads as well as roast beef, turkey and pastrami sandwiches. A full breakfast line is also available. Daily specials are offered as well. An 18-hole golf course right outside their door provides entertainment for many visiting customers. In addition they have a proshop and driving range on the premises. Groups and large parties are always welcome providing advance notice is given. Tee-off times must be arranged ahead of time in order to avoid delays, especially on weekends. The restaurant provides a unique service by preparing outdoor barbecues for local and fly-in groups up to 100 people. Airplane parking is available adjacent to the golf course parking lot. For more information about the cafe restaurant call 533-3311. For reserving tee times call 533-3922.

Restaurants Near Airport:

Table Mountain Golf Course   Adj Arpt.   Phone: 533-3311

Lodging: Motel 6 (3 miles) 534-9666; Wonderland Motel (3 miles) 533-2121.

Meeting Rooms: None reported

Transportation: Taxi service: Yellow Cab 533-4141; Rental cars: A-1 Rent-A-Car 533-2234.

Information: Chamber of Commerce, 1789 Montgomery Street, Oroville, CA 95965, Phone: 533-2542.

Attractions:

Table Mountain Golf Course (18 hole, pro shop and driving range) is situated adjacent to the Oroville Municipal Airport. Airplane parking available adjacent to the golf course parking lot. For tee off times call 533-3922.

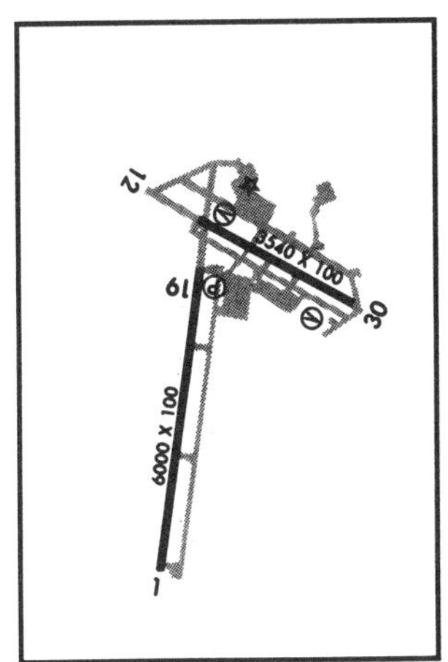

Airport Information:

OROVILLE - OROVILLE MUNICIPAL AIRPORT (OVE)
3 mi southwest of town   39-29-24N 121-37-06W   Elev: 190   Fuel: 80, 100LL
Rwy 01-19: H6000x100 (Asph)   Rwy 12-30: H3540x100 (Asph)   Attended: 1600-0100Z
Unicom: 122.8
FBO: Oroville Aviation, Inc.   Phone: 533-1313

CA-OXR - OXNARD
OXNARD AIRPORT

(Area Code 805)

64

Hangar 5:

The Hangar 5 Restaurant is positioned adjacent to the terminal building on the Oxnard Airport, and is within easy walking distance from the aircraft parking area. This is a combination family-style and fine dining establishment. The restaurant hours are 7 days a week from 11:30 a.m. until 2 p.m. for lunch, and 5 p.m. to 10 p.m. for dinner. Their menu specializes in entrees like BBQ items prepared in front of the restaurant for customers on the go. Additional menu items include chicken, pork ribs, beef ribs, and sausages. Porterhouse steaks, 16-ounce T-bone and rib-eye steaks as well as seafood are available. A luncheon buffet is featured Monday through Friday, as well as on weekends for breakfast, lunch and dinner. Sunday brunch is served 10 a.m. to 2 p.m. Their main dining room can accommodate up to 80 people with a total seating of 165 persons at their location. The restaurant exhibits a theme with a history of aviation. A view of the airport can be enjoyed through large windows. Seating for banquets up to 45 persons can be arranged. Groups and fly-in clubs are welcome. In-flight catering is also provided with advance notice. For more information about the Hangar 5 Restaurant call 984-0994.

Restaurants Near Airport:

Hangar 5	On Site	Phone: 984-0994
TC-Cords	On Site	Phone: 985-3445

Lodging: Casa Sirena Resort (Free trans) 985-6311; Embassy Suites (Free trans) 984-2500; Radisson Suite (Free trans) 988-0130.

Meeting Rooms: Casa Sirena Resort (Convention facilities) 985-6311; Embassy Suites (Convention facilities) 984-2500; Radisson Suite (Convention facilities) 988-0130.

Transportation: Taxi service: Yellow Cab 483-2444; Also rental cars: Budget 483-0145; Hertz 985-0911; National 985-6100; Rent-A-Wreck 486-2694.

Information: Visitors Center, 715 South A Street, Oxnard, CA 93030, Phone: 483-7906.

Attractions:

CEC/Seabee Museum displays memorabilia of the United States Navy Seabees with underwater diving displays, World War II dioramas, weapons and artifacts. For information you can contact the museum at The Naval Construction Battalion Center, Channel Islands Blvd & Ventura Road, Southwest off US 101 in Port Hueneme. Admission is free. Phone: 982-5163 or 982-5167; **Channel Islands Harbor** is located at the end of Peninsula road off Channel Island Blvd. and has beaches, charter boats, bicycle rentals. Also at this location is **Fisherman's Wharf** which is a New England styled village containing restaurants and shops.

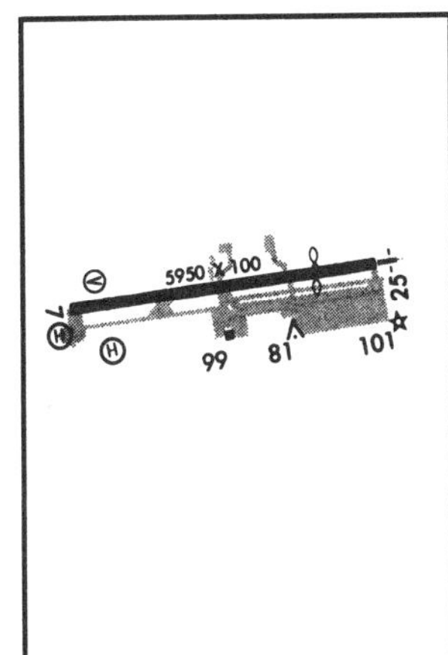

Airport Information:

OXNARD - OXNARD AIRPORT (OXR)
1 mi west of airport   N34-12.05 W119-12.43   Elev: 43   Fuel: 100LL, Jet-A
Rwy 07-25: H5950x100 (Asph)   Attended: continuously   Atis: 118.05   Tower: 120.0   Gnd Con: 121.9
FBO: Venco Pacific Aviation   Phone: 984-4121   FBO: Oxnard Aircraft Serv.   Phone: 984-1424

CA-UDD - PALM SPRINGS BERMUDA DUNES

65

Murph's Gaslight:

The Murph's Gaslight Restaurant is situated just 100 yards west of the Bermuda Dunes Airport. Fly-in guests can and do walk to the restaurant from the aircraft parking ramp. The restaurant is open 11 a.m. to 9 p.m. Monday through Saturday and from 3 p.m. to 9 p.m. on Sundays only. This restaurant is well known for their pan fried chicken served with all the trimmings. Also a famous dish is their Martini-burgers along with several other entrees. Luncheon and daily specials are available, along with one dinner special nightly. The decor and atmosphere of the restaurant is fashioned after an Irish Pub. Murph's Gaslight restaurant will also prepare anything on their menu for carry-out. For more information please call the restaurant at 345-6242.

(Area Code 619)

Restaurants Near Airport:

Macario's Restaurant	1 mi E.	Phone: 342-5649
Murph's Gaslight	On site	Phone: 345-6242

Lodging: Bermuda Dunes New Inn 345-2577; Best Western Date Tree Inn (1 mi) 347-3421; Palm Desert Inn 345-2547

Meeting Rooms: Available at airport. Call the airport manager at 345-2558 for information.

Transportation: Payless Rental Car 360-2277; Taxi Service: A-Valley Cab Service 340-5845; VIP 328-0222.

Information: Palm Springs Desert Resorts Convention and Visitors Bureau, 255 N. El Cielo Road, Suite 315, Palm Springs, CA 92262, 619-327-8411, 800-333-7232.

Attractions:

There are numerous resorts and golf courses located within the Palm Springs Area. See "Information" for convention & Visitors bureau address and phone number.

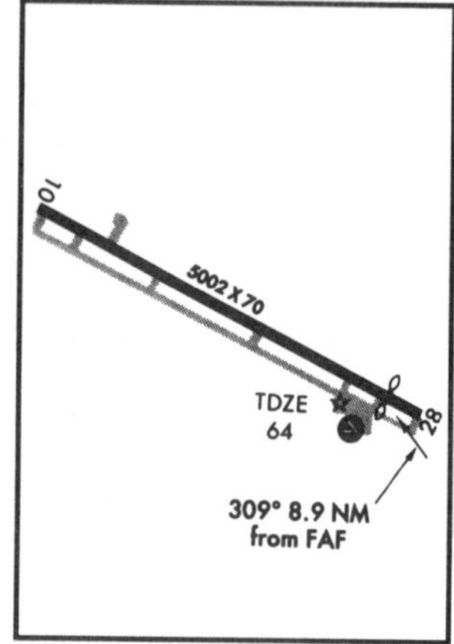

Airport Information:

PALM SPRINGS - BERMUDA DUNES (UDD)

13 mi east of town N33-44.91 W116-16-49 Elev: 73 Fuel: 100LL, Jet-A Rwy 10-28: H5002x70 (Asph) Attended: Sat-Thu 1500-0400Z, Fri 1500-0500Z Unicom: 122.8 Public phone 24hrs; Notes: Landing fee: singles $5.00, twins: $8.00, turbo props: $15.00, Jets: $20.00. Ramp overnight parking: Singles $10.00 Twins: $12.00 Turbo Props $20.00, Jets: $25.00, Fuel available 1500-0400Z daily.

FBO: Airport Manager Phone: 345-2558

Photo by: Doubletree Resort

CA-PSP - PALM SPRINGS
PALM SPRINGS REGIONAL AIRPORT

(Area Code 619)

66, 67, 68

CA1 Services:

The CA1 Services operates a food service facility within the center of the main terminal building at the Palm Springs Regional Airport. You can park your aircraft at AMR Combs FBO and walk 500 feet to the restaurant. Hours of operation for this family dining establishment are December through April from 6:30 a.m. to 7:30 p.m. and May through November between 7 a.m and 4 p.m. Specialties of the house include their California club sandwich, Coachella club sandwich and Cobb salad. Average prices run $6.00 for breakfast, $7.50 for lunch and dinner. Daily specials are featured and vary throughout the week. The decor of this restaurant is contemporary with table and counter space that allows seating for up to 160 persons. In flight catering can also be arranged through AMR Combs on the field. For more information call CA1 Services at 327-4161.

Doubletree Resort:

The Doubletree Resort at Desert Princess Country Club is located about 5 miles from Palm Springs Regional Airport. The resort will offer free transportation to and from the airport. Doubletree's four-story hotel offers 289 comfortable guest rooms and suites, plus 200 elegant two or three bedroom condominiums with fully equipped kitchens. Hotel accommodations feature built-in refrigerators, radios, hair dryers, remote-control televisions, computerized safes, alarm clocks, spacious makeup areas, individual climate control, and a balcony or terrace. Doubletree Resort features a men's and women's hair salon, a gift shop, golf pro shop, laundry and dry cleaning. Babysitters are available.The resort also features a private, on-site, 27-hole championship golf course, driving range, putting greens, 10 tennis courts (5 of which are lighted), 2 swimming pools and whirlpools, a fitness center and racquetball courts. An on-site massage therapist, and golf and tennis pros are available.The resort offers both casual and elegant dining, as well as nightly entertainment and dancing. The Promenade Cafe serves breakfast, lunch, dinner and Sunday brunch in a casual, open-air setting with a great view of the golf course.The Prince Restaurant serves fresh seafood and exquisite California specialties in a formal atmosphere. After dinner, guests can relax in the Oasis Lounge and enjoy drinks, entertainment and dancing every night of the week. For those traveling on business, the resort offers 14,600 square feet of meeting space, including a 7,400-square-foot Royal Ballroom (divisible into two to five sections), a 4,554-square-foot Desert Ballroom, and four Canyon Suites for smaller groups. For banquets, the resort's catering staff will serve just about any size group. Ask about special meeting packages. Group rates are available on request. For more information about rates and accommodations at Doubletree Resort, call 322-7000.

Restaurants Near Airport:

CA1 Services	Trml Bldg	Phone: 327-4161
Doubletree Resort	5 mi	Phone: 322-7000
Million Air Deli	On Site	Phone: 320-0978

Lodging: Doubletree Resort 322-7000; Courtyard by Marriott 322-6100; Golden Palm Villa 327-1408; Palm Tree 327-1293; Spa Hotel & Mineral Springs 325-1461; Hilton 320-6868; Marquis 322-2121; Wyndham 322-6000; La Mancha Villas 323-1773. Also, there is a courtesy phone desk in the terminal building listing the surrounding hotels/resorts located near the airport.

Meeting Rooms: Doubletree Resort 322-7000; Courtyard By Marriott 322-6100; Palm Tree 327-1293; Spa Hotel & Mineral Springs 325-1461; Hilton (Convention facilities) 320-6868; Marquis (Convention facilities) 322-2121; Wyndham (Convention facilities) 322-6000; La Mancha Villas Resort 323-1773.

Transportation: Rental cars: Avis 327-1353; Budget 327-1404; Dollar 325-7333; General Rent-A-Car 778-1084; Hertz 327-1523; National 327-1438.

Information: Convention and Visitors Bureau, 69930 CA 111, Suite 201, Rancho Mirage, CA 92270, Phone: 770-9000.

Million Air Deli:

The Million Air Deli is located within walking distance to the Million Air Fixed Base Operation located on the Palm Springs Regional Airport. This cafe is reported to be open between 8 a.m. and 6 p.m. However, their hours may change in the near future. Please call them for current hours of operation. Their menu includes a variety of entrees including specialty hot and cold sandwiches, hamburgers, soup and salad. Average prices run between $4.00 and $5.00 for most items. The restaurant has a country-style decor with a lively atmosphere. Seating in this cafe is about 20 people. Meals can be prepared-to-go as well. In-flight catering is still another service available through the restaurant and the Million Air line service. For more information about this facility, call them at 320-7704 or 320-0978.

Attractions:

Palm Springs Air Museum, Palm Springs, FL. A collection of 17 or more famous aircraft including a Grumman F4F Wildcat, F6F Hellcat, F7F Tigercat, F8F Bearcat, P47, B-17, Spitfire, Avenger, Lightning and many more. Hours: Wed-Mon 10 a.m. to 5 p.m. Palm Springs Regl. Arpt. Admission: $7.50 adults, $3.50 per child; Gift shop, tours, and special events. Call 619-778-6262.

There are other activities to enjoy within the Palm Springs area, such as horseback riding, shopping along nearby Palm Canyon Drive, the Palm Springs Desert Museum, Indian Canyons, Moorten Botanical Garden, Joshua Tree National Monument, Oasis Water Resort, Camelot Family Fun Center and the Palm Springs Aerial Tramway to Mt. San Jacinto.

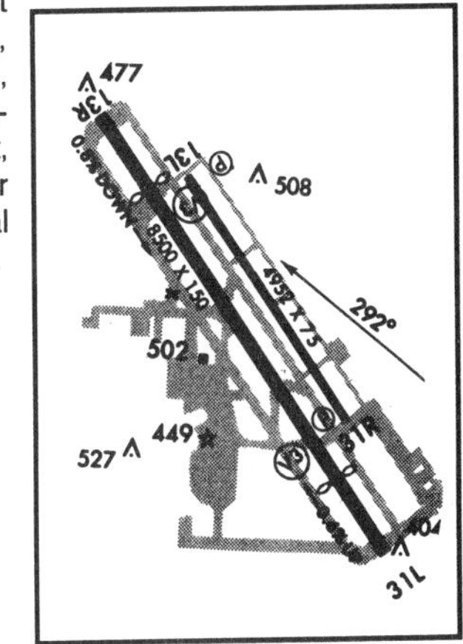

Airport Information:

PALM SPRINGS - PALM SPRINGS REGIONAL AIRPORT (PSP)

2 mi east of town N33-49.72 W116-30.34 Elev: 462 Fuel: 100LL, Jet-A
Rwy 13R-31L: H8500x150 (Asph-Pfc) Rwy 13L-31R: H4952x75 (Asph) Attended: 1400-0700Z
CTAF: 119.7 Atis: 118.25 Unicom: 122.95 App/Dep Con: 126.7, 118.85 L.A. Center App/Dep Con: 128.15 Tower: 119.7 Gnd Con: 121.9 Clnc Del: 128.35 Public Phone 24hrs Notes: Overnight parking fees are $7.50 for singles and $12.50 for twins.

FBO: AMR Combs Palm Springs **Phone: 327-1201**
FBO: Million Air Palm Springs **Phone: 320-7704**

Palm Springs Air Museum

Palm Springs, CA (CA-PSP)

(Information provide by Museum)

Located on the Palm Springs Regional Airport

Hear the pounding roar of the mightiest piston engines ever built! Climb up and look in the cockpits of the legendary fighters and bombers of WWII! See the actual planes that won the greatest war in history. And more.

The Palm Springs Air Museum is dedicated to the restoration, preservation and operation of America's legendary fighters, bombers and trainers. It contains one of the world's largest collections of flying WWII airplanes, including the Robert J. Pond Collection.

Special events include exciting fly-overs and aviation celebrities on Memorial Day, Veterans Day, Armed Forces Day, Pearl Harbor Day, VE Day, VJ Day, Naval Aviation Day, Army Air Force Day and more. Call 619-778-6262 for recorded schedules and details.

Catered events and site rentals. Imagine a theme party or other special event with the nostalgic flavor of Glenn Miller and America's Shining Hour in the history of the western world. You bring the people, they will bring the food, music, furnishings and fun.

Museum hours and admission: Hours are Wednesday through Monday 10 a.m. to 5 p.m. Closed Tuesday. Admission: Adults age 13-65 $7.50; children ages 6-12, $3.50; children 5 and under free. Military with I.D. $5.95, Seniors age 65+ $5.95. Guided tours are conducted every Saturday and Sunday at 12 noon and 2 p.m. Private group tours also available.

Post Exchange Gift Shop: hundreds of unique aviation items including books, models, videos, hats, pins, flight jackets, posters, patches and more. Memberships are offered in six different levels. Benefits ranging from the museum newsletter, admission and gift shop discounts to bronze pins, logo Tee-shirts and free admission are offered. For information about the museum call 619-778-6262.

Aircraft on display include:

Grumman Wildcat
Grumman Hellcat
Grumman Tigercat
Grumman Bearcat
Grumman Avenger
Bell King Cobra
Supermarine Spitfire
Boeing Stearman
Vought Corsair
North American Texan
North American Mitchell
Lockheed Lightning
Curtis Warhawk
Boeing Flying Fortress
Republic Thunderbolt
North American Mustang
Douglas Invader

CA-PAO - PALO ALTO
PALO ALTO OF SANTA CLARA CO.

(Area Code 415)

69

Harry's Hof Brau Restaurant:

Harry's Hof Brau Restaurant is situated across the street from the Palo Alto Santa Clara County Airport. This combination cafeteria and family style establishment is open 7 days a week for breakfast, lunch and dinner between 7 a.m. and 8 p.m. during the summer and 7 a.m. to 6 p.m. during the winter. Their menu includes items like roast beef and turkey dinners, corn beef and ham sandwiches, hamburgers and hot dogs as well as a complete breakfast selection. Most of their prices run between $1.75 and $7.24. The main dining room can seat 120 persons. The restaurant has many windows and allows a nice view of the 18 hole public golf course adjacent to the restaurant. The tee-off area is only 50 feet from the door. Harry's Hof Brau Restaurant provides in-flight catering with advance notice, as well as meals-to-go. For more information call 856-6133.

Restaurants Near Airport:

Harry's Hof Brau	Adj 100 yds.	Phone: 856-6133
Ming's Villa	1/4th mi	Phone: 856-7700
Scott's Seafood Grill	1/4 mi	Phone: N/A

Lodging: Best Western Creekside Inn (Arpt trans) 493-2411; Hyatt Rickey's (Arpt trans) 493-8000.

Meeting Rooms: Best Western Creekside Inn 493-2411; Hyatt Rickey's (Convention facilities) 493-8000.

Transportation: Taxi Service: Merit Cab 571-0606; Yellow Cab 321-1234; Rental Cars: Avis 493-8888; Budget 493-6000; Hertz 493-2009; National 493-3012.

Information: Chamber of Commerce, 325 Forest Avenue, Palo Alto, CA 94301, Phone: 324-3121.

Attractions:

Palo Alto Municipal Golf Course is located right across the street from the Palo Alto Airport. For information call 856-0881.

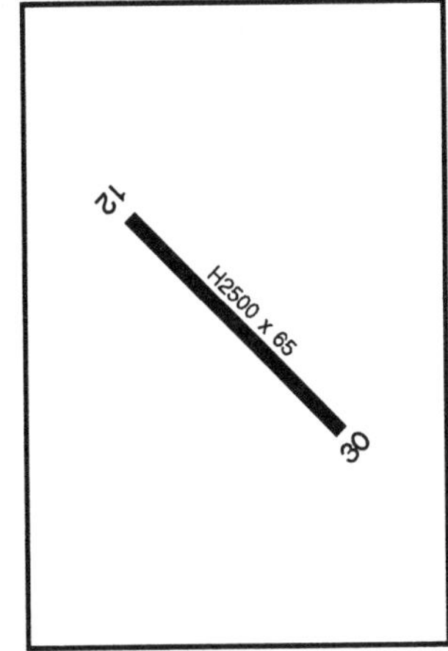

Airport Information:

PALO ALTO - PALO ALTO OF SANTA CLARA COUNTY (PAO)
0 mi east of town N37-27.66 W122-06.90 Elev: 05 Fuel: 80, 100LL
Rwy 12-30: H2500x65 (Asph) Attended: 1500-0500Z Atis: 120.6 Unicom: 122.95
Tower: 118.6 Gnd Con: 125.0 Public Phone 24hrs Notes: Overnight parking $5.00/aircraft
FBO: Main Air Maintenance Phone: 494-6556 FBO: Stanford Flying Club Phone: 858-2200
FBO: Rossi Aircraft Phone: 493-3326

CA-PRB - PASO ROBLES
PASO ROBLES MUNICIPAL AIRPORT

(Area Code 805)

70

Amelia's Food & Drink Restaurant:

Amelia's Food & Drink Restaurant is situated within the terminal building at the Paso Robles Municipal Airport. This deli styled restaurant is open from 9 a.m. to 4 p.m. 7 days a week. Their basic menu includes such items as the "Grinder" sub sandwiches, turkey on white bread, roast beef on sour dough bread, vegetable sandwiches, as well as a selection of dinner and chef salads. They also feature Barbecued items during the week and on weekends like ribs, top sirloin, chicken and pork loin meals. The dining room can seat up to 100 persons. Groups are also welcome. Advance notice would be appreciated for larger parties or fly-ins. In-flight catering is yet another service presented to fly-in costumers. Box lunches, deli trays and breakfast trays can all be prepared if notice is given ahead of time. The airport has a variety of active sky divers, ultralights and radio controlled model airplanes that provide added visual entertainment to restaurant customers, and draw many spectators from the area. For more information about Amelia's call 239-3902.

Restaurants Near Airport:

Amelia's Food & Drink	On Site	Phone: 239-3902

Lodging: Adelaide Motor Inn (4 miles) 238-2770; Black Oak (Best Western (4 miles) 238-4740; Padre Oaks Inn (5 miles) 238-2550; Paso Robles (5 miles) 238-2660.

Meeting Rooms: Black Oak (Best Western) 238-4740; Paso Robles 238-2660.

Transportation: Taxi Service: Dial-A-Ride 239-8747; Shuttle 239-8938; Rental Cars: Enterprise 239-0628.

Information: Chamber of Commerce, 1225 Park Street, Paso Robles, CA 93446, Phone: 238-0506.

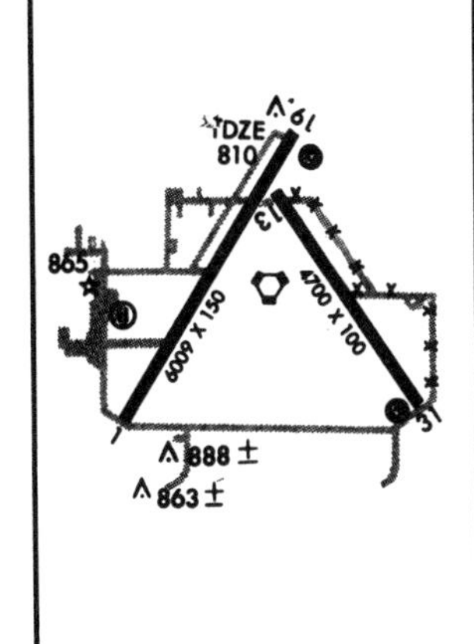

Airport Information:

PASO ROBLES - PASO ROBLES MUNICIPAL AIRPORT (PRB)
4 mi northeast of town N35-40.37 W120-37.62 Elev: 836 Fuel: 100LL, Jet-A
Rwy 01-19: H6009x150 (Asph) Rwy 13-31: H4700x100 (Asph) Attended: 1500-0200Z
Unicom: 123.0
Paso Robles Airport Phone: 237-3877

CA-PTV - PORTERVILLE
PORTERVILLE MUNICIPAL ARPT.

(Area Code 209) 71

Restaurants Near Airport:

Annie's Restaurant	On Site	Phone: 784-8208
Golden Corral Stake Hse	6 mi NE	Phone: 781-0195
Oak Pit Restaurant	5 mi E	Phone: 781-7427
Palace Hotel Dining Rm	4 mi NE	Phone: 784-7086

Lodging: Sundane Inn (5 miles) 676 North Main 784-7920; Motel 6, (5 miles) 935 West Morton 781-7600

Transportation: United Cab 782-0408; Dial-A-Ride 781-8104; Rental Cars: Billingsley Ford 784-6000; PTV. Chrysler 784-9512; Enterprise Car Rental 783-0125.

Information: California Office of Tourism, 1121 L Street, Suite 103, Sacramento, CA 95814, Phone: 800-TO-CALIF.

Annie's Restaurant:

Annies Restaurant is located in the terminal building at the Porterville Municipal Airport. You can taxi right up to the apron at the terminal building and the restaurant is within 50 feet from that location. This family style restaurant is open from 9 a.m. to 3 p.m. Tuesday through Friday and 8 a.m. to 3 p.m. on Saturday and Sunday. They are closed on Monday. Annie's offer a complete menu for breakfast or lunch. The lounge open from noon to midnight also serves food as well. A daily salad bar is also offered. Average prices run $4.00 for breakfast and $5.00 for lunch. The restaurant has recently been remodeled with a modern decor. Large windows provide a view overlooking the apron and runways. There is even a outside deck for fresh air dining. This facility specializes in banquets and parties with accommodations for up to 60 people. Carry out meals from fruit trays to hot dinners can be arranged. A grass camping area is located adjacent to the restaurant complete with showers and a covered BBQ patio area. The new owners are happy to accommodate your needs. Give them a call at 784-8208.

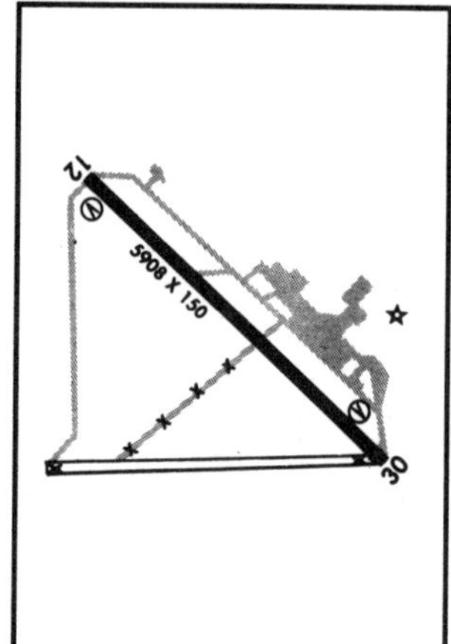

Airport Information:

PORTERVILLE - PORTERVILLE MUNICIPAL AIRPORT (PTV)
3 mi southwest of town N36-0178 W119-03.76 Elev: 444 Fuel: 80, 100LL, Jet-A
Rwy 12-30: H5908x150 (Asph) Attended: May-Oct 1500-0300Z, Nov-Apr 1600-0100Z
Unicom: 122.8 Public Phone 24hrs Notes: Overnight parking, Singles: $2.00 and Twins: $2.50.
FBO: City Airport Phone: 781-0305
FBO: Rays Aircraft Phone: 784-9110

CA-RIU - RANCHO MURIETA
MURIETA AIRPORT

(Area Code 916) 72

Restaurants Near Airport:

Ellen Coffee Shop	1/4 mi	Phone: 354-0210
Riders Steakhouse	1/2 mi	Phone: 354-2878

Lodging: Days Inn 635-0666; Rancho Murieta Resort (5 min) 354-3400;

Meeting Rooms: Riders Steakhouse 1/2 mi 354-2878; Rancho Murieta Resort (5 min) 354-3400.

Transportation: Contact FBO's for transportation.

Riders Steakhouse:

Riders Steakhouse is reported to be located about 1/2 of a mile from the Rancho Murieta Airport within the Rancho Murieta Plaza towards Highway 16. Transportation can be arranged by calling the restaurant in advance. They are open 7 days a week for lunch between 11:30 a.m. and 3 p.m., then again for dinner between 5 p.m. and 10 p.m. Their lunch menu features items like Chinese selections, chicken salad, New York steak sandwiches, garlic and filet melts. Their dinner menu contains selections like steak, prime rib and filet mignon, baked mostaccioli, chicken and dumplings, and chicken fried steak. On Tuesday and Wednesday evenings, they have special Bar-B-Qued items. They also offer specials throughout the week as well. The Riders Steakhouse is decorated with pictures of horses, riding events and has a theme displaying many items associated with horse back riding and the skill of the equestrian rider. Accommodations for small and large groups can be arranged within their banquet area. For more information call the Riders Steakhouse at 354-2878.

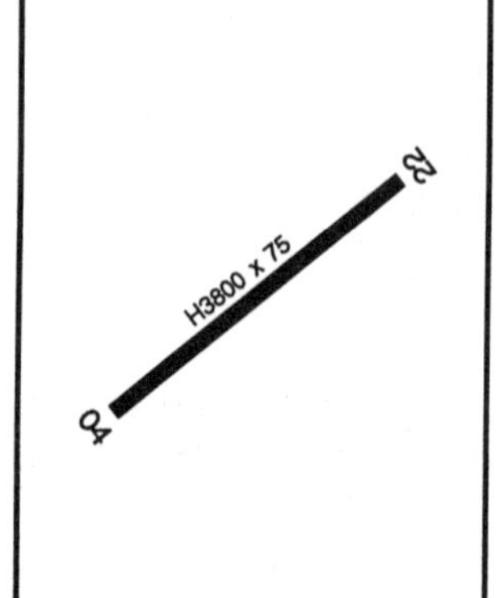

Airport Information:

RANCHO MURIETA - RANCHO MURIETA AIRPORT (RIU)
1 mi west of town N38-29.33 W121-06.15 Elev: 142 Fuel: 100LL, Jet-A Rwy 04-22: H3800x75 (Asph) Arttended: 1600-0100Z Unicom: 122.8
FBO: Rancho Murieta Aviation Phone: 966-8181 or 985-4111
FBO: Pacific Jet Charter Phone: 354-3222 or 800-655-FLYY
FBO: Rancho Murieta Airport Phone: 354-2940

CA-RBL - RED BLUFF
RED BLUFF MUNICIPAL AIRPORT

(Area Code 916) **73**

BJ's Airport Restaurant:

BJ's Restaurant is located on the Red Bluff Municipal Airport north of the hangers. This combination cafe and family style restaurant is situated in the upstairs portion of the terminal building. The restaurant is open 7 a.m. to 2 p.m. 7 days a week. Breakfast and lunch specials are prepared daily. Average prices run $4.15 for breakfast, and around $4.29 for lunch. On Friday they feature a fish fry. Groups and flying associations can arrange catered meals as well. Catering services and meals to go for private or corporate pilots can also be arranged. For more information about BJ's Restaurant call 529-6420.

Restaurants Near Airport:

BJ's Arpt. Restaurant	On Site	Phone: 529-6420
Green Barn	3 mi	Phone: 527-3161
Peking Restaurant	3.5 mi	Phone: 527-0523
Wild Bill's Steakhouse	3 mi	Phone: 529-0342

Lodging: Buttons & Bows Bed & Breakfast 3 mi 527-6405; Flamingo (Free trans) 527-3545; Best Western Grand Manor Inn 5 mi 529-7060; Lamplighter (Free trans, 2 miles) 527-1150; Sky Terrace Motel (2 miles) 527-3645.

Meeting Rooms: None Reported

Transportation: Taxi Service: Red Bluff 529-2219; Page Rental Cars 527-6211.

Information: Red Bluff-Tehama County Chamber of Commerce, 100 Main Street, P.O. Box 850, Red Bluff, CA 96080, Phone: 527-6220.

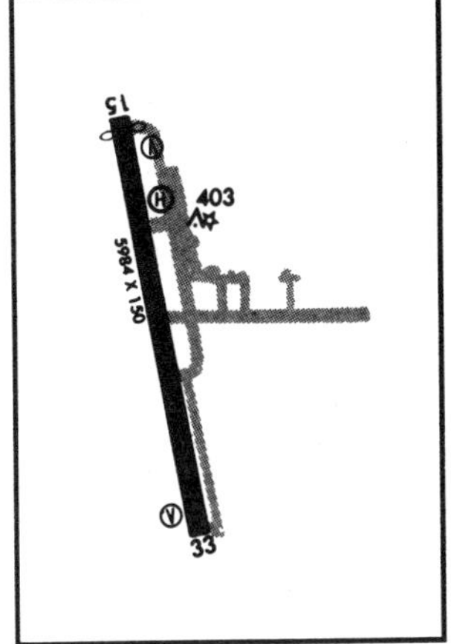

Airport Information:

RED BLUFF - RED BLUFF MUNICIPAL AIRPORT (RBL)
2 mi south of town N40-09.06 W122-15.14 Elev: 349 Fuel: 80, 100LL, Jet-A
Rwy 15-33: H5984x150 (Asph) Attended: 1500Z-dusk Unicom: 122.8
FBO: DZ Phone: 527-6211

CA-O85 - REDDING
BENTON FIELD AIRPORT

(Area Code 916) **74**

Airport Cafe:

The Airport Cafe is located in the Hillside Aviation Building at the Benton Field Airport. This cafe is open weekdays from 7 a.m. to 3 p.m. and on weekends from 8 a.m. to 3 p.m. Their menu contains a complete selection of breakfast and lunch items. Greek and American dishes are featured as their specialty. Average prices run $4.50 for breakfast and $5.00 for lunch. The restaurant contains an aeronautical theme and has accommodations for groups and parties. Catering for pilots on-the-go can also be arranged with cheese trays, sandwiches and hot meals. For more information call the restaurant at 241-7934.

Attractions:

Lake Shasta Caverns guided tours include a boat ride on McCloud Arm lake followed by a transport bus up the mountain to the enterance of the cavern. This attraction is located approx. 16 miles north of the town of Redding by taking I-5 then 1-1/2 miles east on Shasta Cavern Road. For information call 238-2341.

Restaurants Near Airport:

Airport Cafe	On Site	Phone: 241-7934
C.R Gibbs	3-5 mi W	Phone: 221-2335
JD Bennetts	3-5 mi NW	Phone: 221-6177
Red Lobster	3-5 mi NW	Phone: 222-6191

Lodging: Red Lion Inn 221-8700; Holiday Inn Holidome 221-7500; Best Western Hilltop 221-6100; Days Hotel Redding 221-8200

Meeting Rooms: All facilities listed under "Lodging" contain accommodations for meeting space.

Transportation: Hillside Aviation may provide limited courtesy transportation to nearby facilities with advance notice 241-4204; ABC Cab 246-0577; Redding Yellow Cab 222-1234; Airport Bus 222-5456; Car Rental: Avis 221-2855; Hertz 222-4620; National 222-2662.

Information: Convention and Visitors Bureau, 777 Auditorium Drive, Redding, CA 96001, Phone: 225-4100 or 800-874-7562.

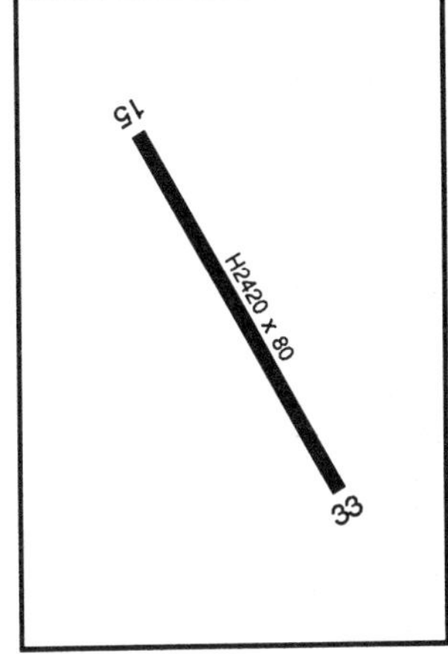

Airport Information:

REDDING - BENTON FIELD AIRPORT (O85)
1 mi west of town N40-34.49 W122-24.48 Elev: 719 Fuel: 100, Jet-A
Rwy 15-33: H2420x80 (Asph) Attended: 1400Z-dusk Unicom: 122.8 Public Phone 24hrs
Notes: No landing fee. Transient (Single) $4.00, (Twin) $5.00, (Heli) $5.00.
FBO: Hillside Aviation Phone: 241-4204

CA-RDD - REDDING
REDDING MUNICIPAL AIRPORT

(Area Code 916)

75

Restaurants Near Airport:

Chu's Restaurnat	On Site	Phone: 222-1364
C.R. Gibbs	3-5 mi W	Phone: 221-2335
JD Bennetts	3-5 mi NW	Phone: 221-6177
Red Lobster	3-5 mi NW	Phone: 222-6191

Lodging: Red Lion Inn 221-8700; Holiday Inn (Holidome) 221-7500; Hilltop Inn Best Western 221-6100, Days Hotel Redding 221-8200.

Meeting Rooms: Red Lion Inn 221-8700; Holiday Inn (Holidome) 221-7500; Hilltop Inn Best Western 221-6100; Days Hotel Redding 221-8200.

Transportation: Airport bus 222-5456; Taxi Service: ABC Cab 246-0577; Redding Yellow Cab 222-1234; Rental Cars: Avis 221-2855; Hertz 221-4620; National 221-2662.

Information: Convention and Visitors Bureau, 777 Auditorium Drive, Redding, CA 96001, Phone: 225-4100.

Chu's Restaurant:

Chu's Restaurant is located on the Redding Municipal Airport. Fly-in guests can park their aircraft near the terminal building and walk to the restaurant. at the restaurant. This is a family style restaurant. This dining facility is open for lunch 11 a.m. to 2:30 p.m. and for dinner 4:30 p.m. to 9 p.m. 7 days a week. The menu features Mandarin dishes. Daily specials are also provided. The main dining room can seat 150 people. In the rear portion of the restaurant is additional seating for 100 people. Groups and parties can easily be accommodated. For more information call the restaurant at 222-1364.

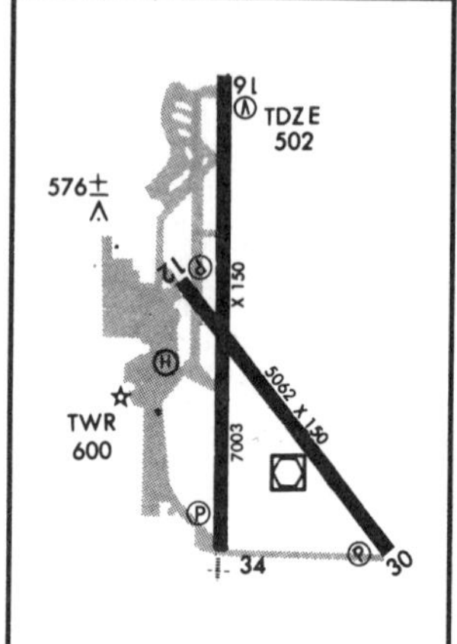

Airport Information:

REDDING - REDDING MUNICIPAL AIRPORT (RDD)

6 mi southeast of town N40-30.54 W122-17.60 Elev: 502 Fuel: 100LL, Jet-A Rwy 16-34: H7003x150 (Asph-Pfc) Rwy 12-30: H5062x150 (Asph) Attended: dawn to dusk Atis: 124.1 Unicom: 122.95 Tower: 119.8 Gnd Con: 121.7 Public Phone 24hrs Notes: No landing fees for GA aircraft; Transient $4.00 single, $5.00 twin & $5.00 for heli; CAUTION: Extensive Ultralight operations within 1 nautical mile radius of Redding Sky Ranch from surface to 1000 feet AGL. Also 4.5 northwest in vicinity of Enterprise Skypark.

Airport Manager	**Phone: 224-4321**
FBO: American Propeller Service	**Phone: 221-4470**
FBO: IASCO (Flight Center)	**Phone: 222-0100**
FBO: Redding Aero Enterprises	**Phone: 224-2300**

CA-L67 - RIALTO
RIALTO MUNICIPAL (MIRO FIELD)

(Area Code 714)

76

Restaurants Near Airport:

Dee Dee's Restaurant	On Site	Phone: 823-9166

Lodging: California 6 Motel 877-2611; El Rey Motel (4 miles) 875-0134; Fiesta Motel (3 miles) 875-4953; Ontario Airport Inn (1 mile) 988-0602; Travel Lodge (2-4 miles) 824-1520.

Meeting Rooms: Ontario Airport Inn 988-0602; Travel Lodge 824-1520.

Transportation: Rental Cars: Agency 889-9561; Budget 889-0076.

Information: California Division of Tourism, P.O. Box 1499, Sacramento, CA 95812, Phone: 800-862-2543.

Airport Diner

The Airport Diner is located only a few feet from the parking area at the Rialto Municipal (Miro Field) Airport. This cafe styled restaurant has a 1950's theme, and decorated with some automobile memorabilia, photo's etc. Also according to the management antique and classic car shows are held nearby. The restaurant is open 7 days a week between 7 a.m. and 3 p.m. They specialize in breakfast and lunch selections. Some of the items on their menu include ham steak, biscuits & gravy, omelets, specials like scrambled egg dishes, hamburgers, steak sandwiches, soups, salads, desserts and pies. Daily lunch specials are also prepared. The dining area can seat 65 to 70 persons and offers a great view of the airport from inside the restaurant through large windows. They also have an outdoor patio that seats an additional 60 persons, and is a favorite with many of their guests. Meals can also be prepared-to-go if requested. For more information about Dee Dee's Restaurant call 823-9166.

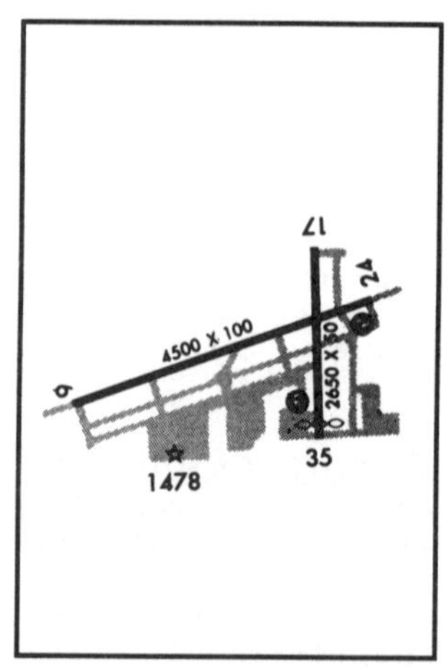

Airport Information:

RIALTO - RIALTO MUNICIPAL (MIRO FIELD) (L67)

3 mi northwest of town 34-07-44N 117-24-02W Elev: 1455 Fuel: 80, 100, 100LL, Jet-A Rwy 06-24: H4500x100 (Asph) Rwy 17-35: H2650x60 (Asph) Attended: 1600-0100Z Unicom: 122.8

FBO: Air Comm Systems, Inc.	**Phone: 824-8860**
FBO: Art Scholl Aviation	**Phone: 874-5800**
FBO: Sunland Aviation	**Phone: 877-2608**
FBO: Western Helicopters	**Phone: 829-1051**

CA-RAL - RIVERSIDE
RIVERSIDE MUNICIPAL AIRPORT

(Area Code 909)

77

D & D Airport Cafe:

The Airport Cafe is located adjacent to the terminal building on the west side of the airport. Pilots can park their aircraft right outside the restaurant. This cafe styled restaurant is open between 6 a.m. and 9 p.m. 7 days a week. Specialties of the house are a full complement of breakfast selections, homemade soups, fish, ribs, sandwiches, steaks, toast turkey and desserts. A specials of the day are also served like meatloaf or Mexican dishes. The restaurant has lots of booths that allow a nice view of the runways. Outside dining is also available. For larger groups there is seating for 16 to 20 people. In-flight catering is also provided. Call the restaurant and they will deliver to the FBO, or place your order in person and take it with you. For more information about the D & D Airport Cafe call them at 688-3337.

Restaurants Near Airport:

Bob's Big Boy	1 mi	Phone: 359-9151
D & D Airport Cafe	On Site	Phone: 688-3337
Food Connection	3 mi	Phone: 689-0755
Harry C's	7 mi	Phone: 686-2212

Lodging: Airport Inn (Adj Arpt) 689-3391; American Inn (4 miles) 351-0355; Arlington Motor Inn (Adj Arpt) 351-9990; Best Western (3-1/2 miles) 359-0770; Holiday Inn (8-10 miles) 682-8000;

Meeting Rooms: Airport administrative offices conference room available 351-6113; Also Holiday Inn 682-8000;

Transportation: Riverside Air Service (FBO) can provide courtesy transportation to nearby facilities 688-8600. Yellow or Red Cab 684-1234; RTA Bus 682-1234; Rental Cars: Enterprise Rent-A-Car 352-9477.

Information: Visitors and Convention Bureau, 3443 Orange Street, Riverside, CA 92501, Phone: 787-7950; Also contact City of Riverside's Parks and Recreation Department at 782-5301.

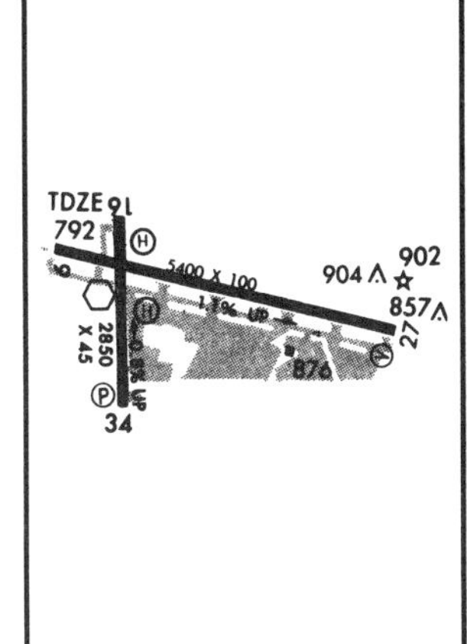

Airport Information:

RIVERSIDE - RIVERSIDE MUNICIPAL AIRPORT (RAL)
4 southwest of town N33-57.11 W117-26.71 Elev: 816 Fuel: 100LL, Jet-A
Rwy 09-27: H5400x100 (Asph) Rwy 16-34: H2850x50 (Asph) Attended: Mon-Fri 1500-0200Z, Sat-Sun 1500-0100Z Atis: 128.8 Unicom: 122.95 Tower: 121.0 Gnd Con: 121.7
Public Phone 24hrs Notes: Overnight parking fees reported: singles $5.00; twins $7.50; Jets $10.00
FBO: Riverside Air Service Phone: 689-1160

CA-RIR - RIVERSIDE (RUBIDOUX)
FLABOB AIRPORT

(Area Code 909)

78

Silver Wings Cafe:

The Airport Cafe is located mid-point to the taxiway 06-24, at the Riverside Flabob Airport. You can taxi up and park your airplane right by the restaurant. This cafe is open from 6:30 a.m. to 5 p.m. daily. Their menu contains a variety of delicious entrees as well as breakfast, lunch and dinner specials. On Friday they offer corned beef and cabbage. Prices run about $4.00 for selections off the menu during breakfast, lunch and dinner. The decor is aviation related with pictures of airplanes and pilots, as well as a fireplace and plenty of seating for customers. On Thursday evenings, they stay open until 8 p.m., and feature specialties like Cajun whitefish, steak & enchiladas and Tri-tip filet. The Silver Wings Cafe can accommodate private parties for up to 75 people. After hours, the restaurant can also be made available for special planned group get-togethers. For more information call 683-9066.

Restaurants Near Airport:

Cask & Cleaver	3 blks W.	Phone: 682-4580
Gay & Larru's (Mex).	1/4 mi N.	Phone: 684-0645
Palace of the Dragon	1/4 mi NW.	Phone: 684-0123
Silver Wings Cafe	On Site	Phone: 683-9066

Lodging: (No pickup service provided by hotels), Sheraton Riverside Hotel, 1 mile east, Phone: 784-8000; Holiday Inn, 2 miles north on University Ave., Phone: 800-465-4329;
Conference Rooms: Conference rooms available at hotels listed above. (See Lodging listed above)
Transportation: Taxi or rental cars: Budget Rent-A-Car, 653-7017; Red Cab Company, 684-1234; Riverside Taxi Company, 684-1234
Information: Visitors and Convention Bureau, 3443 Orange Street, Riverside, CA 92501, Phone: 787-7950.

Attractions:

Indian Hills Country Club (Golf, 2 miles West), at 57 Club House Drive, Phone: 685-7443.

Airport Information:

RIVERSIDE (RUBIDOUX) - FLABOB (RIR)
3 mi northwest of town N33-59.38 W117-24.64 Elev: 764 Fuel: 80, 100LL
Rwy 06-24: H3200x50 (ASPH) Attended: Tue-Sun 1630-0100Z Unicom: 122.8 Public phone 24 hrs Notes: CAUTION, (Land at your own risk) Rwy 06-24 numerous cracks; eroded edges and rough surface. Avoid flying over the trailer park 1000' east of Rwy. Rwy 24 after takeoff turn 10 degrees; stay north of river bed. Call airport manager at 683-2309 for information about runway conditions. Stray dogs on runway, also numerous birds from landfill 1 mile south of airport. 1,340' mountain 3/4 mile SE. of airport. (See Airport Facility Directory for further comments about airport)
FBO: Flabob Airport, Inc. Phone: 683-2309

H3200 x 50
06
24

CA-L00 - ROSAMOND
ROSAMOND SKYPARK AIRPORT

(Area Code 805) 79

Golden Cantina Restaurant:

The Golden Cantina Restaurant is located right on the southeast side of the field at the Rosamond Skypark Airport. After landing, you can taxi right up to the front of the restaurant where there is parking space for aircraft. It's about 40 feet from the runway. This restaurant specializes in Mexican and seafood entrees, as well as a variety of salads, appetizers, soups and desserts. They offer a weekly buffet Wednesday through Friday from 11:00 a.m. to 2:00 p.m. and a Tuesday dinner buffet from 5 p.m. to 8 p.m. The decor is modern southwestern. If planning to fly-in with a group, you can bring as many as 100 of your friends. Accommodations for luncheons, weddings, business meetings etc., will be gladly provided. Catering for pilots on-the-go include Mexican entrees, hot meals, appetizers, etc. The restaurant is open Monday through Wednesday 11 a.m. to 9 p.m. and Friday and Saturday from 11 a.m. to 10 p.m. and Sunday 10 a.m. to 9 p.m. For information call 256-6737.

Restaurants Near Airport:

Golden Cantina	On Site	Phone: 256-6737
Villa Basque	2 mi SW	Phone: 256-4182

Lodging: Devonshire Inn, three miles from airport, Phone: 256-3454

Transportation: None Reported

Information: None Reported

Attractions: Willow Springs International Raceway, Edwards Air Force Test Facility, Exotic Feline Compound, World's International Chili Cookoff.

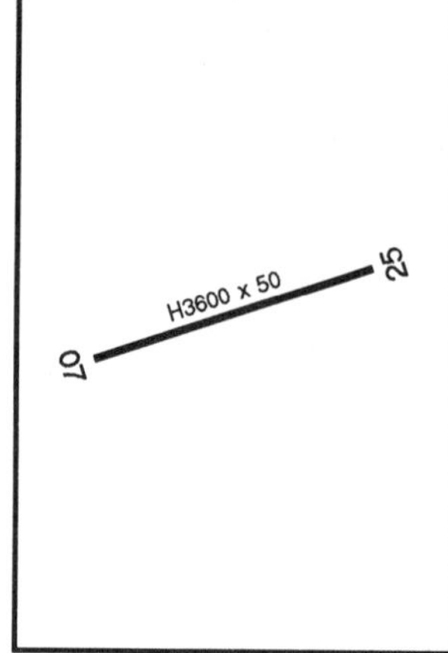

Airport Information:

ROSAMOND - ROSAMOND SKYPARK (L00)
3 mi west of town N34-52.25 W118-12.55 Elev: 2415 Fuel: 100LL
Rwy 07-25: H3600x50 (ASPH) Attended: 1500Z-0100Z
Public Phone 24 hrs CTAF: 122.9 Notes: Intensive glider operations on airport. (Gliders use Rgt. tfc. pattern Rwy 25)
FBO: Airport Manager Phone: 256-4965

CA-Q95 - RUTH
RUTH AIRPORT

(Area Code 707, 916) 80

Flying AA Ranch Restaurant:

We were told that this establishment will have a new management. We have retained the previous information as a reference. We recommend you check with the new owners prior to use. The Flying AA Ranch is located only 500 yards from the Ruth Airport, and is only a five minute walk to the ranch. Courtesy transportation is also available by van. The restaurant is a family style facility which is open 7 days a week between 7 a.m. and 9 p.m. during the summer season from Memorial day to Labor Day, and 8 a.m. to 8 p.m. in the off season. Their menu includes prime rib specials, steak and lobster, prawns, 3 or 4 different types of choice steaks, salad bar from 6 p.m. to 9 p.m. and a full breakfast selection. Average prices run $4.85 for breakfast, $2.95 to $6.95 for lunch and $13.95 and up for dinner. Specials are offered in addition to their Friday prime rib dinners and Saturday barbecued chicken and ribs. The dining room has a western decor and seating for about 50 persons. This ranch offers a variety of activities including guided tours on horse back, tennis, bike rentals, swimming in their pool, trap shooting, outdoor barbecues, camping, fishing in nearby streams and lakes as well as many other sporting activities. For information about the restaurant or ranch, call the Flying AA Ranch at 574-6227 or 574-6417.

Restaurants Near Airport:
Flying AA Ranch Adj Arpt. Phone: 574-6227 or 623-1365

Lodging: Flying AA Ranch 574-6227 or 574-6417.
Meeting Rooms: Conference rooms are available at the Flying AA Ranch 574-6227 or 574-6417.
Transportation: It is only a 5 minute walk to the Flying AA Ranch. However, courtesy transportation is available by van.
Information: Flying AA Ranch Ruth Star Route, Box 700, Bridgeville, CA 95526, Phone: 574-6227 or 574-6417.

Attractions:

The Flying AA Ranch comes equipped with its own airport only 500 yards from the main lodge. Its "Don't fence-me-in" size, appeals to all ages on this honest-to-goodness working cattle ranch, deep in the heart of Northern California's Coast Range Mountains. Accommodations include a modern motel, ranch style dining room, banquet room for special parties in addition to a cocktail lounge and dance hall. All types of outdoor or indoor activities are also available. For information call 574-6227 or 574-6417.

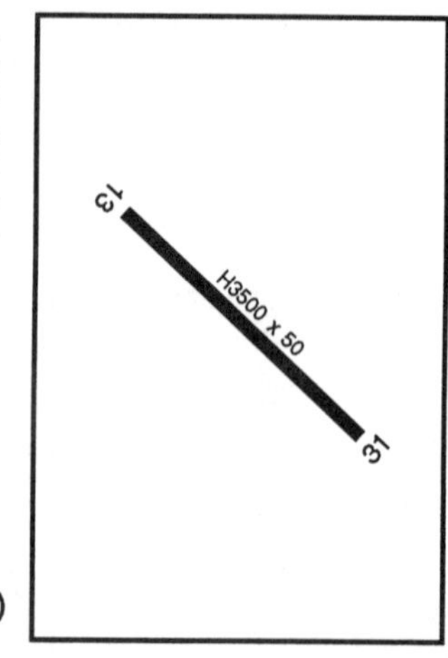

Airport Information:

RUTH - RUTH AIRPORT (Q95)
7 mi south of town N40-12.68 W123-17.85 Elev: 2781 Fuel: 100LL
Rwy 13-31: H3500x50 (Asph) Attended: unattended Unicom: 122.8 Notes: Overnight parking $2.00 CAUTION: High terrain surrounds arpt. **NOTE: (Check with new management prior to use)**
Ruth Airport (Flying AA Ranch) Phone: 707-574-6227 or 916-623-1365

CA-SAC - SACRAMENTO
SACRAMENTO EXECUTIVE ARPT.

(Area Code 916) **81, 82**

Restaurants Near Airport:
Marie Callendar Rest. 1/2 mi Phone: 391-4300
Tailspin Deli On Site Phone: 399-8973

Marie Callendar Restaurant:

The Marie Callendar Restaurant is situated about 1/2 mile from the Sacramento Executive Airport. This family style facility is open Monday through Thursday from 7 a.m. to 10 p.m., Friday and Saturday from 7 a.m. to 11 p.m. and Sunday between 7 a.m. and 10 p.m. Their menu features a nice variety of Italian selections like, fettucini, tortellineis, pastas, spaghetti, hot sandwiches, chili, hamburgers, soups and salads. The main dining area is decorated with brick floors and can accommodate 80 people. The restaurant offers casual dining in a comfortable atmosphere, and is furnished with booths and tables. Large groups and parties are welcome with advance notice. Meals can also be prepared to go on request. For more information call Marie Callendar Restaurant at 391-4300.

Tailspin Deli:

The Tailspin Deli restaurant is situated within the main terminal building at the Sacramento Executive Airport (SAC) For information on hours and services call 399-8973.

Lodging: Beverly Garland Motor Lodge (7 miles) 929-7900; Hilton Inn Sacramento (7 miles) 922-4700; Holiday Inn (5 miles) 446-0100; Paul Bunyan Lodge (2 miles) 422-3760; Red Lion Motor Inn (7 miles) 929-8855; Sacramento Inn (7 miles) 922-8041; Sky Riders (Adj arpt) 421-5700.

Meeting Rooms: Beverly Garland Motor Lodge 929-7900; Hilton Inn Sacramento (Convention facilities) 922-4700; Holiday Inn 446-0100; Red Lion Motor Inn 929-8855.
Transportation: Taxi Service: Camelia City 381-6868; Carey Limousine Service 485-7268 or 635-3748; Courtesy 448-8237; Greyhound 443-3961; Yellow Cab 444-2222; Rental Cars: Senator Ford 427-1279.
Information: Convention & Visitors Bureau, 1421 K Street, Sacramento, CA 95814, Phone: 264-7777.

Attractions:

Executive Flyers, Inc. (FBO) has a pilots shop reported on the premises, 427-1888.

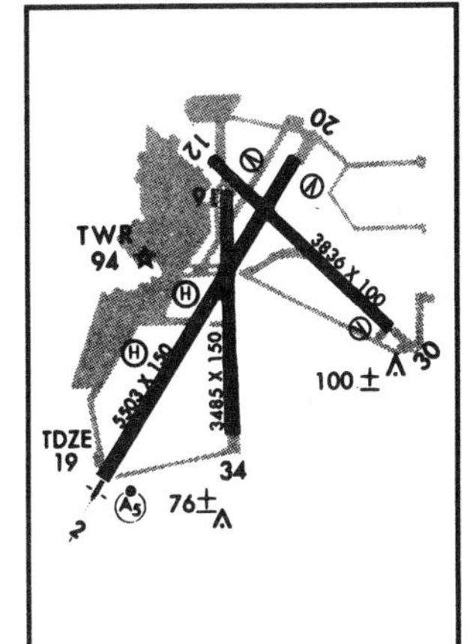

Airport Information:

SACRAMENTO - SACRAMENTO EXECUTIVE AIRPORT (SAC)
3 mi southwest of town N38-30.75 W121-29.61 Elev: 21 Fuel: 100LL, Jet-A
Rwy 02-20: H5503x150 (Asph) Rwy 12-30: H3836x100 (Asph) Rwy 16-34: H3485x150 (Asph)
Attended: 1400-0500Z Atis: 125.5 Unicom: 122.95 App Con: 127.4, 125.25, 119.1, 118.8
Dep Con: 127.4, 118.8, 125.25 Executive Tower: 119.5 Gnd Con: 125.0
FBO: C.F.I. **Phone: 427-7707**
FBO: Flight Operations **Phone: 429-3333**
FBO: Patterson Aviation Co. **Phone: 428-8292**

CA-SMF - SACRAMENTO
SACRAMENTO METRO ARPT.

(Area Code 916) **83**

Restaurants Near Airport:
Vista Dining Room (Host Intl) On Site Phone: 922-8071

The Vista Dining Room (Host Intl.):

This family style restaurant is located in the terminal building at the Sacramento Metropolitan Airport. We were told that guests can park their aircraft over by the general aviation ramp and obtain a courtesy shuttle to the restaurant. This restaurant offers casual dining and is open from 11 a.m. to 3 p.m. for lunch and from 5 p.m. to 9 p.m. for dinner. This facility may be closed on weekends. Items on their menu include sandwiches, French dip, grilled chicken, express lunches, and for dinner, they have prime rib, chicken teriaki, catch of the day, as well as soups and salads. Average prices run $4.95 to $6.95 for most items, and up to $14.95 for choice steaks. The restaurant can accommodate 50 to 60 persons and has large windows allowing guests to watch passenger loading and unloading. In addition to the restaurant, Host International also provides lodging in their hotel across the street. This complex contains 84 units as well as 9 meeting rooms able to serve 10 to 400 people. For information call 929-9596 or 922-8071.

Lodging: Host International Hotel (On Site) 922-8071; Best Western Harbor Inn (Free trans) 371-2100; Best Western Sandman (Free trans) 443-6515; Beverly Garland Hotel (Free trans) 929-7900; Clarion (Free trans) 482-6971; Days Inn (Free trans) 447-3621; Discovery Motor Inn (Free trans) 442-6971; Fountain Suites (Free trans) 441-1444; Hilton Inn Sacramento (Free trans 922-4700; Hotel El Rancho Resort/Conference Center (Free trans) 371-6731; Radisson (Free trans) 922-2020; Red Lion Motor Inn (Free trans) 929-8855; Red Lion Sacramento Inn (Free trans) 922-8041; Vagabond Inn (Free trans) 446-1481;
Meeting Rooms: All hotels listed above have accommodations for meeting rooms. The following have convention facilities: Hotel El Rancho Resort/Conference Center 371-6731; Hilton Inn Sacramento 922-4700; Radisson 922-2020;
Transportation: Avis 922-5601; Budget 927-2425; Dollar 924-1100; Hertz 927-3882; National 927-3644.
Information: Convention & Visitors Bureau, 1421 K Street, Sacramento, CA 95814, Phone: 264-7777

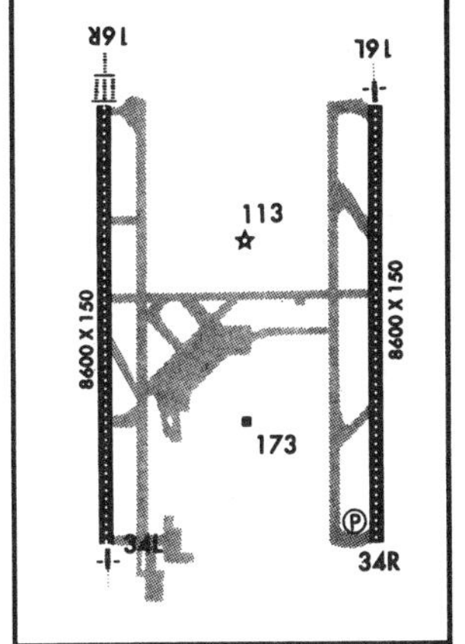

Airport Information:

SACRAMENTO - SACRAMENTO METROPOLITAN AIRPORT (SMF)
10 mi northwest of town N38-41.73 W121-35.45 Elev: 25 Fuel: 100, Jet-A
Rwy 16R-34L: H8600x150 (Asph-Pfc) Rwy 16L-34R: H8600x150 (Conc-Grvd) Attended: continuously App Con: 127.4, 119.1, 120.45, 124.5, 125.6, 125.25, 118.8 Dep Con: 127.4, 125.25, 124.5 Metro Tower: 125.7 Gnd Con: 121.7 Clnc Del: 121.1 Public Phone 24hrs Notes: No landing fee, $6.25 overnight parking fee.
FBO: No fixed base operation reported
Sacramento Metropolitan Airport **Phone: 929-5411**

CA-SNS - SALINAS
SALINAS MUNICIPAL AIRPORT

(Area Code 408)

84

Salinas Airport Bar & Grill:

The Salinas Airport Bar & Grill is situated right next door to available transient aircraft parking. This family style restaurant is open 7 days a week Monday through Wednesday 7 a.m. to 6 p.m. and Thursday through Sunday 7 a.m. to 9 p.m. They specialize in preparing American and Chinese food, including steaks, chicken and seafood dishes. Average prices run $4.25 for breakfast, $5.25 to $5.95 for lunch and $8.50 to $16.00 for dinner. Specials each day usually include one American and one Chinese dish. The restaurant can seat up to 120 persons with accommodations up to 100 persons for larger groups or parties. Everything on their menu can be ordered-to-go if requested. In-flight catering is a service of this facility as well. For more information call the Salina's Airport Bar & Grill at 422-0519.

Restaurants Near Airport:
Salinas Airport Bar & Grill On Site Phone: 422-0519

Lodging: Appling Inn (1-2 miles) 422-6486; Hi-Way Center Lodge (1 mile) 424-1741; Laurel Inn Motel (2 miles) 449-2474; Motel 6 (1 mile); Ramada Inn (1-2 miles) 424-8661.

Meeting Rooms: Laurel Inn 449-2474; Ramada Inn (1-2 miles) 424-8661.

Transportation: Taxi Service: Yellow Cab 443-1234; Rental Cars: American Auto Leasing 757-5144; Budget 422-7488; Trans Plus 424-8918.

Information: Chamber of Commerce, 119 East Alisal Street, P.O. Box 1170, Salinas, CA 93902, Phone: 424-7611.

Attractions:

Salinas Fairways Golf Course (1/4 mile from airport); Monterey Peninsula approx. 18-20 miles from airport.

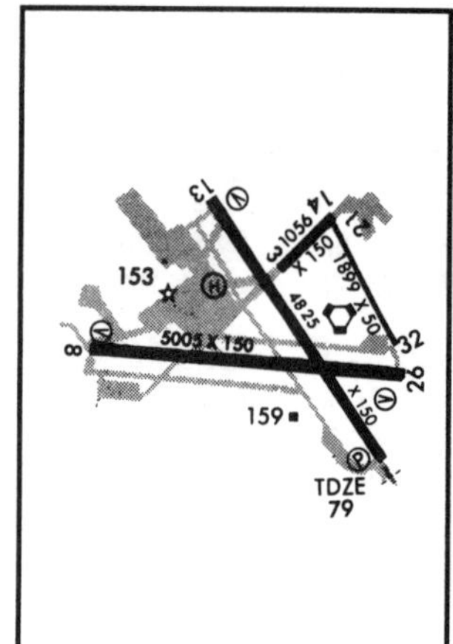

Airport Information:

SALINAS - SALINAS MUNICIPAL AIRPORT (SNS)
3 mi southeast of town N36-39.79 W121-36.38 Elev: 84 Fuel: 100LL, Jet-A
Rwy 08-26: H5005x200 (Asph) Rwy 13-31: H4825x150 (Asph) Rwy 14-32: H1899x50 (Asph)
Attended: continuously Atis: 124.85 Unicom: 122.95 Tower: 119.4 Gnd Con: 121.7
Public Phone 24hrs Notes: Overnight tie-down fees, singles $3.00/night, twins $5.00/night.

Salinas Municipal Airport	**Phone: 758-7214**
FBO: Advancetech Aircraft Maint.	**Phone: 422-2142**
FBO: Air Trails	**Phone: 757-5144**

CA-SQL - SAN CARLOS
SAN CARLOS AIRPORT

(Area Code 415)

85

Sky Kitchen Restaurant:

This cafe is located on the northeast end of the San Carlos Airport adjacent to the transient parking area. It is open Monday through Friday 6:30 a.m. to 4:30 p.m. and Saturday and Sunday 6:30 a.m. to 3 p.m. They specialize insserving breakfast and luncheon selections. Average prices run $5.00 for breakfast and $6.00 for lunch. Daily specials are also offered. The restaurant is decorated with aviation related items. Fly-in guests are welcome. For information you can call 595-0464.

Restaurants Near Airport:

Holiday Inn of Belmont	1 mi NW	Phone: 591-1471
Sky Kitchen Restaurant	On Site	Phone: 595-0464
Sofitel Hotel	1 mi NW	Phone: N/A
Taqueria	1/2 mi W	Phone: 591-3520

Lodging: Holiday Inn (1 mile) 591-1471; Sofitel Hotel (1 mile); Meeting Rooms: Holiday Inn (1 mile) 591-1471.

Transportation: Avis 592-1000; Budget 592-7362; Discount Rental Cars 592-8014; Hertz located in lobby at airport.

Information: Chamber of Commerce, 325 Forest Avenue, Palo Alto, CA 94301, Phone: 324-3121

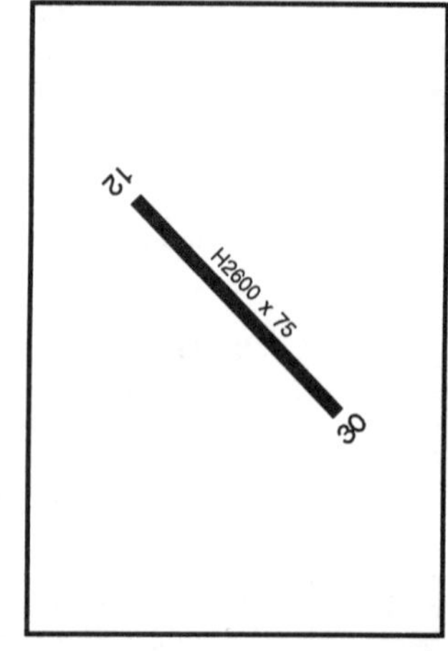

Airport Information:

SAN CARLOS - SAN CARLOS AIRPORT (SQL)
2 mi northeast of town N37-30.66 W122-14.98 Elev: 02 Fuel: 100, 100LL, Jet-A
Rwy 12-30: H2600x75 (Asph) Attended: 1500-0700Z Atis: 125.9 Unicom: 122.95
Tower: 119.0 Gnd Con: 121.6 Public Phone 24hrs Notes: No landing fees, overnight parking $6.00/night
San Carlos Airport Phone: 573-3700

CA-MYF - SAN DIEGO MONTGOMERY FIELD

(Area Code 619)

86, 87

94th Aero Squadron:

The 94th Aero Squadron is located adjacent to the San Diego Montgomery Field. You can reach the restaurant by cab or shuttle from Gibbs Flying Service (FBO) or Crown Air (FBO). Lunch includes homemade bread & choice of soup or salad; dinner includes homemade bread, soup and salad. They have a large selection of appetizers, desserts, and a full service bar. Prices run about $8.00 for lunch and $17.00 for dinner. The restaurant is patterned after a WW-II European villa with authentic photos, posters and Armed Forces material including original airplane wings (And a tri-wing Faulker in the front yard). They will cater either sit down lunches, dinner, or brunches as well as finger food buffets for parties up to 150 persons. While dining, you can enjoy a full panoramic view of the entire runway area from your booth, dining area or their lounge. For more information call 560-6771.

Casa Machado:

This family style restaurant is located adjacent to the transient parking area on Montgomery Field in San Diego. They specialize in Mexican style food, in addition to many other items like appetizers, desserts, salads, soups and various sandwiches. Daily specials are included on their menu along with a special happy hour serving horsdoeuvres, and brunch on Sunday. Prices range from $4.95 for lunch to about $6.50 for dinner. The restaurant is open on Monday through Saturday from 11 a.m. to 10 p.m., Sunday from 9 a.m. to 9 p.m. (Closed on Easter, Thanksgiving Day, Christmas and New Year's Day). There is a partially enclosed all year around patio able to accommodate up to 100 guests, in addition to the main dining room. The decor is primarily Mexican in style with models of aircraft hanging from the ceiling. Fly-in groups often visit this restaurant in groups of 20 or more. Catering for wedding receptions, business meetings and retirement parties can be arranged, upon request. For information call 292-4716.

Restaurants Near Airport:

94th Aero Squadron	On Site	Phone: 560-6771
B & B Deli,	Adj Arpt.	Phone: 292-1636
Casa Machado	On Site	Phone: 292-4716
Tlengu Japanese Rest.	Adj Arpt.	Phone: 292-0140

Lodging: Holiday Inn (On field, Montgomery), courtesy transportation, Phone: 277-8888; Quality Suites (4 miles) call for transportation. (Telephones in terminal building)

Meeting Rooms: Holiday Inn (Montgomery Field), Phone: 277-8888

Transportation: General Rent-A-Car, 278-8795; Yellow Taxi, 234-6161; San Diego Bus (Information), 239-8161.

Information: San Diego Convention & Visitors Bureau, International Visitor Center, 11 Horton Plaza, 1st & F street, San Diego, CA 92101. Phone: 263-1212; Recorded information about daily events call, Phone: 239-9696.

Attractions:

San Diego Zoo: (8 miles), One of the most spectacular and largest zoo in the United States, subtropical gardens containing over 800 species 100 acres of natural surroundings, moving sidewalks, aerial tramway, 40 minute guided tours, Phone: 234-3153; San Diego Sea World: (7 miles), This marine park contains 135 acres with 7 shows and more than 30 exhibits on display, featuring ocean and sea creatures from whales to sea lions in a spectacular and sometimes comical role. Phone: 226-3901 or (800-325-3150 except CA residents); Reuben H. Fleet Space Theater and Science Center: (8 miles), OMNIMAX theater, more than 50 permanent exhibits available for tantalizing the imagination of natural phenomena. (Summer and Winter shows) Phone: 238-1168; San Diego Aerospace Museum: (8 miles), Full scale exhibits of original and static reproductions of space vehicles and aircraft in addition to the Aerospace Hall of Fame, Phone: 234-8291; San Diego Wild Animal Park: (30 miles), 1,800 acre wild life park and preservation area containing over 2,400 species of African & Asian animals roaming freely. Shows, guided tours, recreated Nairobi Village and botanical exhibits. Phone: 480-0100.

Airport Information:

SAN DIEGO - MONTGOMERY FIELD (MYF)
6 mi north of town N32-48.96 W117-08.42 Elev: 423 Fuel: 100LL, Jet-A Rwy 10L-28R: H4600x150 (Asph) Rwy 05-23: H3402x150 (ASPH) Rwy 10L-28R: H3400x150 (ASPH) Rwy 10R-28L: H3399x60 (ASPH) Attended: 1330-0530Z
Atis: 126.9 Unicom: 122.95 App Con: 124.35 Dep Con: 128.6 Tower: 119.2, 125.7 Gnd Con: 121.9 Clnc Del: 127.45 Public Phone 24 hrs Notes: Overnight parking (single or twin) $5.00; Landing fee (Part 135) $10.00;
FBO: Crown Air Phone: 277-1453
FBO: Gibbs Flying Service Phone: 277-0310

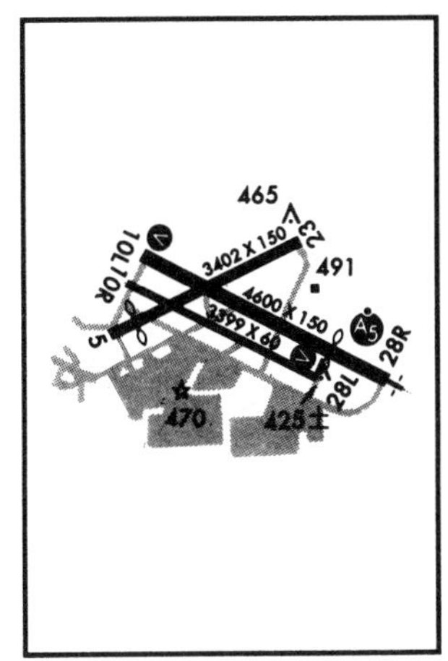

CA-SAN - SAN DIEGO
SAN DIEGO INTL-LINDBERGH FLD.

88

(Area Code 619)

Marriott Host:

Marriott Host manages and operates eateries, cafes and snack bars on the San Diego International Lindbergh Airport. A sit-down restaurant with accommodations for 150 persons is located in the terminal building. This facility is open between 6 a.m. and 9 p.m., and offers full service with a variety of entree selections to choose from. Average prices run $5.99 for most selections. Tables and booths make up most of the seating arrangements for this establishment. Meals can be prepared to carry-out in addition to the standard items on their menu. "A number of fast food establishment are also located throughout the terminal areas. Sky-Chef provides in-flight catering for commercial flight operations as well as private and corporate customers. For catering information, call 231-5490. For more information about the restaurant, call 231-5100.

Attractions: There are many points of interest and attractions within this area. A few of the prominent sites include the San Diego Zoo 234-3153; The Reuben H. Fleet Space Theater and Science Center with 50 permanent exhibits and OMNIMAX theater 238-1168; San Diego Aerospace Museum displaying full scale aircraft 234-8291; International Aerospace Hall of fame 232-8322; Sea World 226-3901, and the San Diego Harbor Excursion 234-4111; And the San Diego Wild Animal Park with over 2,400 wild animals roaming freely on the premises (Animal shows, guided tours, and hiking trails) 480-0100.

Restaurants Near Airport:

Marriott/Host	On Site	Phone: 231-5100
Sky-Chef In-flight cat.	On Site	Phone: 231-5490

Numerous restaurants are located near airport.

Lodging: Best Western Posada Inn (Shuttle service) 224-3254; Best Western Shelter Island (Shuttle service) 222-0561; Howard Johnson Lodge (Shuttle service) 696-0911; Humphrey's Half Moon (Shuttle) 224-3411; Seapoint Hotel (Shuttle service) 224-3621; Sheraton Grand Harbor Island (Shuttle service) 291-6400; Sheraton Harbor Island Hotel (Shuttle service) 291-2900; Travelodge-San Diego Airport (Shuttle service) 232-8931; Viscount Hotel-San Diego (Shuttle service) 291-6700.

Meeting Rooms: All lodging facilities listed above have accommodations for meeting's and conferences.

Transportation: Taxi Service: Yellow Cab 234-6161; Rental Cars: Avis 231-7171; Budget 297-3851; Hertz 231-7000; National 231-7100; Rent-A-Wreck 224-8235.

Information: The San Diego Convention & Visitors Bureau, International Visitors Center, 11 Horton Plaza, 1st & F Streets, San Diego, CA 92101, Phone: 263-1212.

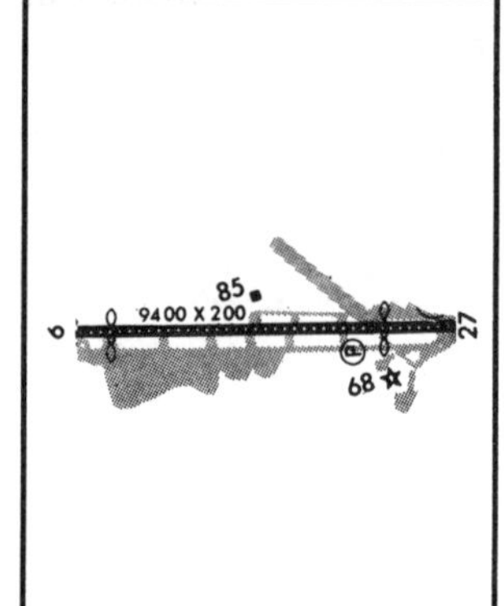

Airport Information:

SANDIEGO - SAN DIEGO INTL-LINDBERGH FLD. (SAN)

2 mi west of town   N32-44.01 W117-11.38   Elev: 14   Fuel: 100LL, Jet-A

Rwy 09-27: H9400x200 (Conc-Asph-Grvd)   Attended: continuously   Atis: 134.8   Unicom: 122.95

App Con: 124.35   Dep Con: 123.9   Lindbergh Tower: 118.3   Gnd Con: 123.9   Clnc Del: 125.9   Notes: No landing fees for private or corporate aircraft, FBO sets their own service fees.

FBO: Jimsair Aviation Services   Phone: 298-7704

CA-SJC - SAN JOSE
SAN JOSE INTERNATIONAL AIRPORT

(Area Code 408) 89, 90

94th Aero Squadron:

The 94th Aero Squadron is located adjacent to the San Jose International Airport. You can reach the restaurant by cab or shuttle from San Jose Jet Center. Turn right on Airport Blvd, right on Coleman Avenue, and the restaurant is located on the right side about 1/4 mile down the street. This facility is open Monday through Saturday from 11 a.m. to 3 p.m. for lunch, with dinner hours from 5 p.m. to 11 p.m. Lunch includes homemade bread and choice of soup or salad; dinner includes homemade bread, soup and salad. They have a large selection of appetizers, desserts and a full service bar. Prices run about $8.00 for lunch and $17.00 for dinner. They also have a buffet-style brunch on Saturday and Sunday. The hours are 11 a.m. to 2:30 p.m. on Saturday and 9 to 2:30 p.m. on Sunday. Champagne is served with Sunday brunch. The restaurant is patterned after a WW-II European villa with authentic photos, posters and Armed Forces material including original airplane wings (and a tri-wing Faulker in the front yard). They will cater either sitdown lunches, dinner, or brunches as well as finger food buffets for parties up to 150 persons. While dining, you can enjoy a full panoramic view of the entire runway area from your booth, dining area or their lounge. For more information call 287-6150.

Av Bon Pain (CA1 Services):

This food service facility is part of the CA1 Services operation. It is located in Terminal A on the San Jose International Airport. It specializes in serving customers takeout items and light fair. Deli sandwiches are their specialty. This establishment is open between 5:30 a.m. and 9:30 p.m. Prices average $4.50 for breakfast, $5.30 for lunch and $6.50 for dinner. For more information call 277-3434.

Restaurants Near Airport:

94th Aero Squadron	On Site	Phone: 287-6150
CA1 Services	Terml A	Phone: 277-3434
Flying Gift Shop & Deli	On Site	Phone: 292-5117
Jora's Restaurant	On Site	Phone: 995-5672

See following page for additional Information about this Airport.

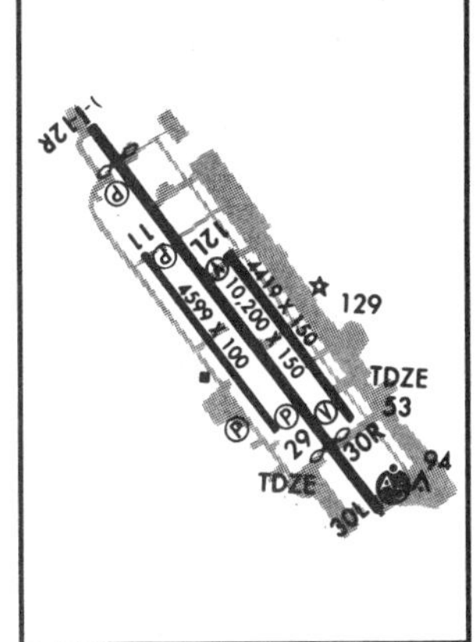

Airport Information:

SAN JOSE - SAN JOSE INTERNATIONAL (SJC)
2 mi northwest of town N37-21.72 W121-55.68 Elev: 58 Fuel: 100LL, Jet-A Rwy 12R-30L: H10200x150 (Asph-Grvd) Rwy 11-29: H4599x100 (Asph) Rwy 12l-30R: H4419x150 (Asph) Attended: continuously Atis: 126.95 (1400-0800Z) CTAF:124.0 Unicom: 122.95 Tower: 124.0, Rwy 12R-30L, 120.7, Rwy 12L-30R (1400-0800Z) Gnd Con: 121.7 Clnc Del: 118.0 Pre Taxi Clnc: 118.0 Public phone: 24hrs

FBO: ACM Aviation,	**Phone:286-3832**	**FBO: Advanced Aviation**	**Phone: 292-0517**
FBO: San Jose Jet Center	**Phone:297-7552**	**FBO: Aris Helicopters**	**Phone: 998-3266**

Photo by: Judy McAlister/Owner

Fly-in Gift Shop located on San Jose Intl. Airport

CA-SJC - SAN JOSE
SAN JOSE INTERNATIONAL AIRPORT

(Area Code 408) 91, 92

Flying Gift Shop and Deli:

The Flying Gift Shop and Deli is located on the first floor of the Jet Center at the San Jose International Airport. This gift shop and deli is open Monday through Thursday, 7:30 a.m. to 7:00 p.m., Friday 7:30 a.m. to 6:00 p.m., Saturday 8:00 a.m. to 5:00 p.m., and Sunday 10:00 a.m. to 5:00 p.m. It offers plenty of pilot supplies, flying gifts, sandwiches, salads, desserts, and beverages. Choose from a wide variety of delicious sandwiches, such as the Gulf Stream - with turkey, ham, salami, swiss and American cheese, or the A-35 - with bacon, lettuce and tomato, or the Lear - with hot pastrami and swiss cheese. Kids will love the J-3 Cub - with lots of peanut butter and jelly. For lighter fare, try Orville's Garden Salad with mixed greens, tomato, mushrooms, cucumber, croutons and pine nuts or the Captains Chef Salad with fresh garden salad, turkey, ham, cheese, egg and artichoke. Try a cool fruit salad and cottage cheese or a hot bagel with the soup of the day. Afterward, top off the meal with a scrumptious sweet treat from the Deli Showcase. Choose from a variety of desserts, such as carrot cake, brownies, eclairs, muffins, chocolate cake, etc. Choose from a variety of hot and cold beverages, including gourmet coffee, Espresso, Cappuccino, Cafe Latte, tea and fountain drinks. The Flying Gift Shop and Deli also does full service corporate and private aviation catering. For more information, call the Flying Gift Shop and Deli at 292-5117.

Jora's Restaurant:

Jora's Restaurant is located in the San Jose Jet Center at the San Jose International Airport. This family-style Italian cafe is open from 11 a.m. to 2 p.m., Monday through Friday for lunch. (Note: At the time of the interview, we were told that they will also be opening for dinner and breakfast in the near future.) Some of the specialties include: shishkabobs with brown mushroom saute, prawns with Bordelaise sauce, breast of chicken with Zaffron sauce and Fettucine Alfredo. Average meal prices are around $9.00. The restaurant has a modern cream, mauve and green decor with a great view of the runways. Three separate banquet rooms are available for larger groups. The first features a two-sided view of the airport and can accommodate up to 100 people. The second is a conference room that holds up to 20 people, and the third offers living room confort and can handle up to 10 people (very private). Jora's also offers in-flight catering services and will handle special orders. With 20 minutes notice via Unicom: 122.95, the restaurant will provide free courtesy transportation to and from the Jet Center. For more information about Jora's Restaurant, call 995-JORA (5672).

Restaurants Near Airport:

94th Aero Squadron	On Site	Phone: 287-6150
CA1 Services	Terml A	Phone: 277-3434
Flying Gift Shop & Deli	On Site	Phone: 292-5117
Jora's Restaurant	On Site	Phone: 995-5672

Lodging: Transportation is furnished by the following (less than 3 miles): Best Western Gateway Inn 435-8800; Comfort Inn-Airport 453-1100; Holiday Inn-Airport 453-5340; Howard Johnson 453-3133; Hyatt 993-1234; The Le Baron 453-6200; Radisson 452-0200 or 298-0100; (Additional facilities); Airport Plaza Inn 243-2400; Residence Inn by Marriott 559-1551; Campbell Inn 374-4300; Holiday Inn Park Center Plaza 998-0400; Beverly Heritage 943-9080; Embassy Suites 942-0400; The Fairmont 998-1900; Sheraton Silicon Valley East 943-0600; Marriott Hotel 988-1500; Courtyard by Marriott 441-6111; Red Lion Hotel 453-4000.

Convention Facilities: Convention facilities are available at the following: The Fairmont; The Le Baron; Meeting rooms available at the following: Comfort Inn-Airport; Holiday Inn-Airport; Howard Johnson; Residence Inn by Marriott; Holiday Inn Park Center Plaza; Beverly Heritage; Hyatt; Radisson; Sheraton Silicon Valley East. (See "lodging" listed above for phone numbers)

Transportation: San Jose Jet Center (FBO) can arrange transportation on the airport. Also, shuttle service is available to other facilities on the airport from this same location. Rental Cars: Avis 993-2224; Budget 286-1072; Dollar 280-2210; Hertz 437-5725; National 295-1344; Alamo, 453-8180; Taxi Service: Airline Cab 998-8294; Alpha Cab 436-1010; American Cab 954-1300; Delta Cab 441-9100; Express Cab 441-6300; Golden Star Cab 280-1510; South Bay Cab 296-1700; United Cab 243-2220; Yellow Cab 293-1234.

Information: Convention & Visitors Bureau, 333 West San Carlos Street, Suite 1000, San Jose, CA 95110, Phone: 295-9600 or 295-2265 for a 24 hour recorded message, or phone the Visitor Information Center at 283-8833.

See previous page for additional Information about this Airport.

Attractions:

Paramount's Great America, (3 mi), 100-acre amusement park facility, phone: 988-1776; Children's Discovery Museum, (3 mi), phone: 298-5495; Japanese Friendship Garden In Kelly Park, (6 mi), 6-1/2 acre Japanese strolling garden on two levels with waterfalls, 3/4 mile paved walkways displaying Japanese gardens, symbolic figures, bridges, lanterns and tea house, phone: 295-8383; San Jose Historical Museum, (6 mi), exhibits include pioneer homes and settlement with replicas of early Indian, Spanish, & Mexican background, phone: 287-2290; Winchester Mystery House, (7 mi). This mansion was owned by Sarah Winchester, the widow of the famous firearms manufacturer. She was convinced through a medium, that in order to remain alive, construction on her mansion must continue 24 hours a day. A fascinating tour of this bizarre 160 room home exhibits a multitude of eccentric architectural designs containing thousands of windows and doors, stair cases that lead nowhere, hidden and secret passages, trap doors, blind chimneys and a museum of rifles and outdoor gardens, phone 247-2101.

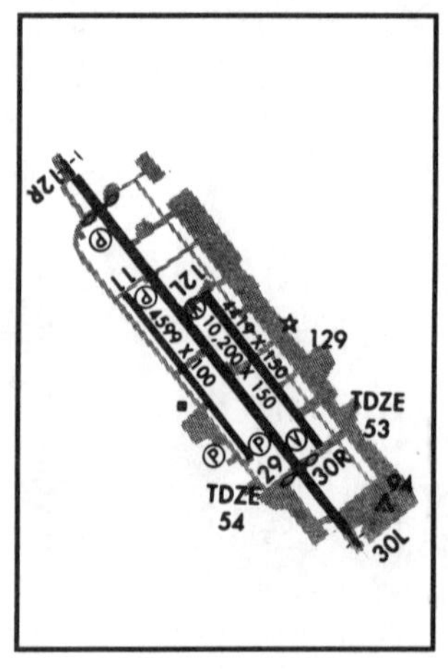

Airport Information:

SAN JOSE - SAN JOSE INTERNATIONAL (SJC)
2 mi northwest of town N37-21.72 W121-55.68 Elev: 58 Fuel: 100LL, Jet-A Rwy 12R-30L: H10200x150 (Asph-Grvd) Rwy 11-29: H4599x100 (Asph) Rwy 12l-30R: H4419x150 (Asph) Attended: continuously Atis: 126.95 (1400-0800Z) CTAF:124.0 Unicom: 122.95 Tower: 124.0, Rwy 12R-30L, 120.7, Rwy 12L-30R (1400-0800Z) Gnd Con: 121.7 Clnc Del: 118.0 Pre Taxi Clnc: 118.0 Public Phone: 24hrs

FBO: ACM Aviation,	**Phone:286-3832**	**FBO: Advanced Aviation**	**Phone: 292-0517**
FBO: San Jose Jet Center	**Phone:297-7552**	**FBO: Aris Helicopters**	**Phone: 998-3266**

CA-SBP- SAN LUIS OBISPO CO. MC CHESNEY FIELD

(Area Code 805) **93**

Restaurants Near Airport:

Spirit of San Luis On Site Phone: 549-9466

Spirit of San Luis:

Located on the San Luis County Airport, two miles from the coast between Los Angeles and San Francisco, this restaurant, classified as a fine dining facility, has it's own access ramp and taxiway. They have a large selection of appetizers, along with an extensive listing of entrees and tempting desserts. They also provide daily specials for lunch and dinner, changed daily. On Sunday, a champagne brunch, from 9:00 a.m. to 3:00 p.m., is served. (Full service sit down brunch). Entree prices range from; brunch $7.95, lunch $6.95 and dinner at about $11.95 to $13.95. This restaurant contains a modern and rustic California decor with a nautical accent., and is frequently visited by aviation clubs and organizations arranging get-togethers. In addition they are happy to serve private and corporate pilots with catering and meals-to-go. Special trays can be prepared like sandwiches, cheese trays, vegetable trays, and fruit trays are available. A very nice dining room and patio provides guests with a panoramic view of the airport from any seat in the house. For information call 549-9466.

Lodging: Best Western Royal Oak, (Free transportation), 544-4410; Sands, (Free transportation), 544-0500; Embassy Suites (Free transportation), 549-0800; Apple Farm, (Free transportation), 544-2040.

Meeting Rooms: Embassy Suites and Sands both contain conference rooms. (See lodging listed above)

Transportation: Rental Cars: Budget, 541-2722; Avis, 544-0630; Hertz, 543-0614; TAXI: Yellow Cab, 543-1234 or 489-1155.

Information: Chamber of Commerce, 1039 Chorro Street, San Luis Obispo, CA 93401-3278, Phone: 781-2777.

Attractions:

Lopez Lake, Avila Beach, Hearts Castle, and Morro Bay

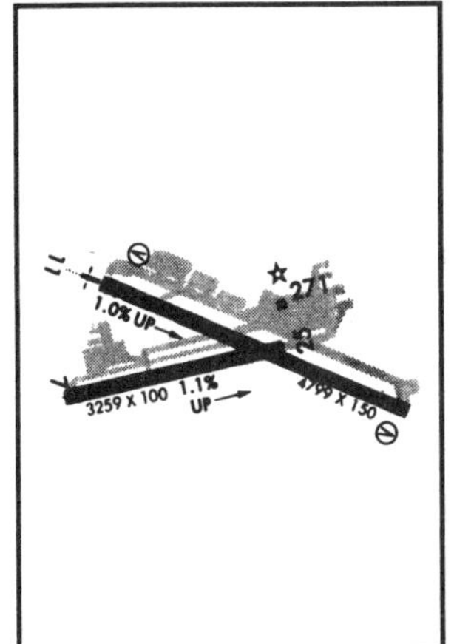

Airport Information:

SAN LUIS OBISPO CO. - MC CHESNEY FIELD (SBP)

3 mi south of town N35-14.22 W120-38.54 Elev: 209 Rwy 11-29: H4799x150 (ASPH) Rwy 07-25: H3259x100 (ASPH) Attended: 1300-0600Z Atis: 120.6 Unicom: 122.95 Tower: 124.0 Gnd Con: 121.6 Public Phone 24hrs

Airport Managers Office Phone: 781-5205

CA-SNA - SANTA ANA JOHN WAYNE ARPT./ORANGE CO.

(Area Code 714) **94**

Restaurants Near Airport:

Host Intl. Restaurant On Site Phone: 252-6125
McDonald's On Site Phone: 252-6100

Orange Grill Restaurant & Bar (Host Marriott.):

The Orange Grill Restaurant & Bar is located in the terminal building at the John Wayne/Orange County Airport, and is open from 6 a.m. to 7 p.m. Monday, Tuesday and Wednesday, 6 a.m. to 8 p.m. Thursday and Friday, 6 a.m. to 6 p.m. on Saturday and 6:30 a.m. to 7 p.m. on Sunday. This sit down restaurant is situated within an open air section of a food court that also offers a variety of different eateries. These are McDonald's Restaurant, TCBY's yogurt delights, Mrs. Field's candies and Pizza Hut. The Orange Grill offers a family style atmosphere and serves entrees like chicken sandwiches, hamburgers, salads, soft shell tacos, chicken tacos as well as other Mexican dishes. Continental breakfast, omelets and egg dishes are also available. Average prices run around $6.00 for most selections. The Orange Grill has seating for 80 to 100 people, with a modern decor, planting areas, palm trees, high beamed ceilings and large windows. Meals can be prepared-to-go if requested. For more information, call Host Marriott at 252-5006 or the restaurant at 252-6125.

Lodging: Best Western Irvine Host (Free trans) 261-1515; Comfort Suites (Free trans) 966-5200; Compri Hotel at Hutton Center (Free trans) 751-2400; Embassy Suites (Free trans) 241-3800; Quality Suites (Free trans) 957-9200; Ramada (Free trans) 966-1955.

Meeting Rooms: Best Western Irvine Host 261-1515; Comfort Suites 966-5200; Compri Hotel at Hutton Center 751-2400; Embassy Suites 241-3800; Ramada 966-1955.

Transportation: Martin Aviation can provide courtesy transportation to nearby facilities; Also airport coach bus 491-3500; Orange county taxi 546-1311; Rental Cars: Avis 549-7313; Budget 252-6240; Dollar 756-6100; General 252-6210; Hertz 756-0780; National 852-8389.

Information: Chamber of Commerce, P.O. Box 205, Santa Ana, CA 92702, Phone: 541-5353.

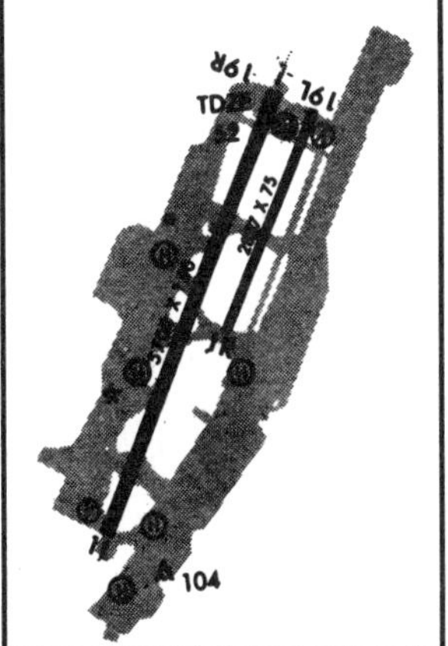

Airport Information:

SANTA ANA - JOHN WAYNE AIRPORT/ORANGE COUNTY (SNA)

4 mi south of town N33-40.54 W117-52.09 Elev: 54 Fuel: 100, 100LL, Jet-A Rwy 01L-19R: H5700x150 (Asph-Pfc) Rwy 01R-19L: H2887x75 (Asph-Pfc) Attended: continuously Atis: 126.0 Unicom: 122.95 Orange County Tower: 119.9, 128.35 Gnd Con: 120.8 Clnc Del: 118.0, 121.85 App Con: 121.3, 124.65, 132.7 Public Phone 24hrs

Notes: CAUTION: Birds on and in vicinity of airport; Transient fees: Under 12,500 lbs $5.00/day, 12,500 and over $15.00/day. See AFD for additional comments.

FBO: Martin Aviation Phone: 800-263-5842 FBO: Sunrise Jet Cntr Phone: 800-500-5061

FBO: Pan Western LTD Phone: 263-8652

CA-SBA - SANTA BARBARA
SANTA BARBARA MUNICIPAL

(Area Code 805)

95, 96

Beachside Bar Cafe:

Located on the beach in Goleta Beach Park, Beachside Bar Cafe is within walking distance of Santa Barbara Municipal Airport. The Beachside is a full service restaurant offering lunch and dinner daily from 11:30 a.m. Monday through Friday and 11:00 a.m. on Saturday and Sunday. There is a heated patio with wood burning fireplace for outside dining as well as a spacious inside dining room with great views of the Channel Islands and Campus Point. The dining room offers a no smoking section. Beachside Bar-Cafe has complete bar service. The menu at lunch includes sandwiches, specialty salads, daily luncheon specials and a daily catch that offers the freshest fish available. At dinner, in addition to the daily dinner specials and daily catch, the Beachside serves steaks, seafood and specialty salads. The Chowder Boat is New England style clam chowder served in a "boat" of sourdough bread. A Sundowner dinner is served nightly from 5:00-6:00 p.m.; a complete meal for $8.00 (not available on holidays or special event days). Although the Beachside does not have a banquet room, Christmas banquets and luncheon and dinner parties may be arranged. For reservations please call 964-7881

Elephant Bar Restaurant:

The Elephant Bar Restaurant is located on the Santa Barbara Municipal Airport. This facility is reported to be within walking distance from the aircraft parking ramp on the general aviation side. Their restaurant hours are 11 a.m. to 10 p.m. 7 days a week. This unique establishment decorates a portion of its lounge with elephant tusks and displays a decor depicting an African jungle safari camp. Pictures and items of interest decorate the restaurant and add to the atmosphere. Menu items include sizzling fajita's, stir fried sesame chicken, St Louis spare ribs, "elephant barbecued platters", buffalo wings, shrimp, Hawaiian chicken, pastas, salads and appetizers. Average prices run $4.95 for lunch and between $7.95 and $13.95 for dinner selections. The main dining area can accommodate at least 100 persons. A banquet room also provides an additional 150 placements. Group and fly-in clubs are welcome with advance notice appreciated. Meals can also be prepared-to-go as well as in-flight catering. A 10% discount is offered to pilots. For information call 964-0779.

Restaurants Near Airport:

Beachside Bar Cafe	Walk Dist.	Phone: 964-7881
Carrows Restaurant	On Site	Phone: 964-4682
Elephant Bar Restaurant	On Site	Phone: 964-0779
Good Earth Restaurant	1 mi N.	Phone: 683-6101
Spike's Restaurant	1/4 mi N	Phone: 964-5211

Lodging: Best Western Pepper Tree Inn (free trans) 687-5511; Best West South Coast Inn 967-3200; Holiday Inn (2 mi) 964-6241; Hollister Inn (On site) 967-5591; Pilot House Motel (On site) 967-2336; Quality Suites (free trans) 683-6722; El Encanto Hotel & Garden Villas (free trans) 687-5000; Fess Parker's Red Lion Resort (free trans) 564-4333.

Meeting Rooms: Best Western Pepper Tree Inn (free trans) 687-5511; Quality Suites (free trans) 683-6722; El Encanto Hotel & Garden Villas (free trans) 687-5000; Fess Parker's Red Lion Resort has convention facilities (free trans) 564-4333.

Transportation: Courtesy car available; Shuttle busses; Santa Barbara Airport Taxi Service 968-7222; Yellow Cab 965-5111; Rental Cars: Avis 964-4848; Budget 964-6791; Hertz 967-0411; National 967-1202.

Information: Conference & Visitors Bureau, 510-A State Street, Santa Barbara, CA 93101, Phone: 966-9222 or 800-927-4688.

Airport Information:

SANTA BARBARA - SANTA BARBARA MUNICIPAL (SBA)

7 mi. west of town N34-25.57 W119-50.42 Elev: 10 Fuel: 100LL, Jet-A, Rwy 07-25: H6049x150 (Asph-Grvd) Rwy 15R-33L: H4183x100 (Asph) Rwy 15L-33R: H4179x75 (Asph) Attended: 1330-0600Z Atis: 127.8 Unicom: 122.95 Tower: 119.7 Clnc Del: 132.9 Gnd Con: 121.7 Notes: Fee for fuel after hours call 805-964-6733 or 967-5608

FBO: Mercury Air Cntr. Phone: 964-6733 FBO: Stratman Aero Serv. Phone: 967-8096
FBO: Santa Barbara Avia. Phone: 967-5608

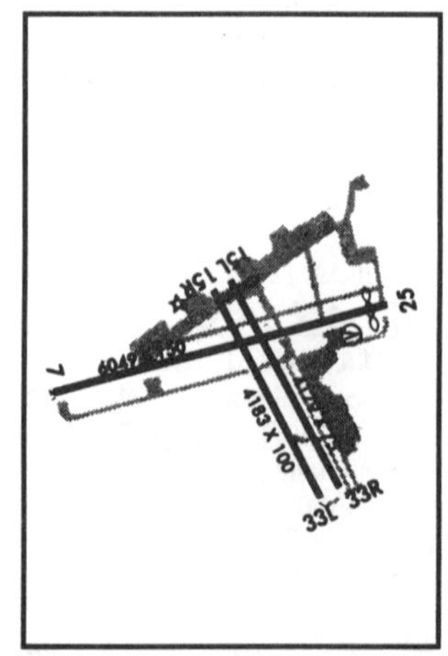

CA-SMX - SANTA MARIA
SANTA MARIA PUBLIC AIRPORT

(Area Code 805)

97

Restaurants Near Airport:

Hilton Garden Cafe	On Site	Phone: 928-8000
Pepper Garcia's	On Site	Phone: 928-4088

Lodging: Santa Maria Airport Hilton, (On Airport) 3455 Terminal Drive, Phone: 928-8000

Meeting Rooms: Santa Maria Airport Hilton, (On Airport), Phone: 928-8000

Transportation: You can taxi right up to the transient parking area next to the terminal building or in front of the Hilton Hotel. Also: Avis 922-4533; Budget 922-2158; Hertz 928-4409; Yellow Cab 925-2727.

Information: Chamber of Commerce, 614 South Broadway, Santa Ana, CA 93454, Phone: 925-2403 or 800-331-3779.

Pepper Garcia's:

The Pepper Garcia's Restaurant is located in the terminal building at the Santa Maria Public Airport. You can taxi your aircraft right up to the parking area adjacent to the restaurant. This family style restaurant is open from 6 a.m. to 10 p.m. and adjoins by a bar. The specialties of the house consist primarily of Mexican cuisine. Popular entrees include their daily specials like "Pollo Balanco Enchiladas", "Fajita's burrito's", "Slauta's" as well as many other items. On Wednesday night a Mexican all you can eat buffet is offered for only $6.95. Prices run about $4.00 for breakfast, $4.50 for lunch and $7.00 for dinner. In addition, they offer daily specials and fish on Friday. The decor of the restaurant is done up in a Mexican motif. Large groups are welcome provided advance arrangements are made. Catering services are also available. The Hilton Hotel, located next door, provides overnight accommodations. For information you can call this restaurant at 928-4088.

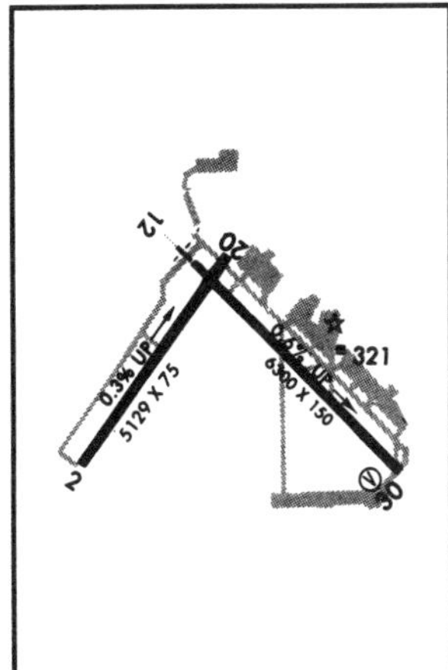

Airport Information:

SANTA MARIA - SANTA MARIA PUBLIC AIRPORT (SMX)

3 mi south of town N34-53.94 W120-27.45 Elev: 259 Fuel: 80, 100LL, Jet-A
Rwy 12-30: H6300x150 (Asph-Grvd) Rwy 02-20: N5129x75 (Asph) Attended: 1400-0600Z, attendant for other hours call 928-0303, or 928-9451 Public Phone 24hrs Atis 121.15
Unicom 122.95 Tower 118.3 Gnd Con: 121.9

FBO: Central Coast Aviation **Phone: 928-7701**
FBO: Goldenwest Air Terminals, Inc. **Phone: 928-9431**
FBO: Skyway Aviation Fuels **Phone: 928-0303**

CA-SMO - SANTA MONICA
SANTA MONICA MUNICIPAL (SMO)

(Area Code 310)

98,99,100

DC3 Restaurant:

The DC3 Restaurant at the Santa Monica Airport is available to cater your special events at the adjacent Museum of Flying. From a meeting luncheon in the Donald Douglas Board Room to a dinner and dancing extravaganza on the main floor of the Museum, DC3 has the ability and experience necessary to satisfy all your needs. DC3's professional and experienced staff will gladly assist to create a memorable occasion. In addition to fine cuisine, DC3 Catering offers complete event planning services including rentals, decor, lighting, entertainment and more. DC3's convenient location provides the flexibility to provide a superb menu for museum events. Chef William Hufferd has created a style of cuisine for DC3 based on traditional American foods with an international flair. Specialties include grilled chicken pancake with Serrano chiles and grapefruit sauce, half charred tuna steak and charred rack of lamb. To complete your fabulous meal, their creative pastry chef Jackie Ravel-Knezevich offers many desserts made on the premises including chocolate hazelnut truffle torte and raspberry creme brulee. For information regarding catering and private parties please contact their catering sales manager at 213-399-2323.

Spitfire Grill:

The Spitfire Grill is located on the south side of the airport and is within a five minute walk of the tiedown ramp. This cafe and family style restaurant serves meals from 6:30 a.m. to 10:00 p.m. on weekdays and 8 a.m. to 10 p.m. on weekends. Their menu carries a nice selection for breakfast lunch and dinner. Daily specials are prepared, as well as a Sunday Brunch, Sunday night family dinners, and for Monday night football. Prices range from $5.00 for breakfast, $6-$8.00 for lunch and $10.00 and up for dinner entrees. A 1940's Pilots Club or meeting spot within the restaurant offers a friendly atmosphere with a service oriented view of the airport. Private parties, club fly-ins are all welcome. Carry-out meals are also available for pilots on-the-go. For more information call 397-3455.

Restaurants Near Airport:

DC-3	On Site	Phone: 399-2323
Spitfire Grill	On Site	Phone: 397-3455
Typhoon	On Site	Phone: 390-6565

Lodging: Gateway Hotel, (Free Transportation), Phone: 829-9100

Meeting Rooms: Gateway Hotel (See listing above); Bayview Holiday Inn, 530 West Pico Blvd, Phone: 399-9344; Radisson Huntly Hotel, 111 Second Street, Phone: 394-5454.

Transportation: Supermarine of Santa Monica, 396-6770; Lighting Taxi, 453-2636; Red Top, 395-3201; Yellow Cab, 827-2933

Information: All restaurants listed above are reported to be within walking distance from their respective parking ramps. Contact airport manager for more information. Phone: 458-8591; Convention and Visitors Center, P.O. Box 5278-M, Santa Monica, CA 90405, Phone: 393-7593.

Attractions:

The Santa Monica Museum of Flying is located at the Santa Monica Airport. This museum exhibits aviation memorabilia as well as aircraft on display. Many of the exhibits depict aviation history along with current contributions. There are special events and exhibitions held Thursday through Sunday. For more information call 392-8822; Penmar Golf Course, Phone: 396-6228.

Typhoon Restaurant:

The Typhoon Restaurant is located on the Santa Monica Municipal Airport on the south side of the field across from the control tower. According to the restaurant manager you can park your aircraft close to the door. This is an Asian styled restaurant specializing in serving oriental cuisine. They are open Monday through Friday between 12 p.m. to 3 p.m. for lunch, Monday through Saturday from 5:00 p.m. to 10:30 p.m. for dinner and open for Sunday brunch between 11:30 and 3:00 p.m. The decor of the restaurant is decorated in cherry wood with windows allowing a view overlooking the parking ramp. Items on their menu include deep fried catfish served with black bean sauce, baked salmon, "Bungress " crab, "Potstickers" consisting of 5 different sauteed dishes, beef, lamb, pork, and chicken. Tie-Garlic short ribs, as well as deserts with cobblers, brownies, lemon cheese cake and more are offered. Fruit platters and a specialty Indonesian fried banana are also available. The restaurant can seat up to 120 persons excluding their full bar and lounge area. In-flight catering as well as carry out orders can be arranged. Groups are also welcome. For information call the Typhoon restaurant at 390-6565.

Airport Information:

SANTA MONICA - SANTA MONICA MUNICIPAL (SMO)

3 mi east of town 34-00-57N 118-27-01W Elev: 175 Fuel: 100LL, Jet-A
Rwy 03-21: H4987x150 (CONC) Attended: continuously Atis: 119.15 Unicom: 122.95
Tower: 120.1 (1500-0500Z) Gnd Con: 121.9 Public Phone 24hrs
FBO: California Aviation, Phone 397-2188
FBO: Gnnnell Aviation, Phone 396-6770

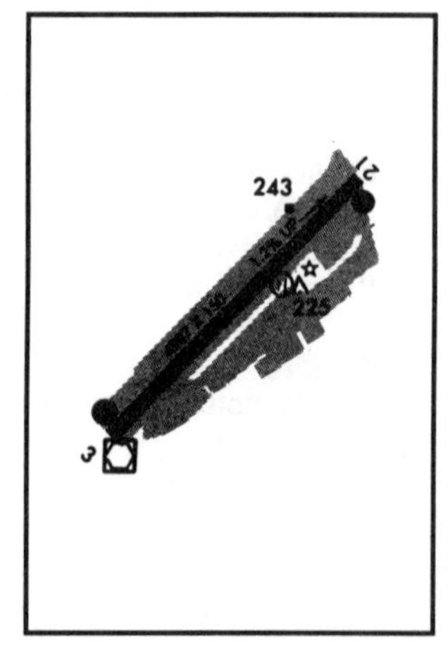

Museum of Flying

Southern California's newest aviation museum is located at the Santa Monica Airport on virtually the same spot where Douglas Aircraft Co. was founded in 1922. The Museum of Flying, housed inside the contemporary 53,000 square foot Supermarine structure of steel and glass, looms dramatically as you approach the museum property.

Fly-in guests can taxi their aircraft to any one of several fixed base operators on the field and obtain courtesy transportation to the museum. Gunnell Aviation and Supermarine are situated adjacent to the museum property. Clover Field Service and Krueger Aviation are located right across the runway from the museum and will be happy to transport their customers.

Within the Courtyard and main entrance to the Museum of Flying, the first sight, is a full scale replica of the Voyager aircraft suspended from the Courtyard's ceiling with vintage biplanes below. Spanning the complex overhead is the critically-acclaimed DC-3 restaurant with a newly-opened Club Lux, a private party room whose oversized sofas, chairs and tulip-shaped wall sconces create the panache of a vamped up men's club.

Santa Monica Airport, once known as Clover Field, acts as a backdrop for the Museum of Flying's extensive display of aviation past, present and future. Facing the tarmac on the main floor is a panoramic-sized hangar door which is opened for visitors to observe many of the WW-II planes start up, taxi, fly and land on the runway outside. Other planes in various stages of restoration are available for observation.

Many of the museum's regular docents and supporters have flown some of the aircraft on exhibit and share first-hand with visitors the history of Warbirds and aviation. Video stations positioned by most of the exhibits show dramatic footage of historic planes in action, narrated by Hal Fishman, well-known local newscaster and aviation buff.

Also on view, are over 120 wood and metal Douglas production models of concept planes, ranging from the Douglas M1 to current fighters like the F15E Eagle, and an outstanding collection of model aircraft from WW-I to the present. A fully equipped theater shows such classic aviation films as "The Great Air Race of 1924", "Blue Angles", "Blackbird SR-71", and first flight footage of the "B-2 Stealth Bomber".

Recently the Museum kicked off a welcome to the Cockpit, a Beverly Hills aviation related clothing store which set up shop alongside the museum's gift merchandise. Now, the annex of the "Cockpit" offers visitors twice the diversity of shopping for personal, birthday, and holiday gifts. Of special interest are leather flight jackets, nose art tee shirts, and nostalgic and current styles of aviation flight suits.

Special events facilities are available on all three levels. Capacity crowd inside the museum is 1,200 with 32,000 sq. ft. For larger parties, they tent on the tarmac. The Museum of Flying can also accommodate smaller parties for 20 persons in the Donald Douglas boardroom or up to 150 persons in the 3rd level Patron's area. The museum staff welcomes receptions, wedding, business conferences, screening, office parties, wrap/industry parties and conventions. Admission to the museum is $7.00 for adults and $3.00 per child. For hours and museum information call 310-392-8822.

DC-3 Restaurant

The DC-3 restaurant is located right on the museum premises and provides fine cuisine, serving their customers within a beautiful private dining and banquet facility able to accommodate small or large groups.

You may consider utilizing both of these wonderful facilities when planning your next group event by beginning with a private screening of vintage film or a museum tour followed by dinner in the banquet room of DC3 Restaurant overlooking the runways of Santa Monica Airport and the entire South Bay. For information regarding the Museum of Flying call 310-392-8822. (Information submitted by museum).

Aircraft available for display or suspended from the ceilings include:

1924 Douglas World Cruiser "New Orleans" - First Around the World Curtiss JN-4 Jenny
Curtiss Robin
Curtiss P-40 Warhawk "Burma Rascal"
Douglas DC-2
Douglas DC-3
Douglas AD-6 Skyraider
Douglas A-4 Skyhawk
Fairey Swordfish
North Ameican P-51D Mustang
North American P-51 Racing Mustang "Dago Red"
Supermarine Spitfire MkIX
Supermarine Spitfire MkXIV

CA-SZP - SANTA PAULA
SANTA PAULA AIRPORT

(Area Code 805)

101

Logsdon Restaurant:

The Logsdon Restaurant is situated within walking distance from aircraft parking at the Santa Paula Airport. This combination family style and fine dining facility is open between 11 a.m. and 4 p.m. for lunch and 5:00 p.m. to 9:30 p.m. for dinner. On weekends they are open until 10:30 p.m. Specialties on their menu include prime rib, lobster, frog legs, top sirloin, fresh fish, chicken fried steaks and home-made desserts. They also offer "early bird" specials between 5:00 p.m. and 7:00 p.m. The decor of the restaurant is contemporary with a rock fireplace and three separate and different dining rooms. They even have a lounge area that offers entertainment and dancing. Larger groups and parties are welcome with advance notice. Accommodations for business luncheons and banquets are also available to handle up to 100 persons. In conjunction with this establishment is a coffee shop on the premises that is open 7 days a week from 7 a.m. to 3 p.m. Meals can also be prepared for carry-out as well. For information about the Logsdon Restaurant, call 525-1101.

Restaurants Near Airport:

Carrow's Restaurant	1/4 mi W.	Phone: 525-0966
Familia Diaz Restaurant	1/4 mi E.	Phone: 525-2813
Logsdon Restaurant	On Site	Phone: 525-1101

Lodging: Mountain View Lodge (1 mile) 525-4743; Royal Oak Motor Inn (1 mile) 525-6661; The Glen Tavern Inn (1 mile) 525-6658; Travel Lodge (1-1/2 miles) 525-1561.

Meeting Rooms: Logsdon's Airport Restaurant has banquet rooms available 525-1101.

Transportation: C.P. Aviation 525-2138, and Santa Paula Flight Center 525-3561 both provide courtesy transportation to nearby facilities; Also rental cars available: Gould Ford 647-5656; Bridges Chevrolet 647-2756.

Information: California Division of Tourism, P.O. Box 1499, Sacramento, CA 95812, Phone: 800-862-2543.

Attractions:

Elkins Ranch Golf Course (8 miles east) 524-1440; Also Mount View Golf Course (16799 South Mountain Rd., Santa Paula) 525-1571.

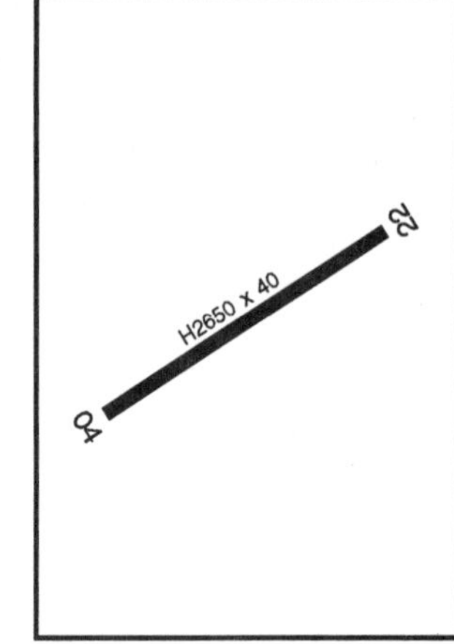

Airport Information:

SANTA PAULA - SANTA PAULA AIRPORT (SZP)

1 mi southeast of town N34-20.83 W119-03.67 Elev: 245 Fuel: 80, 100LL

Rwy 04-22: H2650x40 (Asph) Attended: dawn to dusk Unicom: 122.9 Public Phone 24hrs

Notes: No landing fees, overnight parking fees $3.00 per night, after 10 days $15.00/night. Several maintenance and repair facilities on the airport or have access. Also Helicopter operation requires prior written permit.

FBO: Aerobatic Unlimited	**Phone: 525-0111**	**FBO: Krybus Aviation**	**Phone: 525-8764**
FBO: C.P. Aviation	**Phone: 525-2138**	**FBO: Screaming Eagle**	**Phone: 525-7121**

(Area Code 707)

102, 103

CA-STS - SANTA ROSA SONOMA COUNTY AIRPORT

Sellini Grille & CaSeneo:

The Sellini Grille Restaurant is located in the terminal building on the Sonoma County Airport. It is open 7 days a week between 11 a.m. to 2:30 p.m. on Monday and Tuesday, 11 a.m. to 9:30 p.m. on Wednesday through Friday, and on Saturday and Sunday from 10:30 a.m. to 11 p.m. They feature a Sunday brunch between 10 a.m. and 2 p.m. Specialties of the house include Mediterranean & Greek selections along with pasta dishes. The restaurant has seating for about 150 persons indoors and 40 on their outdoor patio area. They offers casual dining during the day while at night a more elegant decor atmosphere is presented with lanterns on each table. On Friday and Saturday evenings, background musical entertainment is featured for their customers. A portion of the seating in the restaurant is located within their solarium. For more information call 537-6900.

Skylane Deli:

This restaurant is located 1 block east of the field, on Sanomà County Airport Blvd., 400 feet north on Skylane Blvd. It is an easy walk to the restaurant. This Deli serves soups, salads, sandwiches, salad bar and daily hot specials. Average prices for meals run about $4.50. The restaurant is open from 6 a.m. to 6 p.m. Monday through Friday. The decor is modern. Fly-in groups planning get-togethers are welcome if prior notice is given. Cheese trays, meat trays, vegetable trays, sandwich trays, box lunches, salads or just about any item on their menu is available to go. For information about this restaurant please call 573-8993.

Restaurants Near Airport:

Cricklewood	2 mi E.	Phone: 527-7768
Hungry Hunter	6 mi SE	Phone: 542-5705
Sellini Grill	On Site	Phone: 573-6900
Skylane Deli	1/4 mi E.	Phone: 573-8993

Lodging: (Transportation provided) Fountain Grove Inn, (6 miles south), 101 Fountain Grove Pkwy, Santa Rosa, Phone: 800-222-6101 or 578-6101; Los Robles Lodge (10 miles south), 925 Edwords Ave., Santa Rosa, Phone: 545-6330; Days Inn, (11 miles south), 175 Railroad Street, Santa Rosa, Phone: 800-325-2525, 573-9000; Red Lion Inn, (16 miles south), 1 Red Lion Drive, Rohnert Park, Phone: 800-547-8010 or 584-5466.

Meeting Rooms: Fountain Grove Inn, Days Inn, Red Lion Inn, Los Robles Lodge. (See Lodging listed above)

Transportation: Aerowood & Skylane deli are within walking distance. Rental Cars Available: Hertz, 523-3524; Avis, 571-0465; Taxi: George's Taxi, 546-3322; Country Cab, 546-0370; Occidental Taxi, 874-2361; Yellow Cab, 544-4444; Transit Bus: Sonoma County Transit bus, 345-7433.

Information: Sonoma County Convention and Visitors Bureau, 5000 Roberts Lake Road, Suite A, Rohnert Park, CA 94928, Phone: 586-8100 or 800-326-7666.

Attractions:

The Russian River Resort Area is located a few miles west of the airport. There is fishing and canoeing along the river as well as numerous motels and bed and breakfast establishments. **Windsor golf club** is located 2 miles north of the field. Their address is 6555 Skylane Blvd., Windsor CA, Phone: 838-7888; **Lake Sonoma**, which provides fishing, water skiing, boat rentals and picnicking, is located approximately 20 miles north of the airport. off Hwy 101. Lake Sonoma Marina, Phone: 433-2200; **Armstrong Redwoods State Reserve**, home to giant California coastal redwoods, is located approximately 17 miles southwest of the airport, in the Russian River Resort area. Their address is 17000 Armstrong Woods Road., Guerneville, CA, Phone: 865-2391; **Horseback pack rides** are also offered at Armstrong Woods. The address for Lake Sonoma is 3333 Skaggs Springs Road. **Beaches** offering rugged seascapes and views of local marine life such as sea lions, harbor seals, herons, and migrating whales are located approximately 30 miles southwest of the airport, take River Road to Hwy 116 to Coast Hwy 1.

Airport Information:

SANTA ROSA - SONOMA COUNTY AIRPORT (STS)
6 mi northwest of town N38-30.54 W122-48.77 Elev: 125 Fuel: 80, 100LL, Jet-A
Rwy 14-32: H5115x150 (Asph-Pfc) Rwy 01-19: H5002x150 (Asph)
Attended: 1330-0700Z Atis: 120.55 Unicom 122.95 Santa Rosa Tower: 118.5
Gnd Con: 121.9 Public Phone 24 hrs Notes: No landing fee except airline A/C; tiedown fees less than 42' wingspan, tail to tail tiedown $4.00/night, All taxi through tiedowns less than 60' wing span, $12.00/night over 60' wing span $15.00/night.
FBO: Manny's Sonoma Aviation **Phone: 528-7400**
FBO: Redwood Aviation/Let's Fly, **Phone: 546-5546**

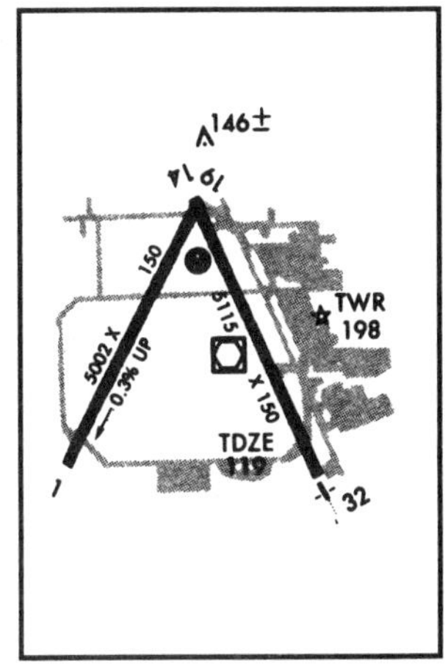

CA-IZA - SANTA YNEZ
SANTA YNEZ AIRPORT

104

Santa Ynez Attractions & Recreation:

The Santa Ynez Valley is a California coastal region, nearly 20 miles wide, nestled between the Santa Ynez and San Rafael mountain ranges. It is easily accessible; just 20 air miles north of Santa Barbara. Blessed with one of the finest climates in the state of California, the smog free Santa Ynez Valley boasts a year round climate in which sunshine prevails. Summer daytime temperatures range in the mid 80's and 90's, evenings average in the low to mid 60's with overnight lows in the 30's. The Santa Ynez Valley is comprised of five unique turn of the century towns, all within 10-12 minutes of the airport. This valley is renowned for its quality horse breeding facilities, art galleries, and prize winning wineries. The quiet beauty of the valley has inspired celebrities, world and business leaders to make the valley their home. Scattered throughout are quaint little towns noted for their fine dining, shops and hotels. The Alisal Guest Ranch (805-688-6411) has been recognized as a world famous 10,000 acre retreat providing two 18 hole championship golf courses, tennis, sail boating, hayrides, horseback riding, trail rides, nightly entertainment with dancing, and winery tours. Nearby, Lake Cachuma Recreational Area provides limitless facilities for lake fishing (trout, bass, catfish) while the Los Padres National Forest offers its hidden delights for the wilderness seeker. The "less adventurous but activity oriented" will delight in the ample golf and tennis facilities. When visiting this regional attraction by air, you will want to land at the Santa Ynez Valley Airport (IZA). The airport is made up of a 126 plus acre facility, with a 2,850-foot, hard surface, lighted runway, and is fog free 90% of the time. Amenities at the airport include fueling and tie-down areas, maintenance and service.

Attractions:

Santa Ynez Valley attractions include resorts, golf courses, state parks, fishing lakes, etc. Some additional attractions include:

- *PCPA Theaterfest, Solvang* - Rotating repertory, six plays "outdoors under the stars";
- *The Honen, Solvang* - A turn of the century trolley pulled by two Belgian horses, tour the Village area;
- *Parks Plaza Theater, Buellton* - 3 screen movie theater;
- Gambling - *Santa Ynez Indian Casino*, Santa Ynez;
- *Wineries* - 23 wineries throughout the Valley (maps available);
- *Art Galleries* - Los Olivos - 12 galleries (maps available);
- *Apple Orchards* - Roadside stands (map available);
- *Horse Ranches* - Tours and demonstrations (list available);
- *Museums - Santa Ynez:*
  Parks-Janeway Carriage Museum,
  Santa Ynez Valley Historical Society;
- *Museums - Solvang:*
  Elverhoy Danish Heritage and Fine Arts Museum;
  Hans Christian Andersen;
  Old Mission Santa Ines;

Airport Information:

SANTA YNEZ - SANTA YNEZ AIRPORT (IZA)

1 mi southeast of town N34-36.41 W120-04.53 Elev: 671 Fuel: 100LL, Jet-A Rwy 08-26: H2804x75 (Asph) Attended: 1500-0300Z Unicom: 122.8 L.A. Center App/Depp Con 124.15 Notes: No landing fees. Overnight parking fees: Single Engine $4.00, Twin Engine $8.00

FBO: Santa Ynez Air Center **Phone: 688-2437**
FBO: Santa Ynez Airport **Phone: 688-8390**

(Area Code 805)

Restaurants Near Airport:

Painted Lady & Western	1 mi	Phone: N/A
Victorian Village	1 mi	Phone: 686-5442
Red Barn Restaurant	1 mi	Phone: 688-4142
Longhorn Cafe/Bakery	1 mi	Phone: 688-5912
Mortensen's Bakery	1 mi	Phone: 688-8373
Olsen's Village Bakery	1 mi	Phone: 688-6314
Uno Mas Cafe	1 mi	Phone: 688-6899
Alisal Guest Ranch	6 mi	Phone: 688-6411

Lodging:
Three Crown's Inn & Cottages (3 mi) 688-4702; Marriott Hotel (6 mi) 688-1000; Ramada Inn (6 mi) 688-8448 or 800-288-2828; (Courtesy transportation is provided by facility.)

Meeting Rooms:
Santa Ynez Air Center-(on airport) 68802437; Royal Scandia Lounge-(Solvang, CA) 688-8000; Ramada Inn-(Buellton, CA) 688-8448. Alisal Guest Ranch has excellent accommodations for combining pleasure with business. For information call 688-6411.

Transportation:
Transportation to nearby restaurants and nearby facilities by contacting Santa Ynez Air Center 688-2437; Available public transportation is also available. Taxi service: Yellow Cab 688-0069; Shuttle Bus: Call Santa Ynez Valley Transit 688-5452; Alisal Guest Ranch will pick-up pilots and their passengers at the airport by calling 688-6411.

Information:
Contact the Solvang Conference & Visitors Bureau, 1511-A Mission Drive, P.O. Box 70, Solvang, CA 93463, or call 800-468-6765. Also, you can obtain information by calling or writing: Santa Ynez Valley Airport Authority, Inc. (IZA), P.O. Box 1572, 900 Airport Road, Santa Ynez, CA 93460-1572, Phone: 688-8390.

Alisal Guest Ranch:

This is a combination ranch/resort situated on a 10,000-acre parcel of land. This working ranch contains 2,000 head of cattle and a large private lake. Guests can enjoy a large number of amenities, including: golfing, boating, horseback riding, nightly entertainment, trail rides and cookouts, hayrides, and tours throughout the area. For information, call Alisal's Guest Ranch at 805-688-6411.

Recreation - Parks, Golf Courses, Lakes, Airport

- Nojoqui Fall County Park - picnic areas, BBQ, ball field, playground
- Hans Christian Andersen Park - picnic areas, fitness track, public tennis
- Lake Cachuma - fishing, boating, rentals, camping, pool, playgrounds, food concessions, picnic & group areas, BBQ, Eagle tours (boat holds a full tour bus).
- Zaca Creek Golf Course, Buellton - 9 holes
- River Course at the Alisal, Solvang - 18 holes
- Glider Rides, Santa Ynez Airport - 7 days a week
- Bike Rentals, Solvang - Surrey Bikes, mountain bikes, tandem

The town of Solvange is noted for its Danish heritage and the following bakeries represent that heritage very well:

- Olsen's Danish Village Bakery & Coffee Shop at 1529 Mission Drive 688-6314.
- Mortensen's Bakery at 1588 Mission Drive 688-8373.

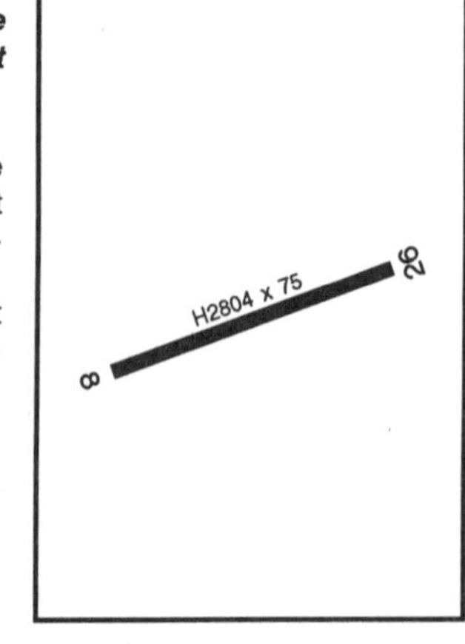

Not to be used for navigational purposes

The Alisal Guest Ranch & Resort:

The Alisal's combination of fresh air, mild climate and scenic beauty provide the perfect backdrop for enjoying a full range of outdoor activities. At the center of the resorts 10,000 acres of wide open space, is their 90-acre spring-fed lake. Here, hungry bass and bluegill abound. Sailboats, pedal boats, and windsurfing boards stand ready to whisk you across the quiet blue waters, and of course, their heated pool and spa offer year-round swimming.

Nature lovers can also find hiking trails and plenty of wildlife. The Alisal Guest Ranch and Resort, tucked away in a quiet corner of the picturesque Santa Ynez Valley, is one such rare retreat. Here, the towering oak and quiet brooks give testimony to The Alisal's rich history. It is a place where the thunder of hooves and the songs of cowboys still echo across a place of extraordinary beauty offering an opportunity for both quality leisure time and productive meetings.

Horseback riding: The Alisal is a horse lover's paradise with spirited horses matched to the skills of the rider. All this makes riding at The Alisal a one-of-a-kind experience. And there is much more... like their early morning breakfast rides to a historic abode camp, half-day lunch rides, and their much talked about moonlight dinner rides to their private lake.

As a golf resort: the Alisal ranks among the finest. Two championship 18-hole courses provide plenty of challenge. The Ranch Course (exclusively for members and guests) winds through aged oaks and sycamores. The River Course, recently built, stretches along the Santa Ynez River and provides a panoramic view of the foothills. Both courses offer private and group lessons by PGA and LPGA professionals who use the latest in split-screen video analysis.

Tennis: The Alisal also has seven tennis courts complete with pro shop. Their resident pros offer private and group lessons and clinics using the latest teaching techniques.

Lodging: There are 73 cottages that are decorated in California ranch design with high beamed ceilings, spacious sitting rooms, handsomely appointed private baths and wood-burning fireplaces. All cottages offer a garden view and a charming covered porch.

The Alisal operates on a modified American plan (breakfast and dinner included). Breakfasts feature lavish buffets brimming with fresh fruit, homemade baked goods and your favorite morning entrees. Dinners are a time to dress up and enjoy their daily menus featuring frontier-size portions. To round out your evening, The Oak Room serves before and after-dinner drinks with live entertainment nightly for dancing. During the day, luncheon far is served at the poolside snack bar and golf course grills. A Western barbecue and fish fries are also available for guests.

Meeting Facilities: At the Alisal, you will find a variety of function areas ranging from their intimate library setting to their light and airy 3,000 square foot Sycamore Room, with meeting space for 200. Also their lake front deck and creekside patio are especially popular for informal gatherings.

How to get there: Santa Ynez Airport (IZA) is located about 18 statute miles northwest of Santa Barbara, CA. and along the 277 degree radial from the San Marcus VOR. The airport itself is only a few miles from the resort, or about 10 minutes by car. Leaving the airport by car, you will want to turn left onto highway 246. Upon entering the town of Solvang, you will come to the intersection of 246 and Alisal Road. Turn left. In 1-1/2 miles you will see the entrance way to the Alisal Guest Ranch and Resort. Please be sure to call the resort prior to your visit, so they will arrange someone to be available to pick you up at the airport. For information you can call the resort at 805-688-6411. *Information obtained through The Alisal Guest Ranch & Resort.*

CA-CA51 - SEA RANCH
SEA RANCH (Association)

(Area Code 707) 105

Restaurants Near Airport:
The Sea Ranch Lodge 1 mi. Phone: 785-2371

The Sea Ranch:

Perched on a wild and lovely stretch of Sonoma Coast, is The Sea Ranch Lodge. Their rooms have no phones or TV's, relieving you from the routines and stresses of day-to-day life. Arresting in its architecture and dramatic location on a bluff overlooking the Pacific, the lodge is an outstanding addition to The Sea Ranch, an internationally famous second-home colony. Points, at The Sea Ranch Lodge, offers fine cuisine featuring fresh local fare and an outstanding wine list drawing heavily on the bounty of the nearby Sonoma, Mendocino and Napa wine country. Their store will entice you with its selection of apparel, gift ideas and unique merchandise. Explore the shoreline and tide pools with its abundant marine life. Observe the sea lions and seals sunning themselves on the rocky shores or watch California Grey Whales, spouting on their annual passage from the Arctic and back. There are miles of trails for walking, hiking and biking, including a continuous bluff trail along the entire 10 mile length of The Sea Ranch, offering a variety of forest and coastal vistas. Their Scottish style Links course offers a challenge to your golfing skills. For information call The Sea Ranch at 785-2371 or 800-SEA-RANCH.

Lodging: The lodge consists of twenty lodge rooms with a variety of accommodations within the lodge itself, call 785-2371.
Meeting Rooms: The Sea Ranch has seminar rooms offered, comfortable board room seating for up to 18 persons and theater style seating for up to 25 persons. For information call 800-732-7262.
Transportation: The Sea Ranch Lodge & Golf Links staff will provide transportation to and from their airport facility. Call 785-2371.
Information: The Sea Ranch, P.O. Box 44, The Sea Ranch, CA 95497. Phone: 785-2371 or 800-SEA-RANCH.

Attractions:

Try your skills on the Links style Golf Course and the Robert Muir Graves designed course, (total 18 holes) at The Sea Ranch Lodge Resort and Golf Links. Special packages are available with discounts. Their "Golf Package Experience Plus"; "Pure Golf"; and "Midweek Getaway" packages allow for accommodations in the way of lodging, meals and gifts. For information call 785-2468.

NO AIRPORT DIAGRAM AVAILABLE

Airport Information:

THE SEA RANCH - THE SEA RANCH - (Association) (CA51)
This is a private airport reported to be owned and operated by the Sea Ranch developement association. (Open to the public) located about one mile from the Sea Ranch Resort. **Note:** Call The Sea Ranch at 785-2371 or 800-SEA-RANCH for airport and runway contitions prior to use.
The Sea Ranch Phone: 785-2371 or 800-SEA-RANCH

CA-0Q5 - SHELTER COVE
SHELTER COVE AIRPORT

(Area Code 707) 106

Restaurants Near Airport:

Camp Ground Deli	1 blk SE	Phone: 986-7474
Cove Restaurant	1 blk N.	Phone: 986-1197
Marina Bar & Grill	1 blk SE	Phone: 986-1199
Shelter Cove Golf Links	1 blk N.	Phone: 986-7000

Shelter Cove (points of interest):

The town of Shelter Cove is situated about 50 miles due south of Eureka/Arcata. The King Mountain Range offers spectacular views for the visitor. The Shelter Cove Airport is located only a block from several dining establishments which makes it a popular location for many fly-in visitors. A 9 hole golf course surrounds the airport property. This 33 par course is known by some as the "Pebble Beach of the North." In addition to the golfing, Shelter Cove contains a marina located just off the threshold of their runway. This marina provides charter boats for deep sea fishing. Tidal pools are abundant within the area displaying yet another sightseeing attraction. The restaurants at this location can be reached by walking a block or two. You can park your aircraft at either end of the runway where tie-down spots are available. Talking with the airport manager we learned that this is a very popular airport with many pilots. The Cove Restaurant, open Thursday through Sunday from 11:30 a.m. to 9 p.m., offers a full service menu. The Marina Bar & Grill 986-1199 also provides a large selection of entrees. The Shelter Cove Golf Links & Pub Restaurant 986-7000 serves many golfers with meals. And the Camp Ground and Deli 986-7474 is famous for their fish and chip selections.

Lodging: Beach Comber 986-7733; Mario's Marina 986-7432; Shelter Cove Motor Inn 986-7521.
Meeting Rooms: None reported
Transportation: Most facilities within walking distance. No rental cars reported.
Information: Arcadia Chamber of Commerce, 388 W. Huntington Drive, Arcadia, CA 91007 818-447-2159; Eureka Chamber of Commerce, 2112 Broadway, Eureka, CA 95501, 707-442-3738.

Attractions:

A nine-hole 33 par golf course surrounds the airport and is known as the "Pebble Beach of the North" offers golfers spectacular views. Camping is also adjacent to airport.

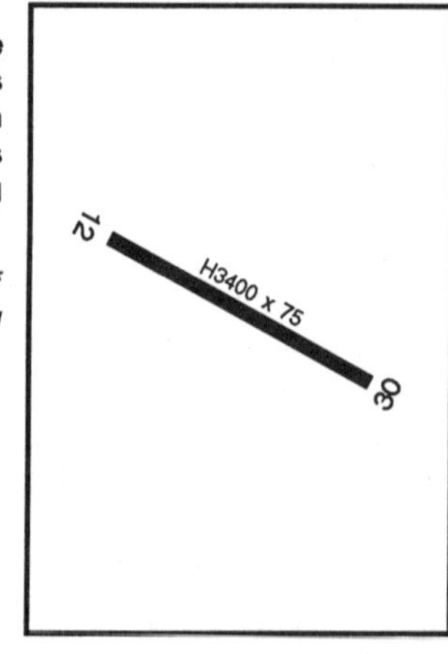

Airport Information:

SHELTER COVE - SHELTER COVE (0Q5)
1 mi west of town N40-01.66 W124-04.40 Rwy 12-30: H3400x75 (Asph) Attended: unattended
Unicom: 122.9
Shelter Cove Airport Mgr. Phone: 839-5402

CA-0Q9 - SONOMA
SONOMA SKYPARK

(Area Code 707) 107

Dining at the Sonoma Mission Inn and Spa:

Sonoma Mission Inn and Spa is located about two miles from historic Sonoma, in Northern California. This luxury resort and European-style spa is situated about 10 miles from Sonoma Skypark, in the heart of California's Wine Country. When guests dine at the Inn, they will enjoy tasty, healthy cuisine. The Grille, located just off the lobby, features a seasonal menu of Wine Country Cuisine prepared with fresh locally grown products. An international wine list features over 200 premium selections from Sonoma and Napa counties. The Grille, which offers a romantic, casually elegant atmosphere, is open daily for lunch, dinner and Sunday Brunch. Poolside dining is available, weather permitting. Reservations recommended. The Cafe is located at the north end of the resort at the corner of Boyes Boulevard and Highway 12. This restaurant features Italian cuisine and California specialties for lunch and dinner in a casual bistro setting. A variety of Sonoma and Napa Valley wines by the glass or bottle are also available. Cafe breakfasts are renowned for being delicious, all-American and abundant. The Cafe is open daily for breakfast, lunch and dinner. Reservations also recommended at this restaurant. The Cafe also features the Cafe Bar which is also open daily. The Lobby Bar, which is located adjacent to the Grille, is open daily and serves complimentary hors d'oeuvres and entertainment nightly in the lobby. As an alternative to dining out, room service is offered daily for breakfast, lunch and dinner. A selection of wines and Spa cuisine is also available. For more information about restaurants, rates and accommodations at the Sonoma Mission Inn and Spa, call 800-862-4945 or 938-9000.

Restaurants Near Airport:
Sonoma Mission Inn and Spa 10 mi Phone: 938-9000

Lodging: Sonoma Mission Inn and Spa (10 miles) 938-9000; El Pueblo Motel (3 miles) 966-3651; nmrs Bed and Breakfast Inns (2 1/2 miles)
Meeting Rooms: Sonoma Mission Inn and Spa 938-9000
Transportation: Sonoma Mission Inn and Spa will provide transportation to and from the airport for a fee. Taxi Service: Checker 996-6734; Sonoma 996-6733; Yellow 996-6733; Rental Cars: Sonoma Airporter 938-4774; Sonoma Trucks/Auto 996-4521
Information: Sonoma Valley Visitors Bureau, 453 1st St.E., Sonoma, CA 95476, Phone: 996-1090

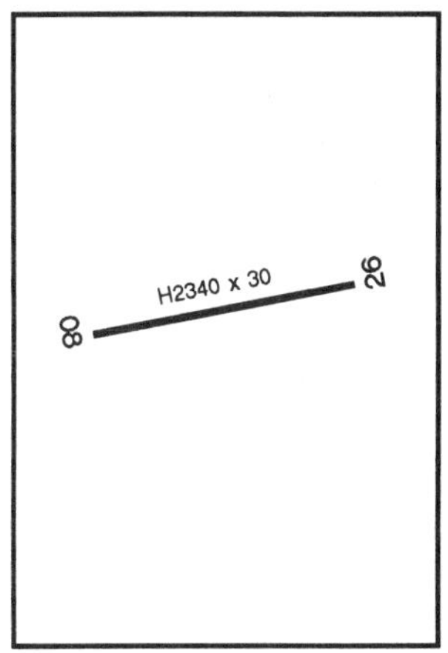

Airport Information:

SONOMA - SONOMA SKYPARK (0Q9)
3 mi southeast of town N38-15.46 W122-26.07 Elev: 20 Fuel: 100LL, MOGAS Rwy 08-26: H2340x30 (Asph) Attended: 1700-0100Z CTAF/Unicom: 122.8 Notes: Rwy 08-26 W 160' CLOSED indefinitely.
FBO: Sonoma Skypark Phone: 996-2100

Sonoma Mission Inn and Spa

Sonoma, CA (CA-0Q9)

Sonoma Mission Inn and Spa is located about two miles from historic Sonoma, in Northern California. This luxury resort and European-style Spa is situated on eight secluded acres of eucalyptus-shaded grounds in the heart of California's Wine Country.

Since the mid-19th Century, Sonoma Mission Inn and Spa has been a haven for relaxation, rejuvenation and romance. The Inn has a history that is rich with colorful lore of Sonoma Valley, enchantingly named Valley of the Moon by the indigenous Indians. These Indians, who were drawn by the curative powers of the site's underground springs, were the first to discover its benefits and used it as a sacred healing ground.

From the mid-1800's to the mid-1920's, the Inn went through a series of owners and was twice destroyed by fire. In 1927, the main building rose from the ashes as an architecturally accurate replica of a California Mission, complete with arcade and bell towers. It quickly became a resort mecca for Northern Californians before entering a long period of decline after World War II. In 1980, a major restoration returned this wine country landmark to its 1920's glory. One year later, the elegant European-style Spa was built, thus attracting vacationers, business travelers and the fitness-minded from all over the world.

In 1991, the Inn embarked on a two-year search for the legendary mineral waters that originally made the resort famous. A new source of 135-degree natural hot artesian mineral water was discovered 1,100 feet directly beneath the Inn. This magical water is now used in the Inn's two pools, as well as in the indoor and outdoor whirlpools.

While Sonoma Mission Inn and Spa is renowned for its world-class spa, it is also famous for its superb dining, and award-winning service and amenities. It features 170 comfortable rooms, many with fireplaces and terraces. For recreation, the Inn has two lighted championship tennis courts. Professional instruction is available by reservation. There are two swimming pools available for guests. The Spa exercise pool for adult guests of the Inn and a large main pool for guests and supervised children are both heated year-round with natural hot artesian mineral water. Lounge chairs and bath towels are complimentary.

The Spa is considered one of the finest fitness and beauty facilities in the country and is open to adult guests of the Inn and to Spa members. It is located directly behind the tennis courts at the north end of the Inn. The highly trained Spa staff includes experts in aerobics, fitness, tennis, beauty, massage, yoga and nutrition. The bathhouse is open from 7:00 a.m. to 9:00 p.m. Sunday through Thursday, and from 7:00 a.m. to 10:00 p.m. Friday and Saturday. Treatment hours are from 8:00 a.m. to 8:00 p.m. daily. The coed bathhouse facilities include an aerobic studio, sauna and steam rooms, indoor and outdoor hot mineral water whirlpools, outdoor mineral water exercise pool, two gyms with weight and cardiovascular equipment, and complete locker rooms with showers. Robes and thongs are available at the Spa reception desk.

The Spa also offer guests the skills of highly trained massage providers. They give full body massages, including Aromatherapy massages given in the Swedish/Esalen style to relieve stress and increase circulation. Luxurious herbal wraps enclose the body in fra-

Photo by: Sonoma Mission and Spa

Front view of the beautiful Spanish-colonial building at the Sonoma Mission Inn and Spa in Sonoma, CA.

grant, steaming Irish linens suffused with herbs to help eliminate toxins and leave the body relaxed. Seaweed body wraps envelop the body in an algae and mud mixture to rehydrate and nutrify it. Other body treatments, include: body scrub, European back treatment and the Revitalizer. Note: advance reservations are strongly recommended for all treatments.

The spa's beauty specialists provide rehydrating manicures, Pedicures, European facials, and full hair salon services. Note: advance reservations are strongly recommended for all treatments.

Daily sceduled exercise classes are offered by professional instructors and include gentle stretch, yoga, limber and tone, and moderate to advanced aerobics, including low impact, morning and afternoon hikes at one of the scenic locales in Sonoma Valley. Note: advance reservations are strongly recommended for the hikes.

The Spa's two exercise gyms are equipped with up-to-date exercise conditioning equipment, including Stairmaster, Life Cycles treadmill, rowin machine, free weights and low inertia-variable resistance weight machines. For guests who are unfamiliar with those machines, the Spa recommends a consultation with one of the fitness instructors who will be happy to explain their use. Private instruction is available. The Exercise Pavilion, located at the Main Pool, also has a complete selection of cardiovascular exercise equipment.

The Inn's Boutique features exercise and Spa apparel, logo t-shirts, bathing suits, and the Inn's own line of products used in the Spa treatments. The Boutique is open from 9:00 a.m. to 7:00 p.m. Monday through Friday, and from 8:00 a.m. to 7:00 p.m. Saturday and Sunday.

Guests who love to go exploring can visit nearby wineries for tours and wine tastings, play golf, or go horseback riding, hot air ballooning or picnicking. The Inn's concierge will offer directions, information and suggestions about these activities and any of Sonoma County's many other attractions. Or, guests can visit the historical landmarks of Sonoma, explore its picturesque plaza, fabulous shopping and locally produced food specialties.

Speaking of food, dining at Sonoma Mission Inn and Spa is a special occasion, with each exquisitely prepared to keep everyone happy and healthy. The Grille, located just off the Lobby, features a seaonal menu of Wine Country Cuisine prepared with fresh locally grown products. Spa Cuisine is also available at lunch and dinner, offering low-calorie, low-sodium and low-cholesterol dishes. The Grille, which offers a romantic, casually elegant setting, is open daily for lunch, dinner and Sunday Brunch. Poolside dining is also available, weather permitting. Reservations are recommended.

The Lobby Bar, which is located adjacent to the Grille, is open daily and provides complimentary hors d'oeuvres and entertainment nightly in the Lobby.

The Cafe is located at the north end of the resort at the corner of Boyes Boulevard and Highway 12. This restaurant features regional Italian cuisine and California specialties for lunch and dinner in a casual bistro setting. The Cafe is open daily for breakfast, lunch and dinner. Reservations are recommended at this restaurant, as well. The Cafe Bar, which is located at the Cafe, is open daily and offers a varietyof Sonoma Valley wines by the glass, draught beer and a full line of spirits and mixed drinks.

The SMI Market, located adjacent to the Cafe, is open daily and offers a vast assortment of items. Such as, specialty food items, cookbooks, kitchenware, baskets and deli items for picnics, Spa apparel and logo merchandise, and sundries. Gift wrapping and shipping is provided.

As an alternative to dining out, guests can order Room Service which offers breakfast, lunch and dinner daily. A selection of wines, champagne, and Spa Cuisine is also available.

Sonoma Skypark Airport is located about 10 miles from the Sonoma Mission Inn and Spa. It has a 2,340'x30 asphalt runway. The Inn will provide transportation to and from the airport for a fee. The overnight parking fee for both singles and twins is $3.00. For more information about activities, rates and accommodations at the Sonoma Mission Inn and Spa, call 800-862-4945 or 938-9000. (Information submitted by Sonoma Mission Inn and Spa)

CA-TVL - SOUTH LAKE TAHOE
LAKE TAHOE AIRPORT

108

Harvey's Resort Hotel & Casino:

This resort is located about 8 miles from the Lake Tahoe Airport and can be reached by shuttle van running between the airport and various other facilities in the area ($5.00/person each way). If driving yourself turn right on Hwy 50 to the "Y" junction; turn right on Hwy 50 to Stateline; Its the first resort casino on the left. Harvey's Resort contains 8 restaurants within their complex ranging from snack bars to their distinctive steak and seafood restaurants. The Sage Room offers one of the most elegant dining experiences in the area and specializes in items like Sauteed Prawns Mediterranean, Filet of Sole Irene and exotic desserts like Bananas Foster including over 100 other items available on their menu with average prices of $16.25 to $28.50. The Sage Room is open Monday through Sunday from 6 p.m. to 11 p.m. The Seafood Grotto is yet another fine restaurant in a quaint environment and features delectable seafood and Chinese specialties. Convention services and catering depart ments will serve the needs of small parties or groups up to 1000 persons. Nightly entertainment in the Emerald Party Lounge and Emerald Theater includes 88,000 square feet of gaming space in addition to the 740 hotel rooms to accommodate their guests. For information call 702-588-2411 or 800-553-1022.

(Area Code 916)

Restaurants Near Airport:

Harvey's Resort	7 mi NE	Phone: 702-588-2411
Skyroom	On Site	Phone: N/A
Snack Bar	On Site	Phone: N/A
The Lookout	On Site	Phone: 542-6080

Lodging: Best Western Station House 916-542-1101; Harrah's (Free Airport Transportation) 702-588-6611; Harvey's Resort 702-588-2411; Horizon Casino Resort 702-588-6211; High Sierra Hotel 702-588-6211; Inn by the Lake 916-542-0330; Lakeland Village Ski Resort 916-541-7711; Tahoe Villa 916-544-3041.

Meeting Rooms: Convention Facilities: Harrah's 702-588-6611; Harvey's Resort 702-588-2411.

Transportation: Taxi: Bills 916-544-1789; Lake Tahoe Limo 916-577-2727; REO Limo 916-544-3333; RTS Shuttle 916-544-5555; Sierra Taxi 916-577-8888; Sunshine 916-544-5565; Tahoe Ready Cab 916-542-2424; Yellow Cab 916-544-5555; Rental Cars: Avis 916-541-7800; Budget 916-541-5777; Hertz 916-544-2327.

Information: Lake Tahoe Visitors Center, 1156 Ski Run Blvd., South Lake Tahoe, CA 96150, Phone: 800-AT-TAHOE.

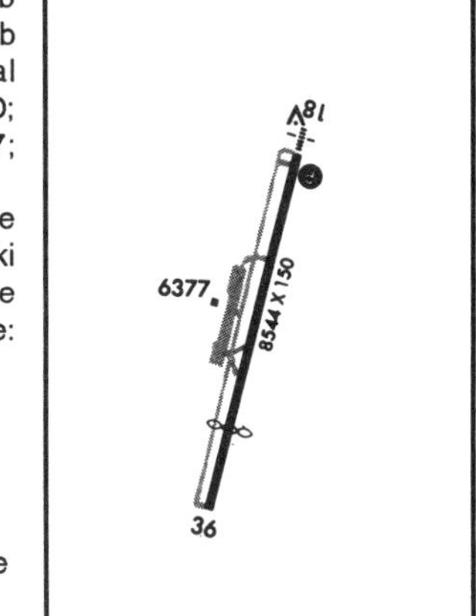

Airport Information:

SOUTH LAKE TAHOE - LAKE TAHOE AIRPORT (TVL)
3 mi southwest of town N38-53.63 W119-59.72 Elev: 6264 Fuel: 100LL, Jet-A
Rwy 18-36: H8544x150 (Asph-Grvd) Attended: 1500-0500Z Unicom: 122.95 Tower: 118.4 (1600-0400Z) Gnd Con: 121.9 Notes: CAUTION - Down drafts may be encountered close to the mountains (Refer to Airport Facility Directory for additional flight precautions etc.)
FBO: Airport Manager Phone: 542-6080

Photo by: Harveys Resort Hotel/Casino

Harveys Resort Hotel and Casino is one of several famous entertainment spots located at the Lake Tahoe's South Shore Area.

With nothing more than two rope tows, a chair lift, and a small base hut, Heavenly first opened its doors to skiers on December 15, 1955. And there's been no looking back.

Today, Heavenly is one of the largest ski resorts in North America - an international destination of incredible magnitude. Skiers come from continents away to explore their mountain, the snow, and the breathtaking views of Lake Tahoe - clearly one of Mother Nature's greatest accomplishments.

Generations of people with a love for skiing and a strong commitment to Heavenly have contributed to this evolution. For the past 40 years, they have applied their talents and energies to establish Heavenly as a world-class resort. The sensational snow and the magnificent mountain...the scenic beauty and the boundless activities...the attention to skier comforts and the focus on pure fun...all combine to create a ski experience unlike any other.

Standing high above Mott Canyon - at 10,000 feet - pause for a moment to enjoy the quiet. Feel the cool, crisp air on your face-savor the spectacular beauty of your surroundings. Take a deep breath...then jump into 3,500 vertical feet of pure, unadulterated bliss.

This is what Heavenly is all about. Here you'll find international caliber skiing...terrain to dive into, a terrain to glide on...awe-inspiring views of a sapphire blue Alpine lake...and the splendor of mountains that span the border between California and Nevada.

Catch a ride on one of 25 lifts, including three high-speed, detachable quads. They'll carry you to 79 trails spread out over 4,800 acres. Sample the radical steeps in Mott and Killebrew canyons...the wide-open cruisers on Dipper and Ridge runs...the challenging moguls on world-famous Gunbarrel.

Heavenly snow lives up to its name - it's light, its's dry, and it's deep. It falls to the rune of about 350 inches a year, and they serve it up any way you like it. Ski it groomed...ski it untracked... whatever strikes your fancy.

Amazingly - even with all this snow Heavenly has sunshine and blue skies about 80 percent of the time. Average daytime temperatures are in the mid-30s, so you can bask in the winter sun to your heart's content.

Heavenly is located smack dab on Lake Tahoe's South Shore - so close to the heart of the action that early morning shadows cast by the mountains eclipse the town. Tahoe's South Shore features a variety of hotels, motels, and lodges...dining options that range from a casual snack to an elegant meal...casinos that pulse around the clock...live entertainment and tons of outdoor activities - all within minutes of Heavenly.

Dining and Skiing Mountain Services: Heavenly has three base lodges and four on-mountain facilities offering skiers easy and convenient access to a variety of dining options and skier facilities throughout the mountain.

CALIFORNIA: California Lodge: is located at the base of the mountain at the corner of Wildwood and Saddle, off Ski Run Blvd. It has a cafeteria, California bar with sushi bar, ski shop, and ski school. **Top of the Tram:** is located at Top terminal of the Aerial Tram. Features include: **Monument Peak Restaurant and cocktail lounge** is located at the top of the tram. Services include: cafeteria, outdoor deck, ski school office, accessory shop. **Patsy's Hut:** is located near the base of Patsy's Lift. There is a snack shop located there. **Sky Meadows:** is located Mid-mountain at the base of the Sky Express Quad and contains an outdoor BBQ and grill facility and snack shop.

NEVADA: Boulder Lodge: is located at the base of the mountain at the end of South Benjamin, off Kingsbury Grade, Stateline. Facilities include a cafeteria, Black Diamond Mexican Cantina, outdoor deck, bar ski shop, & ski school. **Stagecoach Lodge:** is located on Tramway off upper Kingsbury Grade, Stateline (Intermediate and advanced skiers only. Beginner skiers should enter through either the Boulder Lodge or the California Lodge). Facilities include a cafeteria, Slice of Heaven Pizza Pub, bar and ski shop. **East Peak Lodge:** is located mid-mountain at the base of Comet Express Quad and the Dipper Express. Facilities include a cafeteria, deli hut, bar Cappuccino bar, outdoor BBQ, and pizzeria.

First Time Skiers: Heavenly's ski school offers something for every skier - adventure, excitement, and an atmosphere of fun. Their skilled instructors are a dedicated group, and making sure that everyone has a great time is tops on their agenda. They offer a diversity of specialized programs or they can put one together that's just right for you. "First Timers" lessons are designed for brand-new skiers, while Novice Turners is for second-day skiers. Group lesson, all-day equipment rental, and novice lift access are included. (One-day session, 3 hours are about $50.00). Additional lesson packages: "Five-sessions" $125.00; Three-session packages $78.00; And "Single sessions" (2 hours) $29.00.

Accommodations: For entertainment around the clock you can light up your nights with the dazzle of casino excitement at Ceasars, Harrah's, Harveys, and others. Heavenly's live entertainment includes some of the biggest names in show business.

Getting There: South Lake Tahoe Airport (TVL) is only 7 miles from Heavenly. Taxi service, limousine and rental cars are available. If flying by commercial or air carrier into Reno/Tahoe International Airport, you can arrange shuttle service using Trans World Express offering daily non-stop service from Southern California and San Francisco to South Lake Tahoe Airport. For more information about Heavenly Lake Tahoe call at 702-586-7000. (Information for articles, submitted by Heavenly Lake Tahoe).

Lake Tahoe's South Shore

If luxury can be defined as having an abundance of choices, Lake Tahoe must be one of the most luxurious ski destinations in America. Fifteen ski resorts ring the Lake Taho basin with a short, scenic drive from one to the next.

Heavenly, America's largest ski resort, offers 79 trails, 24 lifts including a 50passenger aerial tram and the "Comet" high speed detachable quad. More access at this bi-state resort means skiers spend more time enjoying the mountain

Thanks to the world's largest snow making system, Heavenly has great skiing all season, regardless of the hand dealt by Mother Nature. All lifts on the California side, as well as five lifts on the Nevada side can operate without the benefit of natural snowfall (temperature permitting). Lake Tahoe receives an average annual snow fall of 300 to 500 inches, so snow making is considered an auxiliary measure.

Kirkwood continues to draw skiers of every level to its outstanding mountain, great conditions and impeccable service. With a base elevation of 7,800 feet, the highest in North California, Kirkwood receives plenty of light dry snow that stays fresh through an extended season. The past summer has been spent on detailed slope grooming to create the best possible ski surface.

While 35% of Kirkwood's terrain is for advanced skiers, special attention is also paid to beginning, intermediate and young skiers. Sierra Ski Ranch is widening the lower half of the 3.5 mile Sugar & Spice run, popular with advanced beginners. Width on lower Castle Way, an intermediate run, is also being increased. Expanded snow making will enhance conditions in higher traffic areas at the resort. At the base lodge, a full renovation of the main cafeteria kitchen will mean more food stations and faster service.

Lake Tahoe basks in sunny days 75% of the year. The deep waters of North America's largest Alpine lake are made sapphire blue by reflecting the clear skies. Daytime temperatures are in the 30's, and except during powder-falls, the climate is generally dry.

Pilots flying into South Lake Tahoe Airport should refer to the Airport Facility Directory for current airport remarks as well as other official and currently published documentation regarding proper flight precautions and procedures.

The South Lake Tahoe Airport is served by American and American Eagles Airlines. Those carriers, and most other major airlines, also serve the Reno Cannon International Airport just 58 miles away. Tahoe is also accessible by seven all-weather highways.

Skiers staying at the South Shore can take advantage of free ski shuttles to the slopes, as well as complimentary shuttles to the famous casinos, Harrah's, Harvey's Caesars, Horizon (formerly the High Sierra), Lakeside Inn & Casino, Bill's, and the Tahoe Nugget - where the gaming excitement and entertainment continues a round the clock.

Skiers also have the opportunity to experience over a dozen other ski resorts scattered around the Lake Tahoe basin.

For a free Travel Planner and Ski Package Planner containing complete information on winter and ski vacations at the South Shore, call the Lake Tahoe Visitors Authority toll free at (800) AT-TAHOE. Operators can connect callers directly with over 100 hotels, motels, lodges, and property management companies on the South Shore. (Information submitted by Lake Tahoe Visitors Authority).

Photo by: Lake Tahoe Vistors Authority

Stateline Spendor perched along the California/Nevada border at Lake Tahoe's South Shore are seven exciting casino's offering gaming, accommodations, dining and entertainment against a background of the Sierra Nevada mountains.

CA-TOA - TORRANCE
TORRANCE MUNICIPAL AIRPORT

(Area Code 310) 109, 110

CoCo's Bakery And Restaurant:

CoCo's Family style restaurant is situated kitty-corner to the Torrance Municipal Airport. We were told to reach the restaurant you can walk 1 or 2 blocks south then head west to the restaurant. This family restaurant is open Saturday and Sunday from 7 a.m. to 11 p.m. and Monday through Friday 6:30 a.m. to 11 p.m. Specialties of the house include a variety of breakfast items as well as grilled chicken, sandwiches, hamburgers, cheeseburgers, steaks and shrimp. Freshly baked pies, cookies and muffins are prepared daily. For more information about this restaurant call 373-6316.

Del Conte's Restaurant:

The Del Conte's Restaurant is situated adjacent to the Torrance Municipal Airport. This fine dining restaurant is open for lunch from 11 a.m. to 3 p.m. and for dinner from 4 p.m. to 11 p.m. On Sunday they are only open for dinner from 3:30 p.m. to 10 p.m. Items on their menu include prime rib, steaks, lobster, crab legs, fresh fish daily, sandwiches of all types as well as salads. They also provide combo soup and salad specials with their menu. Average prices for standard entrees run $4.95 to $10.95 for lunch and $7.95 to $29.95 for dinner. The main dining area can accommodate 175 persons. The decor is classified as classic and contemporary. In addition to the restaurant they also have 3 separate banquet rooms that can seat between 10 and 230 persons. For more information call the Del Conte's Restaurant at 326-0880.

Restaurants Near Airport:

CoCo's Bakery & Restaurant	1/2 mi	Phone: 373-6316
Del Conte's Restaurant	Adj Arpt	Phone: 326-0880

Lodging: Holiday Inn (2 miles) 542-0565; Howard Johnsons Lodge (1 block) 325-0660; Marriott Hotel (2 miles) 316-3636; Quality Inn (2 miles) 378-8511.
Meeting Rooms: Del Conte's Restaurant (Adj Arpt) 326-0880; Marriott Hotel 316-3636.
Transportation: Limousine and taxi service reported.
Information: Chamber of Commerce, 3400 Torrance Blvd., Ste. 100, Torrance, CA 90503, Phone: 540-5858. Greater Los Angeles Visitors & Convention Bureau, Manulife Plaza, 515 South Figueroa Street, Los Angeles, CA 90071, 310-624-7300.

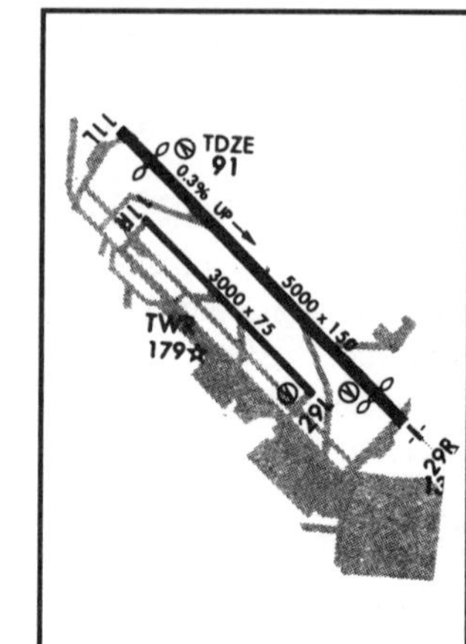

Airport Information:

TORRANCE - ZAMPERINI - (TORRANCE MUNICIPAL) (TOA)
3 mi southwest of town N33-48.20 W118-20.38 Elev: 101 Fuel: 80, 100, 100LL
Rwy 11L-29R: H5000x150 (Asph-Conc) Rwy 11R-29L: H3000x75 (Asph)
Attended: 1300-0600 Atis: 125.6 Unicom: 122.95 Tower: 135.6 (North), 124.0 (South)
Gnd Con: 120.9 Notes: CAUTION: Farm equipment operating near all runways and taxiways.
FBO: Rolling Hill Aviation Phone: 326-3213
FBO:FBO: South Bay Aviation Phone: 326-5050

Not to be used for navigational purposes

CA-O86 - TRINITY CENTER
TRINITY CENTER

(Area Code 916) 111, 112

The Sasquatch Cafe:
This restaurant is located on the corner of Mary Ave. and Airport Rd. and is within walking distance from the (south) end of the Trinity Center Airport. A public phone is available near the airport hangars for courtesy transportation. This colorful restaurant serves the North Trinity Lake area and makes an entertaining as well as refreshing stop for travelers and vacationers. Their big screen TV, pool table and dart board is enjoyed by many customers. As the name suggests, this restaurant is devoted to "Big Foot" (Sasquatch) parapherna-lia. Here you can pick up your map of "Big Foot" sightings, eat a great chicken dinner or enjoy a cold beverage at the bar. Specialties include broasted chicken, pizza, and a variety of specials that are prepared through the week. Prices range from $4.95 for lunch and $8.50 for dinner. The restaurant walls are covered with memorabilia of Old Trinity Center with many historic photographs of gold mining and logging camps. You are invited to enjoy the relaxed and friendly country atmosphere. This restaurant is open Tuesday through Friday 11 a.m. to 9 p.m., Saturday from 8 a.m. to 9 p.m. and Sunday 8 a.m. to 3 p.m. (Closed on Mondays) For information and restaurant hours call 266-3250.

Trinity Center Inn (Bed & Breakfast):
This facility is located about 200 yards from the tie-downs at the (north) end of the airport. You can also call the Bed & Breakfast from the airport phone located near the rest rooms area on the field. The Trinity Center Bed & Breakfast Inn caters to pilot types and is very popular with many general aviation travelers. Reserved dining can be arranged in advance for those not planning to spend the night.. Fixed priced meals are prepared. Their full service lounge and dining room is decorated in tones of gray and burgundy. The area with its many attractions makes this Bed & Breakfast an excellent place to arrange your next vacation. For more information call 266-3223.

Attractions:

You can find Trinity Center Airport on the Klamath Falls sectional. There are 54 paved tiedowns available at the southwest end of the runway (Bring your own ropes). Please keep your traffic pattern over the lake (800 feet AGL). If you plan to dine at the Airporter Inn Restaurant, you can call them on Unicom 122.9, which they are permanently monitoring. They will be glad to pick you up. Restrooms and phones are located at both ends of the field, and during the summer season, most restaurants and resorts will be happy to come out and pick you up if you let them know you are coming.

The Trinity Alps: Much like in Switzerland, the Trinity countryside is embedded between mountains covered in meadows and deep green and peaceful forests. Thirty miles north of Weaverville, you will find a paradise for vacationing. The lake invites leisure boaters, fishermen, and water-skiers, while the mountains and forests attract many hiking, horseback and fly-fishing enthusiasts. In this non congested region it is common to see hundreds of deer in herds grazing or brown bear playing with their cubs on Coffee Creek Road. Prospectors still pan for gold nuggets while working their claims in small mountain streams within this region. During the winter, experienced vacationers take advantage of the hundreds of cros- county skiing and snowmobiling trails and roads. Whether you are arriving by car on route 3, or by plane and landing at the Trinity Center Airport, you will find everything you need to make your stay most enjoyable. Restaurants and dinner clubs, motels, housekeeping cabins, and even houseboats, along with gift shops and grocery stores are all available to you during your stay.

For you fishermen: The ideal conditions provide some of the finest fishing anywhere. Rainbow and German brown trout, large and small mouth bass and kokanee are all found in this northern California region. Approximately 75,000 trout are planted annually by the Department of Fish and Game. Trinity Lake holds the record for the largest small mouth bass ever caught in the state of California at 9 lbs 1 oz. Fly-fishermen are in seventh heaven on the clear cold mountain lakes. During the entire summer the eastern brookies and golden trout strike hard in the shallower parts. The more adventurous fisherman can hike up the mountain where the undisturbed surrounding makes it all worth while.

Restaurants Near Airport:

The Sasquatch Cafe	1/2 mi W.	Phone: 266-3250
Trinity Center Inn	On Site	Phone: 266-3223
Yellowjacket	1/2 mi W.	Phone: 266-3569

Lodging: Airporter Inn Resort, 266-3223 (Adj. Airport); Wyntoom Resort, 266-3337; Carriville Inn, (Bed & Breakfast), 266-3511; Enright Gulch Cabins, 266-3600; Bonanza King Resort, 266-3305; Coffee Creek Guest Ranch, 266-3343.
Transportation: Airporter Inn Resort and Sasquatch are within walking distance. Also free pick up service; No rental cars stationed at airport, at this time.
Information: Chamber of Commerce, 317 Main Street, Box 517, Weaverville, CA 96093, Phone: 623-6101.

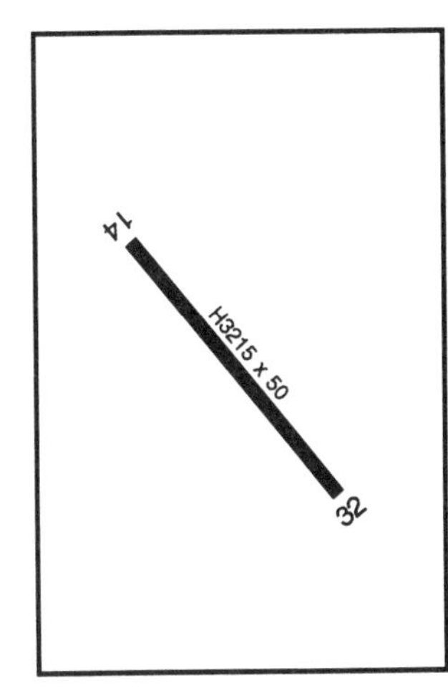

Airport Information:

TRINITY CENTER - TRINITY CENTER AIRPORT (O86)
0 east of town N40-58.99 W122-41.65 Elev: 2390 Rwy 14-32: H3215x50 (ASPH) Unattended CATF: 122.9 Public Phone 24hrs Notes: No landing fee, However, a $2.00 donation or higher would be greatly appreciated by the volunteers and members who maintain the airport. $2.00/ night, $10.00/month; "Seasonally open to tourists, fishermen, hunters, hikers; Off season, better be prepared to rough it; Some camping near southwest end; Tiedowns not officially anchored." **FBO: No Fixed Base Operator on field. However, contact Trinity County Public Works Department for questions about airport. Phone: 916-623-1365 or 266-3487 also (266-3350, local pilot).**

CA-TRK - TRUCKEE
TRUCKEE-TAHOE AIRPORT

(Area Code 916) 113

The Restaurants of Northstar-at-Tahoe

Northstar-at-Tahoe ski resort i s located only three miles from theTruckee-Tahoe Airport. It is halfway(six miles) between the North Shore of Lake Tahoe and Truckee, CA on Highway 267, situated on Mt. Pluto. Free shuttle bus service from Truckee airport to Norhstar is available with 24-hour notice. This resort has a base village that features a choice of restaurants. Timbercreek Restaurant, which has a casually elegant atmosphere, serves breakfast, lunch, and dinner with children's menu . Pedro's Pizza, newly remodeled, serves chili, salads, and of course, pizza , for lunch and dinner. The Basque Club serves five-course family-style dinners, plus it offers sleigh rides. In addition to the village restaurants, try the Big Springs Day Lodge, featuring an on-mountain cafeteria and barbecue, or the Nordic Cafe for lunch at the cross-country center. If you plan to ski and have intermediate skiing ability, you can have access to the mountain-top Summit Deck & Grille. They provide outdoor seating on a 5,000 square-foot deck with views of Lake Tahoe. A free shuttle will pick you up from the airport . For more information, contact Northstar-at-Tahoe at 562-1010.

Restaurants Near Airport:
Northstar-at-Tahoe 3 mi Phone: 562-1010

Lodging: Northstar-at-Tahoe (3 miles) 562-1010; Truckee Super 8 Lodge (3 miles) 587-8888; Best Western Truckee Tahoe (1 mile) 587-4525; Donner Lake Village Resort 587-6081; Resort At Squaw Creek 583-6300
Meeting Rooms: None Reported
Transportation: Free shuttle bus service from Truckee-Tahoe Airport to Northstar is available with 24-hour notice. Taxi service: Donner 587-0600; North Shore 546-3181; Vet Cab 582-8294. Rental cars: Budget 562-1010; A & A 582-8282; Airport Auto 587-2688
Information: Truckee Chamber of Commerce, 12036 Donner Pass Road, Truckee, CA 9616, Phone: 587-2757

Attraction:

Northstar-at-Tahoe ski resort, just 3 miles from Truckee-Tahoe airport, features downhill and cross-country skiing, and has a base village with shops and restaurants. Call 562-1010 for more information.

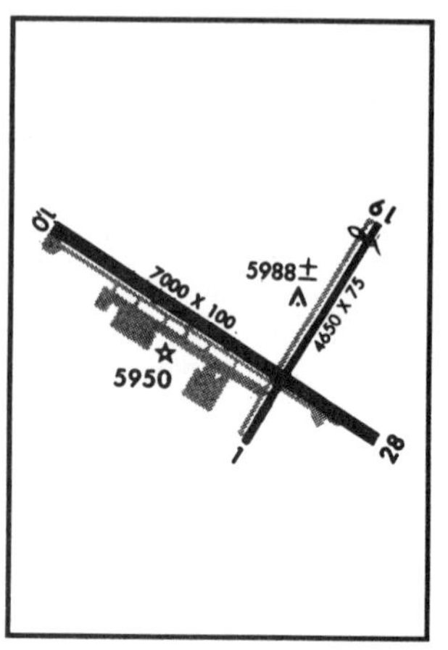

Airport Information:

Truckee - Truckee-Tahoe Airport (TRK)
2 mi east of town N39-19.20 W120-08.37 Elev: 5900 Fuel: 80, 100LL, Jet-A1+ Rwy 10-28: H7000x100 (Asph) Rwy 01-19: H465x75 (Asph) Attended: continuously CTAF/Unicom: 122.8 Notes: Rwy 19 sailplanes left traffic. Ultralight activity on and in vicinity of airport.
FBO: Truckee Tahoe Phone: 587-4119

Northstar-at-Tahoe

Truckee-Tahoe, CA (CA-TRK)

Northstar-at-Tahoe ski resort is located halfway (6 miles) between the North Shore of Lake Tahoe and Truckee, California on Highway 267. The base of the mountain is at 6,330 feet above sea level and the summit is at 8,610 feet, allowing a vertical drop of 2,280 feet. Northstar is a fun vacation getaway for all ages. Its winter season starts from Thanksgiving and goes through mid-April, and the summer season starts from Memorial Day weekend and goes through October (weather permitting). The resort offers downhill, cross-country skiing, snowshoeing, snowmobiling, and snow skating, on-site lodging (some slopeside), a base village with shops, bars, and restaurants, horseback trail rides, and horse-drawn sleigh rides. During the milder season, there other activities such as, 18-hole golf, tennis, swimming, mountain biking, guided nature hiking, and outdoor concerts. There are also meeting and conference facilities.

More than ninety percent of the 2,000 acres of downhill ski terrain is accessible by eleven ski lifts, including four express lifts. There are 60 runs, including eight mile-long advanced runs (on the backside of Mt. Pluto) and a 2.9 mile run. Snowmaking facilities are available from the top to the bottom of the mountain, covering fifty percent of the ski runs. Seven lifts serve those snowmaking runs.

Ski and snowboard lessons, with instructors certified by Professional Ski Instructors of America, are available for all levels of skiers. Specialty clinics are offered throughout the season, including Starkids all-day lesson program (for ages 5-12), and three-day specialty clinics, women's ski clinics, seniors' ski clinics, breakthrough ski clinics, and snowboard improvement clinics. There are free one-hour clinics for men and women every Tuesday morning, for senior skiers (60+) every Wednesday morning, and for all skiers every Thursday morning. (Note: free clinics are not offered during holiday periods, and require a lift ticket to participate). Northstar's Cross-Country and Telemark Ski Center is located adjacent to the downhill runs and has 65 kilometers of groomed trails. The Cross-Country center offers track, skating and telemark lessons (on downhill runs), along with striding, skating, and telemarking rentals. Skiers also enjoy Northstar's popular electronic frequent skier program, Club Vertical. Members get privileges including discounts and members-only lines at each lift.

Take a break from skiing and visit Northstar's base village, which contains shops and restaurants.The Northsport Ski Shop is a full service shop that offers equipment, fashions, gifts and accessories, demo skis and boots, and ski tuning and repair. Northsport also has a special children's department that offers kid size equipment, clothing and accessories. The Ski Rental Shop offers skis, boots, poles, high-performance equipment, snowboards, snowshoes and ski clothing. The Village Food Company offers a full-service deli, cappuccino bar, gourmet groceries, video rentals, and an ATM.

Hungry? Timbercreek restaurant serves breakfast, lunch and dinner in a casual, yet elegant environment. Pedro's

Photo by: Northstar-at-Tahoe

Skiers take to the slopes at Northstar-at-Tahoe.

Pizza, which has been newly remodeled, serves lunch and dinner. The Basque Club Restaurant, at the golf complex, serves five-course family-style dinners, plus a full bar and sleigh rides. The village also features the apres ski Alpine Bar, as well as other bars and lounges.

In addition to the village restaurants, visit the Big Springs Day Lodge(on mountain cafeteria and barbecue), have lunch at the Nordic Cafe(at the cross-country center), or the mountain-top Summit Deck and Grille, with outdoor seating on a 5,000 square-foot deck and views of Lake Tahoe.

To keep the little ones busy, Northstar offers Minors' Camp, a licensed child care center, which is open daily in the winter season for children 2-6 years of age. The program includes recreational and educational activities, lunch and snacks, and learn-to-ski options.

Time to relax? Northstar offers 250 lodging units, ranging from hotel-type rooms to condominiums to mountainside homes scattered throughout the resort. All rooms are equipped with a television and VCR, and most feature fireplaces and full kitchens with microwaves and dishwashers. As an extra treat, a recreation center with outdoor spas, saunas, an exercise room and a game room is available for lodging guests. There is a minimum of a two-night stay. Room deposits must be made within 10 days from verbal confirmation of reservation. Reservations booked within 7 days of arrival must be confirmed with a major credit card. Policies may vary for group reservations. Be sure to inquire about Northstar's various economical ski packages, as well.

Reno Cannon Int'l Airport is about 45 miles from Northstar and is serviced by most major air carriers. Car rentals are available there as well. However as an alternative, the Truckee-Tahoe Airport is just 3 miles away, and it has a 7,000 foot runway. Free shuttle bus service to and from Truckee airport is available with 24-hour notice. Free shuttles also operate throughout the resort, transporting guests from lodging units to the base village, sleigh rides, and recreation center. For information about rates and accommodations, contact Northstar at 800-GO-NORTH (800-466-6784). For other information, call 562-1010 (8 a.m. to 8 p.m., 7 days a week). (Information submitted by Northstar-at-Tahoe)

CA-TLR - TULARE
MEFFORD FIELD AIRPORT

114

Pitching Wedge Restaurant:

The Pitching Wedge Restaurant is situated adjacent to the Mefford Field Airport. Fly-in guests can easily walk to the restaurant from the airport. Their restaurant hours are between 7 a.m. and 2:30 p.m., 7 days a week. The menu contains a wide variety of items like steak sandwiches, hamburgers, cheeseburgers shrimp dishes, salads and also offers a full breakfast selection. Average prices run around $5.00 for most choices. The dining room can accommodate up to 200 persons within a country club setting. Groups and large parties are welcome. A public 18 hole golf course is located right outside this establishment, and makes for a fine location to enjoy both a fine meal and a game of golf. For more information call the Pitching Wedge Restaurant at 686-0270.

(Area Code 209)

Restaurants Near Airport:

Lyles Cafe	Adj Arpt	Phone: N/A
Lynns Cafe	Adj Arpt	Phone: 686-5271
Pitching Wedge	Adj Arpt	Phone: 686-0270

Lodging: Best Western Town & Country Lodge 688-7537; Motel 6 686-1611; Stardust Motel (Adj arpt); Travel Lodge Agri-Center (1 mile) 688-6671.

Meeting Rooms: Best Western Town 7 Country Lodge 688-7537.

Transportation: Taxi Service: Dial-A-Ride 688-5706.

Information: California Division of Tourism, P.O. Box 1499, Sacramento, CA 95812, Phone: 800-862-2543.

Attractions:

Golf course is located adjacent to airport.

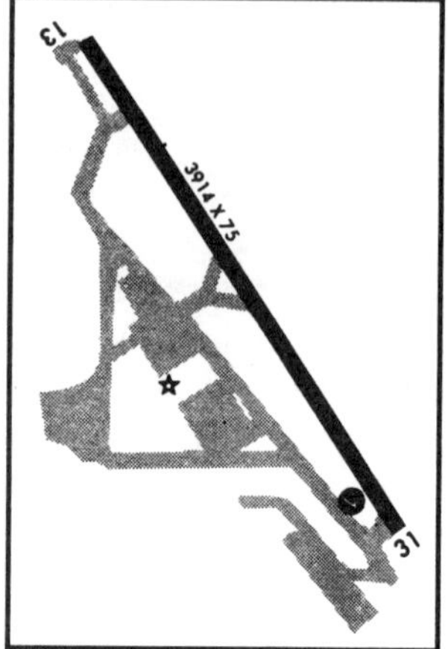

Airport Information:

TULARE - MEFFORD FIELD AIRPORT (TLR)
3 mi southeast of town N36-09.38 W119-19.57 Elev: 271 Fuel: 100LL
Rwy 13-31: H3914x75 (Asph) Attended: 1600Z-dusk Unicom: 122.7
Mefford Field Airport Mgr. Phone: 685-2300

CA-UKI - UKIAH
UKIAH MUNICIPAL AIRPORT

115

Beacon Restaurant:

The Beacon Restaurant is located across the street and west of the Ukiah Municipal Airport. This family style restaurant is open Monday through Friday from 6 a.m. to 8 p.m. and Saturday and Sunday from 6 a.m. to 3 p.m. Their menu contains a varied and extensive selection of different items including chicken fried steak (large portion), extra large choice steaks, pork chops, seafood, sandwiches, soups, and much more. Average prices for a meal run about $5.00 for breakfast or lunch, and between $7.00 to $8.00 for dinner. Daily lunch specials are frequently offered during the week. The Beacon Restaurant is situated in a building that was constructed in the 1940's and can accommodate 100 people in their main dining room as well as 20 in their banquet room. According to the restaurant management, there are a large number of fly-in customers that make this establishment a regular stopping place. For more information call the Beacon Restaurant at 462-3164.

(Area Code 707)

Restaurants Near Airport:

Beacon Restaurant	Adj Arpt	Phone: 462-3164

Lodging: Best Western Inn (Free trans, 1 mile) 462-8868; Best Western Willow Tree Lodge (1 mile) 462-8611; Discovery Motel (1 mile) 462-8873; Holiday Lodge (1 mile) 462-2906; Manor Inn (3 miles) 462-7584; Motel 6 (1 block) 462-8763.
Meeting Rooms: Best Western Inn 462-8868; Discovery Motel 462-8873.
Transportation: Taxi Service: Dial-A-Ride 462-3881; M.T.A. 462-3881; Rental Cars: Hertz 468-0537; Thrifty 462-4759.
Information: Greater Ukiah Chamber of Commerce, 495-E E Perkins Street, Ukiah, CA 95482, Phone: 462-4705.

Attractions:

Some of the attractions within this region include: Ukiah Golf Course, Lake Mendocino, Redwood Noves, Parducci Winery, Fetzer Winery, Bed and Breakfast lodging, historical monuments, etc., all within 15 miles of the Ukiah Municipal Airport. (See Information listed above).

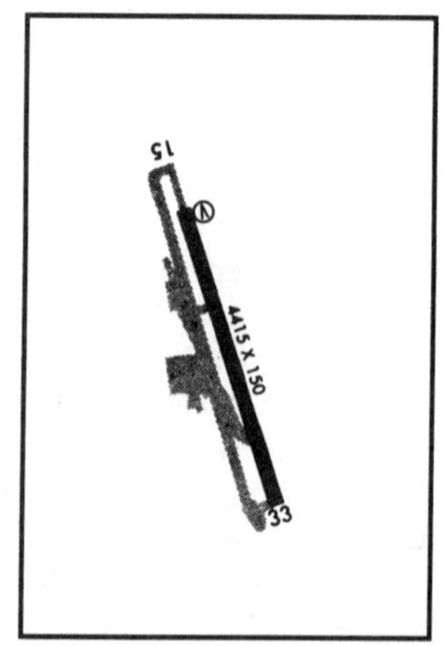

Airport Information:

UKIAH - MUNICIPAL AIRPORT (UKI)
1 mi south of town N39-07.56 W123-12.05 Elev: 614 Fuel: 100LL, Jet-A
Rwy 15-00: H4415x150 (Asph) Attended: 1600Z-dusk CTAF: 123.6 Unicom: 123.0
Public Phone 24hrs
FBO: City of Ukiah Phone: 463-6293

Vichy Springs Resort

Vichy Springs Resort, which is open year-round, is located in the Mendocino foothills in Ukiah, northern California. It is the oldest continuous operating mineral water resort in California and the only naturally carbonated warm water spa in North America. Vichy was named after the world-famous springs first discovered by Julius Caesar in France. The resort's virtually identical waters surge from miles deep within the earth. These crystal clear, sparkling "Champagne Baths" are naturally warm and soothing, and they are filled with minerals and energy renowned for their healing and restorative qualities.These therapeutic waters are also bottled for drinking and are abundantly available for bathing and swimming at the resort.

The resort, which opened in 1854 and is now a California Historical Landmark, was a favorite retreat of writers Mark Twain, Robert Louis Stevenson and Jack London. It was also a favorite of presidents Ulysses S. Grant, Benjamin Harrison and Teddy Roosevelt, as well as pugilists John L. Sullivan and "Gentleman" Jim Corbett.

Today, Vichy Springs Resort has been restored and renovated to successfully combine its natural and historic charm with modern comforts and conveniences. Twelve individually decorated rooms with private baths date from the 1860's. Two cottages with fully equipped kitchens, one and two bedrooms, and living rooms were built in 1854. They are the two oldest standing structures in Mendocino County.

All accommodations have their own heating and air conditioning, plus queen or twin-size beds. Just steps away are the renovated indoor and outdoor bathing tubs, therapeutic massage building, hot tub, and mineral Olympic-size swimming pool.

During their stay, guests are invited to explore the 700-acre ranch where wildlife abounds in woods, meadows, streams and hills. They can visit the old Cinnabar Mine shaft, or visit the falls where the ferns are always green. They can picnic in the forest by Little Grizzly Creek.

Other attractions are easily accesible to the resort. The Mendocino coast, the lakes and wineries of Sonoma Lake, the redwood forests, the Grace Hudson Museum, and the famous "Skunk" train to Ft. Bragg. Sailing, wind surfing, water and jet skiing are all within reach. Salmon and steelhead fishing in winter and trout and striped bass fishing in summer are also close by.

For transportation, Ukiah Municipal Airport is located about 10 miles from Vichy Springs Resort. The airport has a 4, 415'x150 asphalt runway. The resort will provide free transportation to and from the airport. For those traveling on business, meeting areas are available only with approval of the proprietor. Advance reservations are recommended. For more information, call Vichy Springs Resort at 462-9515. (Information submitted by Vichy Springs Resort)

Photo by: Vichy Springs Resort Hot Pool with replica of Monet's Bridge crossing Vichy Creek.

Photo by: Vichy Springs Resort Chemisal Falls is a half-hour walk upstream on the Vichy Springs Ranch.

CA-CCB - UPLAND
CABLE AIRPORT

(Area Code 714) 116

Restaurants Near Airport:

Cable Airport Cafe	On Site	Phone: 985-0177
Charley's Grill & Pub	1/2 mi	Phone: 982-4513
Joey's Bar-B-Que	3/4 mi	Phone: 982-2128

Lodging: Griswolds Inn (2 miles) 626-2411; Uplander Motor Hotel (2 miles) 982-8821.
Meeting Rooms: Griswold's Inn 626-2411.
Transportation: Cable Airport has one loaner car for local use on first come first serve basis; Also Taxi Service: Yellow Cab 986-1138.
Information: California Division of Tourism, P.O. Box 1499, Sacramento, CA 95812, Phone: 800-862-2543.

Cable Airport Cafe:

The Cable Airport Cafe is located adjacent to the aircraft parking ramp only 100 feet away. This facility is reported to be a fine dining establishment, and is open 7 days a week between 6 a.m. and 5 p.m. There are two levels in the restaurant with an upstairs observation area and the main dining room on the ground floor. Their menu provides a variety of breakfast items with names like the "Controller" served with sliced French toast and eggs; the "Hungry Ace" complete with 2 hot cakes, meat and 3 eggs; or the "Pre-Flight" special including 2 hot cakes, sausage and 1 egg; For lunch, their "Jet Burger's" with a double meat patty,are a big success . In addition to these selections, they also offer patty melts, tuna melts, ham and turkey sandwiches, steak with eggs, soups and salads and much more. Average prices run $2.50 to $5.95 for breakfast and about the same for lunch and early dinner. The dining room has three rows of booths with pictures on the wall including a historical 4' x 3' photograph of the airport during its earlier days. Seating for between 125 and 130 persons is available. Larger groups and parties are welcome with advanced notice. In addition, they also serve meals on their 40 foot by 18 foot outdoor patio which can accommodate an additional 45 people, and great for watching the airport activity as well as the arriving and departing aircraft. In-flight catering is also a service provided. For information call the Cable Airport Cafe at 985-0177.

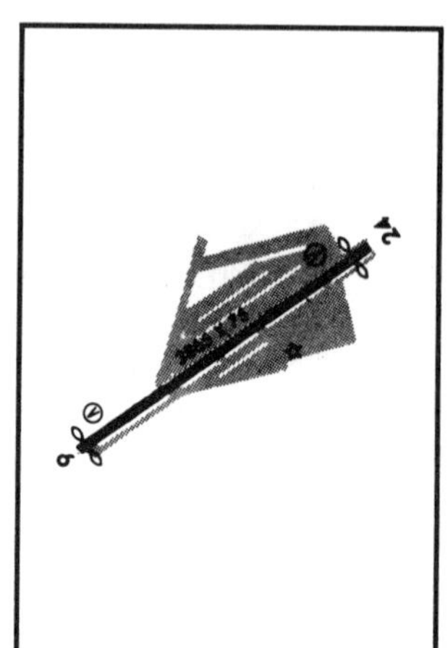

Airport Information:

UPLAND - CABLE AIRPORT (CCB)
2 mi northwest of town N34-06.69 W117-41.20 Elev: 1439 Fuel: 80, 100LL
Rwy 06-24: H3865x75 (Asph) Attended: dalight hours Unicom: 123.0 Public Phone 24hrs
Notes: $3.00 overnight parking fee
FBO: Cable Airport Inc. Phone: 982-1579
FBO: Foothill Aircraft Phone: 985-1977

CA-O45 - VACAVILLE
NUT TREE AIRPORT

(Area Code 707) 117

Restaurants Near Airport:

Coffee Tree	1/2 to 1 mile est.	Phone: 451-9000
Numerous Rest.	Across overpass	N/A

Lodging: Marriott Courtyard 451-9000; Quality Inn (3 miles) 446-8888; Va-Capri (1 mile) 448-8453.
Meeting Rooms: Marriott Courtyard has accommodations for meetings. For information call 451-9000.
Transportation: Courtesy car is available at the airport with advance notice appreciated. Call Blue Ridge Aeronautics FBO at 451-4400. Also, rental cars are available.
Information: Blue Ridge Aeronautics FBO 451-4400;

Attractions:

A Factory outlet shopping mall containing many stores is located within walking distance to the Marriott Courtyard and Coffee Tree Restaurant.

Marriott Courtyard & Coffee Tree Restaurant:

During our conversation with the airport management we learned that the Marriott Courtyard is a new facility located a short distance from the airport on the other side of the overpass. Transportation by courtesy car from the airport is recommended and easily obtained by calling Blue Ridge Aeronautics in advance of your arrival. The Marriott Courtyard has 278 units some of which face the center of the building. The Courtyard has planting areas, swimming pool, hot tub and exercise area. The Coffee Tree Restaurant is a sister facility to the Marriott Courtyard and is located within the same parking lot . It was once owned by the Nut Tree establishment and continues to be a great place to enjoy a meal. The top of the restaurant has a roof that resembles a circus tent with brown and orange colors, which makes it easy to spot. The decor of this restaurant has a casual atmosphere. The entrance area resembles an old airport lobby. The Coffee Tree offers a full course menu containing many choices. Prices average $8.00 to $11.00 for dinner selections. Bread is baked daily and they even make candy on the premises. After a fine meal you can walk a short distance to the factory outlet mall. Each year this complex containing dozens of stores continues to grow in size. There is plenty to see and do when visiting the area. For information about the Marriott Courtyard or Coffee Tree Restaurant call 451-9000.

Nut Tree Restaurant:

At the time of research we learned that the Nut Tree Restaurant, a very popular dining location for many years, has been closed. We were told that the property might be purchased by new owners. For information call the Blue Ridge Aeronautics FBO at 451-4400.

Airport Information:

VACAVILLE - NOT TREE AIRPORT (O45)
2 mi northeast of town N38-22.61 W121-57.75 Elev: 114 Fuel: 100LL, Jet-A
Rwy 02-20: H0000x75 (Asph) Attended: May-Oct 1530-0330Z and Nov-Apr 1600-0100Z
Unicom: 122.7 Public Phone 24hrs Notes: No landing fees, Overnight parking, Single: $4.00; Multi up to 12,500 lbs $6.00; Multi over 12,500 lbs $8.00
FBO: Blue Ridge Aeronautics Phone: 451-4400

CA-VNY - VAN NUYS
VAN NUYS AIRPORT

(Area Code 818)

118

Restaurants Near Airport:

94th Aero Squadron	On Site	Phone: 994-7437
Denny's Restaurant	Adj. W.	Phone: 994-0952
Landings Restaurant	On Site	Phone: 997-7676

Lodging: Airtel Plaza Hotel, (On Airport & Airport Van) 7277 Valjean Avenue, Phone: 997-7676; Carriage Inn, (Free Transportation) 5525 Sepulveda Blvd., Phone: 787-2306; Carriage Inn (Airport Van) 5525 Sepulveda Blvd., Phone: 787-2300;

Meeting Rooms: Airtel Plaza Hotel, (Best Western) has convention facilities available, Phone: 997-7676.

Transportation: Valley Cab 787-1900; United Cab 995-4343; Celebrity Cab 988-8515.

Information: Chamber of Commerce, 14540 Victory Blvd., Suite 100, Van Nuys, CA 91411, Phone: 989-0300.

Landings Restaurant:

The Landings Restaurant is located in the Airtel Plaza Hotel right on the Van Nuys Airport. You can taxi off the runway to their private tie-down area. From there you simply walk across the ramp to the restaurant. They serve lunch Monday through Friday from 11 a.m. to 3 p.m. and dinner on Tuesday through Saturday from 5 p.m. to 10 p.m. On Sunday they also serve a champagne buffet brunch from 10 a.m to 2 p.m. Their menu features contemporary California continental cuisine - everything from appetizers through desserts. Prices range from $9.95 for lunch to about $14.95 for dinner. The decor of the restaurant is modern yet traditional. They welcome fly-in groups large or small. Pilots can arrange for catering by making advance reservations. For the second year in a row, the Landings Restaurant has achieved a place among "Restaurant Hospitality Magazine's" top 500 restaurants in the country. For more information about this facility call 997-7676.

Attractions:

Van Nuys Golf Course, (Off airport south), 6550 Odessa Street Van Nuys, CA 91406 Phone: 785-8871

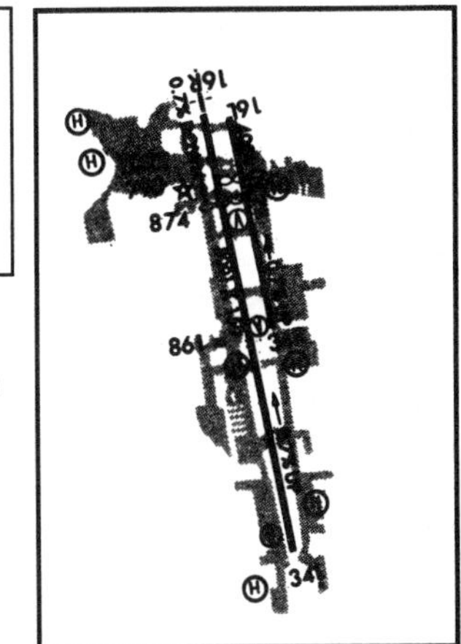

Airport Information:

VAN NUYS - VAN NUYS AIRPORT (VNY)

3 mi northwest of town N34-12.59 W118-29.40 Elev: 799 Fuel: 100LL, Jet-A

Rwy 16R-34L: H8001x150 Rwy 16L-34R: H4000x75 (Asph) Attended: continuously

Public Phone 24hrs Atis: 118.45 Unicom: 122.95 Tower: 119.3, 120.2, 119.0 (helicopters)

Gnd Con: 121.7 Clnc Del: 126.6 Notes: No Landing fee, overnight fee range for singles;

CAUTION: See AFD or AIM for information)

FBO: Air Sources	**Phone: 786-6906**	**FBO: Raytheon Aircraft Serv.**	**Phone: 756-2160**
FBO: Clay Lacy Aviation	**Phone: 989-2900**	**FBO: Skytrails Aviation**	**Phone: 901-9550**
FBO: Flight Works	**Phone: 782-0523**	**FBO: The Jet Center**	**Phone: 988-2800**
FBO: Million Air Van Nuys	**Phone: 994-4990**	**FBO: Van Nuys Flight Cntr.**	**Phone: 994-7300**
FBO: Peterson Aviation	**Phone: 989-2300**		

CA-VIS - VISALIA
VISALIA MUNICIPAL AIRPORT

(Area Code 209)

119

Restaurants Near Airport:

Apple Annie's	3 mi E.	Phone: 739-1646
Marco Polo Restaurant	3 mi E.	Phone: 732-8355
Picific Grill	1/4 mi E.	Phone: 651-5000
The Lamp Lighter Inn	4 mi E.	Phone: 732-4511

Lodging: Holiday Inn & Brass Elephant Restaurant (1/4 mile,) 651-5000; The Lamp Lighter Inn (4 mi east) 732-4511.

Meeting Rooms: The airport has a conference room available, call 738-3201; Also Holiday Inn 651-5000; The Lamp Lighter 732-4511; Marco Polo 732-8355.

Transportation: Budget 651-3092; Hertz 651-1300; Taxi Service: Checker 734-5808 Dial-A-Ride 627-2077; Yellow Cab 732-8294; Limousine 733-9245.

Information: Convention & Visitors Bureau, 815 W. Center Street, Visalia, CA 93277, Phone: 738-3435.

Picific Grill:

The Picific Grill restaurant is located in the Holiday Inn, about 1/4 mile east of the Visalia Municipal Airport. This combination family and fine dining facility is open 7 days a week between 6 a.m. and 10 p.m. Their menu includes shrimp scampi, chicken piccata, captain's platter, prime rib, New York steak and filet mignon, soups and a delicious 30 item salad bar. They also specialize infull breakfast selections during the morning hours. Average prices run $4.00 for breakfast, $6.00 for lunch and between $13.00 and $14.00 for dinner. A champagne brunch is also featured on Sunday between 10 .m.. and 2 p.m. Their dining area can seat 60 people and offers an elegant decor with candle lit tables, wood, and carpeted floors, two large planting areas and large windows on the south side of the building. In-flight catering is another service available through the Picific Grill. The Holiday Inn has 258 spacious guest room and suites available. For information call 651-5000.

Attractions:

Valley Oak Golf, 1800 South Plaza, (On airport property) 651-1441; Sequoia National Park (45 miles east).

Airport Information:

VISALIA - VISALIA MUNICIPAL AIRPORT (VIS)

4 mi west of town N36-19.12 W119-23.57 Elev: 292 Fuel: 100LL, Jet-A

Rwy 12-30: H6543x150 (Asph-pfc) Attended: Sept-May 1500-0300Z, June-Aug 1500-0400Z

Unicom: 123.0 Public Phone 24hrs Notes: No landing fee, overnight fee $3.00

FBO: Visalia Municipal **Phone: 651-1131**

CA-WVI - WATSONVILLE
WATSONVILLE MUNICIPAL ARPT.

(Area Code 408) 120

Restaurants Near Airport:
Zuniga's Mexican Food   On Site   Phone: 724-5788

Zuniga's Mexican Food:

The Zuniga's Mexican Food Restaurant is situated in the terminal building on the Watsonville Municipal Airport. Fly-in guests can park their airplanes near the restaurant and walk to the terminal building. This family style restaurant is open 7 days a week between 11 a.m. and 9 p.m. Specialty items off their menu include many Mexican delights as well as a wide selection of other choices. Some dishes are cheese enchiladas served with rice and beans, Chili Verde plates, super salads, taco salads, steaks, barbecued beef, chicken and BBQ'd rib platters and much more. Average prices run $6.00 to $7.00 for lunch and between $5.00 and $12.95 for dinner. Their dining room can accommodate 110 to 115 persons and provides a casual and comfortable atmosphere. It is decorated with southwestern pictures, aviation photographs, model airplanes hanging from the ceiling, as well as a view of the airport parking ramp and runways. Large groups and parties are welcome, with advance reservations appreciated. Meals can be prepared-to-go if requested, and in-flight catering is also available. During our conversation with the restaurant manager, we learned that Zuniga's Mexican Restaurant happens to be the oldest Mexican restaurant in the Monterey Bay area, and is popular with many fly-in customers. For information call 724-5788.

Lodging: Best Western Inn (Est. 1 mile) 724-3367; National 9 Motel (Est. 2-3 miles) 724-1116;

Meeting Rooms: None Reported

Transportation: Taxi Service: Yellow Cab 724-3871; Rental Cars: Freedom 722-5048.

Information: San Jose Convention & Visitors Bureau, 333 West San Carlos Street, Suite 1000, San Jose, CA 95110, Phone: 295-9600.

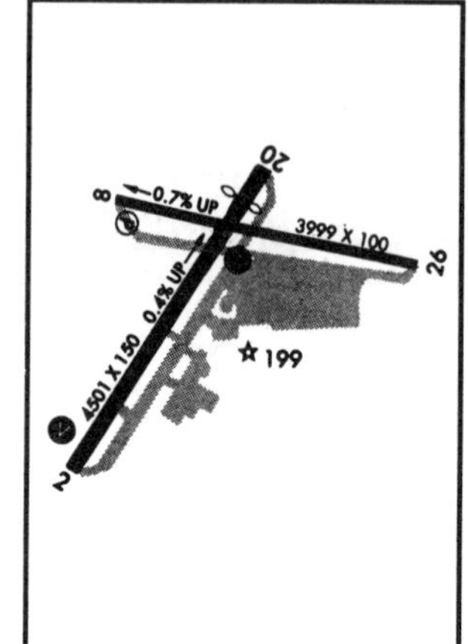

Airport Information:

WATSONVILLE - WATSONVILLE MUNICIPAL AIRPORT (WVI)
3 mi northwest of town   N36-56.14 W121-47.38   Elev: 160   Fuel: 80, 100LL, Jet-A
Rwy 02-20: H4501x150 (Asph)   Rwy 08-26: H3999x100 (Asph)   Attended: 1500-0300Z
Unicom: 122.8
FBO: Strawberry Aviation, Inc.   Phone: 722-1126

CA-WLW - WILLOWS
WILLOWS-GLENN CO. AIRPORT

(Area Code 916) 121

Restaurants Near Airport:

Blue Gum	7 mi N	Phone: 934-9837
Franco's Restaurant	2-3 mi E.	Phone: 934-4273
Nancy's Cafe	Adj Arpt	Phone: 934-7211
Willow Brook	1/4 mi E.	Phone: 934-2878

Willow Brook Restaurant:

The Willow Brook Restaurant is located about 300 yards across Interstate 5 from the Glenn County Airport. This establishment is within walking distance. However, free shuttle service is also available if fly-in customers will call 934-4603. This is a combination family style and fine dining establishment that is open from 11 a.m. to 10 p.m. and Sunday between 10 a.m. to 2 p.m. Their lounge is also open from 10 a.m. to 1:30 a.m. The Sunday brunch 10 a.m. to 2 p.m. features many different items to choose from. Menu selections include daily specials appetizers, desserts, and pastries. Average prices run $5.95 for lunch and $12.95 for dinner. The dining room features a rustic decor and has table side service. The tavern and lounge has a special menu. An indoor and outdoor waterfall, garden room, patio and deck area all add to the restaurants relaxed atmosphere. The garden solarium is available for individual dining or accommodations for groups up to 45 persons. For information about the Willow Brook Restaurant call 934-2878.

Lodging: Golden Pheasant (1 mile, east side of freeway) 934-4603; Blue Gum Inn (7 miles north, courtesy car) 934-5401.
Meeting Rooms: Willows Airport Office & Pilots Lounge southeast corner of tarmac. Call Willows Glenn-County Airport manager at 934-4689.
Transportation: Jimmie's Cab 934-2114; Greyhound 934-7447; Limousine Service 800-KNIGHT3; Shell Car Rental 934-8811.
Information: Forest Supervisor, 410 West Sycamore Street, Willows, CA 95988, Phone: 934-8150.

Attractions:

Glenn Golf & Country Club 10 miles north on Club County road 39. Phone: 934-9918; Also Sacramento Wildlife Refuge, 7 miles south on I-5, Phone: 934-2801.

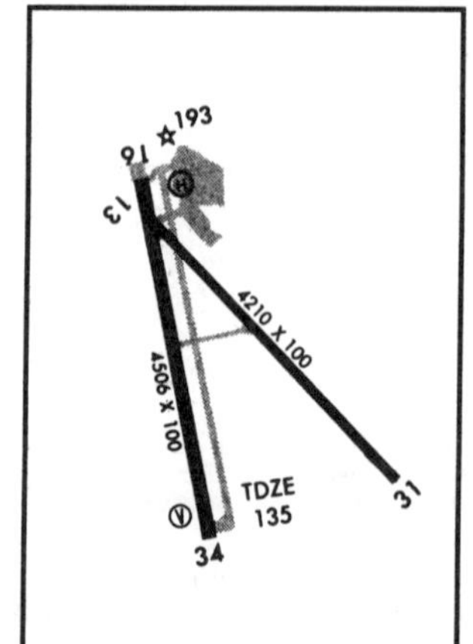

Airport information:

WILLOWS - WILLOWS-GLENN COUNTY AIRPORT (WLW)
1 mi west of town   N39-30.98 W122-13.05   Elev: 139   Fuel: 80, 100LL
Rwy 16-34: H4506x100 (Asph)   Rwy 13-31: H4210x100 (Asph)   Attended: 1630-0030Z   Unicom: 122.8   Public Phone 24hrs   Notes: Phone number for attendant after hours is located at fuel station, with a service charge. Overnight tie down $2.00, monthly $15.00. Pilot supplies and flight training center on airport. Also a pilots lounge with shower located southwest corner of tarmac. Aerial photography operation on site.
FBO: Willows Arpt. Office   Phone: 934-6489

CA-O42 - WOODLAKE WOODLAKE AIRPORT

(Area Code 209) 122

Woodlake Outpost:

The Woodlake Outpost is reported to be located on or very near the Woodlake Airport, which is a private residential airpark. During our conversation with the restaurant personnel, we learned that fly-in guests can easily walk to their facility. This cafe styled restaurant is open 7 days a week from 6 a.m. to 2 p.m. Their menu contains items like a full breakfast selection, homemade biscuits and gravy, chili, burritos, which happens to be available all day as well as sandwiches and other items made to order. Daily specials are also available. The restaurant is located next to the river and can seat 55 persons, exhibiting a homey and friendly atmosphere. A very nice person by the name of Velma who has worked for this establishment for over 15 years, helped answer all our questions and seemed very proud of the Woodlake Outpost Restaurant, while providing customers with efficient and friendly service. For more information you can call this establishment at 564-3244.

Restaurants Near Airport:
Woodlake Outpost On Site Phone: 564-3244

Lodging: Keweah Motel (11 miles) 592-2961.

Meeting Rooms: None Reported

Transportation: None Reported

Information: California Division of Tourism, P.O. Box 1499, Sacramento, CA 95812, Phone: 800-862-2543.

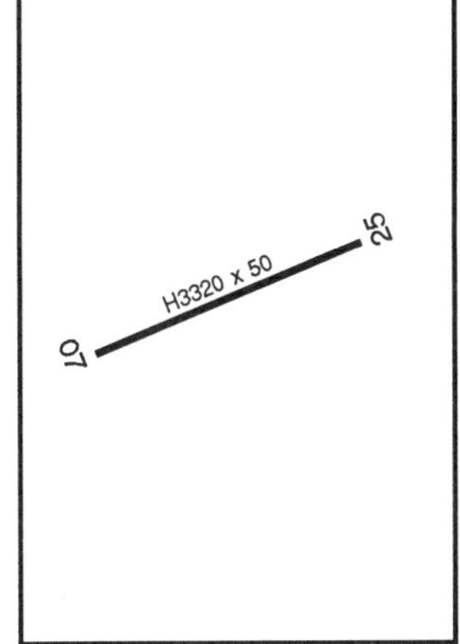

Airport Information:

WOODLAKE - WOODLAKE AIRPORT (O42)
2 mi south of town N36-23.93 W119-06.44 Elev: 425 Fuel: 100LL
Rwy 07-25: H3320x50 (Asph) Attended: irregularly CTAF: 122.9 Notes: Residential airpark.
FBO: Woodlake Airport Phone: 564-3244

CA-L22 - YUCCA VALLEY YUCCA VALLEY AIRPORT

(Area Code 619) 123

Cross Roads Restaurant:

The Cross Roads Restaurant is located only a 50 foot walk from the aircraft parking area of the Yucca Valley Airport. This bar and grill contains a dining area able to accommodate their guests and serves a variety of selections including hamburgers, hot-dogs, patty melts, BLT's, chili, spaghetti, salads and much more. The restaurant is open Tuesday through Sunday from 10 a.m. to 2 a.m. and Mondays from 6 p.m. to 2 a.m. Average prices run $2.25 for lunch and $3.95 for dinner. Daily specials are also available. This facility contains space for up to 109 persons and also features a variety of game room amenities such as pool tables, dart boards, air hockey, pin ball, laser disk, and a large screen TV. Groups and parties are always welcome. Meals can also be prepared-to-go if requested. For more information, call the Cross Roads Restaurant at 365-5393.

Restaurants Near Airport:
Cross Roads Restaurant On Site Phone: 365-5393

Lodging: Desert View Motel (Free trans, 1 mile) 365-9706; Oasis of Eden Motel (2 miles) 365-6321; Yucca Inn (3 miles) 365-3311.

Meeting Rooms: None Reported

Transportation: Taxi Service: Arrow 365-2001; Rental Cars: Yucca Valley Ford 365-2353.

Information: Palm Springs Convention and Visitors Bureau, Palm Springs, CA 69930, P hone: 619-770-9000, or 800-417-3529. Also: California Division of Tourism, P.O. Box 1499, Sacramento, CA 95812, Phone: 800-862-2543.

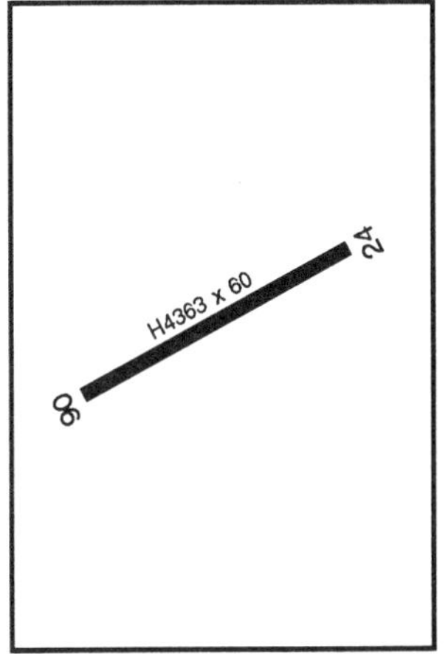

Airport Information:

YUCCA VALLEY - YUCCA VALLEY AIRPORT (L22)
3 mi east of town N34-07.67 W116-24.47 Elev: 3224 Rwy 06-24: H4363x60 (Asph)
Attended: irregularly Unicom: 123.0
Yucca Valley Airport Phone: 228-2588 or 228-1173.

COLORADO

LOCATION MAP

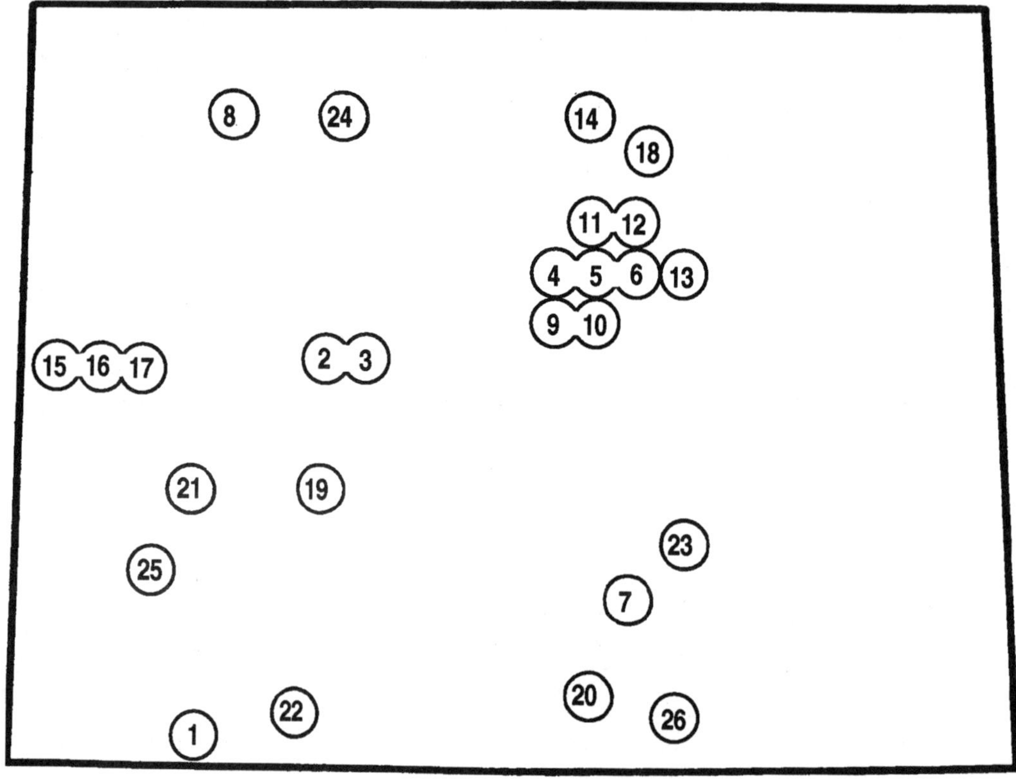

Not to be used for navigational purposes

COLORADO

CROSS FILE INDEX

Location Number	City or Town	Airport Name And Identifier	Name of Attraction
1	Arboles	Navajo Landings Strip (5V9)	Navajo State Park
2	Aspen	Pitkin Co./Sardy Field (ASE)	Creative Croissants
3	Aspen	Pitkin Co./Sardy Field (ASE)	Friedl's Restaurant
4	Aurora	Aurora Airpark (01V)	Bev's Kitchen
5	Aurora	Aurora Airpark (01V)	Coffee Terrace
6	Aurora	Aurora Airpark (01V)	Lulu's Bar & Grill
7	Colorado City	Greenhorn Valley Arpt. (CO22)	Greenhorn Inn
8	Craig	Craig Moffat Arpt. (CAG)	19th Hole Restaurant
9	Denver	Centennial Arpt. (APA)	Perfect Landing
10	Denver	Centennial Arpt. (APA)	Wings Cafe (Clarion Htl.)
11	Denver	Denver Intl. Arpt. (DEN)	CA1 Services
12	Denver	Denver Intl. Arpt. (DEN)	The Galley
13	Denver/Front Range	Front Range Arpt. (FTG)	Front Range Cafeteria
14	Fort Collins	Downtown Fort Collins Arpk. (3V5)	Lincoln Street Grill
15	Grand Junction	Walker Field (GJT)	Olivers Restaurant
16	Grand Junction	Walker Field (GJT)	Sky's Restaurant
17	Grand Junction	Walker Field (GJT)	W.W. Peppers
18	Greeley	Weld Co. Arpt. (GXY)	Barnstormer
19	Gunnison	Gunnison Co. Arpt. (GUC)	Gold Creek Inn
20	La Veta	Cuchara Valley Arpt. (07V)	Positively Main Street
21	Montrose	Montrose Reg. Arpt. (MTJ)	Sun Valley Truck Stop
22	Pagosa Springs	Stevens Field (2V1)	Great Divide, Fairfield
23	Pueblo	Pueblo Mem. Arpt. (PUB)	DC6 Restaurant
24	Steamboat Springs	Bob Adams Field (SBS)	River Bend Inn
25	Telluride	Telluride Reg. Arpt. (TEX)	Restaurants in Telluride
26	Trinidad	Perry Strokes (TAD)	Christina's Restaurant

Articles

City or town	Nearest Airport and Identifier	Name of Attraction
Aspen, CO	Pitkin Co/Sardy Fld. (ASE)	Aspen/Snowmass Ski Area
Denver, CO	Aurora Airpark (01V)	Wings Over Rockies Museum
Pagosa Springs, CO	Stevens Fld. (2V1)	Fairfield Pagosa Resort
Steamboat-Sprgs,CO	Bob Adams Fld. (SBS)	Steamboat Spngs SKi Resort
Telluride, CO	Telluride Regional (TEX)	Telluride Ski & Golf Resort

CO-5V9 - ARBOLES NAVAJO LANDING STRIP

(Area Code 303)

1

Navajo State Park:

At Navajo State Park, visitors have an unparalleled opportunity to capture the history and beauty of southwestern Colorado. Situated outside Arboles, 35 miles south of Pagosa Springs, 45 miles southeast of Durango, the area is unpolluted and sparsely populated. The park's main attraction is the 35 mile long Navajo Reservoir which extends well into New Mexico. The 15,000 acres. including 3,000 acres on the Colorado side offer a challenge to the angler and unlimited pleasure to the boater and waterskier. Navajo boasts Colorado's largest boat ramp - 80' wide, a quarter mile long - and a good recreational airstrip, used frequently by flying clubs and fly-in campers. History lives a Navajo alongside the airplane and the powerboat. The visitor center museum echoes the way of life of the ancient people of the area. Hikers get a feeling of the past as they follow an old stagecoach road or an abandoned railroad bed. Navajo Dam, located in New Mexico, was constructed by the US Bureau of Reclamation in 1962. In Colorado, the Division of Parks and Outdoor Recreation administers the area, which has been managed by the state since 1964. Entrance fee per vehicle (Daily $3.00). In addition to entrance fee camping per night: Primitive $4.00 and $7.00 for developed, with electric $10.00. For reservations call 800-678-2267.

Restaurants Near Airport:

Concessions 3,500 ft. NE of airstrip along park road.
San Juan Marina 1/2 mi Phone: 883-2343

Camping: Adjacent to airport about 1000' east of airstrip
Transportation: None Reported
Information: Navajo State Park, P.O. Box 1697, Arboles, CO 81121, Phone: 303-883-2208.

Attraction:

Also see Navajo Dam, NM. Navajo State Park (1V0). Located about 30 to 35 miles south on the south end of Navajo Lake just west of the Navajo Dam near the Pine River Recreation Area.

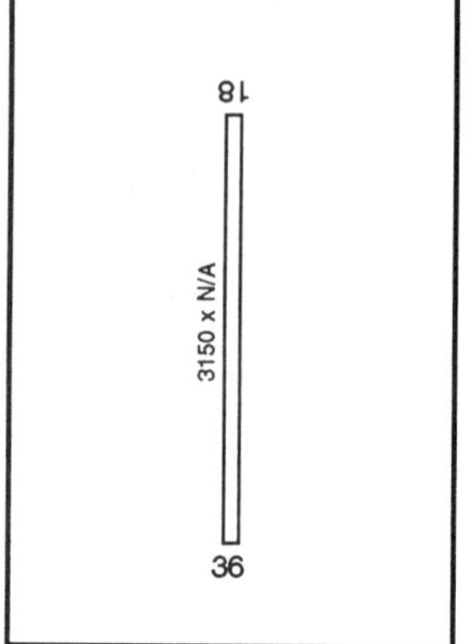

Airport Information:

ARBOLES - NAVAJO LANDING STRIP (5V9)

1 mi southeast of town N37-00.08 W107-25.37 Elev: 6110 Rwy 18-36: 3150 (Turf-Dirt) Attended: Unattended 1' to 3' drainage parallel to centerline both sides of Rwy 18-36. Rwy 36 15' dropoff to lake at thld. Rwy 18-36 soft when wet. Rwy 18-36 weeds on rwy surface. 155' water twr 1/2 mile of Rwy 18 thld. Rwy 18-36 line of sight both ends obstructed due to rwy high point near south end. Communications: 122.9 Note: We recommend that you contact the airport manager for runway conditions prior to use by calling 303-883-2208.

Airport Manager: Phone: 883-2208

CO-ASE - ASPEN PITKIN COUNTY/SARDY FIELD

(Area Code 970)

2, 3

Creative Croissants:

This establishment is located within the main terminal building. They specializes in preparing light fare for travelers. Croissants, muffins, sweet rolls and additional bakery goods. For information call 920-9069.

Friedl's Restaurant:

Friedl's Restaurant is located across the street form the Pitkin County/ Sardy Airport (Well within walking distance). This full service family restaurant is open 7 a.m. to 10 p.m. weekdays and 7 a.m. to 4 p.m. on weekends. Specialties of the house include breakfast served all day long, sandwiches of all types, salad specials, steaks and seafood. Schnitzel is one of the more popular items that Friedl's prepars and is a favorite with many. Average prices run $2.50 to $4.50 for breakfast, $6.50 to $7.95 for lunch and $9.00 to $14.00 for dinner. Indoor as well as out-door dining is available on their deck. For more information call Friedl's Restaurant at 925-9098.

Restaurants Near Airport:

Aspen Aviation In-Flight Catering Phone: 920-2016
Creative Croissants Trml. Bldg. Phone: 920-9069
Friedl's Across Street Phone: 925-9098

Lodging: Aspen Central Reservations (4 miles) 925-9000; Aspen Resort Association (4 miles) 925-1940; Snowmass Resort Association 923-2000; Also: Hotel Jerome (Airport trans) 920-1000; Inn At Aspen (Airport trans) 925-1500; Molly Gibson Lodge (Airport trans) 925-3434; Snowflake Inn (Free trans) 925-3221; Little Nell (Free trans) 920-4600.
Meeting Rooms: Inn At Aspen 925-1500; Molly Gibson Lodge 925-3434; Little Nell 920-4600.
Transportation: Airport courtesy car, van, & bus; Also: Aspen Limo 925-2400; High Mountain 925-8294; Rental Cars: Avis 925-2355; Budget 925-2151; Eagle 925-2128; Hertz 925-7368; National 925-1144.
Information: Aspen Resort Association, 425 Rio Grande Place, Aspen, CO 81611, Phone: 800-26-ASPEN

Attractions: Famous for its outstanding skiing accommodations, with interchangeable multi day ticket purchases for four skiing areas. contact Aspen/Snowmass Nordic council, P.O. Box 10815, Aspen, CO 81611. Aspen Mountain (Vertical drop 3,267 ft.); Buttermilk (Vertical drop 2,030 ft.); Aspen Highlands (Vertical drop 3,800 ft.); Snow Mass (Vertical drop 3,615 ft.) 12 miles NW of town 800-766-9627; Also mining camp tours and ghost towns within region (10 miles south of town) 925-3721; River rafting; and Aspen Historical Society Museum 925-3721.

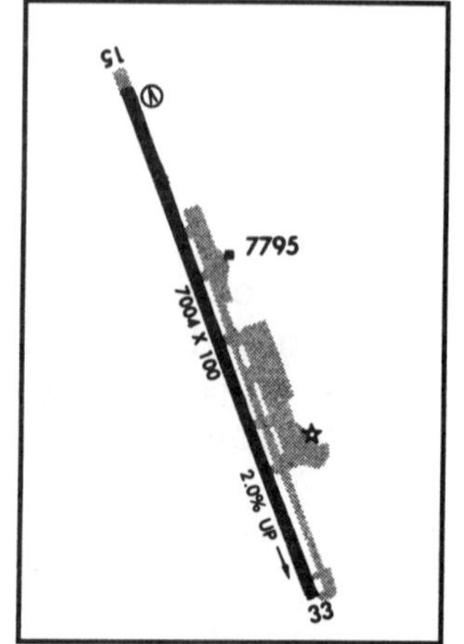

Airport Information:

ASPEN - PITKIN COUNTY/SARDY FIELD (ASE)

3 mi northwest of town N39-13.39 W106-52.13 Elev: 7815 Fuel: 100LL, Jet-A1+ Rwy 15-33: H7004x100 (Asph) Attended: 1400-0600Z Arpt closed 0600-1400Z Atis: 120.4 Unicom: 122.95 Aspen App/Dep Con: 123.8 Denver Center App/Dep Con: 134.5 Tower 118.85 Gnd Con: 121.9 Notes: CAUTION: Airport is located in a high mountain valley with rapidly rising terrain on all sides, Horizontal surface penetrations will not allow normal traffic patterns. Refer to current Airport Facility Directory for critical information.

FBO: Aspen Aviation, Inc. Phone: 925-2522 FBO: Aspen Base Operation Phone: 920-2016

Aspen/Snowmass Ski Area

Aspen, CO (CO-ASE)

Aspen is located in the White River National Forest in Western Colorado. This historic silver mining town offers over 100 years of history, more than 300 retail stores, 30 art galleries and nearly 100 restaurants and bars, as well as an average annual snowfall of 300 inches. Its Victorian architecture, stately commercial buildings and opera house are just a few of the reminders of Aspen's illustrious past. Aspen Mountain, located in the heart of downtown Aspen, has a summit elevation of 11,212 feet and a base elevation of 7,945 feet. It is steep and athletic...the advanced skier's dream! There are 76 trails of bumps, dumps, glades, gullies and ridges. This mountain is not for the weak-kneed! However, beginners do not have to worry, because both Aspen Highlands and Tiehack Ski Area offer spectacular, uncrowded terrain for all levels of skiers. Aspen Highlands, located only 2 miles outside of town, has a summit elevation of 11,675 feet and a base elevation of 8,040 feet. Whereas, Tiehack Ski Area, located approximately 3 miles from downtown Aspen, has a summit elevation of 9,900 feet and a base elevation of 7,870 feet. Aspen Highlands offers magnificent scenery, spectacular steeps, and lots of snow. A great challenge for all skiers. And, no matter what the age, Tiehack is the ideal mountain on which to learn to ski or snowboard and improve every level of technique.

Photo by: Paul Hilts/Aspen Chamber Resort Associaton, Inc.

The Maroon Bells stand majestically around golden Aspen trees and hillsides.

Aspen's neighboring village, Snowmass, offers families another great getaway on the slopes of one of North America's largest ski areas. Snowmass, located only 12 miles from Aspen, has a variety of retail, ski, snowboard and rental equipment shops, as well as over a dozen restaurants. Skiers of all levels of ability can enjoy the 2,500 acres of 72 runs on deep, dry snow. A summit elevation of 12,310 feet helps put Snowmass on top of the world.

Many people associate Aspen with winter and ski slopes, however Aspen offers so much more year-round. Throughout the summer and fall, visitors experience the numerous cultural and oudoor activities, special events and natural attractions. During the summer, music, dance, theatre and art provide a cultural richness that sets Aspen apart. The annual summer Music Festival and School and the Aspen Institute for Humanistic Studies are just two of the many world-class programs that have given Aspen its summer glow. There are other great ways to have fun under the sun, such as whitewater rafting on one of the backyard rivers, taking a leisurely family hike along the Rio Grande trail, or even fly fishing on a cool trout stream. Biking, tennis and golfing are also splendid ways to warm up the afternoon.

Take a golden opportunity to spend a spectacular autumn in Aspen's Colorado Rockies. A time when sports and many cultural activities are at their peak. Culture seekers will enjoy the Aspen Theater, Aspen Art Museum, Aspen Historical Society Museum and over 40 art galleries. Sports enthusiasts will enjoy the Annual Motherlode Volleyball Classic, the Golden Leaf Marathon, and the Annual Aspen Ruggerfest with some of the best rugby players in the world. Fall activities for the whole family include bus tours to the glorious Maroon Bells, Silver Queen Gondola Rides to the top of Aspen Mountain , the Rotary Club's Fall Colors Jeep Tour, and the Aspen Historical Society's HarvestFest. Plus, autumn is also a great time for white water rafting, downhill bicycling, fishing, horseback riding, hot air ballooning and even llama treks!

After all the excitement, it is easy to

Photo by: Burnham W. Arndt/Aspen Chamber Resort Association, Inc.

The Silver Queen Gondola services Aspen Mountain and offers a unique view of Aspen and the surrounding valley.

work up an appetite. Between Aspen and Snowmass, there are 100 restaurants that range from comfortably casual to delightfully formal. Choose from a wide international selection of Italian, Mexican, French, Thai, Chinese and Mediterranean. Sample the fine cuisine at the Sundeck Restaurant on the mountaintop or taste the innovative cooking at Ajax Tavern at the base of the mountain.

A good night's rest is also important after all of those exciting activities. Aspen has a bed base of nearly 9,000 for any budget, in a variety of hotels, inns, bed and breakfasts, lodges and condominiums. Most lodges are located on the free skier shuttle bus route or have private shuttle services. In addition, many of these facilities offer plenty of conference space. For reservations and information, call Aspen Central Reservations at 925-9000. Snowmass has a bed base of 6,000 with 90% ski-in/ ski-out. Snowmass has the second largest meeting facility in the Rocky Mountains. This includes 40,000 square feet of versatile meeting space immediately adjacent to the ski slope. For reservations, call Snowmass Resort Association at 923-2010.

Aspen-Pitkin County/Sardy Field Airport, located 3 miles northwest of the city, has a 7,004'x100 asphalt-porous friction course runway. Overnight parking fees are $10.00 for singles and $15.00 for twins. With advance notice, the FBO will loan out a car for a few hours during the day. For more information, contact the FBO at 925-2522, 24 hours a day. For further information about Aspen/Snowmass, call the Aspen Chamber Resort Assocation at 925-1940 or 800-262-7736 and the Snowmass Resort Association at 923-2000 or 800-598-2003. (Information submitted by Aspen Chamber Resort Association, Inc.)

CO-01V - AURORA
AURORA AIRPARK

(Area Code 303)

4, 5, 6

Bev's Kitchen:

Bev's Kitchen is located right on the Aurora Airpark. Pilots can taxi up and park their aircraft only a few feet from their front door. During our conversation with the management we learned that they are open from 6 a.m. to 8 p.m., 7 days a week. Their menu includes a full selection of breakfast items as well as lunch and dinner selections. All their breads are homemade. Instead of pre-cut patties, the cooks at Bev's Kitchen hand shape their own burgers using nothing less then 80% lean pure beef. In additions to their hamburgers, cheeseburgers and sandwiches, they also serve a variety of Mexican and Italian dishes. Menu prices average $4.00 to $5.00 for most main entrees. Their dining room can seat about 45 persons. Large windows allow a nice view of the parking ramp and active areas on the airport. This is a relatively new restaurant that opened in May of 1996. After lunch at Bev's Kitchen you might enjoy a visit to the Wings Over The Rockies Air and Space Museum, situated about 11 or 12 miles west of the airport by way of Interstate 70. Call the Aurora Airpark manager in advance to arrange for either a rental or courtesy car. For information about Bev's Kitchen call 344-1445.

Coffee Terrace (Holiday Inn):

The Holiday Inn is located about 6 miles east of the Aurora Airpark. This establishment offers its guests a wide variety of services. Restaurant (Coffee Terrace), lounge, gift shops, beauty shops, indoor swimming pool, Jacuzzi and Sauna, 256 rooms (Rates $110 to $115). Ideal for meetings and conventions with 62,000 square feet of space. For information call 371-9494.

Lulu's Bar & Grill:

Lulu's Bar & Grill is a country theme-styled restaurant located about 3 miles from the Aurora Airpark. This combination family and fine dining restaurant is open 7 days a week between 10 a.m. and 2 a.m. Specialties on their menu include New York strip steak, shrimp baskets, chicken dishes, hamburgers, Rocky Mountain Oysters, all types of appetizers along with many other main course selections. What makes this restaurant unique is the rustic country atmosphere with large cooking grills where guests can pick out their particular choice cut of beef, and cook it themselves if they so choose. Indoor and outdoor dining is available. Prices average $9.50 for steaks and $5.00 to $6.00 for other entrees. Two dining rooms allow for casual and upscale dining. Their outdoor patio dining area contains grills and horseshoe pits. Live band entertainment is featured Friday through Sunday evenings. To reach the restaurant, take Interstate 70 east from the airpark about 3 miles until you reach the Watkins Exit. From there go north and the restaurant will be at stop light not far from the expressway. For information call Lulu's Bar & Grill at 261-9672.

Restaurants Near Airport:

Bev's Kitchen	(On Site)	Phone: 344-1445
Coffee Terrace (Holiday Inn)	6 mi W.	Phone: 371-9494
Lulu's Bar & Grill	3 mi E.	Phone: 261-9672

Lodging: Country Manor 3 mi 364-2145; Holiday Inn 6 mi (transprtation with prior arrangements) 256 rooms, lounge, restaurant, gift shop, beauty salon, indoor pool with Jacuzzi and sauna 371-9494.

Meeting Rooms: Holiday Inn 62,000 square feet of convention and meeting facilities.

Transportation: Rental cars can be arranged through Aurora Airpark manager's office; however, advance reservations are necessary. Also a courtesy car is available for limited use. For information call Aurora Airpark, Inc. 361-9630.

Information: Denver Metro Convention & Visitors Bureau, 1555 California Street, Suite 300, Denver, CO 80202, Phone: 303-892-1501 or 892-1112.

Attractions:

Wing's Over The Rockies Air and Space Museum about 11 or 12 miles west from the Aurora Airpark. Flying machines of air and space from World War I to present. For information call 360-5360. (See Article)

Wing's Over The Rockies
Air And Space Museum
(See Article)
12 miles west of Aurora Airpark.
For information call 360-5360.

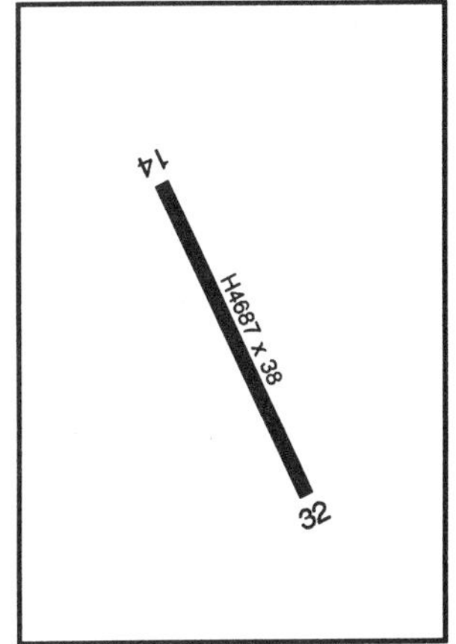

Airport Information:

AURORA - AURORA AIRPARK (01V)
11 mi east of town N39-43.98 W104-39.30 Elev: 5680 Fuel: 100LL, MOGAS
Rwy 14-32: H4687x38 (Asph) Attended: daylight hours Unicom: 122.8 Notes: This airport is reported only 6 miles south of Denver International Airport (DEN). Familiarize yourself with airspace and recommended procedures prior to entry. Also consult AFD for current information.
Aurora Airpark, Inc. Phone: 361-9630

CO-CO22 - COLORADO CITY GREENHORN VALLEY AIRPORT

(Area Code 719)

7

Greenhorn Inn:

The Greenhorn Motel & Lounge is located about 1/4 mile west of the Greenhorn Valley Airport. This family style restaurant is across the street on the west side of Interstate 25. The combination tavern and lodging establishment contains a 57 room motel with swimming pool. This facility can accommodate between 150 and 200 persons within their tavern. Accommodations for large private groups for up to 170 people can also be arranged if advanced notice is given. During our conversation with the new management we learned that the former restaurant establishment at this location may open again for business at anytime. For more information about this establishment, call 676-3315. Note: The Greenhorn Valley Airport is a private use facility. A call to the airport manager would be advised for airport conditions and availability. See Airport Information listed below.

Restaurants Near Airport:

Greenhorn Inn	Adj. Arpt.	Phone: 676-3315
Vicker Station Cafe	200 ft	Phone: 676-3550

Lodging: Greenhorn Inn (Adjacent Airport) 676-3315

Meeting Rooms: None Reported

Transportation: None Reported

Information: Pueblo City Chamber of Commerce, P.O. Box 697, Pueblo, CO 81002, Phone: 542-1704 or the Pueblo Visitor Information Center, 3417 North Elizabeth Street, Pueblo, CO 81002, Phone: 543-1742.

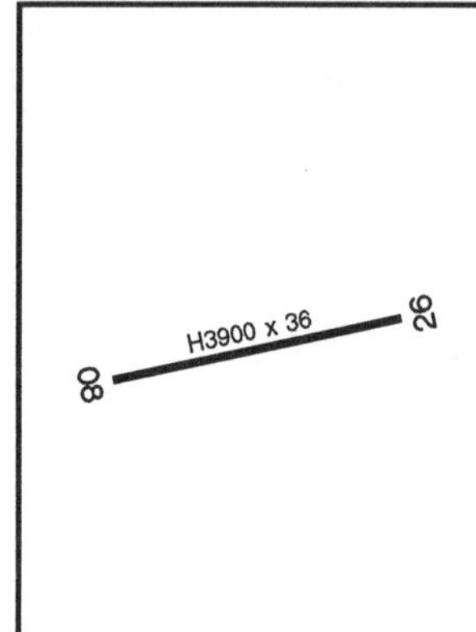

Airport Information:

COLORADO CITY - GREENHORN VALLEY AIRPORT (CO22)
5 mi east of town 37-57-36N 104-47-00W Elev: 5796 Fuel: N/A
Rwy 8-26: H3900x36 (Asph) Notes: Private use facility use at own risk. Landing Fee: $1.00 for maintenance purposes.
Greenhorn Valley Airport Phone: 719-564-9084

CO-CAG - CRAIG CRAIG MOFFAT AIRPORT

(Area Code 970)

8

19th Hole Restaurant:

The 19th Hole Restaurant is located less than 300 yards from the Craig-Moffat Airport. This family style restaurant is open between April 1st and November 1st. Their hours may vary. But for the most part, they provide meals between 7 a.m. and 10 p.m. Their entrees include items like chili, burritos, chicken breast sandwiches, nachos, hamburgers, cheeseburgers, Philly steaks, and grilled ham & cheese sandwiches. A light breakfast menu provides items like donuts and rolls. Average prices run between $3.50 and $6.50 for most items. Daily lunch specials are also available. The restaurant can seat up to 60 persons. There are many windows providing a nice view of the 18 hole golf course situated adjacent to the restaurant. If planning to fly in and play a round of golf, you can even rent clubs as well as driving golf carts at the pro shop connected to the restaurant. For more information call the 19th Hole Restaurant at 824-3764.

Restaurants Near Airport:

19th Hole Restaurant	Adj. Arpt.	Phone: 824-3764

Lodging: A Bar Z Motel (Trans) 824-7066; Best Western Inn 824-8101; Holiday Inn (Holidome) 824-9455.

Meeting Rooms: Holiday Inn (Holidome) 824-9455.

Transportation: None Reported

Information: Greater Craig Area Chamber of Commerce, 360 E Victory Way, Craig, CO 81625, Phone: 824-5689 or 800-864-4405.

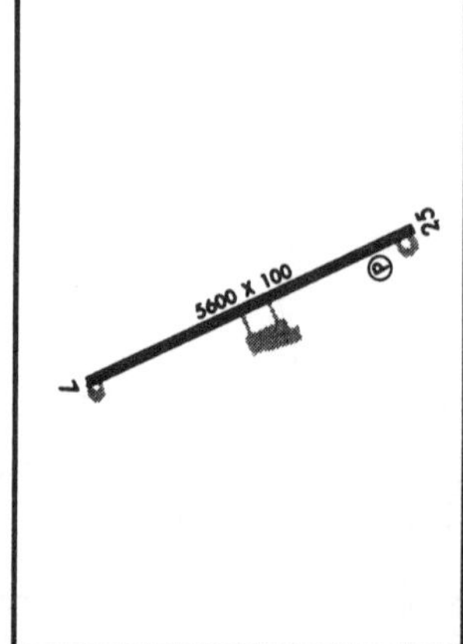

Airport Information:

CRAIG - GRAIG MOFFAT AIRPORT (CAG)
2 mi southeast of town N40-29.71 W107-31.30 Elev: 6193 Fuel: 100LL, Jet-A
Rwy 07-25: H5600x100 (Asph) Attended: Mon-Fri 1500-0000Z Sat-Sun irregularly
Unicom: 122.8 Denver Center App/Dep Con: 128.5
FBO: Mountain Air Spray Company Phone: 824-6335

CO-APA - DENVER CENTENNIAL AIRPORT

(Area Code 303)

9, 10

The Perfect Landing:

The Perfect Landing restaurant is located on the Denver-Centennial Airport (APA). You can park your aircraft right outside of their front door. This up-scale cafe is open 7 a.m. to 6 p.m. Monday through Friday and Saturday and Sunday from 7 a.m. to 3 p.m. Plans to increased hours to include dinner and evening meals are soon to occur. Specialties of the house are their "Perfect Landing Breakfast ", the breakfast burrito, Centennial breakfast, wild chicken salad for lunch, Sam's turkey Reuben, and their chicken quesadrlla. Prices range from $3.00 to $7.00 for most dishes. Daily special include a soup of the day. The view from the restaurant is un-obstructed and provides a nice scene looking out at the mountain range. The Perfect Landing restaurant also has a large outdoor patio that is perfect dining outside. The patio can accommodate about 60 persons with 12 tables available. For more information, call 649-4478.

Wings Cafe (Clarion Hotel Southeast):

The Wings Cafe is located within the Clarion Hotel Southeast. This hotel is situated only a few feet from the tower and provides easy access to air travelers using the Centennial Airport. You can also park your aircraft at either FBO and walk the short distance to the hotel or restaurant. The Wings Cafe is open Monday through Friday from 6 a.m. to 10 p.m. and Saturday & Sunday from 6:30 a.m. to 9:30 p.m. There is also a lounge on the site open from 4 p.m. during the week and from 1 p.m. on weekends until closing time. Entrees provided by this restaurant include items like fresh salmon, filet mignon, New York strip, chicken filets and sirloin steaks. This combination family style and fine dining facility also serves a variety of breakfast selections along with luncheon choices .They provide a breakfast buffet from 6 a.m. to 10 a.m. Average prices run $5.50 for breakfast, $6.95 for lunch and between $10.95 and $17.00 for dinner. The restaurant can seat 80 people in their main dining room. Several private rooms are available for meeting and conventions. Groups between 15 and 250 people can be served within the hotel along with 120 rooms for overnight lodging. In-flight catering is also available at the Holiday Inn Denver South. For more information call 790-7770.

Restaurants Near Airport:

Perfect Landing	On Site	Phone: 649-4478
Pour LaFrance Cafe	On Site	Phone: 790-4321
Wings Cafe	On Site	Phone: 790-7770

Lodging: Clarion Hotel Southeast (On Airport, Also free trans) 790-7770; Denver Hilton South (Nearby) 779-6161; Radisson Hotel-South (Nearby) 799-6200; Residence Inn-South (Nearby) 740-7177; Scanticon Conference Center & Hotel (Nearby) 799-5800.

Meeting Rooms: Clarion Hotel Southeast (Free trans) 790-7770 or 1-800-252-7466 outside Colorado; Scanticon Confrence Center (Nearby) 799-5800.

Transportation: On airport courtesy vans available; Also rental cars: Avis 790-2575; Budget 790-4321; Enterprise 790-4321; Hertz 790-2575.

Information: Chamber of Commerce, 701 West Hampden Avenue, Suite G-34, Englewood, CO 80154, Phone: 789-4473;

Attractions: Several golf courses are available nearby. Castle Pines 5 miles; Inverness Golf Course adjacent; Meridian Golf Course adjacent.

Airport Information:

DENVER - CENTENNIAL AIRPORT (APA)

3 mi southeast of airport 39-34-13N 104-50-56W Elev: 5883 Fuel: 100LL, Jet-A Rwy 17L-35R: H10001x100 (Asph) Rwy 17R-35L: H7003x77 (Asph-Pfc) Rwy 10-28: H4903x62 (Asph) Attended: continuously Atis: 120.3 Unicom: 122.95 Tower:118.9 Gnd Con: 121.8 Clnc Del: 128.6

Notes: No landing fees,

FBO: Aero Services **Phone: 799-0040** **FBO: Denver Jet Center** **Phone: 790-4321**

FBO: AMR Combs **Phone: 790-2575**

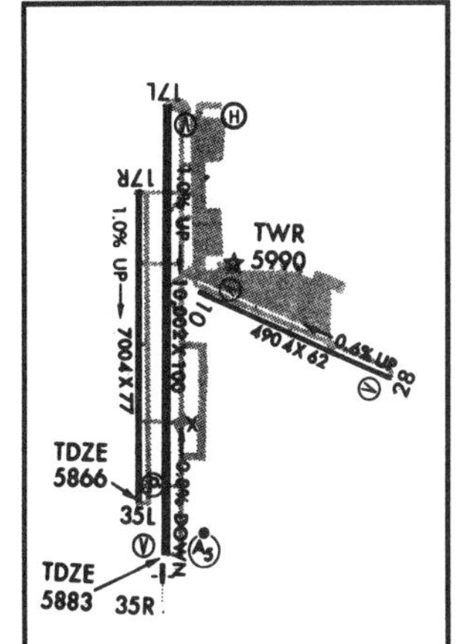

CO-DEN - DENVER
DENVER INTERNATIONAL

Area Code 303) 11, 12

Restaurants Near Airport:

CA1 Services	On Site	Phone: 342-5680
Galley	On Site	Phone: 342-5600

CA1 Services: (Lefty's Red Rock Bar)

Lefty's Red Rock Bar is on the Denver International Airport. Their three locations are near gates 46-49 in the main terminal building on the east side and concourse A, B and C in the main terminal building. This family-style restaurant is open 7 days between 6 a.m. and 8 p.m. Menu specialties include fresh grilled meats and fish along with freshly prepared salads. Prices average $4.25 for breakfast, $5.00 for lunch and $6.00 for dinner. The decor of this restaurant offers a western motif with natural wood and ceramic tiles. On the walls, murals depict mountain settings. If advance notice is given they can prepare catered meals for pilots on the go. For information call 342-5680.

The Galley

The Galley Restaurant is a cafe located at the AMR Combs Terminal. This facility is open from 6 a.m. to 4 p.m. They serve breakfast items, along with lunch selections such as cheeseburgers, grilled cheese sandwiches, club sandwiches, Denver sandwiches, and 10 different types of salads made fresh daily. The restaurant can hold about 30 people in their dining area. Average prices run $5.00 for most of their breakfast and lunch entrees. The restaurants offers its guests a view of the mountains as well as the airport from its location. AMR Combs also specializes in providing catered meals for private or corporate pilots and their crew and passengers. For more information, you can call the restaurant at 342-5600.

Lodging: All facilities listed provide transportation. Comfort Inn Arpt 393-7666; Embassy Suites Arpt. 375-0400; Hilton Inn Arpt. 373-5730; Holiday Inn Arpt. 321-6666; LaQuinta Inn 371-5640; Ramada Inn-Stapleton Arpt. 388-6161; Roadway Inn Arpt. 320-0260; Sheraton Inn Den-Arpt. 333-7711; Stapleton Plaza Hotel 321-3500; Stouffer Concourse Hotel 399-7500; Western Motor Inn 296-6000.

Meeting Rooms: AMR Combs 342-5600; Most lodging facilities listed above contain accommodations for meetings and conferences.

Transportation: Taxi: Carey Limousine Service 693-0732; Metro 333-3333; Ritz 294-9199; Viking 450-8109; Yellow 292-1212; Rental cars: many available on site.

Information: Denver Metro Conventional & Visitors Bureau, 1555 California Street, Ste 300, Denver, CO 80202, Phone: 892-1505 or 892-1112.

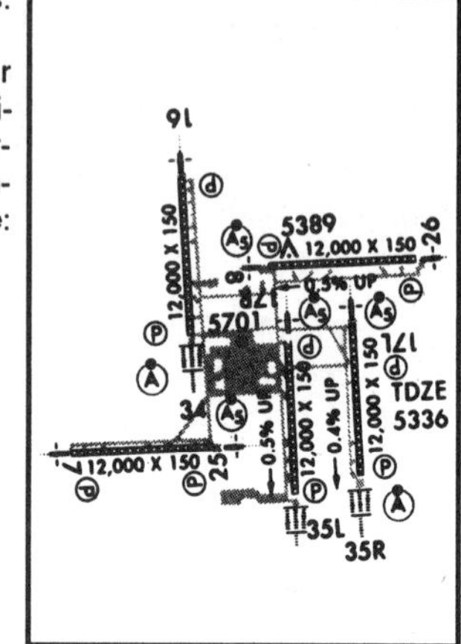

Airport Information:

DENVER - DENVER INTERNATIONAL (DEN)
4 mi east of town N39-51.51 W104-40.02 Elev: 5431 Fuel: 100, 100LL, Mogas
Rwy 07-25: H12000x150 (Conc-Grvd) Rwy 08-26: H12000x150 (Conc-Grvd) Rwy 16-34: H12000x150 (Conc-Grvd) Rwy 17R-35L: H12000x150 (Conc-Grvd) Rwy 17L-35R: H12000x150 (Conc-Grvd) Attended: continuously Atis: 125.6 (Arr), 134.025 (Dep) Unicom: 122.95 App Con 119.3 (North) 124.95 (South) Dep Con: 128.25 (East) 127.05 (North) 126.1 (West) Final Con: 120.8 Tower: 135.3, 133.3, 124.3 Gnd Con: 128.75, 127.5, 121.85 Clnc Del: 118.75
FBO: AMR Combs (Southwest): Phone: 342-5600

Wings Over The Rockies Air And Space Museum

DENVER, CO (CO-01V, DEN)

The Wings Over The Rockies Air and Space Museum is located on East Academy Parkway in Hangar Number 1 at Lowry Air Force Base. More than a score of historic air and spacecraft compete for your amazement. Smallest is a German glider used after WWII to train pilots from the Luftwaffe (powered flight was barred by the Versailles treaty). Next is a D-VII Fokker made famous by Ernst Udet, the highest-scoring surviving German ace of WWI.

Biggest in the hangar is an enormous B-1A bomber, one of only five ever built! You'll also see a huge B-52 Stratofortress, stalwart of the famous Strategic Air Command, standing just outside. It's much too big for the hangar. Newly acquired is an Eaglerock biplane like those manufactured by the Alexander Aircraft Company, on South Broadway in Englewood.

Also: A 7D Corsair; F-86; B-18A Bolo; B-57E Canberra; F-4C and 4E Phantoms; F-102A Delta Dagger; H-21C (Helicopter), the giant Flying Banana; RF-84K Thunderflash; T-33A T-Bird; U3A Blue Canoe; and the "Freedom" Space Module.

Smaller displays include a Norden bomb sight, the famous OX-5 engine, and countless other relics of the birth of flight. In addition, traveling exhibits like the CBI display (China, Burma, India) and one-of-a-kind private collections renew and refresh your visits; there's something new all the time.

A board of 14 volunteer directors, each a distinguished member of the aviation community, governs the museum. More than 200 volunteers maintain the museum, build and clean exhibits, guide tours, and man the store. The museum has no paid employees. Guided tours are available at all times; call 303-360-5360, ext. 21 for arrangements. Groups of 10 or more are admitted for halfprice and may have a free tour guide if you wish. General admission prices run $4.00 for adults, $2.00 for seniors 60 and over, and children 6 through 17, $2.00. Members of the museum and children under 5 years old are admitted free. Hours are Monday through Saturday 10 a.m. to 4 p.m. and Sunday 12 noon to 4 p.m. A gift shop is also on the premises.

Photo by: Wings Over the Rocky's Air & Space Museum F-102A

The store is Richly stocked with aviation and space-oriented items, T-shirts, caps, jacket patches, pins, Aviation-oriented toys, airplane models and window decals. They can provide memorable souvenirs of your visit and hold enchantment for kids of all ages.

When flying in to the Denver, CO area you can land at several nearby community airports. The museum is located about 11 or 12 miles west of the Aurora Airpark (01V). This airport is a non-controlled field along Interstate 70. Rental cars must be arranged in advance through the Airpark manager by calling 303-361-9630. If landing at Denver/ Centennial Airport (APA), rental cars should be no problem. Additional services are also available. Front Range Airport (FTG) and Jeffco (BJC) are also options as well. The museum staff might also be of help in recommending transportation to their location. For information call the museum at 303-360-5360. (Information supplied in part by museum).

Photo by: Wings Over the Rocky's Air & Space Museum A-7D

CO-FTG - DENVER/FRONT RANGE
FRONT RANGE AIRPORT

(Area Code 303) 13

Front Range Cafeteria:

The Front Range Cafeteria is located in the main terminal building on the Front Range Airport. We were told that pilots can park their aircraft near the restaurant on the terminal ramp. This cafe styled facility is open around 10 a.m. to 3 p.m. Monday through Saturday and on Sundays during the same hours depending on business. Entrees include specialties like sandwiches, hamburgers, hotdogs and burrito's. They also feature a salad bar and has plans to include a grill. This will allow a wider variety of entrees on their menu. The seating capacity of this cafe is between 16 and 20 people. For meals on-the-go you can obtain box lunches as well. For more information call Front Range Aviation at 261-9697 or the Airport Authority at 261-9100.

Restaurants Near Airport:

Emilene's Sirloin House	15 mi. W	Phone: 366-6674
Front Range Cafeteria	On Site	Phone: 261-9100
Tomahawk Truck Stop	4 mi SW.	Phone: 366-0877

Lodging: Holiday Inn (Free trans, 15 miles east) 371-9494

Meeting Rooms: Terminal building (On Airport) 261-9100

Transportation: Airport courtesy cars available at times depending on personnel and time of arrival; Also Yellow Cab 777-7777; Metro Cab 333-3333; Zone Cab 444-8888; Professional Car Rental (Airport) 363-0894.

Information: Denver Metro Convention & Visitors Bureau, 1555 California Street, Ste 300, Denver, CO 80202, Phone: 892-1505 or 892-1112.

Airport Information:

DENVER/FRONT RANGE/WATKINS - FRONT RANGE AIRPORT (FTG)
19 mi east of town N39-47.12 W104-32.63 Elev: 5500 Fuel: 100LL, Jet-A Rwy 08-26: H8000x100 (Asph) Rwy 17-35: H8000x100 (Asph) Attended: 1300-0500Z Unicom: 123.0
Notes: Overnight parking $3.00 per night with 3 nights free with fill up of fuel.
Airport Auth. Phone: 261-9100
FBO: Front Range Aviation Phone: 261-9697

CO-3V5 - FORT COLLINS
DOWNTOWN FORT COLLINS AIRPARK

(Area Code 970) 14

Lincoln Street Grill:

This family style restaurant has been in business since 1947 and is located only 1/2 mile from the downtown Fort Collins Airpark. To reach the restaurant, walk 1 block southeast on Airway Drive, then 2 blocks west on Lincoln Avenue. Return transportation can usually be arranged. Their menu contains hamburgers, chicken sandwiches, Mexican selections. Daily specials are also are offered and change daily. Average prices run $5.00 to $7.00 for lunch and $10.00 to $20.00 for dinner entrees. The restaurant has recently been remodeled and offers a very attractive decor. Groups up to 60 people are welcome, with 1-2 days notice. All items on menu are available to-go or take-out. Restaurant hours are 10 a.m. to 10 p.m. Monday through Friday. For information call 482-9934.

Restaurants Near Airport:

Charco Broiler	3/4 mi SW	Phone: 482-1472
Lincoln Street Grill	1/2 mi SW	Phone: 482-9934
Sundance Steak Hse.	3/4 mi SE	Phone: 484-1600

Lodging: Comfort Inn, 1638 E. Mulberry, Ft Collins (3/4 mi) 484-2444; Holiday Inn, 3836 E. Mulberry, Ft Collins (3 mi) 484-4660; Holiday Inn, 425 W. Prospect, Ft Collins (8 mi) 482-2626; Marriott, 350 E. Horsetooth, Ft Collins (10 mi) 226-5200.

Meeting Rooms: Hotels listed above; Colorado State University, Lincoln Center, for information contact Fort Collins Convention and Visitors Bureau. Phone: 482-5821.

Transportation: Community Airpark Association, Inc., Dollar, Rent-A-Car, Econo Car Rental, Hertz Car Rental, Phone 484-4186; Also Shamrock Taxi 224-2222.

Information: Fort Collins Convention & Visitors Bureau, 420 South Howes Street, P.O. Box 1998, Fort Collins, CO 80522-1998, Phone: 482-5821 or 800-274-3678.

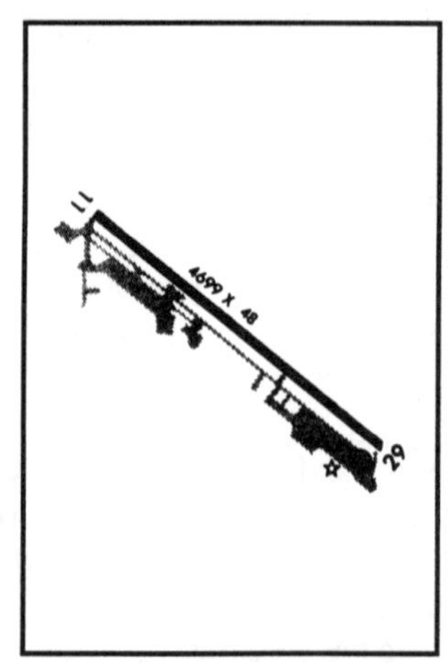

Airport Information:

FORT COLLINS - DOWNTOWN FT COLLINS AIRPARK (3V5)
2 mi east of town N40-35.27 W105-02.45 Elev: 4935 Fuel: 80, 100LL, Jet-A, Mogas Rwy 11-29: H4699x44 (Asph) Rwy: E-W: 2300x50 (Turf) Attended: Arp-Oct 1330-0200Z, Nov-Mar 1400-0100Z Unicom: 123.0 Public phone 24 hrs Notes: Call community Airpark prior to using East-West (Turf) Runway. Overnight tiedown $3.00Runway 29 is the preferred Rwy. for early morning departures, wind and weather permitting.
Fort Collins Downtown Airport Phone: 484-4186

CO-GJT - GRAND JUNCTION WALKER FIELD

(Area Code 970) 15, 16, 17

Oliver's Restaurant:

Oliver's Restaurant is situated within the Ramada Inn 1/2 mile south of Walker Field. Ramada courtesy vans will provide guests with courtesy transportation. The restaurant is open from 6 a.m. to 2 p.m. and 5 p.m. to 10 p.m. This is a fine dining facility that features a salad bar, sandwich bar, bakery, appetizers, desserts and homemade soups. Holiday buffets, breakfast specials and dinner specials are regularly offered. Prices average $5.00 for breakfast, $8.00 for lunch and $12.00 for dinner. The decor displays Victorian furnishings with antiques, in a quiet relaxing atmosphere. Banquet facilities are available for up to 100 people. All orders can be prepared for carry-out. For information you can call 241-8411.

Sky's Restaurant & Lounge:

This cafe, located in the terminal building, is open 6 a.m. to 8 p.m. 7 days a week. Their specialties are build-your-own 1/2 pound hamburger, turkey bacon clubs, turkey sandwiches, roast beef sandwiches, tuna and chicken salad sandwiches. Average prices are $3.00 for breakfast, $4.00 to $5.00 for lunch and dinner. Entree specials vary at the discretion of the cook. From the restaurant, customers can see the activity on the airport. They can seat about 100 guests within the dining room. Groups and fly-in get-togethers are welcome. Catering is available. Anything on their menu can be prepared for carry-out. For more information call the Sky's Restaurant & Lounge at 245-9794.

W.W. Pepper's Restaurant:

This is a fine dining establishment that is located about 1/2 mile south and along the same road that the airport is on. You will see a sign with red letters naming the restaurant. They are open Monday through Friday 11 a.m. to 2 p.m., and re-open for dinner between 4:30 p.m. to 10 p.m., on Saturday from 5 p.m. to 10 p.m.; and Sunday from 5 p.m. to 9 p.m. Specialty items include southwestern cooking, steak & lobster, shrimp and crab Chimichangas, and a variety of burritos and steaks. Average prices run $5.00 to $12.00 for most lunch and dinner choices. Their steak and lobster dinner costs around $30.00. Daily specials include soup and salad bar. The decor of the restaurant is southwestern with lots of wood furnishings and sunburst designs on the walls. Their lounge area displays a collection of old signs adding to the cozy atmosphere. Their main dining room contains table seating to accommodate about 65 persons. They do not accept reservations. However, if planning a large group or fly-in with your association, you should call the restaurant in advance and let them know you are planning to arrive. One room off the main dining area can hold 20 people for banquet seating. For more information about W.W. Pepper's call 245-9251.

Restaurants Near Field:

Olivers	1/2 mi S	Phone: 244-8411
Pantuso's	1/2 mi	Phone: 243-0000
Sky's Restaurant	On Site	Phone: 245-9794
Starvin Arvin	1/2 mi	Phone: 241-0430
W.W. Peppers	1/2 mi S	Phone: 245-9251

Lodging: Free transportation to and from airport: Best Western Horizon Inn 245-1410; Best Western Sandman 243-4150; Howard Johnson Motor Lodge 243-5150; Super 8, 248-8080; Holiday Inn 243-6790; Ramada Inn 244-8411; Hilton 241-8888.

Meeting Rooms: West Star Aviation and Junction Jet Center both have meeting rooms, also airport terminal building has a small board room on the second floor and meeting area on the third floor.

Transportation: Both FBOs listed will furnish local transportation to fly-in guests. Rental cars: Avis 244-9170; Budget 244-9155; Hertz 243-0747; National 243-6626; Rent-A-Wreck 241-1671; Thrifty 243-7556. Taxi service: Sunshine Taxi 245-9013.

Information: Grand Junction Visitor and Convention Bureau, 740 Horizon Drive, Grand Junction, CO 81506, Phone: 244-1480 or 800-962-2547.

Attractions:

3 golf courses in area; Fishing on Grand Mesa (30 miles); Ski area in Grand Mesa (30 miles); Colorado National Monument Canyon Rim Drive (8/10 mile west of field).

Airport Information:

GRAND JUNCTION - WALKER FIELD (GJT)
3 mi northeast of town N39-07.35 W108-31.60 Elev: 4858 Fuel: 100LL, Jet-A
Rwy 11-29: H10501x150 (Asph-Pfc) Rwy 04-22: H5502x75 (Asph) Attended: 1200-0630Z
Public phone 24 hrs Atis: 118.55 Unicom: 122.95 Tower: 118.1 Gnd Con 121.7 Notes: No landing fee reported, overnight parking fee: Singles $3.00, Twins $5.00
FBO: West Atar Aviation Phone: 243-7500

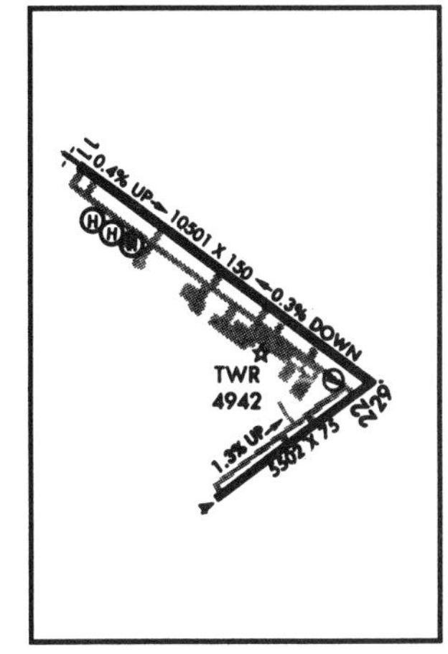

CO-GXY - GREELEY
GREELEY-WELD COUNTY AIRPORT

(Area Code 303)

18

Barnstormer Restaurant:

The Barnstormer Restaurant is located inside the Greeley-Weld Country Airport terminal, on the lower level. At this family-style restaurant, guests dine in an atmosphere of aviation decor. The Barnstormer is open for breakfast and lunch from 7:00 a.m. to 3:00 p.m., 7 days a week. It is closed major holidays. The restaurant offers a full breakfast menu, including delicious omeletes and breakfast burritos (their well-known specialty). Lunch features: daily specials, including juicy double cheeseburgers and tasty burritos with a special sauce (which we were told is popular among patrons). For dessert, the restaurant serves scrumptious homemade pies and "Linda's famous brownies." She told us that her brownies are a "choco-holic's delight!" The average price for breakfast is between $3.50 and $3.95, and for lunch, $4.25. The Barnstormer can cater to parties of 20 or more, as well as to private and corporate pilots on-the-go. For more information about Barnstormer Restaurant, call 356-9141.

Restaurants Near Airport:

Barnstormer Restaurant	(On Site)	Phone: 356-9141

Lodging: The following are within 3 miles of the airport: Greeley Inn 353-3216; Heritage Inn 339-5900; Holiday Inn 356-3000; Ramkota Inn 353-8444
Meeting Rooms: Holiday Inn 356-3000
Transportation: Taxi Service: Shamrock 352-3000; Rental Cars: Airport Terminal 356-9141; Econorate 351-6969; Garnsey and Wheeler 353-1111
Information: Greeley Convention and Visitors Bureau, 1407 8th Avenue, Greeley, CO 80631, Phone: 352-3566

Attractions:

Centennial Village Museum (3 miles); Colorado Air Festival (to be anncd.); Denver Bronco Football Training Camp (8 miles); Greeley Independence Stampede (3 miles); Rocky Mountain EAA Fly-In (June 24-25). Call 352-3566 for more information.

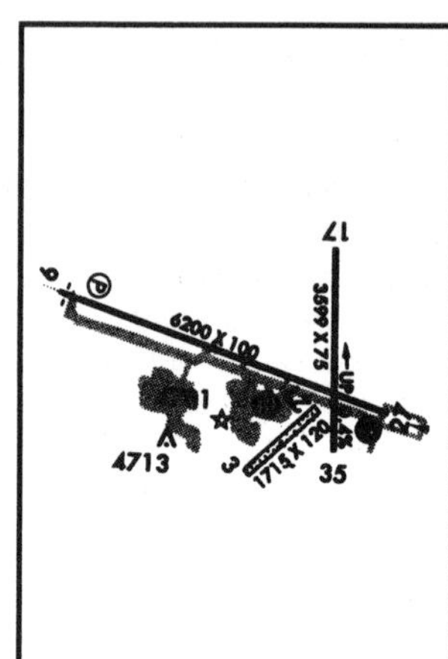

Airport Information:

GREELEY - GREELEY-WELD COUNTY AIRPORT (GXY)
3 mi east of town N40-25.68 W104-37.95 Elev: 4658 Fuel: 100LL, Jet-A, MOGAS Rwy 09-27: H6200x100 (Asph) Rwy 17-35: H3599x75 (Asph) Rwy 03-21: 1715x130 (Grvl-Dirt) Attended: 1400-0200Z CTAF/Unicom: 122.8 Dever Center App/Dep Con: 125.9 Notes: See "Airport Facility Directory" for comments about runway conditions and information. Overnight parking fee: $3.00 (waived with fuel purchase first night), hanger fees: $15.00 unheated and $25.00 heated.

FBO: Harris Aviation	**Phone: 356-6041**
FBO: Precision Propeller Svc., Inc.	**Phone: 352-8578**
FBO: Tailwinds Aviation	**Phone: 353-8378**

CO-GUC - GUNNISON
GUNNISON COUNTY AIRPORT

(Area Code 970)

19

Gold Creek Inn:

The Gold Creek Inn is located 1 mile northeast of the Gunnison County Airport. Courtesy transportation by the restaurant is provided if prior arrangements are made. This fine dining facility is open Tuesday through Saturday from 5:30 p.m. to 10 p.m. and also the 1st Sunday of each month for brunch from 10 a.m. to 3 p.m. Specialties of the house include stuffed artichoke, prime rib, steak Diane, fresh seafood, pecan chicken, and for dessert cheese cake & ice cream parfaits. Their dining room is set with tablecloths, candles, fresh flowers and decorated with antique tools and equipment from an era which has long since passed. A large rock bolder fireplace adds to the warmth. This restaurant will be happy to cater to groups up to 35 persons. This unique facility is also a bed and breakfast located within a historic mining town. Fishing, hiking, 4-wheel drives, ghost towns, skiing and snowmobiling are just some of the activities in this region. For more information about the restaurant call 641-2086.

Restaurants Near Airport:

Cactus Jack's	6 Blks NE	Phone: 641-2044
Cattlemen Inn	1 mi NE	Phone: 641-1061
Gold Creek Inn	1 mi	Phone: 641-2086
The Trough	3 mi	Phone: 641-3724

Lodging: Bennett's Western 641-1722; Comfort Inn Water Wheel 641-1650; Friendship Inn Colorado West 641-1288; Super "8" 641-3068; (All facilities near Gunnison Co Airport with free shuttle service)
Meeting Rooms: Aspinail-Wilson Conference Center 641-2238
Transportation: Courtesy car available through Gunnison Valley Aviaiton 641-0526. Taxi service: Alpine Express 641-5588; Rental Cars: Avis 641-0263; Budget 641-4403; Hertz 641-2881; National 641-5525
Information: Gunnison County Chamber of Commerce, 500 East Tomichi Avenue, Box 36, Gunnison, CO 81230, Phone: 641-1501.

Attractions:

Dos Rios Golf 641-1482; Curecanti National Recreation Area located west on US 50. Elk Creek Visitors Center (18 miles west on Route 50 Mid Apr-Oct) boating, picnicking, camping. For information call 641-0406 or 2337 or write Chief Ranger, 102 Elk Creek, Gunnison, CO 61230.

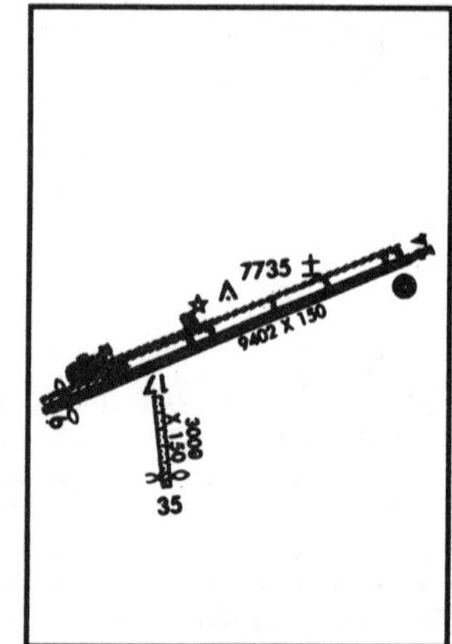

Airport Information:

GUNNISON - GUNNISON COUNTY AIRPORT (GUC)
1 mi southwest of town N38-32.04 W106-55.99 Elev: 7673 Fuel: 100LL, Jet-A Rwy 06-24: H9402x150 (Asph-Pfc) Rwy 17-35: 3000x150 (Turf-Grvl) Attended: daylight hours Unicom: 122.7 Notes: No landing fees daylight, (At night $30.00; Overnight parking: single $4.00, Twin $5.00, Turbine $8.00; Rwy 17-35 CLOSED Dec-May. (See AFD & AIM).
FBO: Gunnison Valley Aviation Phone: 641-0526

CO-07V - LA VETA CUCHARA VALLEY AIRPORT

20

(Area Code 719)

Restaurants Near Airport:

Covered Wagon Rest.	1 mi.	Phone: 742-3679
La Casa Restaurant	1 mi.	Phone: 742-5519
La Veta Lodge	1 mi.	Phone: 742-3700
Positively Main Street	1 mi.	Phone: 742-5505

Lodging: Cuchara Valley Ski Resort (13 miles), Phone: 742-3163; Grandote Golf and Country Club (2 miles), Phone: 742-3123; 1899 Inn B&B (Est. 13 miles) 314 South Main, Cuchara Valley, Phone: 742-3163.

Meeting Rooms: Cuchara Valley Ski Resort (13 miles) Phone: 742-3163; Cuchara Inn (11 miles) Phone: 742-3685; Rio Cucharas Inn, Hwy. 160 west, Phone: 738-1282.

Transportation: FBO will not furnish courtesy cars. However, car rentals can be arranged in advance through National Car Rental, 846-3318; Also guests can call 742-3631 and someone from the town hall can transport them; Taxi service also available through Chamber of Commerce 742-3681.

Information: La Veta Chamber of Commerce, Phone: 742-3681

Attractions:

Grandote Golf And Country Club (2 miles) 742-3123; Cuchara Valley Ski Resort (13 miles) 742-3163; Lathrop State Park (11 miles) 738-2376; Walsenburg Golf Course (11 miles) 738-2730. Also camping on field.

Positively Main Street:

Positively Main Street is a restaurant that is located about 1 mile south of the Cuchara Valley Airport. This unique family dining establishment specializes in serving organic and vegetarian dishes including grass fed beef, poultry, steakes lasagna, grilled fish, chicken, eggplant, seafood and fresh baked bread. All meals are prepared from scratch concentrating on good wholesome food that is not processed and preserved. In addition to dining, this restaurant also features a very complete selection of beers with 14 different assortments, many from the United Kingdom. The restaurant is contained within an Adobe building with a southwestern decor decorated with local artwork. The main dining room can seat about 45 persons. And their lounge can seat 38 people. The owners of this restaurant not only prepare and serve their dinner guests, but also partake in entertaining their customers with music in a festive atmosphere after dinner on weekends. Restaurant hours are 8 a.m. to 8 p.m. Mon-Sat and 9 a.m. to 6 p.m. on Sunday. This is a family-operated business, with limited staff. For those wishing to flyin and obtain free courtesy transportation by the restaurant, we suggest you call them the night before or at least before your departure, in order to give them enough notice to arrange for airport pickup. They will arrange to have someone available when you call them from the Cuchara Valley Airport (07V). Groups planning to fly-in can (With advance notice) arrange catering through the restaurant for up to 40 people. For information call 742-5505.

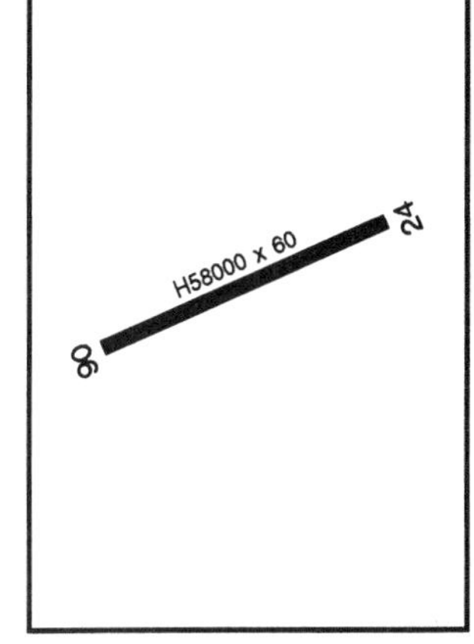

Airport Information:

LA VETA - CUCHARA VALLEY AIRPORT AT LA VETA (07V)
1 mi north of town N37-31.43 W105-00.56 Elev: 7153 Fuel: 100LL, Jet-A
Rwy 06-24: H5800x60 (Asph) Attended: (On call) for attendant call 742-5421 Public phone 24 hrs
Unicom: 122.9 Notes: Wildlife on and in the vicinity of Rwy 06-24 higher occurrence during Jun-Oct; No landing fee at this time, certified mechanic on staff.
Airport Manager Phone: 742-3631

CO-MTJ - MONTROSE MONTROSE COUNTY AIRPORT

21

(Area Code 970)

Restaurants Near Airport:

Casa De Mehas	1 mi S.	Phone: 249-9305
Red Barn Restaurant	3 mi E.	Phone: 249-9202
Sun Valley Truck Stop	On Site	Phone: 249-7343

Lodging: Red Arrow Motel (Best Western, 3 miles) 249-9641; San Juan Inn (3 miles) 249-6644; Will Rogers Motel (1/2 mile) 249-4891.

Meeting Rooms: Conference meeting rooms in commercial terminal. Seating approximately 20, Phone: 249-3203; Montrose Pavilion And Conference Center, Phone: 249-4534.

Transportation: Montrose County Airport and VIP Flyers (FBO's) have courtesy cars; Also Rental Cars: Western Express 249-8880; Budget 249-6083; Hertz 249-9447; Dollar 249-3770; Telluride Transit 249-6993.

Information: Chamber of Commerce, 1519 E Main Street, Montrose, CO 81401, Phone: 800-873-0244.

Sun Valley Truck Stop:

The Sun Valley Truck Stop restaurant is situated behind the general aviation terminal and is well within walking distance to aircraft parking. This family style restaurant is open 24 hours a day. Their menu contains a nice selection of breakfast items as well as hamburgers, chicken, beef steaks, chef salads and homemade soups. Average prices run $2.00 to $3.00 for breakfast, $3.50 to $4.50 for lunch and $5.00 to $6.00 for dinner. They also provide a salad bar as well. This restaurant has a seating capacity for 100 to 125 persons. All meals can be prepared for carry-out or pick-up. For more information you can call 249-7343.

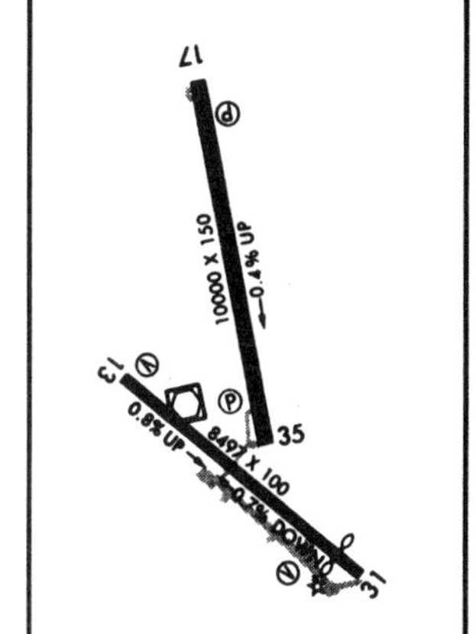

Airport Information:

MONTROSE - MONTROSE REGIONAL AIRPORT (MTJ)
1 mi northwest of town N38-30.53 W107-53.63 Elev: 5759 Fuel: 100LL, Jet-A
Rwy 12-35: H10000x150 (Asph-Grvd) Rwy 13-31: H8497x100 (Asph-Pfc) Attended: 1300-0500Z Unicom: 122.8 Public Phone 24hrs Notes: Conditions permitting takoff Rwy 31 and Land Rwy 13 No landing fee reported for general aviation aircraft. Overnight tie down fee $4.00/night. Five night maximum charged on tie down.
FBO: Montrose Regional Airport Phone: 249-0592

CO-2V1 - PAGOSA SPRINGS STEVENS FIELD

(Area Code 303) 22

Great Divide Restaurant & South Face:

The Great Divide Restaurant and the South Face Dining Room are both fine dining restaurants located within the Fairfield Pagosa Lodge. This facility is situated 1-1/2 miles south of Stevens Field Airport. From the airport, go south on Piedra Road to 160 and turn right. The Great Divide Restaurant is open from 6:30 a.m. to 2:00 p.m. and the South Face Dining Room is open from 5:00 p.m. to 9:00 p.m. There is also the Rendezvous Lounge within this hotel. They run a special breakfast and lunch. The Dinner menu is a "specialty menu" with 4 different specials. Fish, fowl, red meat, and other. Prime rib and pasta are served regularly. They also offer a Sunday Brunch. Breakfast averages around $4.95, lunch around $5.95, and dinner around $14.95. The decor is bright and airy with a 180 degree southwestern view of the beautiful Continental Divide Mountains. The Mountains are snow-covered in the winter and green in the summer. Banquet rooms are available for up to 175 people and can be sectioned into smaller meeting rooms. With advance notice, catering service can also be arranged. For more information about the Great Divide Restaurant and the South Face Dining Room, call 731-4141 or 800-523-7704.

Restaurants Near Airport:

Great Divide	1-1/2mi S.	Phone: 731-4141
Green House	2/10 mi E.	Phone: 731-2021
Moose River Pub	2-1/2mi S.	Phone: 731-5451
Rocky Mtn. Pie Shoppe	7/10 mi E.	Phone: 731-4004

Lodging: Fairfield Pagosa Lodge (Transportation) 1-1/2 mile 731-4141; Oak Ridge Motel, 3 miles 264-4173.
Meeting Rooms: Fairfield Pagosa Lodge 731-4141 & Oak Ridge Motel 264-4173.
Transportation: Pagosa Springs Aviation will provide transportation to nearby facilities. Call 731-2179 or 731-5871. Also, Budget car rental is available at 731-4477.
Information: Chamber of Commerce, 402 San Juan Street, P.O. Box 787, Pagosa Springs, CO 81147, Phone: 800-252-2204 or 264-2360.

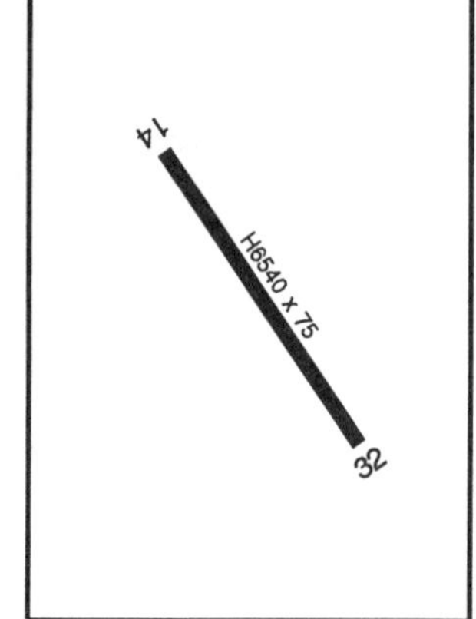

Airport Information:

PAGOSA SPRINGS - STEVENS FIELD (2V1)
3 mi northwest of town N37-16.65 W107-03.35 Elev: 7700 Fuel: 100LL, Jet-A
Rwy 01-19: H6540x75 (Asph) Attended: April-October 1400-0200Z, November-April 1500-0100Z
CTAF/Unicom: 122.8 Public Phone 24hrs Notes: Overnight parking fees: $3 singles and $5 twins.
FBO: FliteCraft Turbo Phone: 731-2127

Fairfield Pagosa Lodge & Resort

Pagosa Springs, CO (CO-2V1)

The Fairfield Pagosa Lodge & Resort is located about 1 mile from Pagosa Springs, Stevens Field (2V1), with free courtesy transportation to the resort. The airport has a 1-19 6,500 x 75 asphalt lighted runway. For airport service call 303-731-2179, 731-5871 or Flite Craft Turbo (FBO) at 303-731-2127.

Nestled in the foothills and valleys of the San Juan Basin, Pagosa Springs offers one of the largest and hottest natural mineral springs in the world. Natural waterfalls are abundant, with many found in the Weminuche Wilderness which is accessed by several local trailheads. River rafting, camping, hiking, mountain biking, hunting, fishing, skiing, snowmobiling, plus activities at their recreation desk will keep any adventurous spirit alive.

The Fairfield Pagosa Lodge and Resort has a 3 story mountain lodge with 100 rooms including suites, with many overlooking Pinon Lake and the mountainous Continental Divide. All rooms have color T.V., cable, phones, air conditioning, and phone message services. Separate check-in and pre-registration for groups is available.

The Great Divide Restaurant offers breakfast, lunch and dinner from 7 a.m. to 10 p.m., with entrees costing an average of between $5.00 to $16.00. Their Rendezvous Lounge is the evening's night spot for relaxing with your favorite liquid refreshment. Every night is $2.00 Margarita night all summer long. Their catering personnel are experts in organizing meeting functions to your specification.

They have a golf pro-shop, tennis pro shop and cross country touring center clubhouse which provides a full line of sports equipment and apparel. In the hotel, is their Emporium gift shop and the Toggery clothing store.

Some of the popular summer time activities include 27 holes of mountain golf, tennis, fishing, hot air balloon rides, guided fishing tours, horseback riding, old fashion BBQ's with horse drawn transportation, bicycle rental, paddle boats, ping-pong, hiking, volleyball, shuffleboard, miniature golf, white water river rafting, mining town tours, jeep tours, Durango/Silverton narrow gage train rides, and Indian cliff dwelling tours.

Winter activities include, snowmobiling, downhill skiing at Wolf Creek ski area, ice fishing, sleigh rides and a complete cross country ski center with more than 15 km of groomed trails.

Additional recreation and services include a health spa, redwood sauna, Jacuzzi, Danish cold plunge, indoor heated pool, video/game room, VCR movie rentals and equipment, and high stakes bingo in Ignacio.

The resort also contains accommodations for meetings and conferences. Three main rooms called the Ponderosa A, B & C. have 888 square feet each for meeting space. Portable stage, dance floor, slide projectors and carrousels, can all be used.

For further information about the Fairfield Pagosa Lodge call 303-731-4141 or 800-523-7704. (Information submitted by Fairfield Pagosa Lodge & Resort).

CO-PUB - PUEBLO
PUEBLO MEMORIAL AIRPORT

DC6 Restaurant:

The Airport Restaurant is located inside the terminal building at the Pueblo Memorial Airport. This family style restaurant is open 7 days a week from 6 a.m. to 5:30 p.m. Future hours may be extended to 9 p.m. The grill shuts down at 4 p.m., however cold sandwiches are available until 5:30 p.m. The restaurant specializes in Mexican cuisine as well as specialty sandwiches, hamburgers, chicken sandwiches, taco salads and some Italian foods. Daily specials are also offered. Average prices run $4.00 for breakfast and lunch. The Airport Restaurant can seat 70 people in their dining area. Guests can watch the aircraft taxiing and taking off from the restaurant while enjoying a fine meal. Group fly-ins are always welcome. Please give advance notice if your group is quite large, so they can better serve you. For more information you can call them at 948-4185.

(Area Code 719) **23**

Restaurants Near Airport:

DC6 Restaurant	On Site	Phone: 948-4185
Holiday Inn	6 mi W.	Phone: 543-8050
Pueblo West Inn	10 mi W.	Phone: 547-2111
Red Lobster	7 mi W.	Phone: N/A

Lodging: Pueblo West Inn (Free trans, 7 miles) 547-2111; Holiday Inn (Free trans, 6 miles) 543-8050.
Meeting Rooms: Flower Aviation FBO (On Airport) has accommodations for meetings and conferences. They also have catering facilities available. For information call 948-2447.
Transportation: Fixed based operators on the airport can provide courtesy transportation to nearby facilities. Also City Cab 543-2525; Hertz 948-3345; National 948-3343.
Information: Chamber of Commerce, P.O. Box 697, Pueblo, CO 81002, Phone: 542-1704. or Pueblo Visitors Information Center (Open May-Sept) at 3417 North Elizabeth Street, 81008 or call 543-1742.

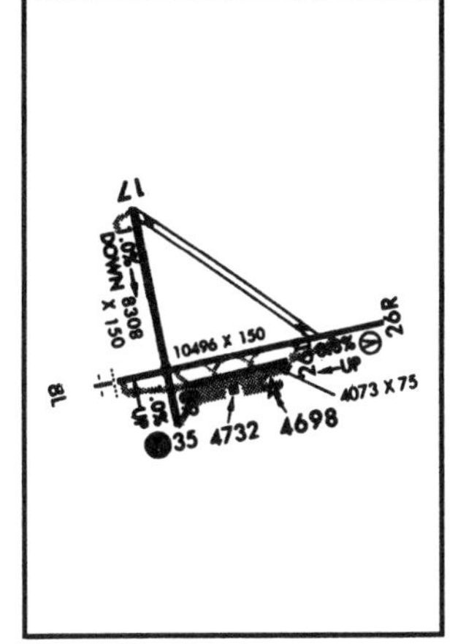

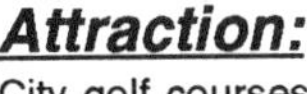
Attraction:

City golf courses nearby; Lake Pueblo 20 miles west has swimming, fishing and boating. For information, contact the Chamber of Commerce or the Pueblo Visitor Information Center listed above.

Airport Information:

PUEBLO - PUEBLO MEMORIAL AIRPORT (PUB)
5 mi east of town N38-17.35 W104-29.79 Elev: 4726 Fuel: 100LL, Jet-A
Rwy 08L-26R: H10496x150 (Asph-Pfc) Rwy 17-35: H8308x150 (Asph-Pfc) Rwy 08R-26L: H4073x75 (Asph) Attended: 1300-0500Z Atis: 125.25 Unicom: 122.95 App/Dep Con: 120.1 (N/S) Tower: 119.1 Gnd Con: 121.9 Public Phone 24hrs (FBO)
Notes: Overnight tiedown $10.00 to $15.00; Landing fee: 23 cents/1000 lbs for non-comercial flights
FBO: Peak Aviation Phone: 948-4560

CO-SBS - STEAMBOAT SPRINGS
BOB ADAMS FIELD

River Bend Inn:

The River Bend Inn is located about 4 miles from the Bob Adams Airport. If you have 4 or more people in your group and plan to fly in and dine at the River Bend Inn Restaurant, they will be happy to provide courtesy transportation. Taxi service is also available from the airport. This family style restaurant is open 7 days a week and has seasonal hours. During the summer they open between 11:30 a.m. and 12 a.m. and during the winter from 4 p.m. to 12 a.m. between the months of November 1st and May 1st. Their menu contains a full assortment of delicious items from barbecued spare ribs, chicken, sandwiches and pizza, to steaks cut to order and lobster tails. The restaurant is decorated with knotty pine walls and has seating for 90 persons. Their outdoor deck provides outdoor dining along with a view overlooking the 9 hole golf course adjacent to the restaurant. Average prices run between $5.00 and $6.00 for lunch and $8.00 and $17.50 for dinner. Combining a golf game with lunch or dinner can be fun and if you have a foursome, your transportation to and from the restaurant will be free. For more information call the River Bend Inn at 879-1615.

(Area Code 970) **24**

Restaurants Near Airport:

River Bend Inn	4 mi	Phone: 879-1615

Lodging: Overlook Hotel (Free trans) 879-2900; Sheraton Steamboat Resort (Free trans) 879-2220; Home Ranch (Free trans) 879-1780; Vista Verde (Free trans) 879-3858.

Meeting Rooms: All lodging facilities listed above have accommodations for meeting rooms. The Sheraton Steamboat Resort has convention facilities available.

Transportation: River Bend Inn will provide courtesy transportation to and from the restaurant if you have 4 or more in your group. Taxi: Alpine 879-2800; Steamboat Taxi 879-3335; Ultimate Limousine 879-8665; Also Rental Cars: Budget 879-3103; Hertz 870-0880; National 879-0800.

Information: Steamboat Springs Chamber Resort Association, P.O. Box 774408, Steamboat Springs, CO 80477, Phone: 879-0880 or 1-800-922-2722.

Attractions:

9 hole golf course located adjacent to the River Bend Inn (4 miles)

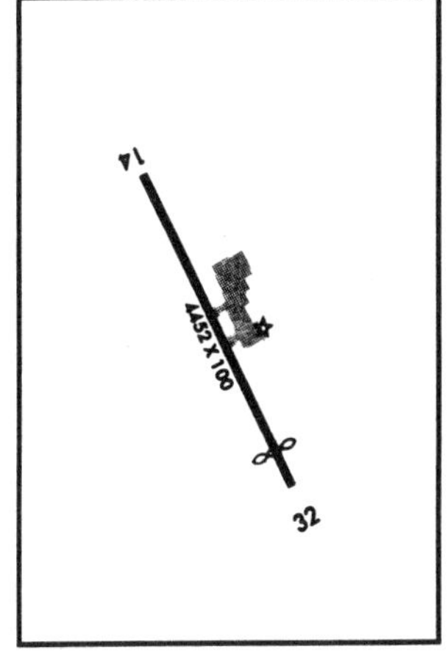

Airport Information:

STEAMBOAT SPRINGS - BOB ADAMS FIELD (SBS)
3 mi northwest of town N40-30.99 W106-51.99 Elev: 6878 Fuel: 100LL, Jet-A
Rwy 14-32: H4452x100 (Asph-Grvd) Attended: 1400-0200Z Unicom: 122.8 Notes: CAUTION: snow removal equipment may be on runway during snow season, for information contact unicom on 122.8.
Mountain Air Xpress Phone: 879-1204

Steamboat Springs Ski Area

Steamboat Springs, CO (CO-SBS)

(Information submitted by Steamboat Ski & Resort Corporation)

Photo by:
Larry Pierce

Steamboat Springs is located in the Yampa River Valley of northwest Colorado, not far from the Continental Divide. It is a complete mountain range of Sunshine Peak, Storm Peak, Thunderhead Peak and Christie Peak. From the top of Mt. Werner, it offers 21 lifts, 107 trails and 7 on-mountain restaurant facilities on 2,500 acres of skiable terrain for all levels of ability. Steamboat is known for its champagne powder snow and its tree skiing which has helped to produce 35 winter Olympians.

Besides downhill skiing, try your skill at skating, track skiing or snowshoeing. Take a guided ice fishing trip, or ride in a four person, padded bobsled that whisks daring riders down a mile-long snow-packed track, over steep hills and through tunnels to an exciting finish. Or, why not try the thrill of Steamboat Powder Cat skiing. The powerful snowcats will accommodate a total of twelve skiers in warmth and comfort for a day of untracked powder on wide open snow fields near the Continental Divide. If you have an urge to see the back country, the Steamboat Sled-Dog Express will zip you across the countryside in open air sleds with a pack of dogs leading the way. For a more modern sledding experience, explore the many miles of trails on one of their snowmobiles. For a change of pace, take a leisurely ride in a hot air balloon and soar above the Yampa Valley to get a bird's-eye view of the ski area. Or, stay down on the ground and go horseback riding.

At the end of the day, before dinner, soak in one of the local hot springs at the Steamboat Health and Rec Center, or take a tour, four miles up, to Strawberry Park Hot Springs for a unique experience in a beautiful outdoor setting. Another popular evening activity is a dinner sleigh ride. Enjoy a unique snowcat sleigh ride over to Ragnar's for a gourmet Scandinavian dinner atop the mountain. Several of the local ranches offer sleigh ride dinners featuring horse-drawn sleighs, live entertainment and home-style western cooking, which includes char-broiled steak.

Steamboat also features over 75 dining facilities, particularly known for their western flair for dining. The BK Corral, located on the third floor of the Thunderhead building, features a full service cafeteria and pizza bar, and it seats up to 550 people, with a barbecue sundeck seating up to 300. The Rendezvous Cafeteria, located in the Rendezvous Saddle facility, is also a full service cafeteria which seats 300 people on the outside deck. Cowpokes will want to kick up their heels for a western BBQ dinner. This exciting evening features live country-western entertainment and an all-you-can-eat family style buffet. It is ideal for families and large groups and reservations must be made in advance. For a lighter fare, the Four Points Hut snack bar, located near the top of teh Four Points lift, serves chips, chili, pastries and other light snacks. Stop in for a casual lunch at the Stoker Bar, which features light salads, snacks and hearty chili and sandwiches. Cafe Thunderhead, also located in the Thunderhead building, serves meals to the children's ski school.

Shoppers will find hours of fun in all three of Steamboat's shopping areas: Gondola Square, Ski Time Square, and the downtown area.

Steamboat has a staff of skiing hosts on the mountain and in the Information Center who offer assistance with directions, activities, lost and found, and general information about Steamboat. Mountain tours are offered Sunday and Monday of each week at 10:30 a.m.

Bob Adams Field Airport is located just 3 miles northwest of town. It has a 4000'x100 asphalt-grooved runway. With advance notice, the FBO will loan out an all-day courtesy car with purchase of fuel. Contact the FBO at 879-1204, 8 a.m. to 5:30 p.m., for further information. As an alternate, the Yampa Valley Regional Airport, which also services major airlines, is located about 22 miles from the resort. Steamboat offers numerous resort, hotel and motel accommodations. For more information about activities and accommodations in Steamboat, contact Steamboat Springs Chamber Resort Association at 800-922-2722 or 879-0880.

CO-TEX - TELLURIDE
TELLURIDE REGIONAL AIRPORT

(Area Code 303) 25

The Restaurants in Telluride:

Telluride Regional Airport is located just 5 miles west of town. Year-round, Telluride offers enough activities to really work up an appetite. Visitors can choose from a wide selection of tasty cuisine, ranging from international fare to all-American home cooking. Dine, on-mountain, at Giuseppe's for mouth-watering Italian dishes served at the mountain's summit, or try the Excelsior or the Campagna for even more delicious Italian dishes. Visit Evangeline's for fine New Orleans Cajun Creole dining in the Mountain Village, just over the ridge from Telluride. Or, spice up your day at Sofio's or the Cactus Cafe for a taste of Mexico. Visit the Floradora, the T-Ride Restaurant and Sports Bar, or the Tavern at the Village and enjoy a variety of great American dishes, such as juicy steaks and succulent fish. But, for distinctive Native American fare, visit Legends at the Peaks. Yet, for a quick meal, the Pacific Street Deli, Village Market, Rose's and the Mercury Cafe serve a variety of sandwiches. Afterward, top off the meal with a chewy, gooey dessert at the Creamery or The Rocky Mountain Chocolate Factory. For more information about the restaurants or activities in Telluride, contact the Telluride Chamber Resort Association at 800-525-3455 or 728-3041.

Restaurants Near Airport:

Restaurants in Telluride	5 mi E	Phone: 728-3041

Lodging: Telluride Accommodations 728-3803; Telluride Central Reservations 728-4431
Meeting Rooms: Telluride Accommodations 728-3803
Transportation: Shuttle bus; limousine; van; Taxi Service: Mountain Limo 728-9606; Skip's 728-6667; Telluride 728-6667; Telluride Transit 728-6000; Western Express 249-8880; Rental Cars: Budget 728-4642; Hertz 728-3163
Information: Telluride Chamber Resort Association, 666 W. Colorado Avenue, Box 653, Telluride, CO 81435, Phone: 800-525-3455 or 728-3041

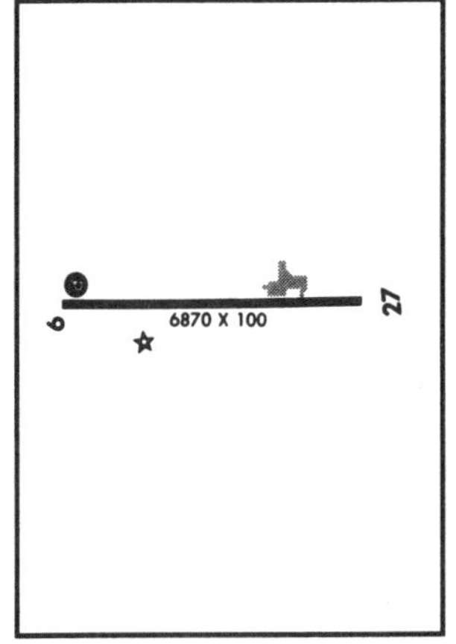

Airport Information:

TELLURIDE - TELLURIDE REGIONAL AIRPORT (TEX)
5 mi west of town N37-57.23 W107-54.51 Elev: 9078 Fuel: 100LL, Jet-A Rwy 09-27: H6870x100 (Asph-Grvd) Attended: 1400-sunset plus 30 minutes. CTAF/Unicom: 123.0 Denver App/Dep Con: 125.35 Notes: Watch for elk on runway. Airport CLOSED 30 minutes after sunset-1300Z or 30 minutes before sunrise (whichever is later). Airport lighting system (emergency use only) 30 minutes after sunset-1300Z or 30 minutes before sunrise. $1.00 landing fee.
FBO: Telluride Executive Services Phone: 728-5051

Telluride Ski and Golf Resort

Telluride, CO (CO-TEX)

Photo by: George H. H. Huey/Telluride Ski & Golf Company

The majestic Rockies provide a breathtaking background for Telluride.

Photo by: T. R. Youngstrom/Telluride Ski & Golf Company

A look at Telluride from a skier's point of view.

Telluride is located in the Uncompahgre National Forest, which is the heart of the 14,000-foot Rockies of Southwestern Colorado. This National Historic District was settled as a gold and silver mining camp in the 1870s, thus earning the name "The Town Without A Bellyache" for its prosperity. Although the colorful mining days are gone, Telluride's rich heritage still lives on. It is predominantly characterized by Victorian architecture among lodges as well as pastel-colored residences which sit squarely in a box canyon cradling two spectacular waterfalls. While Telluride is also famous for its invention of the alternating electric current and the creation of the first aerial tramway, it is best-known for its year-round activities.

Winter activities include: downhill skiing, snowshoeing, cross-country skiing, helicopter skiing, ice-skating, snowmobiling and sleigh rides. Eighty-five percent of its in-town accommodations are liftside or within walking distance to both the Coonskin and Oak Street base facilities. Telluride also offers many other seasonal activities: climbing exhibitions, trout fishing, mountain biking, river rafting, horseback riding trips, camping, hot air balloon rides, paragliding, hockey and much, much more.

Visitors can choose from one of the several on-mountain or mountainside restaurants that feature delectible international and American cuisine. Giuseppe's offers Italian fare served at the mountain's summit, the Gorrono Ranch, a mid-mountain skier cafeteria and grill, serves fine food in a rustic historic homestead. Also, the Cactus Cafe serves Southwestern dining at the base of the Mountain Village, a mid-mountain community that lies just over the ridge from Telluride.

In the Mountain Village, the majority of accommodations are ski-in and ski-out. Choose from several lodges, including a 177-room luxury hotel and spa, as well as a bed and breakfast lodge. The Village also offers six restaurants and bars, an ice skating rink, ski school, a nursery and day care, tennis courts and an 18-hole championship golf course. The Mountain Village combines European-alpine design with the splendor of the Rockies.

Telluride Regional Airport, located just 5 miles west of town, has a 6,870'x100 asphalt-grooved runway. There is a $1.00 landing fee, as well as an overnight parking fee of $7.00 for singles and $9.00 for twins. A shuttle bus and limousine are available, as well as Budget and Hertz rental cars and various taxi services. For more information, contact the FBO at 728-5051, 30 minutes prior to sunrise to 30 minutes past sunset; no earlier than 6 A.M. For reservations, contact Telluride Accommodations at 728-3803. For other information about Telluride, call the Telluride Chamber Resort Association at 800-525-3455 or 728-3041. (Information submitted by Telluride Ski & Golf Company)

CO-TAD - TRINIDAD PERRY STOKES

(Area Code 719) 26

Christina's Restaurant (Best Western Country Club Inn:

Christina's Restaurant is located within the Best Western Country Club Inn located about 8 miles southwest of the Perry Stokes Airport in Trinadad, CO. Christina who manages and owns the restaurant is a pilot herself, and has logged numerous hours flying the mountain ranges throughout the area and Colorado region. Both the restaurant and Best Western Complex make an ideal location to stay while visiting the attractions throughout the area. Infact, a tour trolly stops right at their doorstep on its way to nearby sites. The restaurant is a fine dining facility with linen table cloths and glass ornament centerpieces for each table. The view from this restaurant overlooks I-25 westward toward the Sangre DeCristo Mountains. Their menu contains a fine selection of items specially prepared by their master chef. A gourmet selection on their menu include items like choice steaks and seafood, Beef Arlington, German pastas, pita salads, and apple pancakes. A special luncheon buffet is served between 11 a.m. and 2 p.m Monday through Friday. Three or four main meat selections are available with the buffet. A carver stands ready and will slice just the right cut of your choice. Two different salads complement the buffet along with freshly baked pastries. Even though the restaurant offers an elegant decor, guests enjoy a casual come-as-you-are atmosphere. Average prices run $6.00 for breakfast and lunch and between $8.00 and $10.00 for dinner. The restaurant is open 6 a.m. to 2 p.m., then again from 5 p.m. to 9 p.m., 7 days a week. Christina's Restaurant, combined with the Best Western lodging facility, contains accommodations for business meetings and seminars for as many as 300 individuals. Corporate banquets and group functions can easily be arranged. The Sangre De Cristo Mountain range is situated about 35 miles west of Perry Stokes Airport. "Spanish Peaks" rises to 13,626' above sea level. Less than an hour's drive away from the town will take you from the foot hills up into the mountains. Abandoned gold mining settlements serve as interesting attractions for vacationers. Golf enthusiasts can enjoy a round of golf just up the street from Christina's. The shops the downtown area and Western Art Museum can all be enjoyed as well. For more information about Christina's Restaurant or lodging at the Best Western Country Club Inn call 846-2215.

Restaurants Near Airport:

Chef Liu	N/A	Phone: 846-3333
Christina's Restaurant	8 mi SW	Phone: 846-2215
Neumerous Restaurants	10 mi SW	N/A

lodging:
Best Western Country Club Inn (free trans, 8 mi) 846-2215; Holiday Inn (13 mi) 846-4491.

Meeting Rooms:
Best Western Country Club Inn (free trans, 8 mi) 846-2215; Holiday Inn (13 mi) 846-4491.

Transportation:
Hadad Motors 846-3318

Information:
Trinidad-Las Animas County Chamber of Commerce, 309 Nevada Avenue, Trinidad, CO 81082, Phone: 846-9285.

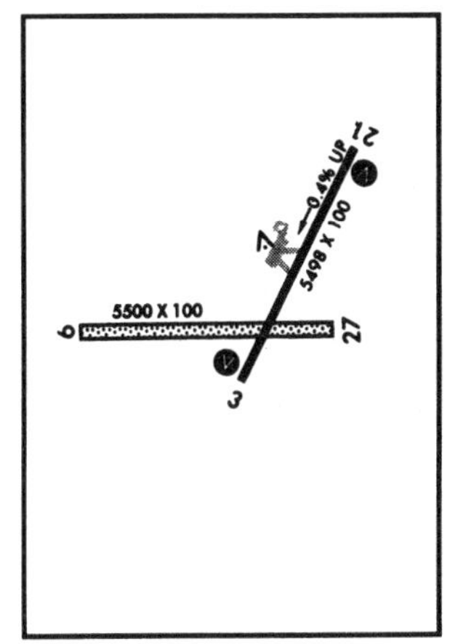

Airport Information:

TRINIDAD - PERRY STOKES (TAD)
10 mi northeast of town N37-15.60 W104-20.40 Elev: 5761 Fuel: 100LL, Jet-A Rwy 03-21: H5498x100 (Asph) Rwy 09-27: 5497x100 (Turf) Attended: continuously Unicom: 122.8 CAUTION: Rwy 09-27 +2'-4' bushes within 5' both sides full length. Rwy 09-27 rough in places.
FBO: Perry Stokes Airport Manager Phone: 846-6271

CONNECTICUT

CROSS FILE INDEX

Location Number	City or Town	Airport Name And Identifier	Name of Attraction
1	Bridgeport	Igor I. Sikorsky Mem. (BDR)	Windsock Restaurant
2	Bridgeport	Igor I. Sikorsky Mem. (BDR)	Wing's Restaurant
3	Danbury	Danbury Muni. Arpt. (DXR)	Moon Dance Restaurant
4	Groton-New London	Groton-New London Arpt. (GON)	Groton Arpt. Restaurant
5	Meriden	Meriden Markham Muni. (MMK)	Mr. D's Restaurant
6	Windsor Locks	Bradley Intl. Arpt. (BDL)	Concorde at Sheraton

Articles

City or town	Nearest Airport and Identifier	Name of Attraction
Groton, CT	Groton-New London (GON)	Mystic Seaport Museum
Groton, CT	Groton-New London (GON)	Nautilus Memorial & Museum
Windsor Locks, CT	Bradley Intl. (BDL)	New England Air Museum

LOCATION MAP

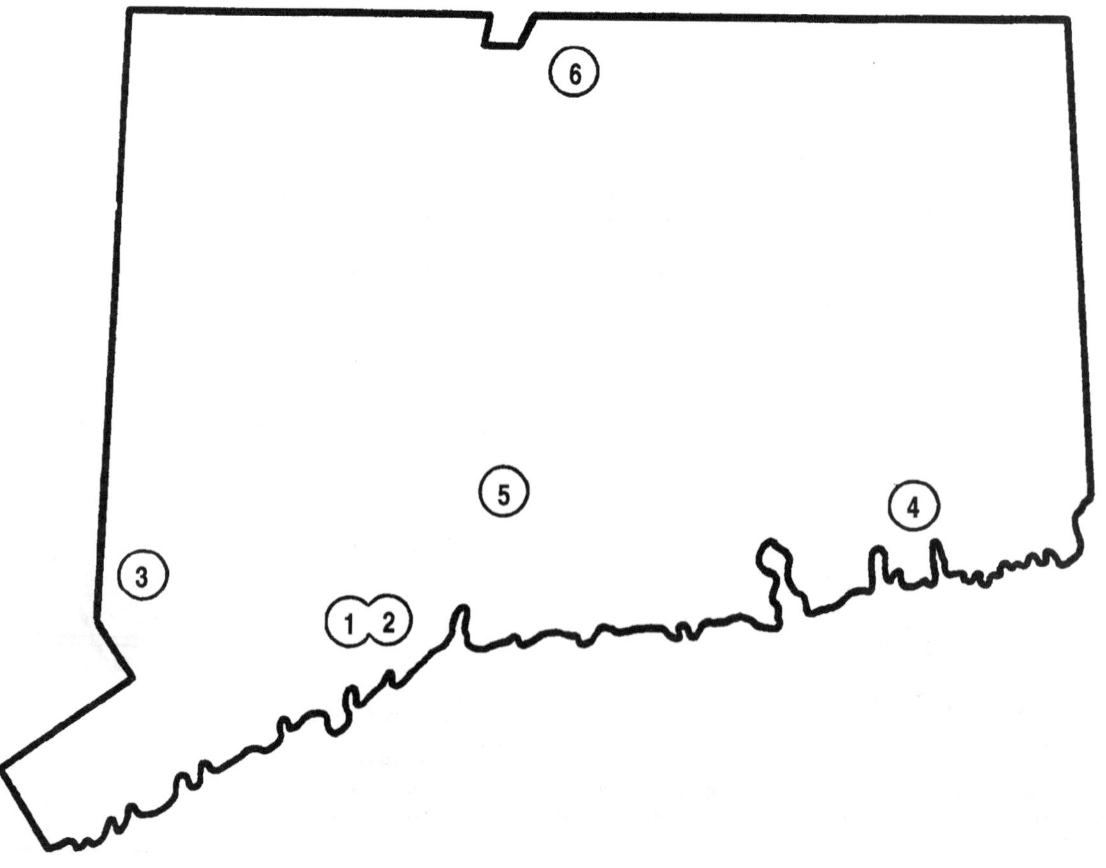

Not to be used for navigational purposes

CT-BDR - BRIDGEPORT
IGOR I. SIKORSKY MEMORIAL

(Area Code 203) **1, 2**

Windsock Restaurant:

The Windsock Restaurant is about 100 yards from the Bridgeport Air Center (FBO). This cafe is open between 10 a.m. and 2 p.m. on the north side of the airport. This is a small cafe and bar. Specialties of the house include hamburgers, hotdogs, turkey clubs, and chili. They also have a selection of sandwiches. The restaurant resembles a Cape Cod Home. It used to be the airport managers house. Groups of 15 or 20 people can be accommodated. For more information call the Windsock at 378-9117.

Wing's Restaurant:

The Wings Restaurant is located on the Sikorsky Memorial Airport. Pilots can park their aircraft near the restaurant. This restaurant and tavern is reported to be open from 11 a.m. to 1 a.m. Their main dining room can seat 60 people. On weekends they feature specials. Along with meal selections appetizers, salad and soup of the day is available. For information call 378-4009.

Restaurants Near Airport:

Windsock Restaurant	On Site	Phone: 378-9117
Wing's Restaurant	On Site	Phone: 378-4009

Lodging: Hilton (Free trans) 344-1234; Marriott (Shuttle available) 378-1400.

Meeting Rooms: Hilton 344-1234; Marriott (Conventions facilities available) 378-1400.

Transportation: Taxi Service: Suburban Limo 377-8294; Also Rental Cars: Avis 377-7390; Hertz 378-0513; National 800-227-7368

Information: Bridgeport Area Chamber of Commerce, 10 Middle Street, Bridgeport, CT 06604, Phone: 335-3800.

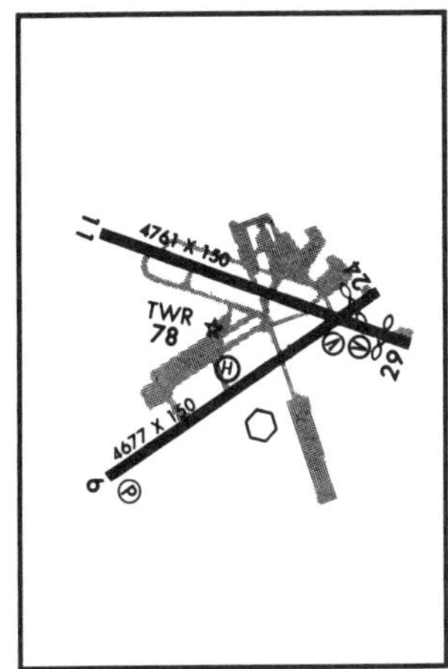

Airport Information:

BRIDGEPORT - IGOR I. SIKORSKY MEMORIAL AIRPORT (BDR)
3 mi southeast of town N41-09.81 W73-07.57 Elev: 10 Fuel: 100LL, Jet-A
Rwy 11-29: H4761x150 (Asph) Rwy 06-24: H4677x150 (Asph) Attended: 1130-0400Z
Atis: 119.15 Unicom: 123.0 Tower: 120.9 Gnd Con: 121.9 Clnc Del: 121.75

FBO: Bridgeport Air Center	**Phone: 375-3329**
FBO: Million Air Bridgeport	**Phone: 377-1100**
FBO: Three Wing Corportation	**Phone: 375-5795**

CT-DXR - DANBURY
DANBURY MUNICIPAL AIRPORT

(Area Code 203) **3**

Moon Dance:

During our interview, this restaurant was receiving new management. Service may vary from the following description. This Restaurant is located on the Danbury Municipal Airport, and is situated along the runway with available parking for transient aircraft. This combination family style and fine dining establishment is open from 11:30 a.m. to 1 a.m. 7 days a week. A variety of favorite entrees include Pasta Primavera, stuffed chicken, Oriental chicken, Cajun fried chicken, shrimp plates, barbecued ribs, Terioki steak, surf and turf, lobster and filet mignon. This restaurant attracts many fly-in customers from all over, and is located within a large hangar which gives this facility a unique appearance. Large 6'x 10' windows allow costumers to see all the activity on the airport while they are enjoying their meal. Seating capacity is around 74 persons in their main dining room. (Groups and parties often fly-in to visit this establishment). A special buffet can be prepared if advance notice is given. Their lounge, located in the lower level of the building, offers live entertainment 6 nights a week from Tuesday through Sunday. For more information about the Moon Dance call 744-4471.

Restaurants Near Airport:

Moon Dance	On Site	Phone: 744-4471

Lodging: Ethan Allen Inn (Free trans) 744-1776; Hilton Inn (Shuttle) 794-0600.

Meeting Rooms: Ethan Allen Inn 744-1776; Hilton Inn (Convention facilities) 794-0600.

Transportation: Taxi Service: Yellow Cab 744-7492; Rental Cars: Avis 744-5450; Hertz 743-6773; National 798-2937.

Information: Housatonic Valley Tourism Commission, 72 West Street, Danbury, CT 06810, Phone: 743-0546.

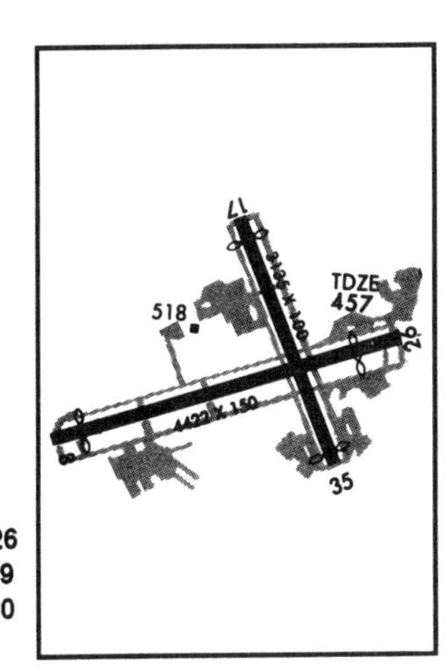

Airport Information:

DANBURY - DANBURY MUNICIPAL AIRPORT (DXR)
3 mi southwest of town N41-22.29 W73-28.93 Elev: 458 Fuel: 80, 100LL, Jet-A
Rwy 08-26: H4422x150 (Asph-Grvd) Rwy 17-35: H3135x100 (Asph) Attended 1200Z-dusk
Atis: 127.75 Unicom: 122.95 Clnc Del: 128.6 Tower: 119.4 Gnd Con: 121.6
Public Phone 24hrs Notes: No landing fees, each FBO has own policy on parking fees.

FBO: Bluebird Aviation	**Phone: 798-7565**	**FBO: Master Aviation**	**Phone: 790-5226**
FBO: Business Arcft Cntr	**Phone: 748-7000**	**FBO: New England Acrft**	**Phone: 748-1449**
FBO: Conn Mooney	**Phone: 744-5010**	**FBO: Reliant Acrft Serv**	**Phone: 743-5100**
FBO: Executive Air Serv, Inc.	**Phone: 790-6800**		

CT-GON - GROTON-NEW LONDON
GROTON-NEW LONDON AIRPORT

(Area Code 860) 4

Groton Airport Restaurant:

The Groton Airport Restaurant is located in the terminal building on the Groton New London Airport. This family style restaurant is open between 5:30 a.m. to 9 p.m. 7 days a week (Closed Christmas). Their menu is extensive and contains specialties like appetizers, roast sirloin of beef, fried chicken, all types of pasta dishes, seafood, chicken salad plate, tuna salad plate, and Greek salads. They also provide different types of sandwiches including club sandwiches. Daily specials are always offered with up to 4 different choices to pick from. The main dining room can seat 84 persons and displays an airport theme. Beige and brown colored walls and many photographs of aircraft add to the atmosphere. Large picture windows allow guests a great view of the airplanes taking off and landing. Groups and parties are also welcome. Please let them know in advance if your group is large. This restaurant can also prepare box lunches and carry-out meals. In addition they also provide a service with catered meals to "U.S. Air". For more information call the Groton Airport Restaurant at 445-9299.

Restaurants Near Airport:
Groton Airport Restaurant On Site Phone: 445-9299

Lodging: Best Western (2-1/2 miles) 445-8000; Gold Star Inn (Resort like activities available) 446-0660; Groton Motor Inn (2 miles) 445-7435; Mystic Hilton Hotel (3 miles) 572-0731; Quality Inn (2 miles) 445-8141; Radisson Hotel (2-1/2 miles) 443-7000.
Meeting Rooms: Gold Star Inn (Resort activities) 446-0660; Quality Inn 445-8140.
Transportation: Taxi service is available, also rental cars: Avis 445-8585; Hertz 446-1200; National 445-7435;
Information: Southeastern Connecticut Tourism District, 27 Masonic Street, P.O. Box 89, New London, CT 06320, Phone: 444-2206 or 800-222-6783.

Attractions:

Mystic Seaport, a 17-acre living history museum is located only 5 miles from Groton, New London Airport. Phone: 860-572-5317.
(See article next page)

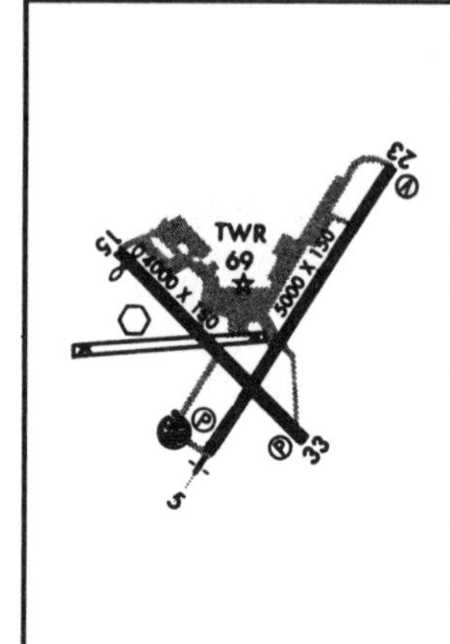

Airport Information:

GROTON-NEW LONDON - GROTON-NEW LONDON AIRPORT (GON)
3 mi southeast N41-19.80 W72-02.71 Elev: 10 Fuel: 100LL, Jet-A
Rwy 05-23: H5000x150 (Asph) Rwy 15-33: H4000x150 (Asph) Attended: May-Oct 1200-0400Z, Nov-Apr 1200-0200Z Atis: 127.0 Unicom: 122.95 Groton Tower: 125.6
Gnd Con: 121.65
FBO: Columbia Air Services, Inc. Phone: 449-1257

Mystic Seaport Museum

Photo by: Judy Beisler
Mystic Seaport Museum

A small part of the waterfront at Mystic Seaport Museum offers a scenic view.

Mystic Seaport, a 17-acre living history museum, is located 5 miles from the Groton-New London Airport in Mystic, Connecticut. The museum stands on a site along the Mystic River that was once lined with ship and boat building yards in the 19th century. Mystic Seaport is open year-round, except Christmas Day. It is a non-profit, educational, maritime museum that is dedicated to preserving American maritime history and its influence on the economic, social and cultural life of the United States. Primary emphasis is on the maritime commerce of the Atlantic coast during the 19th century. There are 60 historic buildings, including homes, shops, and workplaces. The museum is an indoor and outdoor maritime museum which includes: historic ships, boats, a nationally renowned research library, a planetarium, and exhibit galleries.

Historically, the community of Mystic was a shipbuilding center. Mystic shipyards produced some of the fastest clippers, such as the "David Crockett" which made an average over 25 runs around Cape Horn to San Francisco. Mystic is not a town in itself. It is a fire district comprised of sections of the town of Groton on the west bank of the Mystic River and the town of Stonington on the east.

Three major vessels lie at Mystic Seaport wharves and docks where they may be boarded by visitors. The "Charles W. Morgan," (1841) is a National Historic Landmark and America's last surviving wooden whaleship. The "Joseph Conrad," (1882) is a full-rigged training ship which is used in the Seaport's educational programs. The "L. A. Dunton," (1921) is a fishing schooner. Another fine vessel, the steamboat "Sabino," (1908) carries one of the last coal-fired steam engines. It makes passenger runs, including group charters, from mid-May through mid-October on the Mystic River. While on board, crew members tell passengers about "Sabino's" history and the history of the Mystic River. More than 400 small craft, the largest such collection in the United States and one of the largest in the world, are also preserved at Mystic Seaport. Many of the vessels are on display in the Small Boat Exhibit and the North Boat Shed. Some of the smaller vessels are afloat at the museum's docks, including the Noank smack, "Emma C. Berry," the Friendship sloop, "Estell A.," the oyster sloop, "Nellie" and the 1926 fishing dragger, "Florence,"

Several large buidings are devoted to the display of maritime art and artifacts. The three-story Stillman Building contains ship models, paintings and scrimshaw. The coastal life area is intended to give visitors an impression of 19th century seafaring communities. The skills of some of the maritime trades are demonstrated in the shipsmith shop, ship carver's shop and cooperage. Other buildings in this area include: the bank, shipping office, grocery and hardware store, chapel, schoolhouse, rope walk, nautical instrument store, ship chandlery, Thomas Oyster House and New Shoreham Lifesaving Station, Robie Ames Fish House and much, much more. Many of the shops and homes were brought to the area from locations in Mystic or from other locations around New England.

The Children's Museum provides a hands-on environment for children and their parents to explore together. Children of ages 7 and under can swab the deck, move cargo, cook in the galley, dress in sailors' garb and sleep in sailors' bunks.

The Henry B. duPont Preservation Shipyard is a unique and world famous facility which has the equipment and craftsmen required to perform any task in the restoration and preservation of wooden vessels. The shipyard consists of a large main shop, in which a visitors' galley overlooks carpenters' shops, an 85-foot spar lathe, a rigging loft and a large open area where vessels are brought indoors for repair. A paint shop and metal working shop, documentation shop, lumber shed and saw mill are nearby. Central to the facility is a 375-ton capacity lift dock that is capable of raising any of the museum's ships out of the water for repair.

Another highlight of Mystic Seaport is the Planetarium. Since early times, navigators have used the heavenly bodies to determine their ship's position at sea. Even in this electronic age, mariners rely on celestial navigation for position finding. Daily programs in the Planetarium illustrate the night sky for visitors. Groups of children or adults may, by arrangement with the Education Department, have special presentations in the Planetarium. Each year, its staff offers classes in celestial navigation, piloting, dead reckoning, and astronomy for adults and an astronomy class for children.

The G. W. Blunt White Library specializes in American maritime history. It contains more than 560,000 manuscripts and charts. Some of the more unusual items include: a large collection of ships' log-books, the complete New York Maritime Register and an extensive rare books collection.

The Seaport also features the Small Boat Shop which encourages visitors to learn how to construct small sailing and rowing boats. Replicas of historically significant small craft are built by the staff for use on the Mystic River and for the instruction and demonstration of boat-building techniques. The annual Small Craft Workshop, a two-day gathering of traditional boat owners, professional and amateur builders and enthusiasts, allows participants to compare boats and ideas, and to learn more about wooden small craft construction and use. In addition, Mystic Seaport offers a variety of special educational programs in maritime history and other fields of maritime interest. A film presentation on the 19th-century whaling industry, <u>Whales, Whaling and Whalemen</u>, is given daily during the spring and fall. Demonstrations of sail setting and furling, whaleboat rowing and sailing, chanty singing, a breeches buoy rescue drill, fish splitting, salting and drying and open hearth cooking may be seen most of the year on the grounds or on the Mystic River. At specified times, staff will roleplay 19th century characters in one of the village exhibits.

Each year, more than 130 programs and activities take place at Mystic Seaport. Special events include: the Lobsterfest Weekend in May, the Sea Music Festival in June, The Antique & Classic Boat Rondezvous in July, the Schooner Race in September, and the Christmas tours in December.

Hungry visitors have a choice of restaurants at Mystic Seaport. The Seamen's Inne Restaurant, located near mystic Seaport's north entrance, serves lunch and dinner throughout the year. The Samuel Adams Pub offers hearty drinks and entertainment. During the summer, meals are served on the terrace. Private parties, meetings, receptions and summer clambakes may be arranged through the Seaman's Inne Staff. The Galley Restaurant, located near the south green on the museum's grounds, offers fast food service year-round. The menu includes: lobster-in-the- rough, chowder, sea food, as well as hamburgers and hot dogs. Groups can enjoy a clambake served at Lighthouse Point, also located on the museum's grounds. They can also choose from a variety of menus for a custom-catered dinner, luncheon, or cocktail reception. Arrangements can be made through the museum's Catering Department.

The Groton-New London Airport has a 4000'x150 and a 5000'x150 asphalt runway. The airport also provides Avis, Budget, Enterprise, and National rental car services. Taxi service is also available. Contact the FBO at 860-448-1001, 8 a.m. to 6 p.m. during the winter and 8 a.m. to 8 p.m. during the summer, or call 860-449-1257, 5 a.m. to 9 p.m. for further assistance. For more information about Mystic Seaport, call 860-572-5317. (Information submitted by Mystic Seaport).

Nautilus Memorial and Submarine Force Library and Museum

The Nautilus Memorial is located 3 miles from the Groton-New London Airport, and is situated on the Thames River in Groton, Connecticut. The U.S.S. Nautilus is the world's first nuclear-powered submarine and the first ship to go to the North Pole. It is a National Historic landmark and Connecticut's State Ship. The submarine is open year-round, except for Thanksgiving, Christmas, New Year's, and the first full week of May and first two full weeks of December. People of all ages, especially students, will enjoy touring this great attraction.

Upon entering the museum grounds, the first outdoor object that visitors are likely to notice is the large freestanding metal ring, which is a cross-section of the largest portion of the hull of a modern Trident submarine. To the left of the ring, there is a hatch cover and upper portion of a Poseidon missile tube from a missile-carrying submarine. Visitors will also notice that there are four midget submarines that extend from the museum entrance to the river. The Maile submarine is an Italian, WWII swimmer delivery vehicle on which frogmen would ride. Simon Lake's Explorer is an American submarine that was designed to recover items from wrecks and to mine the ocean floor. The German "Seehund" is a German submarine from WWII. Trucks carried Seehunds along the coast until a likely target would be found.The Seehund would then be launched for its attack. The Japanese "Type A" is a short range, two man submarine that was carried by larger ships to its areas of operation. It was usually unsuccessful in its missions.

Once visitors have seen the fascinating outdoor attractions, it is time for them to step inside of the museum's eye-catching interior. In the foyer, a replica of Jules Verne's "Nautilus" from the 1954 Walt Disney movie, 20,000 Leagues Under the Sea, hangs from the ceiling. The mural is taken from an illustration in the first edition of 20,000 Leagues Under the Sea that was published in Paris in 1870. In the main hall, overhead are a series of orange cloth panels (scale, not actual size) that represent cross-sections of Nautilus' hull. The propeller and stern section are closest to the main entrance. Also, in the main hall, visitors will see the interior of a green torpedo that submarines used in the 1960s and 1970s. On the left of the hall are two exhibit rooms. The first consists of a re-created World War II submarine attack center, where visitors can look through three periscopes and see the U.S.S. Nautilus, the Thames River, objects as far out as the museum parking lot, and they might even see one of the Navy's newest

Photo by: Nautilus Memorial Museum

Full view of the Nautilus Memorial and Submarine Force Library and Museum.

nuclear submarines. They will also hear a tape which simulates a World War II torpedo attack by a submarine. The second room recreates a submarine control room where visitors will find the equipment that controlled diving and surfacing, while again listening to a short tape describing the sequence followed in making a dive.

On the right of the main hall is a wall of models of the major types of submarines, ranging from U.S.S. Holland(SS-1), built in 1900, to the present Trident submarines. All models are the same scale. To the right of the Model Wall is the Main Exhibit floor with a variety of entertaining exhibits, including 2 mini-theatres, illuminated panels, static displays and case exhibits. Both theaters seat approximately 10 people and show a continuous 7 minute program, titled A History of Submarines. The illuminated panels trace the history of the submarine up to the present. There are static displays, such as a full-size replica of the Turtle, the first practical submarine that was invented to attack British warships during the Revolutionary War. The Submarine Messenger Buoy was used in the event of an emergency. It contained a telephone for communicating with the crew in a sunken sub. The case exhibits display photos of early submarines under construction in their shipyards, submarine disasters, such as the sinking of the U.S.S. Squalus in 1939 and the development of the fleet boat - the primary type of United States sub used in WWII. A wall mural fills each end of the museum with both black-and-white murals and color murals.

Next, visitors will travel up to the second floor and observe two dominant features: The 50-foot cutaway model of the WWII submarine GATO and a display of 57 large photographs, both in black and white and color, of submariners from 1900 to the present. The exhibit floor also includes the Nautilus Room which contains artifacts, photos and drawings of the illustrious career of the world's first nuclear-powered submarine. It also offers a splendid view of the submarine itself, and the Thames River. Visitors will enjoy The People Wall, where they will see up-close pictures of the faces of the men who served on submarines. Also, the exhibit cases give a first-hand glance at the many contributions from the pioneers of submarine development. It also displays the details of everyday life on submarines during WWII. The Groton-New London Airport has a 4000'x150 and a 5000'x150 asphalt runway. The airport also provides Avis, Budget, Enterprise, and National rental car services. Taxi service is also available. Contact the FBO at 448-1001, 8 a.m. to 6 p.m. during the winter and 8 a.m. to 8 p.m. during the summer, or call 449-1257, 5 a.m. to 9 p.m. for further assistance. For more information about the Nautilus Memorial, call 800-343-0079 or 449-3174. During the summer (mid-April to mid-October), the hours are from 9 a.m. to 5 p.m., daily, except for Tuesdays from 1 p.m. to 5 p.m. During the winter (mid-October to mid-April), the hours are from 9 a.m. to 4 p.m. daily, and closed Tuesdays. (Information submitted by the Nautilus Memorial and Submarine Force Library and Museum)

CT-MMK - MERIDEN
MERIDEN MARKHAM MUNICIPAL

(Area Code 203)

5

Mr. D's Restaurant:

Mr. D's Restaurant is located about 1 mile north of the Meriden Markham Municipal Airport. Although this establishment does not furnish courtesy transportation to and from the airport, Meriden Aviation Services, Inc. (FBO) can provide this service for their customers. Taxi service is also available. This fine dining restaurant is open between 3 p.m. and 10 p.m. 5 days a week, Sunday from 2 p.m. to 8 p.m. and is closed on Monday. Their menu includes veal dishes, chicken, egg plant, steaks, pork chops, linguine with white or red clam sauce, Shrimp Francese, as well as many other delicous items. Average prices run between $5.95 and $13.95 for most selections. Their main dining area has tables and booths and can seat up to 120 persons. It is decorated with many plants and brass items. Groups are always welcome, and meals can also be prepared for carry-out if requested. For more information call Mr. D's Restaurant at 235-1967.

Restaurants Near Airport:

Britannia Spoon	1.5 mi E.	Phone: 265-6199
Mr. D's Restaurant	1 mi N.	Phone: 235-1967
Romano's	1.5 mi S.	Phone: N/A

Lodging: Comfort Inn (Free trans) 276-0736; Days Inn 238-1211; Howard Johnson (Shuttle) 628-0921; Ramada Inn (Free trans) 238-2380.

Meeting Rooms: Comfort Inn 276-0736; Howard Johnson 628-0921; Ramada Inn 238-2300.

Transportation: Meriden Aviation Services, Inc. can provide courtesy transportation to nearby facilities 238-4400; Also Yellow Cab 235-4434.

Information:
Meriden City Hall, 142 E. Main Street, Phone: 630-4105.

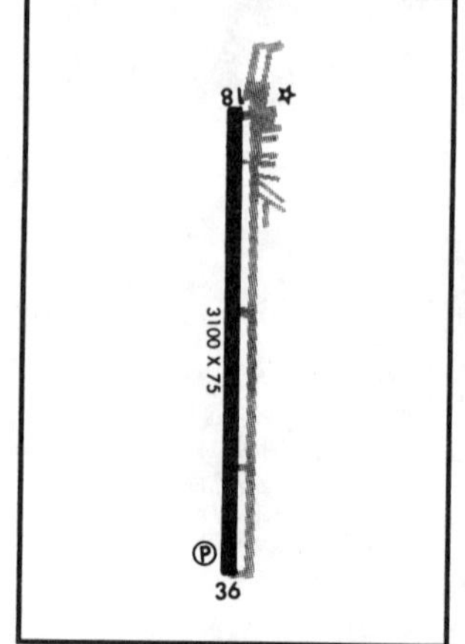

Airport Information:

MERIDEN - MERIDEN MARKHAM MUNICIPAL AIRPORT (MMK)
3 mi southwest of town N41-30.52 W72-49.77 Elev: 103 Fuel: 100LL
Rwy 18-36: H3100x75 (Asph) Attended: 1300Z-dusk Unicom: 122.8 Public Phone 24hrs
Notes: Overnight parking $5.00, Full maintenance facilities are available at this field.
FBO: Meriden Aviation Services, Inc. Phone: 238-4400

CT-BDL - WINDSOR LOCKS BRADLEY INTERNATIONAL ARPT.

(Area Code 203) 6

Concorde's At The Sheraton Hotel:

The Concorde's Restaurant is located within the hotel which is conveniently situated as part of the airport terminal building. Coutresy transportation can be obtained either through AMR Combs, Inc. or Bradley Flight Operations, Inc. This fine dining establishment is open for breakfast between 6:30 a.m. and 2 p.m. then re-opens at 5 p.m. to 11 p.m. on weekdays. Hours vary slightly on weekends. Their menu includes a variety of specialty items like filet mignon, swordfish as well as pasta dishes. Average prices for lunch run $7.00 to $8.00 and around $10.00 to $20.00 for most dinner selections. A breakfast buffet is featured between 6:30 a.m. and 10:30 a.m. for only $8.95. On Sunday they also furnish a brunch between 10:30 a.m. and 2 p.m. as well. Seating capacity in their main dining room is 123 people. There are two large 10'x 30' window panels that provide a paneromic view of the airport and active runway system. The Sheraton Hotel, in addition to the restaurant, contains 237 rooms for overnight travelers. For more information about this convenient airport establishment call 627-5311.

Attractions:

New England Air Museum is located right on the Bradley International Airport. Also the Connecticut Trolly Museum is situated on North Road (Rt 140) in East Windsor, CT aprox 10 miles from the field.

Restaurants Near Airport:

Concorde's at the Sheraton	On Site	Phone: 627-5311
Host International, Inc.	On Site	Phone: 627-3670
Passport International Cafe	1/8 mi N.	Phone: 623-2370
Skyline Restaurant	1/8 mi E.	Phone; 623-9296

Lodging: Sheraton Hotel Airport (On Site) 627-5311; Howard Johnson Conference Center (Free trans) 623-9811; Ramada Inn (Free trans) 623-9411; Ramada Inn Bradley (Free trans, near airport) 623-9494; Holiday Inn (Free trans, near airport) 627-5171.

Meeting Rooms: Sheraton Hotel Airport (On Site) 627-5311; Howard Johnson Conference Center 623-9811; Ramada Inn 623-9411; Ramada Inn Bradley 623-9494; Holiday Inn 627-5171.

Transportation: Travelers can arrange courtesy transportation through AMR Combs, Inc. by calling 627-3300 or Bradley Flight Operations at 623-0087. Also Airport Taxi Co. 627-3210; Alamo 627-7732; Avis 627-3500; Budget 627-3660; Dollar 627-9048; Hertz 627-3850; National 627-3470.

Information: Tobacco Valley Convention & Visitors District, 111 Hazard Avenue, Enfield CT 06082, Phone: 623-2578; or Windsor Lock Chamber of Commerce, P.O. Box 257, Windsor Locks, Ct 06096, Phone: 860-623-9319.

Airport Information:

WINDSOR LOCKS - BRADLEY INTERNATIONAL AIRPORT (BDL)
3 mi west of town N41-56.33 W72-40.99 Elev: 174 Fuel: 100LL, Jet-A
Rwy 06-24: H9502x200 (Asph-Grvd) Rwy 15-33: H6846x150 (Asph) Rwy 01-19: H5141x100 (Asph) Attended: continuously Atis: 118.15 Unicom: 122.95
Bradley App Con: 125.8 Bradley Dep Con: 127.8, 125.35, 123.95 Tower: 120.3 Gnd Con: 121.9
Clnc Del: 121.75 Public Phone 24hrs Notes: Variable landing fees by weight calss - $14.00 per 24 hour parking fee.
FBO: AMR Combs, Inc. **Phone: 627-3300**
FBO: Bradley Flight Operations, Inc. **Phone: 623-3940**

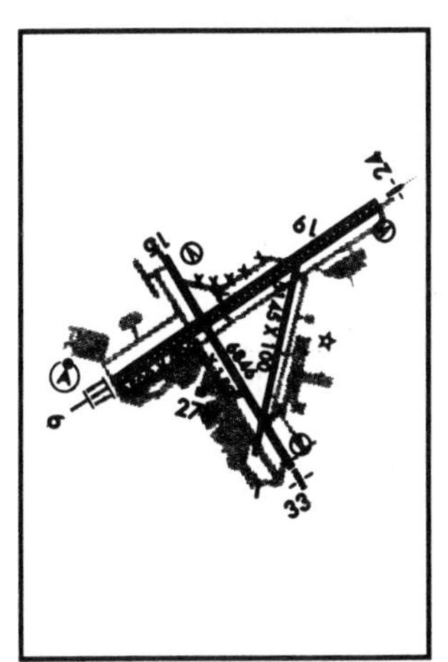

New England Air Museum

The New England Air Museum is located on the north side of the Bradley International Airport (BDL). The museum had its beginning back in the 1960s in a vintage hangar that was donated by the Connecticut Department of Transportation. Then on October 3, of 1979, it was all wiped out. A tornado, packing winds of 150 miles per hour, destroyed a good part of the collection and rendered the hangar unusable. A fabulous museum was reduced to a pile of rubble.

With a lot of help and backing from individuals who cared, and from a large number of area businesses, a new (rebuilt) museum emerged. Just two years after the tornado, the museum opened a 38,000 square foot exhibition building and in 1989 a new 11,000 square foot restoration building was erected.

The museum is a bright cheery place with a wide variety of aircraft on display. Over 42 different types of aircraft and helicopters are featured including many gliders, homebuilts, and civil aircraft as well as military fighters like the famous Mig-15, F-100A Super Sabre, F-105B Thunderchief, Republic P-47 Thunderbolt, XF4U-4 Corsair, Grumman FM-2 Wildcat, F-4B Phantom II and a B-29 bomber are all available to see up close. Ten of the aircraft within the museum are one-of-a-kind treasures. Included in the World War I collection is a Fokker DR-1, Tri-plane (made famous by the Red Baron), and a trophy winning racing aircraft the Marcoux-Bromberg Special which was featured in the movie "Test Pilot" with Clark Gable.

There are several exhibits available for viewing, including the comprehensive accomplishments of aviation pioneer Igor I. Sikorsky. Films are played throughout the day and there is always a guide available to offer information and answer any of your questions. A jet fighter cockpit simulator is also open for children.

The museum runs a number of special events on weekends throughout the year including "Open Cockpit Weekends", several auto shows which are co-sponsored with regional car clubs. Special group tours can be reserved by telephone.

Before leaving, you will want to browse through the gift shop. It's a wonderful place that has posters, prints, models, books for children and adult, toys and souvenirs on sale.

Photo by: New England Air Museum — Guided tours are also provide

The museum is easy to reach by car and even easier to reach by plane, as it is situated on the north edge of the airport. Traveling by car, it's only minutes off I-91. From I-91 take exit 40 to Route 20 and then to Route 75. If planning to fly in to visit the museum, you can park your aircraft at AMR Combs (FBO) and courtesy transportation to the New England Air Museum can easily be obtained.

Hours for the museum are 10:00 a.m. to 5:00 p.m. 7 days a week, year around, except on Christmas and Thanksgiving day. Admission is $5.50 for adults, $2.00 for children between 6 and 11 years of age. Groups rates are available upon request. For a schedule or calendar of events featuring "Open Cockpit Days", tours or antique auto shows held each year, you can call the museum at 860-623-3305. (Information submitted by museum).

Photo by: New England Air Museum — A one-of-a-kind Laird Solition is exhibited

DELAWARE

CROSS FILE INDEX

Location Number	City or Town	Airport Name And Identifier	Name of Attraction
1	Georgetown	Sussex County Arpt. (GED)	Rehoboth Beach
2	Wilmington	New Castle Co. Arpt. (ILG)	Air Transport Command

LOCATION MAP

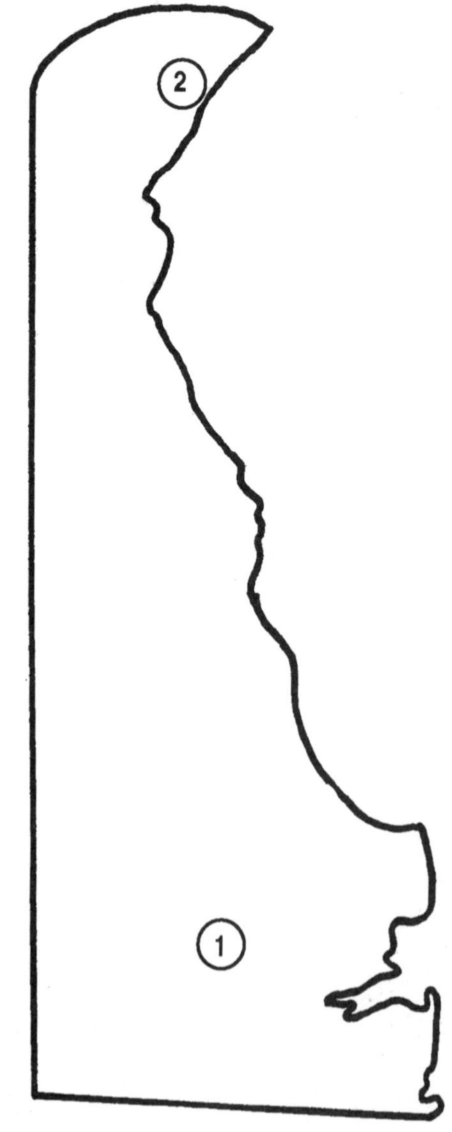

DE-GED - GEORGETOWN SUSSEX COUNTY AIRPORT

(Area Code 302)

1

Rehoboth Beach:

Rehoboth Beach, located in the southeastern portion of Delaware, offers plenty of deep-sea and freshwater fishing, sailing, swimming, biking, dining, shopping and strolling along the Mile-Long Boardwalk. There are several types of accommodations, including hotels, motels, inns and bed and breakfasts. For those who are planning a longer stay, the beach also offers apartments, cottages and condominiums. To help familiarize you with the area, Twin Capes Nature Tours offers several walking tours of Rehoboth each day. The tours explore its plant and animal life, as well as its culture and history. For more information, call 227-5850. Rehoboth Bay offers ideal conditions for deep-sea fishing, small boating, sailing and water skiing. Any area bait and tackle shop will help guests plan their fishing outings. No license is required for tidal waters. Boating and water skiing information can be obtained from any of the local marinas. Biking is a great way to explore the streets of Rehoboth Beach. There are bicycle rentals available. From May 15 to September 15, riding on the Boardwalk may be done between 5:00 a.m. to 10:00 a.m. only. If you enjoy clamming and crabbing, clams and crabs can be found in special locations around Rehoboth Bay. It is recommended that you check with the Delaware Natural Resources and Environmental Control Enforcement Section for proper locations and prohibited shellfish area. Call 739-3440 for more information. You can also go bay fishing and crabbing on Captain K's 49-passenger vessel "Sand Dollar" which departs from Rehoboth Bay Marina. Call 945-3345 for departure times and information. Speaking of seafood, there are plenty of restaurants which serve a variety of fresh seafood, as well as traditional American dishes and international fare. Entertainment for all ages can be found on Rehoboth Beach. The amusements on the Boardwalk are fun for everyone, particularly the young ones. Children's playgrounds, geared to 8-year-olds and younger, are found at Rehoboth's Lake Gerar Park. Throughout the area there are waterslides, go-carts and many other sports activities, such as golfing, surfing, swimming, parasailing, horseback riding and tennis. There is also nightly entertainment at the local restaurants and cocktail lounges. Shopping areas are located in downtown Rehoboth Beach. You will enjoy small town unique specialty shopping, factory outlets and malls. All purchases in Delaware are tax free. The Sussex County Airport is located 2 miles southeast of the center of town. For ground transportation, the Park "N" Ride Transit System runs between Memorial Day and Labor Day, making intermittent stops in the center of town and at the Boardwalk. Call 226-2001. The Jolly Trolley of Rehoboth runs between Rehoboth and Dewey Beaches with stops throughout the area every 30 minutes or less, depending on traffic. Call 227-1197. Also, the Cape May-Lewes Ferry can take you on a scenic trip across the wide mouth of the Delaware Bay. Call 800-64-FERRY (33779) for more information. For more information about activities, rates and accommodations in Rehoboth Beach, call the Rehoboth Beach-Dewey Beach Chamber of Commerce at 800-441-1329 or 227-2233.

Restaurants Near Airport:

Blue Gold Inn	(1 mile)	Phone: 856-7772
Georgetown House	(1 mile)	Phone: 856-6815

Lodging: Classic Motel (2 miles) 856-7532; Atlantic Budget Inn (10 miles) 227-0401; Hickman's Motel (10 miles) 934-8091; Henlopen Hotel (12 miles) 227-2551

Meeting Rooms: Henlopen Hotel 227-2551

Transportation: Rental Cars: Practical 856-4520

Information: Rehoboth Beach-Dewey Beach Chamber of Commerce, 501 Rehoboth Avenue, P.O. Box 216, Rehoboth Beach, DE 19971, Phone: 800-441-1329 or 227-2233

Nearby Attractions:

Mile-Long Boardwalk, Jolly Rover Tall Ship Cruises, train rides (Queen Anne's Railroad), parks, nature cruises, dolphin and whale watching (Fisherman's Wharf), ferry rides (Cape May-Lewes Ferry), and narrated tours (Jolly Trolly of Rehoboth Beach). For more information, call 800-441-1329 or 227-2233.

Airport Information:

GEORGETOWN - SUSSEX COUNTY AIRPORT (GED)

2 mi southeast N38-41.35 W75-21.54 Elev: 51 Fuel: 100LL, Jet-A Rwy 04-22: H5000x150 (Asph) Rwy 13-31: H2325x50 (Conc) Attended: 1200-0400Z CTAF/Unicom: 123.0 Dover App/Dep Con: 128.0 Clnc Del: 125.55 Notes: Parachute jumping in area.

FBO: Delmarva Aircraft, Inc.	**Phone: 855-2355**
Laurel Aero Services, Inc.	**Phone: 855-0326**
Sussex Aero Maintenance, Inc.	**Phone: 856-7059**

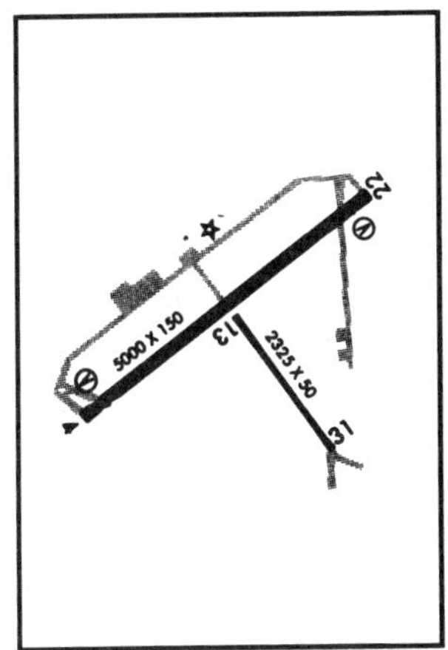

DE-ILG - WILMINGTON NEW CASTLE COUNTY AIRPORT

(Area Code 302)

2

Air Transport Command:

This fine dining facility is located about 500 to 800 feet south of the tower at the New Castle County Airport. The restaurant opens its doors on Monday through Saturday from 11 a.m. to 1 a.m. and Sunday from 10 a.m. to 1 a.m. Specialized entrees include mushrooms in a skillet, beer cheese soup, veal, beef, steak, chops, prime rib, seafood and poultry. All desserts are made on the premises. This restaurant has daily lunch and dinner creations as well as a Sunday brunch buffet. Average prices run $14.95 for brunch, $6.95 for lunch and $16.95 for dinner. An aviation theme dominates the restaurant, with an old Scottish farm house replica with WW-II artifacts, Big Band music in the background, and a panoramic view overlooking the Wilmington Airport. White tablecloths and fine service add to the ambiance of your dining experience. This restaurant can handle up to 150 persons for parties and groups, with banquet menus available upon request. For information call 328-3527.

Restaurants Near Airport:

Air Transport Command	1/4 mi	Phone: 328-3527
Arner's Family Rest.	1/4 mi	Phone: 322-3279
Dutch Pantry	Adj Trml	Phone: 322-4467
Perfect Affair Rest.	On Site	Phone: 328-5562

Lodging: Skyways Motel, 153 N. DuPont Highway, (Walking Dist.) Phone: 328-6666; Christiana Hilton, Phone: 454-1500; Radisson Hotel (10 minute ride), Phone: 655-0400; Christiana Hotel, Phone: 454-1500.

Conference Rooms: Radisson Hotel (See Lodging); Christiana Hotel (See Lodging)

Transportation: Courtesy Cars Available (See FBO's listed); Avis 322-2092; National, 800-227-7368; Yellow Cab, 656-8151.

Attractions:

The historical downtown district of New Castle along Delaware Street, contains a host of interesting buildings, restaurants, pubs, museums and lodging establishments. It is reported less than three miles east from the New Castle County Airport, in Wilmington, DE. Transportation can be obtained by taxi or rental cars. For information call the airport at 322-7423.

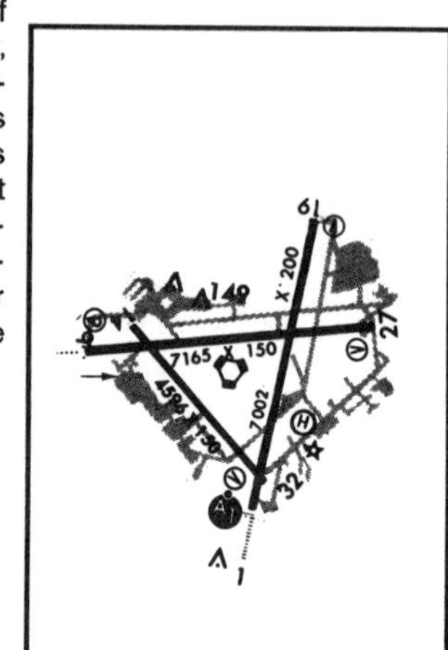

Airport Information:

WILMINGTON - NEW CASTLE CO. AIRPORT (ILG)

4 mi south of town 39-40-42N 75-36-25W Elev: 80 Fuel: 100LL, Jet-A Rwy 09-27: H7165x150 (ASPH) Rwy 01-19: H7002x200 (ASPH-GRVD) Rwy 14-32: H4596x150 (ASPH)
Attended: continuously Atis: 123.95 Unicom: 122.95 Tower: 126.0 Gnd Con: 121.7
Public Phone 24 hrs

FBO: Atlantic Aviation,	**Phone: 322-7000**
FBO: Dawn Aeronautics,	**Phone: 328-9695**
FBO: Dyer Aircraft Service,	**Phone: 328-0848**

DISTRICT OF COLUMBIA

CROSS FILE INDEX

Location Number	City or Town	Airport Name And Identifier	Name of Attraction
1	Washington	Washington Dulles Intl. Arpt. (IAD)	Host Intl.
2	Washington	Washington Dulles Intl. Arpt. (IAD)	J.W. Steak Hse. Marriott
3	Washington	Washington National Arpt. (DCA)	Innovative Aircourts. Inc.

Articles

City or town	Nearest Airport and Identifier	Name of Attraction
Washington, DC	Washington Natl. (DCA)	Smithsonian Air & Space Mus.

LOCATION MAP

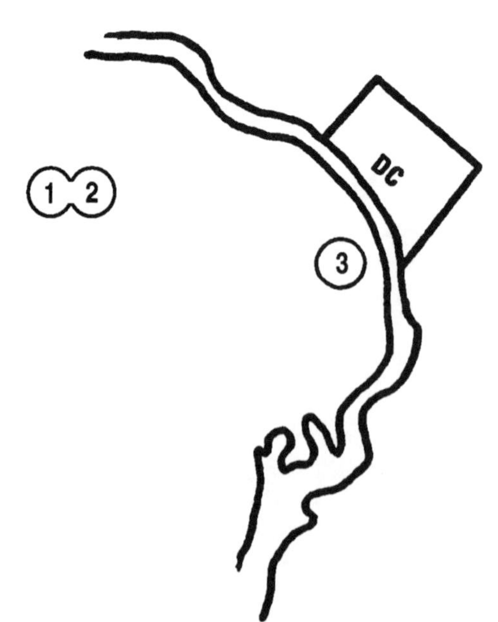

Not to be used for navigational purposes

DC-IAD - WASHINGTON
WASHINGTON DULLES INTL ARPT.

(Area Code 703) 1, 2

Host Intl.:

Host International All Food And Beverage Service, specializes in providing a variety of dining accommodations for the air traveler. Everything from light fare to full service dining establishments are available to those using the Washington Dulles International Airport. Several well known establishment like TGI Friday's restaurant, Burger King, StarBuck Coffee, McDonalds, and Pizza Hut are available. Accommodations for conference rooms can also be arranged for up to 100 persons as well. For information about the Restaurants and meeting room availability call the airport managers office at 661-2710 or 661-2730.

J.W. Steak House (Marriott Hotel):

The Fairfield Inn is located within the Marriott Hotel, which happens to be the only hotel situated directly on the Washington Dullas Airport property. This restaurant can be reached by shuttle sevice either through Page Avejet Aviation Services 471-4450 or Hawthorne-Dulles 661-0150. This family style restaurant is open from 6:30 a.m. to 2 p.m. for lunch and 5 p.m. to 10 p.m. for dinner. Entree selections include specialties like salads, barbecued chicken, rack of lamb, sirloin steaks, grilled salmon, pasta dishes, grilled swordfish, prime rib, filet mignon, and New York strip. Average prices run $8.00 to $10.00 for breakfast, $11.00 for lunch and $14.00 for dinner. A breakfast buffet is also available between 6 a.m. and 10 p.m. Their main dining room can seat 80 people, and is decorated with hand finished wood tables and chairs, chandeliers and etched glass partitions separating the buffet area and the main dining room. Floor to ceiling windows provide a view overlooking flowering Dogwood trees in the foreground. Meals can also be prepared for carry-out. Many people traveling by themselves for private or business reasons, will feel very comfortable dining at the J.W. Steak House. The restaurant is part of the Marriott Hotel which contains 367 guest rooms, 4 suites, 3,500 square feet of conference facilities, 6,000 square feet of ballroom space, and 1,200 feet of outdoor pavilion space. For information about the J.W. Steak House call the Marriott Hotel at 471-9500.

Restaurants Near Airport:

J.W. Steak House Marriott Hotel	On Site	Phone: 471-9500
Host Int'l (All Food/Bev Services)	On Site	Phone: 661-2710
Ramada Renaissance Hotel Rest.	2 mi S.	Phone: 478-2900
Various Local Restaurants Nearby	4 mi E.	Phone: N/A

Lodging: Complimentary shuttle van service to and from main terminal and all local hotel facilities, also contact FBO's for additional information about available transportation; Days Inn (5 miles) 471-6700; Holiday Inn (4 miles) 471-7411; Hyatt (3 miles) 834-1234; Marriott Hotel (On field) 471-9500; Ramada Renaissance (3 miles) 478-2900.

Meeting Rooms: Marriott Hotel (On Site) 471-9500; Also, see hotels listed above for additional meeting and conference accommodations.

Transportation: FBO: (Contact directly for transportation) Page Avjet Aviation Services (Courtesy transportation) 471-4450; Hawthorne (Courtesy transportation) 661-0150; Also Wash. Flyer Taxi 528-4440; Wash Flyer Bus 892-6800; Diplomat Limo 461-6800; Travelers Aid 471-9776; Also taxi on demand 24 hours per day 528-4440. Rental Cars: Avis 800-331-1212; Budget 800-527-0700; Dollar 800-421-6868; Hertz 800-654-3131; National 800-328-4567.

Information: Washington D.C. Convention And Visitors Association, 1212 New York Avenue, Suite 600, Washington, DC 20005, Phone: 202-789-7000.

Attractions:

Contact Fairfax County Parks Authority for park/golf information 246-5700.

Airport Information:

WASHINGTON - WASHINGTON DULLES INTL AIRPORT (IAD)

20 mi west of town N38-56.68 W77-27.35 Elev: 313 Fuel: 100LL, Jet-A

Rwy 01L-19R: H11501x150 (Conc-Grvd) Rwy 01R-19L: H11500x150 (Conc-Grvd)

Rwy 12-30: H10501x150 (Conc-Grvd) Attended: continuously Atis: 134.85

Unicom: 122.95 App Con: 126.1, 124.65, 120.45 Dep Con: 126.65, 125.05

Tower: 120.1 Midfield Ramp Con: 129.55 Gnd Con: 121.9 Clnc Del 127.35

Pre Taxi Clnc: 127.35 Notes: Contact FBO's for fees.

FBO: Hawthorne - Dulles **Phone: 661-0150**

FBO: Signature Flight Support **Phone: 661-0031**

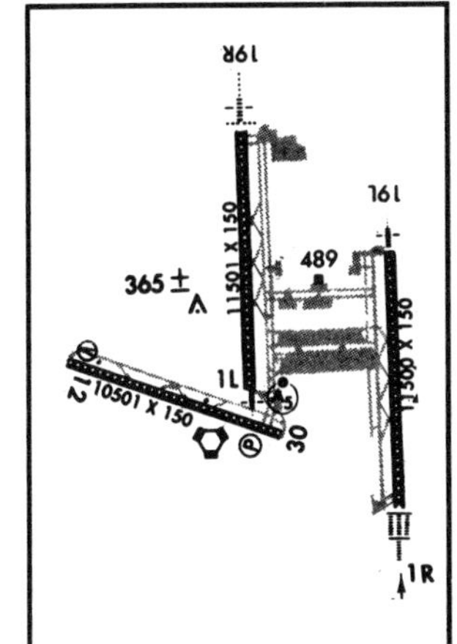

Smithsonian Institution National Air And Space Museum

Articals compiled through information obtained by the National Air And Space Museum.

The Smithsonian's National Air and Space Museum opened in 1976, offers its visitors a dazzling array of flying machines and spacecraft never before assembled in one place. An average of 9 million people visit the museum each year.

Twenty-three exhibit areas house artifacts ranging from the Wright brother's original 1903 Flyer and Lindbergh's "Spirit of St. Louis" to a touchable moon rock and the Skylab Orbital Workshop which visitors may enter.

Also included are dozens of airplanes and spacecraft, missiles and rockets, engines, propellers, models, uniforms, instruments, flight equipment, medals and insignia. These items document most of the major achievements, both historical and technological, of air and space flight.

The Smithsonian's interest in aeronautics dates back to its early years. In 1861, the first Secretary of the Smithsonian, Joseph Henry, recommended to President Lincoln that balloonist Thaddeus Lowe be permitted to demonstrate the potential of the balloon for military observation.

The third Secretary of the Smithsonian, Samuel P. Langley, constructed and tested a number of heavier-than-air models from 1887 to 1903. Two of these unmanned models succeeded in flying under steam power over the Potomac River for more than a half-mile (1 Km).

Interest in rocket research was prompted by Charles Abbot, later the fifth Secretary of the institution, when he supported the early work of the American rocket pioneer Robert H. Goddard. Goddard was one of the first to recognize the potential of the rocket for propelling vehicles through space.

The museum was designed by the architectural firm of Hellmuth, Obata & Kassabaum. The exterior of the 680 foot long by 90 foot tall structure is constructed of Tennessee marble of a pinkish hue. All the aircraft and spacecraft displayed, were actually flown or were used as backup vehicles, unless the label specifically notes an exception.

First Floor Galleries:

Exhibits within the museum are displayed in an array of different galleries. On the first floor, these galleries include: 1) Milestone of Flight from the Wright brother's Flyer and the Spirit of St. Louis to Apollo II and the Viking Lander; 2) Museum Shop; 3) Air Transportation: air transportation of people, mail and cargo; 4) Vertical Flight: helicopters, autogiros and special vehicles; 5) Special Exhibits: rotating exhibition; 6) Golden Age of Flight: history of aviation between the two World Wars (1919-1939); 7) Jet Aviation: traces the evolution of military and commercial jet aircraft; 8) Early Flight: a 1913 indoor air show; 9) South Lobby (Independence Avenue Lobby): aeronautical and astronautical trophies flanked by two large murals - Eric Sloane's "Earthflight En

The Northrop Alpha, seen on display here in the Hall of Air Transportation in the National Air and Space Museum in Washington, D.C., was designed to be a high-performance plane that could carry mail and passengers. The plane was attractive to airlines because of its comparatively high top speed (177 mph for later models) and high reliability. The museum's Alpha, NC11Y, was the third to be built and made its debut in Nov. 1930 (Photo: courtesy of the National Air and Space Museum).

The Winnie Mae, a special Lockheed Model 5C Vega flown by famed aviator Wiley Post, completed two around-the-world record flights and a series of special high-altitude substratospheric research flights, It was named for the daughter of its original owner, F.C. Hall, who hired Post to pilot the Lane, which had been purchased in June 1930. The "Winnie Mae" is new on display in the National Air and Space Museum's Flight Testing Gallery. (Photo: courtesy of the National Air and Space Museum).

vironment" and Robert McCall's "The Space Mural - Cosmic View"; 10) Flight Testing: the history of flight research-research aircraft, flight testing and ground testing; 11) Looking at Earth: Practical uses of aerial photography-from early kite and balloon observations to sophisticated spacecraft and satellite imagery; 12) Stars: a tour of the known universe-from ancient times to the present; 13) Lunar Exploration Vehicles: the Apollo Lunar Module, Lunar Orbiter, Surveyor and Ranger; 14) Rocketry and Space Flight: history of flight from the thirteenth century to the present: rocket engines and space suits; 15) Space Hall: space launch vehicles, manned spacecraft such as the Skylab Orbital Workshop, Apollo-Soyuz and Space Shuttle; and 16) Theater: large-screen motion picture presentations.

Second Floor Galleries:

1) Albert Einstein Planetarium: multimedia presentations; 2) Sea-Air Operations: a history of flight over water, featuring naval aircraft and simulations of an aircraft carrier hangar deck; 3) World War II Aviation: fighter aircraft from five countries; 4) Legend, Memory and the Great War in the Air, on World War I aviation; 5) Exploring Planets: a look at the planets, the tools of exploration and individual space missions. Includes a Voyager spacecraft; 6) Pioneer of Flight: aircraft used on famous first flights and an-exhibit African Americans in aviation; 7) Apollo to the Moon: the triumph of manned space flight, from projected Mercury through the moon landings of the Apollo program; 8) Flight and the Arts: works by leading artists that encompass the theme of flight; and 9) Beyond the Limits: Flight Enters the Computer Age: how computers have revolutionized the aerospace industry.

Albert Einstein Planetarium & Samuel P. Langley Theater:

The Albert Einstein Planetarium is one of the most popular and technically sophisticated sky theaters in the world. At its center is the Zeiss VI planetarium projector, a gift to the United States from the Federal Republic of Germany.

The Zeiss VI can recreate almost every celestial phenomenon visible to the naked eye, from any position on Earth and any time in history, past present or future. It projects about 9,000 stars on the Planetarium's 75 -foot (23 meter) dome and accurately simulates the apparent motions of the sun, moon and five nearest planets. In addition, lasers, video projectors, and hundreds of special effects projectors combine with a six channel sound system to create an unforgettable multi-media experience.

The Samuel P. Langley Theater offers audiences an unparalleled experience in motion-picture viewing. The IMAX projection system uses a 15,000 watt water-cooled projection lamp to project a brilliantly clear image onto a screen that measures 50 x 75 feet. The theater boasts a state-of-the-art digital sound system with six channels of audio and a massive sub-bass speaker array. In addition to IMAX films, the 486-seat theater can present 16-mm, 35-mm and 70-mm films, as well as video, multimedia shows, lectures and seminars. Some of the famous movies specially produced and shown at the Samuel P. Langley Theater are "Blue Planet", "To FLy", "The Dream Is Alive", and the "Living Planet". For information about the National Air And Space Museum call 202-357-2700.

DC-DCA - WASHINGTON
WASHINGTON NATIONAL AIRPORT

(Area Code 703) 3

Innovative Aircourts, Inc:

The food and beverage concessions managed by Innovative Aircourts, are located throughout the entire airport. Regardless of which airline a passenger is using, all terminals house at least one "eatery" within its concourse area. WNA has an extensive ground transport system via shuttle busses to all parking lots, metro, car rental companies and hotels. Eateries and restaurant on the premises include snack bars, cafes, cafeterias, family style restaurants, fine dining establishment and more. From 5:30 a.m. to 11 p.m. there are 25 separate and independent facilities available. A passenger can get a bite or beverage all day. There are 6 bar/lounges available. The WNA menu is varied and extensive. They have everything from bagels and croissants made fresh daily on the premises, to grilled fish platters and brand name products from companies like McDonald's, Frank & Stein, and Jerry's. Average prices run from $1.00 to $6.00 for breakfast, $2.00 to $7.00 for lunch and $3.00 to $9.00 and up for dinner. Many daily specials are offered by each of the independent facilities. Each new dining operation was designed with individuality, eye-catching appeal and warmth in mind, to welcome the weary traveler. Existing locations that were acquired have been given interior renovations and facelifts. There are 4 full-scale kitchens on the premises prepared to accommodate catering for any size group. For more information about the Innovative Aircourts operation and services, call them at 979-1000.

Restaurants Near Airport:

Chesapeake Grill	1 mi W.	Phone: 418-1234
Innovative Aircourts, Inc.	On Site	Phone: 979-1000
Lee Yuan Restaurant	1 mi W.	Phone: 418-3688
Ondine Restaurants & Lounge	1 mi W.	Phone: 418-6800

Lodging: Several hotels in the vicinity of the airport provide courtesy shuttle bus pickup from the airport; Crystal City Marriott 521-5500; Holiday Inn 521-1600; Crystal Gateway Marriott 920-3230; Howard Johnson 684-7200; Hyatt Regency Crystal City 418-1234; Stouffer Concourse 418-6800.

Meeting Rooms: Courtesy shuttle service available by most hotels listed: Crystal City Marriott 521-5500; Holiday Inn 521-1600; Crystal Gateway Marriott 920-3230; Howard Johnson 684-7200; Hyatt Regency Crystal City 418-1234; Stouffer Concourse 418-6800.

Transportation: Airport Taxicab Dispatch Metrorail 202-637-7000; Alamo 800-327-9633; Avis 800-331-1212; Budget 800-527-0700; Dollar 800-800-4000; Hertz 800-654-3131; National 800-3284567. (No courtesy transportation reported by FBO).

Information: Washington D.C. Convention And Visitors Association, 1212 New York Avenue, NW, Washington, DC 20005, Phone: 202-789-7000.

Attractions:

There are many attractions available within and around the Washington D.C. area. After verifying information received by one of our contributors, we learned that pilots landing at the Washington National Airport (DCA) have easy eccess to many famous historical sites located in Washington D.C., only a few miles from the airport. Points of interest like the Arlington Cemetery, the Smithsonian, national monuments, downtown shopping district and much more can be reached using the mass transit system from both the National Airport and College Airport. When landing at the Washington National Airport (DCA), pilots using general aviation aircraft can park at the south end of the field at Signature Flight Support (FBO). From there your party can take a free shuttle bus to the nearby Metro stop. Once there you can select which lines will bring you closest to your destination or what connections you will need to make to reach the point of interest. For example the "Blue Line" should take you to the Arlington Cemetery, and the Blue/Yellow line to the downtown area etc. A handy guide for Metro rates, destinations, and attractions can be obtained by requesting the "Metro System Pocket Guide," as your passport to an exciting array of attractions in the Washington, D.C. area. You can write to: Washington Metropolitan Area Transit Authority 600 Fifth Street, N.W., Washington, D.C. 20001. or call 202-637-7000.

Additional Information about nearby attractions or holiday activities in the nation's Capitol can be obtained by either calling or writing to the Washington D.C. Convention And Visitors Association, 1212 New York Avenue, NW, Washington, DC 20005 or call 202-789-7000

Airport Information:

WASHINGTON - WASHINGTON NATIONAL AIRPORT (DCA)
3 mi south of town 38-51-08N 77-02-17W Elev: 16 Fuel: 100LL, Jet-A
Rwy 18-36: H6869x150 (Asph-Grvd) Rwy 15-33: H5189x150 (Asph-Grvd)
Rwy 03-21: H4505x150 (Asph-Pfc) Attended: continuously Atis: 132.65 Unicom: 122.95
App Con: 118.3 (East) 124.7 (West) Dep Con: 121.05, 118.95, 126.55, 125.65 Tower: 119.1 (120.75 Helicopters) Gnd Con: 121.7 Clnc Del/Pre Taxi Clnc: 128.25 Public Phone 24hrs
Notes: CAUTION: Special Air Traffic Rules in effect, High Density Airport, Prior Reservation Required, see Regulatory Notices! Also see special notices published in Airport Facility Directory, and Airman Information Manual, regarding operations in and about this region. During our conversation with the Signature Flight Support staff, we learned that there is limited parking on their ramp. Those parking at their facility must obtain a pass at the time of parking by security or the Signature staff. Overflow aircraft parking is also available adjacent to their ramp for roughly $12.00/24hrs.
FBO: Signature Flight Support Phone: 419-8440

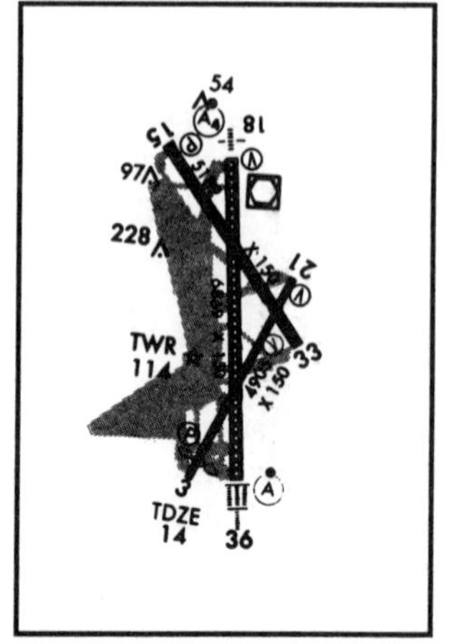

Not to be used for navigational purposes

FLORIDA

LOCATION MAP

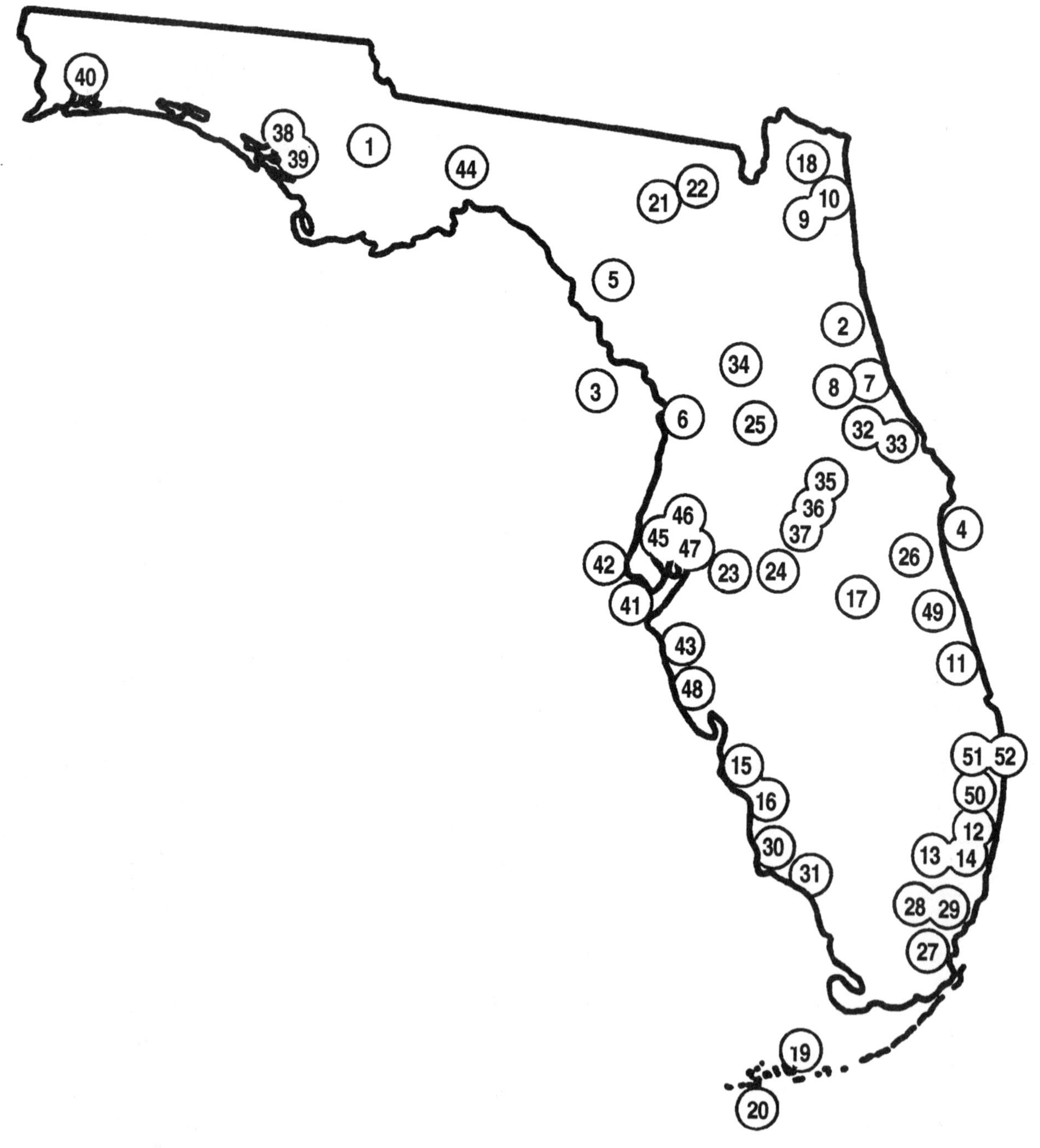

Not to be used for navigational purposes

FLORIDA

CROSS FILE INDEX

Location Number	City or Town	Airport Name And Identifier	Name of Restaurant
1	Blountstown	Calhoun Co. Arpt. (0J9)	Bridge Cafe
2	Bunnell	Flagler Co. Arpt. (X47)	Wings Restaurant
3	Cedar Key	George T. Lewis Arpt. (CDK)	Dining on Cedar Key
4	Cocoa	Merritt Island Arpt. (COI)	Dining on Cocoa Beach
5	Cross City	Cross City Arpt. (CTY)	Cross Cty. Arpt. Rest.
6	Crystal River	Crystal River Arpt. (X31)	Dairy Queen/Brazier
7	Daytona Beach	Daytona Beach Reg. Arpt. (DAB)	Jerry's Restaurant
8	Deland	Deland Muni./Sidney Taylor (DED)	Airport Rest. & Gin Mill
9	Fernandina Beach	Fernandina Beach Muni. (55J)	Amelia Island Plantation
10	Fernandina Beach	Fernandina Beach Muni. (55J)	The Ritz-Carlton
11	Ft. Pierce	St. Lucie Co. Intl. Arpt. (FPR)	Tiki Restaurant
12	Ft. Lauderdale	Ft. Lauderdale Executive (FXE)	Skytel Coffee Shop
13	Ft. Lauderdale	Hollywood Intl. (FLL)	Aviator Tavern & Grill
14	Ft. Lauderdale	Hollywood Intl. (FLL)	CA1 Services.
15	Ft. Myers	Page Field (FMY)	Mikes Landing
16	Ft. Myers	Southwest Florida Reg. (RSW)	Jerry's Restaurant
17	Frostproof	River Ranch Resort (2RR)	River Ranch Inc. Resort
18	Jacksonville	Jacksonville Intl. Arpt. (JAX)	Montegeo's
19	Keywest	Sugarloaf Shores Arpt. (7X1)	Sugar Loaf Rest.
20	Keywest	Keywest Intl. Arpt. (EYW)	Martha's Restaurant
21	Lake City	Cannon Creek Airpark (15FL)	Quail Heights C.C.
22	Lake City	Lake City Muni. Arpt. (31J)	Robert's Dock
23	Lakeland	Lakeland Linder Reg. (LAL)	Tony's Airside Rest.
24	Lake Wales	Chalet Suzanne Air Strip (X25)	Chalet Suzanne B & B
25	Leesburg	Leesburg Muni. Arpt. (LEE)	Captain Bell's Restaurant
26	Melbourne	Melbourne Reg. Arpt. (MLB)	Jerry's Arpt. Restaurant
27	Miami	Kendall Tamiami Exec. (TMB)	(Closed at time of interview)
28	Miami	Miami Intl. (MIA)	Terminal concessions
29	Miami	Miami Intl. (MIA)	Top Of The Port
30	Naples	Naples Muni. Arpt. (APF)	Runway Pub
31	Naples	Port of the Islands (X00)	The Garden Court
32	New Smyrna Beach	New Smyrna Beach Muni. (34J)	Franco's Italian Rest.
33	New Smyrna Beach	New Smyrna Beach Muni. (34J)	Skyline Restaurant
34	Ocala	Ocala Reg./Jim Taylor Fld. (OCF)	Pegasus Arpt. Rest.
35	Orlando	Orlando Exec. Arpt. (ORL)	4th Fighter Group
36	Orlando	Orlando Intl. (MCO)	Host Intl. Restaurant
37	Orlando/Kissimmee	Kissimmee Muni. Arpt. (ISM)	Outback Steakhouse
38	Panama City	Panama City-Bay Co. Arpt. (PFN)	Arpt. Restaurant
39	Panama City	Panama City-Bay Co. Arpt. (PFN)	Smitty's Barbecue
40	Pensacola	Pensacola Reg. Arpt. (PNS)	McGuire's Irish Pub
41	St. Petersburg	Albert Whitted Arpt. (SPG)	Charmain's (Hilton Htl.)
42	St. Petersburg	Clearwater Intl. (PIE)	94th Aero Squadron

CROSS FILE INDEX
(Florida Continued)

Location Number	City or Town	Airport Name And Identifier	Name of Attraction
43	Sarasota	Bradenton Arpt. (SRQ)	Airport Food Court
44	Tallahassee	Tallahassee Reg. Arpt. (TLH)	Jerry's Restaurant
45	Tampa	Tampa Intl. Arpt. (TPA)	CK's Restaurant
46	Tampa	Tampa Intl. Arpt. (TPA)	Tampa Bay Wharf
47	Tampa	Tampa Intl. Arpt. (TPA)	TGI Friday's
48	Venice	Venice Muni. Arpt. (VNC)	Dante's Ristorante
49	Vero Beach	Vero Beach Muni. Arpt. (VRB)	C.J. Cannon's Rest.
50	West Palm Beach	Palm Beach Co. Pk./Lantana (LNA)	The Ark Restaurant
51	West Palm Beach	Palm Beach Intl. (PBI)	391 Bomb Group
52	West Palm Beach	Palm Beach Intl. (PBI)	CA1 Services

Articles

City or town	Nearest Airport and Identifier	Name of Attraction
Cedar Key, FL	George T. Lewis (CDK)	Cedar Key
Cocoa, FL	Merritt Island (COI)	Cocoa Beach
Crestview, FL	Bob Sikes (CEW)	Air Force Armament Mus.
Fernandina Bch., FL	Fernandia Beach Muni. (55J)	Amelia Island Plantation
Key West, FL	Key West Intl. Arpt. (EYW)	Key West
Lake Wales, FL	Lake Wales Muni. (X07)	River Ranch
Naples, FL	Port of the Islands (X00)	Port of the Island Resort
Orlando/Kissimmee, FL	Kissimmee Muni. Arpt. (ISM)	Flying Tigers Museum
Pensacola, FL	Ferguson (82J)	Natl. Mus. of Naval Aviation
St. Petersburg, FL	Clearwater Intl. (PIE)	Florida Military Aviation Mus.
Sugar Loaf Key, FL	Sugar Loaf Shores Arpt.(7X1)	Sugar Loaf Restaurant

FL-0J9 - BLOUNTSTOWN CALHOUN COUNTY AIRPORT

(Area Code 904) 1

Bridge Cafe:

Due to the construction on the Apalachicola River Bridge near the town of Blountstown, Florida, The restaurant that was known as the Riverside Restaurant was re-purchased and has been re-named the Bridge Cafe. This new restaurant is smaller and is mainly open for lunch between 11 a.m. and 2 p.m. This restaurant serves light fare and offers a variety of sandwiches. It is conveniently located well within walking distance and across the street from the tie-down area on the southeast end of the Calhoun County Airport. To confirm restaurant hours, etc. call the Bridge Cafe at 674-1234.

Restaurants Near Airport:
Bridge Cafe Adj Arpt. Phone: 674-1234

Lodging: None Reported

Meeting Rooms: None Reported

Transportation: None Reported

Information: Calhoun County Chamber of Commerce, 340 East Central Avenue, Blountstown, FL 32424 or call 674-4519.

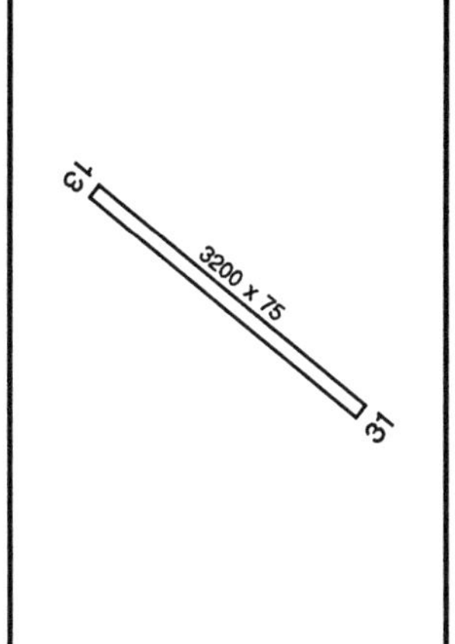

Airport Information:

BLOUNTSTOWN - CALHOUN COUNTY AIRPORT (0J9)
1 mi east of town 30-26-50N 85-01-31W Elev: 56 Rwy 13-31: 3200x75 (Turf)
Attended: unattended CTAF: 122.9
Calhoun County Airport Phone: 674-4545

FL-X47 - BUNNELL FLAGLER COUNTY AIRPORT

(Area Code 904) 2

Wings Restaurant:

The Wings Restaurant is situated on the Flagler County Airport. This family style restaurant is open Tuesday through Saturday and Sunday from 7 a.m. to 8 p.m. and Monday from 7 a.m. to 4 p.m. Menu selections include a variety of breakfast items, sandwiches, specialty 5 ounce hamburgers like their pepper burger, cheeseburgers, and hot plates. Average prices run $1.99 to $6.00 for breakfast, $3.50 to $3.75 for lunch and $7.00 to $12.00 for dinner. Some breakfast specials are offered on week days that run only $1.99 for 2 egg dishes. Their dining room can seat 55 persons. A back party room called the "Wings International Diner Club" offers gourmet German cooking with "Chef Michael" preparing special dishes. This back dining room offers a more elegant atmosphere. It also serves as a comfortable room for business conferences able to hold up to 48 persons. For more information about the Wings Restaurant call, 437-0410.

Restaurants Near Airport:
Wings Airport Restaurant On Site Phone: 437-0410

Lodging: Sheraton Palm Coast (10 miles) 445-3000.

Meeting Rooms: Wings Airport Restaurant, has accommodations for up to 50 persons in their meeting rooms, Phone: 437-0410; Sheraton Palm Coast, has meeting rooms able to accommodate up to 200 persons, Phone: 445-3000.

Transportation: MBL Transportation 437-5466; National Car Rental 437-5466.

Information: Florida Division of Tourism, Visitor Inquiry, 126 Van Buren Street, Tallahassee, FL 32399-2000, 904-487-1462.

Attractions:

Six golf courses within 5 miles of airport; Atlantic Ocean 5 miles; Marineland of Florida 15 miles.

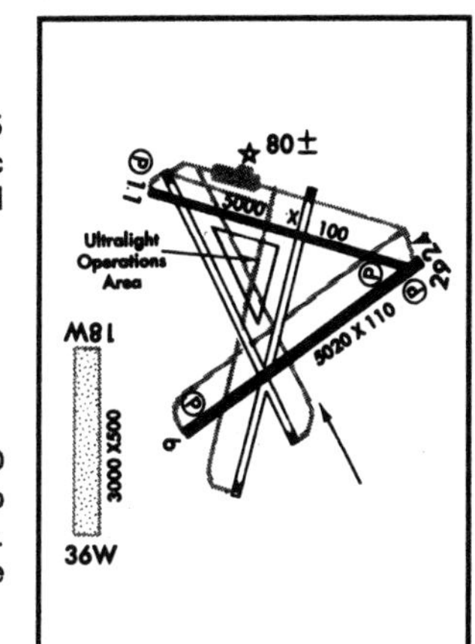

Airport Information:

BUNNELL - FLAGLER COUNTY AIRPORT (X47)
3 mi east of town N29-28.04 W81-12.39 Elev: 32 Fuel: 100LL Rwy 11-29: H5000x150 (Asph) Rwy 06-24: H4755x200 (Asph) Rwy 18-36: 3000 x 500 (Turf) Attended: dawn to dusk Unicom: 123.0 Notes: Parachute jumping. No landing fees, $2.00 overnight parking fee. No touch and go or stop and go landings-intersection or partial runway takeoff. All aircraft must come to a full stop and use airport taxi pattern. Use Caution: Turf Rwy 18-36 reported west of field.
FBO: Flagler County Airport Phone: 437-0401

FL-CDK - CEDAR KEY
GEORGE T. LEWIS AIRPORT

(Area Code 904) 3

Dining On Cedar Key:

Cedar Key is located on the scenic Nature Coast of Florida, just off the Gulf of Mexico. The island is nationally famous for its abundance of seafood, and its commercial fishing industry is still a way of life for many families on the islands. Visitors can talk to the local fishermen and learn about their modern methods of raising and harvesting clams, oysters and other shellfish that hungry visitors may be eating later. The restaurants, which are located in the downtown area, offer plenty of fresh seafood specialties and traditional island dishes fresh from the Gulf, such as heart of palm salad, smoked mullet , fish, clams, shrimp, stone crab claws, blue crabs, soft-shell crabs and oysters. Each year in mid-October, Cedar Key celebrates its bounty with a seafood festival. Thousands of people flock to the island to taste fresh seafood delicacies while enjoying a craft show of artists from the region. George T. Lewis Airport is located just 1 mile west of downtown. Since there is no phone reported at the airport, pilots can call Unicom 122.9 to be picked up by Checker Cab or call 543-5406. For more information about the restaurants and other attractions in Cedar Key, contact the Cedar Key Area Chamber of Commerce at 543-5600.

Restaurants Near Airport:
Restaurants are located downtown. 1 mi E. Phone: 543-5600

Lodging: Beach Front Motel (2 miles) 543-5113; Cedar Cove (2 1/4 miles) 543-5332; Cedar Inn (2 miles) 543-5455; Faraway Inn (2 miles) 543-5330; Gulf Side (2 miles) 543-5308; Island Hotel (2 miles) 543-5111; Island Place (2 miles) 543-5307; Park Place (2 miles) 543-5737
Meeting Rooms: None Reported
Transportation: Pilots can call Unicom 122.9 to be picked up by Checker Cab or call 543-5406.
Information: Cedar Key Area Chamber of Commerce, P.O. Box 610, Cedar Key, FL 32625, Phone: 543-5600

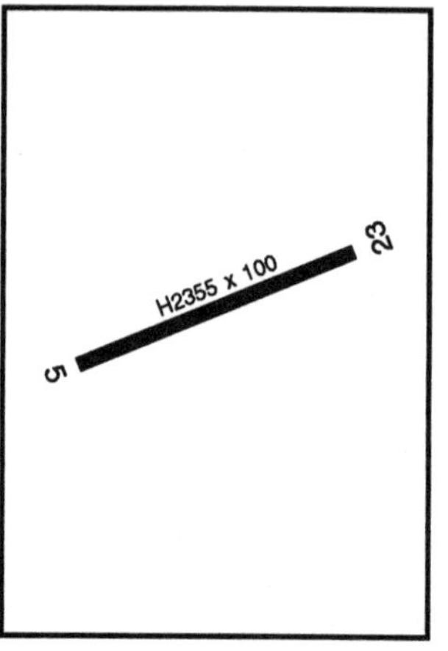

Airport Information:

Cedar Key - George T. Lewis Airport (CDK)
1 mile west of town N29-08.26 W83-02.99 Elev: 7 Fuel: None Rwy 05-23: H2355x100 (Asph) Attended: unattended/no phone, call on unicom freq. 122.9 for transportation or better yet call ahead to arrange transportation. CTAF: 122.9 Notes: See "Airport Facility Directory" for comments about runway conditions and information.
FBO: Airport Manager Phone: 543-5508

Cedar Key

Cedar Key, FL (FL-CDK)

Cedar Key is located on the scenic Nature Coast of Florida, just off the Gulf of Mexico. Cedar Key is filled with hundreds of species of birds and animals, along with 200 years of island history. It is a paradise for both naturalists and history buffs. The Cedar Key Historical Society Museum offers an abundance of information about the island's social and architectural history, including the famous 1000 mile walk of naturalist John Muir who reached his destination to the island in 1867. Also, the Cedar Key State Museum displays exhibits ranging from Indian artifacts to folklore, as well as natural history.

From sunrise to sunset, the shorelines and salt marshes come alive with plants and wildlife. Through the day, thousands of pelicans dive and fish, following fishing boats and usually entertaining all who watch. Ospreys build their nests and feed their young. Great blue herons, egrets, ibis and a myriad of other waders quietly search the waters for food. Frigate birds soar high above, circling the gulf, while dolphins play just off the shore. Occasionally, roseate spoonbills or flocks of rare white pelicans may appear. At dusk, raccoons come out to scavenge the oyster bars and marshes which are home to many species of shellfish and crustaceans.

Cedar Key is nationally famous for its abundance of seafood. Each year in mid-October, Cedar Key hosts a seafood festival, where thousands flock to taste fresh seafood delicacies while enjoying a craft show of artists from the region. In April, Cedar Key celebrates its appreciation for the arts at the Annual Cedar Key Sidewalk Arts Festival. This show attracts artists from all over the country. Crowds of art lovers enjoy a wide variety of fine art as well as fresh seafood in the park. Also, Cedar Key offers plenty of restaurants, which are located in the downtown area, that serve delicious seafood.

After visitors get their fill of fish and fun, they can relax in one of the island's comfortable hotels, motels, cottages or bed and breakfast inns.

For visitors, a walk or bike ride is a fun way to discover the many mysteries of Cedar Key and its inhabitants. The island is located near a variety of parks and preserves. The Cedar Keys National Wildlife Refuge, a group of barrier islands off the coast of Cedar Key, is accessible only by boat. Manatee Springs State Park offers camping, swimming, diving, canoe rentals and an elevated boardwalk through cypress wetlands to the Suwannee River where manatees are often sighted. The Lower Suwannee National Wildlife Refuge offers several hiking trails set within 40,000 acres of unspoiled habitat. Shell Mound Park is a large prehistoric Indian mound that has camping, boating and picnicking facilities. Cedar Key has plenty of public facilities, such as the Cedar Key City Park, a post office, a library, Cedar Key Public Marina and public fishing piers. Canoes, sailboats and motorboats, as well as bicycles and golf carts are available for rental.

The island's George T. Lewis Airport has a 2,355'x100 asphalt runway. Pilots can call Unicom 122.9 to be picked up by Checker Cab or call 543-5406. For information about activities and accommodations in Cedar Key, contact the Cedar Key Area Chamber of Commerce at 543-5600. (Information submitted by the Cedar Key Area Chamber of Commerce)

FL-COI - COCOA MERRITT ISLAND AIRPORT

(Area Code 407) 4

Dining in Cocoa Beach:

Cocoa Beach is located 7 miles from Merritt Island Airport on Florida's scenic Space Coast. In addition to all the sightseeing, sun and fun, it offers plenty of restaurants that range from fine dining to favorite fast foods. Choose from a variety of American or international cuisine to suit everyone's taste. There are several restaurants that offer casual dining, such as the Caravelle Bar and Grille, Coconuts on the Beach, Marlins Good Time Bar and Grill and Gatsby's Dockside Eatery. For those who have an international taste, Cafe Margaux serves fine French cuisine, the Heidelberg Restaurant serves tasty German fare, the Villa Roma offers fine Italian cuisine, and the Red Pepper serves authentic Mexican food. Also, Cedars of Lebanon serves great Middle Eastern fare. For a taste of the Orient, Royal China and TaiHo Japanese Steak, Seafood and Sushi both serve delicious dishes. There are also several steak and seafood restaurants, such as Bernard's Surf, Castaways, Old Fish House, Grandpa's Nebraska-Style Steak House and Gregory's Steak and Seafood Grille. Cocoa Beach also offers a variety of well-known family style restaurants, such as Kentucky Fried Chicken and Shoney's. For more information about restaurants and other facilities in Cocoa Beach, call the Cocoa Beach Area Chamber of Commerce at 459-2200.

Restaurants Near Airport:

Denny's	2 mi	Phone: 453-3050
Olive Garden	2 mi	Phone: 459-0306
Red Lobster	2 mi	Phone: 453-3520

Lodging: Econo Lodge (5 miles) 632-4561; Holiday Inn (1 mile) 452-7711
Meeting Rooms: Cocoa Beach Area Chamber of Commerce 459-2200
Transportation: Rental Cars: Enterprise 453-8710; Public BusTransportation: Space Coast AreaTransit: 633-1878
Information: Cocoa Beach Area Chamber of Commerce, 400 Fortenberry Road, Merritt Island, FL 32952, Phone: 459-2200

Attractions:

Cocoa Beach (7 miles); Kennedy Space Center (5 miles)

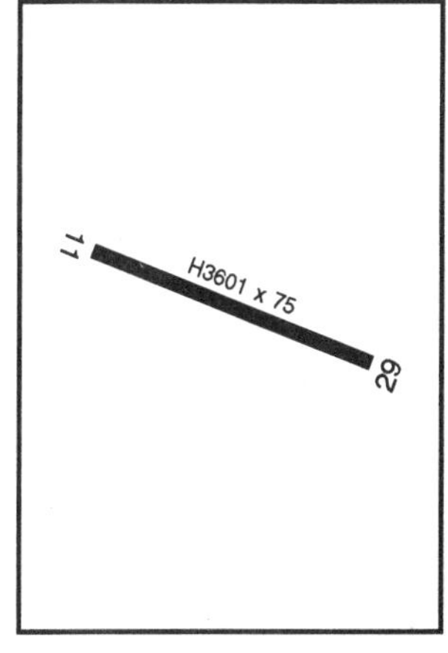

Airport Information:

COCOA - MERRITT ISLAND AIRPORT (COI)
2 miles southeast of town N28-20.50 W80-41.13 Elev: 7 Fuel: 100LL, Jet-A Rwy 11-29: H3601x75 (Asph) Attended: 1300-0100Z CTAF/Unicom: 123.05
FBO: Merritt Island Air Service Phone: 453-2222

Cocoa Beach

Cocoa, FL (FL-COI)

Photo by: NASA

The first flight of the commercially developed SPACEHAB laboratory module begins with the flawless liftoff of the Space Shuttle Endeavour from Launch Pad 39B.

Cocoa Beach (Central Brevard County) is located just 7 miles from Merritt Island Airport on Florida's beautiful Space Coast. A year-round subtropical climate and miles of sandy beaches make Cocoa Beach a vacationer's paradise. Cocoa Beach and Cape Canaveral are linked to Merritt Island and the mainland by State Road 520, a four-lane causeway, and State Road 528, the Bennett Causeway. A bit of interesting history. During the early 1800s, the first commercial building built in Cocoa was erected by B. C. Willard. For many years, he and his brother, C. A. Willard, conducted a general store there. Portions of this building originally faced the Indian River, for which the town was named "Indian River City." The U.S. Postal Authorities claimed the name was too long for use on a postmark. It was in the Willard Store that first news of this was received. Eventually, the "Cocoa" was selected from a box of Baker's Cocoa brought in with some freight. Since then, Cocoa Beach has grown to become a popular tourist attraction. With so much to see and do, people of all ages can have a great time.

NASA's John F. Kennedy Space Center is located just 5 miles from the airport. Visitors can spend hours at Kennedy Space Center Spaceport USA. The center offers guided bus tours of Kennedy Space Center every day of the year except Christmas day. The Galaxy Center (located at the north end of Spaceport U.S.A.) provides visitors with a variety of attractions, such as a Rocket Garden, a space art gallery, a gift shop, an IMAX Theater with a 5-1/2 story high screen, and a Galaxy Theater which features presentations of the exciting adventures of space flight. The two IMAX films shown are: The Dream is Alive and Blue Planet which feature footage shot by NASA astronauts in space. (Note: there is a nominal fee for specific programs such as the films and bus tours.)

The NASA Shuttle Landing Facility is available for viewing, but pilots are not allowed to land there. However, they can get cleared for a low pass over the 15,000-foot runway used by the Space Shuttle. Just ask Patrick Approach at Patrick AFB on frequency 134.95 for the "Cape Tour." The Air Force has scheduled a number of unmanned rocket launches throughout the year and these are usually announced two to three weeks prior to lift-off. Call 867-4636 for NASA's recorded message of launch information. Some of the best viewing sites for the general public are anywhere along the beaches in the Cocoa Beach (Brevard County) area.

Just a few miles down the road from Kennedy Space Center Spaceport USA is the U.S. Astronaut Hall of Fame and U.S. Space Camp. The U.S. Astronaut Hall of Fame displays the human side of space with memorabilia from the original Mercury Seven astronauts. Relive the daring exploits of those heroic men who journeyed into space. Visitors can pilot the Shuttle Simulator and bring Columbia in for a landing. Take a ride on the "Shuttle to Tomorrow," a full scale space shuttle replica with a passenger compartment ready for the whole family. Feel the rumble of lift-off and take a simulated spacewalk. (Note: there is an admission charge to the Hall of Fame.) Visitors may watch as youngsters attending U.S. Space Camp learn what it's like to be part of the future in space.

After a day in space, it's time to come back to earth, kick back and relax. Plan the next day's exciting excursion while resting in one of the area's many oceanfront hotels and motels. When it's time for a bite to eat, Cocoa Beach offers plenty of restaurants which offer everything from fine dining to America's favorite fast foods. Choose from a variety of American or international cuisine to suit every taste.

Photo by: NASA Only a minute after sunrise, the Space Shuttle Endeavour lifts off from Launch Pad 39 A in a halo of light.

For an afternoon of shopping, stop by one of the area's several malls and shops which offer goods in every price range. Also, for a bit of nostalgia, visit historic Cocoa Village. Walk along brick- paved sidewalks and cool, shady lanes with splashing fountains and replicas of old-fashioned gas lamps. Stop by the charming galleries, cafes, gourmet restaurants and emporiums of antiques, jewelry, art, fashion, crafts and gifts. Or, relax and have a picnic in one of the scenic parks.

Before leaving Cocoa, visit the Brevard Museum of History and Naural Science and experience the natural beauty of Florida's environment, or stop by Merritt Island National Wildlife Refuge where some of the nation's rarest and most unusual species can be found.

So, for those who want sun, surf, sand, space, ships and fun, they have come to the right place. Many facilities in the Cocoa Beach area are within a couple of miles from the Merritt Island Airport; however, public bus transportation and rental car service are also available for convenience. Overnight parking fees are $3.00 for singles and $5.00 for twins. For more information about activities and accommodations in Cocoa Beach, contact the Cocoa Beach Area Chamber of Commerce at 459-2200. (Information submitted by the Cocoa Beach Area Chamber of Commerce)

Air Force Armament Museum

The Air Force Armament Museum opened its new building to the public in October 1985. Always a popular attraction to locals and tourists alike, it has become even more so in the past year with many added attractions. Their expanding collection houses not only armament, but aircraft as well, with the platforms for deliverance of many pieces of ordnance. The museum chronicles the development and application of Air Force armament and aircraft from World War I to present state-of-the-art technology to their visitors.

Brightly colored displays now chronicle the path of our Nation's defense. Beginning with early flight, one can progress through history in a logical and interesting sequence, aided by an array of artifacts, maps, dioramas and explanative text. A Desert Storm exhibit has also been added on the main floor, through the collaboration of the exhibits and graphics departments.

Outside exhibits have also been improved upon. The SR-71 Blackbird acquired last year is now surrounded by World War II aircraft moved from behind the museum. The B-17 and B-25 bombers are joined by aircraft recently acquired for the collection, including a B-57, C-131, and the impressive B-52. The future looks bright for the addition of more aircraft as present day fighters and bombers are phased out.

Indoor exhibits include World War II aircraft, Korean conflict aircraft and the Vietnam era F-105. These are surrounded by a variety of armament including the more recent AMRAAM, cluster bombs, as well as TV and laser guided bombs.

To reach the museum by air, pilots can fly into the Crestview, Bob Sikes Airport (FL-CEW). Other nearby airports include Pensacola, Panama City, and the Destin Airport. The museum is located on Route 85 just outside of the Eglin Air Force main gate.

The museum is open seven days a week from 9:30 to 4:30 with free admission. They are closed Thanksgiving, Christmas and New Years. For further information call the Air Force Armament Museum (Eglin Air Force Base) at 904-882-4062 or 904-882-4063. (Information submitted by museum)

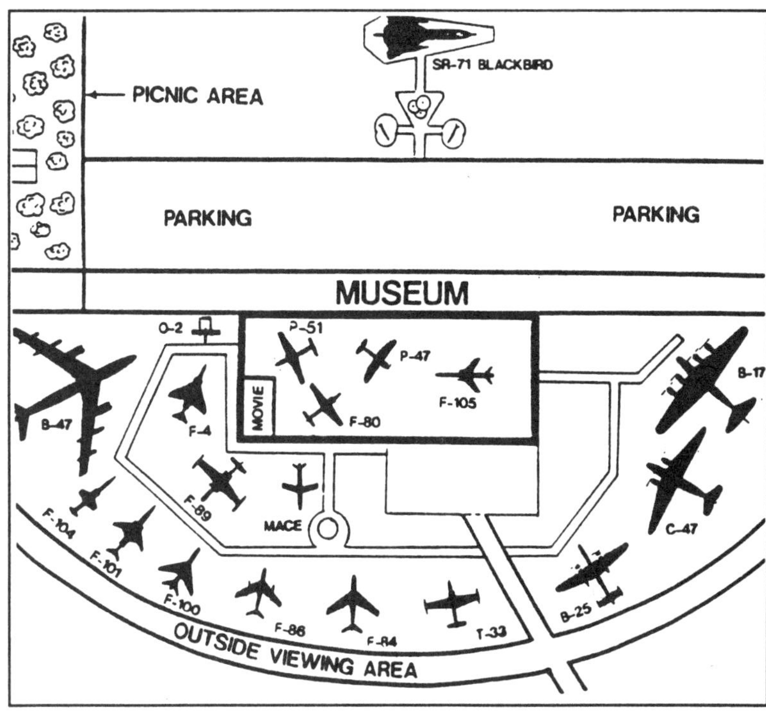

Diagram of outside museum

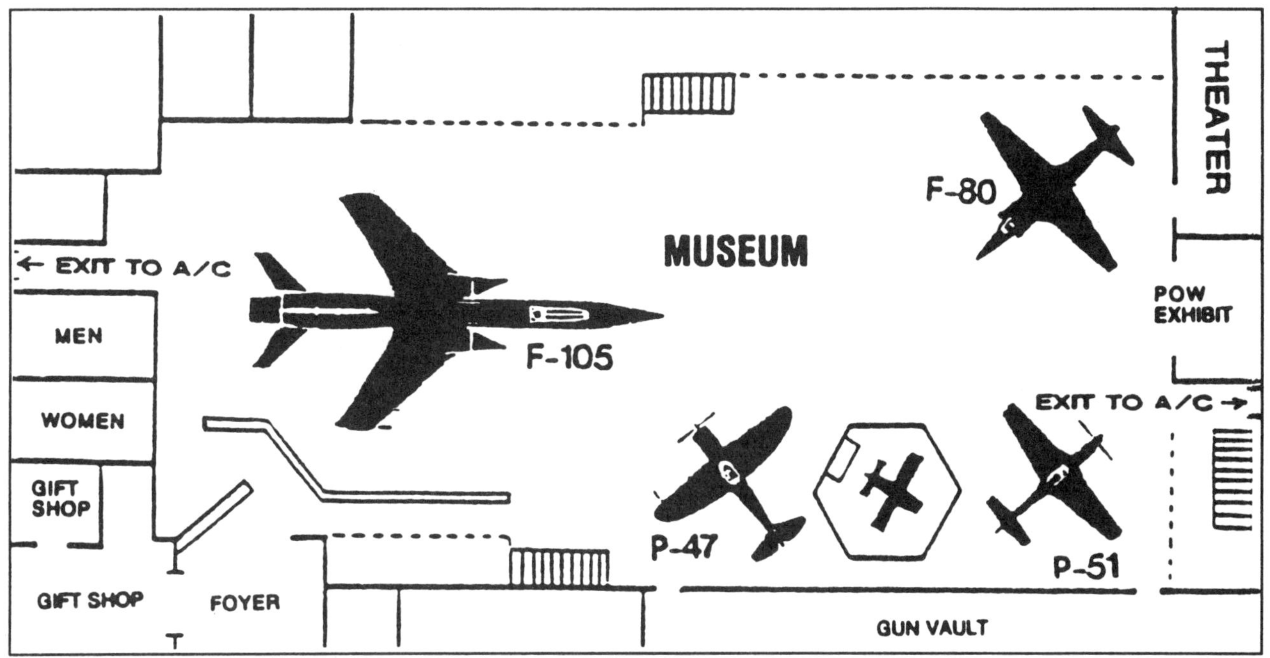

General layout of museum interior

FL-CTY - CROSS CITY
CROSS CITY AIRPORT

(Area Code 904) 5

Cross City Airport Restaurant and Lounge:

The Cross City Airport Restaurant and Lounge is located right on the Cross City Airport. This fine dining restaurant, which has a rustic decor, is open weekdays from 7:00 a.m. to 9:00 p.m., and Friday and Saturday from 7:00 a.m. to 10:00 p.m. Menu items include: a daily buffet, salad bar, fresh king crab, snow crab, lobster, clams, shrimp, frog legs, prime rib, filet, New York strips and charbroiled steaks. On Fridays, the restaurant features an all-you-can-eat Seafood Buffet for $10.95. Meal prices average around $3.00 for breakfast, $4.00 for lunch and $12.00 for dinner. This restaurant also has a lounge which serves all types of cocktails. The Cross City Airport Restaurant can cater to parties of 20 or more, as well as to private and corporate pilots on-the-go. For more information about Cross City Airport Restaurant and Lounge, call 498-2700.

Restaurants Near Airport:

Cross City Aprt. Restaurant	(On Site)	Phone: 498-2700

Lodging: Carriage Inn (1 mile) 498-3910; Eldorado Motel (2 miles) 498-3307

Meeting Rooms: Contact Airport Manager

Transportation: Carriage Inn 498-3910; Eldorado Motel 498-3307

Information: Lafayette County Chamber of Commerce, P.O. Box 416, Mayo, FL 32066, Phone: 294-2705

Attractions:

Horseshoe Beach and Steenhatchee (25 miles); Suwanee town and Suwanee River (30 miles). For more information, call 294-2705.

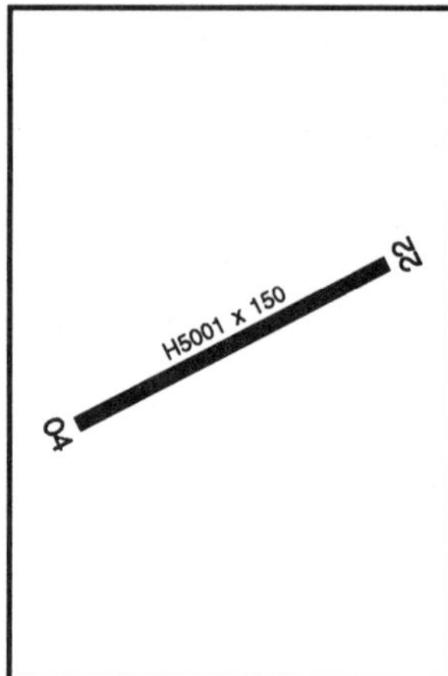

Airport Information:

CROSS CITY - CROSS CITY AIRPORT (CTY)

1 mi east of town N29-38.07 W83-06.34 Elev: 42 Fuel: 100LL Rwy 13-31: H5001x150 (Asph) Rwy 04-22: H4050x150 (Asph) Attended: continuously CTAF/Unicom: 122.8 JAX Center App/Dep Con: 127.8 Public Phone 24hrs Notes: Overnight parking fees are $3.00.

FBO: Cross City Airport, Inc. Phone: 498-3072

FL-X31 - CRYSTAL RIVER
CRYSTAL RIVER AIRPORT

(Area Code 904) 6

Dairy Queen/Brazier:

Dairy Queen/Brazier is just a short walk (approximately 500') from the Crystal Aero Group, Inc. (FBO) office at Crystal River Airport. It is open daily from 10:30 a.m. to 10:00 p.m. This fast food restaurant has a modern oak and brass interior. Menu items include: daily specials, hot, juicy hamburgers, hot dogs, BBQ, chicken, pork loin fritters, fish, French fries, onion rings and well-known cold treats such as Blizzards, banana splits and hard and soft ice cream cones. Prices for lunch and dinner average around $3.00. This restaurant can cater to parties of 20 or more for special occasions, such as birthday parties, ballteam functions, etc. For more information about this facility, call 795-5800.

Restaurants Near Airport:

Best Western Crystal River	(3 miles)	Phone: 795-3171
Dairy Queen/Brazier	(On Site)	Phone: 795-5800
Plantation Inn and Golf Resort	(3 miles)	Phone: 795-4211

Lodging: Best Western Crystal River Resort (3 miles) 795-3171; Plantation Inn and Golf Resort (3 miles) 795-4211; Days Inn (6 miles) 795-2111

Meeting Rooms: Days Inn 795-2111; Plantation Inn 795-4211

Transportation: Taxi Service: Crystal River 563-2909; Rental Cars: Enterprise 563-5511

Information: Chamber of Commerce, 28 NW US 19, Crystal River, FL 34428, Phone: 795-3149

Attractions:

The Plantation Inn and Golf Resort (3 miles) offers deluxe rooms, suites and villas. The resort also features a championship 27-hole golf course, tennis, sport fishing, scuba diving and elegant fine dining. For more information, call 795-4211. The Best Western Crystal River Resort (3 miles) offers affordable accommdations, fabulous dining, a heated swimming pool and jacuzzi, a tiki bar, fitness room, in-room safe, gift shop, boat rental, dive center and dock and ramp. For more information, call 795-3171.

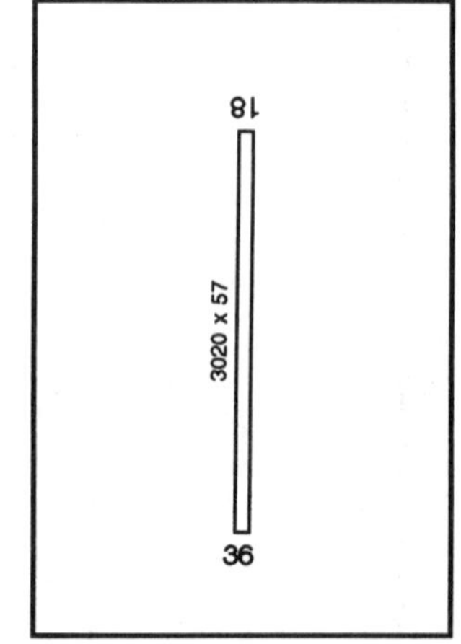

Airport Information:

CRYSTAL RIVER - CRYSTAL RIVER AIRPORT (X31)

3 mi southeast of town N28-52.07 W82-34.47 Elev: 10 Fuel: 100LL, Jet-A Rwy 09-27: H4297x60 (Asph) Rwy 18-36: 3020x57 (Turf) Attended: 1200-0000Z CTAF/Unicom: 122.7 JAX Center Dep/Con: 135.75 Notes: See "Airport Facility Directory" for comments about runway conditions and information.

FBO: Crystal Aero Group, Inc. Phone: 795-6868

FL-DAB - DAYTONA BEACH
DAYTONA BEACH REG. ARPT.

Jerry's Restaurant:

Jerry's Restaurant is situated in the terminal building on the Daytona Beach Regional Airport. This fine dining establishment is open from 11 a.m. to 9:00 p.m. 7 days a week. The restaurant is on the second floor and overlooks the runways and ramp areas. Items featured on their menu include pasta dishes, chicken and veal, seafood selections as well as choice steaks. Seating capacity allows space for 60 persons within a modern and newly built restaurant and dining room. Lots of glass and window space provides for a modern atmosphere. Jerry's Catering is another facility located across the field that is primarily designed for in-flight catering services. Corporate and or business flights can arrange cheese trays, sandwich trays, box lunches, fruit plates and much more by calling 253-0898. Guests planning to dine at the restaurant can call 255-0600.

Attraction: Indigo Lakes Resort & Conference Center (2 miles) 258-6333; Par 3 golf club, (2 miles) 252-3983; Atlantic Ocean (5 miles); Tomoka State Park (15 miles) 677-3931; Disney World (75 miles) 407-824-2600.

Restaurants Near Airport:

Jerry's Catering Services	On Site	Phone: 253-0898
Jerry's Trml. Restaurant	On Site	Phone: 255-0600
The Olive Garden	1/2 mi.	Phone: 252-0639

Lodging: There are over 25 facilities located near the airport. However, it is reported the following will provide shuttle service: Hampton Inn 257-4030; Holiday Inn - Speedway 255-2422; Howard Johnson Lodge Airport 255-7412; Indigo Lakes Resort 258-6333.

Meeting Rooms: The following have accommodations for meeting rooms: Best Western Americano 255-7431; Daytona Inn Broadway 252-3626; Hampton Inn 257-4030; Hilton Daytona Beach 767-7350; Holiday Inn Boardwalk 255-0251; Holiday Inn Oceanside 255-5432; Holiday Inn Speedway 255-2422; Howard Johnson Lodge Airport 255-7412; Indigo Lakes Resort 258-6333; The Reef 252-2581; Travelodge Boardwalk 255-8827; Treasure Island Inn 255-8371.

Transportation: Taxi Service: AAA 253-5222; City 253-0675; Southern Komfort 672-6279; Yellow 255-5555; Rental Cars: Alamo 255-1511; Avis 253-8183; Budget 255-2249; Hertz 255-3681; National 255-3611.

Information: Daytona Beach Convention and Visitors Bureau, 126 E. Orange Avenue, P.O. Box 910, Daytona, Beach, FL 32115, Phone: 255-0415 or 800-854-1234.

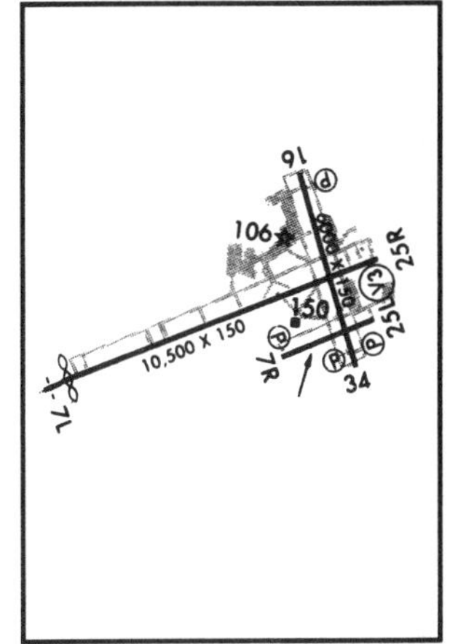

Airport Information:

DAYTONA BEACH - DAYTONA BEACH REGNL. AIRPORT (DAB)
3 mi southwest of town N29-10.80 W81-03.48 Elev: 35 Fuel: 100LL, Jet-A
Rwy 07L-25R: H10500x150 (Asph-Grvd) Rwy 16-34: H6000x150 (Asph-Grvd) Rwy 07R-25L: H3197x100 (Asph) Attended: continuously Atis: 120.05 Unicom: 122.95 App/Dep Con: 118.85, 125.8, 125.35, 123.9 Tower: 120.7, 118.1 Gnd Con: 121.9 Clnc Del: 119.3 Notes: No landing fees. Parking fees: Eagle Flight Center $3.00 singles, $7.00 twins; Sheltair Daytona Beach Jet Center $5.00 singles, twins $7.50.
FBO: Jet Cntr Daytona Beach Phone: 255-0471 FBO: Phil Air Flight Center Phone: 253-9222
FBO: Jet Air Daytona Phone: 248-2473

FL-DED - DELAND
DELAND MUNI-SIDNEY H TAYLOR FLD.

(Area Code 904)

8

Airport Restaurant & Gin Mill:

The Airport Restaurant & Gin Mill is located on the DeLand Municipal Airport and is reported to be situated within walking distance from nearby aircraft tie-down areas. This family style restaurant is open between 11 a.m. and 2 p.m. Monday through Saturday. They are closed on Sunday. Menu items include hamburgers, cheeseburgers, roast beef, tuna, salami, liverwurst and chicken sandwiches as well as many other selections. Average prices run $3.25 for lunch and around $6.00 for most dinner items. Their main dining room can seat 60 persons. 5 tables outside the restaurant along with 6 tables within the restaurant provide a nice view of the airport property. Guests can see aircraft arriving and departing on the runway out in front of this facility. Groups and fly-in clubs are welcome. Meals can be prepared for carry-out as well. Sky diving is a sport frequently carried out at the airport, and serves as entertainment for their guests. For information about the Airport Restaurant & Gin Mill call 734-9755.

Restaurants Near Airport:

Airport Rest. & Gin Mill	On Site	Phone: 734-9755
DeLand Hilton	1 mi W.	Phone: 738-5200
Hampton Restaurant	1 mi W.	Phone: 734-3860
Wally & Julies	N/A	Phone: 738-9343

Lodging: Hilton (Trans) 738-5200; Quality Inn 736-3440; University Inn 734-5711.

Meeting Rooms: Boulevard Motel 734-0716; Hilton 738-5200; Quality Inn 736-3440; University Inn 734-5711.

Transportation: Taxi Service: Bills Veterans Cab 734-6199; City Cab 734-3417; Lucas Cab 734-2401; Orange Cab 734-0545; West Volusia 789-7777; Woody's Cab 734-6500; Rental Cars: Hertz 736-7333.

Information: DeLand Area Chamber of Commerce, 336 N. Woodland Blvd., P.O. Box 629, Deland, FL 32721-0629, Phone: 734-4331 or 800-749-4350.

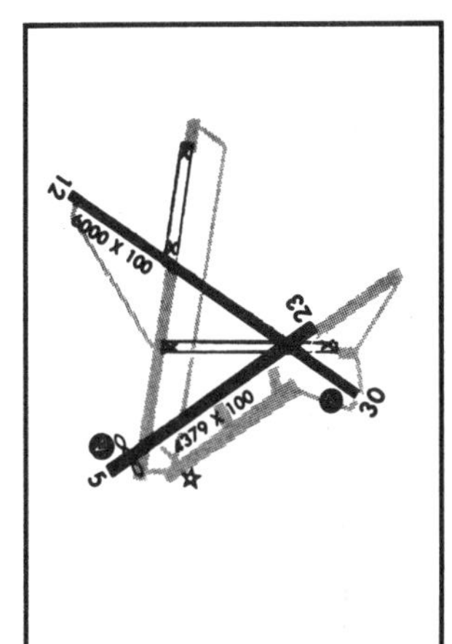

Airport Information:

DELAND - DELAND MUNICIPAL-SIDNEY H TAYLOR FIELD (DED)
3 mi northeast of town N29-04.01 W81-17.05 Elev: 79 Fuel: 100LL, Jet-A
Rwy 12-30: H6000x100 (Asph) Rwy 05-23: H4379x100 (Asph) Attended: continuously Unicom: 122.8 Public Phone 24hrs Notes: Parachute jumping is often in progress at this airport; Also $3.00 overnight parking.
FBO: Deland Aviation Phone: 736-7333

FL-55J - FERNANDINA BEACH
FERNANDINA BEACH MUNICIPAL

(Area Code 904) 9, 10

Dining at Amelia Island Plantation:

Amelia Island Plantation, located just 4 miles south of Fernandina Beach Municipal Airport, offers plenty or restaurants, as well as activities to whet your appetite. Amelia Inn, the resort's premier restaurant, features a stunning view of the ocean and scrumptious international cuisine served in an elegant atmosphere. The Verandah serves fresh seafood and succulent steaks in a pleasant family atmosphere. Children under 12 years of age can eat free at both the Amelia Inn and the Verandah. The Coop offers casual dining inside the restaurant or outside on a tree-shaded deck. For those spending the day at the pool, the Dunes Club features tropical drinks and sandwiches served poolside. Also, the Beach Club Sports Bar is a grill and bar that features casual dining inside or outside by the pool (open seasonally). Upon request, room service will deliver breakfast, lunch and dinner either to the villa or by poolside as well. Roberto's Pizza, which specializes in homemade pizza, is offered through room service. Golfers should enjoy the Golf Shop Restaurant, which overlooks the 18th hole of Oysterbay and serves breakfast and lunch. The Putter Club, which overlooks the beautiful Long Point Golf Course, serves light snack items. For a cool treat, Seaside Sweets serves up delicious, old-fashioned ice cream cones and other frozen specialty treats (open seasonally). The resort will provide a courtesy van to and from the airport. (Note: meeting or conference groups will be charged a shuttle fee.) Also, with a purchase of fuel, the FBO will loan out a courtesy car for a limit of 2 hours. For further information about restaurants and accommodations at Amelia Island Plantation, call 800-874-6878 or 277-5976.

The Ritz-Carlton:

The island, colorful: sapphire skies, azure waters, emerald greens, white sand. The resort, charming: The Ritz-Carlton, Amelia Island. A meeting place where every detail has been designed for convenience. You'll find their location ideal - nestled at the edge of a thirteen-mile beach along the Atlantic Ocean. There also just north of Jacksonville, no more than thirty minutes from Jacksonville International Airport and only 2 miles from Fernandina Beach Municipal Airport (55J). The atmosphere is reminiscent of days past: crystal chandeliers, antiques, 18th and 19th century oils, fresh floral arrangements. Their gracious guest rooms offer private balconies all with breathtaking ocean views with marble baths, honor bars, 24-hour room service. Choose The Ritz-Carlton Club and you'll also have access to a private lounge with a personal concierge and food and beverage presentations throughout the day. The Ritz-Carlton, Amelia Island. For memories past. And future. There's so much to do at The Ritz-Carlton, Amelia Island. You'll stroll along their secluded beach. You'll soak in the sun by their sparkling pool and hot tubs. Or on their sun deck. Play a round of golf on their challenging championship course. Take on an opponent at the Resort Tennis Center. You'll also find a fitness and

Restaurants Near Airport:

Amelia Island Plantation	6 mi S.	Phone: 277-5976
The Ritz-Carlton	3 mi	Phone: 277-1100

Lodging: Amelia Island Plantation (6 mi. trans.) 277-5976; Elizabeth Pointe Lodge (6 mi. trans.) 277-4851; Shoney's Inn (3 mi. trans.) 277-2300; The Ritz-Carlton (3 mi. trans.) 277-1100 or 800-241-3333.

Meeting Rooms: Amelia Island Plantation (6 mi. trans.) 277-5976; The Ritz-Carlton (3 mi. trans) 277-1100 or 800-241-3333.

Transportation: Amelia Island Plantation (6 mi. courtesy shuttle to and from airport) 277-5976; The Ritz-Carlton (3 mi. courtesy shuttle to and from airport) 277-1100 or 800-241-3333.Taxi Service: Benjamin's 261-7278; Rental Cars: Enterprise 261-7890

Information: Amelia Island-Fernandina Beach-Yulee Chamber of Commerce, 102 Centre Street, P.O. Box 472, Fernandina Beach, FL 32034, Phone 277-0717

(The Ritz-Carlton Cont.)

exercise center with its own indoor pool. Do anything you'd Like as their guest. Or nothing at all. The dining - indoors and out - is exceptional. Whether you prefer casual fare poolside, or an elegant dinner for two, you'll find it in one of their four restaurants. The Cafe and The Grill both offer live entertainment. And every afternoon at 3:00 in The Lobby Lounge they present tea and classical music. As their guest, you'll also enjoy another Ritz-Carlton tradition - uncompromising, personal service. They make every meeting an event. When its time for business, they offer meeting facilities for groups of any size. The Ritz-Carlton Ballroom, The Plaza Ballroom and eight meeting rooms have been set apart to afford the ultimate privacy. Pre-function areas are luxuriously furnished and provide gracious settings for coffee breaks or cocktails. They also offer the very latest facilities and audiovisual equipment. And conference services manager to help you with the details even before you arrive. For more information about the services and amenities of The Ritz-Carlton, Amelia Island call 277-1100 or 800-241-3333 (Information submitted by The Ritz-Carlton).

Airport Information:

FERNANDINA BEACH - FERNANDINA BEACH MUNICIPAL (55J)
3 mi south of town N30-36.58 W81-27.64 Elev: 15 Fuel: 100LL, Jet-A Rwy 04-22: H5350x100 (Asph) Rwy 13-31: H5150x150 (Asph) Rwy 08-26: H5000x150 (Asph) Rwy 17-35: H5000x150 (Asph) Attended: 1300Z-dusk CTAF/Unicom: 122.7 Jacksonville App/Dep Con: 127.0 Notes: Trees are at each end of Rwys. Rwys 08-26; 13-31; 17-35 and all taxiways except Rwy 13-31 parallel are cracking with grass and weeds.
FBO: Island Aviation Services, Inc. Phone: 261-7890

NO AIRPORT DIAGRAM AVAILABLE

Amelia Island Plantation

Amelia Island Plantation is located in extreme northeast Florida, across the St. Mary's River from Georgia. This 1,250-acre privately-owned resort and residential community overlooks the deep blue waters of the Atlantic Ocean. The island (named for Princess Amelia, daughter of England's King George II) features sugar-white sand beaches, world-renowned golf and tennis facilities, fine dining, entertainment, shopping and an on-property complimentary transportation system. More than 50 blocks of the downtown area consists of historically registered Victorian homes and businesses which have been restored and refurbished. Many are open for tours. There are also plenty of charming shops, galleries, nautical boutiques and museums.

Year-round, the island maintains reasonably mild temperatures which make everyone's stay that much more enjoyable. There are enough indoor and outdoor activities to keep the whole family busy. Besides 21 on-site swimming pools, more than 9 miles of nature trails and more than 3 miles of Atlantic beaches, the resort also offers biking, fishing, sailing, paddleboating and horseback riding.

The Plantation also features an award-winning youth program, so the children can have a chance to have their "fun in the sun." A great way for the kids to get to know the island is to take the "Discover Amelia" nature tours. They are sure to keep busy at Just for Kids, an activity center for children of ages 3 to 12, which offers a dinner with a children's menu, themed activities and supervision by trained recreation counselors. The resort also offers various aquatic programs, such as beginner, intermediate and advanced levels of swimming lessons. Junior golf, tennis, and racquetball clinics, as well as junior workout and aerobics are also offered. Young adults of ages 13 to 19 can participate in pool parties, beach bonfires, miniature golf and movie trips. For the youngest guests, babysitting service is offered to those who are not quite ready for the youth programs. (24-hour notice is required)

After all of the activities, it is easy to work up a hunger. The resort offers plenty of different types of restaurants from which to choose. The Amelia Inn serves international cuisine in an elegant atmosphere. The Verandah, the Beach Club Sports Bar, and the Coop offer casual family dining. The Dunes Club features tropical drinks and sandwiches served poolside (open seasonally). The Golf Shop Restaurant serves breakfast and lunch while overlooking the 18th hole of Oysterbay. The Putter Club serves light snack items while overlooking the Long Point Golf Course. For a sweet treat Seaside Sweets offers delicious, old-fashioned ice cream cones and other frozen specialty treats (open seasonally).

Photo by: Amelia Island Plantation An aerial stroll along the beaches of Amelia Island.

For meetings and accommodations, the resort has 33,000 square feet of function space to accommodate banquets, conferences and theme parties ranging from 20 to 1,000 people. Lodging includes 17 varying types of accommodations, ranging from deluxe hotel rooms and penthouses to three-bedroom beach townhomes and villas. Guests may choose oceanfront, marsh or fairway views.

Fernandina Beach Municipal Airport is located just 4 miles north of the Plantation. Overnight parking fees are $3.00 for singles and $5.00 for twins. The resort will provide a courtesy van to and from the airport. (Note: meeting or conference groups will be charged a shuttle fee.) Also, with a purchase of fuel, the FBO will loan out a courtesy car for a limit of 2 hours. Otherwise, the fee is $5.00. For more information, call the FBO at 261-7890. For further information about Amelia Island Plantation, call 800-874-6878 or 277-5976. (Information submitted by Amelia Island Plantation.)

FL-FPR - FT PIERCE
ST LUCIE COUNTY INTL.

(Area Code 407) 11

Restaurants Near Airport:
Tiki Restaurant On Site Phone: 489-6859.

Tiki Restaurant:

The Tiki Restaurant is located next to customs in the Fort Pierce/St. Lucie County International Airport. During our conversation with the management, we were told that when pilots fly-in to visit the restaurant, and are unfamiliar with the airport, they just ask for progressive to the Tiki Restaurant. The restaurant is open from 7 a.m. to 3 p.m., 7 days a week. On some special days they stay open until 5 p.m. The restaurant has large solarium-styled windows on two sides that provide a very open atmosphere. The ceiling of the restaurant has a Seminole Indian design thatched roof. One of the walls has mirrors to give an even larger appearance to the restaurant. Specialties of the house include, barbecued beef and pork that are cooked slowly over outdoor cookers. They also are well known for their Saesur salads and fresh seafood catch of the day from local fishermen. Fried, grilled and blackened Mahi Mahi (Dolphin) are very popular. More traditional selections include turkey and stuffing with mashed potatoes. Hamburgers and sandwiches are also prepared to order. Breakfast is served until 11 a.m. Monday through Friday and until 11:30 on weekends. The restaurant can accommodate around 70 people. Group and catered meals can also be arranged. In-flight catering with fruit, cheese and even fresh seafood platters are also available along with traditional sandwich and meat trays. For information call Tiki Restaurant at 489-6859.

Lodging: Holiday Inn-Oceanfront 465-6000; Holiday Inn-Sunshine Parkway 464-5000; Howard Johnson Lodge 464-4500; Sunset Inn 461-3070.
Meeting Rooms: Holiday Inn-Oceanfront 465-6000; Holiday Inn-Sunshine Parkway 464-5000.
Transportation: Rental Cars: Avis 489-2285; Enterprise 468-6106.
Information: Fort Pierce/St Lucie County Chamber of Commerce, 2200 Virginia Avenue, Fort Pierce, FL 34982, Phone: 461-2700.

Airport Information:

FT PIERCE - ST LUCIE COUNTY INTERNATIONAL AIRPORT (FPR)
3 mi northwest of town N27-29.70 W80-22.10 Elev: 25 Fuel: 100LL, Jet-A
Rwy 09-27: H6492x150 (Asph) Rwy 14-32: H4756x100 (Asph) Attended: 1130-0330Z
Atis: 134.825 Miami Center App/Dep Con: 132.25 Ft Pierce Tower: 128.2
Gnd Con: 119.55 Public Phone 24 hrs
FBO: Fort Pierce Air Center Phone: 489-2285, 800-446-7830

NO AIRPORT
DIAGRAM
AVAILABLE

FL-FXE - FT LAUDERDALE
FT LAUDERDALE EXECUTIVE

(Area Code: 305) 12

Restaurants Near Airport:
95th Bomb Group On Site Phone: 491-4595
Annabells at Sheraton On Site Phone: 772-7770
Skytel Coffee Shop On Site Phone: 491-5234

Skytel Coffee Shop:

This family style restaurant is located at the center of the field where the light beacon is situated. According to the airport manager's office, you can taxi your aircraft right up to the restaurant. They offer home cooked specials daily, along with homemade soup, salads, pies, delicious burgers and breakfast served all day. The restaurant is decorated in an aeronautical theme, with a friendly atmosphere. Flying clubs and group get-togethers are always welcome. They also cater to pilots and offer a variety of cheese trays, fruit trays and sandwiches. Prices for meals range from $3.00 for breakfast, to $5.00-$6.00 for lunch. The restaurant is open 7 a.m. to 3:30 p.m. 7 days a week. For more information call the restaurant at 491-5234.

Lodging: Sheraton Execuport; 2440 West Cypress, Fort Lauderdale, FL 33309. (On Airport) Phone: 305-772-7770, 10 other hotels are located within 5 miles of the airport
Transportation:
Cav-Air 491-4454, Banyan 491-3170, Million Air 771-6040, World Jet 772-7444, ATC Jet Center 772-1364, Skytel 491-3300, Mach One 776-0587, Rental Cars: Thrifty 772-1364, Budget 491-3170 or 491-4454, Enterprise 771-6040 or 772-7444
Information:
Greater Fort Lauderdale Convention & Visitors Bureau, 200 E Las Olas Blvd, Suite 1500, Fort Lauderdale, FL 33301, Phone: 765-4466.

Attractions: **Discovery Cruise Line, Inc:** Exciting cruises include dinner dance cruises, theme cruises, and half day cruises. Each trip departs from Port Everglades and Ft Lauderdale. They include meals and on-board entertainment. 1850 Eller Drive, Suite 402, Fort Lauderdale, FL 33316; Phone: 305-525-7800, Fla. 800-226-7800 or U.S. 800-999-7800. **Jungle Queen:** Features a four hour cruise through a tropical paradise. Barbecued and shrimp dinners are served on board along with a variety show and sing along as entertainment. There are also daily sightseeing cruises of the "Venice of America Ft Lauderdale where you stop and see Indian villages, alligator wrestling, rare birds and monkeys. Jungle Queen, Bahia Mar Yachting Center & Hotel, 801 Seabreeze Blvd., Ft. Lauderdale, FL 33316, 305-462-5596. **Ocean World:** Offers seven continuous shows featuring dolphin and sea lion preformances at the Grandstand. A number of fascinating reptiles and birds are also on display including dozens of sharks in the shark moat. 1701 S.E. 17th Street, Fort Lauderdale, FL 33316, Phone: 305-525-6612. Paddle Wheel Queen, Inc. provides luncheon cruises and starlight cruises along the Intracoastal Waterways. Paddle Wheel Queen, 2950 N.E. 32nd Avenue, Fort Lauderdale, FL 33308; 305-564-7659. **Rohr Balloons:** Offer thrilling champagne flights in a hot air balloon. Four people to a balloon. The champagne (for riders) flows freely "AFTER" every flight. Rohr Balloons, 6000 N.W. 28th Way, Fort Lauderdale, FL 33309; 305-491-1774. **Voyager Sightseeing Train:** Provides a relaxing and delightful tour of Fort Lauderdale on the open-air Voyager Tram. You will see the lovely homes on the waterways, fishing fleets' yacht basins and much more. Voyager Sightseeing Train, 600 Seabreeze Blvd., Ft. Lauderdale, FL 33316 305-463-0401 or 467-3149.

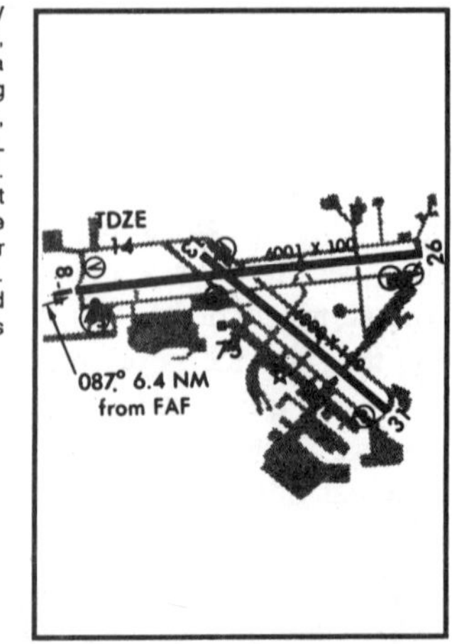

Airport Information: **FT LAUDERDALE - FT LAUDERDALE EXECUTIVE (FXE)**
5 north of town N26-11.84 W80-10.24 Elev: 14 Fuel: 100LL, Jet-A Rwy 08-26: H6001x100 (Asph-Grvd) Rwy 13-31 H3999x100 (Asph) Attended: continuously
Atis: 119.85 Unicom: 122.95 Tower: 120.9 Gnd Con: 121.75 Clnc Del: 127.95 Notes: Flock of birds on and in vicinity of airport. No landing fee, FBO's will charge for overnight parking.
FBO: Banyan Air Service Phone: 491-3170 FBO: World Jet Phone: 772-7444
FBO: Cav-Air Phone: 491-4454 FBO: Additional Operators Available

Not to be used for navigational purposes

FL-FLL - FT LAUDERDALE HOLLYWOOD INTERNATIONAL

(Area Code 954) 13,14

Aviators Tavern & Grill & LaBonne Table Catering:

This restaurant and facility is located under the control tower at the Ft. Lauderdale Intl. Airport. You can tie your airplane right outside the restaurant and use the entrance through the Jet Center. This restaurant is open Monday through Saturday from 10:30 a.m. to 2:00 p.m. Airplane catering is available 24 hours and 365 days a year. The menu consists of items like steaks, chops and seafood, with specials daily. They also feature burgers and chef salad in a shell, along with Caesars made 3 ways - plain, grilled chicken breast and seafood. Aviators features: Daily lunch specials and daily blackboard evening specials. The decor of the restaurant has a casual, modern, nautical and friendly atmosphere. Since the restaurant is located adjacent to the runway, you can see aircraft arriving and departing. Private catering is often done on or off the premises. In fact, they have already done several fly-ins. A private room for formal dining, seating 36 - cocktail parties up to 100 persons is also available. Aviators (LaBonne Table) has a full catering service for corporate or private pilots, serving sandwiches to full course meals. The local people visit this location to watch the planes coming and going. At times you can almost reach out and touch them! For information call 359-0044.

Market Place Restaurant (CA1 Services):

The Market Place Restaurant is part of the CA1 Services organization. It is located in Terminal 2 on the upper level directly behind the U.S. Air ticket counter. This is a family-style restaurant that is open between 6:30 a.m. and 8 p.m. A lounge is situated adjacent to the restaurant. A wide variety of fresh deli meats, soups and salad bar delights are available on their menu. An assortment of pastries are also provided daily. Prices average $5.50 for breakfast, $7.35 for lunch and around $8.95 for dinner. They feature buffets and daily specials. The decor of the restaurant is modern. Groups are welcome with advanced notice. Cheese trays, sandwiches and hot meals can be prepared to go. In-flight catering is also reported. For more information about this restaurant call 359-1500.

Restaurants Near Airport:

Aviators Grill	On Site	Phone: 359-0044
CA1 Services	On Site	Phone: 359-1500

Lodging: Numerous facilities located near airport. Holiday Inn-Intl. Airport, ($85-$109), Free Shuttle Pickup, Phone: 584,4000

Transportation: Yellow Cab 565-5400, Friendly Checker 923-9999, Carey Limousine Service 764-0615 or 920-3996; Rental cars: Airport Yellow Limo, Avis, Budget, Dollar, Herts, National.

Information: Greater Fort Lauderdale Convention & Visitors Bureau, 200 E Las Olas Blvd, Suite 1500, Fort Lauderdale, FL 33301, Phone: 765-4466.

Attractions:

Discovery Cruise Line, Inc: Exciting cruises include dinner dance cruises, theme cruises, and half day cruises. Each trip departs from Port Everglades and Ft Lauderdale. They include meals and on-board entertainment. 1850 Eller Drive, Suite 402, Fort Lauderdale, FL 33316; Phone: 305-525-7800, Fla. 800-226-7800 or U.S. 800-999-7800.

Jungle Queen: Features a four-hour cruise through a tropical paradise. Barbecued and shrimp dinners are served on board along with a variety show and sing along as entertainment. There are also daily sightseeing cruises of the "Venice of America Ft Lauderdale where you stop and see Indian villages, alligator wrestling, rare birds and monkeys. Jungle Queen, Bahia Mar Yachting Center & Hotel, 801 Seabreeze Blvd., Ft. Lauderdale, FL 33316, 305-462-5596.

Ocean World: Offers seven continuous shows featuring dolphin and sea lion performances at the grandstand. A number of fascinating reptiles and birds are also on display including dozens of sharks in the shark moat. 1701 S.E. 17th Street, Fort Lauderdale, FL 33316, Phone: 305-525-6612. Paddle Wheel Queen, Inc. provides luncheon cruises and starlight cruises along the Intracoastal Waterways. Paddle Wheel Queen, 2950 N.E. 32nd Avenue, Fort Lauderdale, FL 33308; 305-564-7659.

Rohr Balloons: Offer thrilling champagne flights in a hot air balloon; four people to a balloon. The champagne (for riders) flows freely after every flight. Rohr Balloons, 6000 N.W. 28th Way, Fort Lauderdale, FL 33309; 305-491-1774

Voyager Sightseeing Train: Provides a relaxing and delightful tour of Fort Lauderdale on the open-air Voyager Tram. You will see the lovely homes on the waterways, fishing fleets' yacht basins and much more. Voyager Sightseeing Train, 600 Seabreeze Blvd., Ft. Lauderdale, FL 33316 305-463-0401 or 467-3149.

Airport Information:

FT LAUDERDALE - HOLLYWOOD INTERNATIONAL AIRPORT (FLL)

3 mi SW of town N26-04.36 W80-09.16 Elev: 11 Fuel: 100LL, Jet-A Rwy 09L-27R: H9001x150 (Asph) Rwy 13-31: H6928x150 (Asph-Grvd) Rwy 09R-27L: H5276x100 (Asph-Grvd) Attended: continously Atis: 135.0 Unicom: 122.95 Tower: 119.3, 120.2 Gnd Con: 121.4, 121.7 Clnc Del: 128.4 Pre Taxi Clnc: 128.4 Landing Fee $1.65/1000 lbs.

FBO: AMR Combs	**Phone: 359-0000**	**FBO: Raytheon Arft Serv**	**Phone: 359-1100**
FBO: Ft Lauderdale Jet Cntr	**Phone: 359-3200**	**FBO: South Florida A/C,**	**Phone: 359-8100**
FBO: National Jet Cntr	**Phone: 359-0066**		

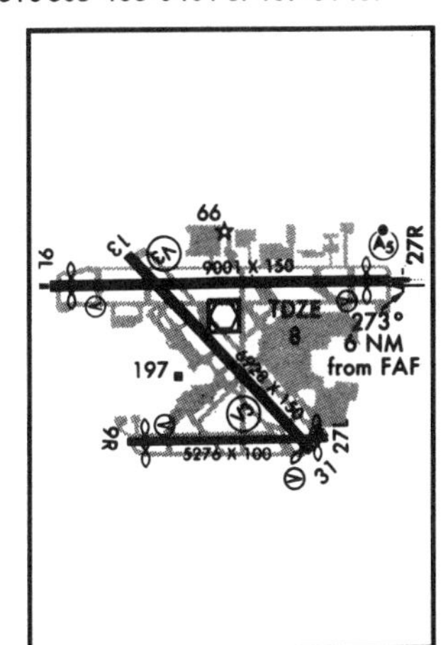

FL-FMY - FT MYERS PAGE FIELD

(Area Code 941) 15

Restaurants Near Airport:

Mikes Landing On Site Phone: 936-0091

Mikes Landing Restaurant:

Mikes Landing Restaurant is situated adjacent to Fort Myers Airways Fixed Base Operation (FBO), on Page Field. This fine dining establishment is reported open for lunch from 11 a.m. to 2:30 Monday through Friday, and for dinner from 4:30 p.m. to 9 p.m. Monday through Thursday and 4:30 p.m. to 10 p.m. Friday and Saturday. A variety of specialty gourmet entrees are available such as roast duck, poached Norwegian salmon, a selection of pasta dishes, rack of lamb, roast pork and much more. Average prices run $3.00 to $8.00 for lunch and $10.95 to $22.50 for dinner. There are three separate dining rooms available for dining, along with their lounge area. Meals can be prepared-to-go if requested. In-flight catering is another service that can be provided if requested. We were told that after 5 p.m. there is a dress code that goes into effect. Jeans & shorts are not permitted after this time. For information call Mikes Landing at 936-0091.

Lodging: Ramada Hotel-Airport (Trans) 936-4300; Ramada Inn (Trans) 332-4888; Sheraton Inn-Harbor Place (Trans) 337-0300.

Meeting Rooms: Ramada Hotel-Airport 936-4300; Ramada Inn 332-4888; Sheraton Inn-Harbor Place 337-0300.

Transportation: Rental Cars: Avis 768-2121; Budget 768-1500; Taxi service, limos & courtesy vans are also available through FBO's.

Information: Lee County Visitors & Convention Bureau, 2180 W 1st Street, Suite 100, Fort Myers, FL 33901, Phone: 335-2631.

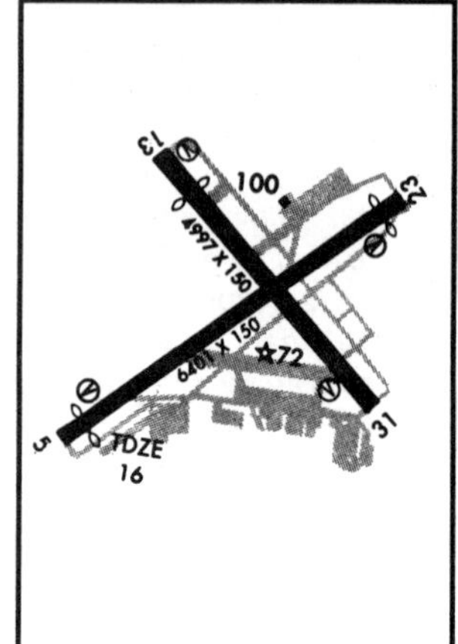

Airport Information:

FT MYERS - PAGE FIELD (FMY)
3 mi south of town N26-35.20 W81-5180 Elev: 18 Fuel: 100LL, Jet-A
Rwy 05-23: H6401x150 (Asph-Pfc) Rwy 13-31: H4997x150 (Asph) Attended: 1200-0300Z
Atis: 135.2 Unicom: 122.95 Ft Myers App/Dep Con: 126.8, 119.75 Tower: 119.0
Gnd Con: 121.7 Clnc Del: 121.7
FBO: Fort Myers Airways, Inc. Phone: 936-2559
FBO: Fort Myers Jet Center Phone: 936-1443

FL-RSW - FT MYERS SOUTHWEST FLORIDA REGIONAL

(Area Code 941) 16

Restaurants Near Airport:

Chart House 10 mi NW. Phone: 332-1881
Jerry's Restaurant On Site Phone: 768-0112

Jerry's Restaurant:

Jerry's Restaurant is situated in the terminal building at the Southwest Florida Regional Airport. This establishment reports a combination cafeteria and fine dining facility. Menu selections include deli sandwiches, pastries, bakery goods, breads and donuts that are made right on the premises. Steam table service with a carver, allows guests to build their own sandwiches. Turkey clubs, shrimp, seafood, taco salads, T-bone steaks, and New York steaks are also offered. A coffee shop at their location provides seating for between 150 and 300 persons. A fine dining restaurant is situated within the restaurant that can accommodate 150 persons. A view of the aircraft ramps and runways are also visible from portions of the dining area. During special times of the year, this restaurant prepares catered lunches for aviation related activities such as their annual "Aviation Day" celebration. In-flight catering is another service provided as well. For information about the services at Jerry's Restaurant call 768-0112.

Lodging: Shuttle service provided by the following: Holiday Inn (Bell Tower, 8 miles) 482-2900; Marriott Courtyard (9 miles) 275-8600; Sheraton Harbor (14 miles) 337-0300; Ramada Inn/Park Inn (10 miles) 936-4300.

Meeting Rooms: Holiday Inn 482-2900; Park Inn 936-4300; Sheraton Harbor 337-0300; Marriott Cortyard 275-8600.

Transportation: Jet South Aviation (FBO) can provide courtesy transportation to nearby facilities 768-3454; Also: Limo and rental cars available: Avis 768-2121; Budget 768-1500; Dollar 786-2223; General 768-1901; Hertz 768-3100; Superior 768-2882.

Information: Lee County Visitors & Convention Bureau, 2180 W 1st Street, Suite 100, Fort Myers, FL 33901, Phone: 335-2631.

Attractions:

Ft. Myers Beach (10 miles); Sanibel Island (20 miles); Gateway Golf Course (3 miles); Edison's winter home museum (14 miles); Sanibel Resort (20 miles); Lakes Park (10 miles).

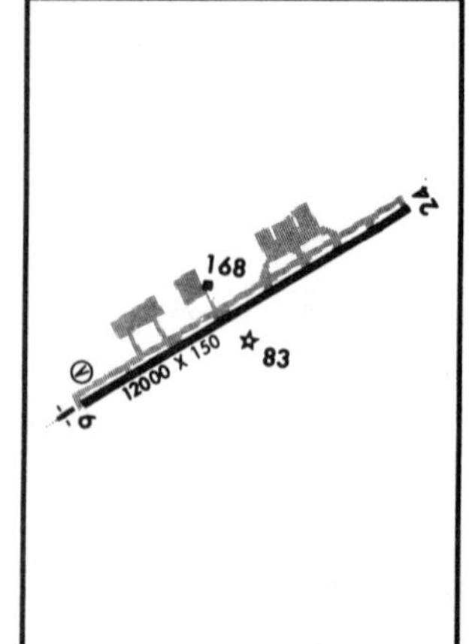

Airport Information:

FT MYERS - SOUTHWEST FLORIDA REGIONAL AIRPORT (RSW)
10 mi southeast of town N26-32.17 W81-45.31 Rwy 06-24: H12000x150 (Asph-Grvd) Attended: continuously Atis: 124.65 Unicom: 122.95 Fort Myers App/Dep Con: 126.8, 119.75, Fort Myers Tower: 128.75 Gnd Con: 121.9 Notes: CAUTION: birds and wildlife on and in vicinity of airport; Landing fees $1.92 per 1000 lbs. Max. gross landing weight; $5.00 overnight parking fees.
FBO: Jet South Phone: 768-3454 or 800-343-5387

FL-2RR - FROSTPROOF RIVER RANCH RESORT

River Ranch Inc. Resort:

The River Ranch Inc. Resort is situated 25 miles east of Lake Wales along Hwy 60. Furnished with its own private airstrip, this establishment hosts numerous recreational activities and amenities within a relaxed and peaceful country atmosphere. The Branding Iron Restaurant located on the premises, is reported to be within walking distance from the airport. Courtesy transportation is also available. This family style restaurant is open 7 days a week from 7 a.m. to 10 p.m. Specials featured on their menu include a Friday night seafood buffet begining at 5 p.m., a Saturday night all-you can-eat BBQ buffet beginning at 5 p.m. until 10 p.m., and a Sunday brunch buffet from 10 a.m. to 2 p.m., very popular with many guests. Reservations are suggested, especially on weekends . Average prices for regular menu selections run $6.00 for breakfast, $5.00 to $6.00 for lunch and $9.50 for dinner. The Branding Iron dining room provides a western decor with wagon wheel chandeliers, cloth covered tables, and a comfortable atmosphere. Outdoor cookouts can also be catered for groups and parties. For more information call the Branding Iron Restaurant at 692-1321

Restaurants Near Airport:

Branding Iron	On Site	Phone: 692-1321
Ranch Harbour	On Site	Phone: 692-1321

Lodging: River Ranch Inc. Resort: A variety of accommodations are available including, motel rooms, suites, efficiencies, one & two bedroom cottages & complete RV facilities. Phone: 692-1321.

Meeting Rooms: River Ranch Inc. Resort: Contains meeting, conference & convention facilities, available for small groups and up to 400 people comfortably.

Transportation: Courtesy transportation is available by the River Ranch Inc. Resort.

Information: Lake Wales Area Chamber of Commerce, 340-West Central Avenue, Lake Wales, FL 33853, Phone: 676-3445.

Attractions: The River Ranch Inc. Resort: is located 25 miles east of Lake Wales, FL, and contains a variety of amenities, including a 4,950x75 lighted & paved airstrip, motel rooms, suites, cottages and complete RV facilities, swimming pools, lighted tennis courts, health spa, golf & miniture golf, a rodeo, western saloon, trail rides, boat rentals, game room, skeet & trap range, swimming pools, tennis courts, all situated on 1,750 acres of private land. Convention Facilities are also available. For information call the resort at 692-1321.

Airport Information:

RIVER RANCH RESORT/FROSTPROOF - RIVER RANCH RESORT (2RR)
17 mi east of town N27-46.94 W81-12.32 Elev: 55 Fuel: 100LL
Rwy 16-34: H4950x75 (Asph) Attended: continuously Unicom: 122.8 Notes: Activate LIRL Rwy 16-34 and rotating beacon - CTAF/Unicom.
River Ranch Inc. Resort **Phone: 692-1321**

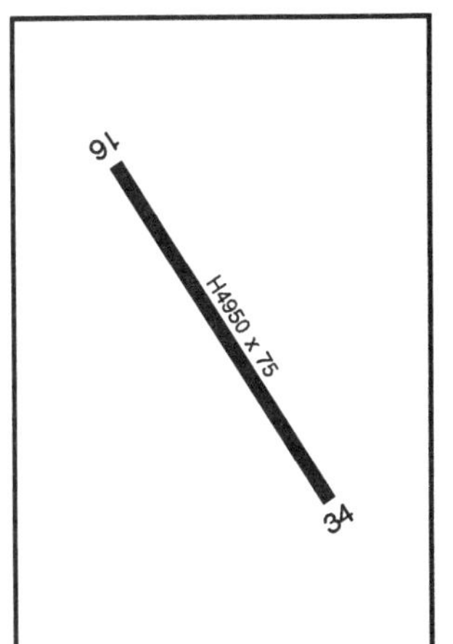

FL-JAX - JACKSONVILLE INTERNATIONAL AIRPORT

(Area Code 904)

18

Montegeo's Restaurant:

The Montegeo's Restaurant is located at the Holiday Inn Airport (500 rooms), about 2 miles east on Airport Road. Complimentary shuttle service is provided for their guests. Open from 6 a.m. to 10 p.m., this facility offers three buffets daily, along with Sunday brunch and dinner selections specializing in steaks and seafood. Prices range from $5.50 for breakfast, $6.60 for lunch and $11.75 for dinner. 11 Banquet rooms are on the premises able to seat up to 300 people. All meals, plus appetizers, can be prepared for carry-out orders. For information call 741-4404

Attractions:

Jacksonville Zoological Park is about 15 minutes by car from the Jacksonville Intl. Airport, at 8605 Zoo Blvd. via Heckscher Drive. 700 mammals, reptiles and birds are on display with safari train rides. Open daily except Jan 1st, Thanksgiving and December 25. Phone: 757-4462 or 4463; Amelia Island Plantation (30 minutes), Phone: 261-6161; Ritz Carlton (30 minutes) 277-2270; Little Talbot Island State Park (30 minutes) Phone: 251-3231.

Restaurants Near Airport:

Days Inn Airport	2 mi E.	Phone: 741-4600
Host International	On Site	Phone: 741-0040
Montegeo's Holiday Inn	2 mi E.	Phone: 741-4404
Radisson Inn Arpt.	On Site	Phone: 741-4747

Lodging: Radisson Inn (On airport property, Free Trans.), Phone: 741-4747; Holiday Inn, (Free Trans.), at I-95 and Airport Road, Phone: 741-4404; Days Inn, (Free Trans.) at I-92 and Airport Road, Phone: 741-4600.

Conference Rooms: Radisson Inn, (On Site), 741-4747; Holiday Inn, (2 miles East), 741-4404; Days Inn, (On Site), 741-4600; Howard Johnson, (Phone number and distance not available).

Transportation: Courtesy transportation provided by "Air Kaman", Phone: 741-2201; Rental Cars: Avis, 741-2327; Hertz, 741-2151; National, 741-4580; Budget, 741-4141; Dollar, 741-4614; Taxi Service: Taxi, 356-8888.

Information: Jacksonville and Beaches Convention and Visitors Bureau, 3 Independent Drive, Jacksonville, FL 32202, Phone: 798-9148

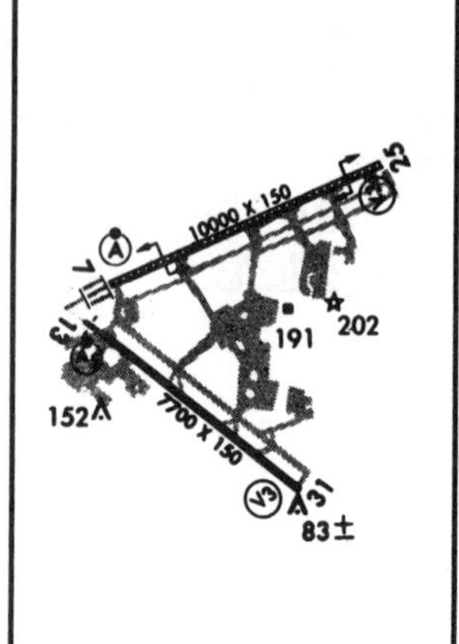

Airport Information:

JACKSONVILLE - JACKSONVILLE INTERNATIONAL (JAX)
9 mi north of town N30-29.64 W81-41.27 Elev: 30 Fuel: 100LL, Jet-A
Rwy 07-25: H10000x150 (Asph-Grvd) Rwy 13-31: H7700x150 (Conc-Grvd)
Attended: continuously Atis: 125.85 Unicom: 122.95 App/Dep Con: 127.0 (North), 118.0 (South), & 124.9 (Southwest) Tower: 118.3 Gnd Con: 121.9 Clnc Del: 119.5
Pre Taxi Clnc: 119.5 Public Phone 24hrs Notes: No landing fee with fuel purchase; Overnight parking $6.00 for (singles) and $10.00 for (twins).
Airport Manager Phone: 741-2000

FL-7X1 - KEY WEST SUGAR LOAF SHORES AIRPORT

(Area Code 305)

19

Sugar Loaf Restaurant:

This establishment is a combination family and fine dining restaurant, along with resort accommodations, located a short walk from the Sugar Loaf Shores Airport. The dining room is open between 7:30 a.m. and 2:30 p.m. and reopens for dinner from 5:00 p.m. to 9:30 p.m. Their menu contains items like breakfast specials, all types of sandwiches, a salad bar, prime rib, fresh local seafood and gourmet cooking specializing in American cuisine. Average prices are $2.00 to $5.00 for breakfast, $2.95 to $6.50 for lunch and $8.95 to $18.00 for dinner. Their main dining room seats 120 people, and has a tropical decor with table cloths, candles, and a spectacular view overlooking the water and dolphin feeding. In addition to the restaurant, their complex includes a 55 room lodge, as well as outdoor activities, tennis courts, a miniature golf course, swimming pool and shuffle board. Airport information can be obtained directly by calling 745-2217. For more Resort information, call the lodge at 800-553-6097 or 745-3211.

Restaurants Near Airport:
Sugar Loaf Restaurant 1/4 mi Phone: 745-3211

Lodging: Sugar Loaf Lodge (1/4 mile) 745-3211

Meeting Rooms: Sugar Loaf Lodge 745-3211

Transportation: Airport is within walking distance of resort.

Information: Greater Key West Chamber of Commerce, 402 Wall Street, Key West, FL 33040, Phone: 294-2587.

Attractions:

Sugar Loaf Lodge provides a host of amenities, including tennis courts, a swimming pool, Dolphin shows, miniature golf, lodging, restaurants and much more. Call 800-553-6097 or 745-3211 for more information.

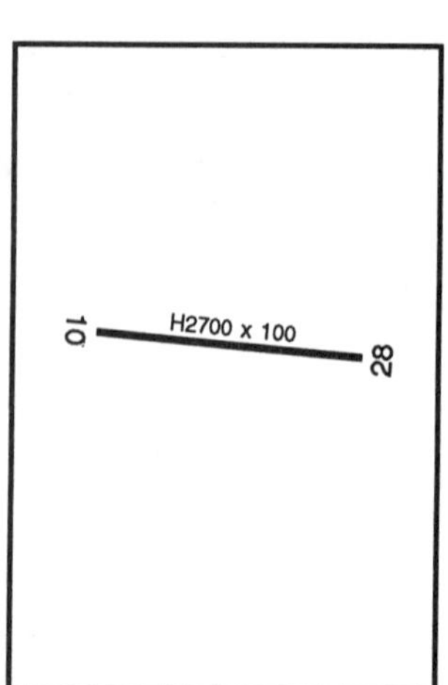

Airport Information:

KEY WEST - SUGAR LOAF SHORES AIRPORT (7X1)
13 mi northeast of town 24-38-54N 081-34-48W Elev: 04 Rwy 10-28: H2700x100 (Asph)
Attended: daylight hours Unicom: 122.8 Notes: Private use facility, use at own risk.
Sugar Loaf Shores Airport Phone: 745-2217
Sugar Loaf Lodge Phone: 745-3211

FL-EYW - KEY WEST
KEY WEST INTERNATIONAL AIRPORT

(Area Code 305) **20**

Martha's Restaurant:

Martha's Restaurant is located 1/4 mile due east of the Key West International Airport, and is within walking distance. Their menu features a fine assortment of steaks, prime rib, and fresh native seafood, including the chefs daily specials. This restaurant is located on the Atlantic Ocean with air conditioned comfort, and to enhance your dining experience, they display four of the most spectacular salt water aquariums in the Florida Keys. Prices for full course dinner selections average $25.00. Restaurant hours are from 5:30 p.m. to 10:00 p.m., 7 nights a week. Located adjacent to the restaurant is the Key West Motel and the Best Western Key Ambassador. For more information about this fine dining facility call 294-3466.

Restaurants Near Airport:

Conch Flyer	On Site	Phone: 296-6333
Benihana	(Adj)	Phone: 294-6400
Marthas	(Adj)	Phone: 294-3466

Lodging: Best Western Key, Phone: 296-3500; Holiday Inn Beachside, (Free transportation) Phone: 294-2571; Pier House, Phone: 296-4600; Marriott's Casa Marina Resort, (Free transportation) Phone: 296-3535.
Transportation: Island City Flying Service, Phone: 296-5422; Five Sixes Phone: 296-6666; Maxi Taxi Phone: 296-1800; Friendly Taxi Phone; 292-0000; Avis Car Rental Phone: 296-8744; Dollar Car Rental Phone: 296-9921
Information: Greater Key West Chamber of Commerce, 402 Wall Street, Key West, FL 33040, Phone: 294-2587

Attractions:

Key West attracts many vacationers each year, This region provides some of the finest fishing in the world. Your choice of charter boats, land fishing from the beach, docks or spear fishing from reefs. There are four public swimming beaches along with private beaches at nearby hotels in the area. Sightseeing tours of the area include walking, auto or bus tours, and even reefs cruises from the North end of Duval Street, which includes a two hour trip in glass bottom sightseeing boats over coral reef (weather permitting). Phone: 296-9535.

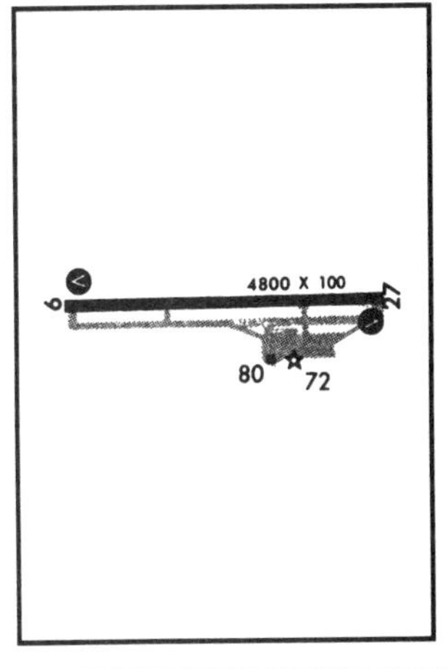

Airport Information:

KEY WEST - KEY WEST INTL. AIRPORT (EYW)
2 mi east of town N24-3337 W81-45.57 Fuel: 100LL, Jet-A Rwy 09-27: H4800x100 (Asph-Grvd) Attended: 1300-2300Z Unicom: 122.95 Navy Key West App/Dep Con: 124.45 Tower: 118.2 Gnd Con: 121.9 Clnc Del: 121.9 Public phone 24 hrs. Notes: Numerous flocks of birds on and in vicinity of airport, No landing fee for private aircraft; Commercial Aircraft: Single $5.00, Multi $6.50.
FBO: Island City Flying Service Phone: 296-5422

Key West

Key West, FL (FL-EYW)

Key West is located at the very tip of the Florida Keys in the Gulf of Mexico. It is an island city of palm-lined streets with glorious Victorian homes, gingerbread conch houses and mansions. John Audubon and Ernest Hemingway once lived there. One had a passion for preservation and the other had a great zest for life. Both of those qualities make up Key West. With an average temperature of 77 degrees, it is one of the most unique places to relax and rejuvenate the spirit. Feel the ambiance of the community when walking on world-famous Duval Street in Old Town Key West. Or, tour the city on foot or by trolley, and discover some of the best-made cigars and aloe products anywhere.

Key West provides some of the finest fishing spots in the world. It also offers breathtaking sunsets, sunny beaches, water activities, historic forts, lighthouses, theaters, museums, galleries, festivals, markets, sidewalk cafes and other restaurants and hotel accommodations.

Dive into the various water activities that Key West has to offer, such as fishing excursions, dive shops, snorkeling and sunset trips on various charters. Enjoy catamaran sailing and snorkeling without the crowds, and take guided reef and backcountry tours. Or, take eco-tours with Mosquito Coast Island Outfitters and explore the beautiful mangrove keys, bays and creeks. Ride the Discovery Glass Bottom Boat and enjoy a 2-hour excursion departing daily from Lands End Marina. Key West offers various boat and watersport rentals, as well as fishing, marine and nautical services.

Discover the diversity of cultural opportunities on this small island. Key West Bight waterfront, Nancy Forrester's Secret Garden and Perkins and Son Chandlery offer fascinating island experiences, while the Key West Aquarium provides an up-close glimpse of the numerous sea critters that inhabit the surrounding waters. The island's many museums and historical attractions document Key West's historical involvement in the arts. Stop by the Audubon House, the Harry S. Truman Little White House, the Ernest Hemingway House and the Key West Lighthouse. Also, take the Currry Mansion Tour and browse through the home of Florida's first millionaire.

Key West enjoys a reputation as an "artsy" community. The galleries exhibit vibrant watercolors of local scenes and marine creatures, as well as collections of African, Haitian and Chinese art. The Wyland Galleries, Gingerbread Square Gallery, Luck Street Gallery, China Clipper and the Haitian Art Company offer fantastic works of art.

Shops are easy to find in Key West. The hardest task is deciding which stores to choose from. Duval Street is the longest street in the world. It runs from the Gulf of Mexico to the Atlantic Ocean. In between are a number of fine stores that offer a range of goods. ACA Joe, Birkenstock, and Spec's are established stores with quality merchandise in clothing, shoes and music. Cross Duval on to Fleming Street to find Island Needlework , the island's most complete selection of needlepoint supplies.

Key West is also filled with dining and nightlife. Indulge in Cuban, Asian, Japanese, Mediterranean, American or Caribbean fare. Plan at least one meal under the tropical stars at a waterside bistro, a rooftop deck, a streetside cafe or a backyard patio. Of course, fresh shellfish and seafood is the specialty at almost every restaurant. Key West has long been famous for its "pink gold," the big pink shrimp found on the Tortugas fishing grounds. During the fall and winter months, Florida lobster (sometimes called crawfish) and stone crabs are at their peak. Conch (pronounced konk), a tough but tasty seafood, is also the name for natives born in Key West. Conch is harvested in the Bahamas and turns up in a tomatoey island treat known as conch chowder. Most dining spots feature a fish of the day, such as dolphin (mahi-mahi), snapper, tuna, group and cobia. Many may be familiar with Key Lime Pie which is the king of island desserts, and is made with natural juices of the tiny yellow-skinned island-grown limes. Stop in at restaurants such as Louie's Backyard, Crab Shack, Dim Sum Exotic Pan Asian Restaurant and Tea House, Lorenzo's Italian Restaurant and Olive Oil's Cafe. Also, for great entertainment, enjoy a casino cruise/dinner on the SeaKruz. The complete entertainment package includes: daily sails, 2 bands, a full dinner buffet, a Las Vegas casino and shipboard bingo. Child attendants are available upon request.

No trip to Key West is complete without the fun, romance and pleasure of island nightlife. Enjoy classical to Caribbean-inspired rock music at various concert halls, clubs, piano bars and watering holes. Visit Sloppy Joe's, Hog's Breath Saloon, Barefoot Bob's, Rum Runners Reggae Bar and Green Parrot for live entertainment.

Key West offers hundreds of comfortable and affordable hotels, motels and guest houses to choose from. Many also provide meeting facilities. Choose from the Curry Mansion Inn (nestled alongside the original 1899 Curry Mansion), the Merlinn Guest House Bed and Breakfast, Duval Gardens, the Blue Marlin Motel, Best Western Hibiscus Motel, Holiday Inn Resort and Convention Center, Marriott's Casa Marina Resort and many more.

Key West International Airport is located 2 miles east of town. The airport has a 4,800'x100 asphalt-grooved runway. Overnight parking fees are $7.00 for singles and $10.00 for twins. Taxi and rental car services are available for transportation. For more information about activities and accommodations in Key West, contact the Greater Key West Chamber of Commerce at 305-294-2587. (Information submitted by the Greater Key West Chamber of Commerce)

FL-15FL - LAKE CITY
CANNON CREEK AIRPARK

(Area Code 904) 21

Quail Heights Country Club:

The Quail Heights Country Club is located 3/4 of a mile west of the Cannon Creek Airpark. Fly-in guests can walk across the golf course to reach the country club or call for courtesy transportation, depending on available staff. There is a snack bar at this location that is open during the summer between 7 a.m. and 3 p.m. and during the winter between 7 a.m. to 4 p.m. Specialties include specials like chicken and rice, hamburgers, cheeseburgers, turkey club sandwiches, roast beef sandwiches, steak sandwiches, along with homemade soups and chili's. Their dining room can seat 28 persons, and provides counter and table service for their guests. Meals can be prepared to go as well. For more information about this establishment call the Quail Heights Country Club at 752-3339.

Attractions:

Quail Heights Golf & Country Club: Golf course located across the street from the airport, Phone: 752-3339; Also tubing at Ichetucknee Springs State Park (20 miles, south) Phone: 497-2511.

Airport Information:

LAKE CITY - CANNON CREEK AIRPARK (15FL)
1 mi southwest of town 30-10-55N W82-34-38W Elev: 125 Rwy 18-36: H3500x50 (Asph)
Rwy 9-27: H2600x60 (Turf) Hours: 24 Owner resides on airport CTAF: 122.75, (FSS 122.6)
Notes: Private use facility, prior permission required. No landing fees. However, donations to local EAA chapter appreciated. Call Kirby Fera (Pres) 904-755-9543.
FBO: Cannon Creek Pilots Assoc. Phone: 752-1957

Restaurants Near Airport:

Fireside Restaurant	2-1/2 mi NW	Phone: 755-6976
Ken's Bar-B-Que	1-1/2 mi N.	Phone: 752-5919
McDonald's Hamburgers	3 mi NW	Phone: 752-7037
Quail Heights Country Club	3/4 mi W.	Phone: 752-3339

Lodging: Holiday Inn (3 miles) 752-3901.

Meeting Rooms: Holiday Inn 752-3901 and Quail Heights Country Club 752-3339.

Transportation: Taxi Service: Express Cab 755-9994; Also Rental Cars: Bullards Rental Cars 755-1454; Ford Rent-A-Car 755-0630.

Information: Columbia County Tourist Development Council, P.O. Box 1847, Lake City, FL 32056, Phone: 758-1165.

NO AIRPORT DIAGRAM AVAILABLE

FL-31J - LAKE CITY
LAKE CITY MUNICIPAL AIRPORT

(Area Code 904) 22

Robert's Dock:

Robert's Dock Restaurant is located adjacent to the Lake City Municipal Airport. Fly-in guests should have no problem reaching the restaurant by walking. This family style establishment is open Tuesday through Friday from 11 a.m. to 8:30 p.m., Saturday from 5 p.m. to 10 p.m. and Sunday from 11 a.m. to 2 p.m. They are closed on Monday. During the winter this restaurant closes at 8:30 p.m. and in the summer they close at 9 p.m., as a rule. Their menu specializes in selections like seafood, fried shrimp, and catfish, as well as hamburgers, chicken and dumplings, fried steaks and chicken & dressing platters. Daily specials are also offered to their customers along with homemade desserts. Their main dining room can seat 135 persons which exhibits a pleasant atmosphere with natural cedar shingled walls. Many fly-in customers pay a visit to this restaurant on a regular basis. Groups and fly-in clubs are also welcome. The Aero Corporation (FBO) building reported as closed at this time, is directly across the street from the restaurant. General aviation customers that would be requiring in-flight catering service can call the restaurant for more information. Meals can be prepared to go as well. To find out more about Robert's Dock Restaurant, call 752-7504.

Restaurants Near Airport:

Robert's Dock	Adj Arpt	Phone: 752-7504

Lodging: Cypress Inn Motel 752-9369; Econo Lodge (Trans) 752-7891; Holiday Inn (Trans) 752-3901; Quality Inn 752-7550; Roadway Inn 752-7720.

Meeting Rooms: Holiday Inn 752-3901; Quality Inn 752-7550.

Transportation: Rental Cars: Roundtree-Moore Ford 755-0630.

Information: Columbia County Tourist Development Council, 601 Hall of Fame Drive, P.O. Box 1847, Lake City, FL 32056, Phone: 758-1312.

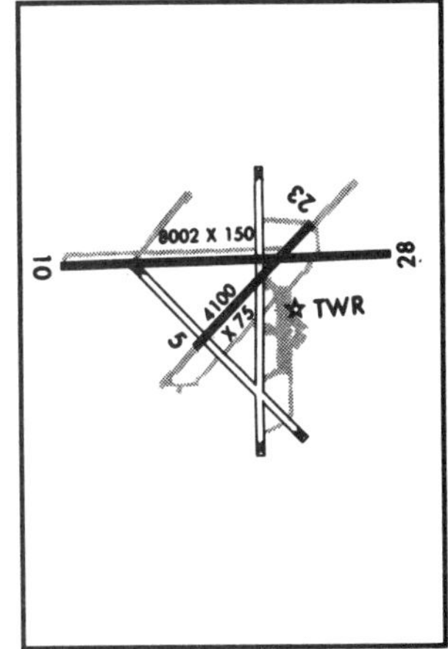

Airport Information:

LAKE CITY - LAKE CITY MUNICIPAL AIRPORT (31J)
3 mi east of town N30-10.92 W82-34.62 Elev: 201 Fuel: 100LL, Jet-A
Rwy 10-28: H8002x150 (Asph) Rwy 05-23: H4100x75 (Asph) Attended: 1300-2300Z
Unicom: 122.7 Aero Tower: 119.2 Gnd Con: 121.9
FBO: Eagle Aviation Phone: 755-4169

FL-LAL - LAKELAND
LAKELAND LINDER REGIONAL

(Area Code 941) 23

Tony's Airside Restaurant:

The Lakeland Linder Regional Airport, home of the annual EAA Sun and Fun Fly-in also contains a restaurant conveniently located at the base of the airport control tower. Tony's Airside Restaurant is open Monday through Saturday 7 a.m. to 9 p.m. and on Sunday from 7 a.m. to 8 p.m. 7 days a week. This restaurant is clasified as a family style and fine dining facility featuring sandwiches like the "Mile High Club", or the "May Day Sub", along with choice cuts of steak and seafood. One specialty of Tony's Airside Restaurant is their fettucini Alfredo with shrimp, prepared to order in a rich creamy Parmesan sauce, served with tossed salad for $11.95. Average prices run $3.00 for breakfast, $4.00 for lunch and $10.00 for dinner. They also offer a salad bar at lunch time. The restaurant decor is simple and clean, with an aviation theme, in addition to a wall mounted TV showing aviation movies. This facility is frequently visited by various aviation groups throughout the year and offers all types of catering to suit their customer's needs. For more information call 644-8684.

Restaurants Near Airport:

Giannini's	2 mi E.	Phone: 647-5977
Holiday Inn South	3 mi E.	Phone: 646-5731
Tony's Airside	On Site	Phone: 644-8684

Lodging: Holiday Inn South, (3 miles), 646-5731; Sheraton Lakeland, (3 miles), 647-3000.

Meeting Rooms: There is a small conference room in the terminal building. Contact airport manager at 644-3538; Holiday Inn South, (3 miles east of airport), Phone: 646-5731; Lakeland Civic Center, 686-7126.

Transportation: Checker Cab, 665-8151; Budget Rent-A-Car, 644-0433.

Information: Chamber of Commerce, 35 Lake Morton Drive, P.O. Box 3607, Lakeland, FL 33802-3607, Phone: 688-8551.

Attractions: Annual event, "Sun and Fun EAA Fly-in" This event has grown substantially in popularity over the years as one of the most popular Experimental Aircraft Association gatherings in the country, second only to the EAA convention held in Oshkosh, Wisconsin. Homebuilts, Ultralights, Warbirds, aircraft manufacturers, aviation workshops and much much more. This event is normally held during the second week in April. For information call 644-2431; Another annual event held in April is the "Orange Cup Regatta" exhibiting Hydroplane races, Phone: 683-3762;

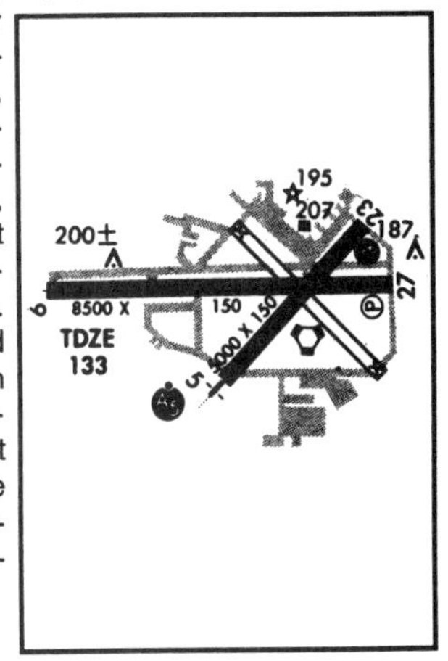

Airport Information:

LAKELAND - LAKELAND LINDER REGIONAL (LAL)
4 mi southwest of town N27-59.34 W82-01.11 Elev: 142 Fuel: 100, Jet-A Rwy 09-27: H8500x150 (Asph-Grvd) Rwy 05-23: H5000x150 (Asph-Grvd) Attended: 1200-0100Z Unicom: 122.95 Tower: 124.5 Gnd Con: 121.4 Public Phone 24 hrs Notes: No landing fee G/A aircraft; Overnight parking fee through FBO.
FBO: Hawthorne Lakeland, Inc. Phone: 644-0433

Photo by: Chalet Suzanne /David Woods

Chalet Suzanne is a unique bed & breakfast facility with its own private airstrip and several nearby popular attractions.

FL-X25 - LAKE WALES
CHALET SUZANNE AIR STRIP

(Area Code 813)

24

Restaurants Near Airport:
Chalet Suzanne On Site Phone: 676-6011

Lodging: Chalet Suzanne (On Site) 676-6011
Meeting Rooms: None Reported
Transportation: Taxi Service: Lake Wales 676-1089; Rental Cars: Enterprise Leasing Co. 294-8090
Information: Lake Wales Area Chamber of Commerce, 340 W. Central Avenue, P.O. Box 191, Lake Wales, FL 33853, Phone: 676-3445

Chalet Suzanne Bed & Breakfast:

Chalet Suzanne Bed & Breakfast is located right in the heart of central Florida. It has its own private airstrip that is within short walking distance of the main office and the dining rooms. This enchanting inn of 30 rooms, nestled on a 70-acre estate, is a gracious oasis amidst the excitement of central Florida attractions. Both Cypress Gardens and Bok Tower Gardens are about 3-5 miles from Chalet Suzanne. Disney World/Epcot is about 45 miles and Busch Gardens is about an hour's drive from the inn. Each Chalet guest room provides you with the comforts of a private entrance, private bath, air conditioning, telephone and television. A sparkling pool and lake are only a few steps from your courtyard or patio. The essence of the Chalet's reputation is its cuisine, particularly its soup, served in a unique setting of five quaint multi-level rooms filled with antiques,stained glass and old lamps. The soup came to the attention of the culinary press and aficionados from all over the country who were soon driving-and flying- to Chalet Suzanne. Among the frequent flyers were the astronauts at Cape Canaveral. Apollo astronaut James Irwin liked the soup so much that he wanted to take it to the moon. So, NASA found a way to freeze-dry it in plastic packets. It went to the moon twice! During your stay, visit the other interesting spots, such as the Swiss Room, Wine Dungeon, Gift Boutique, Autograph Garden, and especially the Soup Cannery, where the Inn's delicious soups are processed for gift giving. For more information about Chalet Suzanne, call 800-433-6011 or 676-6011.

Attractions:

Several major attractions are within an hour's drive from Chalet Suzanne. Estimated driving times are: Bok Tower Gardens - 10 minutes; Cypress Gardens - 10 minutes; Walt Disney World/Epcot Center- 40 minutes; Sea World - 45 minutes; Busch Gardens - 60 minutes. For more information about these attractions, call 676-3445.

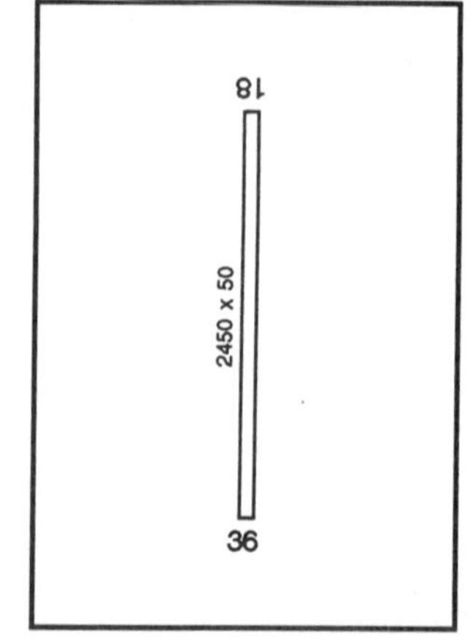

Airport Information:

LAKE WALES - CHALET SUZANNE AIR STRIP (X25)
3 mi north of town N27-57.02 W81-35.99 Elev: 140 Rwy 18-36: 2450x50 (Turf) Attended: 1300-0200Z , other times call 676-6011 CTAF/Unicom: 122.8 **Note**: If an alternate airport with a hard surface runway is desired, the **Lake Wales Municipal Airport (X07)** is attended from 1300Z-dusk. Contact the FBO at 678-3135.
Airport Manager: Chalet Suzanne Phone: 676-6011

River Ranch

Outdoor Resorts Of America, Inc.

"Life on the ranch was never like this. Outdoor Resorts River Ranch offers all that's down-to-earth and warm-hearted. Florida's unique geography sets the scene for a novel jaunt unlike anything you've experienced. Pull out your comfortable duds, sense of adventure and love for the great outdoors - forget your daily routine and settle in for a "good ole time", wrangler style.

We had your vacation enjoyment in mind when we created the nation's first and only Guest Ranch & RV Resort. We've combined the fine quality you expect from Outdoor Resorts of America with down-home fun to create this new vacation paradise.

All of the rugged, good times you'd expect to find are waiting for you here. Enjoy weekly rodeos featuring professional cowboys and champion Brahma bulls. Experience an old-fashioned hay ride with the family or with that special someone for a bit of romantic sparking.

Try your hand at archery, horseshoes and horseback riding on River Ranch's own horses. Test your skill at trap and skeet stations installed by Winchester, the original outfitter of the 19th century American gunsmen. Then, enjoy a game of cards or try your luck at billiards in River Ranch's Mustang Center recreation facility.

You can even play a round of golf on our 9-hole regulation golf course or a set of tennis on our lighted courts.

Relax. Pamper yourself at River Ranch's fully equipped health club with saunas, steam baths and specially designed tanning beds. Take a dip in one of our pools; fish on nearby Lake Kissimmee, well-known for its excellent lunker bass; or hunt wild boar, deer, dove and quail on nearby Fewox Ranch.

If you're hungry, indulge in the best steak in the area at the Branding Iron Restaurant in the main lodge or join in one of the Ranch's famous cookouts or fish fries. For lighter fare, visit the Ranch Harbour Restaurant. Finally, before riding off into the sunset, wind down with your favorite beverage and shuffle your feet to the rhythm of a country-western band in the authentic River Ranch Saloon.

That's right. We offer you all that's warm-hearted and neighborly. If you come by plane, you'll find our private,

Photo by: Outdoor Resorts River Ranch

On various occasions the River Ranch Outdoor Resort hosts a number of exciting events. In fact, the RV club gatherings as shown above, on the airport, is one such popular gathering held annually. Many other outings like the Country Coach Club Rally, Blue bird Rally, Florida Out door Writers Association Convention, and other events including the Lake Amphibian Flyers Annual Fly-in, Southwest Bonanza Society Fly-in and other aviation related gathering are a common site at this resort.

5,000 foot lighted airstrip at the north end of our resort, quite convenient.

Additionally, the Long Horn Convention Center offers groups and seminars a relaxing, fun-loving atmosphere for the business at hand. River Ranch permanent lodging facilities easily accommodate large groups for a down-home adventure worth writing home about.

A variety of fine accommodations are available, including - two-room suites in the River Ranch Inn; quaint one and two bedroom cottages with fireplaces, and efficiency apartments. In addition, vacationing RVers are offered beautifully landscaped, full-service sites shaded by live oaks and Florida palm trees.

We offer the romance and adventure of a real ranch with all the comforts of modern living. Adults and children alike will cherish this vacation to remember.

River Ranch and RV Resort is located on Highway 60 East approximately 65 miles south of Walt Disney World Vacation Kingdom, 50 miles west of Vero Beach and 25 miles west of Lake Wales." For more information call 941-629-1321 or 629-1303. (Information submitted by River Ranch).

FL-LEE - LEESBURG
LEESBURG MUNICIPAL AIRPORT

(Area Code 352) 25

Restaurants Near Airport:
Captain Bell's Rest. 4 blks NW. Phone: 728-3377

Lodging: Mission Inn, (10 miles) Phone: 324-3885; Days Inn, (6 miles) Phone: 787-1210; Econ-O-Lodge 787-3131.

Meeting Rooms: Mission Inn Golf & Tennis Resort, Phone: 324-3885

Transportation: Airport courtesy car available; Central States Rental, 728-2030; Enterprise Rental, 787-1128; Budget Rent-A-Car, 787-5555; City CAB Company, 787-5550.

Information: Leesburg Area Chamber of Commerce, P.O. Box 490309, Leesburg, FL 34749-0309, Phone: 787-2131.

Captain Bell's Restaurant:

This restaurant is located across the highway from the Leesburg Municipal Airport, about 4 blocks northwest of the aircraft parking area. This family style restaurant, with seating for about 102 persons, is open Sunday through Thursday from 11 a.m. to 9 p.m. Friday and Saturday from 11 a.m. to 10 p.m. Their menu lists appetizers, salads, soups, specialized seafood dishes, along with desserts. Prices range from $3.95 to $5.95 for lunch and $6.95 to $22.95 for dinner. The restaurant decor is nautical with tables and booths. For information call 728-3377.

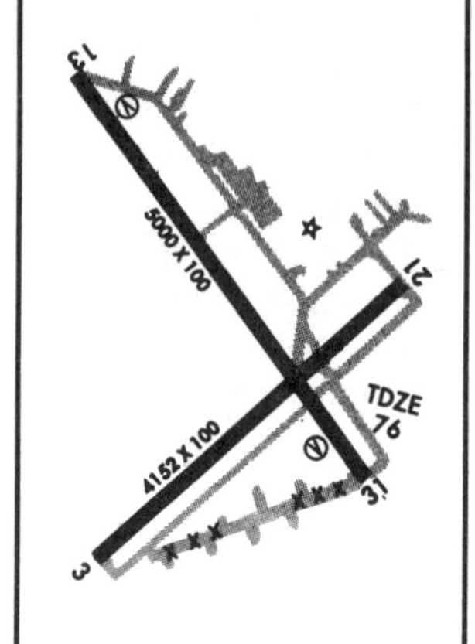

Airport Information:

LEESBURG - LEESBURG MUNICIPAL AIRPORT (LEE)
3 mi northeast of town N28-49.37 W81-48.55 Elev: 77 Fuel: 100LL, Jet-A
Rwy 13-31: H5000-100 (ASPH) Rwy03-21: H4152x100 (ASPH) Attended: 1200-0000Z
Unicom: 122.7 Public Phone 24hrs Notes: No landing fees; overnight tiedown $2.00, several restaurants, fast food service and shoping mall 2 miles east of airport.
FBO: Sunair Aviation, Phone: 787-2211
FBO: Triangle Aviation Serv. Phone: 787-3447

FL-MLB - MELBOURNE
MELBOURNE REGIONAL AIRPORT

(Area Code 407) 26

Restaurants Near Airport:
Jerry's Airport Rest. On Site Phone: 727-3676

Lodging: Courtyard by Marriott (Trans) 724-6400; Hilton-Melbourne Beach (Trans) 777-5161; Hilton Airport (Trans) 768-0200; Holiday Inn-Riverview (Trans) 723-3661; Ramada Inn-Riverfront (Trans) 724-4422.
Meeting Rooms: Courtyard by Marriott 724-6400; Hilton-Melbourne Beach 777-5161; Hilton Inn-Airport 768-0200; Ramada Inn-Riverfront 724-4422.
Transportation: Taxi Service: Yellow 723-1234; Saf-T-Cab 723-4421; Rental Cars: Avis 723-7755; Budget 725-7737; General 984-5393; Hertz 723-3414; National 723-3035.
Information: Greater South Brevard Area Chamber of Commerce, 1005 East Strawbridge Avenue, Melbourne, FL 32901, Phone: 724-5400.

Jerry's Airport Restaurant:

Jerry's Airport Restaurant is reported to be situated within the terminal building at the Melbourne Regional Airport. Fly-in guests can park their aircraft at the fixed based operators (FBO's) and obtain courtesy transportation or taxi service to the restaurant. This cafeteria style facility is open 7 days a week between 5:30 a.m. and 4 p.m. Items on their menu include a full breakfast selection, as well as turkey, pork loin, roast beef, all kinds of chicken dishes, fish sandwiches, and homemade soups. Average prices run $3.95 for breakfast, $4.95 for lunch and $5.95 for dinner. Their dining room can accommodate 200 persons and faces the concourse area of the airport. The decor of the dining room is modern with white walls, blue carpeting and is decorated with photographs. Groups and parties are welcome. Jerry's Airport Restaurant also specializes in In-flight catering. Those interested in this service should contact the restaurant for further information. Meals can be delivered to the aircraft as well. Call Jerry's Airport Restaurant at 727-3676.

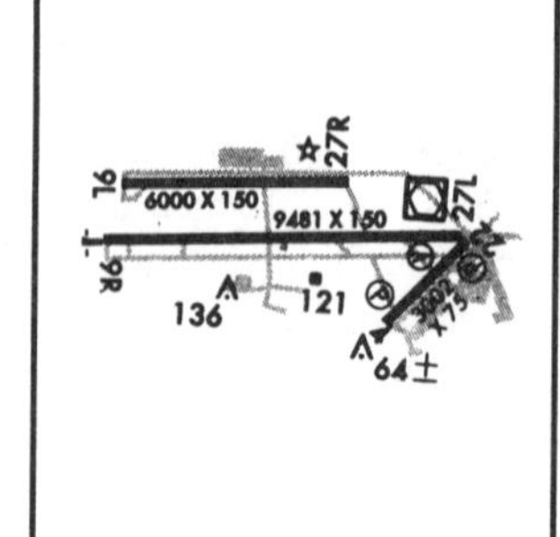

Airport Information:

MELBOURNE - MELBOURNE REGIONAL AIRPORT (MLB)
2 mi northwest of town N28-06.17 W80-38.75 Elev: 35 Fuel: 100LL, Jet-A
Rwy 09R-27L: H9481x150 (Asph) Rwy 09L-27R: H6000x150 (Asph)
Rwy 04-22: H3002x100 (Asph) Attended: continuously Atis: 132.55 Unicom: 122.95
Tower: 118.2, 124.05 Gnd Con: 121.9
FBO: Atlantic Jet Center Phone: 255-7111
FBO: F.I.T. Aviation, Inc. Phone: 727-0461

FL-TMB - MIAMI
KENDALL-TAMIAMI EXECUTIVE

(Area Code 305)

27

Landing Strip Restaurant:

According to the airport management, this restaurant has been closed. We were informed however, that there may be another restaurant establishment re-opening in the future. It is uncertain as to when this may occur.

Restaurants Near Airport:
Landing Strip Restaurant On Site Phone: N/A

Lodging: Marriott-Miami Airport (Trans) 649-5000; Radisson Plaza Hotel (Trans) 261-3800; Wellesley Hotel (Est. 1-2 miles) 270-0359.

Meeting Rooms: Marriott-Miami Airport 649-5000; Radisson Plaza Hotel 261-3800; Wellesley Hotel 270-0359.

Transportation: None Reported

Information: Greater Miami Convention & Visitors Bureau, 701 Brickell Avenue, Suite 2700, Miami, FL 33131, Phone: 539-3000. Public transportation 638-6700.

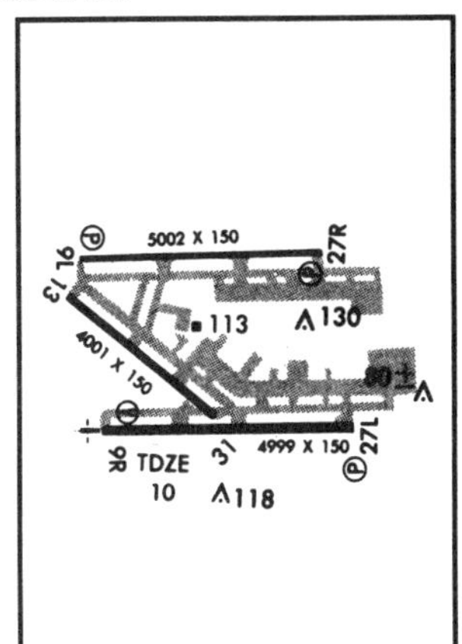

Airport Information:

MIAMI - KENDALL-TAMIAMI EXECUTIVE AIRPORT (TMB)
13 mi southwest of town 25-38-51N 80-25-59W Elev: 10 Fuel: 100LL, Jet-A
Rwy 09L-27R: H5002x150 (Asph) Rwy 09R-27L: H4999x150 (Asph) Rwy 13-31: H4001x150 (Asph) Attended: continuously Atis: 124.0 Unicom: 122.95
Miami App/Dep Con: 125.5 Tower: 118.9, 124.9 Gnd Con: 121.7 Clnc Del: 133.0
Notes: CAUTION: Agriculture aircraft operating in immediate vicinity of airport below 200 feet AGL. Heavy acrobatic practice area 9 MN southwest of airport from surface to 3500 feet, also helicopter training 700 feet south runway 09R-27L and 700 north runway 09L-27R during daylight hours.

FBO: Air Sal, Inc. **Phone: 251-1982**
FBO: Tac Air Service of Miami, Inc. **Phone: 233-0310**
FBO: Tamiami Jet Center **Phone: 233-1111**

FL-MIA - MIAMI
MIAMI INTERNATIONAL

(Area Code 305) 28, 29

Miami Terminal Concessions:

Throughout the horse-shoe shaped terminal complex and its seven passenger concourses, can be found over 50 food and beverage outlets suited for everyone's mood and taste. Full fare restaurants, light-fare food and snack bars, ice cream parlors, coffee shops and juice bars, along with cocktail lounges are carefully dispersed throughout public and passenger areas. A burgerking restaurant is located at the fourth level of the Concourse E Satellite Terminal. A food and snack bar, located within the Airport Pharmacy which is airport wide, remains open 24 hours per day. Miami International Airport terminal complex provides air travelers with all the conveniences and services that one could ask for. For further information contact the Metropolitan Dade County Aviation Department, Miami Intl. Airport, Post Office Box 592075, Miami, Florida 33159.

Top of the Port Restaurant:

In a setting complementing South Florida's tropical climate, the "Top of the Port Restaurant located on the 7th floor of the Miami Intl. Airport Hotel, the only in-airport hotel in Miami, offers fresh seafood and Continental cuisine, with a panoramic view of the airport and the Miami Skyline. The restaurant hours are from 7:00 a.m. to 11:00 p.m., 7 days a week. Their lounge provides a tropical atmosphere with an atrium bar and wide screen televisions. The Poolside Snack Bar serves salads, sandwiches and light snacks. Between checkout and departure relax at at the conveniently located Lobby Bar. In addition to the their dining facilities and lounges, the hotel also contains 260 newly renovated soundproof rooms and suites just steps away from the check-in counters. They also feature a rooftop health club, sauna and steam room, racquet ball court, jogging track, heated swimming pool, whirlpool and even a sun deck. Conference facilities and full service catering is also available. For more information you can call them at 871-4100.

Restaurants Near Airport:

Miami Intl. Arpt. Restaurants	On Site	(Over 50 in Trml. Bldg.)
Top of the Port/MIA Hotel	On Site	Phone: 871-4100

Lodging: Miami Intl. Airport Hotel (Inside the Miami Intl. Airport Terminal-Concourse E, no transportation needed) 871-4100; The following provide shuttle service: Embassy Suites 634-5000; Hilton-Miami Airport 262-1000; Holiday Inn-Intl Airport 885-1941; Holiday Inn-Intl Airport 446-9000; Marriott-Miami Airport 649-5000; Radisson Mart Plaza Hotel 261-3800; Ramada Hotel-Miami Airport 871-1700; Ramada Inn-Palmetto Exp. 261-4230; Regency Hotel-Airport 441-1600; Sheraton Inn-River House 871-3800;

Meeting Rooms: All lodging facilities listed above contain accommodations for meeting or conferences; Also: The Miami Intl. Airport Hotel, right on the airport property, provides an executive conference center able to accommodate 200 people comfortably, as well as two executive board rooms complete with audio/visual equipment 871-4100.

Transportation: Taxi Service: Carey Limousine Service 764-0615 or 920-3996; Rental Cars: Avis 637-4900; Budget 871-3053; Dollar 887-6000; Herts 871-0300; National 638-1026; Value 871-6760.

Information: The Greater Miami Convention & Visitors Bureau, 701 Brickell Avenue, Suite 2700, Miami, FL 33131, Phone: 539-3000 or 800-283-2707. Public transportation 638-6700.

Airport Information:

MIAMI - MIAMI INTERNATIONAL AIRPORT (MIA)
8 mi northwest of town N25-47.59 W80-17.42 Elev: 11 Fuel: 100, Jet-A
Rwy 09R-27L: H13000x150 (Asph-Grvd) Rwy 09L-27R: H10502x200 (Asph-Grvd)
Rwy 12-30: H9355x150 (Asph-Grvd) Attended: continuously Atis: 119.15
Unicom: 123.0 App Con: 124.85, 120.5, 125.75 Tower: 123.9, 118.3 Gnd Con: 127.5, 121.8 Clnc Del: 135.35, 120.35 Dep Con: 125.5, 119.45
FBO: Metro-Dade Aviation Department Phone: 876-7017, 876-7862

FL-APF - NAPLES
NAPLES MUNICIPAL AIRPORT

(Area Code 813) 30

Runway Pub:

The Runway Pub restaurant is located within the terminal building at the Naples Municipal Airport. Fly-in guests should park their aircraft by the fixed base operators on the field. Transportation can be achieved through 4 means. Most of the FBO's provide courtesy vehicles; The Naple Airport Authority reported courtesy vans available, taxi service is also available, and Mulligan's Restaurant said that they would even provide customers with courtesy transportation if required. This pub styled restaurant is open 7 days a week between 6 a.m. and 1 a.m. Their menu contains entrees like corn beef, turkey sandwiches, beef sandwiches, and grilled cheese sandwiches. They also prepare a number of salads like chicken salads, cob salads and shrimp salads. Their dining room can accommodate up to 80 people and exhibits an Irish pub decor, with lively colors of green tile on their bar, and furnishing tables and high backed booths for seating. Guests can enjoy watching the arriving and departing commercial aircraft at the concourse area near the terminal building, only 100 feet away. During our conversation with the management we also learned that in-flight catering may soon be available to corporate and general aviation travelers, depending on the demand. For more information about the Runway Pub restaurant call 643-6553.

Restaurants Near Airport:

Frascatti's	1/2 mi E.	Phone: 643-5709
Nickel Bob's BBQ	Nearby	Phone: N/A
Runway Pub	On Site	Phone: 643-6553

Lodging: La Playa Beach Inn (Trans) 597-3123; Naples Motor Lodge (Trans) 262-1414; Quality Inn-Gulfcoast (Trans) 261-6046.
Meeting Rooms: Naples Airport Authority will allow use of their conference room when available. Clarion Naples 261-5777; Edgewater Beach Hotel 262-6511; La Playa Beach Inn 597-3123.
Transportation: Airport Authority can provide limited courtesy transportation to nearby facilities; Also Taxi Service: Yellow Cab 262-1312; Naples Taxi 775-0505; Gulfshore Taxi 445-9157; Rental Cars: Avis 643-0900; Hertz 643-1515.
Information: Naples Chamber of Commerce, 3620 Tamiami Trail North, Naples, FL 33940, Phone: 262-6141.

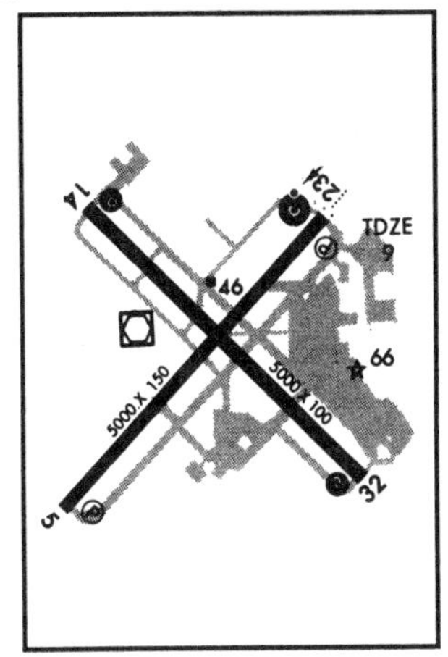

Airport Information:

NAPLES - NAPLES MUNICIPAL AIRPORT (APF)
2 mi northeast of town N26-09.15 W81-46.53 Elev: 9 Fuel: 100LL, Jet-A
Rwy 04-22: H5000x150 (Asph-Grvd) Rwy 13-31: H5000x100 (Asph) Attended: 1030-0300Z
Atis: 134.225 Unicom: 123.0 Tower: 128.5 Gnd Con: 121.6 Public Phone 24hrs Notes: No landing fees. Overnight parking for singles $6.00, twins $7.00, and Jets $8.00 per night plus tax.
Airport Authority (Fuel) Phone: 643-0404

FL-X00 - NAPLES
PORT OF THE ISLANDS

(Area Code 941) 31

The Garden Court:

The Garden Court Restaurant is located within the Port of the Islands Resort & Marina Hotel complex. During our conversation with the staff of the resort, we learned that a private landing strip is situated adjacent to the resort and is well within walking distance (Pvt use at own risk). The Garden Court restaurant is classified as a fine dining facility and is open between 7 a.m. and 10:30 a.m. for breakfast, 11:30 a.m. to 2:00 p.m. for lunch and 6 p.m. to 9 p.m. for dinner. items on their menu include a full breakfast line, 3 different pasta dishes, shrimp scampi, fresh catch of the day, seafood Alfrado, veal selections, chicken, beef dishes, filet mignon, New York strip steaks, as well as appetizers. During lunch hours lighter fare is provide like sandwiches, chicken salad plates, French dip, BLT's, grilled cheese, triple decker sandwiches, hamburger and cheeseburgers. Average prices run $6.95 for breakfast and between $8.95 and $19.95 for dinner. Their dining room exhibits an old Florida ambiance with a Mediterranean flair. Guests will enjoy a view of the swimming pool from the dining room. In addition to their main dining facility, they also have another food service bar and grill located on their property. This restaurant overlooks the harbor and serves lighter fare. For more information about all of the amenities of this resort call 394-3101 or 800-237-4173.

Restaurants Near Airport:

Garden Court (Hotel)	Adj Arpt	Phone: 394-3101

Lodging: Port of the Islands Resort & Marina (Hotel), Phone: 394-3101, or 800-237-4173.
Meeting Rooms: Port of the Islands Resort & Marina (Hotel), has conference rooms available on the premises, Phone: 394-3101 or 800-237-4173.
Transportation: This establishment is reported to be within only a few yards walking distance of the landing strip. A courtesy van can also be arranged for fly-in customers if advance notice of arrival is given to the front desk. Call 394-31-1 or 800-237-4173.
Information: Naples Area Chamber of Commerce, 1700 North Tamiami Trail, Naples, FL 33940, Phone: 262-6141.

Attractions: The Port of the Island Resort (Hotel) contains a variety of activities on their premises, including dining facilities, lodging, tennis courts, skeet & trap range, charter fishing, boat rentals, full service marina, bike rentals, island nature cruises, 2 heated swimming pools, fitness room, and a nearby golf course (8 miles from resort), call 394-3101 or 800-237-4173 for more information.

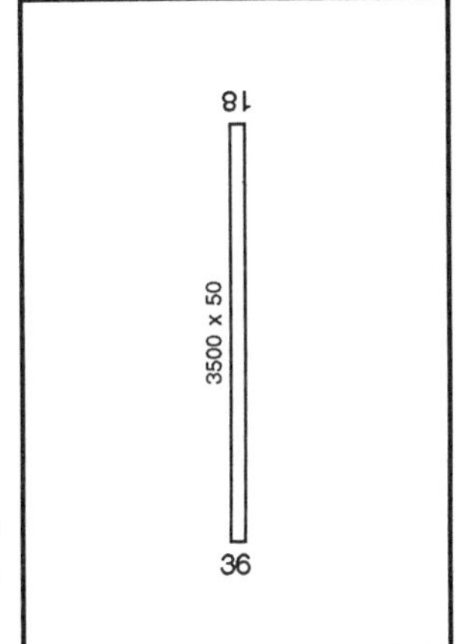

Airport Information:

NAPLES - PORT OF THE ISLANDS (X00)
22 mi southeast of town 25-57-00N 81-30-00W Elev: 06 Rwy 18-36: 3500x50
Attended: unattended Public Phone 24hrs Notes: Private use facility, use at own risk; The airstrip adjacent to the resort is reported to be open for use by the public at the time of this printing. However, operation is restricted to daylight hours. Also check airport status & condition prior to landing.
Port of the Island Resort & Marina (Hotel) Phone: 394-3101 or 800-237-4173.

Port of the Islands Resort & Marina

Naples, FL (FL-X00)

The Everglades - "Sea of Grass" - is recognized as one of the greatest remaining wilderness areas of the United States. It covers 100 miles in length and 50 miles in breadth. Endless grass prairies are interspersed with groves of cypress, palm, and pine trees. It is a place which provides a tremendous sense of peace.

At the boundary between Florida's Everglades and the 10,000 Islands lies a unique and very special resort, Port of the Islands, the Gateway to the 10,000 Islands and the Gulf of Mexico. Surrounded by thousands of square miles of State parks and environmentally protected lands, it is an enclave of sophisticated comfort in a setting of great natural beauty.

Popular for many years with fishermen, naturalists, artists and writers, the "Port" is an ideal place for escaping urban pressures, enjoying a variety of recreational activities, and renewing the soul.

This resort offers a wide selection of entertainment for their guests. Whether you're looking for a quiet place to relax or an active sport, you'll find activities abound at Port of the Islands. Some of their resort amenities include a 3,200 foot airstrip, tennis courts, fitness center, swimming pool, fishing, bicycle and canoe rentals, shuffleboard, billiards, croquet, volleyball, board games, skeet shooting, library, and golfing at a nearby course only 8 miles from the resort.

Entertainment and dining, is presented with constant attention to the highest standards of quality, designed for the discriminating. The Garden Court Restaurant offers Continental Cuisine featuring local and international favorites throughout the week, along with a sumptuous Sunday brunch. They also provide their "Sonny's Chickee" which serves food and grogg in an informal waterside setting. The "Charley's Islander Bar provides an array of libations served by generous bartenders. Live entertainment is the rule most nights during their high season. and always on Friday and Saturday evenings during the off season.

In addition to their many attractions, they also offer island nature cruises which are informative and entertaining. The "Island Princess", their 49-passenger catamaran, takes you on a two-hour tour of the 10,000 Islands. Shelling trips and picnics on uninhabited beaches are available. Refreshments are served on board.

Although Port of the Island exists in a world of its own, it is only 20 miles from the beautiful resort community of Naples, Florida. White beaches, the warm waters of the Gulf of Mexico, and elegant shopping, beckon the vacationer to this jewel-like city. The nearby community of Marco Island also provides a variety of restaurants, shops and beaches. Numerous tourist attractions are available in the area, and the "Port's" staff are happy to provide information and assist in making tour arrangements.

Port of the Islands Resort and Marina owns and operates a private airstrip located on their property. As described for boaters, their outside marker is about 5 miles and 120 degrees from "Coon Key Light" near Marco Island. Resort location #'s (N25-56'-56" W81-30'-4"). For information about this resort, its services and accommodations, please call 800-237-4173 or 941-394-3101. (Information submitted by Port of the Islands Resort and Marina).

Photo by: Port of the Islands Resort & Marina

FL-34J - NEW SMYRNA BEACH
NEW SMYRNA BEACH MUNICIPAL

(Area Code 904) 32, 33

Franco's Italian Restaurant & Seafood Grill:

This restaurant is owned and operated by the same conscientious proprietor, of the Skyline restaurant on the airport. This facility is located 2-1/2 miles south of the New Smyrna Beach Municipal Airport. You can take US 1, from the field, directly to the restaurant. Courtesy transportation is also provided by Fanco's restaurant, as long as prior notice is given. Taxi service from the airport is available if you happen to drop in without prior arrangements. Classified as a family gourmet restaurant, they serve high quality entrees at very reasonable prices, winning the Silver Spoon Awards for 1990 and 1996. Prices range from about $4.00 for lunch to $8.00 for dinner. The decor of the restaurant provides a relaxed, clean and very pleasant atmosphere. Groups and parties planning meetings or get-togethers are welcome. From simple to elaborate arrangements and accommodations, are available to meet the needs of the customer. For information call 423-3600.

Skyline Restaurant & Piano Lounge:

This fine dining facility is located at the east side of the airport about 200 yards from the FBO right at the entrance to the field. Courtesy transportation is also available through the restaurant. Specialized entrees include Escargot, Oysters Rockefeller, Baked Brie & fresh fruit, Rack of Lamb, Black Angus steaks (sold by weight), Beef Wellington, fresh local Grouper, Flounder, Cobia in a variety of sauces, just to name a few. Some entrees are prepared at your table side by your weightier. Piano entertainment on certain nights also adds to your evening enjoyment. Restaurant hours are 4:30 to 10:00 p.m. 7 nights a week. Early bird specials run 4:30 p.m. to 6:30 p.m. and average $7.00 to $10.00. After that time prices during regular dinner hours run about $16.00. The restaurant has an aeronautical theme with WW-I & WW-II miniature replica aeronautical charts embedded in the table tops, and sectional chart on menu covers. The restaurant was once a WW-II Officer's Club on the military base which is now a civilian airport. Clubs and fly-in groups are frequent customers at this restaurant, with accommodations for up to 150 people. This facility, with wooden decking, is surrounded by 4 acres of property. The restaurant is picturesque and contains a lot of history. It is situated across the street from the river, 10 minutes away from the ocean, and a convenient dining spot for pilots. For information call 428-5325.

Restaurants Near Airport:

Franco's Seafood Rest.	2.5mi S.	Phone: 423-3600
Skyline Restaurant	On Site	Phone: 428-5325

Lodging: Mark Charles Oceanfront, Phone: 426-0020; Islander Beach Resort, located at 1601 South Atlantic Avenue, has a lounge with entertainment and dancing, exercise equipment, game rooms, facilities for conference and meeting rooms, picnic tables on the beach. Phone: 427-3452.

Meeting Rooms: See Islander Beach Resort listed above under "Lodging".

Transportation: Airport Taxi, 427-3211; Beachside Taxi, 428-3551

Information: New Smyrna Beach-Edgewater-Oak Hill Chamber of Commerce, at 115 Canal Street, New Smyrna Beach, FL 32168, Phone: 428-2449.

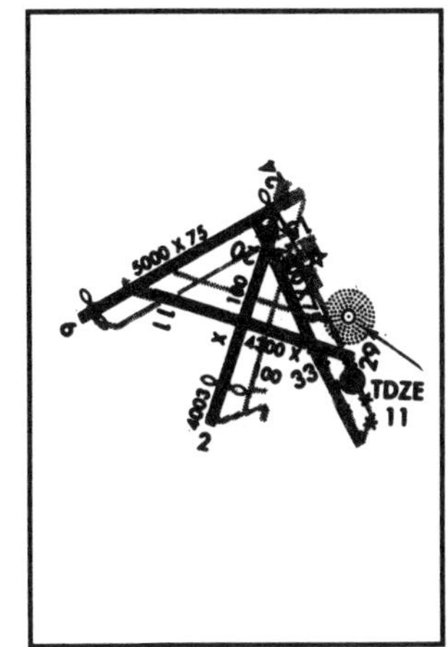

Airport Information:

NEW SMYRNA BEACH - NEW SMYRNA BEACH MUNI. (34J)
3 mi northwest of town N29-03.27 W80-56.89 Elev: 12 Fuel: 100LL, Jet-A
Rwy 06-24: H5000x75 (Asph) Rwy 11-29: H4300x100 (Asph) Rwy 15-33: H3800x75 (Asph)
Rwy 02-20: H4003x100 (ASPH) Attended: 1200-0000Z after 2300Z call 428-4061
Unicom: 122.8 Public Phone 24hrs Notes: no touch and go landings
FBO: Vintage Props and Jets Phone: 423-1773

FL-OCF - OCALA
OCALA REGIONAL/JIM TAYLOR FIELD

(Area Code 904) 34

Pegasus Airport Restaurant/Lounge:

Pegasus Airport Restaurant/Lounge is located at Ocala Regional/Jim Taylor Field in the F.B.O. terminal - Hawthorne Ocala, Inc. This casual family style restaurant is open from 8:00 a.m. to 8:00 p.m., Monday through Saturday, and from 8:00 a.m. to 3:00 p.m. on Sunday. Pegasus serves a wide variety of menu items, and daily breakfast and lunch specials. Items include: omelettes, sandwiches, soups, salads, and all-you-can-eat catfish fillet every Friday night from 5:00 p.m. to 8:00 p.m. Average prices range from $3.00 to $4.00 for breakfast and $4.00 to $5.00 for lunch. Happy Hour specials are offered on Monday, Tuesday and Wednesday from 3:00 p.m. to closing. The restaurant can cater to parties of 20 or more, as well as to private and corporate pilots on-the-go. For more information about Pegasus Airport Restaurant/Lounge, call 237-2161.

Restaurants Near Airport:

Pegasus Airport Rest./Lounge	On Site	Phone: 237-2161

Lodging: Howard Johnson's (2 miles) 237-8000; Budgetel Inn (2 miles) 237-4848; Days Inn (2-1/2 miles) 629-8850; Ocala Hilton (2-1/2 miles) 854-1400
Meeting Rooms: Howard Johnson's 237-8000; Ocala Hilton (2-1/2 miles) 854-1400
Transportation: Taxi Service: Airport 800-999-5851; Best Way 620-8888; Tony's 625-8882
Information: Ocala/Marion County Chamber of Commerce, 110 E. Silver Springs Boulevard, P.O. Box 1210, Ocala, FL 34478, Phone: 629-8051

Attractions:

Numerous attractions are located nearby: Silver Springs Wild Water, Jungle Cruises. Glass bottom boats, Appleton Museum (6 mi.); Silver Springs Wild Waters (7 mi.). For more information about local attractions, call 629-8051.

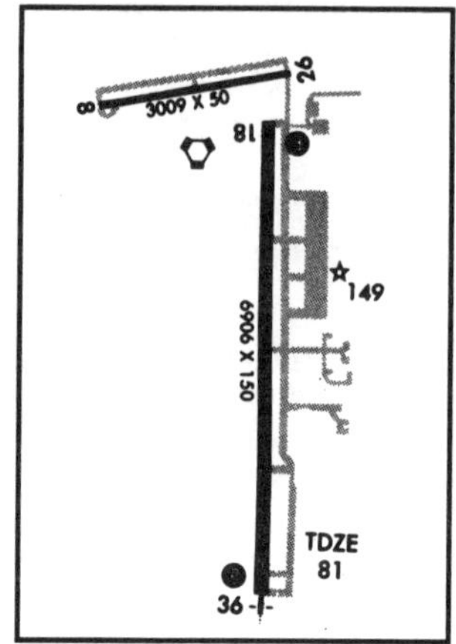

Airport Information:

OCALA - OCALA REGIONAL/JIM TAYLOR FIELD (OCF)
4 mi west of town N29-10.36 W82-13.45 Elev: 90 Fuel: 100LL, Jet-A Rwy 18-36: H6906x150 (Asph) Rwy 08-26: H3009x50 (Asph) Attended: 1230Z-SS CTAF/Unicom: 123.0 JAX Center App Con: 135.75 JAX Center Dep Con: 118.6 Clnc Del: 118.6
FBO: Hawthorne Ocala, Inc. Phone: 237-3444

FL-ORL - ORLANDO
ORLANDO EXECUTIVE AIRPORT

(Area Code 407) 35

4th Fighter Group:

The 4th Fighter Group Restaurant can be reached by shuttle service from Showalter Flying Service (FBO). The other fixed base operators on the field may also provide courtesy transportation. This fine dining establishment is open for lunch between 11 a.m. and 2:30 p.m. Monday through Friday, and for dinner Sunday through Thursday from 5 p.m. to 10 p.m. On Friday and Saturday they serve dinner between 5 p.m. and 11 p.m. Entrees on their menu feature Seafood Imperial, top quality aged steaks, prime rib, chicken dishes, stir fry, New York strip steaks, filet mignon and many other gourmet selections. On Sunday between 10 a.m. and 2:30 p.m. they feature an all-you-can-eat champagne brunch. Daily specials are also provided. Average prices run $10.00 for lunch and $20.00 for dinner. Their main dining room can accommodate 200 persons. This unique aviation theme restaurant depicts an old English farm house during the 1940's and WW-II, when the fighter and bomber action of the 4th Fighter Group was in full swing. Large bay windows allow a great view of the Orlando Executive Airport and its arriving and departing aircraft. For further information about this establishment call 898-4251.

Restaurants Near Airport:

4th Fighter Group	On Site	Phone: 898-4251
Casa Gallardo	1/4 mi	Phone: 896-2167
Bennigan's	1/2 mi E.	Phone: 896-6516
Quincy's Rest.	1/2 mi E.	Phone: 898-1447

Lodging: Colonial Plaza Inn (Trans) 894-2741; Harley Hotel of Orlando (Trans) 841-3220; Sheraton Hotel-Maitland (Trans) 660-9000;
Meeting Rooms: Colonial Plaza Inn 894-2741; Harley Hotel of Orlando 841-3220; Sheraton Hotel-Maitland 660-9000.
Transportation: Showalter Flying Service (FBO) 894-7331 and Executive Air Center (FBO) 896-2799 can provide courtesy transportation to nearby facilities; Also Taxi Service: Carey Limousine Service 855-0442; Sunshine 422-7663; White Rose 855-0564; Yellow Cab 699-9999 or 422-4455; Rental Cars: Avis 896-0721; Hertz 894-7331.
Information: Orlando/Orange County Convention & Visitors Bureau, 7208 Sand Lake Road, suite 300, Orlando, FL 32819; Also Orlando Tourist Info. Center 407-363-5800.

Attractions:

Walt Disney World; Kennedy Space Center; Sea World of Florida; Also Mobil Travel Guide publishes "The Road to Walt Disney World ($10.95) a comprehensive directory of attractions and directions to points of interest within the region. (Available at bookstores).

Airport Information:

ORLANDO - ORLANDO EXECUTIVE AIRPORT (ORL)
3 mi east of town N28-32.73 W81-19.98 Elev: 113 Fuel: 100, Jet-A Rwy 07-25: H6003x150 (Asph-Grvd) Rwy 13-31: H4638x100 (Asph) Attended: 1100-0400Z Atis: 127.25 Unicom: 122.95 Orlando App/Dep Con: 124.8, 120.15, 121.1, 135.3, 119.4 Executive Tower: 118.7 Gnd Con: 121.4 Clnc Del: 128.45 Public Phone 24hrs Notes: Landing fees charged to non-based 135 charter operators. Check with FBO's for overnight parking fees.
FBO: Executive Air Ctr (Fuel) Phone: 896-2799
FBO: Showalter (Fuel) Phone: 894-7331

FL-MCO - ORLANDO
ORLANDO INTERNATIONAL

Host International Concessions:

Host International features a number of eateries located in the terminal building on the Orlando International Airport. There are 3 TVBY's, 2 Nathons, 1 Pizza Hut, 2 Mrs Fields, 1 Cinabun and 3 Burger Kings. For information about about these establishments or other services available call the airport managers office at 825-2001.

Attractions:

Walt Disney World; Kennedy Space Center; Sea World of Florida; For information contact Orange County Convention & Visitors Bureau, or call their information center at 363-5871. (See "Information" listed above).

Restaurants Near Airport: (Area Code 407) 36

Host Intl. Restaurant On Site Phone: 825-2001

Lodging: The following provide shuttle service: Days Inn 859-6100; Days Inn-Landstreet 859-7700; Gold Key Inn 855-0050; Holiday Inn 851-6400; Holiday Inn-Central Park 859-7900; La Quinta Motor Inn 859-4100; Marriott-Orlando Airport 851-9000; Ramada Inn-South 851-2330; Sheraton Inn-Intl Airport 859-2711.

Meeting Rooms: Days Inn-Landstreet 859-7700; Gold Key Inn 855-0050; Holiday Inn 851-6400; Holiday Inn-Crowne Plaza 859-1500; Holiday Inn-Central Park 859-7900; Marriott-Orlando Airport 851-9000; Ramada Inn-South 851-2330; Sheraton Inn-Intl Airport 859-2711.

Transportation: Taxi Service: Limo service 855-0442; Taxi service is available at terminal building; Rental Cars: Americar 859-0818; Avis 851-7600; Budget 855-6660; Dollar 851-3232; Hertz 859-8400; National 855-4170.

Information: Orlando/Orange County Convention & Visitors Bureau, 7208 Sand Lake Road, Orlando, FL 32819; Also call Orlando Tourist Information Center at 363-5871.

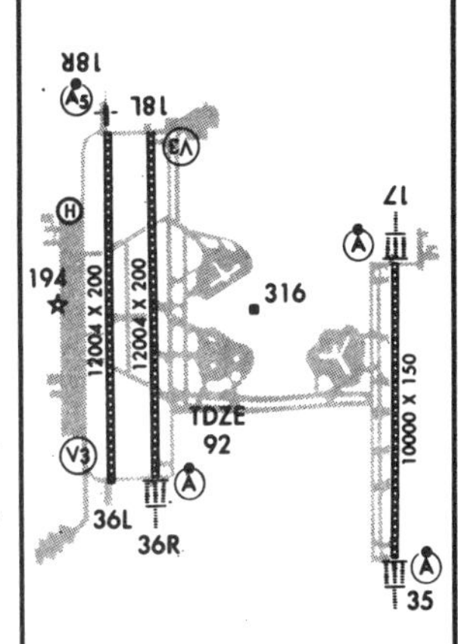

Airport Information:

ORLANDO - ORLANDO INTERNATIONAL AIRPORT (MCO)
6 mi southeast of town N28-25.73 W81-18.96 Elev: 96 Fuel: 100, Jet-A
Rwy 18R-36L: H12004x200 (Conc-Grvd) Rwy 18L-36R: H12004x200 (Asph-Grvd)
Rwy 17-35: H10000x150 (Conc-Grvd) Attended: continuously Atis: 121.25
Unicom: 122.95 App/Dep Con: 124.8, 120.15, 121.1, 135.3, 119.4, Tower: 124.3 (Rwys 18L-36R and 18R-36L), 118.45 (Rwy 17-35) Gnd Con: 121.8 Clnc Del: 134.7
Notes: CAUTION: Birds and deer on and in vicinity of arpt. Taxiway and the west ramp are not clearly visible from tower. Flight Notification Service (ADCUS) available.
FBO: Aircraft Service International, Inc. **Phone: 851-8304**
FBO: Glades Aviation Service **Phone: 924-5696**

FL-ISM - ORLANDO/KISSIMMEE KISSIMMEE MUNICIPAL AIRPORT

Restaurants Near Airport: **(Area Code 407)** 37

Outback Steakhouse 7/8 mi Phone: 931-0033

Outback Steakhouse:

The Outback Steakhouse is situated less than one mile from the Kissimmee Municipal Airport. This family style facility can be reached by FBO's courtesy cars or by taxi service. Their hours are 4 p.m. to 10:30 p.m. Monday through Thursday, Friday and Saturday from 3:30 p.m. to 11:30 p.m., and on Sunday from 3:00 p.m. to 10:30 p.m. Items on their menu include appetizer specialties like their Bloomin Onion, Kookaburra Wings, Grilled Shrimp on the Barbi, and Walkabout Soup. "Down Under Favorites" include Jackeroo Chops, Queensland Chicken'n Shrimp, and Brisbane Shrimp Saute. The "Land Rovers" entrees feature prime rib, the Michael J. "Crocodile Dundee", which is a 14 oz New York strip steak, or their Rockhampton rib-eye 12 ounce steak. Grilled foods such as chicken, ribs, and combination platters, including their "Bontany Bay fish o'the day, features fresh fish lightly seasoned and grilled with vegetables. In addition to the main course meals, they also provide a variety of delicious sandwiches, side dishes, and desserts for your dining pleasure. A children's menu is provided as well. Average prices run $5.00 to $16.95 for dinner. The main dining room can seat 200 persons and displays a unique Australian decor. For more information call 931-0033.

Lodging: Larson's Lodge 846-2713; Rodeway Inn 396-7700; Travelodge 933-2400.
Meeting Rooms: Larson's Lodge 846-2713; Rodeway Inn 396-7700.
Transportation: Taxi Service: Buster Taxi 847-4867; Yellow Cab 846-2222; Also Rental Cars: Budget 847-9095; Kelly 846-6128.
Information: Kissimmee-St Cloud Convention and Visitors Bureau, 1925 E Irlo Bronson Memorial Hwy, P.O. Box 422007, Kissimmee, FL 34742-2007, Phone: 847-5000 or 800-327-9159.

Attraction:

Flying Tigers Warbird Museum: Tom Reilly Vintage Aircraft, operates an aviation museum containing about 20 to 35 vintage WW-II and Korean aircraft on display. Over the past 20 years this facility has primarily been used as a major restoration center for war birds. Four years ago, due to public interest, they began giving guided tours of their facility, which lasts approximately 45 minutes. A small gift shop and 2 rooms filled with artifacts compliment the museum. For information you can call 847-7477.

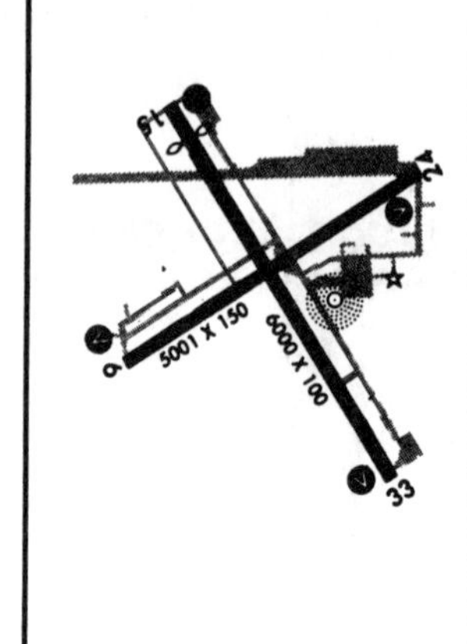

Airport Information:

ORLANDO - KISSIMMEE MUNICIPAL AIRPORT (ISM)
16 mi southwest of town N28-17.41 W81-26.24 Elev: 82 Fuel: 100LL, Jet-A
Rwy 15-33: H6000x100 (Asph-Grvd) Rwy 06-24: H5001x150 (Asph-Grvd)
Attended: 1300-0100Z Unicom: 122.725
FBO: Florida Air Center Phone: 846-4450
FBO: Kissimmee Aviation Services, Inc. Phone: 847-9095
FBO: Marathon Flight School & FBO Phone: 847-6128

Flying Tigers Warbird Museum:

Kissimmee, FL (FL-ISM)

The Flying Tigers Warbird Air Museum is a W.W. II Flying and aircraft restoration facility. Work goes on every day, 7 days a week, all year long. Restoration and major reconstruction projects are always under way. Planes are regularly flown, but on no set schedule; some are test-flown as part of the work, others for the pure pleasure of flight. At Flying Tigers Warbird Air Museum you'll find possibly the largest, most experienced crew of versatile mechanics, sheet-metal and paint artisans ever assembled in one place for commercial restoration of W.W. II aircraft. Work is performed on American warplanes, used by U.S. Army Air Corps, U.S. Navy, and U.S. Marine Corp.

The museum is located twenty-five minutes from Orlando; twelve miles east of Walt Disney Magic Kingdom/Epcot Center. Flying Tigers Warbird Air Museum is located on the Kissimmee Airport one mile south of State Road 192 on Airport Road/Hoagland Blvd. Admission is $6.00 plus tax for adults and $5.00 plus tax for kids (over 60 and under 12) Their hours are 9 a.m. to 5:30 p.m. Monday through Saturday, and Sunday 9 a.m. to 5 p.m. Closed major holidays.

Warbird Weekend

Scheduled on the last weekend of December of each year, is "Warbird Weekend". Aviation enthusiasts are invited to see dozens of flying vintage military aircraft including: TBM Avenger, A-26 Invaders, P-51 Mustangs, F4U Corsair, Mig-17, S-2 Tracker, B-25 Mitchells, Trainers, and many more. Gates open each day from 9:00 a.m. to 5:00 p.m. with free parking for the drive-in public. Tickets for adults in advance are $6.00, and $8.00 at the gate. Kids 12 and under and over 60 advance $4.00; At the gate $6.00. Advance sales tickets on sale at the Flying Tigers Air Museum. Included in the events are flying demonstrations all day, plus military vehicles, classic cars, race boats, warbird rides, aviation fly market, memorabilia and art work. Good food at reasonable prices. For information call the Flying Tigers Air Museum at 407-847-7477. Accommodations can be arranged through the Kissimmee St. Cloud Tourist Development Council by calling 800-333-KISS. (Information sumitted by museum)

FL-PFN - PANAMA CITY
PANAMA CITY-BAY COUNTY AIRPORT

(Area Code 904) 38, 39

Airport Restaurant & Lounge:

The Airport Restaurant & Lounge is located within the terminal building at the Bay County Airport. By parking your aircraft at Sowell Aviation, you can simply walk to the restaurant with no problem, according to our information sources. This full service facility serves hamburgers, hot dogs, subs of all types, grilled cheese, BLT's, cheeseburgers, hamburgers, chicken salad and many other varieties of sandwiches. A luncheon buffet is offered along with daily specials. Their newly remodeled dining room can seat 100 people comfortably. This restaurant offers casual dining in a friendly atmosphere. In-flight catering is a service well preformed by the Skyroom Restaurant. General aviation and corporate pilots can place their orders, and have them delivered to the aircraft by the restaurant. Cheese trays, box lunches, fruit trays and items from their menu are all available. For more information about the Skyroom Restaurant & Lounge call 747-1017.

Smitty's Barbecue & Salad Bar:

Smitty's Barbecue & Salad Bar Restaurant is a very popular spot for the fly-in dining crowd. Guests can easily obtain courtesy transportation through fixed base operators on the field. The decor of the restaurant provides customers with a cozy atmosphere, friendly waitresses, and wall to wall aviation photos and paintings. Large scale WW-II aircraft models cover the ceiling. Their main dining room can accommodate 150 persons and is furnished with tables and booths along the walls. This establishment is open 6 days a week between 11:00 a.m. and 9 p.m. for lunch and dinner (Closed on Sundays). Their menu offers a very nice variety of selections including chicken, ribs, pork, beef and turkey platters, in addition to all types of sandwiches made from fresh cuts of meat and cheeses. Homemade garlic bread compliments their meals as well. One unique attraction that can not go unnoticed is the exterior of the restaurant. A large full scale mockup of an aircraft is imbedded within the roof of this establishment. As a point of interest to aviators, this restaurant should not be missed during your next trip to the Bay County Airport. Large groups and parties are welcome with advance notice. For more information about this facility call Smitty's Barbecue & Salad Bar at 769-3296.

Restaurants Near Airport:

Four Winds	3 mi SE.	Phone: 769-0301
House of Chan	5 mi W.	Phone: 764-9404
Arpt. Restaurant	On Site	Phone: 747-1017
Smitty's Barbecue	2.5 mi SE	Phone: 769-3296

Lodging: Best Western Bayside (4 miles) 763-4622; Holiday Inn (Trans) 769-0000; Marriott (Trans) 234-3307; Ramada Inn (Trans) 785-0561; Travelodge-Panama City 763-5347;

Meeting Rooms: Best Western Bayside 763-4622; Holiday Inn 769-0000; Ramada Inn 785-0561.

Transportation: Taxi Service: Deluxe Coach 763-0211; Executive Limo 832-7230; Yellow Cab 763-4691; Also Rental Cars: Avis 769-1411; Budget 769-8733; Hertz 763-2262; National 769-2383.

Information: Convention & Visitors Bureau, Box 9473, Panama City Beach, Panama City, FL 32417, Phone: 233-6503 or 800-722-3224.

Attractions:

Beautiful beaches, numerous resorts, several excellent golf courses, fresh and salt water fishing and many recreational spots within the area; Also Smitty's Barbeque and Salad Bar Restaurant located 2.5 miles from the Bay County Regional Airport 769-3296.

Airport Information:

PANAMA CITY - BAY COUNTY AIRPORT (PFN)
3 mi northwest of town N30-12.72 W85-40.97 Elev: 21 Fuel: 100LL, Jet-A
Rwy 14-32: H6314x150 (Asph-Grvd) Rwy 05-23: H4888x150 (Asph) Attended: 1230-0300Z Atis: 128.3 Unicom: 122.95 Tyndall App/Dep Con: 119.1 below 4000', 119.75 above 4000' Tower: 120.5 Gnd Con: 121.6 Public Phone 24hrs
Notes: Overnight parking fees determined by FBO's and size of aircraft.
FBO: Sowell Aviation Co., Inc. Phone: 785-4325

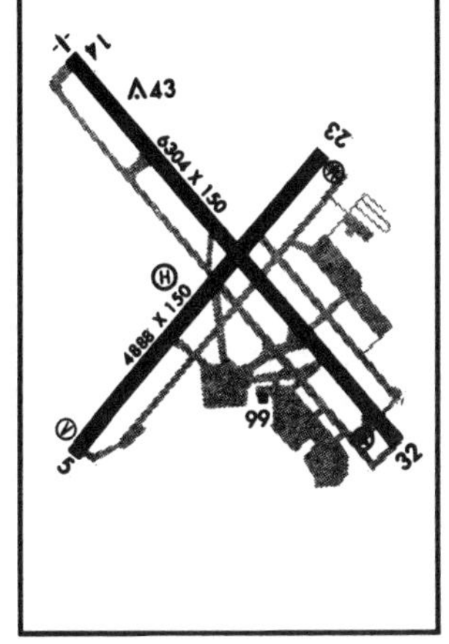

FL-PNS - PENSACOLA
PENSACOLA REGIONAL AIRPORT

(Area Code 904) 40

McGuire's Irish Pub:

One of America's Great Restaurants, McGuire's is located approximately 6 miles south of the Pensacola Regional Airport. Transportation to and from the airport can be arranged by calling Pensacola Aviation Center at 434-0636. They will provide you with a courtesy vehicle. Take Airport Blvd. to 9th Avenue, turn left (south) and follow 9th Avenue to Chase Street. Turn left on Chase Street, go three blocks and take another left at McGuir's Double Decker Bus. You will see McGuire's straight ahead. Extensive Lunch and Dinner menus feature USDA Prime Steaks, fresh Gulf Seafood, Pastas, Traditional Pub Fare as well as Great Burgers and Kosher Sandwiches. Checks average are $9.00 for lunch and $16.00 for dinner. Located in Pensacola's original Firehouse, McGuire's on-premise Oak & Copper brewery produces award winning Stouts, Ales and Porters and their wine cellar house over 7,500 bottles of vintage wine. Over 100,000 dollar bills signed by Irishmen of all Nationalities cover the ceilings. The best Irish entertainment South of Boston begins nightly at 9:00 p.m. McGuire's has been awarded the Florida Trend Golden Spoon Award and is highly rated be AAA & the Mobil Travel Guide. Hours: 11:00 a.m. until the wee hours of the morning, Seven days a week. Reservations are not accepted. For more restaurant information call 433-6789.

Restaurants Near Airport:

Applebee's Restaurant	1 mi	Phone: 479-9208
Jerry's Restaurant	On Site	Phone: 432-2013
McGuire's Irish Pub	6 mi S.	Phone: 433-6789
Scopelos On The Bay	3 mi	Phone: 432-6565

Lodging: The following lodging establishments provide courtesy transportation: Holiday Inn Express (North) 476-7200; Holiday Inn (University Mall) 474-0100; Pensacola Hilton 433-3336; Ramada Inn (Bayview) 477-7155; Ramada Inn-North 477-0711.

Meeting Rooms: Pensacola Civic Center, 201 East Gregory Street., Pensacola, FL, Phone: 432-0800; Lodging facilities listed above also have accommodations for meeting rooms. (See Lodging)

Transportation: Pensacola Aviation Center will provide courtesy vehicles, Phone: 434-0636; Rental Cars: Avis 433-5614; Budget 478-8445; Dollar 434-5431; Hertz 432-2345; National 432-8338.

Information: Visitor Information Center, 1401 East Gregory Street, Pensacola, FL 32501, Phone 434-1234 or 800-874-1234 (Outside FL) and 800-343-4321 (Inside FL).

Attractions:

Recreational areas include: Big Lagoon State Recreation Area (Estimated 25 mi to the northeast) Phone: 492-1595; and Blackwater River State Park (Estimated 25 mi to the southwest) Phone: 623-2363; Both offer, camping, swimming, picnicking, fishing and boating. Fort Barrancs 455-5167 and Fort Pickens 932-9994 are both located on the Gulf Islands National Seashore.

The National Museum of Naval Aviation is located about 15 miles southwest of the Pensacola Regional Airport. To reach the Naval Air Station and the museum, you can take Summit Blvd towards the east. It runs along the south edge of the airport. Once you reach U.S. 90, travel southbound and go about 6 miles until reaching State Route 292. Go southwest about 3-1/2 miles until you come to Navy Blvd (State 295) and turn south. This road (State 295) will take you directly to the Naval Air Station where the museum is located, (3 miles past the main gate). This museum contains more than 50 historical aircraft including exhibits on the progress of flight from the early pioneers to the space age. From the first plane to cross the Atlantic to the modern jet aircraft used today, all are on display. In addition, this museum has scale model aircraft and ships, along with a gift shop, book store, films on aviation, and a Hall of Honor. The museum is open daily except January 1st, Thanksgiving, and December 25th. For more information you can call 452-NAVY (3604) or 800-327-5002.

Airport Information:

PENSACOLA - PENSACOLA REGIONAL AIRPORT (PNS)

3 mi northeast of town N30-28.41 W87-11.20 Elev: 121 Fuel: 100, 100LL, Jet-A
Rwy 17-35: H7002x150 (Asph-Grvd) Rwy 08-26: H6001x150 (Asph-Grvd) Attended: continuously Atis: 121.25 Unicom: 122.95 FSS on Arpt: 122.6, 122.2, 122.1R Tower: 119.9
Gnd Con: 121.9 Clnc. Del: 121.9 (119.0 when Twr. closed) Public Phone: 24 hrs
Notes: Overnight Fee, Single: $5.00; Twin: $7.50; Med Twin: $8.50; Hvy Twin: $10.00
FBO: Pensacola Aviation Center, Phone: 904-434-0636

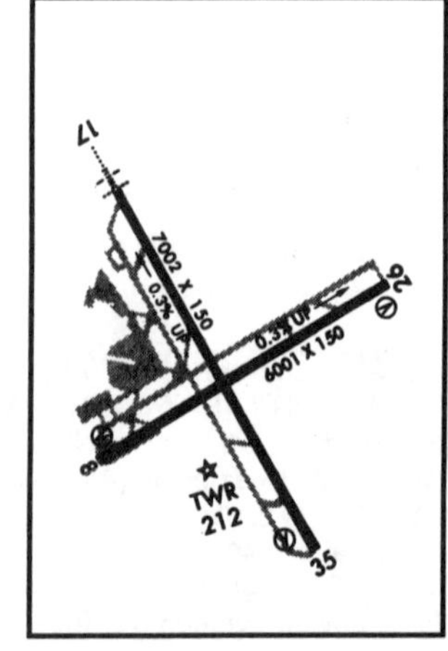

National Museum of Naval Aviation

Pensacola, FL (FL-82J)

The National Museum of Naval Aviation in Pensacola, Florida, is one of the largest air and space museums in the world with 250,000 square feet of exhibit space to display the finest collection of Navy, Marine Corps, and Coast Guard aircraft.

The museum is appropriately located on board the historic Naval Air Station in Pensacola, which is known affectionately as the "Cradle of Naval Aviation". Student naval aviators have trained here for their "Wings of Gold" since 1914. The naval air station is also home to the world-famous Blue Angels flight demonstration team.

Over 600,000 people will venture to Pensacola this year to visit the museum, making it the largest tourist attraction in northwest Florida. President George Bush stopped in for a visit to reminisce about his days as a navy pilot. He saw several of the same types of planes he flew as a naval aviator, such as his trainer the N2S Stearman, and his fleet aircraft, the TBM Avenger. As a special memento, President Bush signed his name to the museum's USS Cadot aircraft carrier island which is similar to the carrier he served on during World War II. Since his visit, the museum has received an N2S Stearman that was actually flown by the President when he was a student pilot.

Museum visitors can see these exhibits and much more. Over 100 authentic aircraft are displayed both inside and outside the museum to show the evolution and history of naval aviation from its days of pioneer flights to the days of supersonic jets and space travel. This extensive collection includes biplanes, blimps, aircraft from the World Wars and Korean Conflict, the fighters of Vietnam and Desert Storm, and a Skylab Command Module. One-of-a-kind aircraft include the first plane to cross the Atlantic, the NC-4; the first F-14 Tomcat, on permanent public display; and the only photo reconnaissance Banshee, used during the Korean war. The aircraft are enhanced with numerous exhibits of memorabilia, scale models, aviation-inspired art and high-tech photography.

The most popular exhibits include a full-scale replica of the USS Cabot aircraft carrier flightdeck and island structure complete with flying signal flags, rotating search lights, catwalks, ladders, and spinning radar. The flightdeck is located in the west wing of the museum which is dedicated primarily to World War II naval aviation. Famous aircraft from this era such as the F4-U Corsair, TBM Avenger, and F6F Hellcat sit parked on the flightdeck, while an F4F Wildcat, SBD Dauntless, and Kingfisher fly overhead.

Another favorite area of the museum is the breathtaking, seven-story glass and steel Blue Angel atrium. It houses four Blue Angel A-4 Skyhawks suspended in a diving diamond formation.

Kids of all ages love the Flight Adventure Deck,--a hands-on aviation-oriented activity center where younger visitors on special tours can suit up in flight gear, climb into jet cockpits, push buttons, turn dials, pull gears, and try their hand at naval aviation.

One of the most recent exhibits is an interactive computerized archive of aviation history known as the National Flight Log. It's the only one of its kind and is capable of storing the histories of thousands of aviators and aviation enthusiasts. Everyone who loves aviation is invited to add his or her name, photograph, and personal history to this everlasting flight roster.

Photo: by Naval Aviation Foundation — F-14 Tomcat at Entrance of museum

Photo: by Naval Aviation Foundation — Original Blue Angels A-4 Skyhawks

Photo: by Naval Aviation Foundation

USS Cabot aircraft carrier flightdeck.

The Naval Aviation museum Foundation (NAMF) is a nonprofit organization established to raise funds for the Museum through donations and memberships which are used for expansion projects and educational programs. For more information about membership to the National Flight Log or other (NAMF) programs, call the museum.

The National Museum of Naval Aviation is located about 4 or 5 miles from the Pensacola - Ferguson (82J) airport. Pilots and their passengers can service their aircraft at Ferguson Flying Service, Inc. (FBO) and call for a taxi cab to take them to the museum. In addition to this is a restaurant called the Chestnut Restaurant & Lounge (904-457-2672) situated across the street from the Fixed Base Operator.

The museum hours are 9 a.m. to 5 p.m. every day of the year, except Thanksgiving, Christmas and New Years Day. Admission is free to the public. For more information about the National Museum of Naval Aviation call 904-452-3604. (Information submitted by museum)

FL-SPG - ST PETERSBURG ALBERT WHITTED AIRPORT

41

Charmain's (Hilton Hotel):

Charmain's Restaurant is located on the lobby level within the Hilton Hotel, about 4 blocks from the Albert Whitted Airport. This family style facility is open 7 days a week between 6:30 a.m. and 11:00 a.m. for breakfast, 11:00 a.m. to 2:00 p.m. for lunch, and from 5 p.m. to 10:00 for dinner. Their menu specializes in a variety of entrees including breakfast plates, luncheon dishes with specials that change monthly, as well as dinner entrees featuring everything from light fare to full course meals. Average prices run $5.00 for breakfast, $6.00 for lunch and $13.00 for dinner. Seating capacity for the restaurant is 150 persons with 3 separate private dining rooms able to accommodate 12 people each for business or catered social events. The restaurant dining area overlooks the hotel swimming pool, and provides an informal brightly lighted atmosphere. Group and party catering as well as in-flight catering can be arranged through the food and beverage director at 894-5000 ext 7064. Lodging accommodations and recreation at the Hilton Hotel complex includes 333 rooms, swimming pool, health facilities, and game room. Fly-in guests can walk to the hotel from the airport, according to the Hilton management. For information about dining, lodging or other services call the Hilton Hotel or Charmain's Restaurant at 894-5000.

Airport Information:

ST PETERSBURG - ALBERT WHITTED AIRPORT (SPG)
0 mi east of town N27-45.91 W82-37.62 Elev: 8 Fuel: 100LL, Jet-A1
Rwy 06-24: H3677x75 (Asph) Rwy 18-36: H2865x150 (Asph) Attended: 1200-0200Z
Unicom: 122.95 Tampa App/Dep Con: 125.3 Tower: 120.4 Gnd Con: 121.8
Public Phone 24hrs Notes: No landing fees; Albert Whitted Airport is situated in downtown St. Petersburg, and is in close proximity to business, museums, and restaurants.
FBO: Bay Air Flying Service Phone: 822-4216
FBO: West Florida Avionics Phone: 896-4325
FBO: West Florida Helicopter Phone: 823-8683 or 823-5200

Restaurants Near Airport: **(Area Code 813)**

Charmain's (Hilton)	4 blks	Phone: 894-5000
Columbia	1 mi	Phone: 822-8000
Ollie O's	8 blks	Phone: 822-6200

Lodging: Hilton Hotel (4 blocks) 894-5000; Presidential Hotel (4 blocks) 823-7552.
Meeting Rooms: Hilton Hotel 894-5000; Presidential Hotel 823-7552.
Transportation: Enterprise Taxi 323-2144; Yellow Cab 821-7777; Also Rental Cars: National 894-3660.
Information: St. Petersburg Area Chamber of Commerce, 100 2nd Avenue North, Box 1371, St Petersburg, FL 33731, Phone: 821-4715; Also "The Pier" 800 2nd Avenue Northeast, St Petersburg, FL 33731, 821-6164

Attractions: The Pier (1 mile) located at 800 2nd Avenue northeast, contains many entertainment facilities including shops, observation deck, restaurants, miniature golf, tourism information center, and the longest pier within the state of Florida 821-6164; Mangrove Bay Gold (4 miles) 893-7800; Twin Brooks 893-7445.

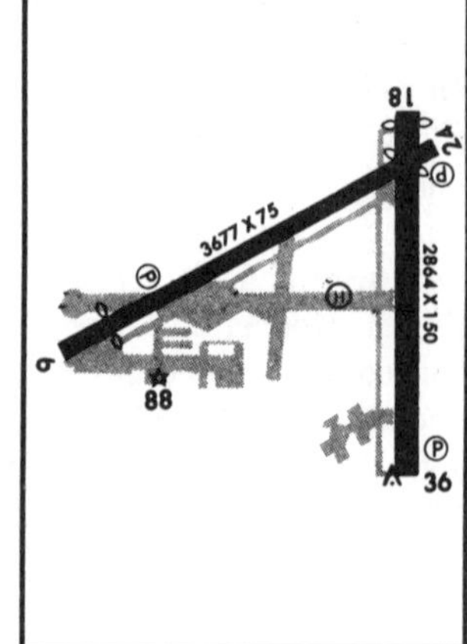

Not to be used for navigational purposes

FL-PIE - ST PETERSBURG CLEARWATER INTERNATIONAL

42

94th Aero Squadron:

The 94th Aero Squadron is situated about 1/2 mile south and adjacent to the Clearwater International Airport. This fine dining establishment can be reached either by courtesy transportation through the fixed base operators on the field, or by taxi service. Restaurant hours are Monday through Friday from 11:00 to 3:30 p.m. with dinner served between 4:30 p.m. and 10 p.m. On Friday & Saturday they begin serving from 5 p.m. to 10:30 p.m. They also feature a Sunday brunch from 10:30 a.m. to 2:30 p.m. and Sunday dinner from 4:30 p.m. to 10 p.m. Items on their menu offer continental cuisine, including prime rib, filet mignon, as well as many other top choices of prime beef and fresh seafood. Several specials are offered to customers like their "Luncheon Express", Luncheon Buffet served weekdays from 11:30 until 2 p.m. or their "Early Bird" special, 7 days a week from 5 p.m. to 6:30 p.m. Average prices run between $12.95 and $19.95 for most main courses. This restaurant can seat 250 persons within its unique surroundings and provides an elegant yet casual atmosphere for its guests. All sorts of photographs and WW-I memorabilia decorates the interior as well as the exterior of this facility. A nearby active runway is situated only 50 to 75 yards from the restaurant. For more information about the 94th Aero Squadron, call 524-4155.

Airport Information:

ST PETERSBURG - CLEARWATER INTERNATIONAL AIRPORT (PIE)
8 mi north of town N27-54.64 W82-41.25 Elev: 11 Fuel: 100, Jet-A, Jet-A+ Rwy 17L-35R: H8500x150 (Asph-Grvd) Rwy 04-22: H5500x150 (Asph) Rwy 09-27: H5165x150 (Asph) Rwy 17R-35L: H3641x75 (Asph) Attended: continuously Atis: 134.5 Unicom: 122.95 Tampa App/Dep Con: 125.3 Tower: 118.3, 128.4 Gnd Con: 121.9 Clnc Del: 120.6 Notes: No landing fees collected by airport; parking fees collected by FBO's.
FBO: Jet Exec. Cntr./Avitat Phone: 530-3453 FBO: Signature Flight Serv. Phone: 531-1441

(Area Code 813)

Restaurants Near Airport:
94th Aero Squadron 1/2 mi N. Phone: 524-4155
Boatyard Village 1/2 mi N. Phone: 535-4678
Las Fontanas 1/2 mi N. Phone: 530-9778
Showboat Dnr. Theater 1/2 mi S. Phone: 537-3777

Lodging: Holiday Inn (Est. 1/2 mile south) 577-9100; La Quinta Inn (Est. 1/2 mile south) 576-7555; Hampton Inn (Est. 1/2 mile south) 577-9200; Days Inn (Est. 1/2 mi south) 573-3334; Residence Inn (Est. 1/2 mile south)573-4444; Radisson Inn (Est. 1/2 mile south) 573-1171;

Meeting Rooms: No information received regarding individual meeting accommodations. Check with above hotels and FBO's.

Transportation: Taxi & Limo service: Airport Express Limo 446-8111; Go Transit Limo 734-7777; The Limo, Inc. 572-1111; Red Line Limo 535-3391; Rental Cars: Avis 530-1406; Hertz 531-3774; National 530-5491; Superior 530-0428.

Information: St. Petersburg Area Chamber of Commerce, 100 2nd Avenue North, Box 1371, St. Petersburg, FL 33731, Phone: 821-4715.

Attractions:

The Florida Military Aviation Museum is located at St. Petersburg-Clearwater International Airport. Also: Sun Coast Beaches, Pinellas County Tourist Development Council 530-6452; Airco Golf (1/2 mile south) 573-4653.

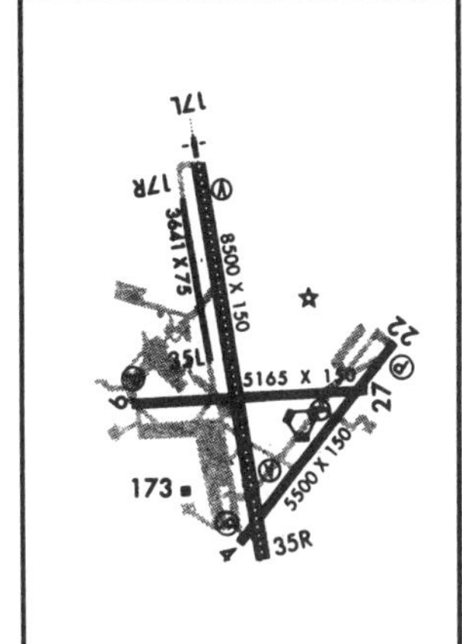

Florida Military Aviation Museum

St. Petersburg, FL (FL-PIE)

The Florida Military Aviation Museum is located at St. Petersburg-Clearwater International Airport. Museum hours are 10:00 a.m. to 4:00 p.m.Tuesday, Thursday, and Saturday, and 1:00 p.m. to 5:00 p.m. Sunday. It is closed on holidays. Admission is $2.00 for adults, $1.00 for children (ages 6-12) and free for children under age 6. The Florida Military Aviation Museum is a non-profit organization that is run by volunteers and is supported by the nominal admission fees, memberships, retail sales and donations. In addition to aircraft, the museum features a collection of military vehicles, weapon systems and a gift shop.

The museum welcomes tour groups, CAP units, church groups, veterans groups, military unit reunions, military organizations, Scouts, JROTC units, ROTC units. There is no charge for pre-arranged groups. For more information about the Florida Military Aviation Museum, call 813-535-9007. (Information submitted by Florida Military Aviation Museum)

Photo by: Florida Military Aviation Museum

Aircraft on display

Fighters, Interceptors & Attack Acft:	U.S. Army L-20 "Beaver"
U.S. Navy A-4C "Skyhawk"	Reconnaissance Aircraft:
U.S. Navy F-4A "Phantom II"	U.S. Army OV-1C "Mohawk"
U.S.A.F. F-86D "Sabre Dog"	Helicopters:
U.S.A.F. F-100 "Super Sabre"	U.S.C.G. H-34 "Seahorse"
U.S.A.F. F-101F "Voodoo"	U.S.C.G. HH-3F "Pelican"
U.S.A.F. F-102 "Delta Dagger"	U.S. Army UH-1H "Iroquois"
U.S.A.F. F-105 "Thunderchief"	Training Aircraft:
Bombers & Long Range Patrol Acft:	U.S.A.A.F. AT-11 "Kansan"
U.S. Navy P2V-3 "Neptune"	U.S.A.F. T-33 "T Bird"
Transport Aircraft:	U.S.A.F. T-37 "Tweety Bird"
U.S.A.A.F. C-47 "Skytrain"	U.S.Army T-41 B "Mescalero"

FL-SRQ - SARASOTA BRADENTON AIRPORT

(Area Code 941) 43

Airport Food Court:

This food court is located on the Central Atrium at the Sarasota Bradenton Airport near the main entrance off DeSoto Blvd. The restaurant hours are 7 days a week from 6 a.m. to 7 p.m. during the season and 6 p.m. off season. The deli & lounge are open until 10p.m. or later. This facility contains several eateries including a Burger King, Pizza Hut, and Healthy Choices deli. Some of restaurants specializes in serving items such as appetizers, sandwiches, salads, chicken, beef entrees, light fare and snacks. Prices average $4-$8.00 for breakfast, and $6-$13.00 for lunch and dinner. Daily specials are also offered along with a large variety of special entrees in addition to a full service deli and snack service. Their facility provides a casual and tropical atmosphere with many plants, patio style furnishings in coral and seafoam with green tones. Special parties or banquet requests are always encouraged subject to availability of space or special party requests. Any requests for special trays/ platters or catering needs are appreciated subject to customer pickup. For information call 359-5380.

Restaurants Near Airport:
Airport Food Court On Site Phone: 359-5380

Lodging: Hampton Inn 351-7734; Holiday Inn 355-2781; Holiday Inn Sarasota South/Venice 966-2121; Hyatt 366-9000.

Meeting Rooms: The Bradenton Airport terminal has 3 conference rooms on the first floor available for rent. Please call 359-5200; Dobbs Houses, Inc 359-5380; Hampton Inn 351-7734; Holiday Inn Sarasota South/Venice 966-2121; Hyatt Hotel 366-9000.

Transportation: Dolphin Aviation 355-7715 and Jones Aviation 355-8100; Taxi: Airport Limo 355-9645; American 355-5127; Diplomat 355-5155; Yellow 955-3341; Rental Cars: Alamo 359-5540; Avis 359-5240; Budget 359-5353; Hertz 355-8848; National 1-800-Car-rent; Superior 355-8864.

Information: Convention and Visitors Bureau, 655 N Tamiami Trail, Atlanta, GA 34236, Phone: 957-1877 or 800-522-9799.

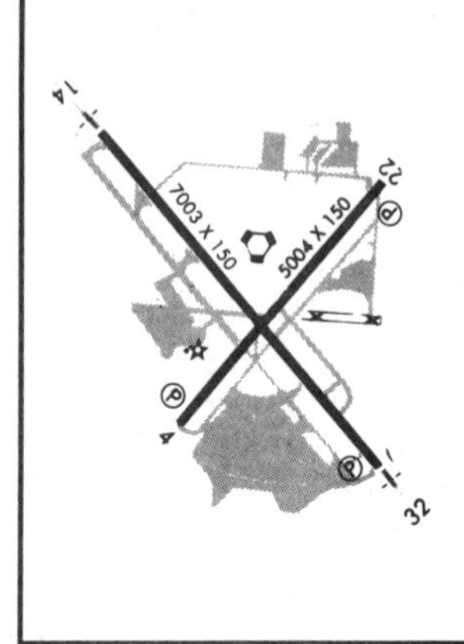

Airport Information:

SARASOTA - BRADENTON AIRPORT (SRQ)
3 mi from town N27-23.72 W82-33.25 Elev: 28 Fuel: 100LL, Jet-A Rwy 14-32: H7003x150 (Asph-Grvd) Rwy 04-22: H5004x150 (Asph) Attended: continuously Atis: 134.15 Unicom: 122.95 App/Dep Con: 120.1 Tower: 120.1 Gnd Con: 121.9 Clnc Del: 118.25
FBO: Dolphin Aviation Phone: 355-2902
FBO: Jones Aviation Phone: 355-8100

Sugar Loaf Lodge

Sugarloaf Key, FL (FL-7X1)

Sugar Loaf Lodge is located on the lower Keys just east of Key West, Florida. The Lodge, which is just 13 miles from Key West, is the home of the Sugarloaf Dolphin Sanctuary dedicated to the release or retirement of previously captive dolphins.

Sugar Loaf comes fully equipped with its own restaurant, cocktail lounge and bar, weekend DJ, live entertainment and dancing, 3,000-foot paved airstrip, airplane rides and sky diving. Other features include: private tennis courts, fresh water swimming pool, salt water swimming in the Gulf of Mexico, ocean fishing, charters and rental boats, kayak tours, back country sport fishing, as well as a full marina and boat ramp and dolphin shows. Power boat rentals are available for half-day or full-day rates. The Lodge also offers a general store, gas station, post office, a bank, and golfing and shopping in Key West.

Sugar Loaf Restaurant offers fine dining in a friendly atmosphere, and is open from 7:30 a.m. until 10:00 p.m. They serve fresh local seafood. They also have a lounge with live entertainment and dancing. A view looking out over the water provides for a pleasurable dining experience.

The Lodge also features "Sugar" their pet Dolphin. The dolphin and showgirl perform daily for guests. Also, the Bat Tower, located on the property, is an interesting historical landmark to visit. All rooms are nicely appointed with quiet, relaxing surroundings. Daily room rates work off the European plan. No charge for 2 children under 12 occupying the same facility as their parents. Pets allowed in designated areas only. For more information about Sugar Loaf Lodge, call 800-553-6097 or 305-745-3211. (Information submitted by Sugar Loaf Lodge)

Photo by: Sugar Loaf Lodge

FL-TLH - TALLAHASSEE
TALLAHASSEE REGIONAL AIRPORT

(Area Code 904)

44

Restaurants Near Airport:
Jerry's Restaurant & Catering On Site Phone: 576-0176

Lodging: Capitol Inn (Trans) 877-6171; Governors Inn (Trans) 681-6855; Hilton (Trans) 224-5000; Howard Johnson Lodge East (Trans) 224-2181; Ramada Inn West 576-6121.
Meeting Rooms: Capitol Inn 877-6171; Governors Inn 681-6855; Hilton 224-5000; Howard Johnson Lodge East 224-2181; Ramada Inn West 576-6121.
Transportation: Taxi Service: Quick Service 224-1121; Tallahassee 224-8313; Yellow Cab 222-3070; Rental Cars: Avis 576-4133; Budget 575-9192; Dollar 575-6460; Hertz 576-1154.
Information: Tallahassee Area Visitor Information Center, New Capitol Bldg., West Plaza, Tallahassee, FL 32302 Phone: 413-9200, 800-628-2866.

Jerry's Restaurant & Catering:

Jerry's Restaurant is located within the terminal building at the Tallahassee Regional Airport. This facility combines a diner and cafeteria within the same restaurant. They are open 7 days a week from 6 a.m. to 10 p.m. The diner resembles an old style dining car on a train that can seat 125 persons. Their menu includes breakfast selections, as well as main lunch and dinner choices like seafood selections, with snapper, grouper, and shrimp dishes. They also feature a variety of steaks including filet mignon, New York steak, and ribeye. Average prices run $3.95 for breakfast, $4.25 for lunch and $12.95 for dinner. The cafeteria portion of the restaurant can seat approx. 150 persons. A snack bar owned and operated by Jerry's is also available near the jet ways on the airport that serves lighter fare. Accommodations for groups are available in the upstairs conference room of the terminal building. This room can seat 500 persons comfortably. In-flight catering is also a specialized service of Jerry's Restaurant. Sandwich trays, box lunches, fruit and cheese trays as well as menu selections are available to all flights and their passengers. For more information about catering services or on-premises dining call 576-0176.

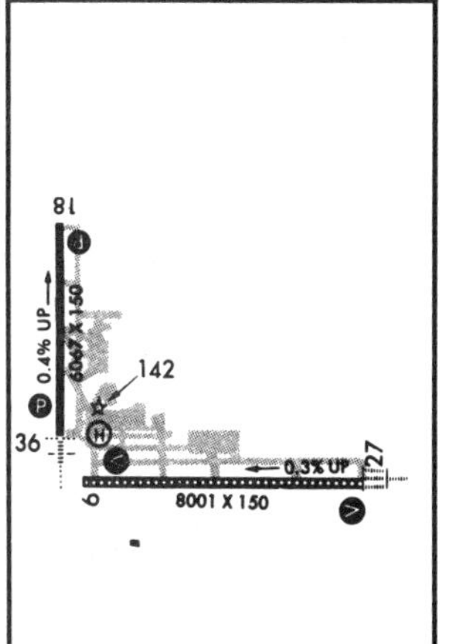

Airport Information:

TALLAHASSEE - TALLAHASSEE REGIONAL AIRPORT (TLH)
4 mi southwest of town N30-23.79 W84-21.02 Elev: 81 Fuel: 100LL, Jet-A Rwy 09-27: H8000x150 (Asph-Grvd) Rwy 18-36: H6066x150 (Asph-Grvd) Attended: 1200-0500 Atis: 119.45 Unicom: 122.95 App/Dep Con: 128.7, 135.8, 133.85 Tower: 118.7 Gnd Con: 121.9 Clnc Del: 126.65
FBO: Flightline Group, Inc. Phone: 574-4444

FL-TPA - TAMPA
TAMPA INTERNATIONAL AIRPORT

(Area Code 813) 45, 46, 47

CK's Restaurant:

CK's Restaurant is positioned atop the Marriott Hotel at the Tampa International Airport. This is a revolving rooftop restaurant that provides a panoramic view for guests. This is a fine dining establishment that is open from 5 p.m. to 10 p.m. Monday through Thursday, Friday and Saturday from 5 p.m. to 11 p.m. and on Sunday from 10:30 a.m. to 2:30 p.m. and again from 5 p.m. to 10 p.m. Specialties of the house are swordfish, Filet Mignon, Lobster as well as many other fine entrees. CK's offers guests casual dining in a elegant and plush atmosphere. Their main dining room can seat around 221 people. Groups and catered meals can be arranged with prior notice. For more information about the CK's Restaurant call 878-6500.

Tampa Bay Wharf (Seafood Restaurant)

The Wharf Restaurant is located on the third level of the main terminal building of the Tampa International Terminal Building. Restaurant hours are from 10:30 a.m. to 9:00 p.m. 7 days a week. This is a family style restaurant specializing in seafood/conch chowder, shrimp, crab legs, oysters, seafood salads, linguine with clam or marinara sauce, sandwiches, cheese bread and key lime pie. Prices range from $8.50 for lunch to about $10.00 for dinner. The restaurant has a nautical atmosphere. For information about this restaurant call 870-8700.

TGI Fridays Restaurant:

This restaurant is located in the main terminal building at Tampa International Airport. You can take a shuttle from most points in the airport as well as courtesy transportation provided by the FBO's. This upscale dining establishment is open from 11 a.m. to 8 p.m. 7 days a week. Specialties include appetizers, salads, soups, hambergers, mexican dishesand many other popular choices. Prices average $7.50 for lunch and $10.50 for dinner. This facility can arrange buffets or brunches for special groups if planned well enough in advance. The dining room is decorated with many interesting items. This restaurant can handle groups up to 100 people for sit down functions. The Marriott Hotel is adjacent to the airport and is connected to the main terminal. For information call the restaurant at 369-8443.

Restaurants Near Airport:

CK's Marriott (Rooftop Rest)	On Site	Phone: 878-6500
Garden Cafe Restaurant	On Site	Phone: 276-3977
Tampa Bay Warf	On Site	Phone: 870-8700
TGI Fridays Restaurant	On Site	Phone: 396-8443

Lodging: Courtyard By Marriott 874-0555; Hampton Inn 287-0778; La Quinta 287-0440; Residence Inn By Marriott 887-5576; Embassy Suites Tampa Airport 873-8675; Guest Quarters 875-1555; Guest Quarters On Tampa Bay 888-8800; Hilton Metro Center 877-6688; Hyatt Regency Westshore 874-1234; Marriott-Tampa Airport 879-5151; Marriott Tampa Westshore 287-2555; Omni At Westshore 289-8200; Sheraton Grand Hotel 286-4400.

Meeting Rooms: Courtyard By Marriott; La Quinta; Residence Inn By Marriott; Guest Quarters; Guest Quarters On Tampa Bay; Hilton At Metrocenter; Hyatt Regency Westshore; Marriott-Tampa Airport; Sheraton; (See phone numbers listed above).

Transportation: Available transportation through FBO's - Hangar One 878-3500 and Suncoast Air Center 872-8324; Also United Cab Co. 253-2424 or Yellow Cab Co. 253-0121. Rental Cars: AVIS 276-3500; Budget 884-1139; Dollar 276-3640; Hertz 874-3232; National 276-3782. (All restaurants listed above are located in the main terminal building at TPA Airport, and can is accessible from all 5 airsides).

Information: Tampa/Hillsborough County Convention & Visitors Assoc, 111 Madison Street, Suite 1010, Tampa, Florida 33602, Phone 223-1111 ext. 44 or 800-44-TAMPA.

Attractions:

Bush Gardens (15 miles), Adventure Island, Gasparilla Festival, Harbour Island, Tampa Bay Downs, Tampa Dog Track, Lowry Park & Zoo, Salvador Dali Museum, Fort Desoto State Park, Walt Disney World (68 miles) Sunken Gardens (17 miles). (See Information listed Above).

Airport Information:

TAMPA - TAMPA INTERNATIONAL AIRPORT (TPA)
3 mi west of town N27-58.53 W82-32.00 Elev: 27 Fuel: 100LL, Jet-A
Rwy 18R-36L: H11002x150 (Conc-Grvd) Rwy 18L-36R: H8300x150 (Asph-Conc-Grvd)
Rwy 09-27: H6998x150 (Asph-Conc-Grvd) Attended: continuously Atis: 126.45 Unicom: 122.95
App/Dep Con 118.15, 119.65, 118.8 Tower: 119.5, 119.05 Gnd Con: 121.7 121.35 Clnc Del: 133.6 Public Phone 24hrs Notes: 1) Single Overnight $7.00, Twin $8.00 landing fee charged only if Part 135; 2) Single Overnight $6.00, Twin $8.00 no landing fee; Shopping complex at TPA by Host International, It includes 15 shopping areas.

FBO: Gulf Coast Avionics, Inc. Phone: 879-9714
FBO: Raytheon Aircraft Services Phone: 878-4500

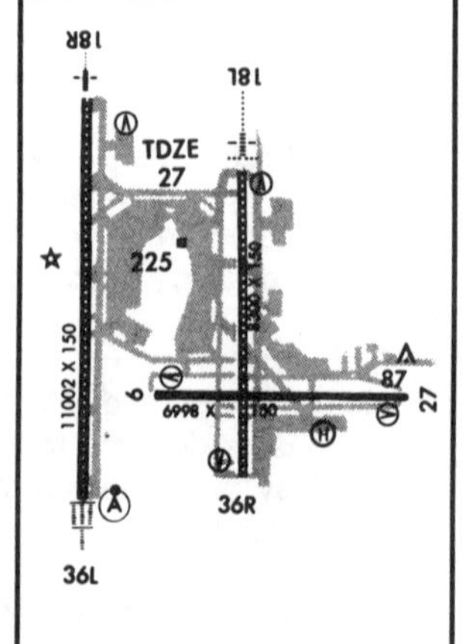

Not to be used for navigational purposes

FL-VNC - VENICE
VENICE MUNICIPAL AIRPORT

48

Dante's Ristorante:

Dante's Ristorante is located on the Venice Municipal Airport within the terminal building. It is reported that fly-in guests can park their aircraft near the terminal building and walk to the restaurant. We were told that after 9 p.m. airport security may have to be notified to get into the building from the ramp area. You can call the airport administration at 485-3311 between 7 a.m. and 7 p.m. This fine dining restaurant is open Tuesday through Thursday from 5 p.m. to 8 p.m., and Friday and Saturday from 5 p.m. to 9 p.m. (Closed Sunday & Monday). They offer a wide variety of over 80 items on their menu and specialize in preparing a nice selection of Italian and pasta dishes. Other selections are available including veal, chicken dishes, choice steaks, seafood and lobster, appetizers and clams. Average dinner prices range from $6.75 to $16.50. Fresh Lobster is listed at market price. The dining room can accommodate up to 90 persons and has 3 separate deck areas that allow an impressive view of the runways, taxi ways and ramp areas especially at night when everything is lit up on the field. Carpeted floors and linen covered tables with individual lamps add to the ambiance of the dining room. On the lower level of the restaurant is the "Runway Club Lounge" with pictures of airplanes, a propeller over the mantle and other aviation related items. Although this restaurant does not open until after 5 p.m., In flight catering can be requested after that time. Reservations for dining and especially on weekends is suggested. For information call 484-7125.

Restaurants Near Airport: **(Area Code 941)**

Dante's Ristorante	On Site	Phone: 484-7125
Sharkey's Restaurant	1/2 mi	Phone: 488-1456

Lodging: Best Western Sandbar Beach Resort Inn (1 mile) 485-5411; Holiday Inn of Osprey (Approx 5 miles) 966-2121; Park Inn Intl. 493-4558; Veranda Inn (1 mile) 484-9559.
Meeting Rooms: Best Western Resort Inn 485-5411; Holiday Inn Sarasota South 966-2121; Park Inn International 493-4558.
Transportation: Sharkey's transportation courtesy van from Venice Flying Service is available. Also Taxi Service K-Cab 485-9211; Yellow Cab 488-0822; Rental Cars Budget 488-8816; Hertz 484-3528.
Information: Venice Area Chamber of Commerce, 257 N Tamiami Trail, Venice, FL 34285 Phone: 488-2236.

Attractions:

Lake Venice Golf Club is located on the Airport. A 27 hole golf course is open to the public 488-3948; Airport is located right on the Gulf ofMexico (Fishing and swimming on Caspersen Beach); Ringling Brothers/ Barnum & Bailey Winter Circus Quarters on the Airport. Annual events include: "Sun Fiesta Airshow" held in October and the "Italian Festival" celebrated in February.

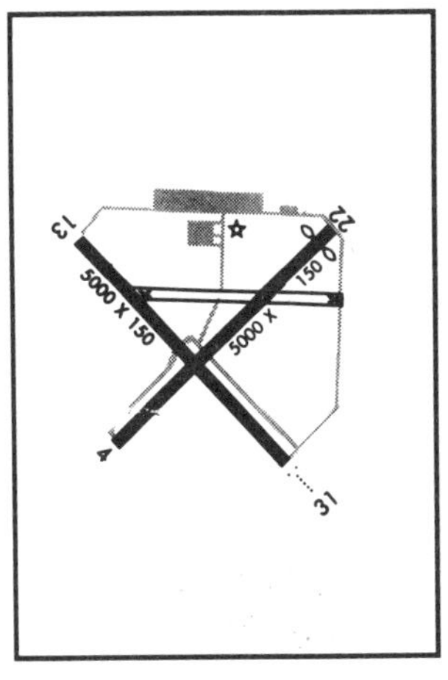

Airport Information:

VENICE - VENICE MUNICIPAL AIRPORT (VNC)
2 mi south N27-04.30 W82-26.42 Elev: 19 Fuel: 100LL, Jet-A
Rwy 04-22: H5000x150 (Asph) Rwy 13-31: H5000x150 (Asph-Grvd) Attended: 1200-0000
Unicom: 122.7 Notes: No landing fee or daytime trancient parking fee reported. Overnight parking $3.50 for singles and $4.50 for twins.
FBO: Venice Flying Service Phone: 484-3528

FL-VRB - VERO BEACH
VERO BEACH MUNICIPAL AIRPORT

49

C.J. Cannon's Restaurant & Lounge:

C.J. Cannon's Restaurant & Lounge is situated within the terminal building at the Vero Beach Municipal Airport. You can park your aircraft in the general aviation areas, either side of the terminal building, and simply walk to the restaurant. This combination family style and fine dining establishment is open 6 days a week from 6:30 a.m. to 9 p.m. On Sunday they close at 2 p.m. Menu selections include breakfast and egg dishes served Monday through Friday until 11 a.m., and all day on Sunday. They also feature many other entrees including fresh fish, prime rib, BBQ ribs, chicken dishes, all types of sandwiches, and salad plates. Average prices run $2.95 for breakfast, $5.00 for lunch and $5.95 to $15.95 for dinner. Daily specials are also available. Their main dining room can seat 150 persons, and exhibits lots of rough sawn cedar, tables and booths, as well as an atrium that allows a good view of the nearby runway. A cocktail lounge adjacent to the restaurant can seat 25 to 30 persons. Fly-in groups and clubs are welcome with advance notice. Accommodations for 40 people can be prepared in the corner of the restaurant. In-flight catering is another service provided. For information call 567-7727.

Restaurants Near Airport: **(Area Code 407)**

C.J. Cannon's	On Site	Phone: 567-7727

Lodging: Days Inn (Free trans) 562-9991; Dodgertown Sports & Conference Ctr. (Trans) 569-4900; Holiday Inn Countryside (Free trans) 567-8321; Holiday Inn Oceanside (Trans) 231-2300.
Meeting Rooms: Days Inn 562-9991; Dodgertown Sports & Conference Ctr. 569-4900; Holiday Inn Countryside 567-8321; Holiday Inn Oceanside 231-2300.
Transportation: Courtesy transportation reported available to nearby facilities; Also City Cab 231-1234; Rental Cars: Hertz 562-4304; National 567-3477.
Information: Beach-Indian River Co. Tourist Council, 1216 21st Street, P.O. Box 2947, Vero Beach, FL 32961, Phone: 567-3491.

Attractions:

Golf courses: (Reported nearby) Dodger Stadium and Dodgertown Dodger Pines.

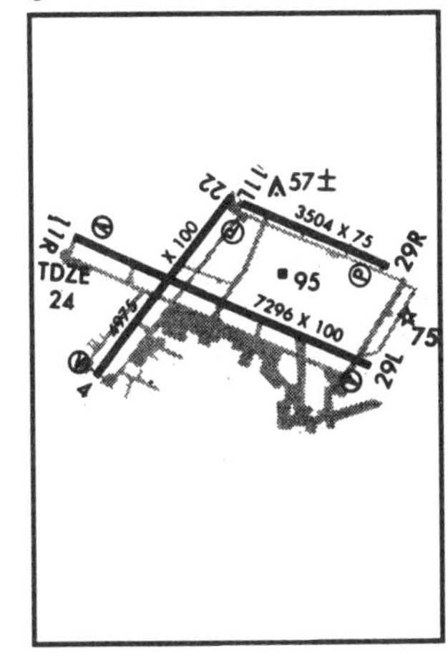

Airport Information:

VERO BEACH - VERO BEACH MUNICIPAL AIRPORT (VRB)
1 mi northwest of town N27-39.33 W80-25.08 Elev: 25 Fuel: 100, Jet-A
Rwy 11R-29L: H7296x100 (Asph-Grvd) Rwy 04-22: H4975x100 (Asph) Rwy 11L-29R: H3504x75 (Asph) Attended: 1200-0200Z Atis: 132.5 Unicom: 122.95
Miami Center App/Dep Con: 132.25 Tower: 126.3, 133.15 Gnd Con: 127.45
Clnc Del: 124.25 Public Phone 24hrs
FBO: Flight Safety Intl. Phone: 567-5178 FBO: Sun Aviation, Inc. Phone: 562-9257
FBO: Pro-Flite Academy Phone: 567-2200 FBO: Vero Beach Arpt Serv. Phone: 562-2848

FL-LNA - WEST PALM BEACH
PALM BEACH CO PARK/LANTANA AIRPORT

(Area Code 407) 50

The Ark Restaurant:

The Ark Restaurant is located only 200 feet east of the Lantana Palm Beach County Airport entrance, and can easily be reached by a 3 or 4 minute walk. Throughout the year they are open for dinner between 4:30 p.m. and 9:30 p.m. During the Winter months (Nov-May), they expand their hours by serving lunch between 11:30 a.m. and 2:30 p.m. House specialties include appetizers, deserts, salad bar, prime rib, seafood, steaks, veal, ribs and chicken. They also prepare a Sunday brunch as well. Average prices run $5.00 for lunch and $11.95 for dinner. Their main dining room exhibits a rustic and nautical decor with a touch of polynesian in a casual atmosphere. Accommodations for 2 to 200 people can be arranged. Meals can also be prepared for carry-out. For information about the Ark Restaurant call 968-8552.

Attractions:

Lion Country Safari, Inc., 640 acre wildlife preserve, auto self guided tours, and over 1000 animals roaming free. Phone: 793-1084;

Restaurants Near Airport:
The Ark Restaurant Adj Arpt Phone: 968-8552

Lodging: Knights Inn (2-1/2 miles) 585-3970; Lantana Lodge (2 miles) 586-9785; Motel Six (1-1/3 mile) 585-5833; Palm Beach Hawaiian (3 mile) 582-5631; White Manor Motel (5 miles) 582-7437.

Meeting Rooms: None Reported; Check with lodging facilities listed above.

Transportation: Taxi Service: Sun Cab 585-1222; Rental Cars: Ajax 586-5544.

Information: Palm Beach County Convention & Visitors Bureau, 1555 Palm Beach Lakes Blvd, Suite 204, West Palm Beach, FL 33401, Phone: 471-3995.

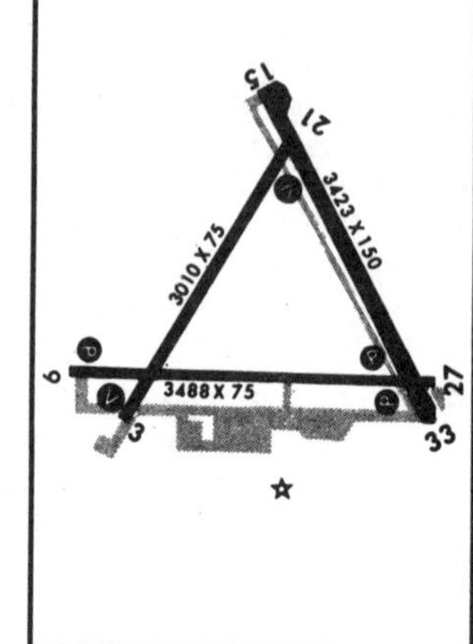

Airport information:

WEST PALM BEACH - PALM BEACH COUNTY PARK AIRPORT (LNA)
6 mi south of town N26-35.57 W80-05.11 Elev: 17 Fuel: 100LL, Jet-A
Rwy 03-21: H3010x150 (Asph) Rwy 15-33: H3423x150 (Asph) Rwy 09-27: H3488x75 (Asph) Attended: 1300-0100Z Unicom: 122.7 App/Dep Con: 127.35
FBO: Florida Airmotive, Inc. (Fuel) Phone: 965-6400

FL-PBI - WEST PALM BEACH
PALM BEACH INTERNATIONAL

(Area Code 407) 51, 52

391 Bomb Group:

The 391 Bomb Group is reported to be located on the south side of the airport on the southern end of Kirk Road. Courtesy transportation can be arranged either through Bizjet, Butler Aviation or Jet Aviation. Taxi service is also available. This fine dining establishment is open for lunch Monday through Friday from 11:30 a.m. to 3:30 p.m. and serves dinner from 4:30 p.m. to 10:00 p.m. during the week. On Saturday they are open from 4:30 p.m. to 11:00 p.m. and Sunday from 4:30 p.m. to 10 p.m. Their specialties include prime rib, porter house steaks, filet mignon, top sirloin, seafood imperial, lamb chops, veal dishes, pork chops, a variety of appetizers, soups salads and homemade desserts. Their famous beer cheese soup is a favorite of many customers. On Sunday they also feature a brunch beginning at 10:00 a.m. to 2:30 p.m. The restaurant is unique in that it exhibits a WW-II motif, complete with 3 full scale aircraft positioned in front of the restaurant along with several army vehicles and artillery pieces. The interior of the restaurant contains many photographs and memorabilia from WW-II. There are separate dining rooms within the premises including an outdoor patio for outdoor dining and cock tails. Guests can enjoy a great view of the airport as well as listen to control tower transmissions using ear phones located at several points throughout the restaurant. For information about the 391 Bomb Group Restaurant call 683-3919.

CA1 Services:

CA1 Services operates a number of convenient dining establishments located right in the terminal building of the Palm Beach International Airport. Restaurants serving specialties like Italian selections, pizzas, French sandwiches, Mexican dishes and ice cream can all be found in the concourse areas. For information about the dining accommodations available, call Concession Air at 697-8140.

Restaurants Near Airport:

391 Bomb Group Restaurant.	On Site	Phone: 683-3919
CA1 Services	On Site	Phone: 697-8140
Gold Coast Pier	On Site	Phone: 686-6542
Lake Worth Deli	On Site	Phone: 686-6542
Manero's Restaurant	3 mi N.	Phone: 686-1901
Raindancer	3 mi N.	Phone: 684-2810
Trader Jack's & Crabhouse	3 mi N.	Phone: 697-0001

Lodging: Comfort Suites (Trans) 689-6888; Hilton Airport (150 Australian, Trans) 684-9400; Hilton Inn Intl. Airport (Trans) 659-3880; Palm Beach Lakes Inn (Trans) 683-8810; Palm Hotel Palm Beaches (Trans) 833-1234 Royce Hotel (1601 Belvedere Rd, Trans) 689-6400; Sheraton Inn West Palm Beach (Trans) 689-6100.

Meeting Rooms: Airport Business Center Building, 1000 Palm Beach International Airport, (PBIA) 640-0980; Also, all lodging facilities listed above have accommodations for meetings and conferences.

Transportation: PB Transportation 689-4222; Taxi Service: Blue Front 842-8294; Carey Limousine Service 471-5466; Palm Beach Taxi 689-2222; Rental Cars: Alamo 684-6806; Avis 233-6440; General 689-7755; Hertz 686-4300; National 233-7350.

Information: Palm Beach County Convention & Visitors Bureau, 1555 Palm Beach Lakes Blvd, Suite 204, West Palm Beach, FL 33401, Phone: 471-3995.

Attractions:

PGA Resort, PGA Sheraton, (20 miles from airport) 627-2000; Lion Country Safari (15 miles from airport) Southern Blvd, State Road 80 West, West Palm Beach, FL. This 640 acre attraction provides a 5 mile self guided auto tour with more than 1,000 wild African, Asian and American animals that are free to roam throughout the preserve. Also many other attractions such as boat rides, petting zoo, nursery for animals, dinosaur exhibits, shops, picnic areas, restaurant and campgrounds are available to the guest. For information call 793-1084.

Airport Information:

WEST PLAM BEACH - PALM BEACH INTERNATIONAL (PBI)
3 mi west of town N26-40.99 W80-05.74 Elev: 19 Fuel: 100LL, Jet-A
Rwy 09L-27R: H7989x150 (Asph Grvd) Rwy 13-31: H6930x150 (Asph-Grvd)
Rwy 09R-27L: H3152x75 (Asph) Attended: continuously Atis: 123.75
Unicom: 122.95 App Con: 124.6 (North) 125.2 (South) Dep Con: 128.3 (North) 127.35 (South)
Tower: 119.1, 118.75 Gnd Con: 121.9 Clnc Del: 121.6 Public Phone 24hrs
Notes: No landing fee unless it is a charter operation. Overnight fees start at $4.71 for aircraft less than 5,000 lbs. and increase to 10,000 lbs.
FBO: Jet Aviation **Phone: 233-7242**
FBO: Signature Flight Support **Phone: 683-4121**

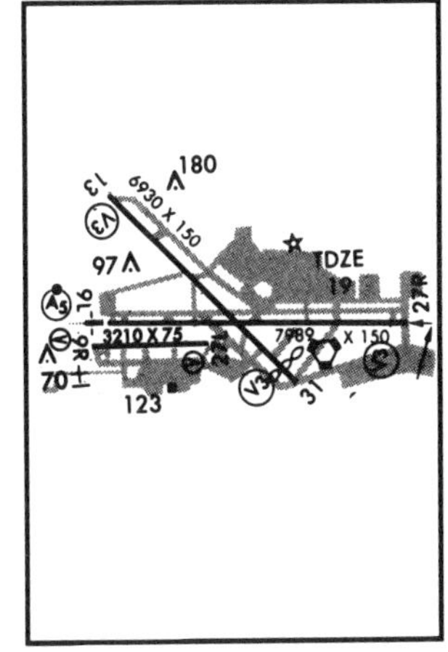

GEORGIA

LOCATION MAP

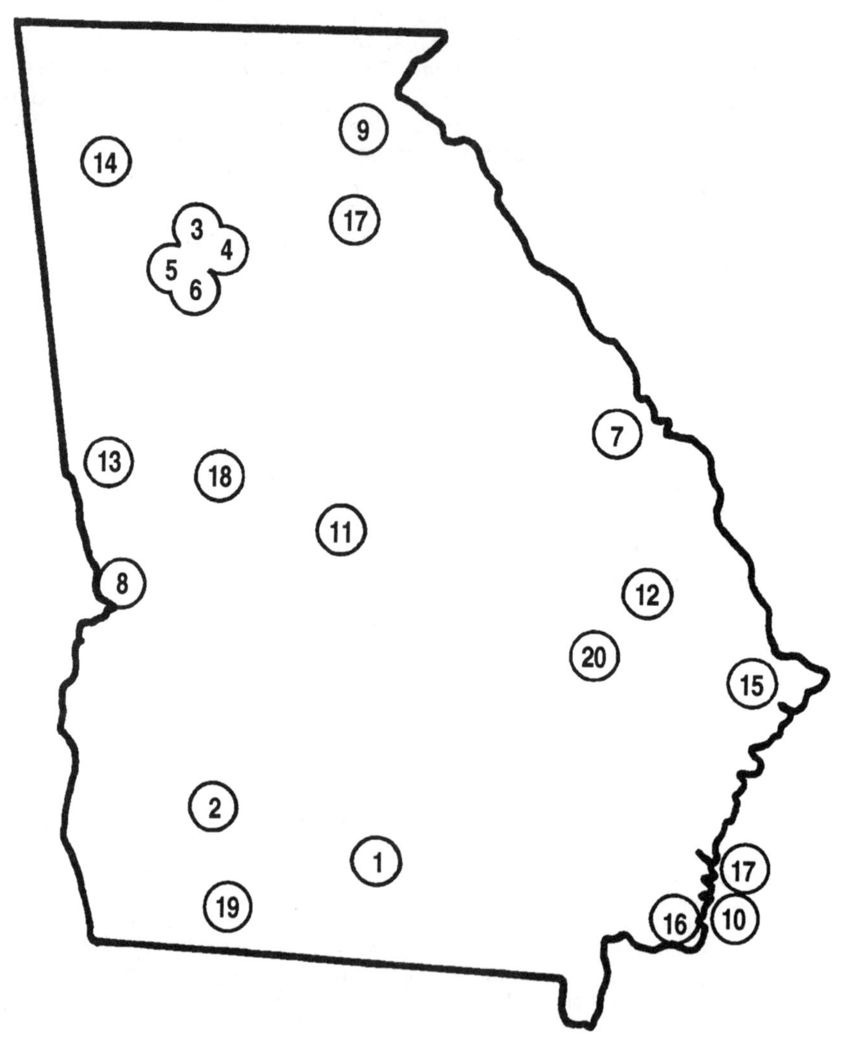

Not to be used for navigational purposes

GEORGIA

CROSS FILE INDEX

Location Number	City or Town	Airport Name And Identifier	Name of Attraction
1	Adel	Cook Co. Arpt. (15J)	Western Sizzlin
2	Albany	Southwest Georgia Reg. (ABY)	Wings Restaurant
3	Atlanta	DeKalb-Peachtree Arpt. (PDK)	57th Fighter Group
4	Atlanta	DeKalb-Peachtree Arpt. (PDK)	Downwind Restaurant
5	Atlanta	Fulton Co. Arpt.-Brown Field (FTY)	Flight Deck Cafe
6	Atlanta	William Hartsfield/Atlanta Intl. (ATL)	CA1 Service
7	Augusta	Bush Field (AGS)	Jerry's Catering
8	Columbus	Columbus Metro. Arpt. (CSG)	Propellers Restaurant
9	Cornelia	Habersham Co. (AJR)	Runway Fish House, Inc.
10	Jekyll Island	Jekyll Island (09J)	Jekyll Island Club Hotel
11	Macon	Middle Georgia Reg. (MCN)	Parachute Grill & Lounge
12	Metter	Metter Muni. Arpt. (MHP)	Western Steer Steak Hse.
13	Pine Mtn.	Callaway Gardens-Harris Co. (PIM)	Callaway Garden Rest.
14	Rome	Richard B. Russell Arpt. (RMG)	Prop Stop Restaurant
15	Savannah	Savannah Intl. (SAV)	Host Marriott
16	St. Marys	St. Marys Arpt. (4J6)	Mary's Seafd. & Stk Hse.
17	St. Simons Is	Brunswick/Malcolm McKinnon (SSI)	St. Simons Island Attrac.
18	Thomaston	Upson County (OPN)	Szechuan Chinese Rest.
19	Thomasville	Thomasville Muni. (TVI)	Holiday Inn
20	Vidalia	Vidalia Muni. Arpt. (VDI)	Shoney's Inn

Articles

City or town	Nearest Airport and Identifier	Name of Attraction
Jekyll Island, GA	Jekyll Island (09J)	Jekyll Island
Macon, GA	Middle GA Reg. (MCN)	Museum of Aviation
Pine Mountain, GA	Callaway Gardens-Harris Co. (PIM)	Callaway Gardens Resort
Brunswick, GA	Malcolm McKinnon (SSI)	St. Simons Island
Brunswick, GA	Malcolm McKinnon (SSI)	The Cloister

GA-15J - ADEL
COOK COUNTY AIRPORT

(Area Code 912)

1

Restaurants Near Airport:

Plaza Restaurant	Adj Arpt	Phone: 567-4596
Western Sizzlin	Adj Arpt	Phone: 896-3663

Lodging: Charles Motel; Comfort Inn (1/2 mile); Davis Brothers; King Frog; Quality Motel (1/2 mile) 896-2244.

Meeting Rooms: Quality Inn 896-2244.

Transportation: Airport courtesy car reported

Information: Adel-Cook County Chamber of Commerce, 100 South Hutchison Avenue, P.O. Box 461, Adel, GA 31620, Phone: 896-2281.

Western Sizzlin:

Western Sizzlin is located 2 blocks from the Cook County Airport and is situated across the street. Their hours are 11 a.m. to 10 p.m. during weekdays and 11 a.m. to 11 p.m. on weekends. Monday through Friday, they feature an all-you-can-eat luncheon buffet from 11 a.m. to 4 p.m. for a very reasonable price. In addition to the buffet, they serve entrees such as soup and salad bar, chicken, hamburgers and sandwiches. They also have a bakery on the premises. Specialties of the house include a variety of steaks as well. The main dining room can accommodate up to 160 persons. A separate dining area can also handle groups or parties. After enjoying your meal, a dessert bar is available. For more information call the Western Sizzlin at 896-3663.

NO AIRPORT DIAGRAM AVAILABLE

Airport Information:

ADEL - COOK COUNTY AIRPORT (15J)
1 mi west of town N31-08.27 W83-27.19 Elev: 235 Fuel: 100LL
Rwy 05-23: H4000x100 (Asph) Rwy 15-33: H4000x100 (Asph) Attended: unattended
Unicom: 122.8
Cook County Airport Phone: 896-2905

GA-ABY - ALBANY
SOUTHWEST GEORGIA REGIONAL

(Area Code 912)

2

Restaurants Near Airport:

Carr's Steak House	3 mi	Phone: 439-8788
Davis Bros. Restaurant	2 mi	Phone: 432-1120
Merry Acres Restaurant	3 mi	Phone: 439-2261
Wings Rest. & Lounge	On Site	Phone: 439-2055

Lodging: Days Inn (Free trans) 888-2632; Sheraton (Free trans, 5 miles) 883-1650; Merry Acres Quality Inn (Free trans, 3 miles) 435-7721; Heritage House Convention Center (Free trans, 3 miles) 888-1910; Holiday Inn (6 miles) 883-8100. Ramada Inn (Free trans) 883-3211.

Meeting Rooms: Merry Acres Quality Inn 435-7721; Ramada Inn 883-3211; Heritage House Convention Center 888-1910; Sheraton Inn 883-1650.

Transportation: Gray Air Service will provide courtesy transportation if advance notice is given. Also taxi: Friendly Cab Co. 436-2764; Veteran's Cab Co. 436-6101; Rental cars: Avis 435-2404; Budget 434-7513; Hertz 435-1751; National 435-0773.

Information: Convention & Visitors Bureau, 225 West Broad Avenue, Albany, GA 31701, Phone: 434-8700.

Wings Restaurant & Lounge:

The Wings Restaurant & Lounge is located within the terminal building at the Southwest Georgia Regional Airport. This facility is open 6 a.m. to 8 p.m. Monday through Thursday, Friday 6 a.m. to 2 p.m. and Saturday 6 a.m. to 1 a.m. Specialties of the house include breakfast served 6 a.m. to 11 a.m., hot wings, sandwiches, hamburgers, and desserts. An all-you-can-eat buffet is served on Sunday between 1 p.m. and 6 p.m. Average prices run $5.50 for breakfast, and $4.50 to $5.50 for lunch. This casual family dining establishment has large windows allowing a nice view of the airport activity. They can seat about 200 people. Catering to small or large groups is no problem. On the weekends during evening hours they feature live entertainment and dancing with their Wings Restaurant also prepares many catered meat, fruit and cheese trays for corporate in-flight customers. For information call Wings Restaurant & Lounge at 439-2055.

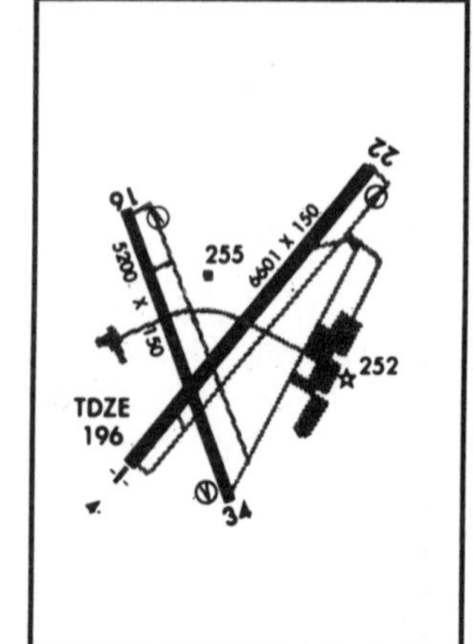

Airport Information:

ALBANY - SOUTHWEST GEORGIA REGIONAL AIRPORT (ABY)
3 mi southwest of town N31-32.13 W84-11.67 Elev: 197 Fuel: 100LL, Jet-A
Rwy 04-22: H6601x150 (Asph-Grvd) Rwy 16-34: H5200x150 (Asph) Attended: 1200-0500Z
Atis 133.05 Unicom: 122.95 Tower: 120.25 Gnd Con: 121.9 Notes: No landing fee for general aviation aircraft operations. Contact FBOs for parking fees.
FBO: Albany Air Center Phone: 434-8787

GA-PDK - ATLANTA
DEKALB-PEACHTREE AIRPORT

(Area Code 770) | 3, 4

57th Fighter Group of Atlanta:

This combination fine dining and family style restaurant is located 1/2 mile from the fixed base operators on the field. Epps Aviation, Air BP and Hangar One, will all provide courtesy shuttle transportation to and from this restaurant. Similar in nature to a 94th Aero Squadron Restaurant, this establishment portrays a bombed out chalet from Italy complete with army vehicles parked out in front, sandbags and bunkers, hundreds of artifacts and displayed souvenirs of the period, as well as over 3,000 pictures and photographs of the 57th Fighter Group from Atlanta. The ambiance of this entire restaurant, exhibits a romantic and lightly lit atmosphere. There are even headphones at some tables allowing guests to listen to the control tower while they dine. Every seat in the restaurant provides the guest with a view of the runways and airport activity. Their menu offers prime rib, steak, and seafood selections. Your three course meal will begin with homemade soup of your choice, followed by a tossed salad with dressing, then the main course served and cooked to perfection. Average prices run $7.95 for lunch and around $15.95 for dinner. The 57th Fighter Group of Atlanta is open from 11 a.m. to 2:00 for lunch, then from 5:00 p.m. to 10 p.m. for dinner, Sunday through Thursday. On Friday and Saturday they stay open until 11 p.m. Groups and/or parties are welcome during the weekdays, however during weekends the restaurant is quite busy. Reservations are also accepted. For information call the restaurant at 457-7757.

Restaurants Near Airport:

57th Fighter Group	1/2 mi	Phone: 457-7757
Downwind Restaurant & Lounge	On Site	Phone: 452-0973

Lodging: Century Center (2-1/2 miles) 325-0000: Quality Inn (2 miles) 451-5231; Radisson Inn (3 miles) 394-5000; Perimeter North (6 miles) 455-1811.

Meeting Rooms: Epps Aviation 458-9851; Air BP 452-0010; Hangar One 452-5000.

Transportation: Transportation by courtesy car is available through,Epps Aviation, Air BP, Hangar 1; Also Avis 458-9851; Enterprises Rental 452-0010; Chamblee Cab: 932-5232; Skyland Cab 455-1750.

Information: Atlanta Convention and Visitors Bureau, 233 Peachtree Street NE, Suite 2000, Atlanta, GA 30303, Phone: 222-6688.

The Downwind Restaurant & Lounge:

The Downwind Restaurant & Lounge is located in the administration building and is well within walking distance from the nearby fixed base operators on the field. This cafe style restaurant provides a casual and friendly atmosphere that attracts many fly-in guests as well as local clientele. This family owned and operated facility is nicely decorated with many photographs of aviation related pictures on the walls. The main dining area can seat 100 people in addition to an outside deck where people can enjoy dining outdoors while watching the airplanes land and take off. The outside deck can hold 50 people. For lunch they offer selections like turkey breast sandwiches, hamburgers, cheeseburgers and much more. During dinner hours they offer choice steaks, seafood and pasta dishes. Daily specials are also available during lunch and dinner. Average prices run $5.00 for lunch and $7.00 for dinner. The restaurant is open 11 a.m. to 11 p.m. Monday through Friday, and Saturday from 12 p.m. to 12 a.m. This restaurant is closed on Sunday. They also specialize in "In-Flight" catering. You can either arrange meals to go through the fixed base operator, or pick-up meals yourself. Groups and parties are welcome with advanced notice. This restaurant has been featured in many flying magazines as well as other publications over the years. For more information you can call the Downwind Restaurant & Lounge at 452-0973.

Airport Information:

ATLANTA - DEKALB-PEACHTREE AIRPORT (PDK)

8 mi northeast of town N33-52.54 W84-18.12 Elev: 1002 Fuel: 100, Jet-A
Rwy 02R-20L: H6001x100 (Conc-Grvd) Rwy 16-34: H3966x150 (Asph) Rwy 02L-20R: H3744x150 (Asph) Rwy 09-27: H3378x150 (Asph) Attended: continuously Atis: 128.4
Unicom: 122.95 Atlanta App/Dep Con: 119.3 Peachtree Tower: 120.9 120.0
Gnd Con: 121.6 Clnc Del: 125.2 Public Phone 24hrs Notes: No landing fees: Check with FBO's for overnight parking fees.

FBO: Air BP Atlanta	**Phone: 452-0010**	**FBO: Prestige Helicopters**	**Phone: 458-6047**
FBO: Epps Air Service	**Phone: 458-0320**	**FBO: Raytheon Aircraft Serv.**	**Phone: 454-5056**
FBO: Execjet Air Transport	**Phone: 982-5444 or 800-267-7538**		

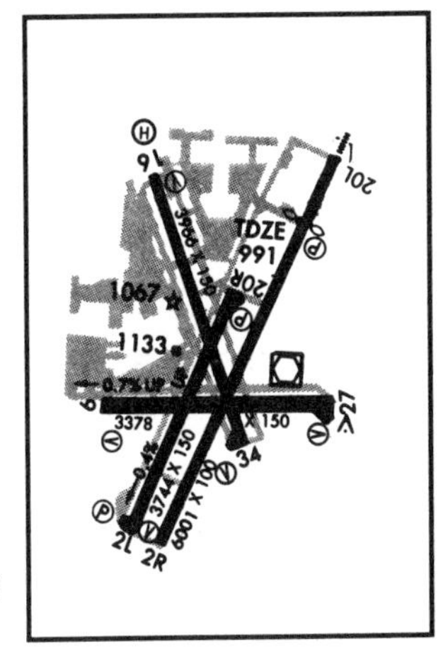

GA-FTY - ATLANTA
FULTON CO AIRPORT-BROWN FLD.

(Area Code 404) 5

Restaurants Near Airport:

Flight Deck Cafe	On Site	Phone: 699-7730
Michael's Restaurant	3/4 mi	Phone: 696-9555
Shoney's Inn	Adj Arpt	Phone: 696-9393

Flight Deck Cafe:

This dining facility is reported to be located in the old terminal building between the fixed base operators on the field. Pilots and their passengers can easily walk to the restaurant from the tiedown areas. The restaurant is open Monday through Friday 7:30 to 3:30 p.m. They are closed on weekends. Home cooked meals with fresh vegetables are the specialty of the house. Good food and clean surrounding are what attracts many customers. Also they have the best view of the activity on the airport. Catering is a specialty of the Flight Deck Cafe. They are owned by one of the largest catering companies in the Atlanta area. For information call 699-7730.

Lodging: Ramada Inn-Six Flags (Free trans) 691-4100; Budget Inn Six Flags 691-9390; Howard Johnson Lodge 696-2274; Mark Inn Six Flags 941-2255; Shoney's Inn 691-2444.
Meeting Rooms: Ramada Inn-Six Flags (Free trans) 691-4100; Budget Inn Six Flags 691-9393; Howard Johnson Lodge 696-2274.
Transportation: Airport courtesy car reported: Avis 691-3330 or 699-9260; Hertz 691-3330 or 699-9260.
Information: Atlanta Convention and Visitors Bureau, 233 Peachtree Street NE, Suite 2000, Atlanta, GA 30303, Phone: 222-6688.

Attractions:

Six Flags Over Georgia, is situated only 3 miles west of the Fulton County Airport-Brown Field. This theme park exhibits more than 100 rides, stage shows, and attractions including many of the latest amusement park thrills. For information call 948-9290 or 739-3400. **Underground Atlanta**, located between Wall, Washington, South Peachtree and Martin Luther King Jr. streets, is situated about 8 miles to the east, and can be reached by taking Interstate 20 from the Fulton County Airport. This attraction covers a six block area. Underground streets, stores and plazas attract many shoppers each year. For information call 523-2311.

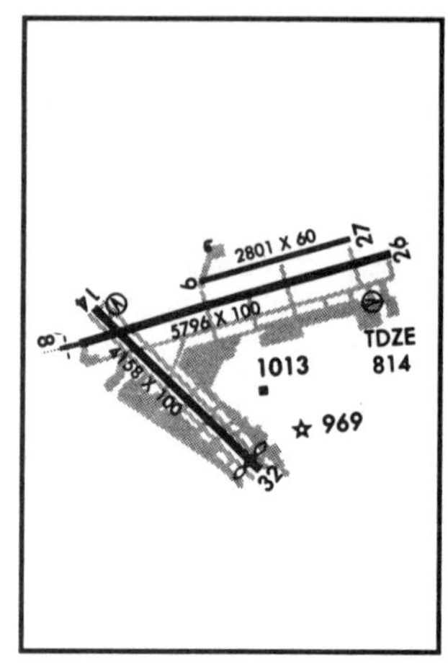

Airport Information:

ATLANTA - FULTON CO AIRPORT-BROWN FIELD (FTY)
6 mi west of town N33-46.75 W84-31.28 Elev: 841 Fuel: 100LL, Jet-A Rwy 08-26: H5796x100 (Asph-Grvd) Rwy 14-32: H4158x100 (Asph) Rwy 09-27: H2801x60 (Asph) Attended: continuously Atis: 120.175 Unicom: 122.95 Atlanta App/Dep Con: 121.0 County Tower: 118.5, 120.7 Gnd Con: 121.7 Clnc Del: 123.7
FBO: Fulton Jet Center Phone: 699-2277 FBO: Hill Aircraft Phone: 691-3330
FBO: Raytheon Aircraft Serv. Phone: 699-9200

GA-ATL - ATLANTA
THE WILLIAM B HARTSFIELD ATLANTA INTERNATIONAL AIRPORT

(Area Code 404) 6

Restaurants Near Airport:

CA1 Services	On Site	Phone: 530-6275
Bentley's	1 mi	Phone: 766-7900
Brentwood Cafe	1 mi	Phone: 761-6500
Grissini	1 mi	Phone: 991-1234
Le Cygne	1 mi	Phone: 762-7676

CA1 Services.

Located on each concourse of the Hartsfield Atlanta International Airport are food services. These range from snack bars to cafe's. Fast food, seafood/deli, meat and vegetable selections are available. Average prices run $5.00 for breakfast, and about $7.00 for lunch and dinner. Hot or cold meals-to-go are also available. For information call 530-6275.

Lodging: Best Western 768-7800; Budgetel Inn (1 mile) 766-0000; Century Airport Hotel 996-4321; Comfort Inn (Atlanta Airport) 991-1099; Days Inn (Airport) 761-6500; Holiday Inn (Airport/North) 762-8411; Holiday Inn (Airport/South) 761-4000.
Meeting Rooms: Accommodations for catered meetings, luncheons and business conferences can be arranged through Dobbs Houses, Inc. At 530-6275. Also many of the nearby hotels and lodging facilities can also provide meeting services.
Transportation: Courtesy car FBO's; Alamo 768-1892; Avis 530-2700; Budget 530-3030; Dollar 530-3100; General 763-2035; Hertz 530-2900; National 530-2800; Value 563-0220.
Information: Atlanta Convention and Visitors Bureau, 233 Peachtree Street NE, Suite 2000, Atlanta, GA 30303, Phone: 222-6688.

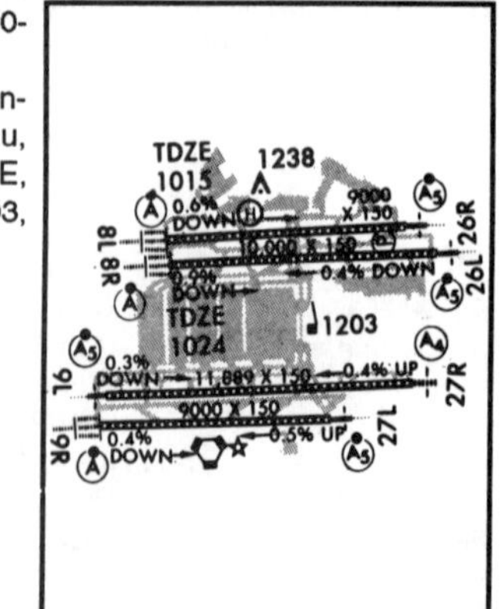

Airport Information:

ATLANTA - WILLIAM B HARTSFIELD ATLANTA INTL (ATL)
6 mi south of town N33-38.43 W84-25.62 Elev: 1026 Fuel: 100, 100LL, Jet-A Rwy 09L-27R: H11889x150 (Conc-Wc) Rwy 08R-26L: H10000x150 (Conc-Grvd) Rwy 08L-26R: H9000x150 (Conc-Grvd) Rwy 09R-27L: H9000x150 (Conc-WC) Attended: continuously Atis: 119.65 Arr, 125.55 dep Unicom: 122.95 App Con: 127.9, 118.35, 126.9, 127.25 Dep Con: 125.0, 125.7 Tower: 119.1, 119.5 Gnd Con: 121.75, 121.9 Clnc Del: 121.65 Pre Taxi Clnc: 121.65
FBO: Lockheed Air Terminal Phone: 530-2030, 530-2054
FBO: Raytheon Aircraft Services Phone: 765-1300

GA-AGS - AUGUSTA BUSH FIELD

(Area Code 706)

7

Restaurants Near Airport:

Jerry's Catering On Site Phone: 790-4208

Jerry's Catering:

Jerry's Catering is located well within walking distance, and is located in the terminal building at the Augusta Bush Field Airport. This cafeteria is open from 6 a.m. to 9 p.m. Monday through Friday and 6 a.m. to 8 p.m. Saturday and Sunday. They offer breakfast as well as a lunch buffet. The breakfast buffet runs from 6 a.m. to 11 a.m. and the lunch buffet runs from 11 a.m. to 4 p.m. Average prices are $4.00 for breakfast, and $5.00 for most lunch and dinner entrees. Their lunch buffet offers beef tips, ribs and home style chicken along with vegetables and other selections. It changes from day to day and is a big draw to many local people as well as fly-in customers. The main dining area can seat between 55 and 60 people. Additional conference rooms can be acquired through this restaurant that can accommodate up to 40 to 45 people. In-flight catering is another main service of Jerry's. In fact during our conversation with the manager, we learned that during the "Masters Golf Tournament" they cater as many as 1,800 aircraft that utilize the airport's facilities. The restaurant has just been remodeled, making it a fine place to stop for a bite to eat. For more information call Jerry's at 790-4208.

Lodging: Continental Airport Hotel (Free trans) 798-5501; Historic Telfair Inn (Free trans) 724-3315; Hornes Motor Lodge (Free trans) 798-2230; Landmark Hotel Augusta (Free trans) 722-5541; Ramada Inn-Airport (Free trans) 722-4344.
Meeting Rooms: Jerry's Catering can accommodate business groups with meeting space. Continental Airport Hotel 798-5501; Historic Telfair Inn 724-3315; Hornes Motor Lodge 798-2230; Landmark Hotel Augusta 722-5541; Ramada Inn-Airport 722-4344.
Transportation: Taxi Service: City Cab 722-3501; Rental Cars: Avis 798-1383; Budget 790-6901; Hertz 798-3970; National 798-5835;
Information: Chamber of Commerce, P.O. Box 1331, Augusta, GA 30903-1331, Phone: 823-6600.

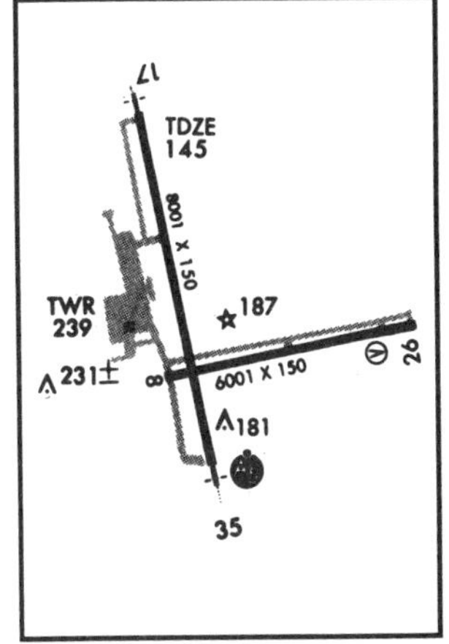

Airport Information:

AUGUSTA - BUSH FIELD (AGS)
6 mi south of town N33-22.20 W81-57.87 Elev: 145 Fuel: 100LL, Jet-A
Rwy 17-35: H8001x150 (Asph-Grvd) Rwy 08-26: H6001x150 (Asph) Attended: continuously Atis: 132.75 Unicom: 122.95 Augusta App/Depp Con: 126.8, 119.15, Augusta Tower: 118.7 Gnd Con: 121.9
FBO: Bush Field Aviation Services Phone: 798-2656

GA-CSG - COLUMBUS
COLUMBUS METROPOLITAN ARPT.

(Area Code 706)

8

Propellers Restaurant:

Propellers Restaurant is situated within the terminal building at the Columbus Metropolitan Airport. This snack bar style restaurant is open from 6 a.m. to 8 p.m. Monday through Friday, and 7 a.m. to 5 p.m. Saturday and Sunday. Their menu provides a full breakfast selection as well as many other choices. They also feature a breakfast and lunch buffet. Most of their sandwiches run between $2.95 and $4.95. Their breakfast buffet runs $6.25, and $7.95 for dinner. The restaurant can accommodate up to 67 persons. Pictures of airplanes as well as propeller decorations add to the aviation theme of this restaurant. There is also a conference room able to handle up to 40 additional people. In-flight catering is available if requested. For more information call 324-5574.

Restaurants Near Airport:
Propellers Restaurant On Site Phone: 324-5574

Lodging: Hampton Inn-Columbus Airport (Free trans) 576-5303; Holiday Inn-Airport (Free trans) 324-0231; Sheraton-Airport (1/2 mile) 327-6868.

Meeting Rooms: Hampton Inn-Columbus Airport (Free trans) 567-5303; Holiday Inn-Airport (Free trans) 324-0231.

Transportation: Airport courtesy car or shuttle and taxi service available; Also Rental Cars: Avis, Budget, Hertz, and National are on the field.

Information: Tourist Department, Convention and Visitors Bureau, 1000 Bay Avenue, Columbus, GA 31902, Phone: 322-1613.

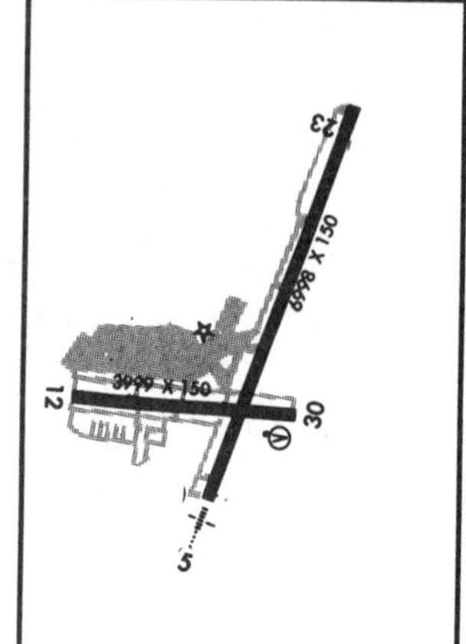

Attractions:

Confederate Naval Museum, located at 201 4th Street. This museum contains exhibits displaying a Confederate gunboat relic, as well as ship models and uniforms along with painting of naval operations. This museum is located about 4 or 5 miles south of the Columbus Metro Airport. Figure on approx. 1 hour to tour museum. For information call 327-9798; Also Fort Benning National Infantry Museum at 1251 Wynnton Road Phone: 322-0400.

Airport Information:

COLUMBUS - COLUMBUS METROPOLITAN AIRPORT (CSG)
3 mi northeast N32-30.98 W84-56.33 Elev: 397 Fuel: 100LL, Jet-A
Rwy 05-23: H6998x150 (Asph-Grvd) Rwy 12-30: H3999x150 (Asph) Attended: continuously
Atis: 127.75 Unicom: 122.95 App/Dep Con: 125.5, 126.55, 126.025 Tower: 120.1
Gnd Con: 121.9
Signature Flight Support Phone: 324-2453

(Area Code 706) 9

GA-AJR - CORNELIA HABERSHAM COUNTY

Runway Fish House, Inc.:

The Runway Fish House is located 1/4 mile from the Milledgeville Baldwin County Airport. You can see the restaurant from the airport. Although you should be able to walk to the restaurant, they will pick you up if you call them. Restaurant hours are Friday & Saturday from 5:00 p.m. to 9:30 p.m. and Sunday from 11:00 a.m. untill 2:30 p.m. Specialties of the house are catfish, bar-b-qued ribs, boiled shrimp. They have crab legs and oysters by the order. An all-you-can eat Sunday dinner buffet includes a variety of meats, (fried chicken, ham, roast beef, catfish, turkey) delicious salad bar, fruit, fresh vegetables and drinks. Average prices run $7.45 for the Sunday buffet and $11.50 for Friday & Saturday evening dinners. The restaurant is decorated with many photographs of aircraft. They can accommodate up to 400 guests in their main dining room and 100 persons in their special banquet area. Although in-flight catering is not available at this time, this facility is very popular with many pilots throughout the area. For information call the Runway Fish House at 706-776-1238.

Restaurants Near Airport:
Runway Fish House 1/4 mi Phone: 776-1238

Lodging: Comfort Inn 778-9573

Meeting Rooms: Runway Fish House 776-1238

Transportation: Rental cars: Dual 776-1950; Taxi: K&L 778-2821.

Information: Gainesville/Hall County Convention & Visitors Bureau, 830 Green Street, Gainesville, GA 30501, Phone: 404-536-5209

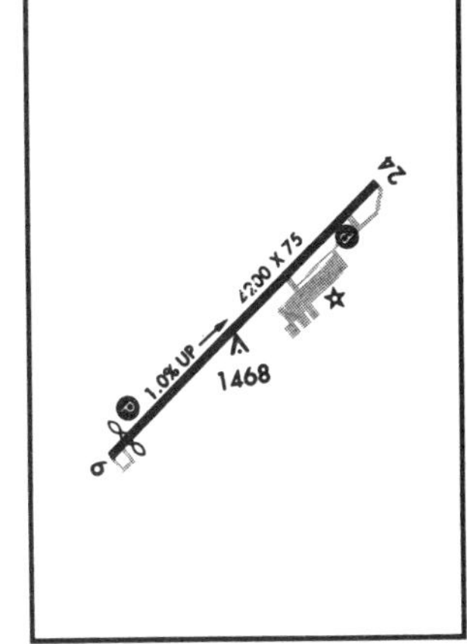

Airport Informaton:

CORNELIA - HABERSHAME COUNTY (AJR)
2 mi southwest of town N34-30.03 W83-33.33 Elev: 1447 Fuel: 100LL, Mogas
Rwy 06-24: H4200x75 (Asph) Attended 1300Z-dusk Unicom: 122.7
FBO: Habersham Aviation, Inc. Phone: 778-9978

Photo by: Runway Fish House (Tom Poole)

The Runway Fish House is located within walking distance from the Habersham County Airport.

GA-09J - JEKYLL ISLAND
JEKYLL ISLAND AIRPORT

(Area Code 912) 10

The Jekyll Island Club Hotel:

Jekyll Island is located six miles off the southeast coast of Georgia. The airport is located on the west side of the island, conveniently accessible to all of the island's attractions. The Jekyll Island Club Hotel, a Radisson Resort, caters to any occasion from a romantic weekend for two to a catered banquet or a grand reception. The guest rooms and suites blend turn-of-the-century comforts with modern conveniences to make every stay more comfortable. Furnishings include: two-poster mahogany beds, armoires, chairs, sofas, desks and tables enhanced by rich fabrics and plush carpeting. Many rooms feature Victorian fireplaces and/or whirlpool tubs, and all rooms feature multiple telephones, AM/FM clock radios and an array of custom bath amenities.The Club also features dining areas.The Grand Dining Room, restored to its historic splendor, features sumptuous gourmet continental cuisine.The Cafe Solterra,a delicatessen/ bakery seves a wide variety of New York-style deli and on-site prepared bakery items. All items are available for carry-out, including Specialty packed baskets for picnics, boating, etc.The Surfside Beach Club offers light snack items at the Club's private beach area. Also, the Poolside Bar is open daily (weather permitting) from Memorial Day through Labor Day. It serves grilled burgers and chicken with side salads and chips. J.P.'s Pub provides live piano entertainment, cocktails and conversation. Guests may have beverage service in any of the public areas, porches or courtyard. For more information about the Jekyll Island Club Hotel, call 635-2600.

Airport Information:

JEKYLL ISLAND - JEKYLL ISLAND AIRPORT (09J)
6 mi southeast of town N31-04.47 W81-25.67 Elev: 12 Fuel: 100LL
Rwy 18-36: H3711x75 (Asph) Attended: Daylight hours CTAF/Unicom: 123.0
Jax Center App/Dep Con: 126.75
FBO: West Aviation Phone: 635-2500

Restaurants Near Airport:

Black Beard's	2 mi	635-3522
Jekyll Club Hotel	1 mi	635-2600
Jekyll Wharf	1 mi	635-3800
Zachery's	2 mi	635-3128

Lodging: Jekyll Island Club Hotel (1 mile) 635-2600; Clarion Resort (3 miles) 635-2261; Comfort Inn (2 miles) 635-2211; Days Inn (3 miles) 635-3319; Holiday Inn (4 miles) 635-3511; Jekyll Estates (2 miles) 635-2256; Jekyll Inn Best Western (3 miles) 635-2531; Ramada Inn (3 miles) 635-2111; Seafarer (2 miles) 635-2202; Villas by the Sea (4 miles) 635-2521

Meeting Rooms: Jekyll Island Club Hotel 635-2600

Transportation: Courtesy van: Jekyll Island Club Hotel 635-2600; Jekyll Wharf 635-3800; Rental Cars: National 635-2500; Rent-A-Wreck 635-2500

Information: Jekyll Island Authority, P.O. Box 3186, Jekyll Island, GA 31527, Phone: 800-841-6586 or 635-3636.

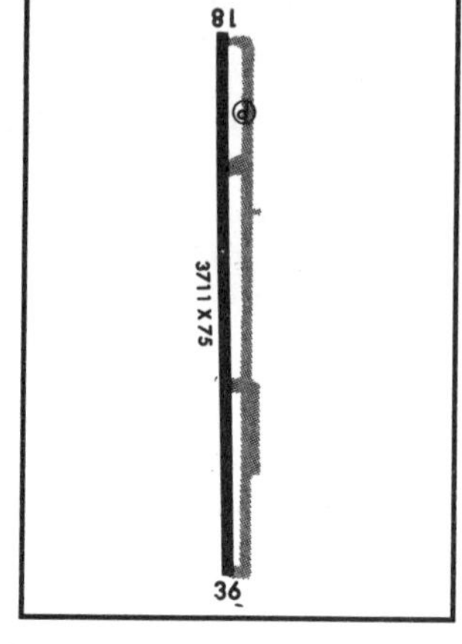

Jekyll Island

Jekyll Island, GA (09J)

Photo by: Jekyll Island Club Hotel

The Jekyll Island Club Hotel is a Registered National Historic Landmark.

Not to be used for navigational purposes

Jekyll Island is located six miles off the southeast coast of Georgia. It is one of the islands that make up the Golden Isles and is midway between Savannah, Ga. and Jacksonville, Fl. This popular vacation getaway spot is rich in history and tradition. The prosperous Jekyll Island Club, which had once privately owned the island, opened for its first official season in January, 1888. During that same year, members began to build private houses on the island. They even consulted some of America's best known architects. In 1947, the state of Georgia bought the island from the Jekyll Island Club, and thereafter established the Jekyll Island Authority to manage the island, which is open to the public. History Buffs can tour the Jekyll Island Club Historic District's restored turn-of-the-century "cottages" that were owned by famous American millionaires. Guided tours aboard spacious trams depart daily from the Museum Orientation Center. Jekyll Island is a refreshing break for anyone who wants to get away from the hustle and bustle of everyday life, and get back into nature. All visitors can enjoy the various recreational activities of the island.

Photo by: Jekyll Island Authority Visitors to the Jekyll Island Club Historic District can step back in time while touring mansion-sized "cottages".

The island, known for its unseasonably mild temperatures, is a haven for golfers, bikers, campers or anyone who just wants to stroll along the beach and watch the sun set on the ocean. Sixty-three holes of golf wind through the island's dunes, woods and lakes. The four golf course layouts, which include three 18-hole courses and one 9-hole course, offer a splendid mix of challenge and playability. The Jekyll Island Tennis Center has 13 clay courts, seven of which are lighted for night play. Deep sea fishing is available at one of the island's two marinas, as well as other fun water activities at Summer Waves Waterpark and the Water Ski Park. There are also activities, such as nature walks, over 30 boutiques to shop, sight-seeing charters, riverboat cruises, several museums to visit and more than 10 restaurants, as well as picnic areas. During the summer, the island hosts The Country by the Sea Music Festival and the Beach Music Festival.

With Jekyll's relatively small size, a bicycle is an interesting way to see the island. There are more than 20 miles of paved bikepaths. Both bike and car rentals are available at the airport, which is located on the west side of the island. Other transportation can also be arranged through several of the island's hotels. The airport accommodates both private and chartered flights, and has a 3,711'x75 asphalt runway. An on-site mechanic is handy for aircraft maintenence. Fly-in groups are welcome, and for a bird's-eye view of the island, airplane tours of up to three people are available. Jekyll is listed in Private Pilot Magazine as one of the top 10 fly-in islands in the country. Jekyll Island has many restaurants to suit both casual and formal tastes. Guests can lodge at one of the island's several fine hotels and rental cottages, as well as utilize the campground. For more information about rates and accommodations, contact the Jekyll Island Convention and Visitors Bureau at 800-841-6586 or 635-3636. They are open from 9A.M to 5P.M., 7 days a week, except for Thanksgiving, Christmas and New Year's. (Information submitted by the Jekyll Island Convention and Visitors Bureau and the Jekyll Island Authority)

Map by: Jekyll Island Convention and Visitors Bureau

Not to be used for navigational purposes

GA-MCN - MACON
MIDDLE GEORGIA REGIONAL

(Area Code 912) 11

Restaurants Near Airport:
Parachute Grill & Lounge On Site Phone: 785-0702

Parachute Grill & Lounge:

The Parachute Grill & Lounge is located in the terminal building at the Middle Georgia Regional Airport. There is a gift shop, lounge pool table, cable TV, vidio and gambling machine on the premises. The restaurant portion of the complex specializes in serving items like Rib-I steak, Phili sandwiches, buffalo wings, Mexican dishes, and chef salads. The dining room allows a nice view of the airport activity. Groups are welcome. In-flight along with on site and on location catering can be arranged. For more information about this establishment call 785-0702.

Lodging: Holiday Inn-Warner Robins (Free trans) 923-8871; Victorian Village (Free trans) 743-3333.

Meeting Rooms: Holiday Inn-Warner Robins (Free trans) 923-8871; Hilton 746-1461; Victorian Village (Free trans) 743-3333.

Transportation: Taxi: Airline Limousine 781-7312; Rental Cars: Avis 788-3840; Hertz 788-3600; National 788-5385.

Information: Macon-Bibb County Convention & Visitors Bureau, 200 Cherry Street. P.O. Box 6354, Macon, GA 31208, Phone: 743-3401 or 800-768-3401.

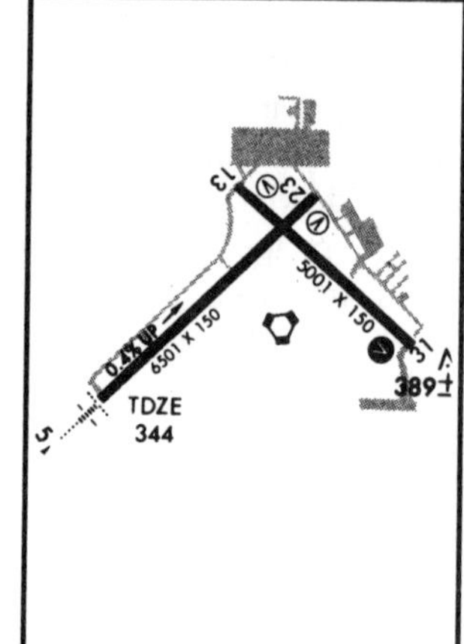

Airport Information:

MACON - MIDDLE GEORGIA REGIONAL AIRPORT (MCN)
9 mi south of town N32-41.57 W83-38.95 Elev: 354 Fuel: 100, Jet-A
Rwy 05-23: H6501x150 (Asph-Conc-Grvd) Rwy 13-31: H5001x150 (Asph-Conc)
Attended: 1000-0300Z Atis: 118.95 Unicom 122.95 Macon App/Dep Con: 119.6, 124.2, 124.8, Macon Tower: 128.2 Gnd Con: 121.65 Notes: For services after hours call 912-994-1066; Control Zone effective continuously.
FBO: Lowe Aviation Company, Inc. Phone: 788-3491

Museum Of Aviation
Robins A.F.B., Macon, Georgia

Macon, GA - Middle Georgia Regional (MCN)

The Warner Air Logistics Center's most ambitious effort under a Heritage Program established in 1981 is the Museum of Aviation at Robins Air Force Base. Three-phased construction of the museum complex is on a 43-acre site just south of the dedication of a 28,000 SF hangar for aircraft display on April 5, 1991. Phase II, a 62,000 square foot, three-story facility planned for interactive exhibits, a historical research center and archives, and 250-seat Vistascope Theater was built entirely with donated funds and was dedicated on July 3, 1992 or beyond.

The Museum of Aviation Phase II building includes a "Home Front Exchange" gift shop, High-Flight Cafe, and the Robert L. Scott Vistascope Theater featuring "To Fly" and "Flyers", both shown at the National Air and Space Museum in Washington. Exhibits include Flying the Hump, Airfield in England, and the Eagle Rotunda featuring a full-size, three-story high diorama with two WW-II aircraft suspended over a modern F-15 Eagle. Other exhibits will be added as time and resources allow.

Thousands of school children tour the museum each year, Vo-Tech students train on museum aircraft, and college students "intern" behind the scenes. As a result of its excellent education and volunteer programs, the Museum of Aviation won the 1992 Regional and National and National Frank G. Brewer Awards. These are Civil Air Patrol's highest awards in the field of aerospace education--the original is located in the Smithsonian. Volunteers at the museum include docent/tour guides, aviation ship staffing, special events, aircraft restoration, etc. They play an important role in museum functions. New volunteers are always welcome and are invited to stop by or call anytime.

In 1992, the Museum of Aviation became the second FAA Resource Center in the State of Georgia and one of ten in the southern region established for distribution of aviation education materials and resources to the public, media, and educational aviation education materials and resources to the public, media, and educational community. Workshop for Houston County educators was conducted at the museum to inspire students to become interested in aviation and space. It is the first aviation-related workshop for teachers in this area, and will expand to include surrounding counties.

Today, the museum welcomes more than 270,000 visitors annually to view more than 85 historic aircraft and missiles, along with static displays. Over 1.5 million have visited since 1984. The museum has grown rapidly from its modest beginning to an economic, educational, and recreational magnet in the state and the only museum of its kind in the southeastern United States.

In April 1989 the Georgia legislature passed a bill establishing the Georgia Aviation Hall of Fame at the museum to

Photo: by Museum of Aviation

Phase II Exhibit Airfield in England, P-51 "Mustang"

honor people, living and dead, who by their extraordinary achievements have made lasting contributions to aviation in the state. Their records, milestones and accomplishments are honored in the Hall of Fame exhibit, a living, growing tribute to Georgia's distinguished aviation history. To date, 19 people have been enshrined in the Hall of Fame.

The impressive array of flying machines on display include an SR-71 Blackbird, U-2 Dragon Lady, British Lightning, and MiG-17 as some of the more unusual attractions. Arrivals within the last year include an RF-101 Voodoo, F-106 Delta Dart, A-37 Dragonfly, T-28 Trojan, and UH-1P Iroquois. Other World War-II, Korea and Vietnam era weapons and missiles complete the inventory.

All three museum buildings are open to the public, free of charge, seven days a week, 10 a.m. to 5 p.m.: closed Thanksgiving, Christmas, and New Year's. There is a small charge for the Vistascope Theater. Fly-in guests can land at Middle Georgia Regional (MCN) approx. 8 miles from museum. Other airports nearby are Herbert Smart Downtown Arpt. (MAC) 15 miles, or Warner Robins Air Park (5A2). For group tours or information call 912-923-6600. (Information submitted by museum)

Photo: by Museum of Aviation

SR-71 Blackbird

Photo: by Museum of Aviation

Arial View Phase II Building, Museum of Aviation

GA-MHP - METTER
METTER MUNICIPAL AIRPORT

(Area Code 912) 12

Western Steer Steak House:

The Western Steer Steak House is situated about 3/4 mile from the Metter Municipal Airport. When speaking to both Tri-Star Aero Service at the airport and the restaurant manager, we learned that Tri-Star will provide courtesy transportation or let you borrow a vehicle to get to the restaurant. This establishment is open from 11 a.m. to 9 p.m. weekdays and from 11 a.m. to 10 p.m. weekends. Their menu offers a very nice selection of choice cuts of sirloin, T-bone, filet mignon, and rib-eye steak. In addition, they also prepare fresh seafood, grilled chicken, and a southern style buffet including items like salad bar, fresh vegetables, meats, soups and desserts. The restaurant can hold 360 persons, with seating for 225 in their front dining room. In addition there are two separate dining rooms in back of the restaurant, that can accommodate up to 70 additional persons each, for private groups and parties. All meals listed on their menu can also be prepared-to-go. Lodging accommodations are available at the Comfort Inn located near this restaurant. For more information about the Western Steer Steak House, call 685-4110.

Airport Information:

METTER - METTER MUNICIPAL AIRPORT (MHP)
2 mi south of town N32-22.43 W82-04.79 Elev: 197 Fuel: 100LL, Jet-A, MOGAS
Rwy 10-28: H3610x75 (Asph) Attended: Mon-Fri 1300-2200Z, Sat-Sun 1400-2200Z
Unicom: 123.0
FBO: Tri-Star Aero Services Phone: 685-4162

Restaurants Near Airport:
Western Steer Steak House 3/4 mi Phone: 685-4110

Lodging: Comfort Inn (3/4 mile); Metter motel (3 miles) 685-2125.

Meeting Rooms: None Reported

Transportation: Airport courtesy car reported; Also rental cars available: Metter Ford 685-2141.

Information: Steatesboro Convention and Visitors Bureau, P.O. Box 1516, Statesboro, GA 30458, Phone: 489-1869.

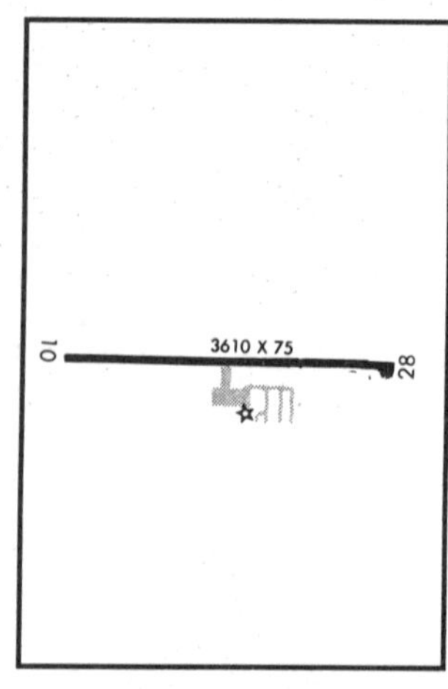

Not to be used for navigational purposes

GA-PIM - PINE MOUNTAIN
CALLAWAY GARDENS-HARRIS COUNTY

(Area Code 706) 13

The Restaurants at Callaway Gardens Resort:

Callaway Gardens Resort is located on U.S. Highway 27 in Pine Mountain, Georgia, and is about 4 miles from the Callaway Gardens-Harris County Airport. While touring the gardens, you are sure to work up an appetite for one of the seven restaurants at this fine resort. Visit The Country Store, atop pine Mountain. At this restaurant, sightseers get their fill during breakfast or lunch on a glass-enclosed porch that overlooks the valley. The Plantation Room, located at the Callaway Gardens Inn, offers generous breakfast, lunch and dinner buffets, as well as a bountiful Friday night Seafood buffet and Sunday brunch. The Gardens Restaurant serves delicious steaks and seafood dishes and offers an appealing menu for lunch. For a taste of Italy, visit The Veranda, and sample fine Italian cuisine. Or, for a lighter fare, The Flower Mill has a soda shop atmosphere that appeals to the whole family, and it serves a selection of sandwiches, salads and pizzas. Champions restaurant features a wide array of sandwiches and salads, and during the warmer months it features outdoor seating. For the ultimate in fine dining, The Georgia Room offers a menu that ranges from delicate pates to juicy steaks and a variety of delicious desserts. With advance notice, the FBO offers a free shuttle to and from the resort. For more information, call 663-5055, between the hours of 8:30 a.m. and 4:45 p.m., 7 days a week or 800-282-8181 for the resort main swichboard.

Restaurants Near Airport:
Callaway Gardens 4 mi Phone: 663-2281

Lodging: Callaway Gardens Resort (4 miles) 663-2281
Meeting Rooms: Callaway Gardens Resort 663-2281
Transportation: With advance notice, the FBO provides free shuttle service to and from the resort, call 663-5055 for more information.
Information: Tourisim Department, P.O. Box 1776, Atlanta, GA, 30301-1776, Phone: 404-656-3590 or 800-VISIT-GA, ext. 1903

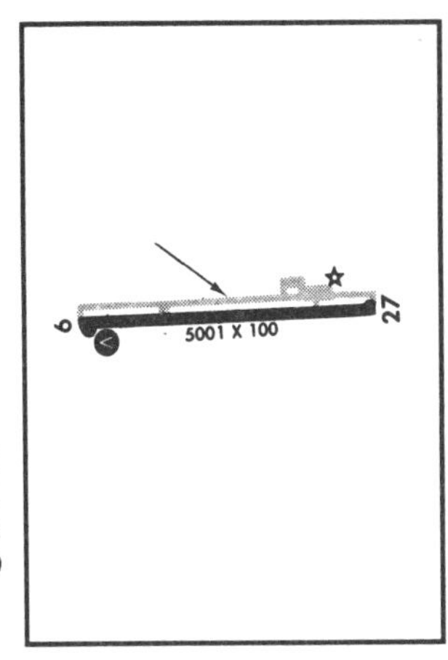

Airport Information:

PINE MOUNTAIN - CALLAWAY GARDENS-HARRIS COUNTY (PIM)
2 mi southwest of town N32-50.44 W84-52.95 Elev: 902 Fuel: 100LL, Jet-A Rwy 09-27: H5001x100 (Asph) Attended: 1330-2145Z CTAF/Unicom: 122.8 Columbus App/Dep Con: 127.7, 126.0 (1200-0400Z) Atlanta Center App/Dep Con: 120.45 (0400-1200Z) Clnc Del: 120.45 Notes: CAUTION-Deer on and in vicinity of airport. Overnight parking fees are $5.00 for singles and $10.00 for twins.
FBO: Callaway Gardens Phone: 663-5055

Callaway Gardens Resort

Pine Mountain, GA (GA-PIM)

Photo by: Callaway Gardens Resort — The Cecil B. Day Butterfly Center

Callaway Gardens Resort is a 2,500-acre, year-round horticultural display garden that attracts more than 750,000 guests annually from throughout the United States and abroad. It is located on U.S. Highway 27 in Pine Mountain, GA, 70 miles south of Atlanta and 30 miles north of Columbus. Callaway Gardens was created by Cason J. Callaway and his wife, Virginia Hand Callaway. It is a public, educational, horticultural and charitable organization that is owned and operated by the non-profit Ida Cason Callaway Foundation.

If you love nature, then this is the place for you! Some of the highlights of this breathtaking attraction include: The Cecil B. Day Butterfly Center, which is the largest glass-enclosed, tropical conservatory for the display of living butterflies in North America. Inside the 854 glass panes, more than 1,000 free-flying Central and South American, Malaysian and Taiwan butterflies, as well as numerous ground and water birds surround the lush tropical foliage, 12-foot waterfall and stream. 1 1/2 acres of wildlife gardens surround the Day Butterfly Center and attract native butterflies and birds. In this garden, guests can learn what to plant in their home gardens so they too can attract butterflies and birds. The Center offers educational displays, as well as an orientation theater which shows the award-winning movie on the life of the butterfly, titled On Wings Of Wonder. The Day Butterfly Center is the centerpiece of Callaway Gardens' 45-acre Meadowlark Gardens area, which contains three walking trails bounded by hollies, cultivated rhododendrons, more than 700 varieties of azaleas and an endless variety of wildflowers.

The John A. Sibley Horticultural Center, named for the late John A. Sibley, an agricultural enthusiast, is one of the most advanced garden/greenhouse complexes in the world. The main conservatory of this five-acre garden features 20,209 square feet of 18 major floral displays each year. The fiberglass roof and surrounding trees provide shade for the plants, while the 22-foot waterfall and pool, along with a misting system, reduce air temperature.The building's southern orientation enables it to draw in the maximum available winter sunlight.

Another highlight of Callaway Gardens is Mr. Cason's Vegetable Garden, which is a model 7 1/2-acre garden producing more than 400 varieties of vegetables, fruits and herbs. The garden is the setting for the Public Broadcasting System television show "Victory Garden South." The upper terrace of the vegetable garden grows varieties of blueberries, muscadine grapes and unusual vegetables. The middle terrace produces seasonable annual vegetables, such as corn, beans, tomatoes, squash, peppers, cauliflower, broccoli, lettuce and radishes. The lower terrace of 11/2-acres features an Herb Garden set in the midst of apple and peach trees. The Vegetable Garden also grows traditional southern crops of okra, field peas and collard greens. These regional favorites are among the vegetables selected for use in Callaway Gardens' restaurants. After you see all of those mouth-watering vegetables, you are sure to work up an appetite.

Callaway Gardens has seven restaurants with selections that range from southern buffets to continental cuisine. Guests can start their day with a delicious breakfast atop Pine Mountain at The Country Store, which is set in a glass-enclosed porch that overlooks the valley. The Plantation Room, located at the comfortable but elegant Callaway Gardens Inn, offers generous breakfast, lunch and dinner buffets, as well as a bountiful Friday night Seafood buffet and Sunday brunch. The Gardens Restaurant and The Veranda, both located in the Gardens overlooking the Lake View Golf Course and Mountain Creek Lake, provide a variety of scrumptious dishes. The Gardens Restaurant serves delicious steaks and seafood and offers an appealing menu for lunch. The Veranda features Italian cuisine in a casual atmosphere. Both the Gardens Restaurant and The Veranda offer outside dining during warmer months. For a lighter fare, The Flower Mill, adjacent to the Callaway Country Cottage meeting facilities, features a wide array of sandwiches, salads and pizzas, and has a fun, soda shop atmosphere that appeals to the whole family. Champions, located in the Mountain View Clubhouse, serves sandwiches and salads, and it features indoor and outdoor seating. For the ultimate in fine dining, The Georgia Room offers a menu that ranges from delicate pates to juicy steaks and a variety of delicious desserts.

Callaway Gardens also features a variety of recreational activities, such as golf, tennis racquetball, boating, fishing, hunting, fitness, swimming, in addition to beach activities at Robin Lake and chidren's playgrounds. For those who like to shop, the resort has 10 stores that feature anything from food products, horticultural and decorative items to apparel, educational materials and much more.

There are three separate meeting facilities: The Convention Center in the Gardens Inn, a 36,000 square-foot Conference Center and the Cottage Meeting Center.

Callaway Gardens Resort is located about 4 miles from Callaway Gardens-Harris County Airport. With advance notice, the FBO provides free shuttle service to and from the resort. Overnight parking fees are $5.00 for singles and $10.00 for twins. For further assistance, call the FBO at 663-5055 between the hours of 8:30 a.m. and 4:45 p.m., 7 days a week. Accommodations are available at the Callaway Gardens Inn, Callaway Country Cottages, and Mountain Creek Villas. For more information about activities and accommodations, contact Callaway Gardens Resort at 800-282-8181 or 663-2281, Monday through Friday, 7:30 a.m. to 10:00 p.m. and Saturday and Sunday, 8:30 a.m. to 6:00 p.m. (Information submitted by Callaway Gardens Resort, Inc.)

Photo by: Callaway Gardens Resort

The John A. Sibley Horticultural Center

GA-RMG - ROME
RICHARD B. RUSSELL AIRPORT

(Area Code 706) 14

Prop Stop Restaurant:

The Prop Stop Restaurant is situated 1/2 mile from the Richard B. Russell Airport. This deli can be reached by several ways. You could either walk on a nice day, call for taxi service or arrange courtesy transportation through one of the fixed base operators or airport commission. This deli is open between 8:30 a.m. and 4:30 p.m. They serve delicious specialty sandwiches made from a wide variety of choice cut meats and cheeses. Sandwiches of all types, including their special steak sandwiches are popular with many customers. Their dining room provides seating that can handle up to 55 persons. Groups and parties are welcome. Meals can also be prepared-to-go. During our conversation with the owner, we learned that many pilots fly in and walk over to the restaurant for lunch. For more information call the Prop Stop Restaurant at 235-3452.

Restaurants Near Airport:
Prop Stop Restaurnat On Site, 1/2 mi Phone: 235-3452

Lodging: Ramada Inn (Free trans, 7 miles) 291-0101.

Meeting Rooms: Ramada Inn (Free trans) 291-0101.

Transportation: Airport courtesy car reported; Taxi: A-1 City 232-5333; Also Rental Cars: AAA 295-7835; Budget 291-0723

Information: Greater Rome Convention & Visitors Bureau, 402 Civic Center Hill, P.O. Box 5823, Rome, GA 30162-5823, Phone: 295-5576.

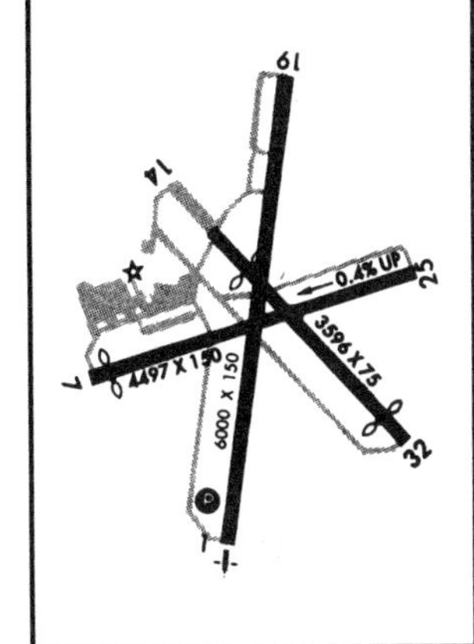

Airport Information:

ROME - RICHARD B. RUSSELL AIRPORT (RMG)
6 mi north of town N34-21.04 W85-09.48 Elev: 644 Fuel: 100, Jet-A
Rwy 01-19: H6000x150 (Asph) Rwy 14-32: H3596x75 (Asph) Rwy 07-25: H4497x150 (Asph) Attended: 1200-0100Z Unicom: 123.0
Floyd County Airport Commission Phone: 295-7835

GA-SAV - SAVANNAH
SAVANNAH INTERNATIONAL

(Area Code 912) 15

Host Marriott:

Host International Restaurant is located in the terminal building at the Savannah International Airport. This facility soon plans on relocating it's establishment to the northeast quadrant of the airport. This is classified as a combination snackbar, lounge and cafeteria. Their menu includes a full breakfast line, seafood gumbo, burgers, sandwiches, salads, and a seafood bar that contains items like shrimp, crab legs, as well as other items. Average prices run $3.99 for breakfast, and $5.50 for lunch & dinner. The main dining room can accommodate up to 100 persons, and depicts an outdoor atmosphere. The restaurant specializes with in-flight catering for airlines or private and corporate aircraft. For more information call 964-7227.

Restaurants Near Airport:
Host Marriott On Site Phone: 964-7227
Quality Inn On Site Phone: 964-1421

Lodging: Quality Inn Airport (On Site, Free trans) 964-1421; Ramada Inn-Airport (Free trans) 748-6464; Hilton-De Soto (Free trans) 232-9000;
Meeting Rooms: Quality Inn Airport 964-1421; Ramada Inn Airport 748-6464; Hilton De Soto (Convention facilities) 232-9000; Hyatt Regency (Convention facilities) 238-1234; Sheraton Savannah Resort & Country Club (Convention facilities) 897-1612.
Transportation: Taxi: Adam 233-8865; Redbird 925-2293; Savannah 925-9188 or 356-1749; Yellow Cab 964-6370; Also Rental Cars available on site: Alamo; Avis; Budget; Dollar; Hertz; National.
Information: Savannah Area Convention & Visitors Bureau, P.O. Box 1628, Savannah, GA 31402-1628, Phone: 944-0456 or 800-444-2427.

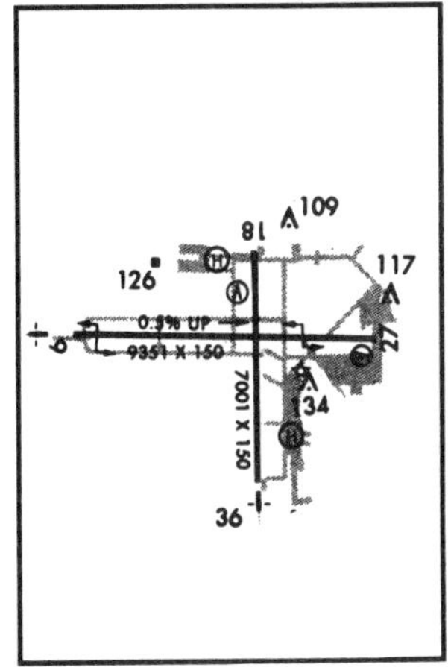

Airport Information:

SAVANNAH INTERNATIONAL AIRPORT (SAV)
7 mi northwest of town N32-07.66 W81-12.13 Elev: 51 Fuel: 100LL, Jet-A
Rwy 09-27: H9351x150 (Asph-Grvd) Rwy 18-36: H7001x150 (Conc-Wc) Attended: 1100-0400Z Atis: 123.75 Unicom: 122.95 App/Dep Con: 125.3, 120.4, 118.4, 121.1
Tower: 119.1 Gnd Con: 121.9 Clnc Del: 119.55 Notes: CAUTION: Birds and deer on and in vicinity of airport., Control Zone effective continuously.
FBO: Savannah Aviation Phone: 964-1022

GA-4J6 - ST MARYS
ST MARYS AIRPORT

16

St Mary's Seafood & Steak House:

St Mary's Seafood & Steak House is located only 2 or 3 blocks from the St. Marys Airport, and should be within easy walking distance. This is a family style restaurant that is open Thursday through Saturday 11 a.m. to 10 p.m. and Sunday through Wednesday 11 a.m. to 9 p.m. They specialize in steak and seafood selections including lobster, as well as more conventional entrees like chicken strips, hamburgers, cheeseburgers, chicken sandwiches, fish sandwiches, soups and salads. Monday through Thursday, they feature an all-you-can-eat crab legs dinner. Their dining room contains many nautical decorations simulating a stroll along the boardwalk, with ropes, fishing nets, as well as many nautical items. The main dining area can seat approx. 100 to 120 persons. This restaurant welcomes guests to come-as-they-are and enjoy a fine dining experience. For more information please call 882-6875.

Restaurants Near Airport: **(Area Code 912)**

Leesgan (Chinese)	1-2 blks	Phone: 882-5169
Sneaky Pete's	4 blks	Phone: 882-6005
St Mary's Steakhouse	2-3 blks	Phone: 882-6875

Lodging: Charter House Inn (1/2 mile) 882-6250; Comfort Inn (6 miles) 729-6979; Days Inn (6 miles) 729-5454; Holiday Inn (6 miles) 729-3000; Riverview Hotel (3 miles) 882-3242; Roadway Inn (6 miles) 729-4363.

Meeting Rooms: None Reported

Transportation: Airport courtesy car reported; Hertz Rental Car 882-2424.

Information: Georgia Department of Industry, Trade and Tourism, P.O. Box 1776, Atlanta, GA 30301-1776, Phone: 404-656-3590 or 800-VISIT-GA.

Airport Information:

ST MARYS - ST MARYS AIRPORT (4J6)
2 mi north of town N30-45.28 W81-33.44 Elev: 24 Fuel: 100LL, Jet-A
Rwy 04-22: H5000x100 (Asph) Attended: 1230-0100Z Unicom: 122.8
FBO: Sharp Aviation Phone: 882-4359

GA-SSI - ST. SIMONS ISLAND BRUNSWICK/MALCOLM McKINNON

(Area Code 912) 17

Restaurants Near Airport:

The Cloister Hotel	5 mi NE	Phone: 638-3611
King & Prince Hotel	3 mi SE	Phone: 638-3631
Sea Palms Resort	3 mi N	Phone: 638-3351

Lodging: The Cloister Hotel 638-3611, County Hearth Inn 638-7805, Days Inn 634-0660, The Island Inn 638-7805, King & Prince Beach Resort 638-3631, Queen's Court 638-8459, Seagate Inn 638-8661, Sea Palms Golf & Tennis Resort 638-3351.
Meeting Rooms: Golden Isles Aviation 638-8617; The Cloister Hotel 638-3611; Days Inn 634-0660; the Island Inn 638-7805; King & Prince Beach Resort 638-3631; And the Sea Palms Golf & Tennis Resort, 638-3351.
Transportation: Courtesy cars and rental cars are available at Golden Isles Aviation 638-8617. Also bicycle rentals are accessible across the street from the airport.
Information: St. Simons' Chamber of Commerce & Visitor Center, 530 B. Beachview Drive, St. Simons Island, GA 31522, Phone: 800-525-8678.

St. Simons Island Attractions:

St. Simons Island is located across the intercoastal waterway east of the town of Brunswick, GA. This island contains its own airstrip and offers many activities for vacationers. A number of upscale resorts and country clubs make this location a golfers paradise. Separated by Village Creek and directly adjacent to St. Simons Island, is Sea Island. The Cloister Hotel is one resort that has become a popular choice. President Bush and other high ranking dignitaries have enjoyed the hospitality of this establishment. The Sea Island Golf Club, located just southwest of the Malcolm McKinnon Airport, is operated by the same owners. A number of other very popular resorts on the island include: the Hampton Club, the King and Prince Resort, and the Sea Palms Resort. McKinnon Airport is situated on the southern part of the island. The downtown district which contains a variety of shops, is only a short distance from the field. Since the island is only 12 miles long, it is easy to reach local attractions. Golden Isles Aviation provides fuel as well as many other services for fly-in guests. Courtesy cars are available to customers for short term use. Rental cars are also on hand. (Avis & Hertz) Visitors can even rent bicycles from a shop located across the street from the airport. For a comprehensive list of area sites and attractions, visit the St. Simons Island Chamber of Commerce at 530 B. Beachview Drive, Neptune Park, St. Simons Island or call 800-525-8678.

NO AIRPORT DIAGRAM AVAILABLE

Airport Information:

BRUNSWICK - MALCOLM McKINNON (SSI)
5 mi east of Brunswick, 1/2 mi downtown St. Simons N31-09.10 W81-23.48 Elev: 20 Fuel: 100LL, Jet-A Rwy 04-22: H5421x150 (Asph) Rwy 16-34: H3313x75 (Asph) Attended: 1200-0100Z CTAF/Unicom: 122.7
FBO: Bill Walker & Assoc. Phone: 638-3191
FBO: Gold Isles Aviation Phone: 638-8617

St. Simons Island, (Brunswick, GA)

Brinswick, St. Simons Island Malcolm McKinnon Airport, GA (GA-SSI)

The live oak trees, marshlands and miles of beaches along St. Simons Island are reason enough for most to choose the island as a home or a vacation spot. The island's extensive history is also a draw for many people who search the shores for signs of Indian life or walk legendary battlegrounds blending history and tradition with present-day life.

But St. Simons' natural beauty coupled with its history and mild year-round weather, make it a recreational haven, with every activity imaginable available from fishing and boating to golf and horseback riding.

St. Simons has many community facilities available such as the Casino Complex & Neptune Park on Beachview Drive. This facility has activity and meeting rooms, miniature golf, a swimming pool, playground, picnic area and bandstand. Several other parks are also situated nearby.

If golf is your favorite pastime, St. Simons will keep you well entertained. Visitors come to the island year-round to challenge its 99 championship holes of golf. Very few days of the year are too cold or too hot to play, thanks to the moderating influence of the sea. The Hampton Club on Tabby Stone is located along the rivers and marshlands of the island's northernmost tip. The club opened in August 1989 and is affiliated with the King & Prince Beach Resort. The course, designed by world-renowned golf architect Joe Lee, was selected by "Golf Magazine" as one of the nation's top 10 resort courses. The course has 18 holes, including four holes located off the main island on small marsh islands.

St. Simons Island Club on Kings Way is a public course, also designed by Lee. A covered bridge leads to the clubhouse and the 18-hole layout. The club is owned and operated by Sea Island Company. Sea Palms Golf & Tennis Resort on Frederica Road offers 27 holes of play. It is consistently ranked among the state's top courses and has been the site of numerous state tournaments.

The Sea Island Golf Club, on Retreat Avenue, is affiliated with Sea Island's Cloister Hotel. The club is at the southern tip of St. Simons on the site of what was once Retreat Plantation. The 36 hole course, with four nine-hole layouts, is also ranked among the state's top courses. In addition, there are three courses in Brunswick and four courses on Jekyll Island.

The recreational opportunities are endless on St. Simons Island. Rental possibilities include: jet skis, rollerblades, bicycles, sailboats, rafts, kayaks and horses for lessons or trail rides. There are also historic island tours by trolley, nature boat rides, air tours and nature walks.

St. Simons Island restaurants offer a wide range of food to fit any taste or budget. From locally caught seafood to continental cuisine to good ol' southern cooking, you can find what you are craving at one of the island's 50 or more restaurants. Shopping opportunities are abundant on St. Simons Island. Close to 10 shopping centers house restaurants, specialty shops, art galleries, antique shops and fashions. Local crafts, island treasures and handmade gifts are also among the finds.

The Cloister

St. Simons Island, Brunswick
Malcom McKinnon Airport, GA (GA-SSI)

The Cloister is located on Sea Island off the scenic southern coast of Georgia.The Cloister on Sea Island is located about 5 miles northeast of Malcolm McKinnon Airport in Brunswick. With 24-hour notice, Cloister will pick up fly-in guests in an executive limousine, or groups using private vehicles. Year-round, Sea Island's climate is usually comfortably moderate. Five miles of sandy beach, championship sports, beautiful gardens, historic sites and 10,000 acres of protected, lush forests and serene marshes make this resort a vacationer's paradise. The Cloister, which is family-owned, puts special emphasis on programs and activities for all ages. There is no charge for children under 19 who share accommodations with their parents, only for meals. Also, there is no charge for their golf or tennis.

The wide, hard-packed beach is ideal for walking, running or just lazing under the sun. Also, the Beach Club, pools and lounges are available for guests to relax and enjoy. The Cloister also features 18 tennis courts, 54 holes of golf, skeet, horseback riding, sailing, fishing and plenty of shopping. The historic sites, artists' colonies and colorful gardens are also a sight to see.

Beach Club privileges are complimentary to Cloister guests and Cottage Club subscribers. Swim lessons, aquatics, scuba and snorkeling are among instruction choices. Guest amenities include salon, lockers, a steam room and a dry sauna. Beach sailing and cabanas are available adjacent to the Beach Club. Windsurfers, catamarans, kayaks and seacycles are available, as well. (Note: At the Beach Club, a cover-up for swimwear is required. Swimsuits and bare feet are not permitted in the hotel lobby or lounges, however a bathers' entrance is provided).

Photo by: The Cloister, Sea Island, GA

Aerial view of The Cloister.

A spa is available to guests so they can relax and indulge in facials, massages, Swiss showers, hydrotherapy and other esthetics treatments. Fitness services include: exercise/ cardiovascular equipment, classes and personal training and assessments.

The Cloister Racquet Club offers fast-dry clay courts that are rested and groomed twice every 24 hours. racquets, balls, clothing and re-string service are available at the clubhouse (adjacent to Main Hotel). Professional tennis instructors are available for arranging matches, round-robins and tournaments. Sea Island holiday guests tournaments occur frequently for those who want a little fun competion. (Note: Appropriate tennis wear is required, including collared shirts for men and tennis (no running) shoes.

The Sea Island Golf Club, located on antebellum Retreat Plantation (once a cotton plantation), offers 36 holes surrounded by seaside breezes and majestic oaks. The resort's Golf Learning Center has an outstanding staff who lead clinics and schools. Custom club fitting is available on-site. (Note: At the Golf Club, golf attire is required. Bermuda and walking shorts may be worn.)

At the riding stables, saddle horses are available for daily beach expeditions, including lunch picnics or evening cookouts. Riding instructors are available for adults and children.

For adults and children, ages two and up, bicycling is available along paths and side streets which offer a tour of beautiful homes. There are also seasonal outings which explore the north end of the island.

All year, Cloister Dock (opposite the hotel motor entrance) offers waterways fishing in saltwater creeks and rivers. From June through September, adjoining inlets and sounds hold trophy tarpon, as well as bass, drum, flounder, whiting, croaker and sheepshead.

For bird-watchers and naturalists, the salt marsh environment is abundant with life, such as waterfowl and bottle-nose dolphin. Accredited guides will direct nature tours.

All meals are included for guests with The Cloister's American Plan. At the Cloister, dining choices cover a unique range of menus and settings. Guests may dress up for an evening of cocktails, dancing and dining at the hotel. Or, they may go casually to their choice of clubs--Beach Club, Sea Island Golf Club and St. Simons Island Club. The Beach Club offers dining by the sea, with indoor and open-air breakfast luncheon buffets, plus a scrumptious seafood dinner buffet. The Golf Clubs offer their disinct personalities and cuisines for both lunch and dinner. The main dining room serves six-course meals accompanied by music and an extensive wine list. Sunday evening buffets offer a dessert extravaganza. (Note: In main dining room, men wear collared shirts w/ jackets for breakfast and lunch and must wear coats and ties for dinner.)

Photo by: The Cloister, Sea Island, GA

Sea Island Beach Club at the Cloister Resort

For evening entertainment, special dance programs and music entertainment by exceptional performers are held throughout the year. Every night, except Sunday, guests can dance to the orchestra during cocktails or after dinner. Ballroom and contemporary dancing are signature activities at The Cloister. Private instruction is available. Also, many evenings feature illustrated talks about local history and the nature of this area of the Georgia coast.

The Cloister offers a variety of accommodations with a wide range of rates appropriate to size and location. Some front the ocean, and others are a few hundred yards back. They also offer special golf or tennis packages, as well as packages for honeymooners, anniversaries, spa visits and holiday periods. The Cloister requires a deposit with reservations and recommends that they be booked early. They do not take credit cards, but will accept checks. For more information about rates, activities and accommodations at The Cloister, call 800-SEA-ISLA (732-4752) or 638-3611. (Information by The Cloister, Sea Island)

GA-OPN- THOMASTON UPSON COUNTY

(Area Code 706) 18

Szechuan Chinese Restaurant:

The Szechuan Chinese Restaurant is located about 4 miles east from the Reginald Grant Memorial Airport. Transportation to this restaurant could be obtained either through airport courtesy transportation, or by taxi. This is a family style facility that is open from 10:30 a.m. to 10 p.m. Monday through Thursday, Friday & Saturday between 10:30 a.m. to 10:30 p.m. and Sunday from 11:30 a.m. to 10 p.m. A luncheon buffet (All you can eat) is served day on Tuesday and Thursday evenings. The main dining room can seat 80 to 120 persons. A separate dining room is able to accommodate up to 16 additional persons for groups or parties. For more information call the Szechuan Chinese Restaurant at 648-3025.

Restaurants Near Airport:

Golden Corral Steak house	4 mi	Phone: 648-6114
Golden Corral	4 mi	Phone: 648-6114
Peking Restaurant	4 mi	Phone: 648-6955
Szechuan Chinese Restaurant	4 mi	Phone: 648-3025

Lodging: Best Western (1/2 mile) 648-2900; Colonial Motel (1 mile) 648-2121; Guest House (3 miles) 647-1203; Upson Hotel (3 miles) 647-7126.

Meeting Rooms: None Reported

Transportation: Taxi Safety 647-5411; Veterans 647-8197; Also courtesy car reported at airport.

Information: Thomaston-Upson County Chamber of Commerce. P.O. Box 827, 201 South Center Street, Thomaston, GA 30286, Phone: 647-9686.

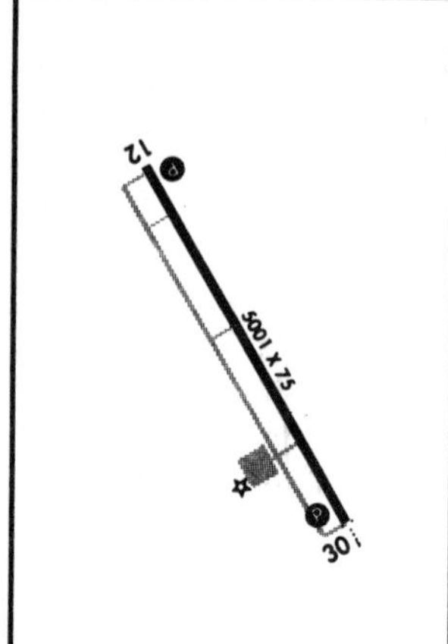

Airport Information:

THOMASTON - UPSON COUNTY AIRPORT (OPN)
5 mi northeast of town N32-57.30 W84-15.87 Elev: 796 Fuel: 100LL, Jet-A
Rwy 12-30: H5001x75 (Asph) Attended: Mon-Sat 1400-2200Z, Sun 1800-2200Z Unicom: 122.8
Airport Manager **Phone: 647-7515**
Upson County Airport **Phone; 647-4500**

GA-TVI - THOMASVILLE THOMASVILLE MUNICIPAL

(Area Code 912) 19

Holiday Inn:

The Holiday Inn along U.S. Highway 19 South is situated about 6 miles from the Thomasville Municipal Airport. One of our readers was kind enough to inform us that this facility will provide transportation for fly-in guests. There is a restaurant combined along with the 147 room lodging establishment. This is a family-style restaurant that is open Sunday through Thursday from 6:30 a.m. to 2:00 p.m. for breakfast and lunch and 5:30 to 9 p.m. for dinner. Friday and Saturdays they are open from 5:30 until 10 p.m. Items on their menu include a full breakfast line along with steaks, shrimp, fish, chicken strips and sandwiches of all types. Fridays and Saturdays they feature a seafood buffet which is very popular with their customers. Average prices run $5.25 for most breakfast and lunch items, including the buffet. Evening entrees run in the neighborhood of $9.95. The restaurant has a contemporary atmosphere with seating for about 40 persons. They also have accommodations for 3 separate meeting rooms. The Holiday Inn has a swimming pool and hot tub. For information you can call 226-7111.

Restaurants Near Airport:

Holiday Inn	6 mi	Phone: 226-7111
Plaza	N/A	Phone: 226-5153

Lodging: Budget Inn 7 mi 226-9585; Days Inn 7 mi 226-6025; Holiday Inn 7 mi 226-7111; Shoney's Inn 7 mi 228-5555.

Meeting Rooms: Holiday Inn 7 mi 226-7111.

Transportation: Rental Cars: Liberty 228-6466; Taxi: Yellow 226-1717.

Information: Thomasville Welcome Center, 109 South Broad Street, P.O. Box 1540, Thomasville, GA 31799 Phone: 225-5222.

Attractions:

Two hour historic bus tours are conducted by the Chamber of Commerce. For information call 226-9600. Also the Pebble Hill Plantation dates back to the 1820s. This plantation has tours, wagon rides, antiques and much more. Call 226-2344. Thomasville Cultural Center, 226-0588.

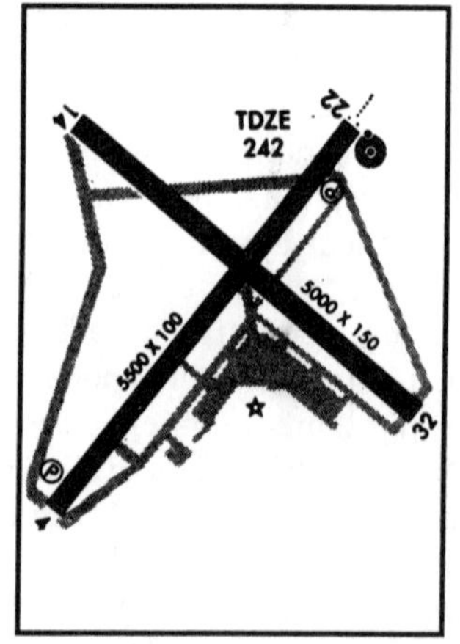

Airport Information:

THOMASVILLE - THOMASVILLE MUNICIPAL (TVI)
6 mi northeast of town N30-54.09 W83-52.88 Elev: 264 Fuel: 100LL, Jet-A Rwy 04-22: H5500x100 (Asph) Rwy 14-32: H5000x150 (Asph) Attended: Mon-Fri 1100-0100Z, Sat-Sun 1300-2300Z Unicom: 122.8
FBO: Thomasville Municipal Airport **Phone: 225-4313**

GA-VDI - VIDALIA
VIDALIA MUNICIPAL AIRPORT

(Area Code 912)

20

Shoney's Inn:

Shoney's Inn and Restaurant is situated adjacent to the Vidalia Municipal Airport about 1/2 mile from the parking ramp. You can call City Taxi at 537-1470, and they will take you over to the restaurant for about $3.00. This fare includes 2 passengers. Additional passengers are charged 25 cents extra. The restaurant is open between 6 a.m. and 11 p.m. 7 days a week, and is part of a motel at the same location. Their dining room can hold 100 people. They specialize in a luncheon and dinner buffet that is offered from 11 a.m. to 2 p.m. and again from 5 p.m. to 9 p.m. On Friday their is an all-you-can-eat seafood buffet for only $9.99. The dining area has a contemporary decor. Accommodations for banquet or catered parties can be arranged. Meals can also be prepared-to-go if requested. For more information about Shoney's Inn you can call 537-0922.

Restaurants Near Airport:

Captain's Corner	1 mi	Phone: 537-8484
Shoney's	1/2 mi	Phone: 537-0922
Shrimp Boat	3 mi	Phone: 537-7469

Lodging: Captain's Inn (3 miles) 537-9251; Shoney's (Adj Arpt) 537-1282; Vidalia Motor Lodge (2 miles) 537-7611.

Meeting Rooms: Shoney's Inn (Adj Arpt) 537-0922.

Transportation: City Taxi 537-1470

Information: Vidalia-Lyons/Toombs County Chamber of Commerce, P.O. Box 1980, 104 East First Street, Vidalia, GA 30474, Phone: 537-4466.

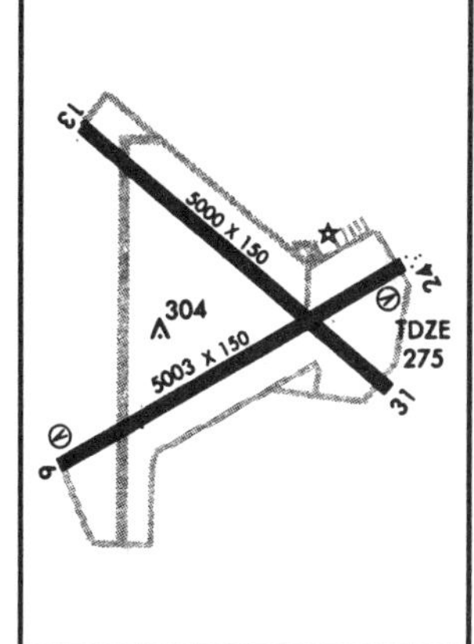

Airport Information:

VIDALIA - VIDALIA MUNICIPAL AIRPORT (VDI)
3 mi southeast of airport N32-11.55 W82-22.32 Elev: 275 Fuel: 100LL, Jet-A1+ Rwy 06-24: H5003x150 (Conc) Rwy 13-31: H5000x150 (Conc) Attended: daylight hours Unicom: 122.8
FOB: Skyway, Inc. Phone: 537-3979

Promote General Aviation Just Take A Friend Flying

IDAHO

LOCATION MAP

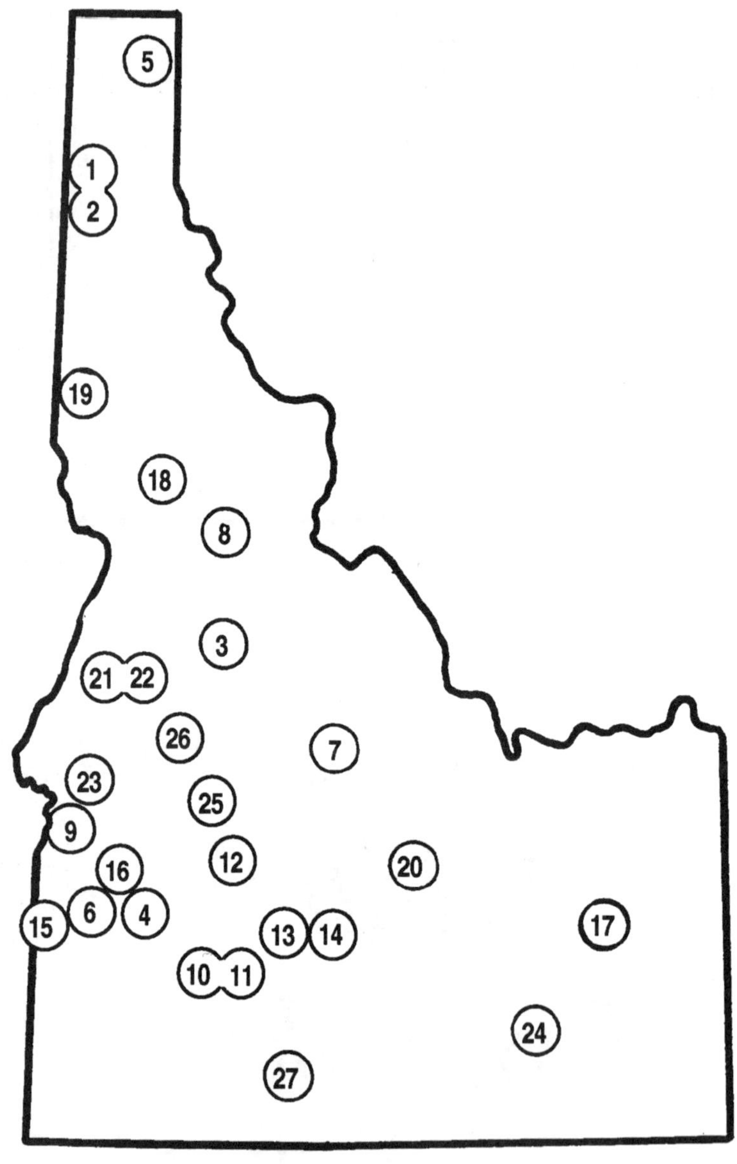

Not to be used for navigational purposes

IDAHO

CROSS FILE INDEX

Location Number	City or Town	Airport Name And Identifier	Name of Attraction
1	Athol	Silverwood (S62)	Silverwood Theme Park
2	Athol/Coeur d'Alene	Silverwood (S62) or Air Trml. (COE)	Coeur d'Alene Resort
3	Big Creek	Big Creek Arpt. (U60)	Big Creek Lodge
4	Boise	Boise Air Terminal (Gowen) (BOI)	Reflections Restaurant
5	Bonners Ferry	Boundry Co. Arpt. (65S)	Beauty's Kitchen
6	Caldwell	Caldwell Industrial Arpt. (EUL)	Cock of the Walk
7	Challis	Challis Arpt. (U15)	Challis Lodge & Lounge
8	Elk City	Elk City Arpt. (S90)	Mother Lode Steak Hse.
9	Emmett	Chuck Sawyer Field/Emmett (S78)	Club House Cafe
10	Fairfield	Camas Co. Arpt. (U86)	The Country Kitchen
11	Fairfield	Camas Co. Arpt. (U86)	Wrangler Drive-In
12	Galena	Smiley Creek (U87)	Smiley Creek Lodge
13	Hailey	Friedman Mem. Arpt. (SUN)	Sun Valley Resort
14	Hailey	Magic Reservoir Arpt. (U93)	Magic Lake Resort
15	Homedale	Homedale Muni. Arpt. (S66)	Ferdinand's Pizza
16	Idaho City	Idaho City USFS (U98)	Idaho City Attractions
17	Idaho Falls	Fanning Field (IDA)	Daskinderhaus Rest.
18	Kooskia	Kooskia Muni. Arpt. (S82)	Rivers Cafe
19	Lewiston	Nez Perce Co. Arpt. (LWS)	Lewiston Arpt. Rest.
20	Mackay	Mackay Arpt. (U62)	Steakhouse Cafe
21	Mc Call	Mc Call Arpt. (MYL)	Shore Lodge (Resort)
22	Mc Call	Mc Call Arpt. (MYL)	SiBueno Mexican Rest.
23	Murphy	Murphy Airport (1U3)	Murphy General Store
24	Pocatello	Pocatello Reg. Arpt. (PIH)	Blue Ribbon
25	Stanley	Stanley (2U7)	Nearby Restaurants
26	Sulphur Creek	Sulphur Creek Ranch (Private)	Sulphur Creek Ranch
27	Twin Falls	Sun Valley Reg./Joslin (TWF)	Hangar Restaurant

Articles

City or town	Nearest Airport and Identifier	Name of Attraction
Caldwell, ID	Caldwell Industrial Arpt. (EUL)	Warhawk Air Museum
Hailey, ID	Friedman Mem. (SUN)	Sun Valley Resort

ID-S62 - ATHOL
SILVERWOOD

(Area Code 208) 1, 2

Restaurants Near Airport:
Silverwood Theme Park On Site Phone: 683-3400

Lodging: Athol Motel (2 mi) 683-3476; Coeur D'Alene Resort On The Lake (12 mi) 765-4000; Holiday Inn (town of Coeur d'Alene12 miles) 765-3200; RV camping at theme park.
Meeting Rooms: Coeur d'Alene Resort On The Lake (12 mi) Convention facilities 765-4000.
Transportation: Dollar Rent-A-Car in Coeur d'Alene (12 mi) Mid-size $33-35.00/day and up. Advance reservations 1 week prefered. Call 664-0682; Also Coeur d'Alene Resort will pick up overnight guests landing at Silverwood Theme Park as well as Coeur d'Alene Air Terminal (COE).
Information: Greater Coeur d'Alene Convention and Visitors Bureau, P.O. Box 1088, Coedur d'Alene, ID 83816, Phone: 664-0587.

Silverwood Theme Park:

Silverwood is a Victorian turn-of-the-century, seasonal theme park. It is the only theme park in the U.S. built around a working private airport. The complex is located on approximately 600 acres of land, 200 of which is developed. The park features 24 rides including their 55 m.p.h. wooden roller coaster, "The Timber Terror." In addition, the Corkscrew Roller Coaster, Skydiver and highly acclaimed Thunder Canyon river raft ride are very popular. Guests may experience all rides as often as they wish with their one-price admission policy. Numerous shows are scheduled daily throughout the park. The Main Street Theatre features, Juggling, and a live stage performance. "Mystical Kingdom On Ice", is a program that features U.S., Canadian and Russian skaters. A new addition to the park is the Silverwood Railroad "Train robbery experience and the Apple Orchard Theatre, home to a new illusion show, "Magic Dimension". The park's retail shops offer a wide selection from souvenir memory items to treasurable gifts. Shops are located on Main Street and in the Country Carnival area. Silverwood offers something for every taste, from their full service menu in Lindy's Restaurant to picnic-style meals in Country Bar BQ. Other locations in the park offer items such as hot dogs and hamburgers. There is also a new Mexican food outlet, "Burrito Bandito," near the wooden coaster entrance. General admission is $20.00 for ages 8 to 64, ages 3-7 and 65+ is $11.00. Under 2 years old, free admission. Special discounts go into effect after 5 p.m. beginning July 1 through September of only $10.00 per person. Under age 2 still free. For information call Silverwood Theme Park at 683-3400.

Coeur d'Alene Resort On The Lake:

This resort is a four star establishment located in the town of Coeur d'Alene, 12 miles from the Silverwood Theme Park. As an alternative vacation planning suggestion, fly-in guests could arrange to land at Silverwood (S62) visit the park for the day, then call the Coeur d'Alene Resort, have them pick your party up. For information about the Coeur d'Alene Resort call 765-4000. Landing at Coeur d'Alene Air Terminal (COE) is another alternative, with courtesy transportation available. (FBO Resort Aviation 772-3731).

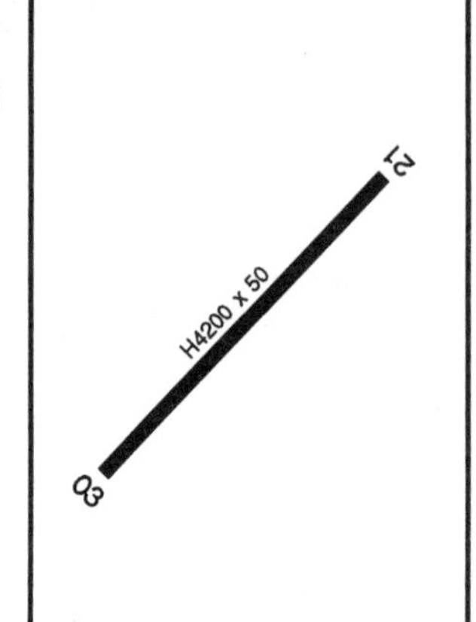

Airport Information:

ATHOL - SILVERWOOD (S62)
2 mi south of town N47-54.49 W116-42.56 Elev: 2350 Fuel: 100, Jet-A Rwy 03-21: H4200x50 (Asph) Attended: irregularly Unicom: 122.7 Notes: Airport CLOSED Nov 1, to May 1. Extensive antique aircraft skydiving, airshow and glider activity on and in vicinity of airport.
Airport Manager/Silverwood Theme Park Phone: 683-3400

ID-U60 - BIG CREEK
BIG CREEK AIRPORT

(Area Code 208) 3

Restaurants Near Airport:
Big Creek Lodge Adj Arpt. Phone: Apt. Mgr. 334-8775

Lodging: Big Creek Lodge, (Adj Arpt) 4 guest rooms and a couple of cabins, Phone: 375-4921.
Transportation: Big Creek Lodge is located within walking distance and adjacent to Big Creek Airport.

Attractions:

The town of Big Creek is the gateway to Idaho's wilderness and comprises a small village with a population of 75 in addition to back country guests.

Big Creek Lodge:

At the time of our latest interview, we learned that this establishment was temporarily closed, however the resort may re-open soon under new management.. For information call the Big Creek Airport manager at 334-8775.

Big Creek Lodge: *is located adjacent to the airport and contains 4 guest rooms in addition to a couple of cabins for overnight guests. In a true wilderness setting, the Big Creek Lodge is nestled in a very rugged yet scenic wilderness location, amongst salmon rivers and mountainous streams with steep to rolling countryside. The lodge can accommodate between 14 to 20 people. The restaurant provides a welcome attraction to visitors and bush pilots working in the region. Built in 1923 this historic structure exhibits hand hewn logs and a atmosphere befitting its location, complete with wooden stove. Many pilots frequently fly in for a hardy breakfast or lunch. Night flights into or out of this region are not recommended. Guests spending the evening can enjoy delicious meals like barbecued country ribs, prime rib, seafood, poultry and Italian dishes. Average prices run around $7.50 for breakfast & lunch and about $15.00 for dinner. Restaurant hours vary as meals are prepared on arrival of their guests. Dinner hours are usually around 7:00 p.m. with accommodation for up to 18 persons. Fly-in groups are welcome, however advance notice must be provided. For information call the airport at 634-7137 or 922-1121*

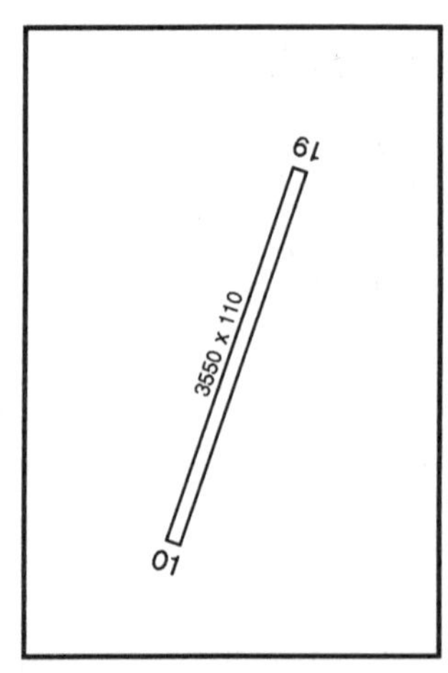

Airport Information:

BIG CREEK - BIG CREEK AIRPORT (U60)
0 mi northeast of town N45-07.99 W115-19.31 Elev: 5743 Rwy 01-19: 3550x110 (Turf) Attended: unattended Ctaf: 122.9 Notes: The Forest Service maintains this airstrip for back country pilots. CAUTION: Recommend land to south, takeoff to north-when conditions allow. Also recommend for experience in high density altitude and turbulent air. No winter maintenance.
Big Creek Airport Phone: 334-8775 Big Creek Lodge Phone: 375-4921

ID-BOI - BOISE
BOISE AIR TERMINAL (GOWEN)

4

Restaurants Near Airport: **(Area Code 208)**
Reflections Restaurant On Site Phone: 383-3233

Reflections Restaurant:

Reflections Restaurant is situated within the terminal building at the Boise Air Terminal Airport. If you park at Boise Air Service you can walk to the restaurant. This family style facility is open from 11 a.m. to 8:30 7 days a week. Their menu includes baked salmon, burgers, chicken, soups and salads. Average prices run between $6.00 and $12.00 dollars for most meals. The decor of the restaurant is modern with available seating for up to 120 persons. A special meeting or party room can also accommodate up to 20 people (V.I.P. Room). The view from the restaurant overlooks the airport. Meals-to-go can also be prepared. For more information call the restaurant at 383-3233.

Lodging: The following facilities provide free shuttle service to and from airport: Best Western Motor Inn 384-5000; Best Western Vista Inn 336-8100; Boisean 343-3645; Comfort Inn 336-0077; Flying J 322-4404; Holiday Inn (1 mile) 344-8365; Quality Inn Airport Suites 343-7505; Rodeway Inn 376-2700; Shilo Inn Airport (1-1/4 miles) 343-7662; Shilo Inn Riverside (9 miles) 344-3521; Super 8 Lodge-Boise Airport 344-8871; Victor's Motor Inn 344-7971; Owyhee Plaza Hotel 343-4611; Red Lion Hotel-Riverside (4 miles) 343-1871; Red Lion Inn Downtowner (4 miles) 344-7691; Compri/Park Center 345-2002; Plaza Suites Heritage 375-7666; Statehouse Inn 342-4622. Vista Inn (On field) 336-8100.

Meeting Rooms: Comfort Inn 336-0077; Holiday Inn 344-8365; Rodeway Inn 376-2700; Shilo Inn Riverside 344-3521; Victor's Motor Inn 344-7971; Owyhee Plaza Hotel 343-4611; Red Lion Hotel-Riverside (Convention facilities) 343-1871; Red Lion Inn Downtowner 344-7691; Statehouse Inn 243-4622.

Transportation: Airport/FBO courtesy car; Taxi: Kwix & Yellow; Rental cars: Avis 383-3350; Budget 383-3090; Dollar 345-9727; Hertz 383-3100; National 383-3210.

Information: Convention and Visitors Bureau, 168 N 9th Street, Suite 200, P.O. Box 2106, Boise, ID 83701, Phone: 344-7777

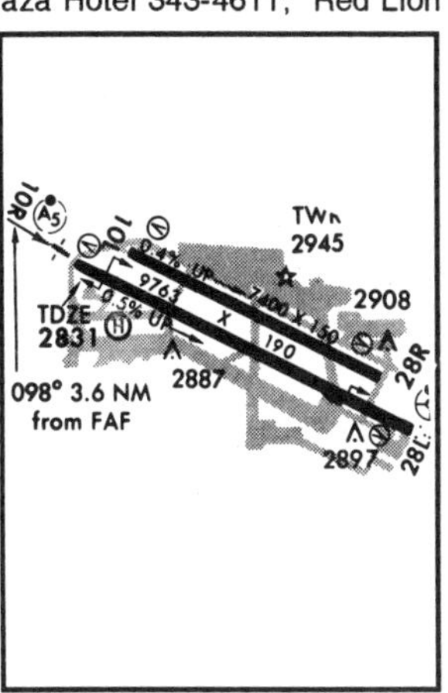

Airport Information:

BOISE - BOISE AIR TERMINAL/GOWEN FIELD (BOI)
3 mi south of town N43-3390 W116-13.51 Elev: 2858
Fuel: 100LL, Jet-A1+ Rwy 10R-28L: H9763x190 (Asph-Pfc)
Rwy 10L-28R: H7400x150 (Asph-pfc) Attended: continuously
Atis: 123.9 Unicom: 122.95 Tower: 118.1, 119.0 Gnd Con: 121.7 Clnc Del: 125.9

FBO: Aviation Air Center	**Phone: 344-4361**	**FBO: Conyan Aviation**	**Phone: 342-1042**
FBO: Boise Air Service	**Phone: 383-3300**	**FBO: Western A/C Main.**	**Phone: 338-1800**
FBO: Boise Executive	**Phone: 383-3191**		

ID-65S - BONNERS FERRY
BOUNDRY COUNTY AIRPORT

(Area Code 208)

5

Beauty's Kitchen Reflections Restaurant:

This restaurant is within a 200 yard walk from the airport on Highway 2. This is a family style restaurant open from 5:30 a.m. to 8 p.m. weekdays and 7 a.m. to 8 p.m. on weekends. Daily homemade specials include soups, pies, rolls, corn bread, and specializes in home cooked meals. The price range for entrees run $4.50 for breakfast, $4.95 for lunch and $7.95 for dinner. This restaurant seats about 30 people and offers a pleasant quality. Fly-in groups are welcome with advance notice preferred. For information call 267-7955.

Restaurants Near Airport:

3-Mile Cafe,	2/10 mi.	Phone: N/A
Beauty's Kitchen	2/10 mi	Phone: 267-7955
Kootenai River Inn	3.5 mi.	Phone: 267-8511
Pan Handle	3.5 mi.	Phone: N/A

Lodging: Kootenai River Inn 3.5 mi. Phone: 267-8511, 47 units, $50.00-$75.00 per night, restaurants on premisses. Swimming pool, accommodations for meeting and/or conferences for the business traveler.

Transportation: Bonners Ferry - Nissan (Rental) Phone: 267-3181 Courtesy car rental (State of Idaho) $5.00 + .30/mi

Information: Bonners Ferry Chamber; P.O. Box 375, Bonners Ferry, ID 83805. Phone: 267-5922

Attractions:

Schweitzer ski area is located about 25 miles southwest from the town of Bonners Ferry along Interstate 95, and offers a dazzling view of Lake Pend Oreille, Schweitzer rises high in the Selkirk Mountains, where Pacific snows bury the slopes in over 200 inches of white delight. Facilities include day lodges, a grocery store, restaurant, lounge and chapel. You can stay overnight on the mountain at one of several luxurious condominiums, or you can stay lakeside in the enchanting resort town of Sandpoint, just 11 miles southeast on the shore of lake Pend Oreille. (Vertical Drop: 2400 Ft., Lifts 7 D-Chairs, 1 T-Lift Runs: 39.) "Idaho State Travel Guide" (See: Sandpoint Airport (S86), Sandpoint, Idaho.)

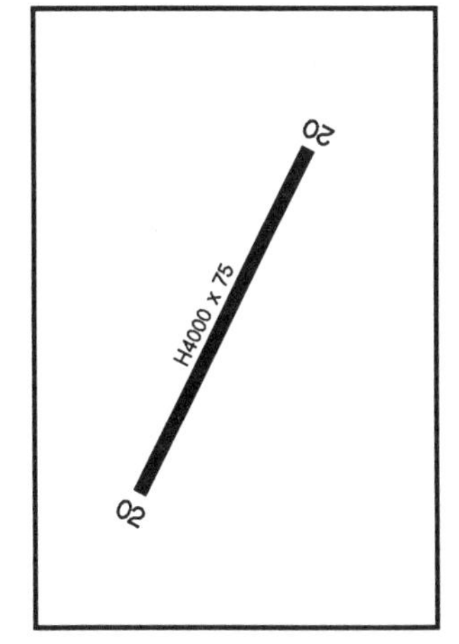

Airport Information:

BONNERS FERRY - BOUNDARY CO. (65S)
2 northeast of town N48-43.58 W116-17.73 Elev: 2331 Fuel: 100LL, Jet A
Rwy 02-20: H4000x75 (ASPH) Attended: 1600-0100Z Unicom: 123.0 Notes: Tiedown $3.00/night - one night FREE with fuel purchase. Camping & shower facility available at FBO.
FBO: Panhandle Rotor & Wing, Phone: 267-3711

Warhawk Air Museum

Caldwell Industrial Airport (Article by Warhawk Air Museum)

The Warhawk Air Museum is located right on the Caldwell Industrial Airport adjacent to the aircraft parking ramp.

Step back in time to the historical period of World War II. Experience the patriotism of the United States, and the bravery of those who fought on fronts around the world. See rare examples of the most advanced technology of the era.

Warhawk Air Museum is the fastest growing World War II museum in the state of Idaho. Visitors have come from around the world to see the rare collection of World War II memorabilia and aircraft that are on display. These unique items are memorials to the brave men and women who fought to preserve freedom.

Many rare and unusual World War II aviation and wartime artifacts are on display including; World War II men's and women's uniforms, World War II aircraft engines, hundreds of photos, aerial cameras, and a Norden bombsight. Other rare items include a magnificent collection of World War II sweetheart and mother's pins, unusual German and Japanese memorabilia, V-Mail and war stamps, a nose art display, a Junior Aircraft Warning Service Kit, P-51B Mustang snow skis...and much more.

Military Aircraft currently on display include a Curtiss P-40 E Kittyhawk; Curtiss P-40N Warhawk; North American P-51B; and a 1917 DR-1 Folker triplane replica. Arrangements can be made to reserve the museum for special groups tours, meetings and private parties. The Warhawk Air Museum is an educational museum whose purpose is to preserve American World War II aviation and wartime history.

The Museum is open to the public. Hours vary throughout the year so please call ahead for current hours. Admission is $2.00 per person donation. For information call 208-454-2854.

ID-EUL - CALDWELL
CALDWELL INDUSTRIAL AIRPORT

(Area Code 208) 6

Cock of the Walk:

The Cock of the Walk is located right next to the Caldwell Industrial Airport terminal. This family-style cafe serves delicious, old-fashioned cooked meals from 7:00 a.m. to 4:00 p.m., 7 days a week. Some of the menu items include: fresh cinnamon rolls, fried potatoes and homemade soups. Breakfast and lunch specials are offered 6 days a week. Menu prices average about $4.50 for breakfast and lunch, and $6.00 for dinner. Every Sunday, a scrumptious country breakfast is served all day for $4.50. With advance notice, the restaurant will cater to groups of up to 20, plus honor a 10% discount. The restaurant will also cater horsdoeuvres, sandwiches and cheese trays to private and corporate pilots-on-the-go. For more information about the Cock of the Walk, call 454-7991.

Warhawk Air Museum

Enjoy a meal at the restaurant on the field and a visit to the WarHawk Air Museum. (See Article)

Restaurants Near Airport:
Cock of the Walk On Site Phone: 454-7991

Lodging: Comfort Inn (3 miles) 454-2222; Sundowner Motel (3 miles) 459-1585; Budget Motel (4 miles) 459-1536; Holiday Motel (4 miles) 459-4678; Shilo Inn (6 miles) 466-8993

Meeting Rooms: Comfort Inn (3 mi) 454-2222; Warhawk Air Museum (on site) can accommodate groups with advanced reservations. Call 454-2854 for information.

Transportation: Taxi service: Caldwell City 459-1619 or 454-8098; Rental cars: Avjet Aviation 459-9455

Information: Chamber of Commerce, 300 Frontage Road, P.O. Box 819, Caldwell, ID 83606, Phone: 459-7493

Attractions:

The Warhawk WWII Museum is located on the airport. Call 454-2854. The Purple Sage Municipal Golf Course is located 5 miles north of Caldwell. Call 459-2223.

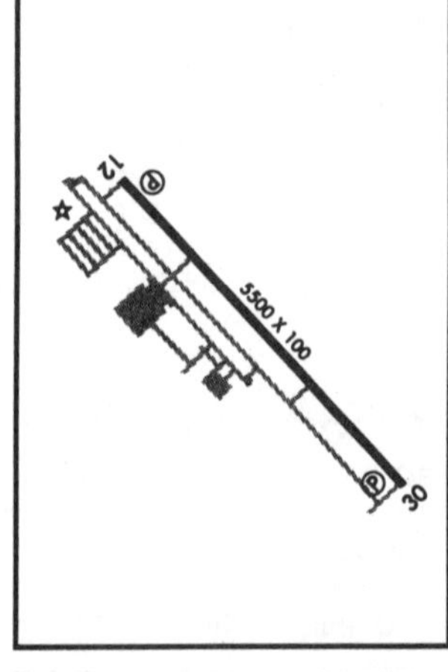

Airport Information:

CALDWELL - CALDWELL INDUSTRIAL AIRPORT (EUL)
3 mi southeast of town N43-38-51 W116-38-12 Elev: 2429 Fuel: 80, 100, Jet-A, MOGAS
Rwy 12-30: H5500x100 (Asph) Attended: Mar-Oct 1500-0200Z, Nov-Feb 1500-0000Z CTAF/
Unicom: 122.8 Boise App/Dep 119.6 Public phone 24 hrs
FBO: Avid Aircraft, Inc. **Phone: 454-2600**
FBO: Aero Flite **Phone: 454-2016**
FBO: Shore & Shore Aviation **Phone: 454-1669**

ID-U15 - CHALLIS
CHALLIS AIRPORT

(Area Code 208)

7

Challis Lodge & Lounge

The Challis Lodge & Lounge is situated on the corner and adjacent to the Challis Airport. This steak house can be reached by courtesy transportation. The restaurant is open from 5 p.m. until the lounge closes, Monday through Saturday, and Sundays from 10 a.m. to midnight. Specialty entrees include steaks and burgers with selections of 8 to 12 oz top sirloin dishes served with baked potato and salad. Average prices range from $5.45 to $8.95. Their dining room can accommodate up to 30 people. If planning to arrange a group fly-out please let them know in advance of your intentions so they may serve your party with the greatest efficiency. In addition to the restaurant, this facility also contains lodging accommodations with 19 units. For more information you can call 879-2251.

Restaurants Near Airport:
Challis Lodge & Lounge   Adj Arpt   Phone: 879-2251

Lodging: Challis Lodge & Lounge (1 mile) 879-2251; Holiday Lodge & Motel (3/4 mile) 879-2259; Northgate Inn (1/2 mile) 879-2490; Village Inn (1 mile) 879-2239.

Meeting Rooms: Northgate Inn 879-2490; Village Inn 879-2239

Transportation: Courtesy transportation is available to nearby facilities, call airport or restaurant.

Information: Challis Chamber of Commerce P.O. Box 1130, Challis, ID 83226

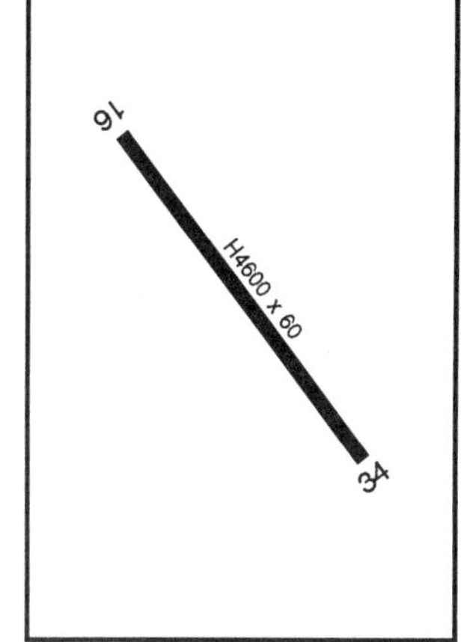

Airport Information:

CHALLIS - CHALLIS AIRPORT (U15)
1 mi northeast of town   N44-31.38 W114-13.05   Elev: 5072   Fuel: 100, Jet-A
Rwy 16-34: H4600x60 (Asph)   Attended: 1400-0200Z   Unicom: 122.8
FBO: Bobs Aircraft, Inc.   Phone: 879-2364

ID-S90 - ELK CITY
ELK CITY AIRPORT

(Area Code 208)

8

Mother Lode Steak House:

The Mother Lode Steak House is situated less than 2 blocks west of the Elk City Airport. This family style restaurant can easily be reached by walking from the airport. Their hours are 3 p.m. to 1 a.m. everyday. There is also a lounge on the premises. The restaurant specializes in steaks as well as a variety of other items including T-Bone, ribs, sirloin, hamburgers, gourmet shrimp, and salads. Average prices for meals run between $5.95 and $10.95. The decor is rustic with pine benches and tables, game room, pool table, and big screen TV. They can seat about 50 people in the dining room. All types of groups are welcome with advance notice. Meals prepared-to-go are no problem. In addition to the restaurant, there is also lodging accommodations with two motels within walking distance in the downtown area. For more information you can call the Mother Lode Steak House at 842-2232.

Restaurants Near Airport:
Elk City General Store   3 Blks NE   Phone: 842-2275
Mother Lode Steak House   3 Blks W.   Phone: 842-2232

Lodging: Elk City Hotel (Free trans, 3 blocks) 842-2452; Elk City Lodge (1/2 mile) 842-2250; Junction Lodge (4 miles) 842-2459.

Meeting Rooms: None reported

Transportation: None reported

Information: None reported

Attractions:

Elk City has a population of about 400 people and had one of Idaho's larger Chinese populations during the days of heavy mining in this region.

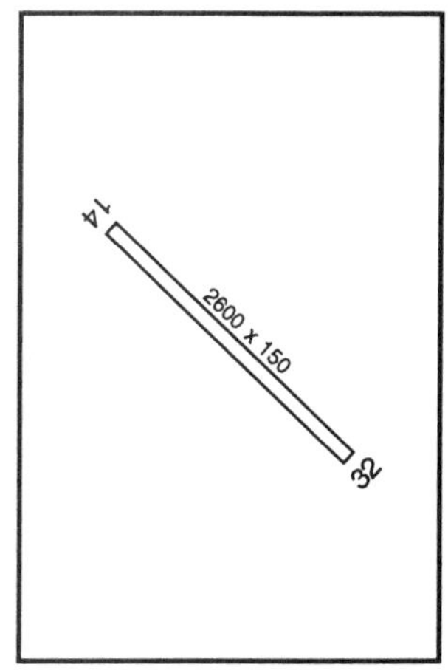

Airport Information:

ELK CITY - ELK CITY AIRPORT (S90)
0 mi southwest of town   N45-49.36 W115-26.39   Elev: 4097   Rwy 14-35: 2600x150 (Turf)
Attended: unattended   Notes: land runway 14, and takeoff runway 35 when wind conditions allow. Runway 14-35 is curved.   CTAF: 122.9   Public Phone 24hrs
Elk City Airport   Phone: 842-2275

ID-S78 - EMMETT
CHUCK SAWYER FIELD/EMMETT

(Area Code 208) 9

Restaurants Near Airport:

Billy Barbs	4 mi NE	Phone: 365-6573
Cloverleaf Cafe	5 mi NE	Phone: 365-6444
Club House Cafe	On Site	Phone: 365-2675
LaFijita Restaurant	3 mi NE	Phone: 365-9910

Lodging: Holiday Motel (Free trans by airport, 3 mi NE) 365-4479

Meeting Rooms: 19th Hole Cafe 365-4598; Billy Barbs Restaurant 365-6573; President Cafe 365-2912; Gem Valley Cafe 365-5549.

Transportation: Transportation can be arranged either through Morris Flying service 365-4598, or City of Emmett courtesy car.

Information: Gem County Chamber, P.O. Box 592, Emmett, ID 83617, Phone: 365-3485.

Club House Cafe:

The Club House Cafe is located on the Chuck Sawyer Field formerly the Emmett Municipal Airport. This combination cafe and family style restaurant can easily be reached by walking from the aircraft tie-down area. Their hours are 8 a.m. to 8 p.m. 7 days a week. The restaurant offers a wide selection of breakfast and lunch and dinner entrees. These include their popular biscuits and gravy, omelets, egg dishes, cinnamon rolls, delicious hamburgers, chicken sandwiches, homemade potato salad, and freshly baked bread. Average prices run $3.00 for breakfast, $3.50 for lunch and about $5.00 for dinner. This cafe has seating for about 60 people. They even have an outdoor patio where guests can watch aircraft operations. A separate room can accommodate 40 people. From the restaurant you can enjoy the view of the airport as well as the 9 hole golf course. Playing a round of golf and enjoying a fine meal while combining the sport of flying can sure make for a fun way to spend the afternoon. For information call the Club House Cafe at 365-2675.

Attractions: The Gem County Golf Course is a 9 hole course located right on the Chuck Sawyer Field/Emmett Municipal Airport; Also a public fishing pond is situated 1/2 mile north of the airport, and 1 mile east of the field; Lyons Park & Black Canyon Dam offers boating, swimming, and picnic areas located about 10 miles northeast of the airport. For information contact the Gem County Chamber listed above under information.

Airport Information:

EMMETT - EMMETT MUNICIPAL (S78)
3 mi southwest of town N43-50.99 W116-32.56 Elev: 2350 Fuel: 80, 100
Rwy 10-28: H2350x50 (Asph) Attended: 1500-0100Z Notes: No landing fees, overnight parking $2.00 per night, $15.00/month.
Airport Manager Phone: 365-4598

10 H2350 x 50 28

ID-U86 - FAIRFIELD
CAMAS COUNTY AIRPORT

(Area Code 208) 10, 11

Restaurants Near Airport:

Country Kitchen	1 blk. NE.	Phone: 764-2256
Wrangler Drive-In	1 blk. N.	Phone: 764-2580

Lodging: Country Kitchen and Inn is located one block N.E. of the airport and has 16 units, Phone: 764-2256.

Transportation: None Listed

Information: Camas County Civic Organization, P.O. Box 337, Fairfield, ID 83372

The Country Kitchen Restaurant:

"The Country Kitchen Restaurant is family owned and operated, serving a full service menu seven days a week from 7:00 a.m. to 9:00 p.m. Our pies are made from scratch, our soups are all homemade, and our giant cinnamon rolls are legendary. Our daily specials include all your favorite home cooked meals and we do take requests. We use only fresh ground beef for our various burgers, and our steaks are top quality. The friendly folks at the Country Kitchen, where the coffee cups are bottomless, invite you to enjoy a meal or a snack at affordable prices, just across the street from the Camas County Airport in Beautiful Fairfield, Idaho situated at the base of Soldier Mountain. Great hunting fishing, hiking, snowmobiling skiing, (Both down hill and cross country, bird watching and rock hunting make Camas County the place you'd love to fly away to". Call 764-2256.

Wrangler Drive-In:

The Wrangler Drive-In, is located across the street (North), next to the market basket general store. Their menu consists of items like hamburgers, Ice cream, finger steaks, and pizza. They feature a large variety of specialty burgers, such as their "RoadKill Pattymelt", "Snow Bunny Burger" and the "Powder Pie Burger". The average price for a lunch or dinner is around $5.00. They are open Monday through Thursday from 11:00 a.m. to 9:00 p.m. and Friday through Sunday from 11:00 a.m. to 9:00 p.m. They will provide bagged lunches (Hot or Cold) with advance notice. For information call 764-2580.

Airport Information:

FAIRFIELD - CAMAS COUNTY AIRPORT (U86)
0 south of town N43-20.24 W114-47.80 Elev: 5058 Rwy 07-25: 2950x40 (Dirt) Attended: unattended CTAF: 122.9 Burley FSS: 1-800-321-0447 Notes: Irregular winter maintenance snow removal, check Rwy. conditions before using. **Airport Manager: 208-764-2261**

Attractions:

The town of Fairfield has a population of 350 people. The Camas County Fair is held in August. The Hidden Paradise Ranch has a nine hole golf course and is located 4 miles west and 3 miles north of the airport. There are several museums, including the Union Pacific Train Depot.

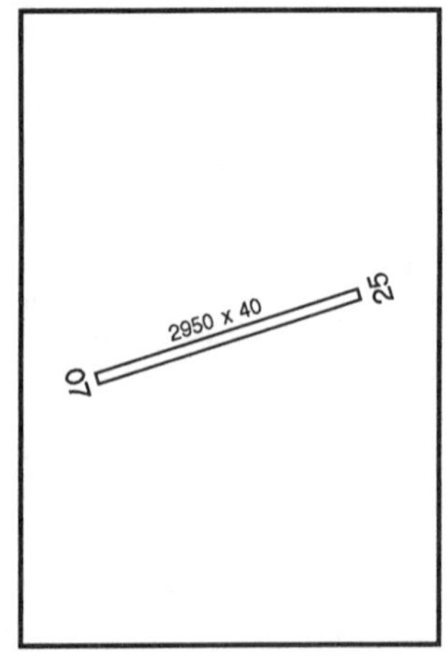

Not to be used for navigational purposes

ID-U87- GALENA SMILEY CREEK

(Area Code 208)

12

Smiley Creek Lodge

Smiley Creek Lodge is located well within walking distance and about 500 yards west from the grass airstrip. During our interview with the management we learned this is a popular destination with many local pilots as well as vacationers. The area contains numerous lakes and a creek that runs adjacent to the property. Smiley Creek Lodge offers accommodations with 3 lodge rooms, 2 cabins, ranging from $40.00 to $70.00 per night, and several tee-pee's fully weather-proofed. Transportation by way of a state courtesy car can be arranged. Mountain bikes can also be rented with advance notice. A camping site adjacent to the lodge area offers picnic tables, stoves, hot showers and modern rest rooms. Fly-in clubs should find this location especially attractive to plan outings for their group. The cafe at Smiley Creek Lodge is open year round. During the winter 9 a.m. to 5 p.m. and summer between 8 a.m. to 9 p.m. The airport is unattended throughout the winter season and is not recommended for use during that time. The cafe offers everything from hamburgers to prime rib. A full breakfast line is served until 11:30 a.m. Daily specials as well as a Sunday brunch are provided as well. The cafe can seat about 40 guests. Large windows allow a beautiful view of the Sawtooth mountain range in the distance. This location offers exceptional outdoor and sight-seeing activities. Hiking, backpacking, mountain bike trails and horseback riding are just some of the most popular activities that attract vacationers each year. Local outfitters can also be hired to guide your party with hunting and fishing trips. For information about Smiley Creek Lodge call 774-3547.

Restaurants Near Airport:
Smiley Creek Lodge Adj Arpt Phone: 774-3547

Lodging: Smiley Creek Lodge offers lodge rooms, cabins and camping. For information call 774-3547.

Meeting Rooms: None reported

Transportation: Courtesy car reported. mountain bike rental also available by calling the lodge at 774-3547.

Information: Idaho Division of Travel Promotion, P.O. Box 83720, 700 West State Street, Boise, ID 83720-0093. Phone: 208-334-2470.

Airport Information:

HAILEY - MAGIC RESERVOIR AIRPORT (U87)

6 mi northwest of town N43-54.91 W114-47.84 Elevation: 7160 Rwy 14-32: 4900x150 (Turf) Unicom: 122.9 Airport Remarks: Unattended. No winter maintenance. Extremely high density altitude conditions exist during summer months. Recommended land Rwy 14, take-off Rwy 32, when wind conditions allow. Be alert for sprinklers/stand pipes on edge of rwy. Rwy 14-32 edges and thresholds marked with white rock. No telephone available at airport.

Airport Manager Phone: 334-8775

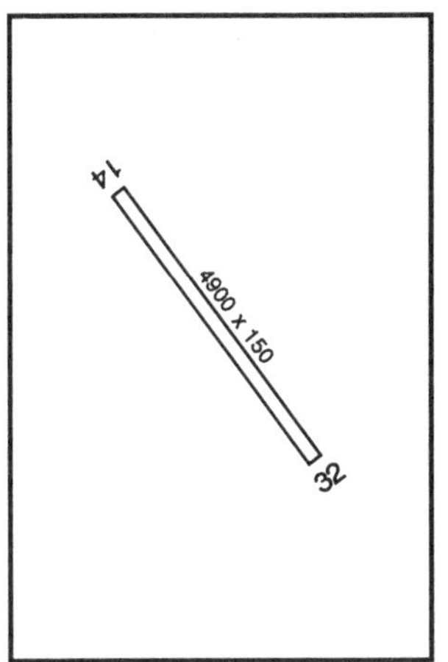

ID-SUN - HAILEY FRIEDMAN MEMORIAL AIRPORT

(Area Code 208)

13

Dining at Sun Valley's Seattle Ridge Lodge:

Seattle Ridge Lodge (open year-round) is one of Sun Valley Resort's highly distinctive day-lodges that is located about 12 miles north of Friedman Memorial Airport. The lodge is a 17,000-square foot log and glass lodge that is perched on a ridge crest at an elevation of 8,680 feet, making it the world's largest high-tech moutaintop day lodge. In addition, its restaurant has literally elevated fine food to new heights. Of course, one of its specialties includes Idaho's own... baked potato with six choices of toppings! The restaurant also serves scrumptious dishes, such as mesquite grilled chicken, salmon, swordfish, prime rib, a variety of soups and salads and stone-fired pizza. Two special recommended entrees are: succulent Salmon Normandy and a mouth-watering classic Idaho baked potato with St. Jacques Sauce. With advance reservations, the resort will provide free transportation to and from the airport. For more information about Seattle Ridge Lodge and other facilities at Sun Valley Resort, call 800-786-8259 or 622-2151.

Restaurants Near Airport:
Sun Valley Resort 12 mi N. Phone: 622-2151

Lodging: Sun Valley Resort (12 miles N.) 622-2151; Airport Inn (adj) 788-2477; High Country Motel (3 miles) 788-2050; Hitchtrack (adj) 788-9980

Meeting Rooms: None Reported

Transportation: With advance reservations, Sun Valley Resort provides free transportation to and from the airport; Taxi Service: A-1 726-9351; Rental Cars: Avis 788-2382; Hertz 788-4548; National 788-3841

Information: Sun Valley/Ketchum Chamber of Commerce, 4th & Main Streets in Ketchum, P.O. Box 2420, Sun Valley, ID 83353, Phone: 726-3423 or 800-634-3347

Attraction:

Sun Valley Resort is a summer and winter retreat located about 12 miles north of Friedman Memorial Airport. Call 622-2151 for more information.

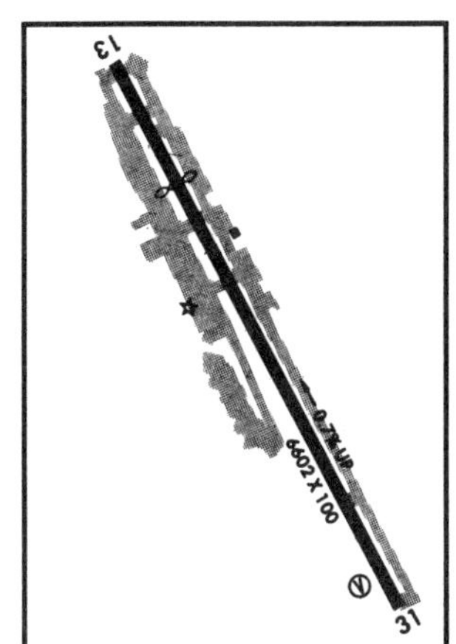

Airport Information:

HAILEY - FRIEDMAN MEMORIAL AIRPORT (SUN)

1 mi southeast of town N43-30.29 W114-17.80 Elev: 5315 Fuel: 100LL, Jet-A1 Rwy 13-31: H6602x100 (Asph-Grvd) Attended: dawn-dusk CTAF: 125.6 Unicom: 122.95 Salt Lake Center App/Dep Con: 118.05 Hailey Tower: 125.6 NFCT(1400-0600Z) All acft within 5 NM of arpt ctc twr 125.6 Gnd Con: 121.7 Notes: See "Airport Facility Directory" for comments about runway conditions and information.

FBO: Sun Valley Aviation Phone: 788-9511

Sun Valley Resort

Sun Valley Resort, often referred to as America's "Queen of Resorts", is nestled in the rugged Sawtooth Mountains (or the American Alps) and is set amid central Idaho's Big Wood River Valley. Sun Valley, open year-round, combines natural beauty with cosmopolitan vivacity. Its mountains tower around a valley with a base elevation of 6,000 feet. Undisturbed nature surrounds the resort, including a vast habitat of elk, deer, beaver, badger, fox, and bear.The desert-montane climate keeps the air crisp and clear in the winter, and warm and dry in the summer. Sun Valley is an ideal spot for families seeking a safe, tranquil retreat to get back in touch with nature.

During the summer seasons, Sun Valley is referred to as "America's Outdoor Treasury" for golfers, hikers, bicyclists, fly-fisherman and other recreationists. It also features America's only continuous oudoor ice skating, therefore, it is frequently visited by some of the world's finest skaters. Other events during the summer include: a classical sympony, a jazz festival and important wine and collector car auctions.

During the winter, Sun valley transforms into a winter wonderland where skiers love to frequent Bald Mountain - Sun Valley's major ski mountain affectionately known as "Baldy". It is widely regarded as one of the best single ski mountains in the U.S. Beginning skiers may find the broad, treeless slopes of nearby Dollar Mountain to be more ideal. Sun Valley also features several cross-country facilities, including the world's first child-sized cross country tracks for ages 3 and up. Sun Valley skiers will enjoy a total of 2,054 acres of skiable terrain with 3,400 feet of vertical drop and perfect pitch.

Like a queen who wears a crown, Sun Valley wears a triple crown of three distinctive, highly sophisticated day-lodge facilities: Warm Springs, Seattle Ridge and River Run Lodges. Warm Springs Lodge is a stunning structure of hand-peeled and hand-stacked huge logs, ancient river rock and soaring glass walls. It was built with masterful technology to provide the utmost in skier comfort and services. The second facility, Seattle Ridge Lodge, is a 17,000-square foot log and glass lodge that is perched on a ridge crest at an elevation of 8,680 feet, making it the world's largest high-tech moutain top day-lodge. In addition, its restaurant has literally elevated fine food to new heights. The third facility, River Run Lodge, is a four-building complex that consists of a day lodge, a skier services building, a mountain operations and maintenance building, as well as a storage facility. It was designed to become the predominant access to Baldy.

In the halls of the stately four-story Sun Valley lodge, plush hand-made carpets display Idaho's wildflowers. Many famous movie actors and actresses have strode down those halls - Gary Cooper, Judy Garland, Clark Gable and Marilyn Monroe. Many films have been shot there, as well. Upstairs, in a second-floor suite, Ernest Hemingway worked on For Whom the Bell Tolls.

While staying at Sun Valley Lodge, guests can sample the fresh, tasty gourmet meals that are served in the resort's lovely chandeliered Lodge Dining Room. And don't forget...a visit to Idaho would not be worth- while without tasting a mouth-watering classic Idaho baked potato! The Seattle Ridge Lodge serves six choices of toppings for those scrumptious potatoes, including their special St. Jacques sauce. The lodge also serves a variety of other meals, including mesquite grilled chicken, salmon, swordfish, prime rib and stone-fired pizza. There are other nearby village restaurants that serve anything from cafeteria style to formal cuisine.

Sun Valley Resort is located about 12 miles north of Friedman Memorial Airport in Hailey, Idaho. It servesboth commercial and private aircraft and has a 6602'x100 asph-grvd runway. There is a parking fee of $5.00/night for singles and $10.00/night for twins. With advance reservations, the resort will provide free transportation to and from the airport. For more information about reservations and accommodations, contact Sun Valley Resort at 800-786-8259 or 622-2151. (Information submitted by Sun Valley Resort)

ID-U93 - HAILEY
MAGIC RESERVOIR AIRPORT

(Area Code 208)

14

Magic Lake Resort:

Magic Lake Resort is located adjacent to the Magic Reservoir Airport and contains accommodations for dining with lodging nearby. Their restaurant is open between 7 a.m. and 9 p.m. 7 days a week. The menu offers hardy breakfast dishes as well as a variety of hamburgers, sandwiches, soups and salads. They also offer bone ham as well as choice cuts of beef. Average prices on their specials run between $3.00 and $4.00 for breakfast, $4.00 to $5.00 for lunch and a 22 oz cut of beef for around $12.50. The restaurant includes a bar with seating for 80 persons. The decor of the restaurant is rustic with barn wood paneling. On Saturday nights there is live entertainment with a band. This facility combines a restaurant, tavern, and 1 cottage for rent, in addition to a trailer park and accommodations for fishing. For more information you can call Magic Lake Resort at 487-2022.

Restaurants Near Airport:
Magic Lake Resort Adj Arpt Phone: 487-2022

Lodging: Magic Lake Resort has one cottage (Adj Arpt) 487-2022. Also: West Shore Motel with 5 units about 2 miles. Phone: N/A.

Meeting Rooms: None reported

Transportation: None reported; Magic Lake Resort is adjacent to Magic Reservoir Airport and should be well within walking distance.

Information: Hailey Visitors Information, P.O. Box 700, Hailey, ID 83333, Phone 788-2700

NO AIRPORT DIAGRAM AVAILABLE

Airport Information:

HAILEY - MAGIC RESERVOIR AIRPORT (U93)
15 mi southwest of town N43-16.94 W114-23.72 Elev: 4844 Rwy 03-21: 4000x100 (Turf-dirt) Rwy 09-27: 1750x100 (Turf) Attended: unattended CTAF: 122.9 Notes: No winter maintenance; When wind conditions allow, land runway 03 or runway 09, and takeoff runway 21 or runway 27 to avoid flying over resort area.
Magic Reservoir Airport Phone: 334-8775

ID-S66 - HOMEDALE
HOMEDALE MUNICIPAL AIRPORT

(Area Code 208)

15

Ferdinand's Pizza:

Ferdinand's Pizza is situated about 1/2 mile from the Homedale Municipal Airport. No courtesy transportation was reported either by the restaurant or airport. However, we were told that this facility is within walking distance. One attractive alternative would be to call Ferdinand's and have them deliver your pizza right to the airport and have a picnic. Restaurant hours are from 11 a.m. to 2 p.m. and from 4:30 to 9 p.m. Monday through Thursday and 4:30 p.m. to 11 p.m. Friday and Saturday. Their menu includes deli sandwiches, pizza (Ferdinand's special 8 toppings), taco pizza, and pizzas with a choice of 18 different toppings available. Average prices are $2.00 to $3.00 for lunch, and $13.00 for a large pizza which can feed six people. They also offer pizza by the slice. Groups planning to visit Ferdinand's restaurant can receive discounts on their meal. The restaurant can seat about 30 to 35 persons. As mentioned before Ferdinand's also delivers meals to the airport. For more information call 337-3323.

Restaurants Near Airport:
Ferdinand's Pizza 1/2 mile Phone: 337-3323

Lodging: Sunnydale Motel (8 units) 337-3302.

Meeting Rooms: None reported

Transportation: None reported

Information: Homedale Chamber of Commerce, P.O. Box 845, Homedale, ID 83628, Phone: N/A

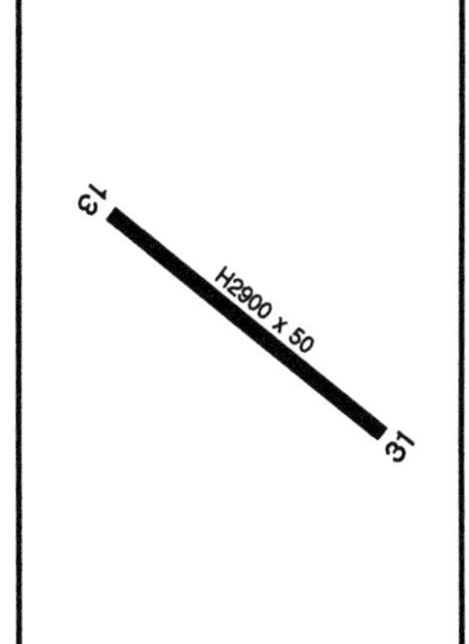

Airport Information:

HOMEDALE - HOMEDALE MUNICIPAL AIRPORT (S66)
1 mi southeast of town N43-36.89 W116-55.29 Elev: 2210 Rwy 13-31: H2900x50 (Asph) Attended: unattended CTAF: 122.9
Homedale Municipal Airport Phone: 337-3865

ID-U98 - IDAHO CITY
IDAHO CITY USFS

(Area Code 208) 16

Restaurants Near Airport:
Restaurants in town   1 to 1-1/2 mi   C.C. Phone: 392-4148

Lodging: Idaho City Hotel 392-4290; Prospector Motel 392-4290.
Meeting: None reported
Transportation: None reported
Information: Chamber of Commerce, P.O. Box 70, Idaho City, ID 83631. Phone: 392-4148

Idaho City: (Attractions)

This town was well known as one of the most famous sites of the great gold rush era. An 18-square-mile area known as the Boise Basin contained deposits of gold sought after by large numbers of prospectors migrating into the region. The town today has a current population of just 372 people. The fascinating history of this town is well-described by the Boise Basin Historical Museum which displays artifacts and memorabilia used by prospectors. Buildings within town have been restored and boardwalks lining the streets depict a taste of a time when the town experienced the fury and anticipation of gold seekers numbering in the thousands. The Museum is open Memorial Day through Labor Day, 7 days a week. May and September they are open weekends and October through April by appointment only. Another point of interest is Boot Hill where many famous gunfight victims of the past remain at rest today. Idaho City depends a great deal on tourism to support businesses and merchants. There are several restaurants within the downtown area. One such establishment, known as the Saparilla Ice Cream parlor on main street, offers customers cool, refreshing homemade ice cream a favorite treat for your pallet especially on a warm summer day. Two lodging establishments in town are the Idaho City Hotel and Prospector Motel. The nearby airstrip offers convenient access for fly-in visitors. For information about the museum, community activities or special events, contact the Idaho City Chamber of Commerce, P.O. Box 70 Idaho City, ID 83631 or call 392-4148.

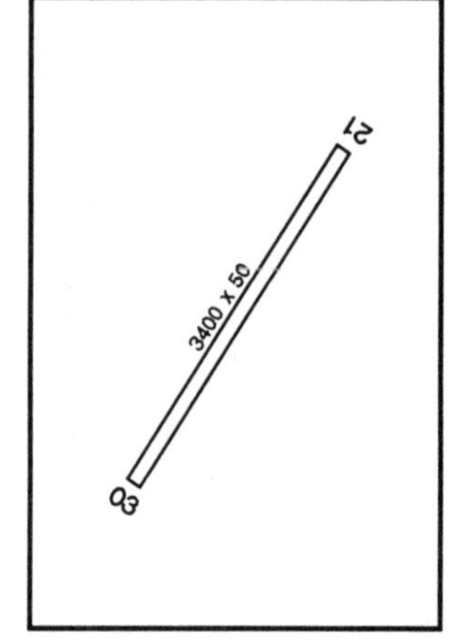

Airport Information:

IDAHO CITY - IDAHO CITY USFS (U98)
1 mi southwest of town   N43-49.24 W115-51.06   Elev: 3920   Attended: unattended   Rwy 03-21: 3400x50 (Dirt-Turf)   CTAF 122.9   Notes: Recommended land Rwy 03, takoff Rwy 21 when wind conditions permit. Rwy 03-21 first 700' turf, remainder dirt. Rwy 03-21 edges and thresholds marked with white rock. No winter maintenance. No telephone available at airport. Recommend you call ahead for airport and runway conditions prior to use.
Airport Information   Phone: 364-4330

ID-IDA - IDAHO FALLS
FANNING FIELD

(Area Code 208) 17

Restaurants Near Airport:
DasKinderhaus Restaurant   On Site   Phone: 523-6065

Lodging: Little Tree Inn (Free trans) 523-5993; Weston Inn (Free trans) 523-6260; Shilo Inn (Free trans) 523-0088.

Meeting: Little Tree Inn (Free trans) 523-5993; Weston Inn (Free trans) 523-6262; Shilo Inn (Free trans) 523-0088.

Transportation: Rental cars: Avis, Budget, Hurtz, all located within the terminal building.

Information: Chamber of Commerce, 505 Lindsay Blvd, P.O. Box 50498, Idaho City, ID 83405, Phone: 523-1010 or 800-634-3246.

Daskinderhaus Restaurant:

Daskinderhaus Restaurant can be found within the terminal building at the Idaho Falls Airport. This unique German dining establishment is open Monday and Tuesday 6:30 a.m. to 8 p.m., and Wednesday through Saturday 6:30 a.m. to 10 p.m. They are closed on Sundays. Their menu contains a variety of delicious German entrees like Jager Schnitzel, Spaetsel, several varieties of sausage, rouladen of beef, chicken Mitweiss Wein, prime rib, seafood as well as a selected European dishes. The decor of the restaurant has a German theme with brightly colored table cloths, and pictures and maps of Germany. On Friday and Saturday beginning around 5:30 or 6:00 p.m. they feature live entertainment with accordian music. This restaurant has a main dining room that can seat about 225 persons allowing a nice view looking out over the airport. Their lounge serves German imported beer on tap as well as domestic beers. They also have a coffee shop on the premises as well. For more information you can call Daskinderhaus Restaurant at 523-6065.

Airport Information:

IDAHO FALLS - FANNING FIELD (IDA)
2 mi northwest of town   N43-3087 W112-04.21   Elev: 4741   Fuel: 100LL, Jet-A1
Rwy 02-20: H9001x150 (Asph-Grvd)   Rwy 17-35: H4050x150 (Asph)   Attended: 1200-0600Z
Unicom: 122.95   Salt Lake App/Dep Con: 128.35   Tower: 118.5   Gnd Con: 121.7
FBO: Aero Mark, Inc.   Phone: 524-1202

Not to be used for navigational purposes

ID-S82 - KOOSKIA
KOOSKIA MUNICIPAL AIRPORT

(Area Code 208)

18

Rivers Cafe:

The Rivers Cafe is a family restaurant reported to be approximately 3 to 4 blocks from the Kooskia Municipal Airport., According to the people managing the airport, this restaurant can be reached by walking. The Rivers Cafe is open from 6 a.m. to 9 p.m. 7 days a week. They serve items like hamburgers, steak, shrimp, pizzas, homemade pies and soup. In addition to their menu, they also have a fresh salad bar available to their guests. Average prices run $3.25 for breakfast, $2.00-$3.50 for lunch and $4.95 to $8.00 for dinner. One of their lunch specials includes fresh homemade soup and salad bar for only $3.25. Usually on Friday and Saturday they also offer a variety of specials like BBQ beef ribs, (1/2 rack) or 1/2 chicken for only $5.95. They also feature shrimp and prime ribs specials as well. The restaurant can seat up to 50 guests and offers a rustic atmosphere with brick and wood cedar walls. Larger groups are always welcome if advance notice is given. This restaurant is situated in town across the street from the"Panky's Grocery Store". For more information you can call the Rivers Cafe at 926-4450.

Restaurants Near Airport:
Rivers Cafe 3-4 blks Phone: 926-4450

Lodging: Ida Lee Motel (1/4th mile) 926-0166

Meeting Rooms: None reported

Transportation: None reported

Information: Kooskia City Hall 926-4684, Also the local Lions Club can furnish you with information regarding this town and annual events.

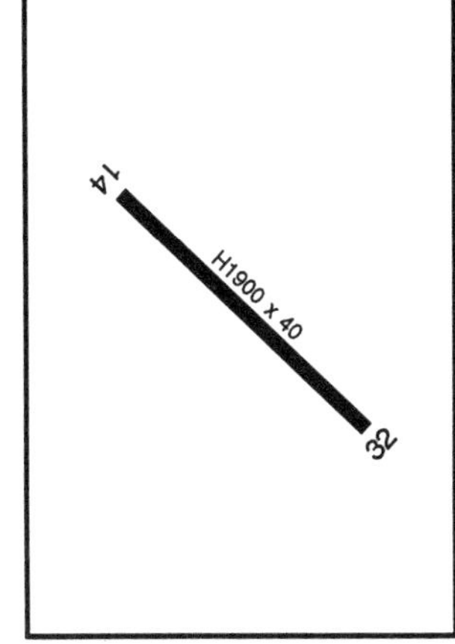

Airport Information:

KOOSKIA - KOOSKIA MUNICIPAL AIRPORT (S82)
1 mi south of town N46-07.96 W115-58.73 Elev: 1263 Rwy 14-32: 1900x40 (Turf)
Attended: unattended Unicom: 122.9 Notes: Road crosses runway 14-32 near center. Runway 14 logs, road and fence on primary surface near threshold. Neumerous obstructions in all quadrants around airport.
Kooskia Airport Phone: 926-4654 or 926-0089

ID-LWS - LEWISTON
NEZ PERCE COUNTY AIRPORT

(Area Code 208)

19

Lewiston Airport Restaurant:

This restaurant is situated on the upper level of the airport terminal building and can easily be reached by courtesy transportation if necessary, obtained through one of the FBO's on the airport. This restaurant specializes in preparing a wide variety of entrees including a Friday night seafood buffet. Regular buffet style selections are available on Saturday and Sunday. On Saturdays they also feature prime rib specials. A large salad bar is also available. They are open for business between 7 a.m. and 8 p.m seven days a week. Entree prices run on an average of $2.25 for breakfast, $3.75 for lunch and $9.00 for dinner. The restaurant has a modern decor with an adjoining banquet room able to seat up to 80 people. Catering is no problem for this facility when planning meetings. For information call 746-9460.

Restaurants Near Airport:
Lewiston Restaurant On Site Phone: 746-9460

Lodging: Ramada Inn; 621 21st street, Lewiston, Free transportation to and from airport, 101 rooms, two swimming pools, cafe 6 a.m. to 10 p.m., Entertainment & dancing in lounge, Meeting rooms, Phone: 799-1000, Quality Inn; 700 Port Drive, Clarkston, Washington 509-758-9500, (9 motels available within a 10 minute drive of the airport).

Transportation: Stout Flying Service Phone: 743-8408, Hertz Rent-A-Car 746-0411, National Car Rental Phone: 743-0176, Budget Car Rental Phone: 746-0488, Lewis Clark Rentals Phone: 746-4726

Information: Lewiston Chamber of Commerce, 2207 East Main Street, Lewiston, ID 83501, Phone: 743-3531 or 800-473-3543.

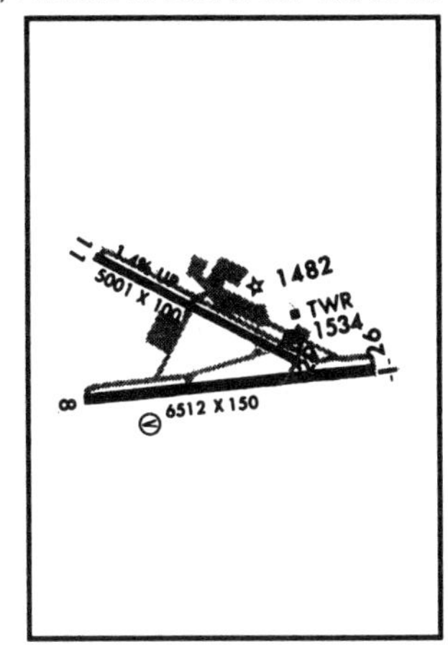

Attractions:

Bryden Canyon Golf Course (On Airport) Phone: 746-0863; Confluence of Snake and Clear Water Rivers (2 miles), Hell Canyon State Park, offers 960 acres of recreation including camping, hiking, swimming, boating, excursion boat tours, paved bicycle trails, Jet boat rides and much more. For information on the park contact Park Manager at 3620A Snake River Avenue, Lewiston, ID 83246, Phone: 743-2363. For Gateway to Hell's Canyon Jet boat rides to Hells Canyon, contact Chamber of Commerce (listed above).

Airport Information:

LEWISTON - NEZ PERCE COUNTY AIRPORT (LWS)
2 mi south of town N46-22.47 W117-00.92 Elev: 1438 Fuel: 100, 100LL, Jet-A
Rwy 08-26: H6512x150 (ASPH-PFC) Rwy: 11-29: H5001x100 (ASPH) Attended: 1330-0500Z Unicom: 122.95 Dep Con: 124.1 Tower: 119.4 Gnd Con: 121.9
Notes: Overnight Parking $2.00
Hillcrest Aircraft Company Phone: 746-8271 FBO: Stout Flying Service Phone: 743-8408,

ID-U62 - MACKAY
MACKAY AIRPORT

(Area Code 208) 20

Steakhouse Cafe & Motel:

The Steakhouse Cafe & Motel is situated, (according to the restaurant) a 3 block walk from the Mackay Airport. This combination cafe and family style restaurant is open 7 days a week from 7 a.m. to 10 p.m. during the summer, and 7 a.m. to 9 p.m. during the winter. Their menu contains items including a full breakfast line, steaks, pork chops, chicken dinners, homemade soups, as well as many other choices. During the week they run many specials for their guests. The restaurant offers a casual atmosphere with seating for about 25 persons. There is a special room in the back of their facility that provides accommodations for groups and parties. The restaurant boasts friendly service with good sized portions. For more information you can call 588-9903.

Restaurants Near Airport:
Steakhouse Cafe & Motel 3 blks Phone: 588-9903

Lodging: Steakhouse Cafe & Motel 588-9903; Wagon Wheel 588-3331; White Knob 588-3201 or 588-3301.

Meeting Rooms: None Reported

Transportation: None Reported

Information: Lost River Valley Chamber, P.O. Box 209, Mackay 83251, Phone: 588-2200.

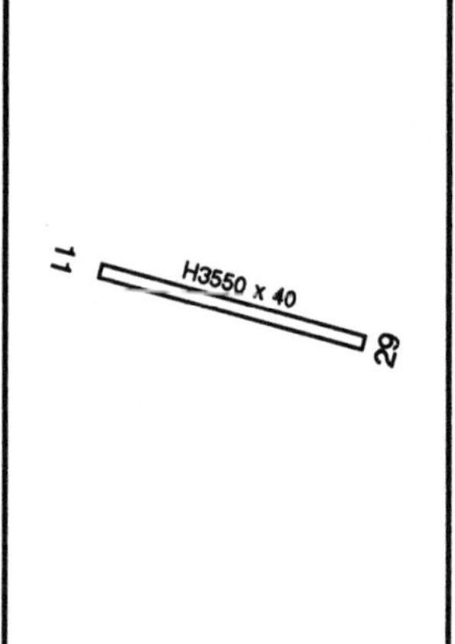

Airport Information:

MACKAY - MACKAY AIRPORT (U62)
1 mi southeast of town N43-54 113-36-00W Elev: 5891 Rwy 11-29: H3550x40 (Dirt)
Attended: unattended CTAF: 122.9
Mackay Airport Phone: 588-2274

ID-MYL - MC CALL
MC CALL AIRPORT

(Area Code 208)

21, 22

Shore Lodge (Resort)

The Shore Lodge Resort is located about 3 or 4 miles from the Mc Call Airport. This facility, if given advance notice will pick people up from the airport. There is a fine dining facility located within the resort, that is open between 7 a.m. to 10 p.m. weekdays and from 7 a.m. to 11 p.m. on weekends. Their entrees are unique with many wild game dishes. In addition, they also serve selections like prime rib, filet mignon, trout, Alaska King crab, King salmon, chicken, as well as soups and salads. Average prices run between $10.00 and $22.00 per person. During the summer months daily specials are also offered. The restaurant overlooks a beautiful lake where guests can experience a fine meal while enjoying the scenery. The decor of the restaurant displays a bright and airy semi-rustic atmosphere with linen covered tables, potted flowers, log and rock walls along with various wild animal trophies. The main dining room can seat 70 person. Their additional separate dining room, able to accommodate up to 250 people is frequently visited by club and association fly-ins throughout the year. In addition to the restaurant, this resort also provides a wide variety of amenities for their guests. Tennis courts, gift shop, racket ball, boat docks, swimming pool and 115 rooms for vacationers. For information you can call Shore Lodge Resort at 634-2244 or 800-657-6464.

Si Bueno Mexican Restaurant:

Si Bueno Mexican Restaurant is located at Mc Call Airport about 1/4 mile on north end of the runway, directly across the street on Deinhard Lane. Hours are 11:00 a.m. to 10:00 p.m. Monday through Friday, and 11:00 a.m. to 11:00 p.m. Saturday and Sunday. Guests will dine in old world Mexican-style decor with an airplane protruding out of the roof. Along with a daily lunch buffet, the restaurant serves homemade mexican meals and specialties, such as tamales, sopapillas, flan, burgers, steaks, seafood, and fajitas. They also serve delicious Margaritas, and Happy Hour appetizer specials. Prices average around $6.00 for lunch and $9.00 for dinner. Si Bueno will open for breakfast for parties of 20 or more, and discounts are available with advance notice only. Reservations are necessary for parties of 15 or more. Also, the restaurant can cater hot, delicious BBQ and "all events" meals to private and corporate pilots on-the-go. For more information about Si Bueno Mexican Restaurant, call 634-2128.

Restaurants Near Airport:

Restaurant	Distance	Phone
Mill Restaurant	1/2 mi	Phone: 634-7683
Pancake House	1/2 mi	Phone: 634-5849
Shore Lodge (Resort)	4 mi	Phone: 634-2244
Si Bueno	1/4 mi N	Phone: 634-2128
Woodsman Cafe	1/2 mi	Phone: 634-8477

Lodging: Mc Call Hotel (1 mile) 634-5728; Woodsman Cafe and Motel (1 miles) 634-7671; Scandia Inn Motel (1 mile) 634-7394; Riverside Motel (2 miles) 634-5610; Shore Lodge (4 miles) 634-2244

Meeting Rooms: Si Bueno 634-2128; Shore Lodge 634-2244

Transportation: Woodsman 634-7671; Shore Lodge 634-2244; Rental Cars: National 634-7137; Pioneer 634-5445

Information: Chamber of Commerce, P.O. Box D, Mc Call, ID 83638, Phone: 634-7631

Attractions:

Frank Church River of No Return Wilderness, Payette Lake (1 mile); Brundage Mountain Ski Area (10 miles); Busiest fishing and hiking season is Jul.-Sept., ski season is Dec-Apr. Call 634-2128.

Airport Information:

MC CALL - MC CALL AIRPORT (MYL)
0 mi south of town N44-53.33 W116-06.09 Elev: 5020 Fuel: 80, 100, Jet-A1+
Rwy 16-34: H6162x75 (Asph) Attended: daylight hours CTAF/Unicom: 122.8 Salt Lake Center App/Dep Con: 128.05 Public Phone 24hrs Notes: See "Airport Facility Directory" for comments about runway conditions and information.
FBO: Mc Call Air Taxi **Phone: 634-7137**
FBO: Pioneer Air Service **Phone: 634-5445**

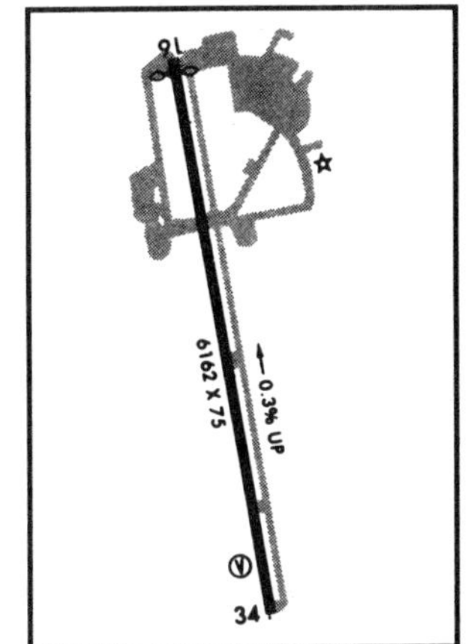

ID-1U3 - MURPHY
MURPHY AIRPORT

(Area Code 208)

23

Restaurants Near Airport:
Murphy General Store Adj. Arpt. Phone: 495-1144

Lodging: None Reported

Meeting Rooms: None Reported

Transportation: None Reported

Information: Convention and Visitors Bureau, 168 N. 9th Street, Suite 200, P.O. Box 2106, Boise, ID 83701, Phone: 344-7777

Attractions:
Museum is located about 2 blocks from the airport. Silver City Mining Town is located about 28 miles. Call 344-7777 for more information.

Murphy General Store:
Murphy is situated in the southwestern portion of Idaho. Murphy General Store is located directly across the street from the Murphy Airport runway. The store features grocery items, soda, beer, etc. There is also a gift shop which sells T-shirts with the Murphy General Store logo. A family-style cafe is open from 8:00 a.m. to 7:00 p.m. Monday through Saturday, and 9:00 a.m. to 5:00 p.m. on Sunday. At this establishment, guests dine in an atmosphere of country decor. The cafe features a fabulous breakfast menu, as well as lunch specialties, such as the "Murph's" burger (a juicy 1/2-pound double-beef, double-cheese, and bacon burger), assorted cold sandwiches, and delicious pies for dessert. At this time, the cafe serves one dinner specialty, which is prawns with French fries on the side for $5.95. Note: We were told at the time of the interview (Sept., 1995) that more dinner items will be coming soon. Breakfast prices average between $4.25 and $4.50. Lunch prices average between $3.50 and $5.00. This restaurant can cater to parties of up to 20 individuals, as well as to private and corporate pilots on-the-go. The managers also informed us that they do provide fuel for pilots in the case of an emergency. Contact the managers for more information. For more information about Murphy General Store, call 495-1144.

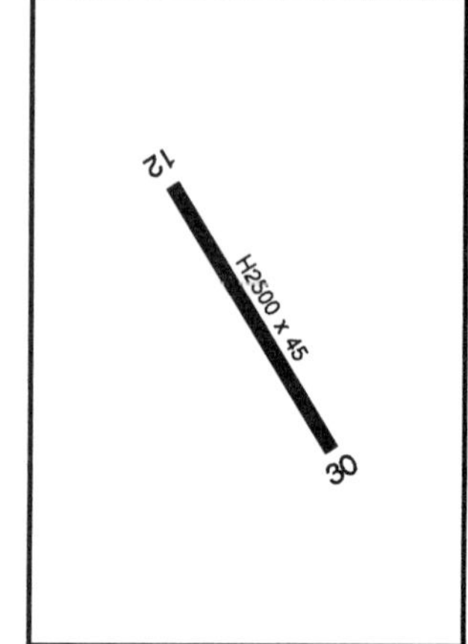

Airport Information:
MURPHY - MURPHY AIRPORT (1U3)
0 mi east of town N43-12.96 W116-32.94 Elev: 2855 Fuel: none reported Rwy 12-30: H2500x45 (Asph) Attended: unattended CTAF: 122.9 Notes: Recommend land Rwy 12, take-off Rwy 30 when wind condition permits.
FBO: Sheriff's Office Phone: 495-1154

ID-PIH - POCATELLO
POCATELLO REGIONAL AIRPORT

(Area Code 208)

24

Restaurants Near Airport:
Blue Ribbon Restaurant & Lounge On Site Phone: 233-8002

Lodging: Little Tree Inn (Free trans) 237-0020; Best Western Cotton Tree Inn (Free trans) 237-7650; Holiday Inn 237-1400; Oxbow Motor Inn (Free trans) 237-3100; Quality Inn Convention Center (Free trans) 233-2200.

Meeting Rooms: Blue Ribbon Restaurant 233-8002; Little Tree Inn 237-0020; Best western Cotton Tree Inn 237-7650; Holiday Inn 237-1400; Oxbow Motor Inn 237-3100; Quality Inn Convention Center 233-2200.

Transportation: Rental Cars: Avis 232-3244; Hertz 233-2970; National 233-6042.

Information: Greater Pocatello Chamber of Commerce, 343 W Center Street, P.O. Box 626, Pocatello, ID 83204, Phone: 233-1525

Blue Ribbon Restaurant & Lounge:
The Blue Ribbon Restaurant is situated within the terminal building on the Pocatello Municipal Airport. This fine dining facility is open monday from 6:45 a.m. to 9 p.m. Tuesday through Friday 6:45 a.m. to 10 p.m., and Saturday from 11 a.m. to 10:30 p.m. (Closed Sunday). Their lounge is open from 11:30 a.m. to 1 a.m. Specialty entrees on their menu include prime rib, steaks, seafood, lobster, crab, poultry, ribs, and catfish, in addition to soups and salad. Average prices run $3.95 for breakfast, $4.95 for lunch and $9.95 for dinner. In addition to their regular menu prices, daily specials are offered as well. The restaurant has a modern decor and has recently been remodeled. The main dining area can seat 100 people while their separate banquet room can seat about the same number. They also have a conference room able to accommodate up to 50 persons. Catered groups and parties can easily be accomplished at the Blue Ribbon restaurant for either friends and family, associations, clubs, or businesses. For more information call 233-8002

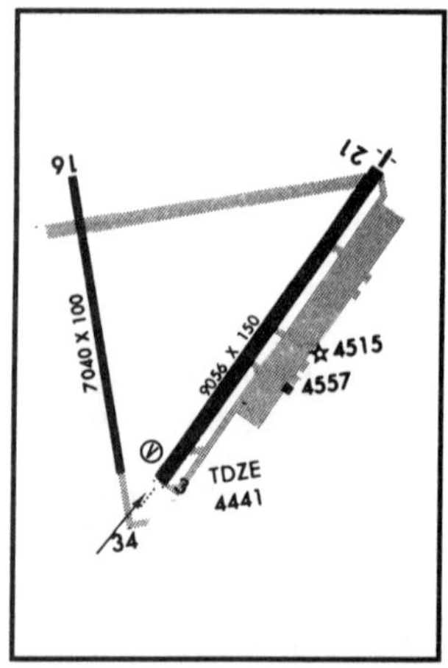

Airport Information:
POCATELLO - POCATELLO REGIONAL AIRPORT (PIH)
7 mi northwest of town N42-54.68 W112-35.75 Elev: 4449 Fuel: 100LL, Jet-A1, A1+
Rwy 03-21: H9056x150 (Asph) Rwy 16-34: H7040x100 (Asph) Attended: 1300-0500Z
Unicom: 122.95 Salt Lake Ctr App/Dep Con: 128.35 Tower: 119.1 Gnd Con: 121.9
FBO: Pacatello Avcenter, Inc. Phone: 234-2141

ID-2U7 - STANLEY
STANLEY

(Area Code 208)

25

Nearby Restaurants & Entertainment:

The town of Stanley is located about 1 mile southeast of the airport. It is situated adjacent to the Salmon River. Activities like river rafting, fishing, camping and backpacking are popular in this location. The Sawtooth National Forest ranger district office is located here. The river contains abundant wild life, abandoned gold mines and caves. Also in the area are several dude ranches that have pack-trips, big-game guides and outfitters. ***Idaho Rocky Mountain Ranch*** *is one of these operations that provides transportation to and from the airport. They have a restaurant open between 7 a.m. and 11 p.m. on the premises. The bar offers entertainment for their guests. Business services and meeting rooms are available. Some of the activities and services at this ranch include horse stables, bicycle rentals, cabins with fireplaces, gift shop, laundry, 9 cabins and 4 rooms in the lodge. For information call the Idaho Rocky Mountain Ranch at 774-3544.* ***Mountain Village Lodge*** *is another establishment that offers transportation for fly-in guests. A restaurant is on site that is open between 7 a.m. and 11 p.m. For information about the Mountain Village Lodge call 774-3661. The Sawtooth Mountain Arts & Craft Fair is held annually on the third weekend of July. For more information about this area call the Chamber of Commerce at 774-3411.*

Restaurants Near Airport:

Idaho Rocky Mountain Ranch	(Trans)	Phone: 774-3544
Mountain Village Lodge	(Trans)	Phone: 774-3661

Lodging: Mountain Village Lodge (Free trans) Phone: 774-3661: Idaho Rocky Mountain Ranch (Free trans) Phone: 774-3544

Meeting Rooms: Mountain Village Lodge (Free trans) Phone: 774-3661: Idaho Rocky Mountain Ranch (Free trans) Phone: 774-3544

Transportation: None reported at airport; Call Stanley chamber of Commerce 774-3411.

Information: Stanley Chamber of Commerce, P.O. Box 8, Stanley, ID 83278. Phone: 774-3411.

Airport Information:

STANLEY - STANLEY AIRPORT (2U7)

1 mi southeast of town N44-12.51 W114-56.07 Elev: 6403 Rwy 17-35: 4300x150 Turf-Dirt Attended: unattended CTAF: 122.9 Notes: No winter maintenance. Airport located in valley surrounded by high mountainous terrain. Numerous air taxi operations during the summer months. Rwy 17-35 rwy edges and threshold marked with white rocks. Due to terrain, recommend land 35 and depart 17 wind permitting.

Airport Management Phone: 334-8775

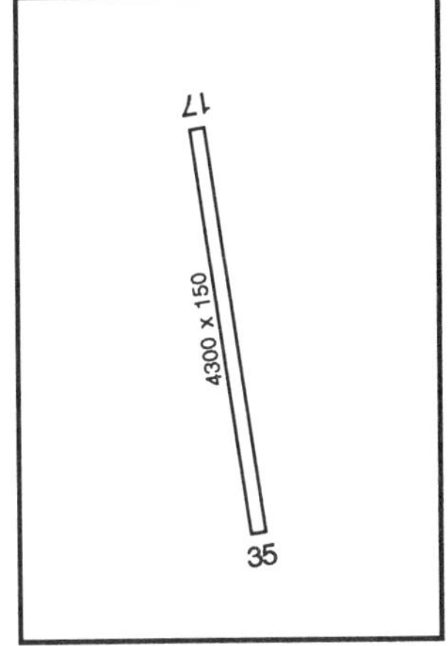

ID-(Private) - SULPHUR CREEK
SULPHUR CREEK RANCH

(Area Code 208)

26

Sulphur Creek Ranch:

Sulphur Creek Ranch is a private guest ranch that contains its own airstrip. This guest ranch has an interesting history dating back to the 1930's. During WW-II it was frequented by military personnel on recreational leave transported by DC-3's from Mountain Home Air Force Base. Today the beauty and serenity of the Sulphur Creek Ranch appeals to visitors because of its natural surrounding within the Boise National Forest. Fly-in guests often make arrangements to spend some quality time, visiting this guest ranch and enjoying its many activities. The owners of this establishment are famous for their huge breakfasts served seven days a week between June 1, through August. Egg dishes of all types along with omelettes are served with bacon, sausage or ham. Other belt buster selections include their delicious biscuits and gravy, pancakes and their special creation known as "Cowboy Benedict". Sulphur Creek Ranch attracts fly-in clubs from all over the region. The guest ranch also serves as an outfitter providing guided hunting and fishing trips. Some of their special hunting trips are designed for big game trophy collectors and can last a week. Trail rides are also offered with over 20 horses available. First time riders will feel at ease as will the experienced equestrian. As this is a private ranch with airstrip, please call the owners in advance prior to use. For information call 377-1188

Restaurants Near Airport:

Sulphur Creek Ranch	On Site	Phone: 377-1188

Lodging: Sulphur Creek Ranch (On site) Phone: 377-1188
Meeting Rooms: Accommodations for group outings can be arranged by calling 377-1188.
Transportation: Not necessary
Information: Write to: Mr. Tom T. Allegrezza, 7153 West Emerald, Boise, ID 83704 or call 377-1188.

Attractions:
The Sulphur Creek Ranch serves as a very popular locations for fly-in guests. A wide variety of ranching activities are provided. Trail rides, outfitters and guides for special hunting and fishing trips, and one of the best known back country breakfast fly-in locations in Idaho. For information call 377-1188.

Airport Information:

SULPHUR CREEK RANCH - SULPHUR CREEK (Private)

Approximate location: 80 miles northeast of Boise, ID; 33 miles east northeast of Cascade Airoprt (U70), and 3 miles southwest of the Morgan Ranch. N44-32.00 W115-21.00 Elev: 5835 Rwy 08-26: 3300x40 (Turf/Gravel) Remarks: Land to west (upstream), Depart to east (downstream) one way strip. Notes: Private use facility, use at own risk. Restrictions: requires prior permision by owner. Owner Tom T. Allegrezza 337-1188.

Airport Manager Phone: 377-1188

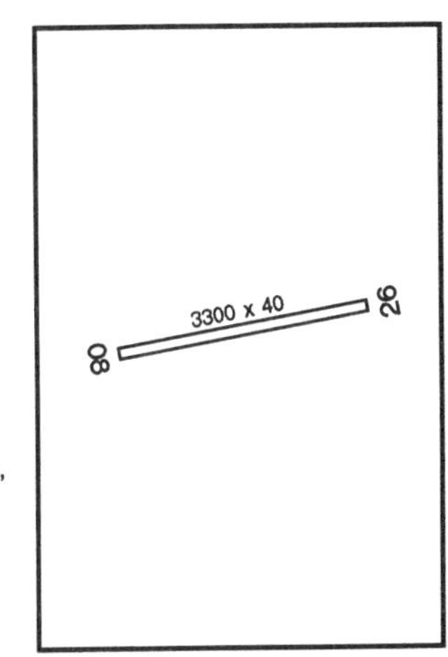

ID-TWF - TWIN FALLS
SUN VALLEY REGIONAL/JOSLIN

(Area Code 208) 27

Approach Control Restaurant:

The Approach Control Restaurant formerly known as the Hanger Restaurant, is situated in the terminal building at the Sun Valley Regional Airport (Joslin Field). At the time of research this restaurant, under new management, was just about to re-open. Services and hours may vary from the description listed below. This establishment is well within walking distance from the aircraft tie-down area. This is a combination cafe and family style restaurant. Their hours are from 6 a.m. to 9 p.m. Monday through Saturday, and 7 a.m. to 6 p.m. on Sunday. Their specialty is pizza with 20 different toppings to choose from. They offer an all-you can-eat special with an assortment of pizzas brought to each table throughout your meal. The theme of this restaurant is unique with items relating to aviation. They have pictures of aircraft on the wall, bombs hanging from the ceiling, and an old aircraft nose protruding through the wall which gives this restaurant a unique quality. The main dining room can hold about 45 persons. Pizza-to-go and carry-out items from their menu are available. For more information you can call the Hangar Restaurant at 734-3147.

Restaurants Near Airport:
Approach Control Restaurant On Site Phone: 734-3147

Lodging: Canyon Springs Inn (Free trans) 734-5000; Weston Plaza (Free trans) 733-0650.
Meeting Rooms: Canyon Springs Inn (Free trans) 734-5000; Weston Plaza (Free trans) 733-0650.
Transportation: Taxi: Yellow Cab 733-9101; First Silver Taxi 736-0100; Rental Cars: Avis 733-5527; Budget 734-4067; Hertz 733-2668; National 733-3646
Information: Chamber of Commerce, 858 Blue Lakes Blvd. N., Twin Falls, ID 83301, Phone: 733-3974 or 800-255-8946.

Attractions:

Shoshone & Twin Falls (Natural falls) that when irrigation is plentiful-excess goes over falls (6 miles); Also overlook Perrine Bridge into canyon north side of Twin Falls; Various landmarks and attractions also located throughout county.

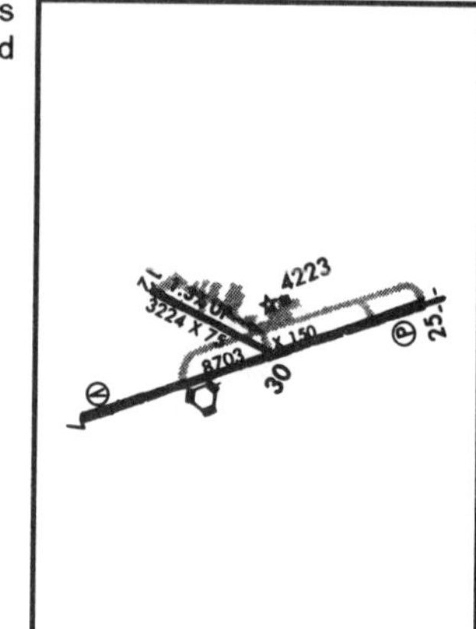

Airport Information:

TWIN FALLS - SUN VALLEY REGIONAL/JOSLIN FIELD (TWF)
4 mi south of town N42-28.91 W114-29.26 Elev: 4151 Fuel: 100LL, Jet-A1+
Rwy 07-25: H8703x150 (Asph-Pfc) Rwy 12-30: H3224x75 (Asph) Attended: continuously
Unicom: 122.95 Tower: 118.2 Gnd Con: 121.7 Public Phone in terminal building daytime-10 p.m.
FBO: AVI Phone: 733-8970
FBO: Reeder Flying Service Phone: 733-5920

ILLINOIS

LOCATION MAP

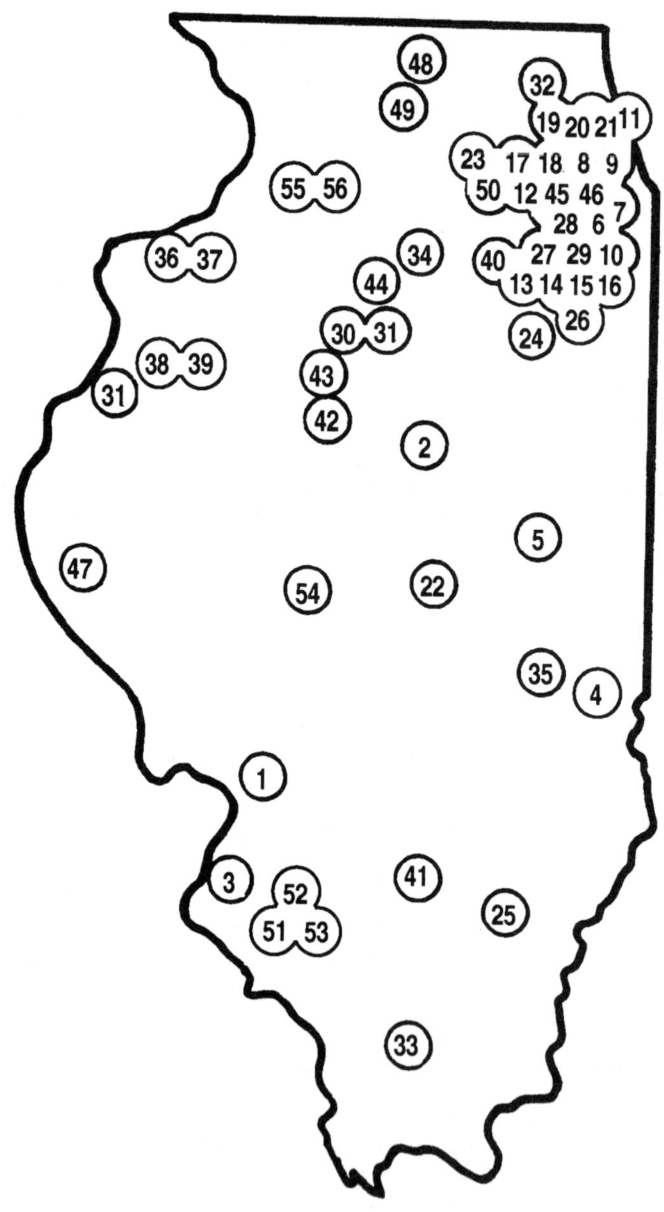

Not to be used for navigational purposes

ILLINOIS

CROSS FILE INDEX

Location Number	City or Town	Airport Name And Identifier	Name of Restaurant
1	Alton/St. Louis	St. Louis Reg. Arpt. (ALN)	Casablanca Restaurant
2	Bloomington	Bloomington Normal Arpt. (BMI)	Arnie's Restaurant
3	Cahokia-St. Louis	St. Louis Downtown-Parks (CPS)	Oliver's Restaurant
4	Casey	Casey Muni. Arpt. (1H8)	Richards Farm
5	Champaign (Urbana)	University of Illinois-Willard (CMI)	Willard's Rest. & Lounge
6	Chicago	Chicago Midway Arpt. (MDW)	Midway Restaurant
7	Chicago	Chicago Midway Arpt. (MDW)	Shipwreck Kelly's
8	Chicago	Chicago O'Hare Intl. Arpt. (ORD)	Hilton Hotel (O'hare Intl.)
9	Chicago	Chicago O'Hare Intl. Arpt. (ORD)	Skybird Meeting Center
10	Chicago	Lansing Muni. Arpt. (IGQ)	Shannon's Landing
11	Chicago	Merrill C. Meigs (CGX)	The Berghoff Restaurant
12	Chicago/Aurora	Aurora Muni. (ARR)	Fishermen's Inn
13	Chicago/Romeoville	Lewis University (LOT)	Baci Restaurant
14	Chicago/Romeoville	Lewis University (LOT)	Empress Casino Joliet
15	Chicago/Romeoville	Lewis University (LOT)	Public Landing
16	Chicago/Romeoville	Lewis University (LOT)	White Fence Farm
17	Chicago/W. Chicago	DuPage Arpt. (DPA)	Kittyhawk Cafe
18	Chidago/W. Chicago	DuPage Arpt. (DPA)	Pheasant Run Resort
19	Chicago/Wheeling	Palwaukee Muni. Arpt. (PWK)	94th Aero Squadron
20	Chicago/Wheeling	Palwaukee Muni. Arpt. (PWK)	LeFrancais Restaurant
21	Chicago/Wheeling	Palwaukee Muni. Arpt. (PWK)	Bob Chinns Crab House
22	Decatur	Decatur Arpt. (DEC)	Main Hangar Restaurant
23	DeKalb	DeKalb Taylor Muni. Arpt (DKB)	Crystal Pistol Beach Club
24	Dwight	Dwight Arpt. (DTG)	Country Mansion
25	Fairfield	Fairfield Muni. Arpt. (FWC)	Bat's Place
26	Frankfort	Frankfort Arpt. (C18)	Die Bier Stube
27	Joliet	Joliet Park District (JOT)	Empress Casino Joliet
28	Joliet	Joliet Park District (JOT)	Stk Hse/Fire Side Resort
29	Joliet	Joliet Park District (JOT)	Town & Country (Days Inn)
30	Lacon	Marshall Co. Arpt. (C75)	Kenyons Place
31	Lacon	Marshall Co. Arpt. (C75)	Sly Fox Pub
32	Lake in the Hills	Lake in the Hills Arpt. (3CK)	Windsock Deli
33	Marion	Williamson Co. Reg. (MWA)	J.W.'s Arpt. Rest.
34	Marseilles	Prairie Lake Hunt Club (68IL)	Prairie Lake Hunt Club
35	Matoon/Charleston	Coles Co. Mem. Arpt. (MTO)	Arpt. Steak House
36	Moline	Quad-City Arpt. (MLI)	CA1 Services
37	Moline	Quad-City Arpt. (MLI)	Skyline Inn Restaurant
38	Monmouth	Monmouth Muni. Arpt. (C66)	Cerar's Barnstormers
39	Monmouth	Monmouth Muni. Arpt. (C66)	Melings Restaurant
40	Morris	Morris Muni. Arpt. (C09)	Runway 47 Restaurant
41	Mount Vernon	Mount Vernon-Outland (MVN)	Stormy's At The Airport
42	Peoria	Greater Peoria Reg. (PIA)	Greater Peoria Arpt. Rest.

CROSS FILE INDEX
(Illinois Continued)

Location Number	City or Town	Airport Name And Identifier	Name of Attraction
43	Peoria	Mount Hawley Auxiliary (3MY)	Shopping Mall Rest.
44	Peru	Illinois Valley Reg./Duncan (VYS)	Red Door Inn
45	Plainfield	Clow Intl. Arpt. (1C5)	Country Aire Restaurant
46	Plainfield	Clow Intl. Arpt. (1C5)	Pancake Cafe
47	Quincy	Quincy Muni. Baldwin Fld. (UIN)	Skyway Arpt. Restaurant
48	Rockford	Cottonwood Arpt. (1C8)	Etta's Family Restaurant
49	Rockford	Greater Rockford Arpt. (RFD)	Terminal Restauant
50	Sandwich	Woodlake Landing Arpt. (C48)	Arpt. Diner
51	Sparta	Sparta Community-Hunter (SAR)	Brandy's Restaurnat
52	Sparta	Sparta Community-Hunter (SAR)	Charlie G's Restaurant
53	Sparta	Sparta Community-Hunter (SAR)	Frontier Steak House
54	Springfield	Capital Arpt. (SPI)	Arena Snack Bar & Lng.
55	Sterling Rockfalls	Whiteside Co. Arpt. (SQI)	Benigan's Restaurant
56	Sterling Rockfalls	Whiteside Co. Arpt. (SQI)	Red Apple Restaurant

Articles

City or town	Nearest Airport and Identifier	Name of Attraction
Chicago, IL	Chicago Midway (MDW)	Museum of Sci. & Industry
Chicago (West Chicago), IL	DuPage Arpt. (DPA)	Museum of Aviation
Chicago (West Chicago), IL	DuPage Arpt. (DPA)	Cantigny
Moline, IL	Quad-City (MLI)	Quad Cities USA
Rantoul, IL	Rantoul Natl. Avia. Cntr. (215)	Aerospace Museum

IL-ALN - ALTON/ST LOUIS
ST LOUIS REGIONAL AIRPORT

(Area Code 618) 1

Restaurants Near Airport:
Casablanca Restaurant On Site Phone: 259-7735

Lodging: Holiday Inn (Trans) 462-1220; Ramada Inn 463-0800.

Meeting Rooms: Holiday Inn 462-1220; Ramada Inn 463-0800.

Transportation: Courtesy car reported; Rental Cars: Available at both Jettronics (FBO) 258-1005, and Premier Jet Air Center (FBO) 259-3230.

Information: Greater Alton/Twin Rivers Convention & Visitors Bureau, 200 Plaza Street, Alton, IL 62002, Phone: 465-6676 or 800-258-6645.

Casablanca Restaurant:

Tar Casablanca Restaurant is located on the Alton/St Louis Regional Airport with available transient aircraft parking reported to be adjacent to their facility. This is classified as a fine dining establishment that is open Monday through Saturday from 11:00 a.m. to 9 p.m., and Sunday from 11 a.m. to 2 p.m. Items on their menu include New York strip steak, prime rib, filet mignon, chicken, seafood, jumbo shrimp, catfish, pasta dishes, and soup and salad bar is served with each full course dinner selection. Sunday brunch is served begining at 11 a.m. until 2 p.m. Verify buffet hours by calling the restaurant. Daily specials are also offered. Average prices run $4.00 to $5.00 for breakfast and lunch and $5.95 to $15.95 for dinner. The main dining room can accommodate up to 100 guests, while 2 separate banquet rooms are equipped to serve 125 persons. The "Red White & Blue" room is aviation decorated, and their "Casa Blanca" room has a softer tone with wicker chairs and a sort of Hawaiian or tropical decor. They even have an outdoor patio available for seating. For more information call the Casablanca Restaurant at 259-7735.

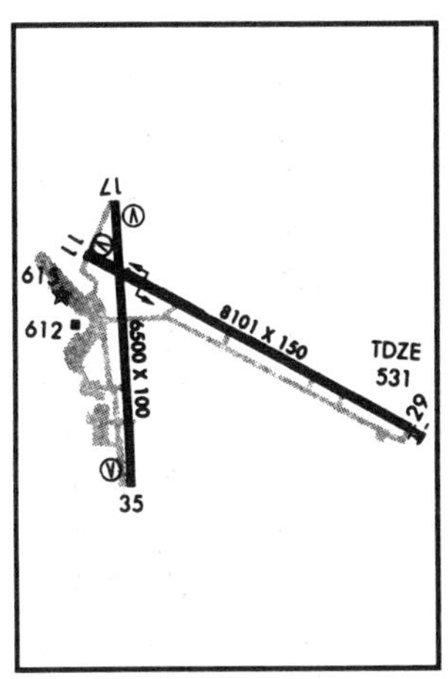

Airport Information:

ALTON/ST LOUIS - ST LOUIS REGIONAL AIRPORT (ALN)
4 mi east of town N38-53.42 W90-02.76 Elev: 544 Fuel: 100LL, Jet-A
Rwy 11-29: H8101x150 (Asph-Grvd) Rwy 17-35: H6500x100 (Asph) Attended: 1200-0400Z Atis: 128.0 Unicom: 122.95 App/Dep Con: 124.2
Clnc Del: 120.2 Regional Tower: 126.0 Gnd Con: 120.2
FBO: National Jet Inc. Phone: 258-1005
FBO: Premier Air Center, Inc. Phone: 259-3230

IL-BMI - BLOOMINGTON
BLOOMINGTON NORMAL AIRPORT

(Area Code 309) 2

Restaurants Near Airport:
Arnie's Restaurant On Site Phone: 662-4212

Lodging: Best Western (Jack & Benny's) (Trans) 663-1361; Best Western University Inn (Trans) 454-4070; Eastland Suites Lodge (Trans) 662-0000; Hampton Inn (Trans) 662-2800; Holiday Inn (Trans) 662-5311; Ramada Inn (Trans) 929-7602; Sheraton Inn (Trans) 452-8300.
Meeting Rooms: Best Western University 454-4070; Eastland Suites Lodge 662-0000; Hampton Inn 662-2800; Holiday Inn 662-5311; Ramada Inn 929-7602; Sheraton Inn 452-8300.
Transportation: Taxi Service: B & N Limousine Service 663-9470; Rental Cars available on airport, Avis, Budget, Hertz, National.
Information:
Bloomington-Normal Visitors Bureau, P.O. Box 1586, Bloomington, IL 61701, Phone: 829-1641.

Arnie's Restaurant:

Arnie's Restaurant is located in the main terminal building on Bloomington Airport, and features a vast array of entrees in a casual dining atmosphere. A full service menu includes breakfast, lunch and dinner selections. Breakfast omelets, burgers, all types of sandwiches, homemade cheese soup and steak dishes are their house specialties. Average prices run $3.25 to $7.95 for breakfast, $3.95 to $8.95 for lunch and $5.45 to $13.95 for dinner. The main dining room can seat 74 people and has ample seating along a large window allowing a great view of the aircraft parking area adjacent to the restaurant. In-flight catering is another service available as well. Reservations are suggested for evening hours except on Sundays. Their hours begin at 7 a.m. to 9 p.m. during the week, Friday and Saturday from 7 a.m. to 10 p.m. and Sunday from 8 a.m. to 9 p.m. Call 662-4212 for further information.

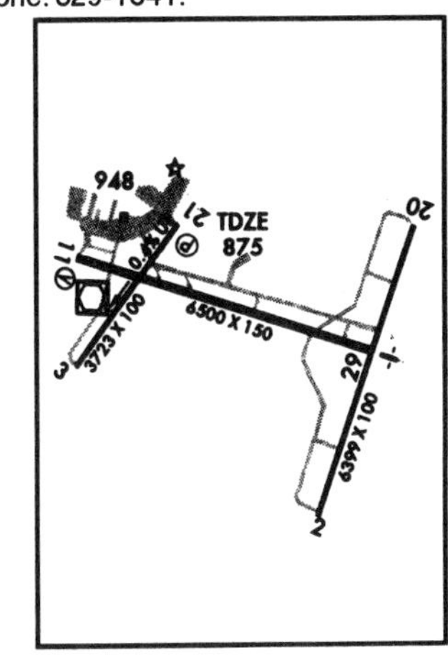

Attractions:

Prairie Aviation Museum, located east of Clark Aviation at the Bloomington-Normal Airport, will now be open to the public on a regular basis with no admission fee. Part of the Prairie Aviation Museum's mission is to "establish and operate a center to display aircraft artifacts and mementos" and to "preserve and display videotapes, films, and oral histories that preserve aviation heritage to present to the public in an educational manner. The museum is open Tuesday evenings 5:00 p.m. to 8:00 p.m., Saturday 11:00 a.m. to 4:00 p.m. and Sunday noon to 4:00 p.m. A-7A and T-38 aircraft display are located next to the building. Call 309-663-7632 for information.

Airport Information:

BLOOMINGTON - BLOOMINGTON NORMAL AIRPORT (BMI)
3 mi east of town N40-28.83 W88-55.43 Elev: 875 Fuel: 100LL, Jet-A
Rwy 11-29: H6500x150 (Conc-Grvd) Rwy 02-20: H6399x100 Rwy 03-21: H3723x100 (Asph)
Attended: 1200-0500Z Atis: 135.35 Unicom: 122.95 Tower: 124.6 Gnd Con: 121.65
FBO: Bloomington Avionics Phone: 663-2713
FBO: Clark Aviation, Inc. Phone: 663-2303

IL-CPS - CAHOKIA-ST LOUIS
ST LOUIS DOWNTOWN-PARKS

(Area Code 618) 3

Restaurants Near Airport:
Oliver's Restaurant On Site Phone: 337-8222

Oliver's Restaurant:

Oliver's Restaurant is located on the St Louis Downtown Parks Airport just southeast of East St. Louis, Illinois. This family style restaurant is open Monday through Thursday from 11 a.m. to 8 p.m., Friday and Saturday from 11 a.m. to 9 p.m. and Sunday from 11 a.m. to 8 p.m. They serve a large selection of entrees, with luncheon specials offered each day. House specialties are pasta dishes and chicken. Average prices run $4.75 for lunch and between $5.00 and $7.00 for most dinner selections. Their lounge is open from 12 p.m. to 10 p.m. According to the restaurant management, this restaurant is situated adjacent to one of the active runways on the airport, and provides a nice view of arriving and departing aircraft. Across the hall from the restaurant, is a small conference room able to accommodate small meetings with a seating capacity of about 10 people. In-flight catering can also be arranged. The phone number for Oliver's Restaurant is 337-8222.

Lodging: Embassy Suites 241-4200; Marriott 421-1776; Radisson 421-4000; Hyatt Regency (Trans) 241-6664.

Meeting Rooms: A small meeting room is available across the hall from Oliver's Restaurant in the terminal building. Call the airport management office for information 337-6060. Also the following contain meeting rooms: Embassy Suites 241-4200; Marriott 421-1776; Radisson 421-4000; Hyatt Regency 241-6664.

Transportation: Taxi service: Laclede Cab 314-652-4435; Metro East 874-0100; Also Rental Cars: Auffenberg Auto Rental 337-6886.

Information: Cahokia Area Chamber of Commerce, 905 Falling Springs Road, Cahokia, IL 62206, Phone: 332-1900.

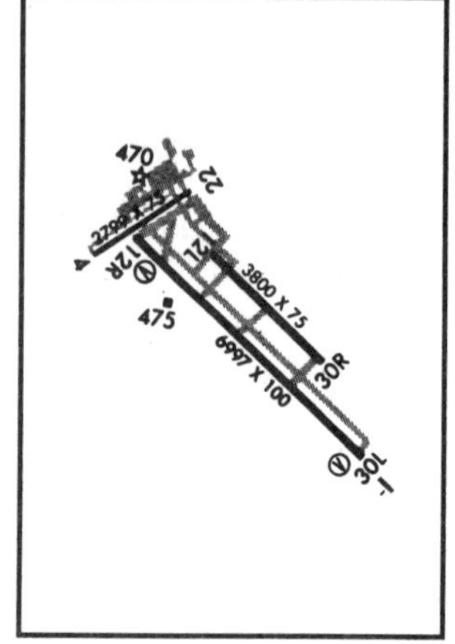

Airport Information:

CAHOKIA-ST LOUIS - ST LOUIS DOWNTOWN-PARKS (CPS)
1 mi east of town N38-34.24 W90-09.37 Elev: 413 Fuel: 100LL, Jet-A Rwy 12R-30L: H6997x100 (Asph) Rwy 12L-30R: H3800x75 (Conc) Rwy 04-22: H2799x75 (Asph) Attended: 1300-0400Z Atis: 127.85 Unicom: 122.95 App/Dep Con: 123.7 Clnc Del: 121.8 Downtown Tower: 120.9 Gnd Con: 121.8
FBO: Air Spirit Arcft Sales Phone: 332-1599
FBO: Helicopters, Inc. Phone: 337-2903
FBO: Avtec, Inc. Phone: 337-7800
FBO: Midcoast Aviation, Inc. Phone: 337-2100
FBO: Corporate Air Center Phone: 337-2903

IL-1H8 - CASEY
CASEY MUNICIPAL AIRPORT

(Area Code 217) 4

Richards Farm Restaurant:

Richards Farm Restaurant is located 2 miles from Casey Municipal Airport. There is a phone available at the airport so you can call the restaurant to pick you up. This casual restaurant is housed in an authentic 1930's hip-roof barn. It is open 11:00 a.m. to 8:00 p.m. Sunday through Thursday, and from 11:00 a.m. to 9:00 p.m. Friday and Saturday. Part of your dining experience at Richards Farm, is exploring the Gift and Craft area. Upon entering the restaurant, you will find a large assortment of unique, original gift items, such as wood designs, jewelry, art creations and clothing. After all that shopping, you are sure to work up an appetite. You can indulge in some of the restaurant specialties: one-pound pork chops (popular item), seafood, chicken, BBQ, steaks (cooked over hardwood coals), sandwiches and a soup and salad bar. A Sunday buffet is offered from 11:00 a.m. to 2:00 p.m. Why not top off the meal with delicious homemade cobblers, peanut butter and pecan pies and persimmon pudding (seasonal). Prices average around $5.00 for lunch and between $10.00 and $14.00 for dinner. Buffet and family-style meals are available for parties of 15 or more. The restaurant has private rooms that can accommodate groups of up to 300 people. They can also cater to private and corporate pilots on the go. For more information about Richards Farm Restaurant, call 932-5300.

Restaurants Near Airport:
Richards Farm Restaurant 2 mi Phone: 932-5300

Lodging: Casey Motel (1 mile) 932-4044

Meeting Rooms: None Reported

Transportation: Richards Farm Restaurant will provide transportation to and from the airport.

Information: Central Illinois Tourism Council, 631 E. Washington Street, Springfield, IL 62701, Phone: 525-7980

NO AIRPORT DIAGRAM AVAILABLE

Airport Information:

CASEY - CASEY MUNICIPAL AIRPORT (1H8)
1 mi northwest of town N39-18.15 W88-00.24 Elev: 654 Rwy 04-22: H4002x75 (Asph) Rwy 18-36: 1965x100 (Turf) Attended: 1400-dusk CTAF/Unicom: 122.8 Hulman App/Dep Con: 125.45
FBO: Sky's The Limit Phone: 932-2078

IL-CMI - CHAMPAIGN (URBANA) UNIVERSITY OF ILLINOIS-WILLARD

(Area Code 217) 5

Willard's Restaurant & Lounge:

Willard's Restaurant & Lounge is located in the terminal building on the Champaign/University of Illinois-Willard Airport, in Savoy, IL. This is a family style restaurant offering a full service menu. Open seven days a week from 5 a.m. to 10 p.m. except on Saturday when they close at 9:00 p.m. They serve breakfast, lunch and dinner and offer daily specials. Aircraft parking is available directly outside of the restaurant. For additional information call 352-0220.

Restaurants Near Airport:
Willard's Restaurant & Lounge On Site Phone: 352-0220

Lodging: Chancellor Hotel (Trans) 352-7891; Holiday Inn (Trans) 359-1601; Howard Johnson Lodge (Trans) 367-8331; Jumers Castle Lodge (Trans) 384-8800; University Inn (Trans) 384-2100.

Meeting Rooms: Chancellor Hotel 352-7891; Holiday Inn 359-1601; Howard Johnson Lodge 367-8331; Jumers Castle Lodge 384-8800; University Inn 384-2100.

Transportation: Taxi Service: Corky's Limo 352-3121; Rental Cars: Avis 359-5441; Budget 398-4490; Hertz 359-5413; National 359-5259.

Information: Convention & Visitors Bureau, 40 East University Avenue, P.O Box Box 1607, Champaign, IL 61820-1607, Phone: 351-4133 or 800-369-6151 in IL.

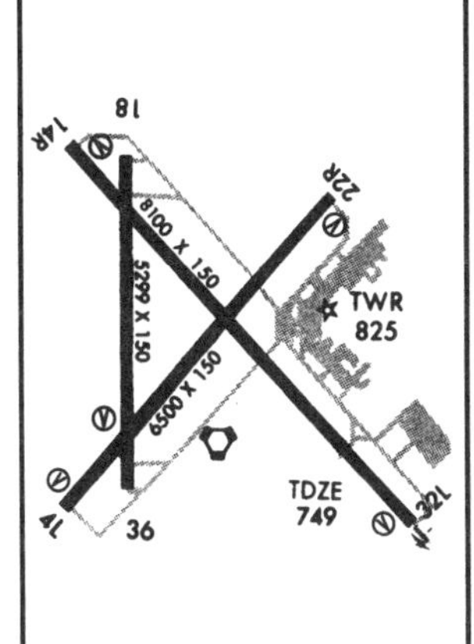

Airport Information:

CHAMPAIGN (URBANA) - UNIVERSITY OF ILLINOIS-WILLARD (CMI)
5 mi southwest of town N40-02.38 W88-16.68 Elev: 754 Fuel: 100LL, Jet-A1+
Rwy 14R-32L: H8100x150 (Conc-Grvd) Rwy 04L-22R: H6500x150 (Conc-Grvd)
Rwy 18-36: H5299x150 (Conc) Attended: continuous Atis: 124.85 Unicom: 122.95
Champaign App/Dep Con: 132.85, 121.35 Tower: 120.4 Gnd Con: 121.8 Clnc Del: 128.75
FBO: Flightstar Phone: 351-7700

IL-MDW - CHICAGO
CHICAGO MIDWAY

(Area Code 312) 6, 7

Midway Restaurant:

The Midway Restaurant is located within walking distance from Midway Airport. This restaurant offers a nice atmosphere with casual family dining. They serve daily specials in addition to many entrees on their menu, which includes steaks, seafood and Italian dishes. The restaurant is open during the week between 6:30 a.m. and 12 a.m. and on weekends between 6:30 a.m. and 1 a.m., and is reported to be situated only 3 blocks south of the airport, at 4801 west 63rd St. Aircraft parking is available at several fixed based operators on the field with courtesy transportation provided by most operators. For restaurant information call 767-1896.

Shipwreck Kelly's & Cafe Volare:

The Shipwreck Kelly's & Cafe Volare, are two restaurants that are situated in the main terminal building at Chicago Midway Airport in Chicago, Illinois. Shipwreck Kelley's has a nautical decor, and prepares a variety of house specialties including hamburgers, broasted chicken and pasta selections, Caesar salads, along with their 16 ounce T-bone steaks. Light fare is also available consisting of grilled food, hamburgers, and a variety of sandwiches etc. This family restaurant is open 7 day a week between 10:30 a.m. and 8:30 p.m. Hours may vary throughout the year. Call to verify hours. Cafe Volare also situated in the terminal building, is open 24 hours a day and serves as a delicatessen offering sandwiches, pastries and continental fare. Both restaurants are operated by the same owner. When flying into Midway Airport, you will need to arrange ground transportation which is available from any one of several fixed base operators located on the airport. For Information you can call the restaurant management at 582-4450.

Attractions:

The City of Chicago contains an endless number of activities and attractions as well as points of interest throughout the region. Museum of Science & Industry and Crown Space Center (9 miles east of airport) 684-1414; Adler Planetarium 322-0300, John G. Shedd Aquarium 939-2438, and Field Museum of Natural History 922-9410 (Est. 10 miles northeast of Midway Airport). Contact the Chicago Tourism Council (See "Information" listed above) for hundreds of additional vacation suggestions available or call 280-5740.

Restaurants Near Airport:

Cafe Volare	On Site	Phone: 582-4450
Midway Restaurant	3 Blks	Phone: 767-1896
Shipwreck Kelly's	On Site	Phone: 582-4450
Top Flight Restaurant	1/4-1/2mi	Phone: 581-1770

Lodging: Hilton-Oak Lawn (Trans) 425-7800; Holiday Inn-Oak Lawn (Trans) 425-7900; Midway Airport Inn (Trans) 581-0500; Quality Inn-Midway (Trans) 423-1100.

Meeting Rooms: Hilton-Oak Lawn 425-7800; Holiday Inn-Oak Lawn 425-7900; Midway Airport Inn 581-0500; Quality Inn-Midway 423-1100. Chicago Convention Facilities: McCormick Place East 23rd Street & South Lake Shore Drive, Phone: 791-7000; Rosemont Horizon 6920 Mannhime Road, Rosemont (Adj O'Hare Airport 708-635-6600.

Transportation: Taxi Service: Checker & Yellow Cabs 829-4222; Rental Cars: Avis 471-3490; Budget 686-6769; Dollar 471-3450; Hertz 372-7600; National 471-3450.

Information: Chicago Office of Tourism, Chicago Cultural Center, 78 E Washington Street, Chicago 60602, Phone: 744-2400, or 800-487-2446. Chicago Tourism Council, Historic Water Tower in-the-Park, 806 North Michigan Avenue, Chicago, IL 60611, Phone: 280-5740.

Airport Information:

CHICAGO - CHICAGO MIDWAY AIRPORT (MDW)
9 mi southwest of town N41-47.16 W87-45.15 Elev: 620 Fuel: 100LL, Jet-A1+
Rwy 13C-31C: H6522x150 (Con-Asph-Grvd) Rwy 04R-22L: H6446x150 (Conc-Asph-Grvd)
Rwy 04L-22R: H5509x150 (Asph) Rwy 13L-31R: H5142x150 (Asph) Rwy 13R-31L: H3859x60 (Conc) Attended: continuously Atis: 132.75 Unicom: 122.95
Chicago App/Dep Con: 118.4, 126.05 Midway Tower: 118.7 (135.2 for Helicopter operations) Gnd Con: 121.7 Clnc Del: 121.85 Pre Taxi Clnc: 121.85
FBO: Aero Services International, Inc. Phone: 582-5333
FBO: Million Air Midway Phone: 284-2867
FBO: Signature Flight Support Phone: 767-4400

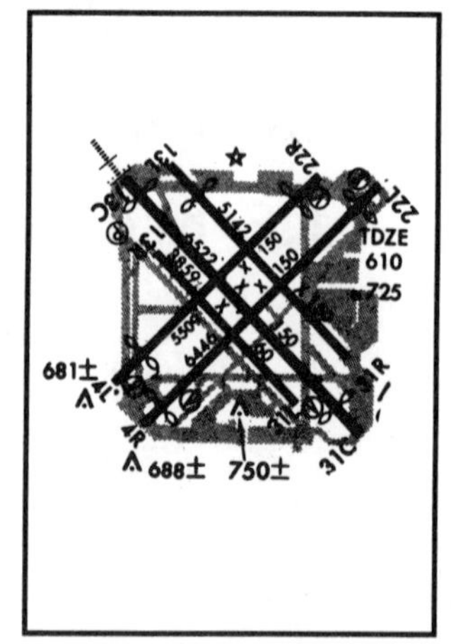

IL-ORD - CHICAGO

CHICAGO - O'HARE INTL.

(Area Code 312)

8, 9

Hilton Hotel- O'Hare Intl. Airport:

The Gas Light Restaurant & Lounge is situated within the Hilton Hotel, located across the street from the main terminal building at the O'Hare International Airport. This restaurant has a Victorian decor, and is decorated in colors of burgundy, gray and forest green. It is open between 11 a.m. and 1 a.m. and is located at the end of the Hilton West Hotel lobby. A lounge is positioned in the center of the restaurant, which supports live entertainment and piano music beginning at 5 p.m. Specialty dishes prepared by the chefs of the Gas Light include a variety of steaks and seafood selections, including strip steak, filet, T-bone, veal, pork chops, boneless breast of chicken, lobster tail, swordfish as well as rack of lamb. The restaurant offers an elegant decor with an exclusive club type ambiance. Proper attire is required. For information call 686-8000 ext. 2427.

Andiamo's Restaurant also located in the Hilton O'Hare, is on the opposite side of the hotel, and offers a more casual decor, and specializes in American and Italian cuisine. These include a variety of past dinners as well as shrimp dinners and all types of sandwiches and hamburger plates. The Hilton O'Hare is within walking distance from the main terminal building. However, for corporate aircraft arriving at Butler Aviation, a courtesy car will have to be arranged. The Hilton Hotel offers excellent accommodations for business or vacation travelers with 858 available rooms. If arranging a conference with clients, hotel staff can provide your party with everything you need. There are 50 separate meeting rooms, 2 main ball rooms and 11 banquet rooms available to serve your needs. For more information about the hotel accommodations, meeting or conference arrangements or restaurant information, call the Hilton O'Hare at 686-8000.

Skybird Meeting Center:

The Skybird Meeting Center is located on the upper level of the circular shaped restaurant building between terminal's 2 & 3 at O'Hare International Airport. This establishment arranges catering for business meeting etc. Arrangement are handled by their catering department. The Skybird dining area has a modern decor, and is constructed with 12 foot high tinted glass panels and mirrors allowing a very nice view of the airport. The seating capacity for this restaurant is between 100 and 150 persons. In addition, there are 5 private VIP meeting rooms situated on the same level. In addition, there are as many as 78 food service facilities and lounges located in the terminal building at O'Hare Airport and are operated through Host International. For general information regarding the food concessions in the terminal building call Host International corporate offices at 686-6123. For more information about the Skybird Meeting Center facility, or if you are interested in reserving a VIP meeting room call 686-6101.

Restaurants Near Airport:

Andiamo-Hilton	Adj Terml.	Phone: 686-8000
Gas Light-Hilton	Adj Terml.	Phone: 686-8000 ext. 2427
Host Intl. Rest.	Terml. Bldg	Phone: 686-6100
Skybird Meeting	Terml. Bldg	Phone: 686-6101

Lodging: Best Western O'Hare (Trans) 296-4471; Best Western O'Hare Inn (Trans) 956-1700; Embassy Suites (Trans) 699-6300; Hilton-O'Hare (Trans, On Airport adj. terminal bldg.) 686-8000; Holiday Inn-DesPlaines (Trans) 296-8866; Holiday Inn-O'Hare (Trans) 671-6350; Howard Johnson Hotel-O'Hare (Trans) 671-6000; Howard Johnson Lodge (Trans) 693-2323; Hyatt Regency-O'Hare (Trans) 696-1234; Marriott-O'Hare (Trans) 693-4444; O'Hare Intl. Hotel (Trans) 678-4800; Plaza Hotel O'Hare (Trans) 693-5800; Radisson Suite Hotel-O'Hare (Trans) 678-4000; Ramada Inn (Trans) 827-5131; Residence Inn By Marriott (Trans) 678-2210; Sheraton Inn-O'Hare (Trans) 297-1234; Sofitel Hotel Chicago (Trans) 678-4488; Travelodge-O'Hare (Trans) 296-5541; Westin (Trans) 698-6000; Winfield Inn-O'Hare (Trans) 678-0670.

Meeting Rooms: There are 5 VIP meeting rooms located in the terminal building on the same level as the Seven Continents Restaurant, situated in the "Round Restaurant Building" between terminal 2 & 3. The Hilton-O'Hare, is right across the street from the O'Hare main terminal building, includes 50 club meeting rooms, 2 ball rooms and 11 banquet rooms on their premises, 686-8000. Also all lodging facilities listed above have reported that they have accommodations for meetings and or conferences. Chicago Convention Facilities: McCormick Place East 23rd Street & South Lake Shore Drive, Phone: 791-7000; Rosemont Horizon 6920 Mannhime Road, Rosemont (Adj O'Hare Airport 708-635-6600.

Transportation: Taxi Service: Their are numerous independent cab companies available on the airport. Also Rental Cars: Avis, Budget, Hertz, and National available at airport.

Information: O'Hare telephone information service is available by calling 686-2200. Also for tourism information contact: Chicago Office of Tourism, 78 E Washington St., Chicago, IL 60602, Phone: 312-744-2400. For information about points of interest or events held within the Suburban communities surrounding the city of Chicago, call 800-851-0014.

Attractions:

There are literally hundreds of attractions and points of interest located within the city of Chicago as well as its surrounding suburbs. A few of the extraordinary attractions include the famous ***Adler Planetarium*** 322-0300; ***John G. Shedd Aquarium*** 939-2438; ***Field Museum of Natural History*** 922-9410; ***Museum of Science and Industry*** 684-1414; and ***McCormick Place Convention Complex*** containing the Nations largest exposition center 791-7000. For information about other attractions within the Chicago land Area, contact the Chicago Office of Tourism at 312-744-2400 or Chicago Suburban Office of Tourism at 800-851-0014. (See "Information" listed above).

Airport Information:

CHICAGO - CHICAGO O'HARE INTERNATIONAL AIRPORT (ORD)

14 mi northwest of town N41-58.76 W87-54.27 Elev: 668 Fuel: 100LL, Jet-A1
Rwy 14R-32L: H13000x200 (Asph-Conc Grvd) Rwy 09R-27L: H10141x150 (Asph-Conc-Grvd)
Rwy 14L-32R: H10003x150 (Asph-Grvd) Rwy 04R-22L: H8071x150 (Conc-Grvd)
Rwy 09L-27R: H7967x150 (Asph-Conc) Rwy 04L-22R: H7500x150 (Asph-Grvd)
Rwy 18-36: H5341x150 (Asph) Attended: continuously Atis 135.4 Unicom: 122.95
Chicago App Con: 119.0, 125.7, 121.15, 124.35, 128.45 O'hare Tower: 126.9 (N) 120.75 (S)
Gnd Con: 121.75 (Outbound) 121.9 (Inbound) Clnc Del: 121.6, 119.25 Pre-Taxi Clnc: 121.6, 119.25 Gnd Metering: 121.675 Chicago Dep Con: 125.0, 125.4, 127.4
Notes: High Density Airport, prior reservations required, see "Regulatory Notices".

Airport Managers Office Phone: 686-2200

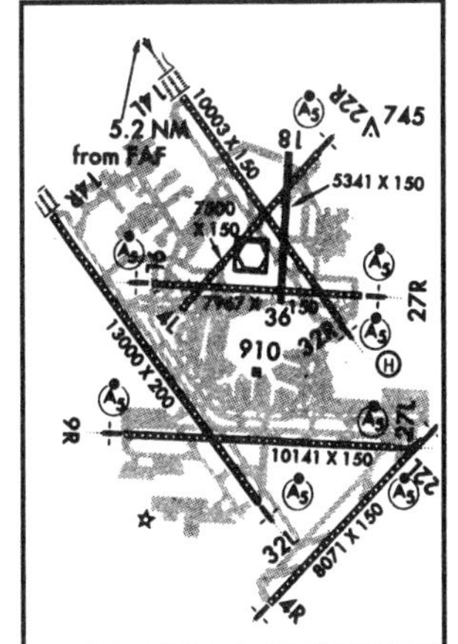

IL-IGQ - CHICAGO LANSING MUNICIPAL

10

Shannon's Landing:

Shannon's Landing Restaurant is an Irish Pub located on Lansing Municipal Airport in Lansing, Illinois. This restaurant serves hot sandwiches, soups, chili, burgers, Reubens, salads, chicken, shrimp, lake perch and steaks. They even make their own potato chips and French fries. Average prices for sandwiches run $4.00 to $5.00. The restaurant is located on the second floor of the administration building, and has seating accommodations for about 150 people. The restaurant serves meals 7 days a week from 11 a.m. until 11 p.m. Their bar is open until 2 a.m. Sunday through Thursday and Friday & Saturday until 3 a.m. Groups up to 25 are welcome, and can make arrangements for parties or club fly-ins. In-flight catering is another service performed with advanced notice appreciated. Aircraft parking is available adjacent to the restaurant. A beautiful airport view can be enjoyed from their second floor location. During the evening they also feature a variety of live bands and entertainment for their guests from Tuesday through Saturday evenings beginning at 9 p.m. For more information about Shannon's Landing Restaurant call 895-6919.

(Area Code 708)

Restaurants Near Airport:
Shannon's Landing On Site Phone: 895-6919

Lodging: Budgetel Inn (6 miles) 596-8700; Fairfield Inn 474-6900; Holiday Inn (5 miles) 474-6300; Lan's Coachman Inn (5 miles) 895-7810.

Meeting Rooms: None Reported

Transportation: Taxi service available; Also Rental Cars: Dollar Rent-A-Car, is reported to have a courtesy phone at the airport.

Information: Chicago Office of Tourism, 78 E Washington St., Chicago, IL 60602, Phone: 312-744-2400. For information about points of interest events held within the Suburban communities surrounding the city of Chicago call 800-851-0014.

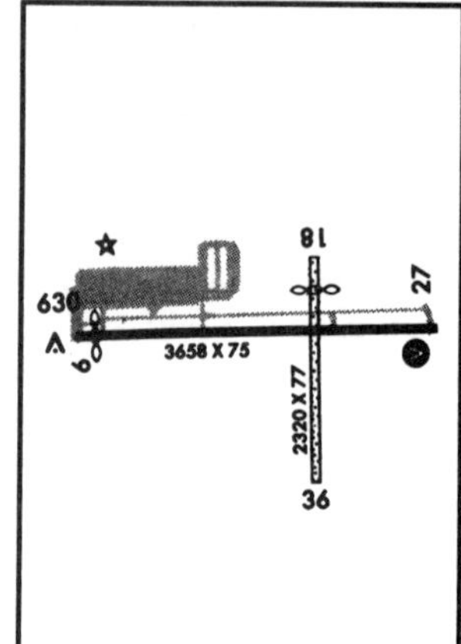

Airport Information:

CHICAGO/LANSING - LANSING MUNICIPAL AIRPORT (IGQ)
21 mi south of town (Chicago) N41-32.39 W87-31.93 Elev: 616 Fuel: 80, 100LL, Jet-A
Rwy 09-27: H3658x75 (Asph) Rwy 18-36: 2320x77 (Turf) Attended: 1300-0100Z
Unicom: 122.7 Notes: CAUTION Rwy 09 pavement end: 7' ditch approximately 100' east.
FBO: AMCORP Flight Center Phone: 895-2666 or 800-845-5826
FBO: Associated Air Activities Phone: 474-6073

A Little Extra Planning Can Make Each One Of Your Excursions More Rewarding

"Just Call Ahead"

Even though we at Aerodine strive to provide the latest information possible at the time of printing, we suggest you take a little time and call ahead to verify that the facility you intend to visit still provides the same services as published. Your comments regarding any changes in these services or about new establishments you have found, are greatly appreciated. With your help, we can include them in our next updated edition.

Aerodine Magazine
P.O. Box 247, Palatine, IL 60078
Phone: 847-358-4355

IL-CGX - CHICAGO
MERRILL C. MEIGS

(Area Code 312) 11

The Berghoff Restaurant:

The Berghoff Restaurant is located 2 miles from Merrill C. Meigs Airport. This fine dining cafe is open Monday through Thursday from 11:00 a.m. to 9:30 p.m., and Friday and Saturday from 11:00 a.m. to 10:00 p.m. It is closed on Sundays and holidays. The decor is set in old-world, turn-of-the-century, with oak paneling and stained glass windows. Some of the specialized entrees include: Sauerbraten, Chicken Dijon, Seafood Brochette, steaks, a variety of salads and vegetarian dishes. Also, with a bakery on the premesis, the sweet tooth won't be disappointed. Choose from items such as the traditional Apple Strudel or the elegant White Chocolate Mousse. Visit the 80-year-old stand-up bar and experience Berghoff's own brewed beers, along with freshly carved turkey, corned beef, roast beef and fish sandwiches. Average prices range from $8.50 for lunch to $14.00 for dinner. Banquet facilities are available. Catering is available for any event, including box lunches and sit-down lunches and dinners for 15 to 5,000 people. For more information about The Berghoff Restaurant, call 427-3170.

Restaurants Near Airport:

Benihana of Tokyo	3-1/2 mi	Phone: 664-9643
Berghoff Restaurant	2 mi	Phone: 427-3170
Gino's East Pizzeria	3-1/2 mi	Phone: 943-1124
Lawry's Prime Rib	3 mi	Phone: 787-5000
Ninety-Fifth	3 1/4 mi	Phone: 787-9596

Lodging: Best Western Grant Park (2 miles) 922-2900; The Blackstone Hotel (2-3/4 miles) 427-4300; Hilton Hotel (1-1/2 miles) 922-4400
Meeting Rooms: Hilton Hotel 922-4400
Transportation: Taxi Service: Yellow Cab 829-4222; Rental Cars: Avis 782-8701
Information: Chicago Office of Tourism, Chicago Cultural Center, 78 E. Washington Street, Chicago, IL 60602, Phone: 744-2400 or 800-487-2446

Attractions:

Field Museum of Natural History 922-9410; John G. Shedd Aquarium 939-2438; Adler Planetarium 322-0300 (all 1 mi); Soldier Field (2 mi) 791-7000; Museum of Science and Industry (7 mi) 684-1414

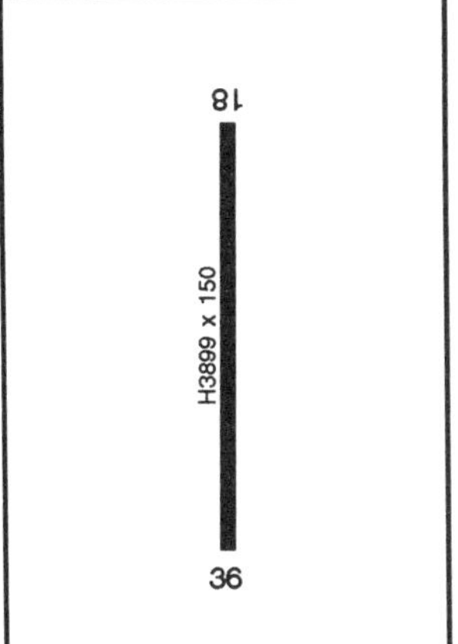

Airport Information:

CHICAGO - MERRILL C. MEIGS (CGX)
2 mi south of town N41-51.53 W87-36.48 Elev: 593 Fuel: 100LL, Jet-A Rwy 18-36: H3899x150 (Asph-Grvd) Attended: 1200-0400Z CTAF: 121.3 ATIS: 127.35 (1200-0400Z) Unicom: 122.95 Chicago App/Dep Con: 118.4 126.05 Meigs Tower: 121.3 (1200-0400Z) Gnd Con: 121.8 Notes: Airport is CLOSED 0400-1200Z daily, and when there are 90 deg. cross winds. CAUTION: Migratory birds, especially gulls in area. Parking fees are $9.00 for singles and $12.00-$15.00 for twins.
FBO: Signature FSO Phone: 922-5454

Museum of Science and Industry

Chicago, IL (IL-MDW)

Photo by: Don Jiskra/ Museum of Science and Industry, Chicago

This United Airlines 727 airplane is the centerpiece of the "Take Flight" exhibit at the Museum of Science and Industry in Chicago, Illinois.

The Museum of Science and Industry is located at 57th Street and Lake Shore Drive in Chicago, Illinois. It offers plenty of fascinating exhibits, as well as exciting demonstrations and visitor activities.

The Museum of Science and Industry makes it easy to get involved with various activities and demonstrations. Science is in full swing up on the balcony of the museum. Visit Grainger Hall and see fascinating science demonstrations which alternate every half hour. Experience the power of air and air pressure-and see how air "pops" up all over, or watch what happens when molecules in everyday objects speed up or slow down. Walk through a 16-foot replica of "The Heart" and see how this vital organ really works! Explore virtual reality and computerized imaging at the"Imaging: The Tools of Science" exhibit.

Visit the "Transportation Zone" and see the spectacular "Take Flight" exhibit. Climb aboard a 727 aircraft and fasten your seat belts as the aircraft makes its way from San Francisco to Chicago in just seven minutes! Or, buckle yourself into an F-14 flight simulator in the "Navy: Technology at Sea" exhibit and prepare for a take-off from an aircraft carrier. Travel through the "Coal Mine" and see what it's like to work hundreds of feet below the surface. Visit the "U-505 Submarine" exhibit and explore the depths of a real German submarine captured in World War II. Take a trip through early twentieth century and walk along "Yesterday's Main Street." Witness nature's miracles as baby chicks peck their way out of their shells. Also, stop by "Colleen Moore's Fairy Castle" and delight yourself with a dazzling collection of precious miniatures.

Experience outer space exploration at the Henry Crown Space Center. Tour the Space Shuttle or the Apollo 8 spacecraft. Afterward, treat yourself to an entertaining film at the Space Center's Omnimax Theater. The Omnimax lets you explore the many wonders of the world without ever leaving your seat. Its five-story screen with a super-sharp picture and six-channel digital sound seems to pull you into the movie. The theater is open 7 days a week, with evening shows on Friday and Saturday.

Take a break from the exhibits and do a little exploring in the museum's three shops. Visit the Museum Shop, located on the main floor, which features educational gifts, souvenirs and "Take Flight" keepsakes. The Holiday Shop, also located on the main floor, offers gifts from all around the world. The Galaxy Shop, located in the Henry Crown Space Center, features space-related gifts, apparel and real astronaut food.

If all that exploring has worked up an appetite, choose from a variety of restaurants. Pizza Hut and Finnigan's Ice Cream Parlor are both located in "Yesterday's Main Street" on the main floor. On the ground floor, the Century Room offers a choice of tasty sandwiches, salads and desserts. Cafe Spectrum features breakfast sandwiches, traditional burgers, hot dogs and fries. The Miner's Stop serves a variety of vending machine items, including sodas, snacks and ice cream bars. Seating is provided for visitors with bag lunches. The Fuel Station (also located on the ground floor), will reserve meals and lunchroom space for large groups. Call 684-1414, Ext. 2290 for more information. The Astro Cafe, located in the Henry Crown Space Center, serves sandwiches, fries, frosties and soft drinks.

The Museum of Science and Industry is open year-round, except for Christmas Day. Between Labor Day and Memorial Day, hours are from 9:30 a.m. to 4:00 p.m., Monday through Friday and to 5:30 p.m. Saturday, Sunday and holidays. During the summer, hours are from 9:30 a.m. to 5:30 p.m., Saturday through Thursday and to 7:00 p.m., Friday.

Merrill C. Meigs Airport is located about 7 miles north of the museum. Meigs offers taxi and rental car services. Also, Chicago Midway Airport is located about 9 miles west of the museum. The FBO, Monarch Air Service, Inc., will loan out a courtesy car for the day. Taxi and rental car services are also available.

For more information about exhibits and admission fees at the Museum of Science of Industry, call 800-GO-TO-MSI (800-468-6674) or 773-684-1414. (Information submitted by the Museum of Science and Industry, Chicago.)

Photo by: Museum of Science and Industry, Chicago

The "Earth Trek" exhibit explores the history of petroleum.

IL-ARR - CHICAGO/AURORA
AURORA MUNICIPAL

(Area Code 708) 12

Fishermen's Inn:

The Fishermen's Inn is located approx 10 miles from the Aurora Municipal Airport. This fine dining establishment is unique in many respects. The restaurant is a converted dairy barn originally built in 1886 on 53 acres of land. The rustic appearance of this establishment offers a elegant atmosphere. The restaurant contains nautical relics and vintage farm implements. There is even a gift shop and bakery on the premises. Their menu specializes in fresh trout. In fact, it's probably the freshest trout you have ever eaten. Located just below the hill from the restaurant are trout ponds interconnected with channels and raceways for the trout to make their way upstream from one cold spring-fed lake to the next. Guests are welcome to stroll along the shaded paths overlooking these ponds. Specialties of the house include fresh Rainbow Trout, Chicken A La Kiev, Buttermilk Battered Fried Chicken, Saute Chicken Marinara, Roast Young Duckling Half and Chicken Pecan Normande, Prime Rib of Beef, NY Strip Steak, Sauteed Calf Liver, Filet Mignon, BBQ Back Ribs, Delmonico Steak, Lamb Chops, New England Styled Scrod, Broiled Orange Roughy, Shrimp De Jonghe, Scallops, Shrimp, Grilled Bar B Qued Salmon, and Broiled Lobster Tail. The Fishermen's Inn can be reached with a drive in the country, by taking Route 30 east from the Aurora Municipal airport to Route 47 north until you reach main street in the town of Elburn. Although this restaurant does not furnish transportation, its well worth the effort to obtain transportation from one of the FBO's at the airport. Restaurant hours are Tuesday through Thursday from 5:00 p.m. to 9:00 p.m., Friday and Saturdays from 5:00 p.m. to 10:00 p.m. and Sundays from 1:00 p.m. to 7:00 p.m. Holiday hours may very. Average dinner prices run $20.00. Banquet accommodations are easily arranged in either of 5 rooms: The Captains Table seating 8-12 persons; The Galleon Room accommodating 30 people; The Cove Room overlooking the countryside with seating for 25 to 70 people and the Main Deck their largest, most scenic banquet room able to serve 50 to 160 guests. Banquet arrangement can be made by calling 365-9697. Reservations for dining or other requests can be made by calling their main phone number at 365-6265.

Restaurants Near Airport:

Fishermen's Inn	10 mi NE	Phone: 365-6265
Prestbury Country	2 mi	Phone: N/A

Lodging: Best Western Fox Valley 7mi 851-2000; Howard Johnson Hotel 7 mi 892-6481; Super 8 Hotel 7 mi 896-0801.

Meeting Rooms: Best Western Fox Valley 7mi 851-2000; Banquet rooms are available at the Fishermen's Inn 365-6265.

Transportation: Rental Cars: Independent 466-7500; National 466-4866; Taxi: Yellow 897-4400; Also Courtesy cars from airport are available.

Information: Aurora Area Convention & Tourism Council, P.O. Box 907, Aurora, IL 60506, Phone: 897-5581.

Attractions:

Hollywood Riverboat Casino is reported located only 3 miles from the Aurora Municipal Airport. Also the Fermilab Particle Accelerator is situated about 10 to 12 miles to the northeast of the airport. Free tours are available by calling 840-3351.

Airport Information:

CHICAGO/AURORA - AURORA MUNICIPAL (ARR)

38 mi west of Chicago N41-46.26 W88-28.37 Elev: 706 Fuel: 100, Jet-A1 Rwy 09-27: H6501x100 (Asph) Rwy 18-36: H3199x75 (Asph) Attended: continuously CTAF: 120.6 Atis: 125.85 Unicom: 123.5 1229.95 Clnc Del: 121.7 Tower: 120.6 Gnd Con: 121.7

FBO: Lumanair Aviation Services: Phone: 466-4866, 800-522-8778
FBO: V.I.P Air Charter: Phone: 466-4800, 800-437-0130
FBO: Viking Express, Inc. Phone: 466-7500

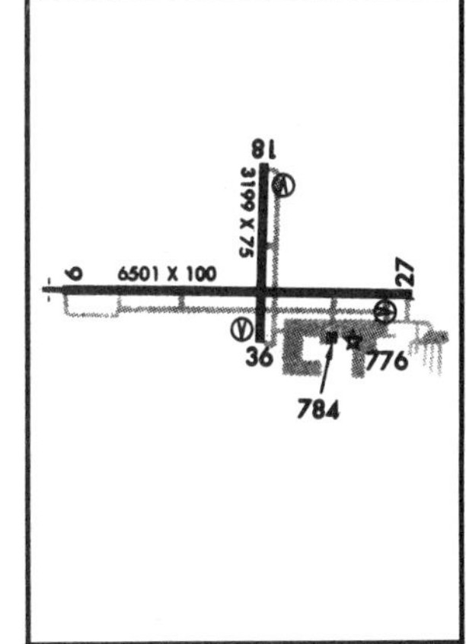

IL-LOT - CHICAGO/ROMEOVILLE LEWIS UNIVERSITY

(Area Code 815)

13, 14, 15, 16

Baci Restaurant:

The Baci Restaurant is a family-style establishment that is located in Plainfield, IL directly west from the Lewis University Airport about 5-1/2 miles along Lockport Road, which borders the northern edge of the airport. You will cross Interstate 55 then continue into town to the restaurant (407 Lockport Street). This restaurant is open 7 days a week, Monday 4 p.m. to 9 p.m.; Tuesday through Thursday 11 a.m. to 9 p.m.; Friday 11 a.m. to 11 p.m.; and Saturday and Sunday 4 p.m. to 9 p.m. Entree specialties include seafood, veal dishes, steaks, ribs and pizzas. Specialties of the house are northern central and southern Italian cuisine. The restaurant is situated in a church. The dining room contains comfortable spacious enclosed booths that offer private dining. The main dining room can seat about 150 people. A party room can be reserved for larger groups. Transportation by courtesy car can be obtained with prior arrangements through the Joliet Port District Office by calling 838-9497. For more information about the Baci Restaurant call 436-3588.

Empress Casino Joliet:

Empress Casino - Joliet will provide your party with free courtesy transportation to and from either Joliet Park District airport, only 5 or 6 miles west of their facility, or Lewis University Airport about 8 miles north of the casino. Get carried away to a place that's far from the everyday, to a world of total entertainment. From the golden grandeur that greets you as you approach the entrance, to the spectacle of sights and sounds in the casino itself. A fantasy, complete with towering walls of hieroglyphics and authentic Egyptian statuary. With off-track betting, 3 different restaurants for your dining pleasure, private party and meeting facilities, a convenient on-site, 102 room hotel, a gift shop and a staff whose highest priority is your comfort and enjoyment. For information call the Casino at 744-9400.

Restaurants Near Airport:

Baci Restaurant	2-1/2 mi.	Phone: 436-3588
Empress Casino	8 mi S. Trans	Phone: 744-9400
Public Landing	2-1/2 mi.	Phone: 838-6500
Tallgrass	N/A	Phone: 838-5566
White Fence Farm	5-1/2 mi.	Phone: 838-1500

Lodging: Comfort Inn 436-5141; Empress Casino - Joliet (trans) 744-9400; Fairfield Inn 800-228-2800.
Meeting Rooms: White Fence Farm Restaurant 838-1500; Empress Casino - Joliet (trans) 744-9400
Transportation: Courtesy cars reported available with prior reservations by calling the Joliet Port District at 838-9497; Also: Rental cars through: Terry's Lincoln Mercury 349-3474.
Information: Lockport Chamber of Commerce, 132 East 9th, Lockport, IL 60441, Phone: 838-3357.

Attractions:

Lewis University Airport (LOT) is the closest airport to the nearby communities of Bolingbrook, Joliet, Oakbrook, Naperville, Orland Park, Argonne National Laboratory, Cog Hill Golf Course which is the home of the Western Open, as well as Illinois top riverboat gaming city and Rialto Theater. **Illinois and Michigan Canal Museum and Pioneer Settlement** situated adjacent to Public Landing Restaurant is open Mid April to October., winter 1 to 4 p.m. (Free admission) This unique settlement offers guided tours by costumed docents. Log cabins, schoolhouse, railroad station, workshop, blacksmith shops and a mid-19th century farmhouse are on display. For information call or write: Illinois and Michigan Canal Museum, Canal Commissioner's Office, 803 South State Street, Lockport, IL 60441 or call Phone: 838-5080. Empress River Casino 345-6789; **Rialto Square Theatre** built in 1926 is a performing arts center famous for its performances conducted in the elaborate and beautiful auditorium featuring bas-reliefs sculpted by the famous artist Eugene Romeo. For information contact the ticket office at 726-6600.

Public Landing Restaurant:

During our conversation with the airport manager, we learned that this restaurant offers its guests a truly unique dining experience. The Public Landing Restaurant is located right on the bank of the Illinois and Michigan Canal offering guests a view of the river and boating activity. This restaurant is classified as an up-scale family and fine dining establishment. The building housing the restaurant is an historic landmark dating back over 150 years. It is one of the earliest structures in the area exhibiting lime stone walls and large hand-hewn wooden beams. Some of the walls in the restaurant contain the original plaster and decorated with beautiful antique quilts. The restaurant's two top floors contain an art gallery and canal museum. Their menu selections include filet of beef, as their specialty, along with other main course items like white fish and salmon together in parchment paper, roast leg of lamb, and some of the most delicious desserts and homemade ice cream. Restaurant hours are Tuesday through Friday 11:30 a.m. to 2 p.m. for lunch; Tuesday through Thursday 5 p.m. to 9 p.m. for dinner; Friday and Saturday 5 p.m. to 10 p.m.; and Sunday 4 p.m. to 8 p.m. (Closed on Monday.) One additional attraction located next to the restaurant is the "Pioneer Village" - a restored canal village that exhibits a general store, train station and blacksmith shop. Transportation from the Lewis University Airport can be arranged through the airport manager's office. If prior arrangements are made, a courtesy car for limited use will be made available. Call the Joliet Regional Port Office at 838-9497. To reach the Public Landing Restaurant from the airport, go south on Route 53 (Route 53 and 7 run together) until Route 7 turns east over the bridge into town. Take Route 7 east over the bridge to State Street and turn left (north). The restaurant is within one block on the left side of the street. You should have no trouble finding it. If you enjoy yourself at the Public Landing Restaurant, you will be happy to know the they also have a sister restaurant called the Tallgrass Restaurant located nearby. For more information about either establishment call the Public Landing Restaurant at 838-6500.

White Fence Farm:

This establishment combines a country style restaurant, museum and antique cars on display. Hours are Tuesday through Saturday 5 p.m. to 8:30 p.m., Sunday 12 noon to 7:30 p.m. Closed Monday. During the winter months of January and February they are closed. White Fence Farm offers a variety of menu selections like shrimp, steak and seafood, but their delicious chicken dishes are what have made them famous over the years and remain their specialty today. Menu prices average $8.95 to $10.95 for most main course meals and up to $14.95 for their largest steaks. Accommodations for groups can easily be arranged. Seating capacity for the restaurant is about 1,000 people including group accommodations. Reservations for groups greater than 12 are recommended. A private dining room can also be reserved for parties of 35 or more. During our conversation with the airport manager we learned that if prior arrangements are made, a courtesy car can be made available for short term use. Call the Joliet Regional Port Office at 838-9497. From the Lewis University Airport take State Route 53 north which is also named Joliet Road. When reaching the intersection where Route 53 splits off to the left towards Bolingbrook at the stop light, do not turn left, but continue straight on Joliet Road for about 1 mile. The restaurant will be on your left side. For information call the restaurant at 838-1500.

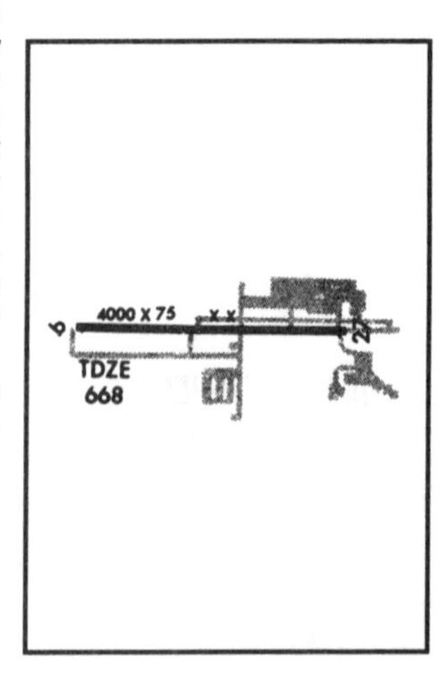

Airport Information:

CHICAGO/ROMEOVILLE - LEWIS UNIVERSITY - (Joliet Port District) (LOT)
20 mi northwest of town N41-36.51 W88-05.46 Elev: 668 Fuel: 80, 100LL, Jet-A Rwy 9-27: H4000x75 (Asph) Attended: 1300-0300Z Notes: Arpt beacon out of service indefinitely
Joliet Regional Port Office Phone: 838-9497 FBO: J.F. Aviation Phone: 838-4848

Photo by: Empress Casino, Joliet, IL

The Alexandria Club dining room at the Empress Palace

Photo by: Empress Casino, Joliet, IL

IL-DPA - CHICAGO (WEST CHICAGO) DUPAGE AIRPORT

(Area Code 630) | 17,18 |

Kittyhawk Cafe:

DuPage Airport has recently constructed a brand new modern terminal facility that contains the Kitty Hawk Cafe. This restaurant provides guest swith a very nice selection of menu items including their full breakfast choices like the popular Denver omelets, egg and sausage , French toast and buttermilk pancakes. For lunch favorites enjoy their "Rickenbocker Ruben", Piper Club sandwich, Falcon chicken breast seasoned with BBQ Teriyaki & lemon, their Glider hamburger and their famous Bowing Burger smothered with onions, green pepper and garlic seasoning. The huge white terminal building can be seen from miles away, and serves as a visual landmark for incoming aircraft. After landing, request taxi instructions to the DuPage Flight Center or terminal building which is one and the same. Aircraft parking is permitted on the terminal ramp in designated areas. The Kitty Hawk Cafe offers a panoramic view of the airport in a modern comfortable setting, complete with aviation photos and models hanging from the ceiling donated by the Air Classics Museum, located on the east side of the field. Restaurant hours are Monday through Saturday 7:30 a.m. to 5 p.m. and Sunday from 7:30 until 3 p.m. Pilots can arrange an afternoon of fun beginning with a meal at the Kittyhawk Cafe, then visit the Air Classics Museum and Pilot Shop adjacent to the museum, and even a round of golf on the "Top Flight Golf Course" adjoining the south side of the airport. Groups and fly-in catered meals as well as in-flight catering are available at the Kitty Hawk Cafe. For information and services at the airport call the DuPage Airport Authority at 584-2211. For restaurant information call the Kittyhawk Cafe at 208-6189.

Restaurants Near Airport:

Colonial Ice Cream	2 mi W.	Phone: 584-4647
Corfu Family Restaurant	1 mi W.	Phone: 584-1099
Kitty Hawk Cafe	Trml Bldg.	Phone: 208-6189
Pheasant Run Resort	Adj Arpt	Phone: 584-6300

Lodging: Best Western Inn (Trans) 584-4550; DuWayne Motel 231-1040; Dunham Inn 584-5300; Pheasant Run Resort (Trans) 584-6300; Super 8 Motel 377-8388.

Meeting Rooms: DuPage Flight Center in the terminal building. Also: J.A. Air Center contains a conference room and pilots lounge 584-3200; Best Western Inn 584-4550; Pheasant Run Resort (Convention facilities) 584-6300.

Transportation: Courtesy transportation is reported available for customers of fixed based operators (FBO's) on the field. Also taxi service: American Cab 232-1363; J.I.L. Limo Service 888-1344; Rental cars: Terry's Rental Cars 584-6200.

Information: Greater St. Charles Convention & Visitors Bureau, 311 N 2nd Street, P.O. Box 11, St. Charles, IL 60174, Phone: 377-6161 or 800-777-4373.

Pheasant Run Resort:

Pheasant Run Resort is located adjacent to the DuPage Airport along North Avenue (Route 64) on the northwest side of the field. Access to the resort can be obtained by a courtesy van either by the resort itself or FBO's on the field. Pheasant Run Resort offers excellent dining and lodging accommodations as well as a host of recreational amenities. The Baker's Wife Restaurant and the Deli are two dining facilities available at their location. The Baker's Wife & Lounge is a charming rustic equestrian theme restaurant, that provides a variety of delicious meals including a light and healthy assortment of entrees. Some of their main courses include boneless midwest pheasant sauteed with juniper berry sauce, prime veal chop with fresh rosemary, fresh linguini tossed with lobster. or try the chef's daily pasta creation. Additional specialties of the house include roast prime rib, filet mignon, grilled New York strip steak as well as grilled center cut pork chops. Average prices run $4.00 for breakfast, $5.00 for lunch and $16.00 for dinner. There are also 4 lounges (some with live entertainment) situated on the premises that also serve food. Restaurant hours at the Pheasant Run Resort are 6:00 a.m. to 10 p.m. Sunday through Thursday and 6:00 to 11:00 p.m. Friday and Saturday. The resort is also fully equipped to handle small, medium or large business conventions, along with a complete catering service on the premises. There is 150,000 square feet of banquet and meeting space and a newly constructed exhibition center. They also can accommodate private or business groups ranging from 20 to as many as 3,000 people. In addition, this resort also contains 474 guest rooms, an 18 hole golf course (open year round), dinner theater and recreation area. For more information call Pheasant Run Resort at 584-6300.

Airport Information:

CHICAGO (WEST CHICAGO) - DUPAGE AIRPORT (DPA)

29 mi west of Chicago N41-54.40 W88-14.91 Elev: 758 Fuel: 100LL, Jet-A
Rwy 01L-19R: H6700x100 (Conc) Rwy 10-28: H4751x75 (Asph) Rwy 15-33:H3401x100 (Asph) Rwy 01R-19L: H3300x75 (Conc) Attended: continuously Atis: 124.8
Unicom: 122.95 Chicago App/Dep Con: 133.5 Tower: 120.9, 124.5 Gnd Con: 121.8
Clnc Del: 119.75

DuPage Flight Center (Fuel, Unicom: 122.95) Phone: 584-2211

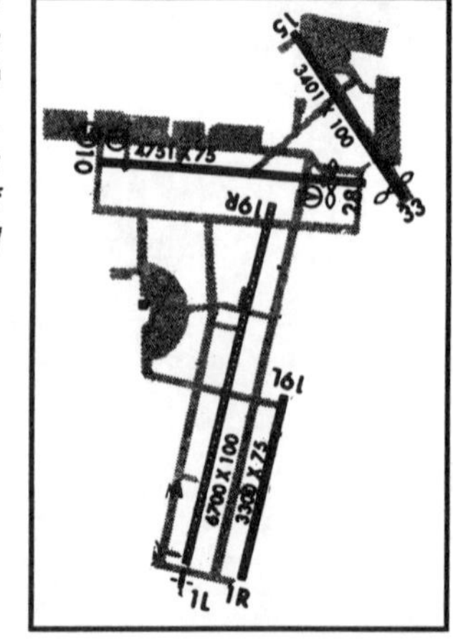

Not to be used for navigational purposes

Air Classics, Inc. Museum of Aviation

Chicago (West Chicago) IL (IL-DPA)

Services at the Air Classics, Inc. Museum of Aviation may change. Call ahead for information.

The excitement and thrill of warbirds are a welcome addition to DuPage Airport. The Air Classics Museum of Aviation celebrated its grand opening on May 21, 1994. "Air Classics features a unique collection of fully operational vintage military aircraft. On display are several aircraft including a P-51 Mustang, TBM "Avenger", Sea Fury, Mig-15, two PT-17 Stearmans, and a newly commissioned F-86 "Sabre Jet", a A-26 Invader, A-7E Corsair, F4B-Phantom, 1/2 scale Thunderbolt, and a T-39 "Sabreliner" are just a few of their aircraft.

The volunteers that service and keep these machines in prime condition devote thousands of hours of meticulous preparation just to keep them flying. Many of the parts are no longer available and must be hand built to tight tolerances. The support and commitment in the way of donations and volunteers can go a long way in helping to preserving these rare examples of our heritage.

By visiting the museum you will witness first hand the planes which shaped history and learn the stories of the gallant people who flew and supported them.

The Air Classics Museum represents a long term commitment to preserving the history of military aviation. As a non-profit organization (5013C) they depend on their membership and volunteer force to provide funding and man power. Their goal is to build a self supporting "World Class" aviation museum to house one of the finest collections of military aircraft anywhere,

Since man first witnessed the soaring bird, he has dreamt of flight. Only in the last hundred years has this dream become reality. Spanning from Kitty Hawk to the outer reaches of the galaxy, nothing has changed our world more than aviation.

Throughout aviation history, man and machine were called upon to protect another dream. The dream of freedom. With tremendous sacrifice and against great odds, young Americans willingly took to hostile skies. The stories of this effort: the people, the planes, the battles and the courage, reflect the heart of America.

It is the mission of the Air Classics Museum to preserve the dream for future generations. Demonstrating the relationship between the dream of flight and the dream of freedom, the museum is committed to chronicling the critical role of military aviation in history. Representation of this history is intended to educate the youth of America and the general public to the significance of these events. It will inspire them to have a lasting appreciation for the wonder of flight, the value of freedom and the spirit of America".

Aircraft parking is available on the ramp out in front of the museum, which is located on the east side of the airport south of J.A. Air Center (red hangars) and north of the fire station. Hours are Mon - Sat 10 a.m. to 5 p.m., Sun 12 noon to 5 p.m. Admission is $3.00 for adults and $1.00 for children. For information about the museum, (Fax 630-584-1889) or call the "Air Classics" information Hot Line at 630-584-1888.

Promote General Aviation Just Take A Friend Flying

Cantigny

Cantigny was the former estate of Colonel Robert R. McCormick, former editor and publisher of the Chicago Tribune. Cantigny covers approximately 500 acres of open and wooded land. This interesting attraction is a source of education and recreation for the public. It is composed of five areas: The Visitors Center, Robert R. McCormick Museum, First Division Museum, gardens, and Cantigny Golf.

The Visitors Center is the best place to start and end your visit with Cantigny. A video presentation highlights the various points of interest and provides a brief history of Colonel McCormick. After touring the grounds, you can return to the Visitors Center for a souvenir from the gift shop or a refreshment from the Tack Room Cafe.

The Robert R. McCormick Museum is an exquisite mansion on the Cantigny estate. It was the home of Colonel McCormick and was established as a museum for public enjoyment. The house has been preserved in McCormick's style and is decorated with many fine European and Oriental antiques. Guided tours treat visitors to a glimpse into the living, entertainment and servants' quarters of the mansion. Tours begin from the Gold Theater which is located on the east side of the building.

The First Division Museum brings history to life through interactive displays, videos and innovative exhibits. A walk through the main gallery treats you to the sight and sounds of division life at places such as the French village of Cantigny, Omaha Beach, and a Vietnam jungle. This facility also includes the Colonel Robert R. McCormick Reserarch Center and a traveling gallery of temporary exhibits.

Cantigny's nearly ten acres of formal gardens, provide both the casual and serious gardener year-round opportunities to study the wide varity of midwestern plant life. Supplied with plantings from Cantigny's greenhouse, the gardens boast one of the largest annual displays in the Midwest. The grounds also include the Idea Garden which demonstrates a variety of growing techniques for adults and fun gardening projects for children. Near the gardens and parking lots are large shaded picnic grounds and the band shell concert area. The peaceful landscape provides a perfect setting for a quiet family picnic or a Sunday afternoon concert.

Both the advanced and occasional player can test their skills on Cantigny's twenty-seven hole golf course. It offers golfers both eighteen and nine hole play in a setting of oak and hickory trees, lakes and streams. The golf complex includes a practice facility, six composition clay tennis courts and a full service clubhouse. The golf shop specializes in contemporary golf fashions, the latest in golf equipment and unique logo apparel.

Following a round of golf or a visit to the museum, Fareways Restaurant provides a relaxed setting for enjoying delicious meals and beverages. On Sundays, the restaurant offers a brunch buffet, which includes a scrumptious variety of the chef's specialties.

Cantigny is located about 10 miles southeast of DuPage Airport. DuPage offers taxi, limousine and rental car service. Also, pilots can check with the FBOs for possible courtesy transportation. Cantigny is closed during the month of January and on Mondays, except for Memorial Day and Labor Day. Note: Hours vary for the gardens and grounds, Visitors Center, and museums. Visitors should call in advance. For more information, call Cantigny at 668-5161. (Information submitted by Cantigny)

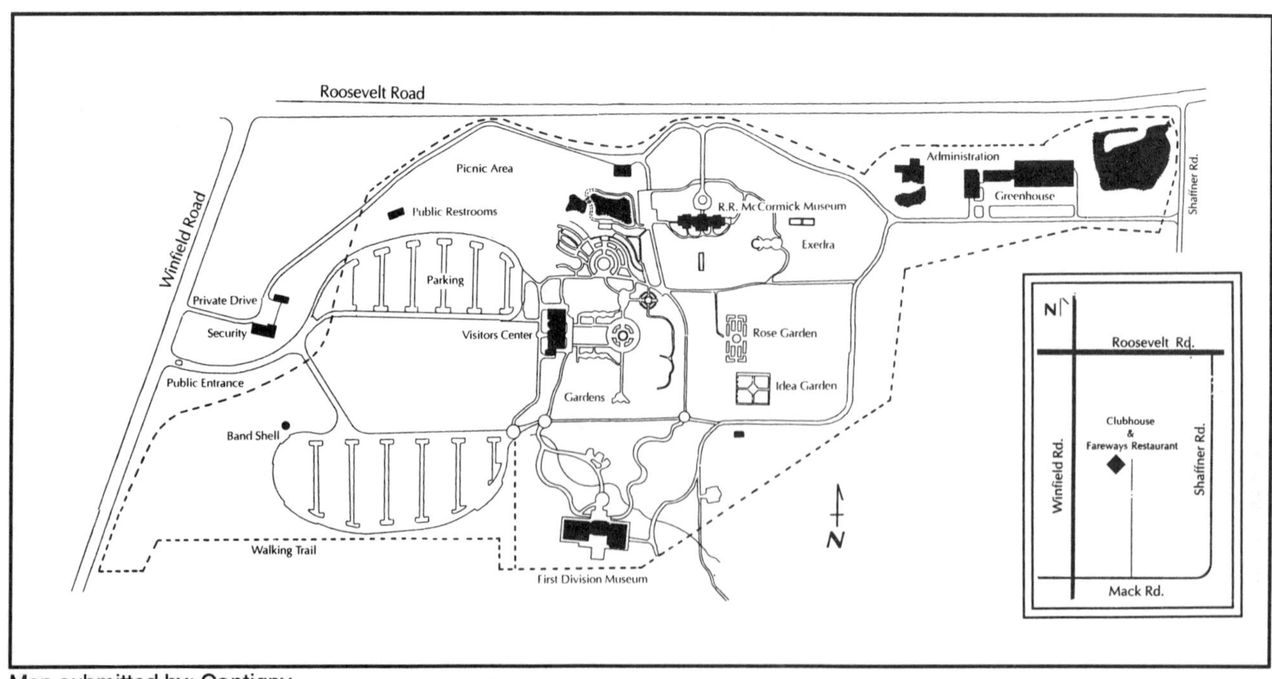

Map submitted by: Cantigny

Not to be used for navigational purposes

IL-PWK - CHICAGO/PROSPECT/WHEELING

(Area Code 847)

19, 20

PALWAUKEE MUNICIPAL

94th Aero Squadron:

The 94th Aero Squadron Restaurant is located on the field at Palwaukee Airport, in Wheeling, Illinois. After parking your aircraft on the main southeast ramp near Priester Aviation, a courtesy car will take you to and from the restaurant. The 94th Aero Squadron has a unique aviation decor which will escort you back in time when silk scarves were worn, and the daring pilots of the 94 Aero Squadron took to the air defending their honor during the great air conflict of World War I. Complete with a reconstructed village farm house near the battle front and decorated with photographs and World War I aviation memorabilia, this restaurant provides guests with delicious entrees combined with an ambiance of intrigue that every aviation enthusiast is bound to enjoy. Large windows facing the Palwaukee airfield allow for a great view of aircraft taking off and landing. Specialties prepared at this establishment include a variety of choice steaks, prime rib, seafood, lobster and pasta dishes. Average prices run $13.00 to $17.95 for most full course dinners. Their dining areas consist of several well appointed rooms, and can serve around 200 dining customers. An outdoor patio on one end of the restaurant , combined with an indoor lounge, also provides a great place to watch the airport activity and enjoy a beverage of your choice. A fee is charged by Priester Aviation for transient parked aircraft. However, this fee is waived if a fuel purchase is made. For information and hours of operation, call the 94th Aero Squadron at 459-3700.

Le Francais:

Le Francais restaurant is located approximately 2 miles from the Palwaukee Airport along Milwaukee Avenue. This fine dining facility is well known as one of the more popular restaurants in the area. They serve a complete menu specializing in contemporary French cooking. Their menu includes the finest in choices of specially prepared entrees like: Dover sole sauteed and served with an infusion of basil; roasted Norwegian salmon served with compote of sweet onions; grilled bass accompanied by natural juices flavored with fresh herbs; lobster and snapper in a broth lightly scented with hazelnut oil. Additional specialties include duck; center cut prime filet served with natural juices; veal medallions with wild mushrooms and rosemary; roasted squab with cabbage accompanied by red wine sauce and combinations of rack of lamb and lamb tenderloin served with vegetable essence. Many appetizers, soups, salads and wonderful French desserts are available as well. A wine list is also provided. Average prices are $25.00 for lunch and $50.00 for dinner. The restaurant is decorated in a traditional sophisticated country French inn styling. Accommodations for group seating are available. The restaurant is open for lunch Tuesday through Friday from 11:30 to 2:00 p.m. and dinner Monday through Saturday from 5:30 to 9:30. Transportation can be arranged at the airport. Le Francais is a 5-Star Mobil, 5-Diamond AAA facility. For information call 541-7470.

Restaurants Near Airport:

94th Aero Squadron	On Site	Phone: 459-3700
Algauer's Inn	1 mi S.	Phone: 934-0093
Bob Chinns Crab House	3/4 mi N.	Phone: 520-3633
Denny's Restaurant	2 blk S.	Phone: 537-3360
Le Francais	1 mi N.	Phone: 541-7470

Lodging: Algauer's Inn (Trans) 934-0093; Days Inn (Trans) 537-9100; Marriott's Lincolnshire Resort (Trans) 634-0100; Ramada Inn (Trans) 298-2525; Sheraton Inn-North Shore (Trans) 498-6500.

Meeting Rooms: Algauer's Inn 934-0093; Days Inn 537-9100; Marriott's Lincolnshire Resort (Convention facilities, Trans) 634-0100; Ramada Inn 298-2525; Sheraton Inn-North Shore 498-6500.

Transportation: Taxi service, courtesy cars, limousines and rental cars are all available at Priester Aviation 537-1200, or 800-323-7887; Also Rental Car Service through: Budget 537-1200; Snappy Car Rental 537-6200.

Information: Wheeling/Prospect Heights Area Chamber of Commerce and Industry, 395 E. Dundee Road, Wheeling, IL 60090, Phone: 541-0170.

Attractions:

Marriott's Lincolnshire Resort is located at 10 Marriott Drive, in Lincolnshire, IL 60069 just off Milwaukee Avenue and 1/2 mile south of Half Day Road. This famous resort contains many entertainment accommodations for vacationers as well as business travelers. The resort provides complete convention facilities, indoor tennis, an 18 hole golf course, gift shops, health rooms, 1 indoor and 2 outdoor swimming pools, restaurants and a 870 seat Theater-In-The-Round that features many musical comedies and theatrical performances by well known entertainers. The resort has 390 rooms within this three story complex. For information about the Marriott's Lincolnshire Resort call 634-0100.

Hangar Restaurant: (Closed)

At the time of updating, we learned that this restaurant has closed. There is no word whether this restaurant plans to re-open under a new name. Check with either Service Aviation 808-9690 or Priester Aviation 537-1200 for information.

See Additional Information (Bob Chinns Crab House, next page)

Airport Information:

CHICAGO/WHEELING - PALWAUKEE AIRPORT (PWK)

18 mi northwest of town (Chicago) N42-06.80 W87-54.05 Elev: 647 Fuel: 100LL, Jet-A1+ Rwy 16-34: H5137x100 (Asph) Rwy 12L-30R: H4397x50 (Asph) Rwy 06-24: H3652x50 (Asph) Attended: continuously Atis: 124.2 Unicom: 122.95 Chicago App/Dep Con: 120.55, 125.0 Tower: 119.9 Gnd Con: 121.7 Clnc Del: 124.7 Notes: Transient parking fee by Priester Aviation is charged: Singles $10.00 waived with fuel purchase of; 10 gal. Retracts 20 gal; Twins $20.00 waived with 40 gal. fuel purchase; Turbo props $30.00 waived with 60 gal. fuel purchase; Small or large turbine jet aircraft fees waived with fuel purchase depending on size. Service Aviation has no daily transient, ramp or landing fee charged at this time.

FBO: Priester Aviation **Phone: 537-1200**
FBO: Service Aviation **Phone: 808-9690**

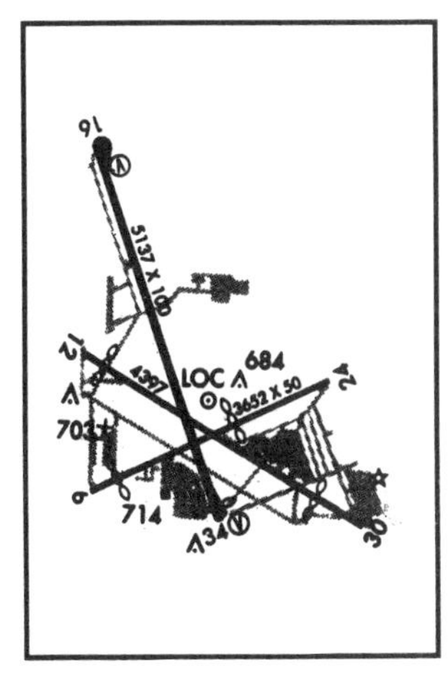

IL-PWK - CHICAGO/PROSPECT/WHEELING PALWAUKEE MUNICIPAL

(Area Code 708)

21

Bob Chinns Crab House:

This restaurant is located only 3/4th of a mile from the Palwaukee Municipal Airport. Transportation can be arranged either through Service Aviation or Priester Aviation. This facility offers a casual atmosphere with a very unique nautical seaboard appearance. Specialties of the house include the freshest in seafood like Dungeness crab, Alaska King crab legs, Alaska King Salmon, New Zealand Orange Roughy, Hawaii "Onaga", Hawaii "Ahi Tuna", Florida black grouper, and Holland Dover Sole, just to mention a few. Traditional choice steaks also included are their 6, 8, and 14 ounce fillet, 11 oz. prime rib and 16 oz. New York Strip steak. Their early bird special offers a delicious salad and oyster bar. Groups and private parties can easily be served. The restaurant can seat up to 630 people. Their hours are 7 days a week serving lunch Monday through Friday from 11:00 to 2:30, and Saturday from 12:00 p.m. to 3: p.m; and dinner until 10:30 p.m. Monday through Thursday, Friday and Saturday to 11:30 p.m; and Sunday from 3:00 p.m. to 10:00 p.m. For information call 520-3633.

Attractions:

CHICAGO/WHEELING - PALWAUKEE AIRPORT (PWK) See previous page for information.

Airport Information:

CHICAGO/WHEELING - PALWAUKEE AIRPORT (PWK)

18 mi northwest of town (Chicago) N42-06.80 W87-54.05 Elev: 647 Fuel: 100LL, Jet-A1+ Rwy 16-34: H5137x100 (Asph) Rwy 12L-30R: H4389x50 (Asph) Rwy 06-24: H3652x50 (Asph) Rwy 12R-30L: H3228x40 (Asph) Attended: continuously Atis: 124.2 Unicom: 122.95 Chicago App/Dep Con: 120.55, 125.0 Tower: 119.9 Gnd Con: 121.7 Clnc Del: 124.7 Notes: Transient parking fee by Priester Aviation is charged: Singles $10.00 waived with 20 gal. fuel purchase; Twins $20.00 waived with 40 gal. fuel purchase; Turbo props $30.00 waived with 60 gal. fuel purchase; Small turbine jet aircraft $50.00 waived with 100 gal. fuel purchase; and large Jets $80.00 with 160 gal. of fuel purchased. Service Aviation has no daily transient, ramp or landing fee charged at this time.

FBO: Priester Aviation Phone: 537-1200
FBO: Service Aviation Phone: 808-9690

Restaurants Near Airport:

94th Aero Squadron	On Site	Phone: 459-3700
Algauer's Inn	1 mi S.	Phone: 934-0093
Bob Chinns Crab House	3/4 mi N.	Phone: 520-3633
Denny's Restaurant	2 blk S.	Phone: 537-3360
Hangar Restaurant	On Site	Phone: 839-1414
Le Francais	1 mi N.	Phone: 541-7470

Lodging: Algauer's Inn (Trans) 934-0093; Days Inn (Trans) 537-9100; Marriott's Lincolnshire Resort (Trans) 634-0100; Ramada Inn (Trans) 298-2525; Sheraton Inn-North Shore (Trans) 498-6500.

Meeting Rooms: Algauer's Inn 934-0093; Days Inn 537-9100; Marriott's Lincolnshire Resort (Convention facilities, Trans) 634-0100; Ramada Inn 298-2525; Sheraton Inn-North Shore 498-6500.

Transportation: Taxi service, courtesy cars, limousines and rental cars are all available at Priester Aviation 537-1200, or 800-323-7887; Service Aviation (Free courtesy cars) 808-9690; Also Rental Car Service through: Budget 537-1200; Snappy Car Rental 537-6200.

Information: Wheeling/Prospect Heights Area Chamber of Commerce and Industry, 395 E. Dundee Road, Wheeling, IL 60090, Phone: 541-0170.

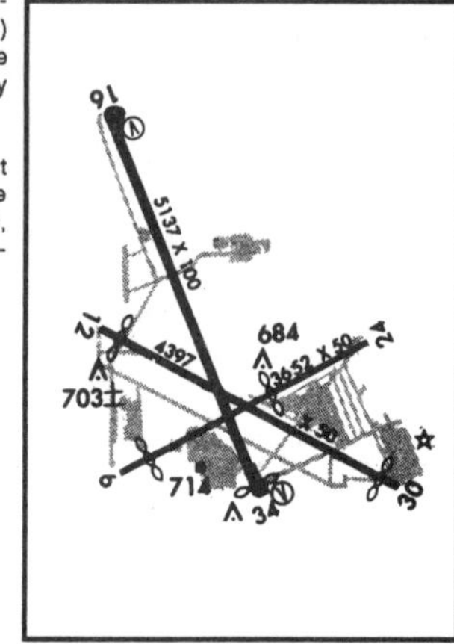

IL-DEC - DECATUR DECATUR AIRPORT

(Area Code 217)

22

Main Hangar Restaurant:

The Main Hangar Restaurant is located on the Decatur Airport within the main terminal building. This restaurant provides its guests with a panoramic view overlooking the main ramp, and has an rustic interior decorated with a variety of aviation related items including large model aircraft hanging from the ceiling. A full menu selection is available for breakfast, lunch and dinner. For lunch they specialize in sandwiches, soups, salads and appetizers. Their dinner menu features steaks, seafood selections along with other delicious entrees. Specials throughout the week include Wednesday fried chicken, Thurday BBQ pork ribs, Friday catfish, Saturday prime rib, and Sunday a buffet from 9 a.m. to 2 p.m. T A private dining room called the "Tower Room" is available for parties, and can seat 75 people. In-flight catering is another service available through the Main Hangar Restaurant. Their hours are Monday through Saturday from 6 a.m. to 9 p.m. in their main dining room and until 11 p.m. in their lounge. On Sunday they are open from 6 a.m. to 2 p.m. Reservations are suggested for parties and groups larger than 8 people between Monday through Thursday. No reservation are accepted on Friday, Saturday or Sunday. For more information call the Main Hangar Restaurant at 429-5956.

Airport Information:

DECATUR - DECATUR MUNICIPAL AIRPORT (DEC)

4 mi east of town N39-50.08 W88-51.99 Elev: 682 Fuel: 100LL, Jet-A
Rwy 06-24: H8496x150 (Asph-Conc-Grvd) Rwy 18-36: H5299x150 (Asph-Grvd)
Rwy 12-30: H6799x150 (Asph-Grvd) Attended: Mon-Fri continuously, Sat-Sun 1300-0300Z
Atis: 126.35 Champaign App/Dep Con: 132.85 Unicom: 122.95 Tower: 118.9
Gnd Con: 121.75 Public Phone 24hrs

FBO: Decatur Aviation, Inc. Phone: 423-9832

Restaurants Near Airport:

Main Hangar Rest.	On Site	Phone: 429-5956

Lodging: Best Western (Trans) 877-7255; Days Inn/Ambassador (Trans) 428-8611; Holiday Inn (Trans) 422-8800; Super 8 Motel (Trans) 877-8888; Courtesy phones for Best Western and Holiday Inn located in terminal building.

Meeting Rooms: A meeting room is reported available for conferences Monday through Thursday in the Main Hangar Restaurant in the main terminal building, for information call 429-5956. Best Western Shelton Inn 877-7255; Budgetel Inn 875-5800; Days Inn/ Ambassador 428-8611; Holiday Inn 422-8800; Super 8 Motel 877-8888.

Transportation: Taxi Service: Yellow Cab 422-1445; Action Cab 422-9999; Park Avenue Limousine 428-4225; Rental Cars: Avis 422-4337; Hertz 429-0414; National 428-5913.

Information: Decatur Area Convention & Visitors Bureau, 202 East North Street, Decatur, IL 62523, Phone: 423-7000 or 800-331-4479.

Attractions:

Nelson Park - golf course, picnic facilities, public swimming pool all located 3-1/2 miles from airport; Scovill Park - children's zoo, picnic facilities, Oriental gardens reported to be situated only 2 miles from the Decatur Municipal Airport.

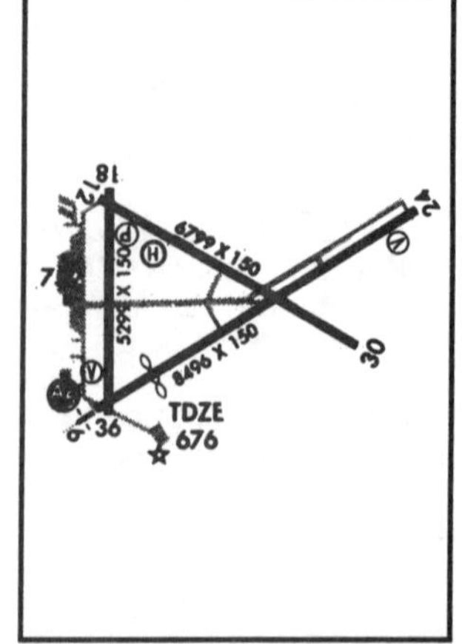

IL-DKB - DE KALB
DE KALB TAYLOR MUNICIPAL AIRPORT

(Area Code 815) 23

Crystal Pistol Beach Club:

Crystal Pistol Beach Club is located 5 miles from De Kalb Taylor Municipal Airport. The restaurant does provide a courtesy van at the airport. This fine dining establishment has an antique, New Orleans decor. Hours are 11:00 a.m. to 2:30 p.m. Tuesday through Sunday for lunch, and 5:00 p.m. to 9:30 p.m. Tuesday through Saturday, and 2:30 p.m. to 8:00 p.m. Sunday for dinner. Menu specialties include: shrimp, steaks, seafood, pork, lamb, creole dishes, as well as homemade soups and desserts. Meal prices average between $5.25 and $6.50 for lunch, and $9.95 and $12.95 for dinner. The restaurant will cater to groups of 20 or more for receptions, business meetings, holiday parties, etc. For more information about the Crystal Pistol Beach Club, call 758-1000.

Restaurants Near Airport:
Crystal Pistol Beach Club 5 mi Phone: 758-1000

Lodging: Days Inn (5 miles) 758-8661

Meeting Rooms: Days Inn 758-8661

Transportation: Crystal Pistol Beach Club does provide a courtesy van at the airport. Rental Cars: Bemis 895-8105

Information: Chamber of Commerce, 127 E. Lincoln Highway, De Kalb, IL 60115, Phone: 756-6306

Attractions:

Ellwood House Museum; Northern Illinois University; Shabbona Lake

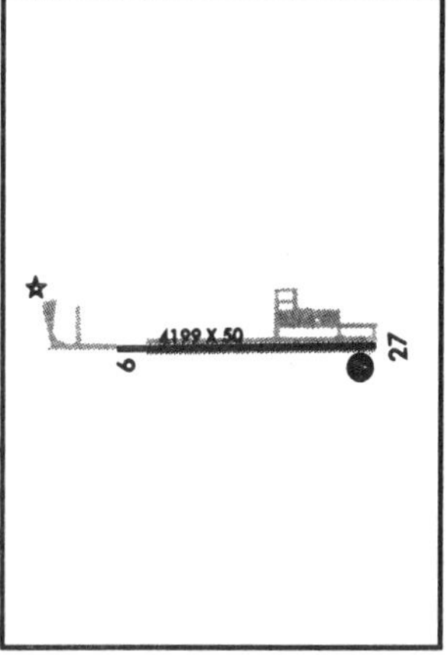

Airport Information:

DE KALB - DE KALB TAYLOR MUNICIPAL AIRPORT (DKB)
2 mi east of town N41-55.79 W88-42.81 Elev: 911 Fuel: 100LL, Jet-A Rwy 09-27: H4199x50 (Asph) Attended: 1300Z-dusk CTAF/Unicom: 122.7 Chicago App/Dep Con: 133.5 Notes: $5.00 overnight parking fee/waived with fuel purchase.
FBO: R & M Aviation Phone: 756-7525, 756-3232

IL-DTG - DWIGHT
DWIGHT AIRPORT

(Area Code 815) 24

Country Mansion:

The Country Mansion is located about 4 miles from the Dwight Airport in Dwight Illinois. When visiting the Mansion, you will enjoy elegant dining in a casual atmosphere. Treat yourself to Sunday brunch from 11 a.m. to 2 p.m. or plan a group fly-in with your friends or local flying club. The restaurant hours are Monday through Saturday from 5 p.m. to 9 p.m. and Sunday from 11 a.m. to 2 p.m. They also have a bakery on the premises offering many freshly made pastries. There are 4 separate dining rooms with available seating for 45 persons. A special banquet room can also be reserved for larger groups. They have a courtesy van that will provide transportation for fly-in guests. Just give them a call from the airport and within minutes they will be out to pick you up. After enjoying a fine meal, you can take a walk through their park adjacent to the restaurant. For reservations or information, call 815-584-2345. For Illinois residents call toll free 1-800-982-5969.

Restaurants Near Airport:
Country Mansion 4 mi N. Phone: 584-2345

Lodging: Moyemont's Carefree Inn 584-3079

Meeting Rooms: Country Mansion contains accommodations for group meeting and banquets 584-2345 or 800-982-5969 for Illinois residents.

Transportation: Dwight Airport courtesy car reported; Also Taxi Service through Dwight Cab at 584-2257.

Information: Chicago Office of Tourism, Chicago Cultural Center, 78 E Washington Street, Chicago 60602, Phone: 744-2400, or 800-487-2446.

Airport Information:

DWIGHT - DWIGHT AIRPORT (DTG)
3 mi north of town N41-08.00 W88-26.45 Elev: 632 Fuel: 100LL Rwy 09-27: H2364x21 (Asph) Rwy 18-36: 2000x92 (Turf) Attended: Mon-Sat 1400-2300Z, Sun 1600-2200 Unicom: 122.8
FBO: Dwight Aero Service Phone: 584-2486

IL-FWC - FAIRFIELD
FAIRFIELD MUNICIPAL AIRPORT

(Area Code 618) 25

Bat's Place:

The Crown Motel is a combination restaurant and lodging facility about 1/4th mile walking distance from the Fairfield Municipal Airport, in Fairfield, IL. This facility offers a family style restaurant that is reported to be open from 6 a.m. to 10 p.m. seven days a week. Hours may vary so call the restaurant to verify. They provide a full service menu with daily specials. This restaurant also offered a smorgasbord on Friday, Saturday and Sunday. For those interested in obtaining courtesy car transportation to the restaurant, you can call Fairfield Municipal airport at 842-9587. For more information about this restaurant please call 842-2695.

Restaurants Near Airport:

Bat's Place	1/4 mi	Phone: 842-2695

Lodging: Crown Motel 842-2695; Uptown Motel (Trans to Airport) 842-2191.

Meeting Rooms: Crown Motel 842-2695; Uptown Motel 842-2191.

Transportation: Courtesy reported at the Fairfield Airport.

Information: Jefferson County Chamber of Commerce, 200 Potomac Blvd., P.O. Box 1047, Mt. Vernon, IL 62864, Phone: 618-242-5725.

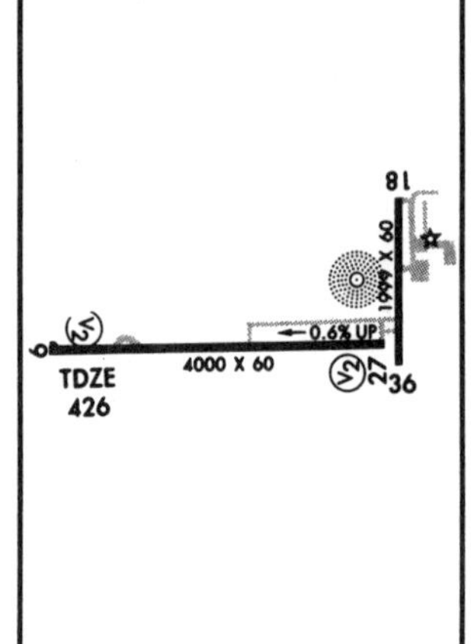

Airport Information:

FAIRFIELD - FAIRFIELD MUNICIPAL AIRPORT (FWC)
2 mi west of town N38-22.72 W88-24.68 Elev: 436 Fuel: 100LL, Jet-A
Rwy 09-27: H4000x60 (Asph) Rwy 18-36: H1999x60 (Asph) Attended: 1400-2200Z
CTAF: 122.9
FBO: Fairfield Municipal Airport Phone: 842-9587

IL-C18 - FRANKFORT
FRANKFORT AIRPORT

(Area Code 815) 26

Die Bier Stube:

Die Bier Stube is located about 1 mile north of the Frankfort Airport. Hours are 11:30 a.m. to 9:00 p.m. Monday through Friday, 11:30 a.m. to 10:00 p.m. Saturday, and 12:00 p.m. to 9:00 p.m. on Sunday. Chef Klaus offers guests Old World German cooking in an authentic German atmosphere. Choose from a fine selection of weiner schnitzels, home-made hearty soups and fabulous German beers and wines. Other specialties include: Bavarian rabbit, venison medallions and a daily salad bar. Meal prices average between $5.00 and $8.00 for lunch, and $12.00 and $17.00 for dinner. The restaurant also offers live German entertainment every Wednesday through Sunday. A festive outdoor beer garden is open during the summer season. Die Bier Stube can cater to parties of 20 or more, as well as to private and corporate pilots on the go. For more information about Die Bier Stube, call 800-320-1188 or 469-6660.

Restaurants Near Airport:

Die Bier Stube	1 mi N.	Phone: 469-6660
Enrico's	1-1/2 mi	Phone: 469-4187
Merichka's	8 mi	Phone: 723-9371
The Rising Sun	1-1/2 mi	Phone: 468-6688

Lodging: Abe Lincoln Hotel (1 mile) 469-5114; Frankfort Inn Motel (1 mile) 469-5061; Super 8 (2 miles) 479-7808; Holiday Inn (5 miles) 708-747-3500

Meeting Rooms: None Reported

Transportation: Taxi Service: Star Cab 755-0312; Sundling Limousine 429-1020; Rental Cars: Enterprise 481-6225; Phillips 469-2323

Information: Northern Illinois Tourism Council, 1740 S. Bell School Road, Cherry Valley, IL 61016, Phone: 332-9626

Attractions:

The following attractions are within 10 miles of the airport: Unincorporated Antiques; World Music Theater; Blacksmith Antiques; Days Gone By Antiques; Pisces Antiques; Riverboat Casinos. Call 800-487-2446 or 744-2400.

Airport Information:

FRANKFORT - FRANKFORT AIRPORT (C18)
1 mile southeast of town N41-28.65 W87-50.43 Elev: 778 Fuel: 100LL Rwy 09-27: H4203x50 (Asph) Attended: Mon-Fri 1330-0200Z, Sat-Sun 1300-0300Z CTAF/Unicom: 122.8 Chicago App Dep/Con: 133.1 Notes: $5.00 landing fee/waived with fuel purchase.
FBO: South Suburban Aviation Phone: 469-2311

IL-JOT - JOLIET
JOLIET PARK DISTRICT

(Area Code 815) 27, 28, 29

Empress Casino Joliet:

Empress opened its doors in June of 1992, and quickly became a favorite entertainment destination for Chicagoland. Empress I and II, their sleek, yacht-styled casinos, offer nearly 1,000 slot machines, blackjack, roulette, craps, mini-baccarat, Caribean Stud Poker and Let It Ride. Guests can choose from 18 daily gaming sessions (19 on Weekends), 365 days a year. Empress Casino - Joliet's pavilion structure features nearly 150,000 square feet of guest amenities. They offer three restaurants: Alexandria (steakhouse), Cafe Casablanca (casual Mediterranean and American fare), and Marrakech Market (international buffet). The Grand Ballroom of the Empress Casino can host groups from 50 to 400, and the Palace Treasures Gift Shop is a popular place to shop for clothing, jewelry and gaming items. Also offered in their pavilion is the Empress OTB, the first off-track betting facility to operate in conjunction with an Illinois casino. The Empress Hotel, a 102-room facility featuring regular rooms, junior and luxury suites, and an indoor pool area. The hotel is located across from their Joliet pavilion, sharing the same spacious parking area, and shuttle bus service is available for casino transport. Since its inception, Empress Casino - Joliet has created over 1,900 new career positions for their area's work force. According to the Will County Chamber of Commerce, Empress ranks as the country's sixth largest employer. Empress Casino is located about 5 to 6 miles east from the Joliet Park District Airport (JOT) and about 8 miles south of the Lewis University Airport (LOT). For more information call the Manager of Public/Community Relations at 815-744-9400 ext. 2275.

Restaurants Near Airport:

Dakota Stk Hse-Fire Side Resort	1/8 mi	Phone: 725-3131
Empress Casino - Joliet	6 mi E. Trans	Phone: 744-9400
Town & Country/Days Inn	1/4 mi	Phone: 744-5454

Lodging: Days Inn (1/4 mile) 725-2180; Fire Side Resort (1/4 mile) 725-3131; Holiday Inn (5 miles) 729-2000.

Meeting Rooms: Empress Casino - Joliet (trans) 744-9400; Days Inn 725-2180; Fire Side Resort 725-3131; Holiday Inn 729-2000.

Transportation: Taxi service: Checker Cab 727-5041; Also rental cars: Budget Rent-A-Car 744-3600

Information: Heritage Corridor Visitors Bureau, 81 N Chicago Street, Joliet, IL 60431, 727-2323 or 800-926-2262.

Attractions:

Empress Casino - Joliet will provide your party with free courtesy transportation to and from either Joliet Park District Airport only 5 or 6 miles west of their facility. Get carried away to a place that's far from the everyday, to a world of total entertainment. From the golden grandeur that greets you as you approach the entrance, to the spectacle of sights and sounds in the casino itself. A fantasy, complete with towering walls of hieroglyphics and authentic Egyptian statuary. With off-track betting, 3 different restaurants for your dining pleasure, private party and meeting facilities, a convenient on-site, 102 room hotel, a gift shop and a staff whose highest priority is your comfort and enjoyment. For information call the Casino at 744-9400.

Dakota Steak House/Fire Side Resort:

The Dakota Steak House Restaurant is a family style establishment that is reported to be a short walk from the Joliet Park District Airport, and located within the Fireside Resort. This restaurant has been in business for over 15 years. Their menus consist of a wide variety of entrees like omelets, pancakes, your favorite sandwiches, luncheon specials, salad bar, seafood, steaks, and much more. The decor is contemporary and very comfortable, with green plants for decoration. Their main dining room can seat 160 people. In addition, they have banquet facilities for up to 150 persons, featuring a buffet style, lunch or dinner, with selections off the menu or any requests welcome. They offer breakfast, lunch and dinner specials as well as their famous "Friday night fish Jamboree." The restaurant is open 7 days a week from 6 a.m. to 11 p.m. on weekdays and 24 hours on weekends, with live entertainment in their lounge. Courtesy transportation is available through the restaurant by calling the resort at 725-0111 or the restaurant at 725-3131.

Town & Country Restaurant/Days Inn:

The Town & Country Restaurant is located within the Days Inn Motel, only a 6 or 7 minute walk from the Joliet Park District Airport. Fly-in guests can park their aircraft on transient parking area and walk towards the Amoco Automobile Service Station, and from there you will be able to see the Days Inn Motel, The restaurant within the motel offers a dinner club atmosphere in quaint yet casual surroundings. The restaurant hours are 6 a.m. to 2 p.m., then from 4 p.m. to 9 p.m., and on weekends from 7 a.m. to 2 p.m. and again from 4 p.m. to 9 p.m.; Their lounge is open from 11 a.m. to 1 a.m. The motel has 181 units, along with a swimming pool and laundry facilities. For more information call the Days Inn and Town & Country Restaurant at 744-5454.

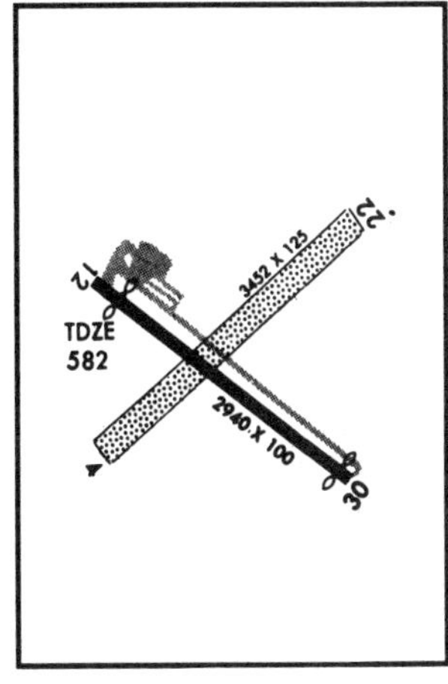

Airport Information:

JOLIET - JOLIET PARK DISTRICT (JOT)
4 mi west of town N41-31.08 W88-10.52 Elev: 581 Fuel: 80, 100LL, Jet-A
Rwy 04-22: 3452x125 (Turf) Rwy 12-30: H2940x100 (Asph) Attended: Aprl-Oct 1300Z-0300Z, Nov-Mar 1300-0100Z Unicom: 122.7
Joliet Park District Phone: 741-7267.

IL-C75 - LACON
MARSHALL COUNTY AIRPORT

(Area Code 309) 30, 31

Kenyons Place:

Kenyons Place is a fine supper club that is located about 1/2 mile from the Marshall County Airport in Lacon, Illinois. Their menu contains a nice choice of entrees consisting of prime steak as well as fresh seafood, Italian cuisine & chicken dishes. They also have sandwiches and light fare. Average prices run $4.50 for lighter fare, $6.75 to $11.95 for most steaks, and seafood selections. In addition to the main dining room,there is a cocktail lounge within the restaurant. This restaurant is open Tuesday through Thursday between 5 p.m. and 8:30 p.m., Friday and Saturday from 4:30 until 9:30 p.m., and Sunday from 11:30 to 8 p.m. For courtesy car transportation information or reservations call the restaurant at 246-3663 or dial 246-FOOD.

Sly Fox Pub:

The Sly Fox Pub is reported to be located within walking distance from the Marshall County Airport. This combination family style and fine dining establishment will even pick your party up from the airport if needed, and if available staff is on duty. They specialize in buffet style selections, including Friday fish and seafood buffet from 5 p.m. to 8:30 p.m. including choices like catfish, walleye, shrimp, clam strips, cod, perch, French fries, rolls, four different salads, as well as cheese and crackers. On Monday/Wednesday from 5 p.m. to 8:30 p.m. they feature a buffet serving ravioli, vegetable, two salads, rolls and brownies. Average prices run between $2.00 and $9.00 for most dinner selections. The Sly Fox Pub has 5 separate dining rooms, each with its own theme, 2 with a view of the airport featuring the aviation room and the sports room. They also have a game room and fitness center in their downstairs level. Accommodations for parties from 2 to 200 people can be arranged. For information call the Sly Fox Pub at 246-2595

Restaurants Near Airport

Kenyons Place	1/2 mi	Phone: 246-3663
Sly Fox Pub	4/10 mi	Phone: 246-2595

Lodging: Pines Motel (1/4 mile east) 246-2595.

Meeting Rooms: Sly Fox Pub & Restaurant located just east of the airport can accommodate groups and meetings by calling 246-2595.

Transportation: Fly-in guests arrange courtesy cars from Aircraft Medics (FBO) on the field by calling 246-8769; Also restaurants listed above can also provide courtesy transportation to their facilities if needed.

Information: Peoria Convention & Visitors Bureau, 403 NE Jefferson, Peoria, IL 61603, Phone: 676-0303 or 800-747-0302.

Airport Information:

LACON - MARSHALL COUNTY AIRPORT (C75)
1 mi east of town N41-01.16 W89-23.19 Elev: 568 Fuel: 80, 100LL
Rwy 13-31: H3200x75 (Asph) Rwy 18-36: H2200x50 (Asph) Attended: 1400Z-dusk
Unicom: 122.8 Public Phone 24hrs Notes: Overnight parking $4.00, one night free with $25.00 fuel purchase for singles and $45.00 for twins. Overnight hangars also available.
FBO: Lacon Aero Service Phone: 246-3700

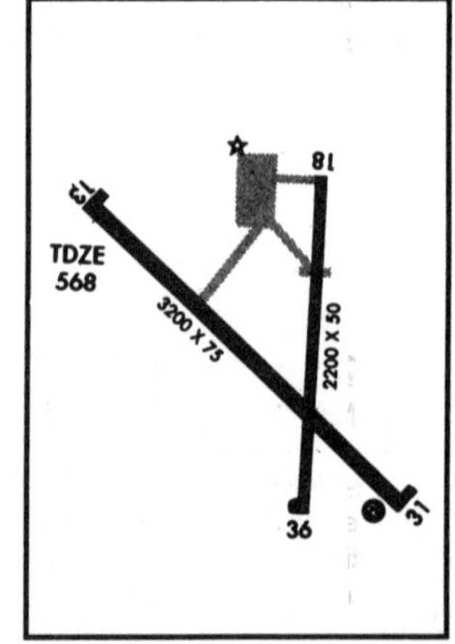

IL-3CK - LAKE IN THE HILLS
LAKE IN THE HILLS AIRPORT

(Area Code 815) **32**

Restaurants Near Airport:
Numerous Rest. 2 miles Phone: N/A
Windsock Deli On Site Phone: 459-DELI

Lodging: Holiday Inn (2 miles) 477-7000; Red Door Inn (1-1/2 mile) 459-6130; Super 8 Motel (1 mile) 455-2388.
Meeting Rooms: Contact Lake in the Hills airport manager's office for information 455-7522.
Transportation: Crystal Lake Taxi 455-0008; Rental Cars: Agency Rent-A-Car 455-9210, Enterprise 455-0003, National 459-4566, R & M Leasing 459-4000.
Information: Chicago Office of Toursim, Chicago Cultural Center, 78 E Washington Street, Chicago, IL 60602, Phone: 312-744-2400 or 800-487-2446.

Windsock Deli:

There is a brand new sandwich and soda shop located right on the Lake in the Hills Airport near Crystal Lake, Illinois. This cafe and deli is open from 8 a.m. to 4 p.m. 7 days a week. Fresh deli sandwiches can be prepared with a variety of meats and cheeses. In addition, their menu also includes their Vienna hot dog "Windsock Style" with chips for only $1.75. Soup of the day, chili and a selection of salads are prepared. Other specials and combinations are regularly featured. Breakfast pastries, along with fountain beverages and soda pop are available. Average prices are around $2.50 for breakfast, and about $4.00 for lunch and dinner. In-flight catering with cheese and sandwich trays is a natural for this establishment. This restaurant has a modern aviation styled decor, and can accommodate fly-in groups as well. A private conference room can be rented at an hourly rate. One additional attraction for fly-in guest is a brand new aviation store within the same building called the Blue Skies Pilot Shop. It contains a variety of pilot related items including books, videos, headsets, radios, jewelry, clothing, and much more. Both of these facilities are situated only a few feet from the aircraft transient parking area. For information call the Blue Skies Pilot shop at 356-8121or the Windsock Deli at 459-DELI or 459-3354.

**Blue Skies
Pilot Shop on field**

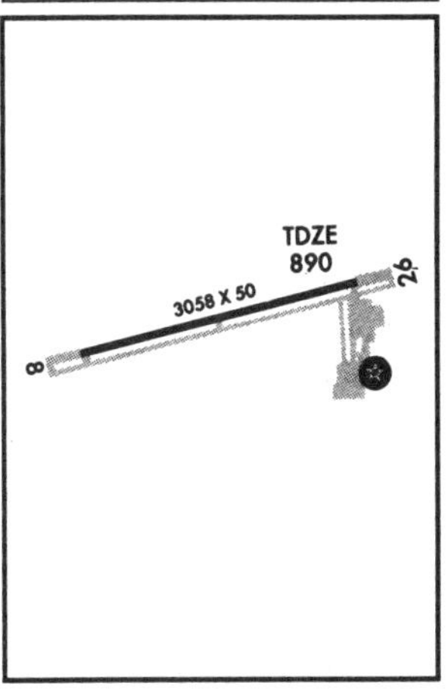

Airport Information:

LAKE IN THE HILLS - LAKE IN THE HILLS AIRPORT (3CK)
2 miles north of town N42-12.41 W88-19.38 Elev: 886 Fuel: 100LL, Jet-A Rwy 08-26: H3058x50 (Asph) Attended: 1300Z-dusk Unicom: 122.8 Notes: Gravel pits 150 feet from centerline north and south of runway. Overnight parking fee $5.00, Runway lights may be activated by pilot between 10 p.m. and dawn. (5 clicks on 122.75 within 5 seconds for medium intensity).
FBO: Northern Illinois Flight Center Phone: 455-7707 or 800-553-7371

IL-MWA - MARION
WILLIAMSON COUNTY REGIONAL

(Area Code 618) **33**

Restaurants Near Airport:
Cracker Barrel 2 mi SE Phone: 993-6306
J.W.'s Restaurant On Site Phone: 997-8086

Lodging: Airport Inn (On airport) 993-3222.
Meeting Rooms: Airport Inn also has accommodations for meetings and conferences, also FAX and secretarial service are available in the airport office, (Terminal building). For information call 993-3353.
Transportation: Aero Flite, Inc. (FBO) can arrange courtesy transportation to nearby establishments; Also taxi service is available: Red Top Cab 997-1098; Marion Cab 993-8181; D & C Cab 942-4880.
Information: Greater Marion Area Chamber of Commerce, 2305 West Main Street, P.O. Box 307, Marion, IL 62959, Phone: 997-6311.

JW's Airport Restaurant:

JW's Airport Restaurant is located in the terminal building on the Williamson County Regional Airport. This establishment is open 7 days a week from 6 a.m. to 9 p.m. Specialized entrees on their menu include veal Parmigiana, meatloaf, roast beef as well as additional special prepared dishes each day. On Saturday prime rib, T-bone, filet and salad bar is featured. On Sunday between 6 a.m. and 6 p.m. they offer a full buffet. Their main dining room can seat 100 persons. Fly-in clubs as large as 40 or 60 people can arrange group parties at JW's Airport Restaurant. If interested in meals-to- go or catered box lunches or platters, you can call the restaurant at 997-8086.

Attractions:

Crab Orchard NWR (2 miles), fishing and recreation at Crab Orchard Lake; 3 golf courses within 10 miles; Little Grassy Lake; and Devils Kitchen Lake located nearby.

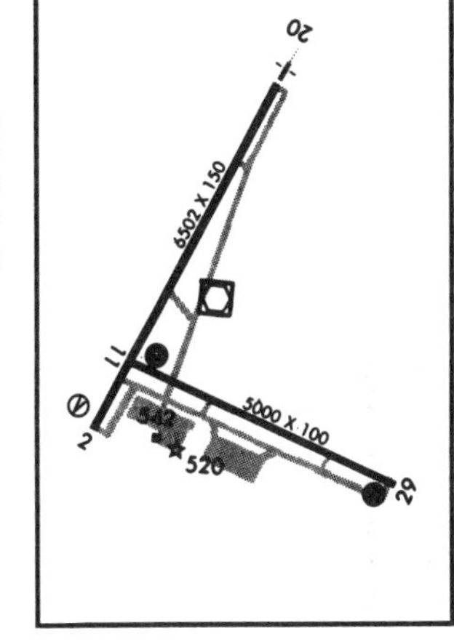

Airport Information:

MARION - WILLIAMSON COUNTY REGIONAL AIRPORT (MWA)
4 mi west of town N37-45.19 W89-00.70 Elev: 472 Fuel: 100LL, Jet-A
Rwy 02-20: H6502x150 (Asph-Pfc) Rwy 11-29: H5000x100 (Asph-Conc-Grvd)
Attended: continuously Unicom: 122.95 Marion Tower: 126.9 Gnd Con: 121.7 Notes: No landing or overnight fees; CAUTION: Migratory water fowl and deer on and in vicinity of airport.
FBO: Aeroflite Phone: 993-2764

IL-68IL - MARSEILLES
PRAIRIE LAKE HUNT CLUB

(Area Code 815) 34

Prairie Lakes Hunt Club:

The Prairie Lakes Resort has been under new ownership now for approximately one year. In that time, there has been extensive remodeling done to the bar/lounge and restaurant area including a new beer garden for summertime enjoyment. The restaurant serves lunch and dinner daily and breakfast on Friday through Sunday. Restaurant hours are 11 a.m. to 2 p.m. for lunch, and 5 p.m. to 9 p.m. for dinner. There is also live entertainment in the lounge on most Friday and Saturday nights. The main dining room can seat up to 75 persons, with additional banquet seating for 100 people. If planning a golf outing for your flying club or business clients, The Prairie Lakes Resort should be able to accommodate your needs with ease. As a hunting club, this establishment can provide excellent hunting grounds for certain types of game. A new golfers pro shop has also been added along with a hunters lodge. The 9 hole golf course has had over 200 new trees added and now receives top-notch maintenance. The restaurant and resort is located very close to aircraft parking and the landing strip which has a north/south layout running between the golf course fairways. Make sure that before landing, there are no golfers playing on the runway. For information you can call 795-5107.

Attractions:

Prairie Lake Hunt Club offers the finest in extended season upland game huntings year round lighted trap shooting, autumn duck and geese hunting and limited deer hunting. Their 750 acre preserve combines covered fields, woodlands and water areas which provide outstanding hunting activities. Prairie Lakes is one of the oldest hunt clubs in the state of Illinois. Founded in 1952, Prairie Lakes has grown over the years to a resort type facility. Amenities such as a full service restaurant with bar and lounge overlook the Prairie Lakes Golf Course with convenient modern lodging facilities adjacent to the restaurant/lounge. Prairie Lakes offers a limited number of individual and corporate memberships. The annual fees include a membership and a hunting fee. All other charges are on an "as used" basis, such as guides, hunting dogs and game birds. Your membership also provides special rates at the Prairie Lakes Lodge, Restaurant bar/lounge and golf course. Their family events include picnics, fishing, golf and special group outings and activities. They extend a cordial invitation for you to visit their club in the near future. To arrange your visit please call their hunt club office at 795-5107. They offer an introductory hunt to aid you in your membership decision. Every aspect of hunting at Prairie Lakes is under the careful scrutiny of their full-time staff to ensure a controlled and safe environment. At the same time, they pledge to maintain the essence of hunting traditions and good sportsmanship.

Restaurants Near Airport:
Prairie Lake Hunt Club On Site Phone: 795-5107

Lodging: Prairie Lake Lodge (On site) two story motel with 13 units. For information call 795-5107.

Meeting Rooms: Prairie Lake Lodge has banquet room able to accommodate up to 80 persons. For reservations call 795-5107.

Transportation: The lodge is reported to be within 100 feet of the aircraft parking area. Transportation is not needed.

Information: Ottawa Chamber of Commerce, 100 West Lafayette Street, P.O. Box 888, Ottawa, IL 61350, Phone: 433-0084 or the Grundy County Association of Commerce & Industry, 112 East Washington Street, Morris, IL 60450, Phone: 942-0113.

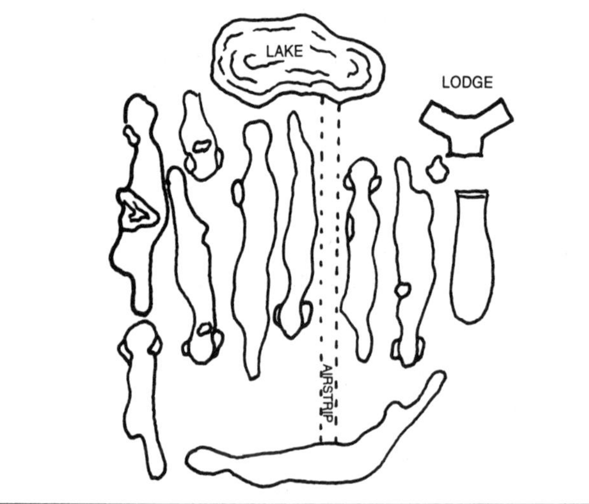

Airport Information:

MARSEILLES - PRAIRIE LAKE HUNT CLUB (68IL)
5 mi north of town N41-23-42 W88-41-00 Elev: 705 Fuel: None reported
Rwy 18-36: 2540x120 (Turf) Attended: Owner lives on property. Notes: Use at own risk, private airport. Reported 18 DME from (JOT) VORTAC & 003 degrees off the Pontiac (PNT) VORTAC.
Prairie Lake Hunt Club Phone: 795-5107

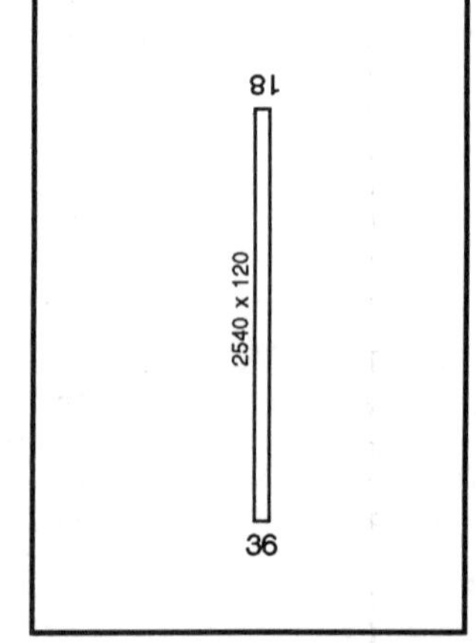

IL-MTO - MATOON/CHARLESTON COLES COUNTY MEMORIAL ARPT

(Area Code 217) 35

Airport Steak House:

The Airport Steak House is located in the main terminal on the Coles County Memorial Airport in Mattoon, Illinois. Fly-in guests can park their aircraft within 20 yards of the restaurant. The Airport Steak House provides a nice view of the runways and aircraft parking area. There is seating for between 70 and 80 people in their main dining room. Pictures of different types of aircraft decorate the restaurant interior. A back party room can also handle up to 40 guests. A full service menu is available for breakfast, lunch and dinner including their specialties like the "Elephant Ear" sandwich with breaded tenderloin and home made pies. Breakfast is served all day. Average prices run $2.00 to $6.00 for breakfast, $1.65 to $5.00 for most sandwiches and $7.00 to $13.95 for dinner choices. Restaurant hours are 7 a.m. to 8 p.m. seven days a week. For more information call 234-9433.

Restaurants Near Airport:

Airport Steakhouse	On Site	Phone: 234-9433
Fat Alberts	4 mi W.	Phone: 234-7337
E.L. Krackers	6 mi E.	Phone: 348-8343

Lodging: Mattoon Holiday Inn (Trans) 235-0313; Charleston Inn 348-8161; L & K Motel 235-4051; Quality Inn (Trans) 235-4161.

Meeting Rooms: Airport Steak House has banquet room available. An airport conference room is also available through the Airport Authority. Call 234-7120. In addition: Holiday Inn Mattoon 235-0313; and Quality Inn 235-4161 have meeting and conference rooms.

Transportation: Foster Aviation has courtesy cars available 235-6611; Taxi Service: Checker Top Cab 234-7474 or 348-5454; Also Car Rental: National (On airport) 235-1898;

Information: Mattoon Association of Commerce, 1701 Wabash Avenue, Mattoon, IL 61938, Phone: 235-5661.

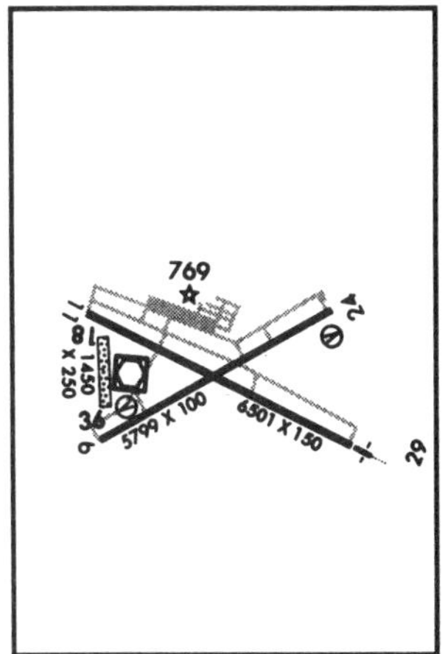

Attractions:

Eagle Creek Resort (Shelbyville, IL); Pleasant Grove Golf Course (Charleston, IL); Also the Lincoln Log Cabin, Fox Ridge & Several lakes all within 30 miles of this airport. See "Information" listed above to receive more data from the Mattoon Association of Commerce or call 235-5661.

Airport Information:

MATTOON/CHARLESTON - COLES COUNTY MEMORIAL AIRPORT (MTO)
4 mi east of town N39-28.68 W88-16.81 Elev: 721 Fuel: 721 Fuel: 100LL, Jet-A
Rwy 11-29: H6501x150 (Conc-Grvd) Rwy 06-24: H5799x100 (Asph-Pfc) Rwy 18-36: 1450x250 (Turf) Attended: Apr-Sep 1300Z-0130Z, Oct-Mar 1300-0030 Unicom: 122.7 Public Phone 24hrs
Notes: Noise abatement - Do not! fly over hospital located 1/4 mile north of airport. No landing fees.
FBO: Central Illinois Air Corporation Phone: 234-8146

IL-MLI - MOLINE QUAD-CITY AIRPORT

(Area Code 309) 36, 37

CA1 Service:

CA1 Services operates a dining facility across from entrance #6, located within the terminal building at the Quad-City Airport in Moline, IL. This family-style restaurant is open between 5:30 a.m. to 8 p.m., 7 day a week. Standard menu listings are available with fast service. Average prices run $5.00 for breakfast, $6.00 for lunch and $7.00 for dinner. A casual atmosphere can be enjoyed. Groups up to 200 are welcome with advance notice appreciated. Full in-flight catering services are provided. For information call 797-4791.

Skyline Inn Restaurant:

The Skyline Inn Restaurant is located just east of the airport entrance. Courtesy transportation can be arranged through Elliott Flying Service (FBO) by calling 799-3183. This fine dining restaurant is open Saturday beginning at 4 p.m. until 11 p.m. and weekdays from 4 p.m. to 10 p.m. (Closed Sundays). Specialty items on their menu include appetizers, salad bar, homemade soups, choice steaks, catfish, prime rib and a variety of seafood. Average prices run $9.00 for most selections. Their dining room provides a modern decor with a casual atmosphere. Meals can also be ordered for carry-out. Reservations are suggested. For more information call 764-9128.

Restaurants Near Airport:

CA1 Services	On Site	Phone: 797-4791
Bender's	1/2 mi NE.	Phone: 797-5375
Harold's On The Rock	2 mi N.	Phone: 764-4813
Skyline Inn Rest.	1/2 mi E.	Phone: 764-9128

Lodging: Hampton Inn (Trans) 762-1711; Holiday Inn (1/2 mile, Trans) 762-8811; Howard Johnson Lodge (Trans) 797-1211; Jumers Castle Lodge (Trans) 359-7141; La Quinta (1/2 mile, Trans) 762-9008; Stardust (Trans) 764-9644.

Meeting Rooms: Elliot Flying Service has a conference room at their location 799-3183; Also: Hampton Inn 762-1711; Holiday Inn 762-8811; Howard Johnson Lodge 797-1211; Jumers Castle Lodge 359-7141; La Quinta Inn 762-9008; Stardust 764-9644.

Transportation: Elliott Flying Service (FBO) has courtesy cars available by calling 799-3183; Also taxi service: Milan Cab Company 788-8341; A/P Transportation & Delivery 764-4949; Bestway Taxi 788-9785.

Information: Cities Convention & Visitors Bureau, 2021 River Drive, Moline, IL 61265, Phone 788-7800 or 800-747-7800.

Attractions:

Quad City Downs, 5005 Morton Drive, East Moline, IL, Phone: 792-0202; Also River boat gambling available, See "Information".

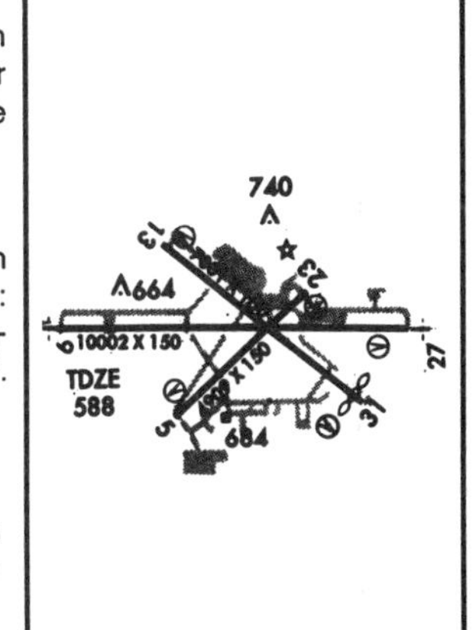

Airport Information:

MOLINE - QUAD-CITY AIRPORT (MLI)
3 mi south of town N41-26.92 W90-30.45 Elev: 589 Fuel: 100LL, Jet-A
Rwy 09-27: H10002x150 (Asph-Conc-Grvd) Rwy 13-31: H7000x150 (Conc) Rwy 05-23: H4909x150 (Asph) Attended: 1200-0400 Atis: 121.2 Unicom: 122.95 App/Dep Con: 118.2, 125.95 Tower: 119.4 Gnd Con: 121.9 Clnc Del: 123.95 Public Phone 24hrs
Notes: Overnight parking: Singles $4.00, Twins $6.00.
FBO: Elliott Aviation Phone: 799-3183

Quad Cities USA

Perhaps you have asked the same question. What in the world is Quad Cities USA? It consists of four U.S. cities that share the Mississippi River: Davenport/ Bettendorf, Iowa and Rock Island/Moline, Illinois. Your next question. What makes these four cities different from the rest? Quad Cities marks the spot where east met west for the first time. In 1856, the first train crossed the Mississippi River into the Quad Cities. This landmark was originally established as a fur trading post, which later became a military outpost. Quad Cities has a population of approximately 370,000 people, with over 2.5 million people within a 100 mile radius. Quad Cities offers lots of history, theater and entertainment.

Step back in time at the Buffalo Bill Cody Homestead, the Colonel Davenport House, the Walnut Grove Pioneer Village and the Black Hawk State Historic Site. Or, stop by the world headquarters of Deere and Company in Moline to hear about the agricultural history of Western Illinois. Hop aboard the Civil War Tram Tours and learn more about the role of the Rock Island Arsenal in the Civil War and in the U.S. military. There are more than a dozen museums that offer 200-million-year-old fossils, as well as two children's museums that offer state-of-the-art fun. The Buffalo Bill Museum, Davenport Museum of Art, Hauberg Indian Museum, the Putnam Museum of History and Natural Science and the Rock Island Arsenal Museum are just to name of few.

After touring the museums, catch a show at one of the theaters. The Circa '21 Dinner Playhouse in Rock Island offers year-round productions and special celebrity nights. The Adler Theatre in Davenport features beautifully restored art deco and offers broadway musicals, symphony, rock and pop concerts and comedy acts. The Quad City Sympony also holds special events throughout the year at the Adler Theatre. The Playcrafters Barn Theatre in Moline presents live performances in a refurbished dairy barn, which run 3 weekends in January, March, May, July, September and November.

For fast-paced excitement, Quad City Downs in East Moline offers exciting simulcast parimutal harness racing all year-round. It's a good bet that you'll have a great time on the mighty Mississippi River while on one of the three riverboat casinos: Casino Rock Island, the President or the Lady Luck Casino Bettendorf. The Casino Rock Island, open year-round, is a 200-foot-paddlewheeler with a red, white and blue theme carried out on three supporting boats that are docked permanently at the Boatworks in Rock Island, 18th Street and Mississippi River. Casino Rock Island offers six cruises Sunday through Thursday and seven on Friday and Saturday. All cruises are free of charge. Or, enjoy the President Riverboat Casino in Davenport, which is the "world's biggest riverboat casino." This registered National Historic landmark offers more than 27,000 square feet of casino space with the largest jackpots on the Mississippi River. It remains dockside except for weekday morning cruises. The Lady Luck Casino Bettendorf provides convenient unlimited gaming action. It offers over 30,000 square feet of 750 slots and 46 table games. Lady Luck's own restaurant features a 70 item international grand buffet.

For guests who just want to take a relaxing cruise, non-gaming excursions are available aboard the Celebration

Photo by: Quad Cities Convention & Visitors Bureau

President Riverboat CasinoThe "biggest in the world".

Cruises in Moline and River Cruises in LeClaire, Iowa.

Quad Cities offers plenty of outdoor recreation. The Great River Trail covers more than six miles of hiking and biking along the Mississippi River from Rock Island to East Moline. Golfers have their choice of over twenty golf courses. There are many outdoor festivals and special events, such as the Quad City Airshow during the month of June or the music festivals and fairs during the month of July.

There are plenty of places to eat and sleep in the Quad Cities. Dining choices range from comfortably formal to elegantly casual. There are more than 4,500 hotel/motel rooms, over a dozen bed and breakfasts, and hundreds of camping spots.

Quad-City Airport is located in Moline, Illinois and has a 8,507'x150 asph-conc-grvd runway, a 6,000'x150 concrete runway, and a 4,909'x150 asphalt runway. Overnight parking is $4.00 for singles and $6.00 for twins. Fee is waived with a fuel purchase. With advance notice, the FBO will provide courtesy cars to local restaurants. Avis car rentals are also available at the airport. Contact the FBO at 799-3183. In addition, Milan Cab Company is available at 788-8341. For more information about attractions and accommodations in the Quad Cities, contact the Quad Cities Convention and Visitors Bureau at 800-747-7800 or 788-7800. (Information Submitted by the Quad Cities Convention and Visitors Bureau.)

Photo by: Quad Cities Convention & Visitors Bureau. Enjoy all kinds of music at the summer music festivals on the banks of the Mississippi River.

IL-C66 - MONMOUTH
MONMOUTH MUNICIPAL AIRPORT

(Area Code 309) 38, 39

Cerar's Barnstormers Restaurant:

Cerar's Barnstormers Restaurant is located 1-1/2 miles west of the Monmouth Municipal Airport and will furnish their dining guests with free courtesy transportation. This restaurant is open Tuesday, Wednesday, Thursday and Friday from 11 a.m. to 2 p.m. and 5 p.m. to 9 p.m. On Saturday they are open from 5 p.m. to 10 p.m. (Closed on Sunday & Monday). Their luncheon menu features "Gourmet" sandwiches; as well as "Diet Watchers" selections. On their dinner menu, specialties of the house include Seafood Parmesan: a combination of char-broiled halibut steak with scallops sauted in a delicious wine and Parmesan cheese sauce; Scallops Au Gratin: a dish containing scallops sauted in Chablis wine sauce, then baked to perfection in aged Swiss cheese; or try the Filet Farci Bearnaise: created by their chef: A sauted beef filet smothered in Bearnaise sauce and fresh mushrooms. In addition, their dinner menu contains appetizers, soups, salads, poultry, seafood, Cajun and diet watcher's entrees. Prices run an average of $4.95 for lunch and $12.00 for dinner. On Tuesday through Friday they feature a luncheon buffet. The decor of this fine dining facility is rustic and the restaurant is decorated with an aviation theme displaying pictures of airplanes on the walls throughout the restaurant. Group fly-in are welcome, given advance notice. For information call 734-9494.

Meling's Restaurant:

Meling's Restaurant is located about 11 blocks west of the Monmouth Municipal Airport in Monmouth, Illinois. This combination restaurant and lodging facility will provide transportation to and from the airport, by calling the motel at 734-2196. The restaurant is a family type restaurant open Monday through Thursday from 6 a.m. to 10 p.m.; Friday and Saturday from 6 a.m. to 11 p.m. and Sunday from 7 a.m. to 8 p.m. This facility contains a dining room, and coffee shop. Their menu includes steaks and seafood as well as a salad bar and buffet. A Sunday buffet is served 8a.m. to 10 p.m. and a luncheon buffet from 11 a.m. to 3 p.m. The coffee shop provides light fare, with daily specials. For information call the restaurant at 734-7965.

Restaurants Near Airport:

Cerar's Barnstormers	1.5 mi W.	Phone: 734-9494
Meling's Restaurant	1.5 mi W.	Phone: 734-7965

Lodging: Meling's Motel is located 1 mile west of the Monmouth Municipal Airport at 1129 North Main Street, (Junction US 34 and 67). This facility contains 55 rooms and will provide courtesy transportation to and from airport. Restaurant on premises (See listing above). Phone: 734-2196

Meeting Rooms: Accommodations for meetings can be arranged with Meling's Motel, Phone: 734-2196

Transportation: Both Meling's Restaurant and Motel as well as Cerar's Restaurant, will provide courtesy transportation to fly-in guests. Heritage Flying Service, Inc. will also provide transportation for their customers, Phone: 734-3411

Information: Monmouth Area Chamber of Commerce, 620 South Main Street, P.O. Box 857, Monmouth, Illinois 61462, Phone: 734-3181.

Attractions:

A golf course is also available about 200-300 yards from the same airport office. With a population of about 11,000 people, Monmuth Illinois is known as the birthplace of the ledgendary Wyatt Earp, and was named after the famous battle of Monmuth, fought during the Revolutionary War in New Jersey. Upon landing at the Monmouth Airport, you will notice that there is an attractive city park located immediately across the road from the airport office. For information on tee off times and reservations you can call 734-9968.

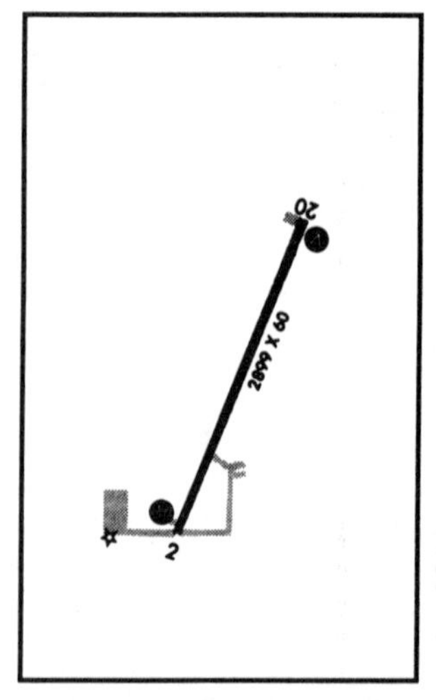

Airport Information:

MONMOUTH - MONMOUTH MUNICIPAL (C66)
2 mi north of town   N40-55.78 W90-37.87   Elev: 753   Fuel: 100LL, MOGAS
Rwy 02-20: H2899x60 (Asph)   Attended: Tues-Sun 1400-2300Z   Unicom: 122.8
Public Phone: 24hrs   Notes: No landing or tiedown fee. Operator states; This is the oldest operating airport within the state of Illinois (Since 1921).
FBO: Monmouth Municipal Airport   Phone: 734-3411

IL-C09 - MORRIS
MORRIS MUNICIPAL AIRPORT

(Area Code 815) 40

Runway 47 Restaurant:

The Runway 47 Restaurant is located on the Morris Municipal Airport and is open 7 days a week between 6 a.m. and 5 p.m. Specialties of the house include a variety of daily specials as well as a Saturday and Sunday buffet for only $5.45 Average prices run $2.50 to $4.50 for breakfast and $2.00 to $5.00 for lunch. Larger groups and parties are welcome with advance notice appreciated. Aircraft parking is available adjacent to the restaurant on the parking ramp. For more information call the Runway 47 Restaurant at 941-4447.

Restaurants Near Airport:
Runway 47 Restaurant On Site Phone: 941-4447

Lodging: Holiday Inn (4 miles) 942-6600; Morris Motel (5 miles) 942-9846; Park Motel (5 miles) 942-1321.

Meeting Rooms: None reported

Transportation: Airport courtesy car available with advance notice appreciated. Call Morris Municipal Airport at 942-1600 or VanReeth Aviation at 941-4200.

Information: Grundy County of Commerce & Industry, 112 East Washington Street, Morris, IL 60450, Phone: 942-0113.

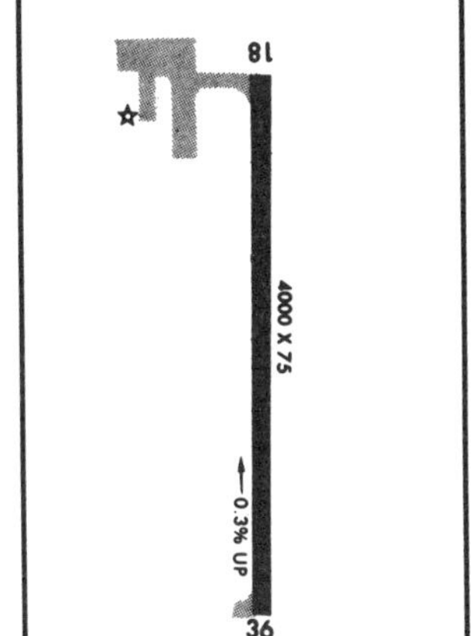

Airport Information:

MORRIS - MORRIS MUNICIPAL AIRPORT (C09)
4 mi north of town N41-25.53 W88-25.12 Elev: 584 Fuel: 80, 100LL
Rwy 18-36: H4000x75 (Asph) Attended: 1400-0200Z Unicom: 122.8
Morris Municipal Airport Phone: 942-1600
FBO: VanReeth Aviation Phone: 941-4200

IL-MVN - MOUNT VERNON
MOUNT VERNON-OUTLAND

(Area Code 618)

41

Stormy's At The Airport:

You can taxi and park your aircraft right out in front of the restaurant. This combination family style and fine dining restaurant is open for lunch 5 days a week between 11 a.m. and 2 p.m. and for dinner on Friday and Saturday from 4 p.m. to 10 p.m. and Wednesday and Thursday from 4 p.m. to 9 p.m. Their specialties are filet and prime rib, rib-eye, New York strip, pork chops, catfish, grilled chicken, Italian spaghetti, soup, salads and sandwiches. Prices average between $3.75 to $3.85 for sandwiches and around $4.95 and $12.95 for dinner items. The decor of the restaurant has an elegant romantic setting with linen covered tables and a flower for each centerpiece. They have one main dining room and a banquet conference room that can be reserved for special occasions. Catering service is another specialty of this establishment. For information call Stormy's at 242-5115.

Restaurants Near Airport:
Stormy's At The Airport On Site Phone: 242-5115

Lodging: Best Western-Inns of America (6 miles) 244-4343; Drury Inn (6 miles) 244-4550; Holiday Inn (6 miles, trans.) 244-3670; Ramada Hotel (6 miles, trans.) 244-7100; Regal 8 Inn (6 miles) 244-2383; Super 8 Motel 242-8800.

Meeting Rooms: Best Western-Inns of America 244-4343; Holiday Inn (trans) 244-3670; Ramada Inn (trans.) 244-7100.

Transportation: Taxi Service: Ace 242-6120; Classic 244-6949; Peoples Taxi 244-1135; Rental Cars: Hertz 244-1215.

Information: Jefferson County Chamber of Commerce, 200 Potomac Blvd, P.O. Box 1047, Mount Vernon, IL 62864, Phone: 242-5725.

Airport Information:

MOUNT VERNON - OUTLAND (MVN)
3 miles east of town N38-19.40 W88-51.51 Elev: 480 Fuel: 100LL, Jet-A Rwy 05-23: H6498x150 (Asph-Pfc) Rwy 15-33: H3149x100 (Asph-Pfc) Attended: continuously Unicom: 123.0
FBO: Fliteline Aero Services Phone: 244-7746

IL-PIA - PEORIA
GREATER PEORIA REGIONAL

(Area Code 309) 42

Greater Peoria Airport Restaurant:

The Greater Peoria Airport Restaurant is located on Greater Peoria Airport near Peoria, Illinois and features a cafeteria styled restaurant with a gift shop nearby. It is open from 5 a.m. to 6 p.m. 7 days a week. Aircraft parking is reported within walking distance. The restaurant is situated within the main terminal building. Daily specials are featured. A meeting room is located downstairs, and can be reserved for catered functions. For information about the Greater Peoria Airport Restaurant call 697-6903.

Restaurants Near Airport:
Greater Peoria Arpt. Rest. On Site Phone: 679-6903

Lodging: Continental Regency Hotel (8 miles, Trans) 674-2500; Holiday Inn & Holidome (Trans) 686-8000; Holiday Inn East (Trans) 699-7231; Jumer's Castle Lodge (4 miles, Trans) 673-8040; Pere Marquette Hotel (8 miles, Trans) 637-6500.

Meeting Rooms: Continental Regency Hotel 674-2500; Holiday Inn & Holidome 686-8000; Holiday Inn East 699-7231; Jumer's Castle Lodge 673-8040; Pere Marquette Hotel 637-6500.

Transportation: Rental Cars: Avis 697-5200; Budget 697-2722; Dollar 697-8267; Hertz 697-0650; National 697-0566.

Information: Peoria Convention & Visitors Bureau, 403 NE Jefferson, Peoria, IL 61603, Phone: 676-0303 or 800-747-0302.

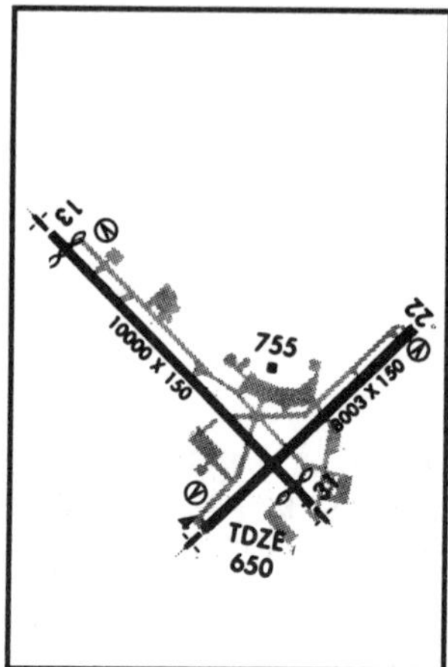

Airport Information:

PEORIA - GREATER PEORIA REGIONAL AIRPORT (PIA)
4 mi west of town N40-39.86 W89-41.60 Elev: 660 Fuel: 100LL, Jet-A
Rwy 13-31: H10,000x150 (Asph-Grvd) Rwy 04-22: H8008x150 (Asph-Grvd)
Attended: continuously Unicom: 122.95 Atis: 126.1 Unicom: 122.95 Peoria App/Dep Con: 125.8, 119.95 Peoria Tower: 119.1 Gnd Con: 121.6 Clnc Del: 121.85
FBO: Byerly Aviation Phone: 697-6300

IL-3MY - PEORIA
MOUNT HAWLEY AUXILIARY

(Area Code 309) 43

Shopping Mall Restaurants:

During our conversation with the staff of North Point Aviation, we were told that there is a shopping mall located within 100 yards of the airport. This complex contains a number of stores including a Builder's Square along with several other shops. There are also 5 fast food facilities including a Hardee's restaurant, subway, little Caesar's Pizza, Taco Bell, and a Kroger Deli. For more information you can call the people at North Point Aviation 693-1908.

Restaurants Near Airport:
5 Fast Food/Shopping Mall Walk Dist. Phone: 693-1908

Lodging: Clayton House Motel (2 miles) 688-8511; Hyatt Lodge (2 miles) 691-4680; Junction City Inn 691-4680.

Meeting Rooms: None Reported

Transportation: Taxi Service: Community Cab 676-0064; Pearlene Bell Cab 674-5956; Yellow Checker 676-0731.

Information: Convention & Visitors Bureau, 331 Fulton, Suite 505, Peoria, IL 61602, Phone: 676-0303 or 800-747-0302.

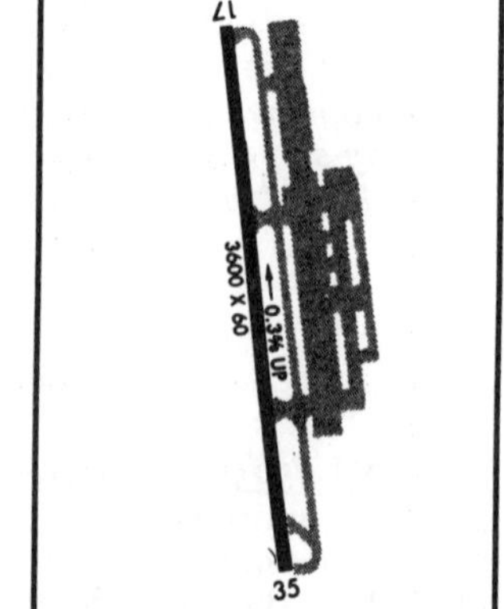

Airport Information:

PEORIA - MOUNT HAWLEY AUXILIARY (3MY)
7 mi north of town N40-47.72 W89-36.80 Elev: 785 Fuel: 100LL, Jet-A
Rwy 17-35: H3600x60 (Asph) Attended: dawn-dusk Unicom: 122.7
FBO: North Point Aviation Phone: 693-1908 or 693-2372

IL-VYS - PERU
ILLINOIS VALLEY REG.-WALTER A DUNCAN FLD.

(Area Code 815) 44

Red Door Inn:

The Red Door Inn Restaurant is a unique restaurant which is located about 3 or 4 miles from the Illinois Valley Regional/Walter Duncan Airport. This restaurant contains three separate main dining rooms in a casual atmosphere, and serves choice steaks, and sea food entrees as well as German cooking. They also have side table service, which offers steaks cooked to perfection at your table. The restaurant is open Monday through Friday from 11 a.m. to 11 p.m. and Saturday 4 p.m. to 12 a.m. and Sunday from 4 p.m. to 10 p.m. For transportation or reservations call 223-2500.

Restaurants Near Airport:
Red Door Inn 4 mi Phone: 223-2500

Lodging: Holiday Inn (Trans) 224-1060; Howard Johnson Lodge 224-2500; Motel 6 224-2785; Super 8 Motel 223-1848.

Meeting Rooms: Holiday Inn 224-1060; Howard Johnson Lodge 224-2500; Super 8 Motel 223-1848.

Transportation: Taxi Service: Starved Rock Taxicab Service 223-2227; Rental Cars: Budget 223-8441; Peterman Rental Cars 224-1655.

Information: Illinois Valley Chamber of Commerce, 300 Bucklin Street, P.O. Box 446, La Salle, IL 61301, Phone: 223-0227.

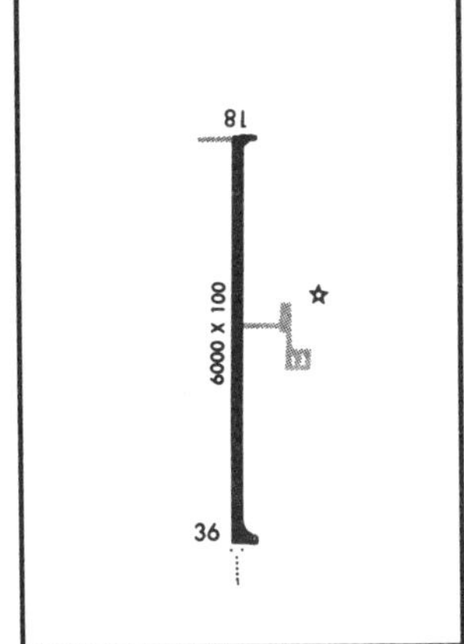

Airport Information:

PERU - ILLINOIS VALLEY REGIONAL-WALTER A DUNCAN FIELD (VYS)
1 mi east of town N41-21.11 W89-09.19 Elev: 654 Fuel: 100LL, Jet-A
Rwy 18-36: H6000x100 (Asph) Attended: 1300-0100Z Unicom/CTAF: 123.0
Illinois Valley Regional Airport **Phone: 223-8441**

IL-1C5 - PLAINFIELD
CLOW INTERNATIONAL AIRPORT

(Area Code 708)

45, 46

Country Aire Restaurant:

The Country Aire Restaurant is a very popular stopping place for many local as well as cross country pilots. This establishment is located right on the Clow International Airport and is situated at the end of a long taxiway that lies perpendicular to the north-south active runway. This same taxiway will lead you to the fuel pumps, as well as the local fixed base operator on the field. The Country Air Restaurant can seat approximately 35 to 40 people, in a very casual and rustic decor, with a come-as-you-are atmosphere. The dining room is decorated with thick dark wooden tables and booths situated along the walls. There are also large windows that provide a nice view of arriving or departing aircraft, which at times, park literally within a few feet of the restaurant. There is limited parking for aircraft on the hard service, but usually enough grass tie-down spots available to accommodate all fly-in guests. The restaurant serves great breakfasts, all types of sandwiches and cheeseburgers as well as other popular dishes. There is always a friendly crowd and plenty of hangar flying to go around. A huge bulletin board running the length of their hallway serves as a favorite place to look for great deals on new or used aviation related items. The Country Aire is open Monday through Thursday from 7 a.m. to 3 p.m., Friday from 7 a.m. to 9 p.m. and Saturday and Sunday from 7 a.m. to 4 p.m. For further information call them at 759-9833.

Pancake Cafe:

The Pancake Cafe is located 8 miles north of Clow International Airport. This family cafe is open from 7:00 a.m. to 10:00 p.m., 7 days a week. Their specialty is not hard to guess! They serve a wide variety of different types of traditional pancakes, such as Buttermilk Old Fashioned Pancakes, Silver Dollar pancakes (which come in stacks of six, twelve, or eighteen!), blueberry, strawberry, banana nut, chocolate chip, bacon, potato, wheat germ, Swedish (served with lingonberries imported from Sweden), and many more. Why not sample their special Apple Pancake, Baked Pecan Pancake, German Pancake, Dutch Baby (small version of the German Pancake) or Vegetable Dutch Pancake. The restaurant also serves a variety of crepes, Belgian Waffles, omelets, eggs, and various salad and sandwich entrees. They serve a special children's menu, as well. With advance notice, the Pancake Cafe can cater to large groups during the week. (We were told that weekends are very busy!) They can also cater to private and corporate pilots on the go. For more information about the Pancake Cafe, call 637-1010.

Restaurants Near Airport:

Country Aire Restaurant	On Site	Phone: 759-9833
Pancake Cafe	8 mi N	Phone: 637-1010

Lodging: Stardust Motel (7 miles); Super 8 Motel (10 min) 759-8880; Holiday Inn - Willowbrook (15 min) 325-6400; Red Roof Inn (15 min) 323-8811

Meeting Rooms: William Tell Inn/Holiday Inn 355-4200.

Transportation: Naperville Cab Service 355-7855; West Suburban Cab 357-4410; Rental Cars: Ed James 312-759-5600

Information: Northern Illinois Tourism Council, 1740 S. Bell School Road, Cherry Valley, IL 61016, Phone: 332-9626

Airport Information:

PLAINFIELD - CLOW INTERNATIONAL (1C5)

6 mi northeast of town N41-41.76 W88-07.75 Elev: 670 Fuel: 80, 100LL Rwy 18-36: H3362x50 (Asph) Attended: 1300-0000Z CTAF: 122.9 Chicago App/Dep Con: 133.5

FBO: A & M Aviation **Phone: 759-1555**

FBO: B & B Aircraft Corporation **Phone: 759-9223**

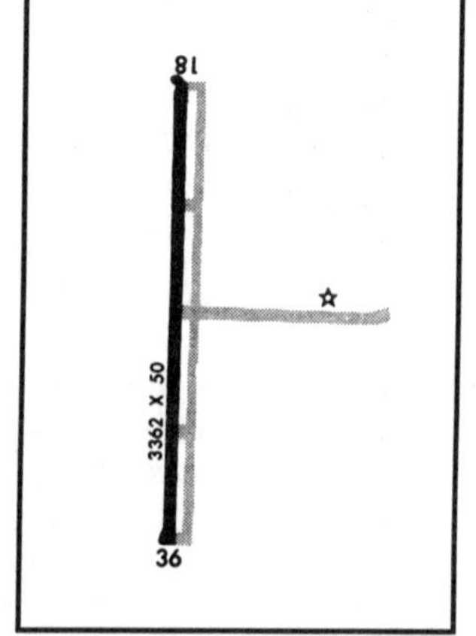

Not to be used for navigational purposes

IL-UIN - QUINCY
QUINCY MUNI. BALDWIN FIELD

(Area Code 217) 47

Skyway Airport Restaurant:

The Skyway Airport Restaurant is a family restaurant that is located on the north end of Quincy Airport. This establishment is open Monday through Saturday 6:30 a.m. to 8 p.m. and Sunday from 7:30 a.m. to 8 p.m. Winter hours may vary slightly. They specialize in serving steaks and seafood along with a nice variety of many other entrees from their menu. On Friday night they feature catfish, as well as rib-eye, and chicken dishes throughout the week. On Sunday they offer a complete salad bar as well. The restaurant layout is a circular glassed in dining room that can seat up to 60 persons and faces the active runways. Accommodations for larger fly-in groups and banquet facilities serving 50 to 60 people can also be arranged with advance reservations. In-flight catering is also possible. Aircraft parking is available within walking distance to the restaurant. For information call 885-3466.

Restaurants Near Airport:
Skyway Restaurant On Site Phone: 885-3466

Lodging: Holiday Inn (Trans) 222-2666; Rodeway Inn (Trans) 223-6780; Travel Lodge-Quincy (Trans) 222-5620.

Meeting Rooms: Holiday Inn 222-2666; Roadway Inn 223-6780; Travel Lodge-Quincy 222-5620.

Transportation: Airport courtesy car reported; Taxi Service: Yellow Cab 222-6820; Also Rental Cars: Hertz 885-3464; National 885-3438.

Information: Chamber of Commerce, 314 Main Street, Quincy, IL 62301, Phone: 222-7980.

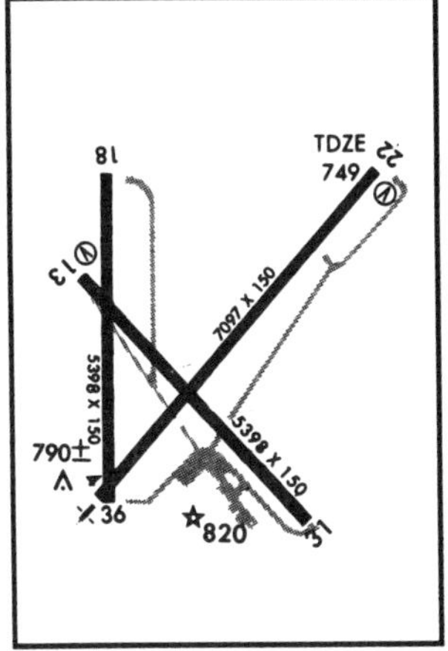

Airport Information:

QUINCY - QUINCY MUNICIPAL BALDWIN FIELD (UIN)
10 mi east of town N39-56.56 W91-11.67 Elev: 769 Fuel: 100LL, Jet-A
Rwy 04-22: H7097x150 (Asph-Grvd) Rwy 13-31: H5398x150 (Asph-Grvd)
Rwy 18-36: H5398x150 (Conc) Attended: 1100-0500Z Unicom: 123.0 Tower: 135.25 Gnd Con: 121.75
Airport Manager Phone: 885-3285

Octave Chanute Aerospace Museum

Rantoul, IL (IL-215)

The Octave Chanute Aerospace Museum, located in Rantoul, Illinois, is a showcase of Illinois Aviation and the 76-year history of Chanute Air Force Base. The museum, which opened April 1, 1994, covers over 126,000 square feet of display space, making it the largest Aerospace Museum in Illinois. Special memorial rooms are dedicated to pioneer aviators of Illinois, and to Chanute AFB commanders and heroes. The museum offers a gift shop, visitors reception suite, library, and guided tours and lectures. Friendly volunteers are there to help too!

As visitors walk through the museum, they may notice artifacts and memorabilia of the Army, Navy, Marine and Coast Guard personnel. Chanute was a leader in "interservice" training and provided training to all the sister services, and in some cases, to civilian personnel of other governmental agencies. Also, International students from many foreign governments received training under various foreign military assistance programs. Several showcases display memorabilia and gifts presented by international students in gratitude for the training and warm hospitality they received in America.

Most of the aircraft on display made their final flight to Chanute, having been sent to serve as trainers in one of the many schools located there. One of the most popular displays is the B-52 nose section. Visitors are allowed to climb all the way up to the upper flight deck, but they must do so carefully because it is a long fall down! They may also enter the C-130 in the outdoor display area.

Many items on display were designed and manufactured by technicians in the Chanute Training Aids Department to support the many varied training programs. The engine cutaways, the F-111 flight controls trainer, and the above ground missile silos are great examples of their skill and expertise, as well as a tribute to them.

In addition to displaying the heritage of Chanute Air Force Base, the museum is chartered to display aviation history within the state of Illinois. Numerous individuals have provided the museum with valuable artifacts on a donation or long term loan basis to be shared with the general public. The David Bunetta display room contains materials dating back to civil war times. Guests will see the aviation pioneers in the Military Aviation Hall of Fame of Illinois. The flight simulators in the Frasca Room are courtesy of Frasca Aviation, a local firm that designs and manufactures general aviation flight simulators for worldwide distribution. A vintage hot-air balloon and the first powered hang glider flown in the state of Illinois are suspended in the hanger bay.

Hours are 10:00 a.m. to 5:00 p.m. on Monday, and Wednesday through Friday. (Closed Tuesday) Also 10:00 a.m. to 6:00 p.m. on Saturday, and 12:00 p.m. to 5:00 p.m. on Sunday. For admission prices and other information, call the Octave Chanute Aerospace Museum at 217-893-1613. (Information submitted by Octave Chanute Aerospace Museum)

Photo by: Chanute Aerospace Museum

Octave Chanute Aerospace Museum, Largest Aerospace Museum in Illinois.

IL-1C8 - ROCKFORD COTTONWOOD AIRPORT

(Area Code 815) 48

Etta's Family Restaurant:

Etta's Family Restaurant is located right on the Cottonwood Airport situated 35 degrees off the Rockford (RFD) VOR, near Rockford, IL. This family style facility is open 7 days a week between 10:00 a.m. and 2 a.m. when their lounge closes. Fly-in guests can park their aircraft just outside the restaurant. A wide variety of selections are offered including breakfast items like their popular biscuits and gravy along with lunch and dinner choices, including steaks, prime rib, New York strip steak, chicken dinners, catfish, cod, perch and shrimp platters, as well as pizza. Average prices run $1.99 to $15.95 for most selections. Friday night specials include perch, cod and shrimp platters. This restaurant has 3 separate dining areas with a lounge. The inside of the restaurant has a southwestern decor along with American and Indian decorations and furnishings. Anything on their menu can be ordered-to-go. For information about this restaurant call 962-8252.

Restaurants Near Airport:
Etta's Family Rest. On Site Phone: 962-8252

Lodging: Conners's Motel (4 miles) 968-0631; Rustic Motel (2 miles) 968-7528.

Meeting Rooms: None Reported

Transportation: Taxi Service: Yellow Taxi 962-5511.

Information: Rockford Area Convention & Visitors Bureau, Memorial Hall, 211 North Main Street, Rockford, IL 61101, Phone: 963-8111, 800-521-0849.

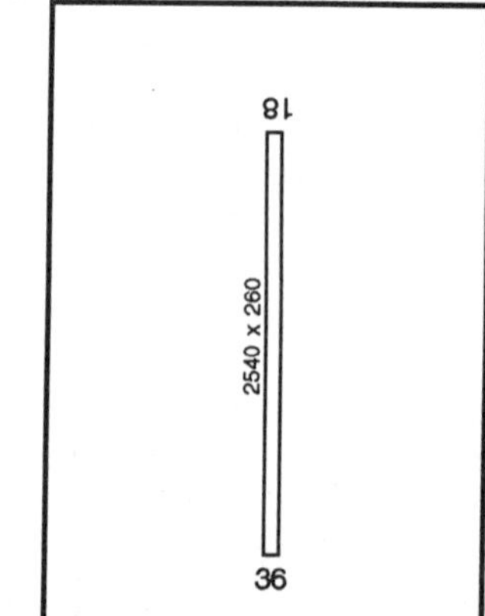

Airport Information:

ROCKFORD - COTTONWOOD AIRPORT (1C8)
2 mi northwest of town N42-17.50 W89-08.17 Elev: 741 Rwy 18-36: 2540x260 (Turf)
Attended: Tues-Sun 1500Z-dusk Unicom: 122.8
Airport Manager Phone: 965-3050

IL-RFD - ROCKFORD
GREATER ROCKFORD AIRPORT

(Area Code 815)

49

Terminal Restaurant: (Temporarily Closed)

A recently constructed terminal building on the Greater Rockford Airport near Rockford, Illinois offers excellent accommodations for travelers. During the time of this writing, we learned that their restaurant has been closed. However we suspect that new owners may re-open this dining establishment. The dining room provides a panoramic view overlooking the main terminal ramp from the upper level, where commuter aircraft arrive and depart during scheduled times. Keep this location on your list of great places to fly and dine. A periodic call or inquiry is well worth your consideration. Call the Airport Management at 965-8639 of updated information as to the re-opening of this facility.

Restaurants Near Airport:
Terminal Restaurant   Trml. Bldg.   Temporarily Closed

Lodging: Comfort Inn-Airport (Trans) 397-4000; Howard Johnson Lodge (Trans) 397-9000; Rockford Motor Inn (Trans) 398-2200.
Meeting Rooms: Comfort Inn-Airport 397-4000; Howard Johnson Lodge 397-9000; Rockford Motor Inn 398-2200.
Transportation: Courtesy cars on field; Also Rental Cars: Avis 962-8447; Budget 962-0331; Hertz 963-5318; National 965-4466.
Information: Rockford Area Convention & Visitors Bureau, Memorial Hall, 211 North Main Street, Rockford, IL 61101, Phone: 963-8111, 800-521-0849.

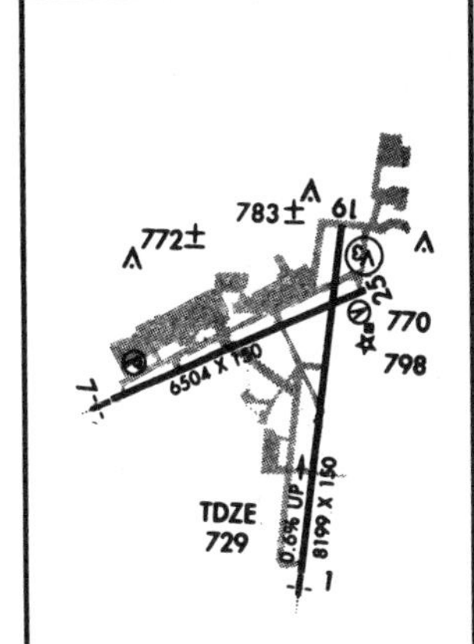

Airport Information:

ROCKFORD - GREATER ROCKFORD AIRPORT (RFD)
4 mi south of town   N42-11.77 W89-05.59   Elev: 736   Fuel: 100LL, Jet-A Jet-A1+
Rwy 01-19: H8199x150 (Asph-Grvd)   Rwy 07-25: H6504x150 (Asph-Grvd)   Attended: continuously   Atis: 126.7   Unicom: 122.95   Rockford App/Dep Con: 126.0 (West) 128.15 121.0 (East)   Rockford Tower: 118.3   Gnd Con: 121.9
FBO: Aero-Taxi Rockford, Inc.   Phone: 963-4444
FBO: Alpine Air Charter   Phone: 800-822-0121
FBO: Courtesy Aircraft, Inc.   Phone: 229-5112
FBO: Emery Air Charter   Phone: 800-435-8090
FBO: Raytheon Aircraft Service   Phone: 987-4100

IL-C48 - SANDWICH
WOODLAKE LANDING AIRPORT

(Area Code 815)

50

Airport Diner: (Temporarily Closed)

The Woodlake Landing Airport, and is a popular stopping point for many local as well as cross country air travelers. This airport has a beautiful new runway and ramp area. At the time of interviewing the airport manager we learned that the restaurant on the field has been temporarily closed. However the restaurant may be re-opened in the future. Aircraft parking is available within only a few feet from the restaurant. This diner was a favorit with many local pilots throughout the region. We suggest that you contact the airport management to obtain an update as to the reopening of the restaurant. For information call 786-7411.

Restaurants Near Airport:
Airport Diner   On Site   Temporarily Closed

Lodging: Harvester Motel (4 miles) 552-8018

Meeting Rooms: None Reported

Transportation: Courtesy car reported available.

Information: Chicago State Office of Tourism, 806 north Michigan Avenue, Chicago, IL 60611, Phone: 312-280-5740.

NO AIRPORT DIAGRAM AVAILABLE

Airport Information:

SANDWICH - WOODLAKE LANDING (C48)
2 mi southwest of town   N41-38.30 W88-38.67   Elev: 677   Fuel: 80, 100, MOGAS
Rwy 08-26: H2988x50 (Asph)   Rwy 18-36: 1750x150 (Turf)   Attended: 1400Z-dusk
Unicom: 122.8   Notes: Parachute jumping. Rwy 18-36 for emergency use only.
FBO: Sandwich Airport, Inc.   Phone: 786-7411

IL-SAR - SPARTA
SPARTA COMMUNITY-HUNTER FLD

(Area Code 618) 51, 52, 53

Brandy's Restaurant:

Brandy's restaurant is located right across the street from the Sparta Community-Hunter Field. This combination bar and grill provides a variety of sandwiches for their customers. Their restaurant hours are reported to be 6 a.m. to 10 p.m. 7 days a week. For information call the restaurant at 443-3899, or Sparta Aero Services, Inc. at 443-2002.

Charlie G's Restaurant:

Charlie G's Restaurant is located between 1 and 2 miles from the Sparta Community-Hunter Field. This establishment is popular with business travelers as well as fly-in customers. A courtesy car from Sparta Aero Services, Inc., located on the field, can easily be obtained for short term use. Charlie G's is open 7 days a week between 6 a.m. and 10 p.m. Their lounge is open until 1 a.m. Specialties of the house include Italian cuisine along with cordon bleu, Italian dishes, filet mignon, poor man's lobster, steaks, pork chops and hickory smoked ham. They also offer full breakfast and lunch selections. Their seating capacity is 185 persons with a separate party room that can accommodate up to 50 persons. The front portion of the restaurant serves as a quaint coffee shop while the back is reserved for full service dining. Average meal price specials run $2.65 for breakfast, $5.00 for lunch and $10.00 for dinner. They also feature a Sunday brunch from 11 a.m. to 2 p.m. For more information call them at 443-4047.

Frontier Steak House:

The Frontier Steak House is located about 700 feet and across the street from the Sparta Community-Hunter Field. This establishment is open from 11 a.m. to 9 p.m. 7 days a week. Specialty items on their menu include steak sandwiches, chicken, and seafood selections. They also have a hot and cold food bar as well as a salad bar and dessert bar. Their steaks include rib-eye, T-bone, porter house, top sirloin, chopped steaks and broiled chicken Monterey. Their dining room offers a casual family atmosphere. Two additional private dining rooms can accommodate 25 and 70 people. A new motel has also been constructed adjacent to this restaurant and airport. For information call the Frontier Steak House at 443-3078.

Restaurants Near Airport:

Brandy's Restaurant	Adj Arpt.	Phone: 443-3899 or 2020
Charlie G's	1-2 mi	Phone: 443-4047
Frontier Steak House	Adj Arpt.	Phone: 443-3078

Lodging: Mac's Motel (2 miles) 443-3614; Poolside Motel (2 miles) 443-3187.

Meeting Rooms: None Reported

Transportation: Courtesy and rental cars are reported available through Sparta Aero Services, Inc. at 443-2002.

Information: Carbondale Convention and Tourism Bureau, 1245 E Main Street, Suite A32, Carbondale, IL 62901, Phone: 618-529-4451 or 800-526-1500.

Airport Information:

SPARTA - SPARTA COMMUNITY-HUNTER FIELD (SAR)
2 mi north of town N38-08.94 W89-41.92 Elev: 538 Fuel: 100LL
Rwy 18-36: H3997x60 (Asph) Rwy 09-27: 2450x135 (Turf) Attended: 1400-0000Z
Unicom: 122.8
FBO: Sparta Aero Services, Inc. Phone: 443-2002

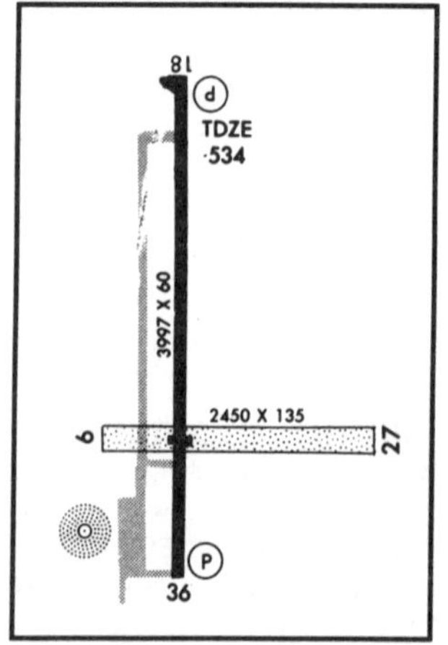

IL-SPI - SPRINGFIELD CAPITAL AIRPORT

(Area Code 217) 54

Arena Snack Bar & Lounge:

The Arena Snack Bar & Lounge is located on Capital Airport in Springfield, Illinois, within the main terminal building. They serve a nice choice of entrees from which to choose. Menu items include sandwiches like chicken salad, tuna salad, ham & egg, and club sandwiches. Fresh baked cookies and donuts are also served. They have and outdoor patio area for dining. Meeting rooms are also available for large functions. The restaurant is open from 5:15 a.m. to 8:00 p.m. on weekdays, 6 a.m. to 3 p.m. on Saturday and from 7 a.m. to 3 p.m. on Sunday. For additional information call 788-1073.

Restaurants Near Airport:
Arena Snack Bar & Lounge On Site Phone: 788-1073

Lodging: Best Western Sky Harbor (Trans) 753-3446; Best Western State House (Trans) 523-5661; Hilton (Trans) 789-1530; Holiday Inn-South (Trans) 529-7131; Mansion View Motel (Trans) 544-7411; Quality Inn (Trans) 522-7711; Ramada Renaissance (Trans) 544-8800; Springfield Travel Inn (Trans) 528-4341.
Meeting Rooms: Best Western Sky Harbor 753-3446; Best Western State House 523-5661; Hilton 789-1530; Holiday Inn-South 529-7131; Mansion View Motel 544-7411; Quality Inn 522-7711; Ramada Renaissance 544-8800.
Transportation: Airport courtesy car available; Taxi Service: A-Diamond 788-5828; Airport Taxi 789-2629; Lincoln Taxi Service 523-2424; Also Rental Cars: Avis 522-7728; Budget 523-7000; Hertz 525-8820; National 544-6300.
Information: Springfield Convention & Visitors Bureau, 109 North 7th, Springfield, IL 62701, Phone: 789-2360 or 800-545-7300.

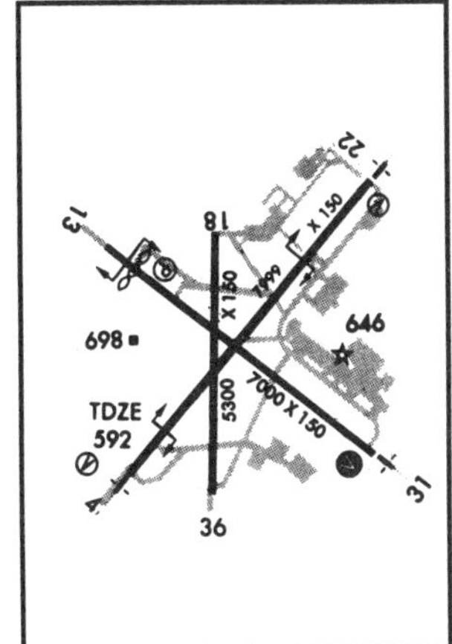

Airport Information:

SPRINGFIELD - CAPITAL AIRPORT (SPI)
3 mi northwest of town N39-50.64 W89-40.66 Elev: 597 Fuel: 100LL, Jet-A
Rwy 04-22: H7999x150 (Conc-Grvd) Rwy 13-31: H7000x150 (Asph-Grvd) Rwy 18-36: H5300x150 (Asph-Conc) Attended: Mon-Fri 1100-0600Z, Sat-Sun 1100-0430 Atis: 127.65
Unicom: 122.95 Springfield App/Depp Con: 118.6, 126.15 Springfield Tower: 121.3
Gnd Con: 121.9 Clnc Del: 121.7
FBO: Garrett Aviation Service Phone: 544-3431

IL-SQI - STERLING ROCKFALLS WHITESIDE CO ARPT-JOS H BITTORF FLD.

(Area Code 815)

55, 56

Benigan's Restaurant:

The Benigan's Restaurant is located about 1-1/2 mile from the Sterling Rockfall Whiteside County Airport. If you call them they will provide free transportaton for fly-in guests. Walking from the airport to the restaurant is not recommended because of a four lane highway between the airport and the restaurant. This facility has undergone a complete renovation. Once known as the Canal House restaurant in conjunction with the Ramada Inn it is now Benigan's Restaurant in conjunction with the Holiday Inn. Benigan's restaurant is an upscale family style dining establishment. Their menu has a wide selection of entrees. Current restaurant hours are 6 a.m. to 10 p.m. Monday through Saturday and 6:30 a.m. to 9 p.m. on Sundays. These hours may vary significantly when the new restaurant has been completed. In additon to the restaurant, the Holiday Inn offers 115 rooms for lodging and up to 5 separate banquet rooms able to accommodate between 250 and 300 persons. These rooms are separated by partitions and can be joined into one large room. For more information you can call 626-1041.

Red Apple Restaurant:

The Red Apple Restaurant has been in business for the past 11 years and is located 1-1/2 miles from the Sterling Rockfalls Whiteside County Airport. Transportation to this facility can be arranged by the airport. This family-style restaurant is open from 5 a.m. to 11 p.m. 7 days a week. A full menu is provided with many items to choose from. Chicken dishes and stir-fry, along with Friday fish fry (Catfish & White fish), are their specialties. Daily specials are also available. Breakfast entrees are served all day long. The Red Apple offers a casual atmosphere with a contemporary decor. Groups are always welcome. For information you can call them at 708-625-5160.

Attractions:

Once a year around the second or third week in September the Annual North Central EAA "Old Fashioned" Fly-in is held. Over the years it has grown to be quite an event for aviation enthusiasts as well as the local community. Some of the events held include: welding workshops, sheet metal workshops, RV Forum, CAFE 150 event, medical's, food vendors, "Young Eagles", fly market, aircraft sales, prizes, pancake breakfast and much more. One item of importance is that this event sponsored by the NCEAA is free to all those in attendance. Donations are accepted and a NCEAA yearbook is available for sale which helps, in part, to fund some of the activities. Everyone with an interest in aviation is welcome. For more information you can call Mr. Dave Christianson at 815-625-6556.

Restaurants Near Airport:

Benigan's (Holiday Inn)	1-1/2 mi	Phone: 626-1041
Red Apple Restaurant	1-1/2 mi	Phone: 625-5160

Lodging: Holiday Inn 1 mi (Free trans.) 626-1041; Motel 8 626-1837.

Meeting Rooms: Holiday Inn 1 mile has accommodations for 250 to 300 persons at their location with 5 separate conference rooms. For information call 626-1041.

Transportation: Airport courtesy cars are available; Rental cars at Garco 625-3761; Taxi Service: Twin City 626-3847.

Information: Illinois Department of Conservation, 2612 Locust Street, Sterling, IL 61081, Phone: 815-625-2968.

Airport Information:

STERLING ROCKFALLS - WHITESIDE CO ARPT-JOSHBITTORF FLD.

2 mi south of town N41-44.57 W89-40.58 Elev: 647 Fuel: 100LL, Jet-A Rwy 07-25: H6500x150 (Asph-Grvd) Rwy 18-36: H3899x100 (Asph-Pfc) Attended: 1400-0200Z, Unattended major holidays Unicom: 122.8

FBO: Aviation Training Professionals	**Phone: 625-9533**
Radio Ranch (Avionics)	**Phone: 622-9000**

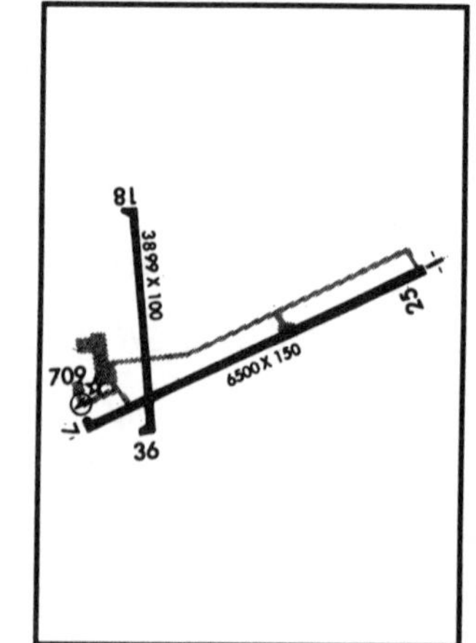

Not to be used for navigational purposes

INDIANA

LOCATION MAP

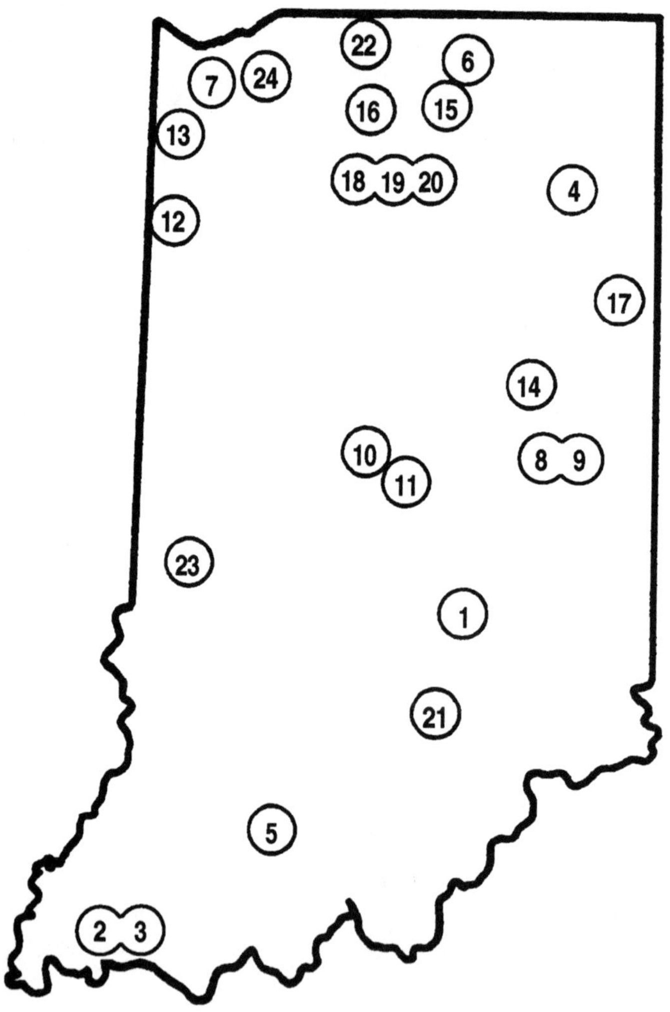

Not to be used for navigational purposes

INDIANA

CROSS FILE INDEX

Location Number	City or Town	Airport Name And Identifier	Name of Attraction
1	Columbus	Columbus Muni. Arpt. (BAK)	Hangar 5 Restaurant
2	Evansville	Evansville Reg. Arpt. (EVV)	Elliott's Steak House
3	Evansville	Evansville Reg. Arpt. (EVV)	Evansville Air Host
4	Fort Wayne	Fort Wayne Intl. Arpt. (FWA)	Ivories Rest. (Hilton)
5	French Lick	French Lick Muni. Arpt. (FRH)	French Lick Sprg. Resort
6	Goshen	Goshen Muni. Arpt. (GSH)	Old Mill Inn
7	Griffith.Merrilville	Griffith-Merrilvill (05C)	Mi Tierra Mexican Rest.
8	Hagerstown	Hagerstown Arpt. (I61)	Generations Restaurant
9	Hagerstown	Hagerstown Arpt. (I61)	Welliver's Restaurant
10	Indianapolis	Eagle Creek Airpark (EYE)	Rick's Cafe Boat Yard
11	Indianapolis	Indianapolis Intl. Arpt. (IND)	Host Marriott Intl..
12	Kentland	Kentland Arpt. (50I)	The Filling Station
13	Lake Village	Lake Village Arpt. (C98)	Farside Restaurant
14	Muncie	Delaware Co.-Johnson Fld. (MIE)	Vince's Gallery
15	Nappanee	Nappanee Muni. Arpt. (C03)	Amish Acres Barn Rest.
16	Plymouth	Plymouth Muni. Arpt. (C65)	Balloon Wurks Rest.
17	Portland	Portland Muni. Arpt. (PLD)	Richard's Restaurant
18	Rochester	Fulton Co. Arpt. (RCR)	Gropps Restaurant
19	Rochester	Fulton Co. Arpt. (RCR)	Karen's Restaurant
20	Rochester	Fulton Co. Arpt. (RCR)	Tony's Restaurant
21	Seymour	Freeman Muni. Arpt. (SER)	Airport Cafe
22	South Bend	Michiana Regl. (SBN)	Air Host Restaurant
23	Terre Haute	Hulman Reg. Arpt. (HUF)	George's Cafe
24	Valparaiso	Porter Co. Muni. (VPZ)	Strongbow Inn

Articles

City or town	Nearest Airport and Identifier	Name of Attraction
French Lick, IN	French Lick Muni. (FRH)	French Lick Spgs. Resort
South Bend, IN	Michianna Regional (SBN)	Studebaker Museum

IN-BAK - COLUMBUS
COLUMBUS MUNICIPAL AIRPORT

Hangar 5 Restaurant:

The Hangar 5 Restaurant is situated within the main terminal building at the Columbus Municipal Airport. This combination cafe and family style restaurant is reported to be within walking distance from aircraft parking. They are open 7 days a week between 7 a.m. and 2 p.m. Specialty items available are soups, salads, a variety of sandwiches and plate lunch specials available Monday through Friday. Average prices run $3.50 for breakfast and $5.00 for lunch. Their dining room is very clean and modern. They also have banquet facilities with two additional rooms that can handle 10 to 100 customers. For more information about the Hangar 5 Restaurant call 378-4070.

Attractions:

Otter Creek Golf Course 579-6585; Brown County State Park; Columbus Architectural Tour 372-1954; Columbus Historical Museum 372-3541.

Airport Information:

COLUMBUS - COLUMBUS MUNICIPAL AIRPORT (BAK)
3 mi north of town N39-15.72 W85-53.78 Elev: 656 Fuel: 100LL, Jet-A
Rwy 05-23: H6401x150 (Asph) Rwy 14-32: H5000x150 (Asph) Attended 1100-0100Z
Unicom: 122.95 Indianapolis App/Dep Con: 134.85 Tower: 118.6 Gnd Con: 121.6
Clnc Del: 121.6 Public Phone 24hrs Notes: No landing fee; Overnight parking $3.00 single, and $4.00 multi engine.
FBO: Rhoades Aviation, Inc. Phone: 372-1819

(Area Code 812) 1

Restaurants Near Airport:

Gropps Fish of Stroh	3 mi S.	Phone: 372-2966
Hangar "5" Restaurant	On Site	Phone: 378-4070
Jonathan Moore's Cafe	6 mi SW.	Phone: 376-3051
Ketchum's Kornucopia	3 mi S.	Phone: 376-4108

Lodging: Holiday Inn (4 miles) 372-1541; Ramada Inn (4 miles) 376-9951; Rodeway Inn (4 miles) 376-9951.

Meeting Rooms: The airport terminal building contains meeting rooms for up to 25 persons as well as banquet and conference rooms for up to 200 people. For information call Rhoades Aviation, Inc. at 372-1819; Also meeting rooms available at Holiday Inn 372-1541; Ramada Inn 376-3051; and Rodeway Inn 376-9951.

Transportation: Courtesy transportation available through Rhoades Aviation, Inc. 372-1819; Also: Taxi Service: Crown Taxi 379-9219; Royal Taxi 376-8360; Rental Cars: Avis 372-5056; National 372-6284; Ugly Duckling 378-3825; Bus Service 376-2506.

Information: Columbus/ Bartholomew County Visitor, Information & Promotion (VIP) Bureau, 825 Washington, Columbus, IN 47202-1477, Phone: 378-2622.

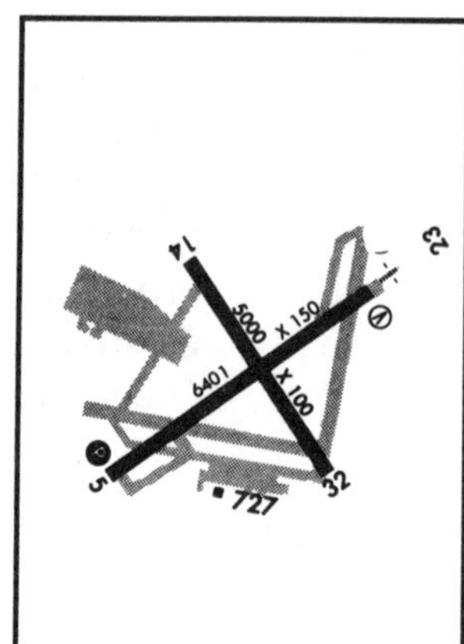

IN-EVV - EVANSVILLE
EVANSVILLE REGIONAL AIRPORT

(Area Code 812)

2, 3

Elliott's Steak House:

Elliott's invites you to come share a unique dining experience with a decor rich in stained glass and exquisitely crafted woodwork gathered from throughout the country. Their menu offers a wide selection of not only choice steaks, but chicken, pork and fresh seafood as well. Begin with their cheese and relish hor d'oeuvre tray, then combine shrimp or a hot meat item to create a combination to suit your taste. Their early evening specials, served Sunday through Friday until 6:30 p.m., appeal to the lighter appetite. Select your entree from their well stocked display case and then you and your guests may enjoy cooking your own steaks on one of their open grills, or you may choose to relax and let their chef do it for you. They can also serve your party in their loft, banquet room, the privacy of their library lounge or in the main dining room. There is table seating by the dance and stage floor to enjoy their dance bands, sports, live music or whatever else they can think of. This restaurant is located across from the Lawndale Shopping Center in Evansville, IN. To reach the restaurant from the Evansville Regional airport (EVV), take Hwy 57 to US 41, south (left) on US 41 to Washington Ave. Turn east (left) on Washington to Green River Road. Turn left and go 1 stop light, then left again and you should see the restaurant shortly. Courtesy transportation can be obtained through Million Aire Aviation by calling 425-4700. This fine dining establishment serves lunch between 11 a.m. and 2 p.m., dinner between 4:30 and 10 p.m. Monday through Saturday and 4:00 to 8:00 on Sundays. Specialties served include appetizers, salads, salad bar, soups and desserts. Main entrees are steaks and seafood. Also one unique feature about this restaurant is that guests can even cook their own steaks to perfection if desired. Average prices run $8.00 for lunch and around $18.00 for most dinner entrees. For information call Elliott's Steak House at 473-3378.

Evansville Air Host:

The Evansville Air Host Restaurant is located in the main terminal at Evansville Dress Regional Airport in Evansville, Indiana. This is a cafe-style restaurant with lounge providing steam table service as well as a variety of sandwiches, soups and salads. Daily specials are also offered. Their main dining room can accommodate 120 persons. Guests are able to enjoy the view and see aircraft from the restaurant dining room. This restaurant can also provide catering service for 35 to 40 people in their banquet room. They can serve private or corporate pilots with In-flight catering. The restaurant hours are 5 a.m. to 6 p.m. Their snack shop is open until 10:30 p.m. A gift shop and bar on the premises is part of the Evansville Air Host. For further information, call 423-1113.

Restaurants Near Airport:

Elliott's Steak House	4 mi	Phone: 473-3378
Evansville Air Host	On Site	Phone: 423-1113

Lodging: Drury Inn 2 mi 423-5818; Days Inn (On Field) 464-1010; Executive Inn 5 mi 424-8000; Holiday Inn (3 mi., Trans) 425-1092; Oak Meadow Lodge 867-6431; Radison Inn 1 mi 867-7999; Ramada Inn (Trans) 424-6400;

Meeting Rooms: Drury Inn 2 mi 423-5818; Days Inn (On Field) has 3 meeting rooms that can be converted into one large room if desired. 464-1010; Executive Inn 5 mi (Arpt. trans) 424-8000; Holiday Inn (3 mi., Trans) 425-1092; Radison Inn (1 mi. Arpt. trans.) 867-7999; Ramada Inn (Trans) 424-6400;

Transportation: Airport Courtesy car: (Million Air FBO 2 hr. max.); Also Taxi Service: River City Taxi 429-0000; Rental Cars: Avis 423-5645; Budget 423-4343; Dollar 425-6020; Hertz 425-7143; National 425-2426.

Information: Convention & Visitors Bureau, 623 Walnut Street, Evansville, IN 47708, Phone: 425-5402 or 800-433-3025.

Airport Information:

EVANSVILLE - EVANSVILLE DRESS REGIONAL AIRPORT (EVV)

3 mi north of town N38-02.28 W87-31.84 Elev: 418 Fuel: 100LL, Jet-A
Rwy 04-22: H8021x150 (Asph-Grvd) Rwy 18-36: H5080x150 (Asph) Rwy 09-27: H3500x100 (Asph) Attended: continuously Atis: 120.2 Unicom: 122.95
App/Dep Con: 126.4, 127.35 Tower: 118.7 Gnd Con: 121.9 Clnc Del: 126.6
FBO: Million Air Phone: 425-4700
FBO: Tri State Aero Phone: 426-1221

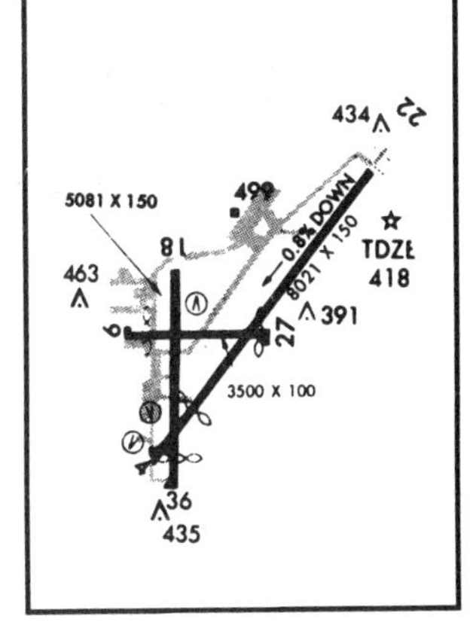

IN-FWA - FORT WAYNE
FORT WAYNE INTL. AIRPORT

(Area Code 219)

4

Ivories Restaurant (Holiday Inn):

Ivories Restaurant is located across the parking lot from the Fort Wayne International Airport in the Airport Holiday Inn. Ivories serves breakfast from 6 a.m. to 11 a.m., lunch from 11 a.m. to 2 p.m. and dinner from 5:30 p.m. to 10 p.m. daily. Specials of the house are served at lunch and weekend nights in a casual atmosphere. In addition to this dining facility, Holiday Inn Airport provides air travelers with many conveniences. They have 146 rooms with family weekend rates, swimming pool, and lounge, as well as tennis and golf privileges. A courtesy van service is available to airport customers. They also provide a limited menu for meals-to-go. Call 747-9171 for information.

Restaurants Near Airport:
Ivories (Holiday Inn) Adj Arpt Phone: 747-9171

Lodging: American Plaza Inn 432-0511; Holiday Inn Airport (On Site, Trans) 747-9171; Hilton Inn Downtown (Trans) 420-1100; Holiday Inn Downtown (Trans) 422-5511; Marriott Fort Wayne (Trans) 484-0411; Sheraton Inn (Trans) 484-9681.

Meeting Rooms: All lodging facilities listed above are reported to contain accommodations for meetings or conferences.

Transportation: Taxi Service: Checker 426-8555; Deluxe 482-3634; Rental Cars: Avis 747-6411; Budget 748-1696; Dollar 747-0849; Hertz 747-6100; National 747-4124.

Information: Fort Wayne County Convention & Visitors Bureau, 1021 S. Calhoun Street, Fort Wayne, IN 46802, Phone: 424-3700 or 800-767-7752.

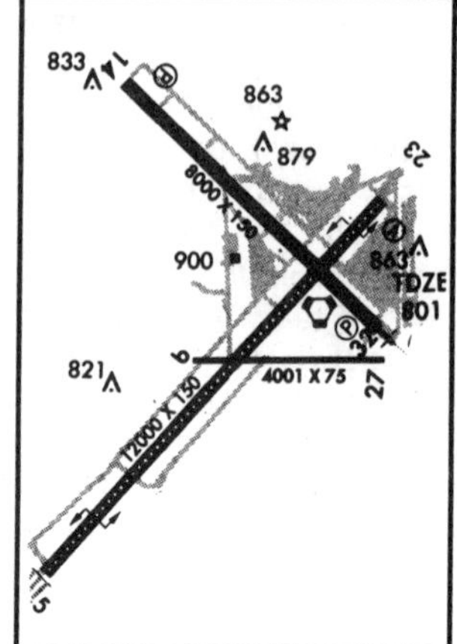

Airport Information:

FORT WAYNE - FORT WAYNE INTERNATIONAL AIRPORT (FWA)
7 mi southwest of town N40-58.70 W85-11.69 Elev: 815 Fuel: 100LL, Jet-A
Rwy 05-23: H12000x150 (Asph-Conc-Grvd) Rwy 14-32: H8500x150 (Asph-Conc-Grvd)
Rwy 09-27: H4001x75 (Asph-Conc) Attended: continuously Atis: 121.25 Unicom: 122.95
App/Dep Con: 132.15, 127.2, 135.325 Tower: 119.1 Gnd Con: 121.9 Clnc Del: 124.75
FBO: Consolidated Airways Phone: 747-1626
FBO: Fort Wayne Air Service Phone: 747-1565

IN-FRH - FRENCH LICK
FRENCH LICK MUNICIPAL ARPT.

(Area Code 812)

5

Restaurants Near Airport:
French Lick Restaurant 4 mi Phone: 936-9300

French Lick Springs Resort Restaurants:

The meals at the French Lick Resort can be enjoyed at several locations on the premises and with a variety of atmospheres from which to choose. The Chez James Gourmet Dining Room features elegant dining at its finest. The Pluto's Pavilion, Hoosier Dining Room for larger groups, and a pizzeria are all situated at different locations on the resort property. In addition to these, is their Golf and Country Club situated nearby which also contains dining accommodations. This four seasons resort located on some 2,600 acres of the Cumberland foot hills, provides excellent accommodations as well as a tremendous selection of entertainment and activities for their guests. Their convention facilities attract many business travelers as well as corporations scheduling conferences for their cliental. Transportation by courtesy van is provided to and from the French Lick Airport 4 miles from the resort complex. For information call the French Lick Springs Golf And Tennis Resort at 936-9300 or 800-457-4042.

Lodging: French Lick Resort (4 miles, Free courtesy transportation provided) 936-9300 or 800-457-4042.
Meeting Rooms: French Lick Resort has accommodations for conventions and meetings, 936-9300 or 800-457-4042.
Transportation: French Lick Resort will pick up their fly-in guests from the French Lick Airport about 4 miles away. Call 936-936-9300 or 800-457-4042.
Information: French Lick-West Baden Chamber of Commerce, P.O. Box 347, French Lick, IN 47432, Phone: 936-2405.

Attractions: French Lick Resort is situated 4 miles from the French Lick Airport. This resort contains 485 rooms, has two private 18 hole golf courses, pro shop, 8 Indoor and 10 lighted outdoor tennis courts, bowling, billiards, horseback riding, chuck-wagon breakfast and dinners held on special occasions, indoor and outdoor swimming pools, spa and health club, live entertainment and stage shows, business and convention facilities able to cater up to 1,200 people, nearby French Lick scenic railway excursions and down hill ski packages at nearby locations, and much more. For information call the resort at 936-9300 or 800-457-4042.

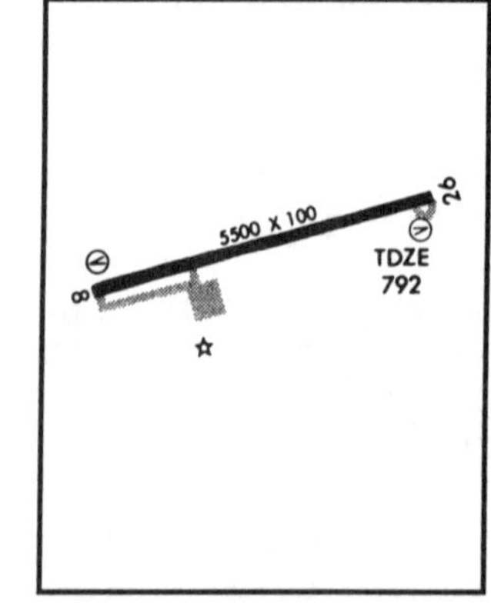

Airport Information:

FRENCH LICK - FRENCH LICK MUNICIPAL AIRPORT (FRH)
3 mi southwest of town N38-30.37 W86-38.22 Elev: 792 Fuel: 100LL, Jet-A
Rwy 08-26: H5500x100 (Asph) Attended: 1500Z-dusk Unicom: 122.8 Notes: The French Lick Resort is located 4 miles from the airport and will furnish a courtesy van to pick their guest up at the airport.
French lick Springs Resort Phone: 936-9300 or 800-457-4042

French Lick Springs Resort

French Lick, IN (IN-FRH)

Located on some 2,600 acres of Cumberland foothills, the French Lick Springs Hotel with its 525 rooms, provides excellent accommodations as well as a tremendous selection of entertainment and activities for their guests.

Two private 18-hole golf courses are made available, consisting of the "Scenic Valley Course", (Par 71) and the championship "Country Club Course", (Par 70) which are both served by a proshop containing rental clubs, club storage, in addition to equipment and sports fashion merchandise available for purchase.

Anyone interested in an exhilarating game of tennis will be able to choose between 25 tennis courts available. More than any other resort hotel in the midwest, French Lick Resort offers 12 indoor and 13 lighted outdoor courts open any time of the day throughout the year. The proshop will fulfill your needs with equipment for sale or rent. Their tennis professional will also help arrange tournaments for small or large groups.

For those guests interested in sharpening their skills in marksmanship, they may enjoy a complete skeet and trap shooting facility at the scenic hilltop location adjacent to the hotel. Gun rental and ammunition is available on the site, along with instruction for beginners, as well as arranging tournaments.

Horseback riding can be a great way to leisurely tour the miles of beautiful bridle trails surrounding the hotel premises. An unforgettable chuck wagon breakfast or dinner in the nearby woods can also be arranged for larger groups.

The French Lick Hotel has indoor sports right up your alley with six bowling lanes complete with automatic pinsetters located in the recreation center. In addition to the activities previously mentioned, guests are encouraged to enjoy themselves with a host of other activities such as bike riding (conventional and tandem bikes for rent); horseshoes; miniature golf; shuffleboard; badminton; volleyball; croquet; surrey rides; pool and billiards; electronic game room and sightseeing programs.

Due to the rejuvenation properties of the rich mineral waters of this region, the French Lick Springs Resort has become famous for its therapeutic mineral baths. "The Spa," a health and beauty care facility, has attributed a great deal to the resort's popularity over the years.

The meals at the French Lick Resort are operated on the American Plan, which means that your appropriate meals are included in the room rate.

Casual attire in the dining room is customary at breakfast or lunch. For dinner, ladies may choose between cocktail dresses or coordinated pantsuits, while gentlemen are required to wear coats or dinner jackets. After enjoying a great meal, you are welcome to partake of the evenings entertainment within French Lick's festive lounges with live entertainment and stage presentations.

Mixing business with pleasure is a general rule rather than an exception at French Lick Springs Resort. The facility contains a flexible complex of 23 meeting and function rooms for groups up to 1,200 persons. Whether it concerns a business conference, banquet or reception, they will accommodate all your needs. For large or small gatherings, they can provide just the right room, ranging in size from 280 square feet to 16,245 square feet.

The French Lick Municipal Airport is located approximately two miles southwest of the city of French Lick, Indiana. This airport is equipped with a (08-26) 5,500 x 100 asphalt runway, with an airport elevation of 792 feet. Runway bearing loads can accommodate aircraft having gross weights up to 60,000 pounds. 100LL and Jet-A is reported available. Limousine service to French Lick Springs Hotel, located about 4 miles from the airport can be obtained by calling the resort at 812-936-9300. (Informationed by French Lick Resort).

Photo by: Aerodine

IN-GSH - GOSHEN
GOSHEN MUNICIPAL AIRPORT

(Area Code 219) 6

Old Mill Inn:

The Old Mill Inn Restaurant is located about 2 miles from the Goshen Municipal Airport in Goshen, Indiana. Transportation is available by using a courtesy car from Medivac Inc., which is the main fixed base operator on the field. The restaurant is a nice family restaurant with a casual rustic country like atmosphere. The menu offers broasted chicken, steaks, house specialty sandwiches, breakfast anytime, as well as many other items available, in a family setting. Prices average $5.50 to $6.00 for meals. They are open Monday through Thursday 5 a.m. to 2 p.m., Friday and Saturday 5 a.m. to 8 p.m. and Sunday from 7 a.m. to 1:30 p.m. This family owned and operated establishment also has banquet rooms available for parties, fly-in groups or business conferences. For more information please call 533-4994.

Restaurants Near Airport:

Old Mill Inn	2 mi	Phone: 533-4994

Lodging: Best Western Inn 533-0408; Checkerberry Inn 642-4445; Goshen Inn 642-4388; Holiday Inn (Trans) 533-9551

Meeting Rooms: Checkerberry Inn 642-4445; Holiday Inn 533-9551.

Transportation: Airport courtesy car reported; Taxi Service: Goshen Cab 533-4510.

Information: Chamber of Commerce, 109 East Clinton Street, Goshen, IN 46526, Phone: 533-2102.

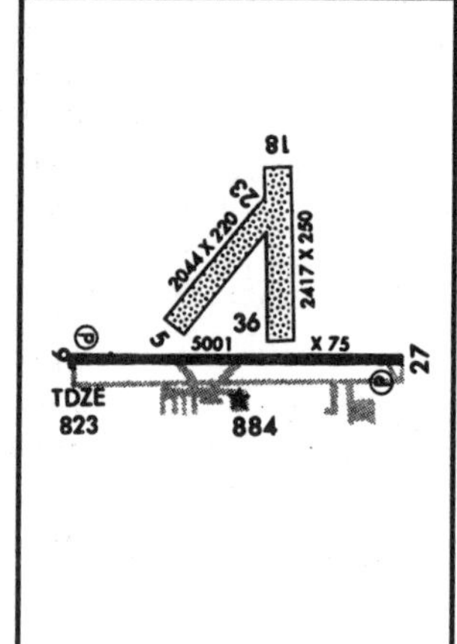

Airport Information:

GOSHEN - GOSHEN MUNICIPAL AIRPORT (GSH)
3 mi southeast of town N41-31.63 W85-47.53 Elev: 827 Fuel: 100LL, Jet-A
Rwy 09-27: H5001x75 (Asph) Rwy 18-36: 2417x220 (Turf) Rwy 05-23: 2044x150 (Turf)
Attended: Mon-Sat 1200Z-dusk, Sun 1300Z-dusk Unicom: 123.0
FBO: Goshen Air Center, Inc. Phone: 642-3123, or 533-8245

IN-05C - GRIFFITH-MERRILVILLE
GRIFFITH-MERRILVILLE AIRPORT

(Area Code 219) 7

Mi Tierra Mexican Restaurant:

This restaurant is located across the street from the Griffith-Merrilvile Airport. You can walk to the restaurant from the airport. This is a family-style facility that is open for business between 10 a.m. and 10 p.m. They specialize in serving authentic Mexican food with a complete selection of entrees. Their menu displays a full assortment of choices. Average prices run $3.75 for breakfast, $4.75 for lunch and $6.00 for dinner. The decor of the restaurant has a Mexican and western style. Mi Tierra Restaurant will also cater to parties with prior notice given. They are also able to accommodate catering for pilots on-the-go if desired. For information you can call the Mi Tierra Restaurant by calling 922-3633.

Attraction:

Southlake Mall is located about 5 to 7 miles from this location. The Star Plaza Theater features famous performers from all parts of the country. Many other facilities are situated near the airport. For information you can call the Merrillville Chamber of Commerce at 769-8180 or 800-252-3948.

Restaurants Near Airport:

Bridges Scoreboard	2 mi	Phone: 924-2206
Excalibur	2 mi	Phone: 924-0304
Jedi's Garden	3 mi	Phone: 838-1155
Mi Terra Mexican	Adj Arpt.	Phone: 922-3633
Stan's Steak House	2 mi	Phone: 924-4767

Lodging: Carlton Lodge-Maryville 5 mi. 756-1600; LaQuinta Inn 5 mi 738-2870; Radisson Hotel Star Plaza 5 mi 769-6311; Red Roof Inn 5 mi 738-2430.

Meeting Rooms: Carlton Lodge-Maryville 5 mi 756-1600; Radisson Hotel Star Plaza 5 mi has convention facilities and meeting rooms available. Call 769-6311.

Transportation: Courtesy car available; Also Rental Cars: Budget 932-1771; Enterprise 924-0707; Hertz 769-0377; Taxi Service: Yellow Cab 931-4400; Limousine Service: 800-676-3631.

Information: Merrillville Chamber of Commerce, 52 W. 80th Place Plaza, Merrillville, IN 46410 Phone: 219-769-8180 or 800-252-3948.

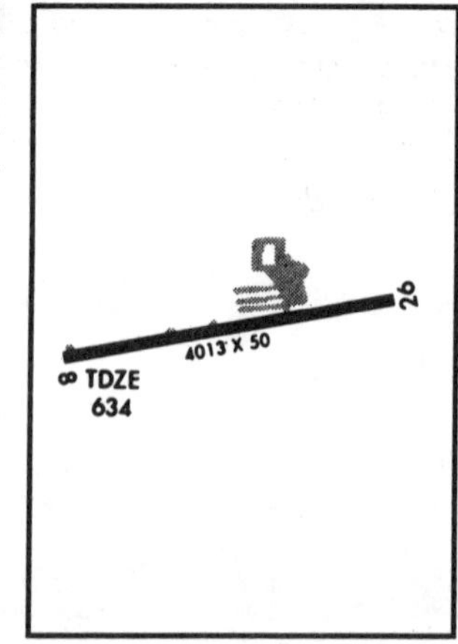

Airport Information:

GRIFFITH-MERRILVILLE - GRIFFITH-MERRILVILLE AIRPORT (05C)
2 mi east of town N41-31.18 W87-24.07 Elev: 634 Fuel: 100LL, Jet-A Rwy 08-26: H4013x50 (Asph) Attended: 1400-0400 Unicom: 123.0
FBO: Griffith Aviation Phone: 219-924-0207

IN-I61 - HAGERSTOWN
HAGERSTOWN AIRPORT

(Area Code 317) | 8, 9

Generations Restaurant:

Generations Restaurant is located approximately 1-1/2 mile from the Hagerstown Airport. Fly-in guests can arrange transportation either through the airport or the restaurant. Once leaving the airport you will take Washington Street to the stop light and turn right. About 3 doors down you will see a blue house. This will be the restaurant. Generations Restaurant is a quaint Victorian-style establishment with their main dining rooms decorated with family memorabilia, a cherrywood fireplace, chandeliers and ceiling fans. There are two dining rooms including a library dining room. Their main menu offers items like garlic chicken, steak, stuffed chicken breasts, 16 oz. Porter House, broiled red snapper, cajun chicken white fish, mushroom topped pork chops, country pork chops, strip steak and prime rib. Lunch specials run $5.50 and average dinner prices range between $9.95 and $15.95. Group accommodations are also available with advance notice. Restaurant hours are Sunday and Monday 11 to 2p.m., Tuesday through Thursday from 11 a.m. to 7p.m., Friday 11 a.m. to 9p.m. and Saturday from 4p.m. to 9p.m. Reservations are suggested. For more information call Generations Restaurant at 489-6116.

Welliver's Restaurant:

Welliver's Restaurant is located one mile from Hagerstown Airport, 300 degrees and 18 miles off the Richmond, Indiana VOR. This restaurant features an all-you-can-eat buffet in addition to a full service menu. It is best known for its extensive salad table and old-fashioned iron skillet cookery. Their main dining area can seat 450 persons. Items on their menu include steamed shrimp, Boston scrod, French fried shrimp, unique pan fried chicken, baked beans, chicken livers and turnips. Prices for the smorgasbord is $12.95 on Friday and Saturday and $10.95 on Sunday. Other menu items run between $4.00 to $8.00 for most meals. Their dining room has a comfortable and casual atmosphere. Restaurant hours are Thursday from 4:30 p.m. until 8 p.m., Friday from 4:30 p.m. to 8:30 p.m., Saturday from 4 p.m. to 9 p.m. and Sunday from 11 a.m. until 8 p.m. They are closed on Monday, Tuesday and Wednesday. Reservations are not usually needed except for large groups. During our conversation with the management we learned that sometimes fly-in guests will walk to the restaurant and then arrange transportation back to the airplane. Transportation can also be obtained by calling Hagerstown Airport Unicom on 123.0 prior to landing. We were told, in order to reach the Welliver's Restaurant, go north on Washington Street up to Main Street (State Route 38) then turn right until you reach the middle of downtown. For more information call Welliver's Restaurant at 489-4131.

Restaurants Near Airport

Generations Restaurant	1 mi	Phone: 489-6116
Welliver's Restaurant	1 mi SW.	Phone: 489-4131

Lodging: None Reported

Meeting Rooms: None Reported

Transportation: Airport courtesy car is reported. Welliver's and Generations Restaurant can both furnish transportation depending on available staff. Call the restaurants to let them know you are coming.

Information: Wayne County Convention and Tourism Bureau, 600 Promenade, Richmond, IN 47374, Phone: 935-8687.

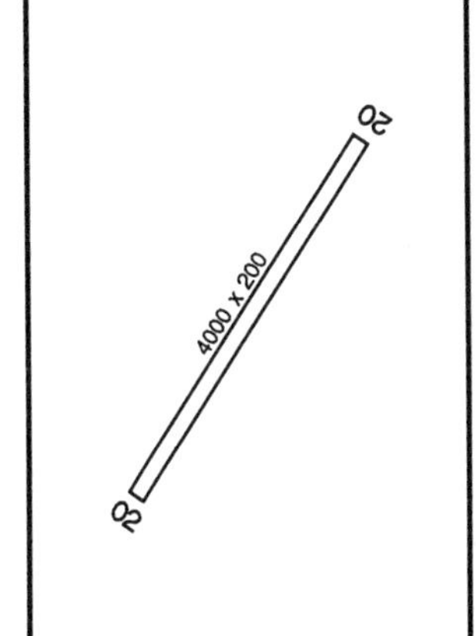

Airport Information:

HAGERSTOWN - HAGERSTOWN AIRPORT (I61)
1 mi south of town N39-53.49 W85-09.75 Elev: 1000 Rwy 02-20: 4000x200 (Turf)
Attended: unattended Unicom: 123.0
Hagerstown Airport Phone: 489-7926, 489-4292

IN-EYE - INDIANAPOLIS
EAGLE CREEK AIRPARK

(Area Code 317)

10

Restaurants Near Airport:
Rick's Cafe Boat Yard   Adj Arpt   Phone: 290-9300

Rick's Cafe Boat Yard:

Rick's Cafe Boat Yard is a new restaurant that is located immediately west of, and across the street from the Eagle Creek Airport. Fly-in guests can walk to the restaurant from the airport. This facility provides guests with a beautiful view overlooking the water. This 12,000 square foot establishment will contain seating for 300 people indoors, and 300 outdoors on their patio. The restaurant property encompasses 10.5 acres of land, and contain its own marina with 120 docks able to accommodate sail boats and pontoon boats. This restaurant provides guests with a popular selection of entrees, some of which are quite unique like their pizza made from scratch than cooked in a wood burning oven. Also featured is their Chicken Cordon Bleu, all types of sandwiches and hamburgers, as well as pasta dishes. Average prices should run in the neighborhood of $6.00 to $18.00 for main selections. For further information about this restaurant you can call the restaurant at 290-9300.

Lodging: Midway Motor Lodge (Trans) 299-8400; Motel "6" 293-3220; Signature Inn West 299-6165.
Meeting Rooms: Eagle Creek Aviation Services, Inc. has accommodations for meetings in addition to a pilot's lounge, 293-6935; Also: Midway Motor Lodge 299-8400; Signature Inn West 299-6165.
Transportation: Courtesy car through Eagle Creek Aviation (FBO); Taxi Service: Yellow Cab 637-5421; Rental Cars: Enterprise Rental Cars 299-0711.
Information: The Indianapolis City Center, 201 S Capitol Ave, Pan Am Plaza, Suite 100, Indianapolis, IN 46225, Phone: 639-4282.

Attractions: The Indianapolis Motor Speedway and Hall of Fame Museum is located about 7 to 8 miles southeast of the airport and contains over 30 vintage race cars, slide presentations, and hundreds of historical items once used by famous race car drivers throughout history. The famous Indianapolis 500 automobile race draws 240,000 spectators each year to this annual extravaganza. Track tours are also available by guided bus that will take your party around the oval race track while explaining the history of the grounds. For information call 241-2500 or 248-6747.

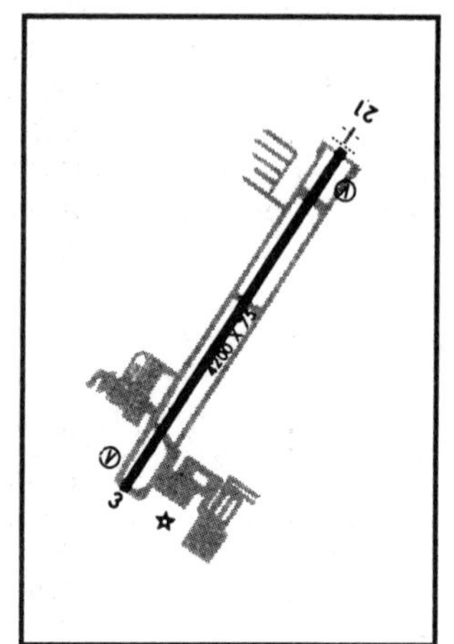

Airport Information:

INDIANAPOLIS - EAGLE CREEK AIRPARK (EYE)
7 mi west of town   N39-49.84 W86-17.66   Elev: 823   Fuel: 100LL, Jet-A
Rwy 03-21: H4200x75 (Asph)   Attended: 1200Z-dusk   Unicom: 122.8   Notes: RAF Limited is a small pilots supply store located within Eagle Creek Aviation Service, Inc. (FBO).
FBO: Eagle Creek Aviation Services, Inc.   Phone: 293-6935

IN-IND - INDIANAPOLIS
INDIANAPOLIS INTL AIRPORT

Restaurants Near Airport: **(Area Code 317)**
Host Marriott Intl.   On Site   Phone: 487-2300

11

Host Marriott International:

Dobbs Houses, Inc. operates a number of food service facilities within the main terminal building at the Indianapolis International Airport. These range in decor and include snack bars, cafes, and a cafeteria. One of these restaurants is always open 24 hours a day, while the others are usually open from 6 a.m. until 9 p.m. Full service cocktail lounges are also available. A variety of meal choices which include fresh made deli sandwiches, Chicago style pizza, Strada, and grilled sandwichs are featured. Average prices run $3.50 for breakfast, $5.00 for lunch and $5.50 for dinner. All of their food service establishments have recently been remodeled. A brand new restaurant will soon be in service and will offer catering facilities. For information call Dobbs Houses, Inc. at 487-2300.

Lodging: Adams Mark Hotel (Trans) 248-2481; Best Western Airport Inn (Trans) 248-0621; Budgetel Inn (Trans) 244-8100; Dillon Inn (Trans) 244-1221; Hilton Inn Airport (Trans) 248-3361; Holiday Inn Airport (Trans) 244-6861; LaQuinta Inn Airport (Trans) 247-4281.
Meeting Rooms: Conference rooms are available within the terminal building. For information call Arpt Manager's Office at 335-2089 or 335-2090. Also at the following lodging facilities: Adams Mark Hotel 248-2481; Best Western Airport Inn 248-0621; Dillon Inn 244-1221; Hilton Inn Airport 248-3361; Holiday Inn Airport 244-6861; LaQuinta Inn Airport 247-4281.
Transportation: Airport courtesy car from FBO's available; Also: Rental Cars: Avis 243-3711; Budget 248-1100; Dollar 241-8206; Hertz 243-9321; National 243-7501.
Information: The Indianapolis City Center, 201 S Capitol Ave, Pan Am Plaza, Suite 100, Indianapolis, IN 46225, Phone: 639-4282.

Attractions:

The Indianapolis Motor Speedway and Hall of Fame Museum is located about 8 to 9 miles northeast of the airport and contains over 30 vintage race cars, slide presentations, and hundreds of historical items once used by famous race car drivers throughout history. The famous Indianapolis 500 automobile race draws 240,000 spectators each year to this annual extravaganza. Track tours are also available by guided bus that will take your party around the oval race track while explaining the history of the grounds. For information call 241-2500 or 248-6747.

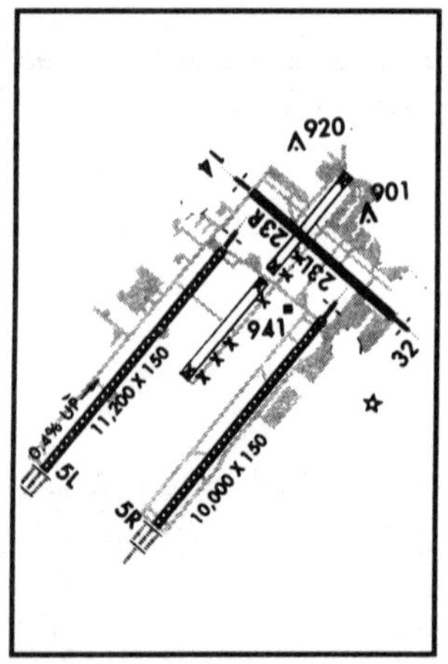

Airport Information:

INDIANAPOLIS - INDIANAPOLIS INTERNATIONAL AIRPORT (IND)
7 mi southwest of town   N39-43.04 W86-17.66   Elev: 797   Fuel: 100LL, Jet-A, A1+
Rwy 05L-23R: H11200x150 (Conc-Grvd)   Rwy 05R-23L: H10000x150 (Conc-Grvd)
Rwy 14-32: H7604x150 (Asph-Grvd)   Attended: continuously   Atis: 124.4   Unicom: 122.95
App Con: 127.15, 124.65, 119.3   Indy Tower: 120.9, 123.95   Gnd Con: 121.9, 121.8
Clnc Del: 128.75   Pre Taxi Clnc: 128.75   Dep Con: 124.95 (East) 119.05 (West)
FBO: AMR Combs-Indianapolis, Inc.   Phone: 248-4900
FBO: Raytheon Aircraft Services   Phone: 800-365-6734

IN-50I - KENTLAND
KENTLAND AIRPORT

(Area Code 219) 12

The Filling Station:

The Filling Station Restaurant is located within 1 or 2 blocks west of the field and is well within walking distance to the Kentland Municipal Airport. This diner styled restaurant is open from 5 a.m. to 9 p.m. Monday through Friday, and on Saturday from 5 a.m. until 3 p.m. (Closed on Sunday). Breakfast is served any time of the day along with house specials including catfish on Fridays, home-made pies and soups, biscuits & gravy, barbecued ribs, ham and beans and meatloaf. Average prices run $2.75 for breakfast, $3.75 for lunch and $3.75 for dinner. Their dining room is uniquely decorated with gas station memorabilia, license plates and 10 gallon gas pumps. Accommodations for parties of 20 to 30 can be provided with no advance notice. Reservations are not accepted. They can make just about anything on their menu to-go. They also deliver if given prior notice. For information about the Filling Station Restaurant call 474-9939 or 5953.

Restaurants Near Airport:

The Filling Station	1/N/A	Phone: 474-9939
Nu Joy Restaurant	N/A	Phone: 474-5672

Lodging: Triway Inn 474-5141.

Meeting Rooms: Nu Joy Restaurant 474-5672

Transportation: None Reported

Information: Indiana Department of Commerce, Tourism Development Division, One North Capitol, Suite 700, Indianapolis, IN 46204-2288, Phone: 800-289-6646.

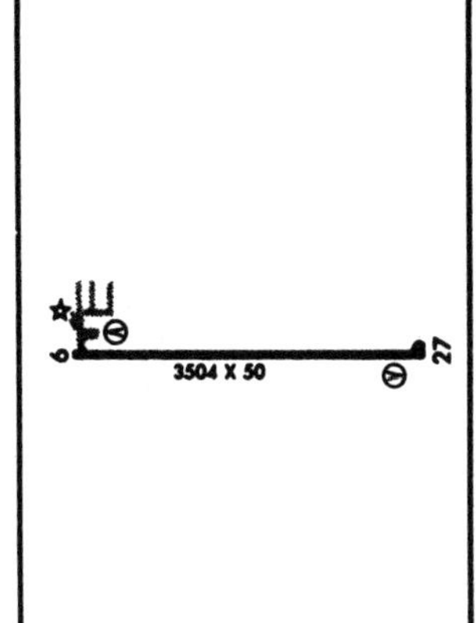

Airport Information:

KENTLAND - KENTLAND AIRPORT (50I)
1 mi southeast of town N40-45.52 W87-25.69 Elev: 698 Fuel: 80, 100LL
Rwy 09-27: H3504x50 (Asph) Attended: irregularly. Airport unattended on holidays.
Unicom: 122.8 Notes: No landing fees or tie-down fees reported. Overnight hangar rental $10.00.
FBO: Kentland Aviation Service Phone: 474-6265

IN-C98 - LAKE VILLAGE
LAKE VILLAGE AIRPORT

(Area Code 219) 13

Farside Restaurant:

The Farside Restaurant is located just down the street from the Lake Village Airport. Fly-in guests can walk to this facility. The town of Lake Village has a population of about 700 people and is situated about 4 miles east of the Indiana/Illinois border along route 41 and about 32 miles south of Hammond, Indiana. This restaurant is a truck stop combined with a restaurant. They are open 24 hours a day. Their menu includes a large selection of entrees including the popular "18 Wheeler" breakfast, meatloaf, perch, pork chops, T-bone, New York strip steak, chicken dinners and chicken strips to mention just a few. Breakfast specials run $3.99 along with lunch specials for only $4.95. For information you can call the Farside Restaurant at 992-9019.

Restaurants Near Airport:

Farside Restaurant	1/4 mi	Phone: 992-9019

Lodging: None reported

Meeting Rooms: None reported

Transportation: None reported

Information: Indiana Department of Commerce & Tourism, One North Capitol Street, Suite 700, Indianapolis, IN 46204 or call 317-232-8860 or 800-289-6646.

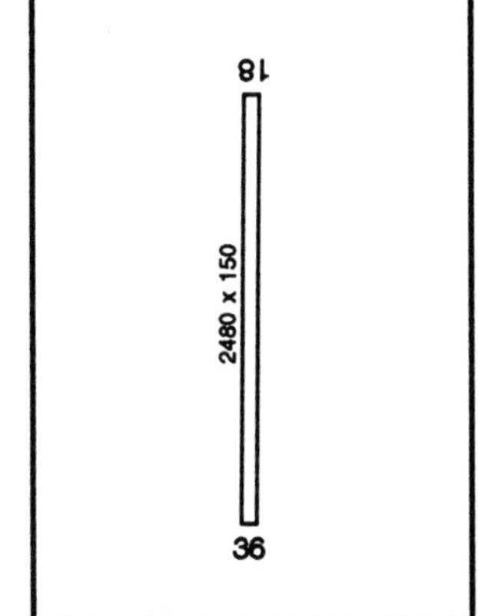

Airport Information:

LAKE VILLAGE - LAKE VILLAGE AIRPORT (C98)
1 mi northwest of town N41-09.00 W87-27.75 Elev: 644 Rwy 18-36: 2480x150 (Turf) Attended: sunrise to sunset CTAF: 122.9
Airport Manager Phone: 992-3100

IN-MIE - MUNCIE
DELAWARE COUNTY-JOHNSON FIELD

(Area Code 317) 14

Vince's Gallery:

Vince's Gallery Restaurant is situated conveniently on the Delaware County-Johnson Field in Muncie, Indiana. This restaurant has a architecturally unique design with its curved beams and glassed-in sections that offer a panoramic view of aircraft moving along the east ramp right in front of the restaurant. This fine dining facility is directly adjacent to aircraft parking and features a wide array of entrees to select from, including filet mignon, pasta, lasagna, chicken Parmigiana and cordon bleu, lobstertail as well as full lobster, and seafood dishes. A variety of vegetarian dishes as well as Ceasar salad and chicken salad can be enjoyed. Some of their favorite appetizers include selections like oysters on the half shell, stuffed mushrooms, and a variety of breaded vegetables and cheese sticks which can start your meal off to a great start. Restaurant hours are 11 a.m. to 10 p.m. Monday through Thursday, 11 a.m. to 11 p.m. on Friday and Saturday, and Sunday from 7 a.m. to 9 p.m. Average prices for a meal run $5.00 to $6.00 for lunch and $10.00 to $15.00 for dinner. Their specials change weekly. The restaurant has a modern design which provides a friendly atmosphere. Flying clubs as well as aviation organizations, will enjoy the convenience of this facility when planning their next fly-out.The management suggests however, that arrangements be made in advance and if possible any time other than Friday and Saturday nights due to the popularity of this restaurant and because these happens to be their busiest times. For the pilot on-the-go, this restaurant also serves as a very handy cross-country stopping point and offers carry-out meals made from anything on their menu. Reservations are not required. However, they are accepted especially on busy nights (during weekends). For more information call 284-6364.

Attractions:

Prairie Creek Reservoir, 15 miles from airport, fine fishing, sail boating, boat docks and bait house, parks and beach area. **Crestview Golf Course,** 5 miles, pro Shop, par 3 and 18 hole course, 289-6952. The **Minnetrista Cultural Center** located at 1200 North Minnetrista Parkway features exhibits in the science, technology and arts of east central Indiana. This 70,000 square foot facility, also contains landscaped lawns, apple orchards, gardens and green houses. For information call 282-4848. Muncie Indiana is located about 50 miles northeast of the city of Indianapolis, Indiana by way of Interstate 69, about an hour and ten minutes away from many attractions located within that area.

Restaurants Near Airport:

Foxfires Restaurant	5 mi SW.	Phone: 284-5235
Szechuan Gardens	3 mi S.	Phone: 289-8007
Vince's Gallery	On Site	Phone: 284-6364
Wheeling Station	3 mi SW.	Phone: 289-4506

Lodging: Delaware Inn 2 miles, 288-9953; Holiday Inn 5 miles, 288-1911; Lee's Inn 5 miles, 282-7557; Muncie Inn 3 miles, 282-5981; Quality Inn 3 miles, 288-9953; Radisson Hotel 5 miles, 741-7777; Signature Inn 5 miles, 284-4200; Super 8 Motel 3 miles, 286-4333; Travelodge 3 miles, 282-5981.

Meeting Rooms: Delaware County Airport Has a conference room available in the administration building at no charge. Please call and make reservations. The following facilities contain meeting rooms for businesses: Holiday Inn 5 miles, 288-1911, Signature Inn 3 miles 284-4200, and the Radisson 3 miles, 741-7777.

Transportation: Delaware County Airport will provide shuttle service through their line department to any hotel, motel or restaurant. Yellow Cab 282-1011, Rental Cars: Budget, 288-7055; National 282-1281; Rent-A-Turkey 282-6633

Information: Muncie-Delware County Convention & Visitors Bureau, 425 North High Street, Muncie, IN 47305, Phone: 284-2700 or 800-568-6862.

Airport Information:

MUNCIE - DELAWARE COUNTY-JOHNSON FIELD (MIE)
3 mi north of town N40-14.54 W85-23.75 Elev: 937 Fuel: 100LL, Jet-A
Rwy 14-32: H6500x150 (Asph-Grvd) Rwy 02-20: H5000x100 (Asph-Grvd) Attended: 1000-0400Z Atis: 133.25 Unicom 122.95 Tower: 120.1 Gnd Con: 121.9 Public Phone 24hrs
Notes: No landing fees.
Muncie Aviation Company, Phone: 289-7141

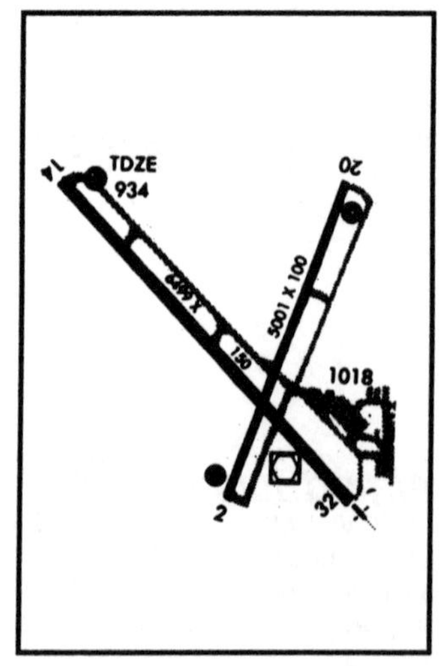

IN-C03 - NAPPANEE
NAPPANEE MUNICIPAL AIRPORT

(Area Code 219) 15

Restaurants Near Airport:
Amish Acres Rest. 4 mi W. Phone: 800-800-4942

Amish Acres Restaurant:

"Amish Acres Resort is located four miles from the Nappanee Municipal Airport. Be sure and enjoy our nationally acclaimed Threshers Style Meal served amidst antique tables and chairs in a 100 year old hand hewn barn. After dining, we suggest you see the Broadway Musical Classic "Plain and Fancy" being presented in the newly reconstructed 1911 Frank Aker Round Barn. For overnight guests Amish Acres offers a 64 room Country Inn complete with rockers on the porch and quilts on the beds. Transportation is no problem. Just call Amish Acres and they will come out and pick you up. Amish Acres is open daily from March 1, through December 30. Call 800-800-4942 for schedules and hours." (Submitted by Mr. Jeff Dorsey General Manager at Amish Acres).

Lodging: Amish Acres Country Inn 800-800-4942; Comfort Inn (3-1/2 miles) 773-2011; Shamrock Motel (3 miles) 773-3193; Victorian Guest House (3 miles, Free trans) 773-4383.
Meeting Rooms: J.B. Air Service has a room adjacent to their main lobby suitable for meetings. Call them at 773-4707 for information.
Transportation: Rental Cars: Jim More Motors, Inc. 773-4171; McCormick Motors, Inc. 773-3134. Until recently free courtesy transportation was always provided by Amish Acres to and from their facility and the airport. This policy might have changed within the past year. Taxi service may be arranged through J.B. Air Service.
Information: Amish Acres Visitor Center, 1600 W Market, Napanee, IN 46550, Phone: 773-4188.

Attractions:

After enjoying an old fashioned feast served up "Family Style", experience a forty-five minute guided tour throughout the farm which will take you to several of the homes all within a short walking distance of each other. You will see working brick ovens used to bake bread and cookies, fruit drying houses, large furnished farm houses with tools and items still very much in use in many of the Amish households. After taking the tour, feel free to stroll at your own pace, and enjoy the peaceful surroundings. They also have horse drawn wagon rides that will take you through the farm and apple orchard nearby. Also the Village Art Festival generally held every year during the 2nd weekend of August draws many visitors and contains over 225 exhibits and hand crafted items. For information call 800-800-4942.

Airport Information:

NAPPANEE - NAPPANEE MUNICIPAL (C03)
3 mi east of town N41-26.77 W85-56.09 Elev: 860 Fuel: 100LL Rwy 09-27: H3000x50 (Asph) Attended: summer 1300-0000Z, winter 1300-2200Z Unicom: 122.8 Notes: J.B. Air Service provides its customers with friendly and efficient service, as well as full maintenance and inspection for general aviation aircraft.
FBO: J.B. Air Service Phone: 773-4707

3000 X 50
9
27

IN-C65 - PLYMOUTH
PLYMOUTH MUNICIPAL AIRPORT

(Area Code 219) 16

Restaurants Near Airport:
Balloon Wurks Restaurant 100 yds Phone: 936-2176

Balloon Wurks Restaurant & Lounge:

The Balloon Wurks Restaurant and Lounge is located on Plymouth Municipal Airport near Plymouth, Indiana and is combined with a Holiday Inn Motor Lodge. The restaurant is situated on the southwest corner of the airport about 100 yards from the main parking ramp. Restaurant hours are 6:30 a.m. to 10 p.m. weekdays, Saturday from 6:30 a.m. to 10 p.m. and Sunday from 7 a.m. to 9 p.m. Their menu contains a full line of entrees with specialties of the house like steaks, seafood and prime rib. The atmosphere of the restaurant is casual with a modern decor. They have a prime rib buffet on Saturday night, and on Sundays, a very nice breakfast buffet between 8 a.m. and 11 a.m. There are accommodations for groups up to 300 persons in a separate room off the restaurant, great for catered fly-ins, business meetings or flying clubs. The restaurant is only a short walk from the airport with no courtesy car transportation needed. For restaurant information call 936-2176.

Lodging: Holiday Inn (100yds) Phone 936-2176; L & K Motel 935-5107; Motel "6" 935-5911.

Meeting Rooms: Holiday Inn 936-2176; L & K Motel 935-5107.

Transportation: Taxi Service: Universal Cab 936-6244; Rental Cars: Amtran Auto Rental 936-4332; Oliver Ford 936-4066; Snyder Auto Rental 936-3415.

Information: Plymouth Area Chamber of Commerce, 120 North Michigan Street, Plymouth, IN 46563, Phone: 936-2323.

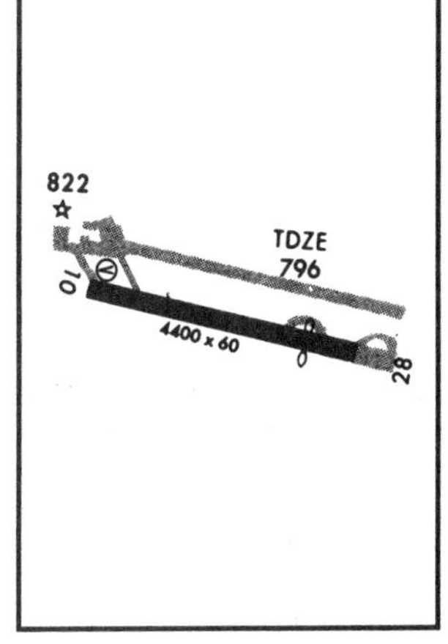

Airport Information:

PLYMOUTH - PLYMOUTH MUNICIPAL (C65)
2 mi north of town N41-21.91 W86-18.11 Elev: 796 Fuel: 80, 100LL, Jet-A
Rwy 10-28: H4400x60 (Asph) Attended: 1300-dusk Unicom: 122.8
Notes: CAUTION: Deer on and in vicinity of airport.
FBO: Plymouth Aviation, Inc. Phone: 935-5152, 936-5172

IN-PLD - PORTLAND
PORTLAND MUNICIPAL AIRPORT

(Area Code 219) 17

Richard's Restaurant:

Richard's Restaurant is located within walking distance (1/4th mile) from the Portland Municipal Airport in Portland, Indiana. This restaurant is a casual family style restaurant serving delicious meals and specializes in chicken dinners. On Monday it's all you can eat chicken dinners and Wednesday all-you-can-eat fish dinners. In addition, their full service menu contains many other selections. Average prices run $2.70 for breakfast, $3.75 for lunch and $5.50 for dinner. They also have a party room situated in back of the restaurant that can provide your group with privacy. Richards Restaurant is open from 5:30 a.m. to 9 p.m. Monday through Saturday and Sunday from 7 a.m. to 8 p.m. Their main dining room can seat 250 persons. Walking from the airport you will notice that the restaurant has brown and light beige colors with white trim and shrubs out in front. For more information call the restaurant at 726-7433.

Restaurants Near Airport:
Richard's Restaurant 1/4 mi Phone: 726-7433

Lodging: Terrace Lodge (Trans) 726-9391.

Meeting Rooms: Richard's Restaurant has a private party room. For information call 726-7433.

Transportation: Courtesy car reported at airport.

Information: Indiana Department of Commerce, Tourism Development Division, One North Capital, Suite 700, Indianapolis, IN 46204-2288, Phone: 800-289-6646.

Attractions:

Golfing 5 miles; Bear Creek Farms; Camping, swimming, live shows and dining.

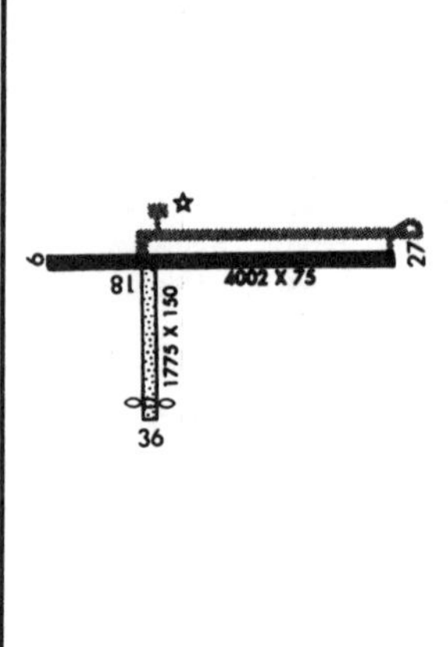

Airport Information:

PORTLAND - PORTLAND MUNICIPAL AIRPORT (PLD)
1 mi northwest of town N40-27.05 W84-59.40 Elev: 926 Fuel: 100LL, Jet-A
Rwy 09-27: H4002x75 (Asph) Rwy 18-36: 1775x150 (Turf) Attended: Mon-Sat 1300-0000Z, Sun 1400-0000Z Unicom: 122.8
Airport Manager Phone: 726-4901

Promote General Aviation Just Take A Friend Flying

IN-RCR - ROCHESTER FULTON COUNTY AIRPORT

(Area Code 219) 18, 19, 20

Gropps Restaurant:

Gropps Restaurant is in north central Indiana and is located adjacent to the Fulton County Airport in Rochester, Indiana. Gropps Restaurant is famous for its fish selections as well as their steaks, chicken, daily specials each evening, and a variety of 12 different homemade salads, and salad bar, along with a separate child's menu. Homemade desserts, pastries, breads and candy are also made right on the premises. Casual dining in this family style facility is accessible by taxiing your airplane to the south side of the field. A short walk across Highway 14 to the restaurant is all that is necessary. There are 2 dining rooms and banquet facilities able to accommodate up to 100 additional persons. They are open from 11 a.m. to 9 p.m. and Sunday to 8 p.m. A daily lunch buffet and Sunday brunch is served between 11 a.m. and 2 p.m. For information call 223-2246.

Karen's Restaurant:

Karen's Restaurant is located about 100 feet from the south side of the Fulton County Airport, and is within walking distance. This family style restaurant is open Tuesday through Saturday 6 a.m. to 9 p.m. and on Sunday from 6 a.m. to 3 p.m. They serve breakfast until 11 a.m. On Friday and Saturday, dinner specials include a 12 and 20 ounce prime rib, catfish, frog legs, in addition to their salad bar, dessert bar and choice of potato. Prices range from $4.50 for a full breakfast, or try their all-you-can-eat salad bar for only $4.25 and $5.95 on Sunday. Dinners range from $5.50 to $13.95 for prime rib selections. Their Saturday and Sunday breakfast buffet beginning at 11 a.m. includes items like eggs, potatoes, sausage links and bacon, sausage biscuits and gravy, fresh fruit, coffee and juice for only $4.50. The Sunday lunch buffet from 11 a.m. to 3 p.m. run $6.95. Karen's Restaurant can also accommodate groups between 20 and 90 people. Their dining area is very clean and comfortable, with carpeting and decorated in mauve colors. They can also prepare anything for carry-out, along with catering for parties of 20 or more. For more information call Karen's Restaurant at 223-5960.

Tony's Restaurant:

Tony's Restaurant is located adjacent to the Fulton Co. Airport, Rochester, Indiana, and hosts a full service menu including an extensive breakfast, steaks, chops, chicken and fish. This combination family style and buffeteria, provides home cooked meals for their guests. Their main dining room can seat 150 persons, complete with 2 dining rooms and a small lounge. Average prices run $2.45 for breakfast, $3.50 for lunch and $6.95 for dinner. Their restaurant hours are between 6 a.m. and 1:30 p.m. onTuesday, Wednesday and Thursday, and on Friday from 6 a.m. to 4 p.m., Saturday from 6 a.m. to 11 a.m. and Sunday from 6 a.m. to 1:30 p.m. (Afternoon and evening hours may vary) They are closed on Monday. For more information call Tonies Restaurant at 223-8706.

Restaurants Near Airport:

Gropps Restaurant	Adj Arpt	Phone: 223-2246
Karens Restaurant	Adj Arpt	Phone: 223-5960
Pizza Hut	Adj Arpt	Phone: N/A
Tony's Restaurant	Adj Arpt	Phone: 223-8706

Lodging: Holiday Inn 936-4013; Motel "6" 935-5911.

Meeting Rooms: A banquet room is available at Gropps Restaurant that can seat up to 100 people, 223-2246; Also: Holiday Inn 936-4013.

Transportation: Courtesy car reported by airport; Also: Auto-Go 233-4290; Hammel Motors 223-2711.

Information: Indiana Department of Commerce, Tourism Development Division, One North Capital, Suite 700, Indianapolis, IN 46204-2288, Phone: 800-289-6646.

Airport Information:

ROCHESTER - FULTON COUNTY AIRPORT (RCR)
2 mi east of town N41-03.95 W86-10.97 Elev: 790 Fuel: 80, 100LL, Jet-A
Rwy 11-29: H4400x60 (Asph) Attended: 1300Z-dusk Unicom: 122.7
FBO: Fulton County Aviation Phone: 223-5384

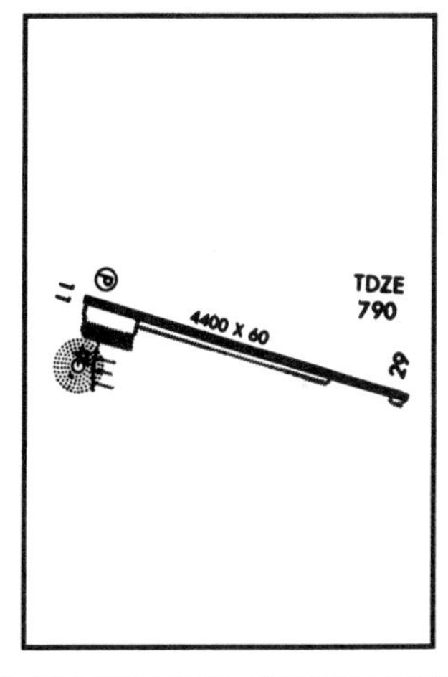

IN-SER - SEYMOUR
FREEMAN MUNICIPAL AIRPORT

(Area Code 812)

21

Airport Cafe:

The Airport Cafe specializes in home cooked meals prepared from scratch. Specialties of the house include five meat selections every day with items such as turkey dishes, fried chicken, salmon, meatloaf, soups and freshly prepared pies made the old fashioned way. Average prices run $3.00 for breakfast, and around $5.00 for lunch and dinner. Their dining room can seat approximately 150 people, along with accommodations for 60 additional persons in their banquet room. This combination family and cafeteria styled restaurant serves daily specials, as well as other selections off their menu. The restaurant is reported to be located about 1/2 miles from the Freeman Municipal Airport. The Airport Cafe has a chalet type architecture with colors in green and white. Their restaurant is open from 7 a.m. to 2 p.m. during the week, and on Sunday from 11 a.m. to 2 p.m. (Restaurant hours may vary). For more information call 522-5300.

Restaurants Near Airport:
The Airport Cafe 4 blks Phone: 522-5300

Lodging: Best Western Seymour Inn 522-8000; Days Inn Seymour 522-3678; Holiday Inn 522-6767.

Meeting Rooms: Days Inn Seymour 522-3678; Holiday Inn 522-6767.

Transportation: None Reported

Information: Columbus/Bartholomew County, Visitor, Information & Promotion (VIP Bureau, 825 Washington, Columbus, IN 47202-1477, Phone: 378-2622.

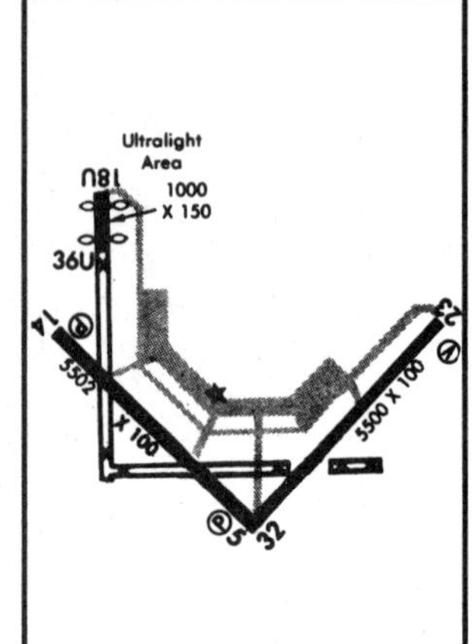

Airport Information:

SEYMOUR - FREEMAN MUNICIPAL (SER)
2 mi southwest of town N38-55.41 W85-54.44 Elev: 583 Fuel: 100LL, Jet-A
Rwy 14-32: H5502x100 (Asph) Rwy 05-23: H5500x100 (Asph) Rwy 18U/36U: H1000x150 (Conc) (by experience of aircraft using the pavement, see AFD) Attended: 1300Z-dusk Unicom: 122.8
FBO: Rhoades International, Inc. Phone: 522-7622

IN-SBN - SOUTH BEND
MICHIANA REGIONAL AIRPORT

(Area Code 219)

22

Air Host Restaurant:

Air Host Restaurant is situated within the center portion of the terminal building at the Michiana Airport in South Bend, Indiana. This establishment could be classified as a full service restaurant combined with a deli, serving breakfast, lunch and dinner selections. A lounge and gift shop are also connected to this facility. Daily specials are offered as well as a full dinner menu. Average prices run between $6.00 and $6.50 for most entree selections. The seating capacity of the Air Host Restaurant is about 95 persons. Aircraft parking at SBN Aviation is adjacent to the restaurant. The restaurant is open weekdays from 6 a.m. to 7:30 p.m. For information call the Air Host Restaurant at 289-8786.

Restaurants Near Airport:
Air Host Restaurant On Site Phone: 289-8786
Tippecano Restaurant 3 to 4 mi Phone: N/A

Lodging: Bed & Breakfast Registry 291-7153; Queen Anne Inn 234-5959; The Beiger Mansion Inn 255-6300; The Book Inn 288-1990; Holiday Inn (Trans) 272-6600; Holiday Inn Downtown (Trans) 232-3941; Marriott 234-2000; Ramada Inn 272-5220; Randalls New Century Inn (Trans) 272-7900.
Meeting Rooms: Holiday Inn 272-6600; Holiday Inn Downtown 232-3941; Marriott 234-2000; Ramada Inn 272-5220; Randalls New Century Inn 272-7900.
Transportation: Taxi service: Airport Cab 272-2902; Allied Cab 232-5323; Courtesy Cab 233-4040; Roseland Cab 277-1095; Yellow Cab 232-5871; Rental cars: Avis 234-1024; Budget 287-2333; Hertz 234-3712; National 234-4878.
Information: South Bend-Mishawaka Convention and Visitors Bureau, 401 East Colfax Avenue, Suite 310, P.O. Box 1677, South Bend, IN 46634, Phone: 234-0051.

Attractions:

Tippecano Restaurant, Studebaker Mansion & Studebaker Museum: A favorite outing suggestion for your flying group is to enjoy dining at the Tippicano Restaurant within the Mansion, followed by a tour of the 93 acre facility and then a short trip to the Studebaker Museum. Transportation can be arranged airport taxi service 233-8285 or in advance through Corporate Wings (FBO) on Michiana Regional Airport by calling 233-8285; Also: University of Notre Dame walking tours 631-5726; College Football Hall of Fame 234-0051; Blackthorn Muni. Golf Course northwest corner of airport along Route 31.

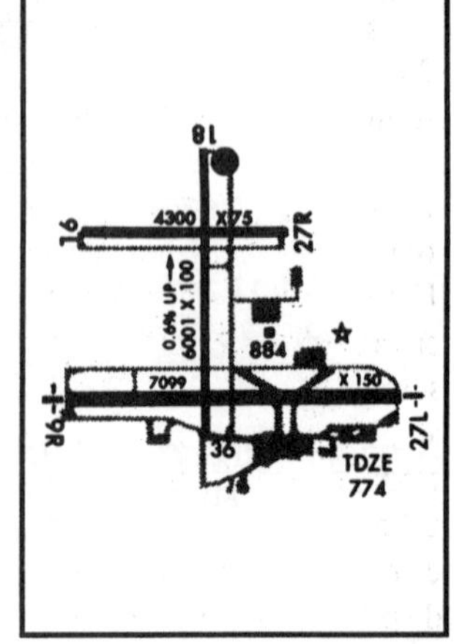

Airport Information:

SOUTH BEND - MICHIANA REGIONAL AIRPORT (SBN)
3 mi northwest of town N41-42.54 W86-19.11 Elev: 799 Fuel: 100LL, Jet-A
Rwy 09-27: H7099x150 (Asph-Grvd) Rwy 18-36: H6001x100 (Asph-Grvd) Rwy 09-27R: H4300x75 (Asph) Attended: continuously Atis: 118.15 Unicom: 122.95 South Bend App/Dep Con: 118.55, 132.05, 124.1 South Bend Tower: 118.9 Gnd Con: 121.7 Clnc Del: 121.9
FBO: Corporate Wings Phone: 233-8285

Studebaker National Museum

Information supplied by South Bend-Misawaka Convention And Visitors Bureau.

Photo by: Rober Beyer

Tippecanoe Place Restaurant within the very same mansion owned and built by the Studebaker family.

In 1852, Henry and Clem Studebaker opened a blacksmith shop in South Bend, Indiana with two sets of tools. During their first years in business, the Studebaker brothers built farm wagons. By the time the United States was 100 years old, the Studebaker Brothers Company was the largest manufacturer of horse-drawn vehicles in the world, delivering on its motto, "Always give more than you promise."

Studebaker was the only wagon-making company to successfully make the transition to automobile production. In 1904, they introduced their first gasoline-powered automobile, a two cylinder, 16 horsepower touring car. Until closing in 1996, Studebaker was a leader in both styling and engineering.

The 114 years of Studebaker history are preserved at the Studebaker National Museum located at 525 South Main Street. Museum's collection contains approximately 75 vehicles on display, including the first and last vehicles produced by Studebaker. Additional exhibits display the carriages of four U.S. presidents and prototype vehicles. The museum also houses an extensive archival collection.

Museum hours: Monday through Saturday 9 a.m. to 5 p.m., Sunday 12 noon to 5 p.m. Admission is $4.50 for adults, $3.50 for senior citizens and students and $2.50 for children 12 and under. While at the museum, explore the gift shop where you'll be able to take home a little piece of history. For information, call the Studebaker National Museum at 800-828-7881.

Tippecanoe Place Restaurant: Dining in the traditional manner at Tippecanoe evolves from a heritage handed down by the famous Studebaker family, who built the mansion a century ago. The restaurant revives the gracious spirit of the past. Its 40 rooms are filled with fine antiques, massive fireplaces and hand-crafted woods. Its award winning fare and beautiful interior will provide a feast for the palate and the eyes. Reservations are suggested. Location of the mansion and restaurant are at 620 West Washington Street. For information and reservations call 219-234-9077.

Transportation: Michiana Regional Airport only about 3-5 miles from the downtown area. Fly-in guests can either obtain rental cars through Corporate Wings FBO on the field by calling 233-8285 or by taxi service. We spoke with Airport Taxi Service 219-233-8285 and were told they will help furnish transportation accommodations to the museum, mansion and restaurant, if given a day or two advance notice.

Directions: To reach the downtown area of South Bend take Route 20 which is Lincoln Way and runs into LaSalle Street in town. Two blocks south from that intersection is Washington Street where the Tippecanoe Place restaurant is reported to be located. To reach the Studebaker National Museum take Route 20 southeast from the airport, which intersects with LaSalle Street in town. Continue east-bound 2 blocks until reaching Main Street. Then head south on Main Street estimated 1/3 to 1/2 mile until reaching the museum. For information on South Bend attractions, contact the South Bend-Mishawaka Convention and Visitors Bureau at 219-234-0051.

IN-HUF - TERRE HAUTE
HULMAN REGIONAL AIRPORT

(Area Code 812) 23

George's Cafe:

George's Cafe, is situated in the terminal building at the Hulman Regional Airport, and adjacent to Mills Aviation (FBO). This is a combination family style and fine dining establishment. This restaurant opens Monday through Thursday 1 a.m. to 3 p.m., Friday 5:30 a.m. to 7 p.m., Saturday 7 a.m. to 1 p.m. reopening at 5 p.m. to 8 p.m. and Sunday 9 a.m. to 1 p.m. (Hours to correspond to arriving commuter service). Their house specialties include pastas, filets, rib-eye steaks, charcoal broiled breast of chicken, shrimp with lime sauce, Oriental chicken, as well as a variety of sandwiches and appetizers. Several of their selections have aviation names attached to them, like their "Runway" cheeseburger, and the "Airstrip" sandwich. They also offer daily specials. The restaurant has a pleasant atmosphere with a contemporary decor, and can seat 85 persons. This facility also provides catering. For further information call the restaurant at 877-6777.

Restaurants Near Airport:
George's Cafe On Site Phone: 877-6777

Lodging: Best Western of Terre Haute 234-7781; Pick of Terre Haute Inn 299-1181.

Meeting Rooms: Best Western of Terre Haute 234-7781; Pick of Terre Haute Inn 299-1181.

Transportation: Airport courtesy car reported; Also: Taxi Service: Ace 235-3262; Vigo Taxi 232-1313; Yellow Taxi 232-0202;
Rental Cars: Avis 232-7120; Hertz 877-9646; National 877-4575.

Information: Terre Haute Convention & Visitor Bureau of Vigo County, 643 Wabash Avenue, Terre Haute, IN 47807, Phone: 234-5555.

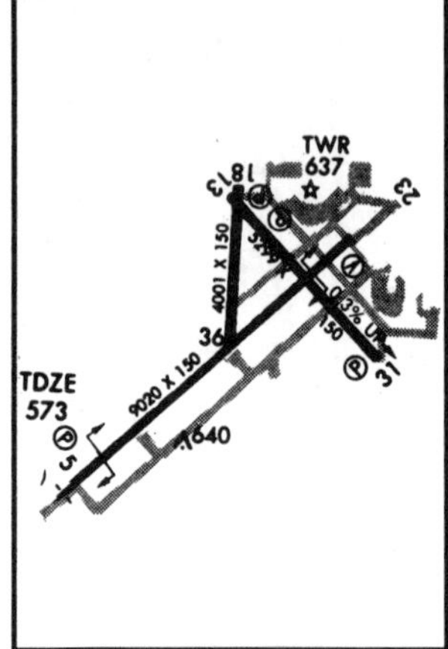

Airport Information:

TERRE HAUTE - HULMAN REGIONAL AIRPORT (HUF)
5 mi east of town N39-27.11 W87-18.53 Elev: 585 Fuel: 100LL, Jet-A
Rwy 05-23: H9020x150 (Asph-Grvd) Rwy 13-31: H5299x150 (Asph) Rwy 18-36: H4001x150 (Asph) Attended: 1100-0300Z Atis: 127.5 Unicom: 122.95
App/Dep Con: 125.45, 119.8 Tower: 118.3 Gnd Con: 121.6
FBO: Mills Aviation Phone: 877-2507

IN-VPZ - VALPARAISO
PORTER COUNTY MUNICIPAL

(Area Code 219) 24

Strongbow Inn:

The Strongbow Inn is located about 2 miles from the Porter County Municipal Airport directly west on U.S. 30. This fine dining facility will provide fly-in guests with free courtesy transportation to and from the airport. The restaurant is open at 11 a.m. every day. For dinner the last seating is at 9 p.m. Monday through Thursday; 9:30 on Saturday and 8 p.m. on Sunday. Specialties include turkey dishes in various forms, along with steaks, seafood and chicken. In addition, they offer homemade breads, pastries, and salads. Their lounge serves sandwiches all day. Wednesday evening they provide a turkey buffet from 5 p.m. to 9 p.m.; Sunday brunch buffets from 11 a.m. to 2 p.m.; daily luncheon features; and perch on Friday. Average prices range from $7.00 for lunch and $13.00 for dinner entrees. Their lounge has an aeronautical theme with model airplanes hanging from the ceiling. The main dining room has a rustic yet elegant look with white tablecloths, flowers and candles on the tables. Private rooms are available for parties of 20 or more individuals. For pilots on-the-go, special box lunches can be arranged if advance notice is given. For information or reservations call the restaurant at 462-5121.

Restaurants Near Airport:

Strongbow Inn	2mi W.	Phone: 462-5121

Lodging: Carlton Lodge (Next door to Strongbow Inn), 111 units with indoor/outdoor swimming pool, Meeting rooms, Phone: 465-1700

Meeting Rooms: The Strongbow Inn contains accommodations for meetings, and banquets. Private rooms available for groups of 20 or more, Phone: 462-5121; Carlton Lodge located adjacent to the Strongbow Inn can also accommodate rooms for meetings and conferences, Phone: 465-1700.

Transportation: A courtesy car is available for free transportation to and from the Strongbow restaurant by calling 462-5121. Additional rental cars are available through AVIS, Phone: 462-6989 and Hertz, Phone: 462-3183.

Information: Chamber of Commerce, 150 West Lincolnway, P.O. Box 330, Valparaiso, IN 46384, Phone: 462-1105.

Additional Information:

Compliments of Strongbow - "Not many folks remember back when, in 1937, tiny but determined Bess Thrun started a turkey farm right here where the Inn is today. For many years after the Highway (Route 30) came right through her land, she served turkey to customers at her 28-seat restaurant. She named her restaurant after a Pottawattomie chief who with his tribe, had lived on the farm a hundred years before. As her fame as a cook spread, she enlarged the restaurant and encouraged her daughters to help while she continued to manage the turkey farm and restaurant until she retired in 1968. Her daughter Caroline and husband Chuck Adams bought the restaurant, and now share ownership with their son, Russ, a graduate of the prestigious Culinary Institute of America. At its peak, Strongbow farm raised 5,000 birds a year. Today, its outdoor-ranged turkeys come from nearby turkey-raisers who carefully follow the Thrun-Adams feeding program. No phosphates or soybean oil for flavor are ever injected into Strongbow's turkeys. "Flavor ought to come from the feed," says Chuck Adams, son-in-law of Bess Thrun. Strongbow was later chosen to do research for Reynolds' oven cooking bags, now on the national market. Strongbow is listed in many prominent directories to fine dining, while Strongbow Turkey Pies are now nationally distributed, and available in many localities throughout the country. From nearby Valparaiso airport come many patrons who fly in just for a real turkey dinner, and take home a whole bird or some Strongbow Turkey Pies and cranberry sauce found in the lobby freezer. Now open every day, Strongbow's seventy employees serve more than 1500 meals on Thanksgiving Day alone; almost as many on other occasions. All breads, rolls, pies and our famous cheesecake are made right here on the premises". Free airport transportation is provided for fly-in guests. Call the restaurant at 462-5121 or 462-3311.

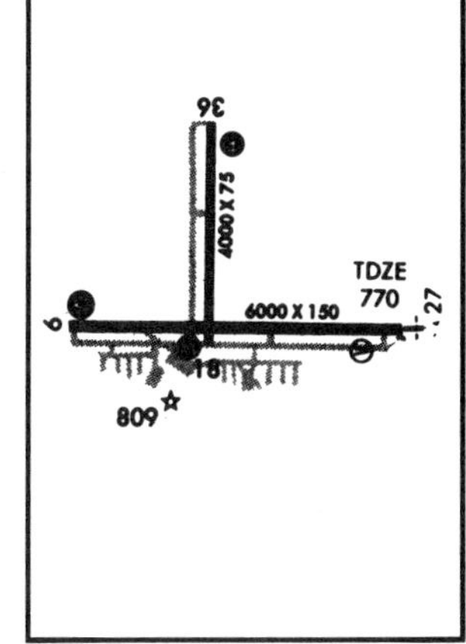

Airport Information:

VALPARAISO - PORTER COUNTY MUNICIPAL (VPZ)
1 mi southeast of town N41-27.15 W87-00.35 Elev: 770 Fuel: 80, 100LL, Jet-A
Rwy 09-27: H6000x150 (Asph) Attended: Mon-Fri 1200-0200Z, Sat-Sun 1400-2400Z Unicom: 122.8
Airport Manager Phone: 800-462-6508

IOWA

LOCATION MAP

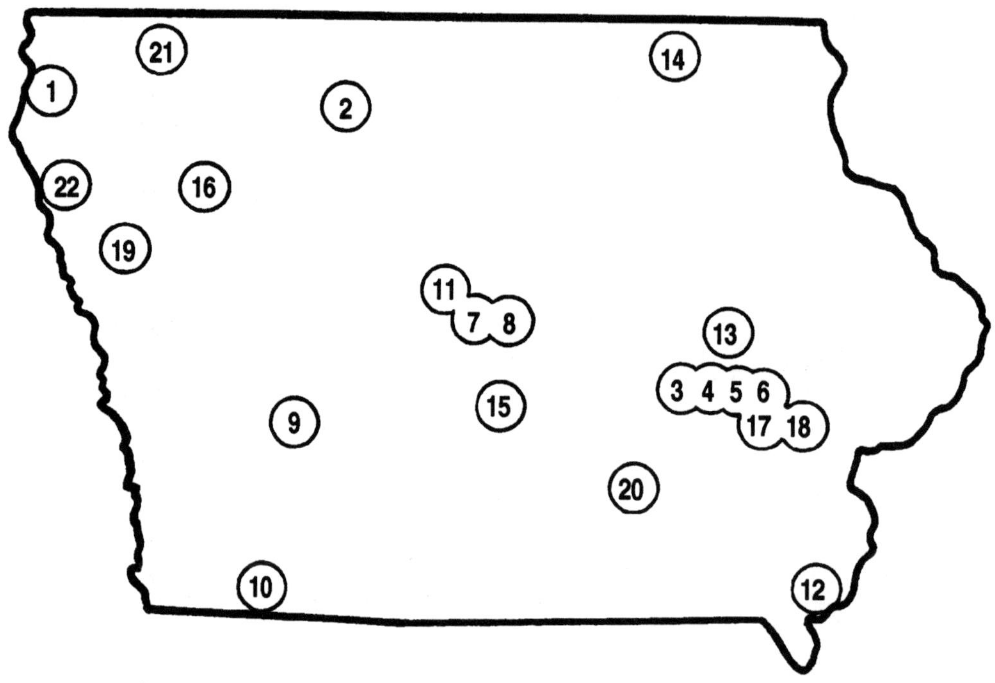

Not to be used for navigational purposes

IOWA

CROSS FILE INDEX

Location Number	City or Town	Airport Name And Identifier	Name of Attraction
1	Akron	Akron Muni. Arpt. (Y40)	Casey's Restaurant
2	Algona	Algona Muni. Arpt. (AXA)	Sister Sarah's
3	Amana	Amana Arpt. (C11)	Amana Barn Restaurant
4	Amana	Amana Arpt. (C11)	Brick Haus Restaurant
5	Amana	Amana Arpt. (C11)	The Colony Inn
6	Amana	Amana Arpt. (C11)	Ox Yoke Inn
7	Ames	Ames Muni. Arpt. (AMW)	Best Wstrn.-Starlight Vlg.
8	Ames	Ames Muni. Arpt. (AMW)	Hickory Park Restaurant
9	Anita	Anita Muni-Kevin Burke Mem. (Y43)	Redwood Steak House
10	Bedford	Bedford Muni. Arpt. (Y46)	O'Hara Restaurant
11	Boone	Boone Muni. Arpt. (BNW)	Country Western Saloon
12	Burlington	Burlington Muni. Arpt. (BRL)	The Tender Trap Rest.
13	Cedar Rapids	Cedar Rapids Muni. (CID)	CA1 Services
14	Cresco	Ellen Church Field (CJJ)	Scooter's
15	Des Moines	Des Moines Intl. Arpt. (DSM)	Host Marriott Services
16	Ida Grove	Ida Grove Muni. (IDG)	Ju Vall's Restaurant
17	Iowa City	Iowa City Muni. Arpt. (IOW)	The Ground Round
18	Iowa City	Iowa City Muni. Arpt. (IOW)	Village Inn Restaurant
19	Mapleton	Mapleton Muni. Arpt. (MEY)	Maple Motel Rest. & Lng.
20	Ottumwa	Ottumwa Industrial Arpt. (OTM)	Arpt. Cafe
21	Sibley	Sibley Muni. Arpt. (ISB)	Krogman's Hwy. 60 Cafe
22	Sioux City	Sioux Gateway Arpt. (SUX)	Arpt. Lounge/Food Bar

Articles

City or town	Nearest Airport and Identifier	Name of Attraction
Ankeny/(Des Moines), IA	Ankeny Muni. (IKV)	Adventureland Pk. & Resort
Blakesburg, IA	Antique Airfield (IA27)	Airpower Museum
Greenfield, IA	Greenfield Muni. (GFZ)	Iowa Aviation Pres. Ctr.

IA-Y40 - AKRON
AKRON MUNICIPAL AIRPORT

(Area Code 712)

1

Restaurants Near Airport:

Casey's Restaurant	Adj Arpt	Phone: 568-3238
Highway Cafe	1/4 mi	Phone: 568-3642
Pizza Ranch	1/2 mi	Phone: 568-3506
Pronto's Restaurant	1/4 mi	Phone: 568-2531

Lodging: None Reported

Meeting Rooms: None Reported

Transportation: None Reported

Information: Sioux City Convention Center/Tourism Bureau, 801 4th Street, P.O. Box 3183, Sioux City, IA 51102, Phone: 279-4800.

Casey's Restaurant:

Casey's Restaurant is located across the street and about 1 block from the Akron Municipal Airport. This facility is a combination convenient store and automobile gas station. A variety of popular items are available throughout the day such as their breakfast croissant sandwiches with egg, sausage or ham and cheese. Homemade donuts and rolls are also available. For lunch they feature a number of items like their pizza bread, ham and cheese sandwiches, tuna or chicken salad sandwiches, all types of deli sandwiches and charbroiled dishes. You can also buy pizza by the slice or order a whole pizza to go. Average prices run between $1.50 and $2.00 for most sandwiches. Casey's Restaurant is open 7 days a week, between 6 a.m. and 11 p.m. Although this establishment does not provide any accommodations for sit down dining, there are many pilots that simply fly in for a bite to eat before continuing on to their destination. For more information about Casey's call 568-3238. There are three other restaurants near the airport that deserves mentioning. Pronto's (568-2531) about 1/4 mile, offers chicken, and barbecued items, specializing is fast service; The Highway Cafe (568-3642) is a family style restaurant with table service located across the street from Pronto's. The Pizza Ranch, (568-3506) is also a family restaurant specializing in preparing a variety of pizza, located about 1/2 mile from the airport.

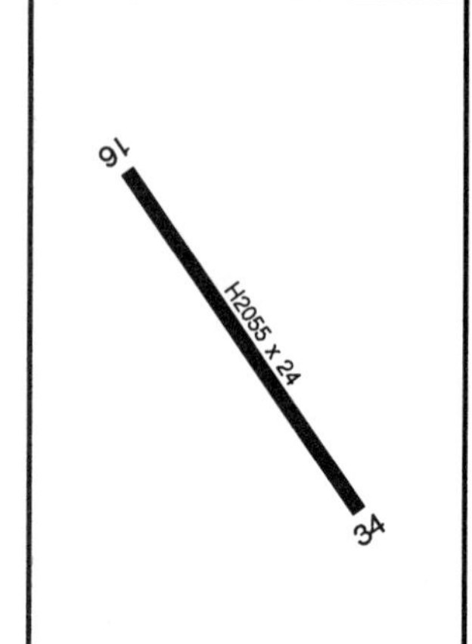

Airport Information:

AKRON - AKRON MUNICIPAL (Y40)
0 mi south of town N42-48.35 W96-33.79 ELev: 1143 Rwy 16-34: H2055x24 (Asph)
Attended: unattended CTAF: 122.9
Arkon Municipal Airport Phone: 568-2735

IA-AXA - ALGONA
ALGONA MUNICIPAL AIRPORT

(Area Code 515)

2

Restaurants Near Airport:

Charlie's Supper Club	3 mi	Phone: 295-3764
Sister Sarah's	2 mi	Phone: 295-7757

Lodging: None Reported

Meeting Rooms: None Reported

Transportation: The airport is reported to have courtesy cars available for use by fly-in guests to nearby facilities.

Information: Algona Chamber of Commerce, 123 E State Street, Algona, IA 50511, Phone: 295-7201.

Sister Sarah's Restaurant:

Sarah's Restaurant is 2 miles from the Algona Municipal Airport. They are located just east of the intersections of Hwy 18 and 169. Their specials are Chicken Kiev, Roast Long Island Duck, and a variety of choice steaks and seafood. Appetizers include Crab Rangoon, nachos Mexicali, Cajun mushroom, mozzarella planks and spicy cheese dip. Their dessert specialties are fresh strawberry & cherry, cheese cake, and apple strudel. On Sunday they offer an all-you-can-eat family style dinner with 3 main meat selections. Average prices run between $5.95 and $12.95 for most entrees. The restaurant has a warm comfortable atmosphere. It also accommodates larger groups with a banquet room that can seat 50 persons. In flight catering as well as on premises catering is also available. Their outdoor beer garden can seat 80 persons. Restaurant hours are Monday through Friday from 11 a.m. to 2 p.m. for lunch and Tuesday through Saturday 5 p.m. to 10 p.m. for dinner. (Closed on Sunday). The restaurant as well as the airport, stated that they would provide courtesy transportation. Call the airport at 295-7492 or contact the restaurant at 295-7757.

Attractions:

The Algona Country Club is located 1/4th miles from the Algona Municipal Airport and has a 9 hole golf course on the premises. This facility is operated by the same people who own Sarah's Restaurant. Catered lunches at the country club can be arranged for larger groups. For information call Sarah's Restaurant at 295-7757.

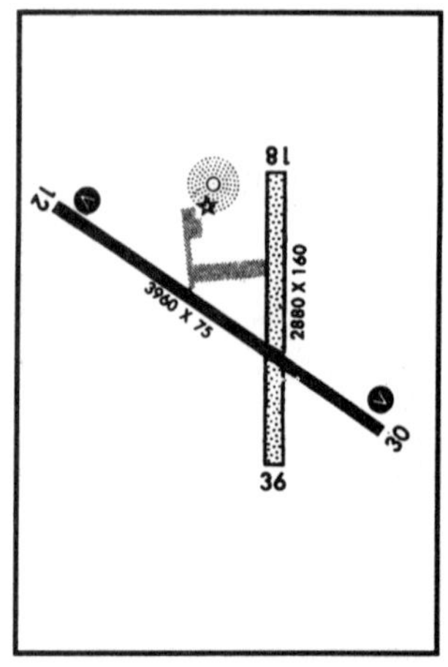

Airport Information:

ALGONA - ALGONA MUNICIPAL AIRPORT (AXA)
2 mi west of town N43-04.67 W94-16.32 Elev: 1219 Fuel: 100LL, Jet-A
Rwy 12-30: H3960X75 (CONC) Rwy 18-36: 2880x165 (Turf) Attended: Mon-Sat 1400-2300Z, Sun 1800-2300Z Unicom: 122.8
FBO: Algona Aviation Phone: 295-7492

IA-C11 - AMANA
AMANA AIRPORT

(Area Code 319)

3, 4, 5, 6

Amana Barn Restaurant:

The Amana Barn Restaurant is located on the east edge of main Amana, and is situated approximately 3 blocks from the Amana Airport in Amana, Iowa. This restaurant's faithfulness to the tradition of Amana, has built this attractive facility with an exterior fashioned with a barn type appearance. The restaurant includes a lounge and banquet room with excellent accommodations for larger groups or business meetings. The restaurant offers traditional German cuisine with items like their famous Amana smoked ham, bratwurst, prime rib, Iowa pork and beef, kassler rippchen (smoked pork chops), barbecued ribs, Barn schnitzel, homemade salads, vegetables and desserts. Traditional Amana cuisine served family style adds to your dining pleasure. The restaurant is open weekdays from 11 a.m. to 8:30 p.m. and Friday and Saturday from 11 a.m. to 9 p.m. They also have a Sunday brunch that is served from 9 a.m. to 2 p.m. as well. For restaurant information call 800-325-2045 or 622-3214. Please park your aircraft in the designated areas.

Brick Haus Restaurant:

The Brick Haus Restaurant is located about 1/4th mile from the Amana Airport in the town of Amana, Iowa. This restaurant mixes a charming blend of traditional heritage and fine German cooking. Their German-American specialties include Wiener schnitzel (veal), bratwurst, kassler rippchen (smoked pork chops), as well as other specialties, including fresh fruit, glazed pies and fresh cream puffs. Their restaurant hours are from 7:30 a.m. to 8 p.m. 7 days a week. They make all their own cinnamon rolls and pies from scratch. This restaurant seats approximately 125 persons and offers a breakfast special that includes all you can eat, eggs, pork sausage, toast, potato, fruit and juice for only $6.35. Dinners average $9.25 and $13.95 for most selections. They also claim to have the only salad bar in town. For restaurant information call 800-233-3441 or 622-3278.

Restaurants Near Airport:

Amana Barn Restaurant	3blks	Phone: 622-3214
Brick Haus Restaurant	1/4 mi	Phone: 622-3278
Colony Inn	Walk Dist	Phone: 622-6770
Ox Yoke Inn	1/2 mi	Phone: 622-3441
Ronneburg Restaurant	1/2 mi	Phone: 622-3641

lodging: Guest House Motor Inn (2 blks) 622-3599; Holiday Inn 668-1175.
Meeting Rooms: Holiday Inn 668-1175
Transportation: Courtesy transportation can be arranged either through the airport or by calling the facility you wish to visit. In most cases there should be no problem. (Please call ahead if possible).
Information: Amana Colonies Convention & Visitors Bureau, Box 303, Amana, IA, 52203 Phone: 622-7622 or 800-245-5465.

Ox Yoke Inn:

The Ox Yoke Inn is located 1/2 mile from the Amana Airport in Amana, Iowa. Menu specialties include German food like Wiener schnitzel, sauerbraten, kassler rippchen (smoked pork chops), pork sausage, five cuts of Iowa grown beef; rhubarb custard pie and pastries baked fresh daily in their own bakery. Their specials include breakfast buffet as well as Friday night whole catfish and Sunday brunch buffet. Antiques and paintings add to the decor of this fine restaurant. Restaurant hours vary throughout the season. Spring & Summer hours are 11 a.m. to 8 p.m. Monday through Saturday, Fall and Winter from 11 a.m. to 2 p.m. then from 5 p.m. to 8 p.m. and Sundays from 9 a.m. to 7 p.m. The restaurant will provide transportation if pre-arranged. Call 800-233-3441 or 622-3441 for reservations.

Attractions:

There are 7 villages within the Amana Colonies, all of which function together as one unit and share a common interest as well as their interesting religious backgrounds. The town of Amana contains many fine establishments including German restaurants, gift and clothing shops, along with a meat, bakery and wine shop. Visitors can also watch craftsmen build custom ordered furniture at the Amana Furniture and Clock Shop right in town. For information call The Amana Colonies Convention & Visitors Bureau at 800-245-5465. Also Amana Golf Course 2 mi 622-6222.

The Colony Inn:

The Colony Inn is a delightful restaurant located within walking distance of the Amana Airport in Amana, Iowa. This restaurant offers German style cooking with specialties like steaks, country fried chicken, Amana cured ham, roast beef, Swiss steak, smoked pork chops, seafood, Amana pork sausages, and Wiener schnitzel. Since 1936 the Colony Inn was the first restaurant in the community to offer family style dinners. The restaurant's policy is "to put plenty of food on the table at a reasonable price." All you can eat breakfast specials for $6.75 are available along with dinners that run between $9.50 and $13.00. The Colony Inn is open daily between 7:00 a.m. and 8:00 p.m. and on Sunday from 7 a.m. to 7:30 p.m. (Closed Christmas Eve and Day). The restaurant offers early American styling with German hospitality. Spend the day while in the colony visiting the attractions like the furniture factory, winery, museums and craft shops all located nearby. For information call 800-227-3471 or 622-6770. For airport information call 622-3251. Please park your aircraft in the designated areas.

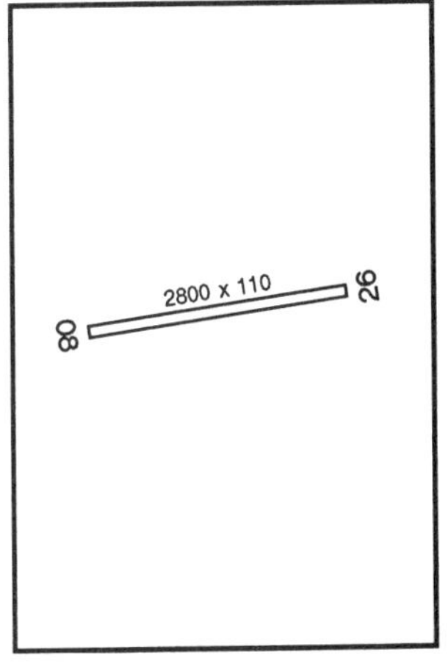

Airport Information:

AMANA - AMANA AIRPORT (C11)
0 mi southeast of airport N41-47.75 W91-52.26 Elev: 712 Rwy 08-26: 2800x110 (Turf)
Attended: Apr-Nov irregularly CTAF: 122.9 Notes: Airport CLOSED Dec-Feb; Please park in the designated general aviation parking areas. For aircraft restricted to hard surface runways we suggest you land at Cedar Rapids Iowa located aprox. 10 miles to the northeast of Amana, Iowa and rent a car to Colonies.
Amana Airport Phone: 622-3251

IA-AMW - AMES
AMES MUNICIPAL AIRPORT

(Area Code 515)

7, 8

Best Western - Starlight Village:

Best Western - Starlight Village has a restaurant by the name of "George L. Larson Dining Room". This family restaurant provides a wide selection of entrees to choose from. The restaurant is open Monday through Thursday from 6 a.m. to 10 p.m., Friday and Saturday 6 a.m. to 11 p.m. and Sunday for brunch. They offer a smorgasbord Monday through Saturday from 11 a.m. to 2 p.m., ($3.85/ person) evenings Monday through Thursdays from 5 p.m. to 9 p.m., Saturday 5 p.m. to 10 p.m. ($6.95/person) and a Friday night seafood buffet from 5 p.m. to 9 p.m. ($9.95/ person). They also have a Sunday brunch from 7 a.m. to 1:30 p.m. ($5.95/person). The restaurant is situated within the motel which offers 131 guest rooms, a pool, tanning bed and sauna along with a lounge. Transportation can be arranged by calling Haps Air Service at 232-4310. For restaurant information call 232-9260 Ext 362.

Hickory Park Restaurant:

Hickory Park Restaurant is located 3/4 of a mile from the Ames Municipal Airport. This is a full service restaurant that is open Sunday through Thursday from 11 a.m to 9 p.m. Friday and Saturday between 11 a.m. and 10 p.m. Specialties include smoked dishes, very popular with local customers barbecue items including ribs and chicken as well as hamburgers and Ice cream selections. For information call 232-8940.

Restaurants Near Airport:

Best Western-Starlight Vlg.	1 mi	Phone: 232-9260
Hickory Park Restaurant	3/4 mi	Phone: 232-8940
Hombre's Restaurant	1 mi	Phone: 232-3410

Lodging: Best Western-Starlight Village (1 mile) 232-9260; Comfort Inn (Trans) 233-6060; Holiday Inn-Gateway Center (Trans) 292-8600; New Frontier Motel (Trans) 292-2056.
Meeting Rooms: Holiday Inn-Gateway Center 292-8600; New Frontier Motel 292-2056.
Transportation: Courtesy transportation reported at Ames airport.
Information: Convention & Visitors Bureau, 213 Duff Avenue, Ames, IA 50010, Phone 232-4032 or 800-288-7470.

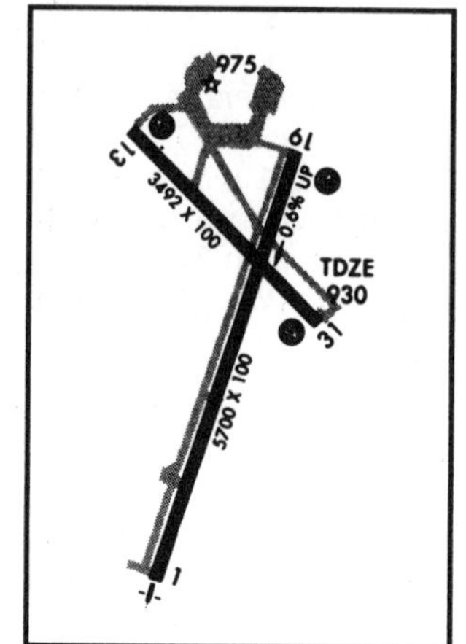

Airport Information:

AMES - AMES MUNICIPAL AIRPORT (AMW)
2 mi southeast of town N41-5952 W93-37.31 Elev: 955 Fuel: 100, Jet-A, MOGAS Rwy 01-19: H5700x100 (Conc) Rwy 13-31: H3492x100 (Asph) Attended 1300-0200Z Unicom: 122.8
FBO: Haps Air Service Phone: 232-4310

IA-Y43 - ANITA
ANITA MUNI-KEVIN BURKE MEM FLD.

(Area Code 712)

9

Redwood Steak House:

The Redwood Steak House is a supper club located adjacent to the Anita Municipal Airport near Anita, Iowa. This supper club is open 7 days a week between 5 p.m. and 10 p.m. The restaurant contains a fine selection of entrees including choice steaks, seafood, chicken, pork chops, ham dinners, sandwiches, crab and shrimp salads along with many other items on their menu from which to choose. The restaurant is decorated with oil paintings suggesting woodland scenes as well as linen covered tables offering a warm yet casual atmosphere. The dining room contains seating for about 110 persons. They also will accommodate larger groups up to 90 persons in their party room complete with fireplace. Everything on their menu can be ordered for carry-out. Even though the restaurant is within walking distance, they will provide a courtesy car if necessary, depending on staff availability. For information or reservations call 762-3530.

Restaurants Near Airport:

Redwood Steak House	Adj Arpt	Phone: 762-3530

Lodging: None Reported

Meeting Rooms: Redwood Steak House (Adj Arpt) has accommodations for private parties or groups, 762-3530.

Transportation: None Reported, Adjacent restaurant reported within walking distance from airport.

Information: The Greater Des Moines Convention & Visitors Bureau, Two Ruan Center, Suite 222, 601 Locust Street, Des Moines, IA 50309, Phone: 286-4960 or 800-451-2625.

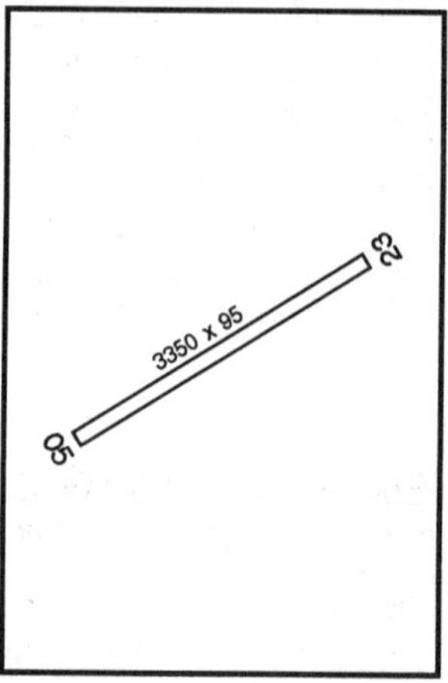

Airport Information:

ANITA - ANITA MUNI-KEVIN BURKE MEM FLD. (Y43)
1 mi south of town N41-26.42 W94-46.18 Elev: 1251 Rwy 05-23: 2825x95 (Turf)
Attended: unattended CTAF: 122.9
Anita Municipal Airport Phone: 762-4105

Adventureland Amusement Park

Adventureland Inn Family Resort:

Adventureland Amusement Park is located just east of Des Moines, Iowa near the intersection of Interstate I-80 and Highway 65, on the southeast corner. This Amusement Park is well known throughout the area and is a popular attraction with many vacationers. There are over 100 rides, shows and attractions within the park property. A variety of vending establishments as well as lodging facilities are nearby. The Adventureland Inn Resort is situated only a couple of minutes away by free shuttle transportation to the park entrance. This is a luxurious resort hotel featuring a large swimming pool, indoor courtyard and whirlpool. The Park View Restaurant on the premises serves a variety of specialties that will satisfy every taste. Amenities at the resort inn include recreational areas, tent and RV camping site. One low admission price includes a pass to all rides in the park. Prices for children 4 to 9 years old are $18.00 plus tax. Senior discounts 65 and older are $15.50. Regular adult admission is $19.50. Second day admission is only an additional $10.00.

During our conversation with the management of the amusement park, the Adventureland Inn and the Ankeny Municipal Airport, we learned that convenient access to the park is available. Guests flying into the area can land at Ankeny Municipal Airport (IKV). Their runway is 18-36: H4,000 x 100 (Conc). Fuel: 100LL, N41-41.53 W93-33.95; Attended: 1300Z-dusk, Unicom: 122.7. Rental cars are available on the field through Altra Car Rental 246-0260; Budget 287-2612; Enterprise 252-3499; and Hertz 285-9650. To reach the park, go south on I-35, take exit to I-80 East, then go about 10 miles and follow the signs to the amusement park. Landing at Des Moines International Airport (DSM) is another alternative, especially if you plan to spend some time visiting the town of Des Moines, IA. For more information call the following: Adventureland Amusement Park 515-266-2121 or 800-532-1286; Recorded information 515-266-2126; Resort Inn 515-265-7321 or 800--910-5382; Ankeny Regional Airport (IKV) Exec 1 Aviation (FBO) 515-965-1020.

IA-Y46 - BEDFORD
BEDFORD MUNICIPAL AIRPORT

(Area Code 712) 10

O'Hara Restaurant:

The O'Hara Restaurant is situated about 5 miles from the Bedford Municipal Airport. This restaurant provides courtesy transportation to fly-in guests. This facility is classified as a fine dining establishment that is open for lunch between 11 a.m. and 2 p.m. Tuesday through Friday and Sunday. Dinner is served Tuesday through Sunday from 5:30 until 9:30 p.m. Entrees featured include prime rib, aged cuts of premium steaks, seafood selections, grilled chicken dishes, pork and many varieties of sandwiches. They also provide a salad bar as well. Average prices run $4.00 for lunch and $9.00 to $14.00 for dinner. Daily specials are also available. Their dining room can accommodate up to 180 people. Linen table cloths, red carpeting, wild life paintings on the walls, as well as Winchester fire arms and related memorabilia, including other antiques, decorate the restaurant. Large groups are welcome, provided advance notice is given. Meals can also be prepared-to-go if requested. For information call the O'Hara Restaurant at 523-3353.

Restaurants Near Airport:
O'Hara Restaurant 5 mi Phone: 523-3353

Lodging: Country Inn (3 miles) 523-3617.

Meeting Rooms: None reported

Transportation: None reported; O'Hara Restaurant will provide transportation for fly-in guests.

Information: Taylor County Historical Museum, Highway 2, Bedford, IA 50833.

18

2710 x 100

36

Airport Information:

BEDFORD - BEDFORD MUNICIPAL AIRPORT (Y46)
2 mi south of town N40-38.27 W94-43.76 Elev: 1201 Rwy 18-36: 2710x100 (Turf)
Attended: unattended CTAF: 122.9 Notes: Sharp drop at both ends of runway 18-36.
Bedford Airport Phone: 523-2385

Airpower Museum, Inc.

Headquarters of Antique Airplane Assoc.

Blakesburg, IA (IA-5C2)

The Antique Airplane Association, Inc. was first formed in August of 1953 by a few persons with a deep interest in old airplanes. At that time, no other association existed that had a specific interest in antique and classic airplanes. No aviation historical groups had yet been formed. The AAA was organized to "Keep The Antiques Flying", and this basic premise has always been their main interest and primary function. They do provide their membership with aviation history and memories of the important parts their own members have played, in this fascinating subject.

The AAA currently has 42 active Chapters with a number more in the formation stage. They maintain a close working relationship with many of the "type clubs". At the present time the AAA, Inc. provides communication and publications for the Interstate, Corben, Fairchild, Great Lakes, Pietenpol, Rearwin, Hatz and Travel Air Clubs. Antique Airfield is the site for numerous "Type Club" fly-ins each season and they welcome their use of Antique Airfield as a practical and economical site for their annual fly-ins and conventions.

The Officers, National and State Directors of the AAA serve without any compensation and all income derived from dues, subscriptions, fly-ins etc., is used for the administration and development of the Association for the benefit of it's members. The AAA is located at Antique Airfield near Blakesburg, Iowa along with the Airpower Museum, Inc., and are both affiliated organizations. The APM has over 20,000 square feet of display and storage space plus tons of many spare engine and aircraft parts being made available to AAA members to assist in their restoration. In addition, the APM owns and sells the Ken/Royce (LeBlond) and Rearwin Cloudster factory remains.

Membership in the AAA is open to anyone, and being a pilot or airplane owner is not a requirement for belonging. During the past 20 years their grass runways, campgrounds and the affiliated Airpower Museum have provided a realistic and pleasant place to visit and participate in antique, classic and unique airplane activities.

Photo: by AAA & APM/ Eric Lundahl

Headquarters of the Antique Airplane Association

The annual APM Reunion and AAA Fly-in is normally held during the end of August and the beginning of September. Contact the AAA for location. In the past, it has been held either on the Antique Airfield or at Bartlesville, Oklahoma.

Antique Airfield is located three miles northeast of Blakesburg, Iowa on the Bluegrass Road and is just 10 miles west of Ottumwa, Iowa. This association welcomes all fly-in visitors with two turf runways. One is 2,200 feet N/S, and their E/W runway of 1,700 feet. Both 80 and 100 octane gasoline is available. Step back in time, visit a facility and organization that provides a realistic program for the finding, restoration and flying of old airplanes. They welcome your personal visits and the opportunity to take you back to the "Good Ole Days" of aviation. Museum hours are 9 a.m. to 5 p.m. Monday through Friday, 10 a.m. to 5 p.m. Saturday and 1 p.m. to 5 p.m. Sunday. Admission: donations requested. For information call 515-938-2773. (Written by AAA & APM)

IA-BNW - BOONE
BOONE MUNICIPAL AIRPORT

(Area Code 515)

11

Country Western Dance & Round Up Saloon:

The Country Western Dance & Round Up Saloon is situated about one mile from the Boone Municipal Airport. Transportation can be obtained during the week through the "Transportation Co." Call the airport at 432-6441 for accommodations. The restaurant will also provide transportation for small groups with advance notice (at least 2 days). Call 432-9866.

Restaurants Near Airport:

Country Western Roundup	1 mi	Phone: 432-9866

Lodging: Imperial Inn (5 miles) 432-4322; Shangri-La Motel (5 miles) 432-6220; Topper Motel (1 mile) 432-2500.

Meeting Rooms: Imperial Inn 432-4322.

Transportation: Boon Country Transportation 432-5038.

Information: Chamber of Commerce, 806 7th Street, Boone, IA 50036, Phone: 432-3342 or 800-266-6312.

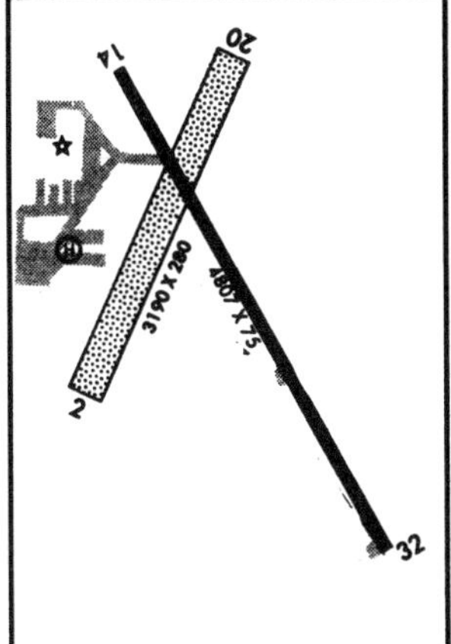

Airport Information:

BOONE - BOON MUNICIPAL AIRPORT (BNW)
2 mi southeast of town N42-02.97 W93-50.85 Elev: 1162 Fuel: 100LL, Jet-A, Mogas Rwy 14-32: H4807x75 (Asph-Conc) Rwy 02-20: 3190x280 (Turf) Attended: 1400Z-Dusk Unicom: 123.0 Notes: CAUTION: Ultralight activity and parachute jumping on and in vicinity of airport.
Boon Municipal Airport Phone: 432-1018

IA-BRL - BURLINGTON
BURLINGTON MUNICIPAL AIRPORT

(Area Code 319)

12

The Tender Trap Restaurant:

The Tender Trap Restaurant is located between 1/4 and 1/2 mile walk on the north side of the Burlington Municipal Airport. This is a family style restaurant that is open 6 days a week from 11 a.m. to 10 p.m. and on Sunday from 2 p.m. to 8 p.m. Items on their menu include smoked beef, pork, chicken, ribs, and all types of sandwiches. A portion of this facility includes a game room and bar. The dining room can seat 76 persons. The front part of the restaurant contains a bar with tables. The back section of the restaurant is often used for parties. We were told that guests can see the end of the runway from the restaurant. Larger groups are welcome if advance notice is given. Meals can also be prepared-to-go as well. For more information about the Tender Trap Restaurant, call 754-4640.

Restaurants Near Airport:

Pzazz J.J. Maguires	(Trans)	Phone: 753-2223
The Tender Trap	3/8 mi N.	Phone: 754-4640

Lodging: Pzazz Motor Inn Resort (Trans) 753-2223; Super 8 Motel 752-9806; The Holiday (Trans) 754-5781.

Meeting Rooms: Pzazz Motor Inn Resort 753-2223; The Holiday 754-5781.

Transportation: None Reported.

Information: Convention & Tourism Bureau, 807-Jefferson Street, P.O. Box 6, Burlington, IA 52601, Phone: 752-6365 or 800-82-RIVER.

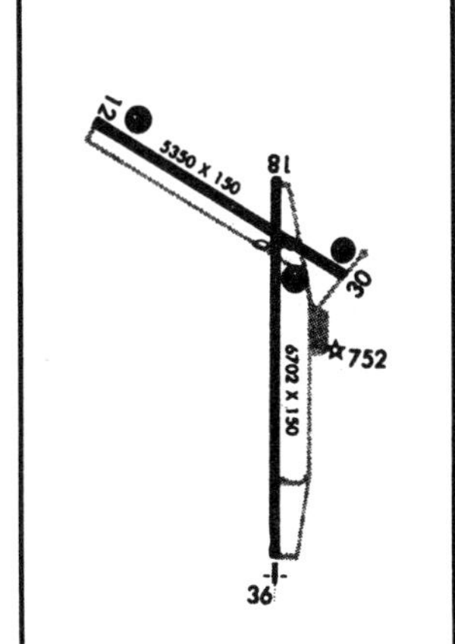

Airport Information:

BURLINGTON - BURLINGTON MUNICIPAL AIRPORT (BRL)
2 mi southwest of town N40-46.99 W91-07.53 Elev: 698 Fuel: 100LL, Jet-A
Rwy 18-36: H6702x150 (Asph-Conc-Grvd) Rwy 12-30: H5350x150 (Asph)
Attended: 1300-0100 Unicom: 123.0
FBO: Remmer's Aviation, Inc. Phone: 754-4601

IA-CID - CEDAR RAPIDS
CEDAR RAPIDS MUNICIPAL

(Area Code 319) 13

CA1 Service:

The Cedar Rapids CA-1 Service, operates a number of public use facilities located on the Cedar Rapids Airport near Cedar Rapids, Iowa. There is a cafe situated within the terminal building that is open from 6 a.m. to 7 p.m. 7 days a week. This cafe offers a complete breakfast selection along with lighter fare all the way up to complete dinner entrees. The cafe can seat approximately 100 people and has a modern decor. A gift shop and lounge is located adjacent to the restaurant. Transportation to the terminal building is available through the FBO's. Catering service can be arranged through one of the fixed base operators on the field. For more information call them at 362-5674.

Restaurants Near Airport:
CA1 Services On Site Phone: 362-5674

Lodging: Best Western Longbranch (Trans) 377-6386; Econo Lodge 363-8101; Holiday Inn (Trans) 365-9441; Roosevelt Hotel (Trans) 364-4111; Sheraton Inn (Trans) 366-8671; Stouffer-Five Seasons (Trans) 363-8161.

Meeting Rooms: Best Western Longbranch 377-6386; Econo Lodge 363-8101; Holiday Inn 365-9441; Roosevelt Hotel 364-4111; Sheraton Inn 366-8671; Stoffer-Five Seasons 363-8161.

Transportation: Taxi Service: Ace 364-0111; Century 365-0505; Yellow 365-1444; Rental Cars: Avis 366-6418; Budget 363-9595; Hertz 365-9408; National 363-0249.

Information: Convention & Visitors Bureau Visitor Information Center, 119 1st Avenue Southeast, P.O. Box 5339, Cedar Rapids, IA 52406-5339, Phone: 398-5009, or 800-735-5557.

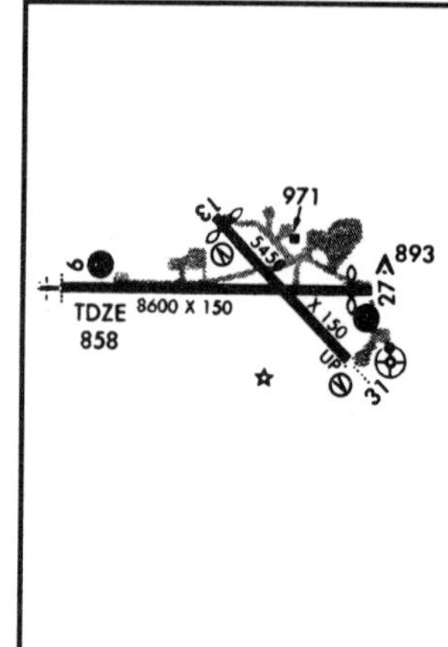

Airport Information:

CEDAR RAPIDS - CEDAR RAPIDS MUNICIPAL (CID)
5 mi southwest of town N41-53.08 W91-42.65 Elev: 864 Fuel: 100LL, Jet-A
Rwy 09-27: H8600x150 (Asph-Conc-Grvd) Rwy 13-31: H5450x150 (Asph-Grvd)
Attended: 1100-0500Z Atis: 124.15 Unicom: 122.95 App/Dep Con: 119.7, 134.05, 119.05 Tower: 118.7 Gnd Con: 121.6 Clnc Del: 125.45
FBO: Signature Flight Support Phone: 366-1925
FBO: Tibben Flight Lines, Inc. Phone: 364-8354

IA-CJJ - CRESCO
ELLEN CHURCH FIELD

(Area Code 319) 14

Scooter's:

Scooter's is about 3/4th of a mile from the Ellen Church Field in Cresco, Iowa. This is classified as a fine dining restaurant, and is open Tuesday through Saturday beginning at 5 p.m. and closing at 9 p.m. during the week and 10 p.m. on weekends. (Closed Monday). Between the months of November and May the restaurant is reported to be open on Sunday from 11 a.m. to 1 p.m. During the rest of the year however, we were informed that this restaurant plans to be closed on Sunday. After November, check with restaurant for hours on Sunday. Entrees on their menu consist of steaks, seafood, boasted chicken & ribs. Soup & salad bar as well as appetizers are also available. Nightly specials include; broasted chicken on Tuesday, BBQ on Wednesday, every other Thursday Mexican or Chinese, Friday fish fry, pike and shrimp and on Saturday prime rib. Sunday's they feature four different entrees to choose from. Prices for dinner entrees run between $5.50 and $24.95, the highest priced plates being for Lobster. The restaurant has a modern decor within 3 levels, and is situated near a river and dam site. Transportation, according to management ,will be provided only if available staff is on duty. Otherwise it is a good 3/4th mile walk from the airport to this restaurant. Be sure to call the restaurant well enough in advance to let them know you are planning to fly in. Their phone number is 547-2080.

Restaurants Near Airport:
Scooter's 3/4 mi Phone: 547-2080

Lodging: Cresco Motel (1/2 mile) 547-2240.

Meeting Rooms: None Reported

Transportation: None reported by airport; Tower Supper Club can furnish transportation only if advance notice is provided, and available staff is on duty.

Information: Decorah Area Chamber of Commerce, 111 Winnebago Street, Decorah, IA 52101, Phone: 382-3990.

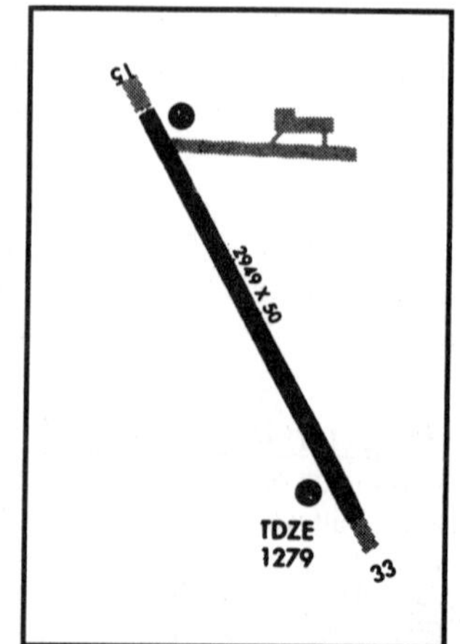

Airport Information:

CRESCO - ELLEN CHURCH FIELD (CJJ)
1 mi southwest of town N43-21.92 W92-07.98 Elev: 1279 Rwy 15-33: H2949x50 (Conc)
Attended: unattended Unicom: 122.8 Notes: Be alert for ultralight activity on and in vicinity of airport.
Ellen Church Field Phone: 547-2357 or 547-4000

IA-DSM - DES MOINES
DES MOINES INTL. AIRPORT

15

Host Marriott Services:

The Host Marriott operate facilities on the upper and lower level of the main terminal building on the Des Moines International Airport. Parking your aircraft at the fixed base operators on the field is suggested when planning to visit the terminal building. FBO's have courtesy transportation available to and from their location and airport sites. A snack bar and cafeteria, along with a lounge provides travelers with a variety of entrees. Such items as sandwiches, salad bar, traditional midwestern selections for breakfast, lunch and dinner, including desserts and appetizers are all available. Average prices run $4.15 for breakfast, $6.50 for lunch and $8.50 for dinner. Each day the cafeteria offer a daily entree special. The decor of these facilities is traditional. They also have a banquet facility to serve up to 250 guests from buffet style to sit down dinners. Meals can also be prepared-to-go as well. On the upper level of the terminal building they report that there are meeting rooms for those who would like to conduct seminars and business meetings. Inquire at the Iowa Reality Business Center located at the ticket counters or call 256-5390. For information about the restaurant or food services call Host Marriott at 256-5360.

(Area Code 515)

Restaurants Near Airport:
Host Marriott Services On Site Phone: 256-5360

Lodging: Airport Inn (Trans) 287-6464; Hampton Inn (Trans) 287-7300; Hilton Inn Airport (Trans) 287-2400; Holiday Inn South (Trans) 283-1711; Ramada Hotel Airport 285-1234.
Meeting Rooms: Meeting rooms are reported to be available on the upper level of the main terminal building. Interested persons can check with the Iowa Reality Business Center located by the ticket counters or call 285-1400 for information; Also: Airport Inn 287-6464; Hampton Inn 287-7300; Hilton Inn Airport 287-2400; Holiday Inn South 283-1711; Ramada Hotel Airport 285-1234.
Transportation: Taxi Service: Capitol Taxi 243-8111; Yellow 282-8111; Rental Cars: Avis 245-2585; Budget 287-2612; Hertz 285-9659; National 285-3359.
Information: Greater Des Moines Convention & Visitors Bureau, Two Ruan Center, Suite 222, 601 Locust Street, Des Moines, IA 50309, Phone: 286-4960.

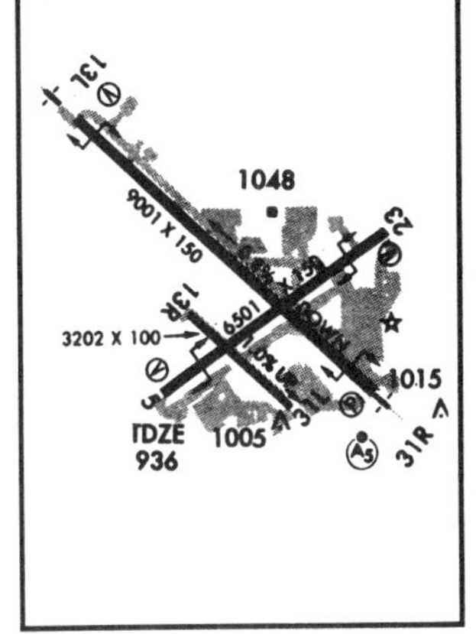

Attractions:

For information about the new location of the Radio Controled exhibition call Byron Original at 515-964-2000.

Airport Information:

DES MOINES - DES MOINES INTL. AIRPORT (DSM)
3 mi southwest of town N41-32.10 W93-39.64 Elev: 957 Fuel: 100LL, Jet-A
Rwy 13L-31R: H9001x150 (Asph-Grvd) Rwy 05-23: H6501x150 (Asph-Grvd) Rwy 13R-31L: H3202x100 (Asph) Attended: continuously Atis: 119.55 Unicom: 122.95
App/Dep Con: 123.9, 135.2, 118.6 Tower: 118.3 Gnd Con: 121.9 Clnc Del: 134.15
FBO: Elliott Flying Serv Phone: 285-6551 FBO: Signature Flt. Support Phone: 256-5330
FBO: Mid-America Jet Centr. Phone: 285-6751

Iowa Aviation Preservation Center

Greenfield, IA (IA-GFZ)

(Information submitted by museum)

The Iowa Aviation Preservation Center is located on Greenfield Municipal Airport and devotes itself to preserving vintage aircraft as well as recognition for outstanding achievements made by Iowa individuals in the aviation field. Fly-in guests are welcome to view early aircraft, including some unique flying machines from the first days of aviation. On display are eight powered airplanes and four gliders.

The Iowa Aviation Hall of Fame, located at the Iowa Aviation Preservation Center is the only place in the state where Iowa men and women contributing to the advancement of aviation are recognized and honored for their achievements. Up to three persons are inducted each year, in the spring. A permanent display salutes each of the inductees. Nomination papers are available at the Center and due each year on February 1. Museum hours are 10 a.m to 5 p.m. weekdays and 1 p.m. to 5 p.m. weekends. For information you can call 515-938-2773.

Photo: by IAPC 1928 Curtiss Robin at the Center. Oldest Robin in existence.

IA-IDG - IDA GROVE
IDA GROVE MUNICIPAL

(Area Code 712)

16

Ju Vall's Restaurant:

Ju Vall's Restaurant is reported to be located across the street from the Ida Grove Municipal Airport. This fine dining establishment is open Monday through Thursday from 5 p.m. to 10 p.m. and Friday and Saturday from 5 p.m. to 11 p.m. Their menu provides selections including appetizers, salads, soups and homemade bread. Their specialties of the house are prime rib steaks and seafood. Every other Friday they offer a special that includes a complete dinner plus all the fish you can eat for only $5.95 per person. The restaurant has a nice party room able to serve groups up to 100 persons with advance notice. This establishment once known as the Camelot Restaurant has relocated across the street from the airport and has changed its name to Ju Vall's Restaurant. Pilots and their guests can simply walk to the restaurant from the airport. For information call 364-3753.

Note: The famous radio controlled exhibition that was held at this location has since moved to it's new location near DesMoines, Iowa. For information see IA-DSM.

Restaurants Near Airport:
Ju Vall's Restaurant Adj Arpt Phone: 364-3753

Lodging: No facilities reported near airport. However, there are lodging accommodations within towns around this location.

Meeting Rooms: None Reported

Transportation: Rental Cars: McCormick Motors (Ida Grove) 263-2179.

Information: Byron Originals-R/C Division, Midwest Industries, Inc., P.O. Box 279, Ida Grove, IA 51445, Phone: 364-3165.

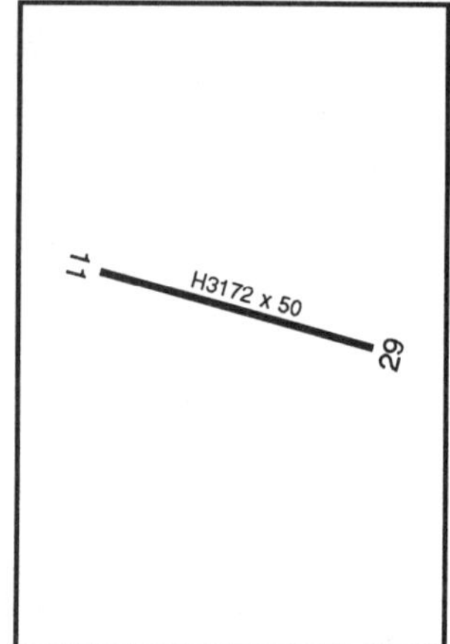

Airport Information:

IDA GROVE - IDA GROVE MUNICIPAL (IDG)
2 mi southeast of town N42-19.96 W95-26.69 Elev: 1245 Fuel: 100LL Rwy 11-29: H3172x50 (Asph) Attended: On call Unicom: 122.8 Notes: 600 foot model airplane runway is located 1/2 mile north of airport. Do not mistake for airport runway.
Ida Grove Airport Phone: 364-9809.

IA-IOW - IOWA CITY
IOWA CITY MUNICIPAL AIRPORT

(Area Code 319)

17, 18

The Ground Round:

The Ground Round Restaurant is located adjacent to and within walking distance, (1/4th mile) to the Iowa City Municipal Airport. This family style restaurant has a casual atmosphere. There is wood, brass and many live plants as well as a glass enclosed dining area. Their menu includes appetizers like soup, beef nachos, buffalo chicken wings, onion rings etc. Entrees include burgers, steaks, seafood, chicken and ribs. They have Mexican & pasta items along with a good selection of desserts. Average prices run $5.00 to $8.00 for lunch and $8.00 to $12.00 for dinner. Restaurant hours are Monday through Thursday 11 a.m. to 12:00 a.m. Friday and Saturday 11 a.m. to 1:00 a.m. and Sunday 11 a.m. to 11 p.m. The Ground Round was the grand prize winner of the "1988 Columbus Rib-Off". They are also known for their buffalo chicken wings. Their telephone number is 351-2370.

Village Inn Restaurant:

The Village Inn is a pancake house that is reported to be located adjacent (and about 2 Blocks) to the Iowa City Municipal Airport near Iowa City, Iowa. This family style restaurant is open 6 a.m. to 3 a.m. 7 days a week and until 1 a.m. on Sunday. Their menu offers a full line of breakfast items as well as lunch and dinner entrees. Their specialties include French toast, pancakes, omelets, country fries, sausage, steak and eggs, hamburgers and a varied selection of sandwiches. Average prices run between $3.00 and $10.00 for most entree selections. The decor of the restaurant is contemporary with a casual atmosphere and seats about 200 people. With advance notice, the restaurant will be happy to accommodate larger groups. In addition to their main dishes, they also serve delicious pies for your dessert selections. The main entrance of the airport can be seen from the restaurant. For more information call 351-1094.

Restaurants Near Airport:

The Ground Round Rest.	Adj Arpt	Phone: 351-2370
Village Inn Restaurant	Adj Arpt	Phone: 351-1094

Lodging: Alxis Park Inn (Adj Arpt) 337-8665; Abbey Retreat (Est. 1-3 miles) 351-6324; Best Western Cantebury Inn (Est. 1-3 miles, Trans provided) 351-0400; Holiday Inn (Est. 2 miles) 337-4058.

Meeting Rooms: Holiday Inn 337-4058.

Transportation: Taxi Service: City or yellow Cab 338-9777; Old Capitol Taxi 354-7662; Rental Cars: Hartwig 337-2101; Hertz 337-3473; Old Capital Motors 354-1101; Winebrenner Ford 338-7811.

Information: Iowa City/Coralville Convention & Visitors Bureau, 325 East Washington Street, P.O. Box 2358, Iowa City, IA 52240, Phone: 337-6592 or 800-283-6592.

Airport Information:

IOWA CITY - IOWA CITY MUNICIPAL (IOW)
2 mi southwest of town N41-38.35 W91-32.79 Elev: 668 Fuel: 100LL, Jet-A Rwy 06-24: H4355x150 (Conc) Rwy 12-30: H3900x150 (Conc) Rwy 17-35: H3875x150 (Conc) Unicom: 122.8 Attended: daylight hours Cedar Rapids App/Dep Con: 119.7 Clnc Del: 119.05
FBO: Iowa City Flying Service Phone: 338-7543, 337-5449

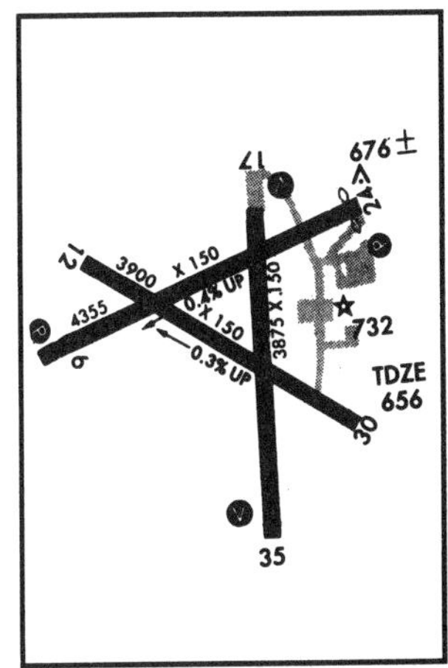

IA-MEY - MAPLETON
MAPLETON MUNICIPAL AIRPORT

(Area Code 712) 19

Maple Motel Restaurant & Lounge:

The Maple Motel Restaurant & Lounge is about 1/4th mile from the Mapleton Municipal Airport and is classified as a dinner club. Fly-in guests can see the motel from the airport, according to the airport management. The menu includes prime rib (Fri-Sat), seafood including lobster & shrimp, pork, beef steaks & chicken. A full salad bar with soup, appetizers & ice cream is available. There are daily specials as well. The decor is Western style with a fireplace in the lounge for cozy conversation. The restaurant can accommodate groups up to 60 persons. The restaurant opens Monday through Saturday at 5 p.m. Courtesy transportation may be available at the airport by calling 882-2764. However, it is not too far of a walk to the restaurant. For more information you can call 882-1271.

Restaurants Near Airport:
Maple Motel Restaurant 1/4th mi Phone: 882-1271

Lodging: Maple Motel (1 mile) 882-1271

Meeting Rooms: None Reported

Transportation: The Maple Motel is reported to be within walking distance. However if courtesy transportation is required, you could call the motel or airport for courtesy transportation.

Information: Sioux City Convention Center/Tourism Bureau, 801 4th Street, P.O. Box 3183, Sioux City, IA 51102, Phone: 279-4800.

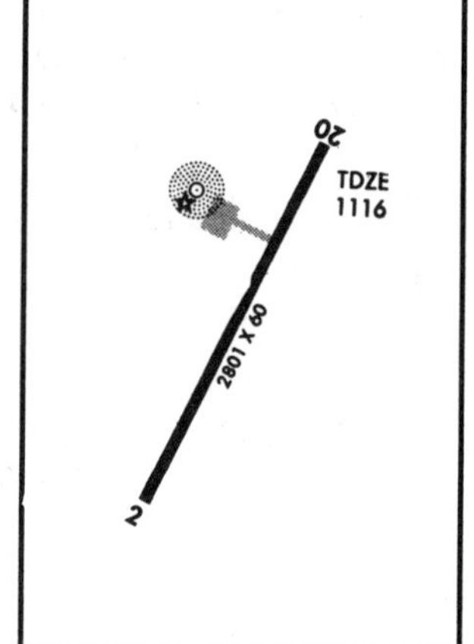

Airport Information:

MAPLETON - MAPLETON MUNICIPAL AIRPORT (MEY)
1 mi north of town N42-10.70 W95-47.62 Elev: 1116 Fuel: 100 Rwy 02-20: H2801x60 (Conc) Attended: Mon-Fri 1400-2300Z Unicom: 122.8
Mapleton Municipal Airport Phone: 882-2764

IA-OTM - OTTUMWA
OTTUMWA INDUSTRIAL AIRPORT

(Area Code 515) 20

Airport Cafe:

The Airport Cafe is located in the terminal building at the Ottumwa Industrial Airport, near Ottumwa, Iowa. This restaurant is a cafe that is open Monday through Friday 5 days a week between 7 a.m. and 3 p.m. It is within walking distance from aircraft parking and offers light fare for breakfast and lunch. Their menu provides a full service breakfast menu as well as luncheon selections like sandwiches, home made soups and pies. The restaurant serves daily specials as well as their main entrees. Fly-in groups are welcome, and carry-out meals can be arranged through catering services at the fixed base operators on the field. For information call the restaurant at 682-1830.

Restaurants Near Airport:
Airport Cafe On Site Phone: 682-1830.

Lodging: Days Inn (Trans) 682-8131; Hartland Inn (Trans) 682-8526; Parkview Plaza (Trans) 682-8051.

Meeting Rooms: Days Inn 682-8131; Hartland Inn 682-8526; Parkview Plaza 682-8051.

Transportation: City Cab 684-4664; Rental Cars: Hertz 682-8187.

Information: Ottumwa Area Convention & Visitors Bureau, 108 East Third, P.O. Box 308, Ottumwa, IA 52501, Phone: 682-3465.

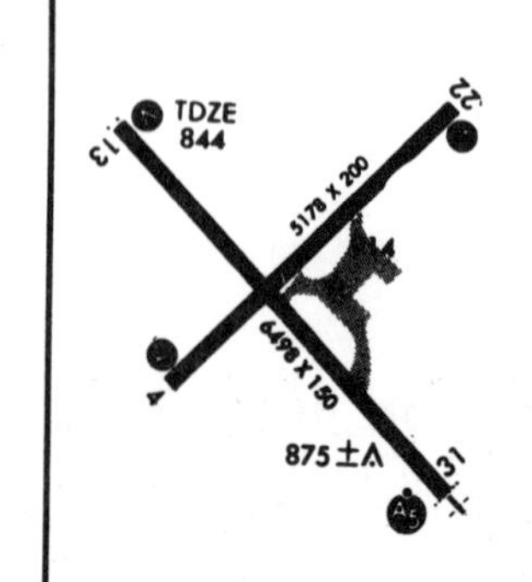

Airport Information:

OTTUMWA, OTTUMWA INDUSTRIAL, (OTM)
5 mi northwest of town N41-06.41 W92-26.90 Elev: 845 Fuel: 80, 100LL, Jet-A Rwy 13-31: H6499x150 (Asph-Conc) Rwy 04-22: H5178x200 (Asph) Attended: 1300-0200Z Unicom: 123.0 Notes: For attendant after hours call 684-7447
Ottumwa Industrial Airport Phone: 682-8044.

IA-ISB - SIBLEY
SIBLEY MUNICIPAL AIRPORT

(Area Code 712) **21**

Restaurants Near Airport:

Krogman's Highway 60 Cafe	Adj Arpt	Phone: 754-2645

Krogman's Highway 60 Cafe:

The Krogman's Highway 60 Cafe is located directly across the street from the Sibley Municipal Airport. This family style restaurant is open between 6:30 a.m. and 8:30 p.m. Monday through Saturday, and from 6:30 a.m. until 2:30 p.m. on Sunday. Specialties on their menu include all types of breakfast dishes, roast beef dinners, hot beef sandwiches, baked and fried ham, taco and chef salads, and a variety of delicious homemade pies. Krogman's Cafe also prepares a special "Hearty Mans" 3/4 lbs beef hamburger made with lean beef and all the trimmings, as well as their famous vegetable burgers. Prices are reasonable with most items running between $1.00 and $5.00. This restaurant has a simple yet comfortable and friendly atmosphere and is decorated with items from the 40's and 50's. The dining room can seat 65 to 75 persons and has paneling, homemade wooden shelves, booths, tables, and coffee counter service. A meeting room was also reported to be available, able to seat 15 to 20 persons with advance notice. Meals can be prepared-to-go as well. One additional service that is frequently used is their In-flight catering operation, with meals to go. Many pilots stop in to pick up sandwiches and desserts and take them on their way. For more information call Krogman's Highway 60 Cafe at 754-2645.

Lodging: None Reported
Meeting Rooms: Krogman's Highway 60 Cafe has accommodations for small meetings. 754-2645.
Transportation: O'Leary Aviation can provide courtesy transportation to nearby facilities, 754-3467.
Information: Iowa Great Lakes Area Chamber of Commerce, US 71, Box 9, Arnolds Park, IA 51331, Phone: 332-2107.

Attractions:

Sibley has a golf course 4 miles from the airport. Call Robert O'Leary fixed base operation at the Sibley Municipal Airport for information 454-3467. Also Spirit Lake resort region 30 east.

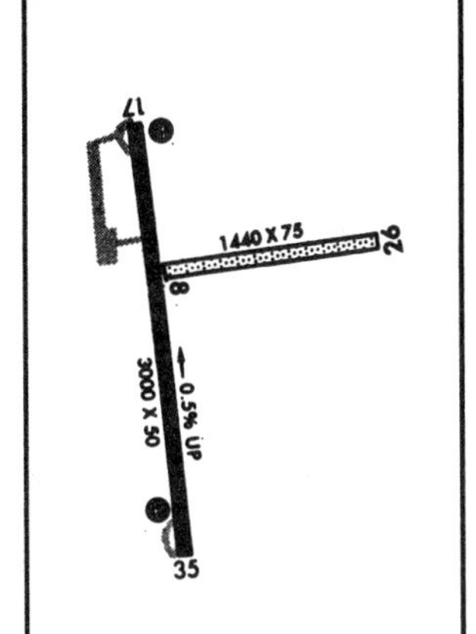

Airport Information:

SIBLEY - SIBLEY MUNICIPAL AIRPORT (ISB)
2 mi south of town N43-22.19 W95-45.55 Elev: 1537 Fuel: 100LL
Rwy 17-35: H3000x50 (Conc) Rwy 08-26: 1420x75 (Turf) Attended: 1200-0000Z
Unicom: 122.8 Public Phone 24hrs
FBO: O'Leary Aviation Phone: 754-3467

IA-SUX - SIOUX CITY
SIOUX GATEWAY AIRPORT

(Area Code 712) **22**

Restaurants Near Airport:

1st Edition	5 mi N.	Phone: 277-3200
Airport Food Bar	On Site	Phone: 255-1187
Hungrys North	5 mi NW.	Phone: 987-3717
Puerto Vallarta	6 mi N.	Phone: 277-9100

Airport Lounge/Food Bar:

The Airport Lounge and Food Bar is located in the terminal building on the Sioux Gatway Airport. This snack bar is open 5 a.m. to 7 p.m. 6 days a week with times varying slightly on Sundays. Items on their menu include eggs and muffins for breakfast, and for lunch and dinner, roast beef, hot turkey, hamburger, hot dogs, pizza, bagels and all types of sandwiches including Swiss, cheddar and American cheese. Prices average $3.00 for most items. The cafe can seat about 50 people. A view of the airport can be enjoyed while having your meal. For information call 255-1187.

Lodging: Best Western Marina (Trans) 494-2441; Best Western Regency (Trans) 277-1550; Hilton Inn (Trans) 277-4101; Holiday Inn (Trans) 277-3211; Howard Johnson Lodge (Trans) 277-9400; Imperial Motel 277-3151.
Meeting Rooms: The Airport Restaurant has reported that they have accommodations for meetings and conference rooms with available seating for 35 to 50 persons. Also: Best Western Marina 494-2441; Best Western Regency 277-1550; Hilton Inn 277-4101; Holiday Inn 277-3211; Howard Johnson Lodge 277-9400; Imperial Motel 277-3151.
Transportation: Airway Services can provide transportation to nearby facilities 258-6563. Also Taxi & Lomo Service: Airline Limo Service 258-8748; Cabs, Inc. 258-0521; Radio Cab 258-0555; Siouxland Taxi 277-0000; Rental Cars: National 255-6629; Budget 255-3533.
Information: Convention & Visitors Bureau, Convention Center, 801 4th Street, P.O. Box 3183, Sioux City, IA 51101, Phone: 279-4800.

Attraction: Green Valley Golf Course,(3 miles) 43 Donner Avenue, Sioux City, 252-2025; Cimmarina Harbor (6 miles) on the Missouri River, 1100 Larsen Park Road 277-2917.

Airport Information:

SIOUX CITY - SIOUX GATEWAY AIRPORT (SUX)
6 mi south of town N42-24.16 W96-23.06 Elev: 1098 Fuel: 100LL, Jet-A
Rwy 13-31: H8999x150 (Asph-Conc-Pfc) Rwy 17-35: H6599x150 (Asph-Pfc)
Attended: continuously Atis: 119.45 Unicom: 122.95 App/Dep Con: 124.6, 134.6
Sioux City Tower: 118.7 Gnd Con: 121.9
Sioux City Airport Phone: 279-6100

KANSAS

LOCATION MAP

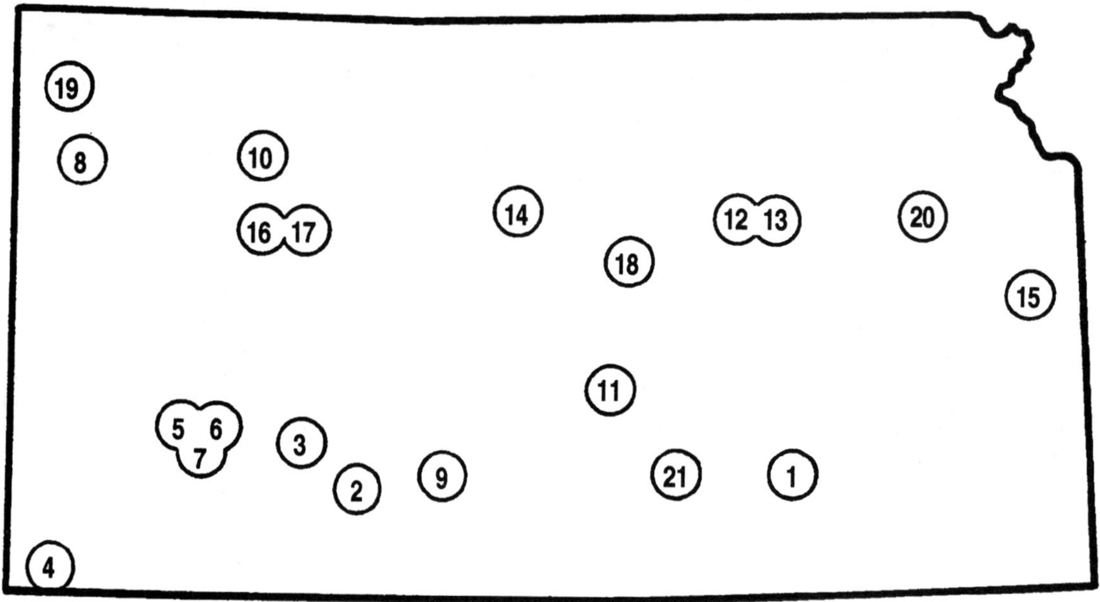

Not to be used for navigational purposes

KANSAS

CROSS FILE INDEX

Location Number	City or Town	Airport Name And Identifier	Name of Attraction
1	Beaumont	Beaumont (Private)	Summit Hse. Cntry. Inn
2	Bucklin	Bucklin Arpt. (8K0)	Baldwin Cafe
3	Dodge City	Dodge City Reg. Arpt. (DDC)	Airport Restaurant
4	Elkhart	Morton Co. Arpt. (EHA)	Spangles Restaurant
5	Garden City	Garden City Muni. Arpt. (GCK)	Flight Deck Restaurant
6	Garden City	Garden City Muni. Arpt. (GCK)	The Grain Bin S.C.
7	Garden City	Garden City Muni. Arpt. (GCK)	Red Baron Restaurant
8	Goodland	Renner Fld./Goodland Muni. (GLD)	Butterfly Cafe
9	Haviland	Gail Ballard Muni. Arpt. (26K)	Cornor Grocery Rest.
10	Hoxie	Sheridan Co. Arpt. (KS01)	Old Sheridan Inn
11	Hutchinson	Hutchinson Muni. Arpt. (HUT)	Arpt. Steak House
12	Junction City	Freeman Field (3JC)	The Imperial Palace
13	Junction City	Freeman Field (3JC)	Taco Bell Family Rest.
14	Lucas	Lucas Arpt. (38K)	K-18 Cafe
15	Osawatomie/Paola	Miami Co. Arpt. (K81)	Brownies Restaurant
16	Quinter	Quinter Airstrip (6KS1)	Q-Inn
17	Quinter	Quinter Airstrip (6KS1)	Tepa Restaurant
18	St. Francis	Cheyenne Co. Muni. (SYF)	Dusty Farmer Restaurnat
19	Salina	Salina Muni. Arpt. (SLN)	Landing Restaurant
20	Topeka	Philip Billard Muni. (TOP)	Mentzer's Restaurant
21	Wichita	Wichita Mid-Continent Arpt. (ICT)	Harvest Land (Host)

KS-BEAUMONT (Private Airport)

1

Restaurants Near Airport: (Area Code 316)
Summit House 1/4 mi Phone: 843-2422

Lodging: Summit House Country Inn and Restaurant (1/4 mi) 843-2422.
Meeting Rooms: None Reported
Transportation: None Reported
Information: Fly-in guests can call Summit House Country Inn and Restaurant for further information about this area 843-2422.

Summit House Country Inn & Restaurant:

The Summit House Country Inn & Restaurant is located within 1/4 mile from a grass landing strip. We were told that some pilots acquainted with the restaurant taxi their aircraft up 116th Street, stopping at the stop sign then proceeding across until they see a dead tree with a prop nailed to it. The sign says "Aircraft Parking." Once arriving at Beaumont, with a population of around 85 persons, you will notice this quaint, friendly town contains a large cypress, wooden water, tower representing an historical landmark, where steam locomotive engines would stop and take on water for their boilers. These trains would transport cattle to the stock yards for market. Today this wooden landmark stands as a proud reminder of the famous cattle drives which took place in the west. Just kitty-corner from the water tower is the Summit House Country Inn & Restaurant. The restaurant is open 10 a.m. to 8 p.m., Tuesday through Saturday and 10 a.m. to 5 p.m. on Sunday. They are closed on Monday. Their menu offers everything from hamburgers to prime rib. Specialties during the week include scampi with linguine, egg plant parmesan, t-bone steak, prime rib, broiled chicken breast, chicken sandwiches, and their popular "Tall grass" beef sandwich and "Summit burger." The restaurant has a cafe's 1950's decor decorated in knotty pine. The Summit House Country Inn also can accommodate overnight guests with 8 rooms. For more information you can call the Summit House at 843-2422.

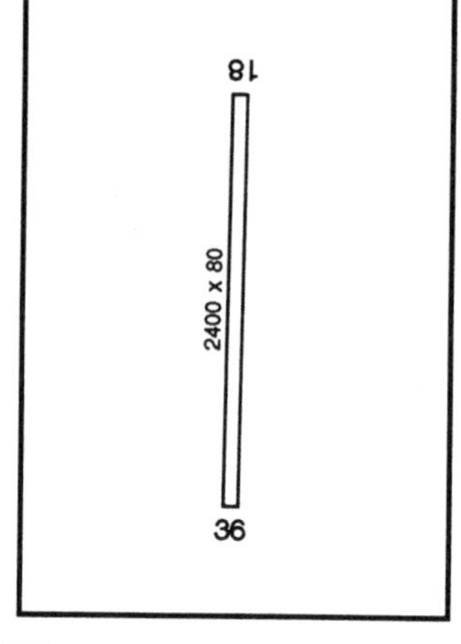

Airport Information:

BEAUMONT - (PRIVATE AIRPORT)
The town of Beaumont is situated about 50 statute miles due east of the Wichita Mid Continent Airport (ICT). It is located under the Eureka High MOA. It is a grass strip that has a windsock located on the northeast corner of the field. The runway has a north-south direction and is reported to be approx. 2,400 feet long with an elevation of 1617 feet MSL. We were also informed that the end of the runway has a rather steep slope for the last 5 or 6 hundred feet of its runway. For information call the Summit House Country Inn at 843-2422. **Notes: (Private use facility use at own risk)**

KS-8K0 - BUCKLIN BUCKLIN AIRPORT

(Area Code 316)

2

Baldwin Cafe:

The Bucklin Fina Mart & Cafe is located 2 blocks from the Bucklin Airport. This cafe is open from 11 a.m. to 7 p.m. Sunday and Monday, and from 7 a.m. to 9 p.m. Tuesday through Saturday. This convenience store is open 6 a.m. to 11 p.m. 7 days a week. This cafe serves items like sub sandwiches, salads and pizza. The dining room can seat 48 persons. Groups and fly-in guests are welcome. Everything on their menu can be prepared for carry-out. This cafe is adjoined by a convenience store primarily used by automobile traffic through the region. For more information call 826-3210.

Restaurants Near Airport:
Baldwin Cafe 2 Blks Phone: 826-3210
Bucklin Cafe 2 Blks Phone: N/A

Lodging: West Side Motel (1/4th mile) 826-3224.

Meeting Rooms: None Reported

Transportation: None Reported

Information: The Travel and Tourism Division, Department of Commerce & Housing, 700 SW Harrison St, Suite 1300, Topeka, KS 66603, Phone: 913-296-2009 or 800-2-KANSAS.

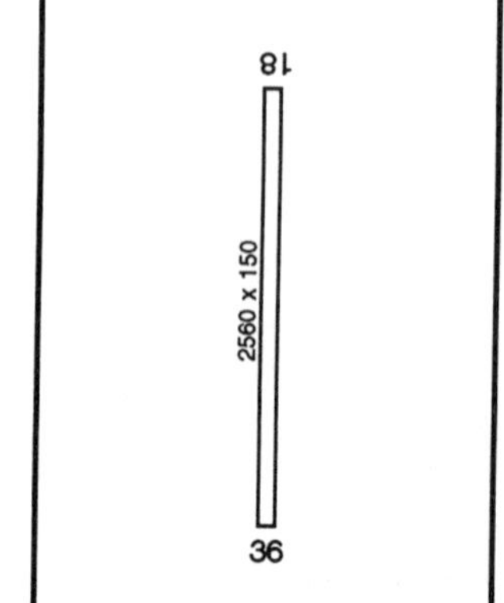

Airport Information:

BUCKLIN - BUCKLIN (8K0)
1 mi southwest of town N37-33.08 W99-38.69 Elev: 2418 Rwy 18-36: 2560x150 (Turf)
Attended: unattended CTAF: 122.9
Bucklin Airport Phone: 826-9954

KS-DDC - DODGE CITY
DODGE CITY REGIONAL AIRPORT

(Area Code 316)

3

Restaurants Near Airport:

Airport Restaurant	On Site	Phone: 227-9885
Jason's Steak & Spirits	2 mi SW	Phone: 255-2288

Lodging: Western Inn (2 miles) 225-1381; Silver Spur Lodge (6 miles) 227-2125

Meeting Rooms: Western Inn 225-1381; Silver Spur Lodge 227-2125.

Transportation: Crotts Aircraft Service can provide transportation to nearby facilities 227-3553; Rental Cars: Hertz 225-4001; Avis 227-3414.

Information: Convention & Visitors Bureau, 4th and Spruce, P.O. Box 1474, Dodge City, KS 67801, Phone: 225-8186.

Airport Restaurant:

The Airport Restaurant is located in the main terminal building at the Dodge City Municipal Airport. This restaurant is open between 11 a.m. and 2 p.m. and again at 5 p.m. to 8 p.m. Tuesday through Saturday and 7 a.m. to 2 p.m. on Sunday for their brunch. Their breakfast selections include egg dishes and pancakes. Lunch and dinner specials include meatloaf, Yankee pot roast , sandwiches, Reuben's, chicken fried steaks, pork chops, salad bar, desserts, pies and icecream. Average prices run $3.00 for breakfast, $3.50 for lunch, and $5.00 for dinner. The main dining room can seat 64 people, with counter service and tables. Customers can watch the activity on the airport as they enjoy their meal. Items off their menu can be prepared-to-go, upon request. For more information call 227-9885.

Attractions:

Boot Hill Museum, on Front Street in Dodge City is located 5 miles from the regional airport. For more informaton call, Phone 227-8188.

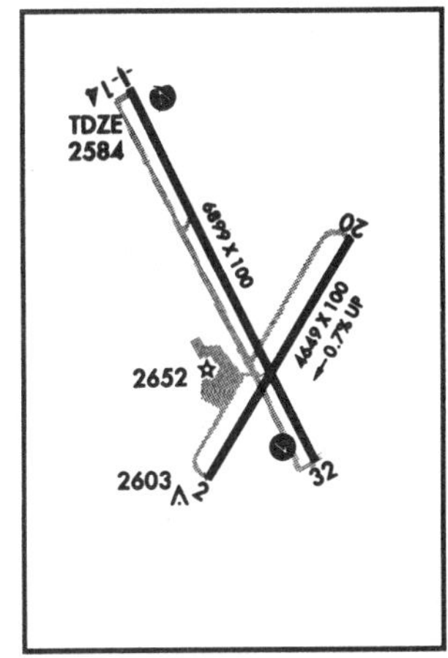

Airport Information:

DODGE CITY - DODGE CITY REGIONAL AIRPORT (DDC)
3 mi east of town N37-45.79 W99-57.93 Elev: 2594 Fuel: 100LL, Jet-A
Rwy 14-32: H6899x100 (Asph) Rwy 02-20: H4649x100 (Asph) Attended: 1300-0400Z
Unicom: 122.7 Kansas City Center App/Dep Con: 125.2 Public Phone 24hrs
FBO: Crotts Aircraft Service Phone: 227-3553

KS-EHA - ELKHART
MORTON COUNTY AIRPORT

(Area Code 316)

4

Restaurants Near Airport:

Pizza Hut	1/2 mi	Phone: 697-4559
Spangles Restaurant	1/2 mi	Phone: 697-9886

Lodging: El Rancho Motel (1 mile) 697-2117

Meeting Rooms: None Reported

Transportation: Courtesy cars and rental cars are available at the airport. Please call in advance to let them know you are coming.

Information: The Travel and Tourism Division, Department of Commerce & Housing, 700 SW Harrison St, Suite 1300, Topeka 66603, Phone: 913-296-2009 or 800-2-KANSAS.

Spangles Restaurant:

The Spangles Restaurant is reported to be about 1/2 to 3/4 of a mile from the Elkhart Country Airport. This family restaurant operates between 6 a.m. and 9 p.m. and serves a variety of entrees. Hand-cut steaks are one of their specialties along with burgers, deep fried vegetable trays, stuffed baked potatoes, shrimp baskets, and a salad bar. Average prices run $2.75 to $4.00 for breakfast, and $5.95 for most lunch and dinner entrees. Their hand cut large rib eye steak runs about $15.75. They also offer a senior citizen discount as well as children portions. The main dining room can seat 60 to 65 persons. They also have a back dining room that can accommodate up to 35 people for groups or parties. The decor of this facility is homey with lots of plants and ferns as well as tables and chairs with black naugahyde trim. For more information, you can call the Spangles Restaurant at 697-9886.

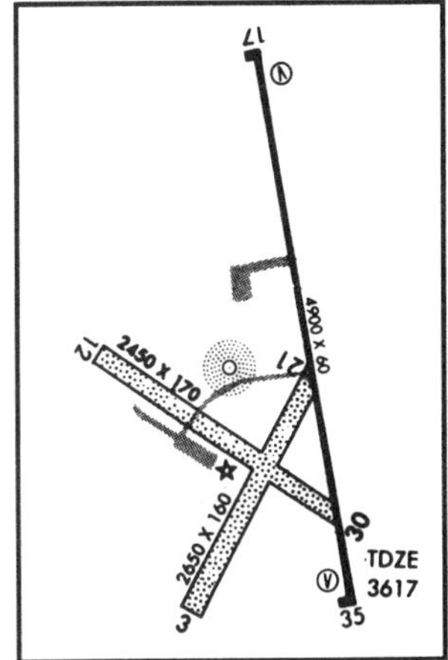

Airport Information:

ELKHART - MORTON COUNTY AIRPORT (EHA)
1 mi east of town N37-00.02 W101-53.03 Elev: 3625 Fuel: 100LL
Rwy 17-35: H4900x60 (Asph) Rwy 12-30: 2450x170 (Turf) Rwy 03-21: 2650x160 (Turf)
Attended: unattended Unicom: 122.8
Morton County Airport Phone: 697-2402 or 697-2016

KS-GCK - GARDEN CITY
GARDEN CITY MUNICIPAL AIRPORT

(Area Code 316)

5, 6, 7

Flight Deck Restaurant:

According to the airport management, the Flight Deck Restaurant is located on the east side of the airport, adjacent to the terminal building. Once entering the terminal, they are situated on the north side of the lobby. This restaurant is open from 8 a.m. to 8 p.m. Monday through Saturday, and 9 a.m. to 3 p.m. on Sunday. Their menu includes a full selection of breakfast entrees as well as specialty items, like their char-broiled burgers, chicken strips, chicken fried steaks and a variety of freshly baked homemade pies. Average prices run $3.00 for breakfast, $4.95 for lunch and $5.95 to $9.00 for dinner. Daily specials are offered along with steak specials on Friday nights. Their main dining room can seat 80 to 85 persons. They also have a back dining room for groups and parties, able to accommodate up to 40 additional customers. The decor of this restaurant offers fine dining in a casual atmosphere. Customers can enjoy a view of the airport and runways from the restaurant. For more information, you can call the Flight Deck Restaurant at 275-0438.

The Grain Bin Supper CLub:

This restaurant is situated about 10 miles west of the Garden City Municipal Airport adjacent to the Wheatlands Motor Inn. Their menu contains over 20 appetizers to choose from as well as a dessert tray, along with the entrees on their menu. The average price for a meal runs about $10.00. This facility is open from 4:00 p.m. to 2:00 a.m., Dinner is served from 6:00 p.m. to 10:30 Monday thorough Friday and 6:30 to 10:30 on Saturday. The decor of this restaurant is designed after the board game "Clue" and parts are decorated with a Victorian atmosphere. For information call 275-5954.

Red Baron Restaurant:

The Red Baron Restaurant is located about 8 miles from the Garden City Municipal Airport. They are open 24 hours a day 7 days a week. Daily luncheons and evening specials like steaks, sandwiches, and salad bar are featured. On Saturday a late night-early morning breakfast buffet is served at 1:00 a.m. Prices run $4.50 for breakfast, $5.50 for lunch and $6.50 for dinner. The restaurant is decorated with WW-II Flyers and planes, which would be of particular interest to pilots flying in for a meal. Located conveniently next door to the restaurant, is their motel. Turn left out of the airport on Hwy 50, and go 8 miles until reaching junction 50-83. The restaurant is located on the right side of the highway. This facility at the time of research, did not provide courtesy transportation, however since then this might have changed. However, Crotts Aviation may help you reach the restaurant. For information call the restaurant at Phone: 275-1797

Restaurants Near Airport:

Dyers Bar-B-Que	11 mi NW	Phone: 275-5003
Flight Deck Restaurant	On Site	Phone: 275-0438
Grain Bin (Wheatlands)	10 mi W.	Phone: 275-5954
Ignazzio's Italian	13 mi	Phone: 275-7556
Red Baron Restaurant	8 mi	Phone: 275-1797

Lodging:
Red Baron Motor Inn (Free transportation to and from airport, see restaurant listing above), Aprox. 8 miles from airport, Phone: 275-4164; Wheatlands Motor Inn, (Airport Transportation) 1311 E. Fulton, Phone: 276-2387; Hilton Inn Garden City, (Free airport transportation), 1911 E Kansas Avenue (US 156), Phone: 275-7471.

Transportation:
Crotts Aviation will help find a ride or arrange rental cars or taxi service to or from restaurants and nearby facilities; Also Quality Cab, Phone: 275-8294; Avis Rental, Phone: 276-2387; Executive Car Rental, Phone: 275-7221; Hertz Rental, Phone: 276-2387.

Conference Rooms: The airport has two meeting rooms for rent. The Flight Deck Restaurant has a large dining room for meetings and dinners. (East/Adj to terminal building).

Information: Chamber of Commerce, 1511 East Fulton, Terrance, KS 67846, Phone: 276-3264

Attractions:

Golden Locket Golf Club is located 6 miles west on highway 50, Phone: 275-1953; Scott County Lake, 40 miles north on 83; Finnup Park & Lee Richards Zoo, south of the city limits, on US 83. This Zoo contains more than 650 animals and birds on display, along with food, gift shops, play ground with picnic area, and museum with artifacts of the early settlers. Phone: N/A (See Information Above)

Airport Information:

GARDEN CITY - GARDEN CITY MUNICIPAL AIRPORT (GCK)
8 mi southeast of town N37-55.65 W100-43.47 Elev: 2890
Fuel: 100LL, Jet-A Rwy 17-35: H7300x100 (Asph-Conc) Rwy 12-30: H5700x100 (Conc)
Attended: dawn-0400Z Unicom: 123.0 Public Phone 24 hrs Notes: landing fee for 129 & 131 operations only; Overnight parking fees are $5.00 to $25.00;
FBO: Crotts Aviaiton, Phone: 275-5055

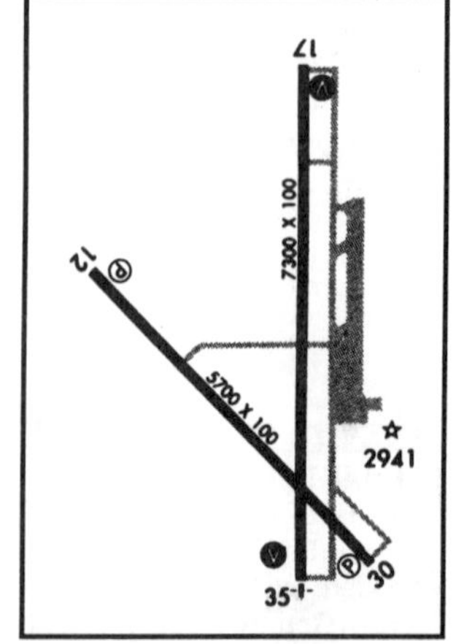

KS-GLD - GOODLAND RENNER FIELD (GOODLAND MUNICIPAL)

(Area Code 913)

8

Butterfly Cafe:

The Butterfly Cafe is located on the Renner/Goodland Municipal Airport. This family style facility is open from 6 a.m. until 3 p.m. Monday through Friday and 6 a.m. to 2 p.m. Saturday and Sunday. They specialize in chicken fried steakes, homemade rolls, salads, pies, desserts and pastries, which are made from scratch. Prices range from $3.00 for breakfast, $3.50 for lunch and $6.50 for dinner. There are daily specials, and a Sunday brunch is featured. The decor of this restaurant is rustic. Fly-in groups are welcome. If you desire carry-out sandwiches can be prepared. They will accommodate your needs. For information call 899-2085.

Restaurants Near Airport:

Buffalo Inn	2 mi	Phone: 899-5057
Butterfly Cafe	On Site	Phone: 899-2085
Rays	1.5 mi.	Phone: 899-2221

Lodging: Buffalo Inn, (2 miles) West Highway 24, Phone: 899-3621

Meeting Rooms: There are meeting rooms available at Butterfly Aviation.

Transportation: Butterfly Aviaiton can provide courtesy transportation; Rental Cars: Finley Motors, Phone: 899-2346.

Information: Convention and Visitors Bureau, 104 West 11th, P.O. Box 628, Goodland, KS 67735, Phone: 899-3515.

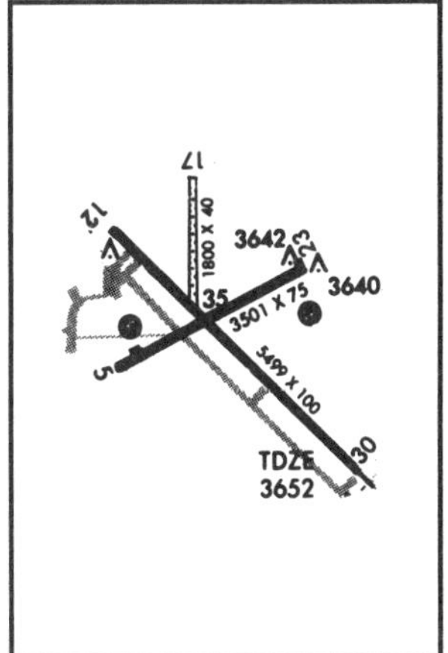

Airport Information:

GOODLAND - RENNER FIELD (GOODLAND MUNICIPAL) (GLD)
2 mi norh of town N39-22.24 W101-41.94 Elev: 3656 Fuel: 100LL, Jet-A
Rwy 12-30: H5499x100 (Conc) Rwy 05-23: H3501x75 (Asph) Rwy 17-35: 1800x40 (Turf)
Attended: daylight hours Unicom: 122.95 Public Phone 24 hrs Notes: For service call 899-5349 or evenings 899-7531.
FBO: Butterfly Aviation, Phone: 899-7531

KS-26K - HAVILAND GAIL BALLARD MUNICIPAL AIRPORT

(Area Code 316)

9

Corner Grocery Store:

This facility contains a convenience store with a snack bar attached, offering light fare. The restaurant is between 1/4 and 1/2 mile from the Gail Ballard Municipal Airport. Even though courtesy transportation may be available through the airport owner, this airport is listed as unattended, and transportation may not be readily available. Snack bar hours vary throughout the year. However, their normal hours are usually 7 a.m. to 9:30 p.m. Their menu includes pizza, along with a variety of pastries, cookies, coffee as well as other snacks. There is seating for 8 people at this time, but they can arrange extra seating for more people if needed. For more information you can call this establishment at 862-5817.

Restaurants Near Airport:

Corner Grocery Store	3/8 mi	Phone: 862-5817

Lodging: None Reported

Meeting Rooms: None Reported

Transportation: Uncertain

Information: The Travel and Tourism Division, Department of Commerce & Housing, 700 SW Harrison St, Suite 1300, Topeka, KS 66603, Phone: 913-296-2009 or 800-2-KANSAS.

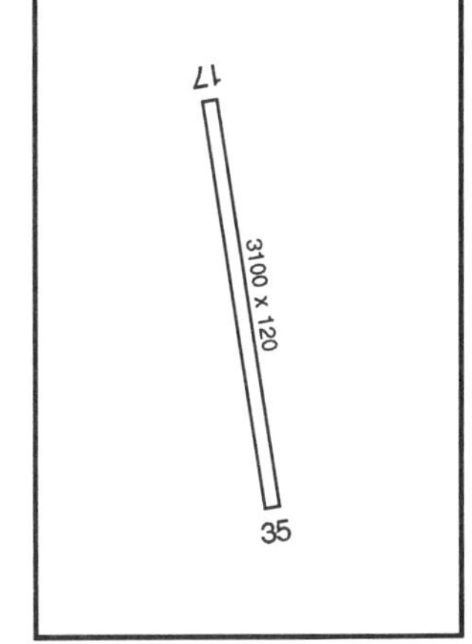

Airport Information:

HAVILAND - GAIL BALLARD MUNICIPAL AIRPORT (26K)
1 mi west of town N37-36.50 W99-06.94 Elev: 2165 Rwy 17-35: 3100x120 (Turf)
Attended: unattended Notes: CAUTION: Circular irrigation system extends across south 400' of runway 35 during growing season.
Gail Ballard Municipal Airport Phone: 862-5211
FBO: Havland Flying Servic Phone: 862-5678 or 862-5211

KS-KS01 - HOXIE
SHERIDAN COUNTY AIRPORT

(Area Code 913)

10

Old Sheridan Inn:

The Old Sheridan Inn is located in the town of Hoxie, about 1/4 mile from the airport, along Highway 23, and is within walking distance. This combination cafe and family style restaurant is open from 7 a.m. to 9 p.m. 7 days a week. Their menu contains selections like sandwiches, pork tenderloin, ground steak burgers, patty melts, roast beef dinners and a wide variety of additional entrees including a salad bar. Average prices for most meals run between $2.50 and $5.00. On Friday they serve Mexican dishes as their specialty. Breakfast selections are served all day. This restaurant can seat 80 to 90 persons in their main dining area. Their back room is designed for groups up to 50 persons. They often cater to local groups and club functions. The restaurant has 2 counter sections, as well as booths along the wall with tables in the middle. Small lanterns decorate the tables along with wall paper in patterns of soft blue colored flowers and chandeliers, that all add to the ambiance, especially during the evening hours. For more information you can call the restaurant at 675-3900.

Restaurants Near Airport:

Hungry Farmer	1/4 Arpt	Phone: 675-2315
Old Sheridan Inn	1/4 Arpt	Phone: 675-3900
Stop And Shop	1/4 Arpt	Phone: 675-3909

Lodging: Cress Vue Motel (1/4 mile) 675-3279; Hoxie Motel (1/2 mile) 675-3055.

Meeting Rooms: None Reported

Transportation: Most facilities are located within walking distance.

Information: The Travel and Tourism Division, Department of Commerce & Housing, 700 SW Harrison St, Suite 1300, Topeka, KS 66603, Phone: 913-296-2009 or 800-2-KANSAS.

NO AIRPORT DIAGRAM AVAILABLE

Airport Information:

HOXIE - SHERIDAN COUNTY AIRPORT (KSO1)
0 mi north of town N39-22.17 W100-26.11 Elev: 2733 Fuel: 100LL
Rwy 17-35: H4400x50 (Asph) Rwy 08-26: 1750x150 (Turf) Attended: Apr-Sep daylight hours, Oct-Mar call 675-2300 CTAF: 122.9 Notes: Rwy 17-35 cracked with loose gravel.
Sheridan County Airport Phone: 675-2300

KS-HUT - HUTCHINSON
HUTCHINSON MUNICIPAL AIRPORT

(Area Code 316) 11

Airport Steak House:

The Airport Steak House is situated in the terminal building on the Hutchinson Municipal Airport. This combination family style and fine dining facility offers a casual atmosphere during breakfast and lunch hours and a more elegant atmosphere in the evening. Their hours are Sunday through Thursday from 8 a.m. to 8:30 p.m., Friday and Saturday from 8 a.m. to 9:30 p.m. Their menu includes a full breakfast, lunch and dinner selection. They offer a breakfast buffet Saturday and Sunday between 8 a.m. and 10:30 a.m. and a lunch buffet Monday through Friday from 11:00 a.m. to 1:30 p.m., featuring an all-you-can-eat hot bar (Sunday hours may vary). Dinner choices provide a salad bar, along with menu choices like, filet mignon, chicken strips, top sirloin, lobster tails, and rib eye steak. Average prices run $4.25 for breakfast, $4.50 for lunch and $9.00 for dinner. The restaurant has seating for 100 persons in their main dining room with additional seating in their coffee shop area. One nice feature about this restaurant is that there is a charcoal grill within the dining area where your steaks are cooked to perfection while you watch. For more information about the Airport Steak House, call 662-4281.

Restaurants Near Airport:

Airport Steak house	On Site	Phone: 662-4281
Giorgio's Italian	2 mi W	Phone: 663-8966
Greg's Rest	1.5 mi SW	Phone: 663-9361
Roy's Hickory Pit	5 mi W.	Phone: 663-7421

Lodging: Budget Motel (Will pick you up, 1.5 miles southwest) 662-1289; Comfort Inn (Will pay for cab fair, 2.5 miles west) 663-7822; Holiday Inn Holidome (Courtesy car, 2.5 miles west) 669-9311; Quality Inn (Courtesy car, 4 miles west) 663-1211; Sundome /Best Western (Courtesy car, 8 miles southwest) 663-4444; Sunset Motel (Courtesy car, 2 miles west) 662-4429. Super 8 Motel (Courtesy car, 2.5 miles west) 662-6394.

Meeting Rooms: Holiday Inn/Holidome 669-9311; Quality Inn 663-1211; Sundome - Best Western 663-4444.

Transportation: Taxi service between 0700 and 2300 hours. Best to prearrange so taxi is waiting upon arrival. Call, City Taxi Service 669-8203; Also Avis car rental on site 665-5353 or 800-831-2847; Taylor Car Rental 669-9510 after hours 663-8197; Conklin Car Rental 665-5999; McCurdy Car Rental 663-2106.

Information: Greater Hutchinson Convention & Visitors Bureau, 117 N. Walnut, P.O. Box 519, 67504, Phone: 662-3391.

Attractions:

Golf Courses: Carey Park Golf Course (Public, 5 miles southwest) 662-9651; Highlands Golf & Supper Club (Private, 10 miles northwest) 694-2698 or 663-5301. **State Parks:** Sand Hills State Park (6 miles north) 663-5272. **Attractions:** Kansas Cosmosphere and Space Center Omnimax Theater and Space Science Exhibits. The Midwest's most comprehensive public science center 1100 North Plum (4 miles east) 662-2305. Dillon Nature Center (2.5 miles north) 663-7411. Kansas State Fairgrounds, home of the Kansas State Fair (Second week in September) (5 miles west by northwest) 662-6611 or 800-362-FAIR; Hutchinson Zoo (In Historic Carey Park) (5 miles southwest) 665-2660.

Airport Information:

HUTCHINSON - HUTCHINSON MUNICIPAL AIRPORT (HUT)
3 mi east of town N38-03.93 W97-51.64 Elev: 1542 Fuel: 100LL, Jet-A
Rwy 13-31: H7001x100 (Asph) Rwy 03-21: H5999x150 (Asph-Conc) Rwy 17-35: H4251x75 (Asph) Attended: 1300-0500Z Atis: 124.25 Unicom 122.95 Tower: 118.5 Gnd Con: 121.9 Public Phone 24hrs Notes: No landing fees, overnight parking fees - tie downs, no charge.
FBO: Hutchinson Aviation Phone: 662-7113
FBO: Well's Aircraft, Inc. Phone: 663-1546

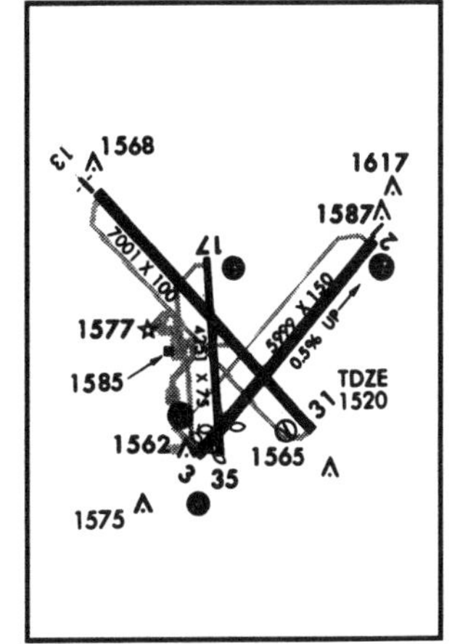

KS-3JC - JUNCTION CITY FREEMAN FIELD

(Area Code 913)

12, 13

The Imperial Palace:

This restaurant serves authentic Chinese food. It is located at 18th and Jackson near the Junction City Freeman Airport. This sit-down restaurant is open for lunch Monday through Friday 11 a.m. to 2 p.m., and for dinner Monday through Saturday 4 p.m. to 9 p.m. They feature a luncheon buffet Monday through Friday between 11:30 a.m. and 1:30 p.m. (Closed Sunday). Daily lunch specials are also available. Their banquet room is available with seating for 70 people. Advanced reservations are suggested. For information call 238-1713. (Tell them you heard about their restaurant in Aerodine).

Taco Bell Family Restaurant:

This restaurant is family owned and operated, and is situated 2 blocks east of the Freeman Airport. This facility is within walking distance and is open between the hours of 9:30 a.m. and 12 midnight. Selections from their menu include family packages of taco's including their 6 and 10 "Taco Pack Special", along with bean burrito's, steak and chicken burrito's, taco salads, nacho's, and Mexican pizza to mention only a few. The restaurant can accommodate up to 100 persons in their main dining room. This restaurant provides counter and carry-out service. However, it is not affiliated with the Taco Bell franchise. There are accommodations for 100 persons in their main dining room with tables, booths and counter seating. Many of their customers place orders for carry-out. Special family pack meals are also prepared and offered at discounts. For more information you can call Taco Bell restaurant at 238-2262.

Restaurants Near Airport:

Burger King	4 Blks E.	Phone: 238-4520
The Imperial Palace	E. of fld.	Phone: 238-1713
Taco Bell (Family Owned)	2 Blks E.	Phone: 238-2262

Lodging: Best Western (Free trans) 238-5188; Days Inn 762-2727; Harvest Inn 238-8101.

Meeting Rooms: Days Inn 762-2727; Harvest Inn 238-8101.

Transportation: Taxi service: A-One Taxi 238-6122; Bell Taxi 238-6161; Robbins Cab 762-2560; Yellow Cab 238-6131; Rental Cars: U-Save Rentals 762-2070; JC Auto Sales 238-8133.

Information: Geary County Convention & Visitors Bureau, 425 N Washington, P.O. Box 1846, Junction City, KS 66441, Phone: 238-2885 or 800-JCT/CITY.

Airport Information:

JUNCTION CITY - FREEMAN FIRLD (3JC)
1 mi northwest of town N39-02.60 W96-50.60 Elev: 1101 Fuel: 100LL, MOGAS
Rwy 18-36: H3495x75 (Asph) Rwy 05-23: 1927x200 (Turf) Rwy 13-31: 1915x140 (Turf)
Attended: 1400-0000Z, Unattended on major holidays. Unicom: 122.8
FBO: Junction City Municipal Phone: 238-2049

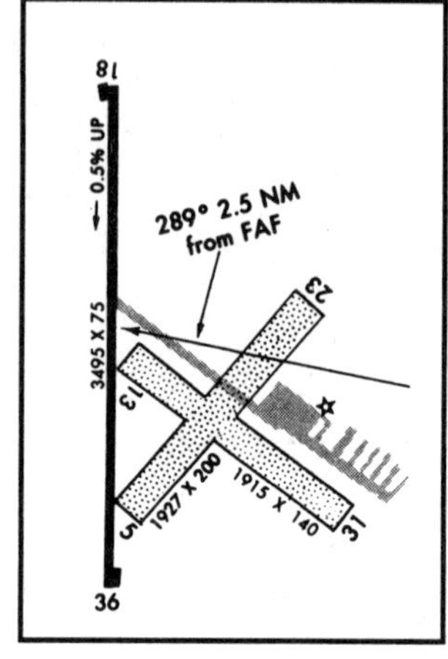

KS-38K - LUCAS LUCAS AIRPORT

(Area Code 913)

14

K-18 Cafe:

The K-18 Cafe is located about 50 yards from the Lucas Airport and is within walking distance. This cafe is open from 6 a.m. to 10 p.m. daily. Their menu includes specialty items consisting of a variety of selections such as, chicken, hamburgers, and baked ham, to mention only a few, along with a full breakfast line. This facility contains 2 separate dining rooms. Reservations are suggested during dinner hours. Seating for 50 persons are available in each portion of the restaurant. Groups and parties are also welcome. Meals can be prepared-to-go on request. For more information, you can call the K-18 Cafe at 525-6262.

Restaurants Near Airport:

K-18 Cafe	50 yds	Phone: 525-6262

Lodging: Lucas Country Inn (1/2 mile) 525-6358.

Meeting Rooms: None Reported

Transportation: Airport courtesy may be available.

Information: The Travel and Tourism Division, Department of Commerce & Housing, 700 SW Harrison St, Suite 1300, Topeka, KS 66603, Phone: 913-296-2009 or 800-2-KANSAS.

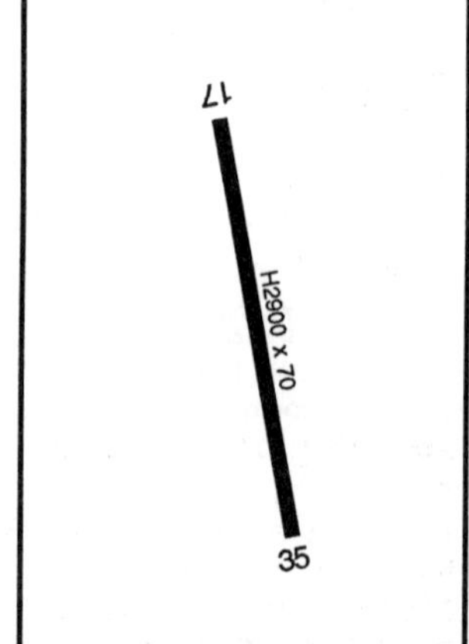

Airport Information:

LUCAS - LUCAS AIRPORT (38K)
1 mi east of town N39-03.72 W98-31.52 Elev: 1485 Fuel: 100LL
Rwy 17-35: H2900x70 (Asph) Attended: daylight hours CTAF: 122.9
Lucas Airport Phone: 525-6366

KS-K81 - OSAWATOMIE/PAOLA MIAMI COUNTY AIRPORT

(Area Code 913) 15

Restaurants Near Airport:
Brownies Restaurant On Site Phone: 755-4006

Lodging: Eastgate Inn (4 miles) 755-3051.
Meeting Rooms: None Reported
Transportation: None Reported
Information: Chamber of Commerce, 526 Main Street, P.O. Box 338, Osawatomie, KS 66064, Phone: 755-4114.

Brownies Restaurant:

Brownies Restaurant is situated right on the Miami County Airport which is near the towns of Osawatomie and Paola, KS. This family style restaurant is reported to be open Wednesday and Thursday between 5:30 a.m. and 2 p.m., Friday and Saturday between 5:30 a.m. to 8 p.m., and Sunday from 5:30 until 4 p.m. The owners first began to serve fly-in guests with grilled foods that were prepared on outdoor grills. As more and more people became aware of this operation, their business quickly increased. The old terminal building is where Brownies Restaurant is now located. Their dining room is furnished with 5 or 6 long tables and 4 regular tables, that can accommodate a total of 30 to 40 persons. The dining area is not large, but offers a festive atmosphere and is furnished with lots of aircraft pictures, unusual calendars, a mounted propeller on the wall, and many big windows allowing a great view of the ramp area and active runways. Items on their menu include breakfast served until 10 a.m., followed by lunch and dinner selections like barbecued beef, ribs, turkey, sausage and chicken. Much of the cooking is still done outside on barbecued grills and cookers. They also carry a nice variety of sandwiches, fish, chicken pot pie and chili. You can park your aircraft within 40 feet of the restaurant. On weekends of pilots fly-in to enjoy a fine meal. They have had as many as 40 to 45 aircraft fly-ins during a Saturday or Sunday. Plenty of hangar flying is also enjoyed by the local and regional based flying clubs that make Brownies Restaurant a regular stopping place. For more information you can call Brownies Restaurant at 755-4006.

NO AIRPORT DIAGRAM AVAILABLE

Airport Information:

OSAWATOMIE/PAOLA - MIAMI COUNTY AIRPORT (K81)
3 mi northeast of town N38-32.25 W94-55.51 Elev: 945 Fuel: 100LL
Rwy 02-20: H2805x25 (Asph) Rwy 15-33: 2700x55 (Turf) Attended: unattended
Unicom: 122.8
Miami County Airport Phone: 755-2345, 755-3249

KS-6KS1 - QUINTER QUINTER AIRSTRIP

(Area Code 913) 16, 17

Restaurant Near Airport:
Q-Inn 1/4 mi Phone: 754-3820
Tepa (Mexican) 1/4 mi Phone: 754-2484

Lodging: Q-Inn (1/4 mile) 754-3337

Meeting Rooms: None Reported

Transportation: Restaurants listed above are well within walking distance from the Quinter Airport.

Information: The Travel and Tourism Division, Department of Commerce & Housing, 700 SW Harrison St, Suite 1300, Topeka, KS 66603, Phone: 913-296-2009 or 800-2-KANSAS.

Q-Inn:

The Q-Inn is situated well within walking distance from the Quinter Airstrip. This family style restaurant is open Monday through Saturday between 6:30 a.m. and 9 p.m. and Sundays 11 a.m. to 2 p.m. There is a 51 room motel adjacent to the restaurant that offers central air-conditioning and cable TV. The restaurant serves a variety of entrees including steaks, buffalo meat, hamburgers, sandwiches, and a salad bar available all day. They also offer a smorgasbord on Sunday from 11 a.m. to 2:30 p.m. Fly-in groups are welcome, and meals-to-go are available for cross-county air travelers. For more information about the motel call 754-3337 or the restaurant at 754-3820.

Tepa Restaurant:

The Tepa Restaurant is located a little closer to the Quinter Airstrip than the Q-Inn. This restaurant serves primarily Mexican food and is highly recommended as is the Q-Inn, by the airport owner as a nice place to eat. For more information call the Tepa Restaurant at 754-2484.

18
2600 x 75
36

Airport Information:

QUINTER - QUINTER AIRSTRIP (6KS1)
1 mi west of town 39-04-00N 100-14-42W Elev: 2675 Fuel: None Reported
Rwy 18-36: 2600x75 (Turf) Notes: This is a private use facility, use at your own risk.
CAUTION: Used by crop spraying aircraft. We recommend you call in advance before using.
Quinter Air Strip Phone: 754-3892 or 754-3611

KS-SYF - ST FRANCIS
CHEYENNE COUNTY MUNICIPAL

(Area Code 913) 18

Dusty Farmer Restaurant & Motel:

The restaurant manager indicated that this family style dining facility is located only one block north from the Cheyenne County Municipal Airport . The restaurant is open 7 days a week from 6:30 a.m. to 9 p.m. They have a full service menu including breakfast, lunch and dinner. They also have 2 daily oriental specials, as well as other specials throughout the week. House specialties include a large fresh salad bar, steaks, sandwiches, homemade pies, cinnamon rolls, desserts and honey stung chicken. Average prices run $4.95 for breakfast, $5.95 for lunch and $8.95 for dinner. The restaurant is decorated with farm equipment advertising, farm implements, tools and a large collection of toy farm tractors on display. Their Tumbleweed Lounge serves mixed drinks. This restaurant also has a small meeting and party room for use by individuals or clubs. Anything on their menu can be prepared and placed in to-go containers for people to pick up. Their own motel is right next door to the restaurant. For information call 332-2231.

Restaurants Near Airport:

Cheyenne Bowl	4 blks W	Phone: 332-2221
Dusty Farmer Restaurant	1 blk N	Phone: 332-2231
Park Hill Restaurant	3 blks NE	Phone: 332-2255
Pizza Hut	5 blks W	Phone: 332-2601

Lodging: Homesteader (1/2 mile) 332-2168; Empire Hotel (3 blocks) 332-2231
Meeting Rooms: Meeting rooms at the Dusty Farmer Restaurant
Transportation: Grace Flying Service, Inc. can accommodate fly-in customers with a courtesy car. Also there is a courtesy car at the airport.
Information: The Travel and Tourism Division, Department of Commerce & Housing, 700 SW Harrison St, Suite 1300, Topeka, KS 66603, Phone: 913-296-2009 or 800-2-KANSAS.

Attractions:

Golf Course (1 mile west) 332-3401; According to Dusty Farmer Restaurant and Hotel manager, there is excellent pheasant hunting in the area which attracts many hunters from all over the country. For information call the restaurant at 332-2231.

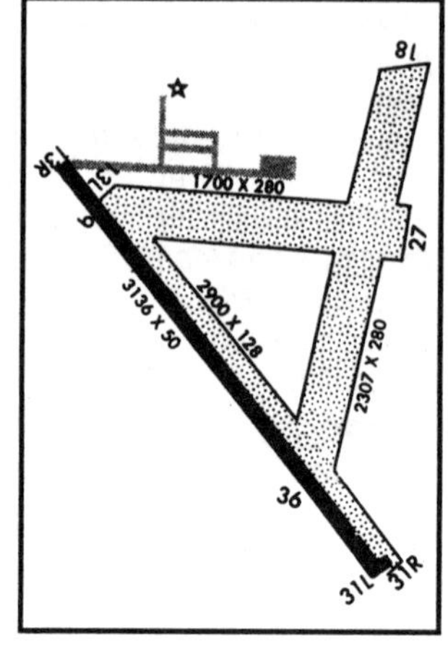

Airport Information:

ST FRANCIS - CHEYENNE COUNTY MUNICIPAL AIRPORT (SYF)
1 mi south of town N39-4566 W101-47.75 Rwy 13R-31L: H3136x50 (Asph) Elev: 3411 Fuel: 100LL Rwy 13R-31L: H3136x50 (Asph) Rwy 13L-31R: 2900x128 (Turf) Rwy 18-36: 2307x280 (Turf) Rwy 09-27: 1700x280 (Turf) Attended: Mon-Sat daylight hours Unicom: 122.8 Public Phone 24hrs Notes: For service call 332-2251.
FBO: Grace Flying Service, Inc. Phone: 332-2251

KS-SLN - SALINA
SALINA MUNICIPAL AIRPORT

(Area Code 913) 19

The Landing Restaurant:

The restaurant previously listed "Landing Restaurant" was closed at the time of our interview. However this facility may reopen in the future under new management. For information call the airport manager at 827-3914.

Restaurants Near Airport:

Brookville Hotel	15 mi SW	Phone: 225-6666
The Landing Restaurant	On Site	Phone: N/A

Lodging: Best Western Mid-America 827-0356; Holiday Inn 823-1739; Howard Johnson 827-5511; Ramada Inn 825-8211.

Meeting Rooms: Best Western Mid-America 827-0356; Holiday Inn 823-1739; Howard Johnson 827-5511; Ramada Inn 825-8211.

Transportation: Some FBO courtesy cars available; Also: Avis 827-2054; Hertz 827-7237.

Information: Chamber of Commerce, 120 West Ash, P.O. Box 586, Salina, KS 67401, Phone: 827-9301.

Airport Information:

SALINA - SALINA MUNICIPAL AIRPORT (SLN)
3 mi southwest of town N38-47.50 W97-39.06 Elev: 1272 Fuel: 100LL, Jet-A, Mogas Rwy 17-35: H13337x200 (Asph) Rwy 12-30: H8500x100 (Asph) Rwy 04-22: H3640x75 (Asph) Attended: continuously Atis: 120.15 Unicom: 122.95 Tower: 119.3 Gnd Con: 121.9
FBO: Flower Aviation Phone: 825-6739
FBO: Moore's Midway Aviation Phone: 825-6261

Not to be used for navigational purposes

KS-TOP - TOPEKA
PHILIP BILLARD MUNICIPAL

(Area Code 913)

20

Mentzer's Family Restaurant:

This restaurant is located within the terminal building at the Topeka Philip Billard Municipal Airport. Customers can park their aircraft right near the entrance to the restaurant. Their hours are from 7 a.m. to 8 p.m. Tuesday through Saturday and 7 a.m. to 2 p.m. Sunday and Mondays. Entrees on their menu include breakfast served all day, chicken fried steaks, pork chops, meat loaf, 6 oz. senior steaks, 10 oz. top sirloin, sandwiches, cheeseburgers and hamburgers. They are also well known for their buffets. A breakfast bar is featured Saturday and Sunday from 8 a.m. to 2 p.m. It includes: scrambled eggs, sausage, baked ham, diced potatoes, biscuits and gravy, French toast stick and donuts. A luncheon buffet is served Monday through Friday between 11 a.m. and 2 p.m. And a supper buffet is served Friday and Saturday. In addition there is an all-you-can-eat salad bar with soup. Average prices range from $4.99 for the breakfast buffet and $5.00 to $7.00 for most other items. Mentzer's Restaurant offers a contemporary decorated in pleasant sky blue colors. The view from the restaurant overlooks the aircraft parking ramp. Groups are welcome. In-flight catering is also provided. For more information you can call the restaurant at 232-4437.

Restaurants Near Airport:
Mentzer's Family Restaurant On Site Phone: 232-4437

Lodging: Clubhouse Inn 7-10 mi. 273-8888; Holiday Inn-City Center 3 mi. 232-7721; Ramada Inn-I-70, 3 mi. 234-5400.

Meeting Rooms: Holiday Inn-City Center 3 mi. 232-7721; Ramada Inn-I-70 has convention facilities, 3 mi. 234-5400.

Transportation: Rental cars: Hertz 233-6677; Taxi Service: Yellow Cab 357-4444.

Information: Topeka Convention & Visitors Bureau, 3 Townsite Plaza, 120 East Sixth Street, Topeka, KS 66603. Phone: 234-1030 or 800-235-1030.

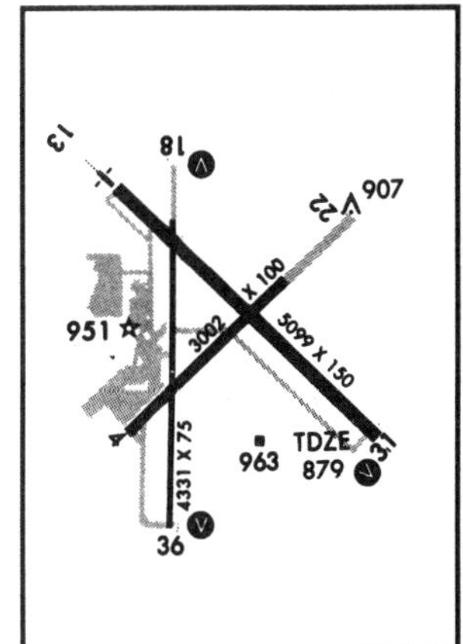

Airport Information:

TOPEKA - PHILOP BILLARD MUNICIPAL (TOP)
3 mi northeast from town N39-04.12 W95-37.35 Elev: 881 Fuel: 100LL, Jet-A Rwy 13-31: H5099x150 (Asph) Rwy 18-36: H4331x75 (Asph) Rwy 04-22: H3002x100 (Asph) Attended: continuously ASOS: 913-234-1591 CTAF: 118.7 Unicom: 122.95 Tower: 118.7 Gnd Con: 121.9 Clnc Del: 121.9
FBO: Ken Godfrey Aviation, Inc. Phone: 233-6677
FBO: T.J. Terminals Phone: 234-2602, 233-0881

KS-ICT - WICHITA
WICHITA MID-CONTINENT AIRPORT

(Area Code 316)

21

Harvest Land (Host Marriott):

This family style restaurant is located on the main concourse near the entrance of the Wichita Mid-Continent Airport. This restaurant is open 7 days a week from 6 a.m. to 10:30 p.m. Their entrees consist of items like Pizza Hut personal pan pizza, mid-west cuisine, a vast assortment of grilled favorites, deli selections, salads and desserts, as well as assorted beverages. They also provide a daily buffet line along with a Friday night fish selection. Average prices run $5.25 for breakfast, $6.25 for lunch and $6.25 for dinner. This restaurants has a modern decor with emphasis on cool colors, brass and glass accents in addition to greenery, marble and tiled floors. Special functions can be arranged through the restaurant for up to 55 persons in the "President Conference Room" located on the premises. Catering is also a service provided by this restaurant to private, corporate and airline travelers. For information call 946-4960.

Restaurants Near Airport:
Harvest Land (Host) On Site Phone: 946-4960

Lodging: (Free Airport Transportation) Country Inn 942-1717; Canterbury Inn 942-7911; Holiday Inn-Airport 943-2181; Imperial Suites 945-2600; Hilton Airport & Executive Conference Center 945-5272;

Meeting Rooms: All lodging facilities listed above contain meeting rooms; Hilton Airport & Executive Conference Center 945-5272 has accommodations for conferences.

Transportation: Taxi Service: American 262-7511; Best 838-1001; Rental Cars: Avis 946-4880; Budget 946-4891; Dollar 943-5095; Hertz 943-3221; National 946-4851.

Information: Wichita Convention & Visitors Buearu, 100 South Main, Suite 100, Wichita, KS 67202, Phone: 265-2800.

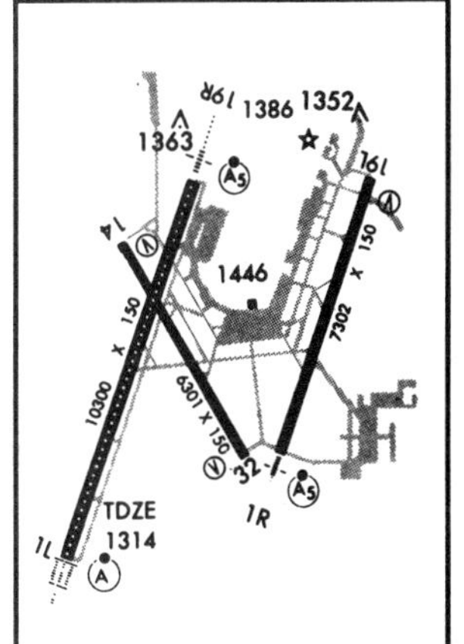

Airport Information:

WICHITA - WICHITA MID-CONTINENT AIRPORT (ICT)
5 mi southwest N37-39.00 W97-25.98 Elev: 1332 Fuel: 100LL, Jet-A
Rwy 01L-19R: H10300x150 (Conc-Grvd) Rwy 01R-19L: H7302x150 (Con-Grvd)
Rwy 14-32: H6301x150 (Conc) Attended: continuously Atis 125.15 Unicom: 122.95
App Con: 134.85, 134.8, 126.7, 125.5 Dep Con: 134.85, 134.8, 126.7 Tower: 118.2
Gnd Con: 121.9 Clnc: 125.7
FBO: Executive Aircraft Corp. Phone: 946-4990
Raytheon Aircraft Service Phone: 946-4300

KENTUCKY

CROSS FILE INDEX

Location Number	City or Town	Airport Name And Identifier	Name of Attraction
1	Berea	Berea-Richmond (I30)	Berea College
2	Bowling Green	Warren Co. Reg. Arpt. (BWG)	Rafferty's Restaurant
3	Cadiz	Lake Barkley State Park (1M9)	Lake Barkley Resort Pk.
4	Campellsville	Taylor Co. Arpt. (AAS)	Airport Grill
5	Danville	Stuart Powell Fld. (DVK)	Bright Leaf Golf Resort
6	Falls-Of-Rough	Rough River State Park Arpt. (2I3)	Rough River State Park
7	Gilbertsville	KY. Dam State Park (M34)	Kentucky Dam Park Rest
8	Lexington	Blue Grass Arpt. (LEX)	Creative Croissants
9	Louisville	Bowman Field (LOU)	Bearno's Little Sicily
10	Louisville	Bowman Field (LOU)	Le Relais Restaurant
11	Louisville	Bowman Field (LOU)	Mazzoni's Cafe
12	Louisville	Standiford Field Arpt. (SDF)	Quilted Cafe (Host Intl.)
13	Mayfield	Graves Co. Arpt. (M25)	Dairy Hill Restaurant
14	Owensboro	Daviess Co. Arpt. (OWB)	Moonlite Bar-B-Q's
15	Paducah	Barkley Reg. Arpt. (PAH)	Flight Deck Restaurant
16	Paducah	Barkley Reg. Arpt. (PAH)	J.R.'s Executive Inn

Articles

City or town	Nearest Airport and Identifier	Name of Attraction
Cadiz, KY	Lake Barkley State Park (1M9)	Lake Barkley Resort Pk
Falls of Rough, KY	Rough River State Park (2I3)	Rough River State Pk.

LOCATION MAP

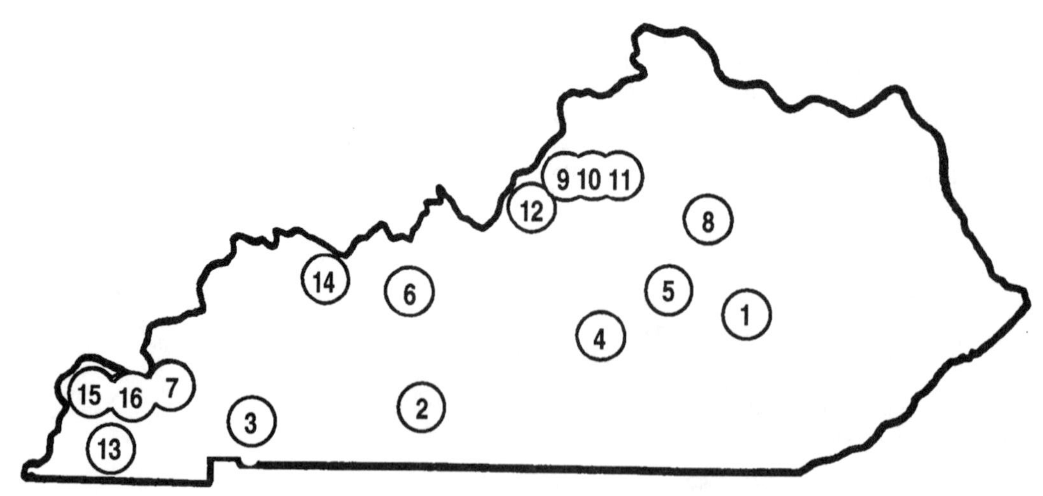

Not to be used for navigational purposes

KY-I30 - BEREA
BEREA-RICHMOND (Private)

(Area Code 606) **1**

Restaurants Near Airport:
Boone Tavern (College) 4 mi. S. Phone: 986-9358
Numerous Restaurants 4-5 mi. S. Old Town Area

Boone Tavern (Berea College):

According to one of our readers, Berea College area has abundant natural beauty, impressive campus buildings and interesting activities. 40 miles south of Lexington, KY. It's a place of natural beauty where the rolling land of central Kentucky meets the foothills of the Cumberland Mountains range. It's also a place where college students learn the value of work and service to others. Each of Berea's 1,500 students is required to work 10-20 hours a week in a college job to help earn money for living expenses (there is no tuition charge at Berea). And two of the areas where students are employed are must-visits - Boon Tavern Hotel and the Student Crafts Program. Boone Tavern, named in honor of Daniel Boone, is well known for its outstanding Southern cuisine. Dining at this white-columned, three-story hotel is an enjoyable experience where such specialties as Chicken Flakes in a Bird's Nest, Spoonbread and Jefferson Davis Pie are genuine delights. Three meals are served daily at the Tavern, which is 80 percent student-staffed, and features 57 air-conditioned rooms. Owned by the college, the Tavern is located in the midst of the Berea College campus and has been an integral part of this Madison County community since 1909. Reservations are suggested by calling 986-9358 or 986-9359. While visiting at the Tavern, you'll want to stop by the Log House Sales Room just around the corner where items from all six College Crafts areas are sold. Berea College is located about 4 miles south of the Berea-Richmond Airport. According to sources, there is courtesy transportation provided by the airport; however, during our research we could not confirm this. Your best bet would be to contact the Berea Chamber of Commerce at 986-9760 or Lackey Flying Service at 986-8566.

Lodging: Boon Tavern Hotel (4 mi. at College) 986-9358; Days Inn 986-7373; Doctor's Inn 986-3042; Howard Johnson Lodge 986-2384; Holiday Motel 986-9311; The Mansion House Bed & Breakfast 986-9851; The Morning Glory Bed & Breakfast 986-8661.

Meeting Rooms: Contact Berea Chamber of Commerce at 986-9760.

Transportation: Contact Berea Chamber of Commerce at 986-9760; or Lackey Flying Service (FBO) at 986-8566.

Information: Berea Chamber of Commerce, P.O. Box 318, Berea, KY 40403. Phone: 986-9760.

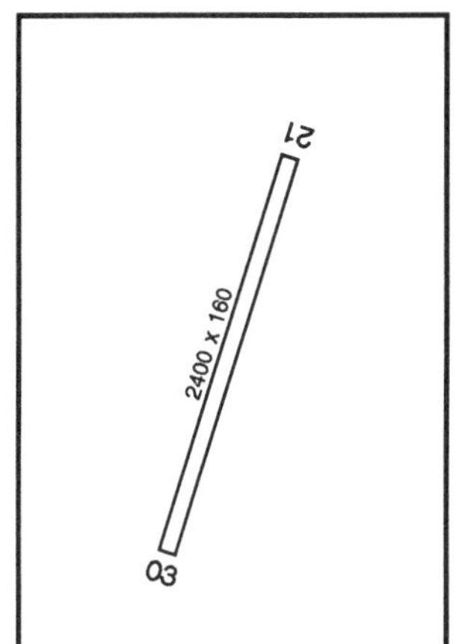

Airport Information:

BEREA - BEREA-RICHMOND (I30)
4 mi north of town N37-38.72 W84-16.98 Elev: 994 Fuel: Auto fuel reported Rwy 3-21: 2400x160 (Turf) **Notes: Private, use at own risk.** Overnight parking fee $2.00; Fence at both ends of runway.
FBO: Lackey Flying Service Phone: 986-8566

KY-BWG - BOWLING GREEN
WARREN COUNTY REGIONAL ARPT.

(Area Code 502) **2**

Restaurants Near Airport:
Rafferty's Restaurant 1/4 mi Phone: 842-0123

Rafferty's Restaurant:

Rafferty's Restaurant is located within 1/4th mile from the Bowling Green/Warren County Airport in Bowling Green, Kentucky. As you are walking towards the restaurant, you should be able to see a large Rafferty's sign nearby. This family styled restaurant has a modern contemporary atmosphere, and is decorated in dark wood, brass and green plants. Their menu displays a wide variety of entrees consisting of meat, fish and barbecued selections. Average prices run between $4.75 and $16.95 for most full course meals. The restaurant is open 11 a.m. to 10 p.m. Sunday through Thursday and 11 a.m. to 11 p.m. on Friday and Saturday. The restaurant can prepare meals-to-go if given advance notice. Transportation is no problem. They will be happy to pick you up from the airport and drive you back. For more information you can call the restaurant at 842-0123.

Lodging: Best Western Motor Inn 782-3800; Greenwood Executive Inn (Trans) 781-6610; Holiday Inn Midtown 842-9453.

Meeting Rooms: Best Western Motor Inn 782-3800; Greenwood Executive Inn 781-6610; Holiday Inn Midtown 842-9453.

Information: Bowling Green-Warren County of Commerce, 812 State Street, P.O. Box 51, Bowling Green, KY 42102, Phone: 781-3200.

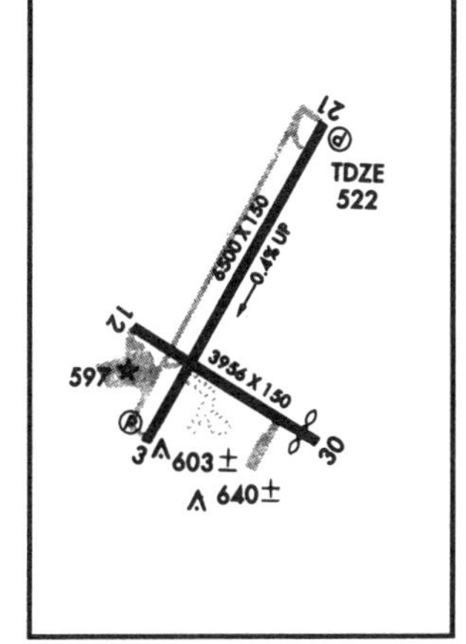

Airport Information:

BOWLING GREEN - WARREN COUNTY REGIONAL AIRPORT (BWG)
2 mi southeast of town N36-57.87 W86-25.18 Elev: 547 Fuel: 100LL, Jet-A
Rwy 03-21: H6500x150 (Asph) Rwy 12-30: H3956x150 (Asph) Attended: continuously
Unicom: 123.0
FBO: Corporate Flight Management Phone: 781-9797

KY-1M9 - CADIZ
LAKE BARKLEY STATE PARK

Lake Barkley State Resort Park:

Lake Barkley State Resort Park has its own private airstrip which provides fly-in guests easy access to the resort for year around enjoyment. The resort's main lodge built with huge timbers, offers a warm rustic atmosphere and contains a very nice restaurant with a beautiful view overlooking a portion of Lake Barkley. The restaurant itself, within the main lodge, can accommodate 330 people and serves breakfast from 7 a.m. to 10:30 a.m., lunch from 11:30 a.m. to 2:30 p.m. and dinner at 5:30 p.m. to 9 p.m. Amenities at the resort include an 18-hole golf course, swimming pool, gift shops, hiking, fishing on Lake Barkley, fitness center and much more. There are two meeting rooms within the lodge and a convention center on the premises for larger groups. Transportation by courtesy car can be obtained by calling the main lodge once reaching the airport. For information call 924-1131 or 1-800-325-1708.

(Area Code 502)

Restaurants Near Airport:
Lake Barkley Resort Park On Site Phone: 924-1131

Lodging: Lake Barkley State Resort Park (On Site), contains accommodations for 330 persons within the lodge, as well as nine executive cottages located in the wooded hills near the lake. For information call 924-1131 or 800-325-1708.

Meeting Rooms: Lake Barkley State Resort Park contains two meeting rooms within the lodge and a convention center on the premises for larger groups. 900 theater style and 500 banquet style. For information call 924-1131 or 800-325-1708.

Transportation: Lake Barkley State Resort Park provides a courtesy car or vans for fly-in guests, 924-1131 or 800-325-1708. If staying in the area to visit the "Land Between The Lakes", Cadiz Motor Company at 522-6601 can be contacted for rental cars.

Information: Cadiz-Trigg County Tourist Commission, P.O. Box 735, Cadiz, KY 42211, Phone: 522-3892.

Attractions:

Lake Barkley State Park Lodge contains its own private airstrip and is located on the eastern edge of Lake Barkley, nestled in the wooded acreage overlooking the shimmering waters of Lake Barkley. This resort offers a modern, yet rustic appearance and contains an 18 hole championship golf course, fitness center, racquetball courts, livery stable and nearby trails for horseback riding, fishing for largemouth, smallmouth, white and Kentucky bass, crappie and bluegill, resort marina with fishing and pontoon boats, trapshooting, swimming pool, business conference accommodations and much more. For information call 924-1131 or 1-800-325-1708. **Land Between the Lakes** (LBL) is 170,000 acres of heavily forested national recreation area situated between Kentucky Lake and Lake Barkley. For information write Land Between the Lakes, Golden Pond, KY 42231 or call 924-5602.

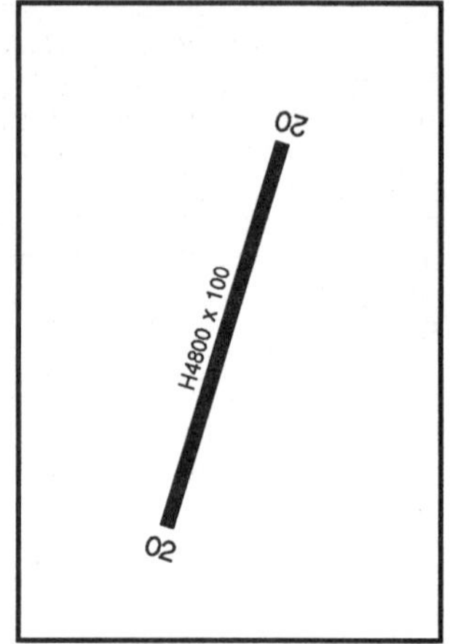

Airport Information:

CADIZ - LAKE BARKLEY STATE RESORT PARK (1M9)
4 mi southwest of town N36-49.14 W87-54.53 Elev: 570 Fuel: 100LL, Jet-A
Rwy 02-20: H4800x100 (Asph) Attended: continuously Unicom: 122.8
Lake Barkley State Resort Airport Phone: 924-1131 or 800-325-1708

Lake Barkley State Resort Park

Cadiz, KY (KY-1M9)

Lake Barkley State Resort Park rests on the shores of one of the world's largest man-made lakes and provides for an array of outdoor activity. Lake Barkley also offers the best, indoors. The fitness center is a "state-of-the-art" facility that can keep you in shape throughout the year.

There are no bad views from Barkley Lodge. Constructed of Western Cedar, Douglas Fir, and three-and one-half acres of glass, the layout of the lodge offer a lake view from private balconies of each of the 120 rooms and four suites. The Little River Lodge, a separate structure from the main lodge, offers 10 rooms and one suite and may be rented as a whole unit. The gift shop located in the lodge lobby offers a large selection of Kentucky handcrafts and souvenirs. Rooms are available by late afternoon, check-out by noon, Central time.

For more private accommodations, enjoy one of the nine two-bedroom, two-bath cottages with lake or wooded views. For rustic charm, Lake Barkley offers four screened-in porches or decks. Tableware, cooking utensils, and linens are provided, with fresh linens available daily. Cottages are available by late afternoon, check-out by 11:00 a.m.

The atmosphere in their dining room is of traditional elegance. The view is beyond compare as is the service and cuisine. This 331-seat dining room serves breakfast, lunch and dinner.

Entertainment at the Lake Barkley State Resort Park comes in many forms. Guests can test their golfing skills year-round on the 18 hole Boots Randolph Golf Course. A full-service pro shop, rental riding cars, pull carts, and golf clubs are available. The course is left open throughout the whole year, weather permitting. A swimming pool adjacent to the lodge is for the exclusive use of lodge and cottage guests. The public beach offers a volleyball court, bathhouse, and hours of swimming fun in the water of Lake Barkley. Grab your racket and enjoy a tennis match. Two lighted courts near the lodge are for use by overnight guests. Additional courts situated closer to the beach area, are available to the general public. A supervised trap shooting range on the resort property is lighted and provides 12-gage shot gun rentals for guests to try out there skills and marksmanship. Or, enjoy the beauty surrounding Lake Barkley on one of the park trails. Three self-guided trails provide for 9 miles of easy to medium hiking. Daily summer activities and year-round special events are available for children and adults under the guidance of a trained recreation director. A picnic shelter near the beach with a gorgeous lake view as well as picnic tables, grills, and playgrounds, located in cottage and camping areas provide for a great outing.

If Planning a fly-in for your group or association, Lake Barkley State Resort Park provides two private meeting rooms in the lodge that can accommodate groups up to 150 people. The Lake Barkley Convention Center is the perfect facility for your large meetings, and can handle banquets with up to 500 persons.

A resort operated airport, has a 4,800 foot paved, lighted air strip, and is located about 3 miles from the main lodge.

Photo by: Lake Barkley State Resort Park.

100LL and jet fuel is available. Transportation to all locations on the resort property are furnished by the resort staff. For more information about Lake Barkley State Resort Park call 502-924-1131. Toll free reservations can also be made by calling 800-325-1708. (Information submitted by Lake Barkley State Resort Park).

KY-AAS - CAMPELLSVILLE TAYLOR COUNTY AIRPORT

(Area Code 502)

4

Airport Grill:

The Airport Grill is a cafe located on Taylor County Airport near Campbellsville, Kentucky. This restaurant serves a nice selection of home cooked meals including breakfast selections, sandwiches, hamburgers plate lunches, and home made pies and desserts. Their menu offers daily specials and on Thursday and Friday, they feature country ham dishes. The restaurant is open from 7 a.m. to 2 p.m. Monday through Friday, 7 a.m. to 4 p.m. on Saturday and 8 a.m. to 4 p.m. on Sunday. If your flying organization is planning a fly-in breakfast meeting or luncheon, the Airport Grill would be happy to make accommodations for your group if given advance notice. Catering for pilots can also be arranged with meals-to-go. For more information call the restaurant at 789-9958.

Restaurants Near Airport:

Airport Grill On Site Phone: 789-9958

Lodging: Best Western 465-7001; Lakeview Motel 465-8139.

Meeting Rooms: Best Western 465-7001.

Transportation: Taxi Service: Taylor Cab 465-4801; Rental Cars: Alex Montgomery Chevy 465-8113; Green River Ford 465-4106.

Information: Taylor County Tourist Commision, Court Street & Broadway, P.O. Box 4021, Campbellsville, KY 42718, 465-3786.

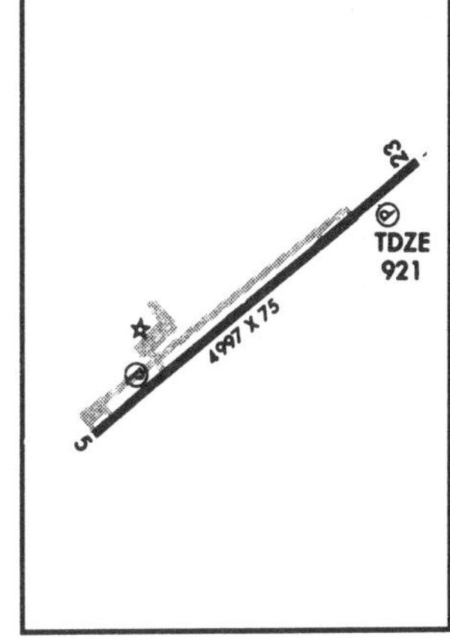

Airport Information:

CAMPELLSVILLE - TAYLOR COUNTY AIRPORT (AAS)

2 mi northeast of town N37-21.50 W85-18.57 Elev: 921 Fule: 100LL, Jet-A

Rwy 05-23: H4997x75 (Asph) Attended: 1400-2200Z Unicom: 122.7

Taylor County Airport Phone: 789-2633

Photo by: Bright Leaf Golf Resort

KY-DVK - DANVILLE STUART POWELL FIELD

(Area Code 606)

5

Bright Leaf Golf Resort:

Bright Leaf Golf Resort is located in Harrodsburg, Kentucky which is just 11 miles north of Stuart Powell Field in Danville. The FBO will provide shuttle service to and from the resort. Bright Leaf, located in the heart of rolling bluegrass country, is a haven for both golfers and history buffs. Harrodsburg is the site of Kentucky's first permanent settlement, Fort Harrod. For added historical interest, the "Legend of Daniel Boone Outdoor Drama" occurs daily. The resort also offers 36 holes of golf for all levels of skill: a 9 hole, par 3, executive course, a 9 hole regulation, and a challenging 18 hole course. Guests can enjoy nighttime golf, as well. After a hard day of golfing, guests can relax in the dry heat sauna or the cool, clear pool. Or, they can pump up with a full line of exercise equipment at the resort's health club. For dining, the 19th Hole Restaurant, which overlooks the golf course and pool, offers fine Southern cuisine and hospitality. Complete banquet and meeting facilities are also provided. The resort offers exciting golf packages in its comfortable motel and golf villas. For more information about rates and accommodations at Bright Leaf Golf Resort, call 734-5481.

Restaurants Near Airport:
Bright Leaf Golf Resort 11 mi N. Phone: 734-5481

Lodging: Bright Leaf Golf Resort (11 mi) 734-5481; Beaumont Inn (12 mi) 734-3381; Best Western (10 mi) 734-9431; Holiday Inn (3 mi) 236-8600; Super 8 Motel (3 mi) 236-8881

Meeting Rooms: Bright Leaf Golf Resort 734-5481

Transportation: FBO will provide shuttle service to and from the resort. Also, taxi service is available at 236-5552, as well as rental car service with Stuart Powell Ford, Inc. at 236-8917.

Information: Harrodsburg/Mercer County Tourist Commission, P.O. Box 283, Harrodsburg, KY 40330, Phone: 734-2364

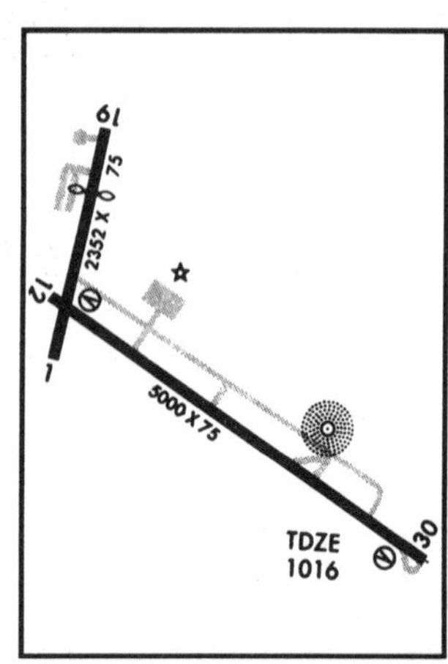

Airport Information:

DANVILLE - STUART POWELL FIELD (DVK)
3 mi south of town N37-34.67 W84-46.17 Elev: 1022 Fuel: 100LL, Jet-A Rwy 12-30: H5000x75 (Asph) Rwy 01-19: H2352x75 (Asph) Attended: Apr-Oct/Mon-Fri 1300-2400Z, Apr-Oct/Sat-Sun 1400-2400Z, Nov-Mar/Mon-Fri 1300-2200Z, Nov-Mar/Sat-Sun 1400-2200Z CTAF/Unicom: 122.8 Lexington App/Dep Con: 120.15
FBO: Aero-Tech, Inc. Phone: 854-6170

KY-2I3 - FALLS-OF-ROUGH ROUGH RIVER STATE PARK ARPT.

6

Restaurants Near Airport:
Rough River Lodge On Site Phone: 257-2311

Lodging: Rough River State Park Lodge (1,600 feet from airport) Phone: 257-2311.
Meeting Rooms: Accommodations for meetings or conferences can be arranged for groups up to 400 persons. For information call 257-2311.
Transportation: A courtesy van can be obtained by calling the Rough River State Park Lodge at 257-2311.
Information: Rough River Dam State Resort Park, Falls of Rough, KY 40119, Phone: 257-2311.

Rough River State Park:
Rough River State Park has its own private airstrip that is located a short walk from the main lodge. A dining room at the lodge on the lower level is available for breakfast, lunch and dinner seven days a week. Breakfast is served from 7 a.m to 10:30 a.m., lunch from 11 a.m. to 2:30 p.m. and dinner from 5 p.m. to 8:30 p.m. Monday through Saturday. The luncheon menu consists of entrees including various sandwiches, salads, soups and fruit plates. Their dinner menu specializes in fish, chicken, and beef selections at very reasonable prices. In addition to the dining facility, Rough River State Park Lodge contains 40 rooms plus 15 cottages. The lodge also has a conference center able to serve 400 guests. Their 9 hole par 3 golf course, swimming pool and sandy beach makes this a popular weekend get-a-way for many travelers. The new terml. bldg. has showers and restrooms for fly-in campers. The main parking ramp is within walking dist. approx. 1,600 feet from the main lodge. A telephone is available at the airport to call the lodge should you desire courtesy transportation. For information call the resort at 257-2311.

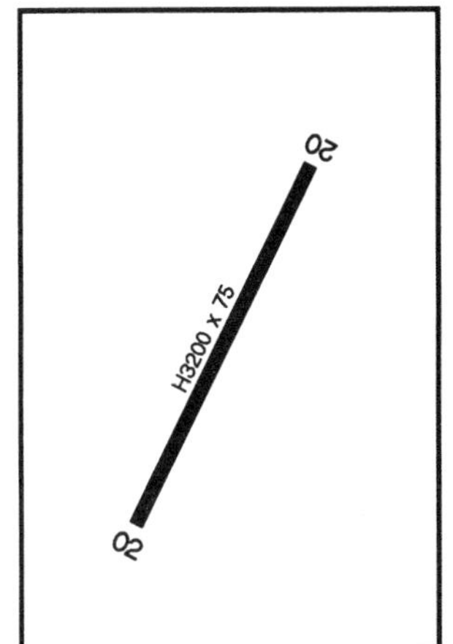

Attractions: Complete with its own airstrip, the Rough River State Resort Park is situated along the western edge of Rough River Lake, approximately 60 miles southwest of Louisville, KY. This complex provides 40 spacious lodge rooms, 15 two-bedroom cottages, its own resort marina, lighted tennis courts and a year round nine hole par-three golf course, which makes it an attractive destination for family, friends or corporate gatherings. Showers/restrooms available for fly-in campers at new terminal building. To learn more about this state park facility call 257-2311.

Airport Information:
FALLS OF ROUGH - ROUGH RIVER STATE PARK (2I3)
3 mi northeast of town N37-36.59 W86-30.42 Elev: 577 Fuel: 100LL Rwy 02-20: H3200x75 (Asph) Attended: continuously Unicom: 122.8 Notes: Their new terminal bldg. has flight planning /observaton area along with showers/restrooms for fly-in campers.
Rough River State Park Phone: 257-2311

Rough River Dam State Resort Park

Falls of Rough, KY (KY-213)

Rough River Dam State Resort Park is secluded in hilly, ruggedly beautiful western Kentucky countryside overlooking a 4,860-acre blue green lake. Rough River Dam offers some of the finest opportunities for fishing and water sports in the state. This beautiful resort contains an 500-seat outdoor amphitheater. With an array of special events and outdoor leisure activities, Rough River Dam Resort is a delightful playground for the entire family. Fly-in campers will be glad to learn that showers and restroom facilities are now available at the new airport terminal building.

Photo by: Rough River Dam State Resort Park — Aerial view of resort

Beautiful lake views enhance the appeal of Rough River Dam Lodge. Each of the 40 rooms feature private patios and balconies for enjoying the gorgeous scenery. While visiting the lodge, browse the lobby gift shop featuring a large selection of Kentucky handcrafted gifts and souvenirs.

For secluded luxury, a two-bedroom cottage is just for you. Fifteen cottages are in wooded areas near the lake. Tableware, cooking utensils, and linens are provided, with fresh linens available daily.

Enjoy the unspoiled beauty surrounding the 66-site campground, next to Rough River.

The dining room, which can accommodate 209 persons, allows you to experience a Kentucky tradition. Courteous service and gracious dining are yours for breakfast, lunch, and dinner.

For contemporary meeting facilities enjoy the Rough River Room in the lodge. This room can be utilized as a conference or banquet-style facility that seats 350 people. Smaller groups may enjoy the Grayson Room or the Breckinridge Room that each seats 125 persons.

Rough River Lake is the perfect location for the water sports enthusiast. Their marina offers 165 open slips, 30 open houseboat slips, 48 covered slips, a launching ramp, and rental fishing boats, pontoon boats, and rowboats. Pedal boats may be rented at the beach area. The avid angler will delight in the abundance of largemouth and smallmouth bass, bluegill, channel catfish, crappie, rough fish, and walleye. The "Lady of the Lake" will take you on a tour of sparkling Rough River Lake. In the summer she makes daily excursions, so hop on for the feel of cruising in an old-fashioned steam boat.

Their nine-hole, par-three course by the lake provides the golfer a challenging game as well as beautiful scenery. A driving range is available to practice the long drive. A fully equipped pro shop offers riding carts, pull carts, and rental clubs. They also have a miniature 18-hole golf course that will provide your family with plenty of entertainment.

Additional activities include tennis, volleyball, and shuffleboard. Several social gatherings are held throughout the year including the "Old Time Fiddlers Contest, their Mint Julep Scale Meet, and the E.A.A. Sports Aviation Weekend. For information about these sensational activities or Rough River Dam State Resort Park accommodations, call 502-257-2311. Toll free reservations can be made by calling 800-325-1713.

Photo by: Rough River Resort — The main lodge at the Rough River Dam State Resort Park

KY-M34 - GILBERTSVILLE KENTUCKY DAM VILLAGE STATE RESORT PARK AIRPORT

7

Kentucky Dam Park Restaurant:

The Kentucky Dam Village State Resort Park Restaurant is located within one mile from their airstrip. This family style restaurant is open 7 day a week between 7 a.m. and 9 p.m. Breakfast is served between 7 a.m. and 10:30 a.m., lunch from 11:30 a.m. until 2:30 p.m. (Sundays at noon), and dinner from 5 p.m. until 9 p.m. (8:00 p.m. from November through February). Their menu specializes in buffet style selections. Breakfast and luncheon buffets usually run about $5.25 and $9.50 for dinner. Their dining room overlooks the lake and can accommodate large groups up to 600 people with banquet facilities. The resort contains many activities for the visitor and makes for a great week or weekend getaway. Their Village Inn contains 72 lake rooms, each with two double beds, and upper level rooms have a balcony; lower rooms have a patio. One, two, and three bedroom cottages are also available including executive cottages able to sleep more individuals. Relax and enjoy a nice game of golf, boating, horse back riding, tennis, mini golf or browse through the gift shop. There are now showers/washroom facilities for fly-in campers. For information call the Park Resort at 362-4271 or for information on reservations call 800-325-0146.

Attractions: The Kentucky Dam Village State Resort Park offers guests a wide variety of accommodations and activities. Some of these include their main dining room, gift shop, 18-hole golf course, campground, tennis courts, game room, miniature golf, paddle boats, airport, marina, and riding stables. Transportation can be obtained once you land at their airport. The lodge and other park related facilities are within 3/4 of a mile from the airport. Camping at the airport include showers and restroom facilities at their new terminal building. For information call the resort at 362-4271 or for reservations only call 800-325-0146.

Airport Information:

GILBERTSVILLE - KENTUCKY DAM VILLAGE STATE RESORT PARK AIRPORT (M34)
1 northwest of town N37-00.57 W88-17.75 Elev: 349 Fuel: 100LL, Jet-A
Rwy 09-27: H4000x100 (Asph) Attended: daylight hours Unicom: 122.8
Notes: Airport is now AWOS equiped. New terml. bldg include showers for campers.
Kentucky Dam Village State Resort Park Airport Phone: 362-4271, ext 377.

(Area Code 502)

Restaurants Near Airport:
KY. Dam State Park On Site Phone: 362-4271

Lodging: Bel-Air Motel 362-4254; Holiday Inn-Kentucky Dam (Trans) 362-4278; Kentucky Dam Village State Resort Park (Trans) 362-4271, for reservations only, call 800-325-0146
Meeting Rooms: Holiday Inn-Kentucky Dam 362-4278; Kentucky Dam Village State Park 362-4271.
Transportation: Courtesy van is available from the airport to the Kentucky Dam Village State Resort Park by calling 362-4271 or the airport at 362-4271, ext 377.
Information: Kentucky Dam Village State Resort Park, P.O. Box 69, Gilbertsville, KY 42044-0069, Phone: 362-4271 ext377.

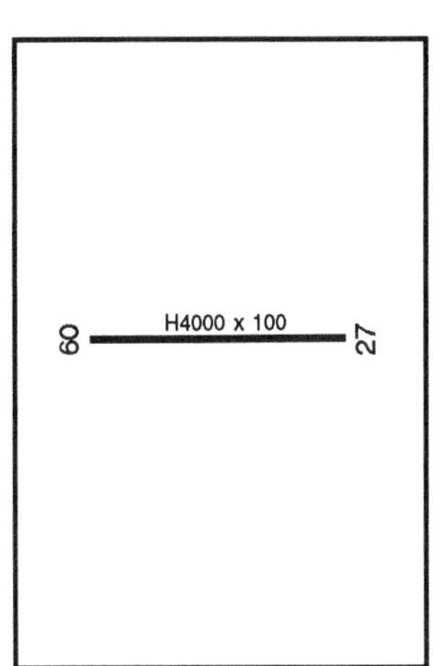

KY-LEX - LEXINGTON BLUE GRASS AIRPORT

8

Creative Croissants:

Creative Croissants is located in the terminal building on the Blue Grass Airport in Lexington Kentucky. This food service facility prepares a variety of delicious sandwiches on freshly baked croissants as well as other light fare selections. At the time of research this establishment was soon to be opened. After landing, you can park your aircraft at the fixed base operator of your choice, and they in turn will take you over to the terminal building. For more information call Creative Croissants at 231-6905.

(Area Code 606)

Restaurants Near Airport:
Creative Croissants On Site Phone: 231-6905
Logans Restaurant 5-7 mi E Phone: N/A
Shooters Restaurant 5-7 mi E Phone: 278-0815

Lodging: Campbell House Inn (Trans) 255-4281; Hilton Inn Lexington (Trans) 259-1311; Hilton Suites-Lex Green (Trans) 271-4000; Hyatt (Trans) 253-1234; Kentucky Inn 254-1177; Marriott Resort (Trans) 231-5100; Radisson Plaza Hotel (Trans) 231-9000; Springs Inn (Trans) 277-5751.

Meeting Rooms: All lodging facilities listed above contain meeting and conference rooms.

Transportation: Taxi service available at airport; Rental Cars: Avis 252-5581; Budget 255-7766; Hertz 254-3496; National 254-8806.

Information: Greater Lexington Convention & Visitors Bureau, 301 East Vine Street, Suite 363, Lexington, KY 40507, Phone: 233-1221 or 800-845-3959.

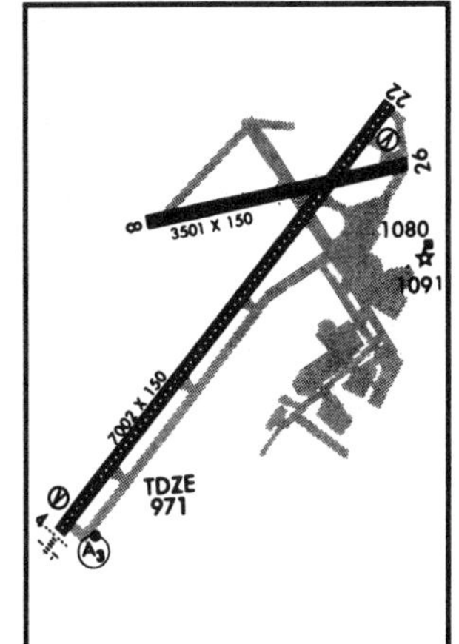

Airport Information:

LEXINGTON - BLUE GRASS AIRPORT (LEX)
4 mi west of town N38-02.22 W84-36.32 Elev: 980 Fuel: 100LL, Jet-A
Rwy 04-22: H7002x150 (Asph-Grvd) Rwy 08-26: H3501x150 (Asph-Conc)
Attended: continuously Atis: 126.3 Unicom: 122.95 Lexington App/Dep Con: 120.75, 120.15, 125.0 Lexington Tower: 119.1 Gnd Con: 121.9 Clnc Del: 132.35
FBO: Southern Jet Phone: 255-7724
FBO: Sprite-Flight Jets Phone: 253-9050

KY-LOU - LOUISVILLE BOWMAN FIELD

(Area Code 502) 9, 10, 11

Bearno's Little Sicily:

Bearno's Little Sicily is a family style restaurant located within walking distance to the Bowman Field in Louisville, Kentucky. Their entrees consist of complete dinner, sandwiches, pizza, soups, and salads for lunch or dinners. Average prices run $4.95 and up. The restaurant is open Monday through Thursday 11:30 a.m. to 10 p.m., Friday and Saturday from 11:30 a.m. to 12 a.m., and Sunday from 4 p.m. to 10 p.m. The restaurant has a modern decor and all menu items are available for carry-out. This restaurant is situated directly across the street from the old terminal building at Bowman Field. For information call 458-8605.

Le Relais Restaurant:

Le Relais Restaurant can be classified as a gourmet restaurant serving traditional French cuisine. This restaurant is located within walking distance from aircraft parking (about 50 feet) and the old terminal building at Bowman Field, Louisville, Kentucky. The restaurant contains a lounge and is open Tuesday through Friday from 11:30 a.m. to 2:30 p.m. and 5:30 p.m. to 10 p.m., Saturday 5:30 p.m. to 11 p.m., Sunday 5:30 p.m. to 9 p.m. The decor of the restaurant is very elegant, with proper dress attire required. Some selections on their menu are grilled steak, filet mignon, seafood, French pastries and a host of delicious soups, salads, and desserts. Prices for dinner range from $14.00 to $18.00. Reservations are requested especially on Friday and Saturday nights. For information call the restaurant at 451-9020.

Mazzoni's Cafe:

Mazzoni's Louisville Famous nostalgic stop for over a century is hosting a full menu including: Southpaw wings, crab Ragoons, fried ravioli, cod fish, fresh veggies, oysters, pasta, seafood, tamales, chili, blacken chicken, Po-Boys, soup and chowder to name a few. Since 1884, Mazzoni's has been serving homemade food and frosty libation in a unique cafe atmosphere. When flying in for a meal, they might suggest you park your aircraft near Central American Airways (Call 502-451-4436 for questions on aircraft parking or available courtesy cars). They invite you to join them and be a part of history. To reach the restaurant you can simply walk across Trylorsville Road. Restaurant hours are from 11 a.m. until 9 p.m. Monday through Thursday , and on Friday and Saturday from 11 a.m. to 10 p.m. and closed on Sundays. Their prices are moderate and catering is available as well as meals-to-go. For more information call Mazzoni's Cafe at 451-4436.

Restaurants Near Airport:

Bearno's Little Sicily	Adj Arpt	Phone: 458-8605
Le Relais Restaurant	On Site	Phone: 451-9020
Mazzoni's Cafe	Adj Arpt	Phone: 451-4436

Lodging: Breckinridge Inn 456-5050; Executive Inn (Trans) 367-6161; Executive West (Trans) 367-2251; Holiday Inn-Hurstbourne (Trans) 426-2600; Holiday Inn-Southwest (Trans) 454-0451; Ramada Inn-East (Trans) 491-4830; Residence Inn By Marriott 425-1821.

Meeting Rooms: Breckinridge Inn 456-5050; Executive Inn 367-6161; Executive West 367-2251; Holiday Inn-Hurstbourne 426-2600; Holiday Inn-Southwest 454-0451; Ramada Inn-East 491-4830; Residence Inn By Marriott 425-1821.

Transportation: Courtesy Cars and Rental cars reported available through fixed base operators; Also: Taxi Service: Car-A-Van 636-0414; Community Taxi 772-2503; Ready 957-5977; Yellow Cab 636-5511.

Information: Louisville Convention & Visitors Bureau, 400 South First Street, Louisville , KY 40202, Phone: 582-3732.

Airport Information:

LOUISVILLE - BOWMAN FIELD (LOU)

5 mi southeast of town N38-13.69 W85-39.80 Elev: 547 Fuel: 100LL, Jet-A
Rwy 06-24: H4312x80 (Asph) Rwy 01-19: H3678x100 (Conc) Rwy 14-32: H3539x80 (Asph) Attended: Mon-Fri 1000-0300Z, Sat-Sun 1200-0100Z Atis: 112.2
Unicom: 122.95 Tower: 119.5 Gnd Con: 121.8 Clnc Del: 118.9

FBO: Cardinal Wings, Inc.	**Phone: 459-6184**
FBO: Central American Airways	**Phone: 458-3211**
FBO: Falcon Aviation	**Phone: 459-5045**
FBO: Trangle Flying Service	**Phone: 452-1185**

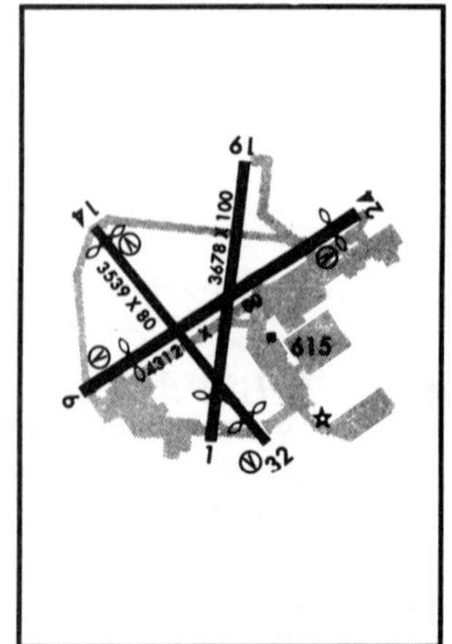

KY-SDF - LOUISVILLE STANDIFORD FIELD AIRPORT

(Area Code 502) 12

Restaurants Near Airport:

Executive Inn	1/4 mi	Phone: 367-6161
Executive Inn West	1/4 mi	Phone: 367-2251
Quilted Cafe (Host Intl)	On Site	Phone: 363-2526

Quilted Cafe (Host Intl):

The Quilted Cafe is located on Standiford Field in Louisville, Kentucky. This restaurant is considered a dinner club with lounge open from 11 a.m. to 8 p.m. 6 days a week. The decor of the restaurant is modern with traditional Kentucky accents, linen covered tables with flowers. Their menu contains various appetizers, choice quality derby steaks, pastry trays, cobb salads and much more. Average prices run between $5.50 and $7.00 for most selections. Many of their entrees are made with authentic Kentucky recipes. They offer daily specials and discounts for larger groups that are booked in advance. The view from the restaurant overlooks the terminal building and airstrip. There are a number of additional food service facilities as well as a lounge, all located within the terminal building and situated near the Quilted Cafe Restaurant. For information you can call the Quilted Cafe Restaurant at 363-2526.

Lodging: Executive Inn Motor Hotel (Trans) 367-6161; Executive West Motor Hotel (Trans) 367-2251; Hilton-East (Trans) 499-6220; Holiday Inn-East (Trans) 452-6361; Holiday Inn-South (Trans) 964-3311; Royce Hotel (Trans) 456-4411.

Meeting Rooms: Executive Inn Motor Hotel 367-6161; Executive West Motor Hotel 367-2251; Hilton-East 499-6220; Holiday Inn-East 452-6361; Holiday Inn-South 964-3311; Royce Hotel 456-4411.

Transportation: Courtesy cars reported available at airport; Taxi Service: Ready 957-5977; Star Community 772-2503; Union 491-3966; Yellow 636-4300; Also Rental Cars: Alamo 361-8522; Avis 361-5688; Budget 363-4300; Dollar 366-6944; Hertz 361-1145; National 361-2515; Thrifty 367-0231.

Information: Louisville Convention & Visitors Bureau has a visitors center, located at Standiford Field. Also contact the Louisville Convention & Visitors Bureau, 400 South First Street, Louisville, KY 40202, Phone: 584-2121.

Airport Information:

LOUISVILLE - STANDIFORD FIELD (SDF)
4 mi south of town N38-10.51 W85-44.01 Elev: 500 Fuel: 100LL, Jet-A Rwy 01-19: H10000x150 (Conc-Wc) Rwy 17-35: H8580x150 (Conc-Grvd) Rwy 11-29: H7249x150 (Conc-Wc) Attended: continuously Atis: 118.15 Unicom: 122.95 App Con: 124.5(S), 123.7(N) 126.55 Dep Con: 124.5(S) 123.7(N) Tower: 120.3 Gnd Con: 121.7 Clnc Del: 126.1
Airport Manager Phone: 368-6524

KY-M25 - MAYFIELD GRAVES COUNTY AIRPORT

(Area Code 502) 13

Restaurants Near Airport:

Dairy Hill Restaurant	1/4 mi	Phone: 247-6866

Lodging: Holiday Inn 247-3700

Meeting Rooms: Holiday Inn 247-3700

Transportation: Taxi: Radio Cab 247-7782

Information: Mayfield-Graves County Chamber of Commerce, 902 Broadway, P.O. Box 468, Mayfield, KY 42066. Phone: 247-6101.

Dairy Hill Restaurant:

The Dairy Hill Restaurant serves light fare and is classified as a roadside snack bar, similar in some ways to a Dairy Queen. It is located less than 1/4 mile across the street from the Graves County Airport, and is well within walking distance from aircraft parking. They are open for business during the late spring and summer months between 10:30 a.m. and 10 p.m. (Closed mid-Nov. thru mid-March). There is no seating within their building but guests are welcome to use the picnic tables outside. Their specialties include made-from-scratch burgers, corn dogs, thick shakes, fresh fruits, soft serve vanilla cones, hot dogs, pork tenderloin, hot ham, Bar-B-Q'd items, fish, chicken, French fries, onion rings, floats and shakes. Average prices run $1.00 to $4.00 for most items. None of their food is cooked until they get your order. This guarantees freshness. This is a popular stopping point with many pilots flying into the area. They have been in business since 1950. This facility will prepare orders for larger groups as well. However they would appreciate advanced notice of 30 minutes, if possible. Mayfield Aviation also provides pilots with services, including a pilot lounge with sleeping room, pilots supplies and maintenance. For more information about the Dairy Hill Restaurant call 247-9387 or Mayfield Aviation at 247-6866.

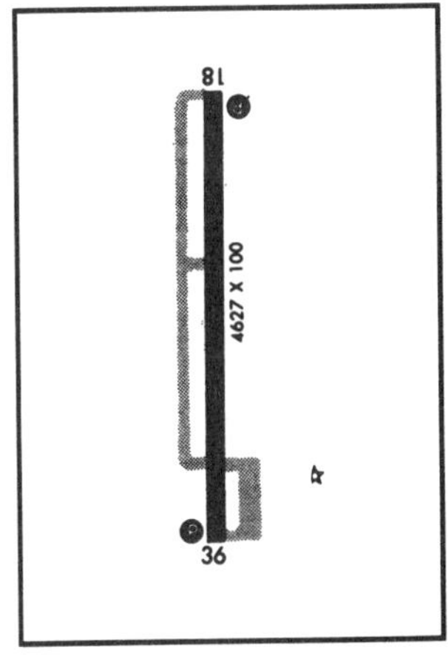

Airport Information:

MAYFIELD - GRAVES COUNTY AIRPORT (M25)
3 mi northeast of town N36-46.15 W88-35.08 Elev: 522 Fuel: 100LL, Jet-A Rwy 18-36: H4627x100 (Asph) Attended: daylight hours Unicom: 122.8
Mayfield Aviation: Phone: 247-6866

KY-OWB - OWENSBORO DAVIESS COUNTY

(Area Code 502)

14

Moonlite Bar-B-Q's

The Moonlite takes pride in being one of Kentucky's finest restaurants. This restaurant was bought by Catherine and Hugh Bosley in 1963, and originated from a road side stand founded in 1949. Today the restaurant seats some 350 people and has been operated by three generations of family members. This restaurant features a menu of Bar-B-Q dinners, catfish, country ham, sandwiches, deliciously seasoned vegetables, homemade salads and desserts. A luncheon buffet is served from 11:00 a.m. until 2:00 p.m. Monday through Sunday and a dinner buffet Monday through Saturday from 4:00 p.m. until 9:00 p.m. The buffet features delicious barbecued mutton, pork, ribs, chicken, ham and beef, numerous vegetables, a salad bar, their famous burgoo soup and a dessert bar of homemade pies and cobblers. Banquet rooms are readily available for luncheons, business meetings or any type of private function. The Moonlite's services also cater to many functions held off their premises as well. In fact, 20,000 pounds of meat are prepared each week for their customers. The restaurant is located 2 miles from the Owensboro Daviess County Airport. Free transportation is provided by the restaurant. For information call the restaurant at 684-8143.

Restaurants Near Airport:
Moonlite Bar-B-Q 2 mi Phone: 684-8143

Lodging: Days Inn 5 mi. 684-9621; Holiday Inn 3 mi. 685-3941; Executive Inn Rivermont (5 mi. Free arpt. trans.) 926-8000.

Meeting Rooms: Executive Inn Rivermont (Free arpt trans) has accommodations for conventions and meetings, 926-8000.

Transportation: Rental cars; Hertz 9261152; Taxi Service: Yellow Cab 683-6262. Courtesy cars can be arranged through the fixed base operators.

Information: Owensboro-Daviess County Tourist Commission, 326 St Elizabeth Street, Owensboro, KY 42301, Phone: 926-1100.

Attractions:

International Bar-B-Q Festival (early May) features Bar-B-Q cooking competition, music, dancing, arts and crafts and more. Call 926-1100 for information.

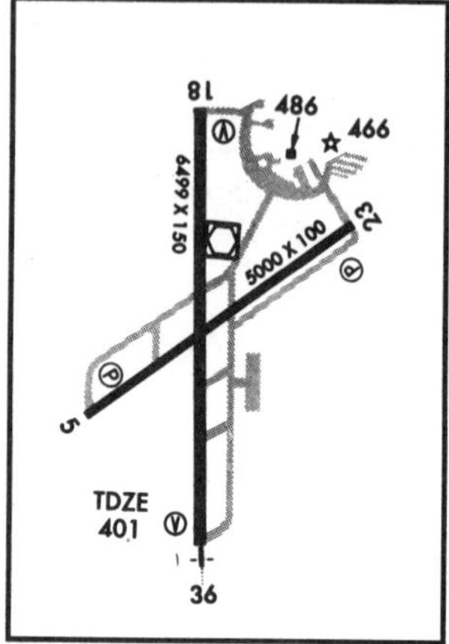

Airport Information:

OWENSBORO - BAVIESS COUNTY (OWB)
3 mi southwest of town N37-44.43 W87-09.98 Elev: 407 Fuel: 100LL, Jet-A Rwy 18-36: H6499x150 (Conc) Rwy 05-23: H5000x100 (Conc) Attended: continuously Unicom: 122.95 Tower: 120.7 Gnd Con: 121.7

FBO: Million Air Owensboro **Phone: 926-6700**
FBO: Singleton Aviation **Phone: 683-3475**

KY-PAH - PADUCAH
BARKLEY REGIONAL AIRPORT

(Area Code 502)

15, 16

Flight Deck Restaurant:

The Flight Deck Restaurant is a cafe that is located on the Barkley Regional Airport in Paducah, Kentucky. The restaurant serves sandwiches, homemade soup, desserts, pies, & cakes, and have certain specials for each day of the week. They are open on Monday through Friday from 6 a.m. to 6:30 p.m., Saturday from 10:00 a.m to 3:00 p.m. and Sunday from 10 a.m. to 3 p.m. The restaurant has a decor which displays a nautical motif. They would also be happy to accommodate club fly-ins or business meetings containing small groups. If requested, they can provide pilots with carry-outs meals or in-flight catering including cheese trays, sandwiches, hot meals, etc. For information call the restaurant at 744-0521.

J.R.'s Executive Inn:

The Patio Room, located inside J.R.'s Executive Inn, offers family style dining at affordable prices. Breakfast,lunch, and dinner buffets are featured daily, along with a wide assortment of delicious ala carte items. The Patio Room's four-story atrium ceiling, cascading fountain, and lush foliage combined with genuine Kentucky hospitality creates the feeling of attending a southern garden party. The Patio Room opens daily at 6:00 a.m. and closes at 9 p.m. on Sunday, 10 p.m. week nights, and 11 p.m. Friday and Saturday evenings. Other attractions in this 434 room facility include two lounges, an olympic size indoor pool, a shopping gallery, and their famous Showroom Lounge which features top-name entertainers such as Wayne Newton, Ricky Van Shelton, Lorrie Morgan, the Commodores, and other artists too numerous to mention. For guest room reservations or show ticket information, call 800-866-3636.

The Kincaid's Crossing and J.R.'s Pub, located inside J.R.'s Executive Inn: *offers Paducah's ultimate in food and spirits. The Celebrity room features classic cuisine in a luxurious atmosphere, ideal for entertaining clients or that special someone. The spectacular view of the majestic Ohio River and the sounds of piano music from J.R.'s Pub will compliment every delicious meal. Open for dinner at 5:30 p.m. Wednesday through Saturday evenings, reservations are accepted. Some Celebrity Room favorites include prime rib, steak Diane "Our Way", filet and lobster, and their "Catch or the Day". Airport transportation is complimentary for guests of this 434-room facility and can be arranged by calling 443-8000 upon arrival at the airport.*

Restaurants Near Airport:

Flight Deck Restaurant	On Site	Phone: 744-0521
J.R.'s Executive Inn	12 mi	Phone: 443-8000

Lodging: Drury Inn 443-3313; Executive Inn 443-8000; Holiday Inn 443-7521.

Meeting Rooms: Executive Inn (Convention Facilities) 443-8000; Holiday Inn 443-7521.

Transportation: Taxi Service: Security Cab 443-4442; Rental Cars: Avis 443-8411; Budget 442-3803; Hertz 443-1234; Also courtesy transportation to Executive Inn with prearranged notice, 443-8000 or 800-866-3636.

Information: Paducah-McCracken County Tourist & Convention Commission, 417 South Fourth, P.O. Box 90, Paducah, KY 42001, Phone: 443-8783 or 800-359-4775.

Attractions:

J.R's Executive Inn located about 12 miles from the Barkley Regional Airport and contains two restaurants, 434 guest rooms, and 55,000 square feet of convention space. In addition to this, they also have a Showroom Lounge able to accommodate 400 people, which features top-name entertainers. For guest room reservations or show ticket information, call 800-866-3636. Please notify them you plan to come, so they can arrange free courtesy transportation from the airport.

Airport Information:

PADUCAH - BARKLEY REGIONAL AIRPORT (PAH)

8 mi west of town N37-03.65 W88-46.42 Elev: 410 Fuel: 100LL, Jet-A
Rwy 04-22: H6499x150 (Asph) Rwy 14-32: H4001x150 (Asph) Attended: 1200-0500Z
Unicom: 123.0 Paducah Tower: 119.6 Gnd Con: 121.7
Barkley Regional Airport Phone: 774-0521
FBO: Midwest Aviation Phone: 744-8600

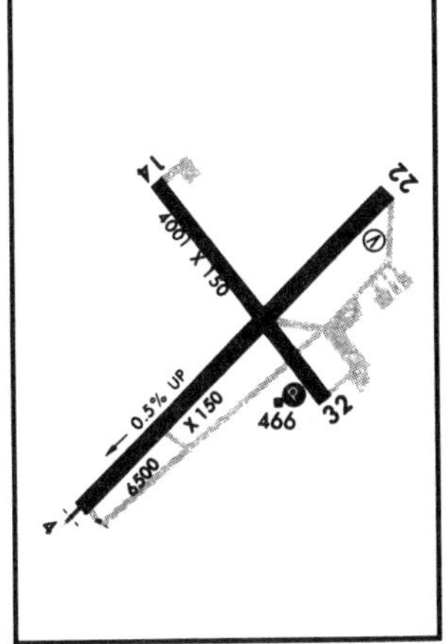

LOUISIANA

LOCATION MAP

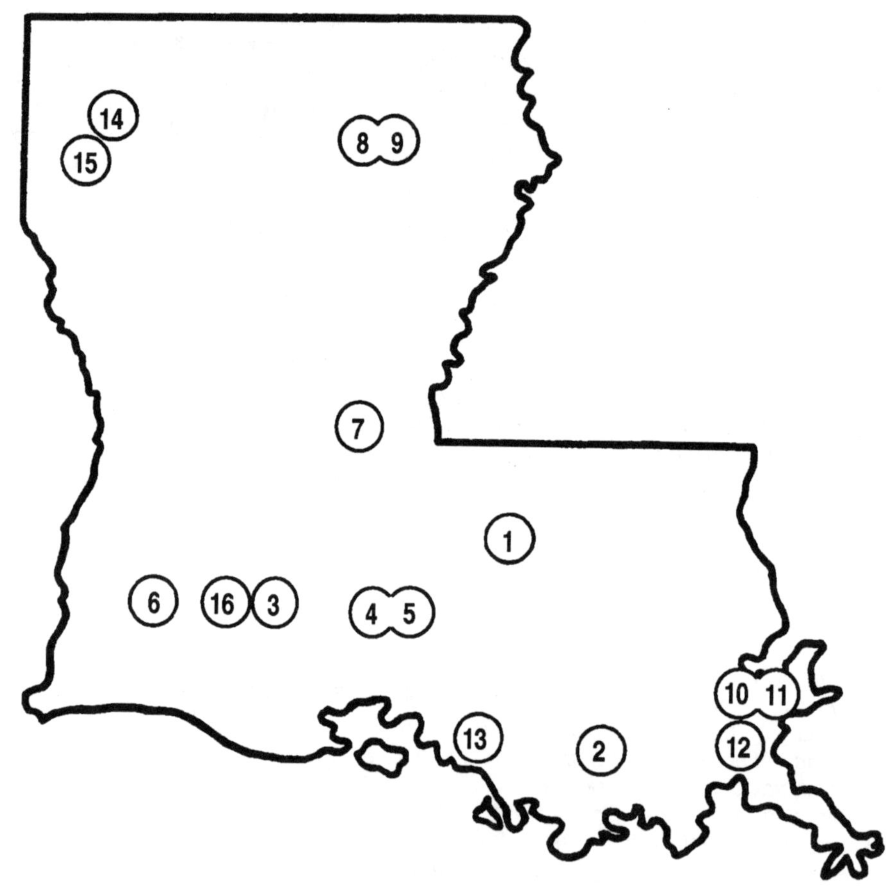

Not to be used for navigational purposes

LOUISIANA

CROSS FILE INDEX

Location Number	City or Town	Airport Name And Identifier	Name of Attraction
1	Baton Rough	Metropolitan, Ryan Field (BTR)	Air Host
2	Houma	Terrebonne Arpt. (HUM)	Highway 24 Seafood
3	Jennings	Jennings Airport (3R7)	Sugar Mill Restaurant
4	Lafayette	Lafayette Reg. Arpt. (LFT)	Blair House Restaurant
5	Lafayette	Lafayette Reg. Arpt. (LFT)	Cafe Vermilionville
6	Lake Charles	Chennault Industrial Airpark (CWF)	Pat's of Henderson
7	Marksville	Marksville Muni. Arpt. (LA26)	Grand Casino Avoyelles
8	Monroe	Monroe Reg. Arpt. (MLU)	Airport Restaurant
9	Monroe	Monroe Reg. Arpt. (MLU)	Red Lobster Restaurant
10	New Orleans	Lakefront Arpt. (NEW)	Commander Palace
11	New Orleans	Lakefront Arpt. (NEW)	Sclafani's Restaurant
12	New Orleans	New Orleans Intl. (MSY)	CA1 Services
13	Patterson	Harry P. Williams Mem. (PTN)	The Eagle's Nest Rest.
14	Shreveport	Shreveport Downtown Arpt. (DTN)	Peggy's Airport Cafe
15	Shreveport	Shreveport Reg. Arpt. (SHV)	Air Host
16	Welsh	Welsh Arpt. (6R1)	Cajun Tales Seafood

Articles

City or town	Nearest Airport and Identifier	Name of Attraction
Patterson, LA	Harry P. Williams Mem. (PTN)	Wedell-Williams Mem.

LA-BTR - BATON ROUGE METROPOLITAN, RYAN FIELD

(Area Code 504) 1

Air Host:

Air Host restaurant is located on the upper level of the terminal building at the Baton Rouge Metropolitan Airport. This combination cafe and cafeteria facility is within walking distance from available aircraft parking areas, according to restaurant personnel. Their hours are from 4:30 a.m. to 10 p.m. 7 days a week. The menu contains a varied selection of entrees including their special Cajun shrimp, seafood gumbo and red beans with rice. This is a self serve establishment with available seating for up to 60 persons. Much of their business is contracted through airline catering. If corporate pilots wish to arrange meals or snack trays for their passengers, they can call the fixed base operators and arrange to have catered meals delivered to the aircraft. For more information you can call Air Host at 355-8898.

Restaurants Near Airport:

Air Host	On Site	Phone: 355-8898

Lodging: Bellemont Hotel (Transportation) 357-8612; Best Western Inn (Transportation) 356-2531; Hilton Baton Rouge (Free trans) 924-5000; Inn On The Lake (Transportation) 346-1482; Ramada Inn (6 miles) 387-1111;

Meeting Rooms: The following contain convention facilities: Hilton Baton Rouge (Free trans, 8 miles) Phone: 924-5000; Ramada Inn (6 miles) 387-1111.

Transportation: Taxi's available at the terminal building, also rental cars are available: Avis 355-4621; Budget 355-0312; Hertz 357-5992; National 357-4467.

Information: Baton Rouge Area Convention & Visitors Bureau, 730 North Blvd., P.O. Box 4149, Baton Rouge, LA 70821, Phone: 383-1825.

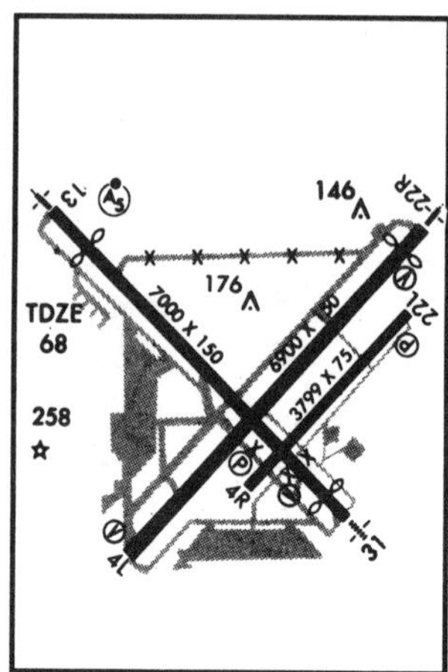

Airport Information:

BATON ROUGE - METROPOLITAN, RYAN FIELD (BTR)
4 mi north of town N30-31.99 W91-08.98 Elev: 70 Fuel: 100, 100LL, Jet-A
Rwy 13-31: H7000x150 (Asph-Grvd) Rwy 04L-22R: H6900x150 (Conc-Grvd)
Rwy 04R-22L: H3799x75 (Asph) Attended: 1100-0600Z Atis: 125.2 Unicom: 122.9
App/Dep Con: 120.3 (West) 126.5 (East) Tower: 118.45 Gnd Con: 121.9
Clnc Del: 119.4

FBO: Baton Rouge Jet Center	**Phone: 358-0111**
FBO: Capitol City Air Service	**Phone: 356-9592**
FBO: Louisiana Aircraft, Inc.	**Phone: 356-1401**
FBO: Pal Aero	**Phone: 355-9052**

LA-HUM - HOUMA TERREBONNE AIRPORT (HUM)

(Area Code 504) 2

Highway 24 Seafood & Restaurant:

The Highway 24 Seafood & Restaurant is located between 1/4 and 1/2 mile from the Terrebonne airport. To reach the restaurant you can either walk toward town or call for taxi service from the airport. This family style facility is open 10:30 a.m. to 9 p.m. Monday through Thursday, 10:30 a.m. to 9:30 p.m. on Friday and Saturday and closed on Sunday. Their menu offers seafood gumbo, seafood platters, catfish, poor boy sandwiches, and a variety of steaks. Daily plate lunches are also available. Their main dining room can seat up to 85 persons. Their banquet room can seat 75 people. Groups and fly-in parties are welcome. Meals can also be prepared-to-go. This restaurant may soon be expanding their facility if their plans proceed as hoped. For more information you can contact this restaurant by calling 851-0341.

Restaurants Near Airport:

East Way East	N/A	Phone: 872-2228
Highway 24 Seafood & Rest.	1/4th mi	Phone: 851-0341
Jeno's	N/A	Phone: 876-4896

Lodging: Holiday Inn (3 miles) 868-5851; Plantation (3 miles) 868-0500; Ramada Inn (3 miles) 879-4871.

Meeting Rooms: The town hall in Houma contains accommodations for meetings and conferences, Phone 873-7571.

Transportation: Taxi's: Courtesy Cab Service 868-2397; White Cab 872-3231; Rental Cars: Hertz 876-0584.

Information: Houma Terrebonne Tourist Commission, 1702 South St Charles Street, P.O. Box 2792, Houma, LA 70361, Phone: 868-2732 or 800-688-2732.

Airport Information:

HOUMA - TERREBONNE AIRPORT (HUM)
3 mi southeast of town N29-34.08 W90-39.64 Elev: 9 Fuel: 100LL, Jet-A
Rwy 18-36: H5001x200 (Conc) Rwy 12-30: 4999x200 (Conc) Rwy 01-19: 1420x75 (Turf)
Rwy 11-29: 1167x75 (Turf) Attended: dawn to dusk New Orleans App/Depp Con: 118.9
Tower 125.3 Gnd Con: 121.8 Atis 120.25 Unicom: 122.95 Clnc Del: 118.35

FBO: Gulf Aire Enterprises Phone: 879-3278
FBO: Hammonds Air Service Phone: 876-0584
FBO: Walker Watts Aviation Phone: 876-6324

Not to be used for navigational purposes

LA-3R7 - JENNINGS
JENNINGS AIRPORT

(Area Code 318) 3

Restaurants Near Airport:
Sugar Mill On Site Phone: 824-5280

Lodging: Holiday Inn (On site) Phone: 824-5280; Travelodge (5 min) 824-6550. Creole Rose Manor Bed & Breakfast 824-3145 or 824-4936.
Meeting Rooms: Holiday Inn (On site) can accommodate 25 to 200 persons. 824-5280;
Transportation: None reported.
Information: Greater Jennings Chamber of Commerce, I-10 Park, P.O. Box 1209, Jennings, LA 70546. Phone: 824-0933.

Sugar Mill Restaurant (Holiday Inn):

The Holiday Inn containing the Sugar Mill restaurant is located on the east side of the Jennings Airport. In fact you can taxi over and tie down right behind the hotel. Transportation is also available if you prefer to park at the other side of the airport. The Restaurant is open from 6 a.m. to 10 p.m. 7 days a week. There is a lounge on the premises open 6 days a week. Specialties on their menu include cajun cooking and fresh Louisiana seafood. There are many other items also available on their menu as well. Noon buffets are served from 11 a.m. to 2 p.m. daily with salad bar, two entrees, vegetables, bread and dessert. They will create a buffet on request for larger groups. They also have a Friday night seafood special. Average prices run $3.00 for breakfast, $6.00 for lunch and $7.00 for dinner. The decor of the Sugar Mill Restaurant is modern and comfortable with mauve, blue and green colors. Fly-in reunions as well as civic clubs and business meetings are easily accommodated in their conference room able to cater, with meals, to groups of 25 people. And seminar seating for up to 200 persons. The Holiday Inn has 132 guest rooms. For information call the Sugar Mill Restaurant at 824-5280.

Attractions:

Stearman Fly-in held in October at Jennings Airport; Zigler art and plantation museum was created in 1963 by Mrs. Ruth Zigler wife of Fred B. Zigler a Jennings industrialist and plilanthropist. 824-0114; W.H. Tupper general merchandise museum an authentic country store of the early 1900's 821-5532; Just ten minutes south of Jennings lies the town of Lake Aurther with a beautiful lakeside park complete with beach, boardwalk and pier. This is a site for many festivals and special events including the Lake Arthur Boat Parade. For information contact the David Parish Tourist Commission at 800-246-5521.

Airport Information:

JENNINGS - JENNINGS AIRPORT (3R7)
1 mi northwest of town N30-14.51 W92-40.32 Elev: 23 Fuel: 100LL, Jet-A Rwy 08-26: H5000x75 (Asph) Rwy 13-31: H3598x75 (Asph) Rwy 17-35: 2000x150 (Turf) Attended: continuously Unicom: 122.8
FBO: Riceland Aviation, Inc. **Phone: 824-1567, 824-5862**

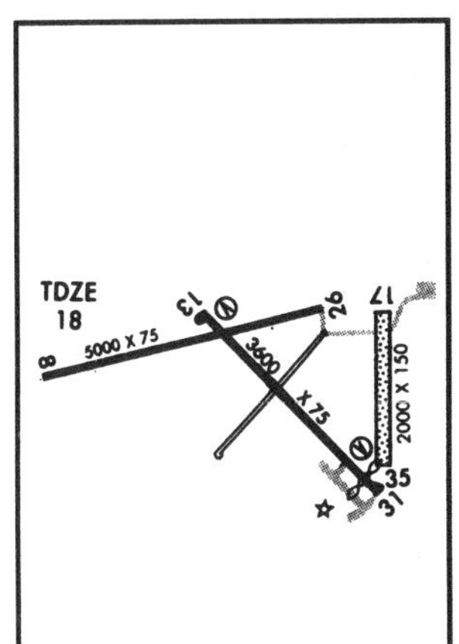

LA-LFT - LAFAYETTE
LAFAYETTE REGIONAL AIRPORT

(Area Code 318) 4, 5

Blair House Restaurant:

This fine dining facility is situated 1 mile north of the Lafayette Regional Airport. Transportation can be arranged either through Cherry Air, Inc. or Paul Fournet Air Service on the field. The restaurant is open Monday through Thursday from 11 a.m. to 10 p.m., Friday from 11 a.m. to 10:30 p.m. and Saturday from 5 p.m. to 10:30 p.m. (Closed Sunday). Specialties of the house feature seafood dishes, prime beef, steaks and veal. Daily lunch specials and evening chef dinner specials are also available. The decor of this facility offers fine dining in a romantic atmosphere. Prices range from $6.95 to $13.00 for lunch and $19.00 to $25.00 for dinner. Accommodations for groups up to 65 persons can be arranged. The Vermilionville attraction (See Attractions listed below) is located only 1/4 mile from this restaurant. For information call 234-0357.

Cafe Vermilionville:

Cafe Vermilionville is situated within an historic house located approximately 2 miles west of the Lafayette Regional Airport. To reach the restaurant you can arrange courtesy transportation in advance either through Cherry Air Inc. or Paul Fournet Air Service at the airport (See FBO listings below). This restaurant is classified as a fine dining facility and is situated within an historic building dating back to 1799. The Cafe Vermilionville is open Monday through Friday from 11 a.m. to 2 p.m. and 5:30 p.m. to 10 p.m. On Saturday their hours are from 5:30 p.m. to 10 p.m. and on Sunday from 11 a.m. to 2 p.m. Their menu consists primarily of French cuisine specializing in freshly prepared seafood dishes as well as other fine entrees. Average prices run $14.00 for lunch and $22.00 for dinner. This restaurant is listed in the National Register of Historic Places and offers its guests a unique dining experience. This restaurant will also cater for groups and parties. For more information or advance reservations you can call the restaurant at 237-0100.

Restaurants Near Airport:

Blair House	1 mi N	Phone: 234-0357
Cafe Bienvenue	On Site	Phone: 266-4400
Cafe Vermilionville	2 mi W	Phone: 237-0100
Ruth's Steak Hse.	1.5 mi W	Phone: 237-6123

Lodging: The following hotels all provide shuttle service and are within 2 to 5 miles from the airport: Holiday Inn Central-Holidome 235-1954; Lafayette Hilton & Towers 235-6111; The Hotel Acadiana 233-8120; Ramada Inn Airport 234-8521.

Meeting Rooms: Conference rooms and meeting rooms are available for rent (Small Fee) in terminal building, call 266-4400.

Transportation: Courtesy transportation available through Cherry Air, Inc. 234-3100 and Paul Fournet Air Service 237-0520; Also rent-a-car agencies available: Southwest Limo 234-7976; Avis 234-6944; Budget 266-4425; Hertz 233-7010; National 234-3170.

Information: Lafayette Convention & Visitors Commission, 1400 NW Evangeline Thrwy, P.O. Box 52066, Lafayette, LA 70505, Phone: 800-346-1958.

Attractions:

Vermilionville: 1600 Surrey Street, Lafayette, LA 70502-2266; (Across from airport) A 23 acre entertainment and living history attraction, features original Acadiana and Creole structures and replications of a plantation house, overseer's cottage, cotton gin, chapel, school house and blacksmith house all accompanied by costumed interpreters. Phone: 233-4077;

New Evangeline Downs Racetrack: I-49 North, Lafayette, LA (10 miles) Thoroughbred racing. Phone: 896-7223;

Tabasco Pepper Sauce Factory: Highway 90 East, New Iberia, LA (30 miles) Tour the early 1900's factory where they still bottle Tabasco brand pepper sauce. Phone: 365-8173;

Lafayette City Golf Course: Mud Avenue, Lafayette, La (5 miles), Phone: 268-5557;

Boat Tours of the Atchafalya Basin: Henderson, LA, Tours departs McGee's Landing and tours Louisiana's great swampland wilderness. Phone: 228-8519;

Se la Houssaye's Atachafalaya Expeditions: 723 Mud Avenue, Lafayette, LA 70505, Swamp tour of the Atachafalaya Basin, hunting and fishing guides and house boat accommodations. Phone: 923-7149.

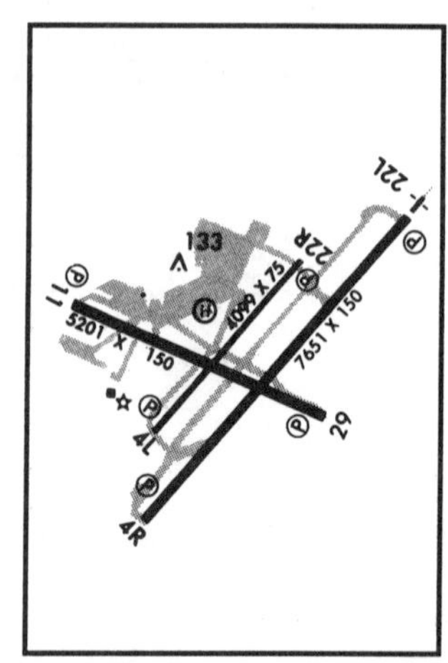

Airport Information:

LAFAYETTE - LAFAYETTE REGIONAL (LFT)
2 mi southeast of town N30-12.32 W91-59.26 Elev: 42 Fuel: 100LL, Jet-A Rwy 04R-22L: H7651x150 (Asph-Grvd) Rwy 11-29: H5201x150 (Asph-Grvd) Rwy 04L-22R: H4099x75 (Asph) Attended: continuously Atis: 120.5 Unicom: 122.95 App/Dep Con: 121.1, 128.7 Tower: 118.5 Gnd Con: 121.8 Clnc Del: 125.55 Public Phone 24hrs
FBO: Lafayette Aero, Inc. **Phone: 234-3100**
FBO: Paul Fournet Air Service **Phone: 237-0520**

LA-CWF - LAKE CHARLES CHENNAULT INDUSTRIAL AIRPARK

(Area Code 318)

6

Pat's of Henderson:

The Pat's of Henderson restaurant is located 1/4 mile off of Interstate 210. According to the restaurant management, they are situated about 1/2 to 1 mile from the Chennault Industrial Airpark. Guests flying into this airport will more than likely need to call a taxi for transportation to and from the restaurant. This fine dining establishment is open from 11 a.m. to 10 p.m.Monday through Thursday, 11 a.m. to 10:30 p.m. Sunday and 11 a.m. to 11 p.m. Friday & Saturday. Selections from their menu include a choice of appetizers including main entrees like craw fish Etouffee, seafood fettucini, U.S. choice rib-eye, broiled snapper filet, fried shrimp, broiled Italian chicken, seafood gumbo, as well as lobster, crab and other special items offered. Average prices range between $7.95 and $21.95 depending on which items are selected. Lunch specials Monday through Friday are offered between 11 a.m. and 2 p.m. This restaurant has a nautical theme and a elegant atmosphere, with wooden floors, brass fixtures and oak chairs and tables. The dining capacity of the establishment is 350 persons, with 4 separate rooms able to accommodate individual parties or large groups. For more information you can call Pat's of Hendersons restaurant at 439-6618.

Airport Information:

LAKE CHARLES - CHENNAULT INDUSTRIAL AIRPARK (CWF)
4 mi east of town N30-12.76 W93-08.61 Elev: 17 Fuel: 100LL, Jet-A
Rwy 15R-33L: H10701x200 (Conc) Rwy 15L-33R: 3700x100 (Turf) Attended: continuously
Lake Charles App/Dep Con: 119.8 Tower: 124.2 Gnd Con: 121.65
Chennault Industrial Airpark Phone: 491-9961
FBO: Transit Aviation of Chennault, Inc. Phone: 478-7722

Restaurants Near Airport:

Harlequin Steaks & Seafood	1-1/2 mi	Phone: N/A
Pat's of Henderson	1/2 mi	Phone: 439-6618
Peking Garden	2-1/2 mi	Phone: N/A

Lodging: Belmont Motel (3 miles) 433-8291; Chateau Charles (transportation) 882-6130; Econolodge (7 miles) 474-5151; Hilton Inn (7 miles) 433-7121; Howard Johnson's (4 miles) 433-5213.
Meeting Rooms: Econo Lodge (7 miles) 474-5151; Howard Johnson (4 miles) 433-5213.
Transportation: Taxi's: Big Dad's 439-9061; Checker & Yellow 433-8282; City Cab 433-6998; Independent Cab 436-6568; Rental Cars: Agency 437-1124; Avis 477-9319; Hertz 477-0616; Thrifty Car Rental 433-0527
Information: Southwest Louisiana Convention & Visitors Bureau, 1211 North Lake Shore Drive, P.O. Box 1912, Lake Charles, LA 70602, Phone: 436-9588 or 800-456-SWLA.

Attraction: Mallard Cove Golf Course is reported to be located adjacent to the airport.

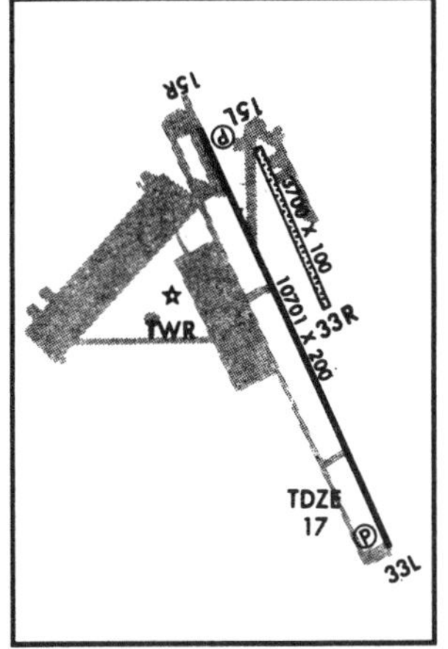

LA-LA26 - MARKSVILLE
MARKSVILLE MUNICIPAL AIRPORT

(Area Code 318) 7

Grand Casino Avoyelles:

Grand Casino Avoyelles is located approximately 1/4 mile from the Marksville Municipal Airport in Marksville, Louisiana. The casino, which is open 24-hours a day, will provide free transportation to and from the airport. This entertainment establishment is owned by the Tunica-Biloxi Indians of Louisiana. They welcome everyone and their families to come and have a great time. Guests will enjoy all the amenities that the casino has to offer. It contains a 38,000 square-foot gaming floor, over 1,100 slot machines, 40 table games featuring Blackjack, Roulette, craps, mini-baccarat, and Caribbean stud poker, and a separate poker room. Grand Casino Avoyelles also offers free admission, free parking, and a Porte Cochere with accompanying valet service at the entry. There are two restaurants: the 354-seat Market Place Buffet which serves 57 items from around the world and the casual 290-seat Roxy's Diner which serves all-American favorites. The casino also has other features, such as the Grand Advantage Players Club, a supervised child care/activity center (ages 6 months to 12 years), a state-of-the-art video arcade (ages 12 and older), and non-smoking gaming areas. The gift shop features Grand Casino logo merchandise and Native American crafts. There are also support areas, such as offices, banking, employee dining and locker rooms. Groups of 30 people, or more, will receive free transportation on the Grand Casino Party Bus with certain requirements. The bus is available from Sunday to 3:00 p.m. Friday. A 5-hour minimum stay at the casino is required, along with a 10-day advance booking with a $400 refundable deposit to hold the reservation (refunded upon departure from the casino). Future development plans at the casino include a 300-room hotel and 250-seat seafood restaurant. For more information about the Grand Casino Avoyelles, call 800-WIN-1-WIN (800-946-1-946) or 253-1946.

Attractions:

Besides the Grand Casino Avoyelles, Marksville has plenty of other attractions to visit. Such as, historic homes, Indian culture, state/national wildlife refuges, agricultural tours and swamp tours. The Tunica-Biloxi Indian Center and Museum features the famous Tunica Treasure which is the most extraordinary collection of Indian and European artifacts from the Colonial Period in the lower Mississippi Valley; The Marksville State Commemorative Area-Prehistoric Indian Park & Museum is a 39-acre park with prehistoric Indian mounds and Indian Village sites with picnic facilities; The Hypolite Bordelon House is an 1820 Creole pioneer dwelling; Le Theatre des Bon Temps "Avoyelles Performing Arts Center" (Fox Theatre) features plays, concerts, etc.; The Avoyelles Parish Courthouse is a 1927 Neo-classical style structure which houses many governmental agencies and tourist information. For more information about the attractions in Marksville, call 253-9222.

Restaurants Near Airport:
Grand Casino Avoyelles 1/4 mi Phone: 253-1946

Lodging: Pine Courts (1 mile) 253-7595; Ranch House (1-1/4 mile) 253-9507; Terrace Inn (1 mile) 253-6528

Meeting Rooms: None Reported

Transportation: Grand Casino Avoyelles will provide free transportation to and from the airport; Taxi Service: Cenis 253-4862

Information: Avoyelles Commission of Tourism Courthouse, 312 North Main Street, Suite D, Marksville, LA, Phone: 253-9222

Airport Information:

MARKSVILLE - MARKSVILLE MUNICIPAL AIRPORT (LA26)
1 mi south of town N31-05.68 W92-04.14 Elev: 79 Fuel: 100LL Rwy 04-22: H3802x75 (Asph) Attended: irregularly CTAF: 122.9 Houston Center App/Dep Con: 135.7 Notes: For fuel after hours, call 253-9574. Airport is CLOSED sunset-sunrise indefinitely.
FBO: Marksville Municipal Airport Phone: 253-9574, 253-9271

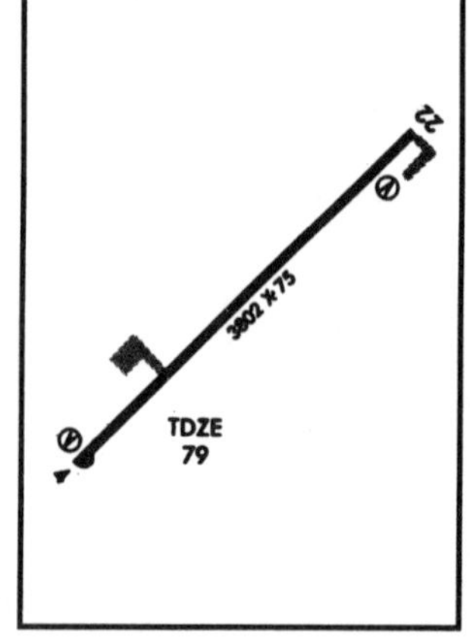

LA-MLU - MONROE
MONROE REGIONAL AIRPORT

(Area Code 318) **8, 9**

Airport Restaurant:

The restaurant is located inside the main terminal building adjacent to the runway at Monroe Regional Airport. This is a family style restaurant that serves soup, seafood gumbo, homemade pies, chicken dumplings, hamburger steak, pork chops, spaghetti, fried chiken, fried fish and fresh vegetables. They also will cater to any number of persons, on or off the premises. Cheese, fruit, sandwiches, or Danish trays can be prepared as well as Hot lunches, breakfasts or anything you request. Average cost for a meal is $5.00 for breakfast, $6.00 for lunch and $7.00 for dinner. The restaurant is open Monday, Thursday & Friday from 5:00 a.m. to 8 p.m., and on Saturday & Sunday from 5:00 a.m. to 4:00 p.m. For information call 323-1574

Restaurants Near Airport:

Airport Restaurant	On Site	Phone: 323-1574
Danken Trail	1 mi	Phone: 343-0773
Frank & Janie's	1 mi	Phone: 343-5860
Red Lobster	2 miS.	Phone: 361-0158

Lodging: Holiday Inn Holidome - Monroe Civic Center (Reservation phone at airport) I-20 at 1051 US Hwy. Shuttle service to and from airport. Phone: 387-5100. LaQuinta Inn - (Reservation phone at airport) 1035 US 165 Bypass South. 3 miles from Monroe Regional Airport, shuttle service. Phone: 322-3900.
Transportation: Fleeman Aviation, Phone: 387-0222, Quachita Cab Service, Phone: 323-9404, Avis Car Rental, Phone: 323-8822, Hertz Car Rental, Phone: 323-8805, National Car Rental, Phone: 387-4477
Information: Monroe-West Monroe Convention and Visitors Bureau, 1333 State Farm Drive, Monroe, LA 71202. Phone: 387-5691

Attractions: **Golfing** (Airport) - Chennault Park Golf Course, 18 holes, Phone: 329-2454. **Fishing;** Bayou Desiard (3 miles); Lake D'Arbonne (20 miles); Ouachita River, Fishing and boating (3 miles).

Red Lobster Restaurant:

The Red Lobster Restaurant is located one mile south of the airport directly down Kansas Lane, adjacent to the airport in the Pecanland Mall. This restaurant serves seafood, steaks, and chicken, as well as appetizers, salads, soups, desserts and pastries. Average price for a meal is $8.00 for lunch and $15.00 for dinner. The decor is modern, comfortable and emits an elegant atmosphere. Fly-in groups are welcome. They will also prepare seafood party trays and cater to pilots on the go. The restaurant is open Sunday through Thursday from 11:00 a.m. to 10:00 p.m. and Friday and Saturday from 11:00 a.m. to 11:00 p.m. For information call 361-0158.

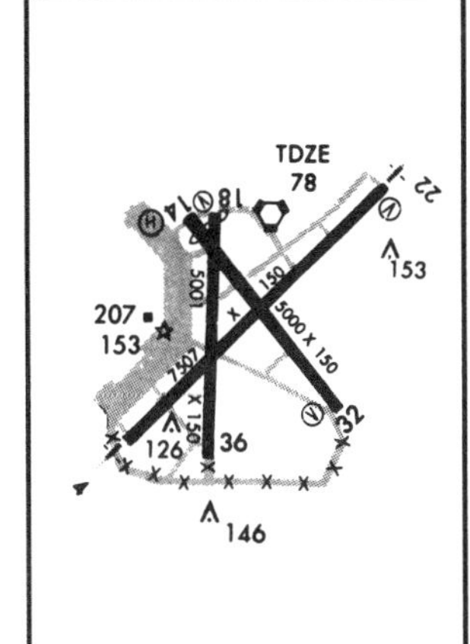

Airport Information:

MONROE - MONROE REGIONAL (MLU)
3 mi. east of town N32-30.65 W92-02.26 Elev: 79 Fuel: 100LL, Jet-A Rwy 04-22: H7507x150 (Asph-Conc-Grvd) Rwy 18-36: H5001x150 (Conc) Rwy 14-32: H5000x150 (Asph) Attended: continuously Atis: 125.05 Unicom: 122.95 Tower: 118.9 Gnd Con: 121.9 Clnc Del: 121.65 **FBO: McMahan Aviation 325-7558** **FBO: Fleeman Aviation 387-0222**

A Little Extra Planning Can Make Each One Of Your Excursions More Rewarding

"Just Call Ahead"

Even though we at Aerodine strive to provide the latest information possible at the time of printing, we suggest you take a little time and call ahead to verify that the facility you intend to visit still provides the same services as published. Your comments regarding any changes in these services or about new establishments you have found, are greatly appreciated. With your help, we can include them in our next updated edition.

Aerodine Magazine
P.O. Box 247, Palatine, IL 60078
Phone: 847-358-4355

LA-NEW - NEW ORLEANS LAKEFRONT AIRPORT

(Area Code 504) 10, 11

Commander Palace Restaurant:

The Commander Palace Restaurant is located about 15 miles from the Lakefront Airport. Transportation can be obtained by taxi or rental car reserved through fixed base operators. This restaurant has been rated by the James Beard Foundation as one of the finest dining establishments in the country according to restaurant management. It is situated in the Historic Garden District 10 minutes west of the famous New Orleans French Quarter. This is a fine dining facility specializing in preparing Haute Creole cuisine. Dishes like turtle soup, Lyonnaise fish, garlic crusted red fish, bread pudding, Tasso stuffed shrimp, wild mushroom ravioli and grilled veal. Average prices for a meal are $45.00. The restaurant is contained in a charming 1880 historic building. The decor is elegant with linen on linen, crystal and center pieces for each setting. Groups can arrange special seatings by contract with the sales office by calling 899-9591. For general information and reservations call 899-8221.

Sclafani's

Sclafani's Restaurant is classified as a fine dining facility located about 5 miles from the New Orleans Lake Front Airport. Most of the FBOs listed below can provide courtesy transportation for customers, in addition to taxi service (listed below). Traveling to the restaurant, you will want to exit east onto Hayne Blvd. along the lake, and go about 3 miles. Sclafani's is open Tuesday through Friday from 11 a.m. to 2 p.m., and Friday and Saturday from 5 p.m. to 9:00 p.m. Specialties include Steak Dauphine, Eggplant Belle Rose, and Veal Parmigiana. In addition, they offer a wide selection of entrees including seafood, prime beef steaks, New Orleans specialties, chicken dishes, pastas and Provimi baby veal dishes. Appetizers, soups and salads are also available. Average prices run $8.95 for lunch and $10.95 for dinner. The decor of the restaurant provides an elegant yet modern atmosphere. Small or large groups from 20 to 80 persons in their dining room or 100 to 350 in their special appointed catering room can be arranged. In fact, Sclafani's has been catering parties in New Orleans for over 25 years. Their rooms are decorated with carpeted floors, crystal chandeliers, linen tablecloths, silk flower arrangements and candles to give guests a special ambience. For information call 241-4472.

Restaurants Near Airport:

Commander Palace	15 mi.	Phone: 899-8221
Deanie's On Hayne	3.5 mi	Phone: 242-9708
Sclafani's	5 mi E.	Phone: 241-4472
Walnut Room	On Site	Phone: 243-4077

Lodging: (All Lodging 3-6 miles from airport) La Quinta Inn, 8400 I-10 Service Road, Crowder, Phone: 800-531-5900; Howard Johnson, 4200 Old Gentilly Road, Phone: 944-0151; Newcourt Inn, 10020 I-10 Service Road, Phone: 244-9115

Conference Rooms: The airport terminal building contains an executive conference room that will hold 14 people. In addition, their board room will accommodate 70 people and their Walnut Room is reserved for larger groups of 100 to 150 persons.

Transportation: FBOs listed below under Airport Information will provide some courtesy transportation. Also rental automobiles can be obtained from FBOs as well. The main terminal building on airport has rental car agencies available to serve your needs. In addition, taxi service is provided: United Cabs, 522-9771; Metry Cabs, 835-4242; Morrison's Cabs, 891-5818; RTA Bus (Public), 569-2600;

Information: Greater New Orleans Tourist & Convention Commission, 1520 Sugar Bowl Drive, New Orleans, LA 70112 or call 566-5011.

Attractions:

The LA Nature Center (6 miles), 246-5672; City Park (7 miles), 482-4888; **New Orleans Museum of Art** at City Park (7 miles), 488-2631; **Audubon Zoo** (13 miles) 861-2537; (Also golf and tennis). **Seasonal Events**: **Mardi Gras,** one of the most popular gala celebrations, is held each year in New Orleans, and includes torchlight parades, street dancing and costumed balls, beginning two weeks before Shrove Tuesday. Information can be obtained by contacting the Greater New Orleans Tourist & Convention Commission listed above. **The New Orleans Jazz and Heritage Festival** is also an event held during an outdoor weekend in late April or early May. This festival features all types of ethnic foods, and music from all corners of the world with 11 stages, and arts and crafts exhibitions. For more information contact, New Orleans Jazz and Heritage Festival at P.O. Box 53407, New Orleans, LA 70153 or call 522-4786.

Airport Information:

NEW ORLEANS - LAKEFRONT AIRPORT (NEW)
4 mi northeast of town N30-02.55 W90-01.70 Elev: 9 Fuel: 100LL, Jet-A Rwy 18R-36L: H6879x150 (Asph-Grvd) Rwy 18L-36R: H3699x75 (Asph)
Rwy 09-27: H3094x75 (Asph) Attended: continuously Atis: 124.9
Unicom: 122.95 Tower: 119.9, 125.65 Gnd Con: 121.7 Clnc Del: 127.4
Public Phone 24 hrs Notes: Landing fee $1.00/1000lbs. gross landing wt. ($6.00 minimum)
Exceptions - (Single Engine) 20 gal or fill, (Light twin) 50 gal or fill. (Airport Manager, Phone: 243-4010)

FBO: Aero Services International	**Phone: 245-1140**
FBO: Aviaport Business Jet Cntr.	**Phone: 242-9496**
FBO: General Aviation of N.O.	**Phone: 241-2700**
FBO: Million Air of New Orleans,	**Phone: 241-2800**

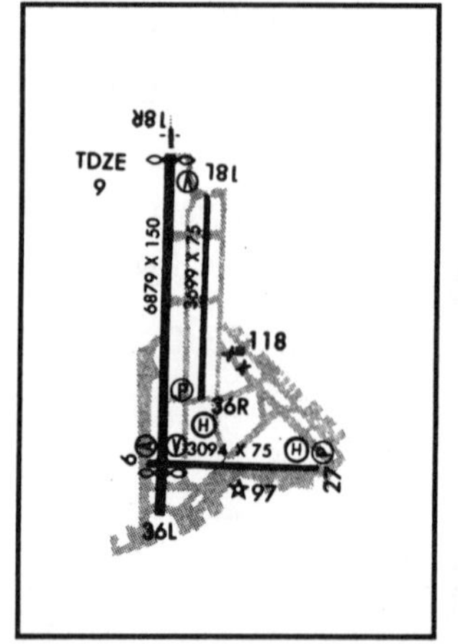

Not to be used for navigational purposes

LA-MSY - NEW ORLEANS
NEW ORLEANS INTL. (MOISANT FLD)

12

Jester Express, East Fast Food: (CA1 Services)

This combination cafe and cafeteria is located at several places within the terminal building at the New Orleans International Airport. You can find them in the east and west lobby as well as down each concourse except "C". They are open between 5:30 a.m. and 9:30 p.m., 7 days a week. Menu specialties include red beans & rice, seafood gumbo, crawfish and corn soup, pizza and fresh made Po-Boy sandwiches. According to the restaurant management, menu prices average $5.00 for breakfast and around $6.25 for lunch and dinner items. The decor of the restaurant is of regional contemporary design. They also can accommodate groups of all sizes. The restaurant has on many occasions catered all types of functions on airport grounds. For more information about Jester, Jester Express, East Fast Food, call 463-5500.

Attractions: There are many attractions within the New Orleans area. Mardi Gras is perhaps one of the most well known events within the United States. It officially opens the day before Lent begins. Torchlight parades, street dancing, masquerades, parties. (Mardi Gras Day, February 20th); Famous is the New Orleans Jazz and Heritage Festival featuring a weekend of specialty foods, art and craft displays, 11 stages used for performing Gospel, blues, ragtime folk and many other types of music. Last weekend in April, to 1st weekend in May. For information call 522-4786; also French Quarter Festival held mid-April, 522-5730. Attractions abound within the Garden District, Central Business District, French Quarter and Faubourg Marigny. For current event schedules contact the Greater Orleans Tourist & Convention Commission 566-6011. (See Information).

Restaurants Near Airport:
Jester Cafe's Trml. Bldg. Phone: 463-5500
Numerous Restaurants nearby Phone: N/A

Lodging: Best Western Inn-Airport 464-1644; Comfort Inn Kenner 467-1300; Holiday Inn 885-5700; Holiday Inn-Airport 467-5611; LaQuinta Inn 456-0003; LaQuinta Inn-Airport 466-1401; New Orleans Airport Hilton 469-5000; Park Plaza Inn 464-6464; Rodeway Inn-Airport 467-1391; Travelodge-New Orleans-Airport 469-7341; all within 5 minutes of airport.

Meeting Rooms: conference rooms available in terminal building. For information about catered meals call 463-5500 or the airport manager's office at 464-0831. Also meeting rooms available at some hotels listed above. See "Lodging."

Transportation: Rental Cars: Alamo 465-3792; Avis 469-5455; Budget 467-2277; Hertz 468-3695; National 46-4335. Also: Taxi and Limo Service: Airport Shuttle 465-9780; Carey Limousine 523-5466.

Information: Greater New Orleans Tourist & Convention Commission, 1520 Sugar Bowl Drive, New Orleans, LA 70112, Phone: 566-5011.

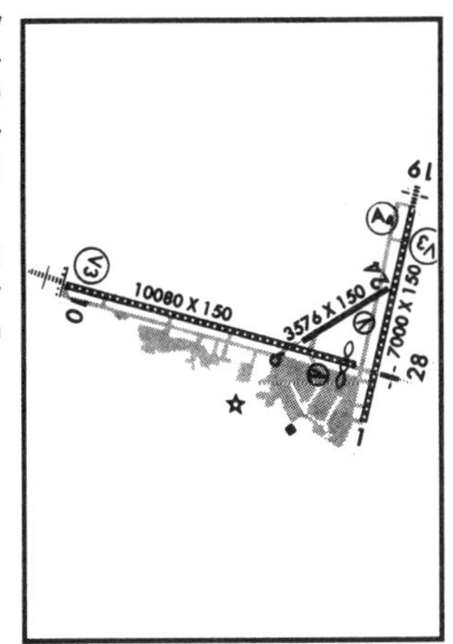

Airport Information:

NEW ORLEANS - NEW ORLEANS INTL. (MOISANT FLD) (MSY)
10 miles west of town N29-59.61 W90-15.48 Rwy 10-28: H10080x150 (Asph-Conc-Grvd) Rwy 01-19: H7000x150 (Asph-Grvd) Rwy 06-24: H3576x150 (Asph) Attended: continuously Atis: 127.55 Unicom: 122.95 New Orleans App/Dep Con: 133.15 (N and E) 123.85 (SE and S) 125.5 (W) Tower: 119.5 Gnd Con: 121.9 Clnc Del: 127.2 Pre Taxi Clnc: 127.2
FBO: General Aviation Corp. Phone: 466-1700 FBO: Transit Aviation Phone: 468-7722

LA-PTN - PATTERSON
HARRY P. WILLIAMS MEMORIAL

(Area Code 504)

13

The Eagle's Nest Restaurant:

This restaurant is located right in the Perry Flying Center FBO (Southeast side of building). The restaurant serves plate lunches Monday through Friday. It is decorated heavily with emphasis on NASA space exploration. Flying clubs and group get-togethers are welcome. Catering is also provided with advance notice. Entrees run about $5.00 for breakfast and lunch items. The restaurant is open Monday through Friday from 7 a.m. to 3 p.m. Weekend hours may vary. If arranging a fly-in with a larger group, if prior arrangements are made, they will open on Sunday to accommodate your needs. In the past they have provided space for as many as 150 persons per group. For information call 395-4501. While on the field, you may want to stop and visit the Memorial Aviation Museum on the airport. (See Attractions).

Restaurants Near Airport:
The Eagle's Nest On Site Phone: 395-4501

Lodging: Acadian Inn, (10 miles) 384-5750; Holiday Inn, (10 miles) 385-2200; Plantation Inn, (3 miles) 395-4511

Transportation: Perry Flying Service, (Rental Cars) Phone: 395-4501

Information: St Mary Parish Tourist Commission, P.O. Box 2332, Morgan City, LA 70381, Phone: 395-4905 or 800-256-2931.

Attractions: Wedell-Williams Memorial Aviation Museum of Louisiand, (On airport), Patterson, PA 70392, Phone: 504-395-7067

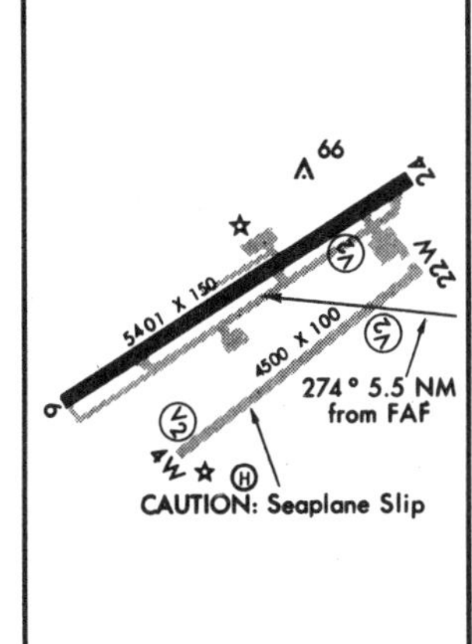

Airport Information:

PATTERSON - HARRY P. WILLIAMS MEMORIAL (PTN)
2 mi NW of town N29-42.65 W91-20.38 Elev: 9 Fuel: 100LL, Jet-A
Rwy 06-24: H5401x150 (ASPH) Attended: dawn to dusk Unicom 122.8
Attended: continuously Notes: CAUTION seaplane landing area (water channel) Southeast of adjacent/parallel runways.
FBO: Parry Flying Center Phone: 395-4501

Wedell-Williams Memorial Aviation Museum of Louisiana

Patterson, LA (LA-PTN)

The Wedell-Williams Memorial Aviation Museum of Louisiana was established by the Louisiana legislature as the official state aviation museum. As such, the museum is responsible for the preservation and exhibition of documentation concerning all of Louisiana's aviation history.

The name Wedell-Williams comes from two of Louisiana's most famous aviation pioneers, Jimmy Wedell and Harry Williams. Together they formed the Wedell-Williams Air Service, based at Patterson, Louisiana. In the early 1930's, Wedell-Williams manufactured low-wing monoplanes which dominated the air races of their time. In the "44", the most famous of the Wedell-Williams racers, Jimmy was the first pilot to officially go over 300 miles per hour in a landplane. Both died in air crashes, Jimmy in 1934, and Harry in 1936. Their deaths brought an end to Louisiana's first commercial airline. Their assets and airmail contracts were sold to a company that was later to become Eastern Airlines. The original Wedell-Williams "44" Racer underwent several modifications during its existence. The airworthy replica on display at the museum, shows it as it appeared when pilot Doug Davis flew it to victory in the 1934 Bendix race from Burbank to Cleveland. A few days later, Doug Davis was killed and the "44" destroyed in a Thompson Trophy Race crash at Cleveland. This beautiful reproduction, on display in the museum, was designed and constructed by Jim Clevenger and Budd Davisson. During his life-time Jimmy held more speed records than anyone else alive. He won more than 48 trophies in his active flying career.

Exhibits dealing with all types of aviation and its history are in the planning stage. The museum has a policy of changing its exhibits so that visitors may return to find new material on display. Coming exhibits include aviation and its role in Louisiana's petroleum and agricultural industries and famous Louisiana military aviators. Museum hours are Tuesday through Saturday from 8:30 a.m. to 5 p.m.. Admission: Adults $2.00 and children are free. Fly-in guests can land at the Harry P. Williams Memorial Airport in Patterson, Louisiana and obtain transportation over to the museum. Special tours may also be arranged by contacting the museum in advance at 504-395-7067. (Information obtained by the Wedell-Williams Memorial Aviation Museum).

LA-DTN - SHREVEPORT
SHREVEPORT DOWNTOWN ARPT.

14

Restaurants Near Airport: **(Area Code 318)**

Casinos nearby	1/4 mi to 3 mi	Phone: N/A
Peggy's Arpt. Cafe	Trml. Bldg.	Phone: 221-2999

Peggy's Downtown Airport Cafe:

Peggy's Downtown Airport Cafe is located within the terminal building on the Shreveport Downtown Airport. This combination cafe and family style restaurant is open from 7 a.m. to 7 p.m., 7 days a week. Specialties of the house include meatloaf, red beans and rice, ribs, enchiladas, tacos and for dessert, cream cheese pie, and apple cobbler. This restaurant prides itself in homemade prepared entrees. Prices average $4.50 to $4.95 for most entrees. The main dining room can seat 60 to 70 people. From the restaurant you can enjoy a great view of the airport and active areas. In-flight catering is also available. Groups are welcome with advance notice. For more information call the restaurant at 221-2999.

Restaurants Nearby:

There are two public airports serving the City of Shreveport. The Downtown Airport to the north near Bossier City and Shreveport Regional Airport to the west of town. The Downtown Airport north of town has a couple of casinos reported within 1/4 mile to 1 mile of this airport. Also a number of lodging facilities in the area containing dining establishments offer free courtesy transportation. Lulu's By the Red used to be a restaurant located right on the airport. However during our interview, we learned this establishment has since been closed. It is possible that this facility may reopen under new management in the future. For information you can call the airport manager at 673-5370 or Downtown Aero Center, Inc. (FBO) at 221-0008.

Lodging: Best Western Airline Inn (transportation) 742-6000; Hilton Inn - Bossier (transportation) 747-2400; Holiday Inn - Bossier City (transportation) 746-8410; LeBossier Hotel (transportation) 747-3000; Residence Inn By Marriott (transportation) 747-6220; Sheraton Inn - Bossier (transportation) 742-9700; Sundowner Inn (Transportation) 746-5050.

Meeting Rooms: Most of the facilities listed under lodging contain accommodations for meetings and banquet rooms.

Transportation: Taxi service: City Cab 221-2222; Yellow Checker 425-7000; Rental cars: Avis 631-1839; Budget 636-2846; Hertz 636-1212; National 636-2743.

Information: Shreveport-Bossier Convention & Tourist Bureau, 629 Spring Street, Box 1761, Shreveport, LA 71166, Phone: 222-9391 or 800-551-8682.

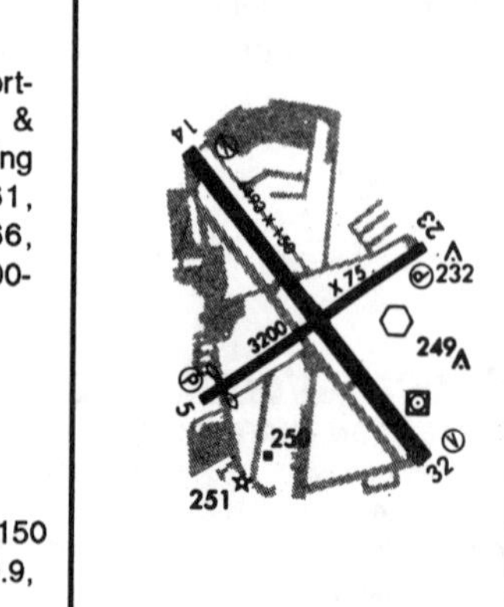

Airport Information:

SHREVEPORT - SHREVEPORT DOWNTOWN AIRPORT (DTN)

3 mi north of town N32-32.39 W93-44.68 Elev: 179 Fuel: 100LL, Jet-A Rwy 14-32: H4493x150 (Asph) Rwy 05-23: H3200x75 (Asph) Attended: 1300-0100 Unicom: 123.0 App/Dep Con: 119.9, 118.6, 121.4

Airport Manager Phone: 673-5370 FBO: Downtown Aero Center Phone: 221-0008

LA-SHV - SHREVEPORT
SHREVEPORT REGIONAL AIRPORT

(Area Code 318) 15

Air Host:

The Air Terminal Services facility contains a family style restaurant located on the second floor of the main terminal building. This restaurant can easily be reached either by courtesy transportation available through the fixed based operators on the field, walking or by taxi service. Restaurant hours are 5 a.m. to 8 p.m. during the week and 5 a.m. to 7 p.m. on Saturday and Sunday. Their menu includes selections like 1/2 pound hamburgers, steakburgers, chicken fried steak, poor-boy shrimp sandwiches, taco salads, appetizers, as well as a full breakfast line. Average prices run $4.00 for breakfast, $4.95 for lunch and $5.95 for dinner. Daily specials are featured each day. The restaurant itself can serve up to 100 persons in their main dining room and about 100 in their lounge. The main dining area is carpeted and contains a southwestern decor with Santa Fe type fixtures complimented by redwood, gray and pink tones. For more information call this restaurant at 636-2511.

Restaurants Near Airport:
Air Host On Site Phone: 636-2511

Lodging: Holiday Inn Airport-Holidome (Free trans) 635-3521; Holiday Inn-Financial Plaza (Free trans) 688-3000; Radisson Hotel Shreveport (Free trans) 222-7717; Ramada Inn Airport (Free trans. 2 blks) 365-7531; Richmond Suites Hotel (Free trans, 2 blks) 635-6431; Super 8 (1 blk) 635-8888; Sheraton Pierremont Plaza (Free trans) 797-9900.

Meeting Rooms: Convention facilities available: Sheraton Pierremont (Free trans) 797-9900; Most other establishments listed above under lodging, have accommodation for meetings and conference rooms.

Transportation: Courtesy cars available by FBO's to local facilities; Also Taxi: Yellow Checker 425-7000; Rental Cars: Budget 636-7438; Dollar 631-6467; Hertz 636-1212; National 636-2734.

Information: Shreveport-Bossier Convention & Tourist Bureau, 629 Spring Street, Box 1761, Shreveport, LA 71166, Phone: 222-9391 or 800-551-8682 outside LA.

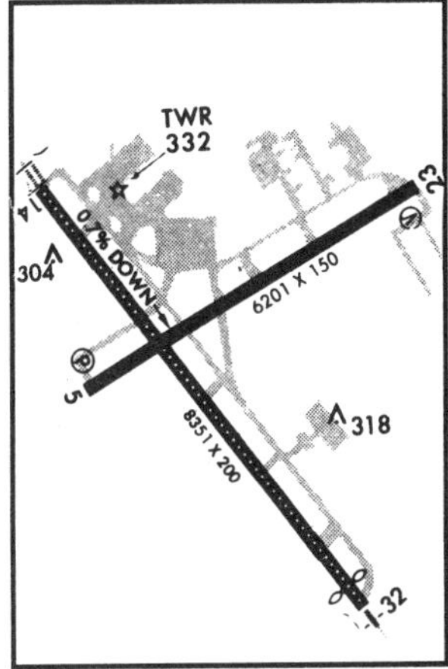

Airport Information:

SHREVEPORT - SHREVEPORT REGIONAL AIRPORT (SHV)
4 mi southwest of town N32-26.80 W93-49.54 Elev: 258 Fuel: 100LL, Jet-A, B
Rwy 14-32: H8351x200 (Asph-Conc-Grvd) Rwy 05-23: H6201x150 (Asph-Grvd) Attended: continuously Atis: 128.45 Unicom: 122.95 Shreveport App/Dep Con: 119.9, 118.6, 121.4 Tower: 121.4 Gnd Con: 121.9 Clnc Del: 124.65 Notes: Landing fee for aircraft over 30,000 lbs.
Shreveport Regional Airport Phone: 673-5370
FBO: TAC Air Phone: 636-1000

LA-6R1 - WELSH
WELSH AIRPORT

(Area Code 318) 16

Cajun Tales Seafood Restaurant:

The Cajun Tales Seafood Restaurant is located about 4 blocks east of the Welsh Airport, and is within walking distance according to the restaurant management. This combination family style and fine dining facility is open 7 a.m. to 10 p.m. on weekends and 7 a.m. to 9 p.m. during weekdays. Selections off their menu include items like seafood gumbo, seafood platters, crawfish, shrimp, crab meat, stuffed catfish, hamburgers, cheeseburgers, poor boy sandwiches, as well as a full line of breakfast choices. Their shrimp omelets are a favorite with many breakfast lovers. In addition to their menu selections, they also provide additional seafood specials. Their main dining room can seat 50 persons. A banquet room is available for groups, parties or special occasions. The main dining room in the front of the restaurant offers a casual atmosphere while the back dining area is somewhat more elegant. They also provide meals-to-go along with special family packages. For more information about this restaurant you can call 734-4772.

Restaurants Near Airport:
Cajun Tales Seafood Restaurant 4 blks E. Phone: 734-4772

Lodging: Holiday Inn (10 miles) 824-5280.

Meeting Rooms: None Reported

Transportation: Airport courtesy car reported.

Information: Southwest Louisiana Convention & Visitors Bureau, 1211 N. Lakeshore Drive, P.O. Box 1912, Lake Charles, LA 70602, Phone: 436-9588 or 800-456-SWLA.

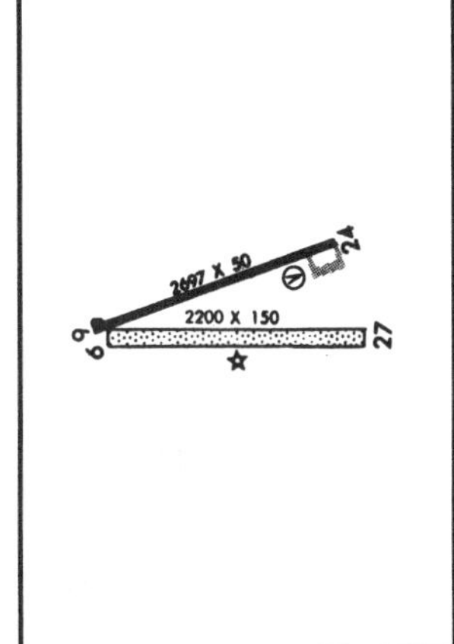

Airport Information:

WELSH - WELSH AIRPORT (6R1)
0 mi northwest of town N30-14.51 W92-49.76 Elev: 18 Fuel: 100LL
Rwy 06-24: H2697x50 (Asph) Rwy 09-27: 2200x150 (Turf) Attended: irregularly
Unicom: 122.8
FBO: Lyon Flying Service, Inc. Phone: 734-2594

MAINE

CROSS FILE INDEX

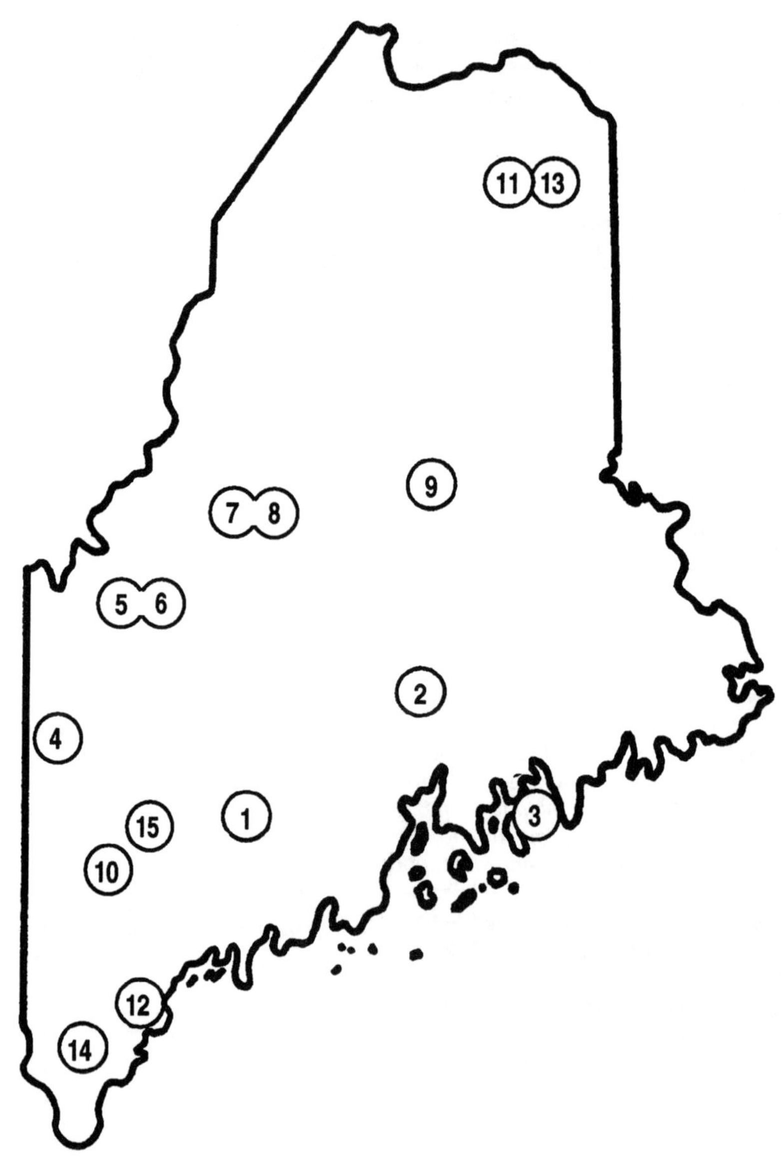

Not to be used for navigational purposes

MAINE

CROSS FILE INDEX

Location Number	City or Town	Airport Name And Identifier	Name of Attraction
1	Augusta	Augusta State Arpt. (AUG)	Ardito's Italian Rest.
2	Bangor	Bangor Intl. Arpt. (BGR)	Wright Brothers Grill
3	Bar Harbor	Hancock Co.-Bar Harbor (BHB)	Gateway Lobster Pound
4	Bethel	Col Dyke Fld. (0B1)	Sunday River Ski Resort
5	Carrabassett	Sugarloaf Reg. (B21)	Sugarloaf Inn
6	Carrabassett	Sugarloaf Reg. (B21)	Sugarloaf Mountain
7	Greenville	Greenville Muni (3B1)/S.P.B. (52B)	Kelly's Landing
8	Greenville	Greenville Muni (3B1)/S.P.B. (52B)	Whitman Hse. B & B
9	Millinocket	Millinocket Muni. Arpt. (MLT)	Lazy 8 Grill
10	Oxford	Oxford Co Reg. (81B)	Maurice Frances
11	Portage	Portage Lake Muni. (S.P.B) (87B)	Deans Motor Lodge
12	Portland	Portland Intl. Jetport (PWM)	Casco Bay Restaurant
13	Presque Isle	Northern Main Reg. (PQI)	Keddy's Inn Solarium
14	Sanford	Sanford Muni. Arpt. (SFM)	Rudy's Cockpit Cafe
15	Turner	Twitchell Arpt. (3B5)	Chick-A-Dee Restaurant

Articles

City or town	Nearest Airport and Identifier	Name of Attraction
Jackman, ME	Newton Fld. (59B)	Sky Lodge

ME-AUG - AUGUSTA
AUGUSTA STATE AIRPORT

(Area Code 207)

1

Ardito's Italian Restaurant:

Ardito's Italian Restaurant is situated within the terminal building at the Augusta State Airport. This restaurant serves Italian food at affordable prices, including seafood, steaks, chicken and prime rib on Friday and Saturday. Within the restaurant is a deli, serving sandwiches. There are daily specials for lunch and dinner as well as special seafood chowder on Friday nights. The decor of the restaurant is modern and provides a beautiful view of the airport runways through large picture windows. They can accommodate groups up to 20 persons if advance notice is given, and will provide meals-to-go consisting of hot or cold sandwiches, fruit trays, vegetable trays, steak and lobster dinners, Italian meals or Antipasto dishes for travelers. This facility has over 40 years experience in the restaurant and catering business. They are open 11 a.m. to 8:30 p.m. Monday through Thursday, 11 a.m. to 9 p.m. Friday and Saturday. (Closed Sundays and major holidays) Average prices are $5.00 for lunch and $8.95 for dinner. For information call 623-2044.

Restaurants Near Airport:
Ardito's On Site Phone: 623-2044

Lodging: Best Western Senator Inn, Phone: 622-5804; Coastline Inn, 622-6371; Howard Johnson, 622-4751; Susse Chalet Motor Lodge, 258-1980

Transportation: New England Taxi, 623-3675

Information: Kennebec Valley Chamber of Commerce, University Drive, P.O. Box E, Augusta, ME 04332, Phone: 623-4559.

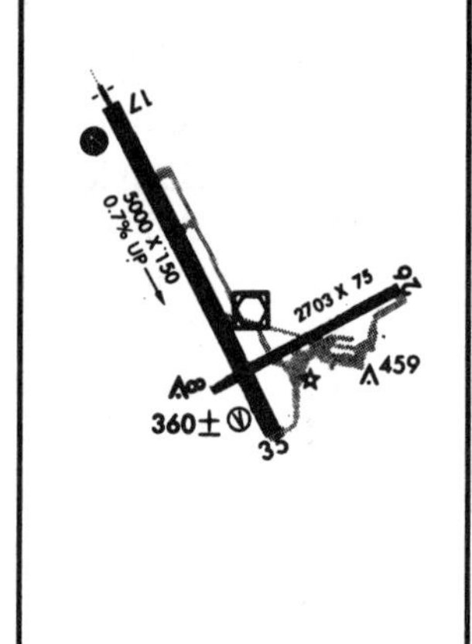

Airport Information:

AUGUSTA - AUGUSTA STATE AIRPORT (AUG)
1 mi NW of town N44-19.24 W69-47.84 Elev: 352 Fuel: 100LL, Jet-A Rwy 17-35: H5000x150 (ASPH) Rwy 08-26: H2703x75 (ASPH) Attended: 1100-0100Z
Unicom: 123.0 Public Phone 24 hrs.
FBO: Maine Helicopters Phone: 622-4643

ME-BGR - BANGOR
BANGOR INTL AIRPORT

(Area Code 207)

2

Wright Brothers Grill:

The Wright Brothers Grill is located within walking distance and adjacent to the Bangor International Airport. Shuttle service is also available through the fixed base operator. This facility offers casual dining and is open for breakfast 6 a.m. to 11:30 a.m., lunch between 11:30 a.m. and 2:30 p.m. Monday through Friday, and Saturday until 2 p.m. For dinner their open from 5 p.m. to 11 p.m. 7 days a week. Their menu includes items like fresh seafood, sirloin steaks, pasta and a variety of sandwiches. Their dining area can seat 42 persons and overlooks the airport. Large or small groups and parties can easily be arranged either through the restaurant or the Marriott Hotel. 101 separate lodging units are available as well as 3 functional meeting rooms able to seat between 10 and 200 guests. According to the restaurant management, they are able to provide in-flight catering as well. For more information call 947-6721.

Restaurants Near Airport:
BAC Coffee Shop Terml. Phone: 947-4375
Pilots Grill 1 mi Phone: N/A
Wright Bro. Grill (Marriott) Adj Arpt Phone: 947-6721

Lodging: Comfort Inn (Shuttle) 942-7899; Days Inn (Shuttle) 942-8272; Econo Lodge (Shuttle) 942-6301; Marriott (on fld) 947-6721; Phoenix Inn (Free Trans) 947-3850; Ramada Inn (Free Trans) 947-6961.
Meeting Rooms: Comfort Inn 942-7899; Econo Lodge 942-6301; Phoenix Inn 947-3850; Ramada Inn 947-6961.
Transportation: Taxi Service: Checker 942-5581; Harold's Taxi 942-8752; Tally Ho Taxi 945-4225; Town Taxi 945-5671 or Yellow Cab 945-6441; Also Rental Cars: Avis 947-8383; Budget 945-9429; Dollar 947-0188; Hertz 942-5519; National 947-0158.
Information: Greater Bangor Chamber of Commerce, 519 Main Street, P.O. Box 1443, Bangor, ME 04401, Phone: 947-0307.

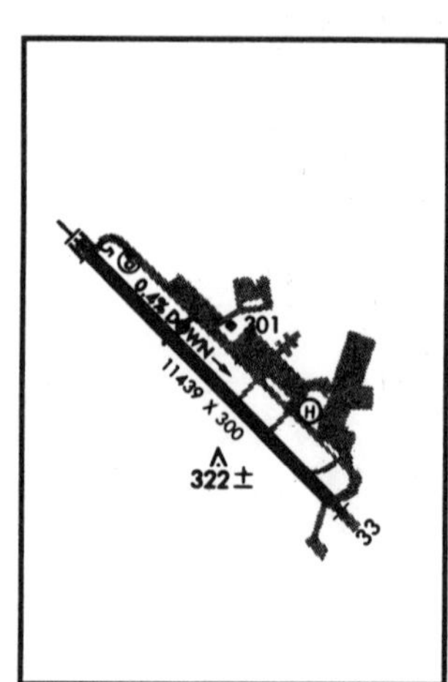

Airport Information:

BANGOR - BANGOR INTERNATIONAL AIRPORT (BGR)
3 mi west of town N44-48.45 W68-49.69 Elev: 192 Fuel: 100LL, Jet-A
Rwy 15-33: H11439x300 (Conc-Grvd) Attended continuously Atis: 127.75 Unicom: 122.95
App/Dep Con: 124.5, 125.3 Tower: 120.7 Gnd Con: 121.9 Clnc Del: 135.9
Notes: Landing fees for all aircraft over 12,500 lbs. and all revenue producing flights.
FBO: Bangor Aviation Service Phone: 947-1251

ME-BHB - BAR HARBOR
HANCOCK CO.-BAR HARBOR ARPT.

(Area Code 207)

3

Gateway Lobster Pound:

This restaurant offers casual family dining and is within an 8 minute walk from the airport. Take the wooded path along the road that parallel sthe airport property. Popular items on their menu include lobster, fresh steamed or fried seafood, shrimp, scallops and clams, along with barbecued steaks, ribs and chicken dishes. Daily specials are also offered. Prices average $8.98 to $9.98 for main entrees. The restaurant can seat about 75 people within the main dining room. An outdoor screened-in deck can seat an additional 60 people. Groups and fly-in associations are always welcome. This restaurant has been in business for the past 27 years. It is a popular stopping place for pilots all across the region. For information call the Gateway Lobster Pound at 667-2620.

Restaurants Near Airport:
Gateway Lobster Rest. 8 min walk Phone: 667-2620

Lodging: Colonial Motor Lodge (6 miles) 667-5548; Holiday Inn (6 miles) 667-9341; Isle View (Trans) 667-5661; Lobster House/ Quality Inn (1 mile, Trans) 667-9506.

Meeting Rooms: None reported

Transportation: Airport Taxi 667-5995; Avis 667-5421; Budget 667-1200; Hertz 667-5017.

Information: Chamber od Commerce, 93 Cottage Street, P.O. Box 158, Bar Harbor, ME 04609, Phone: 288-5103.

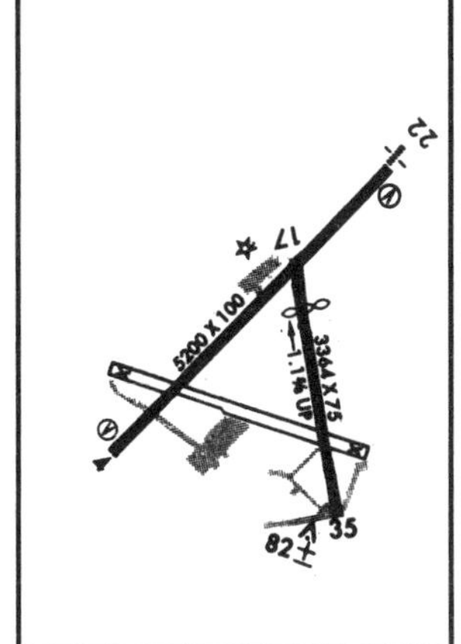

Airport Information:

BAR HARBOR - HANCOCK COUNTY-BAR HARBOR AIRPORT (BHB)
8 mi northwest of town N44-26.99 W68-21.69 Elev: 84 Fuel: 100LL, Jet-A
Rwy 04-22: H5200x100 (Asph) Rwy 17-35: H3364x75 (Asph) Attended: 1200Z-dusk
Unicom: 123.0
FBO: Acadia Air, Inc. Phone: 667-5534

ME-0B1 - BETHEL
COL DYKE FLD.

(Aera Code 207)

4

Sunday River Ski Resort:

Summit Hotel & Conference Center is a 4-story, 230 room complex that is located about 10 minutes or 6 or 7 miles from the Col Dyke Field (0B1). The resort has a restaurant that is open 7 a.m. to 11 a.m., noon to 3 p.m. and 5 p.m. to 10 p.m. Entertainment, gift shop, lighted tennis, 18-hole golf privileges, downhill and cross country skiing on site, and convention facilities able to accommodate 500 people in their banquet room and additional meeting rooms. Taxi service can be arranged by calling 824-6060. Also Bethel Air Service may be able to accommodate transportation needs, 824-4321. Shuttle service is also reported in the area. For information about the resort call 824-3500.

Attractions:

One of Maine's popular recreation areas is the Sunday River Ski Resort situated about 6 miles from the town of Bethel in Newry, ME. In the same area is the Locke Mills, Mount Abram Ski Area well known for its quality groomed snow trails. A number of fine cross country ski centers are located in the area. One additional attraction is the famous "Artists' Bridge" which is known as one of the most painted and photographed covered bridges in the state of Maine.

Restaurants Near Airport:

Bethel Inn & C.C.	N/A	Phone: 824-2175
Sunday River Ski Resort	6-7 mi	Phone: 824-3500

Lodging: Bethel Inn 1 mi 824-2175; Bethel Spa Motel 1 mi 824-3341; Norseman Inn 300 yds 824-2002; Summit Hotel & Conference Center 6-7 miles 824-3500; Bethel Inn & C.C. 824-2175.
Meeting Rooms: Summit Hotel & Conference Center 6-7 miles 824-3500; Bethel Inn & C.C. 824-2175.
Transportation: Taxi Service: 824-6060; Area shuttle bus service originating from town with stops at selected lodging locations; Bethel Air Service can also help with arranging trans. 824-4321.
Information: Bethel Chamber of Commerce, P.O. Box 439, Bethel, ME 04217, Phone: 824-2282.

Special Note:

Pilots that are planning to land at either Portland, or Auburn, Maine will be happy to know that there is a special Rail Express Train that departs Portland on it-way up to Bethel, Maine. It stops at Auburn to pick-up additional travelers. A bus connection will take skiers from the Bethel train station to the Sunday River Ski Resort.

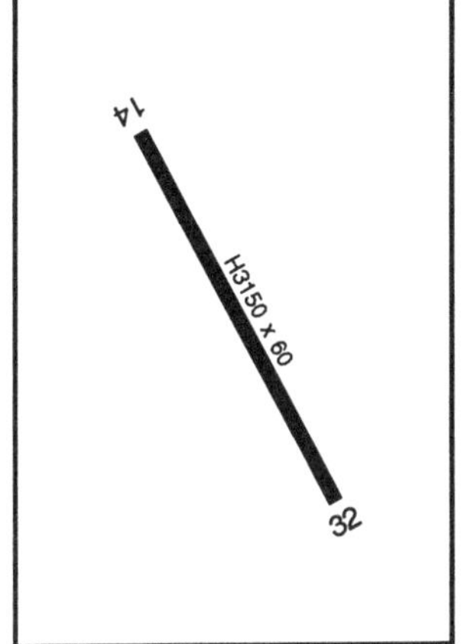

Airport Information:

BETHEL - COLD DYKE FLD (0B1)
2 mi northwest N44-25.50 W70.48.47 Elev: 654 Fuel: 100LL Rwy 14-32: H3150x60 (Asph)
Attended: 1300Z-dusk CTAF: 122.9 Notes: Rwy 32 closed sunset to sunrise. Gravel ramp closed; call 207-824-4321 for parking. Parking and landing fee reported.
FBO: Bethel Air Service Phone: 824-4321

ME-B21 - CARRABASSETT SUGARLOAF REGIONAL

(Area Code 207)

5, 6

Sugarloaf Inn:
Sugar loaf Ski Resort is located about 7 miles northwest of the Sugarloaf Regional Airport. This resort is at its high season during the winter months. However there are many summertime activities like golfing at their 18 hole course. During our conversation with the management, we learned that the base lodge contains all the services needed for skiing. Under the same managemant, Sugarloaf Inn contains 42 rooms and 325 condominiums with 2 to 5 bedrooms. Their dining room is open between 7 a.m. and 10 a.m. for breakfast and 6 p.m. to 9 p.m. for dinner. Meeting rooms are also available. Their services include: down-hill skiing on their premises, x-country skiing adj, fishing, hiking, whitewater rafting, mountain biking rentals, exercise room, whirlpool, sauna and steam room. Fly-in guests are asked to call ahead to let them know you are coming. There is a pay phone at the airport. For information about their services call 237-2000 or 800-843-5623 for ME residents.

Sugarloaf Mountain:
The Sugarloaf Mountain Hotel will provide local airport transportation. This establishment has 110 rooms contained in a 6 story complex. Many activities can be enjoyed from their location. Some of the services available include: family rates and packages for tennis, golf, skiing and rafting. Their restaurant is open 7 a.m. to 10 a.m. for breakfast and 6 p.m. to 9 p.m. for dinner. A lounge provides entertainment and dancing Thursday through Sunday during their skiing season. Meeting rooms are also available. A variety of sporting activities are located on their premises like tennis, downhill and x-county skiing. An 18 hole golf course and putting green is also available. Health club privileges, and a game room can be enjoyed. For information call Sugarloaf Mountain Hotel at 237-2222. ME residents can call 800-527-9879.

Attractions:
Sugarloaf/USA Ski Area: provides 6 Olympic runs and 45 miles of downhill trails. The vertical drop is 2,800 feet and the longest run is 3 miles. There are 65 miles of cross country ski trails in the area. For information call 237-2000. **Carrabassett Valley Ski Touring Center:** Has 50 miles of skiing trails. They also have accommodations including a lunch room, skiing school, ski rentals and a skating rink. For information call 237-2000.

Restaurants Near Airport:

Sugarloaf Inn	6-7 mi	Phone: 237-2000
Sugarloaf Mountain	6-7 mi	Phone: 237-2222

Lodging: Sugarloaf Inn (6-7 mi. trans) 237-2000; Sugarloaf Mountain (6-7 mi. trans) 237-2222.

Meeting Rooms: Sugarloaf Inn (6-7 mi. trans) 237-2000; Sugarloaf Mountain (6-7 mi. trans) 237-2222.

Transportation: Depending on available staff, both the Sugarloaf Inn and Sugarloaf Mountain will provide transportation to and from the Sugarloaf Regional Airport. Call ahead to let them know you are planning to arrive.

Information: Sugarloaf Area Chamber of Commerce, Valley Crossing, Carrabassett Valley, ME 04947, Phone: 235-2100.

Airport Information:
CARRABASSETT - SUGARLOAF REGIONAL (B21)
1 mi north of town N45-05.17 W70-12.97 Elev: 885 Rwy 17-35: H2800x75 (Asph) Attended: unattended Unicom: 122.8 Notes: High terrain 4,237 ft. MSL N/E/W of airport. Use cautions when windy conditions exist. Call ahead for runway conditions during winter season.

Sugarloaf Regional **Phone: 235-2288**
Sugarloaf Ski Resort **Phone: 237-2000**

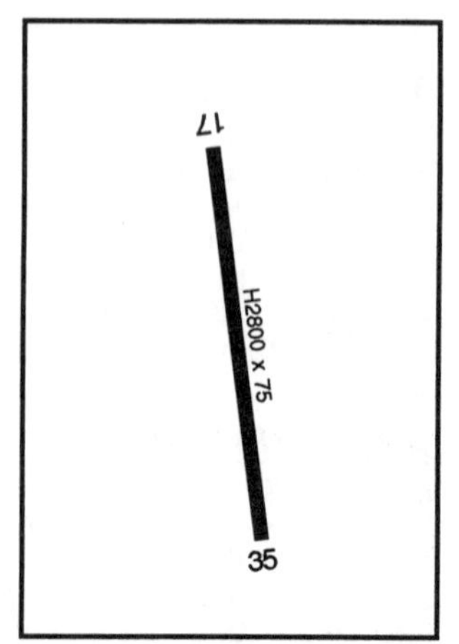

Not to be used for navigational purposes

ME-3B1 & 52B - GREENVILLE
GREENVILLE MUNI & SEAPLANE BASE

(Area Code 207) 7, 8

Kelly's Landing:

Kelly's Landing is a combination restaurant and lodging facility. It is located on the shore of Moosehead Lake in Greenville Junction, Maine. For those landing at (52B) the seaplane can taxi right up to their dock or beach. If planning to land at (3B1) Greenville Municipal Airport, you can call the restaurant and they will come and pick you up. Please let them know in advance you are coming. Kelly's Landing is 2-1/2 miles west on Route 7 to Greenville Junction. Their family style restaurant is open May through November from 7 a.m. to 9 p.m. and the remainder of the year from 11 a.m. to 8 p.m. Appetizers, homemade desserts, homemade style cooking, seafood, steaks and lasagna are their specialties. Sunday breakfast buffets (All you can eat) for $5.95 is a big favorite of local customers. Different daily specials are offered each day. Average prices for entrees run $3.50 for breakfast, $4.00 for lunch and $9.95 for dinner. The decor is modern with matching cedar booths and large tables. The restaurant seats 85 persons and caters to groups and parties. For information call 695-4438.

Whitman House Bed & Breakfast: (Not a restaurant)

The Whitman House is a bed and breakfast facility that is located on a hill overlooking the village of Greenville only a minute from Moosehead Lake. The house is a Georgian Revival buildt in the early 1900's. Enjoy the warm evening breeze on the veranda in the summer, or on those cool fall evenings relax in the living room by a warm, cozy fireplace. Make a selection from their book or movie library, work on the jigsaw puzzle or just relax and enjoy the quiet. A full breakfast is served every morning in the dining room which includes home baked goods by their in-house baker "BASIL". Unusual offerings may include Tennessee Pecan Breakfast Cake, Pennsylvania Fried Mush, hominy grits or whatever the cook feels like experimenting with. Most of their guests find that they need to skip lunch. In the late afternoon relax with a complimentary glass of wine, lemonade, fresh baked cookies or scones. CANOEING: They offer canoes and all the necessary equipment for their guests on Moosehead Lake. Use of the canoes is at no charge for any stay of two or more nights. For reservations at the Whitman House a one night deposit is required for confirmation. For more information call 695-3543 (See Lodging).

Restaurants Near Airport:

Kelly's Landing	2.5 mi W (3B1)	Phone: 695-4438
Kelly's Landing	Adj W (52B)	Phone: 695-4438
The Kineo House	20 mi N	Phone: 534-2293

Lodging: Chalet Moosehead 695-2950; Greenville Inn (Free Pick-up) 695-2623; Kelly's Landing 695-4438; Leisure Life 695-3737; Big Squaw Mountain Resort (Free Pick-up) 695-2272 res. or 800-842-6743. The Whitman House is a B & B located only 1/4 mile from downtown Greenville close to shopping. (Free transportation to and from airport). Call 695-3543.

Meeting Rooms: The Kineo House (20 miles north) 534-2293.

Transportation: Curriers Flying Service can provide courtesy transportation to local facilities, Phone: 695-2778. Kelly's Landing will shuttle guests to their facility. No public or rental car transportation reported by airport manager.

Information: Moosehead Lake Regional Chamber of Commerce, Main Street, P.O. Box 581, Greenville, ME 04441, Phone: 695-2720.

Attractions:

Moosehead Lake, largest in the state, is 40 miles long and 20 miles wide with many bays and inlets, islands, rivers and streams. This area is famous for moose-watching, fishing, camping, hiking and canoeing. In addition, it is a very popular float plane destination with a seaplane base at the southern tip. Kineo Resort & Golf Course is also located on Moosehead Lake; Big Squaw Mountain Ski Area (5 miles NW of town) attracts many skiers and vacationers each year.

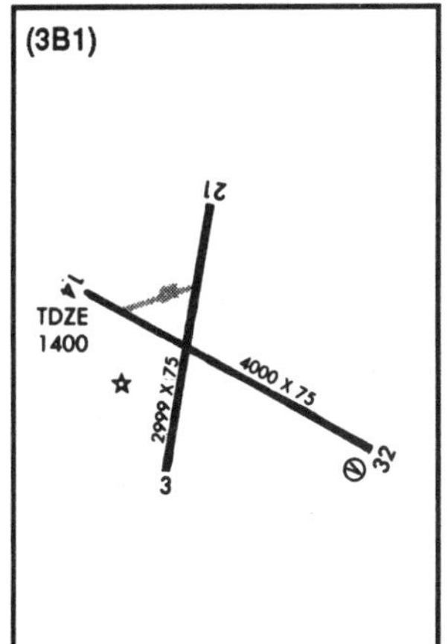

(52B)

Ramp
Ramp
GREENVILLE

Airport Information:

GREENVILLE - GREENVILLE MUNI & SEAPLANE BASE (3B1 & 52B)

(3B1) - 2 mi east of town 45-27-45N 69-33-04 Elev: 1400 Fuel: 100LL, Jet-A
Rwy 14-32: H4000x75 (Asph) Rwy 03-21: H2999x75 (Asph) Attended: unattended
Unicom: 122.8 Notes: Greenville Municipal Land Airport is located 2 miles east of Greenville.
FBO: Curriers Flying Service, Inc. Phone: 695-2778
FBO: Folsom's Air Service Phone: 695-2821

(52B) - 0 mi north of town 45-27-40N 69-35-54W Elev: 1028 Fuel 100LL Rwy 14-32: 6000x1200 (Water) Rwy 18-36: 5000x1000 (Water) Attended: 1300Z-Dusk Unicom: 122.8
Transportation: courtesy car; Notes: pattern altitude 2000' all aircraft.
Airport Phone: 695-2993, 695-2821.

Sky Lodge

The first settler, Captain Samuel Holden, came to Moose River in 1820 and built a cabin of logs. Today there stands on this original site, one of the largest of all log lodges in the northeast. In striking contrast to the first humble abode and over a century later, Richard Sutro of Port Chester, New York, built his Maw Paw Lodge. The corner stone dates to 1929.

The building was two years in construction. The spruce logs were from choice timber cut from nearby Burnt Jacket Mountain and were floated across Bigwood Lake in what is said to be the last log drive on the lake. Some logs used in the structure are more than fifty feet long. A mill and water system were set up to peel, draw, shave and notch corner the logs. The foundation and massive fireplace were built of fieldstone.

The great room with cathedral ceiling and exposed beams the length of the room, is an expansive space, accommodating two bow-shaped staircases leading to a balcony and entrances to the bedrooms.

According to local legends, the history of the Lodge is shrouded in mystery. If you just let your imagination go, you might wonder about the hidden compartments - one of which has never been found, and secret passages. Two of the guest rooms have ingenious false walls that defy detection, leading to stone lined strongholds that don't show on the building plans. Local townspeople talk of a tunnel beginning in the basement, crossing under the open field, and coming out into the woods. Dark and mysterious activities are speculated to have taken place here, but probably the truth behind the tangle of events will forever remain obscured.

In the 1940's the Lodge was sold and renamed Sky Lodge. Sky Lodge has since been a home away from home to many sports people and the traveling public.

Sky Lodge has a number of attractive amenities for their guests. A tranquil atmosphere on 125 acres surrounded by fields, forests, mountains and abundant wildlife; Twenty-seven spacious and comfortable bedrooms; Gym offering basketball, volleyball, ping-pong and more; Meeting room options ranging from cozy couches by a roaring fire, to a formal conference room setting. (Main lodge has ten working fireplaces.); Hot tub when it's cold, outdoor pool when it's warm; Their own professional white water rafting operation available for your service on two nearby rivers; Hunting, fishing, hiking, mountain biking, canoeing, cross country skiing and snowmobiling arranged by their guide staff; a small 9-hole golf course within walking distance, and A sitting room with large-screen T.V. and a video and book library.

Their rates range from their "Standard" package at $59.00 per person per day double occupancy, to their "Deluxe" package rate of $99.00 per person per day single occupancy. Applicable taxes, gratuities, alcoholic beverages, transportation and special activities such as white water rafting, are additional.

Sky Lodge is located about 2-1/2 miles from Newton Field in Jackman, ME. Courtesy airport transportation is provided to fly-in guests. Just let them know you are comming, and they will listen for your arrival on unicom 122.9. Newton field (59B) is 45-37-55N, 70-14-52W. It supports a Rwy 14-32: H2900x60 foot at an elevation of 1176 and is unattended. For more information about Sky Lodge call them at 207-668-2171.

Photo by: Sky Lodge "Luxury in the Rough" Sky Lodge provides a beautifull setting near mountains and lakes.

ME-MLT - MILLINOCKET
MILLINOCKET MUNICIPAL AIRPORT

(Area Code 207) 9

Restaurants Near Airport:
Lazy 8 Grill On Site Phone: 723-8696

Lazy 8 Grill:
The Lazy 8 Grill is situated within the terminal building adjacent to the Plain Air Flying Service (FBO). This snack bar specializes in preparing breakfast during weekends for fly-in customers. The grill is open between 7 a.m. and 11 a.m. on weekends. Specialties of the house include items like, 2 eggs any style with bacon, ham or sausage, and hash browns, or try their 3 egg omelets made with ham, cheese, green pepper and mushrooms. Still another favorite choice is the Texas style French toast. Additional entrees also included are their bacon cheeseburgers, hamburgers and sandwiches which can be prepared as well. This establishment can seat 12 to 15 persons in their dining area. Counter service with 4 stools, basic wood paneling and many windows facing the runway and parking ramp on the north side, providing an excellent view of the airport as well as providing a comfortable and relaxed atmosphere for their guests. For information about the Lazy 8 Grill, call them at 723-8696.

Lodging: Atrium 723-4555; Heritage Motor Inn 723-9777; Pamola Motor Lodge 723-9746.

Meeting Rooms: Atrium 723-4555; Heritage Motor Inn 723-9777.

Transportation: Plain Air Flying Service (FBO) has courtesy car available to nearby facilities; Also fly-in guests are able to walk (3/4 mile) to nearby locations; Lazy 8 Grill located in terminal building (FBO), ground transportation not necessary.

Information: Chamber of Commerce, 1029 Central Street P.O. Box 5, Millinocket, ME 04462, Phone: 723-4443.

Attractions:
Baxter State Park (25 miles northwest); Also West Branch, white water rafting available (35 miles northwest).

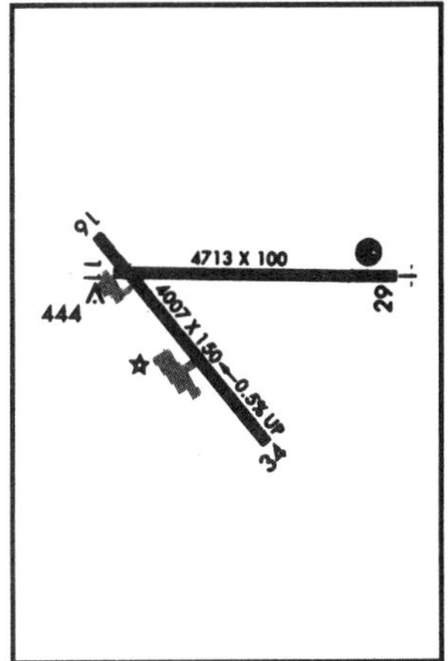

Airport Information:
MILLINOCKET - MILLINOCKET MUNICIPAL AIRPORT (MLT)
1 mi southeast of town N45-38.87 W68-41.13 Elev: 409 Fuel: 100LL
Rwy 11-29: H4716x100 (Asph) Rwy 16-34: H4007x150 (Asph) Attended: 1200Z-dusk
Unicom: 122.8 Notes: No landing fee, Tie-down fee $3.00 per day.
Airport Manager Phone: 723-6649

ME-81B - OXFORD
OXFORD CO REGIONAL

(Area Code 207) 10

Restaurants Near Airport:
Maurice Rest. Frances 2 mi Phone: 743-2532

Maurice Restaurant Frances:
The Maurice Restaurant is about 4 to 5 miles from the airport. We learned about this restaurant when interviewing the owner of a restaurant in New Hampshire with the same name and owned by relatives. This restaurant is classified as a fine dining establishment with unique qualities. Infact, it has been written up in several well-known newspapers like the New York Times, Chicago Tribune, San Francisco Inquirer, Miami Herald and even included as a restaurant in one of Steven King's novels. We were told that the restaurant would provide transportation for guests flying in to the Oxford County Regional airport if advance notice is given and depending on available staff. During the summer months this restaurant is quite busy. It has limited seating, so reservations are highly suggested. Their menu include choices like rack of lamb, duck, chateaubriand, baked stuffed sole, shrimp Alexander, Scampi and over 18 selections. This is a fine dining restaurant with candle lit tables, linen and set-ups. Prices range between $10.50 and $15.95 for complete dinner entrees. A full assortment of appetizers are also available. Escargots, smoked salmon, herring, smoked oysters are just a few. Their largest dining room has six tables, a second dining room can accommodate 4 tables and a third room which is a winterized porch can seat about 25 additional persons. We also were told that many people flyin to this restaurant on a regular basis. Hours of operation are 11:30 a.m. to 1:30 for lunch and 4:30 p.m. to 9:00 p.m. for dinner. For information call the restaurant at 743-2532.

Lodging: Ledgewood Motel 3 mi 743-6347.

Meeting Rooms: None reported

Transportation: Rental cars: Bessey Motors 743-6341

Information: Oxford Hills Chamber of Commerce, P.O. Box 167, South Paris, ME 04281, Phone: 743-2281.

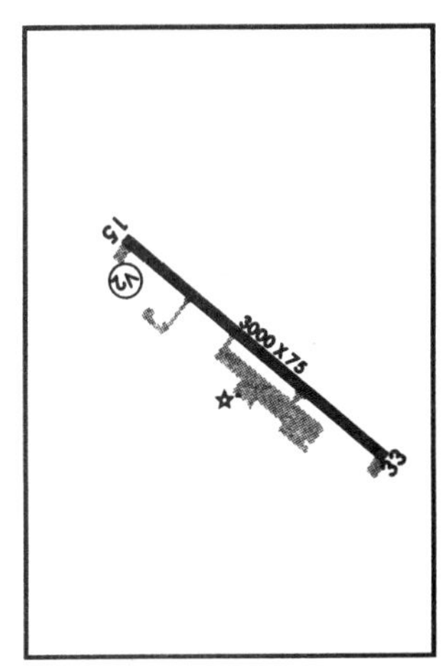

Airport Information:
OXFORD - OXFORD CO REGIONAL (81B)
2 mi east of town N44-09.39 W70-28.80 Elev: 346 Fuel: 100LL, Mogas Rwy: 15-33: H3000x75 (Asph) Attended: 1300-0100Z Unicom: 122.8
Airport Manager Phone: 539-4779

ME-87B - PORTAGE
PORTAGE LAKE MUNICIPAL (SEAPLANE BASE)

(Area Code 207) 11

Deans Motor Lodge:

Deans Motor Lodge is located about 1,000 feet from the Portage Lake Municipal Seaplane Base, and contains a family style restaurant that is open 5 a.m. to 8:30 p.m. 7 days a week. Their menu includes items like steamed and baked seafood selections as well as choice steaks such as prime rib, and sirloin along with a variety of sandwiches, hamburgers, cheeseburgers, soups, salads and home-made desserts. Daily specials are also available. The restaurant is carpeted and even a dance floor used during some weekends. Groups are also welcome, however larger parties should give advanced notice. Meals can also be prepared-to-go. In addition to the restaurant are 9 overnight guest rooms upstairs above the restaurant, 8 motel lodge rooms and 1 cabin able to accommodate 4 or 5 persons. For more information about the Deans Motor Lodge, call 435-3701.

Restaurants Near Airport:
Deans Motor Inn 1000 ft Phone: 435-3701

Lodging: Deans Motor Inn (Walking distance) 435-3701.

Meeting Rooms: Deans Motor Inn 435-3701.

Transportation: None Reported

Information: Presque Isle Chamber of Commerce, P.O. Box 672, Presque Isle, ME 04769, Phone: 764-6561.

NO AIRPORT DIAGRAM AVAILABLE

Airport Information:

PORTAGE - PORTAGE LAKE MUNICIPAL (SEAPLANE BASE) (87B)
0 mi west of town N46-45.75 W68-28.72 Elev: 609 Waterway 02-20: 5000x500 (Water)
Water 15-33: 5000x500 (Water) Unattended CTAF: Unicom: 122.9 Public Phone 24hrs
Portage Seaplane Base Phone: 435-6917

Not to be used for navigational purposes

ME-PWM - PORTLAND
PORTLAND INTL JETPORT

(Area Code 207) 12

Casco Bay Restaurant & Lounge (Host Intl.)

The Casco Bay Restaurant & Lounge operated by Host International, is located on the Portland International Jetport. This family style restaurant is open 7 days a week from 6 a.m. to 8 p.m. Their menu includes a variety of entrees including sandwiches like their lobster roll, Reuben grill, tuna melts, Maine clubs and marinated broiled chicken. For dinner selections, haddock, fisherman's platter, grilled chicken platters as well as fried clam strips, fried shrimp and fresh scallops. In-flight catering is also available from a special menu offering breakfast choices, as well as their "Sandwich Board" selection of lunch entrees along with main entrees for dinner, featuring specialties like the Casco Bay seafood platter, Maine lobster, Signature salad or the Darryl's picnic style chicken plate. Average prices run about $4.00 for breakfast, $5.35 for lunch and $8.95 for dinner. The special discounts of up to 20% at their food services facilities are available to pilots. The Casco Bay Restaurant & Lounge can seat 75 persons in two separate sections of the restaurant. The atmosphere is very casual with seating located near the windows, where guests can enjoy the view of the airport. For more information call 774-6372.

Attractions:

Numerous beaches, Casco Bay Islands, Funtown Amusement Park (20 minutes) 284-5139; Portland Old Port, shopping, art museum, etc. (15 minutes), hiking & autumn foliage, winter skiing, and fishing and hunting are available within this region. (See "Information").

Special Note:

Pilots that are planning to land at either Portland or Auburn, Maine will be happy to know that there is a special Rail Express Train that departs Portland on its way up to Bethel, Maine. It stops at Auburn to pickup additional travelers. A bus connection will take skiers from the Bethel train station to the Sunday River Ski Resort.

Sunday River Ski Resort:
Summit Hotel & Conference Center is a 4-story, 230 room complex that is located about 10 minutes or 6 or 7 miles from the Col Dyke Field (0B1). The resort has a restaurant that is open 7 a.m. to 11 a.m., noon to 3 p.m. and 5 p.m. to 10 p.m. Entertainment, gift shop, lighted tennis, 18-hole golf privileges, downhill and cross country skiing on site, and convention facilities able to accommodate 500 people in their banquet room and additional meeting rooms. Taxi service can be arranged by calling 824-6060. Also Bethel Air Service may be able to accommodate transportation needs, 824-4321. Shuttle service is also reported in the area. For information about the resort call 824-3500.

Additional Attractions in the Bethel area: One of Maine's popular recreation areas is the Sunday River Ski Resort situated about 6 miles from the town of Bethel in Newry, ME. In the same area is the Locke Mills, Mount Abram Ski Area well known for its quality groomed snow trails. A number of fine cross country ski centers are located in the area. One additional attraction is the famous "Artists' Bridge" which is known as one of the most painted and photographed covered bridges in the state of Maine.

Restaurants Near Airport:

Cafe Stroudwater	1/2 mi N.	Phone: 775-2200
Casco Bay (Host Intl.)	On Site	Phone: 774-6372

Lodging: Comfort Inn (Free trans) 775-0409; Hampton Inn (Free trans) 773-4400; Holiday Inn West (Free trans) 774-5601; Howard Inn By The Sea (Shuttle) 799-3134; Johnson (Shuttle) 774-5861; Marriott (Free trans) 871-8000; Sheraton TARA (Free trans) 775-6161; Sonesta (Free trans) 775-5411; Black Point Inn (Resort, Shuttle) 883-4126; Quality Suites (1/2 mile from airport).

Meeting Rooms: Airport conference rooms available at airport; Hampton Inn 773-4400; Holiday Inn West 774-5601; Howard Johnson 774-5861; Marriott (Convention facilities) 871-8000; Sheraton TARA (Convention facilities) 775-6161; Sonesta (Convention facilities) 775-5411; Quality Suites (1/2 mile from airport).

Transportation: Taxi cabs available at main terminal until last air carrier lands (12 a.m.); Jet Service of Portland 775-5635 and Northeast Air 774-6318 both will provide assistance for air travelers; Mainetour 7 Travel 775-4994; Town Taxi 773-1711.

Information: Convention & Visitors Bureau of Greater Portland, 142-Free Street, Portland, ME 04101, Phone: 772-5800.

Airport Information:

PORTLAND - PORTLAND INTL JETPORT (PWM)
2 mi west of town 43-38-46N 70-18-33W Elev: 74 Fuel: 100LL, Jet-A Rwy 11-29: H6800x150 (Asph-Pfc) Rwy 18-36: H5001x150 (Asph-Conc) Attended: 1100-0300Z
Atis: 119.05 Unicom: 122.95 Portland App/Dep Con: 119.75, 132.4 Tower: 120.9
Gnd Con: 121.9 Clnc Del: 121.65 Public Phone 24 hrs Notes: No landing fees reported
FBO: Northeast Air Phone: 774-6318
FBO: Jet Serv. of Portland Phone: 775-5635

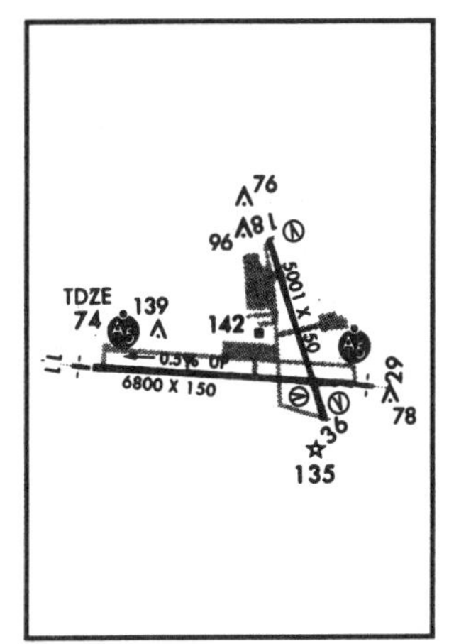

ME-PQI - PRESQUE ISLE NORTHERN MAIN REG. AT PRESQUE ISLE

(Area Code 207)

13

Keddy's Inn Solarium Restaurant:

This restaurant is located about 3 miles south of the Northern Main Regional Airport. Transportation will not be provided by this restaurant. However, you can call "General Aviation" at 764-2555 to see if they will accommodate your party with courtesy transportation. The restaurant is open from 6:30 a.m. to 9:30 p.m. Sunday and Monday and until 10 p.m. the rest of the week. They specialize in buffet style entrees along with a wide variety of selections on their menu, including prime rib, jumbo shrimp scampi, barbecued chicken and ribs. On Tuesday and Friday they serve a luncheon buffet, Sunday brunch and daily specials on Monday, Wednesday and Thursday. The decor is rustic with a solarium providing a view of the Western Aroostook County. Keddy's Inn has several meeting, banquet and convention facilities able to accommodate up to 800 people. Shopping and theaters are also located convenient to this location. For information call 764-3321.

Airport Information:

PRESQUE ISLE - NORTHERN MAIN REG. (PQI)
1 mi northwest of town N46-41.34 W68-02.69 Elev: 534
Fuel: 100LL, Jet-A Rwy 01-19: H7440x150 (Asph) Rwy 10-28: H5994x150 (Asph) Attended: Mon-Fri 1000-0100Z, Sat 1000-2200Z, Sun:1200-2300 Unicom: 122.8 Notes: Landing fee, N/A; Overnight Single $3.00 per night not to exceed $35 per month; Twin, $5.00 per night not to exceed $45 per month; Catering available, heated hangars, tiedowns, plane washing, deicing, and pilots room.
Airport Manager Phone: 764-2250

Restaurants Near Airport:

Carriage House	2 mi S.	Phone: 764-0039
Keddy's Inn	3 mi S.	Phone: 764-3321
Mai Tai	2 mi S.	Phone: 764-4426
Northeastland Hotel	2 mi S.	Phone: 768-5321

Lodging: Keddy's Motor Inn (3 miles south of airport), Phone: 764-3321; Northeastland Hotel (2 miles south of airport), Phone: 768-5321;
Meeting Rooms: Northeastland Hotel, Keddy's Motor Inn, and Carriage House, (See phone numbers listed above)
Transportation: "General Aviation FBO" will provide a courtesy car when able; Rental Cars & Taxi: Star City Taxi, 764-4431; Bill's Taxi, 764-1996; Avis Rental, 768-6761; Budget Rental, 764-1397; Hertz Rental, 768-6761; National Rental, 764-4937.
Information: Chamber of Commerce, P.O. Box 672, Presque Isle, ME 04769, Phone: 764-6561.

Attractions:

PQI Country Club, (5 miles east of airport) Phone: 769-7431; Aroostook State Park and Trans Atlantic Balloon Site: Location where the Double Eagle II was launched, for the first trip by balloon which took place in 1978 across the Atlantic Ocean. Also swimming, fishing, boating and camping in same location and area. (6 miles south of airport) Phone: 768-8341;

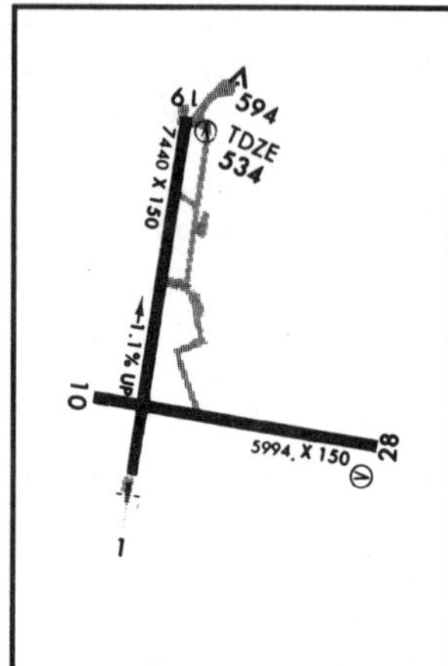

ME-SFM - SANFORD SANFORD MUNICIPAL AIRPORT

(Area Code 207)

14

Rudy's Cockpit Cafe:

Rudy's Cockpit Cafe is located in the terminal building at the Sanford Municipal Airport. This coffee shop is open between 6 a.m. and 2 p.m. Friday and Saturday. Check with operator for other times of operation. Their menu includes all types of sandwiches including cheeseburgers, and hamburgers along with a full selection of breakfast selections. Daily specials are also available. Average prices run around $4.95 for most entrees. According to the management, their main dining room can accommodate 60 people, with a view of airport activities as well. For more information about Rudy's Cockpit Cafe call 324-7332.

Restaurants Near Airport:

Lucas Sub Shop	200 ft.	Phone: 324-5660
Rudy's Cockpit Cafe	On Site	Phone: 324-7332
Weathervane Restaurant	1/2 mi	Phone: 324-0084

Lodging: Bar-H Motel (1/2 mile) 324-4662; Oakwood Inn (1/2 mile) 324-2160.

Meeting Rooms: None Reported

Transportation: Sanford Air, Inc has accommodations for courtesy transportation to nearby facilities. Also Access Transportation 800-233-2032; Sanford Taxi 490-1101; Regal Limousine 603-436-6516.

Information: Sanford-Sprinvale Chamber of Commerce, 261 Min Street, Sanford, ME 04073. Phone: N/A

Attractions:

Kennebunkport Beach (14 miles); Cape Arundel Golf Club (16 miles) 967-2222; Sanford Country Club (3 miles) 324-9712; Wells Beach, President Bush's Summer home.

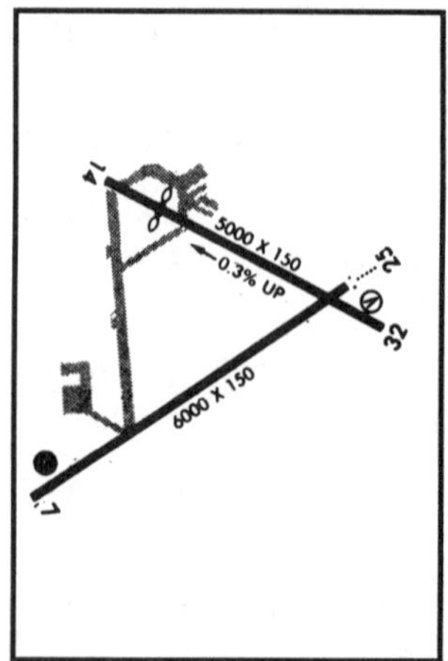

Airport Information:

SANFORD - SANFORD MUNICIPAL AIRPORT (SFM)
4 mi southeast of town N43-23.63 W70-42.48 Elev: 244 Fuel: 100LL, Jet-A
Rwy 07-25: H6000x150 (Asph) Rwy 14-32: H5000x100 (Asph) Attended: 1300Z-dusk
Unicom: 122.8 Clnc Del: 126.05 Notes: Overnight parking: Singles $4.00, Twins $10.00
FBO: American Jet Center Phone: 324-0968 or 800-519-2218
FBO: Sanford Air, Inc. Phone: 324-0905

ME-3B5 - TURNER TWITCHELL AIRPORT

(Area Code 207) 15

Chick-A-Dee Restaurant:

The Chick-A-Dee Restaurant is only a two minute walk from the Twitchell Airport. This family style restaurant is open Sunday, Monday, Wednesday and Thursday from 10 a.m. to 8 p.m. and Friday and Saturday from 10 a.m. to 9 p.m. They are closed on Tuesday. 80% of their menu specializes in seafood selections as well as other specialties of the house, such as fried chicken, steaks and sandwiches along with a variety of soups and chowders. Average prices run $3.95 for lunch and $7.95 to 8.95 for dinner. Daily specials are also available. There are "All you can eat" specials reported on Monday, Wednesday and Thursday. The main dining area can accommodate 150 persons within a recently remodeled room. Booths and tables allow for comfortable seating while a large table provides space for groups up to 30 persons. Take-out and carry out meals can also be arranged. During our conversation we were told that this restaurant has been in business for the past 60 years and continues to provide fine meals for local as well as fly-in customers. For more information about the Chick-A-Dee Restaurant call 225-3523.

Restaurants Near Airport:

Chick-A-Dee	1/4 mi S.	Phone: 225-3523
L & P Variety	1/8 mi	Phone: 225-3752

Lodging: Round House (5 miles) 784-1331.

Meeting Rooms: None Reported

Transportation: Twitchell's Airport has a courtesy car available to nearby facilities 225-3490; Also Rental Cars: Fordland 784-2321; Rent-A-Relic 784-5438.

Information: Androscoggin County Chamber of Commerce, 179 Lisbon, P.O. Box 59, Lewiston, ME 04243-0059, Phone: 783-2249.

NO AIRPORT DIAGRAM AVAILABLE

Airport Information:

TURNER - TWITCHELL AIRPORT (3B5)
4 mi south of town N44-11.25 W70-13.97 Elev: 356 Fuel: 100LL, MOGAS
Rwy 12-30: H2340x50 (Asph) Rwy 11-29: 2200x200 (Turf) Attended: 1200-0000Z
Unicom: 122.8 Public Phone 24hrs
FBO: Turner Aviation Phone: 225-3490

MARYLAND

LOCATION MAP

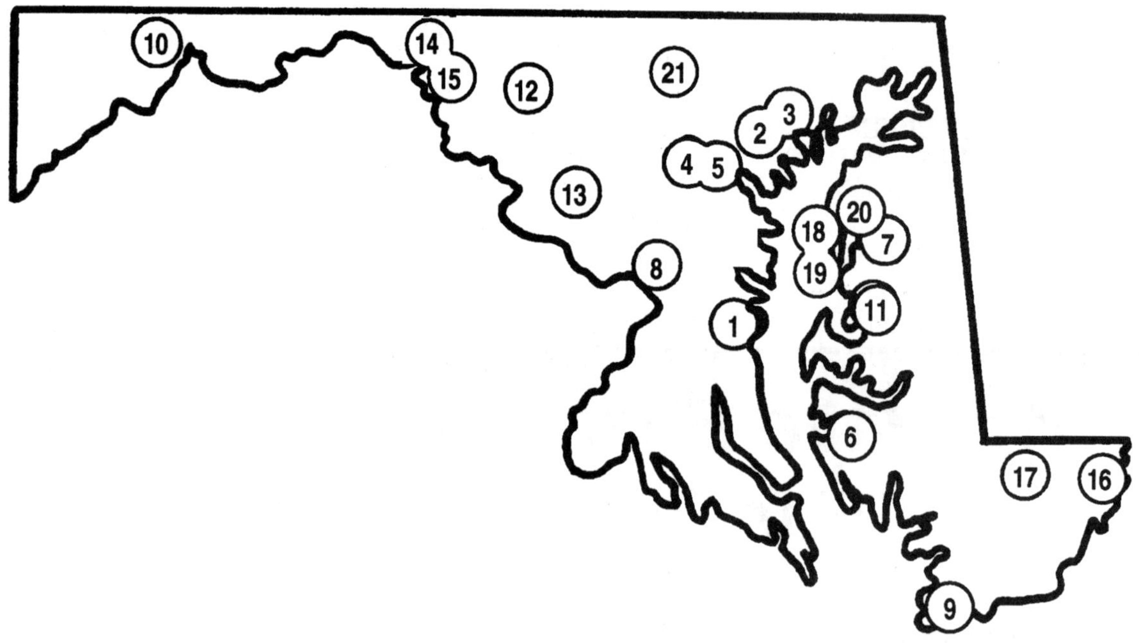

Not to be used for navigational purposes

MARYLAND

CROSS FILE INDEX

Location Number	City or Town	Airport Name And Identifier	Name of Attraction
1	Annapolis	Lee Arpt. (ANP)	Hayman's Crab House
2	Baltimore	Martin State Arpt. (MTN)	Crab Quarters, Inc.
3	Baltimore	Martin State Arpt. (MTN)	River Watch Restaurant
4	Baltimore	Washington Intl. Arpt. (BWI)	Ck's Restaurant
5	Baltimore	Washington Intl. Arpt. (BWI)	Lobby Cafe
6	Cambridge	Cambridge/Dorchester (CGE)	Runway Cafe
7	Chestertown	Scheeler Field Arpt. (0W7)	Buzz's Restaurant
8	College Park	College Park Arpt. (CGS)	94th Aero Squadron
9	Crisfield	Crisfield Muni. Arpt. (W41)	My Fair Lady B & B
10	Cumberland	Cumberland Arpt. (CBE)	Hagenbuch Restaurant
11	Easton	Easton Muni Arpt. (ESN)	Hangar Cafe
12	Frederick	Frederick Muni. Arpt. (FDK)	Airport Cafe
13	Gaithersburg	Montgomery Co. Arpt. (GAI)	Air Cafe
14	Hagerstown	Washington Co. Reg. (HGR)	Colonial Restaurant
15	Hagerstown	Washington Co. Reg. (HGR)	Nick's Airport Inn
16	Ocean City	Ocean City Muni. (N80)	Ocean City Boardwalk
17	Salisbury	Wicomico Co. Reg. (SBY)	Smugglers Cove
18	Stevensville	Bay Bridge (W29)	Hemmingways Rest.
19	Stevensville	Bay Bridge (W29)	Kent Manor Inn
20	Stevensville	Kentmorr Airpark (3W3)	Kentmorr Harbour Rest..
21	Westminster	Carroll Co. Reg. (W54)	Bullock's Airport Inn

MD-ANP - ANNAPOLIS
LEE AIRPORT

(Area Code 410) 1

Hayman's Crab House:

The Hayman's Crab House is located across the street from the Lee Airport in Annapolis, Maryland. This Family style restaurant can easily be reached by walking. Their hours are 11 a.m. to 9 p.m. on weekdays and 11 a.m. to 10 p.m. on weekends. Their menu offers a full seafood selection including hard crab, all types of delicious fresh fish platters, flounder, seafood salads, and homemade crab cakes as well as stuffed lobster. Average prices run $5.95 to $6.95 for lunch and between $8.95 and $17.95 for dinner. The main dining room can accommodate up to 90 persons, and exhibits a clean friendly nautical atmosphere. Everything on their menu can also be ordered to-go. In-flight catering is available as well, by calling the restaurant at 798-9877.

Restaurants Near Airport:

Hayman's Crab House	Adj Arpt	Phone: 798-9877
Paul's Restaurant	5 mi S. of river	Phone: 956-3410

Lodging: Holiday Inn (3 miles) 224-3150.

Meeting Rooms: None Reported

Transportation: Yellow Cab 268-3737

Information: Annapolis & Anne Arundel County Conference and Visitors Bureau, 26 West Street, Annapolis, MD 21401, Phone: 268-TOUR.

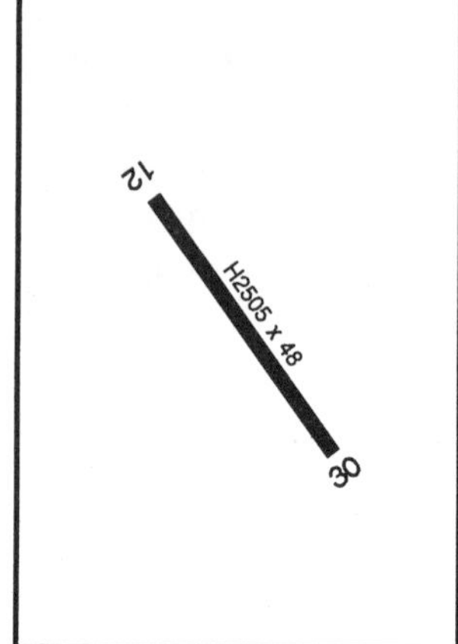

Airport Information:

ANNAPOLIS - LEE AIRPORT (ANP)
5 mi southwest of town N38-56.57 W76-34.13 Elev: 30 Fuel: 100LL
Rwy 12-30: H2505x48 (Asph) Attended: Apr-Oct 1200-0000Z, Nov-Mar 1200-2200Z
Unicom: 122.9
FBO: Chesapeake Aviation Service, Inc. Phone: 956-4129

MD-MTN - BALTIMORE MARTIN STATE AIRPORT

(Area Code 301)

2, 3

Crab Quarters, Inc.

The Crab Quarters Restaurant is located 1-1/2 miles from the Baltimore Martin State Airport. This family style restaurant is open Monday through Thursday from 11:30 a.m. to 11 p.m., Friday from 11:30 a.m. to 12 p.m. and Saturday and Sunday from 1 p.m. to 12 midnight. They serve soups, appetizers, salads, sandwiches, dinners and desserts. They also serve steamed crab, steamed shrimp, oysters, clams, and mussels. All food is prepared fresh daily. Prices average $5.95 for lunch and $13.95 for dinner. Daily lunch and dinner specials are featured. The decor is nautical, with a warm casual atmosphere. They offer a full service bar and eccept Visa, Mastercard and American Express. Fly-in groups are welcome with reservations made in advance. This facility also provides seafood carry-out with fresh fish trays, including shrimp, clams, oysters, mussels, crab meat, lobster and crab salad. For information call 686-2222.

River Watch Restaurant/Marina:

This combination family style and fine dining establishment is located about 4 miles from the Martin State Airport, and is open Monday through Sunday from 11:30 a.m. to 10:30 p.m. Their menu consists of entrees specializing in seafood and steaks. Average prices for a meal run $5.50 for lunch and $15.50 for dinner. Buffets for pre-arranged parties as well as daily specials include fresh fish of the day and chicken dishes. This restaurant has a nautical decor in a casual atmosphere. You can enjoy a meal while enjoying the view of the waterfront. Live entertainment Wednesday through Sunday is also provided. For information call 687-1422.

Attractions:

Rocky Point Beach & Park (5 miles) - swimming & fishing - Rocky Pt. Rd., 574-9732; Rocky Pt. Golf Course (5 miles) - Back River Neck Road, 877-0215; Inner Harbor (9 miles) - dining, paddle boats, aquarium, Science Center, Constellation, shopping, all within this area; The Airport, "offers a friendly home-like atmosphere with a pilots's lounge as comfortable as your living room. Enjoy their famous MD Steamed crabs, take a cruise on the Cheseapeak Bay." For many attractions available within this area, contact the Baltimore Visitors Information Center listed above under "Information".

Restaurants Near Airport:

A-1	3 mi	Phone: 687-6000
Capt. Cafe	1 mi	Phone: 682-4581
Crab Quarters	2 mi	Phone: 686-2222
Riverwatch	4 mi	Phone: 687-1422

Lodging: No lodging will pick up. However, the FBO will take customers to lodging facilities and pickup; Super 8 Motel, 98 Stemmers Run Road, Essex, MD, Phone: 780-0030; Susse Chalet, (4 miles) 8724 Philadelphia Road, Rosedale, MD, Phone: 574-8100

Transportation: Airport has a courtesy van; U-Save Rental Car, 682-8810; Atwater Taxi, 682-2100; Metro-Train, 539-5000; MTA Buses, 539-5000; Marc-Train, 800-325-7245

Conference Rooms: The Airport has meeting rooms available

Information: Baltimore Area Visitors Center, 1E Pratt St, Constellation Pier, MD 21202, Phone: 837-INFO or 800-282-6632.

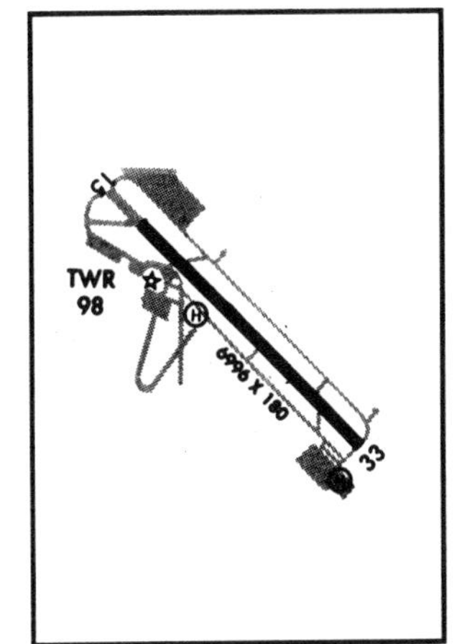

Airport Information:

BALTIMORE - MARTIN STATE AIRPORT (MTN)

9 mi east of town N39-19.54 W76-24.83 Elev: 22 Fuel: 100LL, Jet-A Rwy 15-33: H6996x180 (Conc) Attended: 1200-0400Z Unicom: 122.95 Baltimore App/Dep Con: 119.0 Martin Tower: 121.3 Clnc Del: 121.8 Atis: 124.925 Gnd Con: 121.8

Notes: CAUTION seagulls on and in vicinity of airport.

FBO: Martin State Airport Phone: 682-8810, 682-8800

MD-BWI - BALTIMORE WASHINGTON INTERNATIONAL AIRPORT

(Area Code 410)

4, 5

CK's Restaurant & Lounge (Host International):

CK's Restaurant is located in the main terminal building near the center of the concourse situated behind the ticket counters. Transportation to the terminal building and restaurant can be arranged by Signature Flight Support (FBO) or available taxi service. CK's is classified as a fine dining establishment that is open Monday through Friday from 7 a.m. to 8 p.m. and Saturday and Sunday from 7 a.m. to 7 p.m. Their menu includes specialty seafood dishes like, Maryland crab cakes, Chesapeake chowder, and different types of sandwiches, as well as breakfast items. Average prices run $6.25 for breakfast, $8.95 for lunch and $12.95 for most dinner entrees. The dining area has a modern and contemporary decor, and for groups or parties, additional rooms are made available with advance notice. CK's also provides catering requests. For more information call CK's Restaurant at 859-8350.

Lobby Cafe:

The Lobby Cafe is located within the Baltimore Washington International Marriott Hotel. After arriving at the airport, you can call the hotel shuttle bus and they will pick you up. According to the General Manager it is only a 5 minute ride to the hotel. The Lobby Cafe is a family style restaurant that is open Monday through Friday serving breakfast from 6 a.m. to 11 a.m. and lunch from 11 a.m. to 2 p.m. On Saturday and Sunday they are open from 7 a.m. to 12:00 noon and 5 p.m. to 10 p.m. for dinner. Entree selections include a full menu with soup and salad bar. Seafood is their specialty as well as steaks and chicken dishes. Average prices are $7.00 for breakfast, $9.00 for lunch and $14.00 for dinner. They feature a breakfast buffet on Monday through Friday between 6 a.m. and 9 a.m. for only $7.25 and Saturday and Sunday from 7 a.m. to 12 p.m. for $7.95. The dining room displays soft earth tones and overlooks a waterfall within the swimming pool area. Groups and parties are also welcome with advance notice through the restaurant manager. For more information call 859-8300 ext. 256.

Restaurants Near Airport:

CK's Restaurant	On Site	Phone: 859-8350
Lobby Cafe	1 mi	Phone: 859-8300
Michener's Restaurant	1 mi	Phone: 859-3300
The Rose	6 mi	Phone: 789-9100

Lodging: Sheraton/BWI Airport 859-3300; BWI Holiday Inn 859-8400; BWI Marriott 859-8300; Comfort Inn 789-9100; Guest Quarters 850-0747.

Meeting Rooms: Sheraton/BWI Airport 859-3300.

Transportation: 24 hour taxi service available: GTP Taxi Service 859-1100; Airport Shuttle 859-0800; Rental Cars: Avis 859-1691; Budget 859-0850; Hertz 850-7404; Budget 859-0850.

Information: Baltimore Area Visitors Center, 1E Pratt Street, Constellation Pier, Maryland, MD 21202, Phone: 837-INFO or 800-282-6632.

Airport Information:

BALTIMORE - WASHINGTON INTERNATIONAL AIRPORT (BWI)

9 mi south of town N39-10.52 W76-40.09 Elev: 146 Fuel: 100LL, Jet-A
Rwy 15R-33L: H9519x150 (Asph-Grvd) Rwy 10-28: H10502x200 (Asph-Grvd)
Rwy 04-22: H6005x150 (Asph-Grvd) Rwy 15L-33R: H5000x100 (Asph-Grvd)
Attended: continuously Atis: 115.1, 127.8 Unicom: 122.95 App Con: 119.0, 124.55, 119.7, 128.7 Dep Con: 133.75 Baltimore Tower: 119.4 Gnd Con: 121.9
Clnc Del: 118.05 Public Phone 24hrs Notes: Landing or overnight tiedown fees: Single engine $11.00 min/$10.00, Twin engine $11.00 min/ $10.00 to $20.00
FBO: Signature Flight Support Phone: 859-8393

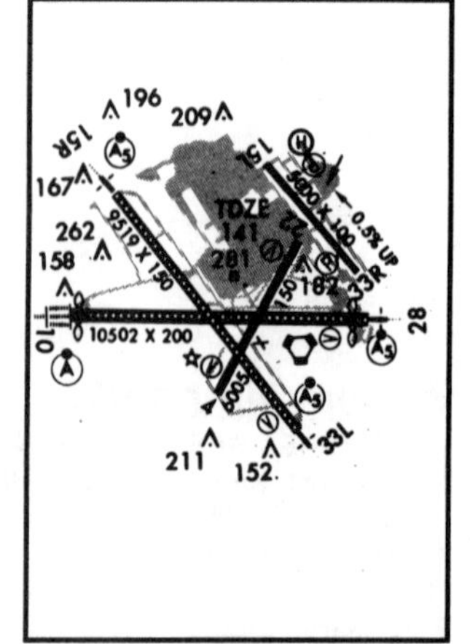

Not to be used for navigational purposes

MD-CGE - CAMBRIDGE CAMBRIDGE/DORCHESTER

(Area Code 410)

6

Runway Cafe:

The Runway Cafe is situated on the Cambridge/Dorchester Airport. This family style restaurant is reported to be open from 6 a.m. to 3 p.m. Monday through Saturday (Closed Sundays). Pilots can park close to the restaurant and walk from the tie-down ramp. This restaurant offers a contemporary atmosphere with a small but clean and well kept facility. They specialize in serving delicious breakfast selections. For lunch they also have a variety of sandwiches, homemade soups and salads available. There are about 12 tables for seating within the restaurant. Fly-in groups are welcome with advance notice preferred. Guests can see the aircraft parking area and airport activity from the restaurant, while enjoying their meal. For more information about this restaurant call the Runway Cafe at 221-0883.

Restaurants Near Airport:
Runway Cafe On Site Phone: 221-0883

Lodging: Econo Lodge 1 mi 221-0800; Quality Inn 1-3 mi 228-6900.

Meeting Rooms: None related

Transportation: Rental Cars: Ocean Hiway Exxon 228-2322; SKS Auto 228-5300.

Information: Cambridge-Dorchester Chamber of Commerce, 203 Sunburst Hwy. Cambridge, MD 21613, Phone: 228-3575.

Attractions:

On the third weekend in May, the Annual Antique Aircraft Fly-in is held featuring vintage and antique aircraft. For information you can call the Cambridge-Dorchester Heritage Museum at 228-5530 or 1899. Or the Cambridge-Dorchester Airport at 228-4571.

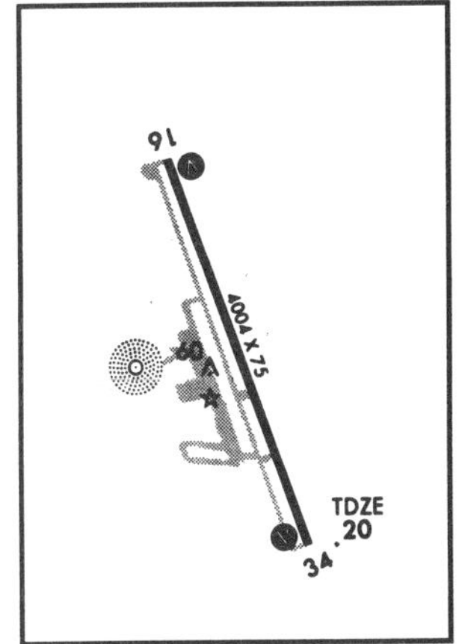

Airport Information:

CAMBRIDGE - CAMBRIDGE DORCHESTER (CGE)
3 mi southeast of town N38-32.36 W76-01.82 Elev: 20 Fuel: 100LL, Jet-A Rwy 16-34: H4004x75 (Asph) Attended: 1300Z-dusk Unicom: 122.7
FBO: Airport Manager Phone: 228-4571

MD-0W7 - CHESTERTOWN SCHEELER FIELD AIRPORT

(Area Code 410)

7

Buzz's Restaurant:

Buzz's Restaurant is located 1 mile from the Scheeler Field Airport. Courtesy transportation is provide by this facility. This is a family style restaurant that is open from 7 a.m. to 9:30 p.m. on weekdays and 7 a.m. to 10 p.m. on Friday and Saturday. A nice variety of entrees are available which include choice steaks such as rib eye, prime rib and New York strip. Seafood items and poultry dishes are also featured, as well as a full breakfast line. A breakfast buffet is also offered on Sunday from 8 a.m. to 11 a.m. which is a favorite with of the locals as well as many fly-in customers. Their dining room can handle about 100 people, and is nicely decorated with red and black paneling and glassed-in windows. During our conversation with the owner, we learned that this particular restaurant is very popular with pilots from near and far. At the time of this writing we also learned that a new airport is in the planning stage fairly near the Scheeler Field Airport. The owner seemed very receptive to providing fly-in customers with transportation, from either airport they decide to land at. For more information call Buzz's Restaurant at 778-1222.

Restaurants Near Airport:
Buzz's Restaurant 1 mile Phone: 778-1222

Lodging: None Reported

Meeting Rooms: None Reported

Transportation: Taxi 778-0088 or Rental Car: Gowo's Automotive Service 778-4361.

Information: Maryland Office of Tourism Development, 217 East Redwood Street, Baltimore, MD 21202, Phone: 800-543-1036.

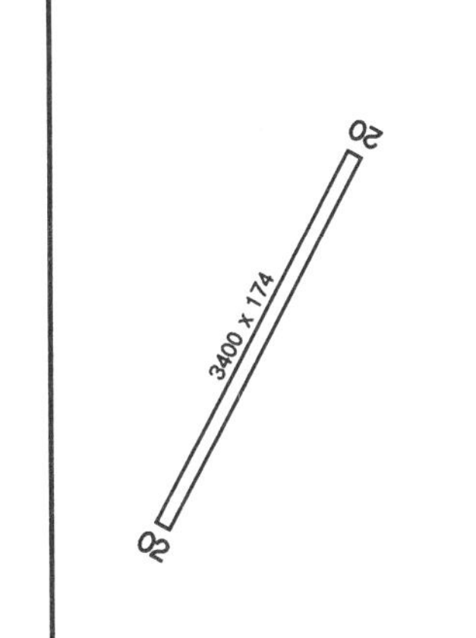

Airport Information:

CHESTERTOWN - SCHEELER FIELD AIRPORT (0W7)
2 mi north of town N39-13.97 W76-04.15 Elev: 70 Rwy 02-20: 3400x174 (Turf) Attended: irregularly Unicom: 122.7 Scheeler
Airport Manager Phone: 778-1222

MD-CGS - COLLEGE PARK
COLLEGE PARK AIRPORT

(Area Code 301)

8

94th Aero Squadron:

The 94th Aero Squadron Restaurant is located about 1/4th of a mile from the aircraft parking area, and can easily be reached by walking, according to the restaurant manager. This unique restaurant is one of several 94th Aero Squadron establishments located across the country, and provides fly-in guests with a choice of quality cuts of beef and steak selections. Their specialties include aged steaks, prime rib, fresh seafood, chicken and pasta dishes. Average prices run $9.00 to $10.00 for lunch and up to $23.00 for some dinner selections. They also provide daily specials. The restaurant is open for lunch between 11 a.m. and 3:30 p.m. and dinner from 5 p.m. to 9:30 p.m. 7 days a week. They can accommodate up to 250 persons within separate rooms all tastefully decorated with WW-I artifacts, phonographs of company squadrons, and pieces of aircraft hanging from walls and ceilings. Large groups are also welcome with advance notice. Meals can be prepared-to-go as well. For more information about this restaurant, call the 94th Aero Squadron at 699-9400.

Restaurants Near Airport:

94th Aero Squadron	On Site	Phone: 699-9400

Lodging: Holiday Inn (2 miles) 345-6700
Meeting Rooms: There is a conference room located at the airport.
Transportation: Taxi Service: Yellow Cab 864-7700; Rental Cars: Enterprise Rental Car 345-6070; Thrifty Car Rental 927-0012.
Information: Prince George's Conference & Visitors Bureau, 9475 Lottsford Road, #130, Landover MD 20785, Phone: 925-8300.

Attractions: Airport Museum located at the College Park Airport 864-1530; Attractions also available throughout the Washington D.C. area only 10 miles from the airport location. We learned from one of our contributors that the College Park Metro stop was commissioned on December 1993 (Green Line). Riders can now walk 1/4 mile to the train station and take the Metro line to downtown D.C. Many attraction including the Smithsonian, Air and Space museum are easily accessible from this location.

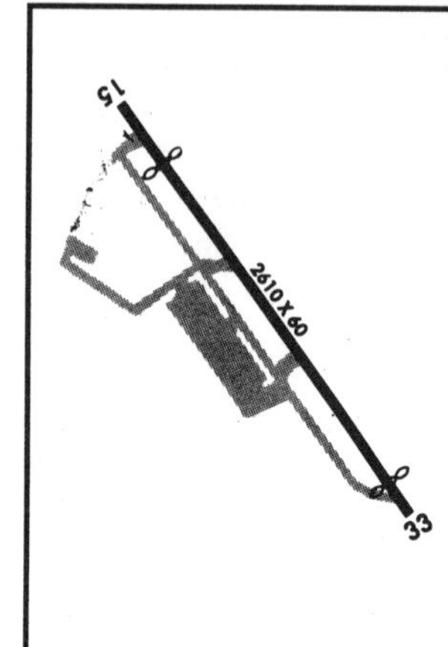

Airport Information:

COLLEGE PARK - COLLEGE PARK AIRPORT (CGS)
1 mi east of town N38-58.84 W76-55.35 Elev: 50 Fuel: 80, 100LL Rwy 15-33: H2610x60 (Asph) Attended: continuously Unicom: 123.0 Public Phone 24hrs Notes: Overnight parking Singles $5.00, and Twins $7.00
FBO: College Park Airport Phone: 864-5844

MD-W41 - CRISFIELD
CRISFIELD MUNICIPAL AIRPORT

(Area Code 410)

9

My Fair Lady Bed and Breakfast:

My Fair Lady Bed and Breakfast is located in Crisfield, on the eastern shore of Maryland. Crisfield Municipal Airport is located about 2 1/2 miles from the Inn. Transportation to and from the airport is provided upon request. Guests stay in an elegant Queen Anne Victorian home and enjoy the modern amenities of a private bath, air conditioning and television in each room. They can swing or sit on the comforable wraparound porch. Or, stroll on the dock and watch the watermen bring in their bounty of crabs. They can also visit the Tawes Museum or the home of the world-renowned Ward Brothers, master wood carvers. Or, take a tour boat ride to Smith Island, Maryland and Tangier Island, Virginia. Boats leave the dock daily at 12:30 p.m. and return in time for the sunset on the bay. The Inn is open year-round, except for January and part of February. Children 14 and over are welcome. Room rates include a full Continental breakfast. Midweek stays (Monday through Thursday) qualify for a 10% discount. A 50% deposit is required on all reservations. For more information about My Fair Lady Bed and Breakfast, call 968-3514.

Restaurants Near Airport:

Capt. Galley	N/A	Phone: 968-3313
Circle Inn	N/A	Phone: 968-1969
My Fair Lady B&B	2 1/2 mi	Phone: 968-3514
Side St. Seafood Market	2 mi	Phone: 968-2442
Waterman's Inn	2 mi	Phone: 968-2119

Lodging: My Fair Lady Bed and Breakfast (2 1/2 miles) 968-3514; Paddle Wheel Motel 968-2220; Pines Motel 968-0900; Somers Cove Motel 968-1900
Meeting Rooms: None Reported
Transportation: My Fair Lady Bed and Breakfast will provide transportation to and from airport. Phone: 968-3514; Taxi Service: Reliance 968-9880
Information: Crisfield Area Chamber of Commerce, P.O. Box 292, Crisfield, MD 21817, Phone: 968-2500

Attractions:

Every year, Crisfield hosts a Crab and Clam Bake which is held on the 3rd Wednesday in July. On Labor Day wknd., the town celebrates with a Crab Derby, colorful parades, boat races and crafts exhibits. Call 968-2500. For information about Tangier Island Cruises in Crisfield, call 968-2338.

NO AIRPORT DIAGRAM AVAILABLE

Airport Information:

CRISFIELD - CRISFIELD MUNICIPAL AIRPORT (W41)
3 mi northeast of town N38-01.01 W75-49.73 Elev: 4 Fuel: 80, 100LL Rwy 06-24: 3440x215 (Turf) Rwy 14-32: H2490x75 (Asph) Attended: Mon, Wed & Fri 0900- 1800Z, and Sat, Sun, Holidays 0900-1900, CTAF/Unicom: 122.8 Notes: Turf areas of airport may be soft. No landing fees, overnight tiedowns $5.00.
FBO: Crisfield Aviation Services Phone: 968-1572

MD-CBE - CUMBERLAND
CUMBERLAND AIRPORT

(Area Code 304) **10**

Hagenbuch Restaurant:

The Hagenbuch Restaurant is located about 1 mile and across the bridge from the Cumberland Airport. Transportation to and from the restaurant can be arranged through the airport FBO's according to the restaurant manager. This combination family style and fine dining facility is open at 8 a.m. to 8 p.m. 7 days a week. Entrees offered on their menu are wide and varied, including such items as their char-broiled steaks, seafood, spaghetti, and different types of sandwiches as well as salads. Average prices run $1.00 to $5.00 for breakfast and around $5.00 to $6.00 for lunch and dinner. Groups and parties are also welcome. There are two separate dining rooms, one able to hold 60 persons, and the other can accommodate about 80 people. When speaking to the owner, we learned that the Hagenbuch Restaurant also provides in-flight catering as well. Just call the restaurant and make arrangements. For more information about this facility call 738-9907.

Restaurants Near Airport:
Hagenbuch Restaurant 1 mile Phone: 738-9907

Lodging: Braddock Motor Inn (7 miles) 729-3300; Continental Motor Inn (7 miles, Trans) 729-2201; Holiday Inn (3 miles) 724-8800; Super 8 (7 miles) 729-6265; Turkey Flight Manor (4 miles) 777-3553.

Meeting Rooms: Continental Motor Inn (7 miles, Trans) 729-2201

Transportation: Taxi Service: Yellow Taxi 722-4050; Allegany Limo 777-8083; Rental Cars: Hertz 722-2522.

Information: Allegany County Tourism & Public Relations, Western MD Station Center, Canal Street, Cumberland, MD 21502, Phone: 777-5905 or 800-50-VISIT.

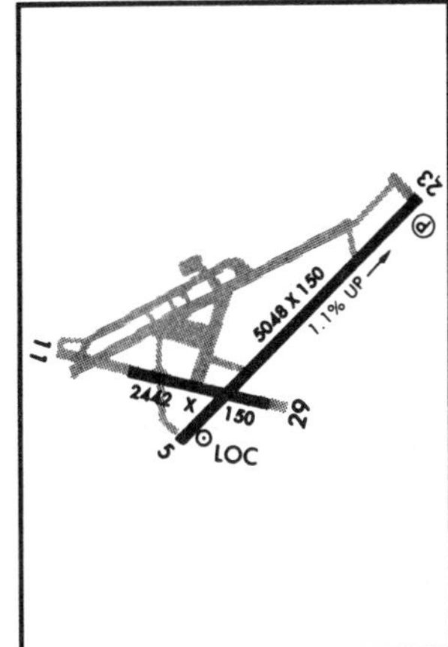

Airport Information:

CUMBERLAND - CUMBERLAND AIRPORT (CBE)
2 mi south of town N39-36.91 W78-45.71 Elev: 776 Fuel: 100LL, Jet-A
Rwy 05-23: H5048x150 (Asph-Grvd) Rwy 11-29: H2442x150 (Asph) Attended: Mon-Thu 1030-0130Z Fri-Sun 1030-0000Z Unicom: 122.8
FBO: Corporate Jets Airport Management Phone: 738-0002
FBO: Summerfield Aviation Phone: 738-2252

MD-ESN - EASTON
EASTON MUNICIPAL AIRPORT

(Area Code 410) **11**

Hangar Cafe:

The Hangar Cafe is located within the terminal building at the Easton Municipal Airport and is only about 30 feet from the aircraft parking area. This cafe is open on weekends from 6:30 a.m. to 3 p.m. and weekdays from 6:30 a.m. to 3:00 p.m. Their menu includes seafood, crab cakes, and tuna dishes. They also offer a nice selection of burgers named after different types of aircraft, such as the Cessna burger, the P-51 burger and much more. 1 or 2 daily specials are always available including seafood platters as well as breakfast entrees. The dining area can accommodate up to 40 persons. Additional seating can easily be arranged in the conference room near the restaurant or within the lobby. Guests can enjoy the view looking out over the tarmac. In-flight catering is also provided. For more information call the Hangar Cafe at 820-6631.

Restaurants Near Airport:

Hangar Cafe	On Site	Phone: 820-6631
The Inn At Perry Cabin	10 mi W.	Phone: 745-2200
Robert Morris Inn	10 mi SW.	Phone: 226-5111
The Trio At The Avalon	3 mi S.	Phone: 822-2500

Lodging: Tidewater Inn (3 miles) 822-1300; Comfort Inn of Easton (2 miles) 820-8333.
Meeting Rooms: There are conference rooms in the airport terminal; Also the Tidewater Inn (3 miles) 822-1300; Harrison Chesapeake House; The Inn At Perry Cabin (10 mi West) 745-2200.
Transportation: Maryland Airlines and Easton Jet Service offer courtesy transportation. Also Taxi Service: Comfort Taxi 820-8629; Rasin's Taxi 822-1048; Scotty's Taxi 822-1475; Thomas's Yellow Top 822-1121; Rental Cars: Avis 822-5040; Hertz 822-1696.
Information: Talbot County Chamber of Commerce, P.O. Box 1366, Easton, MD 21601, Phone: 822-4606.

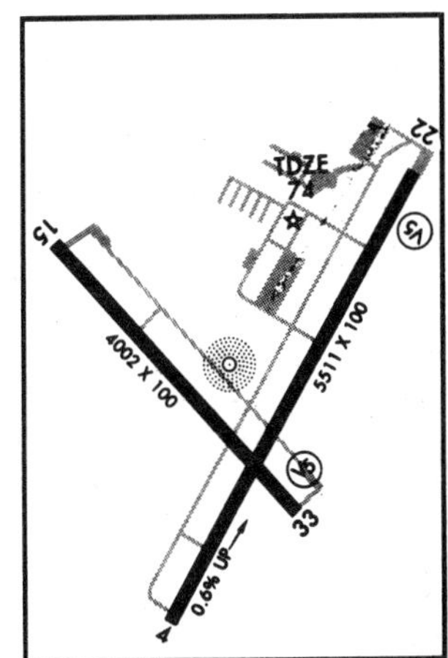

Airport Information:

EASTON - EASTON MUNICIPAL AIRPORT (ESN)
2 mi north of town N38-48.25 W76-04.14 Elev: 74 Fuel: 100LL, Jet-A
Rwy 04-22: H5511x100 (Asph) Rwy 15-33: H4002x100 (Asph) Attended: 1300Z-dusk
Unicom: 122.95 Public Phone 24hrs Notes: Overnight parking is $3.00 for singles and $5.00 for twins.
FBO: Maryland Air Phone: 822-0400 or 800-451-5693
FBO: Maryland Jet Service Phone: 820-8770

MD-FDK - FREDERICK
FREDERICK MUNICIPAL AIRPORT

(Area Code 301)

12

Restaurants Near Airport:
Airport Cafe On Site Phone: 662-3077
Chesapeake Bay(Seafood) 4 mi Phone: 663-7776

Lodging: Days Inn (1-1/2 miles) 694-7500; Econo Lodge (3 miles) 695-6200; Holiday Inn (2 miles) 694-7500; I-70 Motor Lodge (3 miles) 663-0500; Quality Inn (2-1/2 miles) 694-7704.
Meeting Rooms: Days Inn (1-1/2 miles) 694-7500; Quality Inn (2-1/2 miles) 694-7500.
Transportation: Taxi Service: Bowie 695-0333; City Cab 662-2250; Rental Cars: Altra 293-6199; Budget 663-8255; Enterprise 831-4626; Hertz 662-2626 Thrifty (Located on field) 662-2099.
Information: Tourism Council of Frederick County, 19 East Church Street, Frederick, MD 21701, Phone: 663-8687

Airport Cafe:

The Airport Cafe is situated on the Frederick Municipal Airport, and can easily be reached by fly-in customers. This combination snack bar and cafe is open from 7 a.m. to 3:00 p.m. Monday through Friday 7 a.m. to 4 p.m. Saturday and 8 a.m. 4 p.m. on Sunday. Their menu includes a nice variety of selections including huge cheeseburgers, western omelets, sub sandwiches, roast beef, tuna and egg salad sandwiches along with homemade soups and chili served daily. Average prices run $3.30 for breakfast, and $2.95 to $3.95 for lunch. The main dining room can seat between 50 and 60 persons. Carpeted floors, papered walls and pictures of airplanes, give it an aviation theme. Guests can see the activity on the field right from their seats, with windows near the front and rear entrance. For information call 662-3077.

Attractions:

A.O.P.A (Aircraft Owners & Pilots Association) main headquarters are located on the Frederick Municipal Airport. Fly-in guests can take a tour through one of the most prominent general aviation organizations in the world. This facility contains membership services, aviation related publications, in addition to the AOPA Air Safety Foundation with products and services available during business hours. There is also a cafeteria on the premises available for members and staff. For information call 800-USA-AOPA or 301-695-2000.

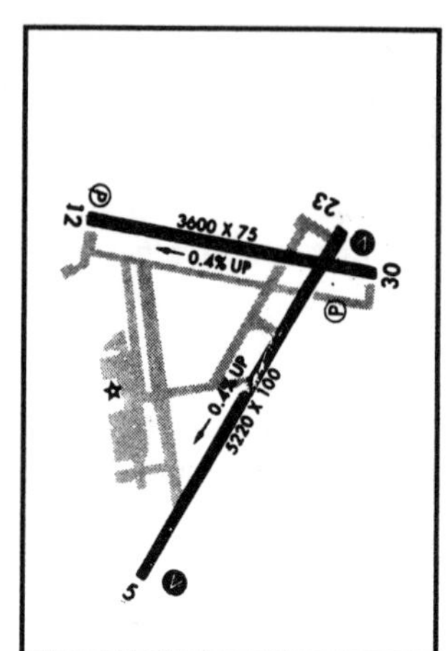

Airport Information:

FREDERICK - FREDERICK MUNICIPAL AIRPORT (FDK)
0 mi east of town 39-24-56N 77-22-34W Elev: 305 Fuel: 100LL, Jet-A
Rwy 05-23: H5200x100 (Asph) Rwy 12-30: H3600x75 (Asph) Attended: 1200-0500Z
Unicom: 123.0
FBO: Frederick Aviation, Inc. Phone: 662-8156

MD-GAI - GAITHERSBURG
MONTGOMERY COUNTY AIRPARK

(Area Code 301)

13

Restaurants Near Airport:
Air Cafe On Site Phone: 330-2222

Lodging: Holiday Inn (2.5 miles) 948-8900

Meeting Rooms: Woodfin Suites (3.5 miles) 590-9880.

Transportation: Taxi: Action Taxi 840-1222; Barwood Taxi 984-1900; Taxi-Taxi 520-6922; Montgomery Taxi 921-0191; Rental Cars: EZ Car Rentals 258-2730; Budget Rental Cars 816-6029.

Information: Chamber of Commerce, 9 Park Avenue, Gaithersburg, MD 20877, Phone: 840-1400.

Air Cafe:

Air Cafe Restaurant is located in the terminal on the first floor. This combination family and fine dining establishment is open from 7:30 a.m. to 9 p.m. 7 days a week. Their menu features a variety of entrees and specialty items like Delmonico steaks, New York strip steaks, 10 ounce burgers, baked Manicotti, and shrimp dishes. A breakfast special usually runs from 8 a.m. to 10 a.m. for only $2.99, lunch prices average around $6.00. The restaurant is decorated with planters, lots of aviation art work and pictures. The restaurant has two large windows providing a view of the runways as well as Sugar Loaf Mountain. Groups often frequent this restaurant. Meals can also be prepared-to-go, and in-flight catering is available for fly-in customers. When speaking to the owner of Air Cafe we learned that he takes pride in providing great food with the friendliest service available. For more information about Air Cafe Landing call 330-2222.

Attractions:

Washington D.C. monuments, Smithsonian Institute, museums, capitol White House, etc. only 30 minutes away by Metro.

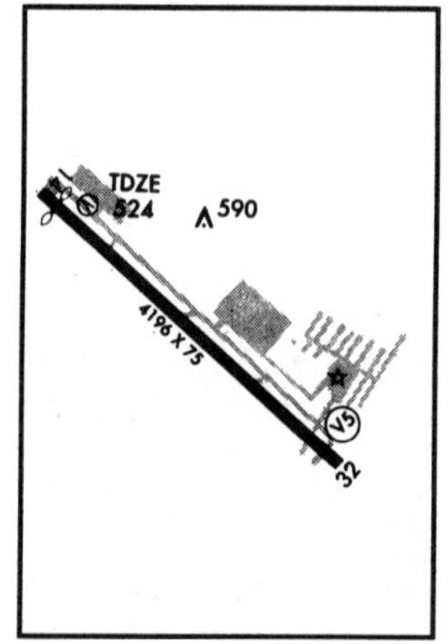

Airport Information:

GAITHERSBURG - MONTGOMERY COUNTY AIRPARK (GAI)
3 mi northeast of town N39-10.10 W77-09.96 Elev: 539 Fuel: 100LL, Jet-A
Rwy 14-32: H4196x73 (Asph) Attended: 1300-0100Z Unattended Thanksgiving, Christmas and New Years. Unicom: 122.7 Notes: Overnight parking $5.00
FBO: Montgomery Aviation Ltd. Phone: 977-5200

MD-HGR - HAGERSTOWN
WASHINGTON CO. REGIONAL

(Area Code 301) | 14, 15

Colonial Restaurant and Lounge:

This full service restaurant is located 1/4 mile from the Washington County Regional Airport. Free courtesy pick-up service is available to fly-in guests. The restaurant is open 8 a.m. to 9 p.m. daily. Specialties of the house include steaks, seafood, prime rib, soups, sandwiches as well as appetizers. Prices for a meal average $3.50 for breakfast, $4.00 for lunch and $8.95 for dinner. Daily specials are available along with their Friday fish fry. Their dining room accommodates 50 people in a casual atmosphere with a country decor. Many local organizations plan get-togethers at this restaurant. Fly-in clubs and organizations are also welcome. Catering service can be arranged for pilots, with cheese trays, sandwiches and hot meals. In addition to the restaurant ,there is also a 26-unit motel located on the premises. For information call 739-0667.

Nick's Airport Inn:

Nicks Airport Inn is located near the west ramp near Aero-Smith FBO about 50 yards from the aircraft parking ramp. This is a fine dining establishment that has been serving customers for the past 35 years. The restaurant is open for lunch Monday through Friday between 11 a.m. to 2:30 p.m. and for dinner 4:30 p.m. to 10 p.m., Monday through Saturday. Specialty items include fresh seafood, crab cakes, tuna, swordfish, fresh veal, steaks, Fillet Mignon, New York strip, and prime rib. Many pilots flyin just for the crab cakes, which is a very popular item. Lunch and dinner specials also include items like soft shell crab and oysters. Selection specials change daily. Entree prices run $15.00 to $30.00 for dinner choices. The restaurant is very upscale with linen-covered tables, and lots of mahogany, brass, etched glass and marble. The main dining room can accommodate up to 400 people. They also provide in-flight catering as well. Nick's Airport Inn is affiliated with the Sheraton Inn Hotel. Although the hotel is not on the premises, the staff will provide courtesy transportation for customers wishing to spend the evening. Simply call the FBO (Aero-Smith, Inc.) or the restaurant to arrange your selection. For more information call Nick's Airport Inn at 733-8560.

Attractions:

Black Rock Golf Course, 791-3040; Fort Frederick State Park (24 miles S.W. of airport) This park contains a revolutionary stone fort erected back in 1756 during the French and Indian War. Historians dressed in costumes and orientation films explain the military personnel and their life style. Also within the State Park are many activities, Call 842-2155.

Restaurants Near Airport:

Black Steer	2 mi.	Phone: N/A
Colonial Inn	1/4 mi.	Phone: 739-0667
Nick's Airport Inn	Adj. Arpt	Phone: 733-8560

Lodging: Air View Motel adj. arpt. 739-7300; Best Western Hagerstown 1-3 mi 791-3560; Best Western Venice Inn 733-0830; Holiday Inn 7 mi 739-9050; Howard Johnson Plaza (Arpt trans) 797-2500; Ramada Inn Convention Center 733-5100. Sheraton Inn Hotel (Arpt trans) 790-3010.

Meeting Rooms: Holiday Inn 739-9050; Sheraton Inn Conference Center (Arpt Trans) 790-3010; Best Western Venice Inn 733-0830; Howard Johnson Plaza (Arpt Trans) 797-2500; Ramada Inn Convention Center 733-5100.

Transportation: Rental Cars: Avis 791-1425; Budget 739-3562; Hertz: 739-6117; Taxi Service: Tri-State 791-3838 or 800-773-3260; Turner's Taxi Service 733-7788. There is also public transportation available.

Information: Washington County Tourism Office, 1826-C Dual Hwy, Hagerstown, MD 21740, Phone: 791-3130, also 24 hr recording 797-8800.

Airport Information:

HAGERSTOWN - WASHINGTON COUNTY REGIONAL (HGR)

4 mi north of town N39-42.48 W77-43.77 Elev: 704 Fuel: 100LL, Jet-A Rwy 09-27: H5451x150 (Asph-Grvd) Rwy 02-20: H3494x100 (Asph) Attended 1015-0430Z Unicom: 122.95 Tower: 120.3 Gnd Con: 121.9

FBO: Aero-Smith, Inc. Phone: 733-3700

FBO: Hagerstown Aviation Phone: 797-4100

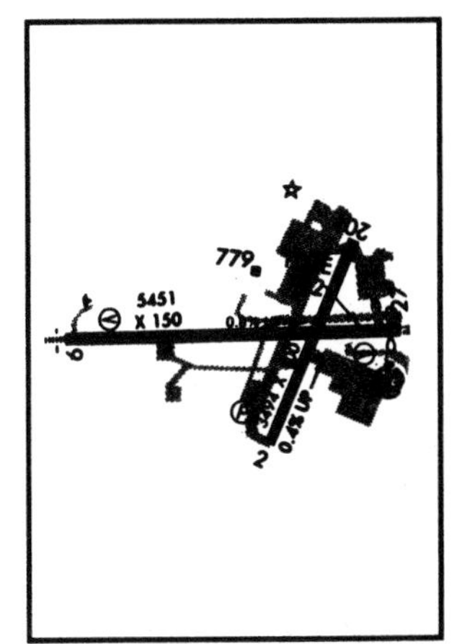

MD-N80 - OCEAN CITY
OCEAN CITY MUNICIPAL

(Area Code 410) 16

Ocean City Beach Boardwalk:

This attraction is located only 3 miles east from the Ocean City Municipal Airport. Shuttle buses regularly depart from the airport during the summer season. Passengers are dropped off one block from the beach and can be picked up at the same spot for the return trip. Ocean City resort community has a ten-mile stretch of wide, sandy beaches. Fishing is one of the major attractions for this area with white or blue marlin, bluefish, tuna and Wahoo. Swimming and watersports are also among the many activities sought after by many visitors. The Boardwalk is what attracts the majority of vacationers. Those who enjoy sampling a variety of dishes will find more than 160 different restaurants serving Italian, French, Chinese and many other ethnic specialties. Among these varieties are wonderful Eastern Shore seafood prepared daily fresh off the docks. Delicacies such as lobsters, crabs, oysters on the half-shell and steamed clams are some of the favorites. In addition to the eateries and fine dining, guests will enjoy a host of night time entertainment. During the evening hours the Boardwalk comes alive. Nightclubs and pubs offer refreshments, while the many specialty shops, amusement parks and arcades provide vacationers with an endless choice of activities. While enjoying the sites, why not try munching on a few of the boardwalk food concessions like cotton candy, fudge or saltwater taffy. In addition to the Boardwalk, there are many more attractions available. Ocean City provides two full-scale amusement parks, water parks, miniature golf, family theatre and Broadway shows. For the golf enthusiast, there are also golf courses nearby. On Labor Day weekend the coastal shores of Ocean City settle down to a relaxed pace where visitors can enjoy the calm ocean breezes and warm autumn air. The town puts on an annual Salt-water Festival. This celebration features food and continuous outdoor family-orientated arts and craft displays. In September the area presents "Sunfest" an annual fall celebration under four circus tents right on the beach. A smorgasbord of delicious foods is offered in addition to arts and crafts. During the Christmas season, Ocean City celebrates the holidays with a special Boardwalk train to view the "Parade of Trees," while the local people and Christmas vacationers enjoy special evening entertainment with the annual "Grand Ball" at the big band ballroom featuring some of the top touring orchestras in the country. For more information about the attractions of this area, contact the Ocean City Visitors & Convention Bureau, Inc. P.O. Box 116, Ocean City, MD 21842 or call 301-289-8181. Also you can contact the Ocean City Public Relations Office at P.O. Box 158, Ocean City, MD 21842 or call 301-289-2800; 800-626-2326.

Restaurants Near Airport: Within the town of Ocean City and along the Boardwalk are numerous restaurants and dining establishments.

Lodging: Castle in the Sand (free trans) 289-6846; Comfort Inn-Boardwalk 289-5155; Comfort Inn-Gold Coast 524-3000; Dunes Manor 289-1100; Quality Inn-Boardwalk 289-4401; Sheraton Fontainebleau 524-3535. Many more establishment are available in the area.

Meeting Rooms: Most lodging facilities have accommodations for meetings and conferences.

Transportation: Taxi Service: Executive 289-0306; Ocean City Taxi 289-8164; Rental Cars: Hertz 289-8355.

Information: Ocean City Visitors & Convention Bureau, Inc. P.O. Box 116, Ocean City, MD 21842 or call 301-289-8181. Also you can contact the Ocean City Public Relations Office at P.O. Box 158, Ocean City, MD 21842 or call 301-289-2800; 800-626-2326.

Airport Information:

OCEAN CITY - OCEAN CITY MUNICIPAL (N80)
2 mi southwest of town N38-18.63 W75-07.44 Elev: 12 Rwy 14-32: H4070x75 (Asph-Conc)
Rwy 02-20: H3200x75 (Asph-Conc) Attended: May-Aug 1300-0100Z, Sept-Apr 1300-2200Z
Unicom: 122.8 Notes: Parking fee after one hour.
FBO: Ocean City Airport Phone: 213-2471

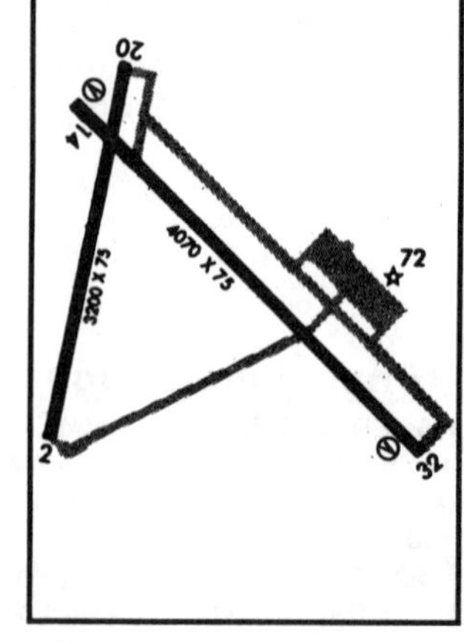

MD-SBY - SALISBURY WICOMICO COUNTY REGIONAL

17

Smugglers Cove:

The Smugglers Cove restaurant is reported to be in the old terminal building located on the Wicomico County Regional Airport. This combination convenient store/restaurant is open 6 a.m. to 6 p.m., 7 days a week. Daily specials are offered including cheese steak sandwiches, cheeseburgers, cold cuts on a Kaiser role, Wing-ding with chicken and fish sandwiches. The restaurant can seat 100 people and has a tropical atmosphere. Large picture windows with palm trees decorate the restaurant. The gift shop adjacent to the restaurant sells souvenirs like T-shirts and gifts of all types. Groups are always welcome. In-flight catering is yet another service performed by this establishment. For information about Smugglers Cove call 548-7137

Attractions:

Ocean City, MD (Beach) 30 miles; Salisbury 200 (5 miles); Ward Wild Fowl Museum (6 miles), largest assembly of bird carvings in the U.S.; Assateage State Park (35 miles); Bay Club (25 miles), Phone: 641-4081; Elk Golf Course (4 miles).

Airport Information:

SALISBURY - WICOMICO COUNTY REGIONAL (SBY)
4 mi southeast of town 38-20-26N 75-30-38W Elev: 52 Fuel 100LL, Jet-A
Rwy 14-32: H5500x150 (Asph-Conc-Pfc) Rwy 05-23: H5000x150 (Asph-Pfc)
Attended: 1100-0300Z Unicom: 122.95 Public phone 24hrs Notes: No landing fees, Tie-down parking available (29 spaces), Singles $2.50/day, Twins $4.00/day
FBO: Bay Land Aviation Phone: 749-0323

(Area Code 410)

Restaurants Near Airport:

Dockside Murphys	4 mi E.	Phone: 742-9221
Goin Nut's Cafe	2 mi	Phone: 860-1164
Imperial Gallery	3 mi E.	Phone: 546-3103
Smugglers Cove	OldTrml Bldg	Phone: 548-7137

Lodging: Comfort Inn (5 miles) Rt. 13 north, Phone: 543-4666; Holiday Inn (5 miles) Rt. 13 north, Phone: 742-7194; Days Inn, (5 miles) Rt. 13 north, Phone: 749-6200; Sheraton (5 miles) 300 S. Salisbury Blvd, Phone: 546-4400
Meeting Rooms: Comfort Inn 543-4666; Holiday Inn 742-7194; Days Inn 749-6200; Sheraton 546-4400.
Transportation: Bay Land Aviation will provide courtesy transportation if advance notice is given, 749-0323. Also the following rental and taxi services are available: Airport Taxi 742-4190; Beach Bound Shuttle 749-9029; Hertz Rent-A-Car 749-2235; Avis 742-8566; National 749-2450.
Information: Wicomico County Convention & Visitors Bureau, Civic Center 500 Glen Avenue, Salisbury, MD 21801, Phone: 548-4914 or 800-332-TOUR; Also: Salisbury Chamber of Commerce, 300 East Main Street, P.O. Box 510, Salisbury, MD 21801, Phone: 749-0144.

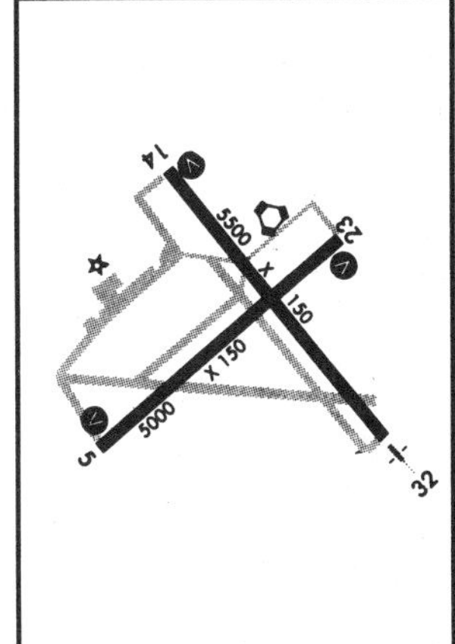

MD-W29- STEVENSVILLE BAY BRIDGE

(Area Code 410) 18, 19

Hemmingways Restaurant:

Hemmingways Restaurant is located about 1/2 mile from the Bay Bridge Airport (W29). This dining establishment offers a unique decor with a fireplace, and tables with maps of the area inlaid on the top. In addition, the restaurant allows a beautiful view looking out over the harbor and directly at the bay bridge. During the summer months guests can enjoy their meal on the outdoor deck which can seat approximately 125 persons. The restaurant is open during the summer 7 days a week from 11 a.m. to 11 p.m. Friday and Saturday, and Sunday through Thursday until 10 p.m. During the winter months they close one hour earlier. Specialty items on their menu include crab cakes, shrimp scallops Dijon, Filet Mignon, Cajun chicken, crab meat tortellini and rosemary smoked duck breasts, to mention a few. Lighter far is also available. Two specials of the day are provided for lunch as well as for dinner. Average prices run $7.95 for lunch and about $16.95 for main dinner selections. Larger groups are also welcome with advanced notice. Transportation from the airport and Hemmingways Restaurant can be arranged with local taxi services or by restaurant courtesy car, depending on available staff. For more information you can call 643-2722.

Kent Manor Inn Restaurant:

This fine dining facility is located across the street from the Bay Bridge Airport (W29) and about 5 miles north of the Kentmorr Airpark (3W3). Transportation is provided by courtesy van if landing at Bay Bridge Airport. Taxi service is also available. (See "Transportation" listed above). The restaurant is open from 10:30 to 9:30 Monday through Saturday. On Sunday they serve brunch from 9:00 a.m. to 2:00 p.m. Selections on their menu for dinner include items like Maryland crab cakes, Northwestern salmon, Veal California, aged U.S. prime sirloin steaks and roasted quail to mention a few. Appetizers, soups, salads and desserts are also offered on their menu. Prices range from $5.25 to $12.95 for lunch and $17.00 to $26.00 for dinner. This restaurant is located within a beautifully restored mansion that provides an elegant, romantic, Victorian atmosphere, furnished with furniture of that period. Adjoining the restaurant are 25 VIP guest rooms, in addition to a veranda that overlooks Thompson Creek. Original Italian marble fireplaces and window seats add additional charm to this facility. Walking trails along the one-and-a-half miles of waterfront and through the farm fields provide nature lovers and fitness buffs with a welcome retreat into peace and quiet. Poolside gazebo bar, volleyball, horseshoes and croquet are other popular warm weather diversions. In any weather, antiques, factory outlet, boutique, local arts and crafts, marine supplies, plus sportsmans shops abound on and off the island. Two additional major shopping centers within a twenty-minute drive make the area a relentless temptation for even the most conservative shopper. Accommodations for conferences, meetings, and seminars can also be arranged at this facility. For more information call 643-7716.

Restaurants Near Airport:

Hemmingways Restaurant	1/2 mi	Phone: 643-2722
Kent Manor Inn & Restaurant	Adj Arpt.	Phone: 643-7716

Lodging: Kent Manor Inn (Transportation by taxi or courtesy van, if needed); Across the street from Bay Bridge Airport (W29). This beautiful Victorian mansion comes complete with 25 VIP guest rooms decorated with Victorian reproductions, poolside gazebo bar, and fine dining restaurant on the premises, Phone: 643-7716

Meeting Rooms: Kent Manor Inn (Free transportation, across the street from Bay Bridge Airport), meeting rooms available for businesses, conferences, and seminars. (See "Lodging" listed above).

Transportation: Kent Island Taxi service 643-2361; Kang Taxi Service 643-1500

Information: Baltimore Visitors Information Centers at 300 W. Pratt Street, Baltimore, MD 21201, Phone: 837-INFO or 800-282-6632.

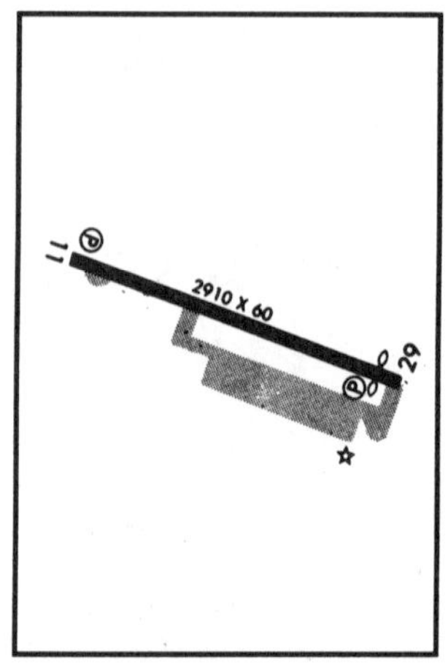

Airport Information:

STEVENSVILLE - BAY BRIDGE (W29)
1 mi west of town N38-58.58 W76-19.78 Elev: 15 Fuel: 80, 100LL Rwy 11-29: H2910x60 (Asph) Attended: 1300-0300Z Unicom: 123.0
FBO: Bay Bridge Aviation Phone: 643-6613

MD-3W3 - STEVENSVILLE KENTMORR AIRPARK

(Area Code 410)

20

Kentmorr Harbour Restaurant and Marina:

This restaurant is located 1 block south of the Kentmorr Airpark. Restaurant hours vary throughout the year. January through February 4 days a week; In March they are open 5 days a week from Wednesday through Sunday at 11:00 a.m.; May through October, 7 days a week from 11:00 a.m. and November through December, 5 days a week on Wednesday through Sunday at 11:00 a.m. Casual dining is offered indoors as well as outdoors in their "Crab House." Daily specials are also provided in this rustic waterfront restaurant. They will arrange accommodations for groups and parties as well as furnishing meals-to-go for their guests. For information call the restaurant at 643-4700.

Restaurants Near Airport:
Kentmorr Harbour Restaurant 1/8th mi S. Phone: 643-4700

Lodging: Comfort Inn 10 mi 827-6767; Kent Manor Inn 5 mi 643-7716.

Meeting rooms: Kent Manor Inn 5 mi 643-7716.

Transportation: Kent Island Taxi service will accommodate you with transportation. Phone: 643-2361; Kang Taxi Service 643-1500

Information: Baltimore Visitors Information Centers at 300 W. Pratt Street, Baltimore, MD 21201, Phone: 837-INFO or 800-282-6632.

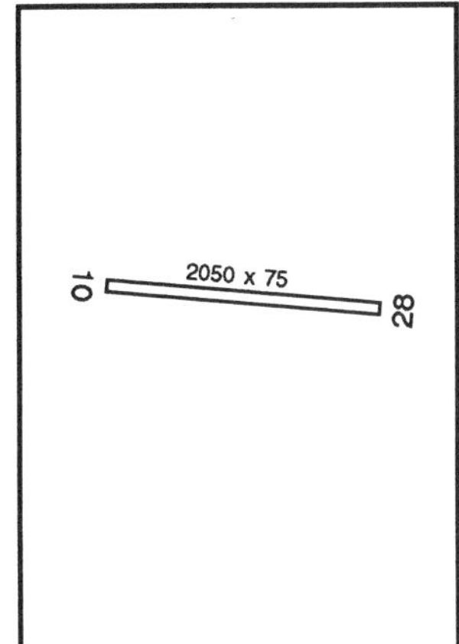

Airport Information:

STEVENSVILLE - KENTMORR AIRPARK (3W3)
5 mi southwest of town N38-55.09 W76-21 Elev: 10 Rwy 10-28: 2050x75 (Turf)
Attended: unattended CTAF: 122.9 Public Phone: At Kentmorr Marina & Restaurant 1/8 mile;
Notes: CAUTION: Rwy 10-28 rough on east end; Rwy soft after rains and in the spring time; Noise abatement - takeoff and land towards Chesapeake Bay (west) to avoid new development of houses at east end of runway whenever possible; Orange cones mark ends of the runway 10-28.
Airport Manager: Phone 643-4741.

MD-W54 - WESTMINSTER CARROLL CO REGIONAL/JACK B POAGE FLD.

(Area Code 410)

21

Bullock's Airport Inn:

Bullock's Airport Inn is located 500 feet from the airport office and main hangar along Airport Drive. Pilots can park their aircraft and walk only a short distance to the restaurant This family style restaurant is open from 7 a.m. to 8 p.m. Monday through Thursday, Friday and Saturday they're open from 7 a.m. to 9 p.m. and Sunday from 8 a.m. to 8 p.m. They offer a complete menu as well as baked goods. A daily buffet is served from 11:00 a.m. to 8:00 p.m. Saturday, a breakfast buffet is served from 7 a.m. to 11:00 a.m. and on Sunday from 8 a.m. to 11 p.m.. Average menu prices run $5.96 for breakfast and lunch and around $8.95 for dinner. Buffets, daily specials, Sunday brunches and Friday fish fries are provided for their customers. The restaurant has an aviation decor with model airplanes hanging from the ceiling. Two party rooms are available for group catering. One can handle 40 persons and the other can serve up to 65 people. In-flight catering and meal-to-go can easily be provided, along with cheese and sandwich trays. For more information about Bullock's Airport Inn you can call them at 857-4417.

Restaurants Near Airport:
Bullock's Airport Inn 500' Phone: 857-4417

Lodging: Comfort Inn 2 mi 857-1900; Days Inn 4-5 mi 857-0500; The Boston Inn 2 mi 848-9095;

Meeting Rooms: Comfort Inn 2 mi 857-1900.

Transportation: Rental Cars: Budget 848-8011, 876-7606; Taxi Service: 898-8833.

Information: Baltimore Area Visitor Center, 300 W. Pratt Street, Baltimore, MD 21201, Phone: 837-INFO or 800-282-6632. Also Tourism Council of Frederick County, 19 E. Church Street, Frederick, MD 21701, 663-8687.

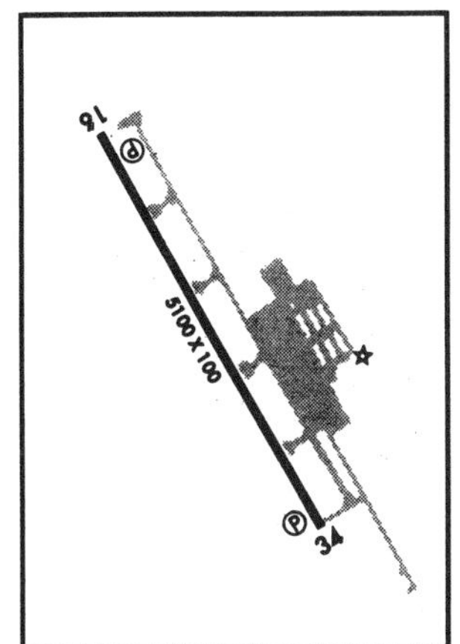

Airport Information:

WESTMINSTER - CARROLL CO REGIONAL/JACK B POAGE FLD. (W54)
3 mi north of town N39-36.22 W77-00.16 Elev: 787 Fuel: 80, 100LL, Jet-A Rwy 16-34: H5100x100 (Asph) Attended: Oct-Apr 1230-2300Z, May-Sept1230-0100Z Unicom: 122.7
FBO: Airport Manager Phone: 876-7200

MASSACHUSETTS

LOCATION MAP

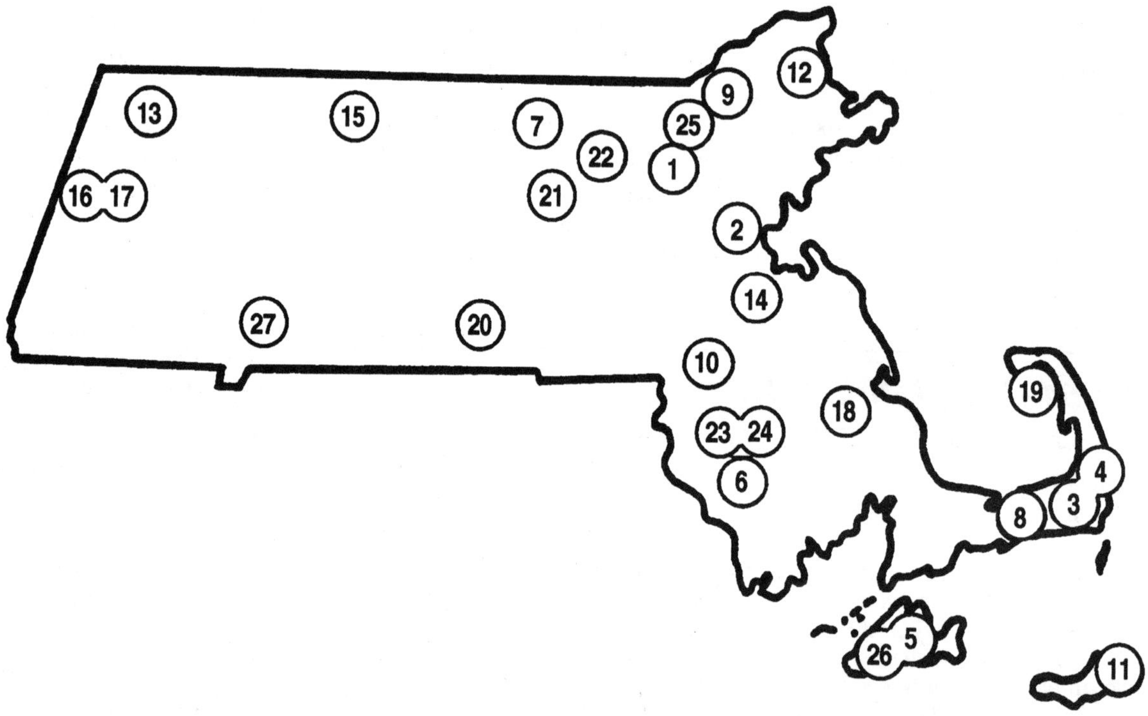

Not to be used for navigational purposes

MASSACHUSETTS

CROSS FILE INDEX

Location Number	City or Town	Airport Name And Identifier	Name of Attraction
1	Bedford	Laurence G. Hanscom Fld. (BED)	Hartwell House
2	Boston	Gen. Edward Lawrence Logan Intl. (BOS)	CA1 Services
3	Chatham	Chatham Muni. Arpt. (CQX)	Crosswind Landing Rest.
4	Chatham	Chatham Muni. Arpt. (CQX)	High Tide Ltd.
5	Edgartown	Katama Airpark (1B2)	Mel's Diner
6	Fall River	Fall River Muni. Arpt. (FLR)	Little Chop Stick
7	Fitchburg	Fitchburg Muni. Arpt. (FIT)	Gene Collette's Rest.
8	Hyannis	Barnstable Muni. (HYA)	Penguins Sea Grill
9	Lawrence	Lawrence Muni. Arpt. (LWM)	Joe's Landing Cafe
10	Mansfield	Mansfield Muni. Arpt. (1B9)	Kings Kitchen
11	Nantucket	Nantucket Mem. Arpt. (ACK)	Hutch's Restaurant
12	Newburyport	Plum Island Arpt. (2B2)	Island Steamer
13	North Adams	Narriman And West Arpt. (AQW)	La Veranda Restaurant
14	Norwood	Norwood Mem. Arpt. (OWD)	Prop Stop Restaurant
15	Orange	Orange Muni. (ORE)	Homestead Fine Foods
16	Pittsfield	Pittfield Muni. (PSF)	Dakota Restaurant
17	Pittsfield	Pittfield Muni. (PSF)	Dakota Restaurant
18	Plymouth	Plymouth Muni. Arpt. (PYM)	Plane Jane's Cafe
19	Provincetown	Provincetown Muni. (PVC)	Mews Restaurant & Cafe
20	Southbridge	Southbridge Muni. Arpt. (3B0)	Windsock Diner
21	Sterling	Sterling Airport (3B3)	Plane Delights Rest.
22	Stow	Minute Man Airfield (6B6)	Izzi's On The Runway
23	Taunton	Taunton Muni. Arpt. (TAN)	Airport Restaurant
24	Taunton	Taunton Muni. Arpt. (TAN)	Taunton House of Pizza
25	Tewksbury	Tew-Mac Arpt. (B09)	Brothers Pizza
26	Vineyard Haven	Marthas Vinyard Arpt. (MVY)	Nunne-Pog Restaurant
27	Westfield	Barnes Muni. (BAF)	Flight Deck

MA-BED - BEDFORD
LAURENCE G. HANSCOM FIELD

(Area Code 617) **1**

Restaurants Near Airport:
Hartwell House On Site Phone: 862-5111

Hartwell House:

The Hartwell House is reported about 1,000 yards from the aircraft parking area. This upscale restaurant has been in business for the past 12 years. It contains two different dining atmospheres. Their main dining room provides a more formal experience with an elegant flair, while the lounge area upstairs offers a casual motif. The restaurant is open Monday through Friday from 11 a.m. to 2:30 p.m. and Monday through Saturday from 5:30 p.m. to 10 p.m. The upstairs lounge and restaurant area offers its own special menu including items like broiled filet mignon, hamburgers, chicken sandwiches, fish and chips, chicken Oscar, popcorn shrimp and shrimp scampi. The dining room area on the main floor offers guests a more formal and elegant atmosphere. Menu selections include fresh fish, scrod, swordfish, salmon, prime rib, prime New York steaks, veal Picatta, and many other choice selections. Main dining room menu prices range from $19.00 and $22.00. On Friday and Saturday evenings they also feature piano background music on their baby grand. In addition to the formal dining room, is a closed-in air-conditioned garden patio room that provides guests with a beautiful view overlooking a pond and wooded area. Reservations are suggested if planning to dine in the formal restaurant. Also proper attire is required (no jeans, shorts etc.) Casual attire however is permitted in the lounge and restaurant upstairs. This is a smoke-free restaurant establishment. Transportation is available through the fixed base operators on the field. For information call this restaurant at 862-5111.

Lodging: FBO's on field can arrange lodging for fly-in guests; Also Stouffer's Bedford Glen Hotel (Free arpt trans) 275-5500.
Meeting Rooms: Both Beechcraft East and Jet Aviation have conference rooms available to business travelers; In addition Stouffer's Bedford Glen Hotel (Free arpt trans) also provides accommodations for meeting and conference rooms 275-5500.
Transportation: Taxi and limousine: Corporate Limousine 274-6200; Hascom Cab 571-2688; Limousine Eighteen 863-8808; Also rental cars: Avis 274-7488; Hertz 274-0030.
Information: Massachusetts Office of Travel and Tourism, 100 Cambridge Street, 13th floor, Boston, MA 02202, Phone: 617-727-3201. Call for free travel guide 800-447-MASS.

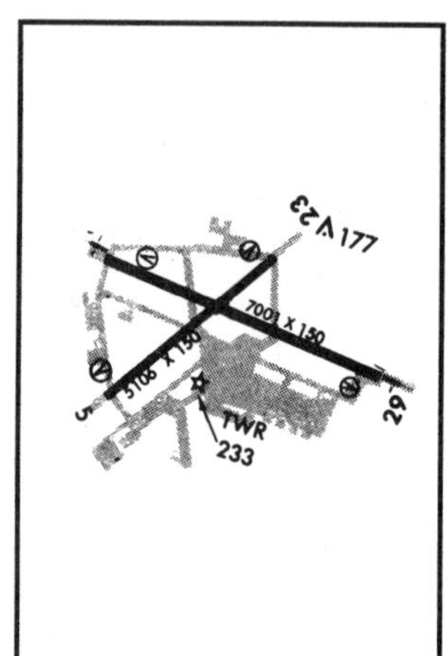

Airport Information:

BEDFORD - LAURENCE G. HANSCOM FIELD (BED)
0 mi northeast of town 42-28-12N 71-17-22W Elev: 133 Fuel: 100LL, Jet-A
Rwy 11-29: H7001x150 (Conc-Asph-Grvd) Rwy 05-23: H5106x150 (Asph) Attended: 1200-0400Z
Atis: 124.6 Unicom: 122.95 Tower: 118.5 Gnd Con: 121.7 Clnc Del: 121.85 Public Phone 24hrs Notes: No landing fee for general aviation aircraft. Night surcharge $36.00 under 12,500 lbs and $236.00 for aircraft over 12,500 lbs. Restaurant and FBO's are closed during night time hours, (11 p.m. to 7 a.m.).
FBO: Beechcraft East Phone: 247-0010
FBO: Jet Aviation Phone: 274-0030

MA-BOS - BOSTON
GENERAL EDWARD LAWRENCE LOGAN INTL.

(Area Code 617) **2**

Restaurants Near Airport:
CA1 Services On Site Phone: 569-2666

CA1 Services:

CA1 Services operates several establishments within the terminal building at the Logan International Airport. According to the restaurant management there should be no problem reaching the restaurant. MassPort shuttle provides transportation from any terminal. Taxi and courtesy transportation can usually be obtained from the local fixed based operator on the field as well. The following establishments are located on the 3rd level of the terminal building. Portside Cafe offers light fare including snacks, sandwiches and beverages. The Portside Bar offers items from their unique Pub Fare Menu for the traveler who is in a hurry with selections like lobster roll, club sandwiches and more. Shipyard Brew Port has 140 seats and is a upscale brew pub restaurant with an outstanding menu selection including seafood, beef, poultry and sandwiches. The Au Pon Pain is a French cafe with assorted croissants, baked goods, salads, coffee, capuccino and more. The Arigato Sushi Bar provides an experience which you will remember. Bean-Town Bento's features a special touch of Japanese food. Commons Bar is a full service bar with a great snack menu including buffalo wings, chicken sandwiches, burgers and more. The Commons Grille features char-broiled items cooked in front of you. Items include burgers, chicken breast, fried foods, salads, fresh fruit and more. Edy's is an ice cream parlor serving grand soft ice cream and yogurt. Sbarro offers Italian cuisine of Boston including lasagna, ziti, pizza and calzone dishes. On the first level of the terminal building CA1 Services manages two establishment: AuBon Pain serves French express items like self serve bakery, coffee, cappuccino and sandwiches. Runways is a lounge. For more information about CA1 Services at Logan International call 569-2666.

Lodging: Bostonian Hotel 523-3600; Hilton Logan Airport Adj 569-9300; Howard Johnson Revere 284-7200; Meriden Boston Hotel 451-1900; Ramada Hotel 569-5250; Harborside Hyatt adjcent arpt 568-1234.
Meeting Rooms: Most hotels and motels listed above contain accommodations for meetings and conferences.
Transportation: Rental cars: Alamo 561-4100; Avis 561-3500; Budget 497-3709; Hertz 569-7272; National 569-6700; Taxi service available, also courtesy car reported at Signature Flight Service by calling 569-5260.
Information: Greater Boston Convention & Visitors Bureau, Prudential Tower, P.O. Box 990468, Boston, MA 02199, Phone: 536-4100.

Airport Information:

BOSTON - GENERAL EDWARD LAWRENCE LOGAN INTERNATION (BOS)
1 mi east of town N42-21.86 W71-00.31 Elev: 20 Fuel: 100LL, Jet-A Rwy 15R-33L: H10081x150 (Asph-Grvd) Rwy 04R-22L: H10005x150 (Asph-Grvd) Rwy 04L-22R: H7860x150 (Asph-Grvd) Rwy 09-27: H7000x150 (Asph-Grvd) Rwy 15L-33R: H2557x100 (Ashp) Attended: continuously Atis: 135.0 Unicom: 122.95 Boston App Con: 120.6 (South) 127.2 (West) 118.25 (North) Boston Dep Con: 133.0 Boston Tower: 128.8, 121.75, 128.8, 119.1 Gnd Con: 121.9 Clnc Del: 121.65 Pre-Taxi Clnc: 121.65 Gate Con: 134.05 Notes: See AFD for current information
FBO: Signature Flight Support Phone: 569-5260

MA-CQX - CHATHAM
CHATHAM MUNICIPAL AIRPORT

(Area Code 508)

3, 4

Crosswind Landing Restaurant:

This restaurant is located at the Chatham Municipal Airport, in the upstairs portion of the terminal building. It is a two minute walk from the airport to the cafe. The Crosswind Landing is open on Monday through Saturday from 8 a.m. to 2:30 p.m., and Sunday for brunch between 8 a.m. and 1:30 p.m. The restaurant provides a gourmet flavor specializing in homemade pastries and desserts. They also serve breakfast served all day and also offer lunch specials. Their menu contains specialties of the house like sword fish, and fresh tuna steaks. Breakfast items including omelets, French toast, and blueberry pancakes are also a favorite with many customers. Prices range from $3.95 for breakfast and $4.95 for lunch. The restaurant is bright and sunny with a nice view of the runway. Pictures and drawings of airplanes decorate the walls. Their upper balcony is also available for outdoor dinning. They will be happy to cater your next fly-in party. Indoor seating can accommodate up to 28 persons. The outdoor deck can seat up to 20 additional people. In fact, you can obtain a special catering brochure from "Pleasant Bay Gourmet" affiliated with this restaurant. For information call 945-5955.

High Tide Ltd:

The High Tide Restaurant is located about 1/2 mile from the Chatham Municipal Airport. To reach this establishment you can either walk or arrange transportation through the airport. If walking, the directions are: left on George Ryder Road to Route 28, then left on 28 about 50 yards to the restaurant which is on the right side of the road. High Tide Restaurant is classified as a fine dining facility that is open at 4:30 p.m. until closing Tuesday through Saturday. Their menu specializes in selections containing beef, seafood, veal and pasta. Average prices run about $15.95 for most diner choices. Sunday brunches are served mid-October through Mothers Day. The restaurant has a warm atmosphere with table linens, fresh flower centerpieces and a fireplace. Groups up to 125 persons can be served with advance notice. They accept Dinners Club, Carte Blanche, Mastercard and Visa. For information call the High Tide Restaurant at 945-2582.

Restaurants Near Airport:

Chatham Square Rest	1-1/2 mi	Phone: 945-0945
Crosswind Landing	On Site	Phone: 945-5955
High Tide Ltd.	1/2 mi	Phone: 945-2582

Lodging: Chatham Bars Inn (3 miles) 945-0096; Town House Inn (3 miles) 945-2180; Wequassett Inn (4 miles) 432-5400; Chatham Bars Inn Resort (Free Shuttle) 945-0096; Wequassett Inn Resort (4 mi, Shuttle) 432-5400.

Meeting Rooms: Ocean Edge Conference Center; Chatham Bars Inn (3 miles) 945-0096;

Transportation: FBO can provide car at minimum cost; Rental Cars: Kelsey's 432-7966. Taxi Service: Eldredge Taxi 945-0068; Nauset 255-3277; Skips 432-7966.

Information: Cape Cod Chamber of Commerce, US-6 and MA-132, Hyannis, MA 02601, Phone: 362-3225.

Attractions:

Monomoy National Wildlife Refuge 945-0594; Chatham Railroad Museum containing a railroad depot, and an impressive collection of model trains and railroad memorabilia. Open Mid-June through mid September, Tuesday through Saturdays. Donations accepted.

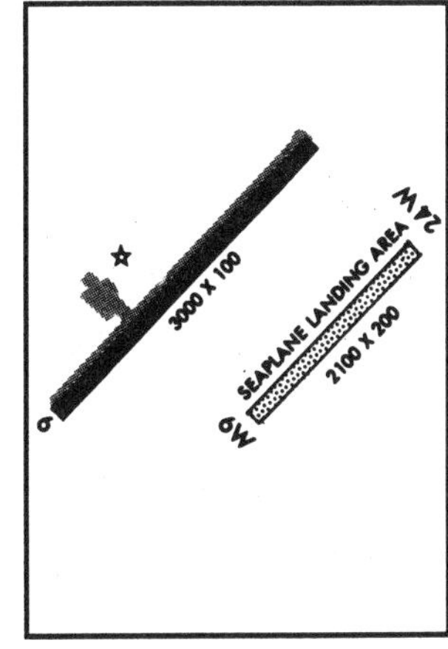

Airport Information:

CHATHAM - CHATHAM MUNICIPAL AIRPORT (CQX)
2 mi northwest of town N41-41.30 W69-59.37 Elev: 68 Fuel: 80, 100LL
Rwy 06-24: H3001x100 (Asph) Attended: 1300Z-dusk Unicom: 122.8 Public Phone 24hrs
Notes: Overnight parking $7.00, Com Landing $15.00
FBO: Cape Cod Aero Marine Phone: 945-9000

MA-1B2 - EDGARTOWN KATAMA AIRPARK

(Area Code 508)

5

Mel's Diner:

This diner is located in the operations building at the Katama Airfield. It opens the Wednesday before Memorial Day and operates on Wednesday through Sunday from 7:30 a.m. to 2:30 p.m. through the month of June. From July until Labor Day it is open 7 days a week during the same hours. They close for the season after Labor Day. Specialized entrees include a full breakfast menu with homemade coffee cakes, muffins, brownies and cookies. Their lunches include sandwiches, salads, diet plates as well as ice cream and snacks. Entrees run about $5.00 for an average meal. The restaurant is rustic with early aviation photos, propellers, and 1st solo cards on the walls. The view from the diner overlooks the three grass runways and 190 acre conservation area as well as the Atlantic ocean at the south end of the field. There is also outdoor dining on their deck. Accommodations for fly-in groups for lunch can be arranged. They can park up to 120 aircraft at the beach parking lot for those who plan to spend the day at the beach. For information call 627-9018.

Restaurants Near Airport:

Beeftender	In town	Phone: 627-8344
Kelley Street Cafe	In town	Phone: 627-4394
Lawry's Seafood Rest	In town	Phone: 627-8857
L'Etoile Restaurant	In town	Phone: 627-5187
Mel's Diner	On Site	Phone: 627-9018
Navigator	In town	Phone: 627-4320
The Wharf	In town	Phone: 627-9966

Lodging: Katama Shores Inn, (1/4 mile from Airport) will give pilots a 10% discount on room rates; located on the ocean with lounge, restaurant, tennis and swimming pool. Phone: 627-4747; Edgartown Heritage, 627-5161 or 800-922-3009 (Exc MA); Charlotte Inn, 627-4751; Many other fine lodging facilities available. Contact Martha's Vineyard Chamber of Commerce, Phone: 693-0085.

Transportation: Island Shuttle bus (Normally stops every 1/2 hour or 1 hour in bad weather); John's Taxi, 627-4677; Rental Cars: Atlantic, 693-0698 summer and 693-9191 off season; Hertz, 693-2402; Bicycles (627-4052) and mopeds (693-5457) available too.

Information: Martha's Vineyard Chamber of Commerce, Beach Road, P.O. Box 1698, Vineyard Haven, MA 02568 or call, Phone: 693-0085

Attractions:

Edgartown was once a major seaport at the time when whaling ships docked within the harbor, displaying towering masts from the wooden decks, and miles of rope and rigging. In those days this town buzzed with activity with tradesmen, merchants and sailors. Today it still remains a busy and active community that is visited by a great many tourists each year.

This quaint village, with its rows of old captain's houses, piers, marinas, restaurants, pubs and unique shops, is all located only a short 3 miles from the Katama Air park. There are two major airports on the island; Katama Air park located right on South Beach and Martha's Vineyard Airport situated near the middle of the island.

By landing at the Katama Air park, you can easily reach the town of Edgartown by either shuttle bus every 1/2 hour, taxi, bicycle, moped or rental car. There are many points of interest that should not go unnoticed by the visitor making the trek to this fascinating island. Dukes County Historical Society, located at Cooke & School streets in Edgartown, contains many items from the whaling era, displaying maritime artifacts, whaling gear, and finely detailed ship models; Cape Island Express Lines, provide bus tours of the island, Phone: 997-1688; Recreation at several sheltered beaches ideal for swimming, are located near Menemsha, Oak bluffs, Edgartown and Vineyard Haven as well as surf swimming on the south shore.

Fishing for striped bass, bonito, bluefish and weakfish is popular with the locals as well as visitors. If golfing is your pleasure, you can play a round at one of two public courses available. Farm Neck Club, Phone: 693-3057 or Mink Meadows, Phone: 693-0600.

At the Katama Airfield, beach parking for airplanes is available for those who enjoy taking in sunshine or going for that refreshing swim. A call to the Martha's Vineyard Chamber of Commerce (693-0085), will provide you with more details about this area.

Airport Information:

EDGARTOWN - KATAMA AIR PARK (1B2)

2 mi south of town N41-21.51 W70-31.47 Elev: 20 Fuel: 100LL
Rwy 03-21: 4000x50 (Turf) Rwy 06-24: 2700x50 (Turf) Rwy 17-35: 2600x100 (Turf)
Attended: May-Oct dawn to dusk Notes: Phone to be installed soon
For airport information call, Roy Nutting. Phone: 627-9018.

NO AIRPORT DIAGRAM AVAILABLE

MA-FLR - FALL RIVER
FALL RIVER MUNICIPAL AIRPORT

(Area Code 508)

6

Restaurants Near Airport:

Little Chop Stick	10 min walk	Phone: 679-9610
Olivers (Lounge)	Adj Arpt S.	Phone: 674-0110

Little Chop Stick:

The Little Chop Stick is a family style Oriental restaurant that is located less than a 10 minute walk from the Fall River Municipal Airport. This restaurant is open weekdays from 11 a.m. to 10 p.m., Friday and Saturday from 11 a.m. to 10:30 p.m. and Sunday from 11:30 a.m. to 10 p.m. A nice variety of entrees are available including specialties of the house like Scallops, shrimp dishes, Oriental chicken, orange beef, as well as many other delicious entrees, including appetizers. Prices run $7.00 to $8.75 for most selections. Specials during the week feature chicken and beef selections as well. This restaurant can accommodate between 90 to 100 persons with a comfortable and casual atmosphere. Groups and parties up to 24 can be served. This restaurant is very popular with the local people in the area and is visited by many fly-in guests. For more information call the Little Chop Stick Restaurant at 679-9610.

Lodging: Airport Inn (Best Western, Adj Arpt) 672-0011; Several others within 4 miles of airport: Days Inn 676-1991; Howard Johnson 678-4545.
Meeting Rooms: Hampton Inn (53 Old Bedford Road, Westport, MD) 675-8500; Days Inn 676-1991; Howard Johnson 678-4545.
Transportation: Budget Rental Cars 677-3113; City Hall (Courtesy Transportation) 674-4633; Rent-A-Ride 675-0558; Vet's 673-5843.
Information: Fall River Area Chamber of Commerce, 200 Pocasset Street, P.O. Box 1871, Fall River, MA 02722, Phone: 676-8226.

Attraction: Battle Ship Cove is situated about 4 miles from the Fall Rivers Municipal Airport. The USS Massachusetts battle ship, and the Lionfish attack submarine are both on display and open for tours for the public. In addition, the PT Boat 796, PT Boat 617, and the USS Joseph P. Kennedy which served in the Korean and Vietnam wars, are also displayed. For information call 678-1100. The Marine Museum is yet another attraction available to the general public located at 70 Water Street in Fall River, MA. Over 130 ship models are on display, telling the story about steam powered shipping since the early 1800's. For information call 674-3533.

NO AIRPORT DIAGRAM AVAILABLE

Airport Information:

FALL RIVER - FALL RIVER MUNICIPAL AIRPORT (FLR)
3 mi north of town N41-45.31 W71-06.60 Elev: 193 Fuel: 100LL, MOGAS
Rwy 06-24: H3948x150 (Asph) Rwy 15-33: H1600x150 (Asph) Attended: 1300Z-dusk
Unicom: 122.8 Public Phone 24hrs Notes: Overnight parking $2.00 per night
FBO: Narragansett Aircraft, Inc. Phone: 676-5153

MA-FIT - FITCHBURG
FITCHBURG MUNICIPAL AIRPORT

(Area Code 508)

7

Restaurants Near Airport:

Chopstick Restaurant	1 mi	Phone: 534-0020
Gene Collettes Airport Rest.	On Site	Phone: 345-1580
Red Checker Restaurant	1 mi	Phone: 534-5117
Sheraton-Leominster	1-1/2 mi	Phone: 534-9000

Gene Collette's Airport Restaurant:

The Airport Restaurant is located in the terminal building on the Fitchburg Municipal Airport. This combination cafe and cafeteria is open 7 a.m. to 2:30 p.m. 7 days a week. Specialties of the house include fish & chips, chicken cordon bleu, sandwiches, a full selection of breakfast items. On Friday they feature fish and chips and clam chowder specials. Daily specials are also offered throughout the week. Most entrees run between $2.00 and $4.00 along with specials like their .99 cent breakfast. The dining area with tables and counter service, can seat 50 persons. All menu choices can be prepared for carry-out. In-flight catering is also available. This establishment prides itself with offering its customers a clean and friendly atmosphere. For more information call Gene Collette's Airport Restaurant at 345-1580.

Lodging: Best Western Westminster (Est 7-8 miles) 874-5911; Holiday Inn - Leominster (2 miles) 537-1661; Suisse Chalet (3 miles) 537-8161.
Meeting Rooms: Best Western Westminster 874-5911; Holiday Inn-Leominster 537-1661.
Transportation: Taxi Service: Fitchburg Taxi 345-4381; Leominster Taxi 537-6331; Also Car Rental: Altra Rental Cars 342-4708; Budget Rental Cars 342-1616.
Information: Chamber of Commerce, Box 7330, Fitchburg, MA 01420, Phone: 343-6487.

Attraction:

Oak Hill Country (10 miles, golf and dining) Oak Hill Road, Fitchburg, MA 342-2717; Monoosnock Country Club (5 miles) Leominster, MA 534-4913.

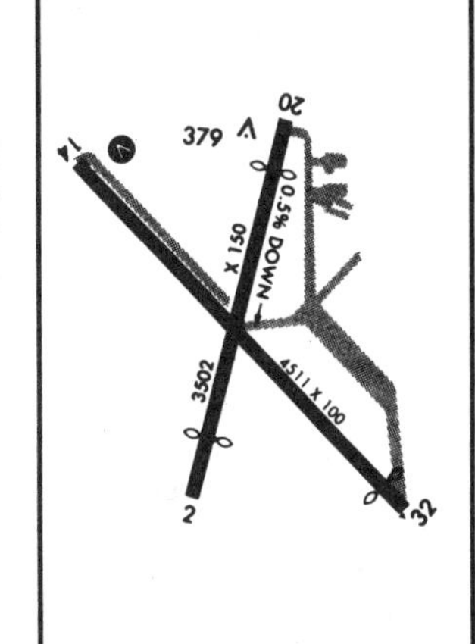

Airport Information:

FITCHBURG - FITCHBURG MUNICIPAL AIRPORT (FIT)
3 mi southeast of town N42-33.25 W71-45.54 Elev: 348 Fuel: 100LL, Jet-A
Rwy 14-32: H4511x100 (Asph) Rwy 02-20: H3502x150 (Asph) Attended: 1300Z-dusk
Unicom: 122.7 Public Phone 24hrs Notes: Landing fee $5.00 for commercial flights. Overnight parking fee $5.00 per night.
FBO: Bullock Charters Phone: 464-2706

MA-HYA - HYANNIS BARNSTABLE MUNI-BOARDMAN/ POLANDO FLD

8

Penguins Sea Grill:

This fine dining establishment is located at the corner of Barnstable Road and Main Street in Hyannis, Massachusetts, between 1 and 2 miles from the Barnstable Municipal Airport. After arriving at your destination you can take a taxi from the airport to the restaurant. Penguins Sea Grill, is open every evening from 5 p.m. to 10 p.m. The entrees on their menu contain a full assortment of seafood specialties. Dinners run about $16.00 to $18.00 on the average. Accommodations for groups can easily be arranged. The restaurant itself, is located about 1 mile from the beautiful beaches and docks where the ferries travel to and from Martha's Vineyard and Nantucket Island. For reservations or information, call the restaurant at 775-2023.

Restaurants Near Airport: (Area Cod 508)

Restaurant	Distance	Phone
Hearth & Kettle	2 mi E.	Phone: 771-3737
Michell's Steak & Rib Hse	1/2 mi S.	Phone: 775-6700
Penguins Sea Grill	2 mi E.	Phone: 775-2023
Windjammer	3/4 mi S.	Phone: 771-2020

Lodging: All lodging facilities listed here are within 5-7 miles of airport. Best Western Heritage House 775-7000; Days Inn 771-6100; Holiday Inn 771-6600; Hyannis Inn 775-0255; Hyannis Regency Inn 775-1153; Sheraton Inn Hyannis 771-3000; Tar Hyannis Resort & Conference Center 775-7775.

Meeting Rooms: Many of the hotels in the area have conference facilities. There is also a room available at the airport (Nominal charge of $25.00), contact airport manager at 775-2020.

Transportation: According to the airport manager: Michell's Steak & Rib House and Windjammer restaurants are within easy walking distance. In addition, there is a taxi stand, as well as several car rental services, at the Barnstable Muni. Airport. Avis: 775-2888; Budget 775-3832; Hertz 775-5825; National 771-4353.

Information: Cape Cod Chamber of Commerce, 1481 Route 132, Hyannis, MA 02601, Phone: 362-5230.

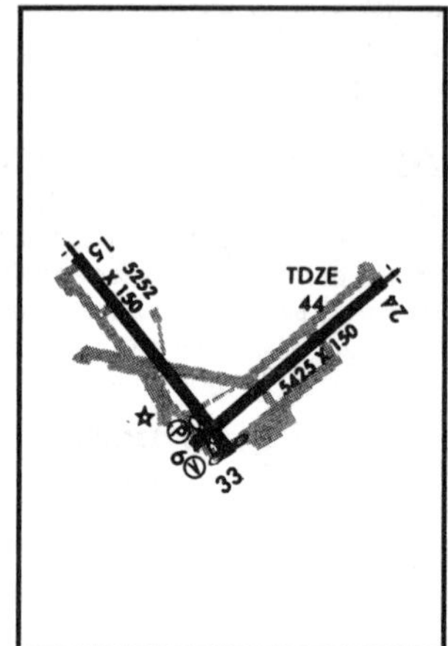

Airport Information:

HYANNIS - BARNSTABLE MUNI-BOARDMAN/POLANDO FLD (HYA)
1 mi north of town N41-40.16 W70-16.82 Elev: 55 Fuel: 80, 100LL, Jet-A Rwy 06-24: H5425x150 (Asph) Rwy 15-33: H5252x150 (Asph-Grvd) Attended: continuously Atis: 123.8 Unicom: 122.95 Tower: 119.5 Gnd Con 121.9 Clnc Del: 125.15 Public Phone: 24hrs
Notes: Fees - Single $6.50 min. $.70/thousand lbs. over 3,500 lbs $9.00 min. up to 6,000 lbs, $.70/ thousand pounds over 6,000.

FBO: Griffin Aviation Phone: 771-2865
FBO: Hyannis Air Service Phone: 775-8171
FBO: Griffin Avionics, Inc. Phone: 771-2638

MA-LWM - LAWRENCE LAWRENCE MUNICIPAL AIRPORT

9

Joe's Landing Cafe & Restaurant:

Joe's Landing Cafe & Restaurant is on the Lawrence Municipal Airport north of the terminal building. This family style restaurant is open between 5:30 a.m. to 9 p.m. 7 days a week. The restaurant facility specializes in serving American and Middle Eastern selections as well as a variety of additional entrees. Their combo breakfast special includes pancakes, bacon or sausage, eggs & toast. In addition to breakfast items, their specialty also include lamb, chicken, sub rolls, chowders, soup of the day and roll up Syrian bread which is a favorite with many customers. The dining area provides seating for 50 people with counter space for about 10 additional customers. Larger groups and parties up to 25 people can be served with advance notice. In-flight catering can be arranged through the Joe's Landing Cafe as well. For more information call 682-8822.

Restaurants Near Airport: (Area Code 508)

Restaurant	Distance	Phone
Bishop's Restaurant	3 mi	Phone: 683-7143
Cedar Crest	3 mi	Phone: 685-5722
China Blossom Rest.	Adj Arpt	Phone: 682-2242
Joe's Landing Cafe	On Site	Phone: 682-8822

Lodging: Andover Inn (4 miles) 475-5903; Merrimack Valley Motor Inn (1 mile) 688-1851; Rolling Green Hotel (6 miles) 475-5400; Marriott Hotel 975-3600.

Meeting Rooms: Andover Inn 475-5903; Merrimack Valley Motor Inn 688-1851; Rolling Green Hotel 475-5400; Marriott Hotel 975-3600.

Transportation: Million Air 685-7692 and Four Star Aviation 686-3412 can provide courtesy transportation to nearby facilities; Also Taxi Service: S. Union Taxi 686-6305; Diamond Taxi 682-9034; Andover Cab 475-2888; Central Yellow Cab 682-6000; Community Taxi 682-0661; King Cab 682-8244; Rental Cars: Automate 794-0520; Budget 475-4408; Sears Rent-A-Car 475-4425; Thrifty 682-6553.

Information: Chamber of Commerce, 264 Essex Street, Lawrence, MA 01840, Phone: 686-0900.

Attractions: Rockingham Park, Salem, NH (10 miles); Hampton Beach, Hampton NH (25 miles); Harold Parker State Park, North Andover, MA (5 miles).

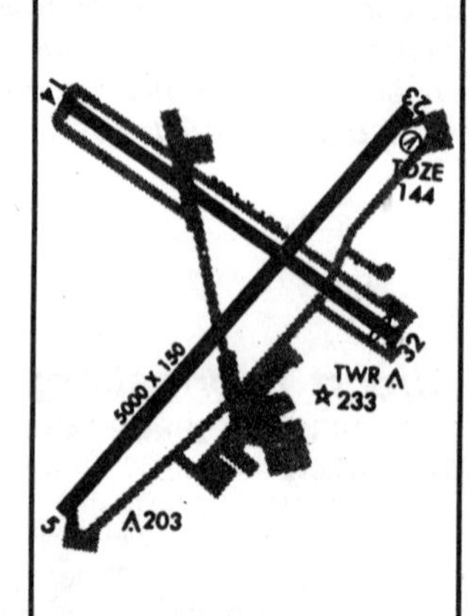

Airport Information:

LAWRENCE - LAWRENCE MUNICIPAL AIRPORT (LWM)
2 mi east of town N42-43.03 W71-07.41 Elev: 149 Fuel: 100LL, Jet-A Rwy 05-23: H5000x150 (Asph) Rwy 14-32: H3901x100 (Asph) Attended: 1300Z-dusk Atis: 126.75 Unicom: 122.8 Tower: 120.0 Gnd Con: 124.3 Public Phone 24hrs Notes: Overnight parking all aircraft $4.00 per night except corporate and commercial aircraft $8.00 for jets and $5.00 for recip. type aircraft.

FBO: Eagle East Aviation Phone: 683-3314
FBO: New England Jet Serv. Phone: 685-7500
FBO: Four Star Aviation Phone: 686-3412

MA-1B9 - MANSFIELD
MANSFIELD MUNICIPAL AIRPORT

(Area Code 508)

10

King's Kitchen: (Closed)

This restaurant has been reported asclosed. During our conversation with airport management we learned that if someone purches the restaurant, it will re-open under a new name.

Restaurants Near Airport:

Anna Marie's Kitchen	1 mi	Phone: 285-5611
Fresh Embassy	1 mi	Phone: 285-8520
Jimmy's Pub	2 mi	Phone: 339-7167
King's Kitchen	On Site	CLOSED
LaDonna's	4 mi	Phone: 261-7000
Taxi-Inn Restaurant	1 mile	Phone: 339-6632

Lodging: Mansfield Host (4 miles) Phone: call King Aviation 339-3624.

Meeting Rooms: None Reported

Transportation: Norton Taxi 285-3993

Information: Massachusetts Office of Travel and Tourism, 100 Cambridge Street, 13th floor, Boston, MA 02202, Phone: 617-727-3201, Also for free travel guide call 800-447-MASS.

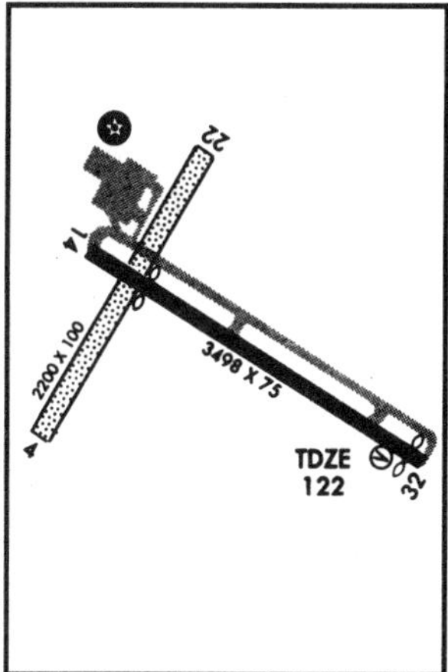

Airport Information:

MANSFIELD - MANSFIELD MUNICIPAL AIRPORT (1B9)
2 mi southeast of town N42-00.01 W71-11.81 Elev: 122 Fuel: 100LL
Rwy 14-32: H3498x75 (Asph) Rwy 04-22: 2200x100 (Turf) Attended: 1300Z-dusk
Unicom: 123.0 Public Phone 24hrs
FBO: King Aviation (Mansfield) Phone: 339-3624

MA-ACK - NANTUCKET
NANTUCKET MEM. AIRPORT

(Area Code 508)

11

Hutch's Restaurant:

Hutch's Restaurant is located in the terminal building on the Nantucket Memorial Airport. This restaurant is open from 6 a.m. to 9 p.m. 7 days a week. Their menu contains a large selections of choices. Items include a complete breakfast selection along with lunch and dinner entrees like T-bone steak, shrimp Scampi, fried chicken, marinated sirloin tips, liver & onions and pork chops. Daily specials are also offered. Average prices run $4.50 for breakfast, $2.50 to $6.95 for lunch and $7.95 to $12.95 for dinner. This restaurant features an open kitchen, 9 stool counter service and seating for about 40 people in their dining area. In-flight catering is also available for private and corporate pilots. The decor of Hutch's Restaurant provides comfortable and casual dining. For information call 228-5550.

Restaurants Near Airport:

Hutch's Restaurant	On Site	Phone: 228-5550
J.C. House	4 mi	Phone: 228-2400
Nantucket Inn	Adj Arpt	Phone: 228-6900
Wings Restaurant	Adj arpt	Phone: 228-6261

Lodging: Nantucket Inn (Adj airport) 27 Macy Lane, 228-6900; J.C. House (4 miles, Call for transportation) 29 Broad Street, 228-2400; The Wauwinet (Approx 6 to 7 miles, Call for transportation) Wausinet Road 228-0145.
Meeting Rooms: Nantucket Inn 228-6900; J.C. House 228-2400; Harbor House 228-5500 (Call for reservations); Also see Lodging listed above.
Transportation: Taxi service and rental cars available at main terminal: Budget 228-5666; Hertz 228-9421; National 228-0300; Thrift 228-1227;
Information: Chamber of Commerce, 48 Main Street, Nantucket Island, MA 02554, Phone: 228-1700, Also general Info: 228-0925.

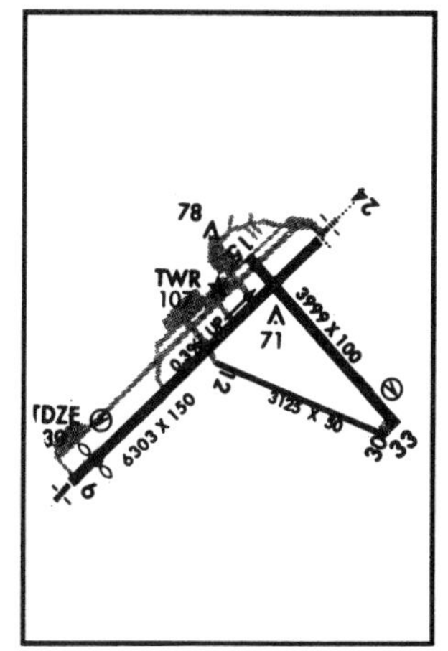

Attractions:

Many resorts as well as numerous attractions and activities are available in this region. The "Historic District" is about 3 miles from the airport, also self guided walking tours as well as guided sightseeing tours are available through Island Tour, Inc. 228-0334 or Barrett's Tours 228-0174. In addition: Sconset Golf (4 miles) 257-6596;

Airport Information:

NANTUCKET - NANTUCKET MEMORIAL (ACK)
3 mi southeast of town N41-15.18 W70-03.61 Elev: 48 Fuel 100LL, Jet-A Rwy 06-24: H6303x150 (Asph) Rwy 15-33: H3999x150 (Asph) Attended: continuously Atis: 126.6 Unicom: 122.95 Tower: 118.3 Gnd Con: 121.7 Cln Del: 128.25 Notes: Landing fee: singles $6.00, Twins $10.00; Parking fee: singles $4.00, Twins $5.00 (All aircraft first two hours Free); After hours fuel service call 508-228-5159 or 228-5125;
Airport Manager Phone: 325-5300
FBO: Coast Air Service Phone: 228-3350

MA-2B2 - NEWBURYPORT PLUM ISLAND AIRPORT

12

Restaurants Near Airport: (Area Code 508)

Island Steamer	1 mi	Phone: 465-0716
Scandia (Gourmet)	1 mi	Phone: 462-2290
Ten Center Street	1 mi	Phone: 462-6652

Island Steamer:

The Island Steamer is located about 1 mile from the Newburyport, Plum Island Airport. We were told that many pilots walk to the restaurant. From the airport you can walk towards the beach. A marshy area exists between the airport and the restaurant. It is the first building on the right that you see past the airport. This is a family style restaurant that is open between May and October 11 a.m. to 9 p.m. Sunday through Thursday and 11 a.m. to 10 p.m. Friday through Saturday. Specialty items include lobster and steamers, fried clams and scallops, lobster rolls, chicken fingers, hamburgers and hot dogs. Average prices run $10.00 to $15.00 for lunch and dinner. The restaurant dining rooms have picnic tables. There is seating for about 40 people. An outdoor deck can seat an addition 50 to 100 people. Beautiful sunsets can be enjoyed. Groups are welcome. For information call 465-0716.

Lodging: Windsor House (Est. 1-1/2 mi) 462-3778; Morrell Palace 462-2808.
Meeting Rooms: Phoenix Room, Firehouse Center, call airport managers office for information 462-2114 or 686-3412.
Transportation: Air Plum Island, Inc (FBO) provides courtesy transportation 462-2114 or 686-3412; Also Port Taxi 465-2333; U-Save Rental Cars 465-1755.
Information: Greater Newburyport Chamber of Commerce, 29 State Street, Newburyport, MA 01950, Phone: 462-6680.

Attractions:

Wildlife refuge: walking trails (1-1/2 miles), beautifully restored historic downtown area, shops, museum, restaurant, performing arts center.

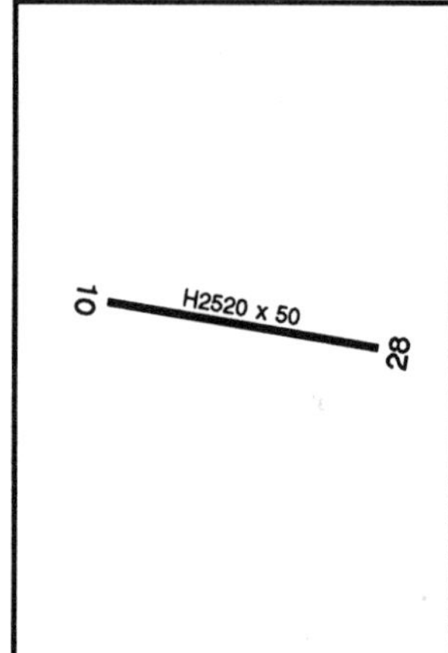

Airport information:

NEWBUARYPORT - PLUM ISLAND AIRPORT (2B2)
1 mi southeast of town N42-47.76 W70-50.47 Elev: 11 Fuel: 100LL Rwy 10-28:H2520x50 (Asph) Attended: Apr 16-Nov 10 Aat-Sun 1300Z-dusk, and May-Oct holidays 1300-dusk Unicom: 123.0 Notes: No public phone reported at airport.
FBO: Air Plum Island, Inc. Phone: 462-2114

MA-AQW- NORTH ADAMS HARRIMAN AND WEST AIRPORT

13

Restaurants Near Airport: Area Code 413)

Four Acres	1-1/5 mi W.	Phone: 458-8158
La Veranda	100 yds	Phone: 663-3321
The Orchards Inn	2 mi W.	Phone: 458-9611
Williams Inn	2-1/2 mi W.	Phone: 458-9371

La Veranda Restaurant:

The La Veranda Restaurant is located about 100 yards in front of the Stop and Shop Convenient Store at the Harriman and West Airport. This family style restaurant is open from 4 p.m. to 9 p.m. Monday through Saturdays. They are closed on Sunday. Their menu features a variety of specialties, such as Seafood Marinara, Chicken Salpimbacca, Shrimp Scampi, Veal Marsala, linquine and New York strip steak. Average prices run between $8.95 and $14.95 for most dinner selections. Daily specials are also available. Their main dining room has a contemporary atmosphere with a beautiful view looking out over their court yard and garden. The decor of the restaurant offers an elegant touch, with carpeted floors, linen table cloths, and candlelit tables. The dining room has seating for up to 70 persons. Larger groups and parties are welcome with advance reservations. This is a family operated and owned establishment eager to satisfy its customers with friendly and efficient service. For more information about La Veranda Restaurant call 663-3321.

Lodging: Four Acres Motel (1-1/5 miles) 458-8158; Redwood Motel (Adj Arpt) 664-4351; The Orchards (2 miles) 458-9611; The 1896 Motel (6 miles) 458-8125; Williams Inn (2-1/2 mile) 458-9371.
Meeting Rooms: Esposito Flying Service (FBO) 663-3330 has accommodations for meetings. Also The Orchards Inn 458-9611, and the Williams Inn 458-9371.
Transportation: Mohawk Motors Car Rental 663-3729; B & L Gulf 458-8269; Norm's Limousine 663-8300; Luxury Limo Service 458-9414.
Information: Northern Berkshire Chamber of Commerce, 40 Main Street, North Adams, MA 01247, Phone: 663-3735.

Attractions:

Numerous summer theatre events, 597-3400; Clark Art Museum (3 miles) 458-9545; Also Taconic Golf Course 458-9669; Waubeeka Golf Course 458-5869; Jiminy Resort and Ski Area 458-5771; Berk Visitor Bureau 443-9186.

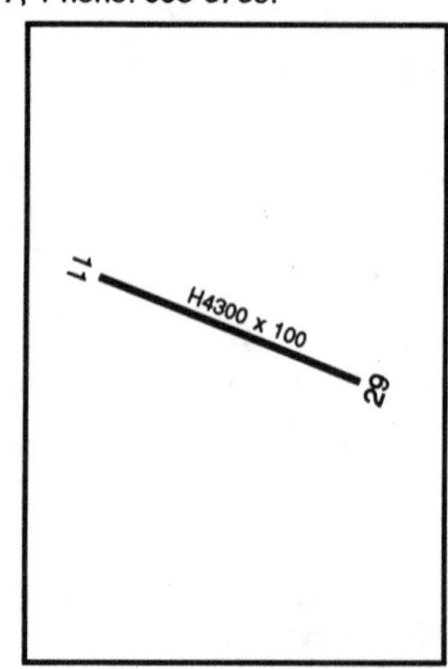

Airport Information:

NORTH ADAMS - HARRIMAN AND WEST AIRPORT (AQW)
3 mi west of town N42-41.75 W73-10.22 Elev: 654 Fuel: 100LL, Jet-A
Rwy 11-29: H4300x100 (Asph) Attended: dawn-dusk Unicom: 122.8 Public Phone 24hrs
Notes: CAUTION: Extensive glider operations sunrise to sunset, surface to 18,000 year around and primarily weekends and holidays. No landing fee; Parking fee $5.00/night or $25/month.
FBO: Turboprop International, Inc. Phone: 664-4585

MA-OWD - NORWOOD
NORWOOD MEMORIAL AIRPORT

(Area Code 617) 14

Prop Stop Restaurant:

The Prop Stop Restaurant is located in a parking lot adjacent to the Norwood Memorial Airport. This is a cafeteria styled restaurant that is open 6 days a week Monday through Saturday between 7 a.m. and 3 p.m. They specialize in preparing breakfast and lunch entrees. Their menu contains selections like omelettes, French toast, homemade soups, sandwiches, fish specials on Fridays, pot roast and chicken dishes. They offer a special choice each day. Their dining room can seat 50 to 55 persons. The decor of this establishment caters to an aviation theme, utilizing aerial pictures of the city and surrounding areas. Groups and parties are always welcome. Meals can also be prepared for carry-out. For more information about the Prop Stop Restaurant call 769-3038.

Restaurants Near Airport:
Prop Stop Restaurant Adj Arpt Phone: 769-3038

lodging: Comfort Inn (2 miles) 326-6700; Holiday Inn (2 miles) 329-1000; Norwood Country Club (Est. 3-4 miles) 769-7000.

Meeting Rooms: Norwood Inn 326-6700; Holiday Inn 329-1000; Norwood Country Club 769-7000.

Transportation: Taxi Service: Norwood Taxi 762-0400; Yellow Cab 769-4100; Also Rental Car Service: Avis 762-6505; Budget 769-8680.

Information: Massachusetts Office of Travel and Tourism, 100 Cambridge Street, 13th floor, Boston, MA 02202, Phone: 617-727-3201. Greater Boster Convention & Visitors Bureau, Prudential Tower, P.O. Box 990468, Boston, MA 02199, Phone: 536-4100.

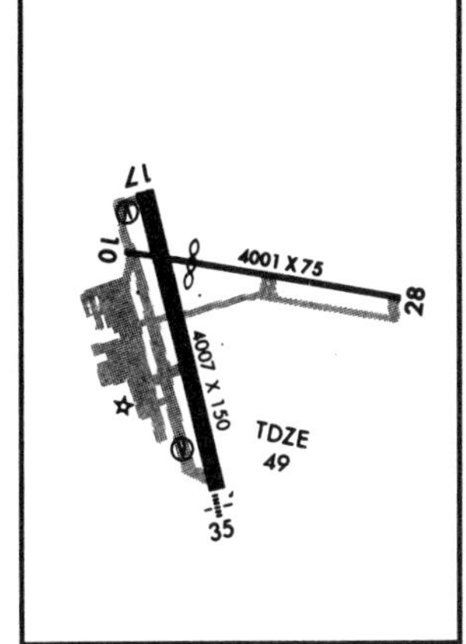

Airport Information:

NORWOOD - NORWOOD MEMORIAL AIRPORT (OWD)
2 mi east of town N42-11.45 W71-10.39 Elev: 50 Fuel: 100LL, Jet-A
Rwy 17-35: H4007x150 (Asph) Rwy 10-28: H4001x75 (Asph) Attended: 1200-0300Z
Atis: 119.95 Unicom: 122.95 Tower: 126.0 Gnd Con: 121.8 Clnc Del: 121.8
FBO: Eastern Air Center, Inc. Phone: 769-8680
FBO: Wiggins Airways, Inc. Phone: 762-5690

MA-ORE - ORANGE
ORANGE MUNICIPAL

(Area Code 508) 15

Homestead Fine Food & Spirits:

The Homestead Fine Food & Spirits Restaurant is located south of the field within walking distance from the Orange Municipal Airport. According to our readers, it's an easy 10 minute walk from aircraft parking. The restaurant is classified as a country farm and family theme dining facility within a rustic 1700s-style tavern. Restaurant hours are lunch served Wednesday through Saturday from 11:30 p.m. to 1:30 p.m., and dinner Wednesday through Thursday from 5:00 p.m. to 8:30 p.m. Friday and Saturday from 5:00 p.m. to 9:30 p.m. and Sunday 12:00 noon to 5:00 p.m. (Closed Monday & Tuesday). Specialties of the house include a large varied menu containing items like Prime rib, steaks, salmon, sword fish, lobster, duck, alligator, chicken and fried steaks. Their lunch buffet is available Wednesday through Friday and runs only $6.95. Their menu includes as many as 12 to 15 daily specials. Average prices run $7.00 for lunch and $10.00 for dinner. Live entertainment is featured every Friday and Saturday night. Reservations can be made for larger groups. In-flight catering is also available. The Homestead Restaurant has been in business for over 10 years, and is popular with many pilots. For information call 544-8949.

Restaurants Near Airport:
Homestead 1/2 mi Phone: 544-8949

Lodging: Bald Eagle 1 mi 544-2101; Bullard Farm Bed & Breakfast 3 mi 544-6959.

Meeting Rooms: None reported

Transportation: Rental Cars: Country Ford 249-3531; Great Escape 544-7507. Taxi Service: Athol 249-2727; Friendly Town Cab 544-3535.

Information: Worcester County Convention & Visitors Bureau, 33 Waldo Street. Worcester, MA 01608. Phone: 508-753-2920.

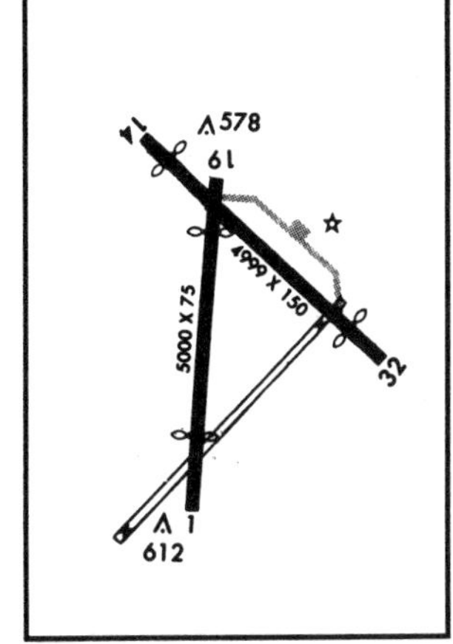

Airport Information:

ORANGE - ORANGE MUNICIPAL (ORE)
1 mi southeast of town N42-34.21 W72-17.32 Elev: 555 Fuel: 80, 100LL Rwy 01-19: H5000x75 (Asph) Rwy 14-32: H4999x150 (Asph) Attended: 1300Z-dusk Unicom: 122.8 Notes: Consult the airport manager and Airport Facility Directory for cautions about runway conditions. Camping on field.
FBO: Orange Municipal Airport Phone: 544-8189
FBO: Wings of New England Phone: 544-6715

MA-PSF - PITTSFIELD PITTSFIELD MUNICIPAL

(Area Code 413) 16, 17

Dakota Restaurant:

This restaurant is a fine dining facility located 1-1/2 miles south-southeast of the Pittsfield Municipal Airport. They specialize in preparing selections like steak and seafood, Teriyaki chicken and sirloin, filet mignon, Dakota grilled sirloin, chicken and shrimp, salmon and sirloin combination plates, wood grilled rainbow trout and live Maine lobster. In addition to these, they also feature 2 separate salad bars. Dakota Restaurant also serves an all you can eat Sunday brunch from 10 a.m. to 2 p.m. specializing in items like Belgium waffles, carver steaks, an omelet line, smoked fish station, fresh fruit and salad bar. Average prices run $11.00 to $19.00 for most selections. This establishment is styled after an Andirondak hunting camp with a big lodge appearance, field stone fireplace, antler trophy mounts and other items on display from the region. Accommodations for groups up to 120 people can easily be arranged. Business rooms for conferences are also available. Restaurant hours are 5 p.m. to 10 p.m. weekdays and 4 p.m. to 11 p.m. on weekends. To reach the restaurant, head east on Dan Fox Drive to Route 7, then make a right and go about 200 yards. It will be on the left side of the street. This is one of the popular establishments in the Berkshire's. For information call 499-7900.

Prop Stop Coffee Shop:

The Prop Stop Coffee Shop is reported to be located on the Pittsfield Municipal Airport at the end of runway 32. It is part of Pittsfield Aviation. This cafe is open Thursdays through Sunday from 9 a.m. to 3 p.m. They serve a full breakfast line along with over stuffed sandwiches, soup & chili. One of our readers also informed us that Pitts Aviation Enterprise offer specials for oil changes for $69.95 and will even buy you free lunch or breakfast. For more information call the restaurant at 499-3548

Restaurants Near Airport:

Dakota	1-1/2 mi	Phone: 499-7900
Jimmy's	5 mi N.	Phone: 499-1288
Lenox	5 mi S.	Phone: 637-4218
Prop Stop Coffee Shop	On Site	Phone: 499-3548
Silver Screen	2-1/2 mi	Phone: 443-5484

Lodging: Hilton Inn 3 mi 499-2000; Quality Inn 637-4244; Yankee Motor Lodge (free trans, 2 mi south) 499-3700;

Meeting Rooms: Hilton Inn 3 mi 499-2000; Jiminy Peak 738-5500; Cranwell Resort (Golf).

Transportation: Lyon Aviation, Inc. has courtesy cars available 443-6700; Also Rental Cars: Enterprise Rent-A-Car 443-6600; Hertz 499-4153; Taxi Service: Rainbow Taxi 499-4300.

Information: Berkshire Visitors Bureau, Berkshire Common, Pittsfield, MA 01201 Phone: 443-9186, 800-237-5747.

Attractions:

Bousquet Ski Resort has a moderate-size ski mountain with a 750 foot drop and 21 trails. This resort has a cafeteria, full bar and lounge on the premises. The resort is located approximately 1 mile from the airport. If you call them from the airport, they will come out and pick you up. For information call 442-8316; Additional attractions in the area include: Norman Rockwell Museum, Tanglewood, Jacobs Pllow. Williams Theatre Festival, Canyon Ranch Resort, Cranwell Resort (Golf), Hancock Shaker Village, Lebanon Valley Speedway. There are 4 public golf courses reported, all within 2 to 10 miles from airport.

Airport Information:

PITTSFIELD - PITTSFIELD MUNICIPAL (PSF)
2 mi west of town N42-25.61 W73-17.58 Elev: 1194 Fuel: 100LL, Jet-A Rwy 08-26: H5000x100 (Asph-Grvd) Rwy 14-32: H3496x100 (Asph) Attended: Mon-Fri 1200-0100Z, Sat 1300-2300Z, Sun 1300-0100Z Unicom: 122.7 Public phone: 24hrs
FBO: Lyon Aviation, Inc. Phone: 443-6700

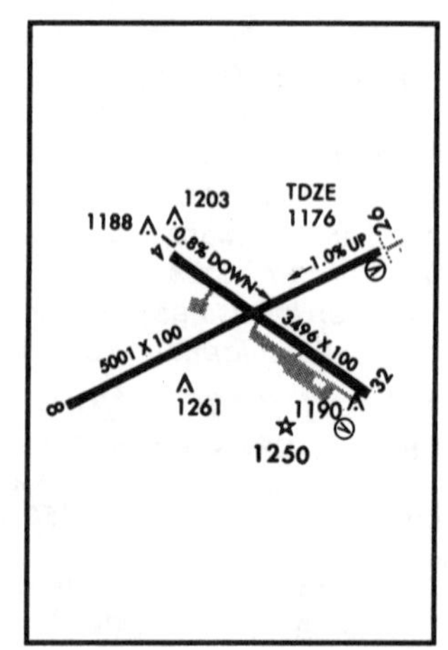

18

MA-PYM - PLYMOUTH
PLYMOUTH MUNICIPAL AIRPORT

(Area Code 508)

Restaurants Near Airport:
Plane Jane's Cafe On Site Phone: 747-9396

Plane Jane's Cafe:

The Plane Jane's Cafe restaurant is situated on the upper level of the terminal building at the Plymouth Municipal Airport. According to the management, aircraft parking is located within easy walking distance to the restaurant. Their hour are 7:30 a.m. to 5 p.m. during weekdays and 6:00 a.m. to 3 p.m. on weekends. The menu features sandwiches, chili and all types of breakfast items served all day including egg dishes, omelets, French toast, and freshly baked muffins. Daily specials are also offered. The restaurant has seating for 30 to 35 persons in addition to outdoor dining on 2 large picnic tables. The view from the restaurant through two large windows allows guests to see all the activity on the airport. The decor of this facility is contemporary and displays many photographs of airplanes on the wall. Average prices run around $2.50 to $3.00 for most selections. Carry-out meals are also available. For more information call the Runway View Restaurant at 747-9396.

Lodging: John Carver Inn (2 miles, free trans) 746-7100; Sheraton Hotel (4 miles, free trans) 746-4900.

Meeting Rooms: John Carver Inn 746-7100; Pilgrim-Sands Motel 747-0900; Sheraton Hotel 746-4900.

Transportation: Taxi Service: Central Cab 746-0018; Blue Taxi 746-2525; Also Rental Cars: Shire Town Ford 746-3400; Thrifty Car Rental 747-2120; Verc Car Rental 746-8933.

Information: Plymouth Area Chamber of Commerce, 225 Water Street, Suite 500, Plymouth, MA 02360, Phone: 830-1620.

Attractions:

Tourist area of America's hometown with historical points of interest such as Plymouth Rock where the Pilgrims first settled, in addition to sporting activities like fresh and salt water fishing within the area.

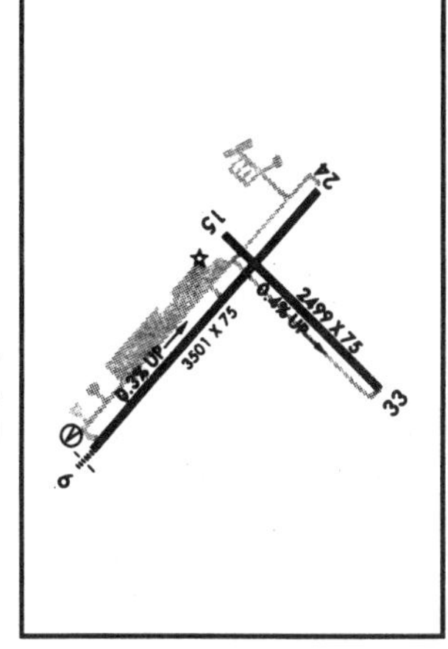

Airport Information:

PLYMOUTH - PLYMOUTH MUNICIPAL AIRPORT (PYM)
4 mi southwest of town 41-54-35N 70-43-46W Elev: 149 Fuel: 80, 100LL, Jet-A, MOGAS Rwy 06-24: H3501x75 (Asph) Rwy 15-33: H2501x75 (Asph) Attended: 1300Z-dusk Unicom: 123.0 Public Phone 24hrs Notes: Overnight parking fees: Twins$10.00, Singles $5.00; (No fee's with fuel purchase).

FBO: Alpha-One Aviation Flight School **Phone: 747-1494**
FBO: Aviation International Flight School **Phone: 746-9326**
FBO: Yankee Services (Maintenance Hangar) **Phone: 746-5511**
FBO: Northeast Maintenance Service **Phone: 746-1112**

19

MA-PVC - PROVINCETOWN
PROVINCETOWN MUNICIPAL

(Area Code 508)

Restaurants Near Airport:

Lobster Pot	3 mi	Phone: 487-0842
Mayflower Cafe	3 mi	Phone: 487-0120
Mews Restaurant	4 mi	Phone: 487-1500
Napi's	3 mi	Phone: 487-1145

Mews Restaurant & Cafe Mews:

This restaurant is very popular with many pilots who enjoy good food and exceptional service. On more then one occasion our readers asked us to include the Mews Restaurant into our directory. To reach the restaurant, you can take Main Road to the center of town. Turn left on Bradford, then right on to Bangs, then right on Commercial to 429. It's on the left. They offer a full menu in their main dining room which includes "scallops Addington" with artichoke hearts, filet mignon, duck, lamb and fresh fish. In their cafe section they have hamburgers, individual pizzas, pork chops, seafood, stew and roasted 1/2 chicken. Average prices run $10.00 for lunch and $30.00 for dinner in the dinning room. Their Sunday brunch features menu items (not a buffet). The cafe provides a view overlooking the harbor. The decor of the restaurant is decorated warmly with mahogany. The main dining room overlooks the beach and contains a light and airy atmosphere with linen-covered tables. Banquet and special events serving up to 120 customers can easily be arranged. For information call The Mews Restaurant & Cafe Mews at 487-1500.

Lodging: Holiday Inn (May-Oct) 3mi 487-1711; Provincetown Inn (July-Aug) 4 mi 487-9500;
Meeting Rooms: Holiday Inn (May-Oct) 3mi 487-1711; Provincetown Inn (Seasonal) 4 mi 487-9500;
Transportation: Rental Cars: Thrifty 487-0243; U-Save 487-1539. Taxi Service: Cape Cab 487-2222; Martins 487-0243.
Information: Provincetown Chamber of Commerce, 307 Commercial Street, P.O. Box 1017, Provincetown, MA 02657. Phone: 487-3424.

Attractions:

Town Wharf (MacMillan Wharf) off Commercial Street at Standish Street; Whale watching charter boats, "Cape Cod Cruises" 747-2400, "Portuguese Princess Whale Watch" 487-2651; Provincetown Museum has exhibits containg whaling equipment, artifacts from shipwrecks, antique memoribelia. 487-1310

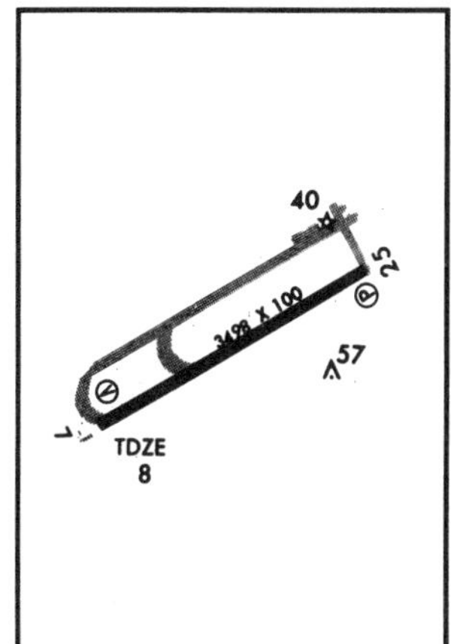

Airport Information:

PROVINCETOWN - PROVINCETOWN MUNICIPAL (PVC)
2 mi northwest of town N42-04.32 W70-13.28 Elev: 8 Fuel: 100LL Rwy 07-25: H3498x100 (Asph) Attended: May-Oct, dalgt hours; Nov-Apr, Mon-Sat 1300-1530Z and 2030-2330Z, Sun 1830-2330Z. Unicom: 122.8

FBO: Cape Air **Phone: 487-0241**

MA-3B0 - SOUTHBRIDGE
SOUTHBRIDGE MUNICIPAL AIRPORT

(Area Code 508) **20**

Restaurants Near Airport:

Public House	5 mi W.	Phone: 347-3313
Windsock Diner	On Site	Phone: 765-0226

Lodging: American Motor Lodge (5 miles) 347-9121; Sir Francis Motel 347-9514; Sturbridge Sheraton (5 miles) 347-7393.

Meeting Rooms: None Reported

Transportation: King Courier Taxi Service 347-7460; Vet's Taxi Service 764-2551; Rental Cars: Budget 764-7965.

Information: Massachusetts Office of Travel and Tourism, 100 Cambridge Street, 13th floor, Boston, MA 02202, Phone: 617-727-3201 or 800-447-MASS for free information booklet.

Windsock Diner:

The Windsock Diner is located right on the parking ramp of the Southbridge Municipal Airport. This dinner is open Thursday and Friday from 11 a.m. to 9 p.m., Saturday 7 a.m. to 4 p.m. and Sunday 7 a.m. to 1 p.m., summer hours are usually longer. Their menu features many items including specialties of the house like their "Tail Dragger" breakfast including 3 eggs, 2 French toasts, a nice slice of ham, 2 strips of bacon, home fries, toast and coffee for only $3.95. Another item which is a favorite with customers is their "Windsock Burger Special" with two 1/4 pound meat patties, 2 strips of bacon, lettuce, tomato, with or without cheese for only $3.50. Other items of interest are their hamburger steak, meat loaf, roast turkey, roast beef, and all types of sandwiches. Most selections run between $4.00 and $5.00. Breakfast is also served all day as well. There are three separate dining areas one of which is located outdoors on their sun deck able to seat up to 40 persons. The view of the entire airport can be enjoyed. Additional seating within the restaurant can accommodate 34 in the front portion, and 28 in the rear portion. Fly-in groups and parties are welcome. Please let them know if your group is large. The owner if this restaurant is dedicated to providing customers with friendly and efficient service and has been at this location for 5 years. Carry-out meals are also available. For more information about the Windsock Diner, call 765-0226.

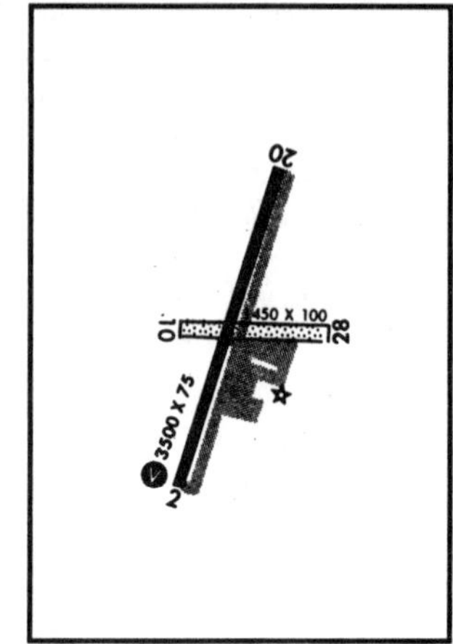

Airport Information:

SOUTHBRIDGE - SOUTHBRIDGE MUNICIPAL AIRPORT (3B0)
2 mi north of town N42-06.06 W72-02.30 Elev: 697 Fuel: 100LL,
Rwy 02-20: H3500x75 (Asph) Rwy 10-28: 1450x100 (Turf) Attended 1300Z-dusk
Unicom: 122.8
FBO: Jim's Flying Service Phone: 765-0226

MA-3B3 - STERLING
STERLING AIRPORT

(Area Code 508) **21**

Restaurants Near Airport:

Country Fare	2 mi	Phone: N/A
Plane Delights Restaurant	On Site	Phone: 422-8860
Sterling Inn	1-1/2 mi	Phone: 422-6333

Lodging: Chocksett Inn 5 mi 422-3355; Sterling Inn 1-1/2 mi 422-6333

Transportation: Courtesy car is available at Sterling Air, Inc. by calling 422-8860.

Information: North Central Massachusetts Chamber of Commerce, 110 Erdman Way, Leominster, MA 01453. Phone: 508-840-4300

Plane Delights Restaurant:

Plane Delights Restaurant is located on the west side of Sterling Airport next to the flight school. Sterling Air, Inc. and the Plane Delights Restaurant are operated by the same owners. Pilots can park their aircraft at the restaurant. This combination snack bar and cafe is open weekdays from 3:30 to dusk and on weekends from 8 a.m. to 1 p.m. Average prices for entrees run around $3.00 for most selections. On weekends they serve a full breakfast as well as sandwiches for lunch. During the week they specialize in ice cream delights. For more information about this facility call the Plane Delights Restaurant at 422-8860.

Attractions:

Wachusett Mountain Ski Area is located 8 miles northwest of the airport. For information you can contact either Sterling Air, Inc. at 422-8860 or the North Central Massachusetts Chamber of Commerce at 508-840-4300.

NO AIRPORT DIAGRAM AVAILABLE

Airport Information:

STERLING - STERLING AIRPORT (3B3)
2 mi north of town N42-27.63 W71-31.08 Elev: 268 Fuel: 100LL, Jet-A, Mogas Rwy: 03-21: H2743x50 (Asph) Rwy 12-30: 1600x50 (Crvl) Attended: May-Oct 1400-2300Z, Nov-Apr 1400-2200Z Unicom: 122.8 Notes: Overnight parking $3.00
FBO: Sterling Air, Inc. Phone: 422-8860

MA-6B6 - STOW
MINUTE MAN AIRFIELD

(Area Code 508) 22

Izzi's On The Runway:

This family style restaurant is located adjacent to the manager's and facilities office on the Minute Man Airfield. It is open from 6:30 a.m. to 3 p.m. 6 days a week (Closed on Mondays). One unique specialty of this restaurant is their famous homemade omelets as well as several other popular daily specials. Prices are very reasonable with large portions. The restaurant has a country setting, beautifully decorated with an aviation atmosphere. They can cater for up to 30 people on the premises after regular restaurant business hours. Preparing meals for pick-up by pilots on the go is also available with advance notice. This restaurant provides fast friendly service in a home style atmosphere and welcomes fly-in customers. For information call 897-5550.

Restaurants Near Airport:
Izzi's On The Runway On Site Phone: 897-5550

Lodging: Bed & Breakfast Inn - Amersoot House, 61 West Action Road, Stow MA 01775, Phone: 897-0660.

Transportation: Rental Cars on field $20/25 per day. Stow Aviation Services, Inc., Phone: 897-3933.

Information: Massachusetts Office of Travel and Tourism, 100 Cambridge Street, 13th floor, Boston, MA 02202, Phone: 617-727-3201 or 800-447-MASS for free information booklet.

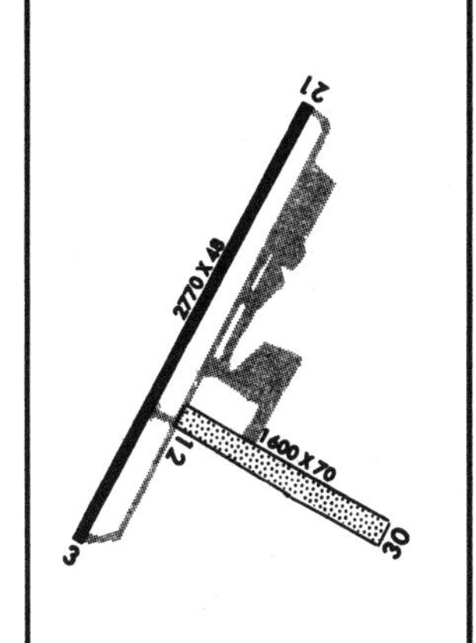

Attraction:

Apple picking 3 miles from airport at local orchards, also 32 miles from Boston MA.

Airport Information:

STOW - MINUTE MAN AIRFIELD (6B6)
2 mi north of town N42-27.63 W71-31.08 Elev: 268 Fuel: 100LL, Jet-A, MOGAS
Rwy 03-21: H2743x50 (Asph) Rwy 12-30: 1600x50 (Grvl) Attended: July-Oct 1400-2300Z, Nov-Jun 1400-2200Z Unicom: 122.8 Public Phone 24hrs Notes: $10.00 parking - part waved if purchasing full.
FBO: Stow Aviation Services, Inc., Phone: 897-3933

MA-TAN - TAUNTON
TAUNTON MUNICIPAL AIRPORT

(Area Code 508) 23, 24

Airport Restaurant: (Temporarily Closed)

The Airport Restaurant is located on the Taunton Municipal Airport and according to the management, can easily be reached by walking from aircraft tie-down areas. This snack bar is temporarily closed. During our conversation with the airport management, they told us that they are looking for someone to cook breakfast and lunch especially on weekends. Once this occurs, the cafe will be re-opened. No further information was available at the time of our research.

Taunton House of Pizza:

The Taunton House of Pizza is reported within 2 miles of the Taunton Municipal Airport. They specialize in preparing an assortment of pizzas as well as other items. For information call 823-6316.

Restaurants Near Airport:
Airport Restaurant On Site Phone: 824-5681
Taunton House of Pizza 2 mi. Phone: 823-6316

Lodging: Swiss Chalet (4 miles); Taunton Regency Inn (5-6 miles) 823-0430; Town & Country Motor Inn (4 miles) 824-8647.

Meeting Rooms: Taunton Regency Inn 823-0430.

Transportation: Taxi Service: Checker Cab 824-5831; Cozy Cab 823-3082; Also Rental Cars: Thrifty 823-9070; Thrust Auto 822-0124.

Information: Massachusetts Office of Travel and Tourism, 100 Cambridge Street, 13th floor, Boston, MA 02202, Phone: 617-727-3201, or call for free travel guide 800-447-MASS.

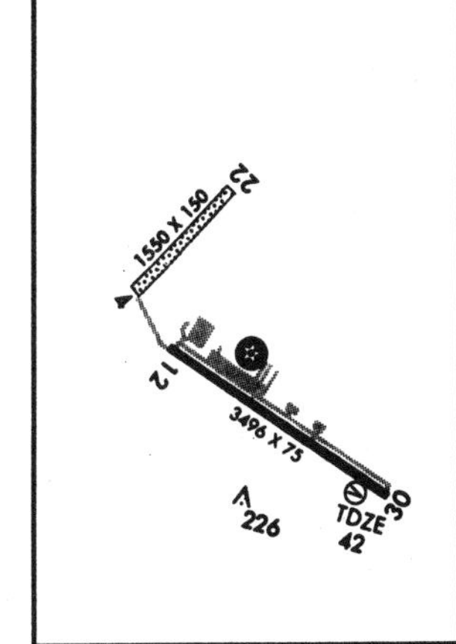

Airport Information:

TAUNTON - TAUNTON MUNICIPAL AIRPORT (TAN)
3 mi east of town 41-52-28N 71-01-03W Elev: 43 Fuel: 100LL
Rwy 12-30: H3496x75 (Asph) Rwy 04-22: 1550x150 (Turf-Grvl) Attended: 1300Z-dusk
Unicom: 122.7
FBO: King Aviation Phone: 823-3682

MA-B09 - TEWKSBURY TEW-MAC AIRPORT

(Area Code 508) 25

Restaurants Near Airport:

Brothers Pizza	On Site	Phone: 851-6713

Brothers Pizza:

The Yesterday's Cafe is located adjacent to the end of runway three at the Tew-Mac Airport. This is a family style restaurant that is open during the summer between 6 a.m. and 10 p.m. They specialize in breakfast (Served all day), and for lunch they serve a variety of sub sandwiches and pizzas as well as soft serve ice cream. Prices range from $3.00 to $4.00 for breakfast and lunch. The decor of the restaurant is rustic, featuring Tew-Mac's early days. Accommodations are available for groups and private parties. Carry-out meals are also provided. For information call 851-6713.

Attractions:

Fun Land Arcade Park reported to b located across the street from the Tew-Mac Airport.

Lodging: Holiday Inn, (3-5 miles) I-495 south to exit 39 (Rt. 133) Victoria's Restaurant and Pub, Boardrooms, Phone: 640-9000; Holiday Inn (3 miles) 1 block south of I-495 along Route 38, Restaurant and lounge on premises, Video Conference rooms are available, Phone: 851-7301; Motel 38, (3 miles) Phone: 851-7378.

Meeting Rooms: Holiday Inn 640-9000; Holiday Inn 851-7301.

Transportation: Mr. Rent-A-Car, Phone: 858-0636; A & L Taxi, Phone: 454-5661.

Information: Northern Middlesex Convention & Visitors Bureau, 45 Palmer Street, Lowell, MA 01852, Phone: 937-9300.

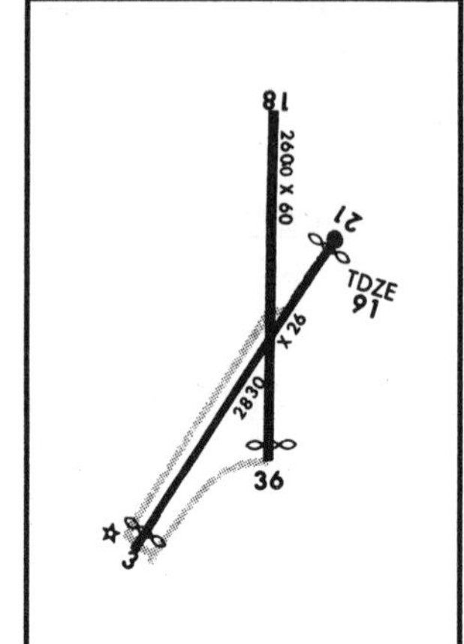

Airport Information:

TEWKSBURY - TEW-MAC AIRPORT (B09)
2 mi southeast of town N42-35.75 W71-12.26 Elev: 92 Fuel: 100LL, MOGAS
Rwy 03-21: H2830x26 (Asph) Rwy 18-36: H2600x60 (ASPH) Attended: 1330Z-Dusk
Unicom: 122.8 Telephone: available when airport office is open Notes: Overnight parking $10.00/night, discount with fuel purchase.
FBO: Tew-Mac Aviation, Phone: 851-9338

MA-MVY - VINEYARD HAVEN MARTHA'S VINEYARD AIRPORT

(Area Code 508) 26

Restaurants Near Airport:

Beef Tender	5 mi	Phone: N/A
Nunne Pog	Trml Bldg.	Phone: 693-3927
Ocean View	5 mi	Phone: N/A

Nunne-Pog Restaurant:

The Nunne-Pog Restaurant is situated within the terminal building on the Martha's Vineyard Airport and according to the management, it is within walking distance. This combination cafe and family style restaurant is open from 7 a.m. to 8 p.m. Monday through Saturday, and 8 a.m. to 5 p.m. on Sunday. They offer a wide selection of entrees for their customers including hamburgers, cheeseburgers, chicken breast and turkey dishes, sword fish burgers, chef salads, spinach and garden salads, homemade soups, seafood gumbo, chowder, homemade pies, and much more. Average prices run $4.95 for breakfast, $5.95 for lunch and around $9.95 for dinner. Daily and Friday night fish fry specials are also available. Their dining room, complete with table, booths and counter service, can seat 50 people. Groups and parties often arrange get-togethers through this restaurant and fly-in, private and corporate in-flight catering is available. In fact, a special menu is provided for catering purposes. A gift shop is also situated at the restaurant. For more information about Nunne-Pog Restaurant call 693-3927.

Lodging: Edgartown Heritage Hotel (5 miles, Edgartown) 627-5161; Harborview (5 miles) 627-4333; Kelly House (5 miles) 627-4394.

Meeting Rooms: Edgartown Heritage Hotel 627-5161; Harborview 627-4333; Kelly House 627-4394.

Transportation: Taxi Service: Jon's 627-4677; Marlene's Taxi 693-0037; Stage Coach 693-9632; Sunset Taxi Service 693-7110; Up Island 693-5454; Also Rental Cars: All Island Rentals 693-6868; Atlantic 693-9191; Budget 693-7322; Hertz 693-4728; National 693-4059.

Information: Chamber of Commerce, Beach Road, P.O. Box 1698, Vineyard Haven, MA 02568, Phone: 693-0085.

Attractions:

See Edgartown - Katama Airpark (MA-MB2)

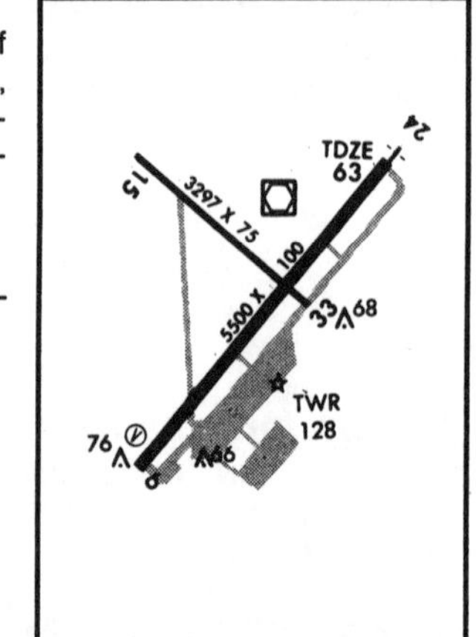

Airport Information:

VINEYARD HAVEN - MARTHA'S VINEYARD AIRPORT (MVY)
3 mi south of town N41-23.58 W70-36.86 Elev: 68 Fuel: 100LL, Jet-A
Rwy 06-24: H5500x100 (Asph) Rwy 15-33: H3297x75 (Asph) Attended: continuously
Atis: 126.25 Unicom: 122.95 Clnc Del: 124.7 Tower: 121.4 Gnd Con: 121.8
FBO: Direct Flight, Inc. Phone: 693-6688
FBO: Flywright Aviation Phone: 693-1067

MA-BAF - WESTFIELD BARNES MUNICIPAL

(Area Code 413)

27

Flight Deck:

Flight Deck is a family style restaurant in the Municipal Building, situated within walking distance, on the Barnes Municipal Airport. Their hours are 8 a.m. to 3 p.m. on Tuesday through Saturday, 8 a.m. to 2 p.m. on Sunday (closed Monday). Specialties of the house are no cholesterol items, full breakfasts, lunch specials, home-made soups and desserts, served each day. Prices run about $5.00 for breakfast and lunch. The restaurant has a home like atmosphere with a seating capacity of 48, clean and bright with tablecloths and fresh flowers on each table. Groups are welcome with advance reservations. Catering is also available for pilots on-the-go. For information call the restaurant at 568-2483.

Restaurants Near Airport:

Burgundy's	2 mi S.	Phone: 568-6320
Gaetano's	3 mi SE	Phone: 568-3946
Flight Deck	On Site	Phone: 568-2483
Foster House	2.5 mi S	Phone: 562-3809

Lodging: Country Court Motel (Adjacent) 562-9790; Edgewood Motel (Adjacent) 562-4662; Westfield Motor Inn (1 mile) 568-2821.
Meeting Rooms: Burgundy's (2 miles south) 568-6320; Holiday Inn (Approx 7-10 miles NE, Holyoke, MA) 534-3311.
Transportation: Mr G's 562-5075; City Cab 568-6177; Charis Air 562-4161.
Information: Greater Westfield Chamber of Commerce, 166 Elm Street, Westfield, MA 01085, Phone: 568-1618, Also Greater Springfield Convention Visitors Bureau, 34 Boland Way, Springfield, MA 01103, Phone: 787-1548.

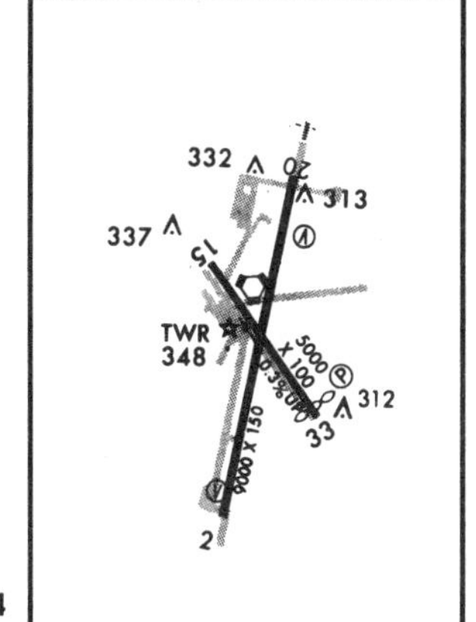

Attractions: East Mountain Country Club, (2 miles) East Mtn Road, 568-1539; Southampton Country Club, (2 miles) Route 10, Southampton, 527-9815; Hampton Ponds (2 miles) on North Road; Stanley Park (4 miles) 200 acres of gardens, ponds, walkways, japanese gardens, (summer concerts, Thur, Sat, Sun, Mid-May through Mid-Oct, Phone: 568-9312).

Airport Information:

WESTFIELD - BARNES MUNICIPAL (BAF)
3 mi north of town N42-09.46 W72-42.94 Elev: 271 Fuel: 80,100LL, Jet-A
Rwy 02-20: H9000x150 (Asph) Rwy 15-33: H5000x100 (Asph) Attended: dawn to dusk
Atis: 127.1 Tower: 118.9 Gnd Con: 121.7 Public Phone 24hrs Notes: Landing and parking fees as follows: (Up to 4000 lbs) No landing fee, $3.00 parking fee; (Up to 5000 lbs) landing fee $3.00, Parking fee $3.00. CAUTION: Deer on and in vicinity of airport.
FBO: Charis Air Corporation Phone: 562-4161 FBO: Northeastern Avionics Phone: 562-5124
FBO: K-C Aviation, Inc. Phone: 562-5860 FBO: Northeastern Air Serv. Phone: 568-8976

Let Us Know About Your Favorite "Prop Stoppers"

If you don't see your favorite fly-in restaurant, resort, or fly-to attraction, simply call us or just drop us a line and let us know about them. (See page 1,019)

Aerodine Magazine
P.O. Box 247, Palatine, IL 60078
Phone: 847-358-4355

MICHIGAN

LOCATION MAP

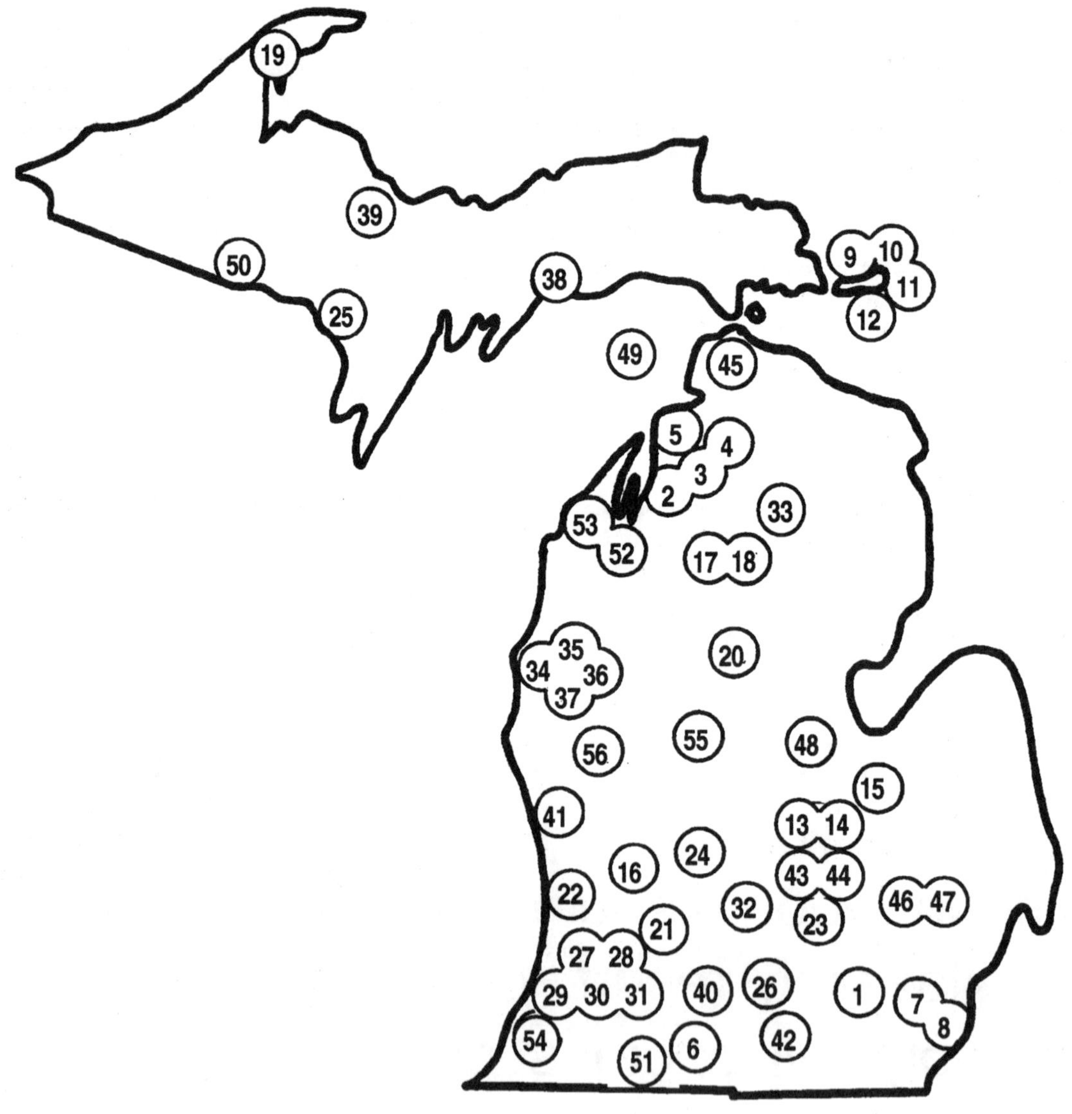

MICHIGAN

CROSS FILE INDEX

Location Number	City or Town	Airport Name And Identifier	Name of Restaurant
1	Ann Arbor	Ann Arbor Muni. Arpt. (ARB)	Trippers Sports Bar
2	Bellaire	Antrim Co. Arpt. (ACB)	Lakeview (Shanty Creek)
3	Boyne City	Boyne City Muni. Arpt. (D83)	Country Star Restaurant
4	Boyne Falls	Boyne Mountain Arpt. (BFA)	Boyne Mountain Lodge
5	Charlevoix	Charlevoix Muni. Arpt. (CVX)	Juilleret's Restaurant
6	Coldwater	Branch Co. Mem. (OEB)	West Arpt. Inn
7	Detroit	Detroit Metro Wayne Co. (DTW)	Marriott Innkeeper Rest.
8	Detroit/Grosse Ile	Grosse Ile Muni. Arpt. (ONZ)	Grosse Ile Racquet Club
9	Drummond Island	Drummond Island Arpt. (Y66)	Bear Track Inn
10	Drummond Island	Drummond Island Arpt. (Y66)	Chuck's Place Bar & Grill
11	Drummond Island	Drummond Island Arpt. (Y66)	Northwood Inn
12	Drummond Island	Drummond Island Arpt. (Y66)	Woodmoor Resort
13	Flushing	Dalton Arpt. (3DA)	Liberty Family Dining
14	Flushing	Dalton Arpt. (3DA)	Squire Creek Restaurant
15	Frankenmuth	William Tiny Zehnders Field (66G)	Bavarian Inn & Zehnder's
16	Grand Rapids	Kent Co. Intl. (GRR)	Marriott's Host Rest.
17	Grayling	Grayling AAF (55D)	Bears Country Inn
18	Grayling	Grayling AAF (55D)	Lone Pine Inn
19	Hancock	Houghton Co. Mem. Arpt. (CMX)	Aero Restaurant
20	Harrison	Clare Co. Arpt. (80D)	Aero Port Restaurant
21	Hastings	Hastings Arpt. (9D9)	Bay Pointe Restaurant
22	Holland	Park Township Arpt. (HLM)	Candlewick Inn
23	Howell	Livingston County Arpt. (OZW)	Tomato Brothers Rest.
24	Ionia	Ionia Co. Arpt. (Y70)	Big Boy's Restaurant
25	Iron Mt./Kingsford	Ford Arpt. (IMT)	The Blind Duck Inn
26	Jackson	Jackson Co.-Reynolds Field (JXN)	Airport Rest. & Spirits
27	Kalamazoo	Kalamazoo/Battle Creek Intl. (AZO)	Bill Knapp's
28	Kalamazoo	Kalamazoo/Battle Creek Intl. (AZO)	Bravo Ristorante
29	Kalamazoo	Kalamazoo/Battle Creek Intl. (AZO)	Gum Ho
30	Kalamazoo	Kalamazoo/Battle Creek Intl. (AZO)	Hawthorne's
31	Kalamazoo	Kalamazoo/Battle Creek Intl. (AZO)	Theo & Stacy's
32	Lansing	Capital City Arpt. (LAN)	Skyway Lng. & Cafeteria
33	Lewiston	Garland Airport (GAR)	Garland Retreat
34	Ludington	Mason Co. Arpt. (LDM)	Gibbs Restaurant
35	Ludington	Mason Co. Arpt. (LDM)	Kuntry Kubbard
36	Ludington	Mason Co. Arpt. (LDM)	Lands Inn Dinner Thetr.
37	Ludington	Mason Co. Arpt. (LDM)	P.M. Steamers
38	Manistique	Schoolcraft Co. (ISQ)	Fireside Inn Restaurant
39	Marquette	Marquette Co. Arpt. (MQT)	Arpt. Rest. & Lounge
40	Marshall	Brooks Field (RMY)	Schuler's Restaurant
41	Muskegon	Muskegon Co. Arpt. (MKG)	Brownstone Restaurant
42	Napoleon	Napoleon Arpt. (3NP)	Napoleon Restaurant

CROSS FILE INDEX
(Michigan Continued)

Location Number	City or Town	Airport Name And Identifier	Name of Attraction
43	Owosso	Owosso Community Arpt. (5D3)	B.J.'s Fine Foods Rest.
44	Owosso	Owosso Community Arpt. (5D3)	Bob Evans Restaurant
45	Pellston	Pellston Reg. of Emmet Co. (PLN)	Brass Rail Restaurant
46	Pontiac	Oakland-Pontiac (PTK)	Cafe Max
47	Pontiac	Oakland-Pontiac (PTK)	Mitch's II Restaurant
48	Saginaw	MBS Intl. (MBS)	The Sky Rm. & Kittyhawk
49	St. James	Beaver Island Arpt. (SJX)	Beaver Island
50	Stambaugh	Stambaugh Arpt. (Y73)	Kermit's Bar
51	Sturgis	Kirsch Muni. Arpt. (IRS)	Taste of Asia
52	Traverse City	Cherry Capital Arpt. (TVC)	Suncatcher Lounge
53	Traverse City	Sugar Loaf Village Arpt. (Y04)	Sugar Loaf Resort
54	Watervliet	Watervliet Muni. Arpt. (40C)	Ma & Pa's Cntry. Kitchen
55	Weidman	Lake Isabella Arpt. (D15)	The Pines
56	White Cloud	White Cloud Arpt. (42C)	Sally's Restaurant

Articles

City or town	Nearest Airport and Identifier	Name of Attraction
Boyne Falls, MI	Boyne Mountain. (BFA)	Boyne Mtn/Boyne Highlands
Detroit, MI	Detroit City (DET)	Hnry. Frd. Musm.-Grnfld. Vill.
Drummond Islnd, MI	Drummond Island (Y66)	Woodmoor Resort
Frankenmuth, MI	Wm "Tiny" Zehnder Fld. (66G)	Town of Frankenmuth
Kalamazoo, MI	Kalamazoo/Battle Creek Intl. (AZO)	Kalamazoo Aviation Museum
Mackinac Island, MI	Mackinac Island (Y84)	Mackinac Island
Traverse City, MI	Sugar Loaf Resort (Y04)	Sugar Loaf Resort

MI-ARB - ANN ARBOR
ANN ARBOR MUNICIPAL AIRPORT

(Area Code 313)

1

Trippers Sports Bar:

Trippers Sports Bar is located 4 blocks from the Ann Arbor Municipal Airport. According to the restaurant management, fly-in guest can see the restaurant from the airport and should have no problem walking. This full service restaurant and combination sports bar is open Monday through Thursday form 11 a.m. to 1 a.m., Friday and Saturday from 11 a.m. to 2 a.m., and Sunday from 11 a.m. to midnight. A variety of house specialties include burgers, Chinese stir fry, burritos, fettucini, and all types of appetizers and sandwiches. Two special entrees are usually offered each day as well as weekly specials. The restaurant combined with a lounge can accommodate 300 guests and provides a variety of atmospheres, from relaxing to exciting and stimulating. Entertainment with big screen sports action, and 36 TV's can bring the action right to your table. The dining room and lounge is decorated with many sports photographs, posters and drawings. A private room called the "Press Box" can seat 45 persons for parties or groups with advance notice required. Meals can also be prepared for carry-out. For further information about Trippers Sports Bar, call 665-1600.

Restaurants Near Airport:
Trippers Sports Bar 4 blks Phone: 665-1600

Lodging: Hilton Berkshire 761-7800; Sheraton Inn University (Trans) 996-0600; Weber's Inn 769-2500.

Meeting Rooms: Hilton Berkshire 761-7800; Sheraton Inn University 996-0600; Weber's Inn 769-2500.

Transportation: Check with fixed base operators for courtesy or available rental cars.

Information: Convention & Visitors Bureau, 120 West Huron, Ann Arbor, MI 48104, Phone: 995-7281.

Airport Information:

ANN ARBOR - ANN ARBOR MUNICIPAL AIRPORT (ARB)
3 mi south of town N42-13.38 W83-44.74 Elev: 839 Fuel: 80, 100LL, Jet-A
Rwy 06-24: H3500x75 (Asph) Rwy 12-30: 2800x120 (Turf) Attended: Nov-Mar 1300-0100Z, Apr-Oct 1300-0100Z Atis: 134.55 Unicom: 123.0 Tower: 120.3 Gnd Con: 121.6 Clnc Del: 121.6
FBO: Aviation Center Phone: 662-8427
FBO: Bijan Air, Inc. Phone: 769-9699

MI-ACB - BELLAIRE
ANTRIM COUNTY AIRPORT

(Area Code 616)

2

Lakeview Dining Room/Shanty Creek: (Resort)

The Lakeview Dining Room is located within the Shanty Creek, situated about 3 miles from the Antrim County Airport. Free courtesy transportation can easily be obtained by calling the resort from the airport. The restaurant is open 7 days a week. Breakfast is served between 7 a.m. and 10 a.m., Lunch from 11:30 to 2:30 p.m. and dinner from 6:00 p.m. to 9:00 p.m. The restaurant has a contemporary lodge setting with a massive field stone fireplace and towering fig trees. A full variety of menu items are prepared by their award winning chef. Average prices run $6.00 for breakfast, $7.50 for lunch, and $17.00 for dinner. Sunday brunch is also featured between 11:30 and 3:00 p.m. Catering is available for groups and business conventions for up to 700 individuals. Shanty Creek offers year around entertainment with a variety of lodging accommodations ranging from lodge rooms to suites to condos to villas. For information about the dining, lodging or recreation, call Shanty Creek at 533-8621 or 800-678-4111.

Restaurants Near Airport:
Mrs. Pete's Place 1/2 mi S. Phone: 533-9901
Shanty Creek 3 mi S. Phone: 533-8621

Lodging: Shanty Creek Lodge (Free trans) 533-8621; Shanty

Meeting Rooms: Shanty Creek Lodge 533-8621.

Transportation: Shanty Creek Lodge provides a courtesy van to pick up guests or diners who fly in to Atrim County Airport, 533-8621. Rental cars can be obtained through the airport manager's office by calling 533-8524; Also Antrim County Transportation (Dial-A-Ride, Monday through Friday only) 533-8644.

Information: Shanty Creek Shanty Creek Road, Bellaire, MI 49615, Phone: 533-8621.

Attractions:

Shanty Creek 4 seasons of entertainment for the entire family. Downhill skiing, cross country skiing, swimming, tennis, golfing, night life and entertainment, dining, lodging and much more. For information about this resort or if requesting free courtesy transportation to and from the airport call 533-8621 or 800-678-4111.

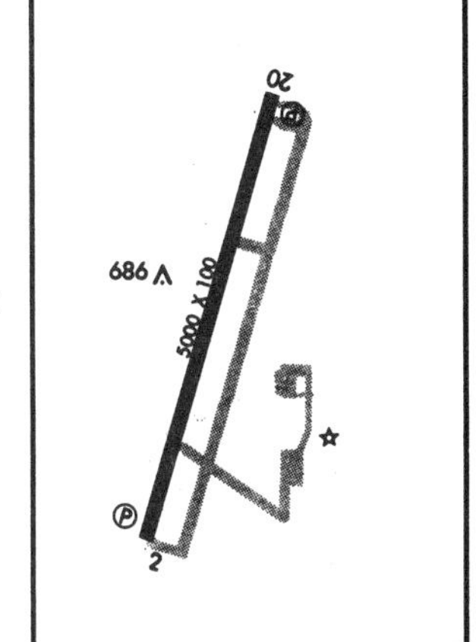

Airport Information:

BELLAIRE - ANTRIM COUNTY AIRPORT (ACB)
1 mi northeast of town 44-59-19N 85-11-54W Elev: 623 Fuel: 80, 100LL, Jet-A
Rwy 02-20: H5000x100 (Asph) Attended: Jun-Aug 1300-0100Z, Sept-May 1300Z-dusk
Unicom: 122.7 Notes: No landing fees; overnight parking: singles $2.50, twins $5.00, turbine $7.50
FBO: Antrim County Airport Phone: 533-8524

MI-D83 - BOYNE CITY
BOYNE CITY MUNICIPAL AIRPORT

(Area Code 616)

3

County Star Restaurant:

The County Star Restaurant is a family style establishment located about 1/4 mile or 2 blocks west from the Boyne City Municipal Airport. This restaurant is open from 7 a.m. to 8 p.m. 7 days a week. They will even pick you up if available staff are available. Their menu consists of a full selection of entrees. Lunch and dinner buffets are featured every day. Specialties of the house include broasted chicken, barbecued ribs, and Friday all you can eat fish fries. A full salad bar, ice cream bar and homemade soups are favorites with many of their customers. Airport activities including arriving and departing aircraft can easily be seen from the restaurant. For more information call 582-2751.

Restaurants Near Airport:
County Star Restaurant 1/4 mi Phone: 582-2751

Lodging: Boyne City Motel 582-6701; Fieldcrest Motel 582-7502; Harborage 800-456-4313; Water Street Inn 800-456-4313.

Meeting Rooms: None Reported

Transportation: Taxi Service: Dial-A-Ride 582-6900.

Information: Boyne City Chamber of Commerce, 28 South Lake Street, Boyne City, MI 40712, Phone: 582-6222.

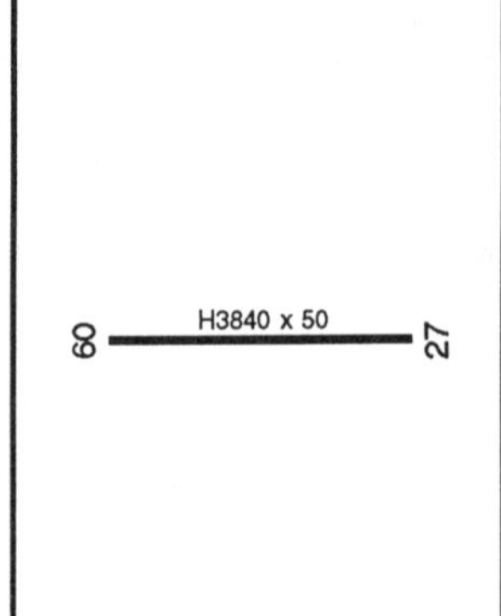

Airport Information:

BOYNE CITY - BOYNE CITY MUNICIPAL AIRPORT (D83)
1 mi southeast of town N45-12.50 W84-59.42 Elev: 657
Rwy 09-27: H3840x50 (Asph) Attended: unattended Unicom: 122.8
Boyne City Municipal AirportPhone: 582-6597, 582-6611

MI-BFA - BOYNE FALLS
BOYNE MOUNTAIN AIRPORT

(Area Code 616)

4

Boyne Mountain Lodge:

Boyne Mountain Lodge contains one main dining room as well as the nearby "Beach House" restaurant located on Deer Lake. Eriksen's Restaurant is conveniently located only 500 yards from the airstrip, and offers unique dining accommodations within a cozy rustic atmosphere, complete with wooden beams and barn wood siding, as well as a great view of the slopes outside thewindow. This particular restaurant is open for breakfast between 7:30 a.m. and 10:00 a.m. and from 12:00 noon to 2:00 p.m. for lunch. Dinner hours begin at 6:30 p.m. until 9 p.m. This restaurant is seasonal and closes down temporarily between April and the first 1/2 month of May, and also during the month of November. Their menu includes a delicious selection. Daily specials along with Sunday buffet are also featured. Fly-in guests, aviation groups and clubs frequently visit the Boyne Mountain Lodge. For more information about their services call the lodge at 549-6000.

Restaurants Near Airport:
Boyne Mountain Lodge Adj Arpt Phone: 549-6000

Lodging: Boyne Mountain Lodge (Shuttle Service available, Adj Arpt) 549-2441.
Meeting Rooms: Boyne Mountain Lodge 549-6000.
Transportation: Courtesy van from Boyne Mountain Lodge is available 549-6000; Also Rental Cars: Bob Mathers 539-6543; Budget 347-7441.
Information: Boyne City Chamber of Commerce, 28 South Lake Street, Boyne City, MI 40712, Phone: 582-6222.

Attractions:

Whether you are a beginner or an expert skier, Boyne Mountain provides down-hill runs from the beginners rope tow, to the famous Hemlock Slopes. There are forty-three kilometers of groomed cross-country ski trails located within the forest on the opposite side of the mountain. Ice skating,swimming in the outdoor heated pool, hayrides and nightly entertainment in the "Snowflake" Lounge are a few of the activities provided for the guests. Convention facilities will accommodate up to 1,200 people and 100 display booths with 13 smaller meeting rooms. A complete audio visual center and banquet facilities are also available. For information call 549-6000.

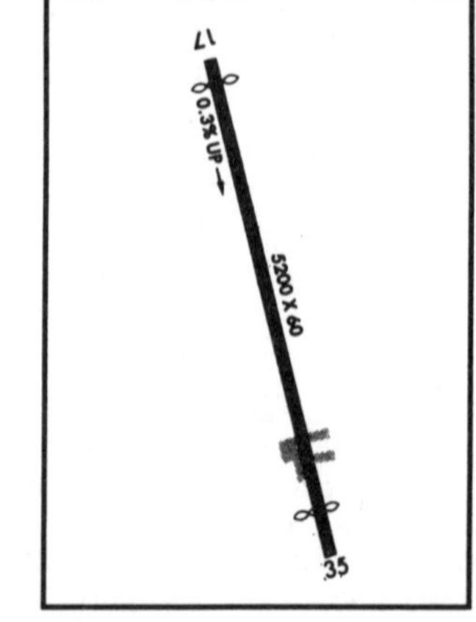

Airport Information:

BOYNE FALLS - BOYNE MOUNTAIN AIRPORT (BFA)
1 mi west of town N45-09.95 W84-55.45 Elev: 717 Fuel: 80, 100LL, Jet-A+
Rwy 17-35: H5200x60 (Asph) Attended: continuously Unicom: 122.8 Notes: Runway not always cleared of snow or ice throughout the winter months. It is imperative that you call the resort or use UNICOM 122.8 to obtain information about runway conditions before landing.
Boyne Mountain Resort Phone: 549-6000

Boyne Mountain & Boyne Highlands

Boyne Falls, MI (MI-BFA)
Harbor Springs, MI (MI-4Y8)

Boyne Mountain's own 4,200-foot jetport is paved, lighted and located an easy walk away from the ski slopes, main lodge, condominiums and restaurants. (But we'll be happy to pick you up. Just give the lodge a call from the airport terminal.) At Boyne Highlands, 25 miles north near Harbor Springs, a 3,800 foot turf strip handles summer flyers just fine. It's well-maintained, and also on resort property. Both Boynes are extremely popular. You'll often see as many as 50 planes parked at our airports...with skis, tennis rackets, golf clubs and fishing rods as baggage. That's because there's so much to see and do in Boyne Country.

Settle in your room, suite, condo or villa, and you can start planning your days. If golf is your game, you're at the right place. We have four world-class championship 18 hole layouts, one rated in the top 100 greatest courses by Golf Digest, and the others worthy candidates for the honor. Two nine-hole executive links, driving ranges and well-equipped pro shops are yours to enjoy, too. And a magnificent Donald Ross Memorial course.

When it comes to skiing, Boyne's challenging groomed slopes are mid-western legends. There's nothing finer, between the Rockies and New England. Boyne Mountain offers 17 runs and 10 chairlifts, while the Highlands features 17 slopes and seven lifts. Austrian ski schools and high-tech snowmaking serve both resorts, and after skiing, you'll enjoy first-class dining facilities and nightly entertainment.

Other Boyne amenities include 18 hard-surface tennis courts, swimming pools, the Deer Lake Beach House where you can swim, fish, sail and dine. Plus jacuzzis, fine restaurants, cocktail lounges and sports shops. More things to do than you possibly have time for.

For flying side-trips and some spectacular scenery, Boyne Country is special. You can cruise over Little Traverse Bay, venture out over Beaver and Fox Island, fly over "Big Mac," the world's longest suspension bridge, view famous Mackinac Island from above - and be back at Boyne in less than an hour.

Flying clubs, business executives and professionals looking for unique fly-in destinations are discovering Boyne Country. Gas up, get in your airplane and come visit. You'll be delighted with what you'll find here. For information call Boyne Mountain at 616-549-6000 or 800-GO-BOYNE. For information about Boyne Highlands call 616-526-2171. Both resorts are owned by the same management. (Information submitted by Boyne USA Resorts).

Photo by: Aerodine — Boyne Mountain Resort

Photo by: Aerodine

Photo by: Aerodine — Boyne Highlands

MI-CVX - CHARLEVOIX
CHARLEVOIX MUNICIPAL AIRPORT

(Area Code 616)

5

Juillerets Restaurant:

Juillerets Restaurant is located about 3 blocks from the Charlevoix Municipal Airport near the town of Charlevoix about 45 miles northeast of Traverse City, MI. This is a family style restaurant with a very casual atmosphere, and is known for specializing in breakfast, served all day. The cinnamon French toast is a favorite, as well as the White Fish, in addition to other entrees on their menu like sandwiches and soups for lunch or dinner. The restaurant is situated across from the airport, along South Bridge Street. They are reported to be open 7 days a week between 5:30 a.m. and 3 p.m. For information call 547-9212.

Restaurants Near Airport:
Juillerets Restaurant 3 blks Phone: 547-9212

Lodging: Lodge of Charlevoix (Trans) 547-6565; Weathervane Terrace Hotel 547-9955.

Meeting Rooms: Weathervane Terrace Hotel 547-9955.

Transportation: Taxi Service: Charlevoix Taxi 547-6129; Quality Limousine 547-9554; Also Rental Cars: Budget 547-6442; Kusina Motors 547-6525.

Information: Chamber of Commerce, 408 Bridge Street, Charlevoix, MI 49720, Phone: 547-2101.

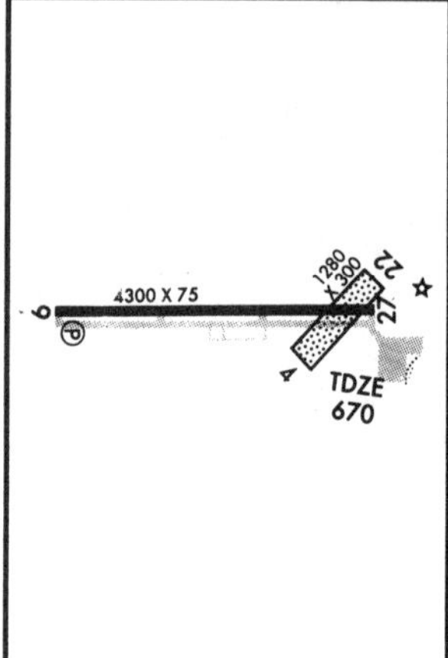

Airport Information:

CHARLEVOIX - CHARLEVOIX MUNICIPAL AIRPORT (CVX)
1 mi southwest of town N45-18.29 W85-16.49 Elev: 670 Fuel: 100LL, Jet-A
Rwy 09-27: H4300x75 (Asph) Rwy 04-22: 1280x300 (Turf) Attended: dawn to dusk
Unicom: 122.8 Notes: Turf runways closed winters.
FBO: Island Airways Phone: 547-2141

MI-OEB - COLDWATER
BRANCH COUNTY MEMORIAL

(Area Code 517)

6

West Airport Inn:

The West Airport Inn is located on Branch County Memorial Airport in Coldwater, Michigan. This is a family restaurant serving a wide variety of delicious entrees contained in their menu. On Fridays through Sunday, a smorgasbord is featured containing an array of dinner selections. Banquet rooms are also available. The restaurant hours are 6 a.m. to 8 p.m. Monday through Saturday and Sunday 8 a.m. to 3 p.m. Winter hours may vary. Aircraft parking is directly in front of the restaurant. Call 278-4673 for information.

Restaurants Near Airport:
West Airport Inn On Site Phone: 278-4673

Lodging: Quality Inn (5 miles) 278-2017; Econo Lodge (3/4 miles) 278-4501.

Meeting Rooms: Banquet rooms reported at the West Airport Inn Restaurant, 278-4673; Quality Inn 278-2017.

Transportation: Branch County Aviation can provide courtesy transportation to nearby facilities, Phone: 278-6516.

Information: Coldwater/Branch County Chamber of Commerce, 20 Division Street, Coldwater, MI 49036, Phone: 278-5985 or 800-968-9333.

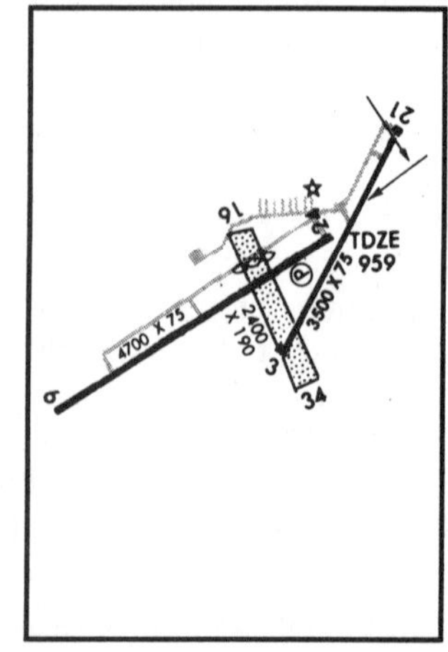

Airport Information:

COLDWATER - BRANCH COUNTY MEMORIAL AIRPORT (OEB)
3 mi west of town N41-56.01 W85-03.16 Elev: 959 Fuel: 100LL, Jet-A
Rwy 06-24: H4700x75 (Asph) Rwy 03-21: H3500x50 (Asph) Rwy 16-34: 2400x190 (Turf)
Attended: 1300Z-dusk Unicom: 122.7
FBO: Coldwater Air Phone: 278-6516

MI-DTW - DETROIT
DETROIT METRO WAYNE COUNTY

(Area Code 313) 7

Marriott Innkeeper Restaurant:

Marriott/Innkeeper Restaurant is located on Detroit Metropolitan Wayne County Airport in Detroit, MI. This elegant restaurant provides a wide selection of fine entrees including house made dishes including char broiled chicken, prime rib & seafood delights. In addition to its wide variety of delicious entrees, they also offer a choice of house salads, and freshly baked breads. The restaurant hours are from 7 a.m. to 10 p.m. Monday through Friday and Saturday and Sunday from 7:30 a.m. to 9 p.m. During evening hours, the decor is quite appealing with soft lighting. For information or reservations call 942-2355.

Restaurants Near Airport:
Marriott/Innkeeper Rest On Site Phone: 942-2355

Lodging: Comfort Inn (Trans) 946-4300; Hilton Inn Airport (Trans) 292-3400; Holiday Inn (Trans) 728-2800; Marriott Detroit Airport (Trans) 941-9400.

Meeting Rooms: Comfort Inn 946-4300; Hilton Inn Airport 292-3400; Holiday Inn 728-2800; Marriott Detroit Airport 941-9400.

Transportation: Courtesy cars, rental cars and taxi & limo service located at the terminal building and fixed base operators.

Information: Metropolitan Detroit Convention and Visitors Bureau, 100 Renaissance Center, Suite 1950, Detroit, MI 48243, Phone: 259-4333 or 800/ DETROIT

Attractions:

There are many attractions within the Detroit area. Contact the Metropolitan Detroit Convention and Visitors Bureau for detailed information, Phone: 259-4333. (See "Information" listed above).

Airport Information:

DETROIT - DETROIT METRO WAYNE COUNTY AIRPORT (DTW)
15 mi south of town N42-12.72 W83-20.93 Elev: 640 Fuel: 100LL, Jet-A
Rwy: 03L-21R: H12001x200 (Conc-Grvd) Rwy 03R-21L: H10000x150 (Conc-Grvd)
Rwy: 09L-27R: H8700x200 (Asph-Conc-Grvd) Rwy: 03C-21C H8500x200 (Asph-Conc-Grvd)
09R-27L: H8500x150 (Conc-Grvd) Attended: continuously Atis: 133.675 Unicom: 122.95 App Con: 125.15 118.575 (East) 124.05 (West) Dep Con: 132.025 (Turbo Jets-East) 134.3 (Turboprops-East) 125.525 (Turbojets-West) 118.95 (Turboprop-West) 118.575 (East) Metro Tower: 135.0 (West) 118.4 (East) Gnd Con: 132.72 (South) 121.8 (West) 119.45 (East) Clnc Del: 120.65 Pre Taxi Clnc: 120.65 Notes: See current AFD for updated airport information.
FBO: Signature Flight Support Phone: 941-7880

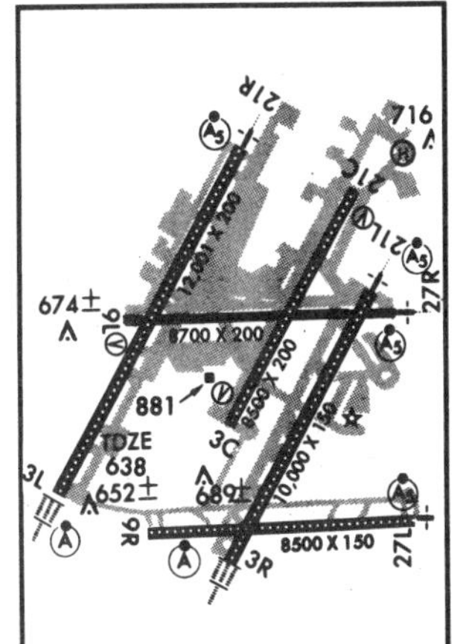

Photo by: Aerodine
Henry Ford Museum

The Henry Ford Museum contains a nice variety of aviation related exhibits including this famous Ford Tri-Motor Aircraft proudly on display.

Henry Ford Museum & Greenfield Village

Detroit, MI (MI-DET)
Okland-Troy, MI (MI-7D2)

Stretching out from an entranceway patterned after Philadelphia's Independence Hall, the museum houses twelve acres of American artifacts and inventions representing 250 years of change. As visitors delight in the elegance of a hand-made crystal goblet or marvel at the massiveness of a 600-ton coal burning locomotive, they discover how technology altered aspects of American life. The museum's world-renowned automobile collection stands transformed into "The Automobile in American Life" as a three dimensional, multi-media mix of cars, video, audio presentations, graphics, and full scale structures that reveal how pervasively the car has shaped the way twentieth-century Americans work, play and conduct their daily lives.

Photo: by Aerodine

Along with more than 100 historically significant cars, the 60,000 square foot exhibition includes such original roadside landmarks as a 1940s Texaco service station and a 1946 diner, a 1950s drive-in movie, and a 1960s Holiday Inn room.

The museum's transportation exhibits also include railroad locomotives and cars, aircraft, horse-drawn vehicles, streetcars, and fire fighting apparatus. The museum's agriculture display showcase is of the most comprehensive collections of American farming tools and machinery anywhere. The museum's colossal accumulation of power machinery includes: the most extensive collection of steam engines in the world; the most complete assemblage of boilers, generators, early motors, transformers and electrical transmission equipment; a notable collection of hot-air engines; and a variety of shop machinery.

Greenfield Village

More than eighty homes, work places, and community buildings from various times and places have been brought to this outdoor museum's eighty-one developed acres to reveal the power of change and the persistence of tradition in American life-styles since the mid-seventeenth century.

Here each new generation can discover the day-to-day processes that helped build this nation as household, community, business, and leisure activities of different periods are presented and demonstrated in many of the buildings.

Thomas Edison's "Invention Factory"

The Menlo Park Laboratory complex sits in Greenfield Village looking much as it did when Edison invented his practical incandescent light. More than 400 inventions, including the phonograph, were created in this "invention factory," recently restored to its 1880 conditions to better preserve it for the enjoyment of generations to come.

Photo: by Aerodine

Dining

A variety of dining experiences await visitors to Henry Ford Museum & Greenfield Village. The Eagle Tavern in the village offers 1850s fare appropriate to each season. A wide assortment of modern-day favorites are served in the museum's neon-lit American Cafe. Fast food snacks are offered throughout the complex as well.

How to get there

When flying into Detroit to visit the Edison Institute, we recommend any one of several airports located near the museum. Detroit Metro is the closest to the museum. However, it is frequented by heavy air-carrier operations for the City of Detroit. Willow Run Airport, southwest of the museum, appears to be an industrial airfield which caters to large transport and corporate activity. Detroit City Airport, located fifteen miles northeast of the museum, provides excellent services for most privately owned and corporate aircraft, as well as rental car accommodations. Troy-Oakland Airport is twenty one miles north of the museum, and Mettetal Airport, is seventeen miles west of the museum and offer a less hectic atmosphere for those of you "Grass Roots" flyers preferring a non-controlled field in which to land your bird. Admission to the Henry Ford Museum is about $11.50 per adult, $10.50 for senior citizen, $5.75 for children between 5 and 12 years old, and free to childeren under 5 years old. Greenfield Village admission is the same as the museum. Two day and several other ticket schedules are available. For information about the Henry Ford Museum & Greenfield Village, you can call 313-271-1620. (Information submitted by museum)

Photo: by Aerodine

MI-ONZ - DETROIT/GROSSE ILE
GROSSE ILE MUNICIPAL AIRPORT

(Area Code 313) 8

Grosse Ile Racquet & Health Club:

(At time of interview the management stated that the cafe has been closed indefinitely).

The Grosse Ile Racquet & Health Club contains a tennis club cafe situated on the Grosse Ile Municipal Airport. The airport is located on an island in the Detroit River, about 18 miles south of Detroit Michigan. The grill serves short orders such as sandwiches, soups and some specials of the day. The Racquet Club has 6 indoor tennis courts, 4 outdoor clay courts and a fitness center available as well as locker room facilities. The club, an interesting old wooden building, was originally an airplane hangar and was built prior to WW-II. The Racquet Club is located in the airport complex and is accessible by walking from the airport office. The grill can accommodate small parties and has a meeting room available, with advance notice. Carry-out orders are welcome. The Club hours are 9 a.m. to 11 p.m. Monday through Friday and Saturday & Sunday from 9 a.m. to 9 p.m. The grill is open from 11 a.m. to 2 p.m. and again at 5 p.m to 8 p.m. Monday through Friday and 11 a.m. to 3 p.m. Saturday. For information call 675-6272.

Airport Information:

DETROIT/GROSSE ILE - GROSSE ILE MUNICIPAL AIRPORT (ONZ)
2 mi south of town N42-05.92 W83-09.66 Elev: 591 Fuel: 80, 100LL, Jet-A
Rwy 04-22: H4978x100 (Asph) Rwy 17-35: H3752x75 (Asph) Attended: 1300-0200Z
Unicom: 123.0 Detroit App/Dep Con: 134.3 Notes: Birds on and in vicinity of airport.
FBO: Eagle Aviation Phone: 676-8880
FBO: Island Aviation Phone: 483-8353

Restaurants Near Airport:
Grosse Ile Racquet & Health Club On Site Phone: 675-6272

Lodging: Best Western Woodhaven Inn 676-8000; Residential Inn 283-4400.

Meeting Rooms: Best Western Woodhaven Inn 676-8000; Residential Inn 283-4400.

Transportation: Taxi Service Suburban Cab 676-1911; Wyandotte Cab 282-2222

Information: Metropolitan Detroit Convention and Visitors Bureau, 100 Renaissance Center, Suite 1950, Detroit, MI 48243, Phone: 259-4333.

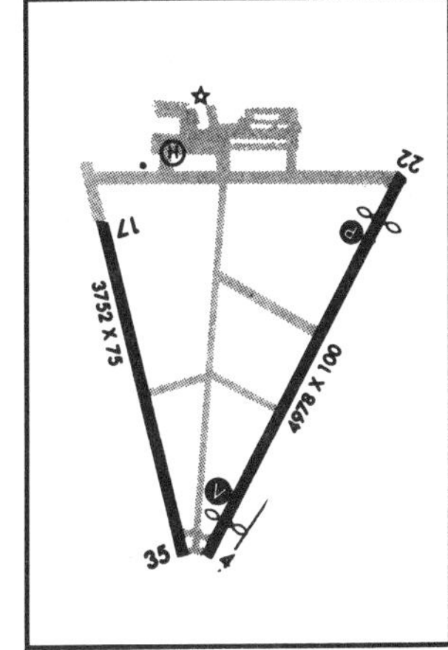

MI-Y66 - DRUMMOND ISLAND
DRUMMOND ISLAND AIRPORT

(Area Code 906)

9, 10, 11, 12

Bear Track Inn:

The Bakery is a family-oriented restaurant located about a quarter of a mile from the Drummond Island Airport in Michigan. This restaurant specializes in a wide variety of home-cooked meals as well as daily specials from their full service menu. The restaurant is open April through November, 7 days a week between 7 a.m. and 8 p.m. (reported closed December through March). For more information call the restaurant at 493-5090.

Chuck's Place Bar & Grill:

Chuck's Place Bar & Grill is located about 4 miles east of the Drummond Island Township Airport. This family-style restaurant can be reached by courtesy transportation either through the airport or the restaurant. The restaurant asks that you contact the airport manager's office first, at 493-5411 to arrange transportation. Restaurant hours are from 12 p.m. to 11 p.m., 7 days a week. Specialty entrees include BBQ ribs, Alaska pollock and white fish. Average prices run $6.00 for lunch and $10.00 for dinner. A Friday fish fry features broiled shrimp and whitefish. Daily specials are also offered . The restaurant exhibits a rustic atmosphere within a log cabin setting. Special arrangements can also be made for parties or groups. For information call 493-5480.

Northwood Inn:

The Northwood Inn is situated about 1 mile south of the Drummond Island Airport, on Drummond Island, Michigan. Transportation can be arranged through the airport by calling 493-5411. This restaurant is open from 11 a.m. to 10 p.m. seven days a week. Their menu contains a nice selection of entrees with specialties including broasted chicken, Lake Huron white fish, 6-ounce hamburgers, soups, salads and relish trays as well as many other items. Average prices run $5.00 for lunch and $11.00 for dinner. Reservations are suggested for larger parties. This restaurant is open during the summer months between May 1 through mid-October. For information call 493- 5282.

Woodmoor Resort:

The Woodmoor Resort is located about 2 to 3 miles northeast of the Drummond Island Airport. This complex encompasses 2,000 acres of beautifully wooded area. Bayside Restaurant which is part of the Woodmoor, is located about 1.2 miles north of the main lodge and provides a nice selection of culinary delights. The Rock Golf Course was designed by Harry Bowers, who crafted each fairway separately covering over 400 acres. There are few, if any, waits. Each group of golfers is in their own game, unaware of any other golfers on the course except the players ahead or behind. They have four tees and therefore, four choices of challenges on each hole. As far as lodging goes, the Woodmoor Resort has a nicely furnished 40-room main lodge. In addition to this, they make available individual homes for rent. Each home is beautifully decorated in a rustic country decor, complete with boulder stone fireplaces, kitchens and bedrooms with private baths. This resort makes an excellent location to hold your business meetings or corporate retreat. The Woodmoor provides it s guests with all the amenities of a 5-star resort. These include lodging, dining, golfing, tennis, fishing, boating, sailing, bowling, hiking, biking and conference and banquet accommodations. For restaurant information or reservations call 493-1014. For information about the resort call their toll free number at 800-999-6343. See the Woodmoor article on the adjoining page.

Airport Information:

DRUMMOND ISLAND - DRUMMOND ISLAND APT (Y66)

1 mi southwest of town N46-00.52 W83-44.79 Elev: 668 Fuel: 100LL, Jet-A, MOGAS
Rwy 08-26: H4000x75 (Asph) Rwy 18-36: 2500x150 (Asph-Turf) Attended: May-Aug Mon-Sat 1300-0100Z, Sep-Apr Mon-Sat 1300-2300Z Unicom: 122.8 Public phone 24 hrs
Notes: Overnight parking fees $2.00 per night
FBO: Marshalls Mobil Phone: 493-5411

Restaurants Near Airport:

Bear Track Inn	1/2 mi N.	Phone: 493-5090
Chuck's Place Bar & Grill	4 mi E.	Phone: 493-5480
Northwood Inn	1 mi S.	Phone: 493-5282
Woodmoor (Bayside Rest.)	3 mi NE.	Phone: 493-1014

Lodging: Woodmoor Resort (2-3 miles NE.) 800-999-6343; The Rock Country Club (3 miles) 493-1000; D I Motel 493-5270; J & R Motel 493-5552; LA Lakes Resort 493-5216.

Meeting Rooms: Woodmoor Resort (2-3 miles NE.) 800-999-6343; The Rock Country Club (3 miles) 493-1000.

Transportation: Courtesy car reported at airport, please give advance notice by calling 493-5411.

Information: The Travel Bureau, Michigan Department of Commerce, P.O. Box 30226, Lansing, MI 48909, Phone: 800-543-2YES

Attractions:

The Rock Country Club contains a championship quality golf course and conference center with hotel. For information call 493-1000; Also the township golf course is reported to be on the Drummond Island Airport property. For information call 493-5406.

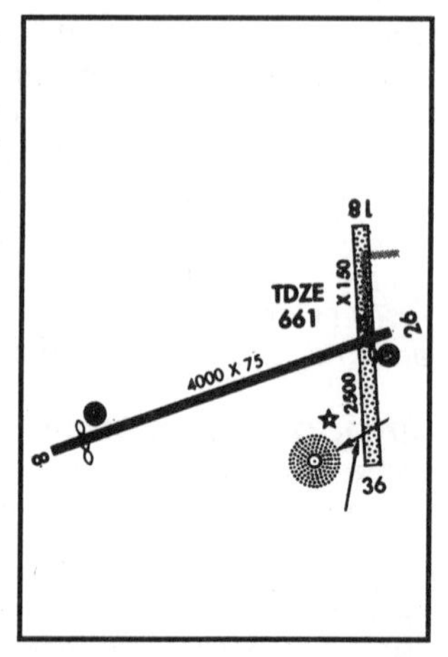

Photo by: Woodmoor Resort

Woodmoor Resort Lodge, Drummond Island, MI

Woodmoor Resort

Drummond Island, MI (MI-Y66)

The Woodmoor encompasses 2000 beautiful acres of woods and water. Originally the site of a hunting and fishing preserve, in the mid-1980s it was purchased by the Domino's Corporation as a corporate retreat. Today, the Woodmoor complex is locally owned and operated, and includes: The Rock, an outstanding golf course; a forty-room log lodge; The Bayside Restaurant serving meals on the waterfront; conference facilities for 10 to 150; and eight unique homes available for rent. Woodmoor is three diamond rated by AAA.

Bayside Restaurant is situated near the shoreline of Potagannissing Bay and about 1.2 miles north of the Woodmoor Lodge. This dining establishment is part of the Woodmoor complex which has been chosen to participate in the highly respected New England Culinary Institute. Included on their menu are appetizers like their Pinenut crusted smoked mozzarella; roasted Portobello mushrooms; seared duck breast; or roasted garlic and potato soup are offered as starters to your meal. Main entrees include pan-seared whitefish; grilled medallions of beef tenderloin; herb-crusted pork loin; grilled cilantro chicken; Vegetable Napoleon; and Angel hair pasta. A variety of salads are also available. In addition to the dinner menu they also have an extensive wine list as well. Prices for main course selections range from $12.00 to $17.00. The hours of operation are from 5 p.m. to 10 p.m. daily. For reservations you can call the restaurant at 493-1014.

The lodging at Woodmoor can be enjoyed by renting homes that offer privacy and comfort, and are ideal for family reunions, a gathering of friends, or corporate retreats. The homes all have stone fireplaces, kitchens, comfortable areas for relaxing and bedrooms with private baths.

Woodmoor's meeting facilities were designed for maximum productivity and creativity. The lodge has two board rooms overlooking scenic ponds and woods. The Annex, a log structure with a great deal of ambience, is perfect for meetings of 15 to 30 people. For the sportsman, hunting and fishing are an integral part of life on Drummond Island. Pan fish can be caught casting off Woodmoor's pier. Small fishing boats and pontoons are also available to rent for cruising the protected waters of Potagannissing Bay. Fall brings bird and duck hunting, followed by deer season. The Rock Golf Course located on the Woodmoor property has been rated on Michigan's top ten list by Michigan Golfer Magazine. The people who love this course play to all levels, and like it because it's an experience, not just a round.

The Drummond Island Airport (Y66) is located within a couple of miles of the Woodmoor Resort. It is attended Monday through Saturday 1300-2200Z. The airport contains two runways. Rwy 08-26: 4,000x75 (Asph) and Rwy 18-36: 2500 (Asph-Turf). For airport information call Marshall's Mobil (FBO) 493-5411.

MI-3DA - FLUSHING DALTON AIRPORT

(Area Code 810)

13, 14

Liberty Family Dining:

This restaurant has been in business for over 24 years and is located adjacent to the Dulton Airport in a brown brick building. This is a family dining facility that is open 6:30 a.m. to 10 p.m., 7 days a week. Their menu is extensive with breakfast, lunch and dinner selections. Anything from light fare to reasonably priced full-course meals are available. Prices average $2.95 to $4.95 for breakfast and $2.00 to $6.95 for lunch and dinner. Daily specials are also prepared. For example, on Wednesday fish and chips are served. The main dining room can seat about 50 people. Groups of 10 or less are welcome anytime. They ask that those planning larger groups to call at least 2 days in advance. For information phone the restaurant at 732-4650.

Restaurants Near Airport:

Liberty Family Dining	Adj Arpt	Phone: 732-4650
Squire Creek	Adj Arpt	Phone: 659-1423

Lodging: Ramada 732-0400; Wallis 789-0400.
Meeting Rooms: Squire Creek Restaurnat reports banquet and catering services for small or large groups. For information call 659-1423.
Transportation: Courtesy car reported available.
Information: Flint Area Tourism Bureau 800-288-8040; Also: The Travel Bureau, Michigan Department of Commerce, P.O. Box 30226, Lansing, MI 48909, Phone: 800-543-2YES

Squire Creek Restaurant:

This establishment is located adjacent to the Dalton Airport in Flushing, Michigan. This facility has undergone extensive renovation, and can be classified as a combination family-style and fine dining restaurant. Hours of operation are 4 p.m. to 11 p.m. Friday and Saturday as well as week nights, except on Sunday they are open from 12 p.m. until 7 p.m. Their house specialties include steaks, seafood and pasta dishes. Daily specials are also offered, as well as weekly specials. Each night they feature something different. All-you-can-eat lobster tail, frog legs or spare ribs is a favorite with many of their customers. Average prices run between $4.95 and $12.95. The layout of this establishment contains a main dining room and bar area able to seat 250 people in the front portion of the building. In addition to this they also have meeting rooms and banquet seating for up to 350 in the back. This restaurant can accommodate in-flight catering services as well. For available banquet service or information about the restaurant call 659-1423.

NO AIRPORT DIAGRAM AVAILABLE

Airport Information:

FLUSHING - DALTON'S AIRPORT (3DA)
2 mi east of town N43-03.42 W83-48.41 Elev: 733 Rwy 18-36: H2510x50 (Asph)
Rwy 09-27: 1330x150 (Turf) Attended: irregularly Unicom: 122.8
Dalton's Airport Phone: 789-8529, 635-2234.

MI-66G - FRANKENMUTH WILLIAM TINY ZEHNDER FIELD

(Area Code 517)

15

Frankenmuth Michigan (Dining):

There are two restaurants which are located near Frankenmuth, Michigan and will be glad to provide their fly-in guests with transportation to and from the Frankenmuth Airport. The Bavarian Inn at 517-652-9941 and the Zehnder's Restaurant at 517-652-9925 both provide excellent meals and specialize in their famous chicken dinners. They also have a very nice selection of German food from which to choose. Both of these restaurants open between 11 a.m. and 9:30 p.m., 7 days a week, and will do their utmost to provide the best of hospitality to their welcome guests. Both the Bavarian Inn and Zehnder's Restaurant serve tens of thousands of customers each year. The town itself comes right out of a storybook, with quaint German-styled architecture serving as a popular attraction. When we flew into the airport we simply called the restaurant, and within minutes we were greeted by a friendly gentleman driving a courtesy car. After a fine meal we walked the town and visited the sights. There are many shops and restaurants, as well as other attractions located within the village. During the summer months, flowers and planting areas line the streets in a colorful display. An additional attraction which is a must to visit, is the Bronner's Christmas Store (652-9931), famous throughout the entire United States for it's extremely large inventory of holiday and Christmas items. Free transportation can usually be easily arranged by the restaurants or through Bronner's when visiting their facility.

Restaurants Near Airport:

Bavarian Inn	2 mi	Phone: 652-9941
Zehnder's Rest.	2 mi	Phone: 652-9925

Lodging: Bavarian Haus Motel (2 miles) 652-6144; Bavarian Inn Motor Lodge (2 miles) 652-6996; Frankenmuth Motel (1 mile) 652-6171; Holiday Inn (2 miles) 755-0461; Red Roof Inn (3 miles) 754-8414.
Meeting Rooms: Bavarian Inn Motor Lodge provides a resort and conference center (2 miles) 652-6996; The restaurants can also provide accommodations for meetings as well. See restaurant description listed above; The Frankenmuth Chamber of Commerce & Visitors Information Center can provide you with all the needed information about attractions, meeting facilities, lodging and much more. See information listed below.
Transportation: During our fly-in visit, we found that many of the establishments within the town of Frankenmuth will provide courtesy transportation to their facilities. Also rental cars: Schaefer & Bierlein 652-9965.
Information: Frankenmuth Chamber of Commerce and Visitors Bureau, 635 S. Main Street, Frankenmuth, MI 48734, Phone: 652-6106.

90 2506 x 100 27

Attractions:

Bronner's Christmas Decorations (1 mile) exhibits one of the largest Christmas stores for decorations in the country, 652-9931; Frankenmuth Historical Museum (2-1/2 miles) 652-9701;

Airport Information:

FRANKENMUTH - WILLIAM TINY ZEHNDER FIELD (66G)
2 mi southeast of town N43-18.84 W83-42.58 Elev: 645 Rwy 09-27: 2506x100 (Turf)
Attended: irregularly Unicom: 122.9 Notes: Snow removal intermittent - verify conditions call 624-5723; Rwy 09-27 soft in spring and after heavy rain. Runway marked with three foot cones.
William Tiny Zehnder Field Phone: 624-5723

Frankenmuth

Somewhere in the far-off lands of the Scottish Highlands, there exists a legend about a certain town that rises out of the mist every one-hundred years and exists but for a single day, only to fade into oblivion, not to reappear until a century has passed. The creator of this imaginary town chose to name it Brigadoon. The town featured in this article is reminiscent of these Grimm Brother's fairytales, However, the town featured in this article is very real, and attracts nearly three million visitors annually. The name of this town is Frankenmuth, and it has been in existence for nearly one hundred and forty years. The pioneers who hewed their community out of the virgin timberland, settled in what is known today as the "Thumb" area of Michigan. The only connection with the outside world was by way of the Cass River which meandered its way across miles of unsettled virgin timberland and hidden Indian trails through dense forests. For many years, this settlement remained undisturbed until the area fell under the control of the timber and lumber industry. From that point on, the land of this region was destined to see changes. The large tracks of land which were cleared by lumbermen, provided access to this region by way of railroads and wagon trails used for shipping lumber.

Photo by: Aerodine

The Bavarian Inn shown here, is one of several fine restaurants within the town of Frankenmuth, Michigan. Zender's Restaurant located across the street from the Bavarian Inn also provides exquisite meals in the German tradition.

In the Spring of 1845, the first settlers were only fifteen missionaries determined to bring the Christian religion to the Indians of North America. By 1846, there were many new arrivals, and within a six year span of time, over eighty cabins and farm houses were erected. Today, Frankenmuth is a thriving community much the same as other communities, except for its proud heritage that has played a large part in its development since its conception. The word "Franken" represents the Province or Franken in the Kingdom of Bavaria from whence the original Frankenmuth settlers came. The "muth" means courage, thus the name "courage of the Franks." The heritage of these people has provided a joyous and festive atmosphere from all parts of the country.

Zehnder's Restaurant and the Bavarian Inn are two of the most prominent restaurants to be found within the town of Frankenmuth, and are open the year around from 11 a.m. until 9:30 p.m. It is said the famous chicken dinners served at Frankenmuth's restaurants have done more to publicize this community than any other product or activity within the area. Here are a few statistics about the quantity of food served, that may be of interest to you: Over 900 persons are employed in the preparation and serving of approximately 1.8 million meals each year. About 80% of these meals are chicken dinners totaling some 1,163,810 pounds of chicken, 227 tons of potatoes, 61,126 heads of cabbage and lettuce, 323,648 loaves of bread, not including all of the other items which make up the fine meals served to their guests.

While in Frankenmuth, the Bronner's Christmas Wonderland is certainly among one of the most interesting attractions within the town. It has become a well-known tourist attraction in the state of Michigan, exhibiting displays of Christmas and all-season decorations for homes, churches, businesses, parades and parties. There are over 30.000 items from 45 nations, including 3,000 glass-blown ornaments, 400 sculptured candles, 500 nativity scenes, along with a host of other colorful decorations to see. While you are visiting this attraction, you are invited to view the all new "World of Bronner's" 10-projector, multi-image presentation. This fascinating 18-minute show is a delight of sights and sounds highlighting the design and production of Bronner's worldwide selections.

Bronner's will provide fly-in guests landing at Frankenmuth Airport, with transportation to and from their facility. The Christmas Wonderland is located approximately one mile south of the Bavarian Inn on Main Street and M-83. Transportation can easily be arranged between the Frankenmuth Airport, Bronner's Christmas Wonderland and the Bavarian Inn, located in the downtown district, by calling either facility.

Early one September morning , we decided to make the trip to the town of Frankenmuth. Our trip originated from Chicago and it took us approximately one hour and forty-five minutes enroute. After a short wait for our ride into town, we were met by a friendly driver that explained about some of the interesting sites and attractions to see in the area. As we approached the downtown area, we crossed the Cass River through a beautifully constructed 239 foot replica of an authentic 19th century covered bridge. Once reaching the other side, it was as if we had been transported to the Kingdom of Bavaria located in Germany. The main street was decorated with beautiful plantings on both sides, and the buildings and shops that lined the streets were of Alpine architecture. There were a great number of people that had come from all over, to partake of the festivities throughout the town. Upon arriving at the Bavarian Inn, we were guided to the Alpine Room, one of seven dining rooms within the huge complex. After being seated for dinner, we enjoyed a sampling of German appetizers which included several relishes, sauerkraut, cottage cheese, chicken noodle soup as well as freshly baked white bread and stollen (fruit bread) with jell -- all of which preceded the main course. After strolling through the town, we were entertained by the Frankenmuth's Glockenspiel and Pied Piper exhibit. The Glockenspiel Tower, on the Bavarian Inn premises, houses a thirty-five bell carillon that was imported from Germany and displays a figurine movement depicting the legend of the Pied Piper of Hamlin. It plays daily at 12:00 noon, 6:00 p.m. and 9:00 p.m.

Photo by: Aerodine

As you enter the town from the main parking area, it will seem as though you were just transported to the Kingdom of Bavaria located in Germany.

If planning to stay the night, there are several fine motels within the Frankenmuth area. The Bavarian Inn Motor Lodge contains a resort and conference center and is located adjacent to the Bavarian Inn Restaurant across from the 240' covered bridge. This 89,000 square foot facility contains 100 guest rooms, all furnished with two double beds each, including eleven suites. Their accommodations will provide brunches and pool-side luncheons for up to one-hundreds and fifty persons. There is also a large meeting room that can seat up to two hundred people, and their lounge displays live entertainment as well.

The activities and attractions of Frankenmuth will make your flying excursion a memorable experience, and the German cuisine will surely entice you to return time and time again.

One of the most popular festivals held each year, is the Bavarian Festival which begins the second Sunday in June and continues through Saturday of that week.

The William 'Tiny' Zehnder Field has a east-west (09-27) runway with a 2,506 x 100 foot turf strip. This airport is situated only 2 miles southeast of the town of Frankenmuth. Transportation to and from the Airport and the Bavarian Inn, Zehnder's Restaurant or the famous Bronner's Christmas outlet, can easily be arranged by calling them at their respective telephone numbers. The airport is listed as being attended irregularly. For information about runway conditions call 517-871-5626. Unicom frequency is given as 122.9. For more information about the town of Frankenmuth and a schedule of social events call the Frankenmuth Chamber of Commerce & Visitors Bureau at 517-652-6106. (Articles prepared in part through information obtained from "A History of Michigan's Little Bavaria" by Irene Zeilinger).

Photo by: Aerodine

Enroute from the William Tiny Zehnder Field Airport, you will cross the Cass River through this beautifully constructed 239 foot replica of an authentic 19th century covered bridge.

MI-GRR - GRAND RAPIDS KENT COUNTY INTERNATIONAL

(Area Code 616)

16

Marriott's Host Restaurant:

The Marriott's Host Restaurant is located on Kent County International Airport in Grand Rapids, MI. It's a cafe style restaurant with lounge that seats approximately 75 persons and serves breakfast, lunch and dinner along with dinner specials. The cafe is located in the terminal building, and is open from 6 a.m. to 10:30 p.m. "Inflight Menus" are a service for business or general aviation pilots wishing package meals for quick turn-around service. Call 949-6654.

Restaurants Near Airport:
Marriott's Host Restaurant On Site Phone: 949-6654

lodging: Best Western Midway Lodge (Trans) 942-2550; Harley Hotel (Trans) 949-8800; Hilton Inn Airport (Trans) 957-0100; Marriott (Trans) 957-1770; Residence Inn (Trans) 957-8111; Signature Inn (Trans) 949-8400.

Meeting Rooms: Best Western 942-2550; Harley Hotel 949-8800; Hilton Inn Airport 957-0100; Marriott 957-1770; Residence Inn 957-8111; Signature Inn 949-8400.

Transportation: Taxi Service: Veterans Cab 459-4646; Rental Cars: Avis 949-1720; Budget 957-4677; Hertz 949-4410; National 949-3510.

Information: West Michigan Tourist Association, 140 Monroe Center NW, Grand Rapids, MI 49503, Phone: 800-678-1859.

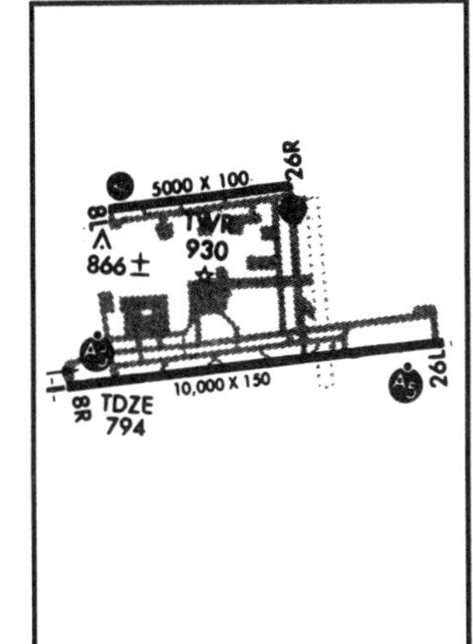

Airport Information:

GRAND RAPIDS - KENT COUNTY INTERNATIONAL AIRPORT (GRR)
6 mi southeast of town N42-52.96 W85-31.44 Elev: 794 Fuel: 100LL, Jet-A
Rwy 08R-26L: H10000x150 (Asph-Conc-Grvd) Rwy 08L-26R: H5000x100 (Asph)
Attended: continuously Atis: 127.1 Unicom: 122.95 Grand Rapids App/Dep Con: 124.6 (North) 128.4 (South) Grand Rapids Tower: 135.65 Gnd Con: 121.8 Clnc Del: 119.3
FBO: AMR Combs Phone: 336-4700
FBO: Rapid Air, Inc. Phone: 957-5050

MI-55D - GRAYLING GRAYLING AAF

(Area Code 517)

17, 18

Bears Country Inn:

The Bears Country Inn is located adjacent to the Grayling Mc Namara Airport on the southern end of the field. This family type restaurant is open Sunday 7 a.m. to 9 p.m., Monday through Thursday 6 a.m. to 9 p.m. and Friday and Saturday 6 a.m. to 10 p.m. Their full service menu contains a breakfast buffet on Saturday, Sunday and a dinner buffet on Friday, Saturday & Sunday. There are 3 different specials offered for lunch and dinner each day. In addition to the restaurant main dining area, a meeting room is also available for larger groups or business meetings with seating for up to 50 persons. For more information call 348-5516.

Restaurants Near Airport:
Bears Country Inn Adj Arpt Phone: 348-5516
Lone Pine Inn Adj Arpt Phone: 348-7312

Lodging: Aquarama Motor Lodge 348-5405; Holiday Inn (Trans) 348-7611; Hospitality House (Trans) 348-8900.

Meeting Rooms: Aquarama Motor Lodge 348-7611; Holiday Inn 348-7611; Hospitality House 348-8900.

Transportation: None Reported by airport

Information: Grayling Area Visitors Council, P.O. Box 217, Grayling, MI 49738, Phone: 800-937-8837.

Lone Pine Inn:

The Lone Pine Inn is located adjacent to the Grayling Mc Namara Airport and offers guests a friendly atmosphere with delicious home style cooking. A few of the many specialties consist of steak, chicken, and seafood selections. The portions will satisfy the most hungry of persons at very reasonable prices. One of the attractions which brings customers back for more, are the homemade pies baked fresh each day. This restaurant can seat 67, and is open during the week between 6:30 a.m. and 2:30 p.m. and on Friday and Saturday from 8:30 to 9 p.m. For more information call 348-7312.

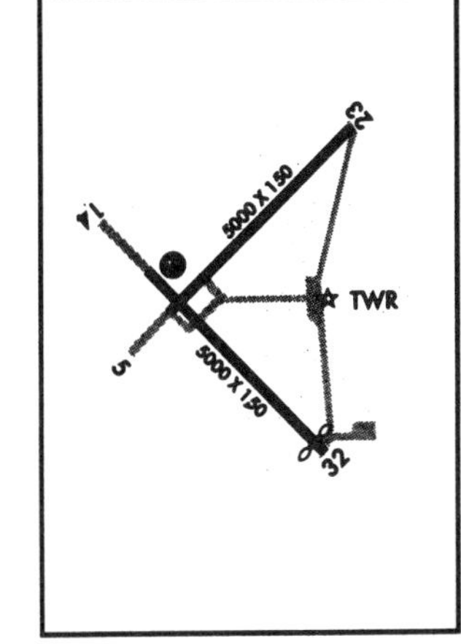

Airport Information:

GRAYLING - GRAYLING AAF (55D)
1 mi northwest of town N44-40.82 W84-43.73 Elev: 1158 Fuel: 100LL, Jet-A
Rwy 05-23: H5000x150 (Conc) Rwy 14-32: H5000x150 (Asph) Attended: Sep-May 1400-2200Z, Jun Aug 1400-0000 Unicom: 122.8 Tower: 126.2 Gnd-Con: 121.9
Grayling AAF Phone: 348-5845

MI-CMX - HANCOCK HOUGHTON CO. MEMORIAL ARPT.

(Area Code 906)

19

Aero Restaurant:

The Aero Restaurant is a cafe situated in a small room within the terminal building on the Houghton County Memorial Airport in Hancock Michigan. We were told that fly-in guests can easily walk to the restaurant from aircraft parking areas. This restaurant can seat approximately 25 persons and serves delicious food. Breakfast is served all day. Steak and eggs French toast and pancakes are specialties on the menu. Lunch entrees include hamburgers, roast beef, steaks, and homemade soups including chicken dumplings, vegetable beef and French onion. Be sure to try their fresh homemade strawberry pie. Prices average $2.75 for breakfast, $2.00 to $3.00 for Lunch. Each day they offer a new special on their menu. The Aero Restaurant is open Monday through Saturday 9 a.m. to 5 p.m. For information call 482-3723.

Attractions:

Calume Golf Club (5 miles north) 337-3911; McClain State Park (8 miles south) 482-0278.

Restaurants Near Airport:

Aero Restaurant	On Site	Phone: 482-3723
Ambassador	6 mi S.	Phone: 482-5054
Gino's Restaurant	5 mi S.	Phone: 482-3020

Lodging: Arcadian Motel (1 mile) 482-0288; Copper Crown Best Western (5 miles) 482-6111; Downtowner (6 miles) 482-4421; Portage Motel (6 miles) 482-2400; Best Western Ramada Inn (6 miles, Free trans) 487-1700; Whispering Pines (1 mile) 482-5887.

Meeting Rooms: There is a small conference room reported on the Houghton County Airport. For information call 482-3970; Also Ramada Inn has meeting rooms available by calling 487-1700.

Transportation: Taxi Service: Neil Taxi 482-5515; Rental Cars: Avis 482-1200; Hertz 482-6503; National 482-6655.

Information: Keweenaw Peninsula Chamber of Commerce, 326 Shelden Avenue, P.O. Box 336, Houghton, MI 49931, Phone: 482-5240 or 800-338-7982.

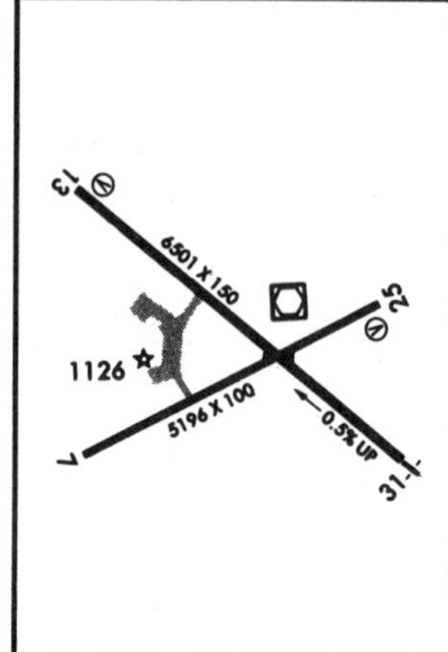

Airport Information:

HANCOCK - HOUGHTON COUNTY AIRPORT (CMX)
4 mi northeast of town N47-10.11 W88-29.34 Elev: 1095 Fuel: 80, 100, Jet-A
Rwy 13-31: H6501x150 (Asph-Grvd) Rwy 07-25: H5169x100 (Asph) Attended: 0900-0500Z
Unicom: 122.7 Notes: See Airport Facility Directory (AFD) for winter runway closing, Rwy 07-25; Landing fees $4.00 to $16.00 reported. Overnight tie down, $3.00 per night.
Houghton County Memorial Airport Phone: 482-3970

MI-80D - HARRISON CLARE COUNTY AIRPORT

(Area Code 517)

20

Aero Port Restaurant:

The Aero Port Restaurant is located adjacent to the Clare County Airport near Harrison Michigan. It is located within walking distance. This Family style facility is open Monday through Thursday from 6 a.m. to 9 p.m., Sunday from 6 a.m. to 6 p.m. and Friday and Saturday 24 hours. Specialties of the house include breakfast selections including 3 eggs, potato's ham, sausage and toast. or their omelets. For lunch some of their customers favorites are, French dip sandwiches, 1/2 pound hamburgers, homemade pies cakes and strawberry short cake. For dinner they feature New York Strip Stake, liver and onions, seafood dishes, supper wet burrito's. Prices average $2.99 for breakfast, $2.59 for lunch and between $8.99 and $7.99 for dinner selections. From inside the restaurant, you can see the aircraft parking ramp. Fly-in groups are welcome. For more information call the Aero Port Restaurant at 539-9887.

Restaurants Near Airport:

Aero Port Restaurant	Adj Arpt	Phone: 539-9887

Lodging: None Reported

Meeting Rooms: None Reported

Transportation: Clare County Transit (Taxi) 539-1473; Mid Michigan Transportaiton (Taxi) 539-6901.

Information: Chamber of Commerce, 809 North 1st Street, P.O. Box 682, Harrison, MI 48625, Phone: 539-6011.

NO AIRPORT DIAGRAM AVAILABLE

Airport Information:

HARRISON - CLARE COUNTY AIRPORT (80D)
2 mi northwest of town N44-03.17 W84-48.75 Elev: 1142
Rwy 18-36: H2780x50 (Asph) Rwy 09-27: 2315x90 (Turf) Attended: irregularly
Unicom: 122.8
Clare County Airport Phone: 539-9235

MI-9D9 - HASTINGS
HASTINGS AIRPORT

(Area Code 616)

21

Bay Pointe Restaurant:

The Bay Pointe Restaurant is located about 9 miles from the Hastings Municipal Airport in Shelbyville, Michigan. It is also located on the shores of Gun Lake, which according to the restaurant management, attracts a number of seaplanes throughout the year, even though this waterway is not listed in the Airport Facility Directory under seaplane bases. The building the restaurant is now located in, was built in 1902 and opened as a restaurant in 1983 offering guests a unique dining experience with a beautiful view overlooking Gun Lake. This fine dining establishment is known for several specialties such as Bay Pointe Chowder, delicious Pork loin Aplet, and award winning pork parmigiana. Arrangements can be made for private luncheon or dinner parties, sales meetings, as well as conferences. Flying groups and clubs are always welcome. In fact this restaurant has seen a number of guests arrive in seaplanes, parking their aircraft right in front of the restaurant. Mr. Roy Martin, owner of Bay Pointe restaurant is a pilot himself and will make a courtesy car available for fly-in guests landing at Hastings Airport when reserved ahead of time. The restaurant is open for lunch between 11 a.m. and 3 p.m. Tuesday through Friday; dinner from 5 p.m. to 10 p.m. Tuesday through Saturday; and 10:30 a.m. to 2:30 p.m. for Sunday brunch. (They are closed on Monday). For reservations or information call 672-5202.

Restaurants Near Airport:
Bay Pointe Restaurant 9 mi Phone: 672-5202
(Notes: Seaplane's can park in front of restaurant)

Lodging: Parkview (3 miles) 945-5111.

Meeting Rooms: Bay Pointe Restaurant has acommodations for meetings, conferences and catered meals on the premisses. For information call 672-5202.

Transportation: Courtesy car reported at airport, 945-5626.

Information: Hastings Area Chamber of Commerce, P.O. Box 236, Hastings, MI 49058, Phone: 945-2454.

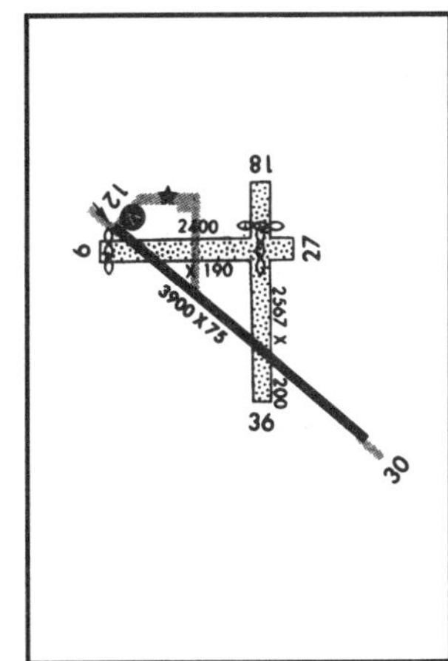

Airport Information:

HASTINGS - HASTINGS MUNICIPAL AIRPORT (9D9)
3 mi west of town N42-39.82 W85-20.78 Elev: 801 Fuel: 80, 100LL
Rwy 12-30: H3900x75 (Asph) Rwy 18-36: 2567x200 (Turf) Rwy 09-27: 2400x190 (Turf)
Attended: 1300Z-0100Z Unicom: 122.8
Hastings Municipal Airport Phone: 945-5626

MI-HLM - HOLLAND PARK TOWNSHIP AIRPORT

(Area Code 616) 22

Candlewick Inn:

The Candlewick Inn is located within one block east of the Park Township Airport on Ottawa Beach Road. This family style restaurant is open for breakfast and lunch between 8 a.m. and 2 p.m. Monday through Friday and 8 a.m. to 1 p.m. on Saturday. Their dinner hours are from 4:30 p.m. to 9 p.m. Monday through Saturday. for breakfast and lunch between 8 a.m. and 2 p.m. Monday through Friday, and 7 a.m. to 1 p.m. on Saturday. Their dinner hours are 4:30 p.m. to 9 p.m. Monday through Saturday. (Closed on Sunday) Specialties of the house include soups, breads, muffins, and pies in addition to fresh salads and a variety of sandwiches for lunch as well as broiled chicken, steaks, stir-fry, and salmon Salibury steak for dinner. Daily specials are also offered during lunch. Average prices run $3.00 for breakfast, $4.00 for lunch and $7.50 for dinner. The restaurant has a warm country decor with oak tables and chairs. Candlelight dining adds to the atmosphere during the dinner hour. Reservations are accepted for groups of 8 or more. All items listed on their menu are available for carry-out. The Candlewick Inn is located three miles from the State Park and Lake Michigan. Camping, fishing, as well as many antique stores and points of interest are located nearby. For more information about this restaurant you can call 399-8460.

Restaurants Near Airport:
Candlewick Inn 1 Blk E. Phone: 399-8460

Lodging: Best Western; Country Hospitality Inn (free pick-up) 396-6677; Days Inn 392-7001; Holiday Inn 394-0111.

Meeting Rooms: Country Hospitality Inn (free pick-up) 396-6677; Holiday Inn 394-0111.

Transportation: Holland Cab Company 392-6270; Rental Cars: Budget 527-0700; R.E. Barber 399-2361.

Information: Holland Area Chamber of Commerce, 272 E 8th Street, Holland, MI 49424.

Attractions:

The Park Township Airport is located on the eastern shoreline of Lake Michigan and just north of the waterway inlet and harbor entrance to the town of Holland Michigan. Rental car transportation can be arranged through the Park Township Airport. Settled on the shores of Lake Michigan, Holland is assured of a vast supply of freshwater to support a variety of fishing, boating, swimming, and beach-combing activities. Holland's Dutch hospitality and friendliness are reflected by the services at its lodgings, restaurants, and shopping facilities. Known around the world for its annual Tulip Time Festival, this historic community also offers museums, historical Cappon House, Dutch-touch factories and gardens, orchards, skiing areas and Hope college with its summer repertoire theater. Some of the following attractions may be of interest to you. Holland State Park contains 1/4 mile of lake- front beach within this 143 acre site. Many activities including camping, swimming and fishing can all be enjoyed within this State Park facility, 399-9390; The Baker Furniture Museum at 147 Columbia Avenue displays a collection of authentic period furniture and accessories from the early sixteenth century to late twentieth century (Open May through September) 392-8761; Brooks Beverage Plant is a major soft drink bottler and offers tours through their plant located at 777 Brooks Avenue, 396-1281: Poll Museum at the Junction of US-31 and New Holland Street, 5 miles north of Holland, contains several antique classic cars, fire trucks, bicycles, coaches, traction engines and model trains-including a 1920 locomobile, a 1921 Pierce Arrow roadster, and a 1929 Marmon roadster. This museum is open May through September. Veldheer Tulip Gardens located On US-31, 4 miles north of the town, and Windmill Island at Seventh Street and Lincoln Avenue both provide activities for the family with working windmill and beautiful gardens. (Information about some of the attractions listed, were obtained through the Michigan Travel Planner available by writing Michigan Travel Bureau, Dept. TPM, P.O Box 30226, Lansing, Michigan 48909 or calling 800-5432 YES).

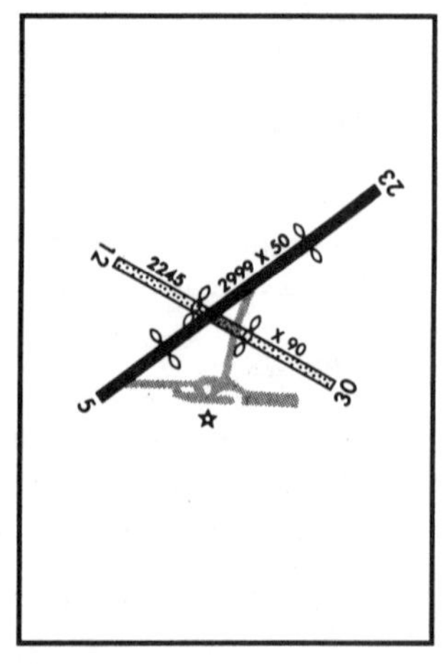

Airport Information:

HOLLAND - PARK TOWNSHIP AIRPORT (HLM)
3 mi northwest of town 42-47-46N 86-09-41W Elev: 602 Fuel: 100LL
Rwy 05-23: H2999x50 (Asph) Rwy 12-30: 2245x90 (Turf) Attended: Mon-Sat 1300-2300Z
Unicom: 122.8 App/Dep: 118.2 Notes: Rwy 12-30 CLOSED winter months; Landing fee waved with fuel purchase.
Airport Manager Phone Number 399-9333.

MI-OZW - HOWELL
LIVINGSTON COUNTY AIRPORT

(Area Code 517)

23

Tomato Brothers Restaurant:

Gus's Greek & Italian Restaurant is located about 1/2 mile from the Livingston County Airport in Howell, MI. This is a family style restaurant specializing in pizza, ribs, Greek salads and pasta dishes. In addition to their full service menu, there are daily specials from which to choose. The restaurant is open from 11 a.m. to 10 p.m. seven days a week. Transportation will be provided upon request. For information call 546-9221.

Restaurants Near Airport:

Gus's Greek & Italian Rest.	1/2 mi	Phone: 546-9221

Lodging: Best Western Of Howell (4 miles) 548-2900; Holiday Inn (4 miles) 546-6800.

Meeting Rooms: Holiday Inn 546-6800.

Transportation: Taxi Service: Arrow 548-3232; Rental Cars: Hiltop Ford 546-2250; Rent-A-Car 227-3530; Rent-A-Wreck 229-5855.

Information: Howell Area Chamber of Commerce, 404 East Grand River, Howell, MI 48843, Phone: 546-3920.

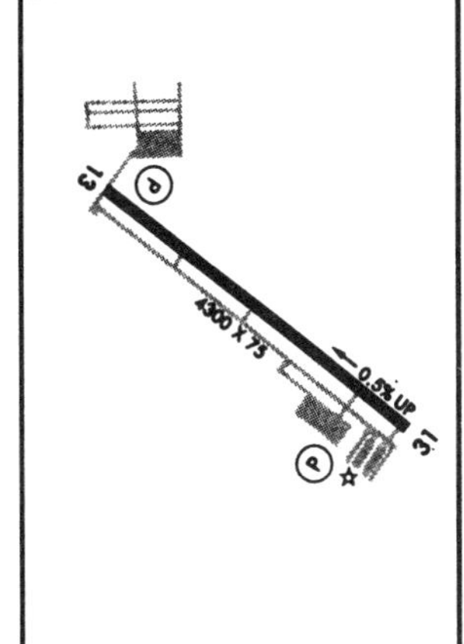

Airport Information:

HOWELL - LIVINGSTON COUNTY AIRPORT (OZW)
3 mi northwest of town N42-37.77 W83-59.05 Elev: 961 Fuel: 100LL, Jet-A
Rwy 13-31: H4300x75 (Asph) Attended: Mon-Fri 1200-0100Z, Sat-Sun 1300-2200Z
Unicom: 123.0
FBO: Livingston County Airport Phone: 546-7379

MI-Y70 - IONIA
IONIA COUNTY AIRPORT

(Area Code 616)

24

Big Boy Restaurant:

Big Boy Restaurant is located about 1/4 mile form the Ionia County Airport at the other side of the K-Mart shopping center. (Call restaurant for directions). This family style facility is open weekdays between 7 a.m. and 11 p.m. and on weekends between 7 a.m. and 12 a.m. They offer a breakfast bar during the week from 8 a.m. to 11 p.m. and on the weekends from 8 a.m. to 2 p.m. A dinner bar is featured on Friday and Saturday night between 5 p.m. and 9 p.m. Specialties of the house include breakfast selections like their delicious hot cakes or French toast with sausage. Lunch and dinner choices include chicken dinners, ground round, shrimp and steak dinners, along with their soup and salad bar. Average prices run $3.99 for breakfast and lunch and around $6.19 for dinner. The restaurant can accommodate 200 persons in addition to meeting area that can be arranged off to the side of the main dining room area. A carry-out menu along with In-flight catering can also be provided with advance notice. For information about this restaurant call 527-3730.

Restaurants Near Airport:

Big Boy	1/4 mi N.	Phone: 527-3730
McDonalds	1/4 mi N.	Phone: 527-1100
Wendy's	3/8 mi N.	Phone: 527-2611

Lodging: Heritage Motel (Adj Arpt) 527-3180; Midway Motel (4 miles) 527-2080; Union Hill Inn (6 miles) 527-0955.

Meeting Rooms: None Reported

Transportation: Caswell Ford (6 miles) 527-3310

Information: West Michigan Tourist Association, Convention & Visitors Bureau, 140 Monroe Center NW, 49503, 800-678-1859

Attractions:

Ionia State Recreation Area (State Park), reported two miles west of airport, Phone: 527-3750.

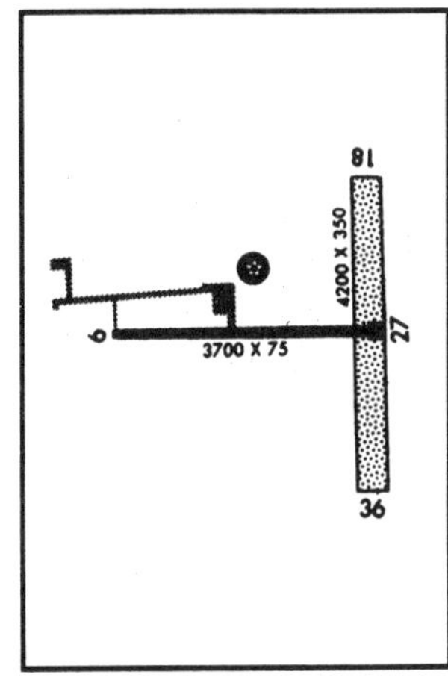

Airport Information:

IONIA - IONIA COUNTY AIRPORT (Y70)
3 mi south of town N42-56.27 W85-03.65 Elev: 812 Fuel: 80, 100LL
Rwy 18-36: 4200x350 (Turf) Rwy 09-27: H3700x75 (Asph) Attended 1400-2200Z
Unicom: 122.8 Public Phone 24hrs Notes: No landing fees, overnight parking is $2.00.
FBO: Benz Aviation, Inc. Phone: 527-9070

MI-IMT - IRON MOUNTAIN/KINGSFORD FORD AIRPORT

(Area Code 906)

25

The Blind Duck Inn:

The Blind Duck Inn is located approximately 300 yards from the Iron Mountain/Kingsford Ford Airport. A beautiful view of Cowboy Lake can be enjoyed by their customers. Their specialty is Mexican cuisine. However, there are American and Italian entrees as well. The restaurant and bar are open from 11:00 a.m. CST to 10:00 p.m. Monday through Saturday. Sunday hours are 5:00 p.m. to 10:00 p.m. The Blind Duck Inn also has a limited number of motel rooms available. During our luncheon visit, we had a great time and enjoyed a superb Mexican lunch. Looking out over Cowboy lake added to the tranquil atmosphere of this restaurant with light pine wooden walls and a pleasant country like decor. For information call The Blind Duck at 774-0037.

Attractions:

Golf Course, fishing and parks all available within this area. For additional information call Superior Aviation, Inc. at 774-0100 or contact the Dickinson County Area Chamber of Commerce under "Information" listed above.

Airport Information:

IRON MOUNTAIN/KINGSFORD - FORD AIRPORT (IMT)
3 mi west of town N45-49.10 W88-06.87 Elev: 1182 Fuel: 100LL, Jet-A
Rwy 01-19: H6500x150 (Asph-Pfc) Rwy 13-31: H3812x75 (Asph) Attended: 1130-0530Z
Unicom: 122.8 Notes: Pilots and customers are welcome to call Superior Aviation, Inc. for additional information, or to have motel or car accommodations arranged for them; CAUTION: Deer on and in vicinity of airport.
FBO: Superior Aviation, Inc. Phone: 774-0400, 800-321-1271

Restaurants Near Airport:

BJ's Food'n Friends	2 mi N.	Phone: 774-1777
The Blind Duck Inn	Adj Arpt	Phone: 774-0037
Fontana's Supper Club	3 mi N.	Phone: 774-0044
Romagnoli's Supper Club	4 mi N.	Phone: 774-7300

Lodging: The Blind Duck has a limited number of motel rooms available located adjacent to airport, 774-0037.
Meeting Rooms: The Blind Duck across from the airport has accommodations for meetings. 774-0037.
Transportation: Superior Aviation, Inc. (FBO) can provide courtesy transportation for their customers to nearby facilities, 774-0400; Also Taxi Service: Twin City Cab 774-7993; Rental Cars: Avis 774-0411; Hertz 774-4506.
Information: Dickinson County Area Chamber of Commerce 600 South Stephenson Avenue, Iron Mountain, MI 49801, Phone 774-2945, 800-236-2447.

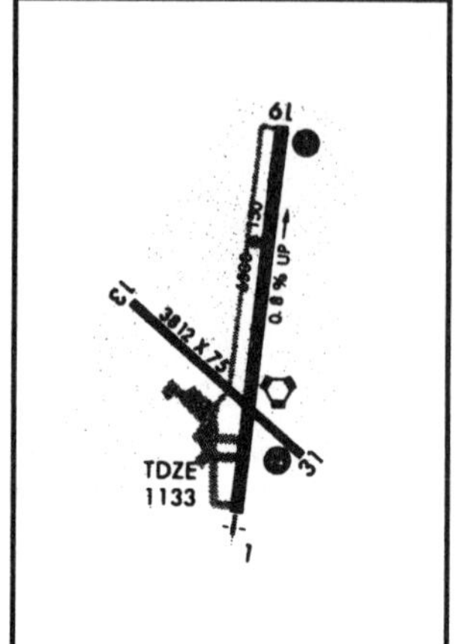

MI-JXN - JACKSON JACKSON CO-REYNOLDS FIELD

(Area Code 517)

26

Airport Restaurant & Spirits:

Don's Airport Restaurant is located on the Jackson County Reynolds Field Airport in Jackson, Michigan. This restaurant offers a wide variety of breakfast, lunch and dinner selections. The house specialties include various steak and seafood entrees along with sandwiches, homemade soups and pies. The seating capacity for this establishment is 100 persons. Large windows offer the visitor a good view of the activities on the airport. Accommodations for groups and parties are also available, as well as meals to-go, and in-flight catering. Restaurant hours are 7 a.m. to 8 p.m. 7 days a week. According to the restaurant management, aircraft parking is available directly in front of the restaurant. For information call 783-3616.

Attractions:

This region contains a number of fascinating attractions including a collection of nineteenth-century buildings, or visit the "Space Center", harness racing, shopping, nature areas, parks, golf courses, as well as the Michigan International Speedway. For information contact the Jackson Convention & Visitors Bureau listed above under "Information".

Airport Information:

JACKSON - JACKSON CO./REYNOLDS FIELD (JXN)
2 mi west of town N42-15.59 W84-27.56 Elev: 1001 Fuel: 100LL, Jet-A
Rwy 06-24: H5344x150 (Asph-Grvd) Rwy 14-32: H3501x100 (Asph) Attended: 1200-0100Z Atis: 127.95 Unicom: 122.95 Tower: 120.7 Gnd Con: 121.9 Clnc Del: 121.9 Notes: CAUTION: Deer and birds on and in vicinity of airport.

FBO: Boorom Aircraft	**Phone: 764-0485**	**FBO: Jackson Executive**	**Phone: 787-5900**
FBO: Day Aviation	**Phone: 784-1881**	**FBO: Skyway Aviation**	**Phone: 787-2460**

Restaurants Near Airport:
Airport Restaurant & Spirits On Site Phone: 783-3616

Lodging: Days Inn 787-1111; Holiday Inn (2 miles) 783-2681

Meeting Rooms: Days Inn 787-1111; Holiday Inn 783-2681.

Transportation: Rental Cars: Avis 782-8218.

Information: Jackson Convention And Visitors Bureau, 6007 Ann Arbor Road, Jackson, MI 49201, Phone: 764-4440.

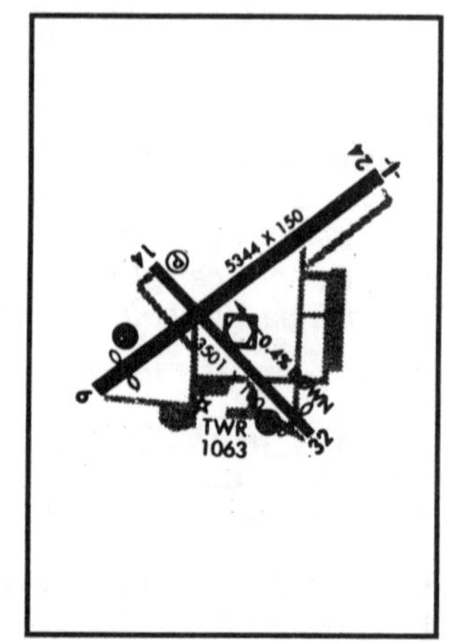

Not to be used for navigational purposes

MI-AZO - KALAMAZOO
KALAMAZOO/BATTLE CREEK INTL.

(Area Code 616)

27, 28, 29, 30, 31

Restaurants Near Airport:

Bill Knapp's	1/4 mi	Phone: 345-8635
Bravo Ristorante	1/4 mi	Phone: 344-7700
Gum Ho	1 blk mi	Phone: 343-1990
Hawthorne's (free pick-up)	4 mi S.	Phone: 323-1327
Theo & Stacy's	1/4 mi	Phone: 345-3000

Lodging: Holiday Inn-Expressway (free trans) 381-7070; La Quinta Motor Inn (Trans) 388-3551; Quality Inn (free trans) 382-1000; Residence Inn by Marriott (free trans) 349-0855; Radisson Plaza-Kalamazoo Center (free trans) 343-3333.

Meeting Rooms: All lodging facilities listed above have accommodations for meeting and conferences. Radisson Plaza-Kalamazoo Center has convention facilities available, 343-3333.

Transportation: Kal-Aero, Inc. (FBO) can provide courtesy transportation to nearby facilities 343-2548; Also taxi service: Rapid Transit 349-9300; Yellow Cab 345-0177; Rental Cars: Avis 381-0555; Budget 381-0617; Hertz 382-4903; National 382-2820.

Information: Kalamazoo Convention And Visitors Bureau, 128 North Kalamazoo Mall, Kalamazoo, MI 49007, Phone: 381-4003.

Bill Knapp's Restaurant:

Bill Knapp's Restaurant is located 1/4th mile from the Kalamazoo County Airport in Kalamazoo, Michigan. The restaurant has a modern decor, and offers a comfortable casual atmosphere for family dining. Seating capacity is around 190 persons. They have a full service menu with specials offered every day. The restaurant hours are Monday through Friday 10:30 a.m. to 10 p.m. and on weekends from 10:30 a.m. to 11 p.m. Aircraft Parking is available at Kal-Aero, Inc. 343-2548. For restaurant information call 345-8635.

Bravo Ristorante:

The Bravo Ristorante has just recently been completely remodeled and is celebrating its newly decorated facility complete with two main dining rooms and a modern Italian decor. They have seating for 180 persons, and a private banquet facility that can provide complete catered services for 15 to 150 people. This restaurant is located across the road from the terminal building and about 100 yards from Kal-Aero (FBO). Their dining room provides a friendly casual atmosphere and serves delicious Italian cuisine seven days a week. They open at 11:30 a.m. to 10 p.m. Monday through Thursday, and 11:30 a.m. to 12 a.m. Friday & Saturday. Daily specials are also available in addition to their Sunday brunch. Average prices run $7.00 for lunch and $16.00 for dinner. For more information about the restaurant, call 344-7700.

Gum Ho Restaurant:

The Gum Ho Restaurant is located within walking distance (one block) from the Kalamazoo County Airport in Kalamazoo, Michigan. This family-style restaurant specializes in Cantonese and Oriental dishes, in addition to their Szechwan (spicy) dishes. They offer a luncheon buffet from 11:30 a.m. to 2 p.m. weekdays and also on Sundays from 12 noon to 5 p.m. Their hours were last reported to be from 11:00 a.m. to 10:00 p.m. Sunday through Thursday and Friday and Saturday from 11 a.m. to 11 p.m. You might want to call and verify these hours. Aircraft parking and courtesy transportation are also available at Kal-Aero, Inc. by calling 343-2548. For more information about the Gum Ho Restaurant call 343-1990.

Attractions:

The Kalamazoo Aviation History Museum is located right on the airport property, and can easily be reached by parking at the museum or from Kal-Aero, Inc. (FBO). Many of the aircraft on display are magnificently restored to original flying condition and perform during various events throughout the year. This museum provides a public awareness about contributors of air power to the Allies' success during World War II. In addition, there are many exhibits and WW-II memorabilia that has been donated for display. For information call the museum at 382-6555;

Theo & Stacy's Restaurant:

Theo & Stacy's Restaurant is a family style restaurant within walking distance from Kal-Aero, Inc., located on the Kalamazoo County Airport in Kalamazoo, Michigan. This fine restaurant specializes in Greek and American foods. They have daily specials in addition to their salad bar and regular entrees including steaks, seafood, Greek dishes, hamburgers, and much more. They also have a banquet room that will comfortably seat 45 people. Their hours are 5:30 a.m. to 10 p.m., 7 day a week. Aircraft parking and courtesy transportation is available at Kal-Aero, Inc. 343-2548. For restaurant information call 345-3000.

Hawthorne's Restaurant & Cafe:

Thanks to one of our readers, we learned about another popular restaurant near Kalamazoo airport. Hawthorne's Restaurant and Cafe is owned by the same party that runs the famous Bay Pointe Restaurant on Gun Lake near Hastings, Michigan. Both of these restaurants are a favorite of many fly-in customers. (Both are Land or Seaplane accessible). Hawthorne's Restaurant offers a cozy hideaway and an elegant dining establishment where you can enjoy a relaxing meal, soft candle light, conversation enhancing atmosphere and front row sunsets reflected in the rippling waters of Portage's West Lake. The furnishings of this restaurant are unique with a Frank Lloyd Wright decor containing oak trim stained glass, a marble bar and dance floor. Two separate menus, and two distinctly different dining areas, are enveloped into a single restaurant. Hawthorn's is located 4 miles directly south of the Kalamazoo Airport along Portage Road, the same road as the airport is on. Tuesday through Friday they are open from 11:30 a.m. to 10:00 p.m., Saturday 5:00 p.m. to 10:00 p.m. and Sunday for their brunch buffet served from 10:30 a.m. until 2:30 p.m. Main entrees include Veal Normandy, Char-broiled lamb chops, Indian fields strip steak, chicken Algonquin, duckling West Lake, prairie grilled pork loin, whitefish chief Pokagan, salmon Taliesin and "Specialties of the chefs." Average prices run $5.00 to $10.00 for lunch and $10.00 to $20.00 for dinner. A large assortment of appetizers, snacks, soups and salads are available as well. Lighter fare is served in their cafe. Daily specials, Sunday brunch and Friday entertainment are provided for their guests. Courtesy transportation from the Kalamazoo Airport is available by calling the restaurant. Also on many occasions seaplane pilots will land their aircraft on the Austin Lake adjacent to the restaurant. For more information call Hawthorne's at 323-1327. **Notes:** Seaplane use: (Seaplane pilots can taxi directly to the restaurant docks on the east side of lake (Sandy bottom, no rocks) Seaplane pilots must contact AZO tower and report their intentions. Departure should be southwesterly if possible and contact tower ASAP when airborne.)

Airport Information:

KALAMAZOO - KALAMAZOO/BATTLE CREEK INTERNATIONAL AIRPORT (AZO)
3 mi southeast of town N42-14.09 W85-33.12 Elev: 874 Fuel: 80, 100LL, Jet-A
Rwy 17-35: H6499x150 (Asph-Grvd) Rwy 05-23: H3999x100 (Asph-Grvd)
Rwy 09-27: H3351x150 (Asph) Attended: continuously Atis: 127.25 Unicom: 122.95
App/Dep Con: 121.2 (173-352), 119.2 (353-172), 123.8 (1100-0400Z) Tower: 118.3
Gnd Con: 121.9 Clnc Del: 121.75
FBO: Kal-Aero, Inc. Phone: 343-2548

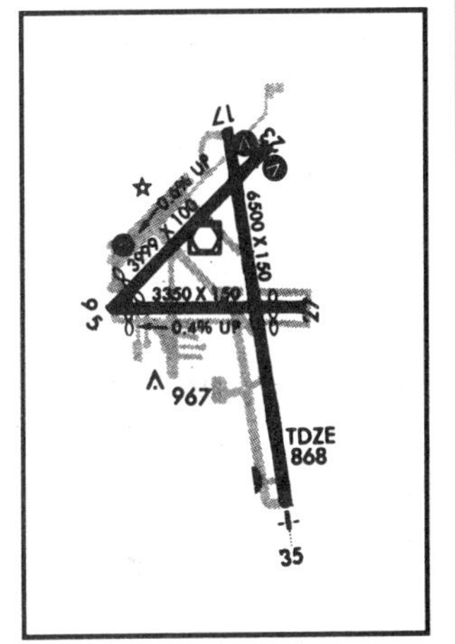

Kalamazoo Aviation History Museum

Kalamazoo, MI (MI-AZO)

New home of Michigan's Aviation Hall of Fame:

The Kalamazoo Aviation History Museum is located right on the Kalamazoo Battle Creek International Airport (AZO). The museum actually opened its doors on November 18, 1979, and expanded its exhibition area from June of 1986 to June of 1987. The "Air Zoo" has 43,000 square feet of display space. This new area exhibits aircraft in an immaculate environment, decorated with insignia banners, aviation photographs and art.

A unique feature of the museum is that many of the aircraft are airworthy and fly on a regular basis. Hourly tours are given in the 30,000 square foot Flight Restoration Center. These activities are held March through September.

The museum's planes have received numerous awards at the Experimental Aircraft Association's (EAA) national convention in Oshkosh, Wisconsin. In fact, the Kalamazoo Aviation History Museum was nicknamed the "Air Zoo," because in years past it was the first museum to possess the only collection of flight-worthy piston-driven Grumman Cats. In recent years, other museums have been fortunate enough to have acquired a few of these rare vintage aircraft as well.

The Kalamazoo Aviation History Museum is the new home of Michigan's Aviation Hall of Fame.

Their "Activity Room" allows visitors to get into a Link Trainer mock-up. Also displayed is a WW-II Link Trainer along with 6 various cockpits on display like the F-106 Delta Dart, C-47, KC-135 Stratotanker, CH-53 Superstallion and DC-3 cockpit.

There are two artifact rooms which display various WW-II memorabilia along with an outstanding model collection of over 200 aircraft displayed. In addition to this, is their Guadalcanal Memorial Museum and Monument, that is dedicated to all of the service people that fought in this "turning point" battle. Within the premises is a video theater showing movies each hour, a gift shop, snack bar and observation lounge. The Air Zoo's climate-controlled observation deck is capable of holding approximately 80-90 people for catered meals.

The Education Department trains and coordinates tour guides, provides educational programs for the community and nearby schools and provides speakers for local organizations. A newsletter is also published quarterly. Members have access to a library approaching 4,000 volumes, including technical manuals. There are also magazines and newspapers on file.

Admission fees for the museum run $4.00 for seniors 60 and above, $5.00 for persons 16-59, $3.00 for children 6 to 15 and free admission age 5 and under. Discounts are available for larger groups, as well as annual and life time members.

When planning to flyin to see the museum, pilots can park their aircraft at the museum. Or taxi to Kal-Aero (FBO) if planning to re-fuel and obtain courtesy transportation to the museum. For more information call 616-382-6555. (Information submitted by museum).

Photo: by Kalamazoo Aviation Museum

MI-LAN - LANSING CAPITAL CITY AIRPORT

(Area Code 517)

32

Skyway Lounge & Cafeteria:

The Skyway Lounge & Cafeteria is located within the main terminal building of the Capital City Airport, near Lansing, Michigan. This restaurant is open for business 7 days a week from 5:30 a.m. to 9 p.m. weekdays and 6 a.m. to 9 p.m. weekends. One of the many specialties available, is their prime rib dinner for only $5.25 and round of beef (Sundays only). They offer daily specials and very comfortable surroundings in a "semi formal" atmosphere, with a view that overlooks the runways. This restaurant can cater from 20 to 200 people for banquets, receptions business meetings, senior groups, and Christmas parties. They also cater to flights; crew meals, sandwich trays, fruit, cheese and cracker trays etc. Their prices are very moderate and the service is very good. The restaurant will not provide transportation. However, this should not pose any problem due to the fact that general aviation aircraft parking is available nearby. For restaurant information call 321-2487.

Restaurants Near Airport:
Skyway Lounge & Cafeteria On Site Phone: 321-2487

Lodging: Clarion Hotel & Conference Center (Trans) 694-8123; Comfort Inn 349-8700; Hilton (Trans) 627-3211; Kellogg Center 355-5090; Radisson Hotel Lansing (Trans) 482-0188; Residence Inn (Trans) 322-7711; Sheraton Inn (Trans) 323-7100.

Meeting Rooms: Clarion Hotel & Conference Center 694-8123; Comfort Inn 349-8700; Hilton 627-3211; Kellogg Center 355-5090; Radisson Hotel Lansing 482-0188; Sheraton Inn 323-7100.

Transportation: Avis 323-9132; Budget 321-2072; Hertz 321-2072; National 321-6777.

Information: Greater Lansing Convention And Visitors Bureau 119 Pere Marquett, P.O. Box 15066, Lansing, MI 48901, Phone: 487-6800.

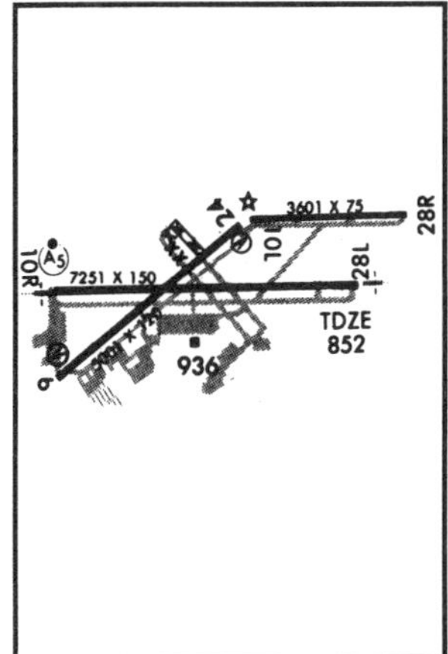

Airport Information:

LANSING - CAPITAL CITY AIRPORT (LAN)
3 mi northwest of town N42-46.72 W84-35.24 Elev: 861 Fuel: 100LL, Jet-A
Rwy 10R-28L: H7251x150 (Asph-Grvd) Rwy 06-24: H5001x120 (Asph-Conc-Grvd)
Rwy 10L-28R: H3601x75 (Asph) Attended: continuously Atis: 119.75 Unicom: 122.95
Lansing App/Dep Con: 118.65 (North) 125.9 (South) Lansing Tower: 119.9 Gnd Con: 121.9
Clnc Del: 120.4
FBO: General Aviation Phone: 321-7000
FBO: Superior Aviation Phone: 800-882-7751 or 321-0224

MI-GAR - LEWISTON GARLAND AIRPORT

(Area Code 517)

33

Garland Recreational and Corporate Retreat:

Garland, located in Lewiston, Michigan, is the ideal four-season retreat for either business or pleasure. It offers 3,500 acres of natural beauty and four challenging golf courses, plus an outdoor recreation pool, an indoor lap pool and three tennis courts. The Inn offers a luxurious executive board-room, comfortable V.I.P. suites and superb dining. During the winter, Garland transforms into a wonderland of seasonal pleasures. Wide groomed cross-country ski trails, indoor and outdoor jacuzzis and gourmet sleigh ride dinners. Garland also offers special golf packages and other various lodging packages. Garland has its own private, 5,000-foot paved runway and ramp area available to all Garland guests who are private pilots. Pilots may call the Inn for current local weather conditions. Also, complimentary shuttle service is provided from the runway to the Inn. For more information about rates and accommodations at Garland Recreational and Corporate Retreat, call 800-968-0042 or 786-2211.

Restaurants Near Airport:
Garland Retreat On Site Phone: 786-2211

Lodging: Garland Retreat (On Site) 786-2211

Meeting Rooms: Garland Retreat 786-2211

Transportation: Garland provides complimentary shuttle service from the runway to the Inn.

Information: Gaylord Area Convention and Tourism Bureau, 101 W. Main, P.O. Box 3069, Gaylord, MI 49735, Phone: 800-345-8621 or 732-6333

Information: Marshall Chamber of Commerce, 109 East Michigan, Marshall, MI 49068. Phone: 781-5163.

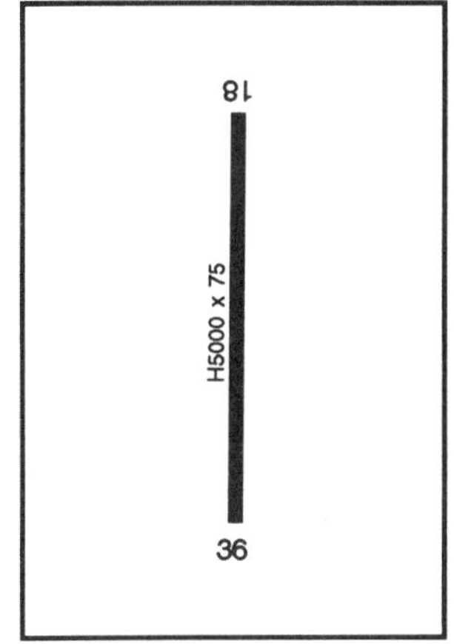

Airport Information:

LEWISTON - GARLAND AIRPORT (Private)
5 mi south of town N44-48.15 W84-15.25 Elev: 1218 Fuel: coming soon Rwy 18-36: H5000x75 (Paved) Attended: daylight hours Unicom: 122.8 Notes: Wildlife, including deer, on the runway perimeter.
FBO: GARLAND RETREAT Phone: 786-2211

MI-LDM - LUDINGTON
MASON COUNTY AIRPORT

(Area Code 616)

34,35,36

Gibbs Restaurant:

Located about 2 miles east of the Mason County Airport, this establishment will transport your party to and from the airport within their courtesy van. This combination colonial and family styled restaurant, provides a casual atmosphere in an elegant setting. Their famous gourmet salad bar contains a great selection of items to satisfy the most demanding of appetites. A desert bar with homemade, pies and other delicious goodies is included with the gourmet salad bar. They also specialize in selections like prime rib, chicken, Swiss steaks, fresh fish, and seafood. No meal is complete without trying one of their outstanding "Sticky Buns" glazed with a special honey and caramel topping, freshly baked and still warm from the oven. Average prices are very reasonable and run between $5.50 for lunch and around $11.00 for a complete dinner. Groups and larger parties can easily be served, with accommodations for up to 85 people offering extensive menu selections as well as separate checks. In-flight catering is also one of their specialties. Hot dinners, meat and cheese trays, cold cuts and box lunches can be prepared-to-go. Their motto is "And come as you are". For more information call Gibbs Restaurant at 845-0311.

Kuntry Kubbard:

The Kuntry Kubbard is the closest restaurant to the Mason County Airport and is located on the southwest corner of the field. This family style restaurant provides many fly-in customers with a nice selection of entrees at very reasonable prices. The restaurant can easily be reached from the main aircraft parking ramp. Fly-in Customers can walk to the main airport gate and down along Hwy 10, (1/4 mile). We were told by some people that you can take a short cut across the corner of the field, about 1/2 the distance to the restaurant, there is a small fence that would have to be scaled. Either way you decide to go, it's worth the effort. The service is friendly and the food is excellent. There are windows on three sides of the restaurant and allows a nice view of the airport, if you sit along the east wall. For more information about the Kuntry Kubbard Restaurant call 845-5217.

Lands Inn Dinner Theater:

During our conversation with the management of the Lands Inn we learned that this lodging establishment will soon be featuring a dinner buffet and stage performance on Friday and Saturday evenings between 6:30 p.m. and 10:00 p.m. Although at the time of interview, this was still in the planning stages, they seemed confident that it would soon be taking place. This establishment is situated about 2 miles east of the Mason County Airport. This Hotel (formerly the Ramada Inn) offers 114 units, banquet and conference rooms, convention accommodation for up to 500 people, indoor swimming pool, sauna, hot tubs and game room. For more information about the service or package family rates or dinner theater performances call 845-7311.

Restaurants Near Airport:

Restaurant	Distance	Phone
Gibbs Restaurant	2 mi E.	Phone: 845-0311
Kuntry Kubbard	1/4 mi W.	Phone: 845-5217
Lands Inn Dinner Thetr.	2 mi E.	Phone: 845-7311
Mc Donalds	1/4 mi. S.E.	Phone: N/A
P.M. Steamers	2-1/2 mi W.	Phone: 843-9555
Scotty's Harbor Hse.	1 mi W.	Phone: 843-4033
Windys Family Rest.	Across St.	Phone: N/A

Lodging: Millers (Trans) 843-2177; Lands Inn (Trans) 845-7311; Viking Arms (Trans) 843-3441. In addition to these establishments, their are numerous other motels and motor lodge facilities that provide exceptional accommodations. For a full list, contact the Mason County Convention & Visitors Bureau listed under "Information" listed below.

Meeting Rooms: Lands Inn (Convention facilities) 845-7311; Viking Armes 843-3441.

Transportation: Taxi Service: Radio Cab 843-2545; Rental Cars: Dick Boyd Ford 843-2049 or 845-5111; Urka Auto Center 845-6282; Also many of the dining and lodging establishments will provide courtesy transportation to their location. The staff at Mason County Airport are also helpful and will try to provide a courtesy car on a first come first serve basis and for short term to nearby locations.

Information: Ludington Area Convention & Visitor Bureau, 5827 West U.S. 10, Ludington, MI 49431, 845-0324 or 800-542-4600.

Attractions:

The town of Ludington has drawn a great many individuals year-round with enough activities to interest just about everyone. The Ludington State Park, with its camping sites, miles of sandy dunes, clean beaches, and secluded hiking trails, all play a significant part in making this region one of the most popular summer vacation spots in the upper midwest region. Many visitors, after enjoying a fine dinner at any one of several exceptional restaurants, can take a romantic stroll out along the break water to the light house and watch the car ferry steaming inbound toward its home port. Or visit the boat landing and catch a glimpse of the fishing boats bringing in their catch of the day. On Friday and Saturday evenings between 6:30 p.m. and 10:00 p.m. a dinner theater at the Lands Inn motel 845-7311 (Formerly Ramada Inn) is featured. This motel is situated only 2 miles east of the Mason County Airport. Transportation for overnight lodging guests is provided to and from the Mason County Airport. Convention meeting space and family entertainment packages are available as well. A travel and entertainment visitors center is also at this same location.

See Following page for more information

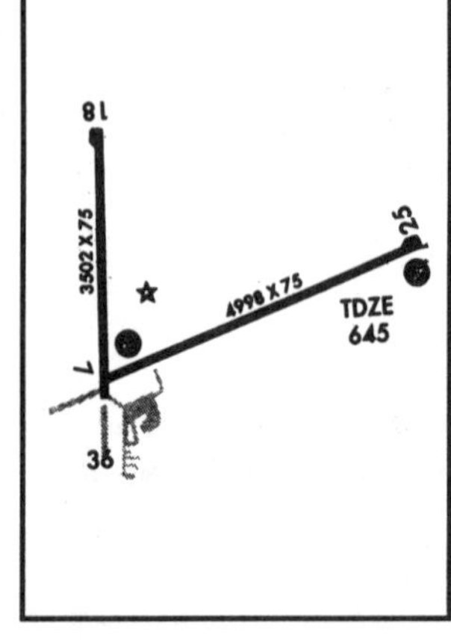

Airport Information:

LUDINGTON - MASON COUNTY AIRPORT (LDM)
2 mi northeast of town N43-57.75 W86-24.48 Elev: 645 Fuel: 80, 100LL, Jet-A
Rwy 07-25: H4998x75 (Asph) Rwy 18-36: H3502x75 (Asph) Attended: 1300Z-dusk Unicom: 123.0 Notes: Through our own personal experience, we were always greeted by friendly and helpful airport personnel, making our stay that much more enjoyable.
Mason County Aviation, Inc. Phone: 843-2049

MI-LDM - LUDINGTON MASON COUNTY AIRPORT

37

(Area Code 616)

P.M. Steamers:

P.M. Steamers is situated 2-1/2 miles west of the Mason County Airport and overlooks the beautiful Ludington City Marina. This dining facility is conveniently located only two blocks from the main shopping district of the downtown area. Its modern wooden structure displays a rustic yet nautical appearance and has a maindining room that is nicely furnished and decorated with a variety of nautical memorabilia and large tinted windows. If using a airport courtesy car, to reach this restaurant, you would take U.S. 10 west through town toward Lake Michigan, then turn left 4 blocks before you reach the lake, and go one block south. P.M. Steamers is at 502 West Loomis. Although their menu contains a nice variety of items, their specialties include Nutty Walleye, prime rib, fresh fish specials served on Friday and Saturday, and a Sunday brunch featured between 10:00 and 2:00 p.m. Average prices run $5.00 for lunch and $12.00 for dinner. A party room is also available and can accommodate up to 70 people for large groups. Lunch is served between 11:30 and 2:00 p.m. while dinner hours are from 5 p.m. to 9 p.m. For more information about P.M. Steamers Restaurant call 843-9555.

Restaurants Near Airport:

Gibbs Restaurant	2 mi E.	Phone: 845-0311
Kuntry Kubbard	1/4 mi W.	Phone: 845-5217
Lands Inn Dinner Thetr.	2 mi E.	Phone: 845-7311
Mc Donalds	1/4 mi. S.E.	Phone: N/A
P.M. Steamers	2-1/2 mi W.	Phone: 843-9555
Scotty's Harbor Hse.	1 mi W.	Phone: 843-4033
Windys Family Rest.	Across St.	Phone: N/A

Lodging: Millers (Trans) 843-2177; Lands Inn (Trans) 845-7311; Viking Arms (Trans) 843-3441.

Meeting Rooms: Lands Inn (Meeting facilities) 845-7311; Viking Armes 843-3441.

Transportation: Taxi Service: Radio Cab 843-2545; Rental Cars: Dick Boyd Ford 843-2049 or 845-5111; Urka Auto Center 845-6282;

Information: Ludington Area Convention & Visitor Bureau, 5827 West U.S. 10, Ludington, MI 49431, 845-0324 or 800-542-4600.

Also See Previous Page

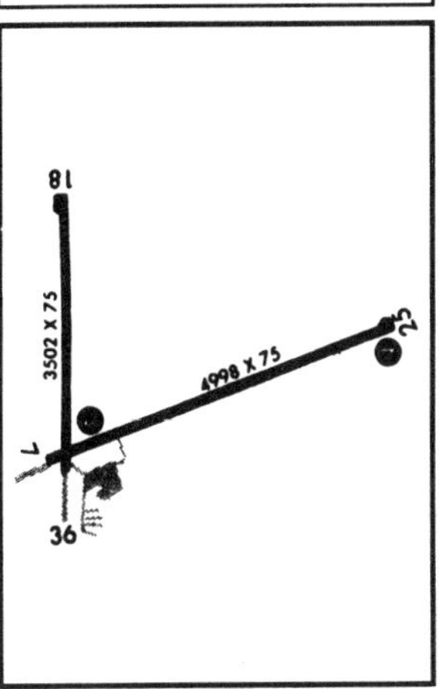

Airport Information:

LUDINGTON - MASON COUNTY AIRPORT (LDM)
2 mi northeast of town N43-57.75 W86-24.48 Elev: 645 Fuel: 80, 100LL, Jet-A
Rwy 07-25: H4998x75 (Asph) Rwy 18-36: H3502x75 (Asph) Attended: 1300Z-dusk Unicom: 123.0 Notes: Through our own personal experience, we were always greeted by friendly and helpful airport personnel, making our stay that much more enjoyable.
Mason County Aviation, Inc. Phone: 843-2049

MI-ISQ - MANISTIQUE SCHOOLCRAFT COUNTY

38

(Area Code 906)

Fireside Inn Restaurant:

The Fireside Inn Restaurant is located just off Schoolcraft County Airport in the Upper Peninsula near Manistique, Michigan. This Supper club is reported to be within walking distance from the airport. They are open Monday through Saturday from 5 p.m. until 9:00 p.m. during the winter season, and 4 p.m. to 10 p.m. during the rest of the year. In the winter season, beginning December 1st, the Fireside Inn Restaurant will be closed on Sundays. Their dining room has a warm and friendly atmosphere as well as a rustic appearance complete with a wood burning brick fireplace. Seating capacity is around 125 persons within their main dining area. Their entree specialties include seafood, whitefish, a variety of steaks, and chicken selections, in addition to many other choices. They also feature a salad bar as well. For information or reservations you can call the Fireside Inn at 341-6332.

Restaurants Near Airport:

Fireside Inn Restaurant	1/2 mi	Phone: 341-6332

lodging: Holiday Motel (Trans) 341-2710; Manistique Motor Inn (Trans) 341-2552; Ramada Inn (Trans) 341-6911

Meeting Rooms: Manistique Motor Inn 341-2552; Ramada Inn 341-6911.

Transportation: Rental Cars: Creigton Ford 341-2123; Curran Chev 341-2141.

Information: Schoolcraft County Chamber of Commerce, P.O. Box 72, Manistique, MI 49854, Phone: 341-5010.

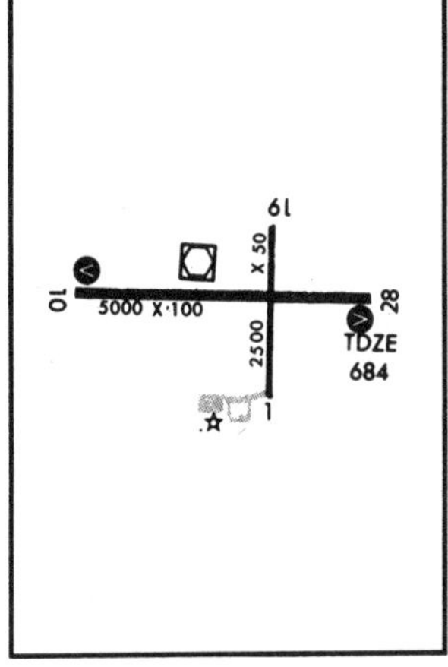

Airport Information:

MANISTIQUE - SCHOOLCRAFT COUNTY AIRPORT (ISQ)
3 mi northeast of town N45-58.48 W86-10.31 Elev: 685 Fuel: 80, 100, Jet-A
Rwy 10-28: H5000x100 (Asph) Rwy 01-19: H2500x50 (Asph) Attended: 1300-2200Z
Unicom: 122.8
FBO: A.N.S. Aviation Phone: 341-5522

MI-MQT - MARQUETTE
MARQUETTE COUNTY AIRPORT

(Area Code 906) 39

Airport Restaurant & Lounge:

The Airport Restaurant & Lounge is located within the terminal building on the second floor. This restaurant is a family styled establishment that is open 5:30 a.m. to 5:30 p.m. on the weekdays and 5:30 a.m. to 5 p.m. on the weekends. Specialty entrees include appetizers, homemade desserts, salad bar, their fabulous Friday fish fry, daily lunch specials, homemade bread and last but not least their famous homemade chili. Average prices run $3.50 for breakfast, $4.75 for lunch and the same for dinner. This is a modern new facility that allows for a very nice view of the airport and its activities. In-flight catering is a service that this restaurant will provide as well. For more information call the Airport Restaurant & Lounge at 475-6702.

Restaurants Near Airport:
Airport Restaurant & Lounge On Site Phone: 475-6702

Lodging: Holiday Inn (Trans) 225-1351; Ramada Inn (Trans) 228-6000; Tiroler Hof Motel 226-7516.

Meeting Rooms: The Airport Restaurant has accommodations for banquets and meetings; Also: Holiday Inn 225-1351; Ramada Inn 228-6000; Tiroler Hof Motel 226-7516.

Transportation: Taxi Service: Superior 226-2521; Rental Cars: Avis 475-4177; Hertz 475-4497; National 475-4717.

Information: Marquette Area Chamber of Commerce, 501 South Front Street, 226-6591.

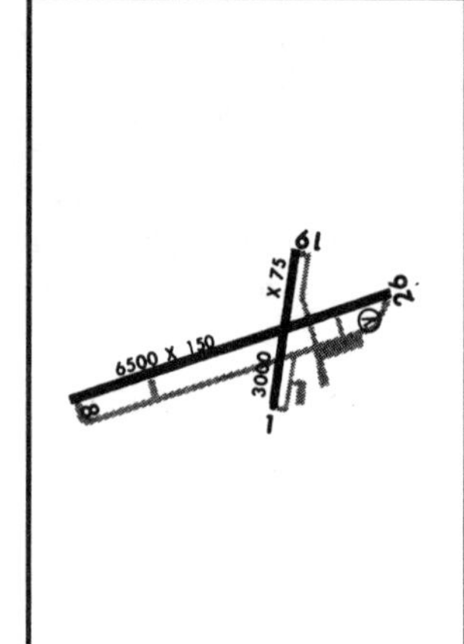

Airport Information:

MARQUETTE - MARQUETTE COUNTY AIRPORT (MQT)
7 mi west of town N46-32.04 W87-33.70 Elev: 1419 Fuel: 100LL, Jet-A
Rwy 08-26: H6500x150 (Asph-Pfc) Rwy 01-19: H3000x75 (Asph) Attended: May-Oct 1100-0600Z, Nov-Apr 1000-0600Z Unicom: 123.0
Marquette County Airport Phone: 475-9651
FBO: Northern Michigan Aviation Phone: 475-4400

MI-RMY - MARSHALL
BROOKS FIELD

(Aera Code 616) 40

Schuler's Restaurant:

Schuler's Restaurant is a fine dining facility located only 3 minutes by restaurant courtesy car from the Brooks Field. This restaurant is frequented by many fly-in customers and makes for an excellent location for planning outings for your flying club or organization. Just give them a call from the airport and they will come out and pick you up. Restaurant hours are 11 a.m. to 11 p.m. Monday through Saturday and 10 a.m. to 10 p.m on Sunday. Their menu includes a wide selection from light fare to their specialties like roast prime rib, rib of beef and daily lunch and dinner specials. They also feature their own bakery with fresh bread every day. Another specialty of the house are their homemade desserts. Prices average $5.00 to $10.00 for lunch and $8.00 to $15.00 for dinner. On Sundays they feature a brunch from 10 a.m. to 2 p.m. Schuler's Restaurant has a traditional English-style decor which is casual and comfortable. Famous sayings and quotes adorn the ceiling beams. Accommodations for meetings, including audio-visual support can easily be arranged. Receptions, banquets and business meetings are one of their specialties. They will even cater to any location as well. Box lunches to go can also be delivered to the airport. Any catering request can be accommodated. Schuler's Restaurant holds an annual Fly-in in July every year. Luncheon, prizes and great fellowship are enjoyed by all. Flyers from around the midwest look forward to this event. For information you can call Schulers Restaurant at 781-0600.

Restaurants Near Airport:

Alwyn Downs	On Site	Phone: 781-3981
Moon Raker	1 mi	Phone: 789-0058
Schuler's	1-1/2 mi	Phone: 781-0600

Lodging: Arborgate Inn 2 mi 781-7772; Howard's Motel 1-2 mi 781-4201; National House Inn 1-2 mi 781-7374;

Meeting Rooms: Schuler's Restaurant has accommodations for meeting and conferences (1-1/2 mi free trans) 781-0600.

Transportation: Rental Cars: Boshear's Ford 781-3981; Caron Motor Sales 781-5151; Taxi Service: Dial-A-Ride 781-3975.

Information: Marshall Chamber of Commerce, 109 East Michigan, Marshall, MI 49068. Phone: 781-5163.

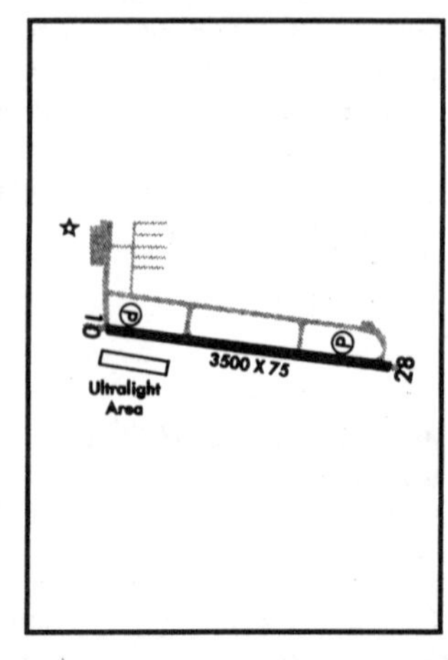

Airport Information:

MARSHALL - BROOKS FIELD (RMY)
1 mi south of town N42-15.07 W84-57.33 Elev: 941 Fuel: 80, 100LL Rwy 10-28: H3500x75 (Asph) Attended: 1300Z-dusk Unicom: 122.8
Brooks Aero, Inc. Phone: 781-3996

MI-MKG - MUSKEGON
MUSKEGON COUNTY AIRPORT

(Area Code 616)

41

Brownstone Restaurant:

The Brownstone Restaurant is located in the main terminal building of the Muskegon County Airport in Muskegon, Michigan. Homemade soups, salads and sandwiches, in addition to several pasta dishes, are their specialties. This restaurant is open Monday through Thursday from 6:30 a.m. to 9 p.m., Friday from 6:30 a.m. to 10 p.m., Saturday from 6:30 a.m. to 10 p.m. and Sunday from 11 p.m. to 5 p.m. Aircraft parking is available at Executive Air Transport. For further information call the restaurant at 798-2273.

Restaurants Near Airport:
Brownstone Restaurant   On Site   Phone: 798-2273

Lodging: Hilton Muskegon Harbor (Trans) 722-0100; Holiday Inn Muskegon 733-2601; Holiday Inn Spring Lake (Trans) 846-1000; Quality Inn Muskegon 733-2651.

Meeting Rooms: Hilton Muskegon Harbor 722-0100; Holiday Inn Muskegon 733-2601; Holiday Inn Spring Lake 846-1000.

Transportation: Taxi Service: Port City 739-7161; United 722-2521; Rental Cars: Budget 798-7983; Hertz 798-2595; National 798-4758.

Information: Muskegon County Convention & Visitors Bureau, 349 West Webster, Muskegon, MI 49440, Phone: 722-3751.

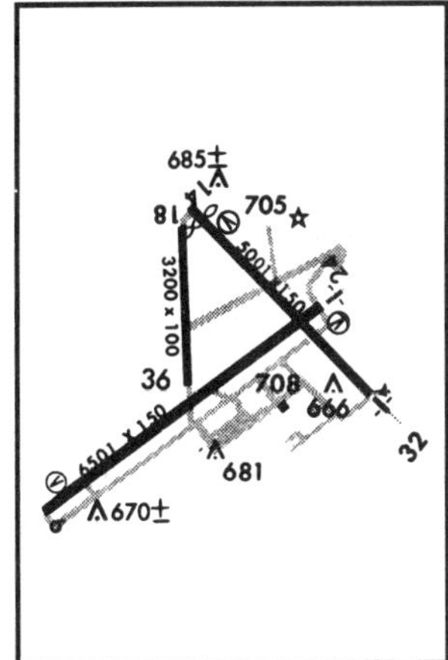

Airport Information:

MUSKEGON - MUSKEGON COUNTY AIRPORT (MKG)
4 mi south of town   N43-10.17 W86-14.29   Elev: 628   Fuel: 100LL, Jet-A
Rwy 06-24: H6501x150 (Asph-Pfc)   Rwy 14-32: H5001x150 (Asph-Pfc)
Rwy 18-36: H3200x100 (Asph-Pfc)   Attended: 1100-0200Z
Atis: 124.3   Unicom: 122.95   App/Dep Con: 118.2 (NE/NW) 119.8 (SE/SW) of Active Runway   Tower: 126.25   Gnd Con: 121.6
FBO: Executive Air Transport   Phone: 798-2126

MI-3NP - NAPOLEON
NAPOLEON AIRPORT

(Area Code 517)

42

Napoleon Restaurant:

The Napoleon Restaurant is reported to be situated 3 city blocks east of the Napoleon Airport in Napoleon, Michigan. This restaurant has an extensive menu including breakfast served all day, lunch entrees, and many choice steak selections. Some of these include their rib-eye steak, large sirloin steak, porterhouse, T-bone and strip steaks. In addition they also serve pork chops, roast beef and pork dishes as well as seafood. On Thursday, Saturday, and Sunday they feature their famous sausage, biscuits and gravy. Every day there is a different special to choose from. Average prices run between $5.95 and $11.95 for most items. The decor of the dining area has a rustic country atmosphere, with wooden seats and booths. Seating capacity is about 75 to 80 persons. Many fly-in customers make a special trip to try their famous breakfast omelets. The restaurant's hours are Friday and Saturday from 5:30 a.m. to 9:30, Tuesday, Wednesday, Thursday and Sunday from 5:30 a.m. to 8:30 p.m. For more information call 536-4244.

Restaurants Near Airport:
Napoleon Restaurant   3 blks   Phone: 536-4244

Lodging: None Reported

Meeting Rooms: None Reported

Transportation: None Reported

Information: Jackson Convention & Tourist Bureau, 6007 Ann Arbor Road, Jackson, MI 49201, Phone: 764-4440.

NO AIRPORT DIAGRAM AVAILABLE

Airport Information:

NAPOLEON - NAPOLEON AIRPORT (3NP)
1 mi northwest of town   N42-10.25 W84-15.58   Elev: 963   Rwy 09-27: 2740x200 (Turf)
Rwy 15-33: 2500x100 (Turf)   Attended: irregularly   CTAF: 122.9
Napoleon Airport   Phone: 536-5353, 783-2119
Skydiving Center   Phone: 536-5252

MI-5D3 - OWOSSO
OWOSSO COMMUNITY AIRPORT

(Area Code 517)

43, 44

BJ's Fine Foods Restaurant:

BJ's Restaurant is located 1/4 mile east of the Owosso Community Airport. This family style facility specializes in good old-fashion home cooking. Daily specials include homemade soups and a variety of freshly baked pies. On Friday they feature cod, perch, catfish or broiled orange roughy. Average prices for specials run $2.75 for breakfast, $2.95 for lunch and $4.95 for dinner. The decor of the restaurant displays a modern yet homey atmosphere, decorated with booths, tables and a non-smoking section. Groups and parties are always welcome. BJ's Fine Foods Restaurant is open at 5 a.m. to 10 p.m. Monday through Thursday, and 5 a.m. to 12 midnight Friday and Saturday. On Sunday they serve meals from 7 a.m. to 8 p.m. They will gladly provide courtesy transportation if you call them from the airport. For more information call 743-6263.

Bob Evans Restaurant:

Bob Evans is situated less than one mile from the Owosso Community Airport. This restaurant is open 6 a.m to 10 p.m. Sunday through Thursday and 6 a.m. to 11:30 p.m. Friday and Saturday. Breakfast specials begin at around $2.99. Breakfast is served all day. Lunch specials run throughout the week beginning at $3.99. Bob Evans Restaurant is famous for his meats and sausages. The restaurant seats about 120 people. No reservations are necessary. For more information call the restaurant at 723-9770.

Attractions:

Curwood Castle located in downtown Owosso about 1.7 miles from the airport and is a architecturally built replica of a Norman castle and museum containing many artifact on display. For information call 723-8844.

Restaurants Near Airport:

BJ's Fine Foods	1/2 mi E.	Phone: 743-6263
Bob Evans	less than 1 mi.	Phone: 723-9770
Fast Food	Neumerous Adj.	Phone: N/A
Risto Bistro	In town - Fine dining	Phone: 723-3143

Lodging: Mulberry House Bed & Breakfast (1/2 mile) 723-4890; Pines Country House (Adj Arpt) 725-5164; R & R Bed & Breakfast 723-2553; Shiakasske House 725-7148; Victoria Splender Bed & Breakfast 725-5168; Welcome Inn (Adj Arpt) 723-5141.

Meeting Rooms: Pines Country House 725-5164.

Transportation: None Reported by airport. However, the BJ's Fine Foods 743-6865 and Pines Country House 725-5164 will provide customers with transportation to their establishment.

Information: Owosso-Corunna Area Chamber of Commerce, 215 N. Water Street, Owosso, MI 48867, Phone: 723-5149.

Airport Information:

OWOSSO - OWOSSO COMMUNITY AIRPORT (5D3)
1.7 mi east of town N42-59.58 W84-08.33 Fuel: 80, 100LL Rwy 10-28: H3800x75 (Asph)
Rwy 18-36: 2575x265 (Turf) Rwy 06-24: 2470x130 (Turf) Attended: 1300Z-Sunset
Unicom: 123.0 Public Phone 24hrs
FBO: Cessna Pilot Center Phone: 723-4166

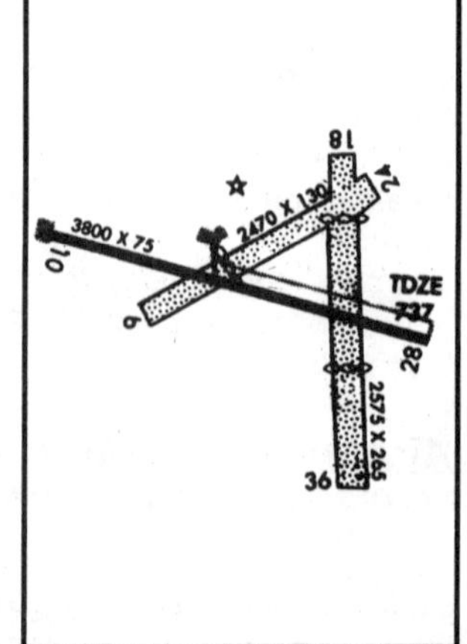

MI-PLN - PELLSTON
PELLSTON REGIONAL AIRPORT OF EMMET CO.

(Area Code 616) 45

Brass Rail Restaurant & Lounge:

The Brass Rail Restaurant is located right on the Pellston Regional Airport of Emmet County. This family style restaurant is situated within the terminal building and is only a short walk from the aircraft parking area. This facility is open from 6:00 a.m. to 2:00 p.m. 7 days a week. (Closed some holidays). Their menu contains a nice selection of entrees along with specials of the day. On Friday they offer fresh lake perch, on Saturday their mouth watering steak and shrimp will delight your pallet and on Sunday as well as during the week, they also offer daily specials for your dining pleasure. Prices range from $5.00 for breakfast and lunch to about $7:50-$10.00 for dinner selections. Group fly-ins are welcome provided your party is not too large and prior arrangements are made with the restaurant. For the pilot on-the-go, the Brass Rail Restaurant will gladly prepare carry out meals consisting of cheese trays, sandwiches and hot meals. For more information you can call the restaurant at 539-8212 or 539-8806.

Restaurants Near Airport:

Brass Rail Restaurant & Lounge	On Site	Phone: 539-8212
Dam Site Inn (Seasonal)	3 mi S.	Phone: 539-8851
Douglas Lake Stk Hse, seasonal	4 mi E.	Phone: 539-8588

Lodging: Arbor Motel (Two miles from airport, Seasonal) US-31, Pellston, MI 539-8622; Holiday Inn (20 miles, pick-up policy varies) Phone: 347-6041; Levering Hotel (6 miles) Phone: 537-4746.

Transportation: Rental Cars: Avis 539-8302; Hertz 539-8404; Taxi Service: Wolverine Stages 539-8635.

Information: Petoskey Regional Chamber of Commerce, 401-East Mitchell Street, Petoskey, MI 49770, Phone: 347-4150 Also you can contact the: West Michigan Tourist Association at 136 East Fulton Street, Grand Rapids, Michigan 49503, Phone: 616-456-8557.

Attraction:

The Pellston Regional Airport of Emmet County is situated within easy access to nearby cities and points of interest throughout this region. Cheboygan 20 mi; Mackinaw City 20 mi; Petoskey 20 mi; Sault Ste Marie 75 mi; Boyne Highlands 16 mi; and Harbor Springs 20 mi. In addition, the Pellston Regional Airport is a frequent stopping point for many aircraft leaving or arriving at Mackinac Island. Since their is no aviation fuel sold on the island, Pellston Airport becomes a particularly attractive location to stop and fill your tanks and grab a bite to eat.

Little Traverse Bay Area: This region located about 20 miles south of the Pellston Airport on U.S. 31 has long been attracting individuals throughout the four seasons with its fine skiing accommodations, as well as its many activities and scenic and peaceful surroundings. ***Harbor Springs:*** is a small community with an "old-fashioned" downtown district, and several very nice shops located along its main street. Through the Christmas and News Years Holidays, its decorated streets are much like what a Christmas card might depict. In the winter months, the town is visited by many of the skiers from the two ski resorts just a few miles to the north. ***Petoskey:*** also about 20 miles from the Pellston Airport on the southern edge of Little Traverse Bay and along U.S. 31, is best known for its downtown Gaslight District, which offers numerous specialty shops.

Winter Sports: There are two major resorts located near the Pellston Regional Airport. During the winter months they attract skiers from all over the midwest. Nubs Nob Ski Resort provides their guests with twenty runs and five chair lifts for the beginner, intermediate or expert. This resort is located only 8 miles by car, southwest of the airport. Boyne Highlands Ski Lodge & Resort is located farther to the west, features 29 runs, 8 chairlifts, 1 rope tow, and accommodations for handling up to 29,000 skiers per hour. This resort covers 200 acres of skiable terrain for down-hill as well as cross-country ski slopes that surround the complex.

Autumn Tours: Flying into this area can give you a Bird'seye view of the beautiful countryside, but to really enjoy this region up close, we recommend taking a scenic trip by car along the country roads and visiting the many camping grounds, fishing spots and State Parks. In Mid-September through Mid-October, the blaze of fall colors is the prime attraction in this region. There are five separate self-tours with recommended easy to follow directions that can be seen by automobile. Information about these tours are available by contacting the Petoskey Regional Chamber of Commerce at 347-4150 and ask for the Autumn Tour Guide pamphlet.

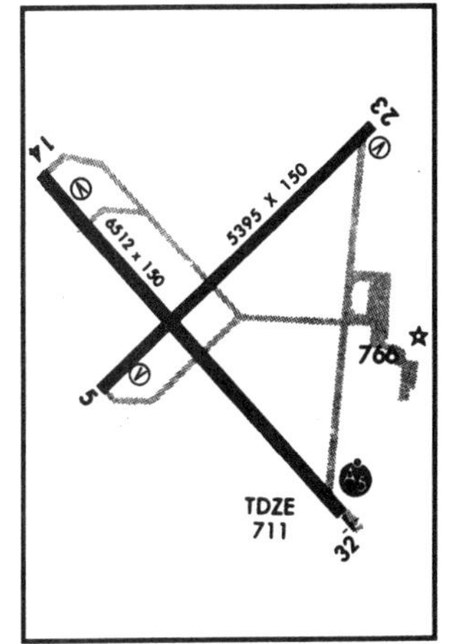

Airport Information:

PELLSTON - PELLSTON REGIONAL ARPT OF EMMET CO. (PLN)
1 mi northwest of town N45-34.26 W84-47.80 Elev: 720 Fuel: 100LL, Jet-A
Rwy 14-32: H6512x150 (Asph-Grvd) Rwy 05-23: H5395x150 (Asph-Grvd)
Attended: 1000-0200Z Unicom: 123.0 Public Phone 24hrs Notes: Landing fee waived with fuel purchase, parking $4.00/night
Pellston Regional Airport of Emmet County, Phone: 539-8441

Mackinac Island

When flying to Mackinac Island, the anticipation of the day's events will begin to unfold as you approach your destination. The great Mackinaw suspension bridge provides an excellent landmark, spanning its way over several miles across shimmering waters, connecting the towns of Mackinaw and St. Ignace, where Lake Michigan meets Lake Huron. For those of you who have never had the opportunity to visit the Island, we can say without a doubt, that your stay will be filled with memorable experiences. The Island offers a casual yet elegant atmosphere amidst an early American setting. When approaching the Island, we suggest you call the airport five or ten miles out, on their unicom frequency of 122.8 for transportation into town. A horse drawn taxi will meet you at the airport office and take your party on a scenic ride along winding roads through the countryside covered with lush green forests. As you approach the downtown area, your taxi will pass the Grand Hotel, one of Mackinac Island's most prominent establishments. Its beautiful surroundings are enhanced with planting areas abundant with brilliant floral arrangements within a park-like setting. After a short stop to let off passengers, the taxi will continue on its way along a tree-lined boulevard busy with horse-drawn vehicles, bicycles and pedestrians. The only sounds of transportation are those made by horses hooves upon the pavement which add to the peaceful atmosphere in this country-like setting. Motor vehicles are not permitted on the Island because the Island's residents and merchants prefer to maintain the early American motif without the disturbing noise of busses and cars. Most all of the houses and buildings on the Island are well maintained with great pride, depicting the early American heritage during the late 1800's.

As your horse drawn taxi enters the downtown district, the streets are alive with people milling through the many souvenir and gift shops. The sights, sounds and especially smells of homemade fudge fill the air, along with the aroma of fresh bakery goods and food from nearby snack shops.

High upon a hill overlooking the town is Fort Mackinac, which in itself is an attraction that should not be missed.

Photo by: Aerodine — The main shopping district of Mackinac Island.

Throughout the day you are bound to hear the report of musket and cannon fire that echoes through the town on hourly intervals. Visitors are encouraged to tour the Fort, which was reconstructed on its original foundation, by the Mackinac Island Park Commission. The Fort portrays military and domestic life during the eighteenth century and was occupied at different periods in time by British and American troops. The history behind the Fort is explained by tour guides dressed in the regalia of that era. The panoramic view overlooking the bay and downtown district is well worth the uphill walk to the Fort's entrance. one inside the Fort, visitors are welcome to stay as long as they like while inspecting the different buildings and witnessing the mock musket and cannon demonstrations within the Fort's surroundings. Guides are always happy to answer any questions you may have about the lifestyle as well as the historic battles fought during the era.

Photo by: Aerodine — The famous Grand Hotel as seen from horse drawn carriage.

Guided & Self Guided Tours:

Since motor vehicles are not permitted on the Island, the visitor is encouraged to take advantage of a number of fine tour and rental facilities located near the downtown district. The guided tours normally provide the guests with a visit to several of the main attractions throughout the Island. You will travel in spacious comfortable covered carriages, visiting such attractions as the Grand Hotel, Antique Livery Display at Surrey Hill, Arch Rock and Fort Mackinac. These tours, usually take between one to two hours with short stops at each attraction, in addition to more than twenty other points of interest discussed during your tour. For those of you who prefer to tour the Island attractions on your own, there are bicycles as well as livery stables with horse-drawn carriages or riding horses for rent. Simple and easy-to-read trail maps will be supplied, with trails marked in different colors depicting approximate lengths in time to complete the tour. Carriages, individual horses and bicycles are all rented to individuals on an hourly and/or daily basis, thus enabling the freedom to visit different attractions at the renter's own pace. There are a number of additional activities provided for the guests of Mackinac Island. Those individuals who enjoy a good game of golf, will be happy to know about two courses in operation in conjunction with the Grand Hotel, and are equipped with putting greens and pro-shop. The Chicago to Mackinac Island Yacht Race and the Port Huron to Mackinac Island Yacht Race are two exciting events normally held each year.

After spending a day visiting the Island's attractions, you will be ready to let yourself wind down while enjoying a fine meal at any one of several restaurants on the Island. As the last ferry leaves for the day back to the mainland, the town becomes very quiet and peaceful. As the twilight sets, in the horse drawn carriages with their lanterns glowing, slowly, make their way carrying passengers between the different hotels and lodging establishments.

Mackinac Island provides an excellent facility for fly-in guests to land right on the Island, utilizing a 3500 foot paved lighted airstrip. There is plenty of aircraft parking available in the grass. However, tiedown ropes and stakes are not provided. There is no fuel sold at the Mackinac Airport. There are several other airports in the area that do. After calling for a taxi on 122.8, allow approximately forty minutes for the taxi to reach the airort from town.

For more information about the accommodations and things to see, call the Mackinac Island Chamber of Commerce at 906-847-6418, or 906-847-3783. The Mackinac Island Airport number is 906-847-3231.

Photo by: Aerodine Bicycle's are used by many visitors

Photo by: Aerodine Mackinac Island Airport

MI-PTK - PONTIAC OAKLAND/PONTIAC

(Area Code 810)

46, 47

Cafe Max:

Cafe Max is located on the Oakland/Pontiac Airport in the terminal building on the east side. This restaurant is open Monday through Saturday from 11 a.m. to 2 p.m. and Sunday from 10 a.m. to 2 p.m. Their menu contains a full selection of choices in addition to specials offered through the week. On Sunday they feature a breakfast buffet served 10 a.m. to 2 p.m. Monday through Friday at happy hour, they have a complimentary buffet. Daily lunch and dinner specials are also offered including Friday night fish fry. Menu prices run $5.99 for breakfast, $5.50 for lunch and $8.50 for evening meals. The restaurant is decorated with sports memorabilia. For larger groups they have a banquet and party room available as well. Carry out and in-flight catering is also available. Live Reggae music is played on Thursdays. D.J.. music is played on Wednesday, Friday and Saturday. For information call Cafe Max at 666-2030.

Mitch's II Restaurant:

The Mitch's II Restaurant is situated across from the airport, 300 feet from the road and approximately a 1/4th mile walk from the Pontiac Oakland Airport. This restaurant specializes in many different types of entrees such as steaks, seafood, pastas and fresh salad creations. Average prices range from $7.00 to $16.00 for most full course dinners. The restaurant also caters to large groups with banquet facilities able to accommodate from 50 to 100 people. The restaurant displays a rustic old tavern decor and is open 6 days a week, Tuesday through Sunday from 11 a.m. to 12 midnight. They are closed on Monday. For more information call 666-4440.

Restaurants Near Airport:

Airport Inn	1/4 mi	Phone: 666-3940
Cafe Max	Trml Bldg.	Phone: 666-2030
Elis Big Boy	1/2 mi	Phone: 674-4631
Lions Den	1 mi	Phone: 674-2251
Mitch's II	1/3 mi	Phone: 666-4440
Ram's Horn	1/2 mi	Phone: 666-8830

Lodging: Comfort Inn-Waterford 12 mi 666-8555; Hilton Suites-Auburn Hills 11 mi 334-2222; Holiday Inn 6 mi 334-2444; Holiday Inn 10 mi 373-4550; Kingsley Inn 7 mi 644-1400; Marriott Courtyard 7 mi 373-4100.

Meeting Rooms: Hilton Suites-Aurburn Hills 11 mi 334-2222.

Transportation: Rental Cars on site: Avis 666-8494; Dollar 666-3630; Hertz 666-4460; Taxi Service: West Bloomfield Cab 360-4616; Limousine Service: Cary 885-5466; Continental 626-8282.

Information: Metropolitan Detroit Convention & Visitors Bureau, 100 Renaissance Center, Suite 1950, Detroit, MI 48243. Phone: 313-567-1170.

Airport Information:

PONTIAC - OAKLAND/PONTIAC (PTK)

5 mi west of town N42-39.90 W83-25.08 Elev: 980 Fuel: 100LL, Jet-A Rwy 09R-27L: H6200x150 (Asph-Pfc) Rwy 09L-27R: H5000x75 (Asph) Rwy 04-22: H2451x75 (Asph) Rwy 18-36: H1856x50 (Asph) Attended: continuously Atis: 125.45 Unicom: 122.95 Tower: 120.5, 123.7 Gnd Con: 121.9 Clnc Del: 118.25 Notes: Customs (Min 3 hrs notice) 313-226-3140); Landing fee for aircraft over 7,500 lbs; The following FBO's dispense fuel.

FBO: Aerodynamics, Inc.	**Phone: 666-3500, 800-235-9234**
FBO: American Flight & Tech. Ctr.	**Phone: 666-4178**
FBO: Chrysler Pentastar Aviation	**Phone: 666-3630**
FBO: Corporate Express	**Phone: 666-9713, 800-521-4406**
FBO: IFL East	**Phone: 666-9600, 800-521-4406**
FBO: Royal Air Freight, Inc.	**Phone: 666-3070**
FBO: Taubman Air Terminals, Inc.	**Phone: 666-4900**

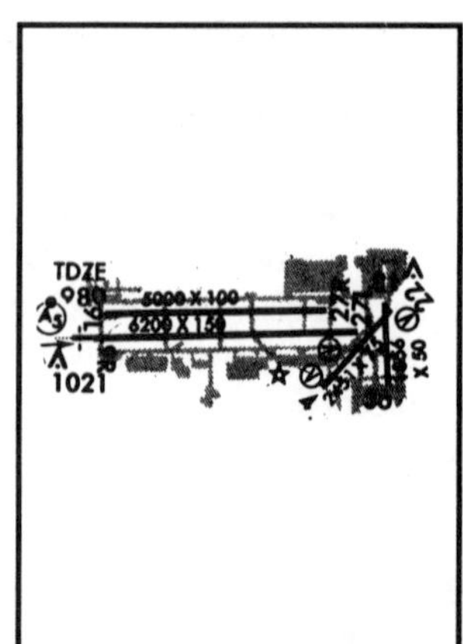

MI-MBS - SAGINAW
MBS INTERNATIONAL

(Area Code 517) 48

The Sky Room & Kittyhawk Snack Bar:

The Sky Room is a banquet center that is located on MBS International Airport near Freeland, MI. It is on the top floor of the terminal building and has recently been specializing in on-premises catering. This catering facility can furnish a variety of services and prepares special menu selections for scheduled social or corporate events. Available entree selections includes steaks, prime rib, and seafood. You can call 695-5391 to reserve times and choice of menu selections. Aircraft parking is located, about 500 feet away. In addition to the Sky Room banquet rooms, the "Kitty Hawk" snack bar is operated by the same enterprise and is especially designed to serve the majority of the airport food service business. This establishment is reported to be situated on the main floor of the terminal building just to the right of the main entrance. The restaurant can seat 80 persons comfortably. Their hours are from 6 a.m. to 7 p.m. and offer selections such as cold sandwiches, grilled specials, homemade soups, chili and pizza. For further information about either of these two facilities, you can call 695-5391.

Restaurants Near Airport:
The Sky Room On Site Phone: 695-5391

Lodging: Best Western Saginaw (Trans) 793-2080; Florentine Inn (Trans) 755-1161; Holiday Inn Saginaw (Trans) 755-0461; Sheraton Inn (Fashion Square) (Trans) 790-5050.

Meeting Rooms: Best Western Saginaw 793-2080; Florentine Inn 755-1161; Holiday Inn Saginaw 755-0461; Sheraton Inn (Fashion Square) 790-5050.

Transportation: Avis: 695-5333; Budget 695-5361; Hertz 695-5587; National 695-5531; Thrifty 695-5308.

Information: Saginaw County Convention & Visitors Bureau, 901 South Washington, Saginaw, MI 48601, 752-7164 or 800-444-9979.

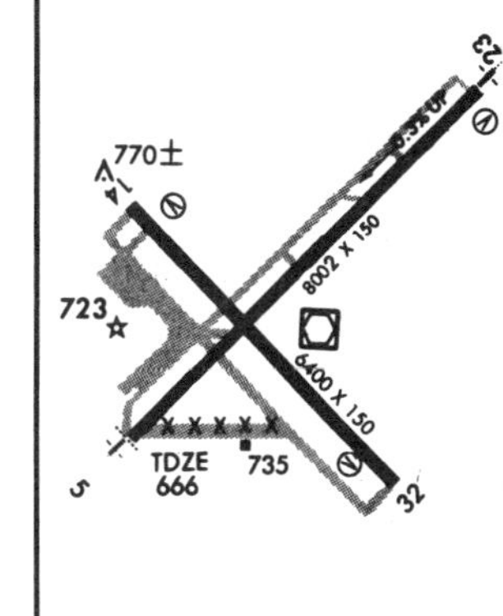

Airport Information:

SAGINAW - MBS International (MBS)
9 mi northwest of town N43-31.97 W84-04.78 Elev: 668 Fuel: 100LL, Jet-A
Rwy 05-23: H8002x150 (Asph-Grvd) Rwy 14-32: H6400x150 (Asph-Grvd)
Attended: 1000-0600Z Atis: 118.6 Unicom: 122.95 Saginaw App/Dep Con: 118.45, 126.45 Saginaw Tower: 120.1 Gnd Con: 121.7 Clnc Del: 121.85
Airport Manager **Phone: 695-5555**
FBO: Aero Services Intl. **Phone: 695-2554 or 800-227-7907**

MI-SJX - ST. JAMES BEAVER ISLAND AIRPORT

(Area Code 616) 49

Beaver Island:

Beaver Island, which measures twelve miles long and five miles wide, is the largest island in both the Beaver Archipelago (consisting of 7 islands) and Lake Michigan. It is also the most remotely inhabited island in the Great Lakes. It has 53 square miles of mostly forested land,with seven inland lakes which offer good fishing. Beaver Island Airport is located 4 miles southwest of St. James Harbor. St. James Harbor, located on the northeast corner of the island, is the center of most business and social activities. It has the museum, post office, bank, community school and the Island's three churches. It is also one of the most beautiful and protected natural harbors in the Great Lakes. Beaver Island offers lodging at motels, tourist courts and cabins. There are also general stores and restaurants. Although island businesses offer everything necessary for comfort, the island is not highly developed. It is the ideal getaway for vacationers who love nature, and yearn for peace and serenity. There are two camping facilities (one in St. James, and the other in PeaineTownship), several hiking trails, beautiful sandy beaches, scenic sunsets, seven nearby islands to explore, two lighthouses and two marinas.The island also offers many activities, such as island tours, sailing, boating, windsurfing, gofing, fishing (and guides), boat and tackle rental, hunting (and guides), hiking, nature tours, plane rides and sunset cruises. If you choose to land at the municipal aiport in Charlevoix, which is 32 miles from the island, Beaver Island Boat Company ferries passengers from the dock in downtown Charlevoix to the dock on Beaver Island in St. James Harbor. It makes two-and -one-quarter-hour trips one to three times a day, April through December. Reservations for the ferry should be made in advance. For sightseeing, some kind of vehicle is required to fully explore the island beyond the village area. Beaver Island Boat Company has guided bus tours available. A bicycle is also an ideal form of transportation around the village area. Cars and bikes can be brought over on the ferry or rented on the island. Reservations for renting a vehicle should be made in advance. Taxi service is also available. In addition, the outlying restaurants will provide rides for their customers. For more information about activities and accommodations on Beaver Island, contact the Beaver Island Chamber of Commerce at 448-2505 (in season) or 547-2101 (off season).

Restaurants Near Airport:

Beaver Island Lodge & Restaurant	4 mi	Phone: 448-2396
Circle Motel & Restaurant	4 mi	Phone: 448-2318
Stoney Acre Grill	4 mi	Phone: 448-2560

Lodging: Beaver Island Lodge & Restaurant (4 miles) 448-2396; Circle Motel & Restaurant (4 miles) 448-2318; Erin Motel (4 miles) 448-2240; Harbor View Motel (4 miles) 448-2201; McCafferty Inn 448-2376 or 448-2238

Meeting Rooms: Beaver Island Lodge & Restaurant (call in adv.) 448-2396

Transportation: Taxi Service: Betty Willis 448-2415; Tim Timsak 448-2317; Rental Cars: Beaver Island 448-2266; Erin Motel 448-2240

Information: Beaver Island Chamber of Commerce, Box 5, St. James - Beaver Island, MI 49782

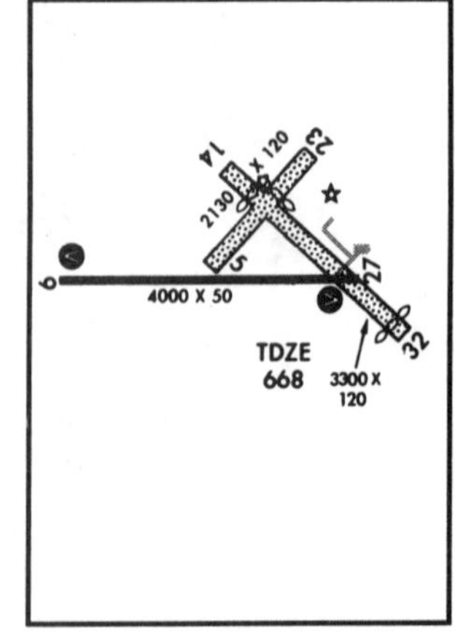

Airport Information:

ST. JAMES - BEAVER ISLAND AIRPORT (SJX)

4 mi southwest of town N45-41.54 W85-33.98 Elev: 669 Fuel: None Reported Rwy 09-27: H4000x50 (Asph) Rwy 14-32: 3300x120 (Turf) Rwy 05-23: 2130x120 (Turf) Attended: irregularly CTAF/Unicom: 122.8 Minneapolis Center App/Dep Con: 134.6 Notes: Rwys 05-23 and 14-32 CLOSED winter months. Rwys 05-23 and 14-32 marked with 3 feet cones.

FBO: Airport Manager Phone: 448-2750

MI-Y73 - STAMBAUGH
STAMBAUGH AIRPORT

(Area Code 906) 50

Kermit's Bar:

Kermit's Bar is a Pizza Pub & Grill located less than 1/4 mile from the Stambaugh Airport, and is reported to be well within walking distance. This combination restaurant and tavern specializes in all types of sandwiches, pizzas and fish dishes. They have seating for about 40 people and can accommodate fly-in groups and parties. Interested fly-in guests can call the restaurant at 265-2790 for further information.

Restaurants Near Airport:

Kermit's Bar	1/4th mi	Phone: 265-2790

Lodging: Crestwood Motel (7 miles) 265-9422; Iron Inn (1 mile) 265-5111; Lakeshore Motel (3 miles) 265-3611.

Meeting Rooms: None Reported

Transportation: Taxi Service: Happy Cab 265-2133, 472-2525.

Information: Iron County Chamber of Commerce, 50 E. Genesee Street, Iron River, MI 49935, Phone: 265-3800 or 800-255-3620; Also: The Travel Bureau, Michigan Department of Commerce, P.O. Box 30226, Lansing, MI 48909, Phone: 800-543-2YES

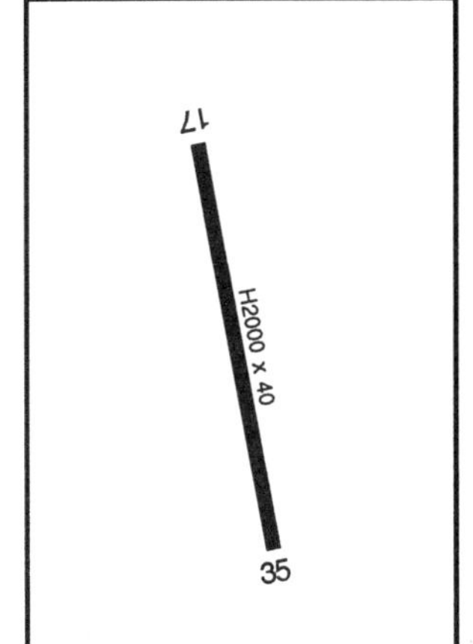

Airport Information:

STAMBAUGH - STAMBAUGH AIRPORT (Y73)
0 mi west of town N46-04.50 W88-37.76 Elev: 1622 Rwy 17-35: H2000x40 (Asph)
Attended: unattended CTAF: 122.9 Notes: Be alert deer in vicinity of runway. Also 100' drop off each end of runway.
Stambaugh Airport Phone: 265-5525, 265-9147

MI-IRS - STURGIS
KIRSCH MUNICIPAL AIRPORT

(Area Code 616) 51

Taste of Asia:

The taste of Asia Restaurant is situated within walking distance from the Kirsch Municipal Airport (Adj Arpt), and is open Monday through Friday 11 a.m. to 2 p.m. and 5 p.m. to 8 p.m. (Closed Sataurday and Sunday). This restaurant specializes in preparing American, Philippine, Chinese, Japanese and Korean cuisine. Breakfast is served all day. Average dinner prices run around $6.00 for most selections. Their main dining room can accommodate up to 50 persons. Groups and parties of 30 to 50 persons can arrange special catering with a three day advance notice required. All items on their menu can easily be ordered to go or packaged for carry-out. In-flight catering is also reported to be available. For more information about the Hackman's Airway Restaurant call 651-4442.

Restaurants Near Airport:

Lake Side Loft	5 mi	Phone: 651-1077
Taste of Asia Restaurant	Adj Arpt	Phone: 651-4442
Welcher Steak & Ribs	N/A	Phone: 651-1800

Lodging: Colonial Motor Inn (Trans) 651-8505; Green Briar Motor Inn (Trans) 651-2361; Holiday Inn 651-7881.

Meeting Rooms: Colonial Motor Inn 651-8505; Holiday Inn 651-7881.

Transportation: Airport courtesy reported; Also Rental Cars: Riley Avn 651-2821 or 651-9045.

Information: Michigan Travel Bureau, Dept TPM, P.O. Box 30226, Lansing, MI 48909, Phone: 800-5432-YES.

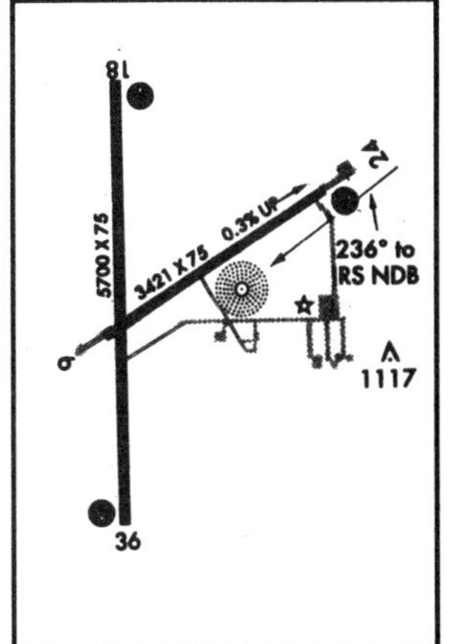

Airport Information:

STURGIS - KIRSCH MUNICIPAL AIRPORT (IRS)
2 mi northwest of town N41-48.77 W85-26.34 Elev: 925 Fuel: 80, 100, Jet-A1+
Rwy 18-36: H5700x75 (Asph) Rwy 06-24: H3421x75 (Asph) Attended: 1300Z-Dusk
Unicom: 123.05
FBO: Riley Aviation Phone: 651-2821

MI-TVC - TRAVERSE CITY CHERRY CAPITAL AIRPORT

(Area Code 616) 52

Suncatcher Bar & Grill:

The Suncatcher Lounge is a family style restaurant that is located on the upper level of the terminal building at the Cherry Capital Airport near Traverse City, Michigan. This restaurant caters to the flying public utilizing the services at the airport. They are open Monday through Friday from 6 a.m. until 8 p.m. Saturday and Sunday from 8 a.m. to 8 p.m. Their entrees consist of continental breakfasts, as well as grilled chicken breasts, burgers & homemade soups along with many other selections. Average prices run $4.50 to $7.00 for most choices. The main dining room can seat 64 persons and contains windows along one whole wall, allowing a nice view of the airport and scenic hills in the background. Watching the sunrises is a particularly pretty time of the day, according to the management. You can even see wildlife on certain occasions. For information call 941-0192.

Restaurants Near Airport:
Suncatcher Lounge On Site Phone: 941-0192

Lodging: Best Western Four Seasons 946-8424; Grand Traverse Resort Village (Trans) 938-2100; Holiday Inn (Trans) 947-3700; Park Place Hotel (Trans) 946-5000; Waterfront Resort Hotel (Trans) 938-1100.

Meeting Rooms: Grand Traverse Resort Village 938-2100; Holiday Inn 947-3700; Park Place Hotel 946-5000; Waterfront Resort Hotel 938-1100.

Transportation: Taxi Service: Classy Cab 946-4400; Rental Cars: Avis: 946-1222; Hertz 946-7051; National 947-1560.

Information: Traverse City Area Chamber of Commerce, 415 Munson, Suite 200, Traverse City, MI 49686, Phone: 947-1120.

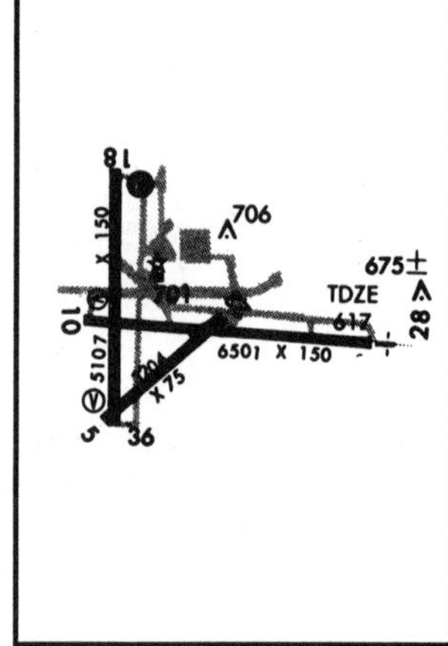

Airport Information:

TRAVERSE CITY - CHERRY CAPITAL AIRPORT (TVC)
2 mi south of town N44-44.45 W85-34.95 Elev: 624 Fuel: 100LL, Jet-A
Rwy 10-28: H6501x150 (Asph-Pfc) Rwy 18-36: H5107x150 (Asph-Pfc)
Rwy 05-23: H3204x75 (Asph) Attended: Jun-Sep 1100-0400Z, Oct-May 1200-0200Z
Atis: 126.0 Unicom: 122.95 Minneapolis Center App/Dep Con: 132.9
Tower: 124.2 Gnd Con: 121.8
FBO: Harbour Air Phone: 929-1126

MI-Y04 - TRAVERSE CITY SUGAR LOAF RESORT

(Area Code 616) 53

Sugar Loaf Resort:

Sugar loaf Resort "located at the highest point of Leelanau County, offers guests an unforgettable view of Lake Michigan, Little Traverse Lake and the Manitou Islands. The 3,700' paved, lighted air strip allows private planes to taxi within 100 yards of the resort. The Four Seasons Dining Room serves breakfast, lunch and dinner featuring American and local delights. They also offer their award winning Sunday Brunch includes over 50 culinary creations with miles of homemade desserts. During the summer months casual dining at the Par Pub, overlooks the Jan Stephenson 18-hole Championship Golf Course, and offers outdoor BBQ's, a variety of sandwiches and your favorite beverages. A variety of additional accommodations are also available for your entertainment pleasure. Call 1-800-968-0576 for resort information.

Restaurants Near Airport:
Sugar Loaf Resort On Site Phone: 800-968-0576

Lodging: Sugar Loaf Resort 800-968-0576

Meeting Rooms: Sugar Loaf Resort contains 22,000 square feet of meeting space, 800-968-0576.

Transportation: Courtesy car reported.

Information: Traverse City Area Chamber of Commerce, 415 Munson, Suite 200, Traverse City, MI 49684, Phone: 947-1120.

Attractions:

Sugar Loaf Village Resort contains 150 hotel rooms, hospitality suites, slope-sided town houses, luxurious Winged-Foot Condominiums, newly remodeled Four Seasons restaurant, lounges, live entertainment, deli, an indoor pool and two outdoor swimming pools and weight training facility. For their guests they also feature a variety of outdoor sporting activities to choose from, including two 18 hole championship golf courses, one of which is their newly constructed Arnald Palmer Course. In addition guests can enjoy their new driving range, tennis courts and for winter activities they excel with their 21 ski runs consisting of one double black diamond, six black diamond, six intermediate and eight beginner slopes. For information call Sugar Loaf Resort at 800-968-0576 or 616-228-5461.

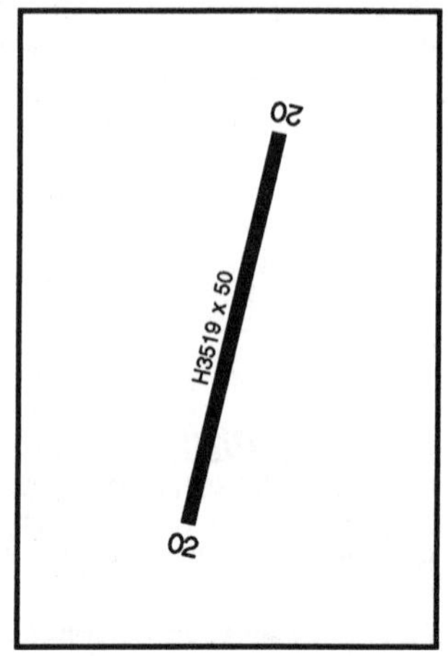

Airport Information:

TRAVERSE CITY - SUGAR LOAF VILLAGE (Y04)
14 mi northwest of town N44-54.75 W85-48.84 Elev: 825 Rwy 02-20: H3519x50 (Asph)
Attended: Apr-Nov., Airport CLOSED winter months. Unicom: 122.8 Notes: ditch in aircraft parking area.
Sugar Loaf Village Resort Airport Phone: 800-968-0576 or 228-5461

Sugar Loaf Resort

Traverse City, MI (MI-Y04)

From check-in to check-out, Sugar Loaf Resort offers the perfect setting for your meeting, special event or family getaway. Located just minutes from Traverse City in Michigan's Leelanau Peninsula, Sugar Loaf is easily accessible by both car and air.

Delectable American cuisine, great entertainment and a staff dedicated to your service are trademarks of Sugar Loaf Resort. Whether you choose to dine in their Four Seasons Dining Room or in one of the many other locations on the grounds, they strive to make your dining experience deliciously enjoyable.

Sugar Loaf Resort provides live entertainment, a pizzeria/deli, indoor pool, whirl-pool spa, weight training facility, two outdoor pools, free jazzercise classes for house guests, mountain bike rentals, "Kid's Klub", Pro Shop, golf lessons, Bavarian Village Ski Shop, and their Sugar Cube Gift Shop.

Summer Activities include golfing on their 18-hole championship golf course, driving range, practice sand traps and putting greens, tennis courts, bike trails, as well as daily excursions to the National Lakeshore and Leland's Historic Fishtown, BBQ's, picnics, and just for the kids there's the "Kid's Klub". Incidentally kid's also sleep and eat free on the two day family package. The beautiful Leelanau Peninsula boasts a variety of activities ranging from beach combing and dune climbing to shopping in the quaint country town and coastal villages.

During the winter season, Sugar Loaf Resort transforms into one of Michigan's most popular skiing resorts, with 21 slopes ranging in expertise; one double-black diamond, six black diamond, six intermediate and eight beginner. They also have a ski school and cross country ski renal as well.

Accommodations for lodging offers guests three alternatives. You can relax in one of their 150 well-appointed guest rooms. Amenities include individual climate control, direct-dial phones with message service, and satellite television; Town houses are located adjacent to the main hotel. Sugar Loaf Resort's town houses are equipped with either two of four bedrooms (each with a full, private bath), living area, dining area, kitchen facilities and satellite television. Their Winged Foot Condominiums offer appointed studio, one-and two-bedroom units overlooking Sugar Loaf Resort's golf course. Each condo is equipped with a living and dining area, fully appointed kitchen or kitchenette, whirlpool bath for two and satellite television.

Photo by: Sugar Loaf Resort

Conference and banquet facilities at Sugar Loaf offers over 22,000 square feet of meeting space to hold your conference or banquet. Twelve versatile meeting rooms can accommodate groups of 10 to 500. In addition, Sugar Loaf's professional convention staff can assist you in planning special events, such as golf tournaments, family reunions, and group Fly-ins for your club or association. Sugar Loaf Resort will also be happy to provide spouse and children's programs and public relations service if your group so desires.

Sugar Loaf Resort is located about 12 miles northwest of Traverse City, Michigan and owns and operates it's own private 3,700 foot paved airstrip which is located just 400 yards from the front desk. Private pilots, flying clubs and corporate jets are all welcome.

For information about the services and amenities at Sugar Loaf Resort call 800-968-0576 res. or 616-228-5461. (Information submitted by Sugar Loaf Resort).

Photo by: Sugar Loaf Resort

MI-40C - WATERVLIET
WATERVLIET MUNICIPAL AIRPORT

(Area Code 616) 54

Ma & Pa's Country Kettle:

The Pa's Country Kettle Restaurant can be found approximately 1000 feet off the north end of the Watervliet Municipal Airport in Watervliet, Michigan or within 1/2 mile from the main ramp area. The restaurant is family owned, and combines a recreational camping area with three small ponds which can be seen from the dining room. The entrees prepared offer good old country cooking. The restaurant is open 7 days a week between 7 a.m. to 9 p.m. The entrees prepared offer good old country cooking. An additional recreational attraction in the area is canoeing down the Paw Paw River. This is a popular activity of many tourists visiting this area. For more information about the Ma & Pa's Country Kettle, call 463-3344.

Restaurants Near Airport:

Ma & Pa's Country Kettle	Adj Arpt	Phone: 463-3344

Lodging: Plaza reported across the street from the airport.

Meeting Rooms: None Reported

Transportation: Ma & Pa's Country Kettle will pick up people fly-in in to visit their restaurant. Call 463-3344; No reported transportation by airport.

Information: St. Joseph/Benton Harbor Area: Comerstone Alliance, 185 East Main Street, P.O. Box 428, Benton Harbor, MI 49023, Phone: 925-6100; Alos: The Travel Bureau, Michigan Department of Commerce, P.O. Box 30226, Lansing, MI 48909, Phone: 800-543-2YES

NO AIRPORT DIAGRAM AVAILABLE

Attractions:

Paw Paw Lake Golf Club in Watervliet, MI, Phone: 463-3831; Also Deer Forest - Paw Paw Lake Road Coloma, MI, Phone: 468-4961.

Airport Information:

WATERVLIET - WATERVLIET MUNICIPAL AIRPORT (40C)

1 mi northeast of town N42-12.00 W86-15.00 Elev: 656 Rwy 02-20: 2600x200 (Turf)
Rwy 07-25: 1975x200 (Turf) Attended: unattended CTAF: 122.9 Public Phone 24hrs
Watervliet Municipal Airport Phone: 463-7130

MI-D15 - WEIDMAN
LAKE ISABELLA AIRPORT

(Area Code 517) 55

The Pines:

The Pines Bar and Grill is located in central Michigan near the Lake Isabella Airport in Weidman, Michigan. The bar and grill is part of the Pines Golf Course. A beautiful 18 hole public golf course hosts the state public matchplay championship. The Pines is located 500 feet from the Airport parking area. The grill serves soups, salads, sandwiches and daily specials. Their grill is open during the golf season, 7 days a week from 11 a.m. until dusk. Greens fees run $20.00 on weekdays, and $25.00 on weekends. For information call The Pines Restaurant and Golf Club at 644-2300.

Restaurants Near Airport:

The Pines	500'	Phone: 644-2300

Lodging: None reported near airport.

Meeting Rooms: None reported near airport.

Transportation: No courtesy cars reported.

Information: Mount Pleasant Convention & Visitors Bureau, 114 East Broadway, Mount Pleasant, MI 48858, Phone: 772-4433 or 800-77-CHIEF; Also: The Travel Bureau, Michigan Department of Commerce, P.O. Box 30226, Lansing, MI 48909, Phone: 800-543-2YES

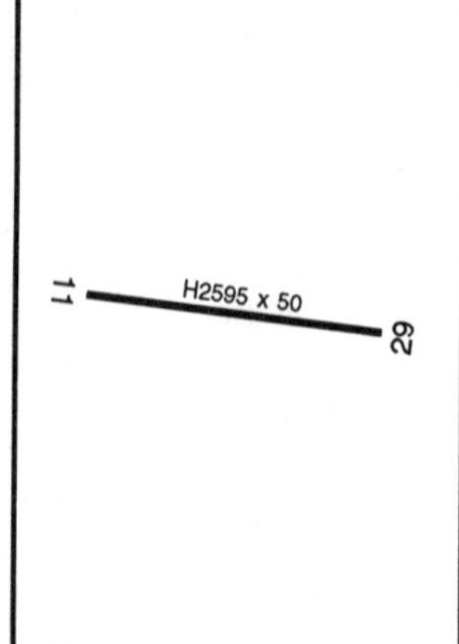

Airport Information:

WEIDMAN - LAKE ISABELLA AIRPARK (D15)

3 mi south of town N43-38.67 W84-58.92 Elev: 886
Rwy 11-29: H2595x50 (Asph) Attended: unattended Unicom: 122.8
Lake Isabella Airpark Phone: 644-2400

MI-42C - WHITE CLOUD
WHITE CLOUD AIRPORT

(Area Code 616)

56

Restaurants Near Airport:

Eaton House	1/2 mi.	Phone: 689-6838
Laningas	1/2 mi.	Phone: 689-1037
Sally's	1/3 mi.	Phone: 689-6560
The Shack	8 mi	Phone: 924-6683

Sally's:

Sally's Restaurant is located 1/3rd mile south of the White Cloud Airport. This family style restaurant is open weekdays between 6 a.m. and 9 p.m., Friday and Saturday from 6 a.m. to 9 p.m., and Sunday from 7 a.m. to 7 p.m. Their dining room can accommodate 100 guests. A variety of entrees are available including specials like their lunch buffet, special Friday night seafood selections, Friday and Saturday breakfast and Sunday brunch buffets, along with other house specials like chicken and ribs. Average prices for these various buffets were reported to be in the neighborhood of $6.25 to $6.50. With advance notice, groups and parties can arrange catered buffet meals as well. This restaurant bakes all their own breads and cinnamon rolls on the premises. For information about Sally's Restaurant call 689-6560.

Lodging: The Shack Bed & Breakfast (8 miles, Trans) provides a unique log cabin complex complete with 26 rooms, 5 hot tub rooms, 100 seat conference room and complimentary home country breakfast, Phone: 924-6683.

Meeting Rooms: The Shack Bed & Breakfast has accommodations for conferences and meetings. For information call 924-6683.

Transportation: Airport can help fly-in customers with courtesy transportation to nearby facilities located beyond walking distance. Most restaurants however, are within walking distance.

Information: The Travel Bureau, Michigan Department of Commerce, P.O. Box 30226, Lansing, MI 48909, Phone: 800-543-2YES

Airport Information:

WHITE CLOUD - WHITE CLOUD AIRPORT (42C)
1 mi north of town N43-33.59 W85-46.45 Elev: 914 Fuel: 100LL, Mogas
Rwy 17-35: H2911x50 (Asph) Attended: irregularly Unicom: 122.8 Public Phone (Across road) Notes: No landing fees, free tie-downs, for information about runway or pavement conditions call airport manager at airport 689-5891 or 689-1621 res.
FBO: White Cloud Corp. Phone: 689-5891

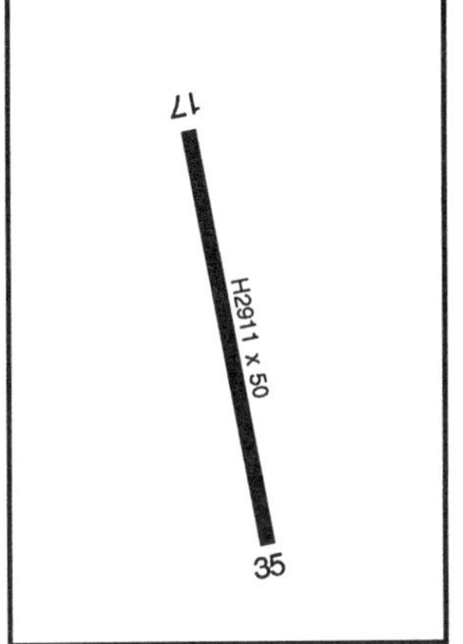

MINNESOTA

LOCATION MAP

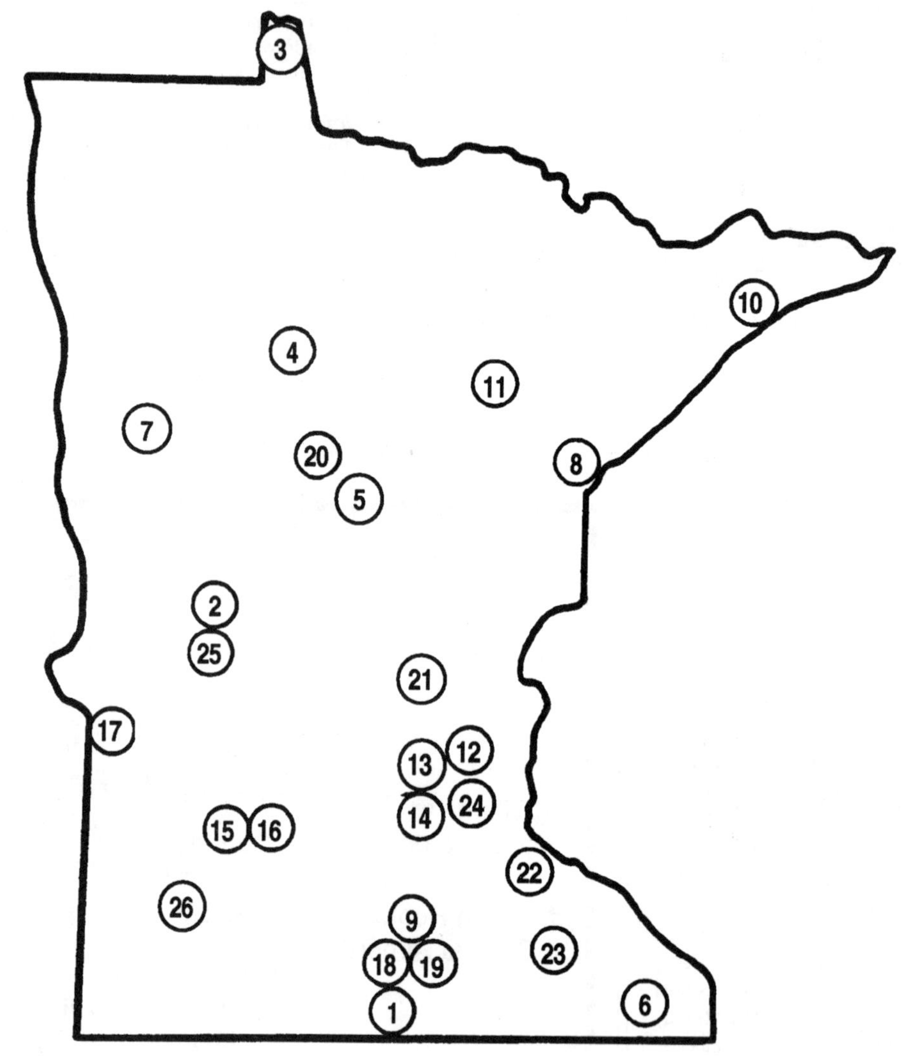

Not to be used for navigational purposes

MINNESOTA

CROSS FILE INDEX

Location Number	City or Town	Airport Name And Identifier	Name of Attraction
1	Albert Lea	Albert Lea Muni. Arpt. (AEL)	Hardee's Restaurant
2	Alexandria	Chandler Field (AXN)	Arrowwood Resort
3	Angle Inlet	Northwest Angle Resort (Private)	Northwest Angle Resort
4	Bemidji	Bemidji-Beltrami Co. Arpt. (BJI)	Gangelhoff's Restaurant
5	Brainerd	Crow Wing Co. Arpt. (BRD)	Arpt. Restaurant
6	Caledonia	Houston Co. Arpt. (CHU)	The Crest Supper Club
7	Detroit Lakes	Detroit Lakes Airport (DTL)	The Fireside Restaurant
8	Duluth	Duluth Intl. (DLH)	Afterburner Dining Room
9	Faribault	Faribault Muni. Arpt. (FBL)	Lavendar Inn & Gallery
10	Grand Marais	Grand Marais/Cook Co. (CKC)	Skyport Lodge
11	Hibbing	Chisholm-Hibbing Arpt. (HIB)	Airway Inn Restaurant
12	Lino Lakes	Surfside (Sea-Plane Base) (8Y4)	Shirley Kayes Restaurant
13	Minneapolis	Crystal Arpt. (MIC)	Embers Restaurant
14	Minneapolis-St. Paul	St. Paul Intl Arpt. (MSP)	Garden Restaurant
15	Olivia	Olivia Reg. Arpt. (Y39)	Chatterbox
16	Olivia	Olivia Reg. Arpt. (Y39)	Sheep Shed, Inc.
17	Ortonville	Ortonville Muni./Martinson (VVV)	Matador Supper Club
18	Owatonna	Owatonna Muni. Arpt. (OWA)	Happy Chef Restaurant
19	Owatonna	Owatonna Muni. Arpt. (OWA)	Ramada Inn
20	Pequot Lake	Myers Field (4MN8)	A-Pine Restaurant
21	Princeton	Princeton Muni. (PNM)	Pine Loft Restaurant
22	Red Wing	Red Wing Muni. Arpt. (RGK)	St. James Hotel
23	Rochester	Rochester Intl. Arpt. (RST)	The Wright Stuff
24	St. Paul	St. Paul Downtown Holman (STP)	Northwinds Restaurant
25	Starbuck	Starbuck Muni. Arpt. (D32)	Waters Edge Restaurant
26	Tracy	Tracy Muni. Arpt. (Y68)	Mediterranean Club

Articles

City or town	Nearest Airport and Identifier	Name of Attraction
Angle Inlet, MN	(Private)	Northwest Angle Resort
Breezy Point, MN	(Private)	Breezy Point Resort
East Gull Lake, MN	East Gull Lake Arpt. (9Y2)	Madden's On Gull Lake
Minneapolis-St. Paul, MN	Minneapolis-St Paul Intl. (MSP)	MN Air Guard Museum

MN-AEL - ALBERT LEA
ALBERT LEA MUNICIPAL AIRPORT

1

Restaurants Near Airport: **(Area Code 507)**

Hardee's	4 blks E.	Phone: 377-1594
Hy-Vee Deli	4 blks E.	Phone: N/A
Northbridge Mall	4 blks E.	Phone: N/A

Hardee's Restaurant:

Hardee's Restaurant is a fast food facility that is situated about 3 or 4 blocks east of the Albert Lea Municipal Airport. Fly-in customers can either walk or obtain a courtesy car from the airport. The restaurant hours are from 6:30 a.m. to 10 p.m. Monday through Thursday, 6:30 a.m. to 11 p.m., on Friday, 6:30 a.m. to 10 p.m. Saturday, and 7 a.m. to 10 p.m. on Sunday. This facility provides a variety of light fare including appetizers, desserts, pastries and salads. Daily specials are also offered. The decor is modern and accommodations for groups can be arranged. A small shopping mall is located adjacent. For more information about Hardee's Restaurant call them at 377-1594.

Lodging: Best Western Albert Lea 373-8291; Green Briar Inn 373-6471; Super 8 Motel 377-0591.

Meeting Rooms: Best Western Albert Lea 373-8291; Green Briar Inn 373-6471.

Transportation: Albert Lea Airport, Inc. can provide courtesy cars for use to local facilities 373-0608.

Information: Albert Lea-Freeborn County Chamber of Commerce/Convention & Visitors Bureau, 202 N Broadway, P.O. Box 686, Albert Lea, MN 56007, Phone: 373-3938, 800-345-8414.

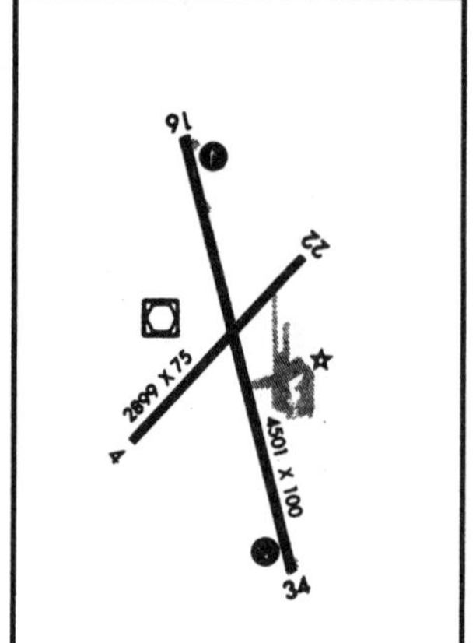

Airport Information:

ALBERT LEA - ALBERT LEA MUNICIPAL AIRPORT (AEL)
3 mi north of town N43-40.89 W93-22.03 Elev: 1259 Fuel: 100LL, Jet-A, MOGAS
Rwy 16-34: H4501x100 (Asph) Rwy 04-22: H2899x75 (Asph) Attended: 1400-dusk
Unicom: 123.0 Public Phone 24hrs Notes: Overnight tie-downs $3.00 per night; Glider activities on field; Northbridge Mall with numerous eating places and shops 4 blocks east of airport.
Albert Lea Airport, Inc. Phone: 373-0608

MN-AXN - ALEXANDRIA
CHANDLER FIELD

2

Restaurants Near Airport: **(Area Code 612)**

Aerowwood Resort	5 mi,(Trans)	Phone: 762-1124
Broadway	1 mi N.	Phone: 763-3999
Depot Express	1-1/2 mi N.	Phone: 763-7712
Perkins Restaurant	1/2 mi S.	Phone: 763-6611

Arrowwood Resort:

The Arrowwood Resort is situated about 5 miles from the Alexandria Chandler Field Airport. This establishment provides a host of activities for the customer. Overnight t accommodations include 200 guest rooms and 24 suites. This 5 story complex contains an indoor and outdoor swimming pool, whirlpool, sauna, dining room that is open from 6:30 a.m. to 10 p.m., 18 hole golf course, private beach, boating and sailing as well as sleighrides and ice skating during the winter season. Live entertainment is also featured at the resort. This is a Three Star Mobil rated resort. Free courtesy transportation to and from the airport is provided by the Arrowwood Resort. For information or reservations you can call them at 762-1124.

Lodging: Arrowwood Resort (5 miles, Trans) 762-1124; Park Inn International (Trans) 763-6577; Super 8 Motel 763-6552. Skyline Motel 763-3175.

Meeting Rooms: A conference room is available in the new terminal building; also Arrowwood Resort (Convention Facilities) 762-1124; Park Inn International 763-6552.

Transportation: Taxi Service: Alex Cab 763-3005; Radio Cab 763-3333; Also Rental Cars: Hertz 763-3553; Steinbring Rentals 762-2114

Information: Chamber of Commerce, 206 North Broadway, Alexandria, MN 56308, Phone: 763-3161.

Attractions:

Arrowwood-A Radisson Resort is located 5 miles from Chandler Field and provides free courtesy transportation. This establishment has 200 rooms, complete with private beach, tennis courts, 18 hole golf course, water sports, live entertainment, and conventions space. Call 762-1124.

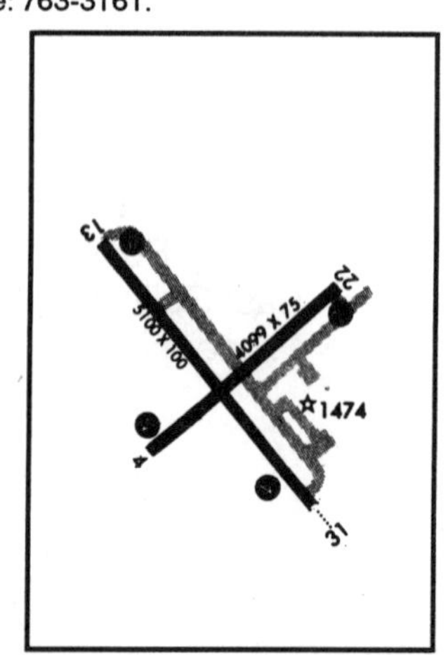

Airport Information:

ALEXANDRIA - CHANDLER FIELD (AXN)
2 mi southwest of town N45-51.98 W95-23.68 Elev: 1424 Fuel: 100LL, Jet-A
Rwy 13-31: H5100x100 (Asph) Rwy 04-22: H4099x75 (Asph) Attended: May-Oct, Mon-Fri 1400-0200Z, Nov-Apr, Mon-Fri 1400Z-dusk, Sat-Sun 1500-2300Z Unicom: 123.0
Notes: Bellanca Aircraft and Weber Aero Repair are both situated on the field.
FBO: Alexandria Aviation, Inc. Phone: 762-2111

MN-ANGLE INLET (Private)
NORTHWEST ANGLE RESORT

(Area Code 218)

3

Northwest Angle Resort:

Northwest Angle Resort is located on the farthest northern tip of Minnesota near Angle Inlet. This town is about 35 air miles north of Warroad, MN. The resort contains its own private 2,380 sod airstrip. Advance notice is required for pilots planning to land there. An alternative airport that contains a 5,400x100 hard surface runway is Warroad International-Swede Carlson Field (RRT). This resort is about 65 to 70 miles by car from the town of Warroad, MN. This establishment offers dining, lodging and recreational amenities for their guests. This fly-in resort offers 14 airconditioned rental units, and a full-service restaurant and lounge open to the public, golf course and excellent fishing accommodations for the sportsperson. The lodge is open between 6 a.m. and 10 p.m. 7 days a week and 180 days of the year, from May 15 to November 1. The restaurant serves light fare, and can handle larger groups from 1 to 50 persons with advance notice. They have their own private airstrip which is 2,380 feet long and 105 feet wide. The resort is located next to the airport and is within walking distance. Before landing, prior permission is required. You can call the airport at 1-800-386-2963 or 223-8511 which, incidentally, is the same phone number for the resort itself. Call for current landing fees, if any, and/or overnight parking rates.

Restaurants Near Airport:
Northwest Angle Resort Adj Arpt Phone: 223-8511

Lodging: Northwest Angle Resort (Adj Arpt) 223-8511 or 800-386-2963.
Meeting Rooms: Contact Northwest Angle Resort for available accommodation for meetings or banquets 223-8511 or 800-386-2963.
Transportation: The resort is reported to be located adjacent to the airport. For information call 223-8511 or 800-386-2963.
Information: Northwest Angle and Islands Chamber of Commerce, Angle Inlet, MN 56711, Phone: 442-5014, Extension 10.

Attractions:

Northwest Angle Resort (Adjacent to airport) 223-8511 or 800-386-2963.

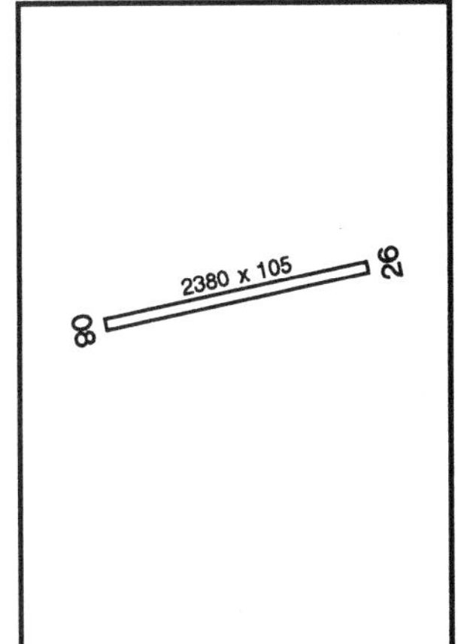

Airport Information:

ANGLE INLET - NORTHWEST ANGLE (Private Airport)
32 mi northeast of town N49-21-06 W95-04-18 Elev: 1071 Fuel: None Reported
Rwy 08-26: 2380x105 (Turf) Attended: daylight Notes: Private use facility, use at own risk.
We learned that this airport is open to resort customers, however you must call in advance for permission and for runway conditions. Call airport manager's office for landing or transient fees.
Northwest Angle Airport Phone: 800-386-2963

Northwest Angle Resort

Angle Inlet, MN (MN-Private)

You will be pleasantly surprised by the comfort and convenience of their accommodations. Their cabins offer privacy, are close to the docks and channel, and some have fireplaces. Their apartments, with private outside entrances, are attached to the lodge building. All units are air conditioned, carpeted, fully furnished, and spotlessly clean. Start your day with breakfast in their lodge, served up with plenty of hot coffee and lively conversation. Stop in later for pizza, snacks, groceries, tackle, or just to relax and reflect on the day's catch. Their heated swimming pool is screen enclosed and has lots of lounge chairs and tables for resort guests.

The Northwest Angle is a magnificent tract of rugged wilderness at the top of the nation (north of Northern Minnesota). If you seek great fishing in clean waters, far from the crowd, this is where you will find it. This complex lake features an outstanding array of game fish including walleye, northern, muskie, and small mouth bass. Lake of the Woods is the most productive walleye lake in Minnesota. Daily limits are the norm. Enjoy fishing the scenic sheltered island area of the lake in Minnesota and Canadian waters. During the summertime "slump" in July, August, and September, fishing on Lake of the Woods is at its best. Let them help you coordinate your Fall fishing and duck hunting trip. Lake of the Woods is a prime stoppingoff spot for northern flights. Experience the magic of Lake of the Woods and you will want to come back again and again.

Fly into their private 2,380 foot sod airstrip, one of Minnesota's finest, for a day or longer of excellent fishing. Enjoy a beautiful flight over the lake and be out fishing in a matter of minutes. The airstrip is only a few steps from their lodge. They do require that you call ahead to check field conditions and to get permission for landing.

Other area highlights include Historic Fort St. Charles, Sunsweep sculpture, mini-trip to Kenora, mini-trip to Winnipeg, golf courses, island and local dining, observe area wildlife including bear, deer, eagles and listen to "loon music," etc. For more information about the Northwest Angle Resort call 800-366-2963 or 218-223-8511.

MN-BJI - BEMIDJI
BEMIDJI-BELTRAMI COUNTY ARPT.

(Area Code 218) 4

Gangelhoff's Restaurant:

Gangelhoff's Restaurant is a very nice supper club located in the Northern Inn and is within walking distance (about 1/4th mile) from the Beltrami County Airport near Bemidji, Minnesota. This restaurant features a rustic decor with a large aquarium in the center of the dining room. All their tables are set with linen table cloths and local artists feature their paintings on display. Their menu contains house specialties like homemade wild rice soup, beef stroganoff, broiled or deep fried shrimp and filet mignon. The restaurant is open for breakfast Monday through Friday from 6 a.m. to 10 a.m. and dinner from 5 p.m. to 10 p.m., Saturday for breakfast 7 a.m. to 11 a.m. and dinners 5 p.m. to 10 p.m., and Sunday 7 a.m. to 2 p.m. A Sunday brunch is served from 10 a.m. to 2 p.m. This facility contains two separate private rooms off the main dining room especially designed for catering to parties of 20 or more people. All selections on their menu can be ordered to go. For information call 751-9508.

Restaurants Near Airport:

Gangelhoff's/Northern Inn	1/4 mi	Phone: 751-9508
Highway Host/Backyard	8 blks SE	Phone: 751-2051
Union Station	5 mi S	Phone: 751-9261

Lodging: Days Inn (Trans) 751-0390; Northern Inn (1/4 mile, Trans) 751-9500; Ruttger's Birchmont Lodge 751-1630.

Meeting Rooms: Northern Inn 751-9500; Ruttger's Birchmont Lodge 751-1630.

Transportation: Taxi Service: Bemidji Cab 759-1368; Rental Cars: National 751-1880; Hertz 751-5230.

Information: Chamber of Commerce, P.O. Box 850, Bemidji, MN 56601, 751-3541 or 800-458-2223.

Attractions:

Lake Bemidji State Park (8 miles northeast); Statue of Paul Bunyan & Babe the Blue-Ox (5 miles south-east); Fishing lakes in all directions.

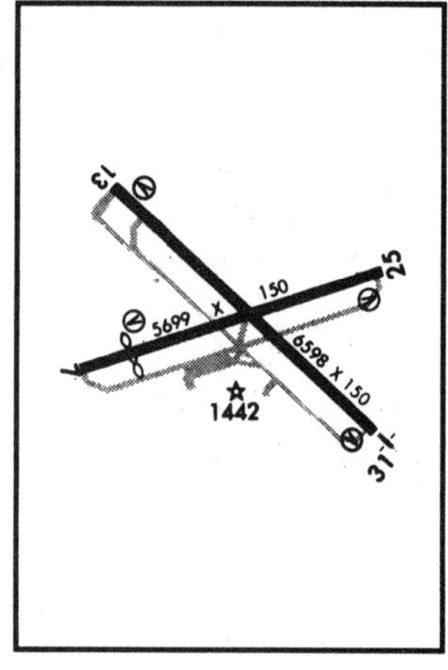

Airport Information:

BEMIDJI - BEMIDJI BELTRAMI COUNTY AIRPORT (BJI)
3 mi northwest of town N47-30.57 W94-56.02 Elev: 1390 Fuel: 100LL, Jet-A
Rwy 13-31: H6598x150 (Asph-Grvd) Rwy 07-25: H5699x150 (Asph) Attended: 1400-0400Z Unicom: 122.8 Notes: No landing fees, overnight parking fee $3.00 or free with fuel purchase.
FBO: Bemidji Aviation Services, Inc. Phone: 751-1880

Breezy Point Resort & Conf. Cntr.

Breezy Point, MN (Private)

Breezy Point Resort & Conference Center is situated only 2 or 3 blocks from the Breezy Point Airport. This airport is privately owned and operated, and as far as we can determine, is not affiliated with the resort. This airport has a north and south asphalt runway of 2500 x 60 feet. After landing, you can walk to the Amaco service station on the southwest side of the field. Transportation can be obtained from the resort by using the pay phone at the service station, or just walk a couple of blocks farther to the resort. A landing and tie-down fee of $10.00 is required for the first day, $5.00 for each additional day, and $25.00 for a weeks stay. This charge goes to help pay for airport maintenance, and is paid at the Amaco Station. For information about airport conditions you can call the owner at 218-562-4986.

Breezy Point Resort on Big Pelican Lake offers you an unparalleled choice of vacation options. Inhabiting 3,000 acres of glorious woods and water, in central Minnesota's famed Brainerd Lakes Area, Breezy Point is a complete four-season vacation resort.

What's your idea of a special place to stay on your vacation? Perhaps it's a deluxe lakeside condominium, complete with jacuzzi, fireplace, VCR and all the luxurious comforts of home. Or maybe you prefer the economy of a modestly-sized unit, close-by to all of Breezy Point's famous activities, including restaurants and indoor pools.

Breezy Point's Traditional Golf Course has been challenging golfers since 1930 with its demanding fairways and challenging greens.

Breezy Center and High Village Spa: Enjoy their four-season recreation facilities. The Center boasts an indoor pool, sauna, whirlpool, table tennis, game room and sunning deck. High Village Spa features a 3/4 Olympic size pool, jacuzzi, and kiddie pool. VIP Condos, Town Houses, and Chalets feature private indoor or outdoor jacuzzi spas.

At Breezy Point, you'll find everything needed to assure a professionally managed, effectively supported, meeting or function. They offer a conference center with options for groups from 7 to 750. Whether it's an intimate private board meeting, large group presentation or a formal banquet with all the finest touches, their meeting professionals will work in close harmony to help plan and execute your best meeting ever.

When your day's itinerary of meetings, recreation and dining has come to an end, it's time to unwind and relax in the company of friends. Here too, Breezy Point offers plenty of exciting options. Their Marina Lounge with its Top 40's entertainment and full slate of menu offerings, or rustic Charlie's Rib Joint, with its variety groups and casual dining. Or, enjoy the cozy ambience of Breezy Club House, or meet at pool side at Captain's Cove. On a warm day you'll especially appreciate the cooling breezes of their waterfront Dockside Lounge. Clearly the possibilities seem endless.

In season, Breezy offers live outdoor entertainment "on-deck,"where you can abandon your briefcase and trade your sportcoat for swimwear.

For further information about this resort call 800-432-3777 or 218-562-7811. (Information submitted by Breezy Point Resort).

MN-BRD - BRAINERD
CROW WING COUNTY AIRPORT

(Area Code 218) 5

Airport Restaurant:

The Airport Restaurant is located on the Brainerd-Crow Wing County/Walter F. Wieland Airport, near Brainerd, Minnesota. This establishment is open Monday through Saturday from 8:00 a.m. to 4:00 p.m. and on Sunday from 9 a.m. to 4 p.m. Their specialties are hamburgers, chicken and turkey sandwiches, club sandwiches, Ruben, steak sandwiches, homemade soups, and French fries. Their menu offers daily specials as well. The view from the restaurant allows customers to see the activity on the airport. Fly-in groups of up to can be accommodated. However, please call in advance. Meals to go are no problem. They also do catering. Transportation is not required due to the convenience of nearby available aircraft parking. For information call the restaurant at 829-3398.

Restaurants Near Airport:
Airport Restaurant On Site Phone: 829-3398

Lodging: Holiday Inn (Trans) 829-1441; Paul Bunyan Motel 829-3571; Riverview Motel (Trans) 829-8771.

Meeting Rooms: J.R.'s Restaurant (1/4 mile) can accommodate groups within the lower level of their facility 829-3487. Holiday Inn 829-1441; Riverview Motel 829-8771.

Transportation: Taxi and Rental Car Service available: Brainerd Taxi, and Budget and National car rental.

Information: Brainerd Lakes Area Chamber of Commerce, 6th & Washington Streets, Brainerd, MN 800-450-2838 in state and 800-950-1162 out of state.

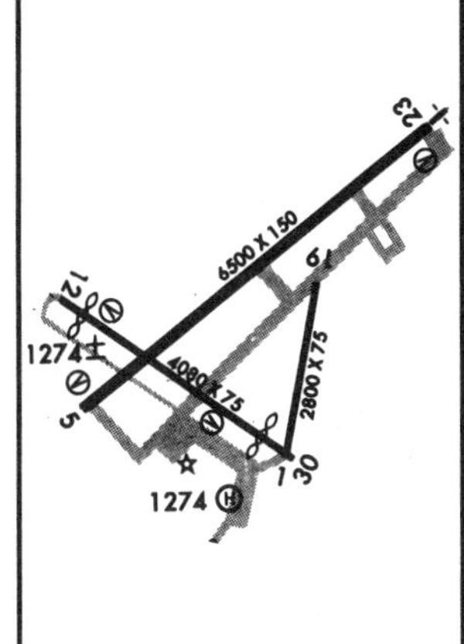

Airport Information:

BRAINERD - BRAINERD CROW WING COUNTY AIRPORT (BRD)
3 mi northeast of town N46-23.87 W94-08.23 Elev: 1226 Fuel: 100LL, Jet-A, MOGAS Rwy 05-23: H6500x150 (Asph) Rwy 12-30: H4080x75 (Asph) Rwy 01-19: H2800x75 (Asph) Attended: May-Sept 1300-0300Z Oct-Apr 1300-0200Z Unicom: 122.7
Notes: CAUTION: Deer and gulls on and in vicinity of airport.
Airport Manager Phone: 829-6873

Madden's On Gull Lake

East Gull Lake, MN (MN-9Y2)
Brainerd, MN (MN-BRD)

Madden's Resort can be reached by using one of two nearby airports. Brainerd Crow Wing County Regional Airport (BRD) phone: 218-829-6873 is 16 miles from Madden's Resort. This airport has 3 hard surface runways and IFR capabilities. Brainerd Airport is served several times daily by Northwest Airlink. East Gull Lake airport (9Y2) phone: 218-828-9279, or 829-5226 has Runway 13-31: which is a 2618 x 130 foot turf strip. This airport is closed during the winter season. However, it is the closest to the Madden's Resort (adjacent) and courtesy transportation is also provided by the resort. The location of East Gull Lake Airport (9Y2) is reported to be 6 miles at 272 degrees from the Brainerd Crow Wing County Airport.

Madden's is synonymous with choice and flexibility. Their three distinctive, integrated resort facilities are all within walking distance of one another, allowing "small resort" atmosphere and privacy, or the versatility of using the entire resort complex if your group is larger.

The accommodations at Madden's offer a scope broad enough to satisfy most any taste or preference. Choose from the rustic rough-hewn wood and stone of Madden's Pine Portage; the gleaming colonial presence of Madden Lodge (where the tradition began over five decades ago); or if you prefer hotel-styled lodging, their Madden Inn & Golf preserves the classic warmth and charm of the 1930's, with all the comforts of today.

Whatever your preference, each accommodation offers guests modern amenities combined with spectacular patio views of either the sparkling waters of Gull Lake, or the manicured greens and fairways of the Madden golf courses.

Madden's offers what no other Midwest resort can: the beauty, variety and challenge of their 45 holes of golf located right on the resort. They support three courses with two pro-shops, a driving range, and most importantly, a professional staff that is at your service. In addition, they also provide guests with sandy beaches, tennis courts, tanning by one of 3 outdoor pools, or feeling the tensions of the work week wash away in one of three spas. If variety is the spice of life, their superb cuisine will flavor every dining function of your group's visit. Each of Madden's three unique resort centers has its own separate dining facilities, with its own accomplished chef and exceptional support staff. Madden's also offers the versatility of a large, modern, central banquet facility, and an informal coffee shop for added convenience. Their outdoor dining option is befitting a resort setting, Enjoy a chicken & rib barbecue, or pig roast in their spacious lakeside cookout pavilion. Or tie in a theme party with live entertainment. The possibilities are limitless, and such options are often included at no additional cost.

Madden's unique arrangement of three separate-but integrated conference facilities allows the ultimate in flexibility. At Madden's you will find 30 meeting rooms totalling over 35,000 square feet in capacity, differing in size and seating options whether it numbers 8, or 800.

For information call toll free 800-642-5363. (Information submitted by Madden's Resort).

Photo by: Madden's Resort

Madden's Resort on Gull Lake has excellent accommodation for their guests.

MN-CHU - CALEDONIA HOUSTON COUNTY AIRPORT

(Area Code 507) 6

Restaurants Near Airport:
The Crest Supper Club 1 mi Phone: 724-3311

Lodging: The Crest Motel & Supper Club 724-3311.

Meeting Rooms: The Crest Motel and Supper Club has accommodations for meetings and banquets 724-3311.

Transportation: The Crest Motel & Supper Club will provide transportation for fly-in guests to and from the airport and their facility 724-3311.

Information: Minnesota Travel Information Center, 100 Metro Square, 121 7th Place East, St Paul, MN 55101, Phone: 612-296-5029 or 800-657-3700 (U.S.) or 800-7-MN-TOUR (Canada).

The Crest Motel & Supper Club:

The Crest Motel & Supper Club is situated approximately 1 mile from the Houston County airport in Caledonia, Minnesota. This dining facility is a supper club with lounge, featuring such entrees as BBQ ribs salad bar, home made soups, Saturday night prime rib and shrimp cocktails, shrimp, lobster, frog legs and steaks. Average prices run in the neighborhood of $10.95 for most steak dinners. The atmosphere of the restaurant is warm and rustic with hard wood floors and a seating capacity of 75 to 100 persons. A small meeting room can also be reserved, that is able to hold about 20 people. In addition to this, is a banquet hall on the lower level of their facility, that can comfortably accommodate 65 additional guests. Restaurant hours are 5 p.m. to 1 a.m. (hours may vary)) Tuesday through Saturday. Groups as large as 100 people can reserve banquet space with advance reservations. One additional attraction is the Ma Cal Grove Country Club, a 9 hole golf course located just across the street from the Crest Motel & Supper Club, and is reported to be open to the public. Fly-in guests can enjoy a great meal as well as a round of golf during their visit. There are no services at the airport. However, we were told that the restaurant will provide courtesy transportation for fly-in guests. Call 724-3311.

Attractions:

Ma Cal Grove Country Club is a 9 hole golf course situated across the street form the Crest Motel & Supper Club. For information call 724-3311.

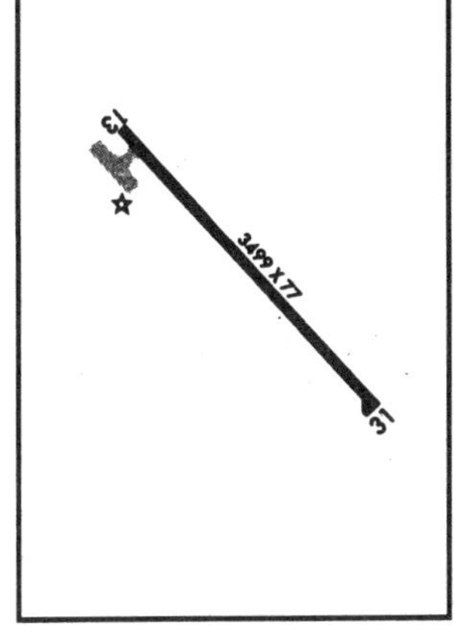

Airport Information:

CALEDONIA - HOUSTON COUNTY AIRPORT (CHU)
3 mi south of town N43-35.78 W91-30.24 Elev: 1179 Rwy 13-31: H3499x77 (Asph) Attended: unattended CTAF: 122.9
Houston County Airport Phone: 724-3925

MN-DTL - DETROIT LAKES DETROIT LAKES AIRPORT

(Area Code 218) 7

Restaurants Near Airport:
The Fireside Restaurant 3 mi Phone: 847-8192
Fair Hills Resort (Est. 10 mi) Phone: 532-2222, 847-7638

Lodging: Best Western Holland Motel 3 mi 847-4483; Fair Hills Resort (trans) 532-2222; Holiday Haven Hotel 6-9 mi 847-5605; Holiday Inn 847-2121; Oak Manor 4 mi 847-4454.
Meeting Rooms: Best Western Holland Motel 3 mi 847-4483; Fair Hills Resort (trans) 532-2222; Holiday Inn 847-2121.
Transportation: Airport courtesy car reported available. Call Detroit Lakes Aircraft (FBO) at 847-3233. Also Rental Cars: Bill Schwartz Auto 847-2601; Taxi Service: Lakes Cab 847-0235; Mahube Taxi Service 847-1674.
Information: Detroit Lakes Regional Chamber of Commerce, Box 348, Detroit Lakes, MN 56502, Phone: 847-9202 or 800-542-3992.

The Fireside Restaurant, Bar & Catering:

For over 50 years The Fireside has been the most popular restaurant in the Detroit Lakes area due to its deserved reputation for great food and great service over that period of time. If you are looking for that special place, The Fireside is nestled along the east shore of Big Detroit Lake and customers enjoy a panoramic view of the beautiful sunsets to the west across the lake. These romantic views are enjoyed not only from an outside patio just a few feet from the lake but also from the entire dining room. The Fireside offers the best in food and beverages including its nationally famous barbecued ribs, steaks and other entrees cooked over a real charcoal fire in full view of dining room patrons and a fine selection of fresh and salt water seafood. Nightly specials are offered to supplement a full menu selection. Your meal will be served by the most experienced waitstaff in the area. Current owners Tom and Jennifer Graham will greet you as you arrive to share The Fireside tradition. On Saturday nights during the summer, take advantage of the expected wait to relax with your favorite beverage by the lake. The wait will be well worth it. Airport courtesy cars are reported available. For information call The Fireside at 847-8192.

Attractions:

Fair Hills Resort is open for business between mid-May and late September. Transportation can be arranged to and from their facility and the Detroit Lakes Airport. This facility has lodging accommodations with 18 rooms in their main lodge and 76 cottages containing 1 to 4 rooms. The Fair Hills Resort establishment has an 18-hole golf course, private beach, heated pool, whirlpool, wading pool, tennis courts, water-skiing, boats and motors, sailboats, entertainment, as well as many other amenities. Their location is 11 miles southwest of town using US 59, then take County 20 3 miles west to their location. For more information about Fair Hills Resort, call 532-2222 or 847-7638.

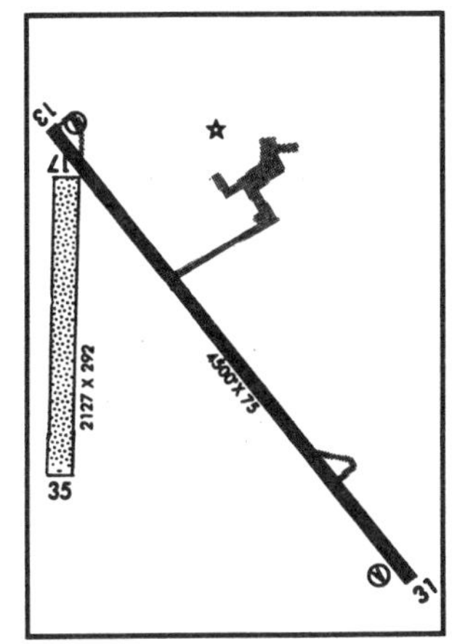

Airport Information:

DETROIT LAKES - DETROIT LAKES AIRPORT (DTL)
2 mi west of town N46-49.51 W95-53.14 Elev: 1396 Fuel: 100LL, Jet-A, MOGAS Rwy 13-31: H4500x75 (Asph) Rwy 17-35: 2127x292 (Turf) Attended: continuously Unicom: 122.8 Notes: Rwy 17-35 CLOSED winter months.
FBO: Detroit Lakes Aviation Phone: 847-3233

MN-DLH - DULUTH
DULUTH INTERNATIONAL

(Area Code 218)

Afterburner Lounge & Dining Room:

The Afterburner Lounge & Dining Room is a supper club located in the terminal building on the Duluth International Airport. This restaurant has modern styling with a leaded glass ceiling and large windows providing a view that overlooks the ramp where planes pull up to load and unload passengers. Their house specialties consist of a variety of steak and shrimp dishes, as well as walleye pike, barbecued ribs, appetizers, soups and desserts. Average prices run between $8.95 and $14.95 for most selections. The restaurant is open Monday through Thursday from 11 a.m. to 4:30 p.m. for lunch and for dinner beginning at 4:30 p.m. to 9 p.m. Friday and Saturday 11 a.m. to 10 p.m. Ans on Sunday they feature a brunch from 11 a.m. to 4:30 p.m. ($9.95 adults, $7.95 Sinors & $4.95 for children) then after the brunch until 7 p.m. they serve Sunday entree specials from their menu. The restaurant does a lot of catering for business associations and can accommodate up to 120 persons. A small private dining room can accommodate groups up to 25 persons. They also can prepare sandwich trays, fruit trays, as well as steak and seafood dinners to go. Their prices are competitive with all the restaurants in town. Courtesy transportation from the parking ramp and FBO to the terminal area can be arranged with North Country Aviation at 727-2911. For restaurant information call 727-1152.

Restaurants Near Airport:
Afterburner Lng & Dining Rm On Site Phone: 727-1152

Lodging: Best Western Edgewater-(East) (Trans) 728-3601; Best Western Edgewater-(West) 728-5141; Holiday Inn-Duluth (Trans) 722-1202; Park Inn International (Trans) 727-8821;

Meeting Rooms: Best Western Edgewater-(East) 728-3601; Best Western Edgewater-(West) 728-5141; Holiday Inn-Duluth 722-1202; Park Inn International 727-8821.

Transportation: Limousine and taxi service available at airport.

Information: Northcentral/West Regional Office, Minnesota Office of Tourism, 1901 South 6th, P.O. Box 443, Brainerd, MN 56401, Phone: 218-828-2335

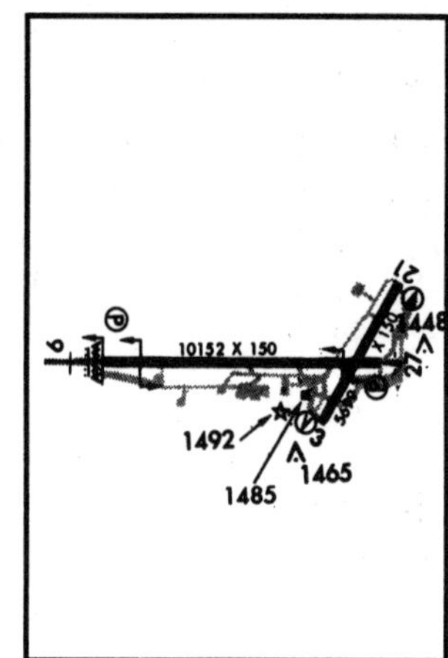

Airport Information:

DULUTH - DULUTH INTERNATIONAL (DLH)
5 mi northwest of town N46-50.52 W92-11.62 Elev: 1428 Fuel: 100, Jet-A
Rwy 09-27: H10152x150 (Conc-Grvd) Rwy 03-21: H5699x150 (Asph-Grvd) Attended: 1200-0600Z Atis: 124.1 Unicom: 122.95 App/Dep Con: 125.45 Tower: 118.3 Gnd Con: 121.9
FBO: North Country Aviation, Inc. Phone: 727-2911

MN-FBL - FARIBAULT
FARIBAULT MUNICIPAL AIRPORT

(Area Code 507)

9

Lavendar Inn & Gallery:

The Lavendar Inn & Gallery is a dinner club which can be found approximately 3/4 mile from the Faribault Municipal Airport. This restaurant contains a lounge on the premises and is open from 11 a.m. to 10 p.m. every day. Their menu contains steaks and seafood entrees as well as daily specials and luncheon specials. To compliment your dining pleasure they offer appetizers, desserts, pastries, salads and soups. Before or after your meal, you are cordially invited to stroll through their art gallery and gift shop adjacent to the restaurant. Transportation to and from the airport and restaurant can be arranged by calling them at 334-3500.

Restaurants Near Airport:
Lavendar Inn & Gallery 3/4 mi Phone: 334-3500

Lodging: Galaxie Motel (3 miles) 334-5508; Lyndale Motel (1 mile) 334-4386; Super 8 (1 mile) 334-1634.

Meeting Rooms: Galaxie Motel 334-5508.

Transportation: Rental Cars: Peoples Express 334-1834.

Information: Faribault Area Chamber of Commerce, 530 Wilson Avenue, P.O. Box 434, Faribault, MN 55021, Phone: 334-4381 or 800-658-2354.

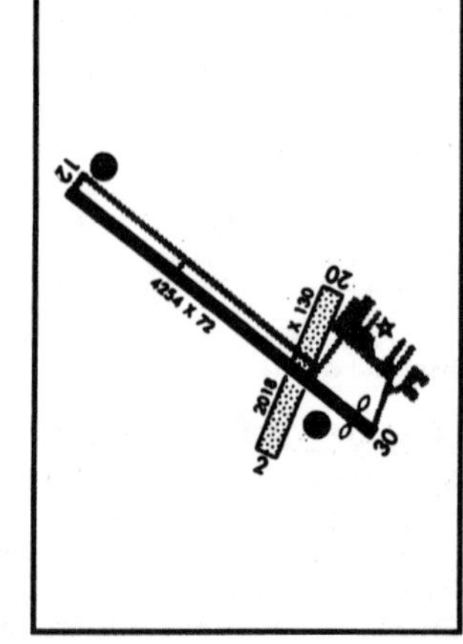

Airport Information:

FARIBAULT - FARIBAULT MUNICIPAL AIRPORT (FBL)
3 mi northwest of town N44-19.48 W93-18.65 Elev: 1060 Fuel: 100LL, MOGAS
Rwy 12-30: H4254x72 (Asph) Rwy 02-20: 2018x130 (Turf) Attended: 1400Z-sunset
Unicom: 122.8
Faribault Municipal Airport Phone: 332-0140

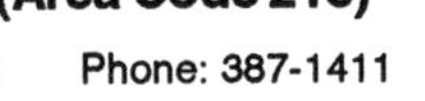

MN-CKC- GRAND MARAIS GRAND MARAIS/COOK COUNTY

(Area Code 218)

10

Restaurants Near Airport:
Skyport Lodge Adj Arpt Phone: 387-1411

Lodging: Skyport Lodge (1/2 mi. Adj Arpt) 387-1411.

Meeting Rooms: None Reported

Transportation: Courtesy car reported; Also Taxi Service: Clydes Taxi 387-1559; Rental Cars: C & S Service 387-1060; Clydes Rental Cars 387-1559.

Information: Northeastern Minnesota Regional Office, Minnesota Office of Tourism, 320 W. 2nd Street, Duluth, MN 55802, Phone: 218-723-4692.

Skyport Lodge (Fishing Resort):

Skyport Lodge is reported to be located about 1/2 mi walking distance from the aircraft parking area at Devils Track Municipal Airport near Grand Marais, Minnesota. This restaurant classified as a family style snack bar, offers a full menu plus daily specials. The restaurant hours are Monday through Thursday 8 a.m. to 10 p.m. offering snacks and lighter fare. On Friday and weekends between 8 a.m. and 1 p.m., they offer a full menu, as well as a salad bar, Friday fresh fish and daily specials. The restaurant provides guests a rustic atmosphere in a log lodge overlooking 7 miles of Devils Track Lake. In addition to the restaurant, this resort also provides accommodations in their motel as well as rustic cabins. Fishing boats, motors and bait are available for those of you interested in fishing. For restaurant information call 387-1411.

Attractions: Skyport Lodge is a fishing resort located on Devils Track Lake. This establishment contains 4 cabins and some motel units. For information about accommodations call the resort at 387-1411.

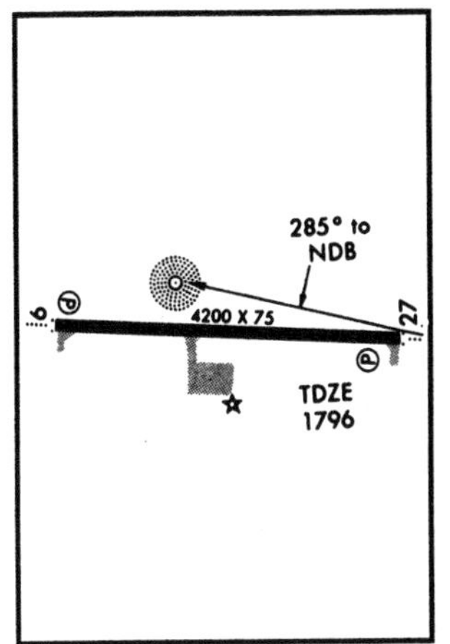

Airport Information:

GRAND MARAIS - GRAND MARAIS/COOK COUNTY (CKC)
7 mi northwest of town N47-50.30 W90-22.99 Elev: 1798 Fuel: 100LL
Rwy 09-27: H4200x75 (Asph) Attended: IRREGULARLY Unicom: 122.8
Grand Marais/Cook County Airport Phone: 387-1081

GRAND MARAIS/COOK COUNTY - SEA PLANE BASE (0G5)
6 miles northwest of town N47-48.99 W90-23.01 Elev: 1635 Fuel: 100LL Waterway 09-27: 15000x1500 (Water) Waterway 03-21: 3000x2000 (Water) Attended: continuously Unicom: 122.8
Grand Marais/Cook County - Sea Plane Base Phone: 387-2721

MN-HIB - HIBBING CHISHOLM-HIBBING AIRPORT

(Area Code 218)

11

Restaurants Near Airport:
Airway Inn 1/4 mi Phone: 263-9801

Lodging: Days Inn 263-8306; Regency Inn 262-3481.

Meeting Rooms: Regency Inn 262-3481.

Transportation: Courtesy car reported; Also Taxi Service: Taxi 263-5065; Rental Cars: Avis 263-5915; Hertz 262-4528; National 262-6641.

Information: Chamber of Commerce, 211 East Howard Street, P.O. Box 727, Hibbing, MN 55746, Phone: 262-3895.

Airway Inn Restaurant:

The Airway Inn Restaurant is situated within walking distance (1/4 mile) from the Chisholm/Hibbing Airport in Hibbing, Minnesota. This family restaurant is open 7 days a week from 11 a.m. to 8 p.m. The main dining area can seat approximately 100 persons. There is also a lounge on the premises that is open from 11 a.m. to 1 a.m. Live entertainment is featured Wednesday through Sunday from 9 p.m. to 1 a.m. The menu for the restaurant offers specialties like homemade soups & chili, sandwiches, along with short order entrees. Steak, chicken, porter house steaks and seafood selections are also available. Average prices run $4.95 for lunch and in the neighborhood of $10.00 for dinners. Small groups are welcome up to 20 persons if prearranged in advance. They will also provide cheese trays and sandwiches for the pilot on-the-go if notified in advance. For information you can call the restaurant at 263-9801.

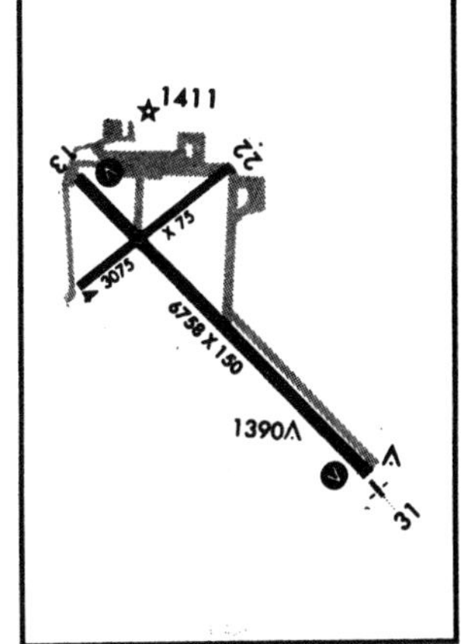

Airport Information:

HIBBING - CHISHOLM/HIBBING AIRPORT (HIB)
4 mi southeast of town N47-23.20 W92-50.34 Elev: 1353 Fuel: 100, Jet-A
Rwy 13-31: H6758x150 (Asph-Grvd) Rwy 04-22: H3075x75 (Asph) Attended: 1100-0500Z Unicom: 123.0
Airport Manager Phone: 262-3451

MN-8Y4 - LINO LAKES SURFSIDE (SEA-PLANE BASE)

(Area Code 612) **12**

Shirley Kayes Restaurant:

Shirley Kayes Restaurant is a sports bar & grill style restaurant located approximately 1/2 mile walk from the Surfside Sea Plane Base (8Y4) situated on Rice Lake, about 18 miles North-Northeast of the Minneapolis/St. Paul International Airport (MSP). This grill includes main entrees like hamburgers, steak sandwiches, barbecued rib sandwiches, grilled chicken and much more. Their dining room has been fully remodeled with a modern decor and is able to seat 65 to 70 persons. A meeting room can be reserved, able to seat 30 additional people. The restaurant is open 6 days a week between 10 a.m. and 1 a.m., and Sunday from 12 p.m. to 1 a.m. An outdoor balcony which could be used for outdoor dining overlooks Rice Lake. Amphibious aircraft can land at the Surfside "SPB" (8Y4) located 1/2 mile east of the restaurant. During our conversation with the airport management, learned that in the future they hope to complete a turf runway for land based aircraft. For airport information call 780-4179. For restaurant information call 780-4181.

Restaurants Near Airport:

49 Club Restaurant	2 mi	Phone: N/A
Shirley Kayes	1/2 mi	Phone: 780-4181

Lodging: Circle Pines (2 miles)

Meeting Rooms: None Reported

Transportation: None Reported

Information: Greater Minneapolis Convention & Visitors Association, 4000 Multifoods Tower, 33 South 6th Street, Minneapolis, MN 55402, Phone: 348-4313 or 800-445-7412; Also: Minnesota Travel Information Center, 100 Metro Square, 121 7th Place East, St Paul, MN 55101, Phone: 296-5029 or 800-657-3700 (US), 800/7-MN-TOUR (Canada)

NO AIRPORT DIAGRAM AVAILABLE

Airport Information:

LINO LAKES - SURFSIDE (SEA-PLANE BASE) (8Y4)
2 mi south of town N45-09.00 W93-07.01 Elev: 880 Fuel: 100LL
Rwy NE-SW: 6500x1000 (Water) Rwy N-S: 5500x1000 (Water) Rwy E-W: 5000x1000 (Water) Attended May-Oct dawn-dusk, unattended Nov-Apr. CTAF: 122.9
Surfside Seaplane Base Phone: 780-4179

MN-MIC - MINNEAPOLIS CRYSTAL AIRPORT

(Area Code 612) **13**

Embers Restaurant:

The Embers Restaurant is within walking distance to Crystal Airport near Minneapolis Minnesota. Open 24 hours a day, this family style restaurant is a favorite gathering place for pilots and airport staff. The entrees served are ribs, chicken, "best broiled scrod in town", steaks, spicy Cajun chicken or fish, burgers, sandwiches, salads and many desserts. One of their many specialties is their clam chowder soup each day and soup De Jour. The restaurant decor is contemporary, and comfortable. Catering for pilots on the go is no problem. Fly-in groups are also welcome, but please call in advance. For information call the restaurant at 537-2809.

Restaurants Near Airport:

Embers Restaurant	Adj Arpt	Phone: 537-2809

Lodging: Budgetel Inn 561-8400; Holiday Inn North (Trans) 566-4140; Sheraton Inn Northwest (Trans) 566-8855.

Meeting Rooms: Holiday Inn North 566-4140; Sheraton Inn Northwest 566-8855.

Transportation: None Reported

Information: Greater Minneapolis Convention & Visitors Association, 4000 Multifoods Tower, 33 South 6th Street, Minneapolis, MN 55402, Phone: 348-4313 or 800-445-7412.

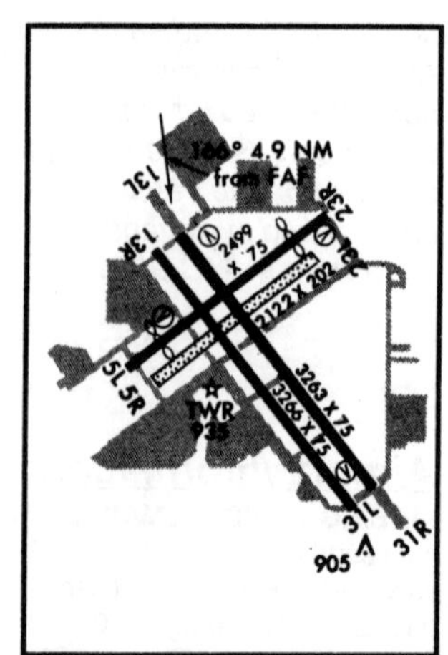

Airport Information:

MINNEAPOLIS - CRYSTAL AIRPORT (MIC)
8 mi northwest of town N45-03.72 W93-21.24 Elev: 869 Fuel: 100LL, Jet-A, MOGAS Rwy 13R-31L: H3266x75 (Asph) Rwy 13L-31R: H3263x75 (Asph)
Rwy 05L-23R: H2499x75 (Asph) Rwy 05R-23L: 2122x202 (Turf) Attended: May-Oct Mon-Fri 1300-0300Z, May-Oct Sat-Sun 1300-0100Z, Nov-Apr Mon-Fri 1300-0100Z Sat-Sun 1300-2300Z
Atis: 125.7 Unicom: 122.95 Tower: 120.7 Gnd Con: 121.6 Clnc Del: 121.6
Notes: CAUTION: refer to current AFD for airport information.
FBO: Crystal Shamrock, Inc. Phone: 533-2214 FBO: Flying Scotchman, Inc. Phone: 537-8485
FBO: Crystal Skyways, Inc. Phone: 537-6611 FBO: Northland Aircraft Phone: 537-1366

14

MN-MSP - MINNEAPOLIS-ST PAUL ST PAUL INTERNATIONAL AIRPORT (WOLD-CHAMBERLAIN)

(Area Code 612)

Garden Restaurant/Host Intl:

The Garden Restaurant is a full service restaurant located within the main terminal building at the Minneapolis St. Paul, Wold-Chamberlain Airport near Minneapolis St. Paul, Minnesota. This restaurant is open 7 a.m. to 9 p.m. through the week. Their entrees are varied, ranging from choice steaks and seafood to lighter fare. House specialties include filet mignon, crab croissant, cobb salad, steak sandwiches, and soups. Their menu offers daily specials. Average prices for most full course meals run about $11.00. The restaurant is glass enclosed, offering a view of the activity on the airport. They also have 2 banquet rooms available for groups of 20 or more. Reservations are suggested. The major fixed base operators on the field are Page Avjet (726-5214) and Van Dusen Airport Services (726-5700). Transportation would have to be arranged with these facilities prior to arriving. For information about the restaurant you can call 726-5341.

Restaurants Near Airport:

Burger King	Trml. Bldg	Phone: 726-5360
Garden Rest.	Main Trml.	Phone: 726-5341
Nathan's Rest.	R&B Concourse	Phone: 726-5360
Pizza Hut	4 locations	Phone: 726-5360
Taco Bell	2 locations	Phone: 726-5360
TCBY	Grn. Concourse	Phone: 726-5360

Lodging: Best Western Thunderbird (Trans) 854-3411; Embassy Suites (Trans) 854-1000; Embassy Suites Hotel (Trans) 884-4811; Hilton Airport 854-2100; Holiday Inn Intl Arpt (Trans) 854-9000; Marriott-Bloomington (Trans) 854-7441; Rodeway Inn Airport (Trans) 854-3400; Sheraton Hotel Airport (Trans) 854-1771;

Meeting Rooms: All lodging facilities listed above contain accommodations for meetings and conferences.

Transportation: Taxi Service available on field: Also Rental Cars: Avis 726-1723; Budget 726-5622; Dollar 726-9494; Hertz 726-1600; National 726-5600.

Information: Greater Minneapolis Convention & Visitors Association, 4000 Multifoods Tower, 33 South 6th Street, Minneapolis, MN 55402, Phone: 348-4313 or 800-445-7412;

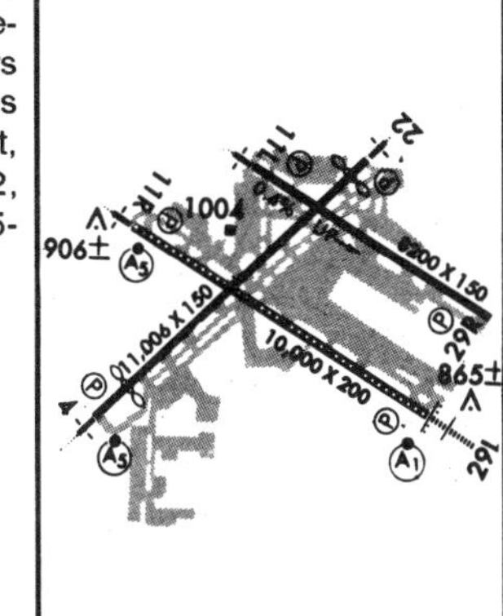

Airport Information:

MINNEAPOLIS ST. PAUL - ST PAUL INTL. WOLD-CHAMBERLAIN AIRPORT (MSP)
6 mi southwest of town N44-53.05 W93-12.90 Elev: 841 Fuel: 100, Jet-A, A1+
Rwy 11R-29L: H10000x200 (Asph-Conc-Grvd) Rwy 04-22: H8256x150 (Conc-Grvd)
Rwy 11L-29R: H8200x150 (Asph-Conc-Grvd) Attended: continuously Atis: 135.35
Unicom: 122.95 App Con: 119.3, 126.96 Tower: 126.7, 123.95 Gnd Con: 121.9, 121.8
Clnc Del: 133.2 Dep Con: 127.925, 124.7 Notes: Waterfowl on and in vicinity of airport. Training prohibited. Only initial departure and full stop termination training flights permitted. (See current AFD for information).

Signature Flight Support Airline Center Phone: 726-5800
Signature Flight Support, Inc. Phone: 726-5700

Let Us Know About Your Favorite "Prop Stoppers"

If you don't see your favorite fly-in restaurant, resort, or fly-to attraction, simply call us or just drop us a line and let us know about them. (See page 1,019)

Aerodine Magazine
P.O. Box 247, Palatine, IL 60078
Phone: 847-358-4355

Minnesota Air Guard Museum

Minneapolis-St.Paul, MN (MN-MSP)

Visiting the museum is to turn back the calendar to mid-1920 when dreams of an aviation squadron in the Minnesota National Guard first took form. Then to follow that dream through many experiences as it grows into the Minnesota Air National Guard as it exists today... and as it readies for the future.

Whether your visit begins outside in the Air Park among vintage to near-current aircraft and equipment operated by the Air Guard - or inside the Main Gallery with its many exhibits, the time spent can be most interesting and inspiring to all ages.

Some of the airplanes on display include a P-51 flown by the 109th Squadron in Europe during WW-II, both the 109th, Twin Cities, and the 179th, Duluth, flew F-89 during the period 1958 to 1966. The sleek F101 "Voodoo" graced the Duluth skies manned by 179th pilots between 1972 and 1976. Beginning with the RF-4C and converting to the F-4D the 179th has also flown the "Mig Killer" since 1976. Also on exhibit is a F-102, F-94, T-33, C-47, C131, C-45, L-4 and even a Pietenpohl. Recently a prestigious new addition to the museum was obtained as the result of much work. Officially assigned to the museum in July of 1990 was the world's fastest aircraft, the SR-71/A-12. The SR-71 was decommissioned after serving more than 25 years as the fastest, highest flying military snoop aircraft in the world. Today it is on display at the Minnesota Air Guard Museum.

The Museum is open to the public from 11 a.m. to 4 p.m., and weekends from mid-April through mid-September. Escorted tours by appointment.

To drive to the Air Guard Base, go south from intersection of Crosstown Hwy 62 and Hwy 55. If flying in to the Minneapolis-St.Paul International World Chamberlain Airport, you can park your aircraft at Signature Flight Support (FBO) 612-726-5700, which is located on the south portion of the airport and obtain a courtesy van or taxi from there to the museum, (Parking fee at FBO waved with fuel purchase). The museum is situated at the north end of the airport. For information you can call the Minnesota Air Guard Museum at 612-725-5609. (Information obtained from museum)

Photograph above is of a diorama depicting the begining of the Minneapolis/St. Paul International Airport. The white oval is Speedway Field in 1915. Built to compete with Indianapolis, running on Labor Day. Constructed of inferior concrete and with little regard to the consequences of Minnesota winters, the track rapidly deteriorated and was abandoned. Soon pilots began using the infield as an airport and in 1921 it became the Guard to receive federal recognition. Model aircraft represent planes flown by the Minnesota Air Guard since its beginning. Behind the diorama is the time line telling the story of the Minnesota Air National Guard. (Photo by: Minnesota Air Guard Museum).

MN-Y39 - OLIVIA
OLIVIA REGIONAL AIRPORT

(Area Code 612)

15, 16

Chatterbox:

The Chatterbox Restaurant is situated within walking distance from the Olivia Regional Airport. This family style restaurant is open 7 days a week between 5:30 a.m. and 9 p.m. Weekend hours may vary. Specialties of the house include a wide variety of selections such as breakfast items, hamburgers, steaks, fish platters, ham and pork dishes, hot beef and shrimp plates. Desserts include homemade pies. Average dinners run between $5.00 and $8.95. Daily specials are often presented. The decor of their dining room offers a clean and attractive appearance with cloth covered tables, lots of oak furnishings and a 12 foot wooden bar. There is seating for 90 persons within their main dining area. For more information about the Chatterbox Restaurant call 523-5384.

Sheep Shed, Inc:

The Sheep Shed Restaurant is reported to be within a 10 minute walk from the Olivia Regional Airport. This combination family style and fine dining facility, resembles an old English pub that is decorated with antiques and artifacts displayed on stucco covered walls and dark wood. Special entrees of the house include steaks, shrimp, prime rib, barbecued ribs, stir fried dishes, fettuccini, as well as a variety of pasta and Mexican selections. Average prices run $5.00 for lunch and $6.00 to $12.00 for dinner. On Sunday they feature a brunch that begins at 10 a.m. and ends at 2 p.m. Their main dining area contains 4 separate rooms that can seat 475 persons. They also can accommodate 238 people in a special banquet room, and often arrange group functions from 70 to 100 persons. All in all, we were told that they have catered as many as 900 banquets in a given year. The restaurant is open for lunch Monday through Friday beginning at 11 a.m. Dinner hours begin every day of the week at 5 p.m. In addition to their dining and group banquet accommodations, they provide lodging as well. This restaurant is adjacent to a 35 unit motel, and has been in business for over 50 years. For information on their lodging facilities call 523-5000. For more information about the Sheep Shed Restaurant, call 523-5555.

Restaurants Near Airport:

Chatterbox	Walk Dist	Phone: 523-5384
Sheep Shed	10 mi walk	Phone: 523-5555

Lodging: Sheep Shed Motel (10 min walk) 523-5000

Meeting Rooms: Sheep Shed Restaurant & Motel; contains several dining rooms as well as banquet facilities, 523-5555 or 523-5000.

Transportation: Both restaurants listed above are reported to be well within walking distance to the Olivia Regional Airport. No transportation is reported by the airport.

Information: Minnesota Travel Information Center, 100 Metro Square, 121 7th Place East, St Paul, MN 55101, Phone: 296-5029 or 800-657-3700 (US), 800/7-MN-TOUR (Canada)

Airport Information:

OLIVIA - OLIVIA REGIONAL AIRPORT (Y39)
2 mi west of town N44-46.71 W95-01.97 Elev: 1076 Fuel: 100LL
Rwy 11-29: H3498x75 (Asph) Attended: 1400-2300Z Unicom: 122.8
Airport Manager Phone: 523-2186

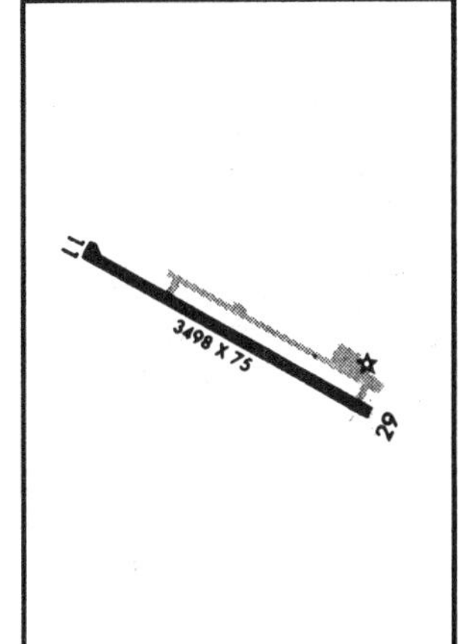

MN-VVV - ORTONVILLE
ORTONVILLE MUNI-MARTINSON FLD.

(Area Code 612) **17**

Restaurants Near Airport:

Dairy Queen	1/2 mi	Phone: 839-3605
Matador Supper Club	1/4 mi	Phone: 839-9981

Lodging: Anchor Motel (1/4 mile) 839-2576; Sunrise Motel (Adj Arpt) 839-2561; Vail-Vu Motel (1 mile) 839-2558.

Meeting Rooms: The Matador Supper Club 839-9981 and the Theatre of Seasons Cafe 839-2261 both have accommodations for meetings and conferences.

Transportation: Rental Cars: Car City 839-3165.

Information: Big Stone Lake Area Chamber of Commerce, 41 Northwest 2nd Street, Ortonville, MN 56278, Phone: 839-3284.

Matador Supper Club:

The Matador Supper Club is located about 1/2th of a mile from the Ortonville/Martinson Municipal Airport near Ortonville, Minnesota. Take a right out of the airport parking lot to the first stop sign, then right again. You should see the restaurant just ahead. Their entrees consist of sirloin steaks, barbecued ribs, seafood, catfish, honey roasted chicken, broiled fish, scampi, as well as a full salad bar and lighter fare like sandwiches and hamburgers. The restaurant has a Spanish/Mexican decor, and offers a separate party room for larger groups planning or arranging meetings or social events. A lounge is also located on the premises. The main dining room seats about 100 people. They also have a banquet room that can seat 250 persons. The restaurant is open Monday through Friday from 11:30 a.m. to 1 p.m. for lunch, and 4:30 p.m. to 12 midnight serving dinner. On Saturday they are open from 4:30 to 12 midnight and Sunday they feature a brunch beginning at 11 a.m. and running until 1 p.m. After that, they re-open for dinner from 5 p.m. to 9 p.m. Old time dancing is also featured in their "Fiesta Room". There is no courtesy transportation provided by the restaurant at this time. However, the airport will provide this service if you call in advance. The airport number is 839-3846. For restaurant information call 839-9981.

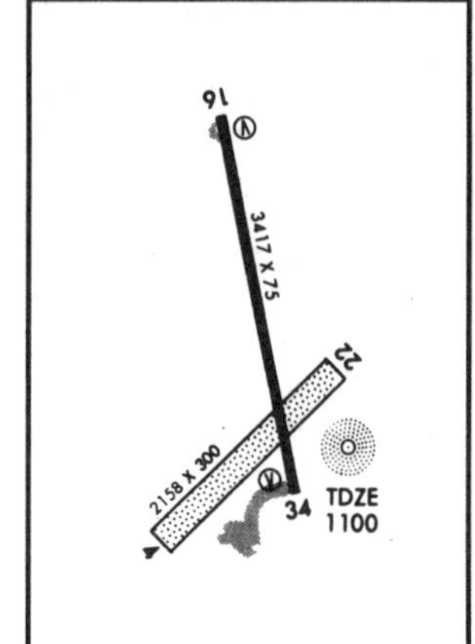

Airport information:

ORTONVILLE - ORTONVILLE MUNI-MARTINSON FIELD (VVV)
1 mi southeast of town N45-18.34 W96-25.47 Elev: 1100 Fuel: 100, MOGAS
Rwy 16-34: H3417x75 (Asph) Rwy 04-22: 2158x300 (Turf) Attended: unattended
Unicom: 122.8
Ortonville Municipal Airport Phone: 839-3846

MN-OWA - OWATONNA
OWATONNA MUNICIPAL AIRPORT

(Area Code 507) **18, 19**

Restaurants Near Airport:

Happy Chef	1/2 mi	Phone: 451-8613
Ramada Inn	1 mi	Phone: 455-0606

Lodging: Country Hearth Motel, 451-8712: Super 8 Motel 451-0380; Western Inn 455-0606.
Meeting Rooms: Super 8 Motel 451-0380; Western Inn 455-0606.
Transportation: Taxi Service: Liberty Cab 455-1000; Also Rental Cars: Budget 451-5600.
Information: Owatonna Area Chamber of Commerce, 320 Hoffman Drive, P.O. Box 331, Phone: 451-7970 or 800-423-6466.

Happy Chef Restaurant:

The Happy Chef Restaurant is a family style restaurant located about 1/2 mile from the Owatonna Municipal Airport in Owatonna, Minnesota. This restaurant is open 24 hours a day and has a menu offering a wide choice of entrees, including light fare for breakfast and lunch like burgers, sandwiches, salads, fish, and chicken. Their dinners have selections like fried chicken, rib eye steak, and chopped steak, to name just a few. Breakfast is served anytime with popular dishes like steak and eggs, golden waffles, omelettes, pancakes and much more. They also feature a all you can eat Friday night fish fry from 5 p.m. to 8 p.m. A breakfast buffet is served Saturday 7 a.m. to 11 a.m. and Sunday 7 a.m. to 1 p.m. This restaurant welcomes fly-in groups and offers catering for pilots-on-the-go. A courtesy car is available through the airport by calling 451-6646. For restaurant information call 451-8613.

Ramada Inn:

Ramada Inn has a casual family restaurant situated about 1 mile from the Owatonna Municipal Airport. The decor offers an informal and friendly atmosphere. Their menu includes specialties of the house like barbecued ribs, fresh Alaskan salmon, walleye pike, and stir fries. Sunday brunch offers breakfast and dinner entrees. Their hours are 6 a.m. to 2 p.m. and 5 p.m. to 9 p.m. on weekdays. On Saturdays they are open 7 a.m. to 2 p.m. and 5 p.m. to 10 p.m. Sunday they open at 7 a.m. until 2 p.m. The restaurant provides catering for small and large groups with a variety of set-ups to accommodate your special needs. For information call 455-0606.

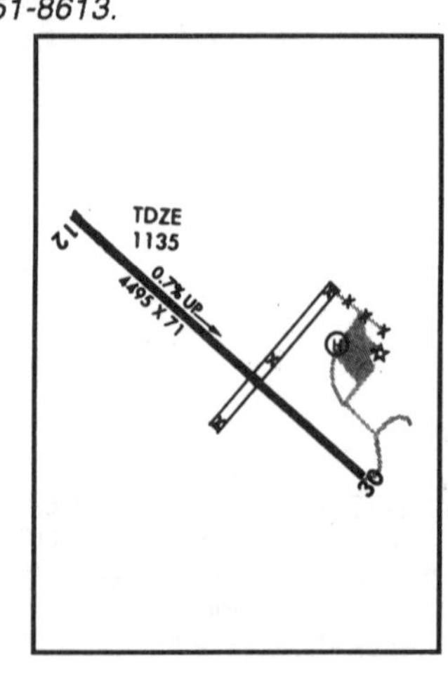

Airport Information:

OWATONNA - OWATONNA MUNICIPAL (OWA)
3 mi northwest of town N44-07.26 W93-15.34 Elev: 1148 Fuel: 100LL, Jet-A
Rwy 12-30: H4495x71 (Asph) Attended: 1400-0200Z Unicom: 122.7
FBO: Owatonna Airport, Inc. Phone: 451-6611

MN-4MN8 - PEQUOT LAKE MYERS FIELD

(Area Code 218) 20

A Pine Restaurant:

The Pine Restaurant is a family style restaurant located within 3/4th of a mile from the Myers Airport near Pequot Lake, Minnesota. This restaurant serves broasted chicken, steaks, sandwiches, salad bar, soups and desserts. They also offer daily luncheon specials. They are open during the winter season from 11 a.m. to 8 p.m. during the week, and 8 a.m. to 10 p.m. Saturday and until 8 p.m. on Sunday. During the Summer season they are open from 8 a.m. to 10 p.m. 7 days a week. The restaurant seating capacity is roughly 87 people and has a rustic decor. This restaurant is nestled in a pine tree forest giving it a very nice quaint and homey appearance. Transportation can be obtained by courtesy car by calling the restaurant at 568-8353.

Restaurants Near Airport:
A Pine Restaurant 3/4th mi Phone: 568-8353

lodging: Motels located in town.

Meeting Rooms: None Reported

Transportation: The "Pine Restaurant" reported that they will provide courtesy transportation for fly-in customers.

Information: Brainerd Lakes Area Chamber of Commerce and Convention and Visitors Bureau, 6th and Washington Streets, Brainerd, MN 56401, Phone: 800-450-2838 in state or 800-950-1162 out of state.

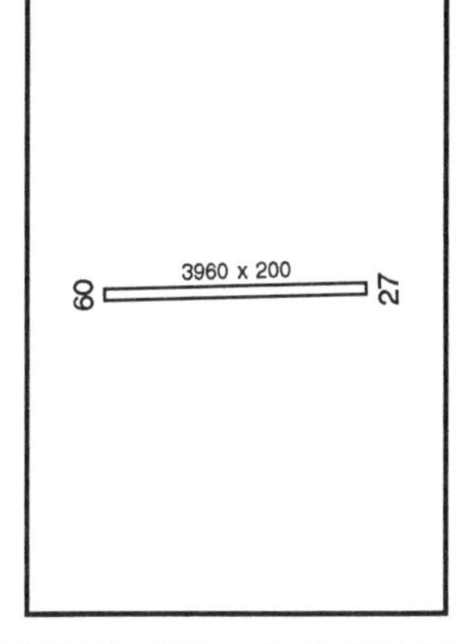

Airport Information:

PEQUOT LAKES - MYERS FIELD (4MN8)
2 mi northwest of town 46-37-06N 94-20-03W Elev: 1300 Fuel: Auto Fuel
Rwy 9-27: 3960x200 (Turf) Attended: daylight Notes: Private use facility open to the public; (Use at own risk) For runway conditions and/or services, call the airport manager at 568-5210. Runway not plowed during the winter months.
Myers Field Airport Phone: 568-5210

MN-PNM - PRINCETON PRINCETON MUNICIPAL AIRPORT

(Area Code 612) 21

Pine Loft Restaurant & Lounge:

When obtaining information about these restaurant, we learned that you can take the taxiway to the far north edge of the airport. After securing your aircraft, you can walk about 1 block (north), less than 500 feet to the restaurant. This fine dining facility is open Monday through Thursday 4 p.m. to 9 p.m., Friday and Saturday 4 p.m. to 10:30 p.m. and Sunday 11 a.m. to 8 p.m. Their lounge features a full sandwich menu. On Sunday they have a champaine lunch buffet from 11 a.m. to 2 p.m. The main dining room provides full American style choices and a selection of fine Italian entrees. Prices run $4.00 to $8.00 with meals served in their lounge and $7.00 to $14.00 for entrees served in the main dining room. Daily lunch and dinner specials are also offered. On Sunday they have baked chicken for their luncheon special. The decor of this restaurant consists of a mixture of rustic northern pines in the lounge and a more modern and open setting in the dining room. If advance notice is given, you can arrange club get-togethers or fly-in's. For information call 389-4762.

Restaurants Near Airport:
Merlins Family Restaurant N/A Phone: 389-3793
Pineloft Restaurant & Lounge 1/4 mi Phone: 389-4762

Lodging: Pine Air Hotel, 1/2 mi., Phone: 389-3120; Pine Air Motel, Phone: 389-2182: Camping on airport.

Transportation: None listed

Information: St Cloud Area Convention & Visitors Bureau, 30 South 6th Avenue, P.O. Box 487, St Cloud, MN 56302, Phone: 251-2940 or 800-264-2940. Minnesota Travel Information Center, 100 Metro Square, 121 7th Place East, St Paul, MN 55101, Phone: 296-5029 or 800-657-3700 (US), 800/7-MN-TOUR (Canada)

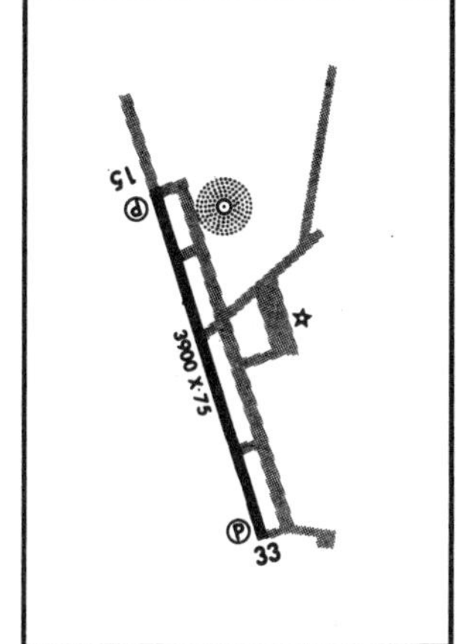

Airport Information

PRINCETON - PRINCETON MUNICIPAL (PNM)
1 mi southwest of town N45-33.59 W93-36.49 Elev: 979 Rwy 15-33: H3900x75 (ASPH)
Attended: unattended Unicom: 123.0 Airport Manager, Phone: 612-389-2040
FBO: Chelcraft Aviation, Phone: 389-5515

MN-RGK - RED WING
RED WING MUNICIPAL AIRPORT

(Area Code 612/715)

22

Restaurants Near Airport:
St James Hotel 5 mi Phone: 612-388-2846.

Lodging: Red Carpet Inn 612-388-1502; St James Hotel (Trans) 612-388-2846; Sterling Motel (Trans) 612-388-3568.

Meeting Rooms: St James Hotel 612-388-2846; Sterling Motel 612-388-3568.

Transportation: Rental Cars: Affordable Used Car Rentals 612-388-1176; Midway Auto Leasing 612-388-8296; Tesdall Motors 612-388-2852.

Information: Red Wing Area Chamber of Commerce, 420 Levee Street, P.O. Box 133, Red Wing, MN 55066, Phone: 612-388-4719 or 800-762-9516.

St James Hotel:

St James Hotel is a very interesting complex that contains two separate and unique dining facilities along with a number of specialty shops. This hotel is located approximately 5 miles from the Red Wing Municipal Airport in Red Wing, Minnesota. The "Veranda Cafe" features daily specials for lighter fare including soups and sandwiches, homemade pies and desserts. The "Port of Red Wing" restaurant and lounge captures the warmth and charm of the river boat era. Restaurant hours are from 11 a.m. to 2:00 p.m. for lunch and 5 p.m. to 9:30 p.m. for dinner. Enjoy an afternoon of shopping and fine dining at the St. James Hotel. For Transportation and restaurant information call 612-388-2846.

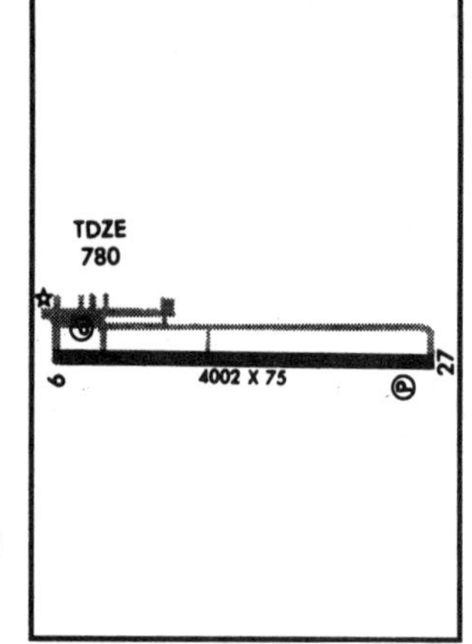

Airport Information:

RED WING - RED WING MUNICIPAL (RGK)
3 mi northeast of town N44-35.41 W92-29.17 Elev: 785 Fuel: 100LL, Jet-A, MOGAS
Rwy 09-27: H4002x75 (Asph) Attended: Mon-Sat1400-2300Z, Sun 1600-2200 Unicom: 123.05
Notes: Red Wing Municipal Airport is physically located in Wisconsin.
FBO: Seifert Skyways Phone: 715-594-3701 or 715-594-3041 or 612-388-6734.

MN-RST - ROCHESTER
ROCHESTER INTERNATIONAL

(Area Code 507)

23

Restaurants Near Airport:
The Wright Stuff On Site Phone: 252-9869

Lodging: Best Western Midway Lodge (Trans) 289-8866; Best Western Soldier Field (Trans) 288-2677; Holiday inn South (Trans) 288-1844; Ramada Inn (Trans) 281-2211.

Meeting Rooms: Best Western Midway Lodge 289-8866; Best Western Soldier Field 288-2677; Holiday Inn South 288-1844; Ramada Inn 281-2211.

Transportation: Taxi Service: Yellow 282-2222; Rental Cars: Avis 288-5655; Budget 288-8769; Hertz 288-2244; National 288-1155.

Information: Rochester Convention & Visitors Bureau, 150 South Broadway, Suite A, Rochester, MN 55904, Phone: 288-4331.

The Wright Stuff:

The Wright Stuff Restaurant is located in the terminal building at the Rochester International Airport. This facility is open 7 days a week between 5:30 a.m. and 6:30 p.m. The restaurant has an aviation decor with seating for about 75 to 100 people. Dark greens, brass, and wood in a pub like atmosphere, decorate the interior of the dining area. A lounge in back of the restaurant can accommodate up to 40 guests. Entree selections include a nice selection of appetizers like cheese curds, mozzarella cheese sticks, and onion rings. Breakfast items are served all day with specials like omelet's, pancakes and egg dishes. Lunch and dinner selections include tems like their 81 percent lean, make-your-own hamburger, adding whatever ingredients you desire from their condiment bar, chicken fingers or strips, sandwiches of all types including egg salad, hot ham & cheese, pizza, soups and three types of salads like their special house salad, taco salad or their delicious pasta salads. Customers can place their orders for meals at the cashier and take them to their seat. There is no waitress to serve meals. All items from their menu are available for carry-out. Fly-in catering can also be arranged. For more information call The Wright Stuff Restaurant at 252-9869.

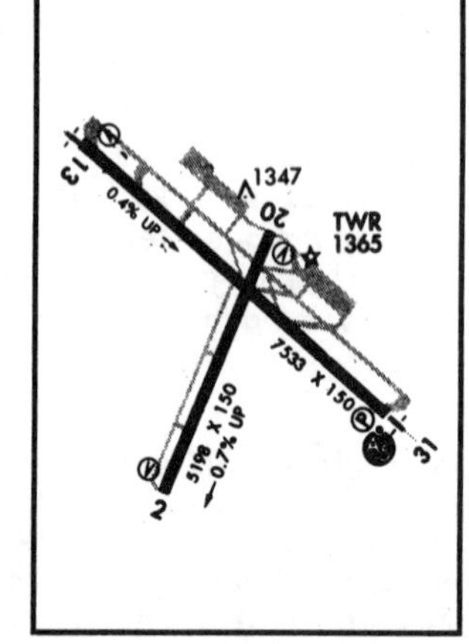

Airport Information:

ROCHESTER - ROCHESTER INTERNATIONAL AIRPORT
7 mi southwest of town N43-54.53 W92-29.88 Elev: 1317 Fuel: 100LL, Jet-A
Rwy 13-31: H7533x150 (Conc-Grvd) Rwy 02-20: H5198x150 (Conc-Wc)
Attended: continuously Atis: 120.5 Unicom: 122.95 App/Dep Con: 119.2, 119.8
Tower: 118.3 Gnd Con: 121.9
FBO: Rochester Aviation Phone: 282-1717, 800-274-1717

MN-STP - ST PAUL
ST PAUL DOWNTOWN HOLMAN FLD.

(Area Code 612)

24

Northwinds Restaurant & Catering:

Northwinds Restaurant & Catering is located on the St. Paul Downtown Holman Field in St. Paul, Minnesota. This restaurant is open from 7 a.m. to 3 p.m. Monday through Friday. Closed Saturday and Sunday. This restaurant is frequented by pilots as well as the airport staff. One of the specialties included on the menu is their famous clam chowder soup and Rueben sandwiches, in addition to many other menu selections, as well as their daily specials. The restaurant offers catering service for pilots on-the-go. They also have accommodations for larger groups like associations, or club fly-ins. Transportation is not a problem. However, if needed, you can arrange a courtesy car through the airport by calling 224-4306 or 726-1892. For restaurant information call 228-1325.

Restaurants Near Airport:
Northwinds Restaurant On Site Phone: 228-1325

Lodging: Embassy Suites (Trans) 224-5400; Holiday Inn Town Square (Trans) 291-8800; Quality Inn Civic Center (Trans) 292-8929; Radisson St Paul 292-1900; Sheraton Midway St. Paul 642-1234.

Meeting Rooms: Embassy Suites 224-5400; Holiday Inn Town Square 291-8800; Quality Inn Civic Center 292-8929; Radisson St. Paul 292-1900; Sheraton Midway St. Paul 642-1234.

Transportation: Taxi Service: City Wide Taxi 292-1601; Rental Cars: National 229-4900.

Information: St. Paul Convention and Visitors Bureau 102 Northwest Center, 55 East Fifth Street, St. Paul, MN 55101-1713, Phone: 297-6985 or 800-627-6101.

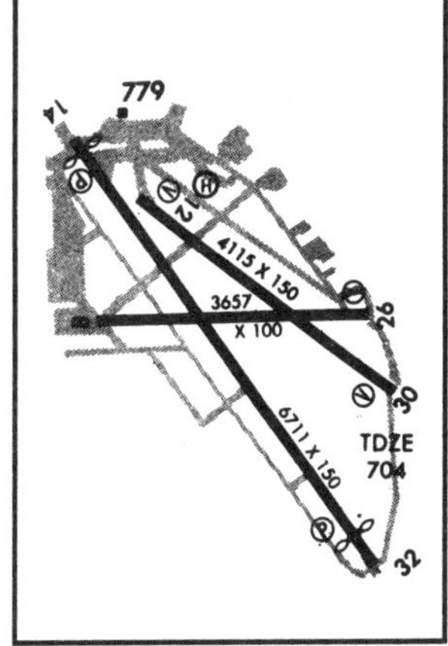

Airport Information:

ST. PAUL - ST. PAUL DOWNTOWN HOLMAN FIELD (STP)
1 mi south of town N44-56.07 W93-03.60 Elev: 705 Fuel: 100LL, Jet-A
Rwy 14-32: H6711x150 (Asph-Grvd) Rwy 12-30: H4115x150 (Asph) Rwy 08-26: H3657x100 (Asph) Attended: continuously Atis: 118.35 Unicom: 122.95
St Paul Tower: 119.1 Gnd Con: 121.7
FBO: Regent Aviation **Phone: 224-1100 or 800-523-7583**

MN-D32 - STARBUCK
STARBUCK MUNICIPAL AIRPORT

(Area Code 612)

25

Waters Edge Restaurant:

The Waters Edge Restaurant is located about 1/4th mile from the Starbuck Municipal Airport near Starbuck, Minnesota. This family style restaurant with lounge is open 7 days a week. On Saturday they are open from 11 a.m. to 10 p.m., Sunday from 4:30 p.m. to 10 p.m. and during the week from 5 p.m. to 10 p.m. For lunch they are open daily from 11:30 a.m. to 1:30 p.m. Their menu contains everything from hamburgers to shrimp, as well as steaks and seafood. There is also a salad bar available. Daily specials are offered as well as Sunday brunch. The restaurant has a contemporary decor, and accommodates groups of 20 or more with advance notice. Meals are also available for carry-out. For more information about this restaurant you can call the restaurant at 239-9117.

Restaurants Near Airport:
Waters Edge Restaurant 1/4th mi Phone: 239-9117

Lodging: None Reported

Meeting Rooms: None Reported

Transportation: None Reported

Information: Morris Area Chamber of Commerce, 507 Atlantic Avenue, Morris, MN 56267, Phone: 589-1242.

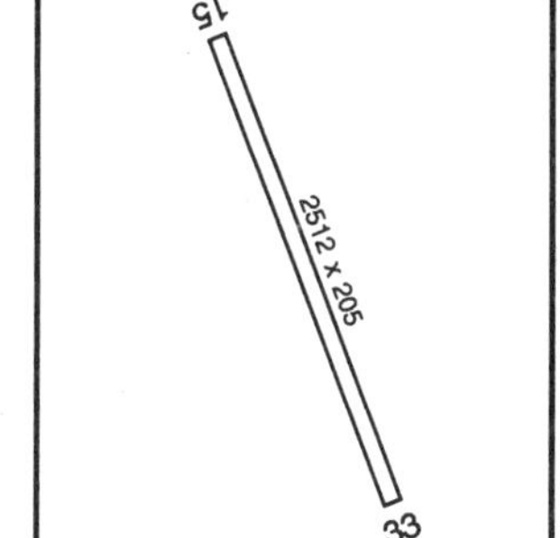

Airport Information:

STARBUCK - STARBUCK MUNICIPAL (D32)
1 mi south of town N45-36.00 W95-32.02 Elev: 1141 Rwy 15-33: 2512x205 (Turf)
Attended: on call 239-2526 CTAF: 122.9
Starbuck Municipal Airport **Phone: 239-2526**

MN-Y68 - TRACY
TRACY MUNICIPAL AIRPORT

(Area Code 507)

26

Mediterranean Club:

The Mediterranean Club is located about 1 mile from the Tracy Municipal Airport in Tracy Minnesota. This dinner club is open from noon until 12 a.m. every day except on Christmas and Thanksgiving. Their menu offers ribs, steaks and seafood selections, as well as a large choice of sandwich, appetizers, soups salads and desserts. On Sundays they have a buffet from 11 a.m. to 1:30 p.m. and Sunday night from 5 p.m. until 8:30 p.m. The buffet also runs from 5 p.m. to 8:30 p.m. on Monday nights. The decor of the restaurant was completely remodeled and displays a contemporary atmosphere. Large groups are welcome with accommodations to handle up to 400 people. Their prices are reasonable with lunch prices that run about $5.00 and dinners about $7.00. Transportation is available through the restaurant by calling them at 629-4400.

Restaurants Near Airport:

Mediterranean Club	1 mi.	Phone: 629-4400
Red Rooster	2 mi.	Phone: 629-9959

Lodging: Cozy Grove Motel (1 miles) 629-3350.

Meeting Rooms: Mediterranean Club is reported to have group banquet accommodations for up to 400 persons. For information call 629-4400.

Transportation: Rental Cars: Bud Hayes Ford 629-3400.

Information: Chamber of Commerce, Prarie Pavilion, 372 Morgan Street, Tracy, MN 56175, Phone: 629-4021.

NO AIRPORT DIAGRAM AVAILABLE

Airport Information:

TRACY - TRACY MUNICIPAL (Y68)
1 mi northeast of town N44-15.00 W95-36.27 Elev: 1340 Fuel: 100LL
Rwy 11-29: H3100x75 (Asph) Rwy 06-24: 2590x200 (Turf) Rwy 17-35: 1918x200 (Turf)
Attended: May-Sep 1400-0000Z, Oct-Apr Mon-Sat on request CTAF: 122.9
FBO: Miller Aerial Spraying Phone: 629-4849

A Little Extra Planning Can Make Each One Of Your Excursions More Rewarding

"Just Call Ahead"

Even though we at Aerodine strive to provide the latest information possible at the time of printing, we suggest you take a little time and call ahead to verify that the facility you intend to visit still provides the same services as published. Your comments regarding any changes in these services or about new establishments you have found, are greatly appreciated. With your help, we can include them in our next updated edition.

Aerodine Magazine
P.O. Box 247, Palatine, IL 60078
Phone: 847-358-4355

MISSISSIPPI

LOCATION MAP

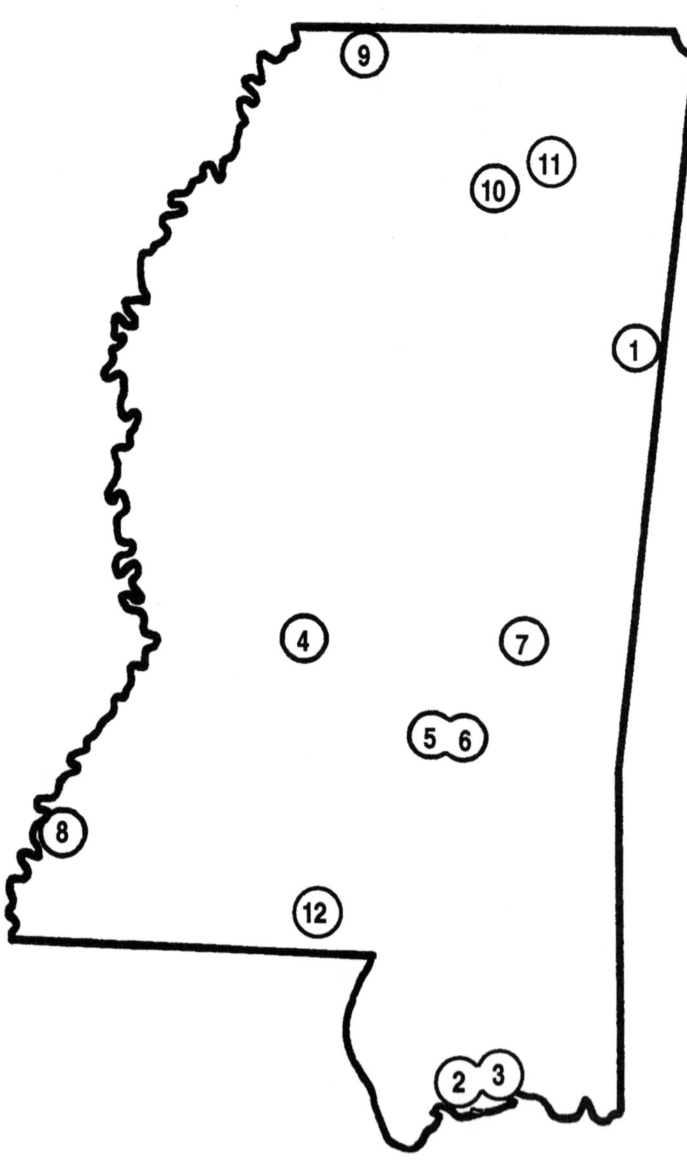

Not to be used for navigational purposes

MISSISSIPPI

CROSS FILE INDEX

Location Number	City or Town	Airport Name And Identifier	Name of Attraction
1	Columbus	Lowndes Co. Arpt. (UBS)	Main Street Bar & Grill
2	Gulfport	Biloxi Reg. Arpt. (GPT)	Armon's Restaurant
3	Gulfport	Biloxi Reg. Arpt. (GPT)	Vrazel's Restaurant
4	Jackson	Jackson Intl. (JAN)	Host Marriott
5	Laurel	Hesler-Noble Field (LUL)	American Foods
6	Laurel	Hesler-Noble Field (LUL)	Hardee's Restaurant
7	Meridian	Key Field Arpt. (MEI)	Queen City Truck Stop
8	Natchez	Hardy-Anders Fld/Adams Co.(HEZ)	LV's Snack Bar
9	Olive Branch	Olive Branch Arpt. (OLV)	Metro Mart & Deli
10	Pontotoc	Pontotoc Co. Arpt. (22M)	Pontotoc Inn Restaurant
11	Tupelo	Tupelo Muni. - CD Lemons (TUP)	Front Porch
12	Tylertown	Paul Pittman Meml (T36)	Stonger's Restaurant

MS-UBS - COLUMBUS LOWNDES COUNTY AIRPORT

(Area Code 601)

1

Main Street Bar & Grill:

This restaurant and tavern facility is located about 3 miles from the Lowndes County Airport. This establishment can be reached by loaner car through Taloney Air Service for $5.00 per hour. Taxi service is also available. The restaurant is open between 4 p.m. and 10 p.m. Wednesday, Thursday and Friday. Saturday they are open from 7 a.m. to 10 p.m. and on closed on Sunday, Monday and Tuesday. There is also a lounge open from 4 p.m. to 1 a.m. The Main Street Bar & Grill formerly named "The Depot" offers a charming atmosphere with a rustic appearance. Artifacts from railroad equipment, antiques and furnishings from the train depot provide a unique backdrop within the lounge area. The main dining room can seat between 100 and 150 people. They also provide a banquet room that can accommodate 200 to 250 persons for special occasions. Catered meals on the premises is also a specialty of theirs. For more information you can call the restaurant at 328-4340.

Restaurants Near Airport:

Main Street Bar & Grill	3 mi NW	Phone: 328-4340
The Deli Gaslight	1 mi N.	Phone: 327-5539
The Kountry Kitchen	2 mi NE	Phone: 327-9207

Lodging: Gilmer Inn 327-1910; Holiday Inn 328-5202.

Meeting Rooms: Holiday Inn 328-5202.

Transportation: Taloney Air Service can provide courtesy transportation to nearby facilities; Also Cab service 329-2041; Tombigbee Tours & Travel (Limo) 328-8282; Avis 327-5957 or 800-331-1212.

Information: Columbus Convention & Visitors Bureau, P.O. Box 789, Columbus, MS 39703, Phone: 329-1191 or 800-327-2686 outside MS.

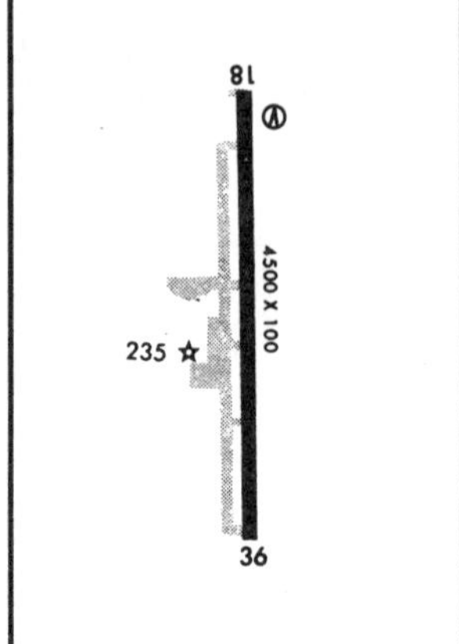

Airport Information:

COLUMBUS - LOWNDES COUNTY AIRPORT (UBS)
3 mi southeast of town N33-27.92 W88-22.82 Fuel: 100LL, Jet-A Rwy 18-36: H4500x100 (Asph)
Attended: daylight hours Unicom: 122.8 Public Phone 24hrs Notes: No landing fees
FBO: Taloney Air Service Phone: 327-6907

MS-GPT - GULFPORT BILOXI REGIONAL AIRPORT

(Area Code 601)

2, 3

Armon's Restaurant:

Armon's Restaurant is located within the main terminal building at the Biloxi Regional Airport. This cafeteria is open 7 days a week from 5:30 a.m. until 11 p.m. The specialty entrees consist of Cajun homemade seafood gumbo, red beans with rice and sausage, soups, desserts, pastries, salads, breakfast and 14 choices of sandwiches prepared on order. Daily specials are served from their buffet line. Average prices run $5.50 for breakfast $7.00 for lunch and dinner. The decor is modern with pictures depicting the many festivals held on the coast at Mississippi beaches, such as Biloxi Seafood Festivals, Gulfport Crayfish Festival, and the Crab Festival. This restaurant offers a flexible, versatile catering service to businesses, clubs, wedding parties, corporate picnics and will prepare meals for up to 500 persons. Armon's catering also provides in-flight catering to commercial airlines, corporate or private planes They will prepare whatever is requested. For information call the restaurant at 863-5350.

Vrazel's:

Vrazel's is located 4 miles south of the Biloxi Regional Airport near Gulfport, Mississippi. This fine dining facility can be reached through U.S. Aviation "FBO"(Ask to speak with Darwin Helms). To reach the restaurant take South Hwy. 49 four miles to Hwy 90. Make a right and go west 1/4 mile. The restaurant will be on your right. They are open Monday through Friday 11 a.m. to 2 p.m. for lunch and Mondaythrough Saturday 5 p.m. to 10 p.m. for dinner. Specialties of the house include Seafood ala Varazel; Veal Anton; Snapper Lenwood or Stuffed Strip Steak Louise Anne consisting of USDA prime sirloin broiled to your liking, stuffed with a delectable combination of mushrooms, bacon, shallots, herbs and a blend of wild rice, or you may want to try their Seafood au Gratin a la Cajun: Fresh Gulf shrimp, oysters, crabmeat and herbs sauteed together till just the right moment, then blended with a spicy rich cream sauce topped with cheese and baked to perfection. In addition, they also provide a selection of appetizers, soups and salads to compliment your choice of entrees. And to complete your dining experience, enjoy their flaming desserts and coffees, prepared by their professionally trained waitstaff. Average prices run $7.00 to $10.00 for lunch and $15.00 to $20.00 for dinner. The decor of the restaurant provides an elegant touch with chandeliers, white linen table cloths. Their beautiful gardens surrounded by majestic Southern oak trees, can be enjoyed looking out from within the restaurant. This restaurant is able to accommodate up to 60 persons if planning a group or business get-together. For information call 863-2229.

Restaurants Near Airport:

Armon's	On Site	Phone: 863-5350
Montana's	3 mi NW.	Phone: 832-1313
Toucans	2 mi W.	Phone: 863-3117
Vrazels	4 mi S.	Phone: 863-2229

Lodging: Holiday Inn 896-6699; Best Western 864-0050; Rozale D'Ikerville 388-6610;

Meeting Rooms: The airport authority can arrange conference space by calling 863-5951 or Holiday Inn has meeting and conference rooms available, call 868-8200.

Transportation: U.S. Aviation will provide courtesy transportation to nearby facilities, call 863-2570; Also, rental cars are available: Avis 864-7188; Budget 864-5181; Hertz 863-2761; National 863-5548; or Taxi Service by: Yellow Cab 864-6801.

Information: Chamber of Commerce, 1401 20th Avenue, P.O. Drawer FF, Gulfport, MS 39502, Phone: 863-2933.

Attractions:

Mississippi Beach is a tourist area providing many family orientated activities. Cruise aboard one of several casino cruise ships for daytime or evening excursions or stay at one of many exclusive beachfront hotels while enjoying golfing, deep sea fishing, swimming or historic tours within this region.

Airport Information:

GULFPORT - BILOXI REGIONAL AIRPORT (GPT)

3 mi northeast of town N30-24.44 W89-04.21 Elev: 28 Fuel: 100LL, Jet-A
Rwy 14-32: H9002x150 (Asph-Grvd) Rwy 18-36: H4950x150 (Asph) Attended: 1130-0500Z
Public Phone 24hrs Atis: 119.45 Unicom: 122.95 App/Dep Con: 124.6, 127.5
Tower: 123.7 Gnd Con: 120.4 Notes: No landing fee, contact fixed base operator for parking fees.
FBO: U.S. Aviation Phone: 863-2570 or 864-2576

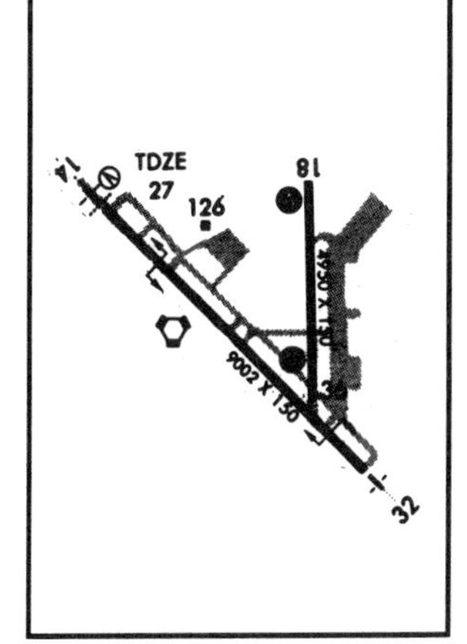

MS-JAN - JACKSON
JACKSON INTERNATIONAL

(Area Code 601) 4

Restaurants Near Airport:

Host Marriott	On Site	Phone: 939-5942

Host Marriott:

Dobbs Houses, Inc. is in charge of several dining facilities located on the Jackson International Airport. A snack bar, cafeteria and a family style restaurant. Food service is available Monday through Friday from 5:30 a.m. to 10:00 p.m. and Saturday and Sunday from 5:30 a.m. to 8:00 p.m. They specialize in "Down Home Cooking" with entrees like fried chicken, and fried catfish. Daily specials are offered Monday through Friday during lunch. Prices average $4.50 for breakfast, and $5.00 to $8.00 for lunch and dinner selections. The restaurants decor has a classical style with marble, ceramic tile and mahogany accents. Their "Skyroom" accommodates private dining available with seating for up to 50 persons. Catering is also provided with advance notice. For information call 939-5942.

Lodging: (Shuttle Service): Holiday Inn Downtown 969-5100; And Ramada Renaissance 957-2800.
Meeting Rooms: Dobbs House located on the airport will provide accommodations for meeting with prior arrangements. Phone: 939-5942
Transportation: FBO will provide transportation to and from Dobbs House. Also Taxi Service: Yellow Cab 354-3441; Deluxe Cab 948-4761; Veterans Cab 355-8319; Airport limo Service 939-1131; Rental Cars: Avis 939-5853; Budget 939-0571; Hertz 939-5312; National 939-7513.
Information: Jackson Chamber of Commerce, 201 S. President Street, Jackson, MS 39205, Phone: 948-7575; Also The Convention & Visitors Bureau, P.O. Box 1450, Jackson MS 39215, Phone: 960-1891 or 800-354-7695.

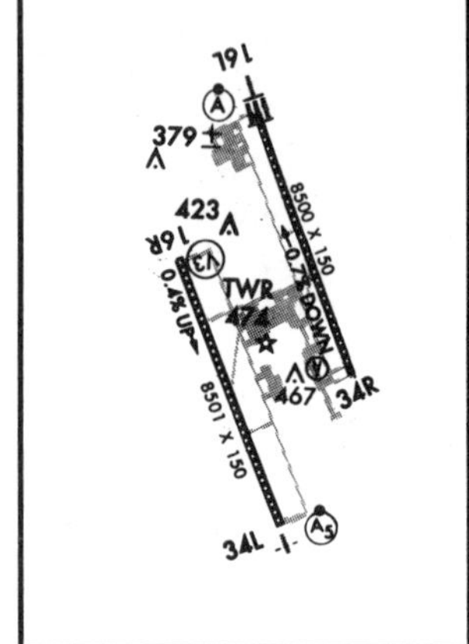

Airport Information:

JACKSON - JACKSON INTERNATIONAL AIRPORT (JAN)
5 mi east of town N32-18.67 W90-04.55 Elev: 347 Fuel: 100, Jet-A
Rwy 16R-34L: H8501x150 (Asph-Con-Grvd) Rwy 16L-34R: H8500x150 (Asph-Grvd)
Attended: continuously Atis: 121.05 Unicom: 122.95 App/Dep Con: 123.9, 125.25
Tower: 120.9 Gnd Con: 121.7 Public Phone 24hrs Notes: Overnight parking fees: Single $4.00 and Twins $6.00 to $10.00 per night.
FBO: Jackson Air Center Phone: 939-9366

MS-LUL - LAUREL
HESLER-NOBLE FIELD

(Area Code 601) 5, 6

Restaurants Near Airport:

American Foods	2 blks	Phone: 428-4419
Charlies Catfish Hs	5 mi	Phone: 428-1442
Hardee's	2 blks	Phone: 649-2723
Shoney's	2 mi	Phone: 426-6596

American Foods:

The American Foods Restaurant is located 2 blocks from the Hesler Noble Airport. This cafeteria style restaurant is open 24 hours a day 7 days a week. Their menu contains items like fried chicken, hamburger steak and gravy, pork chops, red beans & rice, spaghetti and all types of sandwiches, along with a full breakfast line. Seating capacity for this restaurant is 100. For more information call 428-4419.

Hardee's Restaurant:

Hardee's Restaurant is located approx 2 blocks from the airport and is open between 5 a.m. and 10 p.m. 7 days a week. They specialize in combination plates along with specialty hamburgers, roast beef sandwiches and breakfast selections. Average prices run $2.00 for breakfast, and $3.00 for lunch & dinner. Seating capacity for this restaurant is 50 persons. For more information, call Hardee's at 649-2723.

Lodging: Holiday Inn (5 miles) 428-8421; Magnolia Motor Lodge (5 miles) 428-0511; Ramada Inn Sawmill (2 miles) 649-9100; Town House (3 miles) 428-1527.

Meeting Rooms: Days Inn (At jct US 11N, I-59N) 428-8421; Ramada Inn Sawmill (2 miles) 649-9100.

Transportation: Rental Cars: Avis 428-8861; Hertz 649-3807.

Information: Chamber of Commerce, P.O. Box 527, Laurel, MS 39441, Phone: 428-0574.

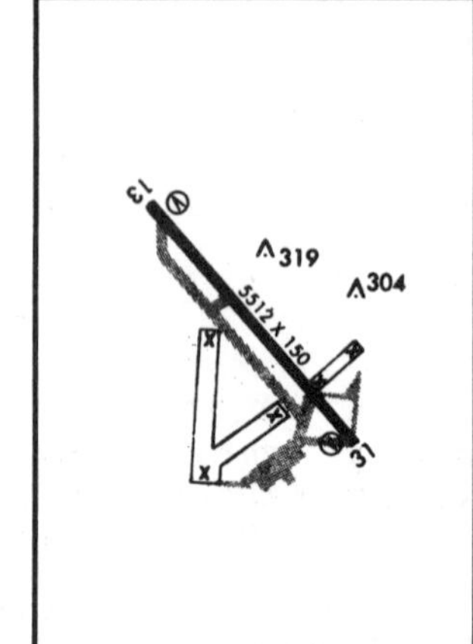

Airport Information:

LAUREL - HESLER-NOBLE FIELD (LUL)
3 mi southwest of town N31-40.35 W89-10.33 Elev: 238 Fuel: 100LL, Jet-A1+
Rwy 13-31: H5512x150 (Asph) Attended 1300Z till dusk Unicom: 122.8
Notes: For service after hours call 426-2626
FBO: Stringer Aviation, Inc. Phone: 426-2626

MS-MEI - MERIDIAN KEY FIELD AIRPORT

(Area Code 601)

7

Queen City Truck Stop:

The Queen City Truck Stop is situated about 1/2 mile from the Meridian Key Field. Meridian Aviation will take fly-in customers to this restaurant. As the restaurant is located at a Philips 66 truck stop, they are open 24 hours a day. Breakfast is served all day. Lunch specials are offered 7 days a week for around $4.00. Additional specials are served for dinner beginning at 8 p.m. Steaks, franks, fish plates and sandwiches of all types. Average prices run between $3.00 to $4.50 for breakfast, $3.00 to $7.00 for lunch and dinner. A plate lunch special is offered every day. They can easily accommodate a dozen fly-in customers. For larger groups of 20 or more, they would appreciate a 2 or 3 day advance notice so they can reserve their private dining room for catering. This restaurant has been in business over the past 11 years. Based on our contributors this restaurant attracts many pilots from the region. For more information about the Queen City Truck Stop you can call them at 482-0259.

Restaurants Near Airport:

Queen City Truck Stop	1/2 mi	Phone: 482-0259
The Patio Restaurant	1 mi S	Phone: 693-4521
The Rustler Steak House	1 mi	Phone: 693-6499

Lodging: Hampton Inn (Free trans) 483-3000; Holiday Inn South (Free trans) 693-4521.
Meeting Rooms: Hampton Inn (Free trans) 483-3000; Holiday Inn South (Free trans) 693-4521.
Transportation: Avis 483-7144; Hertz 485-4774; American Cab Co 482-4900; Meridian Cab Co 693-6338.
Information: Meridian/Lauderdale County Partnership, P.O. Box 790, Meridian, MS 39301, Phone: 483-0083 or 800-748-9970.

Attractions:

Clarko State Park (Fishing Swimming) Hwy 45 South approx. 12 miles; Lakeview Golf Course (City owned) approx. 8 miles; Meridian Museum of Art, downtown Meridian, approx 3 miles.

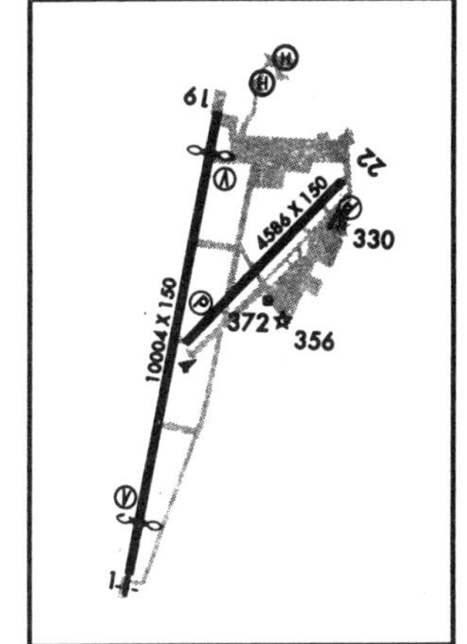

Airport Information:

MERIDIAN - KEY FIELD AIRPORT (MEI)
3 mi southwest of town N32-19.99 W88-45.07 Elev: 297 Fuel: 100, Jet-A
Rwy 01-19: H10004x150 (Asph-Grvd) Rwy 04-22 H4586x150 (Asph) Attended: 1200-0400Z
Unicom: 122.95 Meridian App/Dep Con: 120.5 Tower 119.8 Gnd Con: 121.9
Public Phone 24 hrs Notes: For attendant after hours call 485-8161 or 693-7282.
FBO: Meridian Aviation Phone: 693-7282

MS-HEZ - NATCHEZ HARDY-ANDERS FLD ADAMS CO.

(Area Code 601)

8

LV's Snack Bar:

LV's Airport Snack Bar is located upstairs in the terminal building of the Natches Anders Field Adams County Airport. This restaurant is open 11 a.m. to 2:30 p.m. on weekdays. Their menu contains items like hamburgers, cheeseburgers and French fries. The average price for a meal is between $2.00 and $5.00. The view from the airport terminal overlooks the ramp and runways. Fly-in groups or parties are welcome. Please give advance notice for larger groups. Carry out lunches are also prepared for pilots on the go. For more information call 442-3142.

Restaurants Near Airport:

Cock of Walk	10 mi SW	Phone: 446-8920
LV's Arpt Snack Bar	On Site	Phone: 442-3142

Lodging: Ramada Inn Hilltop (Transportation) 446-6311; Natchez Eola Hotel (Free transportation) 445-6000 res, or 800-888-9140.

Meeting Rooms: Eola Hotel, Ramada Inn Hilltop, and River Park Hotel 446-6688, all provide accommodations for meeting rooms and conferences.

Transportation: Adams County Car (Rental and taxi service) 445-9831

Information: Natchez Convention & Visitors Bureau, 422 Main Street, P.O. Box 1485, Natchez, MS 39120, Phone: 800-647-6724.

Attractions:

Antibellum Houses-Natchez Pilgrimage Tours: More than 24 magnificent homes and mansions are on display with public tours sponsored by the Natchez Pilgrimage Association during the month of October, 800-647-6742; Natchez State Park offers many outdoor activities including camping, fishing and hiking, 442-2658.

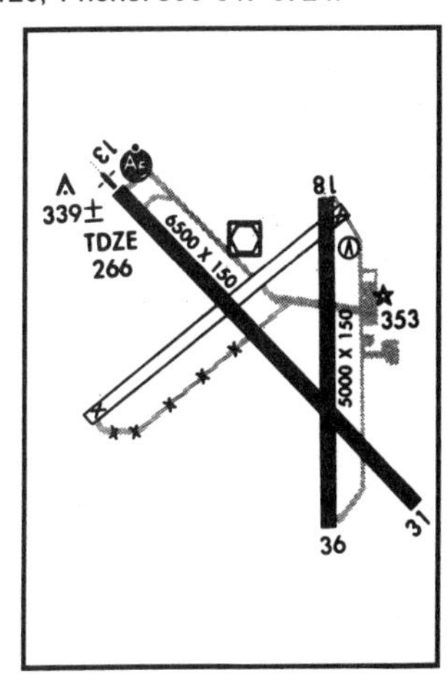

Airport Information:

NATCHEZ - HARDY ANDERS FLD ADAMS CO. (HEZ)
6 mi northeast of town N31-36.82 W91-17.84 Elev: 272 Fuel: 100LL, Jet-A
Rwy 13-31: H6500x150 (Asph) Rwy 18-36: H5000x150 (Asph) Attended: continuously
Unicom: 122.8 Public Phone 24hrs
FBO: Natchez Adams County Airport Phone: 442-3142

MS-OLV - OLIVE BRANCH
OLIVE BRANCH AIRPORT

(Area Code 601)

9

Metro Mart & Deli:

The Metro Mart & Deli is located adjacent to the Olive Branch Airport. This combination convenient store and cafe style restaurant is open between 5 a.m. and 9 p.m. Monday through Friday, 5 a.m. to 7 p.m. Their menu features salisbury steak, spaghetti & meat balls, pepper steak, meat loaf, chicken dishes, meat and vegetables and a full selection of breakfast entrees. Average prices run between $3.00 and $4.00 for most items. Their dining room has seating for 30 people, with a modern atmosphere. Meals can be prepared-to-go as well. For more information about the Metro Mart & Deli, call them at 895-7575.

Restaurants Near Airport:
Metro Mart & Deli Adj Arpt Phone: 895-7575

Lodging: Holiday Inn (Trans) 895-2941; Holiday Inn East (Trans) 682-7881; Ramada Inn (Trans) 362-8010.

Meeting Rooms: Holiday Inn Executive Conference Center 895-2941; Holiday Inn East 682-7881; Ramada Inn 362-8010.

Transportation: Rental cars are available at the airport if advance notice is given. Call Olive Branch Airport at 895-2978.

Information: Division of Tourism, P.O. Box 1705, Ocean Springs, MS 39566, Phone: 800-WARMEST; Also: Mississippi Department of Economic and Community Development, Division of Tourism Development, P.O. Box 22825, Jackson, MS 39205.

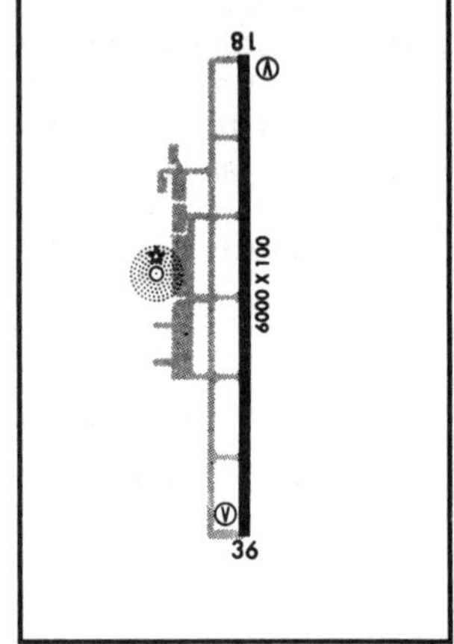

Airport Information:

OLIVE BRANCH - OLIVE BRANCH AIRPORT (OLV)
3 mi northeast of town 34-58.73 W89-47.21 Elev: 401 Fuel: 100LL, Jet-A
Rwy 18-36: H6000x1000 (Asph) Attended: 1300-0200Z Unicom: 122.7
FBO: Metro Aviation Service Phone: 895-2978

MS-22M - PONTOTOC
PONTOTOC COUNTY AIRPORT

(Area Code 601)

10

Pontotoc Inn Restaurant:

The Pontotoc Inn Restaurant is located 2 miles from the Pontotoc County Airport. Transportation to and from the airport can be arranged through the restaurant with advance notice, according to the management. This fine dining facility is open from 6 a.m. to 9 p.m. Monday through Saturday, and on Sunday from 6 a.m. to 2 p.m. Their menu selection primarily features choice steaks and seafood. A full breakfast line is also featured as well as many other items, throughout the day. They also feature a buffet for noon luncheons as well as during the dinner hours. Their Friday night seafood buffet provides a popular selection of choices as well. The main dining room can seat 60 people, while their private dining area offers seating for at least 35 persons. The restaurant exhibits a quiet atmosphere with carpeted floors, linen covered tables and candlelight dining. In addition to the restaurant, accommodations are also available for lodging with a 60 unit motel, adjacent to the restaurant. For more information you can call the Pontotoc Inn Restaurant at 489-5200.

Restaurants Near Airport:
Pontotoc Inn Restaurant 2 mi Phone: 489-5200

Lodging: Pontotoc Inn (2 miles) Hwy 15 & 336, Phone: 489-5200;

Meeting Rooms: Pontotoc Inn (2 miles) Phone: 489-5200;

Transportation: Pontotoc Inn will provide transportation for fly-in guests to and from the airport and their dining and lodging facility, 489-5200.

Information: Division of Tourism, P.O. Box 1705, Ocean Springs, MS 39566, Phone: 800-WARMEST; Also: Mississippi Department of Economic and Community Development, Division of Tourism Development, P.O. Box 22825, Jackson, MS 39205.

Attractions:

Pontotoc Country Club (10 miles east, on Hwy 6); Trace State Park (12 miles east on Hwy 6).

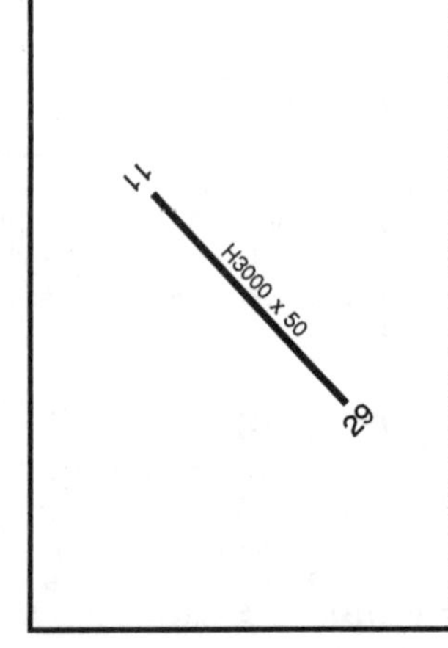

Airport Information:

PONTOTOC - PONTOTOC COUNTY AIRPORT (22M)
2 mi northwest of town N34-16.56 W89-02.30 Elev: 440 Fuel: 100LL
Rwy 11-29: H3000x50 (Asph) Attended: Mon-Fri daylight hours CTAF/Unicom: 122.8
Public Phone 24hrs Notes: Unicom out of service indefinitely
FBO: Pontotoc Airport Phone: 489-1403

MS-TUP - TUPELO
TUPELO MUNICIPAL - C D LEMONS

(Area Code 601)

11

Front Porch:

The Front Porch Restaurant is located about 1/2 to 1 mile from the Tupelo Municipal C D Lemons Airport. According to the management , this family-style restaurant can be reached by turning left to Coley Road, then when you cross Highway 6, the road name changes to Cliff Bookin Blvd; 1/4 mile further and you should see the restaurant on the right side of the street. The restaurant is open from 4 p.m. to 10 p.m. Monday through Thursday and from 4 p.m. to 11 p.m. on Friday and Saturday. They are closed on Sunday. Their menu contains seafood selections, steaks, surf and turf, blackened catfish, shrimp, scallops and oysters. They also provide an assortment of salads and sandwiches. Additional dessert specialties include cheese cake, brownie delight and pecan pie with icecream. Average prices run $6.00 to $7.99 for lunch, and $8.00 to $17.99 for dinner. The atmosphere is casual. The name, Front Porch, describes the decor of the restaurant decorated with cypress wood and a veranda-type deck with rocking chairs and outdoor dining. They can seat between 180 and 200 people. Their bar and grill area has a big-screen TV and dart board. For more information call the Front Porch Restaurant at 842-1591.

Restaurants Near Airport:

Front Porch	1 mi	Phone: 842-1591
Jeffersons Place	3 mi	Phone: 844-8696
Papa Vanelli's	4 mi	Phone: 844-4410
Ruby Tuesday	5 mi	Phone: 844-3383

Lodging: Econo Lodge (3 mi, free trans) 844-1904; Ramada Inn (3 mi free trans) 844-4111; Trace Inn (2 mi free trans) 842-5555.
Meeting Rooms: Ramada Inn (3 mi free trans) 844-4111; Trace Inn (2 mi free trans) 842-5555.
Transportation: Courtesy car reported at airport; Rental Cars: Budget 840-3710; Hertz 844-9148; Taxi Service: Brooks 842-3710; Hertz 844-9148.
Information: Tupelo Convention & Visitors Bureau, 399 E. Main Street, P.O. Box 1485, Tupelo, MS 38801, Phone: 841-6521 or 800-533-0611.

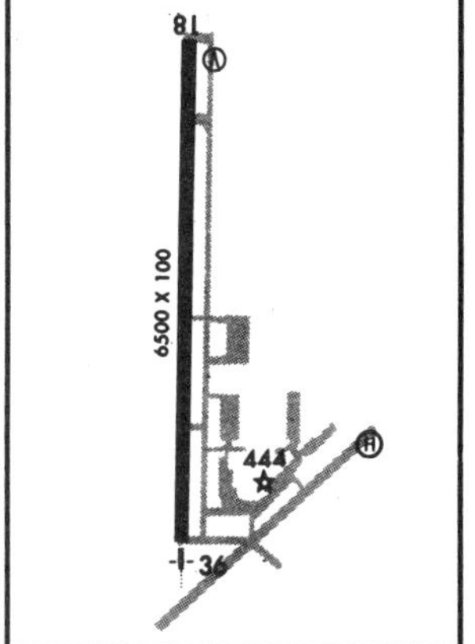

Airport Information:

TUPELO - TUPELO MUNICKPAL - C D LEMONS
3 mi west of town N34-16.09 W88-46.19 Elev: 346 Fuel: 100, Jet A1+ Rwy 18-36: H6500x100 (Asph-Grvd) Attended: 1100-0600Z Unicom: 122.7
FBO: Southernaire, Inc. Phone: 842-6918, 842-6069
FBO: Tupelo Aero, Inc. Phone: 844-9112, 844-3244

MS-T36 - TYLERTOWN
PAUL PITTMAN MEML

(Area Code 601)

12

Stonger's Restaurant:

Stonger's Restaurant is located about 2-1/2 miles east of the Paul Pittman Memorial Airport along Dexter Road. It is said that courtesy transportation is provided by Eagle Aircraft Service (FBO) from the airport. This family restaurant was brought to our attention by one of our readers because it is well known for its seafood. Some of the choice favorites are catfish prepared either whole or filet; oysters; shrimp dishes and many other items including Bar-Be-Qued ribs. Prices run around $7.50. Stonger's Restaurant is a family-owned and operated business that has successfully been serving customers for over 18 years. During our interview we learned that the father and son team actually began by building the restaurant by hand, and take enormous pride in preparing the freshest food anywhere. "No fast junk" but quality food, as they put it, is what they based their popularity on. On Friday nights they feature an "All you can eat" seafood buffet including hush puppies (not the frozen variety, but honest to goodness homemade ones) along with French fries and coleslaw. The restaurant is open from 4 p.m. to 10 p.m. Thursday, Friday and Saturday. For more information call Stonger's Restaurant at 876-5785.

Restaurants Near Airport:

Stonger's Restaurant	2-1/2 mi E.	Phone: 876-5785

Lodging: Holiday Sands Motel 2 mi 876-3454; Hidden Springs Resort 3 mi 876-4151.

Meeting Rooms: Stonger's Restaurant can seat up to 300 people 2-1/2 mi 876-5785.

Transportation: Taxi Service and rental cars as well as courtesy cars for short term use has been reported available through Eagle Aircraft Service 876-4953.

Information: McComb Chamber of Commerce, 202 3rd Street, P.O. Box 83, McComb MS 39648. Phone: 601-684-2291.

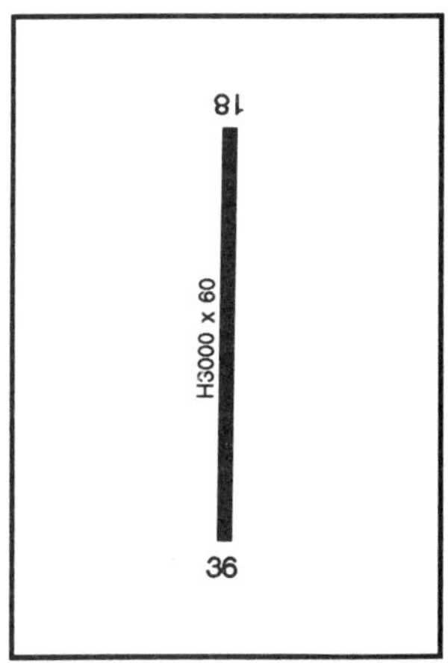

Airport Information:

TYLERTOWN - PAUL PITTMAN MEMORIAL (T36)
3 mi northwest of town N31-08.76 W90-10.09 Elev: 384 Fuel: 100LL, MOGAS Rwy 18-36: H3000x60 (Asph) Attended: continuously Unicom: 122.8
FBO: Eagle Aircraft Service Phone: 876-4953

MISSOURI

LOCATION MAP

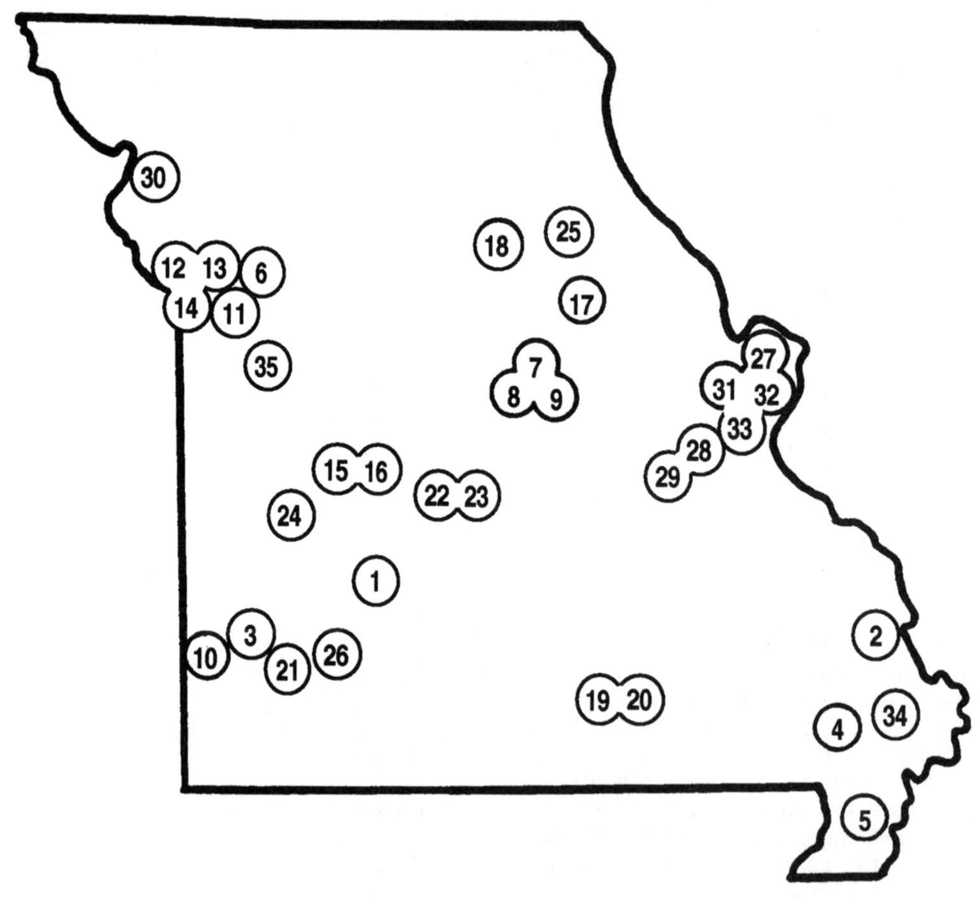

Not to be used for navigational purposes

MISSOURI

CROSS FILE INDEX

Location Number	City or Town	Airport Name And Identifier	Name of Attraction
1	Buffalo	Buffalo Muni. Arpt. (H17)	Maple Street Grill
2	Cape Girardeau	Cape Girardeau Muni. Arpt. (CGI)	Woodards Reg. Diner
3	Carthage	Myers Park Mem. Muni. (H20)	Golden Corral
4	Dexter	Dexter Muni. Arpt. (DXE)	Airways Cafe
5	Hayti	Mid Continent Arpt. (M28)	Pizza Hut
6	Independence	Independence Mem. Arpt. (3IP)	Mrs. A's Country Kitchen
7	Jefferson City	Jefferson City Mem. Arpt. (JEF)	Binghams Restaurant
8	Jefferson City	Jefferson City Mem. Arpt. (JEF)	Carnegie's At The Plaza
9	Jefferson City	Jefferson City Mem. Arpt. (JEF)	Tremains Arpt. Cafe
10	Joplin	Joplin Reg. Arpt. (JLN)	Hunt's Bar-B-Q Rest.
11	Kansas City	Kansas City Downtown Arpt. (MKC)	Savoy Grill
12	Kansas City	Kansas City Intl. (MCI)	Deli & More
13	Kansas City	Kansas City Intl. (MCI)	Final Approach Pub
14	Kansas City	Kansas City Intl. (MCI)	King's Wharf Restaurant
15	Lincoln	Lincoln Muni. Arpt. (MO11)	Bradleys Ribs, Stks
16	Lincoln	Lincoln Muni. Arpt. (MO11)	PaPa Joes Restaurant
17	Mexico	Mexico Mem. Arpt. (H41)	Oligschleger's Rest.
18	Moberly	Omar N. Bradley Arpt. (MBY)	Ramada Inn Moberly
19	Mountain View	Mountain View Arpt. (MNF)	Oak Street Cafe
20	Mountain View	Mountain View Arpt. (MNF)	Ron's Family Restaurant
21	Mt. Vernon	Mt. Vernon Muni. (MO20)	Runway Cafe
22	Osage Beach	Linn Creek/Grand Glaize (K15)	Kenilworth House
23	Osage Beach	Linn Creek/Grand Glaize (K15)	Peace "N" Plenty Cafe
24	Osceola	Osceola Muni. (MO24)	Cecil Pritchetts
25	Paris	Lake Village Arpt. (MU40)	Lake Village Family Rest.
26	Springfield	Springfield Reg. Arpt. (SGF)	Air Host Restaurant
27	St. Charles	St. Charles Co. Smartt (3SZ)	Mary's Restaurant
28	St. Clair	St. Clair Reg. Arpt. (K39)	Lewis Cafe
29	St. Clair	St. Clair Reg. Arpt. (K39)	Pizza Shack, Inc.
30	St. Joseph	Rosecrans Mem. Arpt. (STJ)	Crosswind Cafe
31	St. Louis	Lambert-St. Louis Intl. Arpt. (STL)	94th Aero Squadron
32	St. Louis	Lambert-St. Louis Intl. Arpt. (STL)	Gateway Ribb Cafe
33	St. Louis	Spirit of St. Louis Arpt. (SUS)	Blayneys on the Runway
34	Sikeston	Sikeston Mem. Muni. (SIK)	Lambert's Cafe
35	Warrensburg	Skyhaven Arpt. (9K4)	Fastop Mini Mart & Motel

Articles

City or town	Nearest Airport and Identifier	Name of Attraction
St. Clair, MO	St. Clair Reg. (K39)	Maramec Caverns

MO-H17 - BUFFALO
BUFFALO MUNICIPAL AIRPORT

(Area Code 417) 1

Maple Street Grill:

The Maple Street Grill is situated about 3/4 of a mile from the Buffalo Municipal Airport in Buffalo, Missouri. This family style restaurant has a lounge with a rustic decor, yet the dining room has a more contemporary appearance. The specialties of the house include a wide variety of ethnic choices as well as steaks, seafood, Mexican dishes, hickory smoked BBQ, etc. Their full menu also contains daily specials. The restaurant is open Tuesday 10 a.m. to 2 p.m. and Wednesday through Saturday 10 a.m. to 9 p.m., (Closed on Sunday and Monday). their bar is open Friday and Saturday until 1 a.m. There is courtesy transportation reported to and from the restaurant and airport. For information about the restaurant call 345-5045.

Restaurants Near Airport:

Maple Street Grill	3/4 mi	Phone: 345-5045
Oriental Restaurant	Adj Arpt	Phone: 345-2167

Lodging: Woods Motor Lodge (2 miles) 345-2345.

Meeting Rooms: None Reported

Transportation: Taxi Service: Bob's Taxi 345-8290.

Information: Springfield Convention & Visitors Bureau, 3315 East Battlefield, Springfield, MO 65804-4048, Phone: 417-881--5300 or 800-678-8766; Also Missouri Division of Tourism, 301 W High Street, Box 1055, Jefferson City, MO 65102, Phone: 314-751-4133

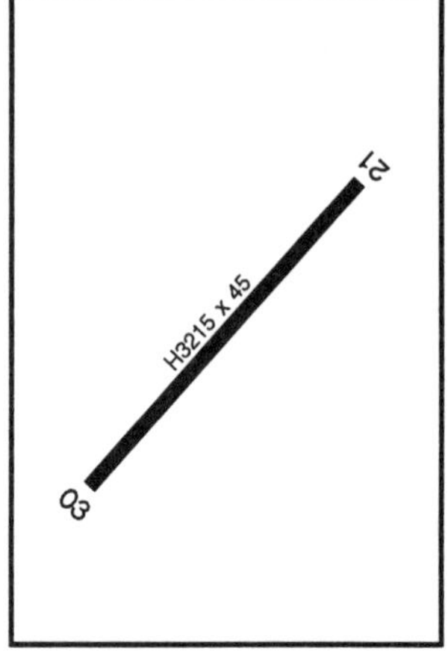

Airport Information:

BUFFALO - BUFFALO MUNICIPAL (H17)
1 mi north of town N37-39.25 W93-05.26 Elev: 1154 Rwy 03-21: H3215x45 (Asph)
Attended: Mon-Fri 1300-2200Z CTAF: 122.9
Buffalo Municipal Airport Phone: 345-8009

MO-CGI - CAPE GIRARDEAU
CAPE GIRARDEAU REGIONAL

(Area Code 573) 2

Woodards Regional Diner

The Woodards Regional Diner is located in the terminal building at the Cape Girardeau Regional Airport, near Cape Girardeau, Missouri. This restaurant has undergone a complete renovation. In-fact during our conversation with the airport management we learned that the entire terminal building complex has also been greatly improved as well. Aircraft parking is available within easy walking distance from the restaurant on the terminal ramp. While you are enjoying your meal, you are able to view the activity on the airport. The restaurant can also provide catering services for pilots, their crews and passengers. For more information call the restaurant at 651-3834.

Restaurants Near Airport:

Newmerous Restaurants	5 mi	Phone: N/A
Woodards Reg. Diner	On Site	Phone: 651-3834

Lodging: Drury Lodge 334-7151; Drury Suites 339-9500 or 800-325-8300Hampton Inn 651-3000; Holiday Inn West Park (trans) 334-4491; Victorian Inn 5 mi 651-4486; Peartree Inn 5 mi 334-3000.

Meeting Rooms: Cape Budget Inn 334-0501; Drury Lodge 334-7151; Holiday Inn 334-4491.

Transportation: Rental and Courtesy car available at FBO; Taxi Service: Yellow Cab 335-5533; Rental Cars: Hertz 335-7013; National 334-7784.

Information: Cape Girardeau Chamber of Commerce 335-3312; Cape Girardeau Convention & Visitors Bureau, 1707 Mt Auburn Road, P.O. Box 617, Cape Girardeau, MO 63701, Phone: 335-1631 or 800-777-0068.

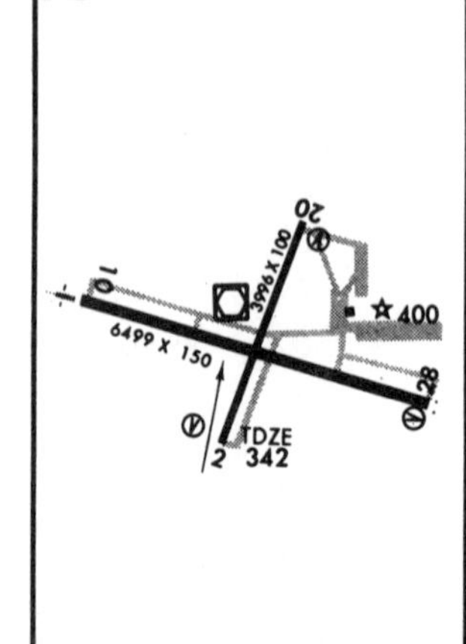

Airport Information:

CAPE GIRARDEAU, CAPE GIRARDEAU MUNI., (CGI)
5 mi southwest of town N37-13.52 W89-34.25 Elev: 342 Fuel: 100LL, Jet-A
Rwy 10-28: H6499x150 (Conc-Grvd) Rwy 02-20: H3996x100 (Asph-Conc)
Attended: Mon-Fri continuously, Sat-Sun 1200-0600Z Unicom: 122.95
Memphis Center App/Dep Con: 128.05 Tower: 119.0 Gnd Con: 121.6
FBO: Air Evac Aviation Phone: 335-6631

MO-H20 - CARTHAGE
MYERS PARK MEMORIAL MUNICIPAL

(Area Code 417)

3

Golden Corral:

Golden Corral Family Steak House is situated across the street from the Myers Park Memorial Municipal Airport next to the Feed Store. This restaurant specializes in all you can eat buffet s along with choice steaks. On weekdays they are open from 11 a.m. to 10 p.m. On weekends their breakfast buffet begins at 7 a.m. to 11 a.m. then the buffet/steak begins at 11 a.m. to 11 p.m. Choice steaks and the "Great Golden Choice Buffet" all you can eat selections is what the Golden Corral Restaurant is best known for. A variety of daily specials are also featured. Friday is their seafood buffet; Sunday they serve a country buffet. with Items like ham, turkey, meat loaf and fried chicken prepared with all the fixen's laid out for the choosing. Large fly-in groups are especially welcome and can be accommodated with ease. Average prices run $4.69 for breakfast, $4.99 for lunch and $5.99 for dinner. According to the restaurant management, we learned that some pilots actually taxi their aircraft across the street from the airport over to the feed store parking lot and walk the short distance to the restaurant. The restaurant warns that vigilance must be particularly observed when taxiing across the street. This practice may or may not be the approved procedure. We suggest that before you taxi over, please make sure this is appropriate and safe. For more information about this popular restaurant call the Golden Corral at 358-1838.

Restaurants Near Airport:

Golden Corrral	Adj Arpt.	Phone: 358-1838
Hardee's	Adj Arpt.	Phone: 358-4759
Wendy's	Adj Arpt.	Phone: 358-1414

Lodging: Econo Lodge 358-3900; Stratford House Inn (adj arpt) 358-2499; Guest Home 3 mi 358-4077.
Meeting Rooms: Econo Lodge 358-3900; Stratford House Inn (adj arpt) 358-2499; Golden Corral can also accommodate groups. 358-1838.
Transportation: Rental Cars: C & C Ford 358-4037; Griffith Brothers Pontiac/GMC 358-5944. Taxi Service: 438-0850.
Informaion: Carthage Chamber of Commerce, 107 East 3rd Street, Carthage, MO 64836. Phone: 358-2373.

Attractions:

Precious Moments Chapel 4 mi has museum gardens, gift shops and cafes 358-7599; The town of Red Oak has a 1930's village including visitor center, general store, Belle Starr museum (free) country school, church, feed & seed store, saw mill and gas station. Also site of maple leaf Festival. Phone: 358-9018.

NO AIRPORT DIAGRAM AVAILABLE

Airport Information:

CARTHAGE - MYERS PARK MEMORIAL MUNICIPAL (H20)
2 mi south of town N37-08.75 W94-18.76 Elev: 1083 Fuel: 100LL, MOGAS Rwy 03-21: H3120x50 (Asph) Rwy 17-35: H2010x46 (Asph) Attended: 1400-0000Z Unicom: 122.8
FBO: Tri-State Aviation Phone: 358-3224

MO-DXE - DEXTER
DEXTER MUNICIPAL AIRPORT

(Area Code 573)

4

Airways Cafe:

Airways Cafe is located on the Dexter Municipal Airport at the north end of the runway adjacent to the taxiway. This cafe contains a pilot's lounge with TV, couch, tables and chairs. (No liquor served). The restaurant is open from 7 a.m. to 2 p.m. 6 days a week (Closed on Sunday). They specialize in home cooking, plate lunches, biscuits and gravy, pancakes, waffles, egg dishes, burgers, BLT's, ham and cheese, grilled cheese, chicken strips, ground sirloin sandwiches, and homemade pies etc. Daily plate lunches are offered. General restaurant seating can accommodate up to 58 people. Buffets for parties of 20 to 40 persons can be arranged after regular restaurant hours, and with prior arrangements. Prices for meals average $3.00 for breakfast and $4.50 for lunch. Catering is often done for the local Pilot's Club based on the field. The town has a population of approximately 12,000 people. There are a variety of sports related activities available, such as duck, goose, deer, and dove hunting, as well as fishing when in season. For more information about the restaurant call 624-4377.

Restaurants Near Airport:

Airways Cafe	On Site	Phone: 624-4377
American Steak House	5 mi NW	Phone: 624-8840
Hickory Log Restaurant	5 mi NW	Phone: 624-4950

Lodging: Dexter Inn, (4 miles) Phone: 624-7465; Hickory House Motor Inn, (8 miles) Phone: 624-3566.

Transportation: Taxi Service: Sue's Taxi 624-6607; Rental Cars: Bud Shell Ford, Phone: 624-7476; Airways Cafe within walking distance. (North end of airport)

Information: Missouri Division of Tourism, 301 West High Stret, Box 1055, Jefferson City, MO 65102, Phone: 314-751-4133. Also: Sikeston Area Chamber of Commerce, 1 Industrial Drive, Sikeston, MO 63801, Phone: 573-471-2498.

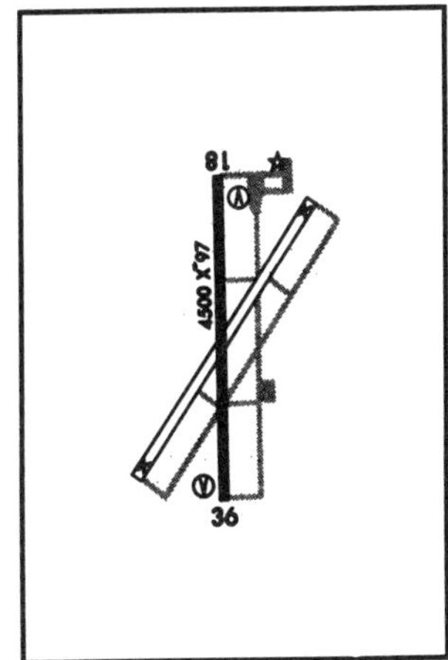

Airport Information:

DEXTER - DEXTER MUNICIPAL AIRPORT (DXE)
2 mi southeast of town N36-46.65 W89-56.47 Elev: 305 Fuel: 100LL, Jet-A
Rwy 18-36: H4500x100 (Asph-Afsc) Attended: 1400-2300Z Unicom: 122.8
Notes: Ultra light and crop dusting operations in vicinity and on airport.
FBO: Rice Aviation Phone: 624-624-1980

MO-M28 - HAYTI
MID CONTINENT AIRPORT

(Area Code 314) 5

Pizza Hut:

For those of you who enjoy the taste of freshly prepared pizza, we might recommend you plan a visit to the Pizza Hut Restaurant situated 1/2 block (Across the street) from the Mid Continent Airport located near Hayti, Missouri. They offer a nice choice of pizzas from the deep dish or thin crust variety, to a deep dish delight, guaranteed to satisfy the hardiest of appetites. This restaurant is open from 11 a.m. to 12 midnight. Sunday through Thursday and Friday and Saturday from 11 a.m. to 1 a.m. In addition to their pizza selections, their menu also includes a wide variety of other entrees as well as a salad and pasta bar. This facility is part of the popular franchise, so well known to pizza lovers all across the United States. They have just recently opened, and provide a "Sun Room" available for parties and large groups. For information call the restaurant at 359-0066.

Restaurants Near Airport:
Pizza Hut Across Street Phone: 359-0066

Lodging: Comfort Inn (1/2 block) 359-0023; Drury Inn (1 mile) 359-2702.

Meeting Rooms: None Reported

Transportation: Airport courtesy car reported; Also Taxi Service: Clyde Jones Taxi 333-2734.

Information: Missouri Division of Tourism, 301 W High St, Box 1055, Jefferson City, MO 65102, Phone: 314-751-4133

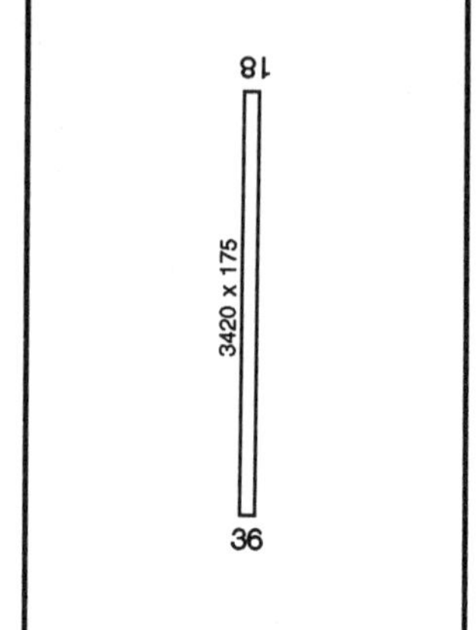

Airport Information:

HAYTI - MID CONTINENT AIRPORT (M28)
2 mi east of town N36-13.50 W89-43.67 Elev: 268 Rwy 18-36: 3420x175 (Turf)
Attended: Mon-Fri 1400-2300Z, Sat 1400-1800Z Unicom: 122.8
Notes: Crop dusting aircraft on and in vicinity of airport. Farm road crosses middle of runway.
FBO: Mid-Continent Aircraft Corp. Phone: 359-0500.

MO-3IP - INDEPENDENCE
INDEPENDENCE MEMORIAL ARPT.

(Area Code 816) 6

Mrs A's Family Restaurant:

Mrs A's Family Restaurant is located about 1/2 mile from the Independence Airport, near Independence, Missouri. The restaurant is situated in a historic two story white home that dates back 100 years, with an appearance of an country general store. According to their directions, turn left out of the Airport entrance. The dining room seats about 50 people. Their hours are Tuesday through Saturday 6 a.m. to 3 p.m. and Sunday from 7 a.m. to 3 p.m. A buffet is served Tuesday through Saturday 6 a.m. to 11 a.m. and Sunday from 7 a.m. to 12 p.m. A few of the house specialties served daily are breakfast and luncheon selections consisting of items like biscuits and gravy, omelets, roast beef sandwiches and much more. All foods are prepared from scratch along with popular freshly baked pies and cakes, which are a favorite with many of her regular customers. In addition to their main dining area they also have a private back room able to seat 35 additional people for parties or meetings. The restaurant is open 7 days a week between 6 a.m. and 3 p.m. For information call 795-8478.

Restaurants Near Airport:
Mrs A's Family Restaurant 1/2 mi Phone: 795-8478

Lodging: Howard Johnson (4 miles) 373-8856, or 800-554-2000; Ramada Inn East (4 miles) 373-8300.
Meeting Rooms: Mrs. A's Country Kitchen (On Site) has a meeting room able to accommodate up to 35 persons; Also: Howard Johnson 373-8856 or 800-554-2000; Ramada Inn East 373-8300.
Transportation: Independence Cab 461-0700; Rental Cars: Enterprise 795-8774.
Information: Independence Tourism Division, 111 East Maple, Independence, MO 64050, Phone: 836-7111.

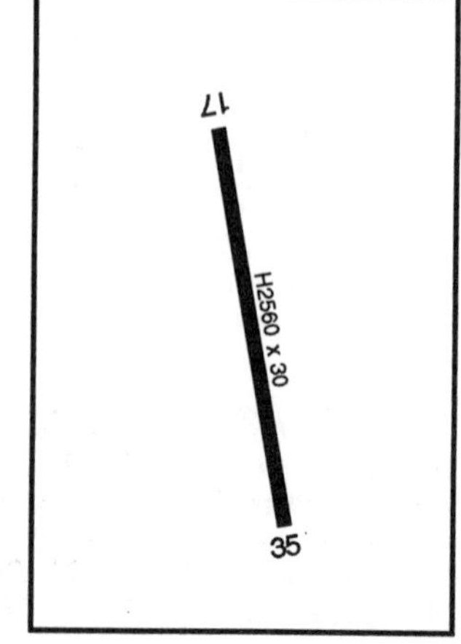

Airport Information:

INDEPENDENCE - INDEPENDENCE MEMORIAL AIRPORT (3IP)
4 mi east of town N39-04.00 W94-20.51 Elev: 756 Fuel: 100LL
Rwy 17-35: H2560x30 (Asph) Attended: 1400-0000Z Unicom: 122.8 Notes: Ultralight activity on and in vicinity of airport.
FBO: Independence Memorial Airport Phone: 795-8774

MO-JEF - JEFFERSON CITY
JEFFERSON CITY MEMORIAL ARPT.

(Area Code 573)

7, 8, 9

Binghams Restaurant:

The Country Squire Restaurant is a fine dining establishment situated 3 miles from the Jefferson City Memorial Airport in Jefferson City, Missouri. This Ramada Inn hotel and dining establishment comes complete with full service lodging, cocktail lounge, game room, fitness room and outdoor pool, in addition to the restaurant. The restaurant serves appetizers, and desserts with specialized entrees that include filets, prime rib, steak and lobster, and orange roughy. Restaurant hours are 7 a.m. to 2 p.m. and 5 p.m. to 10 p.m. weekdays. The lounge is open 11 a.m. to 1 a.m. Monday through Saturday and 12 noon through 10 p.m. on Sunday. Sunday brunch 9:30 a.m. to 2 p.m. Convention/ banquets facilities are able to accommodate 10 to 800 people. Transportation to the restaurant can be obtained by the airport through Jefferson Flying service at 636-5118 or calling the hotel and Binghams Restaurant at 635-7171.

Carnegie's At The Plaza:

Carnegie's At The Plaza Restaurant is a dinner club located approximately 1 mile from the Jefferson City Airport near Jefferson City, Missouri. This restaurant offers specialties of the house like Shrimp Ramaki, fresh Caesar Salad, Steak Diane, Lobster Thermidore, and Lobster Bisque to mention a few. Seafood is flown in twice a week to assure customers the freshest fish selections available along with aged beef cooked to perfection. To compliment your entree they furnish guests with table served tossed salads and delicious French onion soup. The restaurant is furnished with an elegant decor with double top linen covered tables. There is also a private area that can accommodate groups from 8 to 20 people. Carnegie's At The Plaza is open Monday through Saturday from 5:30 to 10 p.m. (Closed on Sunday). This restaurant has received the prestigious award of the 4 diamond rating by the American Automobile Association (AAA). Transportation is available through Jefferson Flying Service by calling 636-5118. For information or reservations call the restaurant at 636-6995 or 635-1234.

Tremains Airport Cafe:

Tremains Airport Cafe is located in the terminal building at Jefferson City Memorial Airport near Jefferson City, Missouri. The restaurant is open Monday through Friday from 5 a.m. to 4:00 p.m. and Sunday from 8 a.m. to 1:30 p.m. They are closed on Saturday. This restaurant serves appetizers, desserts, pastries, salads, complete breakfasts, seafood, steaks, plate lunches and daily specials. The decor is modern and accommodations for larger groups of 25 or more can be scheduled after regular restaurant hours. This is a family operated business with 52 years in the restaurant business. Catering is also provided for pilots requesting meals to go. Courtesy cars are available through Jefferson City Flying Service at 636-5118. For restaurant information call 635-5253.

Restaurants Near Airport:

Binghams Restaurant	3 mi	Phone: 636-7171
Carnegie's At The Plaza	1 mi	Phone: 635-1234
Tremains Airport Cafe	On Site	Phone: 635-5253

Lodging: Best Western Inn 635-4175; Holiday Inn Downtown (Trans) 636-5101; Motel 6 634-4220; Park Inn International (Trans) 636-5231; Ramada Inn (Trans) 635-7171.

Meeting Rooms: Best Western Inn 635-4175; Holiday Inn Downtown 636-5101; Park Inn International 636-5231; Ramada Inn 635-7171.

Transportation: Taxi Service: Veterans 635-0588; Yellow Cab 636-7101; Rental Cars: Hertz 635-6171.

Information: Jefferson City Area Convention & Visitors Bureau, 213 Adams Street, P.O. Box 776, Jefferson City, MO 65102, Phone: 634-3616 or 800-769-4183.

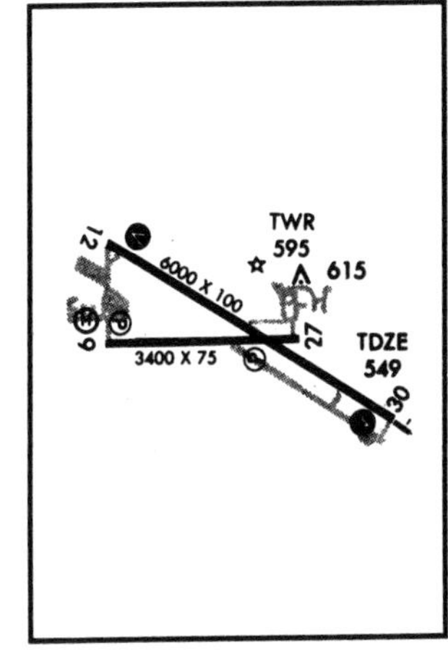

Airport Information:

JEFFERSON CITY - JEFFERSON CITY MEMORIAL AIRPORT (JEF)
2 mi northeast of town N38-35.47 W92-09.37 Elev: 549 Fuel: 100LL, Jet-A
Rwy 12-30: H6000x100 (Asph) Rwy 09-27: H3400x75 (Conc) Attended: 1230-0230Z
Unicom: 122.95 Kansas City Center App/Dep Con: 118.4 Tower: 125.6 Gnd Con: 121.7
FBO: Jefferson City Flying Service Phone: 636-5118

MO-JLN - JOPLIN
JOPLIN REGIONAL AIRPORT

(Area Code 417) 10

Hunt's Bar-B-Q Restaurant:

Hunt's Bar-B-Q Restaurant is situated 1/4th mile south of the Joplin Municipal Airport near Joplin, Missouri, and is within walking distance. Their menu specialties include Bar-B-Q beef, pork, ham, loinback ribs, Polish sausage, as well as a variety of steaks. Their desserts include popular items like peach cobbler and apple dumplings. The restaurant is open Monday to Thursday from 11 a.m. to 8 p.m., Friday and Saturday 11 a.m. to 9 p.m. (Closed on Sunday) Lunch specials are served from 11 a.m. to 2 p.m. The seating capacity of this restaurant is about 100. They take pride in the preparation of all selections on their menu. There is a senior citizen discount offered between 2 p.m. and 5 p.m., with Visa and Mastercard accepted. Courtesy transportation can be arranged either through the airport or the restaurant. The airport phone is 623-1331 and the restaurant phone is 624-3858.

Restaurants Near Airport:
Hunt's Bar-B-Q Restaurant 1/4 mi S. Phone: 624-3858

Lodging: Best Western Hallmark Inn (Trans) 624-8400; Days Inn (Trans) 623-0100; Drury Inn 781-8000; Holiday Inn (Trans) 782-1000; Ramada Inn (Trans) 781-0500; Super 8 Motel 782-8765.

Meeting Rooms: Best Western Hallmark Inn 624-8400; Days Inn 623-0100; Drury Inn 781-8000; Holiday Inn 782-1000; Ramada Inn 781-0500; Super 8 Motel 782-8765.

Transportation: Taxi Service: Taxi 624-4080; Rental Cars: Avis 624-6360; Hertz 623-6242; National 781-9080.

Information: Chamber of Commerce, 222 West 43rd Street, P.O. Box 1178, Joplin, MO 64802, Phone: 625-4789 or 800-657-2534.

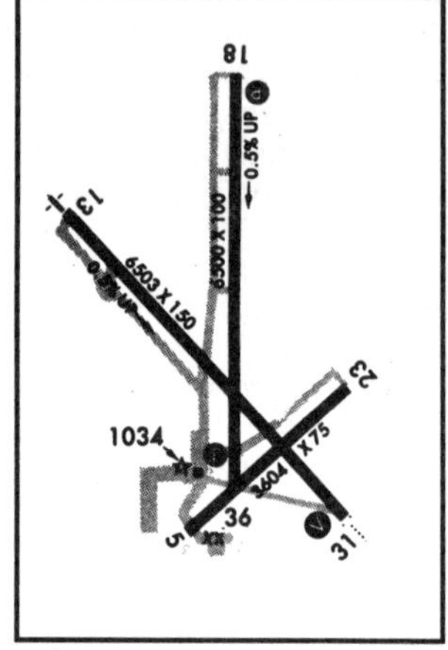

Airport Information:

JOPLIN - JOPLIN REGIONAL (JLN)
4 mi north of town N37-09.03 W94-29.90 Elev: 981 Fuel: 100LL, Jet-A
Rwy 13-31: H6503x150 (Asph-Grvd) Rwy 18-36: H5003x100 (Asph) Rwy 05-23: H3604x75 (Asph) Attended: 1100-0600Z Atis: 120.85 Unicom: 122.95 Kansas City Center App/Dep Con: 128.6 Tower: 119.8 Gnd Con: 121.6
FBO: Mizzou Aviation Phone: 623-1331

MO-MKC - KANSAS CITY
KANSAS CITY DOWNTOWN ARPT.

(Area Code 816) 11

Savoy Grill:

The Savoy Grill is a unique fine dining establishment located 1/2 mile from the Kansas City Downtown Airport. The Savoy Hotel has a turn of the century atmosphere, and contains an elegantly decorated restaurant known as the Savoy Grill. The restaurant first opened the same year the Wright Brothers made their first historic flight in 1903! This restaurant and hotel exhibits "Old World Charm" and has been visited by important political and stage personalities. The hotel exhibits a Bed & Breakfast atmosphere with antique furniture, complete with 3 different size suite accommodations. The restaurant is open Monday through Thursday from 11 a.m. to 11 p.m., Friday and Saturday from 11 a.m. to 12 a.m. and Sunday from 4 p.m. to 10 p.m. House specialties include many elegantly prepared seafood items as well as USDA prime beef selections, dry aged (min. 10 days) and cut on the premises. Average prices for a dinner selection runs about $18.00 to $20.00, with jumbo lobster for two in the neighborhood of $49.75. For a truly fine dining experience visit the Savoy Grill. In-flight catering is also available by calling the restaurant or Executive Beechcraft. Transportation is no problem and can be arranged through the FBO's. For reservations call the restaurant at 842-3890.

Restaurants Near Airport:
Savoy Grill 1/2 mi Phone: 842-3890

Lodging: Alameda Plaza 756-1500; Allis Plaza Hotel 421-6800; Embassy Suites 756-1720; Hyatt Regency 421-1234; Marriott Plaza 531-3000; Raphael Hotel 756-3800; Westin Crown Center 474-4400.
Meeting Rooms: Alameda Plaza 756-1500; Allis Plaza Hotel 421-6800; Embassy Suites 756-1720; Hyatt Regency 421-1234; Marriott Plaza 531-3000; Westin Crown Center 474-4400.
Transportation: Courtesy car reported by FBO's; Taxi Service: Carey Limousine Service 587-4077; Community 474-7474; Northland 741-8300; Yellow 471-5000; Rental Cars: Enterprise 842-8484.
Information: Kansas City Convention & Visitors Bureau, 1100 Main Street, Suite 2550, Kansas City, MO 64105, Phone: 221-5242 or 800-767-7700.

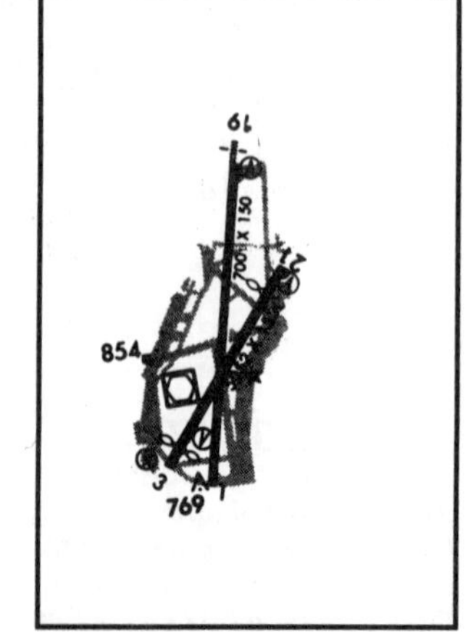

Airport Information:

KANSAS CITY - KANSAS CITY DOWNTOWN (MKC)
0 mi northwest of town N39-07.39 W94-35.56 Elev: 759 Fuel: 100LL, Jet-A
Rwy 01-19: H7001x150 (Asph-Conc-Grvd) Rwy 03-21: H5052x150 (Asph-Grvd)
Attended: continuously Atis: 120.75 Unicom: 122.95 App/Dep: 119.0
Downtown Tower: 133.3 Gnd Con: 121.9 Clnc Del: 118.45 Pre-Taxi Clnc: 118.45
FBO: Baker Flying Service Phone: 221-6677
FBO: Executive Beechcraft, Inc. Phone: 842-8484

MO-MCI - KANSAS CITY
KANSAS CITY INTERNATIONAL

(Area Code 816) 12, 13, 14

Deli & More:

Together the Deli & More and the Final Approach Pub are two facilities that cater to the flying cliental. According to the menu's the Deli & More specializes in catered meals to corporate business pilots. They have a special menu that lists a huge selection of food trays available. They can make small, medium and large trays. Some of these trays include vegetable, fresh fruit, all meat, and cheese trays, pre-made sandwiches, Ramona's Homemade Salad platters, bagel & cream cheese, dessert trays, brownie/cookie combo trays, 2 foot deli subs, and their famous box lunches. Average prices run $12.00 to $30.00 for small trays, $15.00 to $40.00 for medium trays and between $25.00 to $60.00 for large trays. In addition to their selections listed above they also provide hot dishes including BBQ beef or ham, baked beans, soups, chili, meatballs, chicken wings etc. Hours are from 9 a.m. to 5 p.m. For more information about the catering menu call 891-8826.

Final Approach Pub:

The Final Approach Pub combines the entree selection that the Deli & More catering operation provides plus much more. Both operations are operated under the same management. The Final Approach Pub is located 4 miles south along I-29 near the Tiffany Springs Parkway Exit. Restaurant hours are Monday, Tuesday and Saturday from 11 a.m. to 1:30 p.m. and Wednesday through Friday from 11 a.m. to 3 a.m. The decor of the pub is decorated with lots of airline memorabilia including original airline seats at the bar along with many other aviation related items on display throughout the restaurant. Their menu has a very wide selection of appetizers. Hot wings, nachos, mozzarella sticks, homemade soups, salads, as well as a nice selection of sandwiches and freshly baked bakery goods. Average prices run around $5.00 for many selections. To reach this establishment, you many choose to take the free shuttle to the Embassy Suites Hotel and walk the short distance across from the hotel to the pub. For more information you can call the Final Approach Pub at 891-9431.

Restaurants Near Airport:

Deli & More	4 mi S.	Phone: 891-8826
Final Approach Pub	4 mi S.	Phone: 891-9131
King's Wharf Rest.	On Site	Phone: 464-2200

Lodging: Best Western Airport Inn (Trans) 464-2300; Best Western Country Inn 464-2002; Clubhouse Inn 2 mi 464-2423; Comfort Inn-Airport 431-5430; Econo Lodge KCI (Trans) 464-5082; Embassy Suites 1-2 mi 891-7788; Hampton Inn KCI (Trans) 464-5454; Hilton Airport Plaza (Trans) 891-8900; Holiday Inn Intl Airport (Trans) 464-2345; Hyatt Regency Crown Center 421-1234; Marriott KCI Airport (2 mi Trans) 464-2200; Ramada Hotel & Conf. Cntr. 741-9500; Residence Inn (Trans) 891-9009;

Meeting Rooms: Most lodging facilities listed above have accommodations for conferences and meetings. Embassy Suites (1-2 mi. Convention facilities) 891-7788;

Transportation: Taxi Service: Available at airport; Rental Cars: Alamo 464-5151; Avis 243-5760; Blue Springs Ford 464-2100; Budget 243-5756; Dollar 243-5600; Enterprise Leasing 383-1515; Hertz 243-5765; National 243-5770; Thrifty 464-5670.

Information: Kansas City Convention & Visitors Bureau, 1100 Main Street, Suite 2550, Kansas City, MO 64105, Phone: 221-5242 or 800-767-7700.

King's Wharf Restaurant:

King's Wharf Restaurant and the Windjammer Lounge are located in the Marriott Hotel, which is located on the grounds of the Kansas City International Airport. Complimentary shuttle service in available and is just a quick 3 minutes away from the hotel. This restaurant features family style dining and has prime rib, steak, and salmon as the specialties of the house. Breakfast and lunch buffets are offered Monday through Saturday. Their Lakeview breakfast buffet is $7.95 per person, 7 days a week, and the lunch buffet is $6.95 per person and is served Monday through Saturday. The King's Wharf features a fabulous Sunday Brunch. The dining room offers a spectacular view overlooking their beautiful 55 acre lake. This establishment is open from 6:30 a.m. until 11:00 p.m. daily. The Windjammer Lounge is open from 4 p.m. until 12:30 p.m. daily. For more information, call the Marriott Hotel directory at 464-2200.

Airport Information:

KANSAS CITY - KANSAS CITY INTERNATIONAL (MCI)
15 mi northwest of town N39-17.86 W94-43.81 Elev: 1026 Fuel: 100LL, Jet-A
Rwy 01L-19R: H10800x150 (Asph-Grvd) Rwy 01R-19L: H9500x150 (Conc-Grvd) Rwy 09-27: H9500x150 (Asph-Grvd)
Attended: continuously Atis: 128.35 Unicom: 122.95 App/Dep Con: 132.95 (010-190), 124.7 (191-009) Intl Tower: 128.2, 125.75 Gnd Con: 121.8, 121.65
Clnc Del: 135.7
FBO: Executive Beechcraft, Inc. Phone: 243-6440

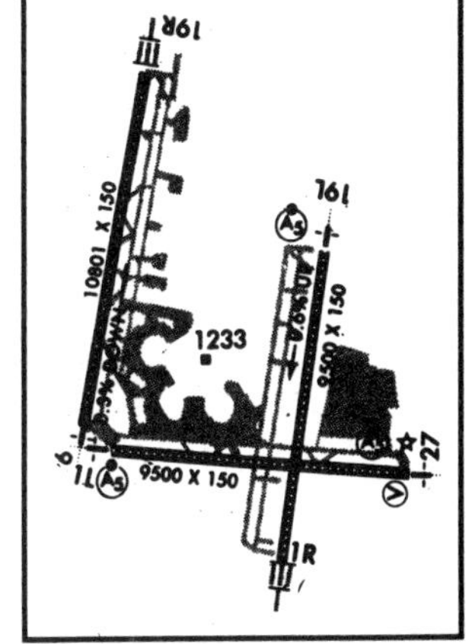

Not to be used for navigational purposes

MO-MO11 - LINCOLN
LINCOLN MUNICIPAL AIRPORT

(Area Code 816) 15, 16

Bradleys Ribs Steaks & What Nots:

Bradleys Ribs Steaks & What Nots is situated about 4 to 5 miles from the Lincoln Municipal Airport. During our conversation with the management we learned that they will provide transportation for fly-in customers. Lunch is served 11 a.m. to 2:30 p.m., and dinner from 4:30 p.m. to 9 p.m. Specialties of the house are baby-back ribs, porter house steaks and grilled chicken. On Sunday they feature a buffet with items like sliced hickory smoked ham, sliced roast beef, omelets made to order and a full salad and dessert bar. Their main dining room can seat 175 people. We were told that the restaurant dining area is divided into quadrants, one of which is their cocktail lounge providing live entertainment on Friday, Saturday and Sunday. For restaurant information call 547-2592.

PaPa Joe's Restaurant:

PaPa Joe's Restaurant is located only 1/2 mile from the Lincoln Municipal Airport. This restaurant is well known with pilots from the area. It's a friendly cafe-styled establishment able to seat 28 people in their dining room. The restaurant is open 5 a.m. to 9 p.m. Tuesday through Saturday, and Sunday 5 a.m. to 5 p.m. They are closed on Monday. You can see the restaurant from the airport located just south of the Pizza Hut restaurant. Specialties on their menu include ham served with breakfast items along with all types of sandwiches and dinner selections. Specials like their Tuesday lasagna, Wednesday meatloaf, Thursday chicken on biscuits and Friday taco salad are provided. Groups are welcome up to 28 people with advanced notice appreciated. For information call the restaurant at 547-2706.

Restaurants Near Airport:

Bradleys Ribs Stks	4 to 5 mi	Phone: 547-2592
PaPa Joe's	1/2 mi	Phone: 547-2706
Pizza Hut	1/2 mi	Phone: N/A

Lodging: Sterett Greek Resort (7 miles) 438-2821; Truman Lodge (11 miles) 438-2882.

Meeting Rooms: Rigby's Restaurant has accommodations for large or small meetings with catering services available, 547-3415.

Transportation: None reported

Information: Warsaw Area Chamber of Commerce, Box 264, 405 Van Buren, Dept. MT-90, Warsaw, MO 65355, Phone: 438-5922. Also: Missouri Division of Tourism, 301 W High Street, Box 1055, Jefferson City, MO 65102, Phone: 314-751-4133

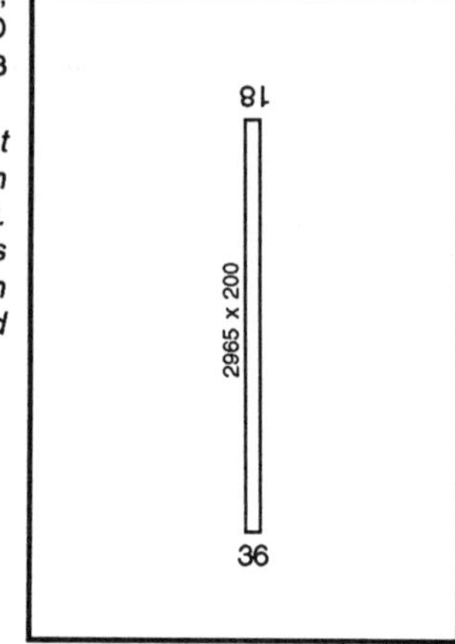

Airport Information:

LINCOLN - LINCOLN MUNICIPAL AIRPORT (MO11)
0 mi north of town N38-24.23 W93-19.98 Elev: 940 Rwy 18-36: 2931x125 (Turf)
Attended: unattended CTAF: 122.9
Lincoln Municipal Airport Phone: Unknown

MO-H41 - MEXICO
MEXICO MEMORIAL AIRPORT

(Area Code 573) 17

Oligschleger's Restaurant:

During the time of interview with Mexico Flying Service (FBO), we learned that the restaurant formerly known as C.C. Sawyers, has just re-opened under new management. Oligschleger's Restaurant is situated 1/4 mile (100 yards) from the Mexico Memorial Airport. You can see the restaurant from the airport and shouldn't have any trouble walking to it. This family style restaurant has a casual atmosphere and is open 7 days a week. Exact hours are unknown. Prices for entree selections are reasonable. Daily specials are also available. The restaurant can accommodate 40 people within their main dining room and up to 100 people in their back room for larger functions such as banquets or catered parties. For further information you can call Mexico Flying Service at 581-3305.

Restaurants Near Airport:

Oligschleger's Restaurant	1/4 mi	Phone: 581-3305

Lodging: Airpark Motel 581-2795; Best Western Stephenson 581-1440.

Meeting Rooms: C.C Sawyers Restaurant (On Site) 581-4100; Airpark Motel 581-2795; Best Western Stephenson 581-1440.

Transportation: None Reported

Information: Mexico Area Chamber of Commerce, 111A North Washington, P.O. Box 56, Mexico, MO 65265, Phone: 581-2765.

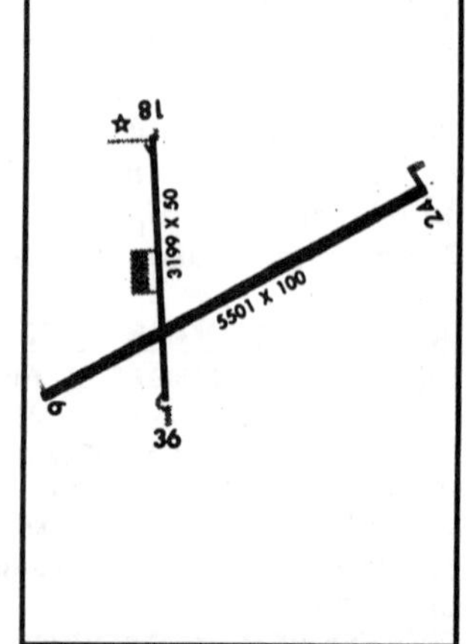

Airport Information:

MEXICO - MEXICO MEMORIAL AIRPORT (H41)
3 mi east of town N39-09.45 W91-49.10 Elev: 823 Fuel: 100LL, Jet-A, MOGAS
Rwy 06-24: H5500x100 (Conc) Rwy 18-36: H3199x50 (Asph-Conc-Afsc) Attended: Mon-Fri 1400-2300Z, Sat 1400-2100Z and Sun 1600-2100Z CTAF: 122.9
FBO: Mexico Flying Service Phone: 581-3305

MO-MBY - MOBERLY
OMAR N BRADLEY AIRPORT

(Area Code 816) 18

Ramada Inn Moberly:
The Ramada Inn Moberly Restaurant is located about 1-1/2 miles from the Omar N. Bradley Airport near Moberly, Missouri. This family style restaurant is open Monday through Sunday from 6:00 a.m. to 10 p.m. There is a lounge on the premises. Their menu contains many delicious items to choose from. They also prepare daily and nightly specials, including fresh seafood. On Monday through Friday they offer a daily lunch and dinner special, and Sunday brunch from 11:00 a.m. to 2:00 p.m. The decor of the restaurant is modern, and has accommodations for party groups of 2 to 150 people if advance notice is given. Menu items can also be prepared for carry-out. The restaurant will pick you up from the airport and take you back. For reservations or information call 263-6540.

Restaurants Near Airport:
Ramada Inn Moberly 1-1/2 mi Phone: 263-6540

Lodging: Noll Motel (Trans) 263-5000; Ramada Inn Moberly (Trans) 263-6540; Super 8 Motel (Trans) 263-8862.

Meeting Rooms: Ramada Inn Moberly 2 mi 263-6540.

Transportation: Moberly Cab Company 263-7800; Rental Cars: Moberly Motor Company 263-6000.

Information: Moberly Area Chamber of Commerce, 211 West Reed, P.O. Box 602, Dept. MT-90, Moberly, MO 65270, Phone: 263-6070

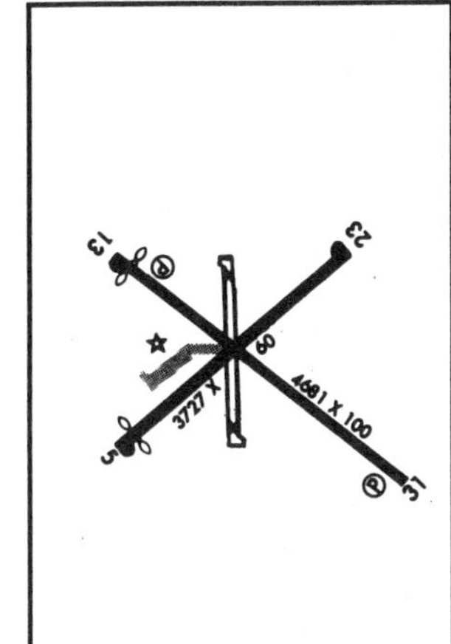

Airport Information:
MOBERLY - OMAR N BRADLEY AIRPORT (MBY)
3 mi north of town N39-27.84 W92-25.66 Elev: 867 Fuel: 100LL, Jet-A
Rwy 13-31: H4681x100 (Asph) Rwy 05-23: H3727x60 (Asph) Attended: Nov-Mar 1400-2300Z, Apr-Nov 1400-0000Z Unicom: 122.7
Airport Manager Phone: 263-4835

MO-MNF - MOUNTAIN VIEW
MOUNTAIN VIEW AIRPORT

(Area Code 417) 19, 20

Oak Street Cafe:
The Oak Street Cafe is a casual family style restaurant situated only 2 blocks from the Mountain View Airport near Mountain View, Missouri. This restaurant is open Sunday through Thursday 5:30 a.m. to 8:30 p.m., Friday and Saturday 5:30 a.m. to 9:30 p.m. Their menu contains items like steaks, catfish, burgers, and home made pie. They also have a small salad bar. Their menu contains daily specials. They also will be happy to cater to small groups. For more information call 934-6389.

Restaurants Near Airport:
Oak Street Cafe 2 blks Phone: 934-6389
Ron's Family Rest. 2-1/2 blks Phone: 934-6574

Lodging: Malone's Motel (2-1/2 blks) 934-2237; Rainbow Motel 934-2386.
Meeting Rooms: Ron's Family Restaurant is reported to have accommodations for meetings or banquets 934-6574.
Transportation: None Reported
Information: Missouri Division of Tourism, 301 West High Street, Box 1055, Jefferson City, MO 65102, Phone: 314-751-4133.

Ron's Family Restaurant:
Ron's Family Restaurant is situated about 2-1/2 blocks from the Mountain View Airport straight down a black top road on Main street, across from a local bank and adjacent to Malone's Motel. This restaurant in open Monday through Saturday from 6 a.m. to 9 p.m. and on Sunday from 6 a.m. to 2 p.m. During the winter their hours vary slightly. Specialty items on their menu include homemade pan fried chicken, a variety of soups and sandwiches, Chinese selections, Mexican foods, Italian spaghetti, along with bakery goods like oven fresh pies, cream pies, cobblers, cinnamon rolls, donuts, and much more. Daily specials are also provided. Their dining room is decorated in an old fashioned decor with wall mounted advertisements from yesteryear. Banquet facilities that can accommodate up to 60 persons are available. For more information call Ron's Family Restaurant at 934-6574.

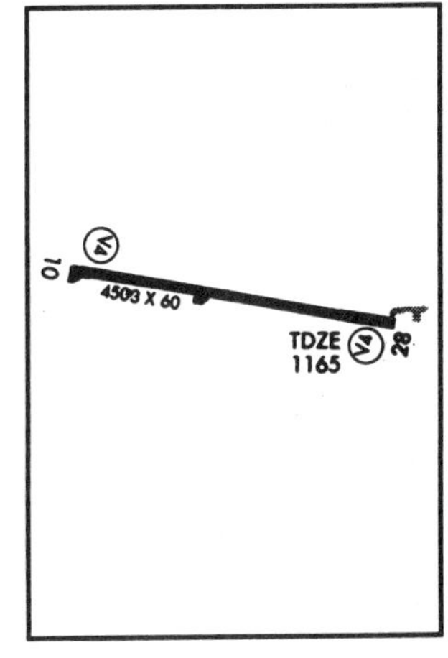

Airport Information:
MOUNTAIN VIEW, MOUNTAIN VIEW, (MNF)
1 mi southwest of town N36-59.57 W91-42.88 Elev: 1181 Fuel: 100LL, Jet-A1+, MOGAS Rwy 10-28: H4503x60 (Asph) Attended: 1400-0000Z Unicom: 122.8
FBO: Smith's Flying Service Phone: 934-6252

MO-MO20 - MT VERNON
MT VERNON MUNICIPAL

(Area Code 417) 21

Runway Cafe:

The Runway Cafe is located right on the Mt. Vernon Municipal Airport. Pilots can park their aircraft just outside the door near the main ramp where the fuel pumps are located. This cafe styled restaurant can accommodate seating for about 32 people. The Runway Cafe specializes in serving delicious breakfasts including many other dishes like homemade biscuits and gravy, hashbrowns, chicken fried steaks, meatloaf, fried chicken, hamburgers, daily dinner specials, and homemade pies. Daily specials run around $3.75. Breakfast specials run between $1.00 to $4.00. Large windows all the way around allow for a great view of the airport parking ramp and active areas. A nice large asphalt parking ramp provides ample parking space. Restaurant hours are 7 days a week from 7 a.m. to 3 p.m. Pilot groups are always welcome. They can also prepare meals from anything off their menu to go. According to the management this restaurant may soon extend their hours so they can be open for dinner. For more information about the Runway Cafe call 466-2820.

Restaurants Near Airport:
Runway Cafe On Site Phone: 466-2820

Lodging: Best Western Bel-Aire 466-2111; Budget Host Ranch 466-2125.

Meeting Rooms: Best Western Bel-Aire 466-2111.

Transportation: Airport courtesy car available by calling 466-2820.

Information: Convention & Visitors Bureau 303 E. 3rd, P.O. Box 1355, Joplin, MO 64802. Phone: 624-0820 or 800-657-2534. Also: Springfield Convention & Visitors Bureau, 3315 E. Battlefield, Springfield, MO 65804-4048. Phone: 881-5300 or 800-678-8766.

Attractions:

Golf course located nearby.

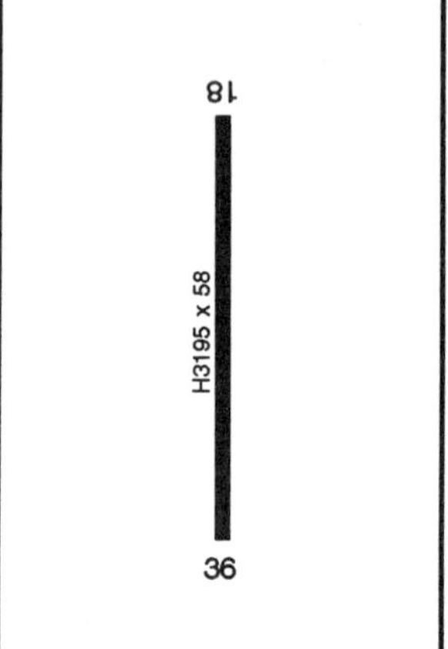

Airport Information:

MT VERNON - MT VERNON MUNICIPAL (MO20)
3 mi southwest of town N37-04.10 W93-53.10 Elev: 1244 Fuel: 100LL Rwy 18-36: H3195x58 (Asph) Attended: irregularly CTAF: 122.9
Airport Manager Phone: 466-2820

Not to be used for navigational purposes

MO-K15 - OSAGE BEACH
LINN CREEK-GRAND GLAIZE MEM

(Area Code 573) 22, 23

Kenilworth House:

The Kenilworth House is situated about 100 yards north of the Linn Creek - Grand Glaize Memorial Airport. If your landing on runway 14, you will fly right over their roof according to the restaurant manager which happens to be a pilot himself. The Kenilworth House can be considered an upscale family dining establishment. They are open 7 days a week. Tuesday through Saturday they are open from 11 a.m. to 9 p.m. and on Sunday and Monday they open for lunch only between 11 a.m. and 3 p.m. Their menu includes choice entrees ranging from soups, salads and sandwiches to prime rib and pork medallions. The decor of this restaurant is unique in that it contains many different items placed on walls and ceilings. Similar to that of a "Fridays" or "Applebee's" restaurant. The restaurant has about 9,000 square feet. 4,000 square feet of this space is used for their gift shop that contains all sorts of interesting items for purchase. In addition to the restaurant and gifts store, the Kenilworth House also provides catering and meeting space for business and social groups wishing to conduct conferences in a friendly and comfortable environment with the availability of food service. For more information about the Kenilworth House call 348-4791.

Peace "N" Plenty Cafe

The Peace "N" Plenty Cafe is located within walking distance, and is reported to be about 1/4 mile east of the Creek/Grand Glaize Memorial Airport near Osage Beach, Missouri. This restaurant is situated within a little shopping center, and offers a warm and friendly atmosphere. Their dining room is decorated with country pictures on the walls and plenty of green plants. They serve a wide variety of deli style sandwiches, salads and wonderful home made soups. They also bake fresh assorted rolls daily, which are a real favorite with many of their customers, as well as local guests around the Lake of the Ozark area. Accommodations for groups between 20 and 60 persons can be easily arranged. Average prices for most meals run between $5.00 and $7.00. Restaurant hours are 11 a.m. to 3 p.m. 7 days a week, year around, from For restaurant information call 348-1462.

Attractions:

Marriott's Tan-Tar-A Resort & Golf Club is situated about 3 miles from the Linn Creek/Grand Glaize Memorial Airport. This exclusive resort contains 365 lodging rooms, 5 swimming pools, restaurant, lounge, meeting and conference rooms, indoor and outdoor tennis, racquetball courts, marina, excursion boats, trap range, and a 27 hole pro golf course. This establishment is situated on 550 acres which makes up a peninsula overlooking the Lake of the Ozark. Free courtesy airport transportation is available by calling 348-3131.

Airport Information:

OSAGE BEACH - LINN CREEK/GRAND GLAIZE MEM (K15)
1 mi southwest of town N38-06.63 W92-40.83 Elev: 875 Fuel: 100LL Rwy 14-32: H3205x60 (Asph) Attended: 1400Z-dusk Unicom: 122.8
FBO: Air Lake Aviation Phone: 348-4469

Restaurants Near Airport:

Kenilworth House	100 yds. N	Phone: 348-4791
Peace "N" Plenty Cafe	1/4 mi	Phone: 348-1462
Tan-Tar-A Resort	3 mi	Phone: 348-3131

Lodging: Inn at Grand Glaize 3 mi 348-4731; Summerset Inn Resort 3 mi 348-5073; Tan Tar-A Hotel (Free arpt trans, 3 miles) 348-3131; Williamsburg Inn (1/4 mile) 348-2267.

Meeting Rooms: Accommodations for conferences available at Tan Tar-A Hotel (3 mi. Conventions) 348-3131; Kenilworth House 100 yrds north of the airport has meeting rooms, 348-4791; Peace "N" Plenty Cafe can arrange business and group luncheons; Summerset Inn Resort 3 mi 348-5073.

Transportation: Taxi Service: Lake Ozark Cab 365-2227; Rental Cars: Available through FBO. Call 348-2444.

Information: Lake Area Chamber of Commerce, P.O. Box 1570, Lake Ozark, MO 65049, Phone: 800-451-4117.

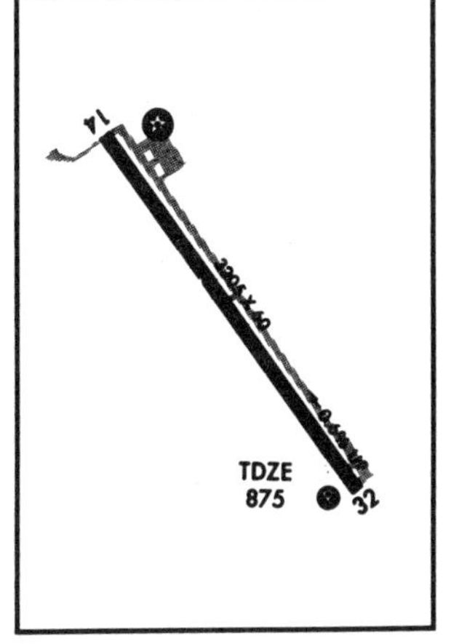

MO-MO24 - OSCEOLA
OSCEOLA MUNICIPAL

(Area Code 417) 24

Cecil Pritchetts:

Cecil Pritchetts is located 3 miles north of the Osceola Municipal Airport. This restaurant specializes in alternative game dishes. Their menu includes items like Alligator Dinner, Hawaiian Style, Rattlesnake, marinated & fried (Blue Ribbon), frog leg dinner, quail dinner served with pecan honey sauce, pan fried rabbit, duck smoked boneless breast, venison in curry sauce, black bear steak, mountain lion steak, zebra steak, and ostrich to mention a few. Combination platters are also available along with smoked sausage dinners, exotic soups and chili. In addition to these exotic dishes, Cecil Pritchetts also provides traditional selections like flame broiled steak, broasted chicken, prime rib aujus and seafood. Average prices range from $10.00 to $30.00 for main entrees and between $19.00 and $25.00 for combination dishes. Individual sandwiches run around $4.00 to $6.00. The restaurant can be classified as a cafe-family style establishment that is decorated with mounted fish, a three-quarter black bear coming out of the wall and black and white zebra covered furniture. Restaurant hours are 11 a.m. to 8 p.m. Sunday through Thursday and 11 a.m. to 11 p.m. Friday and Saturday. Cecil Pritchetts restaurant has been featured on television, cable network, radio and newspapers as providing customers with friendly service and an extremely large selection of exotic wild game food. They will be glad to provide transportation for fly-in customers. Flying groups are also welcome. For information you can call the restaurant at 646-9216.

Restaurants Near Airport:

Cecil Pritchett's	3 mi N.	Phone: 646-9216
Colbys	1 mi	Phone: 646-2620
Dempsey	1 mi	Phone: 646-8988

Lodging: Old Plantation Inn (4 mi) 646-8157.

Meeting Rooms: None reported

Transportation: None reported; Cecil Pritchett's will provide transportation for their guests only, 646-9216.

Information: Springfield Convention & Visitor Bureau, 3315 E. Battlefield, MO 65804-4048. Phone: 881-5300 or 800-678-8766.

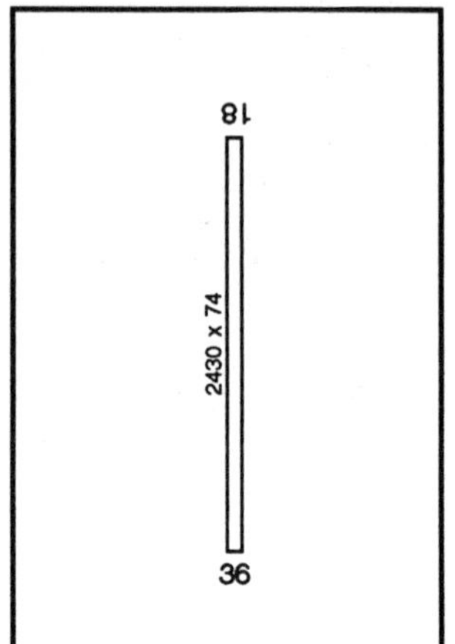

Airport Information:

OSCEOLA - OSCEOLA MUNICIPAL (MO24)

2 mi south of town N38-01.00 W93-42.01 Elev: 900 Rwy 18-36: 2430x74 (Turf-Grvl) Attended: unattended CTAF: 122.9 Notes: South end of rwy soft after rain and in spring. Large rocks and brush south of Rwy 36 thld. Rwy 18-36 25 feet wide grvl strip first 900 fee Rwy 18. See AFD for updated runway information.

Airport Manager Phone: 646-2771

MO-MU40 - PARIS
LAKE VILLAGE AIRPORT

(Area Code 816) 25

Lake Village Family Restaurant:

The Lake Village Family Restaurant is reported to be located within walking distance (1/4 mile) from the Lake Village Airport near Paris, Missouri. This restaurant serves country home cooking and a full service menu. Some of their specialties are, fried chicken, tenderloin, home made pies, and a nice salad bar. The restaurant is decorated in peach/green colors, with oak furniture. They also offer accommodations for groups of 20 or more people. This restaurant is open from 6:00 a.m. to 8:00 p.m. Monday through Thursday, Friday and Saturday 6:00 a.m. to 9:00 and Sunday 6 a.m. to 4 p.m. during the summer and closed on Monday's through the winter season. There is also a motel connected to the restaurant that contains 21 units. Transportation by way of courtesy car can be arranged through the motel. Lake Village is a private airstrip (Use at own risk) and does not have a telephone available at the airport, so we suggest if transportation is needed you call the motel or restaurant in advance and make some sort of arrangements for pick up service. For airport or restaurant information call 327-5151.

Restaurants Near Airport:

Lake Village Family Rest	1/2 to 1 mile	Phone: 327-5151

Lodging: Lake Village Motel (1/2 to 1 mile) 327-5151.

Meeting Rooms: Lake Village Motel 327-5151.

Transportation: The management at the Lake Village Restaurant or Motel will provide courtesy transportation. Notes: There is no telephone reported at airport.

Information: Mark Twain Lake & Cannon Dam Area Development Association, P.O. Box 59, Dept. MT-90, Perry, MO 63462, Phone: 314-565-2228.

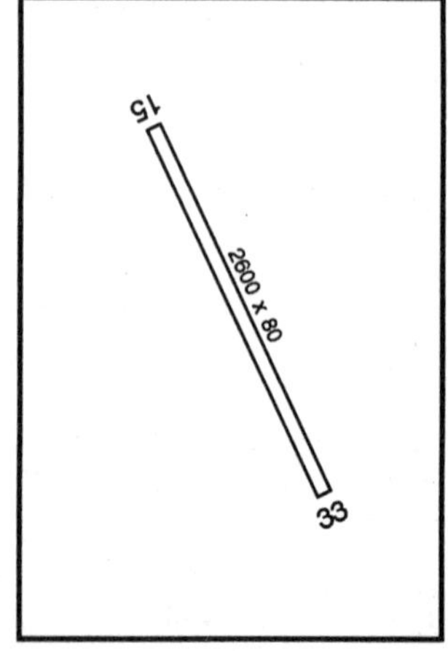

Airport Information:

PARIS - LAKE VILLAGE (MU40)

1 mi south of town N39-27-36 W92-00-36 Elev: 750 Fuel: None Reported
Rwy 15-33 2600x80 (Turf) Attended: unattended Notes: Private Airport (use at own risk).

Lake Village Airport Management Phone: 327-5151

MO-SGF - SPRINGFIELD
SPRINGFIELD/BRANSON REG. ARPT.

26

Restaurants Near Airport: (Area Code 417)

Air Host Restaurant On Site Phone: 862-7295
Lambert's Cafe (SIK) 8-10 mi Phone: 581-ROLL

Air Host Restaurant:

The Air Host Restaurant is a cafe, lounge and deli in the terminal building, located at the Springfield Regional Airport in Springfield, Missouri. The restaurant is open 7 days a week 5:30 a.m. to 7 p.m. and the deli closes at 9 p.m. Their menu includes a full line of selections with appetizers, desserts, pastries, soups and salads along with their main entrees. Catering is made available to both the airlines and the fixed base operators, offering anything from bulk sandwich trays to hot entrees. A courtesy cars is reported available to the restaurant and terminal building from the general aviation service facilities (FBO's). For airport information you can call 869-0300. For restaurant information call 862-7295.

Attractions: Bass Pro Shop is one of the largest sports related attractions in the Midwest containing a restaurant that supports a 30,000 gallon salt water aquarium, trout stream, log cabin, 4 levels of sporting goods related shops, fishing equipment, gift and art gallery, wildlife museum, and much more. This establishment is located at the southwest corner of Sunshine Street and Campbell Avenue on US Hwy 160. This attraction can easily be reached either from Springfield Regional (9 miles) or Springfield Downtown Airport (5-1/2 miles). For information call The Bass Pro Shop at 887-1915. Also Big Cedar Lodge, affiliated with the bass Pro Shop, provides 5 star accommodations. For information call 335-2777.

Lodging: Best Western Coach House (Trans) 862-0701; Big Cedar Lodge 335-2777; Days Inn (Trans) 865-5511; Holiday Inn North (Trans) 865-8000; Holiday Inn University Plaza (Trans) 864-7333; Howard Johnson Lodge (Trans) 866-6671; Quality Inn (Trans) 882-1113; Ramada Inn Hawthorne Park (Trans) 831-3131; Sheraton Inn & Conference Center (Trans) 883-6550.

Meeting Rooms: Big Cedar Lodge 335-2777; Days Inn 865-5511; Holiday Inn North 865-8000; Holiday Inn University Plaza 864-7333; Howard Johnson Lodge 866-6671; Quality Inn 882-1113; Ramada Inn Hawthorne Park 831-3131; Sheraton Inn & Conference Center 883-6550.

Transportation: Courtesy transportation reported by FBO's. and or airport authority; Also Taxi Service: Airport Limo 862-2580; Yellow Cab (On Site) 862-5511; Rental Cars: Avis 865-6226; Budget 831-2662; Hertz 865-1681; National 865-5311.

Information: Springfield Convention & Visitors Bureau, 3315 East Battlefield, MO 65804-4048; Phone: 881-5300, 800-678-8766.

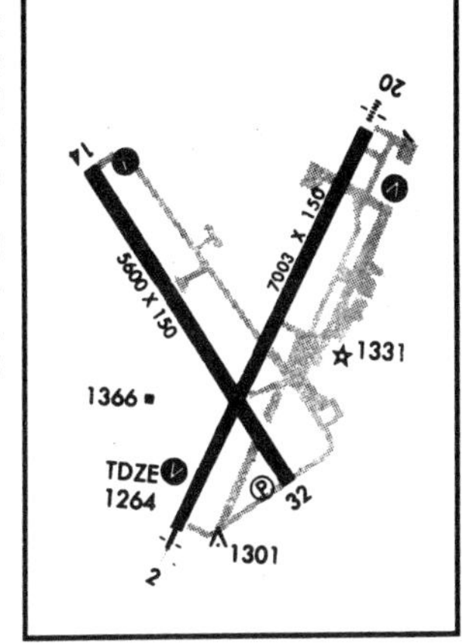

Airport Information:

SPRINGFIELD - SPRINGFIELD-BRANSON REGIONAL AIRPORT (SGF)
5 mi northwest of town N37-14.66 W93-23.21 Elev: 1267 Fuel: 100LL, Jet-A
Rwy 02-20: H7003x150 (Conc-Grvd) Rwy 14-32: H5600x150 (Asph-Pfc)
Attended: continuously Atis: 119.05 Unicom: 122.95 App/Dep Con: 124.95, 121.1
Tower: 119.9 Gnd Con: 121.9
Airport Authority Phone: 869-0300 FBO: World Wide Acrft Serv Phone: 865-1879
FBO: Pro-Flight Air Phone: 864-7229

MO-3SZ - ST CHARLES
ST CHARLES COUNTY SMARTT

27

Restaurants Near Airport: (Area Code 314)

Mary's Restaurant On Site Phone: 250-3665

Mary's Restaurant:

Mary's Restaurant is located within walking distance from aircraft parking on the St. Charles County Smartt Field, in St Charles, Missouri. This snack bar and cafe is open Tuesday through Sunday 12 p.m. to 8 p.m. during the summer season and 12 noon to 6 p.m. in the winter season. They are closed Monday. Their entrees consist of all types of hamburgers "Home of Mary's Flying Hamburgers", double chili cheese burgers, steaks, as well as many other selections like home made vegetable beef soup, chili, and pies. The restaurant is decorated with WW-II photographs and aviation related items. One interesting note is that Mary's A Frame is located next door to the Confederate Air Force Missouri Wing, Hangar & Museum. A combination visit to the museum and lunch at Mary's A Frame would make for a nice way to spend the day. The restaurant can accommodate small groups given advance notice. All items on their menu are available for carry-out. For Information call 250-3663.

Lodging: Best Western Noah's Ark (10 miles) 946-1000; Holiday Inn Saint Peters (12 miles) 928-1500; Ramada Inn Airport West (10 miles) 946-6936.

Meeting Rooms: Contact lodging facilities listed above for possible conference accommodations.

Transportation: Taxi Service: County Cab 281-8080; Saint Charles Yellow Cab 973-1236.

Information: Convention and Visitors Bureau, 230 South Main, P.O. Box 745, St. Charles, MO 63302, Phone: 946-7776 or 800-366-2427.

Attractions: The Confederate Air Force, Missouri Wing, Hangar and Museum is located right on the airport adjacent to Mary's Restaurant. Vintage WW-II aircraft are restored and rebuilt to flyable condition. Flying in to enjoy a visit at this facility along with lunch at Mary's A Frame Restaurant can be arranged for individuals or larger flying clubs and groups. For information call the Airport Manager's office at 258-3200 or the restaurant at 250-3663.

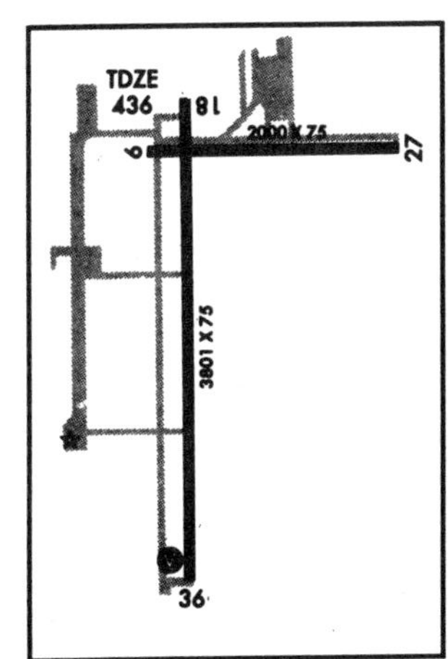

Airport Information:

ST CHARLES - ST CHARLES COUNTY SMARTT FIELD (3SZ)
9 mi northeast of town N38-55-78 W90-25.80 Elev: 436 Fuel: 80, 100LL, MOGAS Rwy 18-36: H3801x75 (Asph-Rfsc) Rwy 09-27: H2000x75 (Asph-Rfsc) Attended: 1400Z-dusk
County Tower 126.3 Gnd Con: 121.6
FBO: C.D. Aircraft Company, Inc. Phone: 250-3665

MO-K39 - ST CLAIR **(Area Code 314)** 28, 29

ST CLAIR REGIONAL AIRPORT

Lewis Cafe

Lewis Cafe is located approximately 1-1/2 miles from the Saint Clair Airport (K39). Transportation can be arranged through the airport manager who lives on the field (629-1400). This restaurant is classified as a cafe and is open from 5 a.m. to 8 p.m. Monday through Saturday and 6 a.m. to 8 p.m. Sunday and holidays. Specialties of the house include home cooked meals with "cut your own meats dishes, daily specials, made from scratch, poppyseed salad dressing and homemade pies. A smorgasbord is served on Sunday from 11 a.m. to 3:30 p.m.. The restaurant has a clean "down homes country look." Average prices run $3.25 for breakfast, $3.85 for lunch and $5.00 for dinner. Catering can also be arranged for groups. To get to the restaurant from the airport, take Hwy 47 south on to St. Clair. Cross over Commercial Street on to Main Street. (3/4 mile). Its a straight stretch from there. For information call the Lewis Cafe at 629-9975.

Pizza Shack, Inc:

The Pizza Shack Restaurant is located within 1 or 2 miles from the St Clair Regional Airport. During our conversation with the airport manager, we learned that courtesy transportation can easily be arranged to nearby facilities, for his customers. The Pizza Shack can be reached by going left (south) on Hwy 47 approx. 1/3 mile, right (West) on Hwy 44 North Service Road approx 3/4 mile to Hwy AB then turn right. Another visual clue to help you find the restaurant are two water towers that are marked "Hot" and "Cold" and can be seen, and used for visual reference when trying to find the restaurant. This family restaurant is open Sunday through Thursday from 11 a.m. to 10 p.m., Friday and Saturday from 11 a.m. to 12 a.m. Specialties of the house include pizza, steak, Mexican and Italian, including a full menu of other items. They also feature a daily soup and salad bar along with homemade desserts. A buffet is available on weekends. Prices average $5.00 for lunch and $7.00 for dinner. They serve a buffet special for only $5.25 Monday through Thursday beginning at 11 a.m. until closing, and Friday, Saturday and Sunday 4 p.m. and 8:30 p.m. for between $6.95 and $7.95. The restaurant was recently remodeled and contains a small meeting room able to seat 30 people. For information about the Pizza Shack call 629-2224.

Restaurants Near Airport:

Lewis Cafe	1-1/2 mi	Phone: 629-9975
Maramec Cavern	15 minutes	Phone: 468-3166
Pizza Shack, Inc.	1-2 mi SW	Phone: 629-2224

Lodging: Arch Motel (3 miles) 629-3030; Budget Motel (1 mile) 629-1000; Super 8 (1 mile) 629-8080.

Meeting Rooms: Unknown. Call airport manager's office at 629-1400 or contact lodging facilities listed above.

Transportation: The airport manager stated that he could provide customers with courtesy transportation to nearby facilities. Also to nearby attractions for minimal fee. For information call 629-1400; Taxi Service: Shorty's 629-1276.

Information: St Louis Convention & Visitors Commission, 10 South Broadway, Suite 1000, St Louis, MO 63102, Phone: 421-1023 or 800-325-7962.

Attractions:

The airport manager lives on the airport and will be happy to arrange courtesy transportation to local facilities or to nearby attractions for a nominal fee. Meramec Cavern is located only 15 minutes by automobile from the St Clair Regional Airport. Six Flags amusment park is only 25 minutes away. Please let the airport manager know you are coming in advance by calling 629-1400. The attractions near this airport as well as the restaurants in nearby St. Clair would make a nice place to plan a group fly-in or association get-together.

Airport Information:

ST CLAIR - ST CLAIR REGIONAL AIRPORT (K39)
2 mi north of town N38-22.47 W90-58.36 Elev: 654 Fuel: 100LL
Rwy 02-20: H3200x60 (Asph-Rfsc) Attended: continuously Unicom: 122.8
St Clair Regional Airport Phone: 629-1400

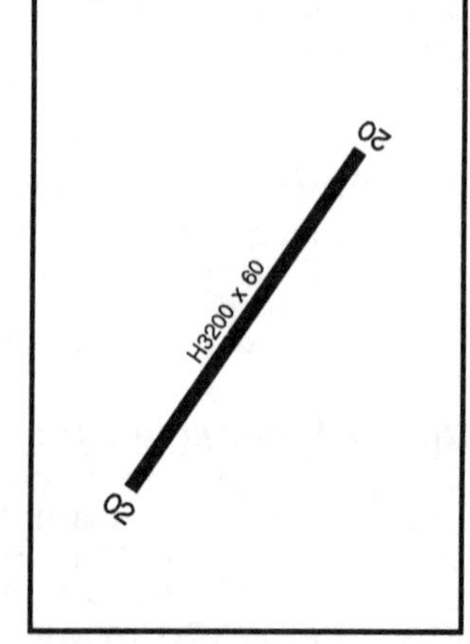

Maramec Caverns

St. Clair, MO (MO-K39)
(Information obtained by Maramec Caverns)

This attraction is one of the most spectacular underground exhibits in the midwest and is only a 15 minute drive from the St. Clair Airport in St. Clair, MO. Beneath the fertile rolling hills of the Meramec Valley, lies a complex of mineral formations color as rare and unique as they are beautiful. These jewels of nature which took millions of years to grow are preserved in the spectacular sights of Meramec Caverns. Guided tours by trained rangers are conducted along well-lighted concrete walkways. All cavern facilities are accessible to the handicapped.

The history of Meramec Caverns is rich with the treasures of time. Going back through the centuries, the Indians revered the cave as the home of their God. An 18th century French miner, Jacques Renault, found the cavern's greatest natural resource, saltpeter, which is used in the manufacture of gunpowder. During the Civil War a federal powder mill in the cave was blown up by Confederate guerrillas of whom Jesse James was a member. Spanish lead miners used the cave as did slaves who were sheltered there as part of the "Underground Railroad." In 1933, Lester B. Dill noted caveoligist, discovered upper levels of the caverns. Further exploration revealed 26 miles of underground passages. Meramec Caverns was opened to the public, as a tourist attraction in 1935. The Stage Curtain, the largest single cave formation in the world, is the crown jewel of Meramec Caverns. This magnificent mineral deposit which measures 70 feet high, 60 feet wide and 35 feet thick is called America's number one cave scene, and estimated to be 70 million years old. The Stage Curtain is the focal point of a dramatic light and musical presentation which climaxes an informative cavern tour.

Accommodations:

Comfortable lodgings are provided at the Meramec Caverns Motel which is AAA approved. Modern units come with television, air-conditioning and electric heat. For reservations call 314-468-4215. The motel and campgrounds are open April through October. A unique gift shop as well as a large restaurant and snack area are conveniently located in the cavern. Meramec Caverns Natural Park holds a cache of scenic beauty and conveniences for visitors. Numerous trees shade the picnic area and riverfront campgrounds where trailer hookups, showers and restrooms, sheltered pavilions, barbecue pits and a concession stand are located. Canoe rentals are also available in season. The cavern is open every day except Thanksgiving and Christmas: March 9 a.m. to 5 p.m.; April 9 a.m. to 6 p.m.; May and June 9 a.m. to 7 p.m.; July through Labor Day 8:30 a.m. to 7:30 p.m.; September 9 a.m. to 6 p.m.; October 9 a.m. to 5 p.m. and November and December from 9 a.m. to 4 p.m. For additional information about accommodations or group tours call the Park office at 314-468-3166. For transportation to the Meramec Caverns call Frank and Billie Pobanz (Airport Manager) at 314-629-1400. Please give them some advance notice so they can make their van available for you.

MO-STJ - ST JOSEPH ROSECRANS MEMORIAL AIRPORT

(Area Code 816) 30

Crosswind Cafe:

The Cockpit Restaurant is situated in the terminal building on the Rosecrans Memorial Airport. This restaurant can be reached by parking your aircraft and walking just 25 feet to their door. The Restaurant is open from 5:30 a.m. to 8:30 p.m. Monday through Thursday, 5:30 until 10 p.m. on Friday and Saturday, and on Sunday from 7 a.m. to 3 p.m. Specialty entrees include the "Single Engine" hamburger, the "Fire Engine Express" with spiced barbecued beef on a bun, the "Piper" turkey club, their "Navaho" hot beef plate with potatoes and gravy, and many other unique selections. They also feature a luncheon buffet that runs Monday through Friday between 11 a.m. and 2 p.m. Their main dining room can accommodate up to 70 people. The totally remodeled restaurant is decorated with aircraft pictures, and aviation related items. The Cockpit Restaurant can serve large or small groups and also specializes in providing in-flight catering for private or corporate pilots on the go. For information you can call this establishment at 364-0319.

Restaurants Near Airport:
Crosswind Cafe — Trml. Bldg. — Phone: 364-0319

Lodging: Best Western Seville Inn 232-2311; Drury Inn 364-4700; Holiday Inn Downtown 279-8000; Ramada Inn 233-6192; Super 8 Motel 364-3031.

Meeting Rooms: Drury Inn 364-4700; Holiday Inn Downtown 279-8000; Ramada Inn 233-6192; Super 8 Motel 364-3031.

Transportation: Taxi Service: Yellow Cab 279-2777.

Information: Chamber of Commerce, 109 South 4th Street, St. Joseph, MO 64502, Phone: 233-6688 or 800-785-0360.

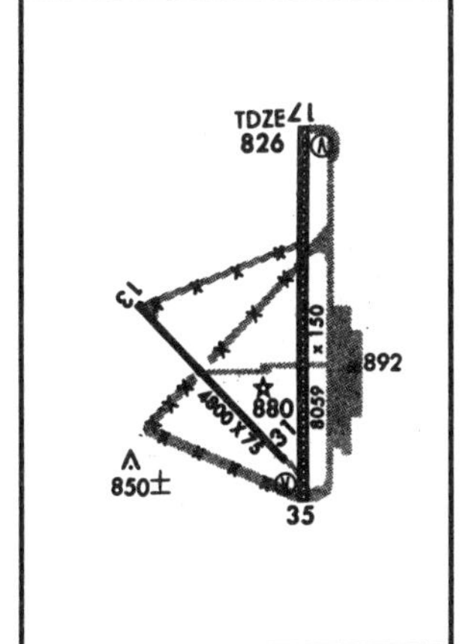

Airport Information:

ST JOSEPH - ROSECRANS MEMORIAL AIRPORT (STJ)
3 mi northwest of town   N39-46.32 W94-54.58   Elev: 826   Fuel: 100LL, Jet-A
Rwy 17-35: H8059x150 (Conc-Grvd)   Rwy 13-31: H4800x75 (Conc)   Attended: 1300-0100Z   Atis: 125.05   Unicom: 122.95   St Joseph Tower: 126.9   Gnd Con: 121.9
FBO: Express Flight, Inc.   Phone: 233-3444

MO-STL - ST LOUIS
LAMBERT-ST LOUIS INTL ARPT.

(Area Code 314) 31, 32

94th Aero Squadron:

The 94th Aero Squadron located on St Louis Lambert International Airport is a very popular restaurant that is conveniently located only a few hundred feet and across the parking lot from Midcoast Aviation, Inc. (FBO). This unique establishment is one of several aviation theme restaurants situated across the country that depicts an old French farm house positioned near the battle front during the great conflict or World War One. The front of the restaurant has cannons, and strategically placed sand bags near the main entrance, along with many fascinating artifacts, photographs and aircraft memorabilia within their dining area itself. The view from their main dining room looks out over the airport and active runway situated only 100 yards from the restaurant. Seating capacity for the 94th is about 250 persons in addition to a patio lounge and a comfortable "Cabaret Lounge" that serves cocktails and assorted beverages. Head phones can be used by their customers to listen to the actual transmissions and conversation between the tower and arriving and departing aircraft. Specialties of the house include prime rib, a fine selection of hand cut steaks, filets and strip steaks. In addition, they also serve delicious chicken dishes, veal chops along with their famous, freshly prepared beer cheese and French onion soup. Average dinner prices run between $14.95 and $19.95. Accommodations for banquets and catered luncheons can also be arranged if advance notice is given. Due to easy access from Midcoast Aviation, this restaurant is frequently used as a destination for fly-in clubs and aviation organizations. Dinner hours are 4:30 p.m. to 10 p.m. on Mondays, Tuesday Wednesday and Thursday from 4:30 p.m. until 11 p.m., Friday and Saturday from 4:30 p.m. to 12 midnight and Sunday from 4 p.m. to 10 p.m. For lunch they are open Monday through Saturday between 11 a.m. and 3 p.m. On Sunday they feature a brunch between 9:30 a.m. and 2 p.m. for only $11.95. For information about the 94th Aero Squadron at Lambert St Louis Intl. Airport call the restaurant at 731-3300.

Restaurants Near Airport:

94th Aero Squadron Rest.	On Site	Phone: 731-3300
Gatway Rib Cafe (Host Intl.)	On Site	Phone: 429-3400
Hangar Restaurant (Marriott)	1/8 mi	Phone: 423-9700

Lodging: Best Western Exec Intl. Inn (Trans) 731-3800; Breckenridge Lambert Hotel (Trans) 427-7600; Drury Inn Airport (Trans) 423-7700; Hilton St Louis Airport (Trans) 426-5500; Holiday Inn North (Trans) 731-2100; Marriott Airport (Trans) 423-9700; Northwest Inn (Trans) 291-4940; Oakland Park (Trans) 427-4700; Ramada Inn (Trans) 426-4700; Rodeway Inn Airport (Trans) 427-5955; Stouffer Concourse Hotel (Trans) 429-1100.

Meeting Rooms: All Lodging facilities listed above are reported to have accommodations for meetings.

Transportation: Taxi Service: Airport Limousine 429-4940; Carey Limousine 946-4114; Taxi Stater 427-0951; Rental Cars: Avis 426-7766; Budget 423-3000; Dollar 423-4004; Hertz 426-7555; National 426-6272.

Information: St Louis Convention & Visitors Commission, 10 South Broadway, Suite 1000, St Louis, MO 63102, Phone: 421-1023 or 800-325-7962; Also 24 hour tourist information call 421-2100. For public transportation call Bi-State Transit at 231-2345.

Gateway Ribb Cafe (Host Intl.):

The Host Intl.-Gateway Ribb Cafe Restaurant is located on Lambert Field in St. Louis, Missouri. There are approximately 31 different customer service facilities situated within the terminal, offering passengers and travelers, accommodations from unique shops and lounges to restaurants providing anything from lighter fare to a complete dining experience, all under the management of Host International. One of the restaurants called the Gateway Ribb Cafe, features gourmet dining. This beautifully decorated and elegant restaurant offers a wide selection of delicious and carefully prepared gourmet meals. The restaurant is open 11 a.m. to 8:00 p.m. 7 days a week. There is also a lounge called the "Cheers Bar" that is a reproduction of the famous television series, located past concourse C & D. This establishment also serves a variety of sandwiches and lighter fare. Transportation can be arranged through the fixed based operators on the field. For reservations and restaurant information call 429-3400.

Airport Information:

ST. LOUIS - LAMBERT-ST LOUIS INTERNATIONAL AIRPORT (STL)
10 mi northwest of town N38-44.86 W90-21.60 Elev: 605 Fuel: 100LL, Jet-A
Rwy 12R-30L: H11019x200 (Conc-Grvd) Rwy 12L-30R: H9003x150 (Conc-Grvd)
Rwy 06-24: H7602x150 (Conc-Grvd) Rwy 13-31: H6286x75 (Asph) Rwy 17-35: H2878x75 (Asph) Attended: continuously Atis: 119.925 Unicom: 122.95
St Louis App Con: 126.5, 125.15, 123.7, 120.05 St Louis Dep Con: 118.95, 119.15, 124.9, 119.75, 120.05 St Louis Tower: 118.5 (South) 120.05 (North) 120.05 (0500-1200Z)
Gnd Con: 121.9, 121.65 Clnc Del: 119.5 Pre-Taxi Clnc: 119.5
FBO: Airport Terminal Services Phone: 731-0400
FBO: Flight Safety Intl Phone: 731-2040
FBO: Midcoast Aviation, Inc. Phone: 731-1915

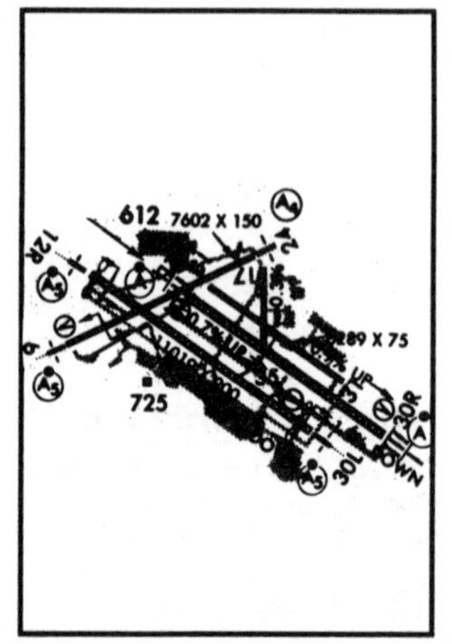

Not to be used for navigational purposes

MO-SUS - ST LOUIS
SPIRIT OF ST LOUIS AIRPORT

33

Blayneys On The Runway:

Blayneys on the Runway is a restaurant that is located on the Spirit of St Louis Airport in Chesterfield, Missouri. When flying in to visit the restaurant, you can taxi right up to the back door. Guests can enjoy a meal while watching the aircraft arriving and departing. Seating capacity is around 50 with additional accommodations for groups up to 150 persons. The restaurant is open from 11 a.m. to 9 p.m. Monday through Saturday and Sunday from 12 p.m. to 9 p.m. They offer a full service menu including selections from hamburgers to steaks, sandwiches, appetizers, and a variety of daily specials. Prices range from $5.00 to $11.00 for most main course meals. The decor of the restaurant is rustic with two wood burning fireplaces creating a warm comfortable atmosphere. For information about the restaurant call 532-7245.

(Area Code 314)

Restaurants Near Airport:
Blayneys On The Rwy   On Site   Phone: 532-7245

Lodging: Breckenridge Frontenac (Trans) 993-1100; Doubletree Hotel & Conference Center (Trans) 532-5000; Holiday Inn St Peters (Trans) 928-1500; Ramada Inn Westport (Trans) 878-1400; Residence Inn (Trans) 537-1444; Sheraton Plaza Hotel (Trans) 434-5010;
Meeting Rooms: On airport conference room facilities can be obtained through the airport administration by calling 532-2222; Also: All lodging establishments listed above have meeting room accommodations.
Transportation: Taxi Service: Carey Limousine Service 949-4114; Chesterfield Cab 537-9330; Rental Cars: Budget 532-0234.
Information: St Louis Convention & Visitors Commission, 10 South Broadway, Suite 1000, St Louis, MO 63102, Phone: 421-1023 or 800-325-7962; Also 24 hour tourist information call 421-2100. For public transportation call Bi-State Transit at 231-2345.

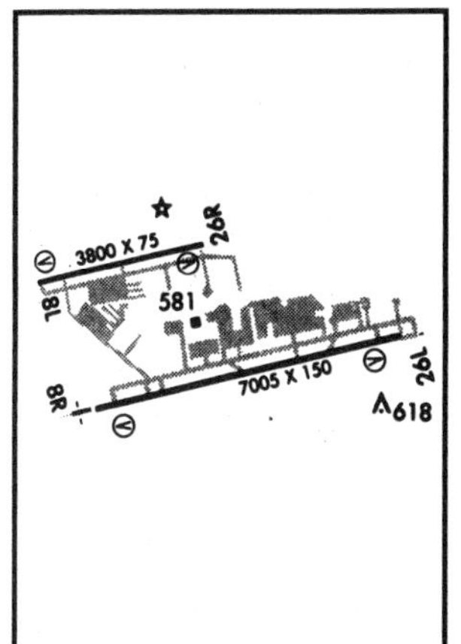

Airport Information:

ST LOUIS - SPIRIT OF ST LOUIS AIRPORT (SUS)
17 mi west of town   N38-39.71 W90-39.07   Elev: 463   Fuel: 100LL, Jet-A
Rwy 08R-26L: H7005x150 (Asph-Rfsc)   Rwy 08L-26R: H3800x75 (Asph-Rfsc)
Attended: continuously   Atis: 134.8   Unicom: 122.95   St Louis App/Dep Con: 126.7   Spirit Tower: 124.75   Gnd Con: 121.7   Clnc Del: 133.1, 121.7 (when twr clsd)   Notes: Spirit of St Louis Airport Administration provides lighted and fenced ramp parking with 24 hour security, pilots lounge, conference room, rental cars and additional pilot services 532-2222.
Airport Admin.   Phone: 532-2222   FBO: Million Air St. Louis   Phone: 532-0404
FBO: Exec. Beechcraft STJ   Phone: 532-4800   FBO: Phoenix viation   Phone: 532-9200

MO-SIK - SIKESTON
SIKESTON MEM MUNICIPAL

34

Lambert's Cafe

Lambert's Cafe is located about 1 mile east of the Sikeston Municipal Airport. The restaurant provides a festive atmosphere with scores of floating balloons, and by musical sounds of Danny Davis an the Nashville Brass. Specialties of the house include poultry, beef, seafood, homemade Okra, white beans and coleslaw . This facility prepares huge quantities of food throughout the year. 211,650 lbs of chicken breasts, 335,400 eggs, 40, 341 lbs of fish and seafood, and 110,619 lbs of choice round beef. However what their most famous for is their "Throwed Rolls". Every week they bake over 2,400 of the biggest, tastiest cinnamon rolls that ever passed your lips. They are so large that they are nicknamed "Hubcaps". Lambert's Cafe is very popular with many fly-in customers. They also have a van that will pick up fly-in guests. For information call the restaurant at 471-4261.

(Area Code 314)

Restaurants Near Airport:

Bo's Pit Bar-B-Que	1 blk	Phone: 471-9927
Lambert's Cafe	1-1/2 mi (free trans)	Phone: 471-4261
Mazzio's Pizza	1 blk	Phone: 471-7120
Mc Donalds	4 blks	Phone: 471-2146
Subway	1 blk	Phone: 472-1033
Taco Bell	1 blk	Phone: 472-4114

Lodging: Best Western 3 mi 4712270; Drury Inn 2 mi 471-8660; Hampton Inn 3-1/2 mi 471-3930; Sikeston Inn 471-4700; Super 8, 2 mi 471-7944.
Meeting Rooms: None Reported
Transportation: Courtesy car reported; Taxi Service: City Cab 471-0685; Friendly Cab 471-0220; Jolly Cab 471-0727; Yellow 471-3422; Rental Cars: Airport managers office can help obtain a rental car by calling 471-9056
Information: Sikeston Area Chamber of Commerce, 1 industrial Drive, P.O. Box 99, Sikeston, MO 63801. Phone: 471-2498.

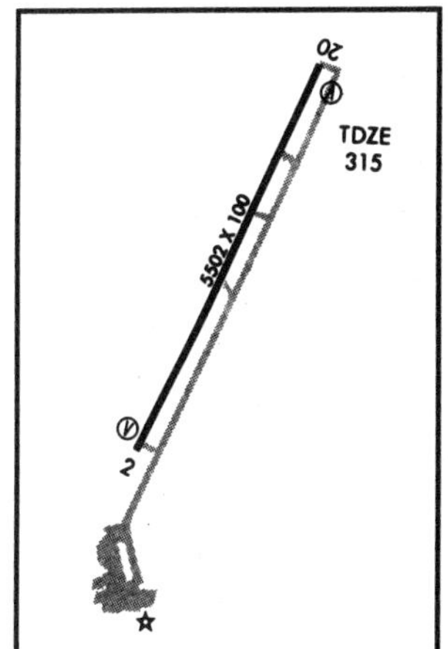

Airport Information:

SIKESTON - SIKESTON MEM MUNICIPAL (SIK)
2 mi northeast of town   N36-53.93 W89-33.70   Elev: 315   Fuel: 100LL, Jet-A   Rwy 02-20: H5502x100 (Asph)   Attended: Mon-Fri 1300-0100Z, Sat-Sun 1500-2300Z.   Unicom: 122.8
Airport Manager   Phone: 471-9056 or 471-7929

MO-9K4 - WARRENSBURG SKYHAVEN AIRPORT

(Area Code 816)

35

Fastop Mini Mart & Motel:

The Fastop Mini Mart & Motel is situated on the southern boundary of the Skyhaven Airport about a 1/4 mile walk from the aircraft parking area. This convenient style snack bar is open 24 hours a day and 365 days of the year. This establishment contains a Conoco filling station, 32 unit motel and a snack bar able to seat about 24 persons. Items available for purchase include chicken dishes, egg rolls, burrito's, and deep fried chicken livers. The grill is located in the middle of the building with the newly remodeled motel stretching out at either ends. For more information about the Fastop Mini Mart & Motel call 747-6131.

Attractions:

Whiteman AFB, Powell Gardens, Knob Noster State Park, Central Missouri State University, Old Drum & Courthouse, 2 golf courses nearby, also wineries. (See "Information" listed above).

Airport Information:

WARRENSBURG - SKYHAVEN AIRPORT (9K4)
3 mi northwest of town N38-47.06 W93-48.15 Elev: 795 Fuel: 100LL, Jet-A
Rwy 18-36: H4206x75 (Asph) Rwy 13-31: H2004x45 (Asph) Attended: dawn-dusk
Unicom: 123.0
FBO: Central MO State Univ. Phone: 543-4921
FBO: Star Aero (Maintenance) Phone: 747-8923

Restaurants Near Airport:

Country Kitchen	3-1/2 mi	Phone: 747-3149
Fastop Mini Mart & Motel	On Site, S.	Phone: 747-6131
Fast food restaurants	3-1/2 mi	Phone: N/A
Vintage House	3-1/2	Phone: 747-6240

Lodging: Skyhaven Motel (Adj Arpt) 747-6131; University Inn (3 miles) 747-5125.

Meeting Rooms: University Inn 747-5125.

Transportation: Taxi Service: Rainbow Taxi 747-3197; Rental Cars: Larson Motors 747-3343; Tally Motors; George Rush, Inc. 747-5175; Freedom Rental 747-3343.

Information: Missouri Division of Tourism, 301 W High Street, Box 1055, Jefferson City, MO 65102, Phone: 314-751-4133.

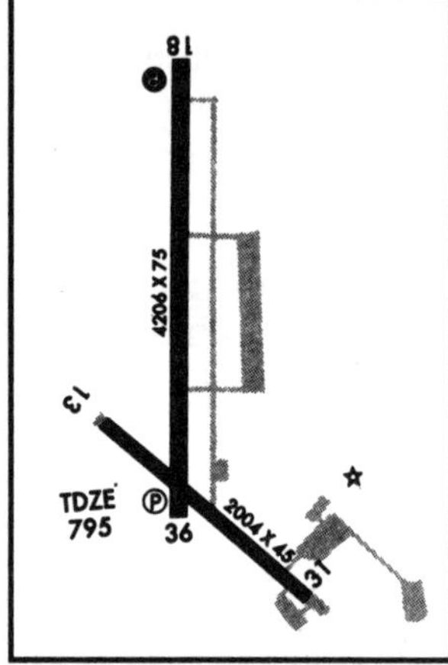

Promote General Aviation Just Take A Friend Flying

Not to be used for navigational purposes

MONTANA

LOCATION MAP

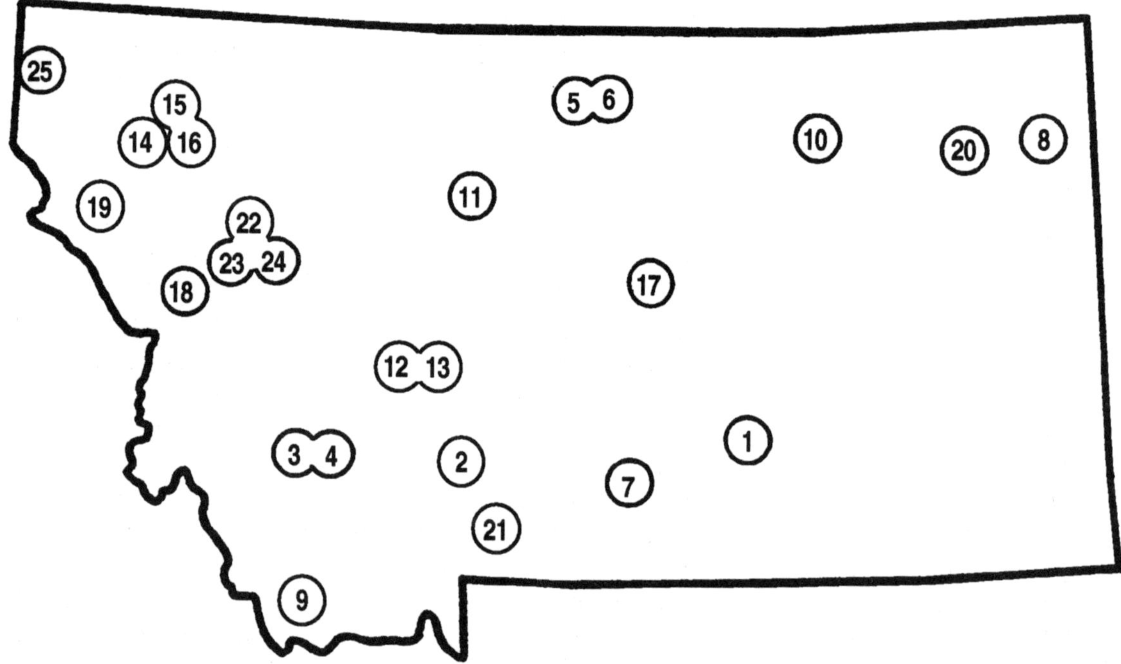

Not to be used for navigational purposes

MONTANA

CROSS FILE INDEX

Location Number	City or Town	Airport Name And Identifier	Name of Attraction
1	Billings	Billings Logan Intl. (BIL)	Skyview Terrace (Host)
2	Bozeman	Gallatin Field Arpt. (BZN)	Skyway Rest. & Lounge
3	Butte	Bert Mooney Arpt. (BTM)	Lydia's Restaurnat
4	Butte	Bert Mooney Arpt. (BTM)	Skyway Restaurant
5	Chinook	Chinook Muni. Arpt. (S71)	Chinook Motor Inn
6	Chinook	Chinook Muni. Arpt. (S71)	Tastee Bite Cafe
7	Columbus	Columbus Arpt. (6S3)	Air Bowl Restaurant
8	Culbertson	Big Sky Field Arpt. (S85)	Wild West Diner
9	Dell	Dell Flight Strip (Private)	Yesterdays Cafe
10	Glasgow	Glasgow Intl. Arpt. (GGW)	Cottonwood Inn
11	Great Falls	Great Falls Intl. (GTF)	Air Host, Inc.
12	Helena	Helena Reg. Arpt. (HLN)	Flyaway Cafe
13	Helena	Helena Reg. Arpt. (HLN)	Landing Strip Restaurant
14	Kalispell	Glacier Park Intl. (FCA)	Cloud Nine
15	Kalispell	Kalispell City Arpt. (S27)	Dos Amigos Restaurant
16	Kalispell	Kalispell City Arpt. (S27)	Mooses Saloon
17	Lewistown	Lewistown Muni. Arpt. (LWT)	Pete's Drive Inn & Fireside
18	Missoula	Missoula Intl. (MSO)	Airport Restaurant
19	Plains	Plains Airport (S34)	Benji's Restaurant
20	Poplar	Poplar Arpt. (42S)	American Legion Club
21	Pray	Chico Hot Springs Airstrip (Private)	Chico Hot Springs Lodge
22	Seeley Lake	Seeley Lake Arpt. (23S)	Lindey's Bayburgers
23	Seeley Lake	Seeley Lake Arpt. (23S)	Lindey's Prime Stk. Hse.
24	Seeley Lake	Seeley Lake Arpt. (23S)	Seasons Restaurant
25	Troy	Troy Arpt. (57S)	Silver Spur

Articles

City or town	Nearest Airport and Identifier	Name of Attraction
Gallatin Gateway, MT	Nine Quarter Circle Ranch (Private)	Nine Quarter Circle Ranch

MT-BIL - BILLINGS
BILLINGS LOGAN INTERNATIONAL

(Area Code 406)

1

Restaurants Near Airport:
Skyview Terrace (Host) On Site Phone: 256-8445

Skyview Terrace (Host Intl.)

The Skyview Terrace restaurant is situated within the main terminal building on the Billings Logan International Airport. According to the people at the restaurant, there is easy access to the restaurant for fly-in guests. FBO courtesy cars are also available. This family style restaurant is open between 11 a.m. to 2 p.m. and 5 p.m. to 8 p.m. 6 days a week, and 11 a.m. to 7 p.m. on Sunday. Their menu featuresfilet mignon, chicken teriyaki, prime rib, and baked Halibut to mention only a few. Average prices run $5.00 to $6.00 for lunch and $9.00 to $16.00 for dinner. A daily luncheon buffet is offered from 11 a.m. to 3 p.m. Sunday buffets are also provided between 11 a.m. and 8 p.m. This restaurant has undergone a complete renovation, with a newly remodeled interior and modern furnishings, able to accommodate up to 75 persons. Banquet facilities are available for large groups up to 50 persons. For more information call the restaurant at 256-8446.

Lodging: Best Western Ponderosa Inn 259-5511; Billings Inn 252-6800; Quality Inn Homestead 652-1320; RimRock Inn 252-7107; Holiday Inn Billings Plaza 248-7701; Rodeway Inn 248-7151; Radisson Northern 245-5121; Sheraton 252-7400.
Meeting rooms: Best Western Ponderosa Inn 259-2511; Rimrock Inn 252-7107; Holiday Inn Billings Plaza 248-7701; Rodeway Inn 248-7151; Radisson Northern 245-5121; Sheraton (Convention facilities) 252-7400.
Transportation: FBO Courtesy cars; Billings Taxi 252-8700; Yellow Cab 245-3033; Avis 252-8007; Budget 259-4168; Hertz 248-9151; National 252-7626; Rent-A-Wreck 252-0219.
Information: Billings Area Chamber of Commerce, 815 South 27th Street, P.O. Box 31177, Billings, MT 59107, Phone: 245-4111 or 800-735-2635.

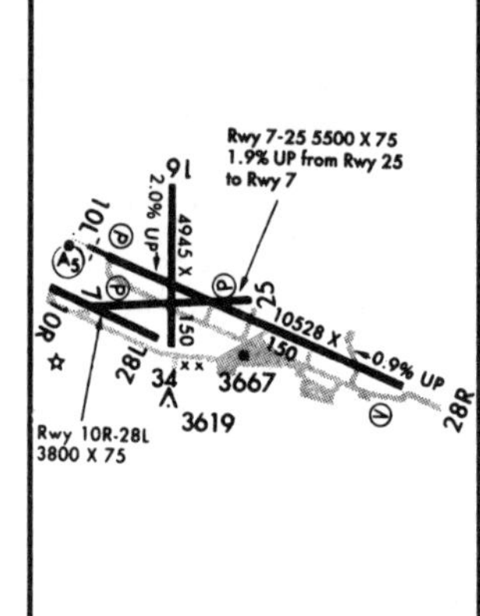

Airport Information:

BILLINGS - BILLINGS LOGAN INTERNATIONAL (BIL)
2 mi northwest of town N45-48.50 W108-32.63 Elev: 3649 Fuel: 80, 100LL, Jet-A, MOGAS Rwy 10L-28R: H10528x150 (Asph-Pfc) Rwy 16-34: H4949x150 (Asph) Rwy 07-25: H5500x75 (Asph-Pfc) Rwy 10R-28L: H3800x75 (Asph) Attended: continuously Atis: 126.3 Unicom: 122.95 App/Dep Con: 120.5 (south) 119.2 (north) Tower: 124.2 Gnd Con: 121.9 Clnc Del: 121.9 Pre Taxi Clnc: 121.9
FBO: Corporate Air Phone: 248-1541
FBO: Lynch Flying Service Phone: 252-0508

MT-BZN - BOZEMAN
GALLATIN FIELD AIRPORT

(Area Code 406)

2

Restaurants Near Airport:

Cantrell's	8 mi. E	Phone: 587-4561
Lounge Cafe	1-1/2 mi E	Phone: 388-6575
Skyway Restaurant & Lounge	On Site	Phone: 388-4565
The Oasis	9 mi W	Phone: 284-6929

Skyway Restaurant & Lounge:

This restaurant facility is located in the main terminal building at the Gallatin Field Airport in Bozeman, Montana. The cafe is open 7 days a week between 6 a.m. and 6:30 p.m. and specializes in serving a full line of breakfast and lunch entrees, as well as some dinner selections. Average prices run $5.00 for breakfast and lunch and $6.50 for dinner. When arriving at the airport you will need to park your airplane at one of the Fixed Base Operators and arrange transportation through the FBO's. The view from the restaurant will enable you to see most of the aircraft operations on the field. Groups are also welcome with advance reservations. Carry-out meals can be prepared to go. For information call the restaurant at 388-4565.

Lodging: Belgrade Super 8 Motel (2 miles) 388-1493; Gran Tree Inn (8 miles) 587-5261; Holiday Inn (8 miles) 587-4561; Bozeman (8 miles) 587-4561. Several Bed & Breakfast facilities are in the area.
Meeting Rooms: There is a small conference room available in the airport terminal building. To reserve call 388-6632.
Transportation: 4x4 Stage Taxi 388-6404; City Taxi 586-2341; Avis 388-6414; Budget Rent-A-Car 388-4091; Hertz 388-6939; National Car Rental 388-6694.
Information: Chamber of Commerce, 1205 East Main, P.O. Box-B, Bozeman, MT 59715, Phone: 586-5421 or 800-228-4224.

Attractions: Cottonwood Hills Public Golf Course, River Road, Bozeman (8 miles) 587-1188; Museum of the Rockies, 600 E. Kagy Blvd, Bozeman (10 miles) 994-2251. Also Gallatin Field is 90 miles from Yellowstone National Park; Great area for fishing and hunting; Big Sky Resort 45 miles from airport; College National Finals Rodeo held during the month of June each year.

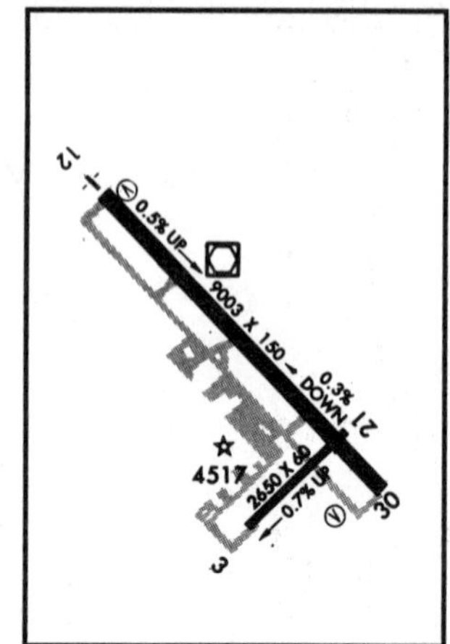

Airport Information:

BOZEMAN - GALLATIN FIELD (BZN)
7 mi northwest of town N45-46.61 W111-09.18 Elev:4474 Fuel: 80, 100, 100LL, Jet-A Rwy 12-30: H9003x150 (Asph-Pfc) Rwy 03-21: H2650x60 (Asph-Pfc) Attended: 1300-0600Z CTAF 123.65 Unicom: 122.95 Public Phone 24hrs Notes: Aircraft operations on turf area north side of Rwy 12-30; Landing Fees for aircraft over 12,500 lbs, $25.00;
Parking Fees: $2.00 per night.
FBO: Arlin's Aircraft Service Phone: 388-1351
FBO: Sunbird Aviation Phone: 388-4152

Nine Quarter Circle Ranch

Gallatin Gateway, MT (MT-Private)

The Nine Quarter Circle Ranch at 7,000 feet is surrounded by National forests containing 2 million acres of primitive wilderness. The ranch provides a mixed pattern of riding, and a select variety of unspoiled trout waters.

The ranch is located in the "high country" of the Montana Rockies alongside a rushing untamed river called Taylor Fork of the Gallatin. It is nestled amongst the Lodge Pole pines overlooking the northwest corner of Yellowstone Park on the east slope of the Continental Divide. The ranch has a "string of 120 head of horses and perpetuates this herd by raising Appaloosa colts with conformation, stamina, color and good disposition.

Among the weekly events at the ranch, the Gym Khana, or "games on horseback", provide an opportunity for everyone to compete and perfect their new riding skills. The Saturday night square dance in the barn "hay mow' will have you dancing and clapping along with the band.

The ranch is one of the last great strongholds of the American spirit. An open place to ride horse-back and fish in an uncluttered and uninhabited wilderness. A vacation in this beautiful country will give you new roots of what it means to be human.

They also offer extended pack trips into Yellowstone Park and the newly created Taylor-Hilfard Wilderness Area. Enjoy photography, fishing and exploring this magnificent country.

The Kiddie Wrangler and Baby Sitter spend most of their time with the kids, teaching them to ride and leading the "Rough Riders" on their own daily trail rides. The weekly picnic and marshmallow roast is also a hit with all the kids. There are volleyball and softball games and a Gym Khana every Saturday at the corral. Mom and Pop will find their responsibilities very limited with lots of time to follow their own interests. Kids will forget TV and be involved with new interests in this land of cowboys and cowgirls. The Ranch Airstrip is 4,000 feet long with border markers. It will accommodate sizable twins. The ranch has 122.8 unicom for two-way aircraft communication. The strip is on the U.S. Great Falls "sectional". It is located at Latitude 45 degrees, 4', Longitude 111 degrees, 17', and approximately 5 miles west of Taylor Fork Creek, Gallatin River confluence. For those interested, please write for separate ranch airstrip pamphlet. If planning to fly in by commercial airline, you will land at Bozeman and West Yellowstone. Their ranch station wagon is available to pick you up at either of these two commercial airports.

Accommodations are secured by advance reservations only. Prior permission is required before using their airport, as this is a private airstrip and is not intended for use by the general public unless reservations include a one week stay. For information send for their informative brochure which includes lots of beautiful pictures and special look at one of the finest fly-in dude ranches available. You can write to: Nine Quarter Circle Ranch, 5000 Taylor Fork Road, Gallatin Gateway, MT 59730 or call 406-995-4276. (Information submitted by Nine Quater Circle Ranch).

Photo by: Nine Quarter Circle Ranch

MT-BTM - BUTTE
BERT MOONEY AIRPORT

(Area Code 406)

3, 4

Lydia's Restaurant:

Lydia's Restaurant is situated 2 blocks south of the Bert Mooney Airport and is well within walking distance. This is a fine dining establishment that is open from 5:30 p.m. until closing time left to the discretion of the proprietor. Their lounge is open from 5:30 until 12 a.m. Their specialties include steaks, lobster, scampi, Italian dishes, pasta, as well as antipasto and relish trays served with every meal. Average prices range about $15.50 for dinners. The decor of this fine restaurant is quite elegant with chandeliers, antique stained glassed, and linen table service. A separate dining room can also provide banquet accommodations for up to 100 people apart from the main dining area which is able to seat approximately 200 guests. If planning a group fly-in or party, please give advance notice. For more information about Lydia's Restaurant you can call 494-2000.

Skyway Restaurant:

Skyway Restaurant is located in the terminal building on Bert Mooney Airport. This family style restaurant can be reached by parking your aircraft adj to the terminal building and walking a short distance to the restaurant. Their hours are from 5 a.m. to 8 p.m. 7 days a week. There is also a lounge open from 11 a.m. to 10 p.m. Specialties of the house include pork chops, grilled fish, French dips, breakfast till noon and homemade chicken noodle soups and salads. They also offer daily specials that change every week as well as Friday night fish fries. Average prices run $3.00 for breakfast, $4.00 for lunch and $5.00 and up for dinner. The restaurant faces a mountain view and statue known as "The Lady of the Rockies." A separate banquet room is also available to accommodate up to 75 people in addition to the main dining area. For information you can call the Skyway restaurant at 494-2186.

Restaurants Near Airport:

Jacyln's Restaurant	5 blks N	Phone: N/A
Lydia's Restaurant	2 blks S.	Phone: 494-2000
Red Rooster	6 blks N	Phone: N/A
Skyway Restaurant	On Site	Phone: 494-2186

Lodging: Copper King Inn (Best Western) Free Transportation Adjacent Airport, 494-6666; Townhouse Inn (Airport Transportation) 494-8850 res or 800-442-4667; War Bonnet Inn (Best Western) Free Transportation, 494-7800;

Meeting Rooms: There is a airport conference room that can accommodate 12 to 20 people, 494-3771; Also all lodging facilities listed above have accommodations with meeting and conference rooms.

Transportation: Butte Aviation has accommodations for courtesy transportation to nearby facilities with advance notice. Also Taxi 723-6511; Hertz 782-1054; Avis 494-3131; Budget 494-7573; Hertz 494-2843; Rent-A-Wreck 723-6171;

Information: Butte-Silver Bow Chamber of Commerce, 2950 Harrison Avenue, Butte, Montana 59701, Phone: 494-5595.

Attractions:

Beef Trail Ski Area (8 miles southwest of town) Butte Ski Club longest run is 1-1/2 miles down hill, with vertical drop of 800 feet, in addition to cross country skiing. Ski school, concessions and cafeteria, Phone: 494-7000; Deerlodge National Forest provides 1,176,450 acres of wilderness with camping, fishing, hunting as well as winter sports. For information call the Forest Supervisor at 496-3400 or write 400 North Main Street, P.O. Box 400, Butte, MT 59701.

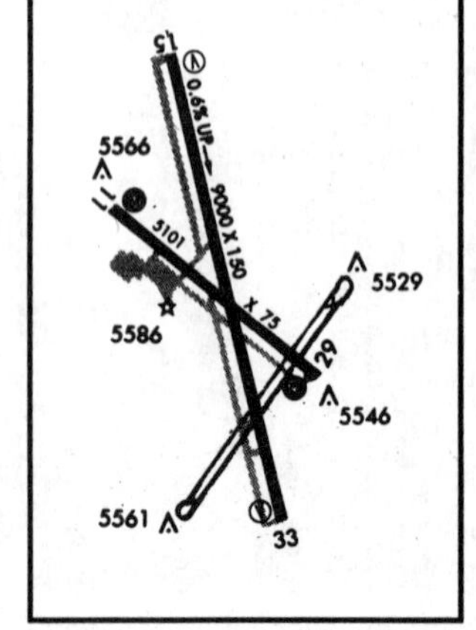

Airport Information:

BUTTE - BERT MOONEY AIRPORT (BTM)

3 mi southeast of town N45-57.29 W112-29.85 Elev: 5545 Fuel: 100LL, Jet-A
Rwy 15-33: H9000x150 (Asph-Pfc) Rwy 11-29: H5101x75 (Asph) Attended: dawn to dusk
Public Phone available dawn to dusk CTAF: 123.6 Unicom: 123.0
Notes: Landing Fee: For aircraft over 11,000 lbs, $1.00/1,000 lbs.
FBO: Butte Aviation Phone: 494-6694

MT-S71 - CHINOOK
CHINOOK MUNICIPAL AIRPORT

(Area Code 406) 5, 6

Chinook Motor Inn:

The Chinook Motor Inn is located 4 blocks from the Chinook Municipal Airport. This family style restaurant is open 6 a.m. to 9 p.m. 7 days a week. Entrees featured on their menu include a full range of entrees, including sandwiches of all types, desserts and salad bar featured on Friday and Saturday. The restaurant's dining room can accommodate up to 60 persons and offers a comfortable decor with carpeted floors and two big picture windows that provide a view facing west. There is a separate dining room designed for banquets able to seat up to 175 people. Meals-to-go including meat and cheese trays can be prepared with advance notice. The service is friendly and courteous. This combination restaurant and lodging facility also offers 38 rooms for overnight guests as well. For more information you can call the Chinook Motor Inn at 357-2248.

Tastee Bite Cafe:

The Tastee Bite Cafe is located about 3 blocks from the Chinook Municipal Airport. This combination cafe and family style restaurant is open weekdays between 6 a.m. and 10 p.m., Sunday from 6 a.m. to 10 p.m. and Friday and Saturday from 6 a.m. to 12 midnight. Entrees include items like homemade soups and sandwiches, steak and shrimp dishes. Average prices run $5.00 for breakfast and lunch, and $7.00 to $8.00 for dinner. They provide a salad bar as well as daily specials. Sunday, they also offer special discounts on their menu selections. Accommodations are available for groups and parties with advance notice. Carry-out meals can also be prepared. For more information you can call the restaurant at 357-9259.

Restaurants Near Airport:

Chinook Motor Inn	3 blks	Phone: 357-2248
Steak House	N/A	Phone: 357-2424
Tastee Bite Cafe	3 blks	Phone: 357-9259

Lodging: Bear Paw (3 blocks) 357-2221; Chinook Motor Inn (3 blks) 357-2248; Hotel Chinook (4 blocks) 357-2231.

Meeting Rooms: Chinook Moter Inn (3 blocks) has accommodations for meeting rooms. 357-2248.

Transportation: Airport courtesy car; Also Doughten Ford 357-2510.

Information: Chamber of Commerce, P.O. Box 744. Chinook, MT 59523, Phone: 357-2100.

Attractions:

The Chief Joseph Battleground State Monument is located about sixteen miles south of town with three self guided trail tours through the battlefields. A visitors center and museum displays many items and firearms used during six day siege between the Nez Perce Indians and US troops. For information contact Big Hole National Battlefield, P.O. Box 237, Wisdom, MT 59761 or call 689-3155.

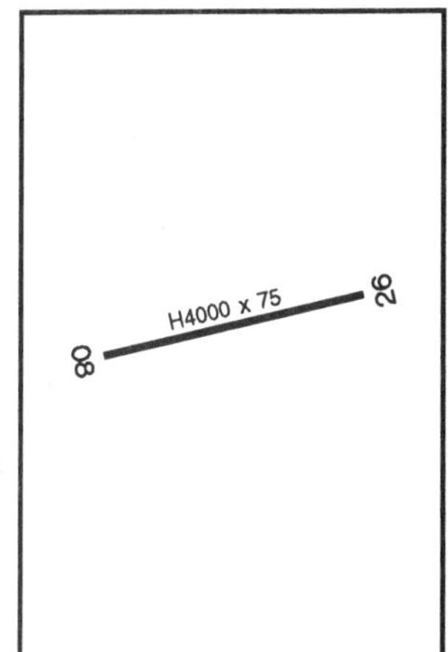

Airport Information:

CHINOOK - CHINOOK MUNICIPAL AIRPORT (S71)
1 mi west of town N48-35.52 W109-14.93 Elev: 2410 Fuel: 100LL
Rwy 08-26: H4000x75 (Asph) Attended 1400-0200Z Unicom: 122.8
FBO: Obie Flying Service Phone: 357-2429

MT-6S3 - COLUMBUS
COLUMBUS AIRPORT

(Area Code 406)

7

Air Bowl Restaurant:

The Air Bowl Restaurant is across the street and right behind the Columbus Airport. You can easily walk to the restaurant from the airport parking area. The Air Bowl specializes in quick efficient service for their customers. The restaurant is open from 10 a.m. to 10 p.m. Monday through Friday, and on weekends from 11 a.m. to 10 p.m. They provide a salad bar available all the time. Menu selections include items like burgers, chicken, pizza, Mexican food, chicken fried steak, fish, T-bone dinners and much more. Weekly specials are also offered. Average prices run $3.50 for lunch and $9.95 for dinner. The restaurant has counter service along with tables and chairs. They also have a little room off to the side that can handle between 12 and 15 persons for parties or groups. Hot or cold meals can also be prepared-to-go for pilots making a quick stop for a bite to eat. There is a bowling alley connected to the restaurant in addition to a car wash next door. When talking to the restaurant owner, we learned that many pilots often fly-in and taxi their aircraft over to the car wash and wash their planes. For more information you can call the restaurant at 322-4780.

Restaurants Near Airport:
Air Bowl Restaurant   Adj Arpt.   Phone: 322-4780

Lodging: Big Sky Motel (740 Pike Avenue) 322-4111; Super 8, (602 E. 8th Avenue) 322-4101.

Meeting Rooms: None reported

Transportation: None reported

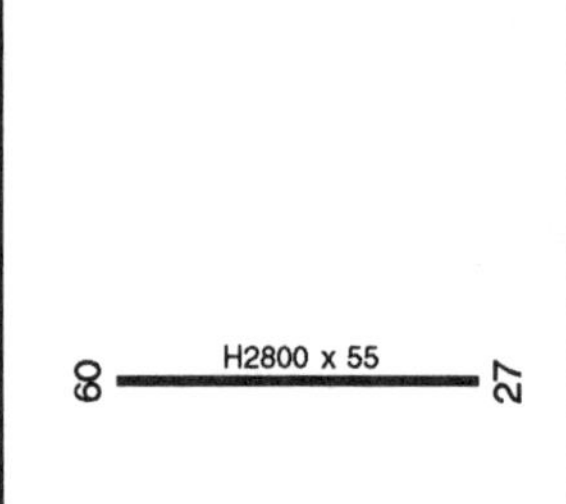

Airport Information:

COLUMBUS - COLUMBUS AIRPORT (6S3)
0 mi southeast of town   N45-37.75 W109-15.04   Elev: 3575   Fuel: 80, 100, MOGAS
RWY 09-27: H2800x55 (Asph)   Attended: Mon-Fri 1500-0000Z   CTAF/Unicom: 122.9
Airport Phone: 322-4111
Airport Manager   Phone: 322-5974

MT-S85 - CULBERTSON
BIG SKY FIELD AIRPORT

(Area Code 406)

8

Wild West Diner:

The Wild West Diner is located 4 blocks south of the Big Sky Airport. This restaurant can be reached either by walking or through courtesy transportation provided by the diner. This is a full service facility open from 6 a.m. to 8 p.m. 7 days a week. Items on their menu include a wide selection of entrees made through good old fashion home style cooking. Daily specials as well as Sunday specials are also offered. On holidays they often provide buffets. Prices average $3.00 to $5.00 for most of the items on their menu. This restaurant is constructed around an old railroad dining car which provides a unique dining experience. The main dining room at this restaurant can accommodate up to 75 persons. Groups planning or arranging parties can call the restaurant for advance reservations. They specialize in good friendly service. For more information you can call the restaurant at 787-5374.

Restaurants Near Airport:
Wild West Diner   4 blks S.   Phone: 787-5374

Lodging: Kings Inn Motel (Adjacent to airport) 787-6277

Meeting Rooms: None reported

Transportation: Wild West Diner is within walking distance, however they will provide courtesy transportation for fly-in guests. Call 787-5374.

Information: Information on points of interest as well as local points of interest may be obtained by calling 1-800-541-1447.

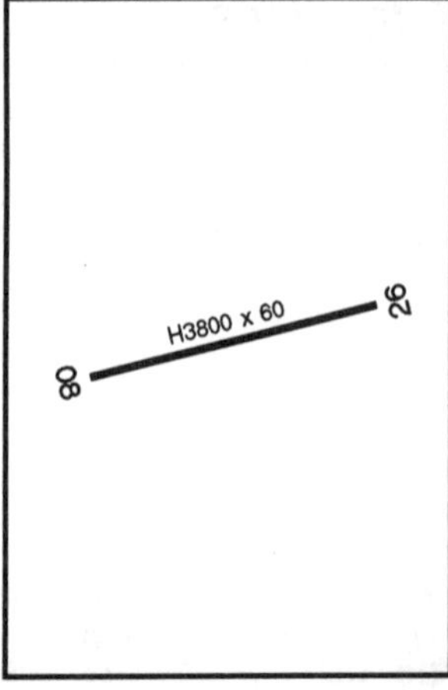

Airport Information:

CULBERTSON - BIG SKY FIELD (S85)
1 mi northeast of town   N48-09.20 W104-30.23   Elev: 1953   Fuel: 100LL
Rwy 08-26: H3800x60 (Asph)   Attended: Mon-Fri 1500-0000Z   Unicom: 122.8
Notes: On call all hours 787-5892
FBO: Modern Aire Flight Service   Phone: 787-6620

MT-(Private) - DELL
DELL FLIGHT STRIP

(Area Code 406) 9

Yesterdays Cafe:

The Yesterdays Cafe is located within walking distance from the airport. The airstrip is on the west side of I-15, Dell is on the east side; 1/2 mile walk from south end of runway. If you call them before going there, then buzz the school house twice so they hear you, they will send a car to the airstrip. Yesterdays Cafe is in a 90-year-old brick school house - one room with a bell tower that was built in 1903. The area around the Yesterday's Calf-A is chock full of antique farm machinery and wagons. The restaurant is open Monday through Saturday from 7 a.m. to 10 p.m. and Sundays from 7 a.m. to 8 p.m. They are closed the 4th of July, Labor Day and Christmas. All their menu items are made on the premises. They are well known for their roast beef, homemade pies and rolls. Homemade hamburger buns and real mashed spuds. On Sunday they offer a salad bar along with daily specials. Average prices run $3.50 for breakfast, $4.00 for lunch and $5.50 for dinner. Larger groups of 20 or more are welcome as long as reservations have been made. If you enjoy fishing, the Rainbow and Brown trout fishing is excellent. For more information about Yesterdays Cafe you can call 276-3319.

Restaurants Near Airport:
Yesterdays Cafe 1/2 mi Phone: 276-3319

Lodging: The town of Dillon 15 to 20 miles north has accommodations for lodging. Best Western Paradise Inn 683-4214; Sundowner Motel 683-2375; Super 8 Motel 683-4288.

Meeting Rooms: None reported

Transportation: None reported. Yesterdays Cafe will provide transportation to their restaurant, for guests only.

Information: Dillon Tourist Information Center, 125 S. Montana, P.O. Box 425 or the Chamber of Commerce, P.O. Box 830, Dillon, MT 59725. 683-5511.

Attractions:

Fishing for Rainbow trout and Brown trout in the red rock river is available a very short distance from the airport. For more information you can call the Yesterdays Cafe for more information 276-3319.

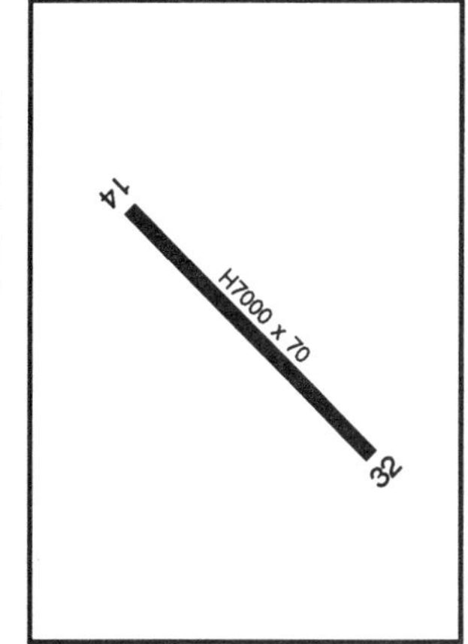

Airport Information:

DELL - (Private) - DELL FLIGHT STRIP (4U9)
1 mi northwest of town N44-44.14 W112-43.20 Elev: 6007 Rwy: 14-32: H7000x70 (Asph)
Attended: Unattended CTAF: 122.9 Notes: Deer on and in vicinity of arpt. Snow removal irregular.
For information you can call Dillin Flying Service in Dillin, MT (DLN) about 15 miles to the north for information (406-683-5242).

MT-GGW - GLASGOW
GLASGOW INTL. AIRPORT

(Area Code 406) 10

Cottonwood Inn:

The Cottonwood restaurant is located 2 miles from the Glasgow International Airport. Free courtesy transportation is provided by both the restaurant (courtesy phone at the airport) and Northern Air Transport. This is a family style restaurant that is open from 6 a.m. to 10 p.m. 7 days a week. entrees include homemade soups, pies and prime rib served nightly. Prices average $3.75 for breakfast, $5.00 for lunch and $8.00 for dinner. The restaurant provides a modern atmosphere. Banquet facilities for up to 250 people can easily be arranged in addition to catering. For information call 228-8213.

Restaurants Near Airport:

Cottonwood Inn	2 mi E	Phone: 228-8213
Elks Lodge	1 mi	Phone: 228-8781
Fort Peck Hotel	20 mi	Phone: 526-3266
Sams's Supper Club	1 mi	Phone: 228-4614

Lodging: Cottonwood Inn (1 mile) 228-8213; Fort Peck (20 miles, at lake) 526-3266.

Meeting Rooms: Cottonwood Inn 228-8213; Fort Peck Hotel 526-3266; Elks Lodge 228-8781.

Transportation: Cottonwood Inn has courtesy van to pick guests up from airport; Northern Air Transport (FBO) provides courtesy transportation to local facilities; Also Budget Rental Cars available with advance notice at the airport.

Information: Chamber of Commerce, P.O. Box 832, Glasgow, MT 59230, Phone: 228-2222.

Attractions:

Fort Peck (20 miles) offers performances with musicians and comedy acts (seasonal mid-June through August), Phone: 228-2222; Fort Peck Reservoir approx. 20 miles from airport provides outdoor activities like fishing, water skiing and sailing; Sunnyside Golf Course And Country Club (1 mile) 228-9937; C.M.R. Game Range contains elk, deer, antelope, big horn sheep and waterfowl.

Airport Information:

GLASGOW - GLASGOW INTL. AIRPORT (GGW)
1 mi northeast N48-12.75 W106-36.89 Elev: 2294 Fuel: 100, Jet-A1+
Rwy 12-30: H4999x100 (Asph-Afsc) Rwy 07-25: H4983x75 (Asph-Pfc) Attended: 1500-0000Z
Unicom: 122.8 Public Phone 24hrs
FBO: Prairie Aviation Phone: 228-4023

MT-GTF - GREAT FALLS
GREAT FALLS INTERNATIONAL

(Area Code 406)

11

Restaurants Near Airport:
Air Host, Inc. On Site Phone: 727-9240

Air Host, Inc.

This family style restaurant is located on the Great Falls International Airport, within the main terminal building. Transportation can be arranged in advance with the fixed base operators on the field. This restaurant is open between 6 a.m. and 6 p.m. 7 days a week. Their menu contains items such as ground round steak, shrimp, cold and hot sandwiches, sweet and sour chicken, side orders, and a full breakfast line, and much more. Average prices run $4.65 for breakfast & lunch selections. Dinner entrees averaging about $6.00 per plate. Daily specials are also offered. The restaurant seats up to 85 persons in addition to their cocktail lounge opening its doors at 10:30 a.m. Meals-to-go can also be prepared for pilots on-the-go. There is even a gift shop with many hand crafted items located near the restaurant. For more information about this restaurant you can call them at 727-9240.

Lodging: Best Western Ponderosa Inn (Free Trans) 761-3410; Best Western Heritage Inn (Free Trans) 761-1900; Sheraton (Free Trans) 727-7200.
Meeting Rooms: Best Western Ponderosa Inn (Free Trans) 761-3410; Best Western Heritage Inn (Free Trans) Convention Facilities, 761-1900; Sheraton (Free Trans) 727-7200.
Transportation: Diamond Cab 453-3241; Avis 761-7610; Budget 454-1001; Hertz 761-6641; National 453-4386;
Information: Chamber of Commerce, 815 2nd Street South, P.O. Box 2127, Great Falls, MT 59403, Phone: 761-4434.

Attractions: Charles M. Russell Museum Complex & Original Studio, Trigg collection of original models and paintings, Browning collection of fine weapons, Phone: 727-8787; Lewis and Clark National Forest: scenic drives through wilderness area with spectacular canyons, mountain, and cliffs. Also fishing, hiking, and big game hunting including many other outdoor activities. For information write to Park Supervisor, 1101 15th Street North, P.O. Box 871, Great Falls, MT 59403, Phone: 791-4434

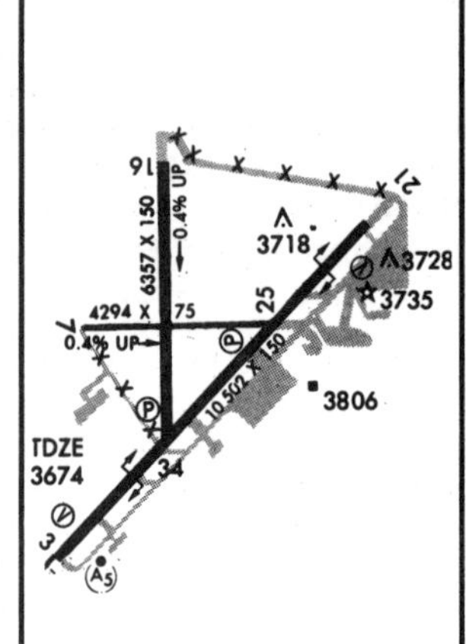

Airport Information:

GREAT FALLS - GREAT FALLS INTERNATIONAL (GTF)
3 mi southwest of town N47-28.92 W111-22.24 Elev: 3674 Fuel: 100, 100LL, Jet-A
Rwy 03-21: H10502x150 (Asph-Pfc) Rwy 16-34: H6357x150 (Asph) RWY 07-25: H4294x75 (Asph-Pfc) Attended: continuously Atis: 126.6 Unicom: 122.95 App/Dep Con: 119.3, 124.15 Tower: 118.7 Gnd Con: 121.7 Clnc Del: 127.55
FBO: Holman Aviation Phone: 453-7613
FBO: Rocky Mountain Air Phone: 761-4040

MT-HLN - HELENA
HELENA REGIONAL AIRPORT

(Area Code 406) 12, 13

Flyaway Cafe:

The Flyaway Cafe is located on the Helena Regional Airport within forty feet from the FBO's in the old terminal building. Ample parking space makes it a convenient place to visit by air. This cafe is open weekday from 6 a.m. to 7 p.m. and Saturday from 7 a.m. to 1 p.m. On Sunday they are open from 9 a.m. to 12 p.m. Their menu includes a nice assortment of breakfast entrees and lunch specials consisting of items like meat loaf, chicken steak, beef and potato selections as well as dinner items like top sirloin, salisbury steak, chicken steak and much more. Daily specials are also offered. Average prices run $3.05 for breakfast, $2.50 to $3.00 for lunch and about $4.00 to 5.50 for dinner. The restaurant looks out upon the hills in the distance from the main dining area. For groups or parties, the Flyaway cafe also provides their "Sunshine Room" as a private dining area, able to accommodate your needs. Also meals prepared to go can also be provided. For more information about this cafe call 443-6472.

Landing Strip Restaurant:

The Airport Cafe is located in the main terminal building on the Helena Regional Airport. According to the restaurant manager there is no problem parking your aircraft near the terminal building and simply walking a short distance to the cafe. This restaurant is open Monday through Friday from 6 a.m. to 9:30 p.m., and Saturday and Sunday from 6 a.m. to 5 p.m. A breakfast and lunch buffet is available between 6 a.m. and 5:30 p.m. There is a lounge located on the premises serving sandwiches and light fare. Specialized entrees include a separate menu for breakfast and lunch as well as luncheon specials served each day. Some of their breakfast entrees include omelets, and hot cake sandwiches. Lunches include entrees like their taco salad, club sandwiches along with different soups and pies made fresh and hot from the oven. Average prices run about $3.50 for breakfast, and lunch. Accommodations for groups and parties can easily be arranged with advance notice. This restaurant often caters to groups like Board of Director meetings as well as Military National Guard functions, in addition to preparing meals and catering to Delta Airlines. For information you can call the cafe at 443-3639.

Restaurants Near Airport:

Flyaway Cafe	On Site	Phone: 443-6472
Landing Strip	On Site	Phone: 443 3639

Lodging: Park Place Motel 443-2200; Colonial Inn 443-2100; Shilo Inn 442-0320; Jorgenson's 442-1770. Aladdin Coach House East Hotel 443-2300;

Meeting Rooms: Accommodations for meeting rooms can be arranged at the airport by calling the Airport Manager 442-2821. Also the following lodging facilities listed above have accommodations for meeting rooms: Aladdin Coach House East Hotel 443-2300; Best Western Colonial Inn 443-2100; Jorgenson's 442-1770.

Transportation: Hertz Rent-A-Car 442-8169: Avis Car Rental 442-4440; National Car 442-8620; Old Trapper Taxi 449-5525.

Information: Helena Area Chamber of Commerce, 225 Cruse Street, Helena, MT 59601, Phone: 442-4120 or 800-7-HEL-ENA, outside MT.

Attractions:

Helena National Forest situated approx. 16 miles north of the town of Helena, encompasses over 900,000 acres of mountainous wilderness, with camping areas, picnic sites as well as scenic drives through the park's interior. For information contact the Park Supervisor at Federal Building, 301 South Park, Room 328, Drawer 10014, Helena, MT 59626 or call 449-5201.

Airport Information:

HELENA - HELENA REGIONAL AIRPORT (HLN)

2 mi northeast of town N46-36.41 W111-58.97 Elev: 3873 Fuel: 80, 100, 100LL Jet-A
Rwy 09-27: H9000x150 (Asph-Pfc) Rwy 05-23: H4643x75 (Asph-Pfc) Rwy 16-34: H2980x75 (Asph) Attended: 1200-0800Z Unicom: 122.95 Tower: 118.3 Gnd Con: 121.9
Public Phone 24hrs Notes: Landing Fees 78.5 cents per 1,000 lbs., Tiedowns - $16.50 per month.

FBO: Exec Air Montana **Phone: 442-2190**
FBO: Montana Coyote, Inc **Phone: 449-3556**
FBO: West Air **Phone: 443-4543**

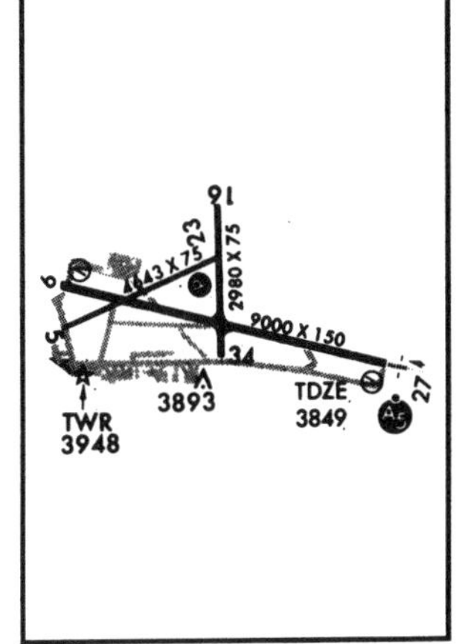

MT-FCA - KALISPELL
GLACIER PARK INTERNATIONAL

(Area Code 406) 14

Cloud Nine:

Cloud Nine Restaurant is located on the Glacier Park International Airport. According to the people at this restaurant, you can walk to their facility from the aircraft parking ramp with no trouble. Their hours are 5 a.m. to 6 p.m. 7 days a week. Items on their menu include muffins, donuts, cinnamon rolls, pies, sandwiches, and home-made soups and specialty sandwiches to order. Specials are also available each day. Average prices run about $3.50 for breakfast, lunch and dinner. The restaurant seats about 20 people. Groups are welcome with advance notice. For more information call them at 752-0980.

Restaurants Near Airport:

Cloud Nine	On Site	Phone: 752-0980
Roccos	1 mile	Phone: N/A

Lodging: Best Western Outlaw Inn 755-6100; Ramada Inn 857-3468; Red Lion Motel 755-6700.

Meeting Rooms: Best Western Outlaw Inn 755-6100

Transportation: Airport Shuttle Service 752-4022; Avis 257-2727; Budget 755-7500; Hertz 257-1266; National 257-7144.

Information: Kalispell Convention & Visitor Association, 15 Depot Park, Kalispell, MT 59901, Phone: 800-543-3105.

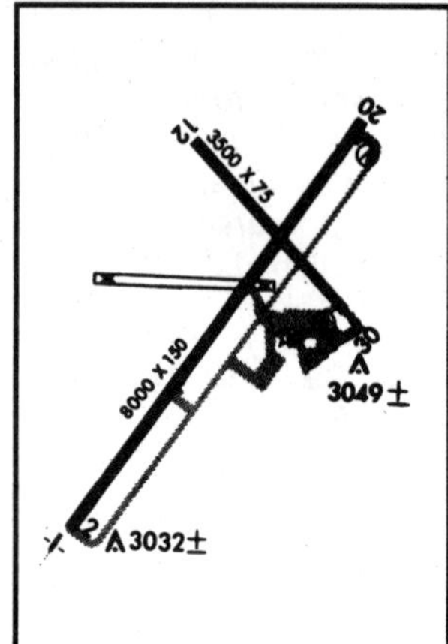

Attractions:

Flathead National Forest borders the west and south sides of Glacier National Park and includes spectacular formations, scenic drives and hiking areas available to the out-doorsman. For detailed information about this region contact the Flathead National Forest Park Supervisor at 1935 3rd Avenue East, Kalispell, MT 59901, or call 755-5401.

Airport Information:

KALISPELL - GLACIER PARK INTERNATIONAL (FCA)

6 mi northeast of town   N48-18.69 W114-15.31   Elev: 2972   Fuel: 80, 100LL, Jet-A
Rwy 02-20: H8000x150 (Asph-Pfc)   Rwy 12-30: H3500x75 (Asph-Pfc)   Attended: 1200-0800Z
Unicom: 123.0
FBO: Holman Aviation   Phone: 755-5362

MT-S27 - KALISPELL
KALISPELL CITY AIRPORT

(Area Code 406)

15, 16

Dos Amigos Restaurant:

Dos Amigos Restaurant specializes in Mexican foods as well as American traditional fare. It may be considered a fine dining facility located about 2 miles from the Kalispell City Airport. Transportation can be obtained by taxi service through either "Kalispell Taxi" or "Eagle Taxi" for approx. $4.00 plus $1.00 for each additional person, one way. The restaurant hours are 11 a.m. to 10 p.m. during the week, 11 a.m. to 11 p.m. on Friday and 11:30 a.m. to 11 p.m. on Saturday and Sunday. Some of their specialty entrees include great chili pasta dishes, Enchilada Suizas, Recoda Enchilada with Cilantro as well as a variety of Chimichangas. Many varieties and combination dishes along with traditional American dishes, including a complete appetizer and dessert selections are also featured. Average prices run $4.00 to $5.00 for lunch and $7.00 to $10.50 for dinner. The decor of the restaurant is in a Spanish theme and exhibits a casual yet colorful atmosphere with tiled floors, plants, cactus and wall decorations. There are three separate dining rooms able to accommodate groups or parties. For information call 752-2711.

Mooses Saloon:

Mooses Saloon is less than 2 miles from the Kalispell City Airport. This establishment is very popular with travelers all across the region. In-fact we were told by local town representatives, that people from all across the country have traveled out of their way to experience this restaurant and saloon. The old western styled decor with a large curved wooden bar, wanted posters on the walls, saw dust on the floor and a large selection of domestic and imported beers (22 on tap) are some of the reasons for its popularity. (Please remember 8 hours from bottle to throttle). The restaurant is located at the intersection of Highway 2 and 93. You will see the swinging doors of the saloon as you approach the restaurant. Their hours are 11 a.m. to 2 a.m. 7 days a week. Entree specialties include a variety of sandwiches, pizza and soup and salad bar featured Monday through Friday 11 a.m. to 3 p.m. Everything on their menu is made from scratch. The restaurant portion seats approximately 200 people. We called the local taxi service and learned that average taxi fares run $4.00 each way plus $1.00 per each additional person. For more information you can call the Mooses Saloon at 755-2337.

Restaurants Near Airport:

The Alley Conn.	2 mi	Phone: 752-7077
Dos Amigos	2 mi	Phone: 752-2711
Mooses Saloon	1 to 2 mi	Phone: 755-2337
The Rose	1/2 mi E	Phone: 752-3246

Lodging: The Outlaw Inn, (1/4th mile) 1701 Highway 93 South, 755-6100; Cavanaugh's (2-1/2 miles) 20 North Main, 752-6660.

Meeting Rooms: The Outlaw Inn can provide accommodations for meetings and conferences, (1/4th mile from airport) 755-6100.

Transportation: Kalispell Taxi 752-4022; Eagle Transit 756-5656; Avis Rent-A-Car 257-2727; Hertz Rent-A-Car 257-1266.

Information: Flathead Convention & Visitor Association, 15 Depot Park, Kalispell, MT 59901, Phone: 800-543-3105.

Attractions:

Flathead National Forest borders the west and south sides of Glacier National Park and includes spectacular geological formations, scenic drives and hiking areas available to the out-doorsman. For detailed information about this region contact the Flathead National Forest Park Supervisor at 1935 3d Avenue East, Kalispell, MT 59901, or call 755-5401.

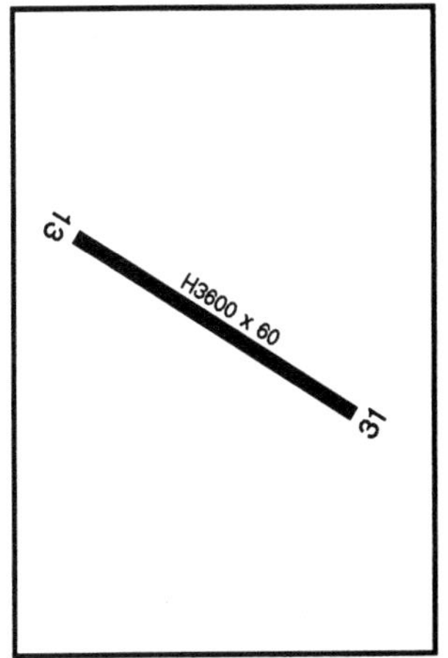

Airport Information:

KAKISPELL - KALISPELL CITY AIRPORT (S27)

1 mi south of town N48-10.71 W114-18.22 Elev: 2932 Fuel: 80, 100LL

Rwy 13-31: H3600x60 (Asph) Attended: daylight hours Unicom: 122.8

Notes: Parking Fee $2.00/day

FBO: Eagle Aviation **Phone: 755-2376**

FBO: Strand Aviation **Phone: 257-7678**

FBO: Stockhill Aviation **Phone: 752-5092**

MT-LWT - LEWISTOWN
LEWISTOWN MUNICIPAL AIRPORT

(Area Code 406) 17

Pete's Drive Inn & Fireside Restaurant:

Pete's Drive Inn & Fireside Restaurant is located about 1 mile east of the Lewistown Municipal Airport. This combination drive-in and family style restaurant can be reached by obtaining a courtesy car from either Central Air Service or Newton Aviation with advance notice. The restaurant is open 5:30 a.m. to 9 p.m. 7 days a week. Their menu specializes in sandwiches of all types, including hamburgers, fish and chicken. For dinner you can enjoy their boasted chicken, rib eye steak, shrimp, or try their steak fingers made from strips of choice beef and lightly breaded in a special batter. Average prices run $4.00 to $5.00 for breakfast & lunch, and $6.00 for dinner. You can either pull your car up and order your meal by speaker phone, or sit in the indoor restaurant with full service and seating accommodations for up to 58 people. The owner has operated this facility for over 25 years and is visited by many local customers as well as fly-in guests. For more information you can call 538-9400.

Restaurants Near Airport:

Pete's Drive Inn & Fireside	1 mi E.	Phone: 538-9400
Pizza Hut	1 mi NE	Phone: 538-5472

Lodging: Mountain View Motel (1 mile east) 538-3457; Yogo Inn (2 miles east) 538-8721; B & B Motel 538-5496.

Meeting Rooms: Yogo Inn (2 miles east) 538-8721

Transportation: Taxi Service: Star Cab 538-3641; Rent-A-Car 538-5457.

Information: Lewistown Chamber of Commerce, P.O. Box 818, Lewistown, MT 59457, Phone: 538-5436.

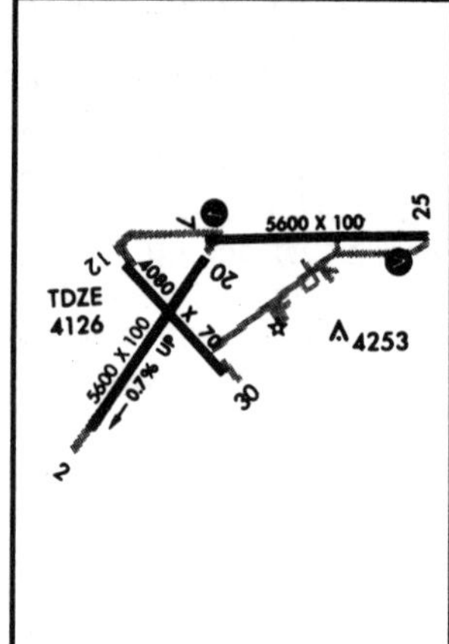

Airport Information:

LEWISTOWN - LEWISTOWN MUNICIPAL AIRPORT (LWT)
3 mi southwest of town N47-02.95 W109-28.00 Elev: 4167 Fuel: 80, 100, Jet-A
Rwy: 02-20: H5600x100 (Asph) Rwy 07-25: H5600x100 (Asph) Rwy 12-30: H4080x70 (Asph)
Attended: Mon-Fri 1400-2300Z Unicom: 123.0
FBO: Newton Aviation Phone: 538-8150, 538-7892
FBO: Skycraft, Inc. Phone: 538-5457

MT-MSO - MISSOULA
MISSOULA INTERNATIONAL

(Area Code 406) 18

Airport Restaurant:

The Airport Restaurant is located on the Missoula International Airport within the terminal building. Transportation arranged through the local fixed base operators will get you to the restaurant. This family-style restaurant is open from 6 a.m. to 7 p.m. 7 days a week. Their menu contains full breakfast and lunch selections. Entrees such as hamburgers, cold sandwiches, Mexican dishes and chicken sandwiches, as well as many other choices, are available to their customers. Average prices for most menu selection will run $4.75. Dinner prices average about $5.25. The dining area is L-shaped and allows privacy for groups planning to visit the restaurant or arrange parties. This facility is also willing to prepare meals from their menu for carry-out. To the best of our knowledge, we learned that within the terminal building, deli food is available 6 am. to 12 a.m., as well as cold sandwiches, frozen yogurt and expresso bar. For more information about the Airport Restaurant you can call 543-8670.

Restaurants Near Airport:

Airport Restaurant	On Site	Phone: 543-8670

Lodging: The following provide free transportation to airport: Holiday Inn (4 miles) 721-8550; Orange Street Budget Motor Inn 721-3610; Quality Inn (3 miles) 543-7231; Red Lion 728-3300; Red Lion Village Motor Inn (4 miles) 728-3300; Reserve Inn (3 miles) 721-0990.

Meeting Rooms: The following lodging facilities provide meeting accommodations as well as courtesy transportation to the airport: Days Inn 721-9776; Orange Street Budget Motor Inn 721-3610; Red Lion 728-3300; Holiday Inn 721-8550; Red Lion Village Motor Inn 728-3100.

Transportation: Airport courtesy car available; Also Yellow Taxi 543-6644; Avis 549-4711; Budget 543-7001; Hertz 549-9511; National 543-3131.

Information: Chamber of Commerce, 825 East Front, P.O. Box 7577, Missoula, MT 59807, Phone: 543-6623

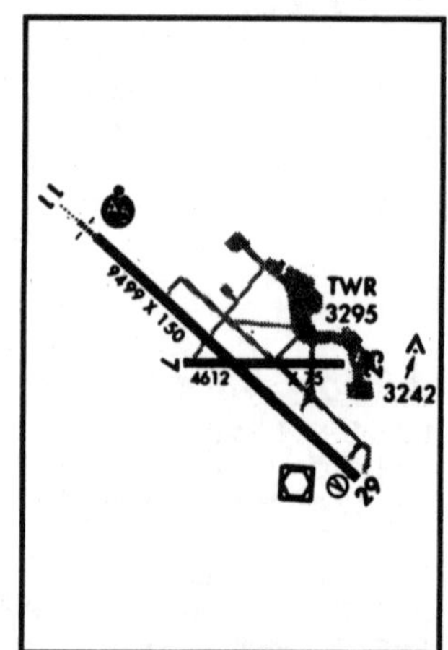

Airport Information:

MISSOULA - MISSOULA INTERNATIONAL AIRPORT (MSO)
4 mi northwest of town N46-54.98 W114-05.43 Elev: 3201 Fuel: 100LL, Jet-A+
Rwy 11-29: H9499x150 (Asph-Pfc) Rwy 07-25: H4612x75 (Asph) Attended: continuously
Atis: 126.65 Unicom: 122.95 Tower 118.4 Gnd Con: 121.9
FBO: Minuteman Aviation Phone: 728-9363
FBO: North Star Air Express Phone: 721-8886

MT-S34 - PLAINS
PLAINS AIRPORT

(Area Code 406) 19

Benji's Restaurant:

Benji's Restaurant is reported 1 mile southwest from the Plains Airport. This restaurant will provide transportation for fly-in guests. They are open from 6 a.m. to 11 p.m. Friday and Saturday and 6 a.m. to 10 p.m. during the week. Sundays they are open from 7 a.m. to 10 p.m. Specialties on their menu include country ham and egg dishes for breakfast. Additional specialties are homemade mashed potatoes, fresh dinner rolls, salad bar, soups and they are especially known for their famous 1/2 pound hamburger. Daily specials feature prime rib on Friday and Saturday. On Friday they also offer scampi, prawns and halibut. The restaurant is decorated with dark cedar wood and decorated with framed mirrors and local artwork. They can accommodate seating for 75 people in their main dining room. Larger groups are welcome. Benji's Restaurant has been serving customers for over 15 years. They have also been featured in several magazines, and are popular with the locals as well as fly-in customers. For information call the restaurant at 826-5662.

Restaurants Near Airport:

Benjis Restaurant	1 mi SW.	Phone: 826-5662
Circle Drive Inn	1 mi	Phone: N/A
Quinn's Resort	12 mi E.	Phone: 826-3150
Wildhore Restaurant	2 mi	Phone: N/A

Lodging: Harwood Motel 2 mi 826-3573; Owl Motel 1 mi 826-3691; Tops Motel 2 mi 8263412; Quinn's Hot Springs Paradise Resort 12 mi 826-3150.

Meeting Rooms: Quinn's Hot Springs Paradise Resort 12 mi 826-3150.

Transportation: Airport courtesy car reported.

Information: Plains Chamber of Commerce, Box 714, Plains, MT 59859. Phone: 826-3605.

Attractions:

Quinn's Hot Springs Paradise Resort is located about 12 miles from the Plains Airport (S34). Outdoor and indoor jacuzzis, hot mineral showers, supper club and bar. Open 7 days a week. 16 cabins, and camping, cabins. Also this facility is currently undergoing an extensive expansion with a new hotel and accommodations for meetings. For information call 826-3150.

NO AIRPORT DIAGRAM AVAILABLE

Airport Information:

PLAINS - PLAINS AIRPORT (S34)
1 northwest of town N47-28.35 W114-54.01 Elev: 2462 Rwy 12-30: H3060x50 (Asph) Rwy 07-25: 1750x100 (Turf) Attended: unattended CTAF: 122.9
Airport Manager Phone: 826-3605

MT-42S - POPLAR
POPLAR AIRPORT

(Area Code 406) 20

American Legion Club:

The American Legion Club is considered a fine dining facility located about 6 blocks from the Poplar Airport. A courtesy car can be obtained through Dallas Aero (FBO) or the airport manager. The restaurant is open on Friday and Saturday from 5 p.m. to 11 p.m. and on Sunday from 4 p.m. to 9 p.m. Menu items include a daily salad bar, with choices of two soups, 6 different appetizers, T-bone steak, filet mignon, sirloin, half cut tenderloin, lobster tail, king crag legs, broiled seafood platter (3 types of fish), jumbo shrimp, breaded seafood platter, halibut, scallops, Walleye and fried oysters. Prime rib specials are featured each Friday night, and a Bar-B-Qued rib special on Saturday nights. The dining room is quite elegant and offers a quiet atmosphere. Carpeted floors and wood paneling along with candles on the tables, leather chairs, wooden tables and chandeliers all add to the abeyance of your dining occasion. The main dining room handles up to 60 people with a separate banquet room able to accommodate as many as 150 to 200 persons. On certain occasions there is live entertainment with dancing. For more information call the American Legion Club at 768-3923.

Restaurants Near Airport:

American Legion Club	6 blks S.	Phone: 768-3923
Buck Horn Cafe	4 blks	Phone: 768-5521
Jasper's Pizza	5 blks	Phone: 768-3316

Lodging: LeAnn's Motel (3 blocks) 768-5442

Meeting Rooms: American Legion Club (See Restaurant Above)

Transportation: Dallas Aero 768-3800

Information: Wolf Point Chamber of Commerce, 201 4th Street South, P.O. Box 237, Wolf Point, MT 59201, Phone: 653-2012

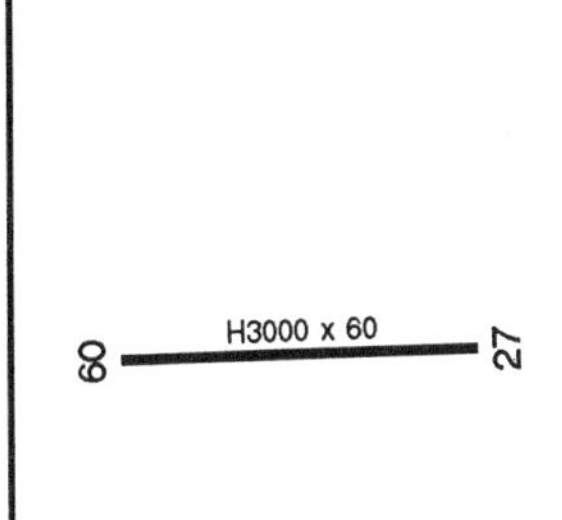

Airport Information:

POPLAR - POPLAR AIRPORT (42S)
0 mi northeast of town N48-07.00 W105-11.28 Elev: 2005 Fuel: 100
Rwy 09-27: H3000x60 (Asph-Pfc) Attended: 1500-0100Z Unicom: 122.8 Public Phone 24hrs
Notes: For fuel after hours call 488-2533
FBO: Dallas Aero Phone: 768-3800

MT-(Private) - PRAY
CHICO HOT SPRINGS AIRSTRIP

(Area Code 406)

21

Chico Hot Springs Lodge:

Chico Hot Springs Lodge is situated in the Rocky Mountains of Pray, Montana. Year-round, you can always find time to relax and enjoy the natural surroundings of this fine resort. Walk up the mountain to the lake or arrange a guided fishing trip on one of Paradise Valley's famous spring creeks. Relax in the natural hot spring pools or treat yourself to a professional massage. Go hiking or mountain biking on Forest Service trails, or rafting down the Yellowstone River. Go horseback riding and take guided hourly or full day tours into the surrounding mountains. During the winter, drive a team of Huskies on a guided dogsled trek, or go cross-country skiing for a day. For fine dining, visit the Chico Inn which offers a rustic, yet elegant atmosphere or visit the Poolside Grille which offers a more casual setting. During the summer, enjoy dining at the Pasta Bar on the deck. For a fun night out; stop by the Chico Saloon which offers a pool table, large screen televisions and live music every weekend. For comfortable lodging, choose from the turn-of-the-century main lodge, rustic cabins, modern motels, or condominiums and houses. There are no telephones or televisions in the rooms, however, Cellular phones are available for rent. If you are planning a special occasion, such as a wedding or a family reunion, Chico's convention center can accommodate 150 people. The sales and catering staff will arrange many kinds of events, such as corporate retreats, informal barbecues and black-tie dinners. For fly-in guests, the lodge uses an automobile highway as its private airstrip. IMPORTANT - see "Airport Information" below for further information about the airstrip. For information about rates and accommodations at Chico Hot Springs Lodge, call 333-4933 or 1800-468-9232.

Comments by a valued contributor:

Not shown on the sectional, but is situated about half way between Gardiner and Livingston Montana. This is apparently an FAA approved landing strip (road). You circle the lodge and can call them on unicom 122.8. They will send out two pickup trucks to block the road, then call you when its ok to land. Field elevation 5,280. The lodge elevation is 5405. (See "Airport Information" for resort-published landing and take-off procedures) Chico has the finest gourmet restaurant in at least 500 miles. Open all year, the pools are fed by natural hot springs. Nothing in the water but heat, and they have horseback riding too. If you're staying overnight, bring your own tie-down gear. Sunday breakfast buffet is unbelievably good.

Restaurants Near Airport:
Chico Hot Springs Lodge On Site Phone: 333-4933

Lodging: Chico Hot Springs Lodge (On Site) 333-4933

Meeting Rooms: Chico Hot Springs Lodge 333-4933

Transportation: Airport is within a short walking distance to Chico Hot Springs Lodge.

Information: Chamber of Commerce, 212 W. Park, Livingston, MT 59047, Phone: 222-0850

Photo by: Chico Hot Springs Lodge

NO AIRPORT DIAGRAM AVAILABLE

Airport Information:

PRAY - CHICO HOT SPRINGS AIRSTRIP (PRIVATE)

On Site N45-22.0 W110-42.0 Elev: 5280 Fuel: None Reported Rwy 14-32: H6000x30 (Asph) Attended: Unattended Unicom: 122.8 Notes: CAUTION - Due to mountain obstruction, pilots must land on Runway 14 and depart on Runway 32. Runway 14-32 is an automobile highway with windsocks at both ends. Chico Hot Springs Lodge has given the following instructions: "You MUST call 'Chico Hot Springs Lodge' on 122.8 at least 10 minutes out so they can block-off road - then - wait for clearance to land before landing Runway 14 (the road)."

FBO: AIRPORT MANAGER Phone: 333-4933

MT-23S - SEELEY LAKE
SEELEY LAKE AIRPORT

(Area Code 406)

22, 23, 24

Lindey's Bayburgers:

This restaurant is operated by the same people who own Lindey's Prime Steak House. "Lindey's Bayburgers By The Bay" is located close to the Lindey's Landing West Sea Plane Base (M35) on Seeley Lake. This facility is open between 11 a.m. and 9 p.m. 7 days a week through the summer season. Their entrees specialize in lighter fare with variations to their famous "Bayburger", along with hotdogs, Polish sausage, nachos with cheese as well as salads, desserts and beverages. Prices run between $2.00 and $4.00 for most selections. For more information, call Lindey's at 677-9229 between Memorial Day through Labor Day.

Lindey's Prime Steak House:

This fine dining facility is located 1-1/2 miles from the Seeley Lake Airport (23S). To reach this restaurant you can call on UNICOM 122.9 and they will come and pick you up. Leaving the airport, you will take the only road going west about 1-1/2 miles until you come to Hwy 83. Lindey's Prime Steak House is located at that intersection. They are open for dinner beginning from 5:00 p.m. to 10 p.m., 7 days a week between Memorial Day through Labor Day. This restaurant specializes in steak. Selections include Lindey's prime sirloin, special sirloin and chopped sirloin, (one pound). Selections on their menu average $15.00. The atmosphere is rustic, with quiet background music, wood panelled interior, fire place and a view overlooking Seeley Lake and nearby mountain range. There is also a lounge area separate from the restaurant. Catering for up to 100 persons can be arranged. For information call 677-9229 between Memorial Day through Labor Day.

Seasons Restaurant At Double Arrow Resort:

The Seasons Restaurant is located at the Double Arrow Lodge, and is approximately 5 miles from the Seeley Lake Airport. To reach the restaurant, take Airport Road to Highway 83, turn left, and go about 2 miles. The lodge will be located at the number 12 mile marker. During the winter months they are open on Wednesday through Saturday from 5:30 p.m. to 9:30 p.m. During the summer months dinner is served from 6 p.m. to 10 p.m. This fine dining facility provides a classic country cuisine emphasizing fresh products & seasonal ingredients. For example: fresh seafood, chicken, beef, appetizers, salads, soups and desserts are just some of the fine selections offered on their menu. Sunday buffet brunch is provided year around from 10 a.m. to 2 p.m., in addition to their barbecued buffet on Sunday, with many of their entrees cooked on a cherrywood grill. Average prices run about $10.95 for brunch and $15.00 for dinner. The restaurant is situated within a historic log building which has been restored to its original elegance complete with linen table- cloths, and beautifully decorated. Accommodations for groups or parties can be arranged. Sporting activities at the resort include golfing and snowmobiling. For information call 677-2777 or 800-468-0777.

Restaurants Near Airport:

Lindey's Bayburgers	1-1/2 mi	Phone: 677-9229
Lindey's Steak Hse	1-1/2 mi	Phone: 677-9229
Seasons Restaurant	5 mi	Phone: 677-2777

Lodging: Seeley Lake Resort 677-2423; Double Arrow Lodge 677-2777

Meeting Rooms: Double Arrow Lodge 677-2777; Lindey's Prime Steak House 677-9229

Transportation: Transportation can be obtained by calling on UNICOM frequency 122.9, No telephone at Seeley Lake Airport.

Information: Missoula Chamber of Commerce, 825 East Front, P.O. Box 7577, Missoula, MT 59807, Phone: 406-543-6623.

Airport Information:

SEELEY LAKE - SEELEY LAKE AIRPORT (23S)

2 mi east of town N47-10.75 W113-26.72 Elev: 4235 Fuel: 100LL, MOGAS
Rwy 16-34: 3475x75 (Turf-Grvl) Attended: unattended Unicom: 122.9 Notes: Takeoffs to north not recommended due to rising terrain. No public phone available at the airport, call for transportation on UNICOM Freq: 122.9 for transportation. Also for fuel call airportmanager at 406-677-9229.
FBO: Lindey's Landing West (SPB) Phone:677-9229, 667-2564

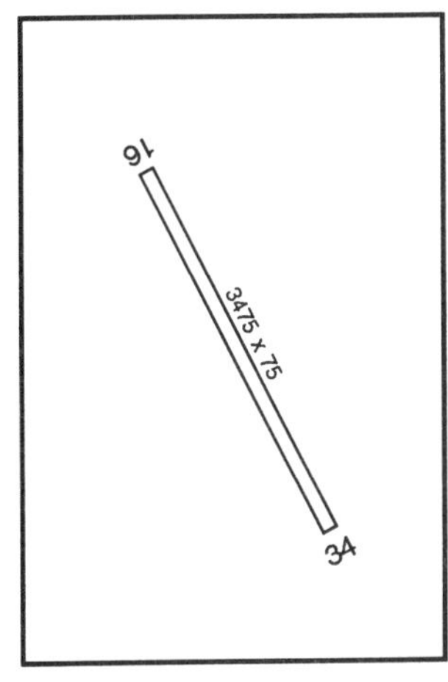

MT-57S - TROY
TROY AIRPORT

(Area Code 406)

25

Silver Spur:

The Silver Spur is a very nice restaurant and bar located near the Troy airport in Troy, Montana. According to the people at Silver Spur restaurant, they are only 1/4 mile on Highway 2 from the airport. This family restaurant is open between 6 a.m. and 9 p.m. 7 days a week. They specialize in a full selection of breakfast lunch and dinner entrees. Steaks, Prawns, sauteed scampi, chicken steaks, spaghetti, and prime cuts of beef are just a few choice selections available. Average prices run $4.95 for breakfast and lunch, and about $4.95 to 7.95 for dinner specials. A complete salad bar is also available with your dinner meal. Daily specials along with buffets from 12:00 p.m. to 6 p.m. are often provided. The interior of the restaurant is decorated with wild animals and wood carved murals from the local artisans, providing a warm rustic atmosphere. Larger groups and parties are welcome provided advance notice is given. Their bar includes a room for playing pool and gaming machines. For more information you can call the Silver Spur at 295-9937.

Restaurants Near Airport:
Silver Spur 1/4 mi Phone: 295-9937

Lodging: Holiday Motel (1 miles) 295-4117

Meeting Rooms: None reported

Transportation: None reported

Information: Libby Chamber of Commerce, 905 W. 9th Street, P.O. Box 704, Libby, MT 59923, Phone: 293-4167

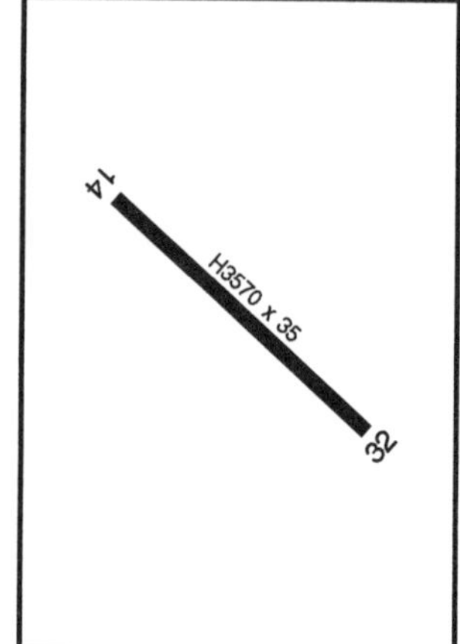

Airport Information:

TROY - TROY AIRPORT (57S)
1 mi northwest of town N48-28.81 W115-54.21 Elev: 2017 Rwy 14-32: H3570x35 (Asph)
Attended: unattended CTAF: 122.9 Notes: Check currrent AFD for runway conditions
Airport Manager: **Phone: 295-4480**

NEBRASKA

LOCATION MAP

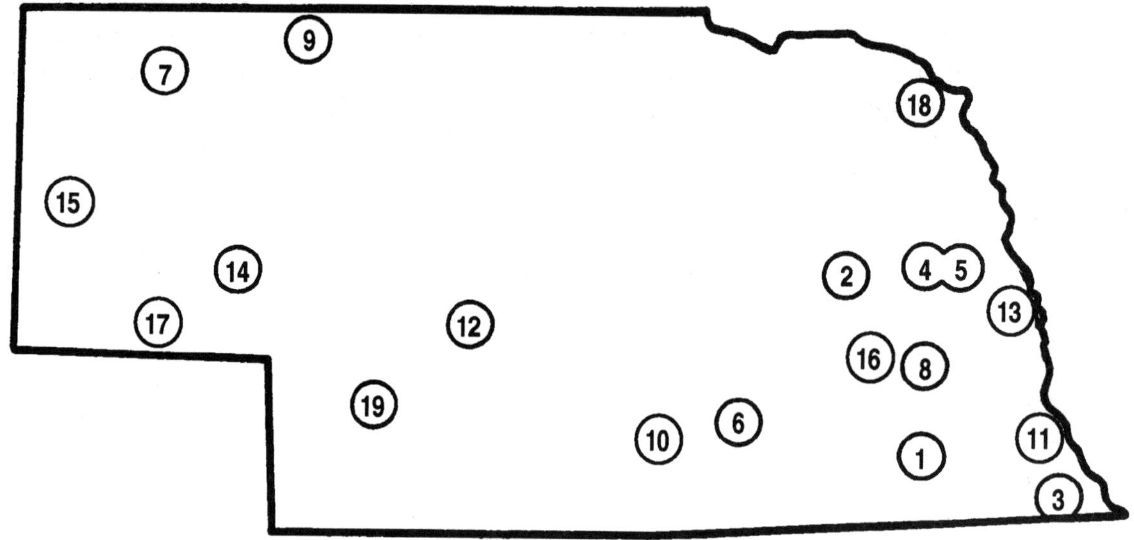

Not to be used for navigational purposes

NEBRASKA

CROSS FILE INDEX

Location Number	City or Town	Airport Name And Identifier	Name of Attraction
1	Beatrice	Beatrice Muni. (BIE)	Beatrice Inn
2	Columbus	Columbus Muni. Arpt. (OLU)	Dusters
3	Falls City	Brenner Field Arpt. (FNB)	The Write Place
4	Fremont	Fremont Muni. Arpt. (FET)	KC's Cafe & Bar
5	Fremont	Fremont Muni. Arpt. (FET)	The Rose Room
6	Hastings	Hastings Muni. Arpt. (HSI)	Village Inn Pancake Hse.
7	Hay Springs	Hay Springs Muni. Arpt. (4V6)	Bob's Bar & Grill
8	Lincoln	Lincoln Muni. Arpt. (LNK)	Air Host, Inc.
9	Merriman	Cole Memorial Arpt. (9V4)	Sands Cafe
10	Minden	Pioneer Village Field (0V3)	Pioneer Village
11	Nebraska City	Grundman Arpt. (3GN)	Valentino's
12	North Platte	Lee Bird Field (LBF)	Airport Inn
13	Omaha	Eppley Airfield (OMA)	Marriott Concessions
14	Oshkosh	Garden Co. Arpt. (OKS)	Cafe Motel & Restaurant
15	Scottsbluff	William B. Heileg Field (BFF)	Skyport Restaurant
16	Seward	Seward Muni. (SWT)	Peppercorn Rest.
17	Sidney	Sidney Arpt. (SNY)	Cabela's
18	South Sioux City	Martin Field (7K8)	Marina Inn
19	Wallace	Wallace Muni. Arpt. (64V)	Wallace Cafe

Articles

City or town	Nearest Airport and Identifier	Name of Attraction
Hastings, NE	Hastings Muni. (HSI)	Hastings Museum
Plattsmouth, NE	Plattsmouth Muni. (PMV)	Strategic Air Museum
Sidney, NE	Sidney Muni. (SNY)	Cabela's Outfitter

NE-BIE - BEATRICE
BEATRICE MUNI

(Area Code 402)

1

Restaurants Near Airport:

Beatrice Inn	2 blks E.	Phone: 223-4074
Bonanza Restaurant	1/2 mi S.	Phone: 228-4345

Beatrice Inn:

Beatrice Inn Restaurant is situated 2 blocks from the Beatrice Municipal Airport, and is within walking distance from the aircraft parking area. Courtesy transportation is also available from the airport or restaurant. When leaving the airport, walk straight east of the airport across highway 77. This facility is open from 6 a.m. to 9 p.m. Monday through Saturday and Sunday for their brunch from 11 a.m. until 2 p.m. They offer a special "Down Home Country" buffet served on Saturday nights. Their Sunday brunch and all you can eat chicken featured on Tuesday nights as well as prime rib on Saturday and Monday nights are very popular with the local people. Prices average $3.50 for breakfast, $3.95 for lunch and $5.95 for dinner. The restaurant offers guests a view overlooking their outdoor heated swimming pool. Groups and parties as well as business seminars are welcome to this facility complete with 3 meeting rooms and accommodations for up to 250 guests. In addition to the restaurant facility the Beatrice Inn also has 63 units for overnight guests. For more information call 223-4074.

Lodging: Beatrice Inn (2 blocks) 223-4074; Holiday House (Adjacent) 223-4074; Super 8 (Adjacent) 223-3536; Victorian Inn (1 mile south) 228-5955

Meeting Rooms: Beatrice Inn (2 blocks) 3 meeting rooms along with the restaurant dining room, Phone: 223-4074

Transportation: Courtesy cars are usually available for use at the airport on a donation basis. Yellow Cab 223-3121.

Information: Chamber of Commerce, 226 South 6th Street, Beatrice, NE 68310, Phone: 223-2338 or 800-755-7745.

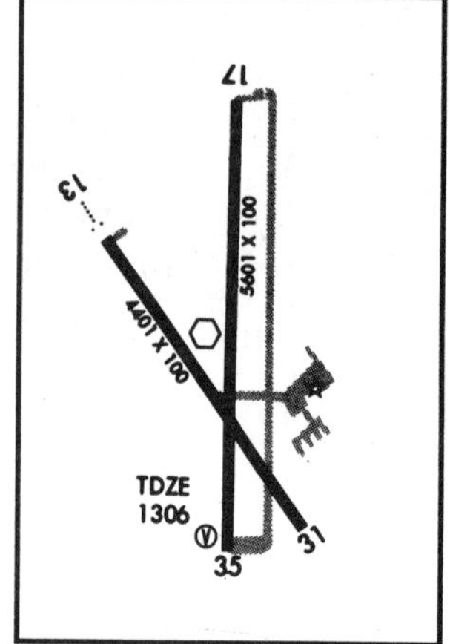

Airport Information:

BEATRICE - BEATRICE MUNICIPAL AIRPORT (BIE)
3 mi north of town N40-18.09 W96-45.25 Elev: 1323 Fuel: 100LL, Jet-A
Rwy 17-35: H5601x100 (Asph-Conc) Rwy 13-31: H4401x100 (Asph) Attended: 1300-0230Z
Unicom: 122.8 Public Phone 24hrs Notes: Tie down $3.00 per night; Hangar-single engine $8.00, Twin $15.00 per night. Courtesy cars are usually available for use and are on a donation basis.
FBO: Beatrice Municipal Airport Phone: 223-5349, 228-4585

NE-OLU - COLUMBUS
COLUMBUS MUNICIPAL AIRPORT

(Area Code 402)

2

Restaurants Near Airport:

Dusters	3-4 mi SW	Phone: 564-8338
Husker House	3 mi SW	Phone: 564-4121
New World Inn	6 mi SW	Phone: 564-1492

Dusters Restaurant:

According to the management, Dusters Restaurant is located about 10 blocks south and 16 blocks west of the Columbus Municipal Airport. If you call the restaurant they will come out to pick you up. If possible, give them advance notice. This restaurant encompasses 12,500 square feet of dining and banquet space. Their hours are 5 p.m. to 10 p.m. Monday through Saturday, and open for Sunday brunch 11 a.m. to 2 p.m. Specialties include prime rib, scallops, shrimp, pasta, veal, rack of lamb, and a variety of appetizers including alligator tail, stuffed mushrooms and much more. The building containing the restaurant has been restored from its original 1920 design. The owner of Dusters Restaurant is very interesting to talk with. In fact, a large mural encompassing the north wall was designed by the owner, and contains a sort of chronological history of the various groups of people that played a significant part in influencing the region. Another interesting fact is that this same building was constructed for the assembly, service and sales of Ford automobiles. Today in addition to the dining area able to seat 78 people, Dusters also contains a banquet room that can accommodate up to 140 people. For more information you can call 564-8338.

Lodging: New World Inn (6 miles) 564-1492
Meeting Rooms: New World Inn (6 miles) 564-1492; Dusters (2 miles) 564-8338.
Transportation: Columbus Aircraft 564-0521 and Flight, Inc. 563-3508 can accommodate courtesy transportation to nearby facilities with advance notice; Johnnie's Steak House will pick up pilots and their guests from the airport when calling 563-3434. Also: City Taxi 563-3334 and Avis Rent-A-Car 564-2846.
Information: Chamber of Commerce, 764 33rd Ave., Box 515, Columbus NE 68601, Phone: 564-2769.

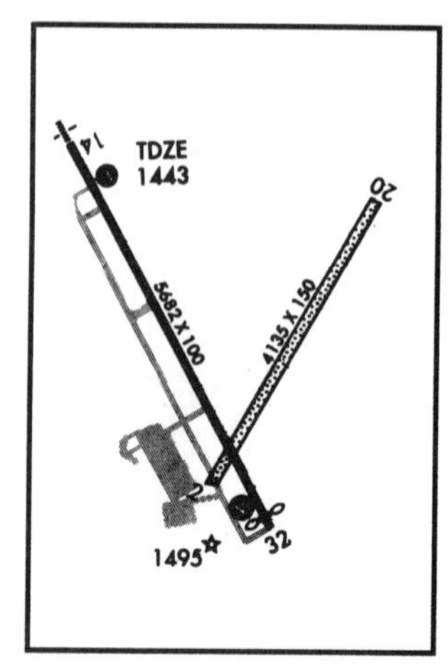

Attractions: Elks Country Club, city golf courses, and Lake North Pawnee Park all provide outdoor sporting activities for visitors. Contact Chamber of Commerce for details. (See "Information" listed above).

Airport Information:

COLUMBUS - COLUMBUS MUNICIPAL AIRPORT (OLU)
1 mi northeast of town N41-26.88 W97-20.42 Elev: 1443 Fuel: 100LL, Jet-A
Rwy 14-32: H5680x100 (Asph-Conc) Rwy 02-20: 4135x150 (Turf) Attended: daylight hours
Unicom: 122.95 Public phone 24 hrs Notes: For assistance after hours call 564-7043 or 9422.
FBO: Avcraft Phone: 564-7884 FBO: Columbus Aircraft Phone: 564-0521

NE-FNB - FALLS CITY BRENNER FIELD AIRPORT

(Area Code 402)

3

The Write Place:

The Write Place Restaurant is located about 1-1/2 miles from the Brenner Field Airport. This fine dining facility can be reached by courtesy car obtained through Falls City Aero Service (FBO) at the airport by calling 245-3715. This family style restaurant is open 7 days a week between 6:30 a.m. and 2 p.m. A Sunday buffet is featured 11 a.m. until 1:30 p.m. Their menu contains a variety of sandwiches, roast beef, hamburger, steak sandwiches, chicken sandwiches, shrimp, seafood salads, taco salads and much more. The main dining room can seat 68 people. The dining room is furnished with dark green table cloths and white napkins. The dining room has an aviation theme with photographs and pictures of antique aircraft. Pin-ups from the U.S. Air Corp. decorate the walls with "Keep Them Flying" mottos. We were told that their menu also uses aviation terms for some of their main dishes. This restaurant is part of the Stevens Hotel which also owns another lodging establishment down the street known as the Stevens Motel. For information call 245-5055.

Airport Information:

FALLS CITY - BRENNER FIELD AIRPORT (FNB)
1 mi northeast of town N40-04.72 W95-35.51 Elev: 984 Fuel: 100LL
Rwy 14-32: H3999x60 (Conc) Rwy 06-24: 1850x250 (Turf) Attended: dawn to dusk
Unicom: 122.8 Public Phone 24hrs.
FBO: Falls City Aero Service Phone: 245-3715

Restaurants Near Airport:

Camp Rulo River Club	9 mi E.	Phone: 245-4096
The Write Place	1 mi W.	Phone: 245-5055

Lodging: Check-In Motel (1 mile) 245-2433.

Meeting Rooms: None Reported

Transportation: Airport courtesy car available to nearby facilities. Falls City Aero Service (FBO) has courtesy car available 245-3715.

Information: Economic Development, Travel and Tourism Division, P.O. Box 94666, 700 South 16th Street, Lincoln, NE 68509. 800-228-4307.

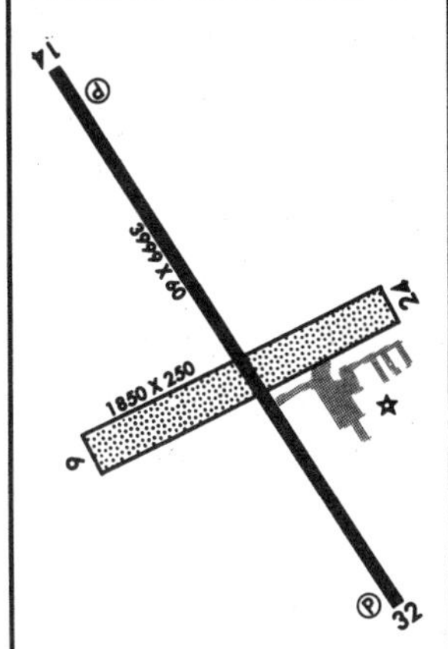

NE-FET - FREMONT
FREMONT MUNICIPAL AIRPORT

(Area Code 402)

4, 5

KC's Cafe & Bar:

KC's Cafe and Bar is located about 3 miles northwest of the Fremont Municipal Airport, within the downtown area. This family-style and fine dining facility specializes in 1/2 pound burgers, home made soups, salads, and for dinner they are well-known for their delicious prime rib and Cajun prime steaks, as well as other beef and steak entrees. In addition, they also serve home-style dinners, sandwiches and a children's menu. Luncheon and dinner specials are offered daily. Buffets are featured twice a year during Mother's Day and Easter. Hours of operation are 11 a.m. to 2 p.m. for lunch, and 5 p.m. to 9:30 p.m. for dinner. They are closed Sunday and Monday. The entire restaurant is furnished with antiques, a large collection of old brewery memorabilia and one room full of antiques from Fremont. A party room that will seat up to 175 people is available to customers planning get-togethers. The owners of this facility did the restoration to the 100 year old building, which originally housed a mortuary. All materials used were obtained from old mansions being torn down. The restoration took two years. For more information call 721-3353.

The Rose Room:

The Rose Room is located in the downtown area of Fremont, NE. This is a quaint dining facility that resembles a tea room nicely decorated with rose bowls on each table. The restaurant can seat about 50 people and serves a complete selection of breakfast and lunch entrees. A courtesy car can be obtained through the airport management or fixed base operator. If driving to this establishment from the airport, their address is 250 East 5th Street, and located 1/2 block east of 5th and Main Street. Restaurant hours are 6:30 a.m. to 3:30 p.m. Monday through Friday, and 7 a.m. to 2 p.m. on Saturday. For information call the restaurant at 721-0101.

Restaurants Near Airport:

Craig's Family Rest.	3 mi	Phone: 727-1095
Happy Inn Restaurant	2 mi.	Phone: 721-4711
KC's Cafe & Bar	3 mi.	Phone: 721-3353
The Rose Room	2 mi.	Phone: 721-0101

Lodging: Best Western/Holiday Lodge, (Free Trans, 3 miles), Jct. US 30 & Old US 275, 100 rooms, heated pool, cafe 6 a.m. to 9:30 p.m., lounge and meeting rooms. Phone: 727-1110

Meeting Rooms: Best Western/Holiday lodge, 727-1110

Transportation: (FBO) Woodaire Ltd., will provide courtesy transportation; Taxicab, 721-2121; AAA Auto Rental, 721-2452.

Information: Fremont Area Chamber, 92 West 5th Street, P.O. Box 182, Fremont, NE 68025, Phone: 721-2641.

Attractions:

Fremont Lakes State Recreation Area, (4 miles from airport on US 30). This park contains 20 lakes on a 650 acre site. Swimming, fishing, boating and picnicking. (Concessions), Phone: 721-8482; Valley View Golf Course, (6 miles from airport RR2), Phone: 721-7772; Fremont and Elkorn Valley Railroad, train rides aboard vintage railroad cars powered by steam locomotive. Trips to the towns of Nickerson and Hooper (Late April-Memorial Day, & Labor Day through late October, daily except Monday), Phone: 727-0615

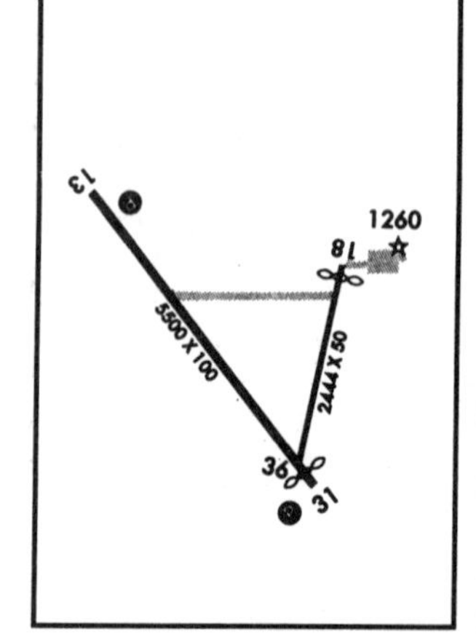

Airport Information:

FREMONT - FREMONT MUNICIPAL AIRPORT (FET)
2 mi northwest of town N41-26.82 W96-31.05 Elev: 1203 Fuel: 100LL, Jet-A
Rwy 13-31: H5500x100 (Asph) Rwy 18-36: H2444x50 (Asph) Attended: 1300-0200Z
Unicom: 122.8 Public phone 24 hrs Notes: Overnight tiedown fee $3.50.
FBO: Fremont Aviation Phone: 721-4520

NE-HSI - HASTINGS
HASTINGS MUNICIPAL AIRPORT

(Area Code 402)

6

Village Inn Pancake House:

The Village Inn Pancake House is situated about 1 block west of the Hastings Municipal Airport, and is well within walking distance. This family style restaurant is open Monday through Saturday from 6 a.m. to 2 a.m. and 7 a.m. to 12 a.m. on Sunday. Their menu includes a full compliment of breakfast items, and specializes in pancakes, omelets, along with burgers, sandwiches and two choices of Serloin steaks. They also provide a nice selection of desserts from which to choose. Average prices for meals run about $3.50 to $5.50 for breakfast and lunch and $5.50 to $6.50 for dinner. The restaurant has booths and tables with seating for 165 persons in their main dining room, as well as additional seating for groups in their atrium with accommodations for up to 24 people. For more information you can call the Village Inn Pancake House at 461-3351.

Restaurants Near Airport:

The Front Porch Restaurant	1 Blk S.	Phone: Out of Service
Village Inn Pancake House	1 Blk S.	Phone: 461-3351
Worlds of Food (Food Mall)	1 Blk S.	Phone: N/A

Lodging: All Within 2 blocks of airport: Budget Host Rainbow (Free trans) 463-2989 or 800-825-7424 res; Holiday Inn Motel (Imperial Mall 1 block south of airport) 800-238-8000; X-L Motel 463-3148; USA Inns 463-1422.

Meeting Rooms: Holiday Inn Motel (1 block south of airport) 800-238-8000.

Transportation: Most of the facilities listed are well within walking distance from the airport. Hasting Aviation can also provide courtesy transportation if needed. Taxi Service: Taxi-80 462-2195.

Information: Convention And Visitors Bureau, P.O. Box 941, Hastings, NE 68901, Phone: 461-2370 or 800-267-2189.

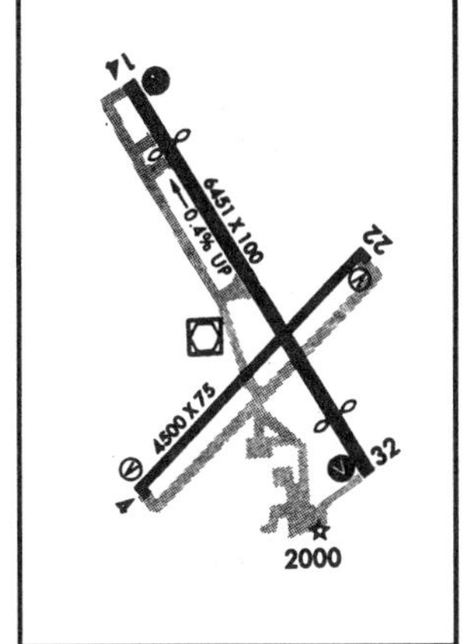

Attractions:

Lochland Country Club (Within 2 miles of airport) 462-4151; Southern Hill County Club (Within 2 miles of airport) 463-8006; Elks County Club (Within 2 miles of airport) 462-6113; Hastings Museum (Within 2 miles of airport) 461-2399; I-Max Theater 800-508-IMAX.

Airport Information:

HASTINGS - HASTINGS MUNICIPAL AIRPORT (HSI)

2 mi northwest of town N40-36.27 W98-25.65 Elev: 1954 Fuel: 100LL, Jet-A
Rwy 14-32: H6451x100 (Conc) Rwy 04-22: H4500x75 (Conc) Attended: dawn to dusk
Unicom: 122.8 Public Phone 24hrs Notes: For attendant after dark call 461-3557.
Airport Manager Phone: 462-6422

Hastings Museum

Hastings, NE (NE-HSI)

The Hastings Museum, located in Hastings in southern Nebraska, will take you on an exciting journey through the diverse world of nature. Many fascinating exhibits show the species of life which share our planet. Imagine yourself standing in a frigid arctic climate and coming face-to-face with the magnificent polar bear. Try gracefully floating from blossom to blossom with a hummingbird or soaring with migrating whooping cranes. Or, look back through time into the primitive, uncharted terrain of an earth dominated by dinosaurs. Dazzle yourself with the spectacular forms, colors and shapes of countless rocks and minerals magically transformed from the earth's crust. Picture endless herds of bison grazing in the mists while exploring the tribal lifestyles of the Native Americans. See the proud history and honored heritage of the people who first called the Great Plains their home. Step into the life of the hardy pioneers who settled the American West. Imagine the courage and spirit of those who left the bustling cities of the east to travel westward across an untamed land.

There's more! Visit the museum's Discovery Center where you will come face to face with nature. See, hear, smell and touch new experiences while opening a door into a world of natural and ethnic history. Hastings Museum also features the 200-seat Lied IMAX Theatre. (Closed Monday evenings.) It has a 70-foot-wide, five story-tall screen that seems to draw you into the film. There are a limited number of IMAX theatres in the world. The amazing combination of visual and audio sensations of an IMAX film lets you explore the wonders of the world without ever leaving your seat. Imagine walking around the world at the South Pole or floating in a shark cage; even flying with a flock of Canada geese or standing on the brink of an erupting volcano. Visit Yellowstone National Park and go wandering along the edges of the Grand Canyon or peeking down the great depths of Old Faithful.

Ever wondered what the other side of the moon looks like? Or, what makes up the rings of Saturn? The J.M. McDonald Planetarium, another of the museum's great attractions, explores these questions and many more. Under the planetarium dome, you get a front row seat to the constellations, solar systems, black holes, white dwarfs, quasars, red giants and many other mysteries of outer space.

The museum, located 2 miles from Hastings Municipal Airport, is open from 9 a.m. to 5 p.m., 7 days a week and is closed Thanksgiving Day and Christmas Day. With advance notice, the FBO will provide courtesy transportation to and from the airport. Overnight parking fees are $1.00-$3.00 for both singles and twins, but are waived with fuel purchase. For more information, call the FBO at 463-6631. For further information about Hastings Museum, call 800-508-IMAX (4629) or 461-2399. (Information submitted by Hastings Museum)

NE-4V6 - HAY SPRINGS
HAY SPRINGS MUNICIPAL AIRPORT

(Area Code 308) **7**

Restaurants Near Airport:

Babosa Cafe	1/2 mi	Phone: N/A
Bob's Bar & Grill	3 blks E.	Phone: 638-4520
Country Boy	1/2 mi	Phone: N/A

Lodging: Marge,s Motel (1 mile) 638-8441.

Meeting Rooms: None Reported

Transportation: None Reported

Information: Chadron Chamber of Commerce, P.O. Box 646, Chadron, NE 69337, Phone: 432-4401; Also: Economic Development, Travel and Tourism Division, P.O. Box 94666, 700 South 16th Street, Lincoln, NE 68509. 800-228-4307.

Bob's Bar And Grill:

Bob's Bar And Grill is located 3 blocks east of the Hay Springs Municipal Airport. This bar and grill is open 8 a.m. to 12 midnight, 6 days a week and closed on Sunday. Their menu has recently been expanded including a variety of sandwiches, finger steaks, chicken filets, fish filets, French fries, gizzards, nacho's and shrimp baskets. Daily lunch specials are also offered. Average prices are $2.75 for lunch and $2.00 to $4.00 for dinner. The main dining room can seat 52 persons. Fly-in clubs and groups are always welcome. Meals can also be prepared-to-go. For more information call Bob's Bar and Grill at 638-4520.

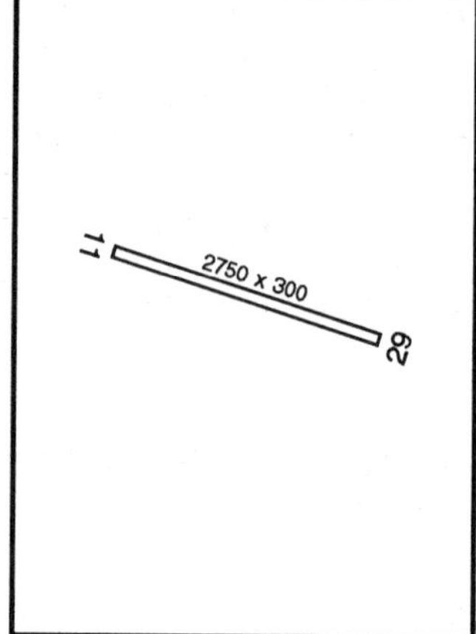

Airport Information:

HAY SPRINGS - HAY SPRINGS MUNICIPAL AIRPORT (4V6)
0 mi southwest of town N42-40.75 W102-42.28 Elev: 3831 Fuel: 100LL
Rwy 11-29: 2750x300 (Turf) Attended: unattended CTAF: 122.9
Hay Springs Municipal Phone: 638-7275 or 638-4566

NE-LNK - LINCOLN
LINCOLN MUNICIPAL AIRPORT

(Area Code 402) **8**

Restaurants Near Airport:

Air Host, Inc.	On Site	Phone: 474-6421

Lodging: The following will provide free transportation: Best Western Villager Motor Inn 464-9111; Best Western Airport Inn 475-9541; Comfort Inn 475-2200; Cornhusker 474-7474; Hilton 475-4011; Holiday Inn-Airport 475-4971; Ramada Inn 475-4400; Residence Inn by Marriott 483-4900; Senate Inn 475-4921;

Meeting Rooms; Cornhusker Hotel has accommodations for conventions; All the rest listed above under lodging, have meeting rooms available except the Senate Inn.

Transportation: Yellow Cab at airport; Also Avis 476-1202; Budget 476-8943; Dollar 435-3322; Hertz 474-4079; National 474-4301.

Information: Lincoln Convention & Visitors Bureau, 1221 N Street, Suite 320 Lincoln, NE 68508, Phone: 434-5335 or 800-423-8212.

Air Host, Inc.

Air Host Restaurant is located in the terminal building at the Lincoln Municipal Airport. This is a combination family style restaurant with snack bar. The restaurant is open from 5:30 a.m. to 3 p.m. 7 days a week. The snack bar opens at 3 p.m. until 9 p.m. They also have a lounge available between 12 p.m. and 6 p.m. The main restaurant offers all types of sandwiches, chicken strips, grilled ham and steak sandwiches, Rib-eye steak as well as fish and chips. Average prices range from $4.00 to $6.00 for most entrees. Their main dining room can seat 80 persons in addition to a separate banquet room available to seat up to 50 persons. For more information you can call the Air Host restaurant at 474-6421.

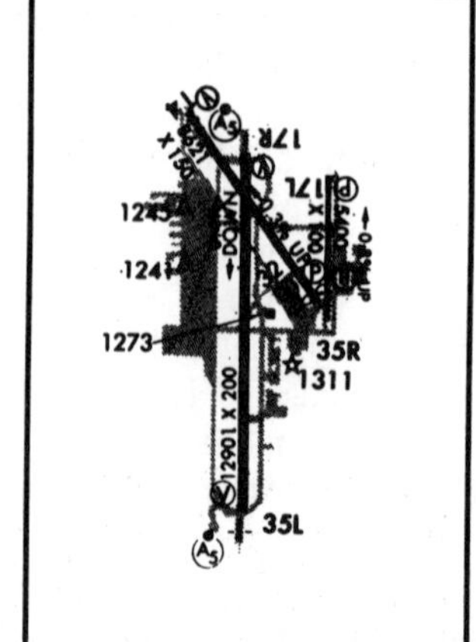

Airport Information:

LINCOLN - LINCOLN MUNICIPAL AIRPORT (LNK)
4 mi northwest of town N40-51.05 W96-45.56 Elev: 1218 Fuel: 100LL, Jet-A
Rwy 17R-35L: H12901x200 (Asph-Conc-Grvd) Rwy 14-32: H8620x150 (Asph-Conc-Grvd)
Rwy 17L-35R: H5400x100 (Asph-Conc-Afsc) Attended: continuously Atis: 118.05
Unicom: 122.95 App/Dep Con: 124.0, 124.8 Tower: 118.5, 125.7 Gnd Con: 121.9
Clnc Del: 120.7
FBO: Capitol Aviation Phone: 475-5444
FBO: Duncan Aviation Phone: 475-2611

NE-9V4 - MERRIMAN COLE MEMORIAL AIRPORT

(Area Code 308) 9

Sands Cafe:

To the best of our knowledge, and at the time of interview, this is the only restaurant that we found where you can still by a cup of coffee for only 25 cents. The Sands Cafe is located 1/4 mile south of the Cole Memorial Airport along highway 20. This family style restaurant is open from 7 a.m. to 8 p.m. Monday through Friday and Saturday until 2 p.m. for their Sunday buffet. Their menu throughout the week offers items like chicken fried steak, T-bone steak, ribs, hamburgers, chicken strips, shrimp and a full breakfast selection. The specials for the day often include roast beef and chicken dishes. Average prices run between $1.50 and $4.25 for breakfast and lunch, and $4.95 to $12.95 for dinner. Their Sunday buffet costs in the neighborhood of $5.50 per person. The main dining room can hold 50 people along with a party room for as many as 50 additional persons. The restaurant has tables and counter service, and is decorated with knotty pine walls. Meals can also be prepared to go. For more information call the Sands Cafe at 684-3389.

Restaurants Near Airport:
Sands Cafe 1/4 mi S. Phone: 684-3389

Lodging: Sands Motel (Adjacent to airport) 684-3330.

Meeting Rooms: None Reported

Transportation: None Reported

Information: Economic Development, Travel and Tourism Division, P.O. Box 94666, 700 South 16th Street, Lincoln, NE 68509. 800-228-4307.

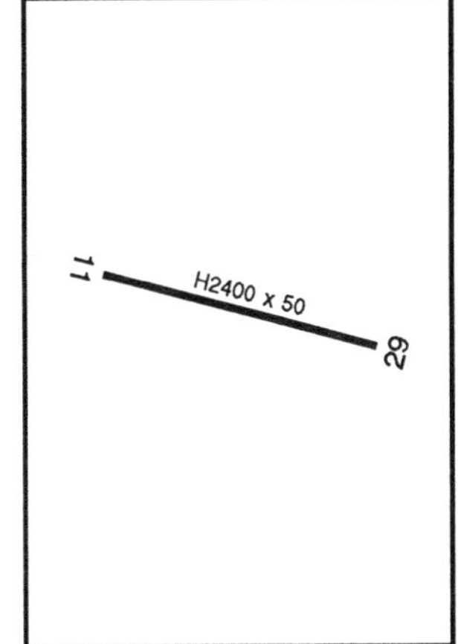

Airport Information:

MERRIMAN - COLE MEMORIAL AIRPORT (9V4)
0 mi northeast of town 42-55-48N 101-42-00W Elev: 3255 Fuel: None reported
Rwy 11-29: H2400x50 (Asph) CTAF: 122.9 Notes: Private use facility, use at your own risk.
Cole Memorial Airport Phone: 684-3330

NE-0V3 - MINDEN PIONEER VILLAGE FIELD

(Area Code 308) 10

Harold Warp Pioneer Village: (Attraction)

The Harold Warp Pioneer Village is a unique and interesting attraction that is popular with many visitors each year. The village contains 30 historic buildings located within a three city block historic area. Some of the buildings include a schoolhouse, a pony express station and even an authentic sod-covered house. Over 100 vintage tractors and locomotive engines are displayed along with 350 antique automobiles. In addition to the fascinating exhibits that chronologically follow man's progress since the 1830s is a collection of 22 vintage flying machines. The Harold Warp Pioneer Village contains a restaurant and motel on the premises. As a mini vacation, pilots could reserve a night's stay at the Pioneer Village Motel, spend the day touring the village, spend the night and, before heading back, play a round of golf at the Minden Country Club golf course (832-1965) located only 1/2 mile from the airport. For details you can call the Harold Warp Pioneer Village at 308-832-1181 or 800-445-4447.

Restaurants Near Airport:
Minden Country Club 1/2 mi Phone: 832-1965
Pioneer Village Restaurant 1 mi Phone: 832-1181

Lodging: Pioneer Village Motel (Trans) 832-2750.

Meeting Rooms: None reported

Transportation: Courtesy transportation can usually be arranged through Harold Warp Pioneer Village with prior notice by calling 832-1181 or 800-445-4447.

Information: Minden Chamber of Commerce, 325 North Colorado Avenue, P.O. Box 375, Minden, NE 68959, Phone: 832-1811.

Attractions:

Harold Warp Pioneer Village contains a huge collection of items dating from the 1830s. including aircraft on display. For information call 832-1181 or 800-445-4447; Also Minden Country Club golf course and restaurant 1/2 mile from the airport. For information call 832-2750.

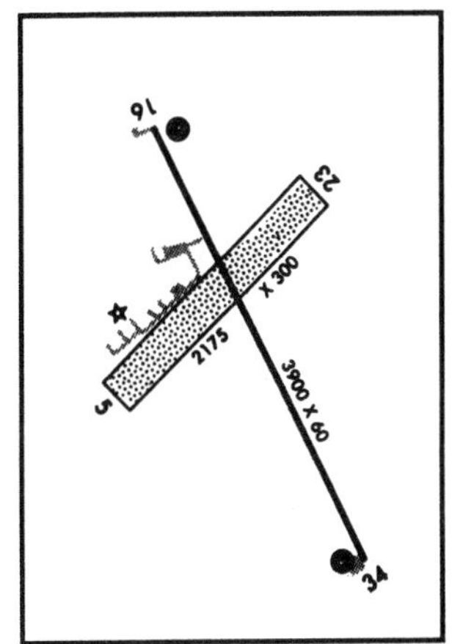

Airport Information:

MINDEN - PIONEER VILLAGE (0V3)
1 mile northeast of town N40-30.89 W98-56.76 Elev: 2159 Fuel: 100LL, MOGAS Rwy 16-34: H3900x60 (Conc) Rwy 05-23: 2175x300 (Turf) Attended: 1300-0100Z Unicom: 122.7
FBO: Classic Aero Phone: 832-0253

NE-3GN - NEBRASKA CITY GRUNDMAN AIRPORT

(Area Code 402)

11

Valentino's

Valentino's Restaurant is located about 2 blocks down the hill from the Grundman Airport along Highway 75. This family style restaurant is open between 7 a.m. and 9 p.m. Monday through Saturday and 10 a.m. to 9 p.m. on Sunday. Their menu provides selections with a variety of pizzas, pasta dishes, all types of sandwiches and their Italian buffet which features many items including lasagna, pizza slices, 6 different pasta sauces, salad bar and much more. This restaurant features an extensive number of buffets. A breakfast buffet runs from 7 a.m. to 10 a.m., then It changes to a luncheon buffet from 10 a.m. to 2 p.m. On Friday and Saturday they feature another buffet that runs from 11 a.m. until 10 p.m., and on Sunday from 11 a.m. to 9 p.m. Average prices for the buffet are $4.99 for lunch and $6.49 for dinner. Sunday brunch is also served between 10 a.m. to 2 p.m. The atmosphere is comfortable and relaxed with seating for up to 65 persons in their main dining room. The restaurant has a new party room for groups. Meals can also be prepared for carry-out. For more information you can call Valentino's restaurant at 873-5522.

Restaurants Near Airport:

Mc Donalds Restaurant	1/2 mile	Phone: N/A
Pizza Hut	1/2 mile	Phone: 873-7761
Valentino's Restaurants	3-4 blks	Phone: 873-5522

Lodging: Arbor Motel (Adj to airport) 873-9920; Stephenson Motel (1 mile) 873-6619.

Meeting Rooms: None Reported

Transportation: Car Rentals: Freshman Ford 873-6622; Rome Motor 873-3375

Information: Chamber of Commerce, 806 First Avenue, Nebraska City, NE 68410, Phone: 873-3000.

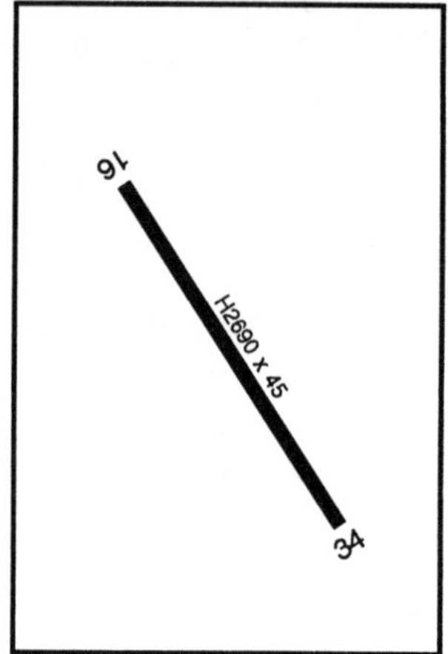

Airport information:

NEBRASKA CITY - GRUNDMAN AIRPORT (3GN)
1 mi southwest of town N40-39.55 W95-51.77 Elev: 1085 Fuel: 100LL
Rwy 16-34: H2690x45 (Asph) Attended: daylight hours CTAF: 122.9
FBO: Grundman Airways Phone: 873-9943 or 873-5836.

NE-LBF - NORTH PLATTE LEE BIRD FIELD

(Area Code 308)

12

Airport Inn:

The Airport Inn is located in the terminal building at Lee Bird Field. This family style restaurant is open 6:30 a.m. to 9:00 p.m. Monday through Saturday and 6:30 a.m. to 8 p.m. on Sunday. Their entrees feature steaks, seafood, fried chicken, home-made pies & soups. All dinners include soup or juice, choice of potato, coffee, tea and dessert. Lunch and evening specials are offered throughout the week. On Sunday they offer a choice of 2 luncheon specials in addition to prime rib dinners available on Friday and Saturday nights. Prices range from $3.50 for breakfast, $4.50 for lunch and $6.25 for dinner. The decor of the restaurant is modern. There is a separate area for private groups and parties that can accommodate up to 40 people. Catering services are also made available to pilots. For information call 534-4340.

Restaurants Near Airport:

Airport Inn	On Site	Phone: 534-4340
American Legion	N/A	Phone: 532-6083

Lodging: Stanford Lodge, (2 miles), Phone: 532-9380; Holiday Inn, (5 miles), Phone: 532-9090; Stockman Inn, (5 miles), Phone: 534-3630.

Meeting Rooms: Conference rooms are available in the airport administration building, and also at the Holiday Inn (5 miles), Phone: 532-9090.

Transportation: Trego Aviation has a courtesy car available, Phone: 532-5860; Avis Rent-A-Car 532-8014; National Rent-A-Car, Phone: 532-3765; Taxi: 532-2345.

Information: North Platte/Lincoln County Convention & Visitors Bureau, 502 South Dewey, P.O. Box 968, North Platte, NE 69101, Phone: 532-4729.

Attractions:

Buffalo Bill Ranch Historical Park, about one mile north of town on Buffalo Bill Avenue. Restored 18 room house with barn and adjoining buildings, open Memorial Day through Labor Day. Phone: 532-4795; Lake Maloney State Park, 6 miles south of town, featuring a 1000 acre lake with fishing, swimming, and camping, For information call 532-7939. There are also three golf courses within this North Platte area.

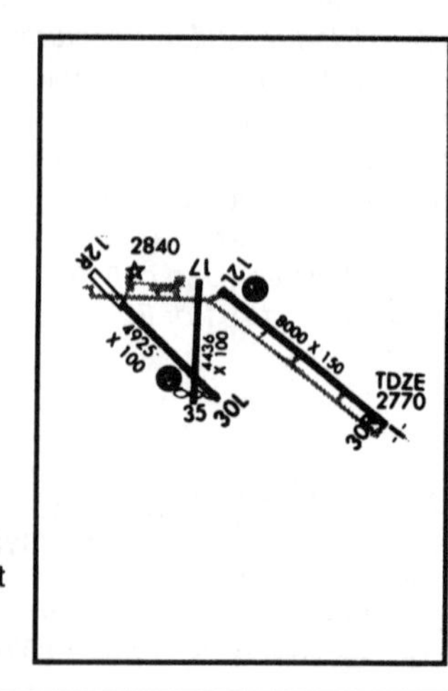

Airport Information:

NORTH PLATTE - LEE BIRD FIELD (LBF)
3 mi east of town N41-07.56 W100-41.23 Elev: 2778 Fuel: 100LL, Jet-A Rwy 12L-30R: H8000-150 (Conc-Grvd) Rwy 12R-30L: H4925x100 (Asph) Rwy 17-35: H4436-100 (Asph) Attended: 1200-0500Z Unicom: 123.0 Clnc Del 132.7 Public Phone: 24hrs Notes: Overnight tiedown fee.
FBO: Trego-Dugan Aviation Phone: 532-5864

NE-OMA - OMAHA
EPPLEY AIRFIELD

(Area Code 402) 13

Restaurants Near Airport:
Marriott Concesions Trml. Bldg. Phone: 422-6382

Marriott Concessions (Food Court):

Within the terminal building areas are two food courts. The North and South concourse of the terminal building include the following eateries. Burgerking, Pizza Hut, Taco Bell, a deli and expresso bar. For information call 422-6382.

Attraction:

Strategic Air Command Museum, founded by SAC in 1959, is located on a section of the Offutt Air Force Base inactive runway. Run by the Air Force until 1970, the museum is now managed by the Nebraska Department of Economic Development's Travel and Tourism Division. The Sac Museum is devoted to preserving the evolution of strategic air power from early World War II operations to the modern operation of SAC today. The museum is 15 to 20 road miles south of the Eppley Airfield via either U.S. 73-75 south to State Route 370 eastbound, or Interstate 29 southbound then exit State Route 370 westbound. For information contact, Strategic Air Command Museum, 2510 Clay Street, Bellevue, Nebraska 68005-3933 or call 402-292-2001.

Lodging: Airport Inn/Best Western (On Airport) 348-0222; Ramada Inn/Airport (Approx. 1 mile from airport) 342-5100.

Meeting Rooms: Eppley Airfield Conference Center 422-6376

Transportation: Elliott Beechcraft (FBO) 422-6789, and Sky Harbor Air Service (FBO) 422-6633, both are able to provide courtesy transportation to nearby facilities. Also Alamo Car Rental 344-0379; American Int'l 342-3375; Avis 422-6480 Budget 422-6610; Dollar 341-5577; Hertz 422-6870; National 422-6565; Safeway Cabs 342-7474; Happy Cab 339-0110.

Information: Greater Omaha Convention & Visitor Bureau, 1819 Farnam Street, Suite 1200, Omaha, NE 68183, Phone: 444-4660 or 800-332-1819.

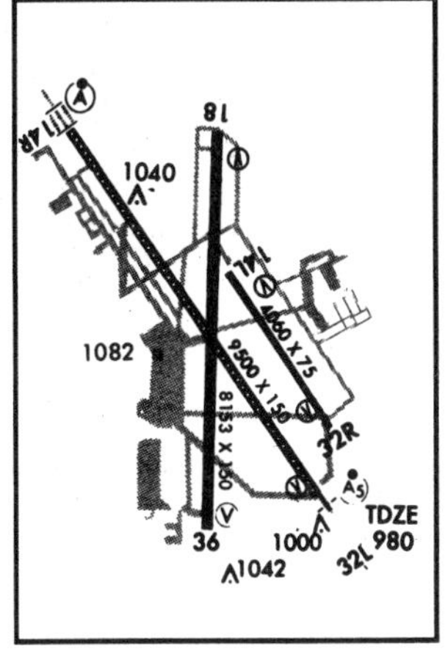

Airport Information:

OMAHA - EPPLEY AIRFIELD (OMA)
3 mi northeast of town N41-18.12 W95-53.62 Elev: 983 Fuel: 100LL, Jet-A
Rwy 14R-32L: H9500x150 (Asph-Grvd) Rwy 17-35: H8153x150 (Asph-Conc-Grvd)
Rwy 14L-32R: H4060x75 (Conc) Attended: continuously Atis: 120.4 Unicom: 122.95
Omaha App/Dep Con: 120.1 (West) 124.5 (East) Omaha Tower: 132.1 Gnd Con: 121.9
Clnc Del: 119.9 Public Phone 24hrs Notes: No landing fee for private aircraft, tie down fees are charged by the FBO's.
FBO: Elliott Aviation Phone: 422-6789
FBO: Sky Harbor Air Service Phone: 422-6633, 800-227-9839

Strategic Air Command Museum

Plattsmouth, NE (NE-PMV)

The Strategic Air Command Museum is located on the Offutt Air Force Base about 10 or 12 miles south of Omaha, Nebraska. Fly-in guests can land at Plattsmouth Municipal Airport (PMV) situated 9 miles south of the Air Force Base and the Strategic Air Command Museum. Rental cars can be obtained through Plattsmouth Municipal Airport by calling 402-298-8468, or by calling Bryant Motors at 402-296-4000.

The Strategic Air Command Museum, founded by SAC in 1959, is located on a section of the Offutt Air Force Base inactive runway. Run by the Air Force until 1970, the museum is now managed by the Nebraska Department of Economic Development's Travel and Tourism Division.

The SAC Museum is devoted to preserving the evolution of strategic air power from early World War II operations to the modern operation of SAC today. They invite you to enjoy the time you spend there, reliving the colorful past, and learning about exciting present-day air power.

The museum is self-supporting from admissions and gift shop sales that include souvenirs for their visitors. Museum improvements are supported by memberships in the SAC Museum Memorial Society.

Offutt Air Force Base has a long and colorful history. Established in 1896 as Fort Crook, an Army Infantry Post, many buildings from the 1800's are still in use.

A landing strip was developed in 1921 on a portion of the fort to refuel cross-country flights. In 1924 it was named Offutt Field to honor 1st Lt. Jarvis Offutt, Omaha's first air casualty in WW-I.

Just west of the current museum site, Glenn L. Martin Co. began production of B-26 Marauder light bombers in 1942. A total of 1,585 B-26s were manufactured before the company switched to production of B-29 Superfortress heavy bombers in 1944. Two of the B-29s produced, the famous "Enola Gay" and "Bock's Car", were used to drop atomic bombs on Hiroshima, Japan and Nagasaki, Japan.

A camp for Italian prisoners-of-war was also located at Fort Crook during World War II.

The installation officially became Offutt Air Force Base in January 1948 and SAC Headquarters moved to the installation from Maryland on November 9, 1948. There are currently more than 14,000 civilian and military personnel stationed at Offutt, including 16 Air Force generals and a Navy admiral.

Today the focal point at Offutt Air Force Base is SAC Headquarters. The complex, of over one million square feet, consist of a four-story main building, a three-story underground work area, and an underground command post.

Anyone interested in touring SAC Headquarters must make arrangements several months in advance.

When arriving at the museum, your path from past to present begins at the bottom of the stairs. Exhibits are grouped by category beginning with World War II and working up through history.

Take time to enjoy information on flying formations and bombs; airborne and underground command posts; SAC weapons and operations today; recon-

Photo by: Strategic Air Command Museum

naissance; evolution of bombers; aircraft engines; air crew trainers; SAC missiles; Medals of Honor; and history and missions of Offutt Air Force Base.

Be sure to include the 15-minute film on SAC's people, equipment and operations shown on the hour in the upstairs theater during your tour. There are short films, also worth viewing, included in the exhibits. The museum staff reminds visitors that many of the aircraft and missiles on display have antennas, flaps, propellers and other pieces protruding outside of the display area. For your safety, please use caution while viewing these items.

Some of the aircraft on exhibit include a B-36 Peacemaker, the first plane on exhibit at the museum, and is one of only four B-36 bombers still in existence. One of the last Peacemakers to fly, the plane was placed on display in 1959. A B-52 Stratofortress, SAC's first B-52, was put in service on June 29, 1955 and placed on display in 1965. Their B-58 Hustler, the famous "Greased Lightning", set and holds three Tokyo-London supersonic flight records. It has been on display since 1969. The XF-85 Goblin, one of only two experimental parasite fighters manufactured in 1948, was placed on display in 1970. The British Vulcan Bomber, one of only three on display in the United States, was a gift from the Royal Air Force. The plane was placed on display in 1982 while Vulcans were phased out of the British inventory. The Royal Air Force used Offutt Air Force Base to train for 26 years. The newest in the collection is the famous SR-71 Blackbird, and billed as the world's fastest airplane, was placed on display in March 1990.

Some planes are painted to represent specific World War II aircraft so that visitors get an idea of the types of colors and markings used by Army Air Corps crew. However, these planes are not the actual aircraft bearing the names shown. SAC Museum planes painted as replicas of specific World War II aircraft are B-17, B-25, B-29 and C-47.

Museum hours are Memorial Day to Labor Day 8:00 a.m. to 8:00 p.m., Labor Day to Memorial Day from 8:00 a.m. to 5:00 p.m. The museum is closed on Thanksgiving and Christmas. Admission is $4.00 for adults and $2.00 for children.

Fly-in guests can land at Plattsmouth Municipal Airport (PMV) situated about 9 miles south of the Air Force Base and the Strategic Air Command Museum. To reach the museum, just travel north on highway 34 from the Plattsmouth Municipal Airport. The AFB will be on your right. Maps are also available from the admissions clerk. For further information call the Strategic Air Command Museum at 402-292-2001.

NE-OKS - OSHKOSH GARDEN COUNTY AIRPORT

(Area Code 308)

14

Cafe Motel & Restaurant:

This facility is a combination cafe, fine dining restaurant & motel, situated one block east of Junction Highway 26 & 27, and is located one block north-northeast of the Garden County Airport. The restaurant hours are from 6 a.m. to 9 p.m. 6 days a week (Closed on Sunday). Cafe style seating is in the front of the restaurant, and the finer dining is in the back with a fire place, antique pictures on the walls, booths and tables. Specialties of the house include steaks, chicken, fish, sandwiches, soup and salad bar along with fresh ground coffee and home baked pies. Dinner specials include prime rib on Friday and Saturday evenings, as well as a Sunday brunch. Daily luncheon specials are offered along with evening dinner specials. Prices run $4.25 for lunch and $9.00 for dinner. They cater to small and l arge groups. Seating for finer dining in the back portion of the restaurant can accommodate up to 83 people while the cafe section in front can hold up to 42 people. If arranging a group fly-in, please call in advance. In addition to the restaurant, they also have a 13 unit motel with reasonable rates, open year around. For information call 772-3350.

Restaurants Near Airport:

Cafe Motel & Rest.	1 Blk NE	Phone: 772-3350
Kwik Stop	1 Blk N	Phone: 772-4510
Ret's Burger Barn	1 Blk NW	Phone: 772-4557

Lodging: S & S Motel (1 block northeast) 772-3350; Shady Rest Motel (1/2 block north & 2 blocks east), 772-4115.

Meeting Rooms: At the airport they have a flight lounge and also a large office room that can be used for meetings or conferences.

Transportation: All restaurants listed above are well within walking distance from airport. For available ground transportation, contact Garden County Airport Authority at 772-4482 or 772-3678.

Information: Economic Development, Travel and Tourism Division, P.O. Box 94666, 700 South 16th Street, Lincoln, NE 68509. 800-228-4307.

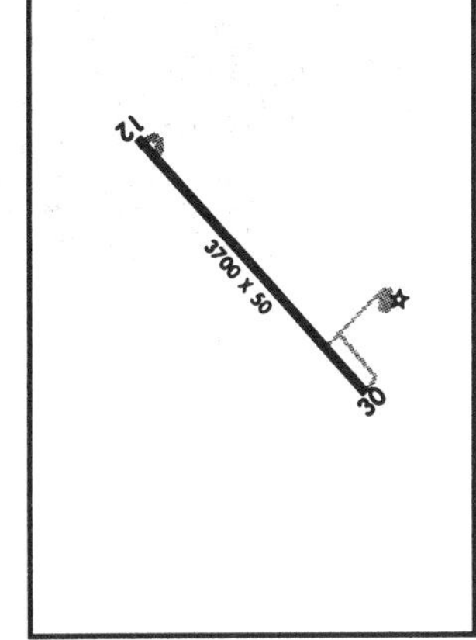

Airport Information:

OSHKOSH - GARDEN COUNTY AIRPORT (OKS)
1 mi southwest of town N41-24.06 W102-21.30 Elev: 3386 Fuel: 100LL
Rwy 12-30: H3700x50 (Conc) Attended: For service after hours call 772-3678 Unicom: 122.8
Public Phone 24hrs
Airport Manager Phone: 772-3236, 772-3515

NE-BFF - SCOTTSBLUFF WILLIAM B. HEILEG FIELD

(Area Code 308)

15

Skyport Restaurant:

The Skyport Restaurant is located within the airport terminal building at the William B. Heileg Field. This family style restaurant is open from 7 a.m. to 6 p.m. Monday through Saturday and from 8 a.m. to 6 p.m. on Sunday. Their menu features a 1/2 pound Skyport burger, croissants sandwiches, homemade soups and salads, full dinner entrees including rib-eye, chicken fried steak, chicken breast platters, and batter fish platters. Average prices run $4.25 for breakfast and lunch entrees and $5.95 for dinner entrees. Their main dining area has seating for 46 persons and displays a southwestern decor. Fly-in groups and clubs are welcome. Larger parties should give advance notice. This restaurant prepares meals to go as well as catering service through Valley Airways (FBO). For more information call the Skyport Restaurant at 632-3673.

Restaurants Near Airport:

Skyport Restaurant	On Site	Phone: 632-3673

Lodging: Budget Host Capri 635-2057; Candlelight Inn 635-3751; Scottsbluff Inn 635-3111; Trail Motel 632-4187

Meeting Rooms: None Reported

Transportation: Cabco Taxi 632-2224; Hertz 632-8174.

Information: Scottsbluff-Gering United Chamber of Commerce, 1517 Broadway, Scottsbluff, NE 69361, Phone: 632-2133.

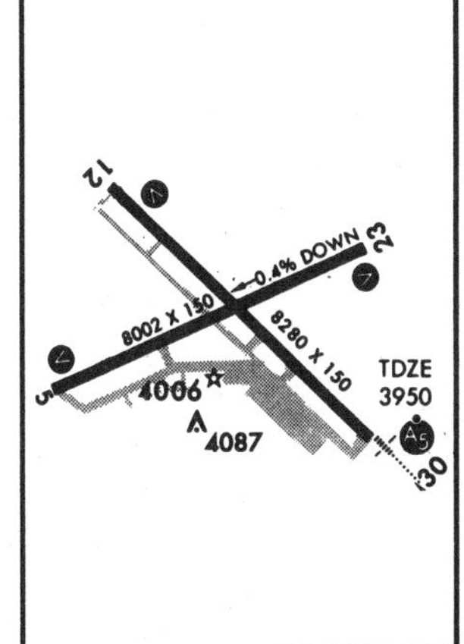

Airport Information:

SCOTTSBLUFF - WILLIAM B. HEILEG FIELD (BFF)
3 mi east of airport N41-52.44 W103-35.74 Elev: 3965 Fuel: 100LL, Jet-A
Rwy 12-30: H8280x150 (Asph) Rwy 05-23: H8000x150 (Asph) Attended: 1500-0300Z
Unicom: 123.0
FBO: Valley Airways, Inc. Phone: 635-1331

NE-SWT - SEWARD
SEWARD MUNICIPAL

(Area Code 402) 16

The Peppercorn Restaurant & Sports Bar:

The Peppercorn Restaurant & Sports Bar is located about 1.5 miles from the Seward Municipal Airport. This is a family restaurant that is situated north of the Seward Municipal Airport along Highway 15 on the left hand side of the road next to the Super 8 Motel. Restaurant hours are Monday through Sunday from 6:30 a.m. to 12:00 midnight Specialties of the house include appetizers, salads, steaks, Tex-Mex, pasta, sandwiches, hamburgers, soup and desserts. Average prices run $5.00 for breakfast, $6.00 for lunch and $9.00 for dinner. They offer a daily soup and sandwich special as well as a nightly beverage and entree special. Friday and Saturday they also feature their prime rib special. The decor of the restaurant exhibits a casual dining experience with a nostalgic sports theme. The Peppercorn Restaurant has three rooms available for parties and meetings that can accommodate 10 to 80 people. Transportation to the restaurant must be arranged through the Seward Airport. A courtesy car is reported available with advance notice by calling the airport manager at 643-2125. For more information, call The Peppercorn Restaurant at 643-9090.

Restaurants Near Airport:
Peppercorn Restaurant 1.5 mi N. Phone: 643-9090.

Lodging: Super 8 Motel 1.5 mi. Phone: N/A; Dandy Lion Inn 643-4517; East Hill Motel 643-3679.

Meeting Rooms: Peppercorn Restaurant has rooms for group gatherings used for catered meals 643-9090.

Transportation: Airport courtesy car reported. Call airport manager at 643-2125 for advance reservations.

Information: Lincoln Convention and Visitors Bureau, 1221 North Street, Lincoln, NE 68508. Phone: 476-7511.

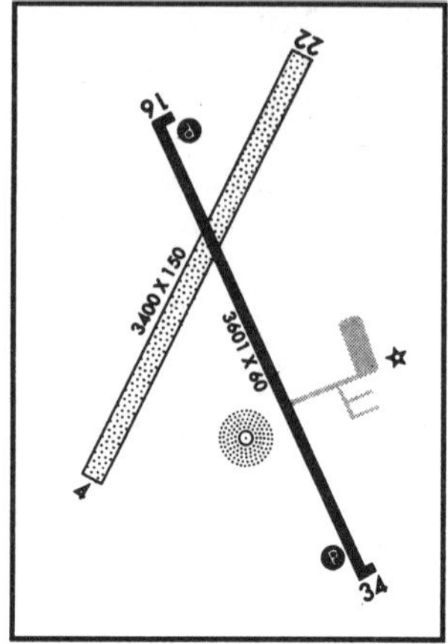

Airport Information:

SEWARD - SEWARD MUNICIPAL (SWT)
3 mi southwest of town N40-51.92 W97-06.56 Elev: 1505 Fuel: 100LL Rwy 16-34: H3601x60 (Conc.) Rwy 04-22: 3400x150 (Turf) Attended: Mon-Sat 1400-2300Z Unicom: 122.8
Airport Manager Phone: 643-2125

NE-SNY - SIDNEY
SIDNEY AIRPORT

(Area Code 308) 17

Cabela's World's Foremost Outfitter:

This establishment has a history as interesting as the thriving business that has become the largest outdoor mail order business in the world. There are two locations from which you can reach the Cabela's outlet stores. The City of Kearney, Nebraska, contains the Kearney Municipal Airport just 2 miles from Cabela's situated west of town. Our article in this issue, however will concentrate on the new World Headquarters located in Sidney, Nebraska. This newly constructed 75,000 square foot extravaganza is a must to visit and is easily reached by courtesy car provided by Cabela's. The High Plains Cache sandwich shop will satisfy your hunger as well as your taste buds, while the magnificent wildlife dioramas and merchandise will satisfy your mind. Everything from fishing, boating, hunting, camping and clothing is on display for your browsing pleasure. Their catalog lists thousands and thousands of items. If you would like a copy just give them a call at 800-331-3454. When landing at Sidney Municipal Airport give the store a call at 254-7889.

Restaurants Near Airport:

Country Kettle	3 mi	Phone: 254-2744
Dude's	3 mi	Phone: 254-9080
Cabela's Restaurant	(Trans)	Phone: 254-7889

Lodging: Days Inn (3 mi.) 254-2121; Econo Lodge (2 mi. free trans.) 254-5011; Super 8 Motel (3 mi.) 254-2081; Fort Sidney Motor Hotel (3 mi.) 254-5863.

Meeting Rooms: Non reported

Transportation: Cabela's will deliver customers to and from their facility 254-7889; Rental Cars: Elwell Motors 254-4547;

Information: Cheyenne County Visitor's Committe, 740 Illinois Street, Sidney, NE 69162.

Attractions:

Cabela's World's Foremost Outfitter 2 mi. from Sidney Municipal Airport (SNY). Free transportation is available by calling 254-7889; Also, there is an 18 hole golf course located 2 miles from airport; Fort Sidney Museum 3 miles from airport; Camping on airport.

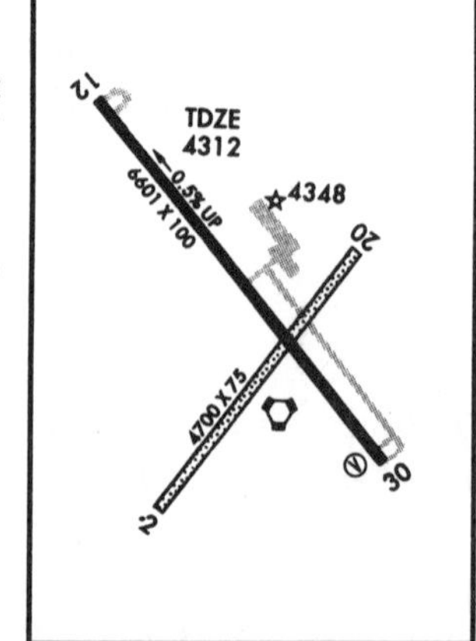

Airport Information:

SIDNEY - SIDNEY MUNICIPAL (SNY)
3 mi south of town N41-06.08 W102-59.12 Elev: 4312 Fuel: 100LL, Jet-A Rwy 12-30: H6601x100 (Conc) Rwy 2-20: 4700 x 75 (Non-hard surface) Attended: 1230-0500Z Unicom: 122.8 Notes: For services after hours call 308-254-3379
FBO: Sidney Aviation Phone: 254-5668

Cabela's World's Foremost Outfitter:

Photo by: Cabela's   An outdoorman's dream: Cabela's World's Formost Outtfitters Retail Store in Sidney, NE.

Cabela's World's Foremost Outfitter displays an attraction of pure sporting enjoyment comprised under one roof. This magnificent museum like retail and catalog enterprise is situated very near the Sidney Airport where fly-in adventures can come in, enjoy a lunch at their "High Plains Cache sandwich shop" and browse for hours the Cabela's retail store. Towering above Interstate 80 on the southern city limits of Sidney stands a tribute to the dedication of the Cabela family - the new 75,000 square-foot retail showplace. Its size is such that it can be seen for several miles in any direction. Acreage around the store contains a customer parking lot large enough to accommodate 450 vehicles, a special parking area for recreation vehicles and trailers that offers water service hookups and waste disposal facilities, and a 3-1/2 acre pond. On the south side of the building, two bronze, double-life-size bull elk in fighting position dominate the yard.

The retail center itself, designed to bring the outdoors inside, is unique in design and arrangement. The entry to the building has been designed for maximum effect. Immediately above is the 52-foot ceiling capped by a skylight and supported by huge pillars covered with Colorado moss rock, each of which holds an elk head of or near record book proportions.

At the opposite end of the building stands a 27-foot tall rock mountain framed in a 48-foot mural of blue sky. The mountain features a waterfall that splits at the base into two ponds and holds 40 life-size game mounts depicted in their natural habitats.

Suspended in the air between the entryway and the mountain is a flock of 16 Canada geese. Other original features include The High Plains Cache sandwich shop; the Cabela's Gun Library where one can see the epitome of the gunmaker's art; and Cabela's own travel service, Outdoor Adventures, where customers can plan and purchase exotic trips to anywhere in the world.

Above the entryway and sandwich shop is a mezzanine area. In the area is more Outdoor Adventures office space, an observation lounge and an art gallery displaying original prints of Cabela's catalog covers. From the observation lounge, it is possible to see every merchandising area for the store, its unique decor and the wildlife mounts.

Cabela's did not begin with an innovative product. Rather, it started with a little creativity and an honest deal. Through the years, incorporated with the company's incredible growth, that honest deals along with unparalleled customer service has remained the guiding force and the reason for Cabela's success.

It took the dreams and dedication of Dick and Jim Cabela to turn a seemingly improbable fantasy into reality and position Cabela's as the leader in the outdoor industry.

Much lies ahead for the company and further progress is not for down the road. But despite the progress and world-famous reputation, the Cabela brothers continue to embrace the original philosophy of ongoing customer service...a philosophy instilled in them by their grandfather, James Cabela, who owned a furniture store in Brainard, NE, and by their parents, A.C. and Marion Cabela, who owned a furniture store in Chappell.

And that's just one of the many reasons Cabela's is today what two brothers always knew it could be - a dream come true.

Transportation: Once landing at Sidney airport just call Cabela's and they will come out and pick you up. For more information call 308-254-7889.

Photo by: Cabela's

NE-7K8 - SOUTH SIOUX CITY MARTIN FIELD

(Area Code 402) 18

Marina Inn:

A restaurant and bar is located within the Marina Inn about 3.5 miles northeast of the South Sioux City Martin Field Airport. Courtesy van transportation is provided by the Inn as well as taxi service at the airport. This restaurant is classified as a fine dining facility with full service and a casual atmosphere. It is open Monday through Thursday from 6:30 a.m. to 10 p.m., Friday & Saturday from 6:30 a.m. to 11 p.m. and Sunday from 7 a.m. to 9 p.m. Their luncheon menu contains items like soups, salads and make your own sandwich bar. Their dinner menu features prime rib, steaks, seafood including and specializing in fresh fish market specials. On Sunday they offer a brunch from 10:30 a.m. to 2 p.m. Average prices are $4-$6.00 for breakfast, $4.50 to $8.00 for lunch and $7.50 to $15.00 for dinner. This modern upscale casual restaurant provides a scenic view that overlooks the Missouri River and downtown Sioux City, Iowa. Casual dress is welcome but formal dress is not out of place. In addition to the restaurant, this facility also contains convention, meeting and banquet facilities within the hotel. For information call 494-4000.

Restaurants Near Airport:

Holiday Inn	4.5 mi NE	Phone: 277-3211
Marina Inn	3.5 mi NE	Phone: 494-4000

Lodging: Marina Inn (3.5 mi NE) Phone: 494-3667; Holiday Inn (4.5 mi NE) Phone: 277-3211

Meeting Rooms: Marina Inn (3.5 mi NE) Phone: 494-3667; Holiday Inn (4.5 mi NE) Phone: 277-3211

Transportation: Both Marina Inn 494-3667, and Holiday Inn 277-3211, will provide courtesy transportation to and from their facility. Also Taxi Service: Radio Cab 712-258-0555; Siouxland Taxi & Limousine Service 712-277-0000.

Information: Chamber of Commerce, 2700 Dakota Avenue, South Sioux City, NE 68776, Phone: 800-793-6327.

NO AIRPORT DIAGRAM AVAILABLE

Attractions:

Arnold Palmer Dakota Doons Championship Golf Course (6 miles); Covington Links Golf Course (2 miles) 494-9841; South Ridge Golf Course (2 miles) 494-4323.

Airport Information:

SOUTH SIOUX CITY - MARTIN FIELD (7K8)

3 mi southwest of town N42-27.25 W96-28.35 Elev: 1100 Fuel: 100LL, Mogas
Rwy 14-32: H3281x22 (Asph) Rwy 04-22: 1950x75 (Turf) Attended: 1400Z-dusk Unicom: 122.8 Public Phone 24hrs Notes: No landing fee, only tie down fee of $3.00 per night; For attendant after hours call 494-3667 or 258-6722.

FBO: Sioux Air, Inc. Phone:494-3667

NE-64V - WALLACE WALLACE MUNICIPAL AIRPORT

(Area Code 308) 19

Wallace Cafe:

The Wallace Cafe is located two blocks north of the Wallace Municipal Airport on Main street. This restaurant is classified as a cafe and family style restaurant that is open Monday through Saturday from 7 a.m. to 8 p.m. They provide a full menu including rolls and pies, with noon and evening specials offered daily. Entrees run about $3.00 for breakfast, $4.50 for lunch and $7.50 for dinner. Fly-in groups are always welcome. They often cater to businesses, weddings, anniversaries, birthday and family reunions. For information call 387-4392.

Restaurants Near Airport:

Butch's Steak Hse.	23 mi E.	Phone: 368-7231
Wallace Cafe	2 blks N.	Phone: 387-4392

Lodging: Prairie View Motel, (4 blocks from airport) Wallace, NE, Phone: 387-4361

Transportation: Wallace Flying Service, Inc., Phone: 387-4662

Information: North Platte/Lincoln County Convention & Visitors Bureau, 502 South Dewey, P.O. Box 968, North Platte, NE 69101, Phone: 308-532-4729.

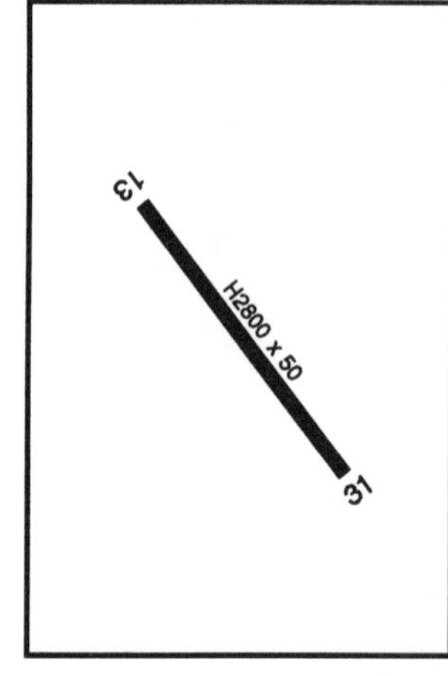

Attractions:

Camp Hayes, Hayes County, (25 miles south); Sutherland Reservoir, (23 miles north), Sutherland, NE.

Airport Information:

WALLACE - WALLACE MUNICIPAL AIRPORT (64V)

1 mi south of town N40-49.93 W101-09.84 Elev: 3101 Fuel: N/A
Rwy 13-31: H2800x50 (Asph) Attended: Apr-Aug dawn to dusk CATF: 122.9
Public Phone 24hrs Notes: Fuel only available during emergency, call 387-4662.

FBO: Wallace Flying Service Phone: 387-4662

NEVADA

LOCATION MAP

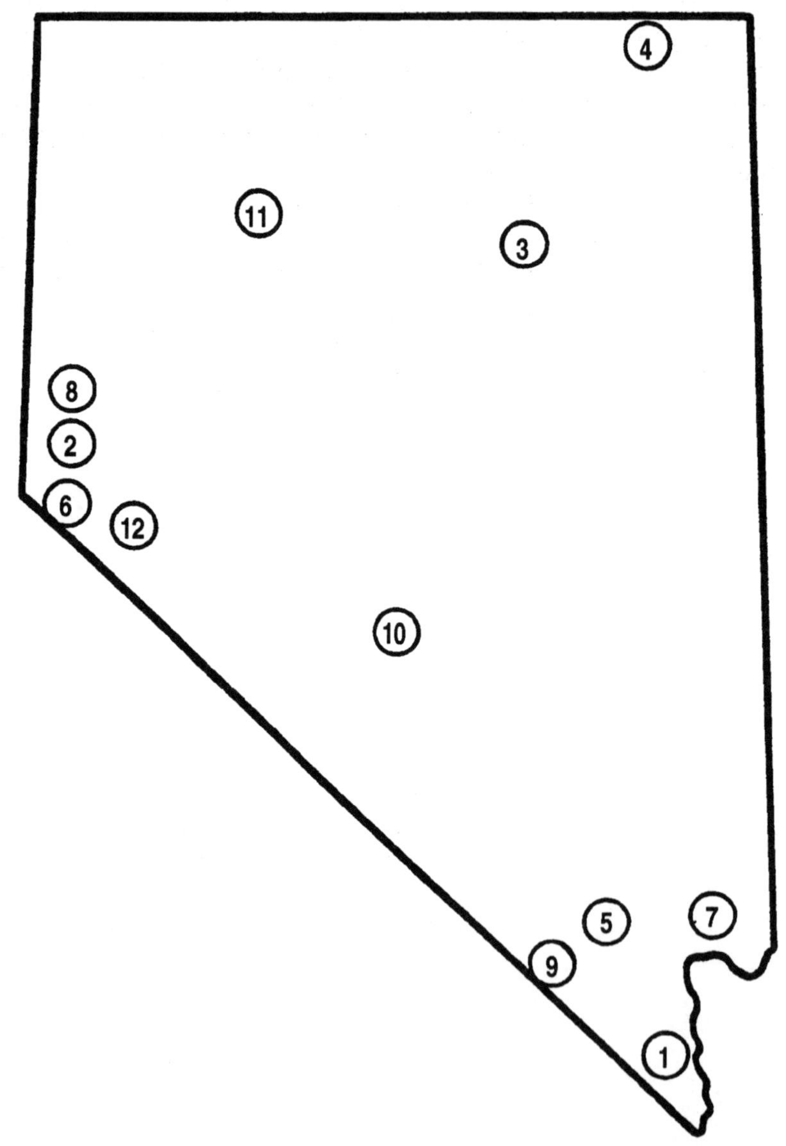

Not to be used for navigational purposes

NEVADA

CROSS FILE INDEX

Location Number	City or Town	Airport Name And Identifier	Name of Attraction
1	Cal Nev Ari	Kidwell Arpt. (1L4)	Cal Nev Ari Restaurant
2	Carson City	Carson Arpt. (O04)	Pookey's Final Approach
3	Elko	Elko Muni.-J.C. Harris Field (EKO)	Cimmaron West
4	Jackpot	Jackpot Arpt. (06U)	Four Jacks Htl. & Casino
5	Las Vegas	North Las Vegas Air Terml. (VGT)	Skyriders Restaurant
6	Minden	Douglas Co. Arpt. (MEV)	Carson Valley Inn
7	Overton	Echo Bay Arpt. (0L9)	Echo Bay Marina/Resort
8	Reno	Reno/Tahoe Intl. (RNO)	Marriott Concessionaire
9	Sandy Valley	Sky Ranch Estates (3L2)	Low Chapparal
10	Tonopah	Tonopah Arpt. (TPH)	Desert Flying Serv. Rest.
11	Winnemucca	Winnemucca Muni. Arpt. (WMC)	Winners Hotel & Rest.
12	Yerington	Yerington Muni. (O43)	Hangar Cafe

NV-1L4 - CAL NEV ARI KIDWELL AIRPORT

(Area Code 702) 1

Cal Ne Vari Coffee Shop & Dining Room:

This combination motel restaurant and casino, is located on the Kidwell Airport and combines a coffee shop and family style restaurant. Just recently they remodeled the restaurant, bar and lounge area. You can taxi your airplane right up to the restaurant. The coffee shop is open 7 days a week from 6 a.m. to 10 p.m., and the main dining room is open from 5 p.m. to 10 p.m. Their menu provides a full line of breakfast selections including, beef, chicken, Mexican dishes, and prime rib. On Friday they feature fish. Mexican food is also offered, Saturday its beef ribs and on Sunday they serve prime rib as their special. Average prices run $2.95 for breakfast, $3.95 for lunch and $8.00 for dinner. The main dining room can seat up to 60 persons. For information call 297-1118.

Restaurants Near Airport:
Cal Nev Ari Restaurant On Site Phone: 297-1118

Lodging: Blue Sky Motel (On Airport) Phone: 297-9289

Meeting Rooms: None Reported

Transportation: Airport courtesy car available

Information: Nevada Commission on Tourism, Capital Complex, Carson City, Nv 89710, Phone: 800-NEVADA-8; Also: Las Vegas Convention & Visitors Authority, 702-892-0711.

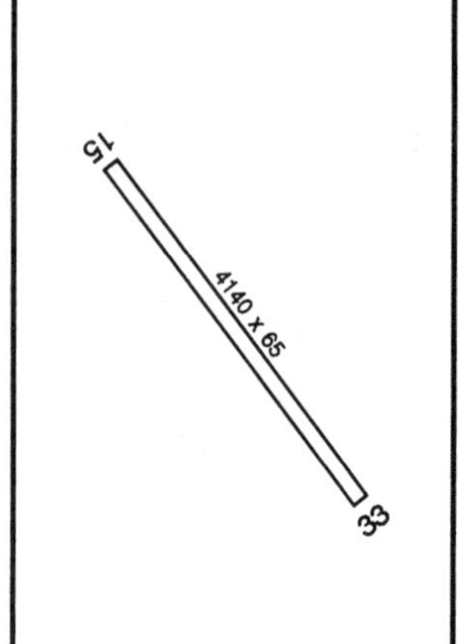

Airport Information:

CAL NEV ARI - KIDWELL AIRPORT (1L4)
0 mi south of city N35-18.33 W114 52.97 Elev: 2605 Fuel: 100LL
Rwy 15-33: 4140x65 (Dirt) Attended: continuously CTAF: 122.9
Kidwell Airport Phone: 297-9289

NV-O04 - CARSON CITY CARSON AIRPORT

(Area Code 702) 2

Restaurants Near Airport:

Carson Nugget	4 mi	Phone: 882-1626
Carson Station	4-1/2 mi	Phone: 883-0900
Pookey's	On Site	Phone: 885-7575
Ranch House	2 mi	Phone: 883-1771

Lodging: Carson Center Motel, 882-5535

Transportation: El Aero Services 883-1500, Also taxi and rental cars available. Transportation provided by some of the restaurants.

Information: Carson City Convention & Visitors Bureau, 1900 S. Carson Street, Suite 200, Carson City, NV 89701, Phone: 687-7410 or 800-638-2321.

Pookey's Final Approach Bar & Biestro:

Tnis newly remodeled facility is located right on the Carson City Airport. Enjoy a wonderful meal while watching planes take off and taxi up to their door step. Wander around and enjoy the large assortment of photos of planes decorating their walls. Breakfast, lunch and dinner is served from 9:00 a.m. to 9:00 p.m. The restaurant is open 7 days a week. Average prices for breakfast and lunch are around $4.50 to $5.00. Dinners start at 4:00 p.m. and feature steaks, chicken and seafood entrees at reasonable prices, averaging about $11.00. Their lounge has live music every weekend from 8:30 p.m. to 1:30 a.m. for your dining pleasure. Banquets of up to 100 people welcome. Live music for weekend banquets is availalible if desired. The FBO next door, provides car rentals so you can travel to Reno or Tahoe both only about 25 minutes away or right downtown Carson which is only 2 miles. For more information call 885-7575."

Attraction: Nevada State Museum is located at North Carson and Robertson Streets. This museum contains a life size recreated ghost town and Indian village along with 300 foot mining tunnel that runs under the museum building, (Open daily except January 1, Thanksgiving, and December 25), slight admission charge, Phone: 885-4810. Nevada State Railroad Museum, South Carson at Fairview drive. 22 freight and locomotives are on display including artifacts and steam train rides. Open June through October, Friday through Sunday and holidays, Phone: 885-5168.

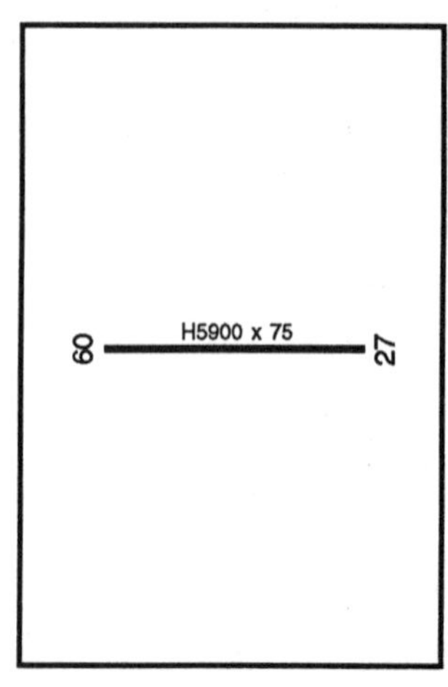

Airport Information:

CARSON CITY - CARSON AIRPORT (O04)
3 mi NE of town N39-11.49 W119-44.14 Elev: 4697 Fuel: 100, Jet-A Rwy 09-27: H5900x75 (Asph) Attended: Jun-Sept 1500-0400, Oct-May 1600-0300Z Unicom: 123.0
Notes: No landing fee, overnight fee.
FBO: El Aero Service Phone: 883-1500

NV-EKO - ELKO
ELKO MUNICIPAL-J C. HARRIS FIELD

(Area Code 702)

3

Cimmaron West:

Cimmaron West Restaurant is a family style establishment located off the airport property but within walking distance to fly-in visitors. Its about 200 yards from the airport and is open from 6 a.m. to 9 p.m. 7 days a week. Their menu contains Italian, Mexican, Oriental, and American cuisine. They also offer a salad bar along with daily specials. Average prices run about $4.50 for breakfast, $5.00 for lunch and $7.95 for dinner. The restaurant can seat up to 92 people in their main dining room. If planning a group fly-out to this establishment your party will be welcome provided advance reservations are made and you limit your group size to about 20 people. Meals-to-go are also available from items on their menu. This facility is comprised of a Texeco gas station, ice cream store and an RV park in addition to the restaurant. For more information call the restaurant at 753-8328.

Restaurants Near Airport:
Cimmaron West 200 yds Phone: 753-8328

Lodging: Red Lion Inn & Casino (Free trans) 738-2111; Thunderbird (Free trans) 738-7115; Stockman's (Free trans) 738-5141.

Meeting Rooms: Stockman's (Free trans) 738-5141.

Transportation: Rental Cars: Avis 738-4426; Hertz 738-5620.

Information: Chamber of Commerce, 1601 Idaho Street, Elko, NV 89801, Phone: 738-7135.

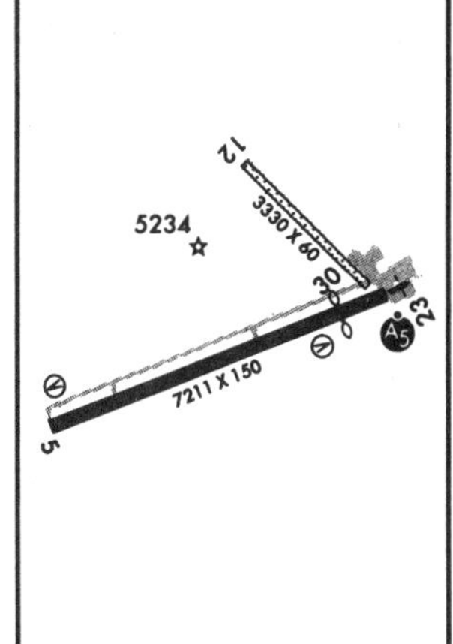

Airport Information:

ELKO - ELKO MUNICIPAL-J C. HARRIS FIELD (EKO)
1 mi west of town N40-49.50 W115-47.47 Elev: 5135 Fuel: 100, Jet-A
Rwy 05-23: H7211x150 (Asph-Pfc) Rwy 12-30: H3331x60 (Asph) Attended: daylight hours
Unicom: 122.7
FBO: El Aero Services Phone: 738-7123

NV-06U - JACKPOT
JACKPOT AIRPORT

(Area Code 702)

4

Four Jacks Hotel & Casino:

This facility is conveniently located approximately three blocks southwest of the Jackpot Airport. The restaurant within the hotel, is a family style facility and is open from 7:00 a.m. to 11 p.m. Courtesy transportation is available by calling Four Jacks. Every dish prepared at the restaurant is made from scratch including pastries and soups, (No outside prepared food). Everyday specials like their N.Y. steak dinner with salad and is offered for only $5.95 and is a favorite many of their regular customers. Another popular dish is their smoked prime rib and rib specials. Prices average $3.00 to $6.00 for breakfast, $4.50 for lunch and $6.00 to $7.95 for dinner selections. Friday specials include steak and shrimp. New York strip specials are offered every day. This is a family owned and operated business with direct owner management of kitchen preparations. By special request, catering to private parties can be arranged. The restaurant will also prepare meals-to-go. For information call 755-2491.

Restaurants Near Airport:

Cactus Pete's Casino	2 blks W	Phone: 755-2321
Barton's Club 93	4 Blks W	Phone: 755-2341
Four Jack's Casino	1/4 mi W	Phone: 755-2491

Lodging: Cactus Pete's Casino Hotel 755-2321; Four Jacks Casino Motel 755-2491; Barton's Club 93 Casino and Motel 755-2341.

Meeting Rooms: Both Cactus Pete's and Club 93 have accommodations for meetings or conventions.

Transportation: Cactus Pete's Casino & Hotel 755-2321; Barton's Club 93 Casino & Motel 755-2341

Information: Jackpot, Nevada Chamber of Commerce, P.O. Box 528, Jackpot, NV 89825, Phone: 755-2321 Ext 6716.

Attractions:

Gambling Casinos within walking distance from the airport. Also Jackpot Municipal Golf Course (18 hole) is located only 1/2 mile from the Jackpot Airport, Phone: 755-2260.

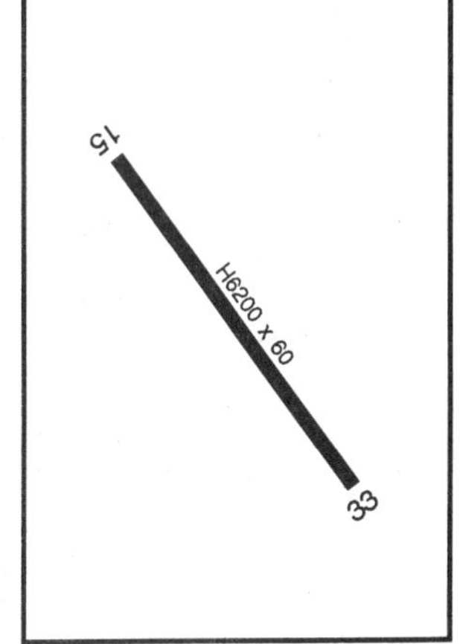

Airport Information:

JACKPOT - JACKPOT AIRPORT (06U)
0 mi from town N41-58.56 W114-39.49 Elev: 5213 Fuel: 100LL
Rwy 15-33: H6200x60 (Asph) Attended: continuously Public Phone 24hrs Unicom: 122.8
Notes: For fuel or taxi service, pilots can call "Cactus Pete's Casino" on unicom frequency of 122.8 or by phone 755-2321. No landing fees. Plenty of tie-down space is available for aircraft.
Airport Manager Phone: 755-2321.

NV-VGT - LAS VEGAS
NORTH LAS VEGAS AIR TERMINAL

(Area Code 702) 5

Skyriders Coffee Shop & Restaurant:

Skyriders Coffee Shop & Restaurant is located on the second floor of the terminal building. Their full service facility is open from 6 a.m. to 10 p.m. 7 days a week. They have an outside terrace as will as a main dining room. This restaurant serves entrees like Italian food, steaks, as well as many standard items. A full breakfast line is also available. Average prices run $4.50 for breakfast, $4.50 for lunch and $5.00 to $9.00 for dinner. Their menu contains daily specials as well as one dinner special. The main dining room can seat up to 130 people along with their outside terrace able to accommodate up to 60 persons. For private parties or business conferences, a special room is available that can hold 12 to 15 persons as well. For more information call the restaurant at 646-6717.

Restaurants Near Airport:
Skyriders Coffee Shop & Restaurant On Site Phone: 646-6717

Lodging: Arizona Charlie's 258-5200

Meeting Rooms: None Reported

Transportation: Taxi: A-North Las Vegas 634-1041; NLV Cab 736-8444

Information: Las Vegas Convention/Visitors Authority, 3150 Paradise Road, Las Vegas, NV 89105, Phone: 892-0711.

Attractions:

Casinos and hotels are located 6 to 12 miles south of airport.

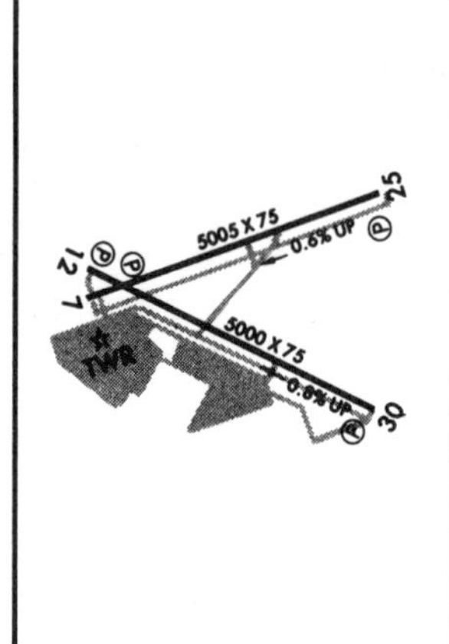

Airport Information:

LAS VEGAS - NORTHLAS VEGAS AIR TERMINAL (VGT)
3 mi northwest of town N36-12.70 W115-11.74 Elev: 2203 Fuel: 100LL, Jet-A
Rwy 07-25: H5005x75 (Asph) Rwy 12-30: H5000x75 (Asph) Attended: 1400-0630Z
Atis: 118.05 Unicom: 122.95 Tower: 125.7 Gnd Con: 121.7 Notes: No landing fees, Overnight parking $4.00 singles and $5.25 twins.
FBO: North Las Vegas Air Terminal Phone: 261-3806
FBO: Vegas Radio, Inc. Phone: 646-0927

NV-MEV - MINDEN
DOUGLAS COUNTY AIRPORT

(Area Code 702) 6

Carson Valley Inn:

The Carson Valley Inn provides a relaxing stay away from the hustle and bustle with 230 luxurious rooms or spacious suites with private spa. Enjoyable excitement may come in many forms while trying your luck at many of the gaming activities or entertainment in store for your enjoyment. The scenic Carson Valley, just 20 minutes from Lake Tahoe, is one of the nation's premier hot air ballooning and soaring areas. You'll also find more down to earth activities like snow skiing, snowmobiling, fishing, water skiing, horseback riding, tennis, trap shooting, pheasant hunting, relaxing in natural hot springs, and of course, sightseeing in an area rich in western history. Plus, Carson Valley Inn has great group golf and hunting packages, along with surprisingly inexpensive winter ski packages for groups and individuals. For your dining pleasure enjoy "Katie's", their 24 hour restaurant which blends friendly attentive service with quality cuisine, all in a cozy garden atmosphere for an unforgettable meal. For an additional dining treat, try Fiona's Restaurant for lunch or dinner featuring superb steaks, seafood and a garden fresh salad bar...plus a relaxing lounge serving appetizers and your favorite beverages. Michael's restaurant is an additional restaurant that offers a tast-tempting Sierra Pinion cuisine along with traditional dinner selections nightly except Tuesdays. This resort establishment majestically nestled between the Sierra mountains to the west and rolling hills to the east, combines accommodations of pleasure and recreation along with a 6,000 foot conventions space for business meetings, executive retreats, banquets or groups up to 400 people. For more information call Carson Valley Inn at 782-9711 in Nevada or 800-321-6983.

Restaurants Near Airport:

Carson Valley Inn	5 mi S.	Phone: 782-9711
Little Monoeaux Lodge	5 mi NW	Phone: 782-8838
Minden McDonalds	4-1/2 mi S	Phone: 782-8822
Pipeline Inn	4-1/2 mi S	Phone: 782-7408

Lodging: Carson Valley Inn Hotel & Casino 782-9711 or 800-321-6983 outside NV.

Meeting Rooms: Carson Valley Inn Hotel & Casino 782-9711 or 800-321-6983 outside NV.

Transportation: Hutt Aviaton, Inc 782-8277; Minden Taxi 782-8294.

Information: Carson Valley Chamber of Commerce and Visitor's Authority, 1524 US Highway 395, Suite 1, Gardnerville, NV 89410; Phone: 800-727-7677 or 702-782-8144.

Attractions: (Information on Carson Valley obtained by Carson Valley Chamber of Commerce)

Carson Valley: Many people use Carson Valley as their headquarters when they want to enjoy northern Nevada. The area offers many great outdoor activities as well as indoor activities. Golf: Choose from two Carson Valley courses or take the short drive to Lake Tahoe, Carson City or Dayton for more golf choices. Bicycling: Stay on the pavement and challenge some of their great grades, or get off road on one of the many mountain-bike trails in the area. Nature Lovers: There are a number of places to go for bird-watching, hiking, camping and spectacular photography. Fishing: The Carson River and Topaz Lake offer great fishing using flies and bait. Snow Skiing: Within 15-30 minute drive are some of the country's best downhill and cross-country skiing. Soaring: Because of ideal winds, the Carson Valley is known as the soaring capital of the West. Take a ride in a glider based at the Douglas County Airport. Hot Air Ballooning: Rise to the occasion with a ride in a hot air balloon, and enjoy the champagne ceremony following the ride. For information and details on these and a wide array of other activities, stop by the Chamber of Commerce office an pick up an Activities brochure. Interested in Golf? Ask for their Golf brochure.

Carson City: Additional attraction in Carson City (Approximately 8 miles north of airport) can be enjoyed such as the State Capitol: Nevada State Museum contains artifacts of antiques, guns, pioneer memorabilia and mining equipment along with a 300 foot mining tunnel which runs beneath the museum, a life size display of a Nevada ghost town, and much more; Warren Engine Company No 1 Fire Museum; and Nevada State Railroad Museum with train rides and railroad memorabilia; Also Carson Valley Inn Hotel & Casino (Reported 5 miles south of the Douglas County Airport) with many activities available for the visitor, Phone: 782-9711 or 800-321-6983.

NO AIRPORT
DIAGRAM
AVAILABLE

Airport Information:

MINDEN - DOUGLAS COUNTY AIRPORT (MEV)
4 mi north of town N39-00.03 W119-45.18 Elev: 4718 Fuel: 100, Jet-A
Rwy 16-34: H7395x100 (Asph) Rwy 12-30: H5289x75 (Asph) Rwy 12G-30G: 2600x20 (Dirt)
Attended: Nov-Feb 1600-0200Z, Mar-Oct, Mon-Fri 1500-0300Z Unicom: 122.8
Public Phone 24hrs
FBO: Hutt Aviation, Inc. Phone: 782-8277

NV-0L9 - OVERTON
ECHO BAY AIRPORT

(Area Code 702)

7

Restaurants Near Airport:

Echo Bay Marina & Resort 2 mi Phone: 394-4000

Lodging: Echo Bay Resort 394-4000.

Meeting Rooms: Echo Bay Marina & Resort 394-4000

Transportation: Courtesy transportation available.

Information: Lake Mead National Recreation Area, 601 Nevada Highway, Boulder City 89005-2426 or call 293-8906; Also: Nevada Commission on Tourism, Capitol Complex, Carson City, Nevada 89710 or call 1-800-NEVADA-8 Ext. 8, Also 1-800-237-0774.

Echo Bay Marina & Resort:

This establishment is located near the western shore of Lake Mead, and as reported by the resort, is approximately 1 to 2 miles to the east of the Echo Bay Airport in Overton, Nevada. We found that resort courtesy transportation is available to fly-in guests. This facility contains 52 rooms, house boats and a family style restaurant. The restaurant hours are from 8 a.m. to 8:30 p.m. during the off season and from 7 a.m. to 9:30 p.m. during the summer season. Their menu includes items like New York steak, trout, halibut, a full line of breakfast entrees as well as soups and salads. Daily specials are offered throughout the day. The decor of the restaurant provides a nautical atmosphere with seating for about 90 persons. A separate dining room can also accommodate up to 80 persons for special events or catered parties and meetings. For more information call the resort at 394-4000.

Attractions:

The Lake Mead National Recreational Area contains a 2,338 square mile region that offers a multitude of attractions and activities for the vacationer. The Hoover Dam creates one of the largest man made reservoirs attracting over eight million people annually. Nearby attractions include Hoover Dam, Davis Dam, Lake Mead Yacht Tours at 293-6180 as well as many additional activities such as camping, swimming, fishing and boating. For information about the Lake Mead attractions and park areas contact: Lake Mead National Recreation Area, 601 Nevada Highway, Boulder City 89005-2426 or call 293-8906.

Airport Information:

OVERTON - ECHO BAY AIRPORT (0L9)

14 mi south of town N36-18.67 W114-27.83 Elev: 1535 Rwy 06-24: H3400x50 (Asph)
Attended: unattended Unicom: 122.8
Echo Bay Airport Phone: 394-4000.

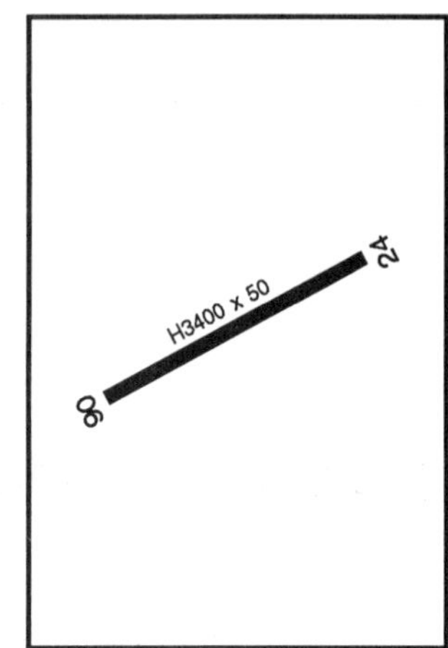

NV-RNO - RENO
RENO/TAHOE INTERNATIONAL

(Area Code 702)

8

Restaurants Near Airport:

Airport Plaza Grill	500 yds.	Phone: 348-6370
Amelia's Restaurant	On Site	Phone: 858-7316
Cattins Restaurant	1/2 mile	Phone: 348-7555
Marriott Concessionaire	On Field	Phone: 785-2587

Lodging: (Free Airport Transportation by the following): La Quinta Inn-Airport 348-6100; Quality Inn Reno 825-4700; Best Western Airport Plaza 348-6370; Bally's 789-2000; Harrah's 648-3773; Peppermill Hotel Casino 826-2121; Ramada Inn 788-2000.

Meeting Rooms: All lodging facilities listed above contain accommodations for meeting and conferences. (See Lodging)

Transportation: All FBO's have courtesy transportation available to nearby facilities; Taxi: Reno-Sparks 333-3333; Whittlesea 323-3111; Yellow 331-7171; Rental Cars: Avis 785-2727; Budget 785-2545; Dollar 348-2888; General 826-2888; Hertz 785-2554; National 785-2756.

Information: Reno-Tahoe Visitors Center, 133 North Sierra Street, or Chamber of Commerce at P.O. Box 3499, Reno, NV 89505 Phone: 329-3558.

Marriott Concessionaire.

Marriott operates several food service facilities at the Reno Cannon International Airport (snack bar, cafe, and cafeteria). These facilities are located in the main terminal building. According to information received, if arriving at Mercury Aviation you can walk to the main terminal building. You might want to varify this. The main lobby is open from 5:30 a.m. to 10:00 p.m. 7 days a week. The concourse snack bars are open from 6 a.m. to 9:30 p.m. 7 days a week. Various hot entrees such as soups, salads, sandwiches, burgers, chicken sandwiches, hot dogs and nacho's are available. Average prices run $4.39 for breakfast, $6.60 for lunch and dinner selections. The dining facilities are modern and decorated with pictures of "Old" Reno and various ski scenes representing Lake Tahoe. Groups are welcome, however please allow at least 48 hours notice prior to meeting. Limited catering can be provided. Interested parties can call 785-2587.

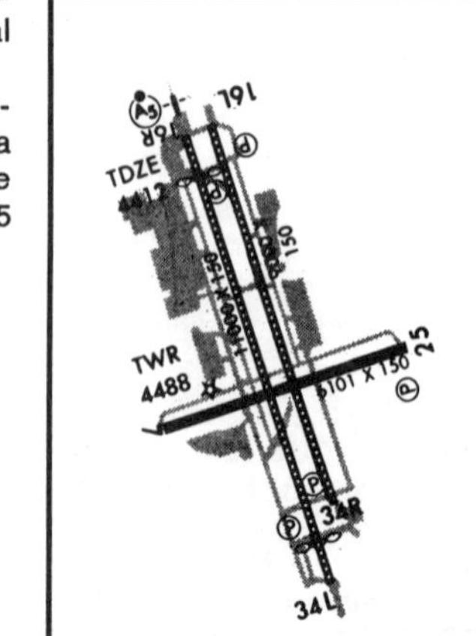

Airport Information:

RENO - RENO/TAHOE INTERNATIONAL AIRPORT (RNO)

3 mi southeast of town N39-29.92 W119-46.08 Elev: 4412 Fuel: 100LL, Jet-A1+
Rwy 16R-34L: H11000x150 (Conc-Grvd) Rwy 16L-34R: H9000x150 (Conc-Grvd)
Rwy 07-25: H6101x150 (Asph) Attended: continuously Atis: 124.35 Unicom: 122.95
App/Dep Con: 126.3, 120.8, 119.2 Reno Tower: 118.7 Gnd Con: 121.9 Clnc Del: 124.9
Public Phone 24hrs Notes: No landing fees for part 91 aircraft - Parking varies by FBO
FBO: Jet West Phone: 825-6400 FBO: Sierra Air Center Phone: 856-8900
FBO: Mercury Aviation Phone: 858-7300

NV-3L2 - SANDY VALLEY SKY RANCH ESTATES

(Area Code 702)

9

Loe Chapparal:

This cafe is located about 1 mile from the Sky Ranch Estates Airport. Dick Clark Aviation/Sandy Valley Aviation at 723-5055 will take you to the restaurant if you let them know in advance that you plan on flying in. This restaurant is open from 8 a.m. to 7:45 p.m. 7 days a week. Their menu contains items like chicken fingers, hamburgers, cheeseburgers, biscuits and gravy, and a full line of breakfast dishes including omelets, pancakes and their popular 99 cent breakfast specials. Average prices for meals run $2.50 for breakfast, $3.75 for lunch and about $4.00 to $5.00 for dinner. The main dining area can seat 25 persons in addition to the bar area. Groups and parties are welcome. For more information you can call the restaurant at 723-5221.

Restaurants Near Airport:
Low Chapparal 1 mi Phone: 723-5221
Sandy Valley Pizza 1-1/2 mi Phone: 723-5400

Lodging: Gold Strike Hotel & Casino 477-5000; Nevada Landing Hotel & Casino 387-5000.

Meeting Rooms: None reported

Transportation: Sandy Valley Aviation courtesy car only available with advance reservation. Phone: 723-5060.

Information: Sandy Valley Sky Ranch Estates 723-5427 or Sandy Valley Aviation 723-5060. Also: Nevada Commission on Tourism, Capitol Complex, Carson City, Nv 89710, Phone: 800-NEVADA-8.

NO AIRPORT DIAGRAM AVAILABLE

Airport Information:

SANDY VALLEY - SKY RANCH ESTATES (3L2)
2 mi southwest of town N35-47.72 W115-37.63 Elev: 2599 Fuel: 100LL
Rwy 12-30: 5850x115 (Dirt) Rwy 03-21: H3340x45 (Asph) Attended: irregularly
Unicom: 122.7
FBO: Sandy Valley Aviation Phone: 723-5060

NV-TPH - TONOPAH TONOPAH AIRPORT

(Area Code 702)

10

Desert Flying Service Restaurant:

This cafe is located in the Desert Flying Service (FBO) on the Tonopah Airport. The restaurant hours are from 8 a.m. to 3 p.m., 6 days a week Monday through Saturday. Their menu offers items such as hamburgers, chicken sandwiches, cheeseburgers, chili, soups, salads, and pies. Average prices for selections run about $4.00 to $5.00. This cafe has seating for about 8 people with two small tables situated near the window where you can see the runways. Carry-out meals are often prepared for pilots on-the-go as well as customers stopping in for fuel and continuing on to their destination. For more information you can call the Desert Flying Service Restaurant at 482-3626.

Restaurants Near Airport:
Desert Flying Service On Site Phone: 482-3626

Lodging: Best Western Hi Desert Inn (Free trans) 482-3511; Jim Buttler Motel 482-3577; Sundowner Motel 482-6224.

Meeting Rooms: None reported

Transportation: None reported

Information: Desert Flying Service 482-3626.

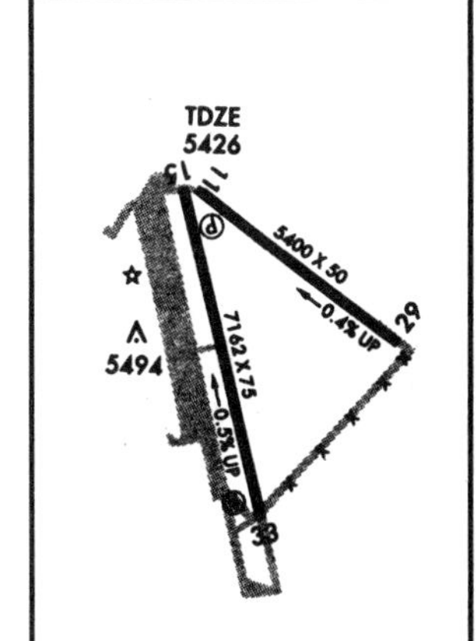

Airport Information:

TONOPAH - TONOPAH AIRPORT (TPH)
7 mi east of town N38-03.48 W117-05.37 Elev: 5426 Fuel: 100, Jet-A
Rwy 15-33: H7162x75 (Asph) Rwy 11-29: H5400x50 (Asph) Attended: daylight hours (On call nights) Unicom: 123.0 Notes: See AFD for runway conditions.
Desert Flying Service Phone: 482-3626

NV-WMC - WINNEMUCCA
WINNEMUCCA MUNICIPAL AIRPORT

(Area Code 702) 11

Winners Hotel - Casino
Pete's Coffee Shop & Grandma's House:

Free shuttle service is available to and from the Winnemucca Municipal Airport. There is a direct line telephone located at the airport. Pete's Coffee Shop is open 24 hours a day seven days a week. Grandma's Restaurant opens its doors at 5:00 p.m. to 10:00 p.m. seven days a week. Pete's Coffee Shop, features a wide variety of entrees such as daily lunch and dinner buffets, brunch buffet on Saturday and Sunday, and a seafood buffet is offered on Friday. The decor exhibits a unique collection of miniature wagons and stagecoaches. Average prices range from $4.00 for breakfast, $5.00 for lunch and $ 8.00 for dinner. Grandma's House is a combination family style and fine dining facility that also offers nightly specials as well as a host of entrees like prime rib, steaks and seafood. Many fine antiques are displayed about the restaurant. Catering is available on the premises for 20 to 75 persons. Winners Hotel-Casino is a full service facility containing 125 hotel rooms and suites, two restaurants, snack bar, lounge, with live entertainment, as well as a variety of gambling machines. For information call 623-2511.

Restaurants Near Airport:

Model T Casino	5 mi NE.	Phone: 623-2588
Red Lion Inn & Casino	5 mi NE.	Phone: 623-2565
Winners Hotel/Casino	5 mi NE.	Phone: 623-2511

Lodging: All three casinos listed above furnish lodging accommodations:

Conference Rooms: All of the casinos listed above furnish conference or meeting rooms.

Transportation: Winnemucca Air Service can provide transportation; All three casinos listed above have shuttle service to and from the airport 24 hours each day; Taxi: Winnemucca Cab, 623-1100.

Information: Humboldt County Chamber of Commerce, 30 West Winnemucca Blvd., Winnemucca, NV 89445, Phone: 623-2225

Attractions:

Local events include: A photographic exhibition of top western photographers held March 7-10; Mule Show & Races displaying performances and pari-mutuel racing held June 1-2; Winnemucca Basque Festival which is a celebration of rich & traditional basque culture, June 8-9; Good Times Street Drags, featuring hot rods and funny cars some in excess of 200 m.p.h., race at the airport, June 29-30; Hot August Nights Winnemucca classic car show, July 27-29 held prior to the Reno celebration; Nevada's oldest rodeo, The Annual PRCA Labor Day Rodeo/Western Art Roundup/Tri-County Fair held August 30-September 2nd.

Airport Information:

WINNEMUCCA - WINNEMUCCA MUNICIPAL AIRPORT (WMC)
5 mi southwest of town N40-53.79 W117-48.36 Elev: 4303 Fuel: 100, Jet-A
Rwy 14-32 H7000x100 (Asph) Rwy 02-20: H4931x150 (Asph) Attended: continuously
Unicom: 122.8 Public Phone 24hrs Notes: No landing fee; $2.50 overnight tie down.
FBO: Winnemucca Air Service, Phone: 623-5091

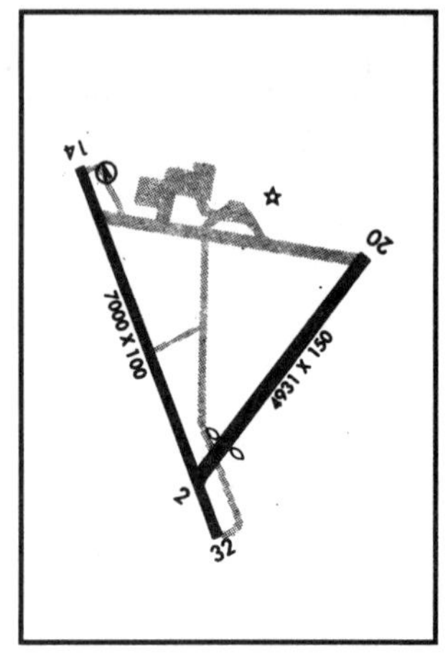

NV-O43 - YERINGTON
YERINGTON MUNICIPAL AIRPORT

(Area Code 702) 12

Hangar Cafe:

The Hangar Cafe restaurant is located on the Yerington Municipal Airport and is within a stones throw away from the aircraft parking ramp. This cafe is open from 6 a.m. to 2 p.m. 7 days a week. Their menu features homemade American dishes as well as freshly baked pies. Daily specials are also provided. Average prices run $2.50 to $5.00 for breakfast, and $3.50 to $5.00 for lunch. The restaurant is decorated with pictures of aircraft on wood paneled walls. Their dining room can seat up to 20 persons. Carry-out items are also available with selections right off their menu. The Hangar Cafe has been in business since 1982 and is within walking distance to town. Visitors can even enjoy the nearby casinos for entertainment. For more information call 463-4830.

Restaurants Near Airport:

Hangar Cafe	On Site	Phone: 463-4830
Mason Co. C.C.	4 mi	Phone: 463-3300
Stage Stop Rest.	4 mi	Phone: 463-3707

Lodging: Casino West 463-2481; Intown Motel 463-2164.

Transportation: Airport courtesy car available; Rental cars: Bill Giles CheveyDealer 463-3456.

Meeting Rooms: None Reported

Information: Mason Valley Chamber of Commerce, Box 227 South Main Street, Yerington, NV 89447, Phone 463-2245; Also Carson City Convention & Visitors Bureau, 1900 South Carson Street, Suite 200, Carson City, NV 89701, Phone: 687-7410 or 800-638-2321.

Attractions:

Mason County Country Club (Golf course 4 miles) 463-3300; Museum open weekends with old jail, black smith shop, school room, kitchens, and Indian displays all within the town of Yerington, NV. For more information contact the Mason Valley Chamber of Commerce at 463-3721; The area contains fishing as well as hiking through nearby ghost towns located within 20-25 miles from the Yerington Municipal airport. (See "Information" listed above)

Airport Information:

YERINGTON - YERINGTON MUNICIPAL AIRPORT (043)
1 mi north of town N39-00.25 W119-09.48 Elev: 4378 Fuel: 80, 100
Rwy 01-19: H5800x75 (Asph) Attended: Mon-Fri 1500-0200Z, Sat-Sun irregularly
Unicom: 122.8 Public Phone 24hrs Notes: Overnight parking $2.00
Yerington Municipal Airport Phone: 463-4545 or 463-4830
FBO: Sorensen Enterprises Phone: 463-4830

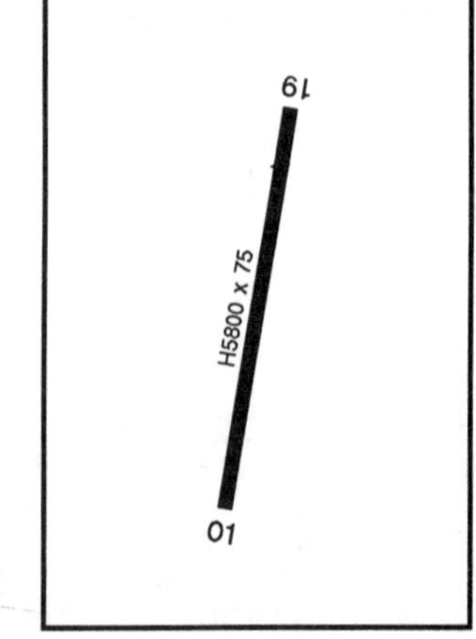

NEW HAMPSHIRE

CROSS FILE INDEX

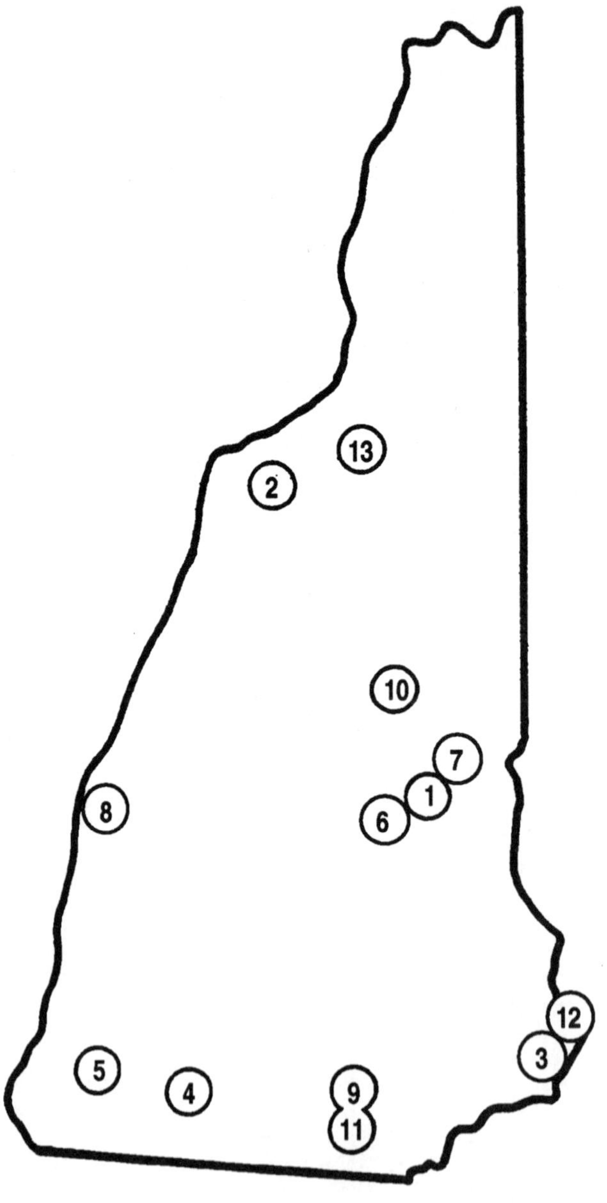

NEW HAMPSHIRE

CROSS FILE INDEX

Location Number	City or Town	Airport Name And Identifier	Name of Attraction
1	Alton Bay	S.P.B. & Ice Arpt. (ALTON)	Shibley's Restaurant
2	Franconia	Franconia Arpt. (1B5)	Franconia Inn
3	Hampton	Hampton Airfield (7B3)	Airfield Cafe
4	Jaffrey	Jaffrey Muni./Silver Ranch (AFN)	Kimball Farm Restaurant
5	Keene	Dillant-Hopkins (EEN)	Campy's Co. Kettle
6	Laconia	Lanconia Muni. (LCI)	B. Mae's Resort Inn
7	Laconia/Wolfeboro	Lakes Region (8B8) S.P.B.	Attractions
8	Lebanon	Lebanon Muni. (LEB)	Tailwind Restaurant
9	Manchester	Manchester/Grenier Airpark (MHT)	Milltowne Grille
10	Moultonboro	Moultonboro Arpt. (NH08)	Moultonborough Inn
11	Nashua	Boire Field (ASH)	The Crosswind
12	Portsmouth	Pease Intl. Tradeport (PSM)	Barnstormers Stkhse.
13	Twin Mountain	Twin Mountain Arpt. (8B2)	Hearty Mountain Rest.

Articles

City or town	Nearest Airport and Identifier	Name of Attraction
Franconia, NH	Franconia Arpt. (Private)	Franconia Inn
Laconia, NH	Laconia Muni. (LCI)	B-Mae's Resort Inn

NH-ALTON - ALTON BAY SEA PLANE BASE & ICE AIRPORT

(Area Code 603)

1

Restaurants Near Airport:

Dockside Rest.	150 yards	Phone: N/A
Shibley's	100 yards	Phone: 875-3636

Lodging: None Reported

Meeting Rooms: Shibley's Restaurant may be able to accommodate meeting and parties with prior notice. Call 875-3636.

Transportation: None required to reach nearby restaurants. Shibley's (100 yds) and Dockside Restaurant (150 yds).

Information: Town Hall 875-2161; Alton, Alton Bay Chamber of Commerce, phone: 875-5777; New Hampshire Office of Vacation Travel, 105 Loudon Road, P.O. Box 856, Concord, NH 03301, Phone: 603-271-2666.

Shibley's:

The town of Alton Bay, NH is located at the southern-most tip of Lake Winnipesaukee. This is where the Alton Bay Sea Plane Base and Ice Airport is reported to be located. Within 100 yards of the ice or water runway is the restaurant. Formerly known as Victoria Pier, Shibley's is the name of the new establishment. We were unable to speak directly to the restaurant owners; however after speaking with several other town officials, we learned that this restaurant offers a very nice view overlooking the water. A person at the town hall mentioned that it has been some time since she remembers seeing a seaplane dock at the pier near the restaurant but boats use it frequently. Although it is likely the new owners have made changes, we have included information about previous services available at this establishment. They are as follows: From October 1st to May 30th, the restaurant is open on Friday from 11 a.m. to 8 p.m., and Saturday and Sunday from 8 a.m. to 8 p.m. The dining area provides a rustic appearance with wooden floors, tables and chairs, and tastefully decorated with hanging plants. On three sides of the restaurant there are large windows providing guests with a spectacular view of Lake Winnipesaukee. Their menu includes a 28 item salad bar, 15 item hot food buffet, appetizers, fried seafood, taco salads, chili, soups and seafood chowder. Their main selections include prime rib, stir fries, broiled entrees, lobster, steamers and 25 seafood dinner choices. Average prices run $3.25 for breakfast, $4.50 for lunch and $9.00 for dinner. They are more than willing to cater to clubs and encourage fly-ins, In fact they will even sponsor a fly-in given the opportunity. Seating is available for up to 78 people. During the summer, it's first come first served for pontoon plane tie-down space at the dock. For conditions or more information about the restaurant, call the new owners at 875-3636.

NO AIRPORT DIAGRAM AVAILABLE

Airport Information:

ALTON BAY - SEA PLANE BASE & ICE AIRPORT

According to a letter we received from the Alton Bay Flying Club, there is a sea plane base and ice airport located in the town of Alton Bay, NH. Their letter reads as follows: "During the winter, the Alton Bay Flying Club maintains an ice runway (Usually 3,000' to 4,000' by 50' to 100' wide) dependent on ice conditions. It is open to the public to use at their own risk as are all private airports. The ice has been good during the last 8 out of 10 years. There are two restaurants that have been open the past many years adjacent to the south end of the ice runway. On occasion there have been as many as five restaurants open during the winter. Alton Bay is primarily a summer resort town and the number open depends upon demand. P.S. there are no FBO's nor fuel available in the ice runway."

Alton Bay Seaplane Base & Ice Airport conditions: Phone: Shibley's 875-3636.

Photo by: Shibley's Restaurant

Shibley's Restaurant, located on the shore of beautiful Lake Winnipesaukee.

NH-1B5 - FRANCONIA
FRANCONIA AIRPORT

Franconia Inn:

The Franconia Inn is situated adjacent and across the street from the Franconia Airport. This fine dining restaurant is open from 6:30 a.m. to 9 p.m. 7 days a week, (Seasonal hours). Their menu lists a very nice selection of entrees including specialties of the house like duck with leek sauce, rack of lamb Dijonaise, veal champagne, filet mignon, scallops with snow crab, chicken Marsala, black Angus beef and shrimp sesame. In addition, a host of other selections for breakfast are also available. Average prices run between $14.00 up to $22.00 for most dinner entrees. Their main dining room can seat 85 persons. The decor of the restaurant depicts a country inn, furnished with Hitcock furniture in a casual atmosphere. The Franconia Inn has 34 rooms for overnight guests along with many package plans for the family. Amenities include a heated swimming pool, hot tub, tennis, bicycle trails, cross-country skiing on their site, down hill skiing 3 miles away, and sleigh rides. There are several package plans including extended stay plans and discount packages available. For more information about the Franconia Inn or their many family plans and incentives, please call 823-5542.

(Area Code 603) 2

Restaurants Near Airport:

Franconia Inn Adj Arpt Phone: 823-5542

Lodging: Franconia Inn (Adj Arpt) 823-5542; Gale River 823-5655; Lovett's Inn By Lafayette Brook 823-7761; Raynor's Motor Lodge 823-9586; Stonybrook Motor Lodge 823-8192; Sugar Hill 823-5621.

Meeting Rooms: Franconia Inn has meeting rooms available for up to 60 persons. For information call 823-5542.

Transportation: No information was available about taxi, courtesy cars, rental cars or public transportation. The Franconia Inn is however reported to be will within walking distance from the airport.

Information: Littleton Chamber of Commerce, 141 Main Street, P.O. Box 105, Littleton, NH 03561, Phone: 603-444-6561.

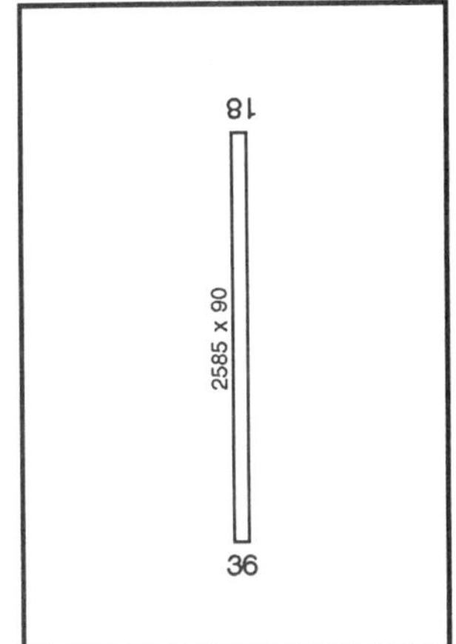

Airport Information:

FRANCONIA - FRANCONIA AIRPORT (1B5)

2 mi south of town 44-11-45N 71-45-00W Elev: 970 Fuel: 100LL

Rwy18-36: 2585x90 (Turf) Attended: May-Nov dawn-dusk, Dec-Apr unattended.

Unicom: 122.8 Notes: Extensive glider activity on and in vicinity of airport. Prior to using airport call 603-823-8881 for airport conditions.

Franconia Airport Phone: 823-8881

Franconia Inn

Franconia, NH (NH-Private)

The Inn, situated on 107 acres in the Easton Valley, affords a breathtaking view of Mount Lafayette, Franconia Notch and the Franconia and Kinsman Ranges of the White Mountains.

The Franconia Inn, originally built in 1868, was destroyed by fire in 1934, then rebuilt by 300 craftsmen in 90 days. The Inn has been in constant service since that time, and is presently owned and operated by the Morris family.

The decor is comfortable and inviting. In the oak paneled private library and spacious living room, are active handsome fireplaces; two dining rooms: the 1st, small and intimate, with it's own fireplace; the other, having a Bermuda ceiling, is airy and boisterous. Each offers views of the mountains. The Inn also boasts 2 porches: the front porch faces east - sunrise over Cannon Mountain. The back porch faces west - the sun sets behind Sugar Hill. Downstairs is the Rathskeller Lounge, movie room, hot tub, and game room.

Photo By: The Franconia Inn

The 35 guest rooms, recently renovated, and decorated simply yet beautifully. All have private baths. Most have double beds, but many have queen and king-size beds. Ten rooms have an additional single bed for a third person. "Family Suite" two rooms connected by one common bath. The "Inn Suite" includes a bedroom with a queen bed, a living room with fireplace, queen-size sleep sofa, balcony and a wet-bar. One of the "Honeymoon Suites" features a queen-size bed and a king-size jacuzzi tub.

The Inn's location provides easy accessibility to villages of Franconia, Sugar Hill and Easton, as well as the charm of quiet country life.

The goal at the Franconia Inn is to offer quality service in an informal atmosphere. The special attention offered guests makes their stay one to remember.

During the winter season: horse-drawn sleigh rides, ice skating, and their own cross-country ski touring center with rentals, sales, and instruction. Three other cross-country touring centers are within 25 minutes. If Alpine skiing is your winter sport, they are just minutes from Cannon Mountain ski area, and within 25 minutes to four other ski areas.

They are not just a Winter Ski Lodge... as the snow melts away in the spring, four beautiful red clay tennis courts pop up and a large sunny pool appears seemingly out of nowhere. The cross-country skis, boots, and poles disappear to be replaced by horses, saddles and stirrups. Cross-country trails are now scenic bridle trails and their friendly cross-country ski instructor is a proficient wrangler. The ski shop that looks like a barn returns to being a barn again. Where snowbanks once reigned, gardens now flourish. The snow-covered airfield with its lonely wind sock becomes an active glider port, catering to both glider pilots as well as fly-in private pilots. In the past guests could even experience glider rides. Check with the Franconia Inn for information. Glider rides cost between $50.00 to $90.00 for various altitudes of 3,000 to 5,000' tows. Airplane rides are available, with 15 and 30 minute flights. Glider instruction is also available. Aviation fuel & oil is on site. For airport information you can call 603-823-8881.

During the Spring, Summer and Fall season, the Inn offers its guests four uncrowded clay tennis courts, a riding stable (for the novice or experienced equestrians), a heated outdoor pool, a 2,200-foot grass air strip, a clear, cool stream for trout fishing, croquet, bicycles for touring, zillions of trails for hiking, and within 15 minutes' drive - two 18-hole golf courses and four 9-hole courses.

As the shadows of dusk stretch across Mount Lafayette and the Kinsman range, the day's last light gives way to a sky turned brilliant by stars.

As night settles in, you will find their living room with its friendly fire and overstuffed wing chairs a comfortable meeting place for family and friends. From their library shelves, choose a mystery or a novel and curl up in quiet satisfaction.

The Inn's dining room is the evening center piece, where unpretentious elegance is the rule, not the exception. Diners seated at tables with flickering candles, view the White Mountains landscape through dozens of small-paned windows. Soft tones of Mozart and Bach set the pace for a leisurely dinner of "Elegant American Cuisine". Their Rathskeller Lounge offers a quiet environment for you to plan the next day's strategies, play a game of darts, or take in the "evening movie".

For information or reservations, call the Franconia Inn at 603-823-5542.

NH-7B3 - HAMPTON
HAMPTON AIRFIELD

(Aera Code 603) 3

Airfield Cafe:

The Airfield Cafe is located on the Hampton Airport. This restaurant is open for breakfast and lunch between 7 a.m. and 3 p.m. Saturday and Sunday, and weekdays from 10:30 a.m. and 2:30 p.m. Homemade muffins, breads and pies are just a few of the most popular items offered on their menu. Lunch entrees include a choice of two soups along with sandwiches made to order. Average prices run around $4.50 for most selections. Besides the delicious meals prepared, the Airfield Cafe has a warm friendly atmosphere with antiques and aviation memorabilia. They even have an outdoor deck with umbrella covered tables for dining. The owners of this restaurant have been serving guests for the past 28 years. Fly-in groups including the 99's have made this restaurant one of their stopping points. For more information about the Airfield Cafe call 964-6749.

Restaurants Near Airport:

Airfield Cafe	On Site	Phone: 964-6749
Country Dinner	1/2 mi	Phone: N/A
Lamie's Tavern	2 mi	Phone: 926-0330
Mc Donalds	1/2 mi	Phone: N/A

Lodging: Hampton Motor Inn 1 mi 926-6771; Lamie's Inn & Tavern 2 mi 926-0330; Pine Haven 964-8187; Villager Motor Inn 1-2 mi 926-3964.

Meeting Rooms: Hampton Motor Inn 1 mi 926-6771; Lamie's Inn & Tavern 2 mi 926-0330.

Transportation: National Rental Car 964-8799; Taxi Service: Colonial 436-0008; A+ Taxi 436-7500; Coastal 926-4334.

Information: Hampton Beach Area Chamber of Commerce, 836 Lafayette Road, P.O. Box 790, Hampton Beach, NH 03842, Phone: 926-8717 or 800-GET-A-TAN.

20
2100 x 170
02

Attractions:

An aviation related Flea Market is featured at the Hampton Airfield the 3rd weekend in May of each year. We, were told that 130 to 160 aircraft attend this event. For information you can call the Airport managers office at 964-6749.

Airport Information:

HAMPTON - HAMPTON AIRFIELD (7B3)
2 mi north of town N42-57.76 W70-49.72 Elev: 93 Fuel: 80, 100LL Rwy 02-20: 2100x170 (Turf) Attended: 1300Z-dusk Unicom: 122.8
FBO: Hampton Airfield, Inc. Phone: 964-6749

NH-AFN - JAFFREY
JAFFREY MUNI /SILVER RANCH

(Area Code 603)

4

Kimball Farm Restaurant:

Addison's Fly-in/Drive-in Restaurant is adjacent to the Jaffrey Municipal Silver Ranch Airport, and is within walking distance along a short pathway, according to the restaurant management. This combination cafeteria and family style establishment is open summer hours between Memorial day to October 12 from 11 a.m. to 9 p.m. During the rest of the season they are open from 11 a.m. to 8 p.m., Closed January and February. This restaurant specializes in seafood, clam dishes, chicken, salads, soups and a wide variety of additional selections. Average prices run up to $8.50 for a complete dinner. The dining area can seat 120 persons with a rustic and homey atmosphere with bench style seating. In addition to the restaurant, there is also a gift shop and candy shop situated nearby. For more information call the restaurant at 532-5765.

Restaurants Near Airport:

Kimball Farm Restaurant	Adj Arpt	Phone: 532-5765
Jaffrey Manor Rest & Inn	N/A	Phone: N/A

Lodging: Benjamin Prescott Inn (1 mile, bed & breakfast) 532-6637; Manadnock Inn (3 miles) 532-7001; Woodboune Inn (3 miles, Free trans) 532-8341.

Meeting Rooms: Woodboune Inn (3 miles, Free trans) 532-8341.

Transportation: Taxi Service: Country Side Limo 924-7229; Rental Cars: Cheshire Motors 924-7777; Hopkins Garage 924-6631; Roland's Exxon 924-3620.

Information: New Hampshire Office of Travel & Tourism, 172 Pembroke Road, P.O. Box 1856, Concord, NH 03302, Phone: 271-2343 or 800-FUN-IN-NH;

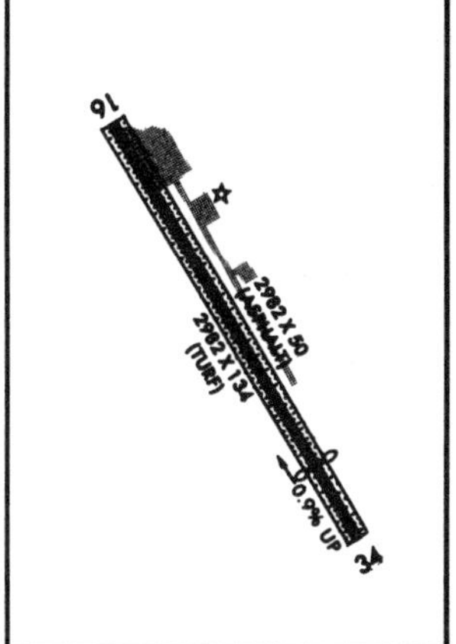

Airport Information:

JAFFREY - JAFFREY MUNI/SILVER RANCH (AFN)
1 mi southeast of town N42-48.31 W72-00.18 Elev: 1040 Fuel: 100LL
Rwy 16-34: H2982x50 (Asph-turf) Attended: 1300Z-dusk Unicom: 122.8
Jaffrey Municipal Arpt (Silver Ranch) Phone: 532-8870 or 532-7763

NH-EEN - KEENE
DILLANT-HOPKINS

(Area Code 603)

5

Campy's Country Kettle:

Campy's Country Kettle is located off the northeast end of the Dillant-Hopkins Airport. During our conversation with the airport managers office, we learned that pilots have taxied their aircraft to the northeast side of the field where they parked their aircraft and walked about 200 feet to the restaurant. Campy's Restaurant is open Monday through Saturday from 6 a.m. to 2 p.m. for lunch and Tuesday, Wednesday, Thursday and Friday night for dinner between 4:40 p.m. and 8 p.m. They also are open on Sunday from 7 a.m. to 2 p.m. Their menu features a full breakfast and many homemade items like meat loaf, chicken pot pie, lasagna, macaroni and cheese, beef stew, and several types of homemade soups including their famous fish chowder soup. Average prices run $1.50 for breakfast, $2.69 for lunch and $3.99 for dinner. Four to six different daily specials are provided as well. The restaurant can seat up to 50 persons and has a western decor with booths and tables. On Friday night they have a dinner buffet which offers different selections. Larger groups and parties are welcome with advance notice. Carry-out items can also be prepared for their customers. For more information about the Campy's Country Kettle, call 357-3339.

Restaurants Near Airport:

176 Main Rest.	176 Main St.	Phone: 357-3100
Campy's Country Kettle	Adj Arpt	Phone: 357-3339
Henry Davids	2-1/2 mi N.	Phone: 352-0608
Libby's Family Rest.	1-1/2 mi S.	Phone: 352-4727

Lodging: Days Inn (3 miles) 352-7616; Ramada Inn (2-1/2 miles) 357-3038; Super 8 Motel (3 miles) 352-9780.
Meeting Rooms: Ramada Inn of Keene 357-3038; Days Inn of Keene 352-7616 or 800-325-2525.
Transportation: Ideal Taxi 352-2525; Monadnock Transport 352-2111; Also: Rental Cars Avis 352-8525; National 357-4045.
Information: Chamber of Commerce, 8 Central Square, Keene, NH 03431, Phone: 352-1303.

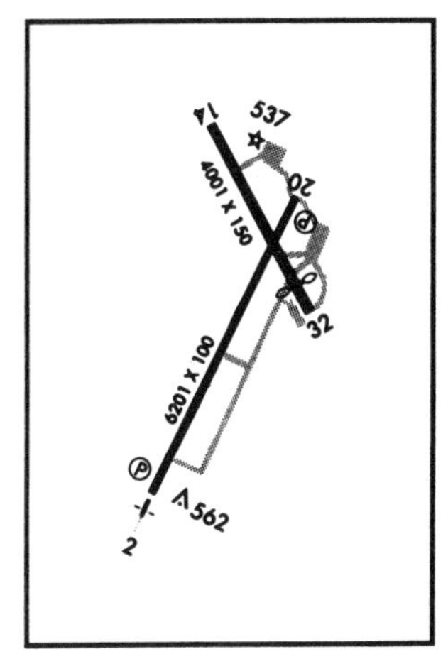

Airport Information:

KEENE - DILLANT-HOPKINS AIRPORT (EEN)
2 mi south of town N42-53.90 W72-16.25 Elev: 488 Fuel: Jet-A
Rwy 02-20: H6201x100 (Asph) Rwy 14-32: H4001x150 (Asph) Attended: 1200-Dusk
Unicom: 123.0 Public Phone 24hrs
Airport Manager Phone: 357-9835 or 357-9812
FBO: C M Lovett, Inc. Phone: 352-8506

B-Mae's Resort Inn & Conference Center

LACONIA, NH (LCI)

B-Mae's Resort Inn & Conference Center is located only 2 miles east of the Laconia Airport on Route 11. Transportation to and from the resort can be arranged by calling the resort. Once reaching the resort, you will be delivered to their main lobby entrance that soars through two levels of wood and glass and has a balcony connecting the second floor wings. Their indoor pool and large whirlpool are right off the main lobby area, and from there you can walk to the outdoor pool, sunning patio and easy nature path leading to a sandy Lake Winnipesaukee beach.

Accommodations at B. Mae's are built for comfort - each spacious room has color cable TV, in-room safe, telephone and private balcony or patio. They also have designer-decorated one bedroom suites in a private wing, each with a kitchen, living/dining area (with queen sleeper), two cable TV's, VCR and its own deck or patio.

Just across the lawn from the Inn is B. Mae's Eating & Drinking Establishment, one of the Lakes Region's most popular gathering spots for breakfast and dinner. Their extensive dinner menu of aged beef, fresh seafood and innovative nightly specials is complemented by an over-80-item bar serving a selection of daily soups, salads, fresh-baked breads and appetizers. The atmosphere is take-your-time casual and a children's menu is available. You'll also enjoy the lively and congenial company you'll find at Bertha's Bar & Grille both before and after your dinner.

In spring and summer there is nothing so relaxing, beautiful and pleasure-filled as a summer in the Lakes Region of New Hampshire. Water sports alone (like sailing, waterskiing, scuba diving, and swimming) can keep you busy for days but you might miss some of the nearby, on-shore family activities. Area attractions including Ellacoya State Beach, Weirs Beach, Surfcoaster Water Park, Gunstock Recreation Area and the NH International Speedway...all within a short drive of B. Mae's. You will also find golfing, tennis, racquetball, bowling, hiking, biking and plenty of tax-free shopping, from antiques to boutiques to outlets. You'll have to come back again and again just to see and do it all.

In the fall, with hundreds of miles of shoreline and mountains, you will be treated to a magnificent display of Mother Nature in her finest hour. View it by taking a relaxing cruise on the MS Mt. Washington that circles the lake several times daily from May through October. Private charter tours by sail or motor boat are also available.

In winter, only 10 minutes from their door, Gunstock Mountain offers a wonderful ski experience for the whole family. With snowmaking on their huge variety of alpine trails for all abilities, and over 30 km of cross country ski trails at the base, you can enjoy a memorable ski season from December to April.

B. Mae's Resort Inn and Conference center has numerous package plans available throughout the year as well as on special holidays, and Conference Packages for 5 to 5 dozen with workshops, lectures round table or classroom accommodations. For information call their resort at 603-293-7526 or 1800-458-3877. (Information for preparing this article was obtained by resort).

NH-LCI - LACONIA
LACONIA MUNICIPAL

(Area Code 603) 6

B. Mae's Resort Inn & Conference Center:

B. Mae's Resort Inn & Conference Center is located only 5 minutes by car or about 2 miles from the Laconia Municipal Airport. This resort contains a restaurant, lounge, entertainment, exercise equipment, whirlpool, game room and bicycles. The Gunstock ski area is only 4 miles from the resort. Lodging accommodations include 82 rooms within a two-story building. Some rooms contain private patios and balconies. Meeting rooms are also available. Due to its close proximity to Lake Winnipesaukee, guests can take advantage of the scenic cruises for breakfast, lunch and dinner aboard the Mount Washington 230-foot tour boat which stops to board passengers at Weirs Beach only a few miles west of the B. Mae's Resort Inn location. Scheduled departure times for the boat are at 9:00 a.m., 12:15 p.m. and 3:30 p.m., and returns about 3 hours later to this same location. For resort information call the resort at 293-7526.

Restaurants Near Airport:

Blackstone's	1 mi	Phone: 524-7060
B. Mae's Resort	2 mi. E.	Phone: 293-7526
Patricks Pub	1 mi	Phone: 239-0841
William Tell	1 mi	Phone: 293-8803

Lodging: B. Mae's Resort Inn 1 mi 293-7526; Inn At Mill Falls 279-7006; Margate Resort 524-5210; Bed & Breakfast: Gunstock Country Inn & Health Club (Gilford, est. 2-3 mi.) 800-654-0180; The Inn at Smith Cove (Gilford, est. 2-3 mi.) 293-1111.

Meeting Rooms: B. Mae's Resort Inn 1 mi 293-7526.

Transportation: Taxi Service: Douglas 524-7028; Richardson 524-0509; Rental Cars: Avis 524-0044; Merchants 528-1400.

Information: Greater Loconia/Weirs Beach Chamber of Commerce 11 Veterans Square, Laconia, NH 03246. Phone: 524-5531 or 800 531-2347.

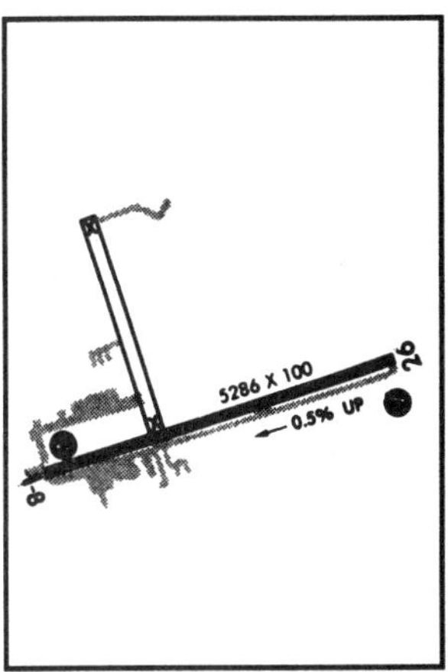

Airport Information:

LACONIA - LACONIA MUNICIPAL (LCI)
3 mi northeast of town N43-34.36 W71-25.13 Elev: 545 Fuel: 100LL, Jet-A Rwy 08-26: H5286x100 (Asph) Attended: 1200-0000Z Unicom: 123.0 Notes: Landing fee multi-engine only
FBO: Emerson Aviation, Inc. Phone: 293-7980
FBO: Sky Bright, Inc. Phone: 800-639-6012 or 528-6818

Attractions:

Lake Winnipesaukee is surrounded by sparkling beaches, rolling hills and towering mountains. It is one of New Hampshire's most popular vacation areas, with activities of all types. The Mount Washington cruise boat can accommodate 1,230 passengers with breakfast, lunch, dinner and even special theme cruises visiting ports along Lake Winnipesaukee. Enjoy the sunset, moonlight, dining and dancing on board this floating night club. Each evening cruise features a delicious dinner buffet and two live bands playing a variety of music for your listening and dancing pleasure. 3-1/2 hour cruises run $14.00 for adults and $6.00 for children. 2-1/2 hour cruises run $12.00 for adults and $5.00 for children. Special family discount rates are also provided. Dinner cruises run $27.00 to $32.00 for adults and $12.00 to $17.00 for children. The boat stops at Weirs Beach, Center Harbor, Wolfeboro and Alton Bay. For scheduled departure times and more information about this attraction call 603-366-BOAT.; Also in the Winnipesaukee Lake region are miles of horseback riding trails commanding magnificent views of lakes and mountains; a smorgasbord of events in the Lakes Region, including the classic antique boat show at Weirs Beach; New Hampshire International Speedway, host of the Winston Cup and other national motorcycle and car races are held at scheduled times; Downhill Skiing and Cross Country Skiing are popular sports for many in the area. For more information contact the Greater Laconia/Weirs Beach Chamber of Commerce at 524-5531 or 800-531-2347.

NH-8B8 - WOLFEBORO
LAKES REGION

(Area Code 603)

The Lakes Region Airport and seaplane base (8B8) is located on the southeast shore of Lake Winnipesaukee and 12 miles east from the town of Laconia. The same attractions and activities for the Laconia region hold true for the town of Wolfeboro and surrounding communities. The Mount Washington tour boat also docks at this location. Departure times are 11:00 a.m. and 2:15 p.m. (See "Attractions" above).

Information:
Wolfeboro Chamber of Commerce, P.O. Box 547, Wolfeboro, NH 03894, Phone: 569-2200.

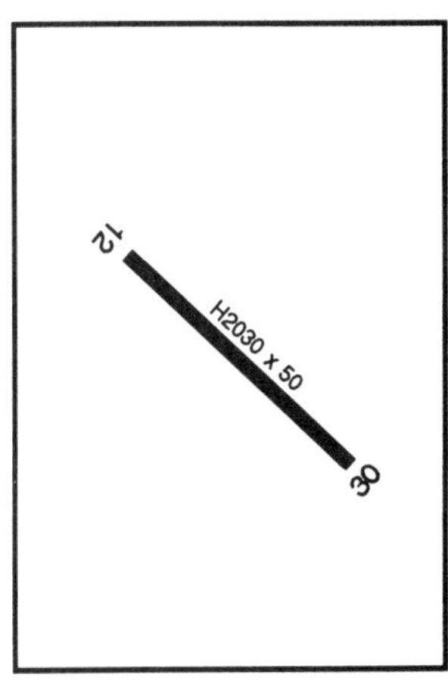

Airport Information: (Land & Seaplane base)

WOLFEBORO - LAKES REGION AIRPORT (8B8)
3 mi west of town N43-35.26 W71-15.97 Elev: 580 Fuel: 100LL Rwy 12-30: H2030x50 (Asph)
Attended: unattended Unicom: 122.8 Notes: Seaplane Base adjacent airport utilizing all ways (no designated sea lane length or width or direction). Winter months contact manager 603-569-1310 for runway conditions.
Airport Manager Phone: 603-569-1310

NH-LEB - LEBANON
LEBANON MUNICIPAL

(Area Code 603)

8

Tailwind Restaurant:

The Tailwind Restaurant is located on the Lebanon Municipal Airport. This dining facility is a combination family-style and fine dining establishment. Hours of operation are 11 a.m. to 9 p.m. Monday through Saturday. Dinner is served between 5 p.m. and 9 p.m. Menu items include fresh catch of the day, chicken dishes, top sirloin, broiled chicken and shrimp, 5 different pasta specials including a vegetarian choice, smoked salmon and spinach in a delightful cream sauce, linguine, beer-battered chicken, sandwiches of all types, some named with aviation titles like their Tailwind Grilled Ruben, Bi-wing hot turkey club sandwich and pilots choice selections. Average prices run $3.00 to $9.00 for lunch and $10.00 to $12.00 for dinner. Lighter fare, including sandwiches, run $3.50 to $6.25. Their special surf and turf dinner runs around $16.00. Guests can view the activity of the terminal ramp and runways from the restaurant. In-flight catering is provided through the Lebanon Jet Center (FBO). Fly-in customers are asked to notify the tower of their intentions, and will be given permission to park their aircraft near the restaurant adjacent to the commercial boarding area. The tower will then call the restaurant and they, in tern will unlock the gate to let their customers enter the restaurant. Fly-in guests are asked not to use the passenger entranceway to the terminal, for security reasons. The restaurant has a very good working relationship with the airport management and tower controllers. For more information call the Tailwind Restaurant at 298-6544.

Restaurants Near Airport:

China Lite	1/2 mi	Phone: 298-8222
Denny's	3/4 mi	Phone: 298-5922
Lui Lui Italian	3/4 mi	Phone: 298-8222
Tailwind	On Site	Phone: 298-6544
Weathervane	3/4 mi	Phone: 298-9845

Lodging: Airport Economy Inn 1/4 mi 298-8888; Days Inn 4 mi 448-5070; Holiday Inn-White River Jct. 3-5 mi 295-3000; Howard Johnson-White River 3-5 mi 295-3015; Sheraton Inn North Century 1/2 mi 298-5906.

Meeting Rooms: Sheraton Inn North Century has accommodations for conferences and conventions 1/2 mi 298-5906.

Transportation: Airport courtesy car reported. Rental Cars: Avis 298-7753; Budget 298-9700; Hertz 298-8927. Taxi Service: Campus Taxi 643-2120; Dartmouth 643-3502; Upper Valley Taxi 448-4639.

Information: New Hampshire Office of Vacation Travel P.O. Box 856 Concord, NH 03301, Phone: 603-271-2666.

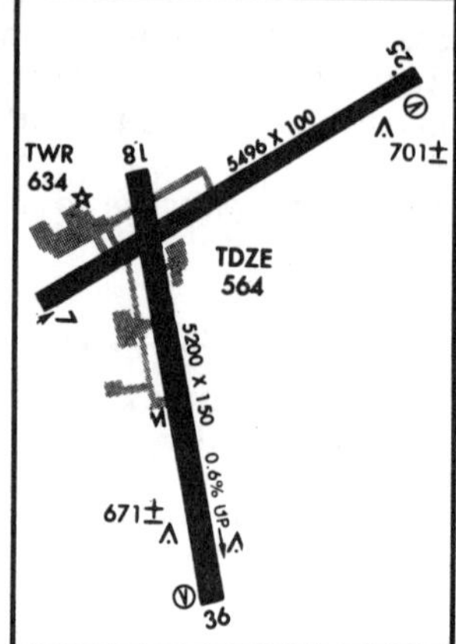

Airport Information:

LEBANON - LEBANON MUNICIPAL (LEB)

3 mi west of town N43-37.58 W72-18.26 Elev: 598 Fuel: 100LL, Jet-A Rwy 07-25: H5496x100 (Asph) Rwy 18-36: H5200x150 (Asph) Attended: 1500-0200Z Atis: 118.65 Unicom: 122.95 Tower: 125.95 Gnd Con: 121.6 Notes: No landing fee reported for non commercial aircraft.

FBO: Lebanon Jet Center Phone: 298-5556 or 298-8728

NH-MHT - MANCHESTER
MANCHESTER /GRENIER AIRPARK

(Area Code 603)

9

Milltowne Grille:

The Milltowne Grille Restaurant is combination family style and fine dining establishment situated in the new terminal building on the upper level, at the Manchester/Grenier Industrial Airpark. This facility is open from 6 a.m. to 5 p.m. Sunday through Friday, and 6 a.m. to 6 p.m. on Saturday (Hours may vary). Selections off their menu include Italian entrees like chicken sun-dried tomato, chicken and lobster tomato, pasta Alfredo, chicken and shrimp pesto in addition to steak and lobster. Their dining room can seat approximately 90 persons, and has a family atmosphere, with table cloths, decorative foliage and lighted trees, dark wood, and many more decorative appointments. For information about restaurant call 625-0256.

Restaurants Near Airport:

McDonalds	Trml. Bldg.	Phone: N/A
Milltowne Grille	Trml. Bldg.	Phone: 625-0256

Lodging: Bedford Village (Shuttle) 472-2602 or 2001; Days Hotel (Shuttle) 668-6110; Sheraton TARA Wayfarer Inn (Shuttle) 622-3766; Holiday Inn-The Center (Shuttle) 625-1000.

Meeting Rooms: Bedford Village 472-2602 or 2001; Days Hotel 668-6110; Sheraton TARA Wayfare Inn 622-3766; Holiday Inn-The Center (Convention facilities available) 625-1000.

Transportation: Taxi: Arrow Cab 668-1388; Londonderry 437-8294; Town & Country 669-8765; Yellow Cab 624-4444; Rental Cars Available: Avis, Budget, Hertz & National. Call airport manager's office for information 624-6539.

Information: Chamber of Commerce, 889 Elm Street, Manchester, NH 03101, Phone: 666-6600.

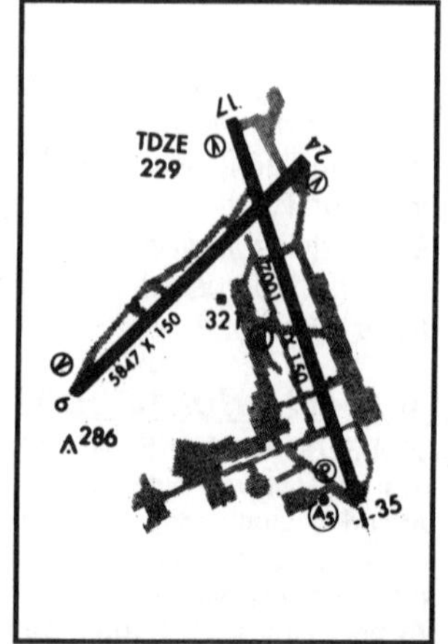

Airport Information:

MANCHESTER - MANCHESTER/GRENIER INDUSTRIAL AIRPARK (MHT)

3 mi south of town N42-56.01 W71-26.26 Elev: 234 Fuel: 100LL, Jet-A Rwy 17-35: H7001x150 (Asph-Grvd) Rwy 06-24: H5847x150 (Asph-Grvd) Attended: continuously Atis: 119.55 Unicom: 122.95 App/Dep Con: 124.9 134.75 Tower 121.3 Gnd Con: 121.9 Clnc 135.9

FBO: Stead Aviation Phone: 669-4363, 669-4360
FBO: Jet Service Phone: 668-0317

NH-NH08 - MOULTONBORO
MOULTONBORO AIRPORT

(Area Code 603) **10**

Maurice Restaurant:

The Maurice Restaurant is located about 1/2 mile from the Moultonboro Airport and is within walking distance. The restaurant will also provide courtesy transportation for fly-in guests if requested. This is a fine dining establishment that is open 4 p.m. to 9 p.m. seven days a week. Their upstairs dining room can accommodate as many as 70 guests. A second dining area on the main floor can seat 25 people and an additional dining room can handle 15 people. Linen covered tables with lighted candles, crystal glassware, and fireplace provide an elegant setting for your evening meal. During the summer months this restaurant is quite popular, so reservations are suggested. Their menu includes choices like rack of lamb, duck, chateaubriand, baked stuffed sole, shrimp Alexander, Scampi and over 18 selections. Prices range between $10.50 and $15.95 for complete dinner entrees. A full assortment of appetizers are also available. Escargot, smoked salmon, herring, smoked oysters are just a few. Fly-in groups are welcome with advanced notice appreciated. Next door to the restaurant is a 17 room lodging facility for travelers wishing to spend some time visiting the areas points of interest. In-flight catering is also a service provided. For more information call Maurice Restaurant at 476-2668.

Restaurants Near Airport:

Maurice Restaurant	1/2 mi	Phone: 476-2668
Village Kitchen	1/2 mi	Phone: N/A
Woodshed	1/2 mi	Phone: 476-2311

Lodging: Moultonborough Inn (1/2 mile) 476-5225; Matterhorn (1-1/2 mile) 253-4314; Red Hill Cabins (1 mile) 253-6712; Rob Roy (100 yards) 467-5571.

Meeting Rooms: Moultonborough Inn 476-5225.

Transportation: Courtesy car reported on field.

Information: New Hampshire Office of Vacation Travel, 105 Loudon Road, P.O. Box 856, Concord, NH 03301, Phone: 603-271-2666.

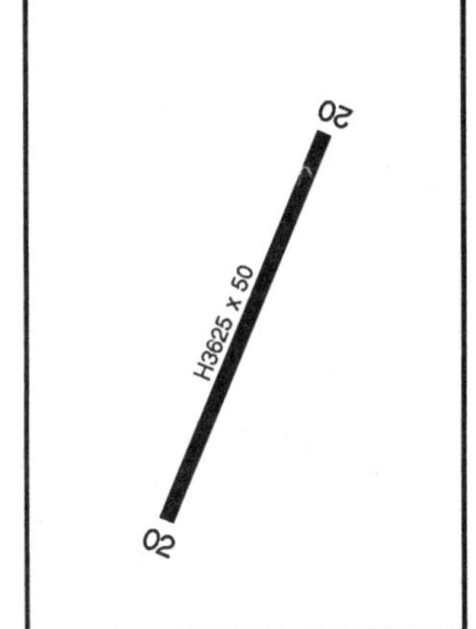

Airport Information:

MOULTONBORO - MOULTONBORO AIRPORT (NH08)
1 mi northeast of town N43-46.11 W71-23.21 Elev: 571 Fuel: 100LL, Jet-A
Rwy 02-20: 3625x50 (Asph) Attended: Jun-Sept 1400-dusk and Oct-May 1400-dusk;
Unicom: 122.8
FBO: Tab Air, Inc. Phone: 476-8801

Photo by: Crosswinds Cafe   The Crosswind Restaurant is on Boire Field at the center ramp.

NH-ASH - NASHUA BOIRE FIELD

(Area Code 603)

11

The Crosswind:

The Crosswind Restaurant is located right on the center ramp area of Boire Field. You only have to walk a few feet to their front door. This cafe is open from 7:00 a.m. to 3 p.m. 6 days a week (Closed Mondays). Their menu includes homemade soups and chowders, appetizers, submarine sandwiches, Italian entrees and burgers, along with a nice selection of desserts. Daily specials are also offered. Average prices run $3.50 for breakfast and $4.50 for lunch. Plenty of windows allow guests a niceview looking out over the airfield. The decore is modern, yet a cozy atmosphere prevails. Green plants, photographs taken by local pilots and paintings adorn the walls. Fly-in groups are welcome with advance notice. For information call the restaurant at 594-0930.

Restaurants Near Airport:

Crosswinds   On Site   Phone: 594-0930

Lodging: Transportation available: Appleton Inn 424-7500; Best Western 888-1200; Comfort Inn 883-7700; Hilton At Merrimack 424-6181; Clarion Somerset Hotel (Free Trans., 1-1/4 miles) 886-1200; Sheraton Tara Hotel 888-9970.

Meeting: Appleton Inn; Hilton at Merrimack; Clarion Somerset; Sheraton Tara.

Transportation: GFW Aero Services can provide courtesy transportation to nearby facilities 883-6372; Also Budget Car Rental 886-9310; Nashua Taxi 882-7444.

Information: Greater Nashua Chamber of Commerce, 188 Main Street, Nashua, NH 03060, Phone: 881-8333.

Attractions:

Anheuser-Busch, Inc. (Estimated 4-6 miles from airport) provides guided tours of their brewery. Also, Clydesdale Hamlet is the home of the famous Busch Clydesdale horses located on this 19th century European style farm, Phone: 595-1202; (Remember 8 hrs from bottle to throttle for you pilots, "Sorry").

Airport Information:

NASHUA - BOIRE FIELD (ASH)

3 mi northwest of town   N42-46.91 W71-30.89   Elev: 200   Fuel: 100LL, Jet-A1+

Rwy 14-32: H5500x100 (Asph)   Attended: 1200-0200Z   Atis 125.1   Manchester App/Dep Con: 124.9   Clnc Del 121.8   Nashua Tower: 133.2 NFCT   Gnd Con/Clnc Del: 121.8

Public Phone 24hrs   Notes: Landing fee/overnight parking fee $5.00 all aircraft

FBO: GFW Aero Services   Phone: 883-6372

FBO: Seyson Airways   Phone: 880-3101 or 598-4526

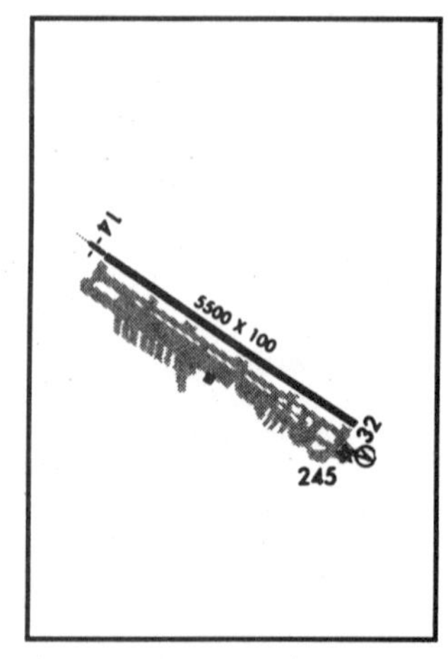

Not to be used for navigational purposes

NH-PSM - PORTSMOUTH
PEASE INTERNATIONAL TRADEPORT

(Area Code 603) 12

Barnstormers Steakhouse:

The Barnstormers Steakhouse is situated about 1 to 2 miles from the Pease International Tradeport Airport. This restaurant combines the decor of a fine dining establishment with reasonable prices found at most family-style restaurants. Items on their menu include choice steaks, prime rib, filet mignon, duck, seafood, lobster, shrimp scampi and combinations like surf and turf. A salad bar is also available. Daily lunch and dinner specials feature items like pasta, blackened pork chops and barbecued chicken, to mention a few. Their 5 star chef has over 17 years of experience in preparing French dishes. Average prices run $4.95 to $7.95 for lunch and from $7.95 to $19.95 for dinner. The restaurant has an aviation theme and is decorated with model aircraft and photos of airplanes. They also have a special function room able to serve 250 to 300 guests for banquets or group dining. The Barnstormers Steakhouse is open from 11:30 a.m. to 9:30 p.m., and until 10:30 p.m. on Friday and Saturday. We were told that transportation can be arranged either through Trans-Oceanic, Inc. (FBO) or the restaurant. For information call the Barnstormers Steakhouse at 433-6700.

Restaurants Near Airport:

Barnstormers Steakhouse	1-2 mi	Phone: 433-6700
Numerous Restaurants	Nearby	Phone: N/A

Lodging: Days Inn 439-5555; Howard Johnson Hotel 436-7600; Sheraton Portsmouth 431-2300; Susse Chalet 436-6363.

Meeting Rooms: Barnstormers Steakhouse has a function room able to serve 250 to 300 guests, 433-6700; Most lodgings listed above also contain accommodations for meetings.

Transportation: Rental Cars: Budget (On field); National 334-6000 or 431-4707. Taxi Service: At airport. Also courtesy transportation reported available for local use, Phone: 427-0350.

Information: Greater Portsmouth Chamber of Commerce, 500 Market Street, P.O. Box 239, Portsmouth, NH 03801, Phone: 436-7678.

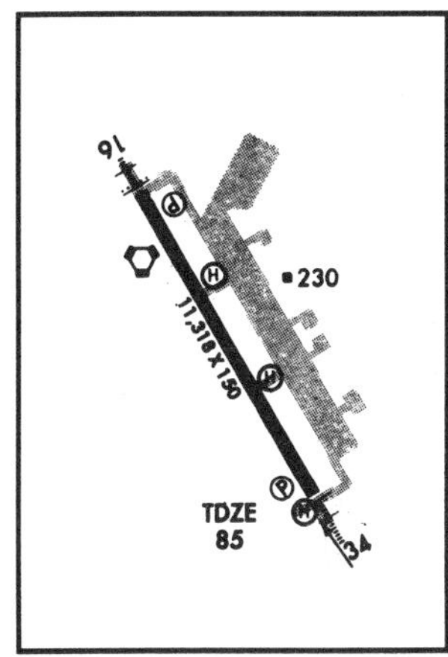

Airport Information:

PORTSMOUTH - PEASE INTERNATIONAL TRADEPORT (PSM)
1 mi west of town N43-04.68 W70-49.40 Elev: 101 Fuel: 100LL, Jet-A Rwy 16-34: H11318x300 (Asph-Conc-Pfc) Attended: Mon-Fri 0930-0230Z; Sat 1000-0130; Sun 1000-0230. Atis: 132.05 Unicom: 122.95 Tower: 128.4 Gnd Con: 120.95 Notes: Use Caution: Littlebrook Airpark located 052 degrees and 4.4 NM, Traffic pattern at 1130 Ft. MSL.
FBO: Trans-Oceanic, Inc. (Fuel) Phone: 427-0350

NH-8B2 - TWIN MOUNTAIN
TWIN MOUNTAIN AIRPORT

(Area Code 603) 13

Hearty Mountain Restaurant:

The Hearty Restaurant is situated within the Charlmont Motor Inn Adjacent to the Twin Mountain Airport. This family style restaurant, is open from 4:30 p.m. to 8:30 p.m. 6 days a week, and Sunday from 2 p.m. to 7 p.m. Their menu includes specialty items like homemade cooked dinners, hot turkey dinners, steaks, seafood and chicken, dishes, filet of soul, prime rib, chicken filet mignon, seafood sandwiches and soups. They also provide a children's menu as well. Average prices run $6.45 to $14.95 for most selections. (In addition, specials are also offered). The dining room can seat 50 persons and has large windows allowing a beautiful view overlooking the distant mountains. Groups and parties are welcome. Meals can also be prepared-to-go. Adjacent to the restaurant is their 40 room motel for overnight travelers. For more information about the Charlmont restaurant and motel, call 846-5549.

Restaurants Near Airport:

Hearty Mountain Restaurant	On Site	Phone: 846-5549
Pizza Pub	300 yds	Phone: 846-5003
Twin View Restaurant	1/4 mi	Phone: New-not listed

Lodging: Charlmont Motor Inn 846-5549; Four Seasons Motor Inn 846-5708; Paquette's Motor Inn 846-5562.

Meeting Rooms: Four Seasons Motor Inn 846-5708.

Transportation: None Reported

Information: Chamber of Commerce, Box 194, Twin Mountain, NH 03595, Phone: 800-245-8946.

09 H2640 x 60 27

Airport Information:

TWIN MOUNTAIN - TWIN MOUNTAIN AIRPORT (8B2)
1 mi southwest of town N44-15.84 W71-32.85 Elev: 1459 Fuel: 100LL
Rwy 09-27: H2640x60 (Asph) Attended: Feb-Sep 1300-0100Z, Oct-Jan 1300-2100Z
Unicom: 122.8 Notes: Airport manegement requests that pilots use paved areas only.
Twin Mountain Airport Phone: 846-5505

NEW JERSEY

LOCATION MAP

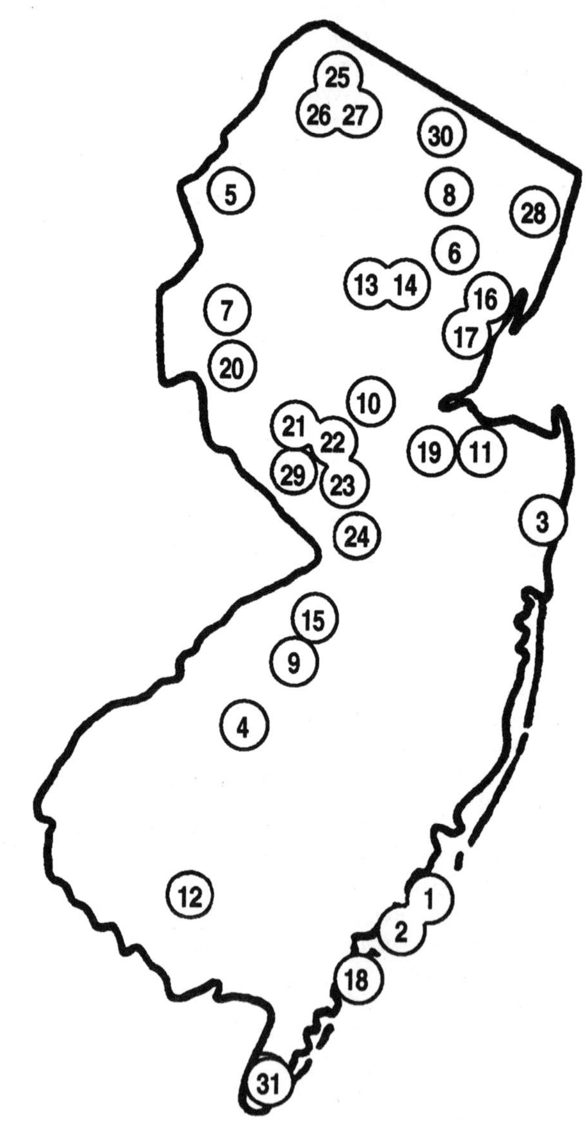

NEW JERSEY

CROSS FILE INDEX

Location Number	City or Town	Airport Name And Identifier	Name of Attraction
1	Atlantic City	Atlantic City Intl. (ACY)	Thrashers Restaurant
2	Atlantic City	Atlantic City Muni. (AIY)	McGettigans Saloon
3	Belmar/Farmingdale	Allaire Arpt. (BLM)	Cafe Allaire
4	Berlin	Camden Co. Arpt. (19N)	Gourmet Rm./Venice Plz.
5	Blairstown	Blairstown Arpt. (1N7)	Runway Cafe
6	Caldwell	Essex Co. Arpt. (CDW)	94th Bomb Group
7	Hammonton	Hammonton Muni. (N81)	Cathy's Cafe
8	Lincoln Park	Lincoln Park Arpt. (N07)	Ready Room Lounge
9	Lumberton	Flying W Arpt. (N14)	Flying W Restaurant
10	Manville	Kupper Arpt. (47N)	Pizza & Pasta
11	Matawan	Marlboro Arpt. (2N8)	Sloppy Joe's Rest.
12	Millville	Millville Muni. Arpt. (MIV)	Flight Line Jug Rest.
13	Morristown	Morristown Muni. (MMU)	Calaloo Cafe
14	Morristown	Morristown Muni. (MMU)	Valentino's Rest.
15	Mount Holly	South Jersey Reg. (VAY)	Airfare Cafe
16	Newark	Newark Intl. Arpt. (EWR)	CA1 Services
17	Newark	Newark Intl. Arpt. (EWR)	Newark Arpt. (Marriott)
18	Ocean City	Ocean City Muni. Arpt. (26N)	Ocean City Arpt. Diner
19	Old Bridge	Old Bridge Arpt. (3N6)	Attractions
20	Pittstown	Sky Manor Arpt. (N40)	Sky Manor Rest.
21	Princeton (Rocky Hill)	Princeton Arpt. (39N)	A & B's
22	Princeton (Rocky Hill)	Princeton Arpt. (39N)	Carvers Cafe
23	Princeton (Rocky Hill)	Princeton Arpt. (39N)	Tiger's Tale
24	Robbinsville	Trenton-Robbinsville Arpt. (N87)	Sky View Country Club
25	Sussex	Sussex Arpt. (FWN)	Dare Devil Deli
26	Sussex	Sussex Arpt. (FWN)	Seasons Hotel Resort
27	Sussex	Sussex Arpt. (FWN)	Sussex Arpt. Diner
28	Teterboro	Teterboro Arpt. (TEB)	Cafe Luberto's
29	Trenton	Mercer Co. Arpt. (TTN)	General Quarters Rest.
30	West Milford	Greenwood Lake	Airport Restaurant
31	Wildwood	Cape May Co. Arpt. (WWD)	Airport Restaurant

Articles

City or town	Nearest Airport and Identifier	Name of Attraction
Teterboro, NJ	Teterboro Arpt. (TEB)	NJ Aviation Hall of Fame

NJ-ACY - ATLANTIC CITY ATLANTIC CITY INTERNATIONAL

(Area Code 609)

1

Thrashers Restaurant:

The Thrashers Restaurant is located within the terminal building at the Atlantic City International Airport. This combination snack bar and cafeteria is open 7 days a week, beginning at 7 a.m. and closing at 12 a.m. Their menu contains such items as hot dogs, cheese steaks, cheeseburgers, sandwiches, chicken wings, salads and homemade soups. They also serve a full breakfast line as well. Their dining room can seat about 100 persons with tables as well as counter service. From the restaurant you can also see the activity on the airport. The Thrashers Restaurant serves in-flight catering for corporate and air carrier operations. For more information call 641-2116.

Restaurants Near Airport

Prima's Ristorante	3 mi SW	Phone: 383-8899
Thrashers Restaurant	On Site	Phone: 641-2116
Tulls Seafood	4 mi SW	Phone: 641-6014

Lodging: Howard Johnson (Trans) 641-7272; Best Western Whittier Inn (Trans) 484-1500; Comfort Inn (6 miles) 646-5000; Fountaine (3 miles) 641-5754; Rex Motel (3 miles) 646-2600;

Meeting Rooms: Howard Johnson 641-7272; Best Western Whittier Inn 484-1500.

Transportation: Budget Rent-A-Car 345-0600; Hertz Car Rental 383-0055.

Information: Greater Atlantic City Convention & Visitors Authority, 2314 Pacific Avenue, Atlantic City, NJ 08401, Phone: 348-7100.

Attractions:

Various casino hotels located approximately 12 miles east of airport.

Airport Information:

ATLANTIC CITY - ATLANTIC CITY INTERNATIONAL AIRPORT (ACY)
9 mi northwest of town N39-27.45 W74-34.63 Elev: 76 Fuel: 100LL, Jet-A
Rwy 13-31: H10000x180 (Asph-Grvd) Rwy 04-22: H6144x150 (Conc-Asph-Grvd)
Attended: Continuously Atis: 108.6 Unicom: 122.95 App/Dep Con 134.25, 124.6
Tower: 120.3 Gnd Con: 121.9 Clnc Del: 127.85 Public Phone 24hrs
FBO: Midlantic Jet Aviation Phone: 344-5555
FBO: Signature Flight Support Phone: 646-5340

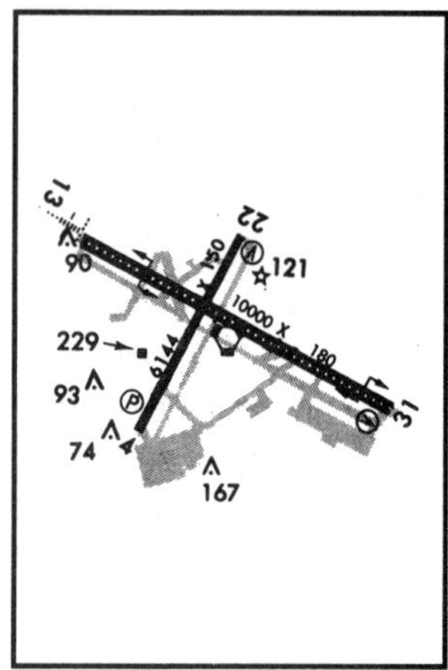

NJ-AIY - ATLANTIC CITY ATLANTIC CITY MUNICIPAL-BADER FIELD

(Area Code 609)

2

McGettigans Saloon:

McGettigans Saloon is within walking distance from the Atlantic City Municipal - Bader Field, according to restaurant personnel. Fly-in guests can walk out of the main terminal building, cross the street (Albany Avenue) turn left and go two blocks, and the restaurant should be on the right side of the street. This family-style restaurant is open for lunch from 11:30 a.m. to 10 p.m. Monday through Friday, and 11:30 a.m. to 5 p.m. on Saturday and Sunday. Specialties of the house include steak, seafood, prime rib, New York strip, baked stuffed flounder, chicken and ribs, barbecued ribs and combination plates. Average prices run between $10.95 to $17.95 for main course dinner selections. Daily specials are also featured as well. The restaurant has an Irish pub decor with lots of dark wood and brass and seating for about 65 people. For information call McGettigans Saloon at 344-3030.

Restaurant Near Airport:

McGettigans Saloon	2 blks	Phone: 344-3030

Lodging: Comfort Inn 645-1818; Econo Lodge 344-2925; Merv Griffin's Resort Casino Hotel 344-6000; Tropworld 340-4000; Trump Plaza Hotel 441-6000. All with 1-2 miles of airport.
Meeting Rooms: Merv Griffin's Resort Casino Hotel (Convention facilities) 344-6000;
Transportation: Taxi Service available at airport.
Information: Greater Atlantic City Convention & Visitors Bureau, 2314 Pacific Avenue, Atlantic City, NJ 08401, Phone: 348-7100.

Attractions:

Atlantic City offers numerous recreational activities. Nearby casino's, Boardwalk at Arkansas Avenue offering a 900 foot 3 deck shopping pier 347-8082; historic town of Smithville, and the Village Greene at Smithville is a restored 18th century village with specialty shops; public beach open Memorial Day through mid-October; fishing; golf courses; bicycling.

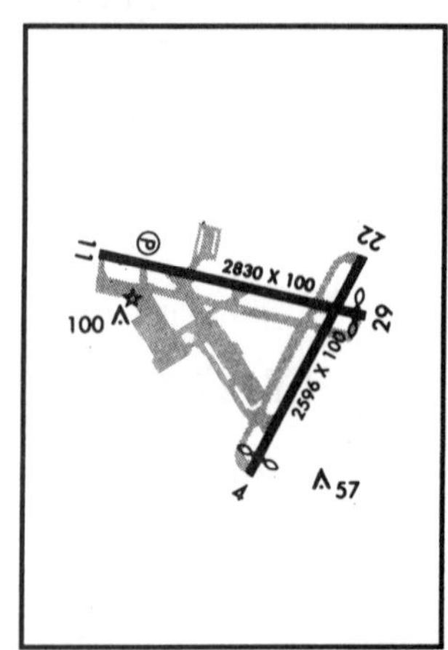

Airport Information:

ATLANTIC CITY - ATLANTIC CITY MUNICIPAL/BADER FIELD (AIY)
1 mi west of town N39-21.60 W74-27.37 Elev: 9 Rwy 11-29: H2830x100 (Asph) Rwy 04-22: H2596x100 (Asph) Attended: unattended Unicom: 123.0 Notes: CAUTION - closed to jet traffic; Numerous cranes (60' to 200') operating on and in vicinity of airport indefinitely. Rwy 4 CLOSED for landings, Rwy 22 CLOSED for takeoffs. Ship masts 35' passing in channel within 200' of all runways. (See Airport Facility Directory for current airport information).
Airport Manager Phone: 345-6402

NJ-BLM - BELMAR/FARMINGDALE ALLAIRE AIRPORT

(Aera Code 908) 3

Cafe Allaire:

The Cafe Allaire is situated only a short walking distance from the terminal building and aircraft parking ramp. This cafe is open for breakfast and lunch Monday through Saturday between 7 a.m. and 3 p.m., and Sunday 8 a.m. to 3 p.m. For dinner they are open on Thursday 4 p.m. to 9 p.m., Friday and Saturday 4 p.m. to 10 p.m. A full-service bar overlooking the airport is available. They feature daily lunch specials including a "dinner menu sampler" with smaller portions of their dinner items at 1/2 the price. Also they provide weekend specials. Average prices run $4.50 for breakfast, $5.00 for lunch and around $15.00 for dinner. The view from the restaurant is a panoramic one of the Allaire Airport. Groups are welcome with their ability to seat up to 30 people. They also are happy to prepare catered meals for pilots on the go. For information you can call Cafe Allaire at 938-7533.

Restaurants Near Airport:
Cafe Allaire — Adj. Terml. Bldg. — Phone: 938-7533

Lodging: Belmar Motor Lodge 8 mi 681-6600; Comfort Inn 10 mi 449-6146; Courtyard By Marriott 8-10 mi 389-2100; Holiday Inn 10-15 mi 544-9300.

Meeting Rooms: Nearby motels and hotels may contain accommodations for meetings. Cafe Allaire 938-7533; Don's Airport Restaurant 938-4067.

Transportation: Taxi service available by calling 223-1114.

Information: Belmar Chamber of Commerce, P.O. Box 297, Belmar, NJ 07719, Phone: 681-2900.

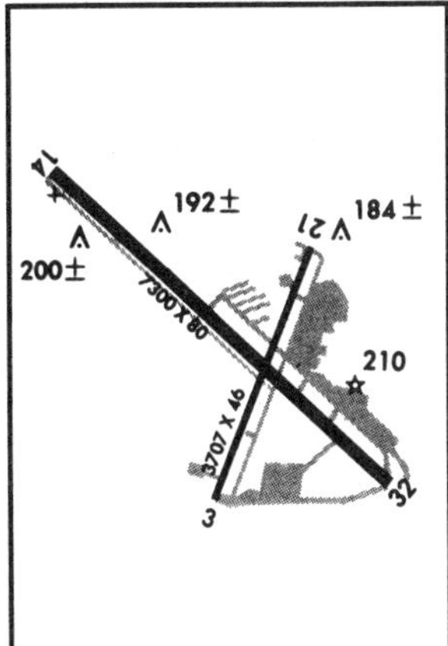

Attractions:

The Allaire Airport is within walking distance to Ed-Brown's Playground (Amusement Park on field); 1/4 mile to Wall Stadium (Car Racing); Golf driving range adjacent to airport and only 10 minutes by car to the beach; Allaire State Park approximately 5 miles west of town.

Airport Information:

BELMAR/FARMINGDALE - ALLAIRE AIRPORT (BLM)
5 mi west of town N40-11.13 W74-07.37 Elev: 157 Fuel: 100LL, Jet-A Rwy 14-32: H7300x80 (Asph) Rwy 03-21: H3707x46 (Asph) Attended: 1200-0200Z Jun-Sept, 1230-2300Z Oct-May Unicom: 123.0 Notes: Landing Fee, Rwy conditions during winter call 908-938-9733.
Allaire Airport Authority — **Phone: 938-4800**
FBO: Eagles View Aviation, Inc. — **Phone: 919-1927**

NJ-19N - BERLIN CAMDEN COUNTY AIRPORT

(Area Code 609) 4

Gourmet Room/Venice Plaza:

The Gourmet Room is located within Venice Plaza, about 4 blocks north of the Camden County Airport. This fine dining facility is open for lunch Tuesday through Saturday beginning at 11 a.m. and until 10 p.m. for dinner. Their menu includes specialty dishes featuring veal, steaks, seafood and pasta. Prices average $14.95 and up for main selections. Daily specials are also offered. The formal dining room can accommodate 50 people and provides for an atmosphere of elegant dining. Linen covered tables, and background music add to the ambiance and fine dining elegance. Live entertainment is featured on Friday and Saturday, with dancing. Proper attire with jackets for the men are the rule. Banquet facilities are also available with catering for 10 to 600 persons within two separate rooms. For more information call the Gourmet Room at the Venice Plaza, 768-0944.

Restaurants Near Airport:
Gourmet Room/Venice Plaza — 4 Blks — Phone: 768-0944

Lodging: Quality Inn (7 miles) 235-5610; Winslow Motor Lodge (5 miles) 561-6200.

Meeting Rooms: Cherry Hill Inn 662-7200

Transportation: Taxi Service: Berlin 767-7700; Car Rental: Berlin Auto Leasing 767-7700.

Information: Cherry Hill Township Public Information Office, 820 Mercer Street, Cherry Hill, NJ 08002, Phone: 488-7847.

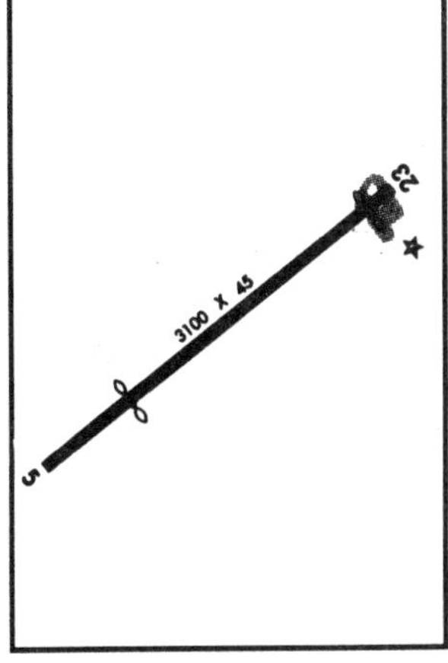

Airport Information:

BERLIN - CAMDEN COUNTY AIRPORT (19N)
1 mi southwest of town N39-46.71 W74-56.87 Elev: 150 Fuel: 100LL, Jet-A Rwy 05-23: H3102x45 (Asph) Attended: 1300-0200Z Unicom: 122.8
FBO: Garden State Aviation — **Phone: 767-1233**

NJ-1N7 - BLAIRSTOWN
BLAIRSTOWN AIRPORT

(Area Code 908) 5

Restaurants Near Airport:
Runway Cafe On Site Phone: 362-9170

Lodging: None Reported

Meeting Rooms: None Reported

Transportation: Rental cars available through Blair Air, Inc., Phone: 362-6263.

Information: State Division of Travel and Tourism, CN-826, Trenton, NJ 08625, Phone: 609-292-2470 or 800-JERSEY-7.

Runway Cafe:

The Runway Cafe is located on the Blairstown Airport, in a building with hangar and fixed base operator all in one. This family style restaurant is open between 7 a.m. and 6 p.m. 7 days a week. Winter hours begin during the time change. During this season they close a 4:30 p.m. They specialize in breakfast and lunch selections. Egg dishes, omelets, and pancakes, as well as a variety of sandwiches including hamburgers, cheeseburgers, Rubin, and chicken dishes are just a few of the choices available. Average prices run between $4.00 and $4.50 for most entrees. Daily specials usually run between $3.50 and $4.95. Their main dining area can seat 44 persons, and has tables, booths, and counter service. Guests can look out over the airport while enjoying a meal. This is a popular restaurant with many of the local people, and often attracts a variety of groups and club functions including fly-in customers. On weekends they are usually quite busy. If organizing a fly-in breakfast or luncheon, with a large number of persons, we were told that if possible plan your function during the week. Please let them know in advance of your intentions. Meals can also be prepared-to-go as well. For more information about the Runway Cafe call 362-9170.

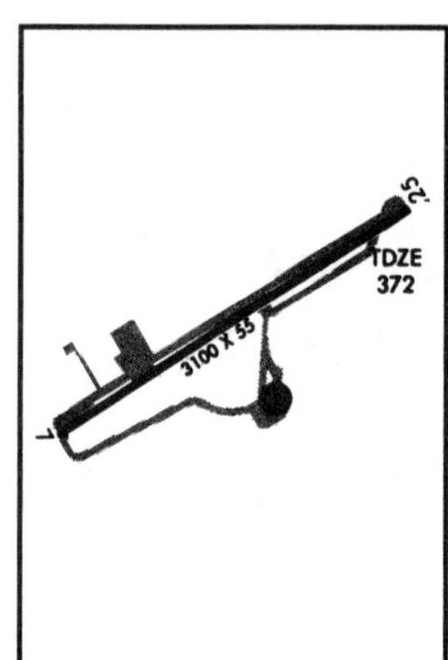

Attractions:

Lake and swimming beach adjacent to field. Paulinskill Trail is a abandoned railroad bead that runs through airport property. Some people enjoy walking or bicycle riding along this path. Also camping sites located within 4 to 5 miles of the airport.

Airport Information:

BLAIRSTOWN - BLAIRSTOWN AIRPORT (1N7)
2 mi southwest of town N40-58.27 W74-59.85 Elev: 372 Fuel: 100LL
Rwy 07-25: H3100x55 (Asph) Attended: dawn to dusk Unicom: 123.0
FBO: Tri-Av, Inc. Phone: 362-6263

NJ-CDW - CALDWELL
ESSEX COUNTY AIRPORT

(Area Code 201) 6

Restaurants Near Airport:

94th Bomb Group	On Site	Phone: 882-5660
Ground Round	1/4 mi	Phone: 227-9862
Sandalwood	1 mi	Phone: 575-1742
Sandalwood East	1 mi	Phone: 882-1111

Lodging: Best Western Executive Inn (1 mile) 575-7700; Holiday Inn (3 miles) 256-7000; Ramada Inn (1 mile) 575-1742; Sheraton Inn (1 mile) 227-9200.

Meeting Rooms: Best Western Executive Inn 575-7700; Holiday Inn 256-7000; Ramada Inn 575-1742; Sheraton Inn 227-9200.

Transportation: Taxi Service: Air Coach Limousine Service 575-6894; Caldwell 226-0884; Mountain Yellow Cab 226-1155; Shamrock Coach Limousine 335-5466; West Caldwell 226-1234; Also Rental Cars: Courier 882-0310; Econo Car Rental 226-6300.

Information: Montclair Chamber of Commerce, 50 Church Street, Montclair, NJ 07042, Phone: 744-7660. Also: Newark Chamber of Commerce, 40 Clinton Street North, Newark, NJ 07100, Phone: 242-6237; Also: State Division of Travel and Tourism, CN-826, Trenton, NJ 08625, Phone: 609-292-2470 or 800--JERSEY-7.

94th Bomb Group:

The 94th Bomb Group is located on the Essex County Airport and according to the restaurant management, is within walking distance from aircraft parking areas. This fine dining establishment is open Tuesday through Friday 11 a.m. to 10 p.m., Sunday and Monday 11 a.m. to 9 p.m. and Saturday 11 a.m. to 11 p.m. Monday through Wednesday during lunch from 11 a.m. to 3 p.m. and dinner from 5 p.m. to 9 p.m., Thursday until 10 p.m. and Friday, and Saturday until 11 p.m. Their menu contains a variety of specially prepared dishes like their 10 oz. and 14 oz. regular or king cut prime rib, chicken dishes marinated in special sauces, veal, filet Medallion, and pepper corn steaks, to mention only a few. Average prices run $6.95 to $9.95 for lunch, and $9.95 to $19.95 for dinner. On Sunday they offer a brunch between 10:30 a.m. and 2:30 p.m. for $16.95 for adults, $8.95 for children 12 and under, and if you are under five years of age you can enjoy the brunch for free. This restaurant has an aviation theme, and depicts an English farm house located on an Air Force base. Several dining rooms within the restaurant are decorated with WW-II artifacts, antiques and photographs of bomber groups and their squadrons. The restaurant can seat approximately 140 persons, and can easily accommodate fly-in groups and parties. There is also an outdoor patio for guests to watch the activity on the airport. For more information call the 94th Bomb Group at 882-5660.

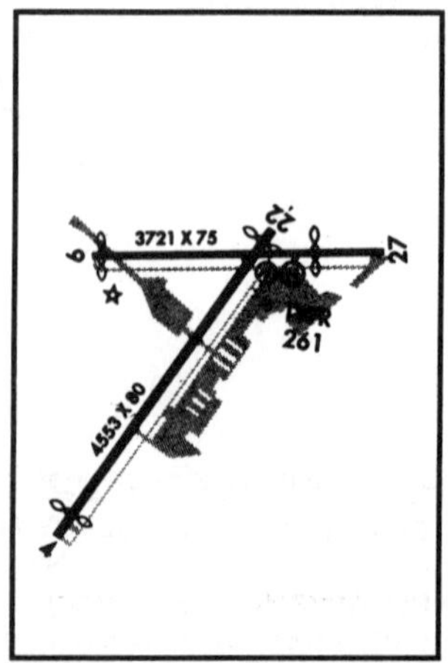

Airport Information:

CALDWELL - ESSEX COUNTY AIRPORT (CDW)
2 mi north of town N40-52.51 W74-16.88 Elev: 173 Fuel: 100LL, Jet-A Rwy 04-22: H4553x80 (Asph) Rwy 09-27: H3721x75 (Asph) Attended: 1200-0400Z Atis: 135.5
Unicom: 122.95 Caldwell Tower: 126.5 Gnd Con: 127.6 Clnc Del: 121.1

Essex County Airport Phone: 227-4567
FBO: Caldwell Air Service Phone: 808-9047
FBO: Mac Dan Aviation Phone: 227-1180
FBO: Mustang Aviation Phone: 575-8807
FBO: Nazarina Aviation Phone: 575-1779

NJ-N81 - HAMMONTON
HAMMONTON MUNICIPAL

(Area Code 609)

7

Restaurants Near Airport:
Cathy's Cafe On Site Phone: 561-0100

Lodging: Lake Front Motel 561-0932; Ramada Inn 561-5700

Meeting Rooms: Non reported

Transportation: Rental cars available through Calderone's Parisi Motors, Inc. 561-0087. Taxi Service: J.P. 561-6033 and Joseph Pino Taxi Service 561-1163.

Information: Division of Travel and Tourism, 20 West State Street, CN 826, Trenton, NJ 08625, Phone: 609-292-2470.

Cathy's Cafe:

This cafe-style restaurant is reported open during the summer month and on weekends from 9 a.m. to 3 p.m. during the winter months. Fly-in guests can park their aircraft on the main apron in front of the restaurant. They specialize in breakfast and lunch items including egg and sausage dishes, pancakes, cheeseburgers, steak sandwiches, hamburgers, tuna sandwiches, chicken sandwiches and an assortment of pies and desserts. The cafe has large windows overlooking the runways. 16 tables along with counter service makes up the seating within the restaurant. This family-operated restaurant has been proudly serving customers for over 28 years. Many people like to fly in to enjoy a meal, and fill their tanks with some of the most economical fuel prices in the area. For information call the Hammonton Municipal Airport Manager at 561-0100.

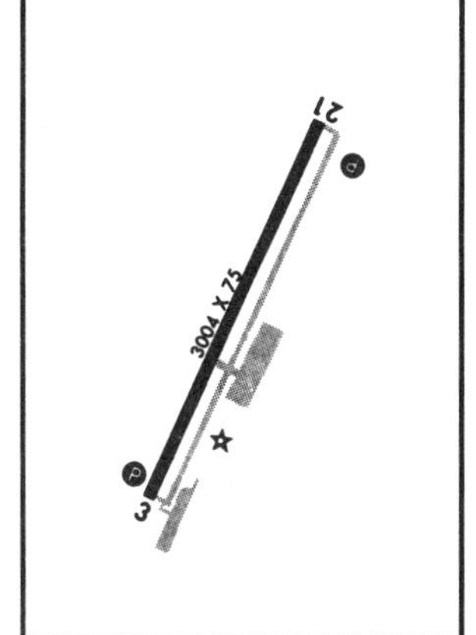

Airport Information:

HAMMONTON - HAMMONTON MUNICIPAL (N81)
3 mi northeast of town N39-40.10 W74-45.45 Elev: 69 Fuel: 100LL, Jet-A Rwy 03-21: H3004x75 (Asph) Attended: 1300Z-dusk Unicom: 122.7 Notes: rotating beacon out of service indefinitely; Glider operations.
FBO: M & D Services, Inc. Phone: 561-0100

NJ-N07 - LINCOLN PARK
LINCOLN PARK AIRPORT

(Area Code 201)

8

Restaurants Near Airport:
Ready Room Lounge On Site Phone: 633-0450

Lodging: B W Fairfield Executive Inn 575-7700; Ramada Inn 575-1742; Sheraton Hotel 227-9200.

Meeting Rooms: None Reported

Transportation: None reported

Information: Division of Travel and Tourism, 20 West State Street, CN 826, Trenton, NJ 08625, Phone: 609-292-2470.

Ready Room Lounge:

This restaurant is located on the Lincoln Park Airport adjacent to Lincoln Park Aviation. It is open 7 days a week. Their menu offers full course meals. Windows along two sides of the restaurant allow for a nice view of the activity on the airport. For more information call the restaurant at 872-0063 or Lincoln Park Aviation at 633-0450.

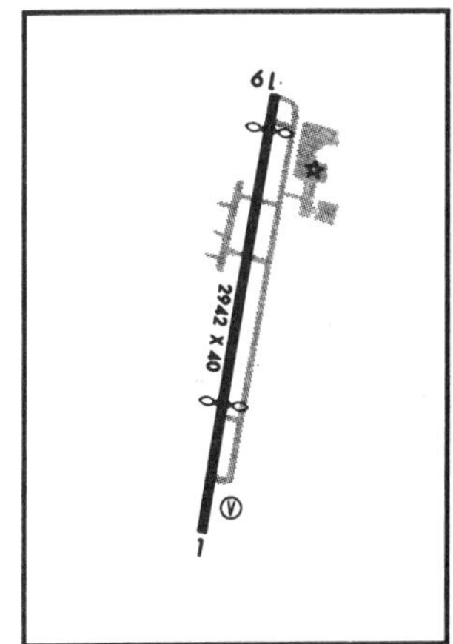

Airport Information:

LINCOLN PARK - LINCOLN PARK AIRPORT (N07)
2 mi north of town N40-56.85 W74-18.87 Elev: 182 Fuel: 100LL, Jet-A, MOGAS Rwy 01-19: H2942x40 (Asph) Attended: 1300Z-dusk Unicom: 122.8 Notes: See AFD for runway condition.
FBO: Lincoln Park Aviation Phone: 633-0450

NJ-N14 - LUMBERTON FLYING W AIRPORT

(Area Code 609)

9

Restaurants Near Airport:

Flying W Ranch	On Site	Phone: 267-8787

Lodging: Flying W Motel (On Site) 267-8787.
Meeting Rooms: Offices and conference room in-flight operations, on the airport. Phone: 267-7673.
Transportation: Taxi: Cherry Hill 235-2584; Eagle Limo Service 723-2000; Medford 383-3232; Rental Cars: Agency 234-8822; Enterprise 386-7522; Medford Ford 654-5166; Miller Ford 267-4466; U-Save 256-0325.
Information: Greater Cherry Hill Chamber of Commerce, 1060 Kings Highway North, Cherry Hill, NJ 08034, Phone: 667-1600.

Attractions:
Flying W Ranch; There is an 18 hole golf course reported adjacent to the airport. Charter boats are also available on Rancocas River.

Flying W Restaurant Airport and Ranch:
Upon the reaction of our contributors, we learned that this establishment ranks very high as a favorite for fly-in destinations, and a must for including in your next planned outing. According to one of our readers the ambiance at this airport is unmatched. The property has a restaurant, catering hall, motel and ranch and even a swimming pool in the shape of an airplane. They also stated that the food is excellent as well. The Flying W Restaurant is located only 100 to 200 feet from the airport, and can easily be reached by walking. This is a very nice family-style restaurant that is open from 11 a.m. to 3 p.m. for lunch and 5 p.m. to 10 p.m. for dinner. The restaurant is closed on Monday. They also feature a Sunday brunch from 9 a.m. to 1 p.m. for only $8.55. Their standard menu contains entrees like steaks, shrimp, rack of lamb, chicken parmesan, spare ribs and chicken dishes. Average prices run $4.95 for lunch and between $8.95 and $12.95 for most dinner selections. The main dining room can seat 165 persons and contains a rustic decor in a barn-like structure with exposed beams, carpeting and large windows where guests can enjoy a view of the airport. Fly-in groups and parties are welcome with accommodations for between 45 and 105 persons in the main dining area. A separate banquet area is also available for larger parties up to 150 persons. The restaurant can prepare box lunches for carry-out as well. In addition to the restaurant, this establishment also contains an 18 hole golf course and motel located adjacent to the airport, which are all situated within a short walk. For more information about the Flying W Restaurant and facilities call 267-8787.

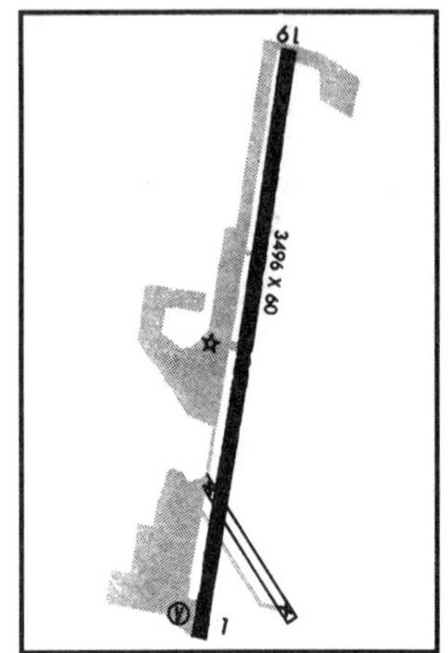

Airport Information:
LUMBERTON - FLYING W AIRPORT (N14)
1 mi southwest of town N39-56.01 W74-48.39 Elev: 50 Fuel: 100LL, Jet-A
Rwy 01-19: H3496x60 (Asph) Attended: 1300-0100Z Unicom: 122.8 Public Phone 24hrs Notes: No landing or parking fees charged. Tethered balloon activity on and in vicinity of airport.
FBO: Aero Prep Gnd. School **Phone: 265-9139**
FBO: Air One Flight School **Phone: 267-6463**

NJ-47N - MANVILLE KUPPER AIRPORT

(Area Code 908)

10

Restaurants Near Airport:

Colonial Farms	8 mi E.	Phone: 873-3990
Espo's	8 mi W.	Phone: 685-9552
Pizza & Pasta	1000 ft. N.	Phone: 725-5522
Red Door	1/2 mi N.	Phone: 722-3667

Lodging: Hillsborough Executive Days Inn 685-9000; Holiday Inn 526-9500; Marriott Hotel 560-0500; All within 5-10 miles.

Meeting Rooms: Marriott Hotel 560-0500; Madison Suites 563-1000. Garden State Convention Center and Exhibit Center.

Transportation: Rental Cars: Dollar 563-9800; American Taxi 526-0055; Franks Limo 874-4258.

Information: Somerset County Chamber of Commerce, 64 W End Avenue, P.O. Box 833, Somerville, NJ 08876. Phone: 725-1552.

Attractions:
Balloon Rides and Bungee jumping on field. Commons shopping mall; colonial park; City of Somerville; Yellow Rose Country Dance Club, are all within 5 miles of the airport. Also Garden State Convention Center and Exhibit Center.

Pizza & Pasta:
The Pizza & Pasta Restaurant is located 1,000 feet from the main airport office. This full service restaurant specializes in gourmet pizza but also provides guests with a full selection of entrees to choose from. The restaurant is contained within a 5,000 square foot building. Front and side windows allow a view of the airport with the ability to see aircraft talking off and landing. Their hours are 11:30 a.m. to 11 p.m. Monday through Saturdays, and between 3 p.m. and 10 p.m. on Sundays. Specialties of the house include pizzas that is baked in a wood burning oven. Many different toppings are available. In addition to their delicious pizza's, guests are welcome to try their pasta dishes, chicken, veal, seafood and sandwiches. Average prices run between $4.45 to $13.00 for pizzas and $8.00 to $9.00 for other main dinner selections. The interior of the restaurant is decorated with green, burgundy and cream colors, Large archways separate the dining rooms from one another. You can even watch them prepare the pasta from one of the dining rooms. For larger groups they have two available and separate dining rooms able to seat 35 and 175 individuals. For information call Pizza & Pasta Restaurant at 725-5522.

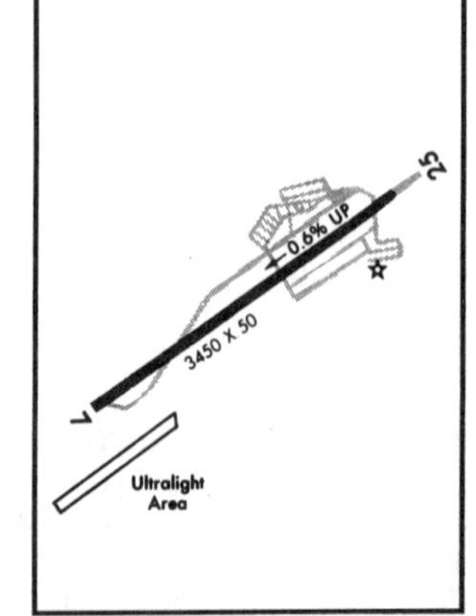

Airport Information:
MANVILLE - KUPPER AIRPORT (47N)
1 mi south of town N40-31.46 W74-35.90 Elev: 86 Fuel: 100LL Rwy 07-25: H3450x50 (Asph) Attended: 1300Z-dusk Unicom: 122.7 Phone: 24hrs Notes: Landing fee $3.00/engine waived with fuel purchase. Overnight parking $5.00 per night
FBO: Tristate Airways **Phone: 526-2822**

NJ-2N8 - MATAWAN MARLBORO AIRPORT

(Area Code 908) 11

Sloppy Joe's Restaurant:

The Sloppy Joe's Restaurant is located within the flight operations building on the Marlboro Airport. Restaurant hours are 6 days a week between 7:30 a.m. to 3:30 p.m. (Closed Mondays). This restaurant has a full line of breakfast items including pancakes, egg and sausage dishes. We were told by the airport manager that the omelet dishes are great! They also serve hamburgers, corn beef, pork chops, chicken sandwiches, club sandwiches and homemade soups. Many of their dishes have names relating to aviation. The restaurant has counter service as well as tables. All seats in the restaurant offer a great view of the active runway. They are only 50 feet from the taxi way and about 100 yards from the runway. They also welcome fly-in groups and club functions. For more information about Sloppy Joe's Restaurant call 591-9805.

Attractions:

Open cockpit biplane rides are given with prior arrangements. For information call the airport manager at 591-1082.

Airport Information:

MATAWAN - AMRLBORO AIRPORT (2N8)
3 mi south of town N40-21.97 W74-15.26 Elev: 122 Fuel: 100LL Rwy 09-27: H2156x50(Asph)
Attended: 1300-2200Z Unicom: 122.7
Airport Manager Phone: 591-1591

Restaurants Near Airport:
Sloppy Joe's Restaurant On Site Phone: 591-9805

Lodging: Howard Johnson 15 mi 671-3400; Ramada Inn 264-2400; Sheraton 10 mi 264-2400; Wellesley Inn 888-2800.

Meeting Rooms: Ramada Inn (in town) 264-2400.

Transportation: None reported

Information: Matawan Chamber of Commerce, P.O. Box 522, Matawan, NJ 07747, Phone: 290-1125.

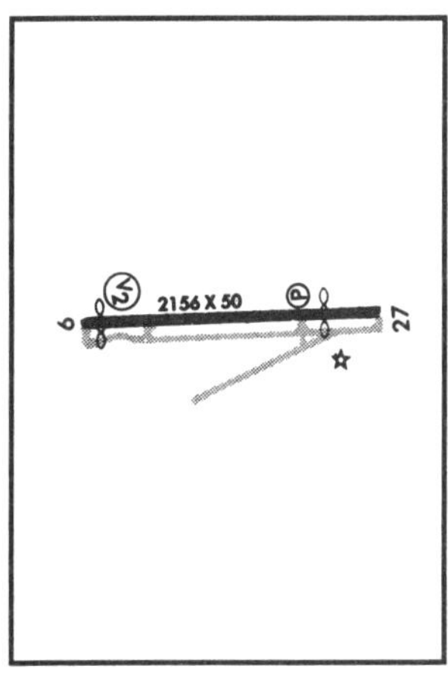

NJ-MIV - MILLVILLE MILLVILLE MUNICIPAL AIRPORT

(Area Code 609) 12

Flight Line Jug Restaurant:

This restaurant is located on the airport flightline between "Airwork" & "Midlantic Jet Facility". You can park your aircraft right in front of the restaurant. The decor is rustic, with a World War II atmosphere. They are open from 6 a.m. to 2 p.m. 7 days a week. Entrees run an average of $3.00 for breakfast, and $4.00 for lunch. This facility will cater to fly-in groups as well as pilots on the go. During our conversation with the management we learned that Midlantic Aviation is located adjacent to their facility. From a quick cup of coffee to start the day, to a stick to your ribs meal to refuel, the Flight Line can accommodate everyone's taste. Home cooking, fast friendly service and a great place to meat. For information about the Flightline Restaurant call 825-3200.

Restaurants Near Airport:
Flight Line Jug Restaurant On Site Phone: 825-3200
Millville Motor Inn 3 mi NE. Phone: 327-3300

Lodging: Days Inn, (5 miles) 696-5000; Millville Motor Inn, (3 miles) 327-3300; Vineland Motor Inn (4 miles) 696-3800
Transportation: Rainbow Aviation, 825-3160; Holly City Cab, 825-9393; Millville Cab, 825-0567.
Information: Chamber of Commerce, 13 South High Street, P.O. Box 831, Millville, NJ 08332, Phone: 825-7000 ext 396.

Attractions:

Millville Army Airfield Musuem is reported to be located on the Millville Municipal Airport. This airport during WW-II served a very important purpose as a P-47 Gunnery school for aviation cadets. The museum has one aircraft on display outdoors as well as many artifacts describing the significance of the airport history. The museum is open Saturday and Sunday from 10 a.m. to 4 p.m. For information call 327-2347.

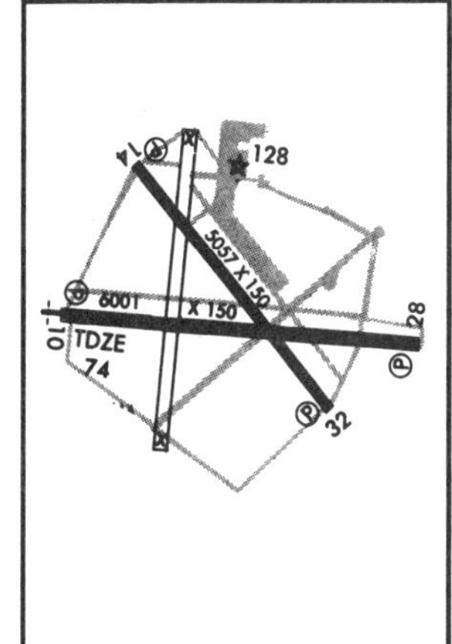

Airport Information:

MILLVILLE - MILLVILLE MUNICIPAL (MIV)
3 mi southwest of town N39-22.08 W75-04.41 Elev: 86 Fuel: 100LL, Jet-A
Rwy 10-28: H6001x150 (Asph) Rwy 14-32: H5057x150 (Conc) Attended: continuous
Unicom: 123.0 Public Phone 24 hrs. Notes: No landing fee, call 825-3160 for parking instructions. Also Automated Flight Service Station (AFSS) on field.
FBO: Rainbow Aviation, Phone: 825-3160
FBO: Midlantic Jet Charter, Phone: 825-5557

NJ-MMU - MORRISTOWN
MORRISTOWN MUNICIPAL

(Area Code 201)

13, 14

Calaloo Cafe:

This restaurant is located about 4 or 5 miles from the Morristown Airport. Transportation can easily be arranged through the fixed base operators on the field. Calaoo Cafe specializes in preparing fresh fish, beef selections, chicken pasta salad, all types of healthy choice salad creations, lamb chops, pork loins, Chinese dishes, cat fish, blackened sword fish, trout and much more. Restaurant hours are Monday through Thursday 11:30 a.m. to 4:30 p.m. for lunch; 4:30 p.m. to 11 p.m. Monday through Thursday for dinner; Friday and Saturday 4:30 p.m. to 12 a.m., and Sunday 4:30 p.m. to 10 p.m. Prices average $12.95 to $14.95 for main dinner selections. Between 11:00 and 3 p.m. they feature a brunch buffet. Selections include omelets, carved meats like turkey and roast beef, cache, Eggs Benedict, and/or a special dish of the day. The decor of the restaurant has a tropical ambience, surrounded by windows. The dining room is L-shaped able to seat about 130 people. Their patio allows outdoor dining under umbrella covered tables amongst tropical trees and flowered arrangements. When ready to return to the airport there are public phones where you can make your call to the FBO for the return trip. Banquet rooms are available downstairs as well. One additional item of special interest is a comedy show that is held each Friday and Saturday evening at the same location. Although this show is a separate attraction from the restaurant, reservations or information can be obtained by calling the restaurant phone number. For more information about the Calaloo Cafe call 993-1100.

Valentino's Restaurant:

Valentino's is a fine dining establishment situated between 3 and 5 minutes by courtesy car away from the Morristown Municipal Airport. Transportation can easily be arranged by the fixed base operators at the airport. This facility is situated within a modest storefront location. The restaurant was recommended to us as a very popular dining facility with the local as well as fly-in clientele. This family-owned operation prepares authentic Northern Italian cuisine. Freshly-made pasta, veal, as well as seafood dishes, are their specialty. Prices average $4.00 to $13.00 for lunch selections and about $12.00 to $22.00 for most dinner choices. The restaurant decor displays an Art Deco styling. The main dining room can accommodate 75 people. A small private and secluded room able to accommodate 6 to 30 persons, serves as a quiet private location for guests to congregate and enjoy themselves apart from the main dining area. This restaurant was the first Italian restaurant to begin business within Morristown. For further information call this restaurant at 993-8066.

Restaurants Near Airport:

Calaloo Cafe	5 to 6 miles	Phone: 993-1100
Valentino's	3 to 5 minutes	Phone: 993-8066

Lodging: Headquarters Plaza (Within 5 miles) 898-9100; Hilton (Within 5 miles) 267-7373; Holiday Inn (Within 5 miles) 994-3500; Madison (Within 5 miles) 285-1800; Roadway Inn (Within 5 miles) 887-9300; The Royce Hotel Governor Morris (Within 5 miles) 539-7300.

Meeting Rooms: Headquarters Plaza Hotel 898-9100; Madison Hotel 285-1800; The Royce Hotel Governor Morris 539-7300;

Transportation: Taxi Service: Livingston 740-1999; Morristown Limo 5538-7575; Ramsey 267-4625; Also rental cars: Avis 292-1300; C & C 539-8500.

Information: Historic Morris Visitors Center, 14 Elm Street, Morristown, NJ 07960, Phone: 993-1194.

Airport Information:

MORRISTOWN - MORRISTOWN MUNICIPAL AIRPORT (MMU)
3 mi east of town N40-47.96 W74-24.89 Elev: 187 Fuel: 100LL, Jet-A
Rwy 05-23: H5999x150 (Asph-Grvd) Rwy 12-30: H3998x150 (Asph-Grvd) Attended: 1145-0330Z
Atis: 124.25 Unicom: 122.95 Tower: 118.1 Gnd Con: 121.7 Clnc Del: 121.2 Notes: Birds and deer in vicinity of airport; Various runways have wind velocity requirements for operation. See current Airport Facility Directory for limitations, Control Zone effective times, and current information. Also landing fee is reported.
FBO: Jet Support System, Inc. Phone: 539-8500
FBO: Lynton Jet Center Phone: 292-1300

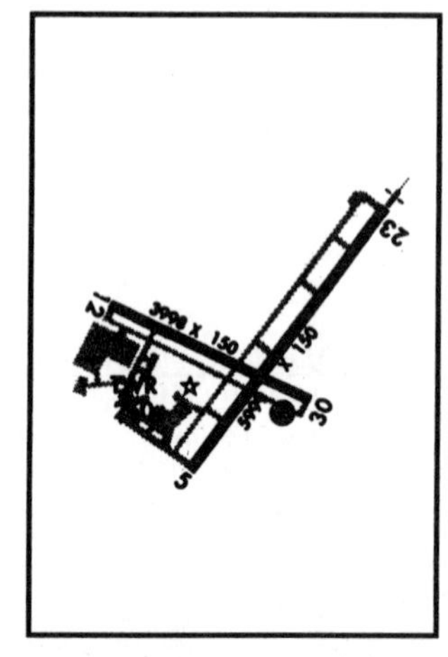

Not to be used for navigational purposes

NJ-VAY- MOUNT HOLLY SOUTH JERSEY REGIONAL

(Area Code 609)

15

Airfare Cafe:

The Airfare Cafe is located on the South Jersey Regional Airport, and is part of the Sabre Flight Services operation. This restaurant is conveniently located only a few feet from the aircraft tie-down area. Classified as a combination snack bar and cafe, the restaurant hours are reported to be open 9 a.m. to 4 p.m. on weekdays and 9 a.m. to 5 p.m. on weekends, 7 days a week. They specialize in deli-style sandwiches including burgers, hogie sandwiches, soups, chili and much more. Average entree selections run between $3.00 and $5.00. Their dining room can seat 20 persons. Guests can also enjoy watching the aircraft on the ramp while eating their meal. Groups can arrange fly-in breakfasts or luncheons as well. In-flight catering is also a part of the overall services available at this establishment, in addition to aircraft fuel and line service for fly-in customers. For more information you can call the Sabre Flight Services at 267-3131.

Restaurants Near Airport:
Airfare Cafe On Site Phone: 267-3131

Lodging: Concord Motel (3 miles) 267-7900.

Meeting Rooms: Accommodations for meeting rooms are available on the South Jersey Regional Airport. For information call 267-3131.

Transportation: Sabre Flight Service will provide courtesy transportation to nearby facilities. Call 367-3131; Also National Car Rental 267-1707.

Information: Burlington Chamber of Commerce, P.O. Box 2006, Willingboro NJ 08046, Phone: 386-1012.

Attraction:

A Golf Course is reported to be located about 2 miles from the South Jersey Regional Airport. For information call the airport manager at 367-3131, or Sabre Flight Services at 267-3131.

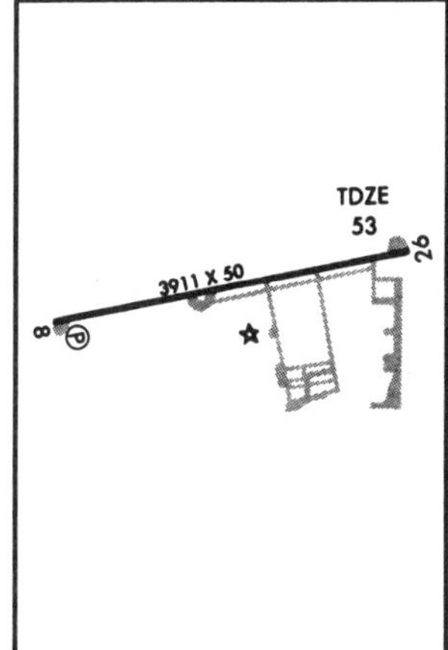

Airport Information:

MOUNT HOLLY - SOUTH JERSEY REGIONAL AIRPORT (VAY)
4 mi southwest of town N39-56.57 W74-50.74 Elev: 53 Rwy 08-26: H3911x50 (Asph)
Attended: 1300-0100Z Unicom: 122.8 Public Phone 24 hrs.
FBO: Sabre Flight Services Phone: 367-3131

NJ-EWR - NEWARK
NEWARK INTL. AIRPORT

(Area Code 201) 16, 17

CA1 Services:

CA1 Services operates numerous food service facilities within terminal C at the Newark International Airport (EWR). ***ABP-I*** *at the C-1 concourse, Gate 70 is open 24 hours a day. Styled after a French Bistro Cafe, this establishment serves fresh pastry, grilled sandwiches, grilled chicken, fresh sandwiches, salads, soups and cappucino;* ***ABP-II*** *is located on the T-4 concourse, and is open between 5:30 a.m. and 9 p.m. The decor and specialties of the house are the same as mentioned for ABP-I.* ***Americo's Pizza*** *is at Gate #130, in the C-4 commuter wing. This is a cafe open between 6 a.m. and 9 p.m. Gourmet pizza, Ceasr salad, fresh pastry, along with sandwiches are offered. Prices average $5.00 to $7.00;* ***The Garden State Diner*** *is located across from Gate 81 in terminal C. This family-style restaurant is open between 6 a.m and 7 p.m. Specialties of the house include breakfast, lunch and dinner selections. Daily specials feature 8 choices. Additional items include grilled chicken, burgers, soups, homemade salads and fresh desserts. Prices average $4.00 to $6.00 for most selections. The restaurant has a modern casual decor. They can accommodate any size group on or off the premises. This restaurant also offers fly-in catering services. This is a family run independent operator;* ***The Grove*** *snack bar is located on the C-1 concourse at gate 81 in terminal C. This facility serves candy, popcorn, jellybeans and various items of this type. If you have a sweet tooth this is the place to go:* ***Jake's Coffee House*** *is located in terminal C, concourse C-1at gate 81. The decor is contemporary. Several round tables with high chairs provide the seating. Fresh pastry, coffee and cappucino are the specialty. Hours are 6 a.m. to 9 p.m.* ***Jake's Coffee House XPress*** *is situated at Gate #75, and offers the same services as Jake's Coffee House; A* ***McDonald's*** *restaurant is located at gate #74, 75 and 90. Hours are 6 a.m. to 9 p.m. Miami Subs specializes in serving gyro, pitas along with other items. Classic cheese steak subs, cold cuts subs and specialized salads, ice cream and chicken wings. Prices run $5.75 to $8.50. The restaurant displays a jazzy tropical decor. Catering is also offered. Nathan's Restaurant at gate #74, 75 and 100 is a cafeteria styled restaurant. Additional eateries include:* ***Sbarro's, Wok & Roll, and World Links.*** *For information about any one of these establishments call 623-2211.*

Restaurants Near Airport:

CA1 Services	On Site	Phone: 623-2211
Newark Arpt. Marriott Hotel	On Site	Phone: 623-0006

Lodging: Holiday Inn Airport (Trans) 355-1700; Holiday Inn Airport North (Trans) 589-1000; Howard Johnson Lodge Airport (Trans) 824-4000; Marriott Newark Airport (Trans) 623-0006; Sheraton Inn Airport (Trans) 527-1327.

Meeting Rooms: Holiday Inn Airport 355-1700; Holiday Inn Airport North 589-1000; Howard Johnson Lodge Airport 824-4000; Marriott Newark Airport 623-0006; Sheraton Inn Airport 527-1327.

Transportation: Taxi service: Elizabeth (Terminal Bldg.) 961-2154; Newark (Terminal Bldg) 961-2154; Rental cars: Avis 961-4300; Budget 961-2990; Dollar-A-Day 824-2002; Hertz 621-2000; National 622-1270.

Information: Convention & Visitors Bureau, One Newark Center, Newark, NJ 07102, Phone: 622-3010.

Newark Airport Marriott Hotel:

Located within the Newark Airport Marriott Hotel, are two dining establishments. Their fine dining facility is called Priscilla's, and is open from 11 a.m. to 2 p.m. for lunch and 5:30 until 10 p.m. for dinner, Monday through Saturday. The Allies American Bar & Grill located next door to Priscilla's has a more casual dining atmosphere. In addition to this, there are also 2 lounges also located on the premises. Both restaurants contain an assortment of excellent selections such as grilled chicken, duck breast Fresno, veal Romano, rack of lamb, filet of beef, shrimp, broiled sword fish, China glazed tuna, and Cajun grilled ribeye steak. In addition to some of the entrees listed above, the Allies American Bar & Grill contains lighter fare; for example, taco salads, pastas and appetizers. Average prices for most meals at Priscilla's run between $15.00 and $25.00. This restaurant is tastefully decorated in burgundy and mauve colors, with light oak wood trim, and can seat up to 85 people, while the Toucan Terrace Dining Room, can accommodate up to 296 persons. The Newark Airport Marriott Hotel have meeting rooms as well as overnight accommodations with 600 separate units. Free courtesy transportation can be utilized to and from their facility. For information call them at 623-0006.

Airport Information:

NEWARK - NEWARK INTERNATIONAL AIRPORT (EWR)

3 mi south of town N40-41.58 W74-10.11 Elev: 18 Fuel: 100LL, Jet-A Rwy 04R-22L: H9300x150 (Asph-Grvd) Rwy 04L-22R: H8200x150 (Asph-Conc-Grvd) Rwy 11-29: H6800x150 (Asph-Conc-Grvd) Attended: continuously Atis: 115.7, 132.45 Unicom: 122.95 New York App Con: 132.8, 128.55, 127.6, 132.7 New York Dep Con: 119.2 Tower: 118.3, 134.05 Gnd Con: 121.8 Clnc Del: 118.85 Pre-Taxi Clnc: 118.85 Gate Hold: 126.15

FBO: Signature Flight Support Phone: 624-1660, 624-2520

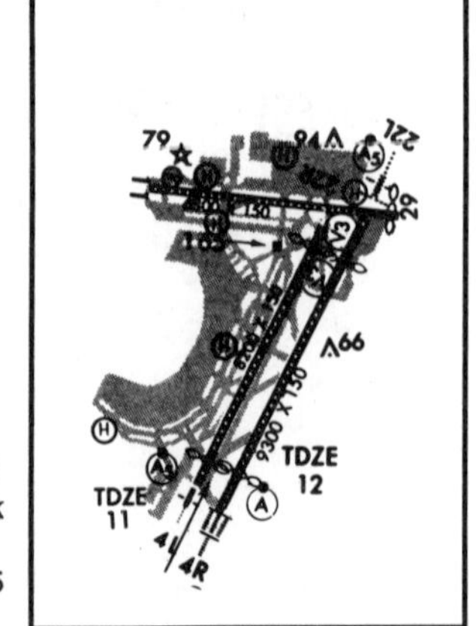

NJ-26N - OCEAN CITY

(Area Code 609)

18

OCEAN CITY MUNICIPAL AIRPORT

Ocean City Airport Diner:

The Augies Airport Diner is located adjacent to the Ocean City Municipal Airport. The restaurant is easily accessible either by walking or by taxi. This family style restaurant is open 7 day a week between 7 a.m. and 4 p.m. during the summer and 7 a.m. to 3 p.m. during the winter. Entree selections include Italian choices, hot subs, cold subs, burgers, all types of sandwiches, soups and salads along with a full line of breakfast items, including hot cakes. Average prices run $2.25 for breakfast and $3.00 for lunch. Daily specials are also offered. The decor of this establishment resembles a country kitchen. The main dining room can accommodate 52 persons. Arts and crafts are used to decorate the walls of the restaurant. Fly-in groups are welcome, and can make arrangements in advance . For more information you can call Augies Airport Diner at 399-3663.

Restaurants Near Airport:
Ocean City Airport Diner On Site Phone: 399-3663

Lodging: Enterprise Bed & Breakfast 398-1698; Port of Call (1 mile) 399-8812.
Meeting Rooms: None reported
Transportation: Jack's Cab 927-7573; P.S. Cab Service 391-1494; City of Ocean City 399-6111 ext 276.
Information: Public Relations Department, City of Ocean City, 9th & Asbury Avenue 399-6111 or 800-BEACH NJ.

Attraction: Beach is 4 blocks from the airport; Boardwalk is reported 6 blocks north of the field. There are eight miles of beach and two and a half miles of boardwalk. This attraction draw many visitors each year. Airport Golf Course and pro shop on site. Ocean City, NJ is a tourist community on the Atlantic Ocean located approximately 12 miles south of Atlantic City with its world renowned Casinos. Ocean City is a family resort area with accommodations and entertainment for all members of the family. There are hundreds of hotels, motels, guest rooms restaurants and entertainment facilities all located throughout Ocean City.

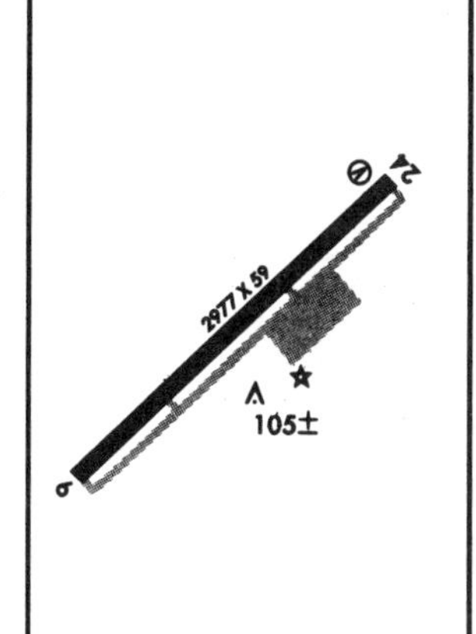

Airport Information:

OCEAN CITY - OCEAN CITY MUNICIPAL AIRPORT (26N)
2 mi southwest of town N39-15.82 W74-3644 Elev: 8 Fuel: 100LL,
Rwy 06-24: H2977x59 (Asph) Attended: 1300-0100Z summer, SR-SS winter. Unicom: 122.7 Public Phone 24hrs Notes: No landing fee. However, parking fees are $5.00/day or $7.00 overnight. We were told by the airport management that if you play a round of golf on their 12 hole course, the aircraft parking fee will be waived. Airport flight operations office is open 7 days a week year round from 8 a.m. to dusk. Pilot activation light in effect.
City of Ocean City Phone: 399-0907

NJ-3N6 - OLD BRIDGE
OLD BRIDGE AIRPORT

(Area Code 908) 19

Photo by Biplane Adventure Tours, Ltd.

Experience the nostalgia and excitement of a ride in an open cockpit bi-plane or WW-II Warbird.

Attractions: Biplane Adventure Tours, Ltd;

At Biplane Adventure Tours Ltd. rides are available in open-cockpit planes (Stearman, Waco) and a North American AT-6. Tours include, but are not limited to, New York Harbor & Statue of Liberty and aerobatic flights. Sight-seeing flights can also be booked in the AT-6, where the passenger may also do some of the flying! Flying season April 21 to October 15, Wednesday through Sunday. Biplane Adventure Tours also has a gift shop and Dixie's Aviation Collectibles in their office. Professional aviation photographs, signed limited editions are also available. For information you can call Biplane Adventure Tours Ltd. at 446-1300.

Attractions: Raceway Park;

Old Bridge Airport (3N6) located 5 to 7 miles east of Amrlboro Airport (2N8) has Raceway Park that schedules a variety of events including drag racing, Funny Car racing, Annual U.S. Diesel Trucking Nationals; All American Jet Car Nationals and Nitrous Oxide Cars; Spring Englishtown Swap Meet & Auto Shows; The annual Yamaha sponsored Raceway Park Championship Motocross Season Opener, Honda Big Bucks Motocross Shootout & Fun Day; Annual $100,000 Tucker-Rocky Championship Motocross Series; Vet & Vintage Nation Reunion; and even their Jet Ski Series Races. For information call 908-446-7800 or write to Raceway Park, 230 Pension Road, Englishtown, NJ 07726.

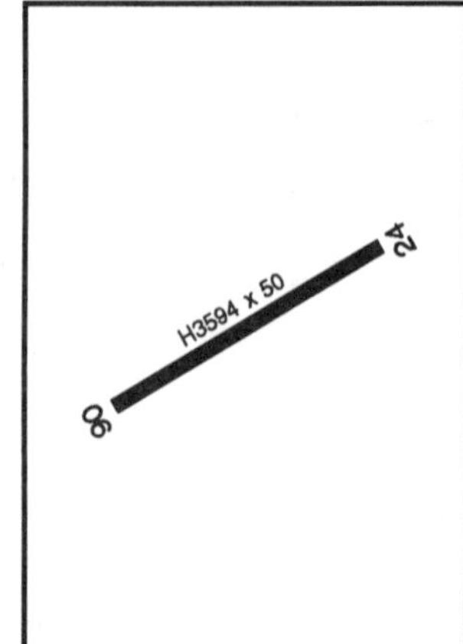

Airport Information:

OLD BRIDGE - OLD BRIDGE AIRPORT (3N6)

5 mi south of town N40-19.79 W74-20.81 Elev: 87 Fuel: 100LL Rwy 06-24: H3594x50 (Asph)
Attended: daylight hours Unicom: 122.8 Notes: Drag Strip located within walking distance and just north of the airport.

Airport Manager Phone: 446-8830 or 446-0303

NJ-N40 - PITTSTOWN
SKY MANOR AIRPORT

(Area Code 908) 20

Sky Manor Restaurant:

The Sky Manor Restaurant is located just off the runway, with aircraft parking available out in front of their facility. The owner of this facility takes pride in providing his customers with selections prepared with the freshest of ingredients. The menu offers 5 or 6 different main entrees including items like fish, chicken, pork and beef. On Saturday they feature a buffet from 9 a.m. to 1 p.m. On Friday their buffet runs from 5 p.m. to 9 p.m. These buffets are very popular with many customers and include soup, salad, dessert, coffee or soda. The restaurant has large glass windows allowing a nice view from within. The decor is rustic with many aviation related pictures hanging on the walls. There is also has outdoor seating for about 25 people on picnic tables. Larger groups are always welcome with advanced notice appreciated. The Sky Manor Restaurant is open during the summer on Monday and Thursday from 11 a.m. to 7 p.m.; Friday 8 a.m. to 9 p.m; Saturday 8 a.m. to 7 p.m; and Sunday 8 a.m. to 7 p.m. During the winter months they are open Monday 11 a.m. to 5 p.m.; Thursday 11 a.m. to 5 p.m.; Friday 11 a.m. to 9 p.m.; Saturday 8 a.m. to 5 p.m.; and Sunday 8 a.m. to 5 p.m. (They are closed on Tuesday and Thursday). For information call the restaurant at 996-3442.

Restaurants Near Airports:
Sky Manor On Site Phone: 996-3442

Lodging: Lodging reported nearby

Meeting Rooms: None Reported

Transportation: None reported

Information: Hunterdon County Chamber of Commerce, Tourism Division, 76 Main Street, Flemington, NJ 08822. Phone: 201-782-5955.

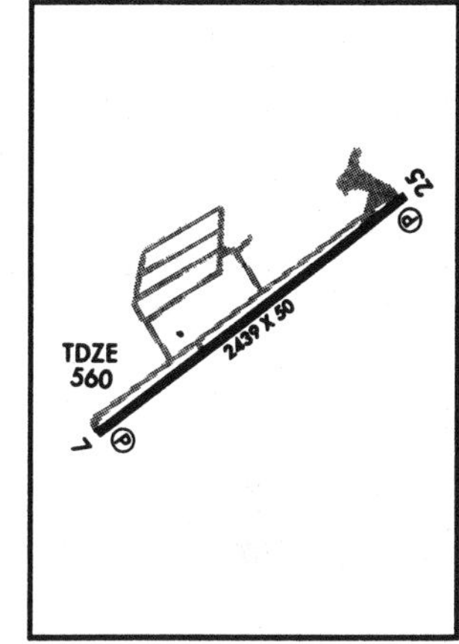

Airport Information:

PITTSTOWN - SKY MANOR AIRPORT (N40)
2 mi southwest of town N40-33.98 W74-58.72 Elev: 560 Fuel: 80, 100LL Rwy 07-25 H2438x52 (Asph) Attended: continuously Unicom: 122.8 Notes: CAUTION: Ulralights fly close in pattern at 860, TRA for low wing acft 1300 (740), high wing acft 1400 (840).
FBO: Royal Karina Air Service, Inc. Phone: 996-7771

Promote General Aviation Just Take A Friend Flying

NJ-39N - PRINCETON (ROCKY HILL) PRINCETON AIRPORT

(Area Code 609)

21, 22, 23

(A & B) Alchemist and Barrister:

The Alchemist and Barrister, better known by the local people as simply A & B's, is a popular restaurant that contains many items on their menu. They are open 7 days a week. Lunch is served Monday through Saturday from 11:30 a.m. to 2:30 p.m. Dinners are served Monday through Thursday 5:30 to 10 p.m. On Sunday a brunch is featured between 12:00 noon and 3:00 p.m. Average prices run between $6.00 to $8.00 for lunch and $15.00 to $25.00 for dinner entrees. Their menu contains items like vegetarian dishes, choice beef, liver, chicken, veal, lamb and seafood. The Alchemist and Barrister (A & B) has an Anglican decor with a comfortable and relaxing atmosphere. They even have a patio for great outdoor dining. For more information you can call 942-5555.

Carvers Cafe:

The Carvers Cafe is located across the street from the Princeton (Rocky Hill) Airport. This deli-styled restaurant is situated within a strip shopping center and is open for business Monday through Friday from 7:30 a.m. to 3:30 p.m. They specialize in preparing many different types of sandwiches. Among popular choices are their breakfast dishes. For lunch they prepare fresh sandwiches made with sliced turkey, roast beef, ham and tuna. Additional selections include specials like meat loaf, lasagna, businessmen lunch and much more. The bread is baked fresh. The restaurant has a small store front with seating for about 80 people. Large groups are welcome with advance notice. Takeout is also available. In-flight catering is available if enough notice is given. For information you can call the airport manager at 921-3100.

Tiger's Tale:

The Tiger's Tale restaurant is reported to be located about 1/2 mile from the Princeton (Rocky Hill) Airport. This full-service family-style restaurant is open between 11 a.m. to 12 midnight 7 days a week (Closed some major holidays). Their menu includes lighter fair like hamburgers and sandwiches, along with full-course meals like fresh fish, steaks and lobster. On Sunday they offer a limited brunch. The restaurant contains a huge bar along with a large dining room decorated with dark wood and tables with lanterns. The restaurant has seating in the dining room for 180 people. According to the management, they serve as many as 1,000 people a day and on Friday and Saturday they prepare meals for 1,400 people. When talking to the management, we were told that their is no dress code. Customers show up in shorts as well as three-piece suits. For more information you can call the Tiger's Tale at 924-0262.

Restaurants Near Airport:

A & B's	Walking dist.	Phone: 924-5555
Carvers Cafe	1/2 mi	Phone: 921-3100
Gd. Time Charley's	2 mi	Phone: 924-7400
Marita's (Mexican)	Nearby	Phone: 924-7855
Nassau Inn	Downtown, 3-4 mi.	Phone: 921-7500
Rusty Scupper	N/A	Phone: 921-3276
Tiger's Tale	1/2 mi	Phone: 924-0262

Lodging: Hyatt Regency Princeton (6 mi.) 987-1234; Nassau Inn est. (2 mi.) 921-7500; Marriott Princeton Ramada Hotel (est. 1-2 mi.) 452-2400; Scanticon Princeton (5 mi.) 452-7800.

Meeting Rooms: Scanticon Princeton (5 mi.) has accommodations for conventions, (100 College Road East) off US 1, in the Princeton Forrestal Center. Phone: 452-7800.

Transportation: Its about 4 miles into town. We were informed that taxi service is available for about $9.00 per person and $2.00 additional for each person. Courtesy transportation also available by FBO's if available. Taxi Service: AAA 921-1177; Mount's 452-0211; Taxi Stand 924-1222; Rental Cars: Econo 924-4700;

Information: Princeton Chamber of Commerce, P.O. Box 431, Princeton, NJ 08542, Phone: 520-1776.

Attractions:

The Pilots Shop is an attraction all by itself. It is located on the Princeton (Rocky Hill) Airport and is owned and operated by Dick, Naomi and Ken Nierenberg at the Raritan Valley Flying School. This unusual pilot supply store contains a huge inventory of items, some of which can't be found anywhere. The proud owners of this facility collect aviation-related items from all parts of the globe. All types of transceivers, navigation radios, head sets, GPS receivers, "Ghost Squadron" and "Ace" patches, a huge assortment of aviation-related Christmas cards, lamps, flying jackets, tee shirts, watches, jewelry, collector's plates, calendars, novelty items, mugs, mail boxes, weathervains, childrens toys, aviation books, kites and teddy bears dressed up for special holiday themes. Naomi seeks out all types of interesting hard-to-obtain items and stocks them for her customers. Like a museum of aviation memorabilia, you will probably find it at the Princeton Airport Pilot Shop. For more information call Dick, Naomi or Ken Nierenberg at 921-3100.

The town of Princeton has many attractions including: Princeton University, (The Putnam Sculptures, McCarter Theatre and Nassau Hall; Bainbridge House, birthplace of commander of the USS Constitution during the War of 1812, Phone: 921-6748; Kuser Farm Mansion and Park 10 miles southeast of town, 22 acre farm of the 1890's with mansion and formal gardens and tours held May through November, Thurs-Sun and February through April on weekends, Phone: 890-3630.

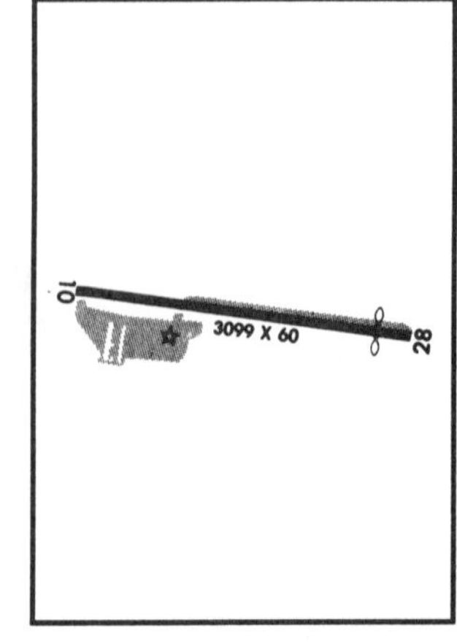

Airport Information:

PRINCETON (ROCKY HILL) - PRINCETON AIRPORT (39N)
3 mi north of town N40-23.90 W74-39.46 Elev: 125 Fuel: 100LL, Jet-A Rwy 10-28: H3099x60 (Asph) Attended: 1300-Dusk Unicom: 122.7 Notes: Noise sensitive area over town of Rocky Hill.

FBO: Princeton Air Corp **Phone: 921-3100**
FBO: Raritan Valley Flying School **Phone: 921-3100**

NJ-N87 - ROBBINSVILLE
TRENTON-ROBBINSVILLE AIRPORT

(Area Code 609) 24

Restaurants Near Airport:
Sky View C.C. & Rest. On Site Phone: 259-0905

Sky View Country Club and Restaurant:

This fine dining establishment is situated within walking distance from the Trenton Robbinsville Airport. Restaurant hours are 11 a.m. to 11 p.m. 6 day a week (Closed on Monday). Their menu contains items like fresh seafood, pastas, chicken, veal, steaks and pork chops. Average prices run $4.95 to $7.50 for lunch, and between $8.95 and $18.00 for dinner selections. The main dining room can accommodate 85 persons. The restaurant exhibits an appearance of a quaint farm house in a country-like setting. Guest can enjoy a fine meal while viewing golfers on the nearby 18 hole course, as well as airport activity. This establishment offers catering to customers within their banquet rooms able to seat up to 200 people. This private country club allows fly-in guest to enjoy many of the unique accommodations available to regular members. These include swimming, tennis, golf, locker room privileges such as steam showers, and much more. A outdoor patio connected to the restaurant also offers a view overlooking the airport. For more information call the restaurant at 259-0905 or the arpt. manager's office at 259-0205.

Lodging: Quality Inn (4 miles) 298-3200; Best Western (4 miles) 298-8000.

Meeting Rooms: Country Club on airport grounds has meeting rooms and banquet facilities. Call airport manager for information 259-0205.

Transportation: AVI (FBO) provides courtesy transportation for fly-in guests to local establishments. Also Cliff's Cab 298-0299.

Information: State Division of Travel and Tourism, CN-826, Trenton, NJ 08625, Phone: 292-2470 or 800-JERSEY7

We learned just prior to printing, that this facility has come under new management. Services might have changed. Call in advance!

Attractions: The owner of this private country club is a pilot himself, and offers a unique service to fly-in customers. For the nominal guest fee charge, pilots and their passengers are able to enjoy the amenities of this facility. Located on the premises is an olympic size swimming pool with a locker room with showers, tennis courts, and 18 hole golf course. The men's locker room is also open to pilots and has a steam shower, towels, shoe shine boy and many other amenities. In addition to all this, there is also a patio that overlooks the runway and a fine dining restaurant all within walking distance. This facility is not open to the general public. However, it is available for pilots who flyin. (I know the lettering is small but its the only way I could fit it all in, sorry!)

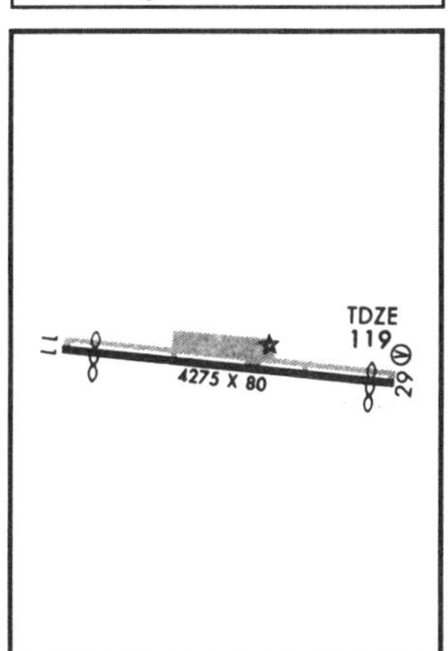

Airport Information:

ROBBINSVILLE - TRENTON-ROBBINSVILLE AIRPORT (N87)
1 mi east of town 40-12-50N 74-36-08W Elev: 119 Fuel: 100LL, Jet-A Rwy 11-29: H4275x80 (Asph) Attended: 1230-0400Z Unicom: 123.0 Notes: Landing fee $5.00 singles and $10.00 for twins; Also the Trenton Robbinsville airport offers unique services, see "Attractions" listed above.
FBO: AVI Phone: 259-0205

NJ-FWN - SUSSEX
SUSSEX AIRPORT

(Area Code 201) 25, 26, 27

Dare Devil Deli:

The Dare Devil Deli is located adjacent to the Sussex Airport. They only have one table within the deli, but they do have picnic tables outside their door where customers can sit outside while having breakfast or lunch. The Deli hours are 6 a.m. to 6 p.m. They specialize in sub sandwiches as well as special cuts of meat. We were told that they were within walking distance. For directions ask the airport manager. For information call The Dare Devil Deli at 702-1900.

Seasons Hotel Resort & Conference Center:

The Seasons Hotel Resort & Conference Center is located about 7 miles from the Sussex Airport. This resort used to be operated by owners of the Playboy organization but now is under new management and attracts visitors from all parts of the region. It is ideally situated within a short distance to the largest ski resort area of New Jersey at the upper most portion of the state. In conjunction with the "Great Gorge Village," it also provides condominium rentals for vacationers. As a full-service resort it offers its own health spa, golfing, swimming, tennis and, of course, skiing. Three ski areas (Vernon Valley, Great George South and Great George North) contains 52 trails and 17 lifts. A variety of ski packages can be arranged along with over-night or weekly rentals. Group business functions and convention arrangements are also a specialty for this establishment. Condominium rentals run from $119 per night to $359 per night off-season. During the prime skiing season, accommodations run $159 per night up to $479 per night, with package and longer term rental discounts. For more information you can call The Seasons Resort and Conference Center at 827-6000.

Sussex Airport Diner:

The Sussex Airport Diner is located on the Sussex Airport property. This family-style restaurant is open between 5 a.m. and 8 p.m. Their menu features a complete breakfast line with omelets and eggs, in addition to cold salad platters, dinner seafood selections, Italian pasta and dinner plates. Prices of some entrees run $0.99 for breakfast specials, $4.95 for lunch and $5.95 for dinner selections. Their dining area can seat 75 persons. Guests can enjoy a fine meal while watching the aircraft move about on the field. Fly-in groups and parties are also welcome. Meals can be prepared-to-go as well. For more information call the Sussex Airport , Inc. at 875-7337.

Restaurants Near Airport:

The Country Meadows	2-1/2 mi	Phone: N/A
Dare Devil Deli	Adj Arpt	Phone: 702-1900
Pizza Plus	Adj Arpt	Phone: N/A
Seasons Resort	7 mi.	Phone: 827-6000
Sussex Airport Diner	On Site	Phone: 875-7337
The Steak Out	1-1/2 mi	Phone; N/A

Lodging: Rolling Hills Motel (3 miles) 875-1270; Seasons Hotel Resort & Conference Center (7 miles) 827-6000; Sussex Motel (3 miles) 875-4191.

Meeting Rooms: Seasons Hotel Resort & Conference Center (7 miles) 827-6000; There is office space reported available at the airport for up to 15 persons for meetings or conferences. Call airport manager at 875-875-7337.

Transportation: Transportation to and from nearby facilities can be arranged through the airport manager's office. Call 875-7337; Also Rental Cars: Capri Motors 875-1077; Condit Motors 383-2800; Franklin Sussex Motors 875-3188; High Point Chev-Geo 875-6101.

Information: Sussex County Chamber of Commerce, 120 Hampton House Road, Newton, HJ 07860, Phone: 579-1811.

Attractions:

High Point State Park; Wild Animal Space Farm; golf courses in the area: High Point 20 min drive; Rolly Green Golf Club 20 min drive; state's largest ski area, Vernon Valley, Great George South and Great George North Ski areas. Seasons Hotel Resort & Conference Center (7 miles) 827-6000;

Airport Information:

SUSSEX - SUSSEX AIRPORT (FWN)
1 mi southwest of town N41-12.01 W74-37.38 Elev: 421 Fuel: 80, 100LL
Rwy 03-21: H3499x75 (Asph) Attended: dawn-0200Z Unicom: 122.7 Public Phone 24hrs Notes: no landing fee, overnight parking single engine $2.00, twins $4.00 per night.
FBO: Sussex Airport, Inc. Phone: 875-7337

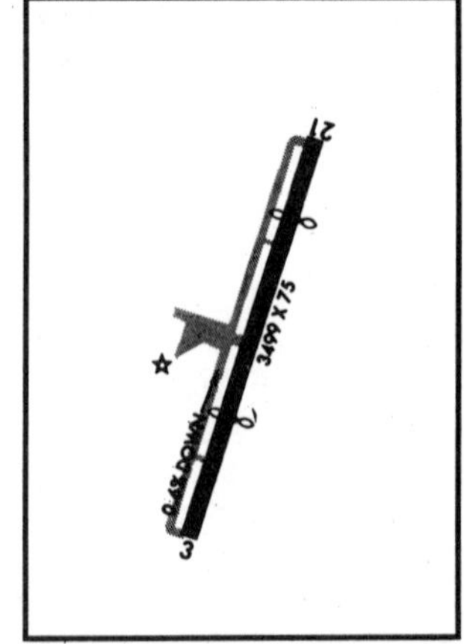

NJ-TEB - TETERBORO
TETERBORO AIRPORT

(Area Code 201)

28

Cafe Luberto's:

The Cafe Luberto's is located 1 mile south of the Teterboro Airport. Courtesy car transportation to the restaurant can be arranged through just about all of the FBO's on the field. Also busses and taxi cabs are available. This combination family style and fine dining facility is open between 11:30 a.m. and 10 p.m. throughout the week except Sunday and Monday night. Their menu includes carefully prepared Italian dishes with authentic sauces prepared by the chefs with much experience in the art of culinary delight. A few additional choices include filet mignon, Peking chicken, and Italian Pizza Siciliano. Average prices run $5.00 to $7.00 for lunch and $6.95 to $17.95 for dinner. Their main dining room can accommodate 84 persons. Soft colors decorated in peach & hunters green compliment the light colored oak walls. Cafe Luberto's provides in-flight catering as well as banquet and group luncheons and dinners. For more information call 438-4747.

Restaurants Near Airport:

Cafe Luberto's	1 mi S.	Phone: 438-4747
Bazzareui Rest.	2 mi SE	Phone: 641-4010
Tracey's	3 mi E.	Phone: 440-1100

Lodging: Embassy Suites 864-7300; Hilton Meadowlands (3 miles) 848-6900; Holiday Inn (1/2 mile) 288-9600; Lowes Glenpointe (3 miles) 836-0600; Marriott (5 miles) 843-9500; Ramada Inn (3 miles) 845-3400; Sheraton Heights (1 mile) 288-6100; Treadway Inn 93 miles) 843-0600.
Meeting Rooms: Embassy Suites 864-7300; Hilton Meadowlands 348-6900; Holiday Inn 348-2000; Loews Glenpointe 836-0600; Marriott Saddle Brook 843-9500; Quality Inn 288-9600; Sheraton Heights 288-6100; Sheraton Inn Meadowlands 896-0500.
Transportation: Fixed base operators can provide courtesy cars to nearby facilities. Also: Teterboro Taxi 288-1950; Cross Country Transport 800-445-TAXI; Public Bus 800-772-2222.
Information: State Division of Travel and Tourism, CN-826, Trenton, NJ 08625, Phone 609-292-2470 or 800-JERSEY7

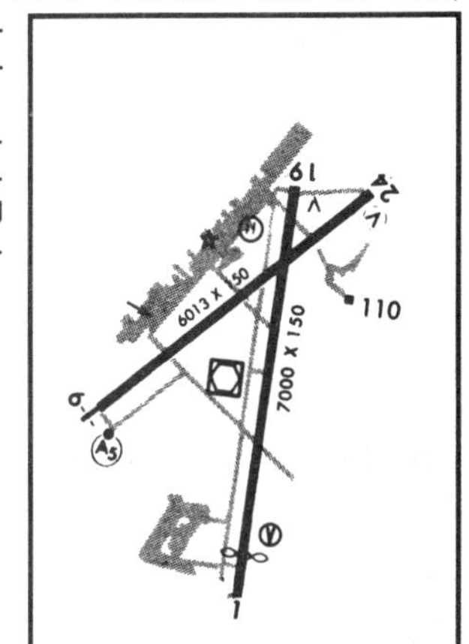

Airport Information:

TETERBORO - TETERBORO AIRPORT (TEB)
1 mi southwest of town N40-51.01 W74-03.65 Elev: 9 Fuel: 100LL, Jet-A
Rwy 01-19: H7000x150 (Asph-Grvd) Rwy 06-24: H6013x150 (Asph-Grvd) Attended: continuously Atis: 132.025, 114.2 Unicom: 122.95 Tower: 119.5, 125.1
Gnd Con: 121.9 Clnc Del: 128.05 Public Phone 24hrs Notes: Overnight parking fees for singles and twins $4.50 and $9.00.

FBO: Atlantic Aviation **Phone: 288-1740**
FBO: First Aviation **Phone: 288-3555**
FBO: Intl. Aviation **Phone: 288-1880**
FBO: Jet Aviation **Phone: 462-4000**
FBO: Million Air **Phone: 288-5040**

Aviation Hall of Fame of New Jersey

Teterboro, NJ (NJ-TEB)

The Aviation Hall of Fame Museum of New Jersey is dedicated to the preservation of the Garden State's distinguished, two-century aviation and space heritage. The men and women, whose outstanding aeronautical achievements have brought worldwide recognition to the state, are enshrined in the Hall of Fame.

The new, exciting museum is located at two opposite sites at Teterboro Airport. The dual locations offer visitors an opportunity to not only learn of the role New Jerseyans have played in our nation's air and space achievements, and to view the museum's fine collection of artifacts, but it also affords them the experience of viewing a busy modern airport in action.

On March 30, 1985, the Aviation Hall of Fame of New Jersey dedicated a new Aviation Educational Center on the east side of Teterboro Airport. The new center supplements the original Hall of Fame museum in the old Teterboro control tower, made famous in the 1950's when entertainer Arthur Godfrey buzzed it in a moment of pique, located on the west side of the airport.

The AHOF is the official aviation museum for the state of New Jersey, and is one of the most unique historical museums in the United States.

In the Aviation Educational Center visitors will see the bronze plaques representing the men and women who have been inducted into New Jersey's only aeronautical hall of fame. They will learn the role New Jerseyans have played in the epic of flight, from the first American balloon ascension in 1793 to the first woman to walk in space in 1985. Young and old that have an aviation enthusiasm, can inspect aircraft piston, jet and rocket engines and even sit in the cockpit of a helicopter and pretend to fly.

A 40-passenger Martin-202 airliner is placed behind the new building on which visitors are welcomed aboard.

On the west side of the field visitors discover the fascinating history of New Jersey's leading airports - Newark, Teterboro, Lakehurst and Hadley. They see films, and inspect the Godfrey aeronautical collection. They may spend hours in the cab of the old tower.

The tour of the two facilities takes approximately one hour and a half. The museum is designed to educate and entertain both the young and old. For information call 201-288-6344. Additional information can be obtained through the Teterboro Airport Managers Office at 201-288-1775.

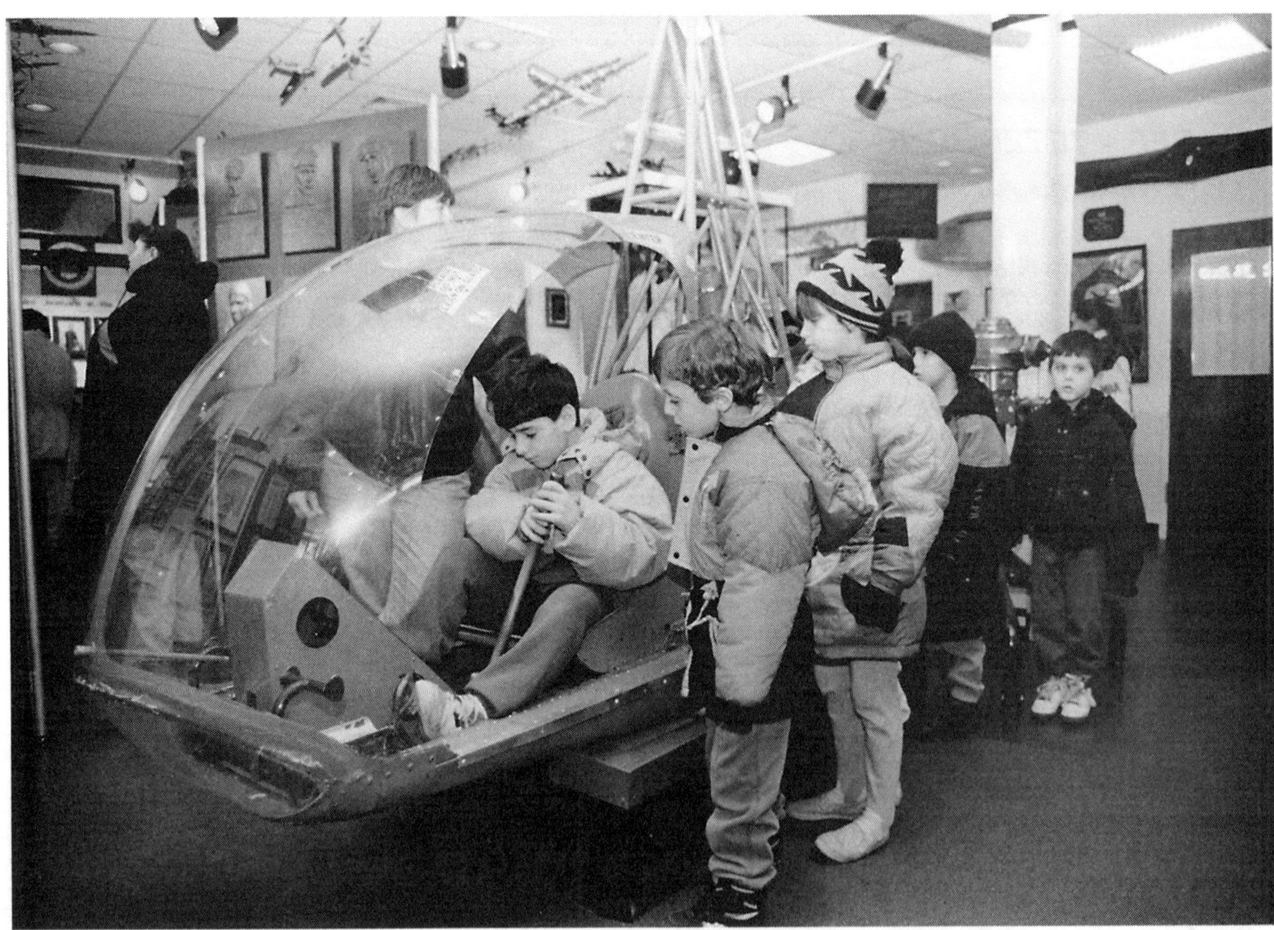

Photo by: Aviation Hall of Fame & Museum of New Jersey

At the New Jersey Aviation Hall of Fame & Museum at Teterboro Airport, NJ children "fly" a helicopter while others look at exhibits such as the glove astronaut Buzz Aldrin wore on the moon.

NJ-TTN - TRENTON MERCER COUNTY AIRPORT

(Area Code 609)

29

General Quarters Restaurant:

The General Quarters Restaurant is located in the main terminal building at the Trenton Mercer County Airport. This restaurant is particularly convenient for scheduled commuter service, However, during our conversation with the airport manager, we learned that private and corporate aircraft must park at the FBO on the opposite side of the airport. FBO courtesy cars are reported, but this depends on their availability. Taxi service is also available from the FBO to the main terminal building. The General Quarters Restaurant is a fine dining establishment open from 9:00 a.m. to 10:00 p.m. Their lounge is open until 11 p.m. Their menu specializes in choice steaks and fresh seafood, along with a wide variety of other entrees. Average prices run around $4.95 for lunch and $11.95 for dinner. There is also an early bird dinner special featuring discounts on meals between 3:30 p.m. and 5:30 p.m. The main dining area can seat 200 persons, and offers a pleasant atmosphere with light pastel colors, a view of the airport activity, carpeted floors, linen table cloths, and flowers on each table. On-site catering for groups or business conferences can also be arranged. For more information call 883-4747.

Restaurants Near Airport:
General Quarters On Site Phone: 883-4747

Lodging: Howard Johnson (6 miles) 896-1100; Hyatt Regency (8 miles) 987-1234; Ramada Inn (10 miles) 452-2400; Stage Depot (4 miles) 466-2000.

Meeting Rooms: Howard Johnson (6 miles) 896-1100.

Transportation: (FBO) Courtesy car & taxi service reported available at airport; Hertz 771-9500.

Information: Mercer County Chamber of Commerce, 214 West State Street, P.O. Box 2708, Trenton, NJ 08608, Phone: 393-4143.

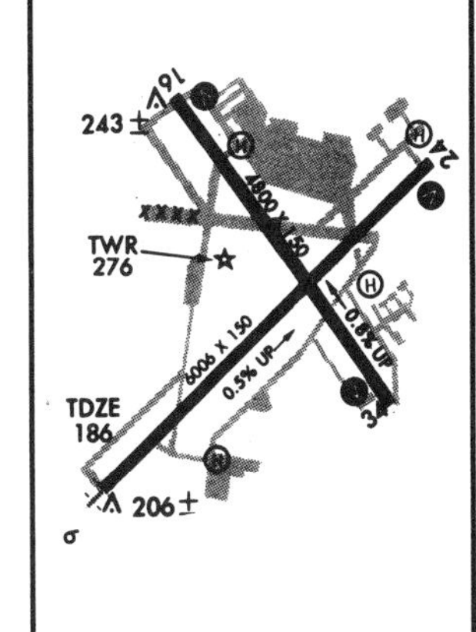

Airport Information:

TRENTON - MERCER COUNTY AIRPORT (TTN)
4 mi northwest of town N40-16.60 W74-48.81 Elev: 213 Fuel: 100LL, Jet-A
Rwy 06-24: H6006x135 (Asph-Grvd) Rwy 16-34: H4800x150 (Asph) Attended: continuously
Atis: 133.7 Unicom: 122.95 Trenton Tower: 120.7 Gnd Con: 121.9 Clnc Del: 121.9
FBO: Air Hangar, Inc. Phone: 882-2010
FBO: Ronson Aviation Phone: 771-9500

NJ-4N1 - WEST MILFORD GREENWOOD LAKE

(Area Code 201)

30

Airport Restaurant:

During our conversation with the airport management we learned that there is a restaurant located right in the terminal building at the Greenwood Lake Airport. Information about this restaurnat can be obtained by calling the airport office at 728-7721. A pilot shop is also located on the field. This pilot shop is unique, being that it is a converted Lockheed Constellation which houses the business. For information call the airport at 728-7721.

Restaurants Near Airport:
Airport Restaurant Trml. Bldg. Phone: 728-7721

Lodging: None Reported

Meeting Rooms: None Reported

Transportation: Rental Cars: Pana's Auto 728-7777; B & D Taxi Service 728-1201

Information: Gateway Regional Tourism Council, 633 Pearl Street, Elizabeth, GA 07202, Phone: 201-351-7100.

Attractions:

A Lockheed Constellation located on the Greenwood Lake Airport contains a pilot shop. For information call the airport at 728-7721.

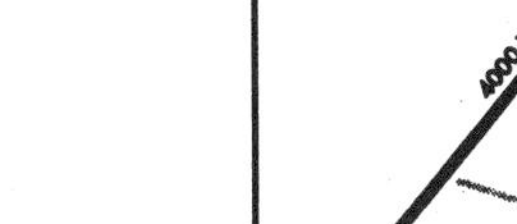

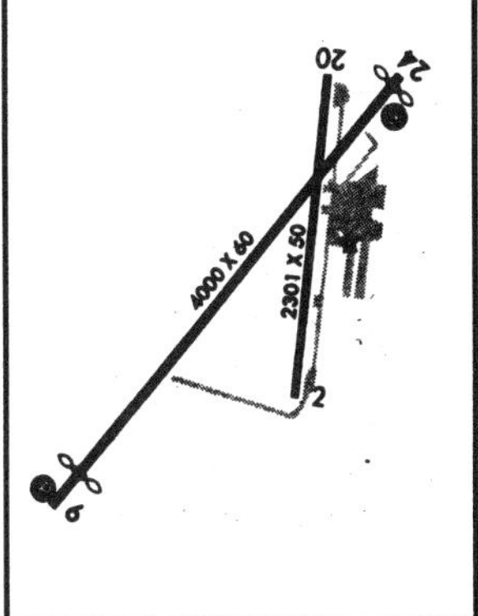

Airport Information:

WEST MILFORD - GREENWOOD LAKE (4N1)
1 mi east of town N41-07.76 W74-20.68 Elev: 791 Fuel: 100LL Rwy 06-24: H4000x60 (Asph) Rwy 02-20: H2301x50 (Asph) Attended: 1300-Dusk CTAF: 122.9 Notes: Arpt lights operate dusk to 0400Z, Rwy 06-24 closed indefinitely.
Airport Manager Phone: 609-886-1755 or 886-4088.

NJ-WWD - WILDWOOD
CAPE MAY COUNTY AIRPORT

(Area Code 609) 31

Airport Restaurant (Temporarely Closed):
The Flight Deck was the name of the previous restaurant located within the terminal building at the Cape May County Airport. This family style restaurant has since closed. However during our conversation with the airport management, we were informed that there is a good chance that new management would reopen the dining facility in the future. Call the airport management office for updated information.

Restaurants Near Airport:
Airport Restaurant On Site Phone: Arpt. Mgr. 886-1755

Lodging: Grand Hotel 729-6000; Port Royal Motor Inn 729-2000; Royal Hawaiian Resort 522-3414.

Meeting Rooms: Grand Hotel 729-6000; Port Royal Motor Inn 729-2000; Royal Hawaiian Resort 522-3414.

Transportation: Taxi Service: High Roller 884-5711; Jones 884-5888; Off Shore Cab 886-9600; Rental Cars: Cape May Rent-A-Car 889-1818. Also Cape Air has courtesy cars.

Information: Greater Wildwood Chamber of Commerce, P.O. Box 823, Wildwood, NJ 08260, Phone: 729-4000.

Attractions:
Cape May National Golf Course; Historical Cape May; Cold Springs Village; And beaches nearby.

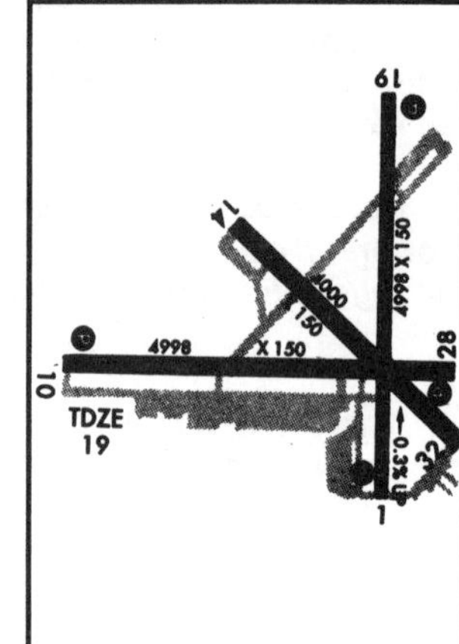

Airport Information:
WILDWOOD - CAPE MAY COUNTY AIRPORT (WWD)
4 mi northwest of town N39-00.51 W74-54.50 Elev: 23 Fuel: 100LL, Jet-A
Rwy 01-19: H4998x150 (Asph) Rwy 10-28: H4998x150 (Asph) Rwy 14-32: H4000x150 (Asph) Attended: Oct-Apr 1300-2200 Unicom: 122.7 Notes: $6.00 charged after first two hours.
Airport Manager Phone: 886-1755, 886-4088
FBO: Classic Air Phone: 889-0300

NEW MEXICO

LOCATION MAP

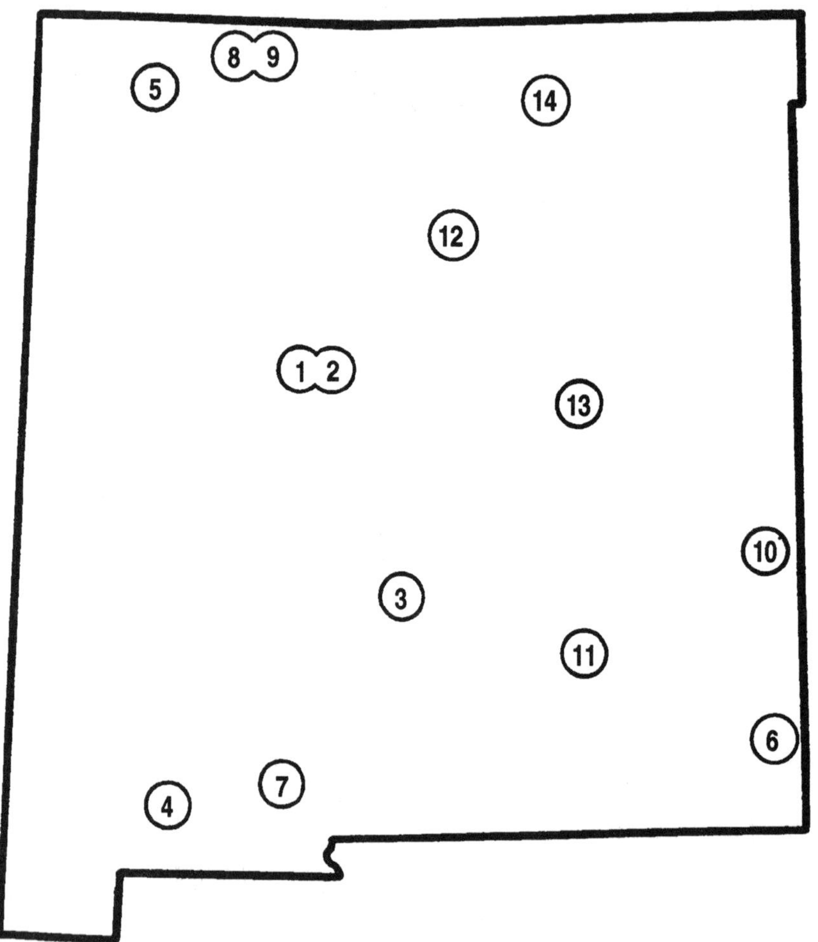

NEW MEXICO

CROSS FILE INDEX

Location Number	City or Town	Airport Name And Identifier	Name of Attraction
1	Albuquerque	Albuquerque Intl. (ABQ)	Airport Sandwich Shop
2	Albuquerque	Albuquerque Intl. (ABQ)	CA1 Services
3	Carrizozo	Carrizozo Muni. Arpt. (Q37)	Barb's East Coast Sub
4	Deming	Deming Muni. Arpt. (DMN)	Grand Motor Inn
5	Farmington	Four Corners Reg. Arpt. (FMN)	Senor Pepper's Rest.
6	Hobbs	Lea Co. (Hobbs) Arpt. (HOB)	Cattle Baron Restaurant
7	Las Cruces	Las Cruce Intl. Arpt. (LRU)	Crosswinds Grill
8	Navajo Dam	Navajo State Park (1V0)	Abe's Motel & Fly Shop
9	Navajo Dam	Navajo State Park (1V0)	Rizuto's San Juan Lodge
10	Portales	Portales Muni. Arpt. (Q34)	El Rancho's Restaurant
11	Roswell	Rowell Industrial Air Cntr. (ROW)	Arpt. Coffee shop
12	Santa Fe	Santa Fe Co. Muni.	Restaurants in Santa Fe
13	Santa Rosa	Santa Rosa Muni. Arpt. (Q58)	Country Pride Restaurant
14	Taos	Taos Muni Arpt. (SKX)	Restaurants in Taos

Articles

City or town	Nearest Airport and Identifier	Name of Attraction
Santa Fe, NM	Santa Fe Co. Muni. Arpt. (SAF)	Santa Fe Ski & Resorts
Taos, NM	Taos Muni. Arpt. (SKX)	Taos Ski Valley

NM-ABQ - ALBUQUERQUE
ALBUQUERQUE INTERNATIONAL

(Area Code 505) 1, 2

Airport Sandwich Shop:

The Airport Sandwich Shop is located at the main concourse & concourse "A" inside the east corner of the Albuquerque International Airport main terminal building. This snack bar is open from 9 a.m. to 9 p.m. 7 days a week. Some of their special entrees include their chili chicken soup, Albuquerque turkey sandwiches, turkey roast, sandwich creations made from all types of delicious items with your choice of breads, cheeses, meats and condiments. Prices average $3.00 for breakfast, $5.00 for lunch and $6.00 for dinner. This cafe features a southwestern motif. Carry-out meals are also available. Business or corporate pilots can arrange, in advance, meals-to-go for their passengers or onboard clients. A variety of sandwiches, salads, soups, fruit trays, cheese and meat trays can be prepared and picked up at the cafe upon arrival. For more information call the Airport Sandwich Shop at 842-4206.

CA1 Services:

CA1 Services operates a food service facility on the third level of the terminal building at the Albuquerque International Airport. This combination lounge and restaurant is open between 6 a.m. and 10 p.m. Their menu contains a variety of southwestern items. Anything on their menu can be prepared for carry-out. CA1 Services also manages a sports bar located on the "A" Concourse. For information about the services available at either locations, or in-flight catering needs call 842-4105.

Attractions:

UNM S. Golf Course, University Blvd. S.E. (North of Runway 17-35), Phone: 265-5636; National Atomic Museum: located about 4 miles east of the Albuquerque. Intl Airport. This museum contains exhibits on the history of nuclear weapons and the Nuclear Energy Science Center. All persons entering the Air Force Base must display appropriate identification. (Driver's licence, [Driver Only], vehicle registration, proof of insurance, and/or car rental paperwork). (No Admission Charge) Phone: 845-6670; Annual Events: International Balloon Fiesta held the first 2 weekends in October each year. (Contact Convention & Visitors Bureau, 243-3696, 800-284-2282).

Restaurants Near Airport:

Airport Sandwich Shop	On Site	Phone: 842-4206
CA1 Services	On Site	Phone: 842-4105
T & C Concessions (Deli)	On Site	Phone: 842-4071
Haagan Daz (Ice Cream)	On Site	Phone: 842-4071
Snack Bar	On Site	Phone: 842-4071

Lodging: The following lodging facilities are within close proximity of airport and provide free courtesy transportation: Best Western Airport Inn 243-0620; Comfort Inn Airport 243-2244; Courtyard By Marriott 843-6600; La Quinta-Airport 243-5500; Radisson Inn Airport 247-0512; AMFAC Hotel 843-7000.

Meeting Rooms: Comfort Inn Airport 243-2244; Courtyard By Marriott 843-6600; La Quinta-Airport 243-5500; Radisson Inn Airport 247-0512; AMFC Hotel 843-7000.

Transportation: Cutter Flying Service 842-4177; Executive Aviation 842-4990; Rental Cars: Avis 842-4080; Budget 842-4021; Dollar 842-4224; General 842-4386; Hertz 842-4235; National 842-4222.

Information: Convention & Visitors Bureau, 121 Tijeras NE, P.O. Box 26866, Albuquerque, NM 87102, Phone: 842-9918 or 800-733-9918. For public transportation call 843-9200.

Airport Information:

ALBUQUERQUE - ALBUQUERQUE INTL. AIRPORT (ABQ)

3 mi southeast of town N35-02.42 W106-36.56 Elev: 5352 Fuel: 100LL, Jet-A, A1, A1+
Rwy 08-26: H13775x300 (Asph-Conc-Grvd) Rwy 17-35: H10000x150 (Asph-Conc-Grvd)
Rwy 03-21: H10000x150 (Conc-Grvd) Rwy 12-30: H5142x150 (Asph) Attended: continuously
Unicom: 122.95 Atis: 118.0 FSS on fld: 122.55, 122.3 App Con: 124.4, 134.8, 123.9, 127.4; Dep Con: 127.4, 124.4, 123.9 Tower: 118.3, 120.3 Gnd Con: 121.9 Clnc Del: 119.2 Notes: Overnight parking fees, contact fixed base operator; All general aviation activity located in the south general aviation area.

FBO: Cutter Flying Service, **Phone: 842-4184, 800-678-5382**
FBO: Executive Aviation, **Phone: 842-4990, 800-593-4990**
Robertson Aircraft **Phone: 842-4999**

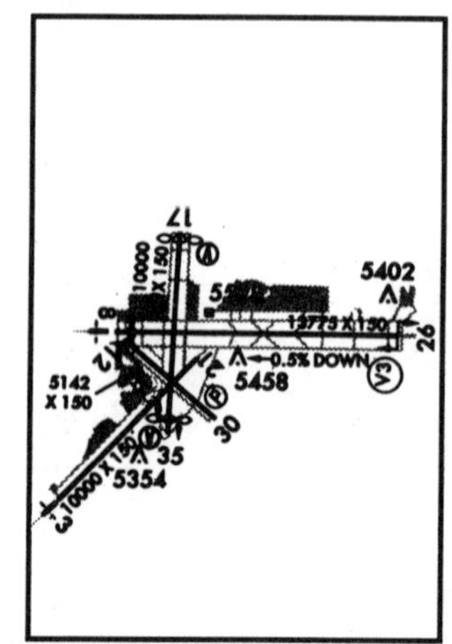

NM-Q37 - CARRIZOZO
CARRIZOZO MUNICIPAL AIRPORT

(Area Code 505) 3

Barb's East Coast Sub Plus:

This is a family style restaurant serving their famous Submarine Sandwiches for the healthy appetite, along with soups, salads and sandwiches such as hamburgers, grilled cheese, etc. for people with smaller appetites. Meals average around $6.00 for lunch and dinner. Their hours are 10:30 a.m. to 9:00 p.m. 7 days a week. Large groups are welcome if giving 24 hr notice. Their sandwiches include their own rolls baked on the premises everyday so advance notice for large parties would be necessary to assure enough rolls are available. All foods can be taken out and they will deliver same to the airport. This restaurant is located 1-1/2 miles south of Carrizozo Municipal airport. When leaving the airport take 8th st. to "E" avenue. Turn right on "E" avenue to Hwy. 54. They are at the corner of "E" & 54. Quote: "Our atmosphere is homey and the customer is our #1 priority. Our prices are affordable so the whole family can eat without getting "sticker-shock". The airport manager, Mr. Hal Marx, has agreed to drive fly-in guests to the restaurant. (Please give him some advance notice if possible) For more information call the restaurant at 648-2155.

Restaurants Near Airport:

Four Winds	1 mi E.	Phone: 648-2964
Barb's East Coast	1-1/2mi S.	Phone: 648-2155
Outpost	2 mi S.	Phone: 648-9994
Tasti-Freeze	1 mi E.	Phone: 648-2442

Lodging: Cross Roads Motel 1 mi. 684-2363; Four Winds Motel 1 mi. 648-2356; Frontier Motel 648-9986

Information: Chamber of Commerce, P.O. Box 567, Carrizozo, NM 88301, Phone: 648-2472

NO AIRPORT DIAGRAM AVAILABLE

Airport Information:

CARRIZOZO - CARRIZOZO MUNICIPAL AIRPORT (Q37)

1 mi. N. of town N33-38.92 W105-53.77 Elev: 5370 Fuel: 100LL Rwy 06-24: H4900x75 (Asph) Rwy 15-33: 2500x90 (Dirt) Attended: continuously Unicom: 122.8 Notes: Drag racing events occur on Rwy 06-24.
Airport Manager, Phone: 648-9996 or 648-2371

NM-DMN - DEMING
DEMING MUNICIPAL AIRPORT

(Area Code 505) 4

Grand Motor Inn:

The Grand Motor Inn also known as the Grand Hotel, is located 1-1/2 miles from the Deming Municipal Airport. The management at this establishment will provide fly-in customers with free courtesy transportation to and from the airport. This restaurant is classified as a combination family style and fine dining establishment. Their hours are from 6 a.m. to 10:00 p.m. 7 days a week. Entrees on their menu include Mexican, Italian, and American dishes. This restaurant also offers a variety of 10 different steak dishes, as well as many seafood entrees to choose from. They also offer a complete salad bar. The main dining room at this restaurant can accommodate up to 100 persons along with a separate banquet room that can provide enough seating for up to 200 persons. According to the management, this facility provides a French Provincial decor with a quaint atmosphere. In addition to the restaurant, the Grand Motor Inn also offer 62 rooms for overnight guests. For more information call 546-2631.

Restaurants Near Airport:

Bell Shore	2 mi	Phone: N/A
Branding Iron	1-3/4 mi	Phone: N/A
Grand Motor Inn	1-1/2 mi	Phone: 546-2631
Si-Senor's	2-1/2 mi	Phone: N/A

Lodging: Grand Motor Inn (Free trans, 1-1/2 miles) 546-2632; Holiday Budget Inn (Free trans) 546-2661.

Meeting Rooms: Deming Flying Service can accommodate space for meetings; Also Grand Motor Inn (Free trans, 1-1/2 miles) 546-2632; Holiday Budget Inn (Free trans) 546-2661.

Transportation: Dart Taxi 546-7505

Information: Chamber of Commerce, 800 East Pine Street, Box 8, Deming, NM, Phone: 546-2674.

Attraction:

Golf course 1/2 mile from airport

8
26
22
6626 X 75
0.3% UP

Airport Information:

DEMING - DEMING MUNICIPAL AIRPORT (DMN)

2 mi southeast of town N32-15.74 W107-43.24 Elev: 4309 Fuel: 100LL, Jet-A1+, MOGAS Rwy 08-26: H6626x75 (Asph) Rwy 04-22: H5657x60 (Asph) Attended: Mon-Fri 1400-0200Z, Sat-Sun 1500-0100Z Unicom: 122.8 Public Phone 24hrs Notes: For airport attendant after hours call 546-9276 or 546-0345.
FBO: Deming Flying Service Phone: 546-3973

NM-FMN - FARMINGTON
FOUR CORNERS REGIONAL AIRPORT

(Area Code 505) 5

Senor Pepper's Restaurant:

The Senor Pepper's Restaurant is located within the terminal building at the Four Corners Regional Airport. This combination family style and fine dining establishment is open from 5 a.m. to 10 p.m. Monday through Thursday, and from 5 a.m. to 10:30 on Friday and Saturday. Their lounge is open 11 a.m. to 2 a.m. Monday through Saturdays. Entrees include chicken dishes, Enchiladas, Huevos Rancheros, stuffed Sopalilla, as well as several delicious egg dishes and Mexican breakfasts. Their restaurant decor exhibits a Spanish style with seating for 75 persons in their main dining room. A private banquet facility and catering service is also available on the premises. This restaurant prides itself in preparing entrees with fresh ingredients. For more information call Senor Pepper's Restaurant at 327-0436.

Restaurants Near Airport:
Senor Pepper's On Site Phone: 327-0436

Lodging: Anasazi Inn 325-4564; Executive Inn & Suites 327-4433; Holiday Inn 327-9811; The Inn (Best Western) 327-5221.

Meeting Rooms: All lodging facilities listed above have accommodations for meetings and conferences.

Transportation: Avis 327-9864; Budget 327-7304; Hertz 327-6093; National 327-0215; Road Runner Taxi 327-1909.

Information: Convention & Visitors Bureau, 203 West Main Street, Farmingtion, NM 87401, Phone: 326-7602 or 800-448-1240..

Attractions:

Pinon Hills Golf Course (5 miles) 326-6066.

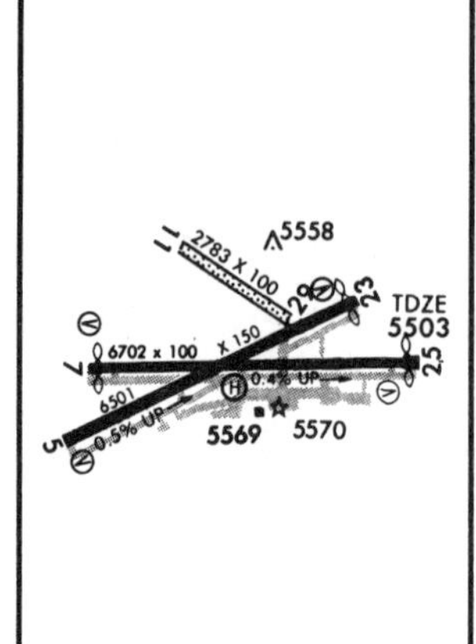

Airport information:

FARMINGTON - FOUR COUNERS REGIONAL AIRPORT (FMN)
1 mi northwest of town N36-44.52 W108-13.79 Elev: 5503 Fuel: 100LL, Jet-A1+, MOGAS Rwy 07-25: H6702x100 (Asph-Pfc) Rwy 05-23: H6501x150 (Asph-Pfc) Rwy 11-29: 2783x100 (Dirt) Attended: continuously Atis: 127.15 Unicom: 122.95 Tower: 118.9 Gnd Con: 121.7 Public Phone 24hrs Notes: No landing fees. Overnight tie down fees are $2.00 for singles and $4.00 for twins. For attendant after hours call 325-2867.
FBO: Four Corners Aviation Phone: 325-2867

NM-HOB - HOBBS
LEA COUNTY (HOBBS) AIRPORT

(Area Code 505) 6

Cattle Baron Restaurant:

The Cattle Baron Restaurant is located about 3 to 5 miles from the Hobbs County Airport. You can reach it by courtesy transportation through the fixed base operator on the field or the airport manager. This family style restaurant is open Monday through Thursday from 11 a.m. to 9:30 p.m., Friday and Saturday from 11 a.m. to 10 p.m. and Sunday from 11 a.m. to 9 p.m. They specialize in steak and seafood dishes. Popular items include fresh seafood, catfish, filet mignon, steak teriyaki, prime rib, and steak & lobster. Average prices run $6.00 for most luncheons and $8.00 to $12.00 for dinners. The main dining room will accommodate up to 180 persons. The restaurant has a southwestern decor with decorations in brass, jade and colors of green and burgundy. Plans for remodeling are in their future plans. For groups, there is also space for up to 60 persons. For more information you can call the restaurant at 393-2800.

Restaurants Near Airport:
Cattle Baron Restaurant 3-5 mi Phone: 393-2800

Lodging: Executive Inn 397-6541; Hobbs Motor Inn 397-3251; Leawood Motel (Arpt trans) 393-4101; Zia Motel 397-3591.

Meeting Rooms: Executive Inn 397-6541; Hobbs Motor Inn 397-3251.

Transportation: Taxi service 393-5151; Rental Cars: Hertz 393-6124; National 393-6424.

Information: Chamber of Commerce, 400 North Marland, Hobbs, NM 88240, Phone: 800-658-6291.

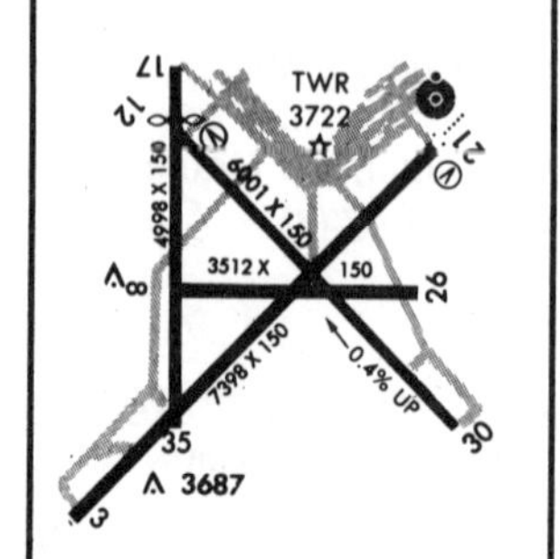

Airport Information:

HOBBS - LEA COUNTY (HOBBS) AIRPORT (HOB)
4 mi west of town 32-41-15N 103-13-00W Elev: 3659 Fuel: 100LL, Jet-A Rwy 03-21: H7398x150 (Asph) Rwy 12-30: H6000x150 (Asph) Rwy 17-35: H4998x150 (Asph) Rwy 08-26: H3512x150 (Asph) Attended: 1400-0100Z Unicom: 122.95 Tower: 120.65 Gnd Con: 121.9
Airport Manager Phone: 393-4943
FBO: Phillips Intl. Aircraft Phone: 397-1747

NM-LRU - LAS CRUCES
LAS CRUCES INTL. AIRPORT

(Area Code 505) 7

Crosswinds Grill:

The Crosswinds Grill is located on the Las Cruces International Airport adjacent to the terminal building and in the same building that the airport manager is situated. This cafe is open 7 days a week between 7 a.m. and 2 p.m. Menu items and specialties of the house include an assortment of breakfast items including sausage, ham and egg dishes. For lunch they prepare hamburgers, cheeseburgers, ham sandwiches, roast beef and turkey dishes. Prices average $2.75 for breakfast and $3.50 to $4.00 for lunch. The decor of the restaurant has a touch of aviation. Pictures and posters of aircraft decorate the walls. These is seating for about 12 persons. Small groups are welcome. Seating for larger groups can also be arranged in their lobby. For information call 524-0705.

Love's Country Store:

The Love's Country Store is located across the freeway from the Las Cruces International Airport. The distance to this cafe by road is about 1 mile. Courtesy transportation is available through North American Aviation at the airport. We were unable to obtain further information about this facility after several attempts. The phone number to the restaurant is 527-5102.

Restaurants Near Airport:

Crosswinds Grill	On Site	Phone: 524-0705
Love's Country Store	1 mi.	Phone: 527-5102

Lodging: Free transportation available by the following: Mission Inn (Best Western) 524-8591; Days Inn 526-4441; Holiday Inn (De Las Cruces) 526-4411; Hilton 522-4300; Meson De Mesilla 525-9212.

Meeting Rooms: Mission Inn (Best Western) 524-8591; Days Inn 526-4441; Holiday Inn (De Las Cruces) 526-4411; Hilton 522-4300.

Transportation: Avis 522-1400; Hertz 523-1171.

Information: Convention & Visitors Bureau, 311 North Downtown Mall, Las Cruces, NM 88001, Phone: 524-8521

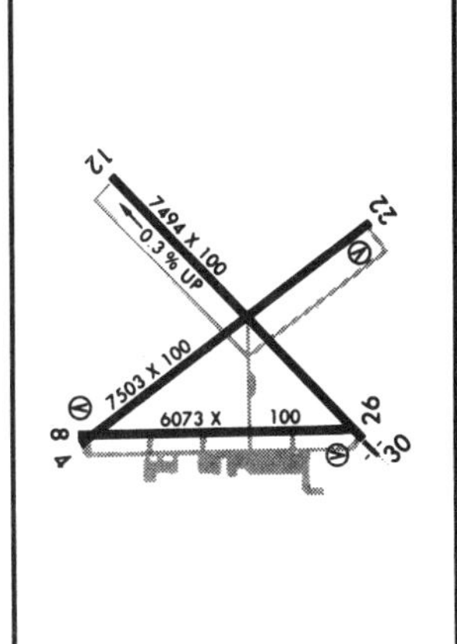

Airport Information:

LAS CRUCES - LAS CRUCES INTL. AIRPORT (LRU)
8 mi west of town N32-17.37 W106-55.32 Elev: 4454 Fuel: 100, 100LL, Jet-A1+, MOGAS Rwy 04-22: H7503x100 (Asph) Rwy 12-30: H7494x100 (Asph) Rwy 08-26: H6073x100 (Asph) Attended: dawn to dusk Unicom 122.7
FBO: Southwest Aviation Phone: 524-8047

NM-1V0 - NAVAJO DAM
NAVAJO STATE PARK

(Area Code 505) 8, 9

Navajo Lake State Park: (Navajo Dam Area)

Navajo is one of New Mexico's largest state parks. The lake is 35 miles long and has over 150 miles of rugged shoreline. The lake surface varies from 13,000 to 15,000 acres. Several species of fish inhabit the lake, including: Rainbow and Brown Trout, Kokanee Salmon, and Channel Catfish, Crappie, Northern Pike and Large-mouth and Smallmouth Bass. Camping fees in the park are: $7.00 for a site with no hookups. $11.00 for a site with electricity and $13.00 per night with a full hookup. They accept no reservations, and operate on a first come first served basis. New Mexico has three distinctive areas of the park on or near the lake. Pine site is the most developed one with showers, electrical. It has a boat ramp and full service Marina. It is located 1/2 mile north of the dam on NM Highway 511. Sims Mesa, like Pine, is located on the lake. It is a more remote ramp, and a full service marina. Its access is through a paved road off of US Highway 64 about 25 miles east of the dam. The San Juan River site includes a beautiful campground located in a large cottonwood grove about 5 miles below the dam. Its access is located 1/4 mile west of the Aztec Bridge on NM 173. For information you can call the State Park Office at 632-2278.

Abe's Motel & Fly Shop:

Abe's Motel and Fly Shop is located about 5 miles west of the Navajo Dam Airport along Highway 511. They have been on the San Juan River since 1958. They are a Family owned and operated business. They were the first to explore the river for trout fishing, the first to guide on the river and the first to fly fish in the winter months. They have a motel with housekeeping amenities that is within easy walking distance to the river and the hungry trout. Most rooms have two double beds and a kitchenette. As an Orvis dealer, they can fill your angling needs offering a full service fly shop. They can also put you in touch with guides for wading or float excursions on the river. For information call Abe's Motel & Fly Shop at 632-2194 or write Box 6428, Navajo Dam, NM 87419.

Rizuto's San Juan River Lodge:

The owner of Rizuto's Fly Shop offers the best in both wading and float fishing trips. They offer two types of trips - floating or wading. MacKenzie River drift boats represent the ultimate in floating the river, ensuring safety, comfort and ease for the angler and guide. They provide plenty of room for storage of gear, food and beverage cookers. Because the majority of the access to the river is off-limits to automobiles, floating is the most ideal way to reach the most productive fishing water not accessible by foot, as well as view the river's beautiful wildlife and scenery. On their float trips, the guides will make stops at some of the riffles to allow you to approach on foot and cast your fly to some of the lunkers in these shallows. Their guides also provide robust streamside lunches with their float trips. For those who don't wish to make use of the boats, Rizuto's offers a fine wade trip from one of the nearby parking areas. Wade trips can provide access to some tributaries where the boats can not access. Rizuto's San Juan River Lodge offers clean spacious rooms, TVs & VCRs in every room. Queen size beds in most rooms, quick access to the river, full service fly tighing store, convenient hangers for rods & waders, fly tying tables and lamps.

Debo's Cafe: Their lodge features Debo's Cafe for your dining convenience. After a refreshing night's rest, join them for a hearty breakfast in their dining room. They call their breakfast "The Gulper". They serve it from 6 a.m. to 9 a.m. You are served quickly and efficiently after your order is taken to enable you to get into the legendary San Juan River to try for their wonderful rainbow trout. Although Debo's Cafe is not open for lunch, they do serve a very nice selection of dinner entrees. These selections include chateau briand, filet mignon, marinated grilled chicken breasts and other choices. For information call 632-1411 or write P.O. Box 6309, 1796 Highway 173, Navajo Dam, NM 87419.

Restaurants Near Airport:

Abe's Restaurant, Motel & Gift Shop	5 mi	Phone: 632-2194
Debo's Cafe	5 mi	Phone: 632-1411
Rizuto's Bed & Breakfast & Fly-Shop	5 mi	Phone: 632-3271
Sportsman's Inn Bar & Cafe	5 mi	Phone: 632-3271

Lodging: Abe's Motel has 54 units available for lodging, 632-2194; Rizuto's Lodge contains 8 units equipped with phones and TV's, 632-3893 along the San Juan River; Navajo Lake State Park has full service camping accommodations, 632-2278.

Transportation: Rita Shuttle Service: Since there is no phone at the airport you will need to call in advance and let Rita know when you will be landing. They will meet you at the airport and take you to whichever lodge facility you request. (Please let them know if you plan to be detained, as they most likely will be waiting for your arrival). You can arrange all your transportation needs through Rita Shuttle Service by calling 632-1506, or once reaching either Abe's Motel or Rizuto's San Juan River Lodge, you can arrange transportation through one of their fishing guides. A complete fishing package with all accommodations are provided. Both Abe's Motel & Fly Shop; Rizuto's San Juan River Lodge & Debo's Cafe; Issies Restaurant; and the Sportsmen's Inn are all located near one another and are all situated about 5 miles west of the Navajo State Park Airport (1V0).

Information: Navajo Lake State Park Manager, Phone: 632-2278

See U.S. Map of area
(By Gov. Printing Office)
Navajo Lake State Park Area
(Next Page)

Airport Information:

NAVAJO DAM - NAVAJO STATE PARK (1V0)

3 mi northeast of town N36-48.50 W107-39.09 Elev: 6475 Rwy 06-24: H4995x60 (Asph)
Attended: unattended CTAF: 122.9 Notes: Arpt. CLOSED sunset-sunrise. Arpt. CLOSED during winter. No snow removal. When snow or ice is on rwy call 505-632-2278. Rwy 06-24 excessive cracking and weed growth in runway, taxiways and apron areas. Use caution.
Airport Manager Phone: 632-2278

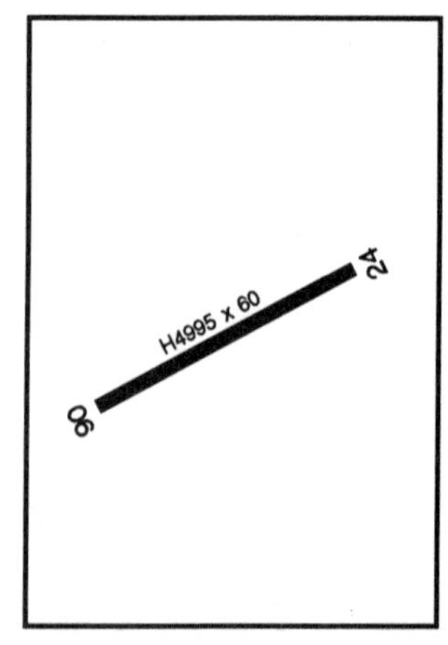

Navajo Lake State Park

(United States Government Printing Office)

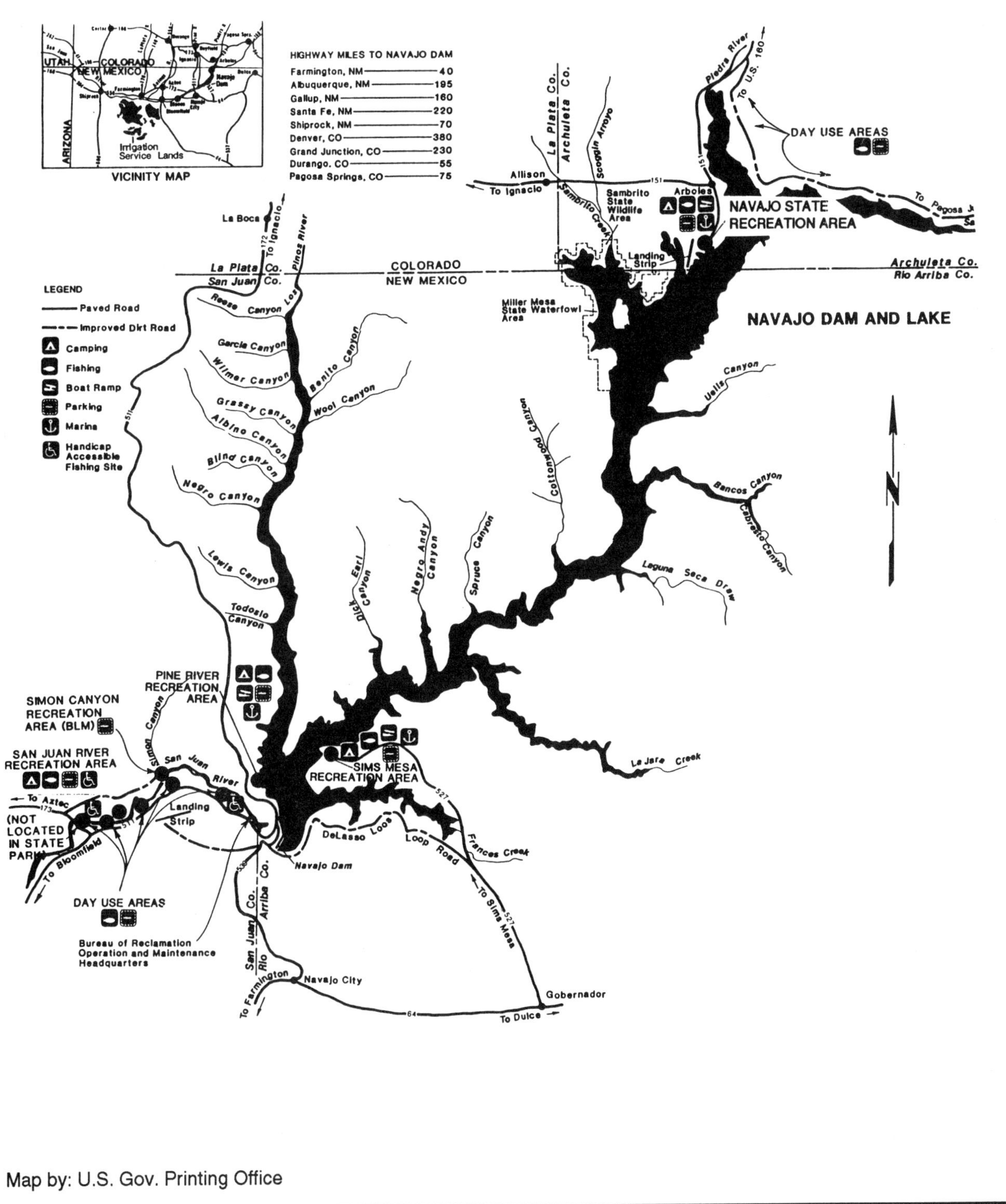

Map by: U.S. Gov. Printing Office

Not to be used for navigational purposes

NM-Q34 - PORTALES
PORTALES MUNICIPAL AIRPORT

10

El Rancho's Restaurant:

El Rancho's Restaurant is situated about 3 or 4 miles from the Portales Municipal Airport. Transportation to and from the restaurant can be arranged only if advance notice is given. When speaking with Mr. Widener of Widener Aviation, we learned that due to his interests in the community and in general aviation, he was kind enough to offer local courtesy transportation to nearby restaurants in the area. He can be reached at 359-1291 during the day or 359-0189 in the evenings. El Rancho's Restaurant is one of several nice local restaurants recommended to us. It is a family style facility open between 10:30 a.m. to 9 p.m. 6 days a week and 10:30 a.m. to 3 p.m. on Sunday. Their menu provides Mexican dishes like their smothered burrito's, "Gorditas", faheta's, chicken fried steak and homemade style hamburgers and cheeseburgers. Average prices run $3.50 for breakfast, $5.00 for lunch and $5.00 for dinner for most selections. Their main dining room can seat 110 persons. This restaurant has been in the family for many years and is located close to motels in the area. For more information about the restaurant call 359-0098.

(Area Code 505)

Restaurants Near Airport:		
Cattle Baron	6 mi N.	Phone: 356-5587
El Rancho's Rest.	5 mi N.	Phone: 359-0098
Portales Inn	6 mi N.	Phone: 359-1208
Recardo's Italian	5 mi N.	Phone: 356-6733

Lodging: Portales Inn (Free trans) 359-1208; Hillcrest Motel (Free trans) 359-1215.
Meeting Rooms: Midway Convention Center 356-5865.
Transportation: When speaking with Mr. Widener of Widener Aviation, we learned that due to his interest in the community and aviation, he would be available to arrange courtesy transportation to local restaurants if given advance notice. Call 359-1291 (Day) and 359-0189 in the evenings; Also: Rental Cars: Thatcher Olds/ Pontiac 356-4419; Trader Horn Motor Company 359-0947.
Information: Roosevelt County Chamber of Commerce, 7th & Abilene Streets, Portales, NM 88130, Phone: 356-8541 or 800-635-8036.

Attractions:

Portales Country Club (2 mi northeast of airport); Oasis State Park (12 mi northeast of airport) 356-5331.

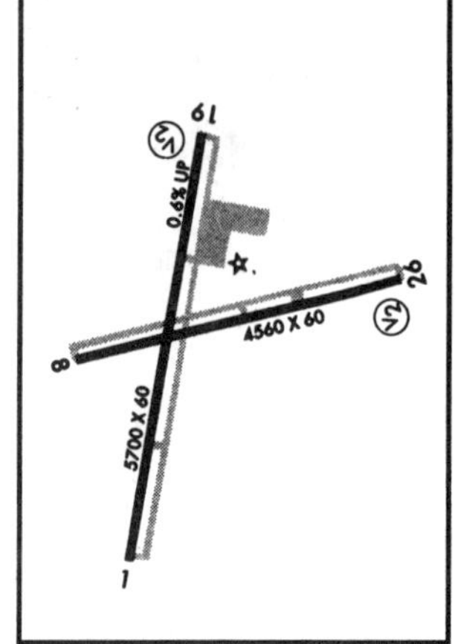

Airport Information:

PORTALES - PORTALES MUNICIPAL AIRPORT (Q34)
4 mi southwest of town N34-08.72 W103-24.61 Elev: 4076 Fuel: 100LL, Jet-A,
Rwy 01-19: H5700x60 (Asph) Rwy 08-26: H4560x60 (Asph) Attended: 1400-0000Z
Unicom: 122.8
FBO: Portales Muni. Airport Phone: 478-2863

NM-ROW - ROSWELL
ROWELL INDUSTRIAL AIR CENTER

11

Airport Coffee Shop (Marriott):

The Airport Coffee Shop is located on the first floor of the terminal building at the Roswell Industrial Air Center. This cafe has just opened this last year and has seating for about 35 people. Their hours are from 7 a.m. to 6:00 p.m., weekdays with a brunch on Saturday and Sunday from 12 p.m. to 2 p.m. Hours may vary. Their menu contains selections like grilled sandwiches and related items, salads, fruit, pastries and beverages. Average prices run $3.25 for breakfast and $4.25 for lunch. The cafe contains a glassed-in roof and is situated in the center of the terminal area within an atrium, and is decorated with live plants and a bright cheery atmosphere. Guests can also see the activity on the airport from this cafe. Additional accommodations can be arranged for groups up to 50 persons. As we mentioned earlier, watch for changes in restaurant hours as they may change in the future. For more information call the snack bar at 624-7196.

(Area Code 505)

Restaurants Near Airport:		
Airport Coffee Shop	On Site	Phone: 624-7196
Cattle Baron Restaurant	5 mi N.	Phone: 622-2465
Cattleman's	4 mi N.	Phone: 623-3500
George's Burger Barn	1/4 mi N.	Phone: 347-2989

Lodging: Roswell Inn (5 miles north) 623-4920; Sally Port Inn (5 miles north) 622-6430; Comfort Inn (5 miles west) 623-9440; Budget Inn (5 miles north) 623-6050; Leisure Inn (5 miles west) 622-2575.
Meeting Rooms: Airport conference room available, call 347-5703; Also Roswell Inn (5 miles north) 623-4920; and Sally Port Inn (5 miles north) 622-6430.
Transportation: Airport Limo Service 347-5522; Roswell Taxi 622-6984; National 347-2323; Hertz 347-2211; Avis 347-2500; Budget 347-2284; Independent 347-2223.
Information: Chamber of Commerce, 131 West 2nd Street, P.O. Drawer 70, Roswell, NM 88201, Phone: 623-5695.

Attractions:

Ruidosa Ski Area 70 miles west; Spring River NM Military Institute Golf Course, 4 miles north; Carlesbad and Bottomless Lakes Park & Wildlife Refuse 70 miles south and 4 miles east.

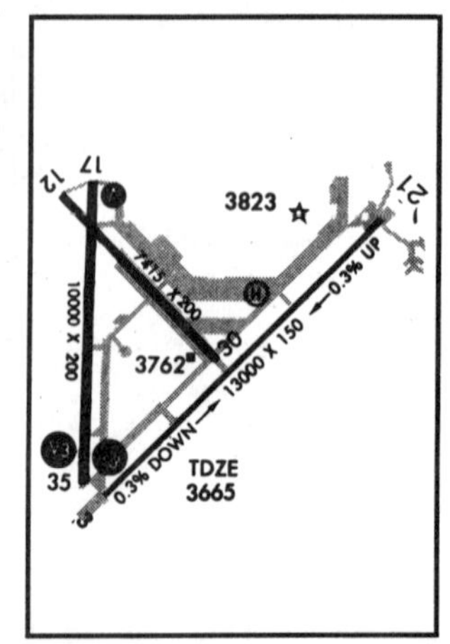

Airport Information:

ROSWELL - ROWELL INDUSTRIAL AIR CENTER (ROW)
3 mi south of town N33-18.09 W104-31.83 Elev: 3669 Fuel: 100LL, Jet-A, A1+
Rwy 03-21: H13000x150 (Asph-Conc) Rwy 17-35: 10000x200 (Asph-Pfc) Rwy 12-30: H7415x200 (Asph-Conc) Attended: 1300-0500Z Atis: 128.45 Unicom: 122.95
Tower: 118.5 Gnd Con: 121.9 Notes: Landing fees for aircraft over 30,000 lbs.
FBO: Great Southwest Aviation Phone: 347-2054, 800-824-0531

NM-SAF - SANTA FE
SANTA FE COUNTY MUNICIPAL

(Area Code 505) 12

Restaurants Near Airport:
Restaurants in Santa Fe On Site Phone: 984-6760

Lodging: El Dorado-Clarion (8 miles) 988-4455; High Mesa Inn (5 miles) 473-2800; Hilton Inn (8 miles) 988-2811; Howard Johnson Plaza Hotel (4 milesP 473-4646; La Quinta Inns (4 miles) 471-1142; Sheraton Santa Fe Inn (7miles) 982-5591; The Inn of the Governors (9 miles) 982-4333
Meeting Rooms: Glorieta Conference Center 757-6161
Transportation: The FBO will provide free all-day courtesy car on first-come, first-serve basis; Taxi Service: Capital City 989-8888; Rental Cars: Avis 982-4361; Hertz 982-1844
Information: Santa Fe Convention and Visitors Bureau, P.O. Box 909, Santa Fe, NM 87504, Phone: 984-6760

Restaurants in Santa Fe:

Among all the wonderful things to do in Santa Fe, the most popular pastime for residents is eating out. The town supports over 200 restaurants that will suit everyone's taste, budget or style. The native New Mexican food, served in half of Santa Fe's restaurants, is as much a part of the city's heritage as adobe architecture.Though the preparation is simple, the food is intensely flavorful and often much hotter than other southwestern and Mexican fare. Most visitors welcome the lively spice of chili peppers; however, there may be times when they get more heat than expected! So, here is a helpful tip. Quench the fire with a bite of something creamy or sweet, rather than with a cold drink. For a taste of traditional New Mexican cuisine, visit the Blue Corn Cafe, Rancho De Chimayo, La Tertulia or Maria's New Mexican Kitchen. Or, for a real taste of the American West, stop by the Cactus Rose There are also many other restaurants that serve International cuisine. Enough for everyone's taste and budget. For more information about the restaurants and other activities in Santa Fe, contact the Santa Fe Convention and Visitors bureau at 800-777-2489 or 984-6760.

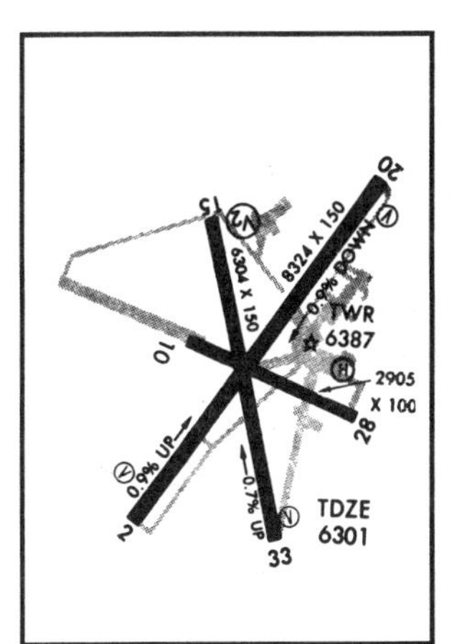

Airport Information:

SANTA FE - SANTA FE COUNTY MUNICIPAL (SAF)
9 miles southwest of town N35-37.01 W106-05.29 Elev: 6345 Fuel: 100LL, Jet-A Rwy 02-20: H8324x150 (Asph-pfc) Rwy 15-33: H6304x150 (Asph) Rwy 10-28: H2905xx100 (Asph) Attended: 1300Z-0500Z CTAF: 199.5 Atis: 128.55 Unicom: 122.95 Albuquerque Center App/ Dep Con: 132.8 Tower: 119.5 (1300-0500Z) Gnd Con: 121.7 Notes: There is a $2.00 parking fee for both singles and twins.
FBO: Santa Fe Aviation Phone: 471-6533
FBO: Capital Aviation of Santa Fe Phone: 471-2525

Santa Fe Ski & Resort Area

Santa Fe, NM (NM-SAF)

Santa Fe is located between the 13,000-foot peaks of the Sangre de Cristo Range of the Rocky Mountains and the valleys of the Rio Grand in northern New Mexico. Throughout the centuries, people from a number of cultures have made Santa Fe their home. Native American farmers, Pueblo Indians (non-tribal), Spanish colonists and governors, other Europeans, descendants of eastern colonists, soldiers marching under the flags of four nations and artists of many kinds. Today, the Pueblo villages still remain. New Mexico's Pueblo Indians trace their immediate roots to the state's 19 surviving pueblos. They are best known for their dances, jewelry and pottery.

Many tourists have walked Santa Fe's crooked-shaped streets. Tourists come to see its fine architecture and art, join in its celebrations, sample its authentic food and observe its customs. The contrast and synthesis of different yet curiously compatible cultures are what sets Santa Fe apart.

The homes and public buildings reflect the Pueblo, Spanish Colonial, Territorial and Victorian cultures in Santa Fe. The Plaza serves as a focal point for the community. It is the center of commerce, gatherings, parades and people-watching. Today, it is flanked by some of Santa Fe's best shops and a wonderfully ornate Victorian structure, the Catron Building. Along the north side is the Palace of the Governors - the oldest government building in the U.S., with construction initiated in 1610. A stroll east of the Plaza on Palace Avenue brings you to Sena Plaza. One of the best preserved large homes of early Santa Fe. Across Palace Avenue from Sena Plaza, at the eastern end of San Francisco Street, stands Saint Francis Cathedral. Its construction began in 1869. A small, older chapel, Capilla de Nuestra Senora la Conquistadora, Reina de la Paz is inside the cathedral and is a stunning example of the simple decorative style of carved and painted wood found in small villages throughout the state. The capel is home to the famous statue "La Conquistadora". Each June, she is removed from her place of honor in the cathedral for a procession to Rosario Chapel, near the intersection of Paseo de Peralta and Guadalupe.

El Zaguan, built in a fortified style with four-foot-thick walls, contains a lovely garden that is open to the public. It was named after Adolph Bandelier, an archeologist and ethnohistorian who pioneered in the southwest and briefly lived at this beautiful architectural dwelling. Those points of interest are just to name a few of the many homes and public buildings in Santa Fe.

Santa Fe is a great place for people who love outdoor activities and sports. Each season provides the right conditions for certain activities, but Santa Fe's generally mild climate also allows many sports to be enjoyed year-round. Fall, spring and summer are usually the best times of the year for hiking, camping, horseback riding, biking, white-water rafting, bird watching and, at the end of an active day, hot-springs bathing.

During the fall, there is little rain; days are warm and nights are cool. It is the time when both nature and northern New mexico's communities are at their best. Chilis are drying on pitched tin roofs, roadside fruit and vegetable stands are bursting at the seams, and glorious color graces the surrounding high country. Above town, on the flanks of Big Tesuque peak, quakin aspen turn a dazzling golden color; and across the Rio Grande Valley in the Jemez Mountains, more strands of aspen set hillsides ablaze. Along streams and rivers, mountain cottonwood, scrub oak, box elder and thicket creeper add dashes of color. Prime time is usually the end of September through mid-October. Hunting season in New Mexico begins in the fall. There is varied typography, sparsely populated countryside and both big and small game, such as deer, elk, bear, quail, pheasant, dove and grouse. Note: Deer hunting is open to anyone buying a license; however, certain restrictions apply to rare game - antelope, bighorn sheep, etc.

During the winter, New Mexico's high mountain ranges capture signifcant amounts of snow, great for both downhill and cross-country skiing. The Santa Fe Ski Area, located just 16 miles northeast of the city, is normally open from Thanksgiving to Easter. It has a vertical drop of 1,650 feet and it has 40 runs for all levels of skiers. It offers daycare/ski program for those with infants and children, as well as rental equipment, lessons, lockers, a day lodge, a ski boutique, a cafeteria and a bar. Cross-country skiing is another popular winter sport. A good local trek is on the Aspen Vista Trail, a Forest Service road closed to traffic in the winter. The trail begins about two-thirds of the way up the road to the Santa Fe Ski Area. The nearby Jemez Mountains also offer an extensive trail system.

Spring is a transitional season in Santa Fe, when many summer and winter activities can be done simultaneously. Such as, skiing in the morning on six inches of new snow, then playing tennis in the afternoon, under the warm sunshine. River and stream fishing picks up with the snow runoff, and opportunities for hiking in the high country become available as the ground clears of snow. Or, simply taking strolls and viewing Santa Fe's blossoming fruit trees, lilacs, irises and other flowering plants and bushes.

The summer brings a warm climate, often challenged by the cooler hig-mountain country around Santa Fe. Of course, swimming is the essence of summer for many people. So are other water activities, such as motorboating, water-skiing, sailing and sailboarding. It is also a perfect time for fishing. Santa Fe is surrounded by waters to the north, east and west in the Sangre de Cristo and Jemez mountains. Summer is also a great time for hiking, backpacking and camping. The 223,000-acre Pecos Wilderness is just one of the many nearby options available for overnight excursions.

Photo by: Don Strel The Museum of Fine Arts, Santa Fe, New Mexico.

Discover and experience a vast range of artistic, cultural and intellectual endeavor at Santa Fe's fine museums: The Museum of New Mexico, Palace of the Governors, Museum of Fine Arts, Museum of International Folk Art, Museum of Indian Arts and Culture, Institute of American Indian Arts Museum, Wheelright Museum of the American Indian, El Rancho de las Golondrinas, the School of American Research and the Santa Fe Children's Museum.

Season after season, Santa Fe is a celebration of music. Spectacular performances of classical, contemporary and experimental music are presented in acoustically excellent spaces, including cathedrals, chapels and outdoor theaters. Santa Fe also hosts a vast array of drama, ranging from the Greek classics to American and European contemporary presented throughout the year.

Among all the wonderful things to do in Santa Fe, the most popular pastime for residents is eating out. The town supports over 200 restaurants that will suit everyone's taste, budget or style. The native New Mexican food, served in half of Santa Fe's restaurants, is as much a part of the city's heritage as adobe architecture. Yet, it is significantly different from the regional cuisines of Mexico and Spain. New Mexicans prepared sauces with red or green chili. Though the preparation is simple, the food is intensely flavorful and often much hotter than other southwestern and Mexican fare. Most visitors welcome the lively spice of chile peppers, however there may be times when they get more heat than expected! So, here is a helpful tip. Quench the fire with a bite of something creamy or sweet, rather than with a drink of something cold.

Besides campsites, there are plenty of hotels and motels in the Santa Fe area; the El Dorado- Clarion, High Mesa Inn, Hilton Inn and the Howard Johnson Plaza Hotel just to name a few. There are also meeting and convention facilities available. For more information about lodging and accommodations, contact Santa Fe Central Reservations at 800-776-SNOW(7669) or 983-8200.

The Santa Fe County Municipal Airport is located 9 miles southwest of the city. It has an 8,324'x150 asphalt-pfc runway, an 6,304'x150 asphalt runway, and an 2,905'x100 asphalt runway. There is a $2.00 parking fee for both singles and twins. The FBO will provide a free all-day courtesy car on a first-come, first-serve basis. For more information, contact the FBO at 471-6533. Rental cars are also available at the airport.

For more information about Santa Fe, contact the Santa Fe Convention and Visitors Bureau at 800-777-2489 or 984-6760, or the Chamber of Commerce at 983-7317. (Information submitted by the City of Santa Fe Convention and Visitors Bureau)

Photo by: Don Strel

A skier glides through the beautiful Santa Fe Ski Area.

NM-Q58 - SANTA ROSA
SANTA ROSA MUNICIPAL AIRPORT

(Area Code 505)

13

Restaurants Near Airport:

Restaurant	Distance	Phone
Adobe Inn Rest.	2-1/2 mi	Phone: 472-3839
Club Cafe	3 mi	Phone: 472-3631
Comet Drive Inn	3-1/4 mi	Phone: N/A
Country Pride	1/4 mi	Phone: 472-3432

Country Pride Restaurant:

The Country Pride Restaurant is located within walking distance or about 1/4th mile to the north from the general aviation parking area. They are open 24hrs a day, 365 day a year. This family style facility is located adjacent to a truck stop and does most of its business with travelers and truckers traveling through the area. Their menu offers a variety of entrees such as rib eye, grilled chicken, several seafood selections, Mexican foods, and many delicious breakfast dishes. This restaurant prides itself in preparing large portions so each and every customer goes away satisfied. They also offer an all you can eat salad bar along with daily specials. Average price for a meal is $4.00 for breakfast, $4.00 to $5.50 for lunch and $5.99 to $11.99 for dinner. The Country Pride Restaurant has just been remodeled and contains tables, booths and counter space. Their main dinning room can seat 122 persons. Groups of 20 or more are welcome with advance notice preferred. We learned that it is possible that several other restaurants may also be added to the truck stop complex. For more information you can call 472-3432.

Lodging: Adobe Inn (Best Western) 472-3446; Scottish Inns 472-3466; Sun & Sands Motel 472-5268; Super 8 Motel 472-5388.

Meeting Rooms: Holiday Santa Rosa 472-5411; Adobe Inn Restaurant 472-3839; Joseph's Restaurant 472-3361.

Transportation: Airport courtesy car available to pilots; Also airport manager can arrange courtesy transportation, Phone: 472-3668.

Information: Chamber of Commerce, 486 Parker Avenue, Santa Rosa, NM 88435, Phone: 472-3763.

Attractions:

Blue Hole scuba diving (3-3/4 mile) 472-3370; Santa Rosa State Parks; Santa Rosa Gulf Course; Pecos River (2 to 4 miles).

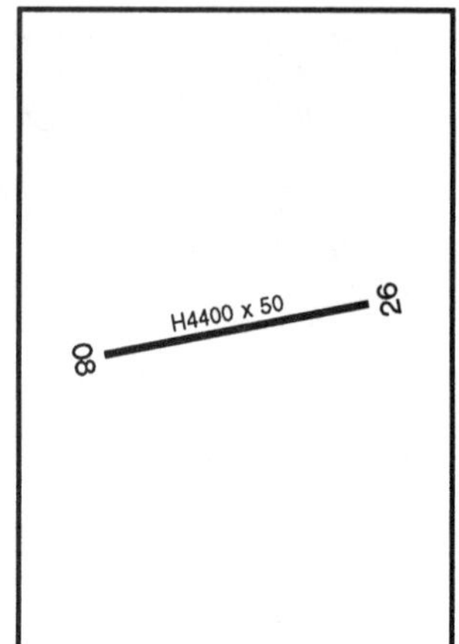

Airport Information:

SANTA ROSA - SANTA ROSA MUNICIPAL AIRPORT (Q58)
3 mi east of town N34-56.37 W104-38.37 Elev: 4782 Fuel: 100LL
Rwy 08-26: H4400x50 (Asph) Attended: 1400-0200 Unicom 122.8 Notes: Fuel is available 24 hours on field 472-4032.
Santa Rosa Municipal Airport Phone: 472-9942

NM-SKX - TAOS
TAOS MUNICIPAL AIRPORT

(Area Code 505) 14

A Taste of Taos (Area Restaurants):

Taos, known as the Soul of the Southwest, is located in the high Rockies of northern New Mexico. The Municipal Airport is located just 6 miles northwest of the city. Taos has plenty of restaurants to spice up your appetite. Sample their mild or hot chile made with red or green peppers. Here is a tip! Before sampling this tasty delicacy, be sure to ask your wait person which is hotter. Or, visit one of the other 50 restaurants, where ambiance is just as varied as the cuisine. Brightly colored playful nooks contrast with more traditional spaces and blazing fires. Skiers enjoy slopeside dining in alpine-style lodges. Twice a year, Taos hosts festivals devoted to the culinary arts. Winemakers, vineyard owners and importers from New Mexico, California and France bring their best vintages to Taos Ski Valley's Winter Wine Festival. Taste of Taos offers a smorgasbord of delicacies from local restaurants. For transportation, Payless Car Rental is located at Taos Municipal Airport. Contact the FBO at 758-9501 (8 a.m. to 5 p.m., or after by prior arrangement) for further information. For more information about Taos Ski Valley, contact the Taos County Chamber of Commerce at 800-732-TAOS (8267) or 758-3873.

Restaurants Near Airport:
Taos Ski Valley 6 mi SE Phone: 758-3873

Lodging: El Monte Lodge (9 miles) 758-3171; Holiday Inn (10 miles) 758-4444
Meeting Rooms: Taos Civic Plaza & Convention Center 800-323-MEET (6338)
Transportation: Rental cars: Payless on field 758-9501; Taxi service: Faust Transportation 758-3410; Pride of Taos 758-8340
Information: Taos County Chamber of Commerce, P.O. Drawer I, Taos, New Mexico 87571, Phone: 800-732-TAOS (8267) or 758-3873

Attractions:

Taos Ski Valley, in New Mexico, invites you to explore the scenery, art, history, skiing, recreation, restaurants and much more. For more information, call the Taos County Chamber of Commerce at 800-732-TAOS (8267) or 758-3873.

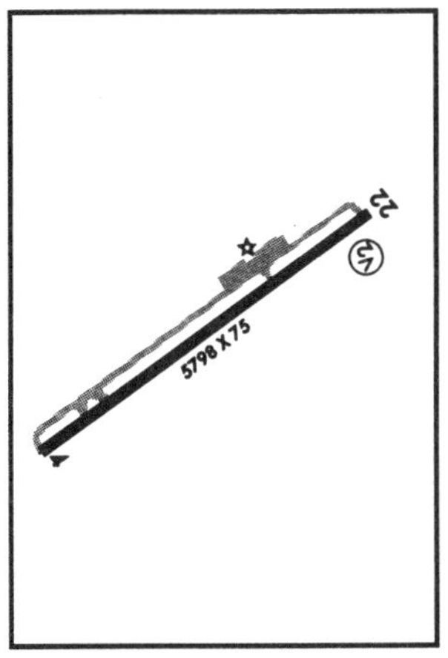

Airport Information:

TAOS - TAOS MUNICIPAL AIRPORT (SKX)
6 mi northwest of town N36-27.49 W105-40.35 Elev: 7091 Fuel: 100LL, Jet-A1 Rwy 04-22: H5798x75 (Asph) Attended: 1500-0000Z CTAF/Unicom: 122.8 Notes: For fuel after hours, call 758-9501 or contact manager on field.
FBO: Horizon Air Service Phone: 758-9501

Taos Ski Valley

Taos, NM (NM-SKX)

The 700 year-old Taos Pueblo is an example of America's earliest high-rise apartment architecture.

Photo by Svat Macha

Taos, known as the Soul of the Southwest, is located in the high Rockies of northern New Mexico. It is a timeless place with scenic vistas and fun in the sun, spiced with the creative spirit and warm hospitality of many cultures. It invites you to explore the scenery, art, history, skiing, recreation and all it has to offer.

People have been drawn to Taos for centuries. Historically, the Spanish settlers and Pueblo Indians farmed the rich valley. In 1680, the Pueblos united to drive out the Spanish. Years later, Don Diego de Vargas subdued the Taos Indians and the Spanish resettled around Taos Pueblo, Taos Plaza and Ranchos de Taos.

Today, Taos Indians still live in their multi-storied Pueblo. The spirit of their cultures are still alive and thriving. In fact, many of their traditional ceremonial dances are open to the public. They proudly preserve their heritage in everyday life, irrigating fields with acequias(canals) in the traditional way, caring for their ancient adobe dwellings and worshipping in historic churches.

Visit the Taos Pueblo and experience the taste of "horno-baked" bread, or explore the simple shops which display beautiful mica-flecked pottery, hand-beaded moccasins and Taos drums. Both Taos Plaza and Ranchos de Taos have many interesting shops and galleries, as well. Interestingly,Taos Plaza, the heart of the community, has survived numerous fires, yet still retains its original shape. Taos also has many museums to explore. Step into the life of a Spanish colonial family at theMartinez Hacienda and travel back to the rugged lifestyle of the 1800's. Visit the home of renowned mountain man, trapper and Indian scout, Kit Carson, at the Kit Carson Home & Museum. Stop by the Millicent Rogers Museum and view the magnificent collection of various Hispanic art forms, as well as Native American jewelry, textiles, baskets, pottery and paintings.

While the visual art and artists of Taos are known world-wide, the performing artists thrive there as well. Each year, the Taos Art Association presents more than 60 national and local performing art events in the TAA Community Auditorium. Every winter, world-famous jazz musicians add pep to the snowy evenings, and every summer, classical musicians add a sense of coolness to the summer heat.

Art, in Taos, is an active excercise for all ages. Visitors can find their favorite artists at the annual Spring Arts Show, as well as many other festivals throughout the year. Taos also has a wide variety of schools and workshops for those who want to pursue their own creative ability. The Taos Institute of Arts offers a summer curriculum that covers sculpture, painting, weaving, jewelry, photography, writing and interdisciplinary expeditions to Anasazi sites. The Fechin Institute hosts 19 painting and sculpture workshops at Branham Ranch. Fort Burgwin Research Center supports an active archaeological program, excavating ruins of a 1,000-year-old pueblo. In addition to these workshops, Taos offers drumming workshops, elderhostels, storytelling, educational lectures and dance workshops.

There is plenty of outdoor recreation in Taos.Try bobbling down the great, brown chasm of the Rio Grande Gorge or hiking through the switchback trails of our nation's first Wild & Scenic Rivers Area, down the 600-foot gorge to the Rio Grande. You'll feel your knees going

Photo by: Ken Gallard Entrance to Taos Ski Valley in the Rockies.

down and your heart and lungs going up as you go mountain biking. Golfers can challenge themselves at the Taos Country Club, which has 18-holes or El Valle Escondido, which has 9-holes. Fishermen can indulge themselves in their hunt for cutthroat trout in the mountain streams and down into the Rio Grande. Looking for a new challenge? Try hot air ballooning, camping or rock climbing. Take a llama trek or horseback ride through the high country.

During the winter, the focus of theTaos experience is the mountain! It transforms into a winter wonderland for skiers and snowmobilers. It offers miles of varied, often challenging terrain in unbeatable sunny weather. Taos offers a total of 72 slopes and 11 chairlifts. The ski season generally runs between the latter part of November through the beginning of April. There are five area ski resorts - Taos, Sipapu, Angel Fire, Red River and Ski Rio. In addition, Taos also offers a reputable ski school for all levels

Explore the flavors of Taos at restaurants that serve tasty authentic Taos cuisine, such as their mild or hot chile made with red or green peppers. Here is a tip! Before sampling this tasty delicacy, be sure to ask your wait person which is hotter. Or, visit one of the other 50 restaurants, where ambiance is just as varied as the cuisine. Brightly colored playful nooks contrast with more traditional spaces with blazing fires. Skiers enjoy slopeside dining in alpine-style lodges. Taos has several comfortable lodging facilities, such as hotels, motels, historic inns, cozy lodges and bed and breakfast inns that will greet visitors with warm hospitality. The Taos Civic Plaza & Convention Center is available for meetings and other events.

Taos Municipal Aiport is located just 6 miles northwest of the city. It has a 5798'x75, asphalt runway. Parking fees are $5.00 for singles and $8.00 for twins. For transportation, Payless Car Rental is located on the field. Contact the FBO at 758-9501 (8 a.m. to 5 p.m.; after by prior arrangement) for further information. Taxi service is available with Faust Transportation at 758-3410 and with Pride of Taos at 758-8340. For more information about Taos Ski Valley, contact the Taos County Chamber of Commerce at 800-732-TAOS(8267) or 758-3873. For meeting information, call 800-323-MEET. (Information submitted by Taos County Lodgers Association in cooperation with Taos County Chamber or Commerce.)

NEW YORK

LOCATION MAP

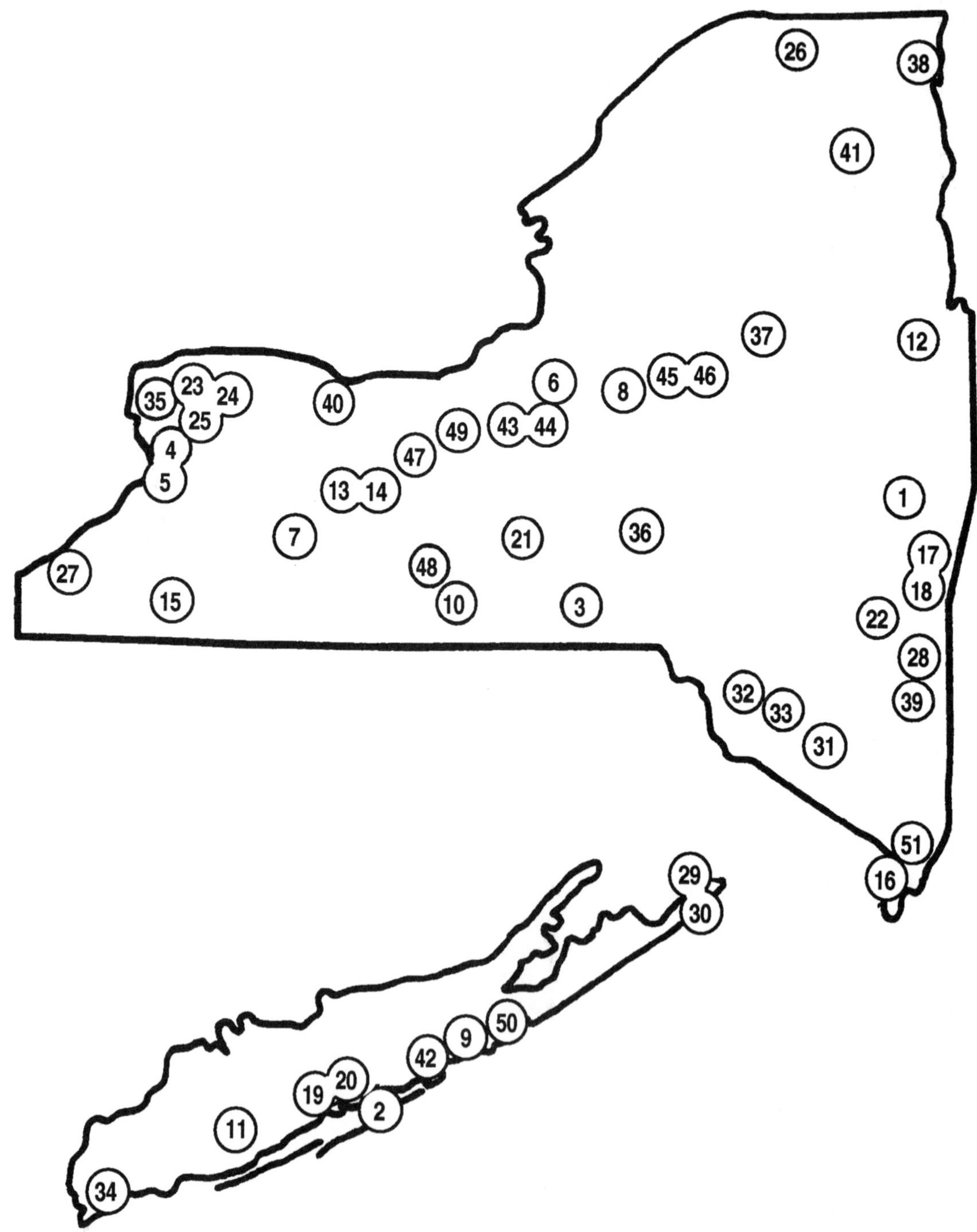

Not to be used for navigational purposes

NEW YORK

CROSS FILE INDEX

Location Number	City or Town	Airport Name And Identifier	Name of Restaurant
1	Albany	Albany County Arpt. (ALB)	Albany Arpt. Trml. Rest.
2	Bayport	Bayport Aerodrome (23N)	The Sayville Inn
3	Binghamton	Binghamton Reg./Edwin link (BGM)	Stephanies Restaurant
4	Buffalo	Greater Buffalo Intl. Arpt. (BUF)	CA1 Services
5	Buffalo	Greater Buffalo Intl. Arpt. (BUF)	Flying Tigers Restaurant
6	Cicero	Michael Airfield (NY10)	Plainville Farms Rest
7	Dansville	Dansville Muni. (DSV)	Buckhorn Family Rest.
8	Durhamville	Kamp Arpt. (NK03)	Suzie's Kitchen
9	East Moriches	Lufker Arpt. (4NY7)	Dominick's Stk. Hse.
10	Elmira	Elmira/Corning Reg. (ELM)	Jennifer's Restaurant
11	Farmingdale	Republic Arpt. (FRG)	56th Fighter Group
12	Glens Falls	Warren Co. Arpt. (GFL)	"Twichell's" coffee shop
13	Gorham	Midlakes Arpt. (92G)	Kamp in the Woods
14	Gorham	Midlakes Arpt. (92G)	Thendara Restaurant
15	Great Valley	Great Valley (N56)	Eddy's Restaurant
16	Greenville	Rainbow Arpt. (NY25)	Rainbow Golf Club
17	Hudson	Columbia Co. Arpt. (1B1)	Kozel's Restaurant
18	Hudson	Columbia Co. Arpt. (1B1)	Meadowgreen Rest.
19	Islip	Long Island Mac Arthur (ISP)	CA1 Services
20	Islip	Long Island Mac Arthur (ISP)	Seasons Restaurant
21	Ithaca	Tompkins Co. Arpt. (ITH)	The Landing Rest.
22	Kingston	Kingston Ulster Arpt. (20N)	Quick Stop (Convenient)
23	Lockport	North Buffalo Suburban (0G0)	Best of Pizza
24	Lockport	North Buffalo Suburban (0G0)	The Inn Field
25	Lockport	North Buffalo Suburban (0G0)	Peppino's
26	Malone	DuFort Arpt. (MAL)	Jammers Fine Foods
27	Mayville	Dart Arpt. (D79)	The Great Escape
28	Millbrook	Sky Acres Arpt. (44N)	Kading's Windsock Cafe
29	Montauk	Montauk Arpt. (MTP)	Blue Moon Restaurant
30	Montauk	Montauk Arpt. (MTP)	Crows Nest Restaurant
31	Montgomery	Orange Co. Arpt. (MGJ)	Orange Co Arpt. Rest.
32	Monticello	Monticello Arpt. (N37)	Russini Restaurant
33	Monticello	Sullivan Co. Intl. Arpt. (MSV)	Airport Coffee Shop
34	New York	John F. Kennedy Intl. (JFK)	CA1 Services
35	Niagara Falls	Niagara Falls Intl Arpt. (IAG)	Goose's Roost
36	Norwich	Lt. Warren Eaton Arpt. (OIC)	Grove Park Restaurant
37	Piseco	Piseco Arpt. (NY43)	Irondequit Inn
38	Plattsburg	Clinton Co. Arpt. (PLB)	Airport Cafe
39	Poughkeepsie	Dutchess Co. Arpt. (POU)	Woronock House
40	Rochester	Gtr. Rochester Intl. (ROC)	Phillips Pastries & Salads
41	Saranac Lake	Adirondack Arpt. (SLK)	Airport Restaurant

CROSS FILE INDEX
(New York Continued)

Location Number	City or Town	Airport Name And Identifier	Name of Attraction
42	Shirley	Brookhaven Arpt. (HWV)	Shirley Ann's Diner
43	Syracuse	Syracuse Hancock Intl. Arpt. (SYR)	Best Western Syracuse
44	Syracuse	Syracuse Hancock Intl. Arpt. (SYR)	CA1 Services
45	Utica	Oneida Co. Arpt. (UCA)	Gabbies Cafe
46	Utica	Oneida Co. Arpt. (UCA)	Horizon Hotel Rest.
47	Waterloo	Airtrek Arpt. (D93)	Nicastro Restaurant
48	Watkins Glen	Schuyler Arpt. (D94)	Castel Grisch Restaurant
49	Weedsport	Whitford's Arpt. (B16)	Whitford's Arpt. Rest.
50	Westhampton Beach	Suffolk Co. (FOK)	Bell's Cafe
51	White Plains	Westchester Co. Arpt. (HPN)	Skytop Restaurant

Articles

City or town	Nearest Airport and Identifier	Name of Attraction
Hammondsport, NY	Penn Yan (PEO)	Glenn H. Curtiss Museum
Red Hook, NY	Red Hook - Sky Park (46N)	Old Rhinebeck Aerodrome
Schenectady, NY	Schenectady Co. (SCH)	Empire Aerosci. Musuem

NY-ALB - ALBANY
ALBANY COUNTY AIRPORT

Restaurants Near Airport: **(Area Code 518)** **1**

Albany Co. Arpt. Trml. Srv. On Site Phone: 869-0351

Albany County Airport Terminal Service:

The Albany County Airport terminal building contains three food service facilities. Schlotzsky's Deli is located within the main entrance to the terminal. It specializes in preparing all types of gourmet sandwiches and specialty pizzas. Near the U.S. Air Terminal is another establishment that serves light fare. It is a bar that is able to serve sandwiches, hamburgers and other items. In addition to these is a gourmet coffee shop that serves many varieties of coffee. During our conversation with the food service management, we learned that food and beverages are available beginning at 5:30 a.m. to at least 10 p.m. in the evening. For more information you can call 869-0351.

Lodging: Americana Hotel (1/2 mile) 869-8100; Holiday Inn Turf (1/2 mile) 458-7250; Albany Marriott (3/4 mile) 458-8444

Meeting Rooms: All lodging facilities listed above have accommodations for conferences and meetings.

Transportation: Page Avjet can accommodate courtesy transportation to nearby facilities, call 869-0253; Also: Airport Taxi 869-9288; Hertz 869-6925; Avis 869-8404; Budget 466-8561; National 785-3247.

Information: Albany County Convention & Visitors Bureau, 52 South Pearl Street, Albany, NY 12207, Phone: 434-1217 or 800-258-3582.

Airport Information:

ALBANY - ALBANY COUNTY AIRPORT (ALB)
6 mi northwest of town N42-44.89 W73-48.18 Elev: 285 Fuel: 100LL, Jet-A
Rwy 01-19: H7200x150 (Asph-Grvd) Rwy 10-28: H5999x150 (Asph-Grvd)
Attended: continuously Atis: 120.45 Unicom: 122.95 App/Dep Con: 125.0, 118.05, 124.7, 127.15 Tower: 119.5 Gnd Con: 121.7 Clnc Del: 127.5 Public phone 24 hrs
Notes: .79 cents per 1000 lbs certificated landing weight.
FBO: Signature Flight Support Phone: 869-0253

NY-23N - BAYPORT
BAYPORT AERODROME

Restaurants Near Airport: **(Area Code 516)** **2**

The Sayville Inn 2 mi Phone: 567-0033

The Sayville Inn:

The Sayville Inn is located about 3 or 4 miles and about a 5 minute drive from the Bayport Aerodrome. Pilots can call D'Angelone Aviation (FBO) at 472-4747, and they will find a way to get you there via courtesy car, restaurant car, etc. This is a well known and very unique restaurant worth the trip. The owner of Sayville Inn is a pilot himself and caters to fly-in cliental. This is a family restaurant with a fine dining atmosphere, and is open during evening hours for dinner between 5 p.m. and 10 p.m. on weekdays, and untill 11 p.m. on weekends. The menu contains gourmet selections like cranberry walnut stuffed chicken, marinated club steak, coconut jumbo shrimp, along with other entrees that change daily. Prices range between $10.95 to $19.95. One of the unique features about this restaurant is that every 7 months or so, they change the theme of the restaurant. One interesting theme is their African Safari decor. Groups are welcome with accommodations for about 15 persons. For information about this restaurant call 567-0033.

Lodging: Contact the staff at D'Angelone Aviation, Inc. for information. Phone: 472-4747.
Meeting Rooms: None reported
Transportation: Call The Sayville Inn 564-0033; Also: Call D'Angelone Aviation, Inc. (FBO) for arranging transportation or courtesy car. Phone: 472-4747.
Information: Contact the staff at D'Angelone Aviation, Inc. for information about attractions, lodging etc. Phone: 472-4747

Notes: Those pilots requiring hard service runways might elect to land at Long Island Mac Arthur Airport (ISP) about 5 miles northwest of Bayport Aerodrome (23N).

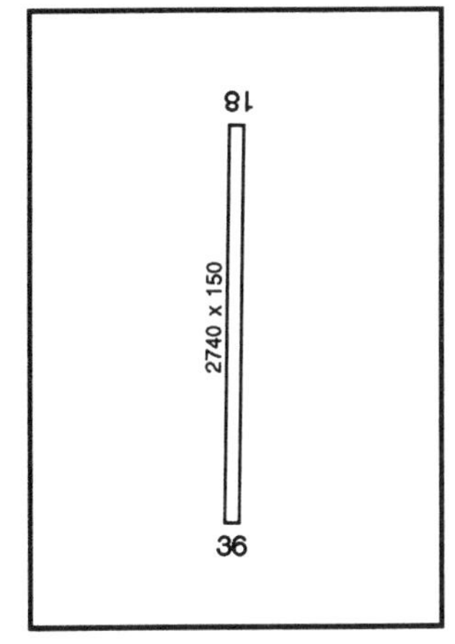

Attractions:

Only a short distance away from The Sayville Inn is Fire Island National Seashore. Some of the attractions in the area include: ferry boat rides, guided walking tours during the summer, nature trails, swimming, fishing, clamming, facilities at "Sailors Haven" sunken forests, Smith Point West Information Center etc. For information you can write to: Fire Island National Seashore, 120 Laurel St., Long Island, NY 11772, Phone: 289-4810; Fire Island Lighthouse Museum 661-4876; Fire Island Ferry Service has charters to the Sunken Forest 665-2115; Sunken Forests 589-8980. Also additional ferry companies include the: Davis Park Ferry Co. 475-1665; and Intra Island Ferry-Island Water Taxi 583-5800.

Airport Information:

BAYPORT - BAYPORT AERODROME (23N)
1 mi northwest of town N40-45.51 W73-03.22 Elev: 41 Fuel: 100LL Rwy 18-36: 2740x150 (Turf) Attended: 1300Z-dusk Unicom: 122.7 Notes: See AFD for special pattern instructions in order to avoid heavy jet traffic pattern activity for Long Island Mac Arthur Airport (ISP). All traffic enter 45 degrees left base for Rwy 36 at 600 Ft. MSL; All traffic enter 45 degree right downwind for Rwy 18 over lakes at 600 ft. MSL.
FBO: D'Angelone Aviation, Inc. Phone: 472-4747

NY-BGM - BINGHAMTON
BINGHAMTON/EDWIN A LINK FLD

(Area Code 607) 3

Stephanies Restaurant:

This restaurant is located at the north end of the terminal building and is within easy walking distance from aircraft parking. This Snack bar and cafe is open Monday through Friday 6 a.m. to 9 p.m., Saturday from 6 a.m. to 7 p.m. and Sunday from 6 a.m. to 7 p.m. Prices range from $3.50 for breakfast, $5.50 for lunch and $8.50 for dinner. In-Flight catering is their specialty, as well as catering for fly-in groups are welcome up to 120 persons. For information call 797-3612.

Restaurants Near Airport:

Airport Inn	1/2 mi S.	Phone: 797-6763
Stephanies	On Site	Phone: 797-3612

Lodging: Holiday Inn Arena, (12 miles) 8 Hawley Street, Binghamton, NY 13901, Phone: N/A; Howard Johnson Lodge, (8 miles) 700 Front Street, Binghamton, NY 13905, Phone: 724-1341; Sheraton, (10 miles) 1 Sarbro Square, Binghamton, NY13901, Phone: 724-7263.

Meeting Rooms: Stephanie's Restaurant can accommodate your needs if planning a conferences or group meetings.

Transportation: Miller Aviation (FBO) will help provide courtesy transportation; Rental Cars: Seafini Trans., 729-0318; Avis, 729-6001; Budget, 729-0833; Hertz, 729-6115; National, 797-2417.

Attractions:

Robertson Center for the Arts & Sciences (Museum), Phone: 772-0660; Chenango Valley State Park, (Swimming, fishing, boat rental, nature trails, 18 hole golf course, & camping); Ross Park Zoo, (75 acre park open early April through Mid-November, daily), Phone: 724-5454; State University of New York, (Performing Arts), Phone: 777-2000 or 777-3535 for recorded events schedule.

Information: Broome County Chamber of Commerce, 49 Court Street, Box 995, Binghamton, NY 13902, Phone: 772-8860. For recorded maessages about Broome County activities call, Phone: 772-8945.

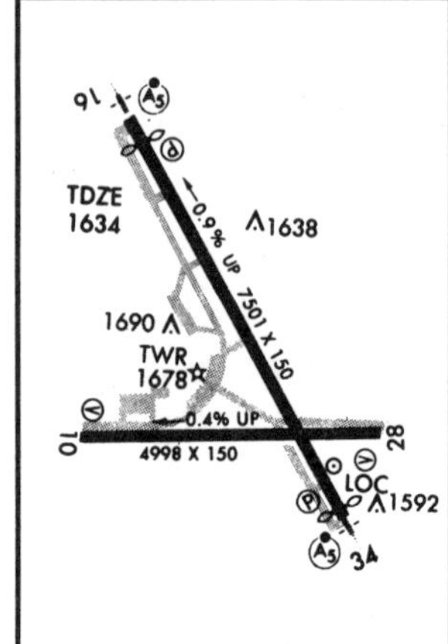

Airport Information:

BINGHAMTON - BINGHAMTON REGIONAL/EDWIN A LINK FLD (BGM)
7 mi north of town 42-12-27N 75-58-46W Elev: 1630 Fuel: 100LL, Jet-A
Rwy 16-34: H7500x150 (ASPH-GRVD) Rwy 10-28: H4999x150 (ASPH-GRVD)
Attended: continuously Atis: 128.15 App/Dep Con: 118.6, 126.1 Tower: 119.3
Gnd Con: 121.9 No 24hr Public Phone Notes: $10.00 per 7,000 lbs or less, $1.50/1000 lbs., No fee assessed with fuel purchase. (Fuel: .05 cents fee)
FBO: Miller Aviation, Phone: 770-1093

NY-BUF - BUFFALO
GREATER BUFFALO INTL. AIRPORT

(Area Code 716) 4, 5

CA1 Cafe And Deli:

This combination cafe, deli and sports bar is located within the terminal building at the Greater Buffalo International Airport. This establishment is open from 5:30 a.m. to 8 p.m. Specialties of the house include their breakfast selections, lunch and dinner daily specials, Friday fish fries, deserts, salads and "buffalo wings." Prices average $3.25 for breakfast, and about $5.50 for lunch and dinner choices. Fly-in groups are welcome. A full catering department is available for in-flight services. For information call 633-5050.

Flying Tigers Restaurant:

The Flying Tigers Restaurant is located across the airport from the fixed base operators, according to the management. CAUTION: Please do not walk across the airport active runway system to reach the restaurant. The airport security is very strict about this. You can arrange courtesy transportation in advance through the FBO or call for taxi service. This fine dining restaurant is open Monday through Thursday for dinner between 4:30 and 9:00 p.m., Saturday until 11 p.m. and Sunday until 10 p.m. On Sunday they also feature a buffet style brunch between 10 a.m. and 2:30 p.m. for $11.95. Please call the restaurant to verify times. Their menu features a variety of choice steaks and seafood selections. Average prices run $7.95 to $9.95 for lunch and $21.00 to $25.00 for most dinner entrees. This restaurant displays a very unique aviation decor within a 1940French farm house.There are a number of separate dining rooms decorated with all sorts of antiques, World War II memorabilia, and photographs. The view from the restaurant looks out over the main runway system, allowing the guests to watch the airplanes land and takeoff while enjoying their meal. For more information call the Flying Tigers Restaurant at 631-3465.

Restaurants Near Airport:

Airway Hotel	1/8th mi	Phone: 632-8400
CA1 Services & Deli	On Site	Phone: 633-5050
Danny's	1/2 mi	Phone: 634-1780
Flying Tigers	Adj Arpt	Phone: 631-3465

Lodging: Airways Hotel (shuttle service) 632-8400. Buffalo Airport Hotel (shuttle) 633-5500; Days Inn (1 mile) 631-0810; Holiday Inn Airport (shuttle) 634-6969; Holiday Inn Cheektowaga (Shuttle) 896-2900; Howard Johnson Lodge (Shuttle) 634-7500; Luxury Budget Inn (Shuttle) 631-8966; Marriott Hotel (Shuttle) 689-6900; Ramada Inn Airport (Shuttle) 634-2700; Ramada Renaissance (Shuttle) 634-2300; Sheraton Inn Airport (Shuttle) 681-2400.

Meeting Rooms: Airways Hotel 632-8400; Buffalo Airport Hotel 633-5500; Holiday Inn Airport 634-6969; Holiday Inn Cheektowaga 896-2900; Marriott Hotel 689-6900; Ramada Inn Airport 634-2700; Ramada Renaissance 634-2300; Sheraton Inn Airport 681-2400.

Transportation: Taxi service call 663-1473; Rental cars: Avis 632-1808; Budget 632-4662; Dollar 631-9880; Hertz 632-4772; National 632-0203.

Information: Greater Buffalo Convention & Visitors Bureau, 107 Delaware Street, Buffalo, NY 14202, Phone: 852-0511.

Airport Information:

BUFFALO - GREATER BUFFALO INTERNATIONAL AIRPORT (BUF)
5 mi east of town N42-56.43 W78-43.93 Rwy 05-23: H8102x150 (Asph-Grvd)
Rwy 14-32: H5376x150 (Asph) Attended: continuously Atis: 135.35 Unicom: 122.95
Buffalo FSS (On site) Buffalo App Dep/Con: 123.8, 126.5, 126.15 Tower: 120.5
Gnd Con: 121.9 Clnc Del: 124.7 Pre-Taxi Clnc: 124.7
FBO: Prior Aviation Services, Inc. Phone: 633-1000

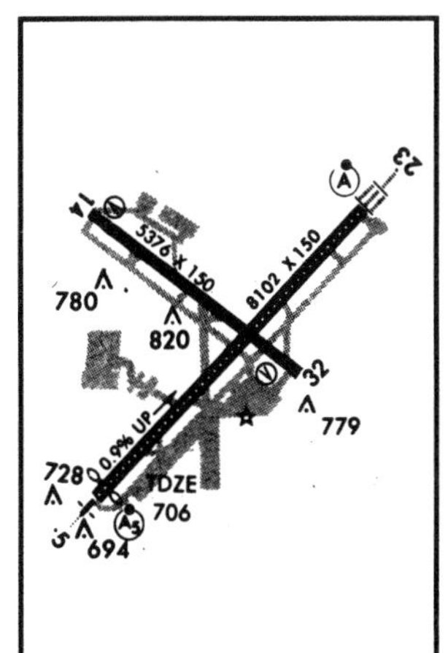

NY-NY10 - CICERO MICHAEL AIRFIELD

(Area Code 315) 6

Plainville Farms Restaurant:

The Plainville Farms Restaurant is located "kitty corner" to the Ononoaga Flight School Airport, and less than 1/10 of a mile. This family style restaurant can easily be reached by just walking from where you tie your plane down. They are open 11 a.m. to 9 p.m. 7 days a week except on Christmas. This establishment raises their own turkeys, and specialize in all kinds of turkey dishes. Their famous roast turkey dinners include soup and salad bar for only $7.50, along with selections like Turkey Teriyaki, Turkey Almandine, turkey sandwiches, turkey melts, fried haddock, 14 ounce T-bone steaks, center cut pork chops, fried scallops and shrimp, homemade desserts, cream pies, Sundays and much much more. They also feature a daily buffet from 11 a.m. to 3 p.m. for only $6.95 and a Sunday buffet from 11 a.m. to 8 p.m. as well. The restaurant can seat up to 190 persons. There are two separate dining rooms decorated in a colonial style with wood and pine furniture, antiques, hand paintings, murals, and pewter chandeliers. This is a very popular restaurant to many of the local people as well as a great place to plan your next party or meeting. There is even a deli and store adjacent to the restaurant which sells all kinds of freshly sliced meats and turkey products. For more information, call the Plainville Farms Restaurant at 699-3852.

Restaurants Near Airport:
Plainville Farms Restaurant Adj Arpt Phone: 699-3852

Lodging: Sundown Motel (1 mile) 699-7283.

Meeting Rooms: Plainville Farms Restaurant 699-3852.

Transportation: Taxi Service: North Area 454-4259

Information: Syracuse Convention & Visitors Bureau, Greater Syracuse Chamber of Commerce, 572 South Salina Street, Syracuse, NY 13202, Phone: 470-1800

10
2500 x 30
28

Airport Information:

CICERO - MICHAEL FIELD (NY10)
00 miles northwest of town N43-10.90 W76-07.67 Elev: 400 Fuel: 80, 100LL
Rwy 10-28: 2500x60 (Asph) Attended: daylight hours Unicom: 122.8
Notes: landing fee reported,
FBO: Onondaga Aviation Phone: 699-5811

NY-DSV - DANSVILLE DANSVILLE MUNICIPAL

(Area Code 716) 7

Buckhorn Family Restaurant:

This restaurant is within walking distance from the Dansville Municipal Airport. You can see it from the main fixed base operator aircraft parking ramp. The Buckhorn is a family restaurant that is open 24 hours each day. Specialty items on their menu include baby back ribs, beef tip platters, weekend breakfast and hot buffet plus a salad bar. They also have a large assortment of sandwiches, soups and homemade pies and desserts. Their breakfast bar runs $4.50 every day. Between 12 p.m. and 10 p.m. they serve a hot buffet for only $5.99. Average prices on their menu are around $4.50 for breakfast and lunch. They have a BBQ rib special (large slab) for only $9.99. If you're watching your weight, enjoy items off their "Light Menu." The Buckhorn Family Restaurant was remodeled in April of 1995. A glass hall atrium was constructed. Oak, glass and brass trim decorate the interior. This restaurant can seat approximately 140 people. Large or small groups can also easily be accommodated. Catered meals can be prepared with advance notice. In addition to the restaurant there is also a Travel Ports of America lodging facility located on the same property. For information about Buckhorn Family Restaurant call 335-6023.

Restaurants Near Airport:

Buckhorn	Adj Arpt.	Phone: 335-6023
Burger King	Adj. Arpt.	Phone: N/A
McDonalds	Adj. Arpt.	Phone: N/A

Lodging: Travel Ports of America (Adj. Arpt.) 335-6023; Dor-Le Modern 1 mi 335-3220; Midtown Motor Lodge 2 mi 335-2259.

Meeting Rooms: None reported

Transportation: Dansville Chrysler Plymouth 335-2227; Taxi service: Bob's 607-335-5223.

Information: Finger Lakes Convention & Visitors Bureau, 904-E. Shore Drive, Ithaca, NY 14850, Phone: 800-284-8422. (US & Canada).

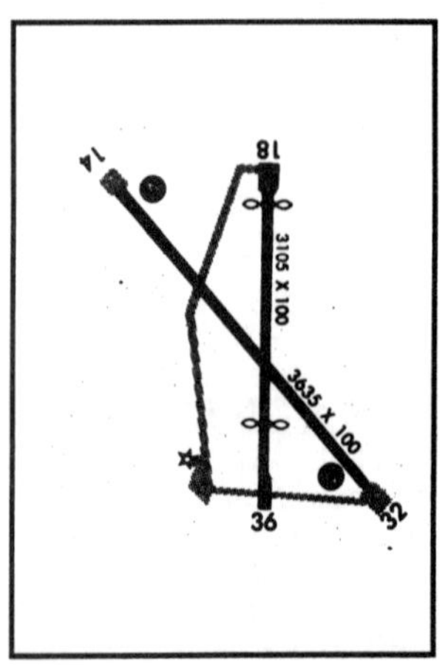

Airport Information:

DANSVILLE - DANSVILLE MUNICIPAL (DSV)
1 mi northwest of town N42-34.25 W77-42.78 Elev: 662 Fuel: 100LL, Jet-A Rwy 14-32: H3635x100 (Asph) Rwy 18-36: H3105x100 (Asph) Attended: 1300Z-dark Unicom: 123.0
Notes: Extensive glider activity.
FBO: Sterling Airways, Inc. Phone: 335-2076

NY-NK03 - DURHAMVILLE KAMP AIRPORT

(Area Code 315) 8

Suzie's Kitchen:

Suzie's Kitchen is located right at the fixed base operator on the Kamp Airport. This snack bar is open from 9 a.m. to 6 p.m. 7 days a week. Items on their menu include French toast, egg dishes, pancakes, English muffins, cheeseburgers, hamburgers, tuna fish sandwiches, hot dogs, chicken patties, fried fish, pizza and French fries. Average prices run $2.00 for breakfast, and $2.75 for lunch and dinner. The restaurant can seat about 17 persons with 8 stools at the counter and three tables. Guests can also enjoy a meal while watching the aircraft on the field. This establishment often features delicious pancake breakfasts throughout the year within their hangar. Seating for up to 150 and 250 is not uncommon. In-flight catering is also one of their specialties. For more information about Suzie's Kitchen call 363-1980.

Restaurants Near Airport:
Suzie's Kitchen At FBO Phone: 363-1980

Lodging: Verona Motel (3 miles) 363-2258.

Meeting Rooms: Meeting room accommodations are available on airport, that can seat approx 10 people. For information call the Kamp Air Aviation, Inc. at 363-1980.

Transportation: Airport courtesy car and rental cars can be obtained by calling Kamp Air Aviation, Inc. at 363-1980.

Information: Oneida Camber of Commerce, 160 Madison Street, Oneida, NY 13421, Phone: 315-363-4300

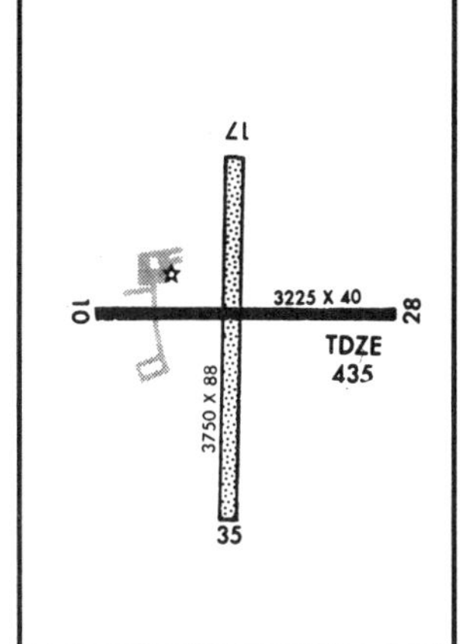

Attractions:

Brandy Brook Golf Course (9 hole course, 1/2 mile) 363-9879; Verona State Beach & Park (5 miles); Sylvan Beach Amusement Park (7 miles).

Airport Information:

DURHAMVILLE - KAMP AIRPORT (NK03)
2 mi north of town N43-08.08 W75-38.93 Elev: 443 Fuel: 100LL, MOGAS
Rwy 17-35: 3750x88 (Turf) Rwy 10-28: H3225x40 (Asph) Attended: daylight hours
Unicom: 122.8 Notes: Overnight parking $3.00; 100LL Avgas, 87 Auto Fuel available, Full Aircraft maintenance, avionics sales & service as well as other services on field.
FBO: Kamp Air Aviation, Inc. Phone: 363-1980

NY-4NY7 - EAST MORICHES LUFKER AIRPORT

(Area Code 516) 9

Dominick's Ribbs & Steak House:

This combination family style and fine dining facility is located across the street from the Lufker Airport on Long Island, New York. They are open Wednesday through Sunday for lunch and dinner. Specialties include items like their barbequed ribs, steaks, chicken, steak feheta's, Porter House steaks, home made smoked sausage, burgers, fried chicken, turkey clubs, homemade desserts, cakes, pies and much much more. Average prices run $3.95 for lunch and between $8.95 and $15.95 for dinner. The main dining room can accommodate up to 65 persons, and displays a cozy atmosphere with a great deal of oak wood, booths and tables, carpeted floors, art work on the walls and a view of the activity across the street on the airport. According to the restaurant personnel, there is quite a lot of parachuting that takes place at the airport. Guests can see this activity if sitting along the front windows. All items from their entire menu can be prepared for carry-out. In flight catering may also be available. Show them your pilots licence and get 10% taken off your meal ticket. For more information, call 878-6464.

Restaurants Near Airport:
Dominick's Ribbs & Steak Hse. Adj Arpt. Phone: 878-6464

Lodging: Riverhead Holiday Inn 369-2200; Riverhead Motor Lodge (10 miles) 727-7800.

Meeting Rooms: None Reported

Transportation: None Reported

Information: Long Island Tourism & Convention Commission, Nassau Coliseum, 1255 Hempstead Tpke, Uniondale, Long Island 11553-1200, Phone: 800-441-4601.

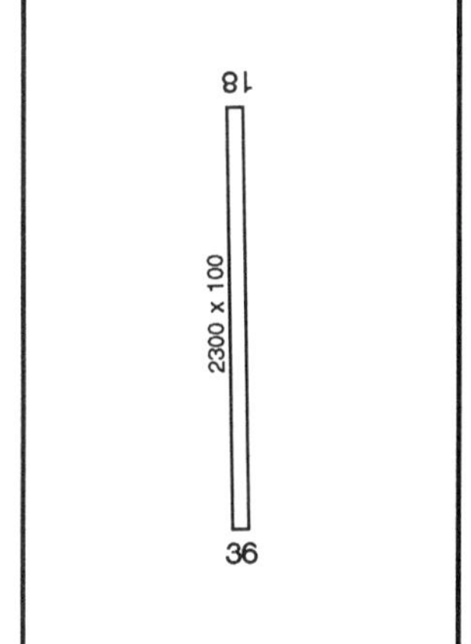

Airport Information:

EAST MORICHES - LUFKER AIRPORT (4NY7)
1 mi northeast of town N40-49.49 W72-45.06 Elev: 57 Rwy N-S: 2300x100 (Turf)
Attended: unattended CTAF: 122.9
FBO: Precision Machine Components, Inc. Phone: 878-6302

NY-ELM - ELMIRA
ELMIRA/CORNING REGIONAL

(Area Code 607) 10

Jennifer's Restaurant:

Jennifer's Restaurant is located within the terminal building at the Elmira Corning Region Airport. This combination family style and fine dining establishment is open Sunday through Friday from 6 a.m. to 8 p.m. and Saturday from 6 a.m. to 3 p.m. Their menu includes taco salads, 5 different varieties of croissant sandwiches served hot or cold, pita bread sandwiches, Greek dishes, New York strip steak, baked lasagna and many other items. In fact, over 80 selections of entrees are available from their menu. On Friday nights they also feature a fish fry (All you can eat) for only $6.25. Average prices run $3.75 to $4.25 for breakfast, $4.25 to $5.75 for lunch and $6.95 to $12.95 for most dinner choices. There are two separate main dining rooms that can seat 150 persons. Guests can watch the activity on the airport while enjoying their meal. Fly-in groups are welcome as well as parties and business gatherings. In-flight catering can also be arranged. For more information about Jennifer's Restaurant, call 739-3760.

Restaurants Near Airport:
Jennifer's Restaurant On Site Phone: 739-3760

Lodging: Corning Hilton (6 miles) 962-5000; Holiday Inn (6 miles) 739-3681; Howard Johnsons (6 miles) 739-5636.

Meeting Rooms: None Reported

Transportation: Taxi Service: Bills Raker's Totem 734-6161; Rental Cars: Avis 739-5689; Hertz 739-3803; National 739-7300.

Information: Chemung County Chamber of Commerce, 215 East Church Street, Elmira, NY 14901, Phone: 734-5137.

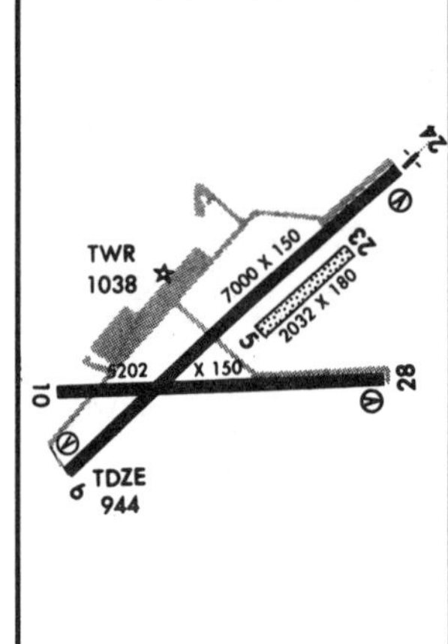

Airport Information:

ELMIRA - ELMIRA/CORNING REGIONAL AIRPORT (ELM)
6 mi northwest of town N42-09.60 W76-53.49 Elev: 955 Fuel: 100LL, Jet-A
Rwy 06-24: H7000x150 (Asph-Grvd) Rwy 10-28: H5202x150 (Asph-Grvd)
Attended: continuously Atis: 109.65 Unicom: 122.95 Elmira App/Dep Con: 118.15, 119.45
Elmira Tower: 121.1 Gnd Con: 121.9
FBO: Elmira Aeronautical Corp. Phone: 739-3597

NY-FRG - FARMINGDALE
REPUBLIC AIRPORT

(Area Code 516) 11

56th Fighter Group:

The 56th Fighter Group is a unique restaurant which is located adjacent to the main terminal building at the Republic Airport on Long Island, New York. This restaurant is open 7 days a week from 11 a.m. to 3 p.m. for lunch during weekdays, and from 4 p.m. to 12 a.m. on weekends. Their menu includes items like farm house chicken, chicken stir-fry, steak and Shrimp Scampi, filet mignon, Seafood Imperial and Broiled Shrimp Brochette. Average dinner prices range between $12.95 and $19.95 for most selections. They also feature a Sunday brunch from 10 a.m. to 3 p.m. This facility can accommodate between 500 and 700 dining guests and provides a unique atmosphere with an aviation theme, displaying numerous WW-II memorabilia along with pictures, antiques and various other items. There are also several separate dining areas within the restaurant allowing ample space for groups and parties. Reservations for larger groups are advised however. For more information about the 56th Fighter Group restaurant call their establishment at 694-8280.

Restaurants Near Airport:
56th Fighter Group Adj Terml. Phone: 694-8280

Lodging: Bar Harbor (3 miles) 541-2000; Heritage Motor Inn (5 miles) 921-6900; Holiday Inn (5 miles) 347-7400; Howard Johnson Plaza Hotel (5 miles) 394-9100; Huntington Hilton (2 miles) 845-1000; Sheraton Inn (8 miles) 231-1100.
Meeting Rooms: Holiday Inn (5 miles) 347-7400; Howard Johnson Plaza Hotel (5 miles) 394-9100.
Transportation: Taxi: Green and White 249-1212; Summit Limousine 756-2545; Also Rental Cars: Budget 420-0270, 752-1776.
Information: Long Island Tourism & Convention Commission, Nassau Coliseum, 1255 Hempstead Tpke, Uniondale, Long Island 11553-1200, Phone: 800-441-4601.

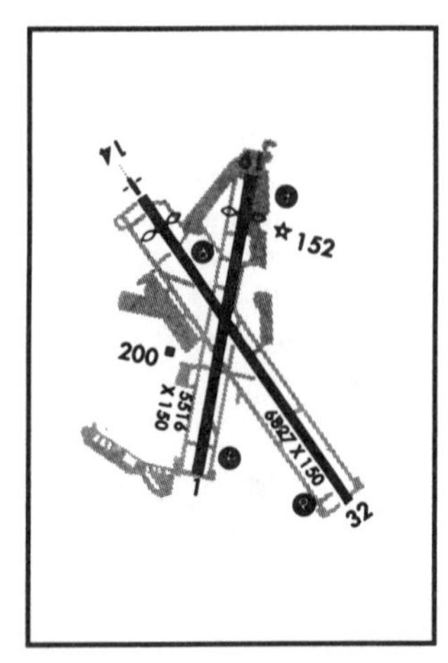

Airport Information:

FARMINGDALE - REPUBLIC AIRPORT (FRG)
1 mi east of town N40-43.73 W73-24.81 Elev: 81 Fuel: 100LL, Jet-A
Rwy 14-32: H6827x150 (Asph) Rwy 01-19: H5516x150 (Asph) Attended: continuously
Atis: 126.65 Unicom: 122.95 Tower: 118.8, 125.2 Gnd Con: 121.6 Clnc Del: 128.25
Notes: Numerous flocks of geese and other birds on and in vicinity of airport. Also refer to current Airport Facility Directory for more information.
FBO: Million Air Farmingdale Phone: 752-9022

NY-GFL - GLENS FALLS WARREN COUNTY AIRPORT

12

(Area Code 518)

Restaurants Near Airport:

Georgian Supper Club	12 mi NW	Phone: 668-5401
Howard Johnsons	2 mi SW	Phone: 793-4415
The Bavarian House	14 mi NE	Phone: 668-2476
Twichell's Coffee Shop	On Site	Phone: 793-6359

Lodging: Alpenhaus Motel (4 miles, Free trans) 792-6941; Howard Johnsons (2 miles) 793-4415; Landmark Motel (Free trans) 793-3441 or 800-453-4511 outside NY.
Meeting Rooms: Howard Johnson 793-4173; Landmark Motel 793-3441.
Transportation: Taxi Service: County 793-9601; Tri County Cab Inc. 793-4646; Also Rental Cars: Avis 792-4779; Hertz 792-8525;
Information: Adirondack Regional Chamber of Commerce, 136 Warren Street, Glens Falls, NY 12801, Phone: 798-1761.

Twichell's Coffee Shoppe":

Tessie Twichell's Coffee Shoppe is located right on the Warren County Airport, and is open 7 days a week from 8 a.m. to 2 p.m. Pilots can park their aircraft near the port area and walk only a few steps to the airport flight building. This restaurant serves breakfast and lunch and has for many years been a favorite stopping place for many local as well as transient pilots. Their menu offers a variety of homemade entrees including their delicious soups, chef's salads, and sandwiches, in addition to breakfast dishes like, 3 egg omelettes, pancakes, and French toast, served with ham, bacon or sausage. They also provide specials throughout the entire week, like macaroni and cheese casseroles as well as goulash dishes etc. Average prices for breakfast run $2.75. Prices for lunch can vary from day to day. The atmosphere of this restaurant is very cheerful and friendly, with lots of "hangar flying" and good conversation. Tessie "Twichell's Coffee Shoppe" is frequently visited by aviation groups and fly-in parties along with customers that stop in during the air show season. They also cater to local or enroute charter flights as well as private and corporate operations, serving light fare such as cold sandwich and coffee. Other items from their menu are also available. However, they would like a days notice if possible to prepare special trays. For more information call the restaurant at 793-6359.

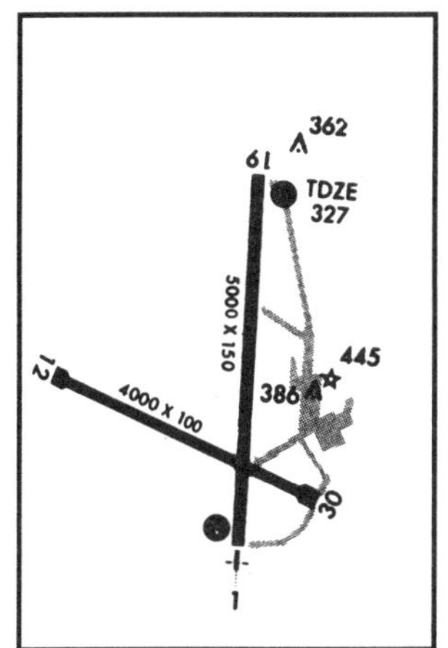

Airport Information:

GLENS FALLS - WARREN COUNTY AIRPORT (GFL)
3 mi northeast of town N43-20.47 W73-36.62 Elev: 328 Fuel: 100LL, Jet-A
Rwy 01-19: H5000x150 (Asph-Grvd) Rwy 12-30: H4000x100 (Asph) Attended: 1300-0100Z
Unicom: 123.0 Public Phone 24hrs Notes: Overnight parking (Singles) $5.00, (Twins) $7.00
FBO: Glen Falls Flight Center **Phone: 793-5605**

NY-92G - GORHAM MIDLAKES AIRPORT

(Area Code 716) 13, 14

Kamp in the Woods:

Kamp In The Woods, is located 1/4th mile from the Midlakes Airport. According to the restaurant management, you can taxi across the road right up to the camp grounds or walk 1/4 mile to their establishment. The restaurant has irregular hours. Fly-in guests should call ahead for information and reservations. The management has featured fly-in breakfasts on many occasions. They usually advertise by mailing out fliers to repeat guests. Should you be interested in finding out when their next social event is scheduled, call them and let them send you information. This facility contains a restaurant, camp ground and antique museum all located in the woods, with very pretty surroundings within the Finger Lakes Region. For more information call them at 554-6996.

Thendara:

Thendara Restaurant provides courtesy transportation to fly-in guests. Located about 2 miles from the Midlakes Airport. This facility offers two separate dining establishments, one of which is a fine dining restaurant. The main dining restaurant is open between 5 p.m. and 10 p.m. and on Sunday from 4 p.m. to 8 p.m. Items on their menu include prime rib, whole nut chicken, Jambalaya, shrimp in the grass, lobster, and fresh seafood specials served every day. Average prices range from $11.95 to $18.95 for most dinner selections. The main dining room is located within a 1906 Victorian building. Accommodations for 192 guests can be arranged in addition to meeting rooms available for business purposes, or social occasions. The second restaurant is called the "Boat House." This facility is situated about 200 feet from the main restaurant along the water's edge. In addition to dining, this establishment also contains 5 quaint rooms in the main cottage for overnight guests. For more information about dining, lodging and available accommodations, call Thendara's at 394-4868.

Restaurants Near Airport:

Kamp in the Woods	1/4 mi	Phone: 554-6996
Thendara	2 mi	Phone: 394-4868

Lodging: Econolodge (5 miles) 394-9000; Sheraton (6 miles) 394-7800; Thendara (2 miles, Free pick-up service) 394-4868.

Meeting Rooms: Thendara (2 miles, Free pick-up service) 394-4868.

Transportation: Taxi Service: Canandaigua Cab Company 394-1378; Also Thendara provides fly-in guests with courtesy transportation, 394-4868.

Information: Geneva Chamber of Commerce, One Lakeside Drive, Box 587, Geneva, NY 14456, Phone: 315-789-1776 or State Department of Economic Development, Division of Tourism, One Commerce Plaza, Albany, NY 12245, Phone: 518-474-4116 or 800-CALL NYS.

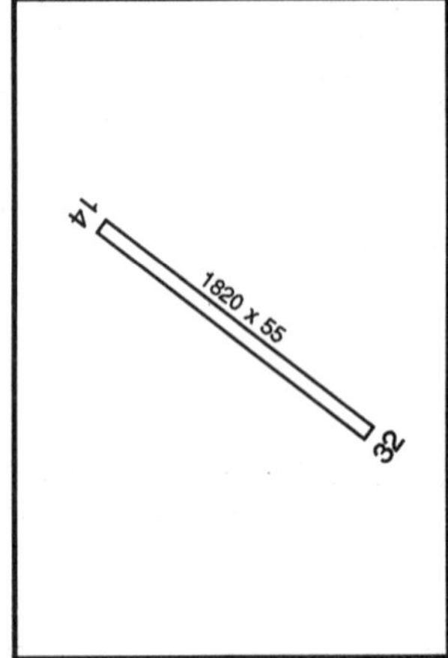

Airport Information:

GORHAM - MIDLAKES AIRPORT (92G)
3 mi west of town N42-48.75 W77-12.23 Elev: 1080 Rwy 14-32: 1820x55 (Turf)
Attended: irregularly Unicom: 122.8
Midlakes Airport Phone: 554-4168

NY-N56 - GREAT VALLEY
GREAT VALLEY AIRPORT

(Area Code 716) 15

Eddy's Restaurant:

Eddy's Restaurant is located about 100 yards east and across the street from the Great Valley Airport. Fly-in guests can easily walk to the restaurant from the aircraft parking ramp. According to customers, Eddy's Restaurant serves great home cooking, famous chicken wings, pizza and Friday fish fries featured along with their salad bar. Eddy's Restaurant is a family restaurant with a modern decor and able to accommodate up to 80 persons in their dining room. Their hours are from 6 :30 a.m. to 11 p.m. 7 days a week. They have a full menu with average prices running between $3.00 and $5.00 for most meals. Groups are welcome. For information you can call Eddy's at 945-5106.

Restaurants Near Airport:
Eddy's Restaurant 100 yds E. Phone: 945-5106

Lodging: Holiday Valley Motel 4 mi. 699-2336

Transportation: Rental cars: Valley Motors 945-5106

Meeting Rooms: For information call airport manager 945-5106.

Information: Olean Chamber of Commerce, 120 N. Union Street, Olean, NY 14760, Phone: 372-4433. (13 mi. S.W. of Great Valley.)

Attractions:

Holiday Valley Ski Resort and Golf Course 4 mi northwest of airport 699-2644. Allegany State Park 7 miles Southwest.

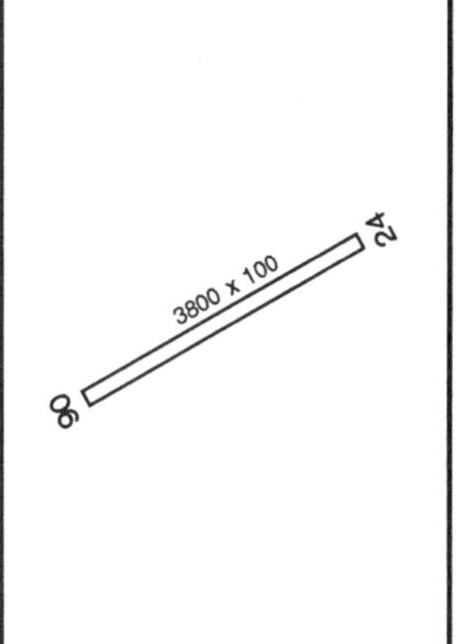

Airport Information:

GREAT VALLEY - GREAT VALLEY AIRPORT (N56)
1 mi southeast of town N42-12.30 W78-38.84 Elev: 1450 Rwy 06-24: 3800x100 (Turf) Attended: dalight hours. CTAF: 122.9 Notes: During winter months call 945-5106 for runway conditions.
FBO: Great Valley Phone: 945-5106

NY-NY25 - GREENVILLE
RAINBOW AIRPORT

(Area Code 518) 16

Rainbow Golf Club:

The Rainbow Golf Club is located right off the fairway about 300 yards from the runway. This fly-in golf club and resort contains a 18 hole U.S.G.A. certified course with sports bar, 6 lodging units with full kitchens, and a restaurant that is open from 7 a.m. to 9:30 p.m. or until the last customer is served. The restaurant offers specialties like their famous Big Mississippi burger, steaks, chicken sandwiches, soups, salads, and all types of special entrees offered each day. Average prices run between $2.35 to $3.25 for breakfast, $2.60 to $4.50 for lunch and around $7.95 for dinner. The main dining room can accommodate 60 people with additional seating for up to as many as 110 persons. The sports bar and restaurant features a rustic decor with fire place, pool table, and a view overlooking the golf course. Fly-in groups are welcome. Special golf packages are also available for overnight guests. For more information call the Rainbow Golf Club at 966-5343.

Restaurants Near Airport:
Rainbow Golf Club 300 yds Phone: 966-5343

Lodging: Rainbow Golf Club & Resort (Adj Arpt) 966-5343.

Meeting Rooms: Accommodations for casual meetings and group parties can be arranged at restaurant, 966-5343.

Transportation: Rainbow Golf Club is located within walking distance form airport. Courtesy pick up service is also available during certain times of the year by calling the resort, 966-5343.

Information: Yonkers Chamber of Commerce, 540 Nepperham Ave, Yonkers, NY 10701, Phone: 914-963-0332; or State Department of Economic Development, Division of Tourism, One Commerce Plaza, Albany, NY 12245, Phone: 518-474-4116 or 800-CALL NYS.

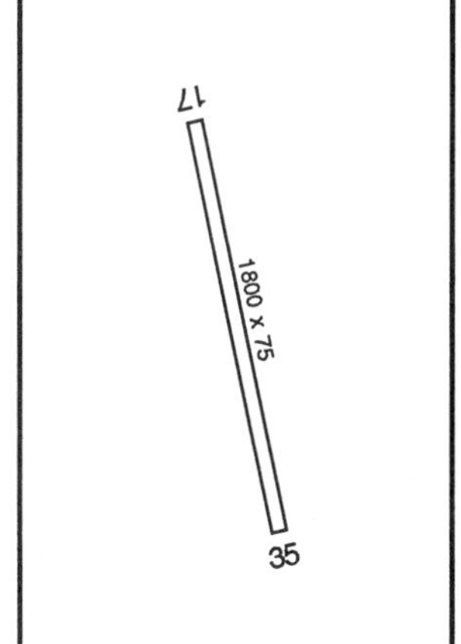

Airport Information:

GREENVILLE - RAINBOW AIRPORT (NY25)
1 mi east of town N42-25.00 W74-00.97 Elev: 840 Rwy 17-35: 1800x75 (Turf) Attended: May-November daylight hours Unicom: 122.8 Notes: Prior permission from November 15 to May 15.
Greenville-Rainbow Airport Phone: 966-5343

Glenn H. Curtiss Museum

The Glenn H. Curtiss Museum of Local History was formally dedicated on May 18th, 1963 with the assistance of many dignitaries and aviation pioneers in attendance. The collection of aircraft and aviation memorabilia soon began to grow. Today this museum contains aircraft on display like the June Bug II, 1912 Curtiss Model D Pusher (Replica), 1918 Curtiss JN-4 Jenny (Fuselage), 1919 Curtiss Robin, 1929 Mercury Chic, 1931 Mercury S-1 (Racer), and the 1949 Ohm Special (Racer).

Their collections also contain several engines dating from 1904 to the 1980's. Included in the aeronautical collection are radios, instruments, flight clothing and many other aviation related items. Another display features Glenn H. Curtiss's involvement with motorcycles. On exhibit are examples of Curtiss motorcycles and motorcycle engines. A 1904 Orient buckboard may also be seen along with numerous displays of local historic interest from vehicles and farm equipment to ladies fashions, China dolls and quilts.

The Curtiss Museum Library and Archives houses one of the foremost Curtiss photo collections encompassing many Curtiss subjects. Included in the library and archives are over 2,000 books, 60 linear feet of periodicals, over 10,000 images, scrapbooks, oral history cassettes, as well as over 150 engine and airplane manuals and catalogs. The library and archives are open to researchers by appointment.

A Curtiss JN-4 "Jenny" on display at the Curtiss Museum in Hammondsport, NY. The Curtiss Jenny was a training plane used during world War I. Photo: by Mike Wakefield; Glenn H. Curtiss Museum

Admission is free to all members. Hours of operation, fee schedule, special group rates and tours are available by writing or phoning the museum at 607-569-2160.

The Penn Yan Airport is the nearest public use airfield to the museum situated about 20 miles to the northeast of the town of Hammondsport. Rental cars can be obtained through Keuka Motors by calling 536-8876. For information about Penn Yan airport call 315-536-4471. (Article submitted in part by the Glenn H. Curtiss Museum).

David R. Fox piloting the "June Bug II" at Hammondsport, NY June 1976. This is a reproduction of Glenn H. Curtiss 1st aeroplane. Photo: by Mike Mandiam

NY-1B1 - HUDSON
COLUMBIA COUNTY AIRPORT

(Area Code 518)

17, 18

Kozel's Restaurant:

Kozel's Restaurant is located at the south side of the Columbia County Airport. You can call the restaurant and they will come and pick you up. This fine dining facility is open Wednesday through Monday from 11 a.m. until they decide to close in the evening. Specialties of the house include steaks, prime rib, fresh seafood, fresh roasted turkey. Luncheon and dinner specials are also offered daily. Average prices run $4.00 and up for lunch and $8.95 and up for dinner. On Sunday they offer a dinner special for only $8.95 including fresh seafood and lobster. Catering and arranging banquets for up to 350 people has been their specialty for 35 years. Meals-to-go are also available for pilots and their passengers. The Kozel's Restaurant has been operated by the family for 3 generations. On some Sunday afternoons they have entertainment with country dancing and/or ballroom dancing. For information call the restaurant at 828-3326.

Meadowgreen Restaurant and Golf Course:

The Meadowgreen Restaurant is situated on the north end of the Columbia County Airport about 1/4th mile or less off the end of the runway. To reach this restaurant, many people park their airplanes at the end of the taxiway and walk about 200 feet to the restaurant. According to the restaurant ,you can call from the main building and they will come over and pick you up by car, however his may not be necessary as most people are easily able to walk the short distance. This family style restaurant is open at 7 a.m. during the golf season and 9 a.m. during the winter season. Their Sunday brunch and buffets start at 11:30 to 3 p.m. Specialties of the house include appetizers, desserts, pastries, salads, and home made soups. Their menu also contains many other selections. Prices average about $3.00 for breakfast, $4.00 for lunch and $8.00 for dinner. The view from the restaurant enables guests to look out over the airport and their 9 hole public golf course. Banquets can easily be arranged for up to 300 persons. Carry out meals can also be prepared. For more information call the restaurant at 828-0663.

Attractions:

Meadowgreens 9 hole public golf course is located within a very short distance from the Columbia County Airport. For information contact the Meadowgreen Restaurant at 828-0663.

Restaurants Near Airport:

Kozel's Restaurant	1 mi	Phone: 828-3326
Meadowgreens	1/2 mi	Phone: 828-0663

Lodging: St. Charles Best Western (5 miles) 828-4165

Meeting Rooms: Both Meadowgreen (1/2 mile) 828-0663; and Kozel's (1 mile) have overnight accommodations.

Transportation: Medowgreens within walking distance (200 feet from end of runway); Kozel's Restaurant will provide free transportation to and from the airport for their guests. Also: Howard's Taxi 828-7673; Star City Taxi 828-3355; C & G Car Rental 828-2289; Fairview Lincoln/Mercury 828-0310.

Information: Columbia County Department of Tourism and Promotion, 401 State Street, Hudson, NY 12534, Phone: 828-3375 or 800-724-1846.

Airport Information:

HUDSON - COLUMBIA COUNTY AIRPORT (1B1)

4 northeast of town   N42-17.48 W73-4262   Elev: 197   Fuel: 100, Jet-A1+

Rwy 03-21: H5350x75 (Asph)   Attended: 1200-0200Z   Unicom: 122.8   Public Phone 24hrs

Notes: No landing fee's, $5.00 overnight parking fee.

FBO: Richmor Aviation, Inc. Phone: 828-9461

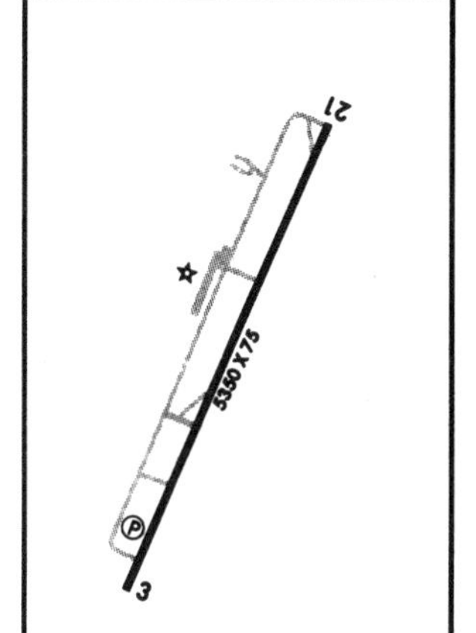

NY-ISP - ISLIP
LONG ISLAND MAC ARTHUR

(Area Code 516)

19, 20

CA1 Services:

CA1 Services manages a lounge located on the Islip/ Ronkonkoma, Long Island Mac Arthur Airport. The operators of the establishment plan to open a restaurant facility in conjunction with the lounge. Hot menu items are currently available, however they are hoping to expand their menu selection depending on future circumstances. Their lounge overlooks the runway allowing a nice view of the activity on the field. For information about this facility call 981-0271.

Seasons Restaurant Holiday Inn:

"An intimate, romantic, spacious and unhurried atmosphere in our hotel, Seasons Restaurant: is a gastronome's delight where hearty breakfast, light lunches and evening feasts share equal billing. Superb gourmet fare is complimented by an equally delightful selection of vintage wines. Dine in a warm, casual environment besides a crackling fire. Our relaxing decor offers plush seating and polished brass railings. Seasons opens at 6:30 a.m. weekdays and 7:00 a.m. on weekends. Larger parties can be accommodated in the library section as well as other banquet facilities available on the property." General prices for meals run between $4.50 for breakfast, $7.85 for lunch and $12.00 for dinner. You can reach the restaurant by calling the Holiday Inn, and they will pick you up in their courtesy van. Or if driving, turn left when leaving the main gate at the airport and go about 3/4th of a mile to the Holiday Inn. Holiday Inn, Mac Arthur Airport Hotel also includes gift shops, car rental desk, exercise facilities, lounge, outdoor pool and VIP Wing all on their premises. For reservations and information, call 585-9500 Ext. 316.

Restaurants Near Airport:

CA1 Services	On Site	Phone: 981-0271
The Sayville Inn	5 mi	Phone: 564-0033
Season-Holiday Inn	1/2 mi	Phone: 585-9500

Lodging: Holiday Inn (1/2 mile) Phone: 585-9500

Transportation: Free transportation to and from the Seasons Restaurant at the Holiday Inn. Also rental cars are available: Avis, 588-6633; Budget, 588-1480; Hertz, 737-9203

Information: Long Island Tourism & Convention Commission, Nassau Coliseum, 1255 Hempstead Tpke, Uniondale, Long Island 11553-1200, Phone: 800-441-4601.

Airport Information:

ISLIP - LONG ISLAND MAC ARTHUR (ISP)
7 mi northeast from town N40-47.72 W73-06.01 Elev: 99 Fuel 100LL, Jet-A
Rwy 06-24: H7002x150 (Asph-Grvd) Rwy 15R-33L: H5186x150 (Asph-Grvd)
Rwy 10-28: H5036x150 (Asph) Rwy 15L-33R: H3212x75 (Asph)
Attended: 1100-0400Z Atis: 128.45 Unicom 122.95 Tower: 119.3 or 124.3
Gnd Con: 135.3 Clnc Del: 121.85

FBO: Garrett Aviation Serv. Phone: 486-3000
FBO: Long Island Jet Cntr. Phone: 588-0303
FBO: Metro Air Phone: 588-0037
FBO: Mid Island Air Serv. Phone: 588-5400
FBO: New York Jet Phone: 588-5400

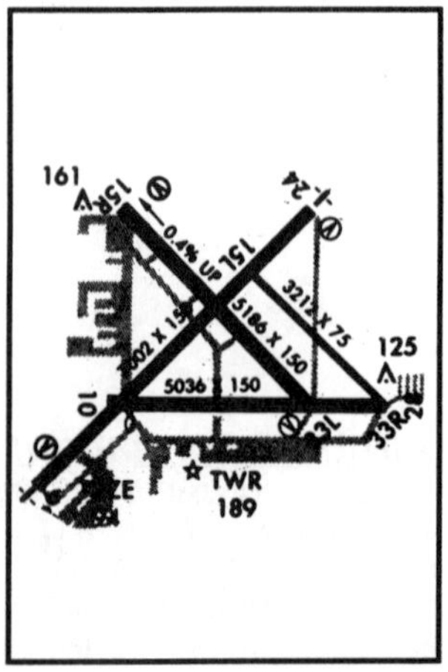

NY-ITH - ITHACA
TOMPKINS COUNTY AIRPORT

(Area Code 607)

21

The Landing Restaurant:

The Landing Restaurant is situated next to the passenger terminal at the Tompkins County Airport, and is well within walking distance from the aircraft parking area. This restaurant is open Monday through Saturday from 11 a.m. to 1 a.m. and serves a full menu until midnight. The decor of the restaurant offers a casual light and airy atmosphere with pictures of local attractions decorating the walls. Specialties of the house include a full menu selection, along with soups, burgers, salads, and buffalo wings. Daily lunch specials are offered as well as Friday night fried and broiled fish. Saturday nights they specialize in prime rib dinners. Average prices run $6.00 for lunch and $9.00 for dinner. This restaurant can accommodate fly-in groups or parties with a full menu to select from. For more information call the restaurant at 266-9783.

Restaurants Near Airport:
The Landing Rest. On Site Phone: 266-9783

Lodging: Sheraton Inn (2 miles) 257-2000; Holiday Inn (2 miles) 257-3100; Ramada Inn (6 miles, in town) 272-1000.

Meeting Rooms: Both the Sheraton and Holiday Inn have conference facilities. (See Lodging)

Transportation: Hertz 272-6622; Budget 257-1975; Ithaca Limo 273-3030.

Information: Ithaca/Tompkins County Convention & Visitors Bureau, 904 East Shore Drive, NY 14850, Phone: 272-1313 or 800-284-8422.

Attractions:

Picturesque Finger Lakes area as well as several State Parks are all within a 10 mile radius of the airport. Cayuga Lake along with steep sloping terrain and surrounding hills add to the beauty of this region.

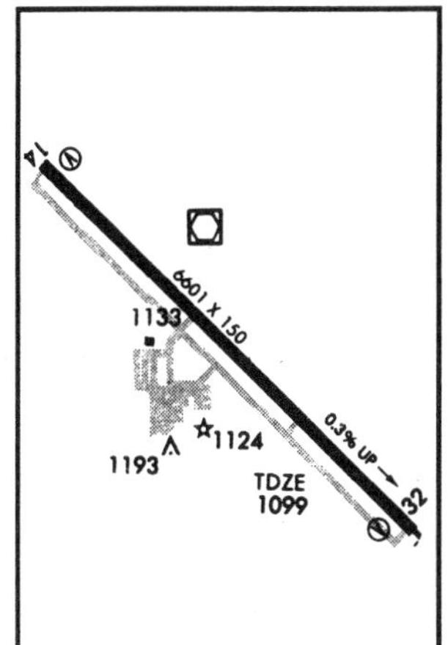

Airport Information:

ITHACA - TOMPKINS COUNTY AIRPORT (ITH)
3 mi northeast of town N42-29.46 W76-27.51 Elev: 1099 Fuel: 100LL, Jet-A
Rwy 14-32: H6601x150 (Asph-Grvd) Attended: 1100-0400Z Atis: 125.175 Unicom: 122.95
Ithaca Tower: 119.6 Gnd Con: 121.8 Public Phone: None Reported
Notes: Landing Fee: Single $2.00, Light Twin $4.00, Med Twins $5.00, Turbine $10.00-$30.00; Parking daily rate same as landing fee's.
FBO: Taughannock Aviation Phone: 257-1666, or 257-7500

NY-20N - KINGSTON
KINGSTON ULSTER AIRPORT

(Area Code 914)

22

Quick Stop (Convenient Store):

The Quick Stop Convenient Store is located about 500 yds north of the Kingston Ulster Airport on Route 32. This sandwich and take-out deli is open 7 days a week between 7 a.m. and 10 p.m. Their menu contain cold sandwiches, macaroni and potato salads, cold cuts, breakfast sandwiches, and hot sandwiches served mostly during the cold weather season. Average prices run $2.50 to $3.00 for most selections. This diner can accommodate up to 12 people in their dining area. Many of their customers order meals-to-go in addition to drinks, chips and groceries. According to the management, the airplanes take off right overhead. For more information about the Quick Stop Convenient Store call 336-8150.

Restaurants Near Airport:
Quick Stop 500 yds Phone: 336-8150

lodging: Costello Motor Court (2 miles) 338-5902; Holiday Inn (4 miles) 338-0400; Howard Johnson (3 miles) 338-4200; Ramada Inn 339-3900; Super 8 338-3076.

Meeting Rooms: Holiday Inn 338-0400; Howard Johnson 338-4200; Ramada Inn 339-3900.

Transportation: Taxi: Serve-All 336-6400; Rental Cars: Hertz (2 miles from airport) call airport manager for information 336-8400.

Information: Chamber of Commerce of Ulster County, 7 Albany Avenue, Kingston, NY 12401, Phone: 338-5100.

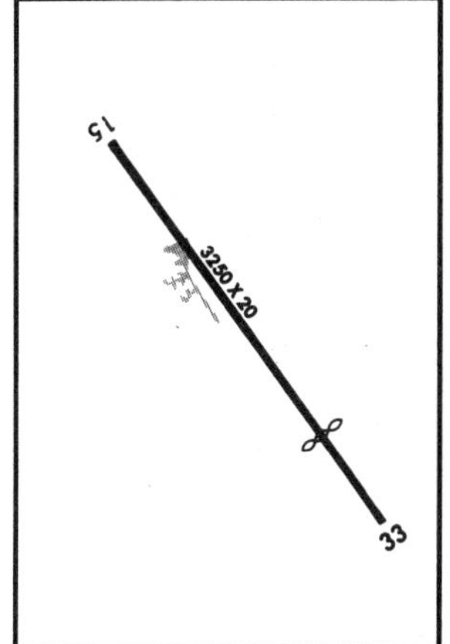

Airport Information:

KINGSTON - KINGSTON ULSTER AIRPORT (20N)
4 mi north of town N41-59.11 W73-57.84 Elev: 149 Fuel: 100LL Rwy 15-33: H3250x20 (Asph) Attended: 1300Z-dusk except Thanksgiving, Christmas and New Years
Unicom: 122.8
FBO: River Aviation Phone: 336-8400

NY-0G0 - LOCKPORT NORTH BUFFALO SUBURBAN

(Area Code 716) **23, 24, 25**

Best Of Pizza:

This restaurant is scheduled to open for business during the Spring of 1996. It will be a carry out establishment specializing in serving an assortment of pizzas as well as other items. It will be located in the terminal building with easy access for fly-in customers. For information about this facility call 625-8111.

The Inn Field:

The Inn Field is reported to be located near Peppino's Restaurant, about a 10 to 15 minute walk from the airport. It is on the same side of the street as the airport. This restaurant opens its doors in April, and displays a sports oriented decor. There is a baseball diamond out back of the restaurant, as well as a miniature golf course. For more information about this restaurant call the airport at 625-8111.

Peppino's:

Peppino's Restaurant is about a 10 or 15 minute walk, and across the street from the main parking ramp of the North Buffalo Suburban Airport. This restaurant serves a selection of contemporary dishes. It is reported to be open at 7:00 a.m. for breakfast and at least through the afternoon. For information you can call this establishment at 625-8203

Restaurants Near Airport:

Best Of Pizza	Trml. Bldg.	Arpt. Mgr. Phone: 625-8111
The Inn Field	1/4 mi.	Arpt. Mgr. Phone: 625-8111
Peppino's	1/4 mi	Phone: 625-8203

Lodging: Best Western Lockport Inn 3 mi 434-6151; Lockport Motel 3 mi. 434-5595.

Meeting Rooms: Best Western Lockport Inn 3 mi 434-6151.

Transportation: Auto Rentals: Bokman 625-8340; Gambino Ford 625-8181. Taxi service: Union 433-2222; Lockcity 433-3100.

Information: Lockport Chamber of Commerce, 151 W. Genessee Street., Lockport, NY 14094 Phone: 433-3828.

Attractions:

Niagara Falls is located within 15 miles from the North Buffalo Suburban Airport. Also Lake Ontario only 8 miles away offers a variety of outdoor watersport activities.

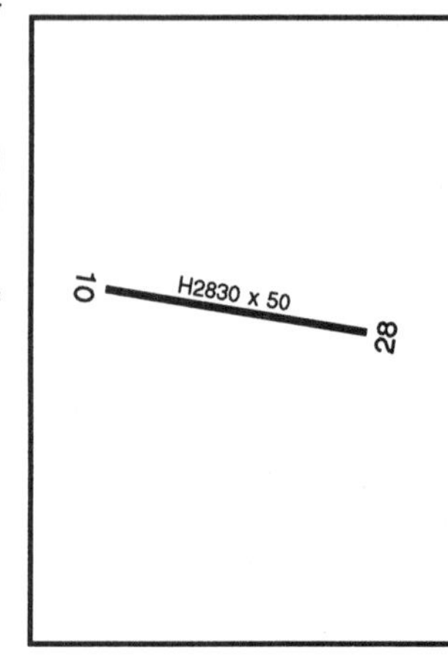

Airport Information:

LOCKPORT - NORTH BUFFALO SUBURBAN (0G0)
3 mi south of town N43-06.20 W78-42.20 Elev: 587 Fuel: 80, 100LL Rwy 10-28: H2830x50 (Asph) Attended: 1330Z-dusk Unicom: 123.0
FBO: Gary Leasing, Inc. Phone: 625-8111
FBO: Quaker Flying Service, Inc. Phone: 625-8111

NY-MAL - MALONE DUFORT AIRPORT

(Area Code 518) **26**

Jammers Fine Food & Spirits:

This fine dining facility is located about 4 miles east of the Malone Dufort Airport straight through the village of Malone and 1/2 mile from the city limits. Transportation can be provided if you phone the restaurant at 483-0711. They can seat 100 persons in the restaurant, and a small lounge is available for gathering. A festive atmosphere abounds within this facility, with entertainment and sing-along enjoyed by all. Jammers specializes in choice prime rib and fresh seafood, but one cannot forget the tantalizing veal and pasta dishes. Prices average $5.00 for lunch to $15.00 for dinner. They currently have a semi-private room to accommodate business meetings or parties for 20 to 35 people. The restaurant is open 11:30 a.m. to 9 p.m. weekdays, Saturday 4 p.m. to 10 p.m. and Sunday 4 p.m. to 9 p.m. (lounge opens at 4 p.m.) For more information call 483-0711.

Restaurants Near Airport:

Hotel Flanagan	2 mi E.	Phone: 483-1400
Jammers	4 mi E.	Phone: 483-0711

Lodging: Four Seasons Motel (1 mile) 483-3490; Econolodge (1 mile) 483-0500; Hotel Flanagan (2 miles) 483-1400.

Meeting Rooms: Jammers Restaurant would be happy to provide meeting accommodations for business or pleasure groups; Hotel Flanagan can also accommodate groups requesting meeting space, 483-1400.

Transportation: City Taxi 483-0798; S&S Rent-A-Car 483-1800; Also taxi service is available: Adirondack Taxi 483-7840; City Taxi 483-0798; North Country Taxi 483-6760; PDQ Taxi 483-8387.

Information: Malone Chamber of Commerce, 170 East Main Street, Malone, NY 12953, Phone: 483-3760.

Attractions:

Malone New York is located in the foot hills of the Adirondack mountains, and approximately 70 road miles from the Canadian border. This town contains a 36 hole public golf course (483-2926) located 4 miles from the Dufort Airport, and the Titus Mountain Ski Center (483-3740) only 8 miles away.

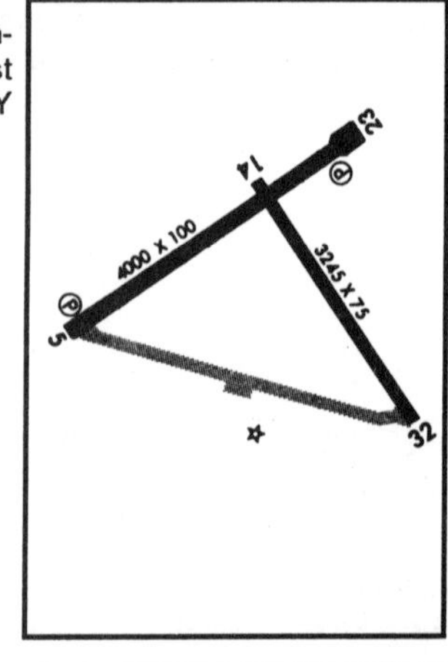

Airport Information:

MALONE - DUFORT AIRPORT (MAL)
2 mi west of town N44-51.22 W74-19.72 Elev: 786 Fuel: N/A Rwy 05-23: H4000x100 (Asph) Rwy 14-32: H3245x75 (Asph) Attended: Apr-Nov, Sat-Sun and Holidays Unicom: 122.8
Airport Manager Phone: 483-1860, 483-7442

NY-D79 - MAYVILLE DART AIRPORT

(Area Code 716)

27

The Great Escape Airport Restaurant And Museum:

The Great Escape Airport Museum and Restaurant is open weekends during the summer between 9 a.m. and 6 p.m., and by chance and/or appointment. A selection of antique airplanes, engines, propellers and memorabilia are on display. When visiting the restaurant or museum, guests can taxi up and park their aircraft right in front of this establishment. The restaurant provides daily specials, sandwiches and speciality ice creams. Breakfast items include eggs, omeletts, pancakes, French toast, breakfast sandwiches, bacon, sausage, home fries and toast. Lunch items include sandwiches like their Cuban, Hamburg, cheeseburgers, bacon cheeseburgers, hot dogs, patty melts, grilled cheese and grilled bacon & cheese sandwiches. Average prices run $2.00 to $3.50 for most items. The decor of the restaurant has an aviation theme with antique aviation items, pictures propellers and model aircraft. There is seating for about 40 people. Groups, aviation clubs and associations are all welcome. In addition to the restaurant and museum, this airport offers other amenities. Glider rides and flight instruction, over 50 "Old Time" aircraft based on the field, ultra light and glider meets, "Old Time" fly-in shows and even a flea market on certain weekends during the summer months. For information during the day call 753-2160.

Airport Information:

MAYVILLE - DART AIRPORT (D79)
2 mi east of town N42-16.09 W79-28.90 Elev: 1330 Rwy 13-31: 2750x50 (Turf)
Rwy 06-24: 1840x80 (Turf) Attended: daylight hours CTAF: 122.9
FBO: R.D. Aircraft, Co. Phone: 753-2160

Restaurants Near Airport:
Great Escape Arpt. Restaurant On Site Phone: 753-2160

Lodging: Snow Ridge Motel 3 mi 753-2712; Webs Captains Inn 4 mi 753-2161; Camping on the field.

Meeting Rooms: Restaurant & Museum can accommodate small groups, 753-2160.

Transportation: None reported

Information: For information you can call the airport at 753-2160.

Attractions:

A number of local attractions are available throughout this region. The town of Mayville is situated on the west edge of Greatsacandaga Lake. Steamboat rides, fishing, wineries, antique shops and more are all located within the area. For information you can call the airport at 753-2160.

NO AIRPORT DIAGRAM AVAILABLE

NY-44N - MILLBROOK SKY ACRES AIRPORT

(Area Code 914)

28

Kading's Windsock Cafe:

The Kading's Windsock Cafe is situated on the Sky Acres Airport. This cafe is open on weekends, only, from 8 a.m. to 4 p.m. This restaurant is owned by Mr. & Mrs. Henry and Anne Kading. They are both hard working individuals with backgrounds varying from Henry working at Central Hudson Gas & Electric for 33 years to owning his own farm and razing cattle, with a love for flying and owning his own Cessna Skyhawk, to Anne's background of 40 years as a registered nurse. Together they both decided to open the restaurant and love to prepare delicious meals for their customers. Their menu includes items like the "Early Departures" which list a variety of breakfast dishes. The "Slide Slip" section displays an assorted choice of muffins, bagels, home fries and other side dishes. The "Pre-Flights" list homemade soups and chili. Their "Cold Fronts and Basic Maneuver" selections list a variety of hamburgers which are famous throughout the area for being especially prepared with the freshest meat around. Other headings listed on their menu include "Magnetic Variations," "Final Checklists" and "Perfect Landings" with homemade pies, a favorite with many customers along with ice cream. Average prices run $3.50 for breakfast and $4.00 for lunch. The restaurant has 5 tables off the lounge area and booths and counter space located in a separate area. This is a non smoking establishment. Aircraft parking may be limited. For information call 677-8174.

Airport Information:

MILLBROOK - SKY ACRES (44N)
6 mi southwest of town N41-42.45 W73-44.28 Elev: 700 Fuel: 80, 100LL Rwy 17-35: H3828x60 (Asph) Attended: Mon-Fri 1430Z-dusk, Sat-Sun 1300Z-dusk Unicom: 122.8
FBO: HerGin Aviation, Inc. (Fuel) Phone: 677-5010
FBO: Styles Aviation, Inc. Phone: 677-8185

Restaurants Near Airport:
Kading Windsock Cafe On Site Phone: 677-8174

Lodging: Edison Motor Inn 7 mi 454-3080; LaGrange Motel 3 mi 635-2141.

Meeting Rooms: None reported

Transportation: Taxi Service: Hopewell 226-5773.

Information: Poughkeepsie Chamber of Commerce, 110 Main Street, Poughkeepsie, NY 12601. Phone: 914-454-1700.

Attractions:

James Baird State Park (Golf, Tennis and Hiking).

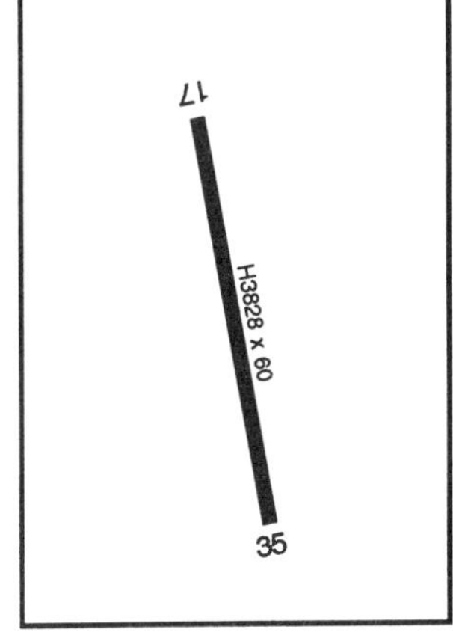

NY-MTP - MONTAUK
MONTAUK AIRPORT

(Area Code 516)

29, 30

Restaurants Near Airport:

Blue Moon	Adj.700'	Phone: 668-1105
Crows Nest	5 mi S.	Phone: 668-2077
Gossman's	7 mi	Phone: 668-5330

Crows Nest Restaurant:

The Crows Nest Restaurant and Inn is located about 5 miles south of the Montauk Airport. This restaurant and lodging establishment will provide courtesy transportation to and from the airport. This restaurant is famous for their delicious lobster and seafood dishes. The Crows Nest restaurant and lodging facility is situated right on Lake Montauk, and have their own private beach area. Unlike other restaurant establishments, the Crows Nest uses it own fishing boats to catch lobster, clams and various types of seafood, providing their customers with the freshest selections around. During our conversation with the owner we learned that this establishment has shark and fish tanks on display. The main dining room can seat approximately 120 people. They also have an outdoor clam bar which is very popular with guests. The view from the restaurant is beautiful looking out over the lake and private beach area. The restaurant hours are 12 p.m. to 12 a.m. Their adjacent motel has 14 units, which are well equipped and contain a jacuzzi in each unit. For larger groups and catering services a banquet area is able to accommodate around 1,000 people. Thanks to our contributor, we believe this establishment is well worth a visit, and one that you will enjoy revisiting time and time again. For information about dining or available lodging call the Crows Nest Restaurant at 668-2077, or their motel at 668-3700

Lodging: Club Montauk is located across the street from the airport. Phone: 668-3200. Also transportation provided by the following: Crows Nest Motel 5 mi south, 668-3700; Montauk Yacht Club Resort Marina, 668-3100; Ocean Beach, 668-4000; Royal Atlantic, 668-5103; Gurney's Inn Resort & Spa, 668-2345.

Meeting Rooms: Conference rooms and accommodations can be arranged at the Montauk Yacht Club Resort Marina, 668-3100 and Gurney's Inn Resort & Spa, 668-2345. Also contact the Chamber of Commerce at 668-2428.

Transportation: MTP Airport Management Corp. will provide courtesy transportation only on the airport premises. Taxi service can be obtained by calling Snowdens Taxi at 668-5511 or Balcuns Service at 668-3449 for rental cars.

Information: Montauk Chamber of Commerce, Montauk Hwy, Box CC, Montauk, L.I., NY 11954 or Phone: 668-2428.

Blue Moon Restaurant:

The Blue Moon Restaurant is located within 700 feet and across the street on the west side of the Montauk airport. This cafe features a Caribbean type decor with an outside patio and patio bar. Specialties of the house include items like their famous Blue Moon chicken or shrimp stir fry, broiled garlic shrimp, sirloin steak, linguini with fresh clams, Seafood Cioppino, lobster and shrimp or broccoli fettuccini. Daily specials feature "right off the boat" lobster, mako, salmon, sword and tuna fish. A wide variety of delicious appetizers, soups, salads and desserts are also available. Prices range from $7.00 for lunch and $12.00 for dinner. Restaurant hours are 12:00 noon for lunch and dinner served until 10 p.m. They can cater up to 125 persons on the premises. Meals prepared for pilots on-the-go can be arranged. For more information call 668-1105.

Photo by: Blue Moon Restaurant

The Blue Moon Restaurant is located across the street and reported only 700 feet from the Montauk Airport.

Attractions:

Montauk State Park is located at the eastern-most tip of Long Island. This park offers fishing, hiking, picnicking and biking. Museum tours, in addition to a lighthouse built in 1795, are some of the attractions, Phone: 668-2461; Hither Hills State Park to the west near Napeaque Bay, contains accommodations for camping (Mid-April through November), Phone: 668-2461; This area has golf courses, state parks, horse back riding and deep sea fishing. Contact the Montauk Chamber of Commerce, 668-2428 for more information. See "Information" listed above.

Airport Information:

MONTAUK - MONTAUK AIRPORT (MTP)

3 mi northeast of town N41-04.59 W71-55.25 Elev: 20 Rwy 06-24: H3480x85 (Asph)

Attended: April-October daylight hours, other times irregularly; Unicom: 122.7 Public phone 24 hrs

Notes: Landing Fee, Private aircraft, single $12, light twin $15, commercial aircraft call for rates. They have a courtesy van to the beach at the end of the runway plus dressing rooms and showers with plenty of hot water. Motel and restaurant located across the street from the airport on Lake Montauk.

FBO: MTP Airport Management Corp., Phone: 668-2233 or 3738

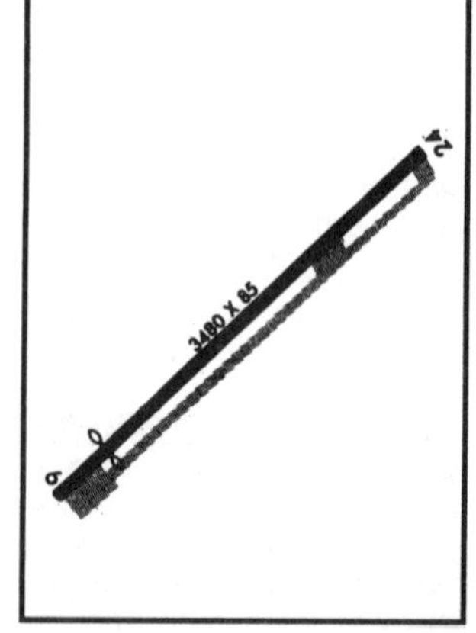

NY-MGJ - MONTGOMERY ORANGE COUNTY AIRPORT

(Area Code 914) 31

Orange County Airport Restaurant:

The Orange County Airport Restaurant is situated within the terminal building at the Orange County Airport. This family style restaurant is open between 8 a.m. and 6 p.m. 7 days a week. Their menu displays items like char-broiled hamburgers, several varieties of sandwiches, pizza, homemade desserts, and a full line of breakfast selections. They also feature daily breakfast and lunch specials. Guests can also view the airport while enjoying a meal. Seating for 50 persons is provide. There is a small pilot's shop located near the restaurant, where the flying public can buy various items of interest. During our conversation, we learned that the operators of this restaurant also cater to a great many fly-in customers as well as local organizations. In-flight catering is also available. For more information you can call this restaurant at 457-5030.

Restaurant Near Airport:

Copperfield's Restaurant	1 mi	Phone: N/A
Crossroads Restaurant	3 mi	Phone: N/A
Orange County Arpt. Rest.	On Site	Phone: 457-5030

Lodging: Holiday Inn (8 miles) Newburgh 565-2100, Middletown 343-1474; Howard Johnson (6 miles) Middletown 342-5822, Newburg 564-4000; Super Eight Motel (3 miles) Montgomery 457-3143.

Meeting Rooms: None Reported

Transportation: Middletown Cab Company 343-1181; Mills Limousine 457-5000; Walden B & D 778-7143; Also Rental Cars: Avis 343-0701; Budget 344-1922; Hertz 800-654-3131.

Information: Eastern Orange County Chamber of Commerce, 47 Grand Street, Newburgh, NY 12550, Phone: 562-5100 or Tourist Information Center, Phone: 567-1467.

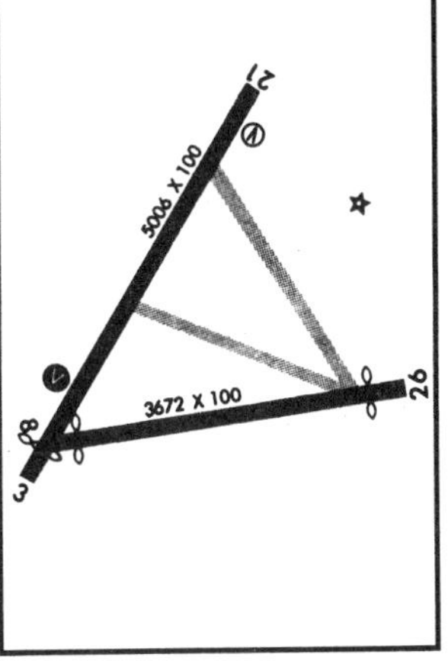

Airport Information:

MONTGOMERY - ORANGE COUNTY AIRPORT (MGJ)
1 mi southwest of town N41-30.60 W74-15.88 Elev: 365 Fuel: 100LL, Jet-A
Rwy 03-21: H5006x100 (Asph-Conc) Rwy 08-26: H3672x100 (Asph-Conc)
Attended: 1200-0200Z Unicom: 122.7
FBO: Eastern Aviation Services, Inc. Phone: 457-9000

NY-N37 - MONTICELLO MONTICELLO AIRPORT

(Area Code 914) 32

Russini Restaurant:

The Russini Restaurant is situated 1/2 mile south, from the Monticello Airport. Courtesy transportation can be arranged through Carl K. Heins (FBO) on the airport, if you let them know you are coming, Phone: 794-6888. This Italian restaurant is open Wednesday and Thursday 5 p.m. to 9 p.m., Friday and Saturday 5 p.m. to 9 p.m. and Sunday 4:30 p.m. to 9 p.m. Beginning September or October their hours vary and days they are open vary. The menu features all homemade items like roast beef, steaks, ribs, seafood, and many delicious Italian pasta dishes. Average prices run from $7.50 to $21.00 for most items. The daily specials offer 3 or 4 complete dinner selections for $10.95 to $12.95. Seating in the restaurant totals about 73 people. The atmosphere is relaxed and friendly. Everything on their menu can also be prepared-to-go as well. In-flight catering is available. For more information call the Russini Restaurant at 794-1620.

Restaurants Near Airport:

Blue Horizon Diner	4 mi N.	Phone: 796-2210
House of Lyons	3 mi Rt42	Phone: 794-0244
Mr. Willy's Restaurant	1 mi Rt42	Phone: 794-0888
Russini Restaurant	1/2 mi S.	Phone: 794-1620

Lodging: Concord Resort Hotel (6 miles, Kiamesha Lake, transportation available) 794-4000; Brossinger Resort (10 miles, Liberty) 292-5000; Kutshers Country Club (5 miles, Kutshers Road, Monticello, transportation available) 794-6000.

Meeting Rooms: It is reported that there are meeting rooms located at the following places: Concord Resort Hotel 794-4000; Brossinger Resort 292-5000; Kutshers Country Club 794-6000.

Transportation: Carl Heins (FBO) can provide courtesy transportation to nearby facilities; Also Rental Cars: Rent-A Wreck 794-5025; U-Save Auto Rental Cars 794-6161.

Information: Sullivan County Government Center, Office of Public Information, 100 North Street, Monticello, NY 12701, Phone: 800-882-2287.

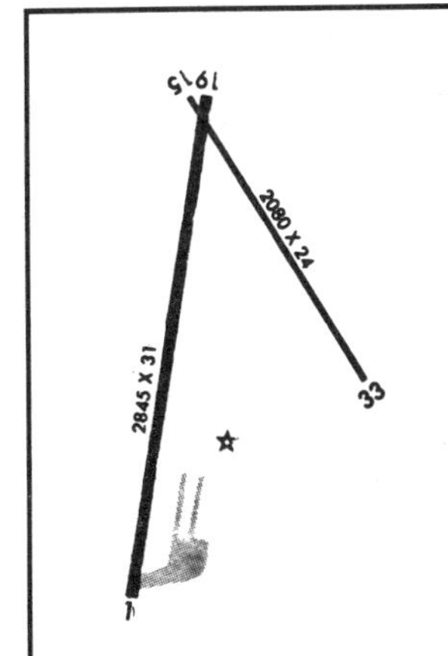

Attractions:

There are a few fine resorts that have been recommended to us. Concord Resort Hotel (6 miles, Kiamesha Lake, transportation available) 794-4000; Brossinger Resort (10 miles, Route 52, Liberty) 292-5000; Kutshers Country Club (5 miles, Kutshers & Monticello, transportation available) 794-6000.

Airport Information:

MONTICELLO - MONTICELLO AIRPORT (N37)
2 mi south of town N41-37.36 W74-42.08 Elev: 1545 Rwy 01-19: H2845x31 (Asph)
Rwy 15-33: H2080x24 (Asph) Attended: daylight hours Unicom: 122.8 Public Phone 24hrs
Notes: $2.00 landing fee and $5.00 overnight parking fee.
FBO: TML Aircraft Phone: 791-5450

NY-MSV - MONTICELLO
SULLIVAN COUNTY INTL. AIRPORT

(Area Code 914) 33

Airport Coffee Shop:

This combination snack bar and family style restaurant is located in the main terminal building at the Sullivan County International Airport. They are open between 7 a.m. and 3 p.m. and are closed on Monday and holidays. Their menu includes a variety of entrees like hot roast beef, hot turkey, shrimp in the basket, soups and salads. Average prices run $5.65 for breakfast and about $5.65 for lunch. Daily specials are also offered. Fly-in groups are always welcome. Larger groups should make advance reservations. There is seating for approx. 50 persons in their main dining room, and in-flight catering is available by calling the restaurant. For more information call the Airport Cafe at 583-6603.

Restaurants Near Airport:
Airport Coffee Shop On Site Phone: 583-6603

Lodging: ElMonaco Motel (4 miles) 583-5260.

Meeting Rooms: None Reported

Transportation: None Reported

Information: Sullivan County Government Center, Office of Public Information, 100 North Street, Monticello, NY 12701, Phone: 800-882-2287.

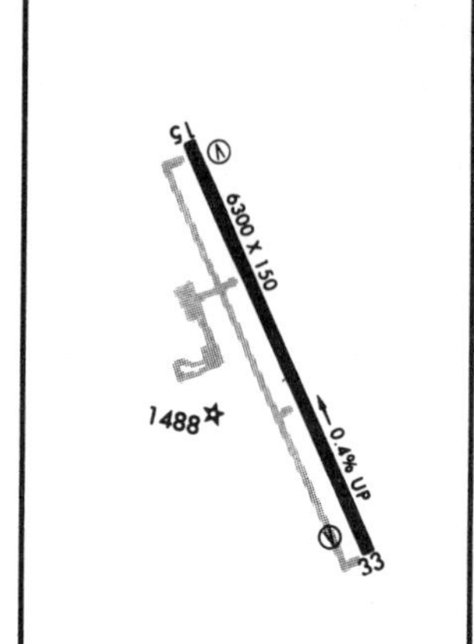

Attractions:

Holiday Mount Ski Area, 3 miles east of town (Longest Run 3,500, Vertical Drop 400 feet) Open December through March daily. 796-3161; Monticello Raceway 794-4100; Woodstock Music Festival Monument, held on the Yasgur's farm.

Airport Information:

MONTICELLO - SULLIVAN COUNTY INTL. AIRPORT (MSV)
6 mi northwest of town N41-42.10 W74-47.70 Elev: 1403 Fuel: 100LL, Jet-A
Rwy 15-33: H6300x150 (Asph) Attended: 1300-2200 Unicom: 122.8
Woodstock Aircraft Serv. Phone: 583-5830

NY-JFK - NEW YORK
JOHN F KENNEDY INTERNATIONAL

(Area Code 718) 34

Restaurants Near Airport:
CA1 Services On Site Phone: 656-6210

CA1 Services:

CA1 Services operates snack bars and cafeterias within the terminal buildings on the John F. Kennedy International Airport. Hours of operation are between 6 a.m. and 10 p.m. Their restaurant offers soups, salads, a nice selection of entrees from which to choose and desserts. Prices run between $5.00 and $7.00 for most selections. In addition to the menu items, they also feature a salad bar, fish fries on Fridays and a sandwich block (make your own v.s. packaged). Throughout the terminal building their restaurant decor varies. On several occasions special catered meals have been arranged for business meetings. Special meal trays and box lunches can also be prepared. A number of other food services are also available within the terminal building. A new Pizzeria as swell as an establishment called "Chock-Full "O" Nuts are also available. For information regarding the food service facilities on the field, or catering services call 656-6210.

Lodging: Hilton JFK Airport (free trans.) 322-8700 or 800-437-7175; Holiday Inn (free trans.) 659-0200 or 800-692-5350; Marriott (free trans) 995-9000; Pan American Motor Inn 446-7676 or 800-937-7374; Travelodge-JFK Airport 995-9000 or 800-578-7878.

Meeting Rooms: Hilton JFK Airport (free trans.) 322-8700 or 800-437-7175; Holiday Inn (free trans.) 659-0200 or 800-692-5350; Marriott (free trans) 995-9000; Pan American Motor Inn 446-7676 or 800-937-7374;

Transportation: Avis 244-5400; Budget 656-6010; Dollar 656-2400; Hertz 800-654-3131; National 800-328-4567.

Information: New York Convention and Visitors Bureau, 2 Columbus Circle, New York City, NY 10019, Phone: 212-397-8222

Attractions:

American Museum of Moving Image 784-0077; Bowne House 359-0528; Flushing Meadow Corona Park - Queens Museum of Art, New York Hall of Science, Shea Stadium; Queens Botanical Garden 886-3800.

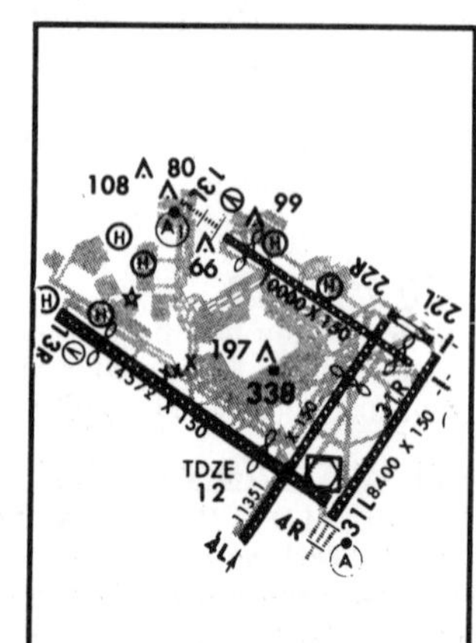

Airport Information:

NEW YORK - JOHN F KENNEDY INTERNATIONAL (JFK)
13 mi southeast of town N40-38.39 W73-46.74 Elev: 13 Fuel: 100LL, Jet-A Rwy 13R-31L: H14572x150 (Asph-Conc-Grvd) Rwy 04L-22R: H1135x150 Asph-Conc-Grvd) Rwy 13L-31R: H10000x150 (Asph-Gvd) Rwy 04R-22L: H8400x150 (Asph-Grvd) Atis: 128.725 (Arr) 117.7 (Arr NE) 115.4 (Arr-SW) 115.1 (Dep) (718-995-8188) Unicom: 122.95 New York App Con: 127.4, 134.35, 132.4, 126.8, 123.7 New York Dep Con: 135.9, 134.35, 124.75, 123.7 Kennedy Tower: 119.1, 123.9 Gnd Con: 121.9, 121.65 Clnc Del/Pre Taxi Clnc: 135.05 Gate Hold: 125.05 Airport Remarks: Refer to the AFD for current information listed above as well as current information about all precautions, notifications and procedures.
Airport Managers Office Phone: 224-4111

NY-IAG - NIAGARA FALLS
NIAGARA FALLS INTL AIRPORT

(Area Code 716)

35

Goose's Roost:

The Goose's Roost restaurant is located adjacent to the Niagra Falls International Airport. We were told that you could simply walk across the street to the restaurant. This combination family style and fine dining establishment is open 7 days a week from 7 a.m. to 9 p.m. during the winter and 7 a.m. to 11 p.m. during the summer. Specialties on their menu include Italian and pasta dishes, chicken wings, roast beef, and homemade soups and salads. They also provide a full breakfast line available all day long. Daily specials run Monday through Friday for breakfast and lunch. Average meal prices are $4.00 for breakfast, $3.99 for lunch and $5.95 to $8.00 for dinner. Their main dining area can seat 150 persons. In addition to the restaurant is a deli with some tables. Everything on their menu can be prepared-to-go. Guests can also see the airport from the restaurant. For more information about the Goose's Roost, call 297-7497.

Attractions:

Niagara Falls Convention & Civic Center, 304 4th Street, Sports events, concerts 278-8130; Niagara Power Project Visitor Center, glassed enclosed observation building 4-1/2 miles north of the falls 285-3211 ext 6661; Fort Niagara State Park: Old Fort Niagara 745-7611, and four mile Creek Park Campground 745-3802.

Restaurants Near Airport:

Goose's Roost	Adj Arpt	Phone: 297-7497

Lodging: Budget Host (Shuttle) 282-1743; Best Western Red Jacket Inn (Shuttle) 283-7612; Comfort Inn-The Pointe (Shuttle) 284-6835; Hoilday Inn-Downtown 285-2521; Howard Johnson-Downtown (Shuttle) 285-5261; Quality Inn Rainbow Bridge (Shuttle) 284-8801; Ramada Inn (Shuttle) 285-2541; Days Inn (Shuttle) 285-9321; Hilton (Shuttle) 285-3361; Red Coach Inn (Shuttle) 282-1459.

Meeting Rooms: Best Western Inn-The Pointe 283-7612; Comfort Inn-The Pointe 284-6835; Holiday Inn-Downtown 285-2521; Quality Inn Rainbow Bridge 284-8801; Ramada Inn 285-2541; Days Inn 285-9321; Hilton (Convention facilities available) 285-3900; Red Coach Inn 282-1459.

Transportation: Lodging establishments listed above advertised available shuttle service to and from airport. Also Rental Cars: Hertz 297-2474.

Information: Convention & Visitors Bureau, 310 4th Street, Niagara Falls, NY 14303, Phone: 285-2400.

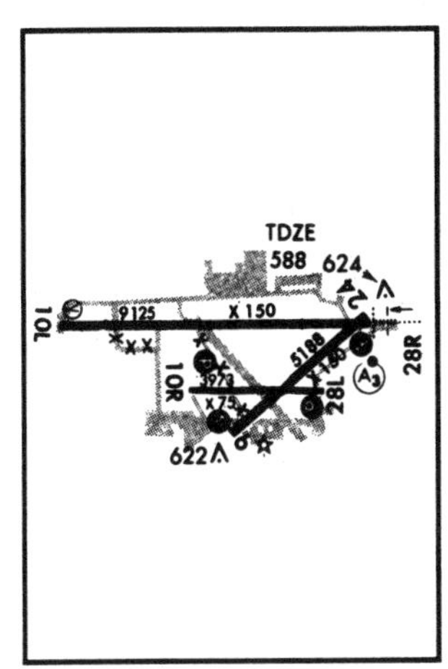

Airport Information:

NIAGARA FALLS - NIAGARA FALLS INTL AIRPORT (IAG)

4 mi east of town N43-06.43 W78-56.73 Elev: 590 Rwy 10L-28R: H9125x150 (Asph-Conc) Rwy 06-24: H5050x150 Rwy 10R-28L: H3973x75 (Asph) Attended: continuously Atis: 120.8 Unicom: 122.95 Tower: 118.5 Gnd Con: 121.7 Clnc Del: 119.25

Notes: CAUTION: Heavy concentration of gulls, blackbirds, starlings up to 5000 AGL.

FBO: Niagara Air Center Phone: 731-9079

FBO: Niagara Falls Arpt Auth. Phone: 297-4494

NY-OIC - NORWICH
LT. WARREN EATON AIRPORT

(Area Code 718)

36

Grove Park Restaurant:

The Grove Park Restaurant is located across from the Lt. Warren Eaton Airport on Route 12 in Norwich, New York. This restaurant specializes in pasta, fish and steak. They also serve a variety of appetizers, desserts, salads and soups. They offer daily specials and buffets. The decor of the restaurant is rustic. If planning a group fly-in, this facility has accommodations for 20 to 80 persons. In conjunction with the restaurant, they also have a 14 unit motel. The restaurant is within walking distance, and is open from Monday through Saturday from 11:30 a.m. to 9:30 p.m. Prices for entree run between $4.95 and $9.95 for lunch and dinner. For information call 334-2251.

Restaurants Near Airport:

Grande Pizza	N/A	Phone: 334-3065
Grove Park	1/2 mi S.	Phone: 334-2251
Lewis	11 mi N.	Phone: 674-9055
Ossie'll	1 mi S.	Phone: 334-5853

Lodging: Howard Johnson Lodge, approx. 2 miles from airport at 75 North Broad Street, on NY 12, 82 units, 3 story bldg., restaurant 6 am to 10 pm, indoor pool, Phone: 334-2200.

Meeting Facilities: Howard Johnson Lodge (See listing above)

Transportation: Norwich Yellow Cab, Phone: 336-3067, Dollar Rent-A-Car, Phone: 336-4700.

Information: Chenango County Chamber of Commerce, 29 Lackawanna Avenue, Norwich, NY 13815, Phone: 334-1400.

Attractions:

Mountaintop Golf Course, approx. 12 miles from airport, route 80, Sherburne, NY, Phone: 674-4005.

Airport Information:

NORWICH - LT. WARREN EATON AIRPORT (OIC)

2 mi north of town N42-33.99 W75-31.45 Elev. 1025 Fuel: 100LL, Jet-A Rwy 01-19: H4724x75 (Asph) Attended: daylight hrs. Unicom 122.8 Public phone 24hrs.

Notes: No landing/overnight fees if you buy gas otherwise $5.00 per night.

Airport Manager Phone: 334-9430

FBO: Flight Service Group, Inc. Phone: 334-9430

NY-NY43 - PISECO
PISECO AIRPORT

(Area Code 518) 37

Irondequit Inn:

The Irondequit Inn is located within walking distance (about 1/8 mile) from the Piseco Airport. During our conversation with the management we learned that this establishment is considered to be a late 1800s or early 1900s country inn located on 640 acres of land. The inn is situated on Piseco Lake and can be seen by its distinctive red metal roof. The lakeshore is wooded and rocky. A beach stretches out in front of the inn. Hiking trails, canoe rentals, tennis courts, camp sites with showers, cabin rentals, and a host of additional activities and amenities are available. The inn is located about 11 miles from town. Shuttle service can be arranged for guests. The lodge contains 9 rooms with accommodations for single or double occupancy and 3 full baths. Cabin rentals have wood burning fireplaces. Rates include breakfast and dinner seatings. Meals are served during certain times of the day. The Inondequit Inn staff serves hearty portions family style. Some of the delicious items prepared are slow baked baby backed ribs, roast turkey with all the trimmings and topped off with homemade apple pie. Vegetarian dishes are also available upon request. To enjoy a peaceful getaway with good company and great food, the Irondequit Inn may just be the place you're looking for. For brochures, or information on rates (FAX 518-548-5500) or call them at 888-497-0350.

Restaurants Near Airport:
Irondequoit Inn 1/8 mi Phone: 888-497-0350

Lodging: Irondequoit Inn provides rooms within the main lodge, cabin rentals and camp sites. Call 888-497-0350.
Meeting Rooms: Accommodations for groups can be arranged at the Irondequoit Inn 888-497-0350.
Transportation: It is reported by the management that guest landing at Piseco Airport can walk to the Irondequoit Inn. Courtesy transportation can also be arranged on request. Shuttle service into town can also be provided.
Information: For information call the Irondequoit Inn at 888-497-0350.

Attractions:

Irondequoit Inn offers a variety of activities including canoing, hiking, swimming, fishing, tennis, camping, cabin rentals and much more. For information call 888-497-0350.

Airport Information:

PISECO - PISECO AIRPORT (NY43)
1 mi north of town N43-27.20 W74-31.06 Elev: 1703 Fuel: 100LL Rwy 04-22: H3100x60 (Asph)
Attended: May-Oct 1300-2100Z Unicom: 122.8 Notes: Airport closed Oct-May, also watch for seaguls and possible wildlife in runway.
Airport Manager Phone: 548-8794

NY-PLB - PLATTSBURG
CLINTON COUNTY AIRPORT

(Area Code 518) 38

Airport Cafe:

The Galley Cafe is reported to be situated on the Clinton County Airport, and is within walking distance from the aircraft parking area. This cafe is open between 7:00 a.m. and 3:00 p.m. 6 days a week. They are closed on Sunday. Their menu includes specialties like homemade bread, pastries, pot roast dinners, chili, hot turkey sandwiches, and a full breakfast line. Average prices run $3.50 for most breakfast and lunch items. A daily special is also offered. On Friday they provide a fish fry as well. The main dining area can seat 60 persons, with a contemporary atmosphere. In-flight catering is also available. For more information call the Galley Cafe at 562-9529.

Restaurants Near Airport:
Airport Cafe On Site Phone: 562-9529

Lodging: Comfort Inn (1/4th mile) 562-2730; Econo Lodge (1 mile) 561-1500; Holiday Inn (1 mile) 561-5000; Howard Johnson Lodge 561-7750.

Meeting Rooms: Holiday Inn 561-5000; Howard Johnson Lodge 561-7750.

Transportation: Avis 563-4120; Hertz 563-2051.

Information: Chamber of Commerce, 101 West Bay Plaza, P.O. Box 310, Plattsburg, NY 12901, Phone: 563-1000.

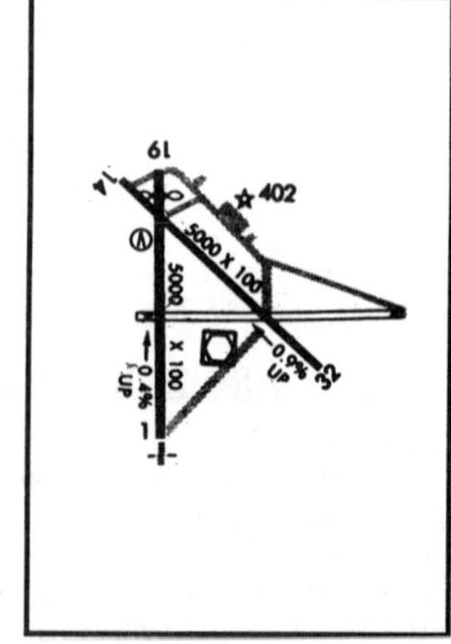

Airport Information:

PLATTSBURG - CLINTON COUNTY AIRPORT (PLB)
3 mi west of town N44-41.25 W73-31.47 Elev: 372 Fuel: 100LL, Jet-A
Rwy 01-19: H5000x100 (Asph) Rwy 14-32: H5000x100 (Asph) Attended: 0900-0500Z
Unicom: 122.7 Notes: Landing and parking fee's reported.
FBO: Flying Nunn's Aviation Phone: 561-3822
FBO: Master Tech, Inc. Phone: 563-1430

NY-POU - POUGHKEEPSIE DUTCHESS COUNTY AIRPORT

(Area Code 914)

39

Restaurants Near Airport:
Mammamia's 2 mi N. Phone: 462-5231
Woronock House 200 ft NE Phone: 462-2220

Lodging: Airport Inn (Adj Arpt) 462-7800; Dorchester Motor Lodge (2 miles) 297-3757; Holiday Inn (3 miles) 473-1151; Radison Poughkeepsie (7 miles) 485-5300; Ramada Inn (3 miles) 462-4600.
Meeting Rooms: Woronock House (200 feet Northeast of airport) 462-2220.
Transportation: Dutchess County Department of Aviation at 462-2600 can provide courtesy transportation to nearby facilities; Also reported are rental cars: Avis 462-7400; Hertz 462-6160.
Information: Chamber of Commerce, 110 Main Street, Poughkeepsie, NY 12601; Phone: 454-1700

Woronock House:

According to our sources, a fine restaurant by the name of Woronock House, is located only 200 feet on the northeast end of the Dutchess County Airport. This combination fine dining and family style restaurant is open from 11:30 a.m. to 10 p.m. Monday through Saturday, and Sunday until 8 p.m. Their menu includes a variety of fresh seafood and choice steaks during dinner hours and many delicious sandwiches for lunch such as their special Rubin, and juicy burgers. Homemade bread is baked right on the premises and served with most meals. The main dining room is located on the upper level of this facility, while their lounge and banquet rooms are situated on the lower level. Several private rooms are available for parties or business conferences. Seating for 200, 65, 25 and 20 can be reserved and catered to your specifications. There is even an outdoor patio where guest can enjoy a meal and watch the aircraft land and take off at the airport. In-flight catering is also available to fly-in customers as well. For more information about the Woronock House, call them at 462-2220.

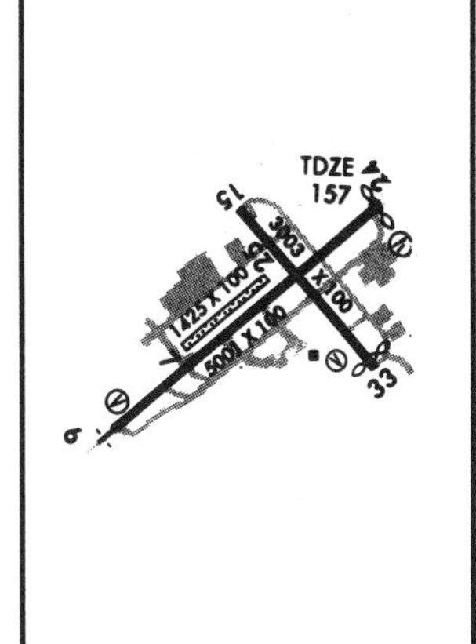

Airport Information:

POUGHKEEPSIE - DUTCHESS COUNTY AIRPORT (POU)
4 mi south of town N41-37.60 W73-53.04 Elev: 166 Fuel: 80, 100LL, Jet-A
Rwy 06-24: H5001x100 (Asph-Grvd) Rwy 15-33: H3003x100 (Asph) Attended: 1200-0230
Atis: 126.75 Unicom: 122.95 Tower: 124.0 Gnd Con: 121.8 Clnc Del: 121.8
Public Phone 24hrs Notes: Landing and or overnight parking fees vary with size of aircraft.
Airport Manager Phone: 462-2600
FBO: Richmor Aviation Phone: 462-2900

Old Rhinebeck Aerodrome

Red Hook-Sky Park, NY (46N)

The Old Rhinebeck Aerodrome presents antique aeroplanes in their natural settings and recaptures the thrill and excitement of old-time flying from the period of 1900 to 1937.

Visitors to the Old Rhinebeck Aerodrome can see outstanding World War I and earlier aircraft in action and watch this colorful era brought back to life amidst the roar of rotary engines and the smell of burnt castor oil. They pride themselves in flying original aircraft or accurate copies powered with original engines.

This attraction is situated in historic Rhinebeck, New York and can be easily reached by car using Taconic State Parkway or the New York Thruway. Pilots flying in can land at Red Hook-Sky Park (46N). Parking and picnicking facilities are free. Be sure to bring along your cameras and vidio recorders.

Old Rhinebeck Aerodrome is open daily from 10:00 a.m. until 5:00 p.m. May 15 through October. Exciting air shows are held every week-end from June 15 through October 15. Sunday shows feature World War I aircraft, and Saturday shows demonstrate the Pioneer and Lindberg Era which consist of two different shows. Show time is 2:30 p.m. to 4:00 p.m. (one performance). Group visits for the shows can be accommodated without advance reservations. Preshow activity starts at 2:00 p.m. During July & August (Mon-Fri) daily tours start at 1:00 p.m. Barnstorming rides in a 1929 open-cockpit biplane are available before and after the shows. Flights are approximately 15 minutes and cost in the neighborhood of $25.00 per person. Daily admission Monday through Friday for adults is $4.00 and $2.00 for children 6 to 10 years old, and Saturday and Sunday Air Shows cost $9.00 for adults and $4.00 for children.

Cole Palen, is the founder and spark plug of the Aerodrome. Old Rhienbeck Aerodrome was conceived in 1951 by the purchase of six World War I aircraft from the famous Roosevelt Field Museum. Late in 1958, they needing a home for these aircraft, and Cole Palen bought up the present property which was then a derelict farm and murder house. This was the rough beginning of a labor of love. However, today it stands as a great aviation attraction where you can see vintage aircraft performing.

A living museum of old airplanes; a dream Mr. Palen envisioned some thirty years ago, is still growing with a small group of dedicated people and the enthusiasm and spirit that started it all.

Before and after the shows, be sure to visit the museum buildings up on the hill in the parking area. These buildings are full of many original and historically significant airplanes from the three eras of aviation depicted in their air shows; Pioneer, World War I and Lindbergh Era. In addition, all types of aircraft engines, cars, motorcycles and related vehicles of the periods are on display. For more information about this attraction call the Old Rhinebeck Aerodrome at 914-758-8610. (Information submitted by museum)

Photo: by Old Rhinebeck Aerodrome

Mr. Cole Palen founder of the Old Rhinebeck Aerodrome, poses along side of a 1930 Great Lakes Biplane, only one of several fine vintage and historically precious aircraft still flying and performing during their airshows.

NY- ROC - ROCHESTER
GREATER ROCHESTER INTERNATIONAL

(Area Code 716) 40

Phillips European Pastries And Salads:

Located at the East terminal building in the food court, this cafe provides many travelers with a delectable selection of European delights. Their menu features, morning pastries,fresh bagels, muffins, salads, specialty sandwiches, European pastries, cappuccino, espresso, and mineral water. Daily salads and soup specials are also provided. Prices range from $1.50 for breakfast, $5.00 for lunch and $8.00 for dinner. The decor of this cafe is European, and is open for business between 5 a.m. and 11 p.m. daily 7 days a week. For information call 328-3390.

Restaurants Near Airport:

Ashley's (Rochester Mtl)	(Adj)	Phone: 235-6030
Greenhouse Cafe (Holiday)	(Adj)	Phone: 328-6000
McDonalds	On Site	Phone: N/A
Phillip's European	On Site	Phone: 328-3390

Lodging: Rochester Host Hotel, 1100 Brooks Avenue Phone: 235-6030; Holiday Inn At Airport, Phone: 328-6000; Marriott At Airport, 1890 Ridge Road, Phone: 225-6880; Holidome (Holiday Inn), 1111 Jefferson Road, Phone: 475-1510, Radisson Inn, 175 Jefferson Road, Phone: 475-1910.
Conference Facilities: Arrangements for meeting rooms and convention facilities can be made with hotels in the area. See lodging listed above.
Transportation: Wilair Services (Mark Craun) will provide courtesy transportation or arrange shuttle service to and from restaurants if utilizing his facilities services. Also, hotel shuttle service will provided transportation to and from their facilities. In addition; Budget 464-6093, Hertz 464-6092, Airport Taxi 464-8209, Avis 464-6094, National 464-6091, Shuffles Limo Service 254-5569.
Information: Greater Rochester Visitors Association, 126 Andrew Street, Rochester, NY 14604, Phone: 546-3070.

Attractions:

Genesee Valley Park Golf Course (10 min drive from airport) 1000 E. River Rd. Phone: 424-2920; Lake Ontario, (Approx. 20 min from airport) Located off of Lake Avenue; Highland Park, (10 min from airport) South Goodman street;

Airport Information:

ROCHESTER - GTR. ROCHESTER INTL. (ROC)
3 mi SW of town N43-07.13 W77-40.34 Elev: 560 Fuel: 100LL, Jet-A Rwy 04-22: H8001x150 (Asph-Grvd) Rwy 10-28: H5500x150 (Asph-Grvd) Rwy 07-25: H4403x150 (Asph) Attended: continuously Atis: 124.825 Unicom: 122.95 Tower: 118.3 Gnd Con: 121.7 Clnc Del: 118.8 Pre Taxi Clnc: 118.8 Landing fees: $1.29 per 1000 lbs; Parking fees: contact FBO
FBO: Wilair Services: 328-2720

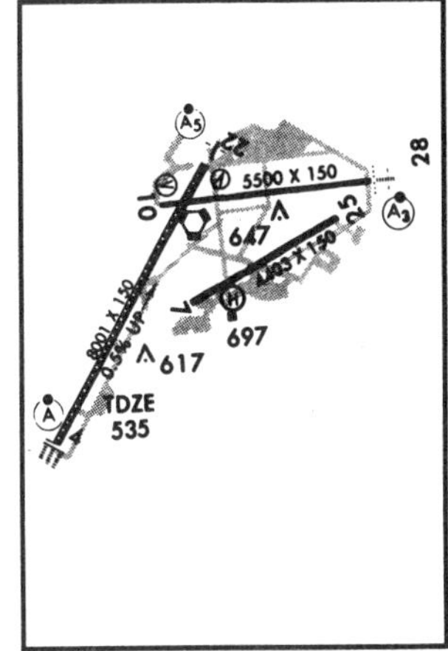

NY-SLK - SARANAC LAKE
ADIRONDACK AIRPORT

(Area Code 518) 41

Airport Restaurant:

This family style restaurant is located on the Adirondack Airport and is open Monday through Friday from 7 a.m. to 3:00 p.m. and 8 a.m. to 3 p.m. Saturday and Sunday. This facility serves daily specials along with breakfast and lunch selections. The Airport Restaurant faces the runway and has a modern yet rustic decor. Prices average $3.25 for breakfast selections and $4.00 for dinner selections. Large fly-in groups or parties are welcome if advance notice is given. Catering can also be arranged as well as meals prepared to go. For information call the airport managers office, 891-9081. The restaurant does not currently have a phone.

Restaurants Near Airport:

Airport Restaurant	On Site	Phone: 891-9081
Hotel Saranac	7 mi SE	Phone: 891-2200
The Lodge	2 miles	Phone: 891-1489

lodging: Hotel Saranac (7 miles) 891-2200; Saranac Inn Golf & Country Club (6 miles) 891-1402; The Lodge (Free transportation, 2 miles) 891-1489.
Meeting Rooms: Hotel Saranac (7 miles) 891-2200; Howard Johnsons 523-2241.
Transportation: Adirondack Regional Airport FBO (Courtesy Car) 891-4600; Adirondack Express 523-2335; Corrow 891-5082; La Vignes Taxi 891-2444; Gene's Taxi 523-3161; Lucky 8 359-3849; M & M Limo 523-3611; Rental Cars: Avis 523-3506; Hertz 891-4075; Super Saver 523-2700.
Information: Saranac Lake Chamber of Commerce, 30 Main Street, Saranac Lake, NY 12983, Phone: 891-1990 or 800-347-1992.

Attractions:

Hunting fishing, hiking, cross country skiing, adjacent to airport; Robert Louis Stevenson Memorial Cottage 891-4480; Six Nations Indian Museum 891-0769.

Airport Information:

SARNANAC LAKE - ADIRONDACK AIRPORT (SLK)
4 mi northwest of town N44-23.12 W74-12.37 Elev: 1663 Fuel: 100LL, Jet-A Rwy 05-23: H6573x150 (Asph-Grvd) Rwy 09-27: H3998x100 (Asph) Attended 1300-0130Z Unicom: 123.00 Public Phone 24 hrs Notes: For airport attendant after hours call 891-2215 or 2659; Landing Fee $4.00 and up for multi engine aircraft, and Parking from $3.50 and up; FBO provides baggage handling, fuel, parking, hangers, tie down, APU, de-ice, pre heat for light to heavy aircraft, (DC-9, 727 etc.)
FBO: Adirondack Regional Airport Phone: 891-4600

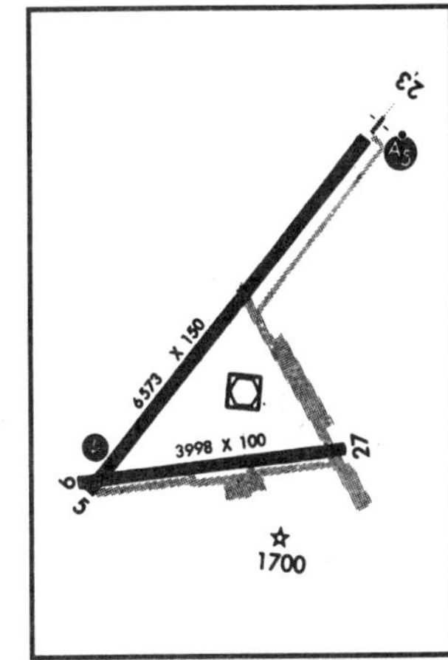

Empire State Aerosciences Museum

Schenectady/Scotia, (NY-SCH)

The Empire State Aerosciences Museum is located on the northwestern perimeter of the Schenectady County Airport next to Fortune Air (FBO). The Museum building houses two main exhibition galleries, a space flight simulator exhibit, a 20-seat film and video theater and, upstairs, a large classroom/meeting room with a small kitchen adjacent.

Outside, the museum has on display a collection of actual aircraft including F-4D Phantom II, F-101F "Voodoo," and F--105G "Wild Weasel" fighter planes, A-4F Skyhawk II, A-10 "Warthog", F-84F Thunderstreak, Huey and Hughes (LOH) helicopters, a World War II era C-47 "Dakota" and Mig-17F among others (including home/kit-built aircraft).

The main galleries inside contain some of their more fragile aircraft, detailed models, dioramas, historical artifacts and memorabilia, and photographic displays. A few of the more popular exhibits are the DePischoff "flying motorcycle," the Amelia Earhart Exhibit, and a 32' scale model of the Japanese aircraft carrier "Akagi." The Museum also contains some hands-on exhibits including a mock-up of a 1910 Von Pomer aeroplane, electronic "spotter" aircraft identification, a small motorized model aircraft/airport exhibit and the space flight simulator (used by appointment only).

The Empire State Aerosciences Museum (*ESAM*) is open Tuesday through Saturday from 10:00 a.m. to 4:00 p.m. year around, and Sundays (May through October only) 12:00 p.m. to 4:00 p.m. This facility is handicap accessible, and admission is $3.00 for adults, $1.00 for children. Admission is free to current *ESAM* members. ($25.00 per year for individuals, and $35.00 for family membership). A small gift shop is located at the front entrance to the museum. No food is sold on site. For more information please call the Museum office at (518) 377-2191 or write to ESAM, 130 Saratoga Road, Scotia, NY 12302-4114.

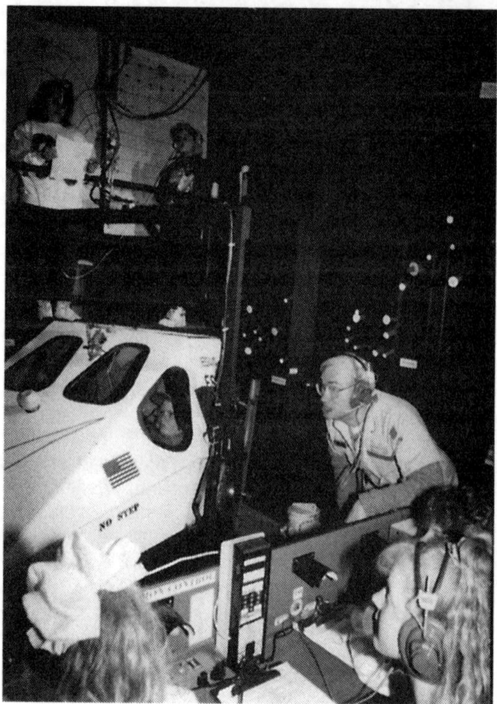

Ace instructor Al Hulstrunk with students in ESAM's "Space Base Alpa" during a "mission" in the Gemini-type space module.

NY-HWV - SHIRLEY BROOKHAVEN AIRPORT

Area Code 516)

42

Restaurants Near Airport:

Guido McMurfi's	3 mi S.	Phone: 399-5353
Leaning Tower of Pizza	3 mi S.	Phone: 399-0888
Shirley Ann's Diner	On Site	Phone: 281-9857
Windmill Diner	5 mi S.	Phone: N/A

Lodging: Smithpoint Motel (5 miles) 281-8887.

Meeting Rooms: None Reported

Transportation: Tony's Taxi 399-5459; Quality Cab 399-0079. Rental cars also available through FBO's on field.

Information: Long Island Tourism & Convention Commission, Nassau Coliseum, 1255 Hempstead Tpke, Uniondale, Long Island 11553-1200, Phone: 800-441-4601.

Shirley Ann's Diner:

Shirley Ann's Diner is located within the terminal building at the Brookhaven Airport and is within walking distance. This diner is open between 8 a.m. and 4 p.m. 7 days a week. Their menu contains selections like a full breakfast line as well as burgers, sandwiches, soups, coffee and desserts. Daily specials are also offered as well. This cafe can seat about 50 persons, and has a simple and friendly atmosphere. Glass windows allowing guests to view the activity on the airport. Outside the restaurant are several picnic tables available for their customers. This restaurant often caters meals for local organizations, as well as fly-in groups. They will even prepare box lunches and handle in-flight catering for private or corporate aircraft. For more information call Shirley Ann's Diner at 281-9857.

Attractions:

Smithpoint Park/Beach-South on William Floyd Parkway, is only a 10 minute drive from airport; Brookhaven National Lab, Upton, NY is a 15 minute drive from airport. Phone: 282-2123.

Airport Information:

SHIRLEY - BROOKHAVEN AIRPORT (HWV)

2 mi west of town N40-49.01 W72-51.72 Elev: 82 Fuel: 100LL, Jet-A
Rwy 15-33: H4325x150 (Asph-Conc) Rwy 06-24: H4200x100 (Asph) Attended: continuously
Unicom: 122.8 Public Phone 24hrs Notes: No landing fee; $2.00 overnight parking fee.

Airport Manager **Phone: 281-5100**
FBO: Brookfield Aviation **Phone: 281-1244**
FBO: Mid-Island Air Serv. **Phone: 281-5400**

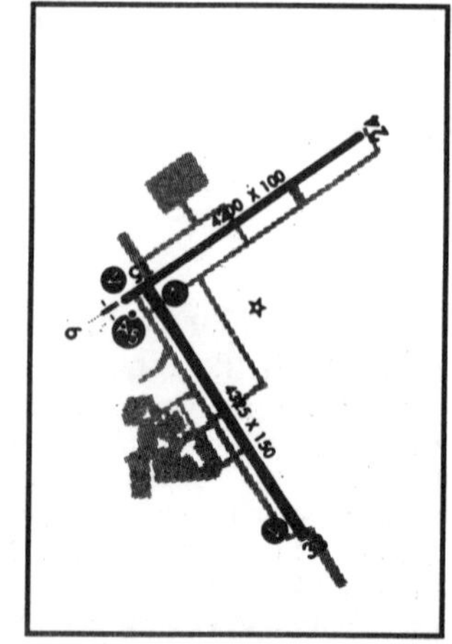

NY-SYR - SYRACUSE
SYRACUSE HANCOCK INTL ARPT.

(Area Code 315) 43, 44

Best Western Syracuse:

This family style restaurant is located on the opposite side of the airport near the fixed base operators. Shuttle service to and from the FBO's can be arranged. The restaurant hours are 7:00 a.m. to 2:00 p.m. and from 5:30 p.m. until 9:30 p.m. 7 days a week. Their hours may vary depending on the scheduled air carrier arrival times. The menu contains a wide variety of entrees for lunch, like fried shrimp platter, tuna platters, and Philadelphia steak. For dinner they serve items like Delmonico steak, broiled pork chops, seafood platters, boneless breast of chicken and shrimp scampi. Average prices for lunch run $4.00 and $5.00. Dinner prices range between $9.50 and $11.75 for most selections. The restaurant is situated within the Best Western Syracuse which contains 94 rooms. Banquet rooms are available for meeting or conferences, able to seat between 15 and 150 persons comfortably. The restaurant, with seating for up to 60 persons, overlooks an outdoor courtyard and swimming pool. For more information you can call them at 455-7362.

CA1 Services:

CA1 Services manages two pizza and bakery establishments on the Syracuse Hancock International Airport. They are both reported to be located on the north and south wings of the terminal building. These restaurants are open between 5 a.m. and 10 p.m. The pizza restaurants offer specialties like spaghetti, salads, freshly baked breads and rolls. Fresh deli meats, cheeses, soups and salads are also available. Prices average $3.00 for breakfast, $4.00 for lunch and $5.00 for dinner. A special 15% airline discount is available. The decor of the pizzeria has brass fixtures and neon lights. Their bakery has a French decor. Groups are always welcome with advance notice appreciated. For information call 455-7444.

Restaurants Near Airport:

Best Western Syracuse	On Site	Phone: 455-7362
CA1 Services	On Site	Phone: 455-7444
Chittela's Restaurant	1-1/2 mi	Phone: 455-1431
Frankie's Steak House	1 mi	Phone: 458-3838

Lodging: Best Western Syracuse (On site, free trans) 455-7362; Days Inn North (Free trans) 451-1511; Quality Inn North (Free trans) 451-1212.

Meeting Rooms: Best Western Syracuse (On site) 455-7362; Days Inn North 451-1511; Quality Inn North 451-1212; Also convention facilities available: Hotel Syracuse 800-255-3892; Sheraton University Inn & Conference Center 475-3000.

Transportation: Avis 455-2461; Budget 458-2017; Hertz 455-2496; National 455-7496.

Information: Convention & Visitors Bureau, Greater Syracuse Chamber of Commerce, 572 South Salina Street, Syracuse, NY 13202, Phone: 470-1800.

Airport Information:

SYRACUSE - SYRACUSE HANCOCK INTL AIRPORT (SYR)
4 mi northeast of town N43-06.67 W76-06.38 Elev: 421 Fuel: 100LL, Jet-A
Rwy 10-28: H9003x150 (Asph-Grvd) Rwy 14-32: H7500x150 (Asph) Attended: continuously
Atis: 132.05 Unicom: 122.95 App/Dep Con: 124.2, 124.6 Tower: 120.3
Gnd Con: 121.7 Clnc Del: 125.05
FBO: Sair Aviation **Phone: 455-7951**
FBO: Syracuse Executive Air **Phone: 455-6617**

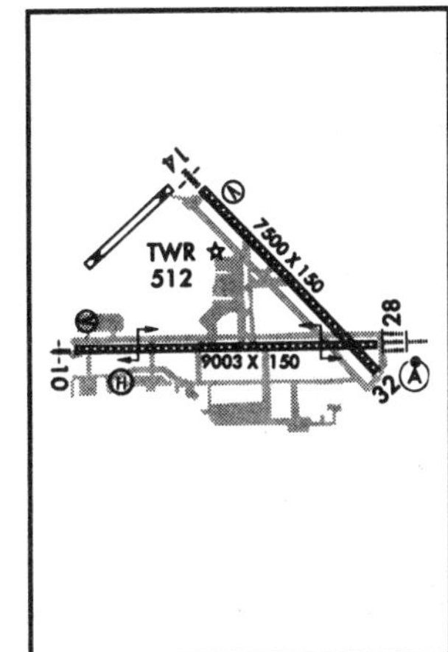

NY-UCA - UTICA
ONEIDA COUNTY AIRPORT

(Area Code 315) 45, 46

Gabbies Cafe:

Gabbie's Cafe is situated within the terminal building at the Oneida County Airport, and is about 1/4 mile from the fixed base operator. Fly-in guests can either walk or take a courtesy shuttle from the FBO. This cafe is open Monday through Friday from 5:30 a.m. to 4 p.m. Deli style sandwiches, daily homemade soups, and hot lunch specials are all available. They are famous for their own style antipasti and their unique breakfasts featuring "frittalata", an Italian open-face omelet with sausage, hot or sweet peppers, potatoes, onions and cheese, served with Italian toast. Menu prices average $2.75 for breakfast, $3.95 for lunch and $4.95 for dinner. Daily specials are also offered along with Friday night dinners featuring fresh haddock for only $4.95. Additional daily specials include items like homemade meatloaf, roast beef dinners, baked ziti with meatballs, chicken and biscuits and much more. The restaurant has a 1950s decor with prints of old-style aircraft. The dining room can seat about 44 persons. Gabby's specializes in preparing catered meals. A special menu describes many delicious entrees like baked Ziti or rigatoni, kielbasa with sauerkraut, ham, turkey and beef trays and roasted chicken. A variety of ethnic foods are available. With one day's notice, Gabby's Catering can prepare delicious moist homemade cakes. Their chef is a culinary graduate of Johnson & Wales College and has 15 years of experience in the art of preparing food. All meals are available for carry-out. For more information about Gabby's Restaurant call 736-3298.

Horizon Hotel (Restaurant):

The Horizon Hotel Restaurant is located across from the terminal building at the Oneida County Airport. This facility can be reached by courtesy van from the fixed base operator. They offer a buffet-style lunch with items like house salads, soup, chicken dishes, hamburgers and cold sandwiches. Their main dining room can seat about 30 persons. Guests can enjoy a meal while watching the activity on the airport. Pink table cloths, carpeting and lots of plants add a nice touch to the decor. Small groups and parties are welcome with advance notice. Meals can also be prepared for carry-out as well. For more information call 736-3377.

Restaurants Near Airport:

Gabby's Cafe	Trml. Bldg.	Phone: 736-3298
Horizon Hotel	Adj Trml.	Phone: 736-3377

Lodging: Consort/Horizon Hotel (Adj. Terminal building) 736-3377.

Meeting Rooms: Consort/Horizon Hotel 736-3377.

Transportation: Avis 337-5454; Hertz 736-5201; National Car Rental 736-7625; Dollar Rent-A-Car 736-0385; Budget Rent-A-Car 736-3365. Also County Air Service can provide courtesy transportation to nearby facilities. Phone: 736-9404.

Information: Oneida County Convention & Visitors Bureau, P.O. Box 551, Utica, NY 13503, Phone: 724-7221.

Attractions:

Shamrock Golf & Country Club (2 miles, on Airport Road) 336-9858; Oriskany Hills Golf Club (2 miles, Route 69) 736-4540; Delta Lake State Park (15 miles, Route 46) 337-4640.

Airport Information:

UTICA - ONEIDA COUNTY AIRPORT (UCA)
6 mi northwest of town N43-08.71 W75-23.03 Elev: 743 Fuel: 100LL, Jet-A
Rwy 15-33: H6001x150 (Asph-Grvd) Rwy 09-27: H5400x150 (Asph-Grvd)
Attended: continuously Atis: 118.7 Unicom: 122.95 Utica Tower: 118.1
Gnd Con/Clnc Del 121.9 Public phone 24 hrs Notes: Landing fee: $1.00 singles and $3.00 for twins; Overnight parking fees: $5.00 and $10.00 for twins.
FBO: County Air Service Phone: 736-9404

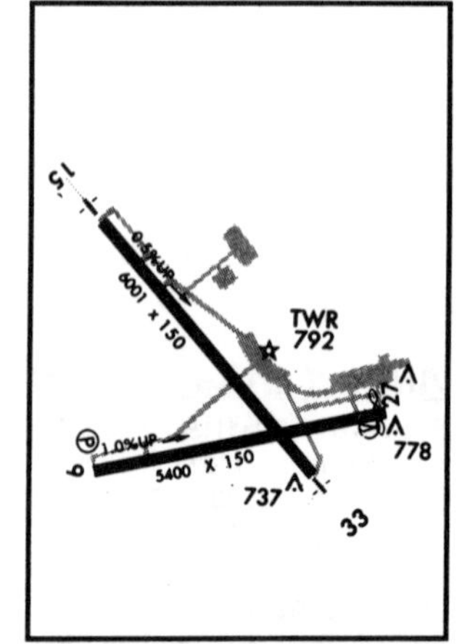

NY-D93 - WATERLOO AIRTREK AIRPORT

(Area Code 315) 47

Nicastro Restaurant:

The Nicastro Restaurant is a family style establishment located about 1000 feet or 1 block from the Airtrek Airport. This facility is also located only 3-1/2 miles from the Seneca Falls Airport (0G7). If landing at the Airtrek Airport, you can simply walk to the restaurant. However, if landing at Seneca Falls, you can call the restaurant and they will come out and pick you up. Their hours are Monday through Friday from 5:30 a.m. to 9 p.m. and Saturday and Sunday from 5:30 a.m. to 3:00 p.m. Their menu includes specialty items like roast pork and dressing, 1/2 chicken, fish, spaghetti, ravioli, barbecued ribs, and all types of omelets as well as a full breakfast line. Average prices run $4.00 for breakfast, $4.40 for lunch and $5.50 for dinner. The main dining area can accommodate about 70 people with counter and table service. According to the management, guest, can see airplanes land and takeoff from the restaurant. Fly-in groups are also welcome. Meals can be prepared for carry-out as well. For more information you can call 539-9577.

Restaurants Near Airport:
Nicastro Restaurant 1 blk Phone: 539-9577

Lodging: Holiday Inn (5 miles) 539-5011

Meeting Rooms: None Reported

Transportation: Taxi Service: Finger Lakes Airport Services 539-2111; Also Rental Cars: Budget 568-9844.

Information: Geneva Chamber of Commerce, One Lakeside Drive, Box 587, Geneva, NY 14456, Phone: 315-789-1776.

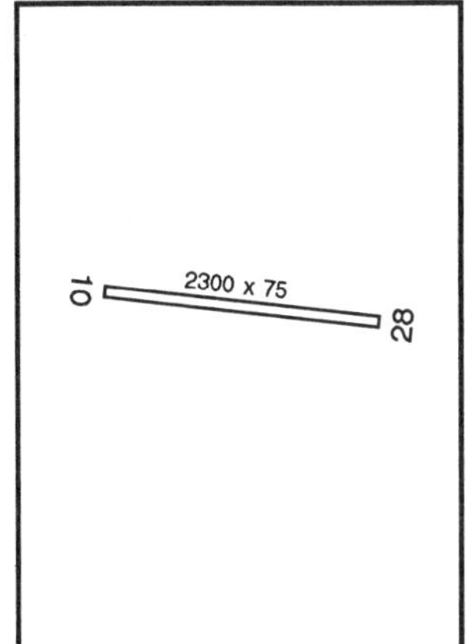

Airport Information:

WATERLOO - AIRTREK AIRPORT (D93)
3 mi south of town N42-51.00 W76-50.98 Elev: 590 Rwy 10-28: 2300x75 (Turf)
Attended: 1300-2100Z CTAF: 122.9
FBO: AirTrek Phone: 539-3670

NY-D94 - WATKINS GLEN SCHUYLER AIRPORT

(Area Code 607) 48

Castel Grisch Winery & Restaurant:

The Castel Grisch Winery & Restaurant is reported to be located about 3 miles southwest of the Schuyler Airport. Transportation can be arranged by calling the airport manager at 535-7392. This gourmet restaurant is open from 11:00 a.m. to 9:00 p.m. every day between May and September. They close down between October and April. The restaurant offers a complete menu featuring Swiss and Austrian specialties. Average prices run $10.00 for lunch and $20.00 for dinner. There are 7 or 8 daily specials to choose from. This unique dining establishment depicts a Swiss chalet with a rustic atmosphere and a large terrace overlooking beautiful Seneca Lake. This combination restaurant and winery provides an attraction for its visitors, with European cooking, tours of the winery and a choice of many items and fine wines that can be purchased for later enjoyment. Fly-in groups are welcome as this establishment is visited by many travelers and vacationers. They also have a bed & breakfast on site as well. For more information call the Castel Grisch Winery & Restaurant at 535-7711.

Restaurants Near Airport:

Castel Grisch	3 mi SW	Phone: 535-7711
Lakeview Inn	1/4 mi NE	Phone: 535-2049

Lodging: Bellevue 535-4232; Castel Grisch Winery & Restaurant now has a bed & breakfast on site 535-7711; Chalet Leon At Hector Falls 546-7171; Chieftain 535-4759; Finger Lakes Motor Inn (Watkins Glen State Park) 535-4800; Longhouse Lodge 535-2565; Queen Catherine 535-2517; Montour House 535-2494.

Meeting Rooms: None Reported

Transportation: Courtesy transportation can be arranged by calling the airport manager (Ron Johnson) at 535-7392.

Information: Schuyler County Chamber of Commerce, 1000 North Franklin Street, Box 330, Watkins Glen, NY 14891, Phone: 535-4300.

Photo by: Castel Grisch

Watkins Glen Estate Winery & Restaurant serves a variety of selections and specializes in Swiss and Austrian cooking.

Attractions:

Lake Breeze golf course (1 mile) 535-4413; Castel Grisch Winery & Restaurant 3 miles, now offers lodging with their Bed & Breakfast on site 535-7711; Bed & Breakfast (Reading House) 1/4 mile 535-9785; Watkins Glen State Park (8 miles) exhibits bridges and paths, working their way through a 700' gorge past rapids and streams, Phone: 535-4511. Cross country skiing, camping, concessions on ground. "Timespell" a sound and laser light show held within the Watkins Glen Gorge, Phone: 535-4960.

Airport Information:

WATKINS GLEN - SCHUYLER AIRPORT (D94) Private Airport

5 mi north of town 42-27-06N 76-54-42W Elev: 870 Rwy 17-35: 2100x50 (Turf) CTAF: 122.9 Attended: daylight Notes: please call the airport manager for airport and runway information. No public phone available, however airport owner lives on field.

FBO: Airport Manager (Ronald G. Johnson) Phone: 535-4173

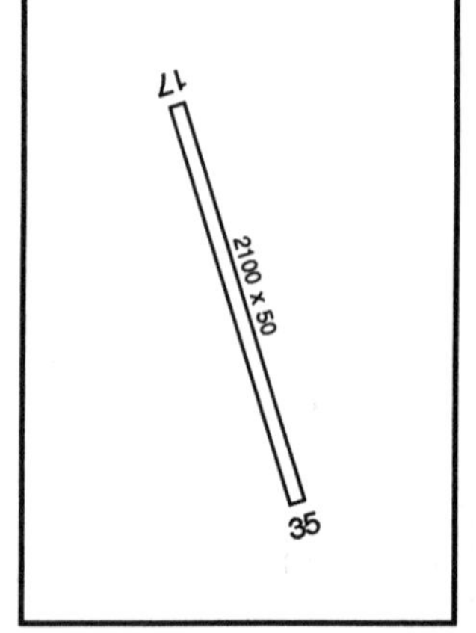

NY-B16 - WEEDSPORT WHITFORD'S AIRPORT

(Area Code 315) 49

Whitford's Airport Club House Restaurant:

This establishment is located on the Whitford's Airport, and is open Saturday and Sunday between 8 a.m. and 2 p.m. During our research we learned that many local people enjoy a pancake breakfast held every other weekend. Fly-in guests can walk to this facility from the aircraft parking area. Service may vary. During our initial interview we were told that the owners serves light fare, and their menu varies throughout the season. A few items prepared include salads, hot dogs, chili, hot soups and sandwiches. They also specialize in serving breakfast. The restaurant can seat 35 persons and has an old fashioned decor with a homey atmosphere. Groups and fly-in parties are also welcome. Call them in advance if your group is a large one. Please call the restaurant facility to assure services. Their phone number is 834-9059.

Restaurants Near Airport:

Ground Round	N/A	Phone: 252-2626
Holiday Inn	8 mi S.	Phone: 253-4531
Old Erie Restaurant	3 mi S.	Phone: 834-6641
Whitford's Arpt Restaurant	On Site	Phone: 834-9059

Lodging: Best Western (3 miles, airport courtesy transportation) 834-6623; Port-40 (3 miles, airport courtesy transportation); Holiday Inn (8 miles, Auburn) 253-4531.

Meeting Rooms: Holiday Inn (8 miles) 253-4531.

Transportation: Letha D. Whitford (FBO) on field can provide courtesy transportation to nearby facilities. Phone: 834-9059.

Information: Geneva Chamber of Commerce, One Lakeside Drive, Box 587, Geneva, NY 14456, Phone: 834-6634.

Attractions:

There are several attractions that were recommended in the nearby area. These are: Waterfront property for camping (on premises); Meadowbrook Golf Course, 4 miles; Owasco Lake Park in Auburn 8 miles from airport, and Fair Haven State Park 20 miles away from airport. For more information you can also call the airport manager at 834-9059.

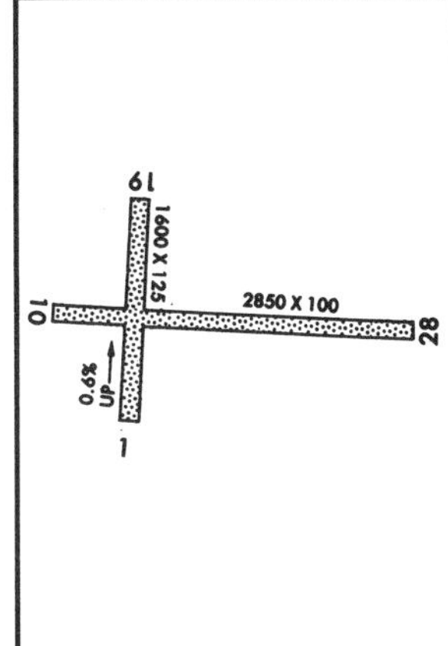

Airport Information:

WEEDSPORT - WHITFORD'S AIRPORT (B16)
2 mi northeast of town N43-04.75 W76-32.48 Elev: 390 Fuel: 80, 100LL
Rwy 10-28: 2850x100 (Turf) Rwy 01-19: 1600x125 (Turf) Attended: daylight hours
Unicom: 122.8 Public telephone available 15 hours a day
FBO: Letha D. Whitford Phone: 834-9059

NY-FOK - WESTHAMPTON BEACH SUFFOLK COUNTY

(Area Code 516) 50

Bell's Cafe:

Bell's Cafe is located right in the Suffolk County Airport terminal building. During our conversation with the restaurant management, we learned that fly-in customers can park their aircraft on the ramp in front of the restaurant. This facility is classified as a luncheonette, and is open from 8 a.m. to 3 p.m. 7 days a week. On weekends they usually stay open later for dinner. They handle a wide variety of hamburgers, sandwiches, Italian food, a full breakfast line served all day as well as different types of club sandwiches and salads. This restaurant was recently remodeled and can seat approximately 30 or 40 people. Everything on their menu can also be prepared-to-go. In-addition, in-flight catering is also offered. For more information about the Bell's Cafe call 288-3927.

Restaurants Near Airport:

Bell's Cafe	On Site	Phone: 288-3927

Lodging: Best Western Circle Inn 727-6200; The Bouy (2 miles) 288-2543; Holiday Inn (6 miles) 369-2200; Westhampton Bath & Tennis 288-2500; Windward Motel (2 miles) 283-6100.

Meeting Rooms: Best Western Circle Inn 727-6200; Holiday Inn 369-2200; Westhampton Bath & Tennis 288-2500.

Transportation: Contact Malloy Air East 288-5410 or Sky East Service, Inc. for taxi or rental car service.

Information: Greater Westhampton Chamber of Commerce, 173 Montauk Hwy, P.O. Box 1228, Westhampton Beach, NY 11978, Phone: 288-3337.

Attractions:

There are numerous beach resorts within the area. (See "Information" listed above).

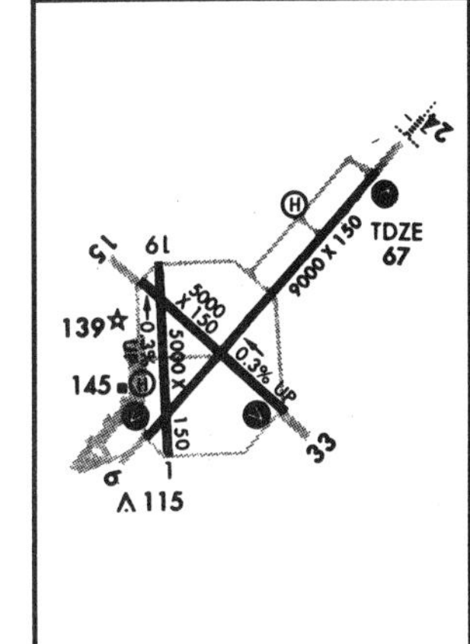

Airport Information:

WESTHAMPTON BEACH - SUFFOLK COUNTY (FOK)
3 mi north of town N40-50.62 W72-37.91 Elev: 67 Fuel: 100LL, Jet-A
Rwy 06-24: H9000x150 (Asph-Conc) Rwy 01-19: H5000x150 (Conc) Rwy 15-33: H5000x150 (Asph-Conc) Attended: 1200-0400Z Unicom: 122.95 Tower: 125.3
Gnd Con: 121.8
FBO: Malloy Air East, Inc. Phone: 288-5410

NY-HPN - WHITE PLAINS
WESTCHESTER COUNTY AIRPORT

(Area Code 914) 51

Skytop Restaurant:
The Skytop Restaurant is located in the new terminal building at the Westchester County Airport. During our conversation we were told that you should be able to walk from nearby aircraft parking areas. Taxi and limo service is also available. This establishment contains a fine dining restaurant and a cafe within the same location. The main dining room is open from 11 a.m. to 10:30 p.m. 7 days a week. Their menu includes New York cut steaks, fresh fish, salmon, tuna, grilled shrimp with peppers and various other seafood plates. In addition, they also feature chicken Florentine, half broiled chicken dinners, roast Long Island duck, Norwegian salmon in a dill and mushroom sauce, and lobster. Daily seafood specials are often presented. The dining area can seat about 85 persons. The decor is modern with an aeronautical accent including linen covered tables and large windows. The Skytop restaurant also provides in-flight catering as well. The coffee shop which makes up part of the total complex, is open from 5:30 a.m. until 9 p.m. and can seat 60 people. For more information about either of these restaurants call 428-0251.

Restaurants Near Airport:
Skytop Restaurant New Trml. Bldg. Phone: 428-0251

Lodging: Holiday Inn Crowne Plaza (Shuttle) 682-0050; Ramada Inn Armonk (5 miles, shuttle) 273-9090; White Plains Hotel (7 miles, shuttle) 761-8100.

Meeting Rooms: Holiday Inn Crowne Plaza 682-0050; Ramada Inn-Armonk 273-9090; White Plains Hotel 761-8100.

Transportation: Limo Service 592-8534; Rental Cars: Avis 946-2669; Hertz 948-1016; National 946-9080.

Information: Westchester Convention & Visitor Bureau, 222 Manaroneck Avenue, White Plains, NY 10605, Phone: 948-0047.

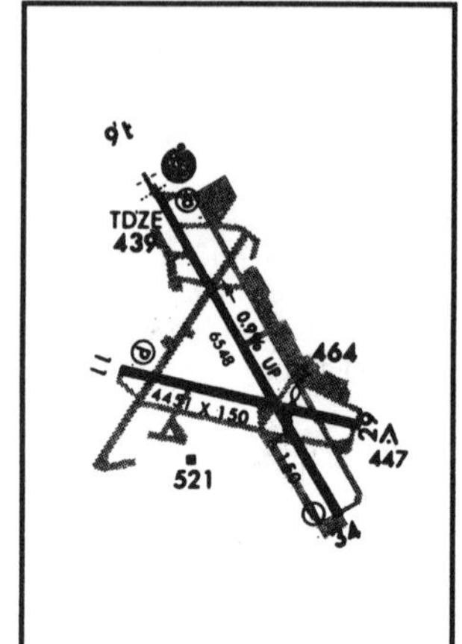

Airport Information:
WHITE PLAINS - WESTCHESTER COUNTY AIRPORT (HPN)
3 mi northeast of town N41-04.02 W73-42.45 Elev: 439 Fuel: 100LL, Jet-A
Rwy 16-34: H6548x150 (Asph-Grvd) Rwy 11-29: H4451x150 (Conc-Grvd) Attended: continuously Atis: 116.6 Unicom: 122.95 Tower: 119.7 Gnd Con: 121.8
Clnc Del: 127.25 Pre-Taxi Clnc: 127.25

FBO: International Aviation Services Phone: 682-7770
FBO: Panorama Flight Service, Inc. Phone: 328-9800
FBO: United Skyport Phone: 761-3200
FBO: Wwstair/Westchester Corp. Phone: 946-0100

Not to be used for navigational purposes

NORTH CAROLINA

LOCATION MAP

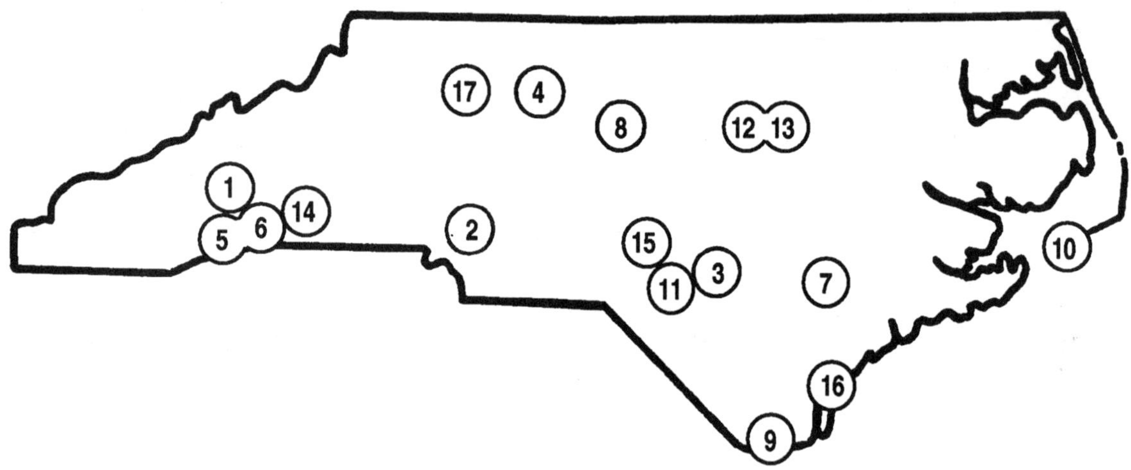

Not to be used for navigational purposes

NORTH CAROLINA

CROSS FILE INDEX

Location Number	City or Town	Airport Name And Identifier	Name of Attraction
1	Asheville	Asheville Reg. (AVL)	Air Host
2	Charlotte	Charlotte/Douglas Intl. (CLT)	Host Marriott
3	Fayetteville	Fayetteville Reg./Grannis Fld. (FAY)	CA1 Services
4	Greensboro	Peidmont Triad Intl. (GSO)	Host Marriott
5	Hendersonville	Hendersonville Arpt. (0A7)	Kelsey's Restaurant
6	Hendersonville	Hendersonville Arpt. (0A7)	Smoke House
7	Kenansville	P.B. Raiford-Duplin Co. (DPL)	The Country Squire
8	Liberty	Causey Arpt. (2A5)	Fran's Front Porch
9	Ocean Isle Beach	Ocean Isle (60J)	Pearl's Island House
10	Ocracoke	Ocracoke Island Arpt. (W95)	Ocracoke Island
11	Raeford	Raeford Muni. (5W4)	O'Baly's Restaurant
12	Raleigh	Raleigh/Durham Intl. Arpt. (RDU)	Angus Barn Restaurant
13	Raleigh	Raleigh/Durham Intl. Arpt. (RDU)	Dobbs Houses, Inc.
14	Rutherfordton	Rutherford Co. Arpt. (FQD)	57 Alpha Cafe
15	Southern Pines	Moore Co. (SOP)	Pine Needles Resort
16	Wilmington	New Hanover Intl. (ILM)	Helnick Corp. Restaurant
17	Winston Salem	Smith Reynolds (INT)	Salem Tavern

Articles

City or town	Nearest Airport and Identifier	Name of Attraction
Asheville, NC	Asheville Reg. (AVL)	Grove Park Inn Resort
Kill Devil Hills, NC	First Flight (FFA)	Wright Brothers Mem.
Southern Pines, NC	Moore Co. (SOP)	Pinehurst-Aberdeen Area

NC-AVL - ASHEVILLE
ASHEVILLE REGIONAL (AVL)

(Area Code 704) 1

Air Host:

Air Host Restaurant is located within the terminal building of the Asheville Regional Airport. This full service restaurant and deli prepares a variety of entrees for air travelers. Their menu includes breakfast selections, salads, cheeseburgers, hamburgers, sliced turkey and club sandwiches, steaks, chicken strips and ham dishes. Average prices run $5.00 for breakfast, $7.00 for lunch and $10.00 to $12.00 for dinner. Their main dining room has large windows on one side, and can hold approx. 60 to 70 persons. Courtesy car transportation from nearby fixed base operators can be arranged. For more information call the restaurant at 687-3780.

Attraction:

The Grove Park Inn Resort is located approximately 18 miles from the Asheville Regional Airport. The resort will provide a shuttle to and from the airport for a fee of $15.00 each way. (See Article next page.)

Airport Information:

ASHEVILLE - ASHEVILLE REGIONAL AIRPORT (AVL)
9 mi south of town N35-26.17 W82-32.51 Elev: 2165 Fuel: 100LL, Jet-A
Rwy 16-34: H8001x150 (Asph-Grvd) Attended: continuously Unicom: 122.95
Atis: 120.2 App/Dep Con: 125.8 (125.8 (340-359 degrees) 124.65 (160-339 degrees)
Tower: 121.1 Gnd Con: 121.9
FBO: Ashville Jet Center Phone: 684-6832 or 800-833-3490

Restaurants Near Airport:

Air Host	On Site	Phone: 687-3780
Waffle House	1/8 mi	Phone: 684-0404

Lodging: Days Inn Airport 684-2281; Econo Lodge Airport (Free trans) 684-1200; Grove Inn Park Inn Resort 18 mi 800-438-5800 or 252-2711; Hilton Great Smokies (Free trans) 254-3211.

Meeting Rooms: Days Inn Airport 684-2281; Grove Inn Park Inn Resort 18 mi 800-438-5800 or 252-2711; Hilton Great Smokies (Free trans) 254-3211.

Information: Asheville Convention & Visitors Bureau, 151 Haywood Street., Box 1010, Asheville, NC 28802-1010, Phone: 258-3858 or 800-257-1300.

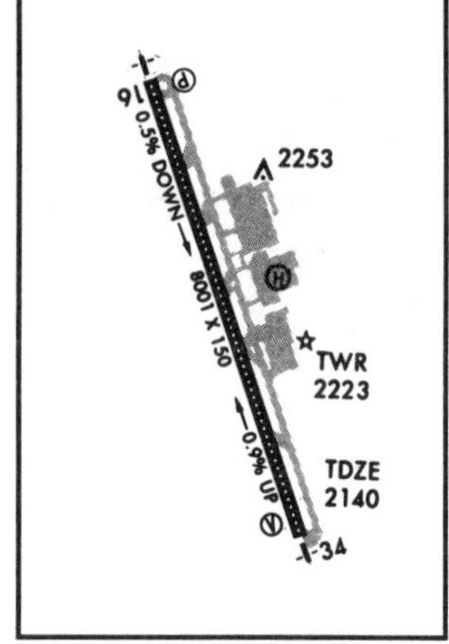

The Grove Park Inn Resort

Asheville, NC (NC-AVL)

(Information submitted by Grove Park Inn Resort)

The Grove Park Inn Resort is located on 140 acres in the beautiful Blue Ridge Mountains atop Sunset Mountain at the crossroads of I-40 and I-240 interstates. The resort was built in 1913. It was listed in the National Register of Historic Places in 1973. It has served as host to many famous guests, including eight American presidents. There are 510 guest rooms, 142 in the historic Main Inn, 202 in the Sammons Wing, 166 in the Vanderbilt Wing (Includes 12 suites in the Vanderbilt Wing, and 28 rooms on the deluxe Club Floor). Handicapped and non-smoking rooms are also available. The Club Floor, which is a private hotel within the larger Grove Park Inn Resort, contains 28 oversized guest rooms with added amenities and Jacuzzis. There is also a lounge with complimentary continental breakfast and cocktail service. (No children are permitted.)

Photo by: The Grove Park Inn Resort, Asheville, NC

For recreation, the resort offers activities for all ages. There is an 18-hole Donald Ross Golf course, 9 tennis courts (3 indoor and 6 outdoor), 2 pools (indoor and outdoor), and a Sports Center with tennis, aerobics, racquetball, squash, Nautilus, Jacuzzis and saunas. There are also supervised activities programs, playground and activities room (TV/VCR, video games, ping pong, toys). Under 16, stay free in room.

For shopping convenience, there are 6 boutiques to choose from: Ancient Page (gifts, newsstand, personal care needs), Gallery of the Mountains (native crafts),

Resort Boutique (casual and formal wear), Resort Photo, tennis and golf shops.

The resort offers an array of dining options, such as the Blue Ridge Dining Room, which serves breakfast, lunch and dinner in a beautiful dining room with a glassenclosed terrace. It also features lavish buffets (Friday seafood, Saturday prime rib, Sunday brunch and Italian buffets) and a la carte dining (American - Continental menu). Casual dress and resort-wear (no pool attire) are acceptable until 6:00 p.m. Casual evening dress (collared shirts and long pants for gentlemen) is requested from 6:00 p.m. until closing. Reservations strongly recommended.

The Sunset Terrace offers majestic views of sunsets over the city skyline and of the mountains beyond. This outdoor dining veranda is open seasonally, and it serves breakfast, lunch and dinner daily, with dinner music and dancing nightly. Casual dress and resort-wear (no pool attire) are acceptable until 6:00 p.m. Casual evening dress (collared shirts and long pants for gentlemen) is requested after 6:00 p.m. Reservations strongly recommended.

Horizons Restaurant serves innovative, classic cuisine in a formal dining room with fantastic views and elegant decor. Horizons is also recognized as one of the top five restaurants in North Carolina. Jacket and tie are required in this dining room. Reservations strongly recommended.

The Carolina Cafe, located in the Main Inn, serves breakfast and all-day dining in a cozy, yet contemporary room which offers great views. It is popular with families and children. One of the inn's massive stone fireplaces is located here and warms the room during the winter. Reservations are required for parties of five or more. Dress code is casual.

The Pool Cabana is an outdoor grill which overlooks the golf course and serves light lunches and drinks. It is located adjacent to the outdoor pool at the Country Club, and it is open daily, in season, as the weather permits. Dress code is very casual.

For pre-dinner and after-dinner entertainment, the Great Hall Bar offers piano concerts nightly in an old-world atmosphere with massive fireplaces and antique "arts and crafts" furnishings. Elaine's, a unique and classy lounge, is open Thursday through Saturday (Friday and Saturday only in January and February). This lounge features a variety of live entertainment and dancing, and it seats 200 on three levels.

For those who are traveling on business, as well as pleasure, there are 40 meeting rooms and 2 ballrooms totalling 50,000 square feet. There are also support services, such as floral and PR Departmens, in-house A/V department, photographers and theme party props.

The Grove Park Inn Resort is located approximately 18 miles from the Asheville Regional Airport. The resort will provide a shuttle to and from the airport for a fee of $15.00 each way. The airport also provides taxi and rental car services. To get to the resort, leave terminal lot and turn left. Cross the bridge onto I-26 west. Take I-26 west to I-240 east. Take the Charlotte Street exit (5B). Turn left at top of the exit. Go 1/2 mile on Charlotte Street. Turn right onto Macon Avenue. The resort is on the left. Guests can inquire about various accommodation packages, such as Romance, Great Gatsby, Golf, Family, Racquet, Easter, Thanksgiving, Christmas, and New Year's. For more information about rates and accommodations at The Grove Park Inn Resort, call 800-438-5800 or 252-2711.

NC-CLT - CHARLOTTE CHARLOTTE/DOUGLAS INTL.

2

Host Marriott:

Host Marriott, at Charlotte Douglas International Airport has a variety eateries that are located within the terminal building concourse. Mexican specialties at Aero Taco, homemade pizza, and grilled delights at the Charlotte Grill are a few of the eating establishments available to the general public. Host Marriott not only offers eating facilities for the air traveler customer, but they also serve your conference needs. They can provide the business traveler with accommodations for planning meetings. In addition they can prepare catered meals, and set up audio visual equipment if requested. All of this of course with advance notice. To reserve accommodation, please call 359-4450.

Attractions:

Pawtuckett Golf Club, (3 miles) 1 Pawtuckett Road, 394-5890; Renaissance Park Golf Course (3 miles) 1525 West Tyvola Road 357-3373.

Airport Information:

CHARLOTTE - CHARLOTTE/DOUGLAS INTERNATIONAL (CLT)
4 mi west of town N35-12.85 W80-56.59 Elev: 749 Fuel: 100LL, Jet-A Rwy 18R-36L: H10000x150 (Conc-WC) Rwy 18L-36R: H8845x150 (Asph-Grvd) Rwy 05-23: H7501x150 (Asph-Conc-Grvd) Attended: continuously Atis: Arr121.15, Dep 132.1 Unicom: 122.95 Tower: 118.1 Gnd Con: 121.9 Clnc Del: 127.15 Public Phone 24hrs Notes: Landing fee $.56 per 1000lbs
FBO: Charlotte Douglas Intl Arpt Phone: 359-4000
FBO: Signature Flight Support Phone: 359-8415

Restaurants Near Airport: **(Area Code 704)**

Host Marriott	On Site	Phone: 359-4450
Gratzi/Marriott Exec. Pk	5 mi N.	Phone: 527-9650
Oscar's/Sheraton Airport Plz	2 mi S.	Phone: 392-1200
Veranda/Royce Hotel	5 mi N.	Phone: 527-8000

Lodging: Holiday Inn Airport (2 miles) 394-4301; Sheraton Airport Plaza (2 miles) 392-1200.

Meeting Rooms: Dobbs Houses, Inc. is a full food company, that can offer event planning for business meetings supply food plus accommodations. Also meeting rooms are available at area hotels, (See Lodging listed above).

Transportation: Taxis, hotels/courtesy shuttles, limousines: Yellow Cab Co. 332-6161; Prestige Cab Co. 332-8001; Charlotte Cab Co. 333-1111; Avis Rent-A-Car 359-4700; Payless Car Rental 359-4640; Hertz Corp. 359-0114.

Information: Charlotte Convention & Visitors Bureau, 122 E Stonewall Street, Charlotte, NC 28202, Phone: 331-2700 or 800-231-4636.

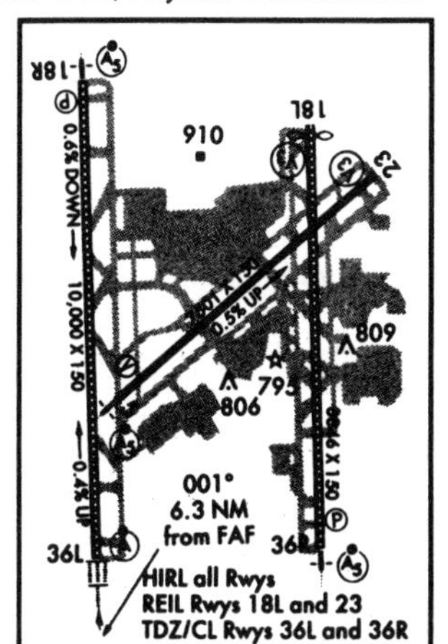

NC-FAY - FAYETTEVILLE
FAYETTEVILLE REG./GRANNIS FLD

3

(Area Code 910)

Restaurants Near Airport:

Ambassador House	3 mi	Phone: 484-4345
CA1 Services	On Site	Phone: 484-2846

CA1 Services:

The CA1 Services Restaurant is situated within the terminal building at the Fayetteville Regional Airport. This facility contains a snack bar, lounge and family style restaurant that caters to air travelers, local customers as well as military personnel from nearby Fort Bragg. Restaurant hours vary according to commercial flight schedules. However, they are open every morning at 6:00 a.m. and sometimes until late at night. The snack shop is usually open between 6 a.m. and 6:00 p.m. or until the last flight comes in. Their main dining area can accommodate up to 60 people, and offers guests a very homey and comfortable atmosphere. The decor exhibits burgundy and pink walls and many plants. Their menu contains a variety of delicious sandwiches including hamburgers, cheeseburgers, hot dogs, hot roast beef and hot turkey plates. They also serve chef salads along with breakfast entrees all day. Daily specials are also prepared during weekdays. Average prices run about $3.00 to $5.50 for most entrees. Group flying clubs and business clients are always welcome. However, please let them know in advance prior to your arrival, so they can prepare your seating arrangements. For more information call Concession Air at 484-2846.

Lodging: Days Inn (Free trans) 483-6191; Holiday Inn (Free trans) 323-1600; Ramada Inn (Free trans) 484-8101; Bordeaux Inn (Free trans) 323-0111; Howard Johnson Hotel (Free trans) 323-8282.

Meeting Rooms: Days Inn 483-6191; Holiday Inn 323-1600; Ramada Inn 484-8101; Bordeaux Inn (Convention Facilities) 323-0111; Howard Johnson Hotel 323-8282.

Transportation: Airport courtesy car reported; Taxi: Big Four 485-1054; Hillsboro 485-1231; Rental Cars: Avis 484-7985; Budget 485-3651; Hertz 483-8808; National 485-2133.

Information: Convention & Visitors Bureau, 245 Person Street, Fayetteville, NC 28301, Phone: 483-5311 or 800-255-8217.

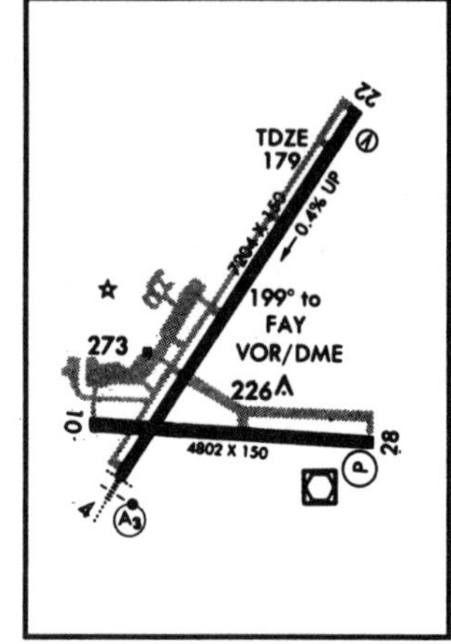

Airport Information:

FAYETTEVILLE - FAYETTEVILLE REGIONAL/GRANNIS FIELD (FAY)
3 mi south of town N34-59.49 W78-52.80 Elev: 190 Fuel: 100LL, Jet-A
Rwy 04-22: H7204x150 (Asph-Grvd) Rwy 10-28: H4802x150 (Asph) Attended: 1100-0500Z
Atis: 121.25 Unicom: 122.95 Tower: 118.3 Gnd Con: 121.7
FBO: Metro Air Center, Ltd Phone: 484-3424
FBO: Piedmont Aviation Phone: 484-2175

NC-GSO - GREENSBORO
PEIDMONT TRIAD INTERNATIONAL

4

(Area Code 910)

Restaurants Near Airport:

Host Marriott	On Site	Phone: 852-9311

Host Marriott Restaurant:

There are two main restaurants located in the terminal building at the Peidmont Triad International Airport. The Lounge Restaurant is open between 12 p.m. and 7 p.m. Sunday through Friday, and Saturday from 12 p.m. to 6 p.m. would be considered an up-scale family style facility. Their menu includes items like turkey, club sandwiches, ground steak burgers, blackened chicken, shrimp cocktails, tuna salad sandwiches, homemade soups of the day, as well as many delicious desserts. Average prices run between $6.95 and $7.95 for most selections. The decor is contemporary with seating for 100 persons. They also have access to a private conference room able to handle up to 60 people. In addition to this restaurant, there are also 2 snack bars and a cafeteria available for travelers. The cafeteria serves hot meals every day including hamburgers, hot dogs, grilled chicken and more. This dining area can also seat up to 100 persons as well as the lounge restaurant. For more information about available dining accommodations, call 852-9311.

Lodging: Ramada Inn Airport 272-6232 or 800-RAMADA; Holiday Inn Airport 668-0421; Marriott Hotel (On Site) 800-852-6450 or 852-6450.

Meeting Rooms: Marriott Hotels Resorts Suites (On Site) 800-852-6450 or 852-6450.

Transportation: Free hotel pick-up service is available; Also Taxi and or limo service: 668-0164, 454-2512, 727-1906; Rental cars: Alamo 665-2540; Avis 665-5700; Dollar 668-0407; Hertz 668-7961; National 668-7657; Triangle 668-3400.

Information: Greensboro Area Convention & Visitors Bureau, 317 South Greene Street, 27401. Phone: 274-2282 or 800-344-2282; Also: Triad Visitor Information Center 668-5612.

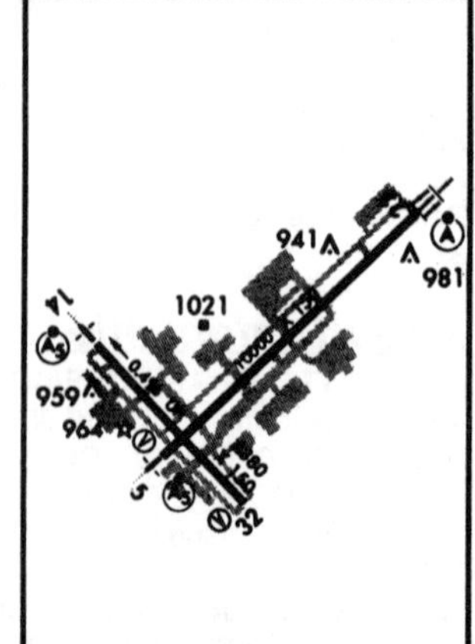

Airport Information:

GREENSBORO - PEIDMONT TRIAD INTERNATIONAL (GSO)
7 mi west of town N36-05.86 W79-56.24 Elev: 926 Fuel: 100LL, Jet-A
Rwy 05-23: H10000x150 (Asph-Grvd) Rwy 14-32: H6380x150 (Asph-Pfc)
Attended: continuously Atis: 128.55 Unicom: 122.95 Tower: 119.1 Gnd Con: 121.9
Clnc Del: 121.75 Public Phone 24hrs Notes: contact FBO's for fees.
Airport Manager Phone: 665-5600
FBO: Atlantic Aero, Inc. Phone: 668-0411

NC-0A7 - HENDERSONVILLE
HENDERSONVILLE AIRPORT

(Area Code 704) 5, 6

Kelsey's Restaurant:

Kelsey's Restaurant is a casual fine dining establishment that is located about 1-1/2 to 2 miles from the Hendersonville Airport. This restaurant provides a very nice assortment of entrees, specializing in prime rib along with all types of beef choices. New York sirloin, ribeyes, fillets, several pasta dishes, fresh mountain trout, shrimp, scallops and grilled chicken salad. They also have appetizers like their Texas Onions, natchos and potato skins to start off your meal. On Sunday they feature a Sunday brunch between 9:30 a.m. to 2:30 p.m. Their dining area displays a warm, elegant atmosphere. The dining area also has non-smoking and smoking sections, as well. Groups up to 30 persons can plan their fly-outs to Kelsey's Restaurant. To reach the restaurant from the airport you can turn right out of the airport entrance onto Airport Rd., then turn right on Spartonsburg Rd. and go about a mile until you reach the restaurant ,which will appear on your right side. Courtesy transportation might be arranged through the airport manager, Aerolina, Inc. (FBO) or museum management. For more information about Kelsey's Restaurant call 693-6688.

The Smoke House and Pros Italian Dining & Pizza:

All three restaurants: Kelsey's, The Smoke House and Pros Italian Dining & Pizza are located in the same area. The Smoke House specializes in serving barbecued items in a unique atmosphere. For information call 692-5300. Pros Italian Dining & Pizza is also a casual family dining establishment. For information call 692-8366. (See Kelsey's restaurant for directions).

Restaurants Near Airport:

Kelsey's	1-1/2 to 2 mi.	Phone: 693-6688
Pro's Italian Dining	1-1/2 to 2 mi.	Phone: 692-8366
The Smoke House	1-1/2 to 2 mi.	Phone: 692-5300

Lodging: Holiday Inn 3 mi. 692-7231; Ramada Inn 3 mi. 692-0521.

Meeting Rooms: Holiday Inn 3 mi. 692-7231;

Transportation: Taxi service: Carolina 693-3221; Rental cars: U-Save Auto Rental Service696-2200.

Information: Hendersonville Chamber of Commerce, 330 North King Street, Hendersonville, NC 28792. Phone: 692-1413.

Attractions:

Western North Carolina Air Museum:

The Western North Carolina Air Museum was founded in 1989 to preserve the aviation heritage of the western North Carolina area. The museum is registered as a corporation in the state of North Carolina and has received its tax exempt status from the Internal Revenue Service. It has over 450 members and is growing rapidly. The Museum is now located in its permanent home at 1340 Gilbert Street in Hendersonville, NC. From the Hendersonville Airport go west on Shepherd Street to Brooklyn Avenue. Turn right onto Brooklyn and follow it to Gilbert Street. The Museum is on the right, just past the stop sign. See award-winning and beautifully restored vintage airplanes, including: 1510 Ornithopter (replica of a design by Leonardo Da Vinci); 1917 replica Nieuport 11 ("BEBE"); 1931 Heath Parasol; 1931 Aeronca C-3; 1931 Piper E-2; 1936 Piper J-2; 1946 Piper J-3 Cub; 1942 Fairchild PT-19; 1942 Stearman N2S-3; 1943 Stearman N2S-4 (1990 Oshkosh Champion); 1943 North American SNJ-5 Texan; 1943 Stinson Reliant; 1952 Ercoupe; and a Corbin Jr. Ace (Asheville, NC Kit Plane). Admission is FREE. Museum hours are March through November: Saturday 10 a.m. to 6 p.m. and Sunday 12 noon to 6 p.m. and Wednesday from 12 noon to 6 p.m. Between December and February they are open on the weekend only from 12 noon to 5 p.m. For information about the museum write to Western N.C. Air Museum, P.O. Box 2343, Hendersonville 28793. Also you can call Aerolina, Inc. (FBO) at 693-3910 or Mr. Jim Granere, a very friendly individual who happens to be an active officer of the museum staff at 704-696-9723.

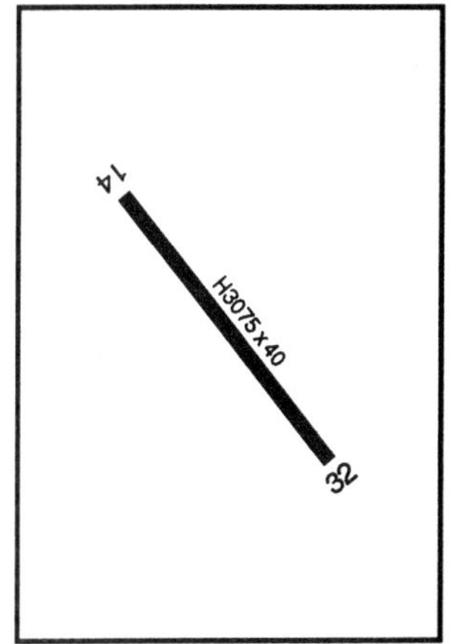

Airport Information:

HENDERSONVILLE - HENDERSONVILLE AIRPORT (0A7)
2 mi east of town N35-18.46 W82-25.99 Elev: 2084 Fuel: 100LL, MOGAS
Rwy 14-32: H3075x40 (Asph) Attended: daylight hours Unicom: 123.0
FBO: Aerolina, Inc. Phone: 693-3910

NC-DPL - KENANSVILLE
P.B. RAIFORD-(Duplin County) (DPL)

7

(Area Code 910)

The Country Squire:

This fine dining facility is located about 3 miles southwest of the Duplin County Airport, on state routes 24 & 50 between the towns of Kenansville and Warsaw and 7 miles from I-40. Transportation is provided by this establishment. Specialties include Korean barbecued beef, fresh seafood, marinated turkey and boneless prime rib. Daily as well as nightly specials are also offered. Entrees average about $5.00 for lunch and $15.00 for dinner. The decor of this restaurant is of a rural setting, that provides for a relaxed atmosphere while enjoying a truly fine meal. This facility is happy to arrange group get-togethers as well as fly-in club meetings. Luncheon is served from 11:30 a.m. to 2:00 p.m. Monday through Friday, and Sunday from 12:00 to 2:00 p.m. For dinner, they are open 5:30 to 10:00 p.m. from Sunday through Thursday, and 5:30 p.m. to 11:00 p.m. on Friday and Saturday. A telephone call is suggested in advance to your arrival, and to verify restaurant hours. For information and reservations call 296-1727.

Restaurants Near Airport:

Josef's Restaurant	3.5 mi SW.	Phone: 296-1368
Taste of Country	9 mi W.	Phone: 293-3213
The Country Squire	3 mi SW.	Phone: 296-1727

Lodging: The Village Inn (3 Miles) southwest of airport, located beside the Country Squire Restaurant.

Meeting Rooms: A large conference room with break room is located at the airport, with facilities available. Refrigerator, ice machine, coffee, drinks, dishwasher and catering available.

Transportation: There is a courtesy car on the airport; Also last reported, restaurants listed above would pick up. (Please call in advance); (Taxi): Carlton 293-4136; Underwood, 293-4985; (Rental Cars): Claudia's Ltd. U-Save 285-7565; Holland Ford, Inc. 293-3031.

Information: North Carolina Travel and Tourism Division, 430 N. Salisbury Street, Raleigh 27603, Phone: 800-VISIT-NC.

Attractions:

18 hole golf course and country club located 1.5 miles from airport.

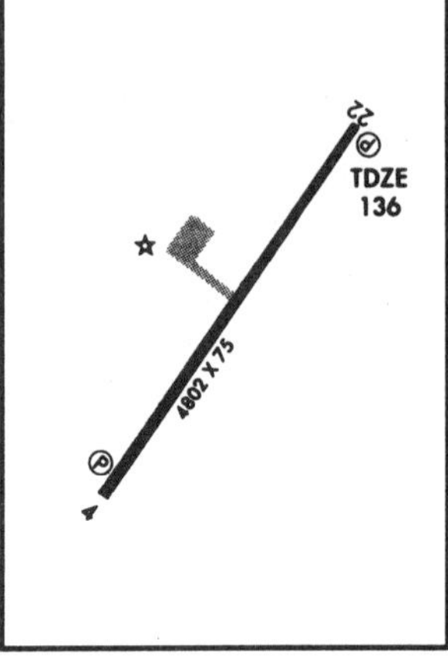

Airport Information:

KENANSVILLE - P.B. RAIFORD (DUPLIN COUNTY) (DPL)
2 mi NW of town N34-59.92 W77-58.97 Elev: 136 Fuel: 100LL, Jet-A
Rwy 04-22: H4802x75 (Asph) Attended: Mon-Sat dawn-dusk, Sun 1800Z-dusk Unicom: 123.0
Public Phone 24 hrs. Notes: No Landing fees; For airport attendant after hours and weekends call 296-2188.
FBO: Duplin Air Phone: 296-2188

Wright Brothers National Memorial:

Kill Devil Hills, NC (NC-FFA)

A thin broken strand of islands curves out into the Atlantic Ocean and then back again in a sheltering embrace of North Carolina's mainland coast and its offshore sounds. These are the Outer Banks of North Carolina. For thousands of years these barrier islands have survived the onslaught of wind and sea. Today their long stretches of beach, sand dunes, marshes and woodlands are set aside as Cape Hatteras National Seashore. It can be a lonely place; you may walk along the beach unseen except by shore birds searching for a meal. Here on the sandy, wind-swept plains of North Carolina's Outer Banks, the Wright brothers discovered nature's secrets of flying, and brought to all the gift of flight.

The principles that were developed, tested and proven by the Wrights at their secluded Kill Devil Hills site laid the foundation upon which all air transportation has been built. The revolution of a new, fast method of travel began here. Few advancements that have so influenced people around the world can be traced back to an episodic beginning. But powered flight can cite as its source December 17, 1903, 10:35 a.m.; the Wright brothers first successful powered flight above the flat sands of Kitty Hawk. It is a heritage that is shared by the entire world.

We suggest upon your arrival, you first stop at the visitor center, where the story of the Wright brothers is told through exhibits and full-scale reproductions of the 1902 glider and the 1903 flying machine. A large granite boulder, at the first flight area near the reconstructed 1903 camp buildings, marks the spot where the first airplane left the ground. Numbered markers indicate the distance of each of the four flights made on December 17, 1903.

One of the 1903 camp buildings duplicates the one used by the brothers as a hangar for the 1903 Flyer. The other is similar to the one used as a workshop and living quarters in 1903. It is furnished with items much like those the Wrights used when they were here. The Wright Memorial Shaft crowns Big Kill Devil Hill, a 990-foot dune of once-shifting sand that has been stabilized with grass. The 60-foot pylon, constructed of gray granite from Mount Airy, North Carolina, honors the Wright brothers and marks the site of the hundreds of glider flights that preceded the first powered flight.

When flying in to visit the Wright Brothers National Memorial, you are able to land at Kill Devil Hills - First Flight Airport (FFA) providing fly-in visitors with the ability to land right at this attraction. The airport was built in 1963 to accommodate small planes. Parking at the airstrips has limited tie-down area and is restricted to 24 consecutive hours or a total of 48 hours during any 30-day period. It's located N36-01.09 W75-40.28 with Runway 02-20: H3000x60 (Asph). This airport is unattended, and is closed 30 minutes after sunset and opens 30 minutes before sunrise. CTAF frequency is 122.9. Use caution for hang and powered gliding within this area. Pilots who wish to stay longer for other purposes may tie down at the Dare County Regional Airport, where gas and rental cars are available. For more information about the Memorial call 919-473-2111, or 24 hrs. aircraft parking permitted 919-441-7430. (Information by Wright Brothers Mem.)

NC-2A5 - LIBERTY CAUSEY AIRPORT

(Area Code 910)

8

Fran's Front Porch:

Frans Front Porch Restaurant is located across the street from the causey Airport. According to the restaurant management we learned that they often see pilots park their aircraft at the end of the runway and just walk across the street. You might want to check with the airport management if this is a standard practice. This restaurant serves strictly southern cooking. Baked ham, chicken pie, roast beef, beef tips and home made desserts are their specialties. A buffet is featured Thursday through Saturday 5 p.m. to 8:30 p.m. and Sunday from 12 p.m. to 2:30 p.m. The buffet runs about $9.00 for adults. The restaurant has a quaint atmosphere with in a farm house setting. There is seating for as many as 100 people within the restaurant as well as outdoor dining. Groups are welcome. For information call 685-4404.

Restaurants Near Airport:
Fran's Front Porch Adj Arpt Phone: 685-4404

Lodging: Holiday Inn (18 miles) 292-9161.

Meeting Rooms: None Reported

Transportation: Airport courtesy car reported.

Information: Burlington/Alamance County Convention & Visitors Bureau, P.O Drawer 519, Burlington, NC 27216, Phone: 910-570-1444 or 800-637-3804; Greensboro Area Convention & Visitors Bureau, 317 South Greene Street, Greensboro, NC 27401, Phone: 910-274-2282 or 800-344-2282; Also: North Carolina Travel and Tourism Division, 430 N. Salisbury Street, Raleigh 27603, Phone: 800-VISIT-NC.

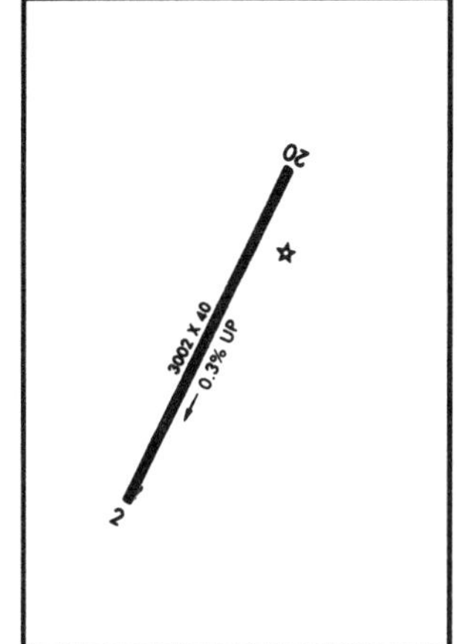

Airport Information:

LIBERTY - CAUSEY AIRPORT (2A5)
4 mi northwest of town N35-54.77 W79-37.04 Elev: 723 Fuel: 100LL, Jet-A
Rwy 02-20: H3002x40 (Asph) Attended: Mon-Sat daylight hours, Sun 1800Z-dusk
Unicom: 122.8
FBO: Causey Aviation Services, Inc. Phone: 685-4423

NC-60J - OCEAN ISLE BEACH OCEAN ISLE AIRPORT

(Area Code 910)

9

Pearl's Island House:

Pearl's Island House is located adjacent to the Ocean Isle Airport. This fine dining facility is primarily a steak and seafood house that offers prime rib, rib eye, New York strip, T-bone, fried chicken and Italian food, in addition to seafood selections. Average prices for most items run about $5.95 to $10.00 and $9.95 to $15.00 for their steaks. The restaurant can be reached by walking across the street from the airport. The dining room has recently been redecorated and displays many plants, decorative wicker baskets, linen covered tables with candles for each setting, and can seat about 200 people. Additional seating within conference room areas are also available to accommodate 30 to 40 and 15 to 30 respectively. Restaurant hours 7 days a week from 3 p.m. until they decide to close depending how busy they are. For more information call Pearl's Island House at 579-3787.

Restaurants Near Airport:

Pearl's Island House	Adj Arpt	Phone: 579-3787
Twin Lakes Seafood	4 mi	Phone: 579-6373

Lodging: Ocean Isle Motel (1 mile) 579-6216; The Winds (1 mile) 579-6275.

Meeting Rooms: Pearl's Island House Restaurant 579-3787.

Transportation: Highland Cab Company 754-6677 or 754-4871.

Information: Cape Fear Coast Convention & Visitors Bureau, 24 N 3rd Street, Wilmington, NC 28401, Phone: 910-341-4030 or 800-222-4757. or North Carolina Travel and Tourism Division, 430 N. Salisbury Street, Raleigh 27603, Phone: 800-VISIT-NC.

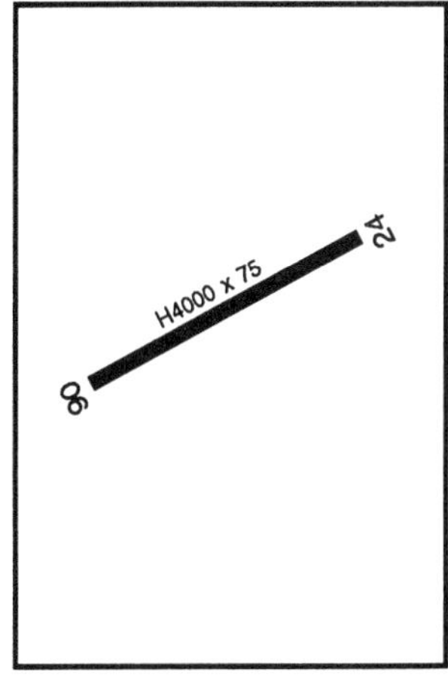

Airport Information:

OCEAN ISLE BEACH - OCEAN ISLE (60J)
1 mi north of town N33-54.51 W78-26.20 Elev: 32 Rwy 06-24: H4000x75 (Asph)
Attended: unattended CTAF: 122.9
Ocean Isle Airport Phone: 579-2166.

NC-W95 - OCRACOKE
OCRACOKE ISLAND AIRPORT

(Area Code 919) 10

Ocracoke Island:

Ocracoke, North Carolina, is part of the scenic Outer Banks - a chain of narow, sandy islands that stretch approximately 175 miles from Cape Lookout to Back Bay, Virginia. Ocracoke was settled in the 17th century, and was, according to legend, once used as headquarters by the pirate, Blackbeard.The airport is located 1 mi east of the Village of Ocracoke and the National Seashore.This island offers good fishing and hunting for wildfowl. Restaurant and lodging facilities are open seasonally. It is recommended that you call ahead to confirm hours of operation.The Back Porch Restaurant is usually open 5:30 p.m. to 9:30 p.m. from mid-April to mid-October. It specializes in crab cakes and fresh fish. Prices range from $7.00 to $19.00. Children's meals are also served.The Island Inn is a motel and restaurant.The restaurant is usually open for breakfast from 7:00 a.m. to 11:00 a.m., and for dinner from 5:00 p.m. to 8:00 p.m. (Lunch hours are seasonal.) It specializes in clam chowder, crab cakes and prime rib.The restaurant is closed December through February, and the motel is open from late May through early September. Many of the motels offer transportation to and from the airport. For more information about Ocracoke Island and its amenities, contact the Chamber of Commerce at 441-8144.

Attractions: National Seashore; National Park Service Beach 1500'; Also Nature Trails; Village of Ocracoke (1 mile)

Restaurants Near Airport:

Back Porch	1 mi	Phone: 928-6401
Island Inn	1 mi	Phone: 928-7821
Pony Island Motel & Rest.	1 mi	Phone: 928-4411

Lodging: Island Inn (1 mile) 928-4351; Pony Island Motel & Restaurant (1 mile) 928-4411; Anchorage Inn (1 mile) 928-1101; Berkley Center Country Inn (1-1/2 miles) 928-5911; Blackbeards Lodge (1 mile) 928-3421; Eugenia's Bed & Breakfast (928-1411); Harborside Motel (1 mile) 928-3111; Pamlico Lodges (1 mile) 928-1661; Sand Dollar Motel & Cottages (1 mile) 928-5571; Silver Lake Motel (1 mile) 928-5731

Meeting Rooms: None reported

Transportation: Most of the island's facilities are within walking distance from the airport. However, courtesy transportation is also provided by: Island Inn 928-4351; Anchorage Inn 928-1101; Eugenia's Bed & Breakfast 928-1411; Pamlico Lodges 928-1661

Information: Chamber of Commerce, P.O. Box 1757, Kill Devil Hills, NC 27948, Phone: 441-8144

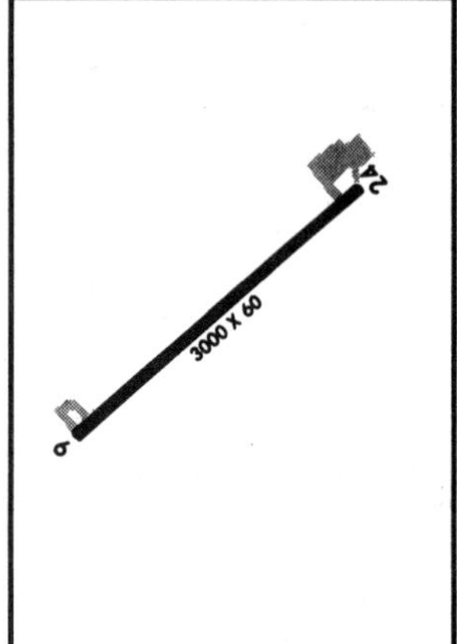

Airport Information:

OCEAN ISLE BEACH - OCRACOKE ISLAND AIRPORT (W95)
1 mi east of town N35-06.07 W75-57.96 Elev: 5 Fuel: None Reported Rwy 06-24: H3000x60 (Asph) Attended: Unattended CTAF: 122.9 Washington Center App/Dep Con: 135.5 Notes: Airport CLOSED 30 minutes after sunset until 30 minutes before sunrise. Flocks of seagulls on and near rwy around standing water after heavy rains. High speed low level military opr in vicinity of arpt. Rwy safety area is loose sand; not suitable for aircraft.
FBO: Pelican Airways Phone: 928-1661

NC-5W4 - RAEFORD
RAEFORD MUNICIPAL

(Area Code 919) 11

O'Baly's Restaurant:

O'Baly's Restaurant is located right on the Raeford Municipal Airport and only feet away from the aircraft parking ramp. This combination cafe and snack bar is open Monday through Friday 7 a.m. to 5 p.m., Saturday 7 a.m. to 7 p.m. and Sunday from 8 a.m. to 5 p.m. The restaurant and airport share a unique affiliation as the home of the famous Golden Knight U.S. Army Parachute Team. Guests can enjoy a meal while viewing the activity on the airport. Parachute drops and banner towing are regularly practiced. Items on the menu include a substantial breakfast selection including egg dishes, gravy and biscuits, bagels, pancakes, French toast and omelets. Their lunch menu contains as many as 15 hot sandwich choices and 7 different cold sandwiches with all the trimmings. Average prices run about $3.00 for breakfast, $4.50 for lunch and $5.00 to $6.00 for special dinner occasions. Many local residents come out to enjoy a fine meal while watching the activity. Groups and clubs often plan outings there as well. For information call O'Baly's Restaurant at 875-5197.

Restaurants Near Airport:

O'Baly's Restaurant	On Site	Phone: 875-5197

Lodging: Raeford Inn 6 mi 875-4524

Meeting Rooms: None reported

Transportation: O'Baly's Restaurant or the airport manager may be able to provide limited use of private van for local use. Snead's Rental Cars 875-2800

Information: North Carolina Division of Travel and Tourism, Dept. of Commerce, 430 N. Salisbury St., Raleigh, NC 27603. Phone: 800-VISIT-NC. In Raleigh, NC call 733-4171.

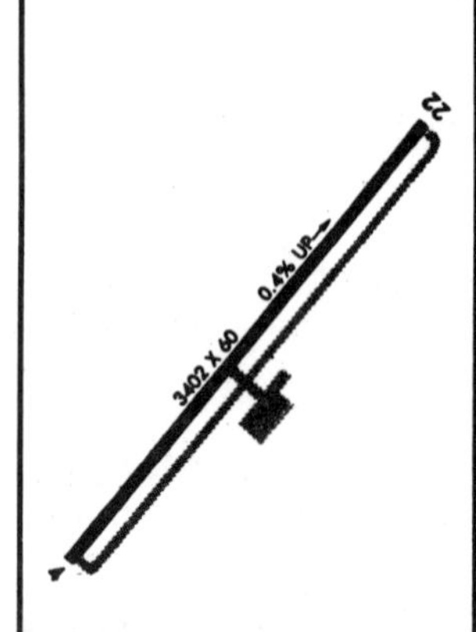

Airport Information:

RAEFORD - RAEFORD MUNICIPAL (5W4)
3 mi northeast of town N35-01.19 W79-11.46 Elev: 304 Fuel: 100LL, MOGAS Rwy 04-22: H3402x60 (Asph) Attended: 1300Z-dusk Unicom: 123.0 (Monitored irregularly) Notes: CAUTION: Low flying military acft in area. Heavy parachute jumping over arpt. Review current AFD cautions and approach procedures prior to use.
Airport Manager Phone: 875-3261

NC-RDU - RALEIGH DURHAM INTERNATIONAL

(Area Code 919)

12, 13

Angus Barn Restaurant:

The Angus Barn Restaurant is located 3 miles north of the Raleigh Durham International Airport. This up-scale fine dining facility will provide transportation for fly-in guests. Their menu features specially prepared beef dishes, BBQ pork ribs, lobster tail, the freshest of seafood, rack of lamb and prime rib, which is most popular with their customers. Their 5 course fixed-price meal is a real winner. They offer a dessert tray with 20 homemade delicious items. They also have a wine cellar containing 45,000 bottles some ranging in price from $15.00 per bottle to literally thousands of dollars per bottle. The restaurant has a rustic decor with a warm fireside dining atmosphere. Average prices run between $13.00 and $30.00 per plate. Restaurant hours are 5 p.m. to 11:30 p.m. 7 days a week. The owners have been serving customers for the past 35 years with bountiful portions. They also welcome larger groups with accommodations for 8 to 250 persons with catered and private dining. This restaurant is one that should be placed on your list of must-try fly-in dining establishments. For information call the Angus Barn at 781-2444.

Dobbs Houses, Inc.

Dobbs Houses restaurants are located in the A & C terminal buildings at the Raleigh/Durham International Airport. There is a snack bar, bakery, cafeteria and two grills, in addition to a fine dining facility known as the First Flight Restaurant. This restaurant is open from 6 a.m. to 12 a.m., in addition to a cocktail lounge on the premises. Their entrees consist of steaks, seafood, appetizers, desserts, soup and salad bar. The grills serve lighter fare such as hamburgers, hot dogs and sandwiches. The bakery will provide items like freshmade croissants, pastries, and soup. The cafeteria offers prime rib, chicken, hamburgers and sandwiches. Average prices at the First Flight restaurant run about $6.00 for breakfast, $8.00 for lunch and $10.00 for dinner. This fine dining facility offers a modern decor, and was winner of an interior restaurant design award. First Flight Restaurant has private rooms for meetings and/or meals fully catered to their clients. They also have the capability for both on-or-off-premises catering, special events catering, and airline employee discounts. For information call 840-4900.

Restaurants Near Airport:

1920 Deli	2 mi NE	Phone: 787-1300
Angus Barn Restaurant	2 mi NE	Phone: 781-2444
Dobbs Houses, Inc.	On Site	Phone: 840-4900

Lodging: Best Western Crown Park 941-6066; Best Western Triangle Inn (On Airport) 840-9000; Budgetel Inn 1-1/2 mile 481-3600; Comfort Suites-Crabtree Hotel 782-6868; Days Inn Raleigh 781-7904; Governors Inn At The Park 549-8631; Marriott Research Triangle 941-6200; Meredith Suites 361-1234; Ramada Inn Blue Ridge 832-4100; Sheraton Hotel Imperial 941-5050.

Meeting Rooms: Dobbs Houses, Inc. can help plan and accommodate your group arrangements with catering as well as services and equipment. Call 840-4900. Most of the lodging facilities listed above contain accommodations for meetings and conferences.

Transportation: Alamo 840-0132 or 800-327-9633; Avis 840-4750 or 800-331-1212; Budget 840-4775 or 800-527-0700; Dollar 840-4850 or 800-544-7891; Hertz 840-4875 or 800-654-3131; National 840-4350 or 800-227-7368; Thrifty 832-9381 or 800-367-2277; Triangle 840-3400. Also Airport Taxi 840-3451

Information: Raleigh Convention & Visitors Bureau, 225 South Hillsborough Street, Suite 400, Box 1879, Raleigh, NC 27602-1879, Phone: 834-5900.

Airport Information:

RALEIGH - DURHAM INTERNATIONAL (RDU)

9 mi northwest of town N35-52.66 W78-47.25 Elev: 436 Fuel: 100LL, Jet-A Rwy 05L-23R: H10000x150 (Conc-Wc) Rwy 05R-23L: H7500x150 (Asph-Grvd) Rwy 14-32: H3550x100 (Asph) Attended: continuously Atis: 123.8 Unicom: 122.95 App Con: 128.3, 124.95, 124.8 Dep Con: 132.35, 125.3 Tower: 119.3 (East), 127.45 (West) Gnd Con: 121.9 (East) 121.7 (West) Clnc Del: 120.1 Public Phone 24hrs Notes: FBO Parking fee. Visibility of beacon shielded to the North.

FBO: Aviation Services, Inc.	**Phone: 840-2200**
FBO: Million Air Raleigh-Durham	**Phone: 840-4300**
FBO: Raleigh Flying Servic, Inc.	**Phone: 840-4400**

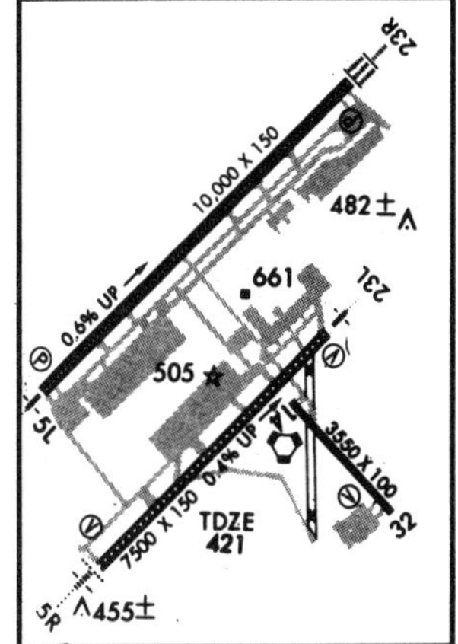

NC-FQD - RUTHERFORDTON RUTHERFORD COUNTY AIRPORT

(Area Code 704)

14

57 Alpha Cafe:

The 57 Alpha Cafe is located next to the airport authority building on the Rutherford County Airport. This cafe styled restaurant is open Tuesday through Saturday from 10 a.m. to 3 p.m. They are closed on Sunday and Monday. This small restaurant can seat only 6 to 8 people within the building itself. However, there are picnic tables outside able to accommodate up to 20 persons. Their menu contains a variety of hamburgers, turkey plates, club sandwiches, gourmet sandwiches, beef stew, hot dogs, salads, and a full breakfast line. Their specialties of the house are Mexican dishes. Average prices run $3.00 for breakfast, and $3.50 to $4.50 for lunch. Many of their customers often order meals-to-go or enjoy a meal on the outside picnic tables while watching the airport traffic. The 57 Alpha Cafe can also prepare cheese trays for corporate air travelers as well. If you plan to use the conference room in the main terminal building,they will also cater your needs. For information about this facility you can call 286-1677.

Restaurants Near Airport:
57 Alpha Cafe 50 yds W. Phone: 286-1677

Lodging: Days Inn (9 miles) 248-3400; Henderson Inn (10 miles) Phone N/A.

Meeting Rooms: There is a conference room located within the terminal building at the airport that can accommodate 15 to 20 persons, if needed.

Transportation: U-Save Auto Rental 287-2464.

Information: North Carolina Travel and Tourism Division, 430 N. Salisbury Street, Raleigh 27603, Phone: 800-VISIT-NC.

Attractions:

Chimney Rock Park Southern Highlands Attraction (Approx 13 miles) 800-277-9611; Rutherford Golf Course (Approx. 5 miles) 287-3406.

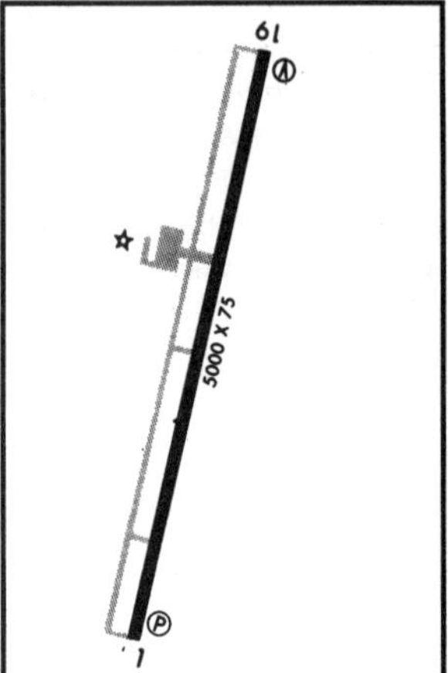

Airport Information:

RUTHERFORDTON - RUTHERFORD CO. AIRPORT (FQD)
3 mi north of town N35-25.69 W81-56.11 Elev: 1078 Fuel: 100LL, Jet-A1+
Rwy 01-19: H5000x75 (Asph) Attended: 1300Z-Dusk Unicom: 122.8 Public Phone 24hrs
Rutherford County Airport Phone: 287-0800

NC-SOP - SOUTHERN PINES
MOORE COUNTY

(Area Code 910)

15

Pine Needles Resort:

Pine Needles Resort is set in the heart of the Pinehurst Area golf community. It is easily accessible by air, car or train (Amtrack, 3 miles). Situated only 3 miles from the Moore County Airport , with free courtesy transportation makes this golf resort an ideal location to plan your next vacation or business event. Pine Needles is your private club away from home offering the finest in accommodations, recreation and dining. The cozy lodges are nestled throughout a natural setting. Golfers, business groups and individual travelers can relax in casual luxury. There are accommodations to suit every need. The Pinehurst/Southern Pines area is known as the Golf Capital of the World. The Pine Needles Resort has one of the most popular courses - a par 71 layout designed by legendary golf course architect Donald Ross in 1927. He skillfully blended the gently rolling countryside into a masterpiece with nature; the rustic and the unique covered practice tee where the celebrated "Golfari" golf schools are conducted. LPGA Teacher of the Year, Peggy Kirk Bell, PGA touring professional, Pat McGowan, and a talented staff offer their own special variety of golf clinics for women, men and juniors. You can also relax with a refreshing dip in the heated pool, play tennis day and night, work out in the weight room or unwind in the whirlpool and sauna. Dining at Pine Needles is a delightful experience, whether it's the breakfast buffet, lunch between your favorite activities or a candlelight dinner in one of their two dining rooms. Their main dining room has a wooden beam ceiling and brick fireplace. White linen table cloths, green napkins and a flower at each table gives a country atmosphere. Meet old friends and make new ones in the Ross Room. Or review the day's events in the adjoining "In the Rough Bar." For those who like to mix business with pleasure, Pine Needles is the perfect meeting facility. The utmost in personal attention is offered in an unsurpassed atmosphere for groups up to 140. The versatile meeting rooms can accommodate sales seminars, executive board meetings or the grand finale banquet. Modern audio-visual equipment is available to help insure the success of your gathering. Pine Needles is a small, ultimate resort for those who desire casual elegance. It's tradition that dates back to an earlier era when warmth, charm and gracious hospitality were a way of life. For information call 692-7111 (Article by Pine Needles Resort).

Resorts Near Airport:

Mid Pines	4 mi. Free trans.	Phone: 692-2114
Pinehurst Resort & C.C.	5 mi. Free trans.	Phone: 295-6811
Pine Needles Resort	3 mi. Free trans.	Phone: 692-7111

Lodging: Holiday Inn 692-8585; Mid Pines Resort 692-2114; Pine Needles Resort 692-7111; Pinehurst Resort & Country Club 295-6811.

Meeting Rooms: Mid Pines Resort 692-2114; Pine Needles Resort 692-7111;

Transportation: Airport courtesy cars reported; Rental cars: National Car Rental 692-4449; Taxi Service: Jones Limousine 692-2011; Thorndale 692-9633.

Information: Pinehurst Area Convention & Visitors Bureau, P.O. Box 2270, Southern Pines, NC 28388, phone: 692-3330 or 800-

Attractions:

Southern Pines (Golf Capital): This area has long been famous for its championship golf courses that attract celebrities from all parts of the country. The resorts in the area play a large part in carrying on the tradition of this fine sport with magnificently groomed fairways and greens. Pinehurst preserves the tradition of golf excellence and serves as an important sight for golf exhibitions. Southern Pines also ranks as a prominent location for golf and equestrian activities. Many of these resorts are within 10 or 15 minutes of the Moore County Airport. In all, there are some 43 championship golf courses reported within, the Southern Pines and Pinehurst region, making this area a golfers mecca. These same resorts also contain excellent accommodations for fine dining and lodging. Transportation to many of the major resorts can easily be arranged. The World Golf Hall of Fame is located southwest of the town of Pinehurst and displays a collection of golf artifacts, and the portraits of golf legends who have been inducted into the Hall Of Fame. For information call the Pinehurst Area Convention & Visitors Bureau at 692-3330 or 800-346-5362.

Airport Information:

SOUTHERN PINES - MOORE COUNTY (SOP)

3 mi north of town N35-14.21 W79-23.49 Rwy 05-23: H5503x150 (Asph) Rwy 14-32: 3100x100 (Turf) Attended: 1200-0200Z Unicom: 122.7 Notes: avoid flying over residential area NE of airport. Noise abatement procedures in effect.

FBO: Moore County Airport Phone: 629-3212

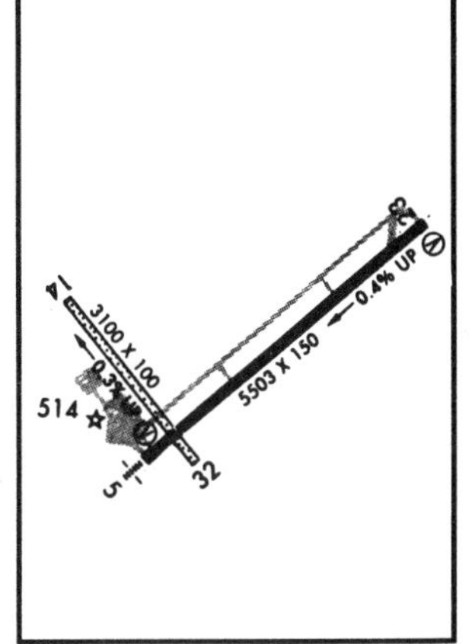

North Carolina's Pinehurst, Southern Pines & Aberdeen Area

Welcome to North Carolina's Village of Pinehurst, Southern Pines, Aberdeen Area, a unique combination of quiet country lanes, friendly southern towns and villages, and world-renowned golf and accommodations blending with the natural ecosystem of the Sandhills region.

Boasting 40 of the world's finest golf courses, the area is, to be sure, steeped in a rich tradition of golfing excellence. But there is so much more to do and see beyond the greens and fairways. You'll find a diversity of equestrian activities from polo to harness racing. Smashing tennis. Watersports, archery, bicycling, even lawn bowling and croquet. You'll find that area dining offers everything from formal resort ambience and dinner theatres to pubs, continental, deli, ethnic and of course, fast-food restaurants.

Visitors can experience warmth and hospitality in a wide variety of accommodations, from cozy bed & breakfast inns to motels, hotels, condominiums and grand resorts.

What, exactly, is it that has made the village of Pinehurst, Southern Pines, and Aberdeen Area synonymous with the game of golf? Is it the sheer number of superb championship courses, some of which are among the most highly rated in the world? Is it the fact that Pinehurst and Southern Pines have been the home to a host of major golf tournaments? Or is it that of major U.S. golf destinations, the Village of Pinehurst, Southern Pines, and Aberdeen Area received top honors in golf course quality, according to "Golf Digest's Places to Play Guide".

For many, it's all of these things and more that account for the area's standing in the world of golf. Perhaps it can best be summarized in one word: tradition.

Nestled in the Sandhills of North Carolina, this area has come to epitomize golf's grandest era. This was an era when legends were born and grew - with names like Nelson, Zaharias, Hogan, Jones, Snead and Palmer, and a time that gave the game some of its finest designers as well: Donald Ross, Ellis Maples, Robert Trent Jones and many more. Today, courses by earlier legends are joined by those of a new generation of designers: Jack Nicklaus, Arnold Palmer, Tom and George Fazio, Dan Maples and Rees Jones just to name a few. All this awaits your return to Golf's Grandest Era.

The "Golf Vacation Planning Guide" published by the North Carolina's Village of Pinehurst, Southern Pines & Aberdeen Area Convention & Visitors Bureau is an excellent reference magazine for planning your accommodations, with pictures of many facilities. For more information, send your requests to 1480 U.S. Hwy. 15-501, P.O. Box 2270, Southern Pines, NC 28388, or call 910-692-3330 or 800-346-5362. The Southern Pines, Moore County Airport (SOP) is located within easy access to major resorts, bed & breakfast inns, hotels and motels and condominium & suite properties all within the area. In most cases, they will be happy to furnish your party with transportation. Information for articles obtained by Convention & Visitors Bureau.

Photo by: Pinehurst Area Convention & Visitors Bureau. Mid-Pines Golf Club

NC-ILM - WILMINGTON NEW HANOVER INTERNATIONAL

(Area Code 910) 16

Restaurants Near Airport:

ACE's Grill	On Side	Phone: 343-1262
Helnick Corp.	On Site	Phone: 343-9881

Helnick Corporation Restaurant:

The Helnick Corp. Restaurant is located within the new terminal building at the New Hanover International Airport. As reported, this combination cafe and cafeteria style restaurant can be reached by walking from nearby aircraft parking areas. The restaurant is open from 6:30 a.m. to 9 p.m. 7 days a week. Their menu contains a varied selection of entrees such as barbecued pork, hambergers, cheese burgers, hot dogs as well as a full compliment of breakfast choices. Average prices run $3.75 to $5.75 for breakfast and $5.00 to $7.00 for lunch as well as dinner. Their main dining room, with modern decor, can seat up to 125 persons, and is situated on the upper level lobby. Guests can watch airplanes takeoff and landing. This establishment also accommodates in-flight catering for corporate business air travelers. Groups or parties with advance notice, can also plan their meetings or fly-ins. For more information about the Helnick Corporation Restaurant, call 343-9881.

Lodging: Holiday Inn Wilmington 799-1440; Holiday Inn Wrightsville Beach 256-2231; Hilton 763-5900; Howard Johnson 392-1101; Shell Island Resort Hotel 256-5050; Blockade Runner Resort Hotel 256-2251.

Meeting Rooms: Airport conference room available with reservations 341-4333.

Transportation: Taxi Brooklyn Cab 763-8522; Letts 548-4754; Port City 726-1165; Top Cat 347-8732; Yellow 762-4464; Rental Cars: Avis 763-3346; Budget 762-9247; Hertz 762-1010; National 762-8000.

Information: Cape Fear Coast Convention & Visitors Bureau, 24 North 3rd Street, Wilmington, NC 28401; Phone: Phone: 341-4030 or 800-922-7117 in NC or 800-222-4757 if calling from the eastern portion of the U.S.

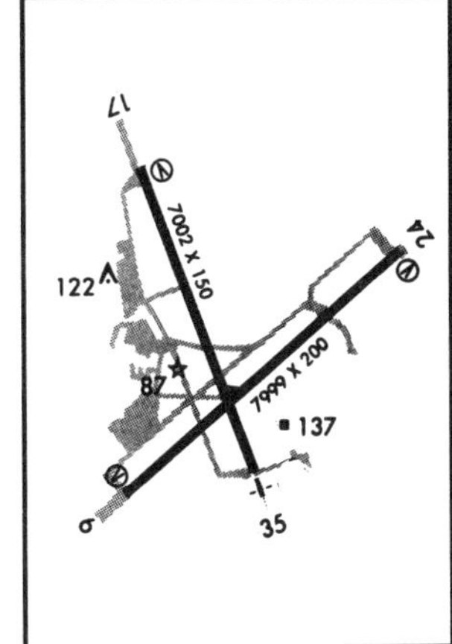

Airport Information:

WILMINGTON - NEW HANOVER INTL. AIRPORT (ILM)

3 mi northeast of town N34-16.24 W77-54.15 Elev: 33 Fuel: 100LL, Jet-A Rwy 06-24: H7999x200 (Asph-Conc) Rwy 17-35: H7002x150 (Asph) Attended: continuously Atis: 121.1 Unicom: 122.95 Wilmington App/Dep Con: 135.75, 118.25, 121.4 Wilmington Tower 119.9 Gnd Con: 121.9 Clnc Del 121.9 Public Phone 24hrs Notes: Possible overnight or ramp parking fees charged by FBO's.

FBO: Aeronautics	**Phone: 763-4691**
FBO: Air Wilmington	**Phone: 763-0146**
FBO: ISO Aero of Willmington	**Phone: 763-8898**

NC-INT - WINSTON SALEM SMITH REYNOLDS

(Area Code 910) 17

Restaurants Near Airport:

La Chaudiere	N/A	Phone: 748-0269
Numerous Restaurants	In town	Phone: 777-3796
Salem Tavern	8 mi	Phone: 748-8585

Salem Tavern:

The Salem Tavern is situated about 8 miles from the Winston Salem-Smith Reynolds Airport. We learned that this restaurant was popular with many of our readers and recommended as a fine place to enjoy a meal. Old Salem contains a treasury of fine historic buildings that were constructed in 1766. Many of these buildings have been restored and serve as a landmark of old tradition. Others have been in continuous operation since that time. After enjoying the hospitality of the Salem Tavern, visitors can walk the streets of Old Salem historic district and take in the sights. To reach the restaurant from the airport take Hwy. 52 south and follow the signs to Old Salem. The restaurant is on Main Street in town. The Salem Tavern is open for lunch between 11:30 a.m. and 2 p.m. on Friday, Saturday and Sunday, and for dinner Monday through Thursday between 5 p.m. and 9 p.m. Specialties of the house include chicken pies, hardy stews, veal dishes, ribeye steaks, seafood, salads, oysters, cache and a full assortment of appetizers. Dinners run $12.00 to $21.00. The Salem Tavern exhibits a warm, cozy atmosphere with "candle light." Outdoor dining is also available as well. For information call 748-8585.

Lodging: Holiday Inn-North 3-5 mi 723-2911; Howard Johnson Lodge 3-5 mi 725-7501; Ramada Inn 2-4 mi 767-8240; Stouffer Winston Plaza 2-4 mi 725-3500; The Marque of Winston-Salem 2-4 mi 725-1234.

Meeting Rooms: The Marque of Winston-Salem has accommodations for conventions and meetings (Est. 2-4 mi) 725-1234.

Transportation: Rental cars: Avis 767-6230; Budget: 767-9100; Hertz 744-0310; Taxi service: Bluebird 722-7121.

Information: Winston-Salem Convention and Visitors Bureau, P.O. Box 1408, Winston-Salem, NC 27102, Phone: 777-3796 or 800-331-7018.

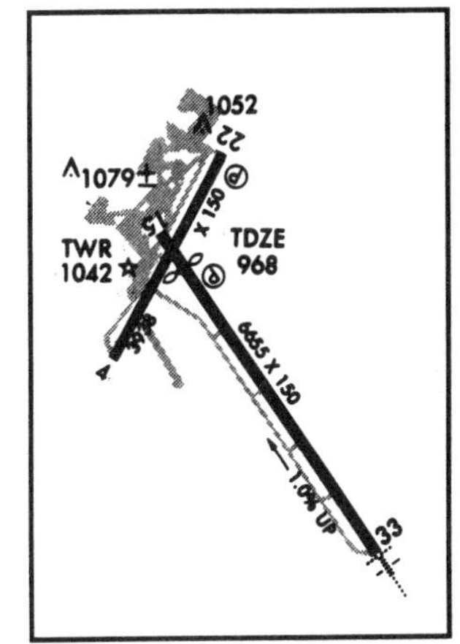

Attractions: Old Salem District contains many historic buildings, art galleries, museums, and art and craft shops. The town of Winston Salem just to the north has numerous attractions: Nature Science Center, Museum of Early Southern Decorative Arts, Southeastern Center for Contemporary Art, Stroh Brewery Company, Whitaker Park and Historic Bethabara Park.

Airport Information:

WINSTON SALEM - SMITH REYNOLDS (INT)

3 mi northeast of town N36-08.02 W80-13.32 Elev: 970 Fuel: 100LL, Jet-A Rwy 15-33: H6655x150 (Asph-Grvd) Rwy 04-22: H3938x150 (Asph) Attended: continuously CTAF: 123.75 Atis: 121.3 (1200-0400Z) Unicom: 122.95 Tower: 123.75 (1200-0400Z) Gnd Con: 128.25

FBO: Piedmont Aviation Service, Inc. Phone: 661-5562 or 661-5570

NORTH DAKOTA

CROSS FILE INDEX

Location Number	City or Town	Airport Name And Identifier	Name of Attraction
1	Bowman	Bowman Muni. (BPP)	Shariver Steak House
2	Fargo	Hector Intl. (FAR)	Barnstomer Restaurant
3	Grand Forks	Grand Forks Intl. (GFK)	Arpt. Cafe
4	Jamestown	Jamestown Muni. Arpt. (JMS)	Gladstone Restaurant
5	Minot	Minot Intl. Arpt. (MOT)	Knight's Bistro
6	Napoleon	Napoleon Muni. (ND45)	Judge's Chambers
7	Plaza	Trulson Field (Y99)	Home Style Cafe
8	Sterling	Top's Airfield (ND61)	Top's Cafe
9	Williston	Sloulin Field Intl. (ISN)	Arpt. Intl. Inn
10	Wishek	Wishek Muni. Arpt. (ND70)	Prairie Winds Restaurant

LOCATION MAP

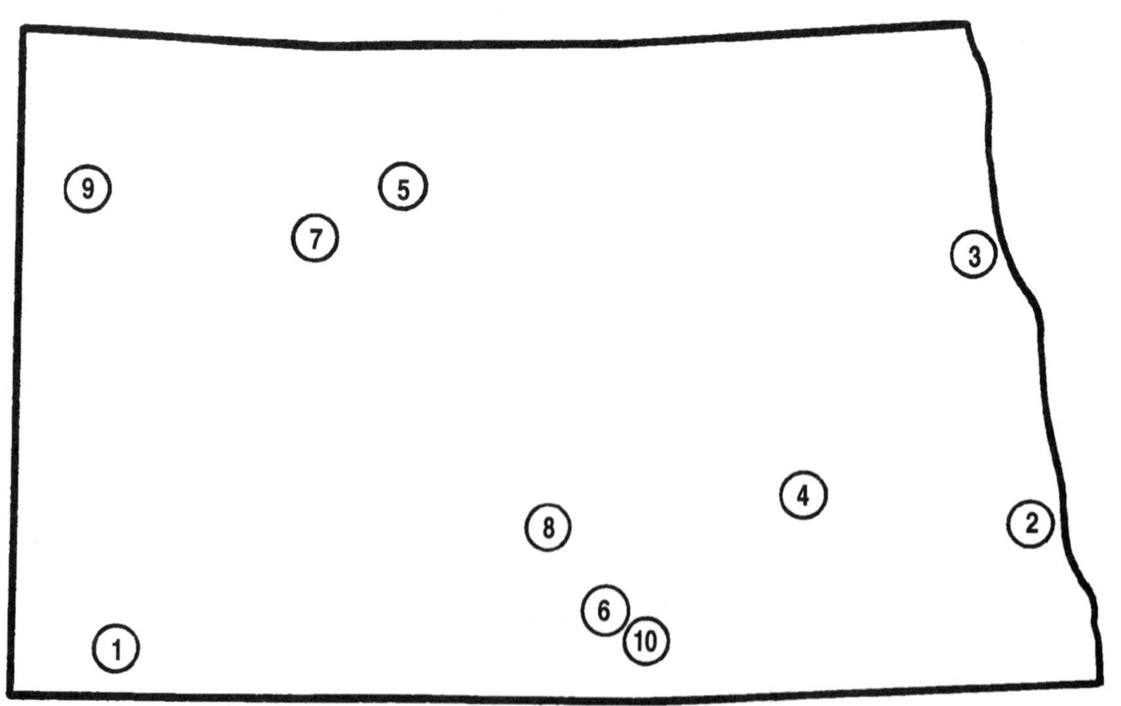

Not to be used for navigational purposes

ND-BPP - BOWMAN
BOWMAN MUNICIPAL AIRPORT

(Area Code 701)

1

Sharivar Steak House:

The Sharivar Steak House is located right in the downtown district of Bowman one block east of main street, about 1 mile east of the Bowman Municipal Airport. This combination family style and fine dining facility can be reached by arranging courtesy transportation with the restaurant itself or through Plains Aviation, Inc. This steak house is open between 5 p.m. and 11 p.m. 6 days a week. (Closed on Sunday). They also have a lounge on the premises. Steaks are their specialty including rib-eye, sirloin, prime rib, along with many other delicious selections such as seafood, lobster, and chicken dishes. Average prices range from $8.95 to $14.95 for most entrees. On Friday and Saturday nights they offer prime rib as their special. The restaurant provides a peaceful, cozy and quiet atmosphere with seating for about 65 people in their main dining area. There is also a banquet room able to accommodate up to 60 persons. The main dining area is situated on the ground level. For more information call the restaurant at 523-5201.

Restaurants Near Airport:

Flagster Terrace	2 mi E.	Phone: 523-3200
Gateway Restaurant	1 mi E.	Phone: 523-5757
Genes Restaurant	1 mi E.	Phone: 523-3137
Sharivar Steak Hse.	1 mi E.	Phone; 523-5201

Lodging: 4-U Motel (Free trans) 523-3243; Northwinds Motel (Free trans) 523-5641; Super 8 lodge 523-5613; Elvue Motel (Free trans) 523-5224;

Meeting Rooms: There are several facilities available nearby, depending on size of meetings. For information call Weather Modifications, Inc. (FBO) 523-3609.

Transportation: Weather Modifications, Inc. (FBO) for courtesy transportation at 523-3609; Also Nordberg Chevrolet 523-5222; Bowman Ford 523-3257.

Information: North Dakota Tourism Department, Capitol Grounds, Bismarck, ND 58505, Phone: 800-435-5663.

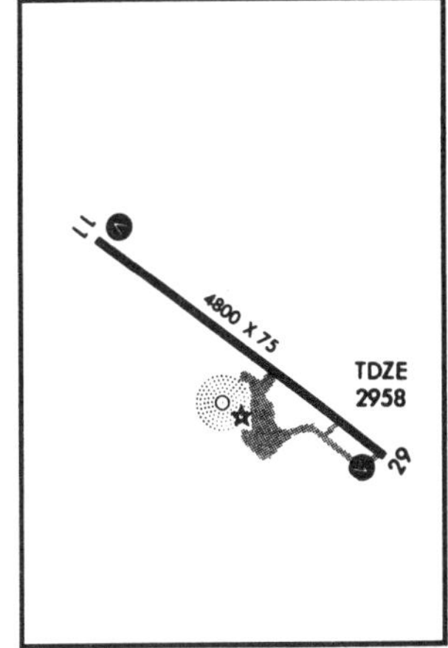

Airport Information:

BOWMAN - BOWMAN MUNICIPAL AIRPORT (BPP)
2 mi west of town N46-11.22 W103-25.69 Elev: 2958 Fuel: 80, 100, Jet-A
Rwy 11-29: H4800x75 (Asph-Afsc) Attended: Mon-Fri 1500-0030Z Unicom: 122.8
Notes: For attendant other hours call 523-5504, 3544,3677. For fuel after hours call 523-5504, also Confirm snow removal with airport manager after major storms.
FBO: Weather Modifications, Inc. Phone: 523-3609

ND-FAR - FARGO
HECTOR INTERNATIONAL AIRPORT

(Area Code 701)

2

Barnstormer Restaurant:

The Barn Stormer Restaurant is located in the newly built terminal building on the second floor near the entrance gate. Courtesy transportation can be obtained to and from the restaurant through Valley Aviation by calling 237-6882. This combination snack bar, cafe and family style restaurant is open between 5:15 a.m. and 9 p.m. 7 days a week. Their menu selections include items like roast chicken, broiled sirloin, prime rib, turkey roast, sandwiches of all types like roast beef, ruben and patty melts etc. Nightly specials are usually offered between 5 p.m. and 8 p.m. as well as Saturday specials. The main dining room can seat 150 persons. From their lounge you can see the aviation ramps. Meals can also be ordered and served in the lounge. This restaurant specializes in catering to small and large groups with advance notice required. For more information call The Barnstormer Restaurant at 241-1559.

Restaurants Near Airport:

Airport Cafe	On Site	Phone: 232-1752
Barnstormer	On Site	Phone: 241-1559
Passages Cafe	4 mi SE.	Phone: 293-6717
Treetop Restaurant	6 mi SE	Phone: 233-1393

Lodging: Radisson Hotel (4 mi SE) 232-7363; Holiday Inn (3 mi S.) 282-2700; Doublewood Inn (3 mi S.) 235-3333; The Madison (8 mi SE) 233-6171. Hotel shuttle phones in Hector Terminal Building.

Meeting Rooms: Radison Hotel, Holiday Inn, Doublewood Inn, The Madison, The Townhouse, Kelly Inn; Hotel shuttle phones in the Hector Terminal Building.

Transportation: Taxi Cab Service 235-5535; Avis Car Rental 241-1580; Budget 241-1574; Hertz 241-1533; National 241-1576; Thrifty 241-1520.

Information: Fargo-Moorhead Convention & Visitors Bureau, P.O. Box 2164, Fargo, ND 58107, Phone: 237-6134.

Attraction:

Edgewood Golf Course located 3 miles east of Hector Terminal 232-2824; Bonanzaville USA, is located on Hwy 10, situated 4 miles southwest of Hector Terminal in West Fargo. This attraction contains over 45 reconstructed buildings, antique vehicle museums, and is home of the Kodak film inventor. Open late May through October daily, Phone: 282-2822.

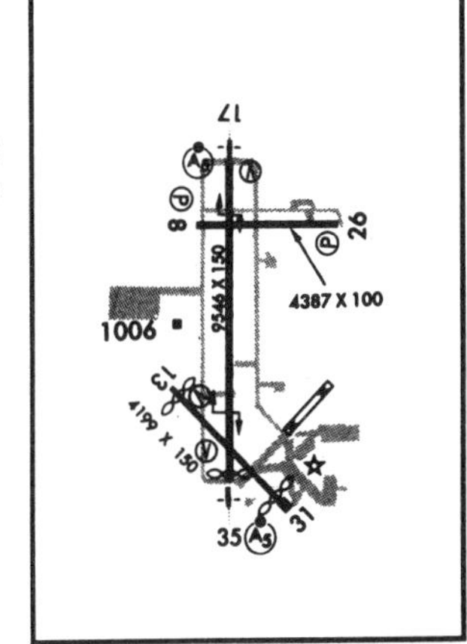

Airport Information:

FARGO - HECTOR INTERNATIONAL AIRPORT (FAR)
3 mi northwest of town N46-55.16 W96-48.90 Elev: 900 Fuel: 100LL, Jet-A Rwy 17-35: H9546x150 (Conc-Grvd) Rwy 08-26: H4387x100 (Conc) Rwy 13-31: H4199x150 (Asph-Conc) Attended: continuously Atis: 124.5 Unicom: 122.95 Fargo App/Dep 120.4, 127.7 Tower: 118.6 Gnd Con: 121.9 Clnc Del: 121.9 Public Phone 24hrs Notes: $3.00 overnight fee/no landing fee for small aircraft. Hotel reservations and shuttle phones are located in the Hector Terminal. U.S. Custom service is available 8:30 a.m. to 5 p.m. or by arrangement, phone: 241-8124.
FBO: Fargo Jet Center Phone: 235-3600, 800-770-0538
FBO: Valley Aviation Phone: 237-6882 or 800-279-8590

ND-GFK - GRAND FORKS
GRAND FORKS INTERNATIONAL

(Area Code 701) 3

Crosswind Cafe:

The Airport Cafe is situated within the terminal building at the Grand Forks International Airport. This family style restaurant is open between 5 p.m. to 11 p.m. Monday through Friday and 5 p.m. to 9:30 p.m. on Saturday and Sunday. Their menu contains items like a French dip sandwich, Denver croissant, Philly sandwiches with roast beef, green peppers and onions and club sandwiches. They also have a variety of soups, and salads including a chef and taco salad. An average price for most entrees runs about $4.00 to $6.00 per selection. Their main dining room has recently been remodeled and can accommodate between 60 and 70 people. The Airport Cafe is capable of catering as well as preparing meals-to-go. Groups planning a party or fly-in are welcome to phone ahead and make reservations. For more information you can call the Airport Cafe at 746-7231.

Restaurants Near Airport:
Crosswind Cafe On Site Phone: 746-7231

Lodging: Holiday Inn (Free trans) 772-7131; Ramada Inn (Free trans) 775-3951; Best Western Fabulous Westward Ho (Free trans) 775-5341.

Meeting Rooms: Holiday Inn (Free trans) 772-7131; Ramada Inn (Free trans) 775-3951; Best Western Fabulous Westward Ho (Free trans) 775-5341.

Transportation: Courtesy car available; Also rental cars: Avis, Hertz and National.

Information: Convention & Visitors Bureau, 202 North 3rd Street, Suite 200, Grand Forks, ND 58203, Phone: 746-0444 or 800-866-4566.

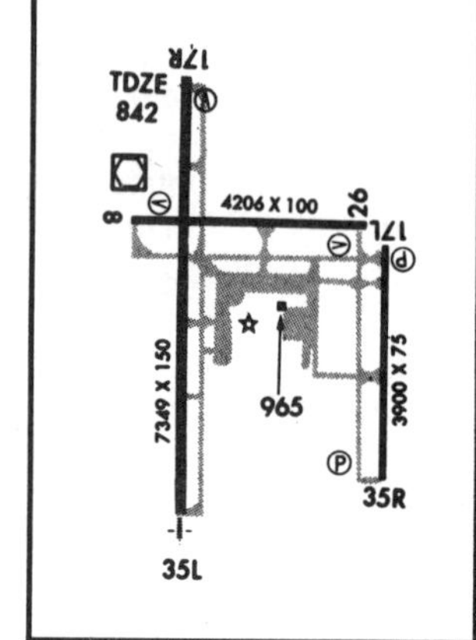

Attractions:

River Cruises on the "Dakota Queen". Evening dinner cruises on the Red River with sightseeing tours, operating between Memorial Day and Labor Day, each day except on Monday. For information call 775-5656.

Airport Information:

GRAND FORKS - GRAND FORKS INTERNATIONAL (GFK)
5 mi northwest of town N47-56.96 W97-10.57 Elev: 844 Fuel: 100LL, Jet-A
Rwy 17R-35L: H7349x150 (Asph-Pfc) Rwy 08-26: H4206x100 (Conc) Rwy 17L-35R: H3900x75 (Conc) Attended: continuously Atis: 119.4 Unicom 122.95 App/Dep Con: 118.1 (Above 4000 ft), 132.3 (4000 ft and below) Tower: 118.4 Gnd Con: 121.9
FBO: GFK Flight Support Phone: 772-5504

ND-JMS - JAMESTOWN
JAMESTOWN MUNICIPAL AIRPORT

Area Code 701) 4

Gladstone Restaurant:

This restaurant is located in downtown Jamestown, 1-1/2 miles southwest of the airport. You can call them and they will provide you with transportation to and from the airport. The restaurant specializes in entrees such as walleye pike, BBQ'd ribs, and nightly specials. On Sunday they offer a 3 meat buffet, Tuesday through Thursday a lunch buffet with breakfast and dinner specials. Their hours are 6:30 a.m. to 10:00 p.m. Monday through Saturday, and from 6:30 a.m. to 3:00 p.m. on Sunday. Entrees average $3.00 for breakfast, $5.00 for lunch, and $11.00 for dinner. The restaurant serves meals on white tablecloths, in a romantic candlelight dinner setting. Banquet facilities are also available for up to 275 people in the hotel adjacent to the restaurant. For more information call 252-0700.

Restaurants Near Airport:
Gladstone Rest. 1-1/2 mi SW. Phone: 252-0700
Serbs Restaurant & Seafood 1/2 mi W. Phone: 251-2900

Lodging: Gladstone Select Inn (Free Trans, 1-1/2 mile southwest of airport), 111 2nd Street NE., 117 rooms, Indoor pool, cafe, meeting rooms, Phone: 252-0700

Meeting Rooms: Conference room located in the terminal building waiting room at Jamestown Airport; Gladstone Select Inn, (See Lodging listed above).

Transportation: Jamestown Aviation will provide courtesy transportation; Avis, 252-2360; Nickel/Dime, 252-0905; Taxi Service, 252-4200.

Information: Jamestown Promotion and Tourism Center, 212 Third Avenue NE., Jamestown, ND 58401, Phone: 252-4835.

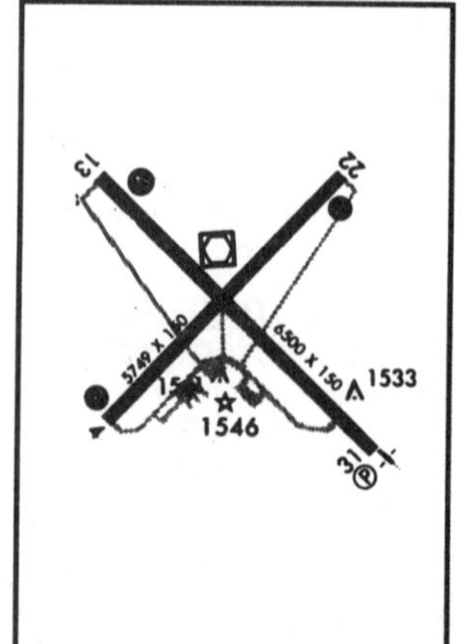

Attractions:

Jamestown Reservoir (Fishing); Pipestem Dam (Fishing); Hillcrest Golf Course, all within 1 mile of Jamestown Airport;

Airport Information:

JAMESTOWN - JAMESTOWN MUNICIPAL AIRPORT (JMS)
2 mi northeast of town N46-55.78 W98-40.69 Elev: 1498 Fule: 100LL, Jet-A
Rwy 13-31: H6500x150 (Asph-Pfc) Rwy 04-22: H5749x150 (Asph) Attended: continuously
Unicom: 123.0 Public Phone 24hrs Notes: landing fee for A/C over 12,500 lbs.
FBO: Jamestown Aviation, Phone: 252-2150

ND-MOT - MINOT
MINOT INTERNATIONAL AIRPORT

(Area Code 701)

5

Restaurants Near Airport:
Jetway Restaurant On Site Phone: 839-5848

Jetway Restaurant:

Knight's Bistro restaurant is a combination family style and fine dining facility. They are located within the upper level of the terminal building. Courtesy transportation to the restaurant is available as well as Taxi service. This restaurant is open between 4:30 a.m. and 4:30 p.m. weekdays and until 10 p.m. on weekends. Their lounge is open until 1 a.m. For breakfast their menu offers all types of omelets, standard egg dishes, pancakes, and muffins.. For lunch 10 different salads are prepared, including Hoagie sandwiches, rubens, and their special prepared quiche of the day. Soup salads and a sandwich bar is also available. A full line of desserts are also prepared. Average prices run $4.00 for breakfast, and $5.50 for lunch. On Sunday they serve a buffet from 11 a.m. to 3 p.m. Daily lunch and dinner specials are also available. Their main dining room can accommodate between 50 and 60 person in addition to banquet and catering services. The restaurant also has a light aviation decor with some photos and a wall propeller decoration. The restaurant provides guests with a view overlooking the city from their main dining room. For more information call the restaurant at 839-5848.

Lodging: American Inn (Adjacent airport) 852-5600; Holiday Inn (Adjacent airport) 852-4161; International Inn-Best Western (3/4 mile) 852-3161; Select Inn (Adjacent airport) 852-3411.

Meeting Rooms: The airport terminal has a complimentary conference room available. Best Western International Inn (Free trans) has accommodations for conventions and is located 3/4 of a mile from the airport, Phone: 852-3161.

Transportation: Ace Taxi 852-1391; Minot Cab 852-8000; Avis 838-7665; Hertz 852-0104; National 852-5115.

Information: Convention & Visitors Bureau, P.O. Box 2066 Minot, ND 58702 or call 857-8206 or 800-264-2626.

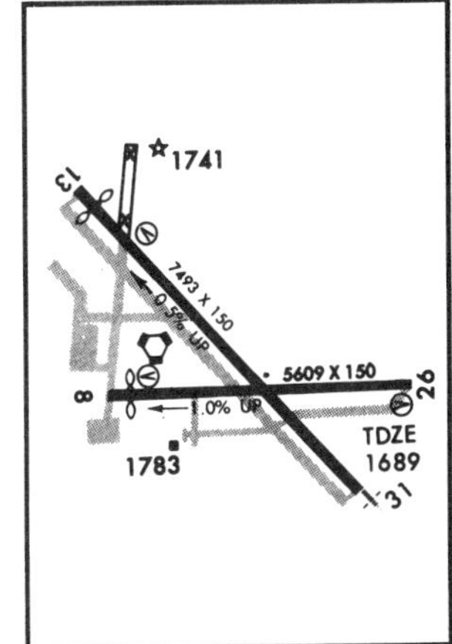

Airport Information:

MINOT - MINOT INTERNATIONAL AIRPORT (MOT)
2 mi north of town 48-15-34N 101-16-51W Elev: 1715 Fuel: 100LL, Jet-A Rwy 13-31: H7493x150 (Asph-Pfc) Rwy 08--26: H5609x150 (Asph-Pfc) Attended: continuously Unicom: 122.95 App/Dep Con: 118.15 Tower: 118.2 Gnd Con: 121.9 Public Phone 24hrs
Minot International Airport Phone: 852-1388 or 857-4724

ND-ND45 - NAPOLEON
NAPOLEON MUNIDIPAL

(Area Code 701)

6

Restaurants Near Airport:
The Judge's Chambers 1/4 mi N. Phone: 754-2797
Wentz Cafe 1/2 mi Phone: 754-2613

The Judge's Chambers:

This restaurant is a restored private home that provides a unique type of dining experience. The Judge's Chambers restaurant is open from 11:00 a.m. to 5:00 p.m. Monday through Saturday. They publish a newsletter featuring "Fun evening theme nights," complete with a special listing of entrees prepared for each day. Some examples include; beef stir fry; pork roast, escalloped apples and caraway potatoes; Chambers chicken salad and fresh rolls; sweet'n sour pork with house salad; chicken divan on rice pilaf; petite shrimp scampi with fresh fruit; salmon loaf with cream pea sauce; chicken alla king on sage dressing; Broiled chicken breast with alfredo cream sauce on rice pilaf; green pepper steak on steamed rice; Mexicali chicken with house salad; crab casserole with house salad. Their selections are so diversified that it would take too much space to list them all. In addition to their special entree for each night they feature a very unique theme on many evenings throughout the entire year. Examples of these include Sweetheart's Night; Farmer In The Dell Night; Surf & Turf Night; Stir-Fri Night at the Chambers; Me Hans A Party; Godfather's Night; Mother's Day Dinner; Nashville Night; April 15th 1040 Taxing Night; and Secretary's Day; They also provide a direct gift service directory that customers can order for special occasions. Fly-in guests can call the restaurant for courtesy transportation. For more information about this unique establishment call 800-525-9363 or 754-2797.

Lodging: Downtowner Hotel & Cafe 754-2260; Fettig Motel 754-2520; The Judge's Chambers (1/4 mi free trans) 754-2797, 800-525-9363.
Meeting Rooms: None reported
Transportation: The Judge's Chambers will provide courtesy for fly-in guests.
Information: Bismarck-Mandan Convention & Visitors Bureau, 523 N Fourth Street, P.O. Box 2274, Bismarck, ND 58502, Phone: 222-4308 or 800-767-3555.

NO AIRPORT DIAGRAM AVAILABLE

Airport Information:

NAPOLEON - NAPOLEON MUNICIPAL (ND45)
1 mi south of town N46-29.67 W99-45.61 Elev: 1985 Rwy 12-30: H3200x60 (Asph) Rwy 08-26: 2500x80 (Turf) Attended: unattended CATF: 122.9 Notes: Rwy 08-26 CLOSED oct-Apr. Confirm winter conditions with arpt manager during day at 754-2226 and evenings 754-2958.
FBO: Napoleon Municipal Airport Phone: 754-2958 or 754-2606

ND-Y99 - PLAZA TRULSON FIELD

(Area Code 701)

7

The Depot:

The Depot restaurant is a cafe situated within a mini mall about 1/4 mile from the Trulson Field Airport. This cafe is open between 7 a.m. and 5:30 p.m. 6 days a week and closed on Sunday. A variety of entrees are available off their menu. Hamburgers, sandwiches, grilled ham, grilled cheese, BLT's, pizza burgers, fish sandwiches, and all sorts of breakfast selections. Average prices run $3.95 for breakfast, $4.15 for lunch and between $4.00 and $5.00 for dinner. Their main dining room can accommodate up to 65 persons. Daily and noon specials are offered on a regular basis. Meals prepared-to-go can also be arranged. For more information about the Home Style Cafe, call 497-3765.

Restaurants Near Airport:
The Depot 1/4 mi. Phone: 497-3765

Lodging: None Reported

Meeting Rooms: None Reported

Transportation: None Reported

Information: North Dakota Tourism Department, Capitol Grounds, Bismarck, ND 58505, Phone: 800-435-5663.

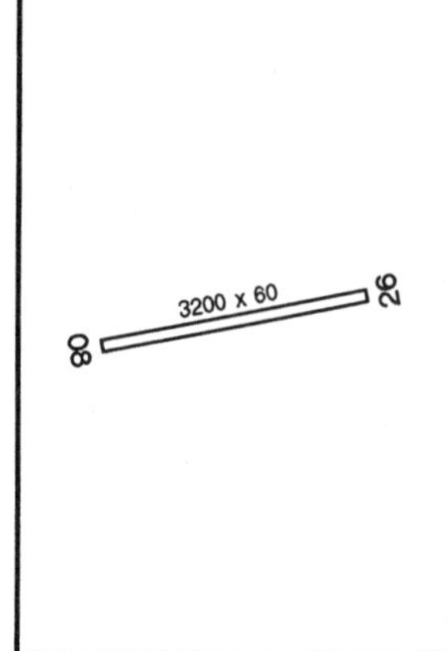

Airport Information:

PLAZA - TRULSON FIELD (Y99)
1 mi northeast of town N48-01.83 W101-57.19 Elev: 2105 Fuel: none reported
Rwy 08-26: 3200x60 (Turf) Attended: unattended CTAF: 122.9 Notes: All traffic remain north of runway 08-26.
Trulson Field Phone: 453-3387

ND-ND61 - STERLING TOP'S AIRFIELD

(Area Code 701)

8

Top's Cafe:

Top's Cafe is adjacent to Top's Airfield, and can easily be reached by walking southwest from the airport. This airport is a private use field, and should be used at your own risk. We talked to the airport owner and he told us that this airport is popular with many pilots and used frequently by people who fly-in to enjoy his restaurant facility. This family style restaurant is open between 6 a.m. and 11 midnight 7 days a week. Their menu includes items like broasted chicken, buffalo burgers, chicken fried steaks, biscuits and gravy, "Curly" burgers and much more. Daily specials are also offered. A special meal they often prepare is called Kuchen, which is a German dish. Average prices from their menu run $1.60 to $5.25 for breakfast, $3.75 to $5.60 for lunch and between $5.00 and $10.00 for dinner selections. Their main dining room can seat 60 people. The restaurant has a contemporary and western decor with pine wood floors, lots of windows and antiques for decoration. Tables, booths and counter space is provided. Fly-in groups are always welcome. Meals-to-go can also be prepared. For more information call the Top's Cafe at 387-4343.

Restaurants Near Airport:
Top's Cafe Adj Arpt Phone: 387-4343

Lodging: Top's Motel (1 mile) 387-4448

Meeting Rooms: None reported

Transportation: Courtesy car may be available, however Top's Cafe is within walking distance.

Information: North Dakota Tourism Department, Capitol Grounds, Bismarck, ND 58505, Phone: 800-435-5663.

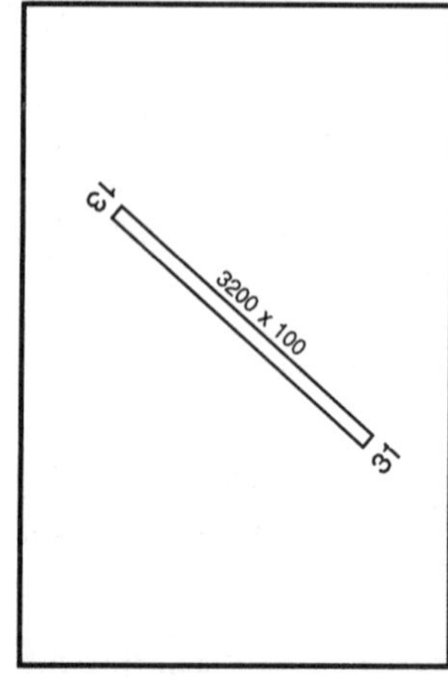

Airport Information:

STERLING - TOP'S AIRFIELD (ND61) - Private Airport
1 mi north of town 46-49-00N 100-17-42W Elev: 1922 Fuel: N/A
Rwy 13-31: 3200x100 (Turf) Attended: unattended Notes: Private use facility, use at own risk.
Top's Airfield Phone: 387-4343

ND-ISN - WILLISTON
SLOULIN FIELD INTERNATIONAL

9

(Area Code 701)

Restaurants Near Airport:

Airport Intl. Inn	2 blk NE.	Phone: 774-0241
El Ranco Motor Hotel	1 mi S.	Phone: 572-6321
Gramma Sharon's Cafe	1/4 mi N.	Phone: 572-1412
Trappers Kettle Rest.	4 blks N.	Phone: 774-2831

Airport International Inn:

The International Inn is located about 2 blocks northeast of the Williston airport. This fine dining facility is open Monday through Saturday from 6 a.m. to 10 p.m. and on Sunday from 6 a.m. to 2 p.m. then from 5 p.m. to 9 p.m. They also have a coffee shop and lounge on the premises. The main dining room provides a variety of dishes including prime rib, chicken cordon bleu, walleye, shrimp platters, steak and shrimp plates, as well as steak and lobster. On Sunday a brunch buffet is served from 10 a.m. to 2 p.m. Average prices for a meal runs $5.00 for breakfast, $7.00 for lunch and $10 for dinner. This establishment contains several facilities in one. A fine dining restaurant able to seat 75 persons, A coffee shop for lighter fare, 3 banquet rooms for private groups and parties as well as complete lodging accommodations with 150 rooms, indoor swimming pool, hot tub, complimentary transportation and a 24 hour desk clerk. For more information call the Airport International Inn at 774-0241.

Lodging: Airport Intl. Inn (2 blocks NE of airport) 774-0241.

Meeting Rooms: Airport Intl. Inn (2 blocks NE of airport) 774-0241

Transportation: Servair Air Taxi can provide courtesy transportation with advance notice 572-3773; Also Basin Cab Company 572-1957; Avis 572-7151; Hertz 572-8442.

Information: Williston Convention & Visitors Bureau, 10 Main Street, Williston, ND 58801, Phone: 774-9041.

Attractions:

Williston Municipal Golf Course (3 miles) 774-1321; Fort Union Trading Post - National historic site (20 miles) 572-9083; Lewis & Clark State Park (20 miles east) 224-4887;

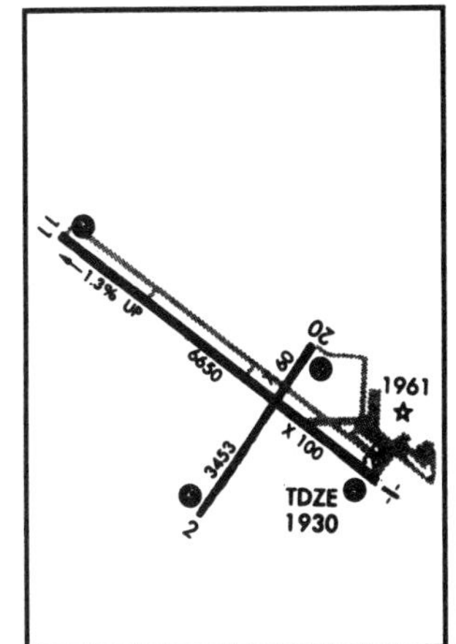

Airport Information:

WILLISTON - SLOULIN FIELD INTERNATIONAL AIRPORT (ISN)
2 mi north of town N48-10.68 W103-38.54 Elev: 1982 Fuel 100LL, Jet-A Rwy 11-29: H6650x100 (Asph-Pfc) Rwy 02-20: H3453x60 (Asph) Attended: Apr-Oct 1300-0300Z, Nov-Mar 1300-0100Z Unicom: 122.8 Public Phone 24hrs Notes: Overnight hangar space available; National Weather Service on airport.
FBO: Servair Air Phone: 572-3773

ND-ND70 - WISHEK
WISHEK MUNICIPAL AIRPORT

10

(Area Code 701)

Restaurants Near Airport:

L & L Restaurant	1/2 mi	Phone: 452-2608
Maggie's Cafe	1/2 mi	Phone: 452-2649
Prairie Winds	1/4 mi	Phone: 452-2495

Prairie Winds Restaurant:

The Prairie Winds Restaurant is located about 1/4 mile west from the Wishek Municipal Airport. This combination cafeteria and fine dining restaurant, is open between 6 a.m. and 9 p.m. 7 days a week. Their lounge opens at 9 a.m. to 1 a.m. Entrees on their menu include steaks and lobster, "Chester" fried chicken, sirloin tips, rib-eye, breaded scallops, a 12 and 16 ounce T-bone steaks as well as a variety of other selections. Friday and Saturday evenings their prime rib specials are a favorite for many local customers. On Sunday they offer three different complete dinner specials. Every day they also provide a buffet that changes daily. The decor of this facility offers elegant dining with chandeliers, carpeting, white linen table service and long stemmed glasses. The main dining room can accommodate between 50 and 60 persons. Provisions for groups and parties are also available. For more information about the Prairie Winds Restaurant, you can call them at 452-2495.

Lodging: Boschee Motel 452-2354; Travel Host Motel 452-4223.

Meeting Rooms: Prairie Winds Restaurant 452-2495; Travel Host Motel 452-4223.

Transportation: Local Police 452-2469.

Information: North Dakota Tourism Department, Capitol Grounds, Bismarck, ND 58505, Phone: 800-435-5663.

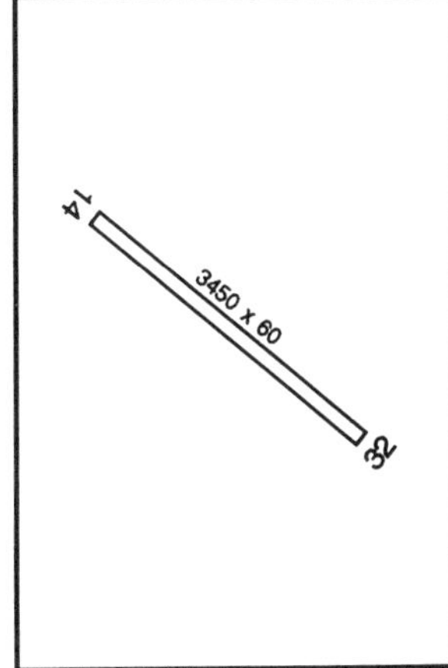

Airport Information:

WISHEK - WISHEK MUNICIPAL AIRPORT (ND70)
1 mi southeast of town N46-14.78 W99-32.27 Elev: 2035 Rwy 14-32: H3450x60 (Grvl-Dirt) Attended: unattended CTAF: 122.9
Wishek Municipal Airport Phone: 452-2364

OHIO

LOCATION MAP

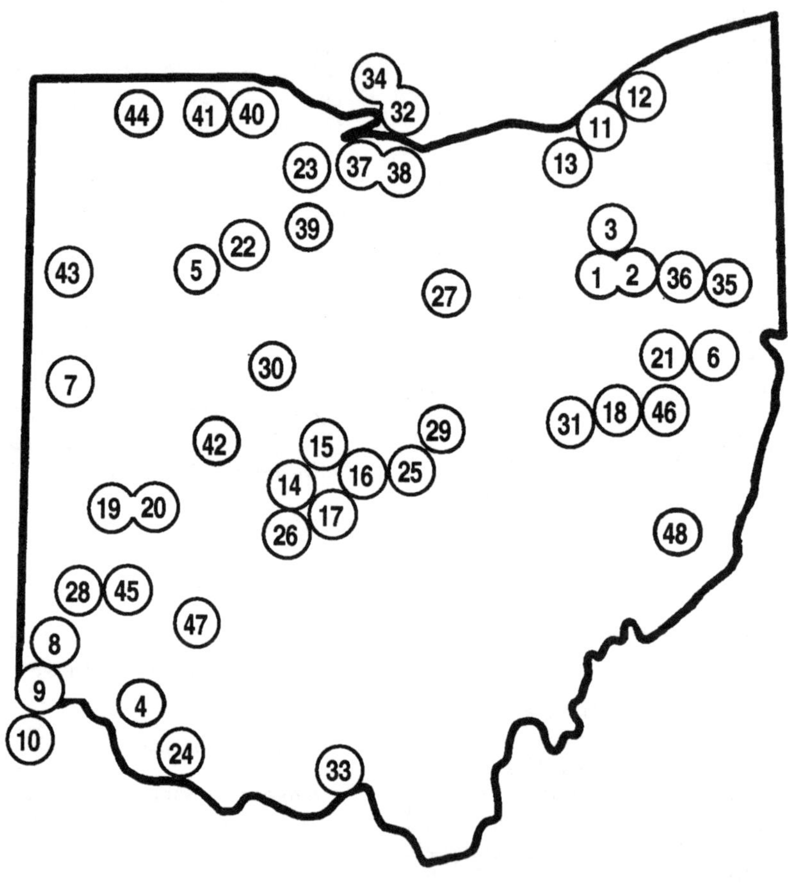

Not to be used for navigational purposes

OHIO

CROSS FILE INDEX

Location Number	City or Town	Airport Name And Identifier	Name of Restaurant
1	Akron	Akron-Canton Reg. Arpt. (CAK)	356th Fighter Group
2	Akron	Akron-Canton Reg. Arpt. (CAK)	Air Host Snack Bar
3	Akron	Akron Fulton Intl. Arpt. (AKR)	Last Quarter
4	Batavia	Clermont Co. Arpt. (I69)	Windows on the Runway
5	Bluffton	Bluffton Arpt. (5G7)	Denny's Restaurant
6	Carrollton	Carroll Co.-Tolson (TSO)	Bluebird Farm & Rest.
7	Celina	Lakefield Arpt. (CQA)	Arnie's Restaurant
8	Cincinnati	Cincinnati-Blue Ash Arpt. (ISZ)	Watson's Brothers
9	Cincinnati	Cincinnati Muni. Arpt./Luken (LUK)	Wings Restauant
10	Cinc./Covington, KY	Cincinnati/Northern KY Intl. (CVG)	CA1 Services
11	Cleveland	Burke Lakefront Arpt. (BKL)	Horn Blower Rest.
12	Cleveland	Cuyahoga Co. Arpt. (CGF)	JB Milano's Restaurant
13	Columbia Station	Columbia Arpt. (4G8)	Columbia Arpt. Rest.
14	Columbus	Bolton Field (TZR)	J.P. Ribs
15	Columbus	Ohio State Univ. (OSU)	Barnstormer Restaurant
16	Columbus	Port Columbus Intl. Arpt. (CMH)	94th Aero Squadron
17	Columbus	Rickenbacker Intl. Arpt. (LCK)	Subway
18	Coshocton	Richard Dowing (I40)	Roscoe Village Inn
19	Dayton	James M. Cox Dayton Intl. (DAY)	Aero Place Deli & Lng.
20	Dayton	James M. Cox Dayton Intl. (DAY)	Kitty Hawk Restaurant
21	Dellroy	Atwood Lodge Arpt. (0I56)	Atwood Lodge Resort
22	Findlay	Findlay Arpt. (FDY)	Rose Villa
23	Fremont	Fremont Arpt. (14G)	Gregs Country Inn
24	Georgetown	Brown Co. (GEO)	Lakewood Restaurant
25	Hebron	Buckeye Executive Arpt. (3I9)	Attraction & Rests.
26	London	Madison Co. (UYF)	Red Brick Tavern
27	Mansfield	Mansfield Lahm Muni. (MFD)	Airport Restaurant
28	Middletown	Hook Field Muni. Arpt. (MWO)	Frish's Big Boy Rest.
29	Mount Vernon	Wynkoop Arpt. (6G4)	Dogwood Inn
30	Mount Victory	Rest. owned arpt. (Private)	The Plaza Inn
31	New Philadelphia	Harry Clever Field (PHD)	Hangar & Arpt. Rest.
32	Port Clinton	Carl R. Keller Field (PCW)	Mon Ami Restaurant
33	Portsmouth	Greater Portsmouth Reg. (PMH)	Skyline Restaurant
34	Put-In-Bay	Put-In-Bay Arpt. (OH30)	Skyway Restaurant
35	Salem	Salem Airpark, Inc. (38D)	Salem Hills Restaurant
36	Sebring	Tri-City (3G8)	The Landing Restaurant
37	Sandusky	Griffing-Sandusky Arpt. (SKY)	Cherokee Inn Restaurant
38	Sandusky	Griffing-Sandusky Arpt. (SKY)	Sawmill Creek Resort
39	Tiffin	Seneca Co. Arpt. (16G)	River View Inn
40	Toledo	Metcalf Fld. (TDZ)	Sallocks Cookhouse
41	Toledo	Toledo Express Arpt. (TOL)	Marriott Host Restaurant

CROSS FILE INDEX
(Ohio Continued)

Location Number	City or Town	Airport Name And Identifier	Name of Attraction
42	Urbana	Grimes Field Arpt. (I74)	Airport Cafe
43	Van Wert	Van Wert Co. Arpt. (VNW)	Golden Corral Stk. Hse.
44	Wauseon	Fulton Co. Arpt. (USE)	Smith's Restaurant
45	Waynesville	Waynesville Arpt. (40I)	Sky Cream And Deli
46	West Lafayette	Try-City Arpt. (80G)	Hickory Flats Club House
47	Wilmington	Hollister Field (3OH9)	Cherrybend Phesnt. Frm.
48	Woodsfield	Monroe Co. Arpt. (4G5)	Katy's Place

Articles

City or town	Nearest Airport and Identifier	Name of Attraction
Columbus, OH	Port Columbus Intl. (CMH)	Ohio History of Flight Museum
Coshocton, OH	Richard Downing (I40)	Roscoe Village
Dayton, OH	Green Co (I19)/James Cox (DAY)	U.S. Airforce Museum
Put-in-Bay/Cedar Pt.	Put-in-Bay (OH30)/Griffing (SKY)	Put-in-Bay/Cedar Pt.

OH-CAK - AKRON
AKRON-CANTON REGIONAL AIRPORT

(Area Code 330) 1,2

356th Fighter Group:

The 356th Fighter Group restaurant is situated on the Akron-Canton Regional Airport property. Courtesy cars can be obtained through the fixed base operators on the field. McKinley Air or Corporate Wing, Ins. (FBO) can both provide transportation, via. courtesy cars. This unique restaurant resembles an old farm house situated in Suffolk England, where the 356th Fighter Group was stationed. In many ways this establishment is similar in appearance to the design of the popular 94th Aero Squadron restaurants situated across the country, complete with jeep and cannon out front of the restaurant and a unique interior containing authentic photographs of WW-II pilots and their aircraft. The specialty of the house is their delicious prime rib of beef au jus, cooked to perfection with a creamy horseradish sauce and complimented with freshly baked bread, salad and baked potato. Other popular dishes include their roast duckling, veal Normandy, and pork chop Americaine, a thick pork chop stuffed with smoked chicken, apples, and bermuda onions sprinkled with seasoned bread crumbs and mushroom sauce. Average prices for complete entrees run $3.00 to $9.00 for lunch and $9.00 to $18.00 for dinner. Specials throughout the week include an all-you-can-eat crab leg dinner that is featured Monday and Tuesday, or their all-you-can-eat prime rib served on Sunday and Wednesday, as well as a Sunday brunch. Fly-in groups are always welcome. Advance notice is appreciated however. The 356th Fighter Group Restaurant is opens 11 a.m. to 10 p.m. weekdays, 11 a.m. to 11 p.m. Friday and 11 a.m. to 12 p.m. on Sunday. Catering services are also reported, consisting of a full menu to-go. For information call the restaurant at 494-3500.

Air Host Snack Bar:

The Air Host Snack Bar is located on the ground floor of the main terminal building at the Akron-Canton Regional Airport. This establishment serves light fare like sandwiches, fries, soups, and salads. There is seating for about 30 to 40 people within the cafe. There is also a small gift shop adjacent to the restaurant. The Air Host Snack Bar is open 6 a.m. to 9 p.m. 7 days a week. A bar next door is also open until 11 p.m. For information call 499-7974.

Restaurants Near Airport:

356th Fighter Group	On Site	Phone: 494-3500
Air Host Snack Bar	Trml Bldg	Phone: 499-7974

Lodging: Hampton Inn 492-0151; Holiday Inn (Trans) 494-2770; Holiday Inn South (Trans) 644-7126; Parke Hotel (Trans) 499-9410; Sheraton Inn-Belden (Trans) 494-6494.

Meeting Rooms: Wings, Inc. (FBO) contains accommodations for meetings and conferences 494-9838; Also: Hampton Inn 492-0151; Holiday Inn 494-2770; Holiday Inn South 644-7126; Parke Hotel 499-9410; Sheraton Inn-Belden 494-6494.

Transportation: Wings, Inc. (FBO) can accommodate air travelers with courtesy cars to nearby locations 494-9838. Phoenix Limo 499-1910; Airport Limo 494-0405; Also Rental Cars: Avis 896-2457; Budget 253-3540; Hertz 896-1331; National 800-442-7368.

Information: Akron/Summit Convention and Visitors Bureau, Cascade Plaza, Sublevel, Akron, OH 44308, Phone: 376-4254 or 800-245-4254.

Airport Information:

AKRON - AKRON-CANTON REGIONAL AIRPORT (CAK)
10 mi southeast of town N40-54.98 W81-26.55 Elev: 1228 Fuel: 100LL, Jet-A
Rwy 05-23: H7598x150 (Asph-Grvd) Rwy 01-19: H6397x150 (Asph-Grvd) Rwy 14-32: H5600x150 (Asph-Grvd) Attended: continuously Atis: 121.05 Unicom: 122.95
App/Dep Con: 125.5, 118.6, 126.4 Tower: 118.3 Gnd Con: 121.7 Clnc Del: 132.05
Notes: CAUTION: Taxiing aircraft on ramp and hangar areas not visible from tower.

FBO: A-Flite, Inc. **Phone: 494-5560**
FBO: ASW Aviation Service **Phone: 494-6104, 800-423-5047**
FBO: Air Camis **Phone: 896-3765**
FBO: McKinley Air Transport **Phone: 499-3316, 800-225-6446**

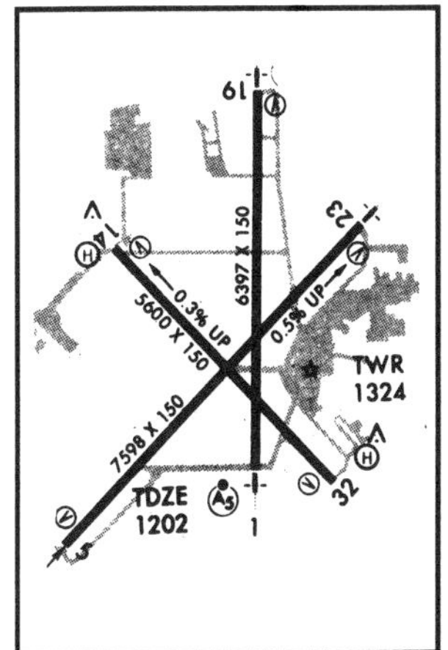

OH-AKR - AKRON
AKRON FULTON INTL. AIRPORT

(Area Code 330)

3

Last Quarter:

The Last Quarter is located approximately 2 blocks from the main terminal building in a small shopping plaza near the Akron Fulton Municipal Airport in Akron, Ohio. This restaurant offers a full service menu consisting of pork chops, steaks, seafood and poultry along with numerous homemade specialties. The main dining room can seat between 50 and 75 people. Groups are welcome with advance notice appreciated for larger parties. A fish fry is featured every Friday evening. This restaurant is open Monday through Friday between 10:30 a.m. and 10 p.m., Saturday only for breakfast between 8 a.m. and 2 p.m. Their lounge remains open until 12 a.m. on Friday and Saturday evenings. Call 784-1108 for information.

Restaurants Near Airport:

Last Quarter	2 blks	Phone: 784-1108

Lodging: Days Inn At Akron West (Trans) 836-8431; Hilton-Quaker (Trans) 253-5970; Hilton Inn West 867-5000; Ramada Inn 666-4131; Residence Inn 666-4811.

Meeting Rooms: Days Inn At Akron West 836-8431; Hilton-Quaker 253-5970; Hilton Inn West 867-5000; Ramada Inn 666-4131; Residence Inn 666-4811.

Transportation: Taxi Service: Yellow Cab 253-3141; Rental Cars: Available through Castle Aviation, Inc. (FBO); Also Thrifty Car Rental 784-3598.

Information: Akron/Summit Convention & Visitors Bureau, Cascade Plaza, Sublevel, Akron, OH 44308, Phone: 376-4254 or 800-245-4254.

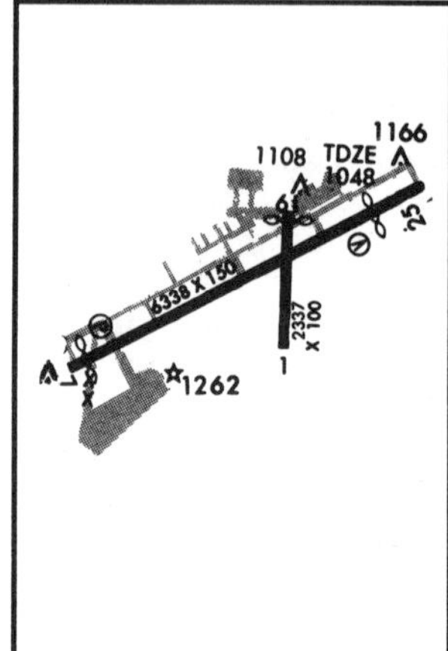

Airport Information:

AKRON - AKRON FULTON INTERNATIONAL AIRPORT (AKR)
0 mi south of town N41-02.24 W81-28.04 Elev: 1068 Fuel: 100LL, Jet-A
Rwy 07-25: H6338x150 (Asph) Rwy 01-19: H2337x100 (Asph) Attended: 1100-0300Z
CTAF: 120.1 Unicom: 122.95 Akron-Canton App/Dep Con: 118.6 Clnc Del: 121.6
FBO: Airspect Air, Inc. Phone: 784-8383, 784-4411.

OH-I69 - BATAVIA
CLERMONT COUNTY AIRPORT

(Area Code 513)

4

Windows on the Runway:

Sporty's Pilot Shop "Windows on the Runway" is on Clermont County Airport in Batavia, Ohio. While not a restaurant, "Windows on the Runway" does offer a variety of hot foods including hamburgers, sandwiches and pizza, as well as salads and desserts, through vending machines. Coffee, ice cream and beverages are also available. In addition, Sporty's cooks free hot dogs and sausages every Saturday at lunch for fly-in customers. Sporty's has plenty of available tie-downs just off the runway, within feet of the door, and is frequented by pilots as well as Sporty's staff. Excellent accommodations for larger groups like associations, or club fly-ins. "Windows On The Runway" was named by aviation journalist Richard L. Collins as he looked down over Sporty's ramp and runway 4-22 through the large windows. Open seven days a week, 8 a.m. to 8 p.m. For more information, call 732-9000.

Restaurants Near Airport:

"Windows on the Runway"	On Site	Phone: 735-9000

Lodging: Holiday Inn (3-1/2 miles), Phone: 752-4400; Ramada Inn (6 miles), Phone: 528-3200

Transportation: "Windows on the Runway" is located within easy walking distance from aircraft parking; Taxi: Batavia Cab, Phone: 732-1933.

Information: Ohio Division of Travel and Tourism, Phone: 800-BUCKEYE.

Attractions:

Sporty's Pilot Shop has been in the business of providing a service to pilots and aviation lovers for over 27 years, and is located right on the Clermont Airport premises. A trip to this airport is not complete without an enjoyable visit to this facility. The complete "Sporty's operation", along with a unique pilots supply store contains an unlimited amount of equipment and supplies available to pilots and general aviation enthusiasts from all across the country. For information call 513-735-9000. For information about their catalog or to place an order from their catalog call 800-543-8633.

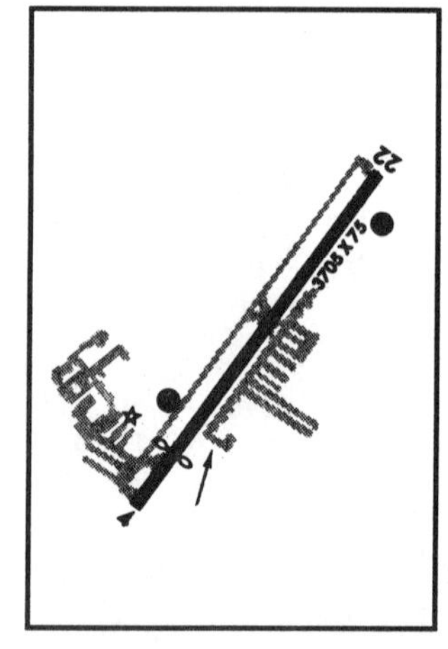

Airport Information:

BATAVIA - CLERMONT COUNTY AIRPORT (I69)
1.7 miles west of town N39-04.70 W84-12.62 Elev: 848 Fuel: 100LL, Jet-A
Rwy 04-22: H3705x75 (Asph) Attended: Mon-Sat 1400Z-dusk, Sun 1600Z-dusk Unicom: 122.7
Cincinnati App/Dep Con 121.0 Clnc Del: 124.9 Airport Phone: 732-2336
FBO: Eastern Cincinnati Aviation Phone: 732-2336

OH-5G7 - BLUFFTON
BLUFFTON AIRPORT

(Area Code 419)

5

Denny's Restaurant:

Denny's Restaurant is situated on Bluffton Airport in Bluffton, OH. This restaurant is located across from the airport parking lot, and is only a 50 yard walk from the airport to the restaurant. The restaurant is open 24 hours. This could be classified as a family style restaurant featuring breakfast specials that run all day. Their vegetable soup and chicken dinners are their specialties with Wednesday and Friday offering their famous "Perch Night". Their main dining room can seat 140 persons. Large groups are always welcome, with advance notice appreciated. Average prices run $3.80 for breakfast, $4.70 for lunch and about $5.50 for dinner. There is a motel that is located only 25 yards from the restaurant which contains 50 rooms. Information about Denny's Restaurant can be obtained by calling them at 358-8581.

Restaurants Near Airport:
Denny's Restaurant On Site Phone: 358-8581

Lodging: HoJo Motel (Adj Arpt) Phone: N/A

Meeting Rooms: None Reported

Transportation: None Reported

Information: Bluffton Area Chamber of Commerce, Town Hall, North Main Street, P.O. Box 142, Bluffton, OH 45817, Phone: 358-5675; Also: Ohio Division of Travel and Tourism, Phone: 800-BUCKEYE.

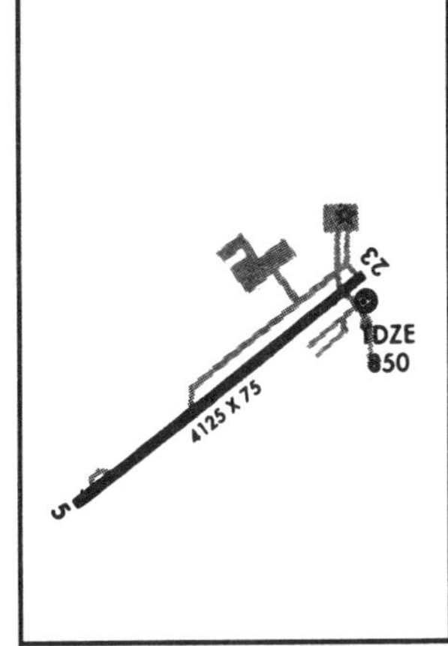

Airport Information:

BLUFFTON - BLUFFTON AIRPORT (5G7)
1 mi southeast of town N40-53.13 W83-52.12 Elev: 850 Fuel: 80, 100LL
Rwy 05-23: H4125x75 (Asph) Attended: 1300Z-dusk Unicom: 122.8
Bluffton Flying Service, Inc. Phone: 358-7045

OH-TSO - CARROLLTON
CARROLL COUNTY-TOLSON

(Area Code 216) **6**

Bluebird Farm Restaurant & Kintner Barn Gift Shop:

The Bluebird Farm Restaurant & Kintner Barn Gift Shop is located across the street from Carroll County-Tolson Airport A scenic path (approximately 1000 feet) leads your way through the woods to the restaurant. The restaurant and gift shop are both situated in a century old farm house and uniquely restored Pre-Civil War era barn. The barn, which is situated several yards from the farm house, features the gift shop with unique gifts and antiques. Its decor includes a brick wood-burning fireplace, large windows with small panes, and a lean-to porch furnished with Amish-made swings, rockers and gliders. The gift shop is open Tuesday through Thursday from 11 a.m. to 5 p.m., Friday and Saturday from 11 a.m. to 8 p.m., and Sunday from 11 a.m. to 3 p.m. The 140-year-old brick farm house, which features the restaurant, has three floors, a deck for outdoor seating and enclosed glass porches. It is open for lunch between 11a.m. to 3 p.m.,Tuesday through Sunday, and for dinner between 5 p.m. to 8 p.m., Friday and Saturday. It serves tasty home-cooked meals.The lunch menu includes: soup, salads, sandwiches and other daytime specials. The evening menu includes: steak, fish, pasta and various evening specials. During the summer and winter, specials may range from fresh fruit and salad dishes to casseroles and hot meat entrees.The Sunday menu features a chicken or beef entree, plus soup, salads and sandwiches. The restaurant also features delicious home-made desserts by the Amish. Average prices range from $6.50 for lunch to $10.95 for dinner. With reservations, the restaurant will provide a special menu for parties of 20 or more individuals. Also, pilots who are on-the-go can carry out meals. For more information, call the Bluebird Farm Restaurant and Kintner Barn Gift Shop at 627-7980.

Restaurants Near Airport:
Bluebird Farm Restaurant On-Site Phone: 627-7980

Lodging: Atwood Lake Resort (11 miles) 735-2211; Whispering Pines Bed and Breakfast 735-2824; The Longhouse Bed and Breakfast 627-7900

Meeting Rooms: Atwood Lake Resort 735-2211

Transportation: Bluebird Farm Restaurant and Kintner Barn Gift Shop will provide transportation only if needed for special circumstances. Phone: 627-7980.

Information: Carroll County Chamber of Commerce, P.O. Box 277, Carrollton, OH 44615, Phone: 627-4811

Airport Information:

Carrollton - Carroll County-Tolson (TSO)
1 mi southeast of town N40-33.71 W81-04.65 Elev: 1163 Fuel: 80, 100LL, Jet-A Rwy 07-25: H4300x75 (Asph) Attended: May-Sept 1100-0200Z, Oct-Apr 1100-0100Z CTAF/Unicom: 122.7 Akron-Canton App/Dep Con: 125.5 (1100-0500Z) Cleveland Center App/Dep Con: 134.9 (0500-1100Z) Notes: Deer on and in vicinity of airport.
FBO: Cooter's Carroll County Avgas Phone: 627-5250
FBO: Lamp Aircraft Service Phone: 627-7330

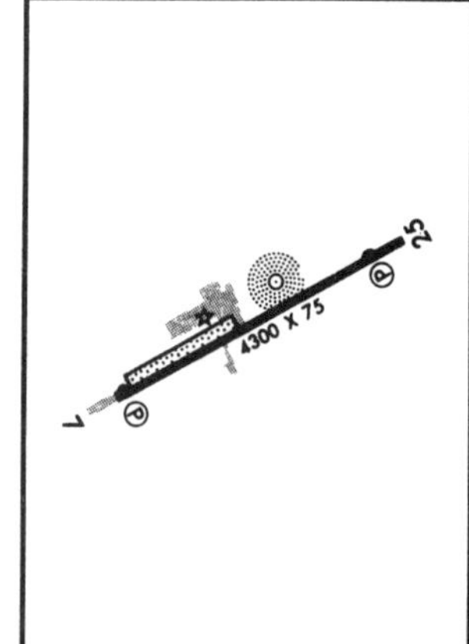

Illustration by: Lynn Fox Bluebird Farm Restaurant & Kintner Barn Gift Shop, Carrollton, OH

OH-CQA - CELINA LAKEFIELD AIRPORT

(Area Code 419)

7

Arnie's Restaurant:

Arnie's Restaurant is located about 1/4 mile east of the Lakefield Airport in Celina, Ohio. The restaurant is situated at the stop light in the center of town. The restaurant serves a full menu with daily specials. There is a full line of breakfast lunch and dinner selections. Specialties of the house include chicken dishes, steaks, pork chops, fish and shrimp. We were told all meats are fresh, not frozen. In addition to the restaurant is a tavern serving beverages of your choice. This family style restaurant has a casual atmosphere, and is open from 8:00 a.m. to 12:00 a.m. week nights, and from 8:00 a.m. to 2:30 a.m. on week-ends. For information call 268-2411.

Restaurants Near Airport:
Arnie's Restaurant 1/4 mi E. Phone: 268-2411

Lodging: None reported

Meeting Rooms: None reported

Transportation: None reported

Information: Celina-Mercer County Chamber of Commerce, 226 North Main Street, Celina, OH 45822, Phone: 586-2219.

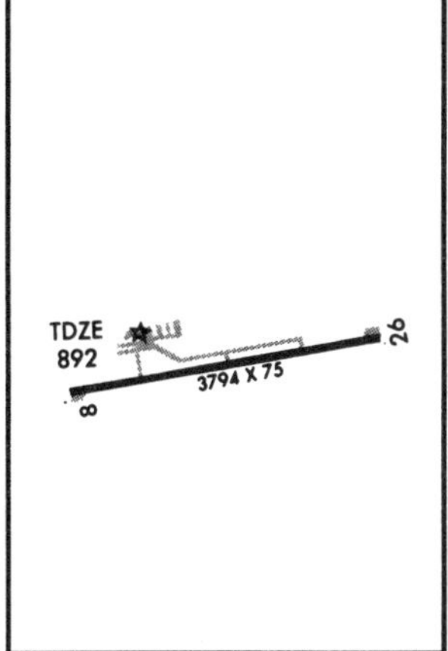

Airport Information:

CELINA - LAKEFIELD AIRPORT (CQA)
6 mi southeast of town N40-29.04 W84-33.61 Elev: 892 Fuel: 80, 100LL
Rwy 08-26: H3794x75 (Asph) Attended: 1300Z-dusk Unicom: 122.8
Lakefield Airport Phone: 268-2190

OH-ISZ - CINCINNATI CINCINNATI-BLUE ASH AIRPORT

(Area Code 513)

8

Watson Brothers Restaurant:

The Watson Brothers Restaurant and Brewhaus is a unique establishment that is located across the street from the Cincinnati Blue Ash Airport. Years ago the Watson brothers were the original owners of the airport. The decor has an upscale casual-styled atmosphere with many aviation-related items on display. The food was described as delicious. Chef daily specials are a favorite choice with local as well as many fly-in customers. Their bar area can seat up to 100 persons. Two separate dining areas can each seat about 100 customers. What's interesting, and makes for a nice addition to your meal, is their patio dining area is able to seat up to 125 people and offers a great view of arriving aircraft on runway 24. They are well known for their beers made right on the premises. They also make their own root beer as well. Carry out and catered meals can be prepared with advance notice appreciated. Lunch entrees run between $5.95 and $9.00. Dinner entrees range from $10.00 to $17.95. Restaurant hours are Monday through Thursday 11 a.m. to 1:30 a.m., Friday and Saturday 11 a.m. to 2:30 a.m., and Sunday 1 p.m. to 12 a.m. Thanks to one of our readers, we were informed about this establishment. Their comments were, "Fabulous new restaurant with aviation decor. Lots of aviation photos (vintage) and memorabilia. The menu is new American. Traffic landing on runway 24 comes right over the patio of Watson's. Great place! For information call 563-9797.

Restaurants Near Airport:
Applebees 3/4 mi NE Phone: 769-6201
Montgomery Inn-Rib King 5 mi E. Phone: 791-3482
Watson Brothers Adj Arpt. Phone: 563-9797

Lodging: Courtyard By Marriott (3/4 mi) 733-4334; Ramada Inn Blue Ash (1 mile) 793-4500; Embassy Suites Blue Ash 733-8900; Red Roof Inn 793-8811.
Meeting Rooms: Courtyard By Marriott 733-4334; Ramada Inn 793-4500; Embassy Suites Blue Ash 733-8900.
Transportation: Co-op Aircraft Service, Inc provides both rental and courtesy cars, 791-8500; Taxi Serv 821-2068.
Information: Greater Cincinnati Convention & Visitors Bureau, 300 West 6th Street, Cincinnati, OH 45202, Phone: 800-CINCY-USA.

Attractions:

Kings Island, an Amusement Park, is reported 8 miles from this airport. This amusement park is quite large and has a variety of entertainment establishments including water park, rides, shows, dining and concession stands. A fireworks display is held during evening hours. There are many lodging facilities available near the park as well. During our conversation with the airport management we learned that shuttle service round trip between the airport and amusement park costs about $18.00 per person. For information call Kings Island Amusement Park at 513-573-5800.

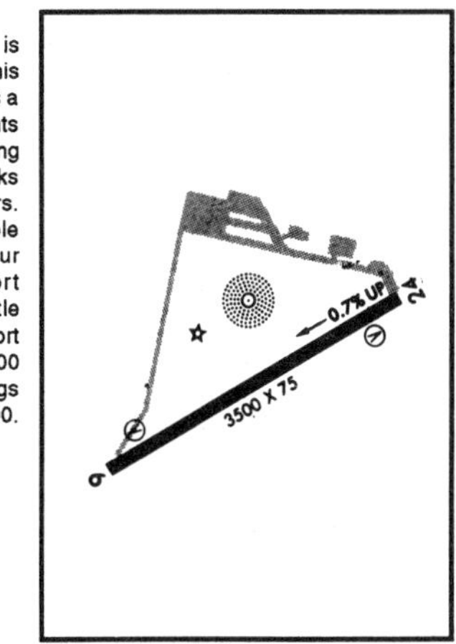

Airport Information:

CINCINNATI - CINCINNATI-BLUE ASH AIRPORT (ISZ)
6 mi northeast of town N39-14.80 W84-23.34 Elev: 856 Fuel: 100LL, Jet-A
Rwy 06-24: H3500x75 (Asph) Attended: Apr-Nov 1130Z-1 hour after dusk, Dec-Mar 1230Z-1 hour after dusk Unicom: 123.0 App/Dep Con: 121.0 Clnc Del: 124.9 Notes: Overnight parking $3.00.
FBO: Co-op Acft Serv. Phone: 791-8500 FBO: Exec Aviation Phone: 984-3881, 984-3882

OH-LUK - CINCINNATI
CINCINNATI MUNI ARPT/LUNKEN FLD

(Area Code 513) 9

Restaurant Near Airport:
Wings Restaurant On Site Phone: 871-7400

Wings Restaurant:

The Sky Galley Restaurant is located on the Lunken Field Airport near Cincinnati, Ohio. It is a combination sports bar andfamily restaurant located in the terminal building. This full service restaurant serves lunch and dinner entrees including daily specials, Alaskan halibut and prime rib selections along with their own homemade soups and pies. Prices for dinners average between $5.75 to $11.99. Large windows in the restaurant provide a nice view of the activity on the field. Aircraft parking is available near the restaurant. The decor of this facility has an aviation theme. Their main dining room can seat 130 people. A separate party room can accommodate up to 50 additional persons. They are open everyday at 11 a.m. until 10 p.m., except on Sunday for their brunch that runs from 10:30 a.m. to 2:30 p.m. For information call 871-7400.

Lodging: Best Western Mariemont Inn 271-2100; Harley House (Trans) 793-4300; Holiday Inn-Eastgate 752-4400; Holiday Inn-Florence 371-2700; Howard Johnson Lodge-East 631-8500; Quality Inn Central (Trans) 351-6000; Red Roof Inn-Central 531-6589.

Meeting Rooms: Best Western Mariemont Inn 272-2100; Harley House 793-4300; Holiday Inn-Eastgate 752-4400; Holiday Inn-Florence 371-2700; Howard Johnson Lodge-East 631-8500; Quality Inn Central 351-6000.

Transportation: Taxi Service: Dispatch 241-2100; East Cab 231-8877; Also Rental Cars: Thrifty 871-8600; Williams 871-2020.

Information: Cincinnati Convention & Visitors Bureau, 300 West 6th St, Cincinnati, OH 45202, Phone: 800-CINCY-USA621.

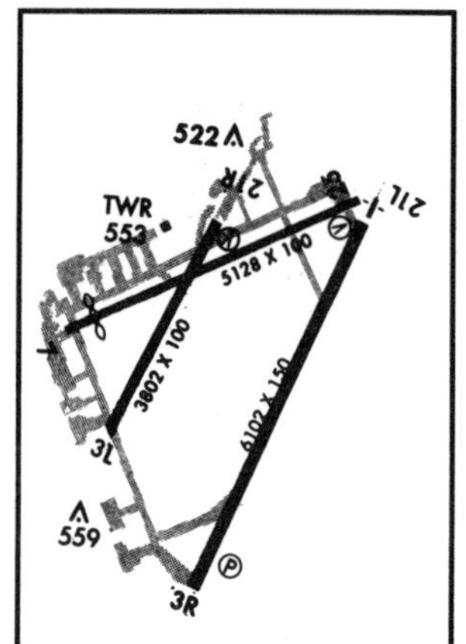

Attractions:

A golf course is reported adjacent to the airport. The Cincinnati Zoo rated as one of top five zoo's in the United States is located only 6 miles from the airport. River Downs Race Track reported 4 miles from the airport. For information call the airport managers office at 321-4132.

Airport Information:

CINCINNATI - CINCINNATI MUNICIPAL AIRPORT/LUNKEN FIELD (LUK)
3 mi southeast of town N39-06.20 W84-25.12 Elev: 483 Fuel: 80, 100LL, Jet-A Rwy 03R-21L: H6102x150 (Asph-Grvd) Rwy 07-25: H5128x100 (Asph-Grvd) Rwy 03L-21R: H3802x100 (Asph) Attended: continuously Atis: 120.25 Unicom: 122.95 App/Dep Con: 121.0 Lunken Tower: 118.7, 133.925 Clnc Del: 124.9 (Use when tower is closed) Gnd Con/Clnc Del: 121.9
FBO: Midwest Jet Center Phone: 871-8600
FBO: Million Air Cincinnati Phone: 871-2020

OH-CVG - CINCINNATI/COVINGTON, KY
CINCINNATI/NORTHERN KY. INTL.

(Area Code 606) 10

Restaurant Near Airport:
CA1 Services On Site Phone: 767-3715

CA1 Services:

CA1 Services manages several food service concessions in the terminal complex at the Cincinnati/northern Kentucky International Airport. Locations include Terminal 1, 2, 3 and concourses A & B. They range from cafes to full service establishments. Lefty's is one such facility that specializes in preparing delicious Santa Fe chicken sandwiches, grilled tuna, cafe espresso, oversized stuffed baked potatoes, over-stuffed deli sandwiches, world links, French links, Texas barbecued links and the famous Chicago hot dog. Prices run $4.00 to $5.00 for most breakfast items and $5.00 to $9.00 for lunch and dinner selections. This restaurant offers casual dining surroundings with historical photos of Cincinnati's waterfront area. There are two meeting rooms and executive dining rooms all overlooking the airport property. CA1 Services can cater groups up to 250 people. They also can provide your in-flight catering needs as well from any of their six different concepts, from deli sandwiches to pizza. For more information call 767-3715.

Lodging: All listed provide free transportation to and from airport: Hampton Inn-Cincinnati South 283-1600; Holiday Inn-Florence 371-2700; Holiday Inn-South 331-1500; Signature Inn 371-0081; Drawbridge Estate 341-2800; Commonweath Hilton 371-4400; Holiday Inn-Cincinnati Airport 371-2233.

Meeting Rooms: All have meeting accommodations: Hampton Inn-Cincinnati South 283-1600; Holiday Inn-Florence 371-2700; Holiday Inn-South 331-1500; Signature Inn 371-0081; Drawbridge Estate 341-2800; Commonweath Hilton 371-4400; Holiday Inn-Cincinnati Airport (Convention facilities) 371-2233.

Transportation: Alamo 800-327-9633; Avis 800-331-1212; Budget 800-527-0700; Dollar 800-800-4000; Hertz 800-654-3131; National 800-328-4567; Taxi service: numerous.

Information: Northern Kentucky Convention and Visitors Bureau, 605 Philadelphia Street, Covington, KY 41011, Phone: 800-336-3535. Also Greater Cincinnati Convention and Visitors Bureau, 300 West 6th Street, Cincinnati, OH 45202, Phone: 800-CINCY-USA.

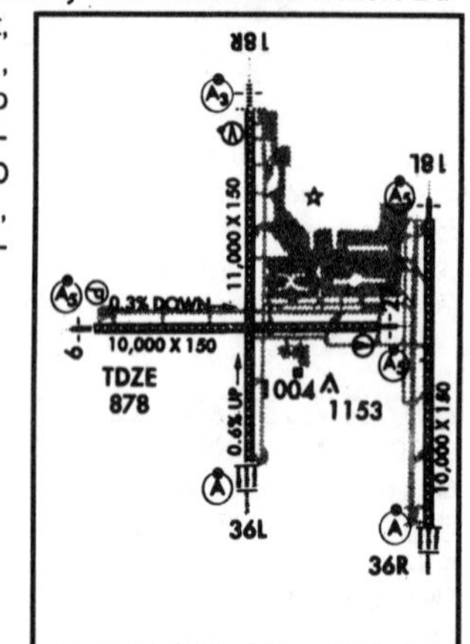

Airport Information: (Also listed in AFD under Covington, KY)

CINCINNATI/COVINGTON, KY - CINCINNATI/NORTHERN KENTUCKY INTL. (CVG)
8 mi southwest of town N39-02.72 W84-39.71 Elev: 897 Fuel: 100LL, Jet-A Rwy 18L-36R: H10000x150 (Conc-Grvd) Rwy 09-27: H10000x150 (Asph-Conc-Grvd) Rwy 18R-36L: H11000x150 (Asph-Grvd) Attended: continuously Atis: 135.3 Unicom: 122.95 App Con: 123.87, 119.7, 121.0 Dep Con: 126.65, 128.7, 121.0 Tower: 118.97 Gnd Con: 121.7 (west) 121.3 (east) Clnc Del: 127.175
FBO: Comair Aviation Phone: 767-3500

OH-BKL - CLEVELAND
BURKE LAKEFRONT AIRPORT

11

Horn Blower Restaurant:

This facility is located on the west side of the airport and adjacent to the terminal building. We were told pilots can park their aircraft at Gate-1 at the terminal building and go through the terminal to the restaurant. Information on available parking can be obtained by calling the airport manager's office at 781-6411. This establishment is classified as a combination family-style and fine dining facility. They are open Tuesday through Thursday 11:30 a.m. to 10 p.m., Friday and Saturday from 11:30 a.m. to 11 p.m., and Sunday from 10:30 a.m. to 9 p.m. A Sunday brunch is featured between 10:30 a.m. to 2 p.m. Prices average $6.50 for lunch and $10.95 to $17.95 for dinner. Daily specials are offered each day. The main dining room can serve 100 to 120 people. In addition, 50 people can be seated in their lounge. Carry-out orders can also be prepared. For information call the Horn Blower's Restaurant at 363-1151

Restaurants Near Airport: **(Area Code 216)**

Alvies At The Stadium	1 mi W.	Phone: 861-5055
Theatrical Bar & Grill	2 mi SW	Phone: 241-6169
Horn Blower	On Site	Phone: 363-1151
New York Spaghetti Hse	2 mi S.	Phone: 696-6624

Lodging: Bond Court Hotel (Trans) 771-7600; Holiday Inn Lakeside (1 mile) 241-5100; Hollenden House (Trans) 621-0700; Howard Johnson Lodge 432-2220; Sheraton City Center (Trans, 1 mile) 771-7600; Stouffer Tower City Plaza (Trans, 2 miles) 696-5600.
Meeting Rooms: Airplane Companies has a small conference room able to seat 6; Cleveland Public Hall and the Cleveland Convention Center can provide accommodations; Also: Bond Court Hotel 771-7600; Holiday Inn Lakeside 241-5100; Hollenden House 621-0700; Howard Johnson Lodge 432-2220; Stouffer Hotel 696-5600.
Transportation: Courtesy cars reported by FBO's. Taxi service: Americab 881-1111; Yellow Cab 623-1500; Carey Limousine Service 267-8282; Yellow Cab 623-1500; Also rental cars: Avis 623-0800; Assured Rental Car 261-6700; Budget 574-9870;
Information: Convention & Visitors Bureau of Greater Cleveland, 50 Public Square, Suite 3100, Cleveland, OH 44113, Phone: 621-4110 or 800-321-1001.

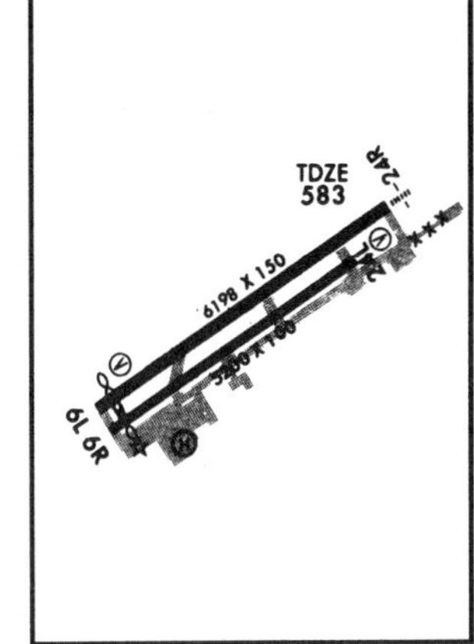

Airport Information:

CLEVELAND - BURKE LAKEFRONT AIRPORT (BKL)
.9 mi north of town N41-31.05 W81-41.01 Elev: 584 Fuel: 100LL, Jet-A
Rwy 06L-24R: H6198x150 (Asph-Grvd) Rwy 06R-24L: H5200x100 (Asph-Grvd)
Attended: continuously Unicom: 122.95 Atis: 125.25 Cleveland App/Dep Con: 125.35 Clnc Del: 121.9 Lakefront Tower: 124.3 Gnd Con: 121.9
Notes: CAUTION: Bird activity on and in vicinity of airport. Also landing fees, if any, determined by city operations per size aircraft, parking fees determined by FBO's.
FBO: Airplane Companies, Inc. Phone: 781-1200
FBO: Million Air Cleveland Phone: 861-2030

OH-CGF - CLEVELAND
CUYAHOGA COUNTY AIRPORT

(Area Code 216) 12

JB Milano's Restaurant:

JB Milano's Restaurant is located on the Cleveland/ Cuyahoga County Airport. This fine dining facility is reported to be situated near Beckett Enterprises, Inc. (FBO). However, courtesy transportation can be arranged through all FBO's on the field. The Restaurant is open between 9 a.m. and 9:30 p.m. Monday through Thursday, and from 7 a.m. to 10:30 p.m. Friday and Saturday. They are closed on Sunday. Items on their menu include Italian dishes including homemade pasta made from scratch, veal dishes, prime beef, specialty sandwiches, appetizers and much more. Average prices run $3.00 for breakfast, $5.00 to $6.00 for lunch and $10.95 to $14.95 for dinner. JB's can handle a variety of groups, ranging from 10 to 40 individuals. This is a family run business that is operated by two people with the names Joan and Bob, thereby giving the restaurant its name JB's. For more information about JB Milano's Restaurant, call 289-4000.

Restaurants Near Airport:
JB Milano's Restaurant On Site Phone: 289-4000

Lodging: Beachwood Inn (Trans) 831-5150; Harley Hotel East (Trans) 944-4300;

Meeting Rooms: Beachwood Inn 831-5150; Harley Hotel East 944-4300.

Transportation: Airport courtesy cars reported; Taxi Service: Northeast 953-0003; Yellow 623-1500; Also: Qua 261-1111; Thrifty 261-5900.

Information: Convention & Visitors Bureau of Greater Cleveland, 50 Public Square, Suite 3100, Cleveland, OH 44113, Phone: 621-4110 or 800-321-1001.

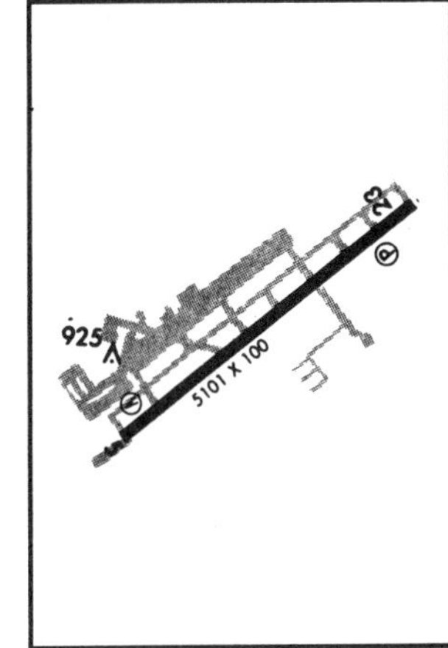

Airport Information:

CLEVELAND - CUYAHOGA COUNTY AIRPORT (CGF)
10 mi east N41-33.91 W81-29.19 Elev: 879 Fuel: 100LL, Jet-A A1+
Rwy 05-23: H5101x100 (Asph-Grvd) Attended: continuously Unicom: 122.95
Cleveland App/Dep Con: 125.35 County Tower: 118.5 Gnd Con: 121.85 Clnc Del: 121.8
FBO: Beckett Enterprises, Inc. Phone: 261-1111
FBO: Corporate Wings Phone:261-5900

OH-4G8 - COLUMBIA STATION COLUMBIA AIRPORT

(Area Code 216) 13

Columbia Airport Restaurant:

Columbia Airport Restaurant is situated on the Columbia Airport in Ohio, and is about twelve miles southwest of downtown Cleveland. This cafe styled restaurant specializes in light fare consisting of sandwiches, hamburgers and pies. For those of you who like a "great bowl of chili", may want to fly in and try their specialty. Their dining room can seat approximately 20 people and offers a quaint atmosphere with tables and counter service. The restaurant is open between 8 a.m. and 10 p.m. with aircraft parking near the door. For more information call 236-8800.

Restaurants Near Airport:
Columbia Airport Restaurant On Site Phone: 236-8800

Lodging: None Reported

Meeting Rooms: None Reported

Transportation: None Reported

Information: Convention & Visitors Bureau of Greater Cleveland, 50 Public Square, Suite 3100, Cleveland, OH 44113, Phone: 621-4110 or 800-321-1001.

NO AIRPORT DIAGRAM AVAILABLE

Airport Information:

COLUMBIA STATION - COLUMBIA AIRPORT (4G8)
1 mi northwest of town N41-19.07 W81-57.63 Elev: 813 Fuel: 80, 100LL Rwy 18L-36R: 3110x270 (Turf) Rwy 02-20: 2580x85 (Turf) Rwy 18R-36L: H2010x40 (Asph) Attended: 1300Z-dusk Unicom: 122.8 Notes: Use hard surface runways during wet conditions.
Columbia Airport Phone: 236-8800.

OH-TZR - COLUMBUS BOLTON FIELD

(Area Code 214) 14

J.P. Ribs:

J. P. Ribs restaurant is located adjacent to the terminal building. The restaurant is open weekdays from 11 a.m. to 9 p.m. and on weekends from 12 noon to 9 p.m. This restaurant is very popular with fly-in customers. The dining room is decorated with airplane memorabilia and aviation-related photographs. Their full service menu lists specialties like ribs and chicken, 8 different types of sandwiches as well as many other items. Prices range between $2.95 and $13.95 for most selections. There is seating for about 40 people within the restaurant. One point of interest about this facility is that it has a covered patio which can accommodate up to 500 additional people. This makes J.P. Ribs an excellent location for large gatherings or catered parties. In fact J.P. Ribs specializes in catering large functions. Yard games are also available. Picnic tables are used on their patio for seating. A view of all the airport activity is just feet away. Guests can also see the ramp and runway from within the restaurant. For information call J.P. Ribs at 878-RIBB.

Restaurants Near Airport:
J.P. Ribs Restaurant On Site Phone: 878-RIBB

Lodging: Days Inn-South 4 mi 871-0065; Holiday Inn 5-7 mi. 771-8999; Ramada Inn-West 3 mi. 878-5301; Ramada Inn-South 4 mi. 871-2990; Red Roof Inn 4 mi. 878-9245.
Meeting: J.P. Ribs Restaurant has a covered patio with picnic tables for outings and group functions as well as yard games.
Transportation: Rental cars: Thrifty 878-2961; Taxi Service available (4 to 6 mi.).
Information: Columbus Visitor Center, 3rd Level of Columbus City Center Shopping Mall, South High St. & South Third St. at Rich St. phone: 800-654-3472. Also a visitor information center is located at Columbus International Airport.

Attractions: There are many points of interest and attractions within the City of Columbus, OH area. Battelle Riverfront Park located at Marconi Blvd. and Broad Street has guided tours of the full scale replica of Christopher Columbus Santa Maria, the flag ship that made the historic voyage in late 1492. (Apr-Nov, Tues-Sun) 645-8760; Ohio Historical Center 297-2300; Ohio Village; Ohio Center of Science & Industry 228-2674; German Village 221-8888.

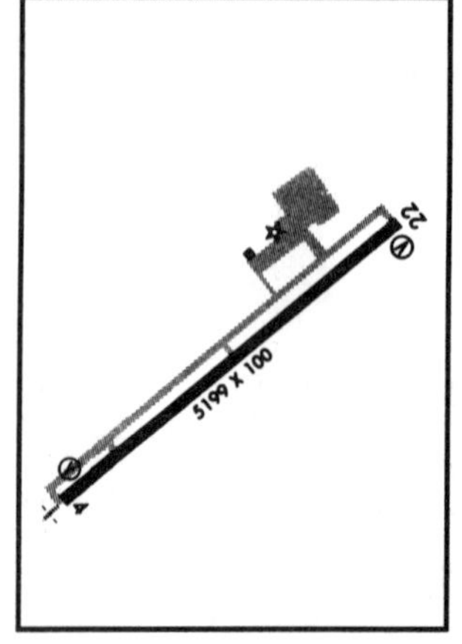

Airport Information:

COLUMBUS - BOLTON FIELD (TZR)
8 mi southwest of town N39-54.05 W83-08.23 Elev: 905 Fuel: 100LL, Jet A1+ Rwy 04-22: H5199x100 (Asph) Attended: Mon-Fri 1100-0500Z, Sat-Sun 1230-0030 Unicom: 122.95 Tower: 119.0 NFCT (1200-0400Z) Gnd Con: 121.8 Notes: Use right traffic when tower closed, avoid Columbus SW and Montoney Airport traffic pattern areas. See AFD for information.
FBO: CMH Aviation Phone: 878-2961 or 878-2050
FBO: Corporate Wings Phone: 878-1200

OH-OSU - COLUMBUS
OHIO STATE UNIVERSITY

(Area Code 614)

15

Barnstormer Restaurant:

The Barnstormer Restaurant is situated on the Ohio State University Airport in Ohio. This restaurant has seating for approximately 40 people, and is open Monday through Friday 7 a.m. to 4:30 p.m., Saturday 7:30 a.m. to 2 p.m. and Sunday from 8:30 to 1 p.m. Specialties of the house include items like meat loaf, spaghetti, and liver and onions along with many other selections. The decor of this restaurant is very casual with pictures of aircraft on the walls and models of airplanes hanging from the ceiling. For information, call 292-5699.

Restaurants Near Airport:
Barnstormer Restaurant On Site Phone: 292-5699

Lodging: Hilton Inn North (Trans) 436-0700; Holiday Inn (Trans) 885-3334; Stouffer Dublin Hotel (Trans) 764-2200;

Meeting Room: Hilton Inn North 436-0700; Holiday Inn Worthington 885-3334; Stouffer Dublin Hotel 764-2200.

Transportation: Rental Cars: Thrifty 292-5580.

Information: Columbus Visitor Center, 3rd Level of Columbus City Center Shopping Mall, South High Street and South Third Street at Rich Street. Phone: 800-345-4FUN. Also Columbus Intl. Arpt. has a information center on site, Phone: 228-1776.

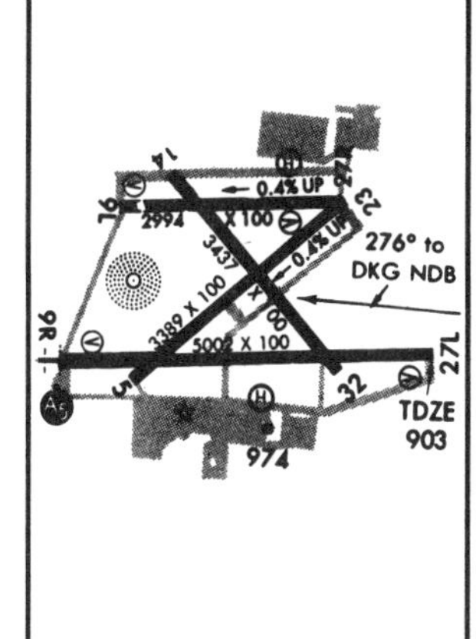

Airport Information:

COLUMBUS - OHIO STATE UNIVERSITY AIRPORT (OSU)
6 mi northwest of town N40-04.79 W83-04.38 Elev: 905 Fuel: 100LL, Jet-A+ Rwy 09R-27L: H5002x100 (Asph-Grvd) Rwy 05-23: H3389x100 (Asph) Rwy 14-32: H3437x100 (Asph) Rwy 09L-27R: H2994x100 (Asph) Attended: continuously Atis: 121.35 Unicom: 122.95 Columbus App/Dep Con: 120.2 Tower: 118.8 Gnd Con: 121.7 Clnc Del: 121.7

Airport Manager **Phone: 292-5460**
FBO: Ohio State University Airport **Phone: 292-5580**

OH-CMH - COLUMBUS
PORT COLUMBUS INTL AIRPORT

(Area Code 614)

16

94th Aero Squadron:

The 94th Aero Squadron is a fine dinner club located on the Port Columbus International Airport in Columbus, Ohio. This restaurant is unique in its decor, exhibiting WW-I memorabilia and surroundings recreating the atmosphere near the battle front, where flying Aces made their fame. This restaurant is open for lunch on Monday through Saturday from 11 a.m. to 3 p.m. and Sunday brunch 9 a.m. to 2:30 p.m. For dinner they are open Sunday through Thursday 4:30 p.m. to 10 p.m., and Friday and Saturday 4:30 p.m. to 11 p.m. They specialize in prime rib, steaks, fresh fish, along with appetizers, and a selective dessert menu. They offer a banquet room able to seat 80 persons. Courtesy transportation should not be a problem with any of the major general aviation fixed base operators on the field. Reservations are suggested by calling the restaurant at 237-8887.

Restaurants Near Airport:
94th Aero Squadron On Site Phone: 237-8887

Lodging: Holiday Inn (Trans) 237-6360; Howard Johnson Lodge East (Trans) 866-1111; Marriott East Columbus (Trans) 861-7220; Quality Inn (Trans) 861-0321; Radisson Hotel Airport (Trans) 475-7551; Sheraton Inn Airport (Trans) 237-2515.

Meeting Rooms: Holiday Inn 237-6360; Marriott East Columbus 861-7220; Quality Inn 861-0321; Radisson Hotel Airport 475-7551; Sheraton Inn Airport 237-2515.

Transportation: Courtesy cars reported to be available; Taxi Service: Carey Limousine Service 228-5466; Hills 221-1313; Northway Taxi 299-1191; Yellow 224-4141; Also Rental Cars: Avis 800-331-1212; Budget 800-527-0700; Dollar 800-421-6868; Hertz 800-654-3131; National 800-227-7368.

Information: Columbus Visitor Center, 3rd Level of Columbus City Center Shopping Mall, South High Street and South Third Street at Rich Street. Phone: 800-345-4FUN. Also Columbus Intl. Arpt. has a information center on site, Phone: 228-1776.

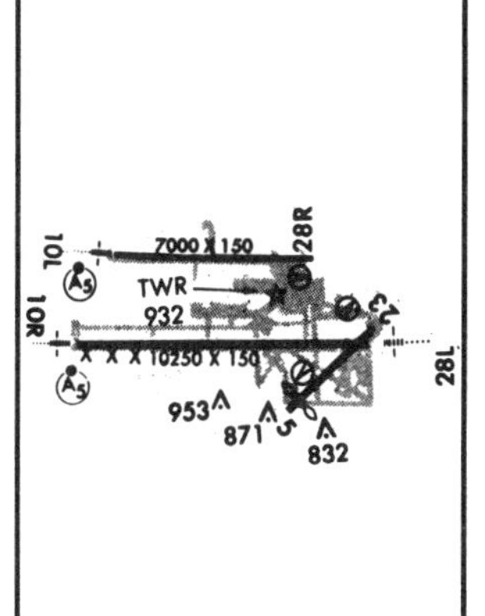

Airport Information:

COLUMBUS - PORT COLUMBUS INTERNATIONAL (CMH)
6 mi east of town N39-59.77 W82-53.34 Elev: 815 Fuel: 80, 100, Jet-A1+ Rwy 10R-28L: H10250x150 (Asph-Grvd) Rwy 10L-28R: H7000x150 Rwy 05-23: H3908x150 (Asph) Attended: continuously Atis: 124.6 Unicom: 122.95 Columbus App/Dep Con: 119.15, 132.3, 125.95, 118.2, 119.65 Columbus Tower: 132.7 Gnd Con: 121.9 Clnc Del: 126.3 Notes: CAUTION: Model aircraft traffic within 1 NM radius of a point 8 NM on a 010 degree bearing from the airport, Surface to 5,000 feet.

FBO: Columbus Jet Center **Phone: 237-6600**
FBO: Executive Jet Aviation **Phone: 239-5500**
FBO: Lane Aviation **Phone: 237-3747**
FBO: PDQ Air Service **Phone: 237-9777**

Ohio History of Flight Museum

Columbus, OH (OH-CMH)

Located on Port Columbus International Airport in Columbus, Ohio the Ohio, History of Flight Museum's newly completed 27,000 square-foot facility displays many vintage aircraft and aircraft engines and a number of aviation artifacts and memorabilia.

Aircraft on display includes a Curtiss Model D pusher, built in Norwalk, Ohio in 1911 and recognized as one of the oldest surviving aircraft in the United States; Waco Models 9 and 10 biplanes built in Troy, Ohio in the late 1920's; Culver "V" and "Cadet" monoplanes built at Port Columbus; a Taylor E-2 "Cub" which was the forerunner of the world renowned Piper J-3 aircraft; an Aeronca C-2 which was built in Middletown, Ohio in 1928; and a very rare Alliance "Argo."

Of particular interest is the Goodyear "Inflato-plane." Built in the mid-50s, the original prototype displayed here pioneered the use of rubberized fabric in aircraft manufacture, and was the world's first inflatable airplane.

All of the museum's aircraft are displayed indoors, with the exception of the French-built "Caravelle" cargo jet-liner which is located on the airport adjacent to the museum.

In the museum's collection of aircraft engines are examples of liquid and air cooled in-line rotary and radial types. Curtiss OX-5 and Le Rhone rotary engines from World War I days and Allison, Jacobs and Pratt & Whitney engines of later years are displayed.

Although basically a museum of general/commercial aviation, some attention is given to military aerospace accomplishments in Ohio. A full-scale mock-up of the Rockwell International "Redhead/Roadrunner" target missile for the U.S. Army, and a large model of the Rockwell U.S. Navy A3J fighter bomber which was capable of delivering an atomic bomb are displayed.

Pieces of the original fabric from the Wright brothers first airplane and Linbergh's "Spirit of St. Louis" are exhibited.

The museum has a well stocked gift shop which features aviation-related items, videotapes and a fine collection of aviation books.

The museum's research library contains many books and periodicals covering all aspects of aviation history.

Photo: by Ohio History of Flight Museum

An extensive video tape library is maintained by the museum and tapes are shown to visitors upon request.

The museum is open on weekdays from 9:00 a.m. to 4:00 p.m. Saturday 12 noon to 4 p.m. and Sunday 1 p.m. to 4 p.m. Evening and weekend tours are available by appointment. Admission is by donation: $2.00 for adults, and $1.50 for children. Visitors can fly in and park their planes at Lane Aviation (Unicom 122.95), or PDQ Air Services (128.85). Both are located near the museum. For museum information call 614-231-1300.

Photo: by Ohio History of Flight Museum

OH-LCK - COLUMBUS RICKENBACKER INTL. AIRPORT

(Area Code 614) 17

Subway:

Subway Restaurant is situated across the street from the entranceway to Rickenbacker International Airport, and is reported to be located about 4 blocks from the aircraft parking ramp. This combination gas station, mini mart, and sandwich shop, serves a variety of sub style sandwiches. Average prices run between $2.50 and $5.00 for most entrees. Carry-out service makes up most of their business. However, they do have seating for about 10 people. We were told that you can see the Rickenbacker Restaurant from the airport. For more information call 491-6833.

Attractions:

Steeple Chase Golf Course is located adjacent to the airport property. Numerous attractions are available within the Columbus area. Scioto Downs Race Track 2 miles; Santa Maria Replica is a full scale replica of Christopher Columbus flagship. Costumed guides give tours of the ship. This attraction is located at Battelle River Front Park. (Apr-Jan daily except Mondays) 645-8760.

Airport Information:

COLUMBUS - RICKENBACKER INTERNATIONAL AIRPORT (LCK)
10 mi south of town N39-48.83 W82-55.67 Elev: 744 Fuel: 100LL, Jet-A
Rwy 05R-23L: H12102x200 (Asph-Conc) Rwy 05L-23R: H12001x150 (Asph) Rwy 06-24: H3244x60 (Asph) Attended: Mon-Fri 1100-0300Z, Sat-Sun 1300Z-dark Atis: 132.1
Unicom: 122.95 Columbus App/Dep Con: 119.15 Rickenbacker Tower: 120.05
Gnd Con: 121.85 Public Phone 24hrs Notes: No fees with fuel purchase;
FBO: Rickenbacker Aviation Center Phone: 497-1276

Restaurants Near Airport:

Bombay Bicycle Club	6 mi N.	Phone: 864-6455
Marriott East	6 mi N.	Phone: 861-7220
Subway	1/2 mi	Phone: 491-6833

Lodging: Air Haven Motel 491-7923; Cross Country Inn Southwest 871-9617; Hilton Inn East (Trans) 868-1380; Marriott Inn East (6 miles north, Trans) 681-7220; Residence Inn East Columbus 864-8844.

Meeting: U.S Cargo & Courier Service (RAC Parent Company) has a conference room available located on airport, 497-1276; Hilton Inn East 868-1380; Marriott East Columbus 861-7220.

Transportation: Taxi Service: Northway Cab 299-1191; Yellow Cab 224-4141; Also Rental Cars: Ricar & Ford Car Rental 836-5321.

Information: Columbus Visitor Center, 3rd Level of Columbus City Center Shopping Mall, South High Street and South Third Street at Rich Street. Phone: 800-345-4FUN. Also Columbus Intl. Arpt. has a information center on site, Phone: 228-1776.

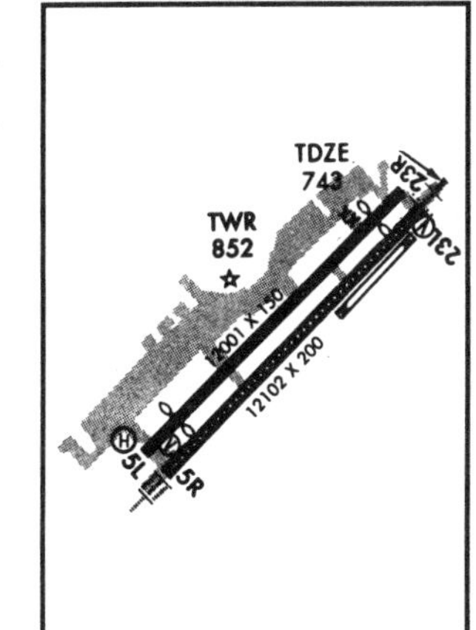

OH-I40 - COSHOCTON RICHARD DOWNING

(Area Code 614) 18

Roscoe Village Inn & Nearby Area:

Roscoe Village contains numerous gift and specialty shops, country inns, several restaurants and a number of historic buildings to investigate. This town creates a quaint living museum of an 1830s Ohio-Erie Canal town. There are many unique and special events that are featured throughout the year. Village walking tours that will take you through a one room school house, 19th-century print shop, Township hall, blacksmith's shop, as well as a number of period homes of 1833 including the Dr. Maro Johnson Home, Toll House and Craftsman House. While visiting the village, you're invited to enjoy a delicious meal at the Roscoe Village Inn, which happens to be one of the most popular dining establishments in the area. Free shuttle transportation is provided. On Sundays during the month of November they have been reported to feature a scrumptious Sunday brunch between 10 a.m. to 2 p.m. For information you can call 800-877-1830.

Restaurants Near Airport:

Old Warehouse	2 mi	Phone: 622-4001
Roscoe Village Inn	2 mi	Phone: 622-2222

Lodging: Roscoe Village Inn 2 mi. 622-2222 or 800-237-7397.

Meeting Rooms: Roscoe Village Inn 2 mi 622-2222 or 800-237-7397.

Transportation: Free transportation is available from the Richard Downing Airport. Call the airport at 622-2252 or Roscoe Village Inn at 622-2222 or 800-237-7397.

Information: Roscoe Village Foundation 381 Hill Street, Coshocton, OH 43812, Phone: 622-9310 or 800-877-1830. or Coshocton County Conv. & Visit. Bureau, P.O. Box 905, Coshocton, OH 43812. Phone: 622-9310, 622-9315 or 800-338-4724.

Attractions: Roscoe Village is conveniently located about 2 miles from the Coshocton Richard Downing Airport (I40). There are many things to see and do in the village. This 1830s Ohio-Erie Canal town depicts the life styles during that period. For information you can call the Roscoe Village Foundation at 614-622-9310 or 800-877-1830. or the Coshocton County Convention & Visitors Bureau at 622-9310, 9315 or 800-338-4724.

Airport Information:

COSHOCTON - RICHARD DOWNING (I40)
3 mi northwest of town N40-18.55 W81-51.20 Rwy 04-22: H4100x75 (Asph) Attended: 1230Z-dusk Unicom: 123.0
Airport Manager Phone: 622-2252

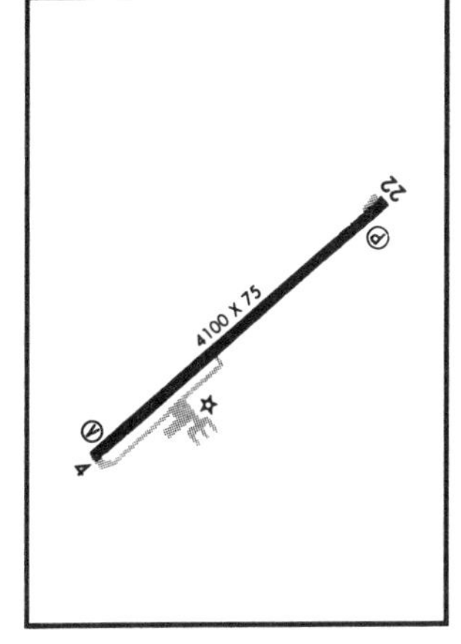

Roscoe Village

The Roscoe Village story begins with the a rich history of a canal town that was laid out in 1816, originally called Caldersburgh by its founder, James Calder. But in 1830, two men of ambition and farsightedness, Leander Ransom and Noah Swayne, petitioned the state legislature to rename the village "Roscoe" in honor of William Roscoe, the famous English author and abolitionist of the time.

The opening of the Ohio & Erie Canal in Caldersburgh in 1830 was heralded when the canal boat, the Monticello, arrived from Cleveland and docked for a few days above the aqueduct. The impact of the canal on the community of Roscoe was to transform it from a backwoods settlement to a thriving port on the Ohio & Erie Canal.

Roscoe was just one of the many ports on the canal, which ran from Cleveland on Lake Erie to Portsmouth on the Ohio River, a distance of 308 miles. The canals opened up the isolated interior of the state, providing cheap transportation for people and goods, resulting in a great economic boom in the first half of the nineteenth century. The canal continued to operate until the great flood of 1913, but the railroads marked the passing of the heyday of the canal.

Roscoe's prosperity declined with the demise of the canal industry in Ohio. The once thriving, important canal port slowly decayed, and its beautiful Greek Revival buildings rapidly deteriorated.

The idea of a historical restoration in Roscoe came to prominence in 1960 at the dedication of the Canal Days mural, painted by the distinguished American Artist, Dean Cornwell, for Coshocton County's 1961 Sesquicentennial Celebration. Cornwell chose a robust 1850s canal scene from Roscoe Village as the subject for his mural. This beautiful 24 by 8 foot painting today hangs in Bank One, while a slightly smaller reproduction now graces the lobby of Roscoe Village's Visitor Center. The painting fascinated and inspired Coshocton industrialist, Edward E. Montgomery, and his wife, Frances, and the dream for the restoration of the old town took root.

On August 28, 1968, the restoration that would end the deterioration of the Roscoe area got under way when the Montgomerys purchased the 1840 Toll House. The remaining examples of canal-era architecture were now to be preserved. The dream of the Montgomerys was becoming a reality. Roscoe Village would be, as Mr. Montgomery stated, "a living museum so that the people of the 20th century and succeeding ones could enjoy a visit back to the 19th century where aged brick buildings, hoop-skirted women and quaint shops would bring the canal areas back to life."

Roscoe Village today is a result of 27 years of dedicated work. Open year-round, the village has a relaxing atmosphere of days gone created by brick sidewalks, pocket gardens and canal-era buildings.

The village features old time shops with one-of-a-kind gifts, a 51-room country inn and four restaurants. With the educational programs offered in Roscoe Village, one can take a fascinating tour of 19th century buildings complete with costumed interpreters and craft demonstrations, as well as attend a variety of weekend festivals and special events.

In addition, a 45-minute ride aboard a horse-drawn canal boat along a restored section of the Ohio & Erie Canal System is offered by the Coshocton City and County Park District and operates May through October.

In 1992, a new Visitor Center was opened. This dramatic structure houses a multi-projector theater, an exhibit hall and a Founders Gallery, the latter honoring the village's founding family, the Montgomerys. Adjacent to the building is an elegant Memorial Garden, created in memory of Frances B. Montgomery.

The restoration project is carried on by The Roscoe Village Foundation, a private, non-profit organization under the guidance and direction of a board of trustees. Funding is derived from private sources; contributions; revenues from their shops, restaurants and inn; ticket sales from their Living History Building Tour; and membership revenues.

The Richard Downing Airport (I40) is located only 3 miles from town. Free shuttle service daily from the airport to Roscoe Village is provided. For information call 800-877-1830.

The village has a number of events held throughout the year. Summer Fest is held during June, July and August. The Coshocton Art Show & Sale is held the middle of June, as well as Blacksmith Weekend the latter part of July. An Old Time Music Fest is featured in late September. Apple Butter Stirrin', is held late in October, and on the first second and third week in December the village celebrates Christmas Candlelightings.

For more information about Roscoe Village contact the Roscoe Village Foundation 381 Hill Street, Coshocton, OH 43812 or call 614-622-9310 or 800-877-1830. (Information supplied by Roscoe Village Foundation).

Photo by: Roscoe Village Foundation

Visit the many gift and specialty shops in town or take a horse drawn carrage or canal tour.

OH-DAY - DAYTON
JAMES M COX DAYTON INTL.

(Area Code 513) 19, 20

Aero Place Deli & Lounge:

The Aero Place Deli & Lounge is located within the terminal building at Dayton International Airport. This facility is open 5 a.m. to 11 p.m. 7 days a week, and is situated near the center concourse. The Aero Place Lounge is open Monday through Friday between 11 a.m. and 9 p.m., Saturday from 11 a.m. to 6 p.m. and Sunday from 1 p.m. to 9 p.m. Private conference rooms located on the premises can accommodate up to 40 persons. These rooms can also be equipped to handle as few as 6 persons. Aircraft parking is located across the field from the terminal building at the fixed base operators. Transportation would have to be arranged through the FBO's. For information about the Aero Place Deli & Lounge call 898-3593.

Kitty Hawk Restaurant:

The Kitty Hawk Restaurant located near the Dayton Airport Inn is a combination coffee shop, lounge and dining room with seating for 150 persons. This establishment is located on James M. Cox Dayton International Airport in Dayton, Ohio. Transportation to this restaurant can be obtained through the fixed base operators located across the field from the main terminal building. They are open 7 days a week at 5 a.m. serving a continental breakfast then provide a full breakfast line beginning at 7 a.m. They stay open throughout the day until 10 p.m. It is reported that you can see one of the main runways from their location. Entrees consist of a wide variety of American cuisine with choice cuts of beef, in addition to lighter fare. We were told that the decor was elegant in Victorian motif and offers a dinner club atmosphere. For information or reservations please call the restaurant at 898-1000.

Attractions:

Dayton Air Force Museum is located on Wright Patterson Air Force Base, six miles northeast of downtown Dayton. Over 150 aircraft are exhibited inside the Museum's main building. In addition, there are thousands of artifacts on display, including hardware, documents, photographs, diaries, and personal memorabilia. For additional information write: USAF Museum, Wright Patterson AFB, OH 45433-6518 or call 513-255-3284.

Restaurants Near Airport:

Aero Place Deli & Lounge	On Site	Phone: 898-3593
Kitty Hawk Restaurant	On Site	Phone: 898-1000

Lodging: Days Inn North 898-4946; Dayton Airport Hotel (Trans) 898-1000; Hampton Inn Dayton Northwest (Trans) 832-2222; Hilton Daytonian (Trans) 461-4700; Holiday Inn Dayton Northwest (Trans) 832-1234; Ramada Inn Dayton North (Trans) 890-9500; Residence Inn (Trans) 898-7764.

Meeting Rooms: Dayton Airport Hotel (Trans) 898-1000; Hampton Inn Dayton Northwest (Trans) 832-2222; Hilton Daytonian 461-4700; Holiday Inn Dayton Northwest 832-1234; Ramada Inn Dayton North 890-9500.

Transportation: Rental Cars: Avis 898-5835; Budget 898-1396; Dollar 898-5765; Hertz 898-5806; National 898-0100.

Information: Dayton Area Chamber of Commerce, Chamber Plaza, Fith & Main, Dayton, OH 45402-2400, Phone: 226-1444; Also: Dayton/Montgomery County Convention & Visitors Bureau, One Chamber Plaza, Fifth & Main, Dayton, OH 45402-2400, Phone: 226-8211.

Airport Information:

DAYTON - JAMES M. COX DAYTON INTERNATIONAL AIRPORT (DAY)

9 mi north of town N39-54.14 W84-13.16 Elev: 1009 Fuel: 100, Jet-A
Rwy 06L-24R H10900x150 (Asph-Conc-Grvd) Rwy 18-36: H8500x150 (Asph-Conc-Grvd)
Rwy 06R-24L: H7000x150 (Asph-Conc-Grvd) Attended: continuously Atis: 125.8
Unicom: 122.95 Dayton App/Dep Con: 118.85, 127.65, 134.45, 118.0, 126.5
Dayton Tower: 119.9 Gnd Con: 121.9 Clnc Del: 121.75
FBO: Aviation Sales Phone: 898-3927
FBO: Stevens Aviation, Inc. Phone: 454-3400, 800-359-7232
FBO: Wright Brothers Aero Phone: 890-8900

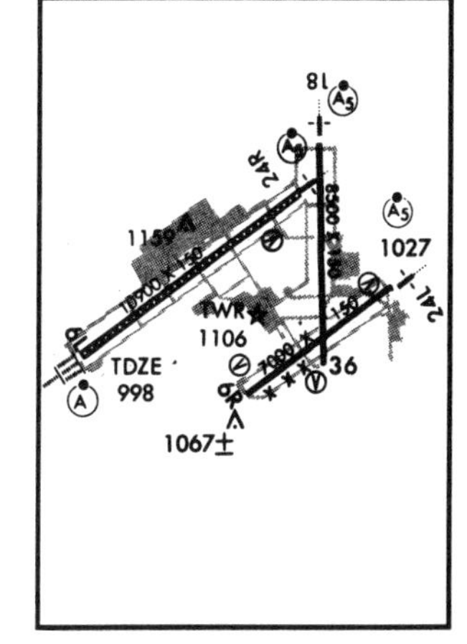

United States Air Force Museum

Dayton, OH (OH-I44), (OH-DAY) (OH-I73), (OH-I19)

Photo by: U.S. Air Force Museum

The U.S. Air Force Museum, near Dayton, Ohio, is the world's largest aviation museum with over 10 acres of aircraft and other exhibits under roof.

The United States Air Force Museum is internationally acclaimed as the world's largest and oldest military aviation museum. It is located at Wright-Patterson Air Force Base, near Dayton, Ohio, the home of the Wright Brothers.

The Museum's origin dates back to 1923 where it started in the corner of an aircraft hangar at McCook Field near downtown Dayton. From the informal showing of World War I planes and equipment of both the United States and foreign governments, the collection has grown to over 300 aircraft and major missiles, plus thousands of aviation artifacts.

Dayton has an early acquaintance with aviation. The Wright Brothers developed their 1903 flyer in Dayton and continued flying at nearby Huffman Prairie between 1904 and 1910. Experimental flying was conducted by the Army at McCook Field during and after World War I.

When area residents donated 4,000 acres of land in the 1920s for the establishment of Wright Field as a research center to replace the outgrown McCook Field, the museum was also moved. Between 1927 and 1935, the museum occupied 1,500 square feet of space in a laboratory building at Wright Field, six miles from downtown Dayton.

In 1935, the museum got its first real home in the form of a specially designed building at Wright Field costing $235,000. It was paid for through the Works Progress Administration (WPA). By this time, the museum collection included about 2,000 items. But the new home was converted to wartime use in 1941, and the collection went into storage.

After the war, the museum program was directed towards collection of items for re-opening the museum. The curator at that time was also given the task of locating aircraft for the National Air and Space Museum of the Smithsonian Institution. Collection efforts continued, and in April of 1954 the museum again opened to the public. This time it was located at adjoining Patterson Field in a World War II structure that had housed an engine-overhaul facility. Attendance in 1954 totaled 10,000 visitors. Since then attendance has spiraled, averaging one million visitors from 1972 through 1986, 1.3 million in 1987, nearly 1.5 million in 1988 and 1989 and reaching an all-time record in 1990 with over 1.6 million.

The museum changed in the early 1960s from a warehouse display to a uniquely designed interior "maze" floor plan which directed visitors along a controlled walkway, unfolding the story of military aviation in chronological sequence.

That converted WW-II building was outgrown in the early 1960s. Further, it was neither fireproof nor air-conditioned and was unsuitable for properly protecting and displaying the growing, priceless collection. Support posts every 16 feet in one direction and every 50 in another, greatly restricted how and where aircraft could be exhibited.

Thanks to the Air Force Museum Foundation, a philanthropic, non-profit organization founded in 1960, the longstanding need for a new building was finally met when a new $6 million museum building was completed on a 400-acre site at historic Wright Field. Formal dedication ceremonies were held with President Richard M. Nixon in September 1971. The 800 x 240 foot building was paid for entirely by public contributions. It was designed specially for display of aircraft and provides indoor protection for nearly 100 aircraft. A $1 million Visitor Reception Center was added in 1976, again through contributions by the public to the Museum Foundation.

A major museum expansion, the Modern Flight Hangar, opened in April 1988, and houses over 50 aircraft including a Boeing B-52D "Stratofortress" and the museum's experimental aircraft collection. It is parallel to and similar in size as appearance to the 1971 museum building. The new $10.8 million building was funded jointly by the federal government and the Air Force Museum Foundation. Whereas the 1971 building retains the chronological layout, the Modern Flight Hangar uses subjective layouts for its exhibits.

An aircraft Annex display, housing about 35 aircraft, was opened in 1977 on the old Wright Field flight line, about one mile from the main museum complex. This twin-hangar storage facility is also open for visitors to view aircraft that are either awaiting restoration or have recently been completed by the museum's restoration staff. Free shuttle bus transportation is provided for museum visitors to this auxiliary building.

The main museum complex and annex provide 10-1/2 acres or 461,470 square feet of indoor exhibition space--a far cry from the 1,500 square feet of the 1927-35 era. Further, the collection has grown from 2,000 items to more than 40,000 items with only a portion on exhibit at any one time.

The Museum also has expanded to provide support to military and civilian

Photo by: U.S. Air Force Museum

This Consolidated B-24D "Liberator now on display at the U.S. Air Force Museum, disappeared on a mission from North Africa in April 1943 and was found later in the Libyan Dessert in May of 1959.

Photo by: U.S. Air Force Museum

Artifacts and planes from WW-II era can be seen in the USAF Museum's Air Power Gallery.

museums around the world. This assistance includes the loan of about 1,300 aircraft, 200 missiles and 22,000 other aviation artifacts. In addition, the museum conducts special workshops for children and operates a free audio-visual loan program for teachers. School tours are conducted for the museum by volunteers for the Wright-Patterson AFB Officers' Wives Club. Among the many special events hosted by the museum each year is an aviation classic film festival and guest lecture series.

During the 1980s, the museum supervised the development of a Memorial Park on a portion of its 400-acre site. As the decade came to a close, more then 175 memorials had been erected to commemorate the military service of individuals and of organizations. Each memorial, whether a tree with a simple plaque or an elaborate granite monument, was financed through donations of concerned and interested citizens.

In October 1989, a $5,7 million contract was awarded to the B.G. Danis Company/Building Division of Dayton by the Air Force Museum Foundation for the construction of an IMAX theater, in front of and connected to the existing museum buildings opened in May 1991. An 80-foot-high dome glass atrium over the expanded lobby serves as the architectural focal point for the entire complex.

Although the museum is operated by the United States Air Force, its IMAX theatre, gift shop, book store, model shop and cafe are run by the Air Force Museum Foundation. Proceeds are used to support museum activities and to remodel or expand museum facilities. "Friends of the Air Force Museum," created by the Foundation in 1978, is an organization of aviation enthusiasts who support the museum. For a $24 annual fee, members receive a newsletter, discounts in the museum shops, a well as a number of other benefits.

The museum may be reached by taking the Harshman Road exit off of Ohio Route 4 (About six miles northeast of Dayton) and following Harshman Road to Springfield Pike (east). The museum is open to the public from 9 a.m. to 5 p.m. seven days a week and is closed only on Thanksgiving, Christmas and New Years Day. Admission and parking are free.

The evolution of the United States Air Force museum will continue. The Museum has a long-range plan to add three parallel buildings to the main complex by the year 2020.

Due to the fact that the museum is located on an Air Force Base, general aviation aircraft are not permitted to land on the field. (Exceptions to this are sometimes made to open the field one day out of the year). If flying in to visit the museum, pilots can land at four nearby civilian fields. These airports are; Dayton-New Lebanon (I44) is about

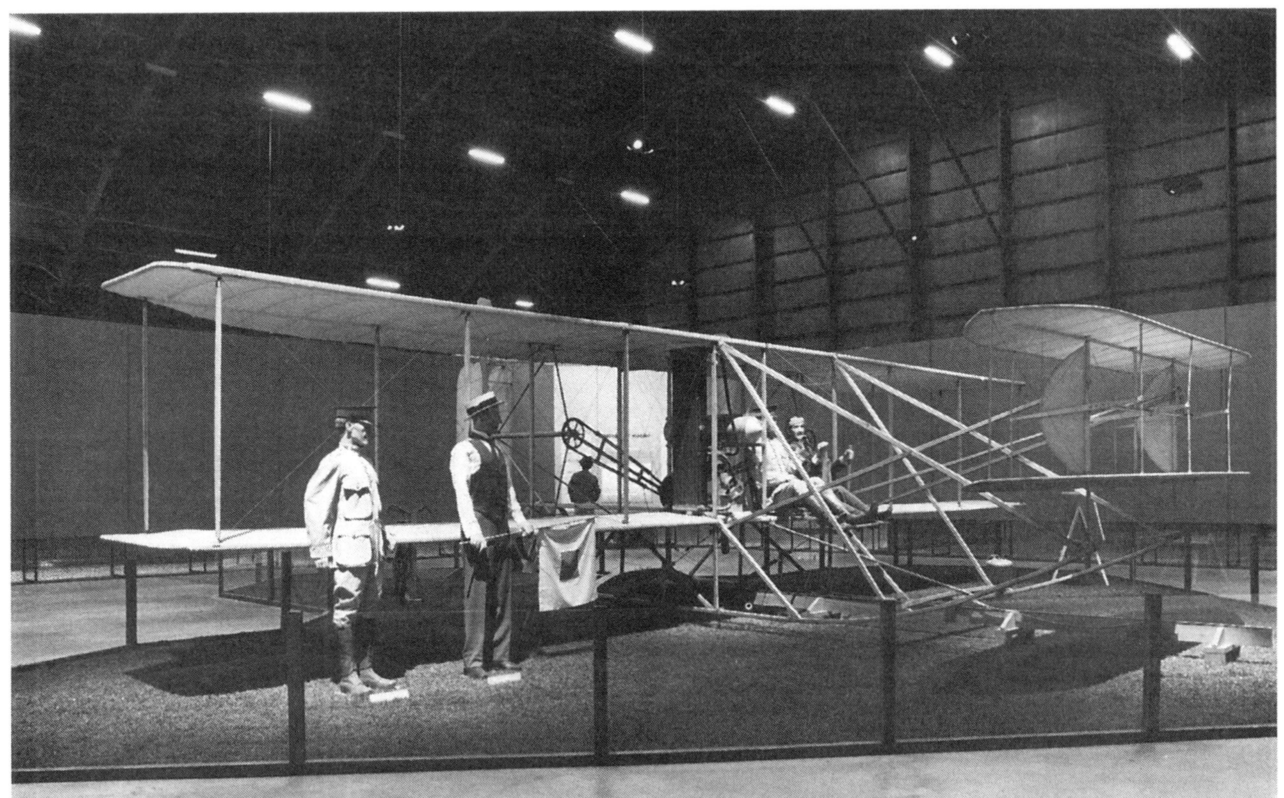

Photo by: U.S. Air Force Museum

Exact reproduction of the world's first military aircraft, purchased by the U.S. from Dayton's Wright Brothers

9 miles west of the city of Dayton, OH; James M. Cox Dayton International (DAY); Dayton-Moraine Air Park (I73) located southwest of city of Dayton and 10 to 12 miles from the museum; and Dayton-Greene County Airport (I19) located southeast of Dayton and approx. 10 miles from the museum. For further information about the museum and its services, contact the Public Affairs Division at 937-255-4704 or their general number 937-255-3286. (Information submitted by United States Air Force Museum).

Photo by: U.S. Air Force Museum

The F-117A "Stealth" fighter, the world's first operational aircraft designed to exploit low observable stealth technology and so successful in Desert Storm, is now in display at the USAF Museum.

OH-0156 - DELLROY
ATWOOD LODGE AIRPORT

(Area Code 330)

21

Atwood Lodge Resort:

The Bryce Browning dinning room within the lodge, serves breakfast, lunch and dinner and exhibits an elegant atmosphere in a rustic decor, complete with large wooden beams, chandeliers, fire place and large glass windows. The resort has excellent accommodations for their guests, including catered meals available for large or small groups from 10 to 400 persons. Some of the amenities of their resort include 104 deluxe guest rooms with either balconies or terraces along with 17 four-bedroom lakeside cottages, each with 1-1/2 baths and complete kitchens. An 18 hole golf course along with a lighted 9 hole par 3 course, putting green and driving range provides the golfing enthusiast with a relaxing way to spend an afternoon along tree-lined fairways. Indoor and outdoor swimming pools combined with whirlpool and sauna, are also available for anyone wishing to take advantage of their use. Their Swiss-style Chalet and Marketplace features a game room, deli, bake shop plus snack bar. Due to its convenient location adjacent to Atwood Lake, activities like sailing, water skiing and fishing can also be enjoyed. During the winter months, the resort attracts many sports-minded individuals with activities and cross country skiing. A conference and convention center can also be reserved. After landing dial "0" at their airport phone and request courtesy transportation. For information call 735-2211.

Restaurants Near Airport:
Atwood Lodge Restaurant   On Site   Phone: 735-2211

Lodging: Atwood Lodge Resort (On Site) 735-2211.
Meeting Rooms: Atwood Lodge Resort (Convention facilities, on site) 735-2211.
Transportation: Free shuttle van available to fly-in guests 735-2211.
Information: Atwood Resort, P.O. Box 96, Dellroy, OH 44620, Phone: 735-2211.

Attractions:

Atwood Resort offers year around activities for the visitor along with many additional attractions within the area. The Muskingum Watershed Conservancy District of the State of Ohio has created man made lakes and reservoirs for flood control. Atwood Lake and Atwood Lake Park situated near the resort contains hiking trails, wooded campsites, picnic shelters, swimming beaches as well as excellent fishing with catches of northern pike, largemouth bass, crappies along with blue gills and yellow perch. For information call 735-2211.

Airport Information:

DELLROY - ATWOOD LODGE AIRPORT (0156)
2 mi southwest of town   N40-31.94 W81-14.29   Elev: 1108   Rwy 12-30: 3158x100 (Turf)   Attended: unattended   CTAF: 122.9   Notes: Runway 12-30 has a 500 foot grass area on the northwest end marked with yellow barrels and a 106 foot grass area on the southeast end marked with yellow barrels.
Atwood Lodge Resort   Phone: 735-2211

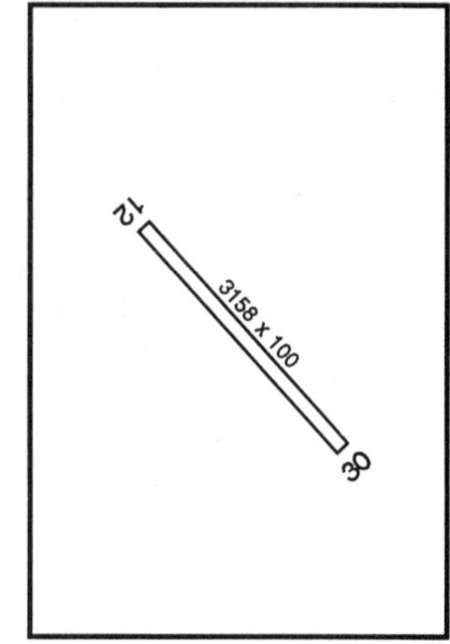

OH-FDY - FINDLAY
FINDLAY AIRPORT

(Area Code 419)

22

Rose Villa:

The Rose Villa is located across the street from the Findlay Airport near the gas pump and weather reporting station. This is a family dining establishment that is open 11 a.m. to 9 p.m. Monday through Thursday, and on Friday and Saturday until 10 p.m. Their menu contains items like steaks, sizzler t-Bone, rib-eye, steak and shrimp combination plates, chicken and noodles, spaghetti, pork chops, ham, fish selections like shrimp and perch, as well as an assortment of breakfast items that are served all day. Specials are also offered each day. Their salad bar is another feature popular with customers. The restaurant dining room is decorated with a pink-colored decor synonymous with the name "Rose Villa." Seating within the restaurant is accomplished with booths and tables. This restaurant caters to groups and also furnishes in-flight catering. Anything on their menu can be prepared for carry-out. The owners of Rose Villa restaurant have been serving customers for the past 50 years. For more information call the restaurant at 424-9284.

Restaurant Near Airport:
Rose Villa   Adj Arpt   Phone: 424-9284

Lodging: Days Inn 2 mi 423-7171; Country Hearth Inn 2 mi 423-4303; Cross Country Inn 2 mi 424-0466; Findlay Inn & Conference Center 2 mi 422-5682; Holiday Inn 2 mi 423-8212; Imperial House Motel 423-7171; Knights Stop 2 mi 422-5516.

Meeting Rooms: Country Hearth Inn 2 mi 423--4303; Cross Country Inn 2 mi 424-0466; Fairfield Inn & Conference Center 2 mi 422-5682.

Transportation: Hertz Rental Cars 422-3933 or 800-654-3131. Also taxi service: Johnston Taxi 424-3233; Harold's Taxi Service 423-3787.

Information: Hancock County County Convention and Visitors Bureau, 123 East Main Crossing Street, Findlay, OH 45840, Phone: 422-3315.

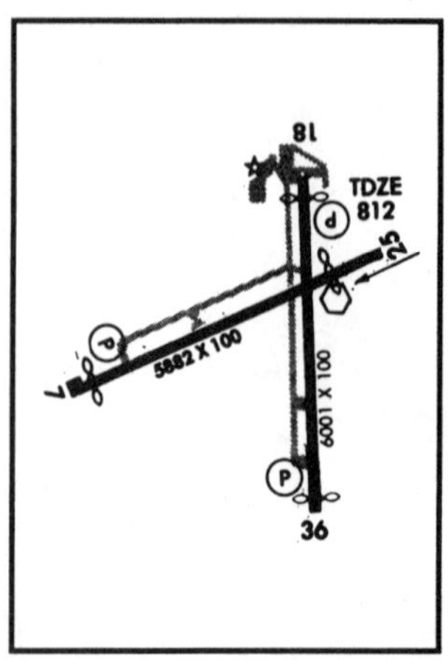

Airport Information:

FINDLAY - FINDLAY AIRPORT (FDY)
1 mi southwest of town   N41-00.81 W83-40.12   Fuel: 100LL, Jet-A   Rwy 18-36: H6001x100 (Asph)   Rwy 07-25: H5882x100 (Asph)   Attended: Mon-Fri 1200-0100Z, Sat-Sun 1400-2300Z   Unicom: 123.0   Notes: CAUTION: No line of sight between runway ends.
FBO: Crow Executive   Phone: 422-4182
FBO: Findlay Aviation Service   Phone: 422-4182

OH-14G - FREMONT
FREMONT AIRPORT

23

(Area Code 419)

Restaurants Near Airport:

Days Inn	5-7 mi.	Phone: 334-9551
Gregs Country Inn	1 mi	Phone: 332-8943
J & R Sons	2-3 mi	Phone: 334-7126
Travel Lodge	5-7 mi.	Phone: 334-9517

Gregs Country Inn:

Gregs Country Inn is a family dining establishment located about 1 mile from the Fremont Airport. According to the restaurant management you want to turn right out of the airport parking lot and continue until you reach the traffic light; once at that intersection make a left and continue on until you reach the restaurant. It is a blue colored building with a wagon wheel out in front. Gregs Country Inn is open Monday through Thursday from 11 a.m. to 9 p.m., Friday from 11 a.m. to 10 p.m., Saturday 8 a.m. to 10 p.m. and Sunday from 8 a.m. to 3 p.m. Specialties on their menu include seafood, pasta and steaks. Chicken Primivera, fillets, pork chops and their orange roughy are just a few favorites customers enjoy. Also try their baked sweet potato if you have a chance. On Friday they feature an all you can eat Alaskan pollock, Saturday their prime rib special after 4 p.m., Thursday all you can eat country style barbecued ribs and Sunday, baked chicken. During the rest of the week they offer a variety of sandwiches for their customers. The restaurant can seat about 120 people. The dining room is bright and cheerfully decorated in colors of pink and teal. They can also accommodate larger groups if given advance notice. For information call 332-8943. Transportation by airport car.

Lodging: Days Inn Fremont 5-7 mi. 334-9551; Holiday Inn 5-7 mi. 334-2682; Travelodge 5-7 mi 334-9517.
Meeting Rooms: Days Inn Fremont 5-7 mi. 334-9551.
Transportation: Airport courtesy car or van reported available with advance notice preferred 332-8037. Also rental cars available.
Information: Sandusky County Convention & Visitors Bureau, P.O. Box 643, Fremont OH 43420, Phone: 332-4470.

Attractions: Hayes Presidential Center is located about 3-4 miles from the Fremont Airport. This attraction draws thousands of visitors each year. This 25-acre wooded estate is where our 19th president and his wife lived and died. Two separate estate tours are provided for guests which feature their home, library and the Hays Museum, containing memorabilia. To reach the estate you must take U.S. 20 and head west until you reach the stop light (Stone Street), then turn right and follow the signs to the Hayes Presidential Center. Admission charged. For hours call 332-2081.

__A new concept:__ is in the planning stages at this airport for drive-in hangars, complete with beds and kitchen accommodations. (Contact Arpt. Manager).

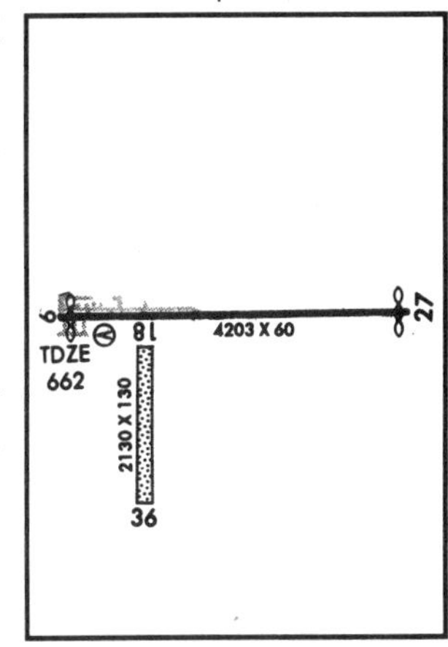

Airport Information:

FREMONT - FREMONT AIRPORT (14G)
2 mi southwest of town N41-19.99 W83-08.52 Elev: 662 Fuel: 80, 100LL, Jet-A Rwy 09-27: H4203x60 (Asph) Rwy 18-36: 2130x130 (Turf) Attended: Mon-Sat 1300Z-dusk, Sun 1700Z-dusk Unicom: 122.8 Notes: For fuel after hours call 419-332-0046.
FBO: Damschroder Sales Co. Phone: 332-8037

OH-GEO - GEORGETOWN
BROWN COUNTY

24

(Area Code 513)

Restaurants Near Airport:

Lakewood Golf & Rest.	1/2 mi	Phone: 378-4200

Lakewood Golf Course & Restaurant:

The Lakewood Golf Course and Restaurant is situated adjacent to the Brown County Airport. Pilots flying in to play a round of golf or for a bite to eat can simply walk across the fairway to reach the restaurant or proshop. If you call them, they will even drive over and pick you up. This is a family restaurant that is open from 11 a.m. to 8 p.m. during the winter and 11 a.m. to 9 p.m. during the summer. They have a full service menu along with appetizers. Some specials on the menu include a variety of sandwiches, chicken breast dinners, ham steak, 12-ounce sirloin, ribeye steak, chicken livers, cod fish dinners, baby backed ribs and prime rib. They feature a buffet Monday through Friday from 11 a.m. to 2 p.m. The restaurant is joined to the pro shop and has a nice view on three sides of the golf course. Restaurant seating is made up of tables and booths as well as a bar on the east side of the restaurant. A party room with sports TVs and main dining area is decorated with pictures of golfers and sports-oriented photos. Aircraft pictures decorate the walls as well. The 18 hole golf course attracts many fly-in golfers. We were told that in addition to the course, they also have tennis courts and a driving range. Reservations for tee off times are not necessary, however we suggest you let them know you are coming anyway. For more information you can call 378-4200.

Lodging: Georgetown Motel 1 mi 378-6789.

Meeting Rooms: None reported

Traansportation: Lakewood Golf Course & Restaurant will provide transportation to and from their facility, Phone: 378-4200. Taxi Service: Lewis Taxi 378-4262.

Information: Clermont County Convention & Visitors Bureau, 4440 Glen Este-Withamsville Road, Cincinnati, OH 45245. Phone: 513-753-7211.

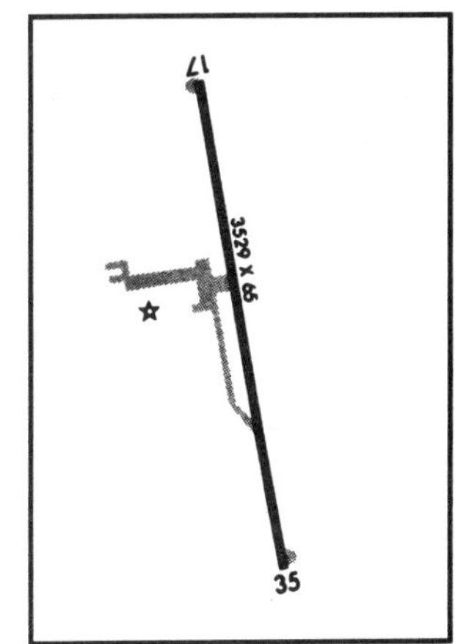

Airport Information:

GEORGETOWN - BROWN COUNTY (GEO)
1 mi northeast of town N38-52.92 W83-52.96 Elev: 957 Fuel: 80, 100LL Rwy 17-35 : H3529x65 (Asph) Attended: Unattended CTAF: 122.9
Airport Manager Phone: 378-9981

OH-3I9 - HEBRON
BUCKEYE EXECUTIVE AIRPORT

(Area Code 614) 25

Restaurants Near Airport:
Nearby restaurant 1/4 mi. Phone: N/A

Lodging: There are two bed & breakfast locations, one upstairs of the Red Baron Cafe (South end ramp) and the Landings Resort, located at Buckeye Lake (4 miles away). Full camping facilities are available at airport, in addition to RV Park, clean rest rooms, new showers and full hookups.

Meeting Rooms: Landings Resort and Buckeye Executive Airport provide accommodations for fly-ins, meetings, private parties, receptions and Camp Fly-ins. For information call the Red Baron Cafe or the airport at 928-5300.

Transportation: Rental Cars are available through the Landings Resort 928-5300. Resort within walking distance from private airstrip.

Information: Landings Resort, 2950 Canal Drive, Millersport, OH 43046, Phone: 928-5300.

Attraction (RC model flying):

During our conversation with the airport management we learned that the owners of the property conduct radio controlled exhibitions at scheduled times each month. This attraction has drawn many visitors from the local community as well as many RC exhibitors and enthusiasts. World Wide Class RC contestants enter in these competitions during this exciting event. The airport is closed during these events. For their safety, pilots should maintain extreme vigilance when entering the area. Prior permission at this airport is mandatory. During our conversation with the property owners that this is quite an attraction to see. All types of model aircraft are flown at these events. Competition jet planes as well as propeller driven model are flown. They even have after dark flights with model helicopters. Traditional air war reenactments draw great enthusiasm with all in attendance. For information call the owners at 928-3083.

Attractions:

Landings Buckeye Lake Resort combined with the Red Baron Cafe and Airport RV Park offers fly-in guests with accommodations for dining, entertainment and lodging all in one location. If planning to fly out for the day or searching for that unique aviation group outing, check out the accommodations available at this fly-in resort. For information call 928-3083.

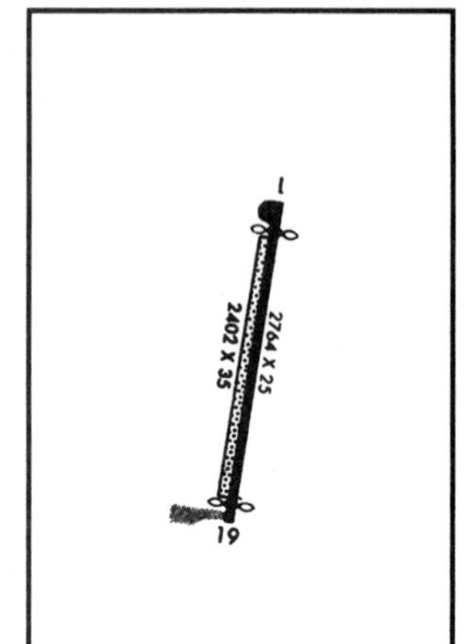

Airport Information:

HEBRON - BUCKEYE EXECUTIVE AIRPORT (3I9) Private Airport
2 mi west of town N39-57.70 W82-32.44 Elev: 914 Fuel: 100LL
Rwy 01-19: H2764x25 (Asph) Attended: continuously Unicom: 123.0 Notes: CAUTION: Do not land at this airport without prior permission. Radio controlled aircraft is operation. Special sceduling for use of airport is necessary. Check runway condition prior to use. Private use at your own risk.
Buckeye Executive Airport Phone: 928-3083

OH-UYF - LONDON
MADISON COUNTY

(Area Code 614) 26

Restaurants Near Airport:
Red Brick Tavern 2 or 3 mi. Phone: 852-1474

Lodging: Red Brick Tavern 2-3 mi 852-1474 or 800-343-6118; Loudon Motel 3 mi 852-9025; Trails Inn 4 mi 852-9415.

Meeting Rooms: Red Brick Tavern 2-3 mi 852-1474 or 800-343-6118.

Transportation: The Red Brick Tavern will provide guests with free courtesy transportation. For information call 852-1474 or 800-343-6118. Also: Rental cars: Buckey Ford Mercury 852-3673; Goodyear Plymouth/Chrysler 852-1432.

Information: London Area Chamber of Commerce, 17 East High Street, London, OH 43140. Phone: 852-2250.

Red Brick Tavern:

Ohio's second oldest inn offers traditional American fare, gracious dining in a carefully preserved historic atmosphere of a centuries' old inn. Since 1837 the tavern has played host to the American traveler, including six presidents. You'll find a wide variety of entrees. plus homebaked cinnamon rolls and biscuits with the old fashioned apple butter. The Red Brick Tavern serves daily 11 a.m. to 9 p.m. Monday through Thursday, 11 a.m. to 10 p.m. Friday and Saturday, and 11 a.m. to 7 p.m. on Sunday. This restaurant is located 2 to 3 miles east of the Madison County Airport. According to some of our readers who have visited this establishment, the service is good and the food is well prepared. The Red Brick Tavern has been named a National Historic Landmark and is registered as such with the National Park Service. Established in 1837 the tavern at Lafayette has been the scene of much history-making. Artist's drawings of six presidents of the US who have visited the Red Brick now hang in the staircase at the tavern. They are: John Tyler, Warren G. Harding, Martin Van Buren, John Quincy Adams, William Henry Harrison and Zachary Taylor. Dining rooms are available for private parties, rehearsal dinners or wedding receptions. If you call the restaurant, they will provide you with transportation to and from the airport. For more information or reservations call 852-1474 or 800-343-6118.

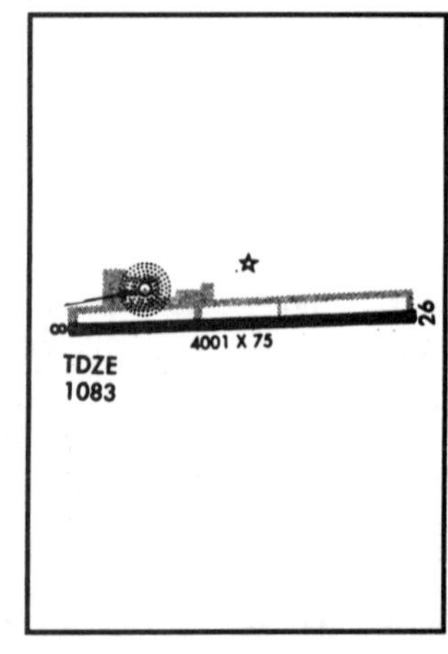

Airport Information:

LONDON - MADISON COUNTY (UYF)
3 mi north of town N39-55.96 W83-27.72 Elev: 1083 Fuel: 80, 100LL, Jet-A Rwy 08-26: H4001x75 (Asph) Attended: Sept and May 1300-0100Z, Oct-Apr 1300-0000Z, Jun-Aug 1300-0200Z. Unicom: 123.0
Airport Manager Phone: 852-5040

OH-MFD - MANSFIELD
MANSFIELD LAHM MUNICIPAL ARPT.

(Area Code 419)

27

Airport Restaurant:

The Airport Restaurant is located about 1/4 mile from Mansfield Lahm Municipal Airport. To reach the restaurant, taxi to Richland Aviation located behind the hangar rows adjacent to, and directly west of the threshold approach end of runway 32. Just follow the signs and you won't have any problem. Once reaching Richland Aviation, you can simply walk along the road about 2 blocks heading south out of the airport. The Airport Restaurant is situated among a group of houses and is located on the east side of the street. This family style restaurant which contains a bar, is open Monday through Friday from 9 a.m. to 8:30 p.m. and Saturdays 9 a.m. to 2 p.m. (Closed on Sunday) The restaurant serves specials like their "Airport Club" which is a 3 decker sandwich. Cheeseburgers, hamburgers, cold deli sandwiches, homemade soups during the winter and a variety of other selections. Carry out meals are also available. The dining area adjoins a bar area and has seating for about 50 persons. Tables can be grouped together for fly-in parties providing ample seating for their guests. The decor of this restaurant exhibits red tablecloths and black chairs, reflecting a relaxed and casual atmosphere. For information call the Airport Restaurant at 526-4510.

Restaurants Near Airport:

Airport Restaurant	1/4 mi	Phone: 526-4510

Lodging: Best Western 589-7118; Days Inn 522-3662; Holiday Inn (Trans) 525-6000; Travelodge 522-5142.

Meeting Rooms: Best Western 589-7118; Days Inn 522-3662; Holiday Inn 525-6000; Travelodge 522-5142.

Transportation: Taxi Service available at airport through Richland Aviation (FBO) 524-4261; Also Rental Cars: Hertz 524-3513.

Information: Mansfield/Richland County Convention and Visitors Bureau, 52 Park Avenue West, Mansfield, OH 44902, Phone: 525-1300 or 800-642-8282.

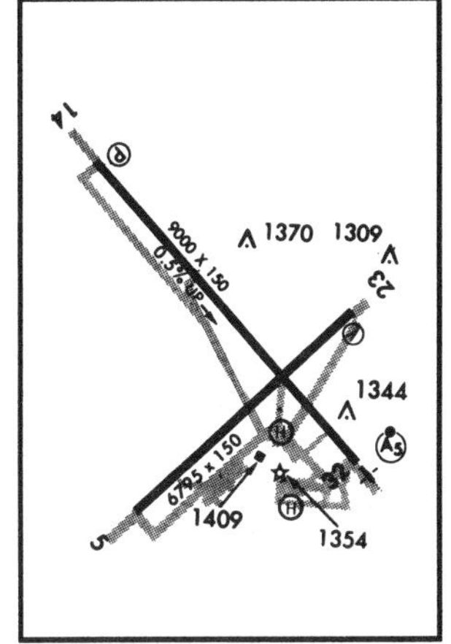

Airport Information:

MANSFIELD - MANSFIELD LAHM MUNICIPAL AIRPORT (MFD)
3 mi north of town N40-49.29 W82-31.00 Elev: 1297 Fuel: 100LL, Jet-A1+
Rwy 14-32: H9000x150 (Asph-Grvd) Rwy 05-23: H6795x150 (Asph-Grvd) Attended: continuously Atis: 125.3 Unicom: 122.95 App/Dep Con: 124.2, 127.35
Tower: 119.8 Gnd Con: 121.8 Notes: Military operations are conducted on field. Tower personnel unable to see FBO parking area from their location. Be sure to obtain taxi clearance from Richland Aviation.
FBO: Richland Aviation Phone: 524-4261

OH-MWO - MIDDLETOWN
HOOK FIELD MUNICIPAL AIRPORT

(Area Code 513)

28

Frish's Big Boy Restaurant:

Frish's Big Boy Restaurant is located across the street from the Hook Field Municipal Airport in southwestern Ohio near the city of Middletown. It is a family-style restaurant having a full menu for breakfast, lunch and dinner. They are noted to have an excellent breakfast and salad bar. You can taxi to within 100 yards of the restaurant. They are open from 7 a.m. to 12 a.m. throughout the week. For information call the restaurant at 423-6596.

Restaurants Near Airport

Frisch's Big Boy	Adj Arpt	Phone: 423-6596

Lodging: Days Inn 424-1201; Regal 8 Inn (Trans) 423-9403; The Manchester (Trans) 422-5481.

Meeting Rooms: Days Inn 424-1201; The Manchester 422-5481.

Transportation: Courtesy Car reported; Rental Cars: Automobile leasing and rental cars available through fixed base operator on airport.

Information: Middletown Area Chamber of Commerce, 30 City Centre Plaza, Middletown, OH 45042, Phone: 422-3030.

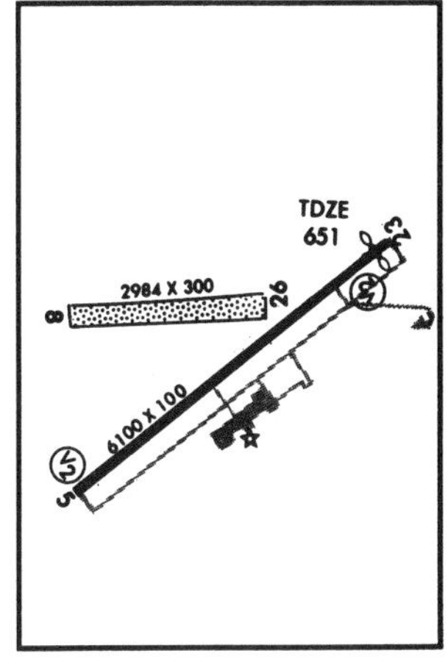

Airport Information:

MIDDLETOWN - HOOK FIELD MUNICIPAL AIRPORT (MWO)
2 mi north of town N39-31.91 W84-23.79 Elev: 651 Fuel: 100LL, Jet-A
Rwy 05-23: H6100x100 (Asph) Rwy 08-26: 2984x300 (Turf) Attended: Sep-Apr 1200-0200Z, May-Aug 1200-0300Z Unicom: 123.0 Notes: CAUTION: Ultralights enter/exit pattern at Rwy 08 to north lower than regular traffic pattern. Ulterlights do not fly south of Rwy 26; Also 895 and 827 foot MSL smoke stacks SW corner of field. (See AFD for current information).
FBO: Hogan Air, Inc. Phone: 423-5757

OH-6G4 - MOUNT VERNON WYNKOOP AIRPORT

(Area Code 614)

29

Dogwood Inn:

The Dogwood Inn is a family style restaurant located about a half mile from the Mount Vernon, Wynhoop Airport. This restaurant is open Sunday from 7 a.m. to 2:30 p.m., Monday 7 a.m. to 2:30 p.m., Tuesday, Wednesday and Thursday from 7 a.m. to 8 p.m. and Friday and Saturday 7 a.m. to 9 p.m. They offer a full line of breakfast, lunch and dinner selections with specials each evening. The decor is of a Colonial atmosphere with casual dining. The Dogwood Inn has a banquet room that can be reserved for 25 or more persons. They can also prepare meals to go. For information call the restaurant at 392-1770. Courtesy car transportation is available at the Wynkoop Airport by calling 392-8351.

Restaurants Near Airport:

Dogwood Inn	1/2 mi	Phone: 392-8351
McDonalds	1/2 mi	Phone: N/A
Rax Roast Beef	1/2 mi	Phone: N/A
Wendys	1/2 mi	Phone: N/A

Lodging: Brookside Motel (1 mile) 397-7414; Hotel Curtis 397-4334.

Meeting Rooms: Dogwood Inn has accommodations for meetings and group parties, call 392-8351.

Transportation: Taxi Service: Kart 392-0161 or 397-8180.

Information: Mount Vernon-Knox County Visitors Bureau, 236 South Main Street, Mount Vernon, OH 43050, Phone: 392-6102 or 393-1111.

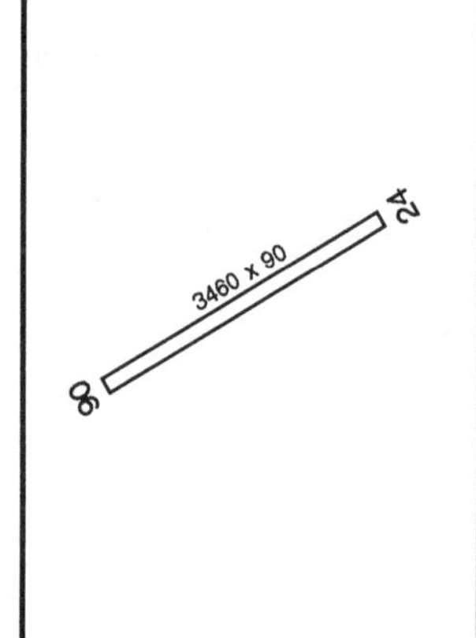

Airport Information:

MOUNT VERNON - WYNKOOP AIRPORT (6G4)
2 mi south of town N40-21.90 W82-29.74 Elev: 1041 Fuel: 80, 100LL
Rwy 06-24: 3460x90 (Turf) Attended: Apr-Sep 1200-0100Z, Oct-Mar 1300-2300Z
CTAF: 122.9
FBO: Antique Aircraft Restoration (Waco) Phone: 393-2243
FBO: Flying Koop Aviation Phone: 392-8351

OH-PLAZA INN AIRSTRIP Mt. VICTORY- (Private Airstrip)

(Area Code 937)

30

The Plaza Inn

The Plaza Inn Restaurant has its own private airstrip and is located about 8 miles southeast of Kenton, 18 miles northwest of Marysville, and about 20 miles west-southwest of Marion, Ohio. The restaurant is situated only 1/4 to 1/2 mile from town and offers 4 different dining rooms. Classified as a family style restaurant, the Plaza Inn is open between 7 a.m. and 9 p.m. 364 days out of the year. They are closed on Christmas Day. Specialties of the house include "Golden Brown" chicken, seafood, pork, farm raised beef and certified Angus steaks. Additional entrees are also featured. On Friday they offer a seafood buffet in addition to their Saturday night buffet featuring a beef carver and salad bar within the elegantly appointed "Coach Room". On Saturday and Sunday between 8 a.m. and 10:30 a.m. they have a breakfast buffet. The decor of the restaurant provides a colonial appearance. Average prices run $3.95 for breakfast, $5.50 for lunch and $7.50 for dinner. Their "Village Green" room can comfortably seat 50 people, with accommodations for up to 150 people during the week for larger gatherings. They also offer in-flight catering. For information about the restaurant or airport call 354-2851.

Restaurants Near Airport:

The Plaza Inn	On Site	Phone: 354-2851

Lodging: Bed & Breakfast (4 miles) Phone: unknown.
Meeting Rooms: The Plaza Inn Restaurant has accommodations for 50 people in their "Village Green" room and seating for up to 150 on weekdays within other portions of the restaurant. (Restaurant is on the airport site) 354-2851.
Transportation: Most of the establishments are reported to be within walking distance from the airport. Additional information about available transportation can be obtained from the Plaza Inn at 354-2851.

Attractions: The town of Mt. Victory contains over 20 unique antique shops which line the streets. On Memorial Day the town celebrates an antique car show. During the last weekend in June and July their "Flea-Market" and Antique Festival is a popular event. For information call the Plaza Inn Restaurant at 354-2851.

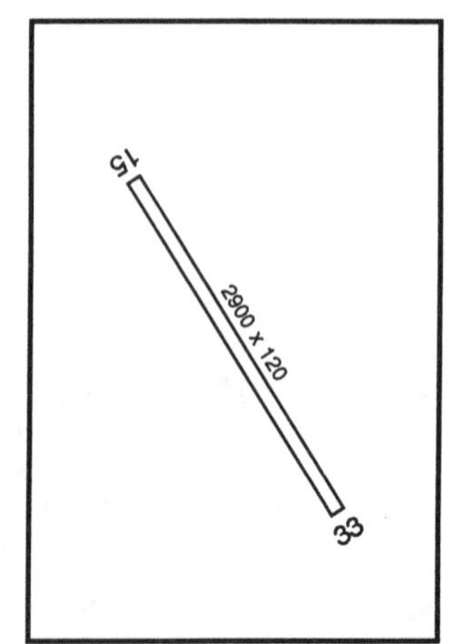

Airport Information:

Mt. Victory - (Private Airstrip)
Adjacent to Mt. Victory, Fuel: none available, Rwy 15-33: 2,900 (Turf) Attended: During restaurant hours 7 a.m. to 9 p.m. 7 days a week. Notes: Use at own risk, private use facility. Call Plaza Inn Restaurant for runway conditions prior to use 354-2851.

OH-PHD - NEW PHILADELPHIA HARRY CLEVER FIELD

(Area Code 330)

31

Hangar Restaurnat Lounge & Arpt. Restaurant:

The Hangar Restaurant Lounge & Airport Restaurant, are both located next to the main terminal area, at Harry Clever Airport, New Philadelphia, in east central Ohio. The AIRPORT RESTAURANT formally a Perkins family restaurant serves breakfast all day with lunch and dinner entrees and daily specials in a casual atmosphere. Their hours are 6:00 a.m. to 9 p.m. 7 days a week. Phone 339-3883. The HANGAR STEAK HOUSE & LOUNGE, a gourmet supper club, features steaks and chops cooked over an open charcoal fire. Other items include seafood, pasta and veal dishes. Restaurant hours are from 4 p.m. until 10 p.m. Monday through Thursday and 4 p.m. to 11 p.m. Friday and Saturday. Reservations are suggested for Fri & Sat evenings. Call 339-4011.

Attractions:

Local attractions include museums, cheese production factories and Amish Country. State Parks include Atwood Dam, Schoenbrunn State Park (Reported on airport), Leesville Dam, Piedmont Dam, Salt Fork Dam and Zoar Golf Course nearby.

Airport Information:

NEW PHILADELPHIA - HARRY CLEVER AIRPORT (PHD)
3 mi southeast of town N40-28.21 W81-25.20 Elev: 895 Fuel: 80, 100LL, Jet-A
Rwy 14-32: H3950x100 (Asph) Rwy 11-29: 2050x100 (Turf) Attended: Apr-Sep 1300-0100Z, Oct-Mar 1300-2200Z Unicom: 122.8 Notes: No landing or tie-down fees with fuel purchase.
FBO: Clever Aircraft Phone: 339-2023

Restaurants Near Airport:

Airport Restaurant	On Site	Phone: 339-3883
Bassetti's Restaurant	1 mile	Phone 339-4212
Hangar Restaurant	On Site	Phone: 339-4011

Lodging: Best Western Valley Inn (Trans) 339-7731; Delphian Motor Inn (Trans) 339-6644; L & K Motel 339-6671.

Meeting Rooms: Best Western Valley Inn 339-7731; Delphian Motor Inn 339-6644; Also check with Air-Delphia, Inc. (FBO) for further information about meeting rooms 339-6078.

Transportation: Air Delphia, Inc has courtesy and rental cars available at their location. 339-6078.

Information: Tuscarawas County Convention & Visitors Bureau, 125 McDonald's Drive Southwest, New Philadelphia, OH 44663, Phone: 339-5453 or 800-527-3387; Also Tuscarawas County Chamber of Commerce, 1323 Fourth Street NW, Box 232, New Philadelphia, OH 44663, Phone: 343-4474.

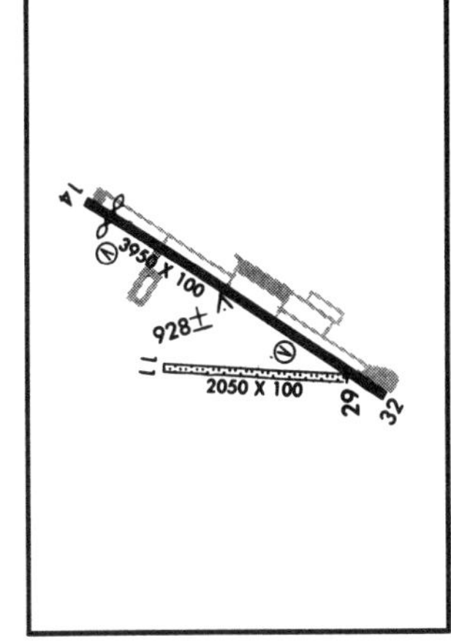

OH-PCW - PORT CLINTON CARL R KELLER FIELD

(Area Code 419)

32

Mon Ami Restaurant:

The Mon Ami Restaurant is located near the Carl R. Keller Airport, Port Clinton, OH. Courtesy transportation to and from the airport is furnished by the restaurant. Fly-in guests will truly enjoy visiting this unique facility which contains not only a fine restaurant but also a winery. Built as a co-op by European immigrants, Mon Ami Winery was constructed in 1872 in the old world tradition, making use of native materials found in the area. Today, Mon Ami produces 26 varieties of wines, from the familiar Catawba to a Cabernet Sauvignon. The restaurant is open Monday through Thursday from 11:30 a.m. to 3 p.m. for lunch and 5:00 p.m. to 9:00 p.m. for dinner. Friday and Saturday they open from 11:30 a.m. to 3 p.m. for lunch and again at 5 p.m. to 10 p.m. for dinner. Average prices run $8.00 for lunch and around $15.00 for dinner. Friday and Saturday nights they feature a prime rib and crab buffet. A Sunday brunch is featured between 11 a.m. and 3 p.m. and runs $10.95 per person. Children discounts are offered. Live Jazz is featured outdoors during the summer months on Sunday between 1 p.m. and 6 p.m., along with a Bar-B-Que. Accommodations for groups and parties can also be arranged. Call Mon Ami Restaurant at 797-4445 or 800-777-4266.

Attractions:

There are numerous attractions located within this region. Middle Bass Island, South Bass Island, Marblehead Peninsula, Catawba Island Peninsula and Cedar Point Amussment Park attracts vacationers from all over the midwest. (See "Information" listed above).

Airport Information:

PORT CLINTON - CARL R KELLER FIELD (PCW)
3 mi east of town N41-30.98 W82-52.12 Elev: 590 Fuel: 100LL, Jet-A
Rwy 09-27: H4996x75 (Asph) Rwy 18-36: H4001x75 (Asph) Attended: May-Aug 1300-0100Z, Sep-Apr 1300-2200Z Unicom: 122.8
FBO: Island Airlines Phone: 734-3149

Restaurants Near Airport:

Greenhouse Restaurant	4 mi	Phone: 797-4411
Mon Ami Restaurant	2 mi	Phone: 797-4445

Lodging: Lakeland Motel (Trans) 734-2101; Old Island House Inn 734-2166; Phils Inn (Trans) 734-4446.

Meeting Rooms: Mon Ami Restaurant and Historic Winery (2 miles) 797-4445; Old Island House Inn 734-2166.

Transportation: Airport courtesy car reported available with advance notice. Taxi Service: "3D" 734-1314

Information: Port Clinton Chamber of Commerce, 130 Jefferson Street, Suite 1B, Port Clinton, OH 43452, Phone: 734-5503; Also Ottawa County Visitors Bureau, 109 Madison Street, Suite E, Port Clinton, OH 43452, Phone: 734-4386.

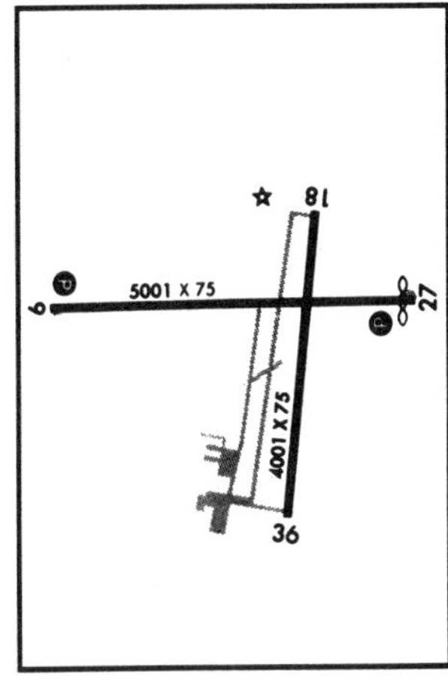

OH-PMH - PORTSMOUTH
GREATER PORTSMOUTH REGIONAL

(Area Code 614) **33**

Skyline Restaurant:

The Skyline Restaurant is located on the Greater Portsmouth Regional Airport and is situated about 5 miles north of the beautiful Ohio River, straight south of Columbus. The restaurant is within the terminal building and provides its guests with a view of the airport runway. A variety of selections for breakfast, lunch and dinner are served seven days a week from 6 a.m. to 8 p.m. during the summer and 7 a.m. to 7 p.m. during the winter months. This is a family style restaurant with specialties like their famous biscuits and gravy, barbecued ribs, meat loaf, sandwiches of all types, hamburgers, cheeseburgers and much more. Breakfast is served all day. Weekly specials run around $3.75 for most dishes. Seating capacity is about 50 persons. For further information, call the Skyline Restaurant at 820-2203.

Restaurants Near Airport:
Skyline Family Restaurant On Site Phone: 820-2203

Lodging: Days Inn 574-8431; Holiday Inn 354-2851; Ramada Inn 354-7711.

Meeting Rooms: Days Inn 574-8431; Holiday Inn 354-2851; Ramada Inn 354-7711.

Transportation: Taxi Service: Yellow 354-4134; Rental Cars: Superior Leasing, Inc. 353-3136.

Information: Portsmouth Convention & Visitors Bureau, 1020 7th Street, P.O. Box 509, Portsmouth, OH 45662, Phone: 353-1116 or 353-7647.

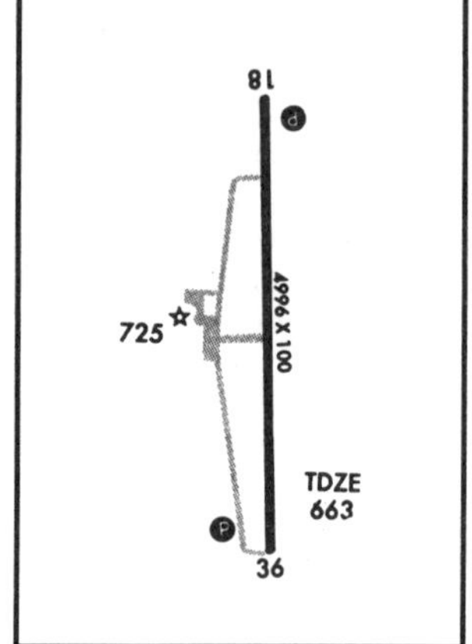

Airport Information:

PORTSMOUTH - GREATER PORTSMOUTH REGIONAL AIRPORT (PMH)
10 mi northeast of town N38-50.43 W82-50.84 Elev: 664 Fuel: 80, 100LL, Jet-A
Rwy 18-36: H4996x100 (Asph) Attended: 1300-0100Z Unicom: 122.8
Public Phone 24hrs Notes: Parking fees $10.00 per day or night, waived with fuel purchase.
Airport Manager Phone: 820-2400

Put-in-bay & Cedar Point, Ohio

Put-in Bay, Ohio (OH30)
Sandusky, Ohio (SKY)
Port Clinton, Ohio (PCW)

Put-in-Bay Island Park, located between the marina and the downtown district

The area around Sandusky, Ohio contains several major attractions. This area is dotted with a number of islands and peninsulas, all adding to the beauty of the surroundings. Kelley's Island, Middle Bass Island, South Bass Island, Marblehead Peninsula, Catawba Island Peninsula and Cedar Point all attract vacationers from all over the Midwest. During the spring, summer and fall, this area is considered a boater's paradise, with a great many marinas lining the shores. Charter fishing is also one of the main attractions.

One of the reasons that so many who fly are attracted to this area, is the availability of airports, some of which are located directly in the islands. Not only is this convenient when visiting the attractions, but in many cases the need for ground transportation is greatly reduced.

The Sandusky area is located between the cities of Toledo and Cleveland, Ohio on the southwestern shore of Lake Erie. There are three areas of interest that bear mentioning. They are, Put-in-Bay Island, Lonz Winery on Middle Bass Island, and Cedar Point Amusement Park located at the tip of Cedar Point. If planning to visit all three attractions, we suggest you allow at least two or three days. There are three airports serving this area: Griffing Sandusky Airport - two miles east of Sandusky; Carl R. Keller Field - three miles east of Port Clinton, and Put-in-Bay Airport conveniently located right on the island.

Put-in-Bay: The island of Put-in-Bay was first chartered in 1789 by a group of unidentified explorers, and later named Put-in-Bay by French and British explorers who used the island harbor to "put-in" for shelter during storms and sudden squalls. During the late 1700s, Admiral Oliver Hazard Perry used the island cliffs to spy on the British fleet before engaging in battle. Perry used this vantage point to gain control over the Great Lakes Region. After this historic conflict, Put-in-Bay would have faded into an uneventful existence if not for the shipping lanes where many steamboats stopped to take on cedar logs for fuel. As time went on, the area became well known as the "Wine Island," with over half of its acreage covered with vineyards which supported several wineries. Because of the scenic surroundings, the area's tourist trade flourished with many of the country's largest summer resorts enticing visitors from Detroit, Cleveland, Toledo and Sandusky, until the days of prohibition began and the great depression forced the resorts and wineries into bankruptcy. Not long after the depression of 1929, Put-in Bay once again began to attract a great number of people due to its beautiful surroundings and excellent bass, walleye and perch fishing. Today, the Put-in-Bay area is alive and well, with several vineyards using the long growing season brought about by the temperate effects of Lake Erie.

The island itself is about four miles north of Catawba Island Peninsula. The downtown district is busy with activity on weekends during the summer season.

There are many souvenir and gift shops which line the main street. The Blacksmith Shop selling nautical antiques and gifts, contains a museum with pictures and island memorabilia; The Shirt Shack, with souvenir T-shirts; The Heritage Shop; The Cargo Net, selling nautical gifts; Bay Fudge Emporium selling candies, cookies and kitchen accessories; The Lone Willow; and The Depot Fudge Company, all of which are only a few of the stores intermixed with pubs and snack shops along the main street. Directly across the street is "Island Park" spotted with shade trees and beautiful planting areas overlooking the Put-in Bay boat harbor filled with sailboats and cabin cruisers of all sizes.

During the summer season there are a number of special events scheduled that make Put-in-Bay particularly interesting and busy, with fishing one of its major assets. The Lake Erie open Walleye Tournament is held toward the beginning of June, where a great many fishing and charter services are on hand. Each year, during the latter part of June, "Founder's Day Weekend" features Ox-roasts, live music and antique car parades which are always held during the last full weekend of the month. During August, the "ILYA Regatta" is a sail and power boat race sponsored by the Put-in-Bay Yacht Club, and promises to be exciting entertainment with over three or four hundred participants entering the contest each season. After the race the entire park and downtown area celebrates the event with a festival, welcoming everyone.

Lonz Winery on Middle Bass Island, only a 15 minute ferry ride from Island Park on Put-in-Bay Island.

The island itself contains several other very interesting attractions such as Perry's Monument, Crystal Cave and Heineman Winery located near the central portion to the island.

Lonz Winery: While visiting Put-in-Bay, your day will not be complete until you take the ferry to Middle Bass Island only one and one-half miles to the north. The Sonny-S-Ferry runs about every thirty to forty minutes and is docked at the marina across from the Island Park. There is a minimal charge for the round trip (keep your ticket stubs for the return trip). Once reaching Middle Bass Island, it is a very short walk to the winery itself. Tours are conducted every

Cedar Point Amusment Park

hour on the half hour from May through October for an admission of $1.00 or $2.00 per person, and begins with a short narrated slide presentation explaining the history of the winery, followed by a guided tour showing the early process of how wine and champagne are made. As you pass the large wooden kegs, which line the cool damp cellars, the tour director will explain the art of making fine red and white wine along with the fermentation process used. Your group will then be guided into rooms where you will learn the process of making champagne and how to determine whether it is a high or low grade. Once completing the tour, you will be invited to sample the wines that are described on the tour. For those of you that will be flying, ask to sample their delicious grape juice -- it is very good. On weekends, there is usually live entertainment featured in a small outdoor pavilion, where baskets of nachos and cheese trays are available. You may also purchase wine by the bottle or case to take home with you. However, we suggest if doing so, you fly at a reasonable low altitude so the corks stay in the bottles to avoid redecorating the interior of your baggage compartment. Transportation near Put-in-Bay Island: There are two ways to reach Put-in-Bay; one is by ferry and the other is by air. At the time of research we found that there are two ferry lines making the trip. One from Port Clinton's downtown district The other from Catawba Peninsula three miles away from the island. Once on the island you can generally hail down a "Taxi-van" and be taken to your destination for only a couple of dollars.

Cedar Point Amusement Park: Cedar Point began its early existence as a resort during 1870. One of the events that added to the area's popularity was pioneer aviator Glen Curtiss, who flew non-stop from Cleveland to Cedar Point in 1910. It was the first long-distance flight ever made over water. During 1956, George Roose acquired control of the resort with plans to turn it into a housing development, but due to public opposition, he decided to give Cedar Point another chance as an amusement park. Funds were appropriated for the site and as time passed, the existing attractions were upgraded as well as new rides added. The Blue Streak roller coaster, Frontiertown, which recreated the era of the Old West, along with the Pioneer Village, all added to the park's popularity. Beginning in 1975, the park began to rapidly expand and soon achieved a modern super-park status. The 1970s and 80s saw the addition of the Ocean Marine Life Stadium, the Cedar Point Cinema, the Corkscrew roller coaster and the Gemini roller coaster, which is considered one of the highest, steepest and fastest in the world. Today, Cedar Point's guests can choose from an entire array of "scream machines." Whether plunging through space on the Demon Drop or screaming with delight on the Gemini racing coaster, everyone is certain to find the excitement they are looking for.

Not only does the park offer a thrill a minute, but also has scenic landscaped surroundings with flower-covered planting areas. A day at Cedar Point will be one of the most pleasurable experiences to remember for years to come. The park opens May 12 through Labor Day from 10:00 a.m. to 10:00 p.m., except on weekdays. Griffing-Sandusky Airport is the closest airport to Cedar Point Amusement Park and offers 100LL and Jet fuel. Although there is no transportation provided by the park staff, car rental is available at the airport. Taxi service normally runs about $4.00 to $5.00 per person each way to Cedar Point.

OH-OH30 - PUT-IN-BAY
PUT-IN-BAY AIRPORT

34

Restaurants Near Airport: **(Area Code 419)**

Numerous Nearby	1 mi	Phone: 285-2832
Skyway Restaurant	On Site	Phone: 285-4331

Lodging: Airport Motel (On Site) 285-3371; Numerous lodging establishments are available on the island. Contact the Put-In-Bay Chamber of Commerce for information, 285-2832.
Meeting Rooms: None Reported
Transportation: Fly-in guests to Put-In-Bay can travel about the island by walking, renting bicycles (Excellent choice), mopeds, or using the services of Island Taxi, which is very reasonable at around $1.00 to $2.00 per person to anywhere on the island.
Information: Put-In-Bay Chamber of Commerce 419-285-2832.

Skyway Restaurant:

The Skyway Restaurant is located at the north end of the airport. The main aircraft parking area is reported to be in the center of the field. However, we were told that pilots could park their aircraft near the restaurant. This family style restaurant offers a rustic appearance with wooden beams and lots of pictures of wild flowers hanging on the walls as decorations. They are open 7 days a week for lunch and dinner, during the summer, and during the months of November through April, only 5 days a week. They are usually closed on Monday and Tuesday. The main dining room can seat 42 persons and contains a bar. Items on their menu include a boneless 8 ounce strip steak, choice rib steak, pork chops, shrimp and walleye platter, Lake Erie perch (When available), homemade soups and salads along with many types of luncheon specials like their Skyway cheeseburger, Reuben, ham sandwiches, and the "Skyway" BLT's. If flying in to visit the island, stop in and enjoy a nice meal at the Skyway Restaurant during your stay. Island taxi service is available from the airport to the downtown district located about one mile away. Bicycle and mopeds can be obtained as well. For more information about the Skyway Restaurant call 285-4331.

A 9 hole golf course is located about 1 block from the airport.

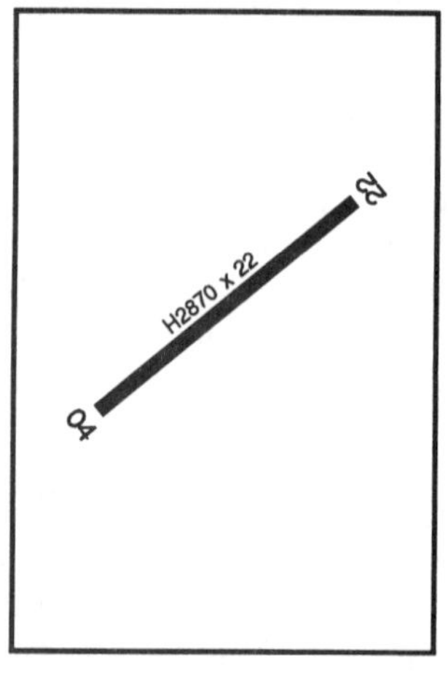

Attractions:

Put-In-Bay Island, and Middle Bass Island, attracts many vacationers during the spring, summer and fall season with a multitude of activities and points of interest within this region. Tourists can either take the ferry or fly in to the islands. The beautiful Island Park adjacent to the boat marina on the north end, provides a festive atmosphere with hundreds of people riding bikes, strolling through the gift shops or picnicking under shade trees overlooking the harbor. Your visit is not complete without a short ferry ride from the marina to Middle Bass Island and taking the tour through the famous Lonz Winery. A variety of fine wines can be purchased by the bottle, or the case. However, we suggest if doing so, you might want to fly back home at a relatively low altitude especially on turbulent days to avoid popping corks and re-decorating the interior or your baggage compartment. Put-In-Bay also features many events each year, like Ox Roasts, Yacht Club Races, Antique Car Parades, and much more. Call the Chamber of Commerce at 285-2832 for information. Also Golf course located adj. to Airport.

Airport Information:

PUT-IN-BAY - PUT-IN-BAY AIRPORT (OH30)
1 mi southwest of town N41-38.00 W82-49.66 Elev: 590 Rwy 04-22: H2870x22 (Asph) Attended: May-Sept 1300-0100Z, Oct-Apr 1230-2230. Unicom: 122.8
Put-In-Bay Airport Phone: 285-3371

OH-38D - SALEM
SALEM AIRPARK, INC.

(Area Code 330) **35**

Salem Hills Restaurant:

Salem Hills Restaurant is located within 1/4 mile from the Salem Airpark, in Salem Ohio. This family style restaurant has bar service available and is open Tuesday through Sunday from 8 a.m. to 9 p.m. Their menu contains appetizers, desserts, pastries, salads, soups as well as steaks and seafood. On Friday they offer a fish fry, and on Sunday a brunch between 11 a.m. and 2:30 p.m. They also have an 18 hole golf course, pool and club room on location. The decor of the restaurant is modern and business groups and club fly-ins are welcome. Meals-to-go can easily be arranged. Courtesy transportation can be obtain through the restaurant by calling 337-3616.

Restaurants Near Airport:
Salem Hills Restaurant 1/4 mi Phone: 337-3616

Lodging: Timber Lanes Motel (3 miles) 337-9901

Meeting Rooms: None Reported.

Transportation: Taxi Service: Columbiana Taxi 482-4965; Paul's Cab 337-7777; Rental Cars: Patterson Chrysler, Inc. 337-3475.

Information: Salem Area Chamber of Commerce, 713 East State Street, Salem, OH 44460, Phone: 337-3473.

Airport Information:

SALEM - SALEM AIRPARK INC. (38D)
3 mi north of town N40-56.89 W80-51.72 Elev: 1162 Fuel: 80, 100LL Rwy 10L-28R: H3482x50 (Asph) Rwy 10R-28L: 2700x84 (Turf) Attended: 1400Z-dusk Unicom: 122.7 Notes: CAUTION: Power line crosses approach end of runway 28L and 28R at threshold; CAUTION: Drag strip 3500 feet southeast of airport; and bird hazard landfill 900 feet east of airport.
FBO: Seidner Aviation Phone: 332-4400

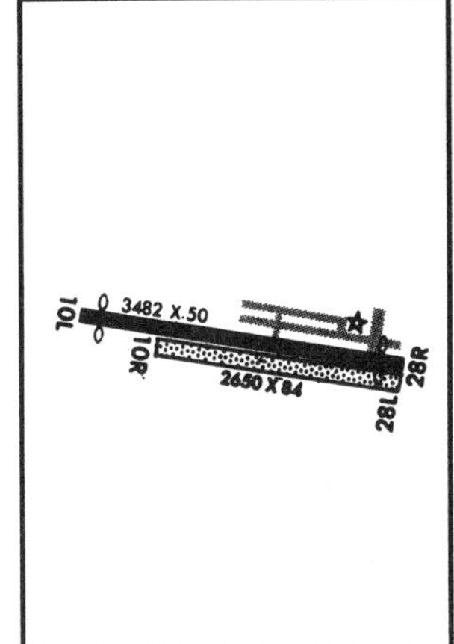

OH-3G6 - SEBRING
TRI CITY AIRPORT

(Area Code 330) **36**

The Landing Restaurant:

The Landing Restaurant is a family style establishment located on the Tri City Airport. We were told by the restaurant management that they are located on the west end of the southern-most hangar building. Their hours are Tuesday through Thursday 11 a.m. to 8 p.m., Friday and Saturday 7 a.m. to 9 p.m., and Sunday from 7 a.m. to 3 p.m. They are closed on Monday. Friday evenings, their beer-battered, baked fish is a popular item. Saturday evenings they serve an 8-ounce center-cut steak. The owners of this restauant takes pride in home-cooked meals and desserts, all made on the premises. Prices average $4.00 for main course lunches and around $6.00 for dinner selections. The view from the restaurant overlooks the active airport ramps, taxiways and runways. They can seat up to 60 persons in their main dining area. An outside deck is also open for dining, weather permitting. Catering on-site as well as in-flight catering is available. For information about the Landing Restaurant call 938-1554.

Restaurants Near Airport:
The Landing Restaurant On Site Phone: 938-1554

Lodging: Best Western (3-5 mi) 821-1933; Comfort Inn 821-1933.

Meeting Rooms: None reported.

Transportation: Airport courtesy car reported

Information: Alliance Chamber of Commerce, 210 East Main Street, Alliance, OH 44601, Phone: 216-823-6260.

Note: Due to late submission, it was necessary to list this airport out of alphabetical order on the index sheet.

Airport Information:

SEBRING - TRI CITY AIRPORT (3G6)
1 mi southeast of town N40-54.36 W81-00.00 Elev: 1192 Fuel: 80, 100LL Rwy 17-35: H2800x60 (Asph) Attended 1300Z-dusk CTAF: 122.8
FBO: Tri-City Aviation, Inc. Phone: 938-1216

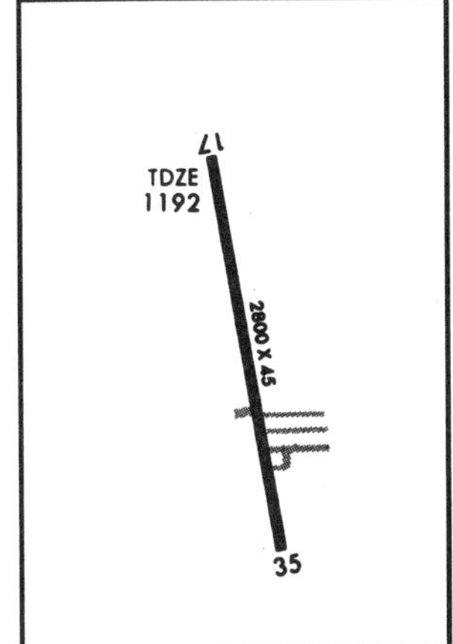

OH-SKY - SANDUSKY
GRIFFING-SANDUSKY AIRPORT

(Area Code 419) 37, 38

Cherokee Inn Restaurant:

The Cherokee Inn Restaurant is a cafe located within the terminal building of the Griffing Sandusky Airport near Sandusky, Ohio. This restaurant is open during the week and on weekends between 8:30 a.m. and 4:30 p.m. Their menu lists such items as eggs dishes, pancaks and breakfast selections, hamburgers, cheeseburgers, chili, homemade soups, smoked sausage sandwiches, fried bologna, French fries and the "best" milk shakes you've ever had. They usually have a special sandwich each day for lunch, like tuna, egg salad and roast beef etc. The decor of the cafe is modern, and can accommodate groups up to 20 people if advance reservations are made. Courtesy transportation is not needed due to the fact that the restaurant is within walking distance from aircraft parking. For information call 626-5161.

Sawmill Creek Resort:

Nestled on the shore of Lake Erie, Sawmill Creek Resort provides a year around setting for business or pleasure. Sawmill Creek is ideally located between Toledo and Cleveland in the heart of Ohio's Vacationland. Experience the beauty and multitude of pleasures that are uniquely Sawmill Creek, Ohio's classic resort. 240 guest rooms & suites; 13 meeting rooms; superb dining from casual to gourmet; challenging 18-hole Fazio golf course, marina, tennis courts, swimming pools and hiking; lounge and entertainment; specialized shopping at Sawmill's 1887 shops, and close to Cedar Point, Lake Erie Islands and other recreational opportunities. Meetings large and small are easily accommodated. Sawmill Creek has 13 meeting rooms (nearly 14,000 square feet); maximum capacity to 700 guests. Conclude your business day by enjoying their challenging golf course and abundant sporting amenities or just relax over a fine meal in The Smuggler's Cove or The Sawmill Steak House. Sawmill Creek is truly one of America's finest, most complete full-service resorts. Free courtesy transportation is provided to and from the Sandusky - Griffing/Sandusky Airport (SKY). For information call the resort at 433-3800.

Attraction:

Sawmill Creek Resort is located just 3-1/2 miles from the Griffing Sandusky Airport and provides year round activities for vacationers as well as business groups. This resort contains 244 lodging units, two restaurants, an 18 hole golf course, indoor and outdoor swimming pools, gift shops, game rooms, exercise rooms, and a lounge with live entertainment. For information call 433-3800 or 1-800-SAWMILL. Cedar Point Amusement Park - See Article about this attraction!

Restaurants Near Airport:

Cherokee Inn Restaurant	On Site	Phone: 626-5161
Sawmill Creek Resort	3-1/2 mi	Phone: 433-3800

Lodging: Econolodge (3 miles) 627-8000; Holiday Inn 626-6671; Radisson Harbour Inn (2 miles) 627-2500; Ramada Inn 626-9890; Sawmill Creek Resort (3-1/2 miles) 433-3800; Sheraton Inn Sandusky 625-6280.

Meeting Rooms: Holiday Inn 626-6671; Radisson Harbour Inn 627-2500; Sawmill Creek 433-3800; Sheraton Inn Sandusky 625-6280.

Transportation: Sawmill Creek Resort will provide courtesy transportation for flying guests landing at Griffing/Sandusky Airport, 433-3800. Also: Taxi Service: Griffing Taxi Service 626-5161.

Information: Sandusky Visitor & Convention Bureau, 231 W. Washington Row, Sandusky, OH 44870, Phone: 625-2984 or 800-255-ERIE.

Attractions:

This particular area is located between the cities of Toledo and Cleveland. Ohio on the southwestern shore of Lake Erie. There are three major points of interest that deserve special mention. They are, Put-in Bay Island, Lonz Winery on Middle Bass Island, and, of course, Cedar Point Amusement Park located at the tip of Cedar Point. If planning to visit all three attractions, we suggest you allow at least two or three days. There are three airports serving this area; Griffing Sandusky Airport - two miles east of Sandusky, Ohio; Carl R. Keller Field - three miles east of Port Clinton, Ohio and Put-in Bay Airport conveniently located right on the island.

Airport Information:

SANDUSKY - GRIFFING/SANDUSKY AIRPORT (SKY)

3 mi southeast of town N41-26.00 W82-39.14 Elev: 580 Fuel: 100LL, Jet-A Rwy 09-27: H3559x60 (Asph) Rwy 18-36: H2593x40 (Asph) Attended: 1300Z-dusk Unicom: 123.0

Note: shuttle service is reported to Cedar Point.

FBO: Griffing Flying Service Phone: 626-5161

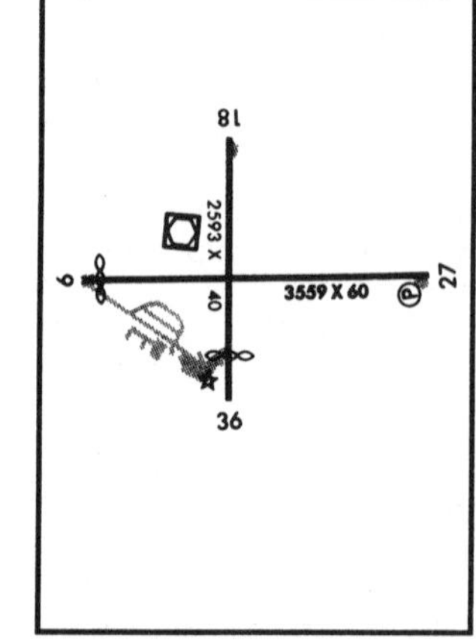

Not to be used for navigational purposes

OH-16G - TIFFIN
SENECA COUNTY AIRPORT

(Area Code 419)

39

River View Inn:

The River View Inn is located approximately one block from the Seneca County Airport, in Tiffin, Ohio. This restaurant is adjoined by a motel containing 70 rooms, and a cocktail lounge. The main restaurant features entrees consisting of gourmet food, with seafood being one of their specialties. Their lounge is open from 4 p.m. until 12 a.m. The main dining room opens for business at 5 p.m. and continues serving until 9 p.m. Monday through Saturday and on Sunday from 7 a.m. until 1 p.m. This establishment is constructed in light brick and should not be hard to locate if walking from the airport. This establishment is situated on the corner of 224 and State Route 53. For information about the motel or restaurant you can call them at 447-6313.

Restaurants Near Airport:
River View Restaurant 1 blk Phone: 447-6313

Lodging: River View Inn 447-6313; L & K Motel 447-7411.

Meeting Rooms: River View Inn 447-6313.

Transportation: Courtesy cars reported available at airport; Taxi Service: Available by calling 447-3232; Rental Cars: Also reported available through Hertz Car Rental, at airport.

Information: Seneca County Convention & Visitors Bureau, 84 Jefferson Street, Tiffin, OH 44883, Phone: 447-5866; Also: Tiffin Area Chamber of Commerce, 62 South Washington Street, Tiffin, OH 44883, Phone: 447-4141.

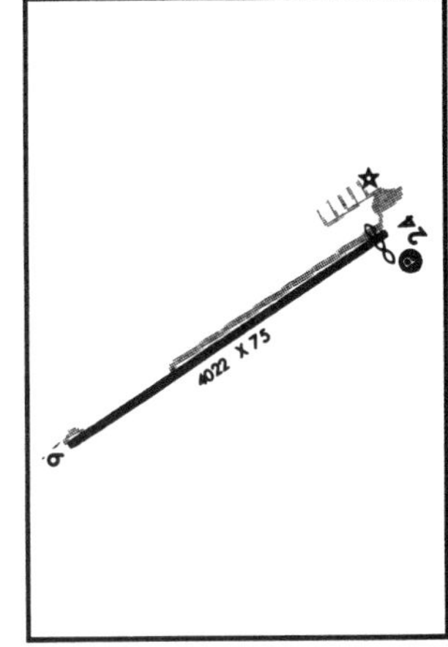

Airport Information:

TIFFIN - SENECA COUNTY AIRPORT (16G)
2 mi southwest of town N41-05.64 W83-12.76 Elev: 787 Fuel: 100LL, Jet-A
Rwy 06-24: H4022x75 (Asph) Attended: 1300Z-dusk Unicom: 123.0
FBO: Tiffin Aire, Inc. Phone: 447-4263

OH-TDZ - TOLEDO
METCALF FIELD

(Area Code 419)

40

Sallocks Family Cookhouse:

This restaurant is located about 1/2 mile from the Metcalf Field. Crow Executive Air (FBO) informed us that transportation to and from the restaurant will be made available to their customers. The Sallocks Family Cookhouse is a family restaurant that specializes as a steak house and prepares Lebanese dishes. The restaurant is open Monday through Thursday from 11 a.m. to 10 p.m., Friday and Saturday from 11 a.m. to 11 p.m. and Sunday from 12 noon to 9 p.m. (confirm Sunday hours) Specialties include prime rib, t-bone steak, sea food, sword fish, shrimp, scallops, broasted chicken and lots more. Lebanese dishes include grape leaves, hummous and Tabouli. Average prices run between $4.00 for light fare and $7.00 to $9.00 for most dinner entrees. Their delicious prime rib is a special on Friday and Saturday. Broasted chicken is also a favorite, with specials on Monday through Wednesday. On Thursdays they feature a steak fest with discounts for selected steak entrees with all the trimmings. The restaurant can seat about 80 customers. The decor of the restaurant has a rustic atmosphere with lots of oak and antique furnishings. Extra room for larger groups can be seated in their upstairs dining area. During the summer months the Sallocks Family Cookhouse also offers outdoor dining on their patio able to seat about 24 people. For more information call 838-7223.

Restaurants Near Airport:
Sallocks Cookhouse 1/2 mi Phone: 838-7223

Lodging: Comfort Inn-South 6 mi 666-2600; Econo Lodge 6 mi 666-5120; Holiday Inn (Perrysburg/French Quarter) 9 mi 874-3111.

Meeting Rooms: None reported. Sallocks Family Cookhouse does have additional space for catering in their upstairs dining area 838-7223.

Transportation: Crow Executive Air, Inc. has a courtesy car available for their customers 838-6921 or 255-2769; Also Taxi service: Express 351-4497, Eagle 255-2323; Rental cars also available at airport. Call Crow Executive Air, Inc. 838-6921 or 255-2769.

Information: Greater Toledo Convention & Visitors Bureau, 401 Jefferson, Toledo, OH 43604, Phone: 321-6404.

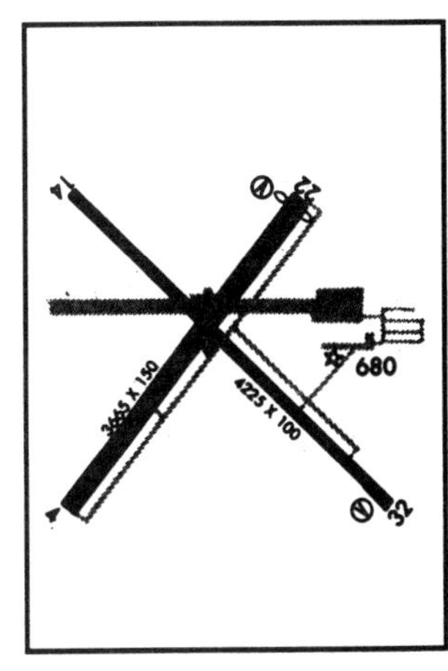

Airport Information:

TOLEDO - METCALF FIELD (TDZ)
6 mi southeast of town N41-33.84 W83-28.87 Elev: 623 Fuel: 100LL, Jet-A Rwy 14-32: H4225x100 (Asph-Conc) Rwy 04-22: H3665x150 (Asph-Conc) Attended: Mon-Fri 1300-2100Z
Unicom: 125.6
FBO: Crow Executive Air, Inc. Phone: 838-6921 or 255-2769

OH-TOL - TOLEDO
TOLEDO EXPRESS AIRPORT

(Area Code 419) 41

Restaurants Near Airport:

Albon Inn	4 mi E.	Phone: 865-8387
Loma Linda's Mexican	1/2 mi E.	Phone: 865-5455
Marriott Host Facilities	On Site	Phone: 865-9484
Mike's Coney Island	1 mi W.	Phone: 826-6453
Valleywood Golf	3 mi W.	Phone: 826-5931

Lodging: Ramada Inn Southwyck (11 miles) 865-1361; Marriott Courtyard (6 miles) 866-1001; Hilton Inn (15 miles) 381-6800.
Meeting Rooms: Executive board/conference room is available at TOL Aviation Corporate Center FBO, 866-9375.
Transportation: TOL Aviation, Inc (FBO) can accommodate fly-in guests with transportation to nearby facilities; Also: PTS Taxi 882-6363; Budget Car Rental 865-8825; Avis Car Rental 865-5541; Hertz Car Rental 866-3400; National Car Rental 865-5513; Airport Limo (Van) 865-4183.
Information: Greater Toledo Convention & Visitors Bureau, 401 Jefferson, Toledo, OH 43604, Phone: 321-6404; Also: Toledo Area Chamber of Commerce, 218 North Huron Street, Toledo, OH 43604, Phone: 243-8191.

Marriott Host Restaurant:

The Marriott Host Restaurant is located on Toledo Express airport in Ohio, and provides a combination buffet and cafeteria (Buffeteria) style dining for their guests. There are usually 2 or 3 main selections offered each day along with additional side dishes. They are located within the main terminal building and are open Monday through Friday 5:15 a.m. to 7 p.m., Saturday and Sunday 6 a.m. to 2:30 p.m. The restaurant is situated near the main entrance and can seat approximately 60 people. Their upper level snack bar serves light fare and is open 7 days a week between 5:15 a.m. and 8 p.m. This snack bar can seat about 16 people with a lounge capable of seating an additional 40 persons. Call 865-9484 for further information.

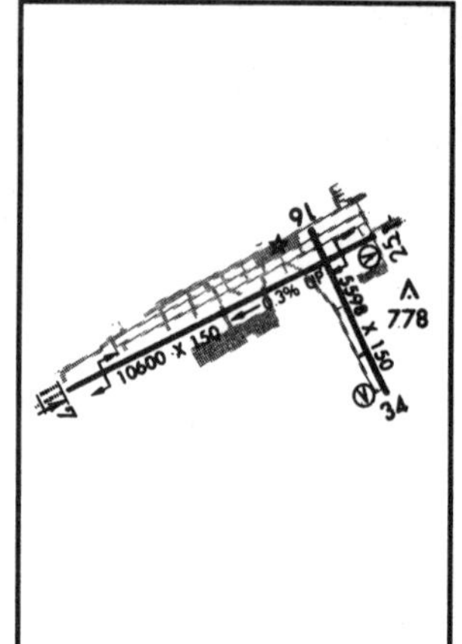

Airport Information:

TOLEDO - TOLEDO EXPRESS AIRPORT (TOL)
10 mi west of town N41-35.21 W83-48.47 Elev: 684 Fuel: 100LL, Jet-A
Rwy 07-25: H10,600x150 (Asph-Grvd) Rwy 16-34: H5598x150 (Asph-Grvd) Attended: continuously Atis: 118.75 Unicom: 122.95 App/Dep Con: 126.1, 128.0
Tower: 118.1 Gnd Con: 121.9 Clnc Del: 121.75 Public Phone 24hrs
Notes: Overnight tie-down $5.50, overnight hangaring varies with size of aircraft.
FBO: Cessna Citation Service Center Phone: 866-6761
FBO: National Flight Service Phone: 865-2311
FBO: TOL Aviation Corporate Center Phone: 866-9375

OH-I74 - URBANA
GRIMES FIELD AIRPORT

(Area Code 513) 42

Restaurants Near Airport:

Airport Cafe	On Site	Phone: 652-2010

Lodging: Logan Lodge Motel 652-2188.

Meeting Rooms: Airport Cafe reports that they have accommodations for groups and banquets, 653-6282.

Transportation: None Reported

Information: Urbana Area Chamber of Commerce, 300 North Main Street, Urbana, OH 43078, Phone: 653-5764.

Airport Cafe:

The Airport Cafe is located on Grimes Airport, Urbana, Ohio, about 40 miles west of Columbus. The restaurant is a cafe with a full menu of home cooked foods including selections like beef and pork which is raised on a nearby farm. In addition to the main course meals this restaurant also serves homemade pies, and hand-dipped ice cream. The restaurant has windows overlooking the field, and is reported to be decorated in an aviation theme. Aircraft parking is available on the adjacent ramp. The Airport Cafe is open Tuesday through Friday from 6:30 a.m. to 7 p.m. and Saturday 8 a.m. to 3 p.m. (Closed Sunday). The restaurant can handle group seating for up to 40 persons. In-flight catering is another service made available to fly-in customers. For more information call 652-2010.

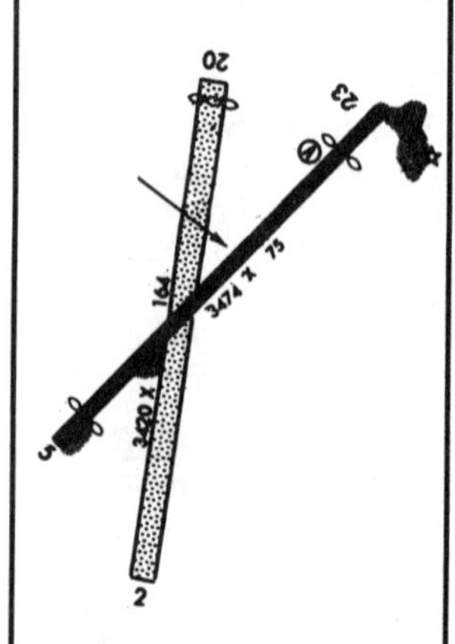

Airport Information:

URBANA - GRIMES FIELD (I74)
1 mi north of town N40-07.79 W83-45.29 Elev: 1060 Rwy 05-23: H3474x75 (Asph)
Rwy 02-20: 3420x164 (Turf) Attended: Mon-Fri 1400-2300Z Unicom: 122.7
City of Urbana Phone: 652-4319

OH-VNW - VAN WERT
VAN WERT COUNTY AIRPORT

(Area Code 419) 43

Golden Corral Family Steak House:

The Golden Corral Family Steak House is located adjacent to the Van Wert County Airport and is reported to be within walking distance. We were told that some fly-in guests park in the grass at the south end of runway 18, and simply walk to the restaurant from there. (Check with the airport management if this is permitted). This establishment offers a variety of steak dinners, including a complete sirloin dinner for $5.99 or their Rib-eye 1/2 pound steak dinner for only $6.99 or their 3/4 pound selection for $8.99 both of which includes potato and beverage. Other selections include chicken dishes, fish, and soup. A salad bar is also available as well. Daily specials are also available. Their main dining room can seat in the neighborhood of 250 persons. The decor has a modern and open atmosphere with available seating for private parties within their back room. For information call the Golden Corral Family Steak House at 238-2154.

Restaurants Near Airport:

Burger King	Adj Arpt	Phone: 238-3675
Golden Corral Steak Hse	Adj Arpt	Phone: 238-2154
Kentucky Fried Chicken	Adj Arpt	Phone: 238-0911
Penguin Point Restaurant	Adj Arpt	Phone: 238-6296

Lodging: Smitty's Motel (1 mile) 238-4693; Days Inn (3 miles) 238-5222; L & K Inn (3 miles) 238-3700.

Meeting Rooms: Contact airport management for information about available meeting or conference facilities, 238-5255.

Transportation: Rental Cars: Bob Dunn Leasing 238-0125; Greve Chrylsler Plymouth Dodge 238-3944; Lee Kinstle Chevrolet/Olds 238-5902.

Information: Van Wert Area Chamber of Commerce, 118 West Main Street, Van Wert, OH 45891, Phone: 238-4390.

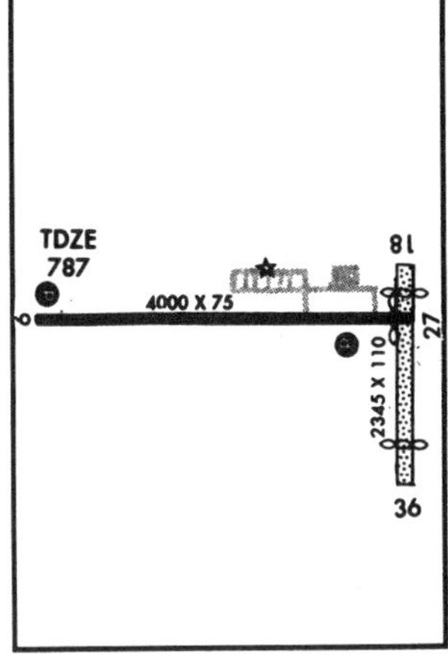

Airport Information:

VAN WERT - VAN WERT COUNTY AIRPORT (VNW)
2 mi southwest of town N40-51.84 W84-36.38 Elev: 788 Fuel: 100LL
Rwy 09-27: H4000x75 (Asph) Rwy 18-36: 2345x110 (Turf) Attended: Mon-Sat 1300-2300Z, Sun 1500-2300Z Unicom: 123.0 Public Phone 24hrs Notes: Overnight tie-down fee $3.00 per night, $5.00 per night for hangar.
FBO: Freedom Air Service Phone: 238-5255

OH-USE - WAUSEON
FULTON COUNTY AIRPORT

(Area Code 419) 44

Smith's Restaurant:

Smith's Restaurant is reported to be within walking distance from two separate airports. Fulton County Airport. is open to the general public and is situated between 1/2 and 1 mile from the restaurant. With prior permission, Exit 3" Airport, which is a private airstrip, is locatted only 100 yards from the restaurant. This restaurant is open 7 days a week between 7 a.m. and 9 p.m. They serve a full menu including daily specials, in addition to a bakery located right on the premises. Smith's Restaurant is famous for their boasted chicken. Average prices for most selections run $3.50 for breakfast, $4.50 for lunch and $8.00 for dinner. Their dining area is newly decorated with clean and comfortable surroundings. Banquet facilities are also available with family style meals, for lunch and dinner. To reach the restaurant from Fulton County Airport, go south on County Road 14, make a right on County J than south on Route 108 under the Turn Pike and on the left side of the street. For information about Smith's Restaurant call 335-4896.

Restaurants Near Airport:

Smith's Restaurant	3/4th mi	Phone: 335-4896

Lodging: Best Western Del Mar (2 miles) 335-1565.

Meeting Rooms: Banquet and board meeting room available at Smith's Restaurant, 335-4896.

Transportation: Airport courtesy car reported at airport. Call FBO's for reservations, Phone: 335-3993.

Information: Wauseon Chamber of Commerce, 115 North Fulton Street, P.O. Box 217, Wauseon, OH 43567, Phone: 335-9966.

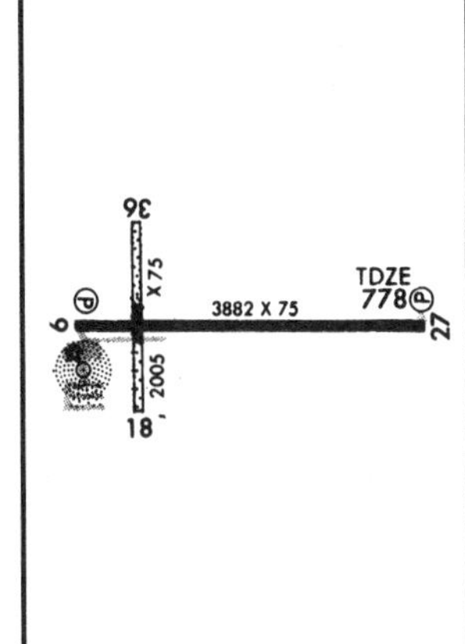

Airport Information:

WAUSEON - FULTON COUNTY AIRPORT (USE)
4 mi north of town N41-36.62 W84-07.63 Elev: 780 Fuel: 80, 100LL
Rwy 09-27: H3882x75 (Asph) Rwy 18-36: 2005x75 (Asph-Turf) Attended: 1300Z-dusk
Unicom: 123.0
Airport Manager Phone: 335-3993

OH-40I - WAYNESVILLE
WAYNESVILLE AIRPORT

(Area Code 513) 45

Restaurants Near Airport:
Sky Cream And Deli On Site Phone: 897-3851

Lodging: None Reported

Meeting Rooms: None Reported

Transportation: None Reported

Information: No chamber number given. However, you can call the Antiques Capitol of the Midwest Organization at 897-8855 or Ceasar's Creek Pioneer Village at 897-1120.

Sky Cream And Deli:

At the time of interview it was uncertain if the Sky Cream and Deli was in operation. The snack bar in the past was open April 1 through October 31 every day from 10 a.m. to 9 p.m. The airport is very active on weekends with gliders, skydivers, and general aviation users. There is even a 18 hole golf course (Holly Hills) across the street. For information about airport services call 800-554-5867 or 897-3851.

Attractions:

Holly Hill 18 hole golf course across the street; Ceasar's Creek Pioneer Village contains 30 pioneer buildings in addition to guided tours and festivals that are held several times each year. For information call 897-1120. 35 different and unique antique shops along with specialty shops and art galleries attract many visitors throughout the entire year. For information call 897-8855.

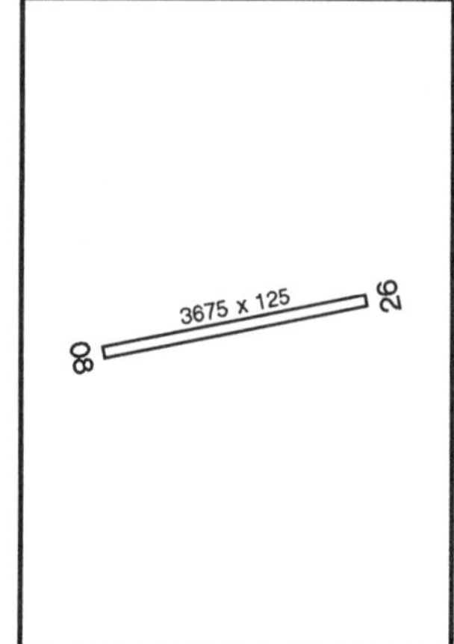

Airport Information:

WAYNESVILLE - WAYNESVILLE AIRPORT (40I)
2 mi southwest of town N39-30.32 W84-07.31 Elev: 955 Fuel: 80, 100LL, MOGAS
Rwy 08-26: 3675x125 (Turf) Attended: 1300Z-dusk CTAF: 122.9 Notes: Parachute jumping on field especially on weekends.
Waynesville Airport Phone: 897-3851

OH-80G - WEST LAFAYETTE
TRI-CITY AIRPORT

(Area Code 614) 46

Hickory Flats Club House:

The Hickory Flats Club House is situated within 1/2 mile from the Tri-City Airport near West Lafayette, Ohio. This restaurant is located adjacent to a golf course, and has a scenic view overlooking pine trees, putting greens and a pond. The restaurant provides seating for about 40 people and serves breakfast, snacks and side orders as well as sandwiches and burgers. The hours are from 6 a.m. to 8 p.m. 7 days a week. Hours may vary throughout the year. Those of you who enjoy golfing, would appreciate the convenience of this facility. For information please call 545-7796.

Restaurants Near Airport:
Hickory Flats Club House 1/2 mi Phone: 545-7796

Lodging: Downtown Motel (6 miles) 662-6607; L & K Motel (7 miles) 622-9823.

Meeting Rooms: None Reported

Transportation: None Reported

Information: West Lafayette Chamber of Commerce, North Kirk Street, P.O. Box 113, West Lafayette, OH 43845, Phone: N/A.

Attractions:

Hickory Golf Club which has an 18 hole course is only 1/2 mile from the Tri-County Airport. For information call the Hickory Flats Club House at 545-7796.

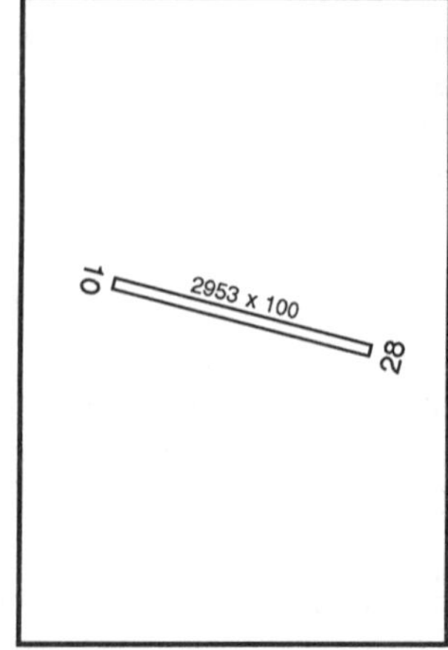

Airport Information:

WEST LAFAYETTE - TRI-CITY AIRPORT (80G)
2 mi southeast of town N40-14.87 W81-44.16 Elev: 844 Rwy 10-28: 2953x100 (Truf)
Attended: daylight hours CTAF: 122.9
FBO: Zimmer Flying Service Phone: 545-9135

OH-3OH9 - WILMINGTON HOLLISTER FIELD

(Area Code 937)

47

Cherrybend Pheasant Farm

Two beautiful, wide grass runways, 2900' and 2100', welcome you to this 368 acre working pheasant farm and hunting preserve. Fly in for noon dinner (Reservations please) prepared by the very able Charlotte and Barb. You won't be disappointed if your tastes lie in exceptionally good farm cooking consisting of pheasant, ham, home grown garden vegetables, and finished off with a slice of one of Charlotte's pies topped by a scoop of homemade ice cream. Friendly hosts and owners, Mary and Holly Hollister, are more than happy to provide a tour of their pheasant production facilities. Holly is a pilot and retired Sperry avionics engineer. He is always looking for an excuse to talk "Flying," and if one's fancy is in the direction of bird hunting, pheasant, quail and chukar hunting, this can be arranged on the preserve proper. Also in season, fresh sweet corn and smoked or plain frozen pheasant can be purchased. Fly-in campers are welcome as there is plenty of soft grass to cushion a sleeping bag "under your wing. Hollister Field (3OH9) is licensed by the state of Ohio. Be sure to call ahead for reservations. For meal reservations and information call: 584-4269. (Submitted to Aerodine by Cherrybend Pheasant Farm and Written by John Lundblad)

Restaurants Near Airport:
Cherrybend Pheasant Farm On Site Phone: 584-4269

Lodging: None available at this location.
Meeting Rooms: None available at this location.
Transportation: Cherrybend Pheasant Farm is within walking distance from Hollister Field.
Information: Cherrybend Pheasant Farm 2326 Cherrybend Road, Wilmington, Ohio 45177, Phone: 584-4269.

Attraction: This attraction is especially popular for the hunting enthusiast or anyone who enjoys the taste of freshly cooked wild pheasant. The Cherrybend Pheasant Farm, is licensed and approved by the Division of Wildlife and the Department of Natural Resources Columbus, Ohio. This picturesque 368-acre Ohio flatland grain farm is stocked with large ringneck pheasants to afford an ideal hunting paradise. Guests are free to roam through fields of clover, across corn fields and along fence rows in a natural habitat for upland wild game. Their new 8 station clay bird range is also provided for your pleasure. If planning to stock your freezer with a plump bird for a dinner feast, or if interested in learning more about the Cherrybend Pheasant Farm call 584-4269.

NO AIRPORT DIAGRAM AVAILABLE

Airport Information:

WILMINGTON - HOLLISTER FIELD (3OH9)
5 east of town N39-26.25 W83-42.50 Elev: 1080 Rwy 05-23: 3225x80 (Turf) Rwy 13-31: 2514x80 (Turf) Attended: daylight hours CTAF: 122.9 Notes: CAUTION: Pheasants released north side of runway for hunting Sep-Apr. Also model aircraft radio control area south of runway 5 near intersection with runway 31.
Cherrybend Pheasant Farm Phone: 584-4269

OH-4G5 - WOODSFIELD MONROE COUNTY AIRPORT

(Area Code 614)

48

Katy's Place:

Katy's Place Restaurant is located about 1-1/2 miles from the Monroe County Airport. This combination family style restaurant and lounge will provide fly-in guests with free transportation to and from the airport. It is situated off the square east in the town of Woodsfield. Their hours are from 8 a.m. to 8 p.m. weekdays and 8 a.m. to 9 p.m. on Friday and Saturday. Menu selections include marinated rib-eyes, marinated pork chops, marinated chicken breasts and the best burgers around. They also make their own French fries along with home baked pies and apple dumplings. Average prices run $2.75 for breakfast, $3.50 for lunch and $7.50 for dinner. Daily specials are also offered. The restaurant exhibits a country decor in an "At-home" atmosphere and is decorated with handcrafted items which are displayed, and all for sale. For information about Katy's Place, call 472-0958.

Restaurants Near Airport:
Katy's Place Restaurant 1-1/2 mi Phone: 472-0958

Lodging: Grandma Betty's Bed & Breakfast (4 miles) 567-3465; Pioneer Motel (Adj to Katy's Place Restaurant); Switzerland of Ohio Inns (Bed & Breakfast) 3 locations 1-1/2 miles from airport. Will provide transportation to and from airport, 800-422-4283 or 472-0002.

Meeting Rooms: Monroe County Airport has a meeting room able to accommodate up to 12 people for private use, call 472-1882.

Transportation: J & M Auto Rental 472-5406; E-Z Ride Bus 472-0006.

Information: Monroe County Chamber of Commerce, P.O. Box 643, Woodsfield, OH 43793, Phone: 472-5499; Also Monroe County Tourism Board, P.O. Box 643, Woodsfield, OH 43793, Phone: 934-2659.

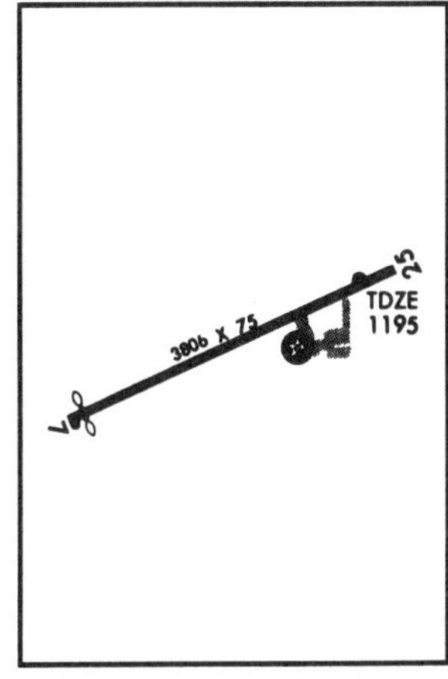

Airport Information:

WOODSFIELD - MONROE COUNTY AIRPORT (4G5)
1 mi north of town N39-46.74 W81-06.17 Elev: 1195 Fuel: 80, 100LL Rwy 07-25: H3806x75 (Asph) Attended: irregularly Unicom: 122.8 Notes: No landing or parking fees.
Monroe County Airport Phone: 472-1882 or 472-2060

OKLAHOMA

LOCATION MAP

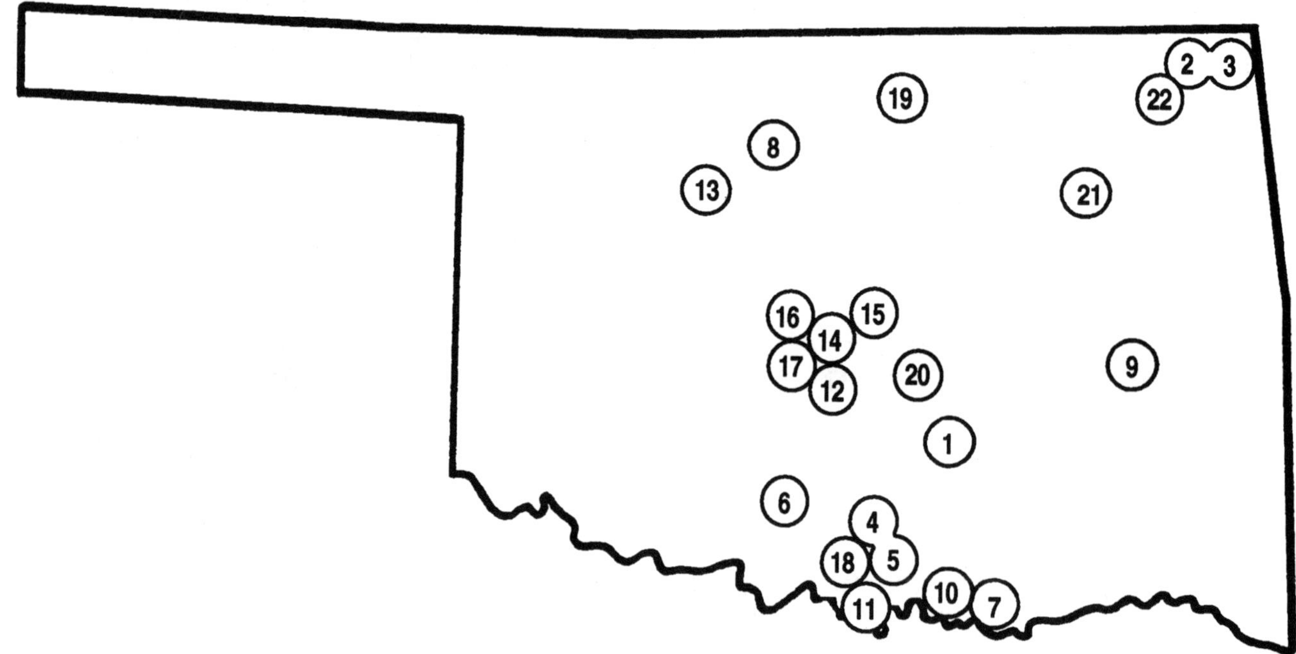

Not to be used for navigational purposes

OKLAHOMA

CROSS FILE INDEX

Location Number	City or Town	Airport Name And Identifier	Name of Attraction
1	Ada	Ada Muni. Arpt. (ADH)	Bob's Bar-B-Que of Ada
2	Afton	Shangri-La Airport (309)	Shangri-La (Resort)
3	Afton	Shangri-La Airport (309)	Touch-N-Go Rest.
4	Ardmore	Ardmore Muni. (ADM)	Airways Cafe
5	Ardmore	Ardmore Muni. (ADM)	Runway Cafe
6	Duncan	Halliburton Fld. (DUC)	Phipp's BBQ
7	Durant	Eaker Field Arpt. (DUA)	Chuck's Bar-B-Que
8	Enid	End Woodring Muni. Arpt. (WDG)	Barnstomer Rest.
9	Eufaula	Eufaula Arpt. (F08)	Salty Pelican Restaurant
10	Kingston	Lake Texoma St. Park Arpt. (F31)	Galley Rest. (Resort)
11	Marietta	McGehee Catfish Rest. Arpt. (T40)	McGehee Catfish Rest.
12	Norman	Univ. of OK Westheimer (OUN)	Ozzie's Diner
13	O'Keene	O'Keene Muni. Arpt. (OK71)	Pizza Inn
14	Oklahoma City	Downtown Airpark, Inc. (2DT)	Downtown Airpark Cafe
15	Oklahoma City	Expressway Airpark (2EJ)	Braum's Ice Cream
16	Oklahome City	Wiley Post Arpt. (PWA)	Runway Cafe
17	Oklahoma City	Will Rogers World Arpt. (OKC)	CA1 Services
18	Overbrook	Lake Murray State Park (1F1)	Fireside Restaurant
19	Ponca City	Ponca City Muni. Arpt. (PNC)	Enrique's Mexican Rest.
20	Shawnee	Shawnee Muni. Arpt. (SNL)	Cinderella Best Western
21	Tulsa	Tulsa Intl. Arpt. (TUL)	CA1 Services
22	Vinita	Vinta Muni. Arpt. (H04)	McDonalds Restaurant

Articles

City or town	Nearest Airport and Identifier	Name of Attraction
Afton, OK	Grand Lake Reg. Arpt. (3O9)	Shangri-La Resort
Kingston, OK	Lake Texoma State Park (F31)	Lake Texoma Resort
Overbrook, OK	Lake Murray State Pk. (1F1)	Lake Murray St. Resort

OK-ADH - ADA
ADA MUNICIPAL AIRPORT

(Area Code 405) 1

Bob's Bar-B-Q of Ada:

Bob's Bar-B-Q restaurant is located at the southwest corner of the Ada Municipal Airport. The airport gives permission for people to park their aircraft near the southwest taxiway and walk to the restaurant from there. (Please stay off grass after a big rain!) It's about a two block walk south on Hwy. 377 & 99. The restaurant is open from 11 a.m. to 9 p.m. Monday through Saturday and Sunday 11 a.m. to 3 p.m. They specialize in Hickory pit Barbecued pork ribs, beef, chopped pork, and chicken served with beans, cole-slaw, fries and bread. Homemade cream pies as well as other types of pies are offered for dessert. Average prices for entrees served for lunch and dinner run between $5.50 and $6.50 per selection. They will serve groups up to 80 persons, however they would like advance notice of when you plan to come, so they can arrange for extra help in the kitchen. For information call the restaurant at 332-6253.

Restaurants Near Airport:
Bob's Barbecue 1/4 mi SW Phone: 332-6253

Lodging: Holiday Inn 332-9000; Indian Hills 332-3883; Raintree Motor Inn (Best Western) 332-6262; Trails 332-4995.

Meeting Rooms: None reported. However some of the lodging facilities listed above might have accommodations for meeting and conference rooms.

Transportation: Bowie Ballard Ford 332-6161; Pronto Rent-A-Car 436-2467; Service Chevrolet 332-4141; Sunshine Rental 332-9000

Information: Chamber of Commerce, 300 West Main, P.O. Box 248, Ada, OK 74820, Phone: 332-2506.

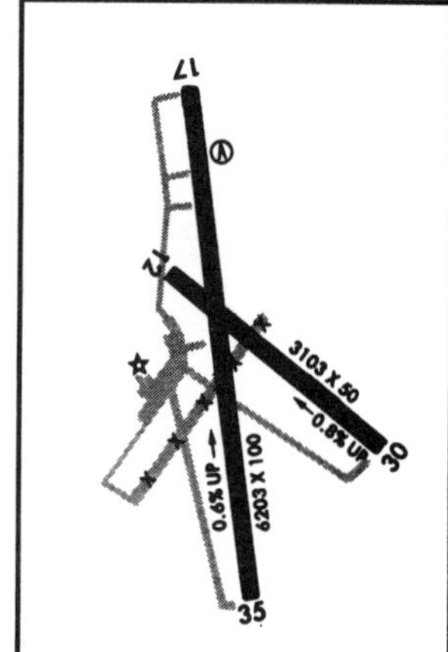

Airport Information:

ADA - ADA MUNICIPAL AIRPORT (ADH)
2 mi north of town N34-48.26 W96-40.28 Elev: 1016 Fuel: 100LL, Jet-A
Rwy 17-35: H6200x100 (Asph) Rwy 12-30: H3103x50 (Asph) Attended: Mon-Sat 1400-2300
Unicom: 122.8
FBO: Ada Aircraft Paint Phone: 332-6086

Not to be used for navigational purposes

OK-309 - AFTON
GRAND LAKE REG. ARPT./
SHANGRI-LA AIRPORT

(Area Code 918)

2, 3

Shangri-La Resort and Conference Center:

Shangri-La Resort and Conference Center is located on Monkey Island on Grand Lake O' the Cherokees, northeast Oklahoma. Shangri-La Airport is located 2 miles north.The resort offers guests complimentary transportation to and from the airport. It is the largest owner and operator of golf courses in the world, with two 18-hole championship golf courses, two putting greens, driving ranges, four indoor and three outdoor tennis courts, a fitness center, four racquetball courts, and four bowling lanes.The resort also features indoor and outdoor swimming pools, a sandy beach and swimming area, bicycle rentals, a body shop and health spa, Bay Club Marina, boat rentals, waverunner rentals, fishing guide service and parasailing. For children, the resort offers a Pirate's Crew program for ages 4-7 and 8-12. Supervised fun and games of all kinds: arts and crafts, group indoor and outdoor games, story time, water games, movies and snacks. 650 wooded acres of running, jogging and walking paths are spread throughout the resort and along the lake shoreline. The resort offers a wonderful collection of boutiques, including a full service florist, women's formal and casual dress and specialty shops. Even more shopping can be found on nearby Main Street in Monkey Island. In addition to all the activities, Shangri-La also has 400 comfortable sleeping rooms (95 suites), 29 meeting rooms, with 50,000 square feet of meeting and function space and 32,000 square feet of exhibit space. The resort also offers plenty of dining choices that will suit every taste. The Bay Club is open for lunch and dinner in season, and it offers juicy steaks and fresh seafood with brilliant sunsets over the lake. Diners can enjoy beverage and food service on the deck overlooking the Marina. The Bay Club also features live entertainment Wednesday through Saturday nights. The Greenery offers breakfast, lunch and dinner in a casually elegant setting. They also offer a delicious Sunday brunch, as well as live weekend entertainment. Pasquale's features hot, bubbling pizza served on site or by room service. R.D.'s Lobby Bar serves burgers, sandwiches and cool drinks in a relaxed atmosphere. They also feature a large screen television. The Recreation Center Snack Bar is ideal for a quick snack between meetings, tennis matches, golf rounds or boating excursions. The resort also features the 19th Hole and the Golden Leaf Snack Bar. For more information about Shangri-La Resort and Conference Center, call 800-331-4060 or 257-4204.

Restaurants Near Airport:

Shangri-La Resort	2 mi S.	Phone: 257-4204
Touch-N-Go	On Site	Phone: 257-8601

Lodging: Shangri-La Resort (2 miles south) 257-4204

Meeting Rooms: Shangri-La Resort 257-4204

Transportation: Shangri-La Resort and Conference Center will provide complimentary transportation to and from the airport. Phone: 257-4204

Information: The Grand Lake Association, 6807 Highway 59 North, Grove, OK 74344, Phone: 786-2289

Attractions:

Northeast Oklahoma has many unique antique shops, art galleries and museums. Historical and Native American heritage inspires such landmarks: Har-Ber Village, Will Rogers Museum, J. M. Davis Gun Museum, Cherokee Heritage Center and Woolaroc Museum and Wildlife Preserve. Entertainment options include: Kountry Kuzins Jamboree, Precious Moments Chapel, "The Man Who Ran" Biblical Drama, Gospel Performance and Blue Ribbon Downs horse racing.

See Article about Shangri-La Resort

Touch-N-Go Deli & Restaurant:

This food service facility is located within the terminal building on the Grand Lake Regional Airport. During our conversation with the airport management, we learned that this deli is open 6 a.m. to 10 p.m. Sunday through Thursday and Friday and Saturday 24 hours. It is a combination convenient store, art gallery, automobile gas station, and airport service establishment. A restaurant is planned to open soon expanding the services of the deli. Seating for about 16 people is available within the deli area and additional seating for 20 people outside on their patio. Menu selections include fresh pizza, Deli subs prepared with meats of your choice including roast beef, smoked turkey and ham. Rueben sandwiches are also available in addition to cheeseburgers and hamburgers. The restaurant soon to open with prepare a wide variety of additional entrees. Full breakfast selections will be provided including selections like biscuits and gravy and egg dishes. The building has a stone face front and is connected to a portion of the airport terminal lobby. For more information about this restaurant call 257-8601 or 257-4204.

Airport Information:

AFTON - GRAND LAKE REG. ARPT/SHANGRI-LA (309)

10 mi southeast of town N36-34.38 W94-52.41 Elev: 792 Fuel: None reported Rwy 17-35: H3965x60 (Conc) Attended: unattended CTAF: 122.7 Notes: At the time of interview, airport information provided to us differs from published information in Airport Facility Directory (AFD).

Airport Management Phone: 257-4204

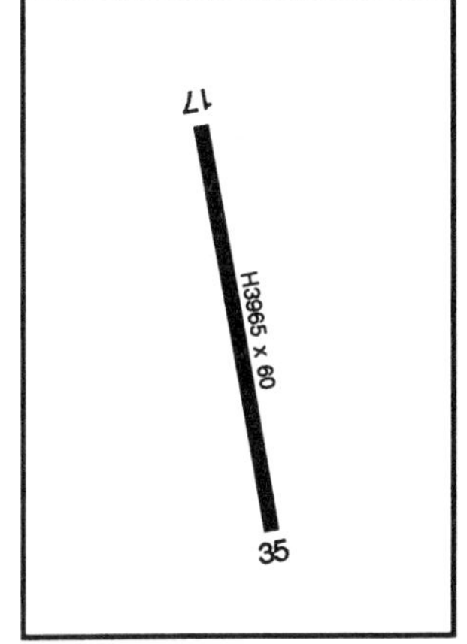

Shangri-La Resort

Afton, OK (309)

On an island surrounded by the Grand Lake o' the Cherokees lies Shangri-La, conveniently located near Tulsa but tucked away in a world of its own. The cool, blue waters of Grand Lake, two championship golf courses, and countless recreational activities, make Shangri-La, a resort destination that is truly unique.

At Shangri-La you may choose from 500 available guest rooms including newly refurbished lodge rooms, suites, or estate homes with golf, lake or country yard views. The Lodge overlooks beautiful Grand Lake and includes a lobby of terraced gardens, flowing water and tropical greenery.

The Golden Oaks complex is characterized by 1, 2, and 3 bedroom suites. Each contains a complete kitchen, living room, and patio.

The entire staff of Shangri-La is at your service. Under the ownership of Club Resorts, Inc., Shangri-La's staff is professionally trained to meet the highest standards of guest satisfaction. So, you are assured of complete comfort and Club level service throughout you visit.

Perhaps what you will notice first about Shangri-La is the golf. Their courses provide a challenge for both beginners and experienced golfers. The 7,000-yard, 18-hole championship Blue Course has been cited by Golf Digest as one of the top five courses in Oklahoma. The new 18-hole Gold Course features tree-studded roughs, irrigated Bermuda fairways and bent-grass greens, in addition to well-placed traps and water hazards. In winter, over seeding of the Blue Course assures great year-round play.

Shangri-La rambles across 650 acres of gently rolling island countryside on the largest and bluest lake in all of Oklahoma. With over 1,300 miles of shoreline, Grand Lake is a water sports paradise. The resort itself features a sandy beach and marina so that you can enjoy boating, water skiing, fishing, and swimming. To add to the fun, take a sunset cruise by riverboat. If you prefer tennis, Shangri-La offers indoor courts. Outdoor courts are lighted for night play.

Whatever your sport, you'll find it's available at the Golden Leaf Recreation Center. They have indoor/outdoor swimming pools, racquetball courts, volleyball, jogging trails, bowling lanes, arcade games and a health spa with gym, whirlpool, sauna, masseuse, aerobics classes, European body wraps and facials.

They also offer organized children's programs. In the Pirates Crew program, children ages 4 to 7 and 8 to 12 will enjoy everything from beach combing to board games to fishing. Teenagers recreation and entertainment programs and baby sitting are also available.

From casual to haute cuisine, Shangri-La offers memorable dining. The Brasserie for a casual breakfast, lunch or dinner; the Lobby Courtyard for refreshments or a complete meal; Top of the Towers for continental cuisine; and Bay West Yacht Club for excellent Italian entrees. Snacks, light fare and beverage are also available in the Recreation Center.

Food, beverages and a panoramic view of the Grand Lake are served up evenings in the Vista Lounge.

The popular Har-Ber Village is just minutes by water shuttle across Grand Lake. From Shangri-La, amphibious "ducks" can transport guests to this village which was created to preserve the heritage of the area typical of the 1800's. You'll find over 100 exhibits, log cabins, and fascinating antique displays.

Shangri-La is also just a short drive from the Will Rogers Museum and the Cherokee Heritage Center. There you can immerse yourself in the history of Oklahoma and the Cherokee nation.

Discover a world of shopping within the resort in their boutiques, pro-shops and sundries shops.

In such a unique setting, Shangri-La is the ideal meeting place. They offer the largest meeting and exhibit space in the state: 54,000 square feet of meeting space including meeting rooms suitable for groups of 10 to 2,000. Shangri-La's expert conference planning staff can make your next meeting your best meeting yet.

By land or by air, Shangri-La is easily accessible. The once Shangri-La Airport (309) is now named the Grand Lake Regional Airport, (Lat 36.34.38N Lon. 94.52.41W) and is reported about 2 miles north of the resort. Runway 17-35: H3965x60 (Conc) and unicom freq: 122.7. We were told by airport management that the terminal building re-opened and offers complimentary shuttle service to the resort. Services at this airport have been expanded including a deli on the premises. Limousine and rental cars can be easily arranged with advanced notice. For information about Shangri-La Resort and its many amenities you can call 800-331-4060 or 918-257-4204. (Information submitted in part by Shangri-La Resort).

Photo by: Shangri-La Resort

OK-ADM - ARDMORE
ARDMORE MUNICIPAL

(Area Code 405) 4, 5

Airways Cafe:

The Airways Cafe is located at the entrance of the Ardmore Municipal Airport, and only 1/4 mile walk from the aircraft parking ramp. This cafe is open Monday through Friday between 7 a.m. and 9 p.m., and Saturday from 9 a.m. to 5 p.m. (Closed Sunday). Their menu features a full breakfast line, a variety of sandwiches and burgers including their fried onion burger, boneless chicken dinners and catfish dinners. Average prices run $3.00 for breakfast, and about $5.00 for most lunch and dinner selections. On Friday they feature catfish specials. The main dining area can seat 200 individuals. All meals on their menu can also be prepared to go. For more information about the Airways Cafe, call 389-5241.

Runway Cafe:

The Runway Cafe under new management is located in the same spot that the Airways Cafe used to be situated. It is positioned next door to Lakeland Aviation along the main ramp area under and adjacent to the control tower. The Runway Cafe specializes in serving a variety of deli sandwiches with all types of meats and cheeses available. In addition they also serve hamburgers and cheeseburgers, baked potatoes and much more. Two specials are usually offered each day. Restaurant hours are Monday through Friday 7:30 a.m. to 3 p.m. and Saturday 10 a.m. to 2 p.m. (Closed Sunday). The decor of this restaurant has an aviation theme with hand-drawn pictures along with photographs of airplanes. The dining room has seating for about 70 people in a friendly and casual surrounding. You can enjoy a nice view of the airport while dining. They also have a conference room able to accommodate 30 to 40 people. Carry-out and catered meals can also be arranged. Just call to order using the Unicom frequency through Lakeland Aviation, and they will place the order with the restaurant ready for pick-up when you arrive. For information call Lakeland Aviation adjacent to the restaurant at 389-9024.

Restaurants Near Airport:

Airway Cafe	On Site	Phone: 389-5241
Runway Cafe	On Site	Phone: 389-9024

Lodging: Dorchester Inn 226-1761; Lake Murray Resort 223-6600.

Meeting Rooms: Contact Airpark Manager's Office at 389-5238 or 389-5280 for information.

Transportation: Sutherland Airmotive provides transportation to nearby facilities 389-5445.

Information: Chamber of Commerce, 410 West Main, P.O. Box 1585, Ardmore, OK 73401, Phone: 223-7765.

Airport Information:

ARDMORE - ARDMORE MUNICIPAL (ADM)
10 mi northeast of town N34-18.13 W97-01.12 Elev: 762 Fuel: 100LL, Jet-A1
Rwy 13-31: H7202x150 (Asph) Rwy 17-35: H6879x150 (Asph) Attended Mon-Fri 1300-0500Z, Sat-Sun 1300-2300Z Unicom: 122.95 Tower: 118.5 Gnd Con: 121.8
Public phone 24 hrs Notes: No landing fees reported
FBO: Lakeland Aviation Phone: 389-5000 or 389-9024

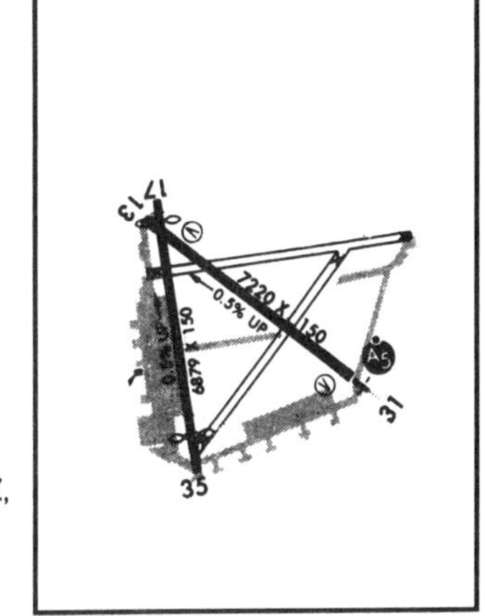

OK-DUC - DUNCAN HALLIBURTON FIELD

(Area Code 405) 6

Phipp's BBQ:

Phillip's BBQ restaurant is a cafe that is located 1/4 mile south and across from the National Guard Armory and is reported to be within walking distance from the Halliburton Airport. This cafe is open Tuesday through Saturday from 11 a.m. to 7 p.m. They are closed Sunday and Monday. This restaurant specializes in preparing ribs, pork, beef, hot links, polish sausage and the biggest steaks in town. Fast and friendly service has been their main objective when serving their customers. The restaurant has been in business since 1966. Average prices run $5.00 for most items on their menu. This is a family restaurant, can seat 55 guests, and offers a casual atmosphere. Groups are always welcome. For information call Phillip's BBQ at 255-5443.

Restaurants Near Airport:

El Palacio Mexican Rest.	1-1/2 mi	Phone: 252-1314
Phipp's BBQ	1/4 mi	Phone: 255-5443

Lodging: Duncan Inn 252-5210; Heritage Inn 252-5612.

Meeting Rooms: None reported

Transportation: None reported

Information: Ducan Chamber of Commerce, 911 Walnut, Duncan, OK 73533. Phone: 255-3644.

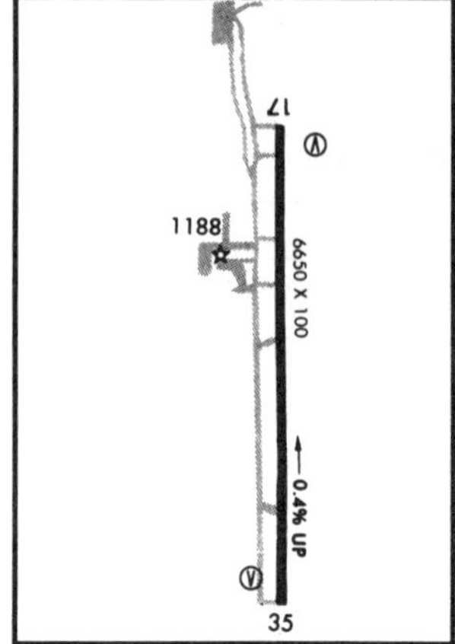

Airport Information:

DUNCAN - HALLIBURTON FIELD (DUC)
2 mi south of town N34-28.33 W97-57.59 Elev: 1113 Fuel: 100LL, Jet-A MOGAS
Rwy 17-35 H6650x100 (Conc) Attended: 1300-0200Z Unicom: 122.8
Airport Manager Phone: 255-1790

OK-DUA - DURANT EAKER FIELD AIRPORT

(Area Code 405) 7

Restaurants Near Airport:

Chuck's BBQ	2 mi SW	Phone: 434-5859
Willie's Catfish Rest.	2 mi NW	Phone: N/A

Chuck's Bar-B-Que:

This family style restaurant is reported to be 1 to 2 miles southwest of the Eaker Field Airport. Courtesy transportation to the restaurant can be arranged through Bestway Aviation at 924-5359. Directions given by airport manager is as follows: (1 mile west of airport to Hwy 69-75 south one mile - first exit Calera, OK). The restaurant is open Tuesday through Thursday 11 a.m. to 8 p.m., Friday and Saturday 11 a.m. to 9 p.m. and Sunday 12 p.m. to 8 p.m. Specialties include barbecued ribs, beef, ham, sausage, catfish served nightly with homemade cobblers and pies. Prices for lunch average $7.00 and $9.00 for dinner. Their daily specials run about $3.99. The restaurant has been remodeled in a western style decor. Full service catering is also provided with advance notice. For information call 434-5859.

Lodging: Markita Inn (Best Western, 4 miles) 60 rooms, 2501 West Main, Durant, Phone: 924-7676;

Meeting Rooms: Markita Inn has seating for up to 120 persons, Their restaurant is located adjacent to the meeting room facilities. Phone: 924-7676.

Transportation: Bestway Aviation (Courtesy car) 924-5359; Taxi: C & S Cab 924-2323.

Information: Chamber of Commerce, 215 North 4th Street, P.O. Box 517, Durant, OK 74701, Phone: 924-0848.

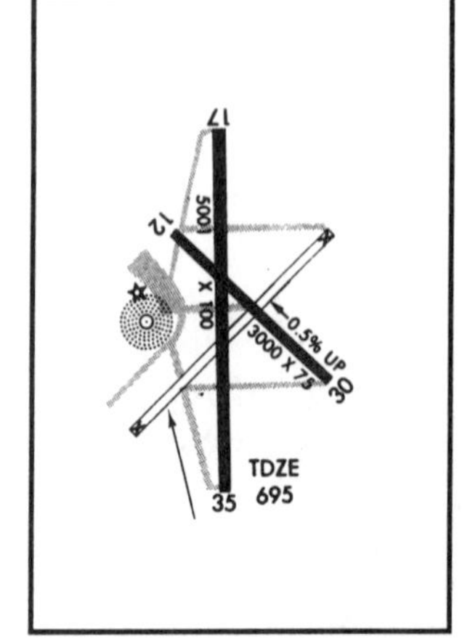

Airport Information:

DURANT - EAKER FIELD AIRPORT (DUA)
3 mi southwest of town N33-56.54 W96-23.67 Elev: 698 Fuel: 100LL
Rwy 17-35: H5000x100 (Asph) Rwy 12-30: H3000x75 (Conc) Attended: 1500-0000Z
Unicom: 122.8 Public Phone 24hr Notes: No landing fee or overnight hangar fee with purchase of fuel.
Airport Manager Phone: 920-0574
FBO: Wings Sales Phone: 920-0574

OK-WDG - ENID

ENID WOODRING MUNICIPAL AIRPORT

(Area Code 405) **8**

Barnstormer Restaurant:

The Barnstormer Restaurant is located on the Enid Woodring Municipal Airport within the terminal building. This cafe style restaurant, is open between 8 a.m. and 2 p.m. Monday through Friday, and Saturday 7 a.m. to 2 p.m. Their menu provides items like chicken, fried chicken steak, hambergers and steak burger sandwiches, a full breakfast line, bisquits and gravy as well as homemade desserts and a salad bar. Average cost for meals run $3.00 to $4.50 for breakfast and lunch. Their main dining room can accommodate up to 50 persons. Guests can enjoy a view of the airport taxiways and runway systems while dining. Fly-in clubs and groups are also welcome. Meals can be prepared-to-go or for carry-out. For more information you can call the Woodring Airport Restaurant at 234-5476 or 234-9913.

Restaurants Near Airport:

Barnstomer Restaurant	On Site	Phone: 234-5476
Gateway Restaurant	3 mi NW	Phone: 234-0930
Holland House Buffet	10 mi W	Phone: 233-4424
Sage Room	8 mi SW	Phone: 233-1212

Lodging: Holiday Inn (Trans available) 233-6600; Ramada Inn (Trans available) 234-0440.

Meeting Rooms: Enid Conference Center 234-1919.

Transportation: Airport shuttle ($2.00 for 1st mile and $1.00 per mile thereafter), Phone: 234-5476.

Information: Chamber of Commerce, 210 Kenwood Blvd, P.O. Box 907, Enid, OK 73702, Phone: 237-2494.

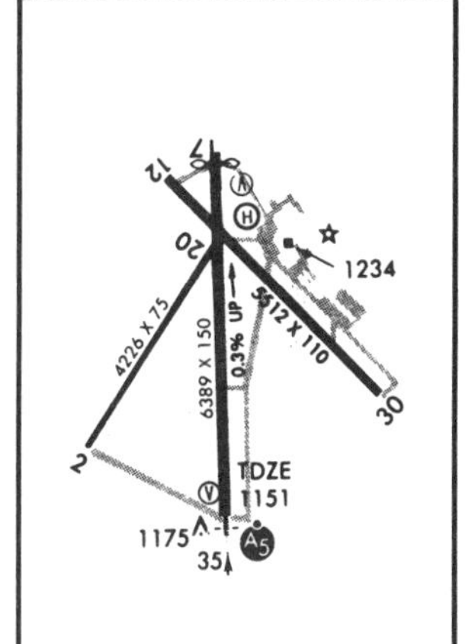

Airport Information:

ENID - ENID WOODRING MUNICIPAL AIRPORT (WDG)
4 mi southeast of town N36-22.75 W97-47.47 Elev: 1167 Fuel: 100LL, Jet-A Rwy 17-35: H6389x150 (Asph) Rwy 12-30: H5512x110 (Asph) Rwy 02-20: H4226x75 (Asph) Attended: Mon-Fri 1130-0500Z, Sat 1130-0300Z, Sun 1300-0300Z Unicom: 122.95 Tower: 118.9 Gnd Con: 121.9 Public Phone 24hrs Notes: No landing fees reported except for scheduled carriers, overnight parking $2.00 on ramp. Overnight hangars range from $10.00 to $50.00.
FBO: Northwest Aero Services (Maintenance) Phone: 233-4531

OK-F08 - EUFAULA

EUFAULA AIRPORT

(Area Code 918) **9**

Salty Pelican Restaurant:

The Salty Pelican Restaurant is located 4 miles east of the Eufaula Airport. This fine dining facility is open March through October, 7 days a week and serves a wide variety of entrees. Some of their specialties include lobster, king crab, prime rib, KC strip steak, shrimp, halibut, chicken and scallops. Daily specials are also offered. Prices range from $5.00 for lunch and $10.00 for diner. The decor of the restaurant is rustic with a nautical theme. Dinning can be enjoyed either indoors or on their outdoor deck. Transportation to and from the airport is provided by the restaurant as well as the airport manager. They will gladly cater to fly-in groups if given advance notice. For information call 689-4455.

Restaurants Near Airport:

JM's	3 mi W	Phone: 689-9474
Lakeside	4 mi E	Phone: 689-5466
Salty Pelican	4 mi E	Phone: 689-4455
Spur	3 mi W	Phone: 689-5451

Lodging: Fountainhead Resort (10 miles) located on Lake Eufaula. Over 200 units in five story complex with 14 cottages, swimming, golfing, tennis, poolside service, bellhops, etc. Phone: 689-9173 (See Eufaula Municipal Airport (0F7) for information).
Meeting Rooms: Fountainhead Resort (10 miles) 689-9173
Transportation: George Didlott Airport Administration can arrange courtesy transportation to nearby facilities, call 689-2444; Also from 8 a.m. to 5 p.m. City bus is available; City Police give rides from airport to town.
Information: Greater Eufaula Area Chamber of Commerce, 64 Memorial Drive, Eufaula, OK 74432, Phone: 689-2791.

Attractions:

Eufaula Cove Marina and Salty Pelican Floating Restaurant are both located together on Lake Eufuala, one of the largest man-made lakes in the world fed by the Canadian River. This facility is made up of floating piers and decks which support a restaurant, marina, and ships store. Sunseeker Houseboat are also a part of the floating complex. 689-4455; Fountainhead Resort, 10 miles to the north, provides fly-in guests with a wide variety of accommodations, complete with its own 3,000 foot paved airstrip. 689-9173 res. or 800-826-3973 if outside OK.

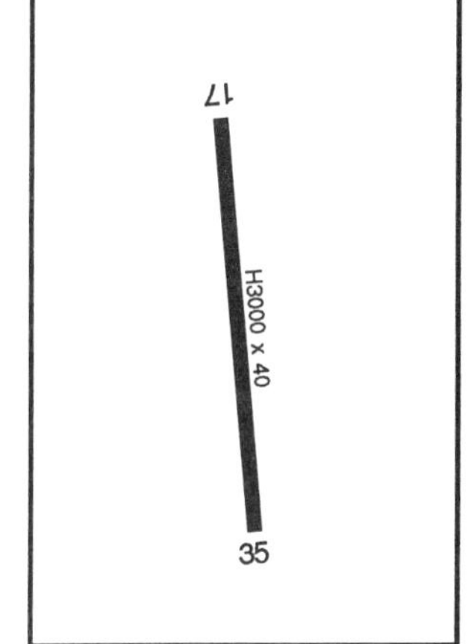

Airport Information:

EUFAULA - EUFAULA AIRPORT (F08)
2 mi west of town N35-17.76 W95-37.52 Elev: 635 Rwy 17-35: H3000x40 (Asph) Attended: unattended CTAF: 122.9 Public Phone 24hrs
Airport Manager Phone: 689-2534
Eufaula Muni. Arpt. Phone: 689-2444

Lake Texoma Resort

Kingston, OK (OK-F31)

Photo by: Fred W. Marvel-Oklahoma Tourism Texoma State Resort features guest rooms, poolside patio cabannas & lakeview cottages.

Welcome to southern Oklahoma's Lake Texoma Resort and State Park for an exciting adventure in the land of beautiful water, big fish and great golf. Overlooking magnificent 93,000 acre Lake Texoma, the Resort and State Park accommodates the most discriminating angler and water enthusiast with fishing guide service, a full-service marina, boat ramps, a fish cleaning station and an enclosed fishing dock. Lake Texoma holds the world record for blue catfish at 118-1/2 pounds and is ranked nationally for big Striper catches.

Activities abound for land-lovers with hiking trails, tennis, horseback riding, hayrides, archery, interpretive tours with the park naturalist, go-carts, miniature golf, bicycle and water sports rentals. An indoor Recreation and Fitness Center offers a daily schedule of recreation and theme programs for guests of all ages.

The Atrium Resort Hotel features guest rooms with one or two beds, terrace rooms with a sun deck or pool-side patio cabanas with king size beds, sitting area and wet bar, Two-bedroom lake-view cottages accommodate four to eight people; each features a kitchenette, living area, fireplace, central heat and air, telephone, and color TV. One-room "studio" cottages for one to four people offer similar amenities. All accommodations have maid service. State Park Rangers provide 24-hour security and guest assistance year around.

The Galley Restaurant serves regional favorites, "Healthy Heart" and children's entrees for breakfast, lunch and dinner. Try their outrageously delicious Galley Fudge Cake when you visit. Join a terrace fish fry, a cookout or the Tom Sawyer Fishing Adventure for fun outdoor dining. Pool-side guests can relax in the colorful Waterfront Lounge for light lunch and snacks or gather in the evening for cocktails and conversation. Browse the gift shop for souvenir shopping. Grab a partner for crafts and games or relax in the sauna and whirlpool in the Recreation and Fitness Center.

Meeting accommodations range from the informal to the functionally sophisticated, enabling you to choose the atmosphere that best accomplishes your meeting objectives. Their ballroom can be divided into three rooms and is equipped with a permanent, 28' x 24' stage. Their Virgie White conference area may be divided into two rooms by means of a trac-air-wall-system. Each function room has individual controls for climate. On the mezzanine floor, comfortable conference suites are available for small groups of up to 30 people.

Lake Texoma Resort is conveniently located half way between I-35 and U.S. 75 on U.S. 70, 5 miles east of Kingston, VT. It's equil distance from Oklahoma City and Dallas.

Kingston Lake Texoma State Park Airport is located adjacent to, and just west of the Lake Texoma State Park Resort. Their runway 18-36: is 3,000 x 50 feet and has an asphalt surface which is lighted and has an elevation of 693 ASL. The airport is unattended. However, if you call them on Unicom (122.8), they will come out and pick you up. Next time you are flying through the area stop in and visit the Lake Texoma State Resort or for further information call 404-564-2311. (Information submitted by Lake Texoma and Oklahoma's Resorts Tourism & Recreation Dept.).

OK-F31 - KINGSTON
LAKE TEXOMA STATE PARK ARPT.

(Area Code 405) 10

Galley Restaurant At Lake Texoma Resort:

The Lake Texoma Resort is located within the Texoma State Park. This facility is served by a 3,000 foot lighted paved airstrip with unicom and courtesy transportation service, located only 1 block from the resort. The Galley Restaurant at the resort serves regional favorites as well as "Healthy Heart" and children's entrees for breakfast, lunch and dinner. In addition to the many fine menu selections available, you are invited to enjoy a unique dining experience with their terrace fish fries or their Tom Sawyer Fishing Adventure for fun outdoor dining. Poolside guests can relax in the colorful Waterfront Lounge for light lunch and snacks. In Addition to the Galley Restaurant this resort hotel also features guest rooms with one or two beds, terrace rooms with a sun deck or poolside patio cabanas with king size beds. Two-Bedroom lake view cottages are also available. While enjoying your stay you can browse the gift shop for souvenir shopping, or take part in any of the many sporting activities available. For more information call the resort at 564-2311.

Restaurants Near Airport:
Galley Restaurant At Resort 1blk Phone: 564-2311

Lodging: Lake Texoma Resort has rooms in lodge as well as cabins available. Phone: 564-2311

Meeting Rooms: Convention facilities are available at this State Park Resort 564-2311.

Transportation: Courtesy transportation to and from the airport and the resort is provided to fly-in guests by calling 564-2311.

Information: Regional Information: Project Office, Lake Texoma, Route 4, Box 493, Denison, TX 75020 or call 903-465-4990; Also for information about the Lake Texoma Resort call 405-564-2311.

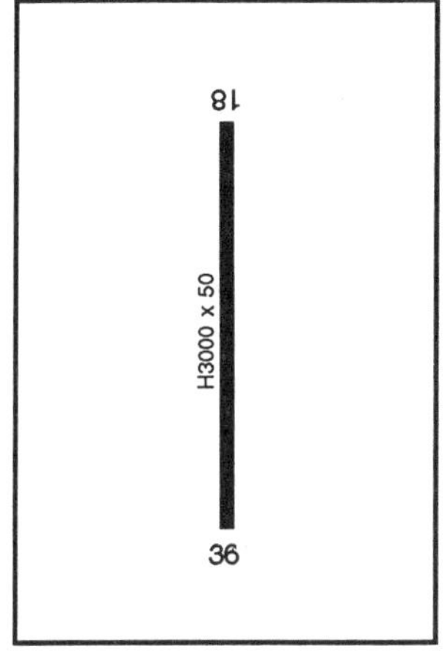

Attractions: The Lake Texoma State Park Resort overlooks Lake Texoma, a 93,000 acre watershed. The resort and State Park accommodates a full-service marina, boat rentals, fishing guides, a fish cleaning station as well as numerous other activities like hiking trails, tennis, horseback riding, golfing on their 18 hole par 71 course, and a complete indoor recreation center. For information call the resort at 564-2311.

Airport Information:

KINGSTON - LAKE TEXOMA STATE PARK AIRPORT (F31)
4 mi east of town 33-59-34N 96-38-31W Elev: 693 Rwy 18-36: H3000x50 (Asph)
Attended: unattended Unicom: 122.8 Public Phone 24hrs Notes: No landing fee
Lake Texoma Resort Phone: 564-2311

Lake Murray State Resort Park

Overbrook, OK (OK-1F1)

During our conversation with the staff at both the Lake Murray Inn and the golf pro-shop, we learned that the Lake Murray State Resort Park has a hard surface lighted runway 14-32, that is 2,500 x 50 feet. This airport is unattended. However, after landing you can taxi up to the golf pro-shop and park your airplane. A call to the Lake Murray Country Inn about 1 mile away will provide you with a courtesy van to their lodge and restaurant. If flying in for a game of golf, you can park your airplane near the golf pro-shop and walk to the first tee only a short distance away. For information about the runway call the Country Inn at 405-223-6600. If you would prefer to land at the Ardmore Downtown Executive (1F0) Airport about 4 miles north of the State Resort, you can obtain a taxi for $5.00 or $6.00 to the resort. This airport is attended and contains fuel, FBO's etc. For information call 405-223-5500.

Lake Murray State Resort Park which is state owned and operated, contains the Country Inn that offers guests a variety of amenities including a recreation room, game room, restaurant and lodging within the inn or nearby cottages. In addition to this, Lake Murray State Resort Park provides lots of recreational ideas for their guests. Tennis courts, basketball courts, water sports including paddle boats, canoe, sailboats, and pontoon boats, fishing, riding stables, (trail, moonlight and hay rides), bicycle rental, hiking, and the Tucker Tower Nature Center are all available. Overnight guests can rent cabins for $40.00 to $200.00 per evening, depending on the number of people who are planning to stay.

Types of cottages include the: "Small Fisherman", tile floor, no television, sleeps two, bath and kitchenette for $40.00; "Large Fisherman", tile floor, no television, sleeps four, one bedroom, living area with a bed bath and kitchenette; "Small Villa", carpet, television, telephone, sleeps four, one bedroom, living area with a murphy bed, 1 bathroom, has a microwave oven and small refrigerator for $85.00; "Large Villa", is basically the same as the Small Villa except it has a fire place for $10.00 more; Their Duplex has two rooms connecting with a door between, sleeps four, one room has kitchenette, both have carpet, television, and bathroom for $95.00; Additional accommodations include the Heritage cottage #1 and #2 for $125.00 and $195.00 respectively; and the Buzzard's Roost Cabin with stone floor, sleeps fourteen, has kitchen, 1 bedroom has 2 queen beds, 1 bedroom has 1 king bed, 1 bedroom with 2 sets of bunk-beds and 2 sleeper sofas in the living area, and 1 bath for $195.00. Deposits are due 14 days from the date the reservation is made. Refunds may be issued if reservations are cancelled 5 days prior to arrival date.

For more information about Lake Murray State Park Resort call 405-223-6600. (Information submitted by Lake Murray Resort).

OK-T40 - MARIETTA
McGEHEE CATFISH RESTAURANT AIRPORT

(Area Code 405)

11

McGehee Catfish Restaurant:

You can eat in any restaurant and satisfy your hunger, but a meal at McGehee Catfish Restaurant is more than a meal, its an experience. The scenery is part of the entire dining adventure, with wide windows looking out on the Red River bottom far below the restaurant. 170 acres of pecan trees stretch out before you. These ponds guarantee that Mr. and Mrs. Rudolph McGehee's customers will never leave the restaurant without a very full, satisfied stomach. "All you can eat" is not just a printed slogan with them. Dishes on your table continually are refilled, and you are urged to consume as much of the tender fried catfish, hush puppies, French fries and coleslaw that you can hold. Customers take them at their word, because they consume 2,000 to 3,000 pounds of dressed catfish per week. Average prices run $4.95 for lunch and dinner. The restaurant is approximately six miles southwest of the town Marietta, Oklahoma, and is located on the south end of the runway only 200 feet from the aircraft parking area. McGehee's Restaurant is open weekdays from 5 p.m. to 10 p.m. and Saturday and Sunday 1 p.m. to 9:30 p.m. It is closed on Wednesdays. For more information call 276-2751.

Restaurants Near Airport:
McGehee Catfish Restaurant On Site Phone: 276-2751

Lodging: None reported

Meeting Rooms: McGehee Catfish Restaurant has accommodations for meeting and luncheons in a separate dining room able to hold 80 people. Call 276-2751

Transportation: The restaurant is within 200 feet from the aircraft parking area. No transportation is needed.

Information: Love County Chamber of Commerce, 104 West Main, Box 422, Marietta, OK 73448, Phone: 276-3102.

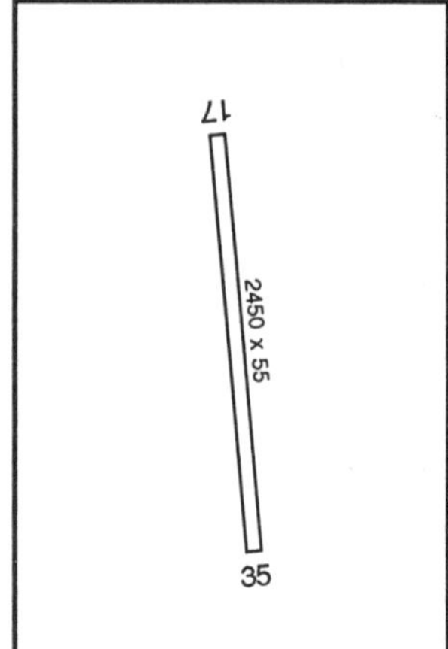

Airport Information:

MARIETTA - McGEHEE CATFISH RESTAURANT AIRPORT (T40)
5 mi southwest of town N33-54.01 W97-10.02 Elev: 760 Rwy 17-35: 2450x55 (Turf)
Attended: Mon-Fri 2300-0330Z, Sat-Sun 1900-0330Z CTAF: 122.9 Telephone inside restaurant
Notes: Rwy 17-35 slippery and soft when wet, also trees near Rwy 17 threshold. Arpt. lighting schedule is dusk to 0400Z
Airport phone at restaurant Phone: 276-2751

OK-OUN - NORMAN
UNIV. OF OK WESTHEIMER AIRPARK

(Area Code 405)

12

Restaurants Near Airport:

Crispy Produce	1-1/2 mi W.	Phone: 360-3164
Little China	1/4 mi S.	Phone: 360-1265
Ozzie's Diner	On Site	Phone: 364-9835
Sooner Bar-B-Q	1/2 mi S.	Phone: 321-5551

Ozzie's Diner:

Ozzie's Diner is located in the University of Oklahoma Airpark terminal building, and is within 100 feet from the aircraft parking area. This diner is open 7 a.m. to 9 p.m. Monday through Saturday, and Sunday 7 a.m. to 3:30 p.m. Their selections include chicken fried steak dinners, hamburger steak dinners, marinated chicken breast dinners, chili, beans and cornbread, hamburgers and cheeseburgers as well as a full breakfast line with omelets pancakes and egg dishes. Some of their specials include all-you-can eat selections. The main dining room can seat 40 to 50 persons. A view of the aircraft parking ramp and runways can be seen through windows on one side of the restaurant. Meals prepared to go, as well as catering service is available. When speaking with the owner, we learned that the restaurant prides itself in providing fast and convenient service for air travelers. For more information call Ozzie's Diner at 364-9835.

Lodging: Sheraton Hotel (1 mile west) 364-2882; Holiday Inn (1-1/4 mile south) 329-1624; Days Inn (2-1/4 mile south) 321-0110.
Meeting Rooms: Sheraton Hotel 364-2882; Holiday Inn 329-1624; Days Inn 321-0110.
Transportation: Cruise Aviation, Inc. 350-3900; Also City Cab Co. 321-0454; Yellow Cab 329-3333; Checker Cab 329-3335; Rental Cars: Reynolds Ford 321-2411.
Information: Chamber of Commerce, 115 East Gray, P.O. Box 982, Norman, OK 73070, Phone: 321-7260.

Attractions:

Westwood Swimming Pool & Westwood Golf Course 1/4th mile west and south 321-0433; Lake Thunderbird, 10 miles east.

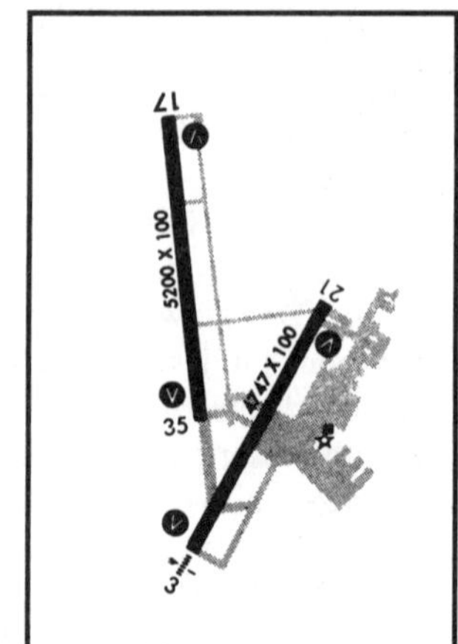

Airport Information:

NORMAN - UNIVERSITY OF OK WESTHEIMER AIRPARK (OUN)
3 mi northwest of town N35-14.73 W97-28.33 Elev: 1182 Fuel: 100LL, Jet-A
Rwy 17-35: H5200x100 (Asph) Rwy 03-21: H4750x100 (Asph) Attended 1300-0200Z
Unicom: 122.95 OKE City App/Dep Con: 120.45 Tower: 118.0 Gnd Con: 121.6
Public Phone 24hrs Notes: No landing fees, 1st night parking free, if fuel purchased. If no purchase $2.00 per night.
Cruise Aviation, Inc. Phone: 360-3900

OK-OK71 - OKEENE
O'KEENE MUNICIPAL AIRPORT

(Area Code 405)

13

Restaurants Near Airport:

Pizza Inn	5-6 Blks W.	Phone: 822-4499
Top Ten	1/2 mi	Phone: 822-3247

Pizza Inn:

The Pizza Inn Restaurant is located 5 or 6 blocks west of the O'keene Municipal Airport. This family style restaurant is open Sunday through Thursday 11 a.m. to 9 p.m. and Friday and Saturday 11 a.m. to 10 p.m. Their specialty is pizza with many varieties and toppings available. They also provide a varied selection of additional entrees such as chicken fried steak dinners, sandwiches, fish, barbecued items, cheeseburgers, hamburgers, and sub sandwiches. There is also a salad bar available, along with a luncheon buffet served on Friday from 5 p.m. to 8 p.m. (Buffet hours may change. Call ahead to confirm times.) The restaurant can seat up to 85 persons in their main dining room. There is also a back roomto accommodate parties and groups with advance reservations. For more information call the Pizza Inn at 822-4499.

Lodging: Okeene Inn (1 mile) 822-3244; Okeene Motel (1 mile) 822-4491.

Meeting Rooms: None Reported

Transportation: Rental Cars, Jim Dobrinski Chev 822-4455.

Information: Oklahoma Tourism & Recreation Department, Literature Distribution Center, P.O. Box 60789, Oklahoma City, OK 73146, Phone: 521-3831 or 800-652-6552.

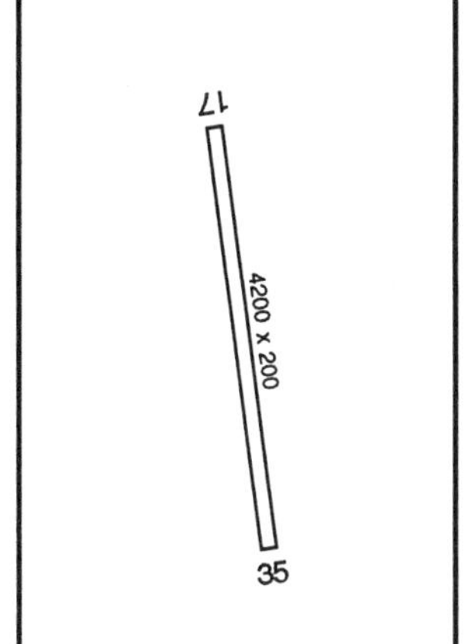

Airport Information:

O'KEENE - OKEENE MUNICIPAL AIRPORT (OK71)
1 mi southeast of town N36-06.75 W98-18.52 Elev: 1205 Rwy 17-35: 4200x200 (Turf)
Attended: unattended CTAF: 122.9
O'keene Municipal Airport Phone: 822-3031

OK-2DT - OKLAHOMA CITY
DOWNTOWN AIRPARK, INC.

(Area Code 405)

14

Restaurants Near Airport:

Downtown Airpark Cafe	On Site	Phone: 632-5288

Downtown Airpark Cafe:

The Downtown Airpark Cafe is a family owned and operated facility that has been serving air travelers and local clientele since 1954. This combination cafeteria and family style restaurant is located in the terminal building at the Oklahoma City Downtown Airpark, and is easily within walking distance from the aircraft parking ramp. Their hours are from 6:30 a.m. to 4:30 p.m. Monday through Friday and are closed on the weekend. Their menu includes a full breakfast line, homemade cinnamon rolls, biscuits and gravy, country fried steaks, pot roast, and a assortment of fresh vegetables served with each dinner, in addition to cobblers and desserts. Nightly specials are also featured, like chicken Cordon Bleu on Monday, meat loaf on Tuesday, Wednesday Mexican foods, Thursday chicken dinners and on Friday Cajun style fish plus chicken fry or pot roast. Three main meats are always served nightly, one of which changes each day. Their soup and salad bar is available from 11 a.m. to 4:00 p.m. and a luncheon buffet is served from 11 a.m. to 2 p.m. The restaurant can seat 50 people in their main dining area. Guests can also watch aircraft take off and land from the restaurant. For more information call 632-5288.

Lodging: Hilton West (Trans, 4 miles) 947-7681
Meeting Rooms: Hilton West 946-7681; Holiday Inn 942-8514; Embassy Suites 682-6000.
Transportation: Yellow Cab Company 232-6161; National Car Rental 634-1456.
Information: Oklahoma City Convention and Visitors Bureau Four Santa Fe Plaza, Oklahoma City, OK 73102, 278-8912 or 800-225-5652.

Attractions: There are many attractions located within this region that would satisfy the interests of almost everyone. One of these is the "45th Infantry Division Museum" located at 2145 N.E. 36th Street in Oklahoma City, about 9 miles to the northeast. Take I-35/40 and exit 36th street going east, just past the golf course on the right side. This museum exhibits large static displays of weaponry, aircraft, artillery, uniforms, vehicles, and an extensive collection of firearms dating back to the American Revolution. The museum is open Tuesday through Friday from 9 a.m. to 5 p.m., and Saturday from 10 a.m. to 5 p.m. (Closed Monday) Admission FREE. For information call 424-5313. Also: Kirkpatrick Center contains seven museums including the Oklahoma **Air Space Museum** and Red Earth Indian Center; Intl. Photography Hall of Fame Museum; Kirkpatric Planetarium; and the Omniplex Science Museum. For information call 427-5461.

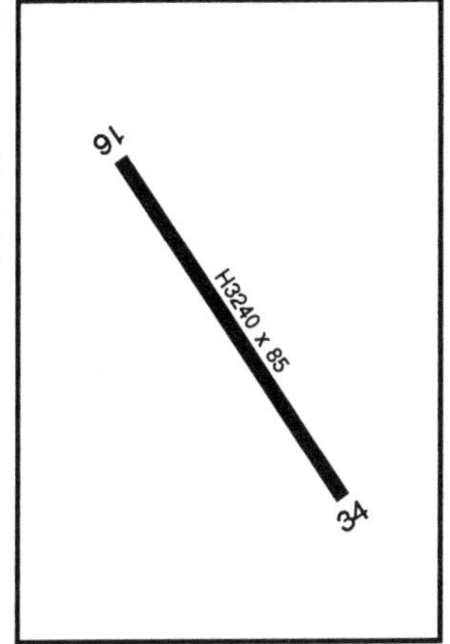

Airport Information:

OKLAHOMA CITY - DOWNTOWN AIRPARK (2DT)
2 mi southwest of town N35-26.95 W97-31.99 Elev: 1180 Fuel: 100LL, Jet-A
Rwy 16-34: H3240x85 (Asph) Attended 1200-0400Z Unicom: 122.8 Public Phone 24hrs
Notes: Overnight parking $3.00 all aircraft; Overnight Hangar $10.00
FBO: Downtown Airpark Phone 634-1456

OK-2EJ - OKLAHOMA CITY EXPRESSWAY AIRPARK

(Area Code 405)

15

Braum's Ice Cream & Dairy Store:

Braum's Ice Cream & Dairy Store is located across the street on the south side of the Expressway Airpark. This facility specializes in selling a wide variety of ice cream, yogurt and soda fountain delights. In fact they even make their own cones from scratch. This particular store has been rated within the top 100 restaurants of its kind, and is one of 252 similar stores across the country. In addition to their dairy products they also provide many traditional entrees for breakfast and lunch. These include a full country breakfast, in addition to items like buttermilk pancakes, cinnamon rolls, and muffins. For lunch, they also offer a nice selection of sandwiches. The restaurant is open Monday through Thursday and on Sunday from 6 a.m. to 10:30 p.m. and Friday and Saturday 6 a.m. to 11 p.m. Average prices run between $.80 and $3.00 for most selections. This restaurant provides weekly specials, and each item on their menu can be prepared for carry-out if requested. Seating for 99 persons is available in their main dining room. The decor of this restaurant has a split stone exterior with red oak trim, and can easily be seen from the airport. For more information you can call 478-5138.

Restaurants Near Airport:

Braum's Ice Cream Store	Adj Arpt.	Phone: 478-5138
Oklahoma Line Barbecue	1-1/2 mi W	Phone: 478-4955

Lodging: Remington Land Inn (Trans available) 478-3365; Santa Fe Inn (Trans available) 848-1919; Hotel Central Park 528-7563.

Meeting Rooms: Airport manager reported that there are meeting and conference accommodations in the Downtown Oklahoma City area, but was not specific. Contact area Chamber of Commerce or area Convention and Visitors Bureau for this information. (Listed Below).

Transportation: Taxi service is provided by the FBO at a nominal charge of $2.00/person. Expressway Airpark, Inc also provides rental cars if needed. In addition, there is public taxi service available: Yellow Cab 232-6161; Safeway Cab 235-1431.

Information: Oklahoma City Convention and Visitors Bureau Four Santa Fe Plaza, Oklahoma City, OK 73102, 278-8912 or 800-225-5652.

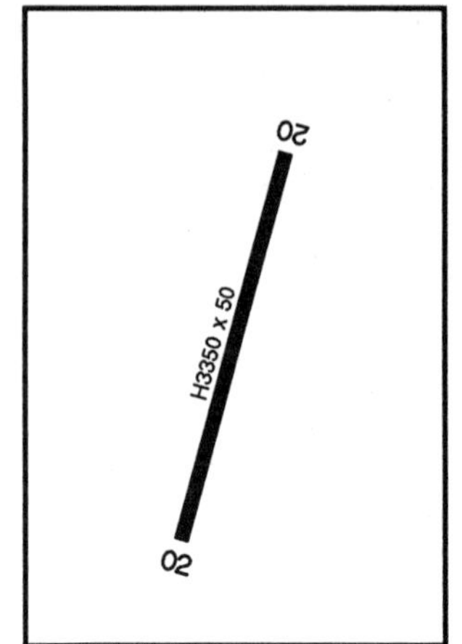

Attractions:

Remington Park - Horse racing, 2 miles west of airport, 424-1000; Oklahoma City Zoo, rated one of the top ten in the country, located only 2 miles west of the airport, 424-3344; Various museums located 2 miles west of field. (Also refer to OK-OKC for attractions)

Airport Information:

OKLAHOMA CITY - EXPRESSWAY AIRPARK (2EJ)

5 mi northeast of town N35-32.48 W97-27.19 Elev: 1070 Fuel: 100LL, Jet-A, MOGAS

Rwy 02-20: H3350x50 (Asph) Attended: 1400-2300, Mar-Oct 1200-0400Z

Unicom: 123.0 Notes: $5.00 in lieu of fuel purchase, after first night $3.00/night. Also: Check runway conditions, AFD reports cracking, asph breaking up.

FBO: Expressway Airpark, Inc. Phone: 478-1413

OK-PWA - OKLAHOMA CITY WILEY POST AIRPORT

(Area Code 405)

16

Runway Cafe:

The Tower Restaurant is located in the main terminal building where the control tower is located. You can park your airplane on the apron located on the west side of restaurant, (Within walking distance). This is a family style restaurant that is open Monday through Fridays from 5:30 a.m. to 2:30 p.m. The specialties of the house are chicken fried steak with country gravy and their homemade cream pie and cobblers in addition to the many other items listed on their menu. Daily specials are offered with average prices running about $3.00 for breakfast and $5.00 for lunch. The decor is modern with accommodations for groups and parties if advance notice is given. Catering is also provide with selections from their menu. For Information call the restaurant at 787-3188.

Restaurants Near Airport:

Airport Manager lists 25 restaurants located near airport.

Harry's Oyster Bar	1-1/2 mi NE	Phone: 721-6802
Olive Garden Italian Rest.	1-1/2 mi NE	Phone: 721-6071
Runway Cafe	On Site	Phone: 787-3188

Lodging: Crosswinds Inn Northwest 942-7730; Hilton Inn Northwest 848-4811; Holiday Inn Northwest 947-2351; Marriott 842-6633; Waterford Hotel 848-4782.

Meeting Rooms: Crosswinds; Hilton Inn; Holiday Inn Northwest; Marriott; Waterford Hotel.

Transportation: Hughes Aviation 495-5520 and MillionAir Aviation 787-4040 can arrange and provide courtesy and rental car transportation to nearby facilities.

Information: Oklahoma City Convention and Visitors Bureau Four Santa Fe Plaza, Oklahoma City, OK 73102, 278-8912 or 800-225-5652.

Attractions:

There are many attractions within the Oklahoma City area. The following have been recommended: Remington Park; OKC Zoo; Air Museum; Omniplex; State Capitol; Botanical Tube; Mike Monroney Aeronautical Center; And the Cowboy Hall of Fame. See "Information" listed above. (See OK-OKC, 45 Infantry Division Museum)

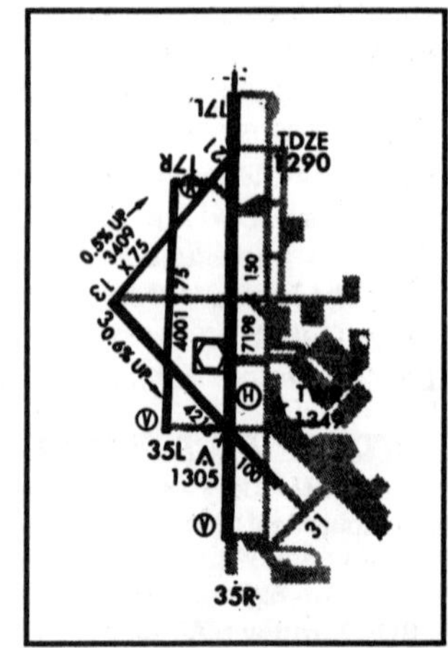

Airport Information:

OKLAHOMA CITY - WILEY POST AIRPORT (PWA)

7 mi northwest of town N35-32.06 W97-38.83 Elev: 1299 Fuel: 100LL, Jet-A

Rwy 17L-35R: H7198x150 (Conc) Rwy 13-31: H4213x100 (Conc) Rwy 03-21: H3409x75 (Asph) Rwy 17R-35L: H4232x75 (Asph-Conc) Attended: continuously Atis: 113.4 Unicom: 122.95 OKE City APP/DEP Con: (See AFD) Tower: 126.9 Gnd Con: 121.7

Public Phone 24hrs Notes: Public Tiedowns ($2.00 Singles, $4.00 Twins).

FBO: MillionAir Phone: 787-4040, 495-5520

OK-OKC - OKLAHOMA CITY
WILL ROGERS WORLD AIRPORT

(Area Code 405) 17

CA1 Services:

CA1 Services operates food establishment in addition to other services within the terminal building on the Oklahoma City Will Rogers World Airport. Transportation to and from the fixed base operator and terminal building is provided by AAR Oklahoma, Inc. customers. There are two deli buffeteria centers with cocktail lounges adjoining, 2 snack shops, 1 ice cream/pizza parlor, 1 World Links sausage shop and 2 full service news and gift shops. Menu specialties for the restaurants include chicken fried steak, homemade pizzas, frozen yogurt, World Links hot dogs and sausages, made to order deli sandwiches. Prices average $5.00 to $7.00 for breakfast and between $7.00 and $9.00 for lunch and dinner. Daily specials are also offered at both buffeterias. The decor is open and airy. They can provide on-site catering to groups up to 60 people in a banquet facility that is rented from the airport and is located on the third floor of the terminal building. Their main kitchen is located directly below this facility on the second floor. They also provide catering to private aircraft through AAR Oklahoma, Inc., the main fixed base operator on the field. CA1 Services can tailor catering to meet any need. They currently provide extensive food services through AAR. Orders can be placed through AAR. Your order will then be picked up at CA1 Services and deliver direct to your aircraft. They can also provide any food service you wish including hot meal service if your aircraft is equipped to reheat or hold hot foods. They pride themselves in home-cooked meals and prepare almost everything they serve from scratch, on site. They are widely known for their chicken fried steak which they prepare from scratch. CA1 Services also opened the very first World Links operation in an airport on December 6, 1996, featuring sausage and hot dogs from around the world. Their gift shop features a large selection of products that are made in Oklahoma for that special gift to take back home. For information call 681-5566.

Attractions:

There are many attractions located within this region, that would satisfy the interests of almost everyone. One of the many museums we thought might be of interest, is the 45th Infantry Division Museum located at 2145 N.E. 36th Street in Oklahoma City. This museum exhibits large static displays of weaponry, aircraft, artillery, uniforms, vehicles, and an extensive collection of firearms dating back to the American Revolution. The museum is open Tuesday through Friday from 9 a.m. to 5 p.m., and Saturday from 10 a.m. to 5 p.m. (Closed Monday) This museum is located approximately 15 to 20 miles northeast of the Will Rogers World Airport. Take I-240 east to I-35 and go north 10 or 12 miles until you reach exit 36th street. Exit 36th street going east. You will first pass a golf course, then the museum will be on your right hand side. Admission FREE. For information call 424-5313.

Restaurants Near Airport:
CA1 Services On Site Phone: 681-5566

Lodging: Courtesy vehicle to these facilities: Comfort Inn 681-9000; Courtyard By Marriott 946-6500; Days Inn Oklahoma City 947-8721; Dillon Inn Associates 682-2080; Embassy Suites 682-6000; Fifth Season Inn 843-5558; Saddleback Inn 947-7000; Hilton Inn Northwest 848-4811; Hilton Inn West 947-7681; LaQuinta Motor Inn 631-8661; Lexington Hotel Suites 943-7800; Lincoln Plaza Hotel 428-2741; Marriott Hotel 842-6633; Meridan Plaza 685-4000; Ramada Inn South 631-3321; Residence Inn by Marriott 942-4500; Santa Fe Inn 848-1919; Sheraton Century Center 235-2780; Sheraton-Norman 364-2882; Waterford Hotel 848-4782.

Lodging Within 2 Miles: Courtyard by Marriott, Dillion Inn, Meridian Plaza. (See listing above for phone numbers).

Meeting Rooms: Most of the lodging facilities listed above have accommodations for meetings or conferences.

Transportation: Public Van Service Program: Airport Express 524-8007; Express Shuttle 840-4944; Metro Airport Transportation, Inc. 387-5107; Metro Express, Inc. 842-0764; Royal Coach, Ltd. 685-5466.

Information: Oklahoma Tourism and Recreation Dept, 500 Will Rogers Building, Oklahoma City, OK 73105, Phone: 521-2409; Also Oklahoma City Chamber of Commerce, One Santa Fe Plaza, Oklahoma City, OK 73102; Oklahoma City Convention and Visitors Bureau, Four Santa Fe Plaza, Oklahoma City, OK 73102, Phone: 278-8912 or 800-255-5652.

Airport Information:

OKLAHOMA CITY - WILL ROGERS WORLD AIRPORT (OKC)
6 mi southwest of town N35-23.59 W97-36.04 Elev: 1295 Fuel: 100LL, Jet-A
Rwy 17L-35R: H9802x150 (Asph-Conc-Grvd) Rwy 17R-35L: H9800x150 (Conc-Grvd)
Rwy 13-31: H7800x150 (Asph-Conc-Grvd) Rwy 18-36: H2975x75 (Asph)
Attended: continuously Atis: 125.85 Unicom: 122.95 OKE City App/Dep Con: 124.6, 120.45, 124.2, 126.65, Rogers Tower: 119.35, 120.25 Gnd Con: 121.9 Clnc Del: 124.35 Pre-Taxi Clnc: 124.35 Public phone 24hrs Notes: Landing fees: $.74 per thousand pounds of maximum approved landing weight.
FBO: AAR Oklahoma, Inc. Phone: 681-3000

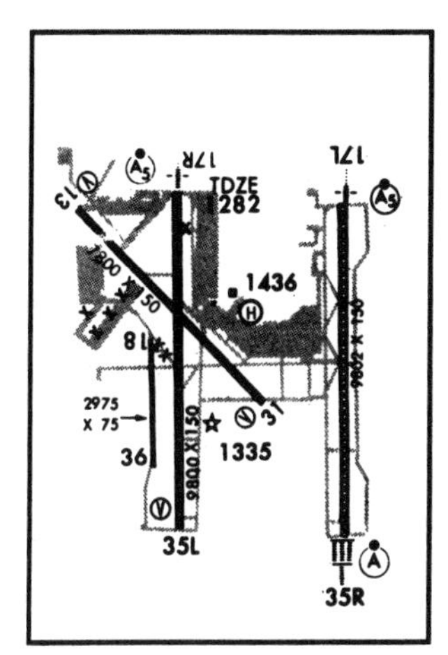

OK-1F1 - OVERBROOK
LAKE MURRAY STATE PARK

(Area Code 405)

18

Fireside Restaurant:

The Fireside Restaurant is located across from the Lake Murray State Resort Park golf course. Guests can park their aircraft at the golf club house at the resort and walk to the restaurant. The Fireside Restaurant staff is also happy to provide courtesy transportation if you call them from the airport. This is an upscale family dining establishment. It has an elegant decor with linen table cloths, candles and flower arrangements for each table. They specialize in serving prime rib. Additional selections of beef are also available with 6 different entrees including t-bone, strip, and fillets. In addition they serve lobster, shrimp, catfish, salmon, orange roughy, chicken, two types of pasta dishes and even a child's menu. Daily specials are provided daily. Prices range from $11.95 and $16.95. The Fireside Restaurant is open between 5 p.m. and 10 p.m. Tuesday through Saturday. There is seating for about 85 people in their main dining room. Additional seating is available in their side rooms for meetings or conferences. Catered meals are available. This restaurant is very popular with many fly-in customers who enjoy a fine meal after a game of golf. For information call the Fireside Restaurant at 226-4070.

Airport Information:

OVERBROOK - LAKE MURRAY STATE PARK (1F1)
2 mi east of town N34-04.51 W97-06.40 Elev: 817 Rwy: 14-32 H2500x50 (Asph)
Attended: unattended Unicom: 122.8
Airport Manager Phone: 223-4044 or 232-6601

Restaurants Near Airport:

Country Inn	1 mi.	Phone: 223-6600
Fireside Restaurant	1/2 mi.	Phone: 226-4070

Lodging: Lake Murray State Park provides accommodations at their lodge as well as guest cottages. Phone: 223-6600.
Meeting Rooms: Lake Murray State Park (1 mi.) has meeting rooms available. Phone: 223-6600. Also Fireside Restaurant has a room off the main dining area for catered meals. Phone: 226-4070.
Transportation: Courtesy cars are available by Lake Murray State Park Resort to their location, 223-6600. Also the Fireside Restaurant will pick up guests, 226-4070.
Information: Ardmore Chamber of Commerce, 6 E Main, P.O. Box 1585, Ardmore, OK 73401. Phone: 223-7765

Attractions:

Lake Murray State Resort Park is only 1 mile from this airport. Park your aircraft at the 18 hole golf course pro shop. The resort is situated about 1 mile away on a 5,728 acre lake. The resort has swimming, paddleboats, 18 hole golf course, miniature golf, sports facilities, lawn games, gift shops, cottages and meeting rooms. For information call the resort at 223-6600.

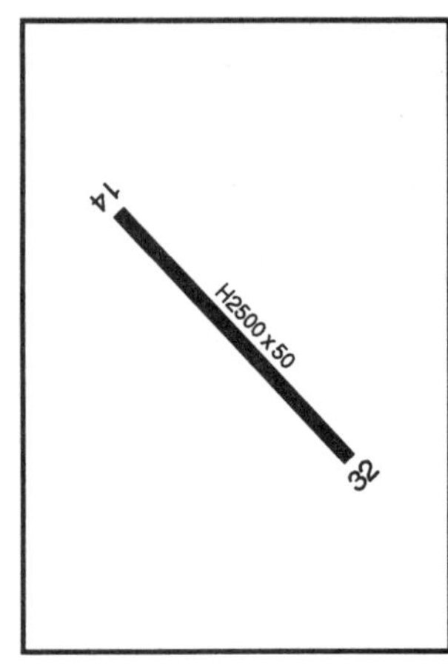

OK-PNC - PONCA CITY
PONCA CITY MUNICIPAL AIRPORT

(Area Code 405)

19

Enrique's Mexican Restaurant:

Enrique's Restaurant is at the Ponca City Municipal Airport at the west side of the field inside the terminal building. This restaurant is positioned about 100 feet from the runway. Large windows allow guests to see the arriving and departing airplanes at the airport while enjoying their meal. This restaurant is considered a family style and fine dining facility open from 11 a.m. to 2 p.m. and 4:30 p.m. to 8 p.m. Monday through Thursday, Friday same hours but open until 9 p.m. and Saturday from 11 a.m. to 9 p.m. throughout the entire year. Their menu contains 17 different items, all of which are freshly made including their corn chips and floured tortillas. Daily lunch specials are offered for $4.25. Average prices run $4.50 for lunch and $7.00 for dinner. The restaurant has a Spanish decor. Fly-in groups and aviation associations are all welcome as well as business travelers. The restaurant caters to pilots on the go providing anything from their menu that they want. This facility is visited by many fly-in customers each year and is very popular with the local towns people. For information call 762-5507.

Restaurants Near Airport:

Enrique's Restaurant	On Site	Phone: 762-5507

Lodging: Marland Estate Hotel 767-0422

Meeting Rooms: Marland Estate Conference Center 767-0422

Transportation: Airport Service Company can accommodate courtesy transportation to nearby facilities; Also Hertz Car Rental is also available at 765-2573

Information: Convention & Visitors Bureau, Box 1109, Ponca City, OK 74602, Phone: 765-4400 or 800-475-4400.

Attractions: Lew Wentz Golf Course (East of city, 5 miles) 762-5156; Lake Ponca (East of city, 5 miles); Marland Estates (3 mile) 55 room mansion of oil baron E.W. Marland features famous art work and painted ceilings, with tours given daily 767-0420 or 0422; Pioneer Woman State Museum (2 miles) honoring the women and their courage during the pioneering days, 765-6108; Kaw Lake (10 miles) 168 miles of shoreline featuring camping, water sports, hunting and boating 762-5611. (See information listed above)

Airport Information:

PONCA CITY - PONCA CITY MUNICIPAL AIRPORT (PNC)
2 mi northwest of town N36-43.84 W97-05.99 Elev: 1007 Fuel: 100LL, Jet-A
Rwy 17-35: H6201x150 (Conc-Grvd) Attended: 1300-0300Z Unicom: 123.0 Public Phone 24hrs
FBO: Greenwood Aviation Phone: 762-2580

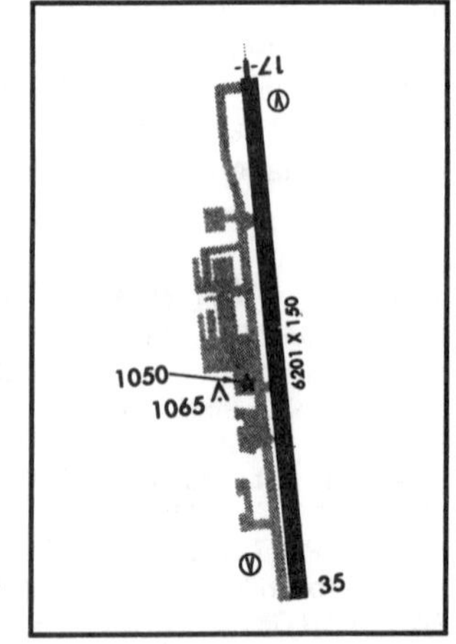

OK-SNL - SHAWNEE
SHAWNEE MUNICIPAL AIRPORT

(Area Code 405)

20

Cinderella Best Western:

This restaurant is classified as a fine dining establishment, and is located 1/2 mile south of the Shawnee Municipal Airport off of 177. Fly-in customers can obtain transportation to and from this restaurant either through the local fixed base operator at the airport, or by calling the restaurant. Their hours are from 6 a.m. to 10 p.m. 7 days a week. Their entrees include a complete breakfast line, including country steaks, rib-eyes, filet mignon, catfish, shrimp, all types of sandwiches, Reubens, patty melts, desserts and fresh baked pies. They also serve a Sunday buffet from 11 a.m. to 2 p.m. as well as a daily buffet Monday through Friday from 11 a.m. to 2 p.m. Their main dining room is elegant with green and mauve colors, linen service, silk plants, and can seat up to 80 persons. Meeting rooms are also available to accommodate groups or parties containing between 20 to 140 people. This complex has just been remodeled and offers lodging for travelers. There are 92 rooms connected to this establishment. A heated swimming pool and whirlpool are available to guests as well. For more information call the Cinderella Best Western at 273-7010.

Restaurants Near Airport:

Amigo's	1 mi SE.	Phone: 275-5552
Anneliese's (German)	3 mi S.	Phone: 273-3041
Cinderella Best Western	1/2 mi S.	Phone: 273-7010
El Burrito Mexican Food	1/2 mi E.	Phone: 273-1682
Holiday Inn	1.5 mi NE.	Phone: 275-4404

Lodging: Cinderella Best Western (1/2 mile south) 273-7010; Holiday Inn (1-1/2 miles northeast) 275-4404.

Meeting Rooms: Cinderella Best Western (1/2 mile south) 273-7010; Holiday Inn (1-1/2 miles northeast) 275-4404.

Transportation: Air Flite, Inc 275-4388 can provide transportation to nearby facilities; Yellow Cab 273-2211; Budget Rentals 275-4388.

Information: Chamber of Commerce, 131 North Bell, P.O. Box 1613, Shawnee, OK 74801, Phone: 273-6092.

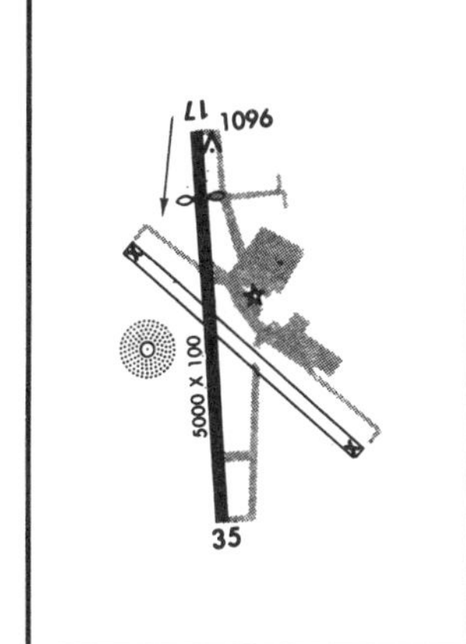

Airport Information:

SHAWNEE - SHAWNEE MUNICIPAL AIRPORT (SNL)
2 mi northwest of town N35-21.33 W96-56.57 Elev: 1073 Fuel; 100LL, Jet-A
Rwy 17-35: H5000x100 (Asph) Attended 1330-0030Z Unicom: 122.7 Notes: For fuel after hours call 800-234-7388. No landing fees
FBO: Air Flite Flightline Phone: 275-4390 or 878-1532
FBO: Air Flite, Inc. Phone: 275-4388

OK-TUL - TULSA
TULSA INTERNATIONAL AIRPORT

(Area Code 918) 21

CA1 Services:

The CA1 Restaurant at Tulsa International Airport is located within the airport terminal building on concourse "A", and can be reached by courtesy transportation through any of the fixed base operators on the field. This combination cafe and buffeteria is open at 5:30 a.m. and closes around 8 p.m. or when the last customer has been served. Their menu provides a large assortment of entrees from which to choose, along with daily specials. Popular items on their menu include chicken spread, turkey and ham and cheese sandwiches on rye, fresh bagels and croissants, cinnamon rolls, Espresso and Cappucino. Prices average $4.50 for breakfast and $5.50 for lunch and dinner. There are 2 separate dining areas available. The main dining area used most often for travelers has accommodations for 160 people. The decor of the restaurant offers a modern atmosphere with background jazz music. A separate dining area especially designed for groups and banquets can seat 40 persons. Guests can enjoy watching the activity on the airport while they dine. In-flight and on site catering needs can also be satisfied. For more information about this restaurant call 838-5163.

Attractions:

Mohawk Golf Course (1 mile north); Tulsa Zoological Organization (1 mile); There are several lakes within 20 miles of airport that provide recreation for the public.

Restaurants Near Airport:

CA1 Services	On Site	Phone: 838-5163

Lodging: The following provide free transportation: Airporter Inn 438-0780; Days Inn 665-6800; Hawthorn Suites 663-3900; Holiday Inn-East Airport 437-7660; Howard Johnson Lodge 665-0220; LaQuinta 254-1626; LaQuinta Motor Inn 836-3931; Ramada Inn-Airport 438-7700; Holiday Inn Central 663-4541; Lexington Hotel Suites 627-0030; Park Plaza Inn 622-7000; Sheraton Inn-Tulsa Airport (On Airport) 835-9911; Doubletree-Downtown 587-8000; Doubletree Hotel At Warren Place 494-1000; Embassy Suites 622-4000; Marriott 627-5000; The Westin Hotel Williams Center 582-9000.

Meeting Rooms: Tulsair Beechcraft, Inc. 835-7651, has a conference room available on the airport; All lodging facilities listed above also contain accommodations for meeting and conference rooms. The following facilities have convention facilities on site: Park Plaza Inn 622-7000; Doubletree Hotel At Warren Place 495-1000; Marriott 627-5000.

Transportation: All fixed base operators (FBO's) on the field will provide local courtesy transportation to nearby facilities. Also, Taxi service: American 321-3539; Checker 582-6611; Green Country Transportation 838-3838; M.Y. 587-6161; Tulsa Airport Taxi 446-6644; Yellow 582-6161; Rental Cars: Alamo 836-0775; Avis 800-331-1212; Avis 800-522-3711; National 800-227-7368; Thrifty 838-3333.

Information: Tulsa International Airport (Information) 838-5000; The Metro Tulsa Chamber of Commerce, 616 South Boston Avenue, Tulsa, OK 74119; Phone: Tulsa Convention & Visitors Bureau, 616 south Boston Avenue, Tulsa, OK 74119; Phone: 585-1201.

Airport Information:

TULSA - TULSA INTERNATIONAL AIRPORT (TUL)
5 mi northeast of town N36-11.90 W95-53.29 Elev: 677 Fuel: 100LL, Jet-A, A1, B
Rwy 18L-36R: H10000x200 (Conc-Grvd) Rwy 08-26: H7695x150 (Conc-Grvd)
Rwy 18R-36L: H6101x150 (Asph) Attended: continuously Atis: 124.9 Unicom: 122.95
App/Dep Con: 120.7 (175-354 degrees), 119.1 (355-174 degrees) Tower 118.7 (Rwy 18R-36L) 121.2 (Rwy 18L-36R and Rwy 08-26) Gnd Con: 121.9 Clnc Del: 134.05 Pre-Taxi Clnc. 134.05 Public Phone 24hrs Notes: No landing fee's for general aviation aircraft. The tiedown fees range form free to $8.00 per night.

FBO: Biz-Jet Intl.	**Phone: 832-7733**
FBO: Intl Business Aircraft	**Phone: 836-8895**
FBO: Million Air, Tulsa	**Phone: 836-6592**
FBO: Sparks Aviation	**Phone: 835-2048**

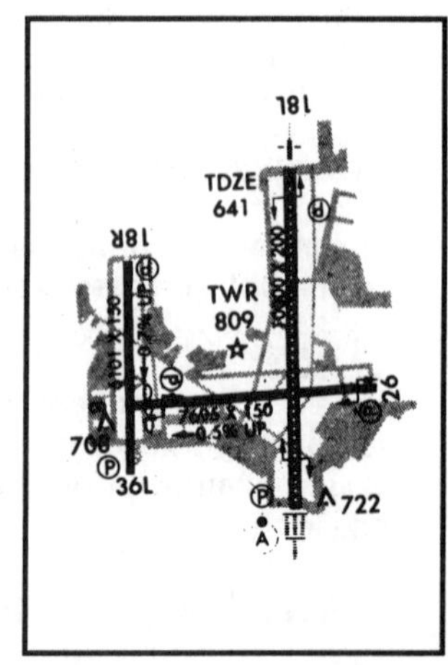

OK-H04 - VINITA
VINITA MUNICIPAL AIRPORT

(Area Code 918)

22

McDonalds:

This McDonalds restaurant is located adjacent to the Vinita Municipal Airport and can easily be reached by walking. Their summer hours are from 5:30 a.m. to 12 a.m. Sunday through Thursday and 5:30 a.m. to 1 a.m. Friday and Saturday; During the winter, their restaurant hours are from 6 a.m. to 11 p.m. Sunday through Thursday and 6 a.m. to 12 a.m. on Friday & Saturday. This family style restaurant is one of the largest, if not, the largest McDonalds fast food restaurant in the country. Seating capacity in their main dining room can accommodate 450 persons. Meeting rooms are also available to handle 50 people. Groups and parties can easily be served. All meals can be prepared for carry-out. Their menu is not unlike that of the standard McDonalds franchise, including items like the famous Big Mack, 1/4 pounder, cheeseburgers, hamburgers, chicken McNuggets, Crispy Chicken Deluxe, Fish Filet Deluxe, as well as breakfast items like scrambled eggs, sausage, pancakes, toast and biscuits. Average prices run $3.25 for breakfast, $3.90 for lunch and dinner. For more information call them at 256-5571.

Restaurants Near Airport:

McDonalds	Adj Arpt	Phone: 256-5571
Subway	3/4 mi	Phone: N/A

Lodging: Deward & Pauline's (2-1/2 miles) 256-6492; Holiday Motel (2-1/2 mile) 256-2369; Park Hill Motel (3 miles) 256-5511; Vinita Inn (1-1/2 mile) 256-2369; Western Motel 256-7542.

Meeting Rooms: McDonalds Restaurant (Adj. Arpt) 256-5571.

Transportation: Howe's Taxi 256-5503; Rental Cars: C.R. Moore Motor Co 256-6455; Green Country Ford 256-7525.

Information: Chamber of Commerce, 104 East Illinois, P.O. Box 882, Vinita, OK 74301, Phone: 256-7133.

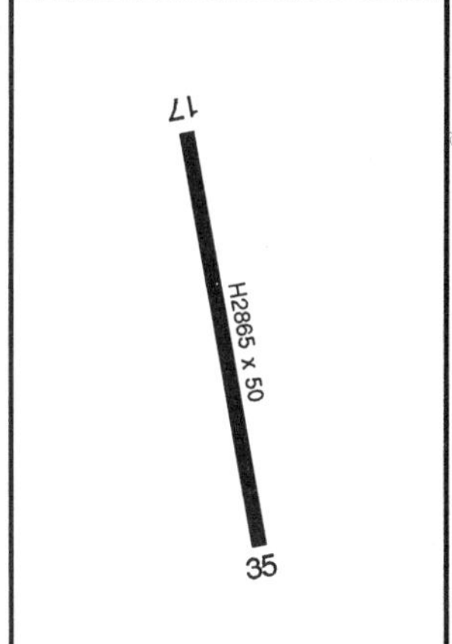

Airport Information:

VINITA - VINITA MUNICIPAL AIRPORT (H04)
2 mi southeast of town N36-37.09 W95-08.86 Elev: 696
Rwy 17-35: H2865x50 (Asph) Attended: unattended Unicom: 122.8 Notes: Check AFD for runway condition; For fuel on request call 256-8552 or 256-6414
Vinita Municipal Airport Phone: 256-8552 or 256-6414.

OREGON

LOCATION MAP

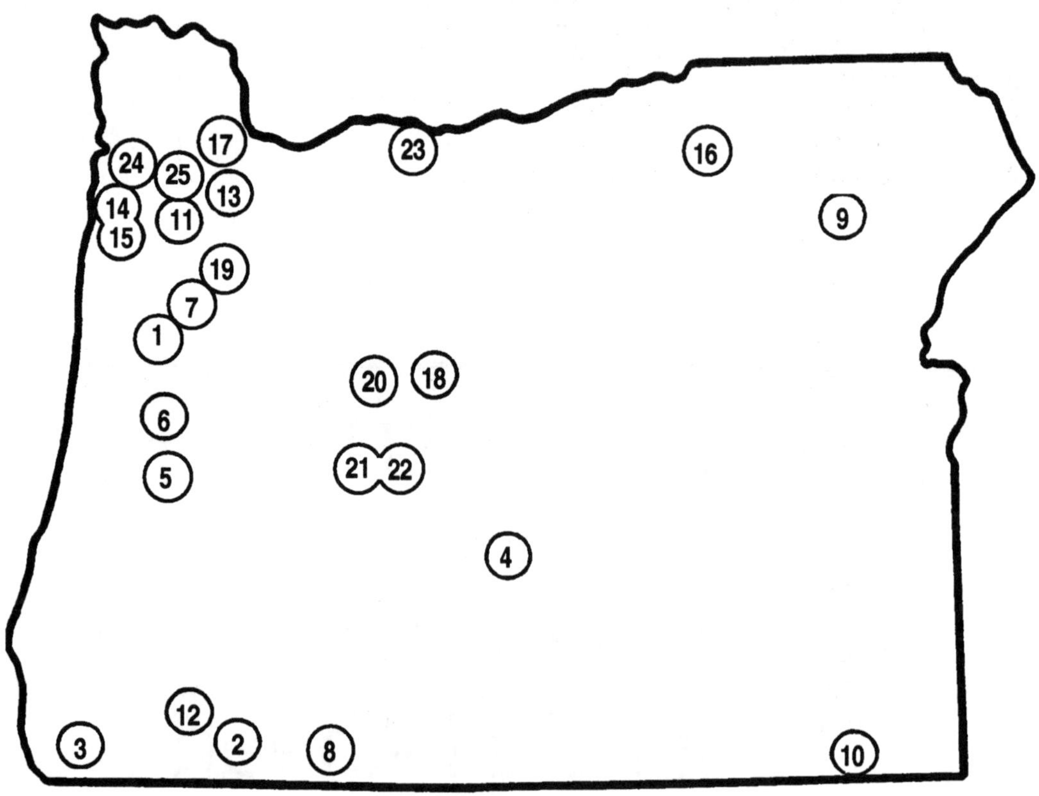

Not to be used for navigational purposes

OREGON

CROSS FILE INDEX

Location Number	City or Town	Airport Name And Identifier	Name of Attraction
1	Albany	Albany Muni. Arpt. (S12)	Burgundy's Restaurant
2	Ashland	Ashland Muni. Summer Fld. (S03)	Omar's Seafood & Stks.
3	Cave Junction	Illinois Valley (3S4)	Stevereno's Arpt. Rest.
4	Christmas Valley	Christmas Valley Arpt. (62S)	Christmas Valley Lodge
5	Cottage Grove	Cottage Grove State (619)	Village Green
6	Eugene	Mahlon Sweet Field (EUG)	Flight Line Inn
7	Independence	Independence State (7S5)	Annie's Restaurant
8	Klamath Falls	Klamath Falls Intl. (LMT)	Satellite Restaurant
9	La Grande	Minam Ldg. H.C. Outfitters (6OR9)	Minam Lodge
10	Mc Dermitt	Mc Dermitt State Arpt. (26U)	Say When Cafe
11	Mc Minnville	Mc Minnville Muni. Arpt. (MMV)	The Red Caboose
12	Medford	Rogue Valley Intl.-Medford (MFR)	Red Barn Restaurant
13	Newberg	Sportsmans Airpark (2S6)	Jay's Restaurant
14	Pacific City	Pacific City State Arpt. (PFC)	Fat Freddy's
15	Pacific City	Pacific City State Arpt. (PFC)	Loscaporales Mex. Rest.
16	Pendleton	Eastern Oregon Reg. (PDT)	Hangar Snack Bar
17	Portland	Portland-Hillsboro Arpt. (HIO)	Eddie Rickenbacker's
18	Redmond	Roberts Field (RDM)	Mrs. Beasley's
19	Salem	Mc Nary Field (SLE)	Flight Deck Restaurant
20	Sisters	Sisters Eagle Air (6K5)	Cascade Cntry. Inn B&B
21	Sunriver	Sunriver Arpt. (S21)	Meadows Restaurant
22	Sunriver	Sunriver Arpt. (S21)	Provision Company
23	The Dalles	The Dalles Muni. (DLS)	Buzzin'in Cafe & Cakes
24	Tillamook	Tillamook Arpt. (S47)	Blimp Hangar (Attraction)
25	Yamhill	Flying "M" Ranch (OR05)	Flying "M" Ranch

Articles

City or town	Nearest Airport and Identifier	Name of Attraction
Baker City, OR	Baker City Muni. (BKE)	Oregon Trail Center
Sunriver, OR	Sunriver Arpt. (S21)	Sunriver Resort
Tillamook, OR	Tillamook Arpt. (S47)	Blimp Hangar & Air Mus.

OR-S12 - ALBANY
ALBANY MUNICIPAL AIRPORT

(Area Code 541)

1

Restaurants Near Airport:

A Taste of Thai At Burgundy's	On Site	Phone: 926-0198
Novak's Hungarian Rest.	2 mi W.	Phone: 967-9488
Wah Lee Restaurant	2 mi W.	Phone: 967-1862
Yaquima Bay Restaurant	1 mi W.	Phone: 967-8420

Lodging: Pony Soldier Motel 928-6322; Motel Orleans 926-0170.

Meeting Rooms: Pony Soldier Motel 928-6322; Motel Orleans 926-0170.

Transportation: Albany Taxi 926-5588; Albany Yellow Cab 926-2263; Timber Town Taxi 926-5588.

Information: Visitors Association, 300 Southwest 2nd Avenue, P.O. Box 965, Albany, OR 97321, Phone: 928-0911or 800-526-2256.

A Taste of Thai At Burgundy's:

This restaurant is located on the Albany Municipal Airport. After landing at the airport, customers can take the taxiway to a private tie down area that is open to the public, and is situated very close to the restaurant. This facility is a combination family style and fine dining establishment that is open from 7 a.m. to 9 p.m. on weekdays and from 7 a.m. to 10 p.m. on weekends. Their menu includes a full breakfast line as well as hamburgers, Mexican foods, a variety of salads, fettucini, scallops, steaks and seafood selections. They also feature a Sunday brunch that is served between 10 a.m. and 2 p.m. Average prices run $4.95 for breakfast and lunch and $6.95 to $7.95 for dinner. The decor of the restaurant is casual yet elegant with soft background music, chandeliers and lots of large windows to see the activity on the airport. On special occasions they offer linen service. There are 5 separate banquet rooms available for anyone planning a party or group fly-in. Banquet and catering service is one of their specialties. For more information about Burgundy's Restaurant you can call them at 926-0198.

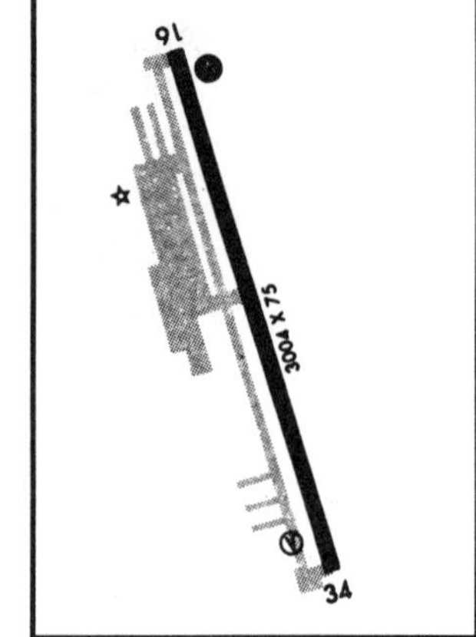

Airport Information:

ALBANY - ALBANY MUNICIPAL AIRPORT (S12)
3 mi east of town N44-38.27 W123-03.57 Elev: 223 Fuel: 80, 100LL
Rwy 16-34: H3000x75 (Asph) Attended: 1600-0100Z Unicom: 122.8 Public Phone 24hrs
FBO: Reliant Aviation **Phone: 928-3232**

OR-S03 - ASHLAND
ASHLAND MUNICIPAL SUMMER PARKER FLD.

(Area Code 541)

2

Restaurants Near Airport:

Ashland Hills Inn	1/2 mi W.	Phone: 482-8310
Beasy's Back Room	3 mi NE.	Phone: 482-2141
The Copper Skillet	1 mi W.	Phone: 482-2684
Omar's	2 mi NW.	Phone: 482-1281

Lodging: Ashland Hills Inn (Free Pick-up, 1/2 mile west) 482-8310
Meeting: Ashland Hills Inn (Free Pick-up) has accommodations for meetings. Restaurant on premises, 482-8310.
Transportation: Courtesy car available at Ashland Air, Inc. 503-488-1626. Also Ashland Hills Inn & restaurant will provide transportation for pilots and their guests, 482-8310.
Information: Chamber of Commerce, 110 E Main Street, P.O. Box 1360, Ashland, OR 97520, Phone: 482-3486.

Omar's Fresh Seafood & Steaks:

Omar's restaurant is a fine dining facility that is situated 2 miles west of the Ashland Municipal Airport. Leaving the airport, take highway 66 to the intersection of Hwy 99 (Siskiyou Blvd). Their specialty is fresh seafood with 6 or more choices each evening and a choice of beef. They offer a complete menu with numerous daily specials including appetizers, soups and desserts. They also offer a full service lunch weekdays from 11:30 to 2 p.m. and dinner from 5 p.m. to 10 p.m. every night. On Saturday night they feature prime rib. Prices average $5.00 for lunch and $10.00 for dinner. Established in 1946, Omar's restaurant is the oldest continually operated restaurant in Ashland. It provides a traditional atmosphere reminiscent of the 40's, 50's and 60's. Old photos, menus, and table side juke boxes, add to the lively atmosphere. For information call 482-1281.

Attractions:

Oak Knoll Golf Course, 1 mile south 482-4311; Emigrant Lake Recreation Area, 4 miles east 776-7001; Oregon Shakespeare Festival 3 miles north 482-4331.

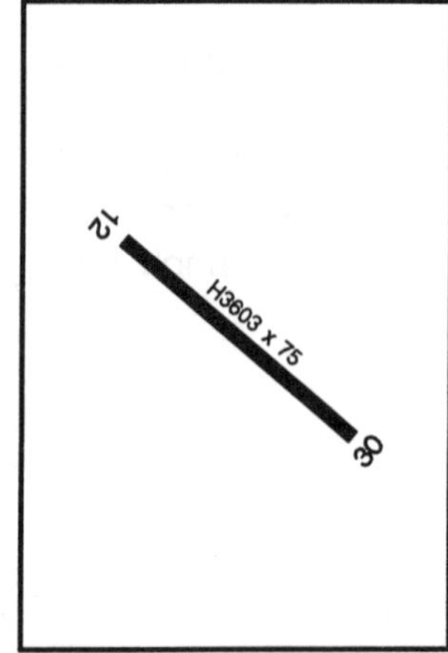

Airport Information:

ASHLAND - ASHLAND MUNI. SUMMER PARKER FLD. (S03)
2 mi east of town N42-11.42 W122-39.64 Elev: 1894 Fuel: 80, 100LL, Jet-A
Rwy 12-30: H3603x75 (Asph) Attended: Oct-Apr 1600-0100Z, May-Sept 1600-0300Z, If attendant unavailable, call 482-5096. Unicom: 122.8 Public Phone 24hrs Notes: Overnight parking fees: $3.00 singles, $5.00 twins.
FBO: Steve Green Aircraft Refinishing **Phone: 482-2635**

Oregon Trail Interpretive Center

Baker City, OR (OR-BKE)

The Oregon Trail Historical Site is a unique attraction designed to educate and inform the general public about the fascinating journey and heroic adventures of pioneers that made the epic trek across the country by wagon train. As a pilot you can appreciate the almost unbelievable contrast between conventional means of travel 200 years ago compared with the ease in hopping into your flying machine and traveling 150 miles for a hamburger. What takes literally minutes by air took the pioneers weeks and months to accomplish. The significance of the Oregon Trail Historical Site encompasses a 23,000 square foot facility that tells the life stories of actual travelers taken from diaries of those who made the historic journey.

After landing at Baker City Municipal Airport, you will need to call Baker City Cab at 523-6070 for transportation over to the Historical Center. Its about 3 to 4 miles and will cost about $19.00 (Round Trip) for the day. There is no additional charge for extra persons.

Once reaching the Oregon Trail Interpretive Center, you will begin your tour by experiencing a life size diorama complete with covered wagon, landscaping, sage brush and 23 different types of animals, birds and reptiles synonymous with the region. As you make your way through the museum, you will watch a movie presentation about a pioneer town, then travel on your way with more dioramas exhibiting a wagon train river-crossing, trading camp, and farming exhibits. After your tour of the indoor portion of the Interpretive Center, you will travel outdoors to actually visit a portion of preserved Oregon Trail. Saturday and Sunday local volunteers dress in period costume and re-enact the actual wagon train life-style. Although there is no admission to the Interpretive Center, a contribution of your choice would be greatly appreciated. For more information about the Oregon Trail Interpretive Center call 503-523-1843.

Photo by: Oregon Trail Interpretive Center

OR-3S4- CAVE JUNCTION ILLINOIS VALLEY

3

Stevereno's Airport Restaurant:

This restaurant has recently come under new management and is located on the Illinois Valley Airport. Pilots can land and taxi right up and park their aircraft in front of the restaurant. Hours of operation are Tuesday and Wednesday 7 a.m. to 4 p.m.; Thursday, Friday and Saturday 7 a.m. to 9 p.m.; and Sunday 8 a.m. to 5 p.m. Specialties of the house include breakfast dishes like omelets, ham and egg dishes, 8 different omelet choices, French toast, waffles, and biscuits and gravy. Lunch and dinner selections include items like BLT sandwiches, roast beef, tuna melts, French dip sandwiches, chicken breasts, Phili sandwiches, BBQ beef, 6 different types of hamburgers, chili burgers, and chef salads. During our conversation with the new owner we learned that since menu selection and service has greatly improved since the previous owner, the restaurant has seen an increase in fly-in business. The inside of the restaurant has also been remodeled with a pleasant and homey atmosphere. Many hand-crafted items are on display as well as antiques. The dining room can accommodate up to 50 people. Fly-in groups are welcome with advance notice, please. Plans for the future include an outdoor dining patio with gazebo and water fountain equipped with lighting for evening dining. For information call Stevereno's Airport Restaurant at 592-2244.

Restaurants Near Airport: **(Area Code 541)**

Chalet Dinner House	4.5 mi N	Phone: 492-4299
Stevereno's Arpt. Rest.	On Site	Phone: 592-2244

Lodging: Junction Inn (60 rooms, 4 miles) 592-3106; Holiday Motel (18 rooms, 5 miles) 592-3003;
Meeting Rooms: Accommodations at airpaort can be arranged for up to 60 people; House of Haywood Restaurant at airport can also provide an additional 50 seats. Phone: 474-5285 for airport and 592-3572 for House of Haywood Restaurant.
Transportation: House of Haywood can provide (free) local transportation to nearby motels, 592-3572; "Tours, Co." 592-4765.
Information: Illinois Valley Chamber of Commerce, 201 Caves Hwy, P.O. Box 312, Cave Junction, OR 97523, Phone: 592-3326

Attractions:

Local golf course open to public (5 miles north) 592-3525; State Park 4 miles north; Oregon Cave 18 miles N.E. of arpt. 592-3400;

Airport Information:

CAVE JUNCTION - ILLINOIS VALLEY (3S4)

4 mi southwest of town N42-06.26 W123-40.94 Elev: 1389
Rwy 18-36: H5200x75 (Asph) Attended: dawn to dusk Unicom: 122.8 Public Phone 24 hrs
Notes: Gasoline & repair, hangar space, tie downs, 14 hotel accommodations, (bring own bedding), RV park, large new showers & restrooms, free to public. Also sky jumper training available at airport. Phone: 592-2874.
Airport Manager (Parks Dept.) Phone: 474-5290

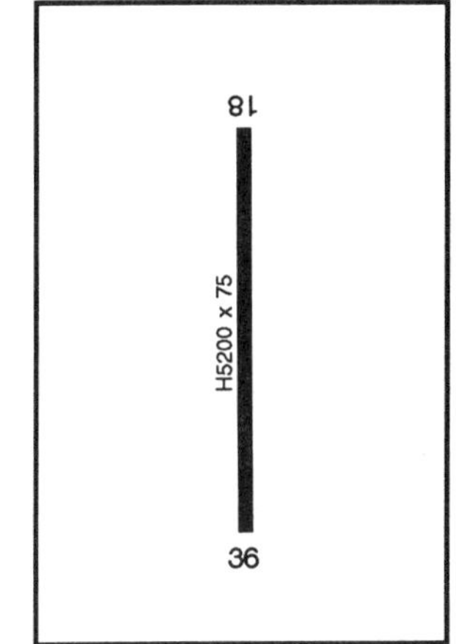

OR-62S - CHRISTMAS VALLEY
CHRISTMAS VALLEY AIRPORT

(Area Code 541) 4

Christmas Valley Lodge:

Christmas Valley Lodge is located about 1/2 mile from the municipal airport. This establishment should be within walking distance. However, if courtesy transportation is desired, you can arrange this in advance. The restaurant is open from 7 a.m. to 9 p.m. 7 days a week. Their menu includes items like their "Captains Plate", steaks, liver and onions, veal, cod, oysters, clam strips, chicken strips and beef strips. A full line of breakfast foods are available, along with a salad bar, and daily specials. Everything is made from scratch, nothing out of the box. Christmas Valley Lodge has its own 9 hole golf course with the first tee off only a few feet from their back door. Fly out and enjoy a game of golf, then a fine meal at Christmas Valley Lodge. For more information call them at 576-2333.

Restaurants Near Airport:

Christmas Valley Lodge	1/2 mi NW	Phone: 576-2333
Lakeside Terrace	1-1/4 mi NW	Phone: 576-2309
The Trail Cafe & Tavern	1/3 mi NW	Phone: 576-2345

Lodging: Desert Inn (1/2 mile) 576-2262; Lakeside Terrace (1-1/4 mile northwest) 576-2309.

Meeting Rooms: Accommodations are available for small groups at Christmas Valley Lodge, (1/2 mile northwest) 576-2333.

Transportation: Arrangements for courtesy transportation to Christmas Valley Lodge should be made prior to arrival by calling them at 576-2333.

Information: State of Oregon Economic Development Department Tourism Division, 775 Summer Street N.E., Salem, OR 97310, Phone: 1-800-547-7842.

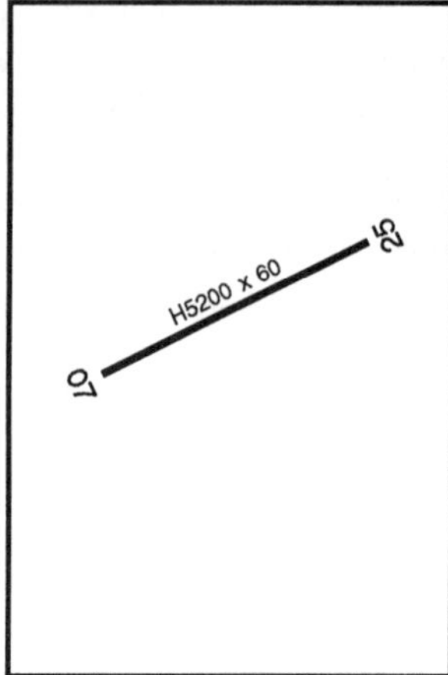

Airport Information:

CHRISTMAS VALLEY - CHRISTMAS VALLEY AIRPORT (62S)
1 mi southeast of town N43-14.19 W120-39.97 Elev: 4317 Fuel: 100, Jet-A, MOGAS
Rwy 07-25: H5200x60 (Asph) Attended: daylight hours Unicom: 122.9
FBO: G.A.A.S., Inc. Phone: 576-2525

OR-619 - COTTAGE GROVE
COTTAGE GROVE STATE

(Area Code 541) 5

Village Green (Best Western):

The Village Green Motel complex contains a coffee shop, formal dining room, banquet facilities, 96 ground floor lodging units, swimming pool and nearby recreational amenities including golfing, nature trails and fishing all within a mile of the Cottage Grove State Airport. The Coffee Shop within the complex is open 6:30 a.m. to 9 p.m. daily and serves a full entree selection: omelets, Belgium waffles, chicken pot pie, hamburgers, sub sandwiches, steaks and even prime rib. The coffee shop serves breakfast, lunch and dinner specials and can seat about 30 to 45 persons. The Castadia Dining Room provides a more formal and elegant dining experience for guests. This restaurant is open 5 p.m. to 10 p.m. Wednesday through Sunday. Specialties of the house include an assortment of appetizers like prawn cocktail, oyster cocktail and French onion soup. Main course items include roast prime rib, New York steak, filet mignon, roasted rack of lamb, North Pacific salmon, Northwest halibut and chicken dishes. Dinners include soup and salad and choice of baked, roasted or red potato. The view from the restaurant is beautiful overlooking the pool area. When talking to Cottage Grove Aviation (FBO) we were informed that an extended taxiway and a small aircraft parking area allows pilots to park their aircraft across the street to the motel. Also they mentioned that a stream winding its way around the airport provides a nice location to do some rainbow trout fishing. A camping area is also located near the remote tie-down spot as well. Also adjacent to the airport is a golf course. Transportation can be arranged by Cottage Grove Aviation as well as Village Green guests. For information about Village Green call 942-2491 or 800-343-7666.

Restaurants Near Airport:

Village Green Castadia	Adj.	Phone: 942-2491
Village Green Coffee Shop	Adj.	Phone: 942-2491

Lodging: Village Green, 96 units, across the street from the airport using extended taxiway. 942-2491 or 800-343-7666.

Meeting Rooms: Village Green Motel has banquet and meeting room facilities available. Phone: 942-2491 or 800-343-7666.

Transportation: Airport courtesy reported. Taxi service: Sunflower Cottage Grove 942-0839.

Information: Cottage Grove Area Chamber of Commerce, 710 Row River Road, P.O. Box 587, Cottage Grove, OR 97424, Phone: 942-2411.

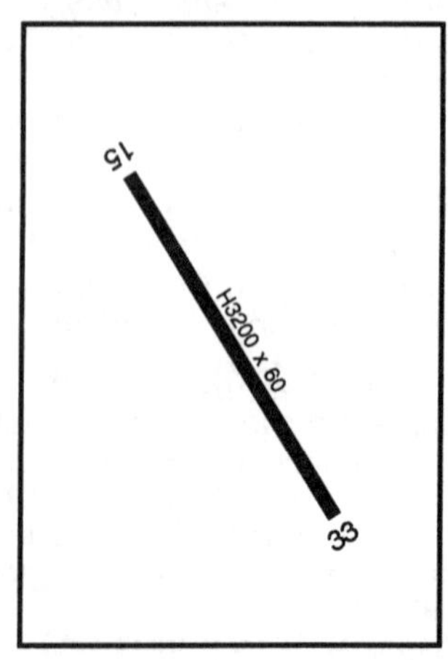

Airport Information:

COTTAGE GROVE - COTTAGE GROVE STATE (61S)
1 mi east of town N43-47.99 W123-01.74 Elev: 640 Fuel: 80, 100LL Rwy 15-33: H3200X60 (Asph) Attended: dawn to dusk Unicom: 122.8
FBO: Cottage Grove Aviation Phone: 942-0663

OR-EUG - EUGENE
MAHLON SWEET FIELD

(Area Code 541) 6

Restaurants Near Airport:
Flight Line Inn On Site Phone: 688-9433

Flight Line Inn:

The Flight Line Inn Restaurant is located in the terminal building on the Mahlon Sweet Field Airport near Eugene Oregon. To reach the restaurant, you can enter the access gates to the terminal building off the main ramp or arrange courtesy transportation if parking your aircraft at one of the fixed base operators on the field. The terminal building includes 2 snack bars and a combination family style and fine dining restaurant. Flight Line Inn restaurant is open between 5:30 a.m. and 7:00 p.m. 7 days a week. Winter hours may vary slightly. Their menu includes several specialized items, such as four basic varieties of chicken and poultry specials, 7 different types of hamburgers, Mexican dishes, and their "Clubhouse Steak," a popular choice of many customers. Average prices run $5.50 for breakfast; $6.00 for lunch and up to $7.50 for dinner. The decor of the restaurant has an aviation theme and is decorated with as many as 50 beautiful line drawings of models and vintage airplanes. Natural wood paneling and carpeted floors add to the atmosphere of this restaurant. Aviation groups and clubs often make fly-in arrangements for their organizations. A combination gift and travelers shop is also located near the restaurant, and is available for visitors to browse through. For more information call the Flight Line Inn at 688-9433.

Lodging: Nendels Inn (12 miles) 726-1212; Red Lion Eugene (10 miles) 342-5201; Red Lion Springfield (12 miles) 726-8181; Holiday Inn (10 miles) 342-5181; Shilo Inn (12 miles) 747-0332; Valley River Inn (12 miles) 341-3460; Eugene Hilton (15 miles) 342-2000.
Meeting Rooms: None Reported
Transportation: Avis 688-9053; Budget 344-4645; Hertz 688-9333; National 688-8161; Also taxi service is available at the airport.
Information: Eugene/Springfield Convention & Visitors Bureau, P.O. Box 10286, Eugene, OR 97440, Phone: 484-5307.

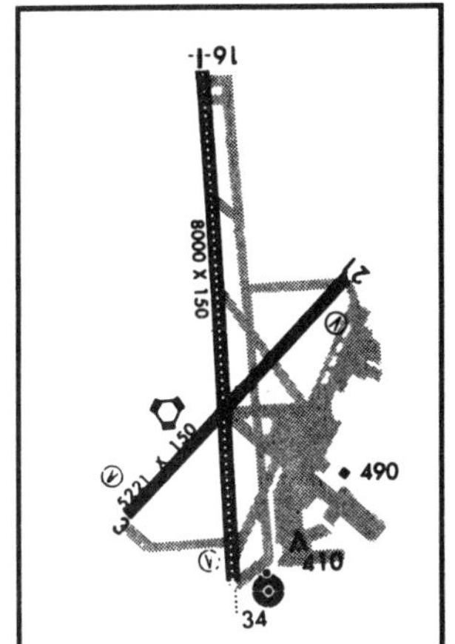

Airport Information:

EUGENE - MAHLON SWEET FIELD (EUG)
7 mi northwest of town N44-07.40 W123-13.12 Elev: 365 Fuel: 100LL, Jet-A
Rwy 16-34: H8000x150 (Asph-Grvd) Rwy 03-21: H5221x150 (Asph) Attended: continuously
Atis: 125.2 Unicom: 122.95 Tower: 118.9 Gnd Con/Clnc Del: 121.7 Public Phone available between 5:30 a.m. and Midnight
FBO: Aerial Communications Phone: 689-3331
FBO: Flightcraft, Inc. Phone: 688-9291

OR-7S5 - INDEPENDENCE
INDEPENDENCE STATE

(Area Code 503) 7

Restaurants Near Airport:
Annie's Restaurant On Site Phone: 838-5632

Annie's Restaurant:

Annie's Restaurant is located on the Independence State Airport. You can park your airplane on the ramp at the fixed base operator and walk to their front door only a few feet away. This is a popular restaurant for many pilots. A redwood deck that overlooks the main ramp can seat 20 people for outdoor dining. Large windows allow a nice view from within the restaurant. Their hours of operation are from 8 a.m. to 3 p.m., 7 days a week. Breakfast and lunch entrees are their specialty. Freshly baked muffins can be enjoyed, along with other morning delights, such as three-egg omelets, pancakes and eggs, waffles, French toast, oat meal and specially prepared hashbrowns made from red potatoes. Their luncheon entrees include 9 deli style sandwiches, along with 7 different types of burgers. Their "Maxi-burger" is a 1/3rd pound beef patty topped with Monterey Jack cheese and served with guacamole and sour cream. Other selections include: the "Garden Burger", stuffed tomatoes, and 5 different salads. They also make their own salsa. Desserts include: 5 different ice cream sundaes, and homemade pies and cobblers that are prepared daily. Annie's Restaurant offers catering for groups for up to 40 people, as well as for groups of up to 20 people on their outdoor deck. In-flight catering is also available for pilots-on-the-go, with advance notice preferred. Average prices run $5.00 to $8.00 for most breakfast or lunch selections. Daily specials are served Monday through Friday. Some favorites include: tropical chicken salad, lasagna and beef stew. When speaking with the manager, we also learned that there are several nearby golf courses and wineries in the area that give tours. For information, call Annie's at 838-5632.

Lodging: Howell's Bed & Breakfast (Courtesy trans) Phone: 838-2085.
Meeting Rooms: Catering at Annie's Restaurant 838-5632.
Transportation: Rental cars available; Agency 362-2616. Also, check with Airport manager's office by calling 378-4880.
Information: Salem Convention & Visitor Association, 1313 Mill Street S.E., Salem, OR 97301, Phone: 581-4325.

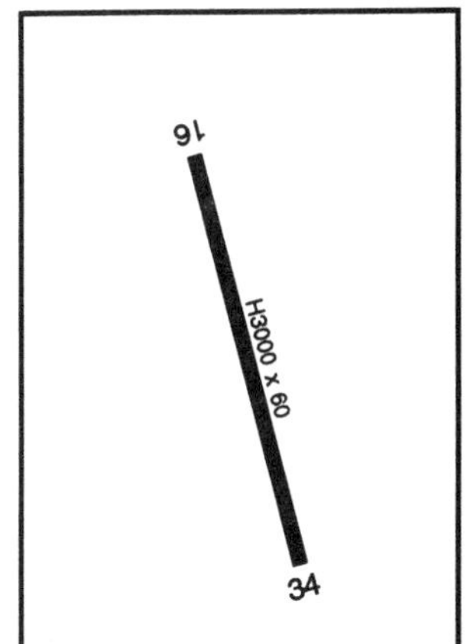

Airport Information:

INDEPENDENCE - INDEPENDENCE STATE (7S5)
1 mi northwest of town N44-52.01 W123-11.90 Elev: 176 Fuel: 80, 100 Rwy 16-34: H3000x60 (Asph) Attended daylight hours CTAF/Unicom: 122.8 Notes: Residential airpark
FBO: Buswell Flying Service: Phone: 838-3737
FBO: Mac's Aircraft Service: Phone: 838-0164
FBO: Thomson Aviation, Inc. (Fuel) Phone: 838-0313

OR-LMT - KLAMATH FALLS
KLAMATH FALLS INTERNATIONAL

(Area Code 503) 8

Satellite Restaurant & Lounge:

The Satellite Restaurant & Lounge is situated within the terminal building at the Klamath Falls International Airport. Pilots can park their aircraft within a short distance of the restaurant. This is a family dining establishment that is open from 7:30 a.m. to 9:00 p.m. 7 days a week. A lounge area is located within the restaurant. Specialties on their menu include prime rib and scampi, steaks and seafood. Average prices run $4.00 for breakfast, $4.25 for lunch and around $11.00 for dinner selections. Large windows all around allow a great view of the airport active areas. The interior of the restaurant is decorated in earth tones. Fly-in groups as well as business clients are welcome. Catering service is also provided as well. Many local customers drive in just to watch the air traffic while enjoying a fine meal. For more information about the Satellite Restaurant & Lounge call 882-5509

Restaurants Near Airport:
Satellite Restaurant On Site Phone: 882-5509

Lodging: Best Western Klamath Inn 3 mi 882-1200; Best Western Olympic Inn 3 mi 882-9665; Cimarron Motel 3 mi 882-4601; Comfort Inn 3 mi 884-9999; Thunderbird Motel 3 mi 882-8864.

Meeting Rooms: Best Western Klamath Inn 3 mi 882-1200; Comfort Inn 3 mi 884-9999.

Transportation: Airport courtesy reported; Also: Taxi service: A & B's 885-5607; Rental cars: Avis 882-7232; Budget 885-5421; Hertz 882-0220.

Information: Klamath County Department of Tourism, 1451 Main St., Klamath Falls, OR 97601, Phone: 884-0666.

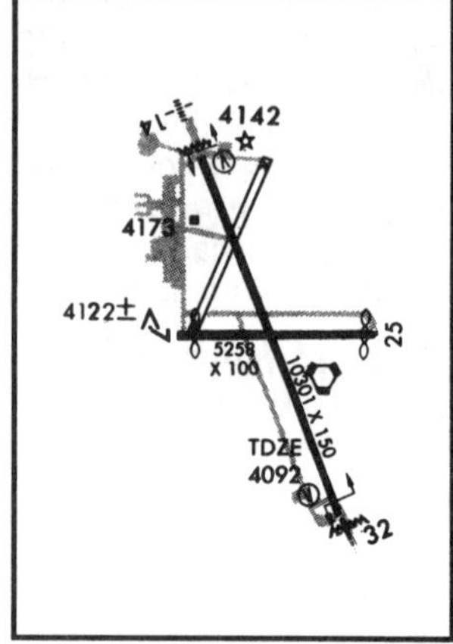

Airport Information:

KLAMATH FALLS - KLAMATH FALLS INTERNATIONAL (LMT)
4 mi southeast of town N42-09.37 W121-43.99 Elev: 4092 Fuel: 100LL, Jet-A Rwy 14-32: H10301x150 (Asph-Conc-Pfc) Rwy 07-25: H5258x100 (Asph-Pfc) Attended: 1500-0600Z Atis: 126.5 Unicom: 122.95 Tower: 118.5 Gnd Con: 121.9
FBO: Klamath Aircraft, Inc. Phone: 882-4681

OR-6OR9 - LA GRANDE
MINAM LODGE
HIGH COUNTRY OUTFITTERS

(Area Code 541) 9

Restaurants Near Airport:
Minam Lodge 500 yds Phone: 432-9171

Lodging: Minam Lodge - High Country Outfitters, 432-9171

Meeting Rooms: Not Reported

Transportation: Airport within walking distance (500 yards) to Minam lodge, 432-9171.

Information: High Country Outfitters, Minam Lodge, Box 26, Joseph, Oregon 97846, Phone: 503-432-9171.

Minam Lodge:

Minam Lodge is located in the Eagle Cap Wilderness. This facility is accessible only by horseback or airplane. Their rustic cabins have showers, bathrooms and wood heat. There is a large eating lodge with a fireplace. Everyone enjoys the exhilarating freedom of the great outdoors: fresh air, clean water, streams, brisk early mornings and the warmth of good companionship... they are all a part of the unique and friendly Minam Lodge. The Minam River flows through the property so fishing is close by and Beaver Lake is 1/2 mile away with excellent fishing. They have their own private airstrip if you wish to fly your own plane in. Their airstrip is about 2600 feet long. It is a two way dirt & sod strip. Reds Horse Ranch strip is just above theirs so you need to fly over the strips to see if there are any other planes landing or departing and transmit on 122.9 and 122.8 giving your intentions of landing or departing. If you wish their pilots to fly you in they fly out of LaGrande, Oregon and Enterprise, Oregon. If you wish to ride in on Horseback, they will pick you up at Moss SP Campground which is 8 miles from Cove, Oregon. If you are riding through or flying, you can stop for a meal and fine company at the Minam Lodge. Prices for breakfast & lunch runs $10.00 per person and $15.00 for dinner. For more information about lodging and entertainment, overnight pack trips, hunting trips, summer drop camps, and summer progressive trips call Minam Lodge at 432-9171.

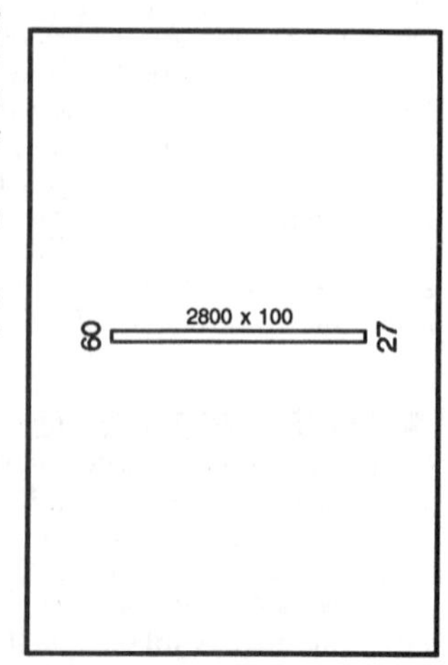

Airport Information:

LA GRANDE - HIGH COUNTRY OUTFITTERS (6OR9) Private Airport
22 mi east of town 45-20-30N 117-37-30W Elev: 3600 Fuel: None reported
Rwy 9-27: 2800x100 (Turf-Gravl) Attended: not reported Notes: See "Restaurant description above." Private use facility, use at own risk. Call Minam Lodge for runway information.
Minam Lodge Phone: 432-9171

OR-26U - MC DERMITT
MC DERMITT STATE AIRPORT

(Area Code 503 for airport)
(Area Code 702 for town)

10

"Say When Cafe":

The "Say When Cafe" is located 1/4 mile from the Mc Dermitt State Airport, and is situated well within walking distance from the airport. This cafe is open 24 hours, and is the only restaurant within the town. Their menu contains a large variety of breakfast, lunch and dinner selections. Breakfast is served all day. Some of their specialty items include their special "Say When Steaks," a variety of sandwiches and breakfast specials, pancake specials, and clam chowder soup served on Friday. Average prices run $3.50 for breakfast, $4.00 for lunch and $6.00 for dinner. The decor is very casual and comfortable. Their motto is "come as you" are. The main dining room can seat up to 100 people. Art displays and pictures made by local artists decorate the walls. In addition to the restaurant, this establishment also contains a casino with 21 gaming tables available. The area code for the airport and town differ due to the fact that they are situated on either side of the Oregon state border. For more information you can call the restaurant at 702-532-8515, and the airport at 503-378-4880.

Restaurants Near Airport:
"Say When Cafe" 1/4 mi Phone: 702-532-8515

Lodging: Mc Dermitt Motel, Phone: 702-532-8588

Meeting Rooms: None Reported

Transportation: "Say When Cafe" will pickup fly-in guests if requested. However, you can easily walk to the restaurant from the airport (Approx. 1/4 mile).

Information: The Oregon Department of Economic Development, Tourism Division, 775 Summer Street N.E., Salem, OR 97310, Phone: 800-547-7842.

One Free Beverage
Show proof that you saw this write-up in Aerodine's National Fly-in Restaurant Guide, and receive one free beverage of your choice.

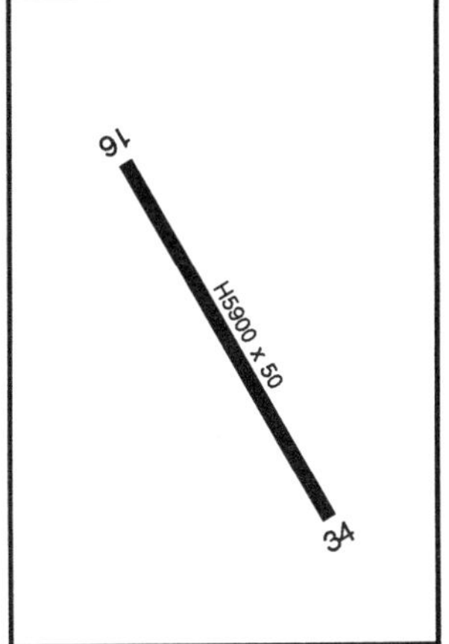

Airport Information:

Mc DERMIT - MC DERMITT STATE AIRPORT (26U)
0 mi west of town N42-00.13 W117-43.39 Elev: 4481 Rwy 16-34: H5900x60 (Asph)
Attended: unattended CTAF: 122.9 Public Phone 24hrs
Mc Dermit Airport Phone: 503-378-4880

OR-MMV - MC MINNVILLE
MC MINNVILLE MUNICIPAL AIRPORT

(Area Code 503)

11

The Red Caboose:

The Red Caboose is a deli that is located about 2 miles west of the Mc Minnville Municipal Airport. Their hours of operation are from 5:30 a.m. to 6:00 p.m. Monday through Thursday; 6:30 till 10 p.m. on Friday nights, and 9 a.m. to 4 p.m. on Saturday. If you give them a call, they will come out and pick you up at the airport. Their menu includes items like hamburgers, cold sandwiches, chicken, shrimp, and pies. All sorts of items are available to help build your sandwich like ham, bacon, lettuce, tomatoes, pickles, and onions to mention a few. Average prices for sandwiches should run about $3.00. The restaurant decor is unique with all kinds of model railroad trains from "G" scale to "Z" scale as well as antique rail road memorabilia dating back when the rail system passed through this town and supported many of its people. The restaurant also has an outdoor patio for dining purposes. For more information call the Red Caboose at 472-8720.

Restaurants Near Airport:
Flying "M" Ranch Resort 15 mi NW Phone: 662-3222
The Red Caboose 2 mi W Phone: 472-8720
Rogers Seafood Restaurant 5 mi NW Phone: 472-0917

Lodging: Paragon Motel (Free trans, 4 miles) 472-9493

Meeting Rooms: None reported

Transportation: Shamrock Taxi 472-5333; Chuck Colvin Ford (Rental Cars) 472-6124.

Information: Mc Minnville Chamber of Commerce 417 N. Adams, Mc Minnville, OR 97128, Phone: 472-6196.

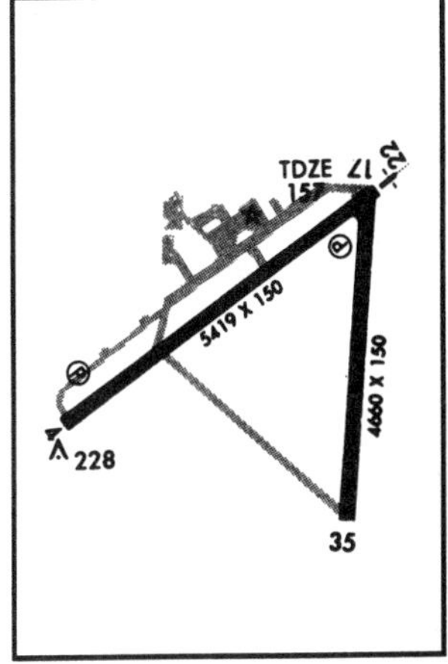

Airport Information:

Mc MINNVILLE - Mc MINNVILLE MUNICIPAL AIRPORT (MMV)
3 mi southeast of town N45-11.67 W123-08.16 Elev: 159 Fuel: 80, 100LL, Jet-A
Rwy 04-22: H5419x150 (Asph) Rwy 17-35: H4660x150 (Asph) Attended: 1600Z-dusk
Unicom: 123.0 Public Phone 24hrs Notes: $2.00 overnight tie-down fee for singles or twins. Glider instruction available.
Mac Air Flite Service Phone: 472-0558

OR-MFR - MEDFORD
ROGUE VALLEY INTL. - MEDFORD

12

Restaurants Near Airport: **(Area Code 541)**

Jacksonville Inn	7 mi W	Phone: 899-1900
Red Baron Restaurant	On Site	Phone: 772-7978

Lodging: Free transportation by the following: Red Lion Inn (3 miles) 779-5811; Horizon Inn 779-5085; Quality Inn (1 mile) 770-1234; Nendels (2 miles) 779-3141; Shilo Inn (2 miles) 770-5151; Windmill Inn (1 mile) 779-0050;

Meeting Rooms: Nendels (2 miles) 779-3141; Windmill Inn (1 mile) 779-0050.

Transportation: Taxi: Courtesy Yellow Cab 772-6288; Metro Taxi 773-6665;

Information: Visitor and Convention Bureau, 101 East 8th Street, Medford, OR 97501, Phone: 779-4847 or 800-599-0039.

Red Baron Restaurant/Lounge:

The Red Baron Restaurant is located within the terminal building at the Rogue Valley Intl. Airport. This fine dining facility can be reached with no problem when flying into this airport. Their hours are from 6:00 a.m. to 9:00 p.m. 7 days a week. The lounge is open from 10 a.m. to midnight. Their specialties include pasta, steaks, chicken, seafood and salad bar. Selections on their menu include a full line of breakfast specialties and "make your own omelets", eggs Benedict, chicken fettucini, shrimp, mahimahi fish filet, 15 different types of sandwiches, filet mignon, weekend prime rib specials, as well as Sunday and holiday buffets. Average prices will run about $5.00 for breakfast, $6.50 for lunch and $ 10.00 to $12.00 for dinner. During the evening hours the lights within the restaurant are dimmed, bringing out the intensity of the runway lighting system. From every table in the house you can see the activity on the taxiways, runways, and ramps. The decor of the restaurant takes on an elegant appearance during the evening dinner hours with linen service on each table, carpeted floors, large booths and forest green colored chairs. The main dining area can accommodate up to 75 persons while the lounge can hold about 40 more people if needed. Carry-out meals and inflight catering can also be arranged in advance. For information call the Red Baron Restaurant & Lounge at 772-7978.

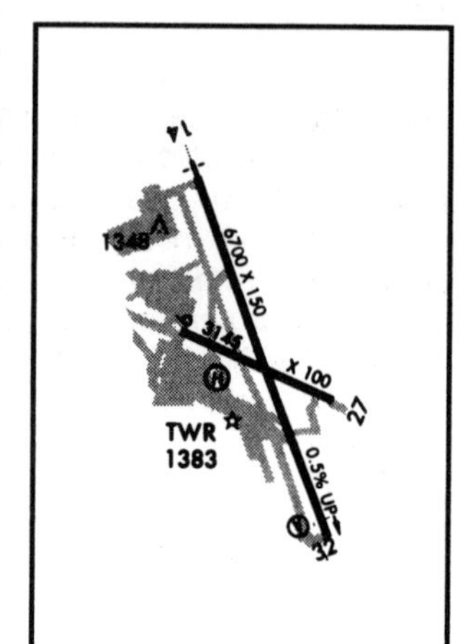

Airport Information:

MEDFORD - ROGUE VALLEY INTERNATIONAL - MEDFORD (MFR)
3 mi north of town N42-22.34 W122-52.36 Elev: 1331 Fuel: 80, 100, 100LL, Jet-A1+
Rwy 14-32: H6700x150 (Asph-Pfc) Rwy 09-27: H3145x100 (Asph) Attended: 1230-0500Z
Atis: 127.25 Unicom: 122.95 Medford Tower: 119.4 Gnd Con: 121.8 Public
Phone 24hrs Notes: No landing fee, $3.00 overnight parking.

FBO: Jet Center	**Phone: 770-5314**	**FBO: Medford Air**	**Phone: 779-5451**
FBO: Logan & Reavis Air	**Phone: 779-7633**	**FBO: Pacific Flights**	**Phone: 779-5445**

OR-2S6 - NEWBERG
SPORTSMANS AIRPARK

(Area Code 503) **13**

Restaurants Near Airport:

Burger King	1/2 mi N	Phone: 538-2371
Jay's	5/8 mi NW	Phone: 538-5925

Lodging: Shiloh Inn (Free trans, 3/8 mile) 537-0303; Partridge Farm (Bed & Breakfast, free trans) 4300 East Portland Road, Phone: Not reported.

Meeting Rooms: None Reported

Transportation: Taxi: Shamrock 538-8855; Rental Cars: Newberg Ford 538-2171.

Information: Chamber of Commerce, 115 North Washington Street, Newberg, OR 97132, Phone: 538-2014.

Jay's Restaurant:

Jay's Restaurant is a family style restaurant located 5/8th of a mile from Sportsman Airpark. We have learned from the proprietor that courtesy transportation can be arranged through the fixed base operator at the airport. This restaurant is open between 6 a.m. to 10 p.m. 7 days a week. Their menu offers a full breakfast line as well as lunch and dinner selections like pasta, fettucini Alfrado, top sirloin, halibut, fish and chips, barbecued chicken, enchiladas, taco salad, and all types of sandwiches and hamburgers. They also specialize in 14 different types of homemade pies. On Saturday nights their special is barbecued ribs, and on Friday is seafood with the fresh catch of the day. Thursday, Friday and Saturday nights they feature prime rib. Average prices run $4.00 for breakfast, $5.50 for lunch and $7.00 for dinner. The main dining room can accommodate a total of 144 persons. Their banquet section is designed to handle as many as 40 individuals. The restaurant has large windows and a natural wood roof. Next to the restaurant is the Shilo Inn complete with 60 units, see "lodging" listed above. For more information about the J's Restaurant, call 538-5925.

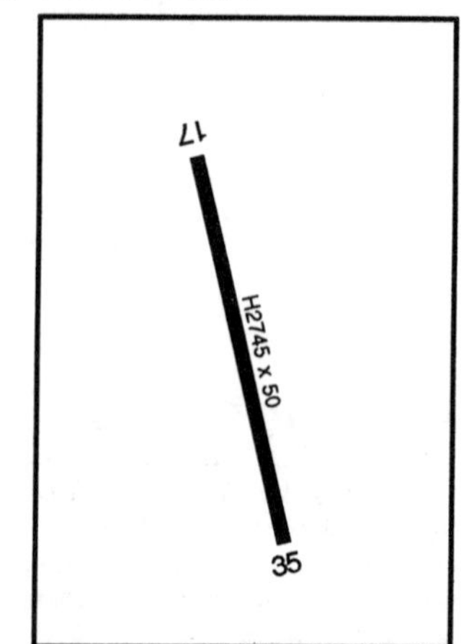

Airport Information:
NEWBERG - SPORTSMAN AIRPARK (2S6)
1 mi southeast of town N45-17.74 W122-57.32 Elev: 178 Fuel: 100LL, Jet-A
Rwy 17-35: H2745x50 (Asph) Attended: dawn-dusk CTAF: 122.9 Airport public phone available between 0700 to 1800Z Notes: parking overnight: single $3.50, over 4000 lbs gross weight $4.50
FBO: Sportsman Airpark, Inc. Phone: 538-2134

Not to be used for navigational purposes

OR-PFC - PACIFIC CITY
PACIFIC CITY STATE AIRPORT

(Area Code 503) 14, 15

Fat Freddy's

Fat Freddy's is a cook-to-order fast food establishment located on the north end of the runway at the Pacific City State Airport. Restaurant hours undetermined. Fat Freddy's prepares a wide selection of foods including burgers, broasted chicken, seafood, fish and chips, hotdogs, chili-burgers, Jo-Jo's, and a variety of shakes and beverages. Average prices run about $4.00 for most meals. The restaurant has about 1600 square feet of floor space and can seat approx. 40 persons. It is situated at the end of the runway so its fun to watch the airplanes fly right overhead. For more information call 965-6012.

Loscaporales Mexican Restaurnat:

Loscaporales Mexican Restaurant is situated 100 yards from the Pacific City State Airport. This family style restaurant is open between 11 a.m. and 9 p.m. 7 days a week. They specialize in Mexican entrees. In addition they also feature seafood, steaks and lobster. Prices average between $7.00 and $10.00 for most main selections. The restaurant can accommodate up to 72 persons. The decor of the restaurant is southwestern with Mexican styled hats and wall decorations. They also have a couple of tables outdoors for dining on their porch. For more information call 965-6999.

Attractions:

Pacific City is a coastal town located only 1/4 mile from local beaches, fishing and even hang gliding.

Restaurants Near Airport:

Fat Freddy's	Adj Arpt	Phone: 965-6012
Loscaporales Mexican Rest.	100 yds	Phone: 965-6999

Lodging: Three Capes Motel (Adj. Airport) Phone:965-6464; O'Shannon Motel, (Adj. Airport) Phone: 965-6464

Meeting Rooms: None Reported

Transportation: None Reported

Information: Pacific City Chamber of Commerce, Phone: 965-6161; Also: The Oregon Department of Economic Development, Tourism Division, 775 Summer Street N.E., Salem, OR 97310, Phone: 800-547-7842.

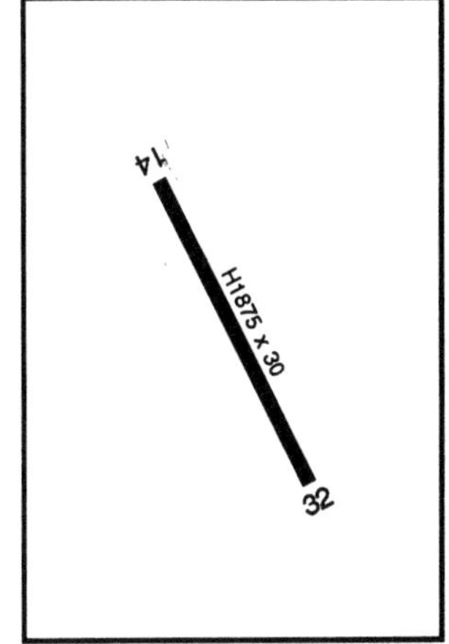

Airport Information:

PACIFIC CITY - PACIFIC CITY STATE AIRPORT (PFC)
1 mi south of town N45-11.99 W123-57.74 Elev: 5 Rwy 14-32: H1875x30 (Asph)
Attended: unattended CTAF: 122.9 Notes: Rwy may be under water during high tides.
Owner advises contact with State Aeronautics Division 503-378-4880 prior to use.
Pacific City State Airport Phone: 378-4880

OR-PDT - PENDLETON
EASTERN OREGON REGIONAL

(Area Code 541)

16

Hangar Lounge & Snack Bar:

This facility contains a snack bar serving light fare. A new lounge called the Hangar is planned to open by the time this edition goes to press. The Hangar will include a limited menu with specials offered. Together the snack bar, lounge and car rental facility make up the services at the Eastern Oregon Regional at Pendleton. For information call 278-0584.

Restaurants Near Airport:

Hangar Lounge	Trml. Bldg.	Phone: 278-0584

Lodging: Best Western Pendleton 276-2135; Chaparral Motel 276-8654; Econo Lodge 276-5252; Longhorn Motel 276-7531; Motel 6 276-3160; Red Lion Inn 276-3160; Tapadera Inn 276-3231; Traveler's Inn 276-6231.

Meeting Rooms: Red Lion Inn 276-3160; Tapadera Inn 276-3231

Transportation: Hertz 276-3183.

Information: Pendleton Chamber of Commerce, 25 Southeast Dorion, Pendleton, OR 97801, Phone: 276-7411 or 800-547-8911.

Attractions:

The Umatilla Indian Reservation is a Native American community created by the Walla Walla Valley Treaty of 1855. The historic traditions and significant life-style of the Umatilla Tribe are explained within this settlement. One of the oldest Catholic missions in the United States is located here. For information call 276-3873.

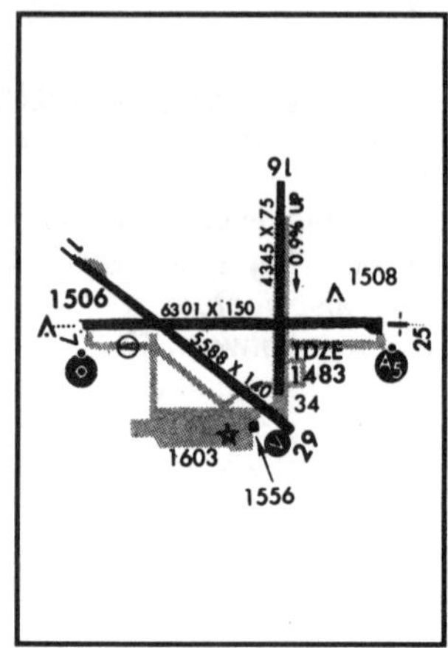

Airport Information:

EASTERN OREGON REGIONAL AT PENDLETON (PDT)

3 mi northwest of town N45-41.71 W118-50.50 Elev: 1493 Fuel: 80, 100LL, Jet A1+, Mogas Rwy 07-25: H6301x150 (Asph-Pfc) Rwy 11-29: H5588x140 (Asph) Rwy 16-34: H4345x75 (Asph) Attended: 1400-0400Z Unicom: 122.95 Pendleton Tower: 118.8 Gnd Con: 121.9

Notes: CAUTION: Pilots shall exercise extreme caution at intersection of ramp and Rwy 29 north end of terminal building. Area obstructed from view of tower by terminal building.

FBO: General Aircraft Service Phone: 276-3554, 278-1358

OR-HIO - PORTLAND
PORTLAND-HILLSBORO AIRPORT

(Area Code 503)

17

Eddie Rickenbacker's:

This family restaurant is located on the second floor within the terminal building at the Portland-Hillsboro Airport. Their hours are from 11 a.m. to 9 p.m 7 days a week. Specialties of the house are a variety of Italian dishes. Aditional menu items include chicken, fettucini, hamburgers, cheeseburgers, steakes, and seafood. Average prices for a meal run about $5.00 for lunch and between $8.00 and $15.95 for dinner. Live music is featured on Friday and Saturday evenings. A dance floor is even available for evening entertainment. Large windows allow a nice view of the airport ramp areas. Their main dining room can accommodate up to 180 persons. For more information you can call the Eddie Rickenbacker's restaurant at 640-9601.

Restaurants Near Airport:

The Brass Horn	1 mi S.	Phone: 640-5527
Dancing Dragon	3/4 mile	Phone: 640-4510
Eddie Rickenbacker's	On Site	Phone: 640-9601
Hallmark Inn	3/4 mi S	Phone: 648-3500

Lodging: Hallmark Inn (3/4 mile, free trans) 648-3500; Shilo Inn (Washington Square, free trans) 620-4320; Embassy Suites 644-4000;

Meeting Rooms: Aero Air, Inc. 640-3711; Hallmark Inn 648-3500; Embassy Suites 644-4000.

Transportation: Aero Air, Inc. can provide courtesy transportation to nearby facilities as well as rental cars available. Phone: 640-3711; Enterprise 681-8000; National 648-3213; Thrifty 640-6200; Hillsboro Cab, 648-1234; Far West Limousine 640-3223; Prestige Limousine 282-5009.

Information: Portland Visitors Association, 26 Southwest Salmon, Portland, OR 97204, Phone: 222-2223 or 800-345-3214.

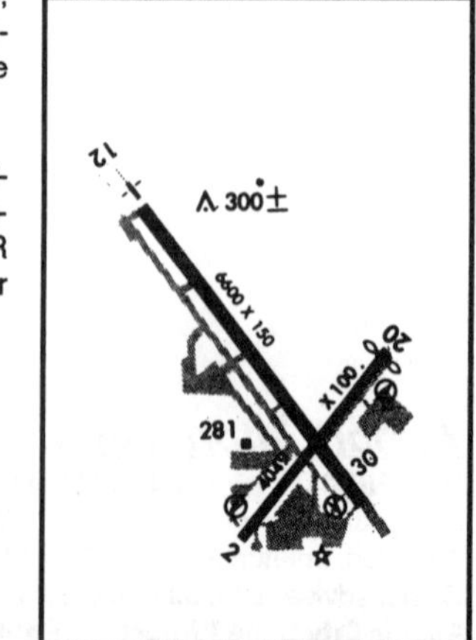

Airport Information:

PORTLAND - PORTLAND-HILLSBORO AIRPORT (HIO)

15 mi southwest of town N45-32.42 W122-56.99 Elev: 204 Fuel: 100LL, Jet-A
Rwy: 12-30: H6600x150 (Asph) Rwy 02-20: H4049x100 (Asph) Attended: 1400-0600Z
Atis: 127.65 Unicom: 122.95 App/Dep Con: 126.0 Tower: 119.3 Gnd Con: 121.7
Public Phone 24hrs

FBO: Aero Air, Inc. Phone: 800-448-2376 or 640-3711

OR-RDM - REDMOND ROBERTS FIELD

(Area Code 541) 18

Mrs. Beasley's:

This family style restaurant is situated about 3 miles from Roberts Field, in Redmond, Oregon. Transportation may be arranged either through taxi service or local FBO. Their hours are 6 a.m. to 11 p.m., 7 days a week. There is a lounge on the premises open from 11 a.m. to 11 p.m. Their menu is quite extensive. Breakfast selections are numerous including pastries, cakes, and pies. Saturday they feature seafood. Daily specials are available along with Sunday brunch between 9:30 and 2 p.m. In addition to their selections, they also specialize in prime rib, halibut, fish & chips, hamburgers, cheeseburgers, homemade soups and a salad bar served between 11 a.m. and 9 p.m. 7 days a week. Average prices run $4.25 for breakfast, $5.50 for lunch and $7.95 to $8.95 for dinner. The main dining room can seat up to 100 people. They also have a coffee shop that can seat 80 persons. Accommodations can be arranged for party and group get-togethers. For information call Mrs. Beasley's restaurant at 548-4023.

Restaurants Near Airport:
Caynon Club/Eaglecrest Resort 15 mi N Phone: 923-2453
Mrs. Beasley's 3 mi W Phone: 548-4023

Lodging: Village Square (Free trans) 548-2105; Nendels New Redmond (Free trans) 923-7378.

Meeting Rooms: Nendels New Redmond (Free trans) 923-7378.

Transportation: Taxis: Call-A-Cab 923-0091; Redmond taxi 548-8830.

Information: Chamber of Commerce, 446 SW 7th Street, Redmond, OR 97756, Phone: 923-5191 or 800-574-1325.

Airport Information:

REDMOND - ROBERTS FIELD (RDM)
1 mi southeast of town N44-15.24 W121-09.00 Elev: 3077 Fuel: 100LL, Jet-A
Rwy 04-22: H7040x150 (Asph-Grvd) Rwy 10-28: H6999x100 (Asph-Grvd) Attended: 1330Z-dusk CTAF: 123.6 Unicom: 122.95 Public Phone 24hrs
FBO: Butler Aviation Phone: 548-8166

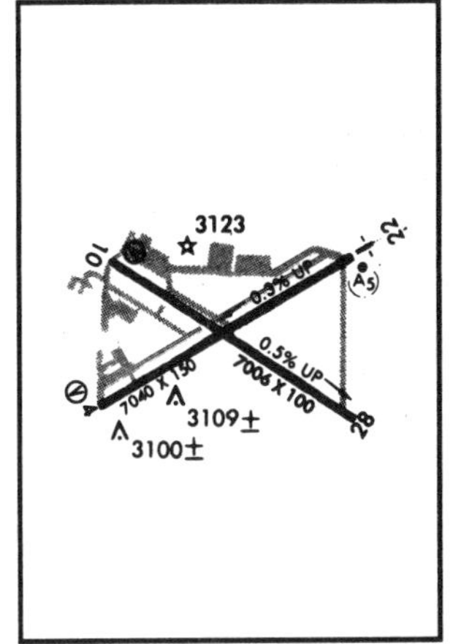

OR-SLE - SALEM MC NARY FIELD

(Area Code 503) 19

Flight Deck Restaurant:

The Flight Deck is a family style restaurant located right on the Salem McNary Airport. Aircraft parking is available in front of this facility without the need for transportation. Restaurant hours are Monday through Thursday 7 a.m. to 8 p.m. and Friday & Saturday 7 a.m. to 9 p.m. Their specialties include and soups, salads, sandwiches, steaks, chicken, and seafood. Daily dinner specials and Friday prime rib, as well as week-day luncheon specials are offered. Prices average around $5.00 for breakfast and lunch and $7.50 for most dinner selections. The restaurant decor exhibits aircraft memorabilia and aircraft paintings. While dining, you can view the activity on the airport. If planning a group fly-in, you should provide 1 weeks advance notice. Catering is also available. For more information call 581-5721.

Restaurants Near Airport:
Flight Deck Restaurant On Site Phone: 581-5721

Lodging: Executive Inn (3 miles) 363-4123; Chumaree (4 miles) 370-7888; Best Western (3 miles) 581-1559

Meeting Rooms: Meeting rooms are available on the airport for up to 12 people, reservations should be made through the airport manager, call 588-6314.

Transportation: Valco Fuels and Buswell Aviation can provide transportation to local facilities. Also Cherriot Bus stops at the airport; Salem Taxi 362-2411; Rental Cars: Valco Rental cars 362-9328;

Information: Convention & Visitors Association, 1313 Mill Street, Southeast, Salem, OR 97301, Phone: 581-4325 or 800-874-7012.

Attractions:

Oregon State Fair is normally held August 22 through September 2nd, agricultural exhibits, Northwest Balloon Championships, horse racing and exhibits on farm equipment. For information call 378-3247.

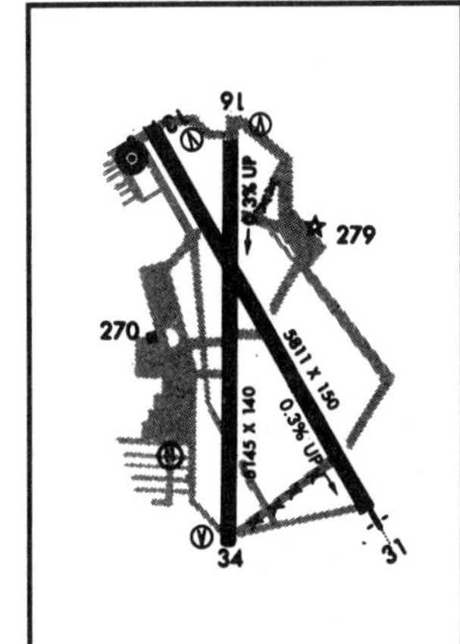

Airport Information:

SALEM - MC NARY FIELD (SLE)
2 mi southeast of town N44-54.57 W123-00.15 Elev: 210 Fuel: 80, 100LL, Jet-A
Rwy 13-31: H5811x150 (Asph-Pfc) Rwy 16-34: H5145x140 (Asph) Attended: 1530Z-Dusk
Atis: 124.55 Unicom: 122.95 Salem Tower: 119.1 Gnd Con: 121.9 Public Phone 24hrs
Notes: Overnight for general aviation $3.00 single, $5.00 multi engine; Home of Oregon Fair and Northwest Balloon Championships.
FBO: Salem Air Center Phone: 364-4158

OR-6K5 - SISTERS
SISTERS EAGLE AIR

20

Cascade Country Inn: (Bed & Breakfast Inn)

Cascade Country Inn is the newest look in elegance and comfort in Sisters, Oregon. Built on 4 acres with the back of the inn to the runway and the front facing the beautiful Cascades, there is hardly a prettier spot. It is convenient to either drive-in or fly-in. You could taxi right up to their front door! They built the inn in 1994 so every room has its own bath. All rooms have 9' ceilings or higher and the tiles and stained glass transoms are custom made. Instead of using wallpaper, there is stencilling and custom murals throughout. The Inn is ideal for anniversaries, birthday celebrations, weddings, group retreats or family reunions. It definitely has a touch of romance for those who wish to spend some time away from the pressures of life. Coming to Sisters is like going back in time. Sisters is the only town in Oregon that Sunset magazine named as one of the most picturesque towns west of the Rockies. It has a western theme and is like stepping into a postcard. All of Central Oregon offers a variety of outdoor activities every season of the year. This will give you a bit of an idea of the ambiance of both Sisters and the Cascade Country Inn. The inn's sumptuous country breakfast will delight you. Homemade quiches, muffins and fresh fruit are typical of their morning fare. If your diet requires special attention, please let them know. They want to make sure one of the many joys you find, is sitting down to a bountiful breakfast in their dining room or on the deck. Don't be surprised if you see deer grazing nearby or hear a flock of geese overhead. For more information call the Cascade Country Inn at 549-INNN

Airport Information:

SISTERS - SISTERS EAGLE AIR (6K5)

1 mi north of town N44-18.27 W121-32.35 Elev: 3168 Rwy 02-20: H3550x50 (Asph) Attended: unattended CTAF: 122.9 Notes: CAUTION: Rwy 02-20 surface covered with loose gravel. Rising terrain off departure end of Rwy 02. Landing fee reported.

Airport management Phone: 549-6011

Restaurants Near Airport: **(Area Code 503)**
Several restaurants are located within the town of Sisters, OR only 1 mile north of the airport. Also when staying overnight at local bed & breakfasts a morning meal is usually a treat that many visitors really enjoy.

Lodging: Cascade Country Inn (On Site) 549-INNN; Ponderose Lodge 1-1/2 mi 549-1234; Sisters Motor Lodge 1 mi 549-2551.
Meeting Rooms: Cascade Country Inn (On Site) contains accommodations for groups, 549-INNN.
Transportation: None reported
Information: Sisters Area Chamber of Commerce, P.O. Box 467, Sisters, OR 97759, Phone: 549-0251 or 549-4253.

Attractions:

Sisters and the surrounding area offer world-class recreation every season of the year. Spring, summer and fall offer mountain biking, hunting, rock climbing at world famous Smith Rock, or fishing in the Jetholius River and the nearby lakes. Don't let us forget to mention golf, horse-back riding or even hiking on some of the lava flows that formed the region. Based on a western town with the quaint architecture, the shopping is a relished pastime for many visitors. Clothing, art, crafts and specialty shops abound. The restaurants range from barbecue and wild west fare to fine dining.

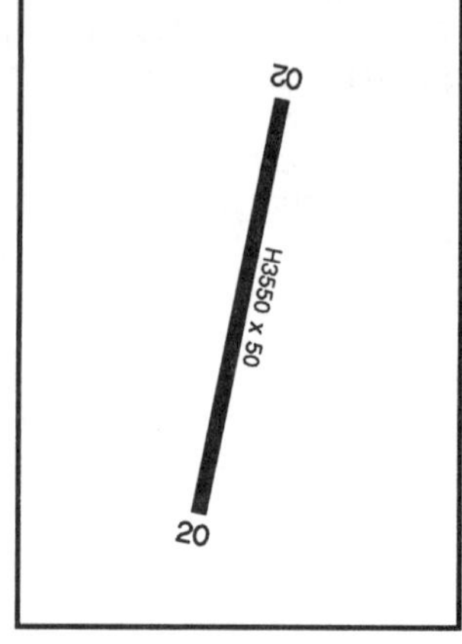

Photo by: Cascade Inn

Enjoy the hospitality at the Cascade Country Inn B & B, a truly unique Fly-in Bed & Breakfast establishment.

OR-S21 - SUNRIVER
SUNRIVER AIRPORT

(Area Code 503)

21, 22

The Meadows Restaurant (Resort):

Transportation to and from this restaurant is available via courtesy van shuttle service (Bell Service). This fine dining facility is open weekdays from 6 to 9 p.m. and weekends from 6 to 10 p.m. The Meadows features "High Dessert Cuisine" which include wild game such as elk, venison and pheasant. Appetizers include fresh oysters on the half shell, hardwood smoked goose with melon and warm Brie dressing. Various desserts are also offered along with their award-winning wine list. Fresh fish and wild game specials are offered daily. Prices run about $26.00 for an average meal. A Sunday champagne brunch is served each Sunday. Located in Sunriver Lodge the Meadows Restaurant has an open and airy atmosphere with a spectacular view of Mt. Bachelor in the Oregon Cascades. There is a large stone fireplace, and the decor is a combination of modern/rustic in keeping with the lodge decor. This (4-star Mobil) restaurant will be happy to accommodate small groups. Larger groups or parties can utilize the Banquet Department and Convention Services. For information call 593-1221.

Restaurants Near Airport:

The Meadows	1/2 mi E.	Phone: 593-1221
Owl's Nest Lounge	1/2 mi E.	Phone: 593-1221
The Provision Co.	1/2 mi E.	Phone: 593-1221

Lodging: Sunriver Lodge and Resort is located 1/2 mile east of the Sunriver Airport. This facility contains 211 units comprised of 1-3 bedroom units available in two story lodge in addition to 100, 1-4 bedroom houses, all with private patios and balconies. Call 1-800-547-3922.

Convention Facilities: Sunriver's convention and banquet staff will provide full service accommodations for large and small businesses with individual meeting rooms, or their newly-built Great Hall Conference Center complete with catering and banquet services. For information call 1-800-547-3922. For information call 1-800-547-3922.

Transportation: Sunriver Lodge and Resort offers its guests complimentary on-call, on property shuttle service. Winter packages include Mt. Bachelor ski shuttle service as well.

Information: Bend Chamber of Commerce, Bend, Oregon 63085, Phone: 382-3221. Also Sunriver Lodge and Resort, P.O. Box 3609, Sunriver, OR 97707 or call 1-800-547-3922 outside Oregon or 1-800-452-6874 inside Oregon.

The Provision Company (Resort):

As with the Meadows Restaurant, the Provision Company can be easily reached by calling the resort for free shuttle service, (See Transportation). This family-style restaurant is open weekdays from 7 a.m. to 9 p.m. and on weekends from 7 a.m. to 10 p.m. Specialized entrees include a variety of seafood, pasta, steak, chicken, sandwiches and salads. Prices range from $6.00 for breakfast, $6.50 for lunch and $10.00 for dinner. Daily lunch and dinner specials are available. This restaurant has a rustic, marketplace theme. Mt. Bachelor, in the Oregon Cascades, offers dining guests a beautiful view. Small groups are welcome during selected hours and with a pre-selected menu. For information call 593-1221.

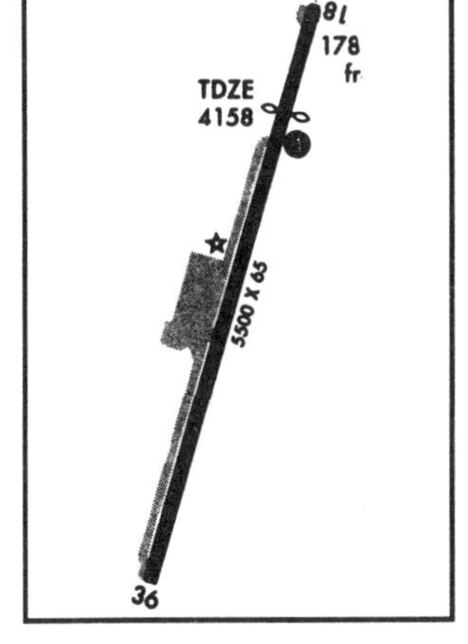

Airport Information:

SUNRIVER - SUNRIVER AIRPORT (S21)

1 mi west of town 43-52-36N 121-27-06W Elev: 4159 Fuel: 80, 100LL, Jet-A
Rwy 18-36: H5500x65 (Asph) Attended: May-Aug 1530-0330Z, Oct-Mar 1630-0030Z, Sep and Mar 1630-0230Z Unicom: 122.8 Emergency fuel available at times other than when airport is attended, call 503-593-1221. **CAUTION:** Important noise abatement procedures: Left traffic runway 36; Right traffic runway 18. Departing runway 36 left turn only to heading 320 degrees; Inbound traffic use Redmond VOR 117.6-24 NM on 176 degree radial.
Resort Phone: 593-1221, 1-800-547-3922 or 1-800-542-6874 in Oregon.

Photo by: Sunriver Resort

Sunriver Resort

Sunriver's lifestyle and luxury strike the ideal balance. From the lodge village bedrooms and suites with wood-burning fireplaces and decks, to a wide range of private homes and condominiums, the resort combines deluxe accommodations with recreation and a variety of entertainment. The resort has 1 indoor and 2 outdoor swimming pools, 28 tennis courts with three indoor pro courts, racquetball, two 18 hole golf courses, driving range, 30 miles of paved bike trails, nature center, skating rink, health club privileges, marina with boat rental, gift shops, grocery, barber and beauty shops. Private 5500' airstrip 1/2 mile east of main lodge across golf course. Once you let yourself be talked into a white water raft trip, you'll have to talk yourself out of doing it again and again. Shooting the Deschutes River is fun. Canoe Sunriver for eight peaceful miles, or amble over to nearby Blue Mountain Lake, where the trout are waiting to hit your flies. Ride horses, jog, hike, or head to either of Sunriver's swimming complexes for a day in the sun. At Sunriver, biking is for everyone who likes the idea of gliding through the woods on paths winding past the fairways and along the river. Bikes are everywhere, and 30 miles of paved paths take you all over the resort. With 28 plexi-paved outdoor tennis courts, Sunriver Lodge really keeps you "on the ball." Plus, there's the Racquet Club for indoor swimming and workouts. With two fine courses, a golfer's dream can come true. Recently rated as one of America's top 25 resort courses by Golf Digest, Sunriver's North Course plays host to the annual Oregon Open Pro/Am. The South Course, with its tree-lined fairways and open meadows, is made even more beautiful by the awesome Cascades in the background. For your dining pleasure, sample the region's finest cuisine at the elegant Meadows Dining Room. Stop by the Provision Company for a memorable meal or snack, or head for the Owl's Nest for live nightly entertainment. **Winter Activities:** When the snow falls, Sunriver transforms into a ski village, with resort shuttle service right to the slopes of neighboring Mt. Bachelor. After taking on the mountain's 3,100 vertical feet, there's ice-skating, horse drawn sleigh rides, cross-country skiing, and after all that activity, you can relax and unwind at the resort and enjoy their hot tubs, saunas or a massage. LOCATION: Sunriver Lodge & Resort is located 15 miles south of Bend, Oregon along U.S. Highway 97. This resort is unique with its own private 5,500 foot airstrip with parking ramps able to accommodate up to 170 aircraft. Sixteen of ramp spaces are designed for multi-engine piston & jet aircraft. (Noise abatement procedures are in affect, see "Airport Information". For resort information call, 503-593-1221. (Article submitted by Sunriver Resort).

Photo by: Sunriver Resort — Sunriver Resort Airport

Photo by: Sunriver Resort — One of Sunriver Resorts lodging units

OR-DLS - THE DALLES
THE DALLES MUNICIPAL

(Area Code 509) 23

Restaurants Near Airport:
Buzzin'in Cafe & Cakes On Site Phone: 767-2229

Buzzin'in Cafe & Cakes:

The Buzzin'in Cafe & Cakes restaurant is located in the terminal building at the "The Dalles Municipal Airport" located in the town of "The Dalles" which is actually located in the state of Washington but is listed in the Airport Facility Directory as an Oregon airport location. This cafe is open Wednesday through Friday 9 a.m. to 2 p.m. and Saturday and Sunday 8 a.m. to 2 p.m. Everything on their menu is homemade from scratch. Breakfast is served all day. Lunch entrees are served beginning at 11:00 a.m. Specialties include their freshly baked cinnamon rolls, omelets, hamburgers made with hand pattied high quality beef, daily baked pies like peach, apple, strawberry and rhubarb. Average prices run in the neighborhood of $4.00 to $5.00 for main menu selections. A special luncheon meal is prepared as a daily special, which can be fried chicken, fettuccini, chicken and mushrooms or any one of several substantial main courses. The view from the restaurant allows guests to look out over the runways. The decor of the restaurant has a country theme. During our conversation with the owner we were impressed with the amount of effort that went into making customers feel at home, right down to the homemade curtains and specially prepared foods that contain no preservatives. The Buzzin'in Cafe & Cakes restaurant provides catering as a main part of their operation, including wedding cakes and specially prepared pastries, sandwich and fruit trays and the like. For more information call the restaurant at 767-2229.

Lodging: Best Western (Tapadera Inn) 296-9107; Huntley Inn 296-1191; Inn at The Dalles 296-1167; Oregon Motor Motel 2-5 mi 296-9111; Shilo Inn 4 mi. free trans 298-5161; Tillicum Inn 8 mi free trans 298-5161.
Meeting Rooms: Tillicum Inn 8 mi free trrans 298-5161;
Transportation: Rental cars: Reported available at airport; Brace Bros 503-296-3761; Schalten Motors 503-296-6191; Thomas Motors 296-2271.
Information: The Dalles Chamber of Commerce, 404 W. 2nd Street, The Dalles, OR 97058. Phone: 296-2231.

Attractions: Ft. Dalles Museum: This museum was the actual location of a 1856 pioneer outpost. On display, and the only remaining building, is the Surgeon's Quarters. A unique and rare collection of pioneer equipment along with stagecoaches and covered wagons can be seen. This museum is only 8 miles from the airport and is open March through October daily, and on Wednesday through Sunday the rest of the year. They are closed holidays and the first 2 weeks in January. For information call 296-4547.

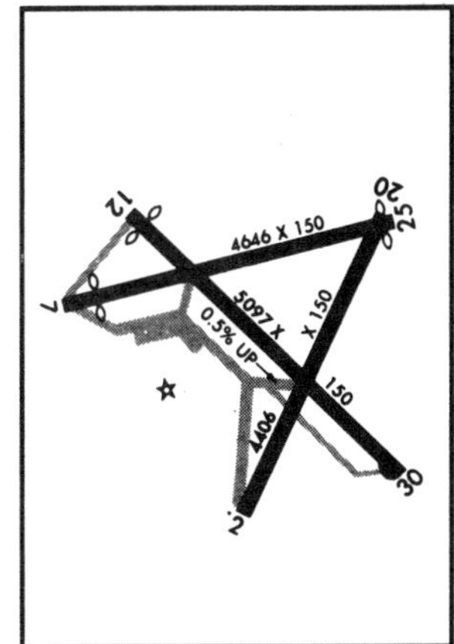

Airport Information:

THE DALLES - THE DALLES MUNICIPAL (DLS)
2 mi northeast of town N45-37.11 W121-10.04 Elev: 243 Fuel: 80, 100LL, Jet-A Rwy 12-30: H5097x150 (Asph) Rwy 07-25: H4646x150 (Asph) Rwy 02-20: H4401x150 (Asph) Attended: Nov-Feb 1600-0100Z, Mar-Oct 1500-0500Z Unicom": 123.0 Notes: The Airport is physically located in the state of Washington.
FBO: Avjet Aviation II Phone: 767-1134 or 296-5481

WW II Blimp Hangar & Flight Museum: TILLAMOOK, OR (OR-S47)

The WW-II Hangar & Flight Museum is located on the east side of the Tillamook Airport. This museum attracts a great many fly-in visitors throughout the year.

The Tillamook blimp hangar can be seen from miles away. There were 17 blimp hangars of this design built between 1942 and 1943. Only 7 hangars of this type still stand today, and two of the remaining 7 are scheduled for demolition in coming years. The Tillamook Blimp Hangar is the only one open to the general public. Other large blimp hangers of this type at various locations across the United States are either privately owned or situated on military installations, and are not accessible to the public. One of the convenient aspects that attract fly-in visitors, is the ease with which one can taxi up and park their aircraft adjacent to the entrance.

During our conversation with Mr. Ken Manske, the public relations director of this establishment, we learned many interesting and historical aspects associated with the Tillamook hangar and museum. Little information about the history behind the construction and emphasis of these huge hangars survived a half century of time that transpired since the second world war. Mr. Manske through great effort, researched the subject and published a book explaining the story about the Tillamooks blimp hangar and similar hangars built during WW-II. Mr. Manske is a pilot himself, and an author of several other fascinating books relating to WW-II aircraft and their origin.

During our interview we learned that the hangar was a prefabricated design of all wood construction. The assembly and building of this massive structure was accomplished by transporting the raw materials to the sight and bolting large wooden beams and components together.

The Tillamook hangar measures 1,070 feet in length, 260 feet wide and 190 feet high. There is enough floor space to fit 6 football fields within its confines. In fact, if you could lay the Empire State Building sideways, minus the tower, it would easily fit inside.

Today the hangar still is used for storing a variety of modern blimps. In addition, the hangar also contains a museum that exhibits a large number of WW-II military aircraft. Some of the aircraft on display include a F4U -"Corsair", B-25, PBY, ME-109, FM-2 "Wildcat", and TBM-Avenger, and Spitfire just to mention a few. The museum also displays unique exhibits and educational displays. Several new arrivals are planned to become permanent exhibits including a SBD-Dauntless and one or two P-38 Lightnings. Most of the aircraft on display are in flight-ready status, and on some weekends put into action, thrilling local residance as well as those visiting the museum.

Those who plan to fuel or service their aircraft can taxi to the other side of the field where the airport main office and fueling ramp are located. For more information call the WW-II Blimp Hangar & Flight Museum at 800-938-1957. Airport managers office and FBO can be reached by calling 503-842-7152.

OR-S47 - TILLAMOOK
TILLAMOOK AIRPORT

24

WW II Blimp Hangar & Flight Museum:

The town of Tillamook Oregon is situated in the northeast portion of the state, about 50 miles west of Portland. The WW-II Hangar & Flight Museum is located on the Tillamook Airport. This museum attracts many fly-in visitors each year. The blimp hangar is huge and can be seen from miles away. The story behind the blimp hangar and museum is a fascinating one. According to museum officials, this is the only hangar of its type to be open to the general public. Many unique aviation exhibits are on display. Unlike other museums that rope off aircraft, this museum allows close up viewing of the exhibits. Most of the aircraft on display are in flight-ready statice. On weekends and during special occasions visitors can enjoy the experience of seeing some of the aircraft in use. During our conversation with the airport manager we learned that although there is no current dining facility located on the field, plans are being considered for a possible future airport restaurant. For information about the WW-II Blimp Hangar & Flight Museum call 800-938-1957.

(Area Code 503)

Restaurants Near Airport:
Restaurants in town 3 mi S. Phone: N/A

Lodging: Shilo Inn (trans) reported 10 mi or 5 min. from airport, phone: 842-7971.
Meeting Rooms: Check with FBO or Museum.
Transportation: Rental cars: Car Connection 842-2592.
Information: Tillamook Chamber of Commerce, 3705 US 101N, Tillamook, OR 97141, Phone: 842-7525.

Additional Attractions:

Additional attractions include: **Tillamook Country Pioneer Museum** contains replica pioneer homes, blacksmith shop, logging displays and war relics. For information call 842-4553; **Capes Scenic Loop Drive to Cape Meares and Oceanside**, is located west of Tillamook, OR along Bay Ocean Road to Cape Meares. Traveling south on Loop Road will take you to Meares State Park. **Cape Meares** Lake, beach and sand dunes offer a variety of attractions and water activities. Also **Cape Meares Lighthouse and "Octopus" Tree** are popular attractions. For more complete information about the attractions in the region contact the Tillamook Chamber of Commerce at 842-7525.

NO AIRPORT DIAGRAM AVAILABLE

Airport Information:

TILLAMOOK - TILLAMOOK AIRPORT (S47)
3 mi south of town N45-25.12 W123-48.82 Elev: 35 Fuel: 100LL Rwy 13-31: H4990x100 (Asph) Rwy 01-19: H2900x75 (Asph) Attended: 1700-0100Z Unicom: 122.8 Notes: Unlighted blimp mooring mast at 850' from thld 320' left in transition surface.
FBO: Tillamook Airport Phone: 842-7152

OR-OR05 - YAMHILL
FLYING "M" RANCH AIRPORT

(Area Code 503) 25

Flying "M" Ranch:

The Flying "M" Ranch embodies the spirit of the Oregon frontier. From their massive Douglas fir log lodge to scrumptious steak-fry trail rides to glimpses of elk and beaver, the pleasure enjoyed by our earliest settlers are ready and waiting for you. Located in the Oregon Coast Range near the base of the 3,500 foot Trask Mountain, they provide a year round ranch just ten miles west of Yamhill. For pilots, they have their own airstrip. The 2,135 foot turf and gravel runway is (one way) at an elevation of 448 feet. It's on the 251 degree radial from the Newberg VOR. Fuel is available at Newberg and McMinnville airports. Their restaurant seats 180 and is divided into two sections by a huge native stone fireplace. Their restaurant hours are 7 days a week from 8 a.m. to 9 p.m. Monday thru Thursday and 8 a.m. to 10 p.m. Friday, Saturday and Sunday (Closed for Christmas). For banquets and meetings they have seating for well over 200 guests, with a fine menu served in either buffet or sit-down style. Accommodations include their comfortable 24-room Bunkhouse Motel, a number of cozy cabins and campground facilities. Stagecoach and trail rides have long been the Flying "M" Ranch trademark. Their guided horse back rides include hourly to several days, and everything in between, They cater to both novice and advanced riders. Other amenities and activities at the ranch include a swimming pond as long as a city block, tennis, volleyball, live entertainment, horseshoes and basketball. Overnight lodging is not a prerequisite for flying in and enjoying a fine meal. For more information, call the ranch at 662-3222.

Restaurants Near Airport:
Flying "M" Ranch On Site Phone: 662-3222

Lodging: Flying "M" Ranch (On Airport) 662-3222
Meeting Rooms: Flying "M" Ranch (On Airport) 662-3222
Transportation: Not required, well within walking distance.
Information: Flying "M" Ranch, 23029 N.W. Flying "M" Road, Yamhill, Oregon 97148, Phone: 662-3222.

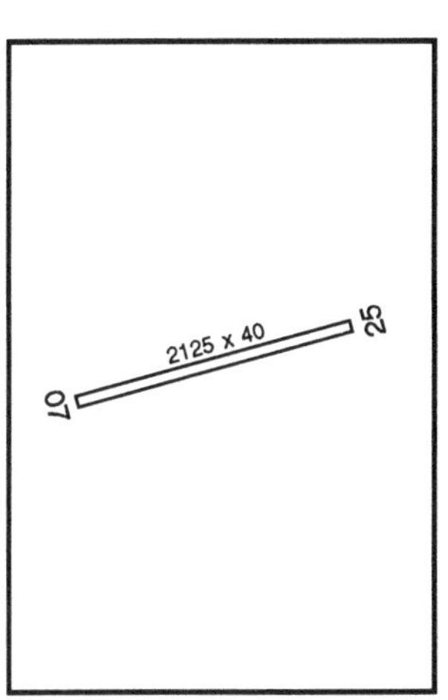

Airport Information:

YAMHILL - FLYING "M" RANCH AIRPORT (OR05) Private Airport
7 mi west of town 45-21-44N 123-21-16W Rwy 07-25: 2135x40 (Turf-Gravl) Elev: 448
Attended: daylight hours CTAF: 122.9 Notes: No landing fees. Excerpt from AFD: Land to west, takeoff to east. No night landings or takeoffs. 6 foot thick timber barrier 25' beyond runway to west. Runway 07-25 LIRL for owners use only. Private use facility, use at own risk.
Flying "M" Ranch Phone: 662-3222

A Little Extra Planning Can Make Each One Of Your Excursions More Rewarding

"Just Call Ahead"

Even though we at Aerodine strive to provide the latest information possible at the time of printing, we suggest you take a little time and call ahead to verify that the facility you intend to visit still provides the same services as published. Your comments regarding any changes in these services or about new establishments you have found, are greatly appreciated. With your help, we can include them in our next updated edition.

Aerodine Magazine
P.O. Box 247, Palatine, IL 60078
Phone: 847-358-4355

PENNSYLVANIA

LOCATION MAP

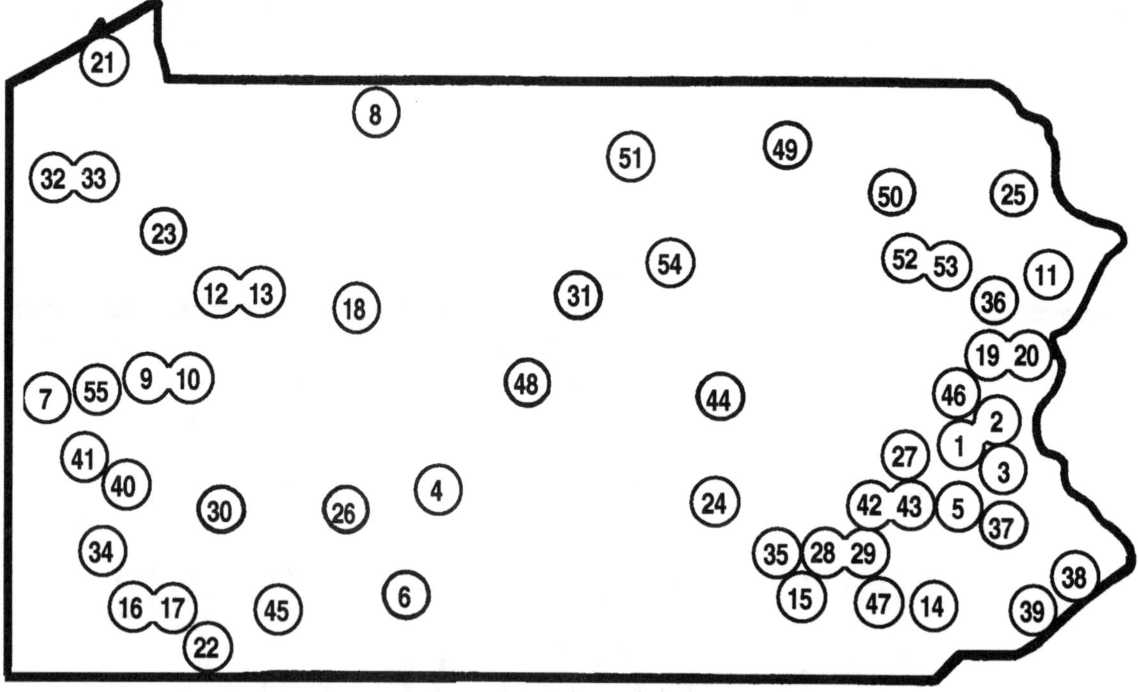

Not to be used for navigational purposes

PENNSYLVANIA

CROSS FILE INDEX

Location Number	City or Town	Airport Name And Identifier	Name of Restaurant
1	Allentown	Allentown-Bethlehem-Easton (ABE)	Creative Croissants
2	Allentown	Allentown-Bethlehem-Easton (ABE)	The Glass Terrace
3	Allentown	Allentown Queen City Muni. (1N9)	Penalty Box Rest.
4	Altoona	Altoona-Blair Co. Arpt. (AOO)	Kitty Hawk
5	Bally	Butter Valley Golf Port (7N8)	Butter Valley Restaurant
6	Bedford	Bedford Co. (B17)	The Arena
7	Bever Falls	Bever Co. Arpt. (BVI)	Charlie's Courtside Rest.
8	Bradford	Bradford Reg. Arpt. (BFD)	Piper Pub & Rest.
9	Butler	Butler Co/K W Scholter Fld. (BTP)	The Runway Restaurant
10	Butler	Butler Co/K W Scholter Fld. (BTP)	Conley's Resort Inn
11	Canadensis	Flying Dollar Arpt. (8N4)	Overlook Inn
12	Clarion Co.	Clarion Co. Arpt. (11D)	Bonanza Family Rest.
13	Clarion Co.	Clarion Co. Arpt. (11D)	Pizza Hut
14	Coatesville	Chester Co. G.O. Carlson (40N)	Flying Machine Cafe
15	Columbia	McGinness Arpt. (8N7)	Columbia Family Rest.
16	Connellsville	Connellsville Arpt. (2G3)	Becker's Shady Side Inn
17	Connellsville	Connellsville Arpt. (2G3)	Valley Dairy (Laurel Mall)
18	Du Bois	Jefferson Co. Arpt. (DUJ)	The Aviator Restaurant
19	East Stroudsburg	Birchwood-Pocono Airpark (ESP)	Birchwood Resort
20	East Stroudsburg	Birchwood-Pocono Airpark (ESP)	Caesar's Pocono Palace
21	Erie	Erie Intl. Arpt. (ERI)	Stonehouse Inn
22	Farmington	Nemacolin Arpt. (9G7)	Nemacolin Woodlands Resort
23	Franklin	Venango Reg. (FKL)	Martino's Delicatessen
24	Harrisburg	Harrisburg Intl. (MDT)	CA1 Services
25	Honesdale	Cherry Ridge Arpt. (N30)	Airport Restaurant
26	Johnstown	Cambria Co. Arpt. (JST)	Rizzo Skyway Rest.
27	Kutztown	Kutztown Aviation Services (N31)	Airport Diner
28	Lancaster	Lancaster Arpt. (LNS)	Lancaster Arpt Rest.
29	Lancaster	Lancaster Arpt. (LNS)	McFlys Pub & Gallery
30	Latrobe	Westmoreland Co. Arpt. (LBE)	Jimmie Monzo's Blue Angel
31	Lock Haven	William T. Piper Mem. (LHV)	Dutch Haven Restaurant
32	Meadville	Port Meadville Arpt. (2G6)	Eddie's
33	Meadville	Port Meadville Arpt. (2G6)	King Family Restaurant
34	Monongahela	Rostraver Arpt. (P53)	Eagles Landing Rest.
35	Mt. Joy/Marietta	Donegal Springs Airpark (N71)	Railroad House Inn
36	Mt. Pocono	Pocono Mountains Muni. (MPO)	The Clam Shack
37	New Hanover	New Hanover Arpt. (N62)	Sunflower Cafe
38	Philadelphia	Northeast Philadelphia (PNE)	94th Aero Squadron
39	Philadelphia	Philadelphia Intl. (PHL)	Airport Restaurant
40	Pittsburgh	Allegheny Co. Arpt. (AGC)	Sky View Restaurant
41	Pittsburgh	Greater Pittsburgh Intl. Arpt. (PIT)	Food Serv. Concessions
42	Reading	Reading Reg./Carl Spaatz (RDG)	Joe's Restaurant

CROSS FILE INDEX
(Pennsylvania Continued)

Location Number	City or Town	Airport Name And Identifier	Name of Attraction
43	Reading	Reading Reg./Carl Spaatz (RDG)	Wild Wings Cafe
44	Selinsgrove	Penn Valley Arpt. (SEG)	Airport Restaurant
45	Seven Spgs Borough	Seven Springs Arpt. (7SP)	Seven Spgs. Mt. Resort
46	Slatington	Slatington Arpt. (69N)	Maple Springs Rest.
47	Smoketown	Smoketown Arpt. (37PA)	T. Burk & Company
48	State College	University Park Arpt. (UNV)	Toftrees Hotel Resort
49	Towanda	Towanda Arpt. (N27)	Pepper Shaker
50	Tunkhannock	Skyhaven Arpt. (76N)	Cross Country Rest.
51	Wellsboro	Grand Canyon State Arpt. (N38)	Coach Stop Inn
52	Wilkes-Barre	Barre Wyoming Valley (WBW)	Colonial Family Rest.
53	Wilkes-Barre	Scranton Intl. Arpt. (AVP)	Intl Coffee Shop
54	Williamsport	Lycoming Co. Arpt. (IPT)	Skyview Restaurant
55	Zelienople	Zelienople Muni. (8G7)	The Plane View Cafe

Articles

City or town	Nearest Airport and Identifier	Name of Attraction
Centre Hall, PA	Penns Cave (N74)	Penn's Cave
E. Stroudsburg, PA	Stroudsburg-Pocono (N53)	Birchwood Resort
Farmington, PA	Nemacolin (Private) (9G7)	Nemacolin Woodlands Resort
Seven Spgs. Borough, PA	Seven Springs (7SP)	Seven Springs Mt. Resort

PA-ABE - ALLENTOWN
ALLENTOWN-BETHLEHEM-EASTON AIRPORT

(Area Code 610) 1, 2

Creative Croissants:

Creative Croissants is located on the second floor (west side) of the Allentown-Bethlehem-Easton Airport terminal building. This restaurant specializes in delicious croissants sandwiches made with all types of fresh ingredients. Breakfast croissants as well as egg sandwiches, fruit muffins, stuffed croissants, chicken, beef and turkey sandwiches are all available. The restaurant can seat about 50 people. They open at 5 a.m. to 8 p.m. 7 days a week. A lounge is reported adjacent to this establishment. For information call 266-8030.

The Glass Terrace:

The Glass Terrace is designed specifically for banquets, group functions, business meetings, weddings and social gatherings. It is located within the ABC Terminal building on the second floor, connected with the lounge and near the A.B.C Coffee Shop. It is ideally suited for companies arranging conferences right on the field especially if your clients or associates happen to be flying in from different locations. In addition to business uses, this facility also caters to many social functions and is well equipped with its own dance floor, speaker podiums, movie screens, plenty of room for live entertainment, discjockeys, bands, as well as banquet and party tables. The Glass Terrace can seat up to 225 persons for auditorium seating, and 185 for banquet or party seating, allowing use of the dance floor and stage area. Their banquet and buffet service runs between $11.95 and $16.75 per person. If food is prepared for your function, there is no charge for the room. Non-catered events are $125.00 for room usage plus $1.00 per person for preparation and cleanup charge. The view from the Glass Terrace overlooks the operations on the airport as well as a beautiful view during sunset and twilight hours. Two week advance notice would be appreciated when arranging your next function. For information call 264-7333 and ask to speak with the banquet coordinator.

Restaurants Near Airport:

Creative Croissants	On Site	Phone: 266-8030
Glass Terrace	On Site	Phone: 264-7333

Lodging: Comfort Inn (Free Pick-up) 391-1500; George Washington Lodge (Free pick-up) 433-0131; Sheraton Jetport (Free pick-up) 266-1000; Hamilton Plaza (Free pick-up) 437-9876; Hilton (Free pick-up) 433-2221.

Meeting Rooms: All facilities listed above under "Lodging" have accommodations for meetings and conferences.

Transportation: DynAir Fueling will provide courtesy transportation to nearby facilities. 266-7343; Also: Avis 264-4450; Budget 266-0667; Hertz 264-4571; National 264-5535; J & J Limousine 776-1516.

Information: Lehigh Valley Convention & Visitors Bureau, P.O. Box 20785, Lehigh Valley, PA 18001, Phone: 882-9200.

Attractions:

The Lock Ridge Furnace Museum is located about 6 miles west-southwest of the Allentown-Bethlehem-Easton Airport. Take State Highway 309 to US Highway 222 southwest. Located in a reconstructed 19th century iron furnace, this museum exhibits the development of the iron and steel industry in this region. Open weekends and holidays call 435-4664 or 5806; Annual events: Lehigh Valley Balloon Festival in late July at the Queen City Airport, Phone: 432-3222.

Airport Information:

ALLENTOWN - ALLENTOWN-BETHLEHEM-EASTON AIRPORT (ABE)
3 mi northeast of town N40-39.14 W75-26.42 Elev: 394 Fuel: 100LL, Jet-A
Rwy 06-24: H7600x150 (Asph-Grvd) Rwy 13-31: H5796x150 (Asph-Grvd)
Attended: continuously Atis: 124.7 Unicom: 122.95 App/Dep Con: 118.2 Tower: 120.5
Gnd Con: 121.9 Clnc Del: 124.05 Public Phone 24 hrs Notes: Landing fees: single $1.00 twin $5.00; Parking: single $2.00, twin $5.00.
FBO: Hawthorne ABE Phone: 266-7343

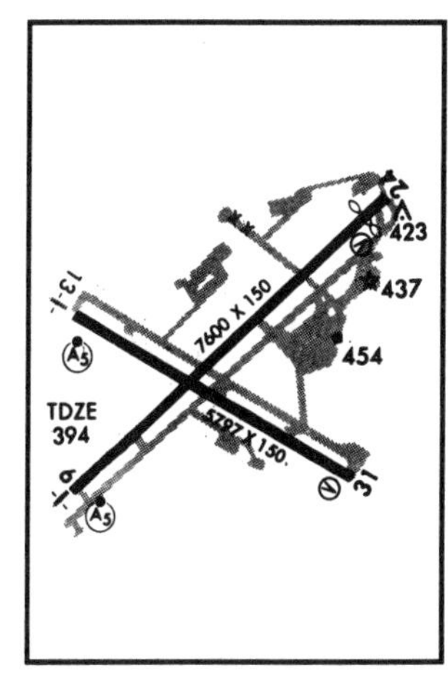

PA-1N9 - ALLENTOWN
ALLENTOWN QUEEN CITY MUNI.

(Area Code 610)

3

Penalty Box Restaurant:

The Penalty Box Restaurant is located about 1/4 mile from the Allentown Queen City Municipal Airport. Courtesy transportation may be available by calling the FBO's on the field. This restaurant provides a unique atmosphere with many plants along with outdoor patio. Accommodations for 220 persons are available within their dining room. Meals can also be prepared- to-go if requested. They will even provide in-flight catering for individual flights on request. For more information about the Penalty Box Restaurant, call 791-4220.

Restaurants Near Airport:

Denny's	1/4 mi	Phone: 797-2176
Penalty Box	1/4 mi	Phone: 791-4220
Ponderosa	1/4 mi	Phone: 797-1411

Lodging: Days Inn Conference Center 395-3731; Hilton Hotel Allentown 433-2221; Motel Allenwood 395-3707.

Meeting Rooms: Days Inn Conference Center 395-3731; Hilton Hotel Allentown 433-2221.

Transportation: Airport courtesy reported; Rental Cars: Thrifty 791-4767;

Information: Lehigh Valley Convention & Visitors Bureau, P.O. Box 20785, Lehigh Valley, PA 18002, Phone: 882-9200.

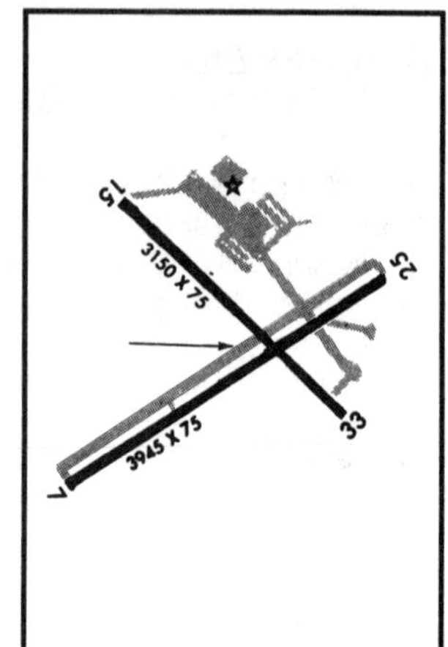

Airport Information:

ALLENTOWN - QUEEN CITY MUNICIPAL (1N9)
2 mi southwest of town N40-34.21 W75-29.29 Elev: 399 Fuel: 100LL, Jet-A
Rwy 07-25: H3945x75 (Asph) Rwy 14-32: H3150x75 (Asph-Grvd) Attended: Mon-Fri 1200-0000Z Sat-Sun 1300-2300Z Summer hours of operation are Mon-Fri 1200-0130Z, Sat-Sun 1300-0100Z
Unicom: 122.7 App/Depp Con: 118.2, 119.65, 124.45 Clnc Del: 118.9
Notes: Landing fee reported
FBO: Airport Manager Phone: 791-4220

PA-AOO - ALTOONA
ALTOONA-BLAIR COUNTY AIRPORT

(Area Code 814)

4

Kitty Hawk:

The Flight Line Restaurant is situated within the terminal building at the Blair County Airport. This family style restaurant is within walking distance from the aircraft parking area. Their hours are from 6 a.m. to 8 p.m. Monday through Friday and 8 a.m. to 9 p.m. weekends. Their menu includes a wide variety of entrees including specialty items like, the Flight Line burger, turkey sandwiches, roast beef, fish, meat loaf, chicken, chicken fried steak and ham dinners, in addition to daily specials offered each day. Average prices run $1.25 to $3.00 for breakfast, $3.00 to $4.00 for lunch and around $5.00 to $6.00 for dinner. The main dining area can seat 58 persons, and exhibits a colonial type atmosphere with floral arrangements, plants and earth tones. Larger groups are also welcome if advance notice is given. They even provide in-flight catering to private and corporate flights as well. For more information, you can call the Flight Line Restaurant at 793-9445.

Restaurants Near Airport:

Kitty Hawk Restaurant	On Site	Phone: 793-9445

Lodging: Altoona-Sheraton (18 miles) 946-1631; Bedford Spring Hotel (22 miles) 623-6121; Days Inn (10 miles) 944-9661; Spring Garden Farm Bed & Breakfast 224-2569.

Meeting Rooms: Days Inn (10 miles) 944-9661.

Transportation: Taxi Service: Yellow Cab 944-6105; Rental Cars: Hertz 793-3983; National 793-3089.

Information: Blair County Convention & Visitors Bureau, Logan Valley Mall, Rte 220 & Goods Lane, Altoona, PA 16602, Phone: 943-4183 or 800-84-ALTOONA.

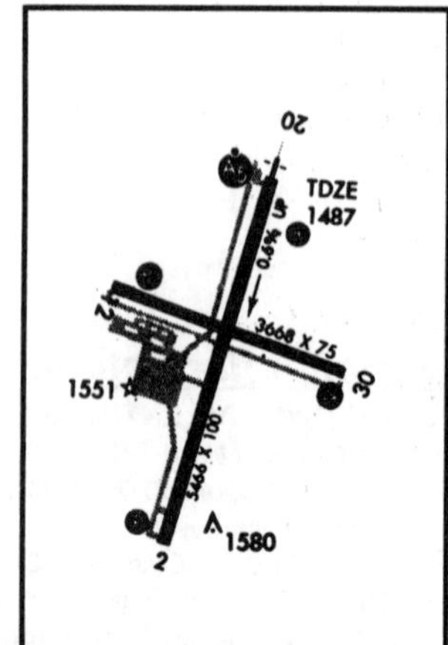

Airport Information:

ALTOONA - ALTOONA-BLAIR COUNTY AIRPORT (AOO)
12 mi south of town N40-17.78 W78-19.20 Elev: 1504 Fuel: 100LL, Jet-A
Rwy 02-20: H5466x100 (Asph-Grvd) Rwy 12-30: H3668x75 (Asph) Attended: 1100Z-dusk
Unicom: 123.0
FBO: Penn-Air, Inc. Phone: 793-2164

PA-7N8 - BALLY BUTTER VALLEY GOLF PORT

(Area Code 610)

5

Butter Valley Restaurant:

The Butter Valley Restaurant is situated adjacent to the airport on the Butter Valley Golf Port. The runway is located in the middle of the golf course with a turf surface and asphalt at the south end. This snack bar is open during the week between 7 a.m. and 6 p.m. and weekends from 6:30 a.m. to 1:30 p.m. Their menu includes, breakfast items, hot dogs, hamburgers, grilled cheese sandwiches, French fries, and ice cream. Average prices run between $2.00 & $3.00 for most selections. The restaurant can seat between 40 and 50 people. Four big bay windows allow for a nice view of the golf course and airport. Larger groups are welcome with advance notice. Many pilots enjoy flying in for a game of golf and a meal at the snack bar. For more information call the Butter Valley Restaurant at 845-2491.

Attractions:

The Butter Valley Golf Course is located adjacent to the airport. The pro-shop, and restaurant are situated together. The pro-shop is being enlarged to accommodate more equipment. For information about the golf course call 845-2491.

Airport Information:

BALLY - BUTTER VALLEY GOLF PORT (7N8)
1 mi east of town 40-23-53N 75-33-53W Elev: 500 Fuel: 100LL, MOGAS
Rwy 16-34: 2420x85 (Asph-Turf) Attended: daylight Hours Unicom: 122.8 Notes: Rwy 16-34 lies in the middle of the golf course, Runway 16-34 1535x24 Asph at south end; remainder turf.
FBO: Butter Valley Aviation Phone: 845-2491

Restaurants Near Airport:
Butter Valley Restaurant On Site Phone: 845-2491

Lodging: Bally Spring Farm Bed & Breakfast 3 mi, 845-7781; Cab Frye Motel (3 miles) 679-5955.

Meeting Rooms: None Reported

Transportation: Airport courtesy car reported.

Information: Pennsylvania Office of Travel Marketing, Department of Commerce, P.O. Box 61, Warrendale, PA 15086, Phone: 800-VISIT-PA.

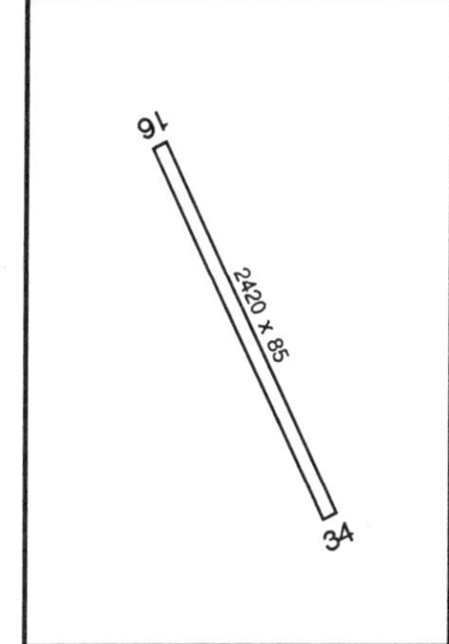

PA-B17-BEDFORD BEDFORD COUNTY

(Area Code 814)

6

The Arena:

The Arena Restaurant is situated about 300 yds or 1/4 mile from the Bedford Airport. To reach the restaurant, turn left out of the airport and go south on highway 220. This is a combination family style and fine dining restaurant that is open between 7 a.m. and 10 p.m. Monday through Saturday and on Sunday from 7 a.m. to 9 p.m. Their menu includes choices like prime rib, filet mignon, choice steaks, seafood, chicken dishes, pasta dishes, and a salad buffet with hot vegetables and steamed shrimp. They also offer a nice selection of breakfast and luncheon dishes as well. A hot lunch buffet, weekly lunch and dinner specials draw a great many customers. Average prices run $3.00 to $4.00 for breakfast, $2.00 to $5.00 for lunch and between $8.00 and $30.00 for dinner. The restaurant decor provides lots of brass, wood and stained glass. Their main dining area can seat between 150 and 175 persons. They also offer a banquet room able to accommodate from 12 to 200 persons. The Arena restaurant combines itself with a Quality Inn with 66 rooms available. Entertainment is featured Tuesday through Saturday in their lounge, and a special "Comedy Night" is presented once a month. For more information call The Arena Restaurant at 623-8074.

Restaurants Near Airport:

The Arena Rest.	1/2 mi S.	Phone: 623-8074
Ed's Steak House	400 yds	Phone: Unknown
Hoss's Steak Hse	1/4 mi	Phone: 623-2793

Lodging: Best Western (1/4 mile) 623-9006; Super 8 Motel (1/4 mile) 800-843-1991; Quality Inn (1/4 mile) 623-5188; All motels just off end of runway.
Meeting Rooms: Best Western 623-9006; Super 8 Motel 800-843-1991; Quality Inn 623-5188;
Transportation: Bun Air Corp can provide courtesy transportation for fly-in guests between 8 a.m. and 5 p.m., by calling 623-8171. Also Rental Cars: Hertz Bed Exxon 623-6897.
Information: Bedford County Tourist Promotion Agency, 141 South Juliana Street, Bedford, PA 15522, Phone: 623-1771.

Attractions:

Bedford Springs Country Club 623-6121; Bed Elks Country Club 623-9314; Down-River Golf Club 652-5193.

Airport Information:

BEDFORD - BEDFORD COUNTY AIRPORT (B17)
3 mi north of town N40-05.12 W78-30.73 Elev 1161 Fuel: 100LL, Jet-A
Rwy 14-32: H4113x75 (Asph) Attended: Mon-Sat 1200-2300Z, Sun 1330-1700Z
Unicom: 122.7 Public Phone located adjacent field Notes: Overnight parking $3.50
FBO: Bun Air Corp. Phone: 623-8171

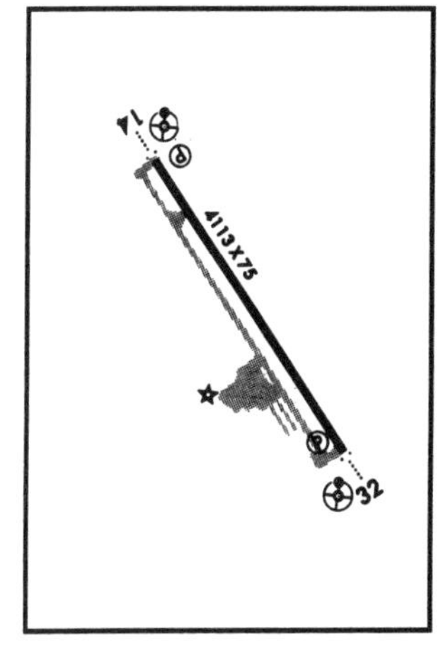

PA-BVI - BEVER FALLS
BEAVER COUNTY AIRPORT

(Area Code 412)

7

Restaurants Near Airport:

Charlie's Restaurant	1 mi	Phone: 846-2072
Flightline	On Site	Phone: 843-9778
Sal's Italian Restaurant	1/2 mi	Phone: 843-4020

Charlie's Courtside Restaurant, Inc:

This fine dining facility is located about 1 mile from the Beaver County Airport. If walking or driving from the airport, turn right at the airport entrance and go about 3 blocks. This restaurant is open Sunday Through Thursday from 7 a.m. to 10 p.m., Friday through Saturday from 7 a.m. to 11 p.m. and their lounge remains open from 11 a.m. to 2 a.m. They have a large salad selection, and main entrees consisting of steak, chicken, fish, and surf & turf. Prime rib is their specialty. All their desserts are homemade. There are daily luncheon specials, as well as dinner specials for $5.95 to $7.95. Their menu prices run an average of $2.00 for breakfast, $4.00 for lunch and $12.00 for dinner. The decor of the restaurant is contemporary. Private banquet rooms are also available. For information call 846-2072.

Lodging: Holiday Inn (10 miles, free shuttle service), Route 18, Beaver Falls, Phone: 846-3700.

Meeting Rooms: There is a small conference room within the main terminal building; Community College Aviation Science Center (On Airport), has an auditorium and two large conference rooms.

Transportation: Beaver Aviation Services, Inc or Prospect Aviation offer courtesy transportation; SOS Taxi, 775-3333; Agency Rental Car, 728-3334; Enterprise Rental Car, Phone: 728-2286

Information: Beaver County Tourist Promotion Agency, 215B Ninth Street, Monaca, PA 15061-2028; Phone: 728-0212 or 800-342-8192.

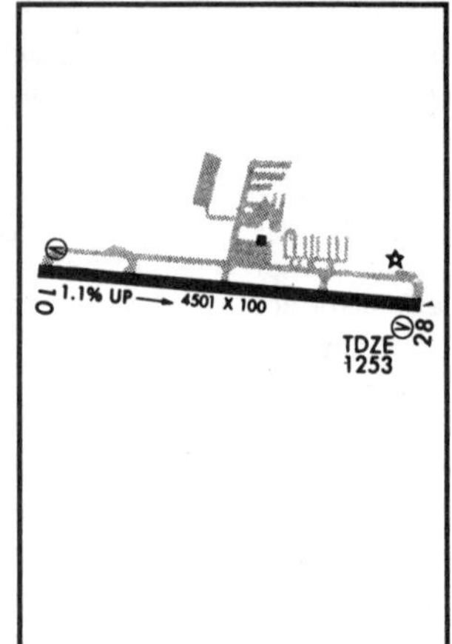

Airport Information:

BEAVER FALLS - BEAVER COUNTY AIRPORT (BVI)
3 mi northwest of town   N40-46.35 W80-23.49   Elev: 1253   Fuel: 100LL Jet-A
Rwy 10-28: H4501x100 (Asph-Grvd)   Attended: 1200-0200Z   Atis: 118.35   Tower: 120.3
Gnd Con: 121.8   Public Phone 24hrs   Notes: Overnight fee $5.00 per night.
FBO: Beaver Aviation Services, Inc., Phone: 843-8600
FBO: Prospect Aviation Phone: 843-3222
FBO: Stensin Aviation, Phone: 846-4900

PA-BFD - BRADFORD
BRADFORD REGIONAL AIRPORT

(Area Code 814)

8

Restaurants Near Airport:

Piper Pub & Restaurant	On Site	Phone: 368-5928
Schooners (Marina)	16 mi SW	Phone: 723-5466
Westline Inn	10 mi	Phone: 778-5103

Piper Pub & Restaurant:

The Airport Restaurant is located in the terminal building at the Bradford Regional Airport. This cafe and family style restaurant features home cooking, along with homemade desserts and pies. Their menu also includes daily specials and Friday night fish frys. Meal prices range from $3.25 for breakfast, and $4.25 for lunch and dinner. Restaurant hours are Monday through Saturday 6:00 a.m. to 9:00 p.m., Sunday 8 a.m. to 9 p.m. They will cater meals if given advance notice. Once expansion is underway, future plans include a lounge added to the restaurant. For information call 368-5928.

Lodging: De Soto Holiday House (Near town, 10 mi), 515 South Avenue, Bradford, PA 16701, 70 rooms, lounge with entertainment on Fri & Sat. Meeting rooms, driving range, miniature golf, Phone: 362-4511. Howard Johnson (Near town, 10 mi) 100 South Davis Street, US 219 exit Elm & Forman Streets., 120 rooms, 3 story, heated pool, Cafe open 7 a.m. to 10 p.m., Lounge 11 p.m. to 2 a.m. Phone: 362-4501.

Transportation: Hertz Rent-A-Car Phone: 362-8800, National Rent-A-Car Phone: 362-4002.

Information: Bradford Area Chamber of Commerce, 10 Main Street, P.O. Box 135, Bradford, PA 16701, Phone: 368-7115.

Attractions:

Kinzua National Park & Dam, 18 mi SW Kinzua, Railroad Bridge & Steam Locomotive Train Ride, Annual Crook Farm County Fair (Settlement, art & crafts, entertainment, exhibits) held last weekend in August, Phone: 362-6730.

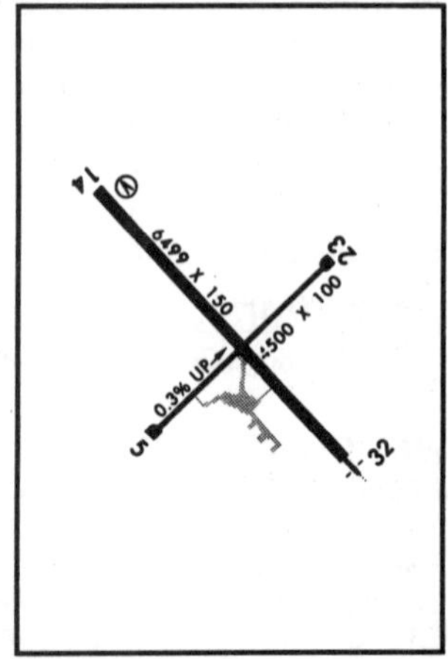

Airport Information:

BRADFORD - BRADFORD REGIONAL AIRPORT (BFD)
9.5 mi south of town   N41-48.18 W78-38.41   Elev: 2143   Fuel: 80, 100LL, Jet-A   Rwy 14-32: H6499x150 (Asph-Grvd)   Rwy 05-23: H4500x100 (Asph)   Attended: 1100-0300Z   Unicom: 122.95   Public Phone 24 hrs   Notes: Landing Fee: (Twins); Light $3.00, Heavy .45/1000 lbs., (Singles); Light $3.00, Parking Fee: singles $3.00, twins $5.00, heavy aircraft $9.00, FREE breakfast on Sundays at airport restaurant with purchase of 10 gal or more of fuel, (April 1st through October 31st).
Bradford Regional Airport Phone: 368-5928
FBO: Hill Top Aviation Phone: 368-8970

PA-BTP - BUTLER
BUTLER CO/K W SCHOLTER FLD.

(Area Code 412)

9, 10

Restaurants Near Airport:

The Runway	On Site	Phone: 586-6599
Conley's Resort Inn	3 mi.	Phone: 586-7711

The Runway:
This restaurant is a fine dining establishment located right on the Butler County airport. Thanks to one of our contributors, we learned that this restaurant was well worth the visit. The meals are prepared with care. The steaks are cooked to perfection, just the way you like them. Prices for full course meals average around $15.00. The dining room has large windows that allow a great view of the aircraft parking area, as well as airport operations. Hours of operation are 11 a.m. to 10 p.m. Tuesday through Saturday, and 11 a.m. to 8 p.m. on Sunday. They are closed on Monday. For information call the restaurant at 586-6599.

Conley's Resort Inn: *This resort is located about 3 miles from the airport. It contains a restaurant that is open 7 a.m. to 10 p.m., lounge 11 a.m. to 2 a.m., and Sunday until midnight, 56 rooms, 10 with kitchen facilities, 18 hole golf course, putting green, tennis courts, indoor swimming pool with 150 foot water slide, whirlpool, sauna, meeting rooms and cross country skiing. We were told that pilots flying in to the Butler County Airport can obtain transportation through "Air Ride" taxi/limo service for a nominal fee. For information call the resort at 586-7711.*

Lodging: Conley's Resort Inn (3 mi.) 586-7711; Days Inn 3-5 mi. 287-6761; MeKee's Motel 3-5 mi. 586-2272; Super 8 (3 mi.) 287-8888; Applebutter Inn (Slippery Rock, PA) 794-1844.
Meeting Rooms: Conley's Resort Inn (3 mi) 586-7711; Days Inn (3-5 mi.) 287-6761.
Transportation: Rental cars reported at FBO; Also "Air Ride" taxi/limo service available.
Information: Butler County Visitors Bureau, 100 North Main Street, P.O. Box 1082, Phone: 283-2222.

Attractions: Conley's Resort Inn is located about 3 miles from the airport. Golf packages. Phone: 586-7711; Morain State Park, 16,180 acre park with lake, fishing, boating, hunting, horseback riding, winter activities and cabin rentals. For information call 368-8811.

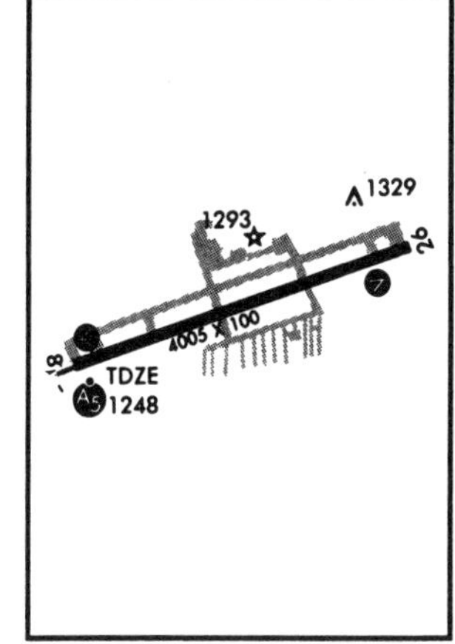

Airport Information:
BUTLER - BUTLER CO/K W SCHOLTER FIELD (BTP)
5 mi southwest of town N40-46.62 W79-56.98 Elev: 1248 Fuel: 100LL, Jet-A Rwy 08-26: H4005x100 (Asph-Grvd) Attended: 1100-0230Z Unicom: 122.8 Notes: Arpt has noise abatement procedures contact airport manager 586-6665. Also three 80 foot lighted towers 2700 feet SW Rwy 08 & 560 feet S Rwy centerline.
FBO: Butler Aviation Serv. Phone: 586-7786
FBO: Butler Air Phone: 586-6023

PA-8N4 - CANADENSIS
FLYING DOLLAR AIRPORT

(Area Code 717)

11

Restaurants Near Airport:

Daniel's Hill Top Lodge	Trans.	Phone: 595-7531
Overlook Inn	Adj Arpt.	Phone: 595-7519

Overlook Inn:
The Overlook Inn is located adjacent to the Flying Dollar Airport, and according to the restaurant manager, is within walking distance from aircraft parking area. This fine dining facility is open Monday through Saturday between 6 a.m. and 9 p.m. and Sunday between 5 p.m. and 8 p.m. Entree selections include, prime steaks, Chateau Briand, Cajun Shrimp, Veal Overlook, grilled rabbit, Rack of Lamb Dijon, and many others. The decor of the dining room provides a country atmosphere with seating for 125 persons, with lanterns on each table. Larger groups are also welcome, if advanced notice is given. All menu selections can be prepared-to-go. The Overlook Inn combines a fine dining restaurant with a 12 room country Bed and Breakfast establishment. A conference room is also available for business guests. For more information call the Overlook Inn at 595-7519.

Lodging: Buck Hill Inn (3-1/2 miles) 595-7441; Daniel's Hill Top Lodge (1 mile) 595-7531; Overlook Inn (Adj Airport) 595-7519; Pines Vacation Resort (1 mile) 595-7172; Sky Top Lodge (1-1/2 mile) 595-7401.

Meeting Rooms: Conference room available at the Overlook Inn able to accommodate between 25 and 30 people. For information call 595-7519.

Transportation: Airport or restaurant will supply trans.

Information: Pennsylvania Office of Travel Marketing, Department of Commerce, P.O. Box 61, Warrendale, PA 15086, Phone: 800-VISIT-PA.

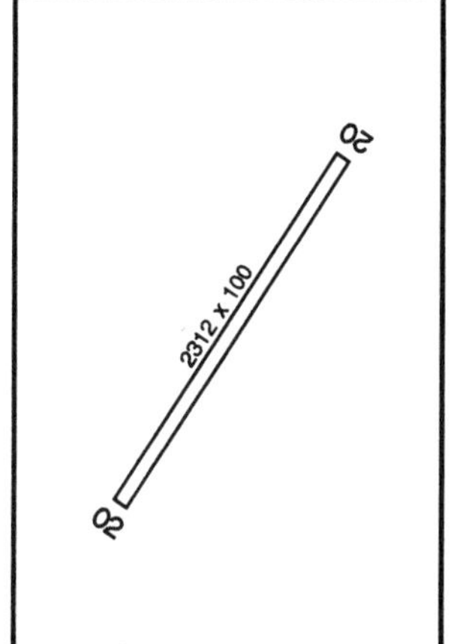

Attractions:
The following activities reported nearby. Golf courese, tennis, swimming, horse back riding etc.

Airport Information:
CANADENSIS - FLYING DOLLAR AIRPORT (8N4)
2 mi north of town N41-13.01 W75-14.98 Elev: 1400 Rwy 02-20: 2312x100 (Turf)
Attended: continuously CTAF: 122.9
Flying Dollar Airport Phone: 595-3465

Penn's Cave

(Information submitted by Penn's Cave).

Among the many things to see and do in Central Pennsylvania is one attraction that will introduce you to underground wonders located only 1/4 to 1/2 mile from the Centre Hall, Penn's Cave Airport (N74). The cavern is the only allwater cavern and wildlife sanctuary. Penn's Cave is a limestone cavern that is rich in history and geology and is a stunning example of nature's flawless beauty. The wildlife sanctuary adjacent, is a natural preserve for North American animals and birds where you can truly take a ride on the wild side.

Centuries ago, the Seneca Indians discovered this natural landmark in the Valley of the Karoondinha (Penn's Valley). The famous legend of the Indian Princess, Nitanee, from whom the famous Penn State Nittany Lion is named, and her lover, Malachi Boyer, has been told around campfires for generations. Unable to marry because of Indian custom, they ran away and were captured, and Malachi was thrown into Penn's Cave to die. Local history also tells of Indians and early explorers using the dry rooms for shelter. The cavern was opened to the public in 1885, and today it has been placed on The National Register of Historic Places.

About 500 million years ago, much of Central Pennsylvania lay beneath a shallow sea. Limestone originally was ocean bottom sedimentation that was compressed into rock and squeezed into folds that have worn away forming valleys in the Ridge and Valley area of the Central Pennsylvania Appalachians. Later, surface water entered and dissolved the limestone to form caves. The unusual feature of Penn's Cave is that the cavern tour is taken on flat-bottom motorboats that float on an underground stream through rooms and passageways filled with stalactites and stalagmites, past pillars and columns ranging in color from soft gray to vibrant red. Well-informed and trained guides enhance your knowledge, plus entertain you with the history and folklore, of the cavern. Beneath the boat swim rainbow, brook and brown trout that make the cavern their home, and as the boat leaves the underground and emerges onto Lake Nitanee, mallard ducks, mute swans and blue herons can be seen in their natural setting. Allow at least one hour for this tour, and be sure to bring a jacket because the temperature is 52 degrees year around.

Photo by: Penn's Cave Undrground boat tours are given through Penn's Cave.

Penn's Cave also offers a guided farm, wildlife and nature tour by vehicle that takes you over approximately 1000 acres.

Seasonal Events: Steam Engine Days are held at Penn's Cave in June and September each year. Sponsored by the Nittany Antique Machinery Association, these shows feature antique tractor and equipment parades, steam engines in operation, horse drawn wagons and equipment, craft sales and demonstrations and a giant flea market. Special homemade food is featured which includes ice cream, apple butter, soups, and pot pie, just to mention a few items.

The cavern is open everyday from the middle of February through November (weekends in December); however, for the daily schedule of all tours, you may want to call ahead. The cavern gift shop has gifts and souvenirs on display. They also have a snack bar that offers light sandwiches, beverages and snacks.

Airport Information: Penn's Cave Airport is attended during daylight hours and is located N40-53.42 W77-36.15 and 2 mi east of town. The field elevation is 1260, with 100LL fuel available. Its active runway is 07-25: H2490x40 (Asph). Unicom is 122.8. A 750 foot mountain 1/2 mile south and 700 foot mountain 1/2 mile north should be noted. For more information write: Penn's Cave, R.R. 2, Box 165A, Centre Hall, PA 16828. Or call 814-364-1664.

PA-11D - CLARION CO./SHIPPENVILLE
CLARION COUNTY AIRPORT

(Area Code 814) | 12, 13

Bonanza Family Restaurant:

This restaurant is located about 1 to 2 miles north of the Clarion County Airport on Route 66. It is classified as a cafeteria and serves a wide selection of steak, chicken and seafood entrees. Daily specials are offered Monday through Friday, with a free beverage refill with meals. Prices range from $3.00 for breakfast, $4.50 for lunch and $6.00 for dinner. There is a separate banquet room for groups and parties. Take out orders are available from anything on their menu. The restaurant is open during the summer, Sunday through Thursday from 6:15 a.m. to 9:00 p.m., and Friday and Saturday from 6:15 a.m. to 10:00 p.m. During the winter they are open Sunday through Thursday 6:30 a.m. to 8 p.m. and Friday and Saturday 6:30 a.m. to 9 p.m. For information call 226-4313.

Restaurants Near Airport:

Bonanza Family Rest.	2 mi N.	Phone: 226-4313
Marianne Towers	2 mi N.	Phone: 226-9600
Pizza Hut	2 mi N.	Phone: 226-5020

Lodging: Days Inn, (4 miles east) 226-8682; Holiday Inn (4 miles east) 226-8850.

Meeting Rooms: Meeting and conference room is located in the airport terminal building, (20'x20'). Also Days Inn and Holiday Inn have accommodations for meetings. (See Lodging listed above)

Transportation: Clarion County Airport Authority will help provide transportation whenever possible. Also: Dick's Taxi, 226-6860; Rental Cars: Gross Motors, 226-7650; Seidle Chevrolet, 226-8300; Sherman Chrysler, 226-9550.

Information: Clarion Area Chamber of Commerce, 41 South Fifth Avenue, Clarion, PA 16214, Phone: 226-9161.

Pizza Hut:

The Pizza Hut restaurant is located about 1 to 2 miles from the Clarion County Airport. To reach the restaurant you take Route 66 north to the restaurant. The airport authority will provide transportation if possible . Taxi service is also available. They are open Sunday through Thursday from 11 a.m. to 10 p.m. and Friday and Saturday 11 a.m. to 12 a.m. They specialize in pizza and pasta dishes, and their prices are reasonable at $3.00 to $5.00 for lunch and dinner. For information call 226-5020.

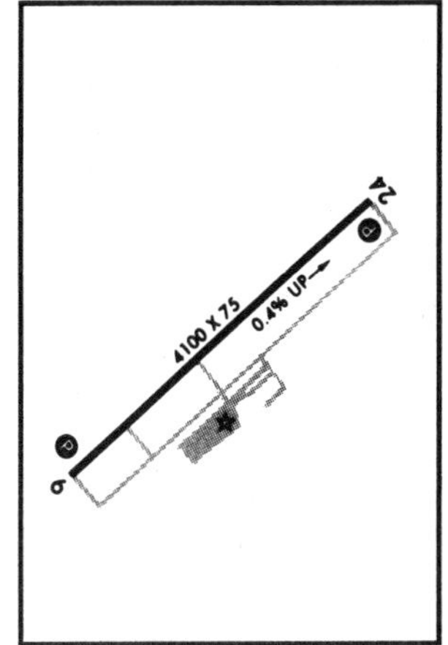

Airport Information:

CLARION COUNTY - CLARION COUNTY AIRPORT (11D)
2.6 mi northwest of town N41-13.55 W79-26.46 Elev: 1458 Fuel: 100LL, Jet-A
Rwy 06-24: H4100x75 (ASPH) Attended: 1300-0100Z Unicom: 122.8 Public Phone 24hrs.
Notes: Overnight parking, Single, $4.00, Multi, $6.00 (waved if fuel is purchased).
Clarion Co. Arpt. Auth. Phone: 226-9993 FBO: Shippenville Aviation Phone: 226-9391

PA-40N - COATESVILLE
CHESTER COUNTY G.O. CARLSON

(Area Code 610) | 14

Flying Machine Cafe:

The Flying Machine Cafe is a fairly new facility that has been in business for about one year since the time of our original interview. It is located within the main terminal building at the Chester County G.O. Carlson Airport. This family dining facility is situated right on the main apron where ample aircraft parking is available. You can see landings and takeoffs as well as most ground activity from within the restaurant. Their menu has a full assortment of delicious meals including breakfast selections. Restaurant hours are Friday and Saturday from 8 a.m. to 12 a.m. and Sunday through Thursday from 8 a.m. to 10 p.m. On Saturdays and Sundays they feature a breakfast buffet between 8 a.m. and 1 p.m. Additional choices listed on their menu, which are favorites with many customers, are their onion soup, a variety of hamburgers, pastas and New York strip steak. After enjoying your main course, try their popular Philadelphia cheese cake. The restaurant seats about 85 people with a combination of tables, booths and counter seating. In-flight catering is yet another specialty of the Flying Machine Cafe. Sandwiches, cheese trays, fruit and just about anything on their menu can be prepared for carry out. If you are planning a large group fly-out the people at the Flying Machine Cafe can even arrange special accommodations for banquets in the next door facility. Smaller groups are easily accommodated within the main restaurant. For more information call 380-7977.

Restaurants Near Airport:

Flying Machine	On Site	Phone: 380-7977

Lodging: Comfort Inn 15-17 mi. 524-8811; Hampton Inn 15-17 mi. 363-5555; Holiday Inn Express 15-17 mi 524-9000; Holiday Inn Hotel & Conference Center 15-17 mi. 363-1100; Tabas Hotel 12 to 14 mi. 269-6000.

Transportation: Car rentals available on airport by calling 384-2497; Taxi service: Downtown Taxi Service 384-2900, 269-3000.

Meeting Rooms: Flying Machine Cafe can arrange meeting accommodations, 380-7977; Also Holiday Inn Hotel & Conference Center (15-17 mi.) 363-1100.

Information: West Chestertown County Chamber of Commerce 384-9550.

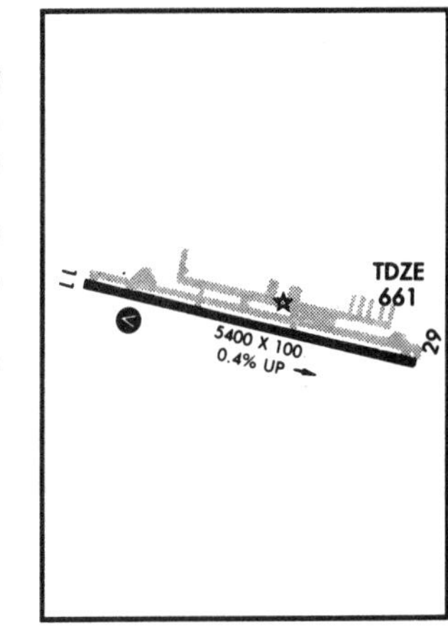

Airport Information:

COATESVILLE - CHESTER COUNTY G.O. CARLSON (40N)
2 mi west of town N39-58.74 W75-51.93 Elev: 661 Fuel: 100LL, Jet-A Rwy 11-29: H5400x100 (Asph-Grvd) Attended: countinuously Unicom: 122.7
FBO: Chester County Aviation Phone: 384-9000

PA-8N7 - COLUMBIA McGINNESS AIRPORT

(Area Code 717) 15

Columbia Family Restaurant:

The Columbia Family Restaurant is located 2 blocks from the McGinness Airport. This family style restaurant can easily be reached by walking, and is open between 5 a.m. and 9 p.m. Monday through Saturday and Sunday from 6 a.m. to 8 p.m. Their menu includes a wide variety of entrees including breakfast items, waffles, broasted chicken, grilled liver, spaghetti and meat balls, sweet and sour pork and much more. Their dining area can seat approx. 150 persons and has a contemporary atmosphere. Selections from their menu can also be prepared-to-go as well. This is a popular restaurant with the flying community. For more information about the Columbia Family Restaurant call 684-7503.

Restaurants Near Airport:
Columbia Family Restaurant 2 blks Phone: 684-7503

Lodging: Pleasant View Motel (2 miles)

Meeting Rooms: None Reported

Transportation: None Reported

Information: Pennsylvania Office of Travel Marketing, Department of Commerce, P.O. Box 61, Warrendale, PA 15086, Phone: 800-VISIT-PA.

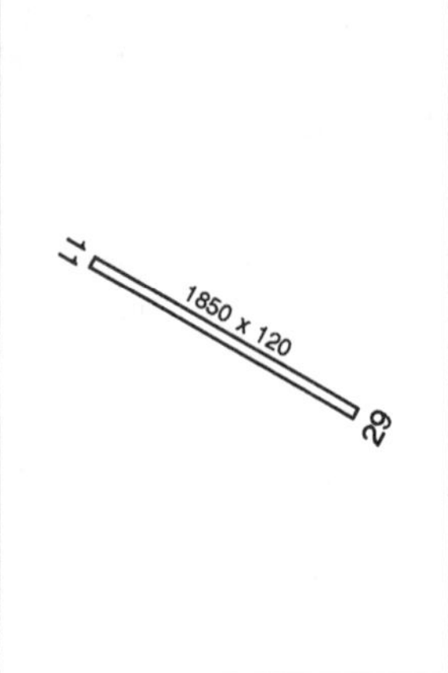

Airport Information:

COLUMBIA - McGINNESS AIRPORT (8N7)
1 mi southeast of town N40-01.51 W76-29.23 Elev: 334 Rwy 11-29: 1850x120 (Turf)
Attended: daylight hours CTAF: 122.9
FBO: McGinness Aviation Service Phone: 684-6157

Not to be used for navigational purposes

PA-2G3 - CONNELLSVILLE CONNELLSVILLE AIRPORT

(Area Code 412)

16, 17

Becker's Shady Side Inn:

Becker's Shady Side Inn is located about 1 mile from the Connellsville Airport. Transportation is available by airport courtesy car, taxi or rental car. This fine dining facility provides elegant dining with carpeted floors, linen covered tables, and chandeliers. Three banquet rooms allow for excellent accommodations for business meetings and luncheons. Their menu includes main entrees such as fresh seafood, veal, beef and chicken including prime steaks and lobster. They serve lunch from 11:30 to 2 p.m. and dinner from 4:30 to 10 p.m. 6 days a week. They are closed on Sunday. For More information call 438-0931.

Valley Dairy (Laurel Mall):

The Valley Dairy Restaurant is located in the Laurel Mall across the street from the Connellsville Airport. This restaurant is within walking distance to the airport and is frequented by many pilots flying into the area. This establishment is open Monday through Saturday between 8 a.m. and 9 p.m. and on Sunday from 9 a.m. to 5 p.m. Their menu includes entrees like spaghetti, salisbury steak, all types of sandwiches, a full breakfast line, and many different types of desserts, including ice cream. They offer breakfast and luncheon specials as well as weekly dinner specials. Average prices run $2.00 to $2.50 for breakfast, $4.50 to $5.50 for lunch and $5.50 to $7.50 for most dinner items. The main dining room can accommodate up to 125 persons with available space for fly-in groups. Please give the restaurant notice if you plan on flying in with a large group. Meals can also be prepared-to-go if requested. For more information about the Valley Dairy Restaurant call 626-1520.

Restaurants Near Airport:

Bakers Shady Side	1 mi	Phone: 438-0931
Silver Leaf	1/2 mi	Phone: 628-9099
Valley Dairy	1/4 mi	Phone: 626-1520
Yee Old Inn	N/A	Phone: 628-9825

Lodging: Holiday Inn (7 miles) 437-2816; Melody Lodge (3 miles) 628-9600; Mount Vernon Inn (5 miles) 437-2704; Silver Leaf Motel (1/2 mile) 628-9099.

Meeting Rooms: Becker's Shady Side Inn (1 mile) 438-0931; Mount Vernon Inn (5 miles) 437-2704.

Transportation: Taxi service available, rental cars, and a airport courtesy car is reported: Avis 626-1610; S.M.E. 626-1610.

Information: Greater Connellsville Chamber of Commerce, 923 W Crawford Avenue, Connellsville, PA 15425, Phone: 628-5500.

Airport Information:

CONNELLSVILLE - CONNELLSVILLE AIRPORT (2G3)
4 mi southwest of town N39-57.54 W79-39.43 Elev: 1265 Rwy 05-23: H3458x100 (Asph)
Rwy 14-32: H2979x100 (Asph) Attended: 1300-0200Z Unicom: 122.8
Connellsville Airport Phone: 626-1610

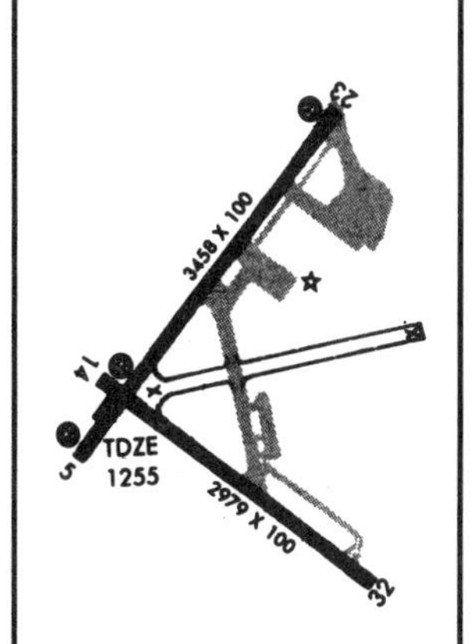

PA-DUJ - DU BOIS
JEFFERSON COUNTY AIRPORT

(Area Code 814) 18

The Aviator Restaurant & Lounge:

This family style restaurant is located within the main terminal building at the Jefferson County Airport. The facility is open Monday through Friday from 6:30 a.m. to 10:30 p.m., and Saturday and Sunday from 7:30 a.m. 10:30 p.m. Homemade soups and cinnamon rolls are served daily. Specialties of the house include Italian, seafood and steak dinners. Included on their full service menu are appetizers and desserts. Breakfast, lunch and dinner specials are offered along with a fish fry every Friday. Average prices run $4.00 for breakfast, $5.00 for lunch and $6.00 for dinner. The restaurant is decorated in a World War II theme displaying many Items and pictures. All selections on their menu may be packaged to go. Meat and cheese trays can also be prepared. Fly-in groups are welcome with accommodations for up to 50 persons. Advance notice is suggested. For information call 328-5281.

Restaurants Near Airport:

The Aviator Restaurant	On Site	Phone: 328-5281
Gateway Lodge	25 mi W.	Phone: 800-843-6862

Lodging: Best Western (9 miles) 800-371-6200; Hilton Motel (10 miles) 849-7344; Holiday Inn (Free transportation, 8 miles) 371-5100; Quality Inn (10 miles) 849-8001; Ramada Inn (Transportation, 11 miles) 371-7070;

Meeting Rooms: Best Western-Penn Rose Motor Inn 800-371-6200; Holiday Inn 371-5100; Ramada 371-7070.

Transportation: Hertz 328-5204; National 371-8171.

Information: Du Bois Area Chamber of Commerce, 71 Beaver Drive, DuBois, PA 371-5010. Phone: 371-5010.

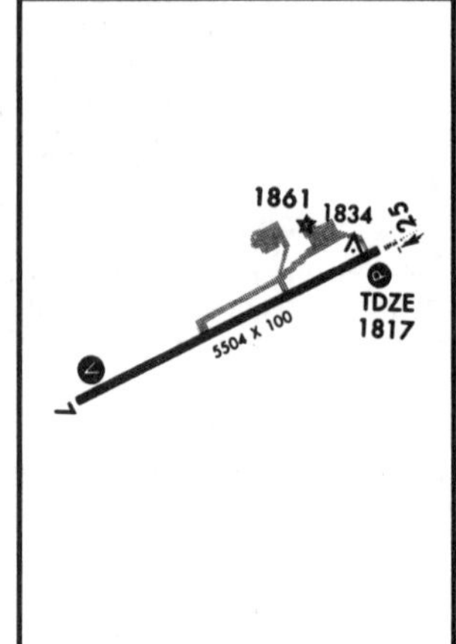

Airport Information:

DU BOIS - JEFFERSON COUNTY AIRPORT (DUJ)
7 mi northwest of town N41-10.70 W78-53.92 Elev: 1817 Fuel: 100LL, Jet-A
Rwy 07-25: H5504x100 (Asph-Grvd) Attended: Sun-Fri 1100-0430Z, Sat 1100-0100Z
Unicom: 122.95 Public Phone 24hrs (Terminal Bldg) Notes: No landing fee for non commercial aircraft, Overnight parking: Single $2.00, Twin $5.00
FBO: Beechwoods Flying Service Inc. Phone: 375-0150

PA-N53- EAST STROUDSBURG STROUDSBURG-POCONO

(Area Code 717) 19, 20

Birchwood Resort:

The Birchwood Resort is situated on the Birchwood Pocono Airport, and is about a 1,000 foot walk from the airport. Within the resort is a fine dining facility open for breakfast during the week from 9 a.m. to 12 p.m. and 6 p.m. to 7:30 p.m. for dinner. On weekends their dinner hours begin at 6 p.m. until 8 p.m. Their menu includes different selections and specials for each night of the week. On Sunday they feature New York sirloin and roast leg of lamb. Monday nights it's country and western with barbecued ribs, Wednesday it's roast prime rib, chicken, seafood scampi and lasagna. Their prices are based on couples and run $17.00 for most breakfast dishes and $37.00 for dinner selections priced for two. The dining room can accommodate 75 persons and is elegantly decorated with linen covered tables and flowers. Groups are also welcome with advance notice preferred. The resort itself encompasses a 400 acre site complete with private airstrip and has been successful in business for over 35 years. Most of the lodging accommodations available are in private chalets. For more information about the Birchwood Resort, call 629-0222.

Caesar's Pocono Palace:

This resort is reported to be located about 7 or 8 miles from the Birchwood-Pocono Airport. The Caesar's Pocono Palace offers lodging with 169 units and 155 suites. Their dining room is open between 10 a.m. and 2 a.m. Recreational amenities include a 9 hole golf course, driving range, putting green, Marina with water skiing and paddle boats. Swimming and fishing can be enjoyed. Lawn games and bicycles are also available. Weight machines, whirlpool, sauna and indoor and outdoor swimming pools, in additional to accessibility to down hill skiing only 3 miles away along with on site cross country skiing. For information call 588-6692.

Restaurants Near Airport:

Birchwood Resort	7-8 mi.	Phone: 629-0222
Caesar's Pocono Palace	7-8 mi.	Phone: 588-6692

Lodging: Birchwood Resort (7-8 miles) 629-0222 Caesar's Pocono Palace (7-8 miles) 588-6692.

Meeting Rooms: None reported

Transportation: Taxi Service, Phone: 421-6068; Car Rental: Avis 800-331-1212; Bruce Price Exxon 421-9102; Budget 421-6913; Freedom 421-5577; Hertz 424-5676.

Information: Pocono Mountains Vacation Bureau, 1004 Main Street, Stroudsburg, PA 18360. Phone: 424-6050 or 800-POCONOS.

Attraction:

Birchwood Resort and Caesar's Pocono Palace are two of several fine resorts within the Stroudsburg area. Alpine Mountain Ski Area provides a vertical drop of 500 feet with 2 quad chairlifts, 595-2150 or 800-233-8240; Also: Canoe the Delaware River by calling Chamberlain Canoes at Phone: 421-0180; Quiet Valley Living Historical Farm depicting a 1765 settlement, Phone: 992-6161; Stroud Mansion with tours given, Phone: 421-7703.

Airport Information:

EAST STROUDSBURG - STROUDSBURG-POCONO-AIRPARK (N53)

3 mi north of town N41-02.15 W75-09.64 Elev: 480 Fuel: 80, 100LL, Jet-A

Rwy 08-26: H3087x30 (Asph) Attended: 1300-dusk Unicom: 123.0 Allentown App/Dep Con: 119.65

Sparta Air Service Phone: 421-8900

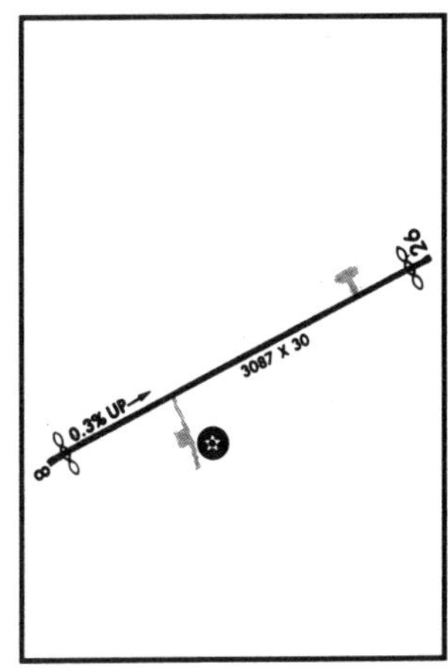

Birchwood Resort

E. Stroudsburg, PA (PA-N53)

Resort Airpark (ESP) temporarily/ permanently closed due to overgrown trees on neighboring property. Land at Stroudsburg-Pocono (N53)

During our conversation with the management of Birchwood Resort & Airpark, we learned that their Rwy 14-32: H2537 x 50 (Asph) airport containing lighting, would be closed for an indefinite period of time due to large trees that are blocking the approach end to their runway. Birchwood Resort had no control over this because the trees in question are situated on a neighboring parcel of property. The owner of that property has thusfar been unwilling or unable to clear the trees. For this reason the airport has been closed. However, Stroudsburg-Pocono Airport (N53) is only 7 or 8 miles away.

Accommodations at Birchwood include 6 different plans. Plan A through F offers lodging in a variety of settings, from private chalets featuring log burning fireplaces and jacuzzi, to separate apartments, and a colonial mansion designed for use by larger groups.

Included in the activities at this resort are indoor miniature golf, outdoor driving range, nearby golfing (2 miles), exercise room, bowling, champagne boat rides, trap shooting, horse drawn carriage and sleigh rides and many outdoor sporting games. Throughout the year, they also plan several social activities as well. For current information about the Birchwood Resort you can call 800-233-8177, or 717-629-0222.

Photo by: Birchwood Resort

PA-ERI - ERIE
ERIE INTERNATIONAL AIRPORT

(Area Code 814) 21

Stonehouse Inn:

The history of the original owners of this English Manor House, is an interesting one, which dates back to the days of prohibition, and the struggle to survive for the Kneidinger family. Built from stone using blocks from a nearby railroad trestle, this restaurant today exhibits the original construction in its European style. Located about 500 yards west of the Erie Airport on Route 5, this fine dinning facility specializes in European dishes with homemade soups, appetizers, and desserts. Selections average in price from $9.95 for lunch, and $16.95 to $22.00 for dinner. The restaurant is open Tuesday through Saturday from 6:00 p.m. to 10:30 p.m. (Closed Sunday & Monday). Groups are also welcome. The restaurant is surrounded by 5 acres of beautiful trees, ponds and flowers. The setting of this restaurant and dining experience will provide you with a tranquil and romantic atmosphere. For information call 838-9296.

Restaurants Near Airport:

Air Host (Erie)	On Site	Phone: N/A
Butch's Place	1 mi E.	Phone: 838-4163
The Hearth	2 mi E.	Phone: 838-1262
Stonehouse Inn	1/2 mi W.	Phone: 838-9296

Lodging: Bel Aire Motel (2 miles), 833-1116; El Patio (2 miles), 838-9772; Holiday Inn Downtown (6 miles), 456-2961; Glass House Inn (2 miles), 833-7751; Holiday Inn South (10 miles), 868-3209; Peek'n Peak Recreation (30 miles), Clymer, NY, 716-355-4141.
Meeting Rooms: Bel Aire Motel, (2 miles), 833-1116
Transportation: Erie Airways, Inc., (Transportation to nearby facilities); Rental Cars and Taxi's: Avis, 833-9879; Budget, 838-4502; National, 838-3041; Erie Cab Co., 452-6090; Erie Limousine, 838-4117; EMTA/City Bus, 452-3515.
Information: Erie Area Chamber of Commerce, 1006 State Street, Erie, PA 16501 or call 454-7191

Attractions:

Presque Isle State Park (5 Miles northeast) invites you to enjoy 3,202 acres of recreation on a seven mile peninsula stretching out into Lake Erie. 6 miles of sandy beaches with swimming, fishing, boating and hiking. For information Call 871-4251. Contact Chamber of Commerce for information on museums and points of interest, (See Information listed above).

Airport Information:

ERIE - ERIE INTERNATIONAL AIRPORT (ERI)
5 mi southwest of town N42-04.92 W80-10.57 Elev: 733 Fuel: 100, Jet-A Rwy 06-24: H6500x150 (Asph-Grvd) Rwy 02-20: H3507x150 (Asph) Attended: continuously Atis: 120.35 Unicom: 122.95 App/Dep Con: 121.0 Tower: 118.1 Gnd Con: 121.9 Clnc Del: 126.8 Public Telephone 24hrs Notes: Twin engine and larger landing fee rate, $.7107 per thousand pounds. ($5.00 Minimum) **FBO: Erie Airways, Inc., Phone: 833-1188**

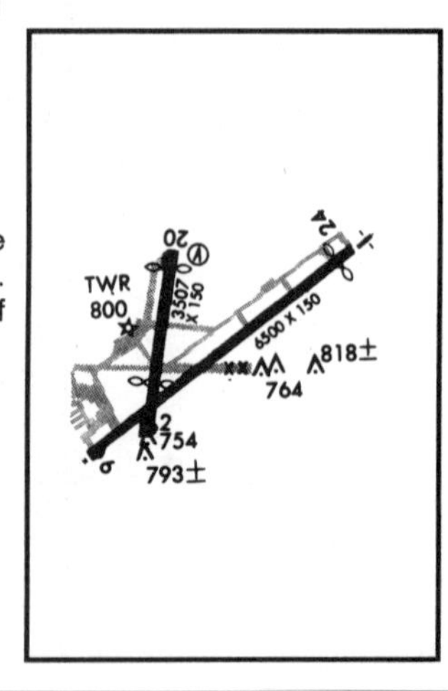

PA-9G7 - FARMINGTON NEMACOLIN AIRPORT

(Area Code 412)

22

Nemacolin Woodlands Resort Restaurants:

*This facility contains 4 full service restaurants: 1) Golden Trout (Fine Dining); 2) Allures; 3) Cafe Woodlands; and 4) Caddy Shack; Their own private airstrip is located adjacent to the resort. With 4 restaurants, they can accommodate any type of dining requirements necessary. They specialize in French, Continental Cuisine. The "**Caddy Shack**" has a casual decor designed for the golfer, with light fare. **"Allures"** provides a full course of famous desserts. Nutritional and low calorie selections are also available. This restaurant provides casual dining in an atmosphere reminiscent of the Art Deco Period. Resort clothes appropriate. **"Cafe Woodlands"** restaurant provides snacks and sandwiches, to complete dinners with casual dining. The **"Golden Trout"** is their premier dining room and offers a challenge to the most discriminating palate. This restaurant has a dress code and a jacket is required with neck tie suggested for the men. Reservations are also a must. This resort facility employs many different types of chefs and make most meals from scratch. Prices range from $10-$21.95 for breakfast, $10-$20 for lunch, and $15-$50 for dinner. Every Sunday from 11 a.m. to 3 p.m. they serve a brunch complete with live entertainment, for $17.95 per person. The Nemacolin Woodlands Resort is a AAA, 4 diamond award winner, and also recently received a Mobil 4 Star Rating. They boast of a world class spa, golf course, golf academy, luxurious accommodations and over 30 activities, with three lakes nearby. For a get-away weekend or a romantic dinner, they will accommodate your special needs. For more information call the resort at 329-8555.*

Restaurants Near Airport:

Allures	Adj	Phone: 329-6958
Caddy Shack	Adj	Phone: 329-6138
Cafe Woodlands	Adj	Phone: 329-6164
Golden Trout	Adj	Phone: 329-6958

Lodging: Nemacolin Woodlands Resort (Adj. Airport), 150 Inn rooms and condos available. For information call the resort at 412-329-8555.

Meeting Rooms: Nemacolin Woodlands Resort (Adj Airport), 38,000 square foot conference center; Groups for 2 to 300 guests; Private meeting rooms; Ballrooms; Exhibit areas; Lecture hall able to accommodate up to 200 people; Audiovisual equipment is available.

Transportation: All fly-in guests will be picked up by courtesy limo or van upon arriving. Courtesy van will take you to all property locations.

Information: Nemacolin Woodlands Resort, Rt. 40, P.O. Box 188, Village of Farmington, Pennsylvania 15437, Phone: 412-329-8555.

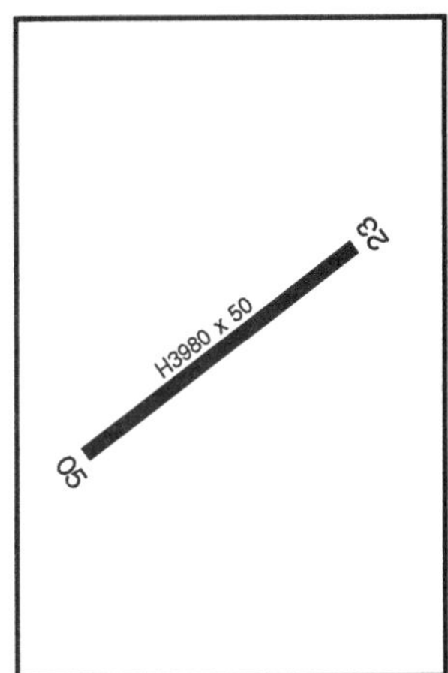

Airport Information

FARMINGTON - NEMACOLIN AIRPORT (9G7)

1 mi east of town 39-48-30N 79-33-00W Elev: 2007 Fuel: None Rwy 5-23: 3980x50 (Asph) Attended: unattended Notes: No FBO on premises (Private), **Permission required prior to landing** call 412-329-8555.

Photo by: Nemacolin Woodlands Nemacolin Woodlands Fly-in Resort & Executive Conference Center.

Photoby Nemacolin Woodlands Resort

Nemacolin Woodlands' 3,980 x 50 foot runway makes this a most accessible resort for those who would like to fly in for the day, a week or longer. And is also great for business conferences.

Nemacolin Woodlands Resort

Farmington, PA (PA-9G7)

Nemacolin Woodlands private airstrip makes this a most accessible resort for those who would like to fly in for the day or a week, for business or a mini getaway. A choice of 4 different but unique restaurants are available on the premises. The guest rooms are spacious and comfortable. Inn accommodations range from attractive standard rooms to their elegantly appointed penthouse suites with jacuzzis. Balconies, whirlpool baths and hospitality areas are some of the available features. An affordable alternative for the whole family is one of their condominiums. Both one and two bedroom units are available with easy access to the Inn, restaurants and all amenities. Condominiums have some or all of the following features: a log burning fireplace, outdoor deck, complete kitchen and laundry facilities. Arranging conferences for your business or group can be easy, when taking advantage of the services at this resort. The Nemacolin atmosphere guarantees the best conditions for learning, training, problem solving and thinking. Conference coordinators will attend to the details and assure that your meetings run smoothly and efficiently. These facilities include accommodations for groups from 2 to 300 guests, a 38,000 square foot conference center, breakout rooms, ballroom, exhibit area, lecture hall that seats 200 people, and advanced audiovisual technology. When its time to play, you will find it at Nemacolin Woodlands. Their assistance can range from organizing an event, to keeping an eye on the children. Just a few of these amenities include: lighted tennis courts, fishing, nature walks, boating and canoeing, shuffleboard, biking, horseback riding, indoor & outdoor pools, cross country skiing, petting zoo and game rooms. Scavenger hunts, mystery weekends, theme parties, and even a hay ride can be arranged. Nearby attractions also include the famous Frank Lloyd Wright's "Fallingwater" architectural masterpiece, the "Laurel Caverns" or White water rafting at Ohiopyle State Park. For information call the resort at (412) 329-8555 or (800) 422-2736

PA-FKL - FRANKLIN VENANGO REGIONAL

(Area Code 814) 23

Restaurants Near Airport:
LaSiesta Restaurant 1/2 mi Phone: 432-1814
Martino's Delicatessen 1/4 mi Phone: 432-2525

Lodging: Franklin Motel (2 miles) 437-3061; Holiday Inn (7 miles) 677-1221; Idlewood (1 mile, trans) 437-3003; Inn at Franklin (2 miles) 437-3031.

Meeting Rooms: Holiday Inn (7 miles) 677-1221; Inn At Franklin (2 miles) 437-3031.

Transportation: Taxi: Baker's Area Transit 437-1997. Rental Cars: Hertz (Adjacent) 432-3515.

Information: Franklin Area Chamber of Commerce, 1256 Liberty Street, Suite 2, Franklin, PA 16323, Phone: 432-5823.

Martino's Delicatessen:

Martino's Delicatessen is located 1/4 mile from the Chess Lamberton Airport. Fly-in guests can walk to this facility with no problem. This is a combination snack bar and family style restaurant that is open 11 a.m. to 8 p.m. 7 days a week. Their menu specializes in Italian dishes like lasagna, pizza, and spaghetti with all their noodles, pizza crusts and sauces make from scratch. They also feature items like meat loaf, turkey, and ham, in addition to many other selections. Specials on meals change daily. The dining area can accommodate between 32 and 40 people, and offers a delicatessen type atmosphere. Fly-in groups are also welcome. Many pilots have made the trip to Martino's a regular destination. For more information call 432-2525.

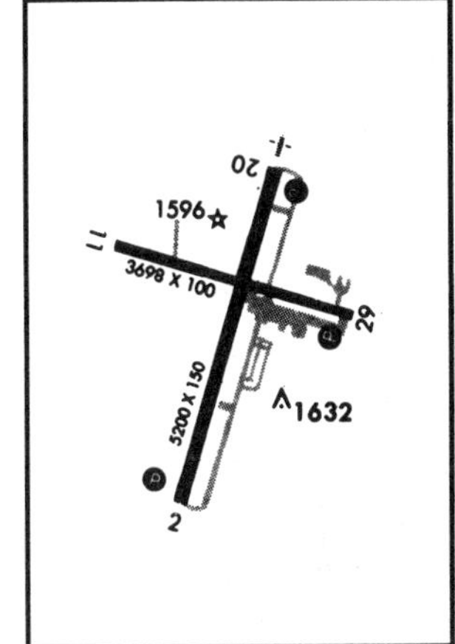

Airport Information:

FRANKLIN - VENANGO REGIONAL (FKL)
2 mi southwest N41-22.67 W79-51.62 Elev: 1540 Fuel: 100LL, Jet-A
Rwy 02-20: H5200x150 (Asph-Grvd) Rwy 11-29: H3698x100 (Asph) Attended: Mon-Fri 1100-0400Z, Sat 1100-0300, Sun 1200-0400Z Unicom: 122.7 Clnc Del: 126.25
Venango Airport Manager Phone: 432-5333

PA-MDT - HARRISBURG HARRISBURG INTERNATIONAL

(Area Code 717) 24

Restaurants Near Airport:
Alfred's Victorian 2 mi Phone: 944-5373
CA1 Services On Site Phone: 948-0967
Sunburst Restaurant 1/2 mi Phone: 944-4895

Lodging: Compri (6 miles) 558-9500; Congress Motel (5 miles) 939-9531; Days Inn Airport (5 miles) 939-1600; Holiday Inn (6 miles) 939-7841; Howard Johnson (6 miles) 564-4730; Marriott (6 miles) 564-5511; Red Roof Inn (6 miles) 939-1331.
Meeting Rooms: Holiday Inn (6 miles) 939-7841; Howard Johnson (6 miles) 564-7430; Marriott (6 miles) 564-5511.
Transportation: Taxi Service: Aero Corp 944-4019; Diamonds 939-7805; Lancaster Limo 732-3533; Yellow 238-7252; Rental Cars: Avis 948-3720; Hertz 944-4088; National 948-3710; Thrifty 848-5710.
Information: Capitol Region Chamber of Commerce, 114 Walnut Street, P.O. Box 969, Harrisburg, PA 17101, Phone: 232-4121 or Harrisburg Hershey-Carlisle Tourism & Convention Bureau, Phone; 232-1377.

CA1 Services:

The CA1 Services Restaurant is located in the Harrisburg International Terminal Building. Shuttle service from the fixed base operators on the field is available. It is at least a 3 block walk from the aircraft parking area to the restaurant. This establishment contains two separate facilities on the premises. A snack bar is open from 6 a.m. to 8 p.m. 7 days a week. Light fare is served such as hotdogs, pizza, popcorn and ice-cream. The main restaurant is down the concourse from the snack bar, and consists of a family style restaurant open between 6 a.m. and 7:30 p.m. 7 days a week. Their menu features a "catch of the day" (seafood), New York strip, burgers, chicken breast dishes, Philadelphia cheese steak, as well as a full breakfast menu. Average prices run $4.50 to $5.00 for breakfast, $5.00 to $6.00 for lunch and between $7.50 and $10.25 for dinner. Their main dining room, with a contemporary atmosphere, can accommodate 118 people. A salad bar is also available throughout the lunch and dinner hours, between 11 a.m. and 7:30 p.m. Larger fly-in groups are welcome with advance notice. In-flight catering is also provided. For more Information call 948-0967.

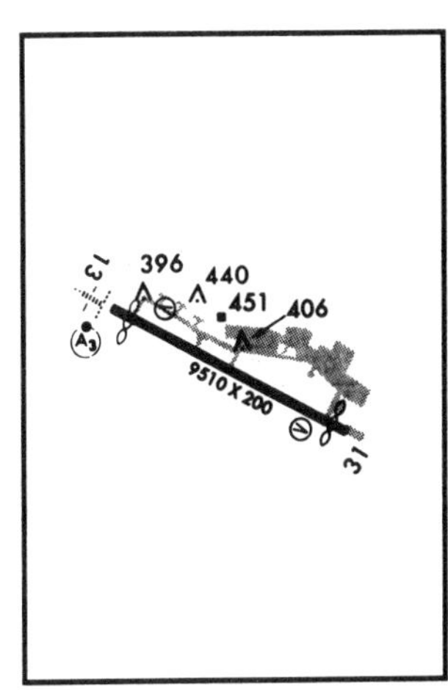

Airport information:

HARRISBURG/MIDDLETOWN - HARRISBURG INTERNATIONAL AIRPORT (MDT)
8 mi southeast of town N40-11.61 W76-45.80 Elev: 310 Fuel: 100LL, Jet-A
Rwy 13-31: H9501x200 (Asph-Conc-Grvd) Attended: continuously Unicom: 122.95
Harrisburg App/Dep Con: 124.1, 126.45, 118.25 Tower: 124.8 Gnd Con: 121.7
FBO: Stambaugh's Air Service Phone: 944-1787

PA-N30 - HONESDALE CHERRY RIDGE AIRPORT

(Area Code 717) 25

Airport Restaurant:

No information was received about this establishment. However we suspect this facility is in operation. Call the Cherry Ridge Airport Managers office for verification. Phone: 253-5833.

Restaurants Near Airport:
Airport Restaurant On Site Phone: N/A
Towne House Diner 3 mi Phone: 253-1311

Lodging: Many in vicinity (Call airport manager's office 253-5833)

Meeting Rooms: None Reported

Transportation: Information on Taxi and Rental Car service through airport manager's office 253-5833

Information: Wayne County Chamber of Commerce, 742 Main Street, Honesdale, PA 18431

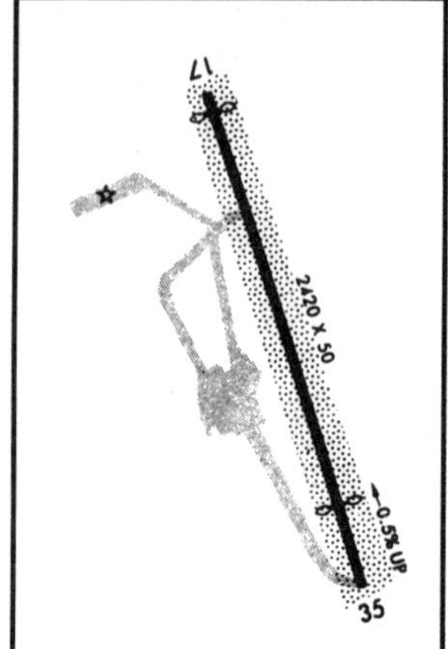

Airport Information:

HONESDALE - CHERRY RIDGE AIRPORT (N30)
3 mi south of town 41-30-55N 75-15-07W Elev: 1357 Fuel: 80, 100LL
Rwy 17-35: H2420x50 (Asph) Attended: 1200-0200Z Unicom: 122.8
FBO: Cherry Ridge Service Phone: 253-5833

PA-JST - JOHNSTOWN CAMBRIA COUNTY AIRPORT

(Area Code 814) 26

Rizzo's Skyway Restaurant:

The Rizzo's Skyway Restaurant is located in the terminal building at the Johnstown Cambria County Airport. This combination family style and fine dining facility is open weekdays from 8 a.m. to 9 p.m., Saturday from 8 a.m. to 10 p.m. and Sunday from 8 a.m. to 8 p.m. Their menu includes selections like egg plant, chicken Sontino, spaghetti and pasta dinners, and much more. Average prices run $2.00 for breakfast, $3.00 to $4.00 for lunch and $6.00 to $11.00 for dinner. Daily specials are offered. Their main dining room can handle 150 persons and offers a great view tof the airport with arriving and departing aircraft through encased windows. Their dining room also has linen covered tables with flower decorations for each setting. Rizzo's Skyway Restaurant also provides in-flight catering in addition to crew meals. If interested in this service or for more information about the restaurant call 539-8829.

Restaurants Near Airport:
Rizzo's Skyway Restaurant On Site Phone: 539-8829

Lodging: Comfort Inn (5 miles) 266-3678; Days Inn (5 miles) 269-3366; Holiday Inn (5 miles) 535-7777; Super 8 Motel (4 miles) 266-8789; Quality Inn (7 miles) 226-5851.

Meeting Rooms: Holiday Inn (5 miles) 535-7777; Quality Inn (7 miles) 226-5851; Super 8 motel (4 miles) 266-8789.

Transportation: Air East, Inc. (Exxon Avitat) can provide courtesy transportation; Also Hertz 536-8755; Budget 266-6088; National 536-0079; Friendly Cab 467-5587; Yellow Cab 535-7737.

Information: Cambria County Tourist Council, 111 Market Street, Johnstown, PA 15901, Phone: 536-7993.

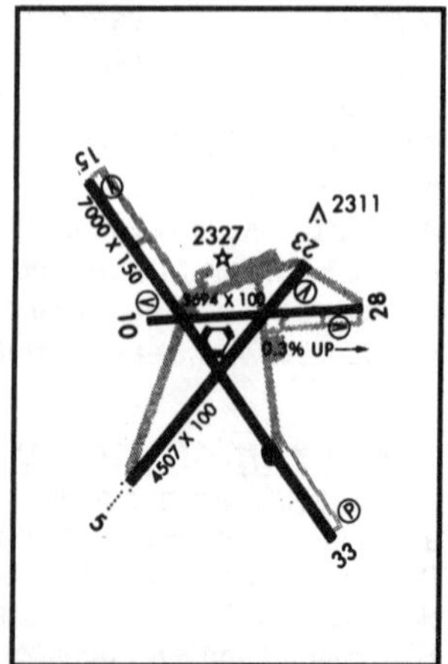

Airport Information:

JOHNSTOWN - CAMBRIA COUNTY AIRPORT (JST)
3 mi northeast of town N40-18.97 W78-50.04 Elev: 2284 Fuel: 100LL, Jet-A
Rwy 15-33: H7000x150 (Asph-Grvd) Rwy 05-23: H4507x100 (Asph-Grvd)
Rwy 10-28: H3694x100 (Asph) Attended 1300-0430Z Unicom: 122.95 Tower: 125.75
Gnd Con: 121.7
Cambria County Airport Phone: 536-0002, 536-5103

PA-N31 - KUTZTOWN
KUTZTOWN AVIATION SERVICES

(Area Code 610)

27

Airport Diner:

The Airport Diner is located only 50 to 100 yards from the Kutztown Aviation Services Airport. This restaurant is open 24 hours, 7 days a week, and specializes in home-made cooking. All of their baking is done right on the premises, with freshly made desserts, pastries appetizers, salads and soups in addition to breakfast, lunch and dinner selections. Daily specials are also featured as well. Average prices run $2.50 for breakfast, $3.00 for lunch and between $5.00 and $7.00 for dinner. The decor of the restaurant follows an old style 50's diner with a modern dining area. Fly-in groups up to as many as 50 people are welcome, with reservations. Meals-to-go and take-out orders can also be provided. The airport and restaurant is located near the Kutztown University in the heart of the Pennsylvania Dutch Valley with many Amish attractions situated within this region. For more information about the Airport Diner call the restaurant at 683-5450.

Restaurants Near Airport:

Airport Diner	On Site	Phone: 683-5450
Fancy Pantry	2 mi W.	Phone: 683-8640
Moselem Springs Inn	5 mi W.	Phone: 944-8213
Whispering Springs	3 mi E.	Phone: 683-5000

Lodging: Lincoln Motel (2 miles, No pick-up service) 683-3456.

Meeting Rooms: Kutztown University, depending on season, does have accommodations for meetings, usually in summer. Call 683-4112 for more information.

Transportation: Ugly Duckling Rental cars 683-8800.

Information: Lehigh Valley Convention & Visitors Bureau, P.O. Box 20785, Lehigh Valley, PA 18002, Phone: 882-9200.

NO AIRPORT DIAGRAM AVAILABLE

Airport Information:

KUTZTOWN - KUTZTOWN AVIATION SERVICES, INC (N31)

1 mi south of town N40-30.21 W75-47.23 Elev: 512 Fuel: 80, 100LL

Rwy 17-35: 2435x240 (Turf-Asph) Rwy 10-28: 2260x150 (Turf) Attended: 1400Z to dusk

Unicom: 122.8

FBO: Kutztown Airport Phone: 683-5666

Photo by: Airport Diner The Airport Diner at Kutztown Aviation Services in Kutztown, PA is popular with many pilots.

PA-LNS - LANCASTER
LANCASTER AIRPORT

(Area Code 717) **28, 29**

Lancaster Airport Restaurant:

This restaurant is located in the terminal building at the Lancaster Airport, and is a short walk from the main ramp. Their hours are from 6:30 a.m. to 8:00 p.m. Monday through Friday, 8:00 a.m. to 4:00 p.m. on Saturday and 9:00 a.m. to 6:00 p.m. on Sunday. Entrees consist of homemade selections including breakfast, soup and sandwiches, and many other specials which change daily. Average prices run, $5.00 for breakfast, $6.00 for lunch and $8.00 for dinner. The restaurant has recently been remodled opening up some walls in order to allow a nice view of the activity on the airport. and increasing the seating from 80 to 170. The dining area is decorated with pictures and models of airplanes, giving it a friendly casual atmosphere. There is also a lounge. The Lancaster Airport Restaurant frequently caters to private groups and organizations arranging get-togethers and parties. They supply US-AIR with 55 crew meals a week and will gladly provide catered meals for all pilots on-the-go. For information you can call 569-4102.

McFlys Pub & Gallery:

This restaurant is a casual yet fine dining establishment that is very popular within the region. McFly's Pub & Gallery offers three separate atmospheres. "Avenues Night Club" offers entertainment; McFly's offers a beer garden with 35 different beers on tap; and The "Gallery" which is their casual yet fine dining restaurant. Their dining room is open 7 days a week between 5 p.m. to 12 a.m. Their dining room has a cozy atmophere. Specialties of the house are pizza, pasta, seafood and steaks. To reach the establishment you can call a taxi service at the airport. We were told Friendly or Yellow taxi are usually used most often. For more information about McFlys Pub & Gallery call 299-3456.

Restaurants Near Airport:

Dutch Apple Dinner Theatre	9 mi. SW.	Phone: 898-1900
General Sutter Inn	3 mi. N.	Phone: 626-2115
Lancaster Arpt. Restaurant	OnSite	Phone: 569-4102
McFlys Pub & Gallery	8 mi. S.	Phone: 299-3456

Lodging:
Eden Resort Inn; 5 mi., S.E., 569-6444, Quality Inn; 9 mi. S.W., 898-2434, Cresthill by Hilton; 5 mi. S.W., 560-0880.

Conference Centers:
Eden Resort Inn; 569-6444, Lancaster Host Golf Resort & Conference Center; 299-5500, Willow Valley Family Resort & Conference Center; 464-2711.

Transportation:
Lancaster Aviation, 569-1221; Romar Aviation, 569-8296; The Friendly Taxi, 392-7327; Yellow Cab 397-8108; Lancaster Limousine 653-8141; Lancaster Co. Taxi, 626-8294.

Information:
Pennsylvania Dutch Convention & Visitors Bureau, 501 Greenfield Road, Lancaster, PA 17601, Phone: 299-8901, 800-723-8824; Lancaster Chamber of Commerce, 397-3531; Pennsylvania Dutch Visitors Bureau, 501 Greenfield Road, PA 17601; Phone: 299-8901.

Attractions:

The Lancaster area blends modern industrial, colonial past and the Pennsylvania Dutch present who reside in the heart of a Dutch-populated region making up a wel- known tourist attraction. Traveling off the main highways, you share the roads with horse drawn carriages and Amish buggies. The Landis Valley Museum at 2451 Kissel Hill road is 2-1/2 miles north of the city, off PA 272. This museum contains the largest collection of Pennsylvania German objects in the United States. Craft Days at Landis Valley Museum, exhibits broom making, candle making and black smiths during June. Harvest Days, held on the 1st weekend in October, demonstrates more than 50 traditional craft and harvest time activities. The museum contains 22 exhibit buildings and two farmsteads, and is open daily except Monday and closed most holidays. For information call 569-0401. Additional attractions in the area include the "Stasburg Railroad Museum of Pennsylvania, exhibiting more than 50 locomotives, freight and passenger cars dating from 1825. (April-Thanksgiving except Monday, 687-8628)., Sightseeing tours by Historic Lancaster Walking Tour 392-1776. Many more activities, shops and attractions are available to the visitor. For more information contact the Pennsylvania Dutch Visitors Bureau, 501 Greenfield Road, PA 17601 or call 299-8901.

Airport Information:

LANCASTER - LANCASTER (LNS)
4.3 north of town N40-07.30 W76-17.77 Elev: 403 Fuel: 100LL, JetA Rwy 08-26: H5398x150(Asph) Rwy 13-31: H4102x100(Asph) Attended Mon-Fri 1100-0400Z, Sat 1200-2345, Sun 1300-0400Z Tower: 120.9 Gnd: 121.8 Unicom: 122.95 Notes: Landing fee waved with fuel purchase.

FBO: Henry Weber Aircraft	**Phone: 569-2691**
FBO: Lancaster Flight Center	**Phone: 569-5341, 800-247-8294**
FBO: Reading Aviation	**Phone: 569-6842**
FBO: Sensenich Propeller Company	**Phone: 569-3711, 800-462-3412**

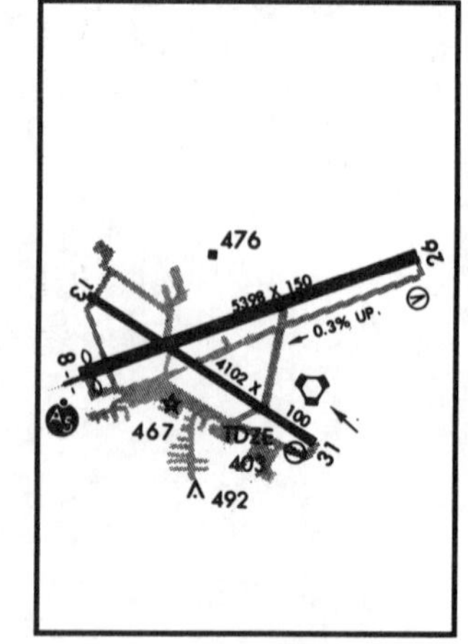

PA-LBE - LATROBE
WESTMORELAND COUNTY AIRPORT

(Area Code 412) 30

Jimmie Monzo's Blue Angel:

This restaurant, located in the main terminal building on the third floor, is situated nearest to Vee Neal and Latrobe Aviation. Through huge glass windows, guests can enjoy a fine meal while viewing the activity and aircraft moving about on the Westmoreland County Airport. Unique in its decor, this facility contains many autographed photos of famous people which decorate the walls. Their menu contains a wide selection of entrees with such items as seafood, veal, steaks, prime rib and all types of pasta dishes, along with soup and salad bar. Sunday brunch begins at 9 a.m. to 2 p.m. for $10.95 and on Friday they feature an Italian and seafood buffet from 5 p.m. to 9 p.m. for $11.95. Seating for this restaurant can accommodate between 200 and 250 people. Conveniently located on the airport, the restaurant is frequented by many fly-in customers and aviation clubs arranging get-togethers. Entrees run about $3.95 for breakfast, $4.25 for lunch and $7.95 to $14.95 for dinners. The restaurant is open from 10 a.m. to 9 p.m. throughout the week and Saturday & Sunday from at 9 a.m. to 9 p.m. Their motto is: "Drive or Fly We Would Love You To Stop By!". For information call 539-3980.

Restaurants Near Airport:
Monzo's Blue Angel On Site Phone: 539-3980

Lodging: Sheraton Inn, Route 30 Greensburg, PA, Phone: 836-6060; Mission Motor Inn (1 mile) 539-1606; Mountain View Hotel (3 miles) 834-5300;

Meeting Rooms: Sheraton Inn (See listing above)

Transportation: Taxi: Veterans 537-7708; Rental Cars: Budget 539-7100; Hertz 539-1512; National 539-9339.

Information: Pennsylvania Office of Travel Marketing, Department of Commerce, P.O. Box 61, Warrendale, PA 15086, Phone: 800-VISIT-PA.

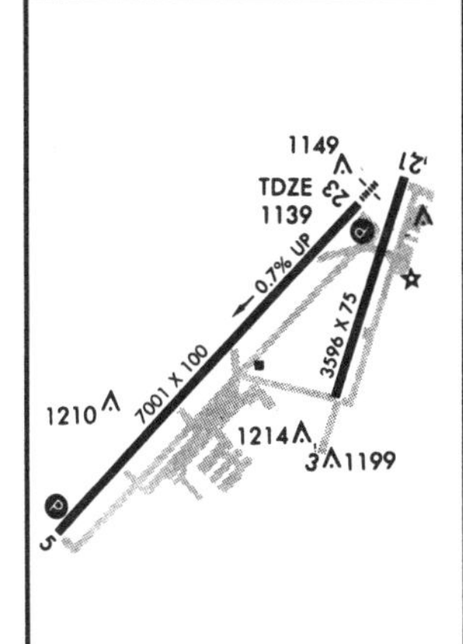

Airport Information:

LATROBE - WESTMORLAND COUNTY AIRPORT (LBE)
2 mi southwest of town N40-16.56 W79-24.29 Elev: 1185 Fuel: 100LL, Jet-A
Rwy 05-23: H7001x100 (Asph-Grvd) Rwy 03-21: H3596-75 (Asph) Attended: 1130-0300Z
ATIS: 118.375 Tower: 125.0 Gnd Con: 121.8 Landing fee: (Singles) no charge; (Twins) $5.00 to $17.00; (No Parking Fees)
FBO: Vee Neal Aviation: Phone: 539-4533

Photo by: Aerodine Magazine, File photo

PA-LHV - LOCK HAVEN WILLIAM T. PIPER MEMORIAL

31

(Area Code 717)

Restaurants Near Airport:

Dutch Haven	1-1/2 mi SW	Phone: 748-7444
Italian Pizza	1-1/2 mi W	Phone: 748-8027
Jeff's Place	1-1/2 mi W	Phone: 748-2234
Rocky Pt Lodge	5.5 mi NW	Phone: 748-1818

Lodging: Comfort Inn 726-4901; Travelers Delite 726-3090; Clintonian Motel 748-8057; Lock Haven Motel 726-4181; Best Western 748-3297; Rocky Point Lodge 748-1818; Schantz's 893-2665; Restless Oaks 769-6035; Days Inn (1 mile) 748-3297; Fallon Queen Hotel & Motel (1 mile) 748-7477; Hoffman's Victorian Bed & Breakfast 748-8688; Keystone Motel (1 mile) 748-8017; Mohawk Hotel (1 mile) 748-4003.

Meeting Rooms: Days Inn (1 mile) 748-3297

Transportation: The airport manager can normally arrange courtesy transportation for fly-in guests. However, advance notice is strongly suggested. Also Rent-A-Wreck is available, call 748-9336.

Information: Clinton County Tourist Promotion Agency, Courthouse, Lock Haven, PA 17745, Phone: 893-4037.

Dutch Haven Restaurant:

The Dutch Haven Restaurant is 1-1/2 miles west of the William T. Piper Memorial Airport. To reach the restaurant you drive on Water Street to the YMCA at Grove Street then turn left and go three blocks. Either the airport or restaurant managers will try to accommodate you if given advance notice you are coming. This fine dining facility is open 7 days a week, Monday through Friday from 11 a.m. to 2 p.m. and 4 p.m. to 10 p.m., Saturday from 4 p.m. to 10 p.m. and Sunday from 11 a.m. to 10 p.m. Casual attire is appropriate. Specialties of the house include, fresh beef, pasta, seafood, grilled and cold sandwiches and salads. Average prices run $5.00 for lunch and $10.00 for dinner. Daily lunch specials, evening specials and chef's choices are available. Accommodations for groups can be made with advance notice. In their lounge they have a piano bar beginning the entertainment at 8 p.m. on Friday and Saturday nights. Carry-out meals and meal deliveries can also be arranged. For information call 748-7444.

Attractions: (Sentimental Journey Fly-in)

Its is very easy to get caught up in the excitement of searching for a facility to house the Piper Aviation Museum. It has become a cause that has generated wide support. The museum showcased an integral part of aviation history as created by the Piper Aviation Corporation. The museum brings tourists to the area which was the corporate home of the Piper firm for over 50 years. Currently the William T. Piper Aviation Museum at Lock Haven Airport, contains a room filled with photographs and memorabilia, several items of special interest in a nearby hangar. Plans are to expand the facility to include a greater display area. (Donations are always welcome). For information call the museum between 9 a.m. and 5 p.m. Phone: 717-748-5123. **Sentimental Journey to Cub Haven Inc.:** This is a very popular event generally held for several days each year in the latter part of June. Over 175 aircraft attend and 4,500 people enjoy this event. Lodging and dining accommodations should be reserved well in advance. For more information you can call 717-748-5123.

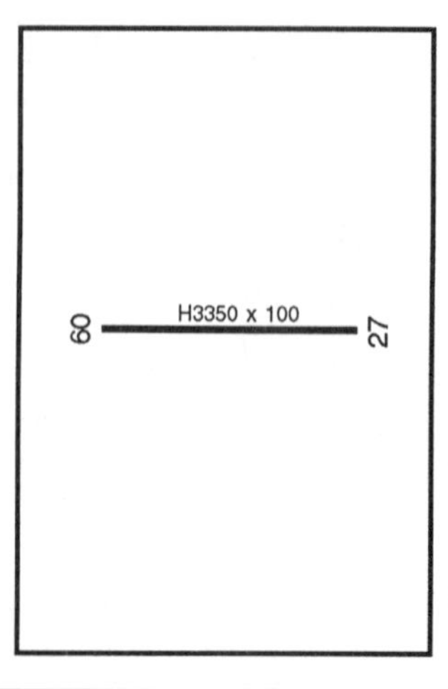

Airport Information:

LOCK HAVEN - WILLIAM T. PIPER MEMORIAL (LHV)
2 mi east of town 41-08-10N 77-25-15W Elev: 555 Fuel: 100LL, Jet-A
Rwy 09-27: H3350x100 (Asph) Attended: Mon-Fri 1300-2200Z, Sat-Sun 1500-1900Z
Unicom: 122.8 Public Phone 24hrs
City Airport Manager Phone: 748-5123

PA-2G6 - MEADVILLE
PORT MEADVILLE AIRPORT

(Area Code 814) 32, 33

Eddie's:

Eddie's is located only 1/8 mile from the Port Meadville Airport. This facility is comprised of a hot dog stand that is open between March and September from 11 a.m. to 10 p.m. Selections off their menu include specialties like foot-long hot dogs, and sloppy joe hamburgers. Located outside the stand are 10 wooden picnic tables for their guests. Average prices for most entrees run between $1.40 to $2.40. The hot dog stand is painted white, and can be reached with only a short walk from the aircraft parking area. For more information call Eddie's at 724-2057.

King Family Restaurant:

King Family Restaurant is located just down the street from Eddie's hot dog stand and about 1/4 mile from the Port Meadville Airport. This family style restaurant is open 24 hours a day and serves a wide variety of selections. Their menu includes a full breakfast line, grilled chicken breast, fish dinners, chopped sirloin, Cajun steak dinners, turkey, club sandwiches, and burgers. Nightly specials are: Monday liver and onions; Tuesday chopped sirloin; Wednesday meat loaf; Thursday fried or baked cod; Friday lemon pepper cod; Saturday veal and Sunday they serve turkey dinners. There are three separate dining areas available. The counter service area, the main dining area, and the green house off to the side of the restaurant. The main dining room contains antiques on display. This restaurant is a favorite with many pilots in the region. For more information call the King Family Restaurant at 333-8938.

Attractions:

Conneaut Lake Resort (10 miles west) camping, fishing swimming, amusement park, numerous restaurants and motels around Conneaut Lake. (See information listed above for Chamber of Commerce address).

Restaurants Near Airport:

Eddie's Foot Long	1/8 mi S.	Phone: 724-2057
King Family Rest.	1/4 mi E.	Phone: 333-8938
Mona Lisa Rest.	1 mi E.	Phone: 333-2889

Lodging: David Mead Inn (4 miles) 336-1692; Days Inn (3 miles) 337-4264; Super 8 (2 miles) 800-843-1991; Wagon Wheel Motel (1 mile) 337-3274.

Meeting Rooms: David Mead Inn 336-1692; Days Inn 337-4264.

Transportation: Airport courtesy car reported; Taxi: LaFayette 724-8600; Rental Cars: Ace Rent-A-Car 337-2277; Mona Lisa restaurant will provide transportation for fly-in customers.

Information: Crawford County Tourist Association, 969 Park Avenue, Meadville, PA 16335, Phone: 333-1258.

Airport Information:

MEADVILLE - PORT MEADVILLE AIRPORT (2G6)

3 mi west of town N41-37.59 W80-12.88 Elev: 1400 Fuel: 100LL, Jet-A
Rwy 07-25: H5002x75 (Asph) Attended: Mon-Fri 1300-2100Z Unicom: 123.0
Public Phone 24hrs

City of Meadville **Phone: 333-2677**
Corporate Charters **Phone: 337-3633, 800-679-3633**

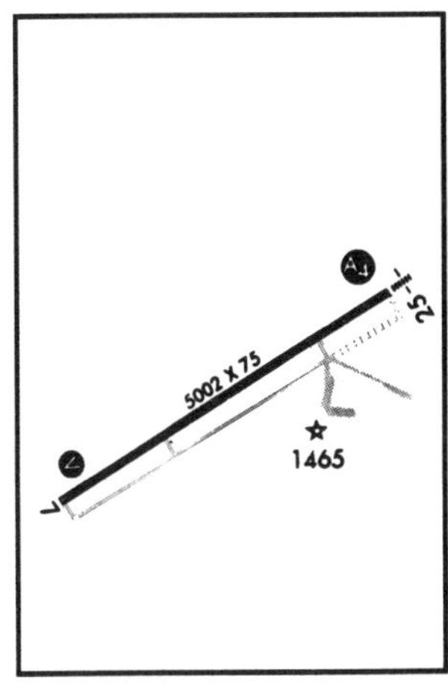

PA-P53 - MONONGAHELA ROSTRAVER AIRPORT

(Area Code 412) 34

Eagles Landing Restaurant:

The Eagles Landing Restaurant is located 15 to 20 miles south of Pittsburgh, PA right on the Rostraver Airport. Pilots can park on the ramp and easily walk to the restaurant only a few feet away. This is a family restaurant that is open from 8 a.m. to 9 p.m. Tuesday through Sunday. They are closed on Monday. Specialties on their menu include spaghetti and pasta dishes, steaks and seafood as well as many other items. They operate their own bakery on the premises, and on any given day prepare 35 different pies, cakes and freshly baked raisin bread, which happens to be a favorite with their customers. Their dining room has its own atrium providing a great view. Pictures of aircraft adorn the walls, some of which hold a special significance for both the owner as well as the fly-public. Eagles Landing Restaurant also has space for groups and can accommodate catered meals. Over the years this facility has expanded to meet its growing popularity. Many pilots enjoy the food and good friendly service while discussing their love of flying. For more information you can call Eagles Landing Restaurant at 379-8830.

Restaurants Near Airport:
Eagles Landing Restaurant On Site Phone: 379-8830

Lodging: Holiday Inn 6 mi 929-4600

Meeting Rooms: None reported

Transportation: Call FBO for available transportation needs at BHL Enterprises, Inc., Phone: 379-8225.

Information: Pittsburgh Convention and Visitors Bureau, 4 Gateway Center, Pittsburgh, PA 15222. Phone: (Mon-Fri) 281-7711 or 800-366-0093.

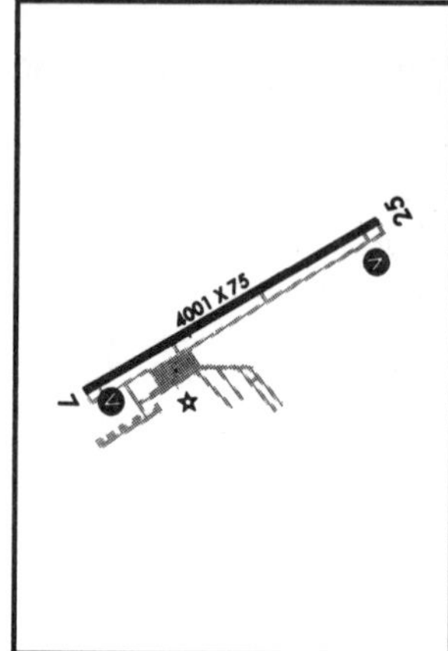

Airport Information:

MONONGAHELA - ROSTRAVER AIRPORT (P53)
5 mi east of town N40-12.58 W79-49.89 Elev: 1230 Fuel: 80, 100LL Rwy 07-25: H4000x75 (Asph-Grvd) Attended: 1300Z-dusk Unicom: 122.8
FBO: BHL Enterprises, Inc. Phone: 379-8225

PA-N71 - MOUNT JOY/MARIETTA DONEGAL SPRINGS AIRPARK

(Area Code 717) 35

Railroad House Inn:

The Railroad House Bed & Breakfast is a restored country Inn located in historic Marietta, along the banks of the Susquehanna River in Lancaster County. This facility contains an outdoor garden, patio as well as ten rooms for lodging. The property also has beautiful flower, vegetable and herb gardens along with antiques for sale. They are located 4 miles from the Mt Joy/Marietta Donegal Springs Airpark, and can be reached either by transportation arranged by the restaurant or Flying Tigers FBO. If you prefer you can even be picked up in style, with a horse drawn carriage by calling the Railroad House. Directions from the airport is as follows: After reaching 743 & 441 intersection go strait through to Market St. then make left on Market St. & go 5 blocks, Make right on Perry Street and take this to the railroad House Inn. The restaurant is open Tuesday through Sunday for lunch and dinner. (Closed Monday). They feature a Sunday brunch between 11 a.m. to 2 p.m. and dinner at 2 p.m. to 9 p.m. (Serving continuously). Prices range from $5.00 for lunch and $19.00 for dinner. Breakfast is available only for Bed & Breakfast guests. They have an American menu with Continental features, including beef, seafood, veal, pasta and poultry. The decor is Victorian with Oriental carpets, antiques, fireplace all in an early 1820's historic Inn. For information call 426-4141.

Restaurant Near Airport:
3 Center Square Inn 2 mi S. Phone: 426-3036
Railroad House 4 mi S. Phone: 426-4141

Lodging: Both restaurants listed are bed and breakfast facilities; Railroad House B&B (4 miles) 426-4141; Three Center Square Inn B&B (2 miles) 426-3036; Also Blue Note Motel (2 miles) 426-1991.

Meeting Rooms: The Railroad House hosts luncheon and dinner meetings and will make accommodations to suit their patrons (4 miles) 426-4141.

Transportation: The Railroad House can arrange a horse and surrey taxi service to pick you up, or courtesy transportation by conventional means. Also Flying Tigers, Inc. (FBO) can usually arrange some type of transportation for their customers.

Information: Pennsylvania Dutch Convention & Visitors Bureau, 501 Greenfield Road, Lancaster, PA 17601, Phone: 299-8901 or 800-723-8824.

Attractions:

The Mount Joy/Marietta - Donegal Springs Airpark (N71) is located within the Pennsylvania Dutch Country, and is less than 20 miles from the Hershey Estates and Amusement Park. With prior notice, rental cars are available by calling 653-8181.

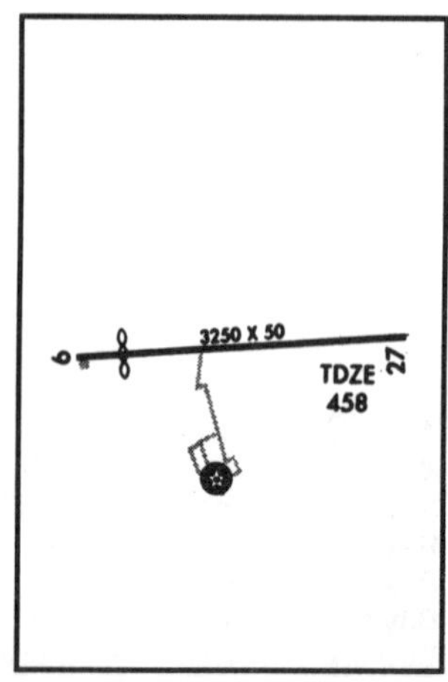

Airport Information:

MOUNT JOY/MARIETTA - DONEGAL SPRINGS AIRPARK (N71)
3 mi southwest of town N40-05.53 W76-34.46 Elev: 458 Fuel: 100LL Rwy 09-27: H3250x50 (Asph) Attended: Mon-Fri 1300Z-dusk, Sat 1400-2300Z, Sun 1700-2200Z Unicom: 122.8 Public Phone 24hrs Notes: No landing fee; Overnight fee $2.00; Rwy lighted until midnight - after midnight key mic 5 times within 7 seconds.
Flying Tigers Inc. Phone: 653-8181

PA-MPO - MOUNT POCONO
POCONO MOUNTAINS MUNICIPAL

(Area Code 717)

36

Restaurants Near Airport:

Bailey's Inn Steak Hse.	1 mi	Phone: 839-9678
The Clam Shack	200 yds	Phone: 839-2526
The Pioneer Diner	1-1/2 mi	Phone: 839-7620

Lodging: Crescent Lodge (5 miles) 595-7486; Highland Park Motel (Adj Arpt) 839-9071; Mount Pocono Motel (1 mile) 839-9407; Pocono Fountain Motel (3 miles) 839-7728; Pocono Manor Inn (3 miles) 233-8150; The Chateau at Camelback 629-5900.

Meeting Rooms: Crescent Lodge (5 miles) 595-7486; The Chateau at Camelback (Free Trans) 629-5900.

Transportation: For taxi service call 421-6068 or 839-2112; Rental Cars: Moyer Aviation 839-7161; Rent-A-Wreck 839-2215; Thrifty 839-6400.

Information: Pocono Mountains Vacation Bureau, 1004 Main Street, Stroudsburg, PA 18360, Phone: 424-6050 or 800-POCONOS.

The Clam Shack:

The Clam Shack Restaurant is a family style facility located only 200 yards from the Pocono Mountains Municipal Airport. This establishment is open during the summer, Thursday through Saturday between 5 p.m. and 10 p.m. and Sunday from 1 p.m. to 8 p.m. During the winter they open Friday and Saturday between 5 p.m. and 10 p.m. Their menu contains a nice variety of seafood dishes including clams, steamed clams, shrimp, and lobster dishes, to mention only a few. Average prices range somewhere between $8.00 and $9.00 per plate. Daily specials are also featured. The main dining area has a nautical theme and can accommodate 85 persons. Private groups are welcome. Carry-out meals can also be prepared if requested. For more information call the Clam Shack at 839-2526.

Attractions:

Pocono International Raceway between May and November features NASCAR, Indy car 500 mile races in addition to modified and midget car racing. For information call 646-2300 or 800/RACE-WAY.

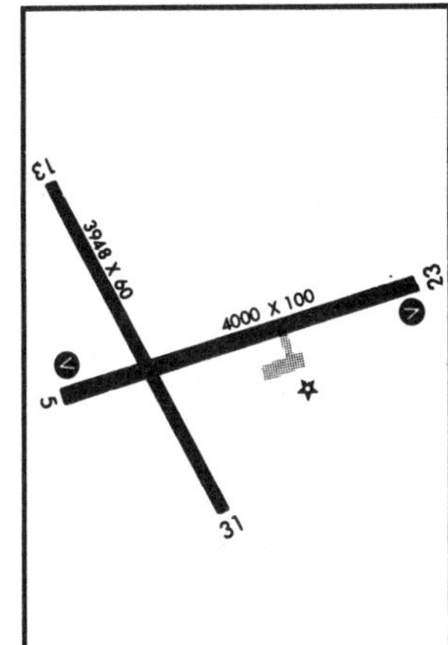

Airport Information:

MOUNT POCONO - POCONO MOUNTAINS MUNICIPAL (MPO)
2 mi northwest of town N41-08.25 W75-22.73 Elev: 1916 Fuel: 100LL, Jet-A
Rwy 05-23: H4000x100 (Asph) Rwy 13-31: H3948x60 (Asph) Attended: 1230Z-dusk
CATF: 122.7 Unicom: 122.7
FBO: Moyer Aviation Phone: 839-7161

PA-N62 - NEW HANOVER
NEW HANOVER AIRPORT

(Area Code 610)

37

Restaurants Near Airport:

Sunflower Cafe	Adj Arpt.	Phone: 323-9667

Lodging: Comfort Inn (4 miles) 326-5000; Downtown Motor Inn (5 miles) 326-7400; Holiday Inn (4 miles) 326-6700.

Meeting Rooms: None Reported

Transportation: Rental Cars: Rhoades Leasing Adjacent Airport

Information: Pennsylvania Office of Travel Marketing, Department of Commerce, P.O. Box 61, Warrendale, PA 15086, Phone: 800-VISIT-PA.

Sunflower Cafe:

The Sunflower Cafe is situated adjacent to the New Hanover Airport . They serve light fare and specialize in breakfast selections. We believe this restaurant is open between 6 a.m. and 6 p.m. When speaking with the operators of the United Parachute Club, we learned that this dining facility is accessible from their location. For information you can call the United Parachute Club, Inc. located on the airport during the weekends, phone 323-9667.

Attractions:

United Parachute Club has been formed solely for the purpose of engaging in and promoting the sport of parachuting. Student training in the art and skill of parachuting is one of their main activities. The purpose of their student training program is not only to get you through the first jump, but to make you into an accomplished skydiver. Three different training programs are available: 1) Static line method; 2) Accelerated free-fall; and 3) Tandem jumps. For more information on how to begin, call 323-9667 on weekends, and ask to speak to a jumpmaster or instructor.

NO AIRPORT DIAGRAM AVAILABLE

Airport Information:

NEW HANOVER - NEW HANOVER AIRPORT (N62)
1 mi west of town N40-18.01 W75-35.40 Elev: 280 Rwy 13-31: 2455x100 (Turf)
Rwy 11-29: 1490x75 (Turf) Attended: irregularly Notes: CAUTION Parachute Jumping and ultralight activity on and in vicinity of airport; Rwy 13-31: and Rwy 11-29: Marked with tires painted white;
FBO: New Hanover Airport Phone: 323-9667

PA-PNE - PHILADELPHIA
NORTHEAST PHILADELPHIA

(Area Code 215) **38**

94th Aero Squadron:

The 94th Aero Squadron is located within walking distance from aircraft parking areas at the Northeast Philadelphia Airport according to the restaurant personnel. Courtesy transportation is also available through Delaware Aviation. This restaurant is privately owned and is open for dinners served from 4:30 p.m. to 10 p.m. Monday through Thursday. Friday and Saturday they are open at 4:30 p.m. until 11 p.m. and on Sunday they close at 9 p.m. This fine dining facility has a unique aviation theme decorated with many reconstructed artifacts and antiques along with photographs of airplanes and fighter pilots of the first World War. Their menu includes specialty items like chicken, fresh fish and seafood, choice steaks, veal and chops along with surf & turf. The main dining area can hold 200 to 250 persons. Fly-in groups are also welcome, with banquet facilities available. They offer a Sunday brunch from 10 a.m. to 2:30 p.m. For information call the 94th Aero Squadron at 671-9400.

Restaurants Near Airport:

94th Aero Squadron	On Site	Phone: 671-9400

Lodging: Hilton (Trans) 638-8300; Holiday Inn-Philadelphia 638-1500; Howard Johnson Lodge 464-9500; Sheraton Inn (Trans) 671-9600.

Meeting Rooms: Hilton (Trans) 638-8300; Holiday Inn-Philadelphia 638-1500; Howard Johnson Lodge 464-9500; Sheraton Inn (Courtesy trans, 1 mile) 671-9600.

Transportation: Airport courtesy car reported by Delaware Aviation 698-3100; Taxi: United 625-2881; Yellow 922-8400; Rental Car: Avis 677-5630; Hertz 331-2314; National 335-4441.

Information: Visitors Center, Philadelphia Convention and Visitors Bureau, 16th Street & John F. Kennedy Blvd, Philadelphia, PA 19102, Phone: 215-636-1666 or 800/537-7676.

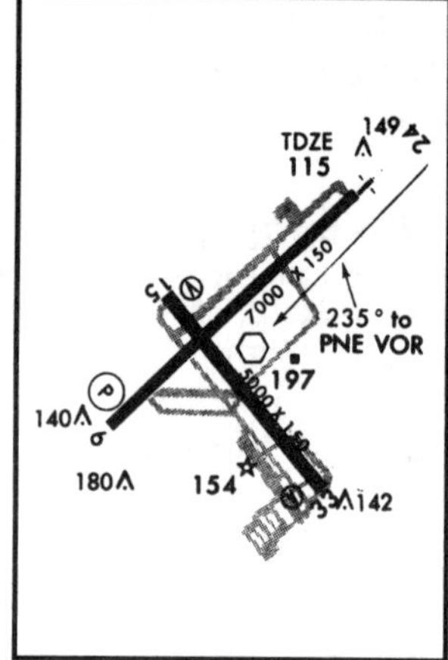

Airport Information:

PHILADELPHIA - NORTHEAST PHILADELPHIA (PNE)
10 mi northeast of town N40-04.92 W75-00.64 Elev: 121 Fuel: 100LL, Jet-A
Rwy 06-24: H7000x150 (Asph-Grvd) Rwy 15-33: H5000x150 (Asph-Grvd)
Attended: continuously Atis: 121.15 Unicom: 122.95 Tower: 126.9 Gnd Con: 121.7
Clnc Del: 127.25
FBO: Delaware Aviation Phone: 698-3100
FBO: Philadelphia Jet Center Phone: 673-9000

PA-PHL - PHILADELPHIA
PHILADELPHIA INTERNATIONAL

(Area Code 215) **39**

Airport Restaurants:

The Philadelphia International airport has a number of nice restaurants located on or near the airport. The Half Shell Tavern is located in Terminal "C" and the Eatery Buffeteria is situated in Terminal "A". Both the Guest Quarters and Marriott Hotel restaurant are 1 mile east of the airport.

Restaurants Near Airport:

Eatery Buffeteria	On Site	Phone: 492-2173
Guest Quarters	1 mi E.	Phone: 365-6600
Half Shell Tavern	On Site	Phone: 492-2181
Marriott Hotel	1 mi E.	Phone: 365-4150

Lodging: Days Inn (Trans) 492-0400; Guest Quarters Suite Hotel (Trans) 365-6600; Hilton-Philadelphia Airport (Trans) 755-9500; Holiday Inn-Philadelphia Airport (Trans) 521-2400; Marriott-Philadelphia Airport (Trans) 365-4150; Quality Inn-Airport (Trans) 755-6500; Ramada Inn-Airport (Trans) 521-9600;

Meeting Rooms: Atlantic Aviation 492-2975 has a meeting room; Days Inn 492-0400; Guest Quarters Suite Hotel 365-6600; Hilton-Philadelphia Airport 755-9500; Marriott-Philadelphia Airport 365-4150; Quality Inn-Airport 755-6500; Ramada Inn-Airport 521-9600.

Transportation: Atlantic Aviation has a courtesy van available 492-2975; Also Taxi Service: Taxi stands on airport; Rental Cars: Alamo 492-3960; Avis 492-2975; Budget 492-9442; Dollar 365-2692; Hertz 492-7200.

Information: Visitors Center of the Philadelphia Convention and Visitors Bureau, 16th Street & John F. Kennedy Blvd, Philadelphia, PA 19102, Phone: 636-1666 or 800-537-7676.

Airport Information:

PHILADELPHIA - PHILADELPHIA INTL. AIRPORT (PHL)
5 mi southwest of town N39-52.22 W75-14.70 Elev: 22 Fuel: 100LL, Jet-A Rwy 09R-27L: H10499x200 (Asph-Grvd) Rwy 09L-27R: H9500x150 (Asph-Grvd) Rwy 17-35: H5459x150 (Asph-Grvd) Attended: continuously Atis: 133.4 Unicom: 122.95 App Con: 128.4, 126.6, 127.35, 126.85, 123.8 Dep Con: 119.75, 124.35 Tower: 118.5, 135.1 Gnd Con: 121.9, 121.65 Clnc Del: 118.85 Notes: Ramp fees waived with quan. fuel purchase. Landing fee's: singles $10.00 twins $18.00; Ramp fee's: singles $25.00, twins $27.00.
FBO: Atlantic Aviation Phone: 492-2975

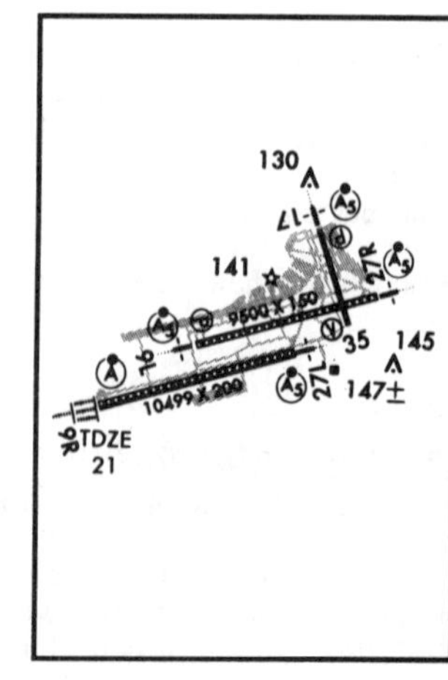

Not to be used for navigational purposes

PA-AGC - PITTSBURGH
ALLEGHENY COUNTY AIRPORT

(Area Code 412)

40

Sky View Family Restaurant:

The Sky View Family Restaurant is situated 1/2 block, from the Allegheny County Airport, and is well within walking distance from nearby aircraft parking ramps. This family style restaurant is open from 11 a.m. to 12 a.m. Monday through Thursday and 11 a.m. to 1 a.m. Friday and Saturday. Sunday 3 p.m. to 8 p.m. They offer a full menu including items like fish sandwiches, hamburgers, cheeseburgers, homemade soups and much more. Average prices run $6.00 to $7.00 for lunch and $8.00 to $9.00 for dinner. Daily specials are also available. Their dining area can accommodate 150 persons within a modern decor. Groups and parties are welcome with advance notice. Everything on their menu can be prepared for carry-out if requested. For more information, call 466-8068.

Restaurants Near Airport:

Century Plaza Inn	Wlk Dist	Phone: 466-8220
Rax Restaurant	1000'	Phone: 469-2421
Sky View Family Restaurant	1/2 block	Phone: 466-8068
Yorkshire Restaurant	2 mi	Phone: 655-7774

Lodging: Century Plaza Inn (Across the street) 466-8220.

Meeting Rooms: None Reported

Transportation: Fix Base Operators will provide transportation. Also: Colonial Cab 531-3500; Yellow Cab 344-8294; Buses 672-9794; Airport Limousine 664-4777; Budget Rental 466-2500; Snappy Rental 4666-2500.

Information: Greater Pittsburgh Convention and Visitors Bureau, 4 Gateway Center, Pittsburgh, PA 15222, Phone: 281-7711 or 800-366-0093.

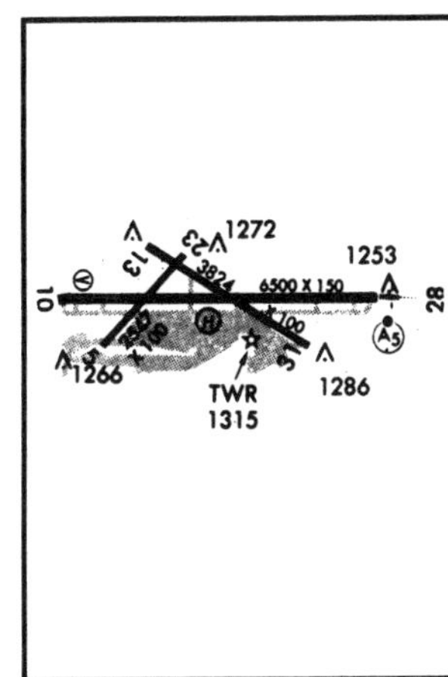

Airport Information:

PITTSBURGH - ALLEGHENY COUNTY AIRPORT (AGC)
4 mi southeast of town N40-21.26 W79-55.81 Elev: 1252 Fuel: 100LL, Jet-A
Rwy 10-28: H6500x150 (Conc) Rwy 13-31: H3824x100 (Asph) Rwy 05-23: H2547x100 (Asph)
Attended: continuously Atis: 120.55 Unicom: 122.95 Pittsburgh App/Dep Con: 119.35 Tower: 121.1 Gnd Con: 121.7 Public Phone 24hrs Notes: No landing fee for aircraft under 5,000 lbs.

FBO: Airburst Helicopters **Phone: 469-3572**
FBO: Corporate Air Management **Phone: 469-6800**
FBO: Corporate Jet **Phone: 466-2500**

PA-PIT - PITTSBURGH
GREATER PITTSBURGH INTL. ARPT.

(Area Code 412)

41

Food Service Concessions:

There are a many food service facilities located within the main terminal building at concourse "A" & "B" at the Greater Pittsburgh International Airport. "BAA Pittsburgh 21st Century Airports" manages the various concessions. within the terminal. Food courts contain popular fast food and beverage counters. Some of the restaurant include: Pub's and Pizzerias, Deli's, Juice and salad bar's, Frozen yogurt, The Great Steak & Potato, La Prema Expresso, McDonalds, Bakery's, a number of TGI Friday's in the Center Core, as well as at concourse A & B. Additional services include many specialty shops, along with several News paper and gift stands. Ground transportation from the general aviation parking ramp can be obtained. For information about the public services available at Greater Pittsburgh International Airport call 472-5180.

Restaurants Near Airport:

Captain's Table	Adj Arpt	Phone: N/A
Food Concessions	On Site	Phone: 472-5180
Glass Tower	3/4 mi	Phone: N/A
Howard Johnson	1/2 mi	Phone: N/A

Lodging: Days Inn Airport (Trans) 771-5200; Hilton Inn Airport (Trans) 262-3800; Holiday Inn Airport (Trans) 262-3600; Marriott Pittsburgh Airport (Trans) 788-8800; Ramada Inn Pittsburgh Airport (Trans) 264-8950; Royce Hotel (Trans) 262-2400.

Meeting Rooms: Days Inn Airport 771-5200; Hilton Inn Airport 262-3800; Holiday Inn Airport 262-3600; Marriott Pittsburgh Airport 788-8800; Ramada Inn Pittsburgh Airport 264-8950; Royce Hotel 262-2400.

Transportation: Taxi Service: Airlines Transportation Company 471-8900; Yellow 665-8100; Rental Cars: Avis 262-5160; Budget 262-1500; Dollar 262-1300; Hertz 262-1705; National 262-2312; Payless 472-0150.

Information: Greater Pittsburgh Convention and Visitors Bureau, 4 Gateway Center, Pittsburgh, PA 15222, Phone: 281-7711 or 800-366-0093.

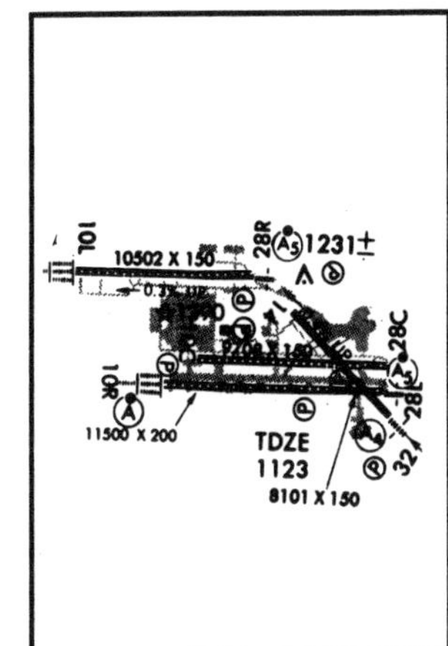

Airport Information:

PITTSBURGH - GREATER PITTSBURGH INTERNATIONAL AIRPORT (PIT)
12 mi northwest of town N40-29.49 W80-13.97 Elev: 1204 Fuel: 100LL, Jet-A
Rwy 10R-28L: H11500x200 (Conc) Rwy 10L-28R: H10502x150 (Conc-Asph-Grvd)
Rwy 14-32: H8101x150 (Asph-Conc-Grvd) Rwy 10C-28C: H9708x150 (Asph-Conc-Grvd)
Attended: continuously Atis: 127.25 Unicom: 122.95 Pittsburgh App Con: 123.95, 120.875, 124.15, 121.25 Pittsburgh Dep Con: 119.35, 124.75, 127.95 Tower: 119.1 Gnd Con: 121.9 (south), 127.8 (north) Clnc Del: 126.75 Pre-Taxi Clnc: 126.75 CAUTION: deer on and near operating surfaces. See Airport Facility Directory for updated and current information.

FBO: Av Center **Phone: 472-6700**

PA-RDG - READING
READING REG./CARL A SPAATZ FLD

(Area Code 610) 42, 43

Joe's Restaurant:

This fine dining facility is located 6 miles from the Reading Regional Airport and can be reached by taxi service or courtesy transportation through Aerodynamics of Reading 373-3000 or Million Air 372-4728. Directions to the restaurant are as follows: Route 183 to Windsor Street, left to 222 (5th Street), right on 5th to Penn Street, turn right and cross bridge to West Reading about 6 blocks. The restaurant should be on the left side of the street. (Verify these directions with FBO). Once reaching Joe's Restaurant, you will be in for a unique dining experience. Their cuisine specializes in wild mushrooms and game dishes. Dinner is served beginning with soup, followed by an intermediate course, then salad dish and finally the main course. Entrees consist of such main items as Mushroom Cracow Style, Filet Mignon with Peppercorn Sauce and Wild Mushrooms, Veal Diccalata, Ragout of Dakota Black Bear with Shiitake and Plantains, Roast Schuykill County Pheasant or Jack's Spicy Spring Casserole with Silver Oyster Mushrooms. Their menu changes regularly to reflect the freshest products seasonally available. Meals average about $58.00 per person. A special "Tasting Menu" choice runs about $75.00 per person and consists of an eight course meal. The decor has a cozy living-room-like atmosphere with Old World charm. The restaurant is open Tuesday through Saturday from 5:30 p.m. to 9:00 p.m. Accommodations for groups are available only by special arrangement. For information call 373-6794.

Wild Wings Cafe:

The Wild Wings Cafe is located in the terminal building at the Reading Regional Airport. After arriving at the airport, you will need to park your aircraft at the FBO and obtain courtesy transportation to the main terminal building. This cafe is open from 8 a.m. to 12 midnight Monday through Saturday, and Sunday from 8 a.m. to 10 p.m. Some of their specialized entrees contain a large variety of items like chicken wings, appetizers, soups, sandwiches, and burgers, salads, as well as main course selections like prime rib on Friday, Saturday, and Sunday. Some of their specials include, Black Diamond steaks, all-you-can-eat chicken wings Monday through Friday from 4 p.m. to 11 p.m. for only $6.95, or try their fresh 7 ounce burgers starting at $4.50. A variety of sandwiches and dinner specials are also offered. Average prices run $1.50 for breakfast, $4.00 for lunch and $4.00 to $10.00 for evening meals. While enjoying your meal you can watch the airplanes landing and taking off with a beautiful view of the runways in front of the restaurant. The Wild Wings Cafe can accommodate groups and parties with catering, providing advance notice is given. Sandwiches and hot meals can also be prepared-to-go for pilots and their passengers. For information you can call 478-1747.

Restaurants Near Airport:

Inn At Reading	2 mi	Phone: 372-7811
Joe's Restaurant	6 mi	Phone: 373-6794
Riveredge	1/4 mi	Phone: 376-6711
Wild Wings Cafe	On Site	Phone: 478-1747

Lodging: Riveredge 376-6711; Dutch Colony 779-2345; Holiday Inn 929-4741; Days Inn 777-7888; Econo Lodge 378-1145; Inn At Reading 372-7811; Sheraton 376-3811; Hampton Inn 374-8100; Wellesley 374-1500

Meeting Rooms: Riveredge; Holiday Inn; Inn at Reading; Sheraton;(See Lodging listed above)

Transportation: Million Air (FBO) and Cap Aviation (FBO) will provide courtesy transportation to local facilities. Also Metro Taxi 374-5111; Barta Bus 921-0601; Avis 372-6636; Hertz 374-1448; National 376-3235.

Information: Reading/Berks County Visitors Bureau, VF Factory Outlet Complex, Park Road & Hill Avenue, P.O. Box 6677, Wyomissing, PA 19610, Phone: 375-4085 or 800-443-6610.

Attractions:

The Mid Atlantic Air Museum is located on the Reading Regional Airport. For information call 372-7333.

Airport Information:

READING - READING REG./CARL A SPAATZ FIELD (RDG)
3 mi northwest of town N40-22.71 W75-57.92 Elev: 344 Fuel: 100LL, Jet-A
Rwy 13-31: H6350x150 (Asph-Grvd) Rwy 18-36: H5151x150 (Asph-Grvd) Attended: 1000-0500Z
Atis: 127.1 Unicom: 122.95 App/Dep Con: 119.25 (north), 125.15 (south) Tower: 119.9
Gnd Con: 121.9 Public phone 24 hrs

FBO: Aerodynamics **Phone: 373-3000**
FBO: Million Air Reading **Phone: 372-4728**
FBO: Reading Flite Acad. **Phone: 376-5447**

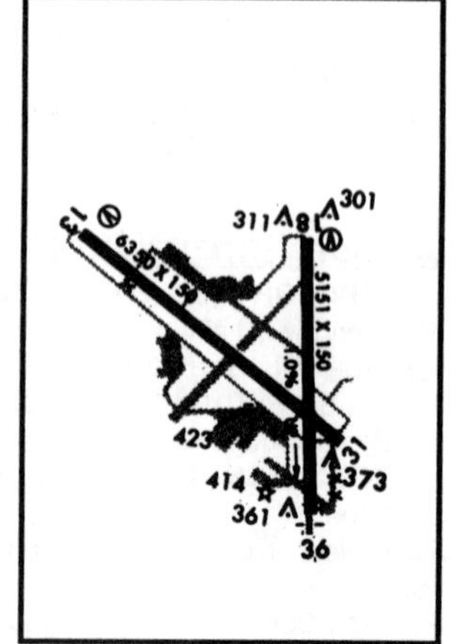

Not to be used for navigational purposes

PA-SEG - SELINSGROVE PENN VALLEY AIRPORT

(Area Code 717)

44

Airport Restaurant:

The Airport Restaurant at the Penn Valley Airport, is about a 300 yard walk across an open field along a foot path. This restaurant is open Monday through Thursday 6 a.m. to 8 p.m., Friday and Saturday 6 a.m. to 9 p.m. and Sunday from 7 a.m. to 3 p.m. Their menu contains items from sandwiches to steaks, homemade pies, including hardy breakfasts. Average prices for meals are $3.50 for breakfast, $4.00 for lunches and $5.50 for dinners. Daily specials, along with breakfast specials are featured. The restaurant has counter service with an attached dining room, able to seat approx. 64 people. Party trays consisting of meats, cheese, salads, and sandwiches are available. Comfort Inn is about 1/2 mile from the restaurant on Route 11 & 15. For more information about this restaurant call 374-5354.

Restaurants Near Airport:

Airport Restaurant	1/2 mi	Phone: 374-5354
Tedd's Landing	6 mi	Phone: 743-1591
Tiffany's	2 mi	Phone: 743-6891

Lodging: Comfort Inn, (Est. 1/2 miles) 374-8880; Days Inn, (3 miles) 743-1111; Blue Lion Inn, (1 mile) 374-2929

Transportation: Penn Valley Rental Cars, 374-7671; Pallis Cab Co., 286-7509; Selinsgrove Motors, 374-8131

Information: Susquenanna Valley Visitors Bureau, Courtyard Offices, Box 2, Route 11 & 15, Selinsgrove, PA 17870; Phone: 1-800-45-VISIT

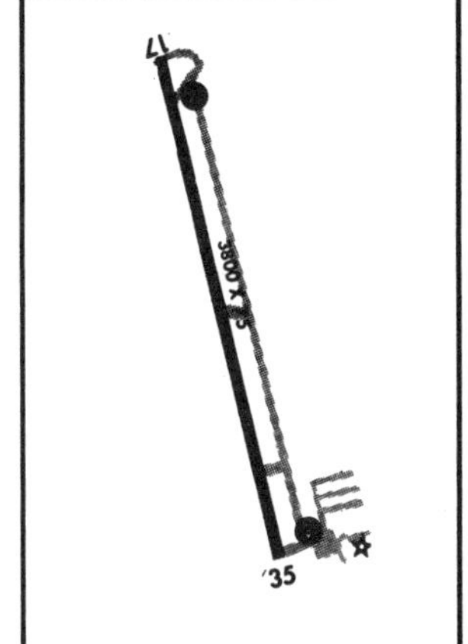

Airport Information:

SELINSGROVE - PENN VALLEY AIRPORT (SEG)
1 mi north of town N40-49.23 W76-51.83 Elev: 450 Fuel: 100LL, Jet-A
Rwy 17-35: H3800x75 (Asph) Attended: 1300-2300Z Unicom: 122.7 Public Phone 24 hrs
Notes: Notes: Rising terrain both sides of approach to runway 17; No charge for overnight parking if purchasing fuel.
FBO: Penn Valley Airport Auth. Phone: 374-7671

PA-7SP - SEVEN SPRINGS BOROUGH SEVEN SPRINGS AIRPORT

(Area Code 814) 45

Dining at Seven Springs Mountain Resort:

Seven Springs' Airport is conveniently located on Seven Springs Mountain Resort, in the heart of the Laurel Highlands in western Pennsylvania. The resort, open year-round, offers several dining choices from gourmet to take-out. The Pizza And Pastry Place serves a variety of fresh dough pizzas, hoagies and a lot of pastries! The Coffee Shop, open from 6 a.m. to 2 a.m. serves breakfast and snacks. For fine dining in a casual atmosphere, visit the Oak Room and feast on elegant cuisine. Or, just off the Oak Room, visit the Slopeside Grill and sample the fresh pastas and seafood specialties along with an elaborate soup, salad and dessert bar, while admiring the view of the ski slopes. For a change in atmosphere, visit Helen's Restaurant, a rustic retreat which serves a medley of classic French, Continental and American cuisine. Seven Springs also features three grand buffets: King Neptune's Friday Seafood Buffet (5 p.m. to 10 p.m.) the Saturday Grand Buffet (5 p.m. to 10 p.m.), and the Sunday Brunch (11 a.m. to 3 p.m.). A free shuttle will pick you up from the resort airport. For more information, call Seven Springs Mountain Resort at 352-7777.

Restaurants Near Airport:
Seven Springs Mountain Resort On Site Phone: 352-7777

Lodging: Seven Springs Mountain Resort (on site) contains 384 hotel rooms, 12 suites and over 200 condominiums. For information call 352-7777

Meeting Rooms: Seven Springs Mountain Resort contains 18 meeting and conference rooms. Phone: 352-7777

Transportation: Free shuttle to and from the resort. Call 352-7777 for further assistance.

Information: Somerset County Chamber of Commerce, 829 N. Center Avenue, Somerset, PA 15501, Phone: 445-6431 or call 800-452-2223.

Attraction:

Seven Springs Mountain Resort is open year-round and it has plenty of activities, including skiing, golfing and horseback riding. For more information, call 352-7777.

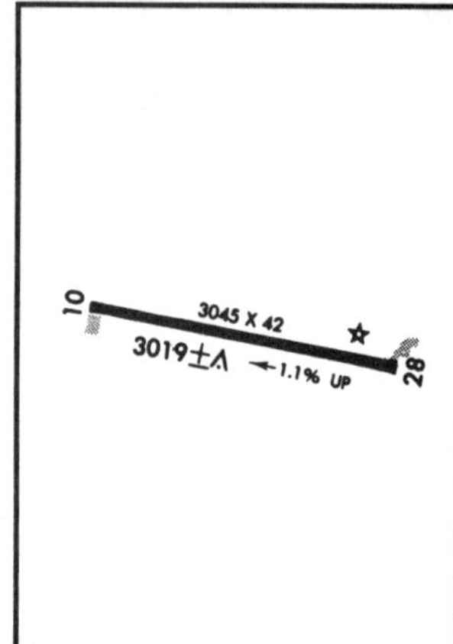

Airport Information:

SEVEN SPRINGS BOROUGH - SEVEN SPRINGS AIRPORT (7SP)
1 Mi southwest of town N40-00.60 W79-19.31 Elev: 2907 Fuel: No Fuel Rwy 10-28:H3045x42 (Asph) Attended: Unattended CTAF: 122.9 Public Phone 24hrs Notes: Airport is open June 1st through Labor Day and closed during winter (weather-pending). Airport is surrounded by trees.

Seven Springs Mountain Resort

Seven Springs Borough PA (PA-7SP)

Seven Springs Mountain Resort is located in the heart of the Laurel Highlands in western Pennsylvania. It is open year-round, and it offers a variety of acitivities to suit almost everyone's taste. History buffs should enjoy visiting nearby Fallingwater Frank Lloyd Wright's historic architectural achievement, or even nearby Ligonier and the 18th Century Hardware Store with its own handmade products. Stop by the glass factories and observe the art of handblown glass, and shop at the large factory outlets that are just minutes away.

During the winter, Seven Springs offers 30 ski slopes and trails, 11 chairlifts, 7 rope tows, complete snowmaking facilities and a certified ski school. During the spring, summer and fall, you can still ride the chairlifts and catch an exciting glimpse of the overall resort. Give tennis and racquetball a swing as well as the 6,360 yard, par 71, 18-hole golf course (complete with a golf pro shop.)

Try your skill at volleyball, shuffleboard and Bocci. Visit the bowling center, indoor miniature golf course and electronic game room, and be sure to take advantage of the year-round indoor, heated swimming pool. There is also an outdoor pool and a wading pool for children. Kids' Korner is a supervised children's play area where they can enjoy each other's company while playing games and participating in other activites.

Go horseback riding and explore the mountains, or rent a bike and look at them from a different perspective. (Note: Horseback riding season is April through November, must be 12 years old, and reservations are required) People of all ages should get a thrill out of 1,800 feet of downhill excitement on the Alpine Slide. You control the speed around the bends and turns of this fun ride. Take guided raft tours down the Youghiogheny River, just minutes from the resort at Ohiopyle.

Go hiking on the nature trails that wind through the hills adjoining the resort. The Laurel Highlands Hiking Trail stretches about 70 miles from Johnstown, PA to the Maryland border. If pre-arranged, the resort will prepare a picnic lunch for you to take on the trails.

Seven Springs offers plenty of places to shop. For example, the Ole Man Winter Leather Shop features jackets, hats, hand bags, wallets, belts and bags. The Good Sport Shop features Seven Springs imprinted sportswear for kids and adults, while the Good Sport 2 Shop features sunglasses, shorts, bathing suits, tee shirts, sweat shirts and more. Mother Nature's Outfitters sells men's and women's sport clothing. The Treasure Haus offers a variety of gifts, ranging from picture frames to an assortment of unique jewelry. For your additional needs, there is also a hair styling salon for both men and women, a flower shop, and a photo shop.

Before dinner, take an early evening ride on the hay wagon (weather permitting). It leaves the main lodge and travels east toward the top of Alpine Slope. Once reaching the top of the mountain, you'll see a panoramic view of the Laurel Highlands of western Pennsylvania. Afterward, select one of Seven Springs' several dining choices, ranging from gourmet to take-out. For fine dining in a casual setting, visit the Oak Room and sample their elegant

Photo by: Seven Springs Mountain Resort

Aerial view of the resort.

cuisine along with an elaborate soup, salad and dessert bar. The Slopeside Grill, just off the Oak Room, offers a view of the slopes, and features fresh pastas and seafood specialties. (Both restaurants offer a breakfast buffet, as well as lunch) The resort also offers three grand buffets: King Neptune's Friday Seafood Buffet (5 p.m.-10 p.m.), Saturday Grand Buffet (5 p.m.-10 p.m.), and Sunday Brunch (11 a.m.-3 p.m.). For a change in atmosphere, Helen's Restaurant, a rustic retreat secluded among timbers along the slopeside, serves a medley of classic French, Continental, and American cuisine. For a lighter fare, visit the Pizza and Pastry Place and the resort's Coffee Shop.

For those who are on business, as well as pleasure, Seven Springs offers 18 meeting rooms ranging from a smaller 13'x 26' to a larger 98'x 119'. They range from forum rooms with tiered levels and centrally focused staging to an auditorium with its own stage, lighting and sound system, which can seat 1200 for a meeting or 900 for dinner. There is also an exhibit hall, complete with a full complement of audio-visual aids.

Lodging ranges from temporary accommodations to permanent living arrangements. Stay at the main lodge of 384 rooms, or one of several condominiums, townhouses, chalets or cabins. All condo units are equipped with a television, full kitchen, dishwasher, washer and dryer. If you plan a permanent stay, The Villages at Seven Springs, a new resort-living community, offers single-family condominiums, townhomes, and courtyard homes.

Photo by: Seven Springs Mountain Resort

Chefs preparing buffet.

Seven Springs provides free shuttle service to and from Seven Springs Airport, located at the top of the mountain. **Note:** The airport is open June 1st through Labor Day, and is closed during the winter season (weather-pending). A public telephone is available. Contact the FBO at 352-7777 for more information. As an alternative, the resort also provides a shuttle to and from Pittsburgh International Airport (60 miles) by prior arrangement with the Hotel Service Department and for an addtional fee.

For information call the Reservations at 800-452-2223 or 814-352-7777, Monday through Saturday from 8:30 a.m. to 9 p.m., and Sunday from 8:30 a.m. to 5 p.m. (By Seven Springs Mtn. Resort).

An outdoor buffet complete with open spit of beef featured at Seven Springs Autumnfest Buffet. Also featured is the Farmer's Market with freshly baked breads and home-made pasta.
Photo by: Seven Springs Mountain Resort

PA-69N - SLATINGTON
SLATINGTON AIRPORT

(Area Code 610) **46**

Maple Springs Restaurant:

The Maple Springs Restaurant is located right at the Slatington Airport entrance and about 500 yards from the aircraft parking area. This restaurant is a family run business with almost everything on the menu made on the premises. They specialize in true Pennsylvania Dutch entrees and their own delicious pies and desserts. Different specials are featured each day. On the weekends they offer extra special items that seem to be a "calling card" that attracts the most business (Very generous portions). Prices range from $2.50 for breakfast, $3.50 for lunch and $4.75 for dinner. The decor is moderately country with a cozy atmosphere. Restaurant hours are Sunday through Wednesday 6 a.m. to 2 p.m. and Thursday, Friday and Saturday 6 a.m. to 9 p.m. They would appreciate it if you could call in advance if your group has 8 or more persons. They strive hard to make each customer's visit a pleasurable dining experience. For information call 767-1456.

Restaurant Near Airport:

Maple Spring Restaurant Adj.Arpt Phone: 767-1456

Lodging: None Reported

Transportation: None Reported; Restaurant within walking distance from airport, about 500 yards from parking ramp at entrance to field.

Information: Pennsylvania Office of Travel Marketing, Department of Commerce, P.O. Box 61, Warrendale, PA 15086, Phone: 800-VISIT-PA.

Attractions:

Appalachian Trail, 2 miles from airport.

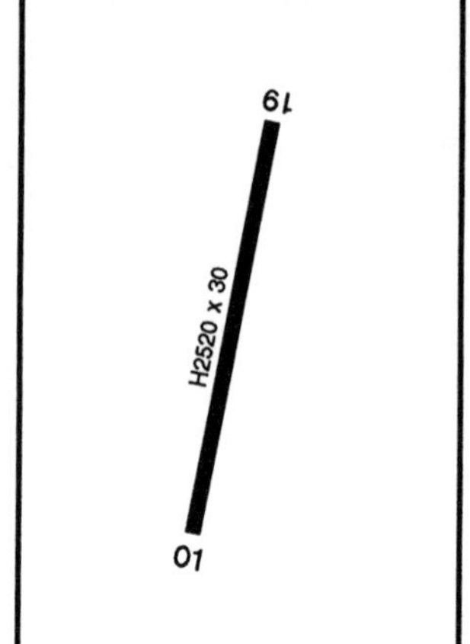

Airport Information:

SLATINGTON - SLATINGTON AIRPORT (69N)
1 mi north of town N40-46.01 W75-35.98 Elev: 380 Fuel: 80, 100LL
Rwy 01-19: H2520x30 (Asph-Turf) Attended: Mon-Sat daylight hours Unicom: 122.8
Public Phone 24hrs Notes: Asphalt portion 2000'x30'; Parking free with fuel purchase.
FBO: Roger P. Sell, Inc. Phone: 767-5881
FBO: Lehigh Valley Aviation Phone: 767-7477 or 767-2104

PA-37PA - SMOKETOWN
SMOKETOWN AIRPORT

(Area Code 717) **47**

Restaurants Near Airport:

Pricilla's N/A Phone: N/A
T. Burk & Company 1/8th mi Phone: 293-0976

T. Burk & Company:

The T. Burk & Company Restaurant is situated about 1/8th mile from the Smoketown Airport. This Deli type restaurant is open from 10 a.m. to 8 p.m. Monday through Saturday, (Closed on Sunday). Their menu includes items such as soups, salads, deli type sandwiches, sweet and sour chicken, crab cakes and homemade desserts. Average prices run between $4.95 and $6.95 for most entree selections. Their main dining room can seat 70 people, within a very comfortable and casual atmosphere. An additional meeting room is available for 20 to 25 people. All meals on their menu can be prepared for carry-out. When interviewing the restaurant personnel, we learned that this restaurant is a very popular fly-in dining establishment with pilots from all over the region. The cook for the restaurant is a pilot himself, and has a great interest in serving pilot and fly-in customers. One of the many selections that seem to be a favorite with costumers are the Friday night crab cakes, a recent addition to their menu. T. Burk & Company also provides in-flight catering as well. For more information about this facility call them at 293-0976.

Lodging: Bird In Hand Motor Inn & Restaurant (2 miles) 768-8271; Millstream Motor Lodge (1 mile) 299-0931; Spruce Lane Motor Inn (Adj Arpt) 393-1991.

Meeting Rooms: None Reported

Transportation: Airport courtesy reported; Taxi: Friendly 392-3727; Yellow 397-8108.

Information: Pennsylvania Office of Travel Marketing, Department of Commerce, P.O. Box 61, Warrendale, PA 15086, Phone: 800-VISIT-PA.

10 H2400 x 50 28

Airport Information:

SMOKETOWN - SMOKETOWN AIRPORT (37PA)
0 mi north of town N40-02.47 W76-12-08 Elev: 370 Fuel: 80, 100LL
Rwy 10-28: H2400x50 (Asph) Attended: 1300-2200Z Unicom: 123.05
FBO: Glick Aviation Ltd. Phone: 394-6476

PA-UNV - STATE COLLEGE UNIVERSITY PARK AIRPORT

48

Toftrees Hotel Resort & Conference Center:

This facility will provide free courtesy transportation and is located only five minutes from State College University Park Airport, The elegant Toftrees Hotel and Resort boasts two restaurants. For the ultimate formal dining experience, the newly remodeled LePapillon offers a Continental menu with a South European flair in a Mediterranean atmosphere, specializing in seafood, veal, chicken, and steaks. Le Papillon features daily specials as well as "heart healthy" entrees prepared with low sodium, low saturated fat and low cholesterol. Prices range from $6.25 for breakfast, $8.50 for lunch and $25.00 for dinner. This restaurant also provides all types of buffets as well as a Sunday brunch. The less formal Eagle Bar & Grille offers lighter fare, perfect for diners-on-the-go. The charming club atmosphere provides a relaxing setting to watch TV or catch a view of one of Pennsylvania's top ten golf courses. A banquet and conference center, able to accommodate 250 guests, is also available and can be used for social as well as business functions. For information call 234-8000.

Restaurants Near Airport: (Area Code 814)

Gamble Mill	6 mi E.	Phone: 355-7764
Toftrees Resort	3 mi W.	Phone: 234-8000
Unimart	Adj W.	Phone: N/A

Lodging: Toftrees Hotel Resort and Conference Center (Free Shuttle) 234-8000; Days Inn 238-8454; Athorton Hilton 231-2100; Hampton Inn 231-1590

Meeting rooms: Toftrees Hotel Resort and Conference Center can accommodate up to 250 persons 234-8000

Transportation: National 355-0874; Hertz 355-0428; Taxi 238-1084; Airport Limo 237-4211. Toftrees Hotel has free transportation to and from the airport. 234-8000.

Information: Center County, Lion Country Visitor & Convention Bureau, 1403 South Atherton Street, State College, PA 16801, Phone: 231-1400.

Attractions:

Toftrees Hotel provides free airport transportation and contains a 18 hole pro-golf course, tennis courts, heated swimming pool and entertainment in addition to their restaurant and lodging facilities. For Information call 234-8000. Pennsylvania State University (5 miles) 865-2501; Historic Bellefonte (6 miles) 355-2761.

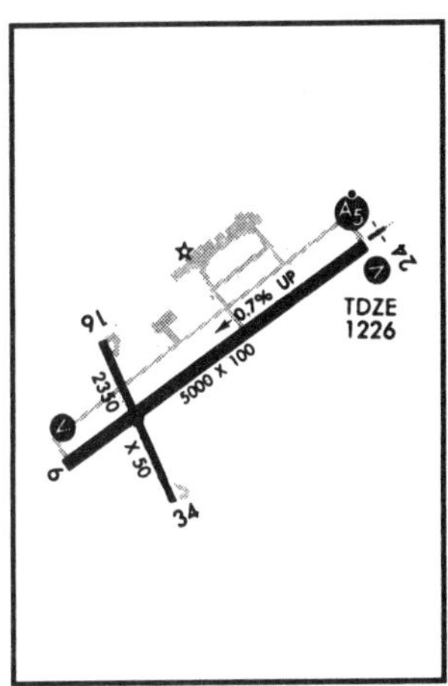

Airport Information:

STATE COLLEGE - UNIVERSITY PARK (UNV)
3 mi north of town   N40-50.93 W77-50.96   Elev: 1239   Fuel: 100LL, Jet-A
Rwy 06-24: H5000x100 (Asph-Grvd)   Rwy 16-34: H2350x50 (Asph)   Attended: 1100-0430Z
Unicom: 122.8   Clnc Del: 118.55   Public Phone 24hrs   Notes: Landing fees for twins & Helos.
FBO: University Park Airport   Phone: 865-5511

PA-N27 - TOWANDA TOWANDA AIRPORT

49

Pepper Shaker:

The Pepper Shaker Restaurant is classified as a combination restaurant, convenient store and gas station. This establishment is adjacent to the airport about 1/4 mile from the Hangars at the southern end of the Towanda airport. This restaurant is open from 5:30 a.m. to 9 p.m. 6 days a week and Sunday 7 a.m. to 9 p.m. During the winter they close one hour earlier. This restaurant is reported to be well within walking distance. They specialize in breakfast, homemade soups made fresh daily, as well as hamburgers and sandwiches. Desserts, pies and cakes are popular with many customers and their specialty. Prices average $3.50 for breakfast, and $4.00 for lunch. Daily specials are offered Monday through Saturday. The decor as expressed by the restaurant manager, is "Down Home Country." Catering for fly-in parties is available for groups of 20-40 persons. Carry-out meal can also be prepared. For information call 265-9919.

(Area Code 717)

Restaurants Near Airport:

Pepper Shaker	Adj Arpt	Phone: 265-9919

Lodging: Towanda Motel 265-2178; Williamston Inn (2 miles) 265-8882.

Meeting Rooms: Williamston Inn 265-8882

Transportation: Northern Tier can provide courtesy transportation to local facilities, Phone: 265-4900.

Information: Endless Mountains Visitors Bureau, RR #6 Box 132A, Tunkhannock, PA 18657-9232, Phone: 836-5431 or 800-769-8999.

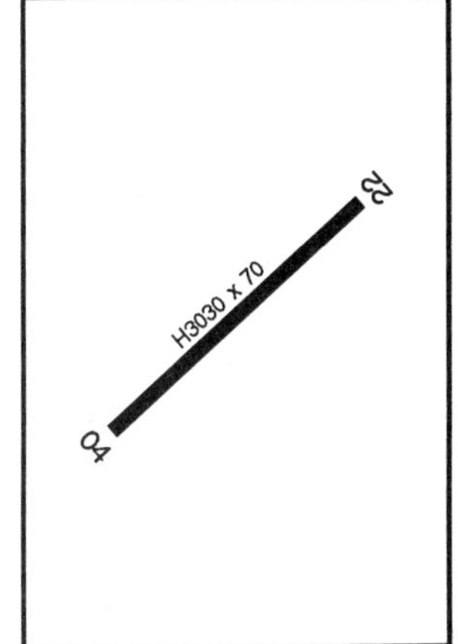

Airport Information:

TOWANDA - TOWANDA AIRPORT (N27)
2 mi south of town   N41-44.67 W76-26.65   Elev: 725   Fuel: 100LL
Rwy 05-23: H3020x70 (Asph)   Attended: 1300-2300Z   Public Phone 24hrs   Unicom: 122.8
Notes: Unicom out of service indefinitely.
Northern Tier Aviation, Inc.   Phone: 265-4900

PA-76N - TUNKHANNOCK SKYHAVEN AIRPORT

(Area Code 717) 50

Cross Country Restaurant:

The Cross Country Restaurant is located adjacent to the Skyhaven Airport. Fly-in guests can easily walk over to the restaurant from the airport. This family style restaurant is open between 7 a.m. and 8 p.m. Monday through Saturday and 7 a.m. to 7 p.m. on Sunday. Their menu displays varied selections, including chicken fingers, cheeseburgers, sandwiches and a full breakfast selection. Average prices run between $5.00 and $7.00 for most items. Their dining room can seat 50 to 75 people with table and counter service. Fly-in groups and parties of 15-20 people are welcome with advance notice. For information call the Cross Country Restaurant at 836-5077.

Restaurants Near Airport:
Cross Country Restaurant Adj Arpt Phone: 836-5077

Lodging: Shadow Brook Resort (2 miles) 836-2151.
Meeting Rooms: Shadow Brook Resort (2 miles) 836-2151.
Transportation: Steven and Barbara Gay owners of the airport have a courtesy car available. Most facilities are well within walking distance.
Information: Pennsylvania Office of Travel Marketing, Department of Commerce, P.O. Box 61, Warrendale, PA 15086, Phone: 800-VISIT-PA.

Attractions:

Shadow Brook Resort is 2 miles and contains a 18 hole golf course, fitness room, and swimming pool 836-2151; Canoe rental is available (5 miles from airport) on the Susquehanna River that flows adjacent to airport property. Skyhaven Airport was built in 1943 by L Charles Gay. Today is owned by his son Steve and wife Barbara. It is one of the few privately owned commercial airports in Pennsylvania. The owner's house is located on the runway for 24 hour airport services. There is an aircraft campground with shower adjacent to the runway. Model airplane flying is done almost every evening. The airport caters to antique and classic aircraft. Full maintenance facility with mechanic who lives adjacent to runway. A shopping mall is also adjacent to runway (IGA) food store open 24hrs. Many people coming there get the "Mom and Pop" treatment not found at larger commercial airports. Airport Phone: 836-4800 or 836-3884.

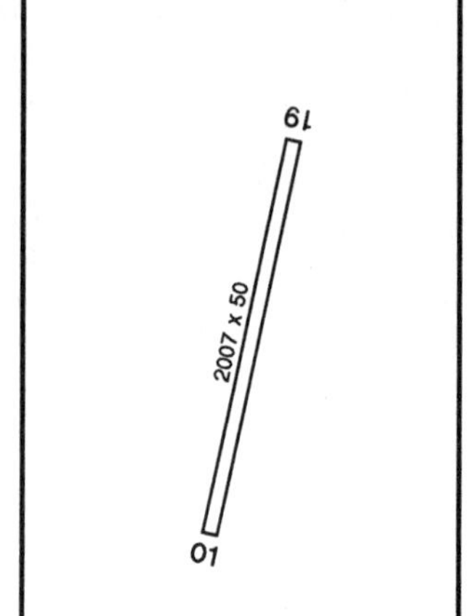

Airport Information:

TUNKHANNOCK - SKYHAVEN AIRPORT (76N)
1 mi south of town N41-31.75 W75-56.81 Elev: 639 Rwy 01-19: 2007x50 (Asph)
Attended: continuously Unicom: 122.8 Public Phone 24hrs Notes: Overnight parking $2.00;
FBO: Skyhaven Airport, Inc. Phone: 836-4800 or 836-3884.

PA-N38 - WELLSBORO GRAND CANYON STATE AIRPORT

(Area Code 717) 51

Coach Stop Inn:

The restaurant at Mount Tom Villa is located 4 miles from the Grand Canyon State Airport. This facility will provide free courtesy transportation for fly-in guests. The restaurant is a family style establishment that is open 7 day a week from 11 a.m. to 9 p.m. and Friday and Saturday until 10 p.m. Their menu includes prime rib, veal Parmesan, baked seafood combo, roast pork, steaks and surf & turf. Specials change on a daily basis, with prime rib featured on Friday and Saturday. Average prices run $4.00 to $5.00 for lunch and $6.95 to $22.00 for dinner. The main dining room can seat 70 to 75 people. The decor is contemporary and the dining area is decorated with wild life pictures. Private rooms are also available which accommodate up to 30 people. The Mount Tom Villa also contains 11 rooms with central air along with bath and shower. For more information call 724-5361.

Restaurants Near Airport:
Coach Stop Inn 4 mi Phone: 724-5361

Lodging: Mount Tom Villa (4 miles, Free trans) 724-5361.

Meeting Rooms: Mount Tom Villa (4 miles, Free trans) 724-5361.

Transportation: Mountain Tom Villa will provide fly-in guests with transportation to and from their facility; Also rental cars are available through Jim West 724-1066.

Information: Wellsboro Area Chamber of Commerce, P.O. Box 733, Wellsboro, PA 16901, Phone: 724-1926.

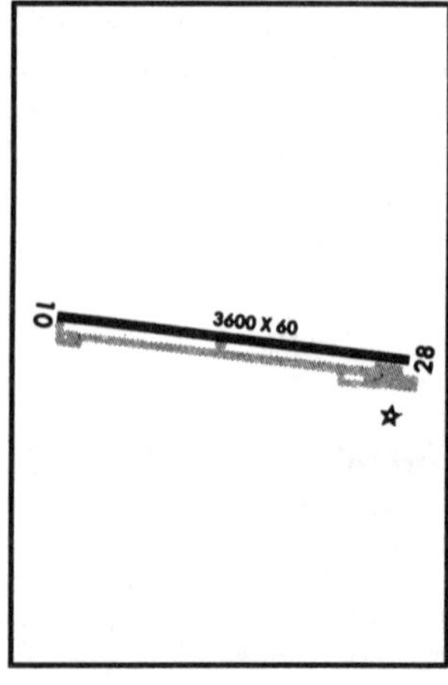

Airport Information:

WELLSBORO - GRAND CANYON STATE AIRPORT (N38)
4 mi southwest of town N41-43.68 W77-23.67 Elev: 1899 Fuel: 80, 100LL
Rwy 10-28: H3600x60 (Asph) Attended: daylight hours Unicom: 122.8
Grand Canyon State Airport Phone: 724-4851

Not to be used for navigational purposes

PA-WBW - WILKES-BARRE BARRE WYOMING VALLEY

(Area Code 717)

52

Colonial Family Restaurant:

The Colonial Family Restaurant is located adjacent to the Barre Wyoming Valley Airport. This family style restaurant is open 7 a.m. to 9 p.m. 7 days a week. Daily specials are offered throughout each day except on Sunday. Their menu includes a wide variety of items like steaks, seafood, liver, Italian dishes, chicken dishes as well as a full breakfast line. Average prices run $3.00 to $4.00 for breakfast, $4.00 to $5.00 for lunch and $5.95 to $7.95 for dinner. The restaurant displays a colonial theme with a somewhat rustic appearance with lots of wood. The dining area can accommodate 120 persons with seating at tables and booths. There is a separate room downstairs for banquets and catered events, which happens to be a large portion of their business. In fact ,we were told that they even do off-site catering as well. During our conversation with restaurant personnel, we also learned that many pilots frequent this establishment, flying in from all over the region. For more information call the Colonial Family Restaurant at 287-2462.

Restaurants Near Airport:

Authur Treacher's Seafood	Adj Arpt	Phone: 288-8727
Burger King Restaurant	Adj Arpt	Phone: N/A
Colonial Family Restaurant	Adj Arpt	Phone: 287-2462
Genetti Hotel & Conv Ctr.	2 mi	Phone: 800-833-6152
McDonalds Restaurant	Adj Arpt	Phone: N/A

Lodging: Best Western Gus Genetti (Trans) 823-6152; Holiday Inn (Trans) 824-8901; Quality Inn (Trans) 824-2411; Red Roof Inn 829-6422; Sheraton-Crossgates 824-7100; The Woodlands Inn & Resort (Trans) 824-9831.

Meeting Rooms: Best Western Gus Genetti 823-6152; Holiday Inn 824-8901; Quality Inn 824-2411; Red Roof Inn 829-6422; Sheraton-Crossgates 824-7100; The Woodlands Inn & Resort 824-9831.

Transportation: America Cab 823-3186; Posten Taxi 823-2111; Pittston Taxi 655-5531.

Information: Tourist Promotion Agency, 201 Hangar Road, Avoca, PA 18641, Phone: 457-1320.

NO AIRPORT DIAGRAM AVAILABLE

Airport Information:

WILKES - BARRE WYOMING VALLEY (WBW)
3 mi north of town N41-17.83 W75-51.07 Elev: 545 Fuel: 80, 100LL, Jet-A
Rwy 06-24: H3376x75 (Asph) Rwy 09-27: 2300x100 (Asph-Turf) Attended: 1330-2200Z
Unicom: 122.8 Public Phone 24hrs Notes: Overnight parking Single $2.00, Twins $3.00; High transmission lines +152 ft 6000 ft from Rwy 24 thld 585 ft left marked with red spheres. See AFD.
FBO: Wyoming Valley Aviation (Arpt Mgr) Phone: 288-3257

PA-AVP - WILKES-BARRE SCRANTON INTERNATIONAL ARPT.

(Area Code 717)

53

International Coffee Shop:

The International Coffee Shop is located in the terminal building on the Scranton International Airport. This family style restaurant is open 7 days a week between 6 a.m. and 8:30 p.m. Their menu includes a full breakfast line as well as many other items such as filet of fish, haddock sandwiches, hamburgers, chicken platters, 10 oz chopped steak, club sandwiches and homemade soups. The main dining area can seat about 80 persons. The restaurant has windows along one side that allow for a very nice view of the airport. Fly-in groups and parties are welcome. This establishment also provides in-flight catering as well. For more information, call the International Coffee Shop at 457-3307.

Restaurants Near Airport:

International Coffee Shop	On Site	Phone: 457-3307

Lodging: Contempri Inn (3 miles, shuttle) 348-1000; Hilton Lackawanna RR Station (9 miles) 342-8300; Holiday Inn (9 miles) 343-4771; Howard Johnson (3 miles, shuttle) 654-3301; Scranton Inn 344-9811; Sheraton Inn-Crossgates (shuttle) 824-7100; The Inn at Nichols Village (14 miles) 587-1135; Woodlands Inn and Resort (5 miles, shuttle) 824-9831.

Meeting Rooms: Contempri Inn 348-1000; Scranton Inn 344-9811; Sheraton Inn (Crossgates) 824-7100; Woodlands Inn 824-9831;

Transportation: Airport courtesy car reported; Also Taxi Service 344-7534 or 800-322-3803; Rental Cars: Avis 654-3318; Budget 654-8911; Hertz 655-1452; National 655-3291.

Information: Tourist Promotion Agency, 201 Hangar Road, Avoca, PA 18641, Phone: 457-1320.

Airport Information:

WILKES-BARRE/SCRANTON INTERNATIONAL AIRPORT (AVP)
5 mi southwest of town N41-20.29 W75-43.46 Elev: 963 Fuel: 100LL, Jet-A
Rwy 04-22: H7501x150 (Asph-Grvd) Rwy 10-28: H4497x150 (Asph-Grvd)
Rwy 16-34: H3699x150 (Asph) Attended: continuously Atis: 111.6 Unicom: 122.95
App/Dep Con: 126.3, 124.5 Tower: 120.1 Gnd Con: 121.9
FBO: Tech Aviation Phone: 457-3400 or 655-5999

PA-IPT - WILLIAMSPORT LYCOMING COUNTY AIRPORT

(Area Code 717) 54

Restaurants Near Airport:

Family Affair Restaurant	1 mi E.	Phone: 368-1181
Hillside Restaurant	3 mi W.	Phone: 326-6779
Hoss's Steak & Seafood	2 mi W.	Phone: 326-0838
Sky View Restaurant	On Site	Phone: 368-2031

Lodging: Econo Lodge 326-1501; Holiday Inn 326-1981; Quality Inn (Trans) 323-9801; Sheraton Inn (Courtesy phone in terminal building) 327-8231.

Meeting Rooms: Airport conference room (12 people); Econo Lodge 326-1501; Holiday Inn 326-1981; Quality Inn 323-9801; Sheraton Inn 327-8231.

Transportation: Courtesy cars or vans available through Lycoming Air Services 368-2651 or Aero Flight, Inc. 368-2721; Billtown Cab Company 322-2222; Avis 368-2683; Hertz 368-1961; National 368-8151.

Information: Lycoming County Tourist Promotion Agency, 454 Pine Street, Williamsport, PA 17701, Phone: 800-358-9900.

Sky View Restaurant & Lounge:

The Sky View Restaurant and Lounge is located right on the Lycoming County Airport in the main terminal building on the second floor. The terminal building is only a 100 foot walk from the aircraft tie-down ramp. This is a combination cafe and fine dining establishment. Their hours are Monday through Friday 7:30 a.m. to 8:30 p.m., Saturday 8 a.m. to 8:30 p.m. and Sunday 8 a.m. to 7 p.m. Their menu contains a full breakfast selection in addition to the lunch and dinner choices. Specialties of the house include prime rib served nightly, Black Diamond steaks, filet mignon, fried shrimp, broiled haddock as well as many other entrees. Prices average $3.25 for breakfast, $3.50 for lunch and $8.95 for dinner. Daily specials are offered, like homemade soups, and Sunday serving full dinner menu from 11:30 a.m. to 7 p.m. Historical items decorate the wall of the restaurant, and a full view is provided with skylights. The Sky View welcomes the opportunity for catering your function. Anything on their menu can be prepared for you. Carry-out meals can also be arranged. We learned that the Little League Baseball World Series is held every summer in Williamsport, PA. For information about the Skyview Restaurant call 368-2031.

Airport Information:

WILLIAMSPORT - LYCOMING COUNTY AIRPORT (IPT)
4 mi east of town N41-14.52 W76-55.31 Elev: 529 Fuel: 100LL, Jet-A
Rwy 09-27: H6449x150 (Asph-Grvd) Rwy 12-30: H4280x150 (Asph) Rwy 15-33: H3502x100 (Asph) Attended: 1100-0400Z Unicom: 122.95 Tower: 119.1
Gnd Con: 121.9 Public Phone 24 hrs Notes: No landing fee for non commercial aircraft. $10.00 fee charged for transient/commercial aircraft. Airport manager 368-2444.
FBO: Williamsport Aircraft Sales Phone: 368-2651

PA-8G7 - ZELIENOPLE ZELIENOPLE MUNICIPAL

(Area Code 412) 55

Restaurants Near Airport:

Plane View Cafe	On Site	Phone: 452-1558

Lodging: Hampton Inn Motel 8 mi 776-1000; Red Roof Inn 8 mi 776-5670; Sheraton Warrendale 8 mi 776-6900; Zelienople Motel 4 mi 452-7900.

Meeting Rooms: None Reported

Transportation: Car rental: AAA 452-5970; Hockenberger Motors 452-8100.

Information: Butler County Visitors Bureau, 100 N. Main Street, Box 1082, Butler, PA 16003-1082 or call 283-2222.

The Plane View Cafe:

The Plane View Cafe is located on the Zelienople Municipal Airport. This restaurant specializes in serving breakfast and lunch. Homemade pies and ice cream delights are popular items with many of their customers. For information about this establishment call 452-1558.

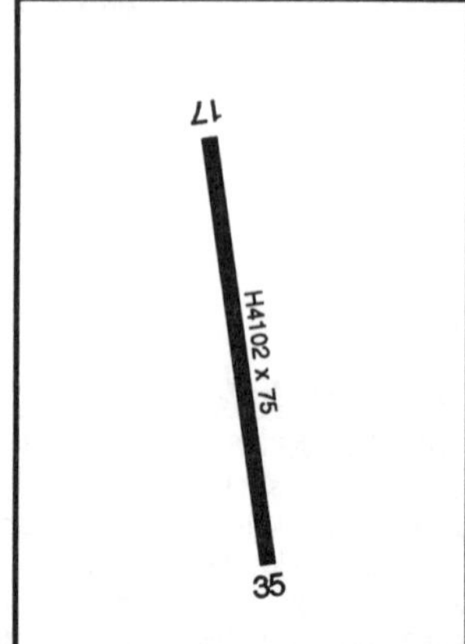

Airport Information:

ZELIENOPLE - ZELIENOPLE MUNICIPAL (8G7)
1 mi west of town N40-48.10 W80-09.64 Elev: 901 Fuel: 100LL Rwy 17-35: H4102x75 (Asph) Attended: Mon-Fri 1300Z-dusk CTAF: 122.9
FBO: Airport Manager Phone: 452-1290

RHODE ISLAND

CROSS FILE INDEX

Location Number	City or Town	Airport Name And Identifier	Name of Attraction
1	Block Island	Block Island State Arpt. (BID)	Block Island Restaurants
2	Block Island	Block Island State Arpt. (BID)	Htl. Manisses Dining Rm.
3	North Kingstown	Quonset State Arpt. (OQU)	Carter's 19th Hole
4	Providence	Theodore Francis Green S. (PVD)	Cowesett Inn
5	Providence	Theodore Francis Green S. (PVD)	Legal Seafood & Pasta
6	West Kingston	Richmond Arpt. (RI04)	Sal's Pizza

LOCATION MAP

Not to be used for navigational purposes

RI-BID - BLOCK ISLAND
BLOCK ISLAND STATE AIRPORT

(Area Code 401) **1, 2**

Block Island Restaurants:

There are a number of fine restaurants on the island, covering a wide variety of services. Most of them are located in town about 1 to 2 mile west of the Block Island Airport. Air transportation commuter service is furnished by New England Airlines 466-5881 between Westerly State Airport and Block Island Airport. During our conversation with the airport manager, we learned that frequent bus and taxi service is available from the airport with no problem. Attractions on the island include the Block Island State Beach; Mohegan Bluffs with light house along 180 foot clay cliffs; New Harbor located 1 mile west of town on Ocean Avenue; also many recreational activities are available like fishing, swimming, picnicking or hiking. Contact the Block Island Chamber of Commerce 466-2982. See "Information".

Restaurants Near Airport:

Beach Head	1-1/2 mi	Phone: 466-2249
Bethenies	Adj Arpt	Phone: 466-3100
Dead Eye Dick	1-1/2 mi	Phone: 466-2654
Ely's Restaurant	1 mi	Phone: N/A
Finn's Seafood Rest.	1-1/2 mi	Phone: 466-2473
Manisses Restaurant	1 mi	Phone: 466-2863
Mohican Restaurant	1-1/2 mi	Phone: 466-5911

Lodging: Ballard's Inn (1 mile) 466-2231; Narragansett Inn (1 mile) 466-2626; National Hotel (1 mile) 466-5577; Seacrest Inn (1 mile) 466-2882; Surf Hotel (1 mile) 466-2241 or 466-5990; The Manisses (1 mile) 466-2421 or 466-2063

Meeting Rooms: None reported

Transportation: Bus; courtesy cars; taxi service: Seacrest 466-2882; Your Taxi 466-5550; Also rental cars: Econo-Car 466-2029; Thrifty 466-2631.

Information: Visitor's Center. P.O. Drawer D, Block Island, PA 02807, Phone: 466-2982.

Hotel Manisses Dining Room:

Manisses Dining Room is a highly rated fine dining establishment. This restaurant specializes in grilled swordfish with tomatilla salsa, filet mignon with shiitake mushroom demi-glace and herb-encrusted salmon. Prices average $9.00 to $22.00 for lunch and $15.00 to $25.00 for dinner. There is an enclosed garden dining room as well as outdoor dining. A panoramic view of Old Harbor can be enjoyed from the restaurant. Weekend hours of operation are 5:30 p.m. to 10 p.m. Saturday, and 11:30 a.m. to 10 p.m. on Sunday. Weekday hours are unknown. For information call 466-2836 or 466-2421.

Airport Information:

BLOCK ISLAND - BLOCK ISLAND AIRPORT (BID)
1 mi west of town N41-10.09 W71-34.67 Elev: 109 Rwy 10-28: H2501x100 (Asph)
Attended: 1200-0400Z Unicom: 123.0
Block Island Airport Phone: 466-5511
FBO: New England Airlines Phone: 466-5881

RI-OQU - NORTH KINGSTOWN
QUONSET STATE AIRPORT

(Area Code 401) **3**

Carter's 19th Hole:

Carter's 19th Hole is a family-style restaurant located about 1 mile from the Quonset State Airport. According to the management, fly-in guests can call the restaurant and they will come out and pick you up at the airport. Please call the restaurant in advance and let them know you are planning to fly in. Their hours are 6 a.m. to 1 a.m., 7 days a week. Specialty items on their menu include prime rib, shrimp, fish, French dip and club sandwiches. Average prices run $3.50 for breakfast & lunch, and $8.50 for most dinner selections. Daily specials are also available. The dining room is combined with a lounge and bar area. One unique feature regarding this establishment is that there is an 18-hole golf, course right outside their door. Fly-in guests could play a round or two of golf and stop to enjoy a meal before heading back to the airport. Groups are also welcome to plan outings or group functions; however advance reservations are strongly suggested for tee-off times, especially on weekends. For more information call Carter's 19th Hole at 294-6460.

Restaurants Near Airport:

Carter's 19th Hole	1 mi	Phone: 294-6460

Lodging: Best Western Monte Vista (3-1/2 miles) 884-8000;

Meeting Rooms: None reported

Transportation: North Kingstown Taxi 885-4488; rental cars: Avis 738-5800; Gorden Chevrolet 294-3351; Hertz 738-7500; Toyota Leasing 884-5438.

Information: Chamber of Commerce, 328 Main Street, P.O. Box 289, Wakefield, RI 02880, Phone: 783-2801; Also: South County Tourism Council, Stedman Government Center, 4808 Tower Hill Road, Wakefield, RI 02879, Phone: 789-4422 or 800-548-4662.

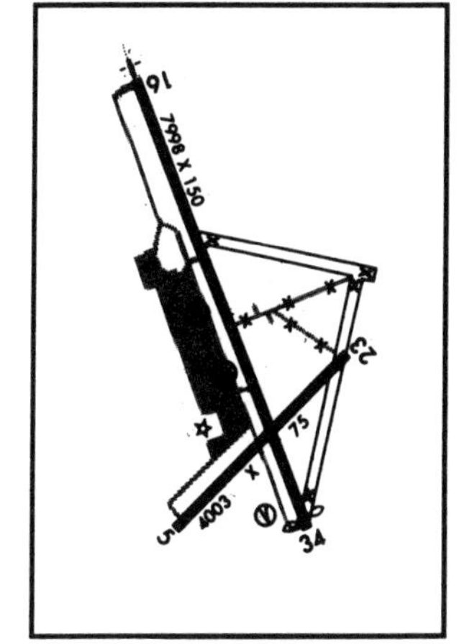

Airport Information:

NORTH KINGSTOWN - QUONSET STATE AIRPORT (OQU)
3 mi northeast of town N41-35.81 W71-24.71 Elev: 19 Fuel: 100LL, Jet-A
Rwy 16-34: H7998x150 (Asph-Conc) Rwy 05-23: H4003x75 (Asph) Attended: 1400-2200Z
Unicom: 122.95 Tower: 126.35 Gnd Con: 134.5 Notes: overnight tiedown fees, singles $3.00, twins $5.00 & jets $10.00. FBO:
FBO: Quonset Airway Phone: 849-6337

RI-PVD - PROVIDENCE
THEODORE FRANCIS GREEN S.

(Area Code 401) 4, 5

Cowesett Inn:

Cowesett Inn is located only 3 to 5 miles from the Theodore Francis Green Airport. It is a very popular establishment with many local people throughout the area as well as airport personnel. This is a casual dining facility open Tuesday through Sunday from 11:30 a.m. to 12 a.m. (closed on Monday). Their menu contains a wide choice of entrees to select from. Specialties of the house include choice steaks and seafood, Prime rib, Black Angus sirloin steaks, baked and stuffed shrimp as well as their fish and ships, hamburgers, salads and delicious appetizers. Prices average $4.95 for lunch specials and $12.00 to $15.25 for main dinner items. This restaurant contains 5 different dining areas with a total seating of about 250 people. The decor of the Cowesett Inn displays lots of oak, dark wood, brass and glass. Two fire place also add to the restaurants ambience. There are also skylights providing plenty of lighting. Catered meals for groups can be arranged with advanced notice. Of site catering is also available . During our conversation with Northstar Aviation (Phone: 738-2600), we learned that they frequently use "Best Taxi Service" (Phone:781-0706), as a source of transportation for fly-in guest. After calling Best Taxi, we were told that their current taxicab rate is $1.60 per mile from the airport. If driving your self, you can reach the restaurant by taking Route 95 south to exit 10B at 117 West Warwick. Stay on this street for 2 miles, then take a left onto Quaker Lane. After merging onto Route 2 South 1/4 mile, take a right onto Route 3 south. The restaurant will be about 1/4 mile down the road. For more information about the Cowesett Inn call 885-2726.

Legal Seafood & Pasta:

The Legal Seafood & Pasta Restaurant is located across from the Theodore Francis Green State Airport. This family style restaurant is open Monday through Thursday 11:30 a.m. to 10 p.m., Friday 11:30 a.m. to 10:30 p.m., Saturday 12 p.m. to 10:30 p.m. and Sunday 12 p.m. to 9 p.m. The restaurant decor is patterned after a New England Seafood establishment with a nautical theme. Specialty dishes include chicken, steaks, prime rib, seafood, scrod, lobster, sword fish, tuna, and Bluefish. Lunch prices run $7.00 to $12.00 and dinner selections run $12.00 to $18.00. There are separate dining areas that can accommodate up to 160 persons in all. The decor is contemporary with an elegant touch. Carpeted and hard wood floors, along with tables and booths add to the comfortable atmosphere. Banquet facilities can also be arranged for up to 60 persons. A hotel next door has 111 rooms for travelers. For more information call the restaurant at 732-3663.

Restaurants Near Airport:

Chelo's Restaurant	5 min walk	Phone: 861-6644
Cowesett Inn	3 to 5 mi	Phone: 885-2726
Fat City Deli & Pub	5 min walk	Phone: 732-9533
Great House	5 min walk	Phone: 739-8600
Gregg's Restaurant	10 min walk	Phone: 831-5700
Legal Seafood	5 min walk	Phone: 732-3663

Lodging: Comfort Inn 732-0470; Crossroads Inn 467-9800; Inn At The Crossings 732-6000; Marriott (Convention facilities) 272-2400; Master Host Inn-Airport (On site) 737-7400; Holiday Inn Downtown (Convention facilities) Omni Biltmore (Convention facilities) 421-0700; Sheraton Tera Airport Hilton 788-4000; Susse Chalet 941-6600; Susse Chalet Smithfield 232-2400.

Meeting Rooms: Marriott (Convention facilities) 272-2400; Master Host Inn-Airport (On site) 737-7400; Holiday Inn Downtown (Convention facilities) Omni Biltmore (Convention facilities) 421-0700; Sheraton Tera Airport Hilton 788-4000.

Transportation: Airport Taxi 737-5550; Cozy Taxi 846-2500; Also Rental Cars: Avis 738-5810; Budget 739-8908; Hertz 738-7500; National 737-4800.

Information: Greater Providence Convention & Visitors Bureau, 30 Exchange Terrace, 4th Floor, Providence, RI 02903, Phone: 274-1636 or 800-233-1636.

Airport Information:

PROVIDENCE - THEODORE FRANCIS GREEN STATE AIRPORT (PVD)

6 mi south of town N41-43.41 W71-25.60 Elev: 55 Fuel: 100LL, Jet-A
Rwy 05-23: H7166x200 (Asph-Grvd) Rwy 16-34: H6081x150 (Asph-Grvd)
Attended: continuously Atis: 124.2 Unicom: 122.95
Tower: 120.7 Gnd Con: 121.9 Clnc Del: 126.65
FBO: Northstar Aviation Phone: 738-2600

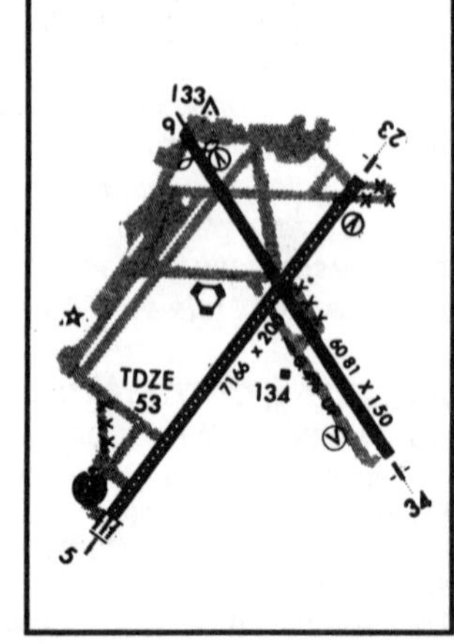

RI-RI04 WEST KINGSTON RICHMOND AIRPORT

(Area Code 401) 6

Restaurants Near Airport:
Sal's Pizza   Adj. Arpt.   Phone: 782-8855

Lodging: Sun Valley Motel 4 mi. Phone: 539-8485

Transportation: Richmond Airport, Inc. (Weekends) Phone: 783-1498

Information: Kingston Chamber of Commerce, 328 Main Street, P.O. Box 289, Wakefield, RI 02880. Phone: 783-2801; Also: South County Tourism Council, Stedman Government Center, 4808 Tower Hill Road, Wakefield RI 02879, Phone: 789-4422 or 800-548-4662.

Sal's Pizza:

Sal's Pizza is located across from the Richmond Airport. As the name implies, Sal's specializes in preparing mouth-watering pizzas with many different toppings. In addition to the traditional cheese, sausage and mushroom pizzas, Sal's pizza creations include a "White Pizza" , vegetable and spinach pizzas which are very popular with many of their customers. This family-style restaurant has seating for about 25 people. Carry-out orders make up a good portion of their orders. The restaurant is open 7 days a week. Friday and Saturday 11 a.m. to 10 p.m., and Sunday through Thursday 11 a.m. to 9 p.m. For information call 782-8855.

Attractions:

A special event held each year, sure to attract aviation enthusiast, is the annual "Hot Air Balloon Festival" held late July or early August, each year at the University of Rhode Island. This university is located 6 miles southeast of the Richmond Airport on Route 138. During this two-day event, there are parachute demonstrations, hot air balloon rides, music, arts and crafts exhibits. For more information call the campus at 792-1000 or the Kingston Chamber of Commerce listed above.

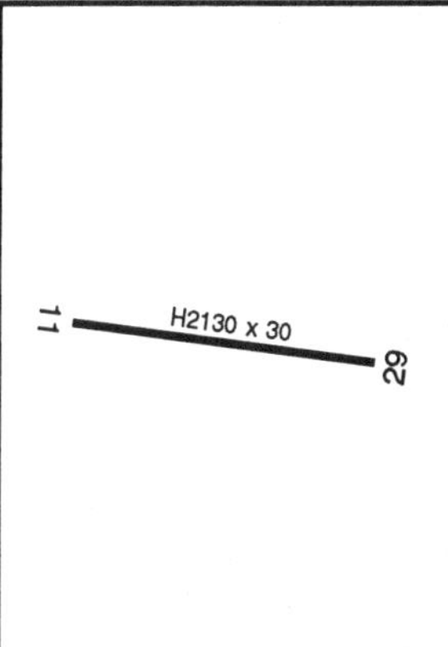

Airport Information:

WEST KINGSTON - RICHMOND AIRPORT (RI04)

3 mi west of town   N41-29.34 W71-37.22   Elev: 130   Fuel: 100LL   Rwy 11-29: H2130x30 (Asph)   Attended: Irregularly   Unicom: 122.8   Notes: Caution-ultralights on and in vicinity of airport. No landing fee, overnight parking $5.00,   24hr public phone

FBO: Richmond Airport, Inc.   Phone: 783-1498
FBO: Richmond Flight Ctr   Phone: 782-8050

SOUTH CAROLINA

LOCATION MAP

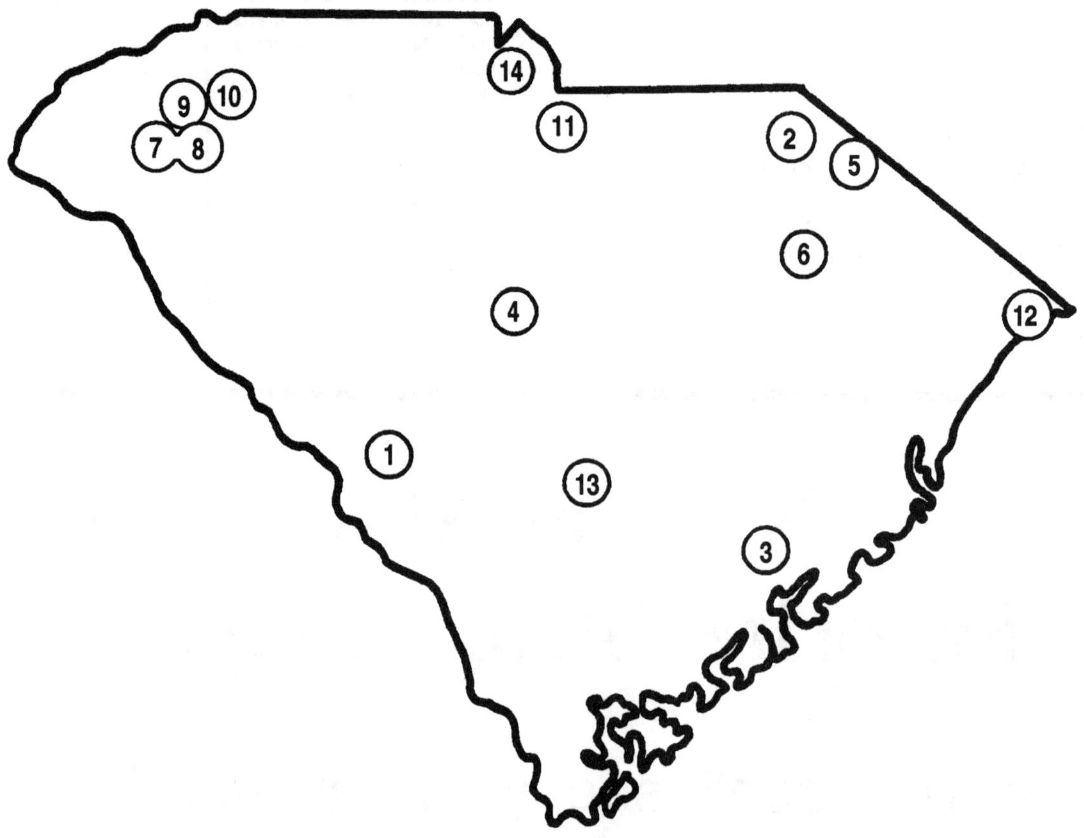

Not to be used for navigational purposes

SOUTH CAROLINA

CROSS FILE INDEX

Location Number	City or Town	Airport Name And Identifier	Name of Attraction
1	Aiken	Aiken Muni. Arpt. (AIK)	Blimpies @ Airport Shell
2	Bennettsville	Stantons BBQ (Private)	Stantons BBQ Rest.
3	Charleston	Charleston AFB/Intl. Arpt. (CHS)	Host Marriott Services
4	Columbia	Columbia Metro. (CAE)	Columbia Concessions
5	Dillon	Dillon Co. Arpt. (DLC)	Hubbard House Rest.
6	Florence	Florence Reg. Arpt. (FLO)	Airport Restaurant
7	Greenville	Donaldson Center Arpt. (7A1)	The Beach House Rest.
8	Greenville	Donaldson Center Arpt. (7A1)	Inflight Catering
9	Greenville	Greenville Downtown (GMU)	The Palms
10	Greer	Greenville-Spartanburg Arpt. (GSP)	Windows Restaurant
11	Lancaster	Lancaster Co/Mc Whirter Fld. (LKR)	Catawba Fish Camp
12	North Myrtle Beach	Grand Strand/Myrtle Beach (CRE)	Jetway Food/Divots
13	Orangeburg	Orangeburg Muni. Arpt. (OGB)	Original Earl Dukes Rest.
14	Rock Hill	Rock Hill Muni./Bryant Fld. (29J)	Tam's Tavern

Articles

City or town	Nearest Airport and Identifier	Name of Attraction
Florence, SC	Florence Reg. (FLO)	Florence Air & Missile Mus.

SC-AIK - AIKEN
AIKEN MUNICIPAL AIRPORT

(Area Code 803)

1

Blimpies @ Airport Shell:

Blimpies @ Airport Shell is a snack bar is located about 4 blocks east, of the Aiken Municipal Airport. This restaurant is open between 6 a.m. and 9:30 p.m. Monday through Friday and 10 a.m. to 9:30 on Saturday and Sunday. This small but quaint snack bar can accommodate about 20 people in the dining area, with seating on picnic tables. Their menu includes a variety of sub-sandwiches with many different toppings. They also serve salads. Prices average around $2.00 to $3.00 for most selections. For more information call them at 648-9835.

Attractions:

Aiken is a resort town offering extensive golf and horse racing facilities, located 8 miles from the Aiken Municipal Airport.

Restaurants Near Airport:

Barber's Country Cafe	4 Blks E.	Phone: 648-8140
Blimpies @ Arpt. Shell	4 Blks E.	Phone: 648-9835
Holiday Inn	4 mi W.	Phone: 648-4272
Waffle House	4 Blks E.	Phone: 648-3470

Lodging: Holiday Inn (4 miles) 648-4272; Comfort Inn (1/2 mile) 642-5692; Deluxe Inn (4 miles) 642-2840.

Meeting Rooms: Holiday Inn (4 miles) 648-4272; Comfort Inn (1/2 mile) 642-5692; Deluxe Inn (4 miles) 642-2840.

Transportation: Aiken Aviation (FBO) can provide fly-in customers with courtesy car: Also: Owens Rental Cars 648-7803; Yellow Cab 642-6055.

Information: Greater Aiken Chamber of Commerce, 400 Laurens Street NW, P.O. Box 892, Aiken, SC 29802, Phone: 649-3161.

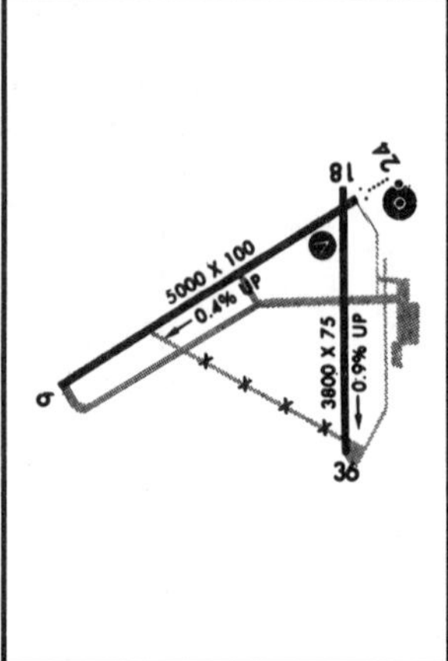

Airport Information:

AIKEN - AIKEN MUNICIPAL AIRPORT (AIK)
6 mi north of town N33-38.97 W81-41.07 Fuel: 100LL, Jet-A Rwy 06-24: H5000x100 (Asph) Rwy 18-36: H3800x75 (Asph) Attended: continuously Unicom: 122.8 Public Phone 24hrs
FBO: Aiken Aviation Phone: 648-7803

SC-(Private) - BENNETTSVILLE
STANTONS BBQ PRIVATE AIRSTRIP

(Area Code 803)

2

Stantons Bar-B-Que Restaurant:

Stantons Bar-B-Que Restaurant is located only 50 to 100 feet from their private grass airstrip located across the road. The name of their establishment and airport is painted right on the roof of the restaurant making it an ideal land mark for pilots planning to drop in for a visit. The restaurant selection of main entrees is synonymous with the name. They specialize in preparing delicious barbecued items. Restaurant hours are Wednesday through Friday from 11:00 a.m. until 2:00 p.m. then they re-open again for dinner between 5:00 p.m. and 9:30 p.m. On Saturday they are open from 11:00 a.m. to 9:30 p.m. and on Sunday from 11:00 a.m. until 3:00 p.m. They are closed on Monday and Tuesday. To find Stanton's Bar-B-Que by air the following navigation aids can be used. Sandhill VOR 111.8, 195 degree Radial, 33 statute miles; Chesterfield VOR 108.2, 84 degree Radial, 34 statute miles; Florence VOR 115.2, 03 degree Radial, 35 statute miles. Roscoe NDB (Hamlet) 182 degrees, 8 statute miles. And three statute miles S.W. of Gibson, NC. on Hwy 79. For more information call Stanton's Bar-B-Que restaurant at 265-4855.

Restaurants Near Airport:
Stanton's Bar-B-Que Adj Arpt. Phone: 265-4855

Lodging: None reported

Meeting Rooms: None reported

Transportation: Unknown

Information: Marlboro County Chamber of Commerce, 300 W. Main Street, P.O. Box 458, Bennettsville, SC 29512, Phone: 479-3941.

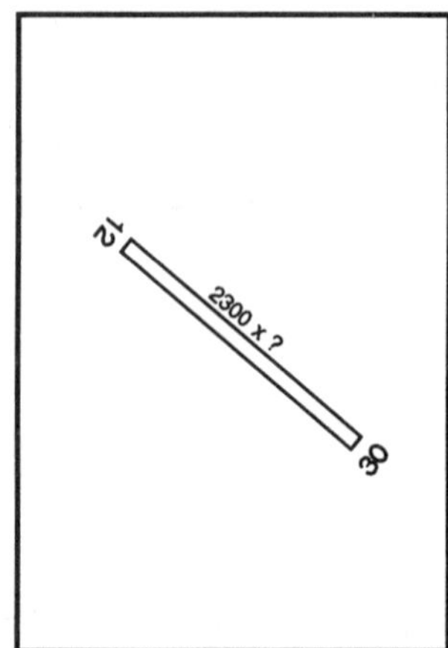

Airport Information:

BENNETTSVILLE - (Private Airstrip)
3 mi southwest of Gibson, NC. This airport is not listed on the sectional. N34-43.9 W79-40-0 Elev: 208 Fuel: None reported Rwy 12-30: 2300 (Grass-turf) Unicom: 122.9 Notes: According to information supplied to us, this airport is owned by Stanton BBQ Restaurant located only 50 to 75 feet across the road. Call restaurant for airport and runway conditions. CAUTION: use at own risk.
Airport Owners Stanton BBQ Phone: 266-4855

SC-CHS - CHARLESTON
CHARLESTON AFB/INTL AIRPORT

Restaurants Near Airport: (Area Code 803)
Host Marriott Services On Site Phone: 767-7054

3

Host Marriott Services.

This facility offers a family style restaurant and snack bar, located in the terminal building at the Charleston International Airport. Restaurant hours are 6 a.m. to 9 p.m. Daily featured entrees include sandwiches, salads, desserts and soups along with daily specials. Average prices run $6.00 for breakfast, and $6.95 for lunch and dinner selections. The theme of this facility provides an attractive blending of the tradition and history of the Charleston area with the contemporary function of a modern airport. Banquet facilities are available for groups up to 20 to 25 persons. A full catering service is also available to accommodate your needs. In addition to this restaurant, there are several other eateries within the terminal concourse open from 6 a.m. to midnight. For more information call 767-7054.

Lodging: Holiday Inn (Airport) 744-1621; Howard Johnson Lodge (Airport) 554-4140; Marriott-Charleston 747-1900; Ramada Inn (Airport) 744-8281; Sheraton Inn (Airport) 744-2501; Northwoods Atrium Inn 572-2200.

Meeting Rooms: Meeting rooms are available at most of the lodging facilities listed above (See Lodging).

Transportation: Avis 767-7030; Budget 767-7051; Dollar 760-1112; Hertz 767-4552; National 767-3078.

Information: Charleston Visitor Reception and Transportation Center, 375 Meeting Street, P.O. Box 975, Charleston, SC 29402, Phone: 853-8000.

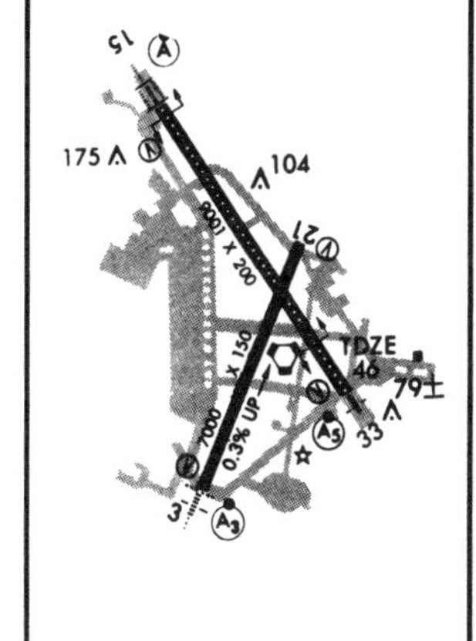

Airport Information:

CHARLESTON - CHARLESTON AFB/INTL AIRPORT (CHS)
9 mi northwest of town N32-53.92 W80-02.43 Elev: 46 Fuel: 100, Jet-A1+
Rwy 15-33: H9001x200 (Asph-Conc) Rwy 03-21: H7000x150 (Asph-Conc)
Attended: continuously Atis: 124.75 Unicom: 122.95 App Con 120.7, 135.8, 119.3
Dep Con: 120.7, 135.8 Tower: 126.0 Gnd Con: 121.9 Clnc Del: 118.0
FBO: New Charleston Aviation Phone: 744-2581

SC-CAE - COLUMBIA
COLUMBIA METROPOLITAN

(Area Code: 803) 4

Columbia Food Concessionaire:

Creative Croissants, headquartered in San Diego, California, will provide the food concession service for the new concourse as well as in the main terminal area once renovations are completed in this location. Columbia Metropolitan Airport will be the eleventh airport location for this company. Creative Croissants has a variety of eateries located in the new food court area of the concourse. A variety of menu choices available in the new food court include an Italian Eatery/Pizza Bar which includes pasta, spaghetti, pizza, colzones, garlic bread; The Grille which features freshly grilled 1/3 pound hamburgers and hotdogs and barbecued sandwiches; TCBY Yogurt which features yogurt and hand-dipped ice cream; Creative Croissants, Bakery & Deli -features a variety of bakery items, gourmet sandwiches on freshly baked breads, salads, hot meal croissants, varieties of bagels. Coffee Bar and Juice Bar which features fresh fruits, vegetable juices and smoothies; Gourmet Coffees Espresso/ Cappucino; The Grove will features nuts, candies and natural snacks. For more information about the concessions at Columbia Metropolitan Airport call 822-5010.

Attractions:

Riverbanks Zoo, approximately ten miles from the airport, has been ranked as one of the top ten zoos in the United States. This zoo exhibits more than 1500 species of mammals and birds that live in a habitat recreated to depict the wild. Lake Murray, located a short drive west of the Columbia Metro Area, contains a 50,000 acre impoundment providing all types of water sports and activities including some of the best fishing around. South Carolina State Museum which features four floors of fascinating exhibits in the fields of history, natural history, science & technology, is open Monday through Saturday from 10:00 a.m. to 5:00 p.m.,(Admission). Sesquicentennial State Park Campgrounds containing 87 sites, is located on U.S. 1, 13 miles N.E.. of Columbia, Call 803-788-2706. Columbia Golf Courses: Lin Rick GC - 18 holes, Par 73, length 6919, Sedgewood 18 holes, Par 72, length 6810, and The Woodlands C.C. - 18 holes, Par 72, length 6500.

Restaurants Near Airport:

Columbia Concessionaire	On Site	Phone: 822-5010
Burger King	1-3/4mi	Phone: N/A
Kettle House	1-3/4mi	Phone: N/A
Lizard Thicket	1-1/2mi	Phone: N/A

Information: Greater Columbia Convention and Visitors Bureau, 301 Gervais Street, Columbia, S.C. 29221 Lake Murray Tourism & Recreation Association, 2184 N. Lake Drive or P.O. Box 210096, Columbia, S.C. 29221, (803) 781-5940.

Lodging: The Marriott 771-7000 Cola, Holiday Inn on #1 Hwy. 794-9440, Holiday Inn CityCenter 799-7800, Embassy Suites 252-8700, and The Sheraton Hotel 731-0300.

Meeting Rooms: Available at the airport administration office, call 822-5010.

Transportation: Eagle Aviation (courtesy car) 822-5555, Columbia Aviation (courtesy car) 822-8332, Yellow Cab, City Bus, Avis 822-5100, Budget 822-8346, Hertz 822-8341, National 822-5180.

Information: Greater Columbia Convention & Visitors Bureau, P.O. Box 15, Columbia, SC 29202-0015, Phone: 254-0479 or 800-264-4884.

Airport Information:

COLUMBIA - COLUMBIA METROPOLITAN (CAE)

5 S.W. of town N33-56.43 W81-07.16 Elev: 236 Fuel: 100LL, JetA
Rwy 11-29: H8602x150 (Asph-Grvd) Rwy 05-23: H8000x150 (Asph-Grvd)
Attended: continuously Atis: 120.15 Unicom: 122.95 Tower: 119.5 Gnd. Con.: 121.9
Clnc. Del.: 119.75 Columbia App/Dep Con: 133.4 Notes: No landing fee. Single engine parking fee $5.00, Twin $7.00 Eagle Aviaiton & Columbia Aviation furnish courtesy transportation.

FBO: Columbia Aviation Phone: 822-8332

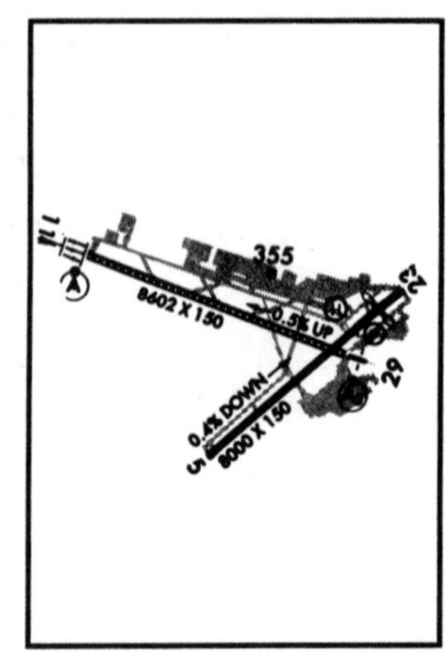

Not to be used for navigational purposes

SC-DLC - DILLON
DILLON COUNTY AIRPORT

(Area Code 803) 5

Hubbard House Restaurant:

The Hubbard House Restaurant is located only 2,000 feet southwest of the Dillon County Airport, at the end of the runway. This fast food restaurant is open from 6 a.m. to 8:30 p.m. 7 days a week. They specialize in American favorites like hot dogs, hamburgers, onion rings, fish and chicken sandwiches, pork chops and a variety of ice cream desserts. Average prices run $3.25 for breakfast and $3.50 for lunch & dinner. Their main dining room can seat 30 persons. The building has a square shape, with large windows. Guests can watch the aircraft landing and taking off. There is even a picnick area with tables outside the restaurant. For more information about the Hubbard House Restaurant, call 774-7781.

Restaurants Near Airport:

Hubbard House Restaurant	2000' SW	Phone: 774-7781
Travel Lodge	2500' SW	Phone: 774-4161
Waffle House	2000' SW	Phone: 774-7836

Lodging: Travel Lodge (2,500 feet from airport) 774-4161.

Meeting Rooms: Travel Lodge 774-4161.

Transportation: Price Flying Service can provide courtesy transportation 774-2636; Also McDonald's Taxi 774-7862; Campbell's Taxi 774-9200; City Cab 774-9560; Rob T. Mc Rae Taxi 774-9111.

Information: Greater Florence Chamber of Commerce, 610 W Palmetto Street, P.O. Box 948, Florence, SC 29503, Phone: 665-0515.

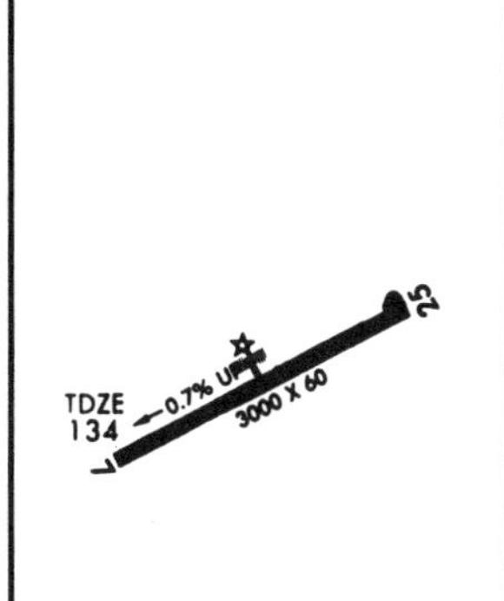

Airport Information:

DILLON - DILLON COUNTY AIRPORT (DLC)
3 mi north of town N34-26.94 W79-22.12 Elev: 134 Fuel: 100LL, MOGAS
Rwy 07-25: H3000x60 (Asph-Afsc) Attended: 1300-2200Z Unicom: 122.8
FBO: Price Flying Service Phone: 774-2636

Florence Air & Missile Museum

Florence, SC (SC-FLO)

For the aviation enthusiast or space buff traveling north or south on Interstate 95 or U.S. 301/76 to Myrtle Beach, a visit to the Florence Air and Missile Museum is a must. Numerous exhibits and displays await young and old.

On the field there are airplanes that represent World War II, Korea, the Cold War and Vietnam. Included in the static displays are a Douglas Torpedo Dive Bomber, B-47 Bomber, North American F-86H Sabre, T-33 Shooting Star, F-104 Stare Fighter, F-101 Voodoo, F-84 Thunderstreak, C-97 Strato Freighter, RB-57 Canberra, Grumman Albatross, and various helicopters, rockets and missiles.

The inside of the museum presents a wonderment of space, aviation, and military artifacts, memorabilia and pictures. For starters, there is a NASA mercury pressure suit, a mock-up of a mercury space capsule with an impact prediction panel, a maze of test consoles from the Apollo/Saturn era and a recently-added tribute to Ron McHair, including various pictures of his first in-flight space suit. There is a remote control Ryan Firebee drone, which flew 11 successful photo reconnaissance missions over north Vietnam.

As the self-guided tour ends, there is a memorabilia and pictures display depicting life at the Florence Army Air Base during World War II and a showcase tribute to Vietnam veterans, Pow/MIAS and much more.

There is an gift shop with items ranging from children aviation and space books to model airplanes and gliders, military veteran pins and patches, posters, postcards and pictures.

Admission is $5.00 for adults and $3.00 for children. Outdoor exhibits and picnic area may be closed if inclement weather exsists.

Their picnic area is usually on a first-come first-served basis, if requested they will reserve it for you. Museum hours are Monday through Saturday 9 a.m. to 5 p.m. and Sunday 10 a.m. to 4:30 p.m. For information call 803-665-5118.

Photo by: Florence Air & Missile Museum

SC-FLO - FLORENCE
FLORENCE REGIONAL AIRPORT

(Area Code 803) 6

Airport Restaurant:

The Airport Restaurant, is a snack bar, located inside the terminal building at the Florence Regional Airport. From the nearest FBO is within walking distance to the restaurant. Entrees include sub sandwiches, club sandwiches, barbecued foods, as well as ham and turkey sandwiches made to order. Soup of the day as well as desserts, pastries, and ice cream are also available. Daily specials include sandwiches, chips and bevarage. Average prices run $2.50 for breakfast, $3.00 for lunch and $ 3.00 for dinner. This facility is open weekdays from 6 a.m. to 8 p.m. and weekends from 8 a.m. to 4 p.m. The decor of the cafe is modern and is aviation oriented. Groups are welcome and sandwich trays can be prepared for pilots on-the-go. For information call the airport managers office at 669-5001.

Restaurants Near Airport:
Airport Restaurant On Site Phone: 669-5001

Lodging: Holiday Inn (5 miles) 669-3251; Quality Inn Downtown (3 miles) 662-6341; Econo Lodge (5 miles) 665-8558; Days Inn East (4 miles) 665-8550.

Transportation: Carolina Air Service and Sutton-Best Aviation can provide courtesy cars with prior notice; Also Rental Cars: Hertz 669-5168; National 662-9077; Avis 669-7695; Budget 667-1117.

Information: Greater Florence Chamber of Commerce, 610 West Palmetto Street, P.O. Box 948, Florence, SC 29503, Phone: 665-0515

Attractions:

Florence Air & Missile Museum is located on the airport. For information call 665-5118. Florence Country Club, 450 Country Club Blvd, Florence 669-3554; Oakdale Country Club, 3700 Lake Oakdale Drive, Florence 669-5301; Lee State Park off I-20 West.

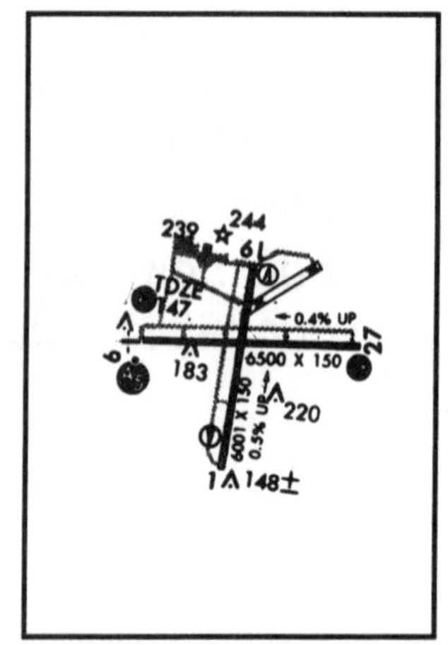

Airport Information:

FLORENCE - FLORENCE REGIONAL AIRPORT (FLO)
3 mi east of town N34-11.12 W79-43.43 Elev: 148 Fuel: 100LL, Jet-A
Rwy 09-27: H6500x150 (Asph) Rwy 18-36: H6001x150 (Asph) Attended: 1130-0300Z
Unicom: 122.95 Florence App/Dep Con: 118.6 (256-074 degrees), 135.25 (075-255)
Tower: 125.1 Gnd Con: 121.9 Public Phone 24hrs Notes: CAUTION: Numerous migrating birds on and in vicinity of airport.
FBO: Carolina Air Service Phone: 667-9627
FBO: Sutton-Best Aviation Phone: 665-2373

SC-7A1 - GREENVILLE DONALDSON CENTER AIRPORT

(Area Code 864)

7, 8

The Beach House Restaurant:

The Beach House Restaurant is located on the Donaldson Center Airport. This snack bar is open between 11 a.m. and 2 p.m. Monday through Friday. We were told fly-in guests must arrange courtesy transportation with Advantage Aviation (FBO) by calling 277-8184. Their menu includes a variety of items including club sandwiches, ham, roast beef, potato salad, and desserts like their homemade cheese cake. This establishment is situated adjacent to "Lockheed" company also on the field.

In-flight Catering:

Vince Perone's catering business can supply your passengers and corporate flights with cheese trays, meat trays, and fruit trays. Contact Advantage Aviation for more information 277-8184.

Attractions:

Donaldson Golf Course which is a 18 hole course, is reported to be located on the Greenville Donaldson Center Airport, Phone: 277-8414; Also Bonnie Brae (1 mile east) 277-9838. Aerobatic flight training and sky-diving are available at the airport.

Restaurants Near Airport:

Applebee's Restaurant	4 mi N.	Phone: 233-9006
The Beach House Rest.	On Site	Phone: 299-1775
Holiday Inn	3 mi N.	Phone: 273-8921
In-flight Catering	On Site	Phone: 277-8184

Lodging: Holiday Inn (3 miles) 277-8921; Greenville Hilton (5 miles north) 232-4747; Ramada South (4 miles north) 277-3734;

Meeting Rooms: There is a conference room at Advantage Aviation (FBO) 277-8184; Holiday Inn 277-8921; Ramada South 277-3734; Palmetto Exposition Hall, Phone N/A

Transportation: Courtesy car through Advantage Aviation 277-8184; Also Rental cars: Hertz 877-4261; All South 370-9057; Agency 235-7895; Enterprise 233-8121.

Information: Greater Greenville Chamber of Commerce, 24 Cleveland Street, P.O. Box 10048, Greenville, SC 29603, Phone: 242-1050.

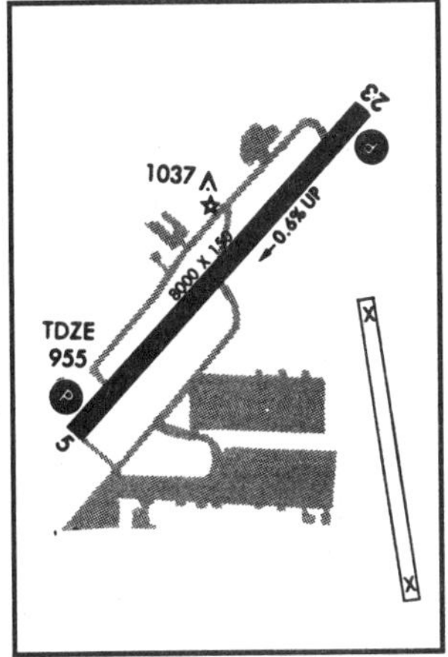

Airport Information:

GREENVILLE - DONALDSON CENTER (7A1)
6 mi south of town N34-45.50 W82-22.59 Elev: 955 Fuel: 100LL, Jet-A Rwy 04-22: H8000x150 (Conc) Attended: 1100-0000Z Unicom: 122.7 Clnc Del 125.95 Public Phone 24hrs
FBO: Advantage Aviation Phone: 277-8184

SC-GMU - GREENVILLE GREENVILLE DOWNTOWN AIRPORT

(Area Code 864)

9

The Palms:

The Palms Restaurant is located adjacent to the Greenville Downtown Airport and can be reached either by walking from the airport, or you can obtain a courtesy van from one of the fixed based operators on the field. This restaurant is classified as a fine dining establishment. It has recently been remodeled and is under new management. For information call 233-4651.

Attractions:

Hartwell Lake 30 miles south on I-85; Table Rock State Park 30 miles northwest 878-9813, 6641; Numerous golf courses in the area.

Restaurants Near Airport:

The Palm Restaurant	Adj Arpt.	Phone: 233-4651

Lodging: Hilton Hotel (Free Transportation) 232-4747; Park Inn International 277-0950; Ramada Inn - Greenville 232-7666; Sheraton Inn - Palmetto 277-8921; The Phoenix Inn (Free Transportation) 233-4651;

Meeting Rooms: Hilton Hotel 232-4747; Phoenix Inn 233-4651; Hyatt Regency 235-1234; Holiday Inn 277-6730.

Transportation: Both Cornerstone Aviation 232-7100, and Greenville Air Center 235-6383 can provide courtesy transportation to nearby facilities; Also Rental Cars: Cornerstone FBO 232-7100; Greenville Air Center 235-6383; Taxi (Airport Limousine) 879-2315; Checker Cab 232-3844; Diamond Cab 235-1713; Yellow Cab 232-5322.

Information: Greater Greenville Chamber of Commerce, 24 Cleveland Street, Box 10048, Greenville, SC 29603, Phone: 242-1050.

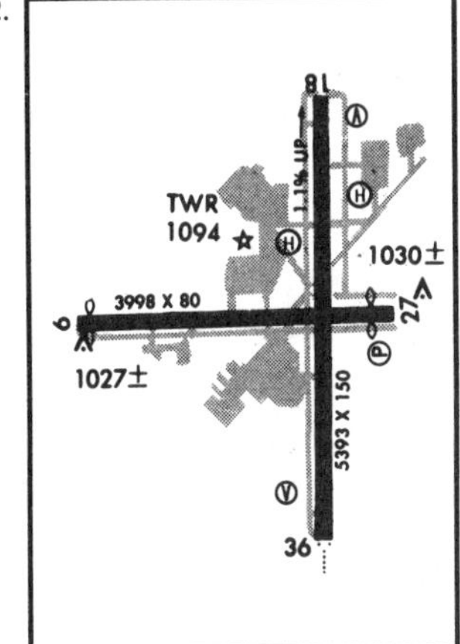

Airport Information:

GREENVILLE - GREENVILLE DOWNTOWN AIRPORT (GMU)
3 mi east of town N34-50.88 W82-21.00 Elev: 1048 Fuel: 100LL, Jet-A
Rwy 18-36: H5393x150 (Asph) Rwy 09-27: H3998x80 (Asph) Attended: 1030-0300Z
Unicom 122.95 App/Dep Con: 118.8 Tower: 119.9 Gnd Con: 121.25
Notes: CAUTION: Aircraft operating in Airport Traffic Area south through east be alert for jet and conventional traffic descending on Greenville-Spartanburg localizer course. (Refer to Airport Facility Directory for further information.) No landing fees; Overnight parking fees determined by FBO's.
FBO: Greenville Air Center Phone: 800-452-0379
FBO: Greenville Aviation Flt. Schl. Phone: 242-4201
FBO: Southern Jet Phone: 232-7100, 800-388-9380

SC-GSP - GREER
GREENVILLE-SPARTANBURG ARPT.

(Area Code 864) 10

Windows Restaurant:

The Windows Restaurant is located at the boarding level of the terminal building on the Greenville Spartanburg Airport. This establishment provides a combination of fine and casual dining from 6:00 a.m. to 9 p.m. 7 days a week. The main dining room opens at 8 a.m., however breakfast counter service is available begining at 6 a.m. Unlike most other airport restaurants, this facility offers a selection of entrees at very reasonable prices, from $3.00 for breakfast, $4.55 for lunch and $5.25 to $14.95 for dinner. Their menu features everything from homemade cookies to Australian lobster tails. All food is freshly made-to-order. Daily specials are also offered, as well as the daily catch of the day seafood special. The dining room is modern with a 3 story glassed in atrium overlooking a sculptured pond and garden with fountain. A 160' mural covers the rear wall of the restaurant, accented by palm and fucus trees, with live background piano music. In addition to the dining area, there is a private dining room that can seat 20 to 25 persons, as well as a conference room for private meetings able to seat 25 to 30 people. In-flight catering through Stevens Aviation is also available. This establishment provides a cafe and lounge in addition to the main dining area. For more information call the Windows Restaurant at 877-7417.

Restaurants Near Airport:

Windows Restaurant On Site Phone: 877-7417

Lodging: Best Western Airport Motel (3 miles) 297-5353; Embassy Suites Greenville (4 miles) 800-362-2779; Hilton (9 miles) 800-445-8667; Hyatt (14 miles) 800-233-1234; Marriott (3 miles) 803-297-0300.

Meeting Rooms: There is a conference room in the terminal building able to accommodate up to 30 people. For information call 877-7426 and ask for ext. #272; Also most of the lodging facilities listed above have conference rooms available.

Transportation: Steven Aviation (FBO) can provide courtesy transportation to nearby locations. Call 879-6000; Also Taxi or limo service 879-2315; Rental Cars: Avis 877-6456; Budget 879-2134; Dollar 848-0209; Hertz 877-4261; National 877-6446.

Information: Greater Greenville Chamber of Commerce, 24 Cleveland Street, P.O. Box 10048, Greenville, SC 29603, Phone: 242-1050.

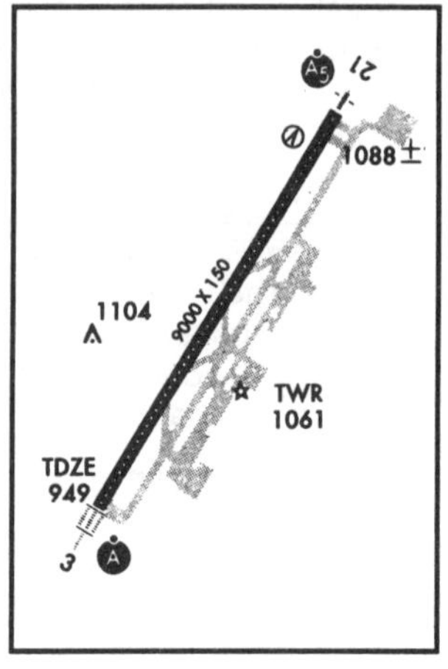

Airport Information:

GREER - GREENVILLE-SPARTANBURG AIRPORT (GSP)
3 mi south of town N34-53.88 W82-13.03 Elev: 964 Fuel: 100LL, Jet-A
Rwy 03-21: H9000x150 (Conc-Asph-Grvd) Attended: continuously Atis: 134.25
Unicom: 122.95 Greer App/Dep Con: 118.8 (West) 119.4 (East) 120.6 (1130-0445Z)
Greer Tower: 120.1 Gnd Con: 121.9 Public Phone 24hrs
FBO: Stevens Aviation Phone: 879-6000, 800-359-7838

Photo by: Windows Restaurant & Spartanburg Airport

Windows Restaurant offers casual and fine diningalong with excellent accommodations for groupmeetings and luncheons.

SC-LKR - LANCASTER
LANCASTER COUNTY-MC WHIRTER FIELD

(Area Code 803)

11

Catawba Fish Camp:

The Catawba Fish Camp is located at the end of the runway, on the other side of a river. Fly-in guests will need to borrow the airport courtesy car which is available through Southland Air (FBO). When speaking to the airport manager, we learned that this restaurant is one of the nicest seafood houses in the entire southeast. This establishment is open from 4 p.m. to 9:30 p.m. Wednesday and Thursday and 11 a.m. to 10:30 p.m. Friday and Saturday. They are closed on Sunday, Monday and Tuesday. Their menu specializes in fresh seafood and chicken entrees. Some of their specialty items are cat fish, cat fish filet, seafood platters, popcorn shrimp, perch, and black bass when available. Some of their specials include all-you-can-eat selections. The dining room can accommodate up to 350 persons with the ability to handle from 4 to 150 in a group. In the past ,they have catered parties as large as 400 persons, at banquets. The restaurant will open on Sunday, Monday or Tuesday for groups scheduling over 100 persons. The decor of the dining room is simple with a light nautical theme. Pictures of ships and fish trophies are displayed on the walls. Carry-out meals make up a large portion of the restaurants business. For more information call the restaurant at 872-4477.

Restaurants Near Airport:

Carriage Inn	4 mi	Phone: 286-6441
Catawba Fish Camp	Adj 1 mi	Phone: 872-4477
Wagon Wheel	3 mi	Phone: 872-4654

Lodging: Best Western (2-1/2 mi) 283-1200; Carriage Inn (4 miles) 286-6441.

Meeting Rooms: Carriage Inn (4 miles) 286-6441.

Transportation: Checker Cab 285-8294; Gerald's 283-2311; Rental Cars: Auto City 283-2045.

Information: Department of Parks, Recreation & Tourism, 1205 Pendleton Street, Columbia, SC 29201, Phone: 803-734-0122.

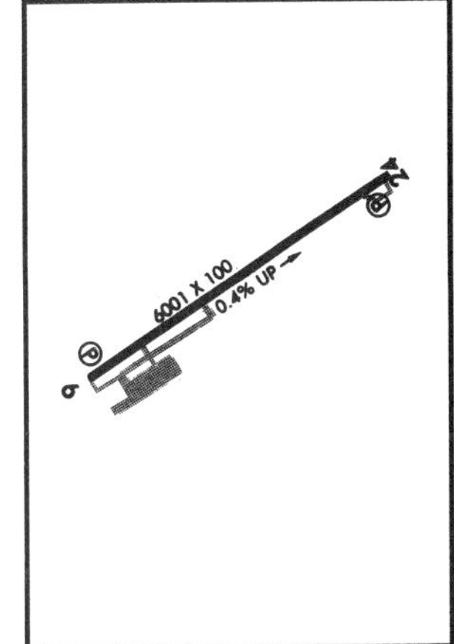

Airport Information:

LANCASTER - LANCASTER COUNTY MC WHIRTER FIELD (LKR)
4 mi west of town N34-43.37 W80-51.28 Elev: 486 Fuel: 100LL, Jet-A, Mogas
Rwy 06-24: H6001x100 (Asph) Attended: 1300-2300Z Unicom: 122.8
FBO: Southland Air Phone: 283-2250

SC-CRE - NORTH MYRTLE BEACH
GRAND STRAND/
MYRTLE BEACH JETPORT

(Area Code 803)

12

Jetway Food/Divots:

This full service restaurant is located on the upper level of the terminal building. They are open from 9 a.m. to 7 p.m. Entrees include appetizers, desserts, pastries, salads, soups, and sandwiches. Daily specials are also offered. Average prices run $6.00 for breakfast, and $7.50 for lunch and dinner. The restaurant has a golfing theme with modern furnishings. Catering is also available. For information call 448-8450.

Attractions:

Myrtle Beach attracts over 11 million vacationers during the summer months. With 60 miles of beach, a 700 foot fishing pier, nature trails, attractions and night life make this area one of the most popular seaside resort towns on the Atlantic Coast.

Restaurants Near Airport:

Arnie's	1 mi	Phone: N/A
Benjamin's	4 mi	Phone: N/A
Damons	1 mi	Phone: N/A
Jetway Food/Divots	On Site	Phone: 448-8450

Lodging: Days Inn 236-1950; Econolodge (1 mile) 272-6196; Firebird Motor Inn 448-7032 or 800-852-7032; Holiday Inn North (2 miles) 272-6153; Myrtle Beach Hilton (3 miles) 449-5000; Sands Beach Club (3 miles) 449-1531.

Meeting Rooms: Many of the lodging facilities have accommodations for meetings, Days Inn, Firebird Motor Inn, Holiday Inn North, etc.

Transportation: Courtesy Car available from FBO's; Coastal Cab 448-3360; Veterans 448-5111; Yellow Cab 448-3181; Rental Cars: Grand Strand Air Service 272-6161; National 272-3509; Ramp 66 272-5337;

Information: Myrtle Beach Area Chamber of Commerce, 1200 North Oak Street, Myrtle Beach SC 29577, Phone: 626-7444 or 800-356-3016.

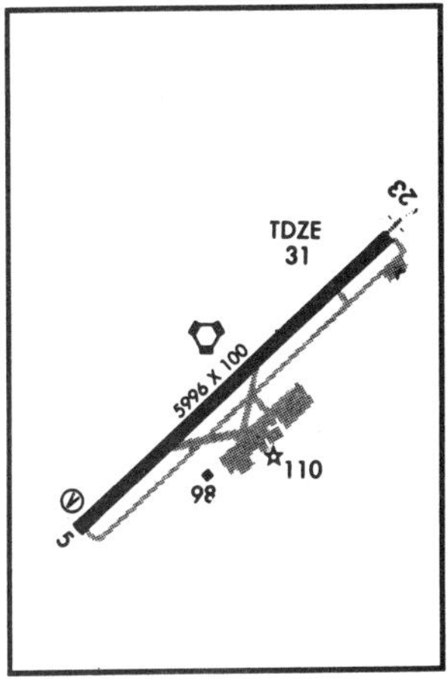

Airport Information:

NORTH MYRTLE BEACH - GRAND STRAND/JETPORT (CRE)
1 mi northwest of town N33-48.71 W78-43.44 Elev: 33 Fuel: 100LL, Jet-A
Rwy 05-23: H5996x100 (Asph) Attended: 1130-0300Z Unicom: 122.95 App/Dep Con: 119.2
Strand Tower: 124.6 Gnd Con: 121.8 Notes: Gulls on and in vicinity of arpt. Extensive banner tow operations from airport along the coastline 10 NM NE to 20 SW after 0500Z.
FBO: Ramp 66 Phone: 272-5337 or 800-433-8918
FBO: Shell Aviation Service Phone: 272-6161 or 800-675-5886

SC-OGB - ORANGEBURG
ORANGEBURG MUNICIPAL AIRPORT

(Area Code 803) **13**

Original Earl Dukes Restaurant:

This restaurant happens to be the original Dukes family owned and operated business, that has been serving the public for over 37 years. This facility is located 1/2 mile from the Orangeburg Municipal Airport. Fly-in guests can acquire a courtesy car from the airport manager with advance notice. The restaurant hours are Thursday through Saturday 11 a.m. to 9 p.m. and Sunday 11 a.m. to 4 p.m. Their menu features many fine barbecued items including pork, ribs, and chicken, in addition to over 70 other items. Meals are served buffet style within a casual and comfortable atmosphere. The main dining room has hardwood floors, brown paneling, and many antiques decorating the walls. Seating capacity is around 100 persons in the main dining area. A separate room is also available for special occasions with the ability to accommodate an additional 100 people. Meals can also be prepared for carry-out if requested. For more information about this restaurant, call 534-4493.

Restaurants Near Airport:

Alexander's Restaurant	2 mi E.	Phone: 536-5244
Original Earl Dukes	1/2 mi	Phone: 534-4493

Lodging: Holiday Inn (2 miles) 531-4600; Best Western (2 miles) 534-7630.

Meeting Rooms: Holiday Inn (2 miles) 531-4600; Best Western (2 miles) 534-7630.

Transportation: Taxi: Carolina Cab 574-7306; Rental Car: Thrifty Car Rental 533-0239.

Information: Orangeburg County Chamber of Commerce, 570 John C. Calhoun Drive, Box 328, Orangeburg, GA 29116-0328, Phone: 534-6821.

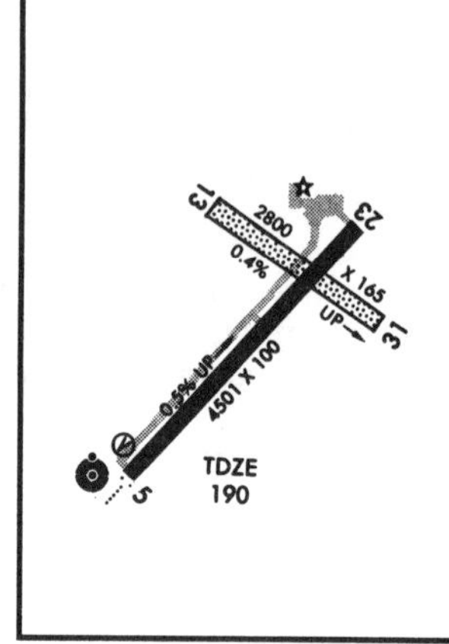

Airport information:

ORANGEBURG - ORANGEBURG MUNICIPAL AIRPORT (OGB)
2 mi south of town N33-27.71 W80-51.47 Elev: 197 Fuel: 100LL, Jet-A
Rwy 05-23: H4501x100 (Asph) Rwy 13-31: 2800x165 (Turf) Attended: 1300Z until dark
Unicom: 122.7 Public Phone 24hrs Notes: FBO: No fees with fuel purchase. Overnight parking fee $3.00/night.
Airport Manager Phone: 534-5545

SC-29J - ROCK HILL
ROCK HILL MUNICIPAL/BRYANT FLD.

(Area Code 803) **14**

Tam's Tavern:

Tam's Tavern is located about 5 miles south of the Rock Hill Municipal/Bryant Field. Courtesy transportation can be arranged through Caro Wings Flight Service (See Airport Information). To reach the restaurant, turn left on Airport Road, left on Museum Road and cross 161 then left on Ebenezer road (274) approx 4 miles, then right on Oakland Avenue, 1/2 block on the right side of street. This is both a cafe and fine dining facility serving lunch from 11 a.m. to 3 p.m. Monday through Saturday, Dinner from 5 p.m. to 10 p.m. Monday through Thursday and 5 p.m. to 10:30 Friday & Saturday (Closed on Sunday). Entrees include Fresh seafood, beef and poultry. Light menu selections are also offered. Prices run about $4.95 for lunch and $10.95 for dinner. Daily lunch specials, as well as nightly fresh seafood specials are offered. The decor of the restaurant is conservative with emphasis on comfort and companionship with soft jazz music in the background. Private rooms for up to 20, and semi private rooms for up to 40 are available. for groups. Hot or cold boxed lunches, along with party trays, can be prepared with 24 hr notice. For information call 329-2226.

Restaurants Near Airport:

El Cancun	6 mi S.	Phone: 366-6996
Jackson's Cageteria	4 mi S.	Phone: 366-6860
Southern Country Barbecue	3 mi S.	Phone: 366-5636
Tam's Tavern	5 mi S.	Phone: 329-2226

Lodging: Howard Johnson Motor Lodge (I-77 & US 21), 329-3121; Ramada Inn (Junction I-77 & US 21), 329-1122.

Meeting Rooms: Both Howard Johnson & Ramada Inn have accommodations for meetings and conferences. (See lodging above)

Transportation: Veteran's Taxi 327-4131; Enterprise Rent 327-9292; U-Save Rent-A-Car 328-2453.

Information: York County Visitor & Convention Bureau, 201 East Main Street, Box 11377, Rock Hill, SC 29731, Phone: 800-866-5200.

Attractions:

Kings Mountain State Park (20 miles west); Carowinds Amusement Park (15 miles North).

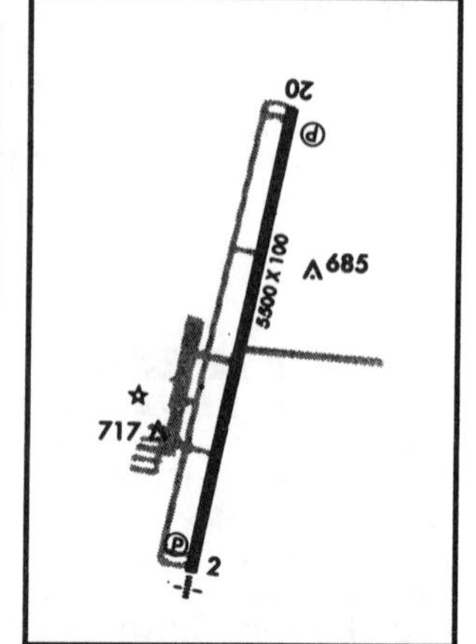

Airport Information:

ROCK HILL - ROCK HILL MUNI./BRYANT FIELD (29J)
4 mi northwest of town N34-59.27 W81-03.43 Elev: 667 Fuel: 100LL, Jet-A
Rwy 02-20: H5500x100 (Asph) Attended: 1300Z-dark Unicom: 122.8 Public Phone 24hrs
Notes: Landing and/or overnight parking fee's: $5.00 single engine, $10 multi engine.
FBO: Caro Wings Flight Service Phone: 366-5108

SOUTH DAKOTA

LOCATION MAP

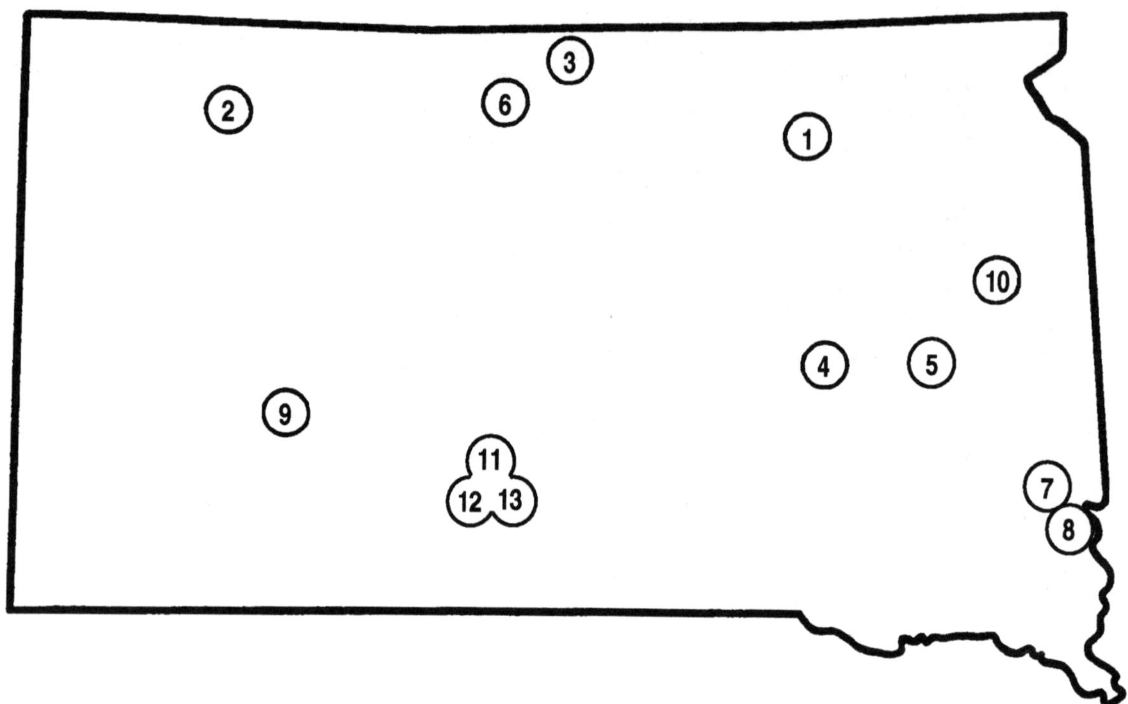

SOUTH DAKOTA

CROSS FILE INDEX

Location Number	City or Town	Airport Name And Identifier	Name of Attraction
1	Aberdeen	Aberdeen Reg. Arpt. (ABR)	Arpt. Cafe & Lounge
2	Bison	Bison Muni. Arpt. (SD07)	Prairie Bowl & Lounge
3	Herreid	Herreid Muni. Arpt. (SD23)	Grandma's Kitchen
4	Huron	Huron Reg. Arpt. (HON)	Hangar Cafe
5	Lake Preston	Lake Preston Muni. Arpt. (Y34)	Four Lake's Supper Club
6	Mobridge	Mobridge Muni. Arpt. (MBG)	The Eagle Club
7	Sioux Falls	Joe Foss Field (FSD)	Airport Inn
8	Tea	Great Planes Arpt. (Y14)	Pat's Steak House
9	Wall	Wall Muni. Arpt. (6V4)	Wall Drugs
10	Watertown	Watertown Muni. Arpt. (ATY)	Ramkota Inn Dining Rm.
11	White River	White River Muni. Arpt. (SD38)	Frontier Restaurant
12	White River	White River Muni. Arpt. (SD38)	Gas-N-Git Cafe
13	White River	White River Muni. Arpt. (SD38)	Quarter Circle Drive-in

Articles

City or town	Nearest Airport and Identifier	Name of Attraction
Wall, SD	Wall Muni. Arpt. (6V4)	Wall Drugstore

SD-ABR - ABERDEEN
ABERDEEN REGIONAL AIRPORT

(Area Code 605) 1

Airport Cafe & Lounge:

The Airport Cafe & Lounge is located in the main terminal building at the Aberdeen Regional Airport. Their menu includes daily breakfast and lunch specials, and Friday "all you can eat fish." The breakfast special features 2 eggs, 2 strips of bacon and 2 sausage links for only $3.42. Specialties include broasted chicken. They also feature a buffet beginning at 4 p.m. on Thursday, Friday and Saturday night. The price range for breakfast is $3.50, lunch $4.50 and dinner $6.00. There is a lounge area where groups up to 30 people can meet. The decor is modern. The restaurant is reported 1 mile from a shopping mall and 1-1/2 miles from a number of lodging facilities. For more information call The restaurant at 225-7210.

Restaurants Near Airport:

Airport Cafe	On Site	Phone: 225-7210
The Flame	3 mi W	Phone: 225-2082
Grain Exchange	3 mi W	Phone: 225-6100
Helen's Kitchen	2 mi SW	Phone: 225-9286
Pirates Cove	1 mi N	Phone: 225-9958
Refuge Lounge	1 mi NW	Phone: 229-2681

Lodging: Aberdeen Inn, 1/2 mile west of airport, free airport pickup, 154 rooms, Phone: 225-3600. Super 8 Motel: (Three locations): Super 8 East, 1 mi. west of airport, Phone: 229-5005, Super 8 (West) 5 mi NW of airport, Phone: 225-1711, Super 8 North, 5 mi. of west airport, Phone: 226-2288. Ramkota Inn, 5 mi NW, Phone: 229-4040.

Transportation: Super 8 Aviation (122.9) Phone: 225-5712, Aberdeen Taxi 225-5712, National Car Rental 225-1384, Avis Car Rental 225-9153, Hertz Car Rental 225-4163.

Information: Convention & Visitors Bureau, 516 S. Main Street, P.O. Box 1179, Aberdeen, SD 225-2414 or 800-645-3851.

Attractions:

Storybook Land & Wylie Park, North Highway 281 6 mi NW., Melgaard Park, S. Melgaard Road 2 mi SW., Lee Park Golf Course NW 8th Avenue, 5 mi NW, Phone: 622-7092, Moccasin Creek Country Club 226-0990., Aberdeen Country Club, NW 8th Avenue, 5-1/2 mi NW, Phone: 225-8135., Richmond Lake 346 acres, 13 mi NW., Mina Lake 13 mi W.

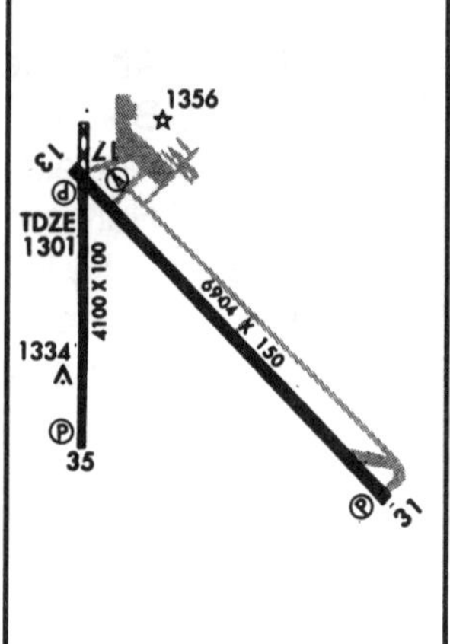

Airport Information:

ABERDEEN - ABERDEEN REGIONAL (ABR)
2 east of town, N45-26.98 W98-25.30 Elev: 1301 Fuel: 100LL, Jet-A, MOGAS
Rwy 13-31: H6904x150 (Asph-Pfc) Rwy 17-35: H4100x100 (Asph)
Attended: 1200-0500Z Unicom: 122.95 Notes: Check AFD for runway conditions; Also: landing fee waved with fuel purchase.
FBO: Aberdeen Flying Serv. Phone: 225-1384
FBO: Quest Aviation Phone: 225-8008

SD-SD07 - BISON
BISON MUNICIPAL AIRPORT

(Area Code 605) 2

Prairie Bowl & Lounge:

The Prairie Bowl & Lounge is located 1/2 mile from the Bison Municipal Airport. According to the restaurant personnel, they will provide courtesy transportation for fly-in guests if they are given advance notice. Another source of transportation would be to call either Mr. Terry Haggart at 244-5423 or Mr Dennis Lewton at 244-5583 from the airport. Please give advance notice in either case. Or on a nice day you might even decide to walk. The Prairie Bowl & Lounge is a combination family style and fine dining establishment, containing a restaurant, bowling alley and bar. The restaurant is open 7 days a week between 10 a.m. and closes at an undetermined time. Their menu includes steaks, fish platters, hamburgers, sandwiches, soups and a salad bar. On Sunday they feature a buffet from 11 a.m. to 2 p.m. Noon specials are also available throughout the week. The restaurant can accommodate up to 100 persons within the main dining room. Groups are also welcome. Fly-in guests might also want to bowl a game or two before or after their meal. For information you can call the Prairie Bowl & Lounge at 244-7207.

Restaurants Near Airport:

Prairie Bowl	1/2 mi	Phone: 244-7207
Truck Stop	1 mi	Phone: 244-5963

Lodging: Country Inn (No trans., 5 blocks from airport) 244-5234.

Meeting Rooms: For special arrangements contact airport management at 244-5423 or 244-5583.

Transportation: Bison Municipal Airport courtesy transportation: Mr. Terry Haggart 244-5423 or Mr. Dennis Lewton at 244-5583. Please call in advance.

Information: South Dakota Department of Tourism, 711 East Wells Avenue, Pierre, SD 57501-3369.

Attractions:

Golf Course 4 miles; Earls Museum 20 miles; State Park & Lake 20 miles; Huge Glass monument (Grizzly Attack) 1/2 mile.

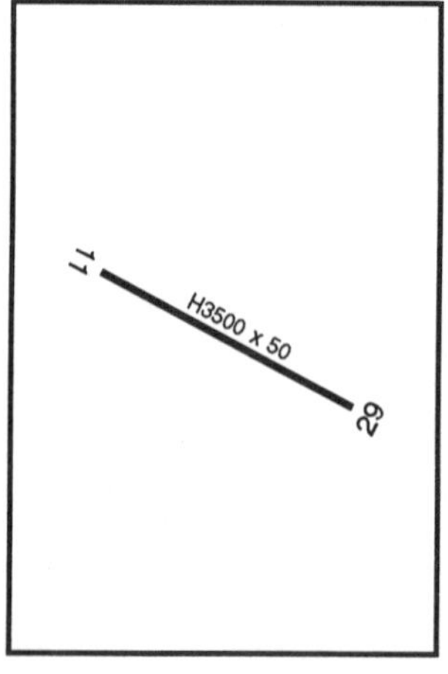

Airport Information:

BISON - BISON MUNICIPAL AIRPORT (SD07)
0 mi southwest of town N45-31.12 W102-28.03 Elev: 2785 Fuel: 100
Rwy 11-29: H3500x50 (Asph) Attended: unattended Unicom: 122.8 Public Phone 24hrs
Bison Municipal Airport Phone: 244-5281

SD-SD23 - HERREID
HERREID MUNICIPAL AIRPORT

(Area Code 605)

3

Grandma's Kitchen:

Grandma's Kitchen is a family style restaurant located 1/4th mile north and within walking distance from the Herreid Municipal Airport, situated at the Herreid Livestock Market. Their hours are from 7 a.m. to 8 p.m. 7 days a week. Several of the specialty items available on their menu include their, pork chops and steaks, seafood, shrimp, and walleye. They also feature a daily noon special, as well as German cooking on Wednesday. On Sunday they serve a buffet between 11:30 a.m. and 2 p.m. A variety of pastries, rolls and breads are prepared and baked fresh each day. According to the restaurant owner, the average price for meals run $3.75 for both breakfast and lunch, and $4.00 for most of their evening selections. When we asked the owner what type of decor the restaurant presented we were told "It looks just like you would picture "Grandma's Kitchen" to look like, neat clean and very friendly. The restaurant dining room has tables in addition to counter service. The main dining room has accommodations for seating up to 50 persons. Clubs and groups of 20 or more are welcome with advance notice. For more information you can call the Grandma's Kitchen at 437-2480.

Restaurants Near Airport:

Grandma's Kitchen	1/4 mi N.	Phone: 437-2480
Patty's Cafe	2 mi S.	Phone: 437-2993

Lodging: None Reported

Meeting Rooms: None Reported

Transportation: None Reported

Information: South Dakota Department of Tourism, 711 East Wells Avenue, Pierre, SD 57501-3369.

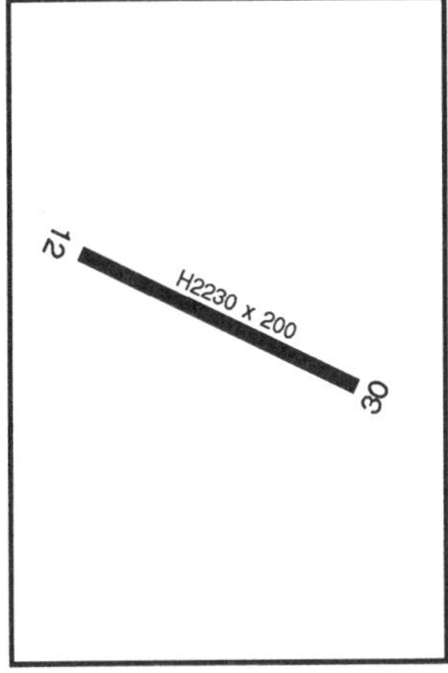

Airport Information

HERREID - HERREID MUNICIPAL AIRPORT (SD23)
1 mi north of town N45-51.25 W100-04.52 Elev: 1725 Rwy 12-30: H2230x200 (Asph-Turf)
Attended: unattended CTAF: 122.9
Herreid Municipal Airport Phone: 437-2302

SD-HON - HURON
HURON REGIONAL AIRPORT

(Area Code 605)

4

Hangar Cafe:

The Hangar Cafe is located within the terminal building at the Huron Regional Airport next to United Express. This family style restaurant is situated within walking distance from the general aviation apron. They are open Monday through Friday from 7 a.m. to 10 p.m. and Saturday and Sunday from 7:30 a.m. to 10 p.m. There is also a lounge on the premises. The menu contains items like prime rib, steaks, fish, and a soup and sandwich bar available all day. Average meal prices run $3.00 for breakfast, $4.00 for lunch and between $5.00 and $8.00 for dinner. On Sunday they offer special selections including roast beef, chicken, turkey, cod, ham and salad bar. The main dining room can accommodate up to 40 persons. Guests can enjoy watching the activity on the airport from the dining room. They also provide two separate meeting rooms in addition to the main dining room, that can seat 12 and 40 persons respectively. Meals from their menu can also be prepared for carry-out. For more information you can call the Hangar Cafe at 352-1639.

Restaurants Near Airport:

Hangar Cafe	On Site	Phone: 352-1639
Library	2 mi S.	Phone: 352-3204

Lodging: Crossroads Hotel and Convention Center, 2 miles south of airport, also Library restaurant is at same location 352-3204.

Meeting Rooms: Crossroads Hotel and Convention Center, 2 miles south of airport, also Library restaurant on location 352-3204.

Transportation: Aero World (Unicom 123.0) provides courtesy transportation to nearby facilities 352-4609; Also Yellow Top Cab Company 352-0444.

Information: Huron Area Convention & Visitors Bureau, 15, 4th Street, Southwest, Huron, PA 57350. Phone: 352-8775.

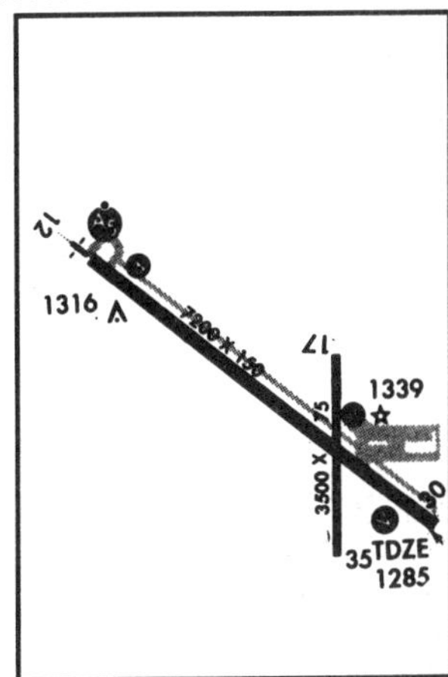

Airport Information:

HURON - HURON REGIONAL AIRPORT (HON)
0 mi northwest of town N44-23.12 W98-13.75 Elev: 1288 Fuel: 100LL, Jet-A
Rwy 12-30: H7200x150 (Asph-Pfc) Rwy 17-35: H3500x75 (Asph) Attended: 1300Z-sunset
CTAF: 123.6 Unicom: 123.0 Public Phone 24hrs
FBO: Skyway, LTD Phone: 352-9262

SD-Y34 - LAKE PRESTON
LAKE PRESTON MUNICIPAL ARPT.

(Area Code 605) **5**

Four Lake's Supper Club:

Four Lake's Supper Club is located only 1/4th of a mile north from the aircraft tie down area, near the Lake Preston Municipal Airport. This supper club is open Tuesday through Saturday 11 a.m. to 2 p.m. and Monday 4 p.m. to 2 p.m. (Closed Sunday). Their dinner selections include items like Prime rib, lobster, crab legs, and poultry to mention a few. Luncheon and evening specials are also offered. Average prices run about $4.00 for lunch and $11.95 for dinner. The main dining room has accommodations for up to 120 persons. Fly-in groups are also welcome if advance notice is given. For more information you can try calling the restaurant at 847-4861.

Restaurants Near Airport:

Four Lake's Supper Club	1/4 mi N.	Phone: 847-4861
J & M Cafe	1/2 mi NE	Phone: 847-4605

Lodging: None Reported

Meeting Rooms: Pat & Carroll's Supper Club 847-4861.

Transportation: Mr. Harley Rauch is the airport manager, and lives 100 yards from the airport and provides local transportation for arriving pilots and passengers. Advance notice is recommended. Call 847-4374.

Information: South Dakota Department of Tourism, 711 East Wells Avenue, Pierre, SD 57501-3369.

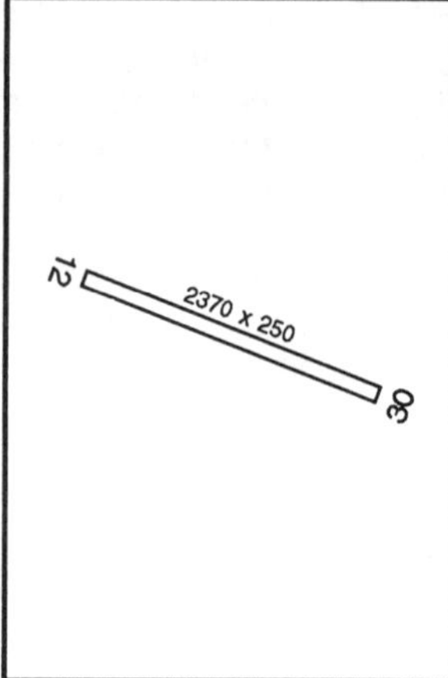

Airport Information:

LAKE PRESTON - LAKE PRESTON MUNICIPAL AIRPORT (Y34)
0 mi southwest of town N44-22.00 W97-23.02 Elev: 1725 Rwy 12-30: 2370x250 (Turf)
Attended: unattended CTAF: 122.9
Preston Municipal Airport Phone: 847-4374

SD-MBG - MOBRIDGE
MOBRIDGE MUNICIPAL AIRPORT

(Area Code 605) **6**

The Eagle Club:

The Eagle Club restaurant is right across the street from the Mobridge Municipal Airport. This steak house is open Monday through Saturday from 5 p.m. to 2 a.m., and on Sunday from 1 p.m. to 12 a.m. Their menu specializes in a variety of steaks including top sirloin, rib eye, chicken fried steaks, prime rib as well as a host of other entrees. They also have a selection of sandwiches available. On Wednesday nights, they usually have specials offered on their menu. The restaurant has a western decor and is often visited by larger groups like weddings and reunions. Fly-in customers are welcome anytime. However, larger groups of 20 or more are requested to make advance reservations. For more information, call the Eagle Club at 845-9126.

Restaurants Near Airport:

The Eagle Club	Adj Arpt.	Phone: 845-9126

Lodging: Mark Motel (2 miles) 845-3681; Super 8 Motel (2 miles) 845-7215; Wrangler (Free trans, 2 miles) 845-3641.

Meeting Rooms: Wrangler Motor Inn (Free trans, 2 miles) 845-3641.

Transportation: Oahe Air (FBO) rental cars, 845-2977.

Information: Chamber of Commerce, 212 Main Street, Mobridge, SD 57601, Phone: 845-2387.

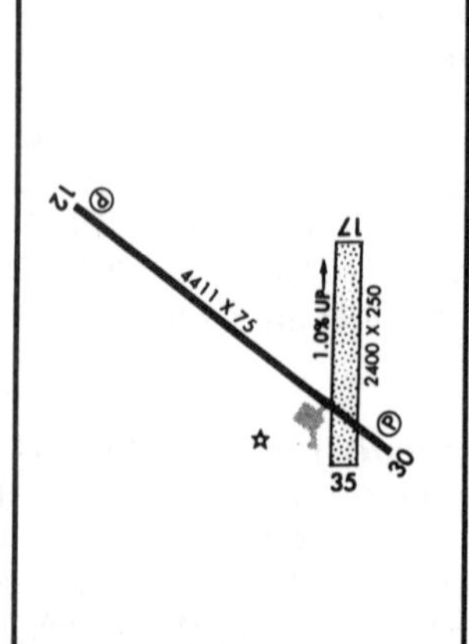

Airport Information:

MOBRIDGE - MOBRIDGE MUNICIPAL AIRPORT (MBG)
1 mi northeast N45-32.79 W100-24.48 Elev: 1715 Fuel: 100LL, MOGAS
Rwy 12-30: H4411x75 (Asph) Rwy 17-35: 2400x250 (Turf) Attended: 1400-0000Z
Unicom: 122.8 Notes: For attendent call 845-7442.
FBO: Oahe Air Phone: 845-2977

SD-FSD - SIOUX FALLS JOE FOSS FIELD

(Area Code 605)

7

Airport Inn:

The Airport Inn Restaurant is located in the main terminal building with available aircraft parking right outside. This family style restaurant is open from 5:30 a.m. to 9 p.m. 7 days a week. There is also a lounge adjacent to the restaurant. This facility serves items like burgers, meat salad sandwiches, a full line of breakfast dishes, hot beef, turkey sandwiches and salad bar. Daily specials are offered along with Friday fish fry and Sunday brunch served between 10 a.m. and 5 p.m. The restaurant can seat 90 persons in the dining room with a view of the aircraft parking area just outside. The decor is of Western style, with booths and tables. Large groups and fly-in clubs are also welcome with advanced notice. Meals can be ordered to go for those in a hurry. For more information call the Airport Inn at 336-0455.

Attractions:

Elmwood Golf Course 1-1/2 mile southwest 339-7092; Lake Madison 35 miles northwest; Newton Hills Park 30 miles south.

Airport Information:

SIOUX FALLS - JOE FOSS FIELD (FSD)
3 mi northwest of town N43-34.88 W96-44.50 Elev: 1429 Fuel: 100LL, Jet-A
Rwy 03-21: H8999x150 (Conc-Wc) Rwy 15-33: H6658x150 (Asph-Pfc) Rwy 09-27: H3152x75 (Conc-Wc) Attended: continuously Atis: 126.6 Unicom: 122.95
Sioux Falls App/Dep Con: 125.8, 126.9 Sioux Falls Tower: 118.3 Gnd Con: 121.9
Public Phone 24hrs Notes: Overnight tie down $5.00
FBO: Business Aviation Phone: 336-7791
FBO: Sioux Falls Aviation Phone: 336-9016

Restaurants Near Airport:

Airport Inn	On Site	Phone: 336-0455
Cracked Pot	1/2 mi S.	Phone: 338-9713
George's Steak Hse.	1 mi W.	Phone: 334-5595
Jack's Grain Bin	1 mi N.	Phone: 339-1264

Lodging: Airport Holiday Inn (1 mi southwest) 336-1020; Holiday Inn (City Center, 2 miles south) 339-2000; Ramkota Inn And Convention Center (1-1/2 miles southwest) 336-0650; Encore Inn (5 miles south) 361-6684.

Meeting Rooms: Ramkota Inn And Convention Center (1-1/2 miles southwest) 336-0650; Howard Johnsons (1-1/2 miles southwest) 336-9000; Holiday Inn (2 miles south) 339-2000.

Transportation: Business Aviation (FBO) has a courtesy car to the Airport Inn; Also: Airport Limo 336-1500; Avis 336-1184; Budget 334-4211; National 332-8111; Hertz 336-8790; Dollar 361-0655.

Information: Chamber of Commerce, P.O. Box 1425, Sioux Falls, SD 57101, Phone: 336-1620.

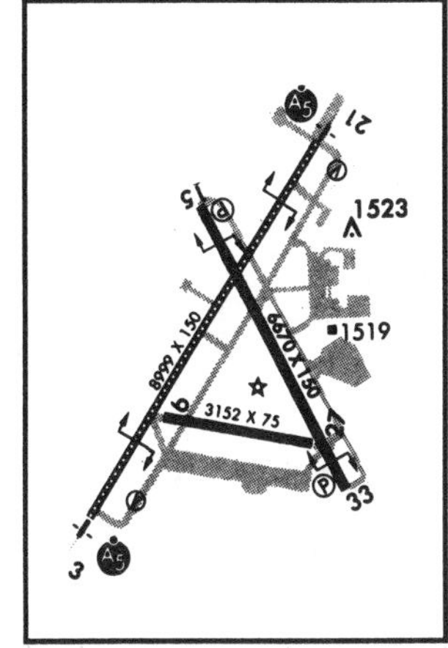

SD-Y14 - TEA GREAT PLANES AIRPORT

(Area Code 605)

8

Pat's Steak House:

Pat's Steak House, according to the restaurant management, is situated within 3/8th of a mile from the Sioux Falls Great Planes Airport. To reach the restaurant, you must walk across the expressway and viaduct. This facility is open Sunday through Thursday 4:30 p.m. to 10 p.m. and Friday and Saturday 4:30 to 12 a.m. Their menu offers a variety of choice steaks including a 32 oz T-bone, 11 oz filet, and a 16 oz prime rib steak. A selection of seafood entrees are also available including the jumbo shrimp platter. A salad bar is featured during the evening dinner hours. Average prices run $9.00 for most dinner selections. Nightly specials are offered as well as a discount for senior citizens and childrens portions. The restaurant is well decorated and has just recently been remodeled. The main dining room can seat 140 people. They also offer additional seating within their banquet rooms having accommodations for between 40 and 100 persons depending on seating arrangements. During the Spring and Fall season they often provide live entertainment for their guest's dining pleasure. For more information about Pat's Steak House you can call 368-2566.

Airport Information:

TEA - Great Planes (Y14)
6 mi southwest of town N43-27.45 W96-48.12 Elev: 1515 Fuel: 100LL
Rwy 16-34: H3650x60 (Asph) Attended: 1400Z-dusk Unicom: 122.8
FBO: Great Planes Aviation Phone: 368-2841

Restaurants Near Airport:
Pat's Steak House 3/8 mi Phone: 368-2566

Lodging: None Reported

Meeting Rooms: None Reported

Transportation: None Reported

Information: South Dakota Department of Tourism, 711 East Wells Avenue, Pierre, SD 57501-3369.

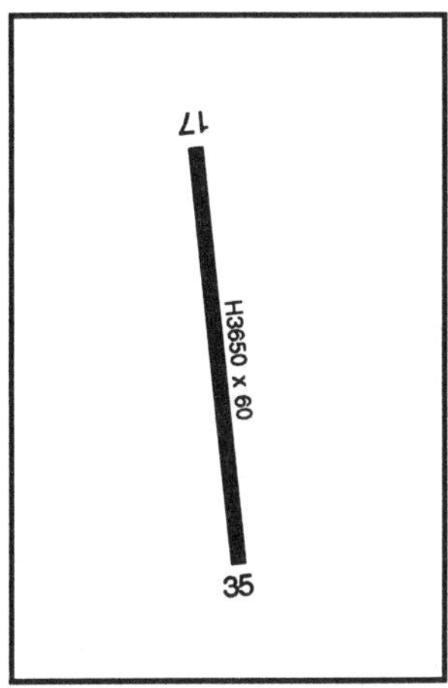

Photo by: Wall Drugs

One view of an interior hall way within the world's most famous drug store. Wall Drugs, located in Wall, South Dakota.

Wall Drugstore

Wall, SD (SD-6V4)

Nestled in the shadows of South Dakota's rugged Badlands is a Wall ... that's a window. It opens onto an area of unparalleled vacation excitement known as "The Great American West". The town of Wall offers all the expected and plenty of the unexpected, with comfortable campgrounds and motels, fine dining at great restaurants, swimming, golf and tennis. Their beautiful city park offers endless entertainment opportunities for young and old alike.

Visit the World's Most Famous Drug Store. You see them advertised on subway trains in London, beside a canal in Amsterdam. Signs all over the world proclaim Wall Drugs as much more than just a drug store.

Ask any of the millions of people who have visited Wall Drugs. They'll tell you Wall Drugs is a drugstore ... and a souvenir, clothing, knick-knack, rock-hound, curio, antique, and unique attraction store all wrapped up in one.

Thousands and thousands of merchandise items are surrounded by walls decorated with over 600 cattle brands, hundreds of historical pictures and items, and a beautiful collection of Indian artifacts.

In addition to Wall Drugs Store, visitors can enjoy many other attractions such as the Wildlife Museum at 510 Main Street. The Wild West History and Wax Museum at 601 Main Street. In addition to these many gift and specialty shops, you will be kept busy for some time. Restaurants like the Cactus Cafe, Dairy Queen, Elkton House, Madre's Pizza Plus and of course the Wall Drugs Cafe can keep your appetite satisfied.

During our conversation with the Wall Drugs management, we were informed that fly-in visitors can land at Wall Municipal Airport located about 1 mile northwest of the town of Wall, South Dakota. This airport supports a (Rwy 12-30) 3,500 x 60 foot asphalt strip. The unicom is 122.9 and the airport elevation is 2810 ASL. The airport is reported unattended. However, you can call Wall Drugs Store at 605-279-2175, and ask for the Public Relations Department or the General Operating Managers office. We were told that they would be happy to furnish your party with transportation to their location. Public transportation is also available by calling 605-279-2325. General information about the town or its many attractions can be obtained by calling the Wall Chamber of Commerce at 605-279-2665.

Photo by: Wall Drugs Famous world wide, Wall Drugs attracts ten's of thousands of tourists passing through each year.

SD-6V4 - WALL
WALL MUNICIPAL AIRPORT

(Area Code 605) 9

Restaurants Near Airport:

Cactus Cafe	1 mi	Phone: 279-2561
Elkton House	1-1/2 mi	Phone: 279-2152
Wall Drugs	1 mi	Phone: 279-2175

Lodging: Elk Motel (1-1/2 mile) 279-2127; Kings Inn (1 mile) 279-2178; Pains Motel (1-1/2 miles) 279-2145; Sands Motel (1-1/2 miles) 279-2121.
Meeting Rooms: Wall Community Center, 503 Main Street, Wall, SD, Phone: 279-2665.
Transportation: We learned that the management of Wall Drugs will furnish courtesy transportation into town from the airport, if you call them at 279-2175.
Information: Wall Community Center & Wall Chamber of Commerce Offices, Box 165, 503 Main Street, Wall, SD 57790-0165. Phone: 605-279-2665.

Wall Drugs:

During the Depression, of 1931, Ted Hustead, a young pharmacist, his wife Dorothy and son Billy moved into the back of a small drug store in Wall, a town of 800 people. After a year they realized they could not stay in business because people in western South Dakota were on hard times. In desperation, Dorothy suggested they advertise free ice water to attract the traveling public. The idea saved the drug store. Because of the Hustead's tenacity, Wall Drug Store slowly grew to be one of the largest drug stores in the world. With a year round population of 812, Wall's summer population swelled, with two million annual visitors. Wall Drugs alone, employs 200 persons to take care of the 15,000 to 20,000 visitors who stop there each day during the summer. Other businesses increased their numbers of employees to provide friendly service at Wall's ten motels, five restaurants, bed and breakfast, seven filling stations, and numerous gift shops. A new Community Center in downtown Wall can accommodate small conventions with seating for 500 and banquet facilities. The Center offers various-sized rooms, sound systems, staging and catering, as well as an Information Center. Dances and other community events are also held there. Wall Municipal Airport, located about 1 mile northwest of town has a paved, lighted 3,500 foot runway. For transportation to and from the airport, you can call the corporate offices of Wall's Drugs at 279-2175. Come fly-in and enjoy the hospitality of Wall Drugs. (Information, compliments of Wall's Drugs)

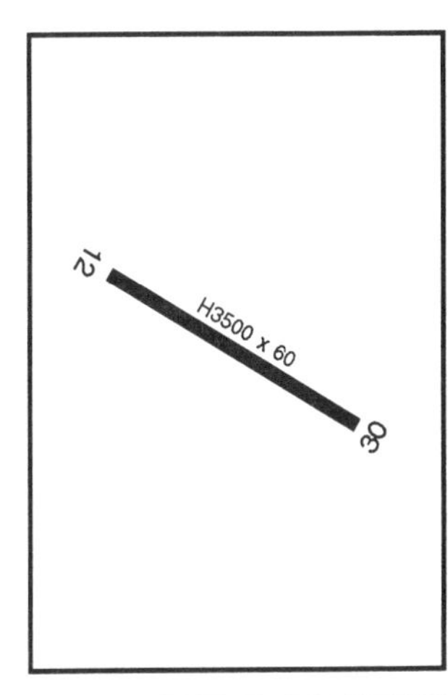

Airport Information:

WALL - WALL MUNICIPAL AIRPORT (6V4)
1 mi northwest of town N43-59.70 W102-15.03 Elev: 2810 Rwy 12-30: H3500x60 (Asph)
Attended: unattended CTAF: 122.8
Wall Municipal Airport Mgr. Phone: 279-2666

SD-ATY - WATERTOWN
WATERTOWN MUNICIPAL AIRPORT

(Area Code 605) 10

Ramkota Inn Dining Room:

The Ramkota Inn is located 5 miles south of the Watertown Municipal Airport and can be reached by courtesy car from the restaurant. There is a direct line telephone located in the terminal building that will put you in touch with the restaurant. Directions to the restaurant are, take highway 20 south to highway 212 and go one mile west. This facility contains a fine dining restaurant and coffee shop. Restaurant hours are Monday through Friday from 6 a.m. to 10 p.m., Saturday from 7 a.m. to 2 p.m. and 5 p.m. to 10 p.m., and Sunday 7 a.m. to 2 p.m. Appetizers, sandwiches, Mexican foods, steaks, seafood, and barbequed ribs are all items featured on their menu along with desserts. Average prices run $3.00 for breakfast, $5.00 for lunch and $7.00 for dinner. This facility has a noon buffet and a Friday night smorgasbord. They also provide a Sunday brunch. The Ramkota Dining Room exhibits a southwestern atmosphere and has accommodations for catering to groups. For more information call 886-8011.

Airport Information:

WATERTOWN - WATERTOWN MUNICIPAL AIRPORT (ATY)
2 mi northwest of town N44-54.84 W97-09.28 Elev: 1748 Fuel: 100LL, Jet-A
Rwy 12-30: H6901x150 (Asph-Pfc) Rwy 17-35: H6895x150 (Asph-Pfc) Attended: May-Aug/Mon-Sat 1400-0200Z, May-Aug/Sun 1400-2300Z, Sep-Apr/Mon-Fri 1400-2300Z, Sep-Apr/Sat-Sun 1500-2300Z Public Phone 24hrs CATF: 123.6 Unicom: 122.95
Notes: Starting at 10,000 lbs. no parking or tie down fee for aircraft.
FBO: Aero Aviation Phone: 882-3488
FBO: Dakota Aviation Phone: 882-5757

Restaurants Near Airport:

Ramkota Inn	5 mi	Phone: 886-8011
Stone Inn	5 mi	Phone: 882-3630
Stockman Cafe	3 mi	Phone: 882-1611
Wheel Inn	3-1/2 mi	Phone: 886-4649

Lodging: Ramkota Inn (5 miles) 886-8011; Guest House (5 miles) 886-8061; Drake Motor Inn 886-8411;
Meeting Rooms: Ramkota Inn (Best Western) 886-8011; Drake Motor Inn 886-8411 or 800-341-8000.
Transportation: According to the airport manager, all restaurants listed above will provide courtesy transportation for fly-in guests. Also Rental Cars: Boldt Brothers Car Rental 886-2732; Hertz Rental 882-1253.
Information: Convention & Visitors Bureau, 26 South Broadway, P.O. Box 1113, Watertown, SD 57201, Phone: 886-5814 or 800-658-4505.

Attractions:

Municipal Golf Course (3 miles) 886-3618; Stokes Thomas Camping (1-1/2 miles) 886-2822; Fishing Lake, Bramble Park Zoo (3 miles); Wild Life Museum (5 miles).

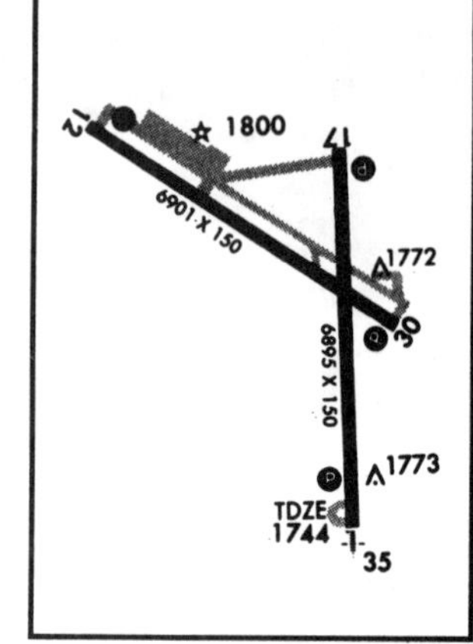

Not to be used for navigational purposes

SD-SD38 - WHITE RIVER
WHITE RIVER MUNICIPAL AIRPORT

(Area Code 605)

11, 12, 13

Frontier Restaurant:

The Frontier Cafe is located 3 or 4 blocks form the airport, and is open between 6:30 a.m. to 10 p.m. This restaurant can seat 50 to 60 persons. Their menu contains selections like steaks, shrimp, and chicken, along with patty melts, sandwiches, roast beef dinners, and a full breakfast line. Average prices for most meals run $3.00 to $5.00. They also have a back room that can accommodate 30 to 40 more people for meetings or parties. For more information you can call the Frontier Restaurant at 259-3140.

Gas-N-Git Cafe:

The Gas-N-Git Cafe is a combination automobile gas station and diner. This cafe specializes in all types of pizzas as well as fried chicken, baked potatoes made with toppings, and deli sandwiches. Their hours are from 7 a.m. to 10 p.m. 7 days a week. Average prices for a full pizza runs about $9.39 and $11.50. you can buy it by the slice, eat it on the spot, or have it packaged-to-go. They even offer a breakfast pizza. For more information about this cafe, call 259-3455.

Quarter Circle Drive-in:

The Quarter Circle Drive Inn is situated adjacent to the White River Municipal Airport. This seasonal restaurant is open between April and October from 11 a.m. to 10 p.m. There is a large sign painted on the roof that says "Drive Inn". You cant miss it. Their menu has items like hamburgers, chicken filets, cheeseburgers, chicken strips, fish sandwiches, and their specialty the "Hoagie" sandwich. On Sunday they feature roast beef or ham dinners. The building is in the shape of a triangle with redwood and white trim. There is seating for about 12 people inside and bench seating for up to 24 persons outdoors. Groups and parties are also welcome. Carry-out meals are their specialty. For more information you can call 259-3431.

Restaurants Near Airport:

E & R Recreation	3 blks N.	Phone: 259-3342
Frontier Restaurant	5 blks N.	Phone: 259-3140
Gas-N-Git (Pizza)	2 blks N.	Phone: 259-3455
Quarter Circle Drive-in	Adj Arpt.	Phone: 259-3431

Lodging: Thoroughbred Lodge (1 block north of airport) 259-3349.

Meeting Rooms: Community Events Center - contact White River School District (4 blocks northeast of airport) 259-3311.

Transportation: Most facilities listed are well within walking distance from the White River Municipal Airport. According to the airport manager, if ground transportation is a necessity, you can contact: The Hon. Mayor Ray Bartlett 259-3342; Mr. Paul Miller 259-3262; or Mr. Joe Krogman 259-3160.

Information: South Dakota Department of Tourism, 711 East Wells Avenue, Pierre, SD 57501-3369.

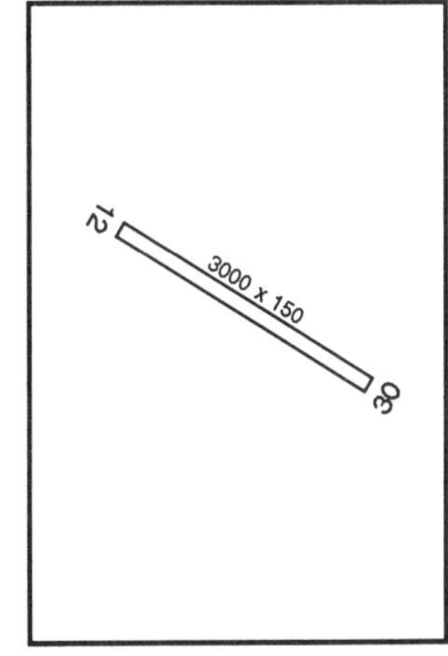

Airport Information:

WHITE RIVER - WHITE RIVER MUNICIPAL AIRPORT (SD38)
1 mi south of town N43-33.70 W100-44.51 Elev: 2151 Fuel: 100LL
Rwy 12-30: 3000x150 (Turf) Attended: unattended CATF: 122.8 Public Phone 24hrs
White River Municipal Airport Phone: 259-3242

TENNESSEE

LOCATION MAP

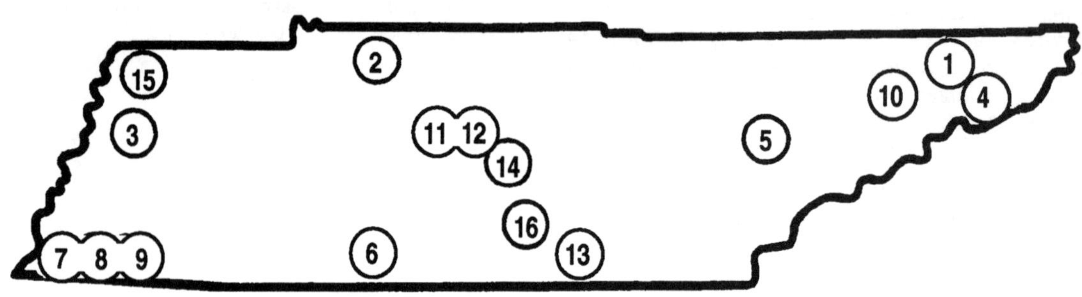

Not to be used for navigational purposes

TENNESSEE

CROSS FILE INDEX

Location Number	City or Town	Airport Name And Identifier	Name of Attraction
1	Bristol/Johnson/King	Tri-City Reg. Arpt. (TRI)	Cafe Rainbow
2	Clarksville	Outlaw Field Arpt. (CKV)	Airport Restaurant
3	Dyersburg	Dyersburg Muni. Arpt. (DYR)	Airport Restaurant
4	Elizabethton	Elizabethton Arpt. (0A9)	Betty's Burger Hut
5	Knoxville	McGhee Tyson (TYS)	Arpt. Hilton Raintree
6	Lawrenceburg	Lawrenceburg Muni. (2M2)	David Crockett St. Park
7	Memphis	Memphis Intl. Arpt. (MEM)	Fred Gang's Restaurant
8	Memphis	Memphis Intl. Arpt. (MEM)	Host Marriott Serv.
9	Memphis	Memphis Intl. Arpt. (MEM)	Jax at Fred's
10	Morristown	Moore-Murrell (MOR)	The Attic Restaurant
11	Nashville	Nashville Intl. Arpt. (BNA)	101st Airborn Rest.
12	Nashville	Nashville Intl. Arpt. (BNA)	CA1 Services
13	Sewanee	Franklin County (UOS)	Jim Oliver's Resort
14	Smyrna	Smyrna Arpt. (MQY)	Landings Restaurant
15	Tiptonville	Reelfoot Lake Arpt. (0M2)	Reelfoot Air Park Inn
16	Tullahoma	Highland Reg. Arpt. (THA)	Western Sizzlin

Articles

City or town	Nearest Airport and Identifier	Name of Attraction
Tiptonville, TN (0M2)	Reelfoot Lake Arpt. (0M2)	Reelfoot Lake St. Resort

TN-TRI - BRISTOL/JOHNSON/KINGSPORT TRI-CITY REGIONAL TN/VA

(Area Code 423)

1

Cafe Rainbow Restaurant:

The Cafe Rainbow is located on the Tri-City Regional Airport. After several attempts we were unable to obtain information from the management. This restaurant can be reached through the Airport Managers office by calling 325-6001.

Restaurants Near Airport:
Cafe Rainbow On Site Arpt. Mgrs Phone: 325-6001

Lodging: Comfort Inn (Kingsport 5 mi West) 239-7447; Sheraton Plaza (est. 7-10 mi.) 282-4611 Super 8 (est. 3-5 mi) 540-466-8800;

Conference Rooms: Check with fixed base operator for available conference or meeting rooms.

Transportation: FBO courtesy car reported; Hertz, 323-6344; Avis, 323-6392; National, 323-6308; Budget, 323-6219; Thrifty, 323-9181; Taxi 245-1351.

Information: Johnson City Convention & Visitors Bureau, 603-E Market Street, P.O. Box 180 37605, Phone: 423-461-8000; Kingsport Convention & Visitors Bureau, 151 E. Main Street, P.O. Box 1403, Kingsport, TN 37662, Phone: 423-392-8820 or 800-743-5282.

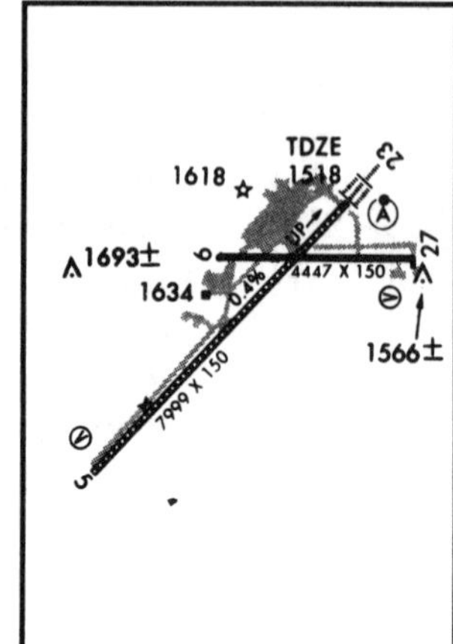

Airport Information:

BRISTOL/JOHNSON/KINGSPORT - TRI-CITY REGIONAL (TRI)
12 miles southwest of town N36-28.51 W82-24.45 Elev: 1519 Fuel: 100LL, Jet-A
Rwy 05-23: H7999x150 (Asph-Grvd) Rwy 09-27: H4447x150 (Asph) Attended: continuously
Atis: 118.25 Unicom: 122.95 Tower: 119.5 Gnd Con: 121.7 Public Phone 24hrs
Airport Manager Phone: 325-6001
FBO: Tri-City Aviation Phone: 325-6261

TN-CKV - CLARKSVILLE OUTLAW FIELD AIRPORT

(Area Code 615)

2

Airport Restaurant:

The Airport Restaurant is located in the Outlaw Field Airport terminal building. This restaurant can be reached by walking if you park at the nearest fixed base operator. This cafe is open between 9 a.m. and 5 p.m. 6 days a week. They are reported as closed on Sunday. Their menu offers hamburgers, cheeseburgers, ham and cheese sandwiches, tuna melts and a full line of breakfast selections served all day long. Average prices run $4.00 for breakfast items and $5.00 for lunch entrees. Daily specials are also offered. This restaurant has recently been remodeled and exhibits a modern decor. There are large windows on all three sides of the dining room, with seating for about 25 persons, along with counter service that faces the kitchen area. They also provide catering for corporate aircraft, with sandwich trays, fruit trays and breakfast items. For more information about this restaurant, you can call them at 431-4170.

Restaurants Near Airport:
Airport Restaurant On Site Phone: 431-4170

Lodging: Holiday Inn (7 miles) 645-9084; Ramada Inn Riverview (Free trans) 552-3331; Roadway Inn (7 miles, Free trans) 645-2100; Skyway Motel (1 mile) 431-5225; Vacation Motor Hotel (6 miles) 645-6483.

Meeting Rooms: Ramada Inn Riverview (Free trans) 552-3331.

Transportation: Budget 552-3082; National 552-2020

Information: Clarksville/Montgomery County Tourist Commission, 180 Holiday Road, Clarksville, TN 37040, Phone: 648-0001.

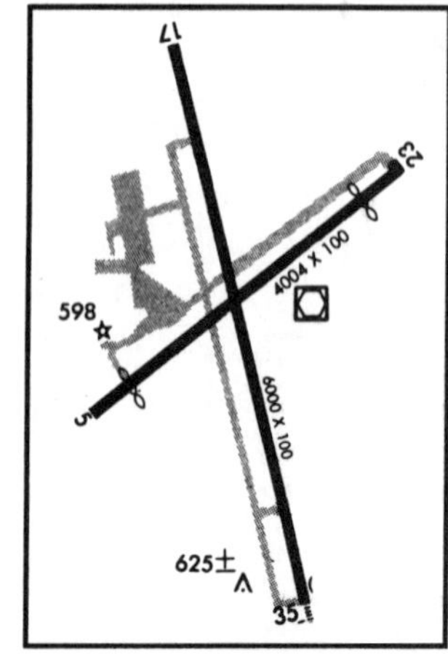

Airport Information:

CLARKSVILLE - OUTLAW FIELD AIRPORT (CKV)
6 mi northwest of town N36-37.31 W87-24.90 Elev: 550 Fuel: 100LL, Jet-A Rwy 17-35: H6000x100 (Asph) Rwy 05-23: H4004x100 (Asph) Attended: 1330-0230Z Unicom: 122.8
Campbell App/Dep Con: 118.1 Notes: Extensive military and civil flight training within airport area.
FBO: Aircraft Maintenance, Inc. Phone: 431-3470
FBO: Volunteer Aviation Phone: 431-9900
FBO: Volunteer Flight Training Phone: 431-4170

TN-DYR - DYERSBURG
DYERSBURG MUNICIPAL AIRPORT

(Area Code 901)

3

Airport Restaurant:

The Airport Restaurant is located right on the Dyersburg Municipal Airport. This restaurant is open 6 a.m. to 2 p.m. Monday through Friday and 11 a.m. to 2 p.m. on Sunday. They are reported as closed on Saturday. They specialize in buffet styled selections, offering a choice of different meats and seafood items, like roast beef, catfish, fried chicken, crab meat salads, and a selection of desserts with fresh strawberries, and cakes. They also feature a complete salad bar as well. Their buffet provides a full meal with beverage, for only $4.00 to $5.00. The restaurant can seat between 75 and 80 people. The decor exhibits a quaint atmosphere with red checkered table cloths. Guests can see the activity on the airport from the restaurant. Fly-in groups and parties are also welcome. However, they should give advance notice especially if they are planning to fly in on Sunday. This is a very busy time, and reservations would be suggested. Cross country air travelers can also arrange catered meals and meal trays to go. For more information about the Airport Restaurant call 286-2477.

Restaurants Near Airport:

Airport Rest.	On Site	Phone: 286-2477
Plaza Rest.	N/A	Phone: 286-0521

Lodging: Colonial Inn (1 mile) 286-0521; Holiday Inn (5 miles) 285-8601;

Meeting Rooms: Colonial Inn (1 mile) 286-0521; Holiday Inn (5 miles) 285-8601.

Transportation: Dyersburg Aviation, Inc. can furnish courtesy transportation to nearby facilities. Also: City Cab 286-4641; Delta Auto 286-4111.

Information: Tennessee Department of Tourist Development, P.O. Box 23170, Nashville, TN 37202, Phone: 615-741-2158.

Attractions:

Dyersburg Municipal Golf Course 286-7620.

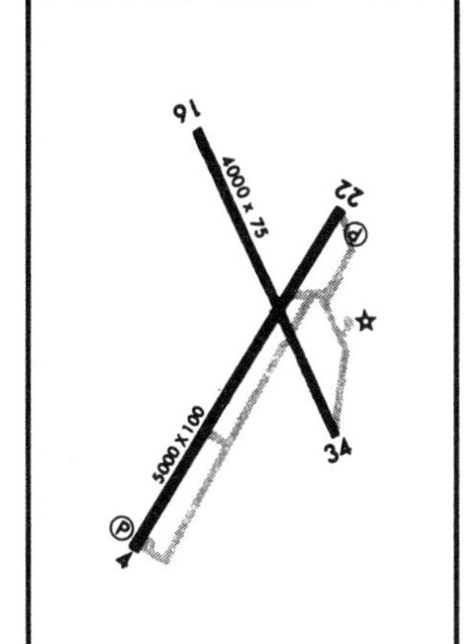

Airport Information:

DYERSBURG - DYERSBURG MUNICIPAL AIRPORT (DYR)
2 mi south of town N35-59.91 W89-24.37 Elev: 338 Fuel: 100LL, Jet-A
Rwy 04-22: H5000x100 (Asph) Rwy 16-34: H4000x75 (Asph) Attended: 1300-0100Z
Unicom: 123.05
Airport Manager **Phone: 286-2233**
Dyersburg Aviation **Phone: 286-2233.**

TN-0A9 - ELIZABETHTON
ELIZABETHTON MUNICIPAL

(Area Code 423)

4

Betty's Burger Hut:

Betty's Burger Hut is located across the street and is within walking distance from the Elizabethton Airport. This family style restaurant is open between 8 a.m. and 10 p.m. 7 days a week. Their menu has a full selection of breakfast items as well as cheeseburgers, hamburgers, hamburger steaks, chicken, club sandwiches, shrimp dishes and much more. Average prices run $2.00 for breakfast and $3.00 to $4.00 for most lunch and dinner items. Their main dining area seats between 32 and 35 persons. There are two basic dining areas, one which contains pin ball machines and video games, and the other dining room is more conventional. Fly-in groups and parties are welcome. This restaurant is frequently visited by pilots flying into Elizabethton Municipal Airport and makes for a convenient stopping place for local pilots on weekends. For more information call Betty's Burger Hut at 543-4561.

Restaurants Near Airport:

Betty's Burger Hut	1/8 mi SE	Phone: 543-4561
Classic Malt Shop	2 mi	Phone: 543-7141
May Flower Seafood Rest.	2 mi	Phone: 542-3667
Western Steer Steak Hse.	3-1/2 mi	Phone: 543-5587

Lodging: Comfort Inn (Free trans between 8 a.m. and 5 p.m.) Breakfast included for corporations, Phone: 542-4466.
Meeting Rooms: Comfort Inn has accommodations for business groups up to 40 people. Phone: 542-4466.
Transportation: East Way Rent-A-Car, Inc. 800-426-7606, 282-1783; Black & White Cab 542-4161; Graham Cabs 542-2171; Yellow Cab 542-9060.
Information: Elizabethton/Carter County Chamber of Commerce, U.S. 19E Bypass, P.O. Box 190, Elizabethton, TN 37644, Phone: 547-3850.

Attractions:

Roan MTN State Park, Watauga Lake, covered bridge 1882; Chamber of Commerce, P.O. Box 190, Elizabethton, TN 37644, Phone: 543-2122.

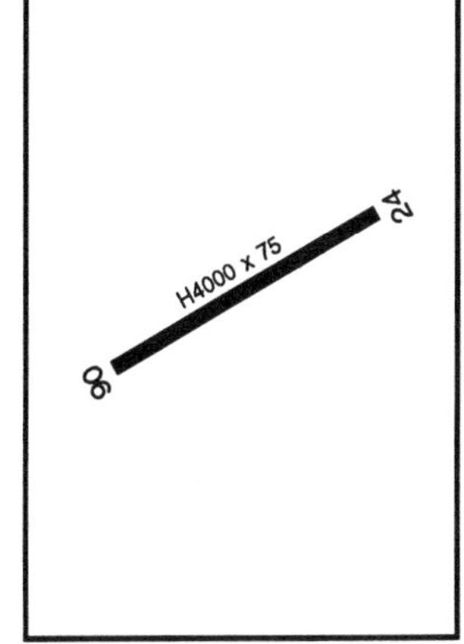

Airport Information:

ELIZABETHTON - ELIZABETHTON MUNICIPAL (0A9)
3 mi northeast of town N36-22.26 W82-10.42 Elev: 1585 Fuel: 100LL, Jet-A
Rwy 06-24: H4000x75 (Asph) Attended: Mon-Fri dalight hours, Sat-Sun 1200Z Unicom: 123.0
Public Phone 24hrs Notes: 1st hangar/tie down free with fill-up, single/twin hangar 1500/2000.
Single and twin tie down fees $3.00/$4.50 per night.
Elizabethton Municipal Airport **Phone: 543-2801**

TN-TYS - KNOXVILLE
McGHEE TYSON

(Area Code 423)

5

Airport Hilton Raintree Restaurant:

The Airport Hilton Raintree Restaurant is located adjacent to the terminal building and can be reached by courtesy transportation by the fixed base operators. Transient parking at the terminal building for general aviation aircraft is not permitted. See "Airport Information." This fine dining facility is open from 6 a.m. to 11 p.m. 7 days a week. Their menu contains A full breakfast line as well as items like prime rib, steamed shrimp and scallops, chicken Rockefeller, and Orange Roughy. There is a lunch buffet served Monday through Friday from 11 a.m. to 3 p.m. On Sunday they serve a brunch also from 11 a.m. to 3 p.m. Average prices range from $6.00 for breakfast, $6.50 for lunch and $10.00 to $16.00 for dinner. Their breakfast buffet runs $5.50 and their lunch buffet runs $6.95. Their main dining room can seat 110 people. The dining room offers a casual atmosphere with many plants, pictures, art work, linen service and a sun room. Accommodations for catered parties, groups, or business meetings, can easily be arranged through the restaurant or the hotel. For information call 970-4300.

Restaurants Near Airport:

Bel Air Grill	1/4 mi	Phone: 981-3788
Cafe Rainbow	On Site	Phone: 970-7327
Raintree Restaurant	On Site	Phone: 970-4300

Lodging: The following provide free transportation to and from airport: Family Inns Of America 970-2006; Quality Inn-Airport 970-3140; Ramada Inn Airport 970-3060; Hilton Inn-Knoxville Airport 970-4300; Hilton 525-6532; Radisson 522-2600.
Meeting Rooms: All lodging facilities listed above contain accommodations for meeting rooms. The Hilton at 501 Church Street has convention services available, 525-6532.
Transportation: Cherokee Aviation and Knox Air, Inc. (FBO) can provide courtesy transportation to nearby facilities. Also Avis: 970-2985; Budget 970-4141; Hertz 970-3010; National 970-2993; Thrifty 970-4407; Limo Service 970-3349.
Information: Knoxville Convention & Visitors Bureau, 810 Clinch Ave, P.O. Box 15012, Knoxville, TN 37901, Phone: 523-2316.

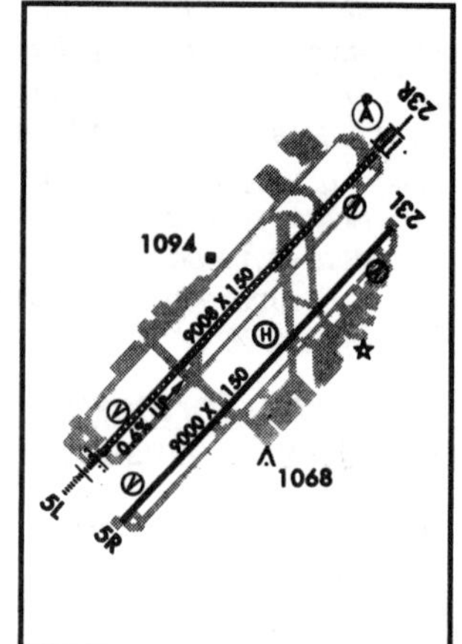

Airport Information:

KNOXVILLE - McGHEE TYSON (TYS)
10 mi south of town N35-48.75 W83-59.57 Elev: 981 Fuel: 100LL, Jet-A
Rwy 05L-23R: H9008x150 (Conc-Grvd) Rwy 05R-23L: H9000x150 (Asph-Grvd) Attended: continuously Atis: 128.35 Unicom: 122.95 Knoxville App/Dep Con: 118.0, 123.9, 120.65, 132.8 Knoxville Tower: 121.2 Gnd Con: 121.9 Clnc Del: 121.65
Notes: For general aviation aircraft, we suggest parking at FBO and use courtesy transportation if flying to visit restaurant or nearby facilities. CAUTION: Birds on and in vicinity of airport.
FBO: Cherokee Aviation Phone: 970-9000

TN-2M2 - LAWRENCEBURG
LAWRENCEBURG MUNICIPAL

(Area Code 615)

6

David Crockett State Park Restaurant:

The David Crockett State Park Restaurant is located about 6-1/2 miles west of the Lawrenceburg Municipal Airport. With notice, and depending on availability, a courtesy car can be obtained at the airport. To get to the state park and restaurant travel west on Hwy 64 through Lawrenceburg and follow the signs to the park. The cafeteria-style restaurant is open Monday through Thursday from 11 a.m. to 2 p.m.; Friday 11 a.m. to 2 p.m. and 5 p.m. to 8 p.m; Saturday 7:30 a.m. to 10 a.m. then again from 11 a.m. to 2 p.m. and 5 p.m. to 8 p.m; Sunday from 7:30 a.m. to 10 a.m and 11 a.m. to 2 p.m. As a state facility, no alcoholic beverages are served. Buffet-style meals specializing in southern cuisine are served on Friday, and Saturday nights. Island seafood is also their specialty. Average prices run $5.25 for breakfast, $6.95 for lunch and $9.55 for dinner. The lodge dining area is modern with three of its sides containing large windows. Guests can enjoy a beautiful view of the lake and wildlife while they are having their meal. There is ample seating within the restaurant. Groups are welcome with advance reservations. Carry-out items off their menu or buffet are also available. For information call 762-9541.

Restaurants Near Airport:

Brass Lantern	2 mi	Phone: N/A
State Park Rest.	6-1/2 mi W.	Phone: 762-9541

Lodging: Days Inn 762-4467; Park View Motel 762-2412; Richland Inn 762-0061; Villa Inn 762-4448.

Meeting Rooms: None reported

Transportation: Airport courtesy car reported 762-5133.

Information: Park Managers Office David Crockett State Park, Lawrenceberg, TN 38464-0398. Phone: 762-9408 (Office) 762-9541 (Restaurant).

Attractions:

David Crockett State Park contains 2 campground locations with 107 sites in all, olympic size pool with modern bathhouse; 40-acre fishing lake; Park naturalist and recreation director hold planned activities and programs. Also the Crockett Museum exhibits life and times of Crocket. No admission charged.

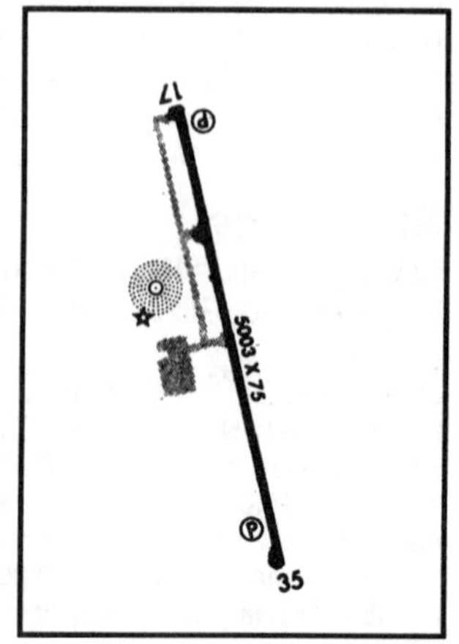

Airport Manager:

LAWRENCEBURG - LAWRENCEBURG MUNICIPAL (2M2)
3 mi northeast of town N35-14.06 W87-15.48 Elev: 936 Fuel: 100LL, Jet-A Rwy 17-35: H5003x75 (Asph) Attended: 1330-2300Z Unicom: 122.8
Airport Manager Phone: 762-5133

TN-MEM - MEMPHIS
MEMPHIS INTERNATIONAL AIRPORT

(Area Code 901) 7, 8, 9

Fred Gang's Restaurant:

Fred Gang's Restaurant is located just minutes (1/2 mile) from Memphis International Airport. They proudly call themselves "The Memphis Prime Rib House" but it doesn't stop there. Specialties of the house include exotic wild game dishes like elk, buffalo, ostrich, kangaroo, and wild bore. Also served are hand cut steaks and a wide variety of grilled fresh fish. Add to this, their is something for everyone. For dessert make sure you leave room for a slice of their homemade pie or dessert. Special request "meals on the go" are also available for corporate fliers, with sufficient notice. Prices range from $8.00 for lunch and $18.00 for dinner. They are easily accessible from the airport and courtesy transportation is provided by AMR Combs and most area hotels. Visit this restaurant and enjoy fine dining in a casual atmosphere. Located at 2872 Airways Blvd., this restaurant serves lunch Monday through Friday from 11 a.m. till 2 p.m. and dinner on Monday through Saturday from 5:30 p.m. until 10 p.m. On Sundays they are open from 5 p.m. to 9 p.m. For more information call 345-3693.

Host Marriott Services:

Host Marriott Services has 19 operating food service facilities located inside the terminal building at the Memphis International Airport, which include snack bars and cafeterias. These facilities are operational 24 hours a day and specialize in pizza, roto chix, salads, burgers and desserts. Daily specials in their "Court Square" include a buffet served in modern surroundings and a southern decor in their Paddle boat Grill. Prices average $3.50 for breakfast, $6.50 for lunch and $6.50 for dinner. For information call 922-8170.

Jax at Fred's:

Jax at Fred's is an east coast style deli located on the upper level above Fred Gang's Restaurant. Courtesy transportation through AMR Combs is provided to this restaurant. Their delicious selections are sliced thin, and piled high using only premium meats & cheeses, freshly baked breads and fresh produce. They serve one of the best sandwiches in Memphis. Jax is open from 11 a.m. to 2 p.m. Monday through Friday. Specialty meat and cheese trays are also available to-go, as well as all their sandwiches. Fly in and try their D.B.R.B., T.W.'s Bird or any of the other sandwiches, with homemade "baked" potato salad or chips and a cool beverage. Prices average about $5.00 for most entrees. Just minutes from the Memphis International Airport or Graceland. For information call 345-3693.

Restaurants Near Airport:

Butcher Shop Stkhse	10 mi W.	Phone: 521-0856
Corky's Barbecue	6 mi E.	Phone: 685-9744
Fred Gang's	1/2 mi W.	Phone: 345-3693
Host Marriott Serv.	Trml. Bldg.	Phone: 922-8170
Jax at Fred's	1/2 mi W.	Phone: 345-3693
Rendezvous	10 mi W.	Phone: 523-2746

Lodging: La Quinta-Airport (Free Shuttle) 396-1000; Holiday Inn-Airport/Graceland (Free Shuttle) 398-9211; Ramada Inn Southwest-Airport (Free Shuttle) 332-3500; Sheraton Inn-Airport (Free Shuttle) 332-2370; Hilton Inn-Memphis Airport (Free Shuttle) 332-1130; Mariott Courtyard (1-1/2 mi west) 396-3600; Radisson (10 mi west) 528-1800; Wilson World (5 mi east) 366-0000;

Meeting Rooms: AMR Combs has a conference room that will accommodate approx. six people. If needed, AMR Combs will arrange meeting rooms at local hotels. Also, the following contain conference rooms: La Quinta-Airport; Holiday Inn-Airport/Graceland; Ramada Inn Southwest-Airport; Sheraton Inn-Airport; Hilton Inn-Memphis Airport;

Transportation: AMR Combs Memphis, Inc. can accommodate courtesy transportation within 1 mile radius of the airport. Also: Yellow Cab 526-2121; Fleetmark Rental 345-4786; Hertz Rental 345-5680; Alamo Rental 332-8412; Avis Rental 345-2847; National Rental 345-0070.

Information: Convention & Visitors Bureau, 47 Union Ave., Memphis, TN 38103, Phone: 543-5300.

Attractions:

Graceland (Elvis Presley's Home) is located only 2 miles west of the Memphis International Airport on 3764 Elvis Presley Blvd 332-3322. Many attractions are available to the visitor within the Memphis area. Contact the Convention & Visitors Bureau for more information. (See "Information" listed above).

Airport Information:

MEMPHIS - MEMPHIS INTERNATIONAL AIRPORT (MEM)
3 mi south of town N35-02.75 W89-58.69 Elev: 332 Fuel: 100LL, Jet-A
Rwy 18R-36L: H9319x150 (Conc-Grvd) Rwy 18L-36R: H9000x150 (Conc-Grvd)
Rwy 09-27: H8936x150 (Asph-Grvd) Rwy 18C-36C: H8400x150 (Conc-Grvd)
Attended: continuously Atis: 127.75 Unicom: 122.95 Gnd Con: 121.9 App Con: 119.1, 125.8
Dep Con: 124.65, 124.15 Tower: 118.3 (Rwy 09-27), 119.7 (Rwy 18L-R, 36R-L)
Clnc Del 125.2 Public Phone 24hrs Notes: No landing fee for general aviation aircraft; Tiedown: Single $7.50, Multi-engined $12.50.
FBO: AMR Combs Memphis Phone: 345-4700

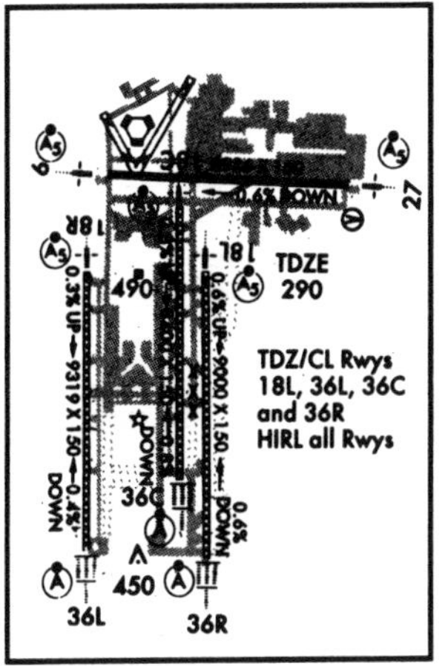

TN-MOR - MORRISTOWN MOORE-MURRELL

(Area Code 423)

10

The Attic Restaurant:

The Attic Restaurant is located about 4 miles west from the Morristown - Moore/Murrell Airport. This restaurant was introduced to us by one of our readers. When talking to the restaurant management we learned that guests can take Route 11-E from the airport. A courtesy car is reported available at the airport. Restaurant hours for lunch are Monday through Saturday from 11 a.m. to 2:30 p.m., then re-opens again from 5 p.m. to 9 p.m. for dinner. On Sunday they are open for lunch only, between 11 a.m. and 2 p.m. Specialties on their menu include Chicken Alexander, Chicken Washington, rib-eye steak, meat loaf Smoky Mountain style and turkey croissants. Average prices run around $5.25 to $6.00 for most dishes, and rib-eye steaks around $10.95. They also offer lunch specials every day. The restaurant can seat about 150 persons in their main dining room. Two additional rooms are available for groups and parties able to accommodate up to 25 people. For more information about The Attic Restaurant call 475-3508.

Restaurants Near Airport:
The Attic 4 mi W. Phone: 475-3508

Lodging: Comfort Suites 1-2 mi 585-4000; Days Inn 2 mi 587-2200; Holiday Inn 1 mi 581-8700; Ramada Inn 8 mi 587-2400.

Meeting Rooms: Holiday Inn 1 mi 581-8700; Ramada Inn 8 mi 587-2400. Also The Attic restaurant has rooms available for groups, parties and catered gatherings. Call 475-3508 for information.

Transportation: It is reported that a courtesy car is available at the airport. Call ahead and confirm your request with the FBO's.

Information: Morristown Chamber of Commerce, 825 W. 1st North St, P.O. Box 9, Morristown, TN 37815. Phone: 586-6382. Note: Area code reported changed from 615 to 423.

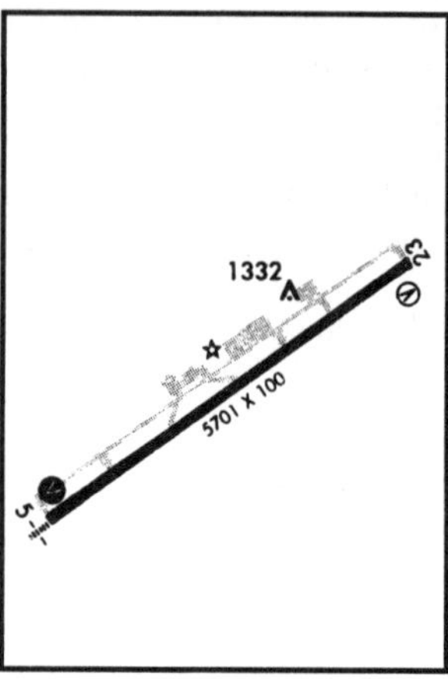

Airport Information:

MORRISTOWN - MOORE/MURRELL (MOR)
4 mi south of town N36-25.07 W81-49.51 Elev: 2240 Fuel: 80 Rwy 05-23: H5701 x100 (Asph) Attended: irregularly Unicom: 122.7
FBO: Alpha Aviation Phone: 581-6583
FBO: Morristown Flying Service Phone: 586-2483 or 586-3082

TN-BNA - NASHVILLE
NASHVILLE INTERNATIONAL

(Area Code 615) | 11, 12

101st Airborne Restaurant:

The 101st Airborne Restaurant is located on the Nashville International Airport. This aviation-theme-style restaurant offers elegant dining in truly enjoyable surroundings. The restaurant can be reached by parking at Stevens Aviation. They provide transportation to and from the restaurant for their customers. Similar in design to the 94th Aero Squadrontype restaurant, the 101st Airborne Restaurant has a replica aircraft parked out in front. As you enter the restaurant you overhear a squadron leader giving the morning's briefing to his pilots. There are 6 rooms that have seating. The lower level has window-side seating, offering a panoramic view of the active runways. The upper level also allows a view of the runways with some seating along the walls facing the windows. Rustic fire-places, replica aircraft parts of all types adorn the walls and ceiling as well as hundreds of photos of war aces. The restaurant hours are Monday through Thursday from 11 a.m. to 2:30 p.m. for lunch and 4:30 p.m. to 10 p.m. for dinner. Friday they are open from 11 a.m. to 2:30 p.m. for lunch and again at 4:30 p.m. to 11 p.m. Saturday they open their doors at 4:30 p.m. and serve dinner until 11 p.m. Their menu includes prime rib, filet mignon, shrimp scampi, broiled lobster tail, crab stuffed roughy, grilled salmon and a special "Jack Daniel Medallion." Average prices run $5.95 to $13.95 for lunch and $13.95 to $29.95 for dinner. In addition to the dining room, the 101st Airborne Restaurant also features the Foxhole Club which is a very cozy and romantically lit lounge with dance floor. There is even an outdoor addition to the restaurant that depicts a bombed-out French chalet with tables and outdoor dining. For more information about this restaurant call 361-4212.

CA1 Services:

CA1 Services owns and operates a fine dining facility located at the Nashville International Airport. This restaurant is situated in the terminal building and is accessible either through courtesy transportation by fixed base operators on the field or by airport taxi service. This establishment is open Monday through Friday between 11:30 a.m. and 7:30 p.m. Menu selections include specialty items like ribeye steak, chicken, catfish, fresh catch of the day including salmon or swordfish, seafood pasta salad, surf and turf, steak and scallops, or scallops fettuccini, to mention only a few. Average prices range from $6.95 to $10.95 for lunch and $6.95 to $17.95 for most dinner choices. There are also specials offered each day. This restaurant contains a two level dining room with seating capacity for up to 70 persons. A cafe located near this fine dining restaurant serves lighter fare and is open 7 days a week from 6:30 to 9 p.m. For more information you can call CA1 Services during normal working hours at 275-2211.

Airport Information:

NASHVILLE - NASHVILLE INTERNATIONAL (BNA)

5 mi southeast of town N36-07.47 W86-40.69 Elev: 599 Fuel: 100LL, Jet-A Rwy 13-31: H11029x150 (Asph-Con-Grvd) Rwy 02R-20L: H8000x150 (Conc-Grvd) Rwy 02C-20C: H8000x150 (Conc-Grvd) Rwy 02L-20R: H7702x150 (Conc-Grvd) Attended: continuously Atis: Arr 135.1 Dep 135.675 Unicom: 122.95 Tower: 128.15, 118.6 Gnd Con: 121.9 (West) 132.95 (East) Clnc Del 126.05

FBO: Signature Flight Support Phone: 361-3000
FBO: Stevens Aviation, Inc. Phone: 360-8100

Restaurants Near Airport:

101st Airborne	1-1/2 mi	Phone: 361-4212
CA1 Services	On Site	Phone: 275-2211
Chinese Garden	3 mi	Phone: 871-0536
Fifth Quarter	3 mi	Phone: 366-4268
New Orleans Manor	1-1/2 mi	Phone: 367-2777
Parkway Cooker	2 mi	Phone: 361-4747

Lodging: All facilities listed here have shuttle service to and from airport, and located within 2 miles of the field: Courtyard by Marriott-Airport 883-9500; Ramada Inn Suites 883-5201; Residence Inn by Marriott 889-8600; Holiday Inn Express 883-1366; Embassy Suites 871-0033; Guest Quarters 889-8889.

Meeting Rooms: All establishments listed under lodging have accommodations for meetings and conferences. Embassy Suites has convention facilities available, phone: 871-0033.

Transportation: Taxi service on airport. Also rental cars: Alamo 275-1050; Avis 361-1212; Budget 366-0847; Dollar 275-1081; Hertz 361-3131; National 361-7467; Rent-A-Wreck 885-8310.

Information: Nashville Area Chamber of Commerce, 161 4th Avenue N., Nashville, TN 37219, Phone: 259-4700; Also: The Nashville Tourist Information Center, I-65 & James Robertson Pkwy, Nashville, TN, 259-4747.

Attractions:

The city and surrounding area of Nashville offers many attractions and points of interest. A few of these include: **The State Capitol**; Fort Nashborough, a pioneer fort at 170 1st Ave. North; **Museum of Beverage Containers and Advertising,** 15 miles north of the city on I-65 to Millersville has more than 30,000 antique soda and beer cans which make up the largest collection of its kind, (Daily; closed Thanksgiving, Dec 25) 859-5236; Car Collectors Hall of Fame 255-6804; **Belmont Mansion** 269-9537; **The Hermitage Mansion** of President Andrew Jackson 889-2941; **Cheekwood/ Museum** and Gardens 8 mi southwest of town offers visitors a collection of 19th and 20th-century American art; **Botanical Hall** with an atrium of vivid tropical plants, greenhouses as well as 5 major gardens. 365-8000; **Country Music Hall of Fame & Museum** 255-5333; Opryland 10 miles east of town displays a 120-acre entertainment showpark that features many forms of music like pop, jazz, blues, Broadway, rock'n roll, country and gospel. This attraction also has craft shops, restaurants, playgrounds and petting zoo. For information call 889-6611; **Grand Ole Opry** tours are available by calling 889-9490; **Belle Carol Riverboats:** provide daytime sight-seeing cruises along the Cumberland River. Information about dinner excursions with entertainment are available by calling 244-3430; **Annual Events:** Music festivals with a number of exciting festive events are held throughout the year. Also the Nashville's Country Holidays, Tennessee State Fair and the Running of the Iroquois. Call the Chamber of Commerce at 259-4700 or The Nashville Tourist Information Center at 259-4747 for further information.

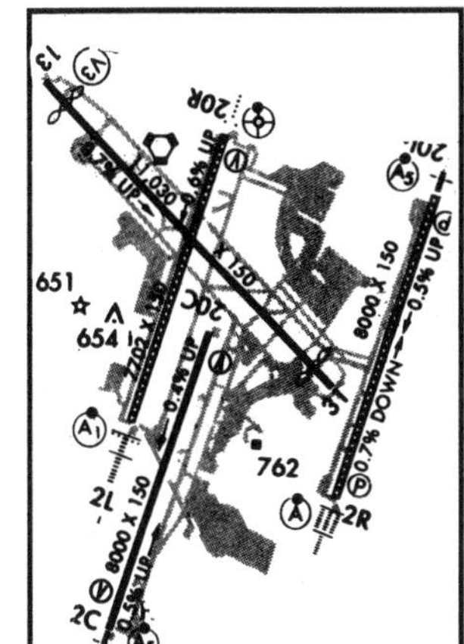

TN-UOS - SEWANEE
FRANKLIN COUNTY

(Area Code 615)

13

Restaurants Near Airport:
Jim Oliver's Smokehouse 3 mi E. Phone: 924-2268

Lodging: Jim Oliver's Smokehouse & Resort. 85 lodge rooms, 14 fully appointed cabins with hot tubs, fire places and kitchens, etc. For information call 924-2268. Also Bed & Breakfasts
Meeting Rooms: Jim Oliver's Smokehouse & Resort has 3,300 square feet of meeting and convention space. Special outdoor barbecues and cookouts can be arranged for your organization. Just call 924-2268 for their accommodations.
Transportation: Sewanee Aviation will provide transportation for their customers. Call 598-5318.
Information: Franklin County Chamber of Commerce, P.O. Box 280, Winchester, TN 373-98, Phone: 615-967-6788.

Jim Oliver's Smokehouse & Resort:

This upscale establishment contains an 85 room lodge, adjacent restaurant, 14 cabins complete with hot tubs, fire places and kitchens, all located on 20 acres of property for pure enjoyment. Their swimming pool, tennis courts, volley ball nearby golf course all add up to a great way to relax and enjoy the surroundings. Jim Oliver's Smokehouse & Resort is located only 3 miles east of the Franklin County Sewanee Airport. According to one of our readers, the people at Sewanee Aviation are very helpful and will arrange transportation to the resort. The Smokehouse restaurant is a full-service facility that is open 6 a.m. to 10 p.m. 7 days a week and 365 days a year. Specialties of the house include, of course, smoked barbecued meat including BBQ pork, hickory smoked prime rib, sugar cured ham as favorites to many of those repeat customers that enjoy home-style cooking. A daily buffet is served in addition to menu items. Their menu includes a fine assortment of additional selections as well as including breakfast items that are served all day. Located only 4 miles off the Interstate, Oliver's Smokehouse & Resort plays host to many business and social gatherings. They even have their own chapel for weddings, and special honeymoon accommodations. They also have 3,300 square feet of meeting and convention space able to accommodate 400 people. Outdoor barbecues and cook-outs can be arranged. As an ideal location to plan your next retreat or vacation, this resort is conveniently situated near many things to see and do. The Monteagle Cellar and Winery is located just across the street. Tours are given, along with wine tasting. If golfing is your pleasure, there is a course not far away. During the first weekend of August and the Last weekend in August, an arts and crafts fair is usually held in town. Directions from the airport to the resort are simple. According to the resort management you can take Hwy 64 & 41A and go right or east about 3 miles. You will see their sign on the right side of the street. For more information about Jim Oliver's Smokehouse & Resort call 924-2268.

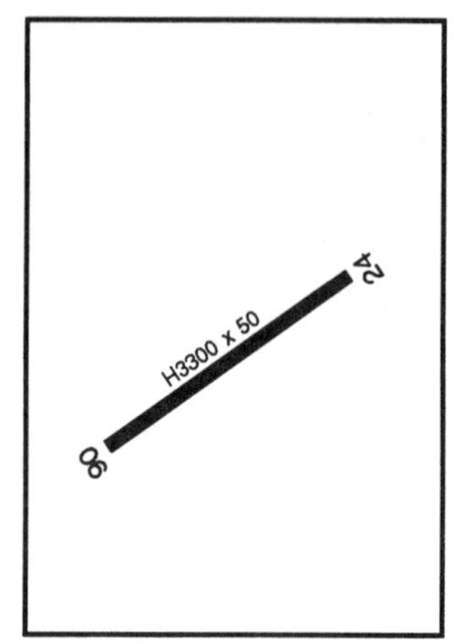

Airport Information:

SEWANEE - FRANKLIN COUNTY (UOS)
1 mi east of town N35-12.24 W85-53.92 Elev: 1950 Fuel: 80, 100LL Rwy 06-24: H3300x50 (Asph) Attended: daylight hours Unicom: 122.8
Airport Manager: Phone: 598-5318

TN-MQY - SMYRNA
SMYRNA AIRPORT

(Area Code 615)

14

Restaurants Near Airport:
Landings Restaurant On Site Phone: 459-0447
Omni Hut 2 mi SW Phone: 459-0236

Lodging: Days Inn (Trans) I-24 & 231 South, Phone: 896-5080.

Meeting Rooms: Airport authority can arrange for meeting and conference rooms for business travelers. Call 459-2651 for information.

Transportation: Smyrna Air Center 459-3337 and Corporate Flight Management 459-8883 can provide courtesy shuttle to nearby facilities; Also: A-One Cab Co. 890-2747; Checker Cab 893-8118; Ideal Cab 896-3939; Able Car Rental 895-2317; Alamo Car Rental 327-9633; Budget Rent-A-Car 896-7420.

Information: Tennessee Department of Tourist Development, P.O. Box 23170, Nashville, TN 37202, Phone: 615-741-2158.

Landings Restaurant:

The Landings Restaurant is situated across the street from the Smyrna Airport. According to the restaurant personnel, if you park your aircraft at the Smyrna Air Center, you can walk to the restaurant. This snack bar style restaurant is open Monday through Friday for lunch between 11 a.m. to 1:30 p.m. and dinner from 2:30 p.m. to 9:00 p.m. Their menu includes hamburgers, cheeseburgers, roast beef, barbecued chicken, chicken nuggets, hot wings and burritos. Average prices for meals range between $2.00 and $4.00. The decor of the restaurant has an aviation theme with pictures of airplanes on the wall. The dining area also contains a pool table off to the side, in addition to a dart board. This establishment can accommodate up to 50 persons. Meals can also be prepared-to-go. For more information call the Landing Restaurant at 459-0447.

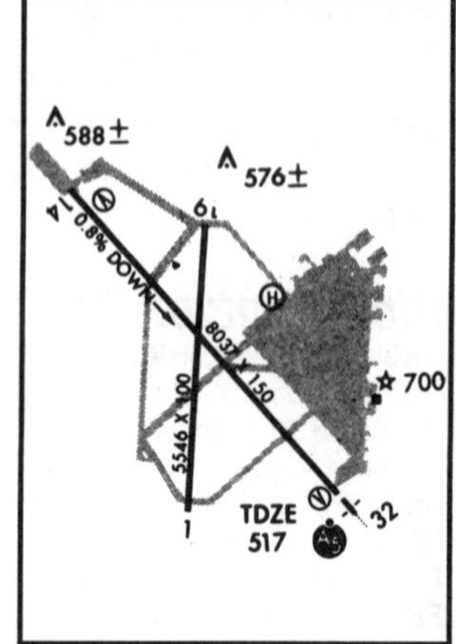

Airport Information:

SMYRNA - SMYRNA AIRPORT (MQY)
2 mi north of town N36-00.54 W86-31.20 Elev: 543 Fuel: 100LL, Jet-A
Rwy 14-32: H8037x150 (Asph) Rwy 01-19: H5546x100 (Asph) Attended: continuously
Unicom: 123.0 Clnc Del: 121.4, 121.7 (When tower closed) Tower: 118.5 Gnd Con: 121.4
FBO: Corporate Flight Management Phone: 459-8883
FBO: Smyrna Air Center Phone: 459-3337

TN-0M2 TIPTONVILLE REELFOOT LAKE AIRPORT

(Area Code 901) 15

Reelfoot Air Park Inn & Restaurant:

The Reelfoot Air Park Inn & Restaurant is located only 100 yards from the Reelfoot Lake Airport. This establishment located within the park, contains a combination family style restaurant is open from 7 a.m. to 8 p.m. Monday through Thursday, and 7 a.m. to 8:30 p.m. on Friday and Saturday. Between July 5th and October 5th, their hours of operation vary. They specialize is buffet style service which includes items like catfish, country ham, cobblers, fried chicken, seafood, as well as a wide variety of other entrees including a full breakfast selection during the morning hours. A salad bar is also available. The restaurant can accommodate 100 persons in their main dining room along with a special room for parties or groups up to 100. Guests can enjoy a view overlooking Reelfoot Lake while they dine. The restaurant has a rustic decor with wooden beams and large glass windows. In addition to the dining establishment, they also provide a 20 unit lodging facility with individual single rooms or suites. For more information you can call 253-7756

Restaurants Near Airport:
Reelfoot Air Park Inn 100 yds Phone: 253-7756

Lodging: Reelfoot Air Park Inn (100 yards from airport) Phone: 253-7756

Meeting Rooms: Reelfoot Air Park Inn (100 yards from airport) Phone: 253-7756.

Transportation: The Reelfoot Air Park Inn and restaurant is located within walking distance (100 yards) from the airport.

Information: Northwest Tennessee Tourist Promotion Council, P.O. Box 963, Martin, TN 38273, Phone: 587-4213.

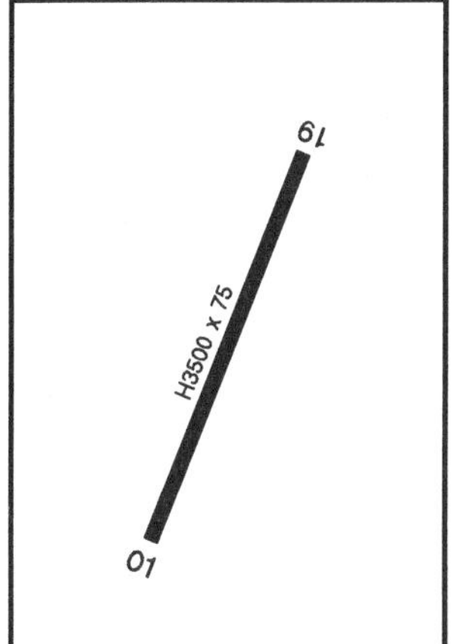

Airport Information:

TIPTONVILLE - REELFOOT LAKE AIRPORT (0M2)
9 mi northeast of town N36-28.52 W89-20.77 Elev: 289 Rwy 01-19: H3500x75 (Asph)
Attended: unattended CTAF: 122.9
Reelfoot Lake Airport Phone: 901-253-7756, or 615-741-3208

Reelfoot Lake State Resort Park

Tiptonville, TN (TN-0M2)

Reelfoot Lake State Resort Park, located in the northwest corner of Tennessee, is one of the greatest hunting and fishing preserves in the nation. The lake encompasses 25,000 acres (15,000 of which are water) and harbors almost every kind of shore and wading bird, as well as the Golden and the American bald eagles. Other animals are also diverse and abundant here. Its many species of flowering and non-flowering plants attract botany enthusiasts from all over the country. Cypress dominate the margins of the lake, but many other trees and shrubs are also present.

History records that Reelfoot was created by a series of severe earthquakes during the bitter cold winter of 1811-12. Landslides swept down bluffs, large areas of land were uplifted, and still larger areas sank. One of these sunken areas filled with water and Reelfoot Lake was born.

Reelfoot Lake State Resort Park is located in Lake and Obion counties. The Park's 280 acres are broken into 10 segments located along 22 miles of the Reelfoot Lake shoreline. The Airpark Inn resort complex is located off State Highway 78, ten miles north of Tiptonville. The other sections of the park - including the visitor/interpretive center and auditorium, picnic, and camping areas - are located along State Highways 21 and 22.

Reelfoot's 20 unit Airpark Inn and Restaurant complex is situated out over the lake, nestled among towering cypress trees. Twelve of the rooms provide double occupancy. The other eight are suites accommodating up to six persons each. Both the inn and 100-seat capacity restaurant are open year-round (except during the Christmas season.) In addition to the Airpark Inn, the park also provide a five-unit motel at the Reelfoot spillway. All units sleep at least three people and three units provide kitchenettes. Inn and motel reservations should be made well in advance by writing or calling the Airpark Inn.

For those who wish to fly in, Reelfoot offers a lighted, all weather landing strip adjacent to the inn. Their runway is 01-19 with a hard surface of 3500' x 75' Asphalt and a unicom of 122.8. This airport is reported unattended. Maintain 1000 feet over lake east of airport (Federal Game Refuge). Check runway conditions before landing.

Reelfoot features two campgrounds with a total of 120 sites. Each site provides a water and electric hook-up, table and grill. One campground is located at the airfield and the other at the south end or Reelfoot Lake. Bathhouses are centrally located at both areas, and dump stations are provided for self-contained camping rigs. The Airpark campground is open all year. Campsites are available on a first-come, first served basis. Reservations cannot be accepted, and maximum stay is two weeks.

One of the main attractions at Reelfoot is its wintering population of bald eagles. From December through March, park naturalists conduct daily eagle tours. Special weekend programs include: slide shows, guest lectures, and bus tours. Reservations for the tours should be made in advance by contacting the park office. During the summer, months seasonal naturalists conduct a variety of interpretive programs. Special interpretive programs may be arranged by contacting the Park Naturalist.

Not surprisingly, fishing and boating are extremely popular at Reelfoot. The lake is recognized as the nation's most abundant natural fish hatchery, and provides fine catches of crappie, bream, and largemouth bass, along with 53 other varieties of fish. All anglers, 16 years of age or above, must be in possession of a valid temporary or annual Tennessee fishing license, as well as a TWRA Preservation Permit. Both bank and boat fishing are popular on scenic Reelfoot. Rental boats are available at the park dock. Privately owned boats and motors are permitted and launch ramps are available.

No visit to the park is complete without a ride on one of the Reelfoot scenic cruise boats. Tours are operated daily from May through September (weather permitting). Shorter tours are also available on each trip to answer questions and to interpret the natural and cultural wonders of the lake. There is a nominal fee for tours, and groups should make reservations in advance.

An adult swimming pool and a children's wading pool are located adjacent to the inn for use by inn guests only. The inn pool is operated from May through August. Other recreational activities at Reelfoot include: swimming, tennis, softball, horseshoes, shuffleboard, pool, ping-pong, badminton, archery, basketball, frisbee throwing, and table games.

Restaurant hours at the Inn are reported to be 4:00 p.m. until 8:00 p.m. on Thursday, 7:00 a.m. until 8:30 p.m. on Friday, 7:00 a.m. till 8:30 p.m. Saturday and 7:00 a.m. until 3:00 p.m. on Sunday. For hours during Monday, Tuesday and Wednesday call the restaurant.

Reelfoot's 400-seat, air conditioned auditorium with kitchen facilities is perfect for banquets and conventions. It is available year-round, and rental cost is small. The adjacent Visitor Center houses interesting exhibits pertaining to the natural and cultural history of Reelfoot, including an earthquake simulator and a variety of audio-visual programs. Admission in free.

Hours of Operation at the park are 8:00 a.m. to 10:00 p.m. during the summer, and 8:00 a.m. to sundown in the winter.

Special summer fishing packages are often featured at very reasonable prices.

For further information and reservations contact the Superintendent's Office or Airpark Inn by calling 901-253-7756. (Information submitted by Tennessee State Parks).

TN-THA - TULLAHOMA HIGHLAND REGIONAL ARPT

(Area Code 615) 16

Restaurants Near Airport:
Western Sizzlin 1/2 mile Phone: 455-2423

Lodging: Steeple Chase Inn (1 mile) 455-4501; Veranda House (2-1/2 miles) 455-7033;

Meeting Rooms: None Reported

Transportation: Courtesy Taxi 455-0044; Ernie's 455-9808; White Top Taxi 455-2604; Rental Cars: U-Save Auto Rental 455-4564, Also Tullahoma FBO has rental and courtesy cars available call 455-3884.

Information: Tennessee Dept of Tourist Development, P.O. Box 23170, Nashville, TN 37202. Phone: 615-741-2158.

Western Sizzlin:

This restaurant is located about 1/2 mile from the Highland Regional Airport. This family style restaurant is open from 11 a.m. to 9 p.m. Sunday through Thursday and 11 a.m. to 10 p.m. Friday and Saturday. They have a food bar that provides a nice selection of entrees with a choice of meats including chicken, catfish, and ham, along with a host of other items. Seventy-five percent of their customers usually order the buffet. In addition, they also serve rib-eye, a 12 ounce sirloin steak, and their 16 ounce T-bone. The decor of this restaurant is modern with carpeted floors, table and booths. Seating for 250 people is available in their main dining room as well as a separate dining area able to accommodate up to 80 people for groups and parties. This restaurant may be a little far to walk to, however, transportation is available through taxi service. Transportation, through the airport, is also possible provided a courtesy car is available at the time. For information you can call the Western Sizzlin at 455-2423.

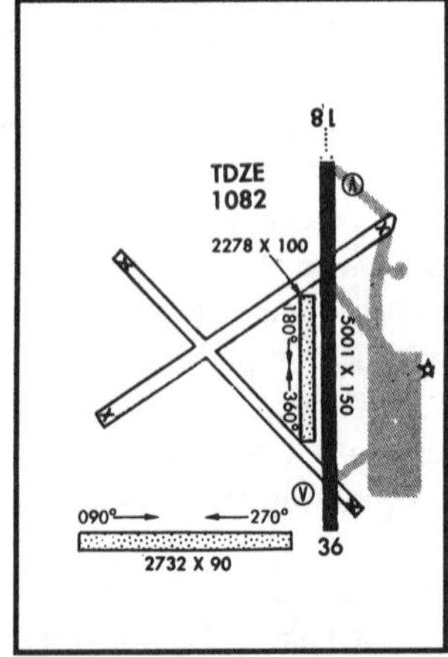

Airport Information:

TULLAHOMA - HIGHLAND REGIONAL AIRPORT (THA)
2 mi northwest of town 35-22-52N 86-14-37W Elev: 1082 Fuel: 80, 100, Jet-A
Rwy 18-36: H5000x150 (Asph-Conc) Rwy E-W: 2732x100 (Turf) Rwy N-S: 2278x100 (Turf)
Attended: daylight hours Unicom: 122.8
FBO: Tullahoma Aviation, Inc. Phone: 455-3884

TEXAS

LOCATION MAP

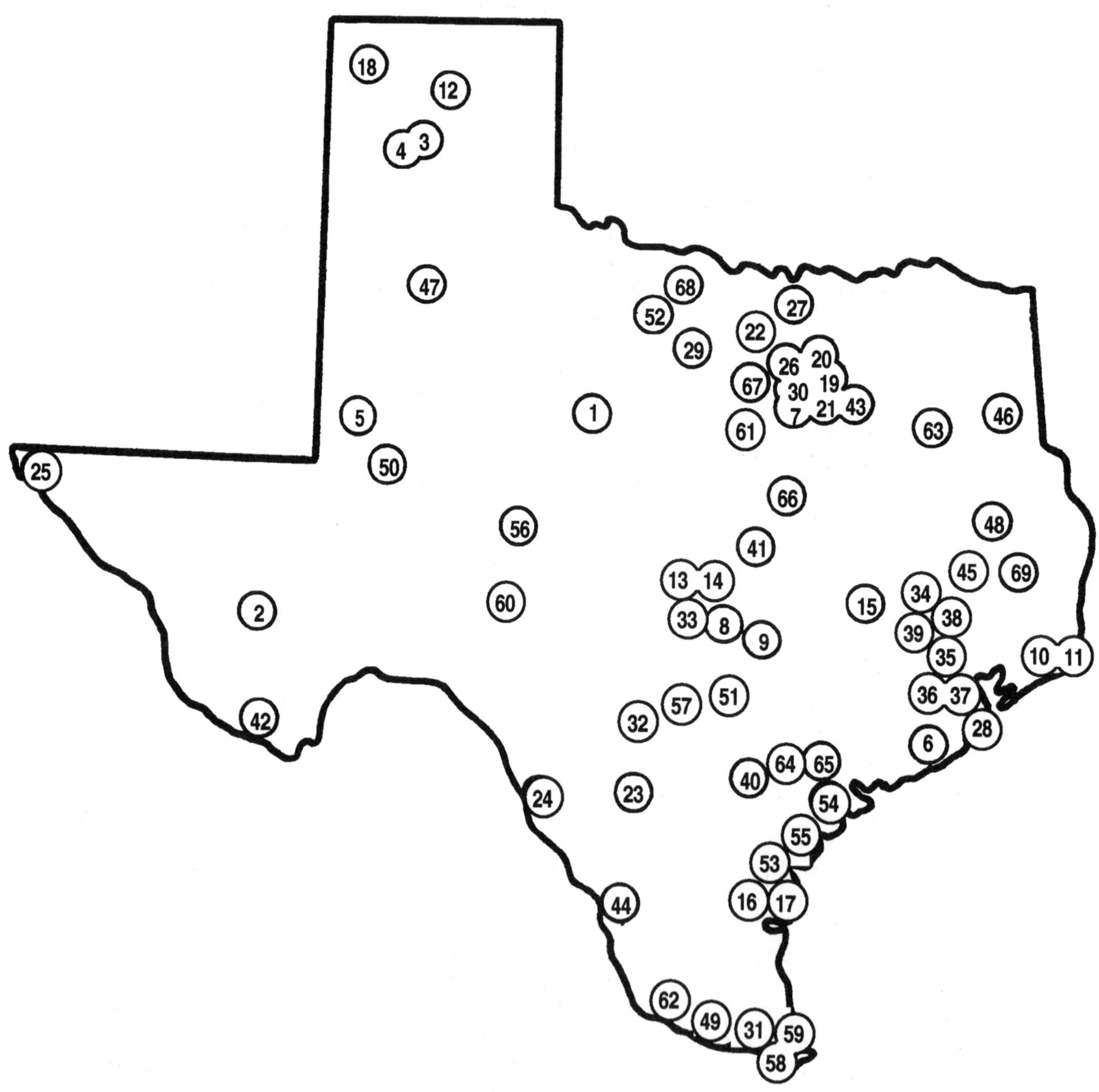

Not to be used for navigational purposes

TEXAS

CROSS FILE INDEX

Location Number	City or Town	Airport Name And Identifier	Name of Restaurant
1	Abilene	Abilene Reg. Arpt. (ABI)	Joe Allen's Restaurant
2	Alpine	Alpine-Casparis Muni. Arpt. (E38)	Reata House
3	Amarillo	Amarillo Intl. Arpt. (AMA)	English Field House
4	Amarillo	Tradewind Arpt. (TDW)	Parachute Bar & Grill
5	Andrews	Andrews Co. Arpt. (E11)	Buddy's Drive Inn
6	Angleton/L. Jackson	Brazoria Co. Arpt. (LBX)	Windsock Grill
7	Arlington	Arlington Muni. Arpt. (F54)	Wings Restaurant
8	Austin	Lakeway Airpark (3R9)	Lakeway Resort
9	Austin	Robert Mueller Muni. Arpt. (AUS)	Host Marriott
10	Beaumont/Pt-Arthur	Jefferson Co. Arpt. (BPT)	Dorothy's Front Porch
11	Beaumont/Pt-Arthur	Jefferson Co. Arpt. (BPT)	The Pickle Barrel
12	Borger	Hutchinson Co. Arpt. (BGD)	Lorene's Mex. Kitchen
13	Burnet	Burnet Muni. Kate Craddock (BMQ)	Highlander Inn
14	Burnet	Burnet Muni. Kate Craddock (BMQ)	Riverwalk Cafe
15	College Station	Easterwood Field (CLL)	Remedies Restaurant
16	Corpus Christi	Corpus Christi Intl. (CRP)	Flight Bites
17	Corpus Christi	Corpus Christi Intl. (CRP)	Republic of Texas
18	Dalhart	Dalhart Muni. Arpt. (DHT)	Ingram Flying Service
19	Dallas	Dallas Love Field (DAL)	Airport Cafe
20	Dallas	Fort Worth Intl. Arpt. (DFW)	Host Marriott
21	Dallas	Redbird Arpt. (RBD)	Redbird Restaurant
22	Decatur	Decatur muni. (8F7)	Mattie's On The Square
23	Dilley	Dilley Airpark (24R)	Dilley Dairy Queen
24	Eagle Pass	Eagle Pass Muni. Arpt. (EGP)	Charcoal Grill
25	El Paso	El Paso Intl. Arpt. (ELP)	CA1 Services
26	Fort Worth	Fort Worth Meacham Arpt. (FTW)	Flightline Cafe
27	Gainesville	Gainesville Muni. Arpt. (GLE)	Wooden Spoon
28	Galveston	Scholes Fld. (GLS)	Dining Moody Gardens
29	Graham	Graham Muni. Arpt. (E15)	Dairy Queen Arpt. Rest.
30	Grand Prairie	Grand Prairie Muni. (GPM)	Final Approach Rest.
31	Harlingen	Rio Grande Valley Intl. (HRL)	Host Marriott
32	Hondo	Hondo Muni. (HDO)	Flightline Cafe
33	Horseshoe Bay	Horseshoe Bay Airpk. (4R2)	Horseshoe Bay Resort
34	Houston	David Wayne Hooks Mem. (DWH)	Aviators Grill
35	Houston	Ellington Fld. (EFD)	Cajun Barbecue Hse.
36	Houston	Houston Gulf (SPX)	Brass Parrot
37	Houston	Houston Gulf (SPX)	Landry's Restaurant
38	Houston	Intercontinental Arpt. (IAH)	Host Marriott
39	Houston	William P. Hobby Arpt. (HOU)	CA1 Services
40	Kenedy	Karnes Co. Arpt. (2R9)	Barth's Restaurant
41	Killeen	Killeen Muni. Arpt. (ILE)	Killeen Arpt. Coffee Shop
42	Lajitas	Lajitas Arpt. (17XS)	Lajitas Rio Grand Resort

CROSS FILE INDEX
(Texas Continued)

Location Number	City or Town	Airport Name And Identifier	Name of Attraction
43	Lancaster	Lancaster Arpt. (LNC)	Happy Landings Cafe
44	Laredo	Laredo Intl. (LRD)	Villa Laredo Restaurant
45	Livingston	Livingston Muni. (00R)	B & B Bar-B-Que
46	Longview	Gregg Co. Arpt. (GGG)	Sunpoint Cafe
47	Lubbock	Lubbock Intl. (LBB)	Host Marriott Restaurant
48	Lufkin	Angelina Co. Arpt. (LFK)	Angelina Co. Arpt. Cafe
49	McAllen	Miller Intl. (MFE)	The Rose Room (Hilton)
50	Midland	Midland Intl. (MAF)	Host Marriott
51	New Braunfels	New Braunfels Muni. (3R5)	Cloud 9 Restaurant
52	Olney	Olney Muni. Arpt. (ONY)	Rodge's Grill & Deli
53	Port Aransas	Mustang Beach Arpt. (2R8)	Port Aransas Island
54	Port Lavaca	Calhoun Co. Arpt. (T97)	Harvey's Rest. & Club
55	Rockport	Aransas Co. Arpt. (RKP)	Back 40 Restaurant
56	San Angelo	Mathis Field Arpt. (SJT)	Mathis Field Cafe
57	San Antonio	San Antonio Intl. Arpt. (SAT)	CA1 Services
58	San Benito	San Benito Muni. Arpt. (T66)	Stars Drive-Inn
59	San Benito	San Benito Muni. Arpt. (T66)	Blue Marlin
60	Sonora	Sonora Muni. Arpt. (E29)	Sutton Cntry. Stk. Hse.
61	Stephenville	Clark Fld. Muni. (SEP)	The Jennie Lee's Buffet
62	Terlingua	Terlingua Ranch Airstrip (Private)	Terlingua Ranch Lodge
63	Tyler	Tyler Pounds Fld. (TYR)	JW Finn's Airline Cafe
64	Victoria	Victoria Reg. Arpt. (VCT)	Daniel's Restaurant
65	Victoria	Victoria Reg. Arpt. (VCT)	Leo's Restaurant
66	Waco	Waco Reg. Arpt. (ACT)	Aerodrome Cafe
67	Weatherford	Parker Co. Arpt. (WEA)	Driver's Diner
68	Wichita Falls	Kickapoo Downtown Arpt. (T47)	Pizza Hut Restaurant
69	Woodville	Tyler Co. Arpt. (09R)	Picket House Restaurant

Articles

City or town	Nearest Airport and Identifier	Name of Attraction
Burnet, TX	Burnet Muni. Kate Craddock Fld. (BMQ)	Highland Lks Sqdn. Mus.
Dallas, TX	Addison Arpt. (ADS)	Cavanaugh Flight Mus.
Dallas, TX	Love Fld. (DAL)	Frontiers of Flight Mus.
Galveston, TX	Scholes Fld. (GLS)	Moody Gardens
Horseshoe Bay, TX	Horseshoe Bay Resort (Private)	Horseshoe Bay Resort
Midland, TX	Midland Intl. (MAF)	Confederate. A.F. Mus.
San Antonio, TX	Stinson Muni. (SSF)	Hangar 9, Brooks A.F.B
Terrell, TX	Terrell Muni. (TRL)	Silent Wings Museum

TX-ABI - ABILENE
ABILENE REGIONAL AIRPORT

(Area Code 915) 1

Joe Allen's Restaurant:

This restaurant is located 3 miles west of the Abilene Regional Airport and can be reached through courtesy transportation furnished by Abilene Aero, Inc. Taxi service is also available. This is a family style restaurant specializing in entrees like barbequed brisket, sausage, chicken, ribs, ham, and ribeye steaks, featured on their dinner menu. In addition to the entrees appearing on their menu, they also have a vegetable buffet that is offered with all meat selections. Prices range from $6.50 for lunch and $12.00 for dinner. Restaurant hours are from 11 a.m. to 9 p.m. Monday through Thursday and 11 a.m. to 9:30 p.m. on Friday, Saturday and Sunday. The decor of the restaurant is rustic with a western theme. Groups of any size are welcome. Carry-out service is available. To reach the restaurant, go into Abilene on Hwy 36 (It's the one the airport is on), take a left at 3rd light and go one block. The restaurant is on the left side of the street. For information call 672-6082.

Restaurants Near Airport:

Airport Restaurant	On Site	Phone: 673-5150
Cahoot's Catfish	2 mi W	Phone: 672-6540
Jo Allen's BBQ	3 mi W	Phone: 672-6082
Zentner's Stk Hse.	7 mi S.	Phone: 672-4290

Lodging: Holiday Inn (2 miles) 673-5271; Days Inn (2 miles) 677-8100; Embassy Suites (7 miles) 698-1234; Kiva Hotel (8 miles) 695-2150; Quality Inn (3 miles) 676-0222;

Meeting Rooms: The Abilene Regional Airport contains a meeting room at the FBO (677-2601) and a press room within the terminal building (675-0392).

Transportation: Transportation is not necessary if visiting the Airport Restaurant (walking distance); Abilene Aero, Inc will provide courtesy transportation to nearby restaurants; Taxi service is available through Classic Cab Co. 677-8294; Rental Cars: Avis 677-9240; Budget 677-7777; Hertz 673-6774; National 673-2553.

Information: Convention & Visitors Council, 1101 North 1st Street, P.O. Box 2281, Abilene, TX 79604, Phone: 676-2556 or 800-727-7704.

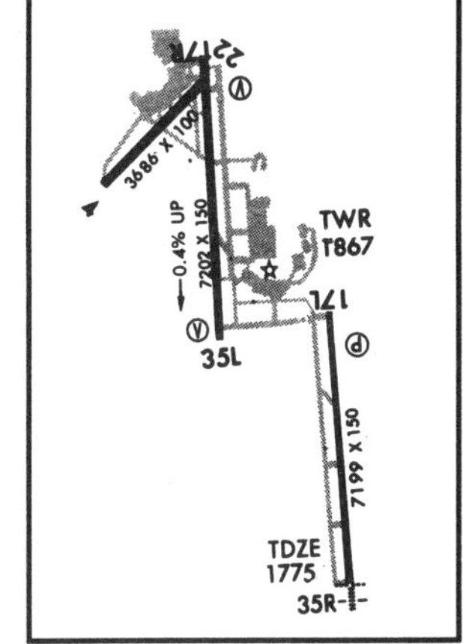

Airport Information:

ABILENE - ABILENE REGIONAL AIRPORT (ABI)
3 mi southeast of town N32-24.68 W99-40.91 Elev: 1790 Fuel: 100LL, Jet-A, A1+
Rwy 17R-35L: H7202x150 (Asph) Rwy 17L-35R: H7199x150 (Asph) Rwy 04-22: H3686x100 (Asph) Attended: continuously Atis: 118.25 Unicom: 122.95 App/Dep Con: 124.1, 125.0
Tower: 120.1 Gnd Con: 121.7 Public Phone 24hrs Notes: No landing fees, Tie-down $4-6 per day
Abilene Aero, Inc. Phone: 677-2601

TX-E38- ALPINE
ALPINE-CASPARIS MUNI. ARPT.

(Area Code 915) 2

Reata Restaurant:

During our conversation with the airport personnel we learned that Reata Restaurant is very popular with many visitors who flyin as well as local customers. It is located about 2 miles from the Alpine-Casparis Municipal Airport. The theme of the restaurant has a western flair, in a truly unique ranch-style home. The main dining room decorated with paintings and western artifacts, can seat about 79 people. An outdoor patio is also used for dining during warm weather months. The name of the restaurant, Reata, means "Rope" in Spanish, which was the name of the majestic ranch in the 1950's epic "Giant". This legendary movie, based on the novel by Edna Ferber, starring James Sean, Rock Hudson and Elizabeth Taylor, captured the true flavor of the west. In order to give their guests a memorable western experience, much of their beef comes from the CF Ranch's Highland Hereford Herd. The CF Ranch, nestled in the Davis and Del Norte Mountains is one of the largest family owned commercial cattle operations in the Southwest. Specialties of the house include: fettucini with crushed tamales and smoked chile cream; pan-seared pepper crusted tenderloin with a port wine glaze; Reata chicken fried steak with mashed potatoes; corn meal crusted pan fried trout with wild rice and jicama; Mesquite-grilled rib eye (14 ounce minimum) steak; roasted pork loin chop with Jim Beam sauteed apples; 16 ounce grilled T-bone; angel hair pasta with grilled shrimp; bar-b-que shrimp enchiladas; or try their smoked 14 ounce prime rib with a cream horse radish. Dessert choices include chocolate torte with blackberry sauce; apple crisp with cajeta; sweet potato custard or their Texas pecan pie. Most of the desserts come with vanilla bean ice cream. Restaurant hours are Monday through Saturday 11:30 a.m. to 2 p.m. for lunch and 5:30 p.m. to 10 p.m. for dinner. We were told that transportation from the airport is no problem. Either Alpine Aviation at 837-2744 or the restaurant will furnish a means to reach Reata's Restaurant. The restaurant is about 2 miles south on the same road (5th Avenue) that the airport is situated along. For more information call Reata's Restaurant at 837-9232.

Restaurants Near Airport:

La Casita	1 mi S.	Phone: 837-9842
Longhorn Cattle Co.	1/2 mi S.	Phone: 837-3692
Reata Restaurant	2 mi S.	Phone: 837-9232
Sunday House Rest.	1.5 mi S.	Phone: 837-9817

Lodging: Sunday House Motor Inn (1.5 miles, east) 837-9817; Mc Farland's Holland Hotel (1/2 mile, south) 837-3455; Siesta Country Inn (1.5 miles, east) 837-2503.

Meeting Rooms: City of Alpine Civic Center, Phone: 837-3301

Transportation: According to the airport management, fly-in guests can call the restaurant and request transportation. Also rental and courtesy cars are available at the airport through Alpine Aviation 837-2744.

Information: Chamber of Commerce, 106 North 3rd Street, Alpine, TX 79830, Phone: 837-2326.

Attractions:

Alpine Municipal Golf Course (1.5 miles, southeast) 837-2752; Davis Mountain Stone Park (30 miles, north) 426-3337; Mc Donald Observatory (40 miles, north) 426-3263; Fort Davis National Historic Site (30 miles, north) 426-3224.

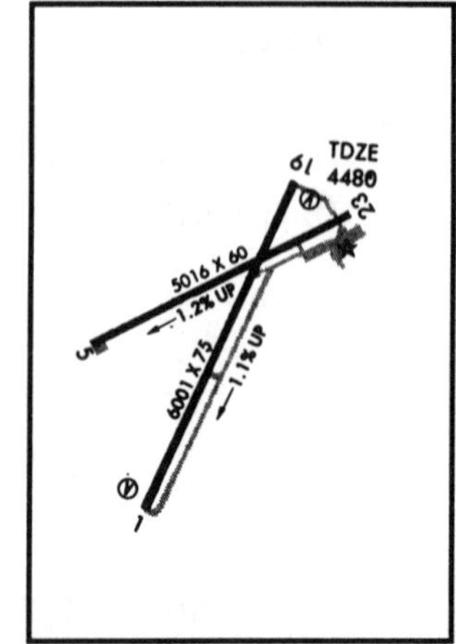

Airport Information:

ALPINE - ALPINE-CASPARIS MUNICIPAL AIRPORT (E38)
2 mi northwest of town N30-23.04 W103-40.99 Elev: 4513 Fuel: 100LL, Jet-A
Rwy 01-19: H6001x75 (Asph) Rwy 05-23: H5016x60 (Asph) Attended: continuously
Unicom: 122.8 Public phone 24 hrs Notes: No landing or parking fees. Alpine Casparis Municipal Airport is situated in the foot hills of the Davis Mountains at an elevation of 4513'. The area is surrounded by beautiful mountain peaks and valleys and offers outstanding recreational and flying opportunities.
FBO: Alpine Aviation Phone: 837-2744

TX-AMA - AMARILLO

(Area Code 806) 3

AMARILLO INTERNATIONAL AIRPORT

English Field House:

The English Field House is situated at Hughes Aviation Services. You can taxi right up to TAC Air (FBO) or they will provide transportation from the main terminal building. The restaurant is open Monday through Friday 7 a.m. to 6 p.m., and Saturday and Sunday 7 a.m. to 5 p.m.(Closed on major holidays). Their menu offers homemade selections as well as freshly baked pies. Daily breakfast and lunch specials are offered. Average prices run $4.00 for breakfast, $5.50 for lunch and $6.00 to $7.00 for dinner. The restaurant has an aviation theme with items of nostalgia. Catering for large or small groups are welcome. Hughes Aviation Services provide not only accommodation for aircraft service and dining facilities but will be happy to transport your party to nearby hotels. For information call 335-9103.

Attractions:

Palo Duro Canyon State Park is located about 15 miles south (As the crow flies) from the Amarillo International Airport. This State park encompasses 16,400 acres and has miniature train rides, hiking trails, horseback riding, picnicking, concessions and a visitors center with campsites. For information you can call 488-2227.

Airport Information:

AMARILLO INTERNATIONAL AIRPORT (AMA)
6 mi east of town N35-13.16 W101-42.36 Elev: 3605 Fuel: 100LL, Jet-A1 + B Rwy 04-22: H13502x300 (Con-Grvd) Rwy 13-31: H7901x100 (Asph-Pfc) Attended: continuously Atis: 118.85 Unicom: 122.95 Tower: 118.3 Gnd Con: 121.9 Public Phone 24hrs **FBO: TAC Air Phone: 335-3551**

Restaurants Near Airport:

Canyon Room	Unknown	Phone: 335-2419
English Field Hse.	On Site	Phone: 335-9103

Lodging: Several hotels are available with free shuttles to airport. Phones located in airport terminal building and at Hughes Aviation, Inc; Best Western 7 miles 372-3511; Fifth Season Inn east 8-1/2 miles 379-6555; Hilton Inn (Airport) 373-3071; Holiday Inn 9 miles 372-8741; Howard Johnson east 8 miles 372-8171; La Paloma Inn 372-8101; La Quinta (Amarilo Airport) 373-7486.
Meeting Rooms: There is a conference room available at the airport manager's office. You can call 335-1671. Also major lodging facilities listed above also contain meeting rooms.
Transportation: Hughes Aviation can provide courtesy transportation to local facilities, with their van. Also Rental cars and taxi service available: Avis 335-2222; Hertz 335-2331; Budget 335-1696; National 335-2311;
Information: Information: Convention and Visitors Council, 1000 Polk Street, P.O. Box 9480, Amarillo, TX 79105, Phone: 374-1479 or 800-692-1338.

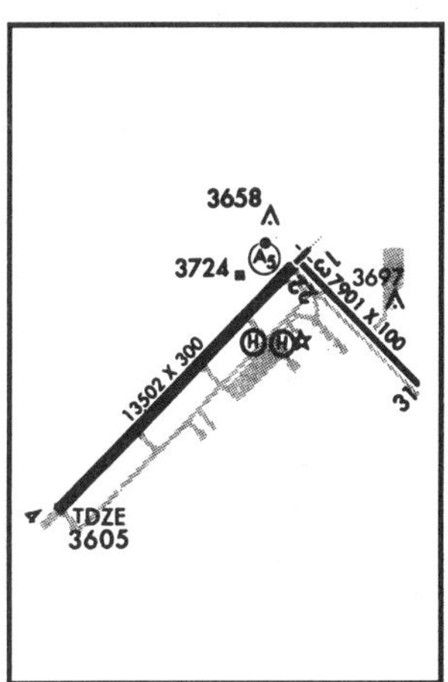

TX-TDW - AMARILLO

TRADEWIND AIRPORT

(Area Code 806)

Restaurants Near Airport:
Parachute Bar & Grill On Site Phone: 376-1008

Parachute Bar & Grill:

This restaurant formerly known as the Tradewind Restaurant is reported to be only 25 feet from the nearby aircraft parking area. Seating within their dining area can accommodate at least 40 persons. The Parachute Bar & Grill at the time of interview was just about to open its door, and is within its final stages of a complete renovation. Meals can also be prepared to go if requested and in-flight catering will most likely be available. For information about this establishment call the airport managers office at 376-1008.

Lodging: Days Inn (Trans) 379-6255; Harvey Hotel (3 miles) 358-7827; La Quinta Inn (Trans, 2 miles) 373-7486; Fifth Season Inn East (2 miles) 379-6555; Fifth Season Inn West (5 miles) 358-7881; Holiday Inn (Free trans) 372-8741; Howard Johnson Plaza (Trans) 358-7881.

Meeting Rooms: Days Inn 379-6255; Harvey Hotel 358-7827; La Quinta Inn 373-7486; Holiday Inn 372-8741; Howard Johnson Plaza 358-7881.

Transportation: Checker Cab 376-8211; Bob's Taxi Service 373-1171; Dependable Cab 372-5509; Rental Cars: Avis 335-2313; Budget 335-1696; Hertz 335-2331; National 335-2311.

Attractions:

Tascosa Country Club (8 miles north) 376-4771; Palo Duro Canyon State Park (North of Amarillo, approx. 11 miles from airport) shows nightly during summer season, Phone: 488-2227.

Information: Convention and Visitors Council, 1000 Polk Street, P.O. Box 9480, Amarillo, TX 79105, Phone: 374-1479 or 800-692-1338.

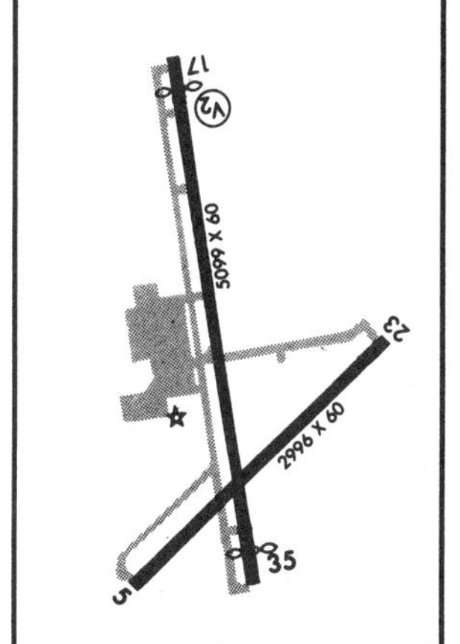

Airport Information:

AMARILLO - TRADEWIND AIRPORT (TDW)
3 mi southeast of town N35-10.19 W101-49.55 Elev: 3648 Fuel: 100LL, Jet-A1+ Rwy 17-35: H5099x60 (Asph) Rwy 05-23: H2996x60 (Asph) Attended: 1100-0500Z Unicom: 122.8 Public Phone 24hrs Notes: $3.00 per day, $15.00 per week, $30.00 per month for tie-down only. No landing fees. (Point of interest: This airport is the home of the prop jet Bonanza).
Airport Manager Phone: 376-1008

TX-E11 - ANDREWS
ANDREWS COUNTY AIRPORT

(Area Code 915)

5

Restaurants Near Airport:

Baron's Park Square	3 mi.	Phone: 523-6285
Buddy's Drive-In	1 mi.	Phone: 523-2840
K-Bobs Steak House	2 mi.	Phone: 523-5851

Buddy's Drive Inn:

During our conversation with airport personnel we were told that local pilots frequent an establishment known as Buddy's Drive Inn. Although is situated about 2 miles form the airport this drive in restaurant brings back memories of better times. Remember the "Dog & Suds" drive-Inn's ? Well Buddy's Drive Inn can be compared as the same, complete with outdoor waitresses. For the past 27 years Buddy's Drive Inn has been satisfying customers with choices like steak fingers, chicken fingers, and hamburger steaks. In-fact while talking with the owners we were told that they prepare over 3,000 pounds of chicken fingers each week. Buddy's Drive Inn has been featured on the CNN network and local television stations as a nostalgic destination by people from all across the region. Restaurant hours are 10 a.m. to 9 p.m. 7 days a week. Prices average under $5.00 for most major menu items. For information call the restaurant at 523-2840.

Lodging: Energy Park Inn (2 miles) 523-6305; Holiday Motel (1/2 mile) 532-5601.

Meeting Rooms: None Reported

Transportation: Airport courtesy car is available. Also, City Taxi 523-5190; Steve Smith Ford Rental Cars 523-2033.

Information: Texas Department of Transportation, P.O. Box 5064, Austin, Texas 78763-5064, Phone: 800-452-9292 or 800-888-8TEX.

Attractions:

Andrews Country Golf Course (Golf Course Road) Phone: 523-2860.

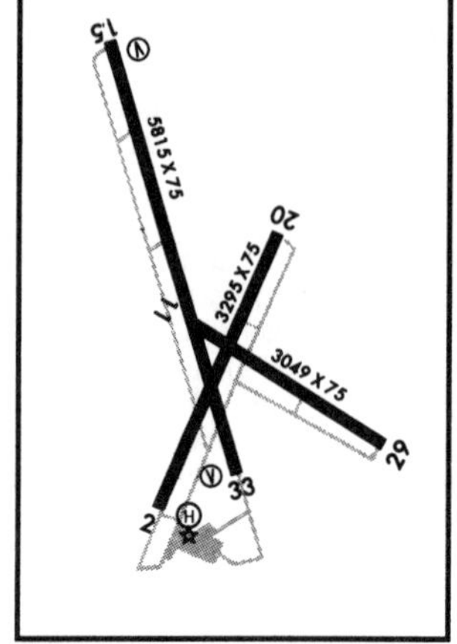

Airport Information:

ANDREWS - ANDREWS COUNTY AIRPORT (E11)
1 mi northeast of town N32-19.79 W102-31.78 Elev: 3178 Fuel: 100LL, Jet-A
Rwy 15-33: H5815x75 (Asph) Rwy 11-29: H3049x75 (Asph) Rwy 02-20: H2395x75 (Asph)
Attended: Mon-Fri 1300-0100Z, Sat-Sun 1400-0000Z Unicom: 122.8 Public Phone 24hrs
FBO: Andrews County Airport Phone: 524-1477

TX-LBX - ANGLETON/LAKE JACKSON
BRAZORIA COUNTY AIRPORT

(Area Code 409)

6

Restaurants Near Airport:

Windsock Grill	On Site	Phone: 849-1221

Windsock Grill:

The Windsock Grill is situated within the terminal building on the Brazoria County Airport. According to the management, you can park your aircraft right out in front of their door and walk only a few steps to the restaurant. This facility would be classified as a short order grill that is open Monday through Friday from 10 a.m. to 2 p.m. (Closed on weekends). Their lunch menu contains a very nice selection of entrees including all types of sandwiches like reuben's, club stake, "Mile high Clubs", hamburger baskets, and cheeseburger baskets (Breakfast not served). They also feature delicious desserts as well. Average prices for most selections run less than $5.00. Seating capacity of the grill is about 48 persons. This facility is very clean. Guests can see the airplanes from the restaurant and there is a small outdoor patio adjacent to the dining area as well. Meals can be prepared-to-go if requested. Fly-in or catering services is another service available through the windsock Grill. Advanced notice is prefered. During our conversation we learned that the owners of this restaurant may relocate to the downtown distric. They informed us that they would be happy tfurnish courtesy transportation to and from their restaurant and the airport. For additional information call the Windsock Grill at 849-1221.

Lodging: Flag Ship Inn (8-10 miles) 297-3031; Hilton (Brazosport, 10 miles) 297-1161; La Quinta Motor Inn (10 miles) 265-7461.
Meeting Rooms: Flag Ship Inn 297-3031; Hilton (Brazosport) 297-1161; La Quinta Motor Inn 265-7461.
Transportation: Taxi Service: AAA Taxi 849-5400; Rental Cars: Budget 265-5955; Enterprize 265-0088; Super Star 265-0911.
Information: Chamber of Commerce, 455 East Mulberry, Box 1356, Angleton, TX 77515, Phone: 849-6443.

Attractions:

Columbia Lakes Resort, located approx. 8 miles west of town, (Airport transportation available) also 18 hole golf course, tennis, swimming pools, entertainment, meeting rooms, boat rental, all located on 1,200 acres of private property including their own private heliport on the premises. Cottages with 2 bedrooms available. For information call 345-5151.

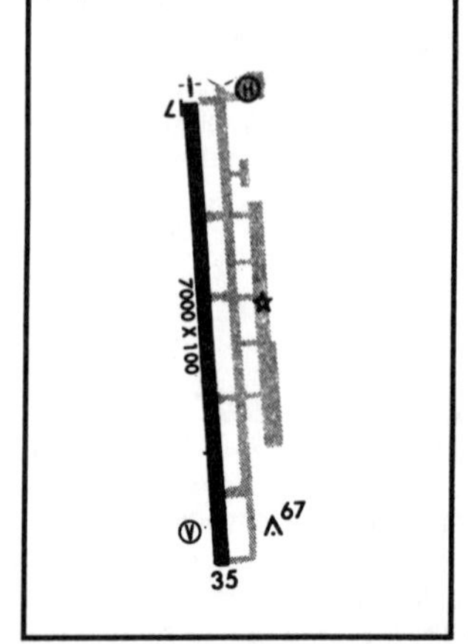

Airport Information:

ANGLETON/LAKE JACKSON - BRAZORIA COUNTY AIRPORT (LBX)
4 mi southwest of town N29-06.60 W95-27.72 Elev: 25 Fuel: 100LL, Jet-A
Rwy 17-35: H7000x100 (Asph-Grvd) Attended: Mon-Fri, 1330-2300Z, Sat-Sun 1400-0000Z
Unicom: 123.0
Brazoria County Airport Phone: 849-5755
FBO: Eagle Air Service Phone: 848-8000

TX-F54 - ARLINGTON
ARLINGTON MUNICIPAL ARPT.

(Area Code Arlington 817 Grand Prairie 214) 7

Wings Restaurant:

The Wings Restaurant is located in the terminal building at the Arlington Municipal Airport. This restaurant is open for business 8 a.m. to 5 p.m. Monday through Saturday. Selections on their menu include full selection of breakfast, lunch and dinner items. A carry out menu is also available. This facility has expanded in size as well as in menu choices. Their dining room can accommodate up to 60 persons. Guests can also enjoy watching the airport activity from the restaurant. Carry-out meals can be prepared if requested. For information call the Wings Restaurant at 465-2188.

Attraction:

Six Flags Over Texas 817-640-8900; Wet & Wild 265-3013; Ranger Station 817-273-5000; Nearby restaurant district is located 5 to 6 miles directly north. Also Wax Museum & wildlife park in nearby Grand Prairie approximately 10 miles northeast of airport.

Restaurants Near Airport:

Wings Restaurant On Site Phone: 465-2188

Lodging: Hampton Inn (Free trans, Est. 1 mile) 214-988-8989; Hilton (Free trans) 817-640-3322; Holiday Inn (Free trans) Phone: 817-640-7712; Quality Inn Arlington Suite Hotel (Free trans) 817-640-4444; Radisson Suite (Free trans) 817-640-0440.

Meeting Rooms: Airport manager's office has a small conference room able to accommodate between 4-6 persons; Also Hampton Inn 214-467-3535; Holiday Inn 817-640-7712; Quality Inn Arlington Suite Hotel 817-640-4444; Radisson Suite 817-640-0440.

Transportation: None reported available at airport; Taxi Service: Super Cab 469-1110; Express Taxi 467-4445; Yellow Checker 534-5555; Rental Cars: Advantage 460-4011; Budget: 261-5531; Enterprise 467-5603; Thrifty: 265-6451.

Information: Arlington Convention & Visitors Bureau, 1250 East Copeland Road, Suite 650, Arlington, TX 76011, Phone: 817-265-7721.

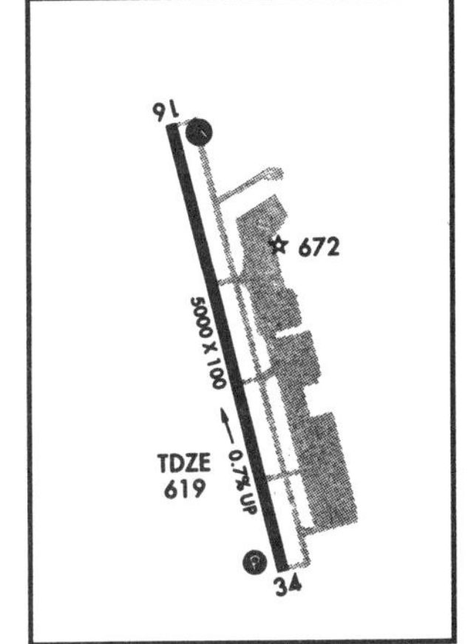

Airport Information:

ARLINGTON - ARLINGTON MUNICIPAL AIRPORT (F54)
4 mi south of town N32-39.75 W97-05.64 Elev: 631 Fuel: 100LL, Jet-A
Rwy 16-34: H5000x100 (Asph) Attended: continuously Unicom: 123.0 Public Phone 24hrs
Notes: No landing fees, parking: single $3.00/night; twin $6.00/night, first night free with fuel purchase.
Arlington Municipal Airport Phone: 817-465-2615 or 817-265-3311

TX-3R9 - AUSTIN
LAKEWAY AIRPARK

(Area Code 512) 8

Travis Dining Room (Lakway Resort):

The Travis Dining Room is situated within the Lakeway Resort. This resort has its own airstrip located about 1 mile from the Inn. Free transportation is provided to all resort guests. You can reach the Inn by taking Lakeway Blvd. from the airport to Lakeway Drive, turn left at the stop sign and follow Lakeway Drive to the end of the street. This will take you directly to Lakeway Inn. The restaurant is open from 7 a.m. to 10 p.m., with a Sunday brunch served between 11 a.m. and 2 p.m. Dinner entrees change daily with 6 to 12 freshly prepared entree choices. Lavish buffets, with soups, salads, appetizers and desserts are prepared, as well as breakfast and luncheon buffets. On Friday nights they have a fish fry with a seafood buffet. The decor of the restaurant has a Southwestern motif. The view from the restaurant provides a panoramic picture of Lake Travis and the Texas hill country. For information call 261-6600.

Restaurants Near Airport:

Lakeway Resort & Conf. Ctr.	1 mi	Phone: 261-7362
Live Oak Golf Snack Bar	1/2 mi	Phone: 261-7573
Travis Dining Room	1 mi	Phone: 261-6600
Yaupon Golf Snack Bar	In resort	Phone: 261-7572

Lodging: The Lakeway Inn and Conference Center, 101 Lakeway Drive, Lakeway, TX 78734, Phone: 261-7362 (Free Transportation)

Meeting Rooms: The Lakeway Inn and Conference Center has accommodations for large and small business groups. For information call 261-7362.

Transportation: Transportation to and from all resort amenities is provided free of charge. Rental cars are also available through Advantage Car Rental by calling 331-1276.

Information: Convention & Visitors Bereau, 201 East 2nd Street, Box 1088, Austin, TX 78767., Phone: 478-0098 or 800-888-8-AUS.

Attractions:

The Lakeway Resort and Conference Center is on the south side of Lake Travis and is located 1 mile from the Lakeway Airpark, and about 15 miles west of the city of Austin, Texas. This facility contains 5,500 acres of land with 3 championship golf courses, driving range, putting green, 3 swimming pools, water sports, charter boats, paddle boats, exercise rooms, a world class tennis school, and a full service marina. The resort has 138 rooms, some with kitchen units, fire places, private patios, balconies, and some town-houses as well. Airport transportation is provided by the resort as well as free courtesy transportation to anywhere on the resort property. For information call the resort at 261-6600.

Photo by: Lakeway Resort & Conference Center

Photo:
The Travis Room is a popular meeting place for celebrating special occasions. Elegant dining and surroundings are a perfect ending to a day at Lakeway.

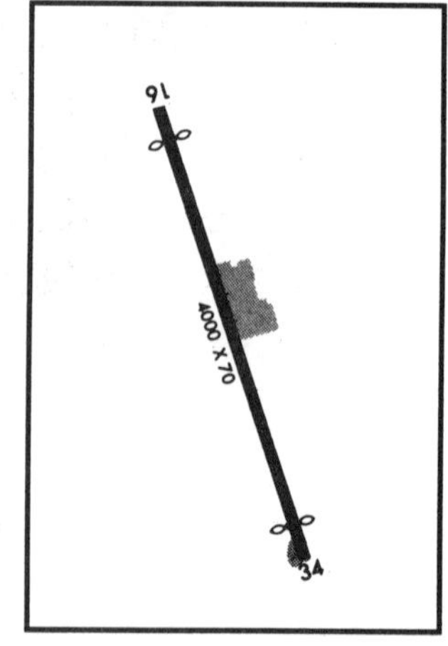

Airport Information:

AUSTIN - LAKEWAY AIRPARK (3R9)

17 mi west of town N30-21.48 W97-59.67 Elev: 905 Fuel: 100LL Rwy 16-34: H4000x70 (Asph) Attended: unattended Unicom: 123.0 Public Phone: 24hrs Notes: No landing fee, first night tiedown free with fuel purchase. After that $8.50 per night. Lakeway is in the middle of the resort.

FBO: Lakeway Airpark, Phone: 261-7250

TX-AUS - AUSTIN (Area Code 512) 9

ROBERT MUELLER MUNICIPAL AIRPORT

Host Marriott:

Host Marriott operates several food service facilities such as snack bar, cafe and cafeteria on the Robert Mueller Municipal Airport in Austin Texas. These facilities are open from 6 a.m. to 11 p.m. and serve a wide variety of foods. Average prices for the entrees in the cafe and cafeteria run about $6.50 for breakfast, $7.50 for lunch and $8.50 for dinner. Daily specials are also offered. If arranged in advance, they will prepare sandwich, vegetable, and cheese trays. Courtesy car transportation is available through Signature Flight Support by calling 426-5451. For information about dining services call 476-2729.

Airport Information:

AUSTIN - ROBERT MUELLER MUNICIPAL AIRPORT (AUS)
3 mi northeast of town 30-17-54N 97-42-05W Elev: 632 Fuel: 100LL, Jet-A Rwy 13R-31L: H7269x150 (Asph-Grvd) Rwy 17-35: H5006x150 (Asph-Grvd) 13L-31R: H3999x75 (Asph) Attended: continuously Atis: 119.2 Unicom: 123.0 App/Dep Con: 124.9, 119.0, 118.8, 118.15 Tower: 121.0 Gnd Con: 121.9 Clnc Del: 125.5 Notes: CAUTION: Airport underlies final approach Rwy 17 Bergstrom AFB.
FBO: Signature Flight Support Phone: 476-5451

Restaurants Near Airport:

Amaya's Toco Village	N/A	Phone: N/A
Host Marriott	On Site	Phone: 476-2729
Jade Fountain	2 mi	Phone; N/A
Pappadeaux	3 mi	Phone: N/A

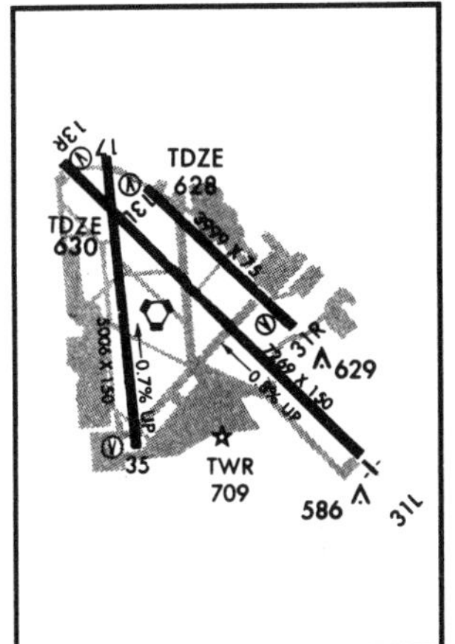

Lodging: (Free transportation by the following) Hotels: Driskill 474-5911; Embassy Suites 469-9000; Embassy Suites-Airport 454-8004 Guest Quarters 478-7000; Hyatt Regency 477-1234; Marriott At the Capitol 478-1111; Radisson Plaza 476-3700; Wyndham Southpark 448-2222; Motor Hotels: Holiday Inn-Townlake 472-8211; Howard Johnson-Austin South Plaza 448-2444.
Meeting Rooms: Howard Johnson-Austin South Plaza 448-4999; Driskill 474-5911; Embassy Suites 469-9000; Guest Quarters 478-7000; Wyndham Southpark 448-2222; Convention Facilities: Marriott At The Capitol 478-1111; Radisson Plaza 476-3700.
Transportation: Courtesy Car; Taxi: American Cab 452-999; Harlem Cab 472-2404; Yellow Checkers 472-1111; Carey Limousine Service 448-3492; Rental Cars: Avis 476-6137; Budget 478-6437; Dollar 480-0048; Hertz 478-9321; National 476-6189.
Information: Convention & Visitors Bereau, 201 East 2nd Street, Box 1088, Austin, TX 78767., Phone: 478-0098 or 800-888-8-AUS.

TX-BPT - BEAUMONT/PORT ARTHUR JEFFERSON COUNTY AIRPORT

(Area Code 409)

10, 11

Dorothy's Front Porch:

Dorothy's Front Porch Restaurant is located about 1-1/2 miles from the Jefferson County Airport. This restaurant is listed under fine dining, and includes such entrees as "Gumbo Fish", shrimp, oysters, barbecued crabs, chicken fried steak, appetizers, soups, freshly-made salad bar, and desserts as well as many other items on their menu. The restaurant overlooks, and is surrounded by, lakes. In fact, you can even feed the fish from their balcony. They are open Tuesday, Wednesday and Thursday from 11:00 a.m. to 9:00 p.m., Friday and Saturday from 11:00 a.m. to 9:30 p.m. and Sundays from 11:00 to 8:30 p.m. Average price for a meal runs $8.00 for lunch and dinner. Transportation is not furnished by the restaurant. However, Jefferson County Fuel Service will provide transportation by calling 722-9203. For information about Dorothy's Front Porch Restaurant call 722-1472.

The Pickle Barrel:

The Pickle Barrel is situated within the Jefferson County Airport Terminal Building. It is within walking distance from aircraft parking, according to the management. The restaurant is next to the luggage pickup area. This is a combination cafe and fine dining establishment. Hours of operation are Monday through Friday 5 a.m. to 7 p.m., and Saturday and Sunday 7 a.m. to 3 p.m. They offer a full service menu including steam table specials for lunch between 11 a.m. and 2 p.m. Breakfast is offered throughout the day. Homemade pies and cakes, shakes, icecream, fried pickles, homemade biscuits, breakfast specials and dinner specials are all available. They have won first place awards for their delicious chicken fried steaks and shrimp gumbo. Prices average $3.50 for breakfast, $4.95 for lunch and $7.00 for dinner. An all you can eat Sunday buffet is served between 11 a.m. and 3 p.m. The decor of the restaurant is contemporary and unique. They can cater up to 150 for groups. In-flight catering is available as they often serve special orders for private aircraft and corporate jets. For information about the Pickle Barrel call 722-1077.

Restaurant Near Airport:

Dorothy's Front Porch	1-1/2 mi NW.	Phone: 722-1472
Casa Ole	1-1/2 mi SE.	Phone: 727-5377
Golden Corral	1-1/2 mi SE.	Phone: 722-8476
Pickle Barrel Restaurant	Trml. Bldg.	Phone: 722-1077

Transportation:
Fuel Service Co. Car, Phone: 727-4045; Avis Rent A Car, Phone: 727-2137; Hertz Rent A Car, Phone: 727-2137; National Car Rental, Phone: 722-6111; Airport Limousine, Phone: 722-8313

Lodging: Park Central Holiday Inn, on Hwy. 69, 3 miles south, Phone: 724-5000, Beaumont Hilton, 842-3600, Holiday Inn Beaumont Plaza, 842-5995.

Information: Convention & Visitors Bureau, 801 Main, P.O. Box 3827, Beaumont, TX 77704.

Airport Information:

BEAUMONT/PORT ARTHUR - JEFFERSON COUNTY (BPT)

9 miles southeast of town, N29-57.05 W94-01.24 Elev: 16 Fuel: 100LL, Jet-A,
Rwy: 12-30 H6751x150 (Conc-Grvd) Rwy: 16-34 H5071x150 (Conc-Asph),
Attended: Continuously Tower: 119.5, Gnd Con: 121.9, Clnc Del: 121.75 Atis: 126.3 Unicom: 122.95 Beaumont App/Dep Con: 124.85, 121.3 Notes: Golf driving range located on Airport - 727-4045, Landing Fees 64 cents per 1,000 pounds/Parking Fee $6.00 Single, $11.00 Twin. Their fully equipped executive suite is available at no charge for use to work or relax, located in Aviation Terminal Building. (Day Bed, Television, etc.)
FBO: Jefferson County Fuel Service Phone: 722-9203, 722-0251

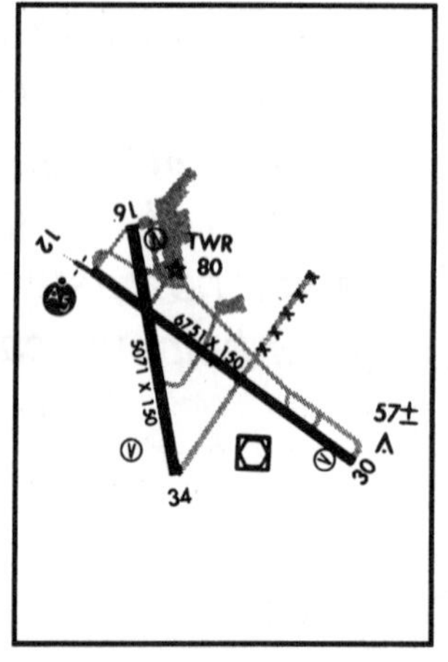

TX-BGD - BORGER
HUTCHINSON COUNTY AIRPORT

(Area Code 806)

12

Lorene's Mexican Kitchen:

The Lorene's Mexican Kitchen is down the street, and about a 1/4 mile walk from the Hutchinson County Airport. This restaurant is open between 5:30 a.m. and 9:00 p.m. This facility specializes in preparing Mexican dishes as well as Italian and American selections. Some of their entrees include steaks, chicken, lasagna, relleno's, and seafood. Luncheon specials are also offered. The restaurant can accommodate up to 100 persons in their main dining area and has recently been remodeled with a southwestern decor. Reservations for larger groups and parties are accepted. This establishment also contains a meeting room called the "Village Room" that can cater between 25 to 30 people. Meals can also be prepared for carry-out if requested. For more information call the restaurant at 273-7106.

Restaurants Near Airport:

Lorene's Mexican Kitchen	1/4 mi	Phone: 273-7106
Nu-Way Cafe	1-1/2 mi	Phone: 273-5321
Stephens Pit Bar-B-Que	1 mi	Phone: 273-6442
Sirloin Stockade	3/4 mi	Phone: 274-5880

Lodging: Travelodge (1-1/2 miles) 273-9556; Gate 1 Inn (3 miles) 273-9511.

Meeting Rooms: Travelodge 273-9556; Borger Chamber of Commerce 274-2211; Also Lorene's Mexican Kitchen can accommodate catered meeting's within their facility for 25-30 persons.

Transportation: City Cab Company 273-2211.

Information: Borger Chamber of Commerce, 613 North Main Street, Borger, TX 79008, Phone: 274-2211.

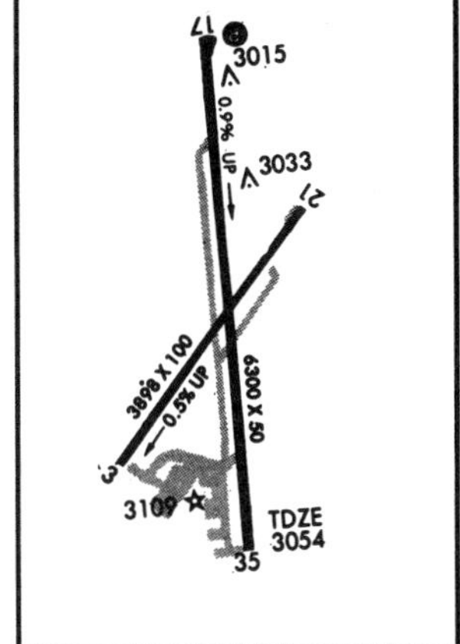

Airport Information:

BORGER - HUTCHINSON COUNTY AIRPORT (BGD)
2 mi north of town N35-42.00 W101-23.64 Elev: 3054 Fuel: 100LL, Jet-A+
Rwy 17-35: H6300x100 (Asph) Rwy 03-21: H3898x100 (Asph) Rwy 10-28: 2900x200 (Turf)
Attended: Mon-Fri 1300-0200Z, Sat-Sun 1400-0100Z Unicom: 123.0 Public Phone 24hrs
Notes: No landing or tiedown fees; hangar $5.00 - $8.00
FBO: Hutchinson County Airport (Fuel) Phone: 273-0137, 273-0138

TX-BMQ - BURNET
BURNET MUNICIPAL
KATE CRADDOCK FIELD

(Area Code 512) 13, 14

Highlander Inn:

The Highlander Inn is located 2 miles north of the airport. The Highlander Inn is an upscale family restaurant that will provide transportation for fly-in guests if they have available staff. Call to confirm. Restaurant hours are 6:30 a.m. to 9:30 p.m. 7 days a week. Specialties of the house are steaks, T-bone, shrimp, chicken, chicken fried steak, burgers, ribs, and linguine. Breakfast is served between 6:30 a.m. and 10:30 a.m. Average prices run $3.00 to $4.00 for breakfast, $6.00 for lunch and $10.00 to $15.00 for dinner. On Friday they provide a buffet between 11 a.m. and 2 p.m. Also on Fridays it's all-you-can-eat catfish served all day. The restaurant can seat 300 people and has several dining rooms in which to cater groups. The Highland Inn decor represents a cozy comfortable dining experience. Plaid table cloths with green napkins decorate each setting. For a truly enjoyable dining experience, try out the Highlander Inn next time you're in the Burnet, TX area. For information call them at 756-7401.

Riverwalk Cafe Restaurant:

The Riverwalk Restaurant is located about 1-1/2 mile from the Burnet Municipal Airport. Courtesy transportation is furnished by the restaurant. This combination cafe and family-style facility is open between 7 a.m. and 9 p.m. Tuesday through Saturday, and 7 a.m. to 2:30 p.m. on Sunday (Closed on Monday). The owner of the Riverwalk has a special interest in fly-in clientele due to the fact that he is an accomplished pilot himself. The menu selection is extensive and offers just about everything you might imagine. Some of the selections include: special homemade recipes for chicken, including grilled chicken breast, Mexican chicken, Fajita chicken, a River Walk Chicken plate or sandwich, BBQ'ed chicken, seafood dishes like stuffed crab or catfish, ribeye steaks, liver and onions, club sandwiches and freshly made bread. Breakfast entrees are served until 10:45 a.m. This is a family owned and operated restaurant, and the lady of the house makes some of the most delicious desserts around. Leave room for homemade pies like chocolate, lemon, coconut and peanut butter. Their main dining room can seat 118 persons and is nicely decorated in a cozy country like atmosphere with blue checkered table cloths. Catered meals with advanced notice can easily be arranged for up to 300 people. A separate private room able to hold up to 30 people can also be reserved for special functions. Next time you're in the Burnet area drop in for a fine meal at the Riverwalk Cafe where the motto of this restaurant states "Only in Burnet, Darn-it! For information call the restaurant at 756-4100.

Restaurants Near Airport:

Highlander Inn	2 mi N.	Phone: 756-7401
Riverwalk Cafe	1-1/2 mi.	Phone: 756-4100

Lodging: Arrowhead Motel 1 mile 756-2146; Ho Jo Inn 2 mi 756-4747; Sundown Motor Inn 1-1/2 mi 756-2171.

Meeting Rooms: Highlander Inn provides catering at their restaurant. Call 756-7401.

Transportation: Courtesy car is reported at airport. Also rental cars: Enterprise 690-8970.

Information: Burnet Chamber of Commerce, 705 Buchanan Drive, P.O. Drawer M, Burnet, TX 78611, Phone: 756-4297.

Attraction:

The Highland Lakes Air Museum is operated by the Highland Lakes Squadron which is an active chapter of the Confederate Air Force. Their museum is located right on the Burnet Municipal Kate Craddock Field (T27). A 100 by 125 foot hanger contains a number of rare and vintage aircraft on display including a restored P-40. For information call 756-2226.

Inks Lake State Park, (Approx. 9 miles SW of Burnet on Hwy 4) contains a 1,200 acre recreational area that provides many activities like golf, fishing, swimming, boating and camping. Phone: 793-2223; Longhorn Cavern State Park is located about 5 miles south of Burnet. (Est. 10-12 miles from airport). This park encompasses 639 acres and provides hiking, picnicking and a museum containing artifacts. The enormous cavern has 8 miles of lighted trails. Phone: 756-4680; Numerous golf courses within 25 mile radius.

Airport Information:

BURNET - BURNET MUNI KATE CRADDOCK FLD (BMQ)
1 mi southwest of town N30-44.34 W98-14.32 Elev: 1283 Fuel: 100LL, Jet-A
Rwy 01-19: H5000x75 (Asph) Attended 1300-0100Z for attendant after hours call 756-6655.
Public Phone 24 hrs Unicom: 122.8
FBO: Faulkner's Air Shop, Inc. Phone: 756-6655

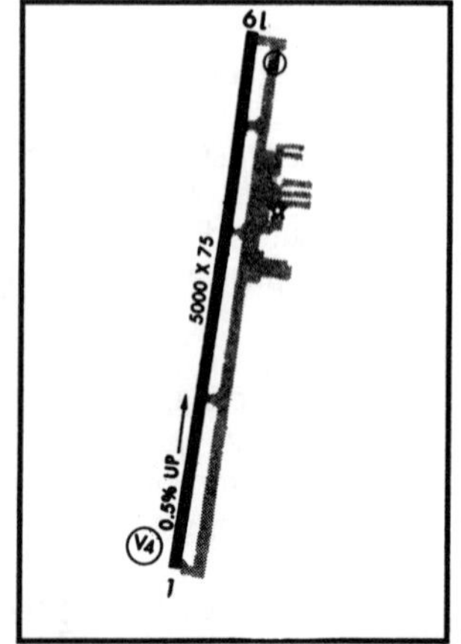

Highland Lakes Squadron Museum Confederate Air Force:

Burnet, TX (TX-BMQ)

The Highland Lakes Squadron is part of the Confederate Air Force, which has their main headquarters in Midland, Texas. The Highland Lakes Squadron Museum is on the Burnet Municipal Airport about 100 miles north of San Antonio, and 50 miles northwest of Austin, Texas. They have a 100 x 125 foot hangar that houses their planes, museum and offices. The museum hours are Saturday from 9 a.m. to 5 p.m., and Sunday noon to 5 p.m. Individuals or groups can request a tour. Some of the private aircraft on display is a P-38 Lightning; four PT-17 Stearmans; a PT-26 Fairchild; L-3 Aeronca; L-4 Piper; Staggerwing Beech; Waco; Curtis Robin; and two YAK-52's. Each year around the middle of April, the Highland Lakes Squadron in conjunction with the Burnet Bluebonnet Festival host an airshow along with other activities. Over forty warbirds take part. The M.A.T.S. Constellation and acts like Tora, Tora, Tora draw thousands. For information call 512-756-2226.

Photo by: Highland Lakes Squadron

P-38 Lightning on dispaly at the Bluebonnet Air.

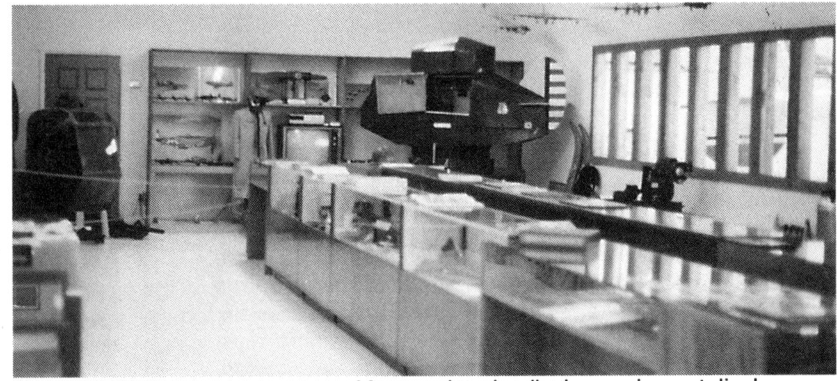

Photo by: Highland Lakes Squadron

Museum interior display equipment display room.

Promote General Aviation Just Take A Friend Flying

TX-CLL - COLLEGE STATION EASTERWOOD FIELD

(Area Code 409) 15

Remedies Restaurant:

On certain occasions you run across a particular restaurant that stands out apart from the run-of-the-mill eating establishments. Well, during our search, we believe we have found a truly unique restaurant that is situated conveniently across from the Easterwood Airport, 1/2 to 1 mile from the entrance. The owner of Remedies is a retired medical professional that has mastered the art of preparing some of the most unique European and American dishes. As a hobby he enjoys sharing his love for cooking with his customers. The meals change often with new creations offered. Dining is by reservation only with 4 to 10 day advance reservations required. Plan to enjoy an average of 3 to 4 hours of fine dining at its best. Once you have arrived your table is yours for the evening. There is one seating available only on Friday and Saturday nights between 6:30 p.m. and 8:30 p.m. and until 12:30 a.m. when the restaurant closes for the night. A 53-year-old mansion serves as the restaurant and is decorated with hardwood floors, Oriental carpets and elegant, yet quaint, furnishings. Place settings are arranged with the finest china and sterling along with fine crystal glasses and heavy linen table cloths. Your dining experience will begin with a first of 6-to 8-course meal ending with some of the most delicious desserts imaginable. Some of the entree choices include Chateau Briand of beef, pork tenderloin, tenderloin of chicken breast, Gulf Coast shrimp tails, steamed artichokes and wine and shrimp Wellington. Specially created sauces and gravies enhance your meal. Dinners are accompanied with vegetables that are purchased from nearby farmer fruit and vegetable stands in the area. No exceptions are made; only the best and freshest ingredients are used in all entrees. Seven-layer salads, Caesar and chef salads are prepared. Potato flour yeast roll or Italian bread sticks accompany your meal. As a final touch, dessert sto kill for are offered, like chocolate carrot cheese cake, the "Incredible Chocolate Experience" or French Silk Pie and finely fresh fruit dessert . Beverages to select from include 4 different gourmet coffees, 6 different teas. Alcoholic beverages are also available, like domestic as well as imported beers and wines. There is no doubt that the owner and chef of this establishment truly loves to cook. For a meal and experience of such elegance and taste one might expect to pay a great deal. However prices are extraordinarily reasonable. Main selections run between $16.50 and $30.00. Prices include everything except alcoholic beverages. Casual dress is appropriate. For more information about Remedies Restaurant or scheduling reservations call 260-1476.

Restaurants Near Airport:
Remedies Restaurant 1/2 to 1 mi. Phone: 260-1476

Lodging: Comfort Inn (Trans) 846-7333; Hampton Inn (Trans) 846-0184; La Quinta (Trans) 696-7777; Manor House (Free trans) 764-9540; Hilton College Station (Free trans) 693-7500; Holiday Inn (Free trans) 693-1736; Ramada Inn (Free trans) 693-9891.

Meeting Rooms: Comfort Inn 846-7333; Hampton Inn 846-0184; La Quinta 696-7777; Manor House 764-9540; Hilton College Station 693-7500; Holiday Inn 693-1736; Ramada Inn 693-9891.

Transportation: Avis 846-9007; Budget 268-8908; Hertz 846-8337.

Information: Bryan/College Station Convention & Visitors Bureau, 715 University Drive East, College Station, TX 77840, Phone: 260-9898 or 800-777-8292.

Airport Information:

COLLEGE STATION - EASTERWOOD FIELD (CLL)
3 mi southwest of town N30-35.32 W96-21.83 Elev: 320 Fuel: 100LL, Jet-A
Rwy 16-34: H7000x150 (Asph-Conc-Grvd) Rwy 10-28: H5160x150 (Asph)
Rwy 04-22: H5149x150 (Conc) Attended: 1200-0400Z Atis: 126.85 Unicom: 122.95
Tower: 118.5 Gnd Con: 121.7
FBO: Easterwood Airport Operations Phone: 845-4811

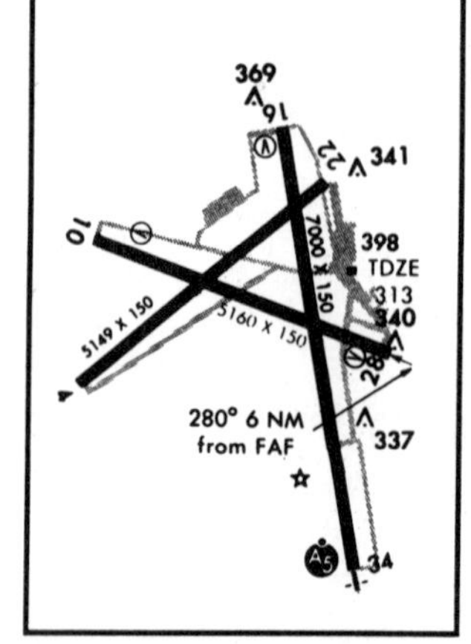

Not to be used for navigational purposes

TX-CRP - CORPUS CHRISTI
CORPUS CHRISTI INTERNATIONAL

(Area Code 512)

16, 17

Flight Bites:

This restaurant is located on the Corpus Christi Airport. We were told that fly-in guests enter the security building entrance way which will take you to the terminal building. This restaurant is open 6 a.m. to 10 p.m., 7 days a week. There is seating for about 100 customers. Menu selections include hamburgers, pizzas, sandwiches, salads, hotdogs, stuffed potatoes, bread sticks, chicken wings, nachos and a variety of beverages such as coffee, beer and wine. From the restaurant you can see the activity on the airport. Flightline catering is available to quick turn-around fly-in corporate and private pilots and their passengers. For information call 289-6967.

Republic of Texas (Omni Bayfront):

This restaurant is located on the 20th floor of the Omni Bayfront Hotel in downtown Corpus Christi, 6 miles southeast of the International Airport. Courtesy transportation is available either by the hotel or the FBO at the airport. The view from this restaurant offers a bird's eye view of the Corpus Christi area. This elegant restaurant specializes in steak selections from their four course menu. They feature 4 kinds of catches every day. Salads are prepared table-side. Daily specials are also available for the guests. Dress code is casual, no ties or coats are required. Restaurant hours are Tuesday through Saturday from 5:30 p.m. to 10:30 p.m. Average prices run about $20.00 per selection. For information call 887-1600.

Restaurants Near Airport:

Flight Bites	Trml Bldg	Phone: 289-6967
Holiday Inn	3 mi SE	Phone: 289-5100
Republic of Texas	6 mi SE	Phone: 887-1600
Wyndham Hotel	6 mi SE	Phone: 887-1600

Lodging: Courtesy cars to all major hotels. Direct phone lines in reservation center bag claim area in terminal: Airport Holiday Inn (courtesy car, 3 miles SE) 289-5100; Omni Bayfront Hotel (courtesy car, 6 miles SE) 887-1600; Wyndham Hotel (courtesy car, 6 miles SE) 887-1600.

Meeting Rooms: Conference facilities are available at hotels listed under "Lodging" See above listing.

Transportation: Both FBO's: Hedrick Beechcraft and Van Dusen have courtesy transportation available for their customers. In addition, taxi and rental cars are available at the airport. Airport Limo Service 289-0191; Checker Yellow 884-3211; Pinkies Taxi 881-5250; Hertz (In terminal) 289-0777; Avis (In terminal) 289-0073; Budget (In terminal) 289-0434;

Information: Greater Corpus Christi Convention & Visitor's Bureau, P.O. Box 2664, 1201 N. Shoreline Drive, Corpus Christi, TX 78403, Phone: 881-5603 or 800-678-6232 or 800-766-2322.

Attractions:

Transform your next meeting or family vacation into a tropical adventure in Corpus Christi...the Isles of Texas! From fishing and golfing to tennis, sailing and more, Corpus Christi is a year-round sports paradise. Corpus Christi International Airport is only minutes away from a wide variety of exciting activities waiting to be discovered! Explore over 130 miles of beautiful gulf beaches. Dive into fun at the **Texas State Aquarium,** located along seven miles of beautiful gulf coast, just northeast of the airport. From the beautiful Flower Gardens Coral Reef to the Island of Steel, you'll be sea deep in fun! Touch a shark, laugh with playful river otters or go nose to nose with endangered sea turtles. For more information, call 1-800-477-GULF. And don't forget the famous ships! All aboard the **USS Lexington,** the most decorated aircraft carrier in U.S. Naval history. Explore multiple areas of the ship, including the flight deck, engine room, captain's quarters and more. Test your wings in the exhilarating Flight Simulator. For more information on the Lexington, located seven miles northeast of the airport, call 1-800-LADY-LEX. And just across the harbor, embark on a Voyage of Discovery aboard the **Nina, Pinta and Santa Maria,** life size reproductions of Christopher Columbus' ships. Learn more about Columbus' voyages next door at the **Corpus Christi Museum of Science and History.** Both the science museum and Columbus ships are six miles northeast of the airport. For more information, call 512-886-4492.

Photo by: Omni Bayfront - Republic of Texas Bar & Grill

Airport Information:

CORPUS CHRISTI - CORPUS CHRISTI INTERNATIONAL (CRP)

5 mi west of town N27-46.22 W97-30.07 Elev: 44 Fuel: 100LL, Jet A, B Rwy 13-31: H7508x150 (Asph-Grvd) Rwy 17-35: H6081x150 (Asph-Grvd) Attended: Continuously Atis: 126.8 Unicom: 122.95 Tower: 119.4 Gnd Con: 121.9 Clnc Del: 118.55 Public Phone: 24hrs Notes: Private & corporate no landing fee; Overnight $3.00 to $10 depending on size.

FBO: Raytheon Aircraft Serv. Phone: 289-1881 or 800-628-2978.

Republic of Texas (20th Floor of the Omni Bayfront Hotel). With a breathtaking view of the city from their spacious rooftop restaurant, makes any evening a special occasion with dinner elegantly prepared.

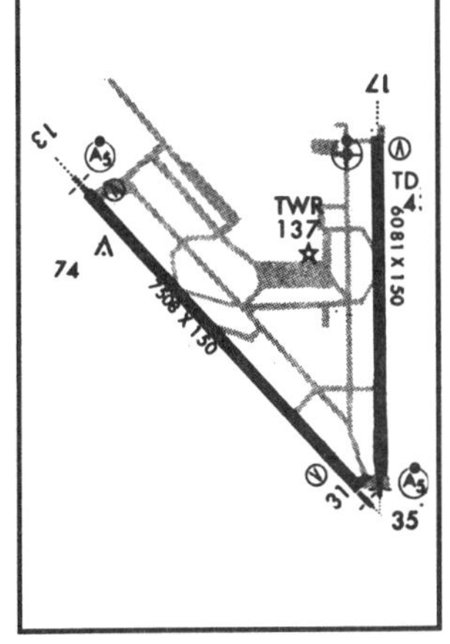

TX-DHT - DALHART
DALHART MUNICIPAL AIRPORT

(Area Code 806) 18

Ingram Flying Service Airport Cafe:

The Airport Cafe is located about 500 feet from the Ingram Flying Service (FBO). This restaurant is open 7 days a week between 9 a.m. and 5 p.m. during the winter, and from 8 a.m. to 6 p.m. during the summer months. Their menu offers homemade soups and sandwiches and daily lunch specials. Average prices run $2.50 for breakfast, $2.95 for lunch and $4.95 for dinner. The dining area can seat 20 persons with 8 counter stools and 6 or 7 booths. Guests can see the aircraft from the restaurant. During our conversation, we learned that they are visited regularly by military helicopter crews that fly into the airport. Menu items can also be prepared for carry-out if requested. For more information call 249-5521.

Restaurants Near Airport:
Ingram Flying Serv. Arpt. Cafe On Site Phone: 249-5521

Lodging: Comfort Inn (Arpt Trans) 249-8585; Travelers Inn (3 miles) 249-4501; Best Western Skies (4 miles, Arpt trans) 249-4538.

Meeting Rooms: Best Western Skies 249-4538.

Transportation: U-Save Auto Rental 249-6768 or 249-6270.

Information: Chamber of Commerce, 102 East 7th Street, P.O. Box 967, Dalhart, TX 79022, Phone: 249-5646.

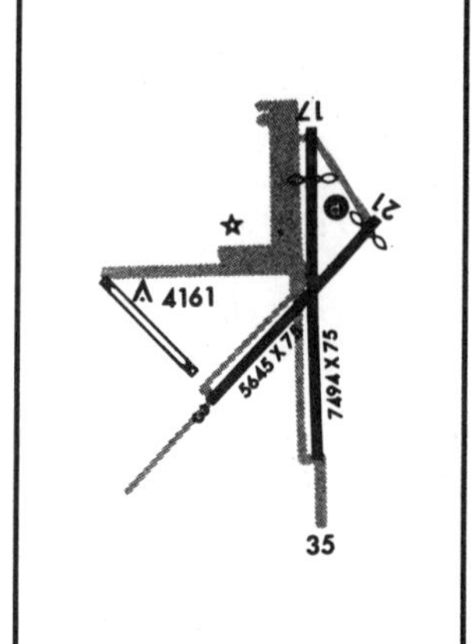

Airport Information:

DALHART - DALHART MUNICIPAL AIRPORT (DHT)
3 mi southwest of town N36-01.35 W102-32.84 Elev: 3989 Fuel: 100LL, Jet-A1
Rwy 17-35: H7494x75 (Asph) Rwy 03-21: H5420x75 (Asph) Attended: dawn-dusk
Unicom: 122.95
FBO: Ingram Flying Service, Inc. Phone: 249-5521

TX-DAL - DALLAS
DALLAS LOVE FIELD

(Area Code 214) 19

Airport Cafe:

The Airport Cafe is located within the main lobby of the terminal building at the Dallas Love Airport. The snack bar is open 7 days a week between 7 a.m. and 8:30 p.m. Items offered on their menu consists mainly of southwestern dishes including enchilada, tacos, and barritos. They also serve a breakfast line as well as lunch items like hamburgers, cheeseburgers, and a variety of salads. Daily specials are also offered. This cafe can seat approx. 50 people. Meals can be prepared to go if requested. Business men can arrange catered meals and make use of two city conference rooms available within the terminal building. On the upper level there are three additional food service establishments including a small snack bar, buffeteria that can seat 20 or 30 people as well as a pizza unit. For information about the Airport Cafe, call 358-1910.

Restaurants Near Airport:

Airport Cafe	Adj Arpt	Phone: 358-1910
Associated Air Center	Adj Arpt	Phone: 350-4111
Aviall Cafeteria	Adj Arpt	Phone: 956-5400
Citijet Cafeteria	Adj Arpt	Phone: 956-1000

Lodging: Clarion Hotel 630-7000; Embassy Suites (Trans) 357-4500; Executive Inn & Conference Center (Trans) 357-5601; Hilton-Dallas Central (Trans) 827-4100; Holiday Inn Brook Hollow (Trans) 630-8500; La Quinta Motor Inn-Regal (Trans) 630-5701; Radisson Hotel-Stemmons (Trans) 351-4477; Ramada-Love Fld. 357-5601; Rodeway Inn-Love Field (Trans) 357-1701; Sheraton Inn-Mockingbird (Trans) 634-8850.
Meeting Rooms: There are 2 city conference rooms available in the main terminal building. All facilities listed above also have accommodations for meeting rooms.
Transportation: Taxi Service available; Rental car service: Avis: 869-2400; Budget 357-1576; Dollar 357-8422; General 399-0900; Hertz: 350-7071; National 352-2413.
Information: Dallas Convention & Visitors Bureau, 1303 Commerce, Dallas, TX 75270, Phone: 746-6679; Also, Terminal Lobby, at Love Field.

Airport Information:

DALLAS - DALLAS LOVE FIELD (DAL)
5 mi northwest of town N32-50.83 W96-51.11 Elev: 487 Fuel: 100LL, Jet-A
Rwy 13R-31L: H8800x150 (Conc) Rwy 13L-31R: H7753x150 (Asph-Grvd)
Rwy 18-36: H6149x150 (Asph) Attended: continuously Atis: 120.15 Unicom: 122.95
Regional App Con: 125.2 (south), 124.3 (north) Love Tower: 123.7, 118.7 Gnd Con: 121.75
Clnc Del: 127.9 Regional Dep Con: 118.55
FBO: AMR Combs Phone: 956-1000, 800-248-4538
FBO: Assoc. Air Cntr. Phone: 350-4111
FBO: Dalfort Aviation Phone: 352-2634
FBO: Dallas Airmotive, Inc. Phone: 353-7000
FBO: Dallas Jet Center Phone: 350-4061
FBO: Jet East, Inc. Phone: 350-8523

Cavanaugh Flight Museum

Addison Airport, Dallas, TX (TX-ADS)

The Cavanaugh Flight Museum encompasses nearly 50,000 square feet of display area and is located on the grounds of the Addison Airport, only minutes from downtown Dallas, or the Dallas-Fort Worth International Airport. The Cavanaugh Flight Museum collects, maintains and flies some of the rarest and most important military aircraft ever produced. First opened in October 1993, the museum is the product of the hard work and financial support of Jim Cavanaugh, creator of Jani-King International, a commercial janitorial services company. Mr. Cavanaugh, a lifelong military aviation enthusiast, purchased his first warbird, a PT-19 Cornell trainer, in 1989. Since then he has added more than thirty aircraft to his collection.

Many of the aircraft have been painstakingly restored to their original, factory-fresh condition and fly today over Dallas as they did over Europe and the Pacific years ago to defend the freedoms that we all enjoy today. The Cavanaugh Flight Museum's collection ranges from replicas of a World War I Fokker D. VIIa and Sopwith Camel, to a Vietnam era McDonnell Douglas F-4C Phantom II, to the Gossamer Penguin, the first manned aircraft to be driven by solar power alone.

The museum has just completed the restoration of a F9F-2B Panther, a U.S. Navy and Marine Corps jet fighter/bomber used during the late 1940s and early 1950s. The museum's Panther is a combat veteran of the Korean War and is the last flying example of its king. The restoration of the museum's B-25J, named "How 'Boot That!?", was also recently completed. This aircraft flew more than 80 combat missions over Italy during World War II and is the most original B-25 flying today. Both the F9F-2B Panther and B-25J have won Grand Champion Warbird at the Experimental Aircraft Association (E.A.A.) Fly-In held in Oshkosh, Wisconsin and the E.A.A. Sun'n Fun Fly-In at Lakeland, Florida.

The Cavanaugh Flight Museum is constantly expanding and exploring new areas of aviation history. The museum houses one of the largest collections of signed aviation artwork in the state of Texas and continues to collect and display historic artifacts which relay the fascinating story of American air power. The museum has a thriving volunteer corps and has recently started a membership program. Through the dedication of Jim Cavanaugh and the museum's staff, the Cavanaugh Flight Museum has become one of the fastest growing aviation museums in the country and will continue to bring America's rich military heritage to life in the skies over north Texas.

Museum hours are Monday through Saturday 9 a.m. to 5 p.m., and Sunday 11 a.m. to 5 p.m. Admission: Adults $5.50, Children ages 6 to 12 $2.75, under 5 years of age admission is free.

The museum is conveniently located right on the Addison Airport. For more information about the museum call 214-380-8800.

TX-DFW - DALLAS FORT WORTH INTL. AIRPORT

20

Host Marriott & Airport Concessions:

Many food service facilities are located within the Dallas Fort Worth International Airport Terminal Building such as snack bars, cafes, cafeterias, and family style restaurants. These facilities offer a wide variety of foods for the air traveler in traditional fare. Prices vary at each facility and cannot be generalized. There are services available 24 hours a day. Host Marriott operates the Burger King and Chili's Restaurants. Additional food service facilities like TGI Fridays and other eateries are operated by individual companies. For information call the airport managers office at 574-3112 or Host Marriott at 574-5601.

Airport Information:

DALLAS - FORT WORTH INTERNATIONAL AIRPORT (DFW) (See Airport Facility Directory For Information)

12 mi northwest of town 32-53-47N 97-02-28W Elev: 603 Fuel: 100LL, Jet-A Attended: continuously Public Phone 24hrs Rwy 17L-35R: H11388x150 (Conc-Grvd) Rwy 17R-35L: H11388x200 (Conc-Grvd) Rwy 18R-36L: H11388x150 (Conc-Grvd) Rwy 18L-36R: H11387x200 (Conc-Grvd) Rwy 13R-31L: H9300x150 (Conc-Grvd) Rwy 13L-31R: H9000x200 (Conc-Grvd) Rwy 18S-36S: H4000x100 (Conc) Notes: CAUTION: Check AFD for current restrictions for general aviation aircraft. "Prior Permission required from airport ops. for general aviation aircraft to proceed to airline terminal gate except to general aviation facility. No General Aviation Facility At Airport, Only Drop Off Area For Transient Passengers. (Airport Manager's Office, 574-3112)

FBO: NONE REPORTED

Restaurants Near Airport: **(Area Code 214)**

Host Marriott Restaurants On Site Phone: 574-5601

Restaurant at many area hotels listed below (See Lodging)

Lodging: (All Within 3 Miles Of Airport): *Motels:* Amerisuites 790-1950; Drury Inn 986-1200; LaQuinta DFW-Irving 252-6546; Lexington Hotel Suite-DFW North 929-4008; Ramada Inn-DFW Airport South 399-2005; *Motor Hotels:* Harvey Suites 929-4499; Holiday Inn-DFW Airport South 399-1010; *Hotels:* Embassy Suites 790-0093; Harvey-DFW Airport 929-4500; Hilton DFW Executive Conference Center 481-8444; Hyatt Regency-DFW 453-1234; Marriott-DFW Airport 929-8800; Sheraton Grand-DFW 929-8400; Wilson World 513-0800.

Meeting Rooms: Convention Facilities at the following facilities: Harvey-DFW Airport; Hilton DFW Executive Conference Center; Hyatt Regency-DFW Marriott-DFW Airport; Sheraton Grand-DFW; All the rest listed above have meeting room accommodations as well. (See Lodging for phone numbers).

Transportation: Free shuttle service provided by most lodging facilities listed above. Taxi: American Cab 451-0444; Carey Limousine 638-4828; Taxi Dallas 634-0661; Terminal Cab 350-4445; Yellow Cab 565-9132; Yellow Checker 534-7777; Car Rental: Avis 574-4110; Budget 574-4121; Hertz 574-2010; National 574-3400.

Information: Dallas Convention & Visitors Bureau, 1303 Commerce, Dallas, TX 75270, Phone: 746-6679.

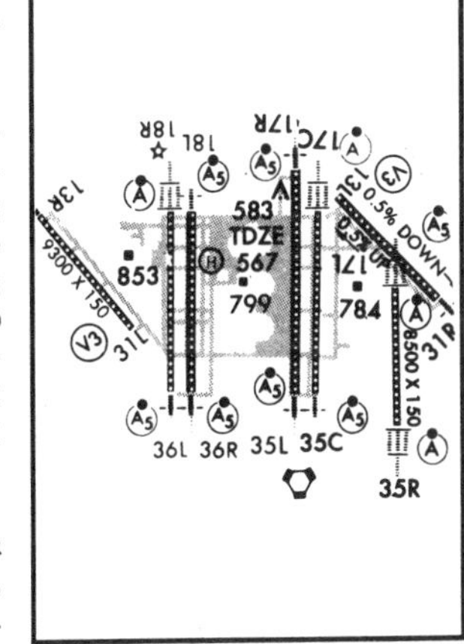

Frontiers of Flight Museum

Love Field, Dallas, TX (TX-DAL)

The Frontiers of Flight Museum contains a history of aviation collections located on Love Field, Dallas Texas, and is dedicated to commemorating the pioneers, their achievements and the aircraft involved in the development of aviation. A collection of rare artifacts including giant propellers from transoceanic airships...a piece of the original fabric from the Wright Flyer... charred remnants of the ill-fated Hindenburg... hundreds of priceless documents... photographs, and models illustrating how flying has changed the world, are all available for inspection. Admission to the museum is $2.00 for adults, and $1.00 for children under 12 years of age. The Frontiers of Flight Museum is located in the terminal building on the airport. Tour guides are on duty, as well as accommodations for groups up to 100 people. Their hours are 10:00 a.m. to 5:00 p.m. Monday through Saturday, and 1:00 p.m. to 5:00 p.m. on Sunday. If you are interested in scheduling a group tour call 214-350-1651. For information about the museum call 214-350-3600.

The Jet Era
Air Transportation
Women in Aviation
World War II
Business Aviation
The Air Ship Era 1900-1937
Space
Aviation Opportunities
The Golden Age
World War I
Gift Shop
Early Concepts of Flight
Entrance

Floor plan layout of the Frontiers of Flight Museum.(Information submitted by museum)

TX-RBD - DALLAS REDBIRD AIRPORT

21

Redbird Restaurant:

The Redbird Restaurant is situated on the Redbird Airport within easy walking distance to nearby aircraft parking ramps. This fine dining establishment is open 6 days a week between 8:30 a.m. and 9 p.m. On Sunday the restaurant is reported to be closed. However, a bar located on the premises remains open. Their menu contains specialties like chicken fried steaks, New York strip steaks, T-Bone steaks, pork chops, German dishes like Wieners schnitzel, soup of the day and house salads. Daily specials are offered as well. The dining room has a very open and airy atmosphere and can seat approx. 50 persons while providing a nice view of the airport and runways. Meals can also be prepared-to-go if requested. In-flight catering is another service available through the Redbird Restaurant. To contact this restaurant, call 337-0477.

(Area Code 214)

Restaurants Near Airport:

Milano's Rest.	3 mi N.	Phone: 709-7123
Redbird Rest.	On Site	Phone: 337-0477
Rudolpho's Rest.	5 mi N.	Phone: 942-1211
Steak & Ale	3 mi N.	Phone: 296-9923

Lodging: Adolphus Hotel 742-8200; Hampton Inn 298-4040; Holiday Inn (Trans) 224-9100; Holiday Inn (Duncanville, 4 mi, Free Trans with prior notice) 298-8911; La Quinta (2 miles) 339-3121; Cliff Inn (2 miles) 375-2511; Lexington Hotel 298-7014.
Meeting Rooms: Adolphus Hotel 742-8200; Holiday Inn 224-9100; Holiday Inn-Duncanville 298-8911; Lexington Hotel 298-7014.
Transportation: FBO courtesy van available; also Taxi Service: Yellow Cab 426-6262; Terminal Cab 350-4445; Taxi Dallas 631-8588; Rental Cars: Redbird 331-1503; Servion 339-2221.
Information: Dallas Convention & Visitors Bureau, 1303 Commerce, Dallas, TX 75270, Phone: 746-6679.

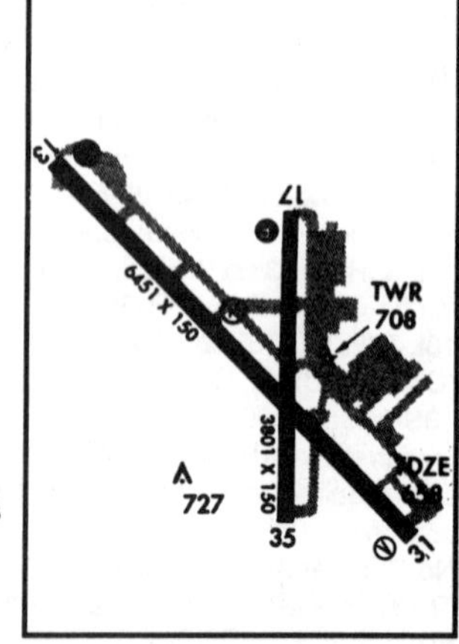

Attractions:

Joe Pool Lake, 10 miles SW; Six Flags Over Texas, 10 mi NW; Wet-N-Wild, 10 mi NW.

Airport Information:

DALLAS - REDBIRD AIRPORT (RBD)
6 mi southwest of town N32-40.85 W96-52.09 Elev: 660 Fuel: 100LL, Jet-A
Rwy 13-31: H6452x150 (Conc) Rwy 17-35: H3801x150 (Conc) Attended: 1230-0330Z
Atis: 126.35 Unicom: 122.95 Tower: 120.3 Gnd Con: 121.7 Clnc Del: 125.45
Regional App Con: 123.9 Regional Dep Con: 125.2 Public Phone 24hrs Notes: No landing fees - No parking fees with fuel purchase.
FBO: Dallas Executive Aviation Phone: 331-1199
FBO: Tri-Star Aircraft Phone: 331-5737

TX-8F7 - DECATUR
DECATUR MUNICIPAL

(Area Code 817)

22

Mattie's On The Square:

Mattie's On The Square is located near the center of town about 1 mile north-northeast from the Court House within historic Decatur. Transportation to and from the airport is provided by the restaurant. This family restaurant is very popular with many pilots. A daily buffet attracts people from all over. A Breakfast Buffet is served on Saturday from 7 a.m. to 2 p.m.; Lunch Buffet Monday through Friday from 11 a.m. to 2 p.m. and an evening seafood dinner buffet Friday and Saturday from 5 p.m. to 9 p.m. To give you an idea of how extensive the buffets are: the lunch buffet features at least three different meats, vegetables, a salad bar, hot rolls and desserts. Specialties include her mouth-watering chicken fried steak, chicken fried boneless chicken, meatloaf, grilled chicken, fried catfish, grilled fish, spaghetti and a marvelous Mexican spread! The Sunday buffet runs $5.95, and the Friday and Saturday seafood buffet costs about $10.95. Mattie's Restaurant hours are Monday through Thursday from 7 a.m. to 3 p.m., Friday and Saturday from 7 a.m. to 9 p.m. After enjoying a fine meal at Mattie's you can stroll around the historic downtown district where antique shops abound, or visit the County Museum. For information call the restaurant at 627-1522.

Restaurants Near Airport:
Mattie's On The Square 2 mi. Phone: 627-1522

Lodging: Best Western 3 mi 627-5982; Comfort Inn 3 mi 627-6919.

Meeting Rooms: Mattie's On The Square has accommodation for groups. For information call 627-1522.

Transportation: Courtesy transportation is available to Mattie's customers by calling 627-1522. Also rental cars can be arranged through Enterprise Car Rental at 627-8180.

Information: Denton Convention & Visitors Bureau, 414 Parkway Street, P.O. Drawer P, Denton, TX 76202, Phone: 382-7895.

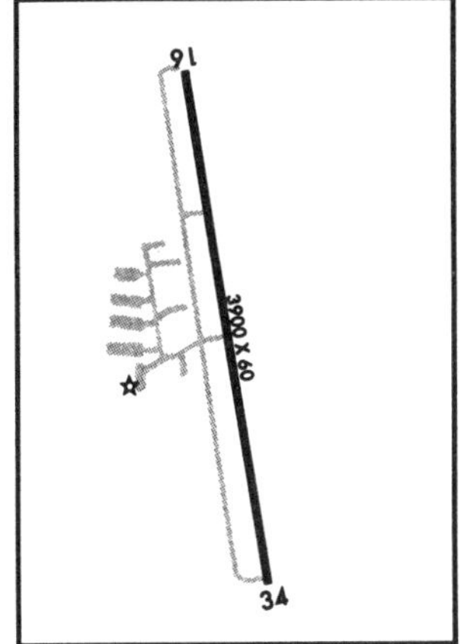

Airport Information:

DECATUR - DECATUR MUNICIPAL (8F7)
2 mi north of town N33-15.28 WW97-34.83 Elev: 1047 Fuel: 100LL, Jet-A Rwy 16-34: H3900x75 (Asph) Attended: 1300-2300Z Unicom: 122.8
FBO: City of Decatur Phone: 627-3342 or 627-9393
FBO: Wise Flying Service Phone: 627-1118

TX-24R - DILLEY
DILLEY AIRPARK

(Area Code 210)

23

Dilley Dairy Queen:

The Dilley Dairy Queen Restaurant is located just behind the Dilley Airpark and is easily accessible by walking. This family style, combination fast food restaurant is open from 7:00 a.m. to 10 p.m. Some of the specialty items on the menu include their popular "Hunger Buster" hamburgers, chicken baskets, steak fingers, taco salads and of course many delicious ice cream products including their famous banana splits. This brand new establishment can seat 75-100 persons in their main dining area. Tables, booths and a soda fountain make up the seating accommodations for this facility. Groups and fly-in parties are always welcome. Meals prepared-to-go is no problem for the Dilley Dairy Queen. For more information call the restaurant at 965-1833.

Restaurants Near Airport:

Dilley Dairy Queen	On Site	Phone: 965-1833
Dilley Hotel B & B	2 mi E.	Phone: 965-1915
Garcia's Cafe	1/2 mi E.	Phone: 965-1127
Pacho Garcia Cafe	1/2 mi E.	Phone: 965-1493

Lodging: Papa's Motel & Restaurant (1 mile south) 965-1521; Safari Motel (1/2 mile north) 965-1541.

Meeting Rooms: None Reported

Transportation: (FBO) Dillards of Dilley, Inc. D.D.I. can furnish courtesy transportation if requested in advance. Also Pipes Chevrolet has rental cars available, Phone: 965-1661.

Information: San Antonio Convention & Visitors Bureau, P.O. Box 2277, San Antonio, TX 78298, Phone: 210-270-8700 or 800-447-3372.

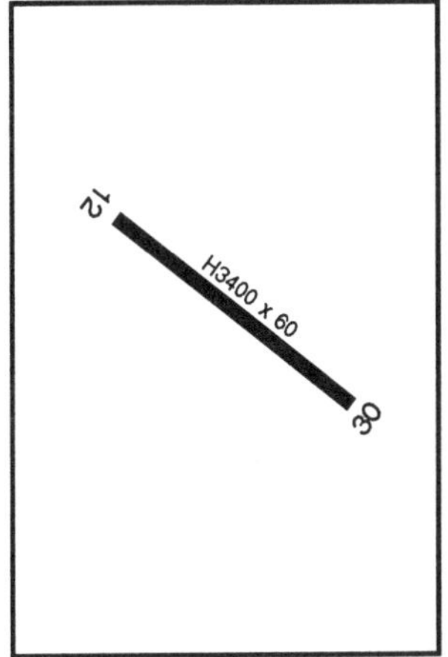

Airport Information:

DILLEY - DILLEY AIRPARK (24R)
2 mi northwest of town N28-41.13 W99-11.35 Elev: 542 Fuel: 100LL
Rwy 12-30: H3400x60 (Asph) Attended: Mon-Fri 1400-2300Z CTAF: 122.9
Notes: No public phone on property, Fuel & Tiedown is available on site.
FBO: Dillards of Dilley (D.D.I.) Phone: 965-1414

TX-EGP - EAGLE PASS
EAGLE PASS MUNICIPAL AIRPORT

(Area Code 210)

24

Charcoal Grill:

The Charcoal Grill is located within a nearby shopping mall about 2 blocks from the Eagle Pass Municipal Airport. This combination family style and fine dining restaurant is situated next to the Walmart department store within the mall. Restaurant hours are 11:30 a.m. to 9 p.m. Monday through Thursday, Friday and Saturday from 11:30 a.m. to 10 p.m. and Sunday from noon to 6 p.m. Average prices for meals run about $5.00. Menu selections include hamburgers, seafood, steaks, Mexican food, Salad Bar that is available all day, and much much more. Daily specials are also provided. Their dining area can seat 130 to 150 persons. The atmosphere is reported to be very nice with a western style decor, wooden tables and is situated within an open area located in the mall. One specialty of the house which has become a favorite of many customers is their charcoal grilled hamburger, just like the ones you cookout in your back yard. Groups of 20 to 40 people can arrange special catered meals. For information about the Charcoal Grill call 773-8023.

Restaurants Near Airport:

Charcoal Grill	2 blks	Phone: 773-8023
Dairy Queen	1.5 blks	Phone: 773-6010
Pizza Hut	1 blk	Phone: 773-7733
Wyatt Cafeteria	2 blks	Phone: 773-1706

Lodging: La Quinta (1 mile) 773-7000; Holy Inn (1/2 mile) 773-9261.

Meeting Rooms: None Reported

Transportation: Bravo Aero Service has a courtesy car when available. Also Benny's Taxi 773-6925; Armadillo's Rental Cars 773-9265.

Information: Chamber of Commerce, 400 Garrison Street, P.O. Box 1188, Eagle Pass, TX 78853, Phone: 773-3224.

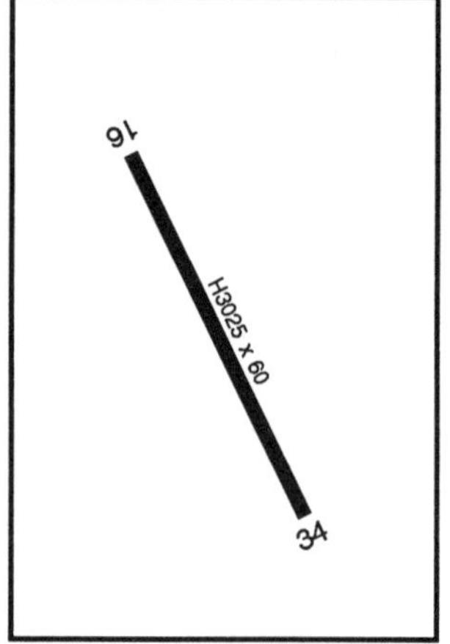

Airport Information:

EAGLE PASS - EAGLE PASS MUNICIPAL AIRPORT (EGP)
1 mi east of town N28-42.02 W100-28.77 Elev: 805 Fuel: 100LL
Rwy 16-34: H3025x60 (Asph) Attended: 1430Z-dusk Unicom: 122.8 Notes: CAUTION: Rwy 16-34 potholes on runway apron and taxiways. Condition very poor. See current AFD for surface contitions. Recomended that you call FBO (Bravo Aero Services 773-9636) to see if conditions have been upgrated.
FBO: Bravo Aero Services Phone: 773-9636

TX-ELP - EL PASO
EL PASO INTL. AIRPORT

(Area Code 915)

25

CA1 Services:

CA1 Services operates a restaurant located on the first floor of the terminal building. CA1 Services also manage a number of other service facilities including snack bars and lounges located on each concourse throughout the El Paso International Airport. Their main dining room facility has a decor that reflects a southwestern atmosphere. The restaurant is open 7 days a week from 6 a.m. until 8 p.m. Specialties of the house include a variety of southwestern Mexican foods. Sandwiches, soups and salads are all available as well as a children's menu. Average prices run $5.40 for breakfast, and $6.75 for lunch and dinner. In-flight catering can be arranged as well, with a full menu of items to choose from. All meals are available "to-go". The CA1 Services restaurants contains news stands and gift shops next to the restaurant that provide air travelers with many items available to make their trip even more enjoyable. For information about the food services or catering menus call their operations at 772-5225.

Restaurants Near Airport:

CA1 Services	On Site	Phone: 772-5225

Lodging: Shuttle service is available to the following lodging facilities; Best Western Airport Inn 779-7700; Best Western Caballero Hotel 772-4231; Embassy Suites 779-6222; Hilton Airport 778-4241; Holiday Inn Airport 778-6411; Howard Johnson Lodge 591-9471; LaQuinta Motor Inn 778-9321; Marriott 779-3300; Residence Inn-El Paso 772-8000; Roadway Inn 778-6611; Travel Lodge 778-6661.

Meeting Rooms: All lodging facilities listed above have accommodations for meetings.

Transportation: Taxi service: Border Cab 533-4245; Checker Cab 532-2626; El Paso Taxi 598-9702; Sun City 544-2211; Texas 562-0022; Yellow Cab 533-5052; Rental cars: Avis 779-2700; Budget 778-5287; Dollar 778-5522; Hertz: 772-4255; National 778-9417.

Information: El Paso Tourist Bureau, 1 Civic Center Plaza, El Paso, TX 79901; 534-0653, 800-351-6024.

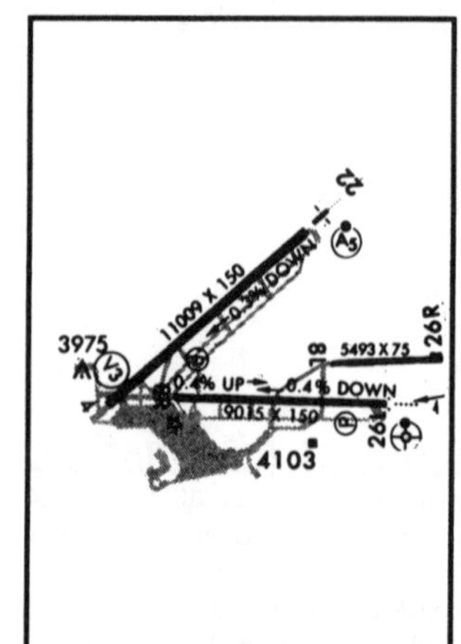

Airport Information:

EL PASO - EL PASO INTERNATIONAL AIRPORT (ELP)
4 mi northeast of town N31-48.40 W106-22.67 Elev: 3956 Fuel: 100LL, Jet-A1+, B+,
Rwy 04-22: H11009x150 (Asph-Grvd) Rwy 08R-26L: H9015x150 (Asph-Grvd) Rwy 08L-26R: H5493x75 (Asph) Attended: continuously Atis: 120.0 Unicom: 122.95 App Con: 124.15, 119.7, 119.1 Dep Con: 119.7 Tower: 118.3 Gnd Con: 121.9 Clnc Del: 125.0
FBO: Aero Freight, Inc. Phone: 772-3273 FBO: Julie's Arcft Srvc Phone: 777-2900
FBO: El Paso Aerol, Inc. Phone: 779-3481 FBO: Oasis Aviation Phone: 775-0833

TX-FTW - FORT WORTH
FORT WORTH MEACHAM AIRPORT

(Area Code 817)

26

Flightline Cafe:

The Flightline Restaurant is located within the terminal building on the Fort Worth Meacham Airport. This cafe-styled facility is open 10 a.m. to 5 p.m. Monday through Friday (Closed weekends). Special group catered functions can be arranged on weekends providing a minimum of 15 to 20 people are guaranteed. Their specialties include hamburger, BLT sandwiches, bacon cheeseburgers, club sandwiches, turkey, pastrami and roast beef sandwiches, as well as salads and homemade soup of the day. Average prices run $4.00 to $5.00 for most selections. The dining room offers casual dining with seating for about 70 people. Large windows allow for a nice view of the airport and active areas. Aircraft parking is available at major FBO's on the field. A flight training school is reported adjacent to the restaurant. For information call the Flightline Cafe at 624-2626.

Restaurants Near Airport:

Baron's (Holiday Inn N.)	4 mi	Phone: 625-9911
Dobbs House	On Site	Phone: 624-8526
Flightline Cafe	On Site	Phone: 624-2626
Main Street (Holiday Inn N.)	4 mi	Phone: 625-9911

Attractions:

Fort Worth Public Events, 870-8150;
Historic Stockyards, 625-1025;
Six Flags over Texas, 640-8900

Lodging: Sandpiper Inn, (On Airport) Phone: 625-5531; Holiday Inn North, 2540 Meacham at I-35W 247 rooms, two restaurants (Main Street & Baron's, see listing above) Phone: 625-9911 or 800-465-4329.
Conference: Small meeting rooms available at FBO: Staci's Jet (On Airport), 625-2366; Holiday Inn North, conference and meeting rooms available, (See lodging listed above).
Transportation: Staci's Jet, 625-2366; Sandpiper Jet, 625-5531; Avis, 624-8438; Budget, 336-6601 Consolidated, 625-2707; American Cab, 429-8829; Yellow Checker, 534-5555; The T (Bus), 870-6200
Information: Fort Worth Convention and Visitors Bureau, Sundance Square area at 415 Throckmorton, TX 76102 Phone: 336-8791 or 800-433-5747.

Airport Information:

FORT WORTH - FORT WORTH MEACHAM (FTW)
5 mi north of town N32-49.16 W97-21.71 Elev: 710 Fuel: 100LL Jet-A Rwy 16L-34R: H7501x150 (Conc-Grvd) Rwy 16R-34L: H4000x75 (Asph) Rwy 09-27: H3677x100 (Asph) Attended: continuously Atis: 120.7 Unicom: 122.95 App/Dep Con: 118.1 (N.) 120.5 (S.) Tower: 118.3 Gnd Con: 121.9 Clnc Del: 124.65 Public phone 24 hr. Notes: Overnight/landing fees: Singles $4.00, Twin $6.00

FBO: Fort Worth Jet Center	**Phone: 625-2366**
FBO: Richardson Aviation	**Phone: 625-1611**
FBO: Sandpiper Airport Inn	**Phone: 625-5531;**
FBO: Texas Jet	**Phone: 624-8438;**

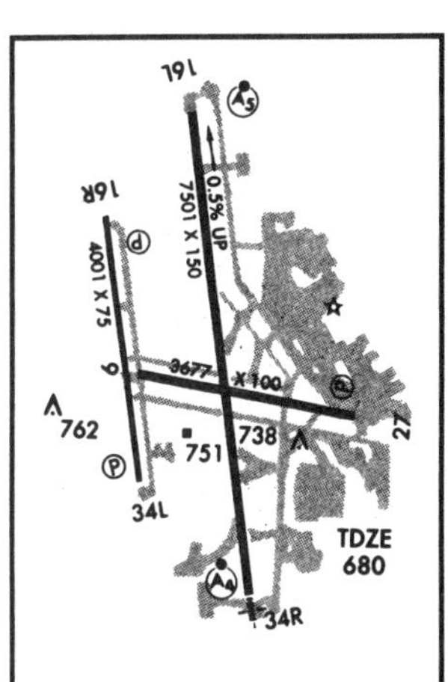

TX-GLE - GAINESVILLE
GAINESVILLE MUNICIPAL AIRPORT

(Area Code 817)

27

Wooden Spoon:

The Wooden Spoon Restaurant is located at least 1 mile from the Gainesville Municipal Airport. Although this restaurant is to far too walk to, fly-in guests can arrange to obtain a courtesy car through Ford Aircraft (FBO) on the field. Taxi service is also available by calling Safeway Taxi. This establishment is classified as a family-style restaurant, and is open from 11 a.m. to 9 p.m., 6 days a week. They are closed on Tuesdays. Menu selections include chicken fried steaks, catfish, fried shrimp, chicken plates, all types of sandwiches including Rueben, clubs, hamburgers and cheeseburgers. All-you-can-eat catfish dinners are featured on Wednesday and Friday. Average meals cost between $5.00 and $8.00 for most selections. Their dining room can seat 150 persons and displays a lot of antiques and green plants hanging from the ceilings and walls. For information about the Wooden Spoon Restaurant call 668-6875.

Restaurants Near Airport:

Smokehouse	1 mi W.	Phone: 665-9052
Wooden Spoon	1 mi W.	Phone: 668-6875

Lodging: Comfort Inn (3 miles) 665-5599; Holiday Inn (3 miles) 665-8800.

Meeting Rooms: Comfort Inn 665-5599; Holiday Inn 665-8800.

Transportation: Ford Aircraft (FBO) has courtesy cars available to nearby facilities 665-3211; Also Safeway Taxi Service is available at 665-4727.

Information: Chamber of Commerce, P.O. Box 518, Gainesville, TX 76240, Phone: 665-2831.

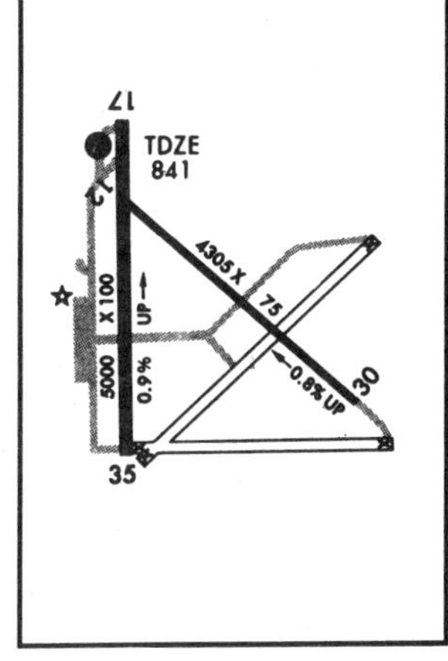

Airport Information:

GAINESVILLE - GAINESVILLE MUNICIPAL AIRPORT (GLE)
3 mi west of town N33-39.08 W97-11.82 Elev: 841 Fuel: 100LL, Jet-A Rwy 17-35: H5000x100 (Asph) Rwy 12-30: H4305x75 (Asph) Attended: 1400Z-dusk Unicom: 123.0 Public Phone 24hrs Notes: $3.00 fee for overnight parking, waived with fuel purchase.
City of Gainesville Phone: 668-4565

TX-GLS - GALVESTON SCHOLES FIELD

(Area Code 409) 28

Dining at Moody Gardens:

Moody Gardens, located about 1 mile from Scholes Field, offers exciting attractions, such as the 55-foot tall Rainforest Pyramid and 3-D IMax Theater. It also offers a wide selection of international and American cuisine in a choice of different dining areas. The Garden Lobby, adjacent to the Rainforest Pyramid, is a sweeping, open area with exotic flamingos, a quiet pond and a brisk waterfall. It is ideal for banquets or receptions. Next to the Lobby, the Garden Restaurant serves delicious gourmet meals with a spectacular view of nightly Dancing Waters fountain displays along the waterfront. Also, the Macadamia Room, adjacent to the Garden Restaurant, offers quiet, intimate dining with a view of the bay. The menus vary from delicious breakfast buffets to scrumptious lunch and dinner entrees. Groups of 100 people, or more, can participate in "themed" buffet seclections, such as the "South of the Border Mexican Buffet", the "Texas Style Hoe-Down", the "Tropical Hawaiian Luau", or the grand "Around the World Buffet" which includes French, Mexican, Italian, Oriental and German cuisine. With advance notice, the FBO will provide a courtesy car to and from Moody Gardens. For more information about the restaurants and other attractions at Moody Gardens, call 800-582-4673 or 331-7256.

Restaurants Near Airport:
Moody Gardens 1 mile Phone: 331-7256

Lodging: Flagship Hotel (4 miles) 762-8681; Gaido's Motor (3 miles) 762--9625; Harbour House (5 miles) 763-3321; Holiday Inn (3 miles) 740-3581; Hotel Galvez Marriott (4 miles) 765-7721; Howard Johnson Suites (adj aprt) 740-1155; San Luis (2 miles) 744-1500; Also, camping is available on field.
Meeting Rooms: Moody Gardens 331-7256
Transportation: Taxi service: Busy Bee 762-8429; Checker 744-5555; Yellow 765-5557; Rental cars: Agency 744-7211; Enterprise 740-0700; Snappy's 744-2002; Super Star 762-5808; Thrifty 744-4413
Information: Galveston Island Convention and Visitors Bureau, 2106 Seawall Blvd., Galveston, Texas 77550, Phone: 763-4311

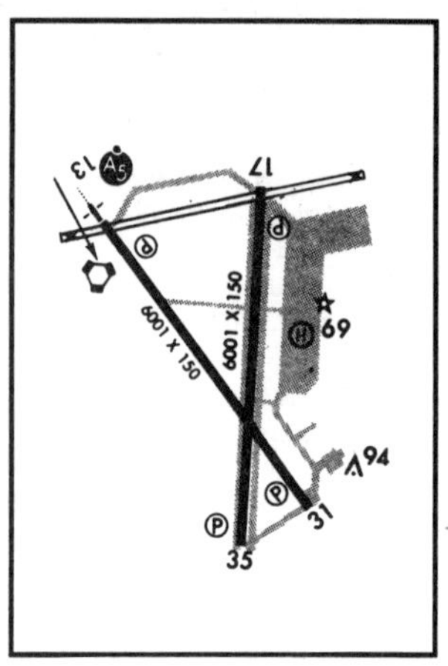

Airport Information:

GALVESTON - SCHOLES FIELD (GLS)
3 mi southwest of town N29-15.92 W94-51.63 Elev: 7 Fuel: 100LL, Jet-A Rwy 17-35: H6001x150 (Conc) Rwy 13-31: H6001x150 (Asph-Conc) Attended: 1200-0400Z CTAF/Unicom: 123.05 Houston App/Cep Con: 134.45 Clnc Del: 135.35 Notes: Flocks of birds in vicinity of airport below 200'. For fuel service after hours, call 740-2737.
FBO: Jet Tech, Inc. Phone: 740-1125

Moody Gardens

Galveston, TX (TX-GLS)

Photo by: Moody Gardens

Children discover a group of curious fish at one of Moody Gardens' many fascinating exhibits.

There is no time like the present to get away from the hustle and bustle of everyday life. Imagine soft white sand and soothing crystal-clear fresh water lagoons surrounded by lush, exotic landscaping. Experience over 2,000 species of exotic plants, animals and butterflies in the rainforests of Africa, Asia and South America. Sound good? Moody Gardens, in Galveston, Texas, has all that and more.

One of the most memorable features of Moody Gardens is the 55-foot tall Rainforest Pyramid. It is a massive jungle full of air-root vines, vibrant flowers that change every season and luscious fruit, such as bananas and papaya. The palm trees are planted in the form of the pyramid, with the tallest tree in the center and descending on either side. The Pyramid is home to thousands of species of birds, butterflies and other exotic animals. The Pyramid is not only a world-class attraction but a unique site for private gatherings.

The Garden Lobby, adjacent to the Rainforest Pyramid, is a sweeping, open area with exotic flamingos, a quiet pond and a brisk waterfall. Convenient for banquets or receptions. Next to the Lobby, the Garden Restaurant serves delicious gourmet meals with a spectacular view of nightly Dancing Waters fountain displays along the waterfront. Also, the Macadamia Room, adjacent to the Garden Restaurant, offers quiet, intimate dining with a view of the bay.

Located west of the Rainforest Pyramid are the sculptured garden terraces filled with an abundance of vegetables. Next to the vegetable and herb gardens is a small vineyard where four grape varieties are planted. These include: Orlando Seedless, Cabernet

Photo by: Moody Gardens

The 55-foot tall Rainforest Pyramid soars above Moody Gardens.

Sauvignon, Chardonnay and Muscat Canelli. Another interesting sight is the Galveston Oleander Collection. This garden holds every oleander variety that can be grown on Galveston Island. The 60 varieties have been planted in groups and flower color, and they are tagged for easy identification.

For a little "fun in the sun," Moody Gardens has created a tropical getaway on its very own Palm Beach. Bask on the white sand beach surrounded by palms mixed with colorful crotons, allamanda, bougainvillea, hibiscus and plumeria. Or, take a ride on the 800 passenger Colonel Paddlewheel Boat.This authentic reproduction of an 1800s Victorian-style paddlewheel boat is docked at Palm Beach and offers daily cruises on Offatts Bayou.

For even more excitement, Moody Gardens hosts an annual two-day festival called IslandFest (usually held in latter part of March), which encompasses the entire complex. The festival features continuous live music, food, a Saturday night concert with laser/fireworks show, water activities, fine arts show and children's activities.

Another fantastic attraction to see is the 3-D IMax Theater. There are only three others in the world. This revolutionary theater complex presents 2-D and 3-D IMAX features with images that come to life on a screen over six stories high. When combined with a wraparound, IMAX digital sound system, the audience feels like it is being pulled into the movie. For state-of-the-art acoustics and theater-style presentations surrounded by natural elegance, visit the smaller preview theater in the same building as the IMAX.

Three other memorable features at Moody Gardens include: the Garden of Life, the Hope Rose Garden and the Vietnam Veterans Memorial. The Japanese inspired Garden of Life symbolically represents the process of birth, death, and then afterlife. Moody Gardens is home to various Hope Therapy Programs designed to assist people with disabilities using physical, occupational, speech and language therapies. The Hope Rose Garden is a quiet retreat for guests and families of Hope Therapy clients to enjoy. The Gardens also feature a Vietnam Veterans Memorial. This monument honors the 75 Galveston County men who died in the Vietnam War. Its six foot black marble columns depict men in military order. The red granite base is depressed and sloped downward to create a 'wound' in the earth, symbolizing the conflicting opinions held by Americans on the U.S. involvement in the war.

Throughout the season, Moody Gardens offers special tours and programs designed for students of all capabilities and ages. For smaller groups such as lectures, luncheons or seminars, the Gardens offer a choice of gathering spaces that are comfortable and well-equipped. For meetings, conventions, or any other type of gatherings, the Moody Gardens Convention Center offers nine fully equipped meeting rooms with movable acoustic walls in 9,500 square feet of flexible space. It also offers a 37,500-square-foot exhibit hall, as well as a gracious pre-function area (ideal for receptions).

For transportation and accommodations, there are plenty of nearby hotels and motels, along with camping facilities available. Moody Gardens is located about 1 mile from Scholes Field. The airport has a 6,001'x150 concrete runway and a 6,001'x150 asphalt-concrete runway. The overnight parking fee is $5.00 for both singles and twins. With advance notice, the FBO will provide a courtesy car. For more information, contact the FBO at 740-1125. For further information about Moody Gardens, call 800-582-4673 or 331-7256. (Information submitted by Moody Gardens- Galveston Island)

TX-E15 - GRAHAM
GRAHAM MUNICIPAL AIRPORT

(Area Code 817) 29

Dairy Queen Airport Restaurant:

The Dairy Queen Restaurant is located across the street from the Graham Municipal Airport. This facility is classified under fast food, and is open 7 days a week Monday through Thursday 7 a.m. to 9 p.m., Friday and Saturday 7 a.m. to 10 p.m. and Sunday 8 a.m. to 9 p.m. Their menu of course specializes in many delicious ice cream products, but doesn't stop there. They also carry a variety of popular entrees like Mexican dishes, chicken fried steak, hamburgers and cheeseburgers, as well as breakfast selections. Their dining area can accommodate between 60 to 65 persons. The restaurant has many large windows that provide a view of the airport across the street. Anything on their menu can be packaged to go if requested. Groups and fly-in clubs are welcome. For information call them at 549-2500.

Restaurants Near Airport:
Dairy Queen Airport Restaurant Adj Arpt Phone: 549-2500

Lodging: Gateway Motel (Trans) 549-0222; Plantation Inn 549-8320; Stevens Motel 549-3221.

Meeting Rooms: Gateway Motel 549-0222.

Transportation: Rental Cars: Davidson Motor Co. 549-2233.

Information: Graham Chamber of Commerce, 608 Elm St, P.O. Box 299, Graham, TX 76450, Phone: 549-3355 or 800-256-4844.

Airport Information:

GRAHAM - GRAHAM MUNICIPAL AIRPORT (E15)
2 mi east of town N33-06.61 W98-33.32 Elev: 1123 Fuel: 100LL, Jet-A
Rwy 03-21: H4200x75 (Asph) Rwy 17-35: H3285x45 (Asph) Attended: Mon-Sat 1400-2300Z, Sun 1900-2300Z Unicom: 123.0
FBO: Glen Air Aviation Phone: 549-6415

TX-GPM - GRAND PRAIRIE
GRAND PRAIRIE MUNI. AIRPORT

(Area Code 972) 30

Final Approach Restaurant & Aleport:

The Wheels Down Restaurant is located right on the Grand Prairie Municipal Airport. Fly-in guests can conveniently park their aircraft very near to the restaurant. This full service cafe and family style restaurant is open 7 a.m. to 3 p.m. every day except Wednesday, Thursday and Friday 7 a.m. to 9 p.m. Their menu includes 120 separate selections including a full breakfast menu and dinner choices like grilled swordfish Felet Mignon, Fajita's, and Teriyaki chicken. Average prices run between \$6.95 to \$12.95 for most items. Daily specials are also offered. The main dining room, with oak tables and wood furnishings, and decorated with aviation pictures that local pilots have donated, can seat 80 persons. A private dining room in the restaurant is ideal for banquet or groups, able to accommodate 40 to 100 persons. They even have an outdoor patio for dining as well. In-flight catering and carry-out meals can also be prepared. For more information call the Wheels Down Restaurant at 660-2378.

Restaurants Near Airport:
Final App. Rest. & Aleport On Site Phone: 660-2378

Lodging: Quality Inn Arlington Suite Hotel (Trans) 640-4444; Radisson Suite Hotel (Trans) 640-0440; Rodeway Inn (Trans) 640-7080.
Meeting Rooms: Quality Inn Arlington Suite Hotel 640-4444; Radisson Suite Hotel 640-0440.
Transportation: Taxi Service: Taxi Cab 817-467-4445; Cab Company 817-429-8829; Also Rental Cars: Grand Prairie Aviation 660-2447; Enterprise/Arlington 467-5603 and 465-0584.
Information: Arlington Convention & Visitors Bureau, 1250 East Copeland Road, Suite 650, Arlington-Grand Prairie, TX 76011, Phone: 817-265-7721; Also: Grand Prairie Convention & Visitors Bureau, 900 Conover Drive, P.O. Box 531227; Grand Prairie, TX 75053, Phone: 263-9588 or 800-288-8386.

Attractions:

Six Flags Over Texas Amusement Park (Within 10 miles); Lake Joe Pool (5 miles); Ripley's Wax Museum (Within 10 miles) Traders Village, Flea Market adjacent to Grand Prairie Municipal Airport.

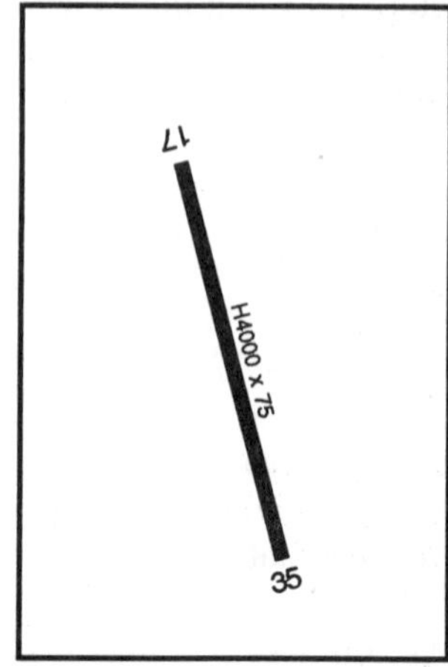

Airport Information:

GRAND PRAIRIE - GRAND PRAIRIE MUNICIPAL AIRPORT (GPM)
3 mi southwest of town N32-41.91 W97-02.80 Elev: 585 Fuel: 100LL, Jet-A
Rwy 17-35: H4000x75 (Conc) Attended: 1300-0300Z Unicom: 122.8 Tower: 128.55
Gnd Con: 121.15 Public Phone 24hrs Notes: Left traffic to Runway 17 - Right traffic to Runway 35; Heavy helicopter traffic on west side of field; Overnight parking \$3.00
FBO: Air Lease Phone: 641-8778
FBO: Howell's Aircraft Service Phone: 988-3171

TX-HRL - HARLINGEN
RIO GRANDE VALLEY INTERNATIONAL

(Area Code 210) 31

Restaurants Near Airport:
Host Marriott On Site Phone: 430-8660

Lodging: Holiday Inn (Free Trans) 425-1810; Hudson House Motel (3 miles) 428-8911; La Quinta (Free Trans) 428-6888; Quality Inn (4 miles) 425-1212; Sun Valley Motel (3 miles) 423-7222.

Transportation: Courtesy Car; Taxi: airport 428-4613; Yellow 423-2212; Car Rental: Advantage 430-8687; Avis 430-8690; Budget 430-8614; Hertz 430-8621; National 430-8687.

Information: Chamber of Commerce, 311 East Tyler Street, Harlingen, TX 78550, Phone: 423-5440 or 800-531-7346.

Host Marriott:

Host Marriott restaurants at the Rio Grande Valley International Airport range in amenities from snack bars and cafes, to family style restaurants and fine dining facilities located on the concourse and main lobby of the terminal building. Their restaurants are open from 5 a.m. and usually remains open until the last departure. Each day they specialize in a wide range of foods with daily specials that change on a daily basis. The decor of their restaurants are decorated with a tropical theme. Host Marriott provides catering for business functions, meetings, parties and business travelers. Transportation from the general aviation fixed base operators to the main terminal building can be arranged. They also cater to private and commercial pilots. For information call 430-8660.

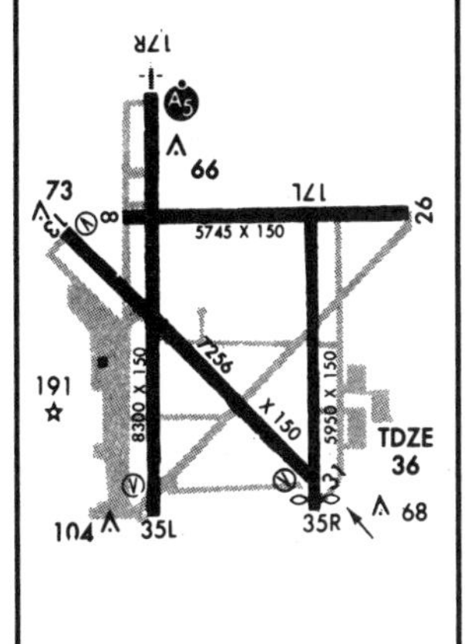

Airport Information:

HARLINGEN - RIO GRANDE VALLEY INTERNATIONAL (HRL)
3 mi northeast of town N26-13.71 W97-39.26 Elev: 36 Fuel: 100LL, Jet-A Rwy 17R-35L: H8300x150 (Asph-Grvd) Rwy 13-31: H7256x150 (Asph) Rwy 17L-35R: H5950x150 (Asph) Rwy 08-26: H5745x150 (Conc-Asph) Attended: 1200-0400Z Atis: 124.85 Unicom: 122.95 Valley App/Dep Con: 120.7 Tower: 119.3 Gnd Con: 121.7
FBO: B/S Aviation Phone: 421-2767 FBO: Gulf Avionics Phone: 423-5770
FBO: Gulf Aviation Phone: 423-7317 FBO: Harlingen Aero Phone: 423-0997

TX-HDO - HONDO
HONDO MUNICIPAL

(Area Code 210) 32

Restaurants Near Airport:
Flightline Cafe On site Phone: 426-4020

Lodging: Armstrong Hotel 1 mi 426-2151; Best Western Alsapian 538-2262; Hondo Motel 1 mi 426-2373; Landmark Inn 538-2133; White Tail Lodge 2 mi 426-3031.

Meeting Rooms: Flightline Cafe offers on site catering for groups. 426-4020.

Transportation: Rental cars are reported available.

Information: San Antonio Convention & Visitors Bureau, P.O. Box 2277, San Antonio, TX 78298, 270-8700 or 800-447-3372.

Flightline Cafe:

The Flightline Cafe is situated on the west side of the field right on the apron facing the runway. Pilots can park their aircraft in front of the restaurant. This combination cafe and family restaurant is open Monday through Thursday from 8:30 a.m. to 2:30 p.m., Friday 8:30 a.m. to 9 p.m., and Saturday and Sunday from 8:30 to 2 p.m. They are closed major holidays. Specials on their menu include: homemade baked bread and rolls, sandwiches given names like: "Gunnership Catfish, Pin-up Girl Chicken Sandwich, U.S.S. MO. Tuna Sandwich, Shirley Tempel, Audie Murphy Burger, Yellow Rose Chicken Fried Steak, Enola Gay Burger" and many more. Average prices run $5.00 or under for breakfast, $6.00 to $7.00 for lunch and around $8.00 to $9.00 for dinner. The restaurant has a theme from out of the forties with memorabilia of sorts on display. A WW-II Jeep makes up their salad bar. Large windows allow for a view of the airport active areas. Two private dining rooms designed for catering groups of 20 and 35 are available if advance notice is given (1 or 2 months). Daily specials are available including a luncheon buffet on Saturday and Sunday, as well as a Friday all you can eat seafood buffet. For information call 426-4020.

Attractions:

There is a golf course located only a couple of blocks west of the airport. Pilots could flyin for a bite to eat and then enjoy a game of golf. For information you can call either Doss Aviation (FBO) 426-3021 or The Flightline Cafe at 426-4020.

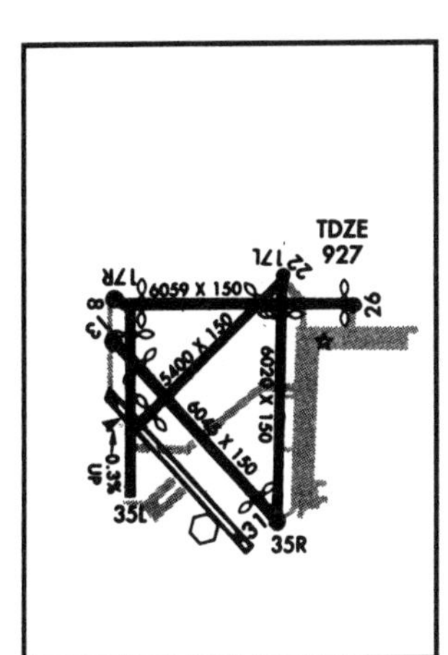

Airport Information:

HONDO - HONDO MUNICIPAL (HDO)
2 mi northwest of town N29-21.58 W99-10.61 Elev: 930 Fuel: 100LL Rwy 08-26: H6059x150 (Conc) Rwy 13-31: H6045x150 (Conc) Rwy 17L-35R: H6020x150 (Conc) Rwy 04-22: H5400x150 (Conc) Rwy 17R-35L: H3662x150 (Asph) Attended: 1400-2300Z Unicom: 122.8
FBO: Doss Aviation Phone: 426-3021

TX-4R2 - HORSESHOE BAY
HORSESHOE BAY AIRPARK

(Area Code 210)

33

Horseshoe Bay Resort and Conference Club:

Horseshoe Bay Resort and Conference Club is located about 1-1/2 miles from the Horseshoe Bay Airpark, a privately owned and professionally operated airport for guests of Horseshoe Bay. This resort, set in the Texas Hill Country on Lake LBJ, features golf courses, indoor and outdoor tennis courts, an equestrian center, a full service marina facility and a conference center. It also features 5 fine dining restaurants: 2 grills in the golf course clubhouses and 3 facilites in the yacht club. The restaurants range from comfortably casual to elegant American and French traditional dining. Average prices range from $7.50 for breakfast, $15.00 for lunch and $25.00 for dinner. Hours of each restaurant vary with the season, but most are generally open from 7 a.m. to 2 p.m. and 6 p.m. to 10 p.m., 7 days a week. The restaurants provide limited catering service to parties of 20 or more, as well as to pilots-on-the-go. Horseshoe Bay Resort offers courtesy shuttle service to and from the airpark. For more information about the restaurants and other resort facilities, call 598-2511.

Restaurants Near Airport:
Horseshoe Bay Resort 1-1/2 mi. Phone: 598-2511

Lodging: Horseshoe Bay Resort and Conference Club (11/2 miles) 598-2511
Meeting Rooms: Horseshoe Bay Resort and Conference Club 598-2511
Transportation: Horseshoe Bay Resort will provide courtesy shuttle service to and from the airport.
Information: Convention & Visitors Bureau, 201 E. 2nd Street, P.O. Box 1088, Austin, TX 78767, Phone: 800-888-8-AUS or 478-0098

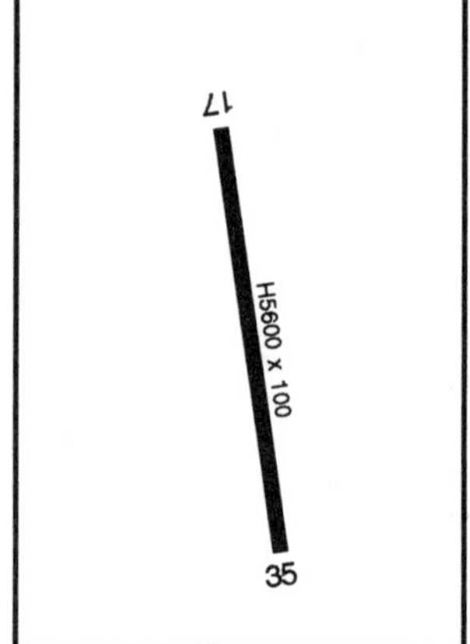

Airport Information:

HORSESHOE BAY - HORSESHOE BAY AIRPARK (4R2) (Private)
11/2 mi from resort N30-31.6 W098-21.5 Elev: 1117 Fuel: AV gas and jet fuel Rwy 17-35: H5600x100 Attended: call resort at 598-2511 for hours CTAF/Unicom: 122.8 Notes: Private use facility use at own risk; CAUTION - Also: Deer and other wildlife on and around runway. Hangar space for overnight parking is available.
Flight Center & Terminal Building: Horseshoe Bay Resort Phone: 598-2511

Horseshoe Bay Resort

Horseshoe Bay Resort and Conference Club is located 1-1/2 miles from Horseshoe Bay Airpark, and is situated on Lake LBJ in the heart of Texas Hill Country. This resort features an assortment of recreational facilities that are set in a relaxing natural environment.

A tennis facility with four covered courts and ten outdoor courts is surrounded by carefully landscaped exquisite Oriental water gardens with waterfalls, fountains, statuary, bridges, lakes and peaceful music from within the trees. A complete Racket Club Pro Shop provides a locker room, sauna, whirlpool, snack bar and a second story atrium-style lounge for pre-arranged social gatherings. In addition, group and individual tennis lessons and private massage therapist services are available. The resort offers three uniquely designed golf courses which have their own beautifully scenic surroundings, such as waterfalls, native rock, stone and architectural plant ornamentation. The two golf clubhouses offer their own creativity as well. The Cap Rock Golf Clubhouse is landscaped atop a four hundred million-year old rock formation that overlooks the lake, hills, greens and fairways. Cap Rock features an adult swimming pool with cascading waterfalls, a cabana and a bathhouse. The Slick Rock Golf Clubhouse also overlooks the lake and hills, and it features a full-service locker facility with sauna whirlpools. Both clubhouses have a fully stocked pro shop and lounge and dining areas.

Photo by: Horseshoe Bay Resort

Breathtaking view of the spa facility.

The Equestrian Center at Horseshoe Bay Resort offers visitors the chance to enjoy the rugged beauty of Texas Hill Country on horseback. The Center features individual and group guided trail rides along Slick Rock Creek.

A full service marina facility offers resort guests various sales and rental services for fishing excursions, sail boats, water skiing and personal watercraft. The marina is located adjacent to the Yacht Club, Norman C. Hurd Conference Center, the Horseshoe Bay Inn and the Horseshoe Bay Beach House. The Yacht Club features three unique dining areas, including a comfortable dining room for casual fare, an elegant dining room that serves traditional American cuisine and a gourmet dining room with French cuisine prepared tableside by a formally trained predominately European staff. Guests can take an after dinner stroll through the waterfall gardens and past the brilliant colored assortment of exotic bird on open-air perches near the Yacht Club. These macaws, parrots, love birds and finches also perch near the spa area, as well as in decorative cages throughout the resort facilities.

The Norman C. Hurd Conference Center hosts corporate meetings and social functions that will accommodate up to 300 people. Horsheshoe Bay Resort also features an outside entertainment area with an Olympic-size black marble pool, fountains, bubblers, waterfalls, a swinging bridge, sport courts, a cabana and bar, and an exotic spa with seating for 25 people. The resort's hotel and condominium facilities offer a wide range of locations, including waterfront, golf course, tennis and Yacht Club areas.

Horseshoe Bay Airpark, a privately owned and professionally operated airport, is located 1-1/2 miles from Horseshoe Bay Resort. It has a 5600'x100 lighted runway. The Airpark Terminal offers tie-down areas, a pilot ready-room, lounge areas and small meeting facilities. The resort offers courtesy shuttle service to and from the airport. For more information, contact Horseshoe Bay Resort and Conference Club at 598-2511 or 800-531-5105. (Information submitted by Horseshoe Bay Resort)

TX-DWH - HOUSTON
DAVID WAYNE HOOKS MEMORIAL

(Area Code 713)

34

Aviators Grill:

The Aviators Grill is located in the terminal building at the David Wayne Hooks Memorial Airport. This family styled restaurant is accessible by taxiing your aircraft up to, and parking it right outside their facility. This restaurant is open Sunday Through Thursday 11 a.m. to 2:30 p.m. and Friday and Saturday 11 a.m. to 9 p.m. Selections off their menu include burgers, grilled dishes, chicken fried steaks, sandwiches made to order, blackin catfish as a special on Friday's, salads and homemade soup. Average prices run $4.50 for breakfast, $4.95 for lunch and $9.95 for dinner. There are 13 large picture windows allowing a very nice view of the airport taxiway and ramp area. The dining area can accommodate 200 people and offers a casual atmosphere. Banquet facilities are also available within the restaurant for between 50 and 60 persons. Meals can be prepared to go if requested. Cheese trays, sandwich trays and anything off the menu can be prepared for in-flight catering. For more information about the Silver Wings Restaurant call 251-6065.

Restaurants Near Airport:
Aviator's Grill On Site Phone: 251-6065

Lodging: Best Western Tomball Inn (8 miles) 351-9700; Days Inn (8 miles) 350-6400; Holiday Inn (Shuttle) 821-2570; Regency Inn (8 miles) 893-5666; Travelodge (8 miles, shuttle) 353-3547; Woodlands Inn (15 miles) 367-1100.

Meeting Rooms: Best western Tomball Inn 351-9700; Days Inn 350-6400; Holiday Inn 821-2570; Travel Lodge 353-3547.

Transportation: Taxi Service: Tomball 351-7294; Ultimate Indulgence Limousine 863-9506 or 353-8051; Rental Cars: AA Car Rental 931-7474; Enterprise 580-3222; Knapp 228-7368.

Information: Greater Houston Convention and Visitors Bureau, 801 Congress, Houston, CA 77002, Phone: 227-3100 or 800-231-7799.

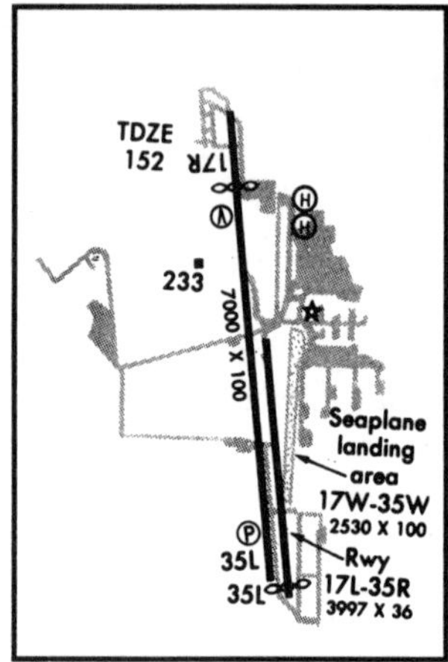

Airport Information:

HOUSTON - DAVID WAYNE HOOKS MEMORIAL AIRPORT (DWH)
17 mi northwest of town N30-03.71 W95-33.16 Elev: 152 Fuel: 100LL, Jet-A
Rwy 17R-35L: H7000x100 (Asph) Rwy 17L-35R: H3997x36 (Asph) Attended: 1200-0400Z
Atis: 124.95 Unicom: 122.95 Hooks Tower: 118.4 Gnd Con: 121.8 Clnc Del: 119.45
FBO: Mort Hall Avionics, Inc. Phone: 370-0550
FBO: National Aviation Phone: 370-5235

TX-EFD - HOUSTON
ELLINGTON FIELD

(Area Code 713)

35

Cajun Barbecue House:

The Cajun Barbecue House is situated about 1/2 mile across the street from Southwest Services (FBO). If you call the restaurant they will provide transportation if available staff are present. Also Southwest Services can help get you to the restaurant. This family restaurant is open Tuesday through Thursday between 9 a.m. to 7 p.m., Friday 9 a.m. to 8 p.m. and Saturday from 10:30 a.m. to 6:30 p.m. They are closed on Sunday and Monday. The Cajun Barbecue House specializes in serving barbecued items as well as Cagun styled entrees. Catfish, gumbo, crawfish, and zydeco are favorites many customers enjoy. They have 2 dining rooms within the restaurant with the ability to seat a total of 300 persons. Groups and associations are welcome. For information call the Cajun Barbecue House at 481-8736.

Restaurants Near Airport:
Cagun Barbecue House 1/2 mi. Phone: 481-8736

Lodging: Days Inn 332-3551; Airport Hilton-Hobby (trans) 645-3000; Holiday Inn-Hobby 943-7979; Holiday Inn-Nasa 333-2500; Ramada Inn 943-3300.

Meeting Rooms: Available at most major lodging facilities listed above. Also the Cagun Barbecue House has additional rooms for group catering 481-8736.

Transportation: Courtesy car; Also rental cars: Thrifty 286-1100; Also taxi service at airport is available.

Information: Greater Houston Convention and Visitors Bureau, 801 Congress, Houston, TX 77002, Phone: 227-3100 or 800-231-7799.

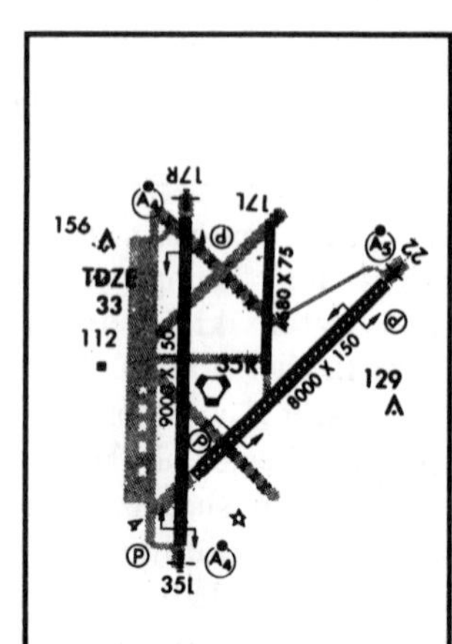

Airport Information:

HOUSTON - ELLINGTON FIELD (EFD)
15 mi southeast of town N29-36.44 W95-09.52 Elev: 34 Fuel: 100LL, Jet A,B+ Rwy 17R-35L: H9000x150 (Conc) Rwy 04-22: H8000x150 (Conc-Grvd) Rwy 17L-35R: H4600x75 (Conc) Attended: continuously Atis: 109.4 Unicom: 122.95 Tower: 126.05 Gnd Con: 121.6 Notes: See AFD for information.
Airport Manager Phone: 481-2828
FBO: Southwest Services Phone: 484-6551

TX-SPX - HOUSTON
HOUSTON GULF

(Area Code 713)

36, 37

Brass Parrot:

The Brass Parrot is located about 6 miles from the Houston Gulf Airport. This family-style restaurant was brought to our attention by one of our readers as a fine place to enjoy a meal. The Brass Parrot is open Sunday through Thursday between 11 a.m. to 10:30 p.m., and Friday and Saturday between 11 a.m. and 11 p.m. They specialize in preparing seafood dishes including catfish, flounder and swordfish. The restaurant has a Caribbean theme with plants and colorful decorations. They have an upper and lower level as well as an outside deck for dining. Inside they have seating for at least 300 people. According to the management, they also have a sister restaurant located next door. A courtesy car is available at the airport as well as taxi service and car rental. For more information about the Brass Parrot call 334-1099.

Landry's Restaurant:

Landry's Restaurant is about 5 to 6 miles from the Houston Gulf Airport. This fine dining establishment is open Monday through Friday from 11 a.m. to 10 p.m. and Saturday and Sunday from 11 a.m. to 11 p.m. Specialties of the house include prime rib, filet mignon, rib-eye, flounder, red snapper and shrimp. Average prices for main entrees run between $12.95 to $20.70. Seafood specials at certain times run between $8.95 and $16.95. This restaurant is located right on the lake. It has dining rooms that have been given special names. The Jimmy Walker room has a veranda and can seat up to 150 persons. The view from the restaurant overlooks the bay. Their Wharf Room is designed to accommodate private parties and small groups up to 15 people. Due to the popularity of this restaurant, reservations are suggested especially on weekends. Out in front of the restaurant there is a 1952 classic Police Car on display. There is a movie theater marquis at the entrance way giving customers the impression they just stepped back into the 1950s. Out in back of the restaurant there is a patio with tables, and along the seawall umbrella covered tables positioned in a tropical setting amongst palm trees and manicured gardens. There are two additional Landry's Restaurant locations in the Galveston, TX area near the Scholes Airport. (GLS). One only 2-1/2 miles east along 53rd Street, 409-740-1010 and another about 6 miles east along 15th Street, 409-762-4261 Both of these additional restaurants are located along the Seawall Blvd. on the south shore of the peninsula facing the Gulf of Mexico. For more information about Landry's Restaurant in Kemah TX, call 334-2513.

Restaurants Near Airport:

Brass Parrot	6 mi	Phone: 334-1099
Flying Dutchman	6 mi	Phone: 334-7575
Landrys	5-6 mi	Phone: 334-2513
Whats Cooking	N/A	Phone: 334-9000

Lodging: Days Inn-NASA 332-3551; Hilton-Nassau Bay 333-9300; Holiday Inn-NASA 333-2500; Ramada Kings Inn of NASA 488-0220; South Shore Harbor Resort 334-1000.

Meeting Rooms: Hilton-Nassau Bay 333-9300;

Transportation: Courtesy car reported at airport; Also taxi service: United Taxi 699-0000; Yellow 236-1111; Rental cars: Thrifty 286-1100.

Information: Greater Houston Convention and Visitors Bureau, 801 Congress, Houston, TX 77002, Phone: 227-3100 or 800-231-7799; Also Texas City Chamber of Commerce, 8419 Emmett F. Lowry Expy., Suite 105, P.O. Box 3330, Texas City, TX 77590, Phone: 409-935-1408 or 713-280-3917.

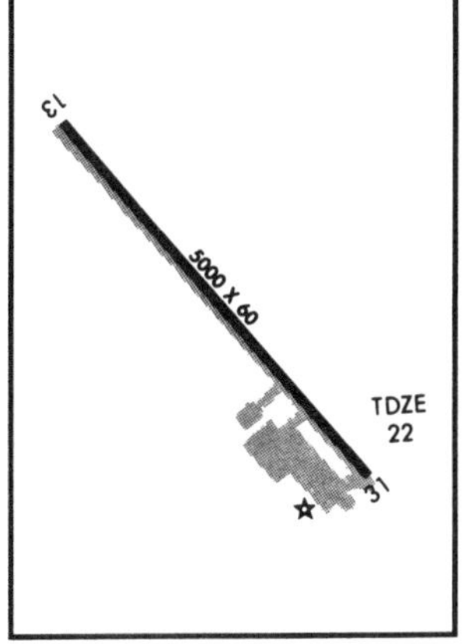

Airport Information:

HOUSTON - HOUSTON GULF (SPX)

26 mi E of town N29-30.50 W95-03.08 Elev: 22 Fuel: 100LL, Jet-A Rwy 13-31: H5000x60 (Asph) Attended: daylight hours Unicom: 122.7

FBO: Statewide Aviation Phone: 337-7827

TX-IAH - HOUSTON INTERCONTINENTAL AIRPORT

(Area Code 713) 38

Host Marriott:

Dobbs Houses restaurants ranging from snack bar, cafeteria, family style and fine dining facilities are located near the concourse area in terminals A, B, C, and IAB. These facilities are available 24 hours a day and specialize in serving items like pizza, hamburgers, and hot dogs for light appetites as well as full course meals. At their fine dining establishment, they specialize in entrees such as seafood selections, fettucine, cajun catfish, etouffee, gumbo, and shrimp dishes. Average prices for a meal vary according to each restaurant and its amenities. Groups traveling with a long lay over or businesses planning luncheons or meetings can arrange catered meals and accommodations through Dobbs Houses, Inc. Food trays and meals-to-go can also be prepared for pilots and/or their passengers if requested. For more information call 443-0764.

Restaurants Near Airport:

Host Marriott	On Site	Phone: 443-0764

Lodging: Quality Inn Intercontinental Airport 446-9131; Marriott-Houston Airport (On Airport) 443-2310.

Meeting Rooms: Quality Inn 446-9131, listed above has meeting rooms, and Marriott Houston Airport 443-2310, has accommodations for meetings and conventions.

Transportation: Courtesy Car; Taxi: Yellow Cab 236-1111; Rental Cars: Avis 443-5850; Budget 449-0145; Dollar 449-0161; General 446-4070; Hertz 443-0800; National 443-8850.

Information: Greater Houston Convention and Visitors Bureau, 801 Congress, Houston, CA 77002, Phone: 227-3100 or 800-231-7799.

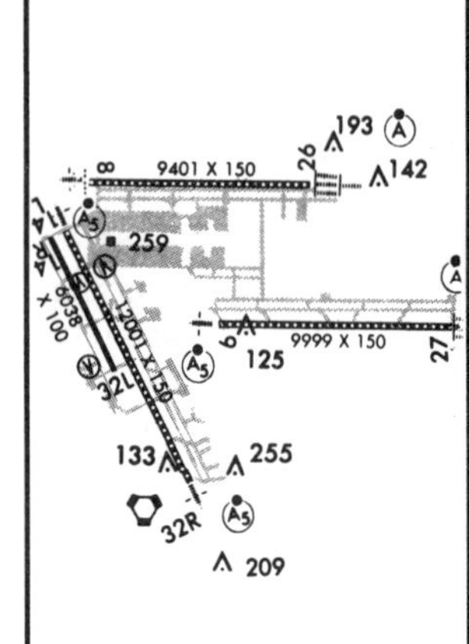

Airport Information:

HOUSTON - INTERCONTINENTAL AIRPORT (IAH)

15 mi north of town N29-58.83 W95-20.38 Elev: 98 Fuel: 100LL, Jet-A Rwy 14L-32R: H12001x150 (Conc-Grvd) Rwy 09-27: H9999x150 (Asph-Grvd) Rwy 08-26: H9401x150 (Asph-Conc-Grvd) Rwy 14R-32L: H6038x100 (Asph-Grvd) Attended: continuously Atis: 124.05 Unicom: 122.95 App Con: 124.35 (W), 120.05 (N&E) Dep Con: 123.8 (W), 119.7 (N), 133.6 (E) Tower: 132.5, 125.35 Gnd Con: 121.7 Clnc Del: 128.1

FBO: Avitat IAH/Qualitron Aero Phone: 443-3434

FBO: Garrett General Aviation Service Division Phone: 230-7800

TX-HOU - HOUSTON WILLIAM P. HOBBY AIRPORT

(Area Code 713) 39

CA1 Services:

CA1 Services is located within the main passenger terminal on the north side of the field, inside on the departures level. This cafeteria styled restaurant is open from 6 a.m. to 9 p.m. daily and offers guests a modern dining room with an attractive view of the airfield. Specialties of the house include made-to-order omelette breakfast bar, grilled sandwiches, deli style sandwiches, fresh soups, fresh cakes and pies. A food court in the terminal offers Colombo yogurt, Mexican specialties, cookies and deep dish pizza. Daily luncheon and dinner specials are attractively priced and feature, taco salads, fresh fruit platters and a bakery on the premisses. Average prices run $5.85 for breakfast, and about $6.30 for lunch and dinner. For groups or parties they also prepare several delicious and reasonably priced party and snack trays. They also have an full In-flight menu including sandwiches, vegetable, fruit trays, hot meals, and sandwich packs for private and corporate clients. Call 644-1312.

Restaurants Near Airport:

CA1 Services	On Site	Phone: 644-1312
Delias Cafe	West side	Phone: 641-0979
Mulberry Tree	On Site	Phone: 644-1261
Plaza Cafe, Hilton	On Site	Phone: 645-3000

Lodging: Hobby Hilton (1 block east of terminal) 645-3000; Concorde Hotel (7777 Airport Blvd) 644-1261; Hobby Airport Holiday Inn (9100 Gulf Fwy) 943-7979; La Quinta Inn (9902 Gulf Fwy) 941-0900; Days Inn (8611 Arpt Blvd) 947-0000.

Meeting Rooms: Aviation Department, Hobby Airport Cloud Room 643-4597; Hotels Listed above have accommodations for meetings and conferences; FBO's have conference rooms as well.

Transportation: Most Fixed Base Operators (FBO's) have courtesy transportation also local major hotels will provide transportation; Taxi service and Bus-Metro service is available; Rental Cars: Avis 641-0531; Hertz 941-6821; National 641-0533.

Information: Greater Houston Convention and Visitors Bureau, 801 Congress, Houston, CA 77002, Phone: 227-3100 or 800-231-7799.

Airport Information

HOUSTON - WILLIAM P. HOBBY AIRPORT (HOU)

8 mi southeast of town N29-38.73 W95-16.73 Elev: 47 Fuel: 100, Jet-A Rwy 04-22: H7602x150 (Conc-Grvd) Rwy 12R-30L: H7601x150 (Asph-Grvd) Rwy 17-35: H6000x150 (Conc-Asph-Grvd) Rwy 12L-30R: H5148x100 (Con-Grvd) Attended: continuously Atis: 124.6 Unicom: 122.95 Houston App Con: 134.45 (south), 124.35 (west), 120.05 (north & east) Hobby Tower: 118.7 Houston Gnd Con: 121.9 Clnc Del: 125.45 Pre-Taxi Clnc: 125.45 Houston Dep Con: 134.45 (south), 123.8 (West), 119.7 (north) Public Phone 24hrs Notes: CAUTION: numerous birds on and in facility of airport; Overnight parking fees determined by FBO's. Landing fees for charter flights $4.41/1,000 lbs; All area codes for Houston is 713; Information about sightseeing and literature are available at FBO's.

FBO: Aero Services Intl Phone: 800-645-4919 FBO: Fletcher Aviation Phone: 649-8700

FBO: Atlantic Aviation Phone: 644-6431 FBO: FlightSafety Texas Phone: 644-1521

TX-2R9 - KENEDY
KARNES COUNTY AIRPORT

(Area Code 210)

40

Barth's Restaurant:

Barth's Restaurant is located a short walk to the east of the Karnes County Airport. If you prefer courtesy transportation, you can call the restaurant and they will come and pick you up. This family style restaurant serves homemade soup, bread and cinnamon rolls as well as pies baked fresh each day. All entrees come with soups salad and homemade bread. Chicken fried steak is their speciality, along with many other entrees available on their menu. Average prices run $4.00 for breakfast, $4.95 for lunch and $6.95 for dinner. On Sunday, turkey and dressing is on the special. Senior citizens discounts are also offered. This restaurant, with a modern decor, has been serving its customers for the past 50 years. Banquet facilities are available for larger groups up to 100 persons. Accommodations can be arranged if given advance notice. The restaurant is open from 5:30 a.m. to 10:00 p.m. 7 days a week. For information call 583-2468.

Restaurants Near Airport:

Barth's Restaurant	1/4 mi NE	Phone: 583-2468
Kenedy's Restaurant	1 mi S.	Phone: 583-3262

Lodging: Antlers Inn, (1/4 mile) adjacent to Barth's Restaurant, Phone: 583-2521.

Transportation: Barr Air Patrol will provide courtesy cars; Rental Cars: Alexander Ford 583-2514.

Information: San Antonio Convention & Visitors Bureau, P.O. Box 2277, San Antonio, TX 78298, Phone: 210-270-8700 or 800-447-3372.

Attractions:

Karnes County Country Club, Hwy 181 south, Kenedy, TX 78119, Phone: 583-3200

Airport Information:

KENEDY - KARNES COUNTY AIRPORT (2R9)
1 mi northwest of town N28-49.50 W97-51.93 Elev: 291 Fuel: 100LL, MOGAS
Rwy 16-34: H3219x60 (Asph) Attended: Mon-Fri daylight hrs. Unicom: 123.0
Public Phone 24hrs Notes: $3.00 overnight parking, no charge if fuel is purchased.
FBO: Stetson Aviation, Inc. Phone: 583-9897

TX-ILE - KILLEEN
KILLEEN MUNICIPAL AIRPORT

(Area Code 817)

41

Killeen Airport Coffee Shop:

The Airport Coffee Shop is situated within the terminal building at the Killeen Municipal Airport. This restaurant is open 6 days a week (Closed on Sunday) from 5:30 a.m. to 6 p.m. Their menu specializes in all types of sandwiches like their bacon burger, club sandwiches, BLT's, chicken salad sandwiches, as well as dinner featuring chicken fried steak, chicken strips, and ham. Most of the items off their menu run between $2.70 and $4.55. The dining room is unique in that it is decorated in early American and western decor with furniture and items of that period. An old piano as well as stuffed animals that decorate the restaurant and give it a light hearted and festive atmosphere. Larger groups and parties are welcome with advance reservations. All of the items available on their menu can be ordered for carry-out. In flight catering is yet another service of the Killeen Airport Coffee Shop. For information call them at 699-4803.

Restaurants Near Airport:

Hallmark Restaurant	1 mi	Phone: N/A
Killeen Arpt. Coffee Shop	On Site	Phone: 699-4803

Lodging: Holiday Inn (Free trans) 634-3101; La Quinta 526-0394; Hilton (Shuttle) 526-4343; Sheraton Plaza (Shuttle) 634-1555.

Meeting Rooms: Holiday Inn 634-3101; La Quinta 526-0394; Hilton 526-4343; Sheraton Plaza 634-1555.

Transportation: Taxi Service: Kelly & Yellow Taxi 699-8294; Rental Cars: Avis 699-5677; Budget 635-5111; Hertz 699-2565; National 699-3113.

Information: Chamber of Commerce, Box 548, Killeen, TX 76540, Phone: 526-9551 or 800-869-8265.

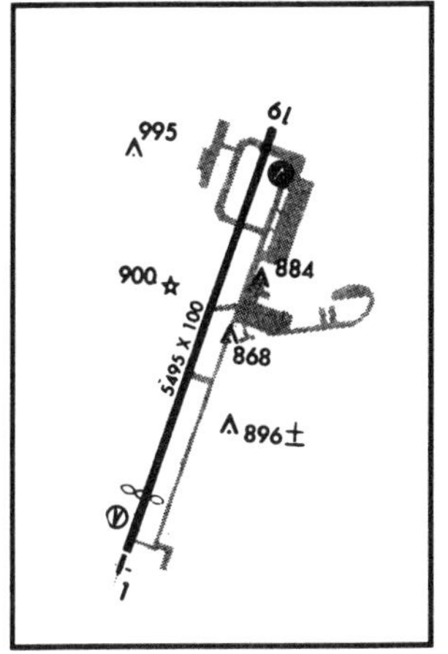

Airport Information:

KILLEEN - KILLEEN MUNICIPAL AIRPORT (ILE)
3 mi east of town N31-05.15 W97-41.19 Elev: 846 Fuel: 100LL, Jet-A
Rwy 01-19: H5495x100 (Asph) Attended: 1100-0600Z Unicom: 122.7
Airport Manager Phone: 699-4509

TX-17XS - LAJITAS
LAJITAS AIRPORT

(Area Code 915) **42**

Lajitas On The Rio Grand (Fly-in Resort)

This establishment contains a family style restaurant that is reported to be situated within walking distance from the Lajitas Airport. Hours are seasonal from 7 a.m. to 2 p.m. and 5 p.m. to 9:30 p.m. throughout the week. Their bar is open all day on Friday and Saturday. A large portion of their menu specializes in breakfast selections as well as choice steaks like t-bone, and sirloin, chicken dinners and fish. Average prices run $ 3.50-$7.50 for breakfast, $4.50 to 9.00 for lunch and $6.50 to $13.95 for dinner. Their large and rustic dining are,a complete with wooden tables, can seat 100 persons comfortably. Six meeting and banquet rooms can satisfy large or small groups with room for 40 to 175 persons. In addition to dining, we learned that they also feature many activities for their guests: swimming pool, tennis courts, riding stable, shopping and beauty salon. Additional activities include river rafting, bicycling, golfing on their 9 hole course, as well as National and State parks nearby. Lodging accommodations include 114 guest rooms, 19 condos, and even 3 or 4 cottages available for rent. For more information about Lajitas On The Rio Grand call 424-3471 or 800-944-9907. Please refer to notes under "Airport Information".

Restaurants Near Airport:
Lajitas On The Rio Grand On Site Phone: 424-3471

Lodging: Lajitas On The Rio Grand, accommodations include 83 rooms, 19 condos and 3 or 4 house rentals, Phone: 424-3471.
Meeting Rooms: Lajitas On The Rio Grand, 6 different meeting and banquet rooms able to accommodate between 40 and 175 persons.
Transportation: Courtesy car, and rental cars reported available.
Information: Texas Department of Transportation, P.O. Box 5064, Austin, Texas 78763-5064, Phone: 800-452-9292 or 800-888-8TEX.

Attractions:

Lajitas On The Rio Grand, provides recreational accommodations for their guests. River rafting, bicycling, swimming, 9 hole golf course, nearby State and National parks, and lodging near airport. The settle ment of Lajitas, TX is a very rustic but pleasant gathering of shops and businesses built around the Lajitas Hotel which built and owns the adjcent airport. One of our readers commented that he had flown in there for the "Great International Terlingua Chili Cookoff" held the first Saturday of November. (Terlingua is a ghost town 14 miles northeast of Lajitas). Phone 915-424-3471.

Airport Information:

LAJITAS - LAJITAS AIRPORT (17XS)
0 mi northeast of town 29-15-54N 103-45-54W Elev: 2364 Fuel: none reported Unicom: 122.9 Rwy 4-22: 4700x60 (Asph/tarred gravel, not reported sticky) Attended: daylight Notes: (Private Use Facility, use at own risk) According to our sources we learned this airport was owned and built by the Lajitas Hotel now a settlement of shops and businesses. Note: CAUTION don't climb out very far upwind to the southwest, or you might cross the border (Rio-Grande river) into Mexico airspace. DEA patrolled. Call 713-869-7800, or Lajitas On The Rio Grand 915-424-3471.
Lajitas Hotel Phone: 915-424-3471 or 800-944-9907

TX-LNC - LANCASTER
LANCASTER AIRPORT

(Area Code 214) **43**

Happy Landings Cafe:

This family style restaurant is located right in the terminal building just off the parking ramp at the Lancaster Airport. Their hours are 7 a.m. to 3 p.m., Tuesday through Sunday (Closed Monday). Specialties of the house include chicken fried steaks with cream gravy, as well as chicken strips, and chopped sirloin steak. Prices run $3.50 for breakfast, and $3.85 for lunch. The restaurant is part of a newly constructed air terminal, and is decorated in an aviation theme. Pictures of local aircraft based at the airport as well as photographs of some of the Confederate Air Force airplanes are displayed within the restaurant. Fly-in groups frequently plan trips to this airport and enjoy a meal at the Happy Landings Cafe while combining a visit to the Confederate Air Force hangar. For more information about this facility you can call the restaurant at 227-5722.

Restaurants Near Airport
Happy Landings On Site Phone: 227-5721

Lodging: Holiday Inn 224-9100; Spanish Trail Inn (4 miles) 224-7501; Great Western Inn 224-8226.

Transportation: Lancaster Airport can provide courtesy transportation to nearby facilities. Also Rental Cars: Snappy 780-7992

Information: Lancaster Chamber of Commerce, 1535 North Dallas Avenue, P.O. Box 1100, Lancaster TX 75146, Phone: 227-2579. Also: Texas Department of Transportation, P.O. Box 5064, Austin, Texas 78763-5064, Phone: 800-452-9292 or 800-888-8TEX.

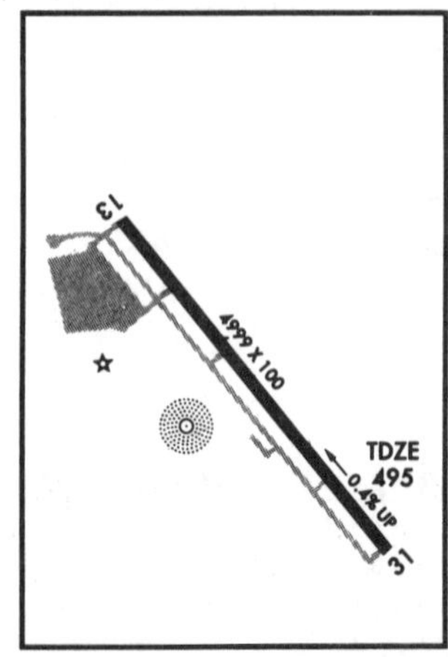

Attractions:

Lancaster Airport is home of the Ghost Squadron of the Confederate Air Force Dallas Ft Worth, 1939 to 1945. Their hangar is open Saturdays with WW-II artifacts and airplanes on display.

Airport Information:

LANCASTER - LANCASTER AIRPORT (LNC)
2 mi south of town N32-34.75 W96-43.14 Elev: 500 Fuel: 100LL, Jet-A
Rwy 13-31: H4999x100 (Asph) Attended: OCt-Apr 1300-0100Z, May-Sept 1300-0200Z
Unicom: 122.7 Public Phone 24hrs
FBO: Lancaster Airport Phone: 227-5721

TX-LRD - LAREDO
LAREDO INTERNATIONAL

(Area Code 210)

44

Villa Laredo Restaurant:

The Villa Laredo Restaurant is located in the terminal building at the Laredo International Airport. This facility specializes Mexican Cuisine. Their hours are 7 days a week from 6 a.m. to 8 p.m. Menu Items include a variety of delicious enchiladas, fahettas, as well as many other choices. Breakfast tacos and are also available. Average prices run $3.75 for breakfast, $4.99 for lunch and $4.99 to $6.95 for dinner. Daily specials are also featured. The main dining area can seat 75 to 80 people. Groups are welcome with advance notice. In-flight catering and carry-out service with items off their menu can also be arranged. For more information call the Villa Laredo Restaurant at 725-3663.

Restaurants Near Airport:
Villa Laredo Restaurant On Site Phone: 725-3663

Lodging: Holiday Inn (Civic Center, 2 miles) 727-5800; La Hacienda (2 miles) 722-2441; La Quinta (2 miles) 722-0511; Mayan Inn (2 miles) 722-8181; La Posada Inn (3 miles) 722-1701; Sheraton Inn (3 miles) 724-8221.

Meeting Rooms: Holiday Inn (Civic Center) 727-5800; La Posada Inn 722-1701; La Quinta 722-0511.

Transportation: Rental Cars: Avis 722-1533; Budget 726-3681; Hertz 722-7607; National 722-2561.

Information: Convention & Visitors Bureau, 2310 San Bernardo Avenue, Box 790, Laredo, TX 78042, Phone: 722-9895 or 800-292-2122.

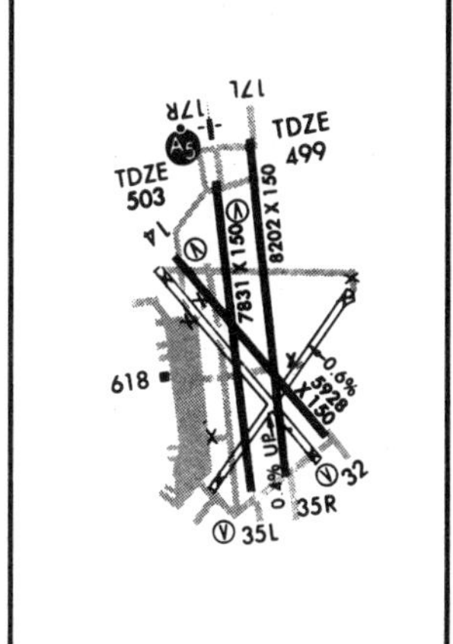

Airport Information:

LAREDO - LAREDO INTERNATIONAL AIRPORT (LRD)
3 mi northeast of town N27-32.68 W99-27.68 Elev: 508 Fuel: 100LL, Jet-A
Rwy 17L-35R: H8201x150 (Asph-Conc) Rwy 17R-35L: H7810x150 (Asph-Conc-Pfc)
Rwy 14-32: H5926x150 (Conc) Attended: 1200-0600Z Unicom: 122.95 Tower: 120.1
Gnd Con: 121.8
FBO: Airport Manager Phone: 795-2000 or 722-4933

TX-00R - LIVINGSTON
LIVINGSTON MUNICIPAL

(Area Code 409)

45

B & B Bar-B-Que:

B & B Bar-B-Que is situated about 140 yards north from the Livingston Municipal Airport. This is a family restaurant that contains a small dining room near the entrance, able to seat about 20 persons. Their side room further back can accommodate about 40 people and is often used as a main dining area for larger groups or when they are busy. The atmosphere is homey and casual with checkered table cloths. Items on their menu include all types of sandwiches like sliced beef, chopped beef and pork. Dinner selections include beef, 1/2 chicken, links, ribs, pork mixed selections, ham and rib-eye. They even sell meat by the pound for customers' carry-out. Groups are always welcome with advanced notice preferred. Average prices run $1.25 to $2.75 for most sandwiches and $5.00 to $8.00 for main dinner items. B & B Bar-B-Que is open Wednesday and Thursday from 10:30 a.m. to 7:00 p.m., Friday and Saturday from 10:30 a.m. to 9:00 p.m., and Sunday from 10:30 to 6:00 p.m. They are closed on Monday and Tuesday. For more information call their restaurant at 967-4108.

Restaurants Near Airport:
B & B Bar-B-Que 140 yds. Phone: 967-4108

Lodging: Park Inn 4 mi 327-2525; Ramada Inn 6 mi 327-3791

Meeting Rooms: None reported

Transportation: Rental cars: Ford/Mercury 327-4327; Loper Chevrolet 327-5220; Taxi service: BLT 327-7414.

Information: Polk County Chamber of Commerce, 516 W. Church (U.S. Hwy. 190W) Livingston, TX 77351, Phone: 327-4929

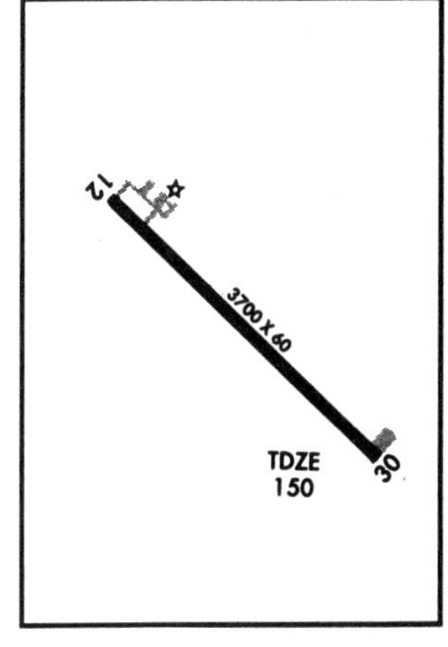

Airport Information:

LIVINGSTON - LIVINGSTON MUNICIPAL (00R)
5 mi southwest of town N30-41.15 W95-01.08 Elev: 151 Fuel: 100LL Rwy 12-30: H3700x60 (Asph) Attended: Mon-Fri 1400-2300Z, Sat-Sun 1800-2300Z Unicom: 122.7
FBO: Burrows Air Service Phone: 566-4229

TX-GGG - LONGVIEW
GREGG COUNTY AIRPORT

46

Restaurants Near Airport: **(Area Code 903)**
Sunpoint Cafe On Site Phone: 643-1189

Lodging: Best Western Longview Inn (Shuttle service) 753-0350; Holiday Inn (Shuttle trans) 758-0700; La Quinta (Shuttle service) 757-3663.

Meeting Rooms: There is a conference room on the second floor of the airport terminal building, also at the fixed based operators (FBO's) on the field. Also at: Best Western Longview Inn 753-0350; Holiday Inn 758-0700; La Quinta 757-3663.

Transportation: Fixed base operators (FBO's) on field, Stebbins Aviation, Eastex Aviation & Omega Jet, Inc. can accommodate courtesy transportation to near by locations. Also: Taxi service through Metro Cab Company 753-5544; Rental Cars: Avis 643-2292; Hertz 643-2291; National 643-3531.

Information: Convention and Visitors Bureau, 100 Grand Blvd, Longview, TX 75606, Phone: 753-3281. Also: Chamber of Commerce, 213 W. Austin, P.O. Box 520, Marshall, TX 75670. Phone: 935-7868.

Sunpoint Cafe: (New management)

Sunpoint Cafe is situated within the terminal building at the Gregg County Airport. This family style restaurant is open between 7 a.m. and 7 p.m. Monday through Friday and closed on Wednesday. Menu selections include hamburgers grilled cheese sandwiches, their special "Super Sport Sandwich" patty melts, cold sandwiches, a salad bar served between 11 a.m. and closing time, as well as a full breakfast line offered from 7 a.m. and 10:30 a.m. The restaurant can seat approximately 80 people and the interior is decorated with all types of airplane pictures. The view of the runways from the restaurant, allows guests to watch aircraft landing and departing the airport. We were told that on certain special occasions, this airport serves as a landing sight for the transport shuttle aircraft by NASA, which happens to draw quite a crowd of spectators. For more information about the Sunpoint Cafe call 643-1189.

Airport Information:

LONGVIEW - GREGG COUNTY AIRPORT (GGG)
3 mi south of town N32-23.09 W94-42.70 Elev: 365 Fuel: 100LL, Jet A
Rwy 13-31: H10000x150 (Asph-Grvd) Rwy 17-35: H6109x150 (Asph) Rwy 04-22: H5202x150 (Asph) Attended: continuously Atis: 119.65 Unicom: 122.95
Longview App/Dep Con: 128.75, 124.67, 118.25 Tower: 119.2 Gnd Con: 121.6
Public Phone 24hrs
FBO: Gregg County Airport Phone: 643-3031
FBO: Omega Jet Phone: 643-0903
FBO: Stebbins Aviation Phone: 643-2621

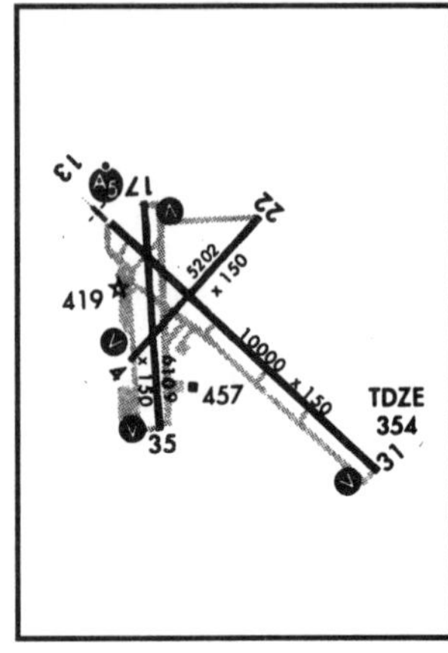

TX-LBB - LUBBOCK
LUBBOCK INTERNATIONAL

47

Restaurants Near Airport: **(Area Code 806)**
Host Marriott On Site Phone: 763-8278

Lodging: Barcelona Court 794-5353; Residence Inn by Marriott 745-1963; Lubbock Inn 792-5181; Lubbock Plaza 797-3241; Holiday Inn-Civic Center 763-1200; Sheraton Inn 747-0171.

Meeting Rooms: Barcelona Court 794-5353; Residence Inn by Marriott 745-1963; Lubbock Inn 792-5181; Lubbock Plaza 797-3241; Sheraton Inn 747-0171.

Transportation: Yellow Cab & Sexton Enterprises 765-7777; Rental Cars: Avis 763-5433; Budget 763-6471; Hertz 762-0227; National 762-2161.

Information: Convention & Toursim Bureau, Box 561, Lubbock, TX 79408 Phone: 747-5232.

Host Marriott Restaurant:

This restaurant is located inside the Lubbock International Airport terminal building. Transportation will have to be arranged through one of the Fixed Base Operators on the airport. This facility is a cafeteria, open from 6 a.m. to 9 p.m. Their entree selections include hot and cold sandwiches as well as a full breakfast. Prices average $3.50 for breakfast, $4.50 for lunch and $4.50 for dinner. Meal trays are available to-go with cold entrees such as cheese, fruit and sandwiches. For information call 763-8278.

Airport Information:

LUBBOCK - LUBBOCK INTL. AIRPORT (LBB)
4 mi north of town N33-39.82 W101-49.37 Elev: 3281 Fuel: 100LL, Jet-A, A1+
Rwy 17R-35L: H11500x150 (Conc-Grvd) Rwy 08-26: H8001x150 (Conc-Grvd)
Rwy 17L-35R: H2869x75 (Asph) Attended: continuously Atis: 125.3 Unicom: 122.95
App/Dep Con: 119.9, West of LBB VOR (165-015 degrees), 119.2 East of LBB VOR (015-165 degrees). ARSA ctc App Con: 124.45 Atis: 125.3 Unicom: 122.95 Tower: 120.5
Gnd Con: 121.9 Clnc Del: 125.8 App Con: 119.9, 119.2 Dep Con: 119.9, 119.2
Public Phone 24hrs
FBO: Horton Aero Phone: 763-5101
FBO: Lubbock Arrow Phone: 747-5101

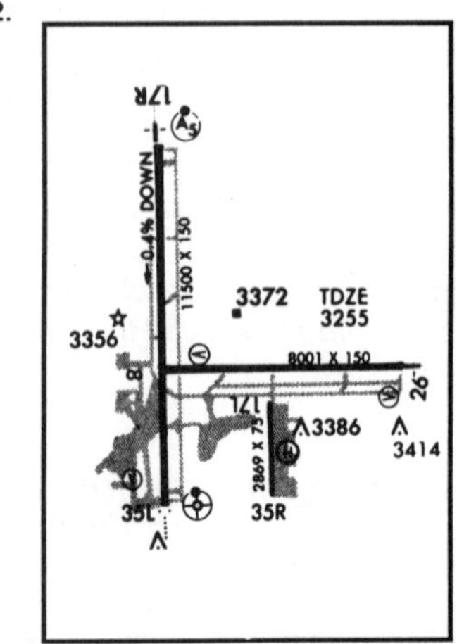

TX-LFK - LUFKIN
ANGELINA COUNTY AIRPORT

(Area Code 409)

48

Restaurants Near Airport:
Angelina Co Arpt Cafe On Site Phone: 634-7511

lodging: Best Western (7 miles) 639-3333; Days Inn 639-3301; Expo Inn 632-7300; Holiday Inn (8 miles, trans) 632-3311; La Quinta 634-3351; Lufkin Inn 800-528-1234; Motel 6 637-7850; Ramada Inn (8 miles) 634-2201; Roadway Inn 639-3301;

Meeting Rooms: Holiday Inn 632-3311; Roadway Inn 639-3301; Expo Inn 632-7300; La Quinta 634-3351.

Transportation: Rental Cars: Agency 634-1640; East TX Van and Bus 632-8267; Greater LFK Rental Cars 632-6611; Hertz 632-2822.

Information: Visitors & Convention Bureau, Box 1606, Lufkin, TX 75902, Phone: 634-6305.

Angelina County Airport Cafe:

The Angelina County Airport Cafe is located next door to the fixed base operation on the field. This cafe is open from 7 a.m. to 3 p.m. Monday through Friday and closed on weekends. Items on their menu include hamburgers, steak sandwiches, steak finger baskets, a variety of other selections including luncheon specials like meat loaf, chicken and dumplings, and chili. They also specialize in making peanut butter cup candy on the premises. Average prices run $4.00 for breakfast and lunch. Seating capacity is 20 persons. Both counter and booth service is available. Meals can be prepared to go if choosing selections off their menu. As an added service, in-flight catering is provided. This restaurant is owned and operated by one individual, devoted to fixing meals and serving the airport employees and guests that fly in for a bite to eat. The Angelina County Airport is located 7 miles from town, which means that in order to operate, they depend largely on fly-in customers to help subsidize this establishment. Next time you are in the area ,why not stop in for a good home cooked meal, and maybe a bag of homemade candy to take back to your friends or family. For information about the Angelina County Airport Cafe call 634-7511.

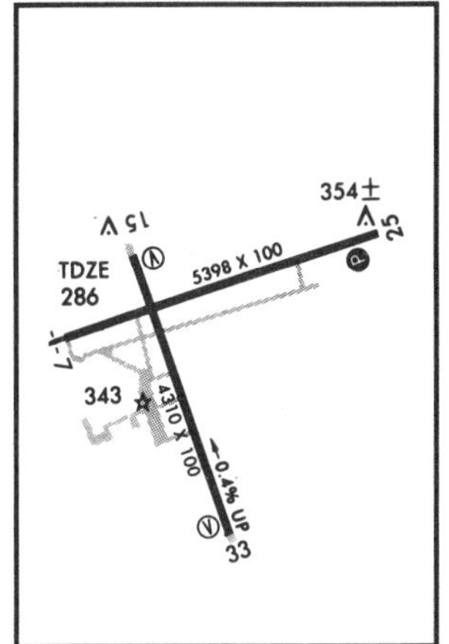

Airport Information:

LUFKIN - ANGELINA COUNTY AIRPORT (LFK)
7 mi southwest of town N31-14.04 W94-45.00 Elev: 296 Fuel: 100LL, Jet-A
Rwy 07-25: H5398x100 (Asph-Grvd) Rwy 15-33: H4310x100 (Asph) Attended: daylight hours Unicom: 123.0
FBO: Angelina County Airport Phone: 634-7511

TX-MFE - McALLEN MILLER INTERNATIONAL

(Area Code 210) 49

The Rose Room and Airport Hilton Inn:

The Rose Room Restaurant is located within the Hilton Inn adjacent to the Miller International Airport. Shuttle transportation is provided to the restaurant by the hotel. Also, McCreery Aviation and Combs Aviation have courtesy vehicles that can transport you to the Hilton Inn. This restaurant is listed as a fine dining facility and offers a full range of items on their menu. Sunday brunch as well as a daily buffet is offered (Except Saturday nights). The decor of the restaurant is formal, with linintable cloths and place settings. If your flying club or organization is planning a meeting or your business associates are arranging a conference, this restaurant can accommodate groups of 5 to 300 persons. Catering is also available with items like muffins, and sandwiches as well as hot meals. The Hilton Inn contains 149 rooms, swimming pool, hot tubs, dancing in their lounge (4 p.m. to 2 a.m.), and lighted tennis courts. Free transportation to the airport, and shopping mall is provided. For more information call 687-1161.

Attractions:

The Santa Ana National Wildlife Refuge is located about 8 miles east of the airport, on I-281. A 2,000 acre preserve with forests and lakes include over 380 different species of birds, auto tours covering 7 miles and 12 miles of walking paths and foot trails. An interpretive tram tour operates between November and April departing from the visitors center. For information write, Santa Ana Natl. Wildlife Refuge, Route 2, Box 202A, Alamo FL 78516 or call 787-3079; There are several golf courses located within town, about 2 to 3 miles north of the airport. County and state parks with boating and fishing on the Rio Grande River are within seven to ten miles from the airport. A One hour drive east will get you to South Padre Island for fishing, swimming and boating.

Restaurants Near Airport:

Beacon Harbor	Adj. Arpt.	Phone: 682-1578
Casa Del Taco	Est. 1/4 mi.	Phone: N/A
Johnney's	Est. 1/4 mi.	Phone: N/A
Rose Room Hilton	Adj. Arpt.	Phone: 687-1161

Lodging: LaQuinta Motor Inn (Free Trans) 1100 South 10th Street, Phone: 687-1101; Compri-Casa DePalmas (Free Trans) 101 North Main Street, Phone: 631-1101; Fairway Resort (Free Trans) 2105 South 10th Street, Phone: 682-2445; Holiday Inn-Civic Center (Free Trans) US 38 at 2nd Street, Phone: 686-2471; Embassy Suites (Free Trans) 1800 South 2nd Street, Phone: 686-3000; Hilton Inn (Free Trans) 2721 South 10th Street, Phone: 687-8651.

Meeting Rooms: All lodging facilities listed above have meeting rooms available to their guests. (See lodging above)

Transportation: McCreery Aviation, 686-1774 and AMR Combs, 687-8171, both provide courtesy transportation. Rental Cars: Avis, 686-4122; Budget, 686-0323; Dollar, 687-7297; Hertz, 687-9564; National, 686-5124

Information: Chamber of Commerce, 10 North Broadway, P.O. Box 790, McAllen, TX 78505, Phone: 682-2871.

Airport Information:

McALLEN - MILLER INTERNATIONAL (MFE)
2 mi south of town N26-10.54 W98-14.31 Elev: 107 Fuel: 100LL, Jet-A
Rwy 13-31: H7108x150 (Asph-Grvd) Rwy 18-36: H2648x60 (Asph) Attended: 1200-0600Z
Atis: 128.5 Unicom: 122.95 Tower: 118.5 Gnd Con: 121.8 Public Phone 24hrs
FBO: MFE International Phone: 687-8446
FBO: McCreery Aviation Phone: 686-1774, 800-999-6195

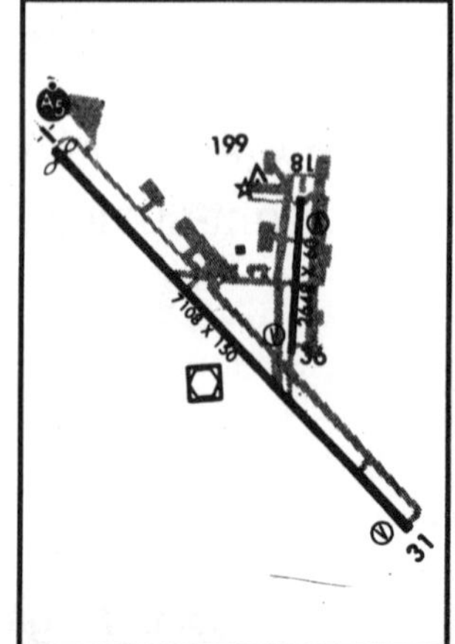

TX-MAF - MIDLAND
MIDLAND INTERNATIONAL

(Area Code 915)

50

Host Marriott:

The Host Marriott cafe is located on the lower level of the Midland International Airport terminal building. This coffee shop is open between 5:30 a.m. and 9 p.m. Specialties of this cafe include chicken fried steaks, Fajitas, and Taco Salad. Average prices run $4.00 for breakfast, $5.00 for lunch and $7.00 for dinner. The restaurant is decorated in a Western theme. Groups and parties are welcome with advance reservations. Pilots on-the-go can arrange carry-out orders like cheese trays, sandwiches, hot meals or just about anything from their menu. A 25% discount is given only to airline pilots. For more information call 563-0860.

Attractions:

Confederate Air Force Headquarters adjacent to airport.

Restaurants Near Airport:

Best Western Restaurant	Adj	Phone: 561-8000
Host Marriott	On Site	Phone: 563-0860
Rosa Cafe	Adj	Phone: N/A
Warfield's Truck Stop	2 mi	Phone: N/A

Lodging: Free transportation to the following: Best Western Airport (Adjacent Airport) 561-8000; La Quinta 697-9900; Plaza Inn 365-3222; Hilton Inn 683-6131.

Meeting Rooms: Best Western Airport (Adjacent Airport) 561-8000; La Quinta 697-9900; Plaza Inn 365-3222; Hilton Inn 683-6131.

Transportation: Courtesy Car; Taxi's: Deluxe 684-9181; M & M 683-2815; Midland 559-5433; Odessa City Cab 337-5501; Western cab 687-4846; Car Rental: Avis 563-0910; Budget 563-1640; Dollar 563-0065; Hertz 563-0110; National 563-0378.

Information: Midland Chamber of Commerce, 109 N. Main, Box 1890, Midland TX 79702, Phone 683-3381 or 800-624-6435.

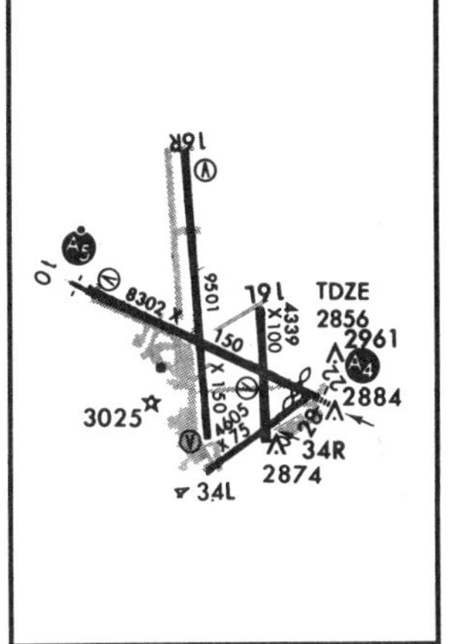

Airport Information:

MIDLAND - MIDLAND INTERNATIONAL AIRPORT (MAF)

8 mi southwest of town N31-56.55 W102-12.12 Elev: 2871 Fuel: 100LL, Jet-A, A1, A1+, B
Rwy 16R-34L: H9501x150 (Asph-Grvd) Rwy 10-28: H8302x150 (Asph-Pfc)
Rwy 04-22: H4605x75 (Asph) Rwy 16L-34R: H4339x100 (Asph) Attended: continuously
Atis: 126.8 Unicom: 122.95 App/Dep Con: 124.6, 121.1 Tower: 118.7 Gnd Con: 121.9
Clnc Del: 118.05

FBO: Avion Flight Center Phone: 563-2033, 800-759-3359

The Confederate Air Force American Airpower Heritage Museum

Midland, TX (TX-MAF)

The origins of the Confederate Air Force date back to the purchase of a surplus Curtiss P-40 Warhawk by Lloyd Nolen, a former World War II Army Air Corps flight instructor, in 1951. In 1957, Nolen and four friends purchased a P-51 Mustang, each sharing in the $2,500 cost of the aircraft. With the purchase of this Mustang, known as "Old Red Nose," the group now known as the Confederate Air Force was unofficially founded.

Legend has it that upon arriving at the Mercedes Airfield in deep south Texas one Sunday morning in 1957, the group found that someone had painted a sign on the fuselage of the P-51 as a joke. The sign read "Confederate Air Force!" All the pilots seemed pleased with the new name, saluted each other and decided it should stay.

Photo by: Paul Hester

In 1958, the group made their second purchase - two Grumman F8F Bearcats for $805 each. With the P-51, this gave the pilots the two most advanced piston-engine fighters to see service with the U.S. Air Force and the U.S. Navy in World War II .

In 1960, the CAF seriously began to search for other World War II aircraft, but it quickly became apparent that very few were still left in flying condition. The CAF Colonels were shocked to find that the aircraft which played such a major role in winning World War II were being rapidly and systematically destroyed. No one, not even the Air Force or Navy were attempting to preserve even one of each type of these historic aircraft for display to future generations!

On September 6, 1961, the Confederate Air Force was chartered as a non-profit Texas corporation in order to restore and preserve World War II-era combat aircraft. By the end of the year, there were nine aircraft in the CAF fleet.

In 1965, the first museum building consisting of 26,000 square feet was completed at old Rebel Field, Mercedes, Texas. The CAF created a new Rebel Field at Harlingen, Texas, when they moved there in 1968, occupying three large buildings. The CAF fleet was rapidly growing and now included medium and heavy bombers such as the B-25, B-26,, B-17 and B-24.

Today, the Confederate Air Force is comprised of more than 8,000 members, several hundred who served as pilots and flight or maintenance crew members committed to preserving World War II American aviation heritage. The year 1991 marked the beginning of a new era for the CAF with the opening of the new Midland headquarters and museum, with better facilities to preserve the CAF fleet, which now numbers over 140 aircraft, for generations to come.

The CAF is an all-volunteer organization, made up of members from all walks of life. Privately funded and totally self-supporting, the non-profit, tax exempt group is dedicated to preserving the military aviation heritage of WW-II.

The CAF includes 94 Wings, Squadrons and Detachments located in 33 U.S. states and districts, and in 4 other countries. Their purpose: is to allow YOU and your fellow Colonels - no matter where you live - to participate in a hands-on way in the activities and events of the Confederate Air Force.

Anyone arriving at the Midland International Airport commercial terminal can hail the Premier parking van outside the baggage area and be transported free to the Confederate Air Force Museum. It is a two minute ride. The Premier van also will pick arrivers up at Andy FBO on the west side of the field, call 563-5911. Those landing at Air Park, Schlemeyer, or the FBO on the south side of MIA, will need to call a cab, hitch a ride, or rent a car and drive a short distance to the museum, that abuts MIA alpha taxiway.

Photo by: Paul Hester

The American Airpower Heritage Museum is open daily, except Christmas. Hours of operation are from 9 a.m. to 5 p.m. Monday through Saturday and from 12 noon to 5 p.m. on Sunday and holidays. For further information call the museum at 915-563-1000.

Annual Airshow:

Each year, on the second full weekend on October, CAF Headquarters host its exciting "AIRSHO". Focus of the annual show is the "Ghost Squadron's" awesome re-enactment of World War II battle scenes. From the chilling attack on Pearl Harbor to the final battles of the Pacific, the sky is filled with re-creations of air battles of European and Pacific conflicts. The explosive sights and sounds of battle are brought to life with an exciting array of pyrotechnics. Spectators enjoy a ring-side seat as approximately 100 vintage aircraft take to the skies over West Texas. (Information submitted by museum)

Photo by: Paul Hester

(Area Code 210)

51

TX-3R5 - NEW BRAUNFELS
NEW BRAUNFELS MUNICIPAL

Cloud 9 Restaurant:

The Cloud 9 Restaurant is reported to be located on the New Braunfels Municipal Airport adjacent to the fixed base operator on the south side of the field. You might want to verify location of the FBO as the main ramp is on the north side of the field. This restaurant is a combination cafe and family style facility. Their hours are 7 a.m. to 3 or 4 p.m. through the week. Specialties of the house include full course breakfasts, tacos, hamburgers, chicken fried steaks, grilled cheese, soup and their special chef salads. They even have a vegetarian selection for those watching their waistline. A lighter children's menu is also available. They also specialize in preparing desserts. The dining room can seat about 30 people with tables and counter service. Two large windows allow a view of the field. Flying groups like the "Fair Weather Flyers" and their 50 members often arrange to have their group meet at Cloud 9 Restaurant for meals. In-flight catering and carry-out can also be easily arranged. The casual and friendly atmosphere of this restaurant attracts fly-in visitors from all around. For information call 629-1700.

Restaurants Near Airport:

Cloud 9 Restaurant On Site Phone: 629-1700

Lodging: John Newcombe's Tennis Ranch Resort (free trans.) 625-9105; Hill Country Inn 6 mi 625-7373; Holiday Inn 4 mi 625-8017; Rodeway Inn 4 mi 629-6991.

Meeting Rooms: None reported

Transportation: Rental cars: Budget 625-8137, 625-6972.

Information: New Braunfels Chamber of Commerce, 390 S. Seguin Avenue, P.O. Box 311417, New Braunfels, TX 78131, Phone: 625-2385 or 800-572-2626.

Attractions:

Landa Park is about 5 miles from the airport and has an 18-hole golf course, miniature golf, glass bottom boat rides and concessions, 629-PARK; John Newcombe's Tennis Ranch is located about 7 miles from the airport. This ranch offers transportation to their facility from the airport. 28 tennis courts as well as entertainment and dancing are available. They also have a 46 room lodge and 10 cottages. For information call 625-9105.

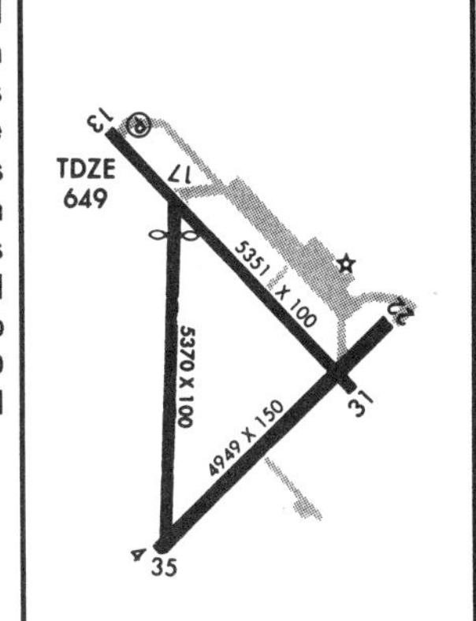

Airport Information:

NEW BRAUNFELS - NEW BRAUNFELS MUNICIPAL (3R5)

4 mi east of town N29-42.18 W98-02.46 Elev: 649 Fuel: 100LL, Jet-A Rwy 17-35: H5370x100 (Asph) Rwy 13-31: H5351x100 (Asph) Rwy 04-22: H4949x150 (Asph) Attended: daylight hours Unicom: 122.7

FBO: Brauntex Aviation Phone: 629-1700

(Area Code 817)

52

TX-ONY - OLNEY
OLNEY MUNICIPAL AIRPORT

Rodge's Grill & Deli:

Rodge's Restaurant is located about 4 miles from the Olney Municipal Airport and can be reached by courtesy car provided through Stark's Aviation (See Airport Information). This family-style restaurant is open Monday through Saturday from 11 a.m. to 8:30 p.m. (Closed Sundays). Specialties of this establishment include a full menu selection, deli sandwiches of all types, chicken fried steak, hamburger steak, cheeseburgers, chicken strips, fish platters, Mexican dinners, Enchiladas and salads. The main dining room has 9 tables and seating for about 36 people. The decor portrays a "Down Home Country" type atmosphere with checkered table cloths. This is a popular restaurant with local customers. Roger, the owner of the restaurant is a pilot himself. Mr. Stark of Starks Aviation has been a loyal customer of this establishment for years and frequents the restaurant almost every day. This comfortable, casual and friendly restaurant is also visited by many fly-in customers landing at Olney Municipal Airport. They will do there best to find a way to get you to the restaurant. It might not be a bad idea if you called or radioed ahead to see if an airport courtesy car can be obtained. For more information about Rodge's Grill and Deli call 564-2056.

Restaurants Near Airport:

Rodge's Grill & Deli 4 mi Phone: 564-2056

Lodging: Olney Inn (Pick-up service) 817-564-5519; Pipeliner Inn (4 miles) 564-5695;

Meeting Rooms: Rodge's Restaurant has a private dining room available to accommodate groups up to 55.

Transportation: Stark's Aviation can provide courtesy transportation to nearby facilities given advance notice. Call 564-2938.

Information: Wichita Falls Convention & Visitors Bureau, P.O. Box 630, Wichita Fall, TX 76307, Phone: 817-723-2741 or 800-799-6732.

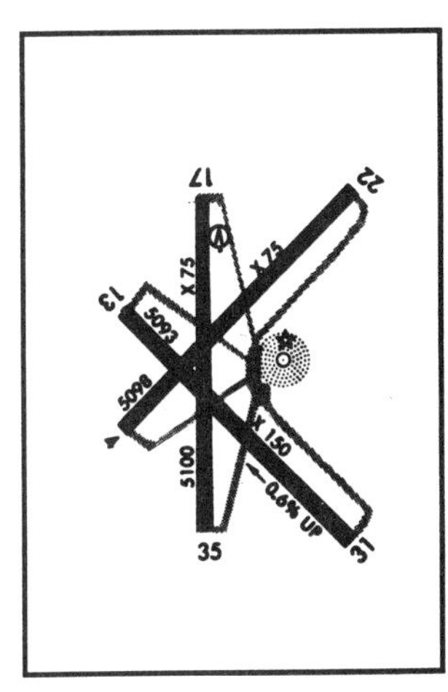

Airport Information:

OLNEY - OLNEY MUNICIPAL AIRPORT (ONY)

3 southwest of town N33-21.05 W98-49.15 Elev: 1274 Fuel: 100LL, Jet-A, MOGAS Rwy 17-35: H5100x75 (Asph) Rwy 04-22: H5098x75 (Asph) Rwy 13-31: H5093x150 (Asph) Attended: 1400-2300Z Unicom: 122.8 Public Phone 24hrs Notes: No Fees for landing or parking

FBO: Stark's Aviation Phone: 564-2938

TX-2R8 - PORT ARANSAS MUSTANG BEACH AIRPORT

(Area Code 512)

53

Port Aransas Island: (Cottage & Condo Rental)

Port Aransas is located on the northern tip of Mustang Island off of the coast of Texas. Mustang Beach Airport is located just 1/6 of a mile from wide, white gulf beaches, swimming, surfing, deep-sea fishing, bird watching or just strolling under the sun. Port Aransas offers many shops with a wide selection of hand-made articles, beachwear, shell and souvenir gifts. Several fine restaurants offer delicious fresh seafood while overlooking the scenic harbor in casual island atmosphere. Accommodations in Port Aransas vary from comfortable rental cottages to condominiums which provide the family an opportunity to vacation without leaving the comforts of home. There are three rental seasons: September through February; March through May; and June through August. Rates vary according to the size of the accommodations and the time of year. Advance reservations are recommended. For more information about activities, rates and accommodations in Port Aransas, contact the Chamber of Commerce at 749-5919.

Restaurants Near Airport:
Port Aransas restaurants 2 mi. Phone:749-5919

Lodging: Aransas Princess Condo (1/6 mile) 749-5118; Courtyard Condos (1/4 mile) 749-5243; Executive Keys (1/2 mile) 749-6272; Island Dunes (1/2 mile) 749-4923; Island Retreat (2 miles) 749-6222; Sea Isle (2 miles) 749-6211

Meeting Rooms: None reported

Transportation: Taxi service: American Transportation 749-5589

Information: Chamber of Commerce, 421 W. Cotter, P.O. Box 356, Port Aransas, TX 78373, Phone: 749-5919

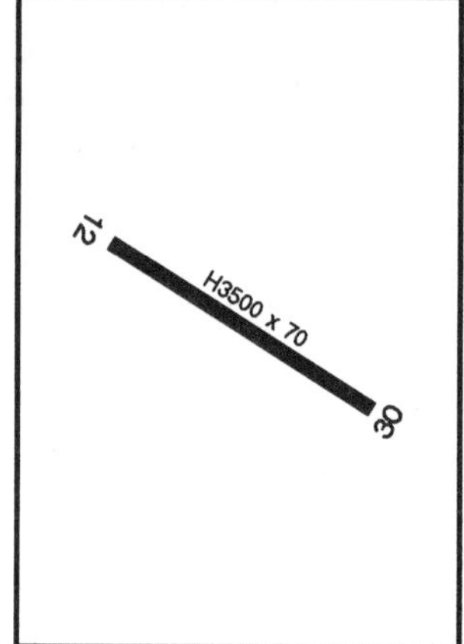

Airport Information:

PORT ARANSAS - MUSTANG BEACH AIRPORT (2R8)
2 mi southwest of town N27-48.69 W97-05.35 Elev: 5 Fuel: None Reported Rwy 12-30: H3500x70 (Asph) Attended: Unattended CTAF: 122.9 Notes: Overnight parking fees are $4.00 for grass and $5.00 for asphalt.
FBO: Airport Manager (City Hall) Phone: 749-4111

TX-T97 - PORT LAVACA CALHOUN COUNTY AIRPORT

(Area Code 512)

54

Harvey's Restaurant & Club:

Harvey's Restauant & Club is situated about 6 miles south of the Calhoun County Airport. This restaurant can be reached by arranging for a courtesy car from Calhoun County Aviation, (552-2933). Specialties of the house include shrimp, flounder (whole & stuffed) appetizers, choice steaks and a large salad bar with all entrees. A lunch buffet is featured every day 11 a.m. to 2 p.m. except on Sunday. Prices for entrees run $5.75 for lunch and $11.00 for dinner. Restaurant hours are from 11 a.m. to 10 p.m. Monday through Saturday. This restaurant specializes in banquet service. Groups planning and arranging a luncheon or evening meal for their fly-in club, business, etc., are welcome. This restaurant is furnished with a variety of antiques. Dining can be enjoyed while overlooking the Lavaca Bay. For information about this restaurant you can call 552-5433.

Restaurants Near Airport:

Crows Nest	15 mi S.	Phone: 552-1964
Harvey's Restauarnt	6 mi S.	Phone: 552-5433
Wagon Train	4 mi S.	Phone: 552-3056

Lodging: Days Inn, Highway 35 Bypass, Phone: 552-4511

Meeting Room: Days Inn conference room, Phone: 552-4511

Transportation: Calhoun County Aviation can provide transportation if advance notice is given to nearby restaurants, etc. Also transportation can be arranged through; Marshall Chev. (car rental), 552-6791 or City Cab, 552-3822.

Information: Port Lavaca-Calhoun County Chamber of Commerce, 2300 TX 35 Bypass, P.O. Box 528, Port Lavaca, TX 77979, Phone: 552-2959.

Attraction:

Port Lavaca Causeway State Recreation Park had an old highway causeway, replaced by a modern span. This has become a popular lighted fishing pier that extends 3,202 feet into the Lavaca Bay. Swimming, boating and saltwater fishing are available to visitors. (A slight fee is charged for pier)

Airport Information:

PORT LAVACA - CALHOUN COUNTY AIRPORT (T97)
3 mi northwest of town N28-39.24 W96-40.88 Elev: 34 Fuel: 100LL, Jet-A Rwy 14-32: H5004x75 (Asph) Attended: 1400-0100Z Unicom: 122.8 Public phone 24hrs
FBO: Calhoun County Aviation Phone: 552-2933

TX-RKP ROCKPORT ARANSAS COUNTY AIRPORT

(Area Code 512)

55

Back 40 Restaurant:

The Back 40 restaurant is located 1 mile south of the Aransas County Airport. To reach the restaurant you take Hwy 35 south approx. 1 mile. The restaurant is on the right side of the street. Courtesy transportation was declined by both the airport and restaurant facility. However, taxi service is available. Perhaps courtesy transportation may be arranged if you call well enough in advance. This family style restaurant is open 7 a.m. to 9 p.m. and specializes in a deluxe salad bar, shrimp salad, homemade soups, seafood and steaks. Breakfast specials run $2.00 from 7 a.m. to 11 a.m. and lunch specials at $3.99 week days from 11 a.m. to 4 p.m. Regular menu selections average $3.00 for breakfast, $5.50 for lunch, and $8.00 for dinner. The restaurant has a Spanish decor with hand painted murals in each dining room. Accommodations for groups of 10 to 70 persons are available. For information call 729-3478.

Restaurants Near Airport:

Back 40 Rest.	1 mi S	Phone: 729-3478
Charlotte	3 mi S	Phone: 729-1185
Puck Inn	6 mi S	Phone: 729-6663
Sand Dollar Pvn	3 mi S	Phone: 729-8909

Lodging: Rockport Best Western (1 mile) 729-8351; Kon-Tiki (2 miles) 729-4975, 800-242-3407; Laquana Reef (7 miles) 729-1742; Sand Dollar Resort (2 miles) 729-2381

Meeting: Rockport Best Western (1 mile) 729-8351;

Transportation: Sand Dollar Pavillion Restaurant (3 miles south) will pick up guests dining at their facility. Also Taxi service available, 729-0025; Avis Rental Cars 790-0141.

Information: Chamber of Commerce, 404 Broadway, Rockport, TX 78382, Phone: 729-6445.

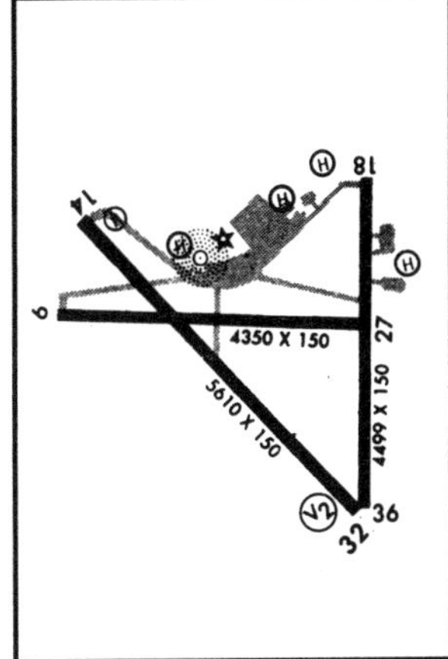

Airport Information:

ROCKPORT - ARANSAS COUNTY AIRPORT (RKP)
4 mi north N28-05.21 W97-02.67 Elev: 24 Fuel: 100LL, Jet-A
Rwy 14-32: H5610x150 (Asph) Rwy 18-36: H4499x150 (Asph) Rwy 09-27 H4350x150 (Asph)
Attended: May-Sept 1300-0100Z Unicom: 122.8 Public Phone 24hrs Notes: Avis cars on airport, automated fuel terminal (100LL) 24hrs a day.
FBO: Aransas County Airport Phone: 790-0141

TX-SJT - SAN ANGELO MATHIS FIELD AIRPORT

(Area Code 915)

56

Mathis Field Cafe:

The Mathis Field Cafe is located in the terminal building on the Mathis Field Airport. This facility specializes in preparing American and Chinese food, and is open Monday through Thursday 11 a.m. to 8 p.m., Friday and Saturday 11 a.m. to 9 p.m. (Closed Sunday). Additional selections available are shrimp plates, homemade soups and oriental meals such as "Hon-sil & Kungbao" chicken dinners with fried rice. Weekly specials are also provided. Their dining room can serve 100 guests, and has an Oriental atmosphere decorated with all types of aviation related pictures. Large groups are welcome with advance notice. Meals can also be prepared-to-go if requested. In-flight catering is another service offered to pilots, their crews and passengers. During our interview with the management, we learned that this restaurant might be the only Chinese restaurant that is actually located right on an airport. For more information about the Mathis Field Cafe call 942-1172.

Restaurants Near Airport:

China Gardens	5 mi N.	Phone: 959-2838
John Zentners Daughter	5 mi NE.	Phone: 949-2821
Mathis Field Cafe	On Site	Phone: 942-1172
Ponchos Restaurant	4 mi NE.	Phone: 949-9010

Lodging: Holiday Inn (10 miles NE, Trans) 658-2828; La Quinta (5 miles N, Trans) 653-1323; Ramada Inn (5 miles N, Trans) 944-2578.

Meeting Rooms: Mathis Field has a conference room in the terminal building. Call 944-1211 for appointment, (Free use) next to cafe which provides catering and will accommodate 30 people.

Transportation: Ranger Aviation is reported to have courtesy cars available 949-3773. Also Taxi Service: All American 658-1982; J & J Cab 658-2444; Yellow Cab 655-3104; Rental Cars: Budget 944-4718; Hertz 944-1221; National 944-9505.

Information: Convention & Visitors Bureau, 500 Rio Concho Drive, San Angelo, TX 76903, Phone: 653-1206 or 800-375-1206.

Attractions:

San Angelo Country Club (5 miles E.) golf, tennis and restaurant on premises 655-3144; Bentwood Country Club (4 miles N.) golf, tennis and restaurant on premises 944-0520.

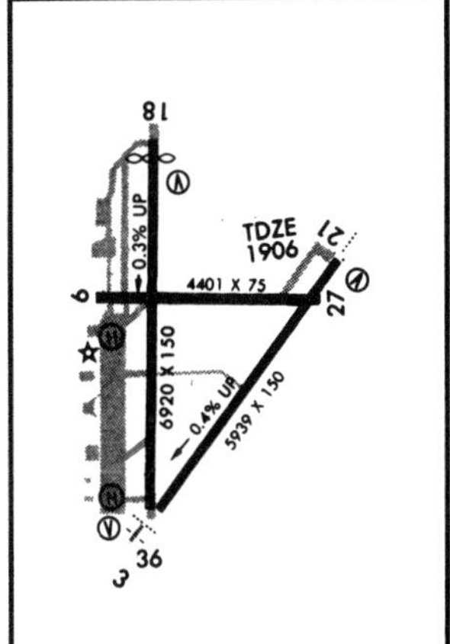

Airport Information:

SAN ANGELO - MATHIS FIELD AIRPORT (SJT)
7 mi southwest of town N31-21.50 W100-29.76 Elev: 1916 Fuel: 100LL, Jet-A
Rwy 18-36: H6920x150 (Asph-Grvd) Rwy 03-21: H5939x150 (Asph-Grvd) Rwy 09-27: H4401x75 (Asph) Attended: 1200-0500Z Atis: 128.45 Unicom: 122.95 Tower: 118.3 Gnd Con: 121.9
Public Phone 24hrs Notes: FSS on field 122.25, operates 24hrs, Weather bureau on field, 24hrs; No landing fees, no tie-down fees reported.
FBO: Ranger Aviation Phone: 949-3773, 800-326-5758
FBO: Southwest Air Center Phone: 944-1543

TX-SAT - SAN ANTONIO
SAN ANTONIO INTL. AIRPORT

Restaurants Near Airport:
CA1 Services On Site

(Area Code 210)
Phone: 821-4800

57

CA1 Services:

CA1 Services situated at the San Antonio International Airport, manages several eateries throughout the airport. During our interview, we learned that a newly opened food court will contain several facilities located both in terminal 1 & 2. Transportation from general aviation fixed based operators to the terminal building, will have to be arranged through the fixed based operators. Taxi service is also available on the airport. Specialties include burgers, barbecued items, pizza, salads, tacos and Chinese dishes. Prices average $4.00 for breakfast and $6.00 for lunch and dinner. Daily specials are also provided. The decor of their restaurants are modern with a western and Italian flair. CA1 Services also provides in-flight catering as a major part of their business. Catered meals can be prepared and are available to both private or business pilots crews as well as passengers. There are 3 FBOs that have accounts with CA1 Services for in-flight catering. Orders may be placed at the fixed based operators and, for a slight fee, delivered to the aircraft. Participating FBOs are Nayak/Million Air 824-7511; Fairchild Gen-Aero 824-2313; and Air Star Aviation 820-8525. For more information about the services available call 821-4800.

Lodging: Amerisuites-San Antonio (1 mile, trans) 342-4800; Courtyard by Marriott (1 mile, trans) 828-7200; Econo Lodge (2 miles, trans) 344-4581; Embassy Suites Airport (2 miles, trans) 525-9999; Executive Guesthoues-Airport (1-1/2 miles) 494-7600; Fountain Plaza (1 mile) 366-2424; Hampton Inn-San Antonio (Trans) 366-1800; Holiday Inn (1 mile, trans) 349-9900; La Mansion Del Norte (1 mile, trans) 341-3535; La Quinta Inn-Airport East (Adj Arpt, trans) 828-0781; La Quinta Inn-Airport West (1 mile, trans) 342-4291; Radisson Hotel Airport (Trans) 340-6060; Ramada Inn-Airport (1 mile, trans) 828-9031;

Meeting Rooms: All hotels and lodging facilities listed above have airport courtesy transportation available.

Transportation: Taxi service available at airport. Also: rental cars: Advantage 341-8211; Alamo 828-7967; Avis 826-6332; Budget 828-5639; Dollar 341-1424; General 822-4975; Hertz 826-0651; National 824-7544; Thrifty 333-7368.

Information: Chamber of Commerce, 390 South Sequin Avenue, P.O. Box 311417, New Braunfels, TX 78131, Phone: 625-2385 or 800-572-2626.

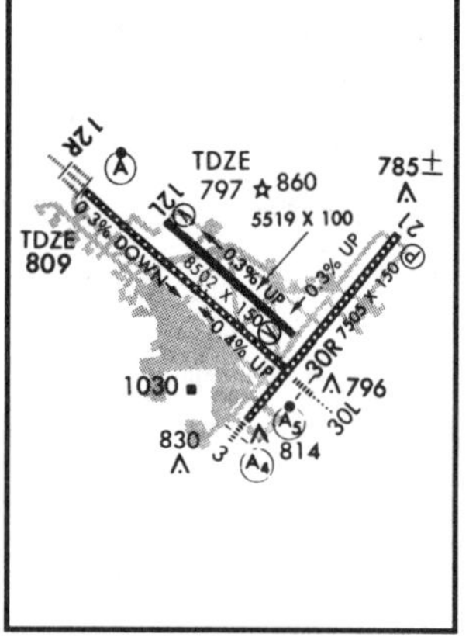

Airport Information:

SAN ANTONIO - SAN ANTONIO INTERNATIONAL AIRPORT (SAT)
7 mi north of town N29-32.02 W98-28.19 Elev: 809 Fuel: 100LL, Jet-A,B
Rwy 12R-30L: H8502x150 (Conc-Grvd) Rwy 03-21: H7505x150 (Conc-Grvd) Rwy 12L-30R: H5519x100 (Asph) Attended: continuously Atis: 118.9 Unicom: 122.95 App/Dep Con: 128.05, 125.1, 124.45, 118.05, 127.1, 125.7 Tower: 119.8 Gnd Con: 121.9 Clnc Del: 126.7

FBO: Air Star Aviation Phone: 820-8525
FBO: Aviation San Antonio Phone: 828-0551
FBO: Fairchild Gen-Aero Phone: 824-2313
FBO: Gen-Aero San Antonio Phone: 800-327-2313
FBO: Hallmark Jet Center Phone: 828-8181
FBO: Million Air Phone: 824-7511
FBO: Raytheon Acft.Serv. Phone: 824-7503

Hangar 9, Brooks A.F.B. Texas

San Antonio, TX (TX-SSF)

Hangar 9 is the oldest wooden aircraft hangar in the United States Air Force. It was built as a "temporary" structure in the winter of 1917-18 when Brooks Field was being constructed to serve as an instructor's training base for the Air Service of the Army Signal Corps. In 1969, a group of local citizens raised funds in the community and arranged to restore the old hangar to existing Air Force construction specifications and return it to the Air Force. Subsequently the hangar has been included in the Texas State Historical Survey, entered in the National Register of Historic Places, and designated a National Historic Landmark.

The hangar was dedicated as a memorial to Astronaut Edward H. White II, a native of San Antonio. It houses the Museum of Flight Medicine and contains exhibits concerning the history of the base, the development of manned flight, and the evolution of aerospace medicine.

As history is made in the aerospace age, the museum will grow, and will at the same time continue to preserve the heritage of the menwho first took to the air when Hangar 9 was new. Any pilot arriving at San Antonio would do best to land at Stinson Field (SSF), which is located one mile west of the Base. Hangar 9 is open 8 a.m. to 4 p.m., Monday through Friday. Closed Saturdays, Sundays and holidays. Admission is free. For information call the museum curator at 210-536-2203. (Information submitted by museum)

Photo by: Hangar 9 Museum Hangar 9, Edward H. White II, Memorial Museum

TX-T66 - SAN BENITO
SAN BENITO MUNICIPAL AIRPORT

(Area Code 210) **58, 59**

Restaurants Near Airport:

Blue Marlin Rest.	4-6 blks	Phone: 399-6412
Cilito Lindo Rest.	4-6 blks	Phone: 399-1145
Stars Drive-In	2 blks	Phone: 399-9007

Lodging: Ramada Inn (5 miles); Rancho Viejo (7 miles); Sheraton Inn; Sun Valley Motor Inn (5 miles).
Meeting Rooms: None Reported
Transportation: Both courtesy and rental cars reported to be available through the airport manager's office, phone: 399-9942
Information: Harlingen Chamber of Commerce, 311 East Tyler Street, Harlingen, TX 78550, Phone: 423-5440 or 800-531-7346.

Stars Drive-Inn:

The Stars Drive-Inn is situated about 2 blocks from the San Benito Municipal Airport. This fast food drive-in is west of the field along business highway 77. According to the airport manager's office, fly-in guests can reach this facility by walking. Even though there are sit down accommodations at this location, fly-in customers can grab a bite to eat, "on the go". Their menu includes an assortment of hamburgers and cheeseburgers, chili dogs, French fries,Onion rings, salads, as well as ice cream and dessert delights. Most of their sandwiches are $2.50 to $3.00. Daily specials offer .99 cent hamburger and $2.59 combo burger specials served with beverage and fries. They have a walk up window where customers can place their orders. For information about the Stars Drive-In call 399-9007.

Blue Marlin:

The Blue Marlin Restaurant is located about 4 to 6 blocks from the San Benito Municipal Airport and provide sit down table service for their customers. During our conversation with the airport manager, we learned that this family style restaurant is a favorite with many locals in the area, and has just been built recently. For information call the Blue Marlin at 399-6412.

NO AIRPORT DIAGRAM AVAILABLE

Airport Information:

SAN BENITO - SAN BENITO MUNICIPAL AIRPORT (T66)
1 mi east of town N26-08.02 W97-36.77 Elev: 31 Fuel: 100LL
Rwy 12-30: H3200x50 (Asph) Rwy 18-36: H1900x30 (Asph) Attended: 1300-0100Z
Unicom: 122.8 Notes: Rwy 18-36 temporarily marked lighted as taxiway, used as crosswind runway indefinitely; Day VFR only.
San Benito Municipal Airport Phone: 399-2948, 399-9942

TX-E29 - SONORA
SONORA MUNICIPAL AIRPORT

(Area Code 915) **60**

Restaurants Near Airport:

La Mexicana Restaurant	1/2 mi	Phone: 387-3401
Sutton County Steak House	1/4 mi	Phone: 387-3833

Lodging: Devil's River Inn (Next to runway) 387-3516

Meeting Rooms: Sutton County Steak House can accommodate business groups and has accommodations for conferences at their facility 387-3833.

Transportation: Free transportation by airport manager is available within immediate vicinity of airport and if advance notice is given. Slight charge to nearby entertainment facilities. Also rental cars are available through Bronco Ford Sales 387-2549.

Information: Chamber of Commerce, 705 North Crockett, Box 1172, Sonora, TX 76950, Phone: 387-2880.

Sutton County Steak House:

This fine dining restaurant is located adjacent to the Sonora Municipal Airport and is open for business Monday through Saturday between 6 a.m. and 2 p.m., and 5 p.m. to 9:30 p.m. On Sunday they are open from 6 a.m. to 2 p.m. The specialties of the house include prime steak dishes, hamburgers, sandwiches, seafood and a different varieties of chicken selections. A special entree is offered every day and every evening, as well as their buffet special on Sunday. Average prices run $4.95 for breakfast, $5.75 for lunch and $7.50 for dinner. The restaurant decor is very modern with a coffee shop and two large dining rooms. They will prepare catered meals for parties, weddings, company meetings Fly-in groups and associations at their facility. For the traveler on-the-go, sandwiches, hot meals, steaks and appetizers can also be prepared for carry-out. For information call 387-3833.

Attractions:

Golf Course located next to runway at Sonora Municipal Airport; Sonora Caverns are 12 miles away and provide unusual rock formations, with guided tours of the area available in addition to camping. For information call 387-3105.

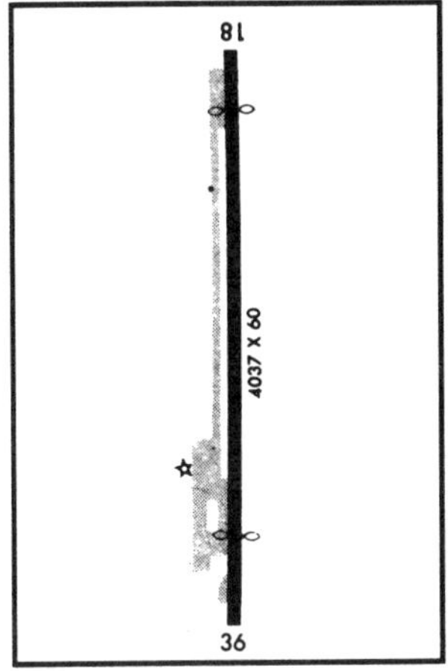

Airport Information:

SONORA - SONORA MUNICIPAL AIRPORT (E29)
1 mi north of town N30-35.14 W100-38.91 Elev: 2139 Fuel: 100LL, Jet-A
Rwy 18-36: H4037x60 (Asph) Attended: continuously Unicom: 122.8 Public Phone 24hrs
Notes: No landing fees; Overnight hanger fee $5.00/night.
Airport Manager Phone: 387-2447

TX-SEP - STEPHENVILLE CLARK FIELD MUNICIPAL

61

The Jennie Lee's Catfish & Shrimp Buffet:

This family style restaurant is located 3 miles southwest of the airport and can be reached either by courtesy car from the airport or by local taxi service. This restaurant is open Tuesday through Saturday from 4:30 p.m. to 9 p.m, Sunday 11 a.m. to 2:30 p.m. They are closed on Mondays. Specialties on their menu include 13 items and appetizers. Jennie Lee's Catfish Restaurant is best known for its popular catfish and shrimp all-you-can-eat buffet served all the time with favorites like fried shrimp, boneless skinless chicken breast, gourmet onion rings and homemade hush puppies. The owners do all the cooking and take pride in preparing the most delicious selections available. The buffet runs about $6.55 plus tax and beverage. Refills are encouraged. The decor of the restaurant is unique with 100 large jigsaw puzzles put together, framed, matted and displayed on their walls, halls and bathrooms. Additional items displayed are collector Coca Cola and Dr. Pepper memorabilia some of which are originals dating back many years. The restaurant has seating for about 115 customers. If planning a large group fly-out their restaurant is closed on Mondays making it a good time to plan your event. For information call 968-0355.

Airport Information:

STEPHENVILLE - CLARK FIELD MUNICIPAL (SEP)
1 mi east of town N32-12.92 W98-10.73 Elev: 1321 Fuel: 100LL, Jet-A Rwy 14-32: H4183x60 (Asph) Rwy 03-21: H2413x50 (Asph) Attended: Mon-Sat 1400-0000Z, Sun 1900-2300Z Unicom: 122.8
FBO: C & F Aviation Phone: 965-2795

Restaurants Near Airport: **(Area Code 817)**
Jennie Lee's Catfish 3 mi S.W. Phone: 968-0355
K-Bob's Steakhouse 2 to 3 mi. Phone: 968-4448

Lodging: Best Western Cross Timbers 1-1/2 mi 968-2114; Holiday Inn 2-1/2 mi 968-5256; Raintree Inn 1/2 mi 968-3392; Texan Motor Inn 3 mi 968-5003;
Meeting Rooms: Holiday Inn 2-1/2 mi 968-5256; Raintree Inn 1/2 mi 968-3392.
Transportation: Airport courtesy car reported; Also rental cars: Enterprise 945-6213; Taxi service 965-7592.
Information: Stephenville Chamber of Commerce, 182 West Wahington, BOx 306, Stephenville, TX 76401. Phone: 965-5313 or 965-5313.

Attractions: Dublin, TX is about eleven miles southwest of Stephenville, TX and has the oldest Dr. Pepper bottling plant in the world. The plant has a museum containing the largest and most complete collections of Dr. Pepper memorabilia anywhere. There are tours given of the plant and museum. For information call the Dublin Chamber of Commerce at 817-445-3422.

NO AIRPORT DIAGRAM AVAILABLE

TX-(Private) TERLINGUA
TERLINGUA RANCH AIRSTRIP

(Area Code 915)

62

Terlingua Ranch Lodge:

Before the 1899 U.S. Geological Survey border expedition, the Big Bend of Texas was known only as desolate country. Discovery of quicksilver at the turn of the century led to the development of the Terlingua mining district, which flourished before and during World War I as the leading source of the then-strategic liquid metal. After the mines watered out, the rugged country may have reverted to almost uninhabited wilderness had it not been for the creation of Big Bend National Park. Many people visited and some fell in love with the unique landscape. One was Dallas businessman David Witt, who purchased Terlingua Ghost Town and the 200,000 acres that eventually became Terlingua Ranch. One of Witt's partners was auto racer Carroll Shelby. When Terlingua Ranch was developed in the late 1960's, the heraldic jackrabbit that adorned Shelby's racing car was retained as part of its logo. Terlingua Ranch Lodge is located deep in the Big Bend country. Whether you arrive by the 16-mile ranch road or their 4,600-foot dirt airstrip, you will be rewarded with a relaxing solitude and intimacy with nature not available in more developed areas around Big Bend National Park. Accommodations include 32 cabin-style motel rooms. RV hookups, and a tent campground. The Ranch restaurant, open all day, seven days a week, offers excellent food served in pleasant surroundings, either inside on the screened front porch, or the stone-terraced patio. Or prepare your own meal using the Texas-size barbecue pit on the patio adjoining their swimming pool. The pool complex includes bathhouses that are also available to campers. Scenic drives take you into Big Bend National Park, Terlingua Ghost Town, or Big Bend Ranch State Natural Area. And their friendly staff can direct you to rafting trips through breathtaking canyons on the Rio Grande, horseback rides to suit skill levels from tenderfoot to top hand, mountain bike tours, or guided hiking trips and bird-watching tours. Explore the Big Bend Country from their secluded base. Hundreds of miles of back roads and trails await your discovery. Bring your horses, bring your bikes, bring your hiking boots. Visit unique Ranch Lodge and truly experience the Big Bend of Texas. For information call them at 371-2416

Restaurants Near Airport:
Terlingua Ranch Lodge On Site Phone: 371-2416

Lodging: Terlingua Ranch Lodge (On site) 32 cabin-style motel rooms, Phone: 371-2416.

Meeting Rooms: Accommodations for group functions and lodging is available, Phone: 371-2416.

Transportation: Terlingua Ranch Lodge has its own dirt airstrip. Rental cars or taxi service not reported.

Information: Alpine Chamber of Commerce, 106 North Third Street, Alpine, TX 79830. Phone: 837-2326.

Attraction:

Terlingua Ranch Lodge 60 miles south of Alpine, TX offers a variety of entertainment including swimming, horse riding, hiking, tours of the Big Bend Country, camping on site and much more. For information call 371-2416.

Airport Information:

TERLINGUA - TERLINGUA RANCH AIRSTRIP (Private)
Private Airstrip Land At Own Risk. Attended: Resort hours.
Notes & Information: (Submitted by resort)
Airstrip headings 210-030 (We strongly recommend landing 210 and take off 030 as the strip has a marked up-slope to the southwest). Length 4,600 feet Elevation 3500 feet, There is a limited number of tie-downs. No services are available, however some flyers do get gas from the regular car gas pumps. The nearest airplane fuel and aircraft services are in Alpine Municipal Airport 60 miles to the north. Airstrip is 180 degrees from Ft. Stockton VOR 100 N.M.; 140 degrees from MARFA VOR 68 N.M., Unicom: 122.8 - 8 a.m.to 5 p.m., We have no rental cars, but the cabins, restaurant and pool are all within walking distance. Call before hand and we will meet you to help with luggage etc. Visit the Big Texas Skies of Terlingua Ranch.
Airport Manager Phone: 371-2416

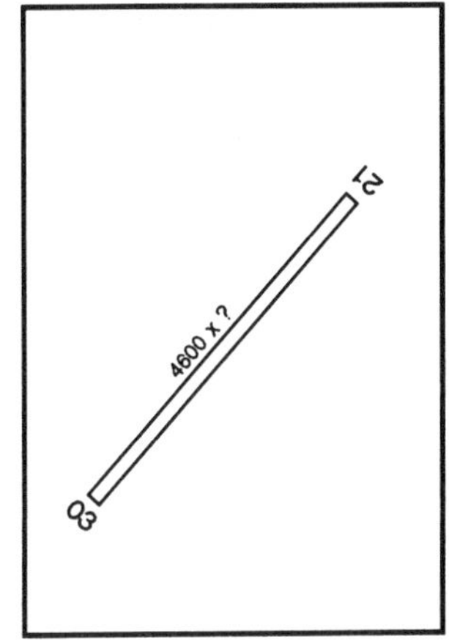

Silent Wings Museum Foundation

Terrell, TX (TRL)

The Silent Wings Museum Foundation is located on the Terrell Municipal Airport in Terrell, Texas. The museum displays a completely restored WWII Waco CG-4A Glider. These gliders were used in the invasions of Normandy, Southern France, Holland, in the Battle of the Bulge (Bastogne), the Rhine River Crossing at Wesel, Germany, as well as seeing action in the China-Burma-India theater.

The museum's beautifully restored Waco CG-4A is the centerpiece of the museum. The restoration took five years of intense effort by the members of the National WW-II Glider Pilots Association. This CG-4A restoration is only the second such restoration in the world, the other one being housed at the Air Force Museum in Dayton, Ohio.

In the Museum's Video Theater, you will have the opportunity to see various showing of WW-II type combat and training film of gliders, glider pilots and airborne troops in action.

In addition to the Video theater, scale model dioramas depict major combat actions in WW-II European Theater of the war. There is also an outstanding collection of WW-II Stars & Stripes newspapers, Yank magazine and hundreds of original documents on WW-II that will be of particular interest to the student and researcher.

The museum is dedicated to the memory of all WW-II airborne personnel. It has a wide appeal, depicting the role of Military Glider Pilots, the Paratroopers, Glider-Borne Troops, Glider Mechanics and Tow Pilots as well as other members of the Air Force's Troop Carrier Command.

Silent Wings Museum Foundation is recognized as a publicly-supported museum non-profit organization. The museum is open 10:00 a.m. to 5:00 p.m. Tuesday through Saturday and 12 noon to 5:00 p.m. on Sunday. Admission Free. Contributions however, are greatly appreciated. For information about this museum, call 214-563-0402 or write to the Silent Wings Museum Foundation, P.O. Box 775, Terrell, Texas 75160. (Submitted by Silent Wings Museum Foundation).

Photo: by Silent Wings Museum Foundation

TX-TYR - TYLER
TYLER POUNDS FIELD

(Area Code 903) 63

Restaurants Near Airport:
JW Finns Airline Cafe On Site Phone: 597-3182

Lodging: Best Western Inn of Tyler (Trans) 595-2681; Holiday Inn-North (Trans) 593-7391; Ramada Inn (Trans) 561-5800; Rodeway (Trans) 595-2451; Sheraton Inn-Tyler (Trans) 597-1301.

Meeting Rooms: Best Western Inn of Tyler 595-2681; Holiday Inn-North 593-7391; Ramada Inn 561-5800; Rodeway Inn 595-2451; Sheraton Inn-Tyler 597-1301.

Transportation: Taxi Service: Rose City 593-8444; Yellow 592-1611; Rental Cars: Avis 592-2613; Hertz 593-2324; National 597-1375; Thrifty 593-6404.

Information: Tyler Convention & Visitors Bureau, 407 North Broadway, Tyler, TX 75702, Phone: 592-1661 or 800-235-5712.

JW Finn's Airline Cafe:

The Airline Restaurant is located in the terminal building at the Tyler Pounds Airport. This combination cafe and family style restaurant is open Monday through Friday 6 a.m. to 8:30 p.m., Saturday and Sunday 7 a.m. to 5:30 p.m. Entrees include breakfast selections, chicken fried steak, all types of sandwiches, homemade desserts as well as a unique item known as their special 4 person hamburger, served on a huge bun baked on the premises, and able to feed 4 people at one time. The dining room furnished with tables and counter service can seat approx. 70 people. Aircraft pictures decorate the walls. Large groups are welcome with advance notice. In-flight catering is another service available on request. For more information call the Airline Restaurant at 597-3182.

Airport Information:

TYLER - TYLER POUNDS FIELD (TYR)
3 mi west of town N32-21.25 W95-24.15 Elev: 544 Fuel: 100LL, Jet-A
Rwy 04-22: H7200x150 (Asph) Rwy 13-31: H5200x150 (Asph-Grvd) Rwy 17-35: H4849x150 (Asph) Attended: 1200-0500Z Atis: 126.25 Unicom: 122.95 Tower: 120.1
Gnd Con: 121.9

FBO: Johnson Aviation Phone: 593-4343
FBO: Tyler Aero Phone: 595-4255
FBO: Tyler Intl. Avia. Schl. Phone: 592-1291

TX-VCT - VICTORIA
VICTORIA REGIONAL AIRPORT

(Area Code 512) 64, 65

Daniel's Restaurant:

Daniel's Restaurant is a family-owned and operated establishment located in the terminal building, at the Victoria Regional Airport. Guests can park their aircraft at the FBO adjacent to the terminal building, and simply walk to the restaurant. This family-style establishment is open from 8 a.m. to 5 p.m. Menu selections include a wide variety of selections including breakfast dishes, juicy hamburger steaks, enchiladas, chicken fried steaks, rib eye steaks, lasagna, shrimp, taco salad and catfish. Guests can also see the activity on the airport from the restaurant. The main dining room can seat 40 persons within the newly-constructed restaurant. In-flight catering can be provided on request. For more information call Daniel's Restaurant at 578-7962.

Leo's Restaurant & Catering Service:

Leo's Restaurant is located on the Victoria Airport about 2 blocks or 1/2 mile from the general aviation parking area. This restaurant is open between 11 a.m. and 11 p.m. 7 days a week. Leo's staff is dedicated to serving the best food and drinks in a congenial and relaxed atmosphere. Their menu contains beef entrees, prime rib, fresh seafood, seafood platters, a diet selection, children and senior citizens menu and last, but not least, their famous Texas Barbecue choices to go. Some of the beef selections include, Leo's Family Style Steak Dinner with flame broiled beef tenderloin; this is the choicest of cuts, sliced and served family style with sauteed fresh mushrooms and onions, baked potato or fries, fresh baked rolls and butter for one $10.95 or for two or more $9.95 each. Additional steaks offered are prime rib, filet mignon, rib-eye steak, Spencer steak, Leo's T-Bone steak, sirloin steak, chicken fried steak, a Texan tradition and hamburger steak. Seafood entrees include a stuffed crab dinner, oyster dinner, catfish, fried shrimp and Half & Half your choice of shrimp, catfish or oysters. A variety of seafood platters are offered, like their combination Reef and Beef, and prime rib and shrimp. Average prices run $6.00 for lunch and $12.00 for dinner. There are 2 main dining rooms. Banquet accommodations can be arranged for 250 people. The restaurant has a distinct western decor, with wooden floors, a rock fireplace, red table cloths with rope ties and even saddles on display. At the time of our interview this restaurant is celebrating its 19th year in business. For more information you can call Leo's Restaurant and Catering Service at 575-3031 or 578-9381.

Restaurants Near Airport:

Daniel's Restaurant	On Site	Phone: 578-7962
Leo's Restaurant	2 blks	Phone: 575-3031

Lodging: Best Western 3 mi 578-9911; Holiday Inn (5 mi Free trans) 575-0251; LaQuinta Inn 7-10 mi 572-3585; Ramada Inn (3 mi free trans) 578-2723

Meeting Rooms: Holiday Inn (5 mi Free trans) 575-0251; LaQuinta Inn 7-10 mi 572-3585; Ramada Inn (3 mi free trans) 578-2723.

Transportation: Taxi service: Allan's Cab 575-8294; Checker Cab 573-6361; Yellow Cab 573-6361; Rental cars: Avis 573-7829; Hertz 575-6502.

Information: Convention & Visitors Bureau, 700 Main Center, Suite 101, Box 2465, Victoria, TX 77902, Phone: 573-5277 or 800-926-5774..

Airport Information:

VICTORIA - VICTORIA REGIONAL (VCT)
5 mi northeast of town N28-51.15 W96-55.11 Elev: 115 Fuel: 100LL, Jet-A Rwy 12L-30R: H9101x150 (Asph-Conc) Rwy 17-35: H4898x150 (Conc) Rwy 12R-30L: H4607x150 (Conc) Rwy 06-24: H4200x75 (Asph) Attended: 1200-0400Z Unicom: 122.7
FBO: Victoria Aviation Service, Inc. Phone: 578-1221

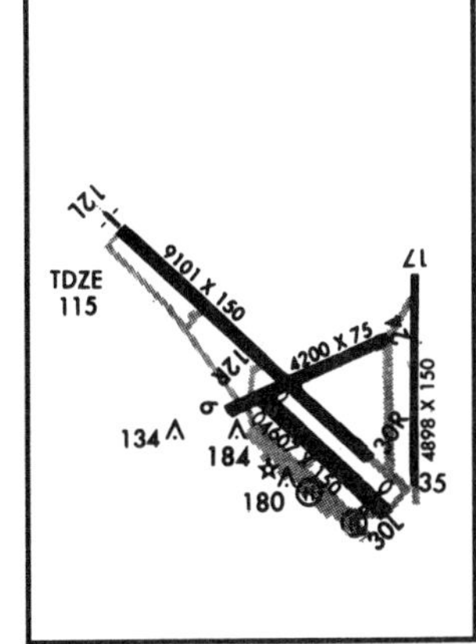

TX-ACT - WACO
WACO REGIONAL AIRPORT

(Area Code 817)

66

Aerodrome Cafe:

The Aerodrome Cafe is located in the terminal building on the Waco Regional Airport. Fly-in guests can park their aircraft at the Texas Aero FBO and walk to the restaurant. This establishment is classified as a snack bar that is open Monday through Saturday from 8 a.m. to 6:30 p.m. and Sunday from 8 a.m. to 3 p.m. Items on their menu include a full breakfast selection as well as sandwiches, hamburgers, hot dogs, cheeseburgers, cookies and all types of snacks. Daily specials are also available. The dining area can accommodate up to 32 persons. Eight tables with checkered table clothes and a simple decor make up the furnishings for this restaurant. Groups of 15 to 20 people can be served in the main dining area. For larger groups of 30 to 50 persons, arrangements can be made for available space in the upper level of the terminal building. For information about the Aerodrome Cafe call 754-4999.

Restaurants Near Airport:

Aerodrome Cafe	On Site	Phone: 754-4999

Lodging: Hilton (Free trans reported) 754-8484.

Meeting Rooms: There is a conference room in the Madison Cooper Terminal building on the field. There is also a smaller meeting room at Texas Aero (FBO).

Transportation: Texas Aero can provide courtesy transportation to nearby facilities 752-9731; Also Taxi Service: Yellow Cab 756-1861; Rental Cars: Avis 756-1921; Hertz 756-5191; National 754-5791.

Information: Waco Tourist Information Center, Box 2570, Waco, TX 76702, Phone: 750-8696 or 800-922-6386.

Attractions:

Texas Rangers Museum (I-35 & Brazos River) This museum exhibits a 150 year history of the Texas Rangers including all types of firearms, and equipment used, including wax figures and exhibits. For information call 754-1433.

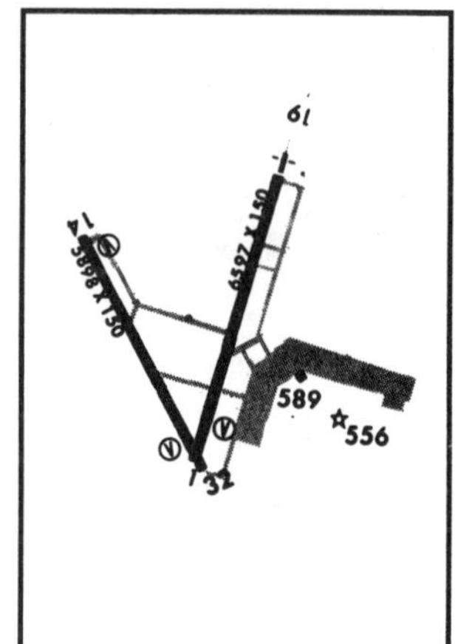

Airport Information:

WACO - WACO REGIONAL AIRPORT (ACT)
5 mi northwest of town N31-36.68 W97-13.83 Elev: 516 Fuel: 100LL, Jet-A
Rwy 01-19: H6597x150 (Asph) Rwy 14-32: H5898x150 (Asph) Attended: 1200-0500Z
Atis: 123.85 Unicom: 122.95 App Con: 135.2 Dep Con: 125.4 Tower: 119.3
Gnd Con: 121.9 Public Phone 24hrs Notes: No landing fee, tie-down fee $2.50 per night for singles and $3.50 for twins.
FBO: Texas Aero Phone: 752-9731

TX-WEA - WEATHERFORD
PARKER COUNTY AIRPORT

(Area Code 817)

67

Driver's Diner:

The Driver's Diner is located about 1\8th of a mile east of the Parker County Airport. This truck stop is open 24 hours a day and is a favorite to many fly-in customers each week. A large variety of menu items can be enjoyed as well as several buffets throughout the week. A luncheon buffet is served every day between 11 a.m. and 3 p.m., Friday night from 5 p.m. to 10 p.m., a seafood buffet is featured. On Saturday and Sunday their breakfast buffet from 7 a.m. to 10 a.m. attracts as many as 50 to 60 fly-in customers. Average prices run between $5.75 and $6.25. Seating capacity of the restaurant is 100 persons with tables, and a small coffee counter. Groups are always welcome and meals can be prepared-to-go. The owner of this establishment is a pilot as well. For more information call the Driver's Diner at 596-8846.

Restaurants Near Airport:

Driver's Diner	1/8 mi E.	Phone: 596-8846

Lodging: None Reported

Meeting Rooms: None Reported

Transportation: None Reported

Information: Chamber of Commerce, 401 Ft Worth Street, P.O. Box 310, Weatherford, TX 76086, Phone: 594-3801.

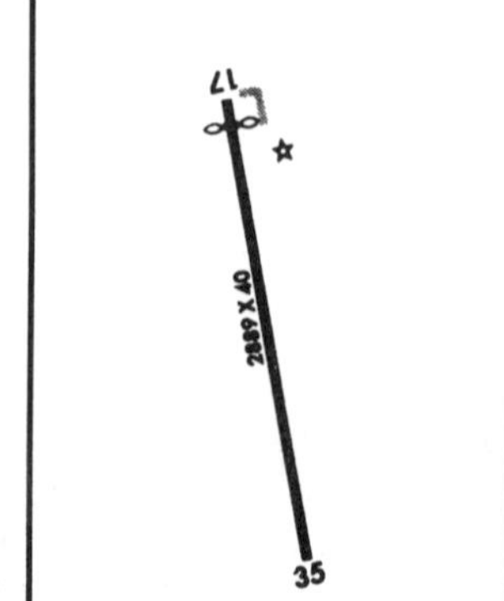

Airport Information:

WEATHERFORD - PARKER COUNTY AIRPORT (WEA)
5 mi east of town N32-44.78 W097-40.95 Elev: 990 Fuel: 100LL
Rwy 17-35: H2889x40 (Asph) Attended: 1400-0200Z Unicom: 122.7 Notes: No landing fee, overnight parking $1.00 to $10.00
FBO: Parker County Aviation Phone: 599-7772, 594-5691

TX-T47 - WICHITA FALLS KICKAPOO DOWNTOWN AIRPARK

(Area Code 817)

68

Pizza Hut Restaurant:

The Pizza Hut Restaurant is reported to be situated 1/4 mile from the Kickapoo Downtown Airpark. This family style restaurant is open Monday through Thursday 11 a.m. to 10 p.m., Friday and Saturday 11 a.m. to 12 a.m. and Sunday 12 p.m. to 10 p.m. This establishment offers a large assortment of freshly made pizzas as well as a host of other dishes. Spaghetti, salad bar, bread sticks and sandwiches are just a few of their menu choices. Daily specials are also available. Their dining room can accommodate 86 persons, and offers a casual and comfortable atmosphere. All of their menu items can be ordered for carry-out. Groups and parties are always welcome. If your group is exceptionally large, please give them advance notice. For more information call Pizza Hut at 761-2222.

Attractions:

Waterfalls (3 miles); Shopping mall (2 miles); Museums (2 miles).

Restaurants Near Airport:

Hacienda Hernandez Rest.	3 mi NE.	Phone: 767-5932
Hunan Chinese Restaurant	2 mi W.	Phone: 691-3900
Pioneer Restaurant SW	2 mi W.	Phone: 692-2170
Pizza Hut Restaurant	1/4 mi	Phone: 761-2222

Lodging: Sheraton Hotel (Courtesy trans reported) 761-6000; Ramada Hotel (Courtesy trans reported) 766-6000.

Meeting Rooms: Kickapoo Airport has a large lobby at their facility as well as pilot lounge, which may be used for meetings or press conferences, call 766-1735.

Transportation: Kickapoo Airport has courtesy vehicles available to local areas with advance notice 766-1735; Also Falls Cab at 691-0219.

Information: Convention and Visitors Bureau, P.O. Box 630, Wichita Falls, TX 76307, Phone: 723-2741 or 800-799-6732.

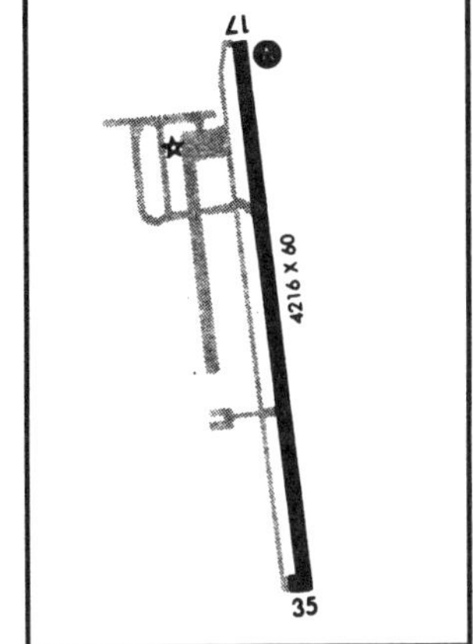

Airport Information:

WICHITA FALLS - KICKAPOO DOWNTOWN AIRPARK (T47)
3 mi south of town N33-51.67 W98-29.43 Elev: 998 Fuel: 100LL, Jet-A
Rwy 17-35: H4216x60 (Asph) Attended: 1200-0300Z Unicom: 122.7 Sheppard App/Dep Con: 120.4 Clnc Del: 121.2 Notes: CAUTION: Do not mistake Sheppard AFB/Wichita Falls Municipal 7 miles north, for Kickapoo Downtown Airpark; No landing fee, $4.00 a night for single engine and $8.00 for twins; Shierry Aviation flight school is also located on the field (Maintance shop).
FBO: Kickapoo Downtown Airpark Phone: 766-1735, 800-671-2992

TX-09R - WOODVILLE TYLER COUNTY AIRPORT

(Area Code 409)

69

Pickett House Restaurant:

The Picket House Restaurant is in an old midway school house, built near the Polk county line in 1909. This restaurant has gained popularity with many pilots in the region, for its country cooking served boarding house style. You can call the restaurant for free pick-up service at the airport. The decor has antique circus posters that line the walls. Looking at the hungry diners seated at long wooden tables topped with checkered cloths, you are certain to find several pilots who have landed at the Woodville Airport to partake of the restaurant's inviting "all you can eat" menu. Selections like chicken and dumplings served everyday, fried chicken, 3 country vegetables, coleslaw, hot homemade biscuits, cornbread, fruit cobbler, watermelon rind preserves, coffee, tea, buttermilk, ribbon cane syrup and east Texas wild honey are all available on their menu. "All you can eat" prices run $8.45 (Adults); $6.95 (Seniors 55 or older); $5.95 for (Children under 12); and $2.50 for children under 6 years of age. (Tax is additional). Restaurant hours are 11 a.m. to 2 p.m. Monday through Thursday and 11 a.m. to 8 p.m. on Friday and Saturday and Sunday 11 a.m. to 6 p.m. For information call 283-3371.

Restaurants Near Airport:

Pickett House	1 mi.	Phone: 283-3371

Lodging: Woodville Inn, 201 N Magnolia, 72 rooms, 283-3741

Meeting Rooms: Woodville Inn, 283-3741

Transportation: Pickett House will pick your party up at the airport and take you back. Call them when you land.

Information: Chamber of Commerce, 201 North Magnolia, Woodville, TX 75979, Phone: 283-2632; Also: Department of Transportation, P.O. Box 5064, Austin, TX 78763-5064, Phone: 800-452-9292.

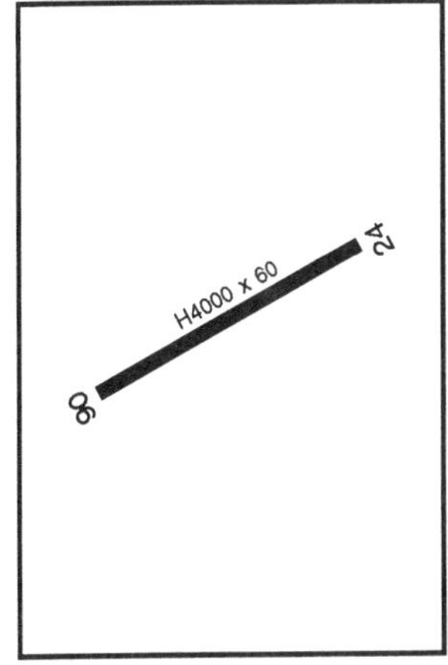

Airport Information:

WOODVILLE - TAYLER COUNTY AIRPORT (09R)
2 mi west of town N30-46.51 W94-27.51 Elev: 388 Rwy 16-34: H4000x60 (Asph)
Attended: unattended CATF: 122.9 Phone daylight hours 283-2141.
Airport Manager Phone: 283-2141

UTAH

LOCATION MAP

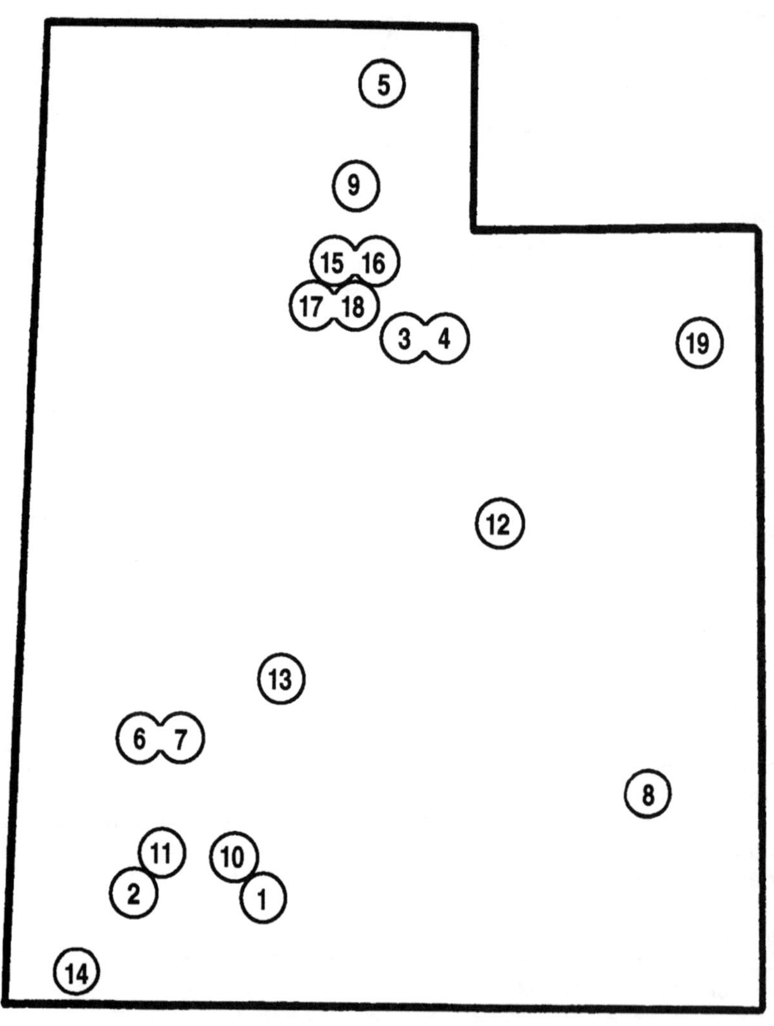

Not to be used for navigational purposes

CROSS FILE INDEX

Location Number	City or Town	Airport Name And Identifier	Name of Attraction
1	Bryce Canyon	Bryce Canyon Arpt. (BCE)	Pinks Cowboy Cafe
2	Cedar City	Cedar City Muni. (CDC)	Wings
3	Heber Valley	Heber Valley Arpt. (36U)	Dock of the Bay
4	Heber Valley	Heber Valley Arpt. (36U)	Hub Cafe
5	Logan	Cache Arpt. (LGU)	Juniper Inn
6	Milford	Milford Muni. Arpt. (MLF)	R & R Diner
7	Milford	Milford Muni. Arpt. (MLF)	Station Restaurant
8	Monticello	Needles Outpost (UT59)	Needles Outpost
9	Ogden	Ogden Hinckley Arpt. (OGD)	Taildragger Cafe
10	Panguitch	Panguitch Muni. Arpt. (U55)	Flying "M" Restaurant
11	Parowan	Parowan Arpt. (1L9)	Jedediah's & Restaurant
12	Price	Carbon Co. Arpt. (PUC)	Days Inn
13	Richfield	Richfield Muni. Arpt. (RIF)	Topfield Lodge
14	Saint George	Saint George Muni. (SGU)	Sullivans Rococo Inn
15	Salt Lake City	Salt Lake City Intl. (SLC)	Encore Grill
16	Salt Lake City	Salt Lake City Intl. (SLC)	Host Marriott (Terrace)
17	Salt Lake City	Salt Lake City Muni. 2 Arpt. (U42)	Deer Valley Resort
18	Salt Lake City	Salt Lake City Muni. 2 Arpt. (U42)	Srein Eriksen Lodge
19	Vernal	Vernal Arpt. (VEL)	Skillet East

Articles

City or town	Nearest Airport and Identifier	Name of Attraction
Salt Lake City/Heber, UT	Slt Lke Cty Muni. 2 (U42) or (36U)	Deer Valley Resort
Salt Lake City/Heber, UT	Slt Lke Cty Muni. 2 (U42) or (36U)	Stein Eriksen Lodge

UT-BCE - BRYCE CANYON
BRYCE CANYON AIRPORT

1

(Area Code 801)

Restaurants Near Airport:

Bryce Canyon Lodge	6 mi SE	Phone: 834-5861
Bryce Canyon Pines	3 mi W	Phone: 834-5264
Pinks Cowboy Cafe	1/2 mi S	Phone: 834-5100
Ruby's Inn	2 mi S	Phone: 834-5341

Lodging: Ruby's Inn (3 miles, Transportation) 834-5341; Bryce Canyon lodge (6 miles) 834-5861, 5361, or 586-7686; Bryce Canyon Pines (3 miles) 834-5336; Bryce Village Resort (Adj airport) 834-5303.

Meeting Rooms: Bryce Village Resort (1/2 mile) can handle single parties or business groups up to 100 persons 834-5303.

Transportation: Bryce Air Service 834-5208; Taxi or Rental cars can also be obtained through Bryce Air Service.

Information: The Visitors Center has complete informatain about the park. Call 834-5322.

Pinks Cowboy Cafe:

This combination family style and fine dining facility is located adjacent to the Bryce Canyon Airport, and is part of a motel, restaurant and gas station complex and part of the Bryce Village Resort containing 54 units along with cabins, RV sites and camping available. You can either walk to the resort or they will pick you up at the airport. Just give them a call after you land. The restaurant itself has a rustic and western decor, and is open 7 days a week between 6 a.m. and 10 p.m. during the summer and 8 a.m. to 9 p.m. winter months. They offer a full menu with Barbecued items, steaks and prime rib as their specialties. Average prices run $6.50 for breakfast, $7.00 for lunch and $13.00 for dinner. Accommodations for up to 100 persons can also be arranged for parties or group get-togethers. Outdoor barbecues and nightly pit bond fires are part of the summer entertainment in addition to live country music Friday and Saturday nights year round. For information call the resort at 834-5100.

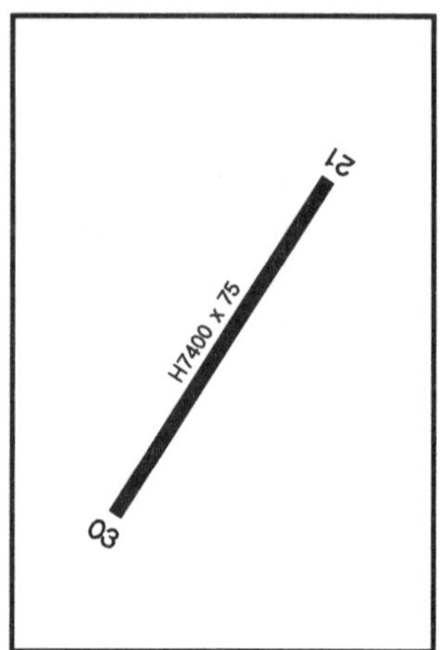

Attractions: Alladin Air Tours is a part 135 operation that offers scenic flights over Bryce canyon, Phone: 834-5555; Bryce Canyon provides spectacular views within the 56 square mile area, exhibiting colorful rock formations, cliffs and bluffs that exhibit shades of orange, red, white, purple, gray and browns as sunlight strike's the rocks at different angles. Hiking, horseback riding on trails as well as tours and lectures are offered. Camping in this region is also a very popular activity. For information contact the Visitors Center at 834-5322.

Airport Information:

BRYCE CANYON - BRYCE CANYON AIRPORT (BCE)

4 mi north of town N37-42.38 W112-08.73 Elev: 7586 Fuel: 100, Jet-A Rwy 03-21: H7400x75 (Asph) Attended: Mon-Sat 1430-0100Z Unicom: 122.8 Public Phone 24hrs Notes: Landing and or overnight parking $5.00 for singles and $10.00 for twins.

Airport Manager Phone: 834-5208, 679-8650

UT-CDC - CEDAR CITY
CEDAR CITY MUNICIPAL

2

(Area Code 801)

Restaurants Near Airport:

Abby Inn	N/A	Phone: 586-9966
Holiday Inn	1 mi	Phone: 586-8888
Town & Country Inn	2 mi	Phone: 586-9900
Wings	On Site	Phone: 586-4358

Lodging: Best Western Town & Country Inn (free trans) 586-9900; Comfort Inn (free trans) 586-2082; Holiday Inn (free trans) 586-8888;

Meeting Rooms: Best Western Town & Country Inn (free trans) 586-9900; Comfort Inn (free trans) 586-2082; Holiday Inn (free trans) 586-8888;

Transportation: Avis 586-3033; National 586-7059

Information: Cedar City Chamber of Commerce, 286 N Main Street, P.O. Box 220, Cedar City, UT 84720, 586-4484

Wings:

Wings restaurant is located at the north part of the main terminal building at the Cedar City Municipal Airport. During our conversation with the restaurant manager we learned that pilots can park their aircraft within 30 feet of the restaurant entrance. Wings is a family style restaurant with a casual relaxed and picnic-style atmosphere. Eight large windows provide guests with a panoramic view of the airport and surrounding countryside. In fact, guests enjoy looking out over the desert and mountain range 80 miles to the west and up to 100 miles to the north. Beautiful sunsets can also be enjoyed during evening hours. This restaurant is open 7 a.m. to 8 p.m. 6 days a week. They are closed on Sunday. The people at Wings restaurant are happy to prepare meals and sandwich trays to go. Please call in advance, if possible for catering requests. On site catering with groups can also be arranged. Average prices for meals range from $1.99 to $5.00 for breakfast items served all day, $2.50 to $5.00 for lunch and $3.99 to $8.50 for dinner items. Favorite breakfast requests include specials featuring 2 large eggs, your choice of bacon or sausage and served with Daves famous hash browns and toast. Additional items are Omelets; buttermilk hot cakes; French toast; and biscuits, sausage and gravy. For lunch their 1/4 pound Mexiburger sounds great, served with mayonnaise, green chili and complemented with two slices of white cheese. Additional sandwiches served are their French dip, BLTs, as well as a host of other sandwiches. Their delicious dinner entrees are a favorite with many pilots. Combination Mexican entrees like their Los Pocos, Los Medios and Los Grandes attract fly-in customers from Las Vegas on a regular basis. For more information about the Wings restaurant call 586-4358.

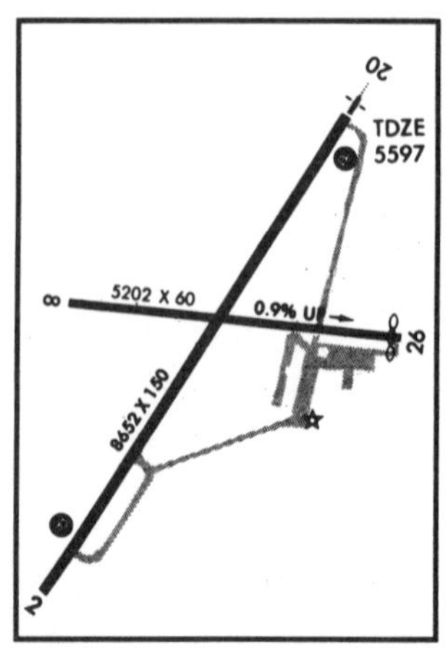

Airport Information:

Cedar City - Cedar City Municipal (CDC)

2 mi northwest of town N37-42.10 W113-05.88 Fuel: 100LL, Jet A Rwy 02-20: H8652x150 (Asph-Pfc) Rwy 08-26: H5202x60 (Asph) Attended: daylight hours Unicom: 122.8 Notes: Rwy 02-20 will be 8652'

FBO: Cedar City Phone: 586-3881

FBO: Scenic Airlines Phone: 586-3881

UT-36U - HEBER VALLEY
HEBER VALLEY AIRPORT

(Area Code 801)

3, 4

Dock of the Bay (Island Resort):

The Island Resort is a state operated "DAY" resort containing a fine dining facility by the name of "Dock of the Bay". This establishment is located 5 miles to the northwest of the Heber Valley Airport. The restaurant management has something in common with air travelers, as they too are pilots and will pick up fly-in guests at the airport and take them to this resort. It is important that you give them advance notice when you will be arriving so they may arrange their schedule accordingly. The restaurant is open 7 days a week from 6 a.m. to 10 p.m. Their menu contains specialty items like halibut, teriyaki chicken, and shrimp dishes in addition to many other items. Average prices run $4.00 to $5.00 for lunch, and $9.50 to $14.50 for dinner. Their steak and lobster dinners average about $25.95 per plate. The restaurant has a rustic and country decor with wooden logs and cedar siding, and is situated right on the waters edge. The main dining room can seat up to 60 persons in addition to banquet facilities for up to 160 persons. On the second floor a private dining room is also available for private parties and groups up to 40 persons. This resort does not contain accommodations for overnight stay. However, there is plenty of recreational activities available as well as rental boats Jet skiing, wave runners, and swimming. For more information you can call 654-2155.

Hub Cafe:

The Hub Cafe is reported about 1/2 to 3/4 of a mile from the Heber Valley Airport. On a nice day you might be able to walk to this restaurant or or if you prefer, you can call for a taxi. (See "Transportation") This restaurant is classified as a combination cafe and family style facility. Their hours are from 5 a.m. to 11 p.m. during the summer months. During the winter months, they are open from 6 a.m. to 10 p.m. Sun, Mon, Tues, Wed, and Thurs, and from 6 a.m. to 11 p.m. on Friday and Saturday. They offer chicken fried steaks, halibut in addition to many other selections for dinner, all types of sandwiches for lunch and a full line of breakfast dishes including eggs and sliced bone ham, biscuits and gravy, as well as a variety of omelets. The portions are large and the price is reasonable. Average entrees run about $4.25 for breakfast & lunch and between $6.95 and $9.95 for dinner. The decor of the restaurant is western with antiques decorating the walls. There are 2 separate rooms available for groups and parties as well as a coffee shop. For more information about this restaurant call 654-5463.

Restaurants Near Airport:

Dock of the Bay	5 mi SE.	Phone: 654-2155
High Country Cafe	3/4 mi	Phone: 654-2022
Hubb Cafe	3/4 mi	Phone: 654-5463

Lodging: Green Acres (1 mile) 654-2202; High Country Inn & Restaurant (Best Western) 654-2022; Stardust (1 mile) 654-0201; Wasatch Motel (1/2 mile) 654-5831.

Meeting Rooms: Both the Dock of the Bay restaurant and Hubb Cafe offer accommodations for meetings and parties.

Transportation: Taxi: Park City Transportation 649-8567; Rental Cars from airport call 654-5831.

Information: Heber Valley Chamber of Commerce, Box 427, Heber, UT 84032, Phone: 654-3666.

Attractions:

Train rides lasting 3-1/2 hours from Heber Valley through Provo Canyon to Vivian Park offers spectacular scenery. Operations begin in early May to Memorial day on weekends and then daily until October. For information write Heber Creeper, P.O. Box 103, Heber City 84032, Phone: 654-2900.

Park City Skiing Area is located approx 15 miles north-north-northwest of Heber Valley Airport and offers 2,200 acres and 82 slopes for novice, intermediate and expert skiers. Facilities include restaurant, & cafeteria, four season resort area, and summer activities as well. For information contact Park City Ski Area, 1345 Lowell Avenue, P.O. Box 39, Park City, UT 84060, Phone: 649-8111, (snow report 649-9571).

See Article on Deer Valley Resort
and Stein Eriksen Lodge
near Park City, UT
Salt Lake City Attractions
Salt Lake City
Municipal 2 Airport (U42)

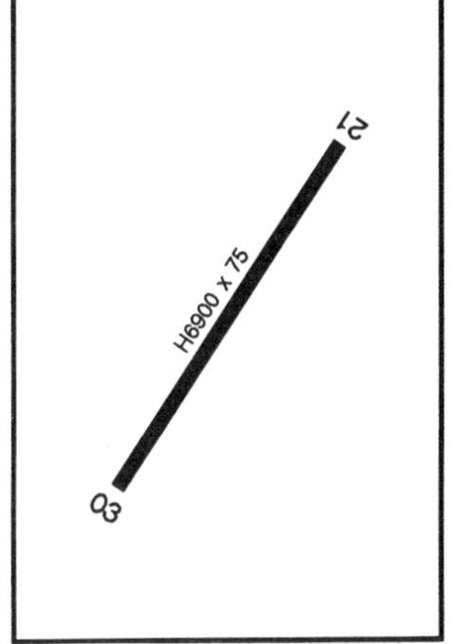

Airport Information:

HEBER VALLEY - HEBBER VALLEY AIRPORT (36U)
1 mi south of town N40-29.08 W111-25.54 Elev: 5632 Fuel: 100, Jet-A, MOGAS
Rwy 03-21: H6900x75 (Asph) Attended: 1500-0300Z Unicom: 122.8
FBO: High County Aviation Phone: 654-5831

UT-LGU - LOGAN CACHE AIRPORT

5

Juniper Inn:

The Juniper Inn is a family style restaurant located 2 miles east of the Logan Cache Airport. Transportation to this establishment can be obtained through Logan Air Service (FBO) by calling 752-5955. They have a loaner car that customers can burrow for short term use. The Juniper Inn is open between 11:30 a.m. to 10:00 p.m. Tuesday through Saturday (Closed Sunday and Monday). Their menu provides a full steak and seafood selection along with sandwiches, soups salads and deserts. For the mighty appetite, one might desire to feast on their special 36 oz. porter house steak, being one of their customers favorite choices. Average prices for light meals run $4.00 to $10.00 and for dinner entrees between $8.00 and $17.00. The restaurant is decorated with a western theme displaying many Indian artifacts. The main dining area can seat 100 persons, however they have 5 additional rooms available for groupsand parties able to accommodate 12, 20, 40, 80, and 180 persons respectively. The "Juniper Inn" also has a sister restaurant by the name of the "Juniper Out" which specializes in catering and carry out service. For more information on either facility you can call 563-3622.

Restaurants Near Airport: (Area Code 801)

The Blue Bird	3 mi SE	Phone: 752-3155
The Copper Mill	3 mi SE	Phone: 752-0647
Frontier Pies	2 mi SE	Phone: 752-9280
Juniper Inn	2 mi E	Phone: 563-3622

Lodging Facilities: The following provide transportation: Baugh Motel (3 miles) 752-5220; Holiday House (3 miles) 752-9141; Weston Inn (3 miles) 752-5700;

Meeting Rooms: Utah State University Conference Center 750-1690.

Transportation: Logan Cab 753-3663

Information: Cache Chamber of Commerce/Brridgerland Travel Region, 160 North Main, Logan, UT 84321, Phone: 752-2161 or 800-882-4433.

Attractions: Smithfield Birch Creek Golf Course (3 miles northeast) 563-6825; Sherwood Hill Resort, (Golf,restaurant, hotel etc., 15 miles southeast) 245-6055; Hyrum State Park (Boating, fishing, waterskiing etc., 10 miles south) 245-6866.

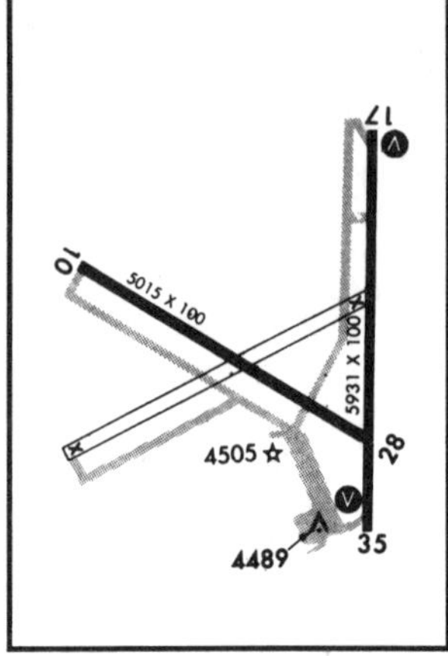

Airport Information:

LOGAN - LOGAN CACHE AIRPORT (LGU)
3 mi northwest of town N41-47.26 W111-51.16 Elev: 4454 Fuel: 100, Jet-A
Rwy 17-35: H5931x100 (Asph) Rwy 10-28: H5015x100 (Asph) Attended: 1500-0200Z
Unicom: 122.8 Notes: For fuel after hours call 750-6563 or 752-0873. No landing fee, Tiedown fees $2.50 per day or $10.00 per month.
FBO: Logan Air Service Phone: 752-5955

Not to be used for navigational purposes

UT-MLF - MILFORD
MILFORD MUNICIPAL AIRPORT

(Area Code 801)

6, 7

R & R Diner:

The R & R Diner restaurant is an authentic 1950's style fast food diner, located about 1-1/2 mile from the Milford Municipal Airport. Courtesy transportation using the airport courtesy car can be arranged in advance. The restaurant is not fancy nor does it have memorabilia or reproduced artifacts depicting the 50's era, but it does contain a certain charm. All furnishing within the restaurant are actually from that period of time, right down to the juke box in the corner of the restaurant. The diner is open 7 days a week form 11:30 a.m. to 6 p.m. Some of the items on their menu include many varieties of cheeseburgers, and hamburgers from 1/4 to 1/2 pound. Hot sandwiches, Mexican food, taco salads, taquitos, which is a corn shell taco with cheese and shredded beef are available. Their onion rings and curly fries are also a favorite with many customers. In addition they provide many delicious soda fountain selections such as malts, shakes, sundays, and desserts. Their dining room contains 6 or 7 stools along the counter, and 5 booths. A juke box, and pinball machine adds to the authenticity of this diner. For information you can call 387-5042.

Station Restaurant:

The Station Restaurant can be reached by courtesy car from the Milford Municipal Airport. This family style restaurant specializes in preparing a variety of Chinese and American dishes. One unique feature offered is their combination Chinese dinners prepared for 2 persons all the way up to 100 persons. In addition, their standard selections include steaks, shrimp dinners, chicken fried steak and much more. Average prices run about $3.00 for breakfast, $4.00 for lunch, and $7.00 for dinner. Every day specials are available right off their menu. The decor of the restaurant is semi-rustic and western. Because the railroad played a significant role in the development of this town, the restaurant displays many old pictures and photos of trains and railroad scenes. The Station Restaurant can seat 145 persons comfortably and welcomes fly-in guests as well as groups and parties. For more information you can call the Station Restaurant at 387-2804.

Restaurants Near Airport:

Hong Kong Restaurant	N/A	Phone: 387-2251
R & R Diner	1-1/2 mi	Phone: 387-5042
Station Restaurant	1-2 mi	Phone: 387-2804

Lodging: Station Motels (2 miles) 387-2481

Meeting Rooms: None reported

Transportation: Airport courtesy car; Also: Speedy Car Rental, (Phone: N/A).

Information: Milford Chamber of Commerce, Phone: 623-5203;

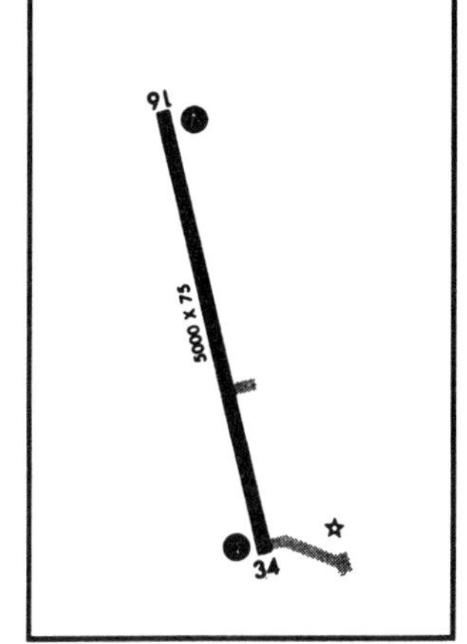

Airport Information:

MILFORD - MILFORD MUNICIPAL AIRPORT (MLF)

2 mi north of town N38-25.60 W113-00.75 Elev: 5039 Fuel: 100LL, Jet-A

Rwy 16-34: H5000x75 (Asph) Attended: 1500-0000Z Unicom: 122.8 Public Phone 24hrs

Milford Airport Phone: 387-2637 or 387-2342

UT-UT59 - MONTICELLO NEEDLES OUTPOST

(Area Code 801)

8

Restaurants Near Airport:
Needles Outpost 1/8th Mi Phone: Unknown

Needles Outpost: (Private Airport)

The Needles Outpost is located about 1/8th mile and only a five minute walk from the airport. The Outpost contains a snack bar in a rustic setting. This is a convenience type store. They try to have a little bit of everything that hikers, campers, and tourists might need, in addition to souvenirs. There are also picnic tables outside in the shade. They have cereals, sweet rolls, and fruit for breakfast. Lunch and dinner items are burgers and sandwiches. A variety of drinks are also available. Rental 4x4 vehicles and jeeps are available on a daily basis, (Reservations are recommended). They are located on the border of Canyonlands National Park, Needles district. A great area to hike or jeep. The outpost is open from 8 a.m. to 7 p.m. Prices for meals average $3.00 for breakfast and $4.00 for lunch and dinner. If pre-arranged, they can provide catering for groups if planning a fly-in or if requesting meals-to-go. During the time of research we learned that the ownership has changed and services available may change. For information you can call the San Juan County Travel Council, 117 S. Main St. P.O. Box 490, Monticello, UT 84535, Phone: 587-3235 or 800-574-4FUN.

Lodging: Camping: Canyon Lands National Park Campgrounds-Needles Outpost (Adj airport, 1/4th mile); Squaw Flats (4 miles).

Transportation: The restaurant is located within 1/8th mile of airport. Transportation not necessary; Rental Cars: 4x4's and Jeep vehicles are for rent. Call 259-2030.

Information: San Juan Travel Council, 117 South Main Street, Monticello, Utah 84535, Phone: 587-3235 or 800-574-4FUN.

Attractions:

This airport, snack bar, and service facility is located on the border of the Canyonlands National Park District. Recreation includes hiking and jeep trails. Also there is a campground on this site equipped with snack bar, camping, gas station, groceries, general store & 4x4 truck and jeep rentals. For information call 259-2030.

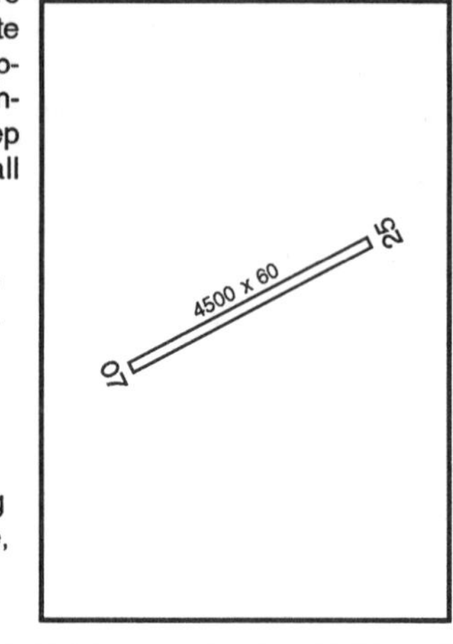

Airport Information:

MONTICELLO - NEEDLES OUTPOST (UT59) (Private Airstrip)
28 mi northwest of town 38-10-36N 109-44-36W Elev: 4950 Fuel: None Reported
Rwy 7-25: 4500x60 (Dirt) Attended: 8 a.m. to 7 p.m. March through October. Notes: No landing fee. However, donations for windsock fund appreciated. Snack bar, camping, groceries, general store, 4x4's for rent. CAUTION: private use facility use at own risk. (Verify airport conditions prior to use).
Airport Information: Phone: 259-8545 or 800-574-4386

UT-OGD - OGDEN OGDEN HINCKLEY AIRPORT

(Area Code 801)

9

Restaurants Near Airport:
Taildragger Cafe On Site Phone: 399-9424

Taildragger Cafe:

The Airport Cafe owned and operated by Jaime Stewart & Ted Elson, is located within the terminal building at the Ogden Hinckley Airport. This cafe is open at 6 a.m. and closes between 5 p.m. and 8 p.m. depending upon customer demand. They serve a wide selection of entrees including chicken fried steak, ground sirloin, hot turkey sandwiches, fish and chips, salads and several different types of burgers and cheeseburgers along with many low cholesterol items. A full breakfast line is offered on their menu and served all day. Daily specials are included in the menu selections as well. The decor of the restaurant is modern and has an aviation theme. Even some of their entrees are named after famous aircraft of the past and present. This cafe can seat about 40 persons. Groups and parties are always welcome. For more information about this cafe, call Jaime or Ted at the Airport Cafe, Phone: 399-9424.

Lodging: Holiday Inn 399-5761; Ogden Park Hotel 627-1190; Radisson Hotel 627-1900;
Meeting Rooms: Holiday Inn 399-5761; Ogden Park Hotel 627-1190; Radison Hotel 627-1900.
Transportation: Ogden Air Service 394-3400 and Spectra Sonics Aviation 392-7533 will provide courtesy transportation to nearby facilities. Also Avis Car Rental is available call 394-5984.
Information: Convention & Visitors Bureau, 2501 Wall Avenue, Ogden, UT 84401, Phone: 627-8288 or 800-ALL-UTAH.

Attractions:

Union Station located at 2501 Wall Avenue provides two attractions with the Browning Firearms Museum and the Browning Kimball Car Museum in addition to a 500 seat theater for musical and theatrical productions 629-8444; Skiing: Snowbasin (Vertical drop 2,400 feet) 399-1135; Powder Mountain 745-3771; Nordic Valley (Vertical drop 1,000 feet) 745-3511; See "Information" listed above to obtain more information about this area.

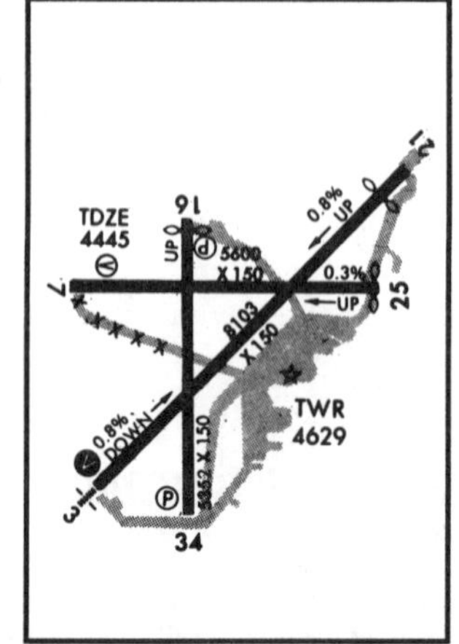

Airport Information:

OGDEN - OGDEN HINCKLEY AIRPORT (OGD)
3 mi southwest of town N41-11.76 W112-00.73 Elev: 4470 Fuel: 80, 100, Jet-A1+
Rwy 03-21: H8103-150 (Asph-Pfc) Rwy 07-25: H5600x150 (Asph) Rwy 16-34: H5352x150 (Asph) Attended: continuously Atis: 125.55 Unicom: 122.95 Salt Lake App/Dep Con: 121.1 Tower: 118.7 Gnd Con: 121.7
FBO: Great Western Aviation Phone: 394-3400
FBO: Ogden Jet Center Phone: 392-7532

UT-U55 - PANGUITCH
PANGUITCH MUNICIPAL AIRPORT

(Area Code 801) 10

Flying "M" Restaurant:

The Flying "M" Restaurant is located about 3 miles southwest from the Panguitch Municipal Airport. We were told that this family style restaurant will provide courtesy transportation for fly-in guests if advance notice is given. Their hours are from 7 a.m. to 9 p.m. 7 days a week during the winter, and 7 a.m. to 10 p.m. during the summer. Specialty entrees include an 8 ounce steak and 4 shrimp for $12.95. In addition they also serve roast beef, fish, trout, Italian spaghetti along with appetizers, homemade pies, bread, soup and salads. Average prices for meals are $3.95 for breakfast & lunch, and $8.25 and up for dinner. The decor of the restaurant is western style with antiques displayed within the dining area. A separate room is available for groups and parties. Meals-to-go can also be prepared. For more information, you can call the Flying M Restaurant at 676-8008

Attractions:

Paunsagaunt Wild Life Museum within town containing 300 animals and birds about 3-1/2 miles from airport. Also: Old Historical Walking Tour of homes within Panguitch. For information call the East Center City Office at 676-8585.

Restaurants Near Airport:

Bishop's Cafe	3 mi SW	Phone: 676-8006
Country Corner Cafe	3 mi SW	Phone: 676-8851
Flying "M" Restaurant	3 mi SW	Phone: 676-8008
Tod's Truck Stop	4 mi SW	Phone: 676-8863

Lodging: Best Western 676-8876; Color Country Motel 676-2386; Proctor Motel 676-2252.

Meeting Rooms: None Reported

Transportation: None reported, except Flying "M" Restaurant is reported to provide courtesy transportation to and from their facility with advance notice.

Information: Panguitch City Corp. East Center City Office, 200 East 25 South, Panguitch, UT 84759, Phone: 676-8585. Also: Chamber of Commerce, 55 South Main Street, Box 400, Panguitch, UT 84759, Phone: 676-2311.

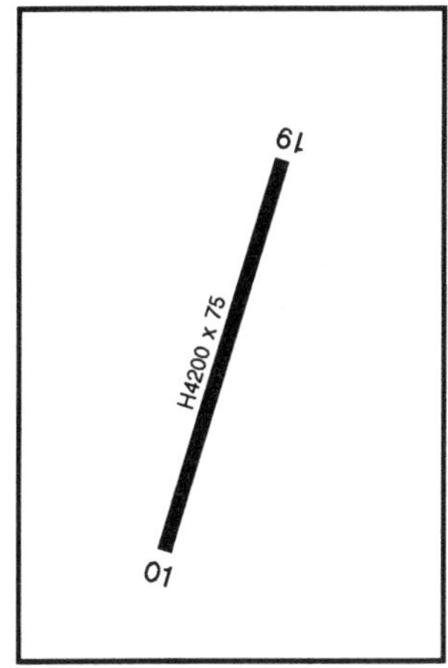

Airport Information:

PANGUITCH - PANGUITCH MUNICIPAL AIRPORT (U55)
3 mi northeast of town   N37-50.72 W112-23.53   Elev: 6757   Rwy 01-19: H4200x75 (Asph)
Attended: unattended   CATF: 122.9
Airport Phone: 676-8585

UT-1L9 - PAROWAN
PAROWAN AIRPORT

(Area Code 801) 11

Jedediah's Inn & Restaurant:

The Jedediah's Inn & Restaurant is situated 2 miles southwest of the Parowan Airport. This fine dining facility is open between 7 a.m. and 10 p.m. 7 days a week, and can be reached with courtesy transportation either through the restaurant or Parowan Aero Service at the airport with advance notice. This restaurant can be classified as a steak house with items such as prime rib, rib-I steaks, Malabu chicken, bay beef liver, honey dipped southern fried chicken, porterhouse steaks and T-bone steaks. Prices are very reasonable and average $5.25 for breakfast & lunch and $8.95 for dinner. They offer a salad bar during lunchtime and through dinner. The restaurant provides a southwestern motif with bleached wood, three old-fashioned carriages including an Amish wagon, harnesses and tackle used as decorations along with antiques and western items. Their main dining room can seat 125 persons while the banquet facilities can accommodate up to 300 people. They also have a smaller room able to accommodate smaller groups of 20 to 30 persons. In addition to the restaurant and banquet facilities, the Jedediah's Inn provides 44 rooms adjacent to the restaurant with 22 of them furnished with king size beds and 22 with two double beds averaging about $55.00 per night. For more information you can call 477-3326

Restaurants Near Airport:

Jedediah's Inn & Rest.	2 mi SW	Phone: 477-3326
Swiss Village Inn	7/10 mi S.	Phone: 477-3391
The Pit Stop	7/10 mi S.	Phone: 477-9990

Lodging: Jedediah's Inn (Free trans) 477-3326; Swiss Village (7/10 mile) 477-3391.

Meeting Rooms: Jedediah's Inn (Free trans) 477-3326.

Transportation: Airport courtesy car is available if advance notice is given through Parowan Aero Service, Phone: 477-8911.

Information: Parowan Visitor Information, City Office, 5 South Main, Parowan, UT 84651, Phone: 477-3331.

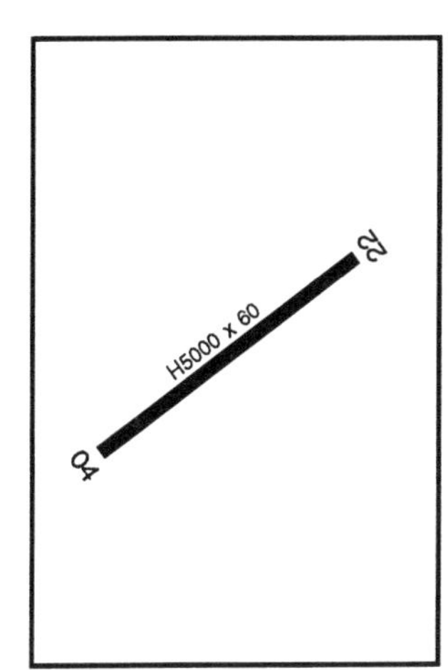

Airport Information:

PAROWAN - PAROWAN AIRPORT (1L9)
1 mi northeast of town   N37-51.58 W112-48.96   Elev: 5930   Fuel: 100, Jet-A
Rwy 04-22: H5000x60 (Asph)   Attended: 1400-0000Z   Unicom: 122.8   Public Phone 24hrs
Notes: Check current AFD for rwy conditions; For fuel after hours call 477-3458; No landing fees, no overnight parking fee. Glider operations in summer and crop dusting operations March through September.
FBO: Parowan Service   Phone: 477-8911

UT-PUC - PRICE
CARBON COUNTY AIRPORT

12

(Area Code 801)

Restaurants Near Airport:

Days Inn	5 mi W	Phone: 637-8880
China City	2-1/2 mi W	Phone: 637-8211
Carriage Inn	2 mi W	Phone: 637-5660
Cowboy Club	6 mi E	Phone: 637-4223

Lodging: Carriage House Inn (Free trans) 637-5660; Days Inn (Free trans) 637-8880.
Meeting Rooms: Days Inn (Free trans, 5 miles west) 637-8880
Transportation: Airport courtesy car through Castle Valley Aviation 637-9705; Also taxi service: Yellow Cab 637-2222; Rental Cars: Hertz 637-0112; Locost Rent-A Car 637-2777.
Information: Carbon County Chamber of Commerce, 31 North 200 East, P.O. Box 764, Price, UT 84501, Phone: 637-2788 or 637-8182.

Attractions: Carbon Country Club Golf Course located nearby, phone: 637-9949; Micro Brewery, Pinnacle Brewery Company 6-1/2 mi. from airport.

Days Inn:

The Days Inn motel is located approximately 5 miles west of the Carbon County Airport and contains a family style restaurant on the premises. Courtesy transportation can easily be arranged either through the Days Inn at 637-8880 or Arrow West Aviation 637-9556. Please call them in advance of your arrival. The restaurant is open from 6 a.m. to 10 p.m. 7 days a week. Specialized entrees include items like seafood fettucini, halibut filet, rib eye steak, chicken teriyaki, steak and shrimp, chicken fried steaks, ground round steaks, liver and onions as well as a variety of sandwiches. On Friday and Saturday they offer prime rib specials. Lunch specials are always available during the week. The restaurant can seat up to 140 persons in their main dining room. The restaurant decor is modern yet somewhat rustic with accents of brass, green plants, skylights and etched glass. A number of banquet and meeting rooms are also available to accommodate between 18 and 200 guests. Full service catering is their specialty. In addition to the restaurant, the Days Inn facility contains 148 rooms, 10 suites, 10 executive suites, an indoor swimming pool, sauna, hot tub, and game room. For information about the restaurant or accommodations for banquets or lodging call 637-8880.

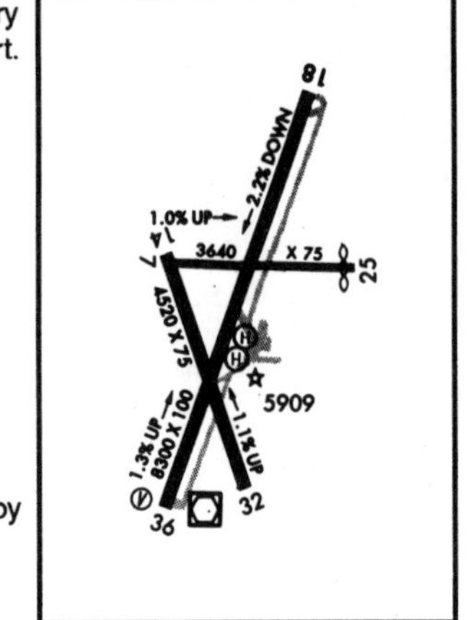

Airport Information:

PRICE - CARBON COUNTY AIRPORT (PUC)
3 mi east of town N39-36.71 W110-45.03 Elev: 5921 Fuel: 100, Jet-A Mogas
Rwy 18-36: H8300x100 (Asph-Pfc) Rwy 14-32: H4520x75 (Asph) Rwy 07-25: H3640x75 (Asph) Attended: continuously Unicom: 122.8 Public Phone 24hrs Notes: Fuel is available by truck as well as at pump; Refuse dumping 1/2 mile SW of runway 36 threshold, occasional smoke and visibility hazard.
FBO: Arrow West Aviation Phone: 637-9556

UT-RIF - RICHFIELD
RICHFIELD MUNICIPAL AIRPORT

13

(Area Code 801)

Restaurants Near Airport:

Days Inn	2 mi N.	Phone: 896-6476
Knights	N/A	Phone: 896-8228
Topfield	1/4 mi N.	Phone: 896-5437
Weston Inn	N/A	Phone: 896-9271

Lodging: Best Western Apple Tree 896-5481; Richfields Western Executive (Free trans) 896-6476; Roadway Inn (Free trans) 896-5491.

Meeting Rooms: Best Western Apple Tree 896-5481.

Transportation: None Reported

Information: Chamber of Commerce, P.O. Box 327, Richfield, UT 84701, Phone: 896-4241.

Topfield Lodge:

The Topfield Lodge is a combination family style and fine dining facility, situated approx. 1/4 mile north of the Richfield Municipal Airport. Fly-in visitors can either walk to the restaurant, obtain a courtesy car from the airport or call the restaurant for transportation. Please call in advance if possible to let them know you are coming and to arrange pick-up service if needed. Their hours of operation are from 5:30 p.m. to 10 p.m. Monday through Saturday. Specialties of the house include prime rib, filet, steak and shrimp dishes, lobster, trout and many seafood and beef combinations. In-fact this restaurant has received the prestigious State of UT "Beef Backer Award". Prices average between $8.00 and $18.00 per plate. They have recently remodeled the restaurant with a new kitchen and dining area. The main dining room can seat 100 people. A separate room available for groups or meetings can seat 35 to 40 people. The restaurant is connected to a 20 unit motel that is well maintained in neat and clean condition, which has also recently been remodeled. For more information, call Topfields Lodge at 896-5437.

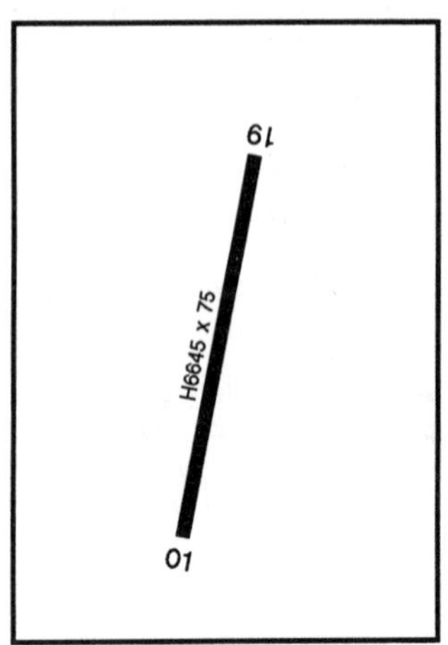

Airport Information:

RICHFIELD - RICHFIELD MUNICIPAL AIRPORT (RIF)
1 mi southwest of town N38-44.50 W112-05.71 Elev: 5279 Fuel: 100, Jet-A
Rwy 01-19: H6645x75 (Asph) Attended: Mon-Fri 1530-0000Z Unicom: 122.8
Notes: For fuel after hours call 896-8918/7258.
Richfield Municipal Airport Phone: 896-9413, 896-8918

Not to be used for navigational purposes

UT-SGU - SAINT GEORGE
SAINT GEORGE MUNICIPAL

(Area Code 801) 14

Restaurants Near Airport:

Budget Inn	1 mi E	Phone: 628-5234
Sullivans (Rococo Inn)	Adj Arpt.	Phone: 673-3305
Holiday Inn	1 mi SW	Phone: 628-4235

Sullivans Rococo Inn:

The Sullivans Rococo Inn is situated across the street from the St George Municipal Airport. To reach the restaurant you will want to park your aircraft on the north end of the field and take the personal access gate directly to the motel located at 511 south Airport Road. This facility serves lunch Monday through Friday 11 a.m. to 3 p.m. They serve dinner 7 days a week between 5 p.m. to 10 p.m. Their selection of entrees are primarily based on choice cuts of beef, steaks, prime rib, and seafood dishes. Average price for a meal will run about $11.95. The restaurant's main dining room faces away from the airport yet overlooks the city from above. the decor of the restaurant is comprised tastefully of white sandstone and lava rock giving it a rustic yet elegant atmosphere. The main dining area can seat 145 persons while two additional rooms can accommodate 80 and 25 persons respectively. catering to private parties and groups is their specialty. For more information about the Rococo Inn call 673-3305.

Lodging: Coronada Family Inn 628-4436; Four Seasons 673-6111; Holiday Inn 628-4235; Rodeway Inn 673-6161; Weston's Lamplighter 673-4861; Hilton Inn 628-0463.
Meeting Rooms: Holiday Inn 628-4235; Weston's Lamplighter 673-4861; Hilton Inn 628-0463.
Transportation: St. George Air Service can provide a courtesy car to nearby facilities 628-0481; Petes Taxis 673-5467; Avis 673-3451; Budget 673-6825; National 673-5098.
Information: Washington County Travel & Convention Bureau, 425 South 700 E, Dixi Center, St. George, UT 84770, Phone; 634-5747 or 800-869-6635.

Attractions:

Snow Canyon State Park provides massive multicolored formations and a flat bottom gorge, with many hiking trails and camping areas. Located approx 7 miles from town. For information call 628-2255;

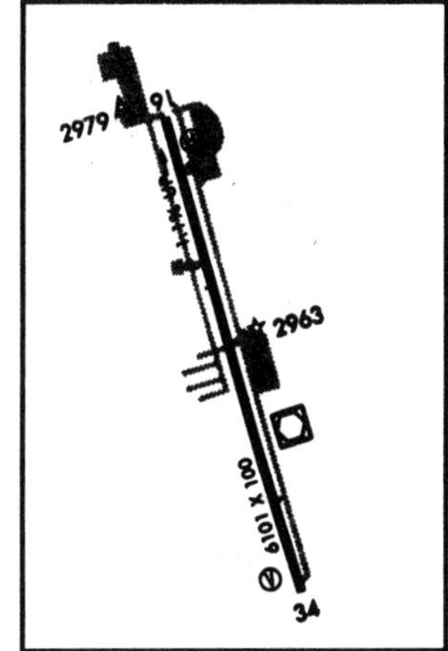

Airport Information:

SAINT GEORGE - SAINT GEORGE MUNICIPAL (SGU)
1 mi west of town N37-05.48 W113-35.58 Elev: 2938 Fuel: 100, 100LL, Jet-A, MOGAS
Rwy 16-34: H6101x100 (Asph-Pfc) Attended: 1330-0230Z Unicom: 122.8
FBO: Aero West Jet Center Phone: 674-1000, 674-0605
FBO: Scenic Jet Center Phone: 628-0481

UT-SLC - SALT LAKE CITY
SALT LAKE CITY INTERNATIONAL

(Area Code 801)

15, 16

Encore Grill:

Encore Grill is located within 150 feet of the Holiday Inn Express approx. 2 to 4 miles from the Salt Lake City Airport. It's about a 4 or 5 minute ride to this facility. Transportation can be arranged by either the fixed base operator at the airport or by taxi. The restaurant is open from 7 a.m. to 10 p.m. Monday through Saturday. Selections from their menu include American, Greek and Italian dishes. Some of their specialties include, meat and vegetarian lasagna, spaghetti, steaks, prime rib, seafood platters, homemade roast turkey, sandwiches, and poultry. Efforts have been made to prepare their foods with healthy, low cholesterol items. Dinner prices average around $10.95 for most main course selections. The atmosphere is very casual, and the main dining room can seat about 104 persons. A private banquet room can accommodate up to 80 people. The Nendel Motor Inn is located next door within 150 feet. For information about Maestro's Grill you can call 534-1996.

Host Marriott: (Terrace Restaurant):

The Terrace Restaurant is located on the 3rd floor of the 1st terminal building next to "A" Gate. Hours of operation for the restaurant are 11 a.m. to 9:30 p.m. Their lounge opens at 10 a.m. Speciality entrees include steaks, New York steaks, chicken dishes, pastas, chef specials of the day and chef salads. Two types of fish selections are offered every day. They have a full service lounge as well. Guests can enjoy a beautiful view of the airport along with the Salt Lake Valley and mountains in the background. The main dining room can seat about 100 persons in addition to 60 seats in their lounge. Accommodations for banquets and group meetings can be reserved. Everything on their menu can be prepared for carry-out. In addition to the Terrace Restaurant, Host Marriott also operates two main food courts that contain well known eateries like snack bars, Pizza Hut, deli's and Cinna-Bun. There is food service available 24 hours a day within the 5 terminal areas on the Salt Lake City International Airport. For information about these establishments or your catering needs, banquet or meeting arrangements, call Host Marriott Human Resources Department at 575-2604.

Restaurants Near Airport:

Encore Grill	3-4 mi	Phone: 534-1996
Lazy Basil	1/2 mi.	Phone: 322-0285
Marriott Arpt Trml	On Site	Phone: 575-2604
Most major hotels	3-5 mi.	See Lodging

Lodging: Free transportation is provided by the following facilities: Days Inn Airport 539-8538; Holiday Inn-Airport 533-9000; Holiday Inn-Downtown 532-7000; La Quinta 566-3291; Mendels Airport Inn (Maestro Grill) 355-0088; Quality Inn 268-2533; Residence Inn By Marriott 532-5511; Royal Executive Inn 521-3450; Comfort Inn 537-7444; Hornes Howard Johnson 521-0130; Reston Hotel 264-1054; Tri-Arc Hotel 521-7373; Doubletree 531-7500; Embassy Suites 539-7800; Hilton 532-3344; Hilton Airport 359-1515; Little America 363-6781; Marriott 531-0800; Peery 521-4300; Red Lion 328-2000; Shilo Inn 521-9500.

Convention Facilities: Tri-Arc Hotel (Free trans) 521-7373; Doubletree (Free trans) 531-7500; Hilton (Free trans) 532-3344; Hilton Airport (Free trans) 539-1515; Little America (Free trans) 363-6781; Marriott (Free trans) 531-0800. Also many of the lodging facilities listed above have accommodations for smaller groups and meetings.

Transportation: Avis 539-2199; Budget 363-1500; Dollar 521-2590; Hertz 539-2683; National 539-0200. Shuttle service provided free of charge to lodging facilities listed above. Also courtesy transportation service is provided by most fixed base operators on the airport to locations nearby.

Information: Salt Lake Convention & Visitors Bureau, 180 South West Temple, Salt Lake City, UT 84101-1493, Phone: 521-2822.

Attractions:

Utah State Fair (State Fairgrounds) begins the first Thursday after Labor day and runs 11 days; Utah Arts Festival (Downtown) demonstrations, exhibits, ethnic foods, and performing arts, held last week in June; There are many attractions and points of interest in and around Salt Lake City. For information on current and social events within this area contact the Salt Lake Convention & Visitors Bureau, 180 South West Temple, Salt Lake City, UT 84101-1493, or call 521-2868. For information on public transportation call the Utah Transit Authority at 287-4636.

Airport Information:

SALT LAKE CITY - SALT LAKE CITY INTERNATIONAL (SLC)

3 mi west of town N40-47.30 W111-58.67 Elev: 4227 Fuel: 80, 100, 100LL, Jet-A1 Rwy 16L-34R: H12003x150 (Asph-Pfc) Rwy 16R-34L: H12003x150 (Conc-Grvd) Rwy 17-35: H9596x150 (Asph-Pfc) Attended: continuously Atis: 127.625, 124.75 Unicom: 122.95 App/Dep 121.1, 124.3, 124.9, 135.5, 125.7, 126.25, 128.1 (See AFD) Tower: 118.3 (Rwy 17-35 and Rwy 14-32) 119.05 (Rwy 16L-34R) 132.65 (Rwy 16R-34L) 127.3 Gnd Con: 121.6 (E of Rwy 17-35) 121.9 (W of Rwy 16L-34R) Clnc Del: 127.3 Pre-Taxi Clnc: 127.3 Pre-Dep-Clnc: 127.3 Notes: CAUTION: Flocks of birds on and in vicinity of airport. (See Airport Facility Directory for further information)

FBO: Salt Lake City Arpt. Auth.	**Phone: 575-2400, 575-2460**
FBO: American Air Academy	**Phone: 537-1537**
FBO: Hudson General	**Phone: 539-2805**
FBO: Million Air of S.L.C.	**Phone: 359-2085, 800-752-5382**
FBO: Salt Lake Jet Center	**Phone: 595-6438, 800-228-9392**
FBO: Westflight Aviation	**Phone: 539-0744**

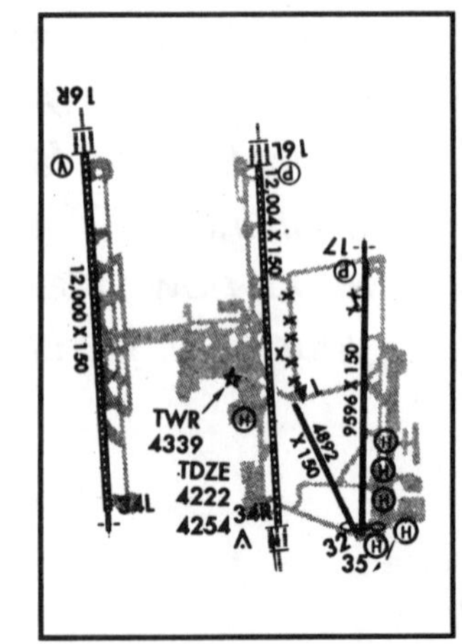

Not to be used for navigational purposes

UT-U42 - SALT LAKE CITY
SALT LAKE CITY MUNI. 2 AIRPORT

(Area Code 801) 17, 18

Deer Valley Resort's Eight Restaurants:

Deer Valley Resort is located in Park City, Utah. From Salt Lake City Municipal 2 Airport, the town of Park City is located about 40 minutes by way of Interstate 80 heading east. Experience Deer Valley's fine cuisine at altitude. It offers eight different restaurants with their own variety of tastes. The Snow Park Restaurant and Seafood Buffet at the base lodge; at mid-mountain, the Silver Lake Restaurant, the Mariposa, McHenry's, the Bald Mountain Pizza Station, along with the Deer Valley Club restaurant; and Snowshoe Tommy's atop Bald Mountain. To start the day, the Snow Park Restaurant offers a delicious Natural Breakfast Buffet, while the Silver Lake Restaurant offers a genuine Continental breakfast. For lunch, McHenry's (adjacent to Silver Lake) serves specialty selections on an outdoor deck. Perfect before or after mountain biking or horseback riding. Pastry Chef Letty Flatt has introduced a high-protein McHenergy Bar for those bikers and skiers on the go. The Silver Lake Restaurant also serves mouth-watering meals for lunch. Also, the Bald Mountain Pizza Station serves Deer Valley's famous tasty pizzas. For a quick snack, Snowshoe Tommy's allows guests to ski up for a hot or cold beverage and a dessert. The Snow Park Lounge offers an early evening of sumptuous dining and entertainment. For dinner, Snow Park's Seafood Buffet features an enormous display of fish. Both the Mariposa and McHenry's also serve delicious dinners. For more about restaurants, rates and other information at Deer Valley Resort, call 800-424-DEER (3337) or 649-1000.

Restaurants Near Airport:

Deer Valley Resort	36 mi S.	Phone: 649-1000
Stein Eriksen Lodge	36 mi S.	Phone: 649-3700

Lodging: Deer Valley Resort (36 miles) 649-1000; Stein Eriksen Lodge (36 miles) 649-3700

Meeting Rooms: Deer Valley Resort 649-1000; Stein Eriksen Lodge 649-3700

Transportation: Taxi service: Canyon Transportation 255-1841; City 363-5014; Midvalley 562-0100; Ute Cab 328-5710; Wasatch Mountain Service 295-4666; West Valley 328-5705; Yellow 521-2100; Rental cars: Eagle (on field) 569-1166

Information: Chamber of Commerce/Convention and Visitors Bureau, 1910 Prospector Avenue, Suite 103, or the Visitor Information Center, 528 Main Street, P.O. Box 1630, Park City, UT 84060, Phone: 800-453-1360 or 649-6100

The Restaurants at Stein Eriksen Lodge:

*Stein Eriksen Lodge is one of several fine lodging and entertainment facilities located near Park City, Utah. From Salt Lake City Municipal 2 Airport, the town of Park City is located about 40 minutes by way of Interstate 80 east. This lodge includes 47 suites, 79 deluxe rooms, swimming pool, Tennis courts, conference center, and access to ski slopes. In addition to all the year-round activities, the lodge offers a myriad of exquisite dining options that will satisfy the palate of every guest. Choices range from contemporary-style cuisine to unique winter selections and casual outdoor dining. The **Glitretind Restaurant** serves contemporary European-style cuisine in mountain side setting. The Glitretind is open year-round for breakfast, lunch and dinner, and it accommodates up to 150 guests. It features spectacular buffet breakfasts from 7:00 a.m. to 10:00 a.m. during the winter. Lunch at the Glitretrind features the acclaimed "Skier's Buffet" which is served from 11:30 a.m. to 2:30 p.m. during the winter. The restaurant also offers al fresco dining during the summer months. **The Forest Room Restaurant** features New American cuisine in an intimate, cozy atmosphere. This restaurant is open during the winter only (December through April), and it serves dinner seven nights a week from 6:00 p.m. to 10:00 p.m. It can accommodate 50 guests. For those who prefer a more casual setting, the **Birkebeiner Cafe** is a casual, comfortable restaurant which accommodates 50 guests. It serves lunch from 11:00 a.m. to 2:30 p.m. during the winter only. The **Troll Hallen Lounge,** which accommodates 60 guests, is a favorite gathering place during ski season for light lunches, drinks, fresh shellfish and apres ski hors d'oeuvre. Winter hours are from 11:00 a.m. to midnight daily. It is also open during the summer in the afternoon and evening hours. As an added amenity to Lodge guests, room service is avaliable during the winter from 6:30 a.m. to 11:00 p.m., and during the summer from 7:00 a.m. to 9:30 p.m. For more about restaurants, rates and other information at Stein Eriksen Lodge, call 800-453-1302 or 649-3700.*

Airport Information:

SALT LAKE CITY - SALT LAKE CITY MUNICIPAL 2 AIRPORT (U42)
7 mi southwest of town N40-37.15 W111-59.57 Elev: 4603 Fuel: 80, 100, Jet-A, MOGAS Rwy: 16-34: H5860x100 (Asph) Attended: 1400-0500Z CTAF/Unicom: 122.7 Salt Lake City App/Dep Con: 120.2, 124.3 Clnc Del: 127.0 Notes: Parachute Jumping often in progress. Flocks of birds on and in vicinity of airport.

FBO: Eagle Aviation	**Phone: 569-1166**
FBO: Salt Lake Avionics	**Phone: 566-2179**
FBO: Hudson General (parking)	**Phone: 539-2805**

Deer Valley Resort

Deer Valley , located in Park City, Utah, is a year-round resort that is situated in the Rocky Mountains' Wasatch Range. It receives an average of 300 inches of the "Greatest Snow on Earth" per year and offers 1,100 acres of skiing.

Ski season usually runs from around the beginning of December through the beginning of April, so there is plenty of time for skiing. There are also plenty of mountains to ski: Bald Eagle Mountain with an elevation of 8,400 feet, Bald Mountain with an elevation of 9,400 feet and Flagstaff Mountain with an elevation of 9,100 feet. While there are some easier trails (ideal for the kids), the more difficult ones provide a real challenge to the avid skier. Bald Eagle Mountain offers ideal terrain for beginner and intermediate skiers. Bald Mountain offers intermediate and challenging skiing with spectacular views. Flagstaff Mountain offers a variety of intermediate and beginner ski trails, especially well suited for family skiing. The resort features an "Experts Only Trail Map" which details all the advanced and expert runs with challenging conditions and terrain, glade skiing, bowls, moguls, powder and steep, narrow chutes. Also, the resort offers two race hills, allowing races to occur simultaneously. Among them,The Stein Eriksen Medalist Challenge (named after the 1952 Olympic Gold Medalist), The Medalist Challenge, the Self-Timed Dual Slalom and Group Races add excitement to the day.

Stein Eriksen, Olympic gold medal winner for the giant slalom in 1952, glides through the powder at Der Valley Resort in Utah. Stein's unique style is the inspiration behind the luxurious lodge that bears his name. Photo by: Deer Valley Resort

Need lessons or sharpening of the skills? Deer Valley offers a myriad of ski school options for both children and adults, including private and group lessons.

As a service, the resort offers the Deer Valley Rental Shop which has high quality equipment in a variety of packages and is serviced by certified technicians. Other services include: basket check, real estate offices, information/ lost and found, photography and video services, as well as complimentary parking, shuttle service, hosted mountain tours and ski storage.

For parents who would like to spend a little time away (but not too far away) from their little ones, the Deer Valley Child Care Center (open 8:30 a.m. to 4:30 p.m. daily) provides indoor supervision and lots of fun activities. For those children who are staying in the center and who are also taking ski lessons, the child care staff and ski school staff work cooperatively to provide constant supervision.

Enough about winter activities! Deer Valley also bursts with activities in the summer. It is easy to forget the everyday stresses of life when soaking in the natural beauty of the Wasatch Mountain range. Enjoy the fresh air while mountain biking, hiking, taking scenic lift rides, horseback riding, in-line skating, fishing, golfing and playing tennis. Bike rentals, helmets and lessons are available.

Park City's Alpine Slide (the world's longest non-snow toboggan ride), as well as hot air ballooning and shopping are all within minutes of Deer Valley Resort. In addition, a nearby reservoir hosts all kinds of water activities, such as swimming, water skiing and jet skiing.

Music lovers with an affinity for the outdoors will delight in Deer Valley's outdoor Utah Symphony concerts. The resort's outdoor amphitheater at Snow Park Lodge is a casual setting for concert-goers to picnic on manicured lawns while listening to this award-winning symphony ensemble. Performances take place most weekends throughout July and August.

Working up an appetite? There are eight restaurants located throughout Deer Valley Resort. Each one offers a different menu choice and environment to satisfy everyone's taste. These include: the Snow Park Restaurant and Seafood

Buffet at the base lodge; at mid-mountain, the Silver Lake Restaurant, the Mariposa, McHenry's, the Bald Mountain Pizza Station, along with the Deer Valley Club restaurant; and Snowshoe Tommy's atop Bald Mountain.

Time for a rest? Deer Valley Resort offers a wide array of guest accommodations, including one to four bedroom condominiums and private homes, the Stein Eriksen Lodge, the Goldener Hirsch Inn and the new Deer Valley Club. Several lodging packages are offered at Deer Valley condominiums, including a "Mountain Biking Package," a "Starry Nights Package" and a "Golf Package." A variety of special summer lodging rates and packages are also offered.

For those visiting on business, both Snow Park and Silver Lake lodges offer a range of meeting and banquet spaces, including a total of over 22,000 square feet of 16 function rooms.

Salt Lake City Municipal 2 Airport (not to be confused with the main airport, Municipal 1) is located 7 miles southwest of Salt Lake City. It has a 5,860'x100 asphalt runway. Park City is located about 40 minutes by way of Interstate 80 eastbound out of Salt Lake City. While in Park City, a complimentary shuttle bus runs from 7 a.m. to midnight, daily, from surrounding points throughout the area, including Deer Valley. For more information about Deer Valley Resort, call 800-424-DEER (3337) or 649-1000. (Information submitted by Deer Valley Resort).

Stein Eriksen Lodge

Salt Lake City, UT (UT-U42)

Photo by: Stein Eriksen Lodge

Eriksen Lodge is nestled mid-mountain at Deer Valley Resort.

The Stein Eriksen Lodge is located in the mid-mountain Silver Lake area at Deer Valley Resort in Park City, Utah. It is surrounded by breathtaking scenery in the Wasatch Mountains. The lodge, which is open year-round, is the proud namesake of the Norwegian skiing legend and 1952 Olympic champion Stein Eriksen. Eriksen has added his own personal touches to help create the internationally acclaimed hotel which first opened in 1982. He serves as host at Stein Eriksen Lodge and is director of skiing for Deer Valley Resort. Frequently, he greets guests and hosts a wine and cheese reception during winter afternoons.

Guests enjoy 145 cozy fireplaces throughout the Lodge, from the lobby and public spaces to the guest rooms and suites. The Lodge features 47 suites and 79 deluxe rooms, all of which are privately owned. The rooms and suites are designed with Scandinavian color schemes and furnishings, including imported European fabrics, and furnishings crafted from heavy brushed pine imported from Spain. Handpainted chandeliers from Italy and hand-crafted kitchen tiles from Portugal simply add to the elegance of each guest room. There are one, two, three and four-bedroom suites, each equipped with a European kitchen, spacious living room, cozy dining area, master bedroom with jetted bathtub and fireplace. Many also have private balconies. The deluxe rooms have either one king or two queen-size beds, jetted tubs and humidifiers. Many have window seats or private balconies. All rooms are fully-equipped with satellite cable television, a radio/alarm clock, spacious closets, gold-plated fixtures, and plush terrycloth robes. Bathroom amenities, include shampoo, conditioner, lotion, lip balm and soaps.

For dining, the lodge offers a variety of superb cuisine choices. The Glitretind Restaurant serves contemporary European-style cuisine in a mountainside setting. It is open year-round for breakfast, lunch and dinner, and it can accommodate up to 150 guests. The Forest Room Restaurant serves New American Cuisine in a cozy atmosphere. It features a unique menu of wild game, seafood and spit roasted meats. The Forest Room is open during the winter only, serving dinner seven nights a week. The Troll Hallen Lounge is a favorite gathering place during ski season for light lunches, drinks, shellfish and apres ski hors d'oeuvre. The Lounge is also open during the summer in the afternoon and evening. The Birkebeiner Cafe is a casual, comfortable cafe that serves lunch during the winter only. The Bald Mountain Deck Grille, which overlooks the ski slopes, serves light entrees and sandwiches outside for lunch during the winter only (weather permitting). Also, for guests, room service is available daily during the winter, and nightly during the summer.

Photo by: Deer Valley Resort Three skiers take the downhill plunge at Deer Valley

Winter is a popular season at the lodge. Guests who are eager to hit the slopes have ski-in/ski-out access to Deer Valley's three mountains with two high-speed quad chairlifts, nine triple chairlifts and state-of-the-art snowmaking capabilities. Cross-country skiing, snowmobiling, sleigh rides, ice skating and hot-air ballooning are within minutes of the Lodge. Guests may also wish to explore Park City, where historic Main Street offers plenty of shopping, dining, and entertainment.

Besides breathtaking scenery, fresh mountain air, scrumptious dining and comfortable luxury accommodations, Stein Eriksen Lodge offers a variety of services and amenities to make a guest's stay more comfortable. Services include: concierge service, valet parking in the heated, underground garage, and shuttle service to and from Deer Valley Resort's Snow Park Lodge, Park City Ski Area, historic Main Street and other areas of Park City. Guests also receive daily newspaper delivery. Other amenities include heated sidewalks, a year-round outdoor heated swimming pool with captivating mountain views, a sauna, hot tub, tennis courts, a state-of-the-art fitness room and massage therapy.

For the culturally-minded, the Park City area offers a variety of summer festivals and events, for "Savor the Summit" and the "Park City Pedalfest" in June to Park City's Old Fashioned July 4th parade, to the Arts Festival and Bluegrass Festival in August. The Utah Symphony performs under the stars on the weekends at Deer Valley's Snow Park Lodge, and Wolf Mountain offers a variety of outddor summer concerts, as well.

Summer is also a favorite time of year for guests. It is a peaceful time. The hillsides of the Wasatch Mountains come to life with lush green grass and fragrant wildflowers. Guests can enjoy Deer Valley's lift-served mountain biking, hiking, scenic lift rides, tennis and horseback riding. Nearby, they can enjoy fly-fishing, wind surfing, gigantic alpine sliding, outdoor symphony concerts and much more.

For those who are traveling on business, as well as pleasure, the lodge features a wide range or meeting facilities appropriate for both business and social functions, perfect for meetings and corporate retreats. The Olympic Conference Center, the Alpine Room, and the elaborate Viking Board Room make up more than 4,700 square feet of meeting space for groups of up to 140 people.

Salt Lake City Municipal 2 Airport (not to be confused with the main airport, Municipal 1) is located 7 miles southwest of Salt Lake City. It has a 5,860'x100 asphalt runway. Park City is located about Salt Lake City Municipal 2 Airport (not to be confused with the main airport, Municipal 1) is located 7 miles southwest of Salt Lake City. It has a 5,860'x100 asphalt runway. Park City is located about 40 minutes by way of Interstate 80 eastbound out of Salt Lake City. While in Park City, a shuttle bus service runs from 7 a.m. to midnight, daily, from surrounding points throughout the area, including Deer Valley. The Stein Eriksen Lodge offers a variety of summer and winter packages. For more information about rates and accommodations at Stein Eriksen Lodge, call 800-453-1302 or 649-3700. (Information submitted by Stein Eriksen Lodge).

UT-VEL - VERNAL
VERNAL AIRPORT

(Area Code 801)

19

Skillet East:

The Skillet East restaurant is located about 1 mile north of the Vernal Municipal Airport. To reach the restaurant turn right out of the airport entrance and drive until you reach main street. the restaurant will be near that intersection. This is a combination type restaurant featuring a cafe in front and a fine dining facility called "Car-19" in the back portion. Their hours are from 5 a.m. to 10 p.m. 7 days a week. The coffee shop in front serves a variety of foods like fried chicken, a 16 oz T-Bone steak for $9.95 and shrimp dishes, while the dining room in back "Car-19" offers a more elegant atmosphere. Such entrees as prime rib, lobster, and crab legs along with a variety of ethnic dishes can also be enjoyed. The decor of their "Car-19" dining room is oblong and is decorated in southwestern style. On Thursday, Friday and Saturday nights there is usually live entertainment. The main dining room can accommodate up to 75 people. Larger groups and parties are welcome with advance notice. For more information call 789-3641.

Restaurants Near Airport:
Skillet East 1 mi N. Phone: 789-3641

Lodging: Econo Lodge (Free airport transportation) 789-0947; Weston Plaza (Airport transportation) 789-9550.

Meeting Rooms: Weston Plaza (Airport transportation) 789-9550.

Transportation: Courtesy Car with advance notice

Information: Dinosaurland Travel Board, 25 East Main Street, Vernal, UT 84078, Phone: 789-6932 or 800-477-5558.

Attractions:

Ashley National Forest is located 15 miles north of town and contains a 1.5 million acre forest as well as the 1500 foot deep Red Canyon and King's Peak with a height of 14,000 feet. The park supervisor's telephone number is 789-1181; Also within this area is Dinosaur National Monument.

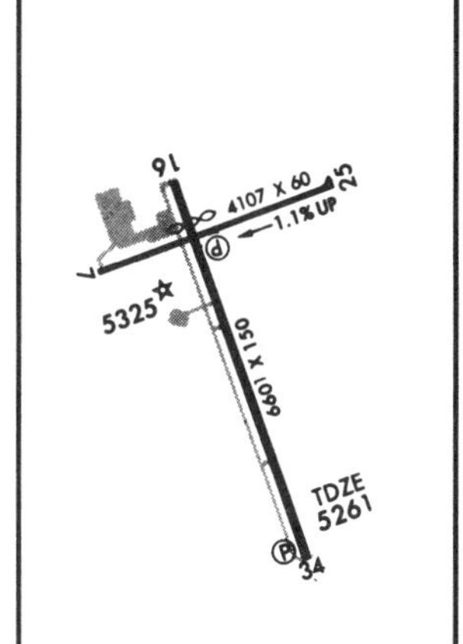

Airport Information:

VERNAL - VERNAL AIRPORT (VEL)
1 mi southeast of town N40-26.47 W109-30.60 Elev: 5274 Fuel: 100LL, Jet-A
Rwy 16-34: H6601x150 (Asph-Pfc) Rwy 07-25: H4107x60 (Asph) Attended: dawn to dusk
Unicom 122.7 Airport Manager 789-3400
FBO: Dinaland Aviation Phone: 789-4612

VERMONT

LOCATION MAP

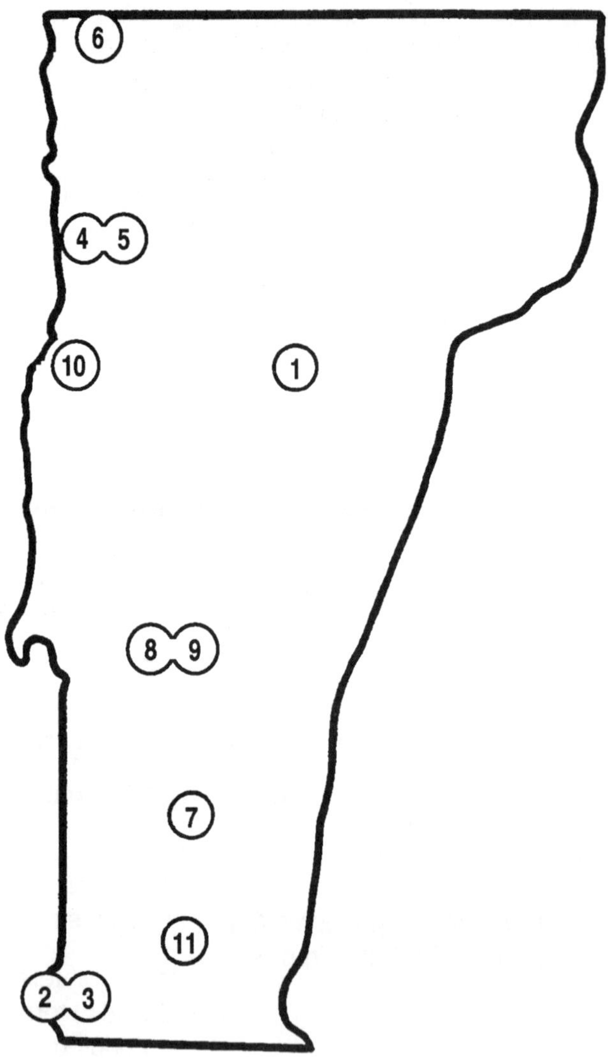

Not to be used for navigational purposes

VERMONT

CROSS FILE INDEX

Location Number	City or Town	Airport Name And Identifier	Name of Attraction
1	Barre-Montpelier	Edward F. Knapp State Arpt. (MPV)	Sambel's Restaurant
2	Bennington	William H. Horse State (5B5)	Four Chimneys Inn
3	Bennington	William H. Horse State (5B5)	Mt. Anthony Country Club
4	Burlington	Burlington Intl. (BTV)	One Flight Up
5	Burlington	Burlington Intl. (BTV)	Windjammer Restaurant
6	Highgate	Franklin Co. State Arpt. (FSO)	Border Air Rest.
7	Londonderry	North Windham Arpt. (VT05)	Tater Hill Country Club
8	Rutland	Rutland State Arpt. (RUT)	Amelia's Canteen
9	Rutland	Rutland State Arpt. (RUT)	Killington Ski Resort
10	Vergennes	Basin Harbor Arpt. (B06)	Basin Harbor Resort
11	West Dover	Mount Snow Arpt. (4V8)	Mt. Snow Country Club

Articles

City or town	Nearest Airport and Identifier	Name of Attraction
Rutland, VT	Rutland State (RUT)	Killington Ski Resort
Vergennes, VT	Basin Harbor (B06)	Basin Harbor Club Resort
West Dover, VT	Mount Snow (4V8)	Mt Snow/Haystack Resort

VT-MPV - BARRE-MONTPELIER
EDWARD F. KNAPP STATE AIRPORT

(Area Code 802) **1**

Restaurants Near Airport:
Sambel's On The Airport On Site Phone: 223-6776
Suzanna's Restaurant 2 mi E. Phone: N/A

Sambel's Restaurant:

Sambel's Restaurant is situated on the Edward F. Knapp State Airport and is located only a few feet from aircraft parking. They are open 7 days a week for lunch from 11:30 a.m. to 2:00 p.m. and dinner from 4:30 p.m. to 9:00 p.m. Their menu displays items like beef, seafood, chicken and veal dishes as their specialty. Selections include rib-eye steak, prime rib, flounder, shrimp, chicken, lobster and clams along with 10 different dinner and lunch specials usually offered each day. On Sunday between 10 a.m. and 2 p.m. they serve a brunch as well. Their dining area can seat 65 to 67 persons, and is divided into two separate sections. Guests can also enjoy watching the airplanes while dining. If advance notice is given larger parties or groups can arrange accommodations with the restaurant. In-flight catering is yet another service provided by this establishment. For more information call Sambel's Restaurant at 223-6776.

Lodging: Comfort Inn (1 mile, trans) 229-2222; La Gue Motel (1 mile, trans) Montpelier, VT 229-5766.
Meeting Rooms: Comfort Inn 229-2222; La Gue Motel (Montpelier) 229-5766.
Transportation: Taxi service: A & D Taxi 476-9408; Norm's Taxi 223-5226; Also rental cars: Avis 229-5922; Barr Ford 479-0136; Budget 476-4724; Hertz 223-3815; National 223-3434.
Information: Central Vermont Chamber of Commerce, P.O. Box 336, Barre, VT 05641, Phone: 229-5711.

Attractions: Located near the airport are some of the largest granite quarries. Self guided tours are available daily 8:30 a.m. to 5:00 p.m., May 1 to October 31 from the Visitor's Center. There is optional shuttle ride tour given June 1 to mid-October, Monday through Friday. An observation deck over Craftsman Center is open weekdays year round. For information call 802-476-3119. Many ski areas are available in the area, approximately 45 minutes by car. State Capitol is located only 4 miles away from airport.

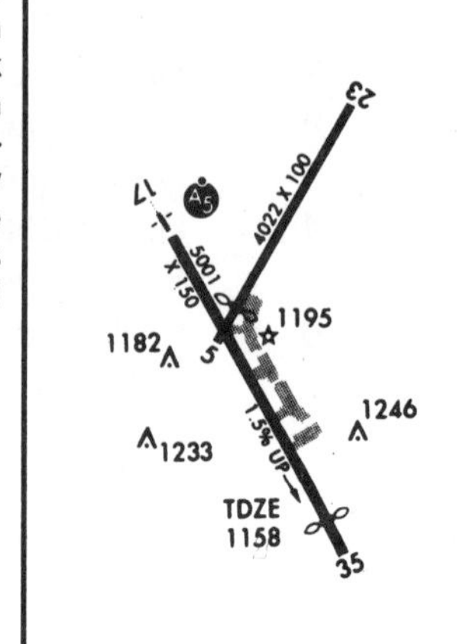

Airport Information:

BARRE-MONTPELIER - EDWARD F. KNAPP STATE AIRPORT (MPV)
3 mi west of town 44-12-12N 72-33-46W Elev: 1165 Fuel: 100LL
Rwy 17-35: H5001x150 (Asph) Rwy 05-23: H4022x100 (Asph) Attended: continuously
Unicom: 122.8 Public Phone 24hrs Notes: No landing fees
Edward F. Knapp State Airport (Manager) Phone: 229-0022
FBO: VT Flying Service Phone: 223-2221

VT-5B5 - BENNINGTON
WILLIAM H. MORSE STATE

(Area Code 802)

2, 3

Four Chimneys Inn:

The Four Chimneys Inn is located only a short distance from the William H. Morse State Airport. This is a combination restaurant and bed and breakfast facility. The restaurant on the premises offers elegant dining with entrees prepared by their master chef. Each meal is a dining experience in elegance. The restaurant itself, is open to the public and is visited frequently by fly-in customers. They serve lunch Tuesday through Sunday from 11:30 a.m. to 2 p.m., and dinner 5 p.m. to 8:30 p.m. everyday. Reservations are suggested. We were told by the owners that you can walk to their establishment on a nice day; however, airport courtesy cars and local taxi service is readily available. You can reach the Four Chimneys Inn by turning left out of the south entrance of the airport, and going east on Walloomsac Road heading towards the Bennington Battle Monument. Then turn right (south) onto Gypsy Lane, then left going east on West Main Street. The Four Chimneys Inn will be on the north side of the street. Once reaching the Four Chimney Inn you will enjoy the parklike setting of this beautiful Georgian estate. Lodging accommodations for overnight guests include rooms with private baths, phones and TV. This is a AAA and Three Diamond Mobile rated establishment.. For reservations call 447-3500.

Mount Anthony Country Club:

The Mount Anthony Country Club has a restaurant, 18 hole golf course and pro-shop. The William H. Morse State Airport is located about 3 miles from the country club. During our interview we learned that the staff will deliver their fly-in guests to and from their establishment depending on available staff. Their family style restaurant serves lunch between 11 a.m. and 3 p.m. and dinner between 5 p.m. and 8:30 p.m. The owner of the restaurant takes great pride in serving freshly prepared food. Some of their specials include roast sirloin, scallops and fettuccini alfredo. Between Tuesday through Friday a dinner special is offered for about $8.00. Normal daily specials are also offered through the week. Their main dining room can seat up to 75 people. There are 4 rooms in all that can be adjoined or partitioned off for banquet or meeting rooms. Guests can see the golf course from the dining room. For more information call the Mount Anthony Country Club at 442-2617.

Restaurants Near Airport:

Four Chimneys Inn	2 mi. SE	Phone: 447-3500
Mt. Anthony C & C	3 mi. NE	Phone: 442-2617
Numerous Restaurants	3-4 mi. E	N/A

Lodging: Bennington Motor Inn 5 mi 442-5479; Best Western New Englander 4 mi 442-6311; Four Chimneys Inn 1 to 1-1/2 mi. 447-3500; Kirkside Motor Lodge 5 mi 447-7596; Knotty Pine Motel 2 mi. 442-5487; Paradise Motor Inn 5 mi 442-8351; Ramada Inn 8 mi 442-8145.

Meeting Rooms: Best Western New Englander 4 mi 442-6311.

Transportation: Rental cars: Hertz 447-0507; National 442-3108; Also taxi service: Bennington Taxi Service 442-6527.

Information: For further information contact the Bennington Information Booth, Veterans Memorial Drive, Route 7, Bennington, VT 05201, Phone: 447-3311, or Fax 447-1163.

Attractions:

If it hadn't been for what transpired near Bennington on August 16, 1777, it is doubtful that there would be an entity known as the State of Vermont...indeed, there might not be a United States of America today! On that date, the Battle of Bennington was fought. Historians have termed it "a turning point of the Revolution" for just reason... The battle foiled General Burgoyne's attempt to cut the colonies in two by halting his advance down the Hudson. Equally important, it revitalized the country's flagging spirit by demonstrating that colonial militia could defeat the finest troops the British could throw against them. By defeating and capturing more than 800 of these regulars-roughly one sixth of Burgoyne's total army - it insured an American victory at the Battle of Saratoga exactly two months later. A visit to the **Bennington Museum** located on West Main Street about 1-1/2 to 2 miles east of the airport, will provide the complete history of the area, plus fine examples of New England furniture, decorative arts, paintings, tools, military artifacts and pottery amongst many other items on display. For museum information call 447-1571. **Areas of Interest:** Bennington, Vermont contains three separate areas containing historic significance. "Old Bennington" is located a short distance southeast of the William H. Morse State Airport. The Victorian and turn-of-the-century buildings downtown; a number of colonial homes and mansions church and commons in Old Bennington; and three covered bridges in North Bennington that span the Walloomsac River: the Silk Road Bridge built in 1840, the Paper Mill Bridge built in 1889, and the Henry Bridge built in 1840. For information about additional lodging, dining, attractions and points of interest contact the **Bennington Area Chamber of Commerce** at Veterans Memorial Drive - Route 7, Bennington, Vermont 05201 or call 447-3311. (Fax 447-1136).

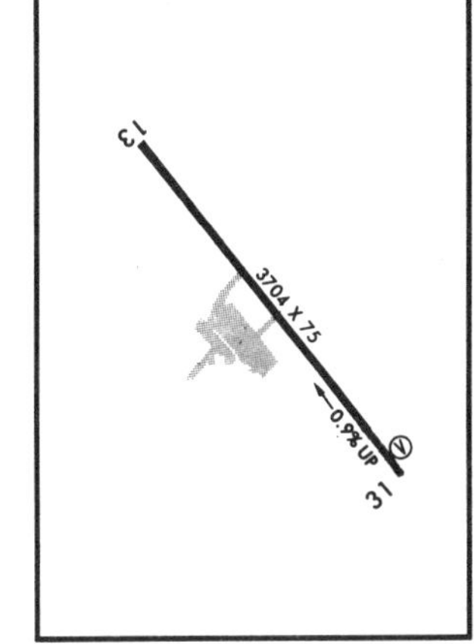

Airport Information:

BENNINGTON - WILLIAM H. MORSE STATE (5B5)

3 mi west of town N42-53.48 W73-14.78 Elev: 826 Fuel: 100LL, Jet-A Rwy 13-31: H3704x75 (Asph) Attended: 1300-2200Z Unicom: 122.8 Notes: Rwy conditions may not be monitored or reported when the airport is unattended. Also for noise abatement, avoid overflying homes SE of airport.

FBO: Business Air, Inc. Phone: 442-3219

VT-BTV - BURLINGTON
BURLINGTON - BURLINGTON INTL.

(Area Code 802) 4, 5

One Flight Up:

If you are looking for ambiance, great cuisine, spectacular views and friendly service, look to One Flight Up Restaurant located in the Burlington International Airport terminal building. Breakfast is served from 6-11 a.m., lunch and dinner daily until closing. This fine dining facility offers more than a meal, it provides a memorable dining experience that is second to none. The cozy atmosphere features a travel and flight theme with aircraft photos, propellers and other travel items decorating the walls. Tableside headphones are available for listing to pilot's conversations. Dressed in their pilot and flight attendants attire, the wait staff adds spark to the restaurant's decor. The menu, designed as a passport, includes both traditional and creative cuisine. Runway Roast Beef, Top Gun Turkey, High Hopes Herb Chicken and Jet Set Chimichangas are just a few delightful dishes. Average prices run $4.50 for breakfast, $6.00 for lunch and $9.00 for dinner. A children's menu is also available offering a variety of pint-size meals. This 152 seat restaurant has a relaxing, full bar and a first class conference and function room. These accommodations are particularly useful for clubs and organizations. Through their in-flight catering facility "Premier Catering" can be called at 862-1819 for reservations. The restaurant hours are 6 a.m. to 8 p.m. daily. Burlington is situated along the eastern shore of Lake Champlain. Backed by the Green Mountains to the east and facing the Adirondacks across the lake, this area offers magnificent scenic panoramas. One Flight Up Restaurant is truly Burlington's best kept secret. For reservations or more information call 862-6410.

Windjammer Restaurant:

The Windjammer Restaurant is located adjacent to the Burlington, Vermont Econolodge 1-1/2 to 2 miles west of the airport on Williston Road. This family style facility is open for breakfast at 6:30 a.m.-10 a.m., lunch from 11:30 a.m. to 2:30 p.m. and dinner from 5 p.m. to 10 p.m., and 4-9 p.m. on Sunday. They also offer a brunch on Sunday from 10 a.m. to 2:30 p.m. Specialized entrees include hand cut steaks, prime rib, fresh seafood and their delicious salad bar. Prices range from $4.00 for breakfast, $6.00 for lunch and $13.00 for dinner. This restaurant has a light nautical decor with booth seating. Banquets and groups can dine in their Pavilion and Gallery rooms, each able to seat up to 70 people. For information call 862-6585.

Restaurants Near Airport:

Holiday Inn	2 mi	Phone: 863-6363
One Flight Up	On Site	Phone: 862-6410
Radisson Burlington	4 mi	Phone: 658-6500
Sheraton Burlington	2 mi	Phone: 862-6576
Windjammer Restaurant	2 mi	Phone: 862-6585

Lodging: Comfort Inn 1 mi 865-3400; Econolodge (See Windjammer Restaurant) 2 miles, 862-6586; Radisson Burlington 4 miles, 658-6500; Sheraton Burlington 2 miles, 862-6576; Holiday Inn 2 miles, 863-6363.

Meeting Rooms: One Flight Up restaurant (terminal bldg.) has accommodations for catered meetings at their facility 862-6410. All lodging facilities listed above have accommodations for conference rooms. (See Lodging)

Transportation: Shuttle busses are available to the Sheraton and Radisson Hotels. FBO's may provide transportation within short distance if given advance notice. Also rental cars are available: Avis 864-0411; Budget 658-1211; Hertz 846-7409; National 864-7441.

Information: Lake Champlain Regional Chamber of Commerce, P.O. Box 453, Burlington, VT 05402. Phone: 863-3489.

Attractions:

The Lake Champlain Transportation Company: This company operates several commercial ferry boats that make three different crossings on Lake Champlain. A 12-minute ferry between Grand Isle, VT and Plattsburgh, NY open all year; a one-hour ferry between Burlington, VT and Essex, NY open April through January, and a 20-minute ferry between Charlotte, VT and Essex, VT., 864-9804. Another water attraction in Burlington is the **"Spirit of Ethan Allen"** a vintage stern-wheeler where guests can cruise Lake Champlain and enjoy daytime, sunset, evening or dinner excursions, 862-9685. **Sport Fishing on Lake Champlain:** There are many charter boats that fish the waters of Lake Champlain. One to six hour fishing trips are normally offered. Everything from bass boats to cabin cruisers are available complete with bait, tackle and all that you will need. **Ethan Allen Homestead:** Vermont began with Ethan Allen and the Green Mountain Boys. Tour Allen's restored 1787 farm house. The orientation center features a multi-media show, exhibits and a gift shop., 865-4556. **Shelburn Museum & Heritage Park:** are located about 12 miles southwest of the Burlington International Airport. This 45 acre facility has 35 historic buildings and is an assembly of everything that symbolizes the New England area. The museum is open daily from mid-May to late October, 9 a.m. to 5 p.m. For information call 985-3344.

Airport Information:

BURLINGTON - BURLINGTON INTL.

3 mi east of town N44-28.29 W73-09.17 Elev: 334 Fuel: 100LL, Jet-A Rwy 15-33: H7807x150 (Asph-Grvd) Rwy 01-19: H3602x75 (Asph) Attended: 1100-0300Z Atis: 123.8 Unicom: 122.95 App/Dep Con: 121.9 Tower: 118.3 Gnd Con: 121.9 Notes: CAUTION: generating plant 2 NM from apch end Rwy 15 produces steam which may obscure visibility on final apch. (See AFD).

FBO: Innotech Aviation **Phone: 658-2200**
FBO: Valet Air Service **Phone: 863-3626 or 800-782-0773**

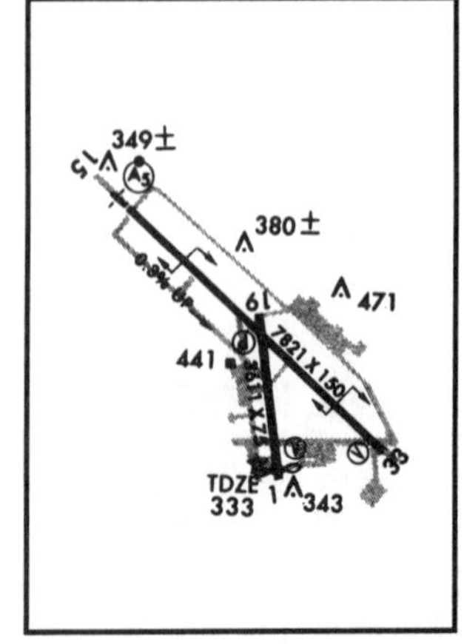

Not to be used for navigational purposes

VT-FSO - HIGHGATE
FRANKLIN COUNTY STATE AIRPORT

(Area Code 802)

6

Border Air Restaurant:

Border Air Restaurant is located within the fixed base operation (FBO) on the Franklin County State Airport. This aviation service facility has a small snack bar that provides light fare for their customers. According to the management, the kitchen is open between 8:30 a.m. and 4:30 p.m. everyday. Their menu contains items like hot dogs, hamburgers, cheeseburgers, soups, salads, beverages, lots of hot coffee and candy bars. Average prices run between $3.00 and $4.00 for most items. Their dining room seats about 12 persons. Meals can also be prepared to go as well. For more information call Highgate Aero, Inc. at 868-2822.

Restaurants Near Airport:
Border Air Restaurant. On Site Phone: 868-2822

Lodging: Swanton Motel (2 miles) 868-4284.

Meeting Rooms: None Reported

Transportation: Ted's Taxi 868-3313; E.J. Barrette & Son Rental Cars 868-3327.

Information: Vermont Department Of Travel And Tourism, 134 State Street, Moutpelier, VT 05602, Phone: 802-828-3236.

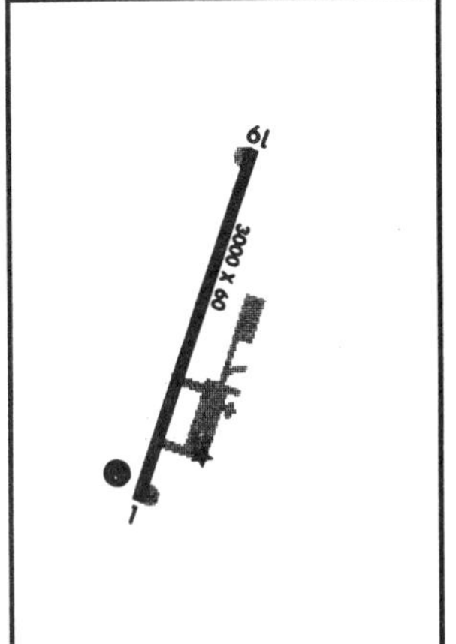

Airport information:

HIGHGATE - FRANKLIN COUNTY STATE AIRPORT (FSO)
3 mi west of town N44-56.42 W73-05.85 Elev: 228 Fuel: 100LL
Rwy 01-19: H3000x60 (Asph) Attended Nov-Mar 1330-2200Z, Apr-Oct 1300-0030Z
Unicom: 122.8
Airport Manager Phone: 868-2822

VT-VT05 - LONDONDERRY
NORTH WINDHAM AIRPORT

(Area Code 802)

7

Tater Hill Country Club:

The Tater Hill Country Club is located adjacent to the North Windham Airport. This country club contains a family style restaurant, 9 hole golf course, swimming pool and tennis courts. The restaurant is open between 11 a.m. and 5 p.m. 7 days a week. They serve hamburgers, hot dogs, grilled ham and cheese sandwiches, chef salads, platters, French fries, onion rings, French fried shrimp and clams. Their main dining room can seat approximately 60 persons and provides a view overlooking their outdoor patio, swimming pool as well as the mountains in the distance. A special breakfast is also served between 8:30 a.m. and 11:30 a.m. on Sunday. Average prices for meals run between $3.00 and $5.00 for most selections. For more information, call the Tater Hill Country Club at 875-4647.

Restaurants Near Airport:
Tater Hill Country Club Adj. Arpt. Phone: 875-4647

Lodging: Dostal's 824-6700; Highland House 824-3019; Inn On Magic Mountain 824-6100; Londonderry 824-5226; Snowdon 824-6047; Swiss Inn 824-3442;

Meeting Rooms: Swiss Inn 824-3442.

Transportation: According to the country club management, fly-in guests can easily walk to the country club from the airport.

Information: Vermont Chamber of Commerce, Box 37, Montpelier, VT 05602 or Vermont Travel Division, 134 State Street, Montpelier, VT 05602, Phone: 802-828-3236.

Attractions:

Tater Hill Country Club championship 18 hole golf course adjacent to the North Windham Airport.

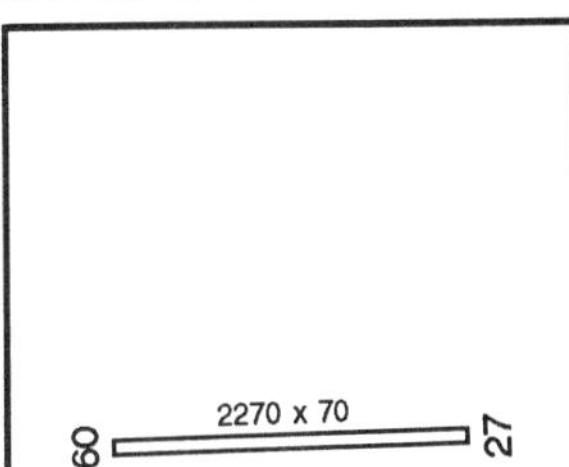

Airport Information:

LONDONDERRY - NORTH WINDHAM AIRPORT (VT05)
4 mi east of town N43-13.29 W72-42.77 Elev: 1750 Rwy 09-27: 2270x70 (Turf)
Unattended CTAF: 122.9 Notes: Ultralights on and in vicinity of airport. Rwy 09-27 no line of sight between runway ends.
North Windham Airport Phone: 875-2517

VT-RUT - RUTLAND
RUTLAND STATE AIRPORT

(Area Code 802) 8, 9

Restaurants Near Airport:

Amelia's Canteen	On Site	Phone: 773-3381
Killington Ski Resort	12 mi.	Phone: 773-1330

Lodging: Killington Ski Resort (12 miles) 773-1330; Holiday Inn (4 miles) 775-1911; Howard Johnsons (4 miles) 775-4303; Rutland Lodge (4 miles) 773-3361
Meeting Rooms: None Reported
Transportation: Taxi service: M&M Travel 775-7565; Rental cars: National 773-3348 (provided by FBO); Avis 773-1317; Hertz 775-3353 (provided by airport)
Information: Chamber of Commerce, 256 N. Main Street, Rutland, VT 05701, Phone: 773-2747

Amelia's Canteen:

This restaurant is situated right on the main ramp where aircraft can park outside their front door. Categorized as a fine dining establishment. Amelia's Canteen provides a full selection of menu items. Specialties of the house include Chicken Winston, duck, Roasted Fillet Mignon, Tomato basal pasta, roasted red pepper (a vegetarian dish), horse radish crusted scrod, salmon braised in white wine and Renne pasta with Portabello mushrooms and spinach salad. Items on their menu change daily. The restaurant can seat about 100 persons and has an aviation theme, decorated with photographs and artist's pictures of aircraft, propellers, model airplanes, and even a collection of original flight jackets on display. Infact, the restaurant is owned by pilots which are very active in aviation. They have recently completed or are in the process of completing a vintage and restored Tuskeegie Stearman for display in the Smithsonian Aviation Museum. During our interview with the management we also learned that the sunsets from Amelia's Canteen are nothing short of spectacular. Their outside dining deck which can seat around 30 persons. Amelia's Canteen is open Friday through Monday 11:30 a.m. to 2:30 p.m. for lunch and 5:00 p.m. to 9 p.m. for dinner. Breakfast is served Saturday and Sunday from 8:30 a.m. to 11 a.m. Hours may vary. For more information call Amelia's Canteen at 773-3381.

Killington Ski Resort:

Killington Ski Resort (open mid-October through early June) is located in central Vermont, and is about 12 miles east of Rutland State Airport. Killington, the largest ski resort in the eastern United States, consists of six mountains interconnected by a system of over 72 miles of a total of 162 trails. Killington is famous for its 2.5 mile, two-stageheated Killington Skyeship. The eight-passenger Killington Skyeship will dazzle you with its colorful exterior created by well-known artists. It features the world's first heated cabin, and it is the fastest model gondola in the world. Killington also features a wide variety of restaurants, ranging from casual to formal American and International cuisine, as well as popular nightspots. It has 118 lodges, country inns, motels and condominiums which offer a variety of accommodations for every budget and lifestyle.The FBO provides National Car Rental Service, and the airport provides both Hertz and Avis Car Rental Services. Contact the FBO at 773-3348 during the daylight hours.For more information about the resort, call the Killington Lodging Bureau at 773-1330 or 800-621-MTNS(6867)

Airport Information:

RUTLAND - RUTLAND STATE AIRPORT (RUT)
5 mi south of town N43-31.76 W72-56.98 Elev: 787 Fuel: 100LL, Jet-A
Rwy 01-19: H5000x150 (Asph) Rwy 13-31: H3170x75 (Asph) Attended: 1230-2330Z CTAF/ Unicom: 122.8 Boston Center App/Dep Con: 135.7 Notes: Runway conditions may not be monitored or reported when the airport is unattended. Parking fee is $5.00/night, and first night is free with fuel purchase.
FBO: Alpine Aviation Phone: 773-3348

Killington Ski Resort

Rutland, VT (VT-RUT)

Killington Ski Resort (open mid-October through early June) is located in central Vermont, and is about 12 miles east of Rutland State Airport. Killington, the largest ski resort in the eastern United States, consists of six mountains interconnected by a system of over 72 miles of a total of 162 trails. There are 10 double black diamond trails, 44 black diamond trails, 39 more difficult trails and 69 easier trails. The six mountains and their summit elevations are: Killington Peak - 4,241 ft.; Snowdon - 3,592 ft.; Rams Head - 3,610 ft.; Skye Peak(the heart of Killington's six mountains) - 3,800 ft.; Bear Mountain - 3,296 ft.; and Sunrise Mountain - 2,456 ft. This six-mountain complex also offers the greatest diversity of ski terrain in the east. The vertical drop is 3,150 feet. Killington also offers the highest capacity lift system in New England. Twenty lifts are located among the six mountains to equally distribute skiers: five double chairlifts; four triple chairlifts; seven quad chairlifts, including two detachables, two surface lifts; and the 2.5 mile, two-stage heated Killington Skyeship.

The eight-passenger Killington Skyeship features the world's first heated cabin. It is the fastest model gondola in the world, and it will whisk skiers from the base of the resort to the summit of 3,800-foot Skye Peak in only 12.5 minutes. Each Skyeship cabin will astound you with its striking colorful exterior design created by world-renowned artists, such as Russell Jacques and George Snyder. The interior contains molded fiberglass seats with armrests, cupholders and a closed-circuit radio system that carries pre-recorded music and spot announcements concerning weather conditions and special events.

Annual snowfall at Killington has averaged 252" per year. Natural snow is supplemented by snowmaking on 44

Photo by: Killington Ski Resort/Jerry Leblond

Two skiers pause to consider their next run at Killington Ski Resort inVermont.

miles of terrain. Killington can make snow on over 522 acres of its trails and has the east's most extensive snowmaking system. Snowmaking services all 20 lifts from the summits of six mountains and inter-mountain connecting trails. Killington maintains a staff of 25 Information Services personnel to assist skiers. This staff also guides a two-hour, complimentary "Meet the Mountains" tour. The resort maintains a staff of 75 Alpine Skiing Ambassadors and five Snowboard Amassadors whose mission is to promote skier/snowboarder education and awareness.

Skiing a little rusty? Killington offers various ski instruction programs for skiers of all ages and abilities. The Introduction to Skiing Program teaches new skiers how to appreciate the art and skill of this exciting sport. The program includes: all-day use of skis, boots and poles, a 1/2-hour introductory film, a 2-hour class lesson, follow-up coaching and ski tips, and a Snowshed and Rams Head area ski pass.The Mountain Ski School allows skiers of all abilities to explore Killington's broad diversity of four acres of specially contoured terrain while developing skill and technique. This program offers two hours of daily instruction and an unlimited use of all 20 operating lifts. The Masters Ski School program is designed to help intermediate skiers get out of that "intermediate rut" and to guide advanced skiers to a new skill level. This program (limited to 5 students per class) includes: three hours of instruction per day, unlimited use of all 20 lifts, plus a videotape analysis.

Last, but certainly not least, the Killington Children's Center, located at the Resort Center at Snowshed offers a variety of Vermont state-certified child care and skiing programs. The Friendly Penguin Daycare Center offers infant and child care for children as young as six weeks, up to six years. The First Tracks Ski Center, for ages three to five, offers a gentle start for beginning skiers. A special practice area has hoops, cones, obstacles and large colorful cut-out figures to create a fun learning environment. Once the beginning skiers have mastered the basic skiing skills, they will be advanced to lessons with other children of similar ability. Superstars Ski School, for ages six to twelve (all skill levels), offers an all-day program which gives kids the skiing confidence they need and never lets them forget that skiing is fun. The Mountain School for Juniors, also for ages six to twelve (all abilities), offers 2-hour lessons and an all-day ski pass.

Hungry or tired from all that skiing? Killington features a wide variety of restaurants, ranging from casual to formal American and International cuisine, as well as popular nightspots. Killington also has 118 lodges, country inns, motels and condominiums which offer a variety of accommodations for every budget and lifestyle. There are several money-saving packages, as well.

The fun doesn't stop in the winter! Killington also offers summer activities from Memorial Day to September, including gondola and chairlift rides, fishing, boating, hiking, backpacking, bicycle, tennis and golf.

Killington is easy to reach from the Rutland State Airport, which has a 5000'x150 and 3170'x75 asphalt runway. Parking fee is $5.00/night, and the first night is free with a fuel purchase. The FBO provides National Car Rental Service, and the airport provides both Hertz and Avis Car Rental Services. Contact the FBO at 773-3348 during the daylight hours. For more information about Killington Ski Resort, call the Killington Lodging Bureau at 800-621-MTNS(6867) or 773-1330. (Information submitted by Killington Ski Resort)

VT-B06 - VERGENNES
BASIN HARBOR AIRPORT

(Area Code 802) 10

Basin Harbor Club Restaurants (Resort):

Basin Harbor Club is open mid May through mid October and is located on the eastern shore of Lake Champlain, and is frequented by many fly-in guests using the resort's own private 3,000 foot turf airstrip. Within this complex are three restaurants to select from. The Red Mill restaurant open from 11 a.m. to 10 p.m., the Ranger Room from 12:30 a.m. to 2:30 p.m., and the Main Lakefront Dining Room from 8 a.m. to 9:30 a.m. for breakfast and again from 7 p.m. to 8:30 p.m. for dinner. Their entrees consist of a variety of New England fare. Daily buffets are served from 12:30 a.m. to 2:30 p.m. during the months of July and August. This facility would be more than happy to provide accommodations for group fly-ins and aviation organizations planning activities for their members. Business travelers can also arrange meetings, conferences and getaway packages for their clients. For more information about these golfing, tennis or special activity packages, you can contact the Basin Harbor Club at 800-622-4000 or 475-2311.

Attractions:

Aside from its beautiful lakeside location and breathtaking views of the Green Mountains and Adirondacks, Basin Harbor Club may be best known for its warm and relaxed hospitality. The atmosphere is often described as one of "attractive tranquility." Since 1886, the Beach family has assured that each guest is treated like an old friend, with thoughtful touches apparent everywhere. Basin Harbor is many things to many people. Couples enjoy its romantic qualities. Families and younger guests enjoy the many special activities and a variety of sports available. Private as well as business groups can also take advantage of the accommodations at the resort, with a reputation for mixing business with pleasure in a pleasant sort of way. But most of all, the atmosphere at this facility is one of friendly wholesome fun in a natural and countryside setting. Accommodations at this resort include a variety of charming lakeview cottages, nestled among lush flowers and foliage, available in a variety of sizes and each one unique in its design. Or you may prefer the comfort of one of their bedrooms in the main lodge, the Champlain House, or in the historic Homestead, all equipped with private baths. After a day of fun, cocktails and conversation in the Champlain Lounge or Red Mill provide the perfect setting for relaxation before dinner. The quiet beauty of the dusky mountains at twilight is complimented by the music of the resorts Basin Harbor Trio. The view from your table in the Lakeside dining room is a fitting prelude to gracious dining. Basin Harbor's classic New England cuisine includes a hardy breakfast and a bountiful buffet lunch. Dinners feature a wide range of tempting entrees, each carefully prepared for your enjoyment.

Restaurants Near Airport:

Basin Harbor Club	On Site	Phone: 475-2311
Red Mill Restaurant	On Site	Phone: 475-2311

Lodging: Basin Harbor Club is a fly-in resort with full accommodations for lodging. Cottages and room rates are available, in addition to numerous package deals including golfing, tennis, bed and breakfast, and seasonal rates. Phone: 475-2311.

Meeting Rooms: Basin Harbor Club has accommodations for all types of executive conferences and meetings. For information call 475-2311 and ask for their conference package.

Transportation: Courtesy transportation is provided by this resort.

Information: Basin Harbor Club, on Lake Champlain, Vergennes, Vermont 05491, Phone: 475-2311

Basin Harbor Club
Open mid-May to mid-October
Airpot Closed late Fall to early Spring

Recreational amenities:

Recreational amenities at this resort allow parents to pursue their interests while the children enjoy activities of their own. Golfers and tennis lovers appreciate the fine facilities and professional staff. The first tee of the scenic 6,513 yard golf course is right at the front door, with putting greens and practice fairways to sharpen your game. Five tennis courts include two Har-Tru and three all weather surfaces. Lake Chaplain's 600 miles of shoreline offer great boating fun. Canoes, rowboats, and windsurfers as well as charter boats for fishing can be rented. Jogging and biking trails, croquet and shuffleboard are also available. Apart from the activities at the resort itself, you are invited to visit and explore the historic nature in this area with a trip to nearby Lake Champlain Maritime Museum. Whatever your pleasure, the Basin Harbor Club will always provide your party with a splendid backdrop during your visit, and each time you return. For more information call 800-622-4000 or 802-475-2311. (Information obtained from Basin Harbor Club)

Airport Information:

VERGENNES - BASIN HARBOR AIRPORT (B06)
4 mi northwest of town N44-11.75 W73-20.98 Elev: 132 Rwy 02-20: 3000x90 (Turf)
Attended: May 15-Oct 15 Unicom: 122.8 Public Phone: 24hrs Notes: Airport CLOSED from mid-October to mid May.
Contact airport manager at 802-475-2311.

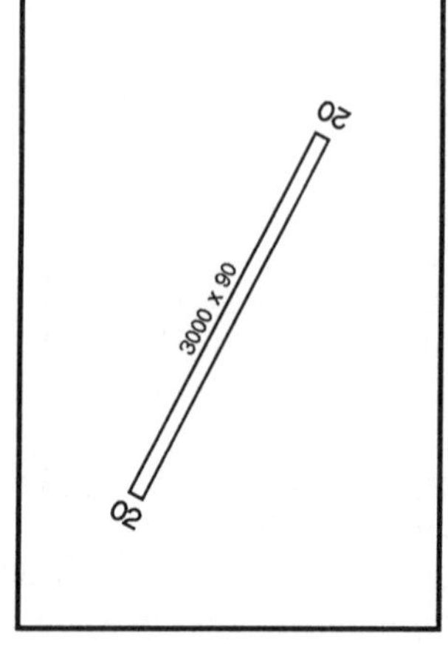

Basin Harbor Club Resort

Once an active shipyard and the home of half-a-dozen vessels that saw action in the War of 1812, Basin Harbor, located on Lake Champlain's southern Vermont coastline, is the site of the Basin Harbor Club, a summer resort unmatched by any other on this magnificent 125-mile long lake. Easily accessible from Boston, New York, Hartford, and Montreal, the Basin Harbor Club is located in Vergennes, VT, 30 miles south of Burlington and 30 miles north of Ticonderoga, New York.

The Basin Harbor Airport (B06) is situated adjacent to the resort and has a runway (2-20) 3,000 x 90 foot turf strip that has an elevation of 132 and is unattended. The airport is reported closed from late Fall to early Spring. The resort is said to be open from May 19 through October 15. However, pilots should call to make sure the field is operational especially during wet periods. The Unicom frequency is 122.8. Runway condition can be obtained through the airport manager's telephone number at 802-475-2311.

The Basin Harbor Club, owned and operated by the Beach family, has a history extending back more than a century. Great Aunt Ardelia Beach first opened her farmhouse doors to visitors in 1886, and a portion of the Basin Harbor property continued to be farmed until the 1950's. However, it was Allen Penfield Beach, Ardelia's son, who had the vision to transform the property into the family resort it is today.

Through four succeeding generations, this vacation destination has embraced old-fashioned charm. Today, Bob and Pennie Beach, with a fifth generation in training, carry on Basin Harbor Club's timeless traditions. Families come to Basin Harbor and return year after year with children and grandchildren, each succeeding generation knowing it will enjoy the same Basin Harbor experience.

For those accustomed to look-alike condos clustered around a pool, Basin Harbor Club is a revelation. Its expansive grounds, extending over 700 well-cared-for acres, afford guests a unparalleled sense of spacious, comfortable privacy. Hundreds of small gardens and flower beds -- 10,000 bulbs are planted annually -- provide a profusion of color throughout the resort.

Randomly scattered around the Basin Harbor Club's grounds are seventy-seven charming cabins of different sizes and decorative appointments, each with its own name like Sunset or Halcyon, and unique features, maybe a deck or it's own secluded terrace that houses the club's 250 overnight guests. Several of these cabins border the club's golf course while others are perched on stone cliffs rising from Lake Champlain or are hidden among clusters of trees. Many of the cabins have been winterized, and nearly half have fireplaces to take the chill off an early Fall evening.

At the club's center is the Lodge, where the resort's main dining room is located. In deference to the club's origins in a more genteel era, linen, china and ties for dinner are still the order of the day. At a typical evening seating, guests must make a difficult choice between eight deli

Photo by Basin Harbor

Basin Harbor Club offers its own grass airstrip, conceived and built by Grandfather A.P. Beach.

Photo by Basin Harbor

Fifty gardens are scattered through Basin Harbor Club's 700 well-cared for acres.

cious entrees, succulent Vermont lamb chops, perfectly broiled salmon and locally grown vegetables for instance, all prepared by Chef Tom Spence, who has been providing Basin Harbor guests with sumptuous American cuisine for almost a decade. If not yet sated, guests can then choose from an array of delectable desserts and pastries, like Basin Harbor's famous apple crisp, created from a recipe originating with the club's founder. Along with dinner, the dining room offers guests spectacular views of Lake Champlain and, in the evening, unforgettable sunsets.

The Lodge also houses a gift shop, the club's offices and comfortable lounging areas that invite visitors to curl up with a book, catch up on world events or just enjoy the ongoing activity.

For those guests who want a more casual fare, there is the Red Mill, an old restored barn. The Red Mill is not only the perfect spot at which to grab a broiled hamburger, lobster roll and French fries, but is also the location for evening entertainment for the younger set.

The third location for culinary delight is the Ranger Room, strategically placed between the golf course and swimming pool. A sumptuous luncheon buffet is served daily offering an extensive selection of gastronomic pleasures, including a choice of hot dishes, homemade breads, and 20 cold salads. Fifty to sixty desserts, ranging from freshly made eclairs to chocolate-dipped strawberries complete the luncheon menu.

Activity choices at the Basin Harbor Club.

The harbor itself is the focus for boaters, water-skiers, wind surfers and those who just want to relax on the beach or enjoy Lake Champlain's crystal clear water. Tennis on one of the three courts or a round of golf on the club's 18 hole course await those sports enthusiasts ready for the challenge. And, if a partner or opponent is needed, one of Basin Harbor Club's staff is always ready to arrange a match. For guests seeking a quieter pace, exploring the club's two nature trails or taking a leisurely bike ride on country roads that weave through rich farmland surrounding the Basin Harbor Club is an ideal recreation.

In July and August, there are organized activities for children between 3 and 10, an optional children's table in the dining room presided over by a counselor, and supervision until 9 o'clock.

The Lake Champlain Maritime Museum, a 150 year old schoolhouse, moved stone by stone to the club's property, houses numerous Lake Champlain's related exhibits that begin during the time of the Indians, continues through the French and Indian War of 1812, and concludes with the days of steamboat commerce. A separate building accommodates a small boat exhibit of birch bark canoes, Adirondack guideboats, rowboats, and small sailboats. In addition, museum volunteers have recently completed a replica of the battleship Philadelphia, lost by Benedict Arnold in the Battle of Valcour Island during the Revolution.

For more about the Basin Harbor's Resort you can call 800-622-4000, or 802-475-2311. (Information submitted by Basin Harbor Resort).

Mount Snow/Haystack Resort

West Dover, VT (VT-4V8)

Mount Snow Vermont offers skiers a chance to try out 127 trails and 24 lifts within the 600 acres of skiing terrain. Most winter vacationers to the Mount Snow region come for Alpine skiing. But Alpine skiing is just one of the many recreational activities available to visitors in the region.

Four cross-country centers, including one with shuttle service from the Mount Snow ski area, offer more than 100 km of groomed tracks. Lessons and rentals are available. The adventurous can ski the three-mile Ridge Trail that connects the summits of Mount Snow and Haystack. Another way to explore the woods is through Mount Snow's Winter Walks Program. Naturalists lead groups on an eye-opening tour of the winter forest. Also offered at Mount Snow, are horse-drawn sleigh rides that cross the base of the mountain. As revelers are whisked across the snow, a brief history of the ski area is told. Bill Adams, fourth generation associate of Mount Snow Resort Association, operates the horse drawn sleighs and even gives rides on his farm nearby where riders wind up at a log cabin heated by wood stoves and lighted by gas lamps. While his wife Sharon serves steaming cups of cocoa, guests entertain themselves around a player piano. Another sleigh ride option is the Matterhorn, which offers a sleigh ride and dinner package. Snowmobile tours, ice fishing, and shopping in the quaint Vermont villages of West Dover and Wilmington, are other vacation alternatives. With all there is to do in the Mount Snow region, you could forget your skis and still keep busy on a winter vacation.

Photo by Mount Snow Resort/Davis Brownell

Kids 12 and under ski free at Mount Snow when their parents buy a five-day package or longer, non-holiday.

With more than 60 lodging options, the Mount Snow region offers something for everyone. Included are several world-class country inns and a deluxe trailside condominium complex.

One of the most prestigious awards a restaurant can receive is the Wine Spectator Grand Award, which recognizes outstanding restaurants with superior wine lists. Of a group of 1074 restaurants world wide, 88 were selected for this award - two in Vermont. These two both are in the Mount Snow region. The Inn at Sawmill Farm in West Dover, and the Hermitage Inn in Wilmington both are situated near Mount Snow/Haystack and provide complete vacation and skiing packages for their guests.

The Inn at Sawmill Farm, which has also been listed for nine years in the exclusive Relais et Chateaux Guide and is a Mobil four-star rated facility, is situated only 1-1/2 miles from the Mount Snow Airport (4V8). This establishment features 21 rooms including 10 fireplace cottages. Originally a working barn, it was bought over two decades ago by its present owners, and converted into one of the most elegant inns in all of New England. Guests come from all over the world. Rates for two people start at $280 per night including breakfast and dinner. Dinner choices include 18 entrees, 14 appetizers and a wine list of 870 selections. For information call 802-464-8131.

The Hermitage Inn, a Spectator Grand Award winner since 1984, also offers an extensive wine list consisting of 2500 labels with an inventory of 37,500. Dining choices include pheasant, duck, goose, wild turkey and partridge that are raised right on the premises. The inn also features a gallery with prints by famous artists as well as hundreds of antique duck decoys; a 500-acre hunting preserve; sporting clay course; a gift shop with wines and homemade jams and jellies; and 40 km of cross-country skiing. Guest rooms number 15, including 10 with working fireplaces. A two-night weekend including breakfast and dinner is $180 per person, based on double occupancy; a five-night ski week is $360. For reservations or information call 802-464-3511.

When it comes to deluxe trailside condominium accommodations, the place is Seasons on Mount Snow. The only trailside condominium at Mount

Snow, Seasons features one to four bedroom units. Located between Mount Snow's Sundance and Carinthia slopes, all units are full ski-in and ski-out. Each unit has a completely equipped kitchen, fireplace, phone and cable TV. The Sports Center features a large indoor pool, sauna, jacuzzi, game room, exercise room and social room. Two-bedroom Seasons units rent for $680 for a weekend, or $720 for a five-night ski week. For reservations, call 800-451-4211.

The Mount Snow region excels in summer activities as well. Golfing packages can be arranged at resort locations. Mount Snow's 140 miles of trails wind through some of the most beautiful areas in the state, and their acclaimed Mountain Bike School is ready to provide you with the skills necessary to gain full advantage of a mountain bike. Let their triple chair lift transport you and your bike to the summit for an unbelievable view and mountain decent. Also available are group tours, specialized mountain bike rentals and child care. For information call 800-451-4211.

Photo by: Mount Snow/Haystack

Mount Snow/Haystack

The Mount Snow Airport (4V8) is located in West Dover, and is situated near the center of the state and about 10 miles north of the Vermont/ Massachusetts border. (42-55-37N & 72-51-58W). Transportation can be arranged through taxi service or through advance notice with facilities in the area. For information about other attractions within the Mount Snow region, contact the Mount Snow/Haystack Resort 802-464-3333 or 800-245-SNOW.

VT-4V8 - WEST DOVER
MOUNT SNOW AIRPORT

(Area Code 802) 11

Restaurants Near Airport:

Deacon's Den Tavern	2 mi	Phone: 464-9361
Elsa's Restaurant	1-1/2 mi	Phone: 464-8425
Mount Snow Country Club	1/2 mi	Phone: 464-3333

Lodging: Snow Den Inn 464-9355; Deerhill Inn 464-3100.
Meeting Rooms: Mount Snow Conference Center & North Real Estate Chalet-(condominium rentals).
Transportation: North Leasing 464-2196 or 464-8481.
Information: Mount Snow/Haystack Region Chamber of Commerce, East Main, Route 9, P.O. Box 3, Wilmington, VT 05363, Phone: 464-8092.

Mount Snow Country Club:

Mount Snow Resort & Country Club is reported to be situated only 4 blocks from the West Dover/Mount Snow Airport. This area contains more than 25 restaurants providing a variety of services and cuisine including American, Italian, French, Chinese and Mexican. Some of these restaurants serve daily specials as well as Sunday brunch. Transportation can be arranged either through taxi service or rental cars with advance notice. Many facilities can accommodate large groups and parties. The Mount Snow Airport is located right on a golf course. Two other golf courses are also available within the area along with additional activities like hiking, mountain biking, summer theatre, boat rides and during the winter Alpine & cross country skiing and sleigh rides are all available to the visitor. For more information about this resort area, contact the Mount Snow Resort in Mount Snow VT 05356 or call the Mount Snow Country Club at 464-3333.

Attractions:

The Mount Snow Ski area north of West Dover, VT is located in Green Mount National Forest and contains numerous ski trails, restaurants and entertainment facilities. The ski season begins in early November and lasts until the beginning of May. The longest of 78 runs in the area is 12,000 feet with a vertical rise of 1,700 feet. For information on accommodations call 464-3333; For snow conditions call 464-2151. Also see Mont Snow/Haystack Region Chamber of Commerce listed above in the "Information" block.

Airport Information:

WEST DOVER - MOUNT SNOW AIRPORT (4V8)
1 mi southwest of town N42-55.63 W72-51.94 Elev: 1953 Fuel: 100LL
Rwy 01-19: H2650x75 (Asph) Attended: unattended Unicom: 122.8 Public Phone 24hrs
Notes: Parking fees: $5.00 for aircraft & pilot, $3.00/passenger, then $5.00 per night after first night.
FBO: NorthAir, Inc. Phone: 464-2196 or 464-8481

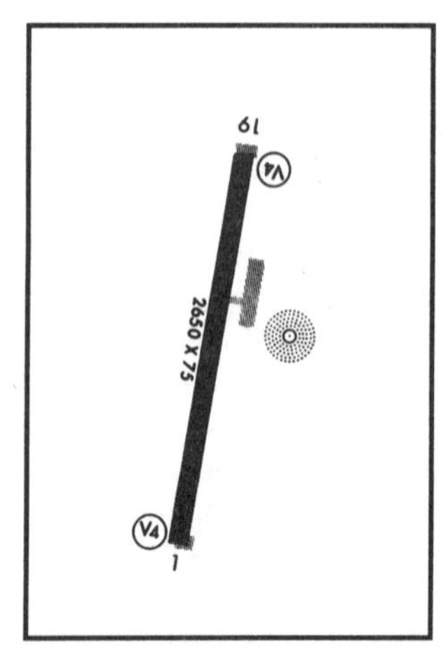

VIRGINIA

LOCATION MAP

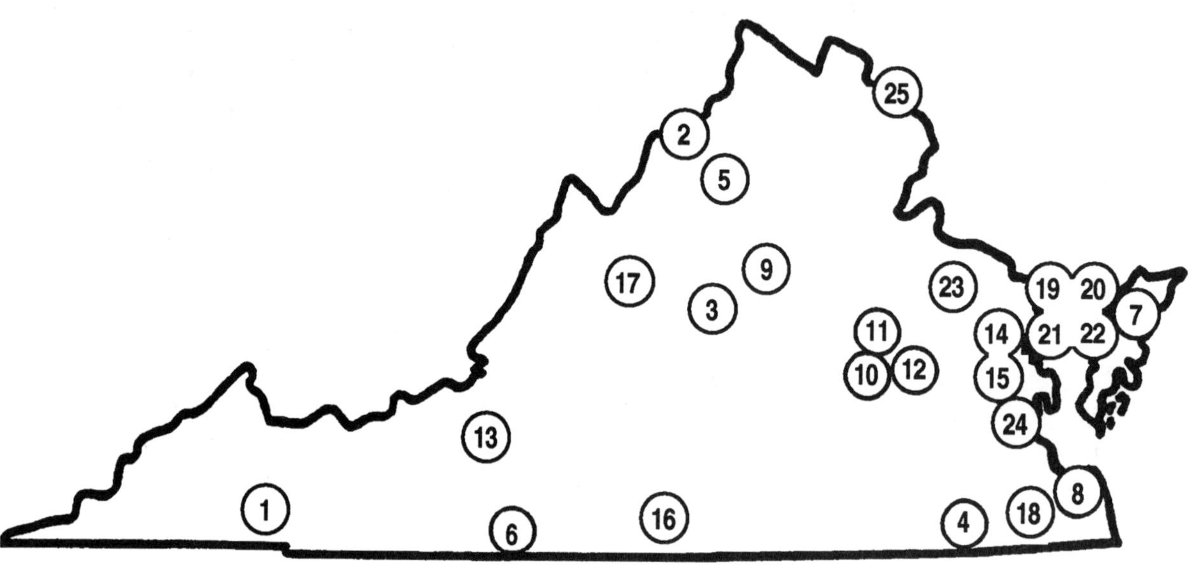

Not to be used for navigational purposes

VIRGINIA

CROSS FILE INDEX

Location Number	City or Town	Airport Name And Identifier	Name of Attraction
1	Abingdon	Virginia Highlands (VJI)	The Martha Washington Inn
2	Basye	Sky Bryce Arpt. (W92)	Bryce Resort
3	Charlottesville	Charlottesville-Albemarle (CHO)	The Boar's Head Inn
4	Franklin	Franklin Muni./Beverly Rose (FKN)	EJ's Landing
5	Luray Caverns	Luray Caverns Arpt. (W45)	Caverns & Coach Rest.
6	Martinsville	Blue Ridge Arpt. (MTV)	Windsock Restaurant
7	Melfa	Accomack Co. Arpt. (MFV)	Paradise Cove
8	Norfolk	Norfolk Intl. Arpt. (ORF)	Arpt. Dining Room
9	Orange	Orange Co. Arpt. (W93)	Mt. View Pizza Shanty
10	Richmond	Chesterfield Co. Arpt. (FCI)	Kings Korner Catering
11	Richmond	Hanover Co. Muni. (OFP)	The Smoky Pig
12	Richmond	Richmond Intl. (RIC)	CA1 Services
13	Roanoke	Roanoke Reg./Woodrum (ROA)	Creative Croissants
14	Saluda	Hummel Field Arpt. (W75)	Tides Lodge & Tides Inn
15	Saluda	Hummel Field Arpt. (W75)	Pilot House & Restaurant
16	South Boston	William M. Tuck (W78)	Ernie's Restaurant
17	Staunton/Wayn/Harr.	Shenandoah Valley Reg. (SHD)	Aero Club Cafe
18	Suffolk	Suffolk Muni. Arpt. (SFQ)	Red Apple Restaurant
19	Tangier Island	Tangier Island Arpt. (TGI)	Fisherman's Corner
20	Tangier Island	Tangier Island Arpt. (TGI)	Hilda - Chesapeake Hse.
21	Tangier Island	Tangier Island Arpt. (TGI)	Islander Seafood Rest.
22	Tangier Island	Tangier Island Arpt. (TGI)	Sunset Inn B & B
23	Tappahannock	Tappahannnock Muni. (W79)	Lawery's Seafood Rest.
24	Williamsburg	Jamestown (JGG)	Charley's
*	Washington	Washington Dulles Intl. (IAD)	See District of Columbia

Articles

City or town	Nearest Airport and Identifier	Name of Attraction
Hampton, VA	Newport News/Williamsburg (PHF)	Air Power Park
Luray Caverns, VA	Luray Caverns (W45)	Luray Caverns
Saluda, VA	Hummel Fld. (W75)	Tides Lodge Resort & C.C.
Saluda, VA	Hummel Fld. (W75)	The Tides Inn
Tangier Island, VA	Tangier Island (TGI)	Tangier Island

VA-VJI - ABINGDON
VIRGINIA HIGHLANDS

(Area Code 703)

1

The Martha Washington Inn:

The Martha Washington Inn is a Four-Star, Four Diamond Hotel and a member of the Historic Hotels Of America. As a recommendation by one of our readers, we obtained information and found that this establishment is most impressive with its unique accommodations and historical furnishings. Transportation can be arranged by calling the inn. Located in the far southwestern corner of Virginia on Daniel Boone's Wilderness Trail is Abingdon's own country inn. Elegant parlors, exquisitely decorated guest rooms, delightful afternoon tea and delicious southern fare are only a sampling of the graceful refinement which characterize the inn. Charming rooms, each with a special decor, featuring special soap, shampoos and cozy monogrammed bathrobes. Room service is yours for the asking from their "First Lady's Table." Should you prefer, settle into one of their deluxe suites with special touches, such as private living areas, beautifully appointed baths and other delights. Guests can partake of Roasted Quail Regent, Fresh Mountain Trout Stuffed with Crabmeat, Scampi Morocco, or Martha's Hot Fudge Cake. Their First Lady's Table is here to please with a sumptuous offering of both continental and traditional southern cuisine. A gracious staff, extensive wine list, fresh flowers and finely set tables set the stage for a dining experience not soon to be forgotten. For entertainment you're invited to dance til the wee hours or slip away for a stolen moment on the veranda. At their Act II Lounge, discover a cozy fireplace, relaxing cocktails and intriguing memorabilia. Should you prefer, visit The Pub with Civil War mementos, live entertainment nightly and a spacious dance floor. A special "Presidents Club Membership" is available and offers special privileges. Members represent a variety of social and business leaders, as well as returning guests, who prefer both privacy and prestigious accommodations. The town of Abingdon, VA contains fine craft and antique shops. Enjoy local festivals, or through November, attend a live performance at the world-renowned Barter Theatre located across the street from the inn. For information call the Martha Washington Inn at 628-3161 or 800-533-1014.

Restaurants Near Airport:
Martha Washington Inn 4 mi. Phone: 628-3161

Lodging: Alpine Motel 6 mi 628-3178; Comfort Inn 2 mi 676-2222; Days Inn 669-9353; Empire Motor Lodge 6 mi 628-7131; Ho Jo Inn 5 mi 669-1151; Holiday Inn Express 6 mi 676-2829; Martha Washington Inn (4 mi. courtesy transportation) 628-3161 or 800-533-1014; Super 8 5 mi 676-3329.

Meeting Rooms: Martha Washington Inn has accommodations for conferences and meetings. For information call 628-3161 or 800-533-1014.

Transportation: Courtesy transportation to the Martha Washington Inn is provided by the Inn by calling 628-3161. Also an airport courtesy car is reported; Taxi and rental cars can also be arranged by calling the airport. FBO: Virginia Highlands Airport Phone: 628-2909 or 628-6030.

Information: Washington County Chamber of Commerce, 179 E. Main Street, Abington, VA 24210. Phone: 628-8141.

Attractions:

The stories abound. A mansion built, perhaps to ensure its children married well. A riderless Yankee horse. A soldier loved and protected by a local schoolgirl, yet ultimately slain. Such tales are as rich and varied as the "Martha's" history. Originally built in 1832 as a magnificent southern mansion to house General Francis Preston, his wife and family of nine, the Martha is elegant testimony to a colorful past. A recent eight million dollar renovation provides visitors with a haven of excellence, yet does nothing to diminish the treasures both real and reminiscent. It is a structure that saw and savored influence during its ownership by General Preston. It was later to become a school for young women called "Martha Washington College." During the Civil War these schoolgirls would become nurses, and the college grounds a billet for the local militia. Ultimately, the Great Depression and typhoid fever would force the school's closing. The Martha would, thereafter, serve to house the now famous and the aspiring, appearing at the renowned Barter Theatre. Later it would become a full-fledged hotel under various managements. Today, under the ownership and considerable investment of The United Company, the Martha lives again to beckon, flirt and intrigue in legendary hospitality and style. For information call 628-3161 or 800-533-1014. (Submitted by Martha Washington Inn).

Airport Information:

ABINGDON - VIRGINIA HIGHLANDS (VJI)
2 mi west of town N36-41.23 W82-02.00 Elev: 2088 Fuel: 100LL, Jet-A Rwy 06-24: H4470x75 (Asph) Attended: 1200-0200 Unicom: 122.8
FBO: Virginia Highlands Airport Phone: 628-2909 or 628-6030

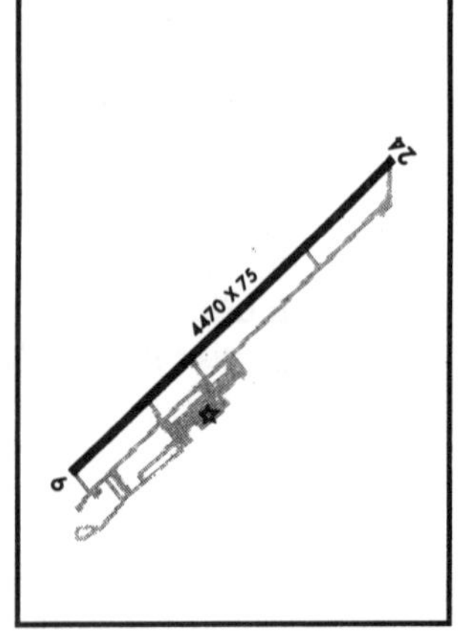

Not to be used for navigational purposes

VA-W92 - BASYE
SKY BRYCE AIRPORT

(Area Code 540)

2

Restaurant Near Airport:

Bryce Resort	1/10 mi	Phone: 856-8082
Sky Chalet Lodging	3 mi/trans	Phone: 856-2147

Bryce Resort:

Bryce Resort is located only a five minute walk from the Sky Bryce Airport. This resort has been in business for 29 years, and contains a wide variety of accommodations including ski packages, golfing, tennis, swimming pools, water sports and conference rooms. In addition, they provide guests with a fine dining facility located on the premises, as well as a cafeteria situated near the ski slopes during the winter season. The Lucio's Ristorante dining room contains seating for 150 persons in addition to a conference or banquet room able to handle up to 250 people. The main restaurant is open between 6 p.m. and 9 p.m. for dining and also during mornings for breakfast. During their evening hours they offer famous German dishes. The main dining room is decorated in a rustic atmosphere with lots of wooden furnishings. Adjoining the dining area is the banquet room. The Bryce Resort makes an excellent choice when planning your next visit within the area for pleasure or on business. For more information call the resort at 856-2121 or the restaurant at 856-8082.

Lodging: Bryce Resort (Adj Airport) 856-2121. Sky Chalet Lodging & Restaurant 3 miles from airport, (Will pick up) 856-2147.

Meeting Rooms: Bryce Resort has accommodations for meetings and conferences. Phone: 856-2121.

Transportation: Bryce Resort is within a 5 minute walk from the airport, Phone: 856-2121. Also The Sky Chalet and Restaurant will provide free courtesy transportation to and from the airport, Phone: 856-2147. (Airport telephone available only when attended).

Information: Bryce Resort can provide travelers with information about attractions within the region. For information call 856-2121.

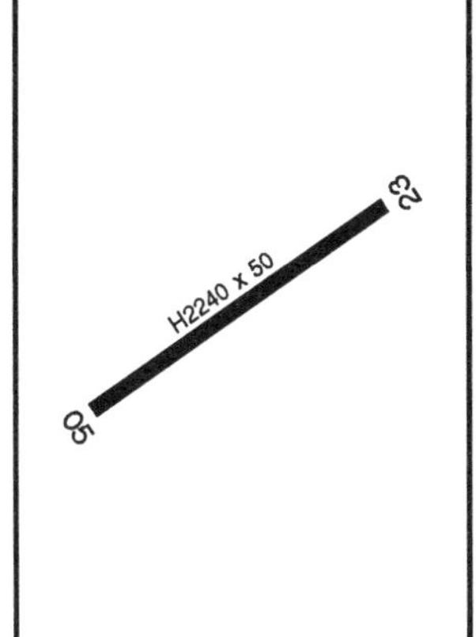

Airport Information:

BASYE - SKY BRYCE AIRPORT (W92) (Private Airport)

1 mi northeast of town 38-48-57N 78-46-14W Elev: 1263 Rwy 05-23: H2240x50 (Asph) Attended: irregularly sunrise-sunset. Unicom: 122.8 Notes: (Private Use Facility, Use at own risk) Airport telephone available only when attended.

Sky Bryce Airport Phone: 856-2121

VA-CHO - CHARLOTTESVILLE
CHARLOTTESVILLE-ALBEMARLE AIRPORT

(Area Code 804) 3

The Boar's Head Inn & Sports Club:

The Boar's Head Inn & Sports Club is located in the foothills of the Blue Ridge Mountains. It is only ten miles from the Charlottesville-Albemarle Airport. The inn is situated on 53 acres with lakes, and it is adjacent to a championship golf course, indoor-outdoor tennis courts, a sports club and four outdoor pools. There are 175 rooms, 48 of them have a view of the lake. For meetings and banquets, the inn features 11 rooms, which can accommodate from 10 to 250 people, including a 3,300 square-foot, oak-floored ballroom. The inn also features three dining areas which have their own atmosphere. The Old Mill Dining Room, the Tavern and the Sports Club. The Old Mill Dining Room features fine cuisine in an elegant atmosphere. This dining room is a restored 1834 waterwheel gristmill. It is one of only twelve Triple A, Four Diamond restaurants in Virginia. It is the only restaurant to hold the honor for seven consecutive years. It is also the consistent winner of the Wine Spectator Award for Excellence. The Tavern Restaurant features lighter fare and entertainment in a relaxed atmosphere, and the Sports Club serves an assortment of delicious sandwiches and entrees in a casual family setting. Outside along a lakeside path to the Sports Club, guests can participate in hot-air ballooning, aerobics, squash, racquetball, paddle tennis, 20 tennis courts, saunas and two swimming pools. Nearby activites include: an 18-hole championship golf course, rafting, hiking and horseback riding. The inn will provide guests with complimentary transportation to and from the airport. For more information about The Boar's Head Inn and Sports Club, call 800-476-1988 or 296-2181.

Restaurants Near Airport:
Boar's Head Inn and Sports Club 10 mi Phone: 296-2181

Lodging: Boar's Head Inn and Sports Club (10 miles) 296-2181; Ramada Inn (5 miles) 977-7700; Holiday Inn (6 miles) 293-9111; The Omni (9 miles) 971-5500; Howard Johnson's (11 miles) 296-8121; The Sheraton 973-2121

Meeting Rooms: Boar's Head Inn and Sports Club 296-2181

Transportation: Boar's Head Inn and Sports Club will provide guests with complimentary transportation to and from the airport. Taxi service: Yellow 295-4131; Rental cars: Avis 973-6000; Budget 973-5751; Hertz 973-8349

Information: Charlottesville/Albemarle Convention and Visitors Bureau, jct I-64 & VA 20, P.O. Box 161, Charlottesville, VA 22902, Phone: 977-1783

Attractions:

There are several nearby attractions to explore: Blue Ridge Mountains, University of Virginia, Jefferson's Monticello, James Monroe's Ashlawn, Madison's Montpelier, Michie Tavern. Plus, antique shops, winery tours and museums.

Photo by: Boars Head Inn — Hot Air balloon rides can be arranged for guests.

Airport Information:

CHARLOTTESVILLE - CHARLOTTESVILLE-ALBEMARLE AIRPORT (CHO)
7 mi north of town N38-08.32 W78-27.17 Elev: 641 Fuel: 100LL, Jet-A Rwy 03-21: H6001x150 (Asph-Grvd) Attended: 1100-0400Z CTAF: 124.5 Atis: 118.425 (Opr twr hrs) Unicom: 122.95 Washington Center App/Dep Con: 135.4 Tower: 124.5 (1200-0400Z) Gnd Con: 121.9 Notes: Deer/dogs/birds on and in vicinity of airport. Men and equipment working adjacent to Rwy 03-21, north and south parallel taxiways indefinitely.
FBO: Corporate Jets Airport Management, Inc. Phone: 978-1474

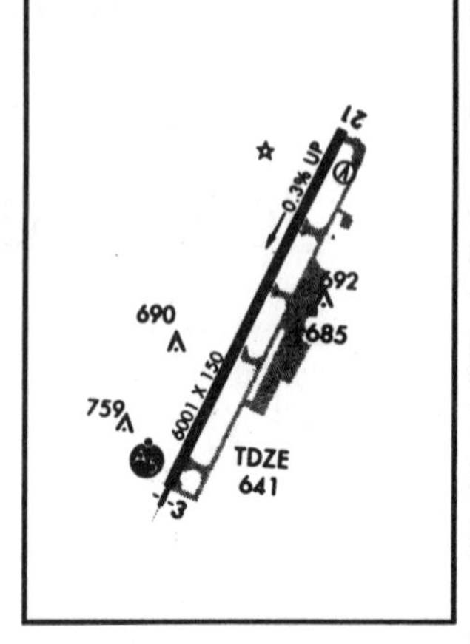

VA-FKN - FRANKLIN
FRANKLIN MUNI-JOHN BEVERLY ROSE ARPT.

(Area Code 804)

4

E J's Landing:

My Teddy Bear Restaurant is situated on the Franklin Municipal Airport. According to the restaurant manager, you can taxi and park your aircraft right next to their facility. This combination family style and fine dining establishment is open from 6:30 a.m. to 9:00 p.m. 7 days a week. Their menu displays a wide variety of entrees and specializes in steak and seafood items. They also provide a full breakfast menu. Average prices run $2.00 to $4.00 for breakfast, $4.95 to $6.95 for lunch and $8.95 to $21.95 for dinner. This restaurant exhibits a unique dining atmosphere with colors of burgundy, blue, mauve and cream. During evening hours flower arrangements are placed atop each of the glass dining room tables. Their main dining room can seat up to 140 persons. Groups and parties are always welcome. For more information about this restaurant call 562-6126.

Restaurants Near Airport:

EJ's Landing	On Site	Phone: 562-6126
Fred's Restaurant	2 mi SW	Phone: 562-2919
Phillips & Company	2 mi NW	Phone: 569-8875

Lodging: Franklin Inn (Best Western) On site and within walking distance, Phone: 562-4100.
Meeting Rooms: My Teddy Bear (Restaurant), On site and within walking distance, Phone: 562-6126.
Transportation: Airport courtesy car depending on availability; Also Buck's Taxi 562-2350; Franklin Taxi 562-5054; Rental Car: National Rental Car 562-4277.
Information: Portsmouth Convention and Visitors Bureau, 505 Crawford Street, Suite 2, Portsmouth, VA 23704. Virginia Division of Tourism, 901 East Byrd Street, Richmond, VA 23219, 804-786-4484. Phone: 804-786-4484.

Attraction:

Cypress Cove Country Club (5 miles) 562-6878; YMCA (4 miles) 562-3491.

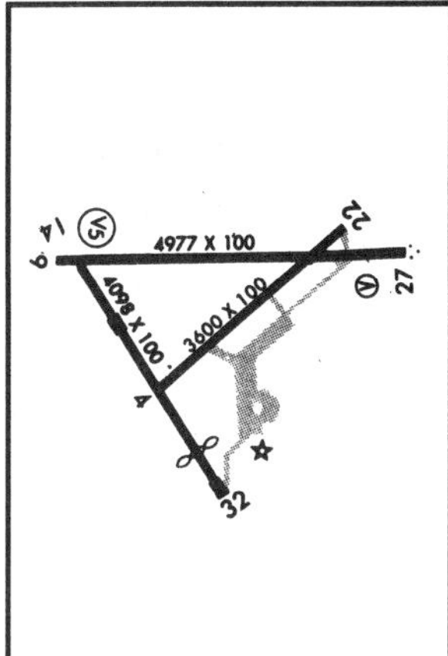

Airport Information:

FRANKLIN - FRANKLIN MUNICIPAL/JOHN BEVERLY ROSE AIRPORT (FKN)
2 mi northeast of town N36-41.89 W76-54.19 Elev: 41 Fuel: 100LL, Jet-A
Rwy 09-27: H4977x100 (Asph) Rwy 14-32: H4098x100 (Conc) Rwy 04-22: H3600x100 (Conc)
Attended: 1300-2200Z Unicom: 122.8 Public Phone 24hrs Notes: No landing fees, overnight parking fees $3.00 per night,
Franklin Municipal Airport Phone: 562-8764

Air Power Park

Hampton, VA - Newport News/Williamsburg Intl. (VA-PHF)

No visit to Hampton is complete without a tour of the Air Power Park. The people at the museum recommend you begin your visit at the park center where you can view the model airplane collection, wind tunnel exhibit and Freedom Shrine. Learn about the vital role Hampton, VA played in America's early exploration and aircraft testing.

Next, use the doors located at the back of the center to enter the park. You will see jet planes, missiles, rockets and space artifacts as you conduct your own self guided park tour. Use the back of this brochure as a guide.

Kids may enjoy the playground area. And feel free to use the park's picnic facilities, located to your right as you enter the park.

The Air Power Park is open year-round, seven days a week (closed Thanksgiving, Christmas and New Year's Day). Hours are 9 a.m. to 4:30 p.m. Free admission and parking.

This is reported to be one of the largest private civilian collections of various aircraft and missiles collected from various branches of the military services.

The Air Power Park is located about 12 road miles southeast of Newport News/Williamsburg International Airport. Take Interstate 64 southeast, exit Mercury Boulevard to the east. Their address is 413 West Mercury Boulevard, Hampton, VA. For information you can call 804-727-1163. (Information supplied in part by Air Power Park).

Nearest Airport to the Air Power Park is: Newport News/Williamsburg International Airport (PHF)

Estimated to be 12 road miles northwest of the park. Take Interstate 64 southeast to Mercury Boulevard.
413 West Mercury Boulevard
Hampton VA 23666
Phone: 804-727-1163

Aircraft & Missiles On Display

1) P. 1127
2) F-86L Sabre
3) Mercury Capsule
4) A-7E Corsair II
5) T-33A Thunderbird
6) Polaris A-2 SLBM
7) F-101F Voodoo
8) F-89J Scorpion
9) Time Capsule
10) RF-4C Phantom
11) F-105D Thunderchief
12) T-33A Trainer
13) Jupiter IRBM
14) Nike SAM (2)
15) Nike Ajax SAM
16) Nike Hercules SAM
17) F-100D Super Sabre
18) Polaris A-2 SLBM
19) Corporal IRBM
20) Little Joe/Mercury
21) Javelin Sounding Rkt.

VA -W45 - LURAY CAVERNS
LURAY CAVERNS AIRPORT

(Area Code 703) 5

Caverns and Coach Restaurant:

The Caverns and Coach Restaurant is located 1 mile from Luray Caverns Airport. Restaurant hours are from 9 a.m. to 4. p.m., 7 days a week. (Note: hours are subject to change.) It offers home-style cooking in a comfortable, modern atmosphere. The restaurant serves breakfast and lunch,with a menu that includes: fried chicken, ham, fish, salisbury steak, a salad bar and a variety of desserts. Average meal prices range from $3.00 for breakfast to $4.00 for lunch. With advance notice the restaurant will cater to parties of 20 or more, as well as to pilots-on-the-go. Special hours can be arranged for scheduled parties. After dining, visit Luray Caverns, just 1 mile from the Caverns and Coach Restaurant. For your convenience, Luray Caverns will provide courtesy transportation to and from the restaurant. For more information about the restaurant or the caverns, call 743-6551.

Restaurants Near Airport:
Caverns and Coach Restaurant 1 mi Phone: 743-6551

Lodging: Luray Caverns Motel - East (1 mile) 743-4531; Luray Caverns Motel - West (1 mile) 743-4536
Meeting Rooms: None reported
Transportation: Courtesy car to Luray Caverns facilities, call 743-6551; Rental car: Luray Motor Company 743-5128
Information: Page County Chamber of Commerce, 46 E. Main Street, Luray, VA 22835, Phone: 743-3915

Attraction:

Luray Caverns, located in Virginia's Shenandoah Valley in the foothills of the Blue Ridge Mountains, is just 1 mile east of the Luray Caverns Airport. The caverns offer guided tours year-round. For more information, call 743-6551. **Caverns Country Club Resort**, 1 mile west of Luray Caverns, is located right in the heart of the fabled Blue Ridge and Massanutten mountains. For information call 743-6551.

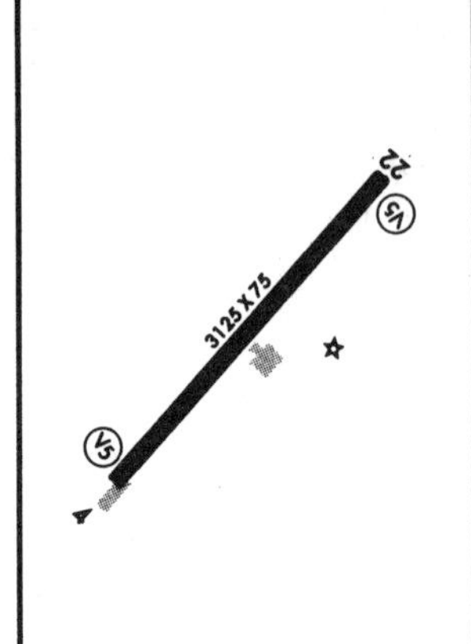

Airport Information:

LURAY CAVERNS - LURAY CAVERNS AIRPORT (W45)
2 mi west of town N38-40.02 W78-30.04 Elev: 902 Fuel: 100LL Rwy 04-22: H3125x75 (Asph) Attended: Apr.-Oct. 1400-2200Z, Nov.-Mar. 1400-2100Z CTAF/ Unicom: 122.8 Washington Center App/Dep Con: 133.2 Public Phone 24hrs
Notes: Runway 22- right-hand traffic. Prevailing winds-southwest. Contact the FBO Manager at 743-6070 (9:00 a.m. to 5:00 p.m. daily).
FBO: Airport Manager Phone: 743-6070

Luray Caverns

Luray Caverns, located in Virginia's Shenandoah Valley in the foothills of the Blue Ridge Mountains, is a U.S. Registered Natural Landmark that is visited by one-half million people each year. Interestingly, the caverns were discovered by two men who felt a cool draft of air coming from a sinkhole. The vast chambers are as large as 25,000 square feet with ceilings as high as 50 feet, and they cover an area of 64 acres. Because of the various sizes, shapes and colors of the formations, the chambers have been given names such as "Giant's Hall," "The Cathedral," and "Pluto's Chasm." Luray Caverns is open year-round (hours vary seasonally) and offers one-hour guided tours every few minutes.

Some of the highlights of the tour include: the Great Stalacpipe Organ, crystal clear lakes and pools, monumental columns and beautiful cascades of glittering, glistening stone. The Great Stalacpipe Organ, invented in 1954 by electronics engineer and organist Leland Sprinkle, plays a repertoire of nearly 20 pieces. The organ is recognized by the Guiness Book of World Records as "the world's largest natural musical instrument." For more musical enjoyment, visit the Luray Singing Tower, located in a scenic park opposite the main entrance to Luray Caverns, and hear the sounds of a carillon of 47 bells that weigh up to 3 1/2 tons. Gaze into mirror-like Dream Lake, a wide pool which reflects thousands of stalactites hanging from above. Or, toss a coin or two into the Luray Caverns Wishing Well, a large subterranean pool of water, approximately six feet deep. Visitors can take a step back in time when they stop by the Luray Cavern's Historic Car & Carriage Caravan, which features fully restored antique cars, carriages, coaches and costumes dating from 1625.

Photo by: Luray Caverns "Giant's Hall," Luray Caverns, Virginia

Huge underground chambers in Luray Caverns hold a profuse variety of natural stone formations. One-half million people annually visit the U.S. registered Natural Landmark located in Virginia's Northern Shenandoah Valley in the foothills of the fabled Blue Ridge Mountains. "Giant's Hall" is the deepest room in the cave at 164 feet beneath the surface of the earth.

If all of that touring has worked up an appetite, visit the Caverns and Coach Restaurant, just 1 mile from the Luray Caverns. It offers home-style cooking in a comfortable, modern atmosphere. The caverns will provide courtesy transportation to and from the restaurant.

For lodging, the **Caverns Country Club Resort**
, 1 mile west of Luray Caverns, is located right in the heart of the fabled Blue Ridge and Massanutten mountains. The resort, which overlooks the Shenandoah River, features an 18-hole, par 72 championship golf course and several tennis courts. Golf vacation packages are also available. Outstanding golf in a beautiful Shenandoah Valley setting awaits you at this resort. High above the banks of the storied Shenandoah River are 6,499 yards of gently rolling fairways which present a challenge to the seasoned golfer and offer an enjoyable experience to the weekend player. If tennis is your game, four courts are located near the spacious and attractive Golf House. Caverns Country Club Resort provides comfortable accommodations in two motels, only one mile from the golf course. The Luray Caverns Motels East And West are conveniently located across from the entrances to the caverns.

Luray Caverns Airport is located 1 mile west of Luray Caverns. It has a 3125'x75 asphalt runway. Tie downs are available. The FBO will provide a courtesy car to Luray Caverns facilities. Also, for your convenience, the Luray Motor Company provides rental cars. Contact the FBO manager at 743-6070, 9 a.m. to 5 p.m., 7 days a week. For more information about attractions and accommodations, call Luray Caverns at 743-6551, from 9 a.m. to 5 p.m., daily. (Information submitted by Luray Caverns)

VA-MTV - MARTINSVILLE BLUE RIDGE AIRPORT

(Area Code 540) 6

Restaurants Near Airport:
Windsock Restaurant On Site Phone: 957-2291

Windsock Restaurant:

The Windsock restaurant is located on the main parking ramp at the Blue Ridge Airport in Martinsville Virginia. This restaurant is unique in the fact that entrees on their menu are all prepared from scratch resulting in true home cooked meals. Many restaurants claim home made food but instead they buy their products from the local bakery; use buttermilk pancake mix; or use bottled Bar-B-Q sauce etc. The cooks at Windsock Restaurant make their pie crust from scratch, slice the apples for their home made apple pie and use real buttermilk poured into their batter for homemade pancakes. They also roast their own pork, cook their own Bar-B-Q sauce and make the coleslaw to top their Bar-B-Q's. Items offered on their menu include light and healthy entree choices. They are always happy to have a fly-in group and frequently plan special cookouts or special menus upon request. While stopping off to enjoy a fine meal at the Windsock Restaurant, don't forget to top your tanks off at Baron Aviation, Inc. This fixed based operation is a down-home mom and pop FBO welcoming pilots to stop in and get their picture in the airport album, or just spend a few minutes to visit and do some hangar flying. At Baron Aviation, Barbara is a "99" and a FAA examiner, while Bob is an ex-Navy pilot and a A & P mechanic. Friendly and good quality service is the specialty at Blue Ridge Airport. For more information call the restaurant or Baron Aviation, Inc. at 957-2291.

Lodging: Best Western, U.S. 220 N. Martinsville, 632-5611; Dutch Inn, 633 Virginia Ave, Collinsville, 647-3721; Econo Lodge, located on U.S. 220 S. Business, (approx 2 mi. south of U.S. 220 Bypass, Collinsville) 647-3941; Martinsville Travel Inn, RFD 3, Ridgeway, 956-3141; Super 8, 666-8888.

Meeting Rooms: Dutch Inn, 633 Virginia Avenue, Collinsville, (1-1/4 miles north on US business 220), 647-3721.

Transportation: Rental Cars: Baron Aviation, 957-2291

Information: For more information you can contact the Martinsville-Henry County Chamber of Commerce at 115 Broad St, P.O. Box 709, Martinsville, Virginia 24114 or call 632-6401; Also the Virginia Division of Tourism, 1021 E. Cary Street, Richmond, VA 23206-0798, 804-786-4484.

Attraction:

Points of interest located near the Blue Ridge Airport include the: *Blue Ridge Farm Museum*, a reconstructed farmstead depicting the history of life in this region during the 1800's, with tours given June-August on weekends or by appointment. Phone: 365-4416: *The Blue Ridge Folklife Festival* is held at this same location each year in late October: *Fairy Stone State Park:* Is a State owned and operated park located about 20 miles by car north-northwest of the Blue Ridge Airport. The park contains a wide selection of outdoor activities including: fishing, boating, public beach with bath house, hiking trails, and bicycle paths. Accommodations for overnight camping as well as cabin rentals are available between May and September. A 160 acre lake situated within this 4,500 acre park attracts many visitors each year. Information on accommodations and activities can be obtained by calling 930-2424. *Philpott Lake:* situated just northeast of the Fairy Stone State Park is Virginia's fourth largest lake and provides water sports as well as camping, hunting and hiking. These two parks make up a portion of the Blue Ridge foothills and provides a scenic backdrop for many activities available through the entire year. If you are interested in the sport of golfing, you will be happy to know that there is a *golf course* approx 2-3 miles from the Blue Ridge Airport.

Photo by: Winsock Restaurant at Baron Aviation

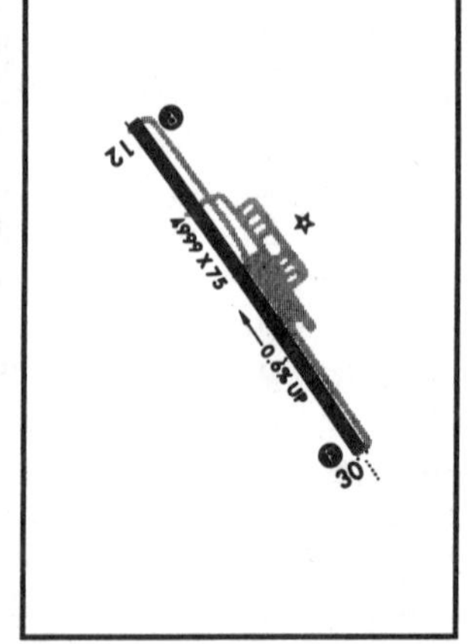

Airport Information:

MARTINSVILLE - BLUE RIDGE AIRPORT (MTV)
8 mi southwest of town N36-37.84 W80-01.10 Elev: 941 Fuel: 100LL, Jet-A
Rwy 12-30: H4999x75 (Asph) Attended: 1300-2300Z Unicom: 122.7 Public Phone: 24hrs
Notes: No landing fee; $2.00 overnight parking waived of you purchase fuel.
FBO: Baron Aviation Inc. Phone: 957-2291

VA-MFV - MELFA
ACCOMACK COUNTY AIRPORT

7

Paradise Cove:

Paradise Cove restaurant is located about 2 miles south of the Accomack County Airport. The restaurant will pick your party up if you give them a call from the airport (Let them know your coming). Directions to the restaurant from the airport is as follows: When leaving the airport make a right and go to 1st red light, make a right and go about 1-1/2 miles. The restaurant should be on the right side of the road. There's a big sign with the restaurants name on it. This family style facility is open at 6 a.m. and closes at 9 p.m. They specialize in dishes featuring Italian, beef, chicken, prime rib, steak, pasta and seafood. Daily specials are also offered. Average prices run $2.95 for breakfast, $3.95 for lunch and $12.95 for dinner. Accommodations for groups up to 50 persons are available in their dining room or their lounge. Accommodations for lodging is also available at a motel located a few feet from the restaurant. For more information call the restaurant at 787-9671 or 787-7381.

(Area Code 804)

Restaurants Near Airport:		
Island House	6 mi E.	Phone: 787-4242
Paradise Cove	2 mi S.	Phone: 787-7381
Ponderosa Steak House	6 mi N.	Phone: 787-5632
Redwood Gables	6 mi N.	Phone: 787-4338

Lodging: Captain's Quarters Motel, (2 miles, Melfa) 787-4545; Anchor Inn (5 miles, Onley) 787-8000; Comfort Inn (5 miles, Onley) 787-7787; Wachapreague Motel (6 miles, Wachapreague) 787-2105.
Meeting Rooms: Eastern Shore Chamber of Commerce Building conference room, Accomack Airport Industrial Park, Route 13, Melfa, VA 23410, Phone: 787-2460.
Transportation: Airport car with driver is available along with Rental cars. Taxi: Mears Taxi 442-9670; Rental Cars: Chandlers Car Rental 787-2828; Four Corner Auto Rental 787-2525.
Information: Eastern Shore Chamber of Commerce, Accomack Airport Industrial Park, Route 13, Melfa, VA 23410, Phone: 787-2460.

Attractions:

There are six charter boats at the Wachapreaque Marina for deep sea fishing excursions 787-4110; Assateaque National Wildlife Refuge (Chincoteaque) 336-6577; Virginia sightseeing flights to Tangier Island (Chesapeake Aviation, Melfa, VA) 787-2901.

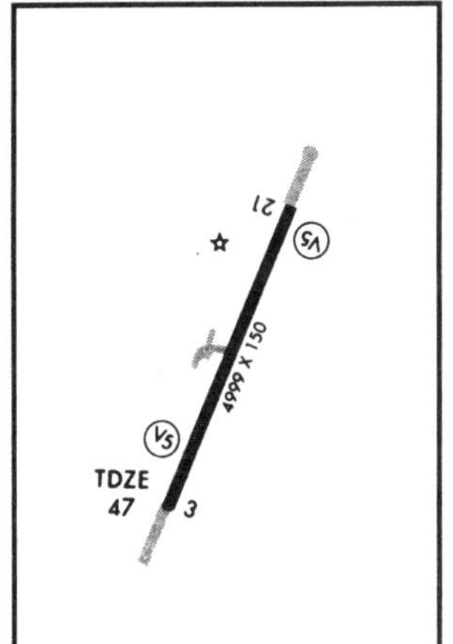

Airport Information:

MELFA - ACCOMACK COUNTY AIRPORT (MFV)
1 mi west of town N37-38.81 W75-45.66 Elev: 48 Fuel: 100LL Rwy 03-21: H4999x150 (Conc)
Attended: May-Oct 1300-0100Z, Nov-June 1300-2300Z Unicom: 122.8 Public Phone 24hrs
Notes: No landing fee - Overnight fee & parking fee $5.00 single, $10.00 & $15.00 twin/jet,
Accomack County Airport Phone: 787-4600

VA-ORF - NORFOLK
NORFOLK INTERNATIONAL ARPT.

8

Airport Dining Room (Ogden Aviation):

The Airport Dining Room is operated through Ogden Aviation, and is located in the main terminal building. This dining facility is open 7 days a week serving breakfast between 7 a.m. and 11 a.m. for breakfast, 11 a.m. to 4:30 for lunch and 4:30 to 7 p.m. for dinner. The restaurant can seat up to 142 persons and exhibits a nautical atmosphere, with a large model ship, paintings, as well as novelties and antiques that go back 30 years or more. Their menu offers a variety of selections for breakfast, lunch and dinner. During the dinner hours guests can enjoy items like Chicken Picatta, seafood, pasta, New York Strip steak as well as vegetarian dishes. Fly-in groups and parties are also welcome, but please call in advance. In addition to the "Dining Room" restaurant, there is a coffee chop and lounge available for lighter fare, as well as other eateries located on each concourse. For more information call Ogden Aviation at 855-0144.

(Area Code 804)

Restaurants Near Airport:		
Dining Room (Ogden Aviation)	On Site	Phone: 855-0144

Lodging: Airport Motor Inn (Shuttle) 855-3355; Hilton-Norfolk Airport (Shuttle) 466-8000; Quality Inn-Lake Wright (Shuttle) 461-6251; Ramada Inn-Newtown (Shuttle) 461-1081; Sheraton Inn-Military Circle (Shuttle) 461-9192.
Meeting Rooms: Hilton-Norfolk Airport has convention facilities available 466-8000; Meeting Rooms: Airport Motor Inn 855-3355; Quality Inn-Lake Wright 461-6251; Ramada Inn-Newtown 461-1081; Sheraton Inn Military Circle 461-9192.
Transportation: Taxi: Andy's Cab 467-4752; Black & White 489-7777; Duke's 583-4079; Eastside 857-4154; Independent 466-5321; Norfolk Checker 855-9009; Taxi Express 468-4355; Yellow 622-3232; Rental Cars: Avis 855-1944; Budget 855-1038; Dollar 855-1988; Hertz 857-1261; National 857-5385; Thrifty 855-5900.
Information: Norfolk Convention & Visitors Bureau, 236 East Plume Street, Norfolk, VA 23510, Phone: 441-5266 or 800-368-3097.

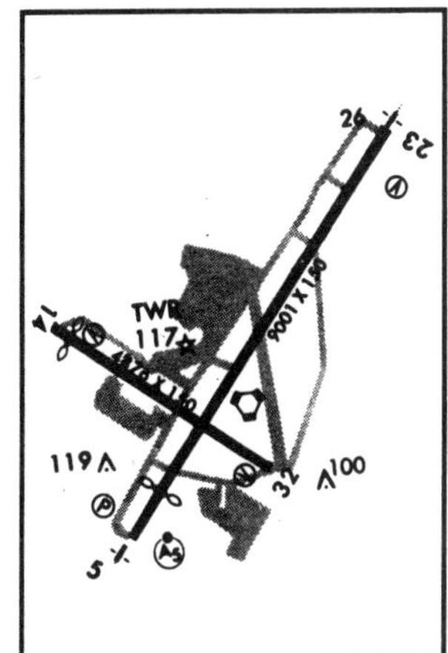

Airport Information:

NORFOLK - NORFOLK INTERNATIONAL AIRPORT (ORF)
3 mi northeast of town N36-53.68 W76-12.08 Elev: 27 Fuel: 100LL, Jet-A
Rwy 05-23: H9001x150 (Asph-Conc-Grvd) Rwy 14-32: H4876x150 (Asph-Grvd)
Attended: continuously Atis 127.15 Unicom: 122.95 Norfolk App Con: 118.9
Norfolk Dep Con: 125.2 Tower: 120.8 Gnd Con: 121.9 Clnc Del: 118.5
FBO: Piedmont Aviation Phone: 857-3463

VA-W93 - ORANGE
ORANGE COUNTY AIRPORT

(Area Code 540)

9

Mountain View Pizza Shanty:

The Mountain View Pizza Shanty is positioned adjacent to the Orange County Airport, and is well within walking distance from aircraft parking areas. This family style restaurant is open between 8 a.m. and 12 a.m. Monday through Wednesday, and 8 a.m. to 12 a.m. Thursday through Saturday. Sunday they are open from 12 p.m. until 8 p.m. The restaurant contains a bar, pool table and game room. Seating for up to 50 persons is available within their dining area. The specialty of the house is of course, pizza. Many different toppings are offered to satisfy the hungriest of appetites. The decor is very casual with tables, chairs, and booths providing a country atmosphere with friendly service. For more information about the Mountain View Pizza Shanty, call 672-1077.

Restaurants Near Airport:
Mountain View Pizza Shanty Adj Arpt Phone: 672-1077

Lodging: Jefferson Motel (4 miles) 672-5159; Hidden Inn 672-3625.

Meeting Rooms: None Reported

Transportation: Taxi Service: Coleman's 672-2338; Maddox 672-1633; Rental Cars: L&W Ford 672-2444; Reynold's Pontiac 672-4855.

Information: Orange County Chamber of Commerce, 205 Caroline Street, Orange VA 22960, Phone: 672-5216; Also: Charlottesville/Albemarie Convention & Visitors Bureau, P.O. Box 161, Charlottesville, VA 22902, 804-977-1783.

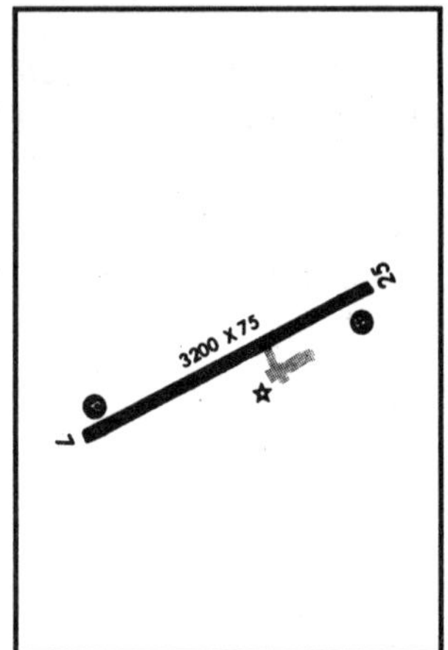

Airport Information:

ORANGE - ORANGE COUNTY AIRPORT (W93)
3 mi east of town N38-14.83 W78-02.74 Elev: 465 Fuel: 100LL Rwy 07-25: H3200x75 (Asph) Attended Oct-Mar 1300-2300Z, Apr-Sep 1300-0100Z Unicom: 122.8
FBO: Orange County Airport Phone: 672-2158

VA-FCI - RICHMOND
CHESTERFIELD COUNTY AIRPORT

(Aera Code 804)

10

Kings Korner Catering:

This facility contains two restaurants in one. A fine dining facility as well as a cafe for lighter fare. They are both located on Chesterfield County Airport, in the main terminal building. This facility serves a wide selection of entrees, such as appetizers, specialty sandwiches, daily lunch and dinner specials, including fresh seafood, steaks, veal and home-made desserts. They also provide a children's menu. Prices run $4-$6.00 for lunch and $5-$14.00 for dinner. Their hours are 11 a.m. to 9 p.m. Monday through Thursday and 11 a.m. to 10 p.m. Friday and Saturday. The lunchroom is modern with a casual daytime flavor, in addition to the dining room and bar area which are more formal. There are several choices for private parties, including rooms for 20 to 30 persons as well as a banquet facility for up to 300 persons in their downstairs location. Catering is also available with light fare, serving cheese and sandwich trays or other items on request. For information call 271-0033.

Restaurants Near Airport:
Kings Korner Catering On Site Phone: 271-0033

Lodging: Days Inn (8 miles) Phone: 748-5871; Holiday Inn (8 miles) Phone: 748-6321; Howard Johnson (8 miles) Phone: 748-2237

Transportation: Taxi service - Charlie Brown, 271-4069; Veterous, 329-1414; Plaza, 271-2211.

Conference Rooms: Conference rooms are available at the airport for $25.00 per day (Reservations required) call airport manager at 743-0771. (Also see Pete's Flightline Restaurant listing)

Information: Convention and Visitors Bureau, 550 East Marshall Street, Box C-250, Richmond, VA 23219, Phone: 782-2777, 358-5511 or 800-365-7272.

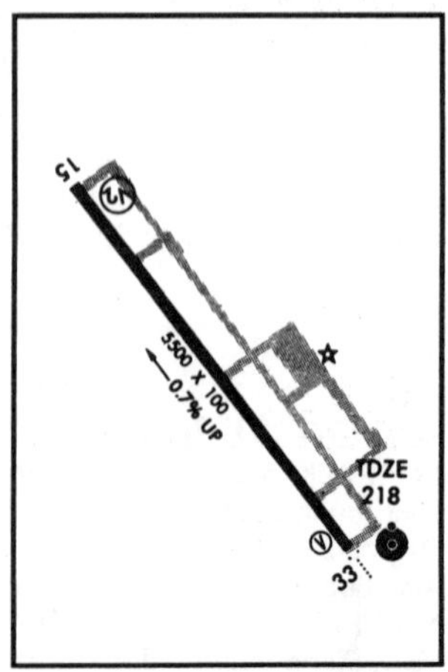

Airport Information:

RICHMOND - CHESTERFIELD COUNTY AIRPORT (FCI)
4 mi southwest of town N37-24.39 W77-31.50 Elev: 237 Fuel: 100LL, Jet-A Rwy 15-33: H5500x100 (Asph-Grvd) Attended: 1200-0300Z Unicom: 123.05 Richmond App/Dep Con: 134.7 Clnc Del: 124.6 Notes: Caution - 400' AGL unlighted tower 5 nautical miles north of airport.
FBO: Air Chesterfield, Inc., Phone: 743-1890;

VA-OFP - RICHMOND/ASHLAND HANOVER COUNTY MUNICIPAL

(Area Code 804)

11

The Smoky Pig:

The Smoky Pig Restaurant is situated about 5 miles from the Hanover County Municipal Airport. This restaurant is considered an upscale steak house specializing in delicious barbecued ribs, barbecued chicken, pork and beef. In addition to these are popular items like crab cakes, fresh fish of the day, soups prepared daily, chef salads and homemade pies and desserts. Specials served include prime rib on weekends, meatloaf on Tuesday, pot roast on Wednesday, beef burgundy on Thursday and 11 or 22 ounce prime rib on Friday, Saturday and Sunday. The main dining room can seat 150 plus customers. It is elegantly decorated with a country atmosphere. Since 1978 The Smoky Pig has been a popular establishment serving many local patrons. From the airport head north on I-95 and west at Ashland exit (Route 54), then go to 3rd light and turn left. 1-1/2 blocks down the road the restaurant should appear on your right side. Confirm these directions with the restaurant, or fixed base operator. A courtesy car can be arranged through Sundance Aviation by calling 798-6500. For information about the restaurant call 798-4590.

Restaurants Near Airport:

The Smoky Pig	5 mi	Phone: 798-4590

Lodging: Hanover House (2 miles) 798-6045; Holiday Inn (5 miles) 798-4231.

Meeting Rooms: None reported

Transportation: Hanover Aviation Co, can provide courtesy car and rental car services. Call 798-8348.

Information: Hanover Visitor Information Center, 112 North Railroad Avenue, Ashland, VA 23005, Phone: 752-6766.

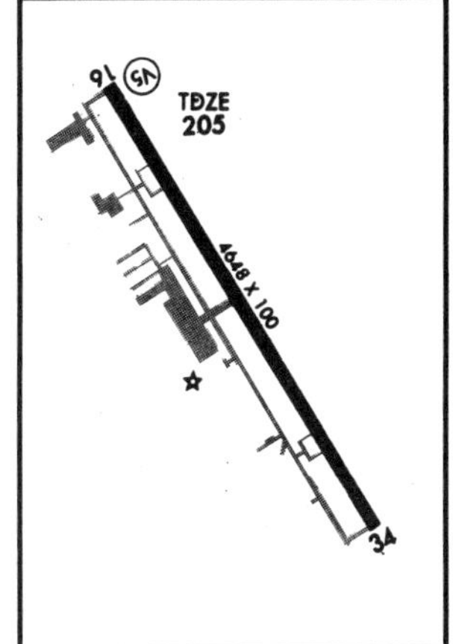

Airport Information:

RICHMOND/ASHLAND - HANOVER COUNTY MUNICIPAL AIRPORT (OFP)
8 mi north of town N37-42.48 W77-26.16 Elev: 205 Fuel: 100LL, Jet-A
Rwy 16-34: H4648x100 (Asph) Attended: Apr-Sep 1200-0200Z, Oct-Mar 1200-000Z
Unicom: 122.7 Richmond App/Dep Con: 134.7 Clnc Del: 125.4
FBO: Sundance Aviation Phone: 798-6500

VA-RIC - RICHMAND RICHMOND INTL.

(Area Code 804)

12

CA1 Services:

The Concession Air Restaurant is located right in the terminal building at the Richmond International/Byrd Field Airport. This family style establishment is open Monday through Friday 5 a.m. to 9 p.m., Saturday 5 a.m. to 6:30 p.m. and Sunday 5 a.m. to 8 p.m. Items on their menu include grilled chicken breast, club sandwiches, chicken, tuna steak sandwich, crab cakes, gourmet burgers, as well as a full breakfast line. Average prices run $4.00 for breakfast, $5.75 for lunch and around $8.50 for dinner. The main dining room can seat 50 persons, along with a downstairs section also available for groups. For more information call 222-1227.

Restaurants Near Airport

Air Maxwells/Sheraton	2 mi	Phone: 226-4300
Argyles/Days Inn	1 mi	Phone: 222-2041
CA1 Services	On Site	Phone: 222-1227
Props/Holiday Inn	1 mi	Phone: 222-6450
Wings/Hilton	1/4 mi	Phone: 226-6400

Lodging: Best Western Airport Inn (Free trans, 1 mile) 222-2780; Days Inn (1 mile) 222-2041; Hampton Inn (1/2 mile) 222-8200; Hilton Airport (Free trans, 1/4 mile) 226-6400; Holiday Inn Airport (Free trans, 1 mile) 222-6450; Sheraton Inn Airport (Free trans, 2 miles) 226-4300.

Meeting Rooms: Best Western Airport Inn (Free trans, 1 mile) 222-2780; Hilton Airport (Free trans, 1/4 mile) 226-6400; Holiday Inn Airport (Free trans, 1 mile) 222-6450.

Transportation: Taxi: service available; Rental cars: Alamo 222-5445; Avis 222-7416; Budget 222-5310; Hertz 222-7228; National 222-7477.

Information: Convention and Visitors Bureau, 6th Street Marketplace, 500 East Marshall Street, Box C-250, Richmond, VA 23219, Phone: 782-2777, 358-5511 or 800-365-7272.

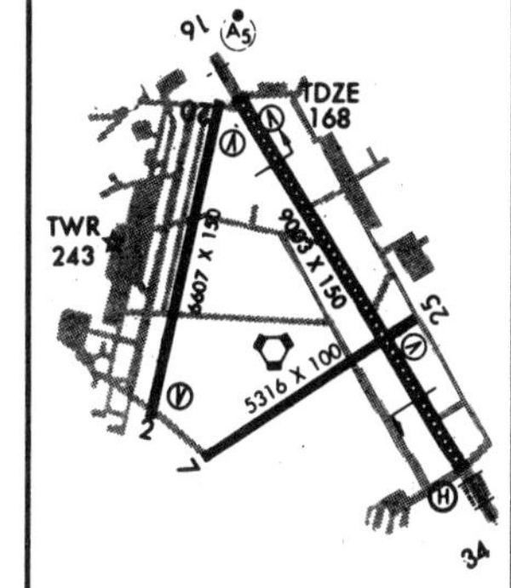

Airport Information:

RICHMOND - RICHMOND INTERNATIONAL (RIC)
6 mi east of town N37-30.31 W77-19.18 Elev: 168 Fuel: 100LL, Jet-A
Rwy 16-34: H9003x150 (Asph-Grvd) Rwy 02-20: H6607x150 (Asph-Grvd)
Rwy 07-25: H5316x100 (Asph-Grvd) Attended: continuously Atis: 119.15 Unicom: 122.95
App Con: 126.8, 126.4, 134.7, 118.2 Dep Con: 126.8, 126.4, 134.7 Tower: 121.1
Gnd Con: 121.9 Clnc Del: 127.55
FBO: Aero Industries/AVITAT-RIC: Phone: 222-7211

VA-ROA - ROANOKE
ROANOKE REG./WOODRUM FLD

13

Creative Croissants:

Creative Croissants is located within the top level of the terminal building at the Roanoke Regional/Woodrum Field. At the time of interview this restaurant was under renovation. Soon to be operational they will operate from 5 a.m. to 8 p.m. 6 days a week and 6 a.m. to 6 p.m. on Saturday. A food serving line provides fast efficient service. Chicken club sandwiches, roast beef croissants, vegetable croissants along with cold salads, grilled items and even a juice and Cappucino gourmet coffee selections is available. Seating for about 100 to 125 people is provided. For more information call 563-0160.

Restaurants Near Airport: **(Area Code 703)**

Charcoal Steak Hse	2 mi	Phone: 366-3710
Coach & Four	2 mi	Phone: 362-4220
Creative Croissants	On Site	Phone: 563-0160
LaMaison du Gourmet	1 mi	Phone: 366-2444

Lodging: Comfort Inn-Airport (Trans) 563-0229; Days Inn-Airport (Trans) 366-0341; Holiday Inn-Airport (Trans) 366-8861; Hotel Roanoke (Trans) 343-6992; Marriott Airport (Trans) 563-9300; Sheraton Inn-Airport (Trans) 362-4500.

Meeting Rooms: Comfort Inn-Airport 563-0229; Days Inn-Airport 366-0341; Holiday Inn-Airport 366-8861; Hotel Roanoke 343-6992; Marriott Airport 563-9300; Sheraton Inn-Airport 362-4500.

Transportation: Taxi: Airport Limousine 345-7910; Blacksburg Limo 951-3973; Cartier Limo 982-5466; Luxury Limo 985-0044; Stat City Limo 366-6390; Yellow Cab 345-7711; Rental Cars: Avis 366-2436; Budget 389-5405; Hertz 366-3421; National 345-7711.

Information: Roanoke Valley Convention & Visitors Bureau, 114 Market Street, Roanoke, VA 24011, Phone: 342-6025 or 800-635-5535.

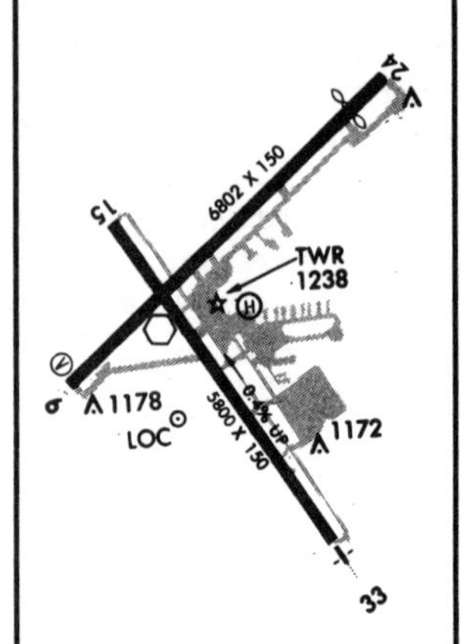

Airport Information:

ROANOKE - ROANOKE REGIONAL/WOODRUM FIELD (ROA)
3 mi northwest of town N37-19.53 W79-58.53 Elev: 1176 Fuel: 100LL, Jet-A
Rwy 06-24: H6802x150 (Asph-Grvd) Rwy 15-33: H5800x150 (Asph-Grvd) Attended: continuously Atis: 118.65 Unicom: 122.95 Roanoke App/Dep Con: 119.05 (360-150 degrees) 126.9 (151-359 degrees) Tower: 118.3 Gnd Con: 121.9 Clnc Del: 119.7
FBO: Piedmont Aviation Phone: 563-4401

VA-W75 - SALUDA HUMMEL FIELD AIRPORT

(Area Code 804)

14, 15

Dining at The Tides Lodge and The Tides Inn:

The Tides Lodge is located at Irvington, in the northern neck of Virginia. It is about eight miles up the Rappahannock River on the western shore of the Chesapeake Bay. The Lodge is located about 10 miles from the Hummel Field Airport. With advance notice, The lodge will provide transportation to and from Hummel Field Airport for a fee. This facility is open from mid-March to December. (Note: check with the Lodge for the exact dates prior to making reservations.) The Lodge features comfortable dining facilities. The formal Royal Stewart Dining Room serves breakfast, lunch and dinner. Breakfast selections include: quiche, Belgian waffles, blueberry pancakes and warm rum buns. Lunch includes: Maryland crab cake sandwiches and chopped sirloin burgers. Dinner includes: scallops, sea trout, soft shell crabs and Virginia ham. The "Lodge Apple Pie", tops off the evening meal. At dinner, Friday, Saturday and Sunday, men are requested to wear a jacket (with or without a tie) with coresoponding attire for ladies and children over 12. Breakfast is casual. The casual, nautical Binnacle Restaurant, which overlooks Carter's Creek and the Lodge's Marina, serves delicious lunch and dinner seafood selections. At this restaurant, men are requested to wear collared shirts for dinner, while ladies dress accordingly. The lodge also offers a Snack Bar/Ice Cream Parlor which features Pina Coladas and Buffalo Burgers. It is open some evenings for very casual dining. The Sandwich Bar features "make your own" sandwiches at the saltwater pool. The Tides Lodge is located across Carter's Creek, about one-quarter of a mile, or five miles away by land from its companion, The Tides Inn. Guests at The Lodge can take advantage of all the facilites of either resort at posed rates. The Inn's restaurants are also available with a surcharge. The Tides Inn offers dining in four locations, including the lovely 127' yacht, "Miss Ann," a la carte Commodore's poolside, Capt B's at The Golden Eagle and the Main Dining Room. For more information about restaurants, rates and accommodations at The Tides Lodge, call 800-248-4337 or 438-6000.

Restaurants Near Airport:

Pilot House and Restaurant	On Site	Phone: 758-2262
The Tides Inn	6 mi	Phone: 438-5000
The Tides Lodge	10 mi	Phone: 438-6000

Lodging: Pilot House and Restaurant (Adj. restaurant at airport) 758-2262; The Tides Inn (6 miles) 438-5000; The Tides Lodge (10 miles) 438-6000; Whispering Pines Motel (3 miles) 435-1101

Meeting Rooms: Pilot House and Restaurant may be able to accommodate business travelers with meeting accommodations. Call 758-2262 for information. Also, The Tides Inn 438-5000 and The Tides Lodge 438-6000 have meeting facilities.

Transportation: With 24-hour notice, The Tides Inn will provide transportation to and from the airport. Call 438-5000. Also, rental cars are often available at the Inn. With advance notice, The Tides Lodge will provide transportation to and from the airport for a fee. Call 438-6000.

Information: Virginia Division of Tourism 1021 East Cary Street, Richmond, Virginia 23219, Phone: 786-4484.

Attractions:

Both The Tides Lodge and The Tides Inn are located in an area that is rich in Virginia history. The original Christ Church (1732), the restored St. Mary's White Chapel (1669), Wakefield (Washington's Birthplace) and Stratford (Lee's Birthplace). Also, one of the few remaining cable drawn ferries will take you across the nearby Corrotoman River. The Lancaster County Court House and Mary Ball (Washington's mother) Museum offer some of the oldest records in America. Williamsburg is a leisurely hour's drive from Irvington. For more information about attractions around the Irvington area, call the Virginia Division of Tourism at 786-4484.

Pilot House and Restaurant:

The Pilot House and Restaurant is located at Hummel Field Airport. Fly-in guests can taxi their aircraft right up to the restaurant. This is a family-style facility that is open between 6 :00 a.m. and 8:00 p.m. 7 days a week. On Saturday nights they offer live entertainment in their lounge. Friday and Saturday they also feature a seafood buffet from 5:00 p.m. to 8:00 p.m. A breakfast bar is provided on weekends from 6:00 a.m. and 11:00 a.m. In addition to these selections, guests can enjoy entrees such as prime rib, soft shell crab dinners, seafood platters, steaks and fried chicken (which is known as one of their most popular items). Average prices are $4.00 for most breakfast and lunch items, and $8.00 for most dinner items. The atmosphere of this establishment is contemporary, with seating for up to 200 people. Pictures of airplanes and sail boats decorate the walls. During their meal, guests can also enjoy the view of the airport and aircraft activity just outside the restaurant. This facility provides lodging for travelers at the Beacon Pilot House adjacent to the restaurant as well. On weekends, many fly-in clubs frequently visit this restaurant, with plenty of good friends and hangar flying to go around. For more information, call the Pilot House and Restaurant at 758-2262.

Airport Information:

SALUDA - HUMMEL FIELD AIRPORT (W75)

6 mi east of town N37-36.01 W76-26.98 Elev: 30 Fuel: 100LL
Rwy 18-36: H2261x45 (Asph) Attended: 1400-2200Z CTAF/Unicom: 123.0 Notes:
Drainage swales full length of Rwy on both sides. Use of exit in front of Hummel Aviation advised. Birds on and in vicinity of airport during winter. Departing Rwy 18-36 climb to 500 ft befor any turn out; arriving acraft use wide pattern to avoid populated areas east and west of airport. Military ops reported in area. (See AFD for updated infjormation).

Airport Manager **Phone: 758-2876**
FBO: Airspray, Inc. **Phone: 758-2165**
FBO: Airwrench, Inc. **Phone: 758-3558**

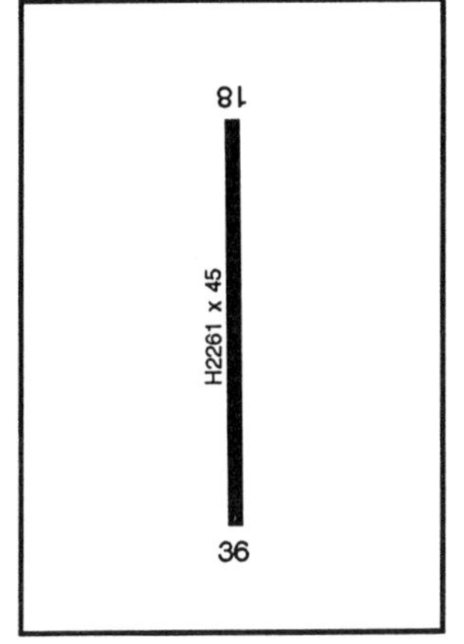

The Tides Lodge Resort & Country Club

Saluda, VA (VA-W75)

Photo by: The Tides Lodge Resort & Country Club A seaplane pilot docks his airplane at The Tides Lodge Resort marina.

The Lodge is located at Irvington, in the northern neck of Virginia. It is about eight miles up the Rappahannock River on the western shore of the Chesapeake Bay. This 60-room resort emphasizes luxury in an informal setting. It offers plenty of fun, rest and relaxation from morning until night. Indulge in a delicious Virginia country breakfast before exploring the lodge's many activities. Play a round of golf on the 18-hole Sir Guy Campbell's Tartan Course, the Golden Eagle or The Tides Inn's Executive Nine. The lodge offers a full-service, 41-slip marina, three tennis courts, two swimming pools (salt and heated fresh water) and an exercise room. You can go fishing, sailing, bicycling, canoeing, outboarding and river exploring. Or, you can just spend the day relaxing in one of the hammocks. For the little ones, the lodge offers supervised children's programs during the summer.

For lunch, enjoy casual dining at the Binnacle Restaurant. Or, after a swim, stop by the lodge's own unique "make your own" Sandwich Bar located at the saltwater pool. Also, visit the Snack Bar/Ice Cream Parlor located beside the fresh water pool. Later, take the family on a sightseeing trip around historic Tidewater Virginia. After the sun goes down, enjoy cocktails while overlooking the marina, and then feast on a delicious dinner in the formal Royal Stewart Dining Room. Dancing is featured three nights a week. (Friday Through Sunday, men are requested to wear a jacket, with or without a tie, with corresponding attire for ladies and children over 12.) Breakfast in the dining room is casual. Or, you can dine on scrumptious seafood delicacies at the Binnacle which overlooks Carter's Creek and the Marina. (At this restaurant, men are requested to wear collared shirts for dinner, while ladies dress accordingly.) After dinner, take a moonlight cruise aboard the 60-foot High Tide II and the 46-foot Highland Fling. If you are still in the mood for sports activities, the lodge even offers lighted tennis and putting. Also, the casual McD's Pub is open nightly, with entertainment on weekends. Later, when it's time to retire, you can relax in your own comfortable suite with a private balcony with a water view, refrigerator, bar, cable television, and terry cloth robes, and a chocolate mint on the pillow.

The Tides Lodge is located across Carter's Creek, about one-quarter of a mile, or five miles away by land from its sister resort, The Tides Inn. Guests at the lodge can take advantage of all the facilites of either resort at posed rates. The inn's restaurants are also available with a surcharge. The Tides Inn offers dining in four locations, including the lovely 127' yacht, "Miss Ann," a la carte Commodore's poolside, Capt B's at The Golden Eagle and the Main Dining Room. This combination of facilities offers guests a greater variety of atmosphere, facilities and services.

The Tides Lodge is located about 10 miles from the Hummel Field Airport. With advance notice, the lodge will provide transportation to and from Hummel Field Airport for a fee. Rental cars are also available. If you own a sea plane you can fly-in and park at their dock along Rappahannock River on the western shore of Chesapeake Bay. This facility is open from mid-March to December. (Note: check with the lodge for the exact dates prior to making reservations.) For more information about rates and accommodations at this facility, call 800-248-4337 or 438-6000. (Information submitted by The Tides Lodge)

The Tides Inn

The Tides Inn is located at Irvington, in the northern neck of Virginia. It is about eight miles up the Rappahannock River on the western shore of the Chesapeake Bay. The Inn features elegance in a casual atmosphere. It is the ideal place to escape from the hustle and bustle of everyday life and enjoy uncrowded luxury. The Tides Inn offers delicious cuisine, 111 comfortable rooms, plenty of shopping, 45 holes of golf, tennis, boating, bicycling, swimming and unique evening entertainment. Enjoy tasty meals in two large dining rooms which offer a scenic waterfront view.

Start with a hardy breakfast before beginning your day of exciting activities. Play George Cobb's Golden Eagle Golf Course, the Executive Nine, or Sir Guy Cambell's Tartan Course. Visit the playroom equipped with a pool table, table tennis and other games. Take a ride on a 60-foot cruising yacht, or sail an electric boat, canoe, paddleboat and sailboat.

Enjoy luncheons and cocktails at Commodore's poolside, or aboard the lovely 127' yacht, "Miss Ann". Or dine at Cap'n B's at the Golden Eagle. Before dinner, indulge in complimentary use of the spa, racquetball and full-range exercise facilities at nearby Oakwood Fitness Center, located 4 miles from the inn. Later, feast on a scrumptious dinner in the Main Dining Room, then dance the night away in the Chesapeake Club. (Jackets with or without ties are required.) Afterward, return to your comfortable room with a scenic view of the water, and then relax and prepare for another exciting day at the inn.

Companion to the inn is The Tides lodge, which is located across Carter's Creek, about one-quarter of a mile, or five miles away by land. Guests at the inn can take advantage of all the facilites of either resort at posed rates. For guests at the inn, the lodge restaurants can be used with a surcharge.

The Tides Inn is located about 6 miles from Hummel Field Airport, located directly across the Rappahannock River. With 24 hour notice, the inn will provide transportation to and from the airport. Also, rental cars are often available at this resort. This facility is open from mid-March to December. (Note: check with the inn for the exact dates prior to making reservations.) For more information about activities, rates and accommodations, call 438-5000 or 800-TIDES-INN (84337-466) (Information submitted by The Tides Inn.)

Photo by: The Tides Inn

The Tides Inn is the ideal place to escape from the hustle and bustle of everyday life and enjoy uncrowded luxury.

VA-W78 - SOUTH BOSTON WILLIAM M. TUCK

(Area Code 804)

16

Restaurants Near Airport:

Ernie's Restaurant	3 mi	Phone: 572-3423
Steve's American Cafe	5 mi	Phone: 572-3106

Lodging: Crestview motor Court (4 miles) 572-3022; Howard House/Best Western (3 miles) 572-4311; Hudson Motel 572-2959; Von Motor Court (4 miles) 572-4941.

Meeting Rooms: None Reported

Transportation: Airport courtesy car reported; Service Cab 572-4521; South Boston Cab 572-3237.

Information: Clarksville Chamber of Commerce, 321 Virginia Avenue. P.O. Box 1017, Clarksville, VA 23927, Phone: 374-2436.

Ernie's Restaurant:

Ernie's Restaurant is located 3 miles from the William M. Tuck Airport. Transportation to their facility can be arranged either by airport courtesy car, taxi or the restaurant will provide fly-in guests with free pick-up service. This combination family style and fine dining facility is open from 11 a.m. to 9 p.m. Tuesday through Sunday. (Closed on Monday) They specialize in an all-you-can-eat Southern buffet that is offered all day long. On Friday and Saturday nights, the daily buffet is replaced by a seafood buffet beginning at 4:00 p.m. Average prices run about $4.95 to $5.95 for the daily buffet and $9.75 for the seafood spread, offering all-you-can-eat crab legs and much more. Their seating capacity is around 200 persons. There are several separate dining areas within the restaurant itself. The main dining room, the small dining room, the porch dining area that can handle 20 persons, and the back dining room that overlooks the lake, able to accommodate up to 100 persons, often used for banquets or larger parties. The restaurant also provides a small petting zoo for children, containing deer, geese, ducks, a lama and a very friendly dog. This establishment has been in existence since 1958 and is well known througout the region. For information call Ernies Restaurant at 572-3423.

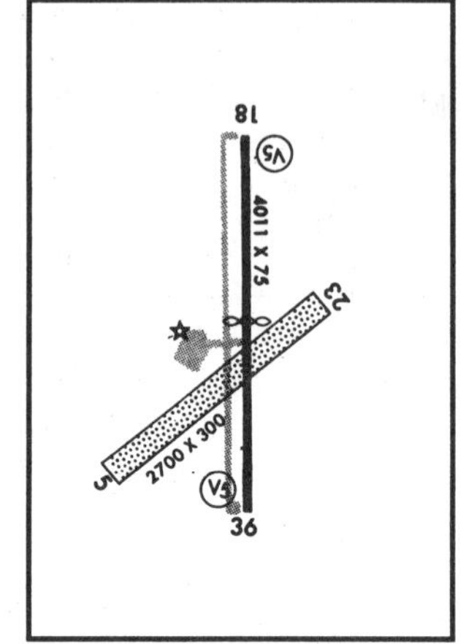

Airport Information:

SOUTH BOSTON - WILLIAM M. TUCK AIRPORT (W78)
3 mi east of town N36-42-36N W78-50.88 Elev: 420 Fuel: 100LL,
Rwy 18-36: H4011x75 (Asph) Rwy 05-23: 2700x300 (Turf) Attended: daylight hours
Unicom: 122.8 Public Phone 24hrs
FBO: Skylark Aviation Company Phone: 572-9961

VA-SHD - STAUNTON/ WAYNESBORO/HARRISONBURG SHENANDOAH VALLEY REGIONAL

(Area Code 540)

17

Restaurants Near Airport:

Aero Club Restaurant	Trml Bldg	Phone: 234-8193
Brook's Restaurant	15 mi S	Phone: 248-1722
Ever's Family Restaurant	20 mi N	Phone: 433-2396

Lodging: Holiday Inn (20 miles north and south in Stauton & Harrisonburg); Sheraton Inn (20 mi north and south in Staunton & Harrisonburg);
Meeting Rooms: Small conference room located on field in GA Building - accommodates 10 people. Large conference room in Hangar 3 - accommodates 75 persons.Both the Holiday Inn and Sheraton Inn have accommodations for meetings and conferences.
Transportation: Al's Cab 949-8245; City Cab-Staunton 8863471; City Cab Harrisonburg 434-2515; Rental Cars: Avis 234-9961; Hertz 234-9411; (No airport courtesy cars available).
Information: Travel Information Service, 1303 Richmond Avenue, Staunton, VA 24401, Phone: 332-3972, 800-332-5219.

Attractions:

Woodrow Wilson Birthplace, Museum of American Frontier Culture, Swannoanoa Palace, Skyline Drive, Blue Ridge Parkway, Natural Chimneys & Grand Caverns Regional Parks, Ingleside/Lakeview/ Swannoanoa Golf Courses.

Aero Club Cafe:

The Farmstead Restaurant is located in the main terminal building on the Shenandoah Valley Regional Airport. This cafe style establishment that is open Monday through Friday 6 a.m. to 4 p.m. Specials are offered throughout the week. Their menu lists items like grilled chicken, steak and cheese sub sandwiches, club sandwiches, and their popular Valley Burger. Special offered through the week include Virginia baked ham sandwiches, lasagna, stuffed green peppers and country fried steak. Their main dining room can accommodate about 35 persons, with booths and provides a quaint, homey and comfortable atmosphere. Groups are welcome. However, advance notice is recommended. Meals prepared-to-go can easily be arranged as well as in-flight catering. The Farmstead Restaurant takes pride in preparing many of their meals from scratch including fresh desserts. For more information call the restaurant at 234-8193.

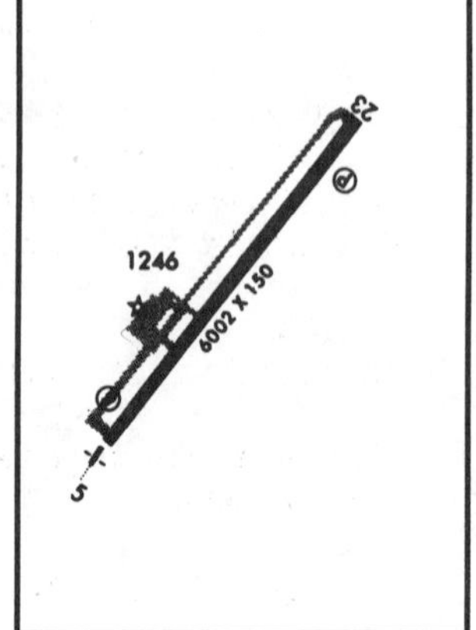

Airport Information:

STAUNTON/WAYNESBORO/HARRISONBURG - SHENANDOAH VALLEY REGIONAL AIRPORT (SHD)
10 mi northeast of town N38-15.83 W78-53.79 Elev: 1201 Fuel: 100LL, Jet-A
Rwy 05-23: H6002x150 (Asph-Grvd) Attended: Mon-Fri 1045-0345Z, Sat 1045-2300Z, Sun 1300-0345Z Unicom: 123.0 Public Phone 24hrs
FBO: Shenandoah Valley Reg Arpt Comm Phone: 234-8304
FBO: Tri-Star Aviation Phone: 234-8998

VA-SFQ - SUFFOLK
SUFFOLK MUNICIPAL AIRPORT

18

Red Apple Restaurant:

The Red Apple Restaurant is within a 100 yard walk from the Suffolk Municipal Airport. To find it, just walk across Route 13/32 (Carolina Road) directly at the approach end of Runway 15. Free courtesy transportation is also provided by this restaurant although it is well within walking distance. This is a family style restaurant combined with a convenient store and gas station that is open 24 hours seven days a week except for Christmas day. Specialties include home style cooking, home style desserts, southern style breakfast any time, or hot and cold sandwiches, in addition to homemade soups and stews. Daily specials are also offered along with seasonal specialties. Prices average $4.00 for breakfast and lunch and $6.00 for dinner. The restaurant depicts a southern style cafe with booths, tables, sit-down counter with a pool table in the back and non-alcoholic beverages on the premises. They have a special menu for their catering service, able to accommodate up to 65 persons served at one sitting. They will even deliver meals to your airplane for parties of 4 or more persons. For more information call the restaurant at 539-9726.

Airport Information:

SUFFOLK - SUFFOLK MUNICIPAL AIRPORT (SFQ)
3 mi southwest of town N36-40.94 W76-36.11 Elev: 72 Fuel: 100LL, Jet-A Rwy 04-22: H5007x100 (Asph) Rwy 07-25: H4700x100 (Asph) Rwy 15-33: H3650x150 (Conc) Attended: Apr-Oct Mon-Fri 1300-0100Z, Sat-Sun 1400-0100Z, Nov-Mar Mon-Fri 1300-2200Z Sat-Sun 1400-2200Z Unicom: 122.7 Public Phone 24hrs Notes: Airport fees waved with purchase of fuel.
FBO: Suffolk Muni Airport Phone: 539-8295 FBO: Cardinals Pilot Shop Phone: 539-0600

Restaurants Near Airport: **(Area Code 757)**

Final Approach	On Site	Phone: 539-8295
George's Steak House	5 mi N.	Phone: 934-1726
Red Apple	100 yds	Phone: 539-9726

Lodging: Comfort Inn (3 miles) 539-3600; Econo Lodge (3 miles) 539-3451; Holiday Inn (7 miles) 934-2311; Camping is available on the airport.
Meeting Rooms: There is a meeting room located in the terminal building that will accommodate up to 30 people, Airport Manager Phone: 539-8295. The Red Apple restaurant also offers luncheons and catering services, Phone: 539-6969.
Information: Portsmouth Convention and Visitors Bureau, 505 Crawford Street, Suite 2, Portsmouth, VA 23704, Phone: 393-5111 or 800-767-8782.

Attractions: Colonial Williamsburg 25 miles; Virginia Beach, VA 35 miles; Great Dismal Swamp 5 miles; Portsmouth Naval Shipyard Museum, on Elizabeth River (Est 20-25 miles). Many artifacts including models, flags and the US Delaware (Ship of the line). For information call 393-8591; Also Norfolk-Portsmouth Harbor Tours (Est 20-25 miles), with 1-1/2 hours tours of the navel shipyard in addition to 2-1/2 hour sunset cruises to navel base and Hampton Roads. For information call 393-4735;

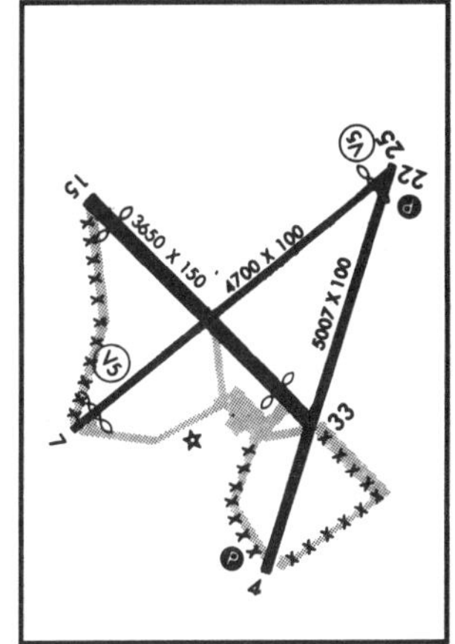

VA-TGI - TANGIER ISLAND
TANGIER ISLAND AIRPORT

(Area Code 804)

19, 20, 21, 22

Restaurants Near Airport:

Fisherman's Corner	1 blk	Phone: 891-1271
Hilda Crockett's Chesapeake Hse.	1/2 mi	Phone: 891-2331
The Islander	1 blk	Phone: 891-2249
Sunset Inn B&B	N/A	Phone: 891-2535

Lodging: Hilda Crockett's Chesapeake House" (1/2 mile) 891-2331; Sunset Inn Bed and Breakfast (3/4 mile) 891-2535
Meeting Rooms: None reported
Transportation: Taxi Service: Pat's 891-2215
Information: You can contact just about any of the businesses on the island to obtain information. They all work together to help promote Tangier Island. Also the Honorable Dewey Crokett the Mayor of Tangier Island. 804-891-2563.

Fisherman's Corner Seafood Restaurant:

The Fisherman's Corner Seafood Restaurant is located within walking distance to the Tangier Island Airport. When leaving the airport bear to the left and go across the long bridge. It's at the end of the lane only about a five-minute walk from the airport. If you call ahead of time and give exact time of arrival, they will meet you at the airport. This fine dining establishment is open Monday through Thursday from 11 a.m. to 7 p.m., and Friday through Sunday from 11 a.m. until 7:30 p.m. Specialties on their menu include crab soup, clam chowder, steamed crabs, clams and shrimp, homemade crab cakes, clam fritters, soft shell crabs, T-bone steak, ham dinners and homemade hamburgers. Average prices run $5.00 for lunch and $11.00 for dinner. They also have daily lunch and dinner specials. The restaurant has seating for about 50 people. Their dining room has a nautical decor with pictures of local "Watermen", old bottles, seashells and old lanterns to complete the seafaring motif. For small groups, they will prepare special seafood platters. When obtaining information, the owner of the Fisherman's Corner Seafood Restaurant told us about a very nice bed & breakfast nearby for those planning on spending the night on the island. For more information about the restaurant call 891-1271.

Hilda Crockett's "Chesapeake House":

Hilda Crockett's "Chesapeake House" is located in the heart of Chesapeake Bay, just 6 miles south of the Maryland-Virginia State Line.The Tangier Island Airport is located within a short walking distance to the Chesapeake House and the center of town. In 1939, Mrs. Hilda Crockett began taking in overnight guests who frequently visited Tangiers, such as traveling salesmen, merchant dealers, traders, etc. As word spread of the fine food and comfortable hospitality, business began to boom. Today, this bed and breakfast still offers the same family-style meals and traditions. The Chesapeake House is open from the 15th of April to the 15th of October, 7 days a week. The meals are prepared from scratch by a delightful kitchen staff. The menu includes items such as, Chesapeake House crab cakes, clam fritters, Virginia baked ham, oven-baked hot corn pudding, potato salad, oven-hot yeast rolls, and all-butter pound cake. Prices for family-style meals are $11.75 for adults and $5.75 for children under eight. For more information about rates and accommodations, contact Hilda Crockett's "Chesapeake House" at 891-2331. Reservations are necessary.

The Islander Seafood Restaurant:

The Islander Restaurant is a locally owned and operated facility specializing in fresh local seafood. It serves a varied menu from hamburgers to seafood platters. The Islander Restaurant is located on Main Street just a few minutes walk from the airport. For your dining comfort, it has an air conditioned dining room as well as a screened deck for outside dining. The menu is especially known for its homemade items, including local family recipes such as clam chowder, crab cake and crab salad, and soft shell crabs. The Islander restaurant is open from 11 a.m. to 8 p.m. Small groups are welcome. If they know that you are planning a small gathering at their restaurant, they will help cater your needs with seafood platters as well as menu items. For information call 891-2249.

Sunset Inn Bed & Breakfast:

The Sunset Inn is a Bed & Breakfast located only 1/2 mile from the beach and not far from the Tangier Airport. This lodging establishment is open all year and contains a private bath, large rooms, cable television, refrigerator and outdoor decks. They are located at 16650 West Ridge Road on Tangier Island. For information call 891-2535.

Attractions:

Tangier Island lies in Virginia's portion of the Chesapeake Bay, mid-center and below Smith Island and the Potomac River. Approximately 700 people live on Tangier Island and 95% of the men are "Watermen" with crabbing, fishing and oystering their main livelihood. Tangier Island is the most southerly of the Chesapeake Islands. It was discovered by Captain John Smith in 1608. The first permanent settlement was established in 1686. In 1969 the Tangier Island Airport was completed and served as a valuable asset to residents needing a quick and efficient way to transport supplies from the mainland. Today, the people on Tangier Island make a living that combines the seafood trade with tourism. During the summer season the island is visited by many tourists. After the last ferry departs the island for the main land, Tangier returns to a very quiet setting. The speed limit on the island is only 15 miles per hour with little over three miles of roadway for bikes, scooters, motorcycles, golf carts and a few mini-size cars and trucks. The streets are 8 to10 feet wide, at best. An additional attraction in the area is the "Crab Derby" held daily at 12:30 p.m. (Except Sundays, Oct-May). And a mail boat, with scheduled trips each day, leaves Crisfield and crosses Sound to Tangier Island. During summer months, a crab-potting boat also takes passengers to the island.

Airport Information:

TANGIER ISLAND - TANGIER ISLAND AIRPORT (TGI)

4 mi west of town N37-49.51 W75-59.87 Elev: 7 Fuel: None Reported Rwy 02-20: H2950x75 (Asph) Attended: Apr-Dec 1300-2200Z CTAF/Unicom: 122.8 Patuxent App/Dep Con: 120.05 (1200-0400Z) Washington Center App/Dep Con: 132.55 (0400-1200Z) Notes: Landing and overnight parking fees. Airport CLOSED sunset to sunrise daily. CAUTION: Restricted area 1 mile west of airport. See "Airport Facility Directory" for further comments.

FBO: Airport Manager Phone: 891-2496

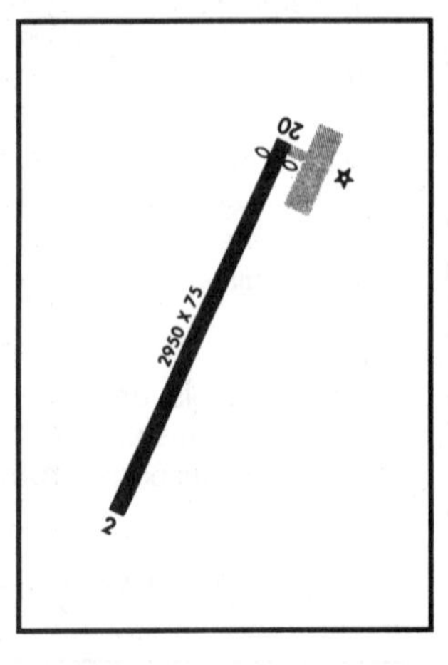

Tangier Island

Tangier Island is a very popular location for pilots from all across the northeast region. The Island was first settled around 1686. Today it has a population of about 700 persons living on its 1 mile wide by 3 mile long real estate. Life on Tangier is very peaceful compared with the larger urban towns in the eastern region. A number of people now living on Tangier Island are dependents of the first settlers back in the late 1600s. The main trade on the island is oystering, clamming and crabbing. We were told that the center of the island is mostly wetland while the outer edges support the population. This island is located 12 miles out in Chesapeake Bay. Many tourists visit the island each season. When talking with a friendly islander, she informed us that at 2 a.m. in the morning the island comes alive with a buzz of activity down by the harbor when the fishing fleet makes ready for another day. At 11:30 a.m. the commercial ferries begin bringing the majority of tourists over from the mainland. After 4 p.m. the island returns to its tranquil setting. Visitors can either rent bicycles at the airport or simply walk to their destinations. We were informed about 3 different restaurants on the island. The Chesapeake House, Fisherman's Corner and the Islander Restaurant. Both the Fisherman's Corner and the Islander Restaurant serve from a menu while the Chesapeake House specializes in family style seafood and steamed selections. Lodging on the island is available either at the Chesapeake House or the Sunset Inn. This island was featured in the back issue of National Geographic November 1973 issue. The Tangier Island Airport has a north-south 2,950' runway that parallels a rocky jetty seawall constructed by the Corps of Engineers to protect the airport from erosion. Tangier Island speed limit is 15 miles per hour with little over three miles of roadway. The heaviest traffic, by far, around Tangier is on the water. Additional attractions in the region can also be experienced, like the famous "Crab Derby." Everyday at 12:30 p.m. (except Sundays, Oct-May), and a mail boat with scheduled trips each day, leaves Crisfield and crosses Sound to Tangier Island. During summer months, a crab-potting boat also takes passengers to the island. For more information about what there is to see and do on the island, you can contact any one of the businesses. They all work together to make Tangier one of the most popular visitor attractions in the Northeast.

Photo by: Islander Seafood Restaurant

One of several fine restaurants on Tangier Island available for the fly-in guest.

VA-W79 - TAPPAHANNOCK TAPPAHANNOCK MUNICIPAL

(Area Code 804)

23

Restaurants Near Airport:

Lawery's Seafood	1/4-1/2 mi	Phone: 443-4314
Stagecoach Rest.	1 mi	Phone: 443-2511

Lodging: Days Inn Tappahannock 443-9200; Super 8 Motel 443-3888.

Meeting Rooms: None Reported

Transportation: Mac Aire (FBO) 443-5885; Also Chandler Chevrolet 443-5100; Tappahannock Ford 443-3381.

Information: Chamber of Commerce, P.O. Box 481, Tappahannock, VA 22560, Phone: 443-5241.

Lawery's Seafood Restaurant:

The Lawery's Seafood Restaurant is located within a few of blocks of the Tappahannock Municipal Airport. If walking, the restaurant is 1/4th mile. By road it's about 1/2 mile. Transportation is available through Mac Aire (FBO) or the restaurant depending on available personnel. The restaurant is open between 7:30 a.m. and 8:30 p.m. This family style facility specializes in seafood dishes as well as other fine choices. Some of their items include seafood platters, crab cakes, soft crab dishes, fried oysters, frog legs, several varieties of steaks, fried chicken and Virginia sliced ham as well as breakfast items. Average prices for a meal run $4.00 to $7.50 for breakfast, $3.50 to $10.00 for lunch and $7.50 to $18.95 for dinner. Daily specials are also offered throughout the week. The main dining room can accommodate between 250 and 300 persons. This restaurant contains a rare collection of automobiles including three 1931 Model-A Fords, a 1910 cadillac and a 1926 Chrysler. Antique cars as well as automobile memorabilia add to the interesting atmosphere of this establishment. The Lawery's Seafood Restaurant has been family owned and operated since 1938. (Three generations) For more information call 443-4314.

Attraction:

Tappahannock is a quaint little town on the Rappahannock River, History, antiques, peace and quiet, fishing, sailing and a relaxed way of life.

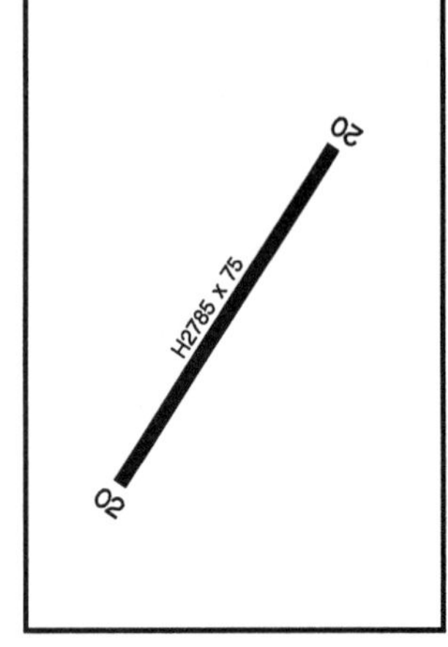

Airport Information:

TAPPAHANNOCK - TAPPAHANNOCK MUNICIPAL AIRPORT (W79)
1 mi west of town N37-55.51 W76-52.30 Fuel: 100LL Rwy 02-02: H2785x75 (Asph) Attended: 1300Z-dusk Unicom: 122.8 Notes: Overnight parking $3.00, no fee with fuel purchase. For fuel after 2300Z call 804-443-5526.
Airport Manager Phone: 443-5885

VA-JGG - WILLIAMSBURG JAMESTOWN

(Area Code 804)

24

Restaurants Near Airport:

Charley's	On Site	Phone: 229-9256

Lodging: Williamsburg Inn (Free trans.) 229-1000; Williamsburg Lodge (Free trans) 229-1000; Colonial Houses (Free trans) 229-1000; Kingsmill Resort 253-1703.
Meeting Rooms: Williamsburg Inn (Free trans.) 229-1000; Williamsburg Lodge (Free trans) 229-1000; Colonial Houses (Free trans) 229-1000; Kingsmill Resort 253-1703.
Transportation: Taxi and rental car service, 229-9256;
Information: Colonial Williamsburg Foundation, P.O. Box 1776, Williamsburg, VA 23187. Phone: 800-HISTORY or 220-7645.

Charley's:

Charley's restaurant is situated at the terminal building on the Jamestown Airport. It was a sincere pleasure talking with the owner of the airport and restaurant. The family-run operation takes great pride in providing the best in services for their customers. Not only does the restaurant and local pilot shop attract fly-in customers, but the historical town of Williamsburg also attracts many vacationers each year. Charley's restaurant is open between 11 a.m. and 3 p.m. 7 days a week. Their menu includes fresh baked breads, along with many homemade items. On Saturdays and Sundays they feature prime rib as a special, along with pork tenderloin. Throughout the week these same dishes are available as well as barbecued selections, seafood bisque, chili and soup of the day. After a fine meal guests can enjoy a choice of several delicious desserts including their famous chocolate or lemon meringue pies, cherry crumb pie, coconut custard pie and "Bumble Berry Pie" which is made with rhubarb, apple and strawberry. Average prices run $5.00 for lunch and $8.00 for dinner. The dining area can accommodate about 38 persons along with additional seating on their outdoor patio, with umbrella covered tables. A special room for groups is also available. Groups up to 20 or 30 persons can easily be served. Charley's can also prepare food trays for pilots on the go. In addition to the restaurant, they have a pilot shop located next door that was nicknamed "Little Sporty's." For more information call Charley's at 229-9256.

Attractions:

Colonial Williamsburg has over 20 nationally acclaimed attractions. Visitors can enjoy Colonial Williamsburg, Bush Gardens, The Old Country, Jamestown, Yorktown, Water Country USA, museums, plantations and much more. For full accommodations within the area you can contact the Williamsburg Hotel & Motel Association by calling 800-446-9244, or the Colonial Williamsburg Foundation at 800-HISTORY.

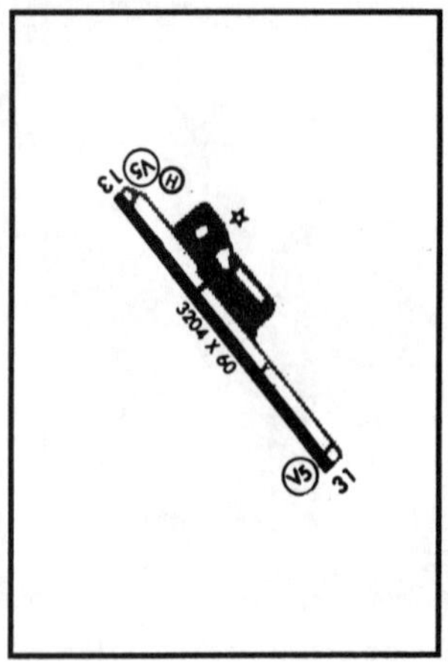

Airport Information:

WILLIAMSBURG - JAMESTOWN (JGG)
3 mi southwest of town N37-14.35 W76-42.97 Elev: 49 Fuel: 100LL, Jet-A Rwy 13-31: H3204x60 (Asph) Attended: 1200Z-dark Unicom: 122.8
FOB: Williamsburg Aviation Phone: 229-7330

WASHINGTON

LOCATION MAP

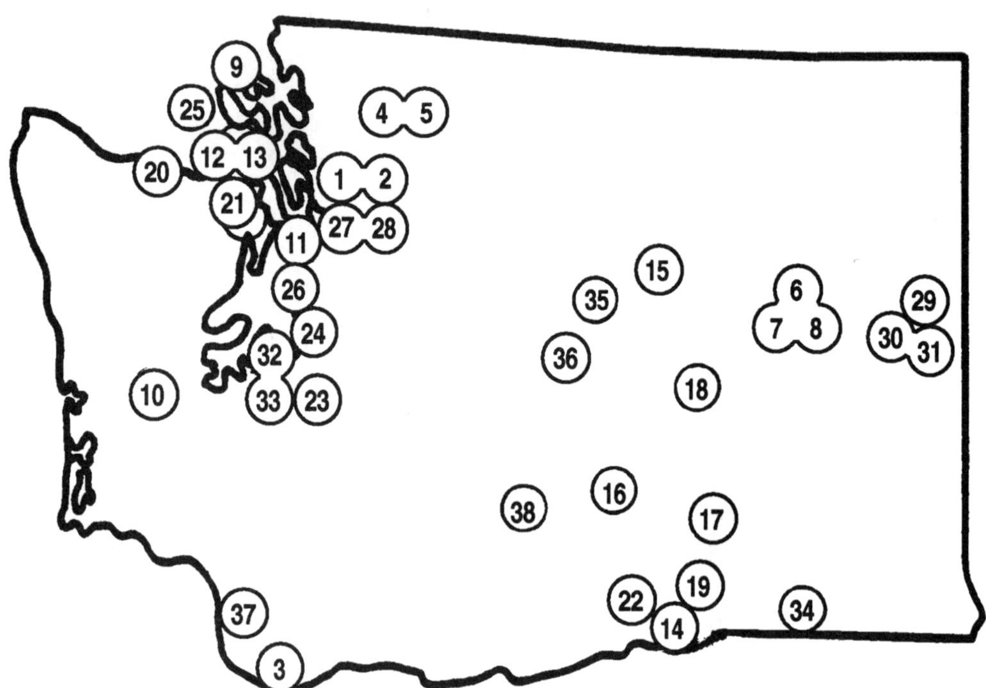

Not to be used for navigational purposes

WASHINGTON

CROSS FILE INDEX

Location Number	City or Town	Airport Name And Identifier	Name of Attraction
1	Arlington	Arlington Muni. Arpt. (AWO)	Aero Book Club
2	Arlington	Arlington Muni. Arpt. (AWO)	Prop Stop Restaurant
3	Camas	Grove Field (WA10)	Lake Side Chalet
4	Concrete	Concrete Muni. Arpt. (WA13)	North Cascade Inn
5	Concrete	Concrete Muni. Arpt. (WA13)	Stephenies Drive-in
6	Davenport	Davenport Arpt. (68S)	Cottonwood Davenport
7	Davenport	Davenport Arpt. (68S)	Ellies Deli
8	Davenport	Davenport Arpt. (68S)	Hangar One Restaurant
9	Eastsound	Orcas Island Arpt. (ORS)	Bilbo's Festiva
10	Elma	Elma Muni. Arpt. (WA22)	The Landing Strip
11	Everett	Snohomish Co. (Paine Fld.) (PAE)	Jet Deck Restaurant
12	Friday Harbor	Friday Harbor Arpt. (FHR)	Cannery House Rest.
13	Friday Harbor	Friday Harbor Arpt. (FHR)	LaCeiba
14	Kennewick	Vista Field (S98)	Boulevard Restaurant
15	Mansfield	Mansfield Arpt. (WA34)	Golden Wheat Cafe
16	Mattawa	Desert Aire (M94)	Desert Flower & Lounge
17	Mesa	Basin City Airfield (97WA)	Frontier Inn
18	Moses Lake	Grant Co. Arpt. (MWH)	Hallmark Resort
19	Pasco	Tri-Cities Arpt. (PSC)	Air Host Restaurant
20	Port Angeles	William R. Fairchild Intl. (CLM)	Hangar Restaurant
21	Port Townsend	Jefferson Co. Intl. (0S9)	Spruce Goose Cafe
22	Prosser	Prosser Arpt. (S40)	The Barn Motor Inn
23	Puyallup	Pierce Co.-Thun Field (1S0)	Hangar Inn
24	Renton	Renton Muni. Arpt. (RNT)	Schumsky's Restaurant
25	Roche Harbor	Roche Harbor Resort Arpt. (9S1)	Roche Harbor Resort
26	Seattle	Boeing Fld./King Co. Intl. (BFI)	CAVU Cafe
27	Snohomish	Harvey Field (S43)	Collector's Choice Rest.
28	Snohomish	Harvey Field (S43)	Harvey's Airport Rest.
29	Spokane	Felts Field (SFF)	Skyway Cafe
30	Spokane	Spokane Intl. (GEG)	Lefty's Northern Grill
31	Spokane	Spokane Intl. (GEG)	Americano's Pizza
32	Tacoma Narrows	Tacoma Narrows Arpt. (TIW)	Fresh Aire Cafe
33	Tacoma Narrows	Tacoma Narrows Arpt. (TIW)	Span Deli Restaurant
34	Walla Walla	Walla Walla Reg. Arpt. (ALW)	Swans at the Arpt.
35	Waterville	Waterville Arpt. (2S5)	Waterville Arpt. (2S5)
36	Wenatchee	Pangborn Mem. Arpt. (EAT)	Apple Shoppe Rest.
37	Woodland	Woodland State (WA71)	Oak Tree Restaurant
38	Yakima	Yakima Air Terml. (YKM)	Restaurant at the Arpt.

Articles

City or town	Nearest Airport and Identifier	Name of Attraction
San Juan Islands, WA	Eastsound or Fri Harbor (ORS/FHR)	San Juan Islands
Seattle, WA	Boeing Fld/King Co. Intl. (BFI)	The Museum of Flight

WA-AWO - ARLINGTON
ARLINGTON MUNICIPAL AIRPORT

(Area Code 360) 1, 2

Aero Book Club:

The Aero Book Club operates several services on the Arlington Municipal Airport. Thursday through Sunday between 10 a.m. and 6 p.m. they have a coffee shop that features gourmet coffee, ice tea and soft drinks. There are custom-made cookies and light lunches served as well. The shop becomes the local pilot social center with much heated discussion about airplanes, flying, pilots, etc. According to the Aero Book Club, the little Book Store attached to the coffee shop carries one of the largest selection of aviation-related books in the western states, in addition to many pilot supplies. Twenty four hour Texaco gas service is available with 80/87, 100LL and auto fuel at some of the lowest prices in the state. Major credit cards accepted, including Texaco. Their location is at the north end of runway 34-16, with plenty of parking available. A deli, just one block east of them, offers great soups, sandwiches and breakfast. This deli is open Monday through Saturday between 7 a.m. and 5 p.m. There is also a youth center about two blocks south of the deli called the (Fly-in J) where one can shower up and use the health facilities. For more information you can call the Aero Book Club at 368-0198.

Prop Stop Restaurant:

The Prop Stop Restaurant is situated right on the Arlington Municipal Airport. This family-style restaurant can easily be reached by walking from the aircraft tie down parking ramp. Their hours are from 7 a.m. to 4 p.m. 7 days a week. Their menu includes entrees like biscuits and gravy, and omelets for breakfast, a wide variety of luncheon items, as well as special diet dishes, like their "Light Eaters Plate." Home-made chili is also one of their specialty items. Their menu contains a nice selection of desserts as well. Daily specials not often listed on their menu include meat loaf, chicken fried steak and macaroni and cheese. The main dining room can seat up to 130 persons with a view of the airport and activity areas. The back of the restaurant can also be blocked off for special occasions and group luncheons, with accommodations for up to 40 persons. They even have outside seating for customers as well. For more information call the Prop Stop Restaurant at 435-5700.

Restaurants Near Airport:

Aero Book Club	On Site	Phone: 368-0198
Flying J. Deli	On Site	Phone: 435-8110
Pie-In-The-Sky	On Site	Phone: 435-5290
Prop Stop Restaurant	On Site	Phone: 435-5700

Lodging: Arlington Motor Inn (3 miles) Phone: 652-9595; Smokey Point Motor Inn (2 miles) Phone: 659-8561.

Meeting Rooms: None reported

Transportation: Aero Book Club can arrange transportation through rental cars with advance notice. Call 368-0198. Marysville Taxi 659-8797.

Information: State Tourism Development Division, Department of Trade and Economic Developement, 101 General Administration Building, P.O. Box 42500, Olympia, WA 98504-2500, Phone: 586-2102, 586-2088 or 800-544-1800.

Attractions:

Just 100 yards south of the Aero Book Club retail store is the famous Glasair Aircraft Manufacturing Facility. This company is open for visitors Monday through Thursday between 8 a.m. and 5 p.m. plus alternate Saturdays. This is a particularly interesting attraction due to its popular affiliation with aviation. For information you can call the Aero Book Club at 368-0198. Also in the area there is great camping, hiking, fishing and skiing all less then a one-hour drive from the airport. Rental cars can also be arranged by calling the Aero Book Club facility at 368-0198.

Airport Information:

ARLINGTON - ARLINGTON MUNICIPAL AIRPORT (AWO)
3 mi southwest of town N48-09.65 W122-09.54 Elev: 137 Fuel: 80, 100, Jet-A+, MOGAS
Rwy 16-34: H5333x100 (Asph) Rwy 11-29: H3500x75 (Asph) Attended: 1600Z-dusk
Unicom: 122.7 Notes: Altralight and Glider activities.
FBO: Arlington Aeronautical Phone: 435-5700
FBO: Arlington Associates Phone: 435-5290

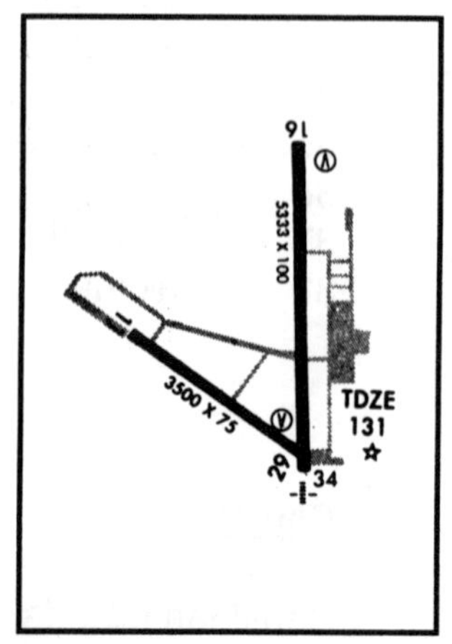

WA-WA10 - CAMAS GROVE FIELD

(Area Code 360) 3

Lake Side Chalet:

The Lake Side Chalet is located about 1-1/2 miles from the Grove Field Airport in Camas WA. This family style restaurant will provide courtesy transportation for fly-in guests provided advance notice is given. There is also taxi service situated only 1/4 milefrom the restaurant. The restaurant is open between 6 a.m. and 9 p.m. 7 days a week. Specialty entrees offered on their menu include a wide variety of sandwiches, hamburgers, cheeseburgers, along with steaks, seafood, and chicken dinners. Average prices are $1-6.00 for breakfast, $2.00 and up for lunch, and $6.00 and up for dinner. Monthly specials are offered where you can buy one meal and get one free. The Lake Side Chalet offers lake view dining within the restaurant or on their outdoor patio. The fire place within the center of the restaurant provides a cozy atmosphere. There is seating for between 60 and 70 people within the main dining room. The Lake Side Chalet can also accommodate fly-in groups and parties, as is also the case with many of the local groups planning luncheons and dinner parties. For more information you can call 834-3430.

Restaurants Near Airport:
Lake Side Chalet 1-2 mi Phone: 834-3430

Lodging: Brass Lamp (5 miles) 835-8591

Meeting Rooms: None Reported

Transportation: Camas Taxi 834-2200.

Information: Vancouver Convention & Visitors Bureau, 404 East 15th Street, Suite 11, Vancouver, WA 986-63, Phone: 360-693-1313 or 800-377-7084. Also: State Tourism Developement Division, Department of Trade and Economic Developement, 101 General Administration Building, P.O. Box 42500, Olympia, WA 98504-2500, Phone: 206-586-2102, 586-2088 or 800-544-1800.

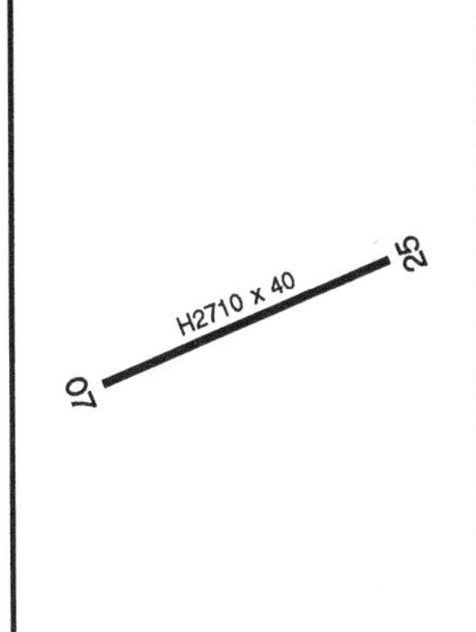

Airport Information:

CAMAS - GROVE FIELD (WA10)
3 mi north of town N45-37.49 W122-24.07 Elev: 420 Fuel: 80, 100
Rwy 07-25: H2710x40 (Asph) Attended: 1700-0100Z CTAF: 122.9
Port of Camas-Washougal (Airport Management) Phone: 835-2196 or 260-6290

WA-WA13 - CONCRETE
CONCRETE MUNICIPAL AIRPORT

(Area Code 360) 4, 5

North Cascade Inn:

The North Cascade Inn is located about 1/2 mile west of the Concrete Municipal Airport along Highway 20. This combination family style and fine dining facility is open 7 days a week between 5 a.m. and 11 p.m. during the summer and 5 a.m. to 9 p.m. during the winter. Their menu offers items like porter house steaks, New York, tenderloin, fish and chips, sandwiches, cod fish, pron, shrimp, oysters along with many steak and seafood dishes. On Wednesday they serve Mexican dishes. There are also daily specialsthroughout the week. Average prices run $5.00 for breakfast & lunch, and under $10.00 for dinner. This restaurant contains seating for about 40 or 50 persons with a private dining area able to accommodate up to 40 people in addition to outdoor dining. Many antiques and pioneer equipment decorate the restaurant as well as a gazebo able to seat 12 people outdoors on their patio. This establishment also provides a 14 unit hotel in conjunction with the restaurant. For more information, you can call the North Cascade Inn at 853-8401.

Stephenies Drive-in:

Daisy's Drive Inn can be classified as a family style restaurant that is well within walking distance to the Concrete Municipal Airport. Their hours are 7 days a week from 10 a.m. to 8 p.m. year around. Entrees on their menu include hamburgers, shakes and fries. Average prices run $2.50 to $5.00for lunch and between $5.00 and $6.00 for dinner. Total seating within the restaurant is 35 and offers a cozy atmosphere. For more information about Daisy's Drive Inn, call 853-8551.

Restaurants Near Airport:

North Cascade Inn	1/2 mi. W	Phone: 853-8771
Stephenies Drive-in	1000 ft	Phone: 853-8551

Lodging: Concrete Motel (Free trans, 1 mile) 853-8771; North Cascade Inn (1 mile) 853-8771.

Meeting Rooms: None Reported

Transportation: None Reported

Information: Sedro Woolley Chamber of Commerce, 116 Woodworth Street, P.O. Box 562, Sedro Woolley, WA 98284, 206-855-1841 or 206-855-0974. Also: State Tourism Developement Division, Department of Trade and Economic Developement, 101 General Administration Building, P.O. Box 42500, Olympia, WA 98504-2500, Phone: 206-586-2102, 586-2088 or 800-544-1800.

Attractions:

Old Fashioned Fly-in: Each year during the middle of May, the town of Concrete celebrates an "Old fashion Fly-in". Many of the merchants and businessmen within the community take part by displaying their goods during this festive occasion. For information you can call the people at Daisy's Drive Inn (853-8551), and they will let you know more about this event. The Town of Concrete is also located near many recreational lakes within 2 miles of the airport as well as state parks providing numerous outdoor activities.

07
H2580 x 60
25

Airport Information:

CONCRETE - CONCRETE MUNICIPAL AIRPORT (WA13)
1 mi south of town N48-31.62 W121-45.49 Elev: 264 Rwy 07-25: H2580x60 (Asph)
Attended: unattended CTAF: 122.9
Concrete Municipal Airport, Phone: 853-8412

WA-68S - DAVENPORT DAVENPORT AIRPORT

(Area Code 509) 6, 7, 8

Cottonwood Davenport:

The Cottonwood Davenport Restaurant is located 6 blocks from the Davenport Airport. This family-style restaurant is open Sunday through Thursday from 7 a.m. to 9 p.m., and Friday and Saturday from 7 a.m. to 10 p.m. Specialties of the house include their 11 oz. and 8 oz. New York steak, 8 and 12 ounce top sirloin, captains plate, scallops and shrimp, chicken breast sandwiches, chicken strips, Philly beef, Mexican selections and a wide variety of additional favorites. Prices average $2.00 to $4.00 for breakfast, $4.00 to $5.00 for lunch and $10.00 to $12.00 for dinner. Daily specials are offered as well as a complete salad bar. The decor of the restaurant is light and airy. They also have a lounge area. Meeting and banquet rooms allow seating for 175 people. For more information call the restaurant at 725-2222.

Ellie's Deli:

Ellie's Deli is situated adjacent to the Davenport Municipal Airport. This combination cafe and family-style restaurant, according to the restaurant personnel, is located east of the field and can be seen from the airport. There is also a sign displaying time and temperature next to the restaurant that will help identify this establishment. Restaurant hours during the summer months are from 6 a.m. to 9 p.m., and 6 a.m. to 8 p.m. during the winter season. Entrees on their menu include a full-service breakfast, 21-piece shrimp plate, fish and chips, BLTs, chicken strips and steak sandwiches. Their belly-buster 1/2 pound burger is a favorite of many customers. Lunch specials are offered every day. Desserts of all kinds are also featured. The decor of the restaurant is contemporary with 12 booths for seating guests. Larger groups should make advance arrangements. Carry-out meals can also be prepared from anything on their menu. For more information about Ellies Deli, call 725-3354.

Hangar One Restaurant:

The Hangar One Restaurant is located about 1/2 mile (6 blocks) from the Davenport Airport. This family-style restaurant has been in business for the past 28 years. Hours of operation are 8 a.m. to 9 p.m. Monday through Saturday, and 8 a.m. to 2 p.m. on Sunday. This is a full-service restaurant with menu items like prime rib and top sirloin. They are very fussy about their selections of meat and cook only the choicest cuts. They feature a Wednesday and Friday "Happy Hour" between 5 p.m. and 7 p.m. There is seating for about 50 in their main dining room and 30 in their lounge. The restaurant decor is cozy with Cape Home Victorian furnishings within this restored 100-year-old building. Their friendly waitresses will serve your every need, as customer satisfaction is guaranteed. Groups and full-catered dinners can easily be arranged. For more information about the Hangar One Restaurant, call 725-6630.

Airport Information:

DAVENPORT - DAVENPORT AIRPORT (68S)
1 mi west of town N47-39.24 W118-10.07 Elev: 2416 Fuel: 100, MOGAS
Rwy 05-23: H3126x50 (Asph) Rwy 03-21: 2185x45 (Grvl) Attended: Mar-July dawn to dusk, Aug-Feb Mon-Fri 1600-0100Z CTAF: 122.9
FBO: Northwest Aviation, Inc. Phone: 725-0011

Restaurants Near Airport:

Cottonwood Inn	6 blocks	Phone: 725-2222
Crestport Deli	N/A	Phone: 725-2737
Ellie's Deli	Adj Arpt	Phone: 725-3354
Hangar One	6 Blocks	Phone: 725-6630

Lodging: Black Bear Motel (Adjacent) 725-7700; Davenport Motel (Adjacent to Airport) 725-7071; Diamond S Motel (1 mile) 725-7742.

Meeting Rooms: Cottonwood Inn has rooms available for catered meetings. Call 725-2222 for information.

Transportation: None Reported

Information: Spokane Convention & Visitors Bureau, W 926 Sprague Avenue, Suite 180, Spokane, WA 99204, Phone: 509-747-3230. Also: State Tourism Development Division, Department of Trade and Economic Development, 101 General Administration Building, P.O. Box 42500, Olympia, WA 98504-2500, Phone: 206-586-2102 or 206-586-2088 or 800-544-1800.

Attractions:

Pioneer Days Museum is located about 6 blocks from the airport. It is located next to the city park. Turn east out of airport and go 6 to 7 blocks until reaching 7th Street. The museum contains items of interest dating back 100 years, including machinery, etc. It is open only during the summer season. For information and to confirm directions call Ellie's Deli at 725-3354 or the Davenport airport manager or Northwest Aviation, Inc. at 725-0011.

NO AIRPORT DIAGRAM AVAILABLE

WA-ORS - EASTSOUND
ORCAS ISLAND AIRPORT

(Area Code 206) 9

Restaurants Near Airport:

Bilbo's Festiva	1 mi	Phone: 376-4728
Bungalow	1 mi	Phone: 376-4338
La Famiglia	1 mi	Phone: 376-2335

Lodging: Landmark Inn (1 mile) 376-2423; Outlook Inn (1 mile) 376-2581; Rosario (6 miles) 376-2222; Smugglers Villa (1 mile) 376-2297

Meeting Rooms: Rosario Resort 6 mi 376-2222, res. 800-562-8820.

Transportation: Adventure Limousine 376-4994; Practical Rent-A-Car 376-4176. Also the airport manager may be able to arrange transportation 376-5285.

Information: San Juan Islands Visitor Chamber of Commerce, P.O. Box 98, Friday Harbor, WA 98250, Phone: 378-5240.

Bilbo's Festiva:

The Bilbo's Festiva Restaurant is located less than one mile from the Orcas Island Airport. This family restaurant can be reached by walking on a nice day or by available transportation. Our readers informed us that this restaurant is known as one of the popular Mexican restaurants in the western portion of Washington state. This family restaurant is open between 5 p.m. and 9 p.m. weekdays and 4:30 p.m. to 9 p.m. on weekends. Their dinner menu includes primarily Mexican dishes including specialties like barbecue mesquite items and their delicious enchiladas. There is seating in their attractive outdoor courtyard for 30 or more people. The restaurant has a warm and friendly atmosphere decorated in a Spanish motif. Groups can arrange catered meals with advance notice. Meals can also be prepared for carry-out. For more information about Bilbo's Festiva call 376-4728.

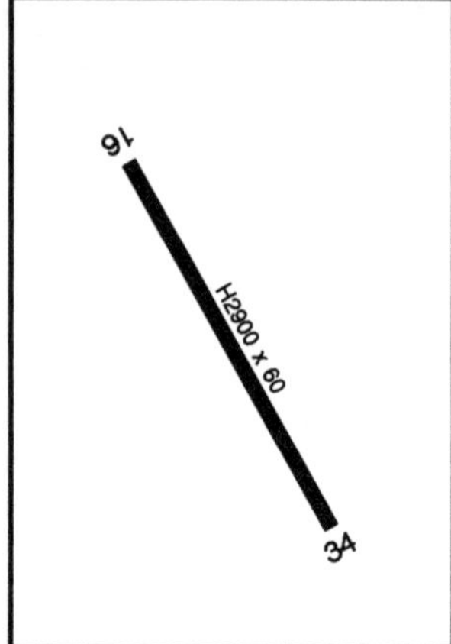

Airport Information:

EASTSOUND - ORCAS ISLAND AIRPORT (ORS)
1 mi north of town N48-42.49 W122-54.83 Elev: 25 Fuel: None Reported Rwy 16-34: H2900x60 (Asph) Attended: 1700-0100Z, Sun 1800-0000Z CTAF: 128.25
FBO: Airport Manager Phone: 376-5285

WA-WA22 - ELMA
ELMA MUNICIPAL AIRPORT

(Area Code 360) 10

Restaurants Near Airport:

The Landing Strip	On Site	Phone: 482-5209

Lodging: Parkhurst Motel (1 mile) 482-2541; Gray's Harbor Pavillion, Phone: N/A

Meeting Rooms: None Reported

Transportation: Car Rental: Day Ford 482-2241.

Informaton: Olympia/Thurston County Chamber of Commerce, P.O. Box 1427, Olympia, WA 98507, Phone: 357-3370 or 800-753-VISIT.

The Landing Strip:

The Landing Strip Restaurant is located on the Elma Municipal Airport. This family style and fine dining facility is open Tuesday through Thursday from 8 a.m. to 3 p.m., Friday and Saturday from 8 a.m. to 8 p.m. and Sunday from 8 a.m. to 5 p.m. (Closed on Monday). This restaurant serves a full line of breakfast items including their popular one pound ham steak and eggs for only $5.25 as well as their steak and eggs special for around $5.00. The menu also features a nice selection of lunch and dinner choices. Daily specials are available throughout the week like their Friday night prime rib special. They also provide a nice assortment of desserts and pastries. Prices for menu items are reasonable. The restaurant has been remodeled, providing a friendly casual atmosphere. This restaurant can easily accommodate fly-in groups. It is not uncommon for as many as 20 different parties to fly-in on Saturday and Sunday mornings. They claim to be one of the busiest airport restaurants within the nearby region, with the best available food and service around. Stan and Vera are the owners of this restaurant well experienced in the art of catering and restaurant management. As an executive chef by profession for over 30 years, stan has trained and worked within many restaurants and hotels throughout the U.S. and in Europe. For more information about the Landing Strip Restaurant, call 482-5209.

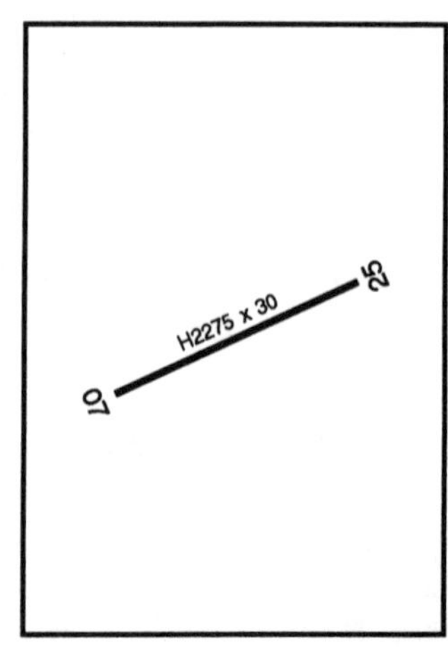

Airport Information:

ELMA - ELMA MUNICIPAL AIRPORT (WA22)
1 mi southwest of town N46-59.42 W123-25.84 Elev: 28 Fuel: 80, 100LL
Rwy 07-25: H2275x30 (Asph) Attended: May-Oct 1600-0400Z Unicom: 122.8
Elma Municipal Airport Phone: 482-2228

WA-PAE - EVERETT
SNOHOMISH COUNTY (PAINE FIELD)

(Area Code 206) **11**

Jet Deck Restaurant:

The Jet Deck is a family-style restaurant that is situated on the Snohomish County (Paine Field) Airport. According to the restaurant management, there is no problem reaching this establishment from nearby aircraft parking areas. Their hours are 10:30 a.m. to 9:00 p.m. during the summer months, and 10:30 a.m. to 8:00 p.m. during the winter months. Selections on their menu include prime rib sandwiches, fish and chips and hamburgers. Breakfast is served only on Saturday and Sunday. Average prices for a meal run $4.95 for lunch and $9.95 for dinner. The main dining room has seating for 175 persons. They frequently cater to fly-in groups with banquet accommodations. Live entertainment with music is also provided on Thursday, Friday and Saturday evenings. For more information about the Jet Deck Restaurant, you can call 743-9500.

Restaurants Near Airport:

Arnie's Restaurant	4 Mi	Phone: N/A
Black Angus Restaurant	2-1/2 Mi	Phone: N/A
Jet Deck Restaurant	On Site	Phone: 743-9500
Zorbas Restaurant	2-1/2 Mi	Phone: N/A

Lodging: All Star Inn (3 miles) 353-8120; Apple Inn (2-1/2 miles) 347-1100; Cypress Inn (3 miles) 347-9099; Quality Inn (3-1/2 miles) 745-2555; Six Motels (1-1/2 miles) 347-2060; Westcoast Everett Pacific Hotel (Airport trans) 339-3333.

Meeting Rooms: Westcoast Everett Pacific Hotel (Airport trans), meeting rooms and convention facilities available 339-3333.

Transportation: Taxi: Airport Connection 659-8797; K-Cab 259-4131; White Top 252-4040: Yellow Cab 259-2121: Car rental: American International (Airport) 259-5058; Budget 252-2422; Hertz 355-6600; U-Save Auto Rental (Airport) 353-5880.

Information: Everett/ Snohomish Convention and Visitors Bureau, P.O. Box 1086, Everett, WA 98206, Phone: 252-5181.

Attractions:

Salty Sea Days is an annual event with festivals, parades and carnivals at the Everett Yacht Basin, held during the beginning of June. There are also many recreational and outdoor activities within the Everett area. For information you can call 259-0300.

Airport Information:

EVERETT - SNOHOMISH COUNTY (PAINE FIELD) (PAE)
6 mi southwest of town N47-54.46 W122-16.90 Elev: 606 Fuel: 80, 100LL, Jet-A Rwy 16R-34L: H9010x150 (Asph-Grvd) Rwy 11-29: H4514x75 (Asph) Rwy 16L-34R: H3000x75 (Asph) Attended: 1500-0500Z Atis: 128.65 Unicom: 122.95 Tower: 121.3, 120.2 Gnd Con: 121.8

FBO: Flightline Services, Inc. Phone: 355-6600
FBO: Regal Air Phone: 353-9123

WA-FHR - FRIDAY HARBOR
FRIDAY HARBOR AIRPORT

(Area Code 360) **12, 13**

Cannery House Restaurant:

The Cannery House Restaurant is situated about 1/2 to 1 mile from the Friday Harbor Airport. It is located at the top of 1st Street. This family-style restaurant is open during the summer from 10:30 a.m. to 8:30 p.m. and in the winter season between 10:30 a.m. and 3:00 p.m. Specialties on their menu include a variety of sandwiches, fresh seafood, Mexican dishes, steaks, appetizers, soups and pastries. Average prices run $6.75 for lunch and $9.95 for dinner. The restaurant has a modern decor and can seat approx. 75 people. Their outdoor deck overlooks the harbor. For more information you can call the Cannery House Restaurant at 378-2500.

La Ceiba:

This restaurant is located about 3/8th of a mile or 5 or 6 blocks from the Friday Harbor Airport. If walking, we were told that you can just take Airport Road out of the airport then right at the next intersection. We suggest you verify these directions. This cafe-styled restaurant is open 11 a.m. to 8 p.m., 6 days a week (closed on Sunday). They specialize in traditional Spanish selections as well as southwestern Mexican and Caribbean foods. They also offer vegetarian dishes. Prices average $5.00 to $7.00 for most items. There is seating for about 30 to 40 people in their main dining room and an additional 30 seats outdoors in their garden screened-in area. They also reserve the outdoor garden area for fund raisers and catered groups. We were told that after a meal many customers enjoy visiting the many shops within a short distance from the restaurant. For more information call 378-8666.

Restaurants Near Airport:

Cannery House	1/2 mi	Phone: 378-2500
Downriggers	1/2 mi	Phone: 378-2700
Ford's Restaurant	1/2 mi	Phone: 378-4747
La Ceiba	3/8th mi	Phone: 378-8666
Roberto's	1/2 mi	Phone: 378-6333

Lodging: Friday Harbor Motor Inn 378-4351; Imperial Gardens (1 mile) 378-2000; Island Lodge 378-2000; San Juan 378-2070

Meeting Rooms: None reported

Transportation: Taxi: Island 378-5545; Primo 378-3550; Rental cars: Friday Harbor 378-4351.

Information: State Tourism Developement Division, Department of Trade and Economic Developement, 101 General Administration Building, P.O. Box 42500, Olympia, WA 98504-2500, Phone: 206-586-2102, 586-2088 or 800-544-1800.

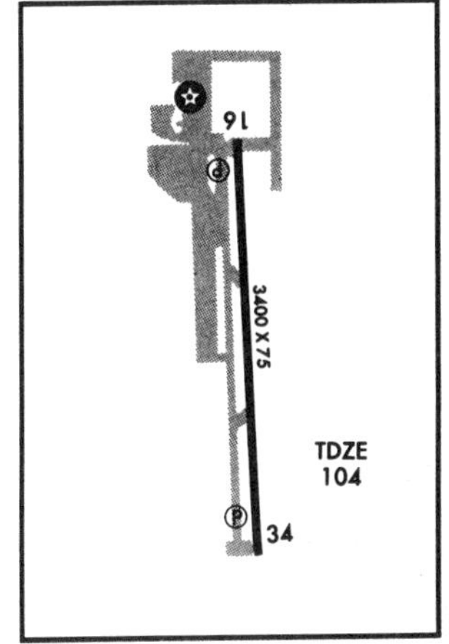

Airport Information:

FRIDAY HARBOR - FRIDAY HARBOR AIRPORT (FHR)
0 mi southwest of town N48-31.32 W123-01.46 Elev: 109 Fuel: 100 Rwy 16-34: H3400x75 (Asph) Attended: 1530-0200Z Unicom: 122.8

Friday Harbor Airport Phone: 378-4724
FBO: Aeronautical Services Phone: 378-2640

WA-S98 - KENNEWICK VISTA FIELD

(Area Code 509) 14

Restaurants Near Airport:

Boulevard Restaurant	3/4 mi N.	Phone: 735-6575
R.F Mc Dougall's	3/4 mi N.	Phone: 735-6418
Cedar's Pier 1	4 mi E.	Phone: 582-2143
Casa Chapala	1/2 mi N.	Phone: 783-8080

Lodging: Cavanaughs Motor Inn (1/4 mile) 783-0611; Nendels Motor Inn 735-9511; Shaniko Inn 735-6385.
Meeting Rooms: Cavanaughs Motor Inn (1/4 mile) 783-0611.
Transportation: There are 2 courtesy cars available at the Kennewick airport, Kennewick Aircraft Sales can arrange courtesy transportation 735-2875.
Information: Kennewick Chamber of Commerce, 1600 North 20th Street, Pasco, WA 99301, Phone: 547-9755; Also: Richland Chamber of Commerce, 511 Lee Blvd., P.O. Box 637, Richland, WA 99352, Phone: 946-1651. (Tri City Area)

Boulevard Restaurant:

The Boulevard Restaurant is a fine dining establishment located about 3/4th of a mile north of the Kennewick Vista Airport. Transportation to and from this restaurant can be obtained through courtesy cars by Kennewick Aircraft Services at the airport. (2 cars available) The restaurant is open Monday through Saturday between 11:00 a.m. and 10 p.m. and 5:00 p.m. to 9:00 p.m. Sundays. Their lounge is open from 11:30 until 1 a.m. weekdays and until 2 a.m. on weekends. Their menu contains a number of fascinating dishes including 4 to 8 selections of fresh fish, prawns, roast lamb, "Tagliatelle Bolognese" which is northern Italian fettucini, prime cuts of midwestern beef, baked chicken Dijon, and sesame chicken salad to mention only a few. The main dining room can seat up to 180 persons with heavy wood and fabric decor that provides a very private and cozy atmosphere. Their lounge on the other hand is bright and airy with live entertainment Thursday, Friday and Saturday evenings. They even host live music Friday and Saturday nights. Larger groups and parties are welcome with advance notice. A portion of the main dining area can be cordoned off for this purpose. For more information about the Boulevard Restaurant you can call 735-6575.

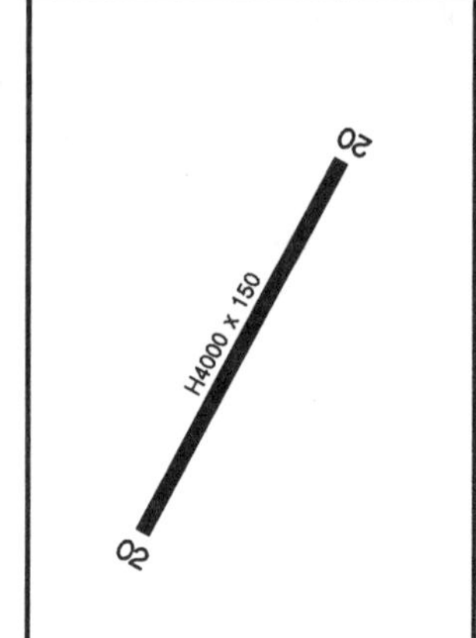

Attractions:

The Oasis Water Park is located only 1/4 mile from the airport (Open summer months); Shopping mall also within walking distance about 1/8th mile away. Columbia Cup Hydro-Plane Races (Transportation provided); Winery tours are available, some with landing strips adjacent, for information call 735-8486.

Airport Information:

KENNEWICK - VISTA FIELD (S98)
3 mi northwest of town   N46-13.24 W119-12.32   Elev: 521   Fuel: 80, 100LL
Rwy 02-20: H4000x150 (Asph)   Attended: daylight hours   CTAF: 122.9
FBO: Kennewick Aircraft Services   Phone: 735-2875

WA-WA34 - MANSFIELD MANSFIELD AIRPORT

(Area Code 509) 15

Golden Wheat Cafe:

The Golden Wheat Cafe is located 1 block down Main Street from the Mansfield Airport, and is within easy walking distance. Their restaurant hours are from 8 a.m. to 7 p.m. weekdays, Sunday and holidays from 9 a.m. to 5 p.m. (Some holidays they are closed). Breakfast is served until noon. Burgers, appetizers, salads and soups are listed on their dinner menu. Daily lunch and dinner specials are offered, along with a Sunday Buffet containing 2 entrees, vegetables, gravy and a full salad bar. Prices run $4.50 for breakfast, $4.95 for lunch and $5.95 for dinner. This restaurant will cater to parties of up to 50-60 people. They frequently cater to groups like the Lions Club, Cattlemen's Association, and Garden Club, Etc. For information call 683-1248.

Restaurants Near Airport:
Golden Wheat Cafe   1 blk.   Phone: 683-1248

Lodging: None Reported

Transportation: None Reported

Information: State Tourism Developement Division, Department of Trade and Economic Developement, 101 General Administration Building, P.O. Box 42500, Olympia, WA 98504-2500, Phone: 206-586-2102, 586-2088 or 800-544-1800.

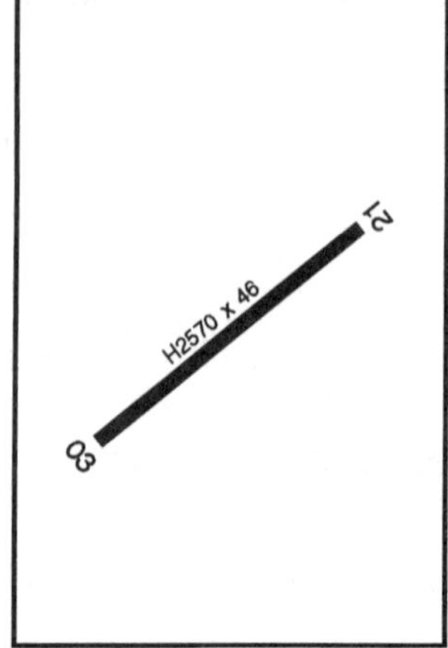

Airport Information:

MANSFIELD - MANSFIELD MUNICIPAL AIRPORT (WA34)
0 mi east of town   N47-48.58 W119-38.24   Elev: 2276   Rwy 03-21: H2570x46 (Asph)
Unattended   CATF: 122.9   Notes: Ultralight activity.
Mansfield Municipal Airport   Phone: 884-9450

WA-M94 - MATTAWA
DESERT AIRE AIRPORT

(Area Code 509)

16

Desert Flower & Lounge:

The Desert Flower & Lounge Restaurant is located about 3 or 4 blocks from the Desert Airport. You can call the restaurant and they will come out and pick you up. This family style restaurant is open 8 a.m. to 9 p.m. 7 days a week. A full line of breakfast entrees are served along with many other items like hamburgers, cheeseburgers, fish, steaks, soups and salads. A specialty of the house and very popular with customers is their delicious smoked ribs. Average prices run about $4.00 for breakfast, $4.95 for lunch and $7.00 to $12.00 for dinner. The lounge area can seat about 40 or 50 people. The main dining room can seat 80 people. Their dining room has been re-decorated in colors of peach and green to reflect a southwestern decore. Larger groups and club gatherings are welcome provided advance notice is given. Items off their menu can be prepared to go or for carry-out. For more information call the Tumbleweed Cafe at 932-4229.

Attractions:

Desert Aire City Development operates a golf course located approx. 1 block from the airport. Wanapum Dam Museum (8 miles).

Airport Information:

MATTAWA - DESERT AIRE (M94)
4 mi southwest of town N46-41.24 W119-55.24 Elev: 570 Fuel: None reported
Rwy 9-27: 3600x40 (Asph)
Desert Aire Airport Phone: 932-4839

Restaurants Near Airport:
Desert Flower & Lounge 3-4 Blks. Phone: 932-4229

Lodging: Desert Aire Motel (1/2 mile)

Meeting Rooms: None Reported

Transportation: None Reported

Information: State Tourism Developement Division, Department of Trade and Economic Developement, 101 General Administration Building, P.O. Box 42500, Olympia, WA 98504-2500, Phone: 206-586-2102, 586-2088 or 800-544-1800.

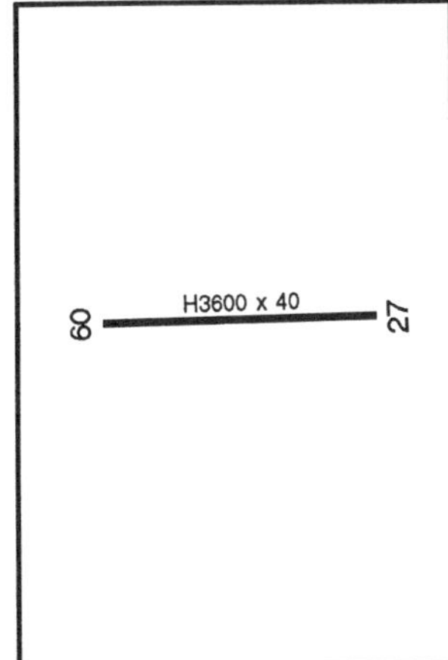

WA-97WA - MESA
BASIN CITY AIRFIELD

(Area Code 509)

17

Frontier Inn:

The Frontier Inn Restaurant is located about 3 blocks from the Basin City Airfield. This restaurant is classified as a cafe and is open between 6:30 a.m. and 9 p.m. Monday through Saturday, and 7 a.m. to 3 p.m. on Sundays. There is a lounge on the premises open from 3 p.m. until closing. Their menu contains a full line of entrees including items like liver and onions, hamburgers, cheeseburgers, and steak sandwiches along with daily specials, Friday night fish fries, and Mexican on Tuesdays. Their main dining room can accommodate up to 50 persons. Separate banquet rooms are also available, that can handle 50-60 guests. For more information call the Frontier Inn at 269-4758.

Airport Information:

MESA - BASIN CITY AIRFIELD (97WA) (Private Field)
5 mi west of town 46-34-54N 119-07-36W Elev: 770 Rwy 04-22: 2300x40 (Grvl-Drt)
Attended: 5 a.m. to 10 p.m. summer, 8 a.m. to 5 p.m. winter Notes: CAUTION Private facility land at your own risk. A/G Aircraft spraying operations in affect.
Call 269-4441 for airport information.

Restaurants Near Airport:
Frontier Inn Restaurant 3 blks Phone: 269-4758

Lodging: None Reported

Meeting Rooms: Frontier Inn Restaurant: Banquet rooms available 269-4758.

Transportation: None Reported

Information: Airport Information 509-269-4441; Also: State Tourism Developement Division, Department of Trade and Economic Developement, 101 General Administration Building, P.O. Box 42500, Olympia, WA 98504-2500, Phone: 206-586-2102, 586-2088 or 800-544-1800.

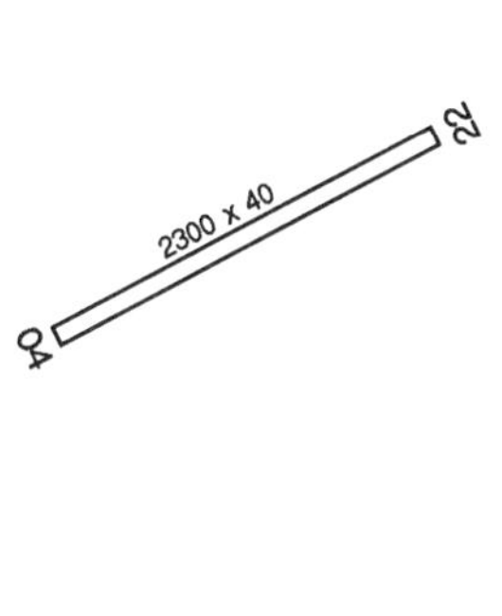

WA-MWH - MOSES LAKE GRANT COUNTY AIRPORT

18

Best Western Hallmark Resort:

The Best Western Hallmark Resort is located about 8 miles from the Grant County Airport. This resort offers free courtesy transportation to and from the airport. This lakeside establishment has beautiful gardens, boat docks, tennis courts, horse stables, swimming pools and all sorts of activities available for their guests. Their restaurant offers a casual and elegant decor. The view from the restaurant provides a panoramic view overlooking Moses Lake. The dining room can seat 80 people. Evening meals are romantic and peaceful. Green plants and colors of hunters green walls give a garden like atmosphere. House specialties include prime rib and King crab specials on Friday and Saturday nights. Dinner menu items include Fettuccini, chicken stirfry, roast rack of lamb, steak Oscar, crab, Hazel Nut Halibut, Teriyaki, Pacific salmon, New York Steak, Filet Mignon and New York rib filet. Petite portions are also available at reduced prices. The hotel has 162 rooms along with hotel suites. Banquet rooms can also be reserved. Their Solar Ball Room has 3,600 square feet and can accommodate 350 people with sit-down dinners. Smaller rooms can seat 60 to 65 people. For more information call 765-9211.

Restaurants Near Airport: **(Area Code 509)**

El Papagayos	1-1/2 mi E.	Phone: 765-1265
Barney Googles	2-1/2 mi W.	Phone: 766-2125
Hallmark Resort	8 mi. (Trans)	Phone: 765-9211

Lodging: Hallmark Inn (Free trans with advance notice) 765-9211; Shilo Inn (Free trans with advance notice) 765-9317.
Meeting Rooms: Meeting room available within terminal building. Hallmark Inn (Free trans with advance notice) 765-9211; Shilo Inn (Free trans with advance notice) 765-9317.
Transportation: Executive Flight (FBO) has courtesy transportation available 762-5350; Lodging facilities listed above will furnish courtesy transportation with advance notice; Also, Taxi: Moses Lake Charter & Limousine Service 765-6976; Rental Cars: Oasis Budget Host Inn 765-8636; U-Save Auto Rental 762-5326.
Information: Chamber of Commerce, 324 South Pioneer Way, Moses Lake, WA 98837, Phone: 765-7888.

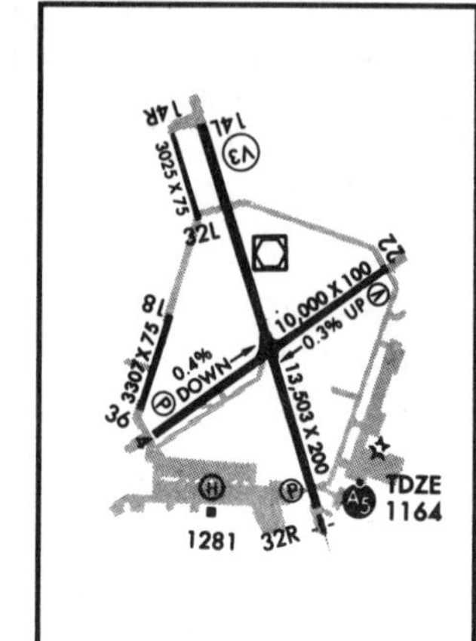

Airport Information:

MOSES LAKE - GRANT COUNTY AIRPORT (MWH)
5 mi northwest of town N47-12.46 W119-19.21 Elev: 1185 Fuel: 80, 100, 100LL, Jet-A
Rwy 14L-32R: H13502x300 (Asph-Conc-Grvd) Rwy 04-22: H9999x100 (Asph-Conc)
Rwy 18-36: H3263x75 (Asph) Rwy 14R-32L: H3025x75 (Conc) Attended: continuously
Atis: 119.05 Unicom: 122.95 Tower: 118.1 (East) 128.0 (West) Gnd Con: 121.9
App/Dep Con: 126.4, 134.35 (1430)00700Z) Public Phone 24hrs
FBO: Air America Services Phone: 762-2222, 2626
FBO: Columbia Pacific Aviation Phone: 762-1016

WA-PSC - PASCO TRI-CITIES AIRPORT

19

Air Host Restaurant:

The Air Host Restaurant is situated within the terminal building at the Tri-City Airport. This family style restaurant is within walking distance to aircraft parking areas, or can be reached by courtesy car from local fixed based operators on the field. The restaurant hours are 6 a.m. to 2 p.m. 7 days a week. Their lounge is open 12 p.m. to 6 p.m. Monday through Friday. Specialty entrees include their "Catch of the Day" featuring fish and seafood items. Steaks, chicken breast, hamburgers, turkey croissant, ham and cheese sandwiches, salads, soups, and club sandwiches are available. Appetizers are also a favorite with many customers Average prices run $5.00 for breakfast, $5.95 for lunch, and about $8.95 for dinner. The restaurant can seat 130 guests and also has accommodations for groups and parties as well as business meetings within their conference room with seating for 25 persons. Large windows within the main dining room allow guests an enjoyable view, looking at the activity and aircraft moving about the airport. In addition to the restaurant, this establishment also contains a gift shop and deli available to traveling passengers. For more information call 545-0632.

Restaurants Near Airport: **(Area Code 509)**

Air Host Restaurant	On Site	Phone: 545-0632

Lodging: Val-U Inn (Airport trans) 547-0791; Red Lion (Airport trans) 547-0701.

Meeting Rooms: Air Host Restaurant can arrange meeting rooms within the airport terminal building, 545-0632; Red Lion Motor Inn can arrange accommodations for conventions, 547-0701.

Transportation: Tri-City Taxi 547-7777; Avis 547-6971; Budget 547-6902; Hertz 547-0111; National 545-9266; U-Save 547-8326.

Information: Chamber of Commerce, 129 North 3rd Street, P.O. Box 550, Pasco, WA 99301, Phone: 547-9755.

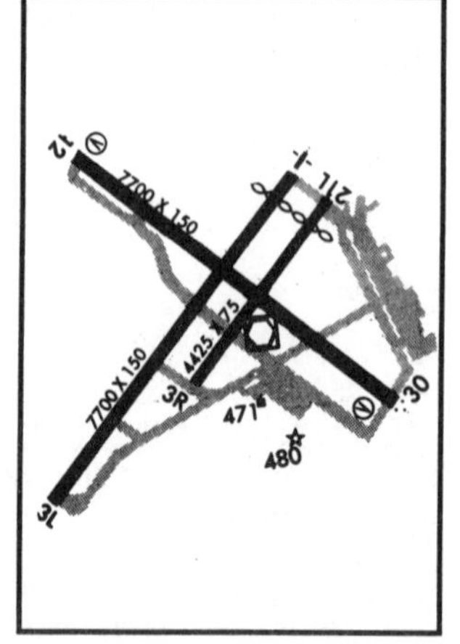

Airport Information:

PASCO - TRI CITIES AIRPORT (PSC)
2 mi northwest of town N46-15.88 W119-07.14 Elev: 407 Fuel: 100LL, Jet-A1+
Rwy 03L-21R: H7700x150 (Asph-Grvd) Rwy 12-30: H7700x150 (Asph-Grvd) Rwy 03R-21L: H4425x75 (Asph) Attended: continuously Atis: 125.65 Unicom: 122.95 Tower: 135.3
Gnd Con: 121.8 Clnc Del: 121.0
FBO: Bergstrom Aircraft Phone: 547-6271

WA-CLM - PORT ANGELES WILLIAM R. FAIRCHILD INTL.

(Area Code 360) 20

Hangar Restaurant:

The Hangar Restaurant is located within the terminal building at the Port Angeles International Airport. This cafe is open during the winter months Monday through Saturday 8 a.m. to 4 p.m. and Sunday 10 a.m. to 4 p.m. During the summer their open weekdays 7 a.m. and 7 p.m. and on Saturday and Sundays between 8 a.m. and 5 p.m. Access to the terminal building is within walking distance. Their entrees include a nice breakfast selection including waffles, biscuits and gravy, along with egg dishes. They also provide a variety of deli and gourmet style sandwiches, homemade soup, delicious cookies, and bread pudding. Cheese cake is also a favorite of many customers. Average prices run between $3.50 and $5.00 for most meals. Seating capacity is about 40 people. For more information about the Hangar Restaurant you can call 452-5877.

Restaurants Near Airport

Hangar Restaurant	On Site	Phone: 452-5877

Lodging: Aggie's Motel (4 miles) 457-8511; Driftwood Motel 452-2393; Aggie's Port Angeles Inn (Transportation) Phone: 457-0471; Red Lion - Bay Shore Inn (4 miles) 452-9215; Super 8 Motel (6 miles) 452-8401; Uptown Motel 457-9434

Meeting Rooms: None Reported

Transportation: Courtesy car through Wright Brothers Aviation 452-7227; Taxi: Angeles Taxicab 452-1717; Blue Top Cab 452-2223; Rental Cars: Budget 452-4774

Information: Chamber of Commerce, 121 E Railroad, Port Angeles, WA 98362, Phone: 452-2363

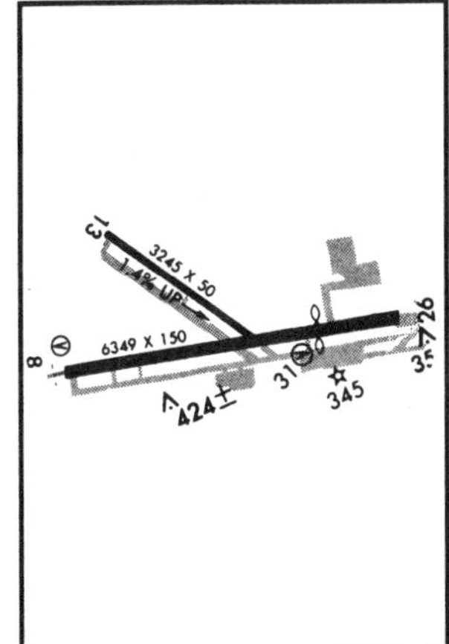

Airport Information:

PORT ANGELES - WILLIAM R FAIRCHILD INTL AIRPORT (CLM)
3 mi northwest of town N48-07.21 W123-29.98 Elev: 288
Rwy 08-26: H6349x150 (Asph) Rwy 13-31: H3245x50 (Asph)
Unicom: 123.0 App/Dep Con 118.2 Clnc Del 124.15
FBO: Rite Brothers Aviation Phone: 800-430-7483, 452-7227

Fuel: 80, 100LL, Jet-A
Attended: 1400-0600Z

WA-0S9 - PORT TOWNSEND JEFFERSON COUNTY INTL.

(Area Code 360) 21

Spruce Goose Cafe:

The Spruce Goose Cafe is located right on the Jefferson County International Airport situated near the fuel pumps, and is well within walking distance from the aircraft parking ramp. This cafe is open between 8 a.m. and 4 p.m. 7 days a week. During the summer season their hours may vary slightly. Some of the popular items on their menu include hamburgers, fish baskets, clams, egg dishes and pancakes as well as specialty omelets. Average prices run $4.50 to $7.00 for breakfast, and $4.00 to $10.00 for lunch. There are daily specials offered throughout the week as well. The restaurant can accommodate up to 28 persons. For more information you can call the Spruce Goose Cafe at 385-3185.

Restaurants Near Airport:

Spruce Goose Cafe	On Site	Phone: 385-4262
Port Hadlock Inn & Marina	4 mi	Phone: 385-5801
Silver Water Cafe	6 mi	Phone: 385-2222
Lanza's Restaurant	6 mi	Phone: 385-6221
A-Jack Cafe	Adj Arpt	Phone: 385-3450

Lodging: Resort At Port Ludlow (Free trans, 12 miles) 437-2222; Port Hadlock Inn & Marina, prefers prior notice (4 miles) 385-5801;
Meeting Rooms: Resort At Port Ludlow (Free trans, 12 miles) 437-2222; Port Hadlock Inn & Marina, prefers prior notice (4 miles) 385-5801.
Transportation: Taxi: 385-5972; Jefferson Transit 385-4777.
Information: Tourist Information Center, 2437 East Sims Way, Port Townsend, WA 98368 Phone: 385-2722.

Attractions:

The following points of interest and attractions are located near the Victorian downtown district of Port Townsend. **Resorts:** Point Hudson Resort, Port Townsend (6 miles) 385-2828; Resort At Port Ludlow (10 miles) 437-2222; **Golf:** Chevy Chase (5 miles) 385-0704; Port Ludlow (12 miles) 437-2222; P.T. Golf Club (7 miles) 385-0752; **State Parks:** Fort Flagler State Park (12 miles) 385-1259; Fort Warden State Park (8 miles) 385-4730; **Fishing:** Sea-Sport Charters (6 miles) 385-3575.

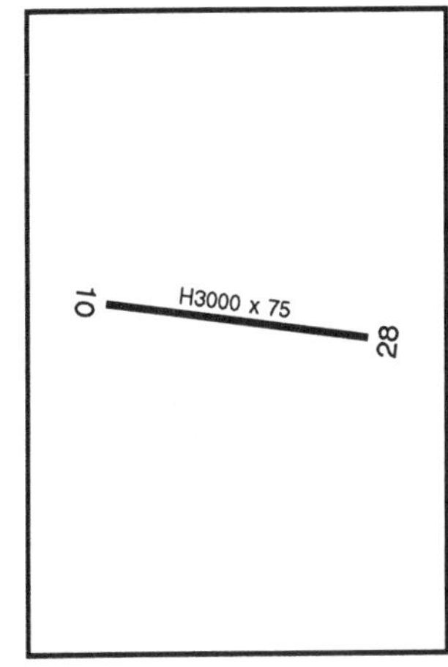

Airport Information:

PORT TOWNSEND - JEFFERSON COUNTY INTERNATIONAL (0S9)
4 mi southwest of town N48-02.99 W122-48.08 Elev: 107 Fuel: 80, 100LL Rwy08-26: H3000x75 (Asph) Attended: 1700-0200Z Unicom: 123.0 Public Phone 24hrs Notes: No landing fees, $2.00 overnight tie-down fee.
Airport Manager Phone: 385-0656
FBO: Tailspin Aircraft Serv. Phone: 385-6394

WA-S40 - PROSSER
PROSSER AIRPORT

(Area Code 509)

22

The Barn Motor Inn:

The Barn Motor Inn Restaurant and RV park is located within walking distance and across the street from the Prosser airport in Prosser, Washington. This combination family style and fine dining facility is open Monday through Thursday from 6 a.m. to 10 p.m. Fridays and Saturday from 6 a.m. to 11 p.m. and Sunday from 6 a.m. to 10 p.m. They specialize in prime rib, New York steak, seafood, chicken, pork chops for dinner selections, and for lunch try their beef stew and corn bread, or delicious cheeseburgers, in addition to many other items offered on their menu. Prices run $4.50 for breakfast, $5.50 for lunch and $12.50 for dinner. Meeting and banquet accommodations, along with a special menu for catering, are available. Eleven different party trays can be prepared for your needs. In addition to the restaurant, this facility also contains a 30 unit motel that provides 28 guest rooms, two suites, outdoor swimming pool,cable TV, air conditioning, room service, banquet rooms and gift shop. For more information call the restaurant at 786-1131 or the motel at 786-2121.

Restaurants Near Airport:
The Barn Motor Inn   Adj Arpt.   Phone: 786-1131

Lodging: The Barn Motor Inn (Adj to airport, free pick-up service) 30 guest rooms, Two suites, outdoor swimming pool, air conditioning, room service, restaurant lounge with piano bar. Phone: 786-2121; Prosser Motel (1 mile) 786-2555.

Meeting Rooms: The Barn Motor Inn (Adj to airport) provides banquet and meeting facilities. Call 786-1131 or 2121

Transportation: Taxi: Prosser Transportation Service 786-1707.

Information: Richland Chamber of Commerce, 511 Lee Blvd., P.O. Box 637, Richland, WA 99352, Phone: 946-1651

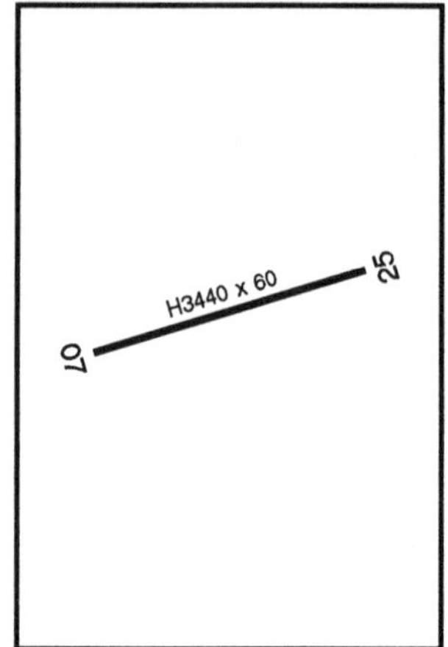

Airport Information:

PROSSER - PROSSER AIRPORT (S40)
1 mi northwest of town   N46-12.74 W119-47.57   Elev: 694   Fuel: 100LL, Mogas
Rwy 07-25: H3440x60 (Asph)   Attended: 1700-0100Z   Unicom: 122.8
FBO: Chuck's Air Service   Phone: 786-3055

WA-1S0 - PUYALLUP
PIERCE CO-THUN FIELD

(Area Code 206)

23

Hangar Inn:

The Hangar Inn is located on the Puyallup Airport, and is situated close to the aircraft parking area. The hours of this family style restaurant are Sunday through Thursday 6 a.m. to 10 p.m. and Friday and Saturday 6 a.m. to 11 p.m. Specialties of the house are a full line of breakfast selections and omelet choices along with other specials each day. rib eye and T-bone steaks as well as prime rib specials on Thursday and Friday evenings are popular dishes with many customers. In addition, they also include a salad bar, homemade pies and plenty of hot coffee. The restaurant is actually an old hangar remodeled into a dining facility with memorabilia of old planes, local artists renderings and a spectacular view of Mt. Rainier through their dining room windows. Seating for 65 people with booths and counter service is available within the restaurant, and fly-in groups and parties are welcome provided advance notice is given. A banquet room can be reserved for 50 people. For more information about the Hangar Inn, call 848-7516.

Restaurants Near Airport:
Hangar Inn   On Site   Phone: 848-7516

Lodging: Holly Hotel (6 miles) 845-9966

Meeting Rooms: None Reported

Transportation: Yellow Cab 848-2930

Information: Puyallup Area Chamber of Commerce, 322 2nd Street, Southwest, P.O. Box 1298, Puyallup, WA 98371, Phone: 845-6755.

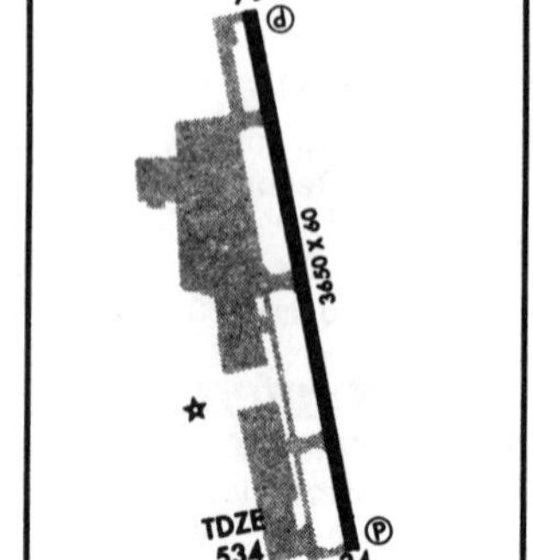

Airport Information:

PUYALLUP - PIERCE CO-THUN FIELD (1S0)
5 mi south of town   N47-06.24 W122-17.23   Elev: 534   Fuel: 80, 100,
Rwy 16-34: H3650x60 (Asph)   Attended: 1600Z-dusk   Unicom 122.8   Notes: No landing fee, overnight donation
FBO: Aero Center   Phone: 848-9349, 800-331-4375
FBO: Spanaflight   Phone: 848-2020

Not to be used for navigational purposes

WA-RNT - RENTON
RENTON MUNICIPAL AIRPORT

24

Schumsky's Restaurant:

Schumsky's Restaurant is situated adjacent and across the street from the Renton Municipal Airport. This family dining facility is open from 8 a.m. to 11 p.m. 7 days a week. The restaurant offers two basic atmospheres for their dining guests. During the day the restaurant menu features items like hamburgers, sandwiches, roast beef, pot roast, and pot pies in addition to many other popular selections. During the evening hours, their menu provides prime cuts of beef, steaks, and seafood selections. The dining room is decorated with antiques and offers a casual decor. Their lounge is open from 11 a.m. to 10 p.m. and offers live entertainment and music for evening guests. There are 3 separate rooms upstairs which can be reserved for group and party functions. Two of the smaller rooms can accommodate between 25 and 30 guests, while the larger room can seat about 120 and can be separated by a movable partition. For more information or reservations call Schumsky's Restaurant at 228-7281.

(Area Code 206)

Restaurants Near Airport:

Schumsky's Brass Rail	1 Blk SE	Phone: 228-7281
Black Angus Restaurant	1 Blk SW	Phone: Not reported
Lermond's Restaurant	1 Blk SW	Phone: Not reported
Sizzler Restaurant	1 Blk SW	Phone: Not reported

Lodging: Holiday Inn (5 blocks south of airport) 226-7700; Westwind (2 blocks south of airport) 226-5060.
Meeting Rooms: Holiday Inn (5 blocks south of airport) 226-7700.
Transportation: Taxi: OK Cab of Renton 255-3000; Rental Cars: All Star Rent-A-Car 431-1531; Car-Temps Rent-A-Car 228-9950; National Car Rental Phone: N/A;
Information: Seattle/King County Convention & Visitors Bureau, 520 Pike Street, Suite 1300, Seattle, WA 98101, Phone: 206-461-5840.

Attractions:

Museum of Flight, King County International Airport: 6 miles west of Renton Airport; Coulon Park: Picnic, boating, fishing, 2-1/2 miles south of Renton Airport; Longacres Race Track: Horse racing, 4 miles south of Renton Airport.

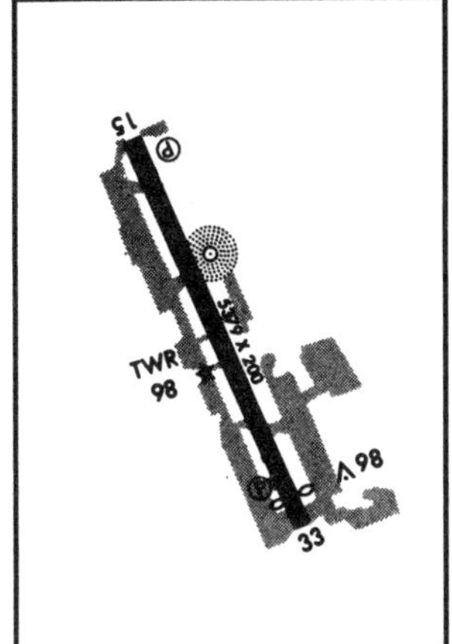

Airport Information:

RENTON - RENTON MUNICIPAL AIRPORT (RNT)
0 mi northwest of town N47-29.59 W122-12.94 Elev: 29 Fuel: 80, 100, 100LL, Jet-A1+
Rwy 15-33: H5379x200 (Asph-Conc) Attended: dawn to dusk Atis: 126.95 Unicom: 122.975 Tower: 124.7 Gnd Con: 121.6 Public Phone 24hrs
Airport Manager Phone: 235-2591

WA-9S1 - ROCHE HARBOR
ROCHE HARBOR RESORT AIRPORT

(Area Code 206) 25

Roche Harbor Resort:

This combination resort and marina facility is situated adjacent to the picturesque Roche Harbor. In 1956 the town was bought by the Tarte family and for over thirty years they have worked to bring their dream of a year-round resort to a reality. This resort contains a restaurant which is a popular local spot for dining and entertainment. Additionally, from early April through October they offer a number of amenities including, cottage rentals within the town, dining in the Roche Harbor Inn, the Olympic-size heated swimming pool, tennis courts and small boat rentals. The summer months open more amenities for your pleasure, with gift shops, sportswear shops and snack bars, both on the wharf and at poolside. Due to the popularity of the area in summer, it is recommended that you make your reservations for any event well in advance. Both English Camp National Park on the northwest side of the island and American Camp on the south end offer picnic areas, hiking trails and beautiful beaches. There are also two-hour ferry trips from San Juan Island. The Roche Harbor Restaurant is 1/2 mile south of airstrip. Fly-in visitors can walk through the archway, past the cottages and chapel. The restaurant will be located on the water's edge. Specialty items are Slow roasted, rock salted prime rib and local fresh seafood. Entree prices run $11.00 to $24.00. The decor is casual/nautical, with views overlooking the marina. Customer seating is around 100. Banquet and meeting facilities and on-sit e catering is available for groups up to 150 persons. Transportation from the airport to and from the restaurant may be available depending on available staff. The airport at Roche Harbor is private, and permission to land may be obtained by phoning the resort in advance. There is a $5.00 landing fee. Also overnight aircraft parking is $5.00. During your stay you can rent mopeds, bicycles or obtain rental cars offered at Friday Harbor on the southeast side of the island. Whether it's brunch, dinner, a personal retreat or a planned business conference, large or small, the professional staff at Roche Harbor Resort is ready to assist you in making your visit a pleasant one. For more information you can call the resort at 378-2155.

Restaurants Near Airport:

Roche Harbor Resort	Adj Arpt.	Phone: 378-2155

Lodging: Roche Harbor Resort contains several accommodations within the Hotel De Haro, nearby condominiums, or their company town cottages, Phone: 378-2155.
Meeting Rooms: Roche Harbor Resort (Pavilion) can accommodate 150 for meetings, banquets, receptions and other special events. For information call 378-2155.
Transportation: Taxi Service: 378-4711; Rental Cars are available by calling 378-2155, or call the resort at 378-2155 for more information.
Information: For more information call Roche Harbor Resort at their reservation office. Phone: 378-2155 or write Roche Harbor, Resort & Marina, P.O. Box 4001, Roche Harbor, WA 98250.

Photo by: Washington State Tourism Development Division

The Hotel de Haro, Roche Harbor Resort

Attractions:

Allow your gathering to benefit from the allure of a 200-acre historic compound surrounded by formal gardens and lawns amidst fir forests on the banks of Roche Harbor in the Puget Sound. All but their modern condominiums were built about 1886. The marina complex that once harbored three-masted schooners on their way around the world, now has all the modern facilities for yachting. The resort offers tennis and swimming in season with golf, fishing and nature tours nearby. For information about accommodations and services of Roche Harbor Resort & Marina call 378-2155 or 800-451-8910.

Airport Information:

ROCHE HARBOR - ROCHE HARBOR RESORT PRIVATE AIRPORT (9S1)
1/2 mi northeast of town N48-28-12 W123-08-12 Elev: 100 Fuel: None Reported
CTAF: 128.25 Rwy 06-24: 4500x35 (Asph) Attended: unattended Notes:The airport at Roche Harbor is private and permission to land may be obtained by telephoning the resort in advance. Also landing fee: $5.00, overnight parking fee $5.00. (Pvt. Arpt. land at your own risk).
FBO: Roche Harbor Resort Phone: 378-2155
ROCHE HARBOR SPB - (WA50)
0 mi southwest of town N48-36.49 W123-09.58 Waterway NE-SW: 5000x1000 (Water)
Waterway NW-SE: 2500x500 (Water) Attended: unattended CTAF: 128.25 Unicom: 123.0
FBO: Roche Harbor Resort Phone: 378-2155

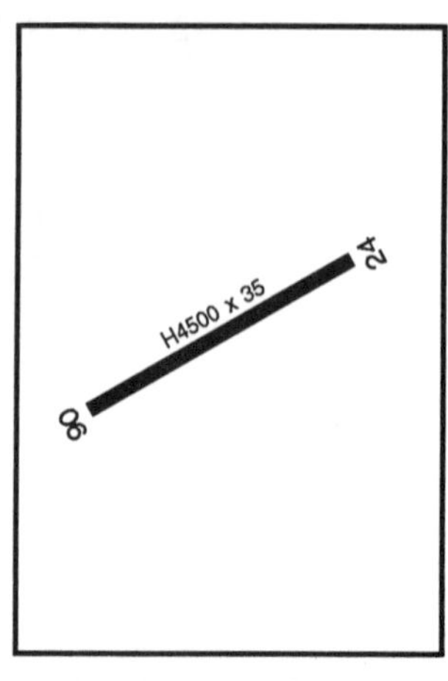

San Juan Islands:

Articles & Information in part by:
San Juan Island Visitors Information Service.

Eastsound, WA (WA-ORS)
Friday Harbor, WA (WA-FHR)
Roche Harbor, WA (WA-Pvt.)

The San Juan Islands of Washington State include: Orcas Island, Lopez Island, San Juan Island and Shaw Island. Surrounding mountain ranges help produce an eternally moderate climate. Temperatures seldom top 80 degrees in the summer or fall below 30 degrees in the winter. The islands also enjoy an average of 247 days of sunshine. When rainfall occurs, it is normally soft and misty, and snowfall is usually a rare treat. Windbreakers, water-resistant footwear and lightweight sweaters can come in handy all year. Each island offers a natural, relaxed environment with a variety of recreational activities. Many of these opportunities are available most months of the year. Hiking, biking, sailing, kayaking, birding, golfing, fishing, scuba diving, museum and gallery exploring and shopping. For a spectacular bird's-eye view of the islands, both Eastsound and Friday Harbor offer guests scenic flight tours. Orcas Aerodrome Inc. even offers biplane adventures for two.

Roche Harbor Resort Airport (9S1) is located on the north end of San Juan Island. The resort offers tennis and swimming in season with golf, fishing and nature tours nearby. Their private 4,500' airstrip is locaed adjacent to the resort. Prior permission for use is obtained by calling 378-2155. Landing fee $5.00, also overnight parking fee of $5.00. The restaurant is located 1/2 mile south of the airstrip. Walk through the archway, past the cottages and chapel. It will be located along the waters' edge overlooking the marina.

Of the four islands, **Orcas Island:** is the largest. It has also been a favorite for generations of vacation seekers. The population is widely dispersed which gives the feeling of privacy. Roads wind through wide valleys and past deep forested coves, and then fan out from the business and social center of Eastsound village. Skippered sailing charters and scheduled whale cruises depart from this island.

The next island, **Lopez Island**, appeals to those seeking quiet relaxation. Its mostly level terrain makes it a favorite for cycling. The landscape includes pastures with scattered sheep and cows, old orchards and weathered barns. The Olympic Mountains serve as a scenic backdrop. Lopez Village, located on Fisherman Bay, is the community hub for shopping and dining.

For those who prefer a little hustle and bustle, **San Juan Island** is the busiest and most populated. The ferry lands at **Friday Harbor** which is the largest town and county seat of all the islands. Friday Harbor is a town, located on the densely forested San Juan Island (a fly-in favorite). It is just a 10-minute walk through the woods from the island's airport (FHR). Of all the airports in the island area, Friday Harbor (FHR) has the most services available. This airport also can become very busy at times. Noise abatement procedures are in effect and strictly enforced. This is a large, mountainous island that offers shops, galleries and museums. Visitors can go biking, or visit the marina and rent a sea kayak or go whale-watching, or even scuba diving. The port bustles all year with fishing boats. Saltwater fishing charters, as well as skippered sailing charters and whale cruises, also depart from there. From mid-May until mid-September, three pods of killer (Orca) whales frequent the islands and may sometimes be observed from land. The Whale Museum in the town of Friday Harbor is open all year. Many of the island's amenities and facilities are within walking distance or available by public transportation from the ferry landing. Public beach access is also available. For history buffs, the San Juan National Historical Park also offers re-enactments of earlier settlers' lives.

Shaw Island is the smallest of the four ferry-served islands. It covers less than 5000 acres, and it does not have any visitor facilities except for a grocery store and a small campground at South Beach. An ideal getaway for the outdoors-man!

For those who have a taste for the arts, concerts, plays, musicals, exhibits and other fun events, there are regularly scheduled shows at the Orcas Center, Eastsound and the San Juan Community Theatre, Friday Harbor. Special events include the popular Jazz Festival on the last weekend in July, the County Fair in August and other small festivals, auctions, bazaars and regattas throughout the year.

Lodging is available year-round on the islands of Orcas, Lopez and San Juan. Choices range from rustic cabins to full service resorts. Guests can choose from fully renovated turn-of-the-century hotels and farmhouses to condominiums and bed and breakfast establishments. Advance reservations are recommended for the summer, early fall, holidays and weekends.

Camping near lakes, saltwater and woods is also another way to enjoy overnight visits. There are many tent sites in county, state and private campgrounds. It is recommended that summer reservations be obtained where they are available (especially for groups).

For those with an appetite for seafood or just plain food, the islands offer several dining-out possibilities, ranging from picnics-to-go to fine cuisine featuring fresh local specialties. Since all restaurants are relatively casual in style, guests my leave their coats and ties at home.

For transportation: Orcas Island Airport (ORS) near Eastsound, WA is the farthest north in the cluster of San Juan Island airports. It is located 1 mile north of the center of town. Roche Harbor Airport (Private Strip) is on the north end of San Juan Island and the furthest west of the island group. Friday Harbor Airport (FHR) is situated on the southeast end of San Juan Island. Lopez Island Airport (Private strip) is the southern most located airport of the group. And Blakely Island also has a private strip. Once on the island of your choice, ferry service can be an alternative for your inter-island connections. Oversized vehicles, bicycles and kayaks are allowed on ferries. Usually, ferries make stops in this order: Lopez (45 min.), Shaw (1 hr.), Orcas (1 hr., 20 min.), and San Juan/Friday Harbor (2 hrs.) The ferry schedule changes several times a year and is not available far in advance. Contact the Washington State Ferries at 800-84-FERRY (33779) or 464-6400 for more information.

For further information about the San Juan Islands, contact the San Juan Islands Visitor Information Service at 468-3663.

WA-BFI - SEATTLE
BOEING FLD/KING CO., INTL.

Restaurants Near Airport: **(Area Code 206)** **26**

CAVU Cafe   Main Trml. Bldg.   Phone: 767-7670

Lodging: Holiday Inn, (Free Transportation), Phone: 762-0300.
Meeting Rooms: Holiday Inn, Phone 762-0300.
Transportation: Budget Rental Car, 763-0350 or 764-6100
Information: Seattle/King County Convention & Visitors Bureau, 520 Pike Street, Suite 1300, Seattle, WA 98101, Phone: 461-5840

Attractions:

Museum of Flight: This museum is located right on the premises of the Boeing/King County International Airport. It contains over 40 aircraft on display, and exhibits the realm of flight from its beginning through the 1930's, as well as modern flight and the exploration of space within the Great Gallery. Transportation can be obtained through one of the FBO's on the field. For more information call 764-5700.

CAVU Cafe:

The CAVU Cafe is situated on the Boeing/King County International Airport within the main terminal lobby. This restaurant has become a favorite of many local folks along with employees on Boeing Field's and fly-in customers traveling through the area and especially those planning a visit to the incredible "Museum of Flight" (Featured Article on next page). The CAVU Cafe serves homemade soups, fresh deli and panini (Italian bread) sandwiches, and beverages including, of course, your favorite espresso drinks. All this can be enjoyed in the pleasant atrium like setting of the lobby, with live tropical plants around you and beautiful stained glass skylights overhead. Or you could take your meal outside to sit by a gently splashing fountain (titled "Crystals", circa 1982) and watch as airplanes of all types take off and land (Boeing Field is a General Aviation airport serving a wide variety of aircraft). Restaurant hours are 6 a.m. to 3:30 p.m. Monday through Friday and 10 a.m. to 3 p.m. on Saturday. So if you're looking for a great little spot to get out of the busyness, visit West Isle Air and the CAVU Cafe at Boeing Field. What could be better than combining a trip to the Museum of Flight and a fine meal at the CAVU Cafe. For information call West Isle Air at 800-874-4434 or the CAVU Cafe at 764-4929.

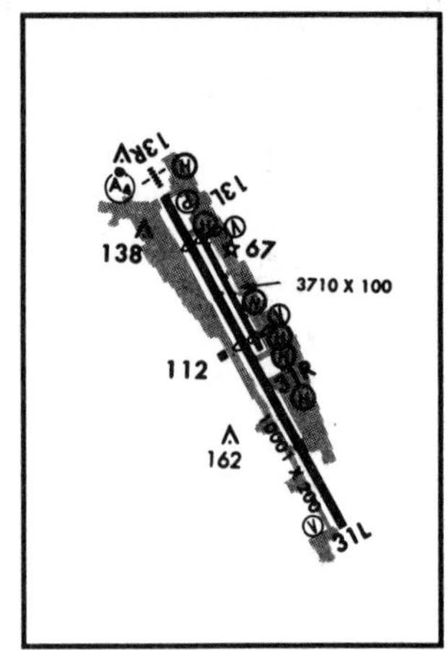

Airport Information:

SEATTLE - BOEING FLD/KING CO INTL. (BFI)
4 mi south of town N47-31.80 W122-18.12 Elev: 18 Fuel: 80, 100, 100LL, Jet-A Rwy 13R-31L: H10001x200 (Asph-Grvd) Rwy 13L-31R: H3710x100 (Asph) Attended: continuously Unicom: 122.95 Atis: 127.75 Boeing Tower: 120.6, 118.3 Gnd Con: 121.9 Clnc Del: 118.9 Notes: $5.00 parking fee 24hrs (First 8 hrs Free); No landing Fee. See aeronautical charts for TCA information.
FBO: Galvin Flying   Phone: 763-0350, 800-341-4102
FBO: Flight Center   Phone: 768-0800, 800-768-1101

A Little Extra Planning Can Make Each One Of Your Excursions More Rewarding

"Just Call Ahead"

Even though we at Aerodine strive to provide the latest information possible at the time of printing, we suggest you take a little time and call ahead to verify that the facility you intend to visit still provides the same services as published. Your comments regarding any changes in these services or about new establishments you have found, are greatly appreciated. With your help, we can include them in our next updated edition.

Aerodine Magazine
P.O. Box 247, Palatine, IL 60078
Phone: 847-358-4355

The Museum of Flight

The Museum of Flight is an independent, non-profit cultural foundation dedicated to the preservation of aircraft and related artifacts, as well as to the knowledge, enjoyment and self-discovery of flight. Founded in 1964 as the Pacific Northwest Aviation Historical Foundation, the museum is located in Seattle at the southwest corner of Boeing Field/King County International Airport, site of Seattle's first powered airplane flight in 1910 and one of the top 15 busiest airports in the country today.

The Museum of Flight opened its first wing at this location in 1983 in the historic "Red Barn," the Boeing Company's original manufacturing plant. Built in 1909, the Red Barn was donated to the Museum of Flight by the Port of Seattle in 1975 and moved to its present location at Boeing Field/King County International Airport that same year.

Restoration of the Red Barn was completed in 1983 and marked the first phase in an extensive two-part program to build a world-class air and space museum in the Pacific Northwest. The second phase, the Great Gallery, opened to the public in July 1987.

Exhibits in the Red Barn trace aviation history from its early beginnings through 1938. Displays include a restored 1917 Curtiss Jenny biplane; a 1929 Curtiss Robin; and authentic recreation of an aircraft manufacturing wood shop; and a working replica of the wind tunnel used by the Wright Brothers.

Exhibits in the Great Gallery chronicle the story of flight from mythology to the early days of wood and all metal-aircraft, to the latest accomplishments in air and space technology. Currently there are over 40 full-size aircraft on display, with 22 of those suspended from the space-frame roof. These exhibits will be expanded and enhanced over the next five years, eventually resulting in displays of approximately 45 air-and-space craft.

The 185,075 square foot Museum of Flight complex, including the Red Barn, also includes a 268-seat theater and auditorium, several special events meeting rooms, extensive educational facilities, a library, and the largest aviation archives on the west coast. The Museum of Flight was made possible by over $30 million in private contributions by individuals and companies around the world.

The Museum of Flight is located at 9404 East Marginal Way South and is open daily 10:00 a.m. to 5:00 p.m. and until 9:00 p.m. on Thursdays. Admission is $8.00 for adults, $4.00 ages 6 through 12, and free for children under 6 years of age. Groups of 10 or more visitors is $4.00 per person. For visitors information please call 206-764-5720. (Information submitted by museum)

Museum Flightfest

The Museum of Flight hosts its annual Emerald City Flight Festival within the month of July each year. The two-day family orientated air show and aviation festival, features acrobatic performances, fly-bys, static aircraft displays, musical entertainment, and hands-on educational programs for all ages. Over 50 aircraft are expected to participate in this event.

Show hours are normally 10:00 a.m. to 5:00 p.m. both Saturday and Sunday. The Flightfest tickets in the past have been priced at $7.00 for adults, $5.00 for children ages 6 through 15 and free for children under six years of age. Automobile parking is included in the admission. The site of the spectator area is normally located on the Museum of Flight property. An additional $1.00 fee is required to access the Museum of Flight Galleries during that particular weekend. For information and current dates, admission fees and airshow schedules call 206-764-5720.

Photo: by Museum of Flight

Photo: by Museum of Flight

The Museum of Flight Collection Includes:

Pioneers:
Boeing B & W (replica)
Lilienthal Glider (replica - 1896)
Wright Glider (replica - 1902)

Military Aircraft:
Aeronca L-3B "Grasshopper" (1941)
Boeing B-17F "Flying Fortress
Boeing B-47E "Sratojet"
Boeing P-12/Model 100
Canadair F86 Sabre
Convair L-13, Curtiss JN-4D "Jenny"
de Havilland DH.115 "Vampire"
Dornier DO.27
Fiat G.91 PAN
Hiller YH-32 (helicopter)
Lockeed A-12 Blackbird
Northrop F-18L (mockup)
Northrop YF-5A
Piasecki H-21B (helicopter)
Stearman PT-13

Naval Aircraft:
Convair XF2Y-1 "Sea Dart"
Douglas A-4F "Skyhawk (Blue Angels)
General Motors FM-2 "Wildcat"
Goodyear FG-1D "Corsair"
Grumman F9F-8 "Cougar"
Gyrodyne QH-50C
Lockheed TV-1 "Shooting Star"
Sikorsky HH-52)USCG helicopter)
Vought XF8U-1 "Crusader"

Spacecraft:
Apollo Command Module (NASA)
Mercury Space Capsule (mock-up)

General Aviation:
Aerocar III, Aeronca C-2
Beech 18
Curtiss Robin
Erco Ercoupe 415-C
Fairchild F-24W
Fournier RF-4D
Howard DGA-15
JAMCO N-62
Lear Fan 2100
Nord 1000 (Me.108)
OMAC-1 (Executive transport)
Stinson SR "Reliant"

Sport & Homebuilt Acrft:
Taylorcraft A
Taylorcraft BC-12
Aero Sport "Scamp"
Benson Gyrocopter B-8M
Bowers Fly Baby
Bowlus Baby Albatross
Cessna CG-2 (Glider)
Durand Mk.V
Eipper Cumulus
Kasperwing 180-B
Let LF-107 Lunak (Sailplane)
Rutan Varieze
Rutan VarViggen
Sorrell Bathtub "Cool Crow"
Task "Silhouette"
Thorp T-18
Wickham B
Wizard J-2
McAllister "Yakima Clipper" (sailplane)
Republican P-47D (replica)
Rotec Rally III-B, Rotorway "Scorpion"
Rutan Quickie

WA-S43 - SNOHOMISH HARVEY FIELD

(Area Code 360) 27, 28

Collector's Choice Restaurant:

This restaurant is located 8-1/2 blocks (across the bridge), from the airport in the heart of the largest antique mall in Snohomish. To reach the restaurant turn right onto First Street and go 4 blocks, turn left onto Union and then right onto Glen. This is a family-style restaurant and is open from 7 a.m. to 9 p.m. The Collector's Choice Restaurant provides delicious home-style meals, reasonable prices, friendly fast service and a homey atmosphere. Breakfasts are hearty. Homemade buttermilk pancakes, bran muffins and fresh-baked biscuits, omelettes and cottage fries will tempt your taste buds. Fresh roasted turkey sandwiches, prime ribs, chicken and crispy salads are only a few choices. Dinner features choice prime rib, New York and sirloin steaks, Filet Mignon, ribeye, T-bone steaks, poultry and fowl selection, prawns, a large seafood listing and a huge fettuccine selection. Prices range from $4.50 for breakfast and lunch. For dinner the average price is $12.95. The decor of this restaurant is elegant and decorated in a Victorian motif with a 3-star rating. For information call 568-1277.

Harvey's Airport Restaurant:

This restaurant is located right on the Snohomish Harvey's Field. This establishment is operated in conjunction with Snohomish Flying Service (FBO). Serving local and fly-in customers Harvey's Airport Restaurant can satisfy your hunger while you fuel up your aircraft. Lodging is also available on site. For information call the restaurant at 568-3970.

Airport Information:

SNOHOMISH - HARVEY FIELD (S43)
1 mi southwest of town N47-54.49 W122-06.32 Elev: 16 Fuel 80, 100, Jet-A
Rwy 14-32: H2660x36 (Asph) Rwy 13-31: 2400x75 (Turf) Attended: Nov-Mar 1530-0200Z Apr-Oct 1530-0500Z Unicom: 123.0 Notes: See AFD for airport information; P-lines Rwy 13 & Rwy 14; No takeoffs Rwy 31. Parachute jumping, Moored balloon opr.
FBO: Snohomish Flying Service Phone: 568-1541

Restaurants Near Airport:

Harvey's At Arpt.	On Site	Phone: 568-3970
Collector's Choice	8.5 blks NE	Phone: 568-1277
Townsend's Deli	1/2 blk N.	Phone: 568-4333
Silver King Cafe	1 block E.	Phone: 568-4589

Lodging: Harvey Lodging (On Arpt) 568-9622; Everett Pacific Hotel (Free Trans.) 800-833-8011; Countryman's Bed & Breakfast (4 Blocks) 568-9622.
Meeting Rooms: Harvey's At The Airport has 3 conference rooms and Everett Pacific Hotel located 6 miles from the airport also provides meeting and conference rooms, 339-3333.
Transportation: Courtesy transportation or walk to restaurants nearby; Snohomish Flying Service 568-1541; Also A #1 Rent-A-Car 259-5058.
Information: Chamber of Commerce, 116 Avenue B, Waltz Building, Box 135, Snohomish, WA, 98290, Phone: 568-2526

Attractions:

Sport parachuting and ballooning is often done at Harvey Field and provides entertainment for visitors; Kenwanda Golf Course (2 miles) 668-1166; 100 stores in this town provide one of the largest, if not the largest antique mall in the northwest region.

NO AIRPORT DIAGRAM AVAILABLE

WA-SFF - SPOKANE FELTS FIELD

(Area Code 509) 29

Skyway Cafe:

The Skyway Cafe is located on Felts Field at the airport terminal building. When arriving at Felts Field, we were told that you can park your aircraft in front of the restaurant within the designated areas. The cafe is open Monday through Friday from 6:30 a.m. to 3:00 p.m. and Saturday and Sunday 6:30 a.m. to 2:30 p.m. Their menu contains items like Rueben sandwiches, hamburgers, steaks and chicken fried steak, sandwiches, soups, salads, desserts, along with a full assortment of breakfast entrees. This cafe offers a comfortable and quaint atmosphere decorated with black and white checkered table cloths, as well as a nice view of the aircraft parking area and ramp right outside their restaurant. This Mom & Pop operation contains smoking and non-smoking sections and can accommodate up to 120 guests for breakfast and lunch. Two rooms divided by a semi-walled partition provide groups and parties with private dining. Several combination meals with meat, vegetable, mashed potatoes, roll and dessert is offered every day along with other specials. For more information call the Skyway Cafe at 534-5986.

Airport Information:

SPOKANE - FELTS FIELD (SFF)
0 mi north of town N47-40.98 W117-19.35 Elev: 1953 Fuel: 80, 100, 100LL, Jet-A1+
Rwy 03L-21R: H4500x150 (Conc) Rwy 03R-21L: H3059x75 (Asph) Attended 1500-0200Z
Atis: 120.55 Unicom: 122.95 Spokane App/Dep Con: 133.35 Tower: 132.5 Gnd Con: 121.7 Public phone 24hrs Notes: No landing fees, Parking fees by FBO's.
FBO: Felts Field Aviation Phone: 535-9011

Restaurants Near Airport:

Skyway Cafe	On Site	Phone: 534-5986

Lodging: Cavanaugh's Inn-Park 326-8000; Cavanaugh's River Inn (Free trans) 326-5577; Ridpath Hotel (Free trans) 838-2711.
Meeting Rooms: All lodging facilities listed above contain accommodations for meeting rooms; Convention facilities: Sheraton Inn (3 blocks W of US 2/395) Phone: 455-9600.
Transportation: Felts Field Aviation 535-9011 and Loranger Aviation 535-8836 both have courtesy cars available to local facilities; Also Spokane Cab 326-4536; Hertz 747-0540; National 624-8995; Avis 747-8081; Budget 838-8662; Dollar 624-4253.
Information: Convention & Visitors Bureau, West 926 Sprague Ave., Suite 180, Spokane, WA 99204, Phone: 747-3230.

Attraction:

Four golf courses within the city; Spokane Riverfront Park contains IMAX theater, opera house, Spokane River, amusement park, picnicking, outdoor amphitheater, petting zoo, restaurants and vendors, 100 acre recreation site with activities for children and adults. For information call 456-5512; Flour Mill adjacent to Riverfront Park, Phone: 838-7970.

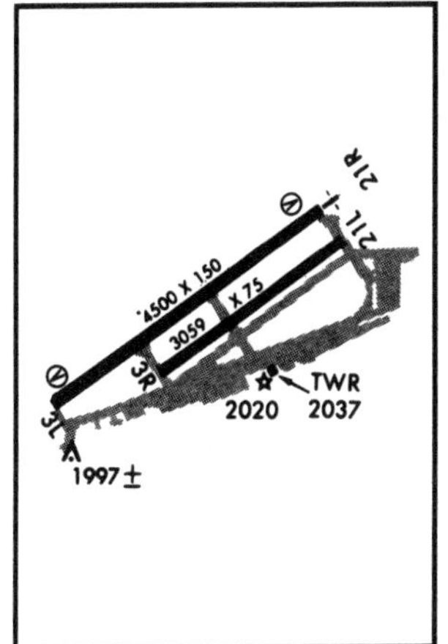

WA-GEG - SPOKANE
SPOKANE INTERNATIONAL

(Area Code 509) **30, 31**

Lefty's Northern Trail Bar & Grill:

Lefty's Northern Trail Bar & Grill is located within the terminal building on the Spokane International Airport. This is considered an upscale family style restaurant. Entrees on their menu include marinated flank steak, grilled chicken, Saesur salads, cheeseburgers, tuna steak sandwiches, a variety of sandwiches along with fresh soups. They even make their own chips. Average prices run $6.50 to $8.50 for most selections. Seasonal entrees are also prepared as well. The decor of this dining establishment is modern and serves as a combination family and sports bar facility. Their main dining room can seat 125 persons. Decorating the walls are a variety of paintings, artwork, and sports related renderings. In-flight catering is also a service provided. For information call Lefty's Northern Trail Bar & Grill at 624-3400.

Americano's Pizza ("C" Concourse):

This restaurant offers a variety of Italian Pizza's and is operated by the same people that runs Lefty's Northern Trail Bar & Grill. For information about either restaurant call 624-3400.

Airport Information:

SPOKANE - SPOKANE INTERNATIONAL (GEG)
5 mi southwest of town N47-37.19 W117-32.00 Elev: 2372 Fuel: 100, 100LL, Jet-A
Rwy 03-21: H9000x150 (Asph-Grvd) Rwy 07-25: H8199x150 (Asph) Attended: 1400-0600Z
Atis 127.8 Unicom: 122.95 App/Dep Con: 133.35 Tower: 118.3 Gnd Con: 121.9
Clnc Del: 127.55 Public Phone 24hrs Notes: No landing fee; Parking charged by FBO's
FBO: Spokane Airways Phone: 747-2017

Restaurants Near Airport:

Lefty's Bar & Grill	Trml Bldg	Phone: 624-3400
Americano's Pizza	Trml Bldg	Phone: 624-3400
Ramada Inn	Adj Arpt.	Phone: 838-5211

Lodging: Cavanaugh's River Inn (5 miles) 326-5577; Holiday Inn (3 miles) 747-2021; Quality Inn (3 miles) 838-1471; Quality Inn Valley Suites 928-5218; Ramada Inn (Adj. Airport) 838-5211; Ridpath Hotel (5 miles) 838-6122; Shilo Inns (8 miles) 535-9000.
Meeting Rooms: Cavanaugh's River Inn 326-5577; Quality Inn 838-1471; Quality Inn Valley Suites 928-5218; Ramada Inn 838-5211; Shilo Inns 535-9000.
Transportation: Courtesy furnished by FBO's: Spokane Airways 838-3658; Flightcraft 747-2017; Also rental cars available: Spokane Cars 326-4536; Hertz 747-0540; National 624-8995; Avis 747-8081; Budget 838-1434; Dollar 624-4253.
Information: The Spokane Regional Convention & Visitors Bureau, West 926 Sprague Ave, Suite 180, Spokane, WA 99204, Phone: 747-3230.

Attractions:

Indian Canyon Golf Course 2 miles; Numerous points of interest in this region. Contact Spokane Regional Convention & Visitors Bureau for information. Phone: 747-3230 (Address listed above).

WA-TIW - TACOMA NARROWS - WASHINGTON (Aera Code 206) 32, 33
TACOMA NARROWS AIRPORT

Fresh Aire Cafe:

A new and unique way to enjoy dining in the Gig Harbor Peninsula area. The restaurant is located at the Tacoma Narrows Airport, which is surrounded by beautiful evergreens. The cafe offers a full breakfast menu. Pilots and associates of the airport also fill the cafe for lunch. The lunch menu lists numerous sandwiches and other mid-day entrees. The dinner menu offers a little for everyone. Seafood, beef and chicken entrees are prepared in ways that will keep you flying back for more. The nightly specials are from the world of fine dining without the fine dining price. There is a separate dining room for groups up to 18 people. The cafe is closed on Monday nights to accommodate larger groups between 40-60 people. The winter hours are Friday and Saturday from 6:30 a.m. to 9:30 p.m., Tuesday & Sunday from 6:30 a.m. to 8:30 p.m.; and Monday from 6:30 a.m. to 3:30 p.m. For reservations call 851-5266.

Span Deli Restaurant:

Span Deli restaurant is located about 1 mile east of Tacoma Narrows Airport. This cafe is a comfortable mom and pop restaurant that serves burgers, sandwiches, shakes, pizza, salads, soups and breakfast selections. They are open Monday through Saturday from 8 a.m. to 8 p.m. and on Sunday from 10:30 a.m. to 8 p.m. Average prices are $3.00 for breakfast, $4.00 for lunch and $4.50 for dinner. The restaurant often caters to organizations and clubs arranging parties, and will provide catering for pilots on-the-go. To reach the restaurant by car, travel north on Airport Road until you come to a stop sign. Turn right and go 2/3 of a mile. The restaurant will provide fly-in guests with transportation if possible. Calling ahead is suggested. The phone number for the restaurant is 206-851-6611.

Attractions:

Charters & Tours; Cascade Trailways Tours & Charters, 2209 Pacific Avenue, Tacoma 98402, 206-383-4615. Cruises & Charters; Adventure Travel, 9021 Pacific Ave, Tacoma 98444, 206-531-1757.

Restaurants Near Airport:

Fresh Aire Cafe	On Site	206-851-5266
Span Deli	1 mi. E.	206-851-6611
Cimarron Restaurant	3 mi. N.	206-851-6665
Shoreline Restaurant	5 mi. N.	206-851-9822

Lodging: LaQuinta Inn 383-0146, 11 mi., Sheraton 572-3200, 8 mi., Sherwoood Inn 535-2800, 12 mi., Shilo Inn 475-4020, 11 mi.

Transportation: Radio Taxi 627-2525, Yellow Cab 472-3303, Budget & API Rentals 851-2381, National Car Rental 851-5577.

Information: Tacoma-Pierce County Visitor & Convention Bureau, 906 Broadway, P.O. Box 1754, Tacoma, WA 98401, 627-2836, 800-272-2662.

Airport Information:

TACOMA - TACOMA NARROWS (TIW)

4 west of city N47-16.08 W122-34.69 Elev: 292 Fuel: 100LL, Jet A,
Rwy. 17-35 H5002x150 (Asph-Afsc) Attended: 1600Z-0400Z CTAF 118.5
Atis 124.05 Unicom 122.9 Tower: 118.5 Gnd Con: 121.8
Notes: Overnight Parking; $2.00/single, $3.00/twin.
FBO: Crossings Aviation Phone: 851-2381, 800-925-1490
FBO: Pavco Flight Center Phone: 851-5577, 800-645-3563

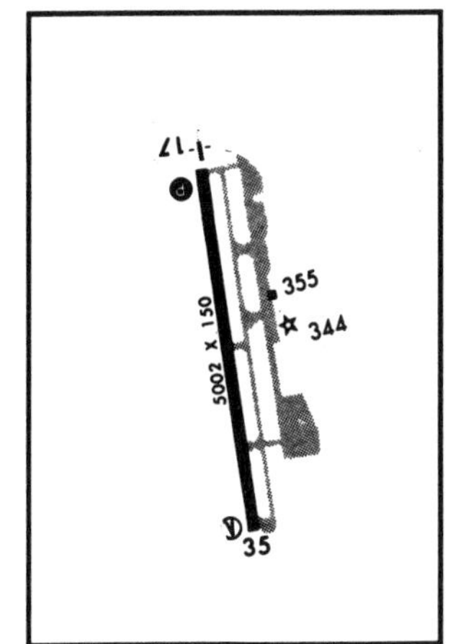

WA-ALW - WALLA WALLA
WALLA WALLA REGIONAL AIRPORT

(Area Code 509) 34

Swans At The Airport:

This restaurant is located next to the terminal building at the Walla Walla Regional Airport. Their restaurant hours are 6 a.m. to 9 p.m. 7 days a week. The lounge is open from Friday and Saturday 6 a.m. to 12:00 a.m. and Monday through Thursday 6 a.m. to 11 p.m. Their menu contains a full breakfast line along with steak and seafood, club sandwiches, hamburgers, soups and pies. They specialize in prime rib on Friday and Saturday night in addition to 1 or 2 specials offered each day. Average prices run $3.50 for breakfast, $4.50 for lunch and $5.50 to $6.95 for dinner. The restaurant can seat 65 to 70 people for dinner. You can enjoy a view of the airport and its activity while having your meal. A special section is available for larger groups able to accommodate up to 40 people. For more information call Swans At The Airport 529-4380.

Restaurants Near Airport:

Swans At The Airport	On Site	Phone: 529-4380
Mr. Ed's Restaurant	1 mi S.	Phone: 525-8440
The Modern Restaurant	1-1/2 mi SW	Phone: 525-8662
Blue Mountain Tavern	1-1/2 mi SW	Phone: 525-9941

Lodging: Whiteman Inn (4 miles, 107 N 2nd) 525-2200;

Meeting Rooms: Mountain States Aviation (FBO) 525-2180; Tommy's At The Airport 529-4380;

Transportation: ABC Taxi 529-7726; A-1 Taxi 529-2525; Valley Transit 525-9140; Budget Rent-A-Car 525-8811; U-Save Auto Rentals 525-1680;

Information: Chamber of Commerce, 29 E. Sumach, P.O. Box 644, Walla Walla, WA 99362, Phone: 525-0850, 800-743-9562.

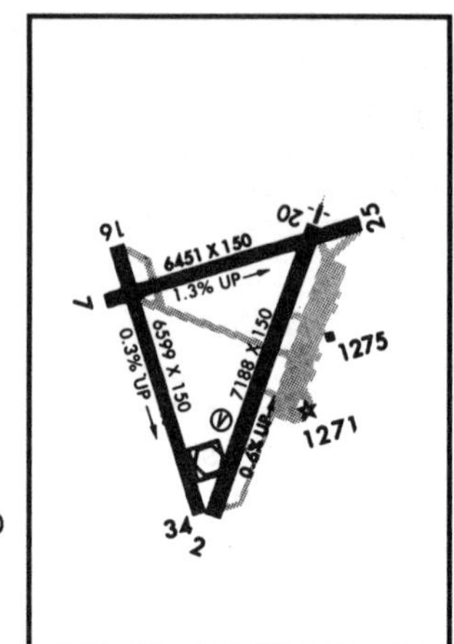

Attractions:

Veterans/Memorial Golf Course (4 miles) 201 E. Rees, Phone: 527-4507; Fort Walla Walla (1 mile west of WA-125, West edge of town) Camping facilities, Fort Walla Walla Museum Complex 14 buildings from the mid 1800's with tours, June-September daily and on weekends in May and October, Phone: 525-7703.

Airport Information:

WALLA WALLA - WALLA WALLA REGIONAL AIRPORT (ALW)
3 mi northeast of town N46-05.67 W118-17.28 Elev: 1205 Fuel: 80, 100LL, Jet-A
Rwy 02-20: H7188x150 (Asph-Pfc) Rwy 16-34: H6599x150 (Asph-Conc) Rwy 07-25: H6451x150 (Asph-Conc) Attended: 1500-0400Z CTAF: 118.5 Unicom: 122.95 Tower: 118.5
Gnd Con: 121.6 Notes: $3.00 per night for single engine, $5.00 per night for twin engine.
FBO: Mountain States Aviation Phone: 525-2180

WA-2S5 - WATERVILLE
WATERVILLE AIRPORT

(Area Code 509) 35

Waterville Cafe & Lounge:

Waterville Cafe & Lounge is a family style restaurant located about 1 mile from the Waterville Airport. This restaurant specializes in good home cooking, and offers a variety of specials on Friday and Saturday. On Friday they feature prime rib. Breakfast selections are available all day. The decor is simple and comfortable. Party and group gatherings are welcome. However, they ask that you give them a weeks notice so they can prepare ahead of time. Meals-to-go can also be arranged. The restaurant is open 6 a.m. to 9 p.m. daily. Prices for meals range from between $5.00 to $8.50. They will be more than happy to furnish transportation to fly-in guests. Just give them a call. We were told that it is possible to obtain a courtesy car at the airport or else walk to either Barns Welding & Machine 745-8588 or Custom Mufflers 745-8241 and use their phone to call the restaurant for transportation. We suggest however, that you call in advance so you can be certain of courtesy transportation. To call the restaurant dial 745-8319.

Restaurants Near Airport:

Kopey's Restaurant	1-1/2 mi.	Phone: 745-8016
Waterville Cafe	1-1/2 mi.	Phone: 745-8319
Knemeyer's Tavern	In Town	Phone: 745-8348

Lodging: Jack's Resort, P.O. Box E, Waterville 98858, Phone: 683-1095

Transportation: None Reported

Information: Waterville Chamber of Commerce, P.O. Box 628, 109 Locust Street, Waterville, WA 98858.

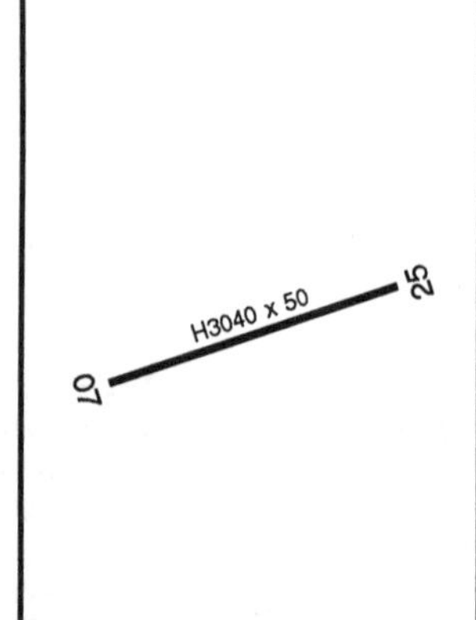

Airport Information:

WATERVILLE - WATERVILLE (2S5)
1 mi NE of town N47-39.24 W120-03.32 Elev: 2640 Rwy 07-25: H3040x50 (Asph)
Attended: Unattended CTAF: 122.9 Notes: Public phone available at Barns Welding 745-8588, or Custom Mufflers 745-8241 located adjacent to airport.
Airport Manager: Douglas County Dept. of Public Works, P.O. Box 100 Waterville, WA 98858, Phone: 745-8595

WA-EAT - WENATCHEE
PANGBORN MEMORIAL AIRPORT

(Area Code 509)

36

Apple Shoppe Restaurant:

The Airport Cafe is located on the far north end of the airport in the new terminal building. This cafe is open between 6 a.m. and 6 p.m. 7 days a week. They serve a full breakfast menu along with a variety of bakery goods, pies, cinnamon rolls and turnovers. For lunch and early dinner they offer a salad bar with hamburgers, specialty sandwiches and deli items like soups, chili, and stew. The restaurant can seat 39 persons and has tables as well as counter service. A conference room is available for business meetings situated within the terminal building near the General Manager's office . For more information call the Airport Cafe at 884-4789.

Attractions:

3 golf courses, and numerous county and state parks located nearby. Winter skiing and several lakes for fishing, boating and water skiing. For more information contact Wenatchee Area Visitor & Convention Bureau, listed above.

Restaurants Near Airport:

Airport Cafe	Adj. Arpt.	Phone: 884-4789
Chieftain Restaurant & Motel	6 mi W.	Phone: 663-7188
David Brown's	2 mi W.	Phone: 884-0514
Horan House	10 mi W.	Phone: 663-0018

Lodging: Wenatchee, West Coast Hotel 1-800-426-0670; Nendels 884-6611; Chieftian, Rivers Inn 884-1474.

Meeting Rooms: Ecexutive Flight (FBO) on the airport has conference room available 884-0533.

Transportation: Courtesy car available through Executive Flight 884-0533 as well as Taxi: Courtesy Cab 662-2126; Woody's Cab 884-0358; Rental Cars: Budget 663-2626; Hertz 884-6900; National 884-8686.

Information: Wenatchee Area Visitor & Convention Bureau, P.O. Box 850, Wenatchee, WA 98801, Phone: 662-4774.

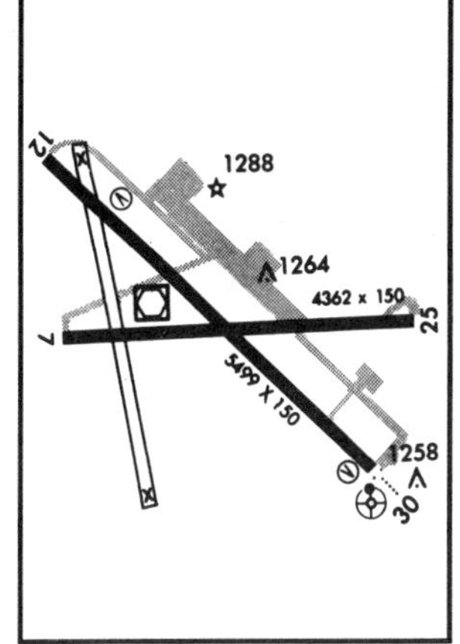

Airport Information:

WENATCHEE - PANGBORN MEMORIAL AIRPORT (EAT)
4 mi east of town N47-23.93 W120-12.41 Elev: 1245 Fuel: 100LL, Jet-A
Rwy12-30: H5499x150 (Asph-Afsc) Rwy 07-25: H4362x150 (Asph) Attended: continuously
Unicom: 123.0 Public Phone 24hrs Notes: No landing or overnight fees for non-commercial aircraft.
FBO: Wings of Wenatchee, Inc. Phone: 886-0233

WA-WA71 - WOODLAND
WOODLAND STATE

(Area Code 206)

37

Oak Tree Restaurant:

Oak Tree Restaurant is located on the approach end to runway 13 and about 1/4 mile north of the Woodland State Airport. You can simply walk to the restaurant from the airport. The Oak Tree Restaurant has been in business for over 30 years. Accommodations include a coffee shop, cocktail lounge, large dining room, banquet and conference facilities, in-house bakery and beautiful appointed gift shop. Their bakery will provide you with delicious pies, cookies, cakes and pastries and their famous cinnamon rolls. Two full time gift and floral consultants on staff are there to help assist you with that special gift. Prime rib is the specialty of the house. The dining room has a contemporary decor. A large fireplace adds atmosphere to the already appealing setting. The Oak Tree Restaurant in Woodland, WA offering more than 10,000 square feet of flexible meeting space and well equipped to handle your banquet, conference and convention needs. For more information about the Oak Tree Restaurant call 887-8661.

Restaurants Near Airport:

Oak Tree Restaurant	1/4 mi N.	Phone: 887-8661

Lodging: There are two motels reported nearby the Oak Tree Restaurant. For information call the restaurant at 887-8661.
Meeting Rooms: Oak Tree Restaurant specializes in accommodations for banquets, meeting, receptions and catered social events on their premises. For information call 887-8661.
Transportation: None reported
Information: Woodland Chamber of Commerce, Tourist Information Center P.O. Box 1012, 1225 Lewis River Road., Woodland, WA 98674. City of Woodland P.O. Box 9, 100 Davidson, Woodland, WA 98674. Phone: 225-8281.

Attractions:

The town of Woodland is known as the gateway to Mount St. Helens. It is located at the junction of Interstate 5 and State Highway 503, just 21 miles north of the Oregon Washington border. Some of the attractions in the area include excellent fishing on the lower Columbia and Lewis rivers and 3 reservoirs northeast along Highway 503. Golfers come from all over to play the 18-hole Lewis River Golf Course 6 miles east of the town of Woodland along Highway 503 to Mount St. Helens; Ape Cave is the longest known lava tube in the United States; Located about 20 miles northeast of Woodland Highway 503 will take you to the lava tubes, and additional attractions including trails that wind down the river or across the slopes of Mount St. Helens tempting day-hikers, backpackers, photographers and nature watchers. Contact the Woodland Chamber of Commerce for more information. (See Information listed above).

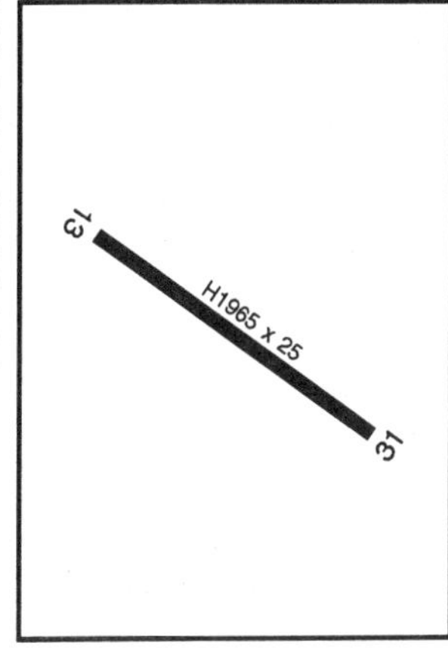

Airport Information:

WOODLAND - WOODLAND STATE (WA71)
1 mi southeast of town N45-53.91 W122-44.24 Elev: 24 Rwy 13-31: H1965x25 (Asph)
Attended: unattended CTAF: 122.9 Notes: Extreme trubulence possible when wind's from the east.
Controling facility: Washington State Division of Aeronautics 206-833-8220 or 800-552-0666 for facility information prior to use. 12' dike NW end. P-lines and building in apch to Rwy 31.

WA-YKM - YAKIMA
YAKIMA AIR TERMINAL

(Area Code 509)

38

Restaurants Near Airport:
Restaurant At The Arpt On Site Phone: 248-4710

The Restaurant At The Airport:

Located on the second floor of the terminal building, this facility provides a panoramic view of the runway and access ramps frequented by many aircraft arriving and departing the airport. This fine dining facility is open Monday through Friday 7:30 a.m. to 1 a.m., Saturday and Sunday from 9 a.m. to 1 a.m. Everything is made from scratch including soups, sauces, bread, desserts, and dressings. Main entrees featured are their seafood, chicken dishes and pastas dinners along with special beverages like their flaming coffee drinks. Prices range between $4.50 and $8.30 for most main entrees. Daily lunch specials run from 11 a.m. to 2 p.m. with a Sunday Brunch between 9 a.m. and 2 p.m. Half price appetizers are featured on special nights in their lounge. The restaurant has an outdoor deck able to seat about 100 people. Their main dining room can seat 80 people. They also have two private rooms able to accommodate 30 and 70 persons. Catering and carry-out items are also available for pilots-on-the-go. For information call the restaurant at 248-4710.

Lodging: Holiday (3 miles) 452-6511; Rio Mirada (3 miles) 457-4444; Red Lion (3 miles) 248-7850; Town Plaza (3 miles) 248-5900; Holiday Motor Inn (3 miles) 248-6666

Meeting Rooms: "Restaurant At The Airport", Holiday, Rio Mirada, Red Lion, Town Plaza and Holiday Motor Inn all have accommodations for meetings and conferences. (See "Information" listed below)

Information: Yakima Valley Visitors & Convention Bureau, 10 North 8th Street, Yakima, WA 98901, Phone: 575-1300.

Attractions:

5 golf courses in this region: Westwood 966-0890; Suntides 966-9065; Fisher Park 575-6075; Elks 697-7177; Country Club 452-2266. Access to Mt. Rainier National Park; White Pass Ski Area; Horse racing at Yakima Meadows (3 miles), Sun Dome events; and many fishing lakes as well as winery tours throughout the area. For more information call 575-1300 or 248-2021.

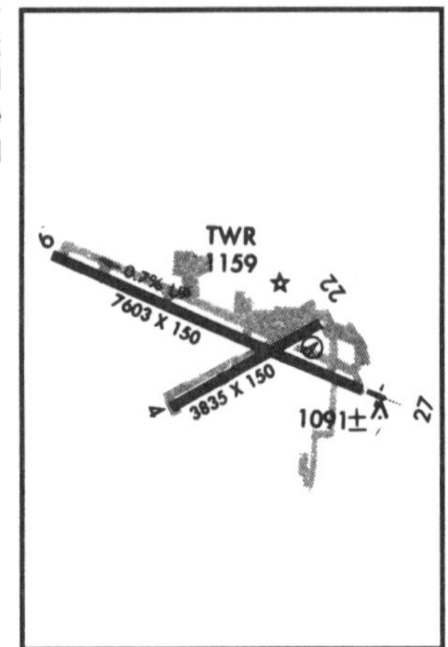

Airport Information:

YAKIMA - YAKIMA AIR TERMINAL (YKM)
3 mi south of town N46-34.09 W120-32.64 Elev: 1095 Fuel: 100LL, Jet-A
Rwy 09-27: H7603x150 (Asph-Pfc) Rwy 04-22: H3835 (Asph-Pfc) Attended: continuously
Public Phone 24 hrs Atis: 125.25 Unicom 122.95 Tower: 133.25 Gnd Con: 121.9
Notes: Parking fee: 0-8 hrs no charge; 8-24 hrs $3.00 charge; each additional 24 hrs $2.00 charge.
FBO: Mc Allister Flying Serv. **Phone: 457-4933**
FBO: Noland Decoto Flying Serv. **Phone: 248-1370, 800-600-0255**

Photo by: Restaurant At The Airport

The Restaurant At The Airport offers guest a panoramic view of the airport

WEST VIRGINIA

LOCATION MAP

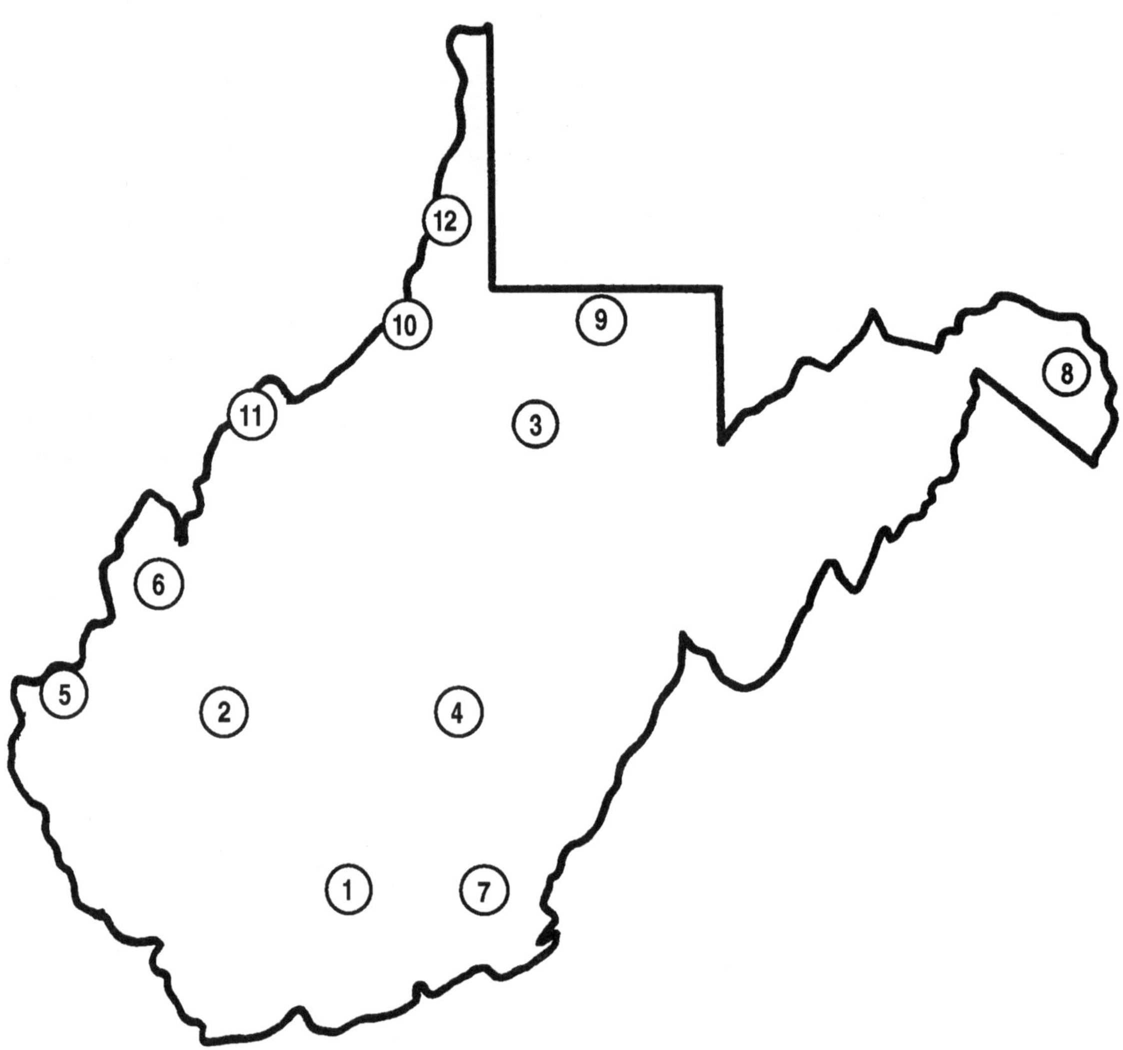

Not to be used for navigational purposes

WEST VIRGINIA

CROSS FILE INDEX

Location Number	City or Town	Airport Name And Identifier	Name of Attraction
1	Beckley	Raleigh Co. Mem. (BKW)	Raleigh Co. Arpt. Rest.
2	Charleston	Yeager Arpt. (CRW)	Banner Service
3	Clarksburg	Benedum Arpt. (CKB)	Aeroclub Restaurant
4	Craigsville	Herold Arpt. (9W2)	Country Inn
5	Huntington	Tri-State/Milton J. Ferguson (HTS)	Red Baron Restaurant
6	leon	Leon Arpt. (WV30)	Country Lanes Mini Mart
7	Lewisburg	Greenbrier Valley Arpt. (LWB)	Ranch Room Steak Hse.
8	Martinsburg	E. West-VA-Reg/Shepherd (MRB)	Redfield's
9	Morgantown	Walter L. Bill Hart Fld. (MGW)	Backbay Restaurant
10	New Martinsville	P.W. Johnson Mem. Arpt. (75D)	Pizza Hut
11	Parkersburg	Wood Co./Gill Robb Wilson (PKB)	Helen's Arpt. Restaurant
12	Wheeling	Wheeling Ohio Co. Arpt. (HLG)	Tail Wind Restaurant

WV-BKW - BECKLEY RALEIGH COUNTY MEMORIAL

(Area Code 304)

1

Raleigh County Airport Restaurant:

The Raleigh County Airport Restaurant is situated within the terminal building, and is open from 8:30 a.m. to 5 p.m. Monday through Friday during the summer and until 3 p.m. in the winter. This facility specializes in items like cheeseburgers, hamburgers, chef salads, hogie sandwiches, chicken breast sandwiches, as well as soup and salad bar. The dining room can accommodate between 75 and 100 persons, and is decorated with red leather chairs, wooden oak tables, a huge quilt draped across one wall and 4 large windows that allow guests to see the airport activity while dining. This facility also provides air travelers with a snack area and gift shop as well. They also provide in-flight catering for business flightswith advance notice. For more information call the airport authority at 255-0476 or the restaurant at 252-9970.

Attractions: Grandview State Park & Country Club; Beaver Creek & Country Club; Glade Springs Resort; Beckley Exhibition Coal Mine; Bluestone Lake and Dam; New River Park; Pipestem State Park; Twin Falls State Park and Golf Winterplace Ski Resort.

Restaurants Near Airport:

Carriage Hse/Beckley Ctr	10 mi N.	Phone: 252-8661
The Char (Fine Dining)	10 mi N.	Phone: 153-1760
Pasquale's (Italian)	6 mi	Phone: 255-5253
Raleigh County Airport Rest.	On Site	Phone: 255-9970

Lodging: Beckley Hotel And Conference Center (10 miles) 252-8661; Holiday Inn 255-1511; Comfort Inn 255-2161; Glade Springs Resort (4 miles) 763-2000.

Meeting Rooms: The airport has a lounge area often used for meetings, etc. Beckley Hotel And Conference Center 252-8661 or 800-274-6010; Holiday Inn 255-1511; Glade Springs Resort (4 miles) 763-2000.

Transportation: Taxi: Beckley Cab Co. 253-3301; Beckley Limousine 253-2254; Glen Morgan Cab 252-5533; Yellow Cab Co. 252-6341; Rental Cars: Avis 253-0277; Hertz 252-2385.

Information: Southern West Virginia Convention & Visitors Bureau, P.O. Box 1799, Beckley, WV 25801, Phone: 252-2244 or outside WV 800/ VISIT-WV.

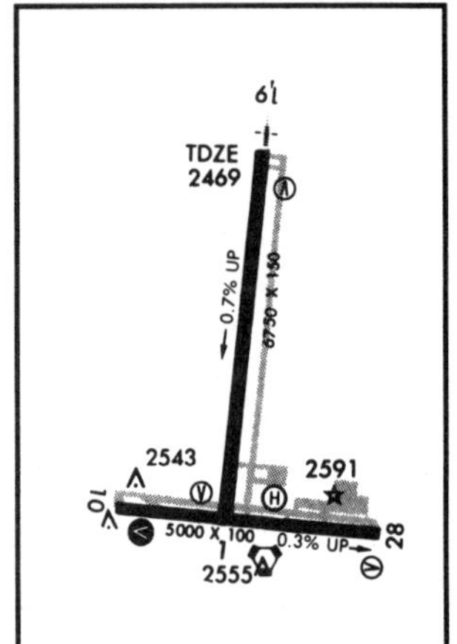

Airport Information:

BECKLEY - RALEIGH COUNTY MEMORIAL AIRPORT (BKW)
3 mi east of town N37-47.24 W81-07.45 Elev: 2504 Fuel: 100LL, Jet-A
Rwy 01-19: H6750x150 (Asph-Grvd) Rwy 10-28: H5000x100 (Asph) Attended: 1100-0300Z Unicom: 123.0 Charleston App/Dep Con: 118.95 Public Phone 24hrs Notes: Landing fee $10.00-$15.00, Parking $3.00-$5.00 per night. There is an industrial park having 218 acres with several profitable businesses located on the park. Several lots are available for purchase or lease. Call the airport manager.
Raleigh County Memorial Airport Phone: 255-0476

WV-CRW - CHARLESTON YEAGER AIRPORT

(Area Code 304)

2

Banner Service:

Banner Service operates a restaurant located within the terminal building at the Charleston Yeager Airport. This family style facility is open between 6:30 am and 7:00 p.m. 7 days a week. Entrees on their menu include such items as marinated chicken breast, ribs, New York strip steak, 5 different types of specialty hamburgers, Ruben, rib eye steaks, ham steaks, chopped beef steak and hot roast beef. In addition, turkey sandwiches, homemade soup and chili can be selected from their menu. Average prices run about $3.55 to $6.25 for most main selections. Their dining area can seat up to 60 persons. Larger groups and parties are welcome with advance notice. Meals can also be prepared to go. In flight catering is available through Executive Air (FBO). For more information you can call them at 342-5231.

Attraction:
Coonskin Park Golf Course (1 mile).

Restaurants Near Airport:

Banner Services	On Site	Phone: 342-5231
Fifth Quarter	3-1/2 mi	Phone: 345-2726
The Hearth	1 mi	Phone: 341-8006
Joey's	3-1/2 mi	Phone; 343-4121

Lodging: Ramada Inn 744-4641; Holiday Inn (Free trans) 343-4661;

Meeting Rooms: Holiday Inn (Free trans) has accommodations for conventions 343-4661

Transportation: Courtesy vans available at airport between 7 a.m. and 11 p.m.; Taxi: C & H Taxi 344-4902; Rental Cars: Avis 343-9446; Budget 343-4381; Hertz 346-0573; National 344-2563.

Information: Convention & Visitors Bureau, Charleston Civic Center, 200 Civic Center Drive, Charleston, WV 25301, Phone: 344-5075 or 800-733-5469.

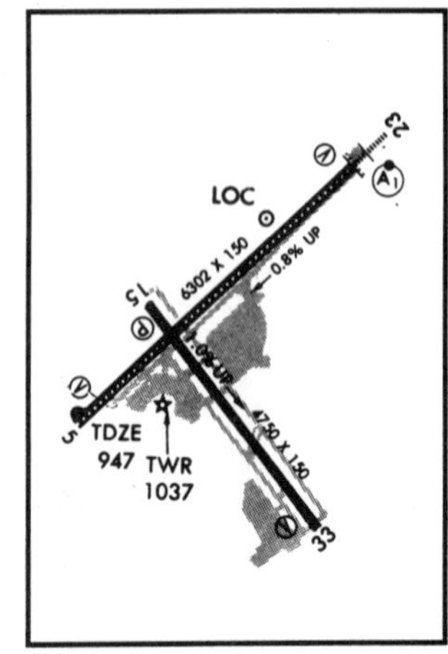

Airport Information:

CHARLESTON - YEAGER AIRPORT (CRW)
3 mi east of town N38-22.39 W81-35.59 Elev: 982 Fuel: 100LL, Jet-A
Rwy: 05-23: H6302x150 (Conc-Grvd) Rwy 15-33: H4750x150 (Asph) Attended: continuously Atis: 127.6 Unicom: 122.95 Charleston App/Dep Con: 119.2 (South) 124.1 (North) 128.5 Tower: 125.7 Gnd Con: 121.8 Clnc Del: 118.55 Public Phone 24hrs
Notes: Overnight fees: $6.50 to $13.00 for non-based aircraft.
FBO: Executive Air Terminal Phone: 343-8818

WV-CKB - CLARKSBURG BENEDUM AIRPORT

(Area Code 304) 3

Restaurants Near Airport:

Aeroclub	On Site	Phone: Closed
Oliverio's	1 mi S.	Phone: 842-7385

Airport Restaurant:

The Aeroclub Restaurant has closed since our last update, however during a recent conversation with the airport manager we learned that they are looking for new owners to manage the restaurant. It is possible that in the near future the restaurant will re-open. For current information call the Airport Managers office at 842-3400.

Lodging: Comfort Inn (3 miles); Days Inn (3 miles) 842-7371; Econo Lodge 842-7381; Holiday Inn (3 miles) 842-5411; Knights Inn (3 miles) 842-7115; Red Carpet (3 miles) 842-7371; Town House East Motel (2 mile) 842-3551.

Meeting Rooms: Airport conference room available; Holiday Inn (3 miles) 842-5411; Red Carpet (3 miles) 842-7371.

Transportation: No Airport courtesy car service reported; Avis 842-3932; Hertz 842-4554; National 842-5666; Taxi: Tom's Taxi 842-6270.

Information: Harrison County Chamber of Commerce, 348 West Main Street, Clarksburg, WV 26301, 624-6331.

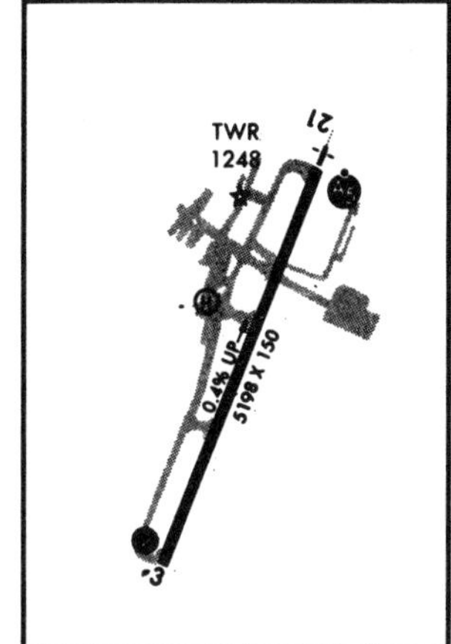

Attraction:

Bel Meadow Country Club (12 miles, Golfing) 623-3702; Cannan State Park (50 miles).

Airport Information:

CLARKSBURG - BENEDUM AIRPORT (CKB)
0 mi northeast of town N39-17.66 W80-13.76 Elev: 1203 Fuel: 80, 100LL, Jet-A
Rwy 03-21: H5198x150 (Asph-Grvd) Attended: 1000-0500Z Atis: 127.825 Unicom: 123.0
Clarksburg Tower: 126.7 Gnd Con: 121.9 Public Phone 24hrs Notes: Fuel not avbl during hours 0500-1000Z, Landing fee for aircraft over 6,500 lbs., No parking fee's.

Airport Manager **Phone: 842-3400**
FBO: KCI Aviation **Phone: 842-3591**

WV-9W2 - CRAIGSVILLE HEROLD AIRPORT (PVT)

(Area Code 304) 4

Restaurants Near Airport:

Country Inn	Adj Arpt	Phone: 742-3853

Country Inn:

The Country Inn Restaurant is located across the street from the Herold Airport in Craigsville, WV. This is a private airstrip. We called the airport and were told that it was open to the public. However, it would be good if you called and let them know of your intentions and obtain permission to land. This will also enable you to find out what the runway conditions are like. The Country Inn is open between 8 a.m. and 9 p.m. 7 days a week. A few of their specialties include hot roast beef sandwiches, soup, lasagna and spaghetti. Their dining room has a country style atmosphere, with a very informal decor, decorated with wooden tables and chairs and seating for up to 50 persons. Fly-in groups are also welcome. Everything on their menu can be prepared-to-go as well. For information you can call the airport at 742-5220 or the restaurant at 742-3853.

Lodging: Midtown Motel (1 mile) 742-5531.

Meeting Rooms: None Reported

Transportation: None Reported

Information: Summerville Chamber of Commerce, 801 West Webster Road, Suite 1, Box 567, Summerville, WV 26651, 304-872-1588; Also: West Virginia Division of Tourism & Parks, State Capitol Complex, Charleston, WV 25305, Phone: 800-225-5982.

18
1450 x 100
36

Airport Information:

CRAIGSVILLE - HEROLD AIRPORT (9W2) (Private Airport)
0 mi north of town N38-20-? W80-39-12 Elev: 2346 Fuel: None Reported
Attended: unattended Rwy 18-36: 1450x100 (Turf) Notes: Private use facility use at own risk.
Herold Airport **Phone: 742-5220.**

WV-HTS - HUNTINGTON TRI-STATE/MILTON FERGUSON

(Area Code 304)

5

Tri State Airport Restaurant:

Located right on the Tri-State Airport, this restaurant is situated in the main terminal building, and is within walking distance from the private terminal. This is a combination family style and fine dining restaurant that serves entrees specializing in chicken and prime pib. Meals run an average of $4.95 for breakfast, $5.95 for lunch and $8.95 for dinner. The restaurant hours are 6:45 a.m. to 7:45 p.m. The restaurant is decorated with WW-1 memorabilia. The Red Barons plane serves as a back drop with murals depicting dog fights. Groups and fly-in guests are always welcome. For information call 453-2196.

Attractions:

Camden Amusement Park, (Approx. 5 miles), US Route 60 west, Huntington, WV, Phone: 429-4231; Beech Fork State Park, (Approx 25 miles), 720 acres, fishing, boating, & hiking. Phone: 522-0303; Greater Huntington Park, (Approx. 10 miles), Phone: 696-5954; Seasonal Event: Tri-State Fair and Regatta: Held June-August, Central Park Festival includes Budweiser Cup and Miller classic speedboat races, Phone: 606-329-8737.

Restaurants Near Airport:

Gino's Pizza	1 mi	Phone: 453-1351
Red Lobster	10 mi	Phone: 529-4042
Rocco's Spaghetti House	3 mi	Phone: 453-3000
Tri State Arpt. Rest.	On Site	Phone: 453-2196

Lodging: Holiday Inn University, (Approx. 10 miles), 1415 5th Avenue, Huntington, WV, Phone: 525-7741; Radisson Hotel, (Approx. 10 miles), 1001 3rd Avenue Huntington, WV, Phone: 525-1001;

Conference Room: Tri-State Airport Authority has a conference room in the private aircraft terminal, available upon request, subject to reservation.

Transportation: Red Baron Restaurant within walking distance. No need for transportation. No courtesy vehicles available at Tri-State Airport. However, taxi service and rental cars are available: Tri-State Cab, 453-6647; Yellow Cab, 529-7131; Avis, 453-1865; National, 453-3524; Hertz, 453-2745.

Information: Cabell-Huntington Convention & Visitors Bureau, P.O. Box 347, Huntington, West Virginia 25708, Phone: 525-7333, 800-635-6329.

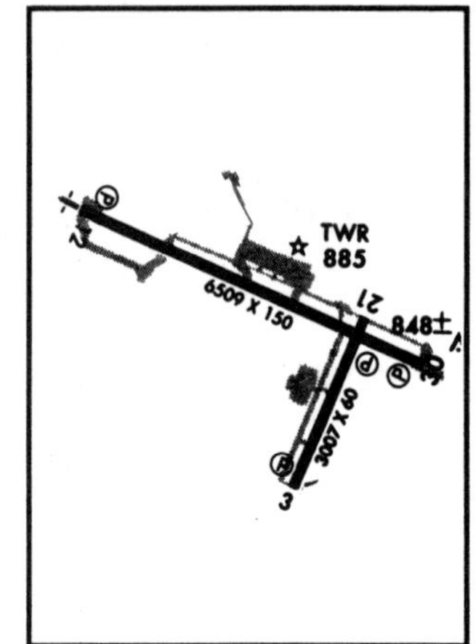

Airport Information:

HUNTINGTON - TRI-STATE/MILTON J. FERGUSON FIELD (HTS)
3 mi south of town N38-22.00 W82-33.48 Elev: 828 Fuel: 100LL, Jet-A
Rwy 12-30: H6509x150 (Asph-Grvd) Rwy 03-21: H3007x60 (Asph-Grvd) Attended: continuously Atis: 125.2 Unicom: 122.95 Tower: 118.5 Gnd Con: 121.9 Clnc Del: 118.05. 121.9 Pre-Taxi Clnc: 121.9 Public Phone 24 hrs Notes: Landing Fee (None for single engine aircraft), Conquest & up $7.00; Overnight Parking, Single $4.50 & up, Twin $7.00 & up.
FBO: Tri-State Airport Phone: 453-6165

WV-WV30 - LEON LEON AIRPORT

(Area Code 304)

6

Country Mart & Lanes:

The Country Lanes Mini Mart is located across the street from the Leon Airport. This establishment contains a deli inside of a grocery store, bowling alley and hardware store all situated within the same complex. One could fly in and bowl a frame or two, then grab a bite to eat before heading back to home base. The snack bar is open between 7 a.m. and 10:30 p.m. weekdays, Friday and Saturday from 7 a.m. to 11 p.m. and Sunday from 8 a.m. to 10:30 p.m. Selections most often ordered include breakfast sandwiches, hot dogs, ham and cheese sandwiches, pizza, pizza bread, and steak hogie sandwiches. Average prices run about $1.80 to $2.89 for most sandwiches, and between $4.50 and $12.00 for small or large pizzas. The seating within the deli itself is limited to 15 or 20 persons. However, many customers place orders to go, or for carry-out meals. For more information call the Country Lanes Mini Mart at 458-1031.

Restaurants Near Airport:

Country Mart & Lanes	Adj Arpt	Phone: 458-1031

Lodging: None Reported

Meeting Rooms: None Reported

Transportation: None Reported

Information: Mason County Area Chamber of Commerce, 305 Main Street, Point Pleasant, WV 25550, Phone: 675-1050.

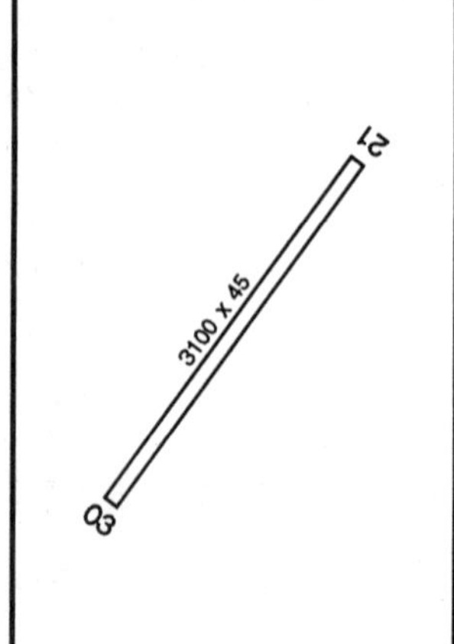

Airport Information:

LEON - LEON AIRPORT (WV30)
3 mi south of town N38-41.71 W81-57.29 Elev: 563 Rwy 03-21: 3100x45 (Turf)
Attended: unattended CTAF: 122.9 Notes: Ultralight activity on and in vicinity of airport.
Leon Airport Phone: 458-1069

WV-LWB - LEWISBURG
GREENBRIER VALLEY AIRPORT

(Area Code 304) 7

Ranch Room Steak House:

The Ranch Room Steak House is situated on the Greenbrier Valley Airport. As you enter the airport lobby they are located to the left. This family style restaurant is open 9 a.m. to 9 p.m. Sunday through Thursday, and 9 a.m. until 10 p.m. Friday and Saturday. Their menu includes a variety of items including steaks and seafood. Average prices run $3.00 for breakfast and lunch and about $6.50 and up for dinner selections. Daily specials are also available. The decor of this restaurant is western. Fly-in groups and parties are always welcome. Carry-out meals can be arranged as well. For more information call the Ranch Room Steak House at 645-3164.

Restaurants Near Airports:

The General Lewis Inn	5 mi S.	Phone: 645-2600
Ranch Room Steak House	On Site	Phone: 645-3164

Lodging: Brier Inn (3 miles) 645-7722.

Meeting Rooms: There is a small conference room available at the airport. Contact the airport manager's office at 645-3961.

Transportation: Taxi Service: Lewisburg Taxi 645-2311; Limousine Service 645-1193; Rental Cars: Avis 645-7243; National 645-3961; Hertz 647-5170.

Information: Lewisburg Visitors Bureau, 105 Church Street, Lewisburg, WV 24901, Phone: 645-1000 or 800-833-2068.

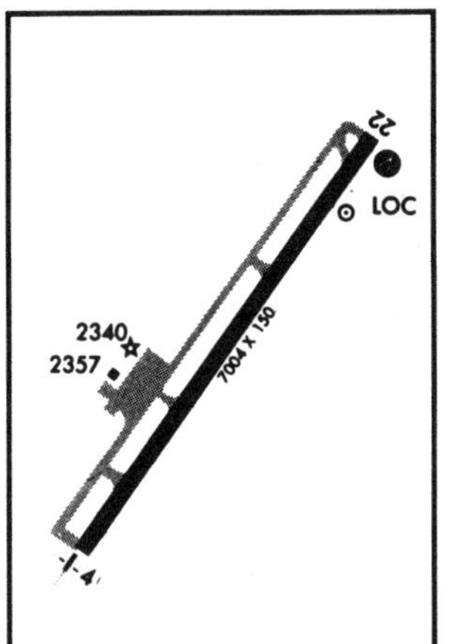

Attractions:

The Greenbrier Hotel (Resort), White Sulphur Springs, West Virginia (13 miles) 536-1110.

Airport Information:

LEWISBURG - GREENBRIER VALLEY AIRPORT (LWB)
3 mi north of town N37-5150 W80-23.97 Elev: 2303 Fuel: 100LL, Jet-A
Rwy 04-22: H7004x150 (Asph-Grvd) Attended: continuously Unicom: 122.95
Washington Center App/Dep Con: 134.4, 127.925 Clnc Del: 120.85 Lewisburg Tower 118.9
Gnd Con: 121.9 Public Phone 24hrs Notes: Landing fee waived if fuel is purchased.
Parking $3.00 Single, $5.00 twin.
FBO: Greenbrier Valley Airport Phone: 645-3961

WV-MRB - MARTINSBURG
EASTERN WEST-VA-REG/SHEPHERD

(Area Code 304) 8

Outback Steak House:

This restaurant is located about 5 miles from the Eastern West Virginia Regional/Shepherd Field. During our conversation with airport personnel we learned that this restaurant is popular in the area and offers a unique atmosphere and, most importantly, good food. Hours of operation are Monday through Friday 4 p.m. to 10:30 p.m. and Saturday 2 p.m. to 10:30. Specialties of the house include 6 different steaks, marinated in their secret blend of seasonings; Porterhouse, New York strip, ribeye, filet and sirloin steaks. One of their popular appetizers is the "Blooming Onion," a one pound battered fried onion. The restaurant has an Australian decor with wooden floors and dark wood walls, with booths in their main dining room. They can seat 250 people. The bar area has wooden mid-high dividers. The restaurant is situated behind the Martinsburg Mall. Directions are left on Airport Rd., right on Route 11, left on Route 9 to the Martinsburg Mall, circle the mall and you should see the restaurant somewhere in the back. Check to see if Aero Smith, Inc. has a courtesy car by calling 262-2507. City Taxi Service (263-4973) will take you from the airport to the Martinsburg Mall for about $7.00 or $8.00 one way plus $1.50 for each additional person. For information about the restaurant call 262-2406.

Restaurants Near Airport:

Heatherfield's	5 mi N.	Phone: 267-5500
Outback Steak Hse.	5 mi N.	Phone: 262-2406
Shoney's	5 mi N.	Phone: 263-8866
Stone Crab Inn	8 mi N.	Phone: 267-6400

Lodging: Sheraton Martinsburg Inn 267-5500; Woods Resort (20 miles) 754-7977.
Meeting Rooms: Sheraton Martinsburg Inn 267-5500; Woods Resort (20 miles) 754-7977.
Transportation: Professional Pilots, Inc. can accommodate customers with courtesy transportation if given advance notice. Also rental car: Hertz 263-7823; Taxi: City Cab 263-4973.
Information: Martinsburg-Berkeley County Chamber of Commerce, 198 Viking Way, Martinsburg, WV 25401, Phone: 267-4841 or 800-332-9007.

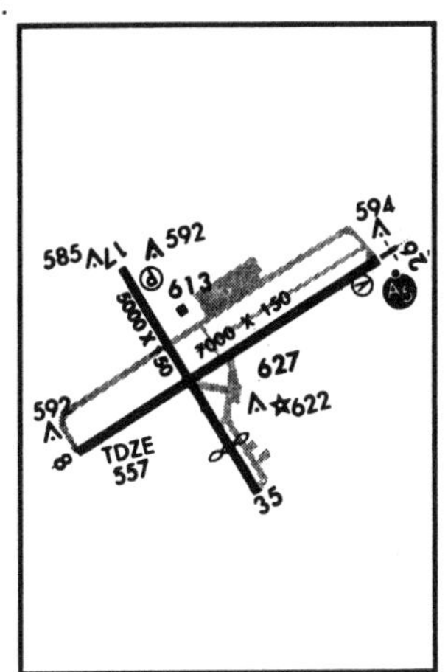

Airport Information:

MARTINSBURG - EASTERN WEST VIRGINIA REG./ SHEPHERD FIELD (MRB)
4 mi south of town N39-24.12 W77-59.07 Elev: 557 Fuel: 100LL, Jet-A
Rwy 08-26: H7000x150 (Asph-Grvd) Rwy 17-35: H5001x150 (Asph-Rfsc) Attended: 1300-2200Z Unicom: 122.95 Martinsburg App/Dep Con: 128.75 Tower: 124.3
Gnd Con: 121.8 Public Phone 24 hrs Notes: No fees if fuel is purchased.
FBO: Aero Smith, Inc. Phone: 262-2507 or 800-550-2507
FBO: Professional Pilots, Inc. Phone: 263-3350 or 800-562-9792

WV-MGW - MORGANTOWN MORGANTOWN MUNICIPAL- WALTER L. BILL HART FIELD.

(Area Code 304)

9

Backbay Restaurant:

The Backbay Restaurant is located about 100 yards or 1/4 mile from the terminal building at the Morgantown Municipal Airport. Fly-in guests can either walk to the restaurant or taxi service from the airport. This fine dining establishment is open on weekdays between 11 a.m. and 9:30 p.m., Saturday from 4 p.m. to 11 p.m. and Sunday from 12 p.m. to 9 p.m. Their choice of entrees are extensive. However, they specilize in fresh seafood shipped in twice a week by air. When speaking to the owner, we learned that the airport not only brings in customers to the nearby region, but also serves as an excellant port of call for the freshest seafood available, and shipped directly to his facility. All types of fish, crab, lobster and shrimp are prepared to perfection for their guests. In addition, prime cuts of beef, prime rib and steaks as well as specialty Cajun dishes are available to the customer. They also feature 6 to 8 luncheon specials throughout the week. Average prices run between $6.00 and $8.00 for lunch and $12.95 to $15.95 for most dinner selections. The Backbay Restaurant is part of a two story building that resembles a New England fish house. Their decor is nautical and somewhat rustic. The main dining room can accommodate up to 175 persons. Groups of 10 or more should make reservations. In flight catering is another service that this restaurant features. For more information you can call 296-3027.

Restaurants Near Airport:

Backbay Restaurant	100yds	Phone: 296-3027

Lodging: Airport Motel (1 mile) 292-7396; Comfort Inn (4 miles) 296-9364; Holiday Inn (4 miles) 599-1680; Holiday Motel (1 mile) 292-3303; Ramada Inn (4 miles, Free trans) 296-3431; Sheraton Lakeview Resort & Convention Center (5 miles, Free trans) 594-1111.

Meeting Rooms: Comfort Inn (4 miles) 296-9364; Holiday Inn (4 miles) 599-1680; Sheraton Lakeview Resort and Conference Center (5 miles, Free trans) 594-1111.

Transportation: Taxi Service: Morgantown Yellow Taxi 292-7441; Rental Cars: Avis 291-5867; Budget 292-3562; Hertz 296-2331.

Information: Morgantown Convention & Visitors Bureau, 709 Beechurst Avenue, Morgantown, WV 26505, 292-5081 or 800-458-7373.

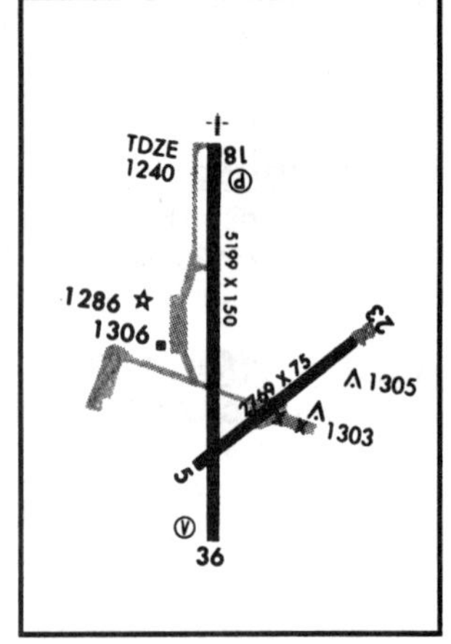

Airport Information:

MORGANTOWN - MORGANTOWN MUNICIPAL-WALTER L. BILL HART FLD. (MGW)
3 mi east of town N39-38.57 W79-54.98 Elev: 1248 Fuel: 100LL, Jet-A
Rwy 18-36: H5199x150 (Asph-Grvd) Rwy 05-23: H2769x75 (Asph) Attended: Mon-Fri 1200-0300Z, Sat 1300-0200Z, Sun 1300-0300Z Unicom: 122.95 Tower: 120.0 Gnd Con: 121.7
FBO: Piedmont Aviation Service, Inc. Phone: 296-2359

WV-75D - NEW MARTINSVILLE P.W. JOHNSON MEMORIAL AIRPORT

(Area Code 304)

10

Pizza Hut:

The Pizza Hut Restaurant is located about 1/3rd mile from the P.W. Johnson Memorial Airport. Fly-in guests can reach this restaurant by walking a short distance through the trailer park located near the airport. We were told that you can see the red roof of the restaurant from the airport during the winter. However, the trees obscure its view during the summer months. The restaurant hours are Monday through Thursday from 11 a.m. to 11 p.m., Friday and Saturday from 11 a.m. to 12:30 a.m. and Sunday from 12 p.m. to 11 p.m. Items like pasta dishes, sandwiches, salad bar, and of course a wide variety of pizzas, including their personal pan pizza, are just some of the many selections offered on their menu. "Meal Deal" specials are also provide, especially for groups. These include your meal and beverage at group discount rates. Their personal pan pizza can be enjoyed for a low price of $1.99 or $2.99. This family dining facility accommodates seating for 105 persons with a very nice decor, comparable with most other Pizza Hut facilities. Groups and fly-in parties are always welcome. Friendly efficient service is provided to all customers. For more information about this establishment you can call 455-4240.

Restaurants Near Airport:

Elby's	1/2 mi	Phone: 455-5600
Pizza Hut	1/3 mi	Phone:455-4240

Lodging: None Reported

Meeting Rooms: None Reported

Transportation: None Reported

Information: West Virginia Division of Tourism & Parks, State Capitol Complex, Charleston, WV 25305, Phone: 800-225-5982.

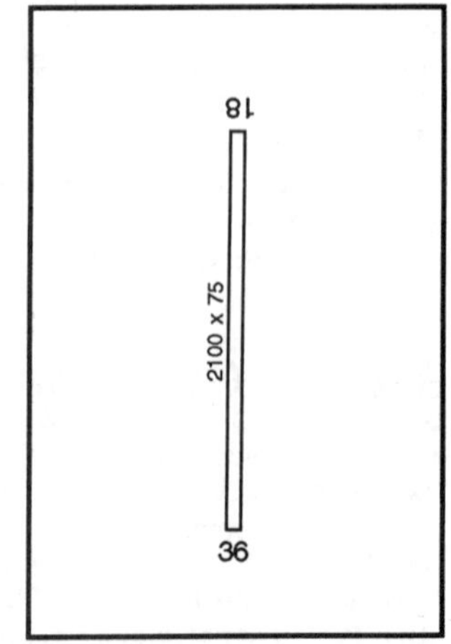

Airport Information:

NEW MARTINSVILLE - P.W. JOHNSON MEMORIAL AIRPORT (75D)
2 mi north of town N39-41.04 W80-51.74 Elev: 632 Rwy 01-19: 2100x73 (Turf) Attended: unattended CTAF: 122.9 Notes: Field is soft when wet. Ultralights on and in vicinity of airport. Ultralight use right traffic for runway 19. Ditch on west side of runway in front of hangers. Use runway exits marked by tires or lights.
Airport Manager Phone: 455-4344

WV-PKB - PARKERSBURG
WOOD CO./GILL ROBB WILSON FLD.

(Area Code 304)

11

Mary's Plane View Restaurant:

Mary's Plane View Restaurant is located within the terminal building at the Wood County Airport. Fly-in guests can just walk to the restaurant from the aircraft parking area, according to the restaurant management. This establishment contains a snack bar and fine dining restaurant. The main restaurant is open 7 days a week from 6:30 a.m. to 2:30 p.m. Their menu consists of home cooked meals including fresh meats, shrimp, seafood, steaks, hot roast beef, spaghetti, ham steak, in addition to a full breakfast line. Average prices for specials run $5.50 for breakfast, $4.50 for lunch and $4.95 for dinner. The decor of this restaurant is very nice with carpeted floors, red table cloths, and candles on each table. They can accommodate about 105 persons. In-flight catering is also provided. For more information about Helen's Airport Restaurant call 464-4413.

Restaurants Near Airport:
Mary's Plane View On Site Phone: 464-4413

Lodging: Blennerhassett Hotel (10 miles) 422-3131; Lafayette Hotel & Restaurant (8 miles) 614-373-5522.

Meeting Rooms: There is a conference room available at the Wood County Airport. For information call airport manager's office at 464-5113.

Transportation: Rental cars: Budget 464-4242; Hertz 464-4402; National 464-5308.

Information: Parkersburg/Wood County Convention & Visitors Bureau, 350 7th Street, Parkersburg, WV 26101, Phone: 428-1130 or 800-752-4982.

Attractions:

Mountwood Park, (15 miles) 679-3611; Golf Club (5 miles) 464-4420; Fenton Art Glass Gift Shop (6 miles) 375-7772.

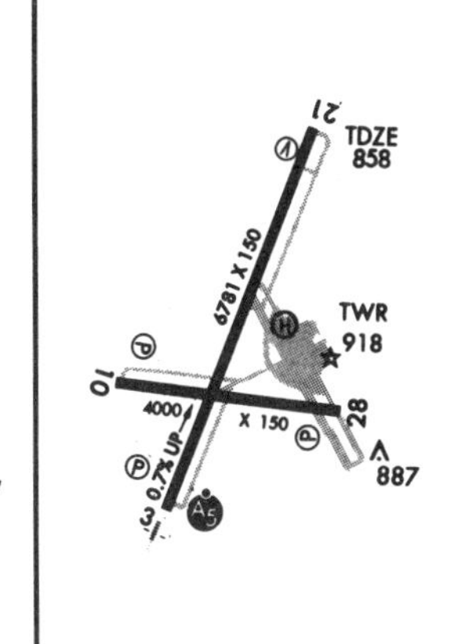

Airport Informaiton:

PARKERSBURG - WOOD COUNTY-GILL ROBB WILSON FIELD (PKB)
6 mi northeast of town N39-20.71 W81-26.35 Elev: 858 Fuel: 80, 100LL, Jet-A
Rwy 03-21: H6781x150 (Asph-Grvd) Rwy 10-28: H4000x150 (Con-Grvd) Attended: continuously
Atis: 124.35 Unicom: 122.95 Indianapolis Center App/Dep Con: 125.55
Parkersburg Tower: 123.7 Gnd Con: 121.7 Notes: Landing fee $5.00 - $52.00, Overnight parking: Single $3.00; Small twin $4.00; Turbo Jet $6.00
FBO: Wood County Airport Auth. Phone: 464-5115

WV-HLG - WHEELING
WHEELING OHIO COUNTY AIRPORT

(Area Code 304)

12

Western Virginia Barbecue Restauant:

Western Virginia Barbecue Restaurant is managed as part of the Ohio County Aviation Center. You can park your aircraft as close as 20 feet from their door. This cafe is open Monday through Thursday 11 a.m. to 4 p.m. and Friday, Saturday and Sunday from 11 a.m. to 9 p.m. The menu includes specialty items such as hamburgers, barbecued ribs, barbecued chicken and pork chops and beef, in addition to side dishes. Average prices run $3.00 to $7.00 for most entrees. The dining area can accommodate about 15 persons. Plate glass windows provide a nice view of the runway and taxiway system at the airport. We were told that catering to general aviation clubs and parties are no problem for this establishment. In fact, we were informed that in the past many local and general aviation related groups have been catered by this facility. During a conversation with the airport manager we were told that a fuel discount is offered to fly-in restaurant guests. Check it out by calling the manager's office. For more information about the restaurant establishment, you can call 277-1601.

Restaurants Near Airport:
Western Virginia Barbecue On Site Phone: 277-1601

Lodging: Downtowner Motel (12 miles) 232-3820; Hampton Inn (10 miles) 233-0440; Holiday Inn (22 miles) 695-0100; McClure House (22 miles, Free trans reported) 232-0330; Wilson Lodge (7 miles) 242-3000.

Meeting Rooms: Hampton Inn (10 miles) 233-0440; McClure House (22 miles, Free transportation reported) 232-0330

Transportation: Wheeling Cab 232-5151; Rental cars: Avis 232-3621.

Information: Convention & Visitors Bureau, 1310 Market Street, Wheeling, WV 26003, Phone: 233-7709.

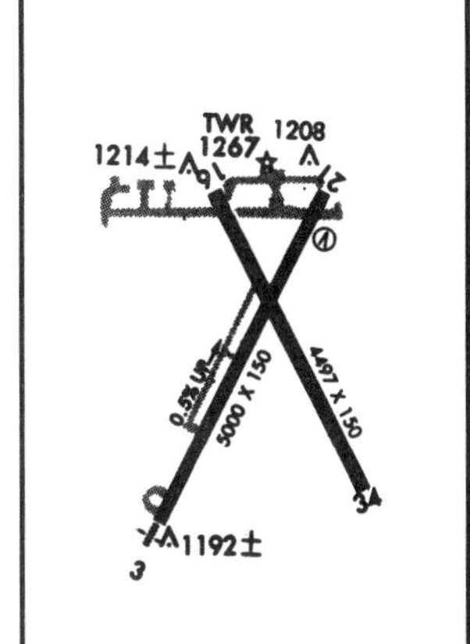

Airport Information:

WHEELING - WHEELING OHIO COUNTY AIRPORT (HLG)
8 mi northeast of town N40-10.58 W80-38.82 Elev: 1195 Fuel: 100LL, Jet-A
Rwy 03-21: H5000x150 (Asph-Grvd) Rwy 16-34: H4499x150 (Asph) Attended: Mon-Fri 1200-0300Z, Sat-Sun 1300-0100Z Unicom: 122.95 Tower: 118.1 Gnd Con: 121.9
Airport Manager Phone: 234-3865
FBO: Ohio County Aviation Sales, Inc. Phone: 277-3499
FBO: Ohio Valley Aviation Sales, Inc. Phone: 277-2121

WISCONSIN

LOCATION MAP

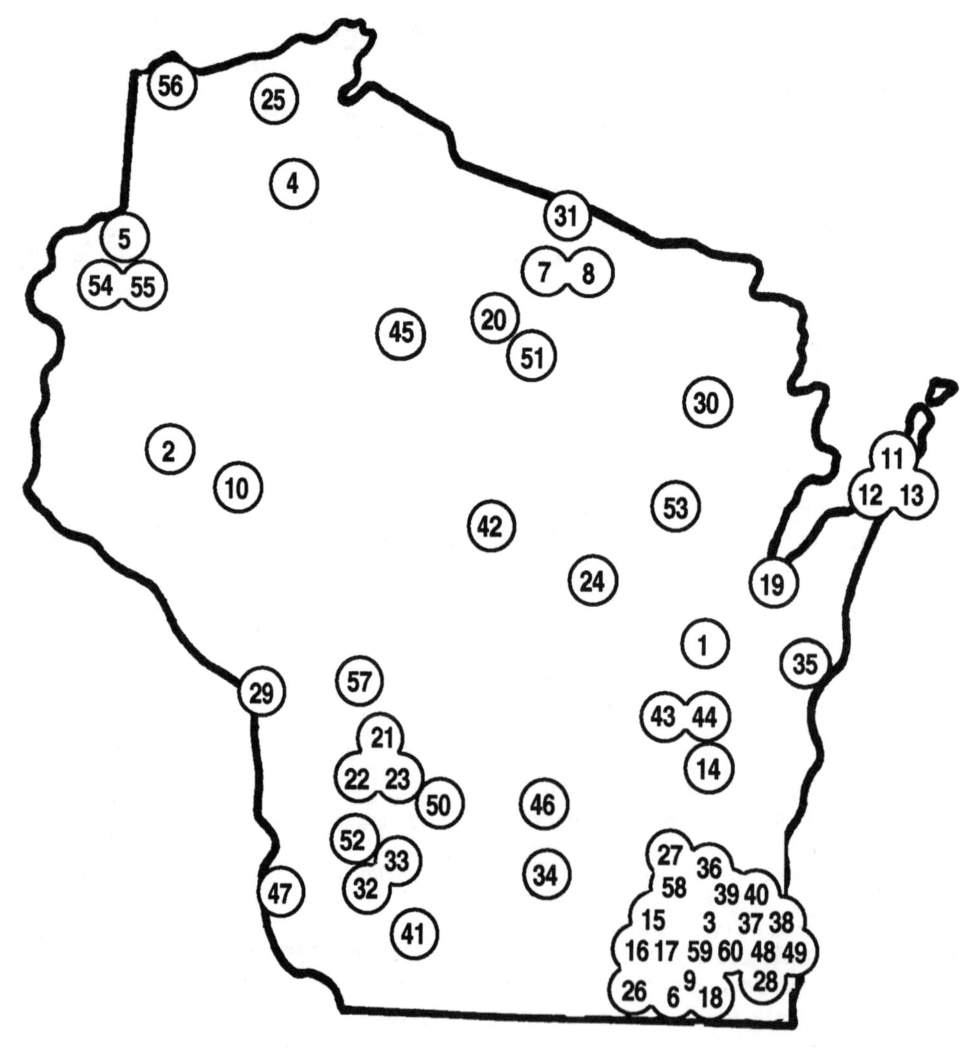

Not to be used for navigational purposes

WISCONSIN

CROSS FILE INDEX

Location Number	City or Town	Airport Name And Identifier	Name of Restaurant
1	Appleton	Outagami Co. Arpt. (ATW)	Creative Croissants
2	Boyceville	Boyceville Muni. Arpt. (WI20)	Cozy Cafe
3	Brookfield	Capitol Arpt. (02C)	Jake's Restaurant
4	Cable	Cable Union (3CU)	Telemark Resort
5	Danbury/Webster	Voyager Village Arpt. (Y05)	Voyager Vill. Resort
6	Delavan	Lake Lawn Arpt. (C59)	Lake Lawn Lodge Resort
7	Eagle River	Eagle River Union Arpt. (EGV)	Aerio Club
8	Eagle River	Eagle River Union Arpt. (EGV)	Betty's Eagle Cafe
9	East Troy	East Troy Muni. Arpt. (57C)	Jackson's Pointe II, Inc.
10	Eau Claire	Chippewa Valley Reg. (EAU)	Connell's II at the Arpt.
11	Ephraim (Door Co.)	Fish Creek (3D2)	C & C Supper Club
12	Ephraim (Door Co.)	Fish Creek (3D2)	Landmark Resort
13	Ephraim (Door Co.)	Fish Creek (3D2)	The White Gull Inn
14	Fond DuLac	Fond DuLac Co. (FLD)	Schreiners Restaurant
15	Fort Atkinson	Fort Atkinson Muni. Arpt. (61C)	Edgewater Restaurant
16	Fort Atkinson	Fort Atkinson Muni. Arpt. (61C)	Fireside Rest. Playhouse
17	Fort Atkinson	Fort Atkinson Muni. Arpt. (61C)	Louise Riverview Rest.
18	Geneva	Grand Geneva Arpt. (Private)	Grand Geneva Resort
19	Green Bay	Austin Straubel Intl. (GRB)	Air Host Restaurant
20	Harshaw	Pinewood Airpark (W539)	Pine Country Club
21	Hillsboro	Joshua Sanford Fld. (HBW)	Alpine Haus
22	Hillsboro	Joshua Sanford Fld. (HBW)	Cornucopia Rest
23	Hillsboro	Joshua Sanford Fld. (HBW)	Country Style Cookin
24	Iola	Central Co. (68C)	Wings Inn Tavern
25	Iron River	Bayfield Co. Arpt. (Y77)	Iron River Trout Haus
26	Janesville	Rock Co. Arpt. (JVL)	C.A.V.U Restaurant
27	Juneau	Dodge Co. Arpt. (UNU)	PJ's Restaurant
28	Kenosha	Kenosha Reg. Arpt. (ENW)	Dairyland Clubhouse
29	La Crosse	La Crosse Muni. Arpt. (LSE)	Amelia's Restaurant
30	Lakewood	Lakewood Country Club (WI31)	Mc Caustin Golf & C.C.
31	Land O' Lakes	Kings Land O' Lakes Arpt. (LNL)	Gateway Lodge (Resort)
32	Lone Rock	Tri-Country Reg. Arpt. (LNR)	Airport Restaurant
33	Lone Rock	Tri-Country Reg. Arpt. (LNR)	House on the Rock
34	Madison	Dane Co. Reg.-Truax Field (MSN)	Jet Room Restaurant
35	Manitowoc	Manitowoc Co. Arpt. (MTW)	Planeview Restaurant
36	Menomonee Falls	Aero Park Arpt. (76C)	Prop Wash Restaurant
37	Milwaukee	General Mitchell Intl. (MKE)	Mitchell's Cafe
38	Milwaukee	General Mitchell Intl. (MKE)	Packing House Rest.
39	Milwaukee	Lawrence J. Timmerman (MWC)	Maxim's Family Rest.
40	Milwaukee	Lawrence J. Timmerman (MWC)	Skyroom Restaurant
41	Mineral Point	Iowa Co. Arpt. (MRJ)	House on the Rock Rest.
42	Mosinee	Central Wisconsin Arpt. (CWA)	Runway Restaurant
43	Oshkosh	Wittman Reg. Arpt. (OSH)	Butch's Anchor Inn
44	Oshkosh	Wittman Reg. Arpt. (OSH)	Pioneer Marina (Resort)

CROSS FILE INDEX
(Wisconsin Continued)

Location Number	City or Town	Airport Name And Identifier	Name of Attraction
45	Phillips	Price Co. Arpt. (PBH)	Harbor View Restaurant
46	Portage	Portage Muni. Arpt. (C47)	Hitching Post
47	Prairie Du Chien	Prairie Du Chien Arpt. (PDC)	Jeffers Black Angus
48	Racine	John H. Batten Field (RAC)	Around The Clock
49	Racine	John H. Batten Field (RAC)	Infucino's Restaurant
50	Reedsburg	Reedsburg Muni. Arpt. (C35)	Longley's Restaurant
51	Rhinelander	Oneida Co. Arpt. (RHI)	Skyview Cafe
52	Richland Center	Richland Arpt. (93C)	Peaches Restaurant
53	Shawano	Shawano Muni. (3WO)	Launching Pad Rest.
54	Siren	Burnett Co. Arpt. (RZN)	Robertson's Family Rest.
55	Siren	Burnett Co. Arpt. (RZN)	Yellow River Inn
56	Superior	Richard Bong Arpt. (SUW)	Bellknap Restaurant
57	Tomah	Bloyer Field (Y72)	Burnstad European Cafe
58	Watertown	Watertown Muni. (RYV)	Streakfire Rest
59	Waukesha	Waukesha Co. (UES)	Waldo Peppers Rest.
60	Waukesha	Waukesha Co. (UES)	Weissgerber Gasthaus

Articles

City or town	Nearest Airport and Identifier	Name of Attraction
Baraboo, WI	Baraboo, WI (C85)	Wisconsin Dells
Cable Union, WI	Cable Union (3CU)	Telemark Lodge Resort
Delavan, WI	Lake Lawn Lodge Arpt. (C59)	Lake Lawn Lodge Resort
Ephraim, WI	Fish Creek Arpt. (3D2)	Landmark Resort
Land O' Lakes, WI	Kings Land O' Lakes (LNL)	Gateway Lodge Resort
Oshkosh, WI	Wittman Reg. (OSH)	EAA Conv. & Avia. Ctr.
Webster, WI	Voyager Village Arpt. (Y05)	Voyager Village C.C.

WI-ATW - APPLETON
OUTAGAMI COUNTY AIRPORT

Restaurants Near Airport: (Area Code 414) 1
Creative Croissants On Site Phone: 830-3393

Lodging: Best Western Midway Motor Inn (Trans) 731-4141; Holiday Inn (Trans) 735-9955; Paper Valley Hotel (Trans) 733-8000; Woodfield Suites (Trans) 734-9231.

Meeting Rooms: Best Western Midway Motor Inn 731-4141; Holiday Inn 735-9955; Paper Valley Hotel 733-8000; Woodfield Suites 734-9231.

Transportation: Taxi service: Fox Valley 734-4546; Yellow Cab 733-4444; Also rental cars: Avis 739-2346; Budget 731-2291; Hertz 734-2032; National 739-6421.

Information: Appleton, c/o Fox Cities Convention & Visitors Bureau, 110 Fox River Drive, Appleton, WI 54915, Phone: 734-3358.

Creative Croissants :

The Creative Croissants is located in the terminal building at the Outagami County Airport. This food service facility specializes in preparing delicious sandwiches made with Croissants. Their hours are weekdays 5 a.m. to 8 p.m. and weekends 6 a.m. to 5 p.m. Items on their menu include a variety of breakfast sandwiches made with ham and eggs. Lunch items include chicken club sandwiches, their special "Mother Earth" sandwich made with turkey, Monterey Jack cheese , lettuce, tomato on a Croissant. Other choices include vegetarian sandwiches, Santa Fe chicken sandwich, pasta and tossed salad, along with fresh homemade soups. The restaurant also contains a juice bar, gourmet coffees and Cappucino. For more information call 830-3393.

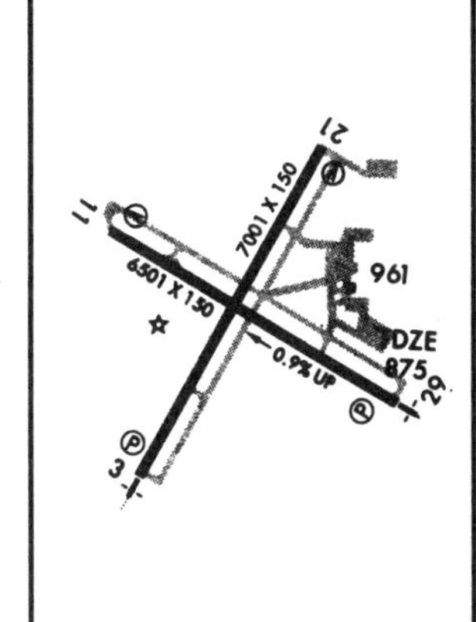

Airport Information:

APPLETON - OUTAGAMI COUNTY AIRPORT (ATW)
3 mi west of town N44-15.44 W88-31.17 Elev: 917 Fuel: 100LL, Jet-A1+, MOGAS
Rwy 03-21: H7001x150 (Conc-Grvd) Rwy 11-29: H6501x150 (Conc-Grvd) Attended: continuously Atis: 127.15 Unicom: 122.95 Appleton Tower: 119.6 Gnd Con: 121.7
FBO: K-C Aviation Phone: 735-7000
FBO: Maxair, Inc Phone: 738-3020

Wisconsin Dells

The Wisconsin Dells area, located in the south-central portion of Wisconsin, has become one of the most popular vacation spots in the midwest. Each year, millions of visitors flock to this region to enjoy the unlimited number of activities available for the entire family. The Dells, rich with its natural beauty along a fourteen mile stretch of the Wisconsin River, exhibits spectacular sculptured cliffs formed by thousands of years of torrential glacial waters through the soft sandstone. Some of these formations extend 100 feet above the water level.

Dells Boat Tours take visitors through the Wisconsin River to view these spectacular formations, while skilled pilots and guides give a running commentary on the area's geology, history and Indian legends. You have a choice of boat tours: The Upper Dells Boat Tour, The Lower Dells Boat Tour or The Complete Dells Boat Tour (a combinaton of the Upper and Lower Dells tours). Dells Boat Tours operate from mid-April through October. Departures are every 20-30 minutes, with less frequent departures during spring and fall. Free parking is available to all boat tour passengers, as well as a courtesy bus for transportation between the Upper Dells and Lower Dells boat docks. Snack shops and public restrooms are near both boat docks, and at all shorelandings. For a bit of history, take a ride on The Original Wisconsin Ducks(open from mid-April through October), amphibious WWII vehicles used during the famous Normandy (D-Day) Invasion, travel over land and water, taking passengers on an 8 1/2 mile, one-hour adventure through the beautiful scenery of Wisconsin Dells.

There are many other exciting activities that Wisconsin Dells has to offer. Take a break from the summer heat and visit the various water amusement parks, such as Family Land, Noah's Ark, and Riverview Park and Waterworld. Or, for a change of pace, relax and laugh while watching an animated stage show at Tommy Bartlett's Country Critter Jamboree; fun for all ages. For hair-raising excitiment, visit Count Wolff Von Baldasars Haunted Mansion, which contains nine dreary dungeons of dastardly illusions.

For the hidden singing sensation in your traveling group, travel to downtown Wisconsin Dells and stop in at On Stage.

Photo by: Wisconsin Dells Visitor And Convention Bureau

Towering sand stone cliffs line the banks along the Wisconsin River.

It offers a fully-equipped recording studio, in which singers can choose from over 100 rock n' roll and country music songs, or Christmas carols to record. Afterward, they can leave with their own professionally recorded song on cassette tape. After making a hit downtown, head to the Tommy Bartlett Ski, Sky and Stage Show on Hwy. 12. Observe an astounding contortionist twist and turn into unimaginable positions, or watch as aerialists make daring mid-air exchanges while swinging from 100-foot sway poles. Speaking of flying, be sure to catch a bird's eye view of the annual "Great Wisconsin Dells Balloon Rally" for two days of colorful flying competition.

Boggle your scientific mind and visit Tommy Bartlett's Robot World (adjacent to the Ski, Sky, and Stage Show), where you'll take a robot-guided tour through a house of the future. Or, stop at the Exploratory, a hands-on scientific and educational center that is filled with over 70 exhibits for explorational fun.

While exploring Wisconsin Dells, visitors will want to stop at the Dells Crossroads, a family entertainment park. Just ten minutes down the road, in Baraboo, Wisconsin, the Circus World Museum comes alive with big top performances, parades, elephant and carousel rides, clown shows, band concerts, a Wild West exhibit, the amazing Theatre of Illusion and tours of historical circus wagons. All Aboard! Visit the Mid-Continent Railway Museum and ride the authentic turn-of-the-century steam train (open through mid-October). The train offers special autumn color tours through the Baraboo River Valley.

For nighttime entertainment, you can

be sure to bet on a good time in Wisconsin Dells if you try your luck at the Ho-Chunk Golden Nickel Casino (open 24-hours a day, 7 days a week), which features 48 Blackjack tables and more than 1,200 Direct Pay slot machines. For fast-paced excitement, Wisconsin Dells Greyhound Racing (open through November) features more than 70 color TV monitors, easy-access betting windows and the choice of either reserved clubhouse or grandstand seating. After the races, take a break at the Kennel Club Restaurant and Bar, which serves both lunch and dinner. Then, liven up your lucky night with some foot-stompin' country music at one of three live country music theatres. The Crystal Grand Music Theatre (open year-round), seats up to 1,500 and features state-of-the-art sound and lighting systems. The Country Legends Music Theatre (open various weekends during fall) speaks for itself. For a real country treat, visit the Wisconsin Opry (open through September) at a working 80-acre farm, which has nightly performances and includes a home-cooked dinner. The Dells also offers many other varieties of music to suit your taste. The Inn of the Dells offers live piano and pop music, or Brother-in-Laws features rock 'n roll dancing and the Tower Pub features jazz sounds of yesterday. If you enjoy banjo playing and sing-a-longs, the Showboat would be the place for you.

When you are simply exhausted from all the sight-seeing and entertainment, Wisconsin Dells offers your choice of several area motels. Love the outdoors? You can stay at one of many campgrounds in the area. If all that touring has worked up an appetite, then a treat for the tastebuds is waiting for you in The Dells. Several area restaurants, including Howie's Huge Breakfast and Nanya's Cafe, have breakfast specials to get your day started. The Patio Restaurant and Dells Grill specializes in delicious homemade rolls, pies, soups and daily specials. Several area supper clubs provide elegant dining experiences. The Crystal Room at Field's Steak N' Stein or Fischer's Supper Club have nightly specials, along with choice steaks, prime rib and seafood. For a bit of entertainment while dining, Fast Molly's performs a light-hearted musical comedy revue simultaneously. For those that love eating out-of-doors during the summer months, Port Vista has great burger specials. Jimmie's Del-Bar offers delicious steak and seafood specialties. The House of Embers garden gazebo features mouth-watering hickory smoked barbeque ribs. Capture a breathtaking view across the table at Ishnala, which overlooks beautiful Mirror Lake. (Note: Ishnala is open only during the summer months) Dine at the Cambrian Lodge or the River Inn for a view of the sandstone rock formations on the Upper Dells. The Lighthouse restaurant provides indoor and outdoor seating, where you can watch the scenic boat tours dock on the Lower Dells.

For your convenience, the Baraboo Wisconsin Dells Airport is located approximately 8 miles south of the Wisconsin Dells downtown district. This airport has a 4795x75' north-south asphalt runway, as well as a 2715x100' northwest-southeast turf strip. If you purchase fuel, there is no tie-down fee, otherwise it is $3.00/night. Country Corner Cars, an on-field car rental service, charges $29.95/day with the first 100 miles free. Call the FBO at 356-2270 for further assistance. For more information about activities and accommodations in Wisconsin Dells, contact the Wisconsin Dells Visitor and Convention Bureau at 800-22-DELLS (800-223-3557). (Information submitted by the Wisconsin Dells Visitor and Convention Bureau.)

Photo by: Aerodine Magazine

The Wisconsin Dells downtown area is many gift shops and attractions on hand

Photo by: Wisconsin Dells Visitor And Convention Bureau

Wisconsin Dells features 3 world-class waterparks for your enjoyment.

WI-WI20 - BOYCEVILLE
BOYCEVILLE MUNICIPAL AIRPORT

(Area Code 715) 2

Cozy Cafe:

The Cozy Cafe is reported to be situated 3 blocks from the Boyceville Municipal Airport. This family style restaurant is open Monday through Thursday from 6 a.m. to 9 p.m., Friday and Saturday 6 a.m. to 10 p.m. and Sunday from 7 a.m. to 8 p.m. Their specialties include breakfast, lunch and dinner dishes with hearty meat and potatoes selections. Turkey, beef, dressing, baked or mashed potatoes, gravy and rolls. Many or these choices are reasonably priced around $3.95 to $4.50. A full breakfast line is also available. Average menu prices range from $2.00 to $9.95. Shrimp and steak dinners usually run around $3.95 to $9.95. They even provide a Sunday brunch beginning at 9 a.m. to 2 p.m. and a Friday fish fry from 5 p.m. to 9 p.m. Their main dining room can seat 65 persons and has a cafe style decor. Larger groups are welcome. However, please let them know how many are in your party so they can serve you more efficiently. Anything on their menu can be prepared for carry-out. For more information, call the Corner Cafe at 643-3314.

Restaurants Near Airport:
Cozy Cafe 3 blks Phone: 643-3314

Lodging: None reported near airport.

Meeting Rooms: None Reported

Transportation: None Reported

Information: Eau Claire Convention Bureau, 2127 Brackett Ave, Eau Claire, WI 5470, (Est. 30 mi S.E. of Boyceville) Phone: 839-2919 or 800-344-FUNN; Menomonie Falls Area Chamber of Commerce, W 168 N8936 Appleton Avenue, P.O. Box 73, Menomonee Falls, WI 53052, (Est. 15 mi S.E. of Boyceville) Phone: 251-2430.

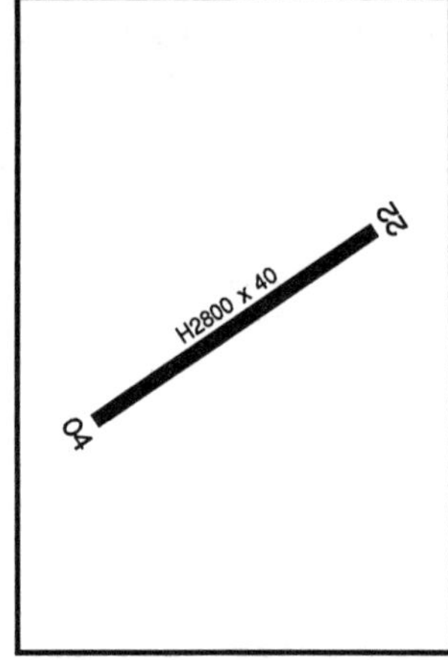

Airport Information:

BOYCEVILLE - BOYCEVILLE MUNICIPAL AIRPORT (WI20)
0 mi southeast of town N45-02.53 W92-01.76 Elev: 960 Fuel: 100LL
Rwy 04-22: H2800x40 (Asph) Attended: 1400-0000 CTAF: 122.8
FBO: Nerling Aviation Phone: 643-6100
FBO: Nor-Wes Aviation Phone: 643-3324

WI-02C - BROOKFIELD
CAPITOL AIRPORT

(Area Code 414) 3

Jake's Restaurant:

Jake's Restaurant is located at the Capitol Airport, Brookfield, Wisconsin in the western suburban area of Milwaukee. In 1960 this restaurant opened its doors for the first time. Back then their specialty was Tenderloin steak smothered with onion rings. As time passed this particular dish is what helped attracted more and more customers. Today their specialty of the house feature a variety of choice steaks and seafood along with roast duckling. The restaurant has a rustic decor with old barn wood finish and a large stone fireplace. Guests can enjoy a casual come as you are atmosphere. The restaurant is open from 4:45 p.m. to 10 p.m. Monday through Sunday. You can park your plane and walk 200 feet or so, across the street to the restaurant. Their telephone number is 781-7995. Reservations are not accepted.

Restaurants Near Airport:
Jake's Restaurant Adj Arpt Phone: 781-7995

Lodging: Budgetel (6 miles) 782-9100; Fairfield Inn (3 miles); Hampton Inn (3 miles); Holiday Inn (3 miles); Knight's Inn (3 miles); Motel 6 (3 miles); Call Brookfield Chamber of Commerce for phone numbers. See "Information" listed below.

Meeting Rooms: None Reported

Transportation: Airport courtesy reported, call airport manager at 781-9550, 781-7809, or 362-3957.

Information: Brookfield Chamber of Commerce, 235 North Executive Drive, #215, Brookfield, WI 53005, Phone: 786-1886.

NO AIRPORT DIAGRAM AVAILABLE

Airport Information:

BROOKFIELD - CAPITOL AIRPORT (02C)
3 mi east of town N43-05.25 W88-10.67 Elev: 850 Fuel: 100LL, MOGAS
Rwy 03-21: H3500x44 (Asph) Rwy 09-27: 3230x90 (Turf) Rwy 18-36: 1525x90 (Turf)
Attended: 1400-dusk Unicom: 122.7 Notes: Rwy 03 and 36 acft ops cannot see Rwy 27 acft ops. See AFD for Rwy conditions and notes about snow removal. Also: Rwy 09-27 and 18-36 not plowed or sanded during winter months, (See Airport Facility Directory).
FBO: Arpt. Mgr, & Eagle Aviation of Milwaukee Phone: 781-9550, 781-0795 or 800-859-7951

WI-3CU - CABLE
CABLE UNION AIRPORT

Telemark Resort:

This four-season resort provides easy access for general aviation travelers, and excellent accommodations for private as well as corporate gatherings. Telemark Lodge, built at the base of Mt.Telemark, offers combined recreation and convention services, and is nestled within 2,500 acres of lush Wisconsin forest land. When it comes down to mixing business with pleasure, this complex provides 48,000 square feet of meeting and exhibit space allowing for tremendous flexibility. Even though the Lodge provides outstanding accommodations for businesses, it also caters heavily to individuals and families, offering special seasonal and weekend package deals. This resort complex offers an 18 hole championship golf course, indoor and outdoor swimming, shopping mall, game rooms, ski school, horseback riding, sleigh rides, sauna, tennis, basket ball, volleyball and many other amenities. The Cable Union Airport is situated only 200 feet from Telemark Resort, at the base of Mt.Telemark. For more information about Telemark Resort call 798-3811.

(Area Code 715) 4

Restaurants Near Airport:

Colosseum Cafeteria	On Site	Phone: 798-3811
Passages (Telemark Resort)	On Site	Phone: 798-3811
Seasons Coffee Shop	On Site	Phone: 798-3811

Lodging: Telemark Resort offers their guests a variety of choices including 200 lodge rooms, their Valhalla townhouses, and the Christiania condos, able to sleep parties of 2 up to groups of 10; For a list of lodging accommodations, call the resort at 798-3811.
Meeting Rooms: Telemark Resort provides convention space along with meeting rooms and banquet facilities. Catered meals can also be prepared for business or group functions. For information call Telemark Resort at 798-3811.
Transportation: Telemark Resort is located adjacent to the Cable Union Airport (Est. 200 feet). Courtesy and rental cars are available with advance notice by calling the airport at 798-3240, or the resort at 798-3811.
Information: (Telemakrk Resort) Mount Telemark, P.O. Box 277, Cable, WI 54821, Phone: 798-3811;

Attractions: Telemark Resort situated only 200 feet from the Cable Union Airport (3CU), Phone: 798-3811.

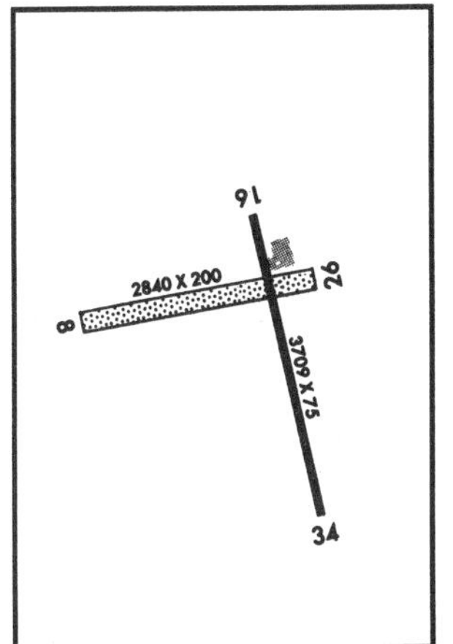

Airport Information:

CABLE - CABLE UNION AIRPORT (3CU)
2 mi southeast of town N46-11.66 W91-14.79 Elev: 1360 Fuel: 80, 100
Rwy 16-34: H3709x75 (Asph) Rwy 08-26: 2840x200 (Turf) Attended: 1400Z-dusk, other hours call 798-3240 Unicom: 122.8 Notes: Rwy 08-26 CLOSED Nov 18-May 1.
FBO: Parod Flying Service Phone: 798-3240

Telemark Resort & Convention Center

Cable Union, WI (WI-3CU)

We want to acquaint you with Telemark Resort, a fly-in resort in Cable, Wisconsin. Cable, Wisconsin is located in the northwestern region of the state, approximately 15 miles northwest of Hayward. This four-season resort is conveniently positioned adjacent to Cable Union Airport, which is equipped with a 3700 foot paved and lighted runway. The resort provides its guests with an outstanding array of winter activities as well as spring, summer and fall recreation.

The lodge itself offers a warm and cheerful atmosphere. The main lobby is constructed of laminated wooden beams, cedar wall planking and a 55 foot high by 14 foot wide fieldstone fireplace with chimney. Accommodations include 200 lodge rooms which are spacious and airy. Each room provides a private balcony, individually controlled heat and air-conditioning, color TV, game table and private bath. Telemark also offers twenty-eight Valhalla townhouses that skirt the tree-lined Valhalla ski hill of

Photo by: Telemark Resort — Telemark Resort during the winter season

Telemark. Each is fully furnished with all the comforts of home, including a fireplace, private balcony, two full baths, and a fully-equipped kitchen. In addition to these, Telemark also offers condominiums available through their vacation ownership program. The Christiania condos are built around the Christiania ski hill and offers plush accommodations sleeping 2 to 10 people. Their vacation ownership program is affiliated with Resorts Condominiums Interna-

Photo by: Telemark Resort

Cable Union Airport only 200 feet from Telemark Resort.

tional, which are world wide vacation ownership suites, that are located inside the resort. These 3 room (2 bedroom) suites offer plush accommodations with full kitchens and jacuzzis. For your dining pleasure, the resort contains a dining room and coffee shop. The Passages dining room is very popular, with economically priced northwoods dinners offering a wide selection of entrees for a fine meal. Seasons coffee shop serves breakfast and lunch to resort guests with daily specials and northwoods favorites. In addition to these restaurants, the Colosseum Cafeteria also provides a quick sandwich or snack, with hamburgers, pizza, chili, donuts, cookies and brownies, to name a few selections. The cafeteria is open during the ski season. During the evening hours, after 9:00 p.m., the Telemark Nite Club provides live entertainment and is an excellent place to gather with friends and dance the night away.

The amenities of the resort provides a great many things to do, including their 18-hole championship golf course. There is also an indoor and outdoor swimming pool and sauna, whirlpool, game rooms and shopping mall. The Telemark Colosseum is in the center of the Telemark ski area, housing a ski school, rental shop and a complete ski shop, and four indoor tennis courts that are also used for volleyball and basketball. Telemark Resort has horseback riding, along with winter activities and sleigh rides for their guests. In addition to the accommodations previously mentioned, Telemark Resort offers banquet and meeting facilities as well. If planning a group fly-in or a corporate convention, Telemark Resort would make an excellent choice. A state licensed day care center is also available for children.

The Cable Union Airport is located at the base of Mt. Telemark, within walking distance (est. 200 feet) of the resort, with a (16-34) 3,709 x 75 paved and lighted runway along with a (08-26) 2,840 x 200 turf strip (turf strip reported closed during the winter season). Aviation 80 and 100LL fuel is available, and their unicom is 122.8. Courtesy and rental cars can be obtained if requested in advance. For information about available services, including fuel and runway conditions, call the airport at 798-3240. For any questions you may have regarding reservations, weekend or seasonal package rates, we suggest you call Telemark Resort in Cable Wisconsin at 798-3811.

WI-Y05 - DANBURY/WEBSTER VOYAGER VILLAGE AIRPORT

(Area Code 715) 5

Voyager Village Country Club:

Voyager Village Country Club is an elegant northland resort home living community in Danbury, Wisconsin, that offers a variety of amenities including 10 scenic lakes located within 6,300 acres of wooded countryside, an 18 hole golf course, plus a par 3, 9 hole course, boating and sailing, and clubhouse complete with indoor olympic size swimming pool, outdoor tennis courts, miniature golf, shuffleboard and a supper club within the main club house. During the summer the restaurant is open from 9 a.m. to 9 p.m. seven days a week and during the winter season from November 1st through April 1st ,they are open 5 days a week on Wednesday through Sunday. Their hours are 9 a.m. to 9 p.m.weekends and from 11 a.m. to 9 p.m. weekdays (closed Monday and Tuesday). Their entrees contain a full breakfast, lunch and dinner selection, as well as a Friday night fish fry. Accommodations for groups up to 50 can be obtained if advance notice is given. The clubhouse containing the restaurant has a view that overlooks Birch Island Lake and private airstrip. Aircraft parking is located within walking distance. For brochures about the country club call 259-3910. For information call the restaurant at 259-3382.

Restaurants Near Airport:
Voyager Village Country Club On Site Phone: 259-3382

Lodging: None Reported
Meeting Rooms: Voyager Village Country Club has accommodations for groups and meeting rooms able to seat up to 20 people. Call 259-3382.
Transportation: None Reported
Information: Webster Chamber of Commerce, P.O. Box 48, Webster, WI 54893, Phone: 866-4251; Also Voyager Village Country Club, 28851 Kilkare Road, Danbury, WI 54830-8506, Phone: 259-3382.

Attractions:

Voyager Village Country Club contains a resort home living community near Danbury Wisconsin. Private airstrip and nearby activities are available including golfing on their 18 hole and par 3, 9 hole courses. For information call 259-3382.

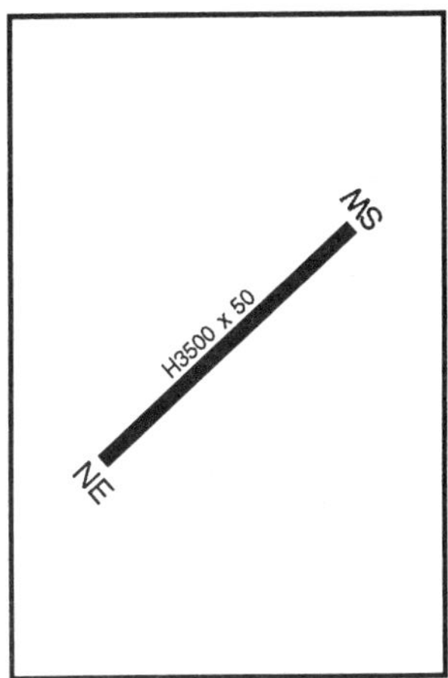

Airport Information:

DANBURY/WEBSTER - VOYAGER VILLAGE AIRPORT (Y05)
10 mi east of town 45-58-00N 92-08-00W Elev: 1020 Fuel: none reported
Attended: N/A Rwy NE-SW H3500x50 (Asph) Notes: (Private: Use at own risk) Contact Voyager Village Resort for airport information prior to use.
Voyager Village Resort Phone: 259-3382.

WI-C59 - DELAVAN LAKE LAWN AIRPORT (RESORT)

(Area Code 414) 6

Lake Lawn Lodge Resort:

Lake Lawn Resort is located on the northern boundary of beautiful Lake Delavan. The resort features fine dining restaurants, coffee shops and a deli as well as several lounges. The restaurants begin serving at 7 a.m. and until 11 p.m. for dinner. Several very popular alternative choices for dining are available. They include breakfast buffets, a fabulous Sunday brunch, Friday fish fry buffet as well as elaborate holiday buffets on special occasions throughout the year. Recreation at Lake Lawn Lodge includes a magnificent new 18-hole golf course, two indoor and one outdoor swimming pools, health club, gift shops, marina, and riding stable. Lodging accommodations include 284 rooms, with special appoitments in some, including unique lofts and suites, all nestled among 275 scenic acres of wooded country side, along the shores of Lake Delavan. In addition, Lake Lawn Lodge also provides banquet facilities and meeting rooms for groups of 10 to 550 persons. Complete with it's own 4,400 x 80 foot hard surface runway, this resort complex rates as one of the highest in the Midwest for fly-in dining and entertainment. Courtesy vans are available, however, it's only a five minute walk from the airport to the main lodge. For more information and reservations, call 728-5511 or 800-338-5253.

Restaurants Near Airport:
Lake Lawn Lodge On Site Phone: 728-5511

Lodging: Lake Lawn Lodge 728-5511.
Meeting Rooms: Lake Lawn Lodge (Convention facilities available) 728-5511.
Transportation: Lake Lawn Lodge is within walking distance and also provides courtesy van transportation from the airport 100 yards to the main lodge.
Information: Delavan-Delavan Lake Chamber of Commerce, 52 East Walworth Avenue, P.O. 384, Delavan, WI 53115, Phone: 414-728-5095

Attractions:

Lake Lawn Lodge attracts literally thousands of fly-in customers each year. The resort is located adjacent to a private airstrip, and is situated along the shores of Lake Delavan in Wisconsin. Phone: 728-5511.

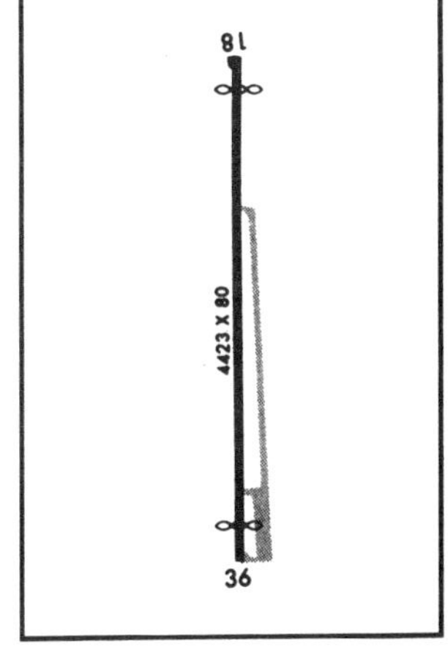

Airport Information:

DELAVAN - LAKE LAWN LODGE (C59)
2 mi east of town N42-38.05 W88-36.07 Elev: 981 Fuel: 100LL, Jet-A
Rwy 18-36: H4423x80 (Asph) Attended: 7 a.m. to 6 p.m. winter, 7 a.m. to 9 p.m. summer; AFD states hours to be: Jun-Aug 1300-0300Z, Sept-Oct 1300-0200Z, Nov-Jan 1300-0000Z, Feb-May 1400-2200Z Unicom: 122.7
FBO: Lake Lawn Lodge Phone: 728-5511

Lake Lawn Lodge

Picture yourself searching for that perfect resort which offers four seasons of activities, exquisite dining and the best in lodging accommodations, along with business and convention facilities. Now imagine this resort with its very own private airstrip, all nestled among 275 acres of the most scenic surroundings imaginable within the Wisconsin Lake Geneva Area. Putting all this together and you have just described a facility by the name of Lake Lawn Lodge.

What sets this particular resort apart from other resorts, is of course its own private 4,400' x 80' paved lighted airstrip, which has made this establishment one of the most popular fly-in dining and entertainment facilities available to the flying public.

Their airport is very well maintained, and is within only a five or ten minute walk, or a 2 minute ride by courtesy van to the lodge. As you approach the main entrance you will see beautiful planting areas and large stone and timber fences on either side of the road, separating an 18 hole golf course spotted with huge oak trees casting their shadows upon the rolling fairways. The resort is made up of several vary attractive yet rustic buildings, all connected to each other by way of glassed in walkways.

Lake Lawn provides a welcome relief from the city traffic and urban congestion. With 2-1/2 miles of scenic lake front, it offers visitors a chance to relax and enjoy themself. Their are 284 rooms, some of which include unique lofts, luxurious suites and spacious guest rooms, all newly renovated. Many rooms are also equipped with lake view patios, balconies, fireplaces, and wet bars, plus cable TV, including a free movie channel. And these accommodations were designed to give you ample space. As many as four people can occupy one of their loft rooms and still enjoy privacy.

Dining in Lake Lawn's "Frontier Dining Room", is an elegant and memorable experience that you won't want to miss. As you dine, and savor their fine cuisine, you can watch sailing and motor boats while overlooking Lake Delavan. If you prefer a light snack or sandwich, you are welcome to dine in the "Courtyard Cafe" for casual contemporary fare, or "Manny's Deli". There are also several unique lounges available for cocktails and mixed drinks.

Photo by: Aerodine Aerial view of lake lawn Resort

In addition to the dining, there are seven unique gift shops that feature top names in fashion, accessories and merchandise including a shop with fresh baked goods and gourmet delicacies. You'll find plenty of recreation too, with an 18 hole golf course with pro shop, tennis courts, horseback riding, cross country skiing, swimming pool, and a private beach with marina for boat rentals. Inside, the lodge, enjoy two tropical pools, a whirlpool, or work out in Lake Lawn's health club - fully equipped with steam, sauna, tanning beds and exercise equipment.

At Lake Lawn, business and pleasure come together and meet with success. The moment you book your group, their professional staff goes to work planning your stay. The staff will work with you, suggesting special activities and teamed events to liven up your agenda. They even help you build team spirit and camaraderie with organized recreation, contests and corporate olympics.

Their meeting rooms are unique, and functional, from the "Geneva Room" to additional conference and breakout rooms, with space for 10 to 550 people. This facility was designed for traffic flow, so your group can move easily from displays to seminars to receptions. Then, to dinner in a beautiful lake view banquet room, all without leaving the facility. If dining outdoors sounds like fun, Lake Lawn can accommodate your needs with outdoor catering, so your group can enjoy the fresh lake breezes and a unique natural setting while you dine. All the resorts amenities are at your disposal when planning your next business conference.

Whether you plan to visit Lake Lawn with your family or friends, or plan to coordinate a business conference to impress your clients, you will find this particular resort the finest choices available. For information call 800-338-5253 or res. 800-338-5296.

Photo by: Aerodine An outside view of one of Lake Lawns main dining rooms

WI-EGV - EAGLE RIVER
EAGLE RIVER UNION AIRPORT

(Area Code 715)

7, 8

Aerio Club:

The Aerio Club Restaurant is located within walking distance (Est. 1/4 mile) from the Eagle River Union Airport. This family style restaurant contains a bar and is open Monday through Saturday for lunch between 11 a.m. and 2 p.m. and for dinner between 4:30 p.m. and 10 p.m. On Sunday they open from 4 p.m. to 10 p.m. Daily dinner specials include: Monday center cut pork loin, Tuesday spaghetti, Wednesday chicken, Thursday barbecued ribs, Friday fish fry, and Saturday prime rib. Their menu contains many selections as well as sandwiches. Average prices run $2.25 to $4.00 for lunch and $4.00 to $8.00 for dinner. Their dining room can accommodate up to 98 persons and provides a cozy atmosphere decorated with knotty pine walls and some aviation pictures. Antiques items decorating the restaurant are for sale. The name Aerio Club Restaurant was selected by the original owners due to its close proximity to the Airport. Even though fly-in guests can not physically see the restaurant from the airport, we were told that the restaurant is situated past a gas station and building that blocks its view. Airport personnel can direct you as well. The restaurant will also prepare meals to-go, or for carry-out. For information about the Aerio Club Restaurant call 479-4695.

Betty's Eagle Cafe:

Betty's Eagle Cafe is located within walking distance from the Eagle River Union Airport. We were told that you can see their establishment from the airport. We were also told that this restaurant is positioned adjacent to a American Heritage Motel. They are open from 5:00 a.m. to 3 p.m. 7 days a week. This family style restaurant provides a rustic appearance with a log cabin exterior, and decorated inside with tongue and groove wood paneling. Seating capacity is 150 persons, with tables and chairs along with a counter with stools. Groups and parties are welcome. Their menu includes a variety of breakfast specials as well as many lunch and dinner items like 4 different chicken dishes, 6 types of hot beef plates along with sandwiches, and their 1/3 pound hamburger. This restaurant is fairly new and provides accommodations for fly-in groups and parties as well as preparing meals-to-go or for carry-out. For more information about Betty's Eagle Cafe, call 479-2766.

Restaurants Near Airport:

Aerio Club Restaurant	1/4 mi	Phone: 479-4695
Betty's Eagle Cafe	1/4 mi	Phone: 479-2766

Lodging: American Budgetel Inn (1/4 mile); Eagle River Inn (3 miles) 479-2000; Hiawatha Motor Lodge (1-1/4 mile) 479-6431; Shoreline (1/2 mile) 479-1508.

Meeting Rooms: Eagle River Inn (3 miles) 479-2000.

Transportation: Airport courtesy car reported; Also Rental Cars: Jer's Auto 479-8353; Ron's Auto 479-7405; Trans North 479-6777.

Information: Eagle River Chamber of Commerce, P.O. Box 1917, Eagle River, WI 54521, Phone: 479-6400, 800-359-6315.

Attractions:

Eagle River hosts a number of activities throughout the year. In January their ***Snowmobile Derby*** kicks off on the 3rd weekend; On the last weekend of February they celebrate their ***"Klondike Day" festival;*** One special event that is a must for aviation enthusiasts is their spectacular ***Eagle River Annual Fly-In***. It is held on the third weekend of June. This event attracts more thatn 100 aircraft including war birds and vintage planes, along with all types of general aviation aircraft. This annual event is open to the public and attracts pilots from all over the midwest region. There is no landing fee or admission charged; Another event is the ***Art'Orama*** which is large art and craft show that is held the 3rd Saturday in July; In August two additional events are scheduled. The ***Vilas County Fair*** and the ***National Muskie Tournament***.. Also during the summer season they have an impressive ***Gun Show*** as well as an ***Antique Show***. In September they feature an***Automobile Show***; and during the month of October their ***Cranberry Festival*** swings into action the 1st weekend of the month. For information call the Eagle River Information Bureau at 715-479-8575 or 800-359-6315.

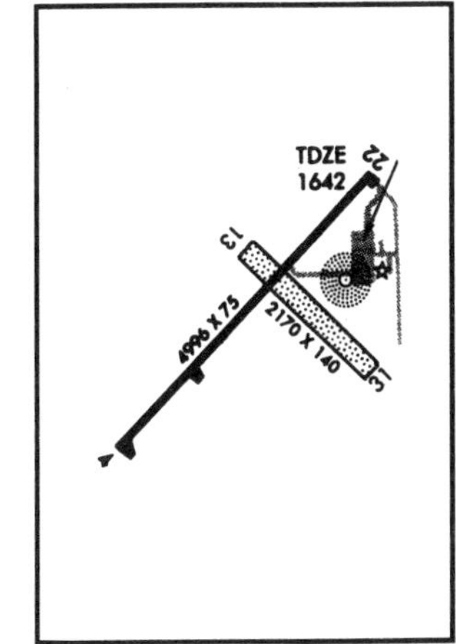

Airport Information:

EAGLE RIVER - EAGLE RIVER UNION AIRPORT (EGV)
0 mi northwest of town N45-55.91 W89-16.14 Elev: 1641 Fuel: 100LL, Jet-A
Rwy 04-22: H4996x75 (Asph) Rwy 13-31: 2170x140 (Turf) Attended: Jun-Aug 1500-0200Z, Sep-May 1500-2300Z Unicom: 122.8
Eagle River Union Airport Phone: 479-7442

WI-57C - EAST TROY
EAST TROY MUNICIPAL AIRPORT

(Area Code 414)

9

Jackson's Pointe II, Inc.

This combination family style and fine dining facility is located about 1 mile west of the East Troy Municipal Airport. This restaurant will provide free transportation for fly-in guests. Ask to speak to either Doug, Joyce or Bob. To get to the restaurant you will take Hwy. L to Hwy. 20 west to ES. Turn right on ES & take it straight to the restaurant. They are located just across Interstate 43 from the airport. The restaurant serves lunch Tuesday through Friday from 11 a.m. to 2 p.m. and dinner at 5 p.m. On Sunday, dinners start at 4 p.m. (Closed on Monday) Their specialties are prime rib, steak, chicken and seafood. They provide a choice of light fare as well as regular portions. Prices average $5.95 for lunch and $8.95 for dinner. On Friday they offer an all-you-can-eat selection featuring Icelandic haddock, homemade potato pancakes, shrimp basket, chicken basket and lake perch. Nightly specials are also offered on their menu. The restaurant's decor is casual with a country atmosphere. Private rooms are available for groups making advance reservations. They can also provide carry-out meals or even deliver to the airport for pilots on-the-go. For information call 642-7348.

Restaurants Near Airport:

Andy's Ranch Inn	2 mi W.	Phone: 642-9070
East Troy House	2 mi W.	Phone: 642-7040
Jackson's Pointe II	1 mi W.	Phone: 642-7348
Obie's Cobblestone	2 mi.	Phone: 642-7128

Lodging: Sky Lark Motel (2 miles), Phone: 642-5001; Alpine Valley Resort, (5 miles) Lodging with 133 rooms available at resort, downhill and cross-country skiing, 288 foot vertical rise with 8 tree lined slopes, longest run 3,300 feet. Accommodations include indoor swimming pool, game room, restaurants & lounges at base of slopes. For information call Phone: 642-7373.

Meeting rooms: Both Jackson's Club Point II & Alpine Valley Resort have accommodations for conferences. (See lodging)

Transportation: Fleet Air, Inc. can help provide their customers with available courtesy transportation. Call 642-9388.

Information: Elkhorn Chamber of Commerce, 9 South Street, P.O. Box 41, Elkhorn, WI 53121, Phone: 723-5788.

Attractions:
Alpine Valley Resort (See Lodging listed above);

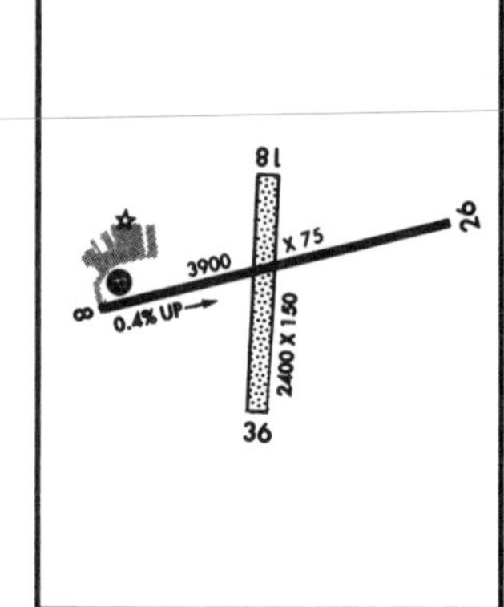

Airport Information:

EAST TROY - EAST TROY MUNICIPAL AIRPORT (57C)
2 mi northeast of town N42-47.83 W88-22.35 Elev: 860 Fuel 80, 100LL, Jet-A
Rwy 08-26: H3900x75 (Asph) Rwy 18-36: 2400x150 (Turf) Attended: 1400-2300Z
Public Phone 24hrs Notes: Rwy 18-36 not plowed during winter months, CLOSED 15 Oct-15 May.
FBO: Base Aviation Phone: 642-4374

WI-EAU - EAU CLAIRE
CHIPPEWA VALLEY REGIONAL

(Area Code 715)

10

Connell's II At The Airport:

Connell's II At The Airport, is a family style restaurant that is situated within the main terminal building on the Chippewa Valley Regional Airport. Their summer hours are from 6 a.m. to 10 p.m. Monday through Thursday and 6 a.m. to 11 p.m. on Friday and Saturday. During the Winter they close at 9 p.m. Monday through Thursday and 10:30 p.m. on Friday and Saturday. Their menu contains everything from light fare to steak and lobster. Daily specials are offered throughout the day and also during the evening hours. Their main dining room can seat 108 persons. Accommodations for groups can easily be arranged. There are 2 banquet rooms that can handle parties from 40 to 100 persons respectively. In-flight catering is another service provided by Connell's II Restaurant. For more information call 833-9400.

Restaurants Near Airport:
Connell's II at the Airport On Site Phone: 833-9400

Lodging: Best Western Midway Motor Inn (Trans) 835-2242; Civic Center Inn (Trans) 835-6121; Holiday Inn (Trans) 834-3181.

Meeting Rooms: Best Western Midway Motor Inn 835-2242; Civic Center Inn 835-6121; Holiday Inn 834-3181.

Transportation: Airport Courtesy car reported; Taxi Service: Limo 835-1413; Yellow Cab 835-6129; Also Rental Cars: Budget 839-7921; Hertz 832-1217; National 832-2152.

Information: Eau Claire Convention & Tourism Bureau, 2127 Brackett Avenue, Eau Claire, WI 54701, Phone 839-2919, 800-344-FUNN.

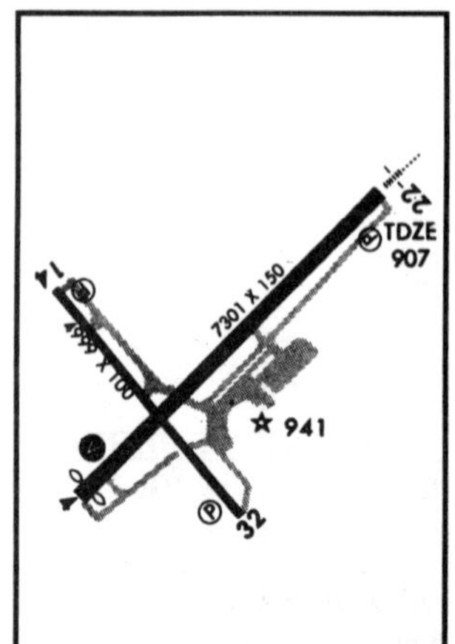

Airport Information:

EAU CLAIRE - CHIPPEWA VALLEY REGIONAL AIRPORT (EAU)
3 mi north of town N44-51.92 W91-29.11 Elev: 907 Fuel: 100LL, Jet-A, MOGAS
Rwy 04-22: H7301x150 (Conc-Wc) Rwy 14-32: H4999x100 (Asph-Conc) Attended 1300-0100Z Unicom: 123.0
Airport Manager Phone: 839-4900
FBO: Heartland Aviation Phone: 835-3181

WI-3D2 - EPHRAIM - (Door County) FISH CREEK

(Area Code 414)

11, 12, 13

C & C Supper Club:

The C & C Supper Club is located about 4-1/2 miles from the Fish Creek Airport. This is a fine dining establishment that is open from 4:45 p.m. to 9:30 p.m. 7 days a week, and on weekends they open their doors at 11:30 for lunch. Specialties of the house are fresh seafood, steaks, pastas and barbecue ribs. They also have a salad bar that is included with all dinner selections. Average prices run $13.00 for main course items. The decor of the restaurant exhibits leaded glass and brass separations in their lounge, and a nautical flair throughout other portions of the restaurant. Linen table cloths, green carpeting and a fire place add to the warm pleasant atmosphere. The C & C Supper Club reported that they would provide transportation to and from the airport for their guests. Airport courtesy transportation may also be available. For more information about the C & C Supper Club call 868-3412.

Landmark Resort Conference Center:

The Landmark Resort is reported about 20 minutes by car from the Fish Creek Airport. This resort is situated along Highway 42. This is a full-service resort and conference center complete with a 27 hole golf course. Accommodations include a restaurant, banquet facilities, 11 meeting rooms, swimming pools, tennis courts and an adjacent golf course. The resort is at 7643 Hillside Road in Egg Harbor, WI. For information about reservations or accommodations call them at 868-3205.

The White Gull Inn:

The White Gull Inn is located 5 or 6 miles from the Fish Creek Airport. This combination family and fine dining establishment is open 7:30 a.m. to 2:30 everyday for breakfast and lunch. During the summer months of May through October they feature a fish boil on Wednesday, Friday, Saturday and Sunday evenings between 5:30 and 7 p.m., and a candle light dinner served on Monday, Tuesday and Thursday evenings 5:30 p.m. to 8:30 p.m. During the winter months the the fish boil is featured on Wednesday and Saturday nights from 5:30 p.m. to 7 p.m. The candlelight dinner is served throughout the week with the exception of Wednesday and Saturday evenings when the fish boil is being offered. Main dinner selections average $15.00 to $20.00. Their fish boil costs about $14.50 per person. The White Gull Inn depicts a beautiful country inn complete with chandeliers, brick floor and walls with decorative woodwork. Their main dining room can seat 85 people. A courtesy car is reported available from the airport for Eagle Harbor Air Service customers. Taxi service is also available. For information about The White Gull Inn call 868-3517.

Restaurants Near Airport:

C & C Supper Club	4-1/2 mi	Phone: 868-3412
The Cookery, Fish Creek	6 mi	Phone: 868-2372
Landmark Resort	20 Min.	Phone: 868-3205
The White Gull Inn	5-6 mi	Phone: 868-3517

Lodging: White Gull Inn 868-3517; Landmark Resort and Conference Center (20 min. by car) 868-3205.

Meeting Rooms: Landmark Resort And Conference Center (20 min. by car) 868-3205.

Transportation: Courtesy car 854-9711; Avis 854-9711; Taxi service 743-3443.

Information: Door County Chamber of Commerce, 1015 Green Bay Road, P.O. Box 406, Sturgeon Bay, WI 54235, Phone: 743-4456.

Attractions:

The town of Ephraim is located at the northern entrance to one of Door County peninsula's spectacular state parks. One of our contributors informed us that Peninsula State Park is situated only 6/10ths of a mile from the Fish Creek Airport. The park is located along a high bluff that jets out into Green Bay. The beautiful State Park Golf Course has an 18-hole course and a restaurant that makes an excellent golfing experience with its scenic surroundings. This is the only state-owned golf course in Wisconsin. There is also a lighthouse at Eagle Bluff located near that site. A number of other attractions draw many people to the region; beach site camping, hiking, cross-country skiing and snowmobiling. If planning to fly north or south along the eastern shore from Washington Island to Sturgeon Bay, WI., you are sure to enjoy the scenery. Passing over Detroit Island, Europe, Rowley Bay, North Bay, Moonlight Bay and Bailey's Harbor, gives the impression of a tropical Caribbean sea shore with underwater landscape that is clearly visible as it slopes away from the peninsula mainland. Fish Creek Attractions: If planning to obtain a courtesy or rental car when visiting Fish Creek, WI., you might want to stop and enjoy seeing an historic village located at the southern entrance to the Peninsula State Park. Old inns and attractive shops, artists galleries, eateries and sailing opportunities abound. Another attraction is the Peninsula Players, a professional resident summer theater company that performs the latest Broadway and Off-Broadway hits. These shows are performed on stage at the "Theater-in-a-Garden," situated between the town of Fish Creek and Egg Harbor. For more information about these and more attractions, you can contact: Peninsula State Park Route 42, Fish Creek, WI 54212 or call 414-868-3258.

Airport Information:

EPHRAIM - FISH CREEK (3D2)

1 southwest of town N45-08.12 W87-11.15 Elev: 773 Fuel: 100LL Rwy 14-32: H2700x60 (Asph) Rwy 01-19: 2370x80 (Turf) Attended: May-Oct 1600-0000Z Unicom: 123.0 Notes: Rwy 01-19 slopes immediately down to South-cannot see one end from the other. Rwy 01-19 ends and edges marked with yellow barrels.

FBO: Eagle Harbor Air Service, Inc. Phone: 854-9711

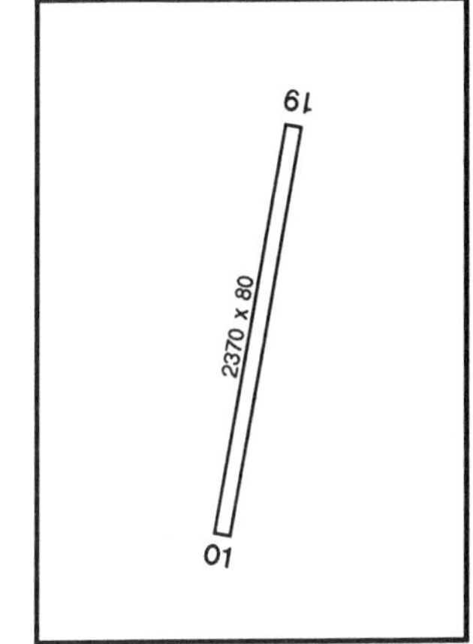

Landmark Resort and Conference Center

Ephraim, WI (WI-3D2)

The Landmark Resort and Door County offer you the beauty of a naturally wooded, bluff-top waterview setting with deluxe condominium accommodations. The Landmark Resort is reported about 20 minutes by car from the Fish Creek Airport. It is one of the most popular establishments in the Ephraim - Door Country, WI. area. This resort is situated along Highway 42. Enjoy the very finest in year-round recreational amenities at a full-service resort. Whatever the occasion... a quiet getaway weekend for two, a family vacation adventure, reunion or business conference... the Landmark Resort welcomes you! Your spacious condominium suite awaits you, with each suite featuring a living room, dining area, a fully stocked kitchen, bedroom and deck or patio.

Recreation: Family relaxation and recreation is what they are best at providing. Join in the fun with "Kamp Landmark," nature walks, arts and crafts, and a full activity schedule. Then enjoy the many amenities like: three outdoor heated pools, a large indoor pool, five indoor whirlpools, basketball courts, new state-of-the-art fitness center, five outdoor tennis courts, shuffleboard and horseshoe, and even outdoor volley ball. For the golfer, they also have a 27-hole golf course adjacent to their facility. Seasonal packages are available as well.

Conference Facilities: Business leaders recognize that productive meetings begin with the ideal setting. The Landmark Resort features eleven meeting rooms and a skilled, professional staff which specializes in groups up to 250. Let them help you organize your audio/visual needs, food and beverage requirements, and coordinate travel and entertainment arrangements during your stay.

Restaurant: Periwinkle's Restaurant, Bar & Grill features a delicious fresh salad and sandwich lunch menu, with dinner favorites including casual American and international entrees. The Egg Harbor Room, located at Periwinkle's caters to your special occasion, weddings, business meetings, and celebrations. For more information call the Landmark Resort at 414-868-3205. For information about conference space call 414-868-2325. (Information supplied by Landmark Resort).

Photo by: Landmark Resort

Landmark Resort offers a naturally wooded, bluff-top setting that overlooks the water.

Photo by: Landmark Resort

One of four swimming pools located on the premises.

WI-FLD - FOND DU LAC
FOND DU LAC COUNTY

(Area Code 414)

14

Restaurants Near Airport:

Country Woods/ Hol. Inn	2 mi	Phone: 923-1440
Gazebo (Dartmoor)	1 mi	Phone: 922-6030
Schreiners Restaurant	1.6 mi	Phone: 922-0590

Lodging: Budgetel Inn 1 mi 921-4000; Dartmoor 1 mi 922-6030; Days Inn 1 mi 923-6790; Economy 2 mi 922-6030; Holiday Inn 1 mi 923-1440; Ramada Inn 3 mil 923-3000; Sheraton Hotel 923-3000.
Meeting Rooms: Holiday Inn (1 mi , Holidome) 923-1440.
Transportation: Rental cars: Abbott 923--4466, Action 923-0003. Taxi service: ABC 923-0858.
Information: Fond du Lac Convention & Visitors Bureau, 19W Scott Street, Fond du Lac, WI 54935, Phone: 923-3010.

Schreiners Restaurant:

The Schreiners Restaurant is located only 1.6 miles from the Fond du Lac County Airport. To reach the restaurant from the airport you go north on W. Frontage road to Hwy 23, then east on 23 over Hwy 41, then south on E. Frontage Road to the restaurant. This establishment is an upscale family style restaurant with a full menu and fast friendly service. Schreiners Restaurant is famous for their New England style clam chowder and fresh baked goods. Daily changing menu specials are offered. Some of their more popular entrees are stewed chicken and dumplings, short ribs of beef and ham loaf. A mini menu at lunch, with specials, is offered between 11 a.m. and 2:30 p.m. Monday through Friday, with smaller portions at smaller prices. Normal menu selections range between $3.00 to $4.00 for breakfast, $4.00 to $6.00 for lunch and $5.00 to $9.00 for dinner. The decor of the restaurant is clean and bright with white and blue interior colors, Seating is accomplished with tables, booths and counter service. Although there are no separate facilities for large groups and no reservations accepted, Schreiners Restaurant should be able to take care of smaller group needs. Box lunches, sandwich and all items listed on their menu can be prepared for carry-out. This restaurant is a particularly popular dining location for pilots flying into the Fond du Lac Airport. For transportation to the restaurant just call the Schreiners staff and they will furnish your party with courtesy transportation. For information call them at 922-0590.

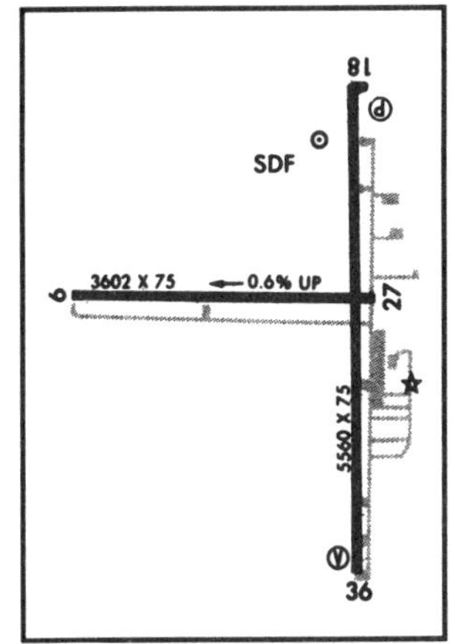

Airport Information:

FOND DU LAC - FOND DU LAC COUNTY (FLD)
1 mi west of town N43-46.25 W88-29.31 Elev: 807 Fuel: 100LL, Jet-A1 Rwy 18-36: H5560x75 (Asph) Rwy 09-27: H3602x75 (Asph) Attended: 1400Z-dusk Unicom: 122.8
FBO: Fond du Lac Skyport, Inc. Phone: 922-6000

WI-61C - FORT ATKINSON
FORT ATKINSON MUNICIPAL ARPT.

(Area Code 414)

15, 16, 17

Restaurants Near Airport:

Edgewater Restaurant	Adj Arpt	Phone: 674-9942
Fireside Playhouse	5 mi	Phone: 563-9505
Louise Riverview Rest.	Walk Dist	Phone: 674-9980

Lodging: Best Western Courtyard Inn (5 mi) 563-6444; Super 8 Motel (9 mi) 563-8444.
Meeting Rooms: None reported
Transportation: Brown Cab Service, Phone: 563-6303.
Information: Fort Atkinson Chamber of Commerce, 89 North Main Street, Fort Atkinson, WI 53538, Phone: 563-3210.

Edgewater Restaurant:

The Edgewater Restaurant is located adjacent to the Fort Atkinson Municipal Airport in Fort Atkinson, Wisconsin. The decor produces a warm rustic atmosphere with beautiful ceilings, pine woodwork and fire place in their main dining room in addition to the porch dining area that provides a beautiful panoramic view overlooking the Rock River. Menu entrees consist of prime steaks and fowl, as well as seafood dishes. Daily specials run around $7.00, and for most full course meals the price range is anywhere from $4.50 to $14.00. The restaurant is open from 4:30 p.m. until 9:30 p.m. every day of the week, except on Tuesday. For restaurant information or reservations call 674-9942.

Fireside Restaurant & Playhouse:

During our conversation with the people at the airport manager's office we learned the Fireside Restaurant is quite a popular establishment. It is considered a fine dining restaurant that features dinner combined with stage acts that are presented on certain evenings throughout the week. Transportation by way of taxi service is available. Brown Cab Service (Phone: 563-6303) runs about $5.00 plus $1.00 for each additional person each way. You can call the Fort Atkinson Municipal Airport for further information 563-7760, or the Fireside Restaurant and Playhouse at 563-9505.

Louise Riverview Restaurant:

The Louise Riverview Restaurant is located within walking distance from the Fort Atkinson Municipal Airport in Fort Atkinson, Wisconsin. This restaurant-pub overlooks the Rock River, and serves fast food dishes including chicken, cheeseburgers and homemade soup, as well as other items. The restaurant seats up to 150 persons and contains a pool table, dart board and video games. They open Tuesday through Friday at 6 a.m. and 10 a.m. on weekends (closed on Monday). They remain open until around 2 a.m. in the morning. For information call 674-9980.

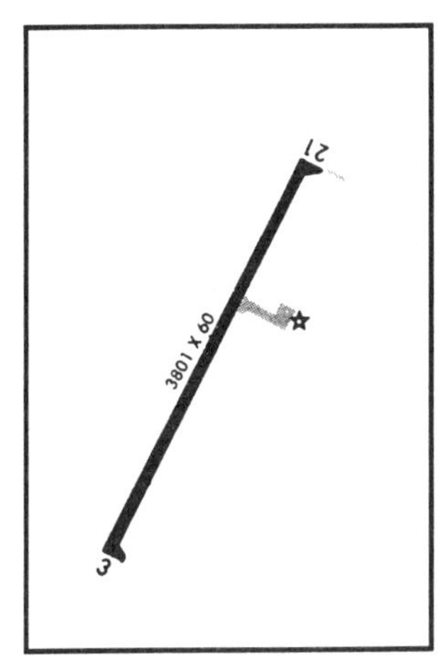

Airport Information:

FORT ATKINSON - FORT ATKINSON MUNICIPAL AIRPORT (61C)
3 mi northeast of town N42-57.79 W88-49.06 Elev: 800 Rwy 03-21: H3801x60 (Asph) Attended: unattended CTAF: 122.9
Fort Atkinson Municipal Airport Phone: 563-7760

WI-(Private) - GENEVA
GRAND GENEVA AIRPORT

(Area Code 414) 18

Grand Geneva Resort & Spa:

The Grand Geneva Resort & Spa is located only a few miles northeast of Lake Geneva in Wisconsin. This resort contains many amenities, including excellent accommodations for pleasure-minded vacationers or business travelers conducting seminars or client/business conferences. The resort offers 13,500 square feet of convention space, 7,680 square feet of ballroom and banquet facilities and 22 meeting and break-out rooms. Some of the services and facility accommodations include: a 36 Hole PGA Championship Golf Course; European Spa & Sports Center, cabaret featuring live entertainment, retail shops, downhill and cross country skiing, tennis courts, indoor/outdoor swimming pools, horseback riding and hay rides. The resort contains three restaurants on their property. One is the Grand Cafe open 6:30 a.m. to 10 p.m. Another is the Newport Grill in operation from 11:30 a.m. to 2:30 p.m. and 5 p.m. to 10 p.m.. And their main dining room the Ristorante Brisago is open between 5:30 p.m. and 10:00 p.m. In addition to the many things to see and do at this resort, there are still nearby attractions that are a must to experience while in the area. Some of these include the popular Gage Marine Boat Tour of Lake Geneva only 3 miles away. The town of Lake Geneva is filled with antique and specialty shops that draw many vacationers during the summer months. Infact, Lake Geneva can be seen from a long way off when flying into the area. Flying over top will give you a bird's eye view of just how popular this lake is to boaters, skiers, fishermen and sight-seeing boats of all types. For more information about the Grand Geneva Resort & Spa call 248-8811 or 800-558-3417.

Restaurants Near Airport:

Grand Cafe	On Resort	Phone: 248-8811
Newport Grill	On Resort	Phone: 248-8811
Ristorante Brisago	On Resort	Phone: 248-8811

Lodging: The Grand Geneva Resort & Spa includes 355 rooms, 37 suites, all with in-room coffee makers, Spa & Sports Center. For information call 248-8811.

Meeting Rooms: The Grand Geneva Resort & Spa has 13,500 feet of convention center, 7,680 square foot of grand ballroom and banquet facilities, and 22 meeting and breakout rooms. For information call 248-8811.

Transportation: The resort has its own private airstrip located within walking distance to the resort and nearby accommodations. For information call the resort at 248-8811 or the airstrip at extension 3812.

Information: Grand Geneva Resort & Spa 7036 Grand Geneva Way at Hwys. 50 East and 12, P.O. Box 130, Lake Geneva, Wisconsin 53147-0130 or call: Phone: 248-8811, Airport is at extension 3812., Fax 414-248-3192.; Also Geneva Lakes Area Chamber of Commerce, 201 Wrigley Drive, Lake Geneva, WI 53147 or call 248-4416 or 800-345-1020.

Attractions:

Excursion and sight-seeing boats tour the 5,230 acre Lake Geneva from Riviera Docks. Two hour round trip and one hour excursions of the lake are a relaxing way to get a close-up view of the private masions and sitealong the shoreline. For information call 245-BOAT.

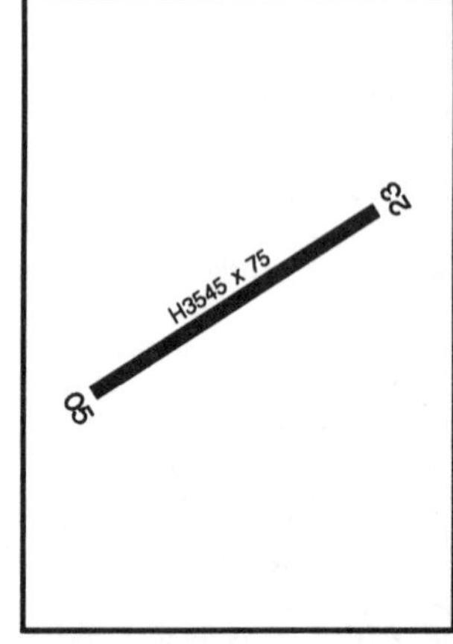

Airport Information:

GENEVA - GRAND GENEVA AIRPORT (Private)

2 mi northeast of town N42-36-53 W88-23-27 Elev: 835 Rwy 5-23: H3545x75 (Asph) Waypoint: BAE-116.40 187 degrees and distance 30.5 Attended: April thru October 7 a.m. to 7 p.m. daily & Nov thru March 9 a.m. to Sundet, daily. Unicom: 122.8 Notes: Pattern Altitude 1835 feet MSL Lighting: Transmitter activated.

Grand Geneva Airport: Phone: 248-8811

WI-GRB - GREEN BAY AUSTIN STRAUBEL INTL.

(Area Code 414) 19

Air Host Restaurant:

Air Host Restaurant is located on the first floor in the terminal building at the Austin Straubel International Airport. This establishment has undergo a total renovation. The new restaurant provide air travelers with complete food and beverage service. The dining room can seat 200 people. The decor is pleasant and casual. Breakfast dishes, hamburgers, sandwiches, homemade soups and chili are their specialties. In-flight catering can also be arranged. The restaurant is open from 5:30 a.m. to 6 p.m. weekdays and 5:30 a.m. to 2 p.m. on weekends. Their lounge is open until 9 p.m. Fly-in costumers can park their aircraft at the fixed base operators on the field and obtain a courtesy car to the restaurant or call for a taxi. For information about this facility call Air Host at 498-5054.

Restaurants Near Airport:
Air Host Restaurant On Site Phone: 498-5054

Lodging: Best Western Midway lodge (Trans) 499-3161; Holiday Inn Southwest (Trans) 499-5121; Howard Johnson Lodge (Trans) 336-0611; Radisson Inn (Trans) 494-7300; Ramada Inn (Trans) 499-0631.

Meeting Rooms: Best Western Midway Lodge 499-3161; Holiday Inn Southwest 499-5121; Howard Johnson Lodge 336-0611; Radisson Inn 494-7300; Ramada Inn 499-0631.

Transportation: Taxi Service: Bay City Cab 432-5588; Packer City Cab 468-9670; Rental Cars: Avis 494-4551; Budget 497-1515; Hertz 498-6400; National 499-3123.

Information: Green Bay Visitors & Convention Bureau, P.O. Box 10596, Green Bay, WI 54307-0596, Phone; 494-9507, 800-236-3976.

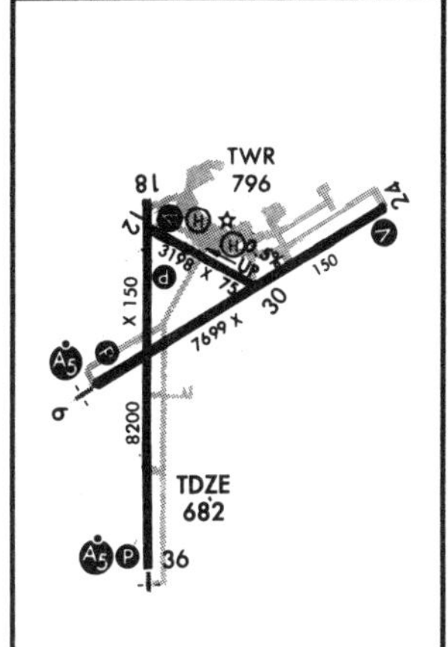

Airport Information:

GREEN BAY - AUSTIN STRAUBEL INTERNATIONAL AIRPORT (GRB)
7 mi southwest of town N44-29.15 W88-07.93 Elev: 695 Fuel: 100LL, Jet-A, MOGAS Rwy 18-36: H8200x150 (Conc-Grvd) Rwy 06-24: H7699x150 (Conc-Grvd) Rwy 12-30: H3198x75 (Asph) Attended: 1100-0400Z Atis: 124.1 Unicom: 122.95 Green Bay App Con: 119.4 Green Bay Dep Con: 126.55 Green Bay Tower: 118.7 Gnd Con: 121.9 Clnc Del: 121.75 Notes: Deer and Birds on and in vicinity of airport.

Airport Manager **Phone: 498-4800**
FBO: Executive Air **Phone: 498-4880**
FBO: Jet Air Corporation **Phone: 497-4900**

WI-W539 - HARSHAW PINEWOOD AIRPARK

(Area Code 715) 20

Pine Country Club:

"Pine Country Club is reported to be located 290 degrees off the Rhinelander, Wisconsin VOR about 9 DME. Our runway is 33/15 and 70'x 2700' turf. We are open from May 1st to October 31 and serve lunches and dinners 11:00 a.m. to 8:00 p.m. daily with a brunch on Sunday from 10 a.m. until 2 p.m. The restaurant and golf course is within walking distance with a scenic trip through the woods over the Bearskin trout stream. Our restaurant overlooks the rolling hills of the front nine of Pinewood Country Club. Our strip is mowed at least weekly and inspected daily. We provide a fun day! Phone 282-5500. Cottage rentals available." (Submitted by restaurant)

Attractions:

Pinewood Country Club contains its own airstrip and has a golf course on the premises. For information call 282-5500

Restaurants Near Airport:
Pinewood Country Club On Site Phone: 282-5500

Lodging: Cottage rentals available through Pinewood Country Club 282-5500.

Meeting Rooms: None Reported

Transportation: Pinewood Country Club is within walking distance from the airport. Available ground transportation unknown.

Information: Rhinelander Area Chamber of Commerce, 135 South Stevens Street, P.O. Box 795, Rhinelander, WI 54501, Phone: 715-362-7464 or 800-236-4386.

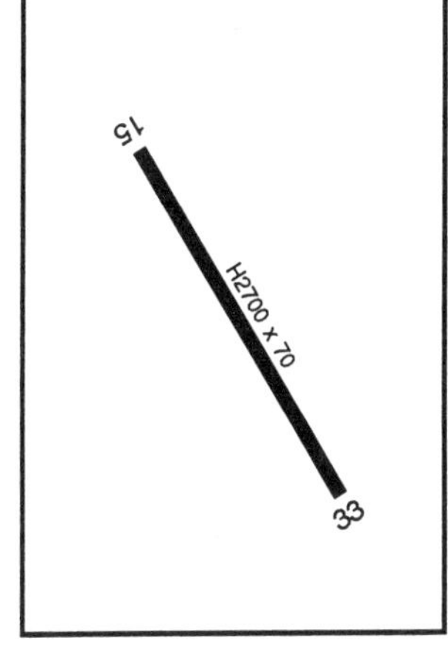

Airport Information:

HARSHAW - PINEWOOD AIRPARK (W539) (Private Airport)
14 mi northwest of town 45-41-59N 89-39-39W Elev: 1635 Fuel: None Reported Attended: unattended Rwy 33-15: 2700x70 (Turf) Notes: CAUTION: Call ahead for runway conditions. Private use facility use at own risk.
Pinewood Airpark Phone: 282-5500

WI-HBW - HILLSBORO JOSHUA SANFORD FIELD

(Area Code 608) 21, 22, 23

Restaurants Near Airport:

Alpine Haus	1/2 mi.	Phone: 489-3888
Cornucopia	1/2 mi	Phone: 489-3896
Country Style Cookin	1/2 mi.	Phone: 489-3539

Lodging: Edgecombe Inn B & B 1 mi. 489-2915; Hilltop B & B Kendall, WI 463-7550; Tiger Inn B & B 489-2918; Garden City Motel 5 mi. 462-8253;
Meeting Rooms: Alpine Haus 489-3888, Cornucopia 489-3896 and Country Style Cookin 489-3539 all have accommodations and welcome groups and catered meals at their restaurant. Please call in advance to let them know you are coming.
Transportation: None reported
Information: Hillsboro Chamber of Commerce, P.O. Box 378, Hillsboro, WI 54634, Phone: 608-489-2264.

Alpine Haus:

The Alpine Haus is well within walking distance about 1/2 of a mile from the Joshua Sanford Field. The Alpine Haus restaurant offers a cozy atmosphere and can be classified as a family-style establishment. The decor of the Alpine Haus exhibits an Austrian-styled setting. During our conversation with Anna Josellis, the owner, we learned that she and her husband designed and decorated the restaurant themselves. Many items are hand made. The restaurant can seat about 40 people. During one of our flights we visited this restaurant and found it as charming as Anna indicated over the phone. Mimors on the wall and ceiling make the small but quaint dining room appear twice as large. Two decorated carousel horses, beer steins of all types, antique plates and pictures are just part of the many interesting memorabilia collected for display. One of the unique qualities are the authentic and colorful attire from Austria and Switzerland worn by the owner and staff. They specialize in preparing German, Swiss and Austrian selections. Included on their menu are wiener; jager and chicken schnitzel; Hungarian goulash; bratwurst; chicken and vegetarian stir fry; French pork chops; Halibut steak; (Yugoslavian Specialty) Civapcici; Italian Creole chicken; Austrian dishes like Linzer Klops, which is lean ground beef with sweet herbs and dill, smothered in a dill-sherry wine sauce; sweet and sour stuffed cabbage and breaded cod. All dinners include fresh bread, homemade soup or tossed salad and choice of baked potato, O'Brien potatoes, dumpling or Hungarian spatzle. Most selections run between $7.00 and $10.00. Their Sunday buffet usually features Polish beef roast or lemon chicken. A back room joining the main dining room is ideally suited for group gatherings. The restaurant is open Friday and Saturday evening from 5 p.m. to 8 p.m. and Sunday for their buffet served between 11 a.m. and 2 p.m. Walk past the cheese factory then right one block and then left three blocks into town where this restaurant and other businesses are located. For information about the Alpine Haus call 489-3888.

Cornucopia:

The Cornucopia is a combination restaurant, antique and art gallery situated only 4 or 5 blocks from the airport at 135 Mills Street. in downtown Hillsboro, Wisconsin. The name Cornucopia represents and signifies prosperity, abundance, horn of plenty. This restaurant contains antiques, paintings and works of art. The restaurant is open Tuesday through Friday 7 a.m. to 5 p.m, and Saturday 9 a.m. to 3 p.m. Specialties on their menu include pasta salad of the day, Caesar salad, Gyros plates, shrimp salad, chicken salad on a pita and a bakery with fresh baked bread, rolls and pastries. Daily specials are also available like beef stroganoff or baked cod. The decor of the restaurant has a 50s, 60s atmosphere with wooden floors and wooden booths. The dining room can seat about 55 people and has paintings for sale by local artists. To reach the restaurant you should walk past the cheese factory at the end of runway 5, then right one block and then left three blocks then right again on Mill Street for one block. You should see a wooden sign with the name Cornucopia carved in it. For information call 489-3896.

Attractions:

This is a quiet friendly town with a population of around 1,300 people and is surrounded by rolling hills and farm country. There are three main restaurants within town all located only 10 minutes walk from the airport. The cheese factory and plant at the end of runway 5 has a retail store across the street where you can buy all types of cheese and cheese products made fresh at their location. A bike path about 300 feet south, runs parallel to the runway which connects several towns in the area. In addition a number of bed and breakfast establishment are located within the area. During our conversation with the airport manager, we learned that the Joshua Sanford Field is a public use airport that is listed within the Wisconsin state aeronautical directory and state printed charts and AOPA Airport USA, however as of the time of our interview this airport has yet to be entered into the AFD. For information call the airport manager at 489-3132.

Country Style Cookin:

This restaurant can be classified as a casual familystyle establishment. Hours of operation are 6 a.m. to 6 p.m. Monday through Thursday, 6 a.m. to 7 p.m. on Friday, and Saturday 6 a.m. to 1:30 p.m. Specialties on their menu include a variety of Czechoslovakia dishes. Additional entrees featured are Shuleke soup, chicken dumplings, roast beef dishes and fresh bread prepared daily. A full breakfast selection is available. Prices average about $4.00 to $6.00 for most selections. After 11 a.m. the restaurant serves food cafeteria style. A back room is available for catered meals. The restaurant is about 3/4 mile from the Hillsboro, Joshua Sanford Field toward town. Walk past the cheese factory then right one block and then left three blocks and this will take you to the downtown area where restaurants and businesses are located. For restaurant information call 489-3539.

Airport Information:

HILLSBORO - JOSHUA SANFORD FIELD (Private) (HBW)
1 mi northeast of town N43-39.40 W090-19.69 Elev: 938 Rwy 5-23: H3,083x50 (Asph)
Attended: unattended Notes: Phone at airport not reported; Formost Cheese Factory at end of runway 5. Ramp parking is limited. Please do not block hangar doors.
Airport Manager Phone: 489-3132

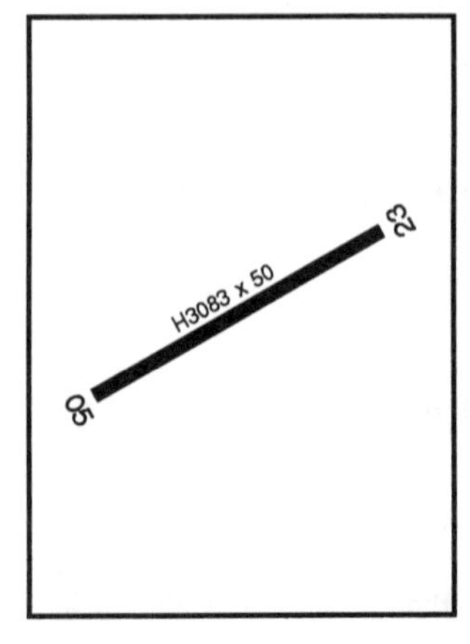

Not to be used for navigational purposes

WI-68C - IOLA CENTRAL COUNTY

(Area Code: is 414 for Ogdensburg, WI and 715 for Iola, WI)

24

Wings Inn Tavern:

The Wings Inn Tavern is situated 1/2 mile from the Iola, Central County Airport. This country tavern is open Tuesday through Saturday beginning at 11 a.m. They serve dinners and specialize in their broasted chicken and sandwich selections. On Friday they feature a fish fry. There is seating for about 35 persons. The Wings Inn Tavern has a rustic decor with all sorts of aviation items on display. Larger groups are welcome, with meeting room space available in their basement. For more information call the airport at 414-244-7850.

Restaurants Near Airport:
Wings Inn Tavern 1/2 mi Phone: 414-244-7850

Lodging: Grand Seasons 715-258-9212; Iola Norseman House 715-445-3300; Simmons Motel (?)-596-2560; Village Inn 715-258-8526; Victorian Bed & Breakfast (?)-596-3643.

Meeting Rooms: None reported; Wings Inn tavern has additional seating in their basement for catered meals, 414-244-7850.

Transportation: None reported

Information: Iola Mills Museum of Pioneer History 300 N. Main St., Iola 54945, 715-445-2900; Iola Old Car Show & Swap Meet, P.O. Box 1, Iola, WI 54945, 715-445-4000; Krause Publications, 700 E. State St., Iola, WI 54945, 715-445-2214.

Attractions: Between the towns of Steven's Point and New London, WI in the central part of the state is the town of Iola, WI. This town has a population of around 1,200 or so. But at certain times of the year it explodes with spectators and enthusiasm. The **"Iola Old Car Show and Swap Meet"** is held on the weekend after the 4th of July. This annual antique auto festival is the largest in the Midwest, and the third largest in the world. As many as 2,500 antique vehicles are displayed and exhibited for more than 100,000 people visiting the three day event. For information about area lodging accommodations they have a HOT line number 800-477-2920. For information about the show call 715-445-4000. In August, after the "Old Car Show," the **"Rod & Kustom Weekend"** features a huge display of vehicles, a 50s-60s dance, swap meet, car corral, camping and a multitude of activities. For information call 715-445-4005. The **"Iola Military Show"** is held around the 17 & 18 of August after the Rod & Kustom Weekend. This event displays a large selection of Military equipment from the past and present. For information call 715-445-4800. Additional attractions are: **"Iola Mills Museum of Pioneer History"** exhibits the Norwegian heritage. For information call 715-445-2900. **"Krause Publications"** is the world's largest publisher of periodicals for the hobbyist. Sample copies of publications like "Antique Auto", comic books, baseball cards and sports collectibles publications are on display. Tours of their complex can be arranged with advance notice by calling 715-445-2214.

NO AIRPORT DIAGRAM AVAILABLE

Airport Information:

IOLA - CENTRAL COUNTY (68C)
4 mi east of the town of Iola N44-30.33 W89-01.51 Elev: 876 Rwy 04-22: 2530x100 (Turf) Rwy 09-27: 1800x120 (Turf) Rwy 13-31: 1745x130 (Turf) Attended: unattended Notes: Ski aircraft only during winter months. Rwy 04-22, Rwy 09-27 and Rwy 13-31 marked with barrels orange white.
Airport Management Phone: 596-3530

WI-Y77 - IRON RIVER
BAYFIELD COUNTY AIRPORT

(Area Code 715) 25

Iron River Trout Haus Bed & Breakfast:

Iron River Trout Haus Bed & Breakfast is located only 1.5 miles from the Bayfield County Airport. Do you love to fish? Particularly for trout? Then this is the place. The bed and breakfast is nestled among forty wooded acres on the outskirts of Iron River, Wisconsin (45 miles east of Lake Superior). The home is a newly remodeled two-story farm-house, built in 1892. Proprietors Ron and Cindy Johnson have worked hard to make sure that each room is uniquely decorated in accordance with a particular theme significant to the area. For example, the Trout Room, which is the largest of the four rooms, includes a private bathroom with a shower; knotty pine paneling, fishing decor and a skylight create a rustic, yet charming atmosphere.The Railroad, Logging and Bird rooms are decorated in their own pleasing manner, as well. Every morning of your stay, you will enjoy the privilege of a warm greeting from the Johnsons, who have been busy preparing the delicious breakfast before sunrise. After selecting your mug of choice from their worldwide collection, you will be offered a cup of freshly brewed coffee, along with delicious, fresh baked muffins. If you register for two nights, you will receive an exquisitely prepared fresh trout breakfast, served with fresh fruit, toast and locally make breakfast sausage. After breakfast, you can go fishing in the privately maintained trout ponds on the grounds. Along the banks of the Iron River lie three springfed trout ponds. Bubbling underground springs keep the ponds open all year. Even in December when the trout season has ended, you can still fish for twelve to twenty-four-inch stocked brown and rainbow trout. Also, for a reasonable fee, anyone can fish. You do not have to be a registered guest to enjoy the Trout Haus. Twice a year, the Trout Haus offers a fly-fishing school, as well as individual fly-fishing lessons. For meetings, there is a 12'x20' conference room, complete with a fireplace and library. We were told that, if available, the Trout Haus will provide transportation to and from the airport; otherwise the airport manager will provide a ride. For more information about rates and accommodations at the Iron River Trout Haus, call 372-4219 or 800-262-1453.

Restaurants Near Airport:

Deep Lake Lodge	2 mi	Phone: 372-4236
Iron River Trout Haus	1-1/2 mi	Phone: 372-4219
Lumberman's Inn	2 mi	Phone: 372-8880

Lodging: Iron River Trout Haus (1-1/2 miles) 372-4219; Lumberman's Inn (2 miles) 372-4515; Rustic Roost (2-1/2 miles) 372-4426

Meeting Rooms: Iron River Trout Haus Phone: 372-4219

Transportation: Iron River Trout Haus will provide transportation to and from airport, otherwise airport manager will provide a ride.

Information: Iron River Area Chamber of Commerce, P.O. Box 448, Iron River, WI 54847, Phone: 372-8558 (Note: we were told that their hours of operation are uncertain.)

Nearby Attractions:

Fishing is abundant in this area. Brule River, located 8 miles west, is known for its abundant rainbow trout fishery. Pike Lake Chain & Chequomegon National Forest are about 3 miles. Other activities such as, hiking, cross-country skiing and snowmobiling are also common in the area. For more information, contact the Iron River Area Chamber of Commerce at 372-8558.

Photo by: Iron River Trout Haus Bed & Breakfast

Airport Information:

IRON RIVER - BAYFIELD COUNTY AIRPORT (Y77)

2 mi northwest of town N46-34.58 W91-27.51 Elev: 1143 Fuel: None Reported Rwy 08-26: 3000x135 (Turf) Attended: irregularly CTAF: 122.9 Notes: CLOSED to wheeled aircraft during winter months. Check with airport manager for runway condition. Occasional wildgame on and in vicinity of airport.

FBO: Airport Manager Phone: 372-5166

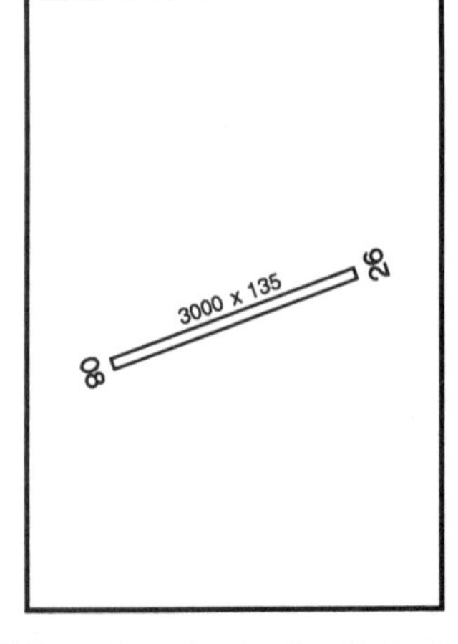

WI-JVL - JANESVILLE ROCK COUNTY AIRPORT

(Area Code 608) 26

C.A.V.U. Restaurant:

Formerly known as Margie's Place,the C.A.V.U. Restaurant is located in the terminal building at Rock County Airport in Janesville, Wisconsin. This restaurant is within walking distance (50 feet) from the general aviation parking area near the terminal building. A full choice of breakfast, lunch and dinner items are listed on their menu at reasonable prices. Their dining room faces the parking ramp and provides a great view of arriving and departing air traffic. The decor is modern and contains tables and chairs that can be pulled together and arranged for larger groups. This is a popular dining spot for many pilots, especially on the weekends. Corporate pilots can also relax and enjoy a nice meal while laying over for a fuel or service stop. This restaurant is open Monday through Thursday 6 a.m. to 2 p.m. Friday 6 a.m. to 9 p.m. and Saturday and Sunday 6 a.m. to 3 p.m. For more information about C.A.V.U. Restaurant call 754-9039.

Restaurants Near Airport:

C.A.V.U Rest. On Site Phone: 754-9039

Lodging: American Inn 752-9411; Janesville Motor Lodge 756-4511; Ramada Inn (Trans) 756-2341; Road Star Inn Janesville 754-0251; Super 8 Motel 756-2040;

Meeting Rooms: American Inn 752-9411; Janesville Motor Lodge 756-4511; Ramada Inn 756-2341.

Transportation: Courtesy cars available through fixed base operators. Also Taxi Service: Caddy Cab 754-1300; JVL Taxi Service 757-1006.

Information: Janesville Department of Information and Tourism, 20 South Main Street, P.O. Box 8008, Janesville, WI 53547, Phone: 757-3160.

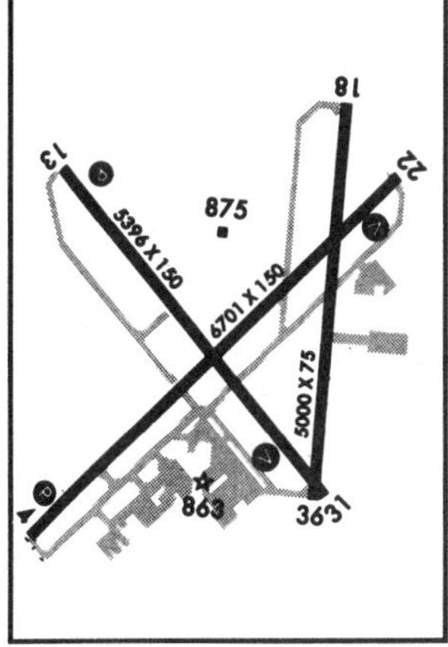

Airport Information:

JANESVILLE - ROCK COUNTY AIRPORT (JVL)
3 mi southwest of town N42-37.18 W89-02.42 Elev: 808 Fuel: 80, 100LL, Jet-A
Rwy 04-22: H6701x150 (Asph) Rwy 13-31: H5396x150 (Asph) Rwy 18-36: H5000x75 (Asph) Attended: continuously Atis: 128.25 Unicom: 122.95
Rockford App/Dep Con: 126.0 Janesville Tower: 118.8 Gnd Con: 121.65
FBO: Blackhawk Airways Phone: 756-1000
FBO: Roessel Aviation Phone: 754-1175
FBO: General Aviation Corp. Phone: 756-1234

WI-UNU - JUNEAU DODGE COUNTY

(Area Code 414) 27

PJ's Restaurant:

This restaurant features old-fashioned country cooking. It is located 1-1/2 miles south of the Dodge County Airport. Farm-fresh eggs, spicy country sausage, and Wisconsin's own unique breakfast entrees top their menu. Daily specials are also featured. Hours of operation are: Monday through Thursday 5:30 a.m. to 8 p.m.; Friday 5:30 a.m. to 9 p.m.; Saturday 6 a.m. to 8 p.m.; and Sunday 7 a.m. to 8 p.m. This restaurant specializes in real home-cooking. For more information call PJ's Restaurant at 386-5691.

Restaurants Near Airport:

P.J's Restaurant 1-1/2 mi Phone: 386-5691
Rita's Country Kitchen 1 mi Phone: 386-2966

Lodging: Beaver Motel (Est. 10 mi.) 887-1112; Best Western Campus Inn 8 mi 887-7171; Country Retreat Bed & Breakfast 1 mi; Royal Oaks Motel 6 mi 485-4489; Super 8 Motel 6-8 mi 887-8880;

Meeting Rooms: None reported

Transportation: Courtesy car reported; Also rental cars: Wisconsin Aviation is reported to have rental cars available 386-2402; Lidtke Motors 887-1661.

Information: Juneau Chamber of Commerce P.O. Box 4, Juneau, WI 53039, Phone: 386-2424; Also Juneau Visitors Bureau, Inc. P.O. Box 377, Necedah, WI 54646, Phone: 565-2180.

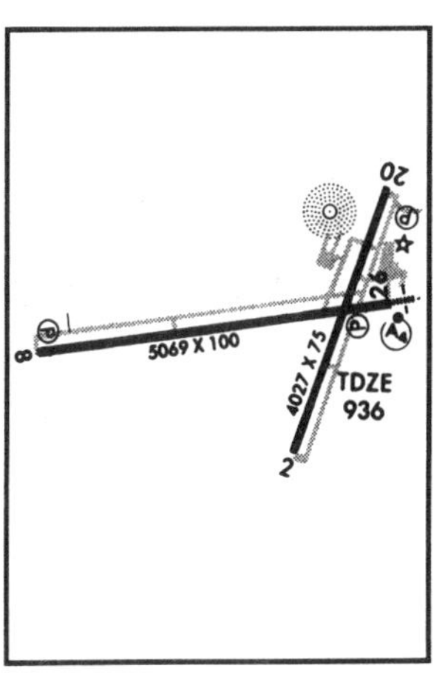

Airport Information:

JUNEAU - DODGE COUNTY (UNU)
1 mi northeast of town N43-25.60 W88-42.19 Elev: 936 Fuel: 100LL, Jet-A, Auto
Rwy 08-26: H5069x100 (Asph) Rwy 02-20: H4027x75 (Asph) Attended: 7 a.m. until sunset Unicom: 122.7
FBO: Wisconsin Aviation, Inc. Phone: 386-2402

WI-ENW - KENOSHA
KENOSHA REGIONAL AIRPORT

Restaurants Near Airport: **(Area Code 414)** **28**
Dairyland Club House 1/2 mi Phone: 800-233-3357

Dairyland Clubhouse (Race Track):

The Clubhouse Restaurant is located within the Dairyland Greyhound Park Race Track, across the street, and less than 1/2 mile away from the airport. From their establishment you can see aircraft landing and departing the airport. This restaurant offers a panoramic view of the track through huge windows that stretch almost the entire length of the building. Their main dining area "Clubhouse" can seat as many as 1,200 people. The restaurant is open Wednesday, Friday and Saturday from 11:45 to 4:00 p.m. and re-opens from 6:00 p.m. to 10:30 p.m., Tuesday and Thursday from 6 p.m. to 10 p.m. and Sunday from 11:30 a.m. to 4:30 p.m. (Closed on Mondays). Specialties of the house includes a delicious 1/2 pound burgers, steak dishes, chicken dishes, sandwiches and a number of other popular entrees. Average prices range from $6.00 to $15.00 for most selections. "Post Times Matinees" begin at 1:00 p.m. Doors open at 11:45 a.m. Evening performances begin at 7:15 p.m., with doors opening at 6:00 p.m. (Closed on Tuesdays). General admission is $1.00, and $3.00 for the clubhouse. Fly-in groups are also welcome. However, reservation are suggested. For more information about race dates or group accommodations call 800-233-3357.

Lodging: Budgetel Inn 857-7911; Holiday Inn 658-3281; Howard Johnson Lodge 857-2311.
Meeting Rooms: Holiday Inn 658-3281; Howard Johnson Lodge 857-2311.
Transportation: Taxi Service: Lambies Luxury Limo 694-4847; Peppies 652-4590; Rental Cars: Avis 656-8158 (On Arpt).
Information: Kenosha Area Tourism Corporation, 800-55th Street, Kenosha, WI 53140, Phone: 654-7307.

Attraction:

Dairyland Greyhound Park Race Track offers year round entertainment with Greyhound racing and live horse and day Simulcast. The general number for information, reservations or group accommodations is 800-233-3357.

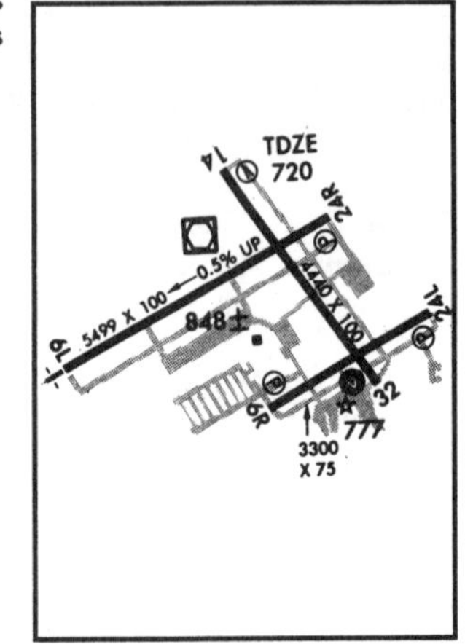

Airport Information:

KENOSHA - KENOSHA REGIONAL AIRPORT (ENW)
4 mi west of town N42-35.74 W87-55.67 Elev: 743 Fuel: 100LL, Jet-A
Rwy 06L-24R: H5499x100 (Conc-Grvd) Rwy 14-32: H4400x100 (Conc-Grvd)
Rwy 06R-24L: H3300x75 (Asph) Attended: 1300-0300Z Atis: 127.175 Unicom: 122.95
Milwaukee App/Dep Con: 119.65 Tower: 118.6 Gnd Con: 121.875
FBO: Kenosha Aero **Phone: 658-2025** **FBO: Northern Airmotive** **Phone: 658-3800**
FBO: Kenosha Jet Center **Phone: 658-0030**

WI-LSE - LACROSSE
LA CROSSE MUNICIPAL AIRPORT

Restaurants Near Airport: **(Area Code 608)** **29**
Amelia's Restaurant On Site Phone: 781-7676

Amelia's Restaurant:

Amelia's Restaurant is located within the terminal building at the La Crosse Municipal Airport. They are open 5:30 a.m. to 11 p.m. during the week and 9 a.m. to 6 p.m. on weekends. Items on their menu includes sorted muffins pastries and continental selections from 5:30 a.m. to 8 a.m. when the restaurant begins preparing a complete breakfast line with eggs, sausage, hot-cakes, along with hot and cold sandwiches, burgers, chicken filet, ham and cheese, hot-dogs, turkey, soups, salads and desserts. Their dining room can accommodate 50 customers and has windows allowing for a nice view of the airport. A conference room is reported to be available through the airport authority also located within the terminal building. For more information call Amelia's Restaurant at 781-7676.

Lodging: Best Western Midway Motor Inn (Trans) 781-7000; Hampton Inn 781-5100; Holiday Inn (Trans) 784-9500; Ivy Motel 784-5440; Radisson Hotel (Trans) 784-6680; Ramada Inn (Trans) 785-0420.

Meeting Rooms: Best Western Midway Motor Inn 781-7000; Hampton Inn 781-5100; Holiday Inn 784-9500; Radisson Hotel 784-6688; Ramada Inn 785-0420.

Transportation: Call fixed base operator to arrange taxi or rental car service.

Information: La Crosse Area Convention & Visitors Bureau, 410 East Veterans Memorial Drive, La Crosse, WI 54601, Phone: 782-2366.

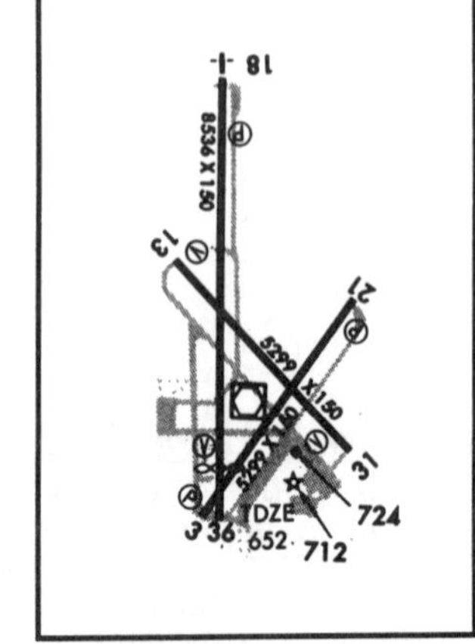

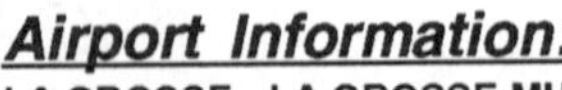

Airport Information:

LA CROSSE - LA CROSSE MUNICIPAL AIRPORT (LSE)
4 mi northwest of town N43-52.75 W91-15.38 Elev: 654 Fuel: 100LL, Jet-A
Rwy 18-36: H8536x150 (Asph-Grvd)) Rwy 13-31: H5299x150 (Asph-Grvd)
Rwy 03-21: H5299x150 (Asph) Attended: 1200-0400Z Atis: 124.95 Unicom: 122.95
Tower: 118.45 Gnd Con: 121.8
FBO: Colgan Air Service **Phone: 783-8359**

WI-WI31 - LAKEWOOD
LAKEWOOD COUNTRY CLUB

(Area Code 715) 30

Mc Caustin Golf & Country Club:

The Mc Caustin Golf & Country Club is located within walking distance of the Lakewood Country Club Airport in Lakewood, Wisconsin. This combination lounge and restaurant is open every day from June through Labor Day, and in the fall season Friday and Saturday. The dining room opens at 5 p.m. and serves a full selection of entrees from their menu. Between 11 a.m. and 2 p.m. their lounge serves lighter fare, with entrees consisting of various sandwich selections. The atmosphere of this family style restaurant is very nice and makes for a great excuse for you duffers to enjoy a fun filled day of fly-in golf and dining. For information call 276-7623.

Attractions:

Mc Caustin Golf & Country Club situated adjacent to airport provides golf course, club house and dining for fly-in guests. For information call 276-7623.

Restaurants Near Airport:

Mc Caustin Golf & C.C. Adj Arpt Phone: 276-7623

Lodging: Unkown

Meeting Rooms: Unknown

Transportation: Country Club is reported to be within walking distance. Available ground transportation unknown.

Information: Lake Country Chamber of Commerce, Box 87, Lakewood, WI 54138, Phone: 276-6500.

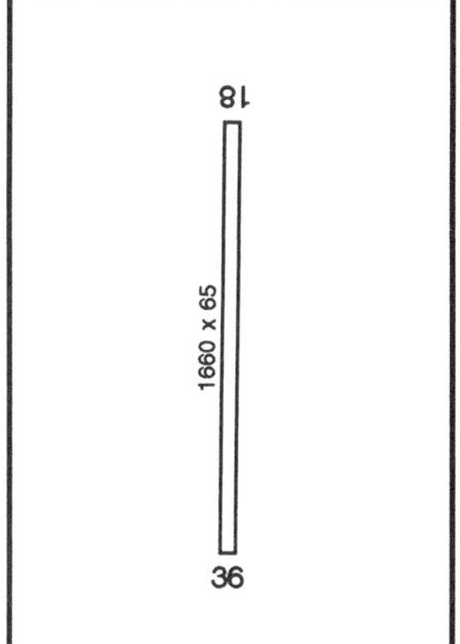

Airport Information:

LAKEWOOD - LAKEWOOD COUNTRY CLUB (WI31)
2 east of town N45-17.67 W88-29.67 Elev: 1229 Rwy 18-36: 1660x65 (Turf)
Attended: May-Nov daylight hours Unicom: 122.8
Mc Caustin Golf & Country Club Phone: 276-7623.

Gateway Lodge

Wisconsin's Northwoods is geared for family vacation activities all year round. At the Gateway Lodge and Recreation Center, you'll enjoy a sporty nine-hole golf course, tennis courts and sprawling grounds to stroll. Nearby are scores of fine fishing lakes and trout streams for fishing and boating. In the winter you'll find an ice skating rink adjoining the lodge, cross country ski and snowmobile trails.

While the northwoods has long been heralded as a summer vacation haven, each of the other seasons are attracting a greater number of travelers. Autumn is lavish in its flamboyant colors that transform the north into a panorama of dazzling fall foliage. Numerous colorama celebrations add to the excitement of that season. In addition, for sportsmen in pursuit of ruffed grouse, deer and ducks.

In the winter, a bright new season beckons to the snowmobiler and cross country skier. Trails for both sports begin on the Gateway grounds, and the snowmobile circuits stretch on for hundreds of miles riding over groomed, marked trails. Cross country ski trails are also open in the famed Sylvania Wilderness tract.

Springtime sees the resurgence of the new season with the lakes opening to offer the best fishing of the year. There are hundreds of lakes to explore and streams to canoe and fish.

The Gateway Lodge is a historic two-story landmark resort, rustic in decor with 72 rooms, suites and studios. All rooms have kitchenettes, cable TV and telephones. Their lobby is centered around a massive stone fireplace to comfort you in a traditional Northwoods fashion. Also adjoining the lodge is one of the largest Trap and Sporting Clay ranges in the Midwest. For those of you that have a private plane, a municipal airport with services adjoins the Gateway property. There are many lakes in the area for fishing and boating. Several have swimming beaches.

The Gateway Lodge will have available to their guests a casino package for use at the Lac Vieux Desert Casino in Watersmeet, MI. Enjoy staying at the Gateway Lodge and visit the casino for your gaming pleasure.

During midweek the Gateway Lodge offers special reduced rates, and large group discounts will be arranged to host your party, club or organization. They also offer fine facilities for banquets and large group meetings and conventions.

Special Accommodations For Fly-in Customers: The Gateway Lodge has a heated indoor pool and hot tub, and low humidity redwood sauna. During your stay enjoy their fine restaurant and lounge. In addition to normal accommodation, pilots receive special care: free tie-down, valet service, 5 gallons of fuel, green fees for 9 holes of golf, a round of sporting clays, two nights' dinner, two breakfasts and two nights' lodging for around $130.00 per person on weekends and $110.00 per person mid-week. These rates are based on 1995 rates and are subject to change. For information about the Gateway Lodge you can call 800-848-8058. (Information in part submitted by Gateway Lodge).

WI-LNL - LAND O' LAKES
KINGS LAND O' LAKES AIRPORT

(Area Code 715) 31

Gateway Lodge:

Emilio's "Gateway to the Mediterranean" is located inside the Gateway Lodge. Situated in a beautiful log dining room, this is Chef Emilio Gervilla and his wife, Ann Marie's expansion to the northwoods. His locations is the Chicago area have been a delight to many patrons. Featuring authentic cuisine of Spain, Italy, France and Greece with a full selection of breakfast, lunch and dinner items. Whether you choose tapas or the more traditional offerings from the menus, you'll find the freshest and finest cuisine anywhere, along with a wide variety of Mediterranean and local wine, beers, after dinner drinks and, of course, their famous sangria from Spain, The restaurant and lounge offers a casual rustic atmosphere with high beamed ceilings, dark wood interior, and a huge fieldstone fireplace in the lobby. The lodge itself has 55 hotel rooms, 24 hour front desk service, indoor heated pool, hot tub, and Finnish-style sauna, on-site trap and sporting clays facility, and adjacent to a 9-hole golf course. Recently renovated, all rooms have queen or twin-sized beds, new carpeting and remote controlled cable television. For information and reservations call 800-848-8058.

Restaurants Near Airport:

Emilio's (Gateway Lodge)	2 blks N.	Phone: 547-3321x315
Pitts Restaurant	2 mi N. 3 mi W.	Phone: N/A
Stateline	Hwy 45&B	Phone: 547-6299

Lodging: Gateway Lodge (2 blocks north) Phone: 800-848-8058; Bel Air (2 blks N. and 2 blks W.), Phone: 547-3343.
Meeting Rooms: Both Gateway Lodge 547-3321 and Stateline 547-6299, have accommodations for meetings, conventions and banquets.
Transportation: Gateway Lodge will pick guests up if requested 547-3321. The lodge is within walking distance of arpt.
Information: Chamber of Commerce, P.O. Box 599, Land O' Lakes, WI 54540, Phone: 800-236-3432.

Attractions:

Gateway Lodge, only 2 blocks north from the airport, provides guests with lodging, dining and a variety of attractions including a 9 hole golf course on the premises, tennis, indoor swimming pool, trap shooting, sport fishing, snowmobiling and cross country skiing. The resort is a short 5 minute walk from the airport. For information call 547-3321.

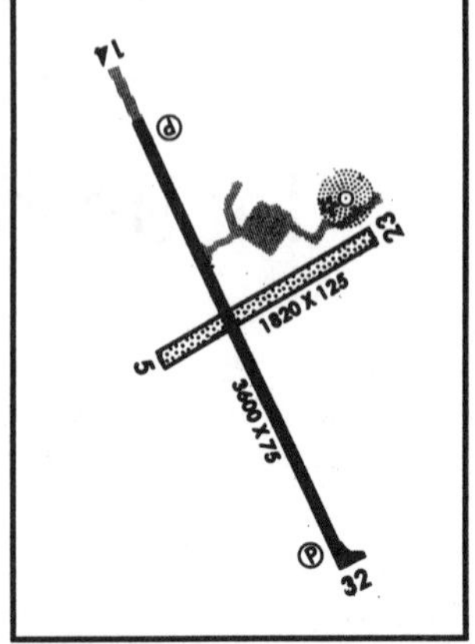

Airport Information:

LAND O'LAKES - KINGS LAND O'LAKES AIRPORT (LNL)
1 mi southeast of town N46-09.23 W89-12.68 Elev: 1706 Fuel: 100LL
Rwy 14-32: H3600x75 (Asph) Rwy 05-23: 1820x125 (Turf) Attended: May-Sep 1500-2300Z, Oct-Apr Sat-Sun on call. Unicom: 122.8 Public phone: at Gateway Lodge
Notes: Parking fee $3.00 per night. Maintenance available with prior notice.
FBO: Barry Aviation Phone: 800-848-8058

WI-LNR - LONE ROCK TRI-COUNTY REGIONAL AIRPORT

(Area Code 608)

32, 33

Airport Restaurant:

The Wild River Cafe was located right on the Tri-County Regional Airport. We learned that this establishment has since closed. However during our conversation with the airport management we were told that they are looking for someone to run the restaurant. Because this facility has a kitchen and cooking equipment on site, it is posible that it may re-open under new management. Contact the airport management for updated information.

House on the Rock Restaurants:

This particular attraction is viewed by tens of thousands of tourists each season from all across the United States. A house perched atop a rocky pinnacle is where your self guided tour begins. From there you will follow carefully designed ground and elevated walkways that will take you through different rooms containing amazing exhibits. Many displays combine vacuum pumps to power musical instruments an orchestra that plays by itself. Indescribable items and collections from all across the world will utterly boggle your mind. Each year this attraction seems to expand in size. Ask anyone who has had the opportunity to visit this attraction and you will get a response, "You have got to see it to believe it." Plan 3 to 4 hours minimum to tour the entire attraction. This attraction is estimated at 15 miles from the Lone Rock, Tri-County Regional Airport. For information about the House On The Rock call 935-3639. There are several food concessions on the premises for your convenience. During a conversation with the airport manager we learned that transportation to and from several attractions within the area can easily be arranged by several means. Rental cars, taxi services and Symons Tours, which specialize in catering to the transportation needs of pilots flying into the area and faring small or larger groups, to their destination at very reasonable prices. Because Symons Tours are located closer to Mineral Point - Iowa County Airport (C32) fairs are usually less expensive and more convenient. Flying into Iowa County Airport might be your best bet if planning to use symons Tours. (See "Transportation").

Also See Mineral Point, WI.
Iowa County Airport (C32)

Restaurants Near Airport:

Arthur's Steak Hse.	5 mi E.	Phone: 588-2521
House on the Rock	15 mi.	Phone: 935-3639
The Round Barn	5 mi E.	Phone: 588-2568
Spring Green Rest.	5 mi E.	Phone: 588-2571
Wild River Cafe	On Site	(Closed)

Lodging: McLaughlin's Country Inn (7 miles) 588-2222; Prairie House (7 miles) 588-2088; Riverside Motel (10 miles) 647-6420; Round Barn (7 miles) 588-2568.

Meeting Rooms: The Spring Green Corp. 588-2571; The Round Barn 588-2568.

Transportation: Lone Stone Taxi 583-2044; Sharp Car Rental 583-7922; Leyda Car Rental 647-2121; Valley Coach-Limos 800-236-8363; Symons Tours (Has been in the business of catering to pilots transportation needs for many years), Call 935-3212.

Information: Spring Green Chamber of Commerce, P.O. Box 3, Spring Green, WI 53588, Phone: 588-2042.

Attractions:

Governor Dodge State Park (15 miles) 935-3368; The ***Springs Golf Course*** (6 miles) 588-7707; House On The Rock (11 miles) 935-3639. The ***"House on the Rock"*** (15 miles) is one attraction that must not be missed if planning to visit the Spring Green area. For information call 935-3639. ***Additional functions:*** that attract the public, is an Art Fair held each year sometime in June. Another event that should be of particular interest to pilots, held right on the airport, is a popular pancake Fly-in Breakfast normally scheduled on the second or third weekend in May, around Mother's Day.

Airport Information:

LONE ROCK - TRI-COUNTY REGIONAL AIRPORT (LNR)
2 mi north of town N43-12.69 W90-10.91 Elev: 717 Fuel: 100LL, MOGAS
Rwy 09-27: H4002x75 (Asph) Rwy 18-36: H1870x40 (Asph) Attended: 1200-2300Z
Unicom: 123.0 Public Phone 24hrs Notes: Overnight parking $2.50 - Free with any fuel purchase.
FBO: Wisconsin River Aviation Corp. Phone: 583-3385

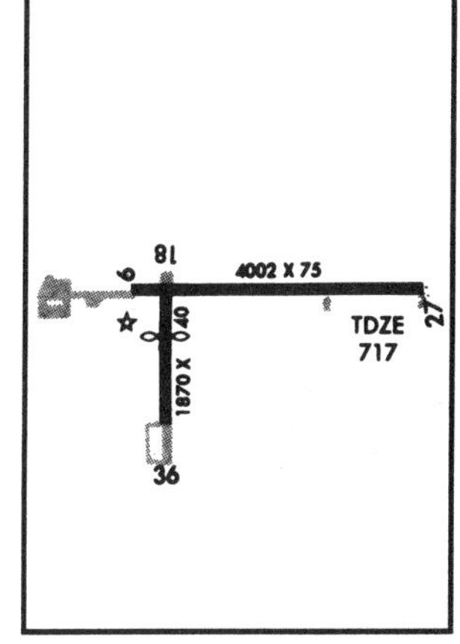

WI-MSN - MADISON
DANE CO. REGIONAL-TRUAX FLD

(Area Code 608) 34

Jet Room Restaurant:

The Jet Room Restaurant is located in the Wisconsin Aviation - Four Lakes general aviation terminal located on the east side of the Dane County Regional/Truax Field Airport in Madison, Wisconsin. This family-style restaurant is open Monday through Friday between 6 a.m. and 6 p.m. and on weekends between 7 a.m. and 2 p.m. The entree selection consists of daily specials, a full line of breakfast items, hamburgers, home-made pies, coffee cakes and other desserts, plus soups and salads. On Friday they feature Wisconsin's famous fish fry. Carry out meals are available upon request. The restaurant seats about 35 persons. For airport/restaurant information, call 249-2189.

Restaurants Near Airport:
Concessionaire Terminal Building Phone: 244-3040
Jet Room Four Lakes Avia. Phone: 249-2189

Lodging: Best Western Inn On The Park (Trans) 257-8811; Concourse Hotel (Trans) 257-6000; Edgewater Hotel (Trans) 256-9071; Holiday Inn - East Towne (Trans) 244-4703; Howard Johnson Plaza Hotel 251-5511; Ramada Inn (Trans) 244-2481; Sheraton Inn (Trans) 251-2300.

Meeting Rooms: All facilities listed above have accommodations for meetings and conferences. Also Four Lakes Aviation has a small meeting room available to handle between 12 to 15 persons.

Transportation: Courtesy car reported; Taxi service: Badger 256-5566; Madison Taxi 258-7458; Union 256-4400; Also Rental Cars: Budget 249-5544; Dollar 241-5100; Hertz 241-3803; National 249-1614.

Information: Chamber of Commerce, 615 East Washington Avenue, P.O. Box 71, Madison, WI 53701, Phone: 256-8348.

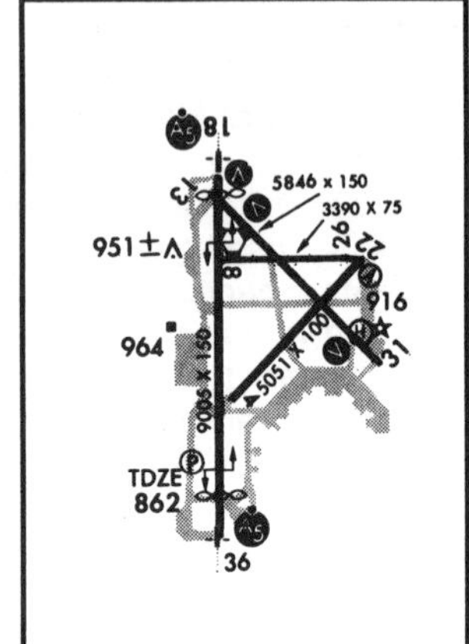

Airport Information:

MADISON - DANE COUNTY REGIONAL-TRUAX FIELD (MSN)
5 mi northeast of town N43-08.37 W89-20.23 Elev: 862 Fuel: 100LL, Jet-A
Rwy 18-36: H9005x150 (Asph-Conc-Wc) Rwy 13-31: H5846x150 (Conc-Wc) Rwy 04-22: H5051x100 (Asph-Afsc) Rwy 08-26: H3390x75 (Asph) Attended: continuously
Atis: 124.65 Unicom: 122.95 Madison App Con: 120.1 (East) 124.0 (West) Madison Dep Con: 126.85 Madison Tower: 119.3 Gnd Con: 121.9 Clnc Del: 121.62
FBO: Wisconsin Aviation - Four Lakes Phone: 249-2189

WI-MTW - MANITOWOC
MANITOWOC COUNTY AIRPORT

(Area Code 414) 35

Planeview Restaurant:

The Planeview Restaurant is a short walk across the street from the terminal at Manitowoc Co. Airport, Wisconsin. During our conversation with the airport manager, we learned that you can park your aircraft on the south end of the field for free, and simply walk about 75 yards to the restaurant. This is a family style restaurant with a full menu, including broasted chicken, broasted pork chops and a number of fresh fish entrees. They specialize in thick juicy hamburgers. Sandwiches run between $2.95 and $3.59. They have seating at tables for 4, 6, and 8 persons. Their hours are Monday through Thursday 6 a.m. to 7 p.m., Friday 6 a.m. to 7:30 p.m., Saturday 6 a.m. to 2:30 p.m. and Sunday 7 a.m. to 7 p.m. Aircraft operations and movement areas can be seen from the restaurant. For information call 682-1001.

Restaurants Near Airport:
Planeview Restaurant Adj Arpt Phone: 682-1001

Lodging: Fox Hills Resort 755-2376; Holiday Inn (Trans) 682-7000; Inn On Maritime Bay (Trans) 682-7000.

Meeting Rooms: Conference room available at Magnus Aviation 682-0043; Holiday Inn 682-6000; Inn On Maritime Bay (Trans) 682-7000.

Transportation: Taxi Service: Clipper City Cab 684-4999; Veteran Cab 682-0000, 684-4444.

Information: Manitowoc-Two Rivers Area Chamber of Commerce, P.O. Box 903, Manitowoc, WI 54221-0903. Phone: 684-5575.

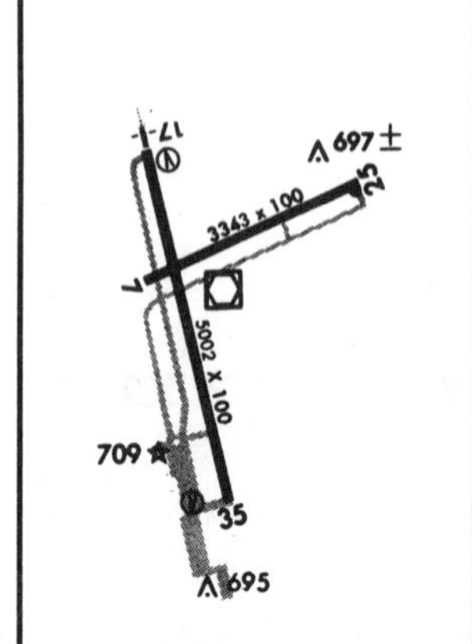

Airport Information:

MANITOWOC - MANITOWOC COUNTY AIRPORT (MTW)
2 mi northwest of town N44-07.73 W87-40.84 Elev: 651 Fuel: 100LL, Jet-A
Rwy 17-35: H5002x100 (Asph) Rwy 07-25: H3343x100 (Asph) Attended: 1330Z-sunset
Unicom: 122.8
FBO: Magnus Aviation Phone: 682-0043

WI-76C - MENOMONEE FALLS AERO PARK AIRPORT

(Area Code 414)

36

Chuck & Judy's Prop Wash Restaurant:

Chuck and Judy's Prop Wash Restaurant is a combination restaurant and tavern and is located on the Aero Park Airport in Menominee Falls, Wisconsin. This tavern offers a casual atmosphere and serves a fine selection of entrees as well as sodas and non-alcoholic beverages. Some of their choices include hot roast beef, submarine sandwiches, as well as pizza. During the winter months they include homemade soups and chili to warm you up. Average prices run $3.50 to $5.00 for most items on their menu. This restaurant is open from 4 p.m. to 10 p.m. Tuesday through Friday and 10 a.m. to 10 p.m. on Saturday and Sunday. Runway 15-33 is a 1880' x 80' turf. The Aero Park Airport has ultralight activity as well as parachuting. Local customers often watch the activity at the airport while enjoying their meal. Their main dining area can seat around 50 persons. Accommodations for meetings or parties up to 100 persons can also be arranged through the restaurant. Runway conditions as well as restaurant information can be obtained by calling 252-4319 or 252-3266.

Restaurants Near Airport:
Chuck & Judy's Prop Wash On Site Phone: 252-4319

Lodging: None Reported

Meeting Rooms: None Reported

Transportation: None Reported

Information: Menomonee Falls Area Chamber of Commerce, W 168 N8936 Appleton Avenue, P.O. Box 73, Menomonee Falls, WI 53052, Phone: 251-2430.

NO AIRPORT DIAGRAM AVAILABLE

Airport Information:

MENOMONEE FALL - AEROPARK AIRPORT (76C)
4 mi southwest of town N43-06.50 W88-09.59 Elev: 850 Rwy 15-33: 1880x80 (Turf)
Rwy 18-36: 1865x110 (Turf) Rwy 05-23: 1340x110 (Turf) Attended: daylight hours
CTAF: 122.9
Airport Manager Phone: 252-3266

WI-MKE - MILWAUKEE GENERAL MITCHELL INTL.

(Area Code 414) 37, 38

Mitchell's Cafe & Billy's Pub:

Mitchell's Cafe & Billy's Pub are located on the second floor of the General Mitchell International Airport terminal, and they overlook one of the airport's busiest runways. The cafe and pub are open from 5:30 a.m. to 7:00 p.m., every day except for Saturdays until 5:00 p.m. Mitchell's Cafe serves various delicious breakfast, lunch and dinner items. Start the day with the 747 Jet - which includes three grade AA farm fresh eggs scrambled together with diced ham, and served with hash browns and toast. For lunch, try the Mitchell's Cafe Club Sandwich - a classic combination of sliced turkey breast, bacon, tomato slices and lettuce, served on a croissant. A steaming bowl of Wisconsin cheese soup and a salad would go nicely with your meal. You can also choose between the Pasta Primavera or Charbroiled Marinated Chicken Breast entrees. For dinner, try the tender Filet Mignon, served with brandy-laced toasted garlic sauce, garnished with homemade haystack onion rings. Also, be sure to ask about the chef's seafood choice of the day, as well as "Fish Fry Friday." There are also children's menu selections, as well as delicious desserts. For larger groups, the cafe features a banquet facility, the Milwaukee Room, which can accommodate up to 130 people. Also, Billy's Pub features delicious sandwiches and other items, such as Bucks, Bango & Backboards - a tortilla bowl filled with corn chips, crisp mixed greens, firehouse chili garnished with guacamole, sour cream, shredded Wisconsin cheddar cheese, diced tomatoes and scallions. Or, try the OGMO special - a quarter pound hot dog served with chopped scallions, pickle relish, tomatoes and a fried chicken wing in honor of the Flight Museum at the airport. The Mitchell Gallery of Flight, located in the north section of the main lobby, features interesting historical exhibits. For more information about Mitchell's Cafe and Billy's Pub, call 747-4630.

Packing House Restaurant:

The Packing House Restaurant is located directly adjacent to General Mitchell Field, in Milwaukee, Wisconsin, and features fine dining with live entertainment. This establishment contains a casual atmosphere and can handle large groups if given advance notice. Entrees include: ribs, steaks, seafood, poultry and veal selections. Lunch hours are from 11:15 a.m. to 2 p.m., Monday through Friday. Their dinner hours are from 5 p.m. to 10 p.m., Monday through Thursday; 4 p.m. to 11 p.m. on Friday; 5 p.m. to 11p.m. on Saturday; and 4 p.m. to 9 p.m. on Sunday. They also offer a Sunday brunch that runs between 10 a.m. and 1:30 p.m. Transportation can be arranged through the FBO on the airport. To confirm restaurant hours and further information, call the Packing House at 483-5054.

Restaurants Near Airport:

Ashley's	8 blks.	Phone: 769-0605
Harold's	5 blks.	Phone: 481-8000
Host Int'l	Terml. Bldg.	Phone: 474-5230
Mitchell's Cafe	Terml. Bldg.	Phone: 747-4630
Packing House	Adj. Arpt.	Phone: 483-5054
Selen's	8 blks.	Phone: 744-7890

Lodging: Quality Inn (adj) 481-2400; Midway Motor Lodge (adj) 769-2100;Super 8 (1/2 mile) 481-8488; The Grand Hotel (1 mile) 481-8000; Holiday Inn South (2 miles) 764-1500; Howard Johnsons (2 miles) 282-7000; Ramada Inn South (2 miles) 764-5300; Budgetel Inn (3 miles) 762-2266

Meeting Rooms: All lodging facilities listed above contain accommodations for meeting rooms. Also contact airport manager's office at General Mitchell International for possible meeting facilities or various services available at the airport. Call 747-5300.

Transportation: Courtesy car reported; Also taxi service: Brew City 263-2739; City Veterans 933-2266; Yellow Cab 271-1800; Rental cars: Alamo 481-6400; Avis 744-2266; Budget 481-2409; Dollar 747-0068; Hertz 747-5200; National 483-9800; Payless 482-0300.

Information: Greater Milwaukee Convention & Visitors Bureau, 510 W. Kilbourn Ave., Milwaukee, WI 53203, Phone: 273-7222 (Mon-Fri) or 800-231-0903. The bureau also has two other visitor centers: General Mitchell Airport (daily) and Grand Ave. Shopping Center (daily). There is also a Fun Line which provides information on daily events, call 799-1177.

Nearby Attractions:

Mitchell Gallery of Flight (Terml. Bldg.); Brewery tours (8 miles); County Stadium (7 miles); County Zoo (10 miles); Museum (6 miles); Summerfest grounds (5 miles)

Airport Information:

MILWAUKEE - GENERAL MITCHELL INTERNATIONAL (MKE)
5 mi south of town N42-56.81 W87-53.82 Elev: 723 Fuel: 100LL, Jet-A
Rwy 01L-19R: H9690x200 (Asph Conc-Grvd) Rwy 07R-25L: H8011x150 (Asph-Conc-Grvd)
Rwy 13-31: H5868x150 (Conc) Rwy 01R-19L: H4182x150 (Conc) Rwy 07L-25R: H3163x100 (Asph) Attended: continuously Atis: 126.4 Unicom: 122.95
Milwaukee App Con: 127.85, 126.5 (A), 118.0 (B) Milwaukee Dep Con: 125.35 (A), 119.65 (B) Milwaukee Tower: 119.1 Gnd Con: 121.8 Clnc Del: 120.8
FBO: Cargo Air Wisconsin Aviation Services Phone: 747-4860
FBO: Milwaukee General Aviation, Inc. Phone: 769-1656
FBO: Signature Flight Support Phone: 747-5100

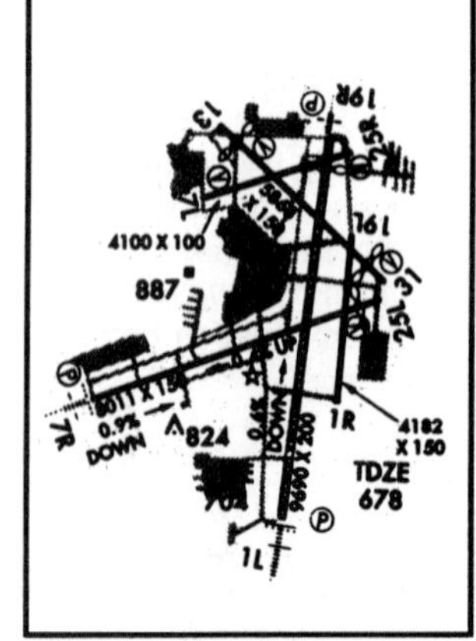

Not to be used for navigational purposes

WI-MWC - MILWAUKEE
LAWRENCE J. TIMMERMAN AIRPORT

(Area Code 414)

39, 40

Maxim's Family Restaurant:

Maxim's Family Restaurant is located on the northeast corner of Lawrence J. Timmerman Airport near Milwaukee, Wisconsin. This restaurant is a pancake house and bakery open 24 hours a day and serves a wide variety of entrees including full breakfast selections, and a luncheon and dinner menu. The restaurant has a modern decor with brass railings and many green plants. The restaurant is divided into two sections with a cocktail lounge. One portion of the restaurant offers a nice view of the airport and main parking ramp located on the north end of the field. Pilots can park their aircraft on the north ramp in front of Gran-Aire, Inc., (Two story brick building). It's only a five minute walk from there to the restaurant along a paved access road. For restaurant information call 462-0541.

Skyroom Restaurant:

The Skyroom Restaurant is located on Lawrence J. Timmerman field in Milwaukee, Wisconsin. This combination restaurant and tavern is situated on the north main ramp of the airport, on the second story above the fixed base operator Gran-Aire, Inc. The restaurant has recently taken on a new look with a unique aviation decor exhibiting corrugated metal siding simulating an airplane hangar, many large WW II aircraft pictures, and a up-scaled yet casual atmosphere. Their entrees consist of a wide selection of choices with a full service menu. Specialties of the house include 20-ounce Porter house steaks, 14 ounce strip steaks, prime rib, Ribeye steaks, jumbo shrimp, chicken parmigiana, broiled flounder and lobster featured as a special on Saturday nights. The restaurant is reported open from 11:00 a.m. to 10 p.m. throughout the week. This restaurant has been in business for over 40 years. The new management has a great interest in general aviation customers, and enjoys providing efficient and friendly service. A great view of the main ramp is available from their location on the second floor. For more information please call the restaurant at 461-5850.

Restaurants Near Airport:

Maxim's Family Restaurant	Adj Arpt	Phone: 462-0541
Skyroom Restaurant	On Site	Phone: 461-5850

Lodging: Best Western Midway Lodge (Trans) 786-9540; Budgetel Inn 535-9540; Days Inn Northwest (Trans) 255-1700; Embassy Suites (West) (Trans) 782-2900; Howard Johnson Lodge West 771-4800; Marriott Milwaukee (Trans) 786-1100; Port Motel (Trans) 466-4728.

Meeting Rooms: Best Western Midway Lodge 786-9540; Budgetel Inn 535-1300; Days Inn North 255-1700; Embassy Suites West 782-2900; Howard Johnson Lodge West 771-4800; Marriott Milwaukee 786-1100.

Transportation: Courtesy cars reported; Also taxi service: Carey Limousine Service 271-5466; Veterans 933-2266; Yellow 271-1800; Rental cars: available at airport - Apple Chevrolet, Uptown Lincoln/Mercury; also Hertz, by advance reservation.

Information: Greater Milwaukee Convention & Visitors Bureau 510 West Kilbourn Avenue, Milwaukee, WI 53203, Phone: 273-7222 or 800-231-0903.

Airport Information:

MILWAUKEE - LAWRENCE J. TIMMERMAN AIRPORT (MWC)

5 mi northwest of town N43-06.66 W88-02.07 Elev: 745 Fuel: 100, jet-A Rwy 15L-33R: H4107x75 (Asph) Rwy 15R-33L: 3251x275 (Turf) Rwy 04L-22R: H3202x75 (Asph) Rwy 04R-22L: 2859x275 (Turf) Attended: May-Sep 1300-0400Z, Oct-Apr 1300-0300Z Atis: 128.3 Unicom: 122.95 Milwaukee App/Dep Con: 125.35 Timmerman Tower: 120.5 Gnd Con: 121.7

FBO: Gran-Aire, Inc. Phone: 461-3222

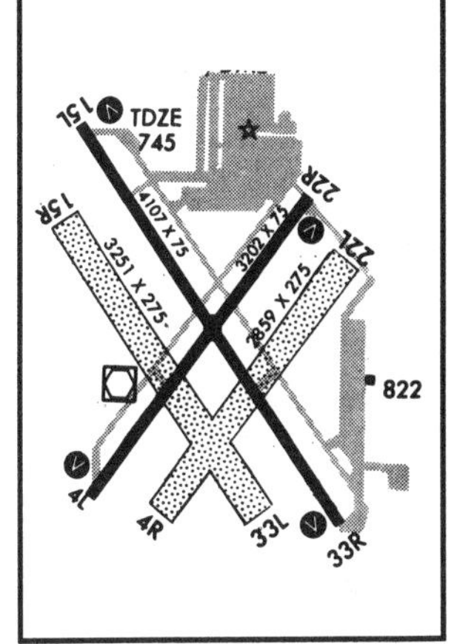

WI-MRJ- MINERAL POINT IOWA COUNTY AIRPORT

(Area Code 608) 41

House on the Rock Restaurants:

This particular attraction is viewed by tens of thousands of tourists each season from all across the United States. A house perched atop a rocky pinnacle is where your self-guided tour begins. From there you will follow carefully-designed ground and elevated walkways that will take you through different rooms containing amazing exhibits. Many exhibits use air pressure to power musical instruments and orchestras that play by themselfs. Indescribable items and collections from all across the world will utterly boggle your mind. Each year this attraction seems to expand in size. Ask anyone who has had the opportunity to visit this attraction and you will get a response, "You have got to see it to believe it." Plan 3 to 4 hours minimum to tour the entire attraction. This attraction is estimated at 15 miles from the Lone Rock, Tri-County Regional Airport. There are several food concessions on the premises for your convenience. During a conversation with the airport manager, we learned that transportation to and from several attractions within the area can be arranged. Rental cars, taxi services and Symons Tours, which specialize in catering to the transportation needs of pilots flying into the area and ferrying small or larger groups to their destination at very reasonable prices. (See "Transportation"). For information about the House On The Rock call 935-3639.

Restaurants Near Airport:
House on the Rock Concessions 20 mi Phone: 935-3639
Lodging: Point Motel (3 miles) 987-3112.
Meeting Rooms: The Spring Green Corp. 588-2571;
Transportation: Airport Courtesy car reported; Rental cars: Franzen Motors 935-9474; Hallada Motors 935-2352; Also Symons Tours (has been in the business of catering to pilots transportation needs for many years), Call 935-3212.
Information: Mineral Point Chamber of Commerce, P.O. Box 78, Mineral Point, WI 53565, Phone: 987-3201.

Attractions:

Historic Mineral Point (3 miles); ***House on the Rock"*** (20 miles) is one attraction that must not be missed if planning to visit the Spring Green area. For information call 935-3639.

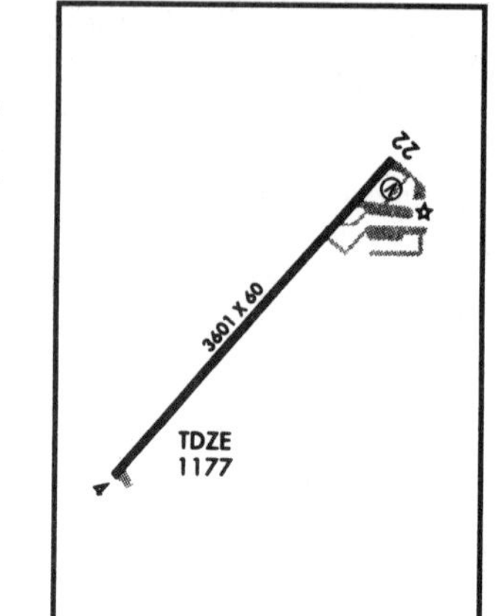

Also See Lone Rock, WI
Tri County Regional Airport (LNR)

Airport Information:

MINERAL POINT - IOWA COUNTY AIRPORT (MRJ)
3 mi northwest of town N42-53.12 W90-13.92 Elev: 1177 Fuel: 100LL, MOGAS
Rwy 04-22: H3601x60 (Asph) Attended: Mon-Fri 1400-2300Z, Sat-Sun 1400-1800Z
Unicom: 122.8
Airport Manager Phone: 987-9931, 935-3069

WI-CWA - MOSINEE CENTRAL WISCONSIN AIRPORT

(Area Code 715) 42

Runway Restaurant:

The Aerodrome Restaurant is located in the main terminal building of Central Wisconsin Regional Airport in Mosinee, Wisconsin with available aircraft parking nearby. The restaurant serves breakfast, lunch and dinner with their menu containing a wide selection of entrees like hamburgers, grilled chicken sandwiches, chicken breast sandwiches, homemade soup made fresh daily along with many other favorites. In-flight catering is also available to pilots on the go. Their dining room can seat between 150 to 175 people. There are windows allowing a nice view of the runways. The restaurant hours and from 5:15 a.m. to 9 p.m. 6 days a week and Friday until 10 p.m. There is a lounge within the restaurant which is open from 11 a.m. to 1 a.m. For information call 693-6122.

Restaurants Near Airport:
Runway Restaurant On Site Phone: 693-6122

Lodging: Best Western Midway Motor Lodge (Trans) 842-1616; Holiday Inn 845-4341; Howard Johnson Lodge (Trans) 842-0711.

Meeting Rooms: Best Western Midway Motor Lodge 842-1616; Holiday Inn 845-4341; Howard Johnson Lodge 842-0711.

Transportation: Taxi Service: Midwest 693-2805; Neda 693-4519; Yellow 845-7346; Rental Cars: Avis 693-3025; Budget 693-6991; Hertz 845-4515; National 693-3430.

Information: Wausau Area Convention & Visitor Council, 300 Third Street, Suite 200, P.O. Box 6190, Wausau, WI 54402, Phone: 715-848-3344, 800-236-9728.

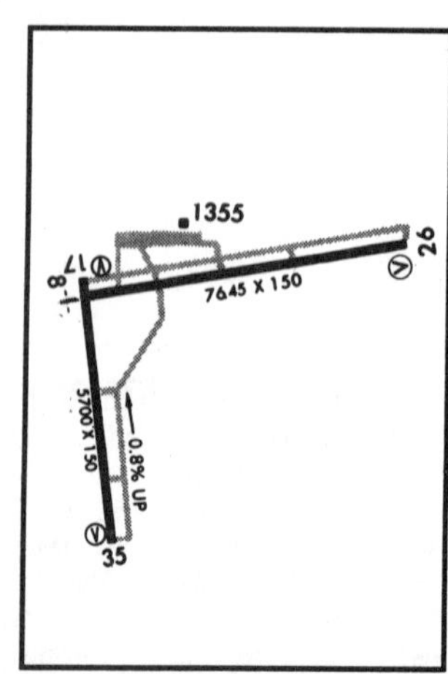

Airport Information:

MOSINEE - CENTRAL WISCONSIN REGIONAL AIRPORT (CWA)
3 mi southeast of town N44-46.70 W89-39.99 Elev: 1277 Fuel: 100LL, Jet-A
Rwy 08-26: H7645x150 (Conc-Grvd) Rwy 17-35: H5700x150 (Conc-Grvd)
Attended: 1100-0300Z Unicom: 122.95 Atis: 127.45 CWA Tower: 119.75
Gnd Con: 121.9
FBO: Central Wisconsin Aviation Phone: 693-6111

WI-OSH - OSHKOSH
WITTMAN REGIONAL AIRPORT

(Area Code 414) **43, 44**

Butch's Anchor Inn:

Butch's Anchor Inn is a unique establishment that is truly a fine dining facility worth special mention. It is located about one half mile from Wittman field, in Oshkosh, Wisconsin. The restaurant will provide courtesy transportation from the main terminal building. This fine restaurant has a nautical decor and serves lunch and dinner with American cuisine, specializing in seafood, steaks, chicken and veal. Private enclosed shelters are available within the dining room that serve as a perfect experience for that romantic occasion or special business conversation. The main dining room is decorated with fishermen nets, oars, harpoons and many other seagoing artifacts. On Sunday between 8:30 a.m. and 2 p.m. try their brunch. They are open seven days a week Monday through Thursday from 11 a.m. to 10 p.m. Friday and Saturday from 11 a.m. to 11 p.m. and Sunday from 10 a.m. to 10 p.m. For reservations, call the restaurant at 232-3742.

Pioneer Inn & Marina (Resort):

The Pioneer Inn & Marina is located about 2 miles north of the Wittman Regional Airport. This resort style establishment contains lodging, restaurants, outdoor swimming pool, marina and business conference and banquet rooms for their guests. Sightseeing cruises, lunch, dinner and even moolight cruises are available during the summer season. Transportation can easily be arranged either through taxi service or by calling the Pioneer Inn & Marina at 233-1980.

Restaurants Near Airport:

Butch's Anchor Inn	1/2 mi N.	Phone: 232-3742
Charcoal Pit	2 mi W.	Phone: 233-7430
Friar Tuck's	2 mi W.	Phone: 231-9555
LaSure's	1 mi W.	Phone: 231-5227
Pioneer Inn & Marina	2 mi N.	Phone: 233-1980

Lodging: Holiday Inn (Trans) 233-1511; Howard Johnson Lodge (Trans) 233-1200; Pioneer Inn (Trans) 288-1980; Radisson Hotel (Trans) 231-5000.

Meeting Rooms: Holiday Inn 233-1511; Howard Johnson Lodge 233-1200; Pioneer Inn 288-1980; Radisson Hotel 231-5000.

Transportation: Courtesy cars available through FBO's depending on available staff; Also Taxi Service: Airport Transit System 426-3900; Oshkosh Taxi 235-7000; Rental Cars: Avis: 235-1111; Budget 235-5900; Hertz 231-0810.

Information: Oshkosh Convention & Tourism Bureau, 2 North Main Street, Oshkosh, WI 54901, Phone: 236-5250 or 800-876-5250.

Attractions:

The ***Experimental Aircraft Association*** better known as the EAA hosts the largest general aviation fly-in anywhere in the world, and is normally held during the last week of July and the beginning of August, each year. This event attracts 800,000 or more aviation enthusiasts during the week long convention. Home built aircraft of every imaginable type, antique airplanes restored to like new condition, military war birds, foreign built aircraft from all parts of the world as well as supersonic transports that fly 1/3 of the way around the world attend this extravaganza. Forums, builder conferences, and a huge "Fly-Market" that takes literally hours to walk through and even longer if researching different new and used equipment for your aircraft. Large display building have the latest in airplane kits for sale, parts, avionics, novelties, books, magazines and anything else you can imagine that remotely relates to aviation. If you haven't yet attended this convention but plan to in the near future, be sure to make lodging accommodations well in advance (up to 1 year). For Information call 426-4800. The ***EAA Air Adventure Museum*** contains an extensive collection of aircraft on display, including, home builts, WW-I and WW-II trainers, fighters, and acrobatic models. In addition, this museum contains four theaters explaining the purpose of the EAA, and it's many available services to the general and home built aviation movement. A very extensive research library is also located on the premises, along with a gift shop, art gallery, and snack room. Transportation to and from the aircraft parking ramp, can usually be arranged through either Bailer Flight Service on the north end of the airport or other FBO's on the field. For more information on hours and admission call the EAA at 426-4800.

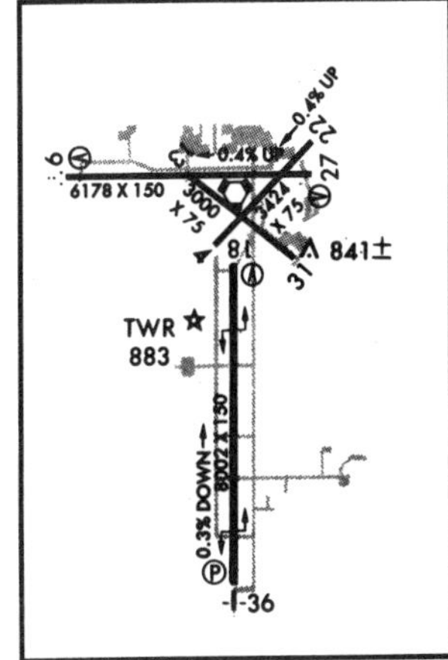

Airport Information:

OSHKOSH - WITTMAN FIELD AIRPORT (OSH)
2 mi south of town　N43-59.06 W88-33.42　Elev: 808　Fuel: 80, 100LL, Jet-A
Rwy 18-36: H8001x150 (Conc-Grvd)　Rwy 09-27: H6180x150 (Asph-Grvd)
Rwy 04-22: H3424x75 (Asph)　Rwy 13-31: H3000x75 (Asph)　Attended: 1300-0200Z
Atis: 125.8　Unicom: 122.95　Unicom: 122.95　Oshkosh Tower: 118.5　Gnd Con: 121.9
FBO: Basler Flight Service　Phone: 236-7827
FBO: Valley Aviation　Phone: 233-2202

EAA Convention, Aviation Center & Air Adventure Museum

The EAA Convention held every year in Oshkosh, Wisconsin, draws over 800,000 participants and spectators, with approximately 14,000 aircraft converging on Wittman Field during the week of the fly-in. The airport is literally a beehive of activity, with exhibitors displaying their products, aircraft homebuilders learning about new construction techniques from one another, and aviation enthusiasts given the chance to escape from the daily routine by enjoying a few days with friends while sharing a common interest. Every year new homebuilt designs are exhibited along with the latest of aviation prototypes, some of which seem to stretch the principles of aerodynamics to the limit. The show provides everyone with a chance to view the world's largest grouping of aviation related flying machines assembled together in one location. Homebuilts, Antiques and Classics, Warbirds Helicopters, and Ultralights, all of which are proudly displayed by the owners who have spent a portion of their lifetime and whose efforts show the enthusiasm behind one of the most gratifying sports known to mankind.

Photo: by Aerodine

During the rest of the year, Wittman Field settles down to its normal daily pace with business as usual. However, in 1983 the EAA Aviation Center opened its doors to all of those interested in the sport of flying, and also offers the aircraft lover a chance to inspect the many

Photo: by EAA Foundation

EAA Aviation Center in Oshkosh, Wisconsin

unusual and unique designs on display throughout the entire year. The building itself combines not only a museum for the general public, but presents a multitude of additional services. The EAA organization, spearheaded by Paul Poberezny and his son Tom have devoted their lives to countless achievements directed toward general aviation and the promotion of homebuilt aircraft. The EAA Aviation Foundation, along with many EAA chapters throughout the United States, have sponsored programs like "Project Schoolflight" and the "EAA Air Academy" as well as the recent "Young Eagle" program designed to build everlasting enthusiasm for the love of aviation in children and young adults. Other significant achievements originated through the EAA, has been the "Kermit Weeks Flight Research Center" devoted to the research and development of programs that have been directed toward enhancing safety and cutting the cost of flying for the average private pilot. One of the most significant achievements recently made through the EAA and other major general aviation organizations, has been the new certification process of small aircraft, designed to ease the prohibitive restrictions forced upon new general aviation manufacturers of aircraft prototypes.

The construction of the EAA Aviation Center not only serves the entire general aviation interest, but also provides a year-round attraction for the public. The EAA Air Adventure Museum, within the Center, contains many exhibits where one can pause and briefly enjoy short entertaining film presentations located at a number of video-briefing stations. A great many aircraft within the museum have been obtained through donations or by loan and remain completely airworthy with their components and engines ready to fly with only minimal preparation. For those aircraft suspended from the ceiling by cables, great care has been taken to maintain the structural integrity so as not to damage spars or ribs within the wings. A variety of different colored trilons throughout the museum marks specific categories of aircraft like Homebuilt aircraft, Antique and Classic, Warbirds exhibits, racing airplanes, acrobatic and special record holding prototypes. An extension to the museum also includes the "Pioneer Airport", a newly constructed facility which gives special recognition to military personnel that served within the armed forces.

Photo: by Aerodine

When planning to fly in to spend the day at the EAA Air Adventure Museum, you can park your aircraft at Basler Flight Service or Valley Aviation and call the museum for courtesy transportation. Hours are 8:30 a.m. to 5 p.m. Monday through Saturday and 11 a.m. to 5 p.m. on Sunday. Admission $7.00 adults and $5.50 for children. For information about the EAA Foundation, scheduled events or museum questions call 414-426-4800. (Information submitted by museum.)

Photo: by Aerodine

WI-PBH - PHILLIPS
PRICE COUNTY AIRPORT

(Area Code 715) **45**

Harbor View Restaurant & Lounge:

The Harbor View Inn is a sports bar located across the street from the Price County Airport in Phillips, Wisconsin. This restaurant serves a full menu including favorits like Ribeye steaks, prime ribsandwiches, barbequed ribs, broasted chicken and homemade pizzas. Average prices run between $5.00 and $8.00 for most main courses. The restaurant offers a cozy atmosphere. The view from the dining room overlooks beautiful Long Lake. They even have additional dining on their outdoor deck which is very popular with many customers. In-flight catering is another service available through the restaurant. This supper club is open Tuesday through Thursday from 6 a.m. to 8 p.m., 7 days a week between 10:30 a.m. and 10:30 p.m. For reservations and information call 339-2626.

Restaurants Near Airport:
Harbor View Rest. Adj Arpt Phone: 339-2626

Lodging: Musky Trail Resort (2 miles) 339-2756; Skyline Motel (Adj Arpt) 339-3086; Timber Inn Motel (Adj Arpt) 339-3071.

Meeting Rooms: None Reported

Transportation: None Reported

Information: Price Chamber of Commerce (Lodging and Resort Information) 339-4100; Also Price County Recreation Department, Normal Building, Phillips, WI 54555, Phone: 339-4505.

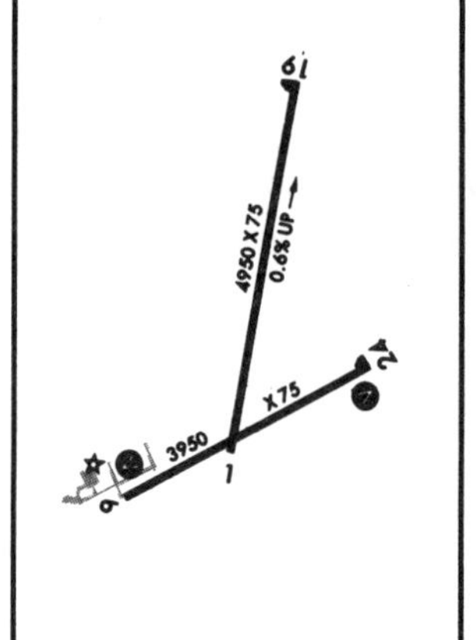

Airport Information:

PHILLIPS - PRICE COUNTY AIRPORT (PBH)
1 mi northwest of town N45-42.33 W90-24.17 Elev: 1471 Fuel: 100LL, Jet-A, MOGAS Rwy 01-19: H4950x75 (Asph) Rwy 06-24: H3950x75 (Asph)
Attended: Mon-Fri 1400-2300Z, Sat 1500-2300Z, Sun 1600-2300Z Unicom: 122.8
Price County Airport Phone: 339-3701

WI-C47 - PORTAGE
PORTAGE MUNICIPAL AIRPORT

(Area Code 608) **46**

Hitching Post:

The Hitching Post Restaurant is within a 4 block walk from the Portage Municipal Airport. We were told by the restaurant management that pilots often park their aircraft next to the Armory and Portage Glass building nearer to the restaurant. You might check this out with the airport management. This is a family style restaurant serving very good food and provides a wide selection of delicious entrees including steaks & seafood choices. The Prime rib melts in your mouth. The dining room offers a casual and friendly atmosphere with wooden beams ceilings, paneling, and a rustic country and western decor. Average prices run $4.95 for lunch and $8.95 for most dinner selections. Daily specials are also available. Accommodations for larger groups can easily be arranged by reservation. This establishment can also provide catering along with meals prepared for carry-out. They are open from 11 a.m. to 11 p.m. Monday through Saturday. They are also open on Mothers day and Fathers day, however we suggest that you make reservations as this is a particularly busy time. The best way to get to the restaurant from the airport, is to walk two blocks north on Silver Lake Drive, then turn right 2 blocks on Frontage road to Wisconsin street unless you park at the location mentioned above. For information call the restaurant at 742-8208..

Restaurants Near Airport:
Hitching Post Restaurant 4 blks Phone: 742-8208

Lodging: Porterhouse Motel (1 mile) 742-2186; Ridge Motel (1 mile) 742-5306; Shady Lawn Motel (4 miles) 742-4218; Super 8 Motel (2 miles) 742-8330.

Meeting Rooms: None Reported

Transportation: Airport van reported; Also Taxi Service: City Cab Company at the airport 742-6669; Rental Cars: Jenkins Motor Cars 742-4112.

Information: Chamber of Commerce, 301 West Wisconsin Street, Portage, WI 53901, Phone: 742-6242 or 800-474-2525.

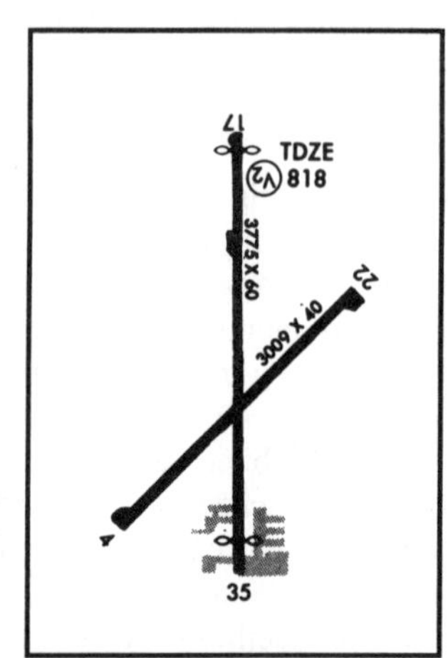

Airport Information:

PORTAGE - PORTAGE MUNICIPAL AIRPORT (C47)
2 mi northwest of town N43-33.61 W89-28.99 Elev: 825 Fuel: 100LL, MOGAS
Rwy 17-35: H3769x60 (Asph) Rwy 04-22: H3009x40 (Asph) Attended: Mon-Sat 1200-0700Z, Sun 1300-0100Z Unicom: 122.7 Notes: CAUTION: High-T Power lines on approach end of runways. Also large hangars and trees 200' west of runway may cause wind shear with strong NW winds. Refer to current AFD for runway conditions, obstructions and airport information.
Portage Municipal Airport Phone: 742-6669
FBO: Services Unlimited Phone: 742-6609

WI-PDC - PRAIRIE DU CHIEN
PRAIRIE DU CHIEN AIRPORT

(Area Code 608) **47**

Restaurants Near Airport:

Jeffers Black Angus	Adj Arpt	Phone: 326-2222

Lodging: Best Western Quiet House (3/4 mile) 326-4777; Brisbois Motor Inn 326-8404; Hidden Valley 326-8476; Holiday Motel 326-2448; Prairie Motel (2 miles) 326-6461.

Meeting Rooms: None Reported

Transportation: Taxi Service: Town Taxi 326-6066; Rental Cars: Rental Cars at airport 326-2118; Southwest Motors, Inc. 326-5121.

Information: Prairie du Chine, Chamber of Commerce, 211 South Main Street, P.O. Box 326, Prairie duChien, WI 53821, Phone: 326-8555 or 800-732-1673.

Jeffers Black Angus:

The Jeffers Black Angus Restaurant is located 500 feet north and directly across from the Prairie du Chien Airport, in Prairie du Chien, Wisconsin. There is always delightful dining in their newly remodeled restaurant, containing 3 separate dining rooms. The decor provides a cozy atmosphere with lots of plants and ample seating for between 150 and 175 people. Their cocktail lounge can also accommodate groups. They feature delicious nightly specials, including their popular Friday fish fry and tempting weekend specials. In addition to the dinner entrees, they also offer a delicious sandwich menu, homemade egg rolls, and Rumaki; or try the famous onion rings or French fries, and Wisconsin cheese curds. Always available is their appetizing "Soup and Salad Well". The Jeffers Black Angus is open daily between 5 p.m. and 10 p.m. and on Sunday from 11:30 a.m. to 10 p.m. For groups large or small call 326-2222.

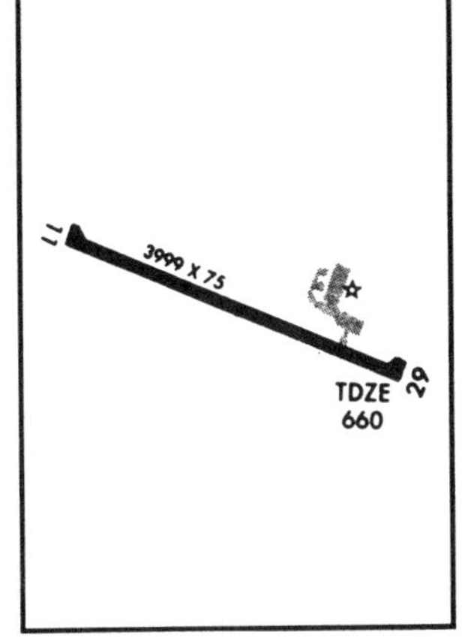

Airport Information:

PRAIRIE DU CHIEN - PRAIRIE DU CHIEN MUNICIPAL AIRPORT (PDC)
2 mi southeast of town N43-01.31 W91-07.48 Elev: 659 Fuel: 100LL, MOGAS
Rwy 11-29: H3999x75 (Asph) Attended: 1600-2200Z Unicom: 122.8
Prairie du Chien Airport Phone: 326-2118

WI-RAC - RACINE
JOHN H. BATTEN FIELD

(Area Code 414) **48, 49**

Restaurants Near Airport:

Around The Clock	1/4 mi	Phone: 632-6566
Infucino's Restaurant	15 min walk	Phone: 633-3173

Lodging: Holiday Inn (Trans) 637-9311; Racine Inn On The Lake (Trans) 633-3551; Sheraton Hotel (Trans) 886-6100.
Meeting Rooms: Holiday Inn 637-9311; Racine Inn On The Lake 633-3551; Sheraton Hotel 886-6100.
Transportation: Rental Cars: American Intl. 553-5422, 637-9562.
Information: Racine County Convention and Visitors Bureau, 345 Main Street, Racine, WI 53403, Phone: 634-3293, 800-C-RACINE.

Around The Clock:

Around The Clock is a restaurant located about a quarter mile from the John H. Batten Field in Racine, Wisconsin. This restaurant is located on Rapids Drive and is open 24 hours a day seven days a week. Their entrees consist of barbecued veal, ribs, chicken, seafood, sandwiches and also a salad bar. On Friday they have an all-you-can-eat fish fry. Each day they also have 2 to 4 specials on their menu. This family style restaurant offers additional space for larger groups. For information call 632-6566.

Infucino's Restaurant:

Infucino's Restaurant is located within a 15 minute walk from the John H. Batten Field, according to the restaurant management. This family restaurant offers a comfortable and casual decor, with a newly carpeted and remodeled dining room decorated in colors of burgundy, and able to seat up to 240 people. They are open seven days a week from 11 a.m. to 12 a.m. and Friday and Saturday until 2 a.m. Their house specialties include Italian and American cuisine, with choices that change daily. The food is very good with large portions. Catered parties and accommodations for larger groups can be held within their back dining room. For information call 633-3173.

Airport Information:

RACINE - JOHN H. BATTEN FIELD (RAC)
2 mi northwest of town N42-45.66 W87-48.82 Elev: 674 Fuel: 80, 100LL, Jet-A, MOGAS Rwy 04-22: H6556x100 (Conc) Rwy 14-32: H4824x100 (Asph)
Attended: continuously Unicom: 123.075
FBO: Racine Commercial Airport Corp. Phone: 631-5620

WI-C35 - REEDSBURG
REEDSBURG MUNICIPAL AIRPORT

(Area Code 608) 50

Longley's Restaurant:

Longley's Restaurant is located across the street from the Reedsburg Municipal Airport in Reedsburg, Wisconsin. This restaurant is open at 5 a.m. to around 10:00 p.m. 7 days a week, with a wide selection of entrees for breakfast, lunch and dinner. The decor of the restaurant is modern with a casual atmosphere. Specials of the house include a delicious prime rib on Saturday evenings. On Sunday they serve a breakfast buffet from 7:30 a.m. to 11:00 a.m., followed by a luncheon buffet from 11:30 a.m. to 3:30 p.m., in addition to their salad bar made fresh daily. They also have a banquet room for up to 100 people, and a cocktail lounge. This establishment attracts many fly-in groups due to its convenient location near the airport. Fly-in customers can park their aircraft and walk across the street to the restaurant. Longley's Restaurant is situated within a strip shopping plaza, and can easily be seen from the airport just kitty-corner to the airport property. For reservations or information call 524-6497.

Restaurants Near Airport:
Longley's Restaurant   Across Street   Phone: 524-6497

Lodging: Reedsburg Motel (Trans) 524-2306; Voyageur Inn 524-6017.

Meeting Rooms: Voyageur Inn 524-6017.

Transportation: Taxi Service: Reedsburg Cab 524-8766; Rental Cars: Koenecke Ford 524-4361.

Information: Reedsburg Chamber of Commerce, 240 Railroad Street, P.O. Box 142, Reedsburg, WI 53959, Phone: 524-2850 or 800-844-3507.

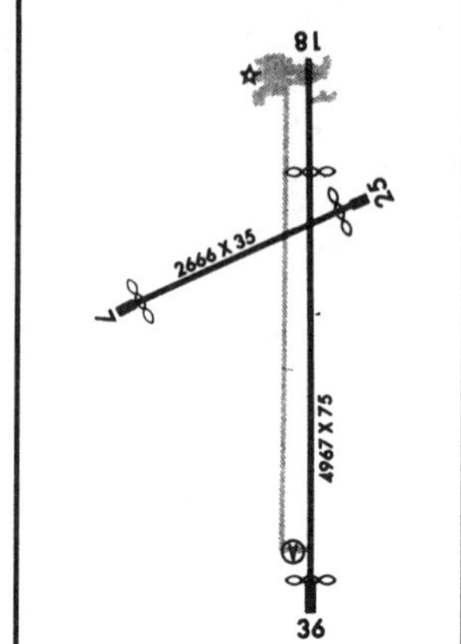

Airport Information:

REEDSBURG - REEDSBURG MUNICIPAL AIRPORT (C35)
1 mi east of town   N43-31.56 W89-58.99   Elev: 907   Fuel: 80, 100LL, Jet-A
Rwy 18-36: H4967x75 (Asph)   Rwy 07-25: H2666x35 (Asph)   Attended: Jun-Aug 1400-0200Z, Sep-May 1400-2300Z   Unicom: 122.8
FBO: T & J Aviation Company   Phone: 524-2396

WI-RHI - RHINELANDER
ONEIDA COUNTY AIRPORT

(Area Code 715) 51

Skyview Cafe & Cocktails:

The Skyview Cafe Restaurant is located in the main terminal building on Oneida County Airport in Rhinelander, Wisconsin. This family style restaurant serves a full selection of entrees for breakfast, lunch & dinner. The restaurant is open 7 days a week from 5 a.m. to 5 p.m., and Sunday from 5 p.m. until closing time depending on arriving flights (8, 9, or 10 p.m.). Hours may vary according to the schedule of the local air-carrier operation. The main dining room can accommodate 40 to 50 persons along with accommodations for groups. Real "home cooked" meals are their specialty, serving unique and delicious breakfasts, real potatoes, omelets, "Big Dipper" beef sandwiches, chicken filets, burgers and fries along with homemade soups and bakery goods. They also provide In-flight catering for transient pilots and their crews or passengers. Aircraft parking is right outside the door. The restaurant and terminal building at the Oneida County Airport, may soon be renovated. Once this happens, new counters and interior for the restaurant will be installed. For information call 365-3440.

Restaurants Near Airport:
Skyview Cafe   On Site   Phone: 365-3440

Lodging: Best Western Claridge Inn (Trans) 362-7100; Holiday Acres Resort (8 miles, Trans) 369-1500; Holiday Inn (1 mile, Trans) 369-3600.

Meeting Rooms: Best Western Claridge Inn 362-7100; Holiday Acres Resort 369-1500; Holiday Inn 369-3600.

Transportation: Airport courtesy reported; Also Taxi Service: Courtesy 369-5411; Yellow 362-3100; Rental Cars: Avis 369-1205; Budget 369-2525; Hertz 369-2434; National 362-2200.

Information: Rhinelander Aera Chamber of Commerce, 135 South Stevens Street, P.O. Box 795, Rhinelander, WI 54501, Phone: 362-7464 or 800-236-4386.

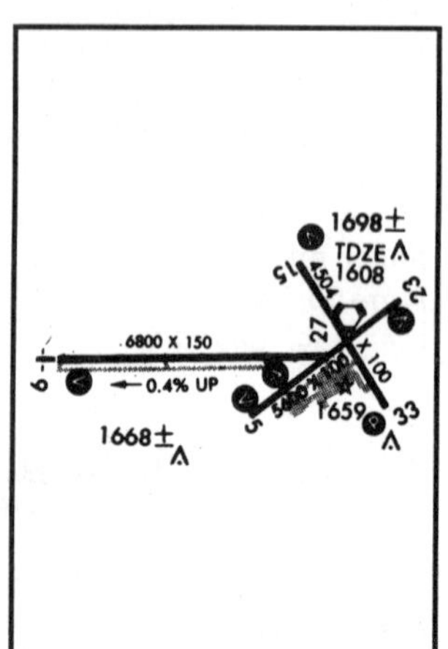

Airport Information:

RHINELANDER - ONEIDA COUNTY AIRPORT (RHI)
2 mi southwest of town   N45-37.85 W89-27.93   Elev: 1623   Fuel: 100LL, Jet-A
Rwy 09-27: H6800x150 (Conc-Wc)   Rwy 05-23: H5600x100 (Asph)   Rwy 15-33: H4504x100 (Asph)   Attended: Oct-Apr 1400-2300Z, May-Sep 1400-0100Z   Unicom: 123.0
FBO: Rhinelander Flying Service, Inc.   Phone: 369-3131.

WI-93C - RICHLAND CENTER RICHLAND AIRPORT

(Area Code 608)

52

Peaches Restaurant:

Peaches Restaurant is located about 1/2 mile and across the highway from the Richland Airport. This combination family style and fine dining establishment is open 11:30 a.m. to 2 a.m. 365 days out of the year. We were told that pilots and their passengers often walk to the restaurant from the airport. If your party would like a ride from the restaurant back to the airport, they will be happy to furnish you with courtesy transportation. They feature a "Noon" buffet along with a Friday "Seafood" buffet, Saturday "Prime-rib" buffet and their special Sunday "Grand" buffet. Their main dining room can seat 110 people. A private dining room can be arranged for groups up to 70 people. For information call Peaches Restaurant at 647-8886.

Restaurants Near Airport:

Peaches Restaurant	1/2 mi	Phone: 647-8886

Lodging: Riverside 647-6420.

Meeting Rooms: None Reported

Transportation: Taxi Service: Richland 647-3114; Rental Cars: Lyeda Ford 647-2122.

Information: Richland Center Chamber of Commerce, 170 West Seminary Street, P.O. Box 128, Richland Center, WI 53581, Phone: 647-6205 or 800-422-1318.

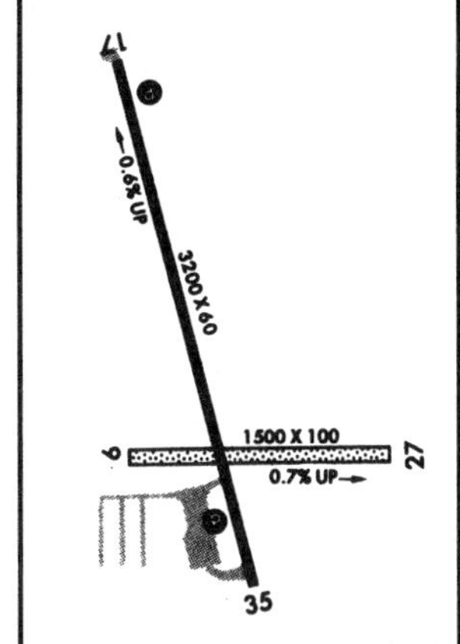

Airport Information:

RICHLAND CENTER - RICHLAND AIRPORT - (93C)
4 mi southeast of town N43-16.98 W90-17.91 Elev: 742 Fuel: 100LL
Rwy 17-35: 3200x60 (Asph) Rwy 09-27: 1500x150 (Turf) Attended: unattended
CTAF: 122.9
Richland Airport Phone: 647-4237, 647-8804

WI-3WO - SHAWANO SHAWANO MUNICIPAL

(Area Code 715)

53

Launching Pad Restaurant:

The Launching Pad Restaurant is located across the street from the Shawano Municipal Airport. We were told that pilots can park their aircraft within 100 feet of the restaurant. This popular fly-in establishment is a favorite with many pilots. They serve daily specials and homemade onion rings. The item they are best known for is their out-of-this-world hamburger. Their 1/3 pound and 1/2 pound burgers are served with all the trimmings. If you have room, you might want to try their famous "Duke Burger." This is a whopping 1-1/2 pound of hamburger meat that is topped with lettuce, tomato, cheese and served on a hard roll. In addition to their delicious burgers, they also offer a 6-ounce tenderloin, chicken sandwich, grilled chicken breast sandwich, ham and cheese sandwich and fish sandwich made with haddock. The staff of the Launching Pad are happy to cater your group needs. There are two back rooms that serve as party and private dining areas. The decor of this combination restaurant and tavern exhibits a festive atmosphere, decorated with knotty pine walls, a pool table and dart board. For information call the Launching Pad Restaurant at 524-4098.

Restaurants Near Airport:

Best Western	1/4 mi	Phone: 526-9595
Launching Pad	100'	Phone: 524-4098
Lee's Truck Stop	3/8th mi	Phone: 526-3515
Perkins	3/8th mi	Phone: 524-2900

Lodging: American 1-1/4 mi 524-5111; Best Western Village Haus Motor Lodge 1/4 mi 526-9595; Pine Acre Motel 1/2 mi 526-5189.

Meeting Rooms: Best Western Village Haus Motor Lodge 1/4 mi 526-9595.

Transportation: Rental cars: Shawano Auto Sales 526-3020; Taxi service: City Taxi 526-6445.

Information: Shawano Chamber of Commerce, 1413 E. Green Bay Street, P.O. Box 38, Shawano, WI 54166, Phone: 524-2139.

NO AIRPORT DIAGRAM AVAILABLE

Airport Information:

SHAWANO - SHAWANO MUNICIPAL (3W0)
1 mi northeast of town N44-47.24 W88-33.59 Elev: 811 Fuel: 100LL Rwy 11-29: H3900x75 (Asph) Rwy 03-21: 1820x75 (Turf) Rwy 09-27: 1600x78 (Turf) Attended: 1400Z-dusk Unicom: 122.8 Notes: Rwy 09-27 and Rwy 03-21 CLOSED to wheeled acft Nov 15 thru Jun 15, Confirm conditions with arpt manager 715-526-2465.
Airport Manager Phone: 526-2465

WI-RZN - SIREN
BURNETT COUNTY AIRPORT

(Area Code 715)

54, 55

Robertson's Family Restaurant:

The Robertson's Family Restaurant can be found just off runway 32 on the Burnett County Airport in Siren, Wisconsin. The folks at the airport suggested that pilots simply park their aircraft well off to the side of the runway and walk to the restaurant. Their establishment combines a dining facility able to accommodate groups between 35 and 40 people in their back room, along with a gift shop, ice cream shop and art gallery. The restaurant is open seven days a week during summer from 7 a.m. to 10 p.m. and 7 a.m. to 9 p.m. during winter. The entrees include sandwiches French dip, patty melts, pizza and hamburgers. Their house specialty is their fried chicken dinners. Every day they have specials and on Friday all-you-can-eat fish and shrimp dinners. Enjoy their freshly baked pies, biscuits, cinnamon rolls and bran muffins. For information call 349-2570.

Yellow River Inn:

Thanks to the airport manager we were informed about this establishment which is located about 8 to 10 miles from the Burnett County Airport. The Yellow River Inn began its tradition of fine food when the original owners founded the business in 1949. They operated the restaurant for 32 years, building a reputation for delicious home cooked meals served with generous portions of friendliness. Since then the new owners have remodeled the entire restaurant and bar. The owners love for antiques are displayed through the restaurant and create a welcoming atmosphere. Three rooms upstairs were turned into turn-of-the-century kitchens to provide private dining. The rooms each with one table accommodating two, four or six people, have wood cook stoves, dry sinks, pantries with jars and cans and cupboards... anything normally found in a kitchen of 80 years ago. The new owners continue the tradition of fine home cooking with their culinary skills. The restaurant is open daily between 4 p.m. and 9 p.m. and during the summer months until 10 p.m. Items on their menu include Top Butt Steak, Porterhouse Steak, T-Bone, Teriyaki Sirloin or chicken, pork chops, liver & onions, and Rib eye steak to mention only a few. Sandwiches of all types as well as combination plates and seafood choices like broiled swordfish, Torsk, Salmon fillet, jumbo shrimp, scallops, Walleyed pike, lobster tail and seafood platters are all available. Evening specials, carry outs and lighter fare selections are also available. A Sunday brunch is prepared for their guests between 11 a.m. and 1:30 p.m. Check with the airport management for available transportation to and from the airport and restaurant. According to the airport management some sort of arrangements can be made for fly-in guests. For information about the restaurant call 866-7375.

Restaurants Near Airport:

Narrows Supper Club	3 mi	Phone: 349-2445
Robertson's Restaurant	Adj Arpt	Phone: 349-2570
Yellow River Cafe	8-10 mi	Phone: 866-7375

Lodging: Forgotten Times Bed & Breakfast 5 mi 349-5837; Pine West Motel 3 mi 349-5225; Webster Motel 3 mi 866-8951.

Meeting Rooms: None Reported

Transportation: Check with airport manager or Burnet County Flying Service at 349-5220 or 349-5362.

Information: Siren Area Chamber of Commerce, P.O. Box 57, Siren, WI 54872, Phone: N/A.

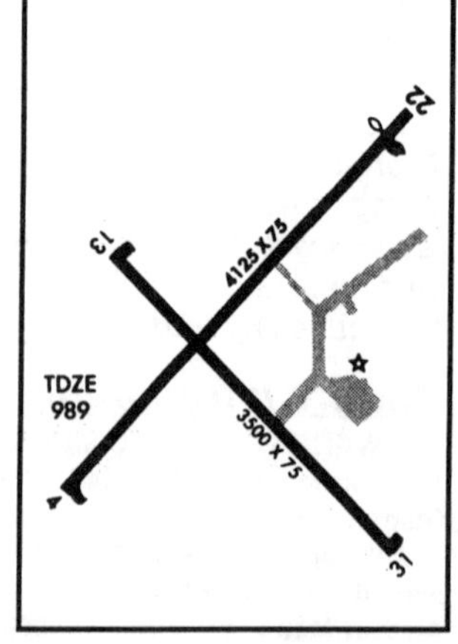

Airport Information:

SIREN - BURNETT COUNTY AIRPORT (RZN)

3 miles north of town N45-49.37 W92-22.34 Elev: 989 Fuel: 100LL
Rwy 04-22: 4125x75 (Asph) Rwy 13-31: H3500x75 (Asph) Attended: 1300Z-dusk
Unicom: 122.8
FBO: Burnett Country Flying Service Phone: 349-5220, 349-5362.

WI-SUW - SUPERIOR
RICHARD BONG AIRPORT

(Area Code 715) 56

Bellknap Restaurant:

Bellknap Restaurant is located on Richard Bong Airport in Superior, Wisconsin, located near the western tip of Lake Superior. The restaurant has large windows on adjoining sides, and at times, guests are able to watch practice parachute landings, while enjoying a fine meal. The restaurant serves real home-style cooking for breakfast, lunch and dinner. There is a banquet room adjoining the restaurant, great for fly-in gatherings. The restaurant hours are Saturday and Sunday 8 a.m. to 9 p.m. andTuesday, through Friday they are open 11 a.m. to 9 p.m. For information call 394-3313.

Restaurants Near Airport:
Bellknap Restaurant On Site Phone: 394-3313

Lodging: Best Western Bridgeview (3 mile) 392-8174; Holiday Inn (3 miles) 392-4783; Radisson Inn (3 miles) 392-7152; Sunshine Motel (1 mile, Trans) 394-7055.

Meeting Rooms: None Reported

Transportation: Taxi Service: Checker 394-5577; Tip Top Taxi 394-6681; Yellow 394-7791; Rental Cars: Debbie's 394-6444.

Information: Superior Tourist Information Center, 305 Harbor View Parkway E, Superior, WI 54880, Phone: 392-2773, 800-942-5313.

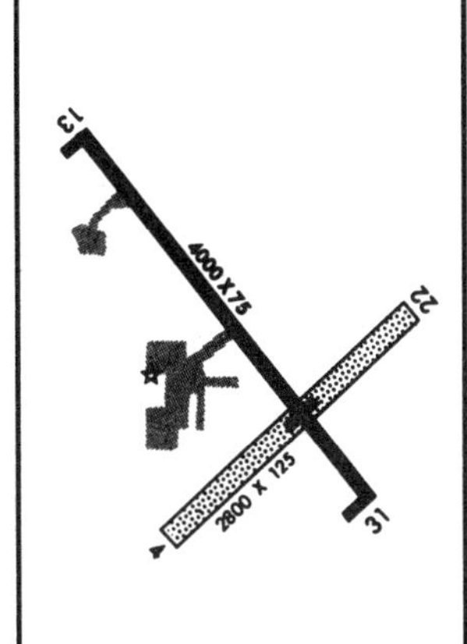

Airport Information:

SUPERIOR - RICHARD BONG AIRPORT (SUW)
3 mi south of town N46-40.99 W92-05.71 Elev: 674 Fuel: 100LL, Jet-A
Rwy 13-31: H4000x75 (Asph) Rwy 04-22: 2800x125 (Turf-Grvl) Attended: 1400Z-dusk
Unicom: 122.7
FBO: Paul Pederson Airmotive, Inc. Phone: 392-3526
FBO: Twin Ports Flying Service Phone: 394-6444.

WI-Y72 - TOMAH
BLOYER FIELD

(Area Code 608) 57

Burnstad's European Cafe:

Burnstad's European Cafe is situated about 1/2 mile from the Bloyer Field Airport in Tomah, Wisconsin. This restaurant can be reached by turning right out of the airport entrance and simply walking about 1/2 mile west along highway 12 & 16. Burnstad's Restaurant is situated within a shopping mall uniquely decorated in a European style with cobblestone walkways and containing several specialty, souvenir and gift shops. Burnstad's is open Monday through Saturday between 8 a.m. and 9 p.m. and 8 a.m. to 8 p.m. on Sunday. Their specialty entree selections include a variety of salads, sandwiches, steaks, seafood, homemade soups prepared from scratch, along with European favorites like Pirozhki, Capelli d' Angelo. They also feature 35 delicious dessert selections created by their experienced chef. Their menu also includes lunch and evening specials. Average prices run $5.95 for lunch and about $5.95 to $14.95 for dinner. The decor of Burnstad's displays a European flair with a touch of elegance. This establishment has recently become popular with many fly-in customers, and has been featured in a number of local and regional publications, including "Midwest Flyer Magazine" (June/July Issue 1992). For information about Burnstad's European Cafe call 372-4040.

Restaurants Near Airport:
Burnstad's European Cafe 1/2 mi W. Phone: 372-4040

Lodging: HoJo's (2 miles) 372-4500; DayBreak Motel (1 mile) 372-5946; Econo Lodge (4 miles) 372-9100; Holiday Inn (4-1/2 miles) 372-3211; Park Motel (1 mile) 372-4655; Rest Well Motel (Adj Arpt) 372-2471; Super 8 Motel (4-1/2 miles) 372-3901.

Meeting Rooms: Holiday Inn 372-3211.

Transportation: Taxi Service: Ace Cab 372-2345.

Information: Greater Tomah Chamber of Commerce, 708 Sourth Superior Avenue, P.O. Box 625, Tomah, WI 54660, Phone: 372-2166.

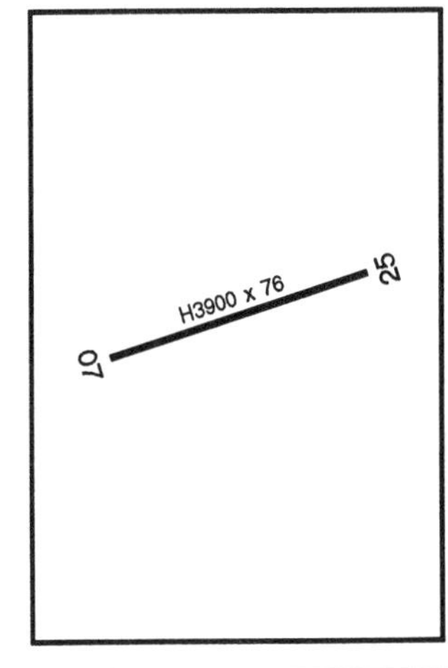

Airport Information:

TOMAH - BLOYER FIELD (Y72)
1 mi east of town N43-58.50 W90-29.01 Elev: 963 Fuel: 180, 00LL, MOGAS
Rwy 07-25: H3900x75 (Asph) Attended: unattended CTAF: 122.9
Airport Manager Phone: 374-7430

WI-RYV - WATERTOWN
WATERTOWN MUNICIPAL

(Area Code 414) **58**

Restaurants Near Airport:

Culver's Restaurant	1/4 mi	Phone: N/A
Steakfire Restaurant	2 blk's W.	Phone: 262-2222

Lodging: Best Western 1/4 mi 261-9010; Flags Inn 2 mi 261-9400; Olympia Resort & Spa 567-0311; Super 8 motel 1/4 mi 800-800-8000.

Meeting Rooms: None reported

Transportation: Airport courtesy reported; Also rental cars can be obtained through Wisconsin Aviation, Inc. (FBO) at 261-4567.

Information: Watertown Chamber of Commerce, 519 E. Main Street, Watertown, WI 53094, Phone: 261-6320.

Steakfire Restaurant:

The Steakfire Restaurant is a new and exciting concept of "Grill your own" dining. They also feature full-service dining. Located 2 blocks west of the airport, they feature open-flame broiling of steaks, chops and seafood. You choose your meat entree from refrigerated display cases and then "do your own thing." The Steakfire is open 7 days a week from 11 a.m. until 10 p.m. On Sunday they feature a brunch that begins at 9:30 a.m. For information you can call the Steakfire Restaurant at 262-2222.

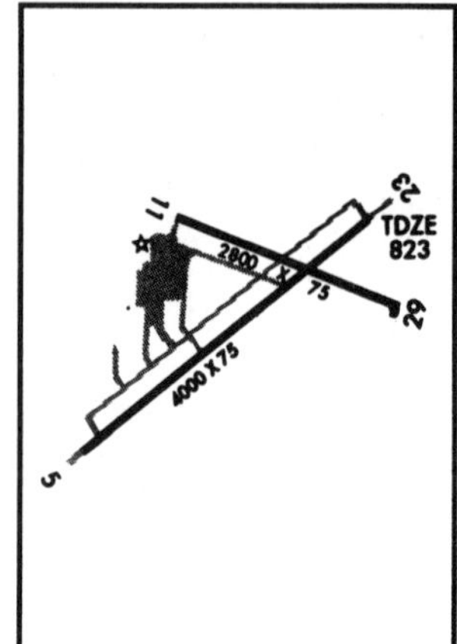

Airport Information:

WATERTOWN - WATERTOWN MUNICIPAL (RYV)

1/2 mi south of town N43-10.18 W88-43.39 Elev: 833 Fuel: 100LL, Jet-A Rwy 05-23: H4000x75 (Asph) Rwy 11-29: H2800x75 (Asph) Attended: 6 a.m. to 10 p.m. daily Unicom: 122.8 Notes: Right hand traffic for Rwy 50; Right hand traffic for Rwy 11.

Central Aviation, Inc. (Aircraft painting interiors etc.) Phone: 261-1880

FBO: Wisconsin Aviation, Inc. Phone: 261-4567 or 800-657-0761

Not to be used for navigational purposes

WI-UES - WAUKESHA
WAUKESHA COUNTY - (Crites Field)

(Area Code 414) **59, 60**

Waldo Peppers:

If you ever saw the movie "Waldo Pepper," you will enjoy this aviation theme restaurant giving tribute to a famous flyer who served as a pilot during WWI, and later plied his skills as a flying barnstormer and airshow pilot across the midwest. Waldo Pepper's restaurant is an upscale family restaurant that is located about 2 miles from the Waukesha Airport. This restaurant is open for breakfast 7 a.m. to 11 p.m., for lunch 11 a.m. to 2 p.m. and for dinner from 2 p.m. until 10 p.m. Their menu is extensive with such items as seafood, shrimp, Mexican dishes, Italian dishes, all types of American selections with sandwiches , burgers and appetizers. The decor of the restaurant has an aviation theme. As you enter the restaurant you will see logos of bi-planes, propellers, clouds hanging from the ceiling, aerial photographs and pictures of airplanes decorating the restaurant. The main dining room is "L" shaped with sections divided off for smoking and non-smoking. In addition to their dining area, they also feature a beer garden and soon expect to add an addition with the ability to seat 70 additional customers. To reach the restaurant turn left out of the airport entranceway and take the frontage road around to the other side of the airport. You will see a sign with the name Peterbuilt (Truck Mfg.) turn left. About 1/4 to 1/2 mile you will see a Denny's Restaurant sign. Turn right at Denny's and take the service road to the end. Waldo Peppers should be on the right side of the street. There are 3 basic ways to reach the restaurants. 1) Airport crew car might be available for short periods if available and not in use. 2) Taxi service: Best Cab or Spring City Taxi for about $7.00 to $9.00 each way depending on time of day, plus $1.00 for each additional person. And 3) Rental car for $30.00 for the day. For information about Waldo Pepper's Saloon and Eatery call 524-9989.

Restaurants Near Airport:

Denny's	2 mi	Phone: 549-4600
Grandview Inn	3 mi	Phone: 549-3824
Maddie's Restaurant	1/2 to 1 mi	Phone: 542-1721
Waldo Pepper's	2 mi	Phone: 524-9989
Weissgerber Gasthaus	2 mi	Phone: 544-4460

Lodging: Country Inn 2 mi 547-0201; Hampton Inn Brookfield 6mi 796-1500; Holiday Inn 4 mi 786-0460.

Meeting Rooms: Weissgerber Gasthaus Restaurant 2 mi, provides meeting accommodations 544-4460; Also Hampton Inn Brookfield 6 mi., has meeting rooms 796-1500.

Transportation: Rental cars through Waukesha Flying Service are available at around $30.00 per day, 549-6150; Taxi Service: Best Cab Company of Waukesha, Inc. 549-6622; Spring City Taxi 524-0711.

Information: Waukesha County Visitors Bureau, N14 W23777 Stone Ridge Drive, Suite 170, Waukesha, WI 53188, Phone: 524-8100 or 800-366-1961.

Attractions:

The Warren O'Brien Air Museum is located in a room, housing Waukesha County Aviation memorabilia, and is situated within the lannon stone administration building/hangar on the northeast corner of Crites Field, Waukesha County Airport. It is under the sponsorship of the Waukesha Aviation club, Inc., and is staffed and open to the public on Sunday from 1:30 to 4:30 p.m. The museum is open Memorial Day through Labor Day, and at other times by special arrangements. It was established in 1985 and named after the first president of the Waukesha Aviation Club, Warren O'Brien. The records start with the first landing and takeoff of an airplane in Waukesha County in 1912 at Stonebank. Important achievements are recorded from 1920 through the present. For information or to arrange special group visits, call 547-7300 or Waukesha Flying Service, Inc. at 549-6150.

Weissgerber Gasthaus:

This is a famous German restaurant that is well known throughout the western Milwaukee area as being one of the finest dining facilities of the region. This restaurant is a fine dining facility with casual but appropriate dress required. The bill of fare provides authentic German cuisine at its finest. Their "Gasthaus Platter" combines delicacies like smoked pork chops and Rouladen. Additional choices include Wiener Schnitzel as well as five other Schnitzel specialties. Stuffed pork chops, pork shank, and many appetizers including Black Forested Vineyard Snails. For your passengers, Weissgerber Gasthaus features some of the finest German beers with 5 famous styles on tap as well as many bottled selections. The restaurant has a warm, elegant atmosphere with oak paneling, plastered ceiling, fireplace, solid mahogany bar and a cathedral ceiling with a lofted dining area. The Weissgerber Gasthaus is a favorite with fly-in business travelers and corporate cliental. Their ability for combining meetings with some of the best German cuisine is a specialty for which they are well prepared to meet your most demanding expectations. To reach the restaurant turn left out of the airport entranceway and take the frontage road around to the other side of the airport. You will see a sign with the name Peterbuilt (Truck Mfg.) turn left. About 1/4 to 1/2 mile you will see a Denny's Restaurant sign. The Weissgerber Gasthaus Restaurant should be near that intersection. There are 3 basic ways to reach the restaurants. 1) Airport crew car might be available for short periods if not in use. 2) Taxi service: Best Cab 549-6622 or Spring City Taxi 524-0711for about $7.00 to $9.00 each way depending on time of day, plus $1.00 for each additional person. And 3) Rental car for $30.00 for the day through Waukesha Flying Service at 549-6150. For information about the Weissgerber Gasthaus call 544-4460.

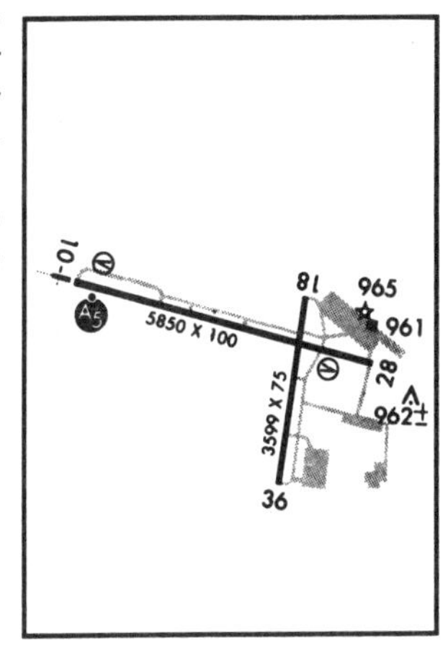

Airport Information:

2 mi north of town N43-02.46 W88-14.22 Elev: 911 Fuel: 100LL, Jet-A Rwy 10-28: H5850x100 (Conc-Grvd) Rwy 18-36: H3599x75 (Asph) Attended: 1200-0300Z Clnc Del. 128.7 Tower: 123.7 Gnd Con 121.6 Unicom: 122.95 Class D airspace 1200-0300Z other times Class G.
FBO: Waukesha Flying Service, Inc. Phone: 549-6150

Voyager Village Country Club

Webster, WI (WI-Y05)

Only 100 miles northeast of the Twin Cities, in the hills of northwestern Wisconsin, you'll find the natural magnificence of Voyager Village. The peaceful surroundings of this vacation property will astound you. So will the amenities. like the 18-hole Championship and Par 3 golf course and club house, an olympic size indoor swimming pool, tennis courts, beaches, marinas, campgrounds, and miles of hiking and snowmobile trails. There's even a 3.500 foot paved, lighted runway. And when you buy a lot at Voyager Village, it's all yours.

A golfers lover's paradise, The Voyager's 18 hole championship golf course is nationally known and has been rated as one of the ten best in the state of Wisconsin. Members play at a discounted rate. Seasonal passes are also available.

Voyager Village is the perfect place for the fishing or boating enthusiast. There are 26 lakes in and around the area, with beaches and excellent fishing or boating.

Of course if you'd prefer to do your swimming indoors, adjoining the clubhouse is an olympic size swimming pool. It comes complete with saunas, it's heated, fully enclosed and open year around.

This is one northern vacation getaway for all seasons. Once they close up the docks for the summer, the winter season is just beginning. You can enjoy cross-country skiing on their trails. There is also snowmobiling and ice fishing. Or you can just relax and admire the wildlife.

Voyager Village Airport is located near Webster, Wisconsin at 45-58-00N latitude and 92-08-45 W Longitude and 1020 feet elevation. The airport site number is 27677.A and location ID is Y05. The runway has a paved surface and is 3,500 feet long by 50 feet wide running NE/SW. The runway is maintained and lighted year round. The airport is located in the heart of Voyager Village Country Club within easy walking distance to all amenities at the club.

Once you see everything Voyager Village has to offer, you'll know why it's the perfect vacation spot. For information call the restaurant at 259-3382. For brochures about the country club call the (POA Office) 259-3910. (Information submitted by Voyager Village).

WYOMING

LOCATION MAP

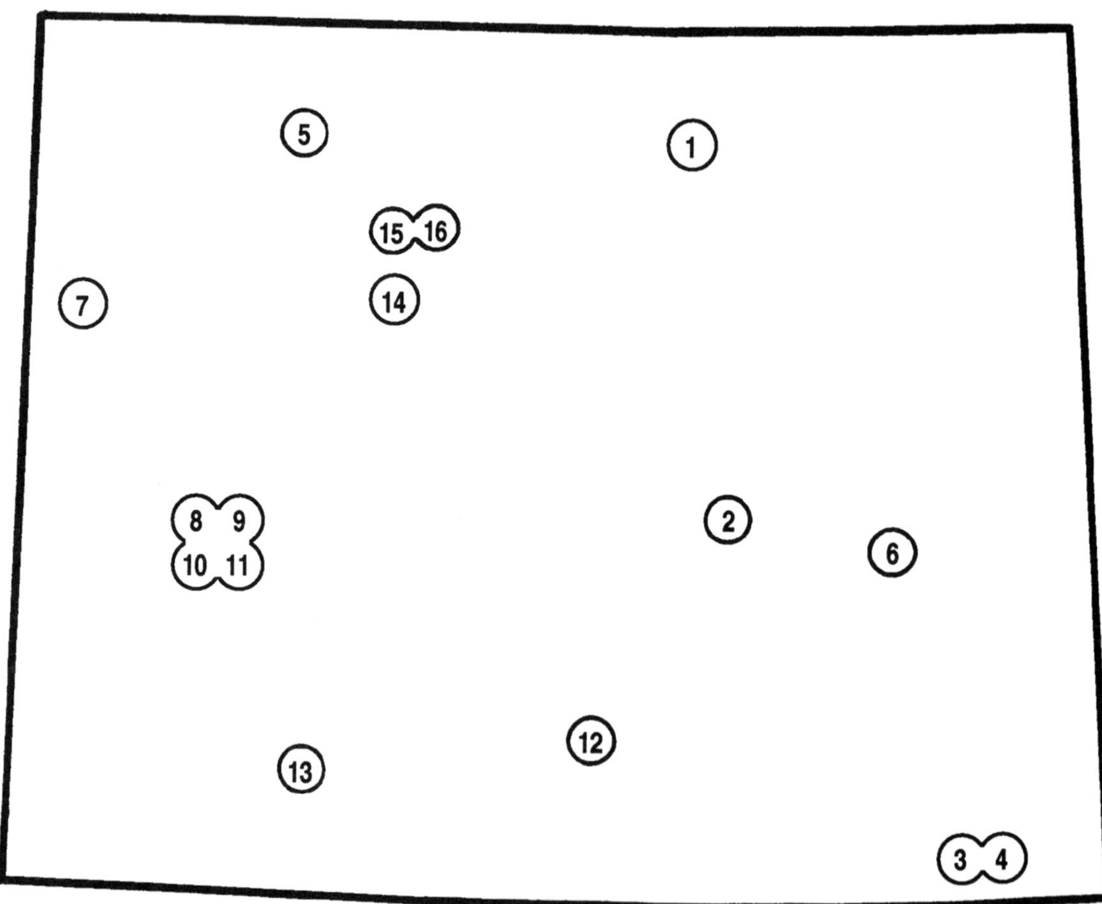

Not to be used for navigational purposes

WYOMING

CROSS FILE INDEX

Location Number	City or Town	Airport Name And Identifier	Name of Attraction
1	Buffalo	Johnson Co. Arpt. (BYG)	Cross Roads Inn
2	Casper	Natrona Co. Intl. (CPR)	Airehart's Restaurant
3	Cheyenne	Cheyenne Arpt. (CYS)	Cloud 9 Restaurant
4	Cheyenne	Cheyenne Arpt. (CYS)	Owl Inn Restaurant
5	Cody	Yellowstone Reg. Arpt. (COD)	Airport Cafe
6	Douglas	Converse Co. Arpt. (DGW)	Chutes Restaurant
7	Jackson Hole	Jackson Hole Arpt. (JAC)	Hanger Canteena
8	Pinedale	Ralph Wenz Fld. (PNA)	Big Sandy Lodge
9	Pinedale	Ralph Wenz Fld. (PNA)	Boulder Lake Lodge
10	Pinedale	Ralph Wenz Fld. (PNA)	Lakeside Lodge Resort
11	Pinedale	Ralph Wenz Fld. (PNA)	Wind River Range (Outfitting)
12	Rawlins	Rawlins Muni. Arpt. (RWL)	Big-G Restaurant
13	Rock Springs	Sweetwater Co. Arpt. (RKS)	Arpt. Snack Bar
14	Thermopolis	Hot Springs Co. (THP)	Legion Supper Club
15	Worland	Worland Muni. Arpt. (WRL)	Antones Supper Club
16	Worland	Worland Muni. Arpt. (WRL)	Worland's Country Club

Articles

City or town	Nearest Airport and Identifier	Name of Attraction
Jackson Hole, WY	Jackson Hole (JAC)	Jackson Hole

WY-BYG - BUFFALO JOHNSON COUNTY AIRPORT

(Area Code 307)

1

Cross Roads Inn:

The Cross Roads Inn is situated 2 miles southeast of the Johnson County Airport. Free transportation is available through the restaurant if advance notice is given. This family style restaurant is open from 6 a.m. to 10:30 p.m. Monday through Thursday, 6 a.m. to 11 p.m. Friday and Saturday and 6 a.m. to 10 p.m. on Sunday during the summer season. Winter season hours vary slightly. Their lounge is open from 3 p.m. to midnight. Their menu include's steak and seafood as well as a wide selection of other breakfast lunch and dinner entrees. Daily specials are offered including a soup and salad bar plus 2 specials Monday through Saturday. In addition they also offer a Sunday smorgasbord from 11 a.m. to 7 p.m. The restaurant is laid out with a cafe in the front and a main dining area in the back. Banquet facilities are available for groups or parties with a separate meeting room provided as well as the space in there main dining room. In addition to the restaurant, their are also lodging accommodations available on the premises. For more information call 684-2256.

Restaurants Near Airport:

Cross Roads Inn	2 mi SE	Phone: 684-2256
Colonea Bozeman's	2 mi	Phone: 684-5555
Pizza Hut	2 mi	Phone: 684-2596
Stage Coach	4 mi	Phone: 684-2507

Lodging: Howard Johnsons-Cross Roads Inn (2 miles) 684-2256; Econo Lodge 684-2219; Mansion House Motel 684-2218; Paradise Guest Ranch (Free Trans) 684-7876; Super 8, 684-2531;

Meeting Rooms: Cross Roads Inn (2 miles) 684-2256; Paradise Guest Ranch (Free Trans) 684-7876.

Transportation: Airport courtesy car available through Johnson Co Aero, 684-9672; Rental Cars: Northside Car Sales 684-5136.

Information: Chamber of Commerce, 55 North Main, Buffalo WY 82834, Phone: 800-227-5122.

Attractions:

Buffalo Golf Courses rated 69.8 white and blue tees 70.9 red tees, Phone: 684-5266; Big Horn National Forest (10 miles) fishing, hunting and camping; Lake DeSmet (12 miles) boat rental and cabins, Phone: 684-9051; Paradise Guest Ranch opens late May through Mid-September, cabins, dining room, fishing guides, entertainment, free arpt trans. 684-7876.

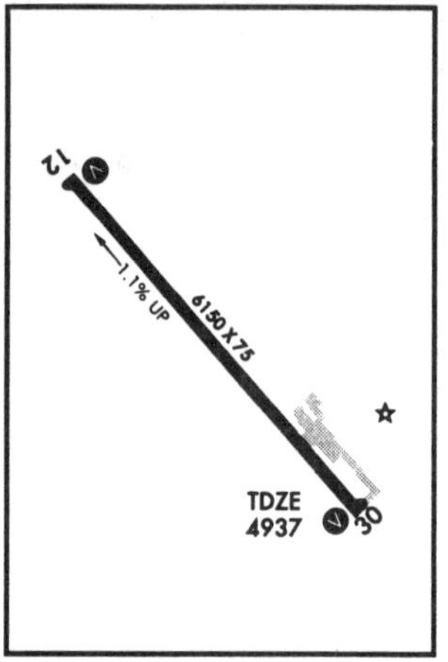

Airport Information:

BUFFALO - JOHNSON COUNTY AIRPORT (BYG)
3 mi northwest of town N44-22.87 W106-43.31 Elev: 4968 Fuel: 100, Jet-A
Rwy 12-30: H6150x75 (Asph) Attended: Mon-Fri 1500-0000Z Unicom: 122.8
FBO: Johnson County Aero Phone: 684-9672

WY-CPR - CASPER NATRONA COUNTY INTERNATIONAL

(Area Code 307)

2

Airehart's Restaurant:

Airhart's Restaurant is located within the terminal building on the Natrona County International Airport. Private and corporate pilots can park their aircraft at Casper Air Service and obtain courtesy transportation over to the terminal. This combination snack bar and fine dining establishment is open 6 a.m. to 9 p.m. 6 days a week and on Sunday for breakfast. Monday through Friday the serve a luncheon buffet as well as selections from their luncheon menu. Dinner entrees consist of items like prime rib, steaks, seafood, chicken, shrimp, in addition to wild came choices like Ostrich, rattle snake and buffalo. Prices average $4.00 for breakfast, $5.25 for lunch and $8.95 to $12.95 for dinner. From the dining room you can enjoy a view overlooking the ramp area through windows on one side of the restaurant. The decor is modern with light muted blue and gray colors. Seating capacity is about 100 in their main dining room and 80 in their lounge. The adjoining snack bar can accommodate up to 60 people. Fly-in groups are welcome. In-flight catering is another service available for pilots on the go. For more information about Airehart's Restaurant call 265-0732.

Restaurants Near Airport:

Airehart's	Trml Bldg	Phone: 265-0732
Benham's	8 mi NW	Phone: 234-4531
El Jarro	8 mi NW	Phone: 577-0538
Kopper Kettle	3 mi NW	Phone: 266-4110

Lodging: Hilton Inn (Free trans) 237-1335; Holiday Inn (Free trans) 235-2531; Shilo Inn (Free trans) 237-1335.

Meeting Rooms: Days Inn 235-6668; Hilton Inn (Free trans) 237-1335; Holiday Inn (Free trans) 235-2531; Shilo Inn (Free trans) 237-1335.

Transportation: Taxi: RC Cab Company 235-5203; Rental Cars: Avis 237-2634; Budget 266-1122; Hertz 265-1355; National 237-7775.

Information: Chamber of Commerce Visitor Center, 500 North Center. P.O. Box 399, Casper, WY 82602, Phone: 234-5311 or 800 852-1889.

Attractions: Alcova Lakeside Marina, provides fishing, swimming, water skiing and camping 234-6821; Casper Municipal Golf Course, 2120 Allendale Blvd; Hogadon Ski Area, 235-8499; Casper Mountain and Beartrap Meadow Parks, offer a Nordic ski area with snowmobile trails and camping.

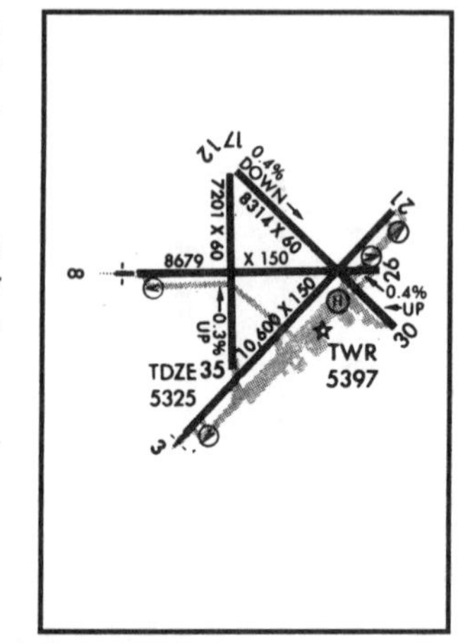

Airport Information:

CASPER - NATRONA COUNTY INTERNATIONAL AIRPORT (CPR)
7 mi northwest of town N42-54.49 W106-27.82 Elev: 5348 Fuel: 100LL, Jet-A
Rwy 03-21: H10600x150 (Asph-Pfc) Rwy 12-30: H8314x60 (Asph) Rwy 08-26: H8679x150 (Asph-Pfc) Rwy 17-35: H7201x60 (Asph) Attended: continuously Atis: 126.15
Unicom: 122.95 Casper App/Dep Con 120.65, 119.0 Tower: 118.3 Gnd Con: 121.9
Clnc Del: 121.9 Public Phone 24hrs
FBO: Casper Air Service Phone: 472-3400 FBO: AVI Air Phone: 234-5566

WY-CYS - CHEYENNE
CHEYENNE AIRPORT

(Area Code 307) 3, 4

Cloud 9 Restaurant & Lounge:

Cloud 9 Restaurant & Lounge is located about 100 yards from the aircraft parking ramp. This combination family style and fine dining restaurant offers items like four different types of steaks, prime rib, a 12 oz. filet mignon, lobster and seafood. Average prices run between $10.00 and $12.00 per plate. In addition to their menu selections, they also provide 2 or 3 daily specials. Their main dining room can seat up to 130 people. A nice view of the airport is available from the restaurant. Hours of operation are from 6 a.m. to 9 p.m. 7 days a week. Delicious homemade soups are prepared daily along with their salads and desserts. For more information call the restaurant at 635-1525.

Owl Inn Restaurant:

The Owl Inn Restaurant is situated about one block southeast from the Cheyenne Airport. Fly-in guests can easily walk to this establishment from their aircraft. This family style restaurant is open from 6 a.m. and closes Sunday through Thursday at 10 p.m. and Friday and Saturday at 11 p.m. Their menu has a wide selection of entrees including a full breakfast line, Mexican dishes, steaks, prime rib, shrimp, cheeseburgers, hamburgers, and ruben sandwiches. They also specialize in homemade soups with two choices each day. While enjoying a fine meal try their delicious cinnamon rolls. Daily specials include a different Mexican dish served each day in addition to their "Square Meal" and sandwich with soup selections. Average prices run $5.00 for breakfast, $6.00 for lunch and $9.00 for dinner. The restaurant is split into two separate sections with a casual family style atmosphere in the front of this facility followed by a couple of step down to the lower portion of the restaurant where a fine dining atmosphere prevails. There is about 62 seats in the front restaurant decorated in a western decor. The rear portion of this facility has a more elegant type atmosphere decorated in a southwestern style able to seat up to 80 people. There is also banquet accommodations available. For more information call the Owl Inn Restaurant at 638-8578.

Restaurants Near Airport:

Cloud 9 Restaurant & Lounge	On Site	Phone: 635-1525
Owl Inn Restaurant	1 Blk SE	Phone: 638-8578

Lodging: Best Western Hitching Post Inn 638-3301; Holding's Little America 634-2771; Holiday Inn 638-4466;

Meeting Rooms: Best Western Hitching Post Inn 638-3301; Little America 634-2771; Holiday Inn 638-4466.

Transportation: Both Aero Ventures & Sky Harbor Air Service can provide courtesy transportation to nearby facilities; Also Taxi Service: Checker 635-5555; Yellow Cab 638-3333; Rental Cars: Avis 632-9371; Hertz 634-2131; National 632-2715; Budget 632-2422.

Information: Cheyenne Convention & Visitors Bureau, 109 West Lincolnway Street, P.O. Box 765, Cheyenne, WY 82003, Phone: 778-3133 or 800-426-5009.

Attractions:

Cheyenne Frontier Days is the last full week of July each year. Frontier Days is one of the largest rodeo in the country. Live concerts each night including big name performers. For information call 778-7290; Also tours of the Warren Air Force Base and Museum are given by appointment. For information call 775-3381.

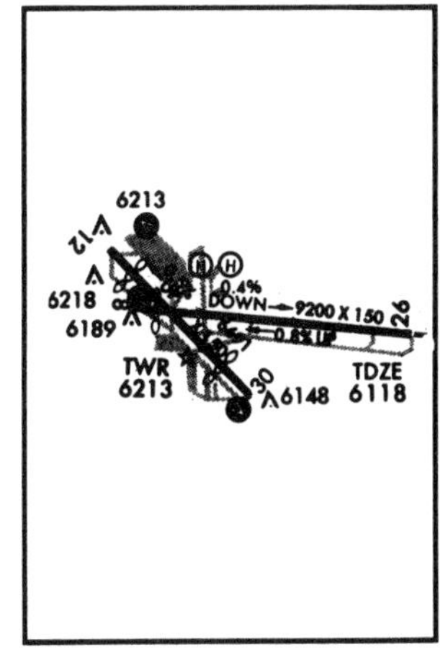

Airport Information:

CHEYENNE - CHEYENNE AIRPORT (CYS)
1 mi north of town N41-09.34 W104-48.77 Elev: 6156 Fuel: 100LL, Jet-A, A1
Rwy 08-26: H9200x150 (Conc) Rwy 12-30: H6691x150 (Asph-Pfc) Attended: 1300-0500Z
Atis: 134.425 Unicom: 122.95 Tower: 118.7 Gnd Con: 121.9
FBO: Sky Harbor Air Service Phone: 634-4417

WY-COD - CODY
YELLOWSTONE REGIONAL AIRPORT

(Area Code 307) 5

Restaurants Near Airport:
Airport Cafe On Site Phone: 587-4755

Airport Cafe:

The Airport Cafe is situated adjacent to the terminal building on the Yellowstone Regional Airport. Transportation is not necessary for fly-in guests. You can simply walk to the restaurant from the aircraft parking area. This cafe can seat about 70 people and is open during the summer from 5 a.m. to 8 p.m. 6 days a week and on Sunday from 7 a.m. to 4:30 p.m. During the winter their hours may vary slightly. The menu selection carries a full variety of dishes for breakfast, lunch and dinner. Average prices run $3.50 for breakfast and lunch and about $5.50 for dinner meals. Every day specials are also offered. For private meeting, there is a board room available within the terminal building that can accommodate up to 20 persons. Carry-out meals are also available from anything on their menu. For more information call the Airport Cafe at 587-4755.

Lodging: Holiday Inn (Free trans) 587-5555; The Irma Hotel (Free trans) 587-4221; The Lockhart (Free trans) 587-6074; Guest Ranches: Blackwater Creek Ranch (Free trans) 587-5201; Castle Rock (Free trans) 587-2076; Crossed Sabres (Free trans) 587-3750; Double Diamond X (Free trans) 527-6276; Rimrock Dude Ranch (Free trans) 587-3970.
Meeting Rooms: Holiday Inn 587-5555; The Irma Hotel 587-4221; Guest Ranches: Castle Rock 587-2076; Double Diamond-X 527-6276. Also Board Rm. in terminal bldg. 587-5096.
Transportation: Taxi: Cody Connection 587-9292; Rental Cars: Avis 587-5792; Hertz 587-2914.
Information: Cody Chamber of Commerce, 836 Sheridan Avenue, P.O. Box 2777, Cody, WY 82414, Phone: 587-2297.

Attractions: Buffalo Bill Historical Center exhibits a group of 4 different museums within the complex along with a gift shop. The Buffalo Bill Museum, Cody Firearm Museum, Whitney Gallery of Western Art and the Plains Indian Museum. This facility is open 7 day a week between May and September, and March, April, October & November daily except on Monday. For information call 587-4771; Also The Olive-Glen 18 hole golf course is located nearby. ***Flying Skytel Guest Ranch:*** is located about 22 miles west of Cody and 28 miles east of Yellowstone National Park. This resort contains a main lodge with lounge and two nice dining rooms, along with six guest cabins, a swimming pool, tennis court, corrals and a picnic/cookout area. The dominant activity is horseback riding with many trails and scenic guided tours available. Even though their private airport has been closed for many years, their unicom is still in use. Overnight fly-in guests can land at Yellowstone Regional Airport and they will pick your party up or furnish a car. For information call 307-587-4029.

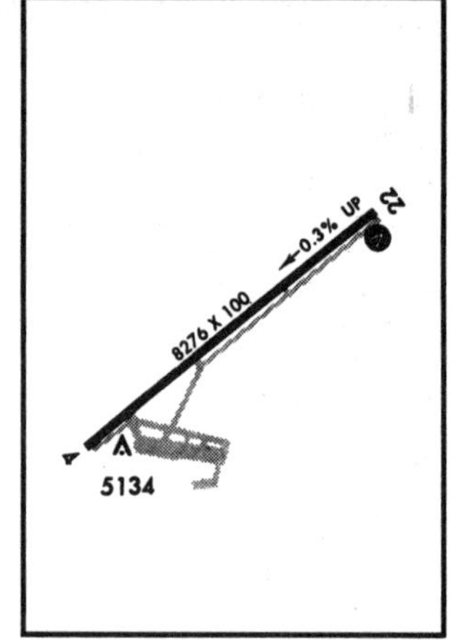

Airport Information:

CODY - YELLOWSTONE REGIONAL AIRPORT (COD)
2 mi southeast of town N44-31.21 W109-01.43 Elev: 5098 Fuel: 100, Jet-A
Rwy 04-22: H8276x100 (Asph-Pfc) Attended: dawn-dusk Unicom: 122.8
FBO: Spirit Mountain Aviation Phone: 587-6732, 587-6932

WY-DGW - DOUGLAS
CONVERSE COUNTY AIRPORT

(Area Code 307) 6

Restaurants Near Airport:

Chutes-Best Western	6 mi	Phone: 358-9790
Clementine's	5 mi	Phone: 358-5554
LaBonte Inn	4-1/2 mi	Phone: 358-9856
Pizza Hut	5 mi	Phone: 358-3657

Chutes Restaurant (Best Western):

Chutes Restaurant is located in the Best Western of Douglas, situated about 6 miles from the Converse County Airport. Courtesy transportation for overnight guests is provided, however at the time we called, dinner guest would have to arrange taxi service through R & G Aircraft Service. The restaurant is open from 6 a.m. to 2 p.m. and from 5:00 p.m. to 10:00 p.m. 7 days a week. Menu selections include seafood dishes like king crab, shrimp, lobster, halibut, and perch. Prices average $6.25 for breakfast, and lunch and $9.95 to $18.95 for dinner. Lunch and dinner buffets are provided along with prime rib featured on Saturday evening. The restaurant seats about 100 people on three levels divided by glassed partitions separating the lounge and dining area. A soup and salad bar is also available. Separate rooms are available for private groups. For more information call 358-9790.

Lodging: Best Western, 1405 Riverbend Drive, (6 miles) 358-9790
Meeting Rooms: Best Western, 1405 Riverbend Drive, (6 miles) 358-9790
Transportation: R & G Aircraft Service (FBO) - will make the call for transportation service; Also: Gubbels Ford 358-3764; Dean Gulley Motors 358-3200; Taxi service available from Holiday Inn and several other restaurants in town.
Information: Douglas Area Chamber of Commerce, 318 1st Street West, Douglas, WY 82633, Phone: 358-2950.

Attractions:

Wyoming State Fair includes special events like rodeos, horse shows etc., held in late August; Ayers Natural Bridge Park on I-25 about 10 miles west of town; Jackalope Warm Spring Plunge 10 miles northwest of town provides artisan spring water pools with a constant temperature of 84 degrees (F). Phone: 358-2820;

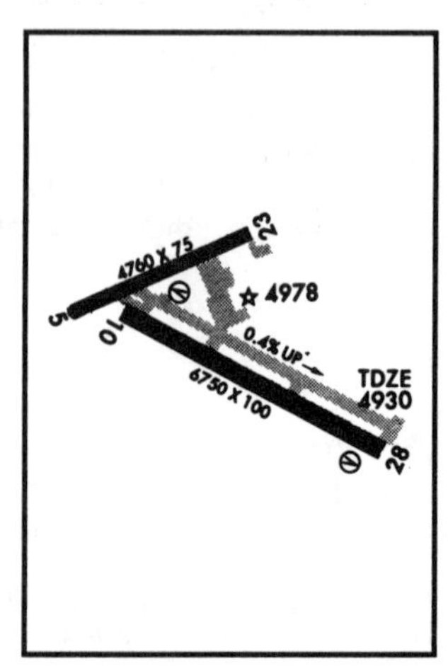

Airport Information:

DOUGLAS - CONVERSE COUNTY AIRPORT (DGW)
3 mi north of town N42-47.84 W105-23.15 Elev: 4929 Fuel: 100LL, Jet-A
Rwy 10-28: H6750x100 (Asph) Rwy 05-23: 4760x75 (Asph) Attended: Mon-Fri 1400-0100Z, Sat-Sun 1500-0000Z Unicom: 122.8 Public Phone 24hrs Notes: Overnight hangers available for twins and single engine aircraft.
Airport Manager Phone: 358-4924

Not to be used for navigational purposes

WY-JAC - JACKSON HOLE
JACKSON HOLE AIRPORT

Hanger Canteena:

This combination snack bar and cafe is located within the terminal building at the Jackson Hole Airport. The cafe is within walking distance from aircraft parking according to the people at the restaurant. Their hours of business are from 7 a.m. to 6 p.m. 7 days a week. Items on their menu include hamburgers, cheeseburgers, buffaloburgers, hotdogs, two different soups each day, grilled cheese as well as hot and cold sandwiches and a full line of breakfast dishes. Carry-out meals can also be arranged. Average prices run $2.00 to $6.00 for breakfast and lunch. Daily specials are also offered. From the restaurant's picture windows, you can see the activity on the airport with arriving and departing aircraft. For information call 733-6063

(Area Code 307) 7

Restaurants Near Airport:
Hangar Canteena On Site Phone: 733-6063

Lodging: Wagon Wheel Village (Free trans) 733-2357; Snow King Resort (Free trans) 733-5200; Wort Hotel (Free trans) 733-2190; R-Lazy S. (Free trans) 733-2655.

Meeting Rooms: Snow King Resort 733-5200; Wort Hotel 733-2190; R Lazy S. 733-2655.

Transportation: Airport courtesy car; Taxi A-1 733-5089; Buckboard 733-1112; JH Trans 733-3135; Teton 733-8898; Tumbleweed 733-0808; Rental Cars: Avis 733-3422; Budget 733-2206; Hertz 733-2272; National 733-4137;

Information: Jackson Hole Area Chamber of Commerce, 532 North Cache, P.O. Box E, Jackson, WY 83001, Phone: 733-3316.

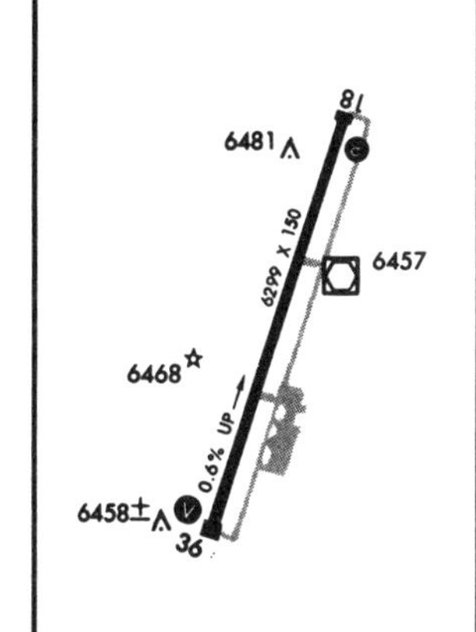

Attractions: Skiing: Snow King Mountain, vertical drop 1,571 feet, 733-5200; Jackson Hole Ski Resort, vertical drop 4,139 feet, also summer activities include golfing, swimming, tennis, hiking and horse back riding, 733-2292; Many river excursions are also available as well as Jeep tours through the national park; 2,4 & 6 day wagon train trips are available through private companies. You can experience the days of pioneering first hand with trips into the surrounding mountains, along with nightly campfire entertainment, square dancing, chuck wagon meals and much more: Wagon Treks at 886-3872 or Teton County Prairie Schooner Holidays, 733-5386; Also Bridger Teton National Forest provides a vast array of outdoor activities and sight seeing trips, mountain climbing and trail excursions. For information contact the forest supervisor at 733-2752.

Airport Information:

JACKSON HOLE - JACKSON HOLE AIRPORT (JAC)
7 mi north of town N43-36.39 W110-44.29 Elev: 6445 Fuel: 100, Jet-A
Rwy 18-36: H6299x150 (Asph-Pfc) Attended: 1300-0500Z Unicom: 122.8
Airport Manager Phone: 733-7682, 733-5454

Jackson Hole

Jackson Hole, snuggled amidst the majestic peaks of the Tetons and the Rocky Mountains in western Wyoming, has been enchanting visitors long before the days of skiing. It has preserved the lifestyle of the Old West. Years ago, frontiersmen, cattle barons and mountain men settled at Jackson Hole. Today, hard working cowboys and ranch hand, still ride the range of old-time ranches scattered throughout the sweeping plains and beneath the breathtaking mountain peaks. Herds of wildlife roam the vast expanses of undiscovered wilderness.

The warmth and charm of Jackson Hole can take the edge off any winter chill. Visitors stroll down the wooden boardwalks that line the Town Square. The Square, adorned with elk antler arches, is surrounded by unique restaurants, art galleries, and boutiques that display anything from fancy designer labels to custom-made local creations. For those who are yearning for more, equally charming Teton Village is located just 12 miles outside of town at the foot of the Jackson Hole Ski Resort. This Village offers quaint wooden chalets, plenty of base lodging, and even a horse-drawn wagon to take you to and from your car. Together, both Jackson and Teton Village offer 34 art galleries which feature the work of local, national and international artists of creations ranging from Western paintings to wildlife bronzes to Native American pottery. There are over 70 restaurants which will satisfy every appetite. Both towns offer plenty of lodging facilities, including rustic cabins, guest ranches, as well as a variety of hotels and motels to meet your styles and needs.

In the Jackson Hole area, there are three major ski resorts which offer a wide range of terrain and snow conditions to suit every skier. Jackson Hole Ski Resort, Grand Targhee Resort and Snow King Resort. Jackson Hole Resort offers fields of powder that spread over two mountains, miles of ungroomed trails and a 4,139-foot vertical drop - the largest in the country. Grand Targhee Ski Resort, located on the west side of the Tetons, offers 1,500 skiable acres, 70 percent of which are intermediate. It also offers its own transportation service. Snow King Resort, located just 6 blocks off the Jackson Town Square, offers skiers a panoramic view of Jackson with more than 400 acres of skiable terrain, in addition to night skiing available five days a week.

There are also other great ways to enjoy winter in Jackson Hole. Grand Teton National Park, set among spruce, fir and lodgepole pine, hosts snowshoeing and cross-country skiing. For something a bit more fast paced, try a dogsled trip. Many of the guides are masters of the famous Alaskan Iditarod Race. Or, try some sightseeing by snowmobile. It is a unique and exhilarating way to view legendary Old Faithful and all of its accompanying steaming mud pots, hot springs and other geothermal wonders. For an up-close encounter with area wildlife, take an old-fashioned sleigh ride on the national Elk Refuge amidst 8,000 wintering elk. Later, take a break from all the activities and enjoy a soak in Granite Hot Springs, a hot mineral pool located in Hoback Canyon, 35 miles south of town.

During the summer, after the snows have melted everywhere except atop the great Teton peaks, Jackson Hole comes to life with color. Vast, rolling plains of green, meadows ablaze with hot pink, yellow and purple wildflowers. Endless skies of blue. Bright orange sunrises, deep red sunsets and glimmering white starlight. Crystal clear rivers, creeks and streams are nestled within these areas. A welcome sight for rainbow, brown, cutthroaat and even the rare and elusive golden trout. The Snake River, which winds its way beneath the Tetons offers incredible opportunities to view wildlife and other local sights while enjoying a quiet, scenic boat trip. Or, catch the Snake a little further outside town where the waters turn to whitewater rapids. There are also many other acitivities to enjoy amidst this scenery between Grand Teton and Yellowstone National parks and Bridger-Teton and Targhee National forests. Hiking, biking, camping and climbing. Many guides are available for tours. While visiting the area, catch three different local events: Old West Days and the Fall Arts and Grand Teton Music Festivals. They each feature everything from old-time mountain men to internationally acclaimed artists and musicians. Quite simply, Jackson Hole will keep visitors busy all year-round.

Jackson Hole Airport, located 7 miles north of Jackson Hole, has a 6,299'x150 asphalt-pfc runway. It also services major airlines. The airport provides public shuttle service to and from certain points between Jackson and Teton Village. Many lodging facilities also offer a free airport shuttle for their guests. In addition, there are numerous rental car and bus services available. For reservations and other information in Jackson Hole, contact Jackson Hole Central Reservations at 800-443-6931. For further information, contact the Jackson Hole Area Chamber of Commerce at 733-3316. (Information submitted by Jackson Hole Ski Corporation)

WY-PNA - PINEDALE
RALPH WENZ FIELD

(Area Code 307)

8, 9, 10, 11

Big Sandy Lodge:

The Big Sandy Lodge is located on the southern end of the Wind River Range, about 56 miles from the Pinedale - Ralph Wenz Field. This remote but scenic lodge was recommended to us by the Pinedale Chamber of Commerce as being a terrific place to visit. During our conversation with Mr. & Mrs. Bernie and Connie Kelly, the owners of the lodge, we learned that their establishment contains 10 one-room log cabins equipped with log-burning stoves, kerosene lanterns and all that is necessary to make your visit enjoyable. If you want to escape the frustrations of the big city, this sounds like the place to stay. The closest power line is about 20 miles away. There are no TV sets, electrically-operated gadgets or telephones, so leave your beepers at home and prepare yourself for a great time. Their "Lodge Package" includes 8 days and 7 nights in their cozy log cabins with meals, guided trail rides (Monday through Saturday) and relaxed evenings in the lodge. Check-in is on Sunday and check out on the following Sunday. Hot showers and washroom facilities are available near each cabin. Transportation to the Big Sandy Lodge can be arranged by calling "Sublette Stage" at 367-6633 for taxi service from the airport to the lodge. To obtain more information about the Big Sandy Lodge call 332-6782.

Boulder Lake Lodge:

The Boulder Lake Lodge is located about 15 miles from the Ralph Wentz Field (PNA) and will provide transportation for fly-in guests. This is one of the oldest and most successful hunting-outfitting operations in the state. It is located in the heart of the Bridger National Forest in the Wind River Range of the Rocky Mountains. The ranch features a beautiful and rustic lodge which serves as the base camp for hunting operations. Within the lodge are 8 guest rooms with private baths. It is located in the center of some of the state's finest big game areas. The ranch is at an elevation of 7300 feet. This is an elaborately equipped camp used primarily for elk hunting, and this gives them over 100 square miles of prime hunting area which is not used by any other outfitter. The area also provides excellent fishing. Visitors hunt out of this camp from September 20 to October 15. At this time, the elk move down to the ranch area. They then hunt out of the lodge from October 16 to October 31. The Boulder Lake Lodge offers these services: restaurant; backpacking; boating and canoeing; cookouts and meals (Family-style meals served in their dining room); Day trips; fishing; float trips; horseback riding & pack trips; photo tours; spot packs and gear drops; and wagon tides. For information call 537-5400 or 800-788-5401.

Lakeside Lodge Resort & Marina:

The Lakeside Lodge Resort & Marina is located about 10 miles form the Pinedale - Ralph Wenz Field. The town of Pinedale is between the airport and the resort, about 5 or 6 miles. The resort is nestled at the south end of Fremont Lake in the beautiful Bridger-Teton National Forest. The resort which includes a restaurant, eight rustic cabins, five motel rooms, RV campground and marina, is situated on over fifteen acres and more than two-thousand feet of shoreline. Western hospitality, privacy, informal comfort and breathtaking views of the Wild River Mountains all add to the pleasant atmosphere of a relaxing, yet fun-filled vacation. Their dining room integrated an appreciation of nature with fine food and spirits in a casual atmosphere. Dine in or out for breakfast, lunch or dinner and breathtaking views of Fremont Lake and the Wind River Mountains. Five motel rooms with private baths have been redecorated to mirror the natural beauty of the wildflower meadows of the region. Cozy comforters adorn the double beds in the rooms that accommodate up to four people. Eight rustic log cabins, which were built in the 1930s, have been redecorated, each with a unique theme and all with quality decor that is representative of the area. Each room has one queen-size bed with a comfortable roll-away bed available if needed. A restroom/shower building is centrally located to the cabins. The marina, at Lakeside Lodge, has a pontoon boat, fishing boats and canoes available to rent. Many hiking trails can be explored or guided trips can be arranged. Transportation to and from the resort can be arranged by calling the resort at 367-2221.

Restaurants Near Airport:
Lakeside Resort 10 mi Phone: 367-2221
McGregors Pub 5 mi Phone: 367-4563

Lodging: Sundance 6 mi 367-4336; Teton Court Motel 6 mi 367-4317; Wagon Wheel 6 mi 367-2871; ZZZ's Inn 6 mi 367-2121; Window on the Winds Bed & Breakfast 367-2600; ***Guest Ranches & Lodges:*** Big Sandy Lodge 56 mi 332-6782; Boulder Lake Lodge 537-5400; Elk Ridge Lodge 35 mi 367-2553; Lakeside Lodge Resort & Marina 367-2221;

Transportation: Airport courtesy car available; Rental cars: Winds Aviation 367-4151; Taxi service: Sublette Stage 367-6633.

Outfitter/Guides: Boulder Lake Lodge 537-5400 or 800-788-5401; Bridger Wilderness Outfitters 367-2268; O'Kelley Outfitting 367-6476; Wind River Hiking Consultants 367-2560.

Information: Pinedale Chamber of Commerce, 32 E. Pine, P.O. Box 176, Pindale, WY 82941. Phone: 367-2242.

Attractions:

Mountain Man Museum is located in town; Also the Annual Green River Rendezvous is a historical pageant held on the 2nd Sunday in July commemorating the meeting of fur trappers, mountain men and Indians with wagon trains at Fort Bonneville.

The Wind River Range (O'Kelley Outfitting):

The Wind River Mountains, located in western Wyoming, are among the highest and most geologically massive of the vast network of Rocky Mountains. Gannett Peak, rising to 13,804 feet, is only one of many peaks reaching over 13,000 feet. Seven of the ten largest glaciers located in the lower 48 states are found here. These glaciers feed many of the 1300 lakes that are filled with a variety of trout including rainbow, golden, cut throat, brown, brook and mackinaw. Also found in these mountains are elk, deer, moose, big horn sheep, antelope, black bear as well as a multitude of other wildlife. Thus the opportunities for hikers, fishermen, horsemen, photographers and anyone who loves the wilderness, are endless. O'Kelley Outfitting owned and operated by Mr. Mark and Kelley Pearson have been in the business of outfitting for many years. They welcome the opportunity to meet each group's or individual's needs. Basic, all-inclusive pack trips begin with a pack-in into the wilderness. A typical day might involve a short ride to a mountain lake to fish for rainbow or golden trout, photography expeditions to spots of wildlife habitat or other scenic splendor, or hike treks up nearby peaks. Bag lunches are prepared to take along, while a hot, home-cooked meal served around the campfire begins and ends the day. Trips can be arranged to accommodate the specific needs of the fisherman, the photographer and the hiker. Group and educational trips can also be arranged emphasizing field biology, geology, wilderness survival and leadership development. Scenic rides for half or full-day are available for those whose time is more limited. If planning your adventure through O'Kelley Outfitting, they will be happy to arrange lodging accommodations for your party. O'Kelley Outfitting is located only 2 or 3 miles from the Pinedale - Ralph Wenze Field. Tranportation can easily be arranged. For information call 307-367-6476.

Airport Information:

PINEDALE - RALPH WENZ FIELD (PNA)
5 mi southeast of town N42-47.73 W109-48.43 Elev: 7085 Fuel: 100LL, Jet-A Rwy 11-29: H7100x100 Attended: daylight hours Unicom: 122.8 Notes: Flying over buildings adjacent to ramp is prohibited.
FBO: Winds Aviation Phone: 367-4151

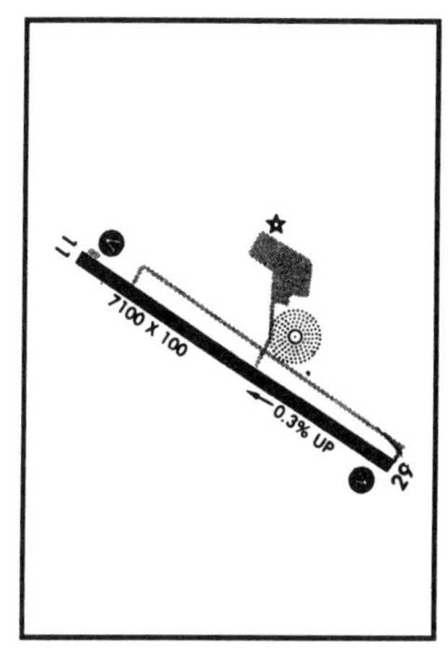

WY-RWL - RAWLINS
RAWLINS MUNICIPAL AIRPORT

(Area Code 307)

12

Big-G Restaurant:

The Big-G Restaurant is located within the Days Inn Motel, about 4 blocks from the Rawlins Municipal Airport. The restaurant is within walking distance from the airport, however, the fixed based operator at the Rawlins field can also arrange transportation if requested. This family style restaurant is open between 5 p.m. and 9 p.m. 6 days a week (Closed on Sunday). Their menu features Chinese and American dishes including hamburgers and sandwiches of all types. On Friday and Saturday they feature prime rib as a special. Average prices run $4.00 for breakfast, $5.00 for lunch and $7.00 for dinner. The restaurant can seat about 130 persons in the main dining room. A separate room can accommodate private parties and groups. Banquet facilities can also be arranged for up to 300 people if necessary. For more information you can call the Big-G Restaurant at 324-6615.

Restaurants Near Airport:

Bel Air Inn	3 MI	Phone: 324-2737
Big-G Restaurant	4 Blks	Phone: 324-6615

Lodging: Best Western Bel Air Inn (3 miles) 324-2737; Days Inn (1/2 mile) 324-6615; Ramada Inn (1 mile) 324-2783.

Meeting Rooms: Best Western Bel Air Inn (3 miles) 324-2737.

Transportation: Airport courtesy car; Also: McGee Murphy Inc. 324-3434.

Information: Rawlins Carbon County Chamber of Commerce, 519 West Cedar, P.O. Box 1331, Rawlins, WY 82301, Phone: 324-4111 or 800-228-3547.

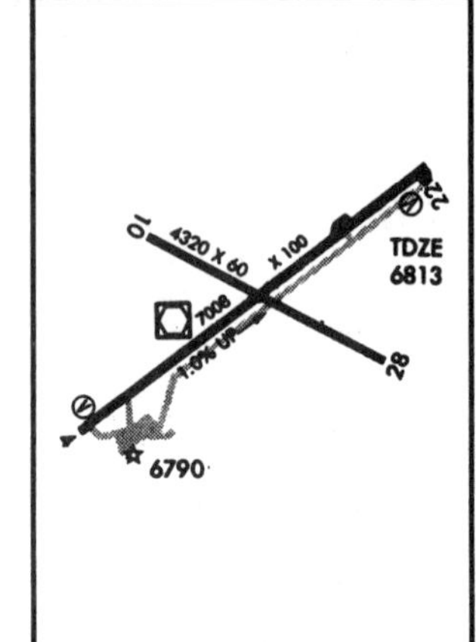

Attractions:

Wyoming Frontier Prison, (now closed) is open for tours between Memorial Day and Labor Day on weekends, (Operated between 1901 and 1981). For information on tours you can call 324-4111.

Airport Information:

RAWLINS - RAWLINS MUNICIPAL AIRPORT (RWL)
2 mi northeast of town N41-48.34 W107-12.00 Elev: 6813 Fuel: 100LL, Jet-A
Rwy 04-22: H7008x100 (Asph-Pfc) Rwy 10-28: H4320x60 (Asph) Attended: 1300-0500Z
Unicom: 123.0
FBO: France Flying Service, Inc. Phone: 324-2361

WY-RKS - ROCK SPRINGS
SWEETWATER COUNTY AIRPORT

(Area Code 307)

13

Airport Snack Bar:

At the time of our interview we spoke with the airport manager told us that the Airport Snack Bar would soon be opening its doors under new management. It is located inside the terminal building, at the Rock Springs, Sweetwater County Airport. Hours of operation had yet to be announced. We suspect that some of their menu items will consist of a variety of hot and cold sandwiches, hamburgers, cheeseburgers, breakfast items, and soups. The restaurant has counter service and specializes in carry-out service and meals-to-go. For information about this establishment call the airport managers office at 352-6888.

Restaurants Near Airport:

Airport Snack Bar (Arpt Mgr)	Trml Bldg	Phone: 352-6888

Lodging: Best Western Outlaw (Free Trans) 362-6623; Holiday Inn (Free Trans) 382-9200; Inn at Rock Springs (Free Trans) 362-9600.

Meeting Rooms: Best Western Outlaw 362-6623; Holiday Inn 382-9200; Inn at Rock Springs 362-9600.

Transportation: Taxi: Sunshine 382-9789; Rental Cars: Avis 362-5599; Hertz: 382-3262

Information: Rock Springs Chamber of Commerce, 1897 Dewar Drive, P.O. Box 398, Rock Springs 82902-0398, Phone: 362-3771

Airport Information:

ROCK SPRINGS - SWEETWATER COUNTY AIRPORT (RKS)
7 mi east of town N41-35 109-03-52W Elev: 6760 Fuel: 100LL, Jet-A1+
Rwy 09-27: H10000x150 (Asph-PFC) Rwy 03-21: H5223x75 (Asph-Pfc)
Attended: 1300-0400Z Unicom: 122.8
FBO: Franklin Aviation Phone: 362-1442

WY-THP - THERMOPOLIS
HOT SPRINGS CO. - THERMOPOLIS

(Area Code 307) 14

Legion Supper Club (Country Club):

The Legion Supper Club is located across the street from the Hot Springs County Airport. This fine dining restaurant is open 7 days a week from 11 a.m. to 2 p.m. and 5 p.m. to 10 p.m. during the Summer season. WInter hours very(Closed Monday's). Their menu primarily offers steak, prime rib and seafood selections. Average price for a meal runs $4.00 to $6.00 for breakfast, and lunch. They offer a Sunday brunch for $7.95 per person. The main dining room can seat about 90 persons with a separate room available for groups and parties which can seat 30 people. There are windows all around the restaurant allowing a view of the golf course. For information about the restaurant or country club call 864-2488.

Restaurants Near Airport:
Legion Supper Club On Site Phone: 864-2488

Lodging: Holiday Inn (Free Trans) 864-3131; Round Top Mountain Motel 864-3126; Rainbow Motel 864-2129; Best Western 864-2321.

Meeting Rooms: Holiday Inn (Free Trans) 864-3131; Legion Country & Sports Club 864-3918.

Transportation: Hot Springs Air can furnish courtesy transportation to nearby facilities; Also Taxi Service: Torrington 532-3561; Rental Cars: Platte Valley Motor Company 532-2114.

Information: Chamber of Commerce, P.O. Box 768, Thermopolis, WY 82443, Phone: 864-3192 or 800-SUN-N-SPA.

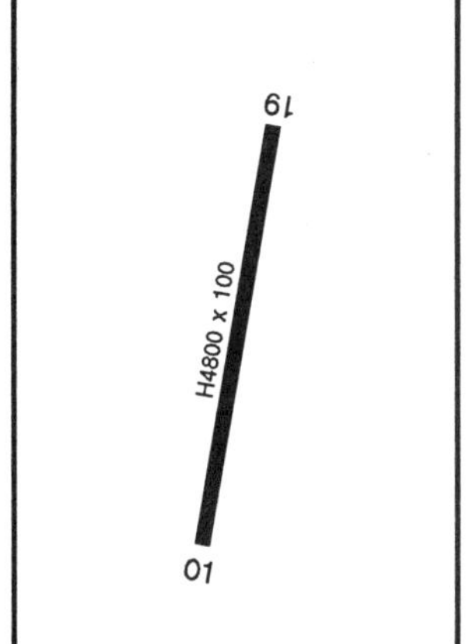

Attractions:

Legion Golf Club is located on the Hot Springs County Airport. Also Hot Springs State Park is located on US 20 displaying many beautiful mineral deposits in the shape of cones and terraces. There are also hiking paths, picnic areas and campgrounds within the park. For information call 864-2176.

Airport Information:

THERMOPOLIS - HOT SPRINGS CO.- THERMOPOLIS (THP)
1 mi north of town N43-39.50 W108-12.79 Elev: 4580 Fuel: 100
Rwy 01-19: H4800x100 (Asph-Pfc) Attended: 1500-0000Z Unicom: 122.8 Public Phone 24hrs
Notes: CAUTION: Due to terrain operations at night are not recommended.
FBO: Hot Springs Co. Airport Phone: 864-2488, 2702

Let Us Know About Your Favorite "Prop Stoppers"

If you don't see your favorite fly-in restaurant, resort, or fly-to attraction, simply call us or just drop us a line and let us know about them. (See page 1,019)

Aerodine Magazine
P.O. Box 247, Palatine, IL 60078
Phone: 847-358-4355

WY-WRL - WORLAND
WORLAND MUNICIPAL AIRPORT

(Area Code 307) 15, 16

Antones Supper Club:

Antones is a combination restaurant and supper club and is located 4 miles north and 1 mile east of the Worland Municipal Airport. Transportation can be arranged in advance through Sky Aviation at 347-6138. This restaurant is classified as a supper club, and is open 11 a.m. to 9 p.m. Monday through Saturday, and on Sunday from 3 p.m. until they decide to close for the evening. A lounge is also located on the premises. Their entrees primarily include steaks and seafood selections. Average prices run $3.50 to 4.50 for lunch and $9.00 to $24.00 for evening meals. A buffet is offered on Wednesday evenings. The restaurant can seat between 150 and 200 people. Their facility is divided into two dining sections. One sections offers a casual decor while the other provides a more elegant appearance. There is a back room that can accommodate groups and private parties. For more information call Antones Supper Club at 347-9924.

Worlands Country Club:

Worland Country Club is located down the street from the Worland Municipal Airport about 600 yards. Sky Aviation can provide courtesy transportation to fly-in customers. However, we were told that you can easily walk to the restaurant. This family style facility is open between 11 a.m. and 2 p.m. and 6 p.m. to 9 p.m. Hours may vary throughout the season, which makes it advisable to call in advance to make sure they will be open. Their specialty entrees include items like steaks, seafood and pasta. Specials vary from day to day. The restaurant can seat up to 200 persons. A view from the restaurant overlooks their 18 hole golf course. The restaurant and golfing pro shop are in the same building. Extra rooms are available for groups planning dinner parties. Also guests may wish to combine an afternoon of golf with a fine meal. For more information or reservations call Worlands Country Club at 347-2695.

Attractions:

Worlands Country Club provides an 18 hole golf course within walking distance to the Worland Municipal Airport. For information call 347-2695.

Restaurants Near Airport:

Antones Supper Club	4 mi NE.	Phone: 347-9924
Rams Horn Cafe	4 mi N.	Phone: 347-6351
Worland Elks	4 mi N.	Phone: 347-4401
Worlands Country Club	Adj Arpt	Phone: 347-2695

Lodging: Settlers Inn, (Best Western) 2200 Big Horn, Phone: 347-8201

Meeting Rooms: Settlers Inn (Best Western) 347-8201; Worland Elks 347-4401.

Transportation: Sky Aviation can provide courtesy transportation to nearby facilities, Phone: 347-6138; Also: Hertz 347-4229; Veronica's Cab 347-8751.

Information: Chamber of Commerce, 120 N 10th Street, Worland, WY, Phone: 347-3226

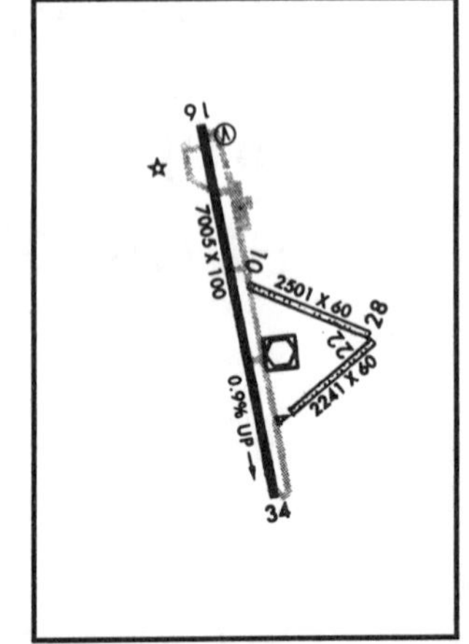

Airport Information:

WORLAND - WORLAND MUNICIPAL AIRPORT (WRL)
3 mi south of town N43-57.93 W107-57.02 Elev: 4245 Fuel: 100LL, Jet-A
Rwy 16-34: H7004x100 (Asph-Pfc) Rwy 10-28: 2500x50 (Turf) Rwy 04-22: 2240x50 (Turf)
Attended: 1500-0000Z CTAF/Unicom: 122.7 Public Phone 24hrs
FBO: Sky Aviation Phone: 347-6138

U.S. BORDER ATTRACTIONS

CROSS FILE INDEX

CANADA

Location Number	City or Town	Airport Name And Identifier	Name of Attraction
1	Cyid-Nova Scotia-Digby	Digby Muni. Arpt.	Pines Resort Hotel
2	Ontario - Eagle River	Eagle River Arpt.	North Shore Lodge

CANADA-CYID - NOVA SCOTIA - DIGBY

(Area Code 902) 1

DIGBY MUNICIPAL AIRPORT

The Pines Resort Hotel:

The Pines Resort Hotel is located in Digby, Novia Scotia, Canada. This summer resort, which is located about 9 miles from Digby Municipal Airport, offers a range of accommodations, including 83 comfortable hotel rooms and suites, and 30 one, two and three-bedroom cottages.The hotel and cottages are surrounded by flower gardens, spacious lawns and woodland trails, set on a hillside overlooking the scenic Annapolis Basin. All the cottages offer an open fireplace, a cozy living room and a covered porch. Some cottages have air-conditioning, mini bars and deluxe furnishings and decor. Guests can enjoy golfing on the 18-hole Stanley Thompson designed golf course or playing tennis, croquet and shuffleboard. They can walk or jog along the wooded trails, work out in the fitness center with sauna, or relax in the large outdoor heated pool. After all the activities, they can dine in the elegant Annapolis Dining Room and sample scrumptious cuisine. The 19th Hole Lounge offers casual dining with scenic views. For meetings, The Pines can accommodate groups of up to 250 people in the well equipped facilities. With advance notice, The Pines will provide a complimentary shuttle to and from the airport. For more information about rates and accommodations at The Pines Resort Hotel, call 245-2511 or 800-667-4637.

Nearby Attractions:

Digby Municipal Airport is located only 4 miles from the Digby shopping area, and it is near the major Port of Digby.There are numerous activities in the area, such as whale-watching cruises on the Bay of Fundy, and deep sea fishing charters for "shucking" scallops. Digby is the home of the largest inshore scallop fleet in the world. Each year, it hosts "Scallop Days", a week long festival in August, which pays tribute the hardy men who harvest this "white gold" from the Bay of Fundy. Digby also features activities, such as antiquing, bird watching, rock hounding, and clam digging. "The French Shore" offers visitors a chance to taste the traditional Acadian dish "Rappie Pie". Upper Clements Theme Park, in nearby Clementsport, will enchant children of all ages. Bear River, the "Switzerland" of Nova Scotia, has homes that are perched stilt-like along the riverbanks. Digby also has the world's highest tides which float boats up against wharves, leaving them "low and dry" six hours later. For more information about attractions, contact the DigbyTourist Information Bureau at 245-5714.

Restaurants Near Airport:
The Pines Resort Hotel 9 mi Phone: 245-2511

Lodging: The Pines Resort Hotel (9 miles) 245-2511

Meeting Rooms: The Pines Resort Hotel 245-2511

Transportation: With advance notice, The Pines Resort Hotel will provide a complimentary shuttle to and from the airport. There are no car rental companies at the airport. However, with advance notice of 1 day, a car rental can be arranged through a local car dealer.

Information: Digby Tourist Information Bureau, Water Street, P.O. Box 641, B0V 1A0, Digby, Nova Scotia, Phone: 245-5714

Airport Information:

NOVA SCOTIA - DIGBY MUNICIPAL AIRPORT (CYID)
4.5 mi south of town N44-32.44 W65-47.20 Elev: 499 Fuel: 100LL Avgas Rwy 06-24: H3950x75 Attended: continuously Unicom: 122.8 Public Phone 24hrs Notes: For aircraft control of Airport Lighting, including rotating Light Key, mike 5 times on Unicom: 122.8 to light windsock, threshold lights, runway, taxiway and apron for 15 minutes.
FBO: Yarmouth Flight Service Phone: 742-6466 (Collect)

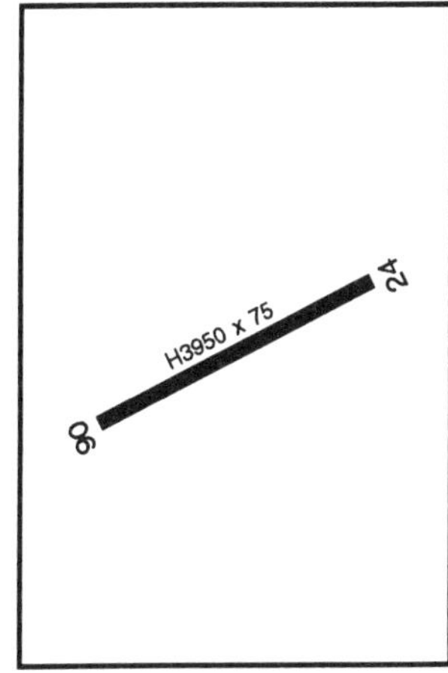

CANADA - ONTARIO - EAGLE RIVER
EAGLE RIVER AIRPORT

(Area Code 807) 2

North Shore Lodge:

North Shore Lodge is located on the east end of Eagle Lake in Ontario, Canada. It contains its own private 2,400' NW-SE turf airstrip. It offers all the comforts of a full service fishing resort, and is located close to some of the best fishing around. The spacious main lodge has a lounge and patio, as well as a fireplace. It's great for playing cards, watching a ball game on satellite TV, or just plain relaxing. The lodge also has a complete tackle shop, souvenir shop and a sundry section with film, snacks, Canadian Jam, along with other items. Home-cooked meals are served in the dining room overlooking Eagle Lake. Homemade bread, soup and pastries are prepared daily. The grounds are covered with pines, birches and spruce. Guests can take a stroll through the 1-1/2 mile fitness/nature trail which winds through the woods along the shore of the lake. In addition to the great fishing, guests can engage in a little friendly competition of horseshoes and shuffleboard. The private cottages are available in a variety of sizes which can accommodate groups up to 12 people with 2 baths. Each cottage has individual beds, electric or propane heat and a refrigerator. The housekeeping cottages are fully equipped with cooking utensils, dishes, linens and towels. Wheeled planes can land at the lodge using the 2400' sod airstrip (soon to be lengthened). Landing and tie-down are free to guests. Incoming U.S. planes should phone or file a flight plan to clear Canadian Customs at Fort Frances, Ontario or at another airport of entry. For reservations and more information about North Shore Lodge, call 807-755-2461 during the summer, 773-794-0545 during the winter or 773-631-5872 year around.

Restaurants Near Resort:
North Shore Lodge On Site 800-976-9779

Lodging: North Shore Resort offers a variety of cottages able to accommodate your party. For information call 800-976-9779.

Meeting Rooms: Their lodge dining room has room for group gatherings.

Transportation: After landing at the airport, guests can walk to the resort located adjacent to the airstrip. (Only 200-400').

Information: (Summer) North Shore Lodge Box 28, Eagle River, Ontario POV1 S0, Phone: 807-755-2441, Fax: 807-755-2461; (Winter) North Shore Lodge 5021 N. Marmora, Chicago, IL 60630, Phone: 312-794-0545, Fax : 312-794-0135; (Year Round) John Guercio, 6764 W. Rascher, Chicago, IL 60656.

Attractions: (North Shore Lodge)

North shore Lodge is located close to some of the best fishing found on Eagle Lake. Walleye Rocks, Spring Bay, Stanton Island and the Barber Pole are very close by. The famous Bear Narrows, Osbourne Bay, Brule Narrows and Niven Bay locations are easily accessible for outstanding musky action and fast spring and fall walleye fishing. Summer fishing at Viking Reef, Eldorado Bay and the Net Island area are only a short boat ride away.

They have recently replaced their boats with new models by Lund and Alumarine, companies which produce boats in limited numbers with great emphasis on quality and heavy duty construction. The resort also features 16-1/2' and 18 ft. lengths with new 30 and 40 H.P. Mercury engines. All boats come equipped with swivel seats, 2 six-gallon gas tanks, paddles, coast guard approved cushions, landing net and bait buckets. Also available are 21 ft. Sylvan Cruisers (with guide service only). Each is powered by a 150 H.P. Mercury engine and comes with trolling motor, live wells, depth finder and canvas top.

When you come fishing in Canada you have the opportunity to enjoy one of the greatest pleasures of the outdoor - the shore lunch! As much as you try, it will be hard to describe how fantastic this simple meal is to those who haven't experienced one themselves. Freshly caught fish fillets accompanied by fried potatoes, brown beans and corn enjoyed in the scenic Beauty of N.W. Ontario is an experience never to be forgotten.

Although the resort is equipped with its own airstrip, North Shore Lodge also draws customers from the Chicago, Illinois area specializing in trouble-free charter bus package trips departing from Niles, IL; Elgin, IL, Rockford, IL; and Madison, WI. locations. For information call 800-976-9779, or refer to the "Information" section above for additonal phone numbers.

Airport Information:

CANADA - EAGLE LAKE - ONTARIO - (EAGLE RIVER AIRPORT) (Private Airstrip)
Wheeled planes can land at the lodge using their private NW-SE 2,400 foot sod airstrip. The airstrip is crowned for good drainage. Landing and tie-down are free to guests. Incoming U.S. planes should phone or file a flight plan to clear Canadian Customs at Fort Frances, Ontario or at another airport of entry. The airport is listed as "Eagle River Airport", on U.S., Canadian and WAC air charts. (Information submitted by North Shore Lodge) **Notes:** (Private use facility, use at own risk) Call the North Shore Lodge in advance to verify runway and airport conditions prior to use.
Airport Management - North Shore Lodge Phone: 800-976-9779

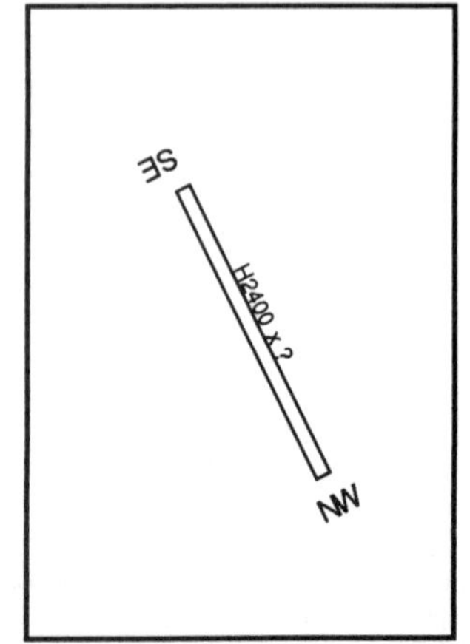

Not to be used for navigational purposes

Aviation Museums

Location Map

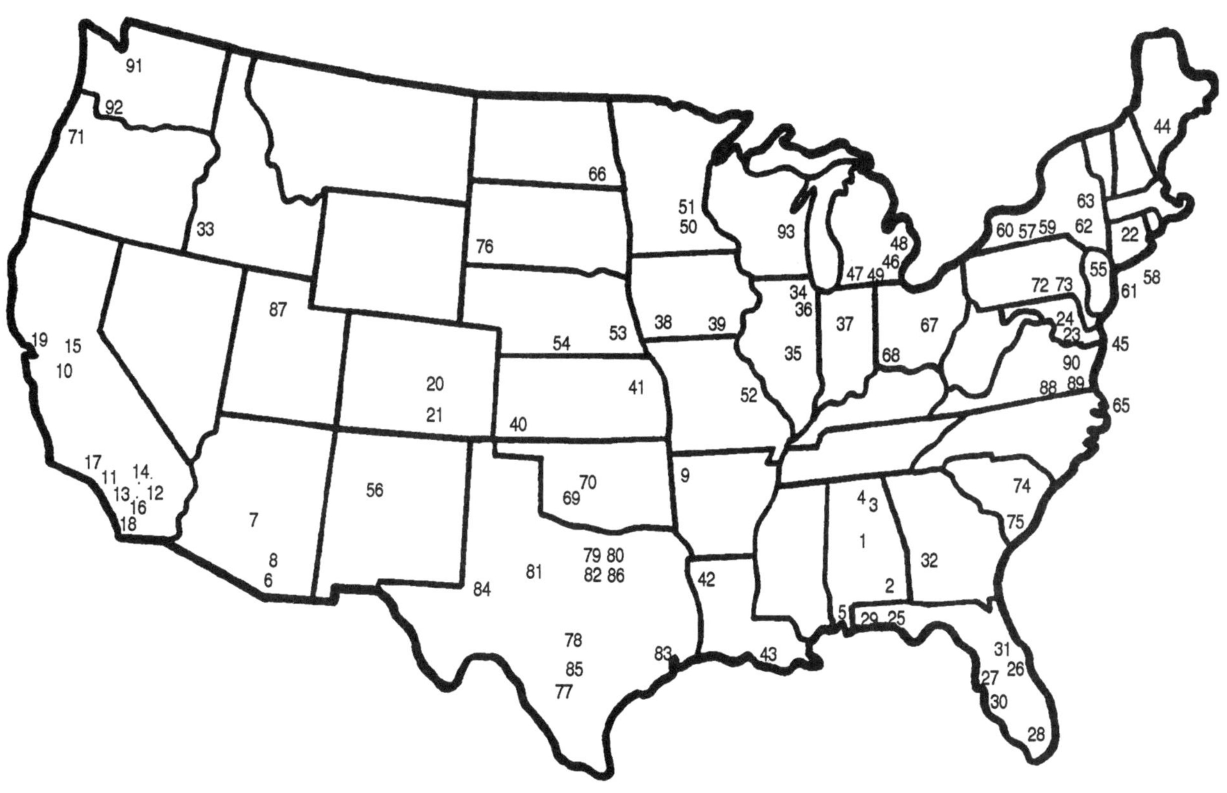

Aviation Museum Listing

Aerodine has compiled a listing of aviation museums that are reported to contain ten or more aircraft on display. The following descriptions include: estimated number of aircraft, general admission prices (note prices may change as time elapses); museum hours; food on premises (vending machines, snack bars, restaurants on premises, etc.); museum location and telephone numbers. A few museums with less than ten aircraft deserving special mention have also been included. We requested information kits from all the museums listed below. Those museums that responded to our request were featured in our book. (See Article) means that there is more detailed information about that museum. See the state chapter for the article.

1 - AL) Southern Museum of Flight:
Birmingham, AL (See Article)
Over 20 aircraft displayed. Exhibits: indoors. Admission: adults $3.00, children $2.00. Museum Hours: Tuesday through Saturday 9:30 a.m. to 5 p.m., and Sunday from 1 p.m. to 4:30 p.m. Dining: restaurant reported nearby. Location: adjacent to Birmingham Municipal Airport (BHM). Phone: 205-833-8226.

2 - AL) U.S. Army Aviation Museum:
Fort Rucker, AL (See Article)
Over 30 aircraft displayed. Exhibits: indoors and outdoors. Admission: free. Museum Hours: open daily 9 a.m. to 4 p.m. Closed on Christmas and New Years. Gift shop on premises. Location: just within the south entrance to Fort Rucker, Alabama. Phone: (Gift shop) 334-598-9965.

3 - AL) Ryder's Replica Fighter Museum:
Guntersville, AL (See Article)
Over 40 WW-I replica aircraft on displey, aircraft engines and propellers. Hours: daily 9 a.m. to 4 p.m., closed some holidays. Admission $5.00 adults and free age 5 and under. For information call 205-549-0351.

4 - AL) U.S. Space And Rocket Center:
Huntsville, AL
Over 24 rockets and spacecraft are on display indoors and outdoors. Admission: adults $9.00 children $6.00. Museum hours: 9 a.m. to 5 p.m. daily. Closed on Christmas. A snack bar and cafeteria are situated on the premises. Location: Huntsville, AL. Exit Altemate 72 from I-65 and go approx. 15 miles east. Museum southwest of city. Phone: 205-837-3400.

5 - AL) U.S.S. Alabama Battleship Memorial Park:
Mobile, AL
Over 13 aircraft displayed along with the U.S.S. Alabama and U.S.S. Drum submarine. Exhibits: indoors and outdoors. Admission: adults $5.00, children $2.50. Museum Hours: open daily 8 a.m. to sunset. Closed Christmas. There is a gift shop and snack bar on the premises. Location: Battleship Parkway Mobile, AL. Phone: 334-433-2703.

6 - AZ) Titan Missile Museum:
Green Valley, AZ
The Titan Missile Museum is located about 25 miles south of Tucson, AZ. This is the only Intercontinental Ballistic Missile (ICBM) complex open to the public. Admission: adults $6.00, children $3.00. Hours: November through April, daily between 9 a.m. and 5 p.m. May and October the museum is open same hours but closed on Mon. & Tues. Last tour begins at 4 p.m. Notes: High heeled shoes not permitted on tour. Phone: 520-625-7736.

7 - AZ) Champlin Fighter Museum:
Mesa, AZ (See Article)
Over 30 aircraft are on display. Exhibits: indoors and outdoors. Admission: adults $5.00, children $2.50, under 6 years free. Hours: 10 a.m. to 5 p.m., 7 days a week. Gift shop on premises. Restaurant located on the airport. Location: Falcon Field, Mesa, AZ. Phone: 602-830-4540.

8 - AZ) Pima Air Museum:
Tucson, AZ (See Article)
Over 200 aircraft on display indoors and outdoors; Admission: adults $6.00, children $3.00, under 10 years old free. Hours: open daily 9 a.m. to 5 p.m. No one will be admitted after 4 p.m. A snack bar is located on the museum premises. The Pima Air Museum is located approx. 5 miles from the Tucson Intl. Airport (TUS). Fly-in visitors can arrange transportation through fixed base operators. Phone: 502-574-9658.

9 - AR) Arkansas Air Museum:
Fayetteville, AR
Over 10 aircraft reported on display. Admission: donation requested. Hours: 9:30 a.m. to 4:30 p.m. daily. Closed on major holidays. Gift shop and food vending machines are available. Location: on Drake Field in Fayetteville, AR. Phone: 501-521-4947.

10 - CA) Castle Air Museum:
Atwater, CA
Over 30 aircraft displayed indoors and outdoors. Admission: free. Hours: 10 a.m. to 4 p.m., Closed on major holidays. Restaurant and gift shop on premises. Location: adjacent to Castle AFB, Atwater, CA. Phone: 209-723-2178.

Aviation Museums Continued

11 - CA) Planes of Fame Air Museum: Chino, CA (See Article)
Two museums on site: Warbird Collection and a separate Fighter Jet Museum. Over 100 aircraft on display indoors and outdoors. Admission: adults $7.95, children $1.95. Combination to both museums are $8.00 for adults and $2.00 for children. Hours: open daily 9 a.m. to 5 p.m. Vending machines on site. Location: on Chino Airport. Phone: 909-597-3722.

12 - CA) General Patton Memorial and Museum: Chiriaco Summit, CA (See Article)
Open 7 days a week between 9 a.m. and 5 p.m. Short video describes Memorial and 6,000 square foot museum complex. Outdoors are 17 tanks and vehicles on display. Admission is $3.50 seniors, $4.00 for adults, under 12 years, free with adult. Chiriaco Summit Airport within 1/4 mile walk to museum and restaurant. For information call 619-227-3483.

13 - CA) Edwards Air Force Base, CA (See Article)
Over 15 aircraft are on display and many more in the restoration process for future display. The closest civilian airport is Fox Field in Lancaster, CA. The museum is open Tuesday through Saturday. Admission is free Phone: 805-277-8050.

14 - CA) March Field Museum: March Air Force Base, CA
Over 40 aircraft on display indoors and outdoors. Admission: free. Hours: Monday through Friday 10 a.m. to 4 p.m., Saturday and Sunday noon to 4 p.m. Restaurant reported near museum. Location: southeast of Riverside near March Air Force Base main entrance. Phone: 909-697-6600, Tours 697-6604.

15 - CA) McClellan Aviation Museum: North Highlands, CA
Over 20 aircraft on display indoors and outdoors. Admission: free. Hours: Monday through Saturday from 9 a.m. to 3 p.m. closed Sundays and holidays. Gift shop on site. Location: at McClellan Air Force Base located northeast of Sacramento. Enter gate 3 for directions and special pass to museum. Phone: 916-643-3192.

16- CA) Palm Springs Air Museum: Palm Springs, CA (See Article)
A collection of over 17 famous aircraft including a Grumman F4F Wildcat, F6F Hellcat, F7F Tigercat, F8F Bearcat, P47, B-17, Spitfire, Avenger, Lightning and many more. Hours: Wed-Mon 10 a.m. to 5 p.m. Palm Springs Regl. Arpt. Admission: $7.50 adults, $3.50 per child; Gift shop, tours, and special events. Call 619-778-6262.

17 - CA) Museum Of Flying: Santa Monica, CA (See Article)
This museum is situated on the Santa Monica Airport. It is located within a 53,000 square foot "Supermarine" structure of steel and glass. There are 3 levels of exhibit space. Over 40 aircraft on display. DC-3 dining room on site. Group catered meals available. Admission: $7.00 adults, $3.00 per child. For information call 310-392-8822.

18 - CA) San Diego Aerospace Museum: San Diego, CA (Balboa Park)
Over 65 aircraft on display indoors and outdoors. Admission: adults $6.00, children $2.00. Hours: 10 a.m. to 4:30 p.m. daily, except holidays. Restaurant and gift shop on premises. Location: Balboa Park area. Phone: 619-234-8291

19 - CA) Travis Air Force Museum: Travis Air Force Base, CA
Over 30 aircraft on display indoors and outdoors. Admission: free. Hours: 9 a.m. to 4 p.m. Monday through Saturday and Sunday 12 noon to 5 p.m. Gift shop and nearby restaurant reported. Location: near Fairfield, CA., Go to Visitor registration building at main entrance to Travis Air Force Base to obtain pass and directions to museum. Phone: 707-424-2619.

20 - CO) Wings Over The Rocky's Air & Space Museum: Denver, CO (See Article)
22 aircraft on display indoors and outdoors. Admission: $4.00 adults, $2.00 children. Hours: 10 a.m. to 4:00 p.m. Monday through Saturday, and 12 noon to 4 p.m. on Sunday. Gift shop on site. Location: 10 miles from Centennial airport (APA) or 15 mi from Front Range airport (FTG). Rental car transportation available. For museum information call 303-360-5360.

21 - CO) Edward J. Peterson Space Command Museum: Peterson AFB, CO
Over 17 aircraft reported on display outdoors. Admission: free. Hours: 8:30 a.m. to 4:30 p.m. Tuesday through Friday, and 9:30 a.m. to 4:30 on Saturday. Closed on Sunday, Monday and holidays. Gift shop on site. Location: adjacent to Colorado Springs. Go to main gate of Peterson Air Force Base at visitors center to obtain directions and pass. Phone: 719-556-4915.

22 - CT) New England Air Museum: Windsor Locks, CT (See Article)
Over 50 aircraft on display indoors and outdoors. Admission: adults $5.50, children $2.00. Hours: 10 a.m. to 5 p.m. daily except on Thanksgiving and Christmas. Gift shop and vending machines reported. Location: adjacent and north of Bradley Intl. Airport. Phone: 860-623-3305.

Aviation Museums Continued

23 - DC) Paul E. Garber Facility:
Smithsonian Institution, Washington, DC
Over 125 aircraft on display indoors. Admission: free. Hours: Tours (Approx. 2 hours in length) begin at 10 a.m. on Monday through Friday, and again at 10 a.m. and 1 p.m. on Saturday and Sunday. Notes: the building that house the aircraft do not have climate control. Location: contact museum for directions. Reservations required. Phone: 202-357-1400.

24 - DC) National Air and Space Museum:
S.W. Washington, DC (See Article)
Over 85 aircraft on display indoors. Admission: free. Hours: 10 a.m. to 5:30 p.m. daily. Closed on Christmas Day. Three gift shops and a restaurant are located on the premises. Location: situated at National Mall adjacent to other Smithsonian museums. Phone: 202-357-2700.

25 - FL) Air Force Armament Museum:
Eglin Air Force Base, FL (See Article)
Over 28 aircraft are on display indoors and outdoors. Admission: free. Hours: 9:30 a.m. to 4:30 p.m. daily. Closed on New Years, Thanksgiving and Christmas. Gift shop on location. Location: near Valparaiso, FL., and situated outside the main entrance to Eglin Air Force Base. Phone: 904-882-4062.

26 - FL) Flying Tigers Warbird Air Museum:
Kissimmee, FL (See Article)
35 to 40 aircraft are on display indoors and outdoors. Admission: adults $6.00, children $5.00. Hours: 9 a.m. to 5:30 p.m. 6 days, Sun 9 a.m. to 5 p.m. Closed major holidays. Gift shop and vending machines on site. Location: northwest corner of the Tampa-St. Petersburg Intl. Arpt. Phone: 407-847-7477.

27 - FL) Sun "n" Fun Aviation Museum:
Lakeland, FL
Over 40 aircraft on display indoors and outdoors. Admission: $4.00 sdults, $2.00 children. Hours: 10 a.m. to 5 p.m.Mon-Fri, Sat 10 a.m. to 4 p.m., Sun 12 p.m. to 4 p.m. Restaurant reported on airport property. Location: on Lakeland Airport. Phone: 813-644-2431.

28- FL) Weeks Air Museum:
Miami, FL
Over 18 aircraft on display indoors and outdoors. Admission: adults $6.95, children (12 and under) $4.95. Hours: 10 a.m. to 5 p.m. daily. They are closed on Thanksgiving and Christmas. Gift shop on premises. Location: situated on the west side of the Kendall-Tamiami Executive Airport. Phone: 305-233-5197.

29 - FL) National Museum of Naval Aviation:
Pensacola, FL - Naval Air Station (See Article)
Over 100 aircraft on display indoors and outdoors. Admission: free. Hours: 9 a.m. to 5 p.m. daily. Closed New Years, Thanksgiving and Christmas. Cafe and gift shop on premises along with film presentation. Location: Pensacola Naval Air Station. Check-in at main gate for directions and pass. Phone: 904-452-3604.

30 - FL) Florida Military Aviation Museum:
St. Petersburg, FL (See Article)
On St. Petersburg-Clearwater International Airport. Hours 10:00 a.m. to 4:00 p.m.Tuesday, Thursday, and Saturday, and 1:00 p.m. to 5:00 p.m. Sunday. Closed on holidays. Admission: $2.00 adults, $1.00 children (ages 6-12), children under age 6 free. In addition to aircraft, the museum features a collection of military vehicles, weapon systems and a gift shop. For more information call 813-535-9007.

31 - FL) Valiant Air Command Museum:
Titusville, FL
Over 20 aircraft on display indoors and outdoors. Admission: $6.00 adults, $4.00 children. Hours: contact museum. Gift shop reported on premises. Also film presentation. Location: situated on the Space Center Executive Airport in Titusville, FL. Phone: 407-268-1941.

32 - GA) Museum of Aviation:
Warner Robins, GA (See Article)
Over 85 aircraft and missiles and Drones on display indoors and outdoors. Admission: free. Hours: 10 a.m. to 5 p.m. daily. Closed major holidays. Snack bar and gift shop on premises. Also a film presentation is available. Location: the museum is on the Robins Air Force Base. Fly-in guests can land at Lewis B. Wilson Airport approx. 8 miles from the museum. Phone: 912-923-6600.

33- ID) Warhawk Air Museum:
Caldwell, ID (See Article)
Located on Caldwell Industrial Airport (EUL). This museum contains a Curtiss P-40E Kittyhawk, Curtiss P-40N Warhawk, North American P-51B and a replica 1917 DR-1 Folker triplane. Restaurant on field. Admission $2.00 per person donation. Museum hours by appointment. Call 208-454-2854.

34- IL) Museum of Science and Industry:
Chicago, IL (See Article)
United 727 Aircraft exhibit indoors along with dramatic flight show presented at scheduled times. Admission: adults $6.00, children $2.50. Hours 9:30 a.m. to 4 p.m. weekdays; Saturday, Sunday and holidays from 9:30 a.m. to 5:30 p.m. 75 exhibit halls plus Henry Crown Space Center open 6 to 9 p.m. on Fri and Sat. Gift shop/

restaurant on premises. Location: Jackson Park just off Lake Shore Drive, on the south side of the city. Phone: 773-684-1414.

35 - IL) Octave Chanute Aerospace Museum: Rantoul, IL (Chanute Air Force Base) (See Article)
Over 35 aircraft on display outdoors. Admission: $3.50 adults, $1.50 children. Hours: Monday through Saturday 10 a.m. to 5 p.m. and Sunday 12 p.m. to 5 p.m. Location: stop at the north gate of the visitors center to obtain a pass and directions to the museum which is located on Chanute Air Force Base near Rantoul, IL. For information write the Octave Chanute Aerospace Museum Foundation (OCAMF), P.O. Box 949, Rantoul, IL 61866 or call 217-893-1613.

36 - IL) Air Classics, Inc., DuPage Airport: West Chicago, IL (See Article)
The Air Classics Museum contains over 12 aircraft on display. Most aircraft are actively being used. During summer season museum hours are Monday through Saturday 9 a.m. to 5 p.m., Winter hours Saturday 10 a.m. to 4 p.m. and Sunday 12 p.m. to 4 p.m. A gift shop is on the premises. The museum is located on the east side of the airport. Admission: $3.00 adults, $1.00 Children. For information about admission or other services please call 630-584-1888.

37 - IN) Grissom Air Museum: Grissom Air Force Base, IN
Over 15 aircraft on display indoors and outdoors. Admission: free. Hours: Tuesday through Saturday 10 a.m. to 4 p.m., outdoor exhibits open 7 a.m. till dusk. Location: Grissom Air Force Base approx 13 miles north of Kokomo, Indiana and about 1 mile west of the town of Bunker Hill along US Hwy 31. For information call 317-688-2654.

38 - IA) Iowa Aviation Preservation Center: Greenfield, IA (See Article)
Over 11 aircraft are on display indoors. Admission: adults $3.00, children $1.50. Hours: 10 a.m. to 5 p.m. Monday through Friday, and 1 p.m. to 5 p.m. Saturday and Sunday. Closed major holidays. Gift shop on premises. Location: on the Greenfield Municipal Airport situated one mile north of the town of Greenfield. Phone: 515-343-7184.

39 - IA) Air Power Museum: Ottumwa, IA (See Article)
Over 25 aircraft are on display indoors. Admission: donations requested. Hours: 9 a.m. to 5 p.m. Monday through Friday, 10 a.m. to 5 p.m. Saturday and 1 p.m. to 5 p.m. on Sunday. Closed major holidays. Gift shop reported on premises. Location: Antique Airfield near Ottumwa/Blakesburg, IA. Phone: 515-938-2773.

40 - KS) Liberal Air Museum: Liberal, KS
Over 90 aircraft displayed indoors and outdoors. Admission: adults $5.00, children $2.00. Hours: 8 a.m. to 5 p.m. Monday through Friday, 10 a.m. to 4 p.m. Saturday, and 1 p.m. to 5 p.m. on Sunday. Closed major holidays. Gift shop reported. Location: on Liberal Municipal Airport. Phone: 316-624-5263.

41 - KS) Combat Air Museum: Topeka, KS
Over 28 aircraft on display indoors and outdoors. Admission: adults $4.00, children $2.50. Hours: 9:00 a.m. to 4:30 p.m. Monday through Saturday, and 10 a.m. to 4:30 p.m. on Sunday. Gift shop reported on premises. Location: south of Topeka at Forbes Field on "J" street, just three blocks south of the air terminal building. Phone: 913-862-3303.

42 - LA) Eighth Air Force Museum: Barksdale Air Force Base, LA
Over 10 aircraft on display. Admission: free. Hours: 9 a.m. to 4 p.m. Monday through Friday, 9:30 a.m. to 4 p.m. daily. Closed Christmas and Thanksgiving. Gift shop on site. Location: Barksdale AFB just east of Shreveport along Interstate 20. Phone: 318-456-3065 or 3067.

43 - LA) Wedell-Williams Memorial Museum: Patterson, LA (See Article)
This museum is located at the Patterson Airport. It was established by the Louisiana legislature as the Official State Aviation Museum to honor Harry P. Williams and James R. Wedell, who held more speed records than anyone else alive. Museum hours are Tuesday through Saturday from 8:30 a.m. to 5 p.m. Admission: adults $2.00, and children free. Phone: 504-395-7067.

44 - ME) Owls Head Transportation Museum: Owls Head, ME
Over 25 aircraft on display indoors and outdoors. Admission: adults $3.00, children $2.00 (under 12 free). Hours: 10 a.m. to 4 p.m. Monday through Friday between November and April, and 10 a.m. to 5 p.m. 7 days a week between May and October. Gift shop and film presentation are provided for guests. Special accommodations with refreshments can be arranged for special groups. Location: Knox County Airport, two miles south of Rockland. Phone: 207-594-4418.

45 - MD) College Park Airport Museum: College Park, MD
"World's Oldest Continually Operated Airport." Established in 1909 when the Wright Brothers taught the first two Army officers to fly. Hours: Wednesday through Friday 11 a.m. to 3 p.m., Saturday and Sunday 11 a.m. to

5 p.m. Closed holidays. Airport listed on National Register of Historic Places. On display: visible foundation of the 1911-12 Army Aviation School hangars, 1910 Rex Smith hangar and original "compass rose" used by first air mail pilots. Also gift shop. (Free admission) Call 301-864-6029 or 301-474-1904.

46 - MI) Henry Ford Museum & Greenfield Village: Dearborn, MI (See Article)

Over 18 aircraft on display indoors. Admission: adults $11.50, children $5.75. Hours: 9 a.m. to 5 p.m. daily except for Christmas and Thanksgiving. Over 60,000 square feet of indoor displays along with Greenfield Village encompassing more than 80 homes, businesses and work places make up this complex. Restaurant/gift shop on premises. Location: pilots can land at Detroit Metro (closest), Willow Run Airport (S.W. of museum), Detroit City Airport (15 mi. N.E.), Troy-Oakland (20 mi. N.) or Mettetal Airport (17 mi W.) Refer to article regarding this attraction. Phone: 313-271-1620.

47 - MI) Kalamazoo Aviation History Museum: Kalamazoo, MI (See Article)

Over 23 aircraft on display indoors and outdoors. Admission: adults $5.00 children $3.00. Hours: 9 a.m. to 5 p.m. Monday through Saturday, and 12 p.m. to 5 p.m. on Sunday. Closed major holidays. Gift shop on premises plus snack area. Restaurants adj. arpt. Location: Battle Creek Intl Arpt., Kalamazoo, MI. Phone: 616-382-6555

48 - MI) Selfridge Military Museum: Selfridge ANG Base, MI

Over 20 aircraft on display outdoors. Admission: donation requested. Hours: Sundays only, 1 p.m. to 5 p.m. between April 1 and November on Sunday only. Closed Easter. Gift shop reported. Location: Selfridge Army Air Field Phone: 818-307-5035.

49 - MI) Yankee Air Force Museum: Ypsilanti, MI

Over 20 aircraft on display indoors and outdoors. Admission: adults $5.00, children $4.00. Summer hours: 10 a.m. to 4 p.m. Tuesday through Saturday, and 12 p.m. to 4 p.m. on Sunday. Winter hours vary; call museum. Gift shop on premises. Location: Willow Run Airport. Phone: 313-483-4030.

50 - MN) Planes of Fame Air Museum: Eden Prairie, MN

Museum states one of largest collection of WWII aircraft in country. Indoor and outdoor displays. Admission: adults $6.00, children $3.00. Hours: Tuesday through Sunday 11 a.m. to 5 p.m. Gift shop on premises. Location: Flying Cloud Airfield (northwest corner). Phone: 612-941-2633.

51 - MN) Minnesota Air Guard Museum: St. Paul, MN (See Article)

Over 10 aircraft on display outside. Admission: donations requested. Hours: 11 a.m. to 4 p.m. on Saturday and Sunday between mid-April through mid-September. Gift shop on premises. Location: Minneapolis St. Paul Intl. Airport (northeast corner). Phone: 612-725-5609.

52 - MO) St. Louis Aviation Museum: St. Louis, MO

Over 15 aircraft on display indoors and outdoors. Admission: $3.00 adults, children free. Hours: 10 a.m. to 4 p.m. Tuesday through Sunday. Gift shop on premises. Location: Creve Coeur Airport. Phone: 314-434-3368 or 878-8575.

53 - NE) Strategic Air Command Museum: Bellevue, NE

Over 30 aircraft on display indoors and outdoors. Admission: adults $4.00, children $2.00. Hours: 8 a.m. to 8 p.m. daily from Memorial Day through Labor Day. 8 a.m. to 5 p.m. the rest of the year. Closed Christmas, New Years and Thanksgiving. Gift shop and vending machines reported. Location: adjacent to Offutt Air Force Base. Phone: 402-292-2001.

54 - NE) Harold Warp Pioneer Village: Minden, NE

Over 15 aircraft on display indoors. Admission: adults $6.00, children $3.00. Hours: 8 a.m. to sundown daily. Gift shop on premises. Location: northwest of Minden, NE near intersection of U.S. Highway 6, 34 and State Highway 10. Transportation available. For information call Phone: 308-832-2750.

55 - NJ) Aviation Hall of Fame of New Jersey: Teterboro, NJ (See Article)

This museum is located on the Teterboro Airport (TEB) and is dedicated to the preservation of two-centuries of aviation and space heritage dating back to 1793. The Hall of Fame of New Jersey is part of a new Aviation Education Center on the east side of the field. For information call the museum at 201-288-6344 or the airport managers office at 201-288-5707.

56 - NM) National Atomic Museum: Albuquerque, NM

Over 10 aircraft on display indoors and outdoors. Admission: free. Hours: 9 a.m. to 5 p.m. daily. Closed major holidays. Location: Kirtland Air Force Base. Phone: 505-284-3243.

57 - NY) National Soaring Museum:
Elmira, NY
Over 12 aircraft on display indoors. Admission: adults $3.00, children $2.50. Hours: 10 a.m. to 5 p.m. daily. Gift shop on premises. Location: adjacent to Harris Hill Soaring Field. Phone: 607-734-3128.

58 - NY) Cradle of Aviation Museum:
Garden City, NY
At time of update museum in process of renovation. Over 50 aircraft on display indoors. Admission: donation requested. Hours: May 1 through October 31, Monday through Saturday 9 a.m. to 5 p.m., Sunday 11 a.m. to 5 p.m. Winter hours: Monday through Saturday 10 a.m. to 4 p.m., and Sunday 12 p.m. to 5 p.m. Location: Nassau Community College campus. (Mitchell Air Force Base). Phone: 516-572-0411.

59 - NY) National Warplane Museum:
Geneseo, NY
Over 32 aircraft on display indoors and outdoors. Admission: adults $5.00, children $2.00. Summer hours: May through October 31, Monday through Saturday 9 a.m. to 5 p.m., Sunday 11 a.m. to 5 p.m. Winter hours: November 1 through April 30, Mon-Sat 10 a.m. to 4 p.m. Gift shop on premises. Location: Geneseo Airport. Phone: 716-243-0690.

60 - NY) Glenn H. Curtiss Museum:
Hammondsport, NY (See Article)
Several aircraft on display indoors. Admission: adults $4.00, children $2.00. Hours: May 1 through October 31 Monday through Saturday 9 a.m. to 5 p.m., Sunday 11 a.m. to 5 p.m. winter months Monday through Saturday 12 p.m. to 4 p.m., and Sunday 12 p.m. to 5 p.m. Gift shop and vending machines reported on site. Location: near Chemung County Regional (45 minutes away) or Bath Hammondsport Airfield. Phone: 607-569-2160.

61- NY) Intrepid Sea-Air-Space Museum:
New York, NY
Over 35 aircraft on display indoors and outdoors. Admission: adults $10.00, children $1.00. Hours: 11 a.m. to 5 p.m. Wednesday through Sunday. Closed Monday and Tuesday as well as major holidays. Gift shop and vending machines reported on premises. Location: just off 12th avenue on pier 86 at west side of Manhattan. Phone: 212-245-2533.

62 - NY) Old Rhinebeck Aerodrome:
Rhinebeck, NY (See Article)
Over 12 aircraft on display indoors and outdoors along with airshows on weekends depicting World War I aerial combat and old time flying. Admission: for weekend airshows, adults $9.00, children $4.00. Flights begin June 15 each year, No airshow during weekdays. Admission: adults $4.00, children $2.00. Restaurant and gift shop on premises. Location: Pilots can land at Red Hook Sky Park (46N) or drive in using the Taconic State Parkway or the New York Thruway. Phone: 914-758-8610.

63 - NY) Empire State Aerosciences Museum:
Scotia, NY (See Article)
This museum is located on the Schenectady County Airport next to Fortune Air (FBO). The Museum building houses two main exhibition galleries. Hours: Tuesday through Saturday from 10:00 a.m. to 4:00 p.m., and Sundays (May through October only) 12:00 p.m. to 4:00 p.m. Admission is adults $3.00, and child/$1.00. Gift shop on site. Phone: (518) 377-2191

64- NC) Western North Carolina Air Museum:
Hendersonville, NC
Founded in 1989, to preserve aviation heritage of the western North Carolina area. Adj. Hendersonville Arpt. (0A7). Admission: free. Hours: March through November: Saturday 10 a.m. to 6 p.m., Sunday 12 noon to 6 p.m. and Wednesday from 12 noon to 6 p.m. Between December and February they are open weekends 12 noon to 5 p.m. Call Aerolina, Inc. (FBO) at 693-3910 or museum staff member at 704-696-9723.

65- NC) Wright Brothers National Memorial:
Manteo, NC
On display is a replica of the famous 1902 Wright Glider and 1903 Wright Flyer along with other artifacts. Admission: adults $2.00, children free. Hours: 9 a.m. to 6 p.m. daily between September and June 15th, and 9 a.m. to 7 p.m. June 15th through Labor Day. Memorial open all holidays except Christmas. Gift shop on premises. Location: Kill Devil Hills near U.S. 158. Phone: 919-441-7430.

66 - ND) Bonanzaville, U.S.A.:
West Fargo, ND
Over 20 aircraft on display indoors. Admission: adults $6.00, children $3.00. Hours: 9 a.m. to 5 p.m.daily. Winter hours November through April Monday through Friday 9 a.m. to 5 p.m. Gift shop reported on premises. Location: Bonanzaville, U.S.A. (historical attraction). Phone: 701-282-2822.

67 - OH) Ohio History of Flight Museum:
Port Columbus Intl. Arpt, Columbus, OH (Article)
Over 12 aircraft on display indoors and outdoors. Admission: adults $2.00, children $1.50. Hours: 9 a.m. to 4 p.m. weedays. Saturday 12 p.m. to 4 p.m. and Sunday 1 p.m. to 4 p.m. Gift shop reported on premises. Location: Port Columbus Intl. Airport. Phone: 614-231-1300.

68 - OH) United States Air Force Museum: Wright-Patterson Air Force Base, OH (See Article)

Over 300 aircraft on display indoors and outdoors. Admission: free. Hours: 9 a.m. to 5 p.m. daily. Closed Christmas, New Years and Thanksgiving. Film presentation available on the hour. Cafe and gift shop on premises. Location: Wright Patterson Air Force Base, near Dayton, OH. Phone: 937-255-3286.

69 - OK) Fort Sill Museum: Fort Sill, OK

Over 15 aircraft and missiles are on display indoors and outdoors. Admission: donations requested. Hours: 9 a.m. to 4 p.m. daily. Closed Christmas and New Years. Gift shop reported on premises. Location: two miles north of the town of Lawton, OK. Phone: 405-351-5123.

70 - OK) Oklahoma Air Space Museum: Oklahoma City, OK

Over 20-30 aircraft are on display indoors. Admission: adults $6.50, children $4.00. Hours: Monday through Friday, 9 a.m. to 5 p.m., Saturday 9 a.m. to 6 p.m. and Sunday 12 p.m. to 6 p.m. Restaurant and gift shop on premises. Location: south of Remington Park Race Track and west of Oklahoma City Zoo. Phone: 405-427-5461.

71 - OR) WW-II Blimp Hangar & Flight Museum: Tillamook, OR (See Article)

Located on east side of Tillamook Airport. Only hangar of its type open to the public. Available aircraft parking adjacent. A facinating history is told. The Tillamook hangar measures 1,070 feet in length, 260 feet wide and 190 feet high. There is enough floor space to fit 6 football fields within its confines. Several WW-II aircraft are on exhibit. For information call 800-938-1957.

72- PA) Mid-Atlantic Air Museum: Reading, PA

Over 20 aircraft on display indoors and outdoors. Admission: adults $3.00, children $2.00. Hours: 9:30 a.m. to 4 p.m. daily. Closed major holidays. Gift shop on premises. Location: Reading Airport. Phone: 215-372-7333.

73 - PA) Willow Grove Air Park: Willow Grove Naval Air Sta., PA

Over 10 aircraft on display outdoors. Admission: free. Hours: daylight. Location: Willow Grove Naval Air Station. Special permission and escort by base personnel must be arranged. Phone: 215-443-1776.

74 - SC) Florence Air and Missile Museum: Florence, SC (See Article)

Over 25 aircraft are on display indoors and outdoors. Admission: adults $5.00, children $3.00. Hours: Monday through Saturday 9 a.m. to 5 p.m., and Sunday 10 a.m. to 4:30 p.m. Gift shop on premises. Location: Florence Regional Airport. Phone: 803-665-5118.

75 - SC) Patriots Piont Naval & Maritime Museum: Mt. Pleasant, SC

Over 12 aircraft are on display indoors and outdoors along with five naval vessels. The aircraft carrier Yorktown is also on display. All ships have public tours available. This is known as the "World's largest Naval and Maritime Museum." Admission: adults $9.00, children $4.00. Hours: 9 a.m. to 6 p.m. daily. Closed on Christmas. Cafe and gift shop reported on premises. Location: Off Patriots Point Road from U.S. 17, near Mt. Pleasant, SC. Phone: 803-884-2727.

76 - SD) South Dakota Air and Space Museum: Box Elder, SD

Over 26 aircraft and missiles on display indoors and outdoors. Admission: free. Hours: 8:30 a.m. to 6 p.m. daily between mid-May and mid-September, and 8:30 to 4:30 p.m. from mid-September to mid-May. Closed major holidays. Location: main gate to the Ellsworth Air Force Base. Phone: 605-385-5188.

77 - TX) Hangar 9 Museum: Brooks Air Force Base, TX (See Article)

Hangar 9 Museum exhibits and gives special appreciation to the history of the aerospace medicine industry. Southwest of San Antonio. This museum is reported open between 8 a.m. and 4 p.m. weekdays. Closed weekends. Admission is free. Phone: 210-536-2203.

78 - TX) Highland Lakes Squadron: Burnet, TX - Confederate Air Force, (See Article)

The museum is housed within a 100x125 foot hangar. Hours are Saturday 9 a.m. to 5 p.m., and Sunday 12 noon to 5 p.m. Burnet Bluebonnet Festival held each year features over 40 aircraft. For information call 512-756-2226.

79- TX) Cavanaugh Flight Museum: Dallas, TX (See Article)

Over 40 aircraft on display. Hours: Monday through Saturday 9 a.m. to 5 p.m. Admission: $5.50 adults, $2.75 children. Gift shop on site. Located: Dallas, TX. Addison Airport (ADS) Northeast side of airport. Fly-in guests can park aircraft at Million Air and walk to museum. For information call 214-380-8800.

80 - TX) Frontiers of Flight Museum Dallas, TX (See Article)

The Museum is Located on Love Field, Dallas Texas. It commemorated the pioneers, their achievements and development of aviation. Hours: 10 a.m. to 5 p.m.

Aviation Museums Continued

Monday through Saturday, and 1 p.m. to 5 p.m. on Sunday. Admission: $2.00 adults, $1.00 for children under 12 years old. For information call 214-350-3600.

81 - TX) Dyess Linear Air Park:
Dyess Air Force Base, TX

Over 25 aircraft on display outdoors. Admission: free. Hours: daylight. Location: W. of Abilene, TX., and located on the Dyess Air Force Base. Phone: 915-696-2196.

82 - TX) Pate Museum of Transportation:
Fort Worth, TX

Over 20 aircraft on display outdoors. Admission: free. Hours: 9 a.m. to 5 p.m. Tuesday through Sunday. Closed Monday and major holidays. Location: along U.S. 377 just north of Cresson, TX. Phone: 817-396-4305.

83 - TX) Lone Star Flight Museum:
Galveston, TX

Over 50 aircraft on display indoors. Admission: adults $6.00, children $3.50. Hours: 10 a.m. to 5 p.m. daily. Closed Christmas, New Years, Thanksgiving and Easter. Gift shop on premises. Location: Scholes Field Municipal Airport. Phone: 409-740-7722.

84 - TX) American Airpower Heritage Museum:
Midland, TX (See Article)

This museum is located on the Midland Intl. Airport. This sight is located on 85 acres of the Confederate Air Force Headquarters. Their fleet contains more than 130 active World War II aircraft. The museum is open from 9 a.m. to 5 p.m. Monday through Saturday, and 12 noon to 5 p.m.on Sunday. Admission: $6.00 adult, $4.00 children. In addition their "Airsho" is held each Fallwith re-enactments of WW-II battle scenes. For information call 915-563-1000.

85 - TX) History and Traditions Museum:
San Antonio, TX

Over 50 aircraft on display indoors and outdoors. Admission: free. Hours: 9 a.m. to 5:30 p.m. daily. Closed Christmas, New Years, Easter, and Thanksgiving. Gift shop reported on premises. Location: Lackland Air Force Base. Phone: 210-671-3055.

86 - TX) Silent Wings Museum:
Terrell, TX (See Article)

A special air museum devoted to military glider pilots. Several full size gliders are on display. Admission: donations appreciated. Hours: 10 a.m. to 5 p.m. Tuesday through Saturday, and 12 p.m. to 5 p.m. on Sunday. Closed major holidays. Gift shop on premises. Location: Terrell Municipal Airport. Phone: 214-563-0402.

87 - UT) Hill Air Force Base Museum:
Hill Air Force Base, UT

Over 58 aircraft on display outdoors. Admission: donations. Hours: 9 a.m. to 5:30 p.m. Tuesday through Friday, and 9 a.m. to 5:30 p.m. Saturday and Sunday. Closed Monday, Christmas, New Years, and Thanksgiving. Gift shop and vending machines available. Location: south of Ogden and situated on the Hill Air Force Base. Phone: 801-777-6818.

88 - VA) U.S. Army Transportation Museum:
Fort Eustis, VA

Over 15 aircraft on display indoors and outdoors. Admission: free. Hours: 9 a.m. to 4:30 p.m. daily. Closed Federal holidays and during Easter holiday. Gift shop on premises. Location: adj. to Newport News, VA. Fort Eustis. See guard at main gate. Phone: 804-878-1182.

89 - VA) Air Power Park and Museum:
Hampton, VA (See Article)

Over 17 aircraft and missiles on display outdoors. Admission: free. Hours: 9 a.m. to 4:30 p.m. daily. Closed on some major holidays. Gift shop and vending machines available on premises. Location: near Langley Air Force Base. Phone: 804-727-1163.

90 - VA) Virginia Aviation Museum:
Sandson, VA

Over 15 aircraft on display indoors. Admission: adults $3.00, children $1.00. Hours: 10 a.m. to 4 p.m. Tuesday through Sunday. Closed on Monday. Gift shop on premises. Location: adjacent to Richmond Intl. Airport. Phone: 804-222-8690.

91 - WA) Museum of Flight:
Seattle, WA (See Article)

Over 40 aircraft on display indoors and outdoors. Admission: adults $8.00, children $4.00. Hours: 10 a.m. to 5 p.m. daily and until 9 p.m. on Thursday. Closed on Christmas. Gift shop on premises. Location: Boeing Field/King County Intl. Airport. Phone: 206-764-5720.

92 - WA) Pearson Air Museum:
Vancouver, WA

Over 15 aircraft on display indoors. Admission: adults $4.00, children $1.50. Hours: 10 a.m. to 5 p.m. Wednesday through Sunday during the summer, and 12 p.m. to 5 p.m. Wednesday through Sunday during the winter. Closed Monday and Tuesday throughout the year. Gift shop on premises. Location: on Pearson Airpark. Phone: 360-694-7026.

Aviation Museums Continued

93 - WI) EAA Air Adventure Museum: Oshkosh, WI (See Article)

Over 100 aircraft on display indoors and outdoors. Admission: adults $7.00, children $5.50. Hours: 8:30 a.m. to 5 p.m. Monday through Saturday and 11 a.m. to 5 p.m. on Sunday. Closed Christmas, Easter, New Years Day, and Thanksgiving. Gift shop and vending machines available. Location: on Wittman Field, Oshkosh, WI. Phone: 414-426-4800.

Does Your Airplane Fit Into One Of These Categories?

DON'T LET YOUR AIRPLANE GO TO "POT"

Expand your horizons and discover new points of interest you can visit with the use of your aircraft.

CATEGORY: 1 "The Planter"

- ☐ *Does your aircraft sit for long periods of time on the ground collecting bird doo-doo?*
- ☐ *Have the local field mice and squirrels hung the No Vacancy sign out and taken up permanent residency within the confines of your airframe?*
- ☐ *Are your wheels half round, like tomatoes that have fallen off the vine a month ago?*
- ☐ *Do you see a multitude of floral arrangements growing knee-high around your landing gear?*

CATEGORY: 2 "Ring Around The Airport"

- ☐ *Does your airplane know its way around the pattern so well that your turn and bank has a permanent left sag to it?*
- ☐ *Does your rudder have a layer of bugs only on one side?*
- ☐ *Have you noticed the left sole on your shoes keep wearing out before the right ones do?*

CATEGORY: 3 "The Ping Pong Syndrome"

- ☐ *Do you feel like a ping pong ball traveling back and forth to the same place, time and time again?*
- ☐ *Does your log book have ditto marks running down its pages?*
- ☐ *Do you have ten or more flight plans made up in advance, to the same place?*

WELL THEN BUNKY !!! you need to order your copy of Aerodine's Pilot Travel Guide, and start enjoying the thrill of discovering new places you can visit by using your aircraft.

Order Form

To order your copy of Aerodine's Pilot Travel Guide

Simply mail your check or money order for **$64.95 Plus $6.00 for postage and handling** to Aerodine Magazine, P.O. Box 247, Palatine, IL 60078. We also accept **VISA & MASTERCARD.** For telephone orders, give us a call at 847-358-4355 Allow 2 to 4 weeks for delivery.

Please Print **Include: $64.95 plus $6.00 for postage & handling**

Your name: ______________________

Address: ______________________

City: ____________ State: ______ Zip: ______

Phone Number: Include Your Area Code

Work: ( ) ____________ Home ( ) ____________

VISA or MASTERCARD number Expiration Date:

____

Order Form

To order your copy of Aerodine's Pilot Travel Guide

Simply mail your check or money order for **$64.95 Plus $6.00 for postage and handling** to Aerodine Magazine, P.O. Box 247, Palatine, IL 60078. We also accept **VISA & MASTERCARD.** For telephone orders, give us a call at 847-358-4355 Allow 2 to 4 weeks for delivery.

Please Print **Include: $64.95 plus $6.00 for postage & handling**

Your name: ______________________

Address: ______________________

City: ____________ State: ______ Zip: ______

Phone Number: Include Your Area Code

Work: ( ) ____________ Home ( ) ____________

VISA or MASTERCARD number Expiration Date:

____

If you are planning to purchase several copies of The Aerodine's Pilot Travel Guide within the same order, we offer quantity discount rates. For information call 847-358-4355.

Order Form

To order your copy of Aerodine's Pilot Travel Guide

Please Print **Include: $64.95 plus $6.00 for postage & handling**

Simply mail your check or money order for **$64.95 Plus $6.00 for postage and handling** to Aerodine Magazine, P.O. Box 247, Palatine, IL 60078. We also accept **VISA & MASTERCARD.** For telephone orders, give us a call at 847-358-4355 Allow 2 to 4 weeks for delivery.

Your name: ______________________________

Address: ______________________________

City: ____________________ State: _____ Zip: _______

Phone Number: Include Your Area Code

Work: ( ) ______________ Home ( ) ______________

VISA or MASTERCARD number Expiration Date:

____

- -

Order Form

To order your copy of Aerodine's Pilot Travel Guide

Please Print **Include: $64.95 plus $6.00 for postage & handling**

Simply mail your check or money order for **$64.95 Plus $6.00 for postage and handling** to Aerodine Magazine, P.O. Box 247, Palatine, IL 60078. We also accept **VISA & MASTERCARD.** For telephone orders, give us a call at 847-358-4355 Allow 2 to 4 weeks for delivery.

Your name: ______________________________

Address: ______________________________

City: ____________________ State: _____ Zip: _______

Phone Number: Include Your Area Code

Work: ( ) ______________ Home ( ) ______________

VISA or MASTERCARD number Expiration Date:

____

- -

If you are planning to purchase several copies of The Aerodine's Pilot Travel Guide within the same order, we offer quantity discount rates. For information call 847-358-4355.

Notes

Notes

Notes

Notes

Notes

Notes

Notes

Notes

Tell Us About Your Favorite "Prop Stoppers"

If you know about a special place to fly for dining or enjoyment, please let us know so we inturn may share it with our readers.

Airport Name: ____________________ **Identifier** (if you know it) ________

City: ____________________ State: ________

Name of attraction: ____________________

(Your favorite fly-in restaurant, resort, attraction or point of interest.)

Approximate dist. ________ Direction from airport ________

Comments: ____________________

____

____

Aerodine Magazine, P.O. Box 247, Palatine, IL 60078, Phone: 847-358-4355

Airport Name: ____________________ **Identifier** (if you know it) ________

City: ____________________ State: ________

Name of attraction: ____________________

(Your favorite fly-in restaurant, resort, attraction or point of interest.)

Approximate dist. ________ Direction from airport ________

Comments: ____________________

____

____

Aerodine Magazine, P.O. Box 247, Palatine, IL 60078, Phone: 847-358-4355

Tell Us About Your Favorite "Prop Stoppers"

Airport Name: ______________________ **Identifier** (if you know it) ________

City: ______________________ State: ________

Name of attraction: ______________________
(Your favorite fly-in restaurant, resort, attraction or point of interest.)

Approximate dist. ________ Direction from airport ________

Comments: ______________________

____

____

Aerodine Magazine, P.O. Box 247, Palatine, IL 60078, Phone: 847-358-4355

Airport Name: ______________________ **Identifier** (if you know it) ________

City: ______________________ State: ________

Name of attraction: ______________________
(Your favorite fly-in restaurant, resort, attraction or point of interest.)

Approximate dist. ________ Direction from airport ________

Comments: ______________________

____

____

Aerodine Magazine, P.O. Box 247, Palatine, IL 60078, Phone: 847-358-4355

Tell Us About Your Favorite "Prop Stoppers"

Airport Name: ____________________ **Identifier** (if you know it) ________

City: ____________________ State: ________

Name of attraction: ____________________

(Your favorite fly-in restaurant, resort, attraction or point of interest.)

Approximate dist. ________ Direction from airport ________

Comments: ____________________

Aerodine Magazine, P.O. Box 247, Palatine, IL 60078, Phone: 847-358-4355

Airport Name: ____________________ **Identifier** (if you know it) ________

City: ____________________ State: ________

Name of attraction: ____________________

(Your favorite fly-in restaurant, resort, attraction or point of interest.)

Approximate dist. ________ Direction from airport ________

Comments: ____________________

Aerodine Magazine, P.O. Box 247, Palatine, IL 60078, Phone: 847-358-4355